UNIVERSITY CASEBOOK SERIES

EDITORIAL BOARD

DAVID L. SHAPIRO
DIRECTING EDITOR
Professor of Law, Harvard University

ROBERT C. CLARK
Dean of the School of Law, Harvard University

DANIEL A. FARBER
Professor of Law, University of Minnesota

OWEN M. FISS
Professor of Law, Yale Law School

GERALD GUNTHER
Professor of Law, Stanford University

THOMAS H. JACKSON
President, University of Rochester

HERMA HILL KAY
Dean of the School of Law, University of California, Berkeley

HAROLD HONGJU KOH
Professor of Law, Yale Law School

SAUL LEVMORE
Professor of Law, University of Chicago

ROBERT L. RABIN
Professor of Law, Stanford University

CAROL M. ROSE
Professor of Law, Yale Law School

To Jan

— J.T.

To Lisa, Amy, and David

— R.H.T.

PREFACE

This book is designed to be an educational tool for students learning about complex civil litigation for the first time; a resource for judges, lawyers, and academics struggling with the intractable problems these cases create; and a thesis about the proper roles of — and limitations on — judges, lawyers, and parties involved in large-scale adjudication in our American democratic society. We meet none of these goals perfectly. But we hope that we convey to each of you the great enthusiasm and respect that we have for this most difficult and important subject.

I

Briefly stated, our perspective is this: Complex litigation tests the limits of the adversary system. In complex litigation, the adversarial process functions poorly, if at all; there are so many parties, documents, facts, and/or issues that the lawyers, the litigants, and the jury are simply incapable of performing the tasks which the adversarial process has traditionally assigned to them. To overcome this dysfunction and to preserve the opportunity for rational adjudication, the judge must of necessity step in. The shift toward increased judicial power, however, has at least two untoward effects. First, the complex litigation judge adopts a posture foreign to adversarial theory and to the notions of party autonomy which underlie that theory. Second, as long as the traditional judicial role remains unchanged in routine litigation, the complex litigation judge creates a conflict with one of the bedrock principles of modern procedure: trans-substantivism (*i.e.*, the like procedural treatment of all lawsuits). It is no exaggeration to say that complex litigation presents the critical test for the continued viability of the adversarial system and the modern American procedural system set up around those adversarial norms.

In consequence, the critical questions of complex litigation, and the questions which this book seeks to address, are: (1) How important are adversarial process and party autonomy? (2) How important is the like procedural treatment of all cases? and (3) Under what circumstances is it desirable or even essential to depart from adversarial process and trans-substantive procedure? Although we are on record in our other writings as answering (1) "Important," (2) "Important," and (3) "Not many," we try in our materials merely to shape the questions, rather than to force the readers to accept our conclusions.

We also believe that by framing the issues in these terms, readers can gain new perspectives on fields such as Civil Procedure, Federal Courts, Conflict of Laws, and Mass Torts. A course in complex litigation can act as a bridge linking and synthesizing these fields, and our materials are intended to show the interconnection of procedure and substance in several specific categories of modern civil litigation.

The organization of this book is set out in detail in the Table of Contents. In general terms, however, the book is divided into an introductory chapter and four major parts. The introductory chapter, Chapter One, is essential to a full understanding of the larger themes developed later in the book. The first three subsections of Chapter One give, respectively, theoretical, historical, and comparative perspectives on our present American system of litigation. Each of the subsections also develop important themes for the later materials: the theoretical materials discuss trans-substantivism, efficiency, and formal justice; the historical materials explore the tensions between certainty and discretion, and between judge and jury; and the comparative materials explore the benefits and weaknesses of adversarial process. In a sense, these materials are a reader on procedure. The fourth subsection of Chapter One shifts to the specific problem of complex litigation. We suggest a more formal definition of "complex litigation" that forms the basis for the rest of the book. We suggest that cases can be complex in one of our ways: when the inability to join all interested parties creates the risk of disparate treatment of like persons (joinder complexity); when the mass of information makes it difficult for lawyers left to their own devices to shape the case for trial (pretrial complexity); when the mass of information makes it difficult for the lawyers o present proofs and arguments at trial or for the fact-finder to resolve the case rationally (trial complexity); and when the parties have difficulty implementing a remedy (remedial complexity).

We then devote one Part of the book to each types of complexity. Part One (Chapters Two through Seven) deal with joinder complexity. Part Two (Chapters Eight and Nine) deal with pretrial complexity. Part Three (Chapters Ten and Eleven) deal with trial complexity. Part Four (Chapter Twelve) deals with remedial complexity.

II

A word of caution is in order regarding our editing of cases. First, in editing the cases, we deleted most citations either to other cases, to other materials, and to the record in the case. When other cases or materials were deleted, we usually marked that fact with ellipses. When citations to the record or to prior opinions in the same litigation were deleted, we tended to delete them without ellipses. Second, as is true of many casebooks, we often edited out significant arguments that were tangential to the points for which the particular case was selected. Third, in order to maintain a consistent style throughout the book, we tended to delete some italics found in the cases and to insert others. Finally, on very rare occasions, when absolutely necessary for comprehension of the edited material, we blended two or more paragraphs into one. In short, readers should not rely on the edited cases to be a verbatim reproduction of the cases or the arguments in them. Care was taken in the editing process, however, to ensure that each case, as near as possible, retained its original flavor and style.

We also tried to use gender-inclusive language wherever possible. Sometimes this proved too awkward, so we tended to use "she" to refer to the hypothetical judge, "he" to refer to the hypothetical lawyer, and both pronouns to refer to hypothetical parties.

III

A word about your authors may be in order. Both of us have experience as practicing lawyers in complex litigation, and have been involved in one capacity or another in some of the cases used in this book. When our participation was directly related to the issues under discussion in the text and was significant enough that we believed a reader would wish to know of that participation in evaluating the material, we dropped a short footnote describing our involvement. When our participation was not directly related to the matter under discussion, however, we did not drop a footnote. Nonetheless, you should probably know that one of authors was lead counsel for the United States for a period of time in the *Agent Orange* litigation, and the other author worked as an associate in the *MGM Grand Hotel Fire* litigation. Both cases are discussed at various points in the book.

IV

We tried to make the book as current as possible. Some developments as recent as June, 1998 are contained in the book. In a world of law evolving as rapidly as complex civil litigation, however, the book will already be out-of-date as soon as it arrives in the bookstores. We will try to supplement the book on an annual basis. Should you ever wish to share with us any recent developments, or should you wish to share any questions or thoughts about the materials in this book, please feel free to contact us.

Notre Dame, Indiana
Washington, D.C.
July, 1998

ACKNOWLEDGMENTS

We gratefully acknowledge the contributions of the people who helped to make this book possible. At the risk of neglecting others, we especially thank:

- Our deans — David Link of Notre Dame Law School and Jack Friedenthal of George Washington University — who provided us with support, encouragement, an occasionally reduced teaching load (for one of us) and a sabbatical (for the other). Our law schools and universities also supplied us with research grant support that helped to move this project to completion.
- Our colleagues — especially Joe Bauer, Todd Peterson, Peter Raven-Hansen, John Robinson, and Bob Rodes — whose conversations and reading of drafts of portions of this book were insightful.
- Our research librarians — Dwight King, Leslie Lee, Patti Ogden, Scott Pagel, Lucy Payne, and Warren Rees — who are the best.
- Our research assistants — Elena Baca, Greg Butrus, Joe Butscher, Bill Dittmer, Burke Harr, Pat Iseman, Mike Mlachak, Brian Nestor, Victor Nieto, Susan Sullivan, Steve Wolf, and Gene Zelensky at Notre Dame, and Gretchen Smith, Jessica Dingfelder, Elizabeth Holohan, John Muccifori, Martin Price, and Andrew Gable at George Washington — who provided research, editorial assistance, and technical advice.
- Our secretarial and technical staffs — Kathleen Bradley, Laura Burdick, Becky Hoven, Corinne Karlin, Dan Manier, Rosemary Reiter, and Debbie Sumption — who did everything we asked of them, and more.
- Our students, who put up with eight years of handouts and half-finished thoughts.
- The authors and publishers that permitted us to reprint excerpts of copyrighted works. They are:

American Law Institute, Complex Litigation: Statutory Recommendations and Analysis (1994). Reprinted with permission.

American Law Institute, Restatement (Second) of the Conflict of Laws (1971). Reprinted with permission.

American Bar Association, ABA Report to the House of Delegates from the Commission on Mass Torts (1989). Reprinted with permission.

Bacigal, Ronald J., The Limits of Litigation: The Dalkon Shield Controversy (1990), reprinted with permission of Carolina Academic Press, copyright © 1990.

Baird, Douglas, The Elements of Bankruptcy (rev. ed. 1993), reprinted with permission of Foundation Press, copyright © 1993.

Bone, Robert G., Rethinking the "Day in Court" Ideal and Nonparty Preclusion, 67 N.Y.U. L. Rev. 193 (1992), reprinted with permission of the New York University Law Review, copyright © 1992.

Bone, Robert G., Lon Fuller's Theory of Adjudication and the False Dichotomy Between Dispute Resolution and Public Law Models of Litigation, 75 B.U. L. Rev. 1273 (1995), reprinted with permission of Trustees of Boston University, copyright © 1995. Forum of original publication.

Brazil, Wayne D., Special Masters in Complex Cases: Extending the Judiciary or Reshaping Adjudication, 53 U. Chi. L. Rev. 394 (1986), reprinted with permission of University of Chicago Law Review, copyright © 1986.

Brunet, Edward J., A Study in the Allocation of Scarce Judicial Resources: The Efficiency of Federal Intervention Criteria, 12 Ga. L. Rev. 701 (1978), reprinted with permission, copyright © 1978.

Buchbinder, David L., Fundamentals of Bankruptcy (1991), reprinted with permission of the author, copyright © 1991.

Bush, Robert A., Dispute Resolution Alternatives and Achieving the Goals of Civil Justice: Jurisdictional Principles for Process Choice, 1984 Wis. L. Rev. 893; copyright © 1984 by The Board of Regents of the University of the University of Wisconsin System; Reprinted by permission of the Wisconsin Law Review.

Calkins, Stephen, Summary Judgment, Motion to Dismiss, and Other Examples of Equilibrating Tendencies in the Antitrust System, 74 Geo. L.J. 1065 (1986), reprinted with the permission of the publisher, Georgetown University & Georgetown Law Journal, copyright © 1986.

Casper, Jonathan D., Restructuring the Traditional Civil Jury: The Effects of Changes in Composition and Procedures in Verdict: Assessing the Civil Jury System (Robert E. Litan ed. 1993), reprinted with permission of Brookings Institution, copyright © 1993.

Cecil, Joe S., & Willging, Thomas E., Accepting Daubert's Invitation: Defining a Role for Court-Appointed Experts in Assessing Scientific Validity, 43 Emory L.J. 995 (1994), reprinted with permission of Emory Law Journal, copyright © 1994.

Chayes, Abram, The Role of the Judge in Public Law Litigation, 89 Harv. L. Rev. 1281 (1976), reprinted with permission of the author, copyright © 1976.

Clark, Charles E., Handbook of the Law of Code Pleading (1928), reprinted with permission of West Group, copyright © 1928.

Clark, Charles E., Special Problems in Drafting and Interpreting Procedural Codes and Rules, 3 Vand. L. Rev. 493, (1950), reprinted with permission of Vanderbilt Law Review.

Cover, Robert M., For James Wm. Moore: Some Reflections on a Reading of the Rules 84 Yale L.J. 718 (1975). Reprinted with permission of The Yale Law Journal Company and Fred B. Rothman & Company from *The Yale Law Journal*, copyright © 1975, Vol. 84, pages 718-740.

Deets, Phyllis V. & Gowan Deets, The Application of EIM/OCR Technology to Litigation Case Management 29-32, in Advanced Litigation Support & Document Imaging (V. Mital ed. 1995), reprinted with kind permission from Kluwer Law International, copyright © 1995.

Elliott, E. Donald, Managerial Judging and the Revolution of Procedure, 53 U. Chi. L. Rev. 306 (1986), reprinted with permission of University of Chicago Law Review, copyright © 1986.

Fiss, Owen M., The Allure of Individualism, 78 Iowa L. Rev. 965 (1993) (reprinted with permission), copyright © 1993.

Frankel, Marvin E., The Search for Truth: An Umpireal View, 123 U. Pa. L. Rev. 1031 (1975), reprinted with permission of the author, copyright © 1975.

Glendon, Mary Ann et al., Comparative Legal Traditions (1985), reprinted with permission of the West Publishing Co. and the authors, copyright © 1985.

Glendon, Mary Ann et al., Comparative Legal Traditions (2d ed. 1994), reprinted with permission of the West Publishing Co. and the authors, copyright © 1994.

Green, Michael D., The Inability of Offensive Collateral Estoppel to Fulfill Its Promise: An Examination of Estoppel in Asbestos Litigation, 70 Iowa L. Rev. 141 (1984) (reprinted with permission), copyright © 1984.

Hazard, Goeffrey C., Jr., Ethics in the Practice of Law (1978), reprinted with permission of Yale University Press, copyright © 1978.

Horowitz, Donald L., Decreeing Organizational Change: Judicial Supervision of Public Institutions, 1983 Duke L.J. 1265, reprinted with permission of the author, copyright © 1983.

Horowitz, Irwin A. & Kenneth S. Bordens, The Effects of Outlier Presence, Plaintiff Population Size, and Aggregation of Plaintiffs on Simulated Jury Decisions, 12 L. & Hum. Behav. 209 (1988), reprinted with permission of Plenum Publishing Corp. and the authors, copyright © 1988.

James, Fleming, Jr., et al., Civil Procedure 19, 238-39, 242-44 (4th ed. 1992), reprinted with permission of Aspen Publishers, copyright © 1992.

Kakalik, James S., et al., An Evaluation of Case Management Under the Civil Justice Reform Act, MR-802-ICJ, Santa Monica, CA: Rand, 1996.

Langbein, John, The German Advantage in Civil Procedure, 52 U. Chi. L. Rev. 823 (1985), reprinted with permission of University of Chicago Law Review, copyright © 1985.

Lederer, Frederic I., Technology Comes to the Courtroom, 43 Emory L.J. 1095 (1994), reprinted with permission of Emory Law Journal, copyright © 1994.

Leng, Shao-chuan, Justice in Communist China: A Survey of the Judicial System of the Chinese People's Republic (1967), reprinted with permission of Oceana Publications, copyright © 1967.

Maitland, F.W., Equity, (A.H. Chaylor & W.J. Whittaker eds., 2d ed. 1936), reprinted with permission of Cambridge University Press, copyright © 1936.

Marcus, Richard L., Myths and Reality in Protective Order Litigation, 69 Cornell L. Rev. 1 (1983), reprinted with permission of Cornell Law Review, copyright © 1983.

McGovern, Francis E., & E. Allen Lind, The Discovery Survey, 51 Law & Contemp. Prob. 41, 41-49, 57-62, 66, 69, 72-73 (Autumn 1988), reprinted with permission of Duke University School of Law, copyright © 1988.

Michelman, Frank I., The Supreme Court and Litigation Access Fees: The Right to Protect One's Rights — Part I, 1973 Duke L.J. 1153, reprinted with permission of Duke University School of Law, copyright © 1973.

Millar, Robert W., Civil Procedure of the Trial Court in Historical Perspective (1952), reprinted with permission of New York University Press, copyright © 1952.

Milsom, S.F.C., Historical Foundations of the Common Law (2d ed. 1981), reprinted with permission of Butterworth Press, copyright © 1981.

Nelson, William E., Americanization of the Common Law (1975), reprinted with permission of the author, copyright © 1975.

Plucknett, Theodore F.T., A Concise History of the Common Law (5th ed. 1956), reprinted with permission of Aspen Publishers, copyright © 1956.

Posner, Richard A., Economic Analysis of Law (4th ed. 1992), reprinted with permission of the author, copyright © 1992.

Pound, Roscoe, The Decadence of Equity, 5 Colum. L. Rev. 20, (1905), reprinted with permission of Columbia Law Review, copyright ©1905.

Ragazzo, Robert A., Transfer and Choice of Federal Law: The Appellate Model, 93 Mich. L. Rev. 703 (1995), reprinted with permission of the Michigan Law review and the author, copyright © 1995.

Rawls, John, A Theory of Justice (1971), reprinted by permission of the publisher, Cambridge, Mass.: Harvard University Press, Copyright ©1971 by the President and Fellows of Harvard College.

Resnik, Judith, Managerial Judges, 96 Harv. L. Rev. 374 (1982), reprinted with permission of Harvard Law Review Association, copyright © 1982.

Richey, Danny P., Guidelines and Techniques for Leading and Managing the Litigation Team, 19 Ohio N. L. Rev. 23 (1992), reprinted with permission of the author, copyright © 1992.

Rubenstein, William B., Divided We Litigate: Addressing Disputes among Group members and Lawyers in Civil Rights Campaigns, 106 Yale L.J. 1623 (1997). Reprinted by permission of The Yale Law Journal Company and Fred B. Rothman & Company, from *The Yale Law Journal*, copyright © 1997, Vol. 106, pages 1623-1681.

Saltzburg, Steven A., Lawyers, Clients, and the Adversary System, 37 Mercer L. Rev. 647 (1985), copyright © 1984 Mercer Law Review.

Schwarzer, William W, Judicial Federalism in Action: Coordination of Litigation in State and Federal Courts, 78 Va. L. Rev. 1689 (1992), reprinted with permission of Virginia Law Review Association and Fred B. Rothman & Co., copyright © 1992.

Schwarzer, William W, Managing Antitrust and Other Complex Litigation: A Handbook for Lawyers and Judges (1982), reprinted with permission of Michie, Charlottesville, VA, (800)446-3410, all rights reserved, copyright © 1982.

Silberman, Linda J., Judicial Adjuncts Revisited, 137 U. Pa. L. Rev. 2131 (1989), reprinted with permission of the University of Pennsylvania Law Review, copyright © 1989.

Smith, Thomas A., A Capital Markets Approach to Mass Tort Bankruptcy, 104 Yale L.J. 367 (1994), reprinted with permission of The Yale Law Journal Company and Fred B. Rothman & Company from The Yale Law Journal, copyright © 1994, Vol. 104, pages 367-434.

Sobol, Richard B., Bending the Law: The Story of the Dalkon Shield Bankruptcy (1991), reprinted with permission of University of Chicago Press, copyright © 1991.

Stengel, James L., and Andrew M. Calamari, Complex Litigation (1994), reprinted with permission of the Practising Law Institute, copyright © 1994. Copies of this work may be purchased from the Practising Law Institute, 810 Seventh Avenue, New York, NY 10019. Tel: (800)260-4754.

Steinman, Joan, The Effects of Case Consolidation on the Procedural Rights of Litigants: What They Are, What They Might Be: Part II, Non-jurisdictional Matters, 42 UCLA L. Rev. 967 (1995), reprinted with permission of UCLA Law Review and Fred B. Rothman & Co., copyright © 1995, The Regents of the University of California. All Rights Reserved.

Subrin, Stephen N., How Equity Conquered Common Law: The Federal Rules of Civil Procedure in Historical Perspective, 135 U. Pa. L. Rev. 909 (1987), reprinted with permission of author, copyright © 1987.

Tidmarsh, Jay, Unattainable Justice, 60 Geo. Wash. L. Rev. 1683 (1992), reprinted with permission of George Washington Law Review, copyright © 1992.

Trangsrud, Roger H., Mass Trials in Mass Tort Cases: A Dissent, 1989 U. Ill. Rev. 69, reprinted with permission of the University of Illinois Law Review, copyright © 1989.

Trangsrud, Roger H., Joinder Alternatives in Mass Tort Litigation, 70 Corn. L. Rev. 779 (1985), reprinted with permission of the author, copyright © 1984.

Waltman, Jerold L., Judicial Activism in England, in Judicial Activism in Comparative Perspective (Kenneth M. Holland ed. 1991), copyright © Kenneth M. Holland, reprinted with permission of St. Martin's Press, Incorporated, and with kind permission from Kluwer Law International.

Weinstein, Jack B., Individual Justice in Mass Tort Litigation (1995), reprinted with permission of the author, copyright © 1995.

Zeisel, Hans, & Callahan, Thomas, Split Trials and Time Saving: A Statistical Analysis, 76 Harv. L. Rev. 1606 (1963), reprinted with permission of Harvard Law Review Association, copyright © 1963.

Except for permitting us to reproduce excerpts of their work in this book, all copyright holders have retained all rights in their works.

SUMMARY OF CONTENTS

PREFACE v
ACKNOWLEDGMENTS ix
SUMMARY OF CONTENTS xv
TABLE OF CONTENTS xxi
TABLE OF CASES xli
TABLE OF AUTHORITIES lxxv

CHAPTER ONE: An Overview of Complex Litigation: Theory, History, and Practice 1

Sec.
A. The Fundamental Principles of Civil Procedure 3
B. The Origins of American Civil Procedure 27
   1. English Procedure after the Norman Conquest 28
      a. The Writ System 29
      b. Common Law Procedure 31
      c. The Rise of Equity 36
   2. American Civil Procedure after the Revolution 47
   3. American Procedure from 1938 to the Present: Living in the Shadow of the Federal Rules of Civil Procedure 56
C. Procedural Systems in Practice: A Comparative Perspective 60
   1. Alternative Adversary Systems 61
      a. In the United States — Public Law Litigation 61
      b. In Britain 67
   2. Civil Procedure in Civil Law Countries 68
   3. Civil Procedure in Socialist Countries 74
D. The Nature of Complex Civil Litigation: An Overview 82

PART ONE: JOINDER COMPLEXITY 87

CHAPTER TWO: Joinder, Preclusion, and Litigant Autonomy 91

Sec.
A. Using Joinder Rules to Overcome Joinder Complexity 93
   1. Voluntary Joinder of Plaintiffs under Rule 20 93
   2. Involuntary Joinder of Defendants under Rule 20 109
   3. Rule Permitting Mandatory Joinder 115
      a. Mandatory Joinder under Rule 19 116
      b. Class Actions under Rule 23 132
      c. Statutory and Rule Interpleader 134
   4. Intervention or Participation by Nonparties 136
B. Using Preclusion Rules as an Alternative Way to Overcome Joinder Complexity 155

Sec.

1. Existing Preclusion Rules 156
2. The Limits of Preclusion Law in Complex and Complicated Cases 174
   a. Precluding Parties that Participated in a Prior Case 174
   b. Precluding Persons that Did Not Participate in a Prior Case 207

C. Marrying Party Joinder and Preclusion: The Brave New World of Preclusion after Notice and Opportunity to Intervene 239

CHAPTER THREE: Limitations on the Aggregation of Related Cases in a Federal System 258

Sec.

A. Limitations on Aggregation Imposed by Territorial Jurisdiction . 260
   1. Territorial Jurisdiction over Defendants 262
   2. Territorial Jurisdiction over Plaintiffs 293
B. Limitations on Aggregation Imposed by Subject Matter Jurisdiction 310
   1. The Basic Rules and Their Limits in Complex and Complicated Litigation 311
      a. Federal Question Jurisdiction 312
      b. Diversity Jurisdiction 325
      c. Supplemental Jurisdiction 340
      d. The Eleventh Amendment 360
      e. Case or Controversy 362
   2. Overcoming the Basic Rules to Achieve Aggregation in a Single Court System 372
      a. Removal Jurisdiction 373
      b. Injunctions and Stays that Preclude One Court System from Hearing Claims 389
         i. Injunctions against Suits in Other Courts 390
         ii. Stays of Federal (or State) Proceedings in Favor of State (or Federal) Proceedings: Herein of Abstention 426
            a) Abstention by Federal Courts in Favor of State Proceedings 426
            b) Abstention by State Courts in Favor of Federal Proceedings 437
      c. Cooperation between State and Federal Courts 442

CHAPTER FOUR: Limitations on the Aggregation of Related Cases Pending in a Single Court System 449

Sec.

A. Limitations on Aggregation Imposed by Venue Rules 450
B. Overcoming Venue Limitations to Achieve Aggregation in a Single Forum 457
   1. Injunctions and Stays that Permit the Case to Proceed Only in a Designated Venue 457
      a. The *Forum Non Conveniens* Dismissal 458

Sec.
      b. The *Kerotest* Stay and Related Doctrines 467
   2. Transfer Devices that Aggregate Cases in a Single Venue ... 473
      a. Consolidation 473
      b. Venue Transfers under § 1404 487
      c. Mass Multidistrict Transfers under § 1407 494
C. Beyond the Present Doctrine 525

CHAPTER FIVE: Class Actions 530

Sec.
A. The Advantages and Disadvantages of Class Actions as an Aggregation Device 531
   1. Doctrinal Advantages and Disadvantages 531
   2. Policy Concerns of Class Actions 535
B. Balancing the Benefits and Risks of Class Action: The Present Limits of Rule 23 550
   1. The Mechanics of Certification Practice 550
   2. Litigation Class Actions 555
      a. Existence and Definition of a Class 556
      b. Membership in a Class 559
      c. Numerosity 559
      d. The Critical Elements of Rule 23(a): Commonality, Typicality, and Adequacy of Representation 564
      e. The Final Requirement: Qualifying Under Rule 23(b) ... 583
        i. Class Actions with No Opt-out Right 584
          a) Incompatible Standards and Limited Fund Class Actions 584
          b) Equitable Class Actions: Rule 23(b)(2) 598
          c) Constitutional and Jurisdictional Limitations on Mandatory Class Actions 613
        ii. Class Actions with an Opt-out Right: Rule 23(b)(3) .. 620
          a) Commercial Common Question Class Actions 621
          b) Mass Tort Common Question Class Actions 630
   3. Settlement Class Actions 647
   4. Defendant Class Actions 689
C. The Future of Class Actions 692
   1. The Reform of Rule 23 693
   2. State Court Class Actions 698

CHAPTER SIX: Compulsory Consolidation in Bankruptcy 702

Sec.
A. **Primer on Bankruptcy** 703
   1. Jurisdiction and Procedure 703
   2. Substance 709
B. Stretching Bankruptcy to Meet the Needs of Complex Litigation . 715
   1. Consolidating Present Cases and Claims against a Debtor in a Single Forum 715

Sec.

    2. Using the Bankruptcy Forum to Consolidate Cases and Claims against Other Defendants 730
    3. Using Bankruptcy to Aggregate the Claims of Future Plaintiffs in a Single Forum 752
C. Modifying a Reorganization Plan 769
D. Class Action or Bankruptcy? 778
E. Concluding Thoughts 787

CHAPTER SEVEN: The Impact of Choice of Law on the Joinder of Related Cases 789

Sec.

A. Choice of Law Issues in a Federal System 791
    1. Choice of Law: Basic Principles and Limitations 791
    2. Federal Courts and Choice of Law: Further Confusion or Possible Solution? 804
        a. The Approach in Diversity Cases: The Confusion? 805
        b. The Approach in Federal Question Cases: The Solution? 819
B. Expanding the Solution to Claims Based on State Law: Alternatives and Their Limits 832
    1. Manipulating Traditional Choice of Law Rules in Complex And Complicated Cases 833
    2. Creating Federal Common Law 844
    3. Creating National Consensus Law 855
    4. Using the Law of the Most Restrictive Jurisdiction 865
    5. Choosing a Single Law with a Right to Opt Out or Opt In 868
    6. Creating Federal Choice of Law Principles 869

PART TWO: PRETRIAL COMPLEXITY 875

CHAPTER EIGHT: Selecting Lawyers and Judicial Officers for the Pretrial Stage 878

Sec.

A. Selecting a Counsel Structure 879
    1. The Initial Selection of Counsel 879
    2. The Work and Structure of the Litigation Team 891
    3. Disqualification of Counsel 898
    4. Withdrawal of Counsel 914
B. Selecting Judicial Officers to Manage the Pretrial Process: Judges, Masters, and Magistrates 925
    1. Historical and Theoretical Perspectives on the Judge as Case Manager 926
    2. Choosing the Judicial Officer(s) to Manage the Case 937
        a. Using Multiple Judges for Pretrial Matters 938
        b. Using Masters for Pretrial Matters 939
        c. Using Magistrate Judges for Pretrial Matters 955
    3. Recusal of a Judicial Officer 960

CHAPTER NINE: Narrowing Issues and Discovering Facts 977

Sec.

A. Issue Narrowing Techniques 979
    1. Pleading Requirements in Complex Cases 979
        a. Pleading with Heightened Specificity 979
        b. Ordering Consolidated Pleadings 993
    2. Narrowing the Issues after the Initial Pleadings 1000
        a. Clearing away the Deadwood: Motions to Dismiss and Other Early Dispositive Devices 1000
        b. Common Case Management Techniques: Herein of the Case Management Order 1007
            i. Establishing Early, Firm Deadlines 1010
            ii. Bifurcating Pretrial Issues 1019
            iii. Forcing Pretrial Stipulations 1030
            iv. Adjudicating Disputed Issues 1042
            v. Using Prior Judgments 1079
            vi. Providing (or Withholding) Advice 1083
B. Discovery Techniques 1086
    1. The Discovery Plan 1088
    2. Traditional Discovery: Problems and Possible Solutions ... 1091
        a. Traditional Discovery Devices: A Review 1091
        b. Making the Process of Discovery Efficient in Complex And Complicated Cases 1098
        c. Imposing Limitations on the Quantity of Discovery 1126
        d. Resolving Discovery Disputes Effectively 1136
    3. Non-Traditional Discovery Techniques 1152
        a. Interviews and Surveys in Lieu of Depositions and Interrogatories 1153
        b. Discovery in Foreign Legal Systems 1162
        c. Alternative Means of Obtaining Information from Governmental and Private Sources 1168
        d. Alternative Means of Obtaining Opinions from Experts . 1170
C. Information Technology: The Solution to Pretrial Complexity? . 1173
    1. A Primer on Automated Litigation Support 1173
    2. Legal Issues Involving Automated Litigation Support 1183

PART THREE: TRIAL COMPLEXITY 1197

CHAPTER TEN: Selecting Lawyers, Factfinders, and Judicial Officers for Trial 1200

Sec.

A. Selecting Trial Counsel 1201
B. Selecting the Decision Maker(s) for Trial 1208
    1. Selecting the Factfinder 1209
        a. Background: The Right to a Civil Jury Trial 1209
        b. The Power of the Trial Judge to Strike a Jury in Complex or Complicated Litigation 1219

Sec.

    c. The Power of the Judge to Appoint Alternative Factfinders in Complex or Complicated Bench Trials ... 1245
  2. Selecting the Lawgiver in Complex Cases 1261

CHAPTER ELEVEN: Trying a Complex Case 1265

Sec.

A. Creating the Courtroom 1266
B. Techniques to Limit Information at Trial 1273
  1. Limiting Issues and Claims 1273
  2. Trial by Statistics 1294
  3. Multiple Juries 1316
  4. Time Limits on Trial 1319
  5. Presenting Evidence in Summary or Narrative Form 1326
C. Techniques to Make Trial Information More Comprehensible 1333
  1. Amending the Usual Order and Structure of Trial 1333
  2. Using High-Tech Demonstrative Evidence 1338
  3. Handling Expert Testimony, Court Appointed Experts, and Masters 1347
  4. Questioning and Commenting by Judge and Jury 1359
  5. Jury Notetaking 1373
  6. Fashioning Comprehensible Jury Instructions 1376
  7. Changing Deliberation Patterns: Special Verdicts, Verdicts With Interrogatories, and Sequential Verdicts 1378
D. Concluding Thoughts 1383

PART FOUR: REMEDIAL COMPLEXITY 1385

CHAPTER TWELVE: Declaring and Implementing Remedies 1387

Sec.

A. Defining the Remedy 1387
  1. Injunctive Relief 1388
  2. Monetary Relief 1404
  3. Using Judicial Adjuncts to Assist in the Process of Declaring a Remedy 1419
  4. Methods of Declaring the Remedy that Reduce Intransigence 1422
B. Implementing the Remedy 1423
  1. Injunctive Relief 1424
  2. Monetary Relief 1435
  3. Using Judicial Adjuncts to Assist in the Process of Implementing a Remedy 1443
  4. Removing Roadblocks to the Implementation of the Remedy: Nonparty Intransigence 1448

TABLE OF CONTENTS

Preface v
Acknowledgments ix
Summary of Contents xv
Table of Contents xxi
Table of Cases xli
Table of Authorities lxxv

CHAPTER ONE: An Overview of Complex Litigation: Theory, History, and Practice 1

Sec.
A. The Fundamental Principles of Civil Procedure 3
   John Rawls, *A Theory of Justice* 3
   Notes and Questions 4
   Richard A. Posner, *Economic Analysis of Law* 8
   Notes and Questions 9
   Robert A. Bush, *Dispute Resolution Alternatives and Achieving the Goals of Justice: Jurisdictional Principles for Process Choice* ... 10
   Notes and Questions 12
   Lon L. Fuller, *The Forms and Limits of Adjudication* .. 13
   Notes and Questions 17
   Stephen A. Saltzburg, *Lawyers, Clients, and the Adversary System* 20
   Geoffrey C. Hazard, Jr., *Ethics in the Practice of Law* .. 22
   Notes and Questions 25
B. The Origins of American Civil Procedure 27
   1. English Procedure after the Norman Conquest 28
      S.F.C. Milsom, *Historical Foundations of the Common Law* ... 28
      a. The Writ System 29
      b. Common Law Procedure 31
         Notes and Questions 35
      c. The Rise of Equity 36
         Theodore F.T. Plucknett, *A Concise History of the Common Law* 36
         F.W. Maitland, *Equity* 37
         Theodore F.T. Plucknett, *A Concise History of the Common Law* 38
         Theodore F.T. Plucknett, *A Concise History of the Common Law* 40
         S.F.C. Milsom, *Historical Foundations of the Common Law* 42

Sec.

B. **The Origins of Modern American Adversary Procedure —** Continued

        Notes and Questions 43
        William Holdsworth, *A History of English Law* 44
        Charles S. Christopher, *The Reign of Queen Victoria: A Survey of Fifty Years of Progress* 45
        Notes and Questions 46

  2. American Civil Procedure after the Revolution 47
      Robert W. Millar, *Civil Procedure of the Trial Court in Historical Perspective* 47
      William E. Nelson, *Americanization of the Common Law* 47
      Notes and Questions 48
      Fleming James, Jr., et al., *Civil Procedure* 50
      Charles E. Clark, *Handbook on the Law of Code Pleading* 51
      Notes and Questions 51
      Roscoe Pound, *The Causes of Popular Dissatisfaction with the Administration of Justice* 53
      Roscoe Pound, *The Decadence of Equity* 54
      Roscoe Pound, *Some Principles of Procedural Reform* 54
      Notes and Questions 54

  3. American Procedure from 1938 to the Present: Living in the Shadow of the Federal Rules of Civil Procedure 56
      Stephen N. Subrin, *How Equity Conquered Common Law: The Federal Rules of Civil Procedure in Historical Perspective* 57
      Jay Tidmarsh, *Unattainable Justice: The Form of Complex Litigation and the Limits of Judicial Power* 57
      Notes and Questions 59

C. **Procedural Systems in Practice: A Comparative Perspective** 60

  1. Alternative Adversary Systems 61
    a. In the United States — Public Law Litigation 61
      Abram Chayes, *The Role of the Judge in Public Law Litigation* 61
      Notes and Questions 64
    b. In Britain 67
      Jerold L. Waltman, *Judicial Activism in England* 67
      Notes and Questions 68

  2. Civil Procedure in Civil Law Countries 68
      Mary A. Glendon, Michael W. Gordon & Christopher Osakwe, *Comparative Legal Traditions* 69
      John H. Langbein, *The German Advantage in Civil Procedure* 70
      Notes and Questions 74

Sec.

C. **Procedural Systems in Practice: A Comparative Perspective**
   — Continued
   3. Civil Procedure in Socialist Countries 74
      Mary A. Glendon, Michael W. Gordon & Christopher Osakwe, *Comparative Legal Traditions* 74
      Shao-chuan Leng, *Justice in Communist China* 78
      Notes and Questions 79

D. **The Nature of Complex Civil Litigation: An Overview** 82
   Manual for Complex and Multidistrict Litigation 83
   American Law Institute, *Complex Litigation: Statutory Recommendations and Analysis* 84
   Manual For Complex Litigation, Third 84
   Notes and Questions 85
   Jay Tidmarsh, *Unattainable Justice: The Form of Complex Litigation and the Limits of Judicial Power* 85
   Notes and Questions 86

PART ONE: JOINDER COMPLEXITY 87

CHAPTER TWO: Joinder, Preclusion, and Litigant Autonomy 91

Sec.

A. **Using Joinder Rules to Overcome Joinder Complexity** 93
   1. Voluntary Joinder of Plaintiffs under Rule 20 93
      Mosley v. General Motors Corp. 93
      Grayson v. K Mart Corp. 97
      Aaberg v. ACandS Inc. 101
      Irwin A. Horowitz & Kenneth S. Bordens, *The Effects of Outlier Presence, Plaintiff Population Size, and Aggregation of Plaintiffs on Simulated Civil Jury Decisions* 102
      Notes and Questions 103
   2. Involuntary Joinder of Defendants under Rule 20 109
      Nassau County Association of Insurance Agents, Inc. v. Aetna Life & Casualty Co. 109
      Notes and Questions 111
   3. Rule Permitting Mandatory Joinder 115
      a. Mandatory Joinder under Rule 19 116
         Temple v. Synthes Corp. 116
         Eldredge v. Carpenter 46 Northern California Counties JATC 117
         William B. Rubenstein, *Divided We Litigate: Addressing Disputes among Group Members and Lawyers in Civil Rights Cases* 120

Sec.

A. Using Joinder Rules to Overcome Joinder Complexity —
Continued

        Deborah R. Hensler, *Resolving Mass Toxic Torts: Myths And Realities* 124
        Notes and Questions 126

    b. Class Actions under Rule 23 132

    c. Statutory and Rule Interpleader 134

  4. Intervention or Participation by Nonparties 136
      Cook v. Boorstin 137
      Trbovich v. United Mine Workers of America 144
      Notes and Questions 145

B. Using Preclusion Rules as an Alternative Way to Overcome Joinder Complexity 155

  1. Existing Preclusion Rules 156
      Federated Department Stores, Inc. v. Moitie 156
      Parklane Hosiery Co. v. Shore 160
      Notes and Questions 166

  2. The Limits of Preclusion Law in Complex and Complicated Cases 174

    a. Precluding Parties that Participated in a Prior Case 174
        Cooper v. Federal Reserve Bank of Richmond 174
        Epstein v. MCA, Inc. 179
        Notes and Questions 191
        Hardy v. Johns-Manville Sales Corp. 194
        Notes and Questions 201

    b. Precluding Persons that Did Not Participate in a Prior Case 207
        Richards v. Jefferson County, Alabama 208
        Tyus v. Schoemehl 213
        Hardy v. Johns-Manville Sales Corp. 222
        Lynch v. Merrell-National Laboratories 225
        Notes and Questions 228

C. Marrying Party Joinder and Preclusion: The Brave New World of Preclusion after Notice and Opportunity to Intervene 239

  Martin v. Wilks 240
  42 U.S.C. § 2000e-2(n) 248
  American Law Institute, *Complex Litigation: Statutory Recommendations and Analysis* 249
  Notes and Questions 251

CHAPTER THREE: Limitations on the Aggregation of Related Cases in a Federal System 258

Sec.

A. **Limitations on Aggregation Imposed by Territorial Jurisdiction** 260
   1. Territorial Jurisdiction over Defendants 262
      World-Wide Volkswagen v. Woodson 262
      Asahi Metal Industry Co. v. Superior Court of California 267
      Notes and Questions 272
      In re DES Cases 278
      American Law Institute, *Complex Litigation: Statutory Recommendations and Analysis* 288
      Notes and Questions 289
   2. Territorial Jurisdiction over Plaintiffs 293
      Phillips Petroleum Co. v. Shutts 294
      In re Asbestos Litigation 301
      In re General Motors Corp. Pick-Up Truck Fuel Tank Products Liability Litigation 304
      Notes and Questions 305

B. **Limitations on Aggregation Imposed by Subject Matter Jurisdiction** 310
   1. The Basic Rules and Their Limits in Complex and Complicated Litigation 311
      a. Federal Question Jurisdiction 312
         Osborn v. Bank of the United States 312
         Merrell Dow Pharmaceuticals, Inc. v. Thompson 314
         Notes and Questions 320
      b. Diversity Jurisdiction 325
         State Farm Fire & Casualty Co. v. Tashire 325
         Strawbridge v. Curtiss 327
         Notes and Questions 328
         Zahn v. International Paper Co. 332
         Notes and Questions 337
      c. Supplemental Jurisdiction 340
         In re Abbott Laboratories 349
         Notes and Questions 352
      d. The Eleventh Amendment 360
      e. Case or Controversy 362
         Carlough v. Amchem Products, Inc. 363
         Notes and Questions 370
   2. Overcoming the Basic Rules to Achieve Aggregation in a Single Court System 372
      a. Removal Jurisdiction 373
         In re General Motors Corp. Pick-Up Truck Fuel Tank Products Liability Litigation 374

Sec.

  B. **Limitations on Aggregation Imposed by Subject Matter Jurisdiction** — Continued

        People of the State of California v. Keating 377
        American Law Institute, *Complex Litigation: Statutory Recommendations and Analysis* 379
        Notes and Questions 381

    b. Injunctions and Stays that Preclude One Court System from Hearing Claims 389

       i. Injunctions against Suits in Other Courts 390

           In re Corrugated Container Antitrust Litigation 393
           Notes and Questions 396
           In re Baldwin-United Corp. 401
           American Law Institute, *Complex Litigation: Statutory Recommendations and Analysis* 408
           Notes and Questions 409
           State Farm Fire & Casualty Co. v. Tashire 413
           Notes and Questions 416
           Note on the Bill of Peace 423

       ii. Stays of Federal (or State) Proceedings in Favor of State (or Federal) Proceedings: Herein of Abstention   426

          a) Abstention by Federal Courts in Favor of State Proceedings 426

              Notes and Questions 435

          b) Abstention by State Courts in Favor of Federal Proceedings 437

    c. Cooperation between State and Federal Courts 442

        William W Schwarzer et al., *Judicial Federalism in Action: Coordination of Litigation in State and Federal Courts* 442
        Notes and Questions 446

CHAPTER FOUR: Limitations on the Aggregation of Related Cases Pending in a Single Court System 449

Sec.

A. **Limitations on Aggregation Imposed by Venue Rules** 450

B. **Overcoming Venue Limitations to Achieve Aggregation in a Single Forum** 457

    1. Injunctions and Stays that Permit the Case to Proceed Only in a Designated Venue 457

      a. The *Forum Non Conveniens* Dismissal 458

        Kempe v. Ocean Drilling & Exploration Co. 458
        Notes and Questions 464

Sec.

B. **Overcoming Venue Limitations to Achieve Aggregation in a Single Forum** — Continued

    b. The *Kerotest* Stay and Related Doctrines 467

  2. Transfer Devices that Aggregate Cases in a Single Venue ... 473

    a. Consolidation 473

      Johnson v. Celotex Corp. 473
      Malcolm v. National Gypsum Co. 476
      In re: Repetitive Stress Injury Litigation 482
      Notes and Questions 484

    b. Venue Transfers under §1404 487

      In re Joint Eastern and Southern Districts Asbestos Litigation 487
      Hoffman v. Blaski 489
      Notes and Questions 491

    c. Mass Multidistrict Transfers under § 1407 494

      In re "East of the Rockies" Concrete Pipe Antitrust Cases 495
      In re Asbestos and Asbestos Insulation Material Products Liability Litigation 498
      In re Asbestos Products Liability Litigation (No. VI) 501
      Notes and Questions 509
      Lexecon Inc. v. Milberg Weiss Bershad Hynes & Lerach .. 516
      Notes and Questions 523

C. **Beyond the Present Doctrine** 525

  American Law Institute, *Complex Litigation: Statutory Recommendations and Analysis* 525
  Notes and Questions 527

CHAPTER FIVE: Class Actions 530

Sec.

A. **The Advantages and Disadvantages of Class Actions as an Aggregation Device** 531

  1. Doctrinal Advantages and Disadvantages 531
  2. Policy Concerns of Class Actions 535

    Hansberry v. Lee 535
    Notes and Questions 538
    In the Matter of Rhone-Poulenc Rorer Inc. 540
    Notes and Questions 545

B. **Balancing the Benefits and Risks of Class Action: The Present Limits of Rule 23** 550

  1. The Mechanics of Certification Practice 550
  2. Litigation Class Actions 555

Sec.

B. **Balancing the Benefits and Risks of Class Action: The Present Limits of Rule 23 — Continued**

    a. Existence and Definition of a Class 556
        Rice v. City of Philadelphia 556
        Notes and Questions 558
    b. Membership in a Class 559
    c. Numerosity 559
        Roubidoux v. Celani 560
        Notes and Questions 562
    d. The Critical Elements of Rule 23(a): Commonality, Typicality, and Adequacy of Representation 564
        General Telephone Co. of the Southwest v. Falcon 564
        Dolgow v. Anderson 570
        In re American Medical Systems, Inc. 574
        Notes and Questions 579
    e. The Final Requirement: Qualifying Under Rule 23(b) ... 583
        i. Class Actions with No Opt-out Right 584
           a) Incompatible Standards and Limited Fund Class Actions 584
                In re Greenman Securities Litigation 585
                In re Telectronics Pacing Systems, Inc., Accufix Atrial "J" Leads Products Liability Litigation   589
                In re "Agent Orange" Product Liability Litigation.   593
                Notes and Questions 596
           b) Equitable Class Actions: Rule 23(b)(2) 598
                Allison v. Citgo Petroleum Co. 599
                Cook v. Rockwell International Corp. 606
                Notes and Questions 607
           c) Constitutional and Jurisdictional Limitations on Mandatory Class Actions 613
                Phillips Petroleum Co. v. Shutts 613
                In re Asbestos Litigation 613
                Notes and Questions 613
                In re Federal Skywalk Class 614
                Notes and Questions 616
                Allison v. Citgo Petroleum Co. 617
                Notes and Questions 619
        ii. Class Actions with an Opt-out Right: Rule 23(b)(3) .. 620
           a) Commercial Common Question Class Actions ... 621
                Kirkpatrick v. J.C. Bradford & Co. 622
                Notes and Questions 627
           b) Mass Tort Common Question Class Actions 630

Sec.

B. **Balancing the Benefits and Risks of Class Actions: The Present Limits of Rule 23** — Continued

    Roger H. Trangsrud, *Joinder Alternatives in Mass Tort Litigation* 630
    Jenkins v. Raymark Industries, Inc. 632
    Castano v. American Tobacco Co. 636
    Notes and Questions 643

  3. Settlement Class Actions 647
    In re Baldwin-United Corp. 648
    Notes and Questions 653
    In re Asbestos Litigation 658
    Amchem Products, Inc. v. Windsor 670
    Notes and Questions 684

  4. Defendant Class Actions 689

C. **The Future of Class Actions** 692

  1. The Reform of Rule 23 693
    Proposed Revision to Rule 23 693
    Proposed Revision to Rule 23 695
    Notes and Questions 696

  2. State Court Class Actions 698
    Spitzfaden v. Dow Corning Corp. 698
    Notes and Questions 700

CHAPTER SIX: Compulsory Consolidation in Bankruptcy .. 702

Sec.

A. **A Primer on Bankruptcy** 703

  1. Jurisdiction and Procedure 703
  2. Substance 709
    Douglas G. Baird, *The Elements of Bankruptcy* 710
    David L. Buchbinder, *Fundamentals of Bankruptcy* 711
    Notes and Questions 714

B. **Stretching Bankruptcy to Meet the Needs of Complex Litigation** 715

  1. Consolidating Present Cases and Claims against a Debtor in a Single Forum 715
    A.H. Robins Co. v. Piccinin 715
    In re A.H. Robins Co. 720
    Notes and Questions 723

  2. Using the Bankruptcy Forum to Consolidate Cases and Claims against Other Defendants 730
    In re Dow Corning Corp. 730

Sec.

B. **Stretching Bankruptcy to Meet the Needs of Complex Litigation** — Continued
    Notes and Questions 738
    A.H. Robins v. Piccinin 742
    In re A.H. Robins Co. 746
    Notes and Questions 748
  3. Using Bankruptcy to Aggregate the Claims of Future Plaintiffs in a Single Forum 752
    Grady v. A.H. Robins Co. 752
    In re Johns-Manville Corp. 755
    Thomas A. Smith, *A Capital Markets Approach to Mass Tort Bankruptcy* 757
    Epstein v. Official Committee of Unsecured Creditors, of the Estate of Piper Aircraft Corp. 759
    Notes and Questions 763

C. **Modifying a Reorganization Plan** 769
    In re Joint Eastern and Southern District Asbestos Litigation 771
    Notes and Questions 777

D. **Class Action or Bankruptcy?** 778
    In re: Joint Eastern and Southern District Asbestos Litigation ... 778
    In re Asbestos Litigation 780
    Notes and Questions 785

E. **Concluding Thoughts** 787

CHAPTER SEVEN: The Impact of Choice of Law on the Joinder of Related Cases 789

Sec.

A. **Choice of Law Issues in a Federal System** 791
  1. Choice of Law: Basic Principles and Limitations 791
    Friedrich K. Juenger, *Mass Disasters and the Conflict of Laws* 791
    American Law Institute, *Restatement (Second) of Conflict of Laws* 794
    Notes and Questions 795
    Phillips Petroleum Co. v. Shutts 797
    Notes and Questions 801
  2. Federal Courts and Choice of Law: Further Confusion or Possible Solution? 804
    a. The Approach in Diversity Cases: The Confusion? 805
      Day & Zimmerman, Inc. v. Challoner 805
      Notes and Questions 807
      Ferens v. John Deere Co. 809
      Notes and Questions 816

Sec.

A. Choice of Law Issues in a Federal System — Continued
   b. The Approach in Federal Question Cases: The Solution? 819
      In re Korean Air Lines Disaster of September 1, 1983 820
      American Law Institute, *Complex Litigation: Statutory Recommendations and Analysis* 824
      Robert A. Ragazzo, *Transfer and Choice of Federal Law: The Appellate Model* 824
      Notes and Questions 826

B. Expanding the Solution to Claims Based on State Law: Alternatives and Their Limits 832
   1. Manipulating Traditional Choice of Law Rules in Complex And Complicated Cases 833
      In re Air Crash Disaster near Chicago, Illinois on May 25, 1979 833
      Notes and Questions 841
   2. Creating Federal Common Law 844
      Kohr v. Allegheny Airlines, Inc. 845
      In re "Agent Orange" Product Liability Litigation 847
      Notes and Questions 851
   3. Creating National Consensus Law 855
      In re "Agent Orange" Product Liability Litigation 855
      In the Matter of Rhone-Poulenc Rorer Inc. 860
      Notes and Questions 862
   4. Using the Law of the Most Restrictive Jurisdiction 865
      In re School Asbestos Litigation 865
      Notes and Questions 867
   5. Choosing a Single Law with a Right to Opt Out or Opt In ... 868
   6. Creating Federal Choice of Law Principles 869
      American Bar Association Commission on Mass Torts, *Report To the House of Delegates* 870
      American Law Institute, *Complex Litigation: Statutory Recommendations and Analysis* 870
      Notes and Questions 872

PART TWO: PRETRIAL COMPLEXITY 875

CHAPTER EIGHT: Selecting Lawyers and Judicial Officers for the Pretrial Stage 878

Sec.

A. Selecting a Counsel Structure 879
   1. The Initial Selection of Counsel 879

Sec.

A. **Selecting a Counsel Structure — Continued**

    Richardson-Merrell, Inc. v. Koller 879
    Manual for Complex Litigation, Third 879
    Vincent v. Hughes Air West, Inc. 881
    Notes and Questions 885

  2. The Work and Structure of the Litigation Team 891

    In re: MGM Grand Fire Hotel Litigation 891
    Danny P. Richey, *Guidelines and Techniques For Leading and Managing the Litigation Team* 893
    Notes and Questions 897

  3. Disqualification of Counsel 898

    In re "Agent Orange" Product Liability Litigation 899
    Jack B. Weinstein, *Individual Justice In Mass Tort Litigation* 904
    Notes and Questions 906

  4. Withdrawal of Counsel 914

    Haines v. Liggett Group, Inc. 915
    Notes and Questions 921

B. **Selecting Judicial Officers to Manage the Pretrial Process: Judges, Masters, and Magistrates** 925

  1. Historical and Theoretical Perspectives on the Judge as Case Manager 926

    Report of the Judicial Conference of the United States on Procedure in Anti-Trust and Other Protracted Cases 926
    Handbook of Recommended Procedures for the Trial of Protracted Cases 926
    Manual for Complex Litigation, Third 927
    Notes and Questions 928
    John H. Langbein, *The German Advantage in Civil Procedure* 930
    Judith Resnik, *Managerial Judges* 931
    E. Donald Elliott, *Managerial Judging and the Evolution of Procedures* 934
    Notes and Questions 936

  2. Choosing the Judicial Officer(s) to Manage the Case 937

    a. Using Multiple Judges for Pretrial Matters 938

      Manual for Complex Litigation, Third 938
      Notes and Questions 939

    b. Using Masters for Pretrial Matters 939

      In re "Agent Orange" Product Liability Litigation 939
      Prudential Insurance Co. of America v. United States Gypsum Co. 942
      Notes and Questions 947

Sec.

B. Selecting the Judicial Officer to Manage the Pretrial Process: Judges, Masters, and Magistrates — Continued
- c. Using Magistrate Judges for Pretrial Matters 955
  - *Manual for Complex Litigation, Third* 955
  - *Notes and Questions* 956
- 3. Recusal of a Judicial Officer 960
  - *In re School Asbestos Litigation* 961
  - Jack B. Weinstein, *Individual Justice In Mass Tort Litigation* 968
  - *Notes and Questions* 968

CHAPTER NINE: Narrowing Issues and Discovering Facts 977

Sec.

A. Issue Narrowing Techniques 979
  1. Pleading Requirements in Complex Cases 979
     a. Pleading with Heightened Specificity 979
        - *Nagler v. Admiral Corp.* 980
        - *Northland Insurance Co. v. Shell Oil Co.* 983
        - *Notes and Questions* 987
     b. Ordering Consolidated Pleadings 993
        - *Katz v. Realty Equities Corp. Of New York* .. 994
        - *Notes and Questions* 997
  2. Narrowing the Issues after the Initial Pleadings 1000
     a. Clearing away the Deadwood: Motions to Dismiss and Other Early Dispositive Devices 1000
        - Stephen Calkins, *Summary Judgment, Motions to Dismiss, and Other Examples of Equilibrating Tendencies in The Antitrust System* 1001
        - *Notes and Questions* 1003
     b. Common Case Management Techniques: Herein of the Case Management Order 1007
        - *Manual for Complex Litigation, Third* 1007
        - *Notes and Questions* 1008
        - i. Establishing Early, Firm Deadlines 1010
          - *In re Fine Paper Antitrust Litigation* ... 1010
          - James S. Kakalik et al., *An Evaluation of Judicial Case Management under the Civil Justice Reform Act* 1013
          - *Notes and Questions* 1016
        - ii. Bifurcating Pretrial Issues 1019
          - *In re "Agent Orange Product Liability Litigation* ... 1020

Sec.

A. Issue Narrowing Techniques — Continued

    In re Love Canal Actions 1024
    Notes and Questions 1027

  iii. Forcing Pretrial Stipulations 1030

    United States v. American Telephone & Telegraph Co. 1031
    Notes and Questions 1036

  iv. Adjudicating Disputed Issues 1042

    National Hockey League v. Metropolitan Hockey Club, Inc. 1043
    Notes and Questions 1045
    Poller v. Columbia Broadcasting System, Inc. 1047
    Matsushita Electric Industrial Co. v. Zenith Radio Corp. 1050
    Samuel Issacharoff & George Loewenstein, *Second Thoughts about Summary Judgment* 1057
    Notes and Questions 1061
    Portsmouth Square, Inc. v. Shareholders Protective Committee 1071
    Fidelity and Deposit Co. of Maryland v. Southern Utilities, Inc. 1073
    Notes and Questions 1075

  v. Using Prior Judgments 1079

    Columbia Steel Fabricators, Inc. v. Ahlstrom Recovery 1080
    Notes and Questions 1082

  vi. Providing (or Withholding) Advice 1083

B. Discovery Techniques 1086

1. The Discovery Plan 1088

  Manual for Complex Litigation, Third 1089
  Notes and Questions 1089

2. Traditional Discovery: Problems and Possible Solutions ... 1091

  a. Traditional Discovery Devices: A Review 1091

    Fleming James Jr. et al., *Civil Procedure* 1092
    Notes and Questions 1092

  b. Making the Process of Discovery Efficient in Complex And Complicated Cases 1098

    Manual for Complex Litigation, Third 1098
    In re Three Additional Appeals Arising out of the San Juan DuPont Plaza Hotel Fire Litigation 1099
    Notes and Questions 1103
    United States v. American Telephone & Telegraph Co. ... 1106
    Notes and Questions 1109

Sec.

B. **Discovery Techniques** — Continued

   Klein v. King 1117
   Notes and Questions 1121

  c. Imposing Limitations on the Quantity of Discovery 1126
   Marrese v. American Academy of Orthopaedic Surgeons . 1127
   Notes and Questions 1132

  d. Resolving Discovery Disputes Effectively 1136
   Manual for Complex Litigation, Third 1137
   Notes and Questions 1138
   In re "Agent Orange" Product Liability Litigation 1140
   Notes and Questions 1144

 3. Non-Traditional Discovery Techniques 1152

  a. Interviews and Surveys in Lieu of Depositions and Interrogatories 1153
   Francis E. McGovern & E. Allen Lind, *The Discovery Survey* 1153
   Notes and Questions 1159

  b. Discovery in Foreign Legal Systems 1162

  c. Alternative Means of Obtaining Information from Governmental and Private Sources 1168

  d. Alternative Means of Obtaining Opinions from Experts . 1170

C. **Information Technology: The Solution to Pretrial Complexity?** 1173

 1. A Primer on Automated Litigation Support 1173
  Phyllis V. Deets & Gowan Deets, *The Application of EIM/OCR Technology to Litigation Case Management* . 1174
  Manual for Cooperation between State and Federal Courts .. 1175
  Phyllis V. Deets & Gowan Deets, *The Application of EIM/OCR Technology to Litigation Case Management* . 1176
  James L. Stengel & Andrew M. Calamari, *Complex Litigation* 1176
  Phyllis V. Deets & Gowan Deets, *The Application of EIM/OCR Technology to Litigation Case Management* . 1177
  Notes and Questions 1178
  Active Products Corp. v. A.H. Choitz & Co. 1180
  Notes and Questions 1182

 2. Legal Issues Involving Automated Litigation Support 1183
  Santiago v. Miles 1183
  United States v. American Telephone & Telegraph Co. 1188
  Notes and Questions 1192

PART THREE: TRIAL COMPLEXITY 1197

CHAPTER TEN: Selecting Lawyers, Factfinders, and Judicial Officers for Trial 1200

Sec.

A. **Selecting Trial Counsel** 1201

    Manual for Complex Litigation, Third 1201
    In re Air Crash Disaster at Detroit Metropolitan Airport on August 16, 1987 1202
    Roger H. Trangsrud, *Mass Trials in Mass Tort Cases: A Dissent* 1203
    Notes and Questions 1205

B. **Selecting the Decision Maker(s) for Trial** 1208

  1. Selecting the Factfinder 1209

    a. Background: The Right to a Civil Jury Trial 1209

      Ross v. Bernhard 1213
      Notes and Questions 1216

    b. The Power of the Trial Judge to Strike a Jury in Complex or Complicated Litigation 1219

      In re Boise Cascade Securities Litigation 1219
      In re: Japanese Electronic Products Antitrust Litigation 1223
      ILC Peripherals Leasing Corp. v. International Business Machine Corp. 1232
      Notes and Questions 1233
      Note on the Special Jury 1240
      Note on Voir Dire 1243

    c. The Power of the Judge to Appoint Alternative Factfinders in Complex or Complicated Bench Trials ... 1245

      Reilly v. United States 1246
      Notes and Questions 1252
      LaBuy v. Howes Leather Co. 1254
      Notes and Questions 1257

  2. Selecting the Lawgiver in Complex Cases 1261

    Reed v. Cleveland Board of Education 1261
    Notes and Questions 1263

CHAPTER ELEVEN: Trying a Complex Case 1265

Sec.

A. **Creating the Courtroom** 1266

    Fredric I. Lederer, *Technology Comes to the Courtroom, and* ... 1267
    Notes and Questions 1271

B. **Techniques to Limit Information at Trial** 1273

  1. Limiting Issues and Claims 1273

    In re Bendectin Litigation 1273

Sec.

B. **Techniques to Limit Information at Trial — Continued**

    Roger H. Trangsrud, *Mass Trials in Mass Tort Cases: A Dissent* 1281
    In the Matter of Rhone-Poulenc Rorer Inc. 1283
    Hans Zeisel & Thomas Callahan, *Split Trials and Time Saving: A Statistical Analysis* 1284
    Notes and Questions 1286

  2. Trial by Statistics 1294

    In re Fiberboard Corp. 1294
    Hilao v. Estate of Ferdinand Marcos 1299
    Notes and Questions 1306

  3. Multiple Juries 1316

    William W Schwarzer et al., *Judicial Federalism in Action: Coordination of Litigation in State and Federal Courts* . 1317
    Michael D. Green, *The Inability of Offensive Collateral Estoppel to Fulfill Its Promise: An Examination of Estoppel in Asbestos Litigation* 1318
    Notes and Questions 1319

  4. Time Limits on Trial 1319

    MCI Communications Corp. v. American Telephone and Telegraph Co. 1319
    Notes and Questions 1322

  5. Presenting Evidence in Summary or Narrative Form 1326

    Oostendorp v. Khanna 1327
    Notes and Questions 1328

C. **Techniques to Make Trial Information More Comprehensible** 1333

  1. Amending the Usual Order and Structure of Trial 1333

    Manual for Complex Litigation, Third 1333
    Notes and Questions 1334

  2. Using High-Tech Demonstrative Evidence 1338

    Hinkle v. City of Clarksburg, West Virginia 1338
    In re Air Crash Disaster 1340
    Racz v. R.T. Merryman Trucking Co. 1342
    Van Houten-Maynard v. ANR Pipeline Co. 1342
    Notes and Questions 1343

  3. Handling Expert Testimony, Court Appointed Experts, and Masters 1347

    Hiern v. Sarpy 1348
    Gates v. United States 1351
    Joe S. Cecil & Thomas E. Willging, *Accepting Daubert's Invitation: Defining a Role for Court-Appointed Experts in Assessing Scientific Validity* 1352

Sec.

C. **Techniques to Make Trial Information More Comprehensible** — Continued

    Notes and Questions 1354

  4. Questioning and Commenting by Judge and Jury 1359

    Reserve Mining Co. v. Lord 1359
    In re International Business Machines Corp. 1362
    DeBenedetto v. Goodyear Tire & Rubber Co. 1364
    Notes and Questions 1367

  5. Jury Notetaking 1373

  6. Fashioning Comprehensible Jury Instructions 1376

  7. Changing Deliberation Patterns: Special Verdicts, Verdicts With Interrogatories, and Sequential Verdicts 1378

    Jonathan D. Casper, *Restructuring the Traditional Civil Jury: The Effects of Changes in Composition and Procedures* .. 1378
    Notes and Questions 1382

D. **Concluding Thoughts** 1383

PART FOUR: REMEDIAL COMPLEXITY 1385

CHAPTER TWELVE: Declaring and Implementing Remedies 1387

Sec.

A. **Defining the Remedy** 1387

  1. Injunctive Relief 1388

    Brown v. Board of Education 1388
    Bradley v. Milliken 1389
    Missouri v. Jenkins 1392
    Notes and Questions 1401

  2. Monetary Relief 1404

    Dougherty v. Barry 1404
    Kyriazi v. Western Electric Co. 1406
    Notes and Questions 1408
    Democratic Central Committee of the District of Columbia v. Washington Metropolitan Area Transit Commission 1410
    Notes and Questions 1414

  3. Using Judicial Adjuncts to Assist in the Process of Declaring a Remedy 1419

  4. Methods of Declaring the Remedy that Reduce Intransigence 1422

B. **Implementing the Remedy** 1423

  1. Injunctive Relief 1424

Sec.

B.. Implementing the Remedy — Continued

    Missouri v. Jenkins 1424
    Notes and Questions 1433

2. Monetary Relief 1435

    In re Combustion, Inc. 1435
    Notes and Questions 1441

3. Using Judicial Adjuncts to Assist in the Process of Implementing a Remedy 1443

    Ruiz v. Estelle 1443
    Notes and Questions 1446

4. Removing Roadblocks to the Implementation of the Remedy: Nonparty Intransigence 1448

    United States v. Hall 1448
    In re U.S. Oil and Gas Litigation 1453
    Notes and Questions 1458

TABLE OF CASES

Aaberg v. ACandS Inc., 152 F.R.D. 498 (D. Md. 1994), **101**
In re **Abbott Laboratories**, 51 F.3d 524 (5th Cir. 1995), **349**
ACandS, Inc. v. Godwin, 340 Md. 334, 667 A.2d 116 (1995), 486, 1336
Ackerman v. Ackerman, 219 A.D.2d 515, 631 N.Y.S.2d 657 (1995), 471
Active Products Corp. v. A.H. Choitz & Co., 163 F.R.D. 274 (N.D. Ind. 1995), 886, **1180**
In re Activision Securities Litigation, 621 F. Supp. 415 (N.D. Cal. 1985), 689
Adair v. Sunwest Bank, 965 F.2d 777 (9th Cir. 1992), 1332
Adam v. Saenger, 303 U.S. 59 (1938), 309
Adams v. Robertson, 520 U.S. 83 (1997), 306
Adams-Arapohoe School District No. 28-J v. GAF Corp., 959 F.2d 868 (10th Cir. 1992), 1289
Addamax Corp. v. Open Software Foundation, Inc., 151 F.R.D. 504 (D. Mass. 1993), 906, 912
Adickes v. S.H. Kress & Co., 398 U.S. 144 (1970), 1061
Adsani v. Miller, 1996 WL 531858 (S.D.N.Y.), 1123
Aerojet-General Corp. v. Askew, 511 F.2d 710 (5th Cir. 1975), 217, 223, 224, 230, 234
Aetna Casualty and Insurance Co. v. Ahrens, 414 F. Supp. 1235 (S.D. Tex. 1975), 420, 421
Aetna Insurance Co. v. Lavoie, 475 U.S. 813 (1986), 971, 972, 973
Affiliated Ute Citizens v. United States, 407 U.S. 916 (1972), 1288
Affiliated Ute Citizens of Utah v. United States, 406 U.S. 128 (1972), 622, 624
African American Voting Rights Legal Defense Fund v. Villa, 54 F.3d 1345 (8th Cir. 1995), 213
In re **"Agent Orange" Product Liability Litigation**, 635 F.2d 987 (2d Cir. 1980), **847**, 864, 1020
In re **"Agent Orange" Product Liability Litigation**, 506 F. Supp. 762 (E.D.N.Y. 1980), 593, 634, **1020**, 1123
In re "Agent Orange" Product Liability Litigation, 94 F.R.D. 173 (E.D.N.Y. 1982), **939**
In re "Agent Orange" Product Liability Litigation, 571 F. Supp. 481 (E.D.N.Y. 1983), 920, 922
In re **"Agent Orange" Product Liability Litigation**, 97 F.R.D. 427 (E.D.N.Y. 1983), **1140**
In re **"Agent Orange" Product Liability Litigation**, 100 F.R.D. 718 (E.D.N.Y. 1983), **593**, 863
In re **"Agent Orange" Product Liability Litigation**, 580 F. Supp. 690 (E.D.N.Y. 1984), **855**, 1084
In re "Agent "Orange" Product Liability Litigation, 611 F. Supp. 1290 (E.D.N.Y. 1985), 1170
In re "Agent Orange" Product Liability Litigation, 611 F. Supp. 1296 (E.D.N.Y. 1985), 554
In re **"Agent Orange" Product Liability Litigation**, 800 F.2d 14 (2d Cir. 1986), **899**
In re "Agent Orange" Product Liability Litigation MDL No. 381, 818 F.2d 145 (2d Cir. 1987), 309, 864, 1417
In re "Agent Orange" Product Liability Litigation, 818 F.2d 179 (2d Cir. 1987), 1416, 1417, 1418, 1420
In re "Agent Orange" Product Liability Litigation, 818 F.2d 226 (2d Cir. 1987), 887
In re "Agent Orange" Product Liability Litigation, 821 F.2d 139 (2d Cir. 1987), 1152
In re "Agent Orange" Product Liability Litigation, 689 F. Supp. 1250 (E.D.N.Y. 1988), 1417, 1418, 1420, 1421, 1442
In re "Agent Orange" Product Liability Litigation, 996 F.2d 1425 (2d Cir. 1993), 309, 389, 400, 431, 516, 973, 975
Ahearn v. Fibreboard Corp., 1995 U.S. Dist. LEXIS 11523 (E.D. Tex.), 303, 308
Ahearn v. Fibreboard Corp., 162 F.R.D. 505 (E.D. Tex. 1995), 691
In re A.H. Robins Co. "Dalkon Shield" IUD Products Liability Litigation, 453 F. Supp. 108 (J.P.M.L. 1978), 516

A.H. Robins Co., Inc. v. Piccinin, 788 F.2d 994 (4th Cir. 1986), **715**, 722, 737, 739, **742**, 746

In Re A.H. Robins Co. Inc., 88 B.R. 742 (E.D. Va. 1988), 720

In re A.H. Robins Co., 880 F.2d 709 (4th Cir. 1989), 308, 338, **720**, **746**

In re A.H. Robins Co., 86 F.3d 364 (4th Cir. 1996), 729, 778

Aiken County v. BSP Division of Envirotech Corp., 866 F.2d 661 (4th Cir. 1988), 969, 975

In re Air Crash Disaster, 86 F.3d 498 (6th Cir. 1996), 1016, **1340**

In re Air Crash Disaster at Detroit Metropolitan Airport on August 16, 1987, 737 F. Supp. 391 (E.D. Mich. 1989), 513, 1291, 1292

In re Air Crash Disaster at Detroit Metropolitan Airport on August 16, 1987, 737 F. Supp. 396 (E.D. Mich. 1989), **1202**

In re Air Crash at Detroit Metropolitan Airport, 776 F. Supp. 316 (E.D. Mich. 1991), 169, 203

In re Air Crash at Detroit Metropolitan Airport, Detroit, Michigan, on August 16, 1987, 791 F. Supp. 1204 (E.D. Mich. 1992), 205, 827

In re Air Crash Disaster at Florida Everglades, 549 F.2d 1006 (5th Cir. 1977), 889, 1202, 1203, 1207

In re Air Crash Disaster at Sioux City, Iowa, on July 19, 1989, 734 F. Supp. 1425 (N.D. Ill. 1990), 842

In re Air Crash Disaster Near Chicago, Illinois on May 25, 1979, 644 F.2d 594 (7th Cir. 1981), **833**

In re Air Crash Disaster Near New Orleans, Louisiana, 821 F.2d 1147 (5th Cir. 1987), 462, 463

In re Air Crash Disaster Near Saigon, South Vietnam on April 4, 1975, 476 F. Supp. 521 (D.D.C. 1979), 859

In re Air Crash Disaster at Stapleton International Airport, Denver, Colorado, on November 15, 1987, 720 F. Supp. 1455 (D. Colo. 1988), 1288, 1291, 1329, 1331

In re Aircrash Disaster at Stapleton International Airport, Denver, Colorado, on November 15, 1987, 1988 WL 243502 (D. Colo.), 1104

In re Air Crash Disaster at Stapleton International Airport, Denver, Colorado, on November 15, 1987, 720 F. Supp. 1493 (D. Colo. 1989), 1329, 1330, 1331, 1332, 1333, 1344

In re Air Crash Disaster at Stapleton International Airport, Denver, Colorado, on November 15, 1987, 720 F. Supp. 1505 (D. Colo. 1989), 203, 1205

In re Air Crash off Long Island, New York, on July 17, 1996, 965 F. Supp. 5 (S.D.N.Y. 1997), 511

In re Air Disaster, 819 F. Supp. 1352 (E.D. Mich. 1993), 827

In re Air Fare Litigation, 322 F. Supp. 1013 (J.P.M.L. 1971), 510

Air Line Stewards and Stewardesses Association, Local 550 v. American Airlines, Inc., 490 F.2d 636 (7th Cir. 1973), 611

In re Airline Ticket Commission Antitrust Litigation, 918 F. Supp. 283 (D. Minn. 1996), 1161, 1162

In re Airline Ticket Commission Antitrust Litigation, 1996 WL 585301 (D. Minn.), 1162

Akers v. Bonifasti, 629 F. Supp. 1212 (M.D. Tenn. 1985), 923

Alabama v. Blue Bird Body Co., 573 F.2d 309 (5th Cir. 1978), 639, 643

Albrecht v. Zwaanshoek Holding en Financiering, B.V., 762 P.2d 1174 (Wyo. 1988), 471

Aldinger v. Howard, 427 U.S. 1 (1976), 346, 347, 348

Alemite Manufacturing Corp. v. Staff, 42 F.2d 832 (2d Cir. 1930), 1450, 1451

Alexander v. National Farmers Organization, 687 F.2d 1173 (8th Cir. 1982), 1105

Alexander v. Primerica Holdings, Inc., 822 F. Supp. 1099 (D.N.J. 1993), 906, 911, 912

Alkot Industries, Inc. v. Takara Co., 106 F.R.D. 373 (N.D. Ill. 1985), 114

In re All Asbestos Cases Pending in the United States District Court for the District of Maryland, (D. Md. Dec. 16, 1983), 475

Allegheny County v. Frank Mashuda Co., 360 U.S. 185 (1959), 434

Allen v. McCurry, 449 U.S. 90 (1980), 168

Allen v. R & H Oil and Gas Co., 63 F.3d 1326 (5th Cir. 1995), 339

Allen v. United States, 588 F. Supp. 247 (D. Utah 1984), 1288

Allen v. Wright, 468 U.S. 737 (1984), 364

In re Allied-Signal, Inc., 891 F.2d 967 (1st Cir. 1989), 969, 974, 975

In re Allied-Signal Inc., 891 F.2d 974 (1st Cir. 1989), 973

Allison v. Citgo Petroleum Corp., 1998 WL 244989 (5th Cir.), **599**, **617**

Allison v. Security Benefit Life Insurance Co., 980 F.2d 1213 (8th Cir. 1992), 433

Allstate Insurance Co. v. Hague, 449 U.S. 302 (1981), 799, 800, 801, 803, 842

Allstate Insurance Co. v. Hill, 218 Ga. 430, 128 S.E.2d 321 (1962), 424

Allstate Insurance Co. v. McNeill, 382 F.2d 84 (4th Cir. 1967), 422

Alpine Gulf, Inc. v. Valentino, 563 S.W.2d 358 (Tex.App. 1978), 440

Alton Box Board Co. v. Esprit de Corp., 682 F.2d 1267 (9th Cir. 1982), 410, 411

In re Amatex Corp., 30 B.R. 309 (Bankr. E.D.Pa. 1983), 756

In re Amatex, 755 F.2d 1034 (3d Cir. 1985), 756

Amchem Products, Inc., v. Windsor, 117 S. Ct. 2231 (1997), 370, 371, 400, 582, **670**

In re American Airlines, Inc., 972 F.2d 605 (5th Cir. 1992), 907

In re American Continental Corp./Lincoln Savings and Loan Litigation, 794 F. Supp. 1424 (D. Ariz. 1992), 922

American Dredging Co. v. Miller, 510 U.S. 443 (1994), 466

American Fire & Casualty Co. v. Finn, 341 U.S. 6 (1951), 327, 384

In re American Hardwoods, Inc., 885 F.2d 621 (9th Cir. 1989), 748, 749, 750

American Honda Motor Co. v. Vickers Motors, Inc., 64 F.R.D. 118 (W.D. Tenn. 1974), 954

In re American Honda Motor Co. Dealerships Relations Litigation, 958 F. Supp. 1045 (D. Md. 1997), 830

American Life Insurance Co. v. Stewart, 300 U.S. 203 (1937), 619

In re American Medical Systems, Inc., 75 F.3d 1069 (6th Cir. 1996), 555, 563, **574**, 590, 644

American National Red Cross v. S.G., 505 U.S. 247 (1992), 320

American Pipe & Construction Co. v. Utah, 414 U.S. 538 (1974), 553, 569

American Security Bank v. Bank of Honolulu, 646 F. Supp. 1063 (D. Haw. 1986), 422

Ex parte American Steel Barrel Co., 230 U.S. 35 (1913), 1363

American Telephone & Telegraph Co. v. Grady, 594 F.2d 594 (7th Cir. 1978), 1111

American Well Works Co. v. Layne and Bowler Co., 241 U.S. 257 (1916), 316, 359

In re Amerifirst Securities Litigation, 139 F.R.D. 423 (S.D. Fla. 1991), 562

In re Amino Acid Lysine Antitrust Litigation, 918 F. Supp. 1190 (N.D. Ill. 1996), 887

In re AM International, Inc. Securities Litigation, 108 F.R.D. 190 (S.D.N.Y. 1985), 997

In re Ampicillin Antitrust Litigation, 88 F.R.D. 174 (D.D.C. 1980), 1039, 1288, 1291

Analytica, Inc. v. NPD Research, Inc., 708 F.2d 1263 (7th Cir. 1983), 907, 909

Anderson v. Liberty Lobby, 477 U.S. 242 (1986), 1057, 1063, 1066, 1067, 1086

Andrews v. American Telephone & Telegraph Co., 95 F.3d 1014 (11th Cir. 1996), 629

Angelo v. Armstrong World Industries, Inc., 11 F.3d 957 (10th Cir. 1993), 1288, 1291

Angus v. Shiley, Inc., 989 F.2d 142 (3d Cir. 1993), 385

Anixter v. Home-Stake Production Co., 977 F.2d 1533 (10th Cir. 1992), 1066

Ankenbrandt v. Richards, 504 U.S. 689 (1992), 331, 430

In re AOV Industries, Inc., 792 F.2d 1140 (D.C. Cir. 1986), 776

Apache Products Co. v. Employers Insurance of Wausau, 154 F.R.D. 650 (S.D. Miss. 1994), 493

In re Apex Oil Co, 980 F.2d 1150 (8th Cir. 1992), 740, 741

Applegate v. Dobrovir, Oakes & Gebhardt, 628 F. Supp. 378 (D.D.C. 1985), 1350

Appleton Electric Co. v. Advance-United Expressways, 494 F.2d 126 (7th Cir. 1974), 689

In re Application of Aldunate, 3 F.3d 54 (2d Cir. 1993), 1168

In re Application of Asta Medica, S.A., 981 F.2d 1 (1st Cir. 1992), 1167

Arch v. American Tobacco Co., 175 F.R.D. 469 (E.D. Pa. 1997), 596, 608, 645, 1312

Archer-Daniels Midland Co. v. Phoenix Assurance Co. of New York, 936 F. Supp. 534 (S.D. Ill. 1996), 1065, 1066

In re Armco, Inc., 770 F.2d 103 (8th Cir. 1985), 949, 950, 1258, 1260

Armco Steel Co. v. CSX Corp., 790 F. Supp. 311 (D.D.C. 1991), 1105

Arney v. Finney, 766 F. Supp. 934 (D. Kan. 1991), 889

Arnold v. United Artists Theatre Circuit, Inc., 158 F.R.D. 439 (N.D. Cal. 1994), 604, 609

Arnold v. Eastern Air Lines, Inc., 712 F.2d 899 (4th Cir. 1983), 478

In re Arthur Treacher's Franchise Litigation, 92 F.R.D. 398 (E.D. Pa. 1981), 991

Asahi Metal Industry Co. v. Superior

Court of California, 480 U.S. 102 (1987), **267**, 278, 283, 287
In re Asbestos Bankruptcy Litigation, 1992 WL 423943 (J.P.M.L.), 741
In re Asbestos Cases, 568 F. Supp. 910 (E.D. Va. 1981), 910
In re Asbestos Litigation, 551 A.2d 1296 (Del. Super. 1988), 1241
In re Asbestos Litigation, 623 A.2d 546 (Del. Super. 1992), 1166
In re Asbestos Litigation, 90 F.3d 963 (5th Cir. 1996), **301**, **613**, **658**, 674, 678, 681, 682, 691, 767, **780**
In re Asbestos Litigation, 173 F.R.D. 81 (S.D.N.Y. 1997), 486
In re Asbestos Litigation, 1998 WL 230950 (S.D.N.Y.), 486
In re Asbestos Litigation, 134 F.3d 668 (5th Cir. 1998), 684
In re Asbestos and Asbestos Insulation Material Products Liability Litigation, 431 F. Supp. 906 (J.P.M.L. 1977), **498**
In re Asbestos Products Liability Litigation (No. VI), 771 F. Supp. 415 (J.P.M.L.1991), 476, **501**, 671
In re Asbestos Products Liability Litigation (No. VI), 1996 WL 539589 (E.D. Pa.), 509, 513
In re Asbestos School Products Liability Litigation, 606 F. Supp. 713 (J.P.M.L. 1985), 511
A Sealed Case, 890 F.2d 15 (7th Cir. 1989), 922
Askey v. C. & M. Service, 45 F.R.D. 242 (M.D. Pa. 1968), 107
Asset Allocation and Management Co. v. Western Employers Insurance Co., 892 F.2d 566 (7th Cir. 1989), 468, 469, 470
Associated General Contractors of California, Inc. v. California State Council of Carpenters, 459 U.S. 519 (1983), 989, 990
Association of Data Processing Service Organizations, Inc. v. Camp, 397 U.S. 150 (1970), 364, 365
Atchison, Topeka and Santa Fe Railway Co. v. Buell, 480 U.S. 557 (1987), 988
Atherton v. Federal Deposit Insurance Corp., 519 U.S. 213 (1997), 853
Atkinson v. Arnold, 893 S.W.2d 294 (Tex. App. 1995), 470
Atlantic Coastline R.R. v. Brotherhood of Locomotive Engineers, 398 U.S. 281 (1970), 394, 398, 401, 405, 411, 615
Atlantis Development Corp. v. United States, 379 F.2d 818 (5th Cir. 1967), 148, 151

Atlas Roofing Co. v. Occupational Health and Safety Review Commission, 430 U.S. 442 (1977), 1217
Austin v. Unarco Industries, Inc., 705 F.2d 1 (1st Cir. 1983), 744
Avila v. Van Ru Credit Corp., 1995 WL 41425 (N.D. Ill.), 172, 205

Bahrs v. Hughes Aircraft Co., 795 F. Supp. 965 (D. Ariz. 1992), 383
Baker v. Waterman S.S. Corp., 11 F.R.D. 440 (S.D.N.Y. 1951), 479
Baldwin County Welcome Center v. Brown, 466 U.S. 147 (1984), 988
Baldwin v. Traveling Men's Association, 283 U.S. 522 (1931), 159
In re Baldwin-United Corp., 105 F.R.D. 475 (S.D.N.Y. 1984), **648**
In re Baldwin-United Corp., 770 F.2d 328 (2d Cir. 1985), 397, **401**, 617, 1419
Ballan v. Upjohn Co., 159 F.R.D. 473 (W.D. Mich. 1994), 628
Baltimore S.S. Co. v. Phillips, 274 U.S. 316 (1927), 158
Baltimore & Ohio R. Co. v. Kepner, 314 U.S. 44 (1941), 391
Bank Brussels Lambert v. Credit Lyonnais (Suisse), 160 F.R.D. 437 (S.D.N.Y. 1995), 1146
In re Bankers Trust Co., 61 F.3d 465 (6th Cir. 1995), 1169
Barnes v. Peat, Marwick, Mitchell & Co., 42 A.D.2d 15, 344 N.Y.S.2d 645 (1973), 439, 440, 441
Barnes v. American Tobacco Co., 176 F.R.D. 479 (E.D. Pa. 1997), 609
Barr Laboratories, Inc. v. Abbott Laboratories, 978 F.2d 98 (3d Cir. 1992), 1291
Barron v. Bludhorn, 68 A.D.2d 809, 414 N.Y.S.2d 15 (1979), 441
Bash v. Firstmark Standard Life Insurance Co., 861 F.2d 159 (7th Cir. 1988), 914
Basic, Inc. v. Levinson, 485 U.S. 224 (1988), 627
Bates v. C & S Adjusters, Inc., 980 F.2d 865 (2d Cir. 1992), 453, 454
Bath & Body Works, Inc. v. Luzier Personalized Cosmetics, Inc., 76 F.3d 743 (6th Cir. 1996), 1161
Batoff v. State Farm Insurance Co., 977 F.2d 848 (3d Cir. 1992), 383
Battle v. Liberty National Life Insurance Co., 877 F.2d 877 (11th Cir. 1989), 399
Baughman v. American Telephone & Telegraph Co., 298 S.C. 127, 378 S.E.2d 599 (1989), 424
Baxter v. Palmigiano, 425 U.S. 308 (1976),

1115
Baxter v. Coca-Cola Co., 47 F.R.D. 345 (S.D.N.Y. 1969), 952
Bayges v. Southeastern Pennsylvania Transportation Authority, 887 F. Supp. 108 (E.D. Pa. 1995), 922
Beacon Theatres, Inc. v. Westover, 359 U.S. 500 (1959), 1211, 1212, 1214, 1215, 1216, 1235, 1257, 1284
In re Beard, 811 F.2d 818 (4th Cir 1987), 972, 973, 975
Beckman Industries, Inc. v. International Insurance Co., 966 F.2d 470 (9th Cir. 1992), 146, 155, 1152
Bedingfield v. Jefferson County, 527 So. 2d 1270 (1988), 208
Beecher v. Able, 575 F.2d 1010 (2d Cir. 1978), 1416
In re Beef Industry Antitrust Litigation, 607 F.2d 167 (5th Cir. 1979), 657
Beirne v. Security Heating Clearwater Pools, Inc., 759 F. Supp. 1120 (M.D. Pa. 1991), 1291
Belfiore v. New York Times Co., 654 F. Supp. 842 (D. Conn. 1986), 951
Bell v. Wolfish, 441 U.S. 520 (1979), 690
In re Bendectin Products Liability Litigation, 749 F.2d 300 (6th Cir. 1984), 205, 229, 591, 597
In re Bendectin Litigation, 857 F.2d 290 (6th Cir. 1988), 322, 324, 869, 1202, 1272, **1273**, 1282
Bennett v. Arrington, 806 F. Supp. 926 (N.D. Ala. 1992), 252
Bennett Silvershein Associates v. Furman, 776 F. Supp. 800 (S.D.N.Y. 1991), 908, 909, 910, 912
Benson v. Wanda Petroleum Co., 468 S.W.2d 361 (Tex. 1971), 224
Benson & Ford, Inc. v. Wanda Petroleum Co., 833 F.2d 1172 (5th Cir. 1987), 230
Berger v. United States, 255 U.S. 22 (1921), 1361
Berkey Photo, Inc. v. Eastman Kodak Company, 74 F.R.D. 613 (S.D.N.Y. 1977), 1185, 1186
Berkovitz v. Home Box Office, Inc., 89 F.3d 24 (1st Cir. 1996), 1007, 1077
Berman Enterprises, Inc. v. Jorling, 6 F.3d 602 (2d Cir. 1993), 429
Berman v. Narragansett Racing Association, 414 F.2d 311 (1st Cir.1969), 375
Bernard v. Gerber Food Prods. Co., 938 F. Supp. 218 (S.D.N.Y. 1996), 354
Berner v. British Commonwealth Pacific Airlines, 346 F.2d 532 (2d Cir. 1965), 200
Bernstein v. Universal Pictures, 79 F.R.D. 59 (S.D.N.Y. 1978), 1233
Beshansky v. First National Entertainment Corp., 140 F.R.D. 272 (S.D.N.Y. 1990), 923, 924
Best v. District of Columbia, 291 U.S. 411 (1934), 1074
Bethune Plaza, Inc. v. Lumpkin, 863 F.2d 525 (7th Cir. 1988), 148, 149, 152
In re Beverly Hills Fire Litigation, 695 F.2d 207 (6th Cir. 1982), 1276, 1277, 1278, 1280, 1281
B.F. Goodrich v. Betkoski, 99 F.3d 505 (2d Cir. 1996), 1070, 1077
B.F. Goodrich Co. v. Murtha, 815 F. Supp. 539 (D. Conn. 1993), 991
Biben v. Card, 789 F. Supp. 1001 (W.D. Mo. 1992), 1159, 1162
Bilello v. Abbott Laboratories, 825 F. Supp. 475 (E.D.N.Y. 1993), 975
Bills v. Kennecott Corporation, 108 F.R.D. 459 (D. Utah 1985), 1185
Bing v. Roadway Express, Inc., 485 F.2d 441 (5th Cir. 1973), 596
In re Birmingham Reverse Discrimination Employment Litigation, 20 F.3d 1525 (11th Cir. 1994), 252
Bittinger v. Tecumseh Products Co., 123 F.3d 877 (6th Cir. 1997), 231, 235
In re Bituminous Coal Operators' Association, Inc., 949 F.2d 1165 (D.C. Cir. 1991), 943, 948, 949, 950, 1258, 1260
Black v. Sheraton Corp. of America, 564 F.2d 531 (D.C. Cir. 1977), 1113
Blackie v. Barrack, 524 F.2d 891 (9th Cir. 1975), 627, 629
Blair v. Source One Mortgage Services Corp., 1997 WL 79289 (E.D. La.), 1028
Blake v. Pallan, 554 F.2d 947 (9th Cir. 1977), 147
Bledsoe v. Salt River Valley Water Users' Association, 179 Ariz. 469, 880 P.2d 689 (Ariz. App. 1994), 1345
Blonder-Tongue Laboratories, Inc. v. University of Illinois Foundation, 402 U.S. 313 (1971), 162, 163
Blue Chip Stamps v. Manor Drug Stores, 421 U.S. 723 (1975), 1130
Blue v. United States, 567 F. Supp. 394 (D. Conn. 1983), 1288
Board of Commissioners of Bryan County v. Brown, 520 U.S. 397 (1997), 361
Board of Education v. Nyquist, 590 F.2d 1241 (2d Cir. 1979), 901, 902, 904, 912, 913
Board of Commissioners of Knox County v. Aspinwall, 24 How. 376, 16 L. Ed. 735 (1861), 1429
Board of Education of Oklahoma City

Public Schools v. Dowell, 498 U.S. 237 (1991), 1396, 1403, 1404
Boaz v. Boyle & Co., 40 Cal. App. 4th 700, 46 Cal. Rptr. 2d 888 (Cal. App. 1995), 289, 290
Bodanner v. Graves, 828 F. Supp. 516 (W.D. Mich. 1993), 322, 358, 359
Boggs v. Divested Atomic Corp., 141 F.R.D. 58 (S.D. Ohio 1991), 563, 645
Bogosian v. Gulf Oil Corporation, 738 F.2d 587 (3rd Cir. 1984), 1186
In re Boise Cascade Securities Litigation, 420 F. Supp. 99 (W.D. Wash. 1976), **1219**
Bonnie & Co. Fashions, Inc. v. Bankers Trust Co., 945 F. Supp. 693 (S.D.N.Y. 1996), 1134
Borel v. Fibreboard Paper Products Corp., 493 F.2d 1076 (5th Cir. 1973), 195, 197, 199
Boston & Maine Corp. v. Town of Hampton, 987 F.2d 855 (1st Cir. 1993), 990
Boughton v. Cotter Corp., 65 F.3d 823 (10th Cir. 1995), 1290
Bowles v. Willingham, 321 U.S. 503 (1944), 398
Bowling v. Pfizer, 143 F.R.D. 141 (S.D. Ohio 1992), 658, 688
Boyle v. United Technologies Corp., 487 U.S. 500 (1988), 852, 853, 854
Braddy v. Nationwide Mutual Liability Insurance Co., 470 S.E.2d 820 (N.C. App. 1996), 1293
Bradley v. Maryland Casualty Co., 382 F.2d 415 (8th Cir. 1967), 383
Bradley v. Milliken, 402 F. Supp. 1096 (E.D. Mich. 1975), 1402, 1403, 1421
Bradley v. Milliken, 540 F.2d 229 (6th Cir. 1976), **1389**
Bradley v. Milliken, 585 F. Supp. 348 (E.D. Mich. 1984), 1402
Bradley v. Milliken, 828 F.2d 1186 (6th Cir. 1987), 1402
Bradley v. Milliken, 918 F.2d 178 (Table), 1990 WL 177183 (6th Cir. 1990), 1402
Brand v. NCC Corp., 540 F. Supp. 562 (E.D. Pa. 1982), 923
In re Branded Products, Inc., 154 B.R. 936 (Bankr. W.D. Tex. 1993), 705
Brandenburg v. Seidel, 859 F.2d 1179 (4th Cir. 1988), 429, 435
In re Braniff Insolvency Litigation, 153 B.R. 941 (Bankr. M.D. Fla. 1993), 1149
Brazinski v. Amoco Petroleum Additives Co., 6 F.3d 1176 (7th Cir. 1993), 358
In re Breast Implant Cases, 942 F. Supp. 958 (E. & S.D.N.Y. 1996), 1067
Brennan v. Midwestern Life Insurance Company, 450 F.2d 999 (7th Cir. 1971), 1135
Brennan's, Inc. v. Brennan's Restaurants, Inc., 590 F.2d 168 (5th Cir. 1979), 912, 914
Bright v. Bechtel Petroleum Co., 780 F.2d 766 (9th Cir. 1986), 312
Brisk v. City of Miami Beach, 726 F. Supp. 1305 (S.D. Fla. 1989), 1233
British Airways v. Laker Airways Ltd., 1985 App. Cas. 58, 472
Brock v. American Messenger Service, Inc., 65 B.R. 670 (D.N.H. 1986), 706
Bronson v. Board of Education, 525 F.2d 344 (6th Cir. 1975), 226
In re Brooklyn Navy Yard Asbestos Litigation, 971 F.2d 831 (2d Cir. 1992), 478, 483, 1375
Brotherhood of Railroad Trainmen v. Baltimore & O. R. Co., 331 U.S. 519 (1947), 154, 155
Brown v. Board of Education, 349 U.S. 294 (1955), 2, 82, 1385, **1388**, 1390, 1399, 1427
Brown v. Board of Education, 84 F.R.D. 383 (D. Kan. 1979), 1401
Brown v. Board of Education, 671 F. Supp. 1290 (D. Kan. 1987), 1401, 1404
Brown v. Board of Education, 892 F.2d 851 (10th Cir. 1989), 1401
Brown v. Board of Education, 978 F.2d 585 (10th Cir. 1992), 1401
Brown v. Fauver, 819 F.2d 395 (3d Cir. 1987), 367
Brown v. Keene, 33 U.S. (8 Pet.) 112 (U.S. 1834), 330
Brown v. Superior Court, 44 Cal. 3d 1049, 751 P.2d 470, (1988), 281
Brown v. Ticor Title Insurance Co., 982 F.2d 386 (9th Cir. 1992), 611
Bulow v. von Bulow, 811 F.2d 136 (2d Cir. 1987), 1145
Burford v. Sun Oil Co., 319 U.S. 315 (1943), 427, 428, 429, 430, 435, 436, 439, 447
In re Burg, 103 B.R. 222 (9th Cir. BAP 1989), 1332
Burger King Corp. v. Rudzewicz, 471 U.S. 462 (1985), 269, 271, 283, 284, 287
Burnham v. Superior Court of California, 495 U.S. 604 (1990), 261
Burton v. Sheheen, 793 F. Supp. 1329 (D.S.C. 1992), 1253
In re Bushkin Associates, 864 F.2d 241 (1st Cir. 1989), 907
Butler v. R.J. Reynolds Tobacco Co., 815 F. Supp. 982 (S.D. Miss. 1993), 330, 331
Butterworth v. Smith, 494 U.S. 624 (1990),

1114

Cafeteria and Restaurant Workers Union, Local 473 v. McElroy, 367 U.S. 886 (1961), 1304

Caiafa Professional Law Corp. v. State Farm Fire & Casualty Co., 15 Cal. App. 4th 800, 19 Cal. Rptr. 2d 138 (1993), 439, 440

Cain v. Armstrong World Indus., 785 F. Supp. 1448 (S.D. Ala.1992), 479

California v. Deep Sea Research, Inc., 118 S. Ct. 1464 (1998), 362

Calumet National Bank v. Levine, 179 B.R. 117 (N.D. Ind. 1995), 739, 741

Caminiti & Iatorola v. Behnke Warehousing, Inc., 962 F.2d 698 (7th Cir. 1992), 432

Campos v. Ticketmaster Corp., 140 F.3d 1166 (8th Cir. 1998), 827

Cannon v. Equitable Life Assurance Society of the United States, 106 Misc. 2d 1060, 433 N.Y.S.2d 378 (1980), 441

Capitol Records, Inc. v. Progress Records Distributing, Inc., 106 F.R.D. 25 (N.D. Ill. 1985), 1066

Carden v. Arkoma Associates, 494 U.S. 185 (1990), 330

Cardenas v. Smith, 733 F.2d 909 (D.C. Cir. 1984), 318, 321, 367

In re Cargill, Inc., 66 F.3d 1256 (1st Cir. 1995), 974

Carlough v. Amchem Products, Inc., 834 F. Supp. 1437 (E.D. Pa. 1993), 337, 338, **363**

Carlough v. Amchem Products, Inc., 10 F.3d 189 (3d Cir. 1993), 338, 364, 370, 371, 372, 400, 617

Carnegie-Mellon University v. Cohill, 484 U.S. 343 (1988), 376, 377, 384, 387

Carpenter v. Davis, 424 F.2d 257 (5th Cir. 1970), 558

Carpenters 46 Northern California Counties Joint Apprenticeship and Training Committee and Training Board v. Eldridge, 459 U.S. 917 (1982), 129

Carter-Wallace, Inc. v. Otte, 474 F.2d 529 (2d Cir. 1972), 1172

Cascade Natural Gas Corp. v. El Paso National Gas Co., 386 U.S. 129 (1967), 146, 147

Case v. Continental Airlines Corp., 1992 WL 201080 (10th Cir.), 1105

Cash Energy, Inc. v. Weiner, 768 F. Supp. 892 (D. Mass. 1991), 991

Castano v. American Tobacco Co., 160 F.R.D. 544 (E.D. La. 1995), 958

Castano v. American Tobacco Co., 84 F.3d 734 (5th Cir. 1996), 589, **636**

Caterpillar, Inc. v. Lewis, 519 U.S. 61 (1996), 385

Caterpillar Inc. v. Williams, 482 U.S. 386 (1987), 382

CBS, Inc. v. Fitchelberg, 88 A.D.2d 881, 452 N.Y.S.2d 596 (1982), 440

In re CBS Licensing Antitrust Litigation, 328 F. Supp. 511 (J.P.M.L. 1971), 509

Celestine v. Citgo Petroleum Corp., 165 F.R.D. 463 (W.D. La. 1995), 1290

Celotex Corp. v. Catrett, 477 U.S. 317 (1986), 1057, 1061, 1062, 1067, 1076, 1077

Celotex Corp. v. Edwards, 514 U.S. 300 (1995), 733, 734, 738, 739, 750

In re Cement Antitrust Litigation (MDL 296), 688 F.2d 1297 (9th Cir. 1982), 973, 974

Central Wesleyan College v. W.R. Grace & Co., 6 F.3d 177 (4th Cir. 1993), 645

Central Illinois Public Service Co. v. Allianz Underwriters Insurance Co., 158 Ill. 2d 218, 633 N.E.2d 675 (1994), 1208

Chambers v. NASCO, Inc., 501 U.S. 32 (1991), 1046

Champeau v. Fruehauf Corp., 814 F.2d 1271 (8th Cir. 1987), 1344, 1368

Champion International Corp. v. Liberty Mutual Insurance Co., 129 F.R.D. 63 (S.D.N.Y. 1989), 958

Chan v. Korean Air Lines, 490 U.S. 122 (1989), 828

Chase National Bank v. Norwalk, 291 U.S. 431 (1934), 210, 242, 1450, 1451

In re Chateaugay Corp., 944 F.2d 997 (2d Cir. 1991), 762, 768

In re Chateaugay Corp., 10 F.3d 944 (2d Cir. 1993), 778

Chauffeurs, Teamsters and Helpers Local No. 391 v. Terry, 494 U.S. 558 (1990), 1217, 1234

Chemray Coatings Co. v. United States, 27 Fed.Cl. 470 (1993), 923

Cheng v. GAF Corp., 631 F.2d 1052 (2d Cir. 1980), 906, 909, 910

In re Chevron U.S.A., Inc., 109 F.3d 1016 (5th Cir. 1997), 1288, 1311, 1312

In re Chicago Flood Litigation, 819 F. Supp. 762 (N.D. Ill. 1993), 434

In the Matter of Chicago, St. Paul & Pacific Railroad Co., 974 F.2d 775 (7th Cir. 1992), 768

Chick Kam Choo v. Exxon Corp., 486 U.S. 140 (1988), 399, 401 465

China Trade and Development Corp. v. M.V. Choony Yong, 837 F.2d 33 (2d Cir. 1987), 472

In re Chiropractic Antitrust Litigation, 483 F. Supp. 811 (J.P.M.L. 1980), 515
Chitimacha Tribe of Louisiana v. Harry L. Laws Co., 690 F.2d 1157 (5th Cir. 1982), 970, 992
Christianson v. Colt Industries Operating Co., 486 U.S. 800 (1988), 829
Cimino v. Raymark Industries, Inc., 1989 WL 253889 (E.D. Tex.), 1336, 1358
Cimino v. Raymark Industries, Inc., 751 F. Supp. 649 (E.D. Tex.1990), 1303, 1304, 1307, 1309, 1420
Cinema 5, Ltd. v. Cinerama, Inc., 528 F.2d 1384 (2d Cir.1976), 901, 908
Cipollone v. Liggett Group, Inc., 113 F.R.D. 86 (D.N.J. 1986), 1115, 1116
Cipollone v. Liggett Group, Inc., 785 F.2d 1108 (3d Cir. 1986), 916, 917, 919, 958, 1151
Cipollone v. Liggett Group, Inc., 799 F. Supp. 466 (D.N.J. 1992), 976
City of New York v. Pullman, Inc., 662 F.2d 910 (2d Cir. 1981), 1233
City of Detroit v. Grinnell Corp., 495 F.2d 448 (2d Cir. 1974), 1104
City of Chicago v. International College of Surgeons, 118 S. Ct. 523 (1997), 357, 382
City of Wichita, Kansas v. United States Gypsum Co., 828 F. Supp. 851 (D. Kan. 1993), 1065, 1066
City of Miami Beach v. Miami Beach Fraternal Order of Police, 619 So. 2d 447 (Fla. App. 1993), 440
City of Cleveland v. Cleveland Electric Illuminating Co., 503 F. Supp. 368 (N.D. Oh. 1980), 970, 974
City of Indianapolis v. Chase National Bank of City of New York, 314 U.S. 63 (1941), 328
City of New York v. Exxon Corp., 697 F. Supp. 677 (S.D.N.Y. 1988), 1104
Clark v. Paul Gray, Inc., 306 U.S. 583 (1939), 334
Clark v. Pennsylvania Railroad Co., 328 F.2d 591 (2d Cir. 1964), 1040
Clark v. Universal Builders, Inc., 501 F.2d 324 (7th Cir. 1974), 1135
Cle-Ware Rayco, Inc. v. Perlstein, 401 F. Supp. 1231 (S.D.N.Y. 1975), 106
Clearfield Trust Co. v. United States, 318 U.S. 363 (1943), 848, 849, 850
Clemmon v. Sowders, 34 F.3d 352 (6th Cir. 1994), 1375
Coates v. AC and S, Inc., 844 F. Supp. 1126 (E.D. La. 1994), 1288, 1291
Coats & Clark, Inc. v. Gay, 755 F.2d 1506 (11th Cir. 1985), 1064

Coburn v. 4-R Corporation, 77 F.R.D. 43 (E.D. Ky. 1977), 782
Cohen v. De La Cruz, 118 S. Ct. 1212 (1998), 708
Ex parte Collett, 337 U.S. 55 (1949), 490
Collins v. Associated Pathologists, Ltd., 844 F.2d 473 (7th Cir. 1988), 1070
Columbia Steel Fabricators, Inc. v. Ahlstrom Recovery, 44 F.3d 800 (9th Cir. 1995), **1080**
In re Combustion, Inc., 161 F.R.D. 51 (W.D. La. 1995), 958
In re Combustion, Inc., 968 F. Supp. 1116 (W.D. La. 1997), 554
In re Combustion, Inc., 978 F. Supp. 673 (W.D. La. 1997), **1435**
In re Commercial Explosives Litigation, 945 F. Supp. 1489 (D. Utah 1996), 990
Commercial Union Insurance Co. v. Boston Edison Co., 412 Mass. 545, 591 N.E.2d 165 (1992), 1345, 1346
Commodity Futures Trading Commission v. Wellington Precious Metals, Inc., 950 F.2d 1525 (11th Cir. 1992), 204
Compaq Computer Corp. v. Packard Bell Electronics, Inc., 163 F.R.D. 329 (N.D. Cal. 1995), 1144
In re Complex Asbestos Litigation, 232 Cal. App. 3d 572, 283 Cal. Rptr. 732 (1993), 907
CompuServe, Inc. v. Patterson, 89 F.3d 1257 (6th Cir. 1996), 275
Computer Associates International, Inc. v. Altai, Inc., 126 F.3d 365 (2d Cir. 1997), 170, 179
Congress Factors Corp. v. Meinhard Commercial Corp., 129 Misc. 2d 726, 493 N.Y.S.2d 917 (1985), 440
Conley v. Gibson, 355 U.S. 41 (1957), 987, 990, 1000, 1001
Connecticut v. Doehr, 501 U.S. 1 (1991), 1304, 1305
Consorti v. Armstrong World Industries, Inc., 72 F.3d 1003 (2d Cir. 1995), 486
Consumers Power Co. v. Public Utilities Commission, 270 Mich. 213, 258 N.W. 250 (1935), 439
Continental Grain Co. v. The Barge FBL585, 364 U.S. 19 (1960), 492
Contini v. Hyundai Motor Co., 149 F.R.D. 41 (S.D.N.Y. 1993), 1357
In re Control Data Corp. Securities Litigation, 933 F.2d 616 (8th Cir. 1991), 1040
Cook v. Boorstin, 763 F.2d 1462 (D.C. Cir. 1985), **137**, 234
Cook v. Rockwell International Corp., 151 F.R.D. 378 (D. Colo. 1993), **606**, 1290

Cooney v. Sun Shipbuilding and Drydock Co., 288 F. Supp. 708 (E.D. Pa. 1968), 1144

Cooper v. Federal Reserve Bank of Richmond, 467 U.S. 867 (1984), **174**, 581, 620, 628

Coopers & Lybrand v. Livesay, 437 U.S. 463 (1978), 369, 554, 569

In re Coordinated Pretrial Proceedings in Petroleum Product Antitrust Litigation, 658 F.2d 1355 (9th Cir. 1981), 910

In re Copley Pharmaceutical, Inc., 161 F.R.D. 456 (D. Wyo. 1995), 545, 1288, 1290

Corcoran v. Universal Reinsurance Corp., 713 F. Supp. 77 (S.D.N.Y. 1989), 429

In re Corn Derivatives Antitrust Litigation, 748 F.2d 157 (3d Cir. 1984), 901, 902, 903, 907

In re: Correct Mfg. Corp., 167 B.R. 458 (Bankr. S.D.Ohio 1994), 762

In re Corrugated Container Antitrust Litigation, 643 F.2d 195 (5th Cir. 1981), 661

In re Corrugated Container Grand Jury and Corrugated Container Anti-trust Criminal and Civil Litigation, 659 F.2d 1330 (5th Cir. 1981), 1114

In re Corrugated Container Antitrust Litigation, 659 F.2d 1332 (5th Cir. 1981), **393**, 617, 660

In re Corrugated Container Antitrust Litigation, 659 F.2d 1341 (5th Cir. 1981), 908, 909

In re Corrugated Container Antitrust Litigation, 556 F. Supp. 1117 (S.D.Tex. 1982), 1114

Cotchett v. Avis Rent A Car, 56 F.R.D. 549 (S.D.N.Y. 1972), 583

Cotten v. Witco Chemical Corp., 651 F.2d 274 (5th Cir. 1981), 1233

County of Cook v. Midcon Corp., 574 F. Supp. 902 (N.D. Ill. 1983), 146, 147, 148, 149, 151, 203

County of Imperial v. Munoz, 449 U.S. 54 (1980), 401

County of Suffolk v. Long Island Lighting Co., 907 F.2d 1295 (2d Cir. 1990), 436, 614

Cox v. American Cast Iron Pipe Co., 784 F.2d 1546 (11th Cir. 1986), 626, 1135

Coxe v. Phillips, 95 Eng. Rep. 152 (K.B. 1736), 154

Crabtree v. Academy Life Insurance Co., 878 F. Supp. 727 (E.D. Pa. 1995), 923

Crateo, Inc. v. Intermark, Inc., 536 F.2d 862 (9th Cir.), 1355

Crawford-El v. Britton, 118 S. Ct. 1584 (1998), 988

Crosby v. America Online, Inc., 967 F. Supp. 257 (N.D. Ohio 1997), 354

Crowell v. Benson, 285 U.S. 22 (1932), 948, 1263

CRS Sirrine, Inc. v. Dravo Corp., 213 Ga. App. 710, 445 S.E.2d 782 (1994), 1323

Cullen v. Margiotta, 811 F.2d 698 (2d Cir. 1987), 206

Cybersell, Inc. v. Cybersell, Inc., 130 F.3d 414 (9th Cir. 1997), 275

Daewoo Electronics Company, Ltd. v. United States, 650 F. Supp. 1003 (C.I.T. 1986), 1185

Dairy Queen, Inc. v. Wood, 369 U.S. 469 (1962), 1211, 1214, 1257, 1349

In re Data General Corp. Antitrust Litigation, 490 F. Supp. 1089 (N.D. Cal. 1980), 1029

In re Data General Corp. Antitrust Litigation, 510 F. Supp. 1220 (J.P.M.L. 1979), 514, 516, 1029

Datskow v. Teledyne Continental Motors Aircraft Prods., 826 F. Supp. 677 (W.D.N.Y. 1993), 1340, 1346

Daubert v. Merrell Dow Pharmaceuticals, Inc., 509 U.S. 579 (1993), 1170, 1171, 1355

In re Davis, 730 F.2d 176 (5th Cir. 1984), 751

Davis-Watkins Co. v. Service Merchandise Co., 500 F. Supp. 1244 (M.D. Tenn. 1980), 1233

Day & Zimmerman, Inc. v. Challoner, 423 U.S. 3 (1975), **805**, 852

Day v. NLO, Inc., 144 F.R.D. 330 (S.D. Ohio 1992), 607

Day v. NLO, 851 F. Supp. 869 (S.D. Ohio 1994), 613

Dayton Board of Education v. Brinkman, 433 U.S. 406 (1977), 1402

Dayton Board of Education v. Brinkman, 443 U.S. 526 (1979), 1402

Dean Witter Reynolds Inc. v. Fernandez, 489 F. Supp. 434 (S.D. Fla. 1979), 421, 422

DeAngelis v. A. Tarricone, Inc., 151 F.R.D. 245 (S.D.N.Y. 1993), 1356

DeBenedetto v. Goodyear Tire & Rubber Co., 754 F.2d 512 (4th Cir. 1985), **1364**

DeBoer v. Mellon Mortgage Co., 64 F.3d 1171 (8th Cir. 1995), 611

DeBremaecker v. Short, 433 F.2d 733 (5th Cir. 1970), 558

Decora Inc. v. DW Wallcovering, Inc., 901 F. Supp. 161 (S.D.N.Y. 1995), 909

In re Decorator Industries, Inc., 980 F.2d 1371 (11th Cir. 1992), 386
Deep v. Manufacturuers Life Insurance Co., 944 F. Supp. 358 (D.N.J. 1996), 354
DeJesus v. Sears, Roebuck, Inc., 87 F.3d 65 (2d Cir. 1996), 990
Delaware Tire Center, Inc. v. State of Delaware, 508 A.2d 470 (Table), 1986 WL 16794 (Del. 1986), 439
Democratic Central Committee of the District of Columbia v. Washington Metropolitan Area Transit Commission, 84 F.3d 451 (D.C. Cir. 1996), **1410**
In re Dennis Greenman Securities Litigation, 94 F.R.D. 273 (S.D. Fla. 1982), 1123
In re Dennis Greenman Securities Litigation, 829 F.2d 1539 (11th Cir. 1987), **585**, 617
Department of Game of State of Washington v. Puyallup Tribe, Inc., 86 Wash. 2d 664, 548 P.2d 1058 (1976), 442
In re Department of Investigation of City of New York, 856 F.2d 481 (2d Cir. 1988), 1113
DePinto v. Provident Security Life Ins. Co., 323 F.2d 826 (9th Cir. 1963), 1214
In re DES Cases, 789 F. Supp. 552 (E.D.N.Y. 1992), **278**
In re DES Cases, 142 F.R.D. 58 (E.D.N.Y. & N.Y.Sup.Ct. 1992), 952
In re DES Litigation, 7 F.3d 20 (2d Cir. 1993), 289, 290, 291
Desert Empire Bank v. Ins. Co. of North America, 623 F.2d 1371 (9th Cir. 1980), 112, 113
DeSylva v. Ballentine, 351 U.S. 570 (1956), 853
Deus v. Allstate Insurance Co., 15 F.3d 506 (5th Cir. 1994), 1323, 1326
Dewey v. R.J. Reynolds Tobacco Co., 121 N.J. 69, 577 A.2d 1239 (1990), 819
DeWit v. Firstar Corp., 904 F. Supp. 1476 (N.D. Iowa 1995), 1123
Diamond v. Charles, 476 U.S. 54 (1986), 146, 147
In re Diamond Shamrock Chemicals Co., 725 F.2d 858 (2d Cir. 1984), 864
Diaz v. Hillsborough County Hosp. Authority, 165 F.R.D. 689 (M.D. Fla. 1996), 611
In re Diet Drugs (Phentermine, Fenfluramine, Dexfenfluramine) Products Liability Litigation, 990 F. Supp. 834 (J.P.M.L. 1998), 510, 511
Dilworth v. Riner, 343 F.2d 226 (5th Cir. 1965), 398
DiNardi v. Ethicon, Inc., 145 F.R.D. 294 (N.D.N.Y. 1993), 386, 388

D'Ippolito v. Cities Service Co., 39 F.R.D. 610 (S.D.N.Y. 1965), 1190, 1191
In re Doe, 662 F.2d 1073 (4th Cir. 1981), 1186
Doe v. Abbott Laboratories, 1993 WL 278458 (N.D. Ill. 1993), 384
Doe v. Charleston Area Medical Center, Inc., 529 F.2d 638 (4th Cir. 1975), 563
Doe v. Kerwood, 969 F.2d 165 (5th Cir. 1992), 384
Dolgow v. Anderson, 43 F.R.D. 472 (E.D.N.Y. 1968), **570**
Dolgow v. Anderson, 438 F.2d 825 (2d Cir. 1970), 583
Dombrowski v. Pfister, 380 U.S. 479 (1965), 394, 397, 404
In re Donald J. Trump Casinos Securities Litigation, 7 F.3d 357 (3d Cir. 1993), 997
Donaldson v. United States, 400 U.S. 517 (1971), 146, 147
Dondi Properties Corp. v. Commerce Savings and Loan Assocation, 121 F.R.D. 284 (N.D. Tex. 1988), 907
Donnelly v. Parker, 486 F.2d 402 (D.C. Cir. 1973), 923
Donovan v. City of Dallas, 377 U.S. 408 (1964), 391, 392, 442
Dougherty v. Barry, 869 F.2d 605 (D.C. Cir. 1989), **1404**
Douglas Oil Co. of California v. Petrol Stops Northwest, 441 U.S. 211 (1979), 1113, 1114
Douglas v. New York, N. H. & H. R. Co., 279 U.S. 377 (1929), 438
Dow Chemical Co. v. Castro Alfaro, 786 S.W.2d 674 (Tex. 1990), 465
In re The Dow Company "Sarabond" Products Liability Litigation, 666 F. Supp. 1466 (D. Colo. 1987), 827
In re Dow Corning Corp., 86 F.3d 482 (6th Cir. 1996), 724, **730**
In re Dow Corning Corp., 1996 WL 511646 (E.D. Mich.), 740
In re Dow Corning Corp., 113 F.3d 565 (6th Cir. 1997), 740
Drexel Burnham Lambert Group, Inc. v. Galadari, 127 B.R. 87 (S.D.N.Y. 1991), 1253, 1254
In re Drexel Burnham Lambert Group, Inc., 960 F.2d 285 (2d Cir. 1992), 308, 563, 773, 775, 782, 783
Duchon v. Cajon Co., 791 F.2d 43 (6th Cir. 1986), 992
Duke Power Co. v. Carolina Environmental Study Group, Inc., 438 U.S. 59 (1978), 366
Duncan v. Louisiana, 391 U.S. 145 (1968),

1370
Duncan v. Merrill Lynch Pierce Fenner & Smith, Inc., 646 F.2d 1020 (5th Cir. 1981), 906, 909
Dunn v. Owens-Corning Fiberglass, 774 F. Supp. 929 (D. St. Croix 1991), 1288
Dunn v. HOVIC, 1 F.3d 1371 (3d Cir. 1993), 1409
Dupasseur v. Rochereau, 21 Wall. (88 U.S.) 130 (1875), 169, 170
Duquense Light Co. v. Westinghouse Electric Corp., 66 F.3d 604 (3d Cir. 1995), 1323, 1325, 1326
Durfee v. Duke, 375 U.S. 106 (1963), 167, 183
In re Duval County Ranch Co., 167 B.R. 848 (Bankr. S.D. Tex. 1994), 705

East Motor Freight System v. Rodriguez, 431 U.S. 395 (1977), 612, 681
Eastman Kodak Co. v. Image Technical Services, Inc., 504 U.S. 451 (1992), 1067
In re "East of the Rockies" Concrete Pipe Antitrust Litigation, 302 F. Supp. 244 (J.P.M.L. 1969), **495**
Eckstein v. Balcor Film Investors, 8 F.3d 1121 (7th Cir. 1993), 827, 828
Edelman v. Jordan, 415 U.S. 651 (1974), 361
Edgington v. R.G. Dickinson & Co., 139 F.R.D. 183 (D. Kan. 1991), 580
Edwards v. Bates County, 163 U.S. 269 (1896), 338
Edwards v. City of Houston, 78 F.3d 983 (5th Cir. 1996), 150, 154, 155, 256
EEOC v. University of Notre Dame Du Lac, 715 F.2d 331 (7th Cir. 1983), 1129, 1149
Eisen v. Carlisle & Jacquelin, 479 F.2d 1005 (2d Cir.1973), 1411, 1415, 1417
Eisen v. Carlisle & Jacquelin, 417 U.S. 156 (1974), 299, 300, 551, 552, 594, 625, 640, 641
Eldridge v. Carpenters 46 Northern California Counties JATC, 662 F.2d 534 (9th Cir. 1982), **117**, 151
Electronic Laboratory Supply Co. v. Motorola, Inc., 1989 WL 113127 (E.D. Pa.), 989
Eli Lilly & Co. v. Generix Drug Sales, Inc., 460 F.2d 1096 (5th Cir. 1972), 1012
Epstein v. Unofficial Committee of Unsecured Creditors, of the Estate of Piper Aircraft Corp., 58 F.3d 1573 (11th Cir. 1995), **759**
Epstein v. MCA, Inc., 126 F.3d 1235 (9th Cir. 1997), **179**
In re Equity Funding Corp. of America Securities Litigation, 416 F. Supp. 161 (C.D. Cal. 1976), 997, 1000
Erie Railroad Co. v. Tompkins, 304 U.S. 64 (1938), 277, 391, 806, 807, 812, 820, 1274, 1296, 1297, 1303
ESAB Group, Inc. v. Centricut, Inc., 126 F.3d 617 (4th Cir. 1997), 274
Esser v. A.H. Robins Co., 537 F. Supp. 197 (D. Minn. 1982), 924
In re Estate of Ferdinand E. Marcos Human Rights Litigation, 910 F. Supp. 1460 (D. Haw. 1995), 1313
In re Estate of Ferdinand E. Marcos Human Rights Litigation, 1994 WL 874222 (D. Haw. 1994), 951, 1355
Eubanks v. Billington, 110 F.3d 87 (D.C. Cir. 1997), 603, 610, 614
Eubanks v. Wynn, 420 S.W.2d 698 (Tex. 1967), 1286
Evans v. Artek Systems Corp., 715 F.2d 788 (2d Cir. 1983), 906
Eways v. Governor's Island, 326 N.C. 552, 391 S.E.2d 182 (1990), 439
Executive Software North America, Inc. v. United States District Court for the Central District of California, 15 F.3d 1484 (9th Cir. 1994), 358
Ex parte — See name of party

Facen v. Royal Rotterdam Lloyd S.S. Co., 12 F.R.D. 443 (S.D.N.Y. 1952), 488
In re Factor VII or IX Concentrate Blood Products Litigation, 169 F.R.D. 632 (N.D. Ill. 1996), 1135
Far East Conference v. United States, 342 U.S. 570 (1952), 436
Farber v. Riker-Maxson Corporation, 442 F.2d 457 (2d Cir. 1971), 889, 1203
Farmers Co-op Oil Co. v. Socony-Vacuum Oil Co., 133 F.2d 101 (8th Cir. 1942), 559
Farmers Irrigating Ditch & Reservoir Co. v. Kane, 845 F.2d 229 (10th Cir. 1988), 419, 420
Farmland Irrigation Co. v. Dopplmaier, 48 Cal. 2d 208, 308 P.2d 732 (1957), 439
Farmland Industries, Inc. v. Grain Board of Iraq, 904 F.2d 732 (D.C. Cir. 1990), 1063
Farr v. Thompson, 78 U.S. (11 Wall.) 139 (1871), 391
Faulkner Advertising Associates, Inc. v. Nissan Motor Corp., 905 F.2d 769 (4th Cir. 1990), 991
Fauteck v. Montgomery Ward & Co., 91 F.R.D. 393 (N.D. Ill. 1980), 1194, 1195
Fautek v. Montgomery Ward & Co., 96 F.R.D. 141 (N.D. Ill. 1982), 1195

Fay v. New York, 332 U.S. 261 (1947), 1241

FDIC v. Kahlil Zoom-In Markets, Inc., 978 F.2d 183 (5th Cir. 1992), 383

FDIC v. Jennings, 816 F.2d 1488 (10th Cir.1987), 149

Federal Election Commission v. Akins, 118 S. Ct. 1777 (1998), 371

In re Federal Skywalk Cases, 680 F.2d 1175 (8th Cir. 1982), 398, **614**, 970, 975

Federal Trade Commission v. Intellipay, Inc., 828 F. Supp. 33 (S.D. Tex. 1993), 923

Federated Department Stores v. Moitie, 452 U.S. 394 (1981), **156**, 382, 383

Feltner v. Columbia Pictures Television, Inc., 118 S. Ct. 1279 (1998), 1218

Ferens v. John Deere Co., 494 U.S. 516 (1990), 492, **809**

Fero v. Kerby, 39 F.3d 1462 (10th Cir. 1994), 970, 971

In re Fibreboard Corp., 893 F.2d 706 (5th Cir.1990), 1162, **1294**, 1303, 1306, 1309, 1310

Fidelity & Deposit Co. of Maryland v. United States, 187 U.S. 315 (1902), 1063

Filartiga v. Pena-Irala, 577 F. Supp. 860 (E.D.N.Y.1984), 1301

In re Fine Paper Antitrust Litigation, 617 F.2d 22 (3d Cir. 1980), 887, 914

In re Fine Paper Antitrust Litigation, 685 F.2d 810 (3d Cir. 1982), 493, **1010**

In re Fine Paper Antitrust Litigation, 98 F.R.D. 48 (E.D. Pa. 1983), 887

Finley v. United States, 490 U.S. 545 (1989), 347, 348, 350, 351, 357, 358, 360, 382

Firestone Tire & Rubber Co. v. Risjord, 449 U.S. 368 (1981), 907

Fitzpatrick v. Bitzer, 427 U.S. 445 (1976), 361

Flaminio v. Honda Motor Co., 733 F.2d 463 (7th Cir. 1984), 1323, 1325, 1326

Flast v. Cohen, 392 U.S. 83 (1968), 365, 368

Flatt v. Johns-Manville Sales Corp., 488 F. Supp. 836 (E.D. Tex. 1980), 195

Fleming v. Harris, 39 F.3d 905 (8th Cir. 1994), 924

In re FMC Corp. Patent Litigation, 422 F. Supp. 1163 (J.P.M.L. 1976), 514

In re Folding Carton Antitrust Litigation, 744 F.2d 1252 (7th Cir. 1984), 1416, 1417

Foman v. Davis, 371 U.S. 178 (1962), 988, 992

In re Food Lion, Inc., Fair Labor Standards Act "Effective Scheduling" Litigation, 73 F.3d 528 (4th Cir. 1996), 516, 829, 830

In re Ford Motor Co. Bronco II Products Liability Litigation, 1995 WL 222177 (E.D. La.), 653

In re Ford Motor Co. Bronco II Products Liability Litigation, 1996 WL 28517 (E.D. La.), 1096, 1097, 1151

In re Forty-Eight Insulations, Inc., 149 B.R. 860 (N.D. Ill. 1992), 749, 750

Foster v. Gueory, 655 F.2d 1319 (D.C. Cir. 1981), 137, 138, 139, 140, 141, 142

In re Foundation for New Era Philanthropy Litigation, 175 F.R.D. 202 (E.D. Pa. 1997), 686

Fox v. Taylor Diving & Salvage Co., 694 F.2d 1349 (5th Cir. 1983), 1075, 1076

Fraidin v. Stutz, 68 Md. App. 693, 515 A.2d 775 (1987), 724

Franchi Construction Co. v. Combined Insurance Co. of America, 580 F.2d 1 (1st Cir. 1978), 1277, 1292

Franchise Tax Board v. Construction Laborers Vacation Trust, 463 U.S. 1 (1983), 316, 317, 318, 321, 378

Francosteel Corp. v. M/V Charm, 19 F.3d 624 (11th Cir. 1994), 275

In re Franklin, 179 B.R. 913 (Bankr. E.D. Cal. 1995), 704

Franklin v. Kaypro Corp., 884 F.2d 1222 (9th Cir. 1989), 1456, 1457, 1458

Franks v. Bowman Transportation Co., 424 U.S. 747 (1976), 177, 371, 432

Fraver v. Studebaker Corp., 11 F.R.D. 94 (W.D. Pa. 1950), 1350

Freeman v. Howe, 65 U.S. (24 How.) 450 (1861), 335, 344, 356

Freeman v. Pitts, 503 U.S. 467 (1992), 1395, 1396, 1397, 1398, 1401

Freeport-McMoran Inc. v. K N Energy Inc., 498 U.S. 426 (1991), 113, 331

Fried v. Sungard Recovery Services, Inc., 925 F. Supp. 372 (E.D. Pa. 1996), 612

Friedman v. Bache Halsey Stuart Shields, Inc., 738 F.2d 1336 (D.C. Cir. 1984), 1170

FSLIC v. Griffin, 935 F.2d 691 (5th Cir. 1991), 385

In re FTC Line of Business Report Litigation, 626 F.2d 1022 (D.C. Cir. 1980), 1203

Fugitt v. Jones, 549 F.2d 1001 (5th Cir.1977), 1352, 1358

In re Fulfer, 159 B.R. 921 (Bankr. D. Id. 1993), 705

Funbus Systems, Inc. v. State of California Public Utilities Commission, 801 F.2d

1120 (9th Cir. 1986), 154
Fund of Funds, Ltd. v. Arthur Andersen & Co., 567 F.2d 225 (2d Cir. 1977), 901, 912, 914

GAF Corp. v. Eastman Kodak Co., 415 F. Supp. 129 (S.D.N.Y. 1976), 1067, 1069, 1111, 1112
GAF Corp. v. Eastman Kodak Co., 85 F.R.D. 46 (S.D.N.Y. 1979), 1190, 1191
Galloway v. United States, 319 U.S. (1943), 1210
Galvan v. Levine, 490 F.2d 1255 (2d Cir. 1973), 612
Gannon v. Payne, 706 S.W.2d 304 (Tex. 1986), 470, 472
In re Gap Stores Securities Litigation, 79 F.R.D. 283 (N.D. Cal. 1978), 689, 692
Garber v. Randall, 477 F.2d 711 (2d Cir. 1973), 994
Gary Plastic Packaging Corp. v. Merrill Lynch, Pierce, Fenner & Smith, Inc., 903 F.3d 176 (2d Cir. 1990), 582
Garza v. National American Insurance Co., 807 F. Supp. 1256 (M.D. La. 1992), 354, 357, 358
Gasoline Products Co. v. Champlin Refining Co., 283 U.S. 494 (1931), 1276, 1277, 1283, 1292, 1383
Gates v. United States, 707 F.2d 1141 (10th Cir. 1983), **1351**
Gautreaux v. Pierce, 690 F.2d 616 (7th Cir. 1982), 553
General Atomic Co. v. Felter, 434 U.S. 12 (1977), 391, 392
General Electric Co. v. Joiner, 118 S. Ct. 512 (1997), 1171
General Mill Supply Co. v. SCA Services, Inc., 505 F. Supp. 1093 (E.D. Mich. 1981), 906
General Mill Supply Co. v. SCA Services, Inc., 697 F.2d 704 (6th Cir. 1982), 907
General Motors Corp. v. Buha, 623 F.2d 455 (6th Cir. 1980), 398
In re General Motors Class E Stock Buyout Securities Litigation, 696 F. Supp. 1546 (J.P.M.L. 1988), 817, 828
In re General Motors Corp. Pickup Truck Fuel Tank Products Liability Litigation, 1993 WL 147245 (E.D.Pa.), 374
In re General Motors Corp. Pick-Up Truck Fuel Tank Products Liability Litigation, 55 F.3d 768 (3d Cir. 1995), 304, 553, 656, 657, 674, 677
In re: General Motors Corp. Pick-Up Truck Fuel Tank Products Liability Litigation, 134 F.3d 133 (3d Cir. 1998), 304
General Signal Corp. v. MCI Telecommunications Corp., 66 F.3d 1500 (9th Cir. 1995), 1322, 1323, 1324, 1325, 1326
General Telephone Co. of the Northwest v. Equal Employment Opportunity Commission, 446 U.S. 318 (1980), 563, 567
General Telephone Co. of the Southwest v. Falcon, 457 U.S. 147 (1982), 143, **564**, 576, 578, 625, 633, 681
Georgetown Manor, Inc. v. Ethan Allen, Inc., 753 F. Supp. 936 (S.D. Fla.1991), 1146
Georgia Education Authority (Schools) v. Davis, 227 Ga. 36, 178 S.E.2d 853 (1970), 425
Georgine v. Amchem Products, Inc., 157 F.R.D. 246 (E.D. Pa. 1994), 370, 686, 914
Georgine v. Amchem Products, Inc., 878 F. Supp. 716 (E.D. Pa. 1994), 400
Georgine v. Amchem Products, Inc., 83 F.3d 610 (3d Cir. 1996), 370, 371, 661, 662, 667, 680, 682, 1306
Gerrard v. Larsen, 517 F.2d 1127 (8th Cir. 1975), 216, 218, 226
Getty Oil Co. v. Department of Energy, 865 F.2d 270 (Temp. Emerg. Ct. App. 1988), 155
Ghandi v. Police Dept. of City of Detroit, 74 F.R.D. 115 (E.D. Mich. 1977), 1144
Gibbs v. Lappies, 828 F. Supp. 6 (D.N.H. 1993), 922, 923
In re Gibson Greetings Securities Litigation, 159 F.R.D. 499 (S.D. Ohio 1994), 582
Gilbert v. Bagley, 492 F. Supp. 714 (M.D.N.C. 1980), 991
Gile v. United Airlines, Inc., 95 F.3d 492 (7th Cir. 1996), 1136
Gilman v. BHC Securities, Inc., 104 F.3d 1418 (2d Cir. 1197), 339
Gilmer v. Walt Disney Co., 915 F. Supp. 1001 (W.D. Ark. 1996), 354
Gladhill v. General Motors Corp., 743 F.2d 1049 (4th Cir. 1984), 1339
In re Glenn W. Turner Enterprises Litigation, 521 F.2d 775 (3d Cir. 1975), 398, 617
Glidden v Chromalloy American Corp., 808 F.2d 621 (7th Cir. 1986), 553
Glueck v. Johnathon Logan, Inc., 653 F.2d 746 (2d Cir. 1981), 908
Gnutti v. Heintz, 539 A.2d 118 (Conn. 1988), 439
Goldberg v. Kelly, 397 U.S. 254 (1970), 1206, 1228
Goldblum v. Boyd, 267 So. 2d 610 (La.App.

1972), 442
Golden Rule Insurance Co. v. Harper, 925 S.W.2d 649 (Tex. 1996), 471
Golden State Bottling Co. v. National Labor Relations Board, 414 U.S. 169 (1973), 1458
Goldlawr, Inc. v. Heiman, 369 U.S. 463 (1962), 455, 456
Goldstein v. Fidelity and Guaranty Insurance Underwriters, 86 F.3d 749 (7th Cir. 1996), 1077, 1078
Gonzalez v. Banco Cent. Corp., 27 F.3d 751 (1st Cir. 1994), 217, 218, 230, 231, 232, 234
Gonzales v. Cassidy, 474 F.2d 67 (5th Cir. 1973), 185, 186, 188, 583
Gonzales v. Media Elements, Inc., 946 F.2d 157 (1st Cir. 1991), 429
Good v. Prudential Insurance Co. of America, 1998 WL 244597 (N.D. Cal.), 516
Gould v. Mitsui Mining & Smelting Co., 738 F. Supp. 1121 (N.D. Ohio 1990), 912
Gould Inc. v. Mitsui Mining & Smelting Co., Ltd., 825 F.2d 676 (2d Cir. 1987), 1185
Government of India v. Cook Industries, Inc., 569 F.2d 737 (2d Cir. 1978), 908
Grady v. A.H. Robins Co., 839 F.2d 198 (4th Cir. 1988), **752**, 762
Grand Central Building, Inc. v. New York and Harlem Railroad Co., 59 A.D.2d 207, 398 N.Y.S.2d 888 (1977), 440, 441
Granfinanciera, S.A. v. Nordberg, 492 U.S. 33 (1989), 709, 1217, 1234
In re Grand Jury Investigation, 55 F.3d 350 (8th Cir. 1996), 1114, 1115
In re Grand Jury Proceedings, 851 F.2d 860 (6th Cir. 1988), 1115
Grant v. Sullivan, 131 F.R.D. 436 (M.D. Pa. 1990), 562
Gray v. American Radiator & Standard Sanitary Corp., 22 Ill. 2d 432, 176 N.E.2d 761 (1961), 266
Gray v. Phillips Petroleum Co., 1990 WL 62074 (D. Kan.), 1336, 1375
Grayson v. K Mart Corp., 849 F. Supp. 785 (N.D. Ga. 1994), **97**
Great Global Assurance Co. v. McFarlin, 728 S.W.2d 401 (Tex. App. 1987), 471
Great Northern Railway v. Alexander, 246 U.S. 276 (1918), 378
Great Northern Railway v. Merchants Elevator Co., 259 U.S. 285 (1922), 436
Greater Rockford Energy and Technology Corp. v. Shell Oil Co., 790 F. Supp. 804 (C.D. Ill. 1992), 1039
Green v. Forney Engineering Co., 589 F.2d 243 (5th Cir. 1979), 923

Green v. Wolf, 406 F.2d 291 (2d Cir. 1968), 622
Green v. County School Board, 391 U.S. 430 (1968), 1390
Greenholtz v. Inmates of the Nebraska Penal and Correctional Complex, 442 U.S. 1 (1979), 1228
Greenhouse v. Hargrave, 509 P.2d 1360 (Okla. 1973), 440
Griffin v. Prince Edward County School Board, 377 U.S. 218 (1964), 1426, 1429
Grimes v. Vitalink Communications Corp., 17 F.3d 1553 (3d Cir.), 308
Grode v. Mutual Fire, Marine & Inland Insurance Co., 8 F.3d 953 (3d Cir. 1993), 429
Gross v. Barnett Banks, Inc., 934 F. Supp. 1340 (M.D. Fla. 1995), 656
Growe v. Emison, 507 U.S. 25 (1993), 191
Gruber v. Price Waterhouse, 117 F.R.D. 75 (E.D. Pa. 1987), 873, 874
Grundberg v. Upjohn Co., 137 F.R.D. 372 (D. Utah 1991), 1151
Guaranty Trust Co. v. York, 326 U.S. 99 (1945), 277, 812
Guilden v. Baldwin Securities Corp., 189 A.D.2d 716, 592 N.Y.S.2d 725 (1993), 440, 441
Gulf Oil Corp. v. Gilbert, 330 U.S. 501 (1947), 458, 460, 463, 466
Gully v. First National Bank, 299 U.S. 109 (1936), 321

H.L. Green Co. v. MacMahon, 312 F.2d 650 (2d Cir. 1962), 821
Haas v. Jefferson National Bank, 442 F.2d 394 (5th Cir. 1971), 129
Hagan v. Lucas, 35 U.S. (10 Pet.) 400 (U.S. 1836), 391
Haines v. Liggett Group, Inc., 975 F.2d 81 (3rd Cir. 1992), 915, 916, 917, 922, 923, 924, 925, 960, 971, 976
Haines v. Liggett Group, Inc., 814 F. Supp. 414 (D.N.J. 1993), **915**
Haley v. Medtronic, Inc., 169 F.R.D. 643 (C.D. Cal. 1996), 609, 644, 645
Hall v. Baxter Healthcare Corp., 947 F. Supp. 1387 (D. Or. 1996), 1172, 1252, 1253
Hall v. E.I. DuPont De Nemours & Co., Inc., 345 F. Supp. 353 (E.D.N.Y. 1972), 113, 114
Halmos v. Safecard Services, Inc., 272 Ill. App. 3d 532, 650 N.E.2d 555 (1995), 471
Hammes v. Aamco Transmissions, Inc., 33 F.3d 774 (7th Cir. 1994), 990
In re Hanford Nuclear Reservation Litigation, 780 F. Supp. 1551 (E.D. Wash.

1991), 991
Hanlon v. Chrysler Corp., 1998 WL 296890 (9th Cir.), 686
Hanover Shoe, Inc. v. United Shoe Machinery Corp., 392 U.S. 481 (1968), 1419
Hans v. Louisiana, 134 U.S. 1 (1890), 360
Hansberry v. Lee, 311 U.S. 32 (1940), 162, 185, 186, 193, 208, 210, 211, 212, 222, 229, 230, 231, 242, 297, 299, 302, 535, 571, 573, 578, 580, 581
Hanson v. Denckla, 357 U.S. 235 (1958), 264, 265
Harbolt v. Carpenter, 536 F.2d 791 (8th Cir. 1976), 817
In re Harcourt Brace Jovanovich, Inc. Securities Litigation, 838 F. Supp. 109 (S.D.N.Y. 1993), 958
Hardy v. Johns-Manville Sales Corp., 509 F. Supp. 1353 (E.D. Tex. 1981), 1307
Hardy v. Johns-Manville Sales Corp., 681 F.2d 334 (5th Cir. 1982), **194, 222**
Harkin v. Brundage, 276 U.S. 36 (1928), 391
Harleysville Mutual Insurance Co. v. Sussex County, Delaware, 831 F. Supp. 1111 (D. Del. 1993), 1017
Harlow v. Fitzgerald, 457 U.S. 800 (1982), 988
Harmon v. Adams & Sons Roofing Co., 120 F.R.D. 78 (N.D. Ind. 1987), 923
Harmsen v. Smith, 693 F.2d 932 (9th Cir. 1982), 842
Harrell v. 20th Century Insurance Co., 934 F.2d 203 (9th Cir. 1991), 385
Harris v. Pernsley, 820 F.2d 592 (3d Cir. 1987), 145
Hart v. Community School Board of Brooklyn, 383 F. Supp. 699 (E.D.N.Y. 1974), 1248, 1355
Hart Steel Co. v. Railroad Supply Co., 244 U.S. 294 (1917), 159
Havens Realty Corp. v. Coleman, 455 U.S. 363 (1982), 369
Havoco of America, Ltd. v. Freeman, Atkins & Coleman, Ltd., 58 F.3d 303 (7th Cir. 1995), 169
Hayes v. Gulf Oil Corp., 821 F.2d 285 (5th Cir. 1987), 456
Healy v. Sea Gull Specialty Co., 237 U.S. 479 (1915), 316
Heaven v. Trust Co. Bank, 118 F.3d 735 (11th Cir. 1997), 558, 630
Heck v. Humphrey, 512 U.S. 477 (1994), 169
Heiser v. Woodruff, 327 U.S. 726 (1946), 159
Heller Financial, Inc. v. Midwhey Powder Co., 883 F.2d 1286 (7th Cir. 1989), 492

Helminski v. Ayerst Laboratories, 766 F.2d 208 (6th Cir. 1985), 1277
Hemmings v. United States, 842 F. Supp. 935 (S.D. Tex. 1993), 470
Hemstreet v. Burroughs Corp., 666 F. Supp. 1096 (N.D. Ill. 1987), 1253
Hendrix v. Raybestos-Manhattan, Inc., 776 F.2d 1492 (11th Cir. 1985), 475
Henkel v. ITT Bowest Corp., 872 F. Supp. 872 (D. Kan. 1994), 354
Herb v. Pitcairn, 324 U.S. 117 (1945), 438
Herbert v. Lando, 441 U.S. 153 (1979), 1093, 1130
Hickman v. Taylor, 329 U.S. 495 (1947), 1145, 1186
Hiern v. Sarpy, 161 F.R.D. 332 (E.D. La. 1995), **1348**
Hilao v. Estate of Ferdinand Marcos, 103 F.3d 767 (9th Cir. 1996), 1162, 1287, **1299**, 1420
Hill v. Martin, 296 U.S. 393 (1935), 401
Hillman v. Webley, 115 F.3d 1461 (10th Cir. 1997), 389
Hills v. Gautreaux, 425 U.S. 284 (1976), 1399
Hinkle v. City of Clarksburg, West Virginia, 81 F.3d 416 (4th Cir. 1996), **1338**
Hobbs v. Northeast Airlines, 50 F.R.D. 76 (E.D. Pa. 1976), 620
Hoffman v. Blaski, 363 U.S. 335 (1960), 489, 514
Hohlbein v. Heritage Mutual Insurance Co., 106 F.R.D. 73 (E.D. Wis. 1985), 104
Holcomb v. Aetna Life Insurance Co., 228 F.2d 75 (10th Cir. 1955), 420
Holcomb v. Aetna Life Insurance Co., 255 F.2d 577 (10th Cir. 1958), 1075, 1076
Holman v. State Farm General Insurance Co., 1991 WL 219425 (W.D. Mo.), 113
Holmes v. Continental Can Co., 706 F.2d 1144 (11th Cir. 1983), 611, 614
Holt v. Lockheed Support Systems, Inc., 835 F. Supp. 325 (W.D. La. 1993), 339, 382
Home Indemnity Co. v. Hoechst-Celanese Corp., 99 N.C. App. 322, 393 S.E.2d 118 (1990), 440
Hooker Chemicals & Plastic Corp. v. Attorney General, 100 Mich. App. 203, 298 N.W.2d 710 (1980), 425
Hoptowit v. Ray, 682 F.2d 1237 (9th Cir. 1982), 154, 155, 1446
In re Hotel Telephone Charges, 500 F.2d 86 (9th Cir. 1974), 1415
Howard v. Globe Life Insurance Co., 973 F. Supp. 1412 (N.D. Fla. 1996), 339
Howlett v. Rose, 496 U.S. 356 (1990), 437,

438, 439, 447
Hubbard v. Parker, 994 F.2d 524 (8th Cir. 1993), 1077
Huffman v. Pursue, Ltd., 420 U.S. 592 (1975), 430
Hughes v. United States, 953 F.2d 531 (9th Cir. 1992), 132
Hunt v. Washington State Apple Advertising Commission, 432 U.S. 333 (1977), 339
Hurn v. Oursler, 289 U.S. 238 (1933), 342
Hutto v. Finney, 437 U.S. 678 (1978), 361, 1399
Hydrite Chemicals Co. v. Calumet Lubricants Co., 47 F.3d 887 (7th Cir.1995), 1283, 1291
Hymowitz v. Eli Lilly and Co., 73 N.Y.2d 487, 539 N.E.2d 1069 (1989), 280, 281, 282, 283, 284, 290, 291

Idaho v. Couer d'Alene Tribe of Idaho, 117 S. Ct. 2028 (1997), 361, 362
ILC Peripherals leasing Corp. v. International Business Machine Corp., 458 F. Supp. 423 (N.D. Cal. 1980), **1232**, 1233
Ilhardt v. A.O. Smith Corp., 168 F.R.D. 613 (S.D. Oh. 1996), 842
Illinois v. City of Milwaukee, Wisconsin, 406 U.S. 91 (1972), 852
Illinois Brick Co. v. Illinois, 431 U.S. 720 (1977), 129
In the Matter of — See name of party
INA Underwriters Insurance Co. v. Nalibotsky, 594 F. Supp. 1199 (E.D. Pa. 1984), 910
Industrial Development Corp. v. Mitsui & Co., 671 F.2d 876 (5th Cir. 1982), 461, 462
In re Industrial Diamonds Antitrust Litigation, 167 F.R.D. 374 (S.D.N.Y. 1996), 629
In re Industrial Gas Antitrust Litigation, 1985 WL 2869 (N.D. Ill.), 973, 975
Industry Network System, Inc. v. Armstrong World Industries, Inc., 54 F.3d 150 (3d Cir. 1995), 924
In re Innotron Diagnostics, 800 F.2d 1077 (Fed. Cir. 1986), 1289
In re — See name of party
Inset Systems, Inc. v. Instruction Set, Inc., 937 F. Supp. 161 (D. Conn. 1996), 275
Insurance Co. of the State of Pennsylvania v. Syntex Corp., 964 F.2d 829 (8th Cir. 1992), 433
Insurance Corp. of Ireland v. Compagnie des Bauxites de Guinee, 456 U.S. 694 (1982), 273, 283, 296, 300, 1046

Intercon Research Associates, Ltd. v. Dresser Industries, Inc., 696 F.2d 53 (7th Cir. 1982), 111, 112, 113
International Business Machines, Inc. v. Levin, 579 F.2d 271 (3d Cir. 1978), 908, 911
In re International Business Machines Corp., 618 F.2d 923 (2d Cir. 1980), 969, 970, **1362**
International Controls Corp. v. Vesco, 490 F.2d 1334 (2d Cir. 1974), 398
International Primate Protection League v. Administrators of Tulane Educational Fund, 500 U.S. 72 (1991), 383
International Shoe Co. v. Washington, 326 U.S. 310 (1945), 263, 265, 267, 270, 281, 295, 296, 305
International Union, United Mine Workers of America v. Bagwell, 512 U.S. 821 (1994), 1433
Interstate Properties v. Pyrmaid Co., 547 F. Supp. 178 (S.D.N.Y. 1982), 911
Irving Trust Co. v. Nationwide Leisure Corp., 562 F. Supp. 960 (S.D.N.Y. 1982), 422
Iskander v. Columbia Cement Co., 197 N.J.Super. 169, 484 A.2d 353 (App. Div. 1984), 920
In re Itel Securities Litigation, 89 F.R.D. 104 (N.D. Cal. 1981), 689
IUE AFL-CIO Pension Fund v. Hermann, 9 F.3d 1049 (2d Cir. 1993), 274
In re Ivan Boesky Securities Litigation, 948 F.2d 1358 (2d Cir. 1991), 889
In re Ivy, 901 F.2d 7 (2d Cir. 1990), 515

J & M Turner, Inc. v. Applied Bolting Technology Products, Inc., 1997 U.S. Dist. LEXIS 1835 (E.D. Pa.), 1357
J.R. Clearwater Inc. v. Ashland Chemical Co., 93 F.3d 176 (5th Cir. 1996), 206, 400
Jack Walters & Sons Corp. v. Morton Building, Inc., 737 F.2d 698 (7th Cir. 1984), 948
Jackson v. J.C. Penney Co., 521 F. Supp. 1032 (N.D. Ga. 1981), 911
Jackson v. Johns-Manville Sales Corp., 750 F.2d 1314 (5th Cir. 1985), 192, 854
Jackson v. Motel 6 Multipurposes, Inc., 130 F.3d 999 (11th Cir. 1997), 254
In re Jackson Lockdown/MCO Cases, 568 F. Supp. 869 (E.D. Mich. 1983), 992
Jaguar Cars, Inc. v. Royal Oaks Motor Car Co., Inc., 46 F.3d 258 (3d Cir. 1995), 986
James Julian, Inc. v. Raytheon Company, 93 F.R.D. 138 (D. Del. 1982), 1184
James v. Grand Trunk Western Railroad

Co., 14 Ill. 2d 356, 152 N.E.2d 858, 472
In re: Japanese Electronic Products Antitrust Litigation, 631 F.2d 1069 (3d Cir. 1980), 1070, **1223**, 1259
Jenkins v. McKeithen, 395 U.S. 411 (1969), 1328
Jenkins v. Raymark Industries, Inc., 782 F.2d 468 (5th Cir. 1986), 600, **632**, 640, 661, 1294, 1307
Jennings v. Emry, 910 F.2d 1434 (7th Cir. 1990), 993
In re: Jensen, 995 F.2d 925 (9th Cir. 1993), 762
Jepson, Inc. v. Makita Electric Works, Ltd., 30 F.3d 854 (7th Cir. 1994), 1152
In re Jiffy Lube Securities Litigation, 927 F.2d 155 (4th Cir. 1991), 1456, 1457, 1458
Jim Beam Brands Co. v. Beamish & Crawford Ltd., 937 F.2d 729 (2d Cir. 1991), 204
In the Matter of Johns-Manville Corp., 26 B.R. 405 (Bankr. S.D.N.Y. 1983), 745, 751
In re Johns Manville Corp., 33 Bankr. 254 (S.D.N.Y. 1983), 744, 745
In re Johns-Manville Corp., 36 B.R. 743 (Bankr. S.D.N.Y. 1984), 755, 762, 786
In re Johns-Manville Corp., 40 Bankr. 219, 229 (S.D.N.Y. 1984), 744
In re Johns-Manville Corp., 52 B.R. 940 (S.D.N.Y. 1985), **755**
Johnson v. Ashby, 808 F.2d 676 (8th Cir. 1987), 1325
Johnson v. Celotex Corp., 899 F.2d 1281 (2d Cir. 1990), **473**, 479, 483, 484, 1337
Johnson v. Georgia Highway Express, Inc., 417 F.2d 1122 (1969), 565, 569
Johnson v. General Motors Corp., 598 F.2d 432 (5th Cir. 1979), 611
Johnson v. Indopco, Inc., 846 F. Supp. 670 (N.D. Ill. 1994), 104
Johnson v. Manhattan Railway Co., 289 U.S. 479 (1933), 486, 994
Joico Laboratories, Inc. v. Fuencarral, 1993 WL 332563 (C.D. Cal. 1993), 382
Joint Anti-Fascist Refugee Committee v. McGrath, 341 U.S. 123 (1951), 26
In re Joint Eastern & Southern Districts Asbestos Litigation, 125 F.R.D. 60 (E.D.N.Y. 1989), 476, 480
In re Joint Eastern and Southern District Asbestos Litigation (Eagle-Picher Industries), 134 F.R.D. 32 (E. & S.D.N.Y. 1990), 782
In re Joint Eastern and Southern Districts Asbestos Litigation, 120 B.R. 648 (E. & S.D.N.Y. 1990), 399

In re Joint Eastern and Southern Districts Asbestos Litigation, 769 F. Supp. 85 (E. & S.D.N.Y. 1991), **487**, 501
In re Eastern & Southern Districts Asbestos Litigation, 772 F. Supp. 1380 (E. & S.D.N.Y. 1991), 1336, 1337
In re Joint Eastern and Southern Districts Asbestos Litigation, 129 B.R. 710 (E. & S.D.N.Y. 1991), 591, 771, 854, 865
In re Joint Eastern and Southern District Asbestos Litigation, 982 F.2d 721 (2d Cir. 1992), 305, 306, 307, 308, 309, 337, 682, 728, 771, 779, 782
In re Joint Eastern and Southern District Asbestos Litigation, 993 F.2d 7 (2d Cir. 1993), 777
In re Joint Eastern & Southern District Asbestos Litigation, 134 F.R.D. 32 (E. & S.D.N.Y. 1990), 617
In re Joint Eastern and Southern Districts Asbestos Litigation, 151 F.R.D. 540 (E. & S.D.N.Y. 1993), 954, 1253, 1355, 1356, 1358
In re Eastern and Southern District Asbestos Litigation, 14 F.3d 726 (2d Cir. 1993), 740, **778**, 782
In re Joint Eastern and Southern Districts Asbestos Litigation, 830 F. Supp. 686 (E.& S.D.N.Y. 1993), 1357
In re Joint Eastern and Southern Districts Asbestos Litigation, 878 F. Supp. 473 (E. & S.D.N.Y. 1995), 765, 767, 768, 777
In re Joint Eastern and Southern District Asbestos Litigation, 78 F.3d 764 (2d Cir. 1996), 306, 308, 429, 435, 765, 777
In re Joint Eastern and Southern Districts Asbestos Litigation, 929 F. Supp. 1 (E. & S.D.N.Y 1996), 777
Jonas v. Conrath, 149 F.R.D. 520 (S.D. W.Va. 1993), 113
Jones & Laughlin Steel Corp. v. Pfeifer, 462 U.S. 523 (1983), 1253
Juidice v. Vail, 430 U.S. 327 (1977), 430
Jungquist v. Sheikh Sultan Bin Khalifa al Nahyan, 115 F.3d 1020 (D.C. Cir. 1997), 275
Justice Jackson in Northwest Airlines v. Minnesota, 322 U.S. 292 (1944), 846
Juzwin v. Amtorg Trading Co., 705 F. Supp. 1053 (D.N.J. 1989), 1409

Kabealo v. Davis, 829 F. Supp. 923 (S.D. Ohio 1993), 359
Kahn v. General Motors Corp., 889 F.2d 1078 (Fed. Cir. 1989), 467
Kalmanovitz v. G. Heilman Brewing Co., 610 F. Supp. 1319 (D. Del. 1985), 906
Kamilewicz v. Bank of Boston, 92 F.3d 506

(7th Cir. 1996), 655
Kane v. Johns-Manville Corp., 843 F.2d 636 (2d Cir. 1988), 764
Kapco Manufacturing Co. v. C & D Enterprises, Inc., 637 F. Supp. 1231 (N.D. Ill. 1985), 912
Katz v. Realty Equities Corp. of New York, 521 F.2d 1354 (2d Cir. 1975), 885, **994**
Kaufman v. Edelstein, 539 F.2d 811 (2d Cir. 1976), 1172, 1173
Keene Corp. v. Caldwell, 840 S.W.2d 715 (Tex. Ct. App. 1992), 1152
Keeton v. Hustler Magazine, Inc., 465 U.S. 770 (1984), 269, 283, 284, 287
Kemner v. Monsanto Co., 217 Ill. App. 3d 188, 576 N.E.2d 1146 (1991), 1272
Kempe v. Ocean Drilling and Exploration Co., 876 F.2d 1138 (5th Cir. 1989), **458**
Kennedy v. Tallant, 710 F.2d 711 (11th Cir. 1983), 624, 626
Kennedy v. Silas Mason Co., 334 U.S. 249 (1948), 1070
Kenny v. Scientific, Inc., 512 A.2d 1142 (N.J. Super. Ct., Law Div.), 1233
Kenvin v. Newburger, Loeb & Co., 37 F.R.D. 473 (S.D.N.Y. 1965), 110
Kerotest Manufacturing Co. v. C-O-Two Fire Equipment Co., 342 U.S. 180 (1952), 163, 467, 469
Kerr v. United States District Court, 426 U.S. 394 (1976), 1129
Key v. Wise, 629 F.2d 1049 (5th Cir. 1980), 429
Kian v. Mirro Aluminum Co., 88 F.R.D. 351 (E.D. Mich. 1980), 1233, 1356, 1358
Kimberly v. Arms, 129 U.S. 512 (1889), 952, 1250, 1254
Kimberly-Clark Corp. v. James River Corp. of Virginia, 131 F.R.D. 607 (N.D. Ga. 1989), 1290
Kinoy v. Mitchell, 67 F.R.D. 1 (S.D.N.Y. 1975), 1140, 1141, 1142
Kirkpatrick v. J.C. Bradford & Co., 827 F.2d 718 (11th Cir. 1987), **622**
Klaxon Co. v. Stentor Electric Manfacturing Co., 313 U.S. 387 (1941), 806, 807, 810, 820, 835, 856
Klein v. King, 132 F.R.D. 525 (N.D. Cal. 1990), 958, **1117**
Kline v. Burke Construction Co., 260 U.S. 226 (1922), 391, 405, 406, 407
Kline v. Coldwell, Banker & Co., 508 F.2d 226 (9th Cir. 1974), 546, 548, 691, 1411
Koehlke Components, Inc. v. South East Connectors, Inc., 456 So. 2d 554 (Fla. App. 1984), 440

Kohr v. Allegheny Airlines, Inc., 504 F.2d 400 (7th Cir. 1974), **845**
In re Korean Air Lines Disaster of September 1, 1983, 829 F.2d 1171 (D.C. Cir. 1987), **820**
Koster v. Lumbermens Mutual Casualty Co., 330 U.S. 518 (1947), 460, 463
Kremer v. Chemical Construction Corp., 456 U.S. 461 (1982), 167, 168, 185, 186
Krumme v. West Point-Pepperell, Inc., 735 F. Supp. 575 (S.D.N.Y. 1990), 1173
Kulko v. California Superior Court, 436 U.S. 84 (1978), 263, 264, 265
Kyriazi v. Western Electric Co., 465 F. Supp. 1141 (D.N.J. 1979), **1406**

La Buy v. Howes Leather Co., 352 U.S. 249 (1957), 943, 945, 946, 1249, **1254**, 1349, 1444, 1447
Laker Airways Ltd. v. Pan American World Airways, 568 F. Supp. 811 (D.D.C. 1983), 461
Laker Airways Ltd. v. Sabena, Belgian World Airlines, 731 F.2d 909 (D.C. Cir. 1984), 472
La Mar v. H & B Novelty & Loan Co., 489 F.2d 461 (9th Cir. 1973), 548, 549, 596, 691
Lanehart v. Devine, 102 F.R.D. 592 (D. Md. 1984), 107
Larson v. Dumke, 900 F.2d 1363 (9th Cir. 1990), 188
Laskey v. UAW, 638 F.2d 954 (6th Cir. 1981), 611
League to Save Lake Tahoe v. Tahoe Regional Planning Agency, 558 F.2d 914 (9th Cir. 1977), 112, 113
Leatherman v. Tarrant County Narcotics Intelligence and Coordination Unit, 954 F.2d 1054 (5th Cir. 1992), 988
Leatherman v. Tarrant County Narcotics Intelligence and Coordination Unit, 507 U.S. 163 (1993), 984, 986, 988
Lehman Brothers v. Schein, 416 U.S. 386 (1974), 434
Leiter Minerals v. United States, 352 U.S. 220 (1957), 400
Lemaine v. Texaco, Inc., 496 F. Supp. 1308 (E.D. Tex. 1980), 910
Lempel & Son Co. v. Boden, 1993 WL 256711 (S.D.N.Y.), 202, 1291, 1293
Leroy v. Great Western United Corp., 443 U.S. 173 (1979), 453, 454
In re Letter of Request from Amtsgericht Ingolstadt, Federal Republic of Germany, 82 F.3d 590 (4th Cir. 1996), 1168
Leverence v. PFS Corp., 193 Wis. 2d 317, 532 N.W.2d 735 (1995), 1313, 1314

Lewis v. Goldsmith, 95 F.R.D. 15 (D.N.J. 1982), 583

Lexecon Inc. v. Milberg Weiss Bershad Hynes & Lerach, 118 S. Ct. 956 (1998), **516,** 829, 845

Lightning Tube, Inc. v. Witco Corp., 4 F.3d 1153 (3d Cir. 1993), 991

Liljeberg v. Health Services Acquisition Corp., 486 U.S. 847 (1988), 964, 966, 969, 972, 974

Lindsey v. Admiral Insurance Co., 804 F. Supp. 47 (N.D. Cal. 1992), 922

Link v. Wabash R. Co., 370 U.S. 626 (1962), 1044, 1046

Liptak v. United States, 748 F.2d 1254 (8th Cir. 1984), 1258, 1260

Lis v. Robert Packer Hospital, 579 F.2d 819 (3d Cir. 1978), 1293

Liteky v. United States, 510 U.S. 540 (1994), 969, 971, 972, 974, 976

Livingston v. Jefferson, 15 Fed. Cas. 660 (No. 8411) (C.C.D. Va. 1811), 455

Lloyds Bank PLC v. Republic of Ecuador, 1997 WL 96591 (S.D.N.Y.), 1147

Local 670, United Rubber, Cork, Linoleum and Plastic Workers v. International Union, United Rubber, Cork, Linoleum and Plastic Workers, 822 F.2d 613 (6th Cir. 1987), 132

Local Number 939, International Association of Firefighters v. City of Cleveland, 478 U.S. 501 (1986), 234

Locks v. United States Trustee, 157 B.R. 89 (W.D. Pa. 1993), 766

Long v. District of Columbia, 469 U.S. 927 (D.C. Cir. 1972), 555

Long v. Trans World Airlines, Inc., 761 F. Supp. 1320 (N.D. Ill. 1991), 1314

Loral Corp. v. McDonnell Douglas Corp., 558 F.2d 1130 (2d Cir. 1977), 1234, 1258

Loran v. Furr's/Bishop's Inc., 988 F.2d 554 (5th Cir. 1993), 553

Lore v. Lone Pine, 1 Tox Law Rpt (BNA) 726, 1027, 1029

Los Angeles Branch NAACP v. Los Angeles Unified Sch. Dist., 750 F.2d 731 (9th Cir.1984), 219

Los Angeles Brush Manufacturing Corp. v. James, 272 U.S. 701 (1927), 943

Louisiana v. Texas, 176 U.S. 1 (1900), 149

Louisville, C. & C. R. Co. v. Letson, 43 U.S. (2 How.) 497 (U.S. 1844), 328

Louisville & Nashville RR. Co. v. Mottley, 211 U.S. 149 (1908), 311, 312, 316, 848

Louisiana Power and Light Co. v. City of Thibodaux, 360 U.S. 25 (1959), 427, 434, 447

In re Love Canal Actions, 145 Misc. 2d 1076, 547 N.Y.S.2d 174 (N.Y. Sup. Ct. 1989), **1024**

Lowe v. Philadelphia Newspapers, Inc., 594 F. Supp. 123 (E.D. Pa. 1984), 1293

Lujan v. Defenders of Wildlife, 504 U.S. 555 (1992), 364, 365, 367

Lumbermens Mutual Casualty Co. v. Connecticut Bank & Trust Co., 806 F.2d 411 (2d Cir. 1986), 433

Lusardi v. Xerox Corp., 975 F.2d 964 (3d Cir.1992), 369, 370

Lynch v. Merrell-National Laboratories, 646 F. Supp. 856 (D. Mass. 1986), 225

Lynch v. Merrell-National Laboratories, 830 F.2d 1190 (1st Cir. 1987), 228

Lyne v. Arthur Anderson & Co.. 1991 WL 247576 (N.D. Ill.), 106

MacAlister v. Guterma, 263 F.2d 65 (2d Cir. 1958), 884, 885, 1202, 1203

MacArthur Co. v. Johns-Manville Corp., 837 F.2d 89 (2d Cir. 1988), 749

Mace v. Van Ru Credit Corp., 109 F.3d 338 (1997), 677

Mack Trucks, Inc. v. Conkle, 263 Ga. 539, 436 S.E.2d 635 (1993), 1409

Mackay Construction Corp. v. Brooklyn Union Gas Co., 39 A.D.2d 687, 332 N.Y.S.2d 486 (1972), 441

Madewell v. Downs, 68 F.3d 1030 (8th Cir. 1995), 1077

Madrigal Audio Laboratories, Inc. v. Cello, Ltd., 799 F.2d 814 (2d Cir. 1986), 1260, 1264

Maenner v. St. Paul Fire and Marine Insurance Co., 127 F.R.D. 488 (W.D. Mich. 1989), 1288, 1290, 1292

Mahan v. Gunther, 278 Ill. App. 3d 1108, 663 N.E.2d 1139 (1996), 471

Makah Indian Tribe v. Verity, 910 F.2d 555 (9th Cir. 1990), 129

Malcolm v. National Gypsum Co., 995 F.2d 346 (2d Cir. 1993), **476**

Male v. Crossroads Associates, 320 F. Supp. 141 (S.D.N.Y. 1970), 563

Mallard Bay Drilling, Inc. v. Bessard, 145 F.R.D. 405 (W.D. La. 1993), 1350

Maniar v. Federal Deposit Insurance Corp., 979 F.2d 782 (9th Cir. 1992), 388

In the Matter of Manges, 29 F.3d 1034 (5th Cir. 1994), 778

Marbury v. Madison, 1 Cranch 137 (1803), 310, 1041

Marcera v. Chinlund, 91 F.R.D. 579 (W.D.N.Y. 1981), 690

Marcera v. Chinlund, 595 F.2d 1231 (2d Cir. 1979), 690

Marfia v. T.C. Ziraat Bankski, 874 F. Supp. 560 (S.D.N.Y. 1994), 923

Maritz Inc. v. Cybergold Inc., 947 F. Supp. 1328 (E.D. Mo. 1997), 275

Markeise v. Peck Foods Corp., 556 N.W.2d 326 (Wis. App. 1996), 1314

Markman v. Westview Instruments, Inc., 517 U.S. 370 (1996), 1217, 1218, 1234

Marrese v. American Academy of Orthopaedic Surgeons, 726 F.2d 1150 (7th Cir. 1984), **1127**

Marrese v. American Academy of Orthopaedic Surgeons, 470 U.S. 373 (1985), 168

Mars Steel Corp. v. Illinois National Bank and Trust Co. of Chicago, 834 F.2d 677 (7th Cir. 1987), 654, 657

Martin v. Hunter's Lessee, 1 Wheaton 304 (1816), 302, 310

Martin v. Wilks, 490 U.S. 755 (1989), 209, 210, 212, 231, **240**, 251, 252, 302, 361, 608

Martin v. Reynolds Metals Corp., 297 F.2d 49 (9th Cir. 1961), 1108

Martindell v. International Telephone & Telegraph Co., 594 F.2d 291 (2d Cir. 1979), 1112

Maryland v. United States, 460 U.S. 1001 (1983), 1042

Maryland Staffing Services, Inc. v. Manpower, Inc., 936 F. Supp. 1494 (E.D. Wis. 1996), 993

In re Master Key Antitrust Litigation, 528 F.2d 5 (2d Cir. 1975), 1293

Mathews v. Eldridge, 424 U.S. 319 (1976), 9, 10, 614, 1228, 1304, 1305, 1313

Mathews v. Weber, 423 U.S. 261 (1976), 956

Matsushita Electric Industrial Co. v. Epstein, 516 U.S. 367 (1996), 168, 179, 181, 190, 583, 641, 655, 656

Matsushita Electric Industrial Co. v. Zenith Radio Corp., 475 U.S. 574 (1986), **1050**, 1224, 1235

Matter of Hendrix, 986 F.2d 195 (7th Cir. 1993), 751

Matter of the Petition of Oskar Tiedemann and Co., 183 F. Supp. 129 (D. Del. 1960), 154

Max Daetwyler Corp. v. R. Meyer, 762 F.2d 290 (3d Cir. 1985), 269

Mayo v. Key Financial Services, Inc., 812 F. Supp. 277 (D. Mass. 1993), 354

Maywalt v. Parker & Parsley Petroleum Co., 147 F.R.D. 51 (S.D.N.Y. 1993), 842

McCarthy v. Kleindienst, 741 F.2d 1406 (D.C. Cir. 1984), 1290

In re MCA Shareholders Litigation, 598 A.2d 687 (Del. Ch. 1991), 187

MCI Communications Corp. v. American Telephone and Telegraph Co., 708 F.2d 1081 (7th Cir. 1983), **1319**

McGee v. International Life Insurance Co., 355 U.S. 220 (1957), 263, 264, 269

McKinnon v. Patterson, 568 F.2d 930 (2d Cir. 1977), 612

McKnight v. General Motors Corp., 908 F.2d 104 (7th Cir. 1990), 1323, 1324, 1325, 1326

McLaughlin v. Anderson, 962 F.2d 187 (2d Cir. 1992), 991

Meeks v. Metropolitan Dade County, Florida, 985 F.2d 1471 (11th Cir. 1993), 155

Meeropol v. Meese, 790 F.2d 942 (D.C. Cir. 1986), 954

Mekdeci v. Merrell National Laboratories, 711 F.2d 1510 (11th Cir. 1983), 922

Memorex Corp. v. IBM, 636 F.2d 1188 (9th Cir. 1980), 1233

Menowitz v. Brown, 991 F.2d 36 (2d Cir. 1993), 827, 828

Meranus v. Gangel, 1991 WL 120484 (S.D.N.Y.), 1288

Meredith v. Beech Aircraft Corp., 18 F.3d 890 (10th Cir. 1994), 1409

Merrell Dow Pharmaceuticals, Inc. v. Thompson, 478 U.S. 804 (1986), **314**

Mesa v. California, 489 U.S. 121 (1989), 383

Messick v. Star Enterprise, 655 A.2d 1209 (Del. 1995), 182

Metropolitan Life Insurance Co. v. Taylor, 481 U.S. 58 (1987), 312, 382

In re MGM Grand Hotel Fire Litigation, 570 F. Supp. 913, 917 (D. Nev. 1983), 897, 958

In re: MGM Grand Hotel Fire Litigation, 660 F. Supp. 522 (D. Nev. 1987), **891**, 1125

Michel v. Anderson, 14 F.3d 623 (D.C. Cir. 1994), 154

Middlesex Ethics Commission v. Garden State Bar Association, 457 U.S. 423 (1982), 430

Migra v. Warren City School District Board of Education, 465 U.S. 75 (1984), 166

Migues v. Fibreboard Corp., 662 F.2d 1182 (5th Cir. 1981), 207

Milford Power Ltd. Partnership v. New England Power Co., 896 F. Supp. 53 (D. Mass. 1995), 1147

Miller v. New Jersey Transit Authority Rail Operations, 160 F.R.D. 37 (D. N.J. 1995), 1287, 1291, 1293

Milliken v. Bradley, 418 U.S. 717 (1974),

1389, 1395
Milliken v. Bradley, 433 U.S. 267 (1977), 1389, 1396, 1397, 1401, 1427, 1428, 1429
Milliken v. Bradley, 620 F.2d 1143 (6th Cir. 1980), 1402, 1422, 1423
Milliken v. Meyer, 311 U.S. 457 (1940), 261
Mims v. Duval County School Board, 447 F.2d 1330 (5th Cir. 1971), 1445
Miree v. DeKalb County, 433 U.S. 25 (1977), 848, 850, 852
Missouri ex rel. Southern R. Co. v. Mayfield, 340 U.S. 1 (1950), 438
Missouri v. Jenkins, 495 U.S. 33 (1990), **1394, 1424,** 1443, 1448
Missouri v. Jenkins, 515 U.S. 70 (1995), **1392,** 1410, 1414, 1433
Mitchum v. Foster, 407 U.S. 225 (1972), 398, 401
Mondou v. New York, N. H. & H. R. Co., 223 U.S. 1 (1912), 438
Monotype Corp. PLC v. International Typeface Corp., 43 F.3d 443 (9th Cir. 1994), 1323, 1325
Monroe v. Board of Commissioners, 391 U.S. 450 (1968), 1390
Montana v. United States, 440 U.S. 147 (1979), 210, 216, 229, 230, 231, 242
Mooney v. Fibreboard Corp., 485 F. Supp. 242 (E.D. Tex. 1980), 224
Moore v. New York, 333 U.S. 565 (1948), 1241
Moore v. New York Cotton Exchange, 270 U.S. 593 (1926), 95, 344
Morales v. Turman, 383 F. Supp. 53 (E.D. Tex. 1974), 1423
Morongo Band of Mission Indians v. California State Board of Equalization, 858 F.2d 1376 (9th Cir. 1988), 418
Morrissey v. City of New York, 171 F.R.D. 85 (S.D.N.Y. 1997), 1113
Mortgagelinq Corp. v. Commonwealth Land Title Insurance Co., 142 N.J. 336, 662 A.2d 536 (1995), 132
Moses H. Cone Memorial Hospital v. Mercury Construction Corp., 460 U.S. 1 (1983), 398, 432, 433
Mosley v. General Motors Corp., 497 F.2d 1330 (8th Cir. 1974), **93,** 98, 111, 581
Movie Systems, Inc. v. Abel, 99 F.R.D. 129 (D. Minn. 1983), 113
M.T. Bonk Co. v. Milton Bradley Co., 945 F.2d 1404 (7th Cir. 1991), 1325
Mullane v. Central Hanover Trust Co., 339 U.S. 306 (1950), 210, 263, 297, 299, 302
In re Multi-Piece Rim Products Liability Litigation, 653 F.2d 671 (D.C. Cir. 1981), 1091

In re Murchison, 349 U.S. 133 (1955), 965
Murphy v. Travelers Insurance Co., 534 F.2d 1155 (5th Cir. 1976), 421, 616
Musick, Peeler & Garret v. Employers Insurance of Wausau, 508 U.S. 286 (1993), 853
Myers v. Celotex Corp., 88 Md. App. 442, 594 A.2d 1248 (1991), 1293

NAACP v. Alabama, 357 U.S. 449 (1958), 1129
NAACP v. Hunt, 891 F.2d 1555 (11th Cir. 1990), 169, 217, 230, 234
N.A.A.C.P. v. Seibels, 31 F.3d 1548 (11th Cir. 1994), 252
Nagler v. Admiral Corp., 248 F.2d 319 (2d Cir. 1957), **980**
Nassau County Association of Insurance Agents, Inc. v. Aetna Life & Casualty Co., 497 F.2d 1151 (2d Cir. 1974), **109**
National Association of Radiation Survivors v. Turnage, 115 F.R.D. 543 (N.D. Cal. 1987), 1105
National Auto Brokers Corp. v. General Motors Corp., 1978 WL 1386 (S.D.N.Y.), 970
In re National Developers, Inc., 803 F.2d 616 (11th Cir. 1986), 705, 706
In re National Gypsum Co., 139 B.R. 397 (N.D. Tex. 1992), 768
National Hockey League v. Metropolitan Hockey Club, Inc., 427 U.S. 639 (1976), **1043**
National Organization for the Reform of Marijuana Laws v. Mullen, 828 F.2d 536 (9th Cir. 1988), 1447
National Organization of Women, Inc. v. Scheidler, 510 U.S. 249 (1994), 986
National Organization for Women v. Mutual of Omaha Insurance Co., 612 F. Supp. 100 (D.D.C. 1985), 339
In re Natural Resources Fund, Inc., Securities Litigation, 372 F. Supp. 1403 (J.P.M.L. 1974), 741
National Union Electric Corporation v. Matsushita Electric Industrial Co., Ltd., 494 F. Supp. 1257 (E.D. Pa. 1980), 1185, 1194
National Union Fire Insurance Co. of Pittsburgh, Pa. v. Continental Illinois Corp., 113 F.R.D. 527 (N.D. Ill. 1986), 113
National Wildlife Federation v. Gorsuch, 744 F.2d 963 (3rd Cir. 1983), 226
Nelson v. International Paint Co., 716 F.2d 640 (9th Cir. 1983), 817
Nelson v. Greater Gadsden Housing Au-

thority, 802 F.2d 405 (11th Cir. 1986), 1414
Nemours Foundation v. Gilbane, Aetna, Federal Insurance Co., 632 F. Supp. 418 (D. Del. 1986), 910
Nevada v. Hall, 440 U.S. 410 (1979), 167
In re Newbridge Networks Securities Litigation, 926 F. Supp. 1163 (D.D.C. 1996), 997
In re New Mexico Natural Gas Antitrust Litigation, 620 F.2d 794 (10th Cir. 1980), 973
New Orleans Public Service, Inc. v. Council of City of New Orleans, 491 U.S. 350 (1989), 428, 430
New Orleans Public Service Co. v. United Gas Pipeline Co., 732 F.2d 452 (5th Cir.), 147
In re New York Asbestos Litigation, 1990 WL 100811 (E. & S.D.N.Y.), 1291
In re New York Asbestos Litigation, 145 F.R.D. 644 (S.D.N.Y. 1993), 480
In re New York Asbestos Litigation, 149 F.R.D. 490 (S.D.N.Y. 1993), 1336, 1337
In re New York Asbestos Litigation, 155 F.R.D. 61 (S.D.N.Y. 1994), 1383
New York Central Railroad Co. v. United States, 200 F. Supp. 944 (S.D.N.Y. 1961), 492
New York Life Insurance Co. v. Dunlevy, 241 U.S. 518 (1916), 418
Newman v. Alabama, 559 F.2d 283 (5th Cir. 1977), 1446
Newman-Green, Inc. v. Alfonzo-Larrain, 490 U.S. 826 (1989), 385
Newton Commonwealth Property, N.V. v. G + H Montage GmbH, 261 Ga. 269, 404 S.E.2d 551 (1991), 1324
Nigh v. Dow Chemical Co., 634 F. Supp. 1513 (W.D. Wis. 1986), 1329, 1332
NLRB v. Bildisco & Bildisco, 465 U.S. 513 (1984), 747
In re Norplant Contraceptive Products Liability Litigation, 168 F.R.D. 579 (E.D. Tex. 1996), 106
North Carolina Bd. of Education v. Swann, 402 U.S. 43 (1971), 1430
In re Northern District of California Dalkon Shield IUD Products Liability Litigation, 693 F.2d 847 (9th Cir. 1982), 534, 594
Northern Securities Co. v. United States, 191 U.S. 555 (1903), 154
Northland Insurance Co. v. Shell Oil Co., 930 F. Supp. 1069 (D.N.J. 1996), **983**
Norwood v. Kirkpatrick, 349 U.S. 29 (1955), 492

Nottingham Partners v. Dana, 564 A.2d 1089 (Del. Supr. 1989), 612
Novo Terapeutisk Laboratorium A/S v. Baxter Travenol Laboratories, Inc., 607 F.2d 186 (7th Cir. 1979), 908
Nowell v. Neal, 249 N.C. 516, 107 S.E.2d 107 (1959), 424
Nuesse v. Camp, 385 F.2d 694 (D.C. Cir. 1967), 140, 141, 147, 148, 149

ODC Communications Corp. v. Wenruth Investments, 826 F.2d 509 (7th Cir. 1987), 1065
Ohio Forestry Association, Inc., v. Sierra Club, 118 S. Ct. 1665 (1998), 371
Ohntrup v. Firearms Center, Inc., 802 F.2d 676 (3d Cir. 1986), 923
O'Keefe v. Van Boening, 82 F.3d 322 (9th Cir. 1996), 1077
Olcott v. Delaware Flood Co., 76 F.3d 1538 (10th Cir. 1996), 827
Olds v. Donnelly, 150 N.J. 424, 696 A.2d 633 (1997), 132
Old Time Enterprises, Inc. v. International Coffee Corp., 862 F.2d 1213 (5th Cir.1989), 986
Olsen Associates, Inc. v. United States, 853 F. Supp. 396 (M.D. Fla. 1993), 1258
O'Melveny & Myers v. Federal Deposit Insurance Corp., 512 U.S. 79 (1994), 853, 854
Omni Capital International v. Rudolf Wolff & Co., 484 U.S. 97 (1987), 274, 276, 277
One World Botanicals Ltd. v. Gulf Coast Nutritionals, Inc., 987 F. Supp. 317 (D. N.J. 1997), 274
In re Oracle Securities Litigation, 132 F.R.D. 538 (N.D. Cal. 1990), 887
Oregon Natural Resources Council v. Mohla, 944 F.2d 531 (9th Cir. 1991), 991
Orjias v. Stevenson, 31 F.3d 995 (10th Cir. 1994), 169
Orlich v. Helm Brothers, Inc., 160 A.D.2d 135, 560 N.Y.S.2d 10 (1990), 1166
In the Matter of Orthopedic Bone Screw Products Liability Litigation (MDL No. 1014), 79 F.3d 46 (7th Cir. 1996), 493
In re Orthopedic Bone Screw Products Liability Litigation, 1995 WL 428683 (E.D. Pa.), 105, 106
In re Orthopedic Bone Screw Products Liability Litigation, 176 F.R.D. 158 (E.D. Pa. 1997), 686
Osborn v. Bank of the United States, 22 U.S. (9 Wheat.) 738 (U.S. 1824), **312**, 315, 343
Osei-Afriyie v. Medical College of Pennsylvania, 937 F.2d 876 (3d Cir. 1991), 1287,

1327
In re Otero Mills, Inc., 25 B.R. 1018 (D.N.M. 1982), 744
Ouellette v. International Paper Co., 86 F.R.D. 476 (D. Vt. 1980), 645
Overseas National Airways, Inc. v. United States, 766 F.2d 97 (2d Cir. 1985), 853
Owen Equipment & Erection Co. v. Kroger, 437 U.S. 365 (1978), 344, 346, 347, 348, 355, 357, 358
Owen v. City of Independence, 445 U.S. 622 (1980), 361
Owens-Corning Fiberglas Corp. v. Baker, 838 S.W.2d 838 (Tex. App. 1992), 472
Oxendine v. Merrell Dow Pharmaceuticals, 506 A.2d 1100 (D.C.C.A. 1986), 227

Packard v. Provident National Bank, 994 F.2d 1039 (3d Cir. 1993), 354
Pacor, Inc. v. Higgins, 743 F.2d 984 (3d Cir. 1984), 733
Palsgraf v. Long Island R.R., 248 N.Y. 339, 162 N.E. 99 (1928), 861
In re Pan Am Corp., 16 F.3d 513, 516 (2d Cir. 1994), 737
Pan American Fire & Casualty Co. v. Revere, 188 F. Supp. 474 (W.D. La. 1960), 419, 420
Pan American World Airways, Inc. v. United States District Court for the Central District of California, 523 F.2d 1073 (9th Cir. 1975), 107, 108, 254
Papagiannis v. Pontikis, 108 F.R.D. 177 (N.D. Ill. 1985), 104
Pardo v. Olson & Sons, Inc., 40 F.3d 1063 (9th Cir. 1994), 169
In re Paris Air Crash of March 3, 1974, 399 F. Supp. 732 (C.D. Cal. 1975), 842
In re Paris Industries Corp., 132 B.R. 504 (D. Me. 1991), 768
Parker v. Connors Steel Co., 855 F.2d 1510 (11th Cir. 1988), 969
Parklane Hosiery Co. v. Shore, 439 U.S. 322 (1979), **160**, 196, 199, 200, 201, 202, 203, 205, 207, 222, 229, 242
Parsons v. Bedford, 28 U.S. (3 Pet.) 443 (1830), 1221
Parsons Steel, Inc. v. First Alabama Bank, 474 U.S. 518 (1986), 168, 399
Pasadena City Board of Education v. Spangler, 427 U.S. 424 (1976), 612
In re Pasquariello, 16 F.3d 525 (3d Cir. 1994), 1216
Patterson Enterprises, Inc. v. Bridgestone/Firestone, Inc., 812 F. Supp. 1152 (D. Kan. 1993), 354
Payton v. Abbott Labs, 83 F.R.D. 382 (D. Mass. 1979), 594, 1289, 1291

Pearl Brewing Co. v. Jos. Schlitz Brewing Co., 415 F. Supp. 1122 (S.D. Tex. 1976), 1193, 1194
Pena v. McArthur, 889 F. Supp. 403 (E.D. Cal. 1994), 113
Penn-Central Merger and N & W Inclusion Cases, 389 U.S. 486 (1968), 210, 243, 247
Pennhurst State School & Hospital v. Halderman, 465 U.S. 89 (1984), 361
Pennoyer v. Neff, 95 U.S. 714 (1878), 263, 297
Pennsylvania Association for Retarded Children v. Pennsylvania, 343 F. Supp. 279 (E.D. Pa. 1972), 368
Pennsylvania v. Union Gas Co., 491 U.S. 1 (1989), 1429
Penny v. Southwestern Bell Telephone Co., 906 F.2d 183 (5th Cir. 1990), 436
Pennzoil Co. v. Texaco, Inc., 481 U.S. 1 (1987), 430, 431
People of the State of California v. Keating, 986 F.2d 346 (9th Cir. 1993), **377**
Peretz v. United States, 501 U.S. 923 (1991), 956
Peretz v. Boston Housing Authority, 379 Mass. 703, 400 N.E.2d 1231 (1980), 1421, 1422
Ex parte Peterson, 253 U.S. 300 (1920), 948, 949, 1247, 1248, 1250, 1252, 1259
Petit v. City of Chicago, 766 F. Supp. 607 (N.D. Ill. 1991), 218, 220
Petition of Kinsman Transit Co., 338 F.2d 708 (2d Cir. 1964), 861
Pettway v. American Cast Iron Pipe Co., 576 F.2d 1157 (5th Cir. 1978), 654
Pfizer, Inc. v. Lord, 447 F.2d 122 (2d Cir. 1971), 519
Pfizer Inc. v. Lord, 456 F.2d 532 (8th Cir.1972), 975
Phillips Petroleum Co. v. Shutts, 472 U.S. 797 (1985), 183, 184, 185, 188, 189, 190, 191, 285, **294**, 301, 302, 303, 305, 471, **613**, 641, 692, **797**, 803, 806, 1206
Phoenix Canada Oil Co. v. Texaco, Inc., 842 F.2d 1466 (3d Cir. 1988), 1040
In re Phonometrics, Inc., Electronic Long Distance Call Cost Computer and Recorder Patent Litigation, 1997 WL 83673 (J.P.M.L.), 510
Picard Chemical Inc. Profit Sharing Plan v. Perrigo Co., 1996 WL 739170 (W.D. Mich.), 629
Pifcho v. Brewer, 77 F.R.D. 356 (M.D. Pa. 1977), 1076
Pillsbury Co. v. Conboy, 459 U.S. 248 (1983), 1114, 1115

Pinel v. Pinel, 240 U.S. 594 (1916), 337, 375

Pinemont Bank v. Belk, 722 F.2d 232 (5th Cir. 1984), 1233

Piper Aircraft Co. v. Reyno, 454 U.S. 235 (1981), 458, 459, 460, 461, 462, 463, 464, 465, 821

Piper Airraft Corp. v. Wag-Aero, Inc., 741 F.2d 925 (7th Cir. 1984), 1161

In re Pizza Time Theatre Securities Litigation, 112 F.R.D. 15 (N.D. Cal. 1986), 874

In re Plumbing Fixture Cases, 298 F. Supp. 484 (J.P.M.L. 1968), 506

In re Plumbing Fixtures Litigation, 342 F. Supp. 756 (J.P.M.L. 1972), 821, 828

Plummer v. Chemical Bank, 668 F.2d 654 (2d Cir. 1982), 650

Polaris Public Income Funds v. Einhorn, 625 So. 2d 128 (Fla.App. 1993), 440, 441

Polin v. Dun & Bradstreet, Inc., 634 F.2d 1319 (10th Cir. 1980), 1264

Pollard v. Cockrell, 578 F.2d 1002 (5th Cir. 1978), 217, 224, 230

Poller v. Columbia Broadcasting System, Inc., 368 U.S. 464 (1962), **1047**

Pope v. Federal Express Corp., 974 F.2d 982 (8th Cir. 1992), 970, 971

Portsmouth Square v. Shareholders Protective Comm., 770 F.2d 866 (9th Cir.1985), 1071, 1076, 1077, 1078, 1081, 1082

Portsmouth Redevelopment and Housing Authority v. BMI Apartments Associates, 851 F. Supp. 775 (E.D. Va. 1994), 922, 923

Postal Telegraph Cable Co. v. Newport, 247 U.S. 464, (1918), 209

In re Potash Antitrust Litigation, 896 F. Supp. 916 (D. Minn. 1995), 1114

PPG Industries, Inc. v. Costle, 630 F.2d 462 (6th Cir. 1980), 1346

Premium Products Sales Corp. v. Chipwich, Inc., 539 F. Supp. 427 (S.D.N.Y. 1982), 911

Prezant v. De Angelis, 636 A.2d 915 (Del. 1994), 182, 183, 184, 191

Princess Lida of Thurn & Taxis v. Thompson, 305 U.S. 456 (1939), 391, 412

Principality of Monaco v. Mississippi, 292 U.S. 313 (1934), 360

Provident Tradesmens Bank & Trust Co. v. Patterson, 390 U.S. 102 (1968), 116, 117, 119, 128, 130, 243, 244

In re Proxima Corp. Securities Litigation, 1994 WL 374306 (S.D. Cal.), 628

Prudential Insurance Co. of America v. United States Gypsum Co., 991 F.2d 1080 (3d Cir. 1993), **942**

In re: The Prudential Insurance Co. of America Sales Practices Litigation, 962 F. Supp. 450 (D.N.J. 1997), 842

In re Prudential Securities Inc. Limited Partnerships Litigation, 158 F.R.D. 562 (S.D.N.Y. 1994), 997

In re the Prudential Insurance Co. of America Sales Practices Litigation, 169 F.R.D. 598 (D.N.J. 1997), 1105

Public Citizen v. Liggett Group, Inc., 858 F.2d 775 (1st Cir.1988), 1152

Public Interest Research Group, Inc. v. Powell Duffryn Terminals Inc., 913 F.2d 64 (3d Cir. 1990), 365

Public Interest Research Group of New Jersey, Inc. v. Magnesium Elektron, Inc., 123 F.3d 111 (3d Cir. 1997), 829

Quackenbush v. Allstate Insurance Co., 517 U.S. 706 (1996), 428, 434, 435

Quercia v. United States, 289 U.S. 466 (1933), 1372

Racz v. R.T. Merryman Trucking, Inc., 1994 WL 124857 (E.D. Pa.), **1342**

Railroad Commission of Texas v. Pullman Co., 312 U.S. 496 (1941), 427, 428, 436, 439, 447

Raines v. Byrd, U.S., 117 S. Ct. 2312 (1997), 371

Ralph C. Wilson Industries, Inc. v. American Broadcasting Co., 598 F. Supp. 694 (N.D. Cal. 1984), 1039

Rano v. Sipa Press, Inc., 987 F.2d 580 (9th Cir. 1993), 275

Ratner v. Chemical Bank New York Trust Co., 54 F.R.D. 412 (S.D.N.Y. 1972), 539, 630

Raytech Corp. v. White, 54 F.3d 187 (3d Cir. 1995), 204

In re Real Estate Title and Settlement Services Antitrust Litigation, 869 F.2d 760 (3rd Cir. 1989), 307

In re Recticel Foam Corp., 859 F.2d 1000 (1st Cir. 1988), 1102, 1104

Reed v. Allen, 286 U.S. 191 (1932), 158, 159

Reed v. Cleveland Bd. of Education, 607 F.2d 737 (6th Cir. 1979), 1248, **1261**

Refac International, Ltd. v. Mastercard International, 758 F. Supp. 152 (S.D.N.Y. 1991), 1291

Regal Knitwear Co. v. NLRB, 324 U.S. 9 (1945), 1452

Regions Hospital v. Shalala, 118 S. Ct. 909, 918 (1998), 166

Reilly v. United States, 863 F.2d 149 (1st Cir. 1988), 954, **1246**, 1254, 1263

Reinsurance Co. of America, Inc. v. Administratia Asigurarilor de Stat, 902 F.2d 1275 (7th Cir. 1990), 1163

Reliance Insurance Co. v. Tiger International, Inc., 91 A.D.2d 925, 457 N.Y.S.2d 813 (1983), 440

Renaud v. Martin Mariette Corp., 972 F.2d 304 (10th Cir. 1992), 1253

Renne v. Geary, 501 U.S. 312 (1991), 987

Rentclub Inc. v. Transamerica Rental Finance Corp., 811 F. Supp. 651 (M.D. Fla. 1992), 906

In re Repetitive Stress Injury Cases, 142 F.R.D. 584 (E.D.N.Y. 1992), 957

In re: Repetitive Stress Injury Products Liability Litigation, 1992 WL 403023 (J.P.M.L. 1992), 483

In re: Repetitive Stress Injury Litigation, 11 F.3d 368 (2d Cir. 1993), **482**

Republic Supply Co. v. Shoaf, 815 F.2d 1046 (5th Cir. 1987), 747

Reserve Mining Co. v. Lord, 529 F.2d 181 (8th Cir. 1976), **1359**

In re Residential Doors Antitrust Litigation, 900 F. Supp. 749 (E.D. Pa. 1995), 1112

Resnick v. American Dental Association, 90 F.R.D. 530 (N.D. Ill. 1981), 103

Revere Copper & Brass, Inc. v. Aetna Casualty & Surety Co., 426 F.2d 709 (5th Cir. 1970), 341

R.H. v. Murphy, 984 F.2d 196 (7th Cir.), 154, 155

In the Matter of Rhone-Poulenc Rorer Inc., 51 F.3d 1293 (7th Cir. 1995), **540**, 583, 590, 641, 642, 643, 644, 645, **860**, **1283**

In the Matter of Rhone-Poulenc Rorer Pharmaceuticals, Inc., 138 F.3d 695 (7th Cir. 1998), 516

Rice v. City of Philadelphia, 66 F.R.D. 17 (E.D. Pa. 1974), **556**, 598

Rice v. Nova Biomedical Corp., 38 F.3d 909 (7th Cir. 1994), 274

Richards v. Jefferson County, Alabama, 517 U.S. 793 (1996), 183, 186, 208, 216, 219, 220, 221, 252

Richardson v. Alabama State Board of Education, 935 F.2d 1240 (11th Cir. 1991), 154

Richardson v. Kelly, 144 Tex. 497, 191 S.W.2d 857 (1945), 691

Richardson v. Miller, 101 F.3d 665 (11th Cir. 1996), 170, 214, 215, 216, 219, 220

Richardson-Merrell, Inc. v. Koller, 472 U.S. 424 (1985), 879, 907, 912

In re Richardson Merrell, Inc. "Bendectin" Products Liability Litigation, 624 F. Supp. 1212 (S.D. Ohio 1985), 1242, 1243

Richmark Corp. v. Timber Falling Consultants, 959 F.2d 1468 (9th Cir.), 1167

Richmond v. Weiner, 353 F.2d 41 (9th Cir. 1965), 1279

Riddell Sports, Inc. v. Brooks, 1994 WL 67836 (S.D.N.Y.), 912

Riley v. Simmons, 839 F. Supp. 1113 (D.N.J. 1993), 429, 435

River Cement Co. v. Bangert Bros. Construction Co., 852 F. Supp. 25 (D. Colo. 1994), 705

Rivera v. Fair Chevrolet Geo Partnership, 165 F.R.D. 361 (D. Conn. 1996), 583

In re Riverside Nursing Home, 144 B.R. 951 (S.D.N.Y. 1992), 705

Rivet v. Regions Bank of Louisiana, 118 S. Ct. 921, 926 (1998), 170, 383

Roberts v. Johns-Manville Corp., 45 B.R. 823 (S.D.N.Y. 1984), 717

Roberts v. Heim, 1990 WL 306009 (N.D. Cal.), 951

Roberts v. Heim, 123 F.R.D. 614 (N.D. Cal. 1988), 1149

Robinson v. Audi Aktiengesellschraft, 56 F.3d 1259 (10th Cir. 1995), 275

Robinson v. Michigan Consolidated Gas Co., 918 F.2d 579 (6th Cir. 1990), 733, 734

Rodriguez v. Pacifica of Texas, Inc., 980 F.2d 1014 (5th Cir. 1993), 358, 382

Roe v. Little Company of Mary Hospital, 815 F. Supp. 241 (N.D. Ill. 1992), 384

Rogers v. Platt, 814 F.2d 683, 687 (D.C. Cir. 1987), 321, 359

Rogers v. Societe Internationale, S.A., 278 F.2d 268 (D.C. Cir. 1960), 1258

Rohrbach v. AT&T Nassau Metals Corp., 902 F. Supp. 523 (M.D. Pa. 1995), 959, 974

Rohrbach v. AT&T Nassau Metals Corp., 915 F. Supp. 712 (M.D. Pa. 1996), 974

Rohrbaugh v. Owens-Corning Fiberglas Corp., 965 F.2d 844 (10th Cir. 1992), 1322

Roman v. ESB, Inc., 550 F.2d 1343 (4th Cir. 1976), 555

Romero v. International Terminal Operating Co., 358 U.S. 354 (1959), 316

Romstadt v. Apple Computer, Inc., 948 F. Supp. 701 (N.D. Ohio 1996), 412

In re Ronald Parr, 13 B.R. 1010 (E.D.N.Y. 1981), 969, 970, 974, 975

Rosado v. Wyman, 322 F. Supp. 1173 (E.D.N.Y. 1970), 580

Rosales v. Honda Motor Co., 726 F.2d 259 (5th Cir. 1984), 1287

Rose v. Giamatti, 721 F. Supp. 906 (S.D.

Ohio 1989), 383
Rosen v. Reckitt & Colman Inc., 1994 WL 652534 (S.D.N.Y.), 1291, 1292
Ross v. Houston Independent School District, 699 F.2d 218 (5th Cir. 1983), 992
Ross v. Bernhard, 396 U.S. 531 (1970), **1213**, 1221, 1222
Roubidoux v. Celani, 987 F.2d 931 (2d Cir. 1993), **560**
Rufo v. Inmates of the Suffolk County Jail, 502 U.S. 367 (1992), 1404
Ruiz v. Estelle, 679 F.2d 1115 (5th Cir. 1982), **1443**
Russ v. State Farm Mutual Automobile Insurance Co., 961 F. Supp. 808 (E.D. Pa. 1997), 354
Rutherford v. City of Cleveland, 137 F.3d 905 (6th Cir. 1998), 253
Rutledge v. Electric Hose & Rubber Co., 511 F.2d 668 (9th Cir. 1975), 1240
Ryan v. Dow Chemical Co., 781 F. Supp. 902 (E.D.N.Y. 1991), 389
Ryan v. Dow Chemical Co., 781 F. Supp. 934 (E.D.N.Y. 1992), 383, 387

Safeco Insurance Co. of America v. Norris & Hirshberg, Inc., 640 F. Supp. 712 (N.D. Ga. 1986), 411
Sagebrush Rebellion, Inc. v. Watt, 713 F.2d 525 (9th Cir. 1983), 150
Saint Paul Mercury Indemnity Co. v. Red Cab Co., 303 U.S. 283 (1938), 338, 375, 376, 385, 386
In re Salem Mortgage Co, 783 F.2d 626 (6th Cir. 1986), 735
In re Sam M. Antar, 71 F.3d 97, 101 (3d Cir. 1995), 974
In re San Juan Dupont Plaza Hotel Fire Litigation, 1989 WL 168401 (D.P.R.), 886, 952, 958, 1106
In re San Juan Dupont Plaza Hotel Fire Litigation, 768 F. Supp. 912 (D.P.R. 1991), 1207
In re San Juan Dupont Plaza Hotel Fire Litigation, 142 F.R.D. 41 (D.P.R. 1992), 1104, 1106, 1272
In re San Juan Dupont Plaza Hotel Fire Litigation, 994 F.2d 956 (1st Cir. 1993), 1272
San Antonio Independent School District v. Rodriguez, 411 U.S. 1 (1973), 1427
Sanford v. Johns-Manville Sales Corp., 923 F.2d 1142 (5th Cir. 1991), 1287, 1293
Santiago v. Miles, 121 F.R.D. 636 (W.D.N.Y. 1988), **1183**
Sartor v. Arkansas Natural Gas Corp., 321 U.S. 620 (1944), 1063
Saval v. BL Ltd., 710 F.2d 1027 (4th Cir. 1983), 101, 104
Saverson v. Levitt, 162 F.R.D. 407 (D.D.C. 1995), 1331
Schall v. Joyce, 885 F.2d 101 (3d Cir. 1989), 431
Schauss v. Metals Depository Corp., 757 F.2d 649 (5th Cir. 1985), 469, 470
Schiavone v. Fortune, 477 U.S. 21 (1986), 988
Schneck v. International Business Machine Corp., 1996 U.S. Dist. LEXIS 10126 (D.N.J.), 1290
Schneider v. Lockheed Aircraft Corp., 658 F.2d 835 (D.C. Cir. 1981), 204
In re School Asbestos Litigation, 104 F.R.D. 422 (E.D. Pa. 1984), 634, 635
In re School Asbestos Litigation, 789 F.2d 996 (3rd Cir. 1986), 598, 617
In re School Asbestos Litigation, 921 F.2d 1310 (3d Cir. 1990), 338, 456
In re School Asbestos Litigation, 977 F.2d 764 (3d Cir. 1992), 646, **865**, **961**, 1085, 1086
Schweitzer v. Consolidated Rail Corp., 758 F.2d 936 (3d Cir.), 364
SCM Corp. v. Xerox Corp., 77 F.R.D. 10 (D. Conn. 1977), 1321
SCM Corp. v. Xerox Corp., 463 F. Supp. 983 (D. Conn. 1978), 1335
Scott v. Frazier, 253 U.S. 243 (1920), 334
Scott v. Spangler Brothers, Inc., 298 F.2d 928 (2d Cir. 1962), 1355
In re Seagate Technologies Securities Litigation, 115 F.R.D. 264 (N.D. Cal. 1987), 842
In re Seagate Technology II Securities Litigation, 843 F. Supp. 1341 (N.D. Cal. 1994), 628
In re Seagate Technology II Securities Litigation, 156 F.R.D. 229 (N.D. Cal. 1994), 628, 629
Sea-Land Services v. Gaudet, 414 U.S. 573 (1974), 223
In re Sealed Case, 877 F.2d 976 (D.C. Cir. 1989), 1105, 1146
Seattle Times Co. v. Rhinehart, 467 U.S. 20 (1984), 1151
SEC v. Everest Management Corp., 475 F.2d 1236 (2d Cir. 1972), 164
Securities and Exchange Commission v. International Scanning Devices, Inc., 415 F. Supp. 3 (W.D.N.Y. 1974), 924
Securities and Exchange Commission v. United States Realty & Improvement Co., 310 U.S. 434 (1940), 153
Seguros Comercial America S.A. de C.V. v. American President Lines, Ltd., 105 F.3d 198 (5th Cir. 1996), 465

Self v. General Motors, 588 F.2d 655 (9th Cir.1978), 378
Seminole Tribe of Florida v. Florida, 517 U.S. 44 (1996), 360, 361
Senter v. General Motors Corp., 532 F.2d 511 (6th Cir. 1976), 577, 578
Shaffer v. Heitner, 433 U.S. 186 (1977), 264, 265, 266, 273, 296, 297
Shaid v. Consolidated Edison Co. of New York, 95 A.D. 610, 622, 467 N.Y.S.2d 843, 851 (1983), 425
Shamrock Oil & Gas Corp. v. Sheets, 313 U.S. 100 (1941), 374
Sheldon v. Sill, 49 U.S. (8 How.) 441 (U.S. 1850), 312
In re Shell Oil Refinery, 136 F.R.D. 588 (E.D. La. 1991), 951, 1288, 1289, 1310
In re Shell Oil Refinery, 155 F.R.D. 552 (E.D. La. 1993), 1311, 1314
Shelley v. Kraemer, 334 U.S. 1 (1948), 123
Shelton v. American Motors Corporation, 805 F.2d 1323 (8th Cir. 1986), 1184
Shields v. Barrows, 17 How. (58 U.S.) 130 (1855), 128
In re Shopping Carts Antitrust Litigation, 95 F.R.D. 299 (S.D.N.Y. 1982), 1114
Shores v. Sklar, 647 F.2d 462 (5th Cir. 1981), 624
Shutts, Executor v. Phillips Petroleum Co., 222 Kan. 527, 567 P.2d 1292 (1977), 797
Shutts v. Phillips Petroleum Co., 240 Kan. 764, 732 P.2d 1286 (1987), 801
Sierra Club v. Cedar Point Oil Co., 73 F.3d 546 (5th Cir. 1996), 1096
Sierra Club v. Morton, 405 U.S. 727 (1972), 366
In re Silicone Gel Breast Implants Products Liability Litigation, 793 F. Supp. 1098 (J.P.M.L. 1992), 514, 515
In re Silicone Gel Breast Implant Products Liability Litigation, 1994 WL 578353 (N.D. Ala.), 558
In re Silicone Gel Breast Implant Litigation, No. 92-CV-10000-S (N.D. Ala., May 31, 1996), 1171
Simer v. Rios, 661 F.2d 655 (7th Cir. 1981), 558, 1415
Simon v. Southern Ry., 236 U.S. 115 (1915), 401
Simpson v. Pittsburgh Corning Corp., 901 F.2d 277 (2d Cir.), 1287
Sims v. ANR Freight Systems, Inc., 77 F.3d 846 (5th Cir. 1996), 1384
Sindell v. Abbott Laboratories, 26 Cal. 3d 588, 607 P.2d 924 (1980), 280, 281
Sinicropi v. Milone, 915 F.2d 66 (2d Cir. 1990), 1040
Six (6) Mexican Workers v. Arizona Citrus Growers, 904 F.2d 1301 (9th Cir. 1990), 1415, 1416
Smiley v. Sincoff, 958 F.2d 498 (2d Cir. 1992), 889, 958
Smith v. Gulf Oil Co., 995 F.2d 638 (6th Cir. 1993), 1040
Smith v. Kansas City Title & Trust Co., 255 U.S. 180 (1921), 315, 316, 318, 321
Smith v. MCI Telecommunications Corp., 124 F.R.D. 665 (D. Kan. 1989), 580
Smith v. North American Rockwell Corp., 50 F.R.D. 515 (N.D. Okla. 1970), 94, 98, 100
Smuck v. Hobson, 408 F.2d 175 (D.C. Cir. 1969), 147, 151
Snider v. Consolidated Coal Co., 973 F.2d 555 (7th Cir. 1992), 202
Snyder v. Harris, 394 U.S. 332 (1969), 333, 335, 375
Societe Internationale v. Rogers, 357 U.S. 197 (1958), 1043, 1167, 1168
Societe Nationale Industrielle Aerospatiale v. United States District Court, 482 U.S. 522 (1987), 1165, 1166, 1167, 1168
Soderbeck v. Burnett County, 752 F.2d 285 (7th Cir. 1985), 1233
Sosna v. Iowa, 419 U.S. 393 (1975), 371
South Dakota v. Bourland, 949 F.2d 984 (8th Cir. 1991), 132
Southern Pacific Communications Co. v. American Telephone & Telegraph Co., 556 F. Supp. 825 (D.D.C. 1982), 1039
Southwest Airlines Co. v. Texas International Airlines, 546 F.2d 84 (5th Cir. 1977), 216, 223, 231, 232, 233, 234
Spallone v. United States, 493 U.S. 265 (1990), 1433, 1458
S.P.C.S., Inc. v. Lockheed Shipbuilding & Construction Co., 631 P.2d 999 (Wash. Ct. App. 1981), 1234
Spencer v. Kemna, 118 S. Ct. 978 (1998), 371
Sperberg v. Firestone Tire & Rubber Co., 61 F.R.D. 70 (N.D. Ohio 1973), 533
Spero v. Abbott Laboratories, 396 F. Supp. 321 (N.D. Ill. 1975), 923
Spitzer v. Haims & Co., 217 Conn. 532, 587 A.2d 105 (1991), 1370, 1371, 1373
Spitzfaden v. Dow Corning Corp., 619 So. 2d 795 (La. App. 1993), **698**
Spitzfaden v. Dow Corning Corp., 1995 WL 662663 (E.D. La.), 739
Sporck v. Peil, 759 F.2d 312 (3rd Cir. 1985), 1147, 1184, 1185, 1194
SRI, Int'l v. Matsushita Elec. Corp., 775 F.2d 1107 (Fed. Cir. 1985), 1233, 1235
Stafford v. Mesnik, 63 F.3d 1445 (7th Cir. 1995), 923, 924

Stagl v. Delta Airlines, Inc., 52 F.3d 463 (2d Cir. 1995), 1136
Standard Microsystems Corp. v. Texas Instruments, Inc., 916 F.2d 58 (2d Cir. 1990), 401
State of New Jersey v. Interstate Recycling, Inc., 267 N.J. Super. 574, 632 A.2d 526 (1993), 424
State of Alabama ex rel. Siegelman v. United States Environmental Protection Agency, 911 F.2d 499 (11th Cir. 1990), 202
State Farm Fire & Casualty Co. v. Tashire, 386 U.S. 523 (1967), 325, 413
State v. Hays, 256 Kan. 48, 883 P.2d 1093 (1994), 1368, 1371, 1373
State v. Graves, 907 P.2d 963 (Mont. 1995), 1371
State of Florida v. Jones Chemicals, Inc., 148 F.R.D. 282 (M.D. Fla. 1993), 958
State Distributors, Inc. v. Glenmore Distilleries Co., 738 F.2d 405 (10th Cir. 1984), 113
State v. Levi Strauss & Co., 41 Cal. 3d 460, 224 Cal. Rptr. 605, 715 P.2d 564 (1986), 1410, 1411, 1412
State of West Virginia v. Chas. Pfizer & Co., 440 F.2d 1079 (2d Cir. 1971), 1419
Stauble v. Warrob, Inc., 977 F.2d 690 (1st Cir. 1992), 950, 961, 1258, 1260, 1264
Stauffacher v. Bennett, 969 F.2d 455 (7th Cir. 1992), 275
Steel Co. v. Citizens for a Better Environment, 118 S. Ct. 1003 (1998), 338, 371
Steele v. Guaranty Trust Co. of N.Y., 164 F.2d 387 (2d Cir. 1947), 334
Steelworkers v. R.H. Bouligny, Inc., 382 U.S. 145 (1965), 330
Sterling v. Velsicol Chemical Corp., 855 F.2d 1188 (6th Cir. 1988), 645
Sterling v. Velsicol Chem. Corp., 855 F.2d 1188 (6th Cir.1988), 1306
Stewart v. Walbridge, Aldinger Co., 162 F.R.D. 29 (D. Del. 1995), 1016, 1019
Stine v. Marathon Oil Co., 976 F.2d 254 (5th Cir. 1992), 1333
Stone Age Foods, Inc. v. Exchange Bank, 1997 WL 123248 (N.D. Cal.), 113
In re Storage Technology Corp. Securitites Litigation, 630 F. Supp. 1072 (D. Colo. 1986), 997, 998
Stransky v. American Isuzu Motors, Inc., 829 F. Supp. 788 (E.D. Pa. 1993), 386
Strawbridge v. Curtiss, 3 Cranch 267 (1806), 327, 328, 329, 330, 337
Stringfellow v. Concerned Neighbors in Action, 480 U.S. 370 (1987), 151, 154
Stromberg v. Board of Education of Bratenahl, 64 Ohio St. 2d 98, 413 N.E.2d 1184 (1980), 212, 220
Stromberg Metal Works, Inc. and Comfort v. Press Mechanical, Inc., 77 F.3d 928 (7th Cir. 1996), 353, 354
In re Stucco Litigation, 175 F.R.D. 210 (E.D.N.C. 1997), 645
In re Sugar Antitrust Litigation, 559 F.2d 481 (9th Cir.1977), 543
In re Sugar Industry Antitrust Litigation, 427 F. Supp. 1018 (J.P.M.L. 1977), 1029
In re Sugar Antitrust Litigation, MDL 201, 588 F.2d 1270 (9th Cir. 1978), 388, 424
Sumitomo Bank of California v. Davis, 4 Cal. App. 4th 1306, 6 Cal. Rptr. 2d 381 (1992), 440
Summit Insurance Co. of New York v. Mulherin, 233 Ga. 606, 212 S.E.2d 788 (1975), 425
Sun Oil Co. v. Wortman, 486 U.S. 717 (1988), 802, 803, 811, 862
Sunbelt Corp. v. Noble, Denton & Associates, Inc., 5 F.3d 28 (3d Cir. 1993), 493
In re Sunrise Securities Litigation, 124 F.R.D. 99 (E.D. Pa. 1989), 951
Supreme Tribe of Ben-Hur v. Cauble, 255 U.S. 356 (1921), 176, 327, 331, 337
In re Surinam Airways Holding Co., 974 F.2d 1255 (11th Cir. 1992), 383, 385
Sutliff, Inc. v. Donovan Companies, Inc., 727 F.2d 648 (7th Cir. 1984), 990, 991
Swann v. Charlotte-Mecklenburg Board of Education, 501 F.2d 383 (4th Cir. 1974), 399
Swann v. Board of Education, 402 U.S. 1 (1971), 1390, 1395, 1402, 1427, 1448, 1452
In re Swine Flu Immunization Products Liability Litigation, 495 F. Supp. 1185 (W.D. Okla. 1980), 1358
In re Swine Flu Immunization Products Liability Litigation, 89 F.R.D. 695 (D.D.C. 1981), 1203
SWS Financial Fund v. Salomon Brothers, Inc., 790 F. Supp. 1392 (N.D. Ill. 1992), 912
Syracuse Broadcasting Corp. v. Newhouse, 271 F.2d 910 (2d Cir.1959), 1074
Szeliga v. General Motors Corp., 728 F.2d 566 (1st Cir. 1984), 1344

Tabas v. Tabas, 1996 WL 107848 (E.D. Pa.), 1287, 1289, 1293
Tabas v. Tabas, 166 F.R.D. 10 (E.D. Pa. 1996), 1323, 1326
Tafflin v. Levitt, 493 U.S. 455 (1990), 324
Tapscott v. MS Dealer Service Corp., 77 F.3d 1353 (11th Cir. 1996), 339

Tavoulareas v. Washington Post Co., 111 F.R.D. 653 (D.D.C. 1986), 1116

TBG, Inc. v. Bendis, 36 F.3d 916 (10th Cir. 1994), 1459

T.B. Harms Co. v. Eliscu, 339 F.2d 823 (2d Cir. 1964), 316, 319

Tec Air, Inc. v. Nippondenso Manufacturing USA, Inc., 1995 WL 470243 (N.D. Ill.), 1287, 1291

Technograph Printed Circuits, Ltd. v. Methode Electronics, Inc., 285 F. Supp. 714 (N.D. Ill. 1968), 689

In re Telectronics Pacing Systems, Inc. Accufix Atrial "J" Leads Products Liability Litigation, 172 F.R.D. 271 (S.D. Ohio 1997), **589**, 608, 645

Telectronics Proprietary, Ltd. v. Medtronic, Inc., 836 F.2d 1332 (Fed. Cir. 1988), 910, 912

In re Temple, 851 F.2d 1269 (11th Cir. 1988), 617

Temple v. Synthes Corp., 498 U.S. 5 (1990), **116**, 129, 235

In re Temporomandibular Joint (TMJ) Implants Products Liability Litigation, 97 F.3d 1050 (8th Cir. 1996), 817

In re Temporomandibular Joint (TMJ) Implants Products Liability Litigation, 113 F.3d 1484 (8th Cir. 1997), 1109

Tennessee v. Davis, 100 U.S. (10 Otto) 257 (1880), 374

Terracorn Development Group, Inc. v. Village of Westhaven, 209 Ill. App. 3d 758, 568 N.E.2d 376 (1991), 440

Testa v. Katt, 330 U.S. 386 (1947), 438

Texas Industries, Inc. v. Ratliff Materials, Inc., 451 U.S. 630 (1981), 852, 853, 854, 855

Textile Workers Union of America v. Lincoln Mills of Alabama, 353 U.S. 448 (1957), 317, 320, 851

The Fair v. Kohler Die & Specialty Co., 228 U.S. 22 (1913), 316

Thermtron Products, Inc. v. Hermansdorfer, 423 U.S. 336 (1976), 376, 385, 386

Thiel v. Southern Pacific Co., 328 U.S. 217 (1946), 1241, 1242

In re Thirteen Appeals Arising out of the San Juan Dupont Plaza Hotel Fire Litigation, 56 F.3d 295 (1st Cir. 1995), 890, 891

Thomas v. Albright, 139 F.3d 227 (D.C. Cir. 1998), 614

Thomas v. General Motors Corp., 118 S. Ct. 657 (1998), 1152

Thomas S. v. Flaherty, 902 F.2d 250 (4th Cir. 1990), 1399

Thompson Everett, Inc. v. National Cable Advertising, L.P., 57 F.3d 1317 (4th Cir. 1995), 1070

Thomson v. Continental Ins. Co., 66 Cal. 2d 738, 59 Cal. Rptr. 101, 427 P.2d 765 (1967), 439

In re Three Additional Appeals Arising out of the San Juan Dupont Plaza Hotel Fire Litigation, 93 F.3d 1 (1st Cir. 1996), **1099**

Three J Farms, Inc. v. Alton Box Board, 609 F.2d 112 (4th Cir. 1979), 393, 394

In re Three Mile Island Litigation, 87 F.R.D. 433 (M.D. Pa. 1980), 645

Ticor Title Insurance Co. v. Brown, 511 U.S. 117 (1994), 306, 602, 611

In re TMI Litigation Cases Consolidated II, 922 F. Supp. 997 (M.D. Pa. 1996), 1096, 1097

In re TMI Litigation Cases Consolidated II, 940 F.2d 832 (3d Cir. 1991), 387

In re Tom Watkins, 271 F.2d 771 (5th Cir.1959), 1349

Torres v. Kuzniasz, 936 F. Supp. 1201 (D.N.J. 1996), 1113

Tourangeau v Uniroyal, Inc., 101 F.3d 300 (2d Cir. 1996), 231, 234

Town of Warwick v. New Jersey DEP, 647 F. Supp. 1322 (S.D.N.Y. 1986), 488

In re Trafficwatch, 138 B.R. 841 (Bankr. E.D. Tex. 1992), 705

Trajano v. Marcos, 878 F.2d 1439 (9th Cir.1989), 1299

Transamerica Computer Co. v. International Business Machine Corp., 573 F.2d 646 (9th Cir. 1978), 1146

Transworld Airlines, Inc. v. American Coupon Exchange, Inc, 913 F.2d 676 (9th Cir. 1990), 1064

Travelers Indemnity Co. v. Sarkasian, 794 F.2d 754 (2d Cir. 1986), 382

Traylor v. Husqvarta Motor, 988 F.2d 729 (7th Cir. 1993), 1330, 1347

Trbovich v. United Mine Workers of America, 404 U.S. 528 (1972), **144**, 234

Trevino v. Gates, 99 F.3d 911 (9th Cir. 1996), 170

Tri-Star Pictures, Inc. v. Unger, 171 F.R.D. 94 (S.D.N.Y. 1997), 1134

Tribette v. Illinois Central R.R., 70 Miss. 182, 12 So. 32 (1892), 424

Troy Bank v. G. A. Whitehead & Co., 222 U.S. 39 (1911), 333, 335, 338

Tull v. United States, 481 U.S. 412 (1987), 1218, 1314

Turner Construction Co. v. First Indemnity of America Insurance Co., 829 F. Supp. 752 (E.D. Pa. 1993), 1260

Turpeau v. Fidelity Financial Services,

Inc., 936 F. Supp. 975 (N.D. Ga. 1996), 690

In re Two Appeals Arising Out of the San Juan Dupont Plaza Hotel Fire Litigation, 994 F.2d 956 (1st Cir.1993), 1100, 1104, 1106

Tyus v. Schoemehl, 93 F.3d 449 (8th Cir.1996), **213**, 232

Underwriters National Assurance Co. v. North Carolina Life and Accident and Health Guaranty Association, 455 U.S. 691 (1982), 167

Union City Barge Line, Inc. v. Union Carbide Corp., 823 F.2d 129 (5th Cir. 1987), 1090

Union Light, Heat and Power Co. v. United States District Court, 588 F.2d 543 (6th Cir. 1978), 442

Union Carbide and Carbon Corp. v. Nisley, 300 F.2d 561 (10th Cir. 1962), 1289, 1314

In re Union Carbide Corp. Gas Plant Disaster, 634 F. Supp. 842 (S.D.N.Y. 1986), 842

In re Union Carbide Corp. Gas Plant Disaster, 809 F.2d 195 (2d Cir. 1987), 464, 466

United Mine Workers of America v. Gibbs, 383 U.S. 715 (1966), 95, 342, 343, 396

In re United Mine Workers of America Employee Benefit Plans Litigation, 854 F. Supp. 914 (D.D.C. 1994), 828

In re United States, 816 F.2d 1083 (6th Cir. 1987), 943, 949, 950, 1258

United States v. Agajanian, 852 F.2d 56 (2d Cir. 1988), 1359

United States v. Ajmal, 67 F.3d 12 (2d Cir. 1995), 1371

United States v. American Telephone & Telegraph Co., 461 F. Supp. 1314 (D.D.C. 1978), 959, **1031**, **1106**

United States v. American Telephone & Telegraph Co., 83 F.R.D. 323 (D.D.C. 1979), 1289, 1324, 1331

United States v. American Telephone & Telegraph Co., 642 F.2d 1285 (D.C. Cir. 1980), 1146, **1188**

United States v. American Telephone & Telegraph Co., 88 F.R.D. 47 (D.D.C. 1980), 1036

United States v. American Telephone & Telegraph Co., 552 F. Supp. 131 (D.D.C. 1982), 1037

United States v. Baggott, 463 U.S. 476 (1983), 1113

United States v. Baker, 10 F.3d 1374 (9th Cir. 1993), 1375

United States v. Bush, 47 F.3d 511 (2d Cir. 1995), 1369, 1371

United States v. Callahan, 588 F.2d 1078 (5th Cir. 1979), 1365

United States v. Cassiere, 4 F.3d 1006 (1st Cir. 1993), 1371

United States v. City of Warren, Michigan, 138 F.3d 1083 (6th Cir. 1998), 1408

United States v. Conservation Chemical Co., 106 F.R.D. 210 (W.D. Mo.), 948, 950, 969, 1258

United States v. Dandy, 998 F.2d 1344 (6th Cir. 1993), 970

United States v. Darden, 70 F.3d 1507 (8th Cir. 1995), 1375

United States v. Edwardo-Franco, 885 F.2d 1002 (2d Cir. 1989), 1368

United States v. El Paso Natural Gas Co., 376 U.S. 651 (1964), 147

United States v. Employing Plasterers' Association, 347 U.S. 186 (1954), 991

United States v. Evans, 994 F.2d 317 (7th Cir. 1993), 1368

United States v. Exum, 744 F. Supp. 803 (N.D. Ohio 1990), 1246

United States v. First National City Bank, 379 U.S. 378 (1965), 271

United States v. GAF Corp., 596 F.2d 10 (2d Cir. 1979), 1112

United States v. Gray, 897 F.2d 1428 (8th Cir. 1990), 1368

United States v. Groene, 998 F.2d 604 (8th Cir. 1993), 1371

United States v. Gulf Oil Corporation, 760 F.2d 292 (Em.App. 1985), 1186, 1187

United States v. Hall, 472 F.2d 261 (5th Cir. 1972), 407, 408, **1448**

United States v. Heldt, 668 F.2d 1238 (D.C. Cir. 1981), 970

United States v. Hooker Chemicals & Plastics Corp., 749 F.2d 968 (2d Cir. 1984), 147, 149, 150

United States v. Hooker Chemical and Plastics Corp., 123 F.R.D. 62 (W.D.N.Y. 1988), 952

United States v. International Business Machines Corp., 1995 WL 366383 (S.D.N.Y.), 147

United States v. John Doe, Inc., I, 481 U.S. 102 (1987), 1113, 1114

United States v. Johnson, 319 U.S. 302 (1943), 368, 369

United States v. Johnson, 892 F.2d 707 (8th Cir. 1989), 1368, 1369, 1370

United States v. Kimbell Foods, Inc., 440 U.S. 715 (1979), 853

United States v. Kramer, 770 F. Supp. 954 (D.N.J. 1991), 1288

United States v. Kramer, 953 F. Supp. 592 (D.N.J. 1997), 1006
United States v. Lenox, 1989 WL 143167 (E.D. Pa.), 906
United States v. Lewin, 900 F.2d 145 (8th Cir. 1990), 1371
United States v. Major Oil Corp., 583 F.2d 1152 (10th Cir. 1978), 419
United States v. Mazzilli, 848 F.2d 384 (2d Cir. 1988), 1368
United States v. Mendoza, 464 U.S. 154 (1984), 172
United States v. Microsoft Corp., 56 F.3d 1448 (D.C. Cir. 1995), 971, 975
United States v. Mississippi, 380 U.S. 128 (1965), 95
United States v. Nabisco, Inc., 117 F.R.D. 40 (E.D.N.Y. 1987), 908
United States v. New Castle County, 116 F.R.D. 19 (D. Del. 1987), 1289
United States v. New York Telephone, 434 U.S. 159 (1977), 405, 407
United States v. One Assortment of 89 Firearms, 465 U.S. 354 (1984), 204
United States v. Oxford, 735 F.2d 276 (7th Cir. 1984), 1337
United States v. Polowichak, 783 F.2d 410 (4th Cir. 1986), 1375
United States v. Porter, 764 F.2d 1 (1st Cir. 1985), 1375, 1376
United States v. Quilty, 541 F.2d 172 (7th Cir. 1976), 1377
United States v. Raddatz, 447 U.S. 667 (1980), 948, 956
United States v. Real Property Known as 77 East 3rd Street, New York, New York, 1994 WL 4276 (S.D.N.Y.), 1335
United States v. Reaves, 636 F. Supp. 1575 (E.D. Ky. 1986), 1324, 1325
United States v. Reynolds, 345 U.S. 1 (1953), 1140, 1142
United States v. Rosenberg, 195 F.2d 583 (2d Cir. 1952), 1365
United States v. Saenz, 134 F.3d 697 (5th Cir. 1998), 1368
United States v. Sells Engineering, Inc., 463 U.S. 418 (1983), 1113, 1114
United States v. Shell Oil Co., 1992 WL 144296 (C.D. Cal.) (denying pretrial trifurcation), 1029
United States v. Shonubi, 895 F. Supp. 460 (E.D.N.Y. 1995), 1314
United States v. Standard Oil Co., 332 U.S. 301 (1947), 848, 849, 850
United States v. State of Alabama, 828 F.2d 1532 (1987), 972, 973
United States v. State of Michigan, 1990 WL 46637 (6th Cir.), 154

United States v. State of Michigan, 940 F.2d 143 (6th Cir. 1991), 154, 155
United States v. Students Challenging Regulatory Agency Procedures (SCRAP), 412 U.S. 669 (1973), 364
United States v. Swift & Co., 286 U.S. 106 (1932), 1403
United States v. Sykes, 7 F.3d 1331 (7th Cir. 1993), 970
United States v. Suquamish Indian Tribe, 901 F.2d 772 (9th Cir. 1990), 1258
United States v. Thompson, 76 F.3d 442 (2d Cir. 1996), 1371
United States ex rel. Touhy v. Ragen, 340 U.S. 462 (1951), 1169
United States v. United Mine Workers of America, 330 U.S. 258 (1947), 1451
United States v. United Shoe Machinery Corp., 110 F. Supp. 295 (D. Mass. 1953), 1252
United States v. Western Pacific Railroad Co., 352 U.S. 59 (1956), 436
United States v. Wild, 47 F.3d 669 (4th Cir. 1995), 1375
United States v. Witt, 215 F.2d 580 (2d Cir. 1954), 1365, 1371
United States v. Yonkers Board of Education, 837 F.2d 1181 (2d Cir. 1987), 1287
United States v. York, 888 F.2d 1050 (5th Cir. 1989), 974
United States v. Young, 745 F.2d 733, 761 (2d Cir. 1984), 1329, 1333
In re United States Brass Corp., 194 B.R. 420 (Bankr. E.D. Tex. 1994), 748, 749
In re United States Financial Securities Litigation, 75 F.R.D. 702 (S.D. Cal. 1977), 1233
United States Football League v. National Football League, 605 F. Supp. 1448 (S.D.N.Y. 1985), 909, 910
United States Parole Commission v. Geraghty, 445 U.S. 388 (1980), 369, 371
University of Maryland at Baltimore v. Peat Marwick Main & Co., 923 F.2d 265 (3d Cir. 1991), 429, 433
In re UNR Industries, Inc., 29 B.R. 741 (N.D. Ill. 1983), 756
In re UNR Industries, Inc., 45 B.R. 322 (N.D. Ill. 1984), 717
In re UNR Industries, Inc., 46 B.R. 671 (Bankr. N.D. Ill. 1985), 756
In the Matter of UNR Industries, Inc., 20 F.3d 766 (7th Cir. 1994), 756, 763, 767, 768, 778
Upjohn Company v. United States, 449 U.S. 383 (1981), 1185
In re U.S. Financial Securities Litigation, 609 F.2d 411 (9th Cir. 1979), 1230, 1233,

1235
In re U.S. Oil and Gas Litigation, 967 F.2d 489 (11th Cir. 1992), **1453**

Valentino v. Carter-Wallace, Inc., 97 F.3d 1227 (9th Cir. 1996), 644
Van Dusen v. Barrack, 367 U.S. 612 (1964), 809, 812, 814, 820, 823, 831, 835, 856
Van Houten-Maynard v. ANR Pipeline Co., 1995 WL 317056 (N.D. Ill.), **1342**
Van Gemert v. Boeing Co., 553 F.2d 812 (2d Cir. 1977), 1416, 1417
Van Leirsburg v. Sioux Valley Hospital, 831 F.2d 169 (8th Cir. 1987), 1368, 1372
Vanity Fair Mills, Inc. v. T. Eaton Co., 234 F.2d 633 (2d Cir. 1956), 817
Vanston Committee v. Green, 329 U.S. 156 (1946), 753, 754
Vaughn v. Rosen, 484 F.2d 820 (D.C. Cir. 1973), 1149
In re Vecchio, 20 F.3d 555 (2d Cir. 1994), 778
Veliz v. Crown Lift Trucks, 714 F. Supp. 49 (E.D.N.Y. 1989), 1344
Vendo Co. v. Lektro-Vend Corp., 433 U.S. 623 (1977), 398, 405, 616
Verlinden B. V. v. Central Bank of Nigeria, 461 U.S. 480 (1983), 315, 320
Vicom, Inc. v. Harbridge Merchant Services, Inc., 20 F.3d 771 (7th Cir. 1994), 989, 993
Village of Elm Grove v. Py, 724 F. Supp. 612 (E.D. Wis. 1989), 154
Vincent v. Hughes Air West, Inc., 557 F.2d 759 (9th Cir. 1977), **881**, 1203
In the Matter of VMS Securities Litigation, 103 F.3d 1317 (7th Cir. 1996), 389
Von Hoffman v. City of Quincy, 4 Wall. 535, 18 L. Ed. 403 (1867), 1429

Wade v. Goldschmidt, 673 F.2d 182 (7th Cir. 1982), 147
Wade v. Hopper, 993 F.2d 1246, 1249 (7th Cir. 1993), 993
Walitalo v. Iacocca, 968 F.2d 741 (8th Cir. 1992), 889
Walker v. Action Industries, Inc., 802 F.2d 703 (4th Cir. 1986), 1329, 1333
Walker v. City of Birmingham, 388 U.S. 307 (1967), 246, 1453
Walker v. Liggett Group, Inc., 175 F.R.D. 226 (S.D. W.Va. 1997), 686
Wallace v. SMC Pneumatics, Inc., 103 F.3d 1394 (7th Cir. 1997), 1064, 1069, 1070
Wallis v. Pan American Petroleum Corp., 384 U.S. 63 (1966), 848, 849, 850
Walter E. Heller & Co. v. Cox, 379 F. Supp. 299 (S.D.N.Y. 1974), 424
Ware v. Jolly Roger Rides, Inc., 857 F. Supp. 462 (D. Md. 1994), 354
Warner v. Transamerica Insurance Co., 739 F.2d 1347 (8th Cir. 1984), 1368
Warner-Jenkins Co. v. Hilton Davis Chemical Co., 520 U.S. 17 (1997), 1234
Warth v. Seldin, 422 U.S. 490 (1975), 367
Warwick Administrative Group v. Avon Products, Inc., 820 F. Supp. 116 (S.D.N.Y. 1993), 990
Washington v. Sherwin Real Estate, Inc., 694 F.2d 1081 (7th Cir. 1982), 923
Washington v. Washington State Commercial Passenger Fishing Vessel Association, 443 U.S. 658 (1979), 1458, 1459
Waste Management, Inc. v. Admiral Insurance Co., 138 N.J. 106, 649 A.2d 379 (1994), 290
In re: Waterman Steamship Corp., 141 B.R. 552 (Bankr. S.D.N.Y. 1992), 762, 763
Watkins v. Fiberboard Corp., 994 F.2d 253 (5th Cir. 1993), 1383
Watson v. Shell Oil Co., 979 F.2d 1014 (5th Cir. 1992), 1311
Watson v. Shell Oil Co., 990 F.2d 805 (5th Cir. 1993), 1311
Wayzata Bank & Trust Co. v. A & B Farms, 855 F.2d 590 (8th Cir. 1988), 421
Wedgeworth v. Fibreboard Corp., 706 F.2d 541 (5th Cir. 1983), 751
In re Wells Fargo Securities Litigation, 157 F.R.D. 467 (N.D. Cal. 1994), 887
Weinberger v. Kendrick, 698 F.2d 61 (2d Cir. 1982), 651, 652, 653, 657
West Gulf Maritime Association v. ILA Deep Sea Local 24, 751 F.2d 721 (5th Cir. 1985), 470
In re Westinghouse Electric Corp. Uranium Contract Litigation, 436 F. Supp. 990 (J.P.M.L. 1977), 511
In re Westinghouse Electric Corp. Uranium Contracts Litigation, 405 F. Supp. 316 (J.P.M.L. 1975), 511
Westinghouse Electric Corp. v. Kerr-McGee Corp., 580 F.2d 1311 (7th Cir. 1978), 908, 910, 911, 912
Westinghouse Electric Corp. v. Gulf Oil Corp., 588 F.2d 221 (7th Cir. 1978), 910, 911
In re West of the Rockies Concrete Pipe Antitrust Cases, 303 F. Supp. 507 (J.P.M.L. 1969), 511
Wetzel v. Liberty Mutual Insurance Co., 508 F.2d 239 (3d Cir. 1975), 607
Wheatley v. Phillips, 228 F. Supp. 439 (D.N.C. 1964), 456

Whitcomb v. Chavis, 403 U.S. 124 (1971), 1427
White v. National Football League, 822 F. Supp. 1389 (D. Minn. 1993), 307
White v. National Football League, 41 F.3d 402 (8th Cir. 1994), 307
Whittaker Corp. v. Execuair Corp., 736 F.2d 1341 (9th Cir. 1984), 1016, 1019
Wichita R.R. & Light Co. v. Public Utilities Commission, 260 U.S. 48 (1922), 327, 331, 335
Wildman v. Wills, 81 F.R.D. 588 (E.D. Pa. 1978), 991
Wilhite v. South Central Bell Telephone & Telegraph Co., 426 F. Supp. 61 (E.D. La. 1976), 559
Wilk v. American Medical Association, 635 F.2d 1295 (7th Cir. 1980), 1111
Will v. Michigan Department of State Police, 491 U.S. 58 (1989), 361
Will v. Calvert Fire Insurance Co., 437 U.S. 655 (1978), 432
William Gluckin & Co. v. International Playtex Corp., 407 F.2d 177 (2d Cir. 1969), 467
Williams v. Georgia Department of Human Resources, 789 F.2d 881 (11th Cir. 1986), 1076
Williams v. AC Spark Plugs, 985 F.2d 783 (5th Cir. 1993), 387
Williams v. Lane, 851 F.2d 867 (7th Cir. 1988), 1446, 1447
Williford v. Armstrong World Industries, Inc., 715 F.2d 124 (4th Cir. 1983), 744
Willis v. Celotex Corp., 978 F.2d 146 (4th Cir. 1992), 751
Wilson v. Southwest Airlines, Inc., 880 F.2d 807 (5th Cir. 1989), 1416
In re Winslow, 17 F.3d 314 (10th Cir. 1994), 469
Wilver v. Fisher, 387 F.2d 66 (10th Cir. 1967), 952
Winbourne v. Eastern Air Lines, Inc., 632 F.2d 219 (2d Cir. 1980), 493
Wind v. Eli Lilly & Co., 814 F. Supp. 305 (E.D.N.Y. 1993), 385
Windham v. American Brands, Inc., 565 F.2d 59 (4th Cir. 1977), 1411, 1415
Winkler v. Eli Lilly & Co., 101 F.3d 869 (7th Cir. 1996), 923
Winters v. Diamond Shamrock Chemical Co., 901 F. Supp. 1195 (E.D. Tex. 1995), 383
In re Wirebound Boxes Antitrust Litigation, 128 F.R.D. 250 (D. Minn. 1989), 951, 997, 999
In re Wirebound Boxes Antitrust Litigation, 724 F. Supp. 648 (D. Minn. 1989), 906, 969, 970, 974, 975
In re Wirebound Boxes Antitrust Litigation, 129 F.R.D. 34 (D. Minn. 1990), 1114
Wisconsin Department of Corrections v. Schacht, 118 S. Ct. 2047 (1998), 384
Wolgin v. State Mutual Investors, 265 Pa. Super. 525, 402 A.2d 669 (1979), 441, 442
Women Prisoners of the District of Columbia Department of Corrections v. District of Columbia, 93 F.3d 910 (D.C. Cir. 1996), 1446, 1447
Wood v. Zapata Corp., 484 F.2d 350 (3d Cir. 1973), 494
Woodall v. Drake Hotel, Inc., 913 F.2d 447 (7th Cir. 1990), 924
Woods v. Covington County Bank, 537 F.2d 804 (5th Cir. 1976), 910, 911
Woods Exploration & Producing Co. v. Aluminum Co. of America, 438 F.2d 1286 (5th Cir. 1971), 395, 396
Word of Faith Outreach Center Church v. Sawyer, 90 F.3d 118 (5th Cir. 1996), 990
World-Wide Volkswagen Corp. v. Woodson, 444 U.S. 286 (1980), **262,** 268, 269, 270, 283, 296, 297
Wortman v. Sun Oil Co., 241 Kan. 226, 755 P.2d 488 (1987), 802

Yniques v. Cabral, 985 F.2d 1031 (9th Cir. 1993), 386
Yonkers Racing Corp. v. City of Yonkers, 858 F.2d 855 (2d Cir. 1988), 388
Ex Parte Young, 209 U.S. 123 (1908), 361, 397
Young v. Pierce, 640 F. Supp. 1476 (E.D. Tex. 1986), 1263, 1358
Younger v. Harris, 401 U.S. 37 1 (1971), 394, 397, 427, 430, 431, 435
Yslava v. Hughes Aircraft Co., 845 F. Supp. 705 (D. Ariz. 1993), 612
Yung v. Raymark Industries, 789 F.2d 397 (6th Cir. 1986), 1275, 1280, 1287, 1291

Zahn v. International Paper Co., 414 U.S. 291 (1973), **332,** 349, 360
Zenith Radio Corp. v. Matsushita Electric Industrial Co., 478 F. Supp. 889 (E.D. Pa. 1979), 1337, 1375
Zenith Radio Corp. v. Matsushita Electric Industrial Co., 529 F. Supp. 866 (E.D. Pa. 1981), 1151
Zepeda v. INS, 753 F.2d 719 (9th Cir. 1985), 612
Zylstra v. Safeway Stores, Inc., 578 F.2d 102 (5th Cir. 1978), 906

TABLE OF AUTHORITIES

ABA Antitrust Section, Expediting Pretrials and Trials of Antitrust Cases 135 (1979), 1216, 1358

Walter F. Abbott et al., Jury Research (1993), 1237, 1335, 1346

Edward S. Adams & Rachel E. Iverson, *Personal-Jurisdiction in the Bankruptcy Context: A Need for Reform*, 44 Cath. U. L. Rev. 1081 (1995), 706

John R. Allison, *Ideology, Prejudgment, and Process Values*, 28 New Eng. L. Rev. 657 (1994), 12, 72

American Bar Association Commission on Mass Torts, Report to the House of Delegates, (1989), **870**, 1358

American Bar Association, Mandatory Prediscovery Disclosure: A First Look (1994), 1096

American Bar Association, Obtaining Discovery Abroad (1990), 1167

American Bar Association, Report and Recommendations of the Special Committee on Class Action Improvements, 110 F.R.D. 195 (1986), 697, 701

American Bar Association, Trying Mass Toxic Tort Cases (1989), 1348

American College of Trial Lawyers, Recommendations of Major Issues Affecting Complex Litigation, reprinted in 90 F.R.D. 207 (1981), 929, 951

American Law Institute, Complex Litigation: Statutory Recommendations and Analysis (1994), 84, 129, **249**, 288, 293, 380, 387, 408, **525**, 529, 807, **824**, 841, **870**, 873

American Law Institute, Federal Judicial Code Revision Project, Tent. Draft No. 2 (1998), 349, 355

American Law Institute, Study of the Division of Jurisdiction Between State and Federal Courts (Official Draft, Pt. 1, 1965), 327

American Law Institute, Study of the Division of Jurisdiction between State and Federal Courts (1969), 319, 324, 330, 332, 374, 392, 450

Angelo N. Ancheta, Comment, *Defendant Class Actions and Federal Civil Rights Litigation*, 33 UCLA L. Rev. 283 (1985), 692

James G. Apple et al., Manual for Cooperation between State and Federal Courts (1997), 447, 1090, **1175**

Morris S. Arnold, *A Historical Inquiry into the Right to Trial by Jury in Complex Litigation*, 128 U. Pa. L. Rev. 829 (1980), 1240

Richard S. Arnold, *State Court Power to Enjoin Federal Court Proceedings*, 51 Va. L. Rev. 59 (1965), 390, 391

Thurman Arnold, The Symbols of Government (1935), 26

Thomas C. Arthur & Richard D. Freer, *Close Enough for Government Work: What Happens When Congress Doesn't Do Its Job*, 40 Emory L.J. 1007 (1991), 351

Thomas C. Arthur & Richard D. Freer, *Grasping at Burnt Straws: The Disaster of the Supplemental Jurisdiction Statute*, 40 Emory L.J. 963 (1991), 354

Arthur D. Austin, Complex Litigation Confronts the Jury System (1984), 1337, 1376, 1378

Carl Baar, *Judicial Activism in Canada*, in Judicial Activism in Comparative Perspective (Kenneth M. Holland ed. 1991), 68

Ronald J. Bacigal, The Limits of Litigation (1990), 709, 726, 729

Douglas G. Baird, The Elements of Bankruptcy (rev. ed. 1993), 704, 707, 709, **710**, 727, 766

R.E. Ball, *The Chancery Master*, 77 L.Q. 331 (1961) 947

Susan Bandes, *The Idea of a Case*, 42 Stan. L. Rev. 227 (1990), 147

Kerry Barrett, Note, *Equitable Trusts: An Effective Remedy in Consumer Class Actions*, 96 Yale L.J. 1591 (1987), 1419

Brian Barry, Political Argument (1965), 5

John A. Bauman, *The Evolution of the Summary Judgment Procedure*, 31 Ind. L.J. 329 (1956), 1063

Edward R. Becker & Aviva Orenstein, *The Federal Rules of Evidence after Sixteen Years The Effect of "Plain Meaning"*

Jurisprudence, The Need for an Advisory Committee on the Rules of Evidence, and Suggestions for Selective Revision of the Rules, 60 Geo. Wash. L. Rev. 857 (1992), 1330

Griffin B. Bell et al., *Automatic Disclosure in Discovery The Rush to Reform*, 27 Ga. L. Rev. 1 (1992), 1096

Curtis J. Berger, *Away from the Court House and into the Field: The Odyssey of a Special Master*, 78 Colum. L. Rev. 707 (1978), 1421, 1422

Adam T. Berkoff, Comment, *Computer Simulations in Litigation: Are Television Generation Jurors Being Misled*, 77 Marq. L. Rev. 829 (1994), 1345

Dennis Bilecki, *A More Efficient Method of Jury Selection for Lengthy Trials*, 73 Judicature 43 (June-July 1989), 1245

Bert Black et al., *Science and the Law in the Wake of* Daubert*: A New Search for Scientific Knowledge*, 72 Tex. L. Rev. 715 (1994), 1253, 1254

William Blackstone, Commentaries on the Laws of England (1790), 42

Robert G. Bone, *Lon Fuller's Theory of Adjudication and the False Dichotomy between Dispute Resolution and Public Law Models of Adjudication*, 75 B.U. L. Rev. 1272 (1995), 18, 65

Robert G. Bone, *Rethinking the "Day in Court" Ideal and Nonparty Preclusion*, 67 N.Y.U. L. Rev. 193 (1992), 5, 238, 252

Robert G. Bone, *Rule 23 Redux: Empowering the Federal Class Action*, 14 Rev. Litig. 79 (1994), 698

Robert G. Bone, *Statistical Adjudication: Rights, Justice, and Utility in a World of Process Scarcity*, 46 Vand. L. Rev. 561 (1993), 1316

Mario Borelli, Note, *The Computer as Advocate: An Approach to Computer-Generated Displays in the Courtroom*, 71 Ind. L.J. 439 (1996), 1345

Gary B. Born & David Westin, International Civil Litigation in American Courts (2d ed. 1994), 1163, 1166

Elizabeth B. Brandt, *Fairness to the Absent Members of a Defendant Class: A Proposed Revision of Rule 23*, 1990 B.Y.U. L. Rev. 909, 690, 690

Wayne D. Brazil, *Special Masters in Complex Cases: Extending the Judiciary or Reshaping Adjudication*, 53 U. Chi. L. Rev. 394 (1986), 950, 952, 953

Wayne D. Brazil, *Authority to Refer Discovery Tasks to Special Masters: Limitations on Existing Sources and the Need for a New Federal Rule*, in Managing Complex Litigation 305 (Wayne D. Brazil et al. ed. 1983), 947, 948, 949, 952

Nancy J. Brekke et al., *Of Juries and Court-Appointed Experts: The Impact of Nonadversarial versus Adversarial Expert Testimony*, 15 Law & Hum. Behav. 451 (1991), 1353

Troyen A. Brennan, *Helping Courts with Toxic Torts*, 51 U. Pitt. L. Rev. 1 (1989), 1254

Paul Brodeur, Outrageous Misconduct (1985), 236

Brookings Institution, Justice for All (1989), 929, 1016, 1139

Brookings Institution, Charting a Future for the Civil Jury System (1992), 1336, 1347, 1370, 1373, 1378, 1384

Ralph Brubaker, *Bankruptcy Injunctions and Complex Litigation: A Critical Reappraisal of Non-Debtor Releases in Chapter 11 Reorganizations*, 1997 U. Ill. L. Rev. 959, 751

Edward J. Brunet, *A Study in the Allocation of Scarce Judicial Resources: The Efficiency of Federal Intervention Criteria*, 12 Ga. L. Rev. 701 (1978), 153

Edward J. Brunet et al., Summary Judgment (1994), 1062, 1065, 1066

Stephen B. Burbank, *Interjurisdictional Preclusion, Full Faith and Credit and Federal Common Law: A General Approach*, 71 Corn. L. Rev. 733 (1986), 169

Stephen B. Burbank, *Of Rules and Discretion: The Supreme Court, Federal Rules and Common Law*, 63 Notre Dame L. Rev. 693 (1988), 7, 59

Stephen B. Burbank, *The Rules Enabling Act of 1934*, 130 U. Pa. L. Rev. 1015 (1982), 56

Bureau of Justice Assistance, Differentiated Case Management (1993), 929

Jean W. Burns, *Decorative Figureheads: Eliminating Class Representatives in Class Actions*, 42 Hastings L. J. 165, 167-86 (1990), 581

Robert A. Bush, *Dispute Resolution Alternatives and Achieving the Goals of Civil Justice: Jurisdictional Principles for Process Choice*, 1984 Wis. L. Rev. 893, 10

Jose R. Bustamonte, *Trial and Court Procedures in Ecuador*, in Trial and Court Procedures Worldwide 205 (1991), 74

Stephen Calkins, *Summary Judgment, Motions to Dismiss, and Other Examples of Equilibrating Tendencies*

in the Antitrust System, 74 Geo. L.J. 1065 (1986), **1001**, 1068, 1069, 1070

James S. Campbell and Nicholas Le Poidevin, *Complex Cases and Jury Trials: A Reply to Professor Arnold*, 128 U. Pa. L. Rev. 965 (1980), 1240

Paul D. Carrington, *Making Rules to Dispose of Manifestly Unfounded Assertions: An Exorcism of the Bogy of Non-Trans-Substantive Rules of Civil Procedure*, 137 U. Pa. L. Rev. 2067 (1989), 7, 1066

Paul D. Carrington, *The Seventh Amendment: Some Bicentennial Reflections*, 1990 U. Chi. L.F. 33, 1212, 1219

Jonathan D. Casper, *Restructuring the Traditional Civil Jury: The Effect of Changes in Composition and Procedures*, in Verdict 414 (Robert E. Litan ed. 1993), 1243, 1337, **1378**

Mark C. Cawley, Note, *The Right Result for the Wrong Reasons: Permitting Aggregation of Claims under 28 U.S.C. § 1367 in Multi-Plaintiff Diversity Litigation*, 73 Notre Dame L. Rev. 1045 (1998), 354

Joe S. Cecil & C.R. Douglas, Summary Judgment Practice in Three District Courts (1987), 1068, 1069, 1085

Joe S. Cecil & Thomas E. Willging, *Accepting Daubert's Invitation: Defining a Role for Court-Appointed Experts in Assessing Scientific Validity*, 43 Emory L.J. 995 (1994), **1352**

Joe S. Cecil & Thomas E. Willging, Court Appointed Experts (1993), 1356

Joe S. Cecil et al., Jury Service in Lengthy Civil Trials (1987), 1236, 1376

Zechariah Chafee, Jr., *Bills of Peace with Multiple Parties*, 45 Harv. L. Rev. 1297 (1932), 389, 424

Robert P. Charrow & Veda R. Charrow, *Making Legal Language Understandable: A Psycholinguistic Study of Jury Instructions*, 79 Colum. L. Rev. 1306 (1979), 1376

Abram Chayes, *Foreword: Public Law Litigation and the Burger Court*, 96 Harv. L. Rev. 4 (1982), 66

Abram Chayes, *The Role of the Judge in Public Law Litigation*, 89 Harv. L. Rev. 1281 (1976), **61**, 1402, 1423

Erwin Chemerinsky, Federal Jurisdiction (2d ed. 1994), 330, 339, 344, 371, 433, 948, 1258

Audrey Chin & Mark A. Peterson, Deep Pockets, Empty Pockets (1985), 1217

Charles S. Christopher, *The Reign of Queen Victoria: A Survey of Fifty Years of Progress*, 1 Select Essays in Anglo-American Legal History 516 (1907), **45**

Civil Practice and Litigation in Federal and State Courts (6th ed. Sol Schreiber ed. 1994), 1348

Charles E. Clark, Handbook on the Law of Code Pleading (1928), **51**, **53**, 987, 1063

Charles E. Clark, *Special Pleading in the "Big Case,"*, 21 F.R.D. 45 (1957), 987

Charles E. Clark, *Special Problems in Drafting and Interpreting Procedural Codes and Rules*, 3 Vand. L. Rev. 493 (1950), 43

Kevin M. Clermont & Theodore Eisenberg, *Trial by Jury or Judge: Transcending Empiricism*, 77 Corn. L. Rev. 1124 (1992), 1217

John C. Coffee, Jr., *Class Wars: The Dilemma of the Mass Tort Class Action*, 95 Colum. L. Rev. 1343 (1995), 654, 738, 767, 786

John C. Coffee, Jr., *The Regulation of Entrepreneurial Litigation: Balancing Fairness and Efficiency in the Large Class Action*, 54 U. Chi. L. Rev. 877 (1987), 887

Frank M. Coffin, *The Frontier of Remedies: A Call for Exploration*, 67 Cal. L. Rev. 983 (1979), 1422

Collier on Bankruptcy (15th ed. 1982), 717

Collier on Bankruptcy (15th ed. 1996), 705, 706, 723

Colloquy: *Perspectives on Supplemental Jurisdiction*, 41 Emory L.J. 1 (1992), 348, 349

Comment, *Complex Civil Litigation and the Seventh Amendment Right to a Jury Trial*, 51 U. Chi. L. Rev. 581 (1984), 1240

Conference on "Economic Analysis of Civil Procedure," 23 J. Leg. Stud. 303 (1994), 10

A Constitutional Analysis of Magistrate Judge Authority, 150 F.R.D. 247 (1992), 956

Edward H. Cooper, *Rule 23: Challenges to the Rulemaking Process*, 71 N.Y.U. L. Rev. 13, 68 (1996), 697

Ross D. Cooper, *Civil Procedure: The Korean Air Disaster: Choice of Law in Federal Multidistrict Litigation*, 57 Geo. Wash. L. Rev. 1145 (1989), 830

Robert Cooter & Daniel Rubinfeld, *An Economic Model of Legal Discovery*, 23 J. Leg. Stud. 435 (1994), 1132, 1133

Jessica Copen, *Courts of the Future*, 77 A.B.A.J. 74 (June 1991), 1273

Stephen T.O. Cottreau, Note, *The Due Process Right to Opt Out of Class Actions*, 73 N.Y.U. L. Rev. 480 (1998), 614

Robert M. Cover, *For Wm. James Moore: Some Reflections on a Reading of the Rules*, 84 Yale L.J. 718 (1975), 6, 35, 44, 80

Robert M. Cover, *The Uses of Jurisdictional Redundancy: Ideology, Interest, and Innovation*, 22 Wm. & Mary L. Rev. 639 (1981), 49

Stanley E. Cox, *Back to Conflicts Basics*, 44 Cath. U. L. Rev. 525 (1995), 797

Stephen L. Cummings, Note, *International Mass Tort Litigation*: Forum Non Conveniens *and the Adequate Alternative Forum*, 16 Ga. J. Intl. L. 109 (1986), 465

Brainerd Currie, *Mutuality of Collateral Estoppel: Limits of the* Bernhard *Doctrine*, 9 Stan. L. Rev. 281, 304, 172

David P. Currie, *The Federal Courts and the American Law Institute, Part II*, 36 U. Chi. L. Rev. 268 (1969), 427

Doyle W. Curry & Rosemary T. Snider, *Bifurcated Trials*, 24 Trial 47 (March 1988), 1286, 1289

Kenneth W. Dam, *Class Actions: Efficiency, Compensation, Deterrence, and Conflict of Interest*, 4 J. Leg. Stud. 47 (1975), 539

Mirjan Damaska, The Faces of Justice and State Authority (1986), 81, 1287

Carlo D'Angelo, *The Snoop Doggy Dogg Trial: A Look at How Computer Animation Will Impact Litigation in the Next Century*, 32 U.S.F. L. Rev. 561 (1998), 1345

Kenneth C. Davis, Administrative Law Treatise, 436

Phyllis V. Deets & Gowan Deets, *The Application of EIM/OCR Technology to Litigation Case Management*, in Advanced Litigation Support & Document Imaging 29 (V. Mital ed. 1995), **1174, 1176, 1177**

Ronan E. Degnan, *Federalized Res Judicata*, 85 Yale L.J. 471 (1976), 169

Natalie A. DeJarlais, Note, *The Consumer Trust Fund: A Cy Pres Solution to Undistributed Funds in Consumer Class Actions*, 38 Hastings L.J. 729, 730 (1987), 1419

R. Lawrence Dessem, *The Role of the Federal Magistrate Judge in Civil Justice Reform*, 67 St. John L. Rev. 799 (1993), 960

Developments in the Law — The Civil Jury, 110 Harv. L. Rev. 1408 (1997), 1218, 1240

Patrick Devlin, *Jury Trial of Complex Cases: English Practice at the Time of the Seventh Amendment*, 80 Colum. L. Rev. 43 (1980), 1240

A.S. Diamond, *The Queen's Bench Master*, 76 L.Q. 504 (1960), 947

Edward V. Di Lello, Note, *Fighting Fire with Firefighters: A Proposal for Expert Judges at the Trial Level*, 93 Colum. L. Rev. 473 (1993), 1259

Discovery and Disclosure Practice, Problems, and Proposals for Change (Federal Judicial Center 1997), 1090, 1093, 1096

Disqualification of Judges (The Sarokin Matter): Is It a Threat to Judicial Independence?, 58 Brook. L. Rev. 1063 (1993), 976

Dan B. Dobbs, Law of Remedies (2d ed. 1993), 389

Howard M. Downs, *Federal Class Actions: Diminished Protection for the Class and the Case for Reform*, 73 Neb. L. Rev. 646 (1994), 654

Howard M. Downs, *Federal Class Actions: Due Process by Adequacy of Representation (Identity of Claims) and the Impact of* General Telephone v. Falcon, 54 Ohio St. L.J. 607 (1993), 580

Anna L. Durand, Note, *An Economic Analysis of Fluid Class Recovery Systems*, 34 Stan. L. Rev. 173 (1981), 1419

W. Cole Durham & Johnathan A. Dibble, *Certification: A Practical Device for Screening Spurious Antitrust Litigation*, 1978 B.Y.U. L. Rev. 299, 1028

Ronald Dworkin, *Principle, Policy, Procedure*, in A Matter of Principle 72 (1985), 8

Frank H. Easterbrook, *Discovery as Abuse*, 69 B.U. L. Rev. 635 (1989), 1093

E. Donald Elliot, *Managerial Judging and the Evolution of Procedure*, 53 U. Chi. L. Rev. 306 (1986), **934**, 1066

Phoebe C. Ellsworth, *Are Twelve Heads Better Than One?*, 52 Law & Contemp. Prob. 205 (Autumn 1989), 1239, 1376

Amiriam Elwork et al., *Juridic Decisions: In Ignorance of the Law or in Light of It?*, 1 Law & Hum. Behav. 163 (1977), 1376, 1377

Amiriam Elwork et al., Making Jury Instructions Understandable (1982), 1376

Richard L. Epling, *Are Rule 23 Class Actions a Viable Alternative to the Bankruptcy Code?*, 23 Seton Hall L. Rev. 1555 (1993), 598

Howard M. Erichson, *Interjurisdictional Preclusion*, 94 Mich. L. Rev. 945 (1998), 169, 172

William H. Erickson, *The Pound Conference Recommendations: A Blueprint for the Justice System in the Twenty-First Century*, 76 F.R.D. 277 (1980), 1130

David L. Faigman & A.J. Baglioni, Jr., *Bayes' Theorem in the Trial Process: Instructing Jurors on the Value of Statistical Evidence*, 12 Law & Hum. Behav. 1 (1988), 1239

Richard H. Fallon et al., Hart and Wechsler's The Federal Courts and the Federal System 909 (4th ed. 1996), 49, 322, 426, 427, 704, 807, 854

Margaret G. Farrell, *The Role of Special Masters in Federal Litigation*, in Civil Practice and Litigation in Federal and State Courts (Sol Schreiber ed. 1994), 959

Margaret G. Farrell, *Special Masters*, in Reference Manual on Scientific Evidence 575 (1994), 969

Federal Judicial Center, Manual for Litigation Management and Cost and Delay Reduction (1993), 885, 929, 938, 957, 958

The Federalist (J. Cooke ed. 1961), 1219, 1431, 1433

Kenneth R. Feinberg, *Do Mass Torts Belong in the Courtroom?*, 74 Judicature 237 (1991), 436

Jeffrey T. Ferriell, *The Perils of Nationwide Service of Process in a Bankruptcy Context*, 48 Wash. & Lee L. Rev. 1199 (1991), 706

J. Kendall Few, Trial by Jury (1993), 1237

Martha A. Field, *Abstention in Constitutional Cases: The Scope of the Pullman Abstention Doctrine*, 122 U. Pa. L. Rev. 1071 (1974), 427, 428, 432, 434

Martha A. Field, *Sources of Law: The Scope of Federal Common Law*, 99 Harv. L. Rev. 881 (1986), 854

Owen M. Fiss, *The Allure of Individualism*, 78 Iowa L. Rev. 965 (1993), 1207

Owen M. Fiss, The Civil Rights Injunction (1978), 1435

Owen M. Fiss, Dombrowski, 86 Yale L.J. 1103, 1107 (1977), 397, 426

Owen M. Fiss, *Foreword: The Forms of Justice*, 93 Harv. L. Rev. 1 (1979), 19, 66

Owen M. Fiss & Doug Rendleman, Injunctions (2d ed. 1984), 1434, 1435

Lynne ForsterLee et al., *Effects of Notetaking on Verdicts and Evidence Processing in a Civil Trial*, 18 Law & Hum. Behav. 567 (1994), 1374

Jerome Frank, Courts on Trial (1950), 1210, 1216

Mark A. Frankel, *A Trial Judge's Perspective on Providing Tools for Rational Jury Decisionmaking*, 85 Nw. L. Rev. 221 (1990), 1370

Marvin E. Frankel, *The Search for Truth: An Umpireal View*, 123 U. Pa. L. Rev. 1031 (1975), 26, 1093

Marvin F. Frankel, Partisan Justice (1978), 1346

Richard D. Freer, *Avoiding Duplicative Litigation: Rethinking Plaintiff Autonomy and the Court's Role in Defining the Litigative Units*, 50 U. Pitt. L. Rev. 809 (1989), 255

Richard D. Freer, *Compounding Confusion and Hampering Diversity: Life after* Finley *and the Supplemental Jurisdiction Statute*, 40 Emory L.J. 445 (1991), 349

Jack H. Friendenthal, *Cases on Summary Judgment: Has There Been a Material Change in Standards?* 63 Notre Dame L. Rev. 770 (1988), 1062

Jack H. Friedenthal, *Increased Participation by Nonparties: The Need for Conditions and Limits*, 13 U.C. Davis L. Rev. 259 (1980), 257

Steven I. Friedland, *The Competency and Responsibility of Jurors in Deciding Cases*, 85 Nw. L. Rev. 190 (1990), 1371

Barry Friedman, *When Rights Encounter Reality: Enforcing Federal Remedies*, 65 S. Cal. L. Rev. 735 (1992), 1435

Henry J. Friendly, *In Praise of* Erie — *and of the New Federal Common Law*, 39 N.Y.U. L. Rev. 383 (1964), 807, 854

Henry J. Friendly, *The "Law of the Circuit" and All That*, 46 St. John's L. Rev. 406 (1972), 822

Lon L. Fuller, *The Adversary System*, in Talks on American Law 30 (Harold J. Berman ed. 1961), 18

Lon. L. Fuller, *The Forms and Limits of Adjudication*, 92 Harv. L. Rev. 353 (1978), 13, 64, 108, 608, 1400

Lon L. Fuller, The Problems of Jurisprudence (1949), 19

Brian Galligan, *Judicial Activism in Aus-*

tralia, in Judicial Activism in Comparative Perspective (Kenneth M. Holland ed. 1991), 68

Mary A. Glendon et al., **Comparative Legal Traditions** (1985), 74, 80

Mary A. Glendon et al., **Comparative Legal Traditions** (2d ed. 1994), 67, **69**, 79

Carole E. Goldberg, *The Influence of Procedural Rules on Federal Jurisdiction*, 28 Stan. L. Rev. 395 (1976), 341

Jane Goodman, *Jurors' Comprehension and Assessment of Probabilistic Evidence*, 16 Am. J. Trial Advocacy 361 (1992), 1237

Jane Goodman & Edith Greene, *The Use of Paraphrase Analysis in the Simplification of Jury Instructions*, 4 J. Soc. Behav. & Personality 237 (1989), 1377

Jennifer M. Granholm & William J. Richards, *Bifurcated Justice: How Trial-Splitting Devices Defeat the Jury's Role*, 26 U. Tol. L. Rev. 505 (1995), 1292

Leon Green, Judge and Jury (1930), 1210

Michael D. Green, *The Inability of Offensive Collateral Estoppel to Fulfill Its Promise: An Examination of Estoppel in Asbestos Litigation*, 70 Iowa L. Rev. 141 (1984), 1318

Michael D. Green & Richard A. Matasar, *The Supreme Court and the Products Liability Crisis: Lessons from Boyle's Government Contractor Defense*, 63 S. Cal. L. Rev. 637 (1990), 853

Samuel R. Gross, *Expert Evidence*, 1991 Wis. L. Rev. 1113, 1252, 1358

John Guinther, The Jury in America (1988), 1237, 1336, 1374

Learned Hand, *The Deficiencies of Trials to Reach the Heart of the Matter*, in Lectures on Legal Topics 1921-1922 87 (1926), 55

Learned Hand, *Historical and Practical Considerations Regarding Expert Testimony*, 15 Harv. L. Rev. 40 (1901), 1355

Handbook of Recommended Procedures for the Trial of Protracted Cases, 25 F.R.D. 351 (1960), **926**, 938, 1007, 1252

Milton Handler, *The Shift from Substantive to Procedural Innovations in Antitrust Suits — The Twenty-Third Annual Antitrust Review*, 71 Colum. L. Rev. 1 (1971), 540

Valerie P. Hans & William S. Lofquist, *Jurors' Judgments of Business Liability in Tort Cases: Implications for the Litigation Explosion Debate*, 26 Law & Society Rev. 85 (1992), 1237

Valerie P. Hans & Neil Vidmar, Judging the Jury (1986), 1237, 1370, 1376, 1378

Louis Harris & Associates, *Judges' Opinions on Procedural Issues: A Survey of State and Federal Trial Judges Who Spend at Least Half Their Time on General Civil Cases*, 69 B.U. L. Rev. 731 (1989), 1242, 1293

Thomas H. Hart, III, *Case Preparation in Federal Court: Informal Discovery*, Comment 22 (July-August 1987), 1169

Reid Hastie et al., Inside the Jury 78 (1983), 1376

Bruce L. Hay, *Civil Discovery: Its Effects and Optimal Scope*, 23 J. Leg. Stud. 481 (1994), 1133, 1160

Geoffrey C. Hazard, Jr., *Authority in the Dock*, 69 B.U. L. Rev. 469 (1989), 2

Geoffrey C. Hazard, Jr., *Discovery Vices and Trans-Substantive Virtues in the Federal Rules of Civil Procedure*, 137 U. Pa. L. Rev. 2237 (1989), 7

Geoffrey C. Hazard, Jr., Ethics in the Practice of Law (1978), **22**, 67

Geoffrey C. Hazard, Jr. and Myron Moskovitz, *An Historical and Critical Analysis of Interpleader*, 52 Cal. L. Rev. 706 (1964), 423

Geoffrey C. Hazard, Jr. & Paul R. Rice, *Judicial Management of the Pretrial Process in Massive Litigation: Special Masters as Case Managers*, in Wayne D. Brazil et al., Managing Complex Litigation 103 (1983), 951, 952, 959, 1036, 1037, 1038, 1331

Geoffrey C. Hazard, Jr. et al., Cases and Materials on Pleadings and Procedure (7th ed. 1994), 1210

Deborah R. Hensler, *Resolving Mass Toxic Torts: Myths and Realities*, 1989 U. Ill. L. Rev. 89, **124**, 889, 1169

Charles M. Hepburn, The Historical Development of Code Pleading in America and England (1897), 52

Wilson W. Herndon & Ernest R. Higginbotham, *Complex Multidistrict Litigation An Overview of 28 U.S.C.A. § 1407*, 31 Baylor L. Rev. 33 (1979), 511, 512

Larry Heuer & Steven Penrod, *Increasing Jurors' Participation in Trials: A Field Experiment with Jury Notetaking and Question Asking*, 12 Law & Hum. Behav. 231 (1988), 1370, 1373, 1374

Larry Heuer & Steven D. Penrod, *Instructing Jurors: A Field Experiment with Written and Preliminary Instructions*,

13 Law & Hum. Behav. 409 (1989), 1336, 1377
Larry Heuer & Steven Penrod, *Juror Notetaking and Question Asking during Trials: A National Field Experiment*, 18 Law & Hum. Behav. 121 (1994), 1373, 1374
Larry Heuer & Steven Penrod, *Trial Complexity*, 18 Law and Hum. Behav. 29 (1994), 1237, 1373, 1374, 1377, 1382
William Holdsworth, A History of English Law (1922), **44**, 947
Donald L. Horowitz, The Courts and Social Policy (1977), 1435
Donald L. Horowitz, *Decreeing Organizational Change: Judicial Supervision of Public Institutions*, 1983 Duke L.J. 1265, 1422, 1434, 1446, 1447
Irwin A. Horowitz & Kenneth S. Bordens, *The Effects of Outlier Presence, Plaintiff Population Size, and Aggregation of Plaintiffs on Simulated Civil Jury Decisions*, 12 L. & Hum. Behav. 209 (1988), **102**, 485
Irwin A. Horowitz & Kenneth S. Bordens, *An Experimental Investigation of Procedural Issues in Complex Tort Trials*, 14 Law & Hum. Behav. 269 (1990), 1286, 1335
Morton Horwitz, The Transformation of American Law 1780-1860 (1977), 48
John B. Houck, Restatement of the Foreign Relations Law of the United States (Revised): *Issues and Resolutions*, 20 Int. Law. 1361 (1986), 1163
Joseph M. Howie, Jr., *Applying Imaging: A Survey of the U.S. Law Office Scene*, in Advanced Litigation Support and Document Imaging 35 (V. Mital ed. 1995), 1178

Illinois Manual for Complex Litigation (1991), 1272, 1293
Inside the Jury (Reid Hastie ed. 1993), 1237
Samuel Issacharoff & George Loewenstein, *Second Thoughts about Summary Judgment*, 100 Yale L.J. 73 (1990), **1057**, 1069, 1160
Samuel Issacharoff & George Loewenstein, *Unintended Consequences of Mandatory Disclosure*, 73 Tex. L. Rev. 753 (1995), 1095

Michael S. Jacobs, *Testing the Assumptions Underlying the Debate about Scientific Evidence: A Closer Look at Juror "Incompetence" and Scientific "Objectivity,"* 25 Conn. L. Rev. 1083 (1993), 1237
Fleming James, Jr. et al., Civil Procedure (4th ed. 1992), **50, 273, 1092**
Friedrich K. Juenger, Choice of Law and Multistate Justice (1993), 797, 862
Friedrich K. Juenger, *Mass Disasters and the Conflict of Laws*, 1989 U. Ill. L. Rev. 105, **791**

Marcel Kahan & Linda Silberman, Matsushita *and Beyond: The Role of State Courts in Class Actions Involving Exclusive Federal Claims*, 1996 Sup. Ct. Rev. 219, 656
Marcel Kahan & Linda Silberman, *The Inadequate Search for "Adequacy" in Class Actions: A Critique of* Epstein v. MCA, Inc., 73 N.Y.U. L. Rev. 765 (1998), 656
James S. Kakalik et al., An Evaluation of Judicial Case Management under the Civil Justice Reform Act (1996), 958, 1010, **1013**, 1095
Harry Kalven, Jr. & Hans Zeisel, The American Jury (1966), 1218, 1237, 1372
Harry Kalven, Jr., *The Dignity of the Civil Jury*, 50 Va. L. Rev. 1055 (1964), 1216
Benjamin Kaplan, *Prefatory Note*, 10 B.C. Ind. & Com. L. Rev. 497 (1969), 676, 677
Larry S. Kaplan, Complex Federal Litigation (1993), 910, 912, 924, 1040, 1046, 1244, 1338, 1345, 1346, 1383
Louis Kaplow, *The Value of Accuracy in Adjudication: An Economic Analysis*, 23 J. Leg. Stud. 307 (1994), 1133
Saul M. Kassin & Lawrence S. Wrightsman, The American Jury on Trial 127 (1988), 1236
Saul M. Kassin & Meghan A. Dunn, *Computer-Animated Displays and the Jury: Facilitative and Prejudicial Effects*, 21 Law & Hum. Behav. 269 (1997), 1345
Irving R. Kaufman, *Masters in the Federal Courts: Rule 53*, 58 Colum. L. Rev. 452 (1958), 947, 948, 952
Susan P. Koniak, *Feasting While the Widow Weeps:* Georgine v. Amchem Products, Inc., 80 Corn. L. Rev. 1045 (1995), 686, 914
Larry Kramer, *Choice of Law in Complex Litigation*, 71 N.Y.U. L. Rev. 547 (1996), 808, 841, 863
Samuel Krislov, *The Amicus Curiae Brief: From Friendship to Advocacy*, 72 Yale L.J. 694 (1963), 154

William Lambarde, Archeion (Charles H.

McIlwain & Paul L. Ward ed. 1957) (1591), 42

William M. Landes, *Sequential versus Unitary Trials: An Economic Analysis*, 22 J. Legal Stud. 99 (1993), 1292

Stephan Landsman, *The History and Objectives of the Civil Jury System*, in Verdict 22 (Robert E. Litan ed. 1993), 1210

John H. Langbein, *The German Advantage in Civil Procedure*, 52 U. Chi. L. Rev. 823 (1985), **70**, **930**, 1161

Rogelio A. Lasso, *Gladiators Be Gone: The New Disclosure Rules Compel a Reexamination of the Adversary Process*, 36 B.C. L. Rev. 479 (1995), 1096

Douglas A. Laycock, Modern American Remedies (2d ed. 1994), 1385

Frederic I. Lederer, *Technology Comes to the Courtroom, and . . .*, 43 Emory L.J. 1095 (1994), **1267**, 1346

Richard O. Lempert, *Civil Juries and Complex Cases: Let's Not Rush to Judgment*, 80 Mich. L. Rev. 68 (1981), 1240, 1380

Richard Lempert, *Civil Juries and Complex Cases: Taking Stock after Twelve Years*, in Verdict 181 (Robert E. Litan ed. 1993), 1237, 1239, 1370, 1374

Shao-chuan Leng, Justice in Communist China (1967), **78**

John Leubsdorf, *Theories of Judging and Judicial Disqualification*, 62 N.Y.U. L. Rev. 237 (1987), 968

Pierre N. Leval, *From the Bench*, 12 Litigation 7 (Fall 1985), 1322

Patrick E. Longan, *The Shot Clock Comes to Trial: Time Limits for Federal Civil Trials*, 35 Ariz. L. Rev. 663 (1993), 1324

Peter W. Low & John C. Jeffries, Jr., Civil Rights Actions (2d ed. 1994), 361

Andreas F. Lowenfeld, *Mass Torts and the Conflict of Laws: The Airline Disaster*, 1989 U. Ill. L. Rev. 157, 790, 841

William V. Luneburg & Mark A. Nordenberg, *Specially Qualified Juries and Expert Nonjury Tribunals: Alternatives for Coping with the Complexities of Modern Civil Litigation*, 67 Va. L. Rev. 887 (1981), 1242

Ralph R. Mabey & Jamie A. Gavrin, *Constitutional Limitations on the Discharge of Future Claims in Bankruptcy*, 44 S.Car. L. Rev. 745 (1993), 767

Robert MacCoun, Improving Jury Comprehension in Criminal and Civil Trials (1995), 1239, 1375, 1378

Robert MacCoun, *Inside the Black Box: What Empirical Research Tells Us about Decisionmaking by Civil Juries*, in Verdict 137 (Robert E. Litan ed. 1993), 1237, 1336

Jonathon R. Macey & Geoffrey P. Miller, *Auctioning Class Action and Derivative Lawsuits: A Rejoinder*, 87 Nw. U. L. Rev. 458 (1993), 889

Jonathon R. Macey & Geoffrey P. Miller, *The Plaintiffs' Attorney's Role in Class Action and Derivative Litigation: Economic Analysis and Recommendations for Change*, 58 U. Chi. L. Rev. 1 (1991), 581 888, 889

Henry Maine, Dissertation on Early Law and Customs (1886), 30

F.W. Maitland, Equity (A.H. Chaylor & W.J. Whittaker eds., 2d ed. 1936), **37**

Managing to Reduce Delay (National Center for State Courts 1980), 929

Manual for Complex and Multidistrict Litigation (1970), **83**, 1122

Manual for Complex Litigation (1972), 885

Manual for Complex Litigation (5th ed. 1982), 649

Manual for Complex Litigation (Second) (1985), 447, 1123, 1249

Manual for Complex Litigation, Third, (1995), **84**, 447, 551, 653, **879**, 885, 886, 887, 907, 910, 911, 914, **927**, 929, **938**, 952, 954, **955**, 957, 992, 997, 999, **1007**, 1008, 1016, 1030, 1033, 1035, 1039, 1040, 1062, 1065, 1076, **1089**, 1094, 1095, 1097, **1098**, 1106, 1111, 1122, 1126, 1134, 1136, **1137**, 1147, 1148, 1149, 1150, 1151, 1152, 1162, 1178, 1193 **1201**, 1245, 1246, 1252, 1254, 1272, 1289, 1326, 1332, **1333**, 1337, 1338, 1344, 1346, 13551370, 1375, 1376, 1383

Richard L. Marcus, *Completing Equity's Conquest? Reflections on the Future of Trial under the Federal Rules of Civil Procedure*, 50 U. Pitt. L. Rev. 725 (1989), 66, 1057

Richard L. Marcus, *Conflict Among Circuits and Transfers Within the Federal Judicial System*, 93 Yale L.J. 677 (1984), 821, 822, 830

Richard L. Marcus, *Myth and Reality in Protective Order Litigation*, 69 Corn. L. Rev. 1 (1983), 1111, 1112, 1116

Richard L. Marcus, *Of Babies and Bathwater: The Prospects for Procedural Reform*, 59 Brook. L. Rev. 761 (1993), 7

Richard L. Marcus, *The Perils of Privilege: Waiver and the Litigator*, 84 Mich. L. Rev. 1605 (1986), 1146, 1147

Richard L. Marcus, *The Revival of Fact Pleading under the Federal Rules of Civil Procedure*, 86 Colum. L. Rev. 433 (1986), 991

James A. Martin, *The Proposed "Science Court,"* 75 Mich. L. Rev. 1058 (1977), 1246

Jerry L. Mashaw, *The Supreme Court's Due Process Calculus for Administrative Adjudication in* Mathews v. Eldridge: *Three Factors in Search of a Value*, 44 U. Chi. L. Rev. 28 (1976), 9, 10, 13

John C. McCoid, *A Single Package for Multiparty Disputes*, 28 Stan. L. Rev. 707 (1976), 255

Paula J. McDermott, Note, *Can Statutory Interpleader Be Used as a Remedy by the Tortfeasor in Mass Tort Litigation*, 90 Dick. L. Rev. 439 (1985), 420

Francis E. McGovern, *The Alabama DDT Settlement Fund*, 53 Law & Contemp. Prob. 61 (Autumn 1990), 1288

Francis E. McGovern, *An Analysis of Mass Torts for Judges*, 73 Tex. L. Rev. 1821 (1995), 236, 646

Francis E. McGovern & E. Allan Lind, *The Discovery Survey*, 51 Law & Contemp. Prob. 41 (Autumn 1988), 105, 1153, 1170

Francis E. McGovern, *Resolving Mature Mass Tort Litigation*, 69 B.U. L. Rev. 659 (1989), 236, 647, 725

Francis E. McGovern, *Toward a Functional Approach for Managing Complex Litigation*, 53 U. Chi. L. Rev. 440 (1986), 236

William P. McLauchlan, *An Empirical Study of the Federal Summary Judgment Rule*, 6 J. Leg. Stud. 427 (1977), 1068, 1069

Denis F. McLaughlin, *The Federal Supplemental Jurisdiction Statute A Constitutional and Statutory Analysis*, 24 Ariz. St. L. Rev. 849 (1992), 349, 354

Robert C. McLean, *Pretrial Management in Complex Litigation: The Use of Special Masters in* United States v. AT&T 275, in Managing Complex Litigation (Wayne D. Brazil et al. ed. 1983), 951

Mealey's Litigation Reports: Drugs & Medical Devices (June 13, 1997), 740

Carrie Menkel-Meadow, *Ethics and the Settlement of Mass Torts: When the Rules Meet the Road*, 80 Corn. L. Rev. 1159 (1995), 686, 914

Frank I. Michelman, *The Supreme Court and Litigation Access Fees: The Right to Protect One's Rights Part I*, 1973 Duke L.J. 1153, 12

Robert W. Millar, Civil Procedure of the Trial Court in Historical Perspective (1952), 33, 34, 47

Arthur R. Miller, The August 1983 Amendments to the Federal Rules of Civil Procedure: Promoting Effective Case Management and Lawyer Responsibility (1984), 1001

Arthur R. Miller, *Confidentiality, Protective Orders, and Public Access to the Courts*, 105 Harv. L. Rev. 427 (1991), 1111, 1149, 1152

Arthur R. Miller, *Of Frankenstein Monsters and Shining Knights: Myth, Reality, and the "Class Action Problem,"* 92 Harv. L. Rev. 664 (1979), 531

Arthur R. Miller & David Crump, *Jurisdiction and Choice of Law in Multistate Class Actions After* Phillips Petroleum v. Shutts, 96 Yale L.J. 1 (1986), 308

Geoffrey P. Miller, *Class Actions and Jurisdictional Boundaries: Overlapping Class Actions*, 71 N.Y.U. L. Rev. 514 (1996), 471

Scott D. Miller, Note, *Certification of Defendant Classes Under Rule 23(b)(2)*, 84 Colum. L. Rev. 1371 (1984), 692

S.F.C. Milson, Historical Foundations of the Common Law (2d ed. 1981), 28, 32, 42

Martha Minow, *Judge for the Situation: Judge Jack Weinstein, Creator of Temporary Administrative Agencies*, 97 Colum. L. Rev. 2010 (1997), 1442

Paul J. Mishkin, *The Federal "Question" in the District Courts*, 53 Colum. L. Rev. 157 (1953), 320

James Wm. Moore, Moore's Federal Practice, 119, 222

Karen N. Moore, *The Supplemental Jurisdiction Statute: An Important but Controversial Supplement to Federal Jurisdiction*, 41 Emory L.J. 31 (1992), 354, 356

Nancy Morawetz, *Bargaining, Class Representation, and Fairness*, 54 Ohio St. L.J. 1 (1993), 654

Michelle M. Morgan, *The Denial of Future Tort Claims in* In re Piper Aircraft: *Will the Court's Quick-Fix Solution Keep the Debtor Flying High or Bring It Crashing Down?* 27 Loy. U. Chi. L. Rev. 27 (1995), 768

Stephen E. Morrissey, Note, *State Settlement Class Actions That Release Exclusive Federal Claims: Developing a Framework for Multijurisdictional*

Management of Shareholder Litigation, 95 Colum. L. Rev. 1765 (1995), 656

H. Geoffrey Moulton, Jr., *Federalism and Choice of Law in the Regulation of Legal Ethics*, 82 Minn. L. Rev. 73 (1997), 907

Linda S. Mullenix, *Beyond Consolidation: Post-Aggregative Procedure in Asbestos Mass Tort Litigation*, 32 Wm. & Mary L. Rev. 475 (1991), 646

Linda S. Mullenix, *Class Resolution of the Mass-Tort Case: A Proposed Federal Procedure Act*, 64 Tex. L. Rev. 1039 (1986), 698, 855

Linda S. Mullenix, *Multiforum Federal Practice: Ethics and* Erie, 9 Geo. J. Leg. Ethics 89 (1995), 907

Diane E. Murphy, *Unified and Consolidated Complaints in Multidistrict Litigation*, 132 F.R.D. 597 (1991), 998, 999

James A.R. Nafziger, *Choice of Law in Air Disasters: Complex Litigation Rules and the Common Law*, 54 La. L. Rev. 1001 (1994), 842

National Bankruptcy Conference, Reforming the Bankruptcy Code (1994), 768

National Bankruptcy Review Commission, Treatment of Mass Future Claims in Bankruptcy (1997), 766

Herbert B. Newberg, Newberg on Class Actions (2d ed. 1985), 562

Herbert B. Newberg & Alba Conte, Newberg on Class Actions (3d ed. 1992), 576, 577, 578, 591

William E. Nelson, Americanization of the Common Law (1975), 47

Bruce H. Nielson, *Was the Advisory Committee Right?: Suggested Revisions of Rule 23 to Allow More Frequent Use of Class Actions in Mass Tort Litigation*, 25 Harv. J. Leg. 461 (1988), 698

Kimberly J. Norwood, *Double Forum Shopping and the Extension of* Ferens *to Federal Claims that Borrow State Limitations Periods*, 44 Emory L.J. 501 (1995), 830

Note, *The Case for Special Juries in Complex Cases*, 89 Yale L.J. 1155 (1980), 1241

Note, *The Changing Role of the Jury in the Nineteenth Century*, 74 Yale L.J. 170 (1964), 48

Note, *Claim Preclusion in Modern Latent Disease Cases: A Proposal for Allowing Second Suits*, 103 Harv. L. Rev. 829 (1990), 192

Note, *Collateral Attack on the Binding Effect of Class Action Judgments*, 87 Harv. L. Rev. 589 (1978), 580

Note, *Defendant Class Actions*, 91 Harv. L. Rev. 630 (1978), 692

Note, *Implementation Problems in Institutional Reform Litigation*, 91 Harv. L. Rev. 428 (1977), 1435

Note, *In-Kind Class Action Settlements*, 109 Harv. L. Rev. 810, 812 (1996), 656

Note, *Judicial Abstention and Exclusive Federal Jurisdiction: A Reconciliation*, 67 Corn. L. Rev. 219 (1981), 430

Note, *Preserving the Right to Jury Trial in Complex Civil Cases*, 32 Stan. L. Rev. 99 (1979), 1240

Note *The Right to a Jury Trial in Complex Civil Litigation*, 92 Harv. L. Rev. 898 (1979), 1232, 1240

Note, *The Right to an Incompetent Jury: Protracted Commercial Litigation and the Seventh Amendment*, 10 Conn. L. Rev. 775 (1978), 1236

Note, *The Right to Retain Counsel in Civil Litigation*, 66 Colum. L. Rev. 1322 (1966), 1206

John B. Oakley & Arthur F. Coon, *The Federal Rules in State Courts: A Survey of State Court Systems of Civil Procedure*, 61 Wash. L. Rev. 1367 (1986), 9, 49

A. Peter Parsons & Kenneth W. Starr, *Environmental Litigation and Defendant Class Actions: The Unrealized Viability of Rule 23*, 4 Ecology L.Q. 881 (1975), 692

Robert F. Peckham, *The Federal Judge as a Case Manager: The New Role in Guiding a Case from Filing to Disposition*, 69 Cal. L. Rev. 770 (1981), 929

Mark A. Peterson, *Giving Away Money: Comparative Comments on Claims Resolution Facilities*, 53 Law & Contemp. Prob. 113 (Autumn 1990), 1443

Mark A. Peterson & Molly Selvin, *Mass Justice: The Limited and Unlimited Power of Courts*, 54 Law & Contemp. Prob. 227 (Summer 1991), 1085

Todd Peterson, *Restoring Structural Checks on Judicial Power in the Era of Managerial Judging*, 29 U.C. Davis L. Rev. 41 (1995), 929

James R. Pielemeier, *Due Process Limitations on the Application of Collateral Estoppel Against Nonparties to Prior Litigation*, 63 B.U. L. Rev. 383 (1983), 239

George C. Piper, Note, *Amicus Curiae*

Participation At the Court's Discretion, 55 Ky. L.J. 864 (1967), 154

Julie K. Plowman, Note, *Multimedia in the Courtroom: Valuable Tool or Smoke and Mirrors?* 15 Rev. Litig. 415 (1996), 1273

Theodore F.T. Plucknett, A Concise History of the Common Law (5th ed. 1956), 30, 34, **36**, **38**, 39, **40**

Richard A. Posner, *Coping with the Caseload: A Comment on Magistrates and Masters*, 137 U. Pa. L. Rev. 2215 (1989), 951, 958

Richard A. Posner, Economic Analysis of Law (4th ed. 1992), 8, 1132, 1210

Roscoe Pound, *Some Principles of Procedural Reform*, 4 Ill. L. Rev. 388 (1910), **54**

Roscoe Pound, *The Causes of Popular Dissatisfaction with the Administration of Justice*, 29 A.B.A. Rep. 395 (1906), **53**

Roscoe Pound, *The Decadence of Equity*, 5 Colum. L. Rev. 20 (1905), 54

George L. Priest, *Justifying the Civil Jury*, in Verdict 103 (Robert E. Litan ed. 1993), 1210

George L. Priest, *Private Litigants and the Court Congestion Problem*, 69 B.U. L. Rev. 527 (1989), 1292

Philip M. Pro & Thomas C. Hnatowski, *Measured Progress: The Evolution and Administration of the Federal Magistrate System*, 44 Am. U. L. Rev. 1503 (1995), 960

Proceedings of the Seminar on Protracted Cases, 21 F.R.D. 395 (1957), 928

Proceedings of the Seminar on Protracted Cases for the United States Judges, 23 F.R.D. 319 (1958), 928, 951

Robert A. Ragazzo, Transfer and Choice of Federal Law: The Appellate Model, 93 Mich. L. Rev. 703 (1995), **824**

John Rawls, A Theory of Justice (1971), 3, 5

Martin H. Redish, *The Anti-Injunction Statute Reconsidered*, 44 U. Chi. L. Rev. 717 (1977), 399

Martin H. Redish, Federal Jurisdiction (2d ed. 1990), 426, 437

Martin H. Redish, *Seventh Amendment Right to Jury Trial: A Study in the Irrationality of Rational Decision Making*, 70 Nw. U. L. Rev. 486 (1975), 1217

Reference Manual on Scientific Evidence (1994), 1070, 1112, 1162, 1314, 1347

Alan Reifman et al., *Real Jurors' Understanding of the Law in Real Cases*, 16 Law & Hum. Behav. 539 (1992), 1237, 1376

Report of the Federal Courts Study Committee (1990), 330, 960

Report of the Judicial Conference Ad Hoc Committee on Asbestos Litigation (1991), 436, 504

Report of the Judicial Conference of the United States on Procedure in Anti-Trust and Other Protracted Cases, 13 F.R.D. 62 (1953), **926**, 983, 1007

Report of the National Commission for the Review of Antitrust Laws and Procedures (1979), reprinted in 80 F.R.D. 509 (1980), 929, 951, 1016, 1148

Judith Resnik, *Failing Faith: Adjudicatory Procedure in Decline*, 53 U. Chi. L. Rev. 494 (1986), 56

Judith Resnik, *Managerial Judges*, 96 Harv. L. Rev. 374 (1982), 66, **931**

Judith Resnik, *Revising the Canon: Feminist Help in Teaching Procedure*, 61 U. Cinn. L. Rev. 1181 (1993), 5

Judith Resnik et al., *Individuals Within the Aggregate: Relationships, Representation, and Fees*, 71 N.Y.U. L. Rev. 296, 300 (1996), 654

Restatement of Conflict of Laws (1934), 795

Restatement (Second) of the Conflict of Laws (1971), **794**, 869

Restatement (Third) of Foreign Relations Law of the United States (1987), 1163, 1165, 1167

Restatement (Second) of Judgments (1982), 197, 216, 223, 224, 229, 232

Restatement (Second) of Judgments (Tent. Draft No. 2, Apr. 15, 1975), 163, 164

Restatement (Second) of Judgments, ch. 4 (1980), 210

Richard L. Revesz, *Specialized Courts and the Administrative Lawmaking System*, 138 U. Pa. L. Rev. 1111 (1990), 1260

William L. Reynolds, *The Proper Forum for a Suit: Transnational Forum Non Conveniens and Counter-Suit Injunctions in the Federal Courts*, 70 Tex. L. Rev. 1663 (1992), 458, 465

Paul D. Rheingold, *The MER/29 Story An Instance of Successful Mass Disaster Litigation*, 56 Cal. L. Rev. 116 (1968), 447

Blake M. Rhodes, Comment, *The Judicial Panel on Multidistrict Litigation: Time for Rethinking*, 140 U. Pa. L. Rev. 711 (1991), 510

Charles R. Richey, *A Modern Management Technique for Trials Courts to Improve the Quality of Justice: Requiring Direct Testimony to be Submitted in Written Form Prior to Trial*, 72 Geo. L.J. 73 (1983), 1329

Danny P. Richey, Guidelines and techniques for Leading and managing the Litigation Team, 19 Ohio N. L. Rev. 23 (1992), **893**

Glen O. Robinson, *Collective Justice in Tort Law*, 78 Va. L. Rev. 1481 (1992), 1419

Mark J. Roe, *Bankruptcy and Mass Tort*, 84 Colum. L. Rev. 846 (1984), 784

John M. Rogers, Comment, *Personal Jurisdiction and Defendant Class Actions*, 53 Ind. L.J. 841 (1978), 692

David Rosenberg, *Individual Justice and Collectivizing Risk-Based Claims in Mass-Exposure Cases*, 71 N.Y.U. L. Rev. 210 (1996), 646

David Rosenberg, *Class Actions for Mass Torts: Doing Individual Justice by Collective Means*, 62 Ind. L.J. 561 (1987), 539, 646

Maurice Rosenberg, *The Federal Rules after Half a Century*, 36 Me. L. Rev. 243 (1984), 7

Michel Rosenfeld, *Deconstruction and Legal Interpretation*, in Deconstruction and the Possibility of Justice 187 (1992), 5

Thomas D. Rowe, Jr., *Beyond the Class Action Rule: An Inventory of Statutory Possibilities To Improve the Federal Class Action*, 71 N.Y.U. L. Rev. 186 (1996), 698

Thomas D. Rowe, Jr., *No Final Victories: The Incompleteness of Equity's Triumph in Federal Public Law*, 56 Law & Contemp. Prob. 105 (Summer 1993), 66

Thomas D. Rowe, Jr. et al., *Compounding or Creating Confusion about Supplemental Jurisdiction? A Reply to Professor Freer*, 40 Emory L.J. 943 (1991), 349, 354, 356

Thomas D. Rowe, Jr. & Kenneth D. Sibley, *Beyond Diversity: Federal Multiparty, Multiforum Jurisdiction*, 135 U. Pa. L. Rev. 7 (1986), 332

William B. Rubenstein, Divided We Litigate: Addressing Disputes among Group Members and Lawyers in Civil Rights Campaigns, 106 Yale L.J. 1623 (1997), **120**

George Rutherglen, *Better Late Than Never: Notice and Opt Out At the Settlement Stage of Class Actions*, 71 N.Y.U. L. Rev. 258 (1996), 552, 655

George Rutherglen, *Notice, Scope, and Preclusion in Title VII Class Actions*, 69 Va. L. Rev. 11, 27-28 (1983), 611

Michael J. Saks, Jury Verdicts (1977), 1237

Michael J. Saks, Small Group Decision Making and Complex Information Tasks (1981), 1237, 1239

Michael J. Saks and Peter David Blanck, *Justice Improved: The Unrecognized Benefits of Aggregation and Sampling in the Trial of Mass Torts*, 44 Stan. L. Rev. 815 (1992), 1312

Michael J. Saks & Robert F. Kidd, *Human Information Processing and Adjudication: Trial by Heuristics*, 15 Law & Society Rev. 123 (1980-81), 1316

Stephen A. Saltzburg, *Improving the Quality of Jury Decisionmaking*, in Verdict 341 (Robert E. Litan ed. 1993), 1370, 1373, 1375, 1378, 1377, 1383

Stephen A. Saltzburg, Lawyers, Clients, and the Adversary System, 37 Mercer L. Rev. 647 (1986), **20**

Leonard B. Sand & Steven A. Reiss, *A Report on Seven Experiments Conducted by District Court Judges in the Second Circuit*, 60 N.Y.U. L. Rev. 423 (1985), 1370

Shira A. Scheindlin, *Discovering the Discoverable: A Bird's Eye View of Discovery in a Complex Multidistrict Class Action Litigation*, 52 Brook. L. Rev. 397 (1986), 960

Bryan J. Schillinger, *Preventing Duplicative Mass Tort Litigation Through the Limited Resources Doctrine*, 14 Rev. Litig. 465 (1995), 617

David Schoenbrod, *The Measure of an Injunction: A Principle to Replace Balancing the Equities and Tailoring the Remedy*, 72 Minn. L. Rev. 627 (1988), 1403

Peter Schuck, Agent Orange on Trial (1986), 124, 951, 952

Bernard Schwartz, Administrative Law (3d ed. 1991), 436

William W Schwarzer, *In Defense of Automatic Disclosure in Discovery*, 27 Ga. L. Rev. 655 (1993), 1096

William W Schwarzer, Managing Antitrust and Other Complex Litigation (1982), 929, 930, 1017, 1039, 1245, 1332, 1376, 1378

William W Schwarzer, *Reforming Jury*

Trials, 132 F.R.D. 575 (1991), 1245, 1261, 1336, 1337, 1368, 1371, 1373, 1374, 1383

William W Schwarzer, *Slaying the Monsters of Cost and Delay: Would Disclosure Be More Effective Than Discovery?*, 74 Judicature 178 (1991), 1133

William W Schwarzer, *Structuring Multiclaim Litigation: Should Rule 23 Be Revised?*, 94 Mich. L. Rev. 1250 (1996), 698

William W Schwarzer, *The Federal Rules, the Adversary Process, and Discovery Reform*, 50 U. Pitt. L. Rev. 703 (1989), 1093

William W Schwarzer & Alan Hirsch, The Elements of Case Management (1991), 929

William W Schwarzer & Allan Hirsch, *Summary Judgment after* Eastman Kodak, 45 Hastings L.J. 1 (1993), 1067

William W Schwarzer et al., *Judicial Federalism in Action: Coordination of Litigation in State and Federal Courts*, 78 Va. L. Rev. 1689 (1992), 442, 939, 1317

William W Schwarzer et al., The Analysis and Decision of Summary Judgment Motions (1991), 1064, 1065, 1066

Eugene F. Scoles & Peter Hay, Conflict of Laws (2d ed. 1992), 795, 796, 869

Austin W. Scott & Robert B. Kent, Cases and Other Materials on Civil Procedure (1967), 46

Robert A. Sedler, *The Complex Litigation Project's Proposal for Federally-Mandated Choice of Law in Mass Tort Cases: Another Assault on State Sovereignty*, 54 La. L. Rev. 1085 (1994), 873

David E. Seidelson, *Section 6.01 of the ALI's Complex Litigation Project: Function Follows Form*, 54 La. L. Rev. 1111 (1994), 873

Seminar on Procedures Prior to Trial, 20 F.R.D. 485 (1957), 928

R. Perry Sentell, Jr., *The Georgia Jury and Negligence: The View from the Bench*, 26 Ga. L. Rev. 85 (1991), 1217

Carroll Seron, The Roles of Magistrates (1985), 957

Carroll Seron, The Roles of Magistrates in Federal District Courts (1983), 960

David L. Shapiro, *Class Actions: The Class as Party and Client*, 73 Notre Dame L. Rev. 913 (1998), 548, 913

David L. Shapiro, *Federal Rule 16: A Look at the Theory and Practice of Rulemaking*, 137 U. Pa. L. Rev. 1969 (1989), 929, 1078

David L. Shapiro, *Jurisdiction and Discretion*, 60 N.Y.U. L. Rev. 543 (1985), 426

David L. Shapiro, *Some Thoughts on Intervention Before Courts, Agencies, and Arbitrators*, 81 Harv. L. Rev. 721 (1968), 155

Edward F. Sherman, *Aggregate Disposition of Related Cases: The Policy Issues*, 10 Rev. Litig. 231 (1991), 1316

Edward F. Sherman, *Class Actions and Duplicative Litigation*, 62 Ind. L.J. 507, 528-36 (1987), 398

Edward F. Sherman, *Restructuring the Trial Process in the Age of Complex Litigation*, 63 Tex. L. Rev. 721 (1984), 1038

Gene R. Shreve, *Questioning Intervention of Right — Intervention of Right Toward a New Methodology of Decisionmaking*, 74 Nw. U. L. Rev. 894 (1980), 155

Linda Silberman, *Judicial Adjuncts Revisited: The Proliferation of Ad Hoc Procedure*, 137 U. Pa. L. Rev. 2131 (1989), 948, 953, 957

Linda J. Silberman, *Masters and Magistrates Part I: The English Model*, 50 N.Y.U. L. Rev. 1070 (1975), 947

Linda J. Silberman, *Masters and Magistrates Part II: The American Analogue*, 50 N.Y.U. L. Rev. 1297 (1975), 943, 947, 952, 960

Christopher P. Simkins, Note & Comment, *Class Actions and Supplemental Jurisdiction: Will* Zahn v. International Paper Co. *Remain Viable?* 1996 B.Y.U.L. Rev. 707 (1996), 354

Victoria Slind-Flor, *Tackling High Tech*, Natl. L.J., Oct. 19, 1992, at 1, 1271

Christopher E. Smith, United States Magistrates in the Federal Courts (1990), 957

Gregory E. Smith, *Choice of Law in the United States Courts*, 38 Hastings L.J. 1041 (1987), 796

Thomas A. Smith, *A Capital Markets Approach to Mass Tort Bankruptcy*, 104 Yale L.J. 367 (1994), 757, 764

Richard B. Sobol, Bending the Law: The Story of the Dalkon Shield Bankruptcy (1991), 724, 725, 727, 728, 729, 750

Maureen Solomon & Holly Bakke, *Case Differentiation: An Approach to Individualized Case Management*, 73 Judicature 17 (June/July 1989), 1010

Patricia A. Solomon, Note, *Are Mandatory Class Actions Constitutional?* 72 Notre

Dame L. Rev. 1627 (1997), 309

Charles W. Sorenson, Jr., *Disclosure under Federal Rule of Civil Procedure 26(a) — "Much Ado About Nothing?"* 46 Hastings L.J. 679 (1995), 1095

Special Project, *The Remedial Process in Institutional Reform Litigation*, 78 Colum. L. Rev. 784 (1978), 1421, 1423, 1444

James L. Stengel & Andrew M. Calamari, Complex Litigation, (1994), **1176**, 1179

Allen R. Stein, *Erie and Court Access*, 100 Yale L.J. 1935 (1991), 465

Joan Steinman, *The Effects of Case Consolidation on the Procedural Rights of Litigants: What They Are, What They Might Be Part 1: Justiciability and Jurisdiction (Original and Appellate)*, 42 UCLA L. Rev. 717 (1995), 474, 487

Joan Steinman, *The Effects of Case Consolidation on the Procedural Rights of Litigants: What They Are, What They Might Be Part 2: Non-Jurisdictional Matters*, 42 UCLA L. Rev. 967 (1995), 487, 998, 999, 1206, 1208

Joan Steinman, *Law of the Case: A Judicial Puzzle in Consolidated and Transferred Cases and in Multidistrict Litigation*, 135 U. Pa. L. Rev. 595 (1987), 829

Joan Steinman, *Section 1367 — Another Party Heard From*, 41 Emory L.J. 85 (1992), 354

Joan Steinman, *Supplemental jurisdiction in § 1441 Removed Cases: An Unsurveyed Frontier of Congress' Handiwork*, 35 Ariz. L. Rev. 305 (1993), 382

Jeffrey W. Stempel, *A Distorted Mirror: The Supreme Court's Shimmering View of Summary Judgment, Directed Verdict, and the Adjudication Process*, 49 Ohio St. L.J. 95 (1988), 1062

Richard B. Stewart, *The Reformation of American Administrative Law*, 88 Harv. L. Rev. 1669 (1975), 913

Franklin Stier, *Making Jury Trials More Truthful*, 30 U.C. Davis L. Rev. 85 (1996), 26, 1240

Joseph Story, Equity Jurisprudence (1st ed. 1836), 391

John W. Strong, McCormick on Evidence (4th ed. 1992), 1145, 1329

Susan P. Sturm, *A Normative Theory of Public Law Remedies*, 79 Geo. L.J. 1355 (1991), 1435

Stephen N. Subrin, How Equity Conquered Common Law: The Federal Rules of Civil procedure in Historical Perspective, 135 U. Pa. L. Rev. 909 (1987), **57**

Stephen N. Subrin, *Uniformity in Procedural Rules and the Attributes of a Sound Procedural System*, 49 Ala. L. Rev. 79 (1997), 7

Symeon C. Symeonides, *Choice of Law in the American Courts in 1993 (and in the Six Previous Years)*, 42 Am. J. Comp. Law 599 (1994), 796

Symposium, 29 Judge's J. 1 (Fall 1990), 929

Symposium, 12 Pace L. Rev. 227 (1992), 854

Symposium, 54 La. L. Rev. 833 (1994), 873

Symposium, *Claims Resolution Facilities and the Mass Settlement of Mass Torts*, 53 Law & Contemp. Prob. 1 (Autumn 1990), 1443

Symposium, *A Duty-Oriented Procedure in a Rights-Oriented Society*, 63 Notre Dame L. Rev. 597 (1988), 60

Symposium, *Entire Controversy Doctrine*, 28 Rutgers L.J. 1 (1996), 132

Symposium, *The 50th Anniversary of the Federal Rules of Civil Procedure, 1938-88*, 137 U. Pa. L. Rev. 1873 (1989), 60

Symposium, *The Fiftieth Anniversary of the Federal Rules of Civil Procedure*, 62 St. John's L. Rev. 399 (1988), 60

Symposium, *The Future of Federal Litigation*, 50 U. Pitt. L. Rev. 701 (1989), 60

Symposium, *Issues in Civil Procedure: Advancing the Dialogue*, 69 B.U. L. Rev. 597 (1988), 60

Symposium, *Is the Jury Competent?* 52 Law & Contemp. Prob. 1 (Autumn 1989), 1237

Symposium, *Modern Civil Procedure: Issues in Controversy*, 54 Law & Contemp. Prob. 1 (Summer 1991), 60

Symposium, *Reinventing Civil Litigation: Evaluating Proposals for Change*, 59 Brook. L. Rev. 655 (1993), 60

Symposium, *The Role of the Jury in Civil Dispute Resolution*, 1990 U. Chi. L.F. 1, 1210

Symposium, *The Sixth Abraham L. Pomerantz Lecture*, 61 Brook. L. Rev. 1 (1995), 1260

Symposium, *Turbulence in the Federal Rules of Civil Procedure: The 1993 Amendments and Beyond*, 14 Rev. Litig. 1 (1994), 60

Jeannette E. Thatcher, *Why Not Use the Special Jury?*, 31 Minn. L. Rev. 232 (1947), 1241 *opment (Part II)*, 5 Harv. L. Rev. 295 (1892), 1241

Randall S. Thomas & Robert G. Hansen, *Auctioning Class Action and Derivative Lawsuits: A Critical Analysis*, 87 Nw. U. L. Rev. 423 (1993), 889

William C. Thompson, *Are Juries Competent to Evaluate Statistical Evidence?* 52 Law & Contemp. Prob. 9 (Autumn 1989), 1239, 1316

Jay Tidmarsh, Mass Tort Settlement Class Actions: Five Case Studies and Their Implications for the Reform of Rule 23 (1998), 655, 656

Jay Tidmarsh, Mass Tort Settlement Class Actions (1998), 372, 545, 553, 656, 1423, 1443

Jay Tidmarsh, Unattainable Justice: The Form and Limits of Complex Litigation, 60 Geo. Wash. L. Rev. 1683 (1992), 7, **57**, **85**, 108

Peter M. Tiersman, *Reforming the Language of Jury Instructions*, 22 Hofstra L. Rev. 37 (1993), 1378

Carl Tobias, *In Defense of Experimentation with Automatic Disclosure*, 27 Ga. L. Rev. 665 (1993), 1096

Carl Tobias, *Public Law Litigation and the Federal Rules of Civil Procedure*, 74 Corn. L. Rev. 270 (1989), 155

Carl Tobias, *Standing to Intervene*, 1991 Wis. L. Rev. 415, 142, 152

Carl Tobias, *The Transformation of Trans-Substantivity*, 49 Wash. & Lee L. Rev. 1501 (1992), 7

Tracey L. Trager, *One Jury Indivisible: A Group Dynamics Approach to Voir Dire*, 68 Chi.-Kent L. Rev. 549 (1992), 1243

Roger H. Trangsrud, Joinder Alternatives in Mass Tort Litigation, 70 Corn. L. Rev. 779 (1985), 519, **630**

Roger H. Trangsrud, *The Federal Common Law of Personal Jurisdiction*, 57 Geo. Wash. L. Rev. 849 (1989), 202, 278

Roger H. Trangsrud, Mass Trials in Mass Tort Cases: A Dissent, 1989 U. Ill. L. Rev. 69, **1203**, **1281**

Laurence H. Tribe, American Constitutional Law (2d ed. 1988), 365, 431

Laurence H. Tribe, *Trial by Mathematics: Precision and Ritual in the Legal Process*, 84 Harv. L. Rev. 1329 (1971), 1316

Robert L. Tucker, *The Flexible Doctrine of Spoliation of Evidence: Cause of Action, Defense, Evidentiary Presumption, and Discovery Sanction*, 27 U. Tol. L. Rev. 67 (1995), 1106

Roberto M. Unger, *The Critical Legal Studies Movement*, 96 Harv. L. Rev. 561 (1983), 7

H. Richard Uviller, *The Advocate, The Truth and Judicial Hackles: A Reaction to Judge Frankel's Idea*, 123 U. Pa. L. Rev. 1067 (1975), 26

Uniform Law Commissioners' Model Class Actions [Act][Rule], in 12 Uniform Laws Annotated 27 (Supp. 1994), 701

Allen D. Vestal, *Uniform Class Actions*, 63 A.B.A. J. 837 (1977), 701

Neil J. Vidmar & Regina A. Schuller, *Juries and Expert Evidence: Social Framework Testimony*, 52 Law & Contemp. Prob. 133 (Autumn 1989), 1236

Arthur von Mehren, *Choice of Law and the Problem of Justice*, 41 Law and Contemporary Problems 34 (Spring 1977), 857

Arthur von Mehren, *The Importance of Structures and Ideologies for the Administration of Justice*, 97 Yale L.J. 341 (1987), 82

Laurens Walker & John Monahan, *Social Frameworks: A New Use of Science in Law*, 73 Va. L. Rev. 559 (1987), 1236

Jerold L. Waltman, Judicial Activism in England, in Judicial Activism in Comparative Perspective (Kenneth M. Holland ed. 1991), **67**

W.J. Waluchow, Inclusive Legal Positivism (1994), 5

Mark C. Weber, *The Federal Civil Rules Amendments of 1993 and Complex Litigation: A Comment on Transsubstantivity and Special Rules for Large and Small Cases*, 14 Rev. Litig. 113 (1994), 7

Herbert Wechsler, *Federal Jurisdiction and the Revision of the Judicial Code*, 13 Law & Contemp. Prob. 216 (1948), 320

Stanley A. Weigel, *The Judicial Panel on Multidistrict Litigation, Transferor Courts and Transferee Courts*, 78 F.R.D. 575 (1977), 829

Ernest J. Weinrib, *Legal Formalism: On the Immanent Rationality of Law*, 97 Yale L.J. 949 (1988), 7

Jack B. Weinstein, Individual Justice in Mass Tort Litigation (1995), 888, 890, **904** 968, 969

Jack B. Weinstein, *The Power and Duty of Federal Judges to Marshall and Comment on the Evidence in Jury Trials and Some Suggestions on Charging Juries,*

118 F.R.D. 161 (1988), 1372

Jack B. Weinstein, *Preliminary Reflections on the Law's Reaction to Disasters*, 11 Colum. J. Envtl. L. 1 (1991), 436

Jack B. Weinstein, *What Discovery Abuse: A Comment on John Setear's* The Barrister and the Bomb, 69 B.U. L. Rev. 649 (1989), 1093

Jack B. Weinstein & Margaret A. Berger, Weinstein's Evidence (1988), 1248

Jack B. Weinstein & Karin S. Schwartz, *Notes from the Cave: Some Problems of Judges in Dealing with Class Action Settlements*, 163 F.R.D. 369 (1995), 688

Joseph F. Weis, *The Federal Rules and the Hague Convention: Concerns of Conformity and Comity*, 50 U. Pitt. L. Rev. 903 (1989), 1165

Gary Wells, *Naked Statistical Evidence of Liability: Is Subjective Probability Enough?*, 62 J. Personality and Soc. Psych. 739 (1992), 1239

Michael Wells, *Why Professor Redish is Wrong about Abstention*, 19 Ga. L. Rev. 1097 (1985), 426

Elizabeth C. Wiggins & Steven J. Breckler, *Special Verdicts as Guides to Jury Decision Making*, 14 Law and Psychology Rev. 1 (1990), 1381

Wigmore's Evidence (James H. Chadbourn ed. 1970), 1321, 1359, 1367, 1372

Thomas E. Willging, Court-Appointed Experts (1986), 895, 954

Thomas E. Willging et al., *An Empirical Analysis of Rule 23 to Address the Rulemaking Challenges*, 71 N.Y.U. L. Rev. 74 (1996), 698

Thomas E. Willging et al., Empirical Study of Class Actions in Four Federal District Courts (1996), 534, 550, 554

James R. Withrow and Richard P. Larm, *The "Big" Antitrust Case: 25 Years of Sisyphean Labor*, 62 Corn. L. Rev. 1 (1976), 1033, 1034, 1035

Jeffrey S. Wolfe, *Toward a Unified Theory of Courtroom Design Criteria: The Effect of Courtroom Design on Adversarial Interaction*, 18 Am. J. Trial Advoc. 593 (1995), 1273

Charles W. Wolfram, *The Constitutional History of the Seventh Amendment*, 57 Minn. L. Rev. 639 (1973), 1217

Charles A. Wright, *Estoppel by Rule: The Compulsory Counterclaim under Modern Pleading*, 38 Minn. L. Rev. 423 (1954), 341

Charles A. Wright & Arthur R. Miller, Federal Practice & Procedure, *passim.*

Stephen Yeazell, From Medieval Group Litigation to the Modern Class Action (1987), 424

Hans Zeisel & Thomas Callahan, *Split Trials and Time Saving: A Statistical Analysis*, 76 Harv. L. Rev. 1606 (1963), **1284**

Complex Litigation and the Adversary System

CHAPTER ONE

AN OVERVIEW OF COMPLEX LITIGATION: THEORY, HISTORY, AND PRACTICE

> [T]he expediency of carrying justice, as it were, to every man's door, was obvious, but how to do it in an expedient manner was far from apparent.
>
> Chief Justice John Jay

At this point in your legal education, you have become so steeped in the American system of civil procedure that you take many of its features for granted. You have become accustomed to the dual system of federal and state courts. The complicated rules — constitutional, statutory, common law, and code-based — that govern the way in which these courts resolve disputes no longer mystify you.

A central feature of American procedural systems is an adversarial approach to adjudication: The parties (or, more typically, their lawyers) are in charge of such basic tasks as identifying the issues at stake, discovering the relevant evidence to bolster claims and defenses, and presenting the evidence and arguments to the appropriate decisionmaker (whether judge or jury). Although Americans place great faith in the adversarial process, we also appreciate that unrestrained adversarialism may not always be desirable. We want substantial justice to be done; we want to make sure that the parties get a hearing on the merits of their dispute and do not get hogtied by a superior adversary using procedural technicalities to his or her advantage.

Because we are familiar with what we know, it is easy to forget that our adversarial system is not the only available option. In fact, in civil litigation, our system has significant costs and drawbacks that we could avoid if we chose other methods of handling disputes. Of course, those methods have their own costs and drawbacks.

The ultimate goals of this book are to pinpoint the problems of the procedural choices that our society has made, and to see whether different sets of choices might be more sensible, more just, and more efficient. The vehicle which we will use to ask these questions is complex civil litigation. Procedural scholars first recognized the phenomenon of complex civil litigation about fifty years ago. Although scholars have yet to agree on a precise definition of the subject, for now let us use an intuitive definition: complex civil litigation involves cases which are "bigger" or "more complicated" than the typical suit in which our adversarial procedures work tolerably well. The *AT&T* antitrust litigation, *Brown v. Board of Education* and the host of desegregation and institutional reform suits it spawned, and the thousands of asbestos cases clogging court dockets are the paradigms of complex civil litigation. Cases of these types have thrown the procedural system that we have selected for ourselves — an adversarial system designed for a far simpler type of lawsuit — into crisis.

The causes of the rise of complex civil litigation are many, but several are certainly at the fore. The first is the growth of substantive bodies of law that restrain institutions with the capacity to inflict widespread harm. Antitrust and securities law, constitutional rights litigation, mass torts, and employment discrimination are just a few examples of "new" doctrines that can be invoked by thousands of claimants and can threaten the future of important economic or political entities. Such high stakes to a certain extent justify and inevitably lead to a searching for every adversarial advantage and a "no stone unturned" mentality in litigation. A second factor is the concentration of great power in corporate and government institutions; as a result, the potential that illegal overreaching would have regional or national consequences increased. Third, our own perceptions about the legitimacy of challenging established entities has changed; we have become, in Geoffrey Hazard's words, more willing to put "authority in the dock." See Geoffrey C. Hazard, Jr., *Authority in the Dock*, 69 B.U. L. Rev. 469 (1989). Finally, after the adoption of the Federal Rules of Civil Procedure in 1938, our procedural systems have tended to require less of plaintiffs and defendants at the pleading stage, preferring instead to sort out the issues and facts during a discovery stage; the same rules have provided wide latitude in the joinder of parties and claims in a single suit. The combined force of these changes made big lawsuits easier to bring, costlier to litigate, and harder to dispose of in an expeditious manner.

Whatever the precise causes, complex civil litigation is a wonderful place to begin a study of the strengths and weaknesses of the American procedural system. In order truly to appreciate the challenge that complex litigation poses, however, it is necessary to take a few introductory steps. We must begin with an understanding of the "theory of procedure" — the fundamental principles, if any, to which all procedural systems might aspire. Next, we must step backward and examine the history of the Anglo-American procedural system. This historical survey points out different procedural choices made by our own culture and the defects in those choices that led to reform — information that is highly relevant to an evaluation of our present situation and our legitimate options in the future. Finally, we must step outward and examine the procedural systems of other cultures in order to broaden our understanding of the ways in which procedural principles can be given life.

With those perspectives behind us, we can finally understand the nature of complex civil litigation in our modern procedural system. The last section of the chapter provides an overview of the different ways in which a case can be complex, focusing on whether there is a core theme to complex litigation that transcends its many manifestations.

The book frequently returns to the theoretical, historical, comparative, and lexical insights of this chapter. They lie at the heart of the phenomenon we call complex civil litigation, and the subject cannot be understood without them.

A. THE FUNDAMENTAL PRINCIPLES OF CIVIL PROCEDURE

You are the Tsar of Procedure in a new country with no procedural system at present. Your job is to design a system. You have absolute discretion to do whatever you want, and you want to do it right. One way that you might try to figure out what to do is to ask whether there are certain fundamental norms that any legitimate procedural system must contain. When you approach the question in this way, you are engaging in a normative inquiry. That type of inquiry is the subject of this section.

The answer to the question about whether all legitimate procedural systems possess certain fundamental building blocks is critical to the procedural enterprise generally, but it is particularly crucial to the problem of complex litigation. If complex litigation involves the cases in which our procedural system does not work well, an understanding of these norms can help us to appreciate the ultimate limitations on procedural solutions designed to ameliorate complexity.

John Rawls, A THEORY OF JUSTICE

58, 235-39 (1971)

This impartial and consistent administration of laws and institutions, whatever their substantive principles, we may call formal justice. If we think of justice as always expressing a kind of equality, then formal justice requires that, in their administration laws and institutions should apply equally (that is, in the same way) to those belonging to the classes defined by them.... Formal justice is adherence to principle, or as some have said, obedience to system.

[This] conception of formal justice, the regular and impartial administration of public rules, becomes the rule of law when applied to the legal system.... [W]e can say that, other things equal, one legal order is more justly administered than another if it more perfectly fulfills the precepts of the rule of law. It will provide a more secure basis for liberty and a more effective means for organizing cooperative schemes. Yet because these precepts guarantee only the impartial and regular administration of rules, whatever these are, they are compatible with injustice. They impose rather weak constraints on the basic structure, but ones that are not by any means negligible.

Let us begin with the precept that ought implies can. This precept identifies several obvious features of legal systems. First of all, the actions which the rules of law require and forbid should be of a kind which men can reasonably be expected to do and to avoid.... The rule of law also implies the precept that similar cases be treated similarly.... The precept that there is no offense without a law (*Nullum crimen sine lege*), and the requirements it implies, also follow from the idea of a legal system. This precept demands that laws be known and expressly promulgated, that their meaning be clearly defined, that statutes be general both in statement and intent and not be used as a way of harming particular individuals who may be expressly named (bills of attainder), that at least the more severe offenses be strictly construed, and that penal laws should not be retroactive to the disadvantage of those to whom they apply.

Finally, there are those precepts defining the notion of natural justice. These are guidelines intended to preserve the integrity of the judicial process. If laws are directives addressed to rational persons for their guidance, courts must be concerned to apply and to enforce these rules in an appropriate way. A conscientious effort must be made to determine whether an infraction has taken place and to impose the correct penalty. Thus a legal system must make provisions for conducting orderly trials and hearings; it must contain rules of evidence that guarantee rational procedures of inquiry. While there are variations in these procedures, the rule of law requires some form of due process: that is, a process reasonably designed to ascertain the truth, in ways consistent with the other ends of the legal system, as to whether a violation has taken place and under what circumstances. For example, judges must be independent and impartial, and no man may judge his own case. Trials must be fair and open, but not prejudiced by public clamor. The precepts of natural justice are to insure that the legal order will be impartially and regularly maintained.

Notes and Questions

1. Rawls' views of the minimal content of a procedurally just system seem unassailable. In fact, they are quite controversial. Begin with his development of principles that derive from the concept of formal justice. Are there really normative principles that *every* procedurally just system must maintain? Where do these norms come from? Natural law? Morality? Fundamental human rights? Many legal philosophers — known as positivists — argue that law and morality are distinct and that a legal rule validly adopted by appropriate governmental authorities cannot be invalidated by appeal to supposedly

fundamental or universal norms. See generally W.J. Waluchow, Inclusive Legal Positivism (1994). Is it possible to talk about fundamental procedural norms if the positivists are correct?

2. Even if we assume that Rawls is correct about the existence of normative principles, his views remain controversial. Rawls believes that formal justice, which includes procedural justice, is not an end in itself, but rather is an instrument to achieve substantively just outcomes. For Rawls, legal procedures are an instance of "imperfect" (as opposed to "pure") procedural justice because "there is an independent criterion for the correct outcome, [but] there is no feasible procedure which is sure to lead to it." Rawls, *supra,* at 85-86; see also Brian Barry, Political Argument (1965). Given that no procedure can guarantee the correct outcome, one of Rawls' unresolved problems is to decide how much imperfection in procedure it is permissible to tolerate. Perhaps, however, the problem lies in Rawls' limited view of procedure. The notion of "imperfection" flows from the instrumental role which Rawls sees procedure as performing. Are there independent procedural values (for instance, the opportunity to be heard, the right of jury trial, the right to cross-examine witnesses, or the like procedural treatment of like cases) which are themselves intrinsically good, so that we would wish to uphold them in all cases even if they lead to incorrect outcomes in some cases? Is procedure substance's servant, or its equal? See generally Robert G. Bone, *Rethinking the "Day in Court" Ideal and Nonparty Preclusion,* 67 N.Y.U. L. Rev. 193 (1992).

3. Rawls can also be critiqued from an opposing perspective. Rawls clearly perceives a distinction between formal and substantive justice. Does this distinction really exist? Perhaps there is simply something called "justice" — an aggregate of features, both substantive and procedural — which must always be present in adjudication. To divide that sense of justice into components is to make overly simple a complex inquiry in which substantive and procedural dimensions of justice merge "in a single whole greater than the sum of its parts." Michel Rosenfeld, *Deconstruction and Legal Interpretation,* in Deconstruction and the Possibility of Justice 187 (1992). Put another way, "neutral" procedural rules designed to achieve the correct outcome are neither neutral nor truly procedural, for all rules favor the interests of some over those of others in particular contexts. Concentration on "formal justice" blinds us to the reality of what our legal system is actually doing. See generally Judith Resnik, *Revising the Canon: Feminist Help in Teaching Procedure,* 61 U. Cinn. L. Rev. 1181 (1993) (describing ways in which "neutral" procedural rules affect gender issues).

4. Note the effect that this last conclusion has on the debate about procedure. In essence, it says that we cannot think about procedure independently of the substance of the controversy. It further implies that procedural rules must vary according to the aims of the substantive law they serve. Rather than there being a single set of procedural rules, there might be one set of rules for tort cases, another for civil rights cases, and so forth. This may sound like a radical proposal, but as we shall see shortly, the opposite is true. For most of our Anglo-American history we had substance-specific procedures, and it has only been in the last few decades that we have tried to divorce procedure from substance through a unified set of rules that applies to all bodies of substantive law.

A set of rules that applies equally to all substantive areas is called "trans-substantive." The use of trans-substantive rules, which is one of the cornerstone assumptions of modern American procedure, has been one of the most debated aspects of procedural theory in recent years. The most famous critique belongs to Robert Cover:

> The fine tuning of remedial and procedural instruments for implementing substantive preferences . . . is severely retarded once procedural norms are codified in a trans-substantive structure. . . . It is extraordinary that our legal system holds a divided view of procedure: Our norms for minimal process, expressed in the constitutional rubric of procedural due process, are generally conceded to constitute a substance-sensitive calibrated continuum in which the nature of the process due is connected to the nature of the substantive interest to be vindicated; yet our primary set of norms for optimal procedure, the procedure available in our courts of general jurisdiction, is assumed to be largely invariant with substance. It is by no means intuitively apparent that the procedural needs of a complex antitrust action, a simple automobile negligence case, a hard-fought school integration suit, and an environmental class action to restrain the building of a pipeline are sufficiently identical to be usefully encompassed in a single set of rules which makes virtually no distinctions among such cases in terms of available process. . . .
>
> [T]he manipulation of procedural tools to effectuate substantive objectives is by no means undesirable and often seems necessary. Thus if the Enabling Act* were read to forbid a Federal Rule to have substantive impact, it would create an anomaly. Federal Rules, intended to provide a flexible structure for achieving substantive ends, would remove from the courts a useful arsenal for remedial policy by freezing process in a single posture for all cases. But there is a way of reading the Enabling Act which neither renders it a dead letter, as courts have tended to do, nor construes it as a bulwark against change. Such a reading would start with the premise suggested above, that absent a trans-substantive structure of rules, courts must often justify decisions about procedure with a combination of substantive and procedural objectives and values. The Rules Enabling Act might then be read to mean that the courts, in applying the Federal Rules of Civil Procedure or any subsequently enacted similar body of rules, may not forsake their responsibility to justify substantive impact in terms of substantive values. . . .
>
> Above all, the Rules Enabling Act would not be read to forbid the application of a federal rule because it altered substantive rights. However, it would forbid the reasoning by which a rule altered the right simply because it is a rule of procedure. As part of the repository of our collective procedural imagination the Federal Rules of Civil Procedure would be read to include remedial structures which could be applied where appropriate in light of substantive objectives. . . .
>
> [Of course, one] cannot re-invent a procedural system for every case. And the question of what is to be presumptively or generally available may be best settled by rule. But where the only or primary issues at stake are substantive, justifications in substantive terms may be necessary.

Robert M. Cover, *For Wm. James Moore: Some Reflections on a Reading of the Rules*, 84 Yale L.J. 718, 732-35, 737 (1975). Others critiquing or defending trans-

---

* Cover is referring to the Rules Enabling Act of 1934, which presently states in relevant part: "Such rules [of civil procedure and evidence] shall not abridge, enlarge or modify any substantive right." 28 U.S.C. § 2072(b) (1988). — ED.

substantivism include Maurice Rosenberg, *The Federal Rules after Half a Century*, 36 Me. L. Rev. 243 (1984); Stephen B. Burbank, *Of Rules and Discretion: The Supreme Court, Federal Rules and Common Law*, 63 Notre Dame L. Rev. 693 (1988); Paul D. Carrington, *Making Rules to Dispose of Manifestly Unfounded Assertions: An Exorcism of the Bogy of Non-Trans-Substantive Rules of Civil Procedure*, 137 U. Pa. L. Rev. 2067 (1989); Geoffrey C. Hazard, Jr., *Discovery Vices and Trans-Substantive Virtues in the Federal Rules of Civil Procedure*, 137 U. Pa. L. Rev. 2237 (1989); Jay Tidmarsh, *Unattainable Justice: The Form of Complex Litigation and the Limits of Judicial Power*, 60 Geo. Wash. L. Rev. 1683 (1992); Carl Tobias, *The Transformation of Trans-Substantivity*, 49 Wash. & Lee L. Rev. 1501 (1992); Richard L. Marcus, *Of Babies and Bathwater: The Prospects for Procedural Reform*, 59 Brook. L. Rev. 761 (1993); Mark C. Weber, *The Federal Civil Rules Amendments of 1993 and Complex Litigation: A Comment on Transsubstantivity and Special Rules for Large and Small Cases*, 14 Rev. Litig. 113 (1994); Stephen N. Subrin, *Uniformity in Procedural Rules and the Attributes of a Sound Procedural System*, 49 Ala. L. Rev. 79 (1997).

Would Rawls agree with Cover's claim that big, complex cases like antitrust suits should receive one type of procedure, and easy cases like car accidents should receive another? Would you? This is a theoretical question with enormous practical consequences. In any complex case, novel procedures or methods can be developed to adjudicate that case. But a case-specific approach has the potential to damage the intricate structure of a system of trans-substantive procedural rules. As you proceed through the book, keep asking yourself how the particular problems you are studying affect your view on the desirability of trans-substantive rules.

5. Thus far, we have talked about trans-substantivism as if it were an aspect of civil procedure that could be discarded if we wished. Granting Rawls his assumption that there is such a thing as formal justice, perhaps trans-substantivism is one of those irreducible elements of justice that we cannot eliminate. Rawls himself says that "similar cases [should] be treated similarly." Such an assumption, which many of us would accept without question, might have an effect on the debate over trans-substantivism. Should we tolerate non-trans-substantive rules that result in defeat for the antitrust plaintiff and victory for the car accident plaintiff? Non-trans-substantive rules that permit a plaintiff injured by a product in State A to recover but effectively deny recovery to a plaintiff injured by the same product in State B, which uses the same substantive law as State A? Non-trans-substantive rules that cause the tort claim of a plaintiff to fail but allow her contract claim to succeed? If your answer is "No, like cases and issues must be treated alike," then isn't Cover wrong?

6. Note a point of tension between Rawls and Cover. Rawls' world is formal in the sense that it posits fundamental premises and then tries to deduce from them the necessary state of a procedural system. The consequences of those rules in particular cases are not as important as adhering to a system of rules determined to be just with reference to neutral principles. Cover's world is contextual — it sees law in more relativistic terms in which procedure can change as the distributive and corrective goals of a society change.

You have undoubtedly seen this jurisprudential debate about the appropriateness of formalism carried out in many contexts in law. See generally Roberto M. Unger, *The Critical Legal Studies Movement*, 96 Harv. L. Rev. 561 (1983); Ernest J. Weinrib, *Legal Formalism: On the Immanent Rationality of Law*, 97 Yale L.J. 949 (1988). The debate has an obvious and immediate application to procedure, which is, after all, a system of rules. A problem that confronts theorists, judges, and lawyers is the reconciliation of competing desires to follow procedural rules with a self-referent coherence and to be fair in individual cases. Should we have coherent rules ineluctably deduced from first principles, with all the hardness and certitude of an exact and mercilessly enforced code? Or should the rules be sensitive to context and consequence, with the open texture of mere guidelines for the exercise of wise discretion? Is it possible to have a little of both? Perhaps we could have certitude in easy cases and discretion in complex cases. Or should it be vice versa? In either event, what gives us the right to treat easy and complex cases in different ways?

7. Do Rawls' principles of formal justice require an adversary system? A system of pretrial discovery? How many days should a defendant have to answer a complaint? An obvious weakness of any conception of formal justice is the generality of the formal principles; at some point, they are unable to guide our choice about specific procedural rules. If the principles do not, then what does? Even if the formal approach is indeterminate, is it necessarily invalid? The problem with a non-formal approach to civil procedure is that it might permit the use of horribly unjust procedures — perhaps even adjudication by coin flip — as long as some other perceived good is achieved.

8. If you remain convinced that the idea of formal justice exists, do you agree that Rawls has chosen the right principles? Are there some that you would exclude? Are there others that you would include? See Ronald Dworkin, *Principle, Policy, Procedure*, in A Matter of Principle 72 (1985) (developing somewhat different rights-based procedural principles). The following three readings provide additional insights into these questions.

Richard A. Posner, ECONOMIC ANALYSIS OF LAW

549-50 (4th ed. 1992)

The object of a procedural system, viewed economically, is to minimize the sum of two types of cost. The first is the cost of erroneous judicial decisions. Suppose the expected cost of a particular type of accident is $100 and the cost to the potential injurer of avoiding it is $90 (the cost of avoidance by the victim, we will assume, is greater than $100). If the potential injurer is subject to either a negligence or a strict liability standard, he will avoid the accident — assuming the standard is administered accurately. But suppose that in 15 percent of the cases in which an accident occurs, the injurer can expect to avoid liability because of erroneous factual determinations by the procedural system. Then the expected cost of the accident to the injurer will fall to $85, and since this is less than the cost of avoidance to him ($90), the accident will not be prevented. The result will be a net social loss of $10 — or will it?

We must not ignore the cost of operating the procedural system. Suppose that to reduce the rate of erroneous failures to impose liability from 15 percent to below 10 percent would require an additional investment in the procedural system of $20 per accident. Then we should tolerate the 15 percent probability of error, because the cost of error ($10) is less than the cost necessary to eliminate it ($20).

This type of cost comparison is implicit in *Mathews v. Eldridge*, [424 U.S. 319 (1976),] which held that in deciding how much process is due to someone complaining that the government has deprived him of his property, the courts should consider the value of the property, the probability of erroneous deprivation because the particular procedural safeguard sought was omitted, and the cost of the safeguard. In Hand Formula terms, due process is denied when $B < PL$, where B is the cost of the procedural safeguard, P is the probability of error if the safeguard is denied, and L is the magnitude of the property loss if the error materializes.

Of course, as with the Hand Formula itself, it is rarely possible (or at least efforts are not made) to quantify the terms. But the formula is valuable even when used qualitatively rather than quantitatively.

Notes and Questions

1. At this point in law school you have undoubtedly been exposed to the law and economics movement, but you may not have considered its special application in the context of procedure. As with Rawls, it is difficult to challenge Judge Posner's vision of procedure: We want litigation procedures to be efficient and not distort the substantive aims of the underlying law. Like Rawls, Posner's method is formal, teasing out specific procedural implications from a given first principle. In other regards, however, Posner's vision of procedure is everything that Rawls's vision is not. Most obviously, Rawls develops his system from principles of justice, while Posner develops his from principles of efficiency. Rawls' system is deontological and retrospective, while Posner's system is consequentialist and prospective. Rawls' procedural rules are absolutes, while Posner's rules bend as efficiency dictates. Rawls sees a distinction between formal and substantive justice; Posner puts both procedure and substance to work for a common goal of efficient resource allocation. Rawls treats like cases alike; Posner does so only when efficiency is served.

Does Posner's efficiency approach have more appeal to you than Rawls' justice approach? Consider the following critique of *Mathews v. Eldridge*, which Posner had held out as an exemplar of the efficiency approach:

> The utilitarian calculus is not without difficulties. The *Eldridge* court conceives of the values of procedure too narrowly: it views the sole purpose of procedural protection as enhancing accuracy, and thus limits its calculus to the benefits or costs that flow from correct or incorrect decisions. No attention is paid to "process values" that might inhere in oral proceedings or to the demoralization costs that may result from the grant-withdrawal-grant-withdrawal sequence to which claimants like Eldridge are subjected. . . . As applied by the *Eldridge* court, the utilitarian calculus tends, as cost-benefit analyses typically do, to "dwarf soft variables" and to ignore complexities and ambiguities. . . .
>
> However broadly conceived, the calculus asks unanswerable questions. For example, what is the social value, and the social cost, of continuing disability payments until after an oral hearing for persons initially determined to be ineligible? Answers to those questions require a technique for measuring social value and social cost of government income transfers, but no such technique exists. . . .

Finally, it is not clear that the utilitarian balancing analysis asks the constitutionally relevant questions. The due process clause is one of those Bill of Rights protections meant to insure individual liberty in the face of contrary collective action. Therefore, a collective legislative or administrative decision about procedure, one arguably reflecting the intensity of the contending social values and representing an optimum position from contemporary social perspective, cannot answer the constitutional question of whether due process has been accorded.

Jerry L. Mashaw, *The Supreme Court's Due Process Calculus for Administrative Adjudication in* Mathews v. Eldridge: *Three Factors in Search of a Value*, 44 U. Chi. L. Rev. 28 (1976). Professor Mashaw goes on to suggest that principles of individual dignity, equality, and tradition are better value theories for due process than efficiency.

2. Does Posner's approach either reflect the aspirations we have for a procedural system or explain its present configuration? For instance, what would an efficiency approach say about the maintenance of state and federal court systems with overlapping jurisdiction? Would efficiency favor the use of adversarial process? Aren't juries a hopelessly inefficient method for dispute resolution? A true commitment to efficiency as a first principle might force us to revisit some of our cherished procedural features. See generally Conference on "Economic Analysis of Civil Procedure," 23 J. Leg. Stud. 303-665 (1994).

Many of us might be unwilling to permit these features to be tested in the crucible of efficiency. Indeed, even *Eldridge* accepted adversarial process as the baseline, allowing departures from adversarial process only when there were clear efficiency gains to be had. If some procedural features are untouchable even when inefficient, have you relegated efficiency to a second-class status, providing answers to smaller procedural issues once the basic shape of the system has been roughed in using other norms?

3. Perhaps the answer is that you would like to make principles of efficiency and justice (and perhaps, like Professor Mashaw, other principles as well) co-equal norms. When all the co-equal norms point in the same procedural direction, using each to smooth out the indeterminacy of the others works well. But when the principles disagree, which principle will you credit? If you pick one principle, are the others really "equal"? On the other hand, if you try to work out a compromise faithful to none of the norms, are you also admitting that the normative enterprise is bankrupt? Consider the problem of multiple norms in light of the next reading.

Robert A. Bush, DISPUTE RESOLUTION ALTERNATIVES AND ACHIEVING THE GOALS OF CIVIL JUSTICE: JURISDICTIONAL PRINCIPLES FOR PROCESS CHOICE

1984 Wis. L. Rev. 893, 905, 908, 911-12, 914-15

What are the goals of the civil justice system? What is it that is to be accomplished, what is important to achieve, through the handling of a civil dispute? Without some agreement about the answers to such first order questions it is difficult to formulate policy for or evaluate civil justice reform, because it is not even clear whether any need for reform exists. . . .

1. Resource Allocation

One important societal goal as articulated by economics is the allocation of society's scarce resources among various resource-consuming activities so that the maximum benefit or value is extracted from those resources. . . .

2. Social Justice

Economists who stress the efficiency goal freely admit that by their terms it is possible to attain efficiency in allocation of resources even where 90% of society's resources is held by a very small and very rich minority, and the remaining 10% is divided among a miserably poor majority. Many therefore argue that another societal goal, at least on a par with efficiency, is social or distributional justice — the attainment of equity in the distribution of society's resources, including all forms of wealth and power. . . . [A] process that gives assistance to the relatively disadvantaged party in presenting his case, or otherwise procedurally advantages him, automatically redistributes wealth and power and may result in outcomes that do likewise, in the individual case or prospectively. . . .

3. Fundamental Rights Protection

A society whose goal is to achieve efficient resource use, or social justice, or some measure of both, may nevertheless be insensitive to certain fundamental rights of individuals. In fact it may ignore, tolerate or even sanction violations of those rights when necessary to further one or both of the other goals. Thus, some argue that the articulation and protection of fundamental individual rights should be considered a prime goal of society, no less important (if not more so) than the two above. . . .

4. Public Order

One of the basic conditions for social existence is some degree of public or social order, without which the previous three goals would themselves often be difficult to pursue, much less to attain. Maintenance of order is therefore a basic societal goal. . . .

5. Human Relations

While it is not cited in the civil justice reform debate as often as some of the previous goals, another important societal goal is that the members of a society be able to get along with one another, on the individual and the group level. This involves mutual tolerance, respect, and even appreciation of different points of view and different modes of existence. It also involves a sense of common, shared humanity, and as a result, a sense of social solidarity. Positive human relations and social solidarity are important for their own sake, although they also relate to other goals.

6. Legitimacy

Every society strives to ensure that its governing institutions and structures appear legitimate in the eyes of its members. Note that this goal is defined in terms of appearance and perception, not some objective standard of fairness or political economy.... Thus, this goal is not concerned with fundamental conditions for legitimacy objectively defined — as might be one view of the fundamental rights goal — but rather with the appearance of legitimacy to the society's members.

7. Administration

Minimizing the cost of administration of social enterprises, although rather pedestrian by comparison to the other goals discussed, is a well established and independent societal goal. Even where action must be undertaken in the public interest to achieve desired goals the action should itself be conducted so as to consume as few resources as possible in administrative costs.

Notes and Questions

1. Professor Bush's methodology is familiar to all law students and lawyers. First, he specifies the goals or purposes of the relevant body of law. Second, he selects a rule by testing the competing possibilities against these goals and choosing the possibility that, on balance, best fulfills those goals. This cost-benefit approach is similar to that of Posner, but it also allows for the use of variables which are poorly quantified in an efficiency calculus.

Is it a better method than that of Rawls or Posner? The success of the method depends in the first instance on the identification of the correct goals. Has Bush identified the right variables? Professor Michelman has also sought to articulate proper procedural values, but his list is different:

> I have been able to identify four discrete, though interrelated, types of such values, which may be called dignity values, participation values, deterrence values, and (to choose a clumsily neutral term) effectuation values. *Dignity values* reflect concern for the humiliation or loss of self-respect which a person might suffer if denied the opportunity to litigate. *Participation values* reflect an appreciation of litigation as one of the modes in which persons exert influence, or have their wills "counted," in societal decisions they care about. *Deterrence values* recognize the instrumentality of litigation as a mechanism for influencing or constraining individual behavior in ways thought socially desirable. *Effectuation values* see litigation as an important means through which persons are enabled to get, or are given assurance of having, whatever we are pleased to regard as rightfully theirs.

Frank I. Michelman, *The Supreme Court and Litigation Access Fees: The Right to Protect One's Rights — Part I*, 1973 Duke L.J. 1153, 1172-73; see John R.

Allison, *Ideology, Prejudgment, and Process Values*, 28 New Eng. L. Rev. 657 (1994) (dividing process values into instrumental values of accuracy, efficacy, efficiency, and fairness and non-instrumental values of individual dignity, heuristic goals, and institutional legitimacy). Recall that Professor Mashaw posited somewhat different values for a procedural system. (See pp. 9-10, *supra*.) And Rule 1 of the Federal Rules of Civil Procedure suggests a more modest set of aspirations for procedural rules: "[The Rules] shall be construed to secure the just, speedy, and inexpensive determination of every action." Whose set of goals is right? If we cannot agree on the relevant goals, can we ever agree on the right procedural rules?

2. There are also problems with the multi-goal approach at the second, balancing stage of the approach. How much weight do we give to justice, to speed, and to efficiency when they each point toward a different procedural rule? The pragmatism of the multi-goal approach suggests that we should adopt the rule which best advances the overall social good, but what is the "good"? A pragmatic approach also suggests that we should be willing to experiment with different approaches. Wouldn't desirable procedural goals such as certainty, predictability, and treating like cases alike strongly counsel against a relentlessly pragmatic approach?

3. None of the multi-goal approaches that we have read mentions adversarial process. None mentions jury trial or civil discovery. How valid can the multi-goal approach be when it does not predict the features of the procedural system we actually have? Moreover, doesn't the multi-goal approach suggest that all procedural features can be abandoned in some circumstances? Is this right? Might adversarialism, for instance, be a fundamental dimension of procedure that trumps the pragmatic balancing of Bush, Michelman, and Fed.R.Civ.P. 1?

Lon L. Fuller, THE FORMS AND LIMITS OF ADJUDICATION

92 Harv. L. Rev. 353, 357, 363, 381-86, 388-95, 397-98 (1978)

II. THE TWO BASIC FORMS OF SOCIAL ORDERING

It is customary to think of adjudication as a means of settling disputes or controversies. This is, of course, its most obvious aspect. . . .

More fundamentally, however, adjudication should be viewed as a form of social ordering, as a way in which the relations of men to one another are governed and regulated. Even in the absence of any formalized doctrine of stare decisis or res judicata, an adjudicative determination will normally enter in some degree into the litigants' future relations and into the future relations of other parties who see themselves as possible litigants before the same tribunal. Even if there is no statement by the tribunal of the reasons for its decision, some reason will be perceived or guessed at, and the parties will tend to govern their conduct accordingly.

If, then, adjudication is a form of social ordering, to understand it fully we must view it in its relation to other forms of social ordering. It is submitted that there are two basic forms of social ordering: *organization by common aims* and *organization by reciprocity*. Without one or the other of these nothing resembling a society can exist. . . .

III. Adjudication As a Form of Social Ordering

Adjudication, contract, and elections are three ways of reaching decisions, of settling disputes, of defining men's relations to one another. Now I submit that the characteristic feature of each of these forms of social ordering lies in the manner in which the affected party participates in the decision reached. This may be presented graphically as follows:

Form of Social Ordering	*Mode of Participation by the Affected Party*
Contract	Negotiation
Elections	Voting
Adjudication	Presentation of proofs and reasoned arguments

It is characteristic of these three ways of ordering men's relations that though they are subject to variation — they present themselves in different "forms" — each contains certain intrinsic demands that must be met if it is to function properly. We may distinguish roughly between "optimum conditions," which would lift a particular form of order to its highest expression, and "essential conditions," without which the form of order ceases to function in any significant sense at all. . . .

Now much of this paper will be concerned in carrying through with [an] analysis of the optimum and essential conditions for the functioning of adjudication. This whole analysis will derive from one simple proposition, namely, that the distinguishing characteristic of adjudication lies in the fact that it confers on the affected party a particular form of participation in the decision, that of presenting proofs and reasoned arguments for a decision in his favor. Whatever heightens the significance of this participation lifts adjudication toward its optimum expression. Whatever destroys the meaning of that participation destroys the integrity of adjudication itself. Thus, participation through reasoned argument loses its meaning if the arbiter of the dispute is inaccessible to reason because he is insane, has been bribed, or is hopelessly prejudiced. . . .

VI. The Forms of Adjudication . . .

2. *Is an Adversary Presentation Necessary to Adjudication?*

The Lawyer's Role as Advocate in Open Court

. . . In a very real sense it may be said that the integrity of the adjudicative process itself depends upon the participation of the advocate. This becomes apparent when we contemplate the nature of the task assumed by any arbiter who attempts to decide a dispute without the aid of partisan advocacy. . . .

The Lawyer as a Guardian of Due Process

The lawyer's highest loyalty is at the same time the most intangible. It is a loyalty that runs, not to persons, but to procedures and institutions. The lawyer's role imposes on him a trusteeship for the integrity of those fundamental processes of government and self-government upon which the successful functioning of our society depends. . . .

3. *May the Arbiter Act on His Own Motion in Initiating the Case?*

Certainly it is true that in most of the practical manifestations of adjudication the arbiter's function has to be "promoted" by the litigant and is not initiated by itself. But is this coy quality of waiting to be asked an essential part of adjudication?

It would seem that it is not. . . . Yet I think that most of us would consider such a case exceptional and would not be deterred by it from persisting in the belief that the adjudicative process should normally not be initiated by the tribunal itself. There are, I believe, sound reasons for adhering to that belief. . . . *First*, it is generally impossible to keep even the bare initiation of proceedings untainted by preconceptions about what happened and what its consequences should be. In this sense, initiation of the proceedings by the arbiter impairs the integrity of adjudication by reducing the effectiveness of the litigant's participation through proofs and arguments. *Second*, the great bulk of claims submitted to adjudication are founded directly or indirectly on relationships of reciprocity. In this case, unless the affected party is deceived or ignorant of his rights, the very foundations of the claim asserted dictate that the processes of adjudication would be invoked by the claimant.

4. *Must the Decision Be Accompanied by a Statement of the Reasons for It?*

We tend to think of the judge or arbitrator as one who decides and who gives reasons for his decision. Does the integrity of adjudication require that reasons be given for the decision rendered? I think the answer is, not necessarily. . . . [But by] and large it seems clear that the fairness and effectiveness of adjudication are promoted by reasoned opinions. Without such opinions the parties have to take it on faith that their participation in the decision has been real, that the arbiter has in fact understood and taken into account their proofs and arguments. A less obvious point is that, where a decision enters into some continuing relationship, if no reasons are given the parties will almost inevitably guess at reasons and act accordingly. Here the effectiveness of adjudication is impaired, not only because the results achieved may not be those intended by the arbiter, but also because his freedom of decision in future cases may be curtailed by the growth of practices based on a misinterpretation of decisions previously rendered.

5. May the Arbiter Rest His Decision on Grounds Not Argued by the Parties?

Obviously the bond of participation by the litigant is most secure when the arbiter rests his decision wholly on the proofs and argument actually presented to him by the parties. In practice, however, it is not always possible to realize this ideal. . . . If the ideal of a perfect congruence between the arbiter's view of the issues and that of the parties is unattainable, this is no excuse for a failure to work toward an achievement of the closest approximation of it. We need to remind ourselves that if this congruence is utterly absent — if the grounds for the decision fall completely outside the framework of the argument, making all that was discussed or proved at the hearing irrelevant — then the adjudicative process has become a sham, for the parties' participation in the decision has lost all meaning . . . .

6. Qualifications and Disqualifications of the Arbiter . . .

I shall merely suggest that the problem of securing a properly qualified and impartial arbiter be tried by the same touchstone that has been used throughout — what will preserve the efficacy and meaning of the affected party's participation through proofs and arguments? Obviously, a strong emotional attachment by the arbiter to one of the interests involved in the dispute is destructive of that participation. In practice, however, another kind of "partiality" is much more dangerous. I refer to the situation where the arbiter's experience of life has not embraced the area of the dispute, or, worse still, where he has always viewed that area from some single vantage point. Here a blind spot of which he is quite unconscious may prevent him from getting the point of testimony or argument. . . .

VII. The Limits of Adjudication

1. Introduction

Attention is now directed to the question, What kinds of tasks are inherently unsuited to adjudication? The test here will be that used throughout. If a given task is assigned to adjudicative treatment, will it be possible to preserve the meaning of the affected party's participation through proofs and arguments?

2. Polycentric Tasks and Adjudication . . .

[S]uppose in a socialist regime it were decided to have all wages and prices set by courts which would proceed after the usual forms of adjudication. It is, I assume, obvious that here is a task that could not successfully be undertaken by the adjudicative method. The point that comes first to mind is that courts move too slowly to keep up with a rapidly changing economic scene. The more fundamental point is that the forms of adjudication cannot encompass and take into account the complex repercussions that may result from any change in prices or wages. . . . In such a case it is simply impossible to afford each affected party a meaningful participation through proofs and arguments. It is a matter of capital importance to note that it is not merely a question of the huge number of possibly affected parties, significant as that aspect of the thing may be. A more fundamental point is that each of the various forms that award might take (say, a three-cent increase per pound, a four-cent increase, a five-cent increase, etc.) would have a different set of repercussions and might require in each instance a redefinition of the "parties affected."

We may visualize this kind of situation by thinking of a spider web. A pull on one strand will distribute tensions after a complicated pattern throughout the web as a whole. Doubling the original pull will, in all likelihood, not simply double each of the resulting tensions but will rather create a different complicated pattern of tensions. This would certainly occur, for example, if the doubled pull caused one or more of the weaker strands to snap. This is a "polycentric" situation because it is "many centered" — each crossing of strands is a distinct center for distributing tensions. . . .

It should be carefully noted that a multiplicity of affected persons is not an invariable characteristic of polycentric problems. . . . [R]apid changes with time are not an invariable characteristic of such problems. On the other hand, in practice polycentric problems of possible concern to adjudication will normally involve many affected parties and a somewhat fluid state of affairs. Indeed, the last characteristic follows from the simple fact that the more interacting centers there are, the more the likelihood that one of them will be affected by a change in circumstances, and, if the situation is polycentric, this change will communicate itself after a complex pattern to other centers. . . .

Now, if it is important to see clearly what a polycentric problem is, it is equally important to realize that the distinction involved is often a matter of degree. There are polycentric elements in almost all problems submitted to adjudication. A decision may act as a precedent, often an awkward one, in some situation not foreseen by the arbiter. . . . In lesser measure, concealed polycentric elements are probably present in almost all problems resolved by adjudication. It is not, then, a question of distinguishing black from white. It is a question of knowing when the polycentric elements have become so significant and predominant that the proper limits of adjudication have been reached. . . . If problems sufficiently polycentric are unsuited to solution by adjudication, how may they in fact be solved? So far as I can see, there are only two suitable methods: *managerial direction* and *contract* (or reciprocity).

Notes and Questions

1. Although not published until shortly after his death in 1978, Professor Fuller's article was actually written in 1958. It is perhaps the most famous effort to derive the basic structure of a procedural system from fundamental norms. Indeed, we have come nearly full circle to Rawls, whose notions of justice were in fact influenced by Fuller. The difference is that Rawls begins with abstract principles of justice, while Fuller begins by asking what adjudication

actually is and then attempts to tease further procedural implications out of descriptive fact. Is Fuller's methodology therefore less susceptible to criticism than those of Rawls and Posner on the one hand, and Bush and Michelman on the other?

Start by assuming that Fuller is correct in believing that adjudication has a fundamental form. If that is so, then Fuller is certainly right to reject any procedural implications that are inconsistent with the form and to embrace any implications that are necessary to the form. But what about Fuller's use of "optimal" procedures? If a procedure is not barred by the form of adjudication, can it be excluded from consideration just because it is "non-optimal"? Beyond those few procedural features that he believes to be necessary, is Fuller any different than other procedural pragmatists?

2. Assuming that Fuller is correct in his claim that adjudication has a fundamental form, is Fuller correct in claiming that the natural ordering principle for that form is the parties' ability to participate through proofs and reasoned arguments? As the third section of this chapter will show, Fuller's view of procedure is Anglophilic. Many legal systems do not use an adversarial process, and accord the parties limited rights to participate through proofs and reasoned arguments. Can we accept as central to the form of adjudication an assumption that is absent or only weakly present in many of the world's legal systems?

More critical to adjudication would appear to be a decisionmaker who applies reason to the facts and the law of the case, and then comes to a justifiable conclusion. But recasting adjudication in terms of "reasoned judgment" rather than "reasoned participation" makes the case for an adversarial system more difficult. An adversarial system becomes one way in which the decisionmaker can be informed about the facts and law on which to base a reasoned decision, but other systems would also suffice.

Professor Bone has argued that Fuller linked reasoned participation to reasoned judgment:

> Fuller did not view the adversarial system simply as an arena of combat in which lawyers fought for their respective versions of the facts and law, with truth winning out in the end. This is a view sometimes associated with Fuller, but it is mistaken. In Fuller's theory, . . . [j]udges made law by engaging in a form of moral reasoning — by asking what general principles ought to apply to a particular social setting. Adversarial presentation was essential to this reasoning process, for it allowed the judge to remain both detached and sympathetically engaged.

Robert G. Bone, *Lon Fuller's Theory of Adjudication and the False Dichotomy between Dispute Resolution and Public Law Models of Adjudication*, 75 B.U. L. Rev. 1272, 1309 (1995). On Bone's reading of Fuller, do you agree that adversarial presentation is "essential" to the process of moral reasoning? Is the process of moral reasoning essential to adjudication? If so, are any of the normative principles or goals which we have discussed (justice, efficiency, and the like) more essential to reasoned judgment than party participation?

3. Fuller himself was ambiguous about whether the adversarial method of ensuring participation was a necessary, or merely an optimal, dimension of adjudication. Fuller saw clear benefits in the adversarial system. He thought adversarial process was "perhaps the most effective means we have of combatting the evils of bureaucracy." Lon L. Fuller, *The Adversary System*, in

Talks on American Law 30, 40 (Harold J. Berman ed. 1961). He also believed that adversarial process helped adjudication achieve its maximum moral and persuasive force as a principle of order, and that it was the system which best "lifted [the individual] to the point where he gains the power to view reality through eyes other than his own, where he is able to become[ ] impartial . . . ." Id. at 43; see also Lon L. Fuller, The Problems of Jurisprudence 706-07 (1949). But he never said whether non-adversarial adjudication is normatively illegitimate.

The question has particular importance in complex cases. Remember the intuitive definition that we have given to complex litigation: cases in which adversarial process works poorly. If adversarial process is essential, then we have only two choices in complex cases: either slog along using a process that badly serves the case, or remove complex cases from the realm of adjudication (perhaps through legislative or administrative solutions). If adversarial process is merely desirable, we have a third option as well: use non-adversarial procedures to resolve complex cases. We could justify our departure from adversarial procedures with the argument that we were protecting the reasoned judgment that lies at the true heart of adjudication.

Of course, this third option puts pressure on the trans-substantivity of our procedural rules — unless we adopt a non-adversarial system in cases both simple and complex. Thus, we must face another question: Is trans-substantivism an essential feature of adjudication, or merely an optimal feature? (Perhaps you can now begin to see how complex litigation implicates an interrelated host of normative procedural issues.)

4. Note Fuller's description of "polycentric" cases. Is a "polycentric" case equivalent to a "complex" one? Or are "polycentric" cases a subset of complex cases? Subsequent materials in this book will often involve many-centered disputes that Fuller would likely have thought impossible to resolve through proofs and reasoned arguments. If Fuller is correct, then we should not be adjudicating these disputes. Do you agree in principle that these disputes are impossible to adjudicate? Professor Fiss does not:

> In truth, the individual participation axiom is rooted in a world that no longer exists. . . . A conception of adjudication that strictly honors the right of each affected individual to participate in the process seems to proclaim the importance of the individual, but actually leaves the individual without the institutional support necessary to realize his true self. In fact, the individual participation axiom would do little more than throw down an impassable bar — polycentrism — to the one social process that has emerged with promise for preserving our constitutional values and the ideal of individualism in the face of the modern bureaucratic state — structural reform.

Owen M. Fiss, *Foreword: The Forms of Justice*, 93 Harv. L. Rev. 1, 44 (1979).

5. Another way to think about polycentrism is to consider the roles that Fuller assigns to each of the players in the adversary system. Only three players are necessary — a decisionmaker and two parties — although at least two additional players — the lawyers — are often involved. Fuller contemplates that the lawyers, as the representatives of the parties, will have the greatest role to play; the parties and the decisionmaker(s) are less active until the end of the case, when a judgment is rendered by the decisionmaker(s) and complied with by the parties.

If complex cases are understood as cases in which the adversary system works poorly, is it because something keeps one or more of the players from fulfilling an appointed role? What might that "something" be? Can we remove complexity simply by assigning the difficult role to a player who is more easily able to accomplish it? Would Fuller say that such a role re-definition threatens the heart of adjudication, and thus requires a non-adjudicatory response?

6. Fuller's defense of the adversary system, and his argument for its normative stature, rest upon a vision of the arrangement of institutions that best advance the social order. He does not justify the adversary system with the kinds of arguments (justice, efficiency, or the promotion of dignity, participation, or effectuation values) that we had seen earlier. Nor does he defend the adversary system in terms of its superior ability to find the truth. Is his argument weakened by his failure to consider these matters? The following articles explore other justifications for the adversary system.

Stephen A. Saltzburg, LAWYERS, CLIENTS, AND THE ADVERSARY SYSTEM

37 Mercer L. Rev. 647, 652-56, 658-59, 687, 697-99 (1986)

What is necessary to have an adversary system? The simple answer is that it is necessary to have more than one person with a stake in the outcome of a proceeding who is permitted to attempt to influence the outcome. That is the only definitional prerequisite. . . .

Thus, those who attack the adversary system as failing in a search for truth attack a straw man, the purple prose of appellate courts notwithstanding. The goal of the adversary system is to apply the substantive legal principles so that those who have rights may claim them and those who have liabilities must face them. This the adversary system endeavors to do, while simultaneously announcing that it is an imperfect process. . . .

The American adversary process entrusts the decision whether to bring claims and to make defenses to the litigants who seek to claim substantive rights and defenses or to impose liability. The desire to win is the motivating consideration that prompts litigants to seek out, develop, and offer evidence and to bring relevant and persuasive legal doctrines and precedents to a decisionmaker's attention. In order to win, litigants have the motivation to gather the most persuasive evidence, put forth the best theories available to them, and develop evidence and theories that will enable them to respond to their adversaries. The result is that the decisionmaker hears the strongest argument that each litigant who is trying to win can muster to support a finding of fact or an evaluation of fact and the most devastating response each adversary can make to that argument.

This incentive system is similar, of course, to other free enterprise concepts that govern economic thinking. The notion is that people who stand to gain or lose from a transaction are likely to be motivated to act more effectively than those who are indifferent to the transaction. . . .

Once one abandons the 'search for truth' language in favor of a more accurate statement of the goals of the system, and Americans understand that the desire to win is neither wholly beneficial nor wholly detrimental to a process of proper application of substantive law, the adversary system appears to have much to commend it. . . .

Assuming that the litigants act according to society's highest expectations so that they produce the best evidence and theories for consideration by a competent decisionmaker, it would seem that every chance exists that the substantive law will be applied in an appropriate way. Decisionmakers will make errors, but these errors are inevitable. The adversary process would not appear to exacerbate the problems of dealing with uncertainty in examining and evaluating past events. . . .

The greatest problem facing the adversary system is that lawyers and their clients may want to win so badly that they will violate the rules that govern their conduct in litigation or other tasks. The desire to win has led, and surely will lead, some individuals to risk criminal penalties, disbarment, and disgrace to prevail in a dispute or venture. . . .

The advantages some litigants have over others is [also] cause for concern. It is doubtful, however, that a reasonable way to handicap the judicial process in order to promote greater equality exists. The greater a person's wealth, the more litigation that person can afford. Money can enable some litigants to hire better investigators, better experts, and better lawyers. This ability can increase the chance that the wrong person will win in litigation. . . .

[Nevertheless, the] adversary system has some attributes that might equalize the litigation more than many people realize. The jury, for instance, generally will not be exceptionally wealthy. Corporations and other entities cannot sit on juries. When an individual litigates against an entity with greater resources, the jury might take the disparity in resources into account when it evaluates the evidence and arguments offered by opposing parties. Thus, the guarantee of trial by jury is one way of assuring that those litigants with political power, social influence, and wealth must argue their case before members of the community who most often lack these advantages.

Other aspects of the adversary system might have an equalizing effect. For example, trial judges may impose time limits on opening statements or closing arguments and may exclude cumulative evidence. . . . That one may hire many lawyers and gather an incredible amount of evidence does not necessarily mean that he can use the talent and evidence. . . .

After all, the witnesses to an event might have no testimony to offer that is favorable to the wealthy litigant and money cannot change that possibility. In the courtroom, each side has an equal chance to examine and cross-examine witnesses and to explain its theories to the jury. A wealthy litigant who . . . offers much more evidence than an opponent may find that . . . the more evidence that is offered, the stronger the cross-examination by the opponent. The adversary system provides cross-examination in response to examination; one opening statement in response to another; one side's argument in response to another's. The process treats all litigants equally and does not permit a wealthy litigant to obtain advantages easily.

Geoffrey C. Hazard, Jr., ETHICS IN THE PRACTICE OF LAW

120-23, 126-29, 131-35 (1978)

There is probably no "pure" form of [an adversarial system in operation.] Even the most passive judge in an adversary system sometimes asks questions . . . . Nevertheless, the adversary system is distinctive for the fact that the parties, through their lawyers, investigate the facts, frame the issues, and present the evidence to a passive tribunal that then reaches a decision. . . .

The theory of adjudication in the adversary system, as usually stated, has two linked components. One is that party presentation will result in the best presentation, because each party is propelled into maximum effort in investigation and presentation by the prospect of victory . . . . The other component of the theory is more complex and has to do with the psychology of decisionmaking. It runs essentially as follows: Proof through evidence requires hypothesis; hypothesis requires a preliminary mind-set; if an active judge-interrogator develops the proof, his preliminary mind-set too easily can become his final decision; therefore, it is better to have conflicting preliminary hypotheses and supporting proofs presented by the parties so that the judge's mind can be kept open until all the evidence is at hand.

In this version of the adversary theory, the role of the advocate is central to adjudication, because the advocate is a necessary orchestrator of the proof to be offered by a party. . . . There are other interpretations of the adversary system, however, that attach much less significance to the role of the advocate as an instrument for developing proofs. One of these interpretations emphasizes the importance of party participation, the idea being that a party's presentation of the case on his behalf gives him a sense of involvement and control in the decision procedure. In this conception of the adversary system, counsel is and should be relegated to the role of coach rather than protagonist . . . .

There is still another and more radical theory of the adversary system. On this view, trials are not quests for truth in a serious objective or empirical sense, and cannot be. . . . [I]n the cases that go to trial the evidence is hopelessly ambiguous according to any concept of rational proof, and decision necessarily involves important elements of intuition, predisposition, and bias. On this analysis, a trial is necessarily theatre or ritual to an important extent. . . .

The adversary system has a strange status in the American legal tradition. [I]t is one derivative of fundamental theories of political liberty. . . . In recent years, the Supreme Court has substantially equated adversarial trial with due process in the determination of legal rights. . . . In [some] respects, the adversary system stands with freedom of speech and the right of assembly as a pillar of our constitutional system. On the other hand, the adversary system in practice is known by its practitioners often to be anything but the truth-revealing process that it pretends to be....

[For example, one issue] has long agitated both the bar and its critics. This is whether an advocate should be allowed to aid his client in presenting testimony that the advocate knows to be false....

This issue poses in special form a general question for the adversary system: How can a procedure be justified as best able to yield truth when certain critical maneuvers in the procedure have the purpose and effect of suppressing the truth? This is an old question. The given answer is that society, and therefore the law, values other things in addition to truth....

Paradoxically, the primary benefit of the system is often said to be the promotion of truth. For every instance in which truth is suppressed or distorted by the adversary system, it is thought there are more instances in which the system uncovers truth that otherwise would not have been uncovered. There is no practicable way to test this claim. It is worth considering, however, whether the situation would really be much better if we gave up the adversary system in favor of the interrogative system. But even if the claim were false we might want to keep the rule as it is. Under the present system, using ostensibly open competition for discovery of the truth, the law has troubles with suppression and distortion; what sort of troubles would it have if we depended on *ex officio* procedures for getting the evidence? If the truth suffers from our use of the adversary system, we ought to consider how it might suffer if we used some other system. In our political culture, the interrogative system of trial could well turn out to resemble Congressional hearings.

The real value of the adversary system thus may not be its contribution to truth but its contribution to the ideal of individual autonomy. This is the rationale underlying many rules that obscure the truth, such as the privilege against self-incrimination and the rule that private premises may not be searched without a warrant. The proposition, as applied to the adversary system, is that there is good in being able to say what one wants to say, even if it involves the commission of perjury. Stated baldly, the proposition is shocking. The norms of our society condemn lying, although it is perhaps worth noting that the Biblical rule is the much narrower proposition that one should not bear false witness against a neighbor. At any rate, conventional morality does not openly recognize the value of being able to lie. Still, our commitment to truthfulness may actually go no further than homily; when it comes to serious business such as negotiation and diplomacy, most people accept the utility, the inevitability, and perhaps even the desirability of dissimulation in various forms....

As the situation stands, the advocate is supposed to be both the champion of his client and a gatekeeper having a duty to prevent his client from contaminating the courtroom. In principle, these responsibilities are compatible. The duty to the court simply limits the ways in which a lawyer can champion his client's cause. In practice, however, the duties have come to be in perhaps uncontrollable conflict....

In the American system, ... the advocate['s] relationship to his client's cause is ... dependent and intimate. In litigation involving "repeat business" clients, the advocate or his firm usually is also counsel under retainer to the client. In litigation involving "one shot" clients, such as plaintiff's injury claims, the lawyer's fee is usually contingent on the outcome. In any event, the advocate is expected and permitted to investigate the facts and interrogate witnesses before trial, thus becoming a party to the evidence before its presentation in court. A much wider range of harassing tactics is indulged in American litigation. Hence, the advocate's situation in our version of the adversary system is fairly defined by Shaw's description of marriage: it "combines the maximum of temptation with the maximum of opportunity." It is not difficult to see why the lawyer may be relatively ineffective as a source of restraint on his client. ...

This brings in view another serious problem of the adversary system. The trial lawyer can become completely immersed in his lawsuits, to the point where they become his identity and their outcome the sole criterion of his professional stature. Indeed, it is often only with difficulty that a modern trial specialist can maintain distance between himself and his craft. The whole tendency of his work leads him to hold, with Vince Lombardi, that winning is not the most important thing but the only thing. And the result can be that he becomes incapacitated to give his client detached advice about the prospects of ultimate victory and the advisability of settling through compromise. The problem can be especially severe in "big" cases for and against big corporations, because one such case can for several years be the vocation of a good part of a firm or agency's litigation staff. But it is inherent in the system. An English barrister is reported to have remonstrated, upon the prospect of compromising a bitter suit between heirs to a large fortune, "What? And allow that magnificent estate to be frittered away among the beneficiaries?"

If it is possible that the adversary system can work satisfactorily, and necessary that it must do so because no other system of adjudication is likely to be any better, it remains true that the system in its present form is pretty sick. ... As the institution of adversary adjudication now stands, the advocate has very strong inducements to oblige [a client's expectation that a lawyer be aggressive, guileful, and exploitative].

If the adversary system is to be changed, it will not be a simple undertaking. The system as it exists expresses a number of strongly held beliefs and ideals. One is that justice should be free. It is this proposition that supports the rule that the loser in litigation does not have to pay the winner's expenses. From this in turn follows the contingent fee system and the lack of inhibitions on running up an opposing party's costs, with the corresponding impairment of the advocate's gatekeeper function. Another belief is that entry into the legal profession should be relatively democratic. From this proposition it follows that admission is relatively easy, levels of training uneven, and professional esprit de corps weak. From this it follows that the images of professional lawyers are fuzzy and the potential for self-policing correspondingly low. Another is that litigation should secure not only justice under law but natural and popular justice. From this it follows that litigation often has inherently political, redistributive, and sometimes subversive characteristics, which infuse not only the merits of the controversies but the way they are prosecuted or defended....

Perhaps the problem is this: We can have a system that does not charge user fees, lets everyone play, seeks both law and common justice, and is subject to few inhibitions in style. We can also have a system in which a trial is a serious search for the truth or at least a ceremony whose essential virtue is solemnity. But we probably cannot have both. So long as the advocate in the American system is supposed to be at once a champion in forensic roughhouse and a guardian of the temple of justice, he can fulfill his responsibilities only if he combines extraordinary technical skill with an unusually disciplined sense of probity. That seems to be asking too much of any profession.

Notes and Questions

1. The arguments made by Professors Saltzburg and Hazard in favor of an adversarial system are different from Fuller's argument. Rather than viewing the adversary system as inhering in a fundamental form, their favorable arguments suggest only that adversary adjudication better advances societal goals than other possible systems. The obvious corollary is that, if societal goals change significantly (either overall or in a particular subset of controversies), the adversarial system could be jettisoned.

The exceptions to this corollary are two arguments mentioned by Hazard: that adversarial process is required by a fundamental theory of political liberty, and that adversarial process is required by a fundamental principle of individual autonomy. Two steps are required for the success of these arguments: first, establishing that some principle (whether it be Jeffersonian democracy or Kantian autonomy) is in fact fundamental to human existence; and second, establishing that adversarial process is in fact demanded by that principle. Is adversarial process a fundamental political or human right?

Even if adversarial process cannot be viewed as a fundamental political or human right, might it still be true that, in a democratic society that places high value on individual autonomy (such as modern American society), adversarial process is an essential feature? Under this more limited claim, the adversarial system would not be a universal necessity; but it would be required in those civilizations that organize their political, economic, and social structures to foster individual participation, choice, and decisionmaking in social life.

2. The excerpts from Professors Saltzburg and Hazard also raise some of the most important problems of the adversarial system. Perhaps the most common criticism involves the disincentive to seek the truth. The best-known formulation of this criticism belongs to Judge Marvin Frankel:

> This is a topic on which our profession has practiced some self-deception. We proclaim to each other and to the world that the clash of adversaries is a powerful means for hammering out the truth.... That the adversary technique is useful within limits none will doubt. That it is "best" we should all doubt if we were to be objective about the question. Despite our untested statements of self-congratulation, we know that others searching after facts — in history, geography, medicine, whatever — do not emulate our adversary system. We know that most countries in the world

> seek justice by different routes. What is more to the point, we know that many of the rules and devices of adversary litigation as we conduct it are not geared for, but are often aptly suited to defeat, the development of truth.
>
> We are unlikely ever to know how effectively the adversary technique would work toward truth if that were the objective of the contestants. Employed by interested parties, the process often achieves truth only as a convenience, a byproduct, or an accidental approximation. The business of the advocate, simply stated, is to win if possible without violating the law. . . . His is not the search for truth as such. To put the matter more exactly, the truth and victory are mutually incompatible for some considerable percentage of the attorneys trying cases at any given time.

Marvin E. Frankel, *The Search for Truth: An Umpireal View*, 123 U. Pa. L. Rev. 1031, 1036-37 (1975); see also Thurman Arnold, The Symbols of Government 185 (1935) ("Bitter partisanship in opposite directions is supposed to bring out the truth. Of course, no rational human being would apply such a theory to his own affairs or to other departments of the government."); Franklin Stier, *Making Jury Trials More Truthful*, 30 U.C. Davis L. Rev. 95 (1996) (unfavorably comparing truth-seeking capacity of adversarial system to that of inquisitorial system).

On the other hand, is truth-seeking all that matters? Like Saltzburg, Professor Uviller has argued that non-adversarial systems of fact finding may be better if such systems can discover truth more objectively, but that truth is rarely objectively knowable. H. Richard Uviller, *The Advocate, The Truth and Judicial Hackles: A Reaction to Judge Frankel's Idea*, 123 U. Pa. L. Rev. 1067 (1975). In a different vein, but leading to the same conclusion, Justice Frankfurter remarked in a famous concurrence:

> The heart of the matter is that democracy implies respect for the elementary rights of men, however suspect or unworthy; a democratic government must therefore practice fairness; and fairness can rarely be obtained by secret, one-sided determination of facts decisive of rights. . . . [An opportunity to be heard] should be particularly heeded at times of agitation and anxiety, when fear and suspicion impregnate the air we breathe. . . .
>
> The validity and moral authority of a conclusion largely depend on the mode by which it was reached. Secrecy is not congenial to truth-seeking and self-righteousness gives too slender an assurance of rightness. No better instrument has been devised for arriving at the truth than to give a person in jeopardy of serious loss notice of the case against him and opportunity to meet it. Nor has a better way been found for generating the feeling, so important to a popular government, that justice has been done.

Joint Anti-Fascist Refugee Committee v. McGrath, 341 U.S. 123, 170-72 (1951).

3. Is truth-seeking a fundamental norm of every procedural system? If so, does it follow that we must adopt the approach that best seeks the truth, or are we free to select any approach that does a passably good job? In the same vein, must we select the litigation model that best advances political liberty or individual autonomy, or can we choose an approach that does a passably good job of protecting these interests? If we are free to select "passably good" approaches, it becomes harder to argue that an adversarial model is essential, doesn't it? Of course, we could still argue that an adversarial system is optimal because it advances truth, liberty, and autonomy better than other systems.

4. As Saltzburg and Hazard state, an adversarial system requires elaborate rules of procedure, evidence, and ethics to police the contest; otherwise, the case threatens to dissolve into a vicious, vindictive, and utterly uncooperative affair in which a lawyer's private incentives dictate the flow and outcome of the litigation. Developing and enforcing such rules, however, is a time-consuming matter. Should either Fuller or others who might argue that an adversarial approach is a fundamental dimension of adjudication factor such problems of administration and efficiency into their arguments?

5. You may not be persuaded that fundamental procedural norms exist, or at least that these norms can tell us much about whether we should choose an adversarial or a non-adversarial system of adjudication. Perhaps, then, we can approach the question in a more functional way. In every lawsuit, evidence must be gathered, the law discerned, and the evidence applied to the law. These tasks must be divided among the players in the litigation enterprise. An adversarial system assigns the bulk of the evidence-gathering task to the lawyers, and also charges them with significant responsibility for identifying the law and for suggesting how the evidence should be applied to the law. Non-adversarial systems give primary responsibility for these functions to someone else — typically, the judge. Therefore, a critical difference between adversarial and inquisitorial systems is the amount of power placed in the hands of the judge.

As a functional matter, then, the issue is whether the judge should exercise these powers. The following two sections of the chapter can help us decide this issue. We look first at our own procedural history to see the advantages and drawbacks of a judge charged with significant power to shape issues and determine facts. We then look at other procedural systems to see whether a more inquisitorial, powerful judge offers a better procedural solution. During these historical and comparative inquiries, we will also discover how our history and other cultures have treated some of the other issues on which this first section has touched: the value of trans-substantive rules, the relative merits of procedural discretion and procedural certainty, and the utility of jury trial.

These issues are not academic. In complex cases the modern American procedural system does not work well. Our procedural history, as well as the experiences of other cultures, might give us valuable information about techniques that might — or might not — solve the problem of complex litigation.

B. THE ORIGINS OF AMERICAN CIVIL PROCEDURE

Shakespeare reminds us that "What's past is prologue." With respect to the history of our procedural system, he is certainly correct. Since the Norman invasion of England in 1066, at which the modern history of Anglo-American adjudication begins, our civil adjudicatory system has seen a constant battle between retrenchment and reform. Although the lines on the battlefield have changed over time, the basic issues — adversarial procedure, trans-substantivism, an expansive judicial role, the benefits of discretionary versus certain procedural rules, and the use of juries — have remained remarkably constant. An appreciation of the ways in which the Anglo-American system has worked out issues provides insight into the problems of complex litigation and potential solutions to those problems.

1. English Procedure after the Norman Conquest

Prior to 1066, most disputes in England were settled by communal and seigniorial courts according to local customs that included ordeal, battle, or compurgation. The Normans, with their genius for administration, gradually centralized the adjudicative process, first by making most disputes regarding land (the most important disputes of the day) into pleas of the Crown, then by entrusting exclusive jurisdiction over the disputes to circuit-riding justices in eyre, and finally by establishing permanent royal courts. The royal courts developed procedures for dispute resolution that were unknown in Saxon England. One procedure was the use of persons familiar with the dispute to assist the court. Thus was the jury system begun.

S.F.C. Milsom, HISTORICAL FOUNDATIONS OF THE COMMON LAW

42-44 (2d ed. 1981)

The fertile changes [in early Norman procedure] were those by which the old modes of proof came to be replaced by jury processes.... The court, no longer just presiding over the ritual formulation of a question to be put to an oracle beyond the need of human guidance, but now in some way responsible for the answer, may be inclined to let the defendant depart from the ancient general denial, and to specify his own facts.

This was a larger change than it sounds. The [ancient forms of trial] assumed that the "right" answer would be clear to the court. But, and this is where the rational nature of the new form of trial comes in, consideration of the actual facts requires the expression, for the first time, of rules of law. ...

Such new questions would suggest one kind of answer to the older clerical judges with their Roman learning, and a quite different kind to the up and coming counters [the medieval English attorneys].... [The clerical judges] would not have been dismayed by the emergence of facts which required legal analysis and legal decision. They were accustomed to think in terms of substantive law.... [But] the counters, being unfamiliar with the Roman system, could not adopt ready-made Roman rules. They did not see the law as a system of substantive rules at all. They saw that their ancient pattern of claim and denial had been disturbed because jurymen were fallible, and that in some circumstances the defendant must be allowed a new kind of answer. Upon the infinite details of this problem they concentrated their great abilities; and they never looked up to consider as a whole the substantive system they did not know they were making.

Jury trial in civil cases is perhaps *the* distinctive contribution of Anglo-American procedure. Contrary to our rose-colored modern beliefs, Professor Milsom demonstrates that the wisdom of using juries was by no means universally acknowledged at the time (just as it is not acknowledged today). The common law had two basic choices in dealing with a jury system: either give the jury free range and trust that it would find the right solution for a difficult and messy dispute, or confine the judgment of the jury as much as possible by giving it a set of narrow, easily answerable questions. Milsom argues that, for the most part, medieval lawyers took the latter approach. Hence, it was necessary to construct a procedural system that left as little as possible to the jury's judgment. The system which the medieval lawyers created revolved around two concepts: the writ and the pleadings.

a. The Writ System

Initially a writ was an administrative device, a royal command that a particular person do something or else show cause to the king why he could not do it. During the first century of Norman rule, an increasing number of those writs ordered royal officials either to investigate alleged errors in the local courts or actually to resolve certain matters, particularly disputes over land ownership. As more time passed and permanent royal courts were established, the writ became the formal piece of parchment which authorized one of the king's courts to hear a dispute. Without a writ, a royal court had — to use a somewhat inaccurate modern term — no subject matter jurisdiction over the controversy. The disputants were left to whatever local procedures and remedies were available.

Writs could be obtained only from the Chancellor, who was the king's most senior advisor and, in the early days, also a cleric trained in Roman law. In the beginning there was no particular structure to the writs nor any particular subject matter that automatically entitled a person to a writ; obtaining a writ depended upon being able to convince the Chancellor that the conduct at issue was of concern to the Crown. Over time, however, the subject matter and language of the writs became systematized. Systematization, however, did not mean inflexibility. During the thirteenth century the Chancery (*i.e.*, the office of the Chancellor) created new writs to cover factual circumstances that had slipped between the cracks of existing writs, and existing writs were stretched to cover conduct that had previously been handled only in local courts. Indeed, in 1250, Henry de Bracton, the author of one of England's first legal treatises, stated with confidence that "there will be as many formulas for writs as there are kinds of action; . . . for it is the king's duty to provide an adequate remedy to redress every wrong." Henry de Bracton, Of the Laws and Customs of England f. 413b (c. 1250) (S. Thorne transl. 1968).

For several reasons, history proved Bracton wrong. First, the thirteenth century saw efforts by the nobility to thwart the king's increasing power. One manifestation of that struggle was the effort to prevent the Chancery from issuing new types of writs. The matter was more or less settled in 1285 by the Statute of Westminster, which allowed the Chancery to issue new writs only "*in consimili casu*" (*i.e.*, in cases similar to those for which writs already existed). Under the authority of this statute the Chancery devised several new writs that had close analogs to existing writs, and Parliament on occasion authorized others. But the rapid growth of the jurisdiction of the king's courts, and the legal processes associated with them, had been halted.

Second, during the fourteenth century the judges of the three royal courts (the Exchequer, the King's Bench, and the Court of Common Pleas) succeeded in winning a degree of independence from the Crown. If the Crown, acting through the Chancellor, were able to continue to expand and define the scope of the royal courts, a measure of that independence would have been lost. Hence, in the latter middle ages common law judges frequently quashed writs issued by the Chancery because of their failure to conform to the scope of existing writs. "The common law is therefore beginning to retire to a definite and limited field, resigns its flexibility, and declines to be drawn into attempts to remove its own defects: that will henceforth be the province of Parliament. Still later, when Parliament fails to keep pace with the needs of litigants, it will be the Chancellor who will take up the task." Theodore F.T. Plucknett, A Concise History of the Common Law 159 (5th ed. 1956).

Third, the nature of the common law (*i.e.*, the law administered by the royal courts) made it difficult for the courts to consider new types of controversies:

> [T]he common law was essentially the law of land. The implications of this fact were very far-reaching. Its procedure was designed to reach people who owned land, and consequently was directed principally against the land rather than the person. . . . When the common law of the King's Court was becoming the common law of the country, it had to deal with very different problems. Other heads of law besides real property had to be developed, and litigants of the newer type were not always landowners of any consequence, although they may have had other forms of wealth. . . . With the growing complication of society, law had to deal with people who could not be reached quickly, if at all, by means of a procedure directed against land — with people, that is, who could not be identified with certain acres. [Id. at 177.]

As the jurisdiction of the royal courts became increasingly rigid, substantive thinking became frozen in an embryonic stage. Rather than developing systematic theories of property, contract, tort, or crime, the common law remained a group of independent, loosely associated writs, each of which dealt with specific dimensions of these subjects. There could be no overarching legal theories to reconcile and systematize the legal principles represented by the writs as long as the common law was unwilling to reform itself along substantive lines — a task which it did not undertake until the nineteenth century. As Sir Henry Maine once observed, "[s]o great is the ascendancy of the Law of Actions in the infancy of the Courts of Justice, that substantive law has at first the look of being gradually secreted in the interstices of procedure." Henry Maine, Dissertation on Early Law and Customs 389 (1886). The simple reality is that medieval English lawyers did not conceive of law in the substantive terms that we do today. There were writs and procedures to handle this type of harm to land and different ones to handle that type of harm to persons, but rarely did the common law stop to consolidate substantive or procedural issues that, with the benefit of hindsight, we can see to be conceptually linked.

The need for reform, however, was more apparent in retrospect than it was at the time. For the most part, the writs were sufficient to cover the types of disputes which were common to the age; and local courts filled in many remaining gaps. But the times finally began to run ahead of the forms of action. Despite the emergence of capitalism, it was not until the seventeenth century (and only after centuries of subterfuge) that the common law generally recognized and applied its trial procedures to contracts not under seal — a result at which Roman law had arrived hundreds of years earlier and which had been desperately needed in England for some time. The common law never developed an interest in dealing with most of the legal aspects of uses and trusts, in spite of their frequent employment by the fifteenth century. Although it later tried to co-opt them for its own courts, the common law also initially refused to entertain cases in such important areas as admiralty and law merchant. In short, although the common law's descent into rigidity was sometimes checked by creative interpretation of the writs, its willingness to deal with novel circumstances was uncertain, halting, and often tortuously slow.

The local courts were unable to fill all of the holes of the common law. Although local courts served as important stopgaps in areas such as law merchant, a series of historical circumstances doomed the local courts to virtual extinction: the royal court had already taken over many common controversies; old amount in controversy limitations on royal jurisdiction became meaningless after centuries of inflation; the writ of pone made many controversies removable from the local to the royal court; and local courts were unable to offer such procedural advantages as the jury, an effective process to compel attendance, speedy decisionmaking, and the power of contempt. Rights of appeal from the local to royal court further reduced local autonomy. The loss of an effective competitor to the common law was, according to Plucknett, a costly one: "The very fact of several bodies of law and custom existing in one nation sometimes had fruitful results for legal science. . . . [I]n America to-day the numerous state systems invite and indeed compel a critical appraisal of their respective merits. In England, on the other hand, our too early unification . . . bred up a profession which was only just sufficiently aware of other systems to glory in its isolation." Id. at 105.

b. Common Law Procedure

Although the congealing of the common law writs (or forms of action) presented some difficulties for the vitality of English law, that criticism would not, in itself, have posed insurmountable problems. An equally important difficulty lay in the procedures used by the common law to resolve the cases that the writs brought to the royal courts. Just as the history of the forms of action reflects a transition from flexibility to rigidity, so does the history of common law procedure.

By the fourteenth century the task of the medieval lawyers was plain: to focus the judge and the jury upon a single, straightforward issue that could be answered with ease. Hence, rather than developing systematic bodies of legal doctrine, they directed their efforts to the procedural rules that narrowed the case to a dispositive question. This centuries-long fascination with procedural questions (such as whether a claim of self-defense was a plea which could be made in response a writ of trespass "by force and arms") had the eventual effect of establishing the doctrines of substantive law (*e.g.*, self-defense is a defense to a claim for battery), but it was never the intention of the medieval lawyers to do so. "There was no substantive law to which pleading was adjective. These were the terms in which the law existed and in which lawyers thought." Milsom, Historical Foundations of the Common Law, at 59.

The centerpiece of this adjective, or procedural, law was the pleadings. It is nearly impossible to describe in brief fashion the intricacies of common law pleading, but several generalizations can be made. First, the rules of pleading did not always give a defendant a good sense of the claim against him. From the opening plea the form of action (or writ) under which the plaintiff was proceeding would be fairly obvious, and thus the defendant would also be aware of the procedures that would be used (procedures among writs varied on important matters such as the process available to compel the defendant's attendance, the mode of trial, and the permitted defensive pleas). Typically, however, facts could be pleaded with great generality, and were often fictional.

Second, the pleadings after the opening plea generally proceeded through a series of responses and counter-responses. In general terms, the defendant had several choices by way of response: he could file a dilatory plea when there were defects such as a misjoinder of parties, another pending action, and so forth; he could file a special demurrer if there was a formal defect in the opening plea; he could plead the general issue (a general denial in effect stating "I did not do it"); he could set up a special plea ("I did it, but I was justified because . . ."); or he could file a general demurrer ("I did it, but my action as alleged in the plaintiff's plea was not a wrong in law"). If the defendant pleaded the general issue, the issue was joined and the trial was held on the issue of whether the defendant did the thing alleged in the complaint. For special pleas and demurrers, rules of further pleading were adopted — rules which over the centuries became encrusted with layers of impenetrable technicalities. If those technicalities were avoided, the special plea also resulted in a trial, but limited only to the issue of whether the facts demonstrated the claimed justification. On the other hand, the demurrer led to a judicial decision: assuming the facts of the complaint to be true, did the defendant commit a legal wrong?

Third, in spite of these similarities, the method of pleading each writ varied in its particulars. Put into the terms we have already discussed, common law pleading was the antithesis of trans-substantivism. Each form of action had its own procedures that a lawyer needed to master. Pleading was a game — a very serious game — in which mistakes were common. Specialists in the art of pleading thrived on an opponent's miscues.

These rules of pleading became increasingly rigid as the centuries passed. The earliest form of pleading was oral; both lawyers appeared before the judge in what we might regard today as the long-lost ancestor of the initial pretrial conference. The plaintiff's lawyer described the facts and the plea. The defendant's lawyer suggested the response he would make to the plea. The plaintiff's lawyer might respond to that response. During this give-and-take, the judge would give advice like "If you use that plea, then you lose; but if you use this plea, then you will have a good claim." Having sorted out the judge's sentiments, the parties pleaded the case, the relevant issue was "joined," and the participants proceeded to determine the issue. By the fifteenth century, however, oral pleading was being replaced by written pleading. Litigants were stuck with their lawyers' plea or response; give-and-take among the lawyers and the court ended.

Wrong pleading choices were often fatal, for it was usually impossible to switch to the right choice. Imagine that a defendant was alleged to have injured the plaintiff in a way that arguably was not a legal wrong, and that the defendant also did not do the act alleged. The pleading system put him to a choice: either demur or plead the general issue. If he chose the former, the alleged facts were conclusively established; if he chose the latter, he could never again contest the issue of legal liability. An even greater penalty arose for those who made a pleading misstep. If a lawyer obtained a particular writ but the pleading showed that he had a valid claim under another writ, his client's case was dismissed rather than switched to the proper writ; he had to return to the Chancery for the proper writ. Even more startling was the common law's response to missteps after the opening plea. If a lawyer who claimed self-defense pleaded the general issue rather than correctly entering a special plea in justification, he could not use self-defense to justify his conduct; the only issue at trial would be whether he had hit the plaintiff. If he had, he lost — in spite of the existence of a valid defense. As Professor Millar observed, "[a] mingling of logic and illogic, not untinctured by tricklings of medieval scholasticism, appears throughout the whole discipline [of common law pleading]. It . . . constructed an arcanum of forensic statement penetrable only by the initiate. . . . Except in the simplest cases, the plaintiff can never be quite sure that his demand will attain the stage of trial, the defendant that some inadvertence will not see him cast *in toto*." Robert W. Millar, Civil Procedure of the Trial Court in Historical Perspective 34, 36 (1952).

Although this failure to do individual justice may seem draconian to us, remember that the narrowing of issues was the entire point of common law pleading. Nonetheless, the irrevocable choice of pleas had a number of deleterious consequences. For our purposes, the most important was the increasing ossification of the common law. Just as discretion had yielded to certainty in the creation of the forms of action, so too it yielded in the procedures and doctrines developed under each form of action:

> The lawyers had a maxim that they would tolerate a "mischief" (a failure of substantial justice in a particular case) rather than an

"inconvenience" (a breach of legal principle).... Our common lawyers in fact were beginning to feel the attraction of the "legal mind", the delight of pushing a principle as far as it will go and even further, and were enthusiastic over their first lessons in the *rigor juris*. This was no doubt the first step in legal wisdom (though certainly not the last); the real question which they had to face was how the future of the law should be developed. Was it to be a system of strict rule, mainly procedural, or was there to be a broader principle of conscience, reason, natural justice, equity? Plainly there were two points of view on this matter in the reign of Edward II [1307-27 — ED.], but it must have been fairly evident by the middle of the century that the stricter party had won. The law no doubt grew in content, but its growth was within a framework of technical doctrine and procedure instead of being the outcome of a broad principle of general equity .... [Plucknett, *supra*, at 680.]

The problems with common law procedure extended beyond its pleading rules. Recall that the pleading rules often did not require the parties to divulge the factual details of their cases. After juries became disinterested arbiters rather than witnesses to the facts, it became the responsibility of the parties to present evidence. Therefore, some method by which the parties could discover the relevant facts for trial would have seemed appropriate. Nonetheless, with the exception of a few special writs and the occasional aid of equitable bills, the pleading system allowed for no pretrial discovery of the facts. Undoubtedly this result put a high premium on the quality of the lawyers and on the parties' resources to conduct alternative pretrial investigations.

For those parties who successfully navigated the treacherous straits of the general issue and the special plea, the trial was finally upon them. Trial was usually to the jury, which was initially a group of persons, familiar with the case or with the character of the parties, who provided information to the judge. At an early point juries also began to give advice to the judge, and eventually began to render verdicts. By the fifteenth century, juries ceased to be the witnesses to the event, and were instead expected to be neutral arbiters and render verdicts based on the testimony of others. Lawyers became the examiners of witnesses. By the sixteenth century, cross-examination seems to have become a widely accepted practice. The practical demands on a jury's time and the itinerant nature of many of the king's judges combined with the narrowness of the triable issues to make a single trial with live testimony both necessary and feasible.

In its mature form, the trial was the pride of the common law system. "In the *viva voce* examination and cross-examination of witnesses in open court, with their demeanor and mode of speech directly appreciable by the organs of decision, is present the method that yields all those advantages of orality, immediacy, and publicity to which contemporary Continental reform is already beginning to aspire." Millar, *supra*, at 36. These positive qualities of jury trial, to which the English finally became committed as a political and cultural matter by the seventeenth century, blinded them to the inequities caused by the rigid pleading system that preceded the trial.

The trial had one significant weakness: Its remedies were limited. This problem derived both from the nature of writs and from the jury system itself. Prior to congealing in the thirteenth century, common law writs had typically involved retrospective controversies for which an award of money or declaration of property rights was the appropriate remedy. Moreover, as an ad hoc body, the jury was ill-suited to the task of ordering defendants to do (or refrain from doing) certain activities; its judgments needed to be final, simple, and enforceable by distress rather than contempt. Hence, although many remedies we now call "equitable" had antecedents in the common law, many equitable remedies (such as injunctions and accountings) were largely unavailable at common law.

Appeal, at least in our modern sense of the term, was a late development in English law. The writs of false judgment and certiorari, which ordered justices in eyre to review the work of the local courts, were among the earliest writs issued, and the use of an attaint jury (comprised of 24 jurors) to decide whether the original jury had perjured itself was developed as a check on the testimony (and, later on, verdicts) of the original jury. For the most part, however, juries were left to decide the factual and legal issues raised by the general issue or special plea. Gradually, through devices such as the demurrer to the evidence, judgment *non obstante*, orders for new trials, special verdicts, and the requests of losing parties to have Parliament review the matter, a modern system of appellate review developed. By the eighteenth century, the line between law and fact had become apparent, an appellate structure was firmly in place, and the opportunity to consider law in substantive terms had arrived.

Notes and Questions

1. This history has relevance both to procedural theory and to our present procedural situation. One lesson is the procedural legacy of the jury system. Although we can disagree with the way in which it implemented the insight, the common law correctly understood that the use of a group of lay decisionmakers requires the use of pretrial devices to narrow issues and facts for trial. If you trust the jury to sort out ill-defined issues and ambiguous facts, you might feel less of a need to provide significant issue-narrowing devices; if you have little trust, you might want important pretrial protections against jury discretion. The existence of a jury has important ramifications on any pretrial procedure that you, as the Tsar of Procedure, might design.

It is interesting how one procedural choice (like jury trial) is so intricately connected to other choices. You can never tinker with one part of a procedural system without considering its effects on other, seemingly unrelated parts.

2. The history of common law procedure demonstrates the evils of overly technical and non-trans-substantive procedural rules: Lawyers can become so caught up in the game of procedural manipulation that they fail to appreciate the effect of their efforts on the substantive law. Remember Professor Cover's argument (p. 6, *supra*) that non-trans-substantive rules are better because they foster substantive justice. Our procedural history is a powerful counterpoint to that argument, is it not? Are circumstances today sufficiently different from

circumstances of five hundred years ago that we can trust lawyers with non-trans-substantive rules?

3. The history of the common law also shows the dangers of a system in which the discretion to overlook procedural missteps in the search for substantive justice is squeezed out and ultimately eliminated. But common law procedure, in its mature form, was administratively certain and, for the most part, convenient. Is a system of utter procedural discretion better than a system of certain rules? Is it possible to strike some balance between a rigid set of procedural rules and absolute discretion? If so, how much rigidity and how much discretion? Put differently, how much procedure and how much substance? In the early days of the common law, substance did procedure's bidding. Should procedure simply do substance's bidding? Or are substantive and procedural rules entitled to roughly equal weight and respect? Can you answer these questions without deciding whether independent procedural values exist? See Chapter 1.A, *supra*.

4. To what extent did the adversarial system contribute to the primacy of procedure over substance in common law procedure? In almost every situation, a procedural rule will favor one party and disadvantage another. If a lawyer's primary loyalty is to the client, the lawyer will stand on procedural technicalities — even when they might result in substantive injustice. Is this potential to vault procedure over substance unavoidable in an adversarial system? Is it counterbalanced by the other party's incentive to argue the substantively just position? To the extent that the story of common law procedure is an indictment of the adversarial process, can we be optimistic about the success of any efforts to infuse our present adversarial system with less rigid procedural rules?

c. The Rise of Equity

Theodore F.T. Plucknett, A CONCISE HISTORY OF THE COMMON LAW

681 (5th ed. 1956)

The decline of discretion in the common law courts, therefore, had the effect of throwing increased emphasis upon the discretion which had always been exercised in the council, and so we reached the position, so full of possible dangers, in which justice was partitioned between two bodies, neither of which could completely deal with a matter. Council and Chancery no longer could manage the complicated machinery of writs and pleadings and process; common law courts no longer exercised discretion. This profound schism in the administration of justice had the most momentous effects. Adjudication, like most other questions of human conduct, depends upon a nice balance between law and equity, rule and exception, tradition and innovation. Each of these different principles became exaggerated when it became the badge of an institution, with the result that law and equity instead of being complementary, became rivals in a political upheaval.

As Plucknett suggests, no legal system can utterly lack discretion. As the common lawyers and judges squeezed discretion out of the common law and as local courts waned, the only option for those seeking a recovery barred at common law was relief from the Crown. In this context, the system of equity sprouted and flourished.

Tracing the antecedents of equity is a difficult business, but they certainly lie in the days before the common law hardened. During the twelfth and thirteenth century parties aggrieved by another's conduct often bypassed their common law remedies and appealed directly to the King, his Parliament, or his Chancellor for relief. Since the Chancellor already had the administrative responsibility of issuing common law writs and was trained in Roman and canon law, the obvious place to refer these requests was the Chancery; and typically they were so referred. When a writ covered (or could cover) the petitioner's claim, however, the plaintiff bore the burden of persuading the Chancellor to hear his claim directly.

F.W. Maitland, EQUITY

4-6 (A.H. Chaylor & W.J. Whittaker eds., 2d ed. 1936)

[T]he petitioner . . . complains that for some reason or another he can not get a remedy in the ordinary course of justice and yet he is entitled to a remedy. He is poor, he is old, he is sick, his adversary is rich and powerful, will bribe or intimidate jurors, or has by some trick or some accident acquired an advantage of which the ordinary courts with their formal procedure will not deprive him. . . . Gradually in the course of the fourteenth century petitioners, instead of going to the king, will go straight to the Chancellor, will address their complaints to him and adjure him to do what is right for the love of God and in the way of charity. Now one thing the Chancellor may do in such a case is to invent a new writ and so to provide the complainant with a means of bringing an action in a court of law. But in the fourteenth century the courts of law have become very conservative and are given to quashing writs which differ in material points from those already in use. But another thing that the Chancellor can do is to send for the complainant's adversary and examine him concerning the charge that is made against him. Gradually a procedure is established. The Chancellor, having considered the petition, or "bill" as it is called, orders the adversary to come before him and answer the complaint. The writ whereby he does so is called a subpoena . . . . Then when he comes before the Chancellor he will have to answer on oath, and sentence by sentence, the bill of the plaintiff. This procedure is rather like that of the ecclesiastical courts and the canon law than like that of our old English courts of law. . . . [T]he Chancellor will decide questions of fact as well as questions of law.

I do not think that in the fourteenth century the Chancellors considered that they had to administer any body of substantive rules that differed from the ordinary law of the land. They were administering the law but they were administering it in cases which escaped the meshes of the ordinary courts. . . . However, this sort of thing can not well be permitted. The law courts will not have it and parliament will not have it. . . . And so the Chancellor is warned off the field of common law — he is not to hear cases which might go to the ordinary courts, he is not to make himself a judge of torts and contracts, of property in lands and goods.

But then just at this time it is becoming plain that the Chancellor is doing some convenient and useful works that could not be done, or could not easily be done by the courts of the common law.

Theodore F.T. Plucknett, A CONCISE HISTORY OF THE COMMON LAW

177-78 (5th ed. 1956)

[T]here were matters which could best be settled by securing the prompt personal attendance of parties, and giving them direct personal commands to act or to desist in certain matters. The common law rarely achieved anything so logically direct as this action *in personam*, simply because its main pre-occupation was real property. . . .

Again, the common law was slow to admit the evidence of parties and witnesses. There was in fact little need for such evidence in the early days of the common law, for its main concern was with records and documents . . . or else with such publicly notorious facts as seisin . . . . Here again, the development of law beyond the confines of real property made it desirable to collect evidence, especially from the parties themselves. How useful this could be was apparent from the success with which the canonists were using the written deposition.

If any further reason for using such a method were needed, it could be found by observing the decline of the jury. Especially in the fifteenth century there were complaints that juries were packed, bribed, intimidated, partial and difficult to obtain within any reasonable space of time. Distrust of juries is an important factor in the early popularity of equity.

Finally, there were those who favored as a remedy to all this the direct business methods of the administrator. They felt there were cases which could not be satisfactorily handled by the common law with its writs, its delays, its pleadings, its limited resources in the finding of facts and the awarding of judgment, and its weakness in the face of disorder and corruption. . . . Some of the substantive rules of the common law, defensible enough when considered purely from a technical point of view, seemed unjust to the unlearned who had to suffer from them, and so we need not be surprised that there grew up a desire for more equitable rules as well as more effective procedure.

The procedural system that the Chancellor developed was shaped by a number of factors. One was canon law, which "was impatient of pedantry and inclined to place substance before form." Plucknett, *supra*, at 685. Another, more pragmatic influence was the fact that, until the nineteenth century, the responsibility for final decision was never delegated beyond the Chancellor and his chief assistant, the Master of the Rolls. But the Chancellor was a powerful and busy person, and could not afford the time to travel the countryside, empanel juries, and hear evidence in an ever increasing number of suits (more than 16,000 petitions were pending at one point in the early seventeenth century).

Hence, the procedural system that resulted was in many regards the diametric opposite of common law procedure. In order to help the Chancellor understand the issues, the pleadings were important, and they were often lengthy. At the same time, many of the technical pleading traps of the common law were avoided. The Chancellor, after all, was supposed to get to the equity of the matter; and, since there was no jury, there was no need of pleading devices designed to prevent multiple-issue confusion. In particular, one of the common law's best issue-narrowing devices — restrictive rules of party joinder — was often ignored, for complete justice required the joinder of all interested persons.

Without stringent issue-narrowing devices, however, equitable disputes were often sprawling affairs (at least compared to common law disputes). Obviously, there was a need for procedural devices to obtain the relevant information. The Chancellor had a staff of assistants, known as masters, who collected most of the information. Information-gathering techniques were borrowed from canon law, which had developed an administrative, inquisitorial process of subpoena and deposition. In their depositions, witnesses responded to questions drafted by the Chancellor, the masters, or the lawyers, and their testimony would be reduced to writing. All the information — and eventually the parties' written arguments — would be collected in the Chancellor's files, where he could read it and render a decision in due course.

Thus, unlike the common law, there was no denouement of "trial" at which live evidence was presented and a judgment rendered. Without a jury, and with equity as the only guide, a final, trial-like event to bring the case to closure was simply unnecessary. This lack of closure had important procedural consequences. The Chancellor wished to get the judgment right, so that if he did not have enough information to judge a particular case, he could reopen the record to obtain it. Even the judgment itself was not truly final, for the parties could always request reconsideration in order to permit complete justice to be done.

Since the Chancellor recognized that even his procedures to determine the equities could be as fallible as those of the common law, the notion arose that the Chancellor could work only on the conscience of the litigants. The Chancellor could order the parties what to do, but he could not make the correction occur himself. Hence, the Chancellor's judgments took the form of orders directed to the parties; payment of money or the transfer of property could typically be obtained only from the common law courts. Out of these circumstances arose the great remedial distinction which many first-year law students learn: law provides monetary relief and equity provides injunctions. Although the distinction was never ironclad in practice, it roughly describes the remedial realm of each system.

Theodore F.T. Plucknett, A CONCISE HISTORY OF THE COMMON LAW

684 (5th ed. 1956)

So far, the early history of equity has followed very much the same lines as the history of the common law three hundred years earlier. The common law gradually made a place for itself, although the country was already well provided with an ancient system of law courts; its intervention was at first political and administrative . . .; its process, the original writ, was of administrative origin, and in its oldest form, the *praecipe quod reddat*, undoubtedly encroached upon the sphere of already existing institutions. And so it was with equity. It imposed itself in spite of the existence of a well-ordered common law system: the basis of its intervention was at first the enforcement problem of the later fourteenth and fifteenth centuries, the preservation of order and the defence of the weak against the strong, together with the correction of real or supposed defects of the common law; its process by bill and *sub poena* was not in its origin judicial, but part of the administrative machinery of the Council; and there was no doubt that the common lawyers had grounds for regarding equity as encroaching upon their province.

From this inauspicious beginning, in which the Chancellor merely plugged jurisdictional and procedural holes that the common law refused to address, emerged a mature system of equity whose doctrines and procedures stood in stark contrast to those of the common law. In retrospect, it is easy to see that equity and law should have merged by the end of the middle ages. Their main difference was procedural rather than substantive. Early equity jurisdiction was determined mostly by the perceived procedural deficiencies of the common law — "its slowness, its expense, its inefficiency, its technicality, its abuse by the mighty, its antiquated methods of proof (for it refused to allow parties or any interested persons to testify, and stubbornly maintained wager of law), its suspicion of volunteer witnesses, . . . its inability to compel one party to an action to discover evidence useful to his adversary [and] its inability at this date to give specific relief in actions on contract and tort . . . ." Id. at 689. Furthermore, in spite of points of friction, law and equity often cooperated: Consultation between law and equity on various issues occasionally occurred, common law judges often sat as commissioners in equitable matters, and some Chancellors (such as Thomas More) were common lawyers.

Indeed, during the fifteenth and sixteenth centuries there were some opportunities when law and equity could have merged. Unfortunately, however, there were to be no shortcuts through the tragic lessons of history. Slowly but surely, the scope of equity's jurisdiction increased as the common law refused to incorporate equitable notions. Equity began to plug the substantive deficiencies as well. The Chancellor took over the important field of uses and trusts when the common law did not. He remade the law of mortgages. He enforced ordinary contracts, eventually spurring the common law to do likewise. Beginning with fraudulent contracts under seal, which the common law was forced to honor because its pleading rules did not allow the parties to place fraud in issue, the Chancellor slowly asserted a jurisdiction, after entry of the common law judgment, to remedy frauds, mistakes, accidents, and forgeries with which the common law was procedurally unable (or in later years unwilling) to deal.

The growing disparity in jurisdiction, remedy, and procedure made compromise between law and equity increasingly difficult. By remaining separate, however, law and equity ultimately became locked in a political battle that had little to do with the legal differences between the systems. During the seventeenth century there was an increasing resistance in England to expansive royal power. Although a relatively minor part of the political upheaval that dethroned two monarchs, common law and equity were important symbols in the battle. The common law represented independence from the Crown; its fixed writs, remedies, and procedures, as well as its jury process, were embraced as a buffer against royal prerogative. Common law judges and lawyers were powerful actors in Parliament, which was the seat of political opposition to the King. Equity was everything that the common law was not. The Chancellor was a minister of the Crown; equity's gap-filling of the common law was seen as an effort to increase royal power by marginalizing the common law; looser equitable procedures gave discretion to a royal servant who was thought (often with reason) to be subject to political influence or even corruption.

During the eighteenth century, equity finally emerged as an institution whose power equaled or exceeded that of the common law courts — a victory that was remarkable in view of the triumph of Parliament over the Crown. As Plucknett explains, the reason was simple: "Against Chancery [the common lawyers] had suffered a defeat which was well deserved; their own justice was an inferior product to that of the chancellors." Id. at 197. Although harmonious relations between law and equity were restored (for instance, the Chancellors sometimes referred matters to law for jury trial and law sometimes invoked Chancery jurisdiction to obtain pretrial discovery), the political battles made clear the division between the systems.

At the same time, another influence was driving a wedge between law and equity. As a more mature concept of substantive law developed during the sixteenth century, it became more difficult to hold to the notions that equity was implementing the same sense of justice as law and that the "deficiencies" of law were merely procedural. See Christopher St. Germain, Doctor and Student (c. 1523). English lawyers, however, began to recognize that the substantive principles of law and equity were different as well.

This realization had an indelible effect on equity. In the early phases of equity there was really no sense that the Chancellor's decision in one case acted as a precedent for subsequent cases; each case was determined on its own equities. Now that equity was seen as a system of positive law, it needed to decide whether it would continue to abide by a single principle of equity to decide cases, or develop a more "law-like" set of substantive principles. See William Lambarde, Archeion 46 (Charles H. McIlwain & Paul L. Ward ed. 1957) (1591).

With his famous dictum in Cook v. Fountain, 3 Swanston 585 (1676) ("With such a conscience which is only *Naturalis et interna* this Court has nothing to do; the conscience by which I am to proceed is merely *civilis et politica*, and tied to certain measures; and it is infinitely better for the public that a trust, security or agreement, which is wholly secret, should miscarry than that men should lose their estates by the mere fancy and imagination of a Chancellor"), Lord Nottingham, the Chancellor often called the "Father of Modern Equity," strongly committed equity to the course of fixed, law-like doctrine as opposed to broad equitable discretion. By 1790 Blackstone was able to observe:

> [I]f a court of equity in England did really act as many ingenious writers have supposed it (from theory) to do, it would rise above all law, either common or statute, and be a most arbitrary legislator in every particular.... But the systems of jurisprudence in our courts, both of law and equity, are now equally artificial systems, founded on the same principles of justice and positive law, but varied by different usages in the forms and mode of their proceedings; the one being originally derived (though much reformed and improved) from the feodal customs as they prevailed in different ages in the Saxon and Norman judicatures; the other (but with equal improvements) from the imperial and pontifical formularies introduced by their clerical chancellors.

3 William Blackstone, Commentaries on the Laws of England *432-34 (1790).

S.F.C. Milsom, HISTORICAL FOUNDATIONS OF THE COMMON LAW

94-95 (2d ed. 1981)

The discussion about the relative importance in a legal system of certainty and abstract justice is unending: but it begins at a definite stage of development, namely when the law is first seen as a system of substantive rules prescribing results upon given states of fact. In England this discussion was at once institutionalized: certainty resided in the common law courts, justice in the chancellor's equity. But there were calls for the regularization of equity itself.... What mattered [after the early seventeenth century] was the civil conscience of the court, which was nothing other than a new system of law; and the conscience of the party slowly passed out of consideration. The dialogue between certainty and justice, law and morals, had been acted out in real life; and the end of it was two systems of certainty, two systems of law.

Notes and Questions

1. Whatever equity's failings, its promise was to deliver substantive justice without procedural technicality. Assume for now that this promise is a good thing. To what extent do the descent of common law and equity into rigidity suggest that, however much we might desire a system in which technicalities can be overlooked in the search for substantive justice, it is impossible to maintain a system of procedural and substantive discretion? Or are the histories of the common law and equity sufficiently different from our present situation that we need not worry about the parallels?

Judge Charles Clark, who was a driving force behind the Federal Rules of Civil Procedure, thought that the desire to eliminate procedural rules "substitut[es] aspiration for realistic endeavor." He also noted the tendency of procedural rules, however discretionary, to become increasingly rigid:

> I have suggested a truism that the greater the judge, the more impatient he is with procedure and hence the more likely to come out with a strange procedural principle which does dispose presently of the case before him. . . . It is a serious problem for those who . . . do feel it necessary to labor in the field; for a procedural decision which does terminate unworthy litigation abruptly comes back in its now crystallized form as a rule to plague judicial administration for the future. . . . Unfortunately, by a kind of Gresham's Law, the bad, or harsh, procedural decisions drive out the good, so that in time a rule becomes entirely obscured by its interpretive barnacles. . . .
>
> [I]t appears to be of the essence of procedure that it tends to harden and solidify. This has often been stated, perhaps as succinctly as ever, by . . . Professor Hepburn, in pointing out "the inveterate nature of the incongruity between procedure and substantive law," for "the former petrifies while the latter is in its budding growth," and "the conservatism of the lawyer preserves the incongruity."

Charles E. Clark, *Special Problems in Drafting and Interpreting Procedural Codes and Rules*, 3 Vand. L. Rev. 493, 497-98, 507 (1950).

Do you agree with Judge Clark's pessimistic appraisal about the ability of any discretionary procedural system to maintain itself in the long run? If he is right, then our only alternatives are either to watch our procedural system slowly set into concrete or periodically shake the system up with revolutionary reforms. Neither is especially appealing, is it? Could we steer a middle course in which certainty is constantly tempered by the discretion to do justice? What form might such procedural rules take? Could we aid the chance of their success by relaxing (or eliminating) adversarial process? Or does the history of equity suggest that the entrustment of significant power to judges is the greater evil?

2. The answers you give to these questions have an important impact on the prospect of trans-substantive rules. When a system of absolute procedural discretion exists, trans-substantive procedural rules are impossible. If individualized discretion is impossible to maintain in the long run and if like procedural treatment of like cases is desirable, is there anything to be said for a discretionary procedural system? Conversely, a code of trans-substantive rules, which subjects cases of all types to a single system of procedure, will sometimes frustrate the individualized substantive justice associated with

equity. If the like procedural treatment of like cases prevents "doing justice" in specific cases, is there anything to be said for a trans-substantive code?

Is it possible to make a case for a trans-substantive procedural code on the theory that it has the greater potential to resist the "death by particularization" that Judge Clark describes? Might it be possible to retard the hardening of procedure if we create (as Professor Cover argues (p. 6, *supra*)) presumptively trans-substantive rules sensitive to the justice of particular cases? The possible gains from merging the best of law and equity are great, but the risks of ending up with the undesirable features of both are also great, are they not?

3. Perhaps we should question the assumption that underlies the past two Notes: that achieving substantive justice without tripping over procedural technicalities is a social good. Is it? Doesn't procedure have independent values that also deserve attention? See Chapter 1.A, *supra*. The discretionary, "substantive-justice-only" approach we have ascribed to equity ignores the values that lie behind procedural "technicalities."

4. The balance between law and equity, between rule and discretion, is one of the critical debates of any procedural system. In your opinion, what is the proper balance? We shall frequently recur to this question, and challenge your answer to it, as we see how specific doctrines in complex litigation have sought to resolve this tension.

5. For much of their history, the greatest contrasts between law and equity lay in the areas of procedure and remedy. We have already seen the common law's vices (rigidity, single-issue strait-jacket on complex problems, technicality, inefficiency, lack of pretrial disclosure, jury chicanery, individual injustice, and inadequate remedies) and virtues (certainty, speed, community participation, finality, and independence from the central government). Would the vices and virtues be reversed in a suit in equity?

William Holdsworth, A HISTORY OF ENGLISH LAW

vol. I, 423-28 (1922)

As soon as the business of the court of Chancery began to increase complaints begin to be heard of its defective organization. There is much evidence as to the nature of these defects in the sixteenth and early seventeenth centuries . . . .

It was said in a debate in Parliament in 1623 that 35,000 subpoenas had been issued in one year. This may have been an exaggeration; but it is probable that over 20,000 were issued. It was thus obvious that the work was too much for the Chancellor and the Master of the Rolls. . . . The result was a constantly increasing arrear of causes, and long delays in the administration of justice. This evil was aggravated by the suspicions entertained, not without reason, that the justice when administered was not always pure. Bacon's confession of corruption showed that the Lord Chancellor himself could not always be trusted; and, as we shall now see, matters were much worse in the offices of the court.

The official staff of the court of Chancery was recruited and paid upon exactly the same plan as the official staffs of the courts of common law; and the same results ensued. The officials were appointed for life, and paid by fees upon the business done. Thus, when the business of the court began to increase, the value of these offices rose. . . . It followed that all those who, from their experience of the court, were most competent to reform it, were the most interested in maintaining it in its existing condition. . . .

There were several reasons why this system of appointing and paying officials produced much worse effects in the case of the court of Chancery than in the case of the courts of common law. Firstly, a suit in equity very often lasted very many years. . . . Obviously this gave the officials a great chance of increasing their revenues. . . .

Secondly, the fact that the procedure of the court was wholly written afforded another chance to the official of making money. The suitor was not in a position to object to being compelled to pay for unnecessary copies of unduly lengthened documents. . . .

Thirdly the practice of the court was unsettled, and many of the Chancellors were not competent to settle it. No trouble was taken to distinguish suits which were merely frivolous from those which were real. "Of ten bills," said Norburie, "Hardly three have any colour or shadow of just complaint." Everything was referred to the Masters. Counsel made needless interlocutory motions which entailed new references, commissions to take evidence, or Orders to interrogate the parties. . . . During this period the rules of equity were so vague that enormous scope was left to those who desired to persuade a weak or a corrupt Chancellor.

Fourthly the Chancellor exercised no detailed supervision over his officials. It is true that Chancellors like Bacon or Coventry issued Orders to regulate practice; but they were of little avail. Bacon's Orders of 1618 had specially prohibited general references to the Masters; but Coke in 1621 said that the Chancellor practically made the Masters his deputies by the general character of his references to them.

A tale related by Sir John Branston in his Autobiography is perhaps the best illustration of the effects of the abuses upon the ordinary litigant. He tells us that during the civil war his grandmother had begun a suit in Chancery to recover some tithes to which she was entitled. She died, and he continued the action. The amount in dispute was £4. "It cost, to recover that £4, £200 at least. . . ."

Charles S. Christopher, THE REIGN OF QUEEN VICTORIA: A SURVEY OF FIFTY YEARS OF PROGRESS

Reprinted in 1 Select Essays in Anglo-American Legal History 516, 529 (1907)

At the beginning of January 1839, 556 causes and other matters were waiting to be heard by the Chancellor and Vice-Chancellor. Those at the head of the list . . . had been set down and had been ripe and ready for hearing for about three years. . . . Since in each suit there were on average two hearings, each destined to be separated by a period of something like two years, it was obvious that, even in the most ordinary litigation . . . four years must be wasted in absolute inactivity, and above any delays that might occur in taking accounts or prosecuting inquiries. If, as seemed possible to skilled observers of the day, the Chancellor should prove unable to do more than keep pace with his appellate work, it would be — so they calculated — six years before the last on the list came on for hearing even in its first stage; if a second hearing was required, thirteen or more years would elapse before this was reached; while, if on the final hearing the master's report was successfully objected to, the long process must begin *de novo.* "No man, as things now stand," says in 1839 Mr. George Spence, the author of the well-known work on the equitable jurisdiction of the Court of Chancery, "*can enter into a Chancery suit with any reasonable hope of being alive at its termination, if he has a determined adversary.*"

Notes and Questions

1. The pleading rules of equity also turned out to be woefully deficient. Although it was never as technical as the common law writ, an equity "bill" became increasingly prolix and convoluted. The same was true of the many replies and other pleadings. As Christopher (later Baron Bowen) observed in a different part of his essay, "[n]o layman, however intelligent, could compose the answer [to a bill] without professional aid. It was inevitably so elaborate and long, that the responsibility for the accuracy of the story shifted, during its telling, from the conscience of the defendant to that of his solicitor and counsel, and truth found no difficulty in disappearing during the operation." Id. at 525. A short treatment of equity's pleading rules can be found in Austin W. Scott & Robert B. Kent, Cases and Other Materials on Civil Procedure 116-28 (1967).

2. Extraordinary slowness, incredible expense, lack of finality, enormous power concentrated in a single official who may not be capable of exercising it wisely — these are the vices often attributed to equity. They also sound like the vices that might concern us if we entrusted great power to a judge in complex litigation. Are these vices inherent in any large-scale litigation, or can they be compensated for? The history of equity is relevant to, even if not determinative of, that question.

3. Although the history of equity often focuses on its evils, equity also had positive features. Decisions on the merits rather than on technicalities were more common. Information could be gathered in advance of the decision; "rabbit out of the hat" surprises were rare. The decisionmaker was educated and less likely to be influenced by rhetorical tricks. Decisions were written opinions rather than closed-door verdicts. Remedies were tailored to address the wrongs committed. Multi-party, multi-issue controversies could be dealt with in a complete fashion.

4. On several occasions in these materials we have asked you to consider whether you would rather see the power of decisionmaking located in a judge or a jury. Our procedural history should help us to make a more informed judgment on this issue. With a jury, more rigid issue-narrowing pretrial devices are necessary, and the trial process takes on a flavor of a culminating event. Without a jury, looser pretrial processes are possible, yet the finality of trial

disappears. The jury carries the risk of bamboozlement and intimidation, but the judge carries the risk of raw abuse of power. Can there be a happy medium, or are we simply forced to choose the second worst? In answering this question, you will undoubtedly want to know about the American history of civil procedure and its efforts at reform.

2. American Civil Procedure after the Revolution

Robert W. Millar, CIVIL PROCEDURE OF THE TRIAL COURT IN HISTORICAL PERSPECTIVE

39-42 (1952)

In America, by the opening of the nineteenth century, the crude administration of matters judicial obtaining in the early colonial period . . . has given way to an acceptance more or less complete of the English legal system and with it of English civil procedure. Yet desire for plainer methods, on the one hand, the more pressing because of the undeveloped state of the bar, and a certain jealousy of judicial power, on the other, have produced in the procedure modifications of not inconsiderable moment, the complete history of which even today remains unwritten.

The chancery jurisdiction which was the subject of irregular and intermittent exercise in colonial days . . . is now, for the most part, a regular branch of judicature. Ordinarily, as in the federal judicial system, it is exercised by the same court that has common-law jurisdiction, but as a wholly distinct activity; in certain of the States, however, as in New York, the Court of Chancery is a separate tribunal.

On the common law side, . . . [a]n awakening recognition of the need of discovery in common-law actions has resulted here and there in remedial steps, at first for minor causes as in the case of the South Carolina summary process, later for causes in general, beginning, perhaps, with the Mississippi statute of 1828. Certain jurisdictions (*e.g.*, Connecticut, 1720, 1731) have enlarged the common-law scope of the general issue in particular cases. Moreover, in sundry quarters place has been given to a "brief statement" (*e.g.*, Massachusetts, 1793; Maine, 1831) or notice (*e.g.*, New York, 1801; Massachusetts, 1836) accompanying the general issue, as a substitute for special pleas in bar. . . .

William E. Nelson, AMERICANIZATION OF THE COMMON LAW

78, 87-88 (1975)

By the early nineteenth century, then, the emerging concern in pleading was with substance, not with form. This concern was of great significance, for it compelled the bench and bar to think about law in substantive categories, such as "tort" and "contract," rather than in the old procedural categories of trespass, assumpsit, and the like. . . .

The emergence of substantive categories did far more than merely facilitate the abolition of common law pleading; it transformed the very meaning of law. In the prerevolutionary period, law had been seen merely as a series of writs and procedures manipulated by trained professionals in order to focus questions for resolution by juries in accordance with anticompetitive and other ethical values shared by the community at large. The abolition of common law pleading forced men to abandon such a view of law, while the emergence of a substantive conception forced them to see law as a set of formal standards dictating particular results in particular cases. The new substantive conception thereby forced lawyers arguing in favor of opposite results to a new articulation of the basis of their differences: they could no longer argue about how certain procedures should be manipulated or even about whether those procedures should exist but were forced to debate the question of what values ought to control the disposition of a case.

Notes and Questions

1. The emergence of substance from the shadow of procedure is a step forward for a civilization. But it also has at least one drawback: It makes judges interested in substantive issues, and thus reduces the power of the lay jury. Indeed, the nineteenth century saw a dramatic increase in jury-control devices such as tightened evidentiary rules, denial of the jury's right to decide issues of law (which juries in colonial Massachusetts, for instance, usually had), reclassification of disputes as issues of law rather than issues of fact, and setting aside jury verdicts. See generally Morton Horwitz, The Transformation of American Law 1780-1860 (1977); Note, *The Changing Role of the Jury in the Nineteenth Century*, 74 Yale L.J. 170 (1964). Is the formulation of substantive principles of law worth the price of denigrating the jury's role? Is the jury's ability to decide the terms of the substantive law nonetheless an issue to which procedural systems should be sensitive?

2. One difference between English and American procedure is the system of courts in the United States. Article III of the United States Constitution requires Congress to create a Supreme Court, and also permits Congress to create such lower federal courts as it may "from time to time ordain and establish." Both the lower federal courts, once established, and the Supreme Court are granted original jurisdiction in certain types of cases and controversies. The Supreme Court also enjoys an appellate jurisdiction over those cases not lying within its original jurisdiction, subject to "such Exceptions, and under such Regulations as the Congress shall make." The Constitution does not, however, explicitly prevent state courts from exercising jurisdiction over the types of cases or controversies which lower federal courts can entertain, and Congress rarely makes federal jurisdiction exclusive of the state courts. Hence, it is possible for both state and federal courts to have the jurisdiction to hear a controversy, just as it is possible that more than one state may have the power to hear the controversy.

Nothing in the Constitution mandates that all courts with jurisdiction over a case adopt a single set of procedures to resolve that case. Therefore, the existence of multiple, overlapping courts guaranteed that the American courts would be, albeit unintentionally, a source of procedural innovation. Millar points to some of the early reforms — such as relaxed pleading standards and discovery in actions at law — that later bore fruit in our present procedural system. There were other experiments as well; for instance, several states (mostly in the South) permitted jury trials even in equitable suits. (After passage of the Seventh Amendment, which guaranteed the right of jury trial only in "Suits at common law," this last experiment was not possible in federal court.)

At first, Congress did not put the federal courts at the forefront of procedural experimentation. In equity, Congress provided the Supreme Court with rule-making power as early as 1792; but it was not exercised until 1822, and even then the Supreme Court adopted an incomplete group of rules whose gaps were filled in by traditional equity procedures. In common law cases, Congress required the federal courts to conform to the procedures as of 1789 in the states in which the federal courts were located. There were, however, problems with this type of "static conformity": It did not address the issue of new states admitted later to the Union, and it neglected the fact that the states themselves continually reformed their procedures, so that over time the procedural rules in federal court bore increasingly less resemblance to the procedural rules of the state courts in the same federal district. Congress finally passed the Conformity Act of 1872, which substituted dynamic for static conformity: The federal courts were ordered to use whatever procedural rules were presently operative in the state courts. For a short history of federal procedure in the nineteenth century, see Richard H. Fallon et al., Hart & Wechsler's The Federal Courts and the Federal Court System 656-63 (4th ed. 1996).

3. To what extent does a federal system cure the problem of procedural rigidity? In England, as the local courts were squeezed out and as equity became more "law-like," there was insufficient competition to check the tendency toward technicality. Does the existence of fifty co-equal procedural systems assure procedural regeneration and impede the enslavement of discretion to rule? Or do we end up with fifty sets of hard-and-fast rules?

It seems a reasonable hypothesis that the overlapping system of state and federal courts has the effect of keeping legal rules more flexible. See generally Robert M. Cover, *The Uses of Jurisdictional Redundancy: Ideology, Interest, and Innovation*, 22 Wm. & Mary L. Rev. 639 (1981). If that is so, what should the federal system's role be in the process of developing procedural rules? One concern would be that the demands for conformity of practice within a state (and, in an age of national litigation practices, among states as well) might create pressure on the states to follow the federal system's lead on procedural rules. See John B. Oakley & Arthur F. Coon, *The Federal Rules in State Courts: A Survey of State Court Systems of Civil Procedure*, 61 Wash. L. Rev. 1367 (1986) (23 states have judicially adopted the Federal Rules of Civil Procedure *in toto* and the rules in all but 6 states have been influenced significantly by the Rules). Therefore, national procedural intervention threatens local procedural innovation; and, with no significant competition, federal rules could lead the states down the road of rigidity already traveled by the common law and equity.

This scenario is in no sense inevitable, but it does provide a powerful argument for the type of dynamic conformity which the 1872 Act established. Of course, one of the counter-arguments to dynamic conformity is that, to the extent that federal rights are at stake, the procedures used to adjudicate those rights should be uniform throughout the nation; procedural vagaries should not as a practical matter allow residents of New York to enjoy greater federal rights than residents of California. Dynamic conformity, the argument runs, is an outdated relic in the modern world of extensive federal rights and federal court enforcement of those rights.

Could we have the best of both worlds by adopting uniform procedural rules for claims of federal right, and insisting on dynamic conformity for state-created rights? What happens, though, when a single case includes claims based on both federal and state law? How could you keep the separate procedural rules for the separate claims straight?

4. Because the 1789 Act committed federal courts to outmoded procedural practices at law and the 1872 Act put the federal courts into a procedural lockstep with the states, the states were the only entities likely to initiate significant procedural reform during the 1800's. The most momentous steps occurred between 1846 and 1848, when New York (1) abolished the common law forms of action in favor of more simplified pleadings and more generous rights of joinder, and (2) eliminated the distinction between procedural rules for law and those for equity.

Fleming James, Jr. et al., CIVIL PROCEDURE

19 (4th ed. 1992)

The hardships, delays, and injustices that resulted [from common law procedure] finally led to reform, first in New York State. The movement for it, led by David Dudley Field, culminated in the constitution of 1846 and the Field Code of 1848. The former abolished the court of chancery and paved the way for the merger of law and equity. The code sought to effectuate this merger and abolish the distinctions among the forms of action. It created the civil action in which the parties were to plead the facts constituting the cause of action or defense. The court then was to give judgment according to the law applicable to the facts found.

The code was not intended to change substantive rights or to alter the substantive showing formerly needed for any given remedy. But it was intended to authorize a single court in a single action to draw on the properly applicable rules whether they were formerly denominated legal or equitable, and, if legal, without regard to distinctions among actions. And it was intended to make available *all* the appropriate remedies in that action, even if separate proceedings in law and in equity formerly would have been needed for full relief. The code also sought to liberalize the provisions for joinder of causes and parties.

By 1900 twenty-seven states, particularly west of the Mississippi, had adopted codes having some or all of these features. Others kept the outline of the old system but modified its rigors by various devices such as allowing joinder of different forms of action, or amendment from form to form, or free transfer of cases between law and equity dockets.

Charles E. Clark, HANDBOOK ON THE LAW OF CODE PLEADING

18-19, 29 (1928)

Probably the most important characteristics of the code were the one form of action and the system of pleading the facts. The first remains the crowning achievement of the codes, although in many respects the full benefit of the change has not been completely realized even at the present time. . . . As to the second characteristic, it was planned that the parties should in their pleadings state the facts in simple and concise form. Instead of the *issue pleading* of the common law there was to be *fact pleading*. . . . [T]his part of the plan has worked least successfully of all the reforms made, since the codifiers and the courts failed to appreciate that the difference between statements of fact and statements of law is almost always one of degree only. . . .

If the common law may be termed *issue pleading*, since its main purpose was the framing of an issue, code pleading may be referred to as *fact pleading*, in view of the great emphasis placed under the codes upon getting the facts stated. At present there is advocated what is called *notice pleading*. This is in general a very brief statement, designed merely to give notice to the opponent. . . .

There is not so much a change in the kind of pleadings as a change in emphasis. The common-law pleading both set forth facts and gave notice, but stressed mainly the framing of the issue; the code produced one or more issues and gave notice, but did this while setting forth the facts. So notice pleading, giving some facts, presents a very broad issue.

Notes and Questions

1. The cause of procedural reform in America received a great boost when Great Britain adopted the Judicature Acts of 1873 and 1875. Its rules of joinder and pleading were even simpler and more generous than the Field Code. Law and equity were also brought closer together.

2. Is it as easy to abolish the difference between law and equity as Judge Clark and the code reformers seemed to believe? First of all, there is the problem that a jury right exists for some claims but not for others. As we have seen, the procedural needs in a jury case are different from those in a suit without a jury. In addition, the decisionmaking arrangements between judge and jury needed to be ironed out when factual issues relevant to both the legal claims and the equitable claims were raised.

Second, as a practical matter, how do you merge a system with a tradition of technical pleading, no pretrial discovery, and a final trial event with a system with a tradition of prolix but liberal pleading, written pretrial discovery, and an ongoing decisionmaking process? Remember that common law procedure functioned, in the main, tolerably well for routine cases, and that equity was intended to handle the cases with which the routine procedures of the common law dealt rather poorly. When you stick legal and equitable procedures together, you are going to have to make procedural compromises that are unnecessary or wasteful for a good percentage of the claims merged under a unified code, aren't you?

Third, there is the danger of an even more rapid descent into technicality after the initial set of reforms had taken effect. Joseph Story, for instance, strongly opposed the merger of law and equity, believing that law would lose the beauty of its certainty and equity the beauty of its justice. Story overstated the case, but he had a point. As a single set of substantive principles and a single system of procedure emerged over time, what would keep the merged system from going down the same road to rigidity which neither the common law nor equity had been able to avoid? Would a "new equity" need to spring up as a competitor to the merged system? Is the growth of federal statutory rights and administrative law in this century the law's response to the need for equity?

3. Although the code reformers rejected the common law's strict issue-pleading method of narrowing the case for trial, they were sufficiently captive to its tradition that they did not consider pretrial methods other than pleading to accomplish the narrowing task. The idea of fact pleading was that the pleader was to state the ultimate facts on which each cause of action was based. "Evidentiary" facts and conclusions of law were to be avoided. Unlike the common law, in which pleading rules were designed to narrow the case to a single issue, code pleading permitted multiple causes of action to be joined, and usually allowed only an answer, a counterclaim, and on occasion a reply; thus, multiple issues remained open at the end of the pleading stage. Like the common law, however, no provision was made for pretrial discovery of "evidentiary" facts.

The upshot of these changes was that a party could end up at trial more uncertain about the critical issues and evidence than at common law. Rhetorical skill and quick-wittedness of the lawyers became absolutely crucial to success. Would such a system tend unduly to favor the rich?

4. There were other criticisms of code pleading as well. The Field Code was hardly a model of simplicity and flexibility. In its original form it had nearly 400 sections, and it was incomplete at that. The New York Legislature added many new sections in an effort to clarify ambiguities in the original code. In 1876 it replaced the Field Code with the infamous Throop Code, which was called "reactionary in spirit. . . . Its requirements ran into the most minute and trivial details of practice." Charles M. Hepburn, The Historical Development of Code Pleading in America and England (1897). More and more amendments were added to the Throop Code, so that by 1895, the New York code of civil procedure had expanded to more than 3400 sections!

Penalties for mispleading could be as severe as they were at common law. Unless the pleader stated the ultimate facts on each element of a claim, an opponent could successfully file a demurrer. Consequently, a vast and intricate body of law sprang up around what constituted "ultimate facts," as opposed to mere evidentiary facts and conclusions of law. In retrospect, it seems obvious that the line between evidence, conclusions of fact, and conclusions of law is so thin that pleading defects should have been overlooked — and sometimes they were. But pleading defects could not be entirely ignored.

5. In a different part of his handbook, Clark states the problem of pleading in this way: "The pleader may not know his case before the evidence is produced; and, if he does, he will hardly desire to give it away in advance. His opponent,

and to a certain extent at least, the court will naturally wish to tie him down to a definite declaration before trial." Clark, *supra*, at 151. Is it not the adversary system that encourages lawyers to reveal as little about their own case as possible, and opposing lawyers to use pleading technicalities? Can any procedural reform be successful as long as an adversary system is in place?

Roscoe Pound, who helped to start the wave of twentieth century procedural reform in whose shadow we live, might have been unwilling to concede this point, but he understood that the adversarial system needed to be put on a shorter leash. He proposed a solution to the system's potential for abuse — a solution that would simultaneously exorcize the ghosts of spiraling rigidity and technicality that haunted our history. Beginning with an excerpt from his speech to the 1906 convention of the American Bar Association, we study Pound's efforts to work out the terms of his solution.

Roscoe Pound, THE CAUSES OF POPULAR DISSATISFACTION WITH THE ADMINISTRATION OF JUSTICE

29 A.B.A. Rep. 395 (1906), reprinted in 35 F.R.D. 273, 275, 281 (1964)

The most important and most constant cause of dissatisfaction with all law at all times is to be found in the necessarily mechanical operation of legal rules. This is one of the penalties of uniformity. Legal history shows an oscillation between wide judicial discretion on the one hand and strict confinement of the magistrate by minute and detailed rules upon the other hand. From time to time more or less reversion to justice without law becomes necessary in order to bring the public administration of justice into touch with changed moral, social or political conditions. But such periods of reversion result only in new rules or changed rules. In time the modes of exercising discretion become fixed, the course of judicial action becomes stable and uniform, and the new element, whether custom or equity or natural law becomes as rigid and mechanical as the old. This mechanical action of the law may be minimized, but it cannot be obviated. . . .

A no less potent source of irritation lies in our American exaggeration of the common law contentious procedure. The sporting theory of justice . . . is so rooted in the profession in America that most of us take it for a fundamental legal tenet. . . . So far from being a fundamental fact of jurisprudence, it is peculiar to Anglo-American law; and it has been strongly curbed in modern English practice. With us, it is not merely in full acceptance, it has been developed and its collateral possibilities have been cultivated to the furthest extent. Hence in America we take it as a matter of course that a judge should be a mere umpire, to pass upon objections and hold counsel to the rules of the game, and that the parties should fight out their own game in their own way without judicial interference. We resent such interference as unfair, even when in the interest of justice. The idea that procedure must of necessity be wholly contentious disfigures our judicial administration at every point.

Roscoe Pound, THE DECADENCE OF EQUITY

5 Colum. L. Rev. 20, 36 (1905)

Ihering has told us that we must fight for our law. No less must we fight for equity. Law must be tempered with equity, even as justice with mercy. And if, as some assert, mercy is part of justice, we may say equally that equity is part of law, in the sense that it is necessary to the working of any legal system. We who have the shaping of the law in our hands in this era of the decadence of equity have no less responsibilities than those who pleaded and judged in its founding, its development and its crystallization.

Roscoe Pound, SOME PRINCIPLES OF PROCEDURAL REFORM

4 Ill. L. Rev. 388, 400, 402-03 (1910)

To go back, now to the immediate problem, how shall we make the rules of procedure, rules to help litigants, rules to assist them in getting through the courts, not rules to be made, in the trenchant phrase of Professor Wigmore, "instruments of stratagem for the bar and of logical exercitation for the judiciary?" First of all, I venture to think, we shall do this by making it unprofitable to raise questions of procedure for any purpose except to develop the merits of the cause to the full.... Hence I should propose as the first principles of procedural reform the two following:

I. It should be for the court, in its discretion, not the parties, to vindicate rules of procedure intended solely to provide for the orderly dispatch of business, saving of public time, and maintenance of the dignity of tribunals; and such discretion should be reviewable only for abuse.

II. Except as they exist for the saving of public time and maintenance of the dignity of tribunals, so that the parties should not be able to insist as of right upon enforcement of them, rules of procedure should exist only to secure to all parties a fair opportunity to meet the case against them and a full opportunity to present their own case; and nothing should depend on or be obtainable through them except the securing of such opportunity.

Next in importance to the two principles just stated, but second to them only, I should put the following:

III. A practice act should deal only with the general features of procedure and prescribe the general lines to be followed, leaving details to be fixed by rules of court, which the courts may change from time to time as actual experience of their application and operation dictates.

Notes and Questions

1. Pound believed that there was a science of judicial administration, and that procedure, which he also called "adjective law," should never be used to

frustrate resolution on the substantive merits. To what extent was Pound merely echoing the ideals of Bracton and the medieval Chancellors? Pound's description of the state of the bar in 1906 sounds a lot like Plucknett's criticism of medieval common lawyers (p. 33-34, *supra*). Why did Pound think that we could be more successful in resisting the temptations of the *rigor juris* than they were? Learned Hand was more skeptical:

> The truth is that no rules in the end will help us. We shall succeed in making our results conform with our professions only by a change of heart in ourselves. It is hard to expect lawyers who are half litigants to forgo the advantages which come from obscuring the case and supporting contentions which they know to be false. . . .
>
> And still at times I can have the hope that in America time may at length mitigate our fierce individualism . . . . If through some such conversion we can be taught to abate the intensity of our own wills, to subject our desires to what has been laid down for us, even when we dislike or distrust it, then in this which seems so trivial and minor a detail, the management of our private disputes, we may succeed. But not, I fear, short of something like that; we are made all of a piece, and the cloven hoof will show however well the bestial heart be covered.

Learned Hand, *The Deficiencies of Trials to Reach the Heart of the Matter*, in Lectures on Legal Topics 1921-1922 87, 104, 106 (1926). If Hand is correct, is the benefit of Pound's procedure worth the sacrifice of our national and professional character? Or has our character so changed in the past seventy years that Pound's ideals are now feasible?

2. Pound's solution was to pin his hopes on the generality of procedural rules and the wisdom of trial judges who could overlook procedural technicalities and come to the merits of the controversy. Given that judges are drawn from the ranks of practicing lawyers whose adversarial training makes them expert in procedure, is this a realistic view? Is the process of judging a science, as Pound believed, or an art form? How can we invest judges with discretion and not expect them to manipulate procedural rules to achieve substantive goals? Moreover, we should not accept Pound's discretion-laden judge without considering the costs. Our history of equity has revealed some of these costs. We will see others as we progress through the book.

3. "[T]he controlling reason for a systematic and scientific adjective law," Pound stated in another passage from *Some Principles*, "must be to insure precision, uniformity, and certainty in the judicial application of substantive law." How can broad equitable rules whose details the courts may change case-by-case "insure precision, uniformity, and certainty"?

4. Didn't Pound neglect the existence of procedural values that deserve protection even though they frustrate a resolution "on the merits"? In overlooking procedural concerns such as treating like cases alike, participation, dignitary enhancement, and efficient use of limited court resources, he staked out a radically different position for procedure. Wasn't he also rather wistful? Remember that Judge Clark thought such enterprises "substitut[ed] aspiration for realistic endeavor" (p. 43, *supra*).

5. It is easier to suggest reform than to execute it. How were Pound's concepts to be translated into definite form? Should a defendant have ten days to answer a complaint? Twenty? Should the time lie entirely within the judge's discretion? If Pound was right, then what would be wrong with a procedural

code that was two rules long, the first rule being Pound's first principle of procedural reform and the second rule being his second principle? Even Pound was unwilling to go that far. Why?

6. Pound's call to reform bore important fruit in 1912, when the Supreme Court revised the Federal Equity Rules for the first time in seventy years. The Rules sought to combine the best aspects of common law and equity, and to avoid their deficiencies. In order to avoid the dual problems of prolixity and rigidity, technical forms of pleadings were abolished; a "short and plain statement" of jurisdiction, and a "short and simple statement of the ultimate facts upon which the plaintiff asks relief" usually sufficed for the plaintiff, while an answer which "in short and simple terms set out his defense" and specifically admitted or denied specific allegations sufficed for the defendant. Joinder of all claims against a defendant was permitted; joinder of parties and actions by class representatives were also allowed in some cases. A system of pretrial disclosure permitted discovery of documents, interrogatories, and, in "good and exceptional" instances, depositions. The rules followed the common law tradition and required that testimony of witnesses be taken in open court. See 226 U.S. 627, 649-73 (1912).

If these rules sound vaguely familiar, they should. They became the model for the Federal Rules of Civil Procedure.

3. American Procedure from 1938 to the Present: Living in the Shadow of the Federal Rules of Civil Procedure

The Federal Equity Rules could not be applied to the courts' larger common law jurisdiction, to which the Conformity Act of 1872 still applied. The work of the next generation of procedural reformers was to persuade Congress to repeal the Conformity Act and allow the federal courts to promulgate rules of procedure in all cases. The long struggle to enact such a statute is recounted in an excellent article. See Stephen B. Burbank, *The Rules Enabling Act of 1934*, 130 U. Pa. L. Rev. 1015 (1982),

Congress finally responded with the Rules Enabling Act of 1934, 48 Stat. 1064 (codified as subsequently amended at 28 U.S.C. § 2072). In language reminiscent of the Field Code, the Rules Enabling Act permitted the Supreme Court to "unite the general rules prescribed by it for cases in equity with those in actions at law so as to secure one form of civil action and procedure for both." It also mandated that "[s]aid rules shall neither abridge, enlarge, nor modify the substantive rights of any litigant." In a sense, Pound and his followers had won: The substance of a dispute would no longer influence the procedure, and the procedure would not influence the substance. The challenge was to construct a system that met both parameters. The drafters's work was not always easy. See Burbank, *supra*; Judith Resnik, *Failing Faith: Adjudicatory Procedure in Decline*, 53 U. Chi. L. Rev. 494 (1986). In 1938, the Federal Rules of Civil Procedure ultimately emerged.

Stephen N. Subrin, HOW EQUITY CONQUERED COMMON LAW: THE FEDERAL RULES OF CIVIL PROCEDURE IN HISTORICAL PERSPECTIVE

135 U. Pa. L. Rev. 909, 922-25, 974 (1987)

In the twentieth century, Federal Rules proponents emphasized that they were not suggesting new procedures. They rather insisted that they were just combining the best and most enlightened rules adopted elsewhere. For the most part the proponents were right, but their argument ignores the implications of their choices regarding what the "best" rules were. The underlying philosophy of, and procedural choices embodied in, the Federal Rules were almost universally drawn from equity rather than common law. The expansive and flexible aspects of equity are all implicit in the Federal Rules. Before the rules, equity procedure and jurisprudence historically had applied to only a small percentage of the totality of litigation. Thus the drafters made an enormous change: in effect the tail of historic adjudication was now wagging the dog.

The result is played out in the Federal Rules in a number of different but interrelated ways: ease of pleading; broad joinder; expansive discovery; greater judicial power and discretion; flexible remedies; latitude for lawyers; control over juries; reliance on professional experts; reliance on documentation; and disengagement of substance, procedure, and remedy. This combination of procedural factors contributes to a procedural system and view of the law that markedly differs from either a combined common law and equity system or the nineteenth century procedural code system. The norms and attitudes borrowed from equity define our current legal landscape: expansion of legal theories, law suits, and, consequently, litigation departments; enormous litigation costs; enlarged judicial discretion; and decreased jury power. . . .

When one looks at the disgruntlement over unwieldy cases, uncontrolled discovery, unrestrained attorney latitude, and judicial discretion, . . . the pattern is clear. These are not the complaints about the rigor and inflexibility associated with the common law, but the opposite. The symptoms sound like what one would expect from an all-equity procedural system. The praise for modern litigation as a creator of new rights essential for a humane society is also consonant with this diagnosis.

Jay Tidmarsh, UNATTAINABLE JUSTICE: THE FORM OF COMPLEX LITIGATION AND THE LIMITS OF JUDICIAL POWER

60 Geo. Wash. L. Rev. 1683, 1743-1747 (1992)

In the United States, although the procedures among federal and state courts are hardly uniform, a set of seven shared assumptions has generated a largely homogenous set of rules whose differences (at least in comparison to Continental or Asian systems of procedure) are far less striking than their similarities. The assumptions are "case or controversy," due process, adversarialism, jury trial of cases at law, post-pleading formulation of issues, "transactionalism," and "trans-substantivism."

The first five assumptions are obvious to anyone who has sat through a basic course in civil procedure. The "case or controversy" requirement of Article III of the United States Constitution, together with prudential considerations of standing, ripeness, and mootness, restrict access to federal courts to those persons who have an actual stake in the outcome of a dispute, and bar advisory opinions. The second assumption, due process, is the cornerstone of American procedure. The Due Process Clause, first and foremost, demands that affected persons receive adequate notice and the opportunity to participate in adjudicatory decisions that directly impinge on their rights to life, liberty, or property; a failure of notice and opportunity to be heard eliminates the preclusive effect of any earlier decisions reached in the person's absence. Second, the Clause acts as a limitation on the territorial power of state sovereigns over the person and property of those located elsewhere. Third, due process requires that the decisionmaker use reasoned judgment in arriving at the decision. Fourth, the Clause expresses a preference for those procedures that minimize the sum of litigation costs and error costs. Finally, the Clause expresses a preference for adversarial proceedings.

Even though the third assumption, adversarialism, is to some extent dictated by due process, American procedure has embraced the adversarial model even beyond the bounds of constitutional requirement. . . . Although adversarialism always has been tempered by the need for judicial power to prevent unfettered gamesmanship, the power may be exercised only within a narrow range that keeps the playing field level.

The next assumption — jury trial in cases at law — represents another constitutional cornerstone of American procedure. The form of adjudication does not itself specify the nature of the decisionmaker. The Seventh Amendment of the United States Constitution, like similar provisions in state constitutions, fills the void by dividing the adjudicatory function between judges and juries.

The fifth assumption of American procedure rejects the common law's devotion to pleading as the process for the definition of issues. Recognizing that there must be some way to narrow a dispute to the relevant questions of law and fact, however, modern procedure requires less specific pleadings, followed by an opportunity for the parties to narrow issues and eliminate meritless claims through pretrial informational disclosures that "discover" the true nature of the opponent's case. The requirement of disclosure conflicts, of course, with the strict adversarial ethic; the resulting accommodation allows discovery of information about the factual occurrences in the dispute while protecting attorney advice, attorney impressions, and other materials prepared in anticipation of litigation.

The final two assumptions are less widely known. A reaction against the common law's use of the writ as the unit around which to organize a lawsuit, "transactionalism" holds that the unit around which a lawsuit should be organized is the transaction or series of factual events that give rise to the claim(s) of legal entitlement. Although the writ system's focus on the plaintiff's personal legal entitlement made joinder of other affected parties largely unnecessary and therefore exceedingly difficult, the transactional approach requires rules that also permit the joinder of other persons affected by the same series of events. Thus, transactionalism contemplates the broad joinder of claims, defenses, and parties whenever the event giving rise to the dispute implicates them.

Finally, the Federal Rules of Civil Procedure aspire to be a "trans-substantive" procedural system. Again a rejection of common law procedure, "trans-substantivism" requires that the same set of rules be applicable to all cases; there are no longer separate rules for tort cases, contract cases, and equitable claims. Trans-substantivism, which can perhaps best be summarized by the phrase "all cases treated procedurally alike," does not require precise equivalence of procedures in all cases; rather, it requires that the procedural differences that inevitably occur among cases not influence the outcome of the case. Necessarily, therefore, trans-substantivism implies a certain amount of discretion. . . . Given the infinite patterns of claim and party joinder possible under transactionalism, trans-substantivism appears to work optimally with a set of "general," "loosely textured" rules in which judges have the discretion to shape procedures to ensure that the rules do not unduly influence the outcomes of cases.

Notes and Questions

1. The Federal Rules of Civil Procedure immediately took up the invitation of Congress to abolish the division between law and equity. Rule 2 provides: "There shall be one form of action known as 'civil action.'"

2. Professor Subrin is correct in asserting that the Federal Rules of Civil Procedure were based largely on equity; with the exception of an expansion of deposition rights, the 1938 Federal Rules of Civil Procedure looked remarkably similar to the 1912 Federal Equity Rules. But the 1912 rules were very different from traditional equity practice; the 1912 rules had been greatly influenced (especially with respect to pleading requirements, the allowance of live testimony, and a single trial) by common law procedure, code pleading, and notice pleading. Thus, Subrin's claim that the 1938 Rules were "all-equity" is somewhat overstated. But he is correct in noting the irony of the Rules' heavy reliance on equitable procedure: Procedures designed for the case in which run-of-the-mill process is inadequate were inverted into the norm for all cases.

3. Equity's influence is apparent in the Federal Rules in other ways as well. For example, Subrin identifies nearly 30 (out of 83 in total) rules which lend themselves to or explicitly provide for the use of judicial discretion. Two dimensions of this more powerful judge deserve present attention. First, judicial discretion in matters of procedure threatens to wreak havoc with the trans-substantive aspirations of a procedural code. The reason is simple: When a judge is given the discretion to create case-specific procedures, the like procedural treatment of like cases becomes nearly impossible to achieve. See Stephen B. Burbank, *Of Rules and Discretion: The Supreme Court, Federal*

Rules and Common Law, 63 Notre Dame L. Rev. 693 (1988). Second, the more powerful judge also creates a tension with the adversarial ideal. Adversarialism posits a neutral arbiter who umpires a fight conducted by others; judicial discretion makes judges active players in shaping the basic terms of the fight.

If these observations are accurate, do they suggest that the judge contemplated by the Federal Rules of Civil Procedure is unwise? Or that it is unwise for us to preserve trans-substantivism and adversarialism? Is it possible in the long run to sustain the Federal Rules, which sought to create a trans-substantive, adversarial, *and* discretionary procedural system?

4. If the Federal Rules have tipped too far in the direction of equity, what sort of procedures would bring them back toward the middle? Greater pleading requirements with reduced opportunities for discovery? Limitations on party and issue joinder? Stronger summary procedures to narrow issues? Would the adversarial system find a way to turn these rules into an unacceptably rigid code? Should we therefore head in the other direction and give trial judges *more* discretion to define and narrow issues? How does this latter proposal square with the Seventh Amendment's right to jury trial for non-equitable claims?

5. To what extent might the problems that Subrin claims to have been caused by the 1938 Rules be the result of non-procedural factors such as increasing complexity of law, concentration of power in large institutions, and importance of rights in the modern state? Should a procedural code try to counterbalance those factors or foster their development?

6. What is your long-range prognosis for the litigation system that the Federal Rules established? You can check your intuition against those contained in symposia. See Symposium, *A Duty-Oriented Procedure in a Rights-Oriented Society*, 63 Notre Dame L. Rev. 597 (1988); Symposium, *The Fiftieth Anniversary of the Federal Rules of Civil Procedure*, 62 St. John's L. Rev. 399 (1988); Symposium, *The 50th Anniversary of the Federal Rules of Civil Procedure, 1938-88*, 137 U. Pa. L. Rev. 1873 (1989); Symposium, *The Future of Federal Litigation*, 50 U. Pitt. L. Rev. 701 (1989); Symposium, *Issues in Civil Procedure: Advancing the Dialogue*, 69 B.U. L. Rev. 597 (1988); Symposium, *Modern Civil Procedure: Issues in Controversy*, 54 Law & Contemp. Prob. 1 (Summer 1991); Symposium, *Reinventing Civil Litigation: Evaluating Proposals for Change*, 59 Brook. L. Rev. 655 (1993); Symposium, *Turbulence in the Federal Rules of Civil Procedure: The 1993 Amendments and Beyond*, 14 Rev. Litig. 1 (1994).

7. The Federal Rules of Civil Procedure are the offspring of two divergent trends in our own history: law and equity. The hope was to create a procedural system with all of the strengths of law and equity and none of their weaknesses. The fear was that the Rules might end up with all of the weaknesses of law and equity and none of their strengths. Complex litigation, in which deficiencies and successes are likely to be revealed most dramatically, becomes our vehicle for finding out whether the hopes or fears were more accurate.

C. PROCEDURAL SYSTEMS IN PRACTICE: A COMPARATIVE PERSPECTIVE

Procedural systems around the world provide another source of information about the benefits and costs of departing from adversarialism in complex cases. We begin our tour right here, in the United States, with Professor Chayes' famous description of "public law litigation." As Chayes demonstrates, in public law cases, our system operates differently than we might have been led to believe from our historical study of American procedure. Next, we look at our system's closest procedural cousin, the British system. From there we move to the European continent and South America to examine traditional civil law procedural systems. Finally, we look at the socialist procedural systems of the former Soviet Union and the People's Republic of China.

1. Alternative Adversary Systems

a. In the United States — Public Law Litigation

Abram Chayes, THE ROLE OF THE JUDGE IN PUBLIC LAW LITIGATION

89 Harv. L. Rev. 1281, 1282-84, 1288-90, 1292-94, 1296-98, 1302, 1315-16 (1976)

In our received tradition, the lawsuit is a vehicle for settling disputes between private parties about private rights. The defining features of this conception of civil adjudication are:

(1) The lawsuit is *bipolar*. Litigation is organized as a contest between two individuals or at least two unitary interests diametrically opposed, to be decided on a winner-takes-all basis.

(2) Litigation is *retrospective*. The controversy is about an identified set of completed events: whether they occurred and if so, with what consequences for the legal relations of the parties.

(3) *Right and remedy are interdependent*. The scope of the relief is derived more or less logically from the substantive violation under the general theory that the plaintiff will get compensation measured by the harm caused by the defendant's breach of duty — in contract by giving plaintiff the money he would have had absent the breach; in tort by paying the value of the damage caused.

(4) The lawsuit is a *self-contained* episode. The impact of the judgment is confined to the parties. If plaintiff prevails there is a simple compensatory transfer, usually of money, but occasionally the return of a thing or the performance of a definite act. If defendant prevails, a loss lies where it has fallen. In either case, entry of judgment ends the court's involvement.

(5) The process is *party-initiated* and *party-controlled*. The case is organized and the issues defined by exchanges between the parties. Responsibility for fact development is theirs. The trial judge is a

neutral arbiter of their interactions who decides questions of law only if they are put in issue by an appropriate move of a party. . . .

Whatever its historical validity, the traditional model is clearly invalid as a description of much current civil litigation in the federal district courts. Perhaps the dominating characteristic of modern federal litigation is that lawsuits do not arise out of disputes between private parties about private rights. Instead, the object of litigation is the vindication of constitutional or statutory policies. The shift in the legal basis of the lawsuit explains many, but not all, facets of what is going on "in fact" in federal trial courts. For this reason, although the label is not wholly satisfactory, I shall call the emerging model "public law litigation." . . .

II. THE PUBLIC LAW LITIGATION MODEL

A. *The Demise of the Bipolar Structure*

Joinder of parties, which was strictly limited at common law, was verbally liberalized under the codes to conform with the approach of equity calling for joinder of all parties having an "interest" in the controversy. The codes, however, did not at first produce much freedom of joinder. Instead, the courts defined the concept of "interest" narrowly to exclude those without an independent legal right to the remedy to be given in the main dispute. . . . The proponents of "efficiency" argued for a more informal and flexible approach, to the end that the courts should not have to rehear the same complex of events. This argument ultimately shifted the focus of the lawsuit from legal theory to factual context — the "transaction or occurrence" from which the action arose. This in turn made it easier to view the set of events in dispute as giving rise to a range of legal consequences all of which ought to be considered together.

This more open-ended view of the subject matter of the litigation fed back upon party questions and especially intervention. Here, too, the sharp constraints dictated by the right-remedy nexus give way. And if the right to participate in litigation is no longer determined by one's claim to relief at the hands of another party or one's potential liability to satisfy the claim, it becomes hard to draw the line determining those who may participate so as to eliminate anyone who is or might be significantly (a weasel word) affected by the outcome — and the latest revision of the Federal Rules of Civil Procedure has more or less abandoned the attempt. . . .

B. *The Triumph of Equity*

One of the most striking procedural developments of this century is the increasing importance of equitable relief. . . . [T]he old sense of equitable remedies as "extraordinary" has faded. . . .

At this point, right and remedy are pretty thoroughly disconnected. The form of relief does not flow ineluctably from the liability determination, but is fashioned ad hoc. In the process, moreover, right and remedy have been to some extent transmuted. The liability determination is not simply a pronouncement of the legal consequences in a way that accommodates the range of interests involved....

At the same time, the breadth of interests that may be affected by public law litigation raises questions about the adequacy of the representation afforded by a plaintiff whose interest is narrowly traditional.

C. *The Changing Character of Factfinding* . . .

In public law litigation, . . . factfinding is principally concerned with "legislative" rather than "adjudicative" fact. And "fact evaluation" is perhaps a more accurate term than "factfinding." The whole process begins to look like the traditional description of legislation: Attention is drawn to a "mischief," existing or threatened, and the activity of the parties and court is directed to the development of on-going measures designed to cure that mischief. . . .

The courts, it seems, continue to rely primarily on the litigants to produce and develop factual materials, but a number of factors make it impossible to leave the organization of the trial exclusively in their hands. With the diffusion of the party structure, fact issues are no longer sharply drawn in a confrontation between two adversaries, one asserting the affirmative and the other the negative. The litigation is often extraordinarily complex and extended in time, with a continuous and intricate interplay between factual and legal elements. It is hardly feasible and, absent a jury, unnecessary to set aside a contiguous block of time for a "trial stage" at which all significant factual issues will be presented. The scope of the fact investigation and the sheer volume of factual material that can be exhumed by the discovery process pose enormous problems of organization and assimilation. All these factors thrust the trial judge into an active role in shaping, organizing and facilitating the litigation. We may not yet have reached the investigative judge of the continental systems, but we have left the passive arbiter of the traditional model a long way behind.

D. *The Decree*

The centerpiece of the emerging public law model is the decree. It differs in almost every relevant characteristic from relief in the traditional model of adjudication, not the least in that it *is* the centerpiece. The decree seeks to adjust future behavior, not to compensate for past wrong. It is deliberately fashioned rather than logically deduced from the nature of the legal harm suffered. It provides for a complex, on-going regime of performance rather than a simple, one-shot, one-way transfer. Finally, it prolongs and deepens, rather than terminates, the court's involvement with the dispute. . . .

E. *A Morphology of Public Law Litigation*

The public law litigation model portrayed in this paper reverses many of the crucial characteristics and assumptions of the traditional concept of adjudication:

(1) The scope of the lawsuit is not exogenously given but is shaped primarily by the court and parties.

(2) The party structure is not rigidly bilateral but sprawling and amorphous.

(3) The fact inquiry is not historical and adjudicative but predictive and legislative.

(4) Relief is not conceived as compensation for past wrong in a form logically derived from the substantive liability and confined in its impact to the immediate parties; instead, it is forward looking, fashioned ad hoc on flexible and broadly remedial lines, often having important consequences for many persons including absentees.

(5) The remedy is not imposed but negotiated.

(6) The decree does not terminate judicial involvement in the affair: its administration requires the continuing participation of the court.

(7) The judge is not passive, his function limited to analysis and statement of governing legal rules; he is active, with responsibility not only for credible fact evaluation but for organizing and shaping the litigation to ensure a just and viable outcome.

(8) The subject matter of the lawsuit is not a dispute between private individuals about private rights, but a grievance about the operation of public policy. . . .

IV. Some Thoughts on Legitimacy

More fundamentally, our transformed appreciation of the whole process of making, implementing, and modifying law in a public law system points to sources other than professional method and role for the legitimacy of the new model lawsuit. As we now begin to see it, that process is plastic and fluid. Popular participation in it is not alone through the vote or by representation in the legislature. And judicial participation is not by way of sweeping and immutable statements of *the* law, but in the form of a continuous and rather tentative dialogue with other political elements — Congress and the executive, administrative agencies, the profession and the academics, the press and wider publics. Bentham's "judge and company" has become a conglomerate. In such a setting, the ability of a judicial pronouncement to sustain itself in the dialogue and the power of judicial action to generate assent over the long haul become the ultimate touchstones of legitimacy. . . .

In my view, judicial action only achieves such legitimacy by responding to, indeed by stirring, the deep and durable demand for justice in our society.

Notes and Questions

1. Professor Chayes was well aware of Fuller's *Forms and Limits* (p. 13, *supra*) when he wrote his article on public law litigation; indeed, the "bipolar"

model of litigation that Chayes critiques sounds remarkably like the adjudicatory model that Fuller advocated. Do Chayes' observations about public law litigation convince you that Fuller's claim about the form of adjudication is wrong? Or does Fuller's claim convince you that Chayes' public law model is illegitimate, and, assuming that it states the present reality, should be abandoned? Cf. Robert G. Bone, *Lon Fuller's Theory of Adjudication and the False Dichotomy between Dispute Resolution and Public Law Models of Litigation*, 75 B.U. L. Rev. 1273 (1995) (arguing that the views of Fuller and Chayes can be reconciled).

2. Chayes does not inject any new players into the litigation, but his model does shift the roles assigned to the players by the traditional adversarial model. In particular, the judicial role which Chayes ascribes to the public law judge differs in important ways from the decisionmaker on which the adversarial system is founded. The adversarial system expects the decisionmaker to be neutral, unbiased, and utterly passive — a *tabula rasa* on which the parties write their versions of the law and facts. In contrast, the public law judge becomes intimately involved in the discovery of evidence, the shaping of issues, the compromise of legal interests, and the implementation of remedies. In each of these tasks, the judge takes power from the lawyers (who gather evidence and shape issues in the traditional model), the jury (which finds the facts at trial), and the parties (who implement the remedy). Is it possible for a judge to maintain neutrality of judgment when she is involved in these aspects of a case?

There might also be problems regarding the public law judge's incentives to probe deeply into the evidence; the public law judge has many cases to decide, and only limited time to devote to any given one. An alternative might be to appoint or elect many more judges, but that solution has its own difficulties. The first is a potential dilution in the quality of the bench; a second is the lack of training or expertise of many American judges in the tasks which the public law judge must perform. Moreover, do you want a society with a large professional judiciary, including the bureaucracy that it would entail?

The public law judge also wrests control of the case from the parties. Entirely apart from the greater incentives which your lawyer might have, wouldn't you rather have your own lawyer shape a transaction that is likely to be of importance to you? Don't you feel as though you have participated more in the process? Aren't you more likely to accept an adverse outcome?

Finally, there are concerns about whether the public law judge can serve as an adequate check on government power. Judges are, after all, government officials, and their extensive involvement in cases threatens to turn them into bureaucrats whose reputation and advancement might depend on their abilities to achieve political compromise rather than their abilities to preside neutrally over a confrontation. Can such officials be counted on to identify novel or expansive rights against the government? Professor Fiss is dubious:

> A judge deeply involved in the reconstruction of a school system or prison is likely to lose much of his distance from the organization. He is likely to identify with the organization he is reconstructing, and this process of identification is likely to deepen as the enterprise of organizational reform moves through several cycles of supplemental relief, drawn out over a number of years. There is, however, a deeper and more pervasive threat to judicial independence, one that turns . . . on the desire of the judge

represented by the very attempt to give a remedy, any remedy — the desire to be efficacious.

Judges are not all powerful. They can decree some results but not all. Some results depend on forces beyond their control. . . . Judges realize that practical success vitally depends on the preferences, the will of the body politic.

This perception of dependence has obvious and important implications for the remedy: no judge is likely to decree more than he thinks he has the power to accomplish. . . . He will strive to lessen the gap between declaration and actualization. He will tailor the right to fit the remedy.

Owen M. Fiss, *Foreword: The Forms of Justice*, 93 Harv. L. Rev. 1, 53-54 (1979). For a more thoroughgoing critique of the activist judge, see Judith Resnik, *Managerial Judges*, 96 Harv. L. Rev. 374 (1982).

3. Chayes also states that the trial is no longer the centerpiece of public law litigation. As we shall soon see, the notion of a trial as a culminating, definitive event is peculiarly Anglo-American; in most systems, "trials" occur continuously throughout the litigation as specific factual and legal issues are resolved seriatim. The continuous trial method makes the use of a civil jury nearly impossible, for it is too disruptive to recall average citizens for a few weeks at a time over a period of several years. Because juries are typically required only in actions at law, juries were not involved in the type of equitable public law cases that Chayes described. Wouldn't expanding the public law litigation model to complex cases at law require that we abandon the single trial and the civil jury as we now know them? See generally Richard L. Marcus, *Completing Equity's Conquest? Reflections on the Future of Trial under the Federal Rules of Civil Procedure*, 50 U. Pitt. L. Rev. 725 (1989). Perhaps we could have two procedural systems: one a single-trial, jury-dominated system for private law cases and the other a continuous-trial, judge-dominated system for public law cases. Or perhaps not: Recall the value of trans-substantivite procedure, and our recent escape from the separate systems of law and equity that operated, respectively, as a single-trial, jury-dominated system and a continuous-trial, judge-dominated system.

4. Is Chayes correct that public law judging is on the rise and gathering momentum? See Abram Chayes, *Foreword: Public Law Litigation and the Burger Court*, 96 Harv. L. Rev. 4 (1982) (although hostile to public law model, Supreme Court was nonetheless engaged in some public law judging); Thomas D. Rowe, Jr., *No Final Victories: The Incompleteness of Equity's Triumph in Federal Public Law*, 56 Law & Contemp. Prob. 105 (Summer 1993) (public law model has been stymied by stingy interpretations of jurisdictional doctrines). Assuming that Chayes is right, at least in part, what gives the judge the authority to assert greater power? Chayes suggests that the judge's power is legitimate vis-á-vis the legislature, but how can her "power grab" be defended vis-á-vis the lawyers, the parties, and the jury? Put another way, can the departure from the adversarial system's judicial role be defended normatively? In answering that question, we are unavoidably drawn back to the theoretical issues of the first section, aren't we?

Chayes' enthusiastic description of public law judging largely overlooks the costs of using greater judicial power to remedy the failings of the lawyers, the parties, and the jury. Keep some of these costs in mind as you read about alternatives to the American adversary system.

b. In Britain

Like the American system, the British system is premised on an adversarial process. There are, however, notable differences. In Great Britain, the pleading process is briefer and more specific. Depositions of witnesses are not allowed; the pretrial period is almost entirely a written, documentary process. Unlike the United States, the pretrial process is routinely overseen by a "master" rather than by the trial judge herself. The master attempts to prepare the case for trial or to facilitate settlement by ruling on interlocutory requests for interrogatories, the discovery of documents, and proposed amendments to the pleadings.

Another difference between the systems involves the delivery of legal services. In Britain, trial is typically conducted by trial specialists, called barristers, and not by the lawyers, called solicitors, who control the pretrial process. This arrangement creates a different adversarial dynamic:

> [T]he barrister is insulated from the case in several important ways. An English barrister has no continuing relation with any client; his fee is fixed before trial in negotiations to which he is not a party and on a basis unrelated to eventual victory or defeat; the case is placed with a barrister through a solicitor as intermediary; and barristers as a group are small in number, aristocratic, clannish, and closely tied to the judiciary. The barrister thus is strongly identified as an officer of the court and as a gatekeeper concerning what kind of evidence will be offered.

Geoffrey C. Hazard, Jr., Ethics in the Practice of Law 131 (1978).

Trials in England, like America, are a single event consisting primarily of oral testimony. Unlike her American counterpart, however, the English trial judge often plays an active role in questioning the parties and may even initiate lines of questioning. Moreover, English civil trials today are less affected than American trials by strict rules of evidence, largely because the civil jury has all but disappeared in England.

English courts routinely allow appeals from civil judgments and, like their American counterparts, appellate courts will ordinarily not receive new evidence or disturb the factual findings of trial courts. See Mary A. Glendon et al., Comparative Legal Traditions 609-27, 655-70 (2d ed. 1994).

In one way, however, the British system remains more adversarial than ours: the relative absence of the activist, public law judge.

Jerold L. Waltman, JUDICIAL ACTIVISM IN ENGLAND

Reprinted in Judicial Activism in Comparative Perspective 34-35 (Kenneth M. Holland ed. 1991)

The major barrier to judicial activism is the constitutional system itself, based on the fact of an unwritten constitution and Parliamentary sovereignty. Absent a written statement of fundamental law, there is no standard against which to measure ordinary legislation. The type of activism which eagerly overturns laws enacted by majorities in legislative bodies, much less the kind which finds "rights" in a constitution and orders government to fulfill them, is simply out of the question. . . .

Reinforcing these constitutional theories have been twentieth century British ideas about democracy. The Labour Party has long been wedded to an ideology which emphasized the concept of a mass movement. . . . Conservatives, on the other hand, believed that popular participation served primarily as a check on the actions of the country's leaders. . . . While contrasting sharply, these two ideologies nonetheless converge in vesting enormous authority in the central institutions of government, and leave little scope for meaningful judicial authority, either as a check on power or as an initiator of policy.

Furthermore, strands of the political and legal culture are hostile to judicial activism. Caution and reverence for tradition have long been deeply embedded in the political culture, militating against radical departures in any area of public life. Judges, moreover, were drawn overwhelmingly, indeed almost exclusively, from segments of society in which these outlooks and habits of mind were even more prevalent than in the population as a whole. . . . English judges, in short, were the least likely people imaginable to go on any sort of change-inducing crusade.

Notes and Questions

1. Professor Waldman notes that British courts have become increasingly active in seeking to hold administrative agencies accountable for their misfeasance. But that activism has not spilled over into areas such as civil liberties, protection of minorities, and economic litigation. Moreover, even in administrative law, "English activism hardly even approaches a threshold that might bear that name" when measured against other Western democracies.

The reasons that the British have been reluctant to become more judicially active apparently have not influenced other Commonwealth countries such as Canada and Australia. See Carl Baar, *Judicial Activism in Canada*, and Brian Galligan, *Judicial Activism in Australia*, both reprinted in Judicial Activism in Comparative Perspective (Kenneth M. Holland ed. 1991).

2. If we assume that the only way to handle public law litigation successfully is to increase judicial power (which is admittedly a premise on which people might disagree), are you willing to sacrifice public law litigation in order to save the adversarial ideal? Put differently, can the traditional adversarial model survive in a society without the political and cultural features of England?

2. Civil Procedure in Civil Law Countries

Until now, our focus has been on American theoretical work in the field of civil procedure and on the Anglo-American history of procedure. How would you expect procedure to change in civil law systems?

Mary A. Glendon et al., COMPARATIVE LEGAL TRADITIONS

In civil law countries, civil procedure occupies the same central position in procedural law that the civil law occupies within substantive law. The basic source of law in this area is typically a code of civil procedure. More modern procedural codes stress that judicial proceedings must be public and that, in principle, the control of the allegations and proof belongs to the parties. This latter principle, however, tends to be tempered in practice by the civil law judge's extensive power to supervise and exercise initiative in the proceedings as well as by the role that the public prosecutor can play in private actions.

In a typical civil action, after the pleadings are filed, a period of evidence taking begins. From the outset, several differences from common law civil procedure appear. These differences can be summed up by noting that on the one hand, there is no real counterpart to our pre-trial discovery and motion practice, while on the other hand there is no genuine "trial" in our sense of a single culminating event. Rather, a civil law action is a continuous process of meetings, hearings, and written communications during which evidence is introduced, testimony is taken, and motions are made and decided. During this process, the judge plays an active role in questioning witnesses, and in framing or reformulating the issues. Although the questioning is typically done by the judge, the questions are often submitted by the parties' counsel who sometimes are permitted to question a witness directly. As the action proceeds, the judge may inject new theories, and new legal and factual issues, thus reducing the disadvantage of the party with the less competent lawyer. In addition, the court may obtain certain types of evidence, such as expert opinions, on its own motion. There are no requirements that documents be formally admitted into evidence, nor are there any rules against hearsay and opinion evidence. . . . The weight to be accorded the evidence is for the free evaluation of the court. . . .

Many of the differences between the foregoing model and the usual American trial seem attributable to the absence of the civil jury in civil law countries. The civil law countries have never felt the need to bring the parties, their witnesses, their lawyers and the judge all together on one occasion because they have not had to convene a group of ordinary citizens to hear all the evidence, to resolve factual issues, and to apply the law to the facts. The factor of the civil jury also helps to explain the relatively great number of exclusionary rules in the common law of evidence and the relatively few restrictions on admissibility in the civil law systems. However, recent developments in both systems tend once again in the direction of a certain convergence. American discovery practice and pre-trial hearings bring us close to a situation where, as in the civil law, there are few surprises at trial. Meanwhile, civil law desire for efficiency and economy has led, notably in Germany, to experiments with and widespread use of a single comprehensive hearing model that is said to work well for the relatively simple cases that form the great bulk of civil litigation....

Decisions of the ordinary civil and criminal courts of first instance may as a rule be appealed to an intermediate appellate court.... Unlike a common law appeal of a trial court's decision, the proceedings in this intermediate court may involve a full review *de novo* of the facts as well as the law of the case. The panel of appellate judges initially will make its independent determination of the facts on the basis of the original record. In addition, however, the appellate court may question the witnesses again, or even take new evidence or send out for expert opinions. A party dissatisfied with the results of the appeal may seek review by the highest court which, like a common law appellate court, in theory considers only questions of law. (It may be noted in passing that civil law high courts have not been more successful than common law appellate courts in distinguishing factual from legal issues).

John H. Langbein, THE GERMAN ADVANTAGE IN CIVIL PROCEDURE

52 U. Chi. L. Rev. 823, 826, 830-35, 843-46, 848-50 (1985)

There are two fundamental differences between German and Anglo-American civil procedure, and these differences lead in turn to many others. First, the court rather than the parties' lawyers takes the main responsibility for gathering and sifting evidence, although the lawyers exercise a watchful eye over the court's work. Second, there is no distinction between pretrial and trial, between discovering evidence and presenting it. Trial is not a single continuous event. Rather, the court gathers and evaluates evidence over a series of hearings, as many as the circumstances require....

From the standpoint of comparative civil procedure, the most important consequence of having judges direct fact-gathering in this episodic fashion is that German procedure functions without the sequence rules to which we are accustomed in the Anglo-American procedural world. The implications for procedural economy are large. The very concepts of "plaintiff's case" and "defendant's case" are unknown. In our system those concepts function as traffic rules for the partisan presentation of evidence to a passive and ignorant trier. By contrast, in German procedure the court ranges over the entire case, constantly looking for the jugular — for the issue of law or fact that might dispose of the case. Free of constraints that arise from party presentation of evidence, the court investigates the dispute in the fashion most likely to narrow the inquiry. A major job of counsel is to guide the search by directing the court's attention to particularly cogent lines of inquiry....

Part of what makes our discovery system so complex is that, on account of our division into pretrial and trial, we have to discover for the entire case. We investigate everything that could possibly come up at trial, because once we enter the trial phase we can seldom go back and search for further evidence. By contrast, the episodic character of German fact-gathering largely eliminates the danger of surprise; if the case takes an unexpected turn, the disadvantaged litigant can count on developing his response in another hearing at a later time. Because there is no pretrial discovery phase, fact-gathering occurs only once; and because the court establishes the sequence of fact-gathering according to criteria of relevance, unnecessary investigation is minimized. . . .

The episodic character of German civil procedure — Benjamin Kaplan called it the "conference method" of adjudication — has other virtues: It lessens tension and theatrics, and it encourages settlement. Countless novels, movies, plays, and broadcast serials attest to the dramatic potential of the Anglo-American trial. . . . German civil proceedings have the tone not of the theatre, but of a routine business meeting — serious rather than tense. When the court inquires and directs, it sets no stage for advocates to perform. The forensic skills of counsel can wrest no material advantage, and the appearance of a surprise witness would simply lead to the scheduling of a further hearing. In a system that cannot distinguish between dress rehearsal and opening night, there is scant occasion for stage fright.

In this business-like system of civil procedure the tradition is strong that the court promotes compromise. The judge who gathers the facts soon knows the case as well as the litigants do, and he concentrates each subsequent increment of fact-gathering on the most important issues still unresolved. As the case progresses the judge discusses it with the litigants, sometimes indicating provisional views of the likely outcome. He is, therefore, strongly positioned to encourage a litigant to abandon a case that is turning out to be weak or hopeless, or to recommend settlement. The loser-pays system of allocating the costs of litigation gives the parties further incentive to settle short of judgment. . . .

Adversary control of fact-gathering in our procedure entails a high level of conflict between partisan advantage and orderly disclosure of the relevant information. Marvin Frankel put this point crisply when he said that "it is the rare case in which either side yearns to have the witnesses, or anyone, give *the whole truth.*" . . .

When we cross the border into German civil procedure, we leave behind all traces of this system of partisan preparation, examination, and cross-examination of witnesses. German law distinguishes parties from witnesses. A German lawyer must necessarily discuss the facts with his client, and based on what his client tells him and on what the documentary record discloses, the lawyer will nominate witnesses whose testimony might turn out to be helpful to his client. As the proofs come in, they may reveal to the lawyer the need to nominate further witnesses for the court to examine. But the lawyer stops at nominating; virtually never will he have occasion for out-of-court contact with a witness. Not only would such contact be a serious ethical breach, it would be self-defeating. "German judges are given to marked and explicit doubts about the reliability of the testimony of witnesses who previously have discussed the case with counsel or who have consorted unduly with a party."

No less a critic than Jerome Frank was prepared to concede that in American procedure the adversaries "sometimes do bring into court evidence which, in a dispassionate inquiry, might be overlooked." That is a telling argument for including adversaries in the fact-gathering process, but not for letting them run it. German civil procedure preserves party interests in fact-gathering. The lawyers nominate witnesses, attend and supplement court questioning, and develop adversary positions on the significance of the evidence. Yet German procedure totally avoids the distortions incident to our partisan witness practice. . . .

Equality of representation. The German system gives us a good perspective on another great defect of adversary theory, the problem that the Germans call "'Waffenungleichheit" — literally, inequality of weapons, or in this instance, inequality of counsel. In a fair fight the pugilists must be well matched. . . . The simple truth is that very little in our adversary system is designed to match combatants of comparable prowess, even though adversarial prowess is a main factor affecting the outcome of litigation. Adversary theory thus presupposes a condition that adversary practice achieves only indifferently. It is a rare litigator in the United States who has not witnessed the spectacle of a bumbling adversary whose poor discovery work or inability to present evidence at trial caused his client to lose a case that should have been won. Disparity in the quality of legal representation can make a difference in Germany, too, but the active role of the judge places major limits on the extent of the injury that bad lawyering can work on a litigant. In German procedure both parties get the same fact-gatherer — the judge. . . .

Prejudgment. Perhaps the most influential justification for adversary domination of fact-gathering has been an argument put forward by Lon Fuller: Nonadversarial procedure risks prejudgment — that is, prematurity in judgment. . . .

[Fuller's argument] obtains much of its force from the all-or-nothing contrast that so misdescribes German civil procedure. In a system like the German, which combines judicial fact-gathering with vigorous and continuing adversarial efforts in nominating lines of factual inquiry and analyzing factual and legal issues, the adversaries perform just the role that Fuller lauds, helping hold the decision in suspension while issues are framed and facts explored.

In German procedure counsel oversees and has means to prompt a flagging judicial inquiry; but quite apart from that protection, is it really true that a "familiar pattern" would otherwise beguile the judge into investigating too sparingly? If so, it seems odd that this asserted "natural human tendency" towards premature judgment does not show up in ordinary business and personal decision-making, whose patterns of inquiry resemble the fact-gathering process in German civil procedure. Since the decision-maker does his own investigating in most of life's decisions, it seems odd to despair of prematurity only when that normal mode of decision-making is found to operate in a courtroom. Accordingly, I think that Fuller overstates the danger of prematurity that inheres in allowing the decision-maker to conduct the fact-gathering; but to the extent that the danger is real, German civil procedure applies just the adversarial remedy that Fuller recommends.

Depth. Fuller's concern about prematurity shades into a different issue: How to achieve appropriate levels of depth in fact-gathering. Extra investment in search can almost always turn up further proofs that would be at least tenuously related to the case. Adversary domination of fact-gathering privatizes the decision about what level of resources to invest in the case.... In German procedure, by contrast, these partisan calculations of self-interest are subordinated, for a variety of reasons. The initiative in fact-gathering is shared with the judge; and the German system of reckoning and allocating the costs of litigation is less sensitive to the cost of incremental investigative steps than in our system where each side pays for the proofs that it orders. On the other hand, the German judge cannot refuse to investigate party-nominated proofs without reason, and this measure of party control greatly narrows the difference between the two systems....

[German fact-gathering] does indeed contrast markedly with the inclination of American litigators "to leave no stone unturned, provided, of course, they can charge by the stone." The primary reason that German courts do less fact-gathering than American lawyers is that the Germans eliminate the waste....

Because German procedure places upon the judge the responsibility for fact-gathering, the danger arises that the job will not be done well. The American system of partisan fact-gathering has the virtue of its vices: It aligns responsibility with incentive. Each side gathers and presents proofs according to its own calculation of self-interest. This privatization is an undoubted safeguard against official sloth. After all, who among us has not been treated shabbily by some lazy bureaucrat in a government department? And who would want to have that ugly character in charge of one's lawsuit?

The answer to that concern in the German tradition is straightforward: The judicial career must be designed in a fashion that creates incentives for diligence and excellence. The idea is to attract very able people to the bench, and to make their path of career advancement congruent with the legitimate interests of the litigants.

The career judiciary. The distinguishing attribute of the bench in Germany (and virtually everywhere else in Europe) is that the profession of judging is separate from the profession of lawyering. Save in exceptional circumstances, the judge is not an ex-lawyer like his Anglo-American counterpart. Rather, he begins his professional career as a judge....

The work of a German judge is overseen and evaluated by his peers throughout his career, initially in connection with his tenure review, and thereafter for promotion through the several levels of judicial office and salary grades.... These evaluations by senior judges pay particular regard to (1) a judge's effectiveness in conducting legal proceedings, including fact-gathering, and his treatment of witnesses and litigants; and (2) the quality of his opinions — his success in mastering and applying the law to his cases.

Notes and Questions

1. Civil law procedural systems do not introduce any new players to the litigation enterprise, but the roles assigned to the lawyers, the parties, and the decisionmaker(s) are different from those in the adversarial model. Indeed, the civil law systems sound rather like Chayes' public law model in the roles assigned to various participants, although the civil systems seem to emphasize even more the power of the judge in fact-finding, issue-defining, and trial. Recall some of the potential problems of Chayes' model: bias on the part of the judge, lack of incentive to investigate adequately, lessened feelings of participation, and lack of jury trial. Professor Langbein's description of German procedure addresses many of these criticisms. Are you convinced by his responses?

2. In particular, Langbein suggests that the use of the judge to gather facts and question witnesses is an advantage of the German system. Do you agree? With judicial fact-finding come a decreased need for juries, reduced need for strict rules of evidence, and a different trial process. Assuming that these are desirable changes, is it possible to engraft the German approach onto a judicial system that guarantees a right to jury trial and largely equates "due process" with adversarial process? Would Americans tolerate the bureaucratization of the judiciary that adoption of the German model would entail?

3. The Ecuadoran procedural system, which is based on the Napoleonic Code (by way of the Andres Bello Code of Chile), removes even more power from the lawyers, who are unable to question witnesses or suggest follow-up questions during a hearing. Most of the fact-gathering is done by masters appointed on an *ad hoc* basis. See Jose R. Bustamonte, *Trial and Court Procedures in Ecuador*, in Trial and Court Procedures Worldwide 205 (1991). Is this the logical endpoint of allowing judges greater authority in fact-finding? Are there principled reasons why the German and most other civil systems stop short of this point?

3. Civil Procedure in Socialist Countries

At communism's height in the late 1980's, six of every ten people lived under socialist legal systems. There has been a considerable falloff in these numbers lately, but these procedural systems remain an important source of facts and theories about the nature and possibilities for a procedural system.

Mary A. Glendon et al., COMPARATIVE LEGAL TRADITIONS

889-90, 892-94, 900-07, 911, 915-16, 920 (1985)*

To portray [socialist legal systems] we have chosen the prototypical socialist adversary system — the Soviet.

---

* In order for the edited version of this material to be more accessible to readers, the order of some of the excerpts has been re-arranged. — ED.

Soviet civil procedure ... is motivated in part by ideology and in part by pragmatism. The dominant ideology of this system of rules is systematized collectivism. To the Soviet mind civil procedure is not and could not be devoid of class consciousness. . . . "[T]he principal reflection of the class consciousness of the science of civil procedure is its active role in the promotion of the interests of the working class as well as the toiling people for the purpose of fulfilling the social tasks confronting the civil courts.". . .

Modern Soviet civil procedure, like the procedural systems of the continental European civil law countries, is essentially an adversary process. This is so despite the fact that, by contrast, Soviet criminal procedure is profoundly an inquisitorial process. In designing its systems of civil procedure, the Soviet Union borrowed ideas both from the civil law and [from] the common law traditions. . . . We think that it is much closer to the civil law than it is to the common law. . . .

In the language of Article 2 of the F.P.Civ.P., Soviet civil procedure seeks to further three goals — to protect, to educate and to deter.

The first of these purposes is to protect the legal rights and lawful interests of the Soviet state, public organizations and individual citizens from unlawful encroachments. This goal is achieved principally by making the courts accessible to anyone who wishes to vindicate a legal right or protected interest. An equally important goal of Soviet civil procedure is its educational mission. Through their correct application of civil procedure rules, Soviet courts seek to educate all defendants in the spirit of respect not only for the law but also for the rights and interests of other persons. Whereas the educational function of Soviet civil procedure is aimed specifically at the defendant who is adjudged liable in the action, the deterrent mission of the same judgment is directed at the general citizenry. . . . This goal is . . . furthered by rules which permit non-governmental organizations, which are not parties in interest, to participate actively in civil trials either at their own initiative or at the request of the court. . . .

The first quintessentially socialist feature of modern Soviet civil procedure is the ubiquitous presence of a state official called a procurator throughout the proceedings. The institution of the procuracy is completely unknown to the Anglo-American system. . . . The procurator is perhaps the single most important participant in a Soviet civil action. His domineering presence serves as a check on the actions of all other actors in the process, including but not limited to the judges, the counsel for the parties and the parties in interest. Put quite simply, the procurator is the lamp which is supposed to show that justice prevails in the Soviet civil courts. . . .

The central mission of the procurator is to protect the public interest in the civil litigation. In this capacity the procurator can institute a civil action and prosecute it either without the consent or over the objection of the real party in interest. . . . The system confers upon the procurator powers which in many critical respects go beyond those enjoyed by the real parties in interest. . . .

Modern Soviet rules governing the status and role of parties in a civil action are notably different also from those applicable in the United States.

A fundamental principle of U.S. civil procedure is that a civil suit must be prosecuted by or in the name of the true party in interest. Soviet law on the other hand affords the right to initiate and prosecute a civil suit to a wide range of persons in addition to the parties in interest. Even where an inappropriate party files a suit, under the Soviet system such a party may not be removed as plaintiff either by the court acting *ex proprio motu* or by the proper party, unless he so consents. In such situations the only remedy left to the real party in interest is to be joined as a third party with an independent claim. . . .

After all, to the Soviet legal mind no breach of the law can be regarded as being exclusively "private," in the sense that it would exclude the intervention of a representative of the public authority in the protection of the legal right so violated. For this reason the procurator participates in civil actions so as to protect the social and state structure of the USSR, the socialist system of economy, socialist property relationships, political, labor, housing and other personal and property interests of citizens, as well as the rights and lawful interests of state enterprises and institutions, collective farms and other cooperative organizations, and other social organizations. . . .

When a procurator initiates and prosecutes a civil suit he enjoys all of the following procedural rights during the trial proceedings: unimpeded access to all [pretrial] discovery of evidence, the right to express an opinion regarding the time and place of the trial, the right to nominate other intervening parties that ought to participate in the trial, [and] all other procedural rights enjoyed . . . by all the other participants, *i.e.*, the right to challenge the composition of the court, to participate in the oral arguments, and to suggest proposals for a decision to the court. If the parties in interest submit an out-of-court settlement to the court for its approval, the participating procurator has the right to scrutinize the terms of the proposed settlement for conformity with the law.

The intervention of the procurator at the post-trial stages of the proceedings is as important and pervasive as participation in the earlier stages. . . .

Another notable difference between Soviet and Anglo-American civil procedural systems is the use or non-use of the class action device for the joinder of parties. In its rejection of the class action device, the Soviet system is merely following a tradition that is entrenched in modern civil law countries. . . . In effect the Soviet system substitutes the lack of a need for a real party in interest for a class action. As such the Soviet system deems the class action device to be fundamentally unnecessary.

Turning to the rules governing the filing of claims, one further notices several peculiarities of the Soviet system in contrast to the American system, including the seemingly limitless freedom of the parties in a socialist civil action to amend their claims after the initial filing . . . .

On the question of discovery Soviet law, like American law, makes provisions for [pretrial], pre-suit and pre-pleading discovery of facts. However, . . . the parties in a Soviet civil action do not have anything near [the] dazzling array of discovery devices [available to an American party].

A party in a Soviet civil action may resort to a handful of informal methods of individual discovery of facts in the case, such as inspection of documents and real evidence, written depositions which are used only to take the testimony of written witnesses, and request for admission.

On the other hand, U.S. law has a wider range of undiscoverable information than does Soviet law. . . . Under Soviet law, for example, discoverable information includes information relating to the opponent's trial strategy; defendant's financial ability; expert's information developed for litigation; investigator's notes and written ideas and written as well as oral statements of witnesses obtained by an investigator in preparation for trial. In fact, most of these types of information would be discovered under Soviet law not by the parties themselves, but by the pretrial judge as part of the measures undertaken by him in preparation for trial. . . .

From the perspective of the U.S. lawyer there are many noteworthy features of Soviet law of evidence. This may be attributed to the fact that these rules were designed for a bench trial in which lay and law judges are the fact finders. The general tendency in the U.S.S.R. is to admit all relevant and probative sources of proof in a case. . . .

When one turns to the issue of pleadings it becomes immediately clear that Soviet law, like the laws of the continental European countries, adopts what amounts to notice pleadings and rejects the stringency generally associated with fact pleadings. . . .

Once process has been served on all the prospective persons, the next step is to prepare for the actual trial hearing. One element is the pretrial conference. There are two types of pretrial conference — the tripartite pretrial conference, at which the judge meets with both parties at the same time, and the sequential bilateral pretrial conferences, at which the judge meets separately with the parties. As part of the required pretrial preparation measures, the judge must also familiarize the lay judges with the materials of the case, and bring the case to the attention of potential intervenors. . . .

The Soviet trial hearing is perhaps the one aspect of modern Soviet civil procedure that has been most influenced by the Anglo-American tradition. Nevertheless, it is dissimilar to the U.S. trial in many respects. Among the noteworthy characteristic features of the Soviet trial is the absence of the jury. Because Soviet trials are concentrated, there is an intensive [pretrial] preparation of the case to shape the issues. Thus, in contrast to the civil law systems, . . . preparation for the trial hearing is one of the most critical moments of the entire proceedings. . . .

Under Soviet law the parties merely nominate witnesses to be called in a case. The decision whether or not to call such witnesses, as well as the sequence in which the witnesses are to testify in the trial, is made not by the parties, but by the [pretrial] judge or the court. Consequently, Soviet law does not permit [pretrial] contacts between the counsel and the prospective witnesses . . . . The fact that the parties are not supposed to have [pretrial] contacts with the witnesses does not mean that the parties are uninformed of the contents of the testimony of the witnesses prior to the trial. The parties have full pretrial access to the depositions of the witnesses on both sides. These depositions are generally taken by the [pretrial] judge either personally or, at his request, by a commissioned judge. . . .

In the area of remedies, Soviet law is characterized by two noteworthy features, *i.e.*, the general provision that a court may grant more relief than that which is prayed for by the plaintiff if the interests of justice so demand, and the general prohibition against the award of pecuniary compensation for nonpecuniary harm, unless statute specifically provides otherwise. . . .

Because a socialist court of review does not engage in evidentiary hearings, the scope of review is thus less than *de novo* but more extensive than review for legal errors only. A Soviet court of review verifies not only the correct application of law by the lower court, but also the supportability of the judgment by all the evidence.

Shao-chuan Leng, JUSTICE IN COMMUNIST CHINA

139-40, 171-74 (1967)

"People's lawyers" are public servants and not private practitioners. They all work in Legal Advisory Offices, each of which is under the supervision of a director chosen by the Lawyers' Association. . . .

In civil disputes, the first thing that the "people's lawyer" frequently does is to try to effect some form of compromise or informal settlement through his mediation and persuasion. A number of instances have been reported in which lawyers helped their clients to resolve family, marriage, debt, and property disputes without recourse to court litigation. On occasions, however, the "people's lawyer" does attend the court to act for litigants in civil suits. . . .

[T]he Chinese Communists are by and large not so much concerned with the resolution of individual disputes as with the suppression of crimes. This attitude is actually in accord with the traditional Chinese view that law was primarily an instrument to protect the political and social order rather than a guardian of private rights and interests. . . . In one instance, the Special Office of Yengchow in Fukien province granted divorces to twenty-one couples without having given a hearing to the other party's story. . . .

Inasmuch as no code of civil procedure has been promulgated in Communist China, legal proceedings in civil matters are apparently governed by experimental rules, unpublished regulations and the relevant provisions in the Constitution and the Organic Law of the People's Courts. As a rule, there is no preliminary hearing in a civil suit; otherwise, court activities and procedural guarantees are quite similar to those described in criminal procedure. A civil action is instituted through the filing of a written petition with the court by the plaintiff or his representative. The plaintiff [may] be an individual, institution, enterprise, or organization. Moreover, the Procuracy may initiate or intervene in any civil suit at any stage of the proceedings if it considers the case to be of great political or economic significance. . . .

In handling civil suits, the practice is for the "people's court" or "people's tribunal" to work closely with the masses, rely upon the methods of persuasion and education, and use legal judgment sparingly as a last resort. The overriding objective is to settle internal contradictions by conciliation, uphold law and discipline, facilitate production work, strengthen the unity of the people, and promote the development of socialist virtues. Efforts to mediate disputes are made by the court not only at the first trial but even in the appeal. The court hearings are generally conducted in an informal atmosphere, with the participation of the relatives, friends, neighbors, and co-workers of the litigants in a joint endeavor to resolve the disputes. If matters of major importance are involved in a civil action, then a large-scale "democratic debate meeting" is held so that more people can take part in the discussion to help clarify the issues and reconcile the parties to the suit. It goes without saying that in the process the court conducts propaganda and education among both the litigants and the public at large concerning the obedience to the laws and policies of the state. . . .

Finally, what should not be overlooked in our discussion is the fact that the Chinese Communists have insisted that the class line, too, must be maintained in handling civil disputes. From their standpoint, different classes and strata still exist in the economic life of Chinese society. There is a distinction between the proletariat and the peasantry. There are also differences among poor peasants, lower-middle peasants, and rich middle peasants. Consequently, internal conflicts among the people often reflect contradictions between the road of socialism and the road to capitalism, and must be handled in the interest of socialism and the unity of all the people. Such being the official line, the judges have thus been told to use a clear and firm class viewpoint to analyze the problems when dealing with civil disputes.

Notes and Questions

1. With the collapse of the Soviet Union and the weakening of its Communist Party, and with the slow Westernization of China, would you expect to see changes in their procedural systems? If so, what would the likely changes be? See Mary A. Glendon et al., Comparative Legal Traditions 395-436 (2d ed. 1994). Do such changes prove that rules of procedure are based on cultural and historical factors rather than on fundamental procedural norms, or only that such factors help to flesh out the indeterminacy surrounding those norms?

2. The Soviet and Chinese systems add a new player to the litigation: the procurator. As we move away from the party control associated with the Anglo-American adversarial model, does a procurator make sense? The procurator removes some of the pressure from the public law judge to be both decisionmaker and guardian of the public interest, and it provides an independent check on her work. The procurator also attempts to ensure that substantial justice will be done, evens out unequal counsel, and helps to avoid the inevitable pressures on the parties to obfuscate the truth. In reality, of course, the procurator's office in the Soviet Union was not always successful in achieving its goals. This is the assessment of Professor Glendon and her co-authors:

> On the whole it is fair to say that the Soviet procurator has emerged as an effective protector of what one might call the old public interests, especially in the areas of status and family matters. . . . But in the new areas of social concern such as environmental protection, consumer protection, historical preservation, and protection against hazards posed by the operation of nuclear power stations, the Soviet procurator has shown a lack of political will in the performance of this public trust. It is obviously not good politics for the procurator to institute civil litigation to challenge a government-approved public work project, even if the project is harmful to the public interest.

Glendon et al., *supra*, at 918. The critique of the procurator is remarkably similar to Fiss' critique of the public law judge (p. 65-66, *supra*). Could we have our cake and eat it too if we relied on non-governmental entities (say, the National Wildlife Federation in environmental cases) to fulfill the procurator's role? Or would non-governmental entities be captive to particular interests?

For a study of the fate of the procuracy in the post-Soviet Russia, see Stephen C. Thaman, *Reform of the Procuracy and Bar in Russia*, 3 Parker School J. East Eur. L. 1 (1996).

3. In the Soviet and Chinese systems, judges do not try to separate procedural and substantive justice; rather, they interpret procedural rules with an eye to the substantive justice of the cause. Isn't this precisely what Professor Cover (p. 6, *supra*) said that American courts should do when he argued that they should forsake trans-substantive procedural rules? Are socialist countries so far ahead of us procedurally that they have been practicing for years a procedural convention that we are still arguing about implementing? Or are we the ones who have found the true path to procedural enlightenment? In a socialist society, it is far easier to implement a non-trans-substantive code of procedure because the basic goals of society are better defined and because all law (even procedural law) exists to serve those goals. In a capitalist society, the goals of society are defined largely by private ordering, so that making the rules of procedure serve the diffuse goals of society is far more problematic. Perhaps in a capitalist society we can do no more than establish "neutral" rules of procedure by which everyone must play. But what about public law litigation, which partakes of some socialist qualities in a largely capitalist state? In this type of litigation, do we bend procedure to fit substance, or do we rest on neutral principles designed for the ordering of private disputes?

One way to assure that procedure serves substance is to refuse to adopt any code of procedure, as the Chinese did. Is this a desirable alternative to the extensive rules of procedure needed in an adversarial system? There is the disadvantage of re-inventing the wheel for each case, but the advantage of knowing that the wheel fits. Would Cover's presumptive rules of procedure that can be easily changed if circumstances warrant be a happy medium? This solution, of course, gives great discretion to the individual trial judge. Are certainty, predictability, and like treatment of like cases more or less important than entrusting trial judges with the procedural flexibility to accomplish justice?

4. It seems counter-intuitive that civil and socialist systems, which tend to respect party autonomy and party control less than the common law adversarial system, do not typically permit widespread resort to the class action, while the common law does. Would the adversarial system need the class action device if judges were empowered, as they were in the Soviet system, to award

relief greater than the relief the present parties desire? Would you be willing to give American judges a similar power?

5. Should judges and lawyers be expected to bring about a reconciliation of parties? Should they be expected to use an individual lawsuit to educate the larger society about proper behavior? In performing these tasks, are socialist lawyers and judges acting in the roles assigned to them by the model of adjudication? If not, is there anything wrong with merging the adjudicatory and political roles of lawyers and judges?

6. Professor Damaska has suggested that the world's procedural systems can be explained by two variables: the organization of authority within a state and the extent to which a state attempts to manage social interactions. Mirjan Damaska, The Faces of Justice and State Authority (1986). With respect to the first variable, Damaska identifies two opposing organizational structures: a hierarchical and bureaucratic structure and a "coordinate" structure in which power is diffused widely to autonomous decisionmakers. With respect to the second variable, Damaska identifies two opposing types of state: an activist (or "policy-implementing") state that actively manages social interactions in order to achieve some ideal of the good and a reactive (or "conflict-solving") state that is more laissez-faire, merely resolving disputes about citizens' private orderings. Damaska then combines the variables into a 2x2 matrix:

Type of State

	Policy-implementing	Conflict-solving
Hierarchical	(1)	(2)
Coordinate	(3)	(4)

Organization of Authority

Damaska demonstrates that, within each cell, the optimal procedural features of each type of organization to some extent reinforce the optimal procedural features of that type of state, and to some extent clash with the optimal procedural features of that type of state. Damaska then argues that certain procedural consequences are likely to flow from these complements and tensions, and shows that these predicted features are reflected in the actual procedural systems in use around the world. Damaska contends that the types of procedures expected to be found in Box (1) correspond to socialist civil (and criminal) procedure; the expected features in Box (2) correspond to the procedures found in civil law countries; the expected features in Box (4) correspond to traditional common law procedure; and the expected features in Box (3) correspond to Chayes' public law litigation.

One of the problems of Damaska's approach is it that operates at a level of great generality. There are thousands of different procedural systems in the world, and any effort to classify them into four categories means that the categories must permit considerable room for procedural variation. If it is not possible to deduce the procedural features of a given system from the theoretical constructs which Damaska gives us, where can we search for the answer? See Arthur von Mehren, *The Importance of Structures and Ideologies for the Administration of Justice*, 97 Yale L.J. 341 (1987).

Even though its conclusions should not be accepted uncritically, Damaska's work has obvious ramifications for our study of complex litigation. In the first place, Damaska's analysis suggests that many of the problems we have identified in adversarial process (such as undue partisanship, insufficient incentives for truth-telling, need for extensive controls on evidence, and inequality of counsel) cannot be easily remedied, for the nature of the society in which adversarial process flourishes abets — indeed, even creates — those problems. Second, Damaska's work suggests that, until the nature of a society changes, there are limits on successful procedural change within that society. Third, Damaska's analysis suggests that the wide array of social and political arrangements legitimizes a wide array of procedural systems. This conclusion casts a great cloud over the work of any scholar (whether it be Rawls, Posner, or Fuller) who seeks to orient procedure along a particular theory; and further casts into doubt the enterprise of seeking universal and fundamental norms of procedure.

But Damaska's work does not refute the normative enterprise. Perhaps there remain fundamental principles shared by all of the procedural systems we have studied. Perhaps there still remain limits on the power of the judge, on the disparate treatment of like cases, and on the use of discretion. Comparative analysis broadens our perspective on Fuller's inquiry into the form and limits of adjudication, but it does not answer his question. Comparative analysis cannot decide whether adversary process, notice pleading, and liberal party joinder are the right choices for American society today. Nor can it tell us how to handle complex cases that ill fit the adversarial model. At most, comparative analysis provides us with options that we *might* use to solve the problems we find in our procedural system generally and in complex cases specifically.

D. THE NATURE OF COMPLEX CIVIL LITIGATION: AN OVERVIEW

At a certain point, we can all agree on which litigation is "complex." Some examples are asbestos litigation, in which thousands of claimants have filed suits in federal and state courts; the *AT&T* antitrust litigation, involving tens of millions of pages of documents, thousands of witnesses, a year-long trial, and a remedial plan in whose shadow we all still live; and *Brown v. Board of Education* and other desegregation litigation, which have posed enormous remedial challenges. Is there anything, though, that unites these very different types of litigation? Is every antitrust case complex? Is a consumer class action under the Truth in Lending Act complex?

At the beginning of this chapter we loosely defined complex litigation to be those cases that the modern American adversary system is ill-equipped to handle. Since then we have surveyed normative theory, history, and alternative procedural systems in an effort to determine how critical adversarial process is, and what the advantages and disadvantages of a non-adversarial approach might be — all with an eye toward forming an opinion about how our system should respond to the problems posed by complex litigation. Beginning in the next chapter, we explore the specific problems themselves. Before we turn to those problems, however, it would, obviously, be wise to consider again exactly what "complex litigation" is.

There are two reasons for undertaking this lexical task. The first is pragmatic. As you proceed through the materials in this book, you will notice that the phrase "complex litigation" has a magical quality about it; when a judge becomes convinced that a case is "complex," procedural innovation often replaces procedural conservatism. These innovations might lead to a different result than the result that would have occurred under traditional procedure. As a lawyer, you want to make sure that the judge applies the most favorable procedural rules; and that might require you to be able to convince the judge that your case is (or is not) "complex."

The second reason is broader: We want to know what procedural rules are best. It might be, as Professor Cover has suggested, that there should be different rules for complex and simple cases; indeed, many people would claim that different rules are inevitable. Until we understand exactly what complex litigation is, however, how can we really decide whether these claims are correct? Furthermore, if we choose to create one set of rules for complex cases and another for simple cases, we had better be sure that we give the right cases the right set of rules, hadn't we? Finally, how can we assess arguments that we should abandon assumptions such as adversarialism, transactionalism, or trans-substantivism because of the pressures of complex litigation if we do not know which cases are complex, which cases are not, and whether complexity has anything to do with the problems of the modern procedural system?

We look first at a number of definitions of complex litigation, each of which varies from our initial loose definition. We close by providing our own more formal definition — a definition that serves as the basis for the organization of the remainder of this book.

MANUAL FOR COMPLEX AND MULTIDISTRICT LITIGATION

7-9 (1970)

0.1 *Definitions.*

"Complex litigation," as used in this Manual, includes one or more related cases which present unusual problems and which require extraordinary treatment, including but not limited to the cases designated as "protracted" and "big." . . .

0.22 *Classes of potentially complex cases.*

Cases in the following classification may require special treatment in accordance with the procedures in this Manual: (a) antitrust cases; (b) cases involving a large number of parties or an unincorporated association of large membership; (c) cases involving requests for injunctive relief affecting the operations of a large business entity; (d) patent, copyright, and trademark cases; (e) common disaster cases; (f) individual stockholders', stockholders' derivative, and stockholders' representative actions; (g) products liability cases; (h) cases arising as a result of prior or pending Government litigation; (i) multiple or multidistrict litigation; (j) class actions or potential class actions; or (k) other cases involving an unusual multiplicity or complexity of factual issues.

American Law Institute, COMPLEX LITIGATION: STATUTORY RECOMMENDATIONS AND ANALYSIS

7 (1994)

"Complex litigation" has no fixed definition, and the term sometimes is used to refer to litigation that concerns complex issues even if the dispute takes place only between two parties in a single forum. As used in this Project, however, "complex litigation" refers exclusively to multiparty, multiforum litigation; it is characterized by related claims dispersed in several forums and often involving events that occurred over long periods of time. It presents one of the greatest problems our courts currently confront. Repeated relitigation of the common issues in a complex case unduly expends the resources of attorney and client, burdens already overcrowded dockets, delays recompense for those in need, results in disparate treatment for persons harmed by essentially identical or similar conduct, and contributes to the negative image many people have of the legal system. . . .

Complex cases may arise under state or federal law and in the courts of either system. They are generated by a variety of circumstances — from a single mass disaster such as the collapse of a Hyatt Hotel skywalk, from myriad individual contacts with a hazardous product such as asbestos, or from allegations of antitrust violations committed by one of the world's largest corporations or a number of small ones. The claims in a complex case may accrue all at once as in an air crash, or they may be latent for generations and mature at different times, as in the case of DES. . . . But complex cases share two defining characteristics: they all involve the potential for relitigation of identical or nearly identical issues, and consequently, they all involve the enormous expenditure of resources.

MANUAL FOR COMPLEX LITIGATION, THIRD

3 (1995)

What is complex litigation? . . . A functional definition of complex litigation recognizes the need for management in the sense used here — judicial management with the participation of counsel — does not simply arise from complexity, but is its defining characteristic: The greater the need for management, the more "complex" is the litigation. Clearly, litigation involving many parties in numerous related cases — especially if pending in different jurisdictions — requires management and is complex, as is litigation involving large numbers of witnesses and documents and extensive discovery. On the other hand, litigation raising difficult and novel questions of law, though challenging to the court, may require little or no management, and therefore may not be complex as that term is used here.

Notes and Questions

1. The foregoing definitions or descriptions of complex litigation were arranged in chronological order. Can you see any theme uniting them? Any progression or refinement from one to the other?

2. The *Manual for Complex and Multidistrict Litigation*, published in 1970, was the direct predecessor of the *Manual for Complex Litigation (Second)*, published in 1985. The *Manual (Second)* is the direct predecessor of the *Manual, Third*, published in 1995. Of these three manuals, which suggest procedures that judges and practitioners involved in complex litigation might use, two of them (the original *Manual*, and the *Manual, Third*) provided definitions of complex litigation. These two definitions, however, are quite different. The *Manual (Second)* consciously declined to define complex litigation. Do the changing definitions convince you that the decision of the authors of the *Manual (Second)* was wise? But how can someone write a manual describing what to do in complex litigation without defining what complex litigation is?

3. Recall Professor Fuller's definition of a "polycentric" case: a many-sided dispute in which it is impossible for all parties to participate meaningfully through proofs and arguments (pp. 16-17, *supra*). Assuming that "polycentric" and "complex" are equivalent terms, is Fuller's definition of complex litigation superior to other descriptions? Does Fuller's definition provide the overarching theme — the inability of adversarial adjudication to handle a dispute — that unites these other definitions? If so, must we also accept Fuller's remedy for polycentric cases: their removal from the adjudicatory process? Or can we simply shift to non-adversarial procedure in complex cases? Does our answer to these questions hinge on whether adversarial procedure is normatively required by the form of adjudication? This last question brings us full-circle back to Fuller's concern: What are the essential, optimal, and forbidden procedural features of an adjudicatory system?

Jay Tidmarsh, UNATTAINABLE JUSTICE: THE FORM OF COMPLEX LITIGATION AND THE LIMITS OF JUDICIAL POWER

60 Geo. Wash. L. Rev. 1683, 1801 (1992)

It is now possible to provide a formal definition of complex litigation: Litigation in an adversarial system in which the judicial power necessary to overcome the dysfunction of the lawyers, the jury, or the parties results in procedural disparities that cause substantively disparate outcomes among similarly situated parties, claims, or transactions. The definition contains three essential elements. The first element is dysfunction — the inability of the lawyers, jury, or parties to fulfill the responsibilities for rational adjudication assigned to them by the adversarial system. The second element is curative judicial power — the ability of the judge to establish procedures that remedy this dysfunction and thus allow rational adjudication, albeit in a manner inconsistent with the adversarial model. The third element is that like cases are treated unalike because of the tendency of the selected procedures to cause the nature and quality of evidence, and consequently the substantive outcome, to vary (1) among persons who have experienced the same or similar factual occurrences, (2) among cases seeking recovery under the same legal theory, or (3) among legal theories constituting a party's claim or defense.

Notes and Questions

1. The idea of dysfunction is central to our understanding of complex litigation. Every litigation system expects certain players to perform certain roles. In the adversarial system, the roles of fact-gathering and argument-creating are performed by lawyers; the role of rational decisionmaking is performed by the judge (and sometimes the jury); and the role of complying with the remedy is performed by the parties. As we define complex litigation, at least one party cannot perform the assigned task. The voluminous nature of a case may make it impossible for a lawyer adequately to gather the relevant facts and organize the relevant issues into arguments. When this dysfunction occurs during the pretrial process, we have "pretrial complexity," which is the subject of Part Two of the book. When this dysfunction occurs during the trial process, or when the volume or technicality of the evidence makes it impossible for a decisionmaker to decide rationally, we have "trial complexity," which is the subject of Part Three. When the courts are unable to declare or the parties are unable to implement the remedy, we have "remedial complexity," which is the subject of Part Four. Finally, when lawyers vigorously representing their clients do not join all interested parties in one proceeding, and when that decision means that those left out of the case will either be unable to secure a remedy comparable to those who have been joined or else disrupt the remedy obtained by others, we have "joinder complexity," which is the subject of Part One.

A single case can be — but need not be — complex in more than one way.

2. Our understanding of complex litigation also requires that the dysfunction be curable by the non-adversarial application of judicial power, and that this application of judicial power cause the unequal treatment of like cases. These qualifications return us to Fuller. Even if we do not accept the full thrust of Fuller's argument — that the adversarial system is demanded by the form of adjudication — we might still think that the adversarial system is better than any other. What about our trans-substantive desire to give all cases the same procedural treatment — is that a fundamental norm too? Are there limits on our ability to depart from adversarial and trans-substantive process, so that some complex cases lie beyond the bounds of adjudication? These are the questions that the remainder of this book explores, as we examine the specific ways in which procedural and remedial doctrines affect and are affected by complex litigation. But the answers to these questions lie in this chapter — in the theory of procedure, in its history, and in its many manifestations in the world.

PART ONE

JOINDER COMPLEXITY

One of the lawyers' primary tasks in the prosecution or defense of a lawsuit is the selection of parties to be joined in the case and the forum in which to try the case. Unquestionably the plaintiff's lawyer exercises the greatest influence over this process. The plaintiff is often said to be "master of the complaint" who therefore enjoys the "venue privilege" — in other words, the plaintiff makes the initial decisions about party structure, legal theories, and forum. Within narrow parameters, defense lawyers or the judge can sometimes change these choices.

In making these choices, lawyers are guided by two constraints. The first is the panoply of restrictions found in the relevant constitutions, statutes, and codes of procedure regulating state and federal courts. The second is the adversarial ethic's command to represent a client's interests zealously. Working within the legal rules, the lawyers seek to find the combination of claims, parties, and court that meets their obligation to secure the best outcome for their clients. Typically there will be trade-offs. For instance, a plaintiff's attorney may believe that the best chance of recovery lies in a state court, but the best legal theory lies within the exclusive jurisdiction of the federal courts. Hence, the attorney will need to decide whether the state forum or the federal claim is more important. Conversely, those defending a lawsuit will try to thwart the opposing attorney's choices. For instance, assuming that a plaintiff's lawyer wishes to remain in state court, the defense lawyer may try to find ways to remove the case to federal court.

Whether lawyers are in fact best-suited to make these decisions about selecting parties, theories, and forum is a debatable point. Competent lawyers will make the choice that best protects their clients' interests. But these interests may not match the interests of society in efficiently allocating access to the courts. The "master of the complaint" approach, which is highly consistent with an adversarial system, assumes that litigation is primarily a mechanism that resolves private disputes rather than a public good that must be guarded against socially irrational uses.

Whether the adversarial approach to selection of parties, theories, and forum should continue to be maintained is the main theme of this part. The vehicle through which we will be exploring this theme is complex litigation. We choose complex litigation because it presents the set of cases in which the standard adversarial assumption is weakest. Complex litigation often involves hosts of potential parties and claims. In these cases, certain lawyers are simply unable to represent their clients with the degree of diligence upon which the adversarial system insists. There are various reasons for this "lawyer dysfunction," but they can generally be grouped into two categories:

(1) When numerous individual plaintiffs separately sue a defendant and the defendant's assets are insufficient to pay the total claims against it, the plaintiffs who obtain judgments early will recover in full and later plaintiffs will take nothing. Lawyers for the early plaintiffs may purposely avoid notifying or joining other plaintiffs in order to maximize their own clients' recoveries. The decisions of the early-filing lawyers make it impossible for the late-filing lawyers to obtain any meaningful remedy for their clients, and also result in dissimilar treatment for similarly situated plaintiffs.

(2) When the plaintiff seeks a remedy that would have an adverse effect on nonparties and does not join these non-parties, one of two results will obtain: (a) The non-parties will be barred from later challenging the remedy, so that the rights of the nonparties will effectively have been determined in a lawsuit in which they had no representation; or (b) The nonparties will not be barred from a later challenge, so that the original plaintiffs might find that the rights for which they had fought have vanished, or the original defendant might find that it is now subject to inconsistent obligations. The first outcome is unfair to nonparties; the second is unfair to either the original plaintiffs or the original defendants. This type of dysfunction usually arises in connection with injunctive remedies, but may also arise when there are competing claims with respect to a specific thing.

There exists as well a third category of cases that do not necessarily involve lawyer dysfunction but do test the adversarial assumption. In these cases, large numbers of plaintiffs are injured by the same or similar event, but for tactical or practical reasons wish to sue in different forums at different times. In this situation, the same factual and legal issues will be litigated in hundreds of forums across the country — a possibility that is enormously expensive and may produce docket backlogs in the affected courts. When the costs of individual litigation are great enough to render a defendant insolvent, the first category of lawyer dysfunction discussed above comes into play. Even when the costs are not so great, however, this third category of cases asks whether an adversarial approach to the selection of parties, theories, and forum is too outdated and expensive to justify.

In our nomenclature, the first two categories involve cases that are "complex"; "joinder complexity" prevents lawyers from adequately performing their adversarial functions. Since the lawyers can perform their adversarial tasks without hindrance, most of the third category does not involve "complex" cases; nonetheless, these cases are, for lack of a better word, "complicated." Whether "complex" or "complicated," all three sets of cases present scenarios in which there is a compelling interest in a common resolution in a common forum.

Such a common resolution can, however, have significant side effects, including the reduction of a litigant's autonomy to choose whether, where, and against whom to bring suit; the substitution of group for individual interests; the need to design mechanisms to protect individuals within the group; the expansion of judicial power to effect the appropriate structure of parties, theories, and forum; the need to develop methods for handling multi-party litigation; and the possibility of disparate outcomes between multi-party and individual adjudication. Even if these side effects can be overcome (or at least made palatable), there exist a number of constitutional, statutory, code-based, and common law barriers — such as subject matter jurisdiction, territorial jurisdiction, venue, limited joinder rules, and choice of law rules — that make a common resolution difficult to achieve.

Our exploration of these issues begins with Chapter Two, which begins with an examination of the rules of traditional party joinder and the limitations that these rules impose on the ability to package multiple claims and parties in one suit. The chapter then explores two alternate ways through which the parties and the court can avoid some of these limitations and thus prevent joinder complexity or inefficient re-litigation of common issues. The first alternative would require formal joinder of all interested nonparties. A second alternative would expand the rules of claim and issue preclusion to bind both parties and nonparties to the outcome of a prior case in which comparable claims or issues were litigated.

In Chapter Three we look at the jurisdictional rules that affect a plaintiff's choice of court system, and at the ways in which a defendant or a judge can change the plaintiff's choice. Once again, the existing jurisdictional rules create various impediments to the effective joinder of related cases within one court system.

Chapter Four then examines the constellation of venue rules and related doctrines that govern the choice of a particular court within a court system. Once again, we examine both the rules that affect the plaintiff's choice and the ways in which a defendant or the court can alter that choice of forum. Unfortunately but predictably, these statutes and rules are also limited in their ability to avoid problems of lawyer dysfunction and inefficient packaging.

Chapters Five and Six continue this theme by focusing on two specific mechanisms that might overcome the barriers discovered in the three prior chapters. Chapter Five looks at the class actions as a mechanism to bring related claims before a single court. Chapter Six examines the benefits and limitations of bankruptcy as a means of consolidating a controversy in a single forum.

Chapter Seven serves as a bridge to Part Two, which will examine issues of pretrial complexity. In this chapter we ask whose law should be applied to resolve a case that has been successfully aggregated. As we shall see, the answer to this question has an important effect on the desirability of joinder.

Throughout this Part, we question whether the adversarial assumption of party control over the litigation is appropriate, and whether it is wise to entrust judges with discretion to override the parties' desires. We explore the legitimate boundaries of adjudication. We ask whether the plethora of joinder options renders the like procedural treatment of like cases impossible. Finally, we consider, for the first time, the extent to which notions of federalism should influence our views on adversarialism, trans-substantivism, and judicial discretion. As you read the materials, also ask whether we should respond to "complex" and "complicated" cases in the same way.

CHAPTER TWO

JOINDER, PRECLUSION, AND LITIGANT AUTONOMY

> [U]nder the present . . . rules people allegedly injured under circumstances that have the indicia of being part of a complex dispute have an incentive to remain on the sidelines while litigation is pursued by similarly situated parties.
>
> ALI Complex Litigation Project

In complicated and complex litigation, there often exists a perceived need to bind as many persons as possible to the outcome of a single judgment. In complicated cases, the need is efficiency; it is costly to relitigate essentially identical issues in numerous forums. In complex cases, issues of efficiency may also be involved, but the need for a single resolution derives from lawyer dysfunction; standard adversarial practices will leave some group of plaintiffs either without the remedy for which they have fought or without a remedy comparable to the one that similarly situated plaintiffs have achieved. Obviously the two situations are not equivalent, nor is it clear that the reasons that a single resolution is desirable are equally weighty in both cases.

In theory, binding persons to a particular judgment can be achieved in one of at least two ways. First, a person can be joined as a party to the suit in which the judgment is entered. Second, a person can be forced to accept the findings or outcome of a suit brought by other, similarly situated parties. Under the party joinder alternative, joinder can be either voluntary or involuntary; in other words, a party must either agree to become a party (voluntary joinder) or can be forced to become a party against her will (involuntary joinder). A joined person might fully participate in the litigation, or might have her interests represented by another, similarly situated person. Under the preclusion approach, various alternatives are also possible. For instance, a person might be precluded only if she receives notice or she might be bound even if she does not. Likewise, a person might be precluded only if she has an opportunity to intervene in the case, or a right of intervention might be denied or restricted. These alternatives can be mixed and matched; for instance, there could be preclusion only when there is notice but not a right to intervene, or preclusion only when there is a right to intervene but no notice, preclusion with neither notice nor intervention, or preclusion only with both notice and intervention.

At present, our procedural system rests on the assumption that the primary way — and in nearly all circumstances the only way — in which a person can be bound by a judgment is through party joinder. Therefore, if a single resolution of a controversy is to be achieved, we must begin with the study of the legal rules and constraints surrounding party joinder. Many of these rules and constraints can be found in Rules 19-24 of the Federal Rules of Civil Procedure or comparable state law joinder rules, although some derive from statutes, common law doctrines, or equity practice.

Our present joinder rules rest on at least four additional assumptions. First, our system assumes that each putative plaintiff is "master" of his or her own complaint. In the context of party joinder, this assumption means that a plaintiff has the initial (and usually largest) say in determining who will be the parties in her lawsuit; but it also means that plaintiffs cannot generally be forced to join the lawsuit of other plaintiffs involuntarily. Second, the joinder rules rest on an assumption of "transactionalism" — in other words, the relevant unit for deciding whether persons are properly joined in one suit is whether they all participated in the factual events or series of factual events that resulted in a legal claim. A third assumption is that party joinder rules should be interpreted with an eye to assuring the efficient conduct of litigation. The final assumption is that flexible, discretionary joinder rules applicable to all types of lawsuits are preferable to rules narrowly drawn to deal with specific factual or legal circumstances.

To some extent, these assumptions work at cross-purposes. Allowing the plaintiff, who may have pragmatic reasons not to want broad joinder, to choose the party structure will achieve the transactional assumption only fitfully. Likewise, the combination of the "only parties are bound" and "master of the complaint" assumptions makes it difficult to achieve complete joinder of related claims in one suit, and may lead to significant inefficiencies as multiple suits litigate an essentially common factual scenario.

This chapter examines how well these various assumptions work, or do not work, in complicated and complex litigation. We begin by considering traditional voluntary and involuntary joinder rules, paying particular attention to their shortcomings as means of either packaging complicated cases efficiently or packaging complex cases to avoid lawyer dysfunction. We then examine an alternative to our present rules: expanding the concept of preclusion to prevent re-litigation of claims or issues already decided. Finally, we examine an alternative that blends aspects of both joinder and preclusion: providing persons with an opportunity voluntarily to join the litigation as parties, while binding those that decline to enter the case.

Both of these latter alternatives turn on its head the "only parties are bound" assumption of American procedure, and both impinge on the "master of the complaint" rule. In short, these alternatives challenge our standard adversarial notions of litigant autonomy. Moreover, since the need for different rules is most pressing in complicated and complex cases, these alternatives force us to ask how important the last assumption — the use of trans-substantive rules that provide a single set of joinder rules in all cases — actually is.

Hence, the present rules of party joinder and their alternatives provide a wonderful case study of the modern American procedural system. Is it possible simultaneously to embrace the ideals of litigant autonomy, transactionalism, efficiency, and interpersonal fairness? If not, which one(s) should give way?

A. USING PARTY JOINDER RULES TO OVERCOME JOINDER COMPLEXITY

The Federal Rules of Civil Procedure contain a combination of voluntary and involuntary joinder provisions. We begin by looking at Rule 20, the basic rule for the voluntary joinder of plaintiffs. We then examine the involuntary joinder of defendants under Rule 20, explore other involuntary joinder rules, and then conclude by looking at the ability of a person not joined by the plaintiff to intervene and participate in the suit as a party.

1. Voluntary Joinder of Plaintiffs under Rule 20

MOSLEY v. GENERAL MOTORS CORP.

497 F.2d 1330 (8th Cir. 1974)

■ ROSS, Circuit Judge. Nathaniel Mosley and nine other persons joined in bringing this action individually and as class representatives alleging that their rights guaranteed under 42 U.S.C. § 2000e et seq. and 42 U.S.C. § 1981 were denied by General Motors and Local 25, United Automobile, Aerospace and Agriculture Implement Workers of America [Union] by reason of their color and race. Each of the ten named plaintiffs had, prior to the filing of the complaint, filed a charge with the Equal Employment Opportunity Commission [EEOC] asserting the facts underlying these claims. Pursuant thereto, the EEOC made a reasonable cause finding that General Motors, Fisher Body Division and Chevrolet Division, and the Union had engaged in unlawful employment practices in violation of Title VII of the Civil Rights Act of 1964. Accordingly, the charging parties were notified by EEOC of their right to institute a civil action in the appropriate federal district court, pursuant to § 706(e) of Title VII, 42 U.S.C. § 2000e-5(e).

In each of the first eight counts of the twelve-count complaint, eight of the ten plaintiffs alleged that General Motors, Chevrolet Division, had engaged in unlawful employment practices by: "discriminating against Negroes as regards promotions, terms and conditions of employment"; "retaliating against Negro employees who protested actions made unlawful by Title VII of the Act and by discharging some because they protested said unlawful acts"; "failing to hire Negro employees as a class on the basis of race"; "failing to hire females as a class on the basis of sex"; "discharging Negro employees on the basis of race"; and "discriminating against Negroes and females in the granting of relief time." Each additionally charged that the defendant union had engaged in unlawful employment practices "with respect to the granting of relief time to Negro and female employees" and "by failing to pursue 6a grievances." The remaining two plaintiffs made similar allegations against General Motors, Fisher Body Division. All of the individual plaintiffs requested injunctive relief, back pay, attorneys fees and costs. Counts XI and XII of the complaint were class action counts against the two individual divisions of General Motors. They also sought declaratory and injunctive relief, back pay, attorneys fees and costs.

General Motors moved to strike portions of each count of the twelve-count complaint, to dismiss Counts XI and XII, to make portions of Counts I through XII more definite, to determine the propriety of Counts XI and XII as class actions, to limit the scope of the class purportedly represented, and to determine under which section of Rule 23 Counts XI and XII were maintainable as class actions. The district court ordered that "insofar as the first ten counts are concerned, those ten counts shall be severed into ten separate causes of action," and each plaintiff was directed to bring a separate action based upon his complaint, duly and separately filed. The court also ordered that the class action would not be dismissed, but rather would be left open "to each of the plaintiffs herein, individually or collectively . . . to allege a separate cause of action on behalf of any class of persons which such plaintiff or plaintiffs may separately or individually represent."

In reaching this conclusion on joinder, the district court followed the reasoning of Smith v. North American Rockwell Corp., 50 F.R.D. 515 (N.D. Okla. 1970), which, in a somewhat analogous situation, found there was no right to relief arising out of the same transaction, occurrence or series of transactions or occurrences, and that there was no question of law or fact common to all plaintiffs sufficient to sustain joinder under Federal Rule of Civil Procedure 20(a). Similarly, the district court here felt that the plaintiffs' joint actions against General Motors and the Union presented a variety of issues having little relationship to one another; that they had only one common problem, i.e. the defendant; and that as pleaded the joint actions were completely unmanageable. Upon entering the order, and upon application of the plaintiffs, the district court found that its decision involved a controlling question of law as to which there is a substantial ground for difference of opinion and that any of the parties might make application for appeal under 28 U.S.C. § 1292(b). We granted the application to permit this interlocutory appeal and for the following reasons we affirm in part and reverse in part.

Rule 20(a) of the Federal Rules of Civil Procedure provides:

All persons may join in one action as plaintiffs if they assert any right to relief jointly, severally, or in the alternative in respect of or arising out of the same transaction, occurrence, or series of transactions or occurrences and if any question of law or fact common to all these persons will arise in the action. . . .

Additionally, Rule 20(b) and Rule 42(b) vest in the district court the discretion to order separate trials or make such other orders as will prevent delay or prejudice. In this manner, the scope of the civil action is made a matter for the discretion of the district court, and a determination on the question of joinder of parties will be reversed on appeal only upon a showing of abuse of that discretion. . . . To determine whether the district court's order was proper herein, we must look to the policy and law that have developed around the operation of Rule 20.

The purpose of the rule is to promote trial convenience and expedite the final determination of disputes, thereby preventing multiple lawsuits. . . . Single trials generally tend to lessen the delay, expense and inconvenience to all concerned. Reflecting this policy, the Supreme Court has said:

> Under the Rules, the impulse is toward entertaining the broadest possible scope of action consistent with fairness to the parties; joinder of claims, parties and remedies is strongly encouraged.

United Mine Workers of America v. Gibbs, 383 U.S. 715, 724 (1966).

Permissive joinder is not, however, applicable in all cases. The rule imposes two specific requisites to the joinder of parties: (1) a right to relief must be asserted by, or against, each plaintiff or defendant relating to or arising out of the same transaction or occurrence, or series of transactions or occurrences; and (2) some question of law or fact common to all the parties must arise in the action.

In ascertaining whether a particular factual situation constitutes a single transaction or occurrence for purposes of Rule 20, a case by case approach is generally pursued. . . . No hard and fast rules have been established under the rule. However, construction of the terms "transaction or occurrence" as used in the context of Rule 13(a) counterclaims offers some guide to the application of this test. For the purposes of the latter rule,

> "Transaction" is a word of flexible meaning. It may comprehend a series of many occurrences, depending not so much upon the immediateness of their connection as upon their logical relationship.

Moore v. New York Cotton Exchange, 270 U.S. 593, 610 (1926). Accordingly, all "logically related" events entitling a person to institute a legal action against another generally are regarded as comprising a transaction or occurrence. . . . The analogous interpretation of the terms as used in Rule 20 would permit all reasonably related claims for relief by or against different parties to be tried in a single proceeding. Absolute identity of all events is unnecessary.

This construction accords with the result reached in United States v. Mississippi, 380 U.S. 128 (1965), a suit brought by the United States against the State of Mississippi, the election commissioners, and six voting registrars of the State, charging them with engaging in acts and practices hampering and destroying the right of Negro citizens of Mississippi to vote. The district court concluded that the complaint improperly attempted to hold the six county registrars jointly liable for what amounted to nothing more than individual torts committed by them separately against separate applicants. In reversing, the Supreme Court said:

> But the complaint charged that the registrars had acted and were continuing to act as part of a statewide system designed to enforce the registration laws in a way that would inevitably deprive colored people of the right to vote solely because of their color. On such an allegation the joinder of all the registrars as defendants in a single suit is authorized by Rule 20(a) of the Federal Rules of Civil Procedure. . . . These registrars were alleged to be carrying on activities which were part of a series of transactions or occurrences the validity of which depended to a large extent upon "[questions] of law or fact common to all of them."

Here too, then, the plaintiffs have asserted a right to relief arising out of the same transactions or occurrences. Each of the ten plaintiffs alleged that he had been injured by the same general policy of discrimination on the part of General Motors and the Union. Since a "state-wide system designed to enforce the registration laws in a way that would inevitably deprive colored people of the right to vote" was determined to arise out of the same series of transactions or occurrences, we conclude that a company-wide policy purportedly designed to discriminate against Negroes in employment similarly arises out of the same series of transactions or occurrences. Thus the plaintiffs meet the first requisite for joinder under Rule 20(a).

The second requisite necessary to sustain a permissive joinder under the rule is that a question of law or fact common to all the parties will arise in the action. The rule does not require that all questions of law and fact raised by the dispute be common. Yet, neither does it establish any qualitative or quantitative test of commonality. For this reason, cases construing the parallel requirement under Federal Rule of Civil Procedure 23(a) provide a helpful framework for construction of the commonality required by Rule 20. In general, those cases that have focused on Rule 23(a)(2) have given it a permissive application so that common questions have been found to exist in a wide range of contexts. Specifically, with respect to employment discrimination cases under Title VII, courts have found that the discriminatory character of a defendant's conduct is basic to the class, and the fact that the individual class members may have suffered different effects from the alleged discrimination is immaterial for the purposes of the prerequisite. . . .

The right to relief here depends on the ability to demonstrate that each of the plaintiffs was wronged by racially discriminatory policies on the part of the defendants General Motors and the Union. The discriminatory character of the defendants' conduct is thus basic to each plaintiff's recovery. The fact that each plaintiff may have suffered different effects from the alleged discrimination is immaterial for the purposes of determining the common question of law or fact. Thus, we conclude that the second requisite for joinder under Rule 20(a) is also met by the complaint.

For the reasons set forth above, we conclude that the district court abused its discretion in severing the joined actions. The difficulties in ultimately adjudicating damages to the various plaintiffs are not so overwhelming as to require such severance. If appropriate, separate trials may be granted as to any particular issue after the determination of common questions.

The judgment of the district court disallowing joinder of the plaintiffs' individual actions is reversed and remanded with directions to permit the plaintiffs to proceed jointly. That portion of the district court's judgment that withholds determination of the propriety of the purported class until further discovery is affirmed. . . .

GRAYSON v. K MART CORP.

849 F. Supp. 785 (N.D. Ga. 1994)

■ CARNES, United States District Judge. . . . The eleven plaintiffs in this case are former store managers of defendant K Mart Corporation ("K Mart") who are, or were, employed in defendant's stores located in Alabama, Florida, Georgia, and North Carolina. Each plaintiff seeks relief for alleged age discrimination, pursuant to the Age Discrimination in Employment Act, 29 U.S.C. §§ 621, et seq. ("ADEA"). Each plaintiff also seeks relief for common law intentional infliction of emotional distress, pursuant to the applicable law of each plaintiff's home state.

Plaintiffs have alleged that each plaintiff was demoted by defendant due to the respective plaintiff's ages at the time of their demotions. In support of their claim, plaintiffs point to evidence they believe indicates that each plaintiff was subjected to such adverse action as part of a "pattern and practice" of illegal treatment of K Mart's older employees at all levels. All the plaintiffs were over forty years of age at the time of the demotions and, thus, protected by the ADEA. Notwithstanding plaintiffs' allegations, defendant alleges that the employment decisions made regarding each plaintiff were made based upon the individual circumstances of each plaintiff's employment record and job performance. Plaintiffs, in turn, cite to evidence which tends to indicate that defendant's stated reasons for each employment decision are mere pretext.

Although the Complaint purported to include the claims of each of the eleven plaintiffs "and other similarly situated persons," it was not brought as a class action, and plaintiffs have made no effort to seek representative status or to certify any proposed class. Prior to bringing the instant action, each plaintiff filed an individual complaint with the Equal Employment Opportunity Commission office in his respective state. At the time of the adverse employment actions complained of, pursuant to K Mart's management structure, each plaintiff reported to a district manager and regional manager located in each plaintiff's home state. Each regional manager in turn reported to John Valenti in Troy, Michigan, who was in charge of the operations of some eight hundred K Mart stores in the Southern states.

DISCUSSION

I. Introduction.

Defendant has moved the Court to sever the claims of the various plaintiffs in this case, pursuant to Fed.R.Civ.P. 21 and 42(b) ("Rule 21" and "Rule 42(b)"). Defendant argues that plaintiffs' cases were improperly joined and that defendant is entitled to have the claims severed under Rule 21 and, in the alternative, that, even if plaintiffs cases are properly joined, sufficient reason exists to sever each plaintiff's case for trial under Rule 42(b). Plaintiffs argue in response that joinder was proper under Fed.R.Civ.P. 20 ("Rule 20") because their claims arose out a common "transaction, occurrence, or series of transactions or occurrences" and because there are questions of law or fact common to all" the plaintiffs. Plaintiffs further argue that any prejudice or confusion that may exist, due to their decision to join their claims under Rule 20, can be eliminated through proper instruction to the jury, thus eliminating any justification to sever under Rule 42(b). For the reasons discussed below, the Court concludes that, under the circumstances of these cases, defendant has presented the better argument and that defendant's motion to sever should be granted on either of its proposed alternative grounds.

II. Misjoinder.

In order for plaintiffs' cases to be properly joined, they must satisfy the prerequisites of Fed.R.Civ.P. 20(a) ("Rule 20(a)"). "The rule states two requirements for proper joinder: (1) there must be a right to relief arising out of the same transaction occurrence or series of transactions or occurrences; and (2) there must be a question of law or fact common to all of the plaintiffs which will arise in the action. Both these requirements must be satisfied." Smith v. North Am. Rockwell Corp., 50 F.R.D. 515, 522 (N.D. Okla. 1970) (hereinafter "*Rockwell*"). "In ascertaining whether a particular factual situation constitutes a single transaction or occurrence for purposes of Rule 20, a case by case approach is generally pursued. No hard and fast rules have been established under the rule." Mosley v. General Motors Corp., 497 F.2d 1330, 1333 (8th Cir. 1974) (citation omitted). The Court finds, based upon the factual situation presented by these cases, that plaintiffs' cases satisfy neither requirement for joinder under Rule 20(a) and, thus, that their claims have been misjoined.

A. Common Transaction or Occurrence.

Defendant argues that plaintiffs' cases arise from distinct and unrelated employment actions taken by various management employees in the course of their job responsibilities. Accordingly, under defendant's theory of the cases, each adverse employment decision was a separate transaction or occurrence, not part of some unified series of transactions or occurrences, and not amenable to joinder under Rule 20(a). Plaintiffs argue vigorously that their pattern and practice evidence establishes that each plaintiff's demotion was part of an organized course of conduct by K Mart and, thus, that each demotion was but one transaction or occurrence within a common series of transactions or occurrences. Under plaintiffs' theory of their respective cases, the first prong of Rule 20(a) has been satisfied. While the Court finds the facts of these cases to present a somewhat close question, it concludes that the "common transaction or occurrence" requirement of Rule 20(a) has not been satisfied.

In support of their theory of the cases, plaintiffs have directed the Court's attention to evidence they believe establishes the common transaction requirement under Rule 20(a). This evidence may be categorized into three general types: (1) evidence of motive to discriminate against older employees; (2) anecdotal evidence of age bias within defendant's organization; and (3) statistical evidence of age bias. Plaintiffs paint the picture of a hostile corporate culture for older store managers. Plaintiffs have not, however, directed this Court's attention to any discrete program or procedure employed by K Mart that affected each of the plaintiffs in this litigation. Absent some causal link between a common and identifiable wrongful act on the part of the defendant and the adverse action taken with respect to each plaintiff, the first prong of Rule 20(a) is not satisfied.

Plaintiffs' "motive" evidence relates to defendant's admitted need to improve its profitability during the same time period within which plaintiffs were demoted. . . . Plaintiffs allege that K Mart's demands of improved profitability put increased pressure on regional, district, and store managers to cut costs in order to improve profits. Plaintiffs assert that the need to cut costs caused these managers to make employment decisions based upon the relative costs of retaining one employee over another. In making this argument, however, plaintiffs ignore the fact that each employment decision was made by different managers within the company. The fact that all these managers may have been feeling the same pressure to improve profitability does not mean that all these decisions constitute one unified transaction or occurrence or series thereof.

The anecdotal evidence of discrimination consists of statements made by various K Mart managers at all levels, which plaintiffs assert establishes the existence of a company-wide policy of age bias. Plaintiffs rely in part on public statements made by defendant's chairman, Joseph Antonini, regarding the company's "renewal" and regarding the relatively young age of K Mart's management team to support the existence of such a policy. Plaintiffs also present the anecdotal testimony of various present and former K Mart employees recounting conversations they have had with managers at various levels in which pejorative or derogatory statements were made regarding the age and job performance of other K Mart employees. Assuming, without deciding, that plaintiffs' evidence establishes a general hostility toward older employees, the Court fails to see how such hostility transforms the decisions of the various managers with respect to each of the plaintiffs into one logical transaction or occurrence.

Plaintiffs' reliance on defendant's alleged general bias toward store managers over forty to support joinder of their cases is misplaced, as "litigation of even any purported general policy of defendant, as it might affect each plaintiff here, would inevitably focus in detail on the separate work histories of each plaintiff." *Rockwell*, 50 F.R.D. at 522 . . . . The instant cases involve eleven individuals who live in four states. Each plaintiff worked in a different store, geographically remote from the other plaintiffs. The decision to demote each plaintiff originated with his district manager and was derived within the context of the business circumstances of each plaintiff's store. Three different regional managers participated in the eleven demotion decisions at issue in these cases. While all of these decisions may not be completely unrelated, in that they were made during the same time period and in response to the immense competitive pressures being felt by K Mart at the time, they hardly constitute a single action on the part of the defendant.

Plaintiffs make much of defendant's centralized controls to support their theory that each demotion was part of one logical transaction or occurrence. . . . While the decisions to demote the plaintiffs could not have been implemented without approval by the Southern Regional Vice President, John Valenti, the undisputed evidence establishes that the recommendation to make such a demotion originated with the individual employee's district and regional managers. Taking plaintiffs' reasoning to its logical end, every employment decision made by managers subject to central policies and review would constitute one transaction or occurrence, and any group of aggrieved employees would be entitled to join its claims under Rule 20(a). The Court declines to read the permissive joinder rules so broadly.

Plaintiffs also offer statistical evidence to support their single transaction theory of the case. The Court fails to see, however, how this evidence transforms eleven individual employment decisions into one logical transaction. Primarily, plaintiffs seek to use their statistical evidence in order to create an inference of discrimination. Plaintiffs do not seek to use the evidence in order to establish their cases using a disparate impact theory; rather, they seek to use it as evidence of defendant's intent to discriminate against older employees. While such evidence possibly may be used by each of the plaintiffs to establish intent with respect to the adverse action taken against them, it seems ill-suited for satisfying the single transaction requirement of Rule 20(a). Thus, the Court concludes that plaintiffs' cases do not constitute one logical transaction or occurrence for purposes of Rule 20(a).

B. *Common Question of Law or Fact.*

The Court further finds that no common question of law or fact exists between the plaintiffs' cases, within the meaning of Rule 20(a). "It is, of course, true that plaintiffs have alleged against defendant claims based upon the same general theories of law, but this is not sufficient." *Rockwell*, 50 F.R.D. at 524 . . . . As detailed previously, each demotion decision affecting the plaintiffs in these cases was a discrete act by the defendant. "As indicated, the factual and legal questions between the plaintiffs and the defendant are based upon the wholly separate acts of the defendant with respect to each plaintiff. There is consequently a complete lack of common questions of fact or law, the second element required by Rule 20(a), and the actions must be severed on this ground as well." Id.

III. *Separate Trials under Rule 42(b).*

Defendant has argued, alternatively, that even if plaintiffs' cases were properly joined under Rule 20(a), it would be highly prejudicial to defendant for all the plaintiffs' cases to be presented to one jury. Plaintiffs argue that no undue prejudice to defendant exists, but that each plaintiff's case would be "prejudiced" by having to present evidence common to every case multiple times and because each plaintiff's case will appear more isolated to the juries hearing their cases. . . .

In these cases, there are eleven factual situations and eleven sets of witnesses with testimony pertinent to those situations. Moreover, plaintiffs' state law claims arise under the laws of four different states. The resulting confusion and prejudice from the scenario presented by a common trial of all plaintiffs' claims against the defendant would be intolerable. . . . Accordingly, the Court concludes that defendant's motion for severance should be granted under either Rule 21 or 42(b).

AABERG v. ACandS INC.

152 F.R.D. 498 (D. Md. 1994)

■ SMALKIN, District Judge. This 1,000 plaintiff asbestos case is before the Court on plaintiffs' counsel's response to various defendants' motions to dismiss. . . .

It is . . . clear from the plaintiffs' filing that they do not seek to have this case proceed as a class action, but as a case in which 1,000 plaintiffs are properly joined under Fed.R.Civ.P. 20. The plaintiffs oppose dismissal, even if the Court were to find misjoinder, citing Fed.R.Civ.P. 21 as precluding dismissal on account of misjoinder of parties.

It is plain to this Court that the 1,000 plaintiffs' claims, set forth in this complaint simply as a skeleton claim of maritime exposure to asbestos, without any attempt at individualization or description of the particular circumstances and exposures of the individual plaintiffs, let alone the products and/or defendants alleged to have been responsible, do not satisfy the "same transaction or occurrence" test of Fed. R. Civ. P. 20(a). See, *e.g.,* Saval v. BL Ltd., 710 F.2d 1027, 1031-32 (4th Cir. 1983). This is so plain on the face of the matter as not to require any oral hearing. . . .

The Court is mindful of the strictures of Fed.R.Civ.P. 21 that prohibit dismissal of a case for misjoinder. That same rule however, provides that the Court may, upon its own initiative, drop parties who are misjoined "on such terms as are just."

In this case, it is entirely appropriate and just to drop all but the first named plaintiff, Mr. Aaberg, on condition that their having been dropped from this lawsuit is without prejudice to their institution, individually, of suit against some or all of the present defendants based on the claim or claims attempted to be set forth in the present complaint. Of course, any such filing must be accompanied by the appropriate filing fee, and the complaint must satisfy the jurisdictional, pleading, and venue requirements of federal law and the Federal Rules of Civil Procedure.

Irwin A. Horowitz & Kenneth S. Bordens, THE EFFECTS OF OUTLIER PRESENCE, PLAINTIFF POPULATION SIZE, AND AGGREGATION OF PLAINTIFFS ON SIMULATED CIVIL JURY DECISIONS

12 L. & Hum. Behav. 209, 211-12, 225-26 (1988)

Lawyers have been cognizant of the possibility of differential outcomes in mass trials due to the aggregation of plaintiffs. Concern has been expressed that if a person with less severe injuries is adjudicated along with a very seriously injured individual, prejudice to the *defendant* may occur . . . . Fear has been expressed that jurors will treat all the members of the plaintiff aggregate alike, homogenizing individual claims and overlooking separate defenses of individual defendants . . . . Jurists have also suggested that as the number of plaintiffs increases so does the complexity of the decision-making process . . . . Doubts have been expressed about the jury's ability to effectively keep separate the information about each plaintiff. . . .

Each of these issues just outlined can be evaluated from the perspective of psychological research and theory. [The authors then described a study that they designed, using 66 six-person mock juries, to test these issues. Scripts were prepared and presented to the mock juries on audiotapes. In one set of experiments, each person's case was heard and decided separately. In another set of experiments, aggregation of four plaintiffs occurred. In one subset of the aggregation cases, all four plaintiffs had roughly comparable issues (the "no outlier" condition); in another subset, one of the four plaintiffs had significantly more serious injuries (the "outlier" condition). These subsets were further broken down, so that in one-third of the "no outlier" and "outlier" cases, mock jurors were given no information of other, similarly injured plaintiffs, in one-third of the cases mock jurors were told that 26 other plaintiffs existed, and in one-third of the cases, plaintiffs were told that "hundreds" of similar plaintiffs existed. Jury deliberations were also audiotaped.]

The impact of the independent variable manipulations was observed, as predicted, primarily in the award of punitive damages. Two main effects were significant: The presence of an outlier, a plaintiff with significant injuries as compared to other plaintiffs, increased both the amounts of the punitive awards as well as the variability of those awards; the awards were also increased by the juries' knowledge that the plaintiffs were part of a population that numbered in the hundreds. The same trend, although statistically nonsignificant, was observed in the compensatory awards.

While the presence of an outlier tended to help all plaintiffs, regardless of the severity of their injuries, the plaintiff with the weakest case benefitted most significantly.

The outlier also increased the unpredictability of the verdicts. . . . There were more instances of juries finding for the defendant in the outlier condition . . . . Interestingly, in the instances in which liability was not found, juries tended not to make distinctions between the outlier and the others. One might have reasonably expected a contrast effect, in which the outlier received a significant award and the others little or nothing. Instead, juries seemed to use the judgment of the outlier as a threshold test. . . . The rule seems to have been all-or-none.

The effect of informing the juries about the size of the distal plaintiff population was most clearly realized in the "hundreds" condition. This trend was observed in both the punitive (significant) and compensatory (nonsignificant) parts of the trial . . . The deliberation audiotapes suggest that when juries were informed that hundreds were involved, their imaginations . . . were, in a sense, liberated. When told that "26" others were involved, the ultimate effects of the tort [were] concretized and delimited. . . .

The findings as to the effects of plaintiffs being aggregated or not suggest that a plaintiff with a relatively weak case is [definitely] helped by aggregation; conversely, a plaintiff with quite a strong case . . . appears to be better served by being disaggregated, particularly with reference to punitive damages. As the disaggregated control groups were run under a no information condition (concerning the plaintiff population), we do not know if information as to the distal population would have had an impact on these trials.

Notes and Questions

1. *Mosley* is probably the leading case on the issue of voluntary (or permissive) joinder of plaintiffs. It takes a generous view of joinder; as long as some issues seem to be common, there are economies that can be achieved from common pretrial and trial proceedings, and the plaintiffs consent to joinder, Rule 20(a) will present no obstacle. On rather similar facts, *Grayson* takes a stingier view; it examines closely the extent to which the issues are in fact common, worries a great deal more about the inefficiencies of joining similar but not identical claims, and pays more attention to the harm that joinder might cause to a defendant. Although short on analysis, *Aaberg* seems to suggest that, as the differences among plaintiffs increase, the likelihood of using voluntary Rule 20 joinder to effect a single resolution of a multi-plaintiff controversy decreases.

Therefore, even though *Mosley* is the "leading" case, it is misleading to think that it is the only extant attitude about Rule 20 joinder; rather, it lies at the generous end of a spectrum of attitudes. Indeed, for nearly any case authorizing Rule 20 joinder of plaintiffs on particular facts, it is possible to find a case holding that such plaintiffs are misjoined. See, *e.g.*, Resnick v. American Dental Association, 90 F.R.D. 530 (N.D. Ill. 1981) (sex discrimination case in which plaintiffs alleging denial of promotion and plaintiffs alleging inadequate pay joined; permitting joinder); Johnson v. Indopco, Inc., 846 F. Supp. 670 (N.D. Ill. 1994) (two plaintiffs alleged denial of promotion due to racial and/or sexual discrimination; not permitting joinder); Hohlbein v. Heritage Mutual Insurance Co., 106 F.R.D. 73 (E.D. Wis. 1985) (fraud in various hiring decisions; permitting joinder); Saval v. BL Ltd., 710 F.2d 1027 (4th Cir. 1983) (breaches of federal warranty statute by four owners of same model of car; not permitting joinder); Papagiannis v. Pontikis, 108 F.R.D. 177 (N.D. Ill. 1985) (fraud in investment scheme; not permitting joinder); . For what it is worth, our general impression, formed after reading most of the reported Rule 20(a) decisions in the last twenty years, is that *Mosley* seems in recent years to have lost some of its luster; as *Grayson* and *Aaberg* show, courts today are taking a harder look at voluntary joinder decisions, and are more frequently finding such cases to be misjoined.

2. If economy and convenience were in fact the critical issues in interpreting Rule 20(a), would you expect such variance in the outcomes of the decisions? Does this suggest to you that factors other than economy and convenience are also motivating courts? What might those factors be?

Mosley, *Grayson* and *Aaberg* present two different scenarios in which joinder might be appropriate. If the plaintiffs in *Mosley* succeeded on their claims in separate suits, each might have obtained injunctive relief that would have affected other plaintiffs. Therefore, *Mosley* presented a classic threat of joinder complexity, which the joinder of different claimants in a single suit solved. *Grayson* was a comparable situation, but the plaintiffs apparently did not assert claims for company-wide injunctive relief; hence, the individual relief in *Grayson* created no issues of joinder complexity, and the same need for joinder did not exist. Next, assuming that the defendants were not going to become insolvent, *Aaberg* presented a case in which joinder might have created certain economies, but joinder complexity was not present; again, this powerful reason for joint treatment was not present. On the other hand, assuming that insolvency was likely, the voluntary joinder in *Aaberg* failed to join thousands of other, similar asbestos victims, and therefore did not cure the problem of joinder complexity. In either event, *Aaberg* did not present a case in which joinder would overcome problems of joinder complexity. Therefore, *Mosley*, in which joinder complexity existed, presented a clear need for joinder; *Grayson* and *Aaberg* did not present a clear need.

Of course, the absence of joinder complexity in *Grayson* and *Aaberg* does not necessarily mean that joinder in either case should have been denied. But its absence does mean that a (and maybe the) critical reason for permitting voluntary joinder is not present, so that the burden of justifying joinder is higher.

3. Did the facts in *Grayson* and *Aaberg* meet the burden? Joinder in both cases would have generated certain trial efficiencies and economies. As *Grayson* and *Aaberg* suggest, the joinder of multiple cases also creates counterbalancing inefficiencies in pretrial and trial. Moreover, joinder creates certain difficulties that are reflected in the data from Professors Horowitz and Bordens. Most notably, joinder of multiple plaintiffs appears to have the potential of affecting the outcome of lawsuits — in ways both favorable and unfavorable to defendants. Since the plaintiffs' lawyer is making the joinder decision, he will presumably join cases together only when it is favorable for the plaintiffs to do so. Therefore, defendants will typically be the only parties disadvantaged by the plaintiffs' joinder decision. Should the outcome-determinative potential and asymmetrical use of joinder influence a court in deciding whether joinder is appropriate? Can

you think of factors other than inefficiency, outcome-determinativeness, and unfairness to defendants that should influence a judge's decision on whether joinder is permissible?

One factor that arises a fair amount in the cases is the preservation of subject matter jurisdiction. As we shall see in more detail in the next chapter, the diversity jurisdiction of the federal courts requires, in nearly all cases, that none of the plaintiffs can be a citizen of the same state as any of the defendants. When one plaintiffs and one defendant are citizens of the same state, the court lacks subject matter jurisdiction. The flaw can be cured if the non-diverse plaintiffs (or defendants) are dropped. See F.R.Civ.P. 21 (permitting parties to be dropped on motion or on court's initiative). Conversely, when a plaintiff in state court adds a non-diverse party against whom no real claim exists simply in order to avoid federal jurisdiction, a federal court (after removal of the case from the state court) can drop the non-diverse party in order to preserve its subject matter jurisdiction. See 7 Charles A. Wright et al., Federal Practice & Procedure § 1685 (1986). Note that the first use of Rule 21 creates two lawsuits, thus frustrating the single resolution of claims in cases of dysfunction. The second use, which shifts the lawsuit from a state to a federal forum, is neutral in terms of reduction of dysfunction, although if other similar cases already exist in federal court, it may help to reduce dysfunction.

4. Even if the economy and efficiency of Rule 20 joinder are not dispositive factors, they are important. In order to determine whether a joined suit is more or less efficient than individual suits, however, you would need to know about the types of pretrial, trial, and remedial devices that can be used to handle a joined suit. We will come to those issues in Parts Two, Three, and Four of this book. Nonetheless, it should now be apparent to you that seemingly later-in-the-day decisions about pretrial, trial, and remedial organization influence early-in-the-day decisions on the structure of the lawsuit. Civil procedure is a seamless web.

5. As we shall see in ensuing materials, one of the greatest challenges in achieving global joinder of plaintiffs occurs in mass tort cases like *Aaberg*; other joinder devices are often ill-suited to effect joinder. In particular, we shall see that nearly every joinder or consolidation device has been tried on asbestos litigation, and none has thus far been entirely successful. Should the judge in *Aaberg* have considered this fact in making his ruling?

The largest mass tort voluntary joinder case of which we are aware involved two related suits — one involving 8,500 plaintiffs and one involving 1,300 plaintiffs — that alleged injuries due to exposure to DDT emitted by a pesticide factory. Hagood v. Olin Corp., No. CV-83-C-5917-NE (N.D. Ala.); Wilhoite v. Olin Corp., No. CV-83-C-5021-NE (N.D. Ala.); see Francis E. McGovern & E. Allan Lind, *The Discovery Survey*, 51 Law & Contemp. Prob. 41 (Autumn 1988) (describing case).* Unlike *Aaberg*, there were a limited number of defendants and a common pattern of conduct. But the range of injuries was more varied, the causation issues were more difficult, and the exposure issues were no less complicated. Under *Aaberg*'s analysis, should joinder have been permitted?

Recently, courts in other mass torts have authorized joinder subject to certain limitations. In In re Orthopedic Bone Screw Products Liability Litigation, 1995 WL 428683 (E.D. Pa.), the court permitted joinder as long as

---

* One of the authors of this book was lead counsel for United States in a separate action involving the 1,300 plaintiffs in *Wilhoite*. — ED.

each joined plaintiff received a medical device made by the same manufacturer at the same medical facility. Acknowledging that Rule 20(a) should be read liberally to promote judicial economy and efficiency, the court nonetheless thought that Rule 20(a) "requires at a minimum that the central facts of each plaintiff's claim arise on a somewhat individualized basis out of the same set of circumstances." Id. at *2. In another medical device case, In re Norplant Contraceptive Products Liability Litigation, 168 F.R.D. 579 (E.D. Tex. 1996), the judge rejected the joinder limitations imposed in *Orthopedic Bone Screw*, but did require that every plaintiff in a given case be represented by the same lawyer and also have received the medical device in the same state.

Does the fact that joinder in different mass torts is subject to different restrictions trouble you? Should mass torts receive different joinder rulings than discrimination cases or securities cases? How could we justify disparate treatment among mass torts or between mass torts and other types of cases?

6. *Orthopedic Bone Screw* is also noteworthy for its discussion of the relationship between voluntary joinder of plaintiffs under Rule 20 and class action joinder under Rule 23. It seems to suggest that voluntarily joined plaintiffs must meet a higher burden to justify joint treatment than involuntarily joined class members. Its reasoning is that Rule 23 guarantees class members greater judicial and procedural protections than individually joined plaintiffs receive. 1995 WL 428683, at *2-*3. We are deferring the fuller study of class actions until Chapter Five. But as an initial matter, does this reasoning sound right? Do you agree that the scope of Rule 20 joinder should be influenced by the scope and procedural protections of the other joinder rules?

7. Does Rule 20(a) allow one plaintiff involuntarily to join another putative plaintiff? In Cle-Ware Rayco, Inc. v. Perlstein, 401 F. Supp. 1231 (S.D.N.Y. 1975), a court refused to grant an injunction in a trademark case unless the true owner of the trademark was made an additional plaintiff. The owner was already a third-party defendant, and on the original plaintiff's motion, the court made the owner a plaintiff and issued the injunction. It was not clear from the opinion, however, whether the owner consented to be joined as a plaintiff, or was involuntarily joined. In Lyne v. Arthur Anderson & Co., 1991 WL 247576 (N.D. Ill.), ten individually joined plaintiffs sought either to maintain their case as a class action or, in the alternative, to force the joinder of seven additional plaintiffs that did not give their consent to joinder. After refusing to certify a class, the court then refused to authorize involuntary joinder of the seven potential plaintiffs:

> In considering a Rule 20 motion, the court should examine whether permissive joinder of a party comports with fundamental fairness. . . . Normally, plaintiffs invoke Rule 20 to bring reluctant defendants into an action. When plaintiffs invoke Rule 20 to bring in additional plaintiffs, the additional plaintiffs usually want to participate in the litigation. . . . All prospective class members have been contacted about this action. If any of the seven unnamed prospective class members desired to participate in this litigation, they could have joined with plaintiffs voluntarily or petitioned to intervene. There is nothing fundamentally fair about joining plaintiffs who have expressed no interest in participating in this litigation. Accordingly, plaintiffs' alternative motion for permissive joinder under Rule 20 is denied. [1991 WL 247576, at *3.]

Lyne seems not to have been a case of joinder complexity. Should that make a difference in the outcome of the case?

8. Even assuming that *Lyne* is wrong in cases of joinder complexity, the plaintiffs will not join additional plaintiffs unless it is in their interests to do so. In many cases of joinder complexity, however, the present plaintiffs have no interest in joining others with whom they will need to divide the spoils. Therefore, reliance on plaintiffs to effect the appropriate joinder will avoid joinder complexity only fitfully.

But note that Rule 21 permits a court to drop or add parties not only on the motion of a party, but also "on its own initiative." How much power does this rule give to a defendant or a judge to join additional plaintiffs? In particular, can a defendant request or a judge order *sua sponte* the joinder of all the plaintiffs that are necessary to overcome joinder complexity, despite *Lyne*'s holding that the plaintiffs cannot do so? Such a power would override the adversarial system's preference that each plaintiff have the autonomy to choose the party structure for his or her own case, and a *sua sponte* power would create a judicially-controlled system of involuntary joinder. On the other hand, since the adversarial preference has created a form of dysfunction that threatens to treat like claimants unfairly, is there adequate reason to respect the preference?

Few cases have tested the limits of these issues. With regard to the defendant's right to seek the addition of more plaintiffs, there are a handful of cases in which courts have granted defense motions to join plaintiffs' insurer, which had a subrogation claim. See, *e.g.*, Askey v. C. & M. Service, 45 F.R.D. 242 (M.D. Pa. 1968). Likewise, it seems fairly clear that a court *sua sponte* can add the real party in interest, and can order on its own initiative the joinder of persons that are needed for a just adjudication. See F.R.Civ.P. 17, 19; Wright et al., *supra*, § 1683. But these powers are limited, and would not provide defendants or a court with a broad power of joinder. Does a court possess the broader *sua sponte* power to join plaintiffs in order to prevent prejudice to present plaintiffs, present defendants, and/or putative plaintiffs? Does it also possess the power to join merely in order to prevent a multiplicity of suits? See id. (suggesting such power). In Lanehart v. Devine, 102 F.R.D. 592 (D. Md. 1984), a court added 550 plaintiffs that, but for amount of damages, were identically situated to the original seven plaintiffs. The court noted that joinder would not prejudice defendant, and would "certainly avoid a multiplicity of suits." Id. at 596. In *Lanehart*, however, plaintiffs requested the joinder of the additional plaintiffs, and it appears that the additional plaintiffs might have consented to joinder.

The most analogous case takes a dim view of the court's *sua sponte* joinder power under Rule 21. In Pan American World Airways, Inc. v. United States District Court for the Central District of California, 523 F.2d 1073 (9th Cir. 1975), a district judge before whom a number of cases involving an airplane crash was pending ordered that notice of the lawsuits be given to the personal representatives of all crash victims. Notice is not the same as joinder, but the judge clearly hoped that the notice would induce the estates of other victims to file suit. The airline refused to provide the passenger lists, and sought a writ of mandamus. The court of appeals found that Rule 21 did not give the judge the power to order notice:

> Respondents contend that since this rule authorizes the district court to order joinder of potential plaintiffs on its own motion, it also authorizes notice to such persons. The premise of this argument is untenable, again because it would effectively permit class actions that do not satisfy the requirements of Rule 23. The reasons, however, require some elaboration.

By itself, Rule 21 cannot furnish standards for the propriety of joinder, for it contains none. Hence it must incorporate standards to be found elsewhere. The only standards for proper joinder relevant to this case are Rules 19 and 20 but, as earlier demonstrated, Rule 19 is inapplicable. This leaves Rule 20, which allows persons to join as plaintiffs in a single action if they assert claims arising out of the same occurrence and if those claims share a common question of law or fact. The claims of potential plaintiffs here presumably would meet this test.

Rule 21 has been used to join potential plaintiffs who meet the requirements of Rule 20 and who subsequently consent to be joined. . . . But even if we were to follow these cases, they would not support the notice that would be issued in this case. With two exceptions not relevant here, these cases all involve joinder of four persons or fewer. In the present case, the district court has decided to send notice to the next of kin of several hundred passengers and crew. The effect of notice of this magnitude is the same as notice to an entire class. Such notice will effectively transform the present action into an [unwieldy] pseudo-class-action not authorized by Rule 23. Rules 20 and 21 cannot be read to circumvent the requirements of that rule. [523 F.2d at 1079-80.]

On the assumption that the airline was solvent enough to pay each of the judgments, *Pan Am* was not a case of joinder complexity, although it was a case in which a single resolution of essentially identical liability issues would likely have been quite efficient. Even if *Pan Am* is correct, should the judge possess the power to order involuntary joinder to prevent joinder complexity? If so, why is joinder complexity a more compelling case for the exercise of this power than increased efficiency? See Jay Tidmarsh, *Unattainable Justice: The Form and Limits of Complex Litigation*, 60 Geo. Wash. L. Rev. 1683 (1992).

9. In these notes we have not yet parsed out the precise language of Rule 20, which requires the establishment of two elements: The plaintiffs must assert a right of relief "in respect of or arising out of the same transaction, occurrence, or series of transactions or occurrences," and "any question of law or fact common to all [plaintiffs] will arise in the action." Is the common "question of law or fact" requirement in Rule 20 superfluous? Can you conceive of any claim which arises out of "the same transaction, occurrence, or series of transactions or occurrences" and in which there are no questions of law or fact common to all plaintiffs joined or all defendants joined?

Whatever their exact meaning, phrases such as "transaction, occurrence, or series of transactions or occurrences" and "common question of law or fact" are hardly self-defining, and the cases and notes have suggested some of the deeper reasons that courts might be motivated to interpret these words more or less liberally. Let us add one final consideration — the debate between Professors Fuller and Chayes (see pp. 13-17, 61-64, *supra*). According to Professor Chayes, public law litigation often contains a wealth of separate interests and consequently a sprawling and amorphous party structure; according to Professor Fuller, courts faced with such a messy party structure might attempt to deal with the problem by shoehorning the case into a traditional two-party mold. See Lon. L. Fuller, *The Forms and Limits of Adjudication*, 92 Harv. L. Rev. 353, 401 (1978). Should a court faced with defining "transactions" and "common questions" ensure that the proposed joinder does not suppress the voices of separate interests by shoehorning a multi-interest dispute into a two-party affair? Should the plaintiffs' consent to joinder override these concerns?

10. The typical device by which a misjoinder of plaintiffs is challenged is a motion under F.R.Civ.P. 21. At common law, misjoinder was a fatal defect to the case, and required dismissal. See Wright et al., *supra*, § 1681. Under Rule 21, however, misjoinder does not authorize a judge to dismiss the entire action. The Rule does, however, allow the judge to drop parties from the action "on such terms as may be just," and also allows the judge to sever and proceed separately with claims against a party if severance can cure the problem. In this regard, *Grayson* and *Aaberg*, which ordered the severance of parties, may not have comported with the precise language of Rule 21. The distinction between "dropping" and "severing" is, however, largely a matter of semantics, and in practice courts often sever parties rather than drop them. Id., § 1689.

11. The decision to add or drop parties or to sever claims is reviewed on appeal under an abuse of discretion standard. See id., § 1688. Should a judge's discretion be confined by more specific rules?

2. Involuntary Joinder of Defendants under Rule 20

Rule 20(a) governs not only the circumstances under which plaintiffs can join together, but also the circumstances under which defendants can be joined. The language concerning joinder of defendants mirrors the language concerning joinder of plaintiffs; defendants can be joined if "there is asserted against them jointly, severally, or in the alternative, any right to relief in respect of or arising out of the same transaction, occurrence, or series of transactions or occurrences and if any question of law or fact common to all defendants will arise in the action." Unlike joinder of plaintiffs, this type of "permissive" joinder is hardly "voluntary"; and it is "permissive" only in the sense that the plaintiff gets to choose which defendants to sue. The issue, therefore, is whether essentially identical language for the joinder of plaintiffs and defendants should be interpreted differently to accommodate the distinct issues raised by the voluntary nature of plaintiff joinder and the involuntary nature of defendant joinder. If a different interpretation creates a restrictive attitude toward joinder of defendants, the global resolution of a controversy through permissive joinder becomes more difficult to accomplish — even when the plaintiff(s) want such a resolution.

NASSAU COUNTY ASSOCIATION OF INSURANCE AGENTS, INC. v. AETNA LIFE & CASUALTY CO.

497 F.2d 1151 (2d Cir.), cert. denied, 419 U.S. 968 (1974)

■ LUMBARD, Circuit Judge. Seeking to recover over $3,750,000,000 in treble damages from 164 insurance companies, four unincorporated associations of insurance agents, the Nassau County Association of Insurance Agents, the Suffolk County Association of Insurance Agents, the Independent Insurance Agents Association of Queens, and the Richmond County Association of Insurance Agents, commenced this class action on behalf of member and independent insurance agents and their policyholders in the Southern District on November 3, 1972, alleging that the defendants had terminated or threatened to terminate thousands of agency contracts with the insurance agents on grounds violative of the federal antitrust laws. Specifically, it was alleged that agents were required regularly to sell new lines of insurance, meet higher minimum volume requirements, and maintain a low pay-out ratio on policies sold or face termination. Plaintiffs contended that enforcement of these requirements by the defendant insurance companies represented "illegal coercion, illegal intimidation, illegal restraints of trade, all of which are in violation of the Clayton Act, the Sherman Act, [and] the McCarran-Ferguson Act...."

On July 24, 1973, Judge Stewart dismissed the action on the ground that the plaintiff associations lacked standing to sue under the antitrust laws in either their own or a representative capacity, 361 F. Supp. 967.... We affirm for the reasons given by Judge Stewart and because of the misjoinder of parties.

[After holding that the plaintiffs lacked standing to claim a Clayton Act violation, the court turned to the misjoinder issue.]

[B]y joining the 164 defendant companies in one action [plaintiffs] have failed to comply with Rule 20(a) of the Federal Rules of Civil Procedure relating to joinder of defendants....

Here there has been no showing of a right to relief arising from the same transaction or series of transactions. No allegation of conspiracy or other concert of action has been asserted. No connection at all between the practices engaged in by each of the 164 defendants has been alleged. Their actions as charged were separate and unrelated, with terminations occurring at different times for different reasons with regard to different agents.

Kenvin v. Newburger, Loeb & Co., 37 F.R.D. 473 (S.D.N.Y. 1965) involved a similar, though less extreme situation. There, plaintiff joined four stockholders, who, he alleged, had extended credit to him in violation of Federal Reserve Board Regulations and the Securities Exchange Act. The wrongdoing of each defendant was identical, but the loans and securities involved and the dates on which the transactions were entered into differed. The court held that defendants had been misjoined since plaintiff had merely "alleged against each of the four defendants distinct and unrelated acts which happened to involve violations of the same statutory duty" and the "operative facts" of each transaction were unrelated to those of any other.

Here, unrelated transactions running into the thousands are asserted as the basis of joinder. Indeed, plaintiffs have not limited joinder of insurance companies on the basis of insurance agents whose contracts have been terminated or who have been threatened with termination, but have also sought to join defendants on the basis of policyholders whose policies were cancelled or not renewed because of the termination of the agency contract with their particular agent by one of the defendant insurance companies.

The misjoinder here, resting on thousands of unrelated transactions, is such a gross abuse of procedure that dismissal under F.R. Civ. P. 41(b) for failure to comply with the federal rules is warranted. Although the usual remedy under Rule 21 is severance, that would be inadequate to remedy the present abuse since the result would be thousands of individual actions, in all of which the association, rather than individual agent and policyholders, would be plaintiffs.

Although we affirm Judge Stewart's dismissal of this action, the rights of any aggrieved individuals to seek appropriate relief are in no wise affected.

Notes and Questions

1. Does *Nassau County* pay sufficient attention to the "series of transactions or occurrences" language of Rule 20(a)?

2. *Nassau County* and *Mosley* (p. 93, *supra*) were decided within two days of each other. Do they reflect the same view of the breadth of F.R.Civ.P. 20(a)? Is the difference between the cases best explained as a difference in attitude about how much joinder Rule 20(a) allows, or as a difference in attitude about joinder of defendants as opposed to joinder of plaintiffs? One way to think about answering this question is to imagine the 164 insurance companies voluntarily joining as plaintiffs in an action that sought a declaratory judgment that their conduct did not violate the antitrust laws. Would the Second Circuit have permitted the joinder of the insurance companies in this situation? If so, then the critical variable in *Nassau County* was the unfairness of joining the 164 companies as *defendants*, rather than their joinder *per se*.

3. In an adversarial system, there is a credible argument that the permissive joinder of plaintiffs should be handled differently than the "permissive" joinder of defendants. After all, if a group of plaintiffs agrees to join together, the plaintiffs presumably regard the joinder as fair. A judge should not tamper with their decision about their own best interests unless significant prejudice to the interests of their opponents results. On the other hand, the joinder of defendants is permissive only in the sense that the plaintiff "permits" them to be sued. Since plaintiffs in an adversary system are unlikely to worry about the fairness of joinder to the defendants (and indeed may be attempting to create unfairness to defendants), the court may need to take a somewhat more active role in assuring that the joinder of defendants is not fundamentally unfair.

Some of the leading cases involving joinder of defendants seem intuitively to understand this point. For instance, in Intercon Research Associates, Ltd. v. Dresser Industries, Inc., 696 F.2d 53 (7th Cir. 1982), a plaintiff sued two foreign defendants for breach of contract. Since the defendants had no assets in the United States, the plaintiff also joined as a defendant Dresser Industries, an American company that owed money to the foreign defendants. The plaintiff had no direct claim against Dresser. The court upheld, on an abuse of discretion standard, the district court's dismissal of Dresser:

> [T]he trial court's decision to dismiss Dresser Industries as a defendant promotes one of the goals of the judicial system, which is to ensure fundamental fairness to all parties. The Ninth Circuit recently noted that, when deciding the question of joinder under Rule 20, "a trial court must also

examine the other relevant factors in a case in order to determine whether the permissive joinder of a party will comport with the principles of fundamental fairness." Desert Empire Bank v. Ins. Co. of North America, 623 F.2d 1371, 1375 (9th Cir. 1980). Requiring Dresser Industries to participate as a defendant in this action would have been unfair for several reasons. There existed no privity of contract between Dresser Industries and Intercon, but rather the contract giving rise to this dispute was between Intercon and the [foreign] defendants . . . . [T]here is no evidence that Dresser Industries had acted improperly toward the plaintiff Intercon. Under this fact situation, it would violate principles of fundamental fairness to require Dresser Industries to expend the time and expense of defending in an action brought to merely ensure payment of any judgment rendered against the two principal defendants. Moreover, the plaintiff was not without other legal or equitable remedies to ensure that a potential recovery against [the foreign defendants] could be satisfied; for example, possibly Intercon could have sought an injunction prohibiting [the foreign defendants] from removing any assets from the country. . . . In summary, Rule 20(a) was designed to allow a plaintiff to join only those parties against whom the plaintiff has a legitimate claim, and not to permit a plaintiff to bring all of a defendant's debtors into a lawsuit. [696 F.2d at 57-58.]

Conversely, however, in League to Save Lake Tahoe v. Tahoe Regional Planning Agency, 558 F.2d 914 (9th Cir. 1977), the plaintiff joined both the Tahoe Regional Planning Agency (TRPA), which had allegedly acted illegally in approving the plans of certain developers, and the developers themselves, against whom plaintiffs had no direct claims. If the plaintiff succeeded in its lawsuit against the Tahoe Regional Planning Agency (TRPA), however, it might have had claims against the developers. The court of appeals thought that joinder of the developers was appropriate:

> [T]he primary purpose [of Rule 20 joinder] is to promote trial convenience and to prevent multiple lawsuits. We do not believe that these purposes will be served if the developers are dismissed from this action. The developers were present before the court and they do have an interest in this litigation in that their projects were approved by TRPA which may be declared invalid if appellants succeed on the merits. If the developers are not present before the court, they will not be bound by any decree of invalidity, thereby creating the possibility of future lawsuits.
>
> Moreover, it would appear that the developers were joined in order to afford complete relief to appellants if they are successful on the merits. If these developers are not joined, then, while the court battle over the approvals of the various construction projects is going on, the actual construction would be taking place. Thus the actual harm sought to be prevented, the upsetting of the ecological balance, would have already occurred, thereby denying appellants their requested relief, even if they are successful.
>
> The district court's concern over the absence of any wrongdoing on the part of the developers is not controlling when balanced against the need to afford complete relief to a plaintiff when it is convenient to do so. [558 F.2d at 917.]

Is the difference between *Intercon* and *League to Save Lake Tahoe* explained by their starting points — in *Intercon* the principle of fundamental fairness to defendants and in *League to Save Lake Tahoe* the principle of trial convenience and prevention of multiple lawsuits? Or is the difference between the cases explained by the lack of joinder complexity in *Intercon* and the existence of joinder complexity in *League to Save Lake Tahoe*?

4. Other cases involving joinder of defendants are not entirely consistent. On the pro-joinder side are cases such as Stone Age Foods, Inc. v. Exchange Bank, 1997 WL 123248 (N.D. Cal.) (employee stole and cashed checks; joinder of company that provided background check on employee and bank that cashed check permitted); and Jonas v. Conrath, 149 F.R.D. 520 (S.D. W.Va. 1993) (joinder of negligent doctor and health insurance company that refused to pay insurance bills permitted). On the more cautious side are cases such as Pena v. McArthur, 889 F. Supp. 403 (E.D. Cal. 1994) (joinder of negligent driver and plaintiff's own insurance company not permitted); National Union Fire Insurance Co. of Pittsburgh, Pa. v. Continental Illinois Corp., 113 F.R.D. 527, 531 (N.D. Ill. 1986) (joinder of other parties to counterclaim not permitted; court noted that "[t]hese lawsuits are already complex and bid fair to become unmanageable. Addition of new litigants and new counsel tends to increase the difficulties geometrically rather than arithmetically."); and Movie Systems, Inc. v. Abel, 99 F.R.D. 129, 129-30 (D. Minn. 1983) (joinder, in 18 actions of 99 or 100 defendants each, of 1,795 defendants that pirated plaintiff's microwave signals improper; cases had created "unmanageable administrative problems in the clerk's office and [had] occasioned unfairness, confusion and prejudice to defendants in their efforts to answer plaintiff's complaints, make responsive motions and conduct pre-trial proceedings").

5. As with the joinder of plaintiffs, one of the most common contexts in which the issue of the scope of defendants' joinder arises is in the midst of a jurisdictional squabble. Plaintiffs may have filed a case in state court against diverse defendants; the defendants then remove the case to federal court; the plaintiffs then propose to join a new non-diverse defendant to force the remand of the case back to state court. See Desert Empire Bank v. Insurance Co. of North America, 623 F.2d 1371 (9th Cir. 1980) (permitting joinder); State Distributors, Inc. v. Glenmore Distilleries Co., 738 F.2d 405 (10th Cir. 1984) (denying joinder); Holman v. State Farm General Insurance Co., 1991 WL 219425 (W.D. Mo.) (permitting joinder and listing 8 "equitable" factors to be used in determining whether "joinder is fundamentally fair"). Cf. Freeport-McMoRan, Inc. v. K N Energy, Inc., 498 U.S. 426, 428 (1991) ("Diversity jurisdiction, once established, is not defeated by the addition of a nondiverse party to the action.").

6. The scope of Rule 20 joinder of defendants both influences and is influenced by the underlying substantive law. For instance, in Hall v. E.I. DuPont De Nemours & Co., Inc., 345 F. Supp. 353 (E.D.N.Y. 1972), thirteen children injured by blasting caps in twelve unrelated accidents filed two separate diversity actions. In the first case, ten of the plaintiffs sued six manufacturers of blasting caps and the manufacturers' trade association when they were unable to identify the manufacturer of the caps that injured them. In the second action, two of the plaintiffs had been injured by caps manufactured by DuPont and one by caps manufactured by Hercules; all three brought actions against both companies.

Judge Weinstein reached different conclusions concerning joinder of plaintiffs and defendants in the two cases. For the ten plaintiffs that were unable to identify a manufacturer, he developed a theory of "industry-wide" liability and shifted the burden of proof on causation. Weinstein then permitted joinder of all six defendants on this issue of joint activity, holding that the allegations satisfied both the "transaction or occurrence" and the "common question" requirements of Rule 20(a). This portion of his decision should remind us of the symbiotic relationship between substance and procedure. Joinder of the ten plaintiffs and seven defendants would not have been possible without a theory of industry-wide liability. Conversely, however, such a theory of liability would not have been possible without a rule authorizing joinder of the plaintiffs and defendants.

For the other three plaintiffs in *Hall*, however, Judge Weinstein found that the Rule 20(a) joinder of a second defendant (Hercules in two cases and DuPont in one) that acted as a representative of the industry was impermissible; the actual tortfeasor was known, and it was unfair to make one defendant bear the burden of defending the entire industry on a joint activity claim. What should the result be if the second set of plaintiffs had joined all of the defendants that the first set of plaintiffs had joined?

Does Judge Weinstein's holding concerning the second set of plaintiffs and defendants in *Hall* suggest that Rule 20(a) actually requires that the common questions predominate? That they at least be significant?

7. In *Nassau County* the court dismissed the case under Rule 41(b) for the "gross abuse" of the joinder rules by plaintiffs. Although consistent with the common law remedy for misjoinder of parties, this remedy seems inconsistent with Rule 21. See Note 10, p. 109, *supra*. Should *Nassau County* have paid closer attention to the language of Rule 21? Obviously, since the case was also dismissed on other grounds, it made little difference in the outcome of *Nassau County* itself. But imagine another case just like *Nassau County* in which valid claims were stated. If the court in that case had tried to drop parties or sever claims, what test would the court have used to decide which defendants to drop and which claims to sever? Would breaking the case up into four suits (one for each insurance association), 164 suits (one for each defendant insurance company), or into thousands of separate suits (one for each plaintiff insurance agency) be the most sensible method of proceeding? If either the first or the third option is used, is *Nassau County* a case about improper joinder of defendants, or about improper joinder of plaintiffs?

8. Once sued, defendants can themselves become "plaintiffs" and file counterclaims against the plaintiff, cross-claims against other defendants, and new claims against third-party defendants that are or may be liable to the defendant. See F.R.Civ.P. 13(a), 13(b), 13(g), 14(a). Can a defendant that wants to join additional parties as defendants on a counterclaim or cross-claim do so? As a general proposition, the answer is "yes"; Rule 13(h) permits joinder of new parties "in accordance with the provisions of Rules 19 and 20." The exact boundaries of this joinder power are, however, less than clear, and many tricky and uncharted issues remain. See generally 6 Charles A Wright et al., Federal Practice & Procedure §§ 1434-36 (1990); Alkot Industries, Inc. v. Takara Co., 106 F.R.D. 373 (N.D. Ill. 1985) (permitting joinder of some but not all counterclaim defendants).

9. If the potential for unfair joinder of defendants already requires a court to supervise somewhat carefully the joinder of defendants (see Note 3, *supra*), and if complex litigation involves that subset of cases in which the adversary system does not work well, what should the court's role be in the decision about the joinder of defendants in complex cases? In particular, should a court have a power to establish an appropriate structure for defendants when the plaintiffs fail to do so? In the context of a court's Rule 21 power to join additional

plaintiffs, we have already seen that courts seemed generally unable to override Rule 20's requirement that plaintiffs must consent to joinder. See Note 8, p. 114, *supra*. Rule 21 also gives the court the power to add (or drop) defendants. Since Rule 20 does not presuppose defendants' consent to suit, does a court enjoy a broader Rule 21 power to re-configure the *defendants* in the case? Should the court's power (if any) in complex cases vary with whether it is attempting to drop parties unfairly joined or add parties to achieve a broader resolution of the case?

Thus far, the issue seems not to have been tested; the reported cases involve defendants sought to be joined either on the plaintiffs' motion or, if joined by the court, under circumstances in which Rule 19 compelled joinder. See 7 Charles A Wright et al., Federal Practice & Procedure §§ 1684, 1688 (1986). We turn to the nature of Rule 19 joinder in the following section.

3. Rules Permitting Mandatory Joinder

Rule 20 is the basic and most heavily invoked joinder rule. As we have seen, Rule 20 is a "permissive" joinder rule in the sense that the plaintiff chooses the party structure; other plaintiffs can be joined only if they consent to being in the suit and the plaintiff also agrees, and defendants can be joined only if the plaintiff selects them to be in the suit. Rule 20 (in conjunction with Rule 21) gives the defendant(s) and the court only a very limited power to change the party structure chosen by the plaintiff(s).

In cases of joinder complexity, the inability to join other parties creates inequity; in other complicated cases, the inability to join parties creates inefficiency. Should the defendant(s) or the judge have the power to mandate the joinder of parties that reduce the inequity and/or inefficiency in complex or complicated cases? By significantly constraining the operation of the "master of the complaint" rule, such a power (especially if exercised by the judge) would damage our adversarial approach to litigation. It also damages the notion of individual autonomy to control the timing and placement of a lawsuit. Is the reduction in inequity and/or inefficiency nonetheless worth these harms?

These are the questions that we explore as we look at several joinder devices (Rule 19, interpleader, and Rule 23) that were designed to foster either the joinder of plaintiffs that did not consent to Rule 20 joinder or the joinder of defendants that plaintiff(s) declined to join under Rule 20. With the arguable exception of Rule 23, however, these "mandatory joinder" rules were not written, and are not generally interpreted, with the problems of complex and complicated cases in mind. As you read the materials, consider whether we should create special "complex litigation" or "complicated litigation" glosses on the mandatory joinder rules. Would it be even better if we created separate rules of mandatory joinder for complex cases and complicated cases? How would such a breach of our trans-substantive aspiration to treat cases alike be justified?

a. Mandatory Joinder under Rule 19

TEMPLE v. SYNTHES CORP.

498 U.S. 5 (1990)

■ PER CURIAM.

Petitioner Temple, a Mississippi resident, underwent surgery in October 1986 in which a "plate and screw device" was implanted in his lower spine. The device was manufactured by respondent Synthes, Ltd. (U.S.A.) (Synthes), a Pennsylvania corporation. Dr. S. Henry LaRocca performed the surgery at St. Charles General Hospital in New Orleans, Louisiana. Following surgery, the device's screws broke off inside Temple's back.

Temple filed suit against Synthes in the United States District Court for the Eastern District of Louisiana. The suit, which rested on diversity jurisdiction, alleged defective design and manufacture of the device. At the same time, Temple filed a state administrative proceeding against Dr. LaRocca and the hospital for malpractice and negligence. At the conclusion of the administrative proceeding, Temple filed suit against the doctor and the hospital in Louisiana state court.

Synthes did not attempt to bring the doctor and the hospital into the federal action by means of a third-party complaint, as provided in Federal Rule of Civil Procedure 14(a). Instead, Synthes filed a motion to dismiss Temple's federal suit for failure to join necessary parties pursuant to Federal Rule of Civil Procedure 19. Following a hearing, the District Court ordered Temple to join the doctor and the hospital as defendants within twenty days or risk dismissal of the lawsuit. According to the court, the most significant reason for requiring joinder was the interest of judicial economy. The court relied on this Court's decision in Provident Tradesmens Bank & Trust Co. v. Patterson, 390 U.S. 102 (1968), wherein we recognized that one focus of Rule 19 is "the interest of the courts and the public in complete, consistent, and efficient settlement of controversies." When Temple failed to join the doctor and the hospital, the court dismissed the suit with prejudice.

Temple appealed, and the United States Court of Appeals for the Fifth Circuit affirmed. The court deemed it "obviously prejudicial to the defendants to have the separate litigations being carried on," because Synthes' defense might be that the plate was not defective but that the doctor and the hospital were negligent, while the doctor and hospital, on the other hand, might claim that they were not negligent but that the plate was defective. The Court of Appeals found that the claims overlapped and that the District Court therefore had not abused its discretion in ordering joinder under Rule 19. . . .

In his petition for certiorari to this Court, Temple contends that it was error to label joint tortfeasors as indispensable parties under Rule 19(b) and to dismiss the lawsuit with prejudice for failure to join those parties. We agree. Synthes does not deny that it, the doctor, and the hospital are potential joint tortfeasors. It has long been the rule that it is not necessary for all joint tortfeasors to be named as defendants in a single lawsuit. . . . Nothing in the 1966 revision of Rule 19 changed that principle. The Advisory Committee Notes to Rule 19(a) explicitly state that "a tortfeasor with the usual 'joint-and-several' liability is merely a permissive party to an action against another with like liability." . . . There is nothing in Louisiana tort law to the contrary. . . .

The opinion in *Provident Bank, supra,* does speak of the public interest in limiting multiple litigation, but that case is not controlling here. There, the estate of a tort victim brought a declaratory judgment action against an insurance company. We assumed that the policyholder was a person "who, under § (a), should be joined if 'feasible[,]'" . . . and went on to discuss the appropriate analysis under Rule 19(b), because the policyholder could not be joined without destroying diversity. After examining the factors set forth in Rule 19(b), we determined that the action could proceed without the policyholder; he therefore was not an indispensable party whose absence required dismissal of the suit.

Here, no inquiry under Rule 19(b) is necessary, because the threshold requirements of Rule 19(a) have not been satisfied. As potential joint tortfeasors with Synthes, Dr. LaRocca and the hospital were merely permissive parties. The Court of Appeals erred by failing to hold that the District Court abused its discretion in ordering them joined as defendants and in dismissing the action when Temple failed to comply with the court's order. For these reasons, we grant the petition for certiorari, reverse the judgment of the Court of Appeals for the Fifth Circuit, and remand for further proceedings consistent with this opinion.

ELDREDGE v. CARPENTERS 46 NORTHERN CALIFORNIA COUNTIES JATC

662 F.2d 534 (9th Cir.), cert. denied, 459 U.S. 917 (1982)

■ FLETCHER, Circuit Judge. This is an appeal from the district court's order dismissing the action for failure to join indispensable parties . . . . We reverse and remand. . . .

Plaintiffs Eldredge and Mazur brought suit under Title VII, 42 U.S.C. § 2000e-2, against the Carpenters 46 Northern California Counties Joint Apprenticeship and Training Committee (JATC), alleging sex discrimination in the operation of JATC's apprenticeship program. Plaintiffs brought the suit as a class action, but the district court has not yet considered the question of class certification.

Defendant JATC is a joint labor-management committee established under an agreement that provides for a trust fund contributed to by the parties to the master collective bargaining agreements in the Northern California construction industry. JATC is composed of equal numbers of labor and management representatives, and acts as a board of trustees for the administration of the Carpenters Apprenticeship and Training Trust

Fund for Northern California. It is responsible for establishing, supporting, and maintaining programs to educate and train journeymen and apprentices in all classifications covered by any collective bargaining agreement that requires employer contributions to the trust fund.

Plaintiffs allege that the process by which JATC selects applicants to its apprenticeship training program discriminates against women. Although JATC has employed other selection procedures in the past, it presently relies on what is known as the "unrestricted hunting license" system. Under this system, an individual must first convince an employer to hire him or her as a beginning apprentice. JATC then places the individual's name on its applicant register. The applicant enters into an apprenticeship agreement with JATC and is dispatched through the union hiring hall. An individual needs no prior training to become an apprentice; all that is required is that he or she be 17 years of age and have a high school diploma or its equivalent.

The master collective bargaining agreements under which JATC operates require employers to hire one apprentice for every five journeymen employed. The apprenticeship is a four-year program. Employers are under no obligation to hire beginning as opposed to experienced apprentices. In May of 1976, only thirteen of JATC's 3220 registered apprentices were women.

The essence of plaintiffs' complaint is that, by relying on the unrestricted hunting license system to recruit apprentices, JATC has adopted an entrance requirement for its program which is known to have a discriminatory effect on women. Plaintiffs argue that JATC knows that individual employers do not hire women under the unrestricted hunting license system, and that JATC's use of this system is therefore illegal under Title VII. The district court assumed for the purposes of its rule 19 analysis that plaintiffs had stated a claim on which relief could be granted. . . .

The district court held that the 4500 employers and 60 union locals covered by the master labor agreement, or adequate representatives of their interests, were indispensable to the litigation under the standards imposed by rule 19(b). It ordered them joined within 60 days. Plaintiffs were granted extensions of time in which to explore the possibilities for joinder . . . but joinder of all 4500 employers proved impossible. The plaintiffs then sought to join the Northern California Homebuilders' Conference (NCHBC) to represent the absent employers' interests.[10] The court held this inadequate and dismissed the case.[11] We conclude that the employers are not necessary parties under rule 19(a) and thus cannot be indispensable parties under rule 19(b). . . .

10. The NCHBC is a large employers' organization which negotiated the master labor agreement under which JATC operates. Not all of the employers who subscribe to the master agreement belong to the NCHBC.

11. The plaintiffs also sought to join the United Brotherhood of Carpenters and Joiners of America, the international, to represent the union locals. The district court did not decide whether the international could adequately represent the locals because it decided that the action could not proceed in any case.

Rule 19 requires two separate inquiries. First, are there persons who should be joined, either because their own interests or the interests of the parties might be harmed by their absence? Such persons, referred to as "necessary parties," must be joined if feasible. Fed.R.Civ.P. 19(a). Second, if parties determined to be necessary under rule 19(a) cannot be joined, should the action in "equity and good conscience" be dismissed? Only if the court determines that the action should be dismissed is the absent party labelled "indispensable." Fed.R.Civ.P. 19(b) . . . .

The nature of the rule 19 inquiry is described at some length in Provident Tradesmens Bank & Trust Co. v. Patterson, 390 U.S. 102 (1968). The inquiry should focus on the practical effects of joinder and nonjoinder. Id. at 116 n.12 . . . . Rule 19 was revised in 1966 to emphasize its practical focus and to avoid the inflexible approach taken by many courts under the prior version of the rule. . . .

Rule 19(a) describes two categories of persons who should be joined if feasible. If the absent employers fall into either of these two categories, they are "necessary parties."

The first category comprises those persons in whose absence "complete relief cannot be accorded among those already parties." Fed.R.Civ.P. 19(a)(1). This portion of the rule is concerned only with "relief as between the persons already parties, not as between a party and the absent person whose joinder is sought." 3A Moore's Federal Practice ¶ 19.07-1[1], at 19-128 (2d ed. 1980) . . . . The district court concluded that the absent employers could frustrate any relief granted against JATC, and that complete relief would therefore not be possible unless the employers were made parties. The court reasoned that the employers could defeat any order against JATC by refusing to hire any apprentices, by hiring only unregistered, nonunion apprentices, or by rejecting all female apprentices dispatched to them. We believe that the district court misapprehended the legal inquiry required by rule 19(a)(1).

If JATC's activities violate Title VII, a question not yet decided, then the court has both the power and the duty to enjoin those activities. The possibility that such an injunction may induce employers to avoid JATC's services, or ultimately to disband the training and referral system altogether, should not defeat the present action against JATC. JATC may not avoid its own liability for practices illegal under Title VII by relying on the employers' possible future conduct that might frustrate the remedial purposes of any court-ordered changes in the apprenticeship program. . . .

The district court appears to assume that the employers would refuse to hire women admitted to the apprentice program pursuant to any judgment that may be entered against JATC in this suit. There is no evidence to this effect in the record. On the contrary, the employers have previously participated, apparently successfully, in a state-mandated affirmative action program designed to increase the number of minority apprentices.

While it might be desirable to join all 4500 employers in order to eradicate sex discrimination in the industry, we conclude that relief on plaintiffs' claims against JATC as an entity could be afforded by an injunction against JATC alone. Both sides agree that JATC has the power under the trust fund agreement to structure its apprenticeship program in any way it sees fit. It is quite possible that a court-ordered restructuring of the program could effectively increase the participation of women in the apprenticeship program. . . .

The second inquiry required by rule 19(a) concerns prejudice, either to the absent persons or to those already parties. Rule 19(a)(2)(i) provides that a person should be joined if he claims an interest relating to the subject of the action, and the disposition of the action may "as a practical matter impair or impede his ability to protect that interest."

The district court held that the employers should be joined since they have a right to select their own employees, a substantial interest that they have a right to protect. We disagree. The trust fund agreement grants full authority to JATC to structure the apprenticeship program and to select the apprentices. We conclude that the employers have by contract ceded to JATC whatever legally protectible interest they may have had in selecting apprentices to be trained. On the other hand, without the joinder of the employers, any court order that may be entered to enjoin JATC to institute programs cannot go beyond the authority granted JATC under the trust fund agreement. The absent employers are thus assured that an injunction against JATC will not trench on any rights reserved to the employers under the agreement. We must conclude that the employers' ability to protect whatever interest in employee selection they retain will not be "impaired or impeded" if they are not made parties. They are therefore not necessary parties under rule 19(a)(2)(i).

The district court was understandably concerned that the absent employers might have interests that would be unrepresented in the present suit. Although we have concluded that their interests are not the sort that would make the employers necessary under rule 19, on remand it is possible that some employers, or the NCHBC, may move to intervene. . . .

We hold that the trial court erred in dismissing the case for nonjoinder of necessary parties. We reverse and remand for further proceedings.

Wiiliam B. Rubenstein, DIVIDED WE LITIGATE: ADDRESSING DISPUTES AMONG GROUP MEMBERS AND LAWYERS IN CIVIL RIGHTS CAMPAIGNS

106 Yale L.J. 1623, 1644-48, 1650-53 (1997)

Current procedural and ethical rules encourage group members and attorneys to pursue their own individual paths in filing, pursuing, and constructing test cases. . . .

C. *Individualism in the Pursuit of Goals*

Civil procedure's private law orientation conceptualizes litigation decisions as individual "rights" to be protected from governmental or centralized community control. The guarantee of litigative autonomy is recognized by the "day in court" ideal and realized through the procedural rules that define parties to, and the preclusive effects of, litigation. Because an individual enjoys litigative liberty, it would deprive her of due process to bind her to the results of a case in which she was not heard, or over which she did not have control. If [some plaintiffs litigate their] cases and lose, future plaintiffs are not barred from litigating theirs. These plaintiffs can pursue their self-interest now, others can pursue theirs in the future.

The benefits of the individualist model are several. By safeguarding the day in court ideal, the procedural rules guarantee that each individual can control the legal decisions that govern her life. She can exercise this control as she sees fit and cannot be coerced into a case that she does not want to join. Litigation therefore represents a valuable means of self-definition: Individuals can express themselves through the conflicts that they formalize into litigation and through the manner in which they wage these conflicts. By fostering this self-definition, individualism promotes engagement and avoids the alienation that can result when decisions are yielded to experts. The aggregate result of ensuring these individual litigative freedoms may also be more productive for the community than a single collective litigation; through a multiplicity of cases, the community's common good will be served. . . .

The primary problem with the individualist model is the central downside of liberalism generally: a satisfactory account of its limits. For John Stuart Mill, this rested upon the ability to delineate between self-referring (protected) acts and other-harming (not protected) acts. A strong critique of liberty challenges this line as ultimately incoherent. This critique is powerful when applied to the litigation context. Because preclusion rules bind only the named parties to a lawsuit, the system assures itself that these individuals are only litigating their individual cases and thus are causing no "harm" to anyone else. The plaintiffs' fists have stopped before reaching the other group members' noses. Yet procedural rules actually do not envision present and future litigants to be fully disconnected: The outcome of the initial action, though not preclusive of future litigations, will be authoritative precedent governing them. Hence each initial lawsuit will infringe upon the freedom of other community members to litigate their own individual cases (or to choose *not* to litigate). . . . While the individualist model guarantees the litigant her day in court, that day in court may well deny other community members *their* days in court.

Defenders of the individualist model might point to several aspects of the procedural rules in response. First, the individualist might argue that the preceding account exaggerates the impact of a lawsuit on later cases and thus on other litigants' autonomy; the earlier case may be precedent in later cases, but it would not preclude the filing of such cases. Yet, generally speaking, "the doctrine of *stare decisis* is a *mandate* that courts should give due weight to precedent. It holds that an already established point of law should be followed without reconsideration, provided that the earlier decision was authoritative." . . . The only difference between this precedential effect and pure preclusion is that the later plaintiffs can literally have their day — albeit a short one — in court. The individualists are correct that they have left a scrap of litigative autonomy on the table for future litigants after the resolution of their lawsuits, but it is only a scrap. In practice, the outcome of their lawsuits did harm (or benefit) others within their community. These were therefore not purely self-regarding acts with no externalities.

Beyond invoking the distinction between stare decisis and preclusion, defenders of the individualist model could argue that it enables a "pluralistic" solution to the problem that cases inevitably affect non-parties: Those persons can intervene and add their voices to the action. For [potential members of an affected community who do not want to argue for the result for which others wish to argue], or do not want to do so now, merely allowing intervention in the pending marriage cases hardly protects their autonomy. Such measures may enable them to let the court know of their views, but, of critical importance, their intervention will not enable them to have the underlying claim dismissed. So long as the plaintiffs have standing and a case or controversy, they are proper parties and cannot be foreclosed from litigating. There is no manner in which the intervention rules, or pluralist approaches generally, will satisfy everyone's autonomous choices. . . .

Through rigid adherence to litigative autonomy, [individualist procedural rules] entitle any individual to litigate cases with groupwide effects regardless of the rest of the group's desires. In so doing, the procedural rules exalt the autonomy of the present plaintiff at the expense of the autonomy of nonlitigating parties. This procedural system also rewards those within the group who have access to attorneys and thus to courts: These players, often the community's legal experts themselves, have the power to opt out of the group debate about filing simply by filing at any time they want. The effect of the legal system's preference for the liberal model of adjudication is to pit community members against one another as competitive individualists. In the shadow of this legal regime, group disputes are exacerbated and constituencies are disharmonized. Although the individualist model embodies important principles, it fails to provide a satisfactory framework for addressing group disputes.

D. *Individualism in the Choice of Means*

Disagreements among attorneys over the tactics and strategies employed to further the social group's legal goals could also be addressed by individualist decisionmaking. When [community members] disagree about how to frame [their legal] claims, the individual autonomy model authorizes each private attorney to select the course of action she believes is best, unrestrained by . . . anyone else's . . . recommendation or opinion. Like her client, the attorney enjoys complete liberty within her realm: liberty to frame the "technical and legal tactical issues." Those who espouse the "every lawyer for herself" approach find support for such unilateral action in the traditional vision of lawyering championed by the bar and embodied in the rules of professional responsibility.

The benefits of the individualist model flow from this approach. Because the attorney is entitled to define her own approach to litigation, the manner in which she litigates reflects her individuality; she defines herself through her litigative choices. Individualism induces creativity and permits the attorney a sense of self-definition and connection to, as opposed to alienation from, her work. The model of individual autonomy also creates a diverse set of approaches in test cases, out of which some "best" way of litigating, or ultimate litigation strategy, will emerge. By encouraging each attorney to pursue her own "self-interested" way of framing a case, the individualist model leads to better outcomes for the entire community.

The problems with individualism in litigation-framing parallel the problems with individualism in litigation-filing: litigation is not a "self-regarding" act and thus the framing, as much as the filing, can seriously impair the autonomy of other framers. When Vaughn [the lawyer for the plaintiffs in *Shelley v. Kraemer*, 334 U.S. 1 (1948), in which the Supreme Court invalidated racially restrictive covenants] spent the better part of his Supreme Court argument pursuing his Thirteenth Amendment theory, the lawyers framing the covenant cases as Fourteenth Amendment violations were harmed; they had to amend their approaches to account for Vaughn's idiosyncratic method. . . .

When confronted with the externalities of her professional judgment, the individualist retreats to a central norm of legal ethics: She insists that she may exercise her autonomy unilaterally because she must be loyal to her individual client's interests. She argues that her client's "day in court" envisions the client having "control" of the litigation. These principles are said to support the notion that, for instance, Vaughn's loyalty is to the Shelleys, not to other attorneys or clients; that Vaughn's clients are the Shelleys, not the larger African-American community; and that Vaughn must pursue his own view of what is best for the Shelleys (perhaps developed in concert with the Shelleys), without regard to the consequences for other litigants.

For several reasons, this defense of individualism as an approach to disputes among lawyers in litigation campaigns is unsatisfying. First, the more technical the lawyering decision, the less likely it is that the lawyer has in fact consulted with her client on how to make it. Second, even if the individualist attorney did consult with her individual client, it is not clear that technical decisions are within the client's sphere of control. There is nothing magic about the client's desires on questions of tactics. Indeed, the third problem with the individualist's strict reliance on client loyalty is: Why only that individual client? The individualist attorney knows her case is a test case meant to make law for the entire community. She pursues it for that reason. When her tactics are questioned as possibly harming the entire community for which she hopes to set a precedent, it is inconsistent to defend them on the grounds that they comport with the desires of her individual named client. A more robust vision of client loyalty in this circumstance would ask the litigator to acknowledge the larger client — the community — and thus to consider the consequences of her tactics on the community's interests.

Deborah R. Hensler, RESOLVING MASS TOXIC TORTS: MYTHS AND REALITIES

1989 U. Ill. L. Rev. 89, 91-93, 95-96, 100

II. THE TRADITIONAL TORT VERSION OF REALITY

Beliefs about the traditional tort approach relate to both process and outcomes. As Schuck indicates, the version of legal reality implicit in the traditional tort approach assumes that "private [litigant] control of litigation" and "intimate contact and consultation" between litigants and lawyers "force lawyers to educate their clients, respond to their wishes, and litigate faithfully and vigorously."[9] . . .

According to the traditional tort approach, fair outcomes not only require adequate compensation and similar levels of compensation for similarly situated plaintiffs but also proper attention to defendants' varying degrees of fault. More generally, the deterrence objective of the tort system can only be satisfied, according to modern economic theory, if the full losses of plaintiffs are imposed upon negligent defendants.

III. PROCEDURAL REALITIES

Systematic empirical research on litigation suggests that the tort process in practice diverges substantially from the picture painted above. Although most of the research concerns routine litigation, some involves mass torts. . . .

In a [recent] survey of litigants in personal injury cases involving amounts up to $50,000, respondents were asked how many times they met in person with their lawyer and how many times they talked to their lawyer on the telephone. Table 1 summarizes the results. . . . Because this survey deliberately overrepresented litigants whose cases were resolved after some sort of court intervention . . . these numbers may overestimate the average time spent by lawyers with clients whose cases are more typically resolved through bilateral bargaining. . . . Although [this table shows] significant fractions of litigants do interact multiple times with their attorneys, a sizeable number would seem to have little opportunity to establish the "intimate" relationship envisaged by the traditional tort version of reality. Data from several other studies documenting the modest hours attorneys typically spend on civil cases bolster this interpretation. . . .

Tables 4 and 5 show how litigants summarized their role in the litigation process. Table 4 illustrates that a majority of litigants felt they had little or no control over how their cases were handled. Table 5 shows that about half of those who felt relatively lacking in control attributed this to their lawyers; only a few litigants said they exercised little control by choice. . . .

---

9. [Peter Schuck, Agent Orange on Trial] 263 [(1986)].

TABLE 1
TORT LITIGANTS' INTERACTION WITH LAWYERS

Number	In-person Meetings %	Telephone Calls %
Zero	11	11
One	14	9
Two	15	12
Three	15	9
Four	12	7
Five or more	33	52
Total Number of Cases	363	359

TABLE 4
TORT LITIGANTS' PERCEPTION OF CONTROL OVER THEIR CASE

How Much Control Was Exercised	%
A Lot	18
Some	26
A Little	18
Not Much	38
Total Number of Cases	372

TABLE 5
TORT LITIGANTS' PERCEPTIONS OF WHY THEY LACKED CONTROL

Reason for Lack of Control	%
Court	21
Lawyer	46
Self	8
Lawyer & Court	10
Insurance Company or Other	15
Total Number of Cases	299

None of the research described above deals with mass toxic tort cases, and no one has yet surveyed litigants in these cases. However, descriptions of the mass tort litigation process gives little reason to believe that the traditional tort approach to such cases provides more interaction between lawyers and clients, more intimate relations between lawyers and clients, or more opportunity for clients rather than lawyers to control the litigation process. In fact, the reverse is likely to be true: when lawyers handle cases individually, the already tenuous client relationship described above is attenuated further by the press of the sheer number of claims....

IV. OUTCOME REALITIES

Critics of formal aggregative procedures fear they will impair the equity of outcomes, by impairing the court's ability to match losses and compensation properly. Because most tort cases are settled without formal adjudication and outcomes are regarded as highly sensitive, there is little empirical evidence on patterns of tort outcomes. What evidence there is, however, suggests that in routine as well as mass litigation, claimants with small losses are overcompensated and claimants with large losses are undercompensated. In addition, evidence suggests a considerable variation in compensation not attributable to loss. Moreover, total compensation payments may often not equal the amount that, in principle, would be required to deter negligent behavior on the part of potential defendants.

Notes and Questions

1. The basic idea of Rule 19(a) is to give the present players in the litigation (plaintiffs, defendants, and judge) the ability to force additional persons into the litigation when the plaintiffs either refuse to join the additional persons or because the additional persons refuse the plaintiffs' invitation to join. The basic idea of Rule 19(b) is to decide whether the lawsuit should go forward when these additional parties cannot for some reason (usually because of immunity, lack of personal jurisdiction, or lack of subject matter jurisdiction) be forced into the suit. Although Rule 19(a) does not use this term, those that should be made parties to the suit under Rule 19(a) are often called "necessary" parties. Those necessary parties whose presence is so vital to the suit that it is better to dismiss the suit under Rule 19(b) than to proceed are called, to use Rule 19(b)'s term, "indispensable" parties.

Rule 19 is therefore important both as a practical and as a theoretical matter. At a practical level, the lure of a Rule 19(b) dismissal gives a defendant such as Synthes an incentive to argue for mandatory joinder of additional parties when the defendant knows that there exists an insuperable obstacle (whether based on immunity, jurisdiction, or other ground) to joinder of the necessary party. At a theoretical level, Rule 19's concept of mandatory joinder forces us to confront, as Professor Rubenstein and Ms. Hensler confronted, the value of litigant autonomy and the right of such litigants (usually potential plaintiffs) to control their own destiny.

2. Before we return to the larger theoretical issue, let us try to unpack some of the practical aspects of Rule 19. Begin with the idea of using Rule 19 to force additional plaintiffs into a suit. Which players would want to use Rule 19 in this way? The present plaintiff might, when she is incapable of convincing other plaintiffs to join; but she might also lose control of the litigation as more persons are added (see Horowitz and Bordens, pp. 102-03, *supra*). Clearly a defendant would not normally want additional plaintiffs suing him, and would have an incentive to file a Rule 19(a) motion only in those cases in which (a) the additional plaintiffs could not in fact be brought into the suit, and the defendant thought that he had a very good chance of convincing the court that the additional plaintiffs were indispensable; or (b) the defendant desired complete peace, and dreaded the costs of additional litigation more than the costs of the additional remedy that must be provided to the additional plaintiffs. Neither

plaintiff nor defendant typically has the incentive to seek mandatory joinder merely in order to prevent joinder complexity or inefficient re-litigation; these goals are achieved fitfully when the parties are left with the responsibility for making a Rule 19 motion. The only player with an incentive to seek Rule 19 joinder of additional plaintiffs in order to avoid joinder complexity or inefficiency is the judge. Do we want judges to have a broad Rule 19 joinder power? If so, what is the point of having Rule 20 and its preference for voluntary joinder of plaintiffs? Wouldn't we be better off with a single joinder rule that allowed the judge to pick the plaintiff package that minimized complexity or inefficiency? Moreover, the focus thus far in this paragraph has been on the interests of the present plaintiffs, the defendants, and the court. Shouldn't we also consider the interests of the persons sought to be joined? Does the concern for their autonomy, as well as the related concern for the limited role of a judge in an adversarial system, combine to make a broad power of mandatory joinder of plaintiffs a bad idea?

Now switch to the problem of using Rule 19 to join additional defendants. Which players would want to use Rule 19 in this way? Typically not the present plaintiff; she already had her chance to join additional defendants under Rule 20, and decided for whatever reason not to do so. (This assumes, of course, that Rule 19 joinder is not broader than Rule 20 joinder.) A defendant might want to join additional defendants when (a) the additional defendants could not in fact be brought into the suit, and the defendant thought that he had a very good chance of convincing the court that the additional defendants were indispensable; or (b) the defendant thought that the presence of an additional defendant would reduce or eliminate his own responsibility to the plaintiff, and that this chance of limiting responsibility outweighed the tactical disadvantages (such as the loss of the time-honored trial technique of pointing to the "empty chair") of having additional defendants. Again, neither plaintiff nor defendant has an incentive to use Rule 19 when and only when mandatory joinder is necessary to overcome joinder complexity or inefficiency. Again, the judge might have such an incentive. Is a more powerful, non-adversarial judge desirable in this context? What happened to Rule 20 and the "master of the complaint" principle that underlies it? Do the advantages of such a judge outweigh the costs to the autonomy of present plaintiffs (who chose not to add such defendants), present defendants (who might find their trial strategies upended by the presence of additional defendants), and the putative defendants (who find themselves in a lawsuit in which none of the parties sought their joinder)?

3. The last Note suggests that there are both practical objections (Rule 19 is often used for tactical reasons unrelated to achieving an appropriate joinder of parties) and theoretical objections (harm to the notion of adversarialism, as well as related notions of master of the complaint and litigant autonomy) to an expansive reading of Rule 19. Indeed, these objections seem to have carried the day, both in the text of Rule 19 and the way in which that text has been interpreted. Starting with the text, a person can be a necessary party only when (1) the necessary person's absence makes it impossible to provide complete relief to those already parties, Rule 19(a)(1); (2) the necessary party has an interest in the subject of the action, and the action "may . . . as a practical matter impair or impede the person's ability to protect that interest," Rule 19(a)(2)(i); or (3) the necessary party's interest in the subject of the action leaves a present party "subject to a substantial risk of incurring double, multiple, or otherwise inconsistent obligations," Rule 19(a)(2)(ii).

A quick study of this text leads to three observations. First, the language of Rule 19(a) sounds more restrictive than the language of Rule 20(a). Gone is the notion of joinder when there are common questions of law or fact and a common transaction or occurrence; instead, three specific, narrower circumstances permit joinder. This difference suggests that mandatory joinder, at least in relation to permissive joinder, is disfavored — a suggestion that must be true if Rule 20 permissive joinder is to have a significant scope of operation.

Second, the three circumstances under which a person can be deemed necessary correspond roughly to circumstances in which the plaintiff is prejudiced by non-joinder (Rule 19(a)(1)), the defendant is prejudiced by non-joinder (Rule 19(a)(2)(ii), and the necessary party is prejudiced by non-joinder (Rule 19(a)(2)(i)). Conspicuously missing from the list of players whose interests in mandatory joinder might count is the judge.

Third, these three limited circumstances in which Rule 19(a) mandates joinder sound a great deal like the circumstances in which lawyer dysfunction can cause joinder complexity. Lawyer dysfunction in joinder decisions arises when early-filing plaintiffs make it impossible for later-filing plaintiffs to receive a remedy, when later-filing parties threaten to undo the remedy obtained in the original suit, or when the defendant cannot meet the remedies sought by both the early-filing and the later-filing plaintiffs. See p. 88, *supra*. Although Rule 19(a)(2)(ii) also adds in the notion of double or multiple liability, Rule 19(a)'s concerns with practical impairment to the interests of non-joined parties, plaintiffs' need for complete relief, and defendants' need for consistent remedies seem to echo these types of dysfunction. Note that concerns for efficient packaging of lawsuits in order to prevent unnecessary re-litigation are not generally reflected in Rule 19(a); mandatory joinder is not authorized merely in order to avoid complicated litigation.

4. Although Rule 19(a) sometimes receives a broad interpretation, the standard interpretation of Rule 19 tends to emphasize its narrow scope. Highwater marks for a broad interpretation can be found in language from Shields v. Barrows, 17 How. (58 U.S.) 130 (1855) and Provident Tradesmens Bank & Trust Co. v. Patterson, 390 U.S. 102 (1968). In *Shields*, the Court stated that the purpose of the equitable predecessor to Rule 19 was to join those "persons having an interest in the controversy, and who ought to be made parties, in order that the court may . . . finally determine the entire controversy, and do complete justice, by adjusting all the rights involved in it." 17 How. at 139. But *Shields* is an old case, its discussion of necessary and indispensable parties was largely dicta, and its reasoning concerning necessary and indispensable parties hinged on the harm to absent parties rather than on the court's desire to achieve a sensible packaging of the case. *Provident Tradesmen* involved an absent person that owned a car involved in a fatal crash. When some of the victims of the crash failed to sue the owner, whose presence would have destroyed federal jurisdiction, the court of appeals held that the owner was indispensable, and ordered dismissal of the case. The Supreme Court reversed, holding that the owner was not indispensable. Along the way, the Court "assumed" that the owner was a necessary party in a suit brought by one victim against the owner's insurance company because of the owner's interest in preserving insurance proceeds for other state court suits in which he was involved. Again, the discussion was dicta (the Court ultimately holding that, even if necessary, the owner was not indispensable), and the focus of the analysis was on the harm to an absent party, not on the systemic harm of duplicative

litigation. Any attempt to extrapolate a broader right of mandatory joiner from *Provident Tradesmen* seems to have been stymied by *Temple v. Synthes*.

Another highwater mark is Illinois Brick Co. v. Illinois, 431 U.S. 720, 737-38 (1977), in which the Court, also in dicta, suggested a somewhat broader reading of Rule 19(a) in its description of the interests that underlay mandatory joinder: "the interest of the defendant in avoiding multiple liability for the fund; the interest of the absent potential plaintiffs in protecting their right to recover for the portion of the fund allocable to them; and the social interest in the efficient administration of justice and the avoidance of multiple litigation." *Illinois Brick* does not mention the concern for an incomplete remedy for present plaintiffs (an interest that was not involved on the facts of the case) and reads in a judicial interest in efficient adjudication. Since this last interest is not reflected in the text of Rule 19(a), can a court use this interest to interpret the text of Rule 19(a)? If so, mandatory joinder might be interpreted rather expansively.

Most cases interpreting Rule 19(a), however, have tended to fall in the direction of *Temple* and *Eldridge*, so that the circumstances permitting mandatory joinder have been narrowly construed. As a general matter, the use of Rule 19 to join additional plaintiffs is quite rare, see 7 Charles A. Wright et al., Federal Practice & Procedure §§ 1605-06 (1986); yet the failure to join additional plaintiffs (as opposed to defendants) is a more common cause of joinder complexity. Next, in addition to joint tortfeasors, neither co-conspirators, insureds, insurers, nor plaintiffs suffering similar injuries are usually thought to be "necessary" parties, since (1) their absence does not affect the plaintiff's ability to obtain relief, (2) the lack of any res judicata effects of a judgment entered against the other defendants means that there is no impairment of their interests, and (3) the present parties are not subject to any multiple or inconsistent obligations. See generally id., §§ 1604, 1612-24. Indeed, joinder will usually be required only when it can be shown either that (1) there is a limited extant pie that must be awarded to one of a group of competing interests or divided among numerous competing legally viable interests, see, *e.g.*, Makah Indian Tribe v. Verity, 910 F.2d 555 (9th Cir. 1990), or (2) an absentee plaintiff might suffer (through the operation of collateral estoppel or otherwise) a destruction of their legal rights, see Haas v. Jefferson National Bank, 442 F.2d 394 (5th Cir. 1971). As a result, Rule 19 mandatory joinder has not been a significant factor in achieving joinder in complicated or complex litigation. See American Law Institute, Complex Litigation 24-26 (1994).

5. Note that *Temple* is not a complex dispute. *JATC* would be complex only if the employers would have had a later right to challenge the judgment between the JATC and the plaintiffs; but since the employers retained the right to choose their employees, it is not clear that they had standing or incentive to do so. Cf. Carpenters 46 Northern California Counties Joint Apprenticeship and Training Committee and Training Board v. Eldridge, 459 U.S. 917, 921-22 (1982) (Rehnquist, J., dissenting from denial of certiorari) (asserting that any injunction emanating from *JATC* will be a "'paper' decree"). In both *Temple* and *JATC*, joinder in a single forum would have been efficient and expedient, but these extra-textual concerns might not be enough to overcome our system's preference for autonomous decision making about whom to sue, when to sue, and where to sue. Do these cases, as well as the text and ordinary interpretation of Rule 19(a), reflect that our system does not prefer mandatory joinder in complicated cases, but does permit mandatory joinder in complex cases? If so, why the distinction?

6. One of the problems of Rule 19(a) mandatory joinder is Rule 19(b), which allows a court to dismiss a case when "in equity and good conscience" it cannot continue to be maintained in the necessary party's absence. In determining whether this test has been established, Rule 19(b) lists four factors:

> "first, to what extent a judgment rendered in the person's absence might be prejudicial to the person or those already parties; second, the extent to which, by protective provisions in the judgment, by shaping of relief, or other measures, the prejudice can be lessened or avoided; third, whether a judgment rendered in the person's absence will be adequate; fourth, whether the plaintiff will have an adequate remedy if the action is dismissed for nonjoinder."

Provident Tradesmen recast these factors into four interests served by the indispensable party rule:

> First, the plaintiff has an interest in having a forum. . . . Second, the defendant may properly wish to avoid multiple litigation, or inconsistent relief, or sole responsibility for a liability he shares with another. . . . Third, there is the interest of the outsider whom it would have been desirable to join. . . . Fourth, there remains the interest of the courts and the public in complete, consistent, and efficient settlement of controversies. [390 U.S. at 109-11.]

How different are these interests than the interests that motivate Rule 19(a) (at least after the *Illinois Brick* gloss adding the court's interest as a Rule 19(a) factor)? Certainly these interests must mean something different in the Rule 19(a) and Rule 19(b) contexts, or else the answer to the Rule 19(a) question would determine the Rule 19(b) question.

More fundamentally, what is the reason to have Rule 19(b) at all, at least in complex litigation? One problem with Rule 19 is that the tactical advantages of Rule 19(b) dismissal, rather than the desire to achieve appropriate Rule 19(a) joinder, often drive the use of Rule 19. This tactical use of Rule 19 probably distorts the interpretation of Rule 19(a), since a court will not want to construe Rule 19(a) broadly when the consequence of that interpretation is that the case might need to be dismissed under Rule 19(b). But there is also a larger theoretical problem with Rule 19(b). Assuming that Rule 19(a) roughly corresponds to the circumstances in which joinder complexity exists, and further assuming that these are the circumstances in which joinder is therefore most essential, does it make sense to have a rule like Rule 19(b), in which the court can dismiss some of the very cases that most need to be resolved together? Rather than throwing down another barrier to joinder, as Rule 19(b) does, shouldn't we be working on ways to overcome the barriers that presently exist? In Chapters Three and Four, we examine some of the jurisdictional and venue barriers that create Rule 19(b) problems and some ways in which these barriers might be eliminated. The more that we succeed in eliminating these barriers, the more potent a joinder device Rule 19 becomes. You might wish to keep this fact in mind as you consider the later materials.

In the meantime, however, why exacerbate joinder problems in complex cases? Couldn't we creatively "interpret" the judicial interest factor from *Provident Tradesmen* to preclude Rule 19(b) dismissals in complex cases?

If you agree that we should creatively "interpret" Rule 19 in complex cases, is there as compelling a reason to do so in complicated cases? If the problem of complicated cases is wasteful re-litigation, won't a Rule 19(b) dismissal prevent such re-litigation in many cases?

7. One alternative to Rule 19(b) that would keep present jurisdictional and venue barriers intact would be to achieve as much joinder as possible under Rule 19(a), to notify those that cannot be joined and invite them to join, and then to preclude those that refuse to join from seeking to undo the remedy. This alternative blends aspects of mandatory joinder with aspects of the "notice and preclusion" concept that we explore in Chapter 2.C, *infra*. Of course, the idea does not work in Rule 19(a)(1) cases, in which the plaintiff cannot obtain complete relief without the absent parties. As an initial matter, however, is this solution a better alternative to our present system with regard to Rule 19(a)(2) cases?

8. Assuming that some satisfactory solution to the Rule 19(b) problem can be found, we then need to face the basic issue: Is a broad mandatory joinder rule a good idea? It is probably impossible to know what to think about this issue without a sense of the deeper issues at stake. What is the strongest argument against mandatory joinder? Is it the threat to individual autonomy? If so, how do you account for the work of Ms. Hensler, who shows that many litigants in this present (supposedly autonomy-based) legal system in fact exercise remarkably little control over their cases? How do you respond to the arguments of Professor Rubenstein, who suggests that your autonomy to control your litigation should end when it threatens another's autonomy to control his or her litigation?

Is the strongest argument against mandatory joinder an historical devotion to the adversarial system? But Rule 19 is hardly a modern invention; its roots extend far back into equity practice. Moreover, mandatory joinder does not (at least directly) limit the parties' ability to present proofs and arguments in an adversarial fashion; it merely expands the number of parties capable of making such arguments. Perhaps, expanding on Professor Fuller's point, the problem is that, as more and more parties are added, the dispute becomes "polycentric" and incapable of a rational adjudicatory solution. See pp. 16-17, *supra*. But mandatory joinder does not make the case polycentric; it merely makes the polycentrism plain. To resolve the dispute without the presence of all affected parties, as we do now, is to resolve a dispute through a form (adjudication) that is incapable, according to Fuller, of properly handling the dispute.

Is the strongest argument against mandatory joinder the lack of trans-substantivity? Obviously, this concern could be remedied by requiring mandatory joinder in all cases, big and small. At a certain point, however, requiring complete joinder of all interested parties in one suit would be making mountains out of molehills, so that mandatory joinder is likely to be appropriate only in some cases. If so, we do have a problem with trans-substantivity. How important a value is the like procedural treatment of like cases? Can it be sacrificed as long as there is a good reason (such as the need to overcome lawyer dysfunction) to do so? Is efficient packaging also an adequate reason to abandon trans-substantivity?

Is the strongest argument against mandatory joinder the injustice of a Rule 19(b) dismissal? Can't we amend Rule 19(b) to prevent this injustice while still permitting mandatory joinder in appropriate cases?

Does mandatory joinder threaten other important procedural or constitutional values? Are these values important enough to derail mandatory joinder in complex or complicated cases? Even if none of these arguments is strong enough on its own, does the combined force of the arguments suggest that a rule of broad mandatory joinder is unwise?

9. In answering these questions, you might consider the experience of New Jersey, which has developed something called the "entire controversy" doctrine. The doctrine requires a plaintiff (as well as cross-claim defendants) to join all claims against defendants in one case; if the plaintiff fails to join a defendant, any future case against that defendant is barred. See Mortgagelinq Corp. v. Commonwealth Land Title Insurance Co., 142 N.J. 336, 662 A.2d 536 (1995); Symposium, *Entire Controversy Doctrine*, 28 Rutgers L.J. 1 (1996). The New Jersey Supreme Court has recently indicated that it might make changes to the doctrine, which effectively operates as a mandatory joinder rule. See Olds v. Donnelly, 150 N.J. 424, 440-49, 696 A.2d 633 (1997).

10. According to F.R.Civ.P. 19(c), the plaintiff is supposed to advise the court of any parties that should be joined if feasible, as well as the reasons that they have not been joined. The failure to advise the court of such persons might result in dismissal of the case or the establishment of facts against the plaintiff. See Wright et al., *supra*, § 1625. According to the advisory committee notes to Rule 19(c), the court can notify such a person about the existence of the case and provide the person with an opportunity to intervene (unless, of course, the person's intervention would create jurisdictional difficulties, in which case a Rule 19(b) analysis must be performed). If the person declines to intervene, or if the court otherwise becomes aware of the presence of such a necessary party, the court may have the power under Rule 21 to order the joinder of such a person (at least as long as there are no jurisdictional, venue, or other barriers to joinder). See p. 107, *supra*. A defendant that believes an indispensable party has not been joined is supposed to file a motion to dismiss under Rule 12(b)(7).

11. It is usually thought that the standard of appellate review for a decision regarding Rule 19 joinder is abuse of discretion. See, *e.g.*, South Dakota v. Bourland, 949 F.2d 984 (8th Cir. 1991) (collecting cases), *rev'd on other grounds*, 508 U.S. 679 (1993); but see Local 670, United Rubber, Cork, Linoleum and Plastic Workers v. International Union, United Rubber, Cork, Linoleum and Plastic Workers, 822 F.2d 613 (6th Cir. 1987), cert. denied, 484 U.S. 1019 (1988) (*de novo* review). The Ninth Circuit has created an exception to the abuse of discretion standard when "the determination of whether the movant's interest is impaired under the rule involves an interpretation of law"; here the review of the legal issue is *de novo*. Hughes v. United States, 953 F.2d 531 (9th Cir. 1992).

12. Mandatory joinder under Rule 19 "is subject to the provision of Rule 23." F.R.Civ.P. 19(c)(4). Rule 23 is another mandatory joinder rule — the class action rule. The limitation of Rule 19(c)(4) is sensible. If every member of a class action were required to be individually joined under Rule 19, the concept of class joinder under Rule 23 would be eviscerated.

b. Class Actions under Rule 23

A rather different concept of mandatory joinder is the class action. Unlike Rule 19 joinder, in which individual joinder of each necessary party is contemplated, class action joinder under Rule 23 contemplates that a person or group of persons act as representatives of other, similarly situated persons within the same class. Thus, except for the representative parties, members of the class are not individually joined in the suit, but the members are nonetheless viewed as being parties to the litigation by virtue of their membership in the class.

Because the class action is an important joinder tool in complex and complicated litigation, and because its full power is best understood after an examination of the jurisdictional and venue issues that we explore in Chapters Three and Four, we defer a full examination of class actions until Chapter Five. In order that you understand how class actions generally fit within the pattern of present joinder rules, however, we pause to describe briefly the structure of Rule 23.

Rule 23 can be used to join as parties either a class of plaintiffs or a class of defendants. In order for a class to be judicially acknowledged to exist, a court must enter an order "certifying" the class. Certification occurs when each of the elements of Rule 23(a) and at least one of the elements of Rule 23(b) has been met. The elements of Rule 23(a) are that there is a class, that the class is so numerous that individual joinder is impracticable, that there are questions of law or fact common to the class, that the claims or defenses of the representative parties are typical of those of the class, and that the representative parties fairly and adequately represent the interests of the class. See F.R.Civ.P. 23(a)(1)-(4). Next, Rule 23(b) requires either that separate actions by or against individual class members create a risk of inconsistent or varying adjudications that would establish incompatible standards of conduct for the party opposing the class, see F.R.Civ.P. 23(B)(1)(A); that separate lawsuits would as a practical matter be dispositive of, or at least substantially impair or impede the ability to protect, the interests of class members not party to the lawsuits, see F.R.Civ.P. 23(b)(1)(B); that injunctive relief for the class is appropriate because the person opposing the class has acted on grounds generally applicable to the class, see F.R.Civ.P. 23(b)(2); or that common questions of law or fact predominate and a class action is a superior means of resolving the controversy, see F.R.Civ.P. 23(b)(3).

The Rule 23(b)(1) and (b)(2) class actions are "mandatory," in the sense that class members cannot remove themselves from the class. (In Chapter Five, we explore a couple of possible exceptions to this statement.) The Rule 23(b)(3) class action is an "opt out" class action, which means that class members have the right to remove themselves from the class. Thus, in terms of mandatory joinder, mandatory class actions come closer to accomplishing the goal than the opt-out class action. But note that Rule 23 is not mandatory in the way that Rule 19 is mandatory. Rule 23 does not require that any case be maintained as a class action; someone (whether plaintiff or defendant) must seek class certification.

Why the dichotomy between mandatory and opt-out class actions? Here is one possible explanation. You might note a parallel between Rule 23(b)(1)(A) mandatory joinder and Rule 19(a)(2)(ii) mandatory joinder, and a parallel between Rule 23(b)(1)(B) mandatory joinder and Rule 19(a)(2)(i) mandatory joinder. The relevant pairs of provisions have some differences in wording (what are they?), but in general terms the first pair of provisions addresses the problem of a present party (usually a defendant) that cannot meet the legal obligations that separate lawsuits would impose, while the second pair of provisions addresses the problem of a later-filing party that finds its interests adjudicated in a lawsuit to which it was not a party. To a degree, Rule 23(b)(2) can be seen as a specific application of these two issues in the context of injunctive relief. Rule 23(b)(3) has no parallels elsewhere in the joinder rules. Its closest cousin may be the judicial gloss of fairness and efficiency seemingly imposed on involuntary joinder under Rule 20(a), although the lack of an opt-out right for defendants involuntarily joined under Rule 20(a) makes the analogy less than perfect.

Note that the concerns to which Rules 23(b)(1) and (b)(2) are responsive — inability of defendants to meet obligations to all victims or inability of third persons to protect their interests in later litigation — correspond fairly well to two of the causes of lawyer dysfunction and joinder complexity. Therefore, in both circumstances there is a strong argument for mandatory joinder. Rule 23(b)(3), on the other hand, permits class adjudication when it is efficient to do so. This circumstance corresponds to the category of complicated litigation. Since joinder complexity does not exist, the strongest reason to mandate joinder does not exist. In these complicated cases, the interest in individual autonomy and control outweighs the interest in mandatory joinder, and require an opt-out right for class members.

Does this explanation for the structural divide between mandatory and opt-out class actions sound intuitively correct? In thinking about this question, you might have noticed that the presumptions in opt-out class actions and voluntary joinder situations are reversed: The plaintiff in a class action can join non-consenting plaintiffs upon a demonstration of efficient packaging and then force the non-consenting class member to remove herself, while the plaintiff in a non-class action situation can join other plaintiffs only upon showing that the other plaintiffs affirmatively "opted into" the suit by means of their consent. Should we convert Rule 20 into an "opt-out" rule? Should we change Rule 23(b)(3) into an "opt-in" rule? Or can we defend both the present Rule 20 and the present Rule 23(b)(3)?

The thumbnail sketch of Rule 23 in this section is too incomplete for you to have developed fully formed opinions on these questions. We return to class actions in much greater depth in Chapter Five. For the present, it is both useful and important to understand how Rule 23 fits into the scheme of the joinder rules and how some of the common themes of the joinder rules might influence, and in turn might be influenced by, class actions.

c. Statutory and Rule Interpleader

A final form of mandatory joinder is interpleader. Because it contains certain procedures that can overcome jurisdictional and venue barriers to joinder, we defer a more complete examination of interpleader to Chapter Three. See pp. 325, 413, *infra*. As with class actions, however, this section provides an overview of interpleader in order to locate it within the general framework of the present joinder rules.

Interpleader initially arose in equity to handle the problem of a person that was holding a tangible thing (such as property or a sum of money) to which more than one other individual claimed title. The person holding the thing (often called the "stakeholder") claimed no interest in the thing, but faced the undesirable prospect that each of the individuals would separately sue at common law for the thing (or a monetary equivalent). Assuming that the first person won, the second person would not be bound by that judgment. Therefore, the stakeholder could face the prospect of multiple judgments even though, as a matter of logic, the stakeholder should have been liable only once. In this circumstance, the stakeholder was able to invoke the aid of equity, and sue (or "interplead") the various interested parties in one suit. The chancellor or judge sitting in equity then let the various interested parties present their claims against each other, and the decree deciding the ownership issue bound all the joined parties. Although the decree did not bind interested parties that were not joined, the stakeholder had an obvious incentive to interplead all interested parties.

Although interpleader has been liberalized in various ways over the years, this basic concept remains the heart of interpleader. Whatever its precise contours, interpleader can be seen as a type of mandatory joinder of interested parties — in particular, interested potential plaintiffs. But note again that interpleader is more like Rule 23 mandatory joinder than Rule 19 mandatory joinder: The stakeholder makes a voluntary decision whether to interplead potential plaintiffs and which potential plaintiffs to interplead; he or she cannot be forced to interplead, or to interplead everyone with an interest in the case. Interpleader is also somewhat unique in the sense that the defendant in the underlying dispute strikes preemptively, becoming the plaintiff and converting the underlying plaintiffs into defendants. In cases in which it applies, therefore, the underlying defendant, rather than the plaintiff, becomes the master of the complaint.

In the federal system two separate forms of interpleader exist: "rule interpleader" and "statutory interpleader." Rule interpleader arises under Federal Rule of Civil Procedure 22(1), allows a person against whom claims may be asserted to become an interpleader plaintiff when "the plaintiff is or may be exposed to double or multiple liability," and authorizes an already existing defendant to use interpleader by way of cross-claim or counterclaim. Note the relationship of this language to that of Rules 19(a)(2)(ii) and 23(b)(1)(A). Rule 19(a)(2)(ii) permits mandatory joinder when a person already a party is "subject to a substantial risk of incurring *double, multiple, or otherwise inconsistent* obligations." Rule 23(b)(1)(A) permits a class action to be maintained when separate actions by class members would create a risk of "*inconsistent* or varying adjudications." Rule 22 picks up on the *double* and *multiple* aspects of Rule 19(a)(2)(ii). Is there a difference between Rule 19's "double [or] multiple obligations" and Rule 22's "double or multiple liability"? If not, what does Rule 22 accomplish that Rule 19 does not? Cf. 1966 Advisory Committee Note to Rule 19 (suggesting that defendant's ability to use interpleader may be a factor relevant to Rule 19(b) decision about indispensability of non-joined party).

Statutory interpleader permits a person holding a "note, bond, certificate, policy of insurance, or other instrument of value or amount of $500 or more" to join adverse claimants when two or more of the claimants are of diverse citizenship from each other. 28 U.S.C. § 1335; see also §§ 1397, 2361. Although § 1335 does not recite the "double or multiple liability" language of Rule 22, the requirement of two or more adverse claimants seems to capture the same point in an indirect way. For reasons that we study in Chapter Three, statutory interpleader is often preferable to rule interpleader, but the limitation on the types of "things" (notes, bonds, and so on) to which it applies makes it a somewhat more limited remedy.

Interpleader creates a remedy to deal with one of the circumstances that meets the definition of lawyer dysfunction and joinder complexity: the circumstance that a defendant might be subject to inconsistent obligations. But its remedy operates in an incomplete way. First, as mentioned above, it relies on the underlying defendant to sue and to join all the underlying plaintiffs. Second, the remedy is limited to situations in which the inconsistent obligations relate to a tangible "thing." To be completely effective, the defendant would need to be under some compulsion to join all interested parties (or alternatively the court would need the power to effect appropriate joinder); then the limitation to tangible things would need to be eliminated; and finally forms of inconsistent obligations other than double or multiple liability would need to be included within the remedy. Interpleader points the way toward a regime that could eliminate lawyer dysfunction caused by inconsistent obligations, but it does not establish that regime in full measure. Nor does it even attempt to establish a regime for other forms of lawyer dysfunction that cause joinder complexity. Based on your initial impression, is the interpleader idea worth expanding on, or are its present constraints an appropriate compromise of the competing interests in complete joinder and litigant autonomy?

4. Intervention or Participation by Nonparties

The previous sections of this chapter have shown our procedural tradition prefers that the parties (and in particular, the plaintiff) structure the litigation. The problem with which this tradition leaves us, and which complex and complicated litigation highlights, is that some persons with an interest in the litigation may not be joined; and this failure of joinder, in turn, creates undesirable consequences such as joinder complexity or inefficiency. One solution to this problem is to permit the persons left out of the initial party structure to intervene or participate in the litigation. This solution is at best a partial solution to the problem, since it cannot force those nonparties that wish to remain on the sidelines into the suit. Moreover, this solution is disrespectful of the autonomy of existing parties (especially plaintiffs), at least when the existing party does not consent to the intervention. Intervention shifts the focus from the autonomy interests of the parties to the autonomy interests of nonparties — a theoretical move that requires some justification.

The following materials examine the circumstances under which our present party joinder rules permit nonparties to intervene or otherwise participate in litigation structured by other parties. As you read these materials, ask whether this system of intervention and participation adequately addresses the concerns expressed in the last paragraph. In particular, you might wish to begin thinking about whether nonparties should be required to intervene in some circumstances. The idea of a system of mandatory intervention as opposed to a system of mandatory joinder will be explored in detail in the final section of this chapter. In order to analyze a system of mandatory intervention, however, it is important to understand how much intervention is possible in our present system.

COOK v. BOORSTIN

763 F.2d 1462 (D.C. Cir. 1985)

■ MIKVA, Circuit Judge. This is an appeal by thirty-one black employees and former employees of the Library of Congress, challenging the district court's refusal to allow them to intervene in a Title VII class action brought against the Library. We agree with appellants that our decision in Foster v. Gueory, 655 F.2d 1319 (D.C. Cir. 1981), requires reversal of the district court's order.

I. BACKGROUND

In 1975, Howard Cook, David Andrews, and an organization called the Black Employees of the Library of Congress ("BELC") filed a class action administrative complaint alleging racially and sexually discriminatory employment practices throughout the Library. The Library's final decision, issued more than six years later, concluded that the "investigative file does not support the allegations of discrimination."

In February 1982, Cook and the BELC filed a Title VII class action complaint in the district court. Four months later they filed an amended complaint narrowing their allegations; specifically, they charged that the Library systematically discriminated against its black professional and administrative employees in making promotion and advancement decisions. At the same time, six black Library employees sought to intervene as plaintiffs and additional class representatives. The proposed amended complaint incorporated the claims of the six applicants for intervention and charged the Library with, *inter alia*, basing promotion decisions on "unvalidated tests which disqualify a disproportionate number of minority and female employees" and on "unchecked, unvalidated subjective recommendations of supervisory personnel."

In late 1983, the district court allowed all six employees to intervene. The court found that two of the employees, who had filed separate administrative complaints, were entitled to intervene of right under Rule 24(a)(2) of the Federal Rules of Civil Procedure. Rule 24(a)(2) requires the district court to grant a timely filed application for intervention whenever the applicant claims an interest relating to the property or transaction which is the subject of the action and he is so situated that the disposition of the action may as a practical matter impair or impede his ability to protect that interest, unless the applicant's interest is adequately represented by existing parties.

As to the other four applicants, the court found that intervention of right was unavailable, but nonetheless exercised its discretion to allow permissive intervention under Rule 24(b)(2). That subsection states that a court "may" grant a timely motion to intervene if "an applicant's claim or defense and the main action have a question of law or fact in common." The court also granted leave to file the amended complaint, but denied the plaintiffs' motion for class certification. Plaintiffs moved for reconsideration.

While the motion for reconsideration was pending, the thirty-one appellants in this action filed their motion to intervene. All are or were employed in administrative or professional positions at the Library, and all claim to have been discriminated against in promotion or advancement because they are black. Like the original plaintiffs in the action and the six intervenors, the thirty-one applicants alleged that they had been victimized by systematic discrimination in the Library's personnel practices. In individual affidavits filed with a second proposed amended complaint, each of the applicants claimed experience with the Library's personnel system "very similar" to the claims raised by the plaintiffs.

In June 1984, the district court nonetheless denied the intervention motion. The court's terse order commented only that "the four criteria for intervention under Rule 24(a) have not been satisfied and . . . intervention under Rule 24(b) would subject defendant to undue prejudice and unduly delay the adjudication of the rights of the parties."

On the same date, the district court granted the plaintiffs' motion for reconsideration of the denial of class certification. Instead of certifying the class as requested by plaintiffs, however, the court created six narrow subclasses defined to match closely the particular facts alleged by six of the named plaintiffs. It is unclear which, if any, of the appellants would have fit within any of the subclasses. In any event, counsel informed this court at oral argument that the district court subsequently decertified all but one of the subclasses, retaining class representation only for those black employees who were allegedly not promoted because of the Library's failure to post certain job openings. Although this subclass contains close to 400 members, it apparently does not include any of the appellants. Since many of the appellants never perfected their claims by timely filing of individual administrative complaints, the district court's denial of their motion to intervene effectively precluded them from obtaining any judicial relief for the wrongs they alleged.

II. ANALYSIS

We do not reach appellants' challenge to the district court's discretionary denial of permissive intervention to the thirty-one appellants, because we agree with appellants that our decision in Foster v. Gueory, 655

F.2d 1319 (D.C. Cir. 1981), required the district court to grant them intervention of right. In *Foster*, four union members sued their union and several employers under Title VII, alleging racial discrimination in matters relating to employment as pile drivers. After the district court refused to certify the suit as a class action brought on behalf of all minority victims of racial discrimination with respect to employment as pile drivers, three persons moved to intervene as additional plaintiffs. They alleged that their experience differed from that of the four original plaintiffs only in that racial discrimination had prevented the three movants from even obtaining union membership or apprenticeship training. The district court denied intervention for failure to exhaust administrative remedies, and the movants appealed.

This court reversed, ruling first that the claims raised by the plaintiffs and intervenors were all so similar that the administrative complaint pursued by one of the original plaintiffs had satisfied the exhaustion requirement for the would-be intervenors as well, and second that the three appellants were entitled to intervene of right under Rule 24(a)(2). . . .

The *Foster* panel read Rule 24(a)(2) to establish "four criteria for intervention of right," and determined that the appellants before the court satisfied each of the criteria.

First, the panel considered the requirement imposed by Rule 24(a) that the intervention motion be timely filed. The court found the requirement was satisfied because the appellants' motion had been filed little more than a month after the district court had denied class certification. As the Library tacitly concedes, the timeliness requirement is therefore also satisfied in the present case, because the appellants now before us filed their intervention motion within five weeks of the denial of class certification.

Second, the court addressed the requirement that an intervenor of right claim "an interest relating to the property or transaction which is the subject of the action," Fed. R. Civ. P. 24(a)(2). Noting that "the 'interest' test is primarily a practical guide to disposing of lawsuits by involving as many apparently concerned persons as is compatible with efficiency and due process," 655 F.2d at 1324 (quoting Nuesse v. Camp, 385 F.2d 694, 700 (D.C. Cir. 1967)), the panel concluded that the test was satisfied because

> [a]ppellants are persons who allege that they have suffered injury from the same or very similar wrongful acts as those complained of by the original plaintiffs, and appellants' claims for relief are founded on the same statutory rights as are the claims of the plaintiffs. While the individual acts of discrimination suffered by the plaintiffs and the appellants may differ, they each assert their claims as a result of the same "significantly protectable interest" . . . in being free of racial discrimination in employment.

As discussed below, the Library argues that the current appellants fail to meet this standard.

Third, the *Foster* panel concluded that the appellants' interests might be "practically impaired or impeded" by disposition of the plaintiffs' suit, because appellants and plaintiffs challenged the same practices of the defendants, and the trial court's consideration of the plaintiffs' claims "could result in a determination that certain of these practices as a matter of law do not violate either Title VII or § 1981." The panel noted that *Nuesse v. Camp* had established the sufficiency of such potential stare decisis effects as sufficient to meet the Rule 24(a)(2) requirement. The Library does not argue expressly that the appellants also fail to satisfy this third requirement, but, as discussed below, such an argument may be implied by the Library's contention that the factual variability of the employees' claims renders intervention inappropriate.

Fourth, the court considered the "adequacy of representation" requirement. The court noted that the fourth requirement is met if the representation "may" be inadequate, and that inadequacy was quite possible in the case before the court both (a) because the appellants' cases differed slightly from the plaintiffs' in that the appellants had been unable even to join the union, and (b) because each of the plaintiffs and appellants was seeking back pay (as are the plaintiffs and appellants currently before us), and "there is no way that plaintiffs could represent all of appellants' individual claims adequately." The Library does not dispute that the appellants' motion for intervention satisfied this last criterion.

Although the court's reasoning in *Foster v. Gueory* appears squarely applicable to the appeal now before us, the Library attempts to distinguish Foster based on the relative complexity of the facts involved in the present case and based on a highly creative argument concerning standing. We find neither purported distinction convincing.

1. *Factual complexity*. The Library attempts to distinguish this case from *Foster* based on the variation in the factual situations presented by the appellants in this case and on the sheer number of persons who seek to intervene. In *Foster*, three persons sought to intervene in a suit brought by four others, and all seven claimed discrimination with respect to the same job of pile driver. Here, in contrast, thirty-one persons seek to intervene in a class action brought by seven individual plaintiffs and an organization, and the thirty-eight individuals involved hold a variety of different jobs under different promotion and advancement schemes. The Library suggests that the appellants in this case therefore fail to meet the "interest in the transaction" test for intervention of right under *Foster*, and by implication the Library may be understood also to deny that the appellants' interests could be "practically impaired or impeded" by disposition of the plaintiffs' suit.

We note at the outset that we are far from convinced that the factual circumstances of the plaintiffs and intervenors in *Foster* were significantly more homogeneous than those presented by the plaintiffs and appellants in this case. True, there was only one job at issue in *Foster* — pile driver — and this case involves a myriad of different positions. But in this case all the plaintiffs and intervenors share a common employer; there is only one defendant. In *Foster*, several different employers and labor organizations appear to have been named as defendants. Moreover, this case does not contain the tension between the interests of union members and non-members, a tension explicitly recognized by the court in *Foster*. In any event, even granting that there is more factual variability in this case, we believe *Foster* is still controlling.

(a) *Interest in the transaction.* Like the appellants in *Foster*, the thirty-one appellants in this case, although complaining of separate personnel actions, all allege to have suffered from a system of racial discrimination "the same [as] or very similar [to]" that described in the plaintiffs' complaint. Consequently, each may be said to have "assert[ed] their claims as a result of the same 'significantly protectible interest' . . . in being free of racial discrimination in employment."

Nonetheless, the Library suggests that *Foster* and *Nuesse v. Camp* require a balancing of sorts, and that the balance comes out differently in this case than in *Foster*. *Foster* and *Nuesse* construed the "interest test" to be "primarily a practical guide to disposing of lawsuits by involving as many persons as is compatible with efficiency and due process," and the court ordered intervention in *Foster* only after concluding that "intervenors are indeed concerned persons whose involvement in the suit is compatible with efficiency and due process." The Library suggests that the number of people seeking intervention in this case and the differences in the factual circumstances giving rise to their complaints mean that the involvement of appellants would not be compatible with efficiency and due process.

Despite the general understanding that "[a]n application for intervention of right seems to pose only a question of law," we would ordinarily be inclined to give substantial weight to a trial court's findings with regard to whether intervention would comport with efficiency and due process. In this case, however, there are essentially no factual findings to which to defer; in denying intervention of right the district judge stated only that "the four criteria for intervention under Rule 24(a) have not been satisfied." Consequently, we must make our own determination under *Foster* and *Nuesse*.

We do not think it could be argued seriously that allowing intervention in this case would violate due process, and the Library in any event does not press such an argument. What the Library does argue is that allowing the appellants to intervene would make no sense in terms of judicial efficiency, because at bottom "these are 31 separate disparate treatment cases." The Library recognizes that its efficiency argument depends on a denial of the appellants' claim that their cases will rely on substantially the same evidence as the plaintiffs' case. The "efficiency" issue, therefore, ultimately becomes a question of acceptable methods of proof in Title VII cases.

More specifically, the question is whether a plaintiff bringing a disparate treatment claim against the Library can rely on evidence of Library-wide discrimination or must instead limit his or her proof to evidence of discrimination in the plaintiff's particular job category. Initially, it is clear that statistical evidence — despite its perhaps more familiar use to show disparate impact — can in general also be used to prove disparate treatment claims. As part of his or her prima facie case, a plaintiff alleging disparate treatment may introduce statistics tending to demonstrate a "pattern and practice" of discrimination, i.e., evidence "that racial discrimination was the [defendant's] standard operating procedure — the regular rather than the unusual practice." . . . In addition, a disparate treatment plaintiff may employ statistics concerning the employment practices of the defendant to rebut explanatory defenses as pretextual. . . .

More generally, it is well settled that "tests for the sufficiency of Title VII prima facie case must not be applied in a 'rigid, mechanistic, or ritualistic way.' . . . The ultimate test of sufficiency must remain. . . . [whether] the plaintiffs offer evidence 'adequate to create an inference that . . . employment decision[s] . . . [were] based on a discriminatory criterion illegal under the Act.[']" . . .

We think the appellants are clearly correct that evidence of discrimination throughout the Library is relevant to each of their claims. The plaintiffs and the intervenors all say they plan to make such evidence of systemic discrimination the centerpiece of their case, and their representations in this regard must be accepted as true. . . . Compared to the alternative of forcing those appellants who have exhausted their administrative remedies to bring separate civil actions, allowing intervention by the thirty-one appellants seems fully consistent with, if not mandated by, concerns of judicial efficiency.

Allowing intervention, it need hardly be noted, does not preclude separate trials of particular claims or even issues. If these complaints are ever actually tried, the district court will have broad discretion under Rule 42(b) to order separate trials as appropriate to further the aims of justice.

(b) *Practical impairment of interests.* In *Foster*, the court found that the appellants' interests might be "practically impaired or impeded" by the plaintiffs' litigation because it was possible "that trial of plaintiffs' claims could result in a determination that certain of these practices [challenged both by plaintiffs and the would-be intervenors] as a matter of law do not violate either Title VII or § 1981." That concern is not nearly so strong in this case, given the wide variety of actions challenged by plaintiffs and appellants here. Nevertheless, the reasoning does apply to some extent, since part of what the plaintiffs and intervenors all challenge in this case is the Library's failure to adopt less subjective employment practices.

More importantly, a stare decisis consideration similar but not identical to the one noted by the panel in *Foster* applies to this case quite forcefully: it is possible that trial of plaintiffs' claims could result in a determination that certain statistical evidence, on which both the plaintiffs and the intervenors plan to rely, is inadmissible or insufficient as a matter of law. Consequently, the potential for practical impairment of the appellants' interests seem just as substantial here as in *Foster*.

2. *Standing.* The Library devotes little of its brief to its attempt to distinguish *Foster v. Gueory* based on the relative factual simplicity of that case; by far the main part of the Library's argument on intervention of right is that appellants lack standing to intervene under Rule 24(a). . . . [T]he Library builds an elaborate argument that to intervene of right a party must have standing to challenge or defend the precise actions challenged by the original plaintiffs. . . .

We do not understand the Library to suggest that the appellants in this action would lack standing to assert their Title VII rights in separate actions; indeed, separate actions are apparently just what the government thinks the law requires. The Library's position is instead that the appellants should not be permitted to pursue their interests in this suit, because the basis of their standing differs in some particulars from the basis of the plaintiffs' standing. Such a restriction on intervention finds no support in [any] cases of which we are aware, nor, of that matter, in common sense. The whole point of intervention is to allow the participation of persons with interests distinct from those of the original parties; it is therefore to be expected that an intervenor's standing will have a somewhat different basis from that of the original plaintiffs. . . .

III. CONCLUSION

We therefore vacate the district court's denial of the appellants' motion to intervene, and we remand the case for further proceedings consistent with this opinion.

By way of guidance, we suggest that on remand the district court may wish to reconsider its denial of class certification in light of today's decision. Particularly given the large number of employees who we hold must otherwise be granted intervention of right, it may well make more sense for this case to proceed as a class action. . . .

Title VII embodies a profound national commitment to end the scourge of racism and sexism in our country's workplaces. If our nation is to move with speed toward genuine equality of opportunity, employers, including federal agencies, cannot be allowed to escape the requirements of Title VII by a litigation strategy of divide and conquer. "Careful attention" to the Federal Rules of Civil Procedure of course remains "indispensible," [General Telephone Co. v. Falcon, 457 U.S. 147, 157 (1982)], but those rules, it should be remembered, are to be "construed to secure the just, speedy, and inexpensive determination of every action." Fed. R. Civ. P. 1.

We recognize and are sympathetic to the burdens placed on trial judges by cases involving multiple parties and multiple lawyers. It is fine for commentators and appellate courts to speak of the systemic efficiency of trying one lawsuit in lieu of many, but a multi-party action obviously does little in the short run to alleviate the workload of the individual trial judge to whom it is assigned. Instead, the trial judge faces only the demands of managing a complex proceeding, maintaining order among many litigants, and assembling a coherent record out of a jumble of pleadings, testimony and evidentiary exhibits. We recognize also that the burdens placed on the trial judge can rise geometrically with the number of parties and claims. Nevertheless, the judicial system as a whole benefits substantially when similar complaints are resolved in a single unified proceeding, and the advantages in terms of efficiency and uniformity are simply too great to ignore. In the case before us, we need not strike the balance between these disparate concerns; the balance has already been struck by statute, rule and precedent.

TRBOVICH v. UNITED MINE WORKERS OF AMERICA

404 U.S. 528 (1972)

■ MR. JUSTICE MARSHALL delivered the opinion of the Court.

The Secretary of Labor instituted this action under § 402 (b) of the Labor-Management Reporting and Disclosure Act of 1959 (LMRDA), 29 U.S.C. § 482(b), to set aside an election of officers of the United Mine Workers of America (UMWA), held on December 9, 1969. He alleged that the election was held in a manner that violated the LMRDA in numerous respects, and he sought an order requiring a new election to be held under his supervision.

Petitioner, a member of the UMWA, filed the initial complaint with the Secretary that eventually led him to file this suit. Petitioner now seeks to intervene in the litigation, pursuant to Fed. Rule Civ. Proc. 24 (a), in order (1) to urge two additional grounds for setting aside the election, (2) to seek certain specific safeguards with respect to any new election that may be ordered, and (3) to present evidence and argument in support of the Secretary's challenge to the election. The District Court denied his motion for leave to intervene, on the ground that the LMRDA expressly stripped union members of any right to challenge a union election in the courts, and gave that right exclusively to the Secretary. The Court of Appeals affirmed on the basis of the District Court opinion. We granted certiorari to determine whether the LMRDA imposes a bar to intervention by union members under Rule 24, in a suit initiated by the Secretary. We conclude that it does not, and we remand the case to the District Court with directions to permit intervention.

[The Court first held that the LMRDA prevented a union member from initiating a lawsuit alleging violations of the act, but that the LMRDA permitted a union member to intervene in a suit brought by the Secretary. It then held that intervention was limited just to the theories and violations asserted by the Secretary; no additional theories could be asserted.]

Finally, the Secretary argues that even if the LMRDA does not bar intervention, petitioner has no right to intervene under the terms of Fed. Rule Civ. Proc. 24 (a). Rule 24 (a)(2) gives one a right to intervene if (1) he claims a sufficient interest in the proceedings, and (2) that interest is not "adequately represented by existing parties."

The Secretary does not contend that petitioner's interest in this litigation is insufficient; he argues, rather, that any interest petitioner has is adequately represented by the Secretary. The court below did not reach this question, in light of its threshold determination that Rule 24 had no application to the case. Nevertheless, we think it clear that in this case there is sufficient doubt about the adequacy of representation to warrant intervention.[10]

---

10. The requirement of the Rule is satisfied if the applicant shows that representation of his interest "may be" inadequate; and the burden of making that showing should be treated as minimal. . . .

The Secretary contends that petitioner's only legally cognizable interest is the interest of all union members in democratic elections, and he says that interest is identical with the interest represented by the Secretary in [the LMRDA] litigation. Hence he argues that petitioner's interest must be adequately represented unless the court is prepared to find that the Secretary has failed to perform his statutory duty. We disagree.

The statute plainly imposes on the Secretary the duty to serve two distinct interests, which are related, but not identical. First, the statute gives the individual union members certain rights against their union, and "the Secretary of Labor in effect becomes the union member's lawyer" for purposes of enforcing those rights. . . . And second, the Secretary has an obligation to protect the "vital public interest in assuring free and democratic union elections that transcends the narrower interest of the complaining union member." . . . Both functions are important, and they may not always dictate precisely the same approach to the conduct of the litigation. Even if the Secretary is performing his duties, broadly conceived, as well as can be expected, the union member may have a valid complaint about the performance of "his lawyer." Such a complaint, filed by the member who initiated the entire enforcement proceeding, should be regarded as sufficient to warrant relief in the form of intervention under Rule 24 (a)(2).

The judgment is reversed and the case is remanded to the District Court with directions to allow limited intervention in accordance with this opinion.

[The opinion of JUSTICE DOUGLAS, dissenting in part, is omitted.]

Notes and Questions

1. Rule 24 provides two methods by which nonparties can become litigants: intervention of right (Rule 24(a)) and permissive intervention (Rule 24(b)). Even though the test under Rule 24(b) is less stringent, most would-be intervenors prefer to obtain Rule 24(a) intervention. One practical reason is that, under Rule 24(b), an intervenor's participation is likely to be more circumscribed, in terms of both the issues on which intervention is allowed and the degree of participation on those issues. 7C Charles A. Wright et al., Federal Practice & Procedure §§ 1913, 1922 (1986). Although intervention of right might not guarantee full rights of participation, an intervenor of right is far more likely to be entitled to participate in discovery and trial. See id., § 1922; see also Harris v. Pernsley, 820 F.2d 592, 599 (3d Cir.) ("given the complexity of much public law litigation, permitting courts to limit intervention as of right to discrete phases of the litigation may be necessary in some cases"), cert. denied, 484 U.S. 947 (1987).

Prior to 1990, a second practical reason for preferring intervention of right was that an intervenor of right did not need to have an independent basis of federal jurisdiction for the intervenor's claim (unless the intervenor was an indispensable party), while a person seeking permissive intervention needed to demonstrate an independent basis of federal jurisdiction over the claim. After the passage of 28 U.S.C. § 1367 in 1990, however, a person that seeks intervention of right in a case founded solely on diversity jurisdiction must demonstrate an independent basis of subject matter jurisdiction over the claim in intervention, as must persons seeking permissive intervention. In cases not originally founded solely on diversity jurisdiction, the text of § 1367 seems (by implication) to permit claims for intervention of right without an independent basis of federal jurisdiction, and the same rule seems to be true of claims for permissive intervention. But the issue is unclear, to say the least. See pp. 348-60, *infra* (discussing § 1367); see also Beckman Industries, Inc. v. International Insurance Co., 966 F.2d 470 (9th Cir.) (no need for independent basis of jurisdiction when permissive intervenor did not seek to litigate any claims on the merits), cert. denied, 506 U.S. 868 (1992).

2. Rule 24(a) provides two methods for obtaining intervention of right: when a statute grants intervention of right (Rule 24(a)(1)), and when an interest which is inadequately represented by existing parties might be impaired by their ongoing litigation (Rule 24(a)(2)). Statutes granting intervention of right are rare. See, *e.g.*, 28 U.S.C. § 2403; 42 U.S.C. § 9613(i). Thus, most persons seeking intervention of right, including the parties in *Cook* and *Trbovich*, must invoke Rule 24(a)(2).

3. As *Cook* says, Rule 24(a)(2) is to contain four elements: timeliness of the motion, an "interest relating to the property or transaction which is the subject of the litigation," a practical impairment or impeding of the intervenor's "ability to protect that interest," and inadequate representation by existing parties. The timeliness element has been construed somewhat flexibly, with factors such as the length of the delay in filing the motion, the reasons for delay, and the prejudice to the parties caused by delay in moving for intervention often influencing the court's decision on the issue. See Wright et al., *supra*, § 1916.

4. How flexibly should the "interest" element be interpreted? Here the Supreme Court appears to be of two minds. In Cascade Natural Gas Corp. v. El Paso National Gas Co., 386 U.S. 129 (1967), the acquisition of one natural gas supplier by another was found to have violated the antitrust laws. During the divestiture hearings, the State of California (on behalf of its citizens), a distributor, and a large user all sought to intervene in order to assure that the improperly acquired company be restored as an effective competitor. The Court held that the State and the user were able to intervene under former (and now abrogated) Rule 24(a)(3), which required a property interest in order to intervene. It did not decide whether the distributor could intervene under former Rule 24(a)(3), saying instead that could intervene under the recently amended Rule 24(a)(2). 386 U.S. at 132-35. On the other hand, in Donaldson v. United States, 400 U.S. 517 (1971), the Court refused to permit the target of an Internal Revenue Service investigation to intervene in an enforcement proceeding in which the Service sought the target's employment records from his employer. "What is obviously meant" by Rule 24(a)(2)'s interest requirement, the Court said, "is a significantly protectable interest." 400 U.S. at 531. Since the target could protect his interest in a subsequent trial, the Court felt there was no reason to "unwarrantedly cast doubt upon and stultify the Service's every investigatory move." *Donaldson* did not cite *Cascade*. Can you reconcile the results? See Diamond v. Charles, 476 U.S. 54, 68 (1986) (citing both cases favorably in dicta).

One possible distinction between the cases is that in *Donaldson*, another forum existed to protect the putative intervenor's rights, while in *Cascade*, no other forum existed. A second possible distinction is that in *Cascade*, the United States was dragging its feet with respect to the divestiture proceedings, even though the Court had, in a prior opinion, ordered "divestiture without delay." United States v. El Paso Natural Gas Co., 376 U.S. 651, 662 (1964). Under this distinction, *Donaldson*'s narrower view of "interest" is the correct one, and the Court's willingness in *Cascade* to permit intervention should "be regarded as an extraordinary case, occasioned by the Court's 'splenetic displeasure' with the government's lack of diligence in seeking relief." United States v. Hooker Chemicals & Plastics Corp., 749 F.2d 968, 986 n.15 (2d Cir. 1984) (Friendly, J.). According to this view, *Cascade* is simply an exception to the general, oft-cited rule that private parties seeking to represent the public interest cannot intervene in antitrust litigation prosecuted by the government. See United States v. International Business Machines Corp., 1995 WL 366383 (S.D.N.Y.).

It is also possible to reconcile *Cascade* with *Donaldson* along the following principle: that the term "interest" should be interpreted either broadly or narrowly depending on the public interest involved in permitting intervention. In *Cascade* the public interest favored intervention, and in *Donaldson* the public interest did not favor intervention. One problem with this reconciliation is that any effort "to deduce from those cases rules applicable to ordinary private litigation is fraught with great risks." Wright et al., *supra*, §1908. Moreover, the language of Rule 24(a)(2) speaks in terms of the putative intervenor's "interest," not the public interest. Cf. *Diamond*, 476 U.S. at 68-69 (when party chooses not to continue with litigation, intervenor must possess standing under Article III in order to continue litigation; sidestepping issue whether intervenor still possesses a Rule 24(a)(2) interest). Finally, how would the public interest cut in complex litigation? In favor of allowing intervention when it helps to reduce lawyer dysfunction? Or against allowing intervention when the plaintiff fails to consent to intervention, because broad rights of intervention in this situation threaten the master of the complaint rule? Could efficiency gains from intervention count as an adequate public interest?

As *Cook* states, lower courts have tended to be guided by the practical consideration — first articulated in Nuesse v. Camp, 385 F.2d 694, 700 (D.C. Cir. 1967) — of "involving as many apparently concerned parties as is compatible with efficiency and due process." See also Smuck v. Hobson, 408 F.2d 175 (D.C. Cir. 1969); Blake v. Pallan, 554 F.2d 947, 952 (9th Cir. 1977) ("several courts including this one, have implicitly at least, rejected the notion that Rule 24(a)(2) requires a 'specific legal or equitable interest'"). On the other hand, the Seventh Circuit has stated that Rule 24(a)(2) "requires a direct, significant legally protectable interest in the property or transaction subject to the litigation." Wade v. Goldschmidt, 673 F.2d 182, 185 (7th Cir. 1982). The Fifth Circuit similarly requires a "direct, substantial, legally protectable definition of the required interest." New Orleans Public Service Co. v. United Gas Pipeline Co., 732 F.2d 452, 463 (5th Cir.) (en banc), cert. denied, 469 U.S. 1019 (1984).. See Susan Bandes, *The Idea of a Case*, 42 Stan. L. Rev. 227, 282-83 (1990) (suggesting that federal courts employ a half-dozen different, and sometimes internally inconsistent, tests to determine "interest"). Do any of these tests provide an adequate sense of the types of interest that a putative intervenor needs?

More specifically, would the types of factual circumstances that give rise to lawyer dysfunction meet any of the "interest" tests in the last paragraph? Recall that lawyer dysfunction arises either when there are insufficient assets to cover all judgments, when the declared relief cannot be undone in subsequent litigation by the putative intervenor, or when later-filing litigants cannot undo the judgment entered in the earlier litigation. In which of these circumstances does the putative intervenor have a Rule 24(a)(2) "significantly protectable" interest? In which would intervention be consistent with "efficiency and due process"? The first two categories would seem to satisfy both of these tests. When the third form of dysfunction exists, however, the intervenor would not seem to have a "significantly protectable" interest, even though intervention would be consistent with "efficiency and due process." Does either the "significantly protectable interest" or "efficiency and due process" test adequately address the reasons that we might want intervention to occur in complex cases? Should a separate test for the requisite "interest" be developed for complex cases? Does the "efficiency" language of *Nuesse* already establish the test for complicated cases?

5. The third element for Rule 24(a)(2) intervention is a practical impairment of the interest. The seminal case on the issue of impairment is Atlantis Development Corp. v. United States, 379 F.2d 818 (5th Cir. 1967), in which the court held that the stare decisis effect of a judgment was a sufficient practical impairment interest to justify intervention. The same idea is found in *Cook*. In both *Atlantis* and *Cook*, however, the claims of the intervening parties and the present plaintiffs involved the same basic series of transactions or occurrences. Should other stare decisis effects constitute an impairment for Rule 24(a)(2) purposes? For instance, could a tort plaintiff injured in one accident intervene in a case brought as a result of an unrelated accident merely because the case might unfavorably decide certain legal issues relevant to the tort plaintiff's own case? In Bethune Plaza, Inc. v. Lumpkin, 863 F.2d 525 (7th Cir. 1988), the court took a cautious view, ultimately holding that only the stare decisis effects of an appellate court decision might support intervention, but only in some cases:

> Permitting intervention liberally raises the costs of litigation and makes settlement harder, which may well discourage the initial suit and effectively block the real plaintiff from vindicating its own rights. When a would-be intervenor says that it fears only the stare decisis effect of a decision . . . desire to block a settlement is never a legitimate reason to intervene, because if the case settles the possibility of an authoritative appellate decision vanishes, and with it the only substantial concern of the putative intervenor. . . .
>
> [T]he opinion of a single district judge rarely yields an effect broader than the force its reasoning carries. Such an influence is not reason enough to complicate litigation by adding as parties all who might be concerned about the court's choice of words. Each would-be litigant can conduct its own case when its own dispute comes into focus, and the more persuasive opinions will carry the day. Stare decisis as *Atlantis* and other courts use it for purposes of Rule 24(a)(2) accordingly means the decision of an appellate tribunal. The decision of an appellate court is binding (not just persuasive) on those lower in the hierarchy even if not binding on the parties under principles of preclusion — that is, the parties are free to relitigate but are unlikely to get anywhere.
>
> When should the prospect of an appellate decision cutting off further litigation in the circuit (or the nation as a whole, if the Supreme Court decides the case) be enough to support intervention? "Infrequently" is one response, an essential one if cases are to remain manageable. Trade associations, labor unions, consumers, and many others may be affected by

(and hence colloquially "interested" in) the rules of law established by appellate courts. To allow them to intervene as of right would turn the court into a forum for competing interest groups, submerging the ability of the original parties to settle their own dispute (or have the court resolve it expeditiously). Participation as amicus curiae will alert the court to the legal contentions of concerned bystanders, and because it leaves the parties free to run their own case is the strongly preferred option. Perhaps the right question to ask is: when will participation as amicus curiae be inadequate to present claims to the tribunal? [863 F.2d at 531-33.]

See also FDIC v. Jennings, 816 F.2d 1488, 1492 (10th Cir.1987) (stare decisis effect not enough to justify intervention when plaintiff's and putative intervenor's theories of liability differed, intervenor would inject new issues into trial, and intervention would make already complicated suit even more unmanageable). Can *Cook* be reconciled with *Bethune Plaza* or *Jennings*?

Return to the circumstances that give rise to joinder complexity. In the first two circumstances (insufficient assets or unchangeable relief), the practical impairment to the putative intervenor seems obvious. In the third circumstance of a subsequently changeable judgment, the stare decisis concern does not exist. Is there any other practical impairment?

Recall that in this third circumstance it was also difficult to discover an "interest" that fell within the ambit of Rule 24(a)(2). See Note 4, *supra*. If Rule 24(a)(2) poorly captures one of the three situations in which there might be a pressing need to achieve complete joinder, should the rule be amended? Or should we rely on other joinder doctrines to handle this situation?

6. The final element, upon which *Trbovich* bases its holding, is inadequacy of representation. Note that this element is stated in the negative: Intervention is appropriate unless present parties can prove that representation is adequate; the intervenor does not need to prove that representation is inadequate. See Wright et al., *supra*, § 1909.

Trbovich seems to take a fairly relaxed attitude toward the inadequacy requirement, finding that, at least for those claims that were contained within the Secretary's complaint, some differences in the interests of the putative intervenor and the Secretary of Labor were enough to clear the "minimal" threshold of inadequacy. See also *Nuesse*, 385 F.2d at 703 ("interests need not be wholly 'adverse' before there is a basis for concluding that existing representation of a 'different' interest may be inadequate"). This attitude is generally reflected in the cases, see Wright et al., *supra*, § 1909, but other cases have taken a more restrictive attitude. For instance, in *Hooker Chemicals*, several environmental organizations sought to intervene in an enforcement action brought by the United States and the State of New York when it appeared to the organizations that the proposed environmental remedy might have been inadequate. Judge Friendly ruled that the district court had not abused its discretion in failing to permit intervention of right:

> [The district court's conclusion] was based to a large extent on the fact that the existing parties were governmental entities. We agree with the district court that it is significant to the analysis required by Rule 24(a)(2) that the plaintiffs are governmental entities suing on behalf of their citizens. In such actions, the state or the United States presents itself "in the attitude of *parens patriae*, trustee, guardian or representative of all her citizens." Louisiana v. Texas, 176 U.S. 1, 19 (1900)....

Whether or not it is particularly helpful to speak of a "presumption" of adequate representation by the sovereign in *parens patriae* litigation, we agree with the Third, Fifth and District of Columbia Circuits that, in litigation of this sort, a greater showing that representation is inadequate should be required. It is not enough that the applicant would insist on more elaborate pre-trial or pre-settlement procedures or press for more drastic relief, particularly when the sovereign's interest is in securing preventive relief of the same general sort as the applicant. While it would be going too far to require an applicant to demonstrate collusion, there must be, at least in cases where the applicant has no independent right to sue, a strong affirmative showing that the sovereign is not fairly representing the interests of the applicant....

There is another reason to apply Rule 24(a)(2) narrowly in this case. The emergency powers provisions [under the environmental statutes] confer "broad authority" on the Administrator to provide him with substantial flexibility needed to prevent imminent hazards. This broad authority granted to the Administrator extends not only to the decision to bring a suit, but also to defining what level of a given pollutant constitutes "an imminent and substantial endangerment," and, most importantly, to deciding what the appropriate remedy should be.... The proper exercise of this authority requires that the Administrator's discretion under this provision be left relatively untrammeled.... The diversion of time and resources as well as the risk that a court will err in evaluating the positions of the Administrator and the intervenor on technological and scientific questions at the outer limits of a court's competence, dictates the need to require a strong showing of inadequacy of representation before impairing the Administrator's control over the litigation. [749 F.2d at 984-85, 988-89.]

See also Edwards v. City of Houston, 78 F.3d 983, 1005 (5th Cir. 1996) (describing presumptions in favor of adequate representation when putative intervenor is citizen of governmental entity suing on matter of sovereign interest and when putative "intervenor has the same ultimate objective as a party [and there is no] adversity of interest, collusion, or nonfeasance"). What happens if, as a result of an election or other major political shift, the government switches litigation positions and private parties that were happy with the previous position now wish to intervene in the case? See Sagebrush Rebellion, Inc. v. Watt, 713 F.2d 525 (9th Cir. 1983).

But why is this additional roadblock to joinder imposed at all? One possible answer is suggested by the contrast between class joinder under Rule 23 and intervention of right under Rule 24. We briefly encountered the idea of adequacy of representation in our overview of class actions, see pp. 132-34, *supra*. Note how the idea of representation works in different ways in the class action and intervention contexts: In the context of class actions, adequacy of representation is an essential element of class joinder; while in the context of intervention, adequacy of representation denies joinder in the case. One explanation for the difference is that, in the class action context, the existing parties (*i.e.*, the putative class representatives) threaten to wrest away the class members' control over their cases. Thus, the court needs to be assured that the representative parties will pay adequate attention to the interests of class members and not merely use class members' cases as leverage to advance their own interests. In the intervention context, the intervening party threatens to wrest control of the litigation away from the existing parties. Thus, the court needs to be assured that the intervenors will not dilute the force of the existing parties' own claims or defenses. If this explains the reason for an "inadequacy of representation" requirement in Rule 24(a)(2), should the rule be more explicit about the point of the requirement? Is there some other purpose that the "inadequacy of representation" requirement fulfills?

Indeed, is there any reason to insist on an "inadequacy of representation" requirement in complex litigation, given that the traditional concern for protecting litigant autonomy creates lawyer dysfunction? Even if the "inadequacy of representation" requirement remains, wouldn't it almost automatically be satisfied in complex cases? Recall that the two circumstances presently giving rise to a right to intervene in complex litigation are inadequate assets and unchangeable relief. See Notes 4-5, *supra*. In these circumstances, the present parties would seem to have little practical or legal incentive to raise the issues that the putative intervenor would wish to raise. Note, however, that in complicated cases the "inadequacy of representation" requirement may impose a more significant hurdle to intervention under Rule 24(a)(2).

7. Can a judge impose conditions or restrictions on a person seeking to intervene of right? The text of Rule 24(a) does not suggest so, but the 1966 Advisory Committee Notes to Rule 24 state that intervention of right may be "subject to appropriate conditions or restrictions responsive among other things to the requirements of efficient conduct of the proceedings." The cases are mixed. See Wright et al., *supra*, § 1922 (suggesting that only reasonable "housekeeping" restrictions can be imposed); Stringfellow v. Concerned Neighbors in Action, 480 U.S. 370, 383 (1987) (Brennan, J., concurring) ("restrictions on participation may . . . be placed on an intervenor of right").

8. Since the "interest" and "impairment" language of both rules is nearly identical, is every person who is entitled to intervene under Rule 24(a)(2) also a necessary party under rule 19(a)(2)(i)? In *Eldredge*, p. 117, *supra*, the Ninth Circuit found that the 4500 signatory employers to a collective bargaining agreement were not necessary parties in a case alleging that an apprenticeship program established by the agreement was discriminatory. Since the employers' agreement had "ceded whatever legally protectable interest they may have had in selecting apprentices," the court found no "interest" for purposes of Rule 19(a)(2)(i). But the court went on to note that its decision might lead some employers to move to intervene, after which the district court "may consider whether to permit intervention under Fed.R.Civ.P. 24." 662 F.2d at 538. If the employers had no "interest" for purposes of Rule 19, how can they have an "interest" for purposes of Rule 24? Consider the following discussion in *Smuck v. Hobson*:

> The phrasing of Rule 24(a)(2) as amended parallels that of Rule 19(a)(2) concerning joinder. But the fact that the two rules are entwined does not imply that an "interest" for the purpose of one is precisely the same as for the other. The occasions upon which a petitioner should be allowed to intervene under Rule 24 are not necessarily limited to those situations when the trial court should compel him to become a party under Rule 19. [408 F.2d at 178.]

Does this discussion help you draw the line between Rule 19 "interests" and Rule 24 "interests"? To test your understanding, ask whether a stare decisis effect like that in *Cook* or *Atlantis* is an interest that could justify the Rule 19 mandatory joinder of those potentially subject to the stare decisis effect.

One functional difference between Rule 19 and Rule 24 is that, when jurisdiction cannot be obtained over a necessary party under Rule 19, the party might in some circumstances be deemed indispensable, and the entire case dismissed. When a non-necessary party seeks to intervene under Rule 24 but is unsuccessful, the litigation continues. Hence, in interpreting the terms "interest" and "impairment" for purposes of Rules 19 and 24, courts might be sensitive to the litigative consequences of the interpretation. A second functional difference between Rule 19 and Rule 24 is that, at least in some cases, a Rule 19 necessary party might be forced into the litigation against his or her will. In contrast, a Rule 24 intervenor will, in nearly all circumstances, make a voluntary choice to enter the litigation. To the extent that courts are concerned with forcing people to litigate against their will, there is a second reason to interpret the terms "interest" and "impairment" more generously in the Rule 24 context than the Rule 19 context. Do either of these functional differences persuade you that these terms should receive different readings in the two rules? Can you think of other functional differences that might lead a court to construe the terms differently in the two rules? Are you comfortable with the idea that these terms do not have an immutable, normative meaning in all circumstances? Without such meaning, the only way to fill the terms with meaning is to appeal to the deeper values of procedural and substantive law implicated in your case.

9. On the issue of these deeper values, do you think that *Bethune Plaza* targeted the right set of values — the value of the present parties to control their litigation on their own terms and the value of resolving litigation efficiently and expeditiously? These values are consistent with an adversarial approach to litigation. But these notes have suggested that these values can be trumped in at least some cases. One such trump might occur when lawyer dysfunction exists, and that the present rules concerning intervention might not go far enough in avoiding lawyer dysfunction. What value or values underlie the desire to eliminate lawyer dysfunction? Are these values so strong that they should trump the values underlying adversarial process? Cf. Carl Tobias, *Standing to Intervene*, 1991 Wis. L. Rev. 415 (stating that Rule 24(a)(2) was drafted without public law litigation in mind, and suggesting changes to permit intervention when, *inter alia*, it would help the quality of decisionmaking). Is the desire to eliminate inefficiency in complicated cases also of sufficient weight to trump the values of a party-controlled, adversarial approach to organizing the litigation?

On the assumption that it has selected the right values, do you agree with *Bethune Plaza* that notions of adversarialism and efficiency disfavor broad intervention rules? Professor Brunet does not:

> The approach used in the United States to achieve information input and accurate output is mainly adversarial in nature. . . . The incentive of each party to succeed stimulates input . . . .
>
> But although the adversary system establishes a framework for efficiency, it is understandably inadequate to achieve, by itself, efficient resolution of every dispute. The parties sometimes do not produce the information essential to a just and accurate result. . . . Only efficiency considerations complementing the adversary model can resolve these problems. . . .
>
> [I]t is worthwhile to consider the numerous economies which the general concept of intervention advances. The chief policy advantage of intervention is that it merges into one central dispute additional issues related to the original case and avoids multiple trials on identical or related

issues.... Second, intervention can also prevent inconsistencies in fact finding and law determination that might occur if the decisionmaker separately considered the issues combined for consideration through intervention.... Third, intervention's integration of similar issues into one action can also avoid complicated issues of collateral estoppel....

These efficiency considerations ... are central to a system of dispute resolution with properly allocated resources. The adversary model, the control of information, and the minimization of transaction costs are the three factors that contribute to efficiency....

[M]ost of the essential features of intervention are efficient. The ... representation and impaired interest requirements of [Rule] 24(a) have resulted in an increasing number of good opinions analyzing the incentive and informational input of intervenors.

Other features of Rule 24, however, are potentially inefficient. Absence of an explicit grant of judicial discretion in Rule 24(a) creates the possibility that judges might allow potentially counter-productive intervention.

Edward J. Brunet, *A Study in the Allocation of Scarce Judicial Resources: The Efficiency of Federal Intervention Criteria*, 12 Ga. L. Rev. 701, 711, 713, 719-20, 745-46 (1978) (some paragraphing omitted). Do you accept Brunet's apparent assumption that efficiency, rather than adversarialism, is the most significant procedural value?

10. It may be useful in forming an opinion about our present joinder rules to have a sense of other options for joining persons in a litigation or binding persons to the outcome of that litigation. At this point, we have nearly completed our examination of the rules of party joinder, and are about to move to an examination of preclusion rules. Before we make that move, however, you should be aware of a couple of other joinder possibilities. One is permissive intervention under Rule 24(b). The other is participation as amicus curiae.

Permissive intervention is much easier to establish than intervention of right. Unlike intervention of right, permissive intervention "plainly dispenses with any requirement that the intervenor shall have a direct personal or pecuniary interest in the subject if the litigation." Securities and Exchange Commission v. United States Realty & Improvement Co., 310 U.S. 434, 459 (1940). Instead, Rule 24(b) demands only that the putative intervenor make a timely application and that the intervenor's "claim or defense and the main action have a question of fact or law in common." (Note that the "common question of law or fact" language of Rule 24(b) tracks comparable language in Rules 20(a) and 23(a)(2).) In choosing whether to grant intervention, a court is required under Rule 24(b) to consider "whether the intervention will unduly delay or prejudice the adjudication of the rights of the original parties." The court's decision is also often informed by matters such as the delay in the request for intervention, the desire to avoid a multiplicity of suits, the often-opposing desire to ensure that the original parties receive a fair hearing on their original claims, other forums in which the intervenor's rights can be determined, and other means (including amicus participation) by which the intervenor's interests can be protected or otherwise aired. See Wright et al., *supra*, § 1913.

Like intervention of right, permissive intervention bestows party status on the person intervening. Unlike intervention of right, however, a court has a fairly clear power to place significant limitations on the scope and manner of participation in appropriate circumstances. Id., §§ 1913, 1922.

Participation as an amicus curiae (literally, "friend of the court") provides an even more limited mode of participation. An amicus does not become a party, and typically does not become involved in discovery of the facts. See United States v. State of Michigan, 940 F.2d 143, 163-66 (6th Cir. 1991); but see Hoptowit v. Ray, 682 F.2d 1237, 1260 (9th Cir. 1982) (amicus participated in discovery, trial, and appeal). Rather, the amicus provides input (usually by brief, and sometimes by oral argument) on the legal issues in the case. The lawyer representing an amicus, of course, often presents the issues from the perspective of the lawyer's client, and that perspective may vary from the perspective of any of the present litigants. Nonetheless, because the court is interested primarily in the amicus's views on particular legal issues, the court can, and typically does, limit participation just to the issues raised by the parties. See Richardson v. Alabama State Board of Education, 935 F.2d 1240, 1247 (11th Cir. 1991); but see Michel v. Anderson, 14 F.3d 623 (D.C. Cir. 1994) (court would consider jurisdictional arguments made by amicus but not by parties). Thus, although an amicus may provide a different perspective on the issues in the case, it is less likely that new issues will be injected into the litigation with amicus participation as opposed to participation by intervention.

Participation by amici occurred during the seventeenth century, although the first reported decision of an amicus representing his own (as opposed to the court's) interests seems first to have occurred in 1736. See Coxe v. Phillips, 95 Eng. Rep. 152 (K.B. 1736); Samuel Krislov, *The Amicus Curiae Brief: From Friendship to Advocacy*, 72 Yale L.J. 694 (1963). Since that time, the precise requirements for amicus participation have changed. Initially, an amicus needed to show a sufficient interest in the litigation, and sometimes quite substantial interests were deemed insufficient. See Northern Securities Co. v. United States, 191 U.S. 555 (1903); Matter of the Petition of Oskar Tiedemann and Co., 183 F. Supp. 129 (D. Del. 1960) (members of industry could not participate as amicus in case with potential effects on entire industry; application also untimely). Furthermore, amicus status was often reserved to cases involving public, as opposed to private, interests; and the concept of a "friend" of the court was thought to imply a degree of neutrality that excluded obviously interested partisans. See Funbus Systems, Inc. v. State of California Public Utilities Commission, 801 F.2d 1120, 1124-25 (9th Cir. 1986); Village of Elm Grove v. Py, 724 F. Supp. 612 (E.D. Wis. 1989). The modern trend, however, has been to care less about the precise interests or neutrality of the amicus, and to focus instead on whether the information supplied by the amicus "is timely, useful, or otherwise necessary to the administration of justice." See *United States v. Michigan*, 940 F.2d at 165; Krislov, *supra*; George C. Piper, Note, *Amicus Curiae Participation — At the Court's Discretion*, 55 Ky. L.J. 864 (1967).

11. A decision granting a motion to intervene or to participate as amicus is not a final order, and therefore not immediately appealable. See Wright et al., *supra*, § 1923; United States v. State of Michigan, 1990 WL 46637 (6th Cir.). A decision denying a motion to intervene or to participate as amicus presents a more complicated picture. First, although the rationale for rule varies among the cases, it is generally thought that denial of a motion to intervene of right is immediately appealable. See Brotherhood of Railroad Trainmen v. Baltimore & O. R. Co., 331 U.S. 519, 524 (1947); R.H. v. Murphy, 984 F.2d 196 (7th Cir.), cert. denied, 508 U.S. 960 (1993); *Edwards*, 78 F.3d at 992 & n.16. Nevertheless, when a court denies intervention of right but authorizes permissive intervention, the decision is not immediately appealable. *Stringfellow*, 480 U.S. 370.

Second, when the court denies permissive intervention, the rules are somewhat unclear. In *Brotherhood of Railroad Trainmen*, the Court suggested that a discretionary ruling on permissive intervention is not immediately appealable "if there is no abuse of discretion." 331 U.S. at 525. This caveat has led some courts to develop the "anomalous" rule that an appellate court has "provisional jurisdiction" to review denials of permissive intervention for abuse of discretion; if no abuse is found, the appeal is dismissed for want of jurisdiction rather than affirmed. See *Edwards*, 78 F.3d at 992; see also Wright et al., *supra* § 1923 & 1998 Supp. (suggesting that denial of permissive intervention should be immediately appealable).

Third, the ability to appeal the denial of a motion to participate as amicus seems to have received virtually no attention in the reported cases, although the discretionary nature of such a grant, the lack of party status for an amicus, and the lack of immediate appeal from a grant of amicus participation combine to suggest that a denial of amicus participation is not immediately appealable. See *State of Michigan*, 940 F.2d at 164-65.

12. The standard of review for a decision to grant or deny intervention of right is also less than clear. The general view seems to be that factual findings are reviewed for clear error, some legal aspects of the ruling (such as timeliness) are reviewed under an abuse of discretion standard, and the remaining legal aspects (such as interest, impairment, and adequacy) are reviewed *de novo*. See *Murphy*, 984 F.2d at 200; Getty Oil Co. v. Department of Energy, 865 F.2d 270, 274 (Temp. Emerg. Ct. App. 1988). A decision regarding permissive intervention is reviewed for abuse of discretion. Meeks v. Metropolitan Dade County, Florida, 985 F.2d 1471 (11th Cir. 1993); see *Beckman Industries*, 966 F.2d 470 (9th Cir. 1992) (abuse of discretion is standard, but issues of law presented by permissive intervention reviewed *de novo*). The standard for amicus participation is abuse of discretion. *Hoptowit*, 682 F.2d at 1260.

13. For additional sources on the issue of intervention, see David L. Shapiro, *Some Thoughts on Intervention Before Courts, Agencies, and Arbitrators*, 81 Harv. L. Rev. 721 (1968); Gene R. Shreve, *Questioning Intervention of Right — Toward a New Methodology of Decisionmaking*, 74 Nw. U. L. Rev. 894 (1980); Carl Tobias, *Public Law Litigation and the Federal Rules of Civil Procedure*, 74 Corn. L. Rev. 270 (1989).

B. USING PRECLUSION RULES AS AN ALTERNATIVE WAY TO OVERCOME JOINDER COMPLEXITY

The main concern in Part I of this book is the unfairness or inefficiency caused by the existence or potential existence of multiple lawsuits. In the last section, we examined the ways in which our present rules of party joinder address this concern. An alternative to party joinder also exists: the use of preclusion doctrines. The basic idea of preclusion is that certain claims or issues that were, or could have been, litigated in a prior suit cannot be litigated again. Precluding re-litigation of claims or issues does not bring everyone into a lawsuit, as does joinder, but preclusion does have a comparable effect; claims or issues are decided once, and persons with a stake in the precluded claim or issue are bound by that determination.

You may have already studied the basic preclusion rules in a course in Civil Procedure. Claim preclusion (sometimes called res judicata) focuses on situations in which a plaintiff sues a defendant on a claim that was, or could have been, decided in a prior lawsuit arising out of the same transaction or occurrence. Issue preclusion (sometimes called collateral estoppel) focuses on situations in which a party in a later lawsuit is bound by the factual or legal determinations made in a prior lawsuit. The following subsection reviews these basic rules of claim and issue preclusion in more detail.

It is possible to envision for preclusion a broad role — one in which all persons are bound by the judgments (or the decided issues) in an earlier litigation. With this approach, joinder of interested parties becomes less important; persons must accept the outcome of a judgment even when they were not parties to it. This approach appears to solve many of the problems of inefficiency associated with complicated litigation. Does it also solve the problems of dysfunction associated with joinder complexity? If preclusion does solve some of the problems that complicated and complex litigation pose, does it cut too deeply into the adversarial preference for individual control of litigation? Would creating an approach just for complicated or complex litigation treat unfairly other, more routine cases in which preclusion might not be used? Should limits be put on preclusion's use? These are the issues and questions that we address in the second subsection, in which we explore various efforts to make broader use of preclusion in complicated and complex cases.

1. Existing Preclusion Rules

FEDERATED DEPARTMENT STORES, INC. v. MOITIE

452 U.S. 394 (1981)

■ JUSTICE REHNQUIST delivered the opinion of the Court.

The only question presented in this case is whether the Court of Appeals for the Ninth Circuit validly created an exception to the doctrine of res judicata. The court held that res judicata does not bar relitigation of an unappealed adverse judgment where, as here, other plaintiffs in similar actions against common defendants successfully appealed the judgments against them. We disagree with the view taken by the Court of Appeals for the Ninth Circuit and reverse.

I

In 1976 the United States brought an antitrust action against petitioners, owners of various department stores, alleging that they had violated § 1 of the Sherman Act, 15 U.S.C. § 1, by agreeing to fix the retail price of women's clothing sold in northern California. Seven parallel civil actions were subsequently filed by private plaintiffs seeking treble damages on behalf of proposed classes of retail purchasers, including that of respondent Moitie in state court (*Moitie I*) and respondent Brown (*Brown I*) in the United States District Court for the Northern District of California. Each of these complaints tracked almost verbatim the allegations of the Government's complaint, though the *Moitie I* complaint referred solely to state law. All of the actions originally filed in the District Court were assigned to a single federal judge, and the *Moitie I* case was removed there on the basis of diversity of citizenship and federal-question jurisdiction. The District Court dismissed all of the actions "in their entirety" on the ground that plaintiffs had not alleged an "injury" to their "business or property" within the meaning of § 4 of the Clayton Act, 15 U.S.C. § 15. . . .

Plaintiffs in five of the suits appealed that judgment to the Court of Appeals for the Ninth Circuit. The single counsel representing Moitie and Brown, however, chose not to appeal and instead refiled the two actions in state court, *Moitie II* and *Brown II*. Although the complaints purported to raise only state-law claims, they made allegations similar to those made in the prior complaints, including that of the Government. Petitioners removed these new actions to the District Court for the Northern District of California and moved to have them dismissed on the ground of res judicata. In a decision rendered July 8, 1977, the District Court first denied respondents' motion to remand. It held that the complaints, though artfully couched in terms of state law, were "in many respects identical" with the prior complaints, and were thus properly removed to federal court because they raised "essentially federal law" claims. The court then concluded that because *Moitie II* and *Brown II* involved the "same parties, the same alleged offenses, and the same time periods" as *Moitie I* and *Brown I*, the doctrine of res judicata required that they be dismissed. This time, Moitie and Brown appealed.

Pending that appeal, this Court on June 11, 1979 . . . [held] that retail purchasers can suffer an "injury" to their "business or property" as those terms are used in § 4 of the Clayton Act. On June 25, 1979, the Court of Appeals for the Ninth Circuit reversed and remanded the five cases which had been decided with *Moitie I* and *Brown I*, the cases that had been appealed, for further proceedings . . . .

When *Moitie II* and *Brown II* finally came before the Court of Appeals for the Ninth Circuit, the court reversed the decision of the District Court dismissing the cases. . . .[2] Though the court recognized that a "strict application of the doctrine of *res judicata* would preclude our review of the instant decision," . . . it refused to apply the doctrine to the facts of this case. It observed that the other five litigants in the *Weinberg* cases had successfully appealed the decision against them. It then asserted that "non-appealing parties may benefit from a reversal when their position is closely interwoven with that of appealing parties," . . . and concluded that

---

2. The Court of Appeals also affirmed the District Court's conclusion that *Brown II* was properly removed to federal court, reasoning that the claims presented were "federal in nature." We agree that at least some of the claims had a sufficient federal character to support removal.

"[b]ecause the instant dismissal rested on a case that has been effectively overruled," the doctrine of res judicata must give way to "public policy" and "simple justice." . . . We granted certiorari . . . to consider the validity of the Court of Appeals, novel exception to the doctrine of res judicata.

II

There is little to be added to the doctrine of res judicata as developed in the case law of this Court. A final judgment on the merits of an action precludes the parties or their privies from relitigating issues that were or could have been raised in that action. . . . Nor are the res judicata consequences of a final, unappealed judgment on the merits altered by the fact that the judgment may have been wrong or rested on a legal principle subsequently overruled in another case. . . . As this Court explained in Baltimore S.S. Co. v. Phillips, 274 U.S. 316, 325 (1927), an "erroneous conclusion" reached by the court in the first suit does not deprive the defendants in the second action "of their right to rely upon the plea of *res judicata*. . . . A judgment merely voidable because based upon an erroneous view of the law is not open to collateral attack, but can be corrected only by a direct review and not by bringing another action upon the same cause [of action]." We have observed that "[t]he indulgence of a contrary view would result in creating elements of uncertainty and confusion and in undermining the conclusive character of judgments, consequences which it was the very purpose of the doctrine of *res judicata* to avert." Reed v. Allen, 286 U.S. 191, 201 (1932).

In this case, the Court of Appeals conceded that the "strict application of the doctrine of *res judicata*" required that *Brown II* be dismissed. By that, the court presumably meant that the "technical elements" of res judicata had been satisfied, namely, that the decision in *Brown I* was a final judgment on the merits and involved the same claims and the same parties as *Brown II*. The court, however, declined to dismiss *Brown II* because, in its view, it would be unfair to bar respondents from relitigating a claim so "closely interwoven" with that of the successfully appealing parties. We believe that such an unprecedented departure from accepted principles of res judicata is unwarranted. Indeed, the decision below is all but foreclosed by our prior case law. . . .

This Court's rigorous application of res judicata in [*Reed v. Allen*] makes clear that this Court recognizes no general equitable doctrine, such as that suggested by the Court of Appeals, which countenances an exception to the finality of a party's failure to appeal merely because his rights are "closely interwoven" with those of another party. Indeed, this case presents even more compelling reasons to apply the doctrine of res judicata than did *Reed*. Respondents here seek to be the windfall beneficiaries of an appellate reversal procured by other independent parties, who have no interest in respondents' case, not a reversal in interrelated cases procured, as in *Reed*, by the same affected party. Moreover, in contrast to *Reed*, where it was unclear why no appeal was taken, it is apparent that respondents here made a calculated choice to forgo their appeals. . . .

The Court of Appeals also rested its opinion in part on what it viewed as "simple justice." But we do not see the grave injustice which would be done by the application of accepted principles of res judicata. "Simple justice" is achieved when a complex body of law developed over a period of years is evenhandedly applied. The doctrine of res judicata serves vital public interests beyond any individual judge's ad hoc determination of the equities in a particular case. There is simply "no principle of law or equity which sanctions the rejection by a federal court of the salutary principle of *res judicata.*" Heiser v. Woodruff, 327 U.S. 726, 733 (1946). The Court of Appeals' reliance on "public policy" is similarly misplaced. This Court has long recognized that "[p]ublic policy dictates that there be an end of litigation; that those who have contested an issue shall be bound by the result of the contest, and that matters once tried shall be considered forever settled as between the parties." Baldwin v. Traveling Men's Assn., 283 U.S. 522, 525 (1931). We have stressed that "[the] doctrine of *res judicata* is not a mere matter of practice or procedure inherited from a more technical time than ours. It is a rule of fundamental and substantial justice, 'of public policy and of private peace,' which should be cordially regarded and enforced by the courts. . . ." Hart Steel Co. v. Railroad Supply Co., 244 U.S. 294, 299 (1917). The language used by this Court half a century ago is even more compelling in view of today's crowded dockets:

> "The predicament in which respondent finds himself is of his own making . . . . [W]e cannot be expected, for his sole relief, to upset the general and well-established doctrine of *res judicata,* conceived in the light of the maxim that the interest of the state requires that there be an end to litigation — a maxim which comports with common sense as well as public policy. And the mischief which would follow the establishment of precedent for so disregarding this salutary doctrine against prolonging strife would be greater than the benefit which would result from relieving some case of individual hardship." *Reed v. Allen,* 286 U.S., at 198-199.

Respondents make no serious effort to defend the decision of the Court of Appeals. They do not ask that the decision below be affirmed. Instead, they conclude that "the writ of certiorari should be dismissed as improvidently granted." In the alternative, they argue that "the district court's dismissal on grounds of res judicata should be reversed, and the district court directed to grant respondent's motion to remand to the California state court." In their view, *Brown I* cannot be considered res judicata as to their *state*-law claims, since *Brown I* raised only federal-law claims and *Brown II* raised additional state-law claims not decided in *Brown I*, such as unfair competition, fraud, and restitution.

It is unnecessary for this Court to reach that issue. It is enough for our decision here that *Brown I* is res judicata as to respondents' federal-law claims. Accordingly, the judgment of the Court of Appeals is reversed, and the cause is remanded for proceedings consistent with this opinion.

It is so ordered.

■ JUSTICE BLACKMUN, with whom JUSTICE MARSHALL joins, concurring in the judgment. . . .I, for one, would not close the door upon the possibility that there are cases in which the doctrine of res judicata must give way to what the Court of Appeals referred to as "overriding concerns of public policy and simple justice." . . . But this case is clearly not one in which equity requires that the doctrine give way. . . .

I would [also] flatly hold that *Brown I* is res judicata as to respondents' state-law claims. . . . [R]espondents' failure to allege the state claims in *Brown I* manifestly bars their allegation in *Brown II*. The dismissal of *Brown I* is res judicata not only as to all claims respondents actually raised, but also as to all claims that could have been raised. . . .

■ JUSTICE BRENNAN, dissenting. . . . [The dissent began with an extended argument that removal of *Moitie II* and *Brown II* from state court was improper.]

Even assuming that this Court and the lower federal courts have jurisdiction to decide this case, however, I dissent from the Court's disposition of the res judicata issue. Having reached out to assume jurisdiction, the Court inexplicably recoils from deciding the case. The Court finds it "unnecessary" to reach the question of the res judicata effect of *Brown I* on respondents' "*state*-law claims." "It is enough for our decision here," the Court says, "that *Brown I* is res judicata as to respondents' federal-law claims." *But respondents raised only state-law claims; respondents did not raise any federal-law claims.* Thus, if the Court fails to decide the disposition of respondents' state-law claims, it decides nothing. And in doing so, the Court introduces the possibility — heretofore foreclosed by our decisions — that unarticulated theories of recovery may survive an unconditional dismissal of the lawsuit.

Like JUSTICE BLACKMUN I would hold that the dismissal of *Brown I* is res judicata not only as to every matter that was actually litigated, but also as to every ground or theory of recovery that might also have been presented. . . . An unqualified dismissal on the merits of a substantial federal antitrust claim precludes relitigation of the same claim on a state-law theory. . . . The Court's failure to acknowledge this basic principle can only create doubts and confusion where none were before, and may encourage litigants to split their causes of action, state from federal, in hope that they might win a second day in court.

PARKLANE HOSIERY CO. v. SHORE

439 U.S. 322 (1979)

■ MR. JUSTICE STEWART delivered the opinion of the Court.

This case presents the question whether a party who has had issues of fact adjudicated adversely to it in an equitable action may be collaterally estopped from relitigating the same issues before a jury in a subsequent legal action brought against it by a new party.

The respondent brought this stockholder's class action against the petitioners in a Federal District Court. The complaint alleged that the petitioners, Parklane Hosiery Co., Inc. (Parklane), and 13 of its officers, directors, and stockholders, had issued a materially false and misleading proxy statement in connection with a merger. The proxy statement, according to the complaint, had violated §§ 14 (a), 10 (b), and 20 (a) of the Securities Exchange Act of 1934, 48 Stat. 895, 891, 899, as amended, 15 U.S.C. §§ 78n (a), 78j (b), and 78t (a), as well as various rules and regulations promulgated by the Securities and Exchange Commission (SEC). The complaint sought damages, rescission of the merger, and recovery of costs.

Before this action came to trial, the SEC filed suit against the same defendants in the Federal District Court, alleging that the proxy statement that had been issued by Parklane was materially false and misleading in essentially the same respects as those that had been alleged in the respondent's complaint. Injunctive relief was requested. After a 4-day trial, the District Court found that the proxy statement was materially false and misleading in the respects alleged, and entered a declaratory judgment to that effect. The Court of Appeals for the Second Circuit affirmed this judgment.

The respondent in the present case then moved for partial summary judgment against the petitioners, asserting that the petitioners were collaterally estopped from relitigating the issues that had been resolved against them in the action brought by the SEC.[2] The District Court denied the motion on the ground that such an application of collateral estoppel would deny the petitioners their Seventh Amendment right to a jury trial. The Court of Appeals for the Second Circuit reversed, holding that a party who has had issues of fact determined against him after a full and fair opportunity to litigate in a nonjury trial is collaterally estopped from obtaining a subsequent jury trial of these same issues of fact. The appellate court concluded that "the Seventh Amendment preserves the right to jury trial only with respect to issues of fact, [and] once those issues have been fully and fairly adjudicated in a prior proceeding, nothing remains for trial, either with or without a jury." Because of an intercircuit conflict, we granted certiorari.

I

The threshold question to be considered is whether, quite apart from the right to a jury trial under the Seventh Amendment, the petitioners can be precluded from relitigating facts resolved adversely to them in a prior equitable proceeding with another party under the general law of collateral estoppel. Specifically, we must determine whether a litigant who was not a party to a prior judgment may nevertheless use that judgment

---

2. A private plaintiff in an action under the proxy rules is not entitled to relief simply by demonstrating that the proxy solicitation was materially false and misleading. The plaintiff must also show that he was injured and prove damages. . . . Since the SEC action was limited to a determination of whether the proxy statement contained materially false and misleading information, the respondent conceded that he would still have to prove these other elements of his prima facie case in the private action. The petitioners' right to a jury trial on those remaining issues is not contested.

"offensively" to prevent a defendant from relitigating issues resolved in the earlier proceeding.[4]

A

Collateral estoppel, like the related doctrine of res judicata,[5] has the dual purpose of protecting litigants from the burden of relitigating an identical issue with the same party or his privy and of promoting judicial economy by preventing needless litigation. Blonder-Tongue Laboratories, Inc. v. University of Illinois Foundation, 402 U.S. 313, 328-329 [1971]. Until relatively recently, however, the scope of collateral estoppel was limited by the doctrine of mutuality of parties. Under this mutuality doctrine, neither party could use a prior judgment as an estoppel against the other unless both parties were bound by the judgment. Based on the premise that it is somehow unfair to allow a party to use a prior judgment when he himself would not be so bound,[7] the mutuality requirement provided a party who had litigated and lost in a previous action an opportunity to relitigate identical issues with new parties.

By failing to recognize the obvious difference in position between a party who has never litigated an issue and one who has fully litigated and lost, the mutuality requirement was criticized almost from its inception. Recognizing the validity of this criticism, the Court in *Blonder-Tongue Laboratories, Inc. v. University of Illinois Foundation, supra*, abandoned the mutuality requirement, at least in cases where a patentee seeks to relitigate the validity of a patent after a federal court in a previous lawsuit has already declared it invalid. The "broader question" before the Court, however, was "whether it is any longer tenable to afford a litigant more than one full and fair opportunity for judicial resolution of the same issue." The Court strongly suggested a negative answer to that question:

> "In any lawsuit where a defendant, because of the mutuality principle, is forced to present a complete defense on the merits to a claim which the plaintiff has fully litigated and lost in a prior action, there is an arguable misallocation of resources. To the extent the defendant in the second suit may not win by asserting, without contradiction, that the plaintiff had fully and fairly, but unsuccessfully, litigated the same

---

4. In this context, offensive use of collateral estoppel occurs when the plaintiff seeks to foreclose the defendant from litigating an issue the defendant has previously litigated unsuccessfully in an action with another party. Defensive use occurs when a defendant seeks to prevent a plaintiff from asserting a claim the plaintiff has previously litigated and lost against another defendant.

5. Under the doctrine of res judicata, a judgment on the merits in a prior suit bars a second suit involving the same parties or their privies based on the same cause of action. Under the doctrine of collateral estoppel, on the other hand, the second action is upon a different cause of action and the judgment in the prior suit precludes relitigation of issues actually litigated and necessary to the outcome of the first action. . . .

7. It is a violation of due process for a judgment to be binding on a litigant who was not a party or a privy and therefore has never had an opportunity to be heard. Blonder-Tongue Laboratories, Inc. v. University of Illinois Foundation, 402 U.S. 313, 329; Hansberry v. Lee, 311 U.S. 32, 40 [1940].

claim in the prior suit, the defendant's time and money are diverted from alternative uses — productive or otherwise — to relitigation of a decided issue. And, still assuming that the issue was resolved correctly in the first suit, there is reason to be concerned about the plaintiff's allocation of resources. Permitting repeated litigation of the same issue as long as the supply of unrelated defendants holds out reflects either the aura of the gaming table or 'a lack of discipline and of disinterestedness on the part of the lower courts, hardly a worthy or wise basis for fashioning rules of procedure.' Kerotest Mfg. Co. v. C-O-Two Co., 342 U.S. 180, 185 (1952). Although neither judges, the parties, nor the adversary system performs perfectly in all cases, the requirement of determining whether the party against whom an estoppel is asserted had a full and fair opportunity to litigate is a most significant safeguard." Id., at 329.[10]

B

The *Blonder-Tongue* case involved defensive use of collateral estoppel — a plaintiff was estopped from asserting a claim that the plaintiff had previously litigated and lost against another defendant. The present case, by contrast, involves offensive use of collateral estoppel — a plaintiff is seeking to estop a defendant from relitigating the issues which the defendant previously litigated and lost against another plaintiff. In both the offensive and defensive use situations, the party against whom estoppel is asserted has litigated and lost in an earlier action. Nevertheless, several reasons have been advanced why the two situations should be treated differently.

First, offensive use of collateral estoppel does not promote judicial economy in the same manner as defensive use does. Defensive use of collateral estoppel precludes a plaintiff from relitigating identical issues by merely "switching adversaries." Thus defensive collateral estoppel gives a plaintiff a strong incentive to join all potential defendants in the first action if possible. Offensive use of collateral estoppel, on the other hand, creates precisely the opposite incentive. Since a plaintiff will be able to rely on a previous judgment against a defendant but will not be bound by that judgment if the defendant wins, the plaintiff has every incentive to adopt a "wait and see" attitude, in the hope that the first action by another plaintiff will result in a favorable judgment. Thus offensive use of collateral estoppel will likely increase rather than decrease the total amount of litigation, since potential plaintiffs will have everything to gain and nothing to lose by not intervening in the first action.[13]

A second argument against offensive use of collateral estoppel is that it may be unfair to a defendant. If a defendant in the first action is sued for

---

10. The Court also emphasized that relitigation of issues previously adjudicated is particularly wasteful in patent cases because of their staggering expense and typical length. . . .

13. The Restatement (Second) of Judgments § 88 (3) (Tent. Draft No. 2, Apr. 15, 1975) provides that application of collateral estoppel may be denied if the party asserting it "could have effected joinder in the first action between himself

small or nominal damages, he may have little incentive to defend vigorously, particularly if future suits are not foreseeable. Allowing offensive collateral estoppel may also be unfair to a defendant if the judgment relied upon as a basis for the estoppel is itself inconsistent with one or more previous judgments in favor of the defendant.[14] Still another situation where it might be unfair to apply offensive estoppel is where the second action affords the defendant procedural opportunities unavailable in the first action that could readily cause a different result.[15]

C

We have concluded that the preferable approach for dealing with these problems in the federal courts is not to preclude the use of offensive collateral estoppel, but to grant trial courts broad discretion to determine when it should be applied. The general rule should be that in cases where a plaintiff could easily have joined in the earlier action or where, either for the reasons discussed above or for other reasons, the application of offensive estoppel would be unfair to a defendant, a trial judge should not allow the use of offensive collateral estoppel.

In the present case, however, none of the circumstances that might justify reluctance to allow the offensive use of collateral estoppel is present. The application of offensive collateral estoppel will not here reward a private plaintiff who could have joined in the previous action, since the respondent probably could not have joined in the injunctive action brought by the SEC even had he so desired.[17] Similarly, there is no unfairness to the petitioners in applying offensive collateral estoppel in this case. First, in light of the serious allegations made in the SEC's complaint against the petitioners, as well as the foreseeability of subsequent private suits that typically follow a successful Government judgment, the petitioners had every incentive to

and his present adversary."

14. In Professor Currie's familiar example, a railroad collision injures 50 passengers all of whom bring separate actions against the railroad. After the railroad wins the first 25 suits, a plaintiff wins in suit 26. Professor Currie argues that offensive use of collateral estoppel should not be applied so as to allow plaintiffs 27 through 50 automatically to recover. [Brainerd] Currie, [*Mutuality of Estoppel: The Limits of the* Bernhard *Doctrine,*] 9 Stan. L. Rev. [281,] 304 [1957]. See Restatement (Second) of Judgments § 88 (4), *supra*.

15. If, for example, the defendant in the first action was forced to defend in an inconvenient forum and therefore was unable to engage in full scale discovery or call witnesses, application of offensive collateral estoppel may be unwarranted. Indeed, differences in available procedures may sometimes justify not allowing a prior judgment to have estoppel effect in a subsequent action even between the same parties, or where defensive estoppel is asserted against a plaintiff who has litigated and lost. The problem of unfairness is particularly acute in cases of offensive estoppel, however, because the defendant against whom estoppel is asserted typically will not have chosen the forum in the first action. See, id., § 88 (2) and Comment d.

17. SEC v. Everest Management Corp., 475 F.2d 1236, 1240 (CA2) ("[The] complicating effect of the additional issues and the additional parties outweighs any advantage of a single disposition of the common issues"). Moreover, consolidation of a private action with one brought by the SEC without its consent is prohibited by statute. 15 U.S.C. § 78u(g).

litigate the SEC lawsuit fully and vigorously.[18] Second, the judgment in the SEC action was not inconsistent with any previous decision. Finally, there will in the respondent's action be no procedural opportunities available to the petitioners that were unavailable in the first action of a kind that might be likely to cause a different result.[19]

We conclude, therefore, that none of the considerations that would justify a refusal to allow the use of offensive collateral estoppel is present in this case. Since the petitioners received a "full and fair" opportunity to litigate their claims in the SEC action, the contemporary law of collateral estoppel leads inescapably to the conclusion that the petitioners are collaterally estopped from relitigating the question of whether the proxy statement was materially false and misleading.

II

The question that remains is whether, notwithstanding the law of collateral estoppel, the use of offensive collateral estoppel in this case would violate the petitioners' Seventh Amendment right to a jury trial.

[The Court concluded that it would not violate the Seventh Amendment for findings of fact in a bench trial to estop the defendant from relitigating those facts in a jury trial.]

The judgment of the Court of Appeals is

Affirmed.

■ MR. JUSTICE REHNQUIST, dissenting.

It is admittedly difficult to be outraged about the treatment accorded by the federal judiciary to petitioners' demand for a jury trial in this lawsuit. Outrage is an emotion all but impossible to generate with respect to a corporate defendant in a securities fraud action, and this case is no exception. But the nagging sense of unfairness as to the way petitioners have been treated, engendered by the imprimatur placed by the Court of Appeals on respondent's "heads I win, tails you lose" theory of this litigation, is not dispelled by this Court's antiseptic analysis of the issues in the case. It may be that if this Nation were to adopt a new Constitution today, the Seventh Amendment guaranteeing the right of jury trial in civil cases in federal courts would not be included among its provisions. But any present sentiment to that effect cannot obscure or dilute our obligation to enforce the Seventh Amendment, which was included in the Bill of Rights in 1791 and

---

18. After a 4-day trial in which the petitioners had every opportunity to present evidence and call witnesses, the District Court held for the SEC. The petitioners then appealed to the Court of Appeals for the Second Circuit, which affirmed the judgment against them. Moreover, the petitioners were already aware of the action brought by the respondent, since it had commenced before the filing of the SEC action.

19. It is true, of course, that the petitioners in the present action would be entitled to a jury trial of the issues bearing on whether the proxy statement was materially false and misleading had the SEC action never been brought — a matter to be discussed in Part II of this opinion. But the presence or absence of a jury as factfinder is basically neutral, quite unlike, for example, the necessity of defending the first lawsuit in an inconvenient forum.

which has not since been repealed in the only manner provided by the Constitution for repeal of its provisions.

The right of trial by jury in civil cases at common law is fundamental to our history and jurisprudence. Today, however, the Court reduces this valued right, which Blackstone praised as "the glory of the English law," to a mere "neutral" factor and in the name of procedural reform denies the right of jury trial to defendants in a vast number of cases in which defendants, heretofore, have enjoyed jury trials. Over 35 years ago, Mr. Justice Black lamented the "gradual process of judicial erosion which in one hundred fifty years has slowly worn away a major portion of the essential guarantee of the Seventh Amendment." . . . Regrettably, the erosive process continues apace with today's decision.

Notes and Questions

1. We should begin with a note on vocabulary. Today the favored term for the doctrine that precludes the assertion of certain *claims* in subsequent litigation is "claim preclusion." As the opinions in *Moitie* reflect, the old name for this doctrine is "res judicata"; it has also sometimes been called "merger and bar." The favored modern term for the doctrine that precludes the assertion of certain *issues* in subsequent litigation is "issue preclusion." The old name for this doctrine is "collateral estoppel"; it has also sometimes been called "direct estoppel." Despite this trend, the terms "offensive collateral estoppel" and "defensive collateral estoppel" are often still used to describe these two branches of issue preclusion. In *Moitie* and *Parklane Hosiery*, the Justices used the old terms of "res judicata" and "collateral estoppel," rather than the new terms of "claim preclusion" and "issue preclusion." So far, so good.

The problem is that "res judicata" has also been used as an umbrella term that describes all of preclusion law — both claim preclusion and issue preclusion. Indeed, the Supreme Court itself has not been entirely consistent in its usage of the term "res judicata." As the Court has noted, "[t]his Court on more than one occasion has used the term 'res judicata' in a narrow sense, so as to exclude issue preclusion or collateral estoppel. . . . When using that formulation, 'res judicata becomes virtually synonymous with 'claim preclusion.'" Migra v. Warren City School District Board of Education, 465 U.S. 75, 77 n.1 (1984). "In order to avoid confusion resulting from the two uses of 'res judicata,'" *Migra* used the term "'claim preclusion' to refer to the preclusive effect of a judgment in foreclosing litigation of matters that should have been raised in an earlier suit." Id. Does this definition of "claim preclusion" capture the full scope of the doctrine?

2. As *Moitie*, *Parklane Hosiery*, and *Migra* show, claim preclusion and issue preclusion are distinct doctrines with distinct elements. Claim preclusion bars the subsequent assertion of any claims or defenses that were *actually* presented, or that *should have been* presented, in a prior lawsuit whose judgment has become final. Issue preclusion prevents re-litigation of any issues that were *actually* presented in a prior lawsuit and that were *necessary* to the final judgment in that prior suit. See Regions Hospital v. Shalala, — U.S. —, 118 S.Ct. 909, 918 (1998) ("Absent actual and adversarial litigation about [an issue], principles of issue preclusion do not hold fast"). There are some significant differences in the doctrines. Most obviously, claim preclusion precludes the re-

litigation of entire claims or defenses, while issue preclusion precludes the re-litigation of certain issues. Next, claim preclusion bars the re-litigation of matters that either were or should have been presented in the first case, while issue preclusion bars the re-litigation only of those issues that actually were litigated in the first case. Finally, with a few exceptions that we shall explore later in this chapter, claim preclusion operates only between the two parties to the first litigation. Although the same "mutuality of estoppel" idea used to operate with regard to issue preclusion, *Parklane Hosiery* shows that, with the advent of the concepts of defensive and offensive collateral estoppel, the requirement of mutuality has significantly eroded.

Both claim and issue preclusion involve some difficult questions of line-drawing. With claim preclusion, one troubling question is whether the matter being litigated in the second case is the same "claim" as the matter that was litigated in the first case. A second line-drawing problem is trying to figure out which claims should have been brought in the first proceeding, and which did not need to be brought. The general modern approach to both of these questions is to look at the matter transactionally, so that later claims or defenses are barred when the original and the later claims both arise from a common set of events. 18 Charles A. Wright et al., Federal Practice & Procedure § 4407 (1981). With regard to issue preclusion, there are comparable questions of determining the scope of the issue actually litigated in the first case and the necessity of that issue to the ultimate judgment. Id. §§ 4417, 4419-21.

3. In terms of their ability to prevent re-litigation, claim and issue preclusion suffer from an obvious deficiency: The doctrines apply only when a final judgment has occurred. When the parties settle, however, the court does not usually issue a judgment. (Important exceptions to this rule involve class action settlements and consent decrees.) This limitation on the use of preclusion is somewhat softened by the fact that a settling defendant usually obtains a release from the plaintiff. The release usually provides that the settlement absolves the defendant from any further liability for the events that gave rise to the lawsuit. If a second suit is brought, the question then becomes one of contract interpretation, rather than one of preclusion law. See F.R.Civ.P. 8(c) (requiring that defendant plead release as affirmative defense). Unless there are ambiguities in the language of the release, however, the ultimate effect of a release is roughly equivalent to the claim preclusion effect of a judgment. But note that most settlement agreements do not stipulate to the truth of particular factual issues, so that a settlement does not usually provide any effects equivalent to issue preclusion. In this regard, therefore, preclusion law is inferior to joinder as a means of preventing re-litigation of issues.

4. When the first litigation and all subsequent litigation occur in the same forum, it is obvious that the preclusion law of the forum will determine the preclusive effect of the first judgment. But whose preclusion principles apply when the second litigation is brought in a different forum? There is general agreement that a court in the second forum does not need to give preclusive effect to a prior judgment obtained through the use of procedures that violated due process. See Kremer v. Chemical Construction Corp., 456 U.S. 461 (1982). Likewise, a second court need not give preclusive effect to a judgment that is not "valid." The doctrine on what constitutes invalidity (typically lack of jurisdiction over the subject matter or the person) is not completely clear, but it is straightforward in the main. See Durfee v. Duke, 375 U.S. 106 (1963); Nevada v. Hall, 440 U.S. 410 (1979); Wright et al., *supra*, §§ 4427-31; see also Underwriters

National Assurance Co. v. North Carolina Life and Accident and Health Guaranty Association, 455 U.S. 691 (1982) (when court in first forum has determined, after full and fair consideration, that it has jurisdiction, court in second forum is required by full faith and credit command to accept first court's determination).

In cases in which the first judgment comports with due process and is valid, the effect that the second court must give to the judgment of the first court is rather complicated. The starting point of the analysis is the obligation of the second forum to give full faith and credit to the judgment of the first forum. This full faith and credit command has different sources. Under Article IV of the United States Constitution, state courts must give full faith and credit to the judgments of other state courts. Under 28 U.S.C. § 1738, federal courts must give full faith and credit to the judgments of state courts. Finally, although it is unclear whether the source for this proposition lies in the supremacy clause of Article VI of the Constitution or elsewhere, there is general agreement that state courts must give full faith and credit to the judgments of federal courts. This much is clear; the problem lies in sorting out the implications of the full faith and credit command for claim and issue preclusion.

It is clear that 28 U.S.C. § 1738 generally requires federal courts to give the same preclusive effect to a state court judgment that a court of that state would give to the judgment — even when the claim or issue decided in the state court judgment was a federal one. Allen v. McCurry, 449 U.S. 90 (1980); *Kremer*, 456 U.S. 461; Parsons Steel, Inc. v. First Alabama Bank, 474 U.S. 518 (1986). There is an exception to this rule if a federal remedial scheme expressly or impliedly repeals § 1738, although the circumstances in which this has occurred are rare. See Matsushita Electric Industrial Co. v. Epstein, 516 U.S. 367 (1996). There is also an exception when the state court did not provide a full and fair opportunity to litigate the matter on which preclusion is sought. See *McCurry*, 449 U.S. at 95. As a corollary to this exception, there is also an arguable exception, which the Court has suggested but has not definitively ruled, that a federal court can overlook state preclusion rules that would operate to preclude litigation of a claim that only a federal court would have jurisdiction to hear. See Marrese v. American Academy of Orthopaedic Surgeons, 470 U.S. 373 (1985); cf. *Matsushita*, 516 U.S. 367 (judgment of Delaware state court purported to settle both state and federal claims of class members, even though state court had no jurisdiction over federal claims; in determining preclusive effect of judgment on subsequently filed suit alleging federal claims, federal court must look to law of Delaware).

The same simple rule does not quite pertain with respect to the effect that a court in State B must give to a judgment entered in State A. With respect to claim preclusion, the general rule is the one stated in the last paragraph — that the court in State B must give the same preclusive effect to the judgment as a court in State A. There are some indications, however, that this general rule does not "compel[ ] the conclusion that full faith and credit incorporates every minute detail of res judicata doctrine," so that, for instance, claim preclusion might not apply when it was necessary to resort to the courts in State A first but the courts in State B can provide more complete relief. Wright et al., *supra*, § 4467. The picture with regard to issue preclusion is somewhat more murky. Suppose for instance, that State A permits the use of defensive collateral estoppel, but State B does not. When the losing plaintiff sues a new defendant in State B, must State B extend issue preclusive effect to the judgment from State A? Conversely, suppose that State B recognizes defensive collateral estoppel, but State A does not; may State B give State A's judgment more preclusive effect than it would have in State A? The prevailing wisdom suggests that State B must extend as much preclusive effect to the judgment as State A would give it, but is not constitutionally compelled to extend greater preclusive effect to a judgment than State A would give it. Courts have differed, however, about whether they should give greater effect as a matter of policy or comity. See id.

A third scenario is the effect that one federal court must give to another federal court's judgment. In this scenario, notions of full faith and credit do not come into play; the issue is a straight-forward question of the relevant rules of preclusion. You might think that the answer here is simple: the second federal court should use the federal law of preclusion. With respect to federal question claims, this should be the correct answer, although there is some doubt on the matter. See Orjias v. Stevenson, 31 F.3d 995, 1010 (10th Cir.) (federal preclusion law applies), cert. denied, 513 U.S. 1000 (1994); but see NAACP v. Hunt, 891 F.2d 1555, 1560 (11th Cir. 1990) (federal courts should apply res judicata law of state in which they sit even to federal question claims). But when the first federal court decides a state law claim, should the second federal court use federal preclusion law or the preclusion law of the state whose law is the source of the claim? At present courts differ on the matter, with some deferring to state law and others relying on federal law. See Wright et al., *supra*, § 4472; In re Air Crash at Detroit Metropolitan Airport, 776 F. Supp. 316 (E.D. Mich. 1991) (federal interests in preclusion required use of federal rule of defensive collateral estoppel for diversity claims). The matter is often further complicated by the facts that state law might itself adopt federal preclusion rules and federal law might incorporate the state's preclusion rules. See Pardo v. Olson & Sons, Inc., 40 F.3d 1063 (9th Cir. 1994); Havoco of America, Ltd. v. Freeman, Atkins & Coleman, Ltd., 58 F.3d 303 (7th Cir. 1995).

The final scenario is the effect that a state court must give to a prior federal judgment. This scenario replicates the last scenario, although here issues of full faith and credit (or the supremacy clause) are directly implicated. There remains an old line of cases, decided during the time when federal courts were required to adopt state rules of procedure, that a federal court judgment has the same effect as a state court judgment in the same state. Dupasseur v. Rochereau, 21 Wall. (88 U.S.) 130 (1875). But the modern thinking is that, with respect to federal questions, federal preclusion law applies and states must apply that law. See Heck v. Humphrey, 512 U.S. 477, 488 n.9 (1994); Wright et al., *supra*, § 4468. The picture with respect to claims based on state law is less clear. See id., § 4472.

Would it be better if we had a flat rule that the preclusion law of the court that issues the first judgment always controls the preclusive effects of the judgment? See Ronan E. Degnan, *Federalized Res Judicata*, 85 Yale L.J. 471 (1976); Howard M. Erichson, *Interjurisdictional Preclusion*, 94 Mich. L. Rev. 945 (1998) (proposing rule after empirical analysis); see also Stephen B. Burbank, *Interjurisdictional Preclusion, Full Faith and Credit and Federal Common Law: A General Approach*, 71 Corn. L. Rev. 733 (1986).

5. Some of the complexities of the prior note may have explained the disposition in *Moitie*, in which the Court indicated that claim preclusion barred the re-assertion of federal claims, and then remanded the case for further proceedings. As the dissents pointed out, this was (to say the least) a curious resolution, since the complaint alleged only state law claims. Perhaps the

majority noticed the almost mind-numbing complexity of trying to figure out whose preclusion laws should apply when there is an initial federal judgment followed by a state law suit followed by removal of the state case back to the federal court that issued the original judgment. Is it obvious that federal preclusion law applies here? The majority's solution makes clear that *Moitie II* raised no federal issues, a fact that probably required the federal district court to remand the case to state court. Once returned to state court, the California court could determine whose preclusion rules should govern the state law allegations, and what those rules should be. Note that the majority's approach also avoids the need for the Supreme Court to decide whether *Dupasseur* remains good law. Assuming that this was the majority's rationale, is it a sufficient reason to have disposed of the case as it did? Would it have been more sensible to have held that the case was not removable from state court, as Justice Brennan urged?

Although we reserve to Chapter Three a more detailed look at the concept of removal and remand, see p. 373, *infra*, you might be interested to know that Justice Brennan may have lost the battle in *Moitie* but ultimately won the war. Seventeen years after *Moitie*, the Supreme Court essentially disowned "*Moitie's* enigmatic footnote" 2, and held that "claim preclusion by reason of a prior federal judgment is a defensive plea that provides no basis for removal under § 1441(b)." Rivet v. Regions Bank of Louisiana, — U.S. —, 118 S.Ct. 921, 926 (1998). *Rivet*, however, seemed to stop just shy of expressly overruling *Moitie*.

6. As *Rivet* says, claim and issue preclusion are affirmative defenses that must be pleaded in the answer to a complaint. See 118 S.Ct. at 925; F.R.Civ.P. 8(c). As *Parklane Hosiery* shows, offensive collateral estoppel can be raised on a motion for partial summary judgment, or on other pretrial motions seeking to limit issues. Wright et al., *supra*, § 4405. The question can even be raised by the court acting *sua sponte*. See pp. 1079-83, *infra*. An appellate court reviews the district court's decision on preclusion under a *de novo* standard, while factual findings relevant to the decision are reviewed under a clearly erroneous standard. See Computer Associates International, Inc. v. Altai, Inc., 126 F.3d 365 (2d Cir. 1997); Trevino v. Gates, 99 F.3d 911 (9th Cir. 1996), cert. denied, 117 S.Ct. 1249 (1997); Richardson v. Miller, 101 F.3d 665 (11th Cir. 1996) (conclusion that issue was actually litigated is reviewed under clearly erroneous standard).

7. Despite their doctrinal differences, the doctrines of claim preclusion and issue preclusion respond to a common set of policy arguments. The sense of the doctrines is that a party should be entitled to get only one bite at an apple. Policy arguments — especially the judicial system's interests in finality of judgments, efficient use of scarce resources, and consistent results, as well as the opposing litigant's interest in freedom from defending against the same claims over and over — support this intuition. Notice, however, that these policy arguments play out somewhat differently with regard to various aspects of claim and issue preclusion.

The easiest case may be the preclusion of a claim or defense that was actually litigated in a prior lawsuit involving the same parties and that was necessary to the decision in the prior lawsuit. In these circumstances, the only arguable reason to permit a second bite at the apple is either the discovery of new evidence or some significant defect in the original trial (such as lack of jurisdiction or fraud). Rather than relaxing preclusion rules in these situations, however, we could require that a party claiming new evidence or some defect move to vacate or amend the earlier judgment, or request relief from that judgment. In fact, this latter approach is the method that our system has used to address the problems of new evidence and other defects. See F.R.Civ.P. 59, 60.

The second easiest case for application of preclusion is the preclusion of issues that were actually litigated in a prior lawsuit involving the same parties and that were necessary to the decision in that lawsuit. The arguments for finality, efficiency, and consistency are all compelling. But the concern for multiple and vexatious litigation is somewhat reduced, since the plaintiff has a right to proceed with the second suit. Moreover, it is possible that a factfinder that resolved a factual dispute in the context of the claim asserted in the first case might not have resolved the dispute the same way in the context of the different claim asserted in the second case. Thus, issue preclusion deprives the factfinder of the opportunity to place factual findings into context.

The next, and somewhat less easy, case for preclusion is the application of claim preclusion to bar the re-litigation of claims or defenses that were actually litigated but were not necessary to the decision in the case. As a practical matter such cases are rare, but imagine this hypothetical: A plaintiff brings a case with two claims that would entitle her to identical relief. The jury returns a verdict in her favor on Claim A, and never decides Claim B. After the judgment becomes final, the supreme court of the state declares that parties can get greater relief under Claim B than under Claim A. In this case, the interests in finality, efficiency, and prevention of multiple litigation would still support the use of claim preclusion against a second suit re-asserting Claim B, even though the interests in consistency are somewhat weaker. Since the plaintiff could presumably have appealed on the issue of the scope of Claim B's remedy, however, the application of claim preclusion in this situation does not seem particularly unfair.

In the next situation — the preclusion of a claim that should have been presented, but was not — the policy arguments in favor of preclusion start to become less compelling. Interests in finality and efficiency, as well as the protection of parties from a multiplicity of vexatious suits, are still present. Since the second claim was not litigated in the prior suit, the consistency interest is muted although still implicated in the sense that a favorable finding on the second claim might cast some doubt on the validity of the first judgment. On the other side of the ledger, there is a certain sense of unfairness in denying a person the opportunity to present in some forum a potentially valid claim.

In the next situation — defensive collateral estoppel that permits a nonparty to the first case to use findings in the prior judgment as a shield against the plaintiff's second suit — the arguments become still weaker. Concerns for finality, efficiency, and consistency all pertain, although the fact that different parties are involved on one side of the suit weakens the finality and consistency points. Since the plaintiff is suing a new defendant, the concern for protecting the defendant from multiple and vexatious litigation does not exist, although it is replaced, to a degree, by the desire to prevent the plaintiff from maintaining such litigation. Moreover, there is some potential unfairness in giving to a finding that was made in one factual context preclusive effect in another factual context. The plaintiff's right to jury trial with regard to her case against the defendant in the second suit is also affected.

In the final situation — offensive collateral estoppel that permits a nonparty to the first case to use findings in the prior judgment as a sword against the defendant — the arguments for preclusion are weakest. As *Parklane Hosiery* shows, the efficiency and inconsistency arguments cut both ways with offensive collateral estoppel. As with defensive collateral estoppel, the finality concern does not apply with full force. The concern for multiple and vexatious litigation is not present, but is replaced by a concern for a defendant's multiple denials of responsibility. Since a defendant has a right to insist that a plaintiff be put to her proof, however, it is difficult to regard these denials as "vexatious." Moreover, the jury trial concerns that *Parklane Hosiery* identifies and rejects have some weight. Likewise, there is some measure of unfairness in binding a defendant to the results of a judgment against it when nonparties would not be bound be a judgment in favor of the defendant. Is this asymmetry in risk ameliorated by the requirement that the beneficiary of issue preclusion show that the target had a "full and fair opportunity" to litigate the issue? Finally, the "contextualization" point that we described above is especially relevant with offensive collateral estoppel. How do we know that the findings in the first trial were reliable, especially when the defendant was forced to litigate in a forum that was chosen by his opponent? As footnote 14 in *Parklane Hosiery* discusses, Professor Currie makes the telling point that, if a defendant railroad won the first 25 suits and a plaintiff the 26th suit, we would not estop the defendant from contesting the remaining 24 suits because the verdict in the 26th case was unreliable and aberrational. The rest of Currie's analysis expresses doubt about whether we should estop the defendant in the subsequent 49 suits even when the plaintiff wins the first one. Brainerd Currie, *Mutuality of Collateral Estoppel: Limits of the* Bernhard *Doctrine*, 9 Stan. L. Rev. 281, 304. How do we know that the first verdict is not aberrational? Do the exceptions that *Parklane Hosiery* develops for collateral estoppel adequately address this concern?

Does the analysis in this note suggest that all the forms of preclusion should be recognized? If not, at what point along the line should preclusion doctrine be cut off? Cf. United States v. Mendoza, 464 U.S. 154 (1984) (refusing to apply non-mutual offensive collateral estoppel against government).

8. The joinder doctrines that we examined in the first part of this chapter and the preclusion doctrines that we are now studying are interwoven. We began this chapter with the observation that, in the American procedural system, the primary (and often only) way to bind a person to a lawsuit's outcome is to join that person in the lawsuit. *Moitie* and *Parklane Hosiery* describe some of the basic contours of preclusion for the parties that are joined. Thus, at one level, preclusion law and joinder law should be seen as complementary. The preclusion rules describe the scope of preclusion. The joinder rules then set the outer parameter on the number of persons to whom preclusion might extend, and the plaintiffs (in conjunction to some extent with the defendants and court) then decide the actual parties to whom preclusion in fact extends. At another level, however, the limitations of joinder might make us want to expand our use of collateral estoppel; for instance, note that the decision in *Parklane Hosiery* would have been unnecessary if our joinder rules required the joinder of all claims in the first proceeding. Conversely, the limitations and difficulty of using preclusion on a case-by-case basis may lead us to take a more expansive view of our joinder rules. See Avila v. Van Ru Credit Corp., 1995 WL 41425, *7 (N.D. Ill.) ("a class action remedy for vindicating the rights of thousands of consumers is a more efficient use of judicial resources than forcing those consumers to each file individual actions for statutory damages and assert offensive collateral estoppel" against defendant); Erichson, *supra*, at 954-56, 959 (discussing joinder effects of preclusion).

9. Recall that the great problem on which we are focusing is the dysfunction- or inefficiency-causing re-litigation of claims and issues, and that the solution to this problem requires an ability either to bring into the litigation or to preclude from litigating those putative plaintiffs or defendants that are unwilling or unable to enter the litigation voluntarily. We have already seen that the joinder rules do not provide an adequate solution to this problem. Do standard preclusion rules ameliorate or exacerbate this problem? The answer is rather mixed. First, to the extent that they operate only against the subset of persons that have already been joined, the preclusion rules do not prevent subsequent litigation either by persons that could have been joined but were not or by persons that could not have been joined. Therefore, in order to find a complete answer to the re-litigation problem, some method of dealing with both of these non-joined groups must be found. Second, the doctrines of defensive and offensive collateral estoppel have some litigation-reducing potential; both would reduce the scope of subsequent litigation, and defensive collateral estoppel might operate either to give a plaintiff the incentive to join all defendants in the first suit or to discourage a plaintiff from filing a second suit. Third, both doctrines inject an additional issue into the subsequent litigation, and offensive collateral estoppel may have the counterproductive effect of inducing plaintiffs to remain on the sidelines. Although *Parklane Hosiery* seeks to mitigate this effect by denying sideline-sitters the benefit of collateral estoppel, it is not clear that a court will always successfully ferret out the sideline-sitters.

10. The following subsection examines in more detail some of the limits of preclusion doctrines in addressing the problems of complicated and complex litigation. Before we begin that study, however, you should ask yourself whether the size or complexity of a lawsuit should affect either the policy considerations or the scope of preclusion doctrines described in the earlier notes. To the extent that complicated litigation involves extreme examples of inefficient re-litigation of claims or issues, the complication of the litigation puts a weighty thumb on the scale in favor of broader use of preclusion rules. Indeed, preclusion rules are in many ways a better response to the problem of inefficient multiparty, multiforum litigation than joinder rules, since the joinder of additional persons creates its own inefficiencies. The broader use of preclusion rules in complex litigation, however, would rest on different arguments. Since the central feature of complex litigation is lawyer dysfunction, the only argument for broader preclusion rules is that such rules would eliminate lawyer dysfunction and make the rational adjudication of a dispute possible.

Moitie and *Parklane Hosiery* do not indicate whether there might be a more generous reading of preclusion rules in complicated or complex litigation. Both cases involved multiparty litigation, and in *Moitie* the litigation was also multiforum. Both cases — one an antitrust case and one a securities case — involved legal theories that are often associated with complex litigation, although it is not clear that lawyer dysfunction existed in either case. *Moitie*'s preference for plain rules and its rejection of fairness-oriented exceptions to those rules would seem to argue against the development of broader preclusion rules in complicated or complex litigation, while the concerns for efficiency in both *Moitie* and *Parklane Hosiery* would argue in favor of broader rules in complicated litigation.

Against this background, we now turn more specifically to the uses and limitations of preclusion rules in complex and complicated litigation.

2. The Limits of Preclusion Law in Complex and Complicated Cases

In this subsection we examine efforts that have been made to mold preclusion doctrines to the needs of complex or complicated litigation, and the limits of these efforts. We begin the inquiry by examining the use of preclusion doctrines when the doctrines are invoked against a party that was also a party in a prior case. We then shift our focus to the more difficult — and more critical — issue of using preclusion doctrines to bind nonparties (whether potential plaintiffs or potential defendants) in the prior suit to the judgment or findings of that suit.

a. Precluding Parties that Participated in a Prior Case

COOPER v. FEDERAL RESERVE BANK OF RICHMOND

467 U.S. 867 (1984)

■ JUSTICE STEVENS delivered the opinion of the Court.

The question to be decided is whether a judgment in a class action determining that an employer did not engage in a general pattern or practice of racial discrimination against the certified class of employees precludes a class member from maintaining a subsequent civil action alleging an individual claim of racial discrimination against the employer.

I

On March 22, 1977, the Equal Employment Opportunity Commission commenced a civil action against respondent, the Federal Reserve Bank of Richmond. Respondent operates a branch in Charlotte, N.C. (the Bank), where during the years 1974-1978 it employed about 350-450 employees in several departments. The EEOC complaint alleged that the Bank was violating § 703(a) of Title VII of the Civil Rights Act of 1964 by engaging in "policies and practices" that included "failing and refusing to promote blacks because of race."

Six months after the EEOC filed its complaint, four individual employees[2] were allowed to intervene as plaintiffs. In their "complaint in intervention," these plaintiffs alleged that the Bank's employment practices violated 42 U.S.C. § 1981, as well as Title VII; that each of them was the

---

2. Sylvia Cooper, Constance Russell, Helen Moore, and Elmore Hannah, Jr., sometimes referred to by the District Court as the "intervening plaintiffs" and by the parties as the "Cooper petitioners." . . .

victim of employment discrimination based on race; and that they could adequately represent a class of black employees against whom the Bank had discriminated because of their race. In due course, the District Court entered an order conditionally certifying the following class pursuant to Federal Rules of Civil Procedure 23(b)(2) and (3):

> "All black persons who have been employed by the defendant at its Charlotte Branch Office at any time since January 3, 1974 [6 months prior to the first charge filed by the intervenors with EEOC], who have been discriminated against in promotion, wages, job assignments and terms and conditions of employment because of their race."

After certifying the class, the District Court ordered that notice be published in the Charlotte newspapers and mailed to each individual member of the class. The notice described the status of the litigation, and plainly stated that members of the class "will be bound by the judgment or other determination" if they did not exclude themselves by sending a written notice to the Clerk. Among the recipients of the notice were Phyllis Baxter and five other individuals employed by the Bank. It is undisputed that these individuals — the Baxter petitioners — are members of the class represented by the intervening plaintiffs and that they made no attempt to exclude themselves from the class.

At the trial the intervening plaintiffs, as well as the Baxter petitioners, testified. The District Court found that the Bank had engaged in a pattern and practice of discrimination from 1974 through 1978 by failing to afford black employees opportunities for advancement and assignment equal to opportunities afforded white employees in pay grades 4 and 5. Except as so specified, however, the District Court found that "there does not appear to be a pattern and practice of discrimination pervasive enough for the court to order relief." With respect to the claims of the four intervening plaintiffs, the court found that the Bank had discriminated against Cooper and Russell, but not against Moore and Hannah. Finally, the court somewhat cryptically stated that although it had an opinion about "the entitlement to relief of some of the class members who testified at trial," it would defer decision of such matters to a further proceeding.

Thereafter, on March 24, 1981, the Baxter petitioners moved to intervene, alleging that each had been denied a promotion for discriminatory reasons. With respect to [one of the Baxter petitioners], the court denied the motion because she was a member of the class for which relief had been ordered and therefore her rights would be protected in the Stage II proceedings to be held on the question of relief. With respect to the other five Baxter petitioners, the court also denied the motion, but for a different reason. It held that because all of them were employed in jobs above the grade 5 category, they were not entitled to any benefit from the court's ruling with respect to discrimination in grades 4 and 5. The District Court stated: "The court has found no proof of any classwide discrimination above grade 5 and, therefore, they are not entitled to participate in any Stage II proceedings in this case." The court added that it could "see no reason why, if any of the would be intervenors are actively interested in pursuing their claims, they cannot file a Section 1981 suit next week. . . ."

A few days later the Baxter petitioners filed a separate action against the Bank alleging that each of them had been denied a promotion because of their race in violation of 42 U.S.C. § 1981. The Bank moved to dismiss the complaint on the ground that each of them was a member of the class that had been certified in the Cooper litigation, that each was employed in a grade other than 4 or 5, and that they were bound by the determination that there was no proof of any classwide discrimination above grade 5. The District Court denied the motion to dismiss, but certified its order for interlocutory appeal under 28 U.S.C. § 1292(b). The Bank's interlocutory appeal from the order was then consolidated with the Bank's pending appeal in the Cooper litigation.

The United States Court of Appeals for the Fourth Circuit reversed the District Court's judgment on the merits in the Cooper litigation, concluding that (1) there was insufficient evidence to establish a pattern or practice of racial discrimination in grades 4 and 5, and (2) two of the intervening plaintiffs had not been discriminated against on account of race. The court further held that under the doctrine of res judicata, the judgment in the Cooper class action precluded the Baxter petitioners from maintaining their individual race discrimination claims against the Bank. The court thus reversed the order denying the Bank's motion to dismiss in the Baxter action, and remanded for dismissal of the Baxter complaint. We granted certiorari to review that judgment, and we now reverse.

II

Claims of two types were adjudicated in the Cooper litigation. First, the individual claims of each of the four intervening plaintiffs have been finally decided in the Bank's favor. Those individual decisions do not, of course, foreclose any other individual claims. Second, the class claim that the Bank followed "policies and practices" of discriminating against its employees has also been decided. It is that decision on which the Court of Appeals based its res judicata analysis.

There is of course no dispute that under elementary principles of prior adjudication a judgment in a properly entertained class action is binding on class members in any subsequent litigation. See, *e.g.*, Supreme Tribe of Ben-Hur v. Cauble, 255 U.S. 356 (1921) . . . . Basic principles of res judicata (merger and bar or claim preclusion) and collateral estoppel (issue preclusion) apply. A judgment in favor of the plaintiff class extinguishes their claim, which merges into the judgment granting relief. A judgment in favor of the defendant extinguishes the claim, barring a subsequent action on that claim. A judgment in favor of either side is conclusive in a subsequent action between them on any issue actually litigated and determined, if its determination was essential to that judgment.

III

A plaintiff bringing a civil action for a violation of § 703(a) of Title VII of the Civil Rights Act of 1964, 78 Stat. 255, as amended, 42 U.S.C. § 2000e-2(a), has the initial burden of establishing a prima facie case that his employer discriminated against him on account of his race, color, religion, sex, or national origin. A plaintiff meets this initial burden by offering evidence adequate to create an inference that he was denied an employment opportunity on the basis of a discriminatory criterion enumerated in Title VII.

A plaintiff alleging one instance of discrimination establishes a prima facie case justifying an inference of individual racial discrimination by showing that he (1) belongs to a racial minority, (2) applied and was qualified for a vacant position the employer was attempting to fill, (3) was rejected for the position, and (4) after his rejection, the position remained open and the employer continued to seek applicants of the plaintiff's qualifications. . . . Once these facts are established, the employer must produce "evidence that the plaintiff was rejected, or someone else was preferred, for a legitimate, nondiscriminatory reason." . . . At that point, the presumption of discrimination "drops from the case," and the district court is in a position to decide the ultimate question in such a suit: whether the particular employment decision at issue was made on the basis of race. . . . The ultimate burden of persuading the trier of fact that the defendant intentionally discriminated against the plaintiff regarding the particular employment decision "remains at all times with the plaintiff," and in the final analysis the trier of fact "must decide which party's explanation of the employer's motivation it believes." . . .

In Franks v. Bowman Transportation Co[.], 424 U.S. 747 (1976), . . . we held that demonstrating the existence of a discriminatory pattern or practice established a presumption that the individual class members had been discriminated against on account of race. Proving isolated or sporadic discriminatory acts by the employer is insufficient to establish a prima facie case of a pattern or practice of discrimination; rather it must be established by a preponderance of the evidence that "racial discrimination was the company's standard operating procedure — the regular rather than the unusual practice." . . . While a finding of a pattern or practice of discrimination itself justifies an award of prospective relief to the class, additional proceedings are ordinarily required to determine the scope of individual relief for the members of the class. . . .

The crucial difference between an individual's claim of discrimination and a class action alleging a general pattern or practice of discrimination is manifest. The inquiry regarding an individual's claim is the reason for a particular employment decision, while "at the liability stage of a pattern-or-practice trial the focus often will not be on individual hiring decisions, but on a pattern of discriminatory decisionmaking." . . .

[A] class plaintiff's attempt to prove the existence of a companywide policy, or even a consistent practice within a given department, may fail even though discrimination against one or two individuals has been proved. The facts of this case illustrate the point.

The District Court found that two of the intervening plaintiffs, Cooper and Russell, had both established that they were the victims of racial discrimination but, as the Court of Appeals noted, they were employed in grades higher than grade 5 and therefore their testimony provided no support for the conclusion that there was a practice of discrimination in grades 4 and 5. Given the burden of establishing a prima facie case of a pattern or practice of discrimination, it was entirely consistent for the District Court simultaneously to conclude that Cooper and Russell had valid individual claims even though it had expressly found no proof of any classwide discrimination above grade 5. It could not be more plain that the rejection of a claim of classwide discrimination does not warrant the conclusion that no member of the class could have a valid individual claim. "A racially balanced work force cannot immunize an employer from liability for specific acts of discrimination." . . .

The analysis of the merits of the Cooper litigation by the Court of Appeals is entirely consistent with this conclusion. In essence, the Court of Appeals held that the statistical evidence, buttressed by expert testimony and anecdotal evidence by three individual employees in grades 4 and 5, was not sufficient to support the finding of a pattern of bankwide discrimination within those grades. . . .

The Court of Appeals was correct in generally concluding that the Baxter petitioners, as members of the class represented by the intervening plaintiffs in the Cooper litigation, are bound by the adverse judgment in that case. The court erred, however, in the preclusive effect it attached to that prior adjudication. That judgment (1) bars the class members from bringing another class action against the Bank alleging a pattern or practice of discrimination for the relevant time period and (2) precludes the class members in any other litigation with the Bank from relitigating the question whether the Bank engaged in a pattern and practice of discrimination against black employees during the relevant time period. The judgment is not, however, dispositive of the individual claims the Baxter petitioners have alleged in their separate action. Assuming they establish a prima facie case of discrimination . . ., the Bank will be required to articulate a legitimate reason for each of the challenged decisions, and if it meets that burden, the ultimate questions regarding motivation in their individual cases will be resolved by the District Court. Moreover, the prior adjudication may well prove beneficial to the Bank in the Baxter action: the determination in the Cooper action that the Bank had not engaged in a general pattern or practice of discrimination would be relevant on the issue of pretext. . . .

The Bank argues that permitting the Baxter petitioners to bring separate actions would frustrate the purposes of Rule 23. We think the converse is true. The class-action device was intended to establish a procedure for the adjudication of common questions of law or fact. If the Bank's theory were adopted, it would be tantamount to requiring that every member of the class be permitted to intervene to litigate the merits of his individual claim.

It is also suggested that the District Court had a duty to decide the merits of the individual claims of class members, at least insofar as the individual claimants became witnesses in the joint proceeding and subjected their individual employment histories to scrutiny at trial. Unless these claims are decided in the main proceeding, the Bank argues that the duplicative litigation that Rule 23 was designed to avoid will be encouraged, and that defendants will be subjected to the risks of liability without the offsetting benefit of a favorable termination of exposure through a final judgment.

This argument fails to differentiate between what the District Court might have done and what it actually did. The District Court did actually adjudicate the individual claims of Cooper and the other intervening plaintiffs, as well as the class claims, but it pointedly refused to decide the individual claims of the Baxter petitioners. Whether the issues framed by the named parties before the court should be expanded to encompass the individual claims of additional class members is a matter of judicial administration that should be decided in the first instance by the District Court. Nothing in Rule 23 requires as a matter of law that the District Court make a finding with respect to each and every matter on which there is testimony in the class action. Indeed, Rule 23 is carefully drafted to provide a mechanism for the expeditious decision of common questions. Its purposes might well be defeated by an attempt to decide a host of individual claims before any common question relating to liability has been resolved adversely to the defendant. We do not find the District Court's denial of the Baxter petitioners' motion for leave to intervene in the Cooper litigation, or its decision not to make findings regarding the Baxter petitioners' testimony in the Cooper litigation, to be inconsistent with Rule 23.

The judgment of the Court of Appeals is reversed, and the case is remanded for further proceedings consistent with this opinion.

- JUSTICE MARSHALL concurs in the judgment.
- JUSTICE POWELL took no part in the decision of this case.

EPSTEIN v. MCA, INC.

126 F.3d 1235 (9th Cir. 1997)

- NORRIS, Circuit Judge. This case is before us on remand from the United States Supreme Court. In Matsushita Electric Industrial Co. v. Epstein, [516 U.S. 367] (1996) ("*Matsushita*"), the Court reversed our judgment in Epstein v. MCA, Inc., 50 F.3d 644 (9th Cir. 1995) ("*Epstein I*"), and remanded "for proceedings consistent with this opinion." *Matsushita*, 116 S.Ct. at 884.

The case is a class action brought by former MCA shareholders who surrendered their stock in response to a tender offer by Matsushita. In *Epstein I*, the named plaintiffs ("the Epstein plaintiffs") contended, *inter alia*, that Matsushita's tender offer violated the so-called "all-holder, best-price" rule of SEC Rule 14d-10 by paying a premium for the stock of MCA's chairman and chief executive officer, Lew Wasserman, and MCA's chief operating officer, Sidney Sheinberg. The district court awarded summary judgment to the defendants, and the Epstein plaintiffs appealed.

In *Epstein I* we reversed the summary judgment for Matsushita, holding that [federal securities laws created a private right of action and that there were genuine issues of material fact with regard to Matsushita's alleged violations of these laws.] We also held that the district court had abused its discretion in refusing to certify the class because "[t]he claims of every tendering shareholder turn on identical facts and law — regardless of the identity or circumstances of the particular shareholder." . . .

None of these rulings on the merits of the Rule 14d-10 claims were disturbed by the Supreme Court in *Matsushita*. The Court reversed our judgment and remanded for further proceedings solely on the basis of the first question presented in Matsushita's petition for the writ of certiorari: "Whether a federal court can withhold full faith and credit from a state court final judgment approving a class action settlement simply because the settlement released exclusively federal claims." Matsushita Electric Indus. Co. v. Epstein, 515 U.S. 1141 (1995) (granting certiorari limited to Question 1 presented by the petition for writ of certiorari) . . . .

[The facts that underlay *Matsushita* were these: Prior to the filing of the *Epstein* suit in federal court, a similar class action had been filed in Delaware state court. Since only the federal courts have jurisdiction to hear claims of violation of federal securities laws, the Delaware case pleaded only state law claims. While the district court's judgment in *Epstein I* was on appeal to the Ninth Circuit, the class representatives in the Delaware case agreed to a settlement that specifically released the federal securities claims. In the course of approving the settlement, the Delaware state court entered a final judgment discharging the federal claims of all class members that did not opt out. That judgment was affirmed by the Delaware Supreme Court. Among its other holdings in *Epstein I*, the Ninth Circuit held that the state court could not release or discharge the federal claims, so that its judgment discharging those claims was not entitled to full faith and credit. In *Matsushita*, however, the Supreme Court held that, under the Full Faith and Credit Act, 28 U.S.C. § 1738, the federal court was required to give the state judgment discharging the federal claims the same preclusive effect that a Delaware state court would give the judgment — even though the state court would not have had jurisdiction over the federal claims themselves. The respondents in *Matsushita* were persons that were members of both the state and federal classes and that did not opt out of the state class action.]

On remand, the Epstein plaintiffs press anew an argument that we found unnecessary to address in *Epstein I*: that we should withhold full faith and credit from the Delaware judgment because it was entered into in violation of the due process right of the absent class members to adequate representation at all times. We now turn to that question.

I

Matsushita contends that we are barred from addressing the merits of the Epstein plaintiffs' claims of inadequate representation. Matsushita makes three arguments in support of this contention:

(1) The Supreme Court's decision in *Matsushita* did not leave the issue open on remand;

(2) The issue of the adequacy of representation was fully and fairly litigated in the Delaware Court of Chancery;

(3) The Epstein plaintiffs are estopped from raising the adequacy of their representation collaterally because they did not raise it by intervening in the Delaware proceeding.

A

In arguing that the "[t]he opinion of the Supreme Court leaves no issue open on remand," Matsushita either mischaracterizes or disregards the unambiguous statements in the record to the contrary . . . .

Matsushita, although quoting various excerpts from the Court's opinion, fails to quote the following explicit statement by the Court that it did not address the due process claim:

> We need not address the due process claim [of inadequate representation] . . . because it is outside the scope of the question presented in this Court. . . . While it is true that a respondent may defend a judgment on alternative grounds, we generally do not address arguments that were not the basis for the decision below. . . .

[*Matsushita*, 516 U.S. at 379,] n.5. . . .

In sum, we reject Matsushita's argument that the Supreme Court did not leave the due process issue open on remand. The Court laid out an unambiguous contrary intention in its statement of the question presented and in footnote five, and no voice was raised against Justice Ginsburg's explicit statement that the issue of adequacy of representation "remain[ed] open for airing on remand." 116 S.Ct. at 890 (Ginsburg, J., concurring in part and dissenting in part).

B

Next we address Matsushita's argument that the Delaware settlement judgment precludes the Epstein plaintiffs from "relitigating" the issue of adequacy of representation under Delaware issue preclusion law. It claims that adequacy of representation was actually litigated by objectors at the Delaware fairness hearing, and that other Delaware courts would therefore give preclusive effect to the Chancery Court's determination that representation of the absent class members was adequate. Therefore, Matsushita argues, under 28 U.S.C. § 1738, we too must attach issue preclusion.

The Epstein plaintiffs argue in response that the Delaware judgment raises no issue preclusion bar to the question of constitutional adequacy of representation. First, they contend, the objectors did not actually litigate the issue at the Delaware fairness hearing, as is required under Delaware issue preclusion law. More broadly, the Epstein plaintiffs contend that individual, uncertified objectors in a class action cannot constitutionally bind absent class members on the issue of adequacy of representation. We consider each contention in turn.

1

Under Delaware law, issue preclusion attaches only when a question of fact essential to the judgment has been actually litigated and determined by a valid and final judgment. See Messick v. Star Enterprise, 655 A.2d 1209, 1211 (Del. 1995) ("The test for applying collateral estoppel requires that (1) a question of fact essential to the judgment, (2) be litigated and (3) determined (4) by a valid and final judgment.") . . . . The Delaware record shows clearly that the issue of adequacy of representation was not litigated during the settlement proceedings.

First, the notice to class members said nothing about adequacy of representation. Instead, the notice stated that the purpose of the settlement hearing was to determine "(a) the fairness, reasonableness, and adequacy *of the terms of the . . . Settlement,* and (b) whether an order and final judgment should be entered approving the proposed settlement." Supplemental Record ("SR") 354 (emphasis added). Whether the class was adequately represented by the named plaintiffs or by class counsel was not an issue noticed for hearing. Thus, absent class members were not on notice that they could have objected to the adequacy of representation at the settlement hearing.

Not surprisingly, the objectors who did appear at the settlement hearing did not litigate the adequacy of their representation. Objector Marion Minton focused solely on the issue of inadequate notice. Objector Pamela Minton de Ruiz, in her memorandum to the Chancery Court, framed her objection in terms of collusion, arguing that "[t]he second proposed settlement is collusive and should not be approved." Likewise, the Minton objectors argued at the settlement hearing that "this two-cent settlement is collusive." Neither of the Minton objectors focused on the much broader issue of whether representation was constitutionally adequate. Finally, objector William A. Krupman did submit an affidavit to the Chancery Court stating that he opposed the settlement because "the purported class representatives . . . had proposed a settlement that benefitted no one but their own attorneys. They did not provide adequate representation." However, this single blanket statement conflating the non-constitutional question of the fairness of the settlement with the constitutional question of the adequacy of representation hardly qualifies as "actual litigation" of the constitutional issue. Indeed, in his argument at the settlement hearing, objector Krupman did not address the constitutional adequacy of the representation, but argued only that the terms of the settlement were unfair.

Since the issue of adequacy of representation was never actually litigated in Chancery Court, no Delaware court would attach preclusion to the issue of adequate representation of the absent class members. . . . [6]

---

[6]. It also appears that Delaware courts would not attach preclusion to the Delaware judgment because the Vice Chancellor failed to make a finding, supported by reasons and evidence on the record, that the requirements of Delaware Rule 23 were satisfied. In Prezant v. De Angelis, 636 A.2d 915 (Del. 1994), the Delaware Supreme Court held that a Court of Chancery is required to "articulate on the record its findings regarding the satisfaction of the Rule 23 criteria and

2

Even if adequacy of representation had actually been litigated by objectors at the fairness hearing, and even if Delaware law would allow an individual objector to bind an absentee on the issue of adequacy of representation — however improbable that might seem — we still could not give full faith and credit to such a judgment because it would violate due process of law. As the Epstein plaintiffs aptly put it, "[o]bjectors are objectors, not class representatives." Binding absentees to any part of a class action judgment "is an act of judicial power," *Epstein I*, 50 F.3d at 667, and that power can only be exercised over absentees when their interests have, in fact, been adequately represented by parties lawfully authorized to represent them. See, *e.g.*, Richards v. Jefferson Cty., Ala., 517 U.S. 793 (1996) ("[O]ne is not bound by a judgment in personam in a litigation in which he is not designated as a party . . . [except, in a class action, where he] has his interests adequately represented."). It would defy this fundamental principle of our jurisprudence to allow the due process right of absent class members to adequate representation to be litigated by random, volunteer objectors.[7]

Not surprisingly, Matsushita offers no persuasive authority in its attempt to argue against this basic principle. Some of the cases that it cites involve individual litigants, not class members. In Durfee v. Duke, 375 U.S. 106, (1963), for example — upon which Matsushita relies heavily — the Supreme Court held that an individual who has unsuccessfully challenged subject matter jurisdiction in an initial action can be precluded from raising the issue in a collateral attack on the judgment. *Durfee* was not a class action and says nothing about the rights of absent class members. Some of Matsushita's other cases pre-date Phillips Petroleum v. Shutts, 472 U.S. 797 (1985), the controlling Supreme Court precedent on the rights of absent class members. See infra, Section I.C. . . .

Finally, Matsushita raises the alarmist cry that it will sound the death knell to finality in class actions if individual objectors cannot bind absentees on the issue of adequate representation. We of course reject this hyperbole. So does Delaware. In Prezant v. De Angelis, 636 A.2d 915 (Del. 1994), the Delaware Supreme Court points out that prudent class action defendants can protect themselves from collateral attack. Although they cannot foreclose a subsequent collateral action absolutely, they can minimize the risk by asking for a judicial finding, supported by reasons and evidence in

supporting reasoning" before it approves a class action settlement. Id. at 925. The only mention of Rule 23 that the Chancery Court ever made in this case was contained in a pro forma statement supported by neither reasons nor evidence in the record. See Chancery Court's Order and Final Judgment, at 2 ("[I]t is hereby . . . determined that the plaintiffs in these Actions, as representatives of the Settlement Class, have fairly and adequately protected the interests of the Settlement Class and that the maintenance of this action as a class action meets all the requirements of Rule 23(a) and (b)(3) of the Court of the Chancery"). While we need not decide the issue, we are doubtful that this pro forma recital satisfies *Prezant*.

7. Absent class members are, of course, bound by a judgment on the merits of the class action issues, as for example, the fairness of the settlement.

the record, that the plaintiffs' "due process right to adequate representation has been satisfied." *Prezant*, 636 A.2d at 925-26. Such a finding will "help insure" that judgments will be subject to collateral attack only under extraordinary circumstances like those that exist in this case. See id. Thus, we disagree with Matsushita that finality of settlements will come to an end if volunteer objectors are not vested with the authority to bind absentees on the issue of the adequacy of class representation. . . .

C

Finally, Matsushita argues that because of the procedures used in the Delaware Chancery Court, the Epstein plaintiffs cannot bring a collateral attack on adequacy of representation. This argument comes in two parts. First, Matsushita argues, the settlement hearing provided a "full and fair opportunity" for absentees to contest the adequacy of their representation. The absentees had a duty to intervene in that hearing if they wished to protect their rights, Matsushita claims, and having failed to do so, they are estopped from bringing a collateral challenge. Second, and more broadly, Matsushita argues that the procedures Delaware had in place foreclose us from ever hearing a collateral challenge to adequacy of representation. Matsushita argues that we are limited to reviewing the sufficiency of the procedures that Delaware had in place to ensure adequate representation, rather than the adequacy of the representation itself. "[T]he Chancery Court's adherence to Rule 23 procedures satisfies the Due Process Clause as a matter of law," Matsushita continues, and an absent class member's claim on "the merits" of inadequate representation "is far outside the scope of the [collateral] review permitted by . . . the case law of this Court." We agree with the Epstein plaintiffs that both of these arguments are meritless.

1

Matsushita argues that class members who wish to contest adequacy of representation must intervene during the course of the class action proceedings and do battle with their own representatives in an adversarial contest over the way they are discharging their fiduciary duties. This argument ignores the clear teaching of Phillips Petroleum Co. v. Shutts, 472 U.S. 797 (1985), that a class member is not required to do anything during the course of a class-action proceeding. . . . As the Court put it in *Shutts*, "Unlike a defendant in a normal civil suit, an absent class-action plaintiff is not required to do anything. He may sit back and allow the litigation to run its course, *content in knowing that there are safeguards provided for his protection*." Id. at 810 (emphasis added). Those "safeguards", as enumerated in *Shutts*, are (1) "notice," (2) "an opportunity to be heard and participate in the litigation," (3) "an opportunity to remove himself from the class" by opting out, and (4) "adequate represent[ation]" "*at all times*." Id. at 812 (emphasis added). Thus, *Shutts* admonishes absent class members that they will be bound by the merits of a judgment — including the fairness of a court-approved settlement — if it is a product of adequate representation and their other due process safeguards. But *Shutts* promises in return that they need not monitor this proceeding from afar: if the litigation culminating in the judgment violated their due process rights, then absent class members will not be bound by it.

Gonzales v. Cassidy, 474 F.2d 67 (5th Cir. 1973) — a precursor to *Shutts* — is square authority against Matsushita's intervene-or-be-estopped argument. In *Gonzales*, the Fifth Circuit rejected the very argument that Matsushita now urges upon us . . . .

As the Court stated in *Shutts*, . . . it is the prerogative of absentees to remain just that: *absent* from a proceeding in which they are "parties" only virtually, through their class representatives. The "continuing solicitude for their rights" entitles absent class members to refrain from intervening, "content in knowing that there are safeguards provided for [their] protection." Id. at 810. [F]orcing an absent class member to monitor a proceeding and intervene to challenge the adequacy of representation that he is still in the process of receiving would defeat the purpose of having such safeguards. . . .

2

Matsushita attempts to avoid *Shutts* by arguing that Kremer v. Chemical Constr. Corp., 456 U.S. 461 (1982) prevents absentees from ever collaterally challenging adequacy of representation when the forum state uses a procedure like Delaware Chancery Court Rule 23. This attempt gets Matsushita nowhere. We reiterate the fundamental principle that *Shutts* established: absent class members have a right to adequate representation "at all times," and they have no duty to intervene in the initial proceeding in order to protect that right. *Shutts*, 472 U.S. at 812. There is nothing in *Kremer* to the contrary.

In *Kremer*, the Court reaffirmed the bedrock principle that a judgment must satisfy the requirements of due process in order to receive full faith and credit. In the specific case before it, the Court held that a New York administrative proceeding was entitled to full faith and credit because the procedures it employed satisfied due process. Matsushita argues that *Kremer* likewise limits absent class members to a "procedures only" approach when they seek to challenge adequacy of representation. . . .

We categorically reject this simplistic application of *Kremer* to the class action context. The Court fashioned *Kremer*'s "procedures only" approach to apply to collateral challenges of judgments in traditional litigation, where individual parties are bound by virtue of their presence before the court. *Kremer* was not a class action and did not address the special due process problems of binding persons not parties to the action. *Shutts*, in contrast, which was a class action, held that absentees have a right to adequate representation "at all times," 472 U.S. at 812, and that they need not intervene to enforce that right. No procedure can reliably protect an absent plaintiff who does not in fact have an adequate representative in court championing his cause. The Court recognized this salutary principle in Hansberry v. Lee, 311 U.S. 32 (1940), and it has never retreated from it. . . .

Nonetheless, Matsushita argues, the absent class members in this case received notice, an opportunity to be heard (at the objection hearing), and the right to opt out of both the class action proceeding and the proposed settlement. Surely, Matsushita complains, these protections fully satisfied the "minimum procedural requirements" of *Kremer*, and due process does not require anything more.

The Supreme Court, however, could not have been more clear in requiring more. Indeed, if settled law defeats Matsushita's contention that absent class members have a duty to intervene or be estopped from challenging the adequacy of their representation, then this contention faces a veritable fortress of authority.... In addition to Shutts, the case law is consistent that adequate representation *in fact* is required to bind absent plaintiffs. See Richards v. Jefferson Cty., 517 U.S. 793 (1996); *Matsushita*, 116 S.Ct. at 885 (Ginsburg, J., concurring in part and dissenting in part); *Hansberry*, 311 U.S. at 41-43 . . . .

In sum, neither caselaw nor common sense supports Matsushita's position that the mere existence of procedures like Rule 23 can foreclose an absentee from receiving his day in court on the issue of adequacy of representation. . . .

II

We now turn to the merits of the adequacy of representation issue. Following the model provided by *Gonzales*, we conduct a "two-pronged inquiry," *Gonzales*, 474 F.2d at 72. First, we determine whether there was a disabling conflict of interest between Delaware counsel and the MCA shareholders who tendered their shares. Second, we review the actual conduct of Delaware counsel in discharging their fiduciary duty to protect the interests of those shareholders.

A

The essence of the Epstein plaintiffs' position on the claimed conflict of interest is that the Delaware settlement was the product of a one-sided bargaining process because their representatives went to the table with no credible bargaining power. Not surprisingly, Matsushita makes no serious attempt to challenge this position, relying almost exclusively on their arguments as to why we cannot reach the merits. It is axiomatic that a plaintiff's power to negotiate a reasonable settlement derives from the threat of going to trial with a credible chance of winning. . . .

The Delaware class plaintiffs and their counsel could not carry out a threat to litigate the federal claims in this case, and Matsushita knew it.

The inability of the class representatives to exercise any leverage on behalf of the Epstein plaintiffs was the result of three basic facts. First, they could not litigate the federal claims because Congress has said that Exchange Act claims may not be litigated in state courts. . . . Moreover, there was no discovery on those claims; indeed, the Delaware plaintiffs probably were unable to conduct any discovery on the federal claims because the facts relevant to those claims had no apparent relevance to the subject matter of the state law claim that the MCA directors had breached their fiduciary duties in failing to maximize shareholder value upon a change of corporate control. See *Epstein I*, 50 F.3d at 659; Del. Chancery Court Rule 26(b)(1). Finally, Matsushita would have had reason to discount the value of any settlement made with the state plaintiffs against the risk that a state court judgment releasing Exchange Act claims would not survive a collateral attack on the ground that the Delaware courts had no jurisdiction to release exclusively federal claims especially in light of the absence of any overlapping issues of fact between the state and federal claims. . . . The denouement was predictable: Matsushita used its infinitely superior bargaining power vis-a-vis the state class representatives to settle the Exchange Act claims at a rock bottom price.[13]

Second, the class representatives not only lacked the bargaining power that comes with a credible threat of going to trial and winning, they also lacked the ability to make a credible threat that they could put Matsushita at risk by going to trial on the state claims and proving facts material to the federal claims that would be binding upon Matsushita through issue preclusion. Because the state and federal claims shared no common issues of material fact, a judgment on the state claims could not be used as an "offensive" estoppel in future litigation of the federal claims. See *Epstein I*, 50 F.3d at 665-55. While the Delaware class representatives lacked the muscle to put Matsushita at risk on the federal claims, the existence of their state class action, however worthless standing alone, served to provide Matsushita with an opportunity to try to get rid of the federal claims at a bargain basement price. If the parties could get court approval of a settlement that released the federal claims, Matsushita would have at least a fair shot of using the judgment to block the federal action with a full faith and credit argument. That is, of course, exactly what Matsushita did as soon as the judgment became final. We had the Epstein plaintiffs' appeal of the district court's summary judgment under submission when Matsushita notified us of the Delaware settlement judgment and argued that we should give it preclusive effect.

Third, Matsushita had a further bargaining advantage, quite apart from its knowledge that the Delaware plaintiffs could not put it at risk on the federal claims. Matsushita also knew that class counsel had an extraordinary incentive to settle and settle *quickly* because that was the *only* way they could extract a fee out of the federal claims. Class counsel could not benefit from the federal claims by going to trial for the obvious reason that the federal claims could not be litigated in state court. Moreover, the pendency of a parallel action in federal court — the *Epstein*

---

13. Indeed, it would not be an exaggeration to say that the Delaware plaintiffs were kept in state court entirely at the sufferance of Matsushita. As we discuss below, the Delaware Vice Chancellor, in rejecting the first settlement, determined that the state law claims were "extremely weak" and had "little or no value" because no such state cause of action existed. See In re MCA Shareholders Litigation, 598 A.2d 687, 694 (Del. Ch. 1991) . . . . Matsushita could have, but did not move the Chancery Court to dismiss the state action. Rather, it chose to use it as a vehicle for seeking an inexpensive release of the federal claims. . . .

case — meant that Delaware class counsel were at risk of being "beaten to the punch" and getting no return on the federal claims at all. Matsushita knew that it was negotiating a release of the federal claims with class counsel who could not litigate those claims and whose self-interest gave them an incentive to settle and settle fast.

What all this demonstrates is that there was a jarring misalignment of interests between class counsel and members of the federal class. It was plainly in the best interest of counsel to settle the federal claims at any price. For them, any settlement was better than no settlement because settlement was the only way they could make any money on the federal claims — indeed, given that the state claims were essentially worthless, it was the only way that Delaware counsel could get any compensation at all. Delaware counsel were not, after all, serving as pro bono counsel to the MCA shareholders who tendered their shares.

It was not, in contrast, in the best interest of the clients — the MCA shareholders— to settle their Exchange Act claims at any price. Their interest lay in settling those claims for a sufficient amount to make it imprudent to take the risk of litigation. That risk, of course, would have to be realistically assessed in terms of the chances of prevailing on either or both of their claims that Matsushita had violated SEC Rules 10b-13 and 14d-10 . . . . Indeed, the misalignment of interests and incentives between class counsel and their clients in these extraordinary circumstances was so great that it is fair to say that counsel's interests were more in line with the interests of Matsushita than those of their clients.

This was not the adequate representation of absent class members that due process requires "at all times." *Shutts*, 472 U.S. at 812. As we have said, "An adequate representative must . . . be free from economic interests that are antagonistic to the interests of the class." Larson v. Dumke, 900 F.2d 1363, 1367 (9th Cir. 1990). . . . Here, there is no question that there was antagonism between the interests of the lawyers and the interests of their clients. That antagonism made their representation of the MCA shareholders who tendered their shares inadequate as a matter of law.

B

In addition to the argument that Delaware counsel had a disabling conflict of interest, the Epstein plaintiffs contend that the actual conduct of Delaware counsel in settling the federal claims fell far short of the representation that due process requires. Rather, they claim, Delaware counsel completely failed to investigate or develop their federal claims and basically "rolled over" during settlement negotiations, ultimately entering into a settlement that was essentially worthless except for their own fees. This course of conduct, they conclude, falls well below the level of representation that is required to bind absentees. We agree.

Adequate representation requires that counsel "vigorously and tenaciously protect[ ] the interests of the class." *Gonzales*, 474 F.2d at 75. "Vigorous" and "tenacious" protection requires, at a minimum, that counsel pursue their clients' claims, make a reasonable effort to assess the fair settlement value of those claims, and pursue a settlement that approximates that value, always taking into account the ever-present risks of litigation. The inadequacy of Delaware counsel's representation is brought into sharp focus by their vigorous *disparagement* of the federal claims throughout the course of the settlement proceedings. Indeed, Delaware counsel's representation of those claims surpassed inadequacy and sank to the level of subversion. Counsel consistently sought to convince, not only their clients, but their adversaries and the Chancery Court itself that the federal claims had no merit. They repeatedly and summarily dismissed those claims as "frivolous" without ever conducting any discovery or any meaningful analysis of the legal issues, much less presenting the claims in a favorable light. In sharp contrast, the Epstein counsel earnestly pursued those same claims in federal court, recognizing their merit and successfully demonstrating that merit in persuading this court to reverse an adverse summary judgment ruling below. This contrast makes it all the more clear that Delaware counsel's representation of the MCA shareholders who tendered their shares fails even the most minimal standards of adequacy. . . .

[After a lengthy review of the litigation and settlement proceedings, the court concluded that the representation of the Delaware counsel] was not merely "inadequate" representation, it was hostile representation that served the interests of counsel in getting a fee, but did not serve the interests of the MCA shareholders in getting a settlement based upon a thorough and fair assessment of their Exchange Act claims. To bind the Epstein plaintiffs to the Delaware judgment under these circumstances would violate their due process right to have their interests adequately represented at all times.

III

The Epstein plaintiffs also contend that we may withhold full faith and credit from the Delaware judgment because the Vice Chancellor did not adequately supervise the settlement proceedings. They argue that adequacy of judicial supervision is intricately bound up with adequacy of representation and, hence, that it rises to the level of a due process requirement. In effect, they argue that we should add adequacy of judicial supervision to the four safeguards that *Shutts* guarantees to absent class members. . . .

Because we hold that the absent class members were denied due process because of inadequate representation, we need not reach this novel constitutional question. . . .

We reverse the judgment and remand for proceedings consistent with Parts I, II, III, V & VI of *Epstein I*.

■ O'SCANNLAIN, Circuit Judge, dissenting. . . . The argument urged upon us by the Epstein plaintiffs certainly engenders sympathy and has some force. Irrespective of whether the Delaware attorneys' conduct in the state court rose to the level of constitutional deprivation, their act of referring, in a single breath, to their own clients' claims as "fraught with uncertainty," "weak," and "horrendous" suggests less than dynamic advocacy. Regrettably, however, and unlike my colleagues, I do not believe that we are in a position to pass judgment on the merits of this appeal. . . .

I do agree with my colleagues that the Supreme Court did not conclusively resolve the due process issue before it remanded the case to us. . . . However, the fact that the Supreme Court chose not to reach the due process challenge does not inexorably lead to the conclusion that this court may decide the issue. Quite the contrary, after reviewing the record, the Supreme Court concluded — in three separate passages and in no uncertain terms — that the Delaware courts had already conclusively resolved the due process issue. First, in Part I, in which it described the procedural posture of the case, the Court stated, rather matter-of-factly, that "[a]fter argument from several objectors, *the [Chancery] Court found the class representation adequate* . . . ." [516 U.S. at 371] (emphasis added). Several pages later, the Court reiterated its conclusion: citing the decisions of the Delaware courts approving the second MCA settlement, the Supreme Court specifically found that the Chancery Court, in accordance with Delaware Court of Chancery Rule 23, had "*determined* that the plaintiffs[,] . . . as representatives of the Settlement Class, have fairly and adequately protected the interests of the Settlement Class." [516 U.S.. at 378-79] . . . . Finally, in its now famous footnote five, the Court expressed its skepticism at plaintiffs' decision even to press the due process issue "*in spite of the Chancery Court's express ruling*, following argument on the issue, that the class representatives fairly and adequately protected the interests of the class." [516 U.S. at 379] n.5 (emphasis added). . . .

I conclude, as did the United States Supreme Court, that the question of adequate representation (1) was actually litigated before the Delaware Chancery Court and (2) was decided by that court in a valid and final judgment. Although the plaintiffs in this action were not themselves present before the Vice Chancellor, their grievances were ably litigated through their surrogates, objectors Krupman and Minton de Ruiz. Moreover, as the settlement notice made explicit, the plaintiffs themselves were presented with a "full and fair opportunity" to participate personally in the settlement hearing if they so desired. Consequently, under long-established principles of Delaware preclusion law, I believe that the Delaware courts would give collateral estoppel effect to the Chancery Court's judgment and would forbid plaintiffs from relitigating the merits of the inadequacy issue. . . . Pursuant to the plain — and now universally acknowledged — meaning of the Full Faith and Credit Act, 28 U.S.C. § 1738, we must do the same. . . .

As to the majority's last-gasp invocation of Phillips Petroleum Co. v. Shutts, 472 U.S. 797 (1985), to deny the Delaware judgment issue preclusive effect, I most emphatically protest. The court cites *Shutts* in support of its per se rule that class settlement objectors — such as Krupman and Minton de Ruiz — may never, consistent with the Due Process Clause, finally litigate absent class plaintiffs' rights to adequate representation. *Shutts* simply cannot, in my view, bear the weight of such an extreme interpretation. The concerns that impelled the *Shutts* Court's recognition of the prerogative of absent plaintiffs generally to "sit back and allow the litigation to run its course," *Shutts*, 472 U.S. at 810, plainly are not in play in this case.

The *Shutts* Court was motivated by a concern for fairness to parties who, without the right to "sit back," might be forced to forfeit their claims altogether. The *Shutts* Court found that in light of financial constraints, some plaintiffs, if forced to litigate their own claims, might "have no realistic day in court." Id. at 809. However, . . . the Epstein plaintiffs (quite unlike the "absent" class plaintiffs in *Shutts*) absented themselves from the Delaware fairness hearing not for financial reasons, but for tactical reasons . . . . What is more, the Epstein plaintiffs lost absolutely nothing by not attending the settlement hearing. As they sat idly by, content in the notion that they had preserved their right collaterally to attack the Delaware judgment, their substantive arguments were, as detailed above, simultaneously being presented by objectors Krupman and Minton de Ruiz. (Indeed, this fact very likely was known to the Epstein lawyers, in light of objector Krupman's lawyer's admission that his client's objection had originally been drafted by the attorneys representing the Epstein plaintiffs.) . . .

The Epstein plaintiffs have managed, quite literally, to have their cake and eat it too. They now get two bites at the proverbial apple. Today, this court not only *condones* such gluttony, it *constitutionalizes* it. . . .

Matsushita, after all, did precisely what the *Prezant* court (and now this court) instructed it to do: It asked for and got a judicial finding — an "express ruling," in the words of the United States Supreme Court — that the representation of the plaintiff class had been constitutionally adequate. Curiously, today this court tells both Matsushita and the Delaware judiciary that, alas, they did not do enough.

Because I believe that today's decision not only threatens finality, but also contravenes "the elementary principles of federalism and comity," Growe v. Emison, 507 U.S. 25, 35 (1993), that animate the Full Faith and Credit Act, I respectfully dissent.

Notes and Questions

1. Both *Cooper* and *Epstein* deal with the problem of claim preclusion in a second suit between the same parties. As a general proposition, claim preclusion between the same parties does not frequently arise in complex or complicated litigation, although there are two situations in which the issue tends to come up with regularity. One is in the context of a latent-injury mass tort, in which a person may suffer a present injury from an exposure to a toxic substance, and is also at risk of developing a further injury at some point in the future. Under traditional notions of claim preclusion, a plaintiff could not "split" the claims into two by bringing one suit for the first injury and then a second suit for the second injury, should it develop. The rule against claim-splitting thus put a plaintiff to a difficult choice: either bring a claim for a minor but certain injury and forego the ability to recover for a major but uncertain injury, or wait for the major injury to occur and allow the statute of limitations to run on the minor injury. Courts have begun to loosen the usual preclusion rules, or else have

created an exception to the relevant statute of limitations, in order to permit claim-splitting in this context. See Jackson v. Johns-Manville Sales Corp., 750 F.2d 1314 (5th Cir. 1985); Note, *Claim Preclusion in Modern Latent Disease Cases: A Proposal for Allowing Second Suits*, 103 Harv. L. Rev. 829 (1990).

The second situation in which the claim preclusion issue tends to come up is the context reflected in *Cooper* and *Epstein*: a member of a plaintiff class seeks to pursue a claim against the same defendant after the conclusion of the first suit, and the defendant tries to defend by claiming that the matter was concluded in the first suit. *Cooper* and *Epstein* establish several propositions relevant to the use of claim preclusion in this context.

2. First, *Cooper* establishes the proposition that the only claims that a class member is precluded from asserting in the second suit are those that were (or, presumably, could have been) asserted on behalf of the class as a whole; individual claims for relief that are based on grounds not generally applicable to the class survive the judgment in the class action. Next, *Epstein* ultimately seems to stand for two propositions: (1) that a class member cannot be bound by a judgment on the class's claims in a case in which she was not adequately represented, and (2) unless the issue of adequate representation was litigated by the class representatives and actually decided by the court in the first case, the class member is free to challenge the adequacy of the representation in the second case. Of these three propositions, the first proposition in *Epstein* is a bedrock, incontrovertible principle of American procedure.

The remaining propositions are more controvertible. On one level, the proposition in *Cooper* seems entirely unremarkable and fair on the facts of *Cooper* itself because the relevant class members (the Baxter petitioners) had been denied an opportunity to intervene and press their claims. On another level, however, this proposition creates an exception to the usual rule of claim preclusion, which holds that a party must bring all the claims that she has against a defendant in the first suit or forever find them barred. In order to take advantage of *Cooper*'s exception, must a class member seek to intervene and be denied? Or does *Cooper*'s exception apply to all class members, so that the attempts of the Baxter petitioners to intervene is an interesting but ultimately irrelevant fact? Does *Cooper*'s exception ultimately rest on the inefficiency that the assertion of individual claims in a class action would create? Or does the exception ultimately rest on the unfairness of precluding the assertion of individual claims for which class members had received inadequate representation from the class representatives? Which justification is stronger in your judgment? Which does *Cooper* emphasize?

Epstein's second proposition, which is less a matter of claim preclusion than issue preclusion, is even more controvertible; at this writing, it is not yet clear what the ultimate fate of *Epstein* will be. Consider *Epstein* in light of the justifications that seem to support *Cooper*. Like *Cooper*, the adequate representation justification disfavors the use of claim preclusion. The efficiency justification presents a more mixed scenario. On the one hand, the preclusion of the federal claims prevents the litigation of a set of issues that would require significant and costly discovery; on the other hand, a new federal class action based on new evidence would not lead to the re-litigation of old issues. As the dissent argues, a third justification — the concerns for a properly functioning federal system — also affect the fate of *Epstein*.

3. How can the defect that the majority in *Epstein* identifies be corrected? The majority's reasoning seems to suggest that it could have been corrected if the

class representatives (who, unlike the objectors, were in theory representing the interests of Epstein) had litigated the issue and the Delaware state court had made more detailed findings on the point. But would either the class representatives or the defendant — both of whom want to settle the case — have an incentive to litigate the adequacy of representation issue with sufficient vigor? If they had litigated the issue, couldn't Epstein simply have shifted his argument and contended that the representatives did not adequately represent him on the adequacy of representation issue? Should a finding of the court that the representation was adequate preclude this argument? Cf. Hansberry v. Lee, 311 U.S. 32 (1940) (class member can subsequently challenge judgment on theory that class representative was inadequate; no full faith and credit issue presented). Moreover, if *Epstein* is correct, wouldn't every class member be entitled to bring an individual challenge to the adequacy of representation? Or would MCA eventually be able to invoke some variation of defensive collateral estoppel against class members? If defensive collateral estoppel were invoked, is there a risk that MCA might recruit a class member to bring a collusive suit to establish the adequacy of representation?

Do these difficulties in implementing *Epstein*'s holding prove that the case is wrong, or do they instead prove the wisdom of the adversarial system's goal of individualized representation for each person's interests?

4. At a deeper level, what seems to be at stake in both *Cooper* and *Epstein* is the fate of the class action as a mandatory joinder device. No mandatory joinder device that is incapable of precluding subsequent litigation has a chance of being successful. But the problem of the class action, in comparison to other mandatory joinder devices such as Rule 19(a) joinder, is that individuals within the class do not have the opportunity to present individual proofs and arguments; their interests are represented by others. This breach of the adversarial ideal is somewhat palatable as long as the interests of the class representatives have a high degree of identity with the interests of the class members. When that identity no longer exists, the representation becomes inadequate, the class action collapses, and the efficacy of the class action as a means of avoiding re-litigation is destroyed.

5. Should the extent of the preclusive effect of a class judgment be the same in complex litigation and in complicated litigation? In complex litigation, the existence of lawyer dysfunction means that changes will need to be made in the standard adversarial approach. In complicated litigation, adversarial process creates some inefficiencies, but can still be utilized. Thus, the case for a broader rule of preclusion for class actions is different in complex litigation than in complicated litigation.

Neither *Cooper* nor *Epstein* seems to have been a complex case; neither involved problems of insufficient assets, relief that nonparties could later undo, or relief that nonparties would be forced to accept. Consequently, neither case presented the argument that a departure from an individualistic, autonomy-based approach to preclusion was needed to assure the rational adjudication of the claims of all interested persons. This does not necessarily mean that the result in both cases is correct; some might argue that the federalism and arguable efficiency concerns in *Epstein* are as weighty as the concern for rational adjudication. But it does mean that one compelling reason for changing our present adversarial system's rules of preclusion does not exist.

Nevertheless, it is possible to imagine that class members, if they were to file a second suit, could effectively create two of the three types of lawyer dysfunction: their second suit could force a re-allocation of limited assets in their favor, or the second suit could threaten to undo relief that the first suit had secured. Should the limitations that *Cooper* and *Epstein* place on the operation of claim preclusion be removed in these cases? If so, which of the limitations should be removed? For instance, in a complex case comparable to *Cooper*, should the rules be reformed to preclude a class member from bringing any individual claims, or only from bringing individual claims when the class member intervened? Likewise, in a complex case comparable to *Epstein*, should the rules be reformed to preclude a class member from bringing claims for which she was inadequately represented, or only from bringing claims in which the representation was adequate in fact but the quality of the representation had not been actually litigated and decided?

Reforming preclusion rules to deal with these two instances of lawyer dysfunction may well have a counterproductive effect. Recall that the third form of dysfunction arises when the class relief in an earlier suit makes it impossible for a subsequent claim for relief to be maintained. If we reshape our preclusion rules to prevent class members from re-allocating limited assets or otherwise undoing the relief obtained in the first suit, we will have actually created the third form of dysfunction! The only way to sidestep this conundrum would be to force the class members to bring their individual claims in the first suit — which is exactly what the dicta in *Cooper* says that class members do not have to do. Does this analysis suggest that *Cooper*'s dicta should be disregarded in complex cases? Does it also suggest that a mandatory joinder approach is superior to a preclusion approach in complex litigation?

6. As mentioned above, *Epstein* can be viewed as a case of issue preclusion. This view of *Epstein* raises an important practical point — even if claim preclusion does not for some reason operate in the second suit between the same parties, issue preclusion might. We now turn to the limits of using issue preclusion against a party in an earlier litigation.

HARDY v. JOHNS-MANVILLE SALES CORP.

681 F.2d 334 (5th Cir. 1982)

■ GEE, Circuit Judge. This appeal arises out of a diversity action brought by various plaintiffs — insulators, pipefitters, carpenters, and other factory workers — against various manufacturers, sellers, and distributors of asbestos-containing products. The plaintiffs, alleging exposure to the products and consequent disease, assert various causes of action, including negligence, breach of implied warranty, and strict liability. The pleadings in each of the cases are substantially the same. No plaintiff names a particular defendant on a case-by-case basis but, instead, includes several-often as many as twenty asbestos manufacturers-in his individual complaint. . . .

Defendants' interlocutory appeal under 28 U.S.C. § 1292(b) is directed . . . at the district court's amended omnibus order dated March 13, 1981, which applies collateral estoppel to this mass tort. The omnibus order is, in effect, a partial summary judgment for plaintiffs based on nonmutual offensive collateral estoppel and judicial notice derived from this court's opinion in Borel v. Fibreboard Paper Products Corp., 493 F.2d 1076 (5th Cir. 1973), cert. denied, 419 U.S. 869 (1974) (henceforth *Borel*). Borel was a diversity lawsuit in which manufacturers of insulation products containing asbestos were held strictly liable to an insulation worker who developed asbestosis and mesothelioma and ultimately died. The trial court construed *Borel* as establishing as a matter of law and/or of fact that: (1) insulation products containing asbestos as a generic ingredient are "unavoidably unsafe products," (2) asbestos is a competent producing cause of mesothelioma and asbestosis, (3) no warnings were issued by any asbestos insulation manufacturers prior to 1964, and (4) the "warning standard" was not met by the *Borel* defendants in the period from 1964 through 1969.[1] . . . The sole issue on appeal is the validity of the order on grounds of collateral estoppel or judicial notice.

In Flatt v. Johns-Manville Sales Corp., 488 F. Supp. 836 (E.D. Tex. 1980), the same court outlined the elements of proof for plaintiffs in asbestos-related cases. There the court stated that the plaintiff must prove by a preponderance of the evidence that

1. Defendants manufactured, marketed, sold, distributed, or placed in the stream of commerce products containing asbestos.
2. Products containing asbestos are unreasonably dangerous.
3. Asbestos dust is a competent producing cause of mesothelioma.
4. Decedent was exposed to defendant's products.
5. The exposure was sufficient to be a producing cause of mesothelioma.
6. Decedent contracted mesothelioma.
7. Plaintiffs suffered damages. . . .

The parties agree that the effect of the trial court's collateral estoppel order in this case is to foreclose elements 2 and 3 above. Under the terms of the omnibus order, both parties are precluded from presenting evidence on the "state of the art" — evidence that, under Texas law of strict liability, is considered by a jury along with other evidence in order to determine whether as of a given time warning should have been given of the dangers knew or should have known of the dangerous propensities of their products

---

1. The omnibus order states in relevant part:

> 1. Relying upon the Court's opinions in Flatt v. Johns-Manville Sales Corporation, 488 F. Supp. 836 (E.D. Tex. 1980) and a contemporaneously entered memorandum in the *Hardy* case, collateral estoppel in some form shall be entered in each of the foregoing cases. Issue preclusion may extend to the ultimate issue of marketing an unreasonably dangerous product or be limited to cluster issues depending upon the particular facts of the case.
>
> 2. In any event, no evidence shall be introduced on the issue of whether asbestos causes either asbestosis or mesothelioma.
>
> 3. Further, no evidence shall be introduced on the issue of knowledge as it may relate to a duty to warn due to the res judicata and/or collateral estoppel effect of [*Borel*]. In essence, no evidence shall be admitted with respect to a state of the art defense. . . .

and therefore should have warned consumers of these dangers, defendants being precluded from showing otherwise. On appeal, the defendants contend that the order violates their rights to due process and to trial by jury. Because we conclude that the trial court abused its discretion in applying collateral estoppel and judicial notice, we reverse.

CHOICE OF LAW

An initial question presented on appeal is what law governs the application of collateral estoppel in a diversity suit involving a prior federal judgment. Appellants argue that the trial court's choice of federal law was incorrect. According to appellants, these cases, couched in terms of Texas law of strict liability and negligence, should be governed by Texas rules of collateral estoppel. The choice of law question is supposedly of significance because, according to appellants, Texas strictly adheres to the doctrine of mutuality, *i.e.*, neither party can use a prior judgment to estop another unless both parties were bound by the prior judgment. If this view of Texas law is correct, the plaintiffs here, none of whom were parties to *Borel*, would of course be unable to invoke collateral estoppel.

We need not resolve the question of whether appellants' view of Texas law of collateral estoppel is correct, however, since the district court was bound under the law of our circuit to apply federal law.... [T]he principle of finality essential to a court's authority demands that "federal law determine the effects under the rules of res judicata of a judgment of a federal court."...

Having determined that federal law of collateral estoppel governs, we next turn to an examination of just what that law is. [After discussions of *Parklane Hosiery Co. v. Shore*, 439 U.S. 322 (1979) (p. 160, *supra*) and of the use of offensive collateral estoppel against fourteen defendants that were not party to *Borel* (p. 222, *infra*), the court turned to the use of offensive collateral estoppel against the six defendants that had been party to *Borel*.]

THE *BOREL* DEFENDANTS...

The party asserting the estoppel must show that: (1) the issue to be concluded is identical to that involved in the prior action; (2) in the prior action the issue was "actually litigated"; and (3) the determination made of the issue in the prior action must have been necessary and essential to the resulting judgment.

> If it appears that a judgment may have been based on more than one of several distinctive matters in litigation and there is no indication which issue it was based on or which issue was fully litigated, such judgment will not preclude, under the doctrine of collateral estoppel, relitigation of any of the issues.

Federal Procedure, Lawyers Ed. § 51.218 at 151 (1981)....

Appellants argue that *Borel* did not necessarily decide that asbestos-containing insulation products were unreasonably dangerous because of failure to warn. According to appellants, the general *Borel* verdict, based on general instructions and special interrogatories, permitted the jury to ground strict liability on the bases of failures to test, of unsafeness for intended use, of failures to inspect, or of unsafeness of the product. Strict liability on the basis of failure to warn, although argued to the jury by trial counsel for the plaintiff in *Borel*, was, in the view of the appellants, never formally presented in the jury instructions and therefore was not essential to the *Borel* jury verdict.

Appellants' view has some plausibility. The special interrogatories answered by the *Borel* jury were general and not specifically directed to failure to warn. Indeed, as we discussed at length in our review of the *Borel* judgment, the jury was instructed in terms of "breach of warranty." . . . Although the jury was accurately instructed as to "strict liability in tort" as defined in section 402A of the Restatement (Second) of Torts, that phrase was never specifically mentioned in the jury's interrogatories. It is also true that the general instructions to the *Borel* jury on the plaintiff's causes of action did not charge on failure to warn, except in connection with negligence. Yet appellants' argument in its broadest form must ultimately fail. We concluded in *Borel*:

> The jury found that the unreasonably dangerous condition of the defendants' product was the proximate cause of Borel's injury. This necessarily included a finding that, had adequate warnings been provided, Borel would have chosen to avoid the danger. . . .

Indeed, the first sentence in our *Borel* opinion states that that case involved "the scope of an asbestos manufacturer's duty to warn industrial insulation workers of dangers associated with the use of asbestos." . . . Our conclusion in *Borel* was grounded in that trial court's jury instructions concerning proximate cause and defective product . . . . Close reading of these instructions convinced our panel in *Borel* that a failure to warn was necessarily implicit in the jury's verdict. While the parties invite us to reconsider our holding in *Borel* that failure to warn grounded the jury's strict liability finding in that case, we cannot, even if we were so inclined, displace a prior decision of this court absent reconsideration en banc. Further, there is authority for the proposition that once an appellate court has disposed of a case on the basis of one of several alternative issues that may have grounded a trial court's judgment, the issue decided on appeal is conclusively established for purposes of issue preclusion. . . . Nonetheless, we must ultimately conclude that the judgment in *Borel* cannot estop even the *Borel* defendants in this case for three interrelated reasons.

First, after review of the issues decided in *Borel*, we conclude that *Borel*, while conclusive as to the general matter of a duty to warn on the part of manufacturers of asbestos-containing insulation products, is ultimately ambiguous as to certain key issues. As the authors of the Restatement (Second) — Judgments § 29, comment g (1982), have noted, collateral estoppel is inappropriate where the prior judgment is ambivalent:

> The circumstances attending the determination of an issue in the first action may indicate that it could reasonably have been resolved otherwise if those circumstances were absent. Resolution of the issue in question may have entailed reference to such matters as the

intention, knowledge, or comparative responsibility of the parties in relation to each other.... In these and similar situations, taking the prior determination at face value for purposes of the second action would extend the effects of imperfections in the adjudicative process beyond the limits of the first adjudication, within which they are accepted only because of the practical necessity of achieving finality.

The *Borel* jury decided that Borel, an industrial insulation worker who was exposed to fibers from his employer's insulation products over a 33-year period (from 1936 to 1969), was entitled to have been given fair warning that asbestos dust may lead to asbestosis, mesothelioma, and other cancers. The jury dismissed the argument that the danger was obvious and regarded as conclusive the fact that Borel testified that he did not know that inhaling asbestos dust could cause serious injuries until his doctor so advised him in 1969. The jury necessarily found "that, had adequate warnings been provided, Borel would have chosen to avoid the danger."... In *Borel*, the evidence was that the industry as a whole issued no warnings at all concerning its insulation products prior to 1964, that Johns-Manville placed a warning[ ] label on packages of its products in 1964, and that Fibreboard and Rubberoid placed warnings on their products in 1966....

Given these facts, it is impossible to determine what the *Borel* jury decided about when a duty to warn attached. Did the jury find the defendants liable because their warnings after 1966, when they acknowledged that they knew the dangers of asbestosis, were insufficiently explicit as to the grave risks involved? If so, as appellants here point out, the jury may have accepted the state of the art arguments provided by the defendants in *Borel* — i.e., that the defendants were not aware of the danger of asbestosis until the 1960's. Even under this view, there is a second ambiguity: was strict liability grounded on the fact that the warnings issued, while otherwise sufficient, never reached the insulator in the field? If so, perhaps the warnings, while insufficient as to insulation workers like Borel, were sufficient to alert workers further down the production line who may have seen the warnings — such as the carpenters and pipefitters in this case. Alternatively, even if the *Borel* jury decided that failure to warn before 1966 grounded strict liability, did the duty attach in the 1930's when the "hazard of asbestosis as a pneumoconiotic dust was universally accepted," ... or in 1965, when documentary evidence was presented of the hazard of asbestos insulation products to the installers of these products?

As we noted in *Borel*, strict liability because of failure to warn is based on a determination of the manufacturer's reasonable knowledge .... [A] determination that a particular product is so unreasonably hazardous as to require a warning of its dangers is not an absolute. Such a determination is necessarily relative to the scientific knowledge generally known or available to the manufacturer at the time the product in question was sold or otherwise placed in the stream of commerce.

Not all the plaintiffs in this case were exposed to asbestos-containing insulation products over the same 30-year period as plaintiff Borel. Not all plaintiffs here are insulation workers isolated from the warnings issued by some of the defendants in 1964 and 1966. Some of the products may be different from those involved in *Borel*. Our opinion in *Borel*, "limited to determining whether there (was) a conflict in substantial evidence sufficient to create a jury question," did not resolve that as a matter of fact all manufacturers of asbestos-containing insulation products had a duty to warn as of 1936, and all failed to warn adequately after 1964. Although we determined that the jury must have found a violation of the manufacturers' duty to warn, we held only that the jury could have grounded strict liability on the absence of a warning prior to 1964 or "could have concluded that the (post-1964 and post-1966) 'cautions' were not warnings in the sense that they adequately communicated to Borel and other insulation workers knowledge of the dangers to which they were exposed so as to give them a choice of working or not working with a dangerous product." . . . [O]ur opinion in *Borel* merely approved of the various ways the jury could have come to a conclusion concerning strict liability for failure to warn. We did not say that any of the specific alternatives that the jury had before it were necessary or essential to its verdict. . . . Like stare decisis, collateral estoppel applies only to issues of fact or law necessarily decided by a prior court. Since we cannot say that *Borel* necessarily decided, as a matter of fact, that all manufacturers of asbestos-containing insulation products knew or should have known of the dangers of their particular products at all relevant times, we cannot justify the trial court's collaterally estopping the defendants from presenting evidence as to the state of the art.

Even if we are wrong as to the ambiguities of the *Borel* judgment, there is a second, equally important, reason to deny collateral estoppel effect to it: the presence of inconsistent verdicts. In *Parklane Hosiery v. Shore*, 439 U.S. at 330-31, the Court noted that collateral estoppel is improper and "unfair" to a defendant "if the judgment relied upon as a basis for the estoppel is itself inconsistent with one or more previous judgments in favor of the defendant." . . . Not only does issue preclusion in such cases appear arbitrary to a defendant who has had favorable judgments on the same issue, it also undermines the premise that different juries reach equally valid verdicts. . . . One jury's determination should not, merely because it comes later in time, bind another jury's determination of an issue over which there are equally reasonable resolutions of doubt. . . .

On appeal, the parties inform us that there have been approximately 70 similar asbestos cases thus far tried around the country. Approximately half of these seem to have been decided in favor of the defendants. . . . [T]he appellants inform us of several products liability cases in which the state of the art question was fully litigated, yet the asbestos manufacturers were found not liable. Although it is usually not possible to say with certainty what these juries based their verdicts on, in at least some of the cases the verdict for the defendant was not based on failure to prove exposure or failure to show an asbestos-related disease. . . . This court takes judicial notice of these inconsistent or ambiguous verdicts pursuant to Fed.R.Evid. 201(d). We conclude that the court erred in arbitrarily choosing one of these verdicts, that in *Borel*, as the bellwether.

Finally, we conclude that even if the *Borel* verdict had been unambiguous and the sole verdict issued on point, application of collateral estoppel would still be unfair with regard to the *Borel* defendants because it is very doubtful that these defendants could have foreseen that their $68,000 liability to plaintiff Borel would foreshadow multimillion dollar asbestos liability. As noted in *Parklane*, it would be unfair to apply collateral estoppel "if a defendant in the first action is sued for small or nominal damages (since) he may have little incentive to defend vigorously, particularly if future lawsuits are not foreseeable." 439 U.S. at 330. While in absolute terms a judgment for $68,000 hardly appears nominal, the Supreme Court's citation of Berner v. British Commonwealth Pacific Airlines, 346 F.2d 532 (2d Cir. 1965), cert. denied, 382 U.S. 983 (1966) (application of collateral estoppel denied where defendant did not appeal an adverse judgment awarding damages of $35,000 and defendant was later sued for over $7 million), suggests that the matter is relative. The reason the district court here applied collateral estoppel is precisely because early cases like *Borel* have opened the floodgates to an enormous, unprecedented volume of asbestos litigation. According to a recent estimate, there are over 3,000 asbestos plaintiffs in the Eastern District of Texas alone and between 7,500 and 10,000 asbestos cases pending in United States District Courts around the country. The omnibus order here involves 58 pending cases, and the many plaintiffs involved in this case are each seeking $2.5 million in damages. Such a staggering potential liability could not have been foreseen by the *Borel* defendants. . . .

The trial court's application of issue preclusion to the "fact" that asbestos is in all cases a competent producing cause of mesothelioma and asbestosis involves similar problems. *Borel* dealt with the disease-causing aspects of asbestos dust generated by insulation materials. That case did not determine as a matter of fact that because airborne asbestos dust and fibers from thermal insulation materials are hazardous, all products containing asbestos — in whatever quantity or however encapsulated — are hazardous. The injustice in precluding the "fact" that the generic ingredient asbestos invariably and in every use or mode causes cancer is clearest in the case of appellant Garlock. Garlock points out that its products, unlike the loosely woven thermal insulation materials in *Borel* that, when merely handled, emitted large quantities of airborne asbestos dust and fibers, are linoleum-type products in which the asbestos is encapsulated in a rubber-like coating. According to Garlock, its gasket products do not release significant amounts of dust or fibers into the air and have never been demonstrated to be dangerous in installation, use, or removal. Certainly, defendants ought to be free, even after *Borel*, to present evidence of the scientific knowledge *associated with their particular product* without being prejudiced by a conclusive presumption that asbestos in all forms causes cancer. The court regarded collateral estoppel in this context as precluding merely the "can it" question rather than the "did it" question. . . . The problem is that the "can it" and "did it" questions cannot in this instance be so easily segregated, and a determination that asbestos generally is hazardous threatens to undermine a defendant's possibly legitimate defense that its product was not scientifically known to be hazardous, now or at relevant times in the past. If the trial court's application of issue preclusion on the generic danger of asbestos is not meant to burden a defendant's ability to present such evidence, then we fail to see the intended usefulness of the court's action.

For much the same reasons, the court's alternative justification for this aspect of its omnibus order — relying upon judicial notice of adjudicative fact under Fed.R.Evid. 201(b)(2) and (c) — is likewise improper. . . . [J]udicial notice applies to self-evident truths that no reasonable person could question, truisms that approach platitudes or banalities. The proposition that asbestos causes cancer, because it is inextricably linked to a host of disputed issues — *e.g.*, can mesothelioma arise without exposure to asbestos, is the sale of asbestos insulation products definitely linked to carcinoma in the general population, was this manufacturer reasonably unaware of the asbestos hazards in 1964 — is not at present so self-evident a proposition as to be subject to judicial notice. The rule of judicial notice "contemplates there is to be no evidence before the jury in disproof." Fed.R.Evid. 201, Adv.Comm. Note g (1975). Surely where there is evidence on both sides of an issue the matter is subject to reasonable dispute. Judicial notice was therefore inappropriate here.

[W]e . . . sympathize with the district court's efforts to streamline the enormous asbestos caseload it faces. None of what we say here is meant to cast doubt on any possible alternative ways to avoid reinventing the asbestos liability wheel. We [invite] district courts to attempt innovative methods for trying these cases. We hold today only that courts cannot read *Borel* to stand for the proposition that, as matters of fact, asbestos products are unreasonably dangerous or that asbestos as a generic element is in all products a competent producing cause of cancer. To do otherwise would be to elevate judicial expedience over considerations of justice and fair play.

Reversed.

Notes and Questions

1. As a practical matter, the scope of offensive collateral estoppel is the critical preclusion issue in complex and complicated litigation. Although direct preclusion in a second case between parties that were both involved in a prior lawsuit and defensive collateral estoppel against a plaintiff in a prior lawsuit arise with some frequency, the fact that defendants in complex and complicated litigation often engage in a pattern of conduct that allegedly injures many persons makes offensive collateral estoppel the form of issue preclusion that is most useful in eliminating dysfunction- or inefficiency-causing re-litigation. Indeed, without a strong doctrine of offensive collateral estoppel, the hope that preclusion law can solve the problems of re-litigation will have vanished, and we will need to resort to either mandatory joinder or some other solution.

2. *Hardy* presents a panoply of reasons that offensive collateral estoppel cannot be used. These reasons are a fairly straight-forward application of two of the important exceptions to collateral estoppel raised in *Parklane Hosiery* — inconsistent prior verdicts and insufficient incentive to contest the issue in the first litigation. *Hardy* also bases its holding on a third reason — the ambiguity in the jury's verdict in *Borel*. This third ground is generally applicable to all arguments for issue preclusion, although, due to the fact that at least one new

party is involved, the ground may come up more frequently in cases of defensive or offensive collateral estoppel. If *Hardy* interprets these grounds correctly, the ability to use offensive collateral estoppel in mass tort or other large-scale litigation will be seriously impeded. See Roger H. Trangsrud, *Joinder Alternatives in Mass Tort Cases*, 70 Corn. L. Rev. 779, 815 (1985) ("while offensive collateral estoppel may contribute to the fair and efficient adjudication of some cases, its limited utility in most mass tort cases makes it unsuitable as a primary technique for the management of mass tort litigation").

3. Do you see any flaws in *Hardy*'s analysis and application of offensive collateral estoppel? Probably the most debatable point is whether the earlier $68,000 *Borel* case provided adequate incentive for the *Borel* defendants to litigate the issue vigorously. Note, however, that if *Hardy* had come out differently on the point, defendants facing the potential of massive future litigation will really prolong the pretrial and trial processes in the first litigation, and might even create pretrial or trial complexity. Is this fair to the first litigant? With respect to *Borel*'s concern for the ambiguity of the jury's verdict, it would have been possible to avoid some of the ambiguity in the jury's verdict if a special verdict or general verdict accompanied by interrogatories had been used. We look more generally at these devices when we examine techniques to reduce trial complexity. See p. 1378, *infra*.

The observations in the last paragraph raise two important points. First, the possible solutions to one form of complexity may raise other, equally intractable forms of complexity. Second, and conversely, the solution to one form of complexity may also be a solution to another form of complexity. To some extent, therefore, it is necessary to reserve judgment on the use of doctrines designed to eliminate joinder complexity until we study the remaining forms of complexity.

4. *Hardy* does not discuss two other limitations on offensive collateral estoppel mentioned in *Parklane Hosiery*: procedural opportunities that the *Borel* defendants might not have enjoyed in the *Borel* litigation and *Hardy*'s opportunity to join the *Borel* litigation. See pp. 164-65, *supra*. Since both *Borel* and *Hardy* were tried in federal court, it is unlikely that the "lack of procedural opportunity" exception would have come into play in *Borel* itself. The exception does, however, arise in certain circumstances. First, the judge in the first case had declined to admit evidence that was deemed to be important to the defense in the second case. See Snider v. Consolidated Coal Co., 973 F.2d 555 (7th Cir. 1992), cert. denied, 506 U.S. 1054 (1993). A second "lack of procedural opportunity" scenario occurs when an issue is litigated and decided in a multiparty suit, a party is joined on claims that do not require the party to litigate that issue, and the issue is decided in a way generally adverse to the party's interests. In a second suit, another plaintiff now wishes to use the findings against the party. The usual rule is that no issue preclusion consequences attach. See State of Alabama ex rel. Siegelman v. United States Environmental Protection Agency, 911 F.2d 499 (11th Cir. 1990). A third, related scenario occurs when the claims against a party in the first suit are severed, so that the first party cannot participate in the trial at which findings adverse to the party's interests are made. Not surprisingly, issue preclusion does not usually attach in this situation. See Lempel & Son Co. v. Boden, 1993 WL 256711 (S.D.N.Y.) ("parties in complex litigation who are not directly involved in the litigation of an issue are not bound by findings made with respect to that issue, unless they fully participated in proceedings and were thus

afforded the opportunity to speak to those issues"); but see County of Cook v. Midcon Corp., 574 F. Supp. 902 (N.D. Ill. 1983) (finding that party that had remained in litigation to contest unrelated issue was subject to issue preclusion in second suit because it had participated on other issues and had opportunity to contest the issue in dispute). We will examine in Chapters Nine and Eleven the circumstances under which a court can sever claims for pretrial and trial purposes. See pp. 1019, 1273, *infra*. You might wish to keep in mind severance's effects on the ability to use preclusion when we come to that material.

For other circumstances invoking the "lack of procedural opportunities" exception, see 18 Charles A. Wright et al., Federal Practice and Procedure § 4423 (1981).

5. How about *Parklane Hosiery*'s other limitation — the opportunity to join the original litigation? Suppose that Hardy had been injured at the same time as Borel, and knew about Borel's suit. Should that knowledge, combined with the arguable ability of Hardy to intervene in *Borel*, preclude Hardy from using the findings of *Borel* against the *Borel* defendants? See In re Air Crash Disaster at Stapleton International Airport, Denver, Colorado, on November 15, 1987, 720 F. Supp. 1505, 1523 (D. Colo. 1989), rev'd on other grounds, 964 F.2d 1059 (10th Cir. 1992) ("We find that in cases not consolidated for trial, justice, fairness and equity weigh against permitting 'wait and see' plaintiffs to assert non-mutual offensive collateral estoppel."); In re Air Crash at Detroit Metropolitan Airport, Detroit, Michigan, on August 16, 1987, 776 F. Supp. 316, 325-26 (E.D. Mich. 1991) (issue preclusion in favor of "wait and see" plaintiffs permitted when plaintiffs would have been unable to participate in trial even had they filed suit earlier).

Presumably, this limitation should not be enforced against Hardy if Hardy either (a) had not been injured at the time of *Borel*; (b) had no notice of *Borel*; or (c) was unable to join the suit. With respect to this last factor, would Hardy have been able to join the original suit? The only apparent basis for joinder would be intervention under Rule 24. Note how the scope of the law of joinder may be inversely proportional to the scope of offensive collateral estoppel: the easier that it is for the plaintiff to join the prior suit, the less successful the plaintiff's claim of offensive collateral is likely to be; while the harder joinder is, the easier the collateral estoppel argument is. How should this fact affect our attitude toward liberalizing joinder rules?

More generally, why should some nonparties to the first litigation be able to invoke offensive collateral estoppel, but not others? If we cared about preventing re-litigation of issues, wouldn't we want to preclude all future litigation on these issues — even when plaintiffs like Hardy knew of the litigation and could have intervened? Is the reason that we do not permit some plaintiffs to use offensive collateral estoppel the unfairness of allowing a plaintiff that could have intervened the benefit of favorable findings when the same plaintiff would not be bound by adverse findings? Does that reason suggest that we should refuse to use collateral estoppel, or that we should bind plaintiffs that could have joined the litigation to the litigation's findings? See Chapter 2.C, *infra*.

6. Although also not raised in *Hardy*, another common problem with the application of all forms of issue preclusion, including offensive collateral estoppel, is the question whether there exists an "identity of issues" in the first and second proceedings. Discerning whether the relevant issues in the two proceedings are the same may appear to be an easy task, but there are some

difficult questions. First, courts generally hold that there is not an identity of issues when the legal significance of the relevant facts is different in the two cases. See Raytech Corp. v. White, 54 F.3d 187, 191 (3d Cir.), cert. denied, 116 S.Ct. 302 (1995) (difference in legal standards must be "substantial"); Jim Beam Brands Co. v. Beamish & Crawford Ltd., 937 F.2d 729 (2d Cir. 1991). A second common situation in which the issues are not deemed to be identical is when the burdens of proof in the two proceedings differ. See United States v. One Assortment of 89 Firearms, 465 U.S. 354 (1984); Commodity Futures Trading Commission v. Wellington Precious Metals, Inc., 950 F.2d 1525 (11th Cir.), cert. denied 506 U.S. 819 (1992).

A third situation arises when the issue in the first litigation is heavily fact-bound, so that the finding in the first litigation would not necessarily carry over to a somewhat different set of factual circumstances in the second case. For instance, in Schneider v. Lockheed Aircraft Corp., 658 F.2d 835 (D.C. Cir. 1981), cert. denied, 455 U.S. 994 (1982), plaintiffs that had allegedly suffered serious injuries during the explosive decompression of an airplane cabin sought to use the favorable verdict in a case involving another passenger that suffered the same injuries to estop the defendant from contending that their injuries had been caused by the decompression. The court of appeals held that, although the prior case had established the fact that decompression could cause the type of injury from which the plaintiffs suffered, it could not be used to establish that the plaintiffs' injuries were in fact caused by the decompression:

> The very heart of the collateral estoppel doctrine is the requirement that the issue to be precluded must be substantially the same as the issue previously litigated. . . . Delineating the proper scope of the estopped issue is often a difficult and delicate task. The court must weigh the burden of repetitious litigation against the risk of denying a party his day in court. Many of the criteria we look to in determining "substantial identity of issues" have been met here: evidence of the accident is the same for each case; the claims are closely related; the arguments and issues of law are virtually identical. But the cases are also different in one important respect: they involve different individuals, each with his own physical constitution and developmental history, and each alleging a particular set of symptoms caused by the accident. [658 F.2d at 852.]

7. A number of courts involved in mass tort litigation have recently been experimenting with a unique form of issue preclusion that raises "identity of issues" questions. Assume that a court has before it the cases of 5,000 plaintiffs. Under this form of preclusion, the court tries general liability issues, and also tries the individual causation and damages issues for a selected sample of plaintiffs. The court then uses the judgments in the sample cases to determine the causation and damages issues for the remaining plaintiffs. For example, assume that the cases of 25 of the plaintiffs were tried, and that the average judgment was $50,000. The court would therefore award $50,000 to each of the 4,975 plaintiffs whose cases had not yet been tried. We examine this practice in detail in Chapter Eleven. See p. 1294, *infra*. When you read that material, you will see that the courts do not usually analyze the practice in terms of offensive collateral estoppel. But isn't that what the court is doing? Does this practice seem to be an appropriate use of offensive collateral estoppel?

8. *Hardy* and some of the other cases described in these notes show that the use of offensive collateral estoppel is problematic in complex and complicated litigation — and especially problematic in the mass tort area. But at least

offensive collateral estoppel remains a theoretical possibility. In studied dicta, however, the Sixth Circuit seems to have eliminated even this theoretical possibility for mass tort cases, stating that "[i]n *Parklane Hosiery*, the Supreme Court explicitly stated that offensive collateral estoppel could not be used in mass tort litigation." In re Bendectin Products Liability Litigation, 749 F.2d 300, 305 n.11 (6th Cir. 1984). As support for its dicta, *Bendectin* cited footnote 14 of *Parklane Hosiery* (p. 164, *supra*). Did the Sixth Circuit correctly read *Parklane Hosiery*? Is this decision consistent with the trans-substantive aspiration of our procedural rules? Can the decision nonetheless be defended?

9. Recall that the arguments for direct issue preclusion in a second suit between the same parties and for defensive collateral estoppel are somewhat stronger than those for offensive collateral estoppel. See pp. 170-72, *supra*. Should courts therefore be more receptive to the use of direct issue preclusion and defensive collateral estoppel than they have been to the use of offensive collateral estoppel? In In re Air Crash at Detroit Metropolitan Airport, Detroit, Michigan, on August 16, 1987, 791 F. Supp. 1204 (E.D. Mich. 1992), *aff'd* 86 F.3d 498 (6th Cir. 1996), the plaintiffs brought suit against numerous defendants allegedly involved in an airline crash. In these proceedings, one defendant, Northwest Airlines, filed a cross-claim against another defendant, McDonnell Douglas (MDC). Northwest also filed a separate property damage suit against MDC for its own loss of the airplane. MDC eventually settled all its claims with crash victims, but some of the cases against Northwest went to trial. The jury found Northwest liable for the crash, and on the cross-claims between Northwest and MDC found Northwest 100% at fault. When Northwest continued to pursue its property damage claim against MDC, MDC argued that the prior verdict required dismissal of the property damage suit. The court held that issue preclusion should apply. In so holding, the court "rejected Northwest's contention that collateral estoppel should not be applied in mass disaster litigation." 791 F. Supp. at 1214. Instead, the court interpreted *Bendectin*, 749 F.2d 300, "as precluding the utilization of offensive estoppel in a mass tort litigation situation . . . in which its application would be unfair to the defendant. The contours of when offensive collateral estoppel would be unfair — even in mass tort litigation — should be developed on a case-by-case basis. Invoking the term 'mass tort litigation' is meaningless without contextual analysis. The teaching of *Parklane Hosiery* is that the issue is delicate and must be handled in this manner." Id. at 1215. "More importantly," the court concluded, "MDC is principally relying upon the defensive use of collateral estoppel, as to which the *Parklane Hosiery* and *Bendectin* language does not apply." Id.

10. In Note 5, *supra*, we suggested that the issues of joinder and issue preclusion are intertwined, and that the reasons for issue preclusion contract as joinder rules expand. A variation on that theme can be found in Avila v. Van Ru Credit Corp., 1995 WL 41425, *7 (N.D. Ill.). In *Avila*, the court decided to certify a class action in part because it thought that a class action was more efficient than the filing of thousands of individual suits in which the issue of offensive collateral estoppel would be raised. Is *Avila* correct that mandatory joinder rules such as class actions are generally more efficient than preclusion rules? If so, why don't we just create stronger rules of mandatory joinder? One reason is that we do not wish to do violence to a litigant's autonomy. If so, then the broader use of offensive collateral estoppel is, from plaintiffs' viewpoint, a preferable solution to mandatory joinder, for it preserves plaintiffs' right to decide when to bring suit, while making the suit more economical to bring. Whether a broader use of

offensive collateral estoppel preserves defendants' autonomy to contest the case of each plaintiff is another matter.

There are also other relationships between joinder and preclusion. For instance, in Cullen v. Margiotta, 811 F.2d 698, 733 (2d Cir.), cert. denied, 483 U.S. 1021 (1987), the defendants argued that the plaintiffs, who had unsuccessfully sought to maintain a class action in state court, were collaterally estopped from arguing that they were entitled to maintain a class action in federal court. The court rejected the argument because of a lack of "identity of issues"; "the standards governing the propriety of the suit as a class action in the state court and the federal court differed significantly." Id. at 733. What result if the state and federal standards are identical? Cf. J.R. Clearwater Inc. v. Ashland Chemical Co., 93 F.3d 176 (5th Cir. 1996) (federal court cannot enjoin plaintiffs that unsuccessfully sought certification in federal court from commencing state court action also seeking class certification).

11. Should the complication or complexity of the litigation affect the scope of the interpretation that we give to defensive or offensive collateral estoppel? From the viewpoint of complicated litigation, any doctrine that can prevent the inefficient re-litigation of issues should be favorably regarded. But courts do not always take a broad reading of estoppel; indeed, if efficiency is the primary criterion for using defensive or offensive collateral estoppel, there is good reason to believe that *Hardy* is wrongly decided.

From the viewpoint of complex litigation, the issue is not whether issue preclusion can prevent inefficiency, but whether it can prevent lawyer dysfunction, which arises when later parties can undo an earlier judgment, when insufficient assets exist, or when later parties are otherwise precluded from obtaining meaningful relief. A more expansive view of defensive or offensive collateral estoppel does little to prevent lawyer dysfunction. In the first place, these doctrines do not address the problem of the re-opening of a prior judgment in a way that deprives earlier parties of their relief. Nor do the doctrines operate in a way that prevents later-filing parties from obtaining a fair share of the defendants' assets or other meaningful relief, unless (a) the reason that later filing parties cannot obtain their share of the relief is that the defendant has insufficient assets or capacity to provide that relief, and (b) the use of offensive collateral estoppel would so streamline the later lawsuits that the defendants' assets or capacity would now become adequate. Indeed, in some ways a broader use of offensive collateral estoppel might exacerbate the problem of insufficient assets, since such a doctrine creates an incentive to file later suits, and therefore might exacerbate the problem of dysfunction.

In short, cases like *Hardy*, which do not take an expansive view of offensive collateral estoppel, are hard to reconcile with the principle that courts should seek to reduce inefficient re-litigation. They are, however, consistent with the principle that courts should not depart from the standard adversarial model (under which both parties — plaintiffs *and* defendants — have the right in each case to present the proofs and arguments relevant to that case) unless (1) the adversarial model cannot deliver a rational resolution of the dispute, but (2) changes in legal doctrine can achieve a rational resolution of the dispute. Condition (1) may pertain in cases like *Hardy*; due to the insufficiency of assets, the adversarial system's goal of preserving to each plaintiff the right to choose the timing of his or her suit means that some similarly situated plaintiffs will receive full compensation while others will receive no compensation (and thus no effective adjudication) for their claims. Nonetheless, condition (2) has not been satisfied; although it may preserve more assets for plaintiffs' use, a broader use of collateral estoppel will not remove the problem of insufficient assets that the asbestos controversy posed.

Assuming that the observations in this Note are accurate, it would provide a descriptive argument for the present state of the law. It does not, however, provide a normative argument for the present state of the law. Are there good reasons to maintain a traditional adversarial approach to complicated litigation? What would be the reasons to depart from that approach in complex litigation?

12. Offensive collateral estoppel is not the only "preclusion" doctrine that might apply in complex or complicated cases. Another doctrine that does some of the same work is stare decisis. In an opinion decided shortly before *Hardy*, the Fifth Circuit refused to hold that *Borel* was stare decisis under Texas law on the issue of the dangerousness of asbestos. At most, the Fifth Circuit said, *Borel* established that a reasonable jury could find such dangerousness, not that every reasonable jury would necessarily so find. Migues v. Fibreboard Corp., 662 F.2d 1182 (5th Cir. 1981). *Migues* is nonetheless instructive. If a party can succeed in convincing a judge that an issue decided by a court whose decisions bind the judge was an issue of law or an issue of fact that no reasonable jury could dispute, stare decisis might bind later parties (whether they were involved in the prior litigation or not) to the finding on the issue.

In the following section we turn more generally to the idea of binding nonparties to a prior litigation to the findings in that litigation. Before we do, however, two comments might be in order. First, remember that stare decisis is a prudential doctrine of judging, not an absolute command; hence, the preclusive effect of stare decisis is weaker than that of res judicata or collateral estoppel. Second, recall that stare decisis effects are often thought to be grounds for intervention of right under Rule 24, and may be grounds for requiring the joinder of affected parties under Rule 19. See pp. 129, 148-49, *supra*. If judges start to take a broad view of stare decisis, won't they also need to be prepared to handle sprawling, many-sided cases? How should judges handle the problem of nonparties that never knew about the original case, or whose claim might indeed not even have arisen at the time that the original case is decided? Do these difficulties suggest that a broad construction of stare decisis is undesirable?

b. Precluding Persons that Did Not Participate in a Prior Case

In the last subsection we examined the limits of using preclusion doctrines against persons that had been involved in prior litigation. Even if preclusion doctrines were broadly construed in this context (and they often are not), these doctrines would still be an incomplete response to the problems posed by complex and complicated litigation. The reason is that these preclusion doctrines run only against *parties* to a prior litigation; they do not run against *nonparties* to that litigation. To use *Parklane Hosiery* as an example, suppose that Parklane Hosiery had prevailed in the securities case brought against it by the government. The company now faces an identical suit from individual investors, and would like to use the judgment or the factual determinations from the government action against the investors. Obviously, if the company is permitted to do so, the subsequent litigation will be significantly pared down, and possibly even avoided altogether. At the same time, persons that did not participate in the prior case will find themselves bound to a result in which they did not participate in the shaping of the proofs and arguments — the right that is, according to Professor Fuller, the cornerstone of any adversarial system.

Are there circumstances in which this adversarial right should give way to the concerns of joinder complexity? Should the right also give way in order to avoid the inefficient re-litigation of claims or issues? Should it make a difference whether we are seeking to prevent the assertion of an entire claim, as opposed to the litigation of certain factual issues?

RICHARDS v. JEFFERSON COUNTY, ALABAMA

517 U.S. 793 (1996)

 JUSTICE STEVENS delivered the unanimous opinion of the Court.

In Hansberry v. Lee, 311 U.S. 32 (1940), we held that it would violate the Due Process Clause of the Fourteenth Amendment to bind litigants to a judgment rendered in an earlier litigation to which they were not parties and in which they were not adequately represented. The decision of the Supreme Court of Alabama that we review today presents us with the same basic question in a somewhat different context.

I

Jason Richards and Fannie Hill (petitioners) are privately employed in Jefferson County, Alabama. In 1991 they filed a complaint in the Federal District Court challenging the validity of the occupation tax imposed by Jefferson County Ordinance 1120, which had been adopted in 1987. That action was dismissed as barred by the Tax Injunction Act, 28 U.S.C. § 1341. They then commenced this action in the Circuit Court of Jefferson County.

Petitioners represent a class of all nonfederal employees subject to the county's tax. Petitioners alleged that the tax, which contains a lengthy list of exemptions, violates the Due Process and Equal Protection Clauses of the Fourteenth Amendment and similar provisions of the Alabama Constitution. Because $10 million of the annual proceeds from the county tax have been pledged to the Birmingham-Jefferson Civic Center for a period of 20 years, the court permitted the Center to intervene and support Jefferson County's defense of its tax.

The county moved for summary judgment on the ground that petitioners' claims were barred by a prior adjudication of the tax in an earlier action brought by the acting director of finance for the city of Birmingham and the city itself. That earlier action had been consolidated for trial with a separate suit brought by three county taxpayers, and the Supreme Court of Alabama upheld the tax in the resulting appeal. See Bedingfield v. Jefferson County, 527 So. 2d 1270 (1988). After examining the course of this prior litigation, the trial court granted the county's motion for summary judgment as to the state constitutional claims, but refused to do so as to the federal claims because they had not been decided by either the trial court or the Alabama Supreme Court in *Bedingfield*.

On appeal, the county argued that the federal claims as well as the state claims were barred by the adjudication in *Bedingfield*. The Alabama Supreme Court agreed. The majority opinion noted that in Alabama, as in most States, a prior judgment on the merits rendered by a court of competent jurisdiction precludes the relitigation of a claim if there is a "substantial identity of the parties" and if the "same cause of action" is presented in both suits. . . . Moreover, the court explained, the prior judgment is generally "'res judicata not only as to all matters litigated and decided by it, but as to all relevant issues which could have been but were not raised and litigated in the suit.'" . . .

We now conclude that the State Supreme Court's holding that petitioners are bound by the adjudication in *Bedingfield* deprived them of the due process of law guaranteed by the Fourteenth Amendment.

II

State courts are generally free to develop their own rules for protecting against the relitigation of common issues or the piecemeal resolution of disputes. . . . We have long held, however, that extreme applications of the doctrine of res judicata may be inconsistent with a federal right that is "fundamental in character." . . .[4]

The limits on a state court's power to develop estoppel rules reflect the general consensus "'in Anglo-American jurisprudence that one is not bound by a judgment *in personam* in a litigation in which he is not designated as a party or to which he has not been made a party by service of process.' *Hansberry v. Lee*, 311 U.S. [at] 40 . . . . This rule is part of our 'deep-rooted historic tradition that everyone should have his own day in court.' . . ." *Martin v. Wilks*, 490 U.S. 755, 761-62 (1989). As a consequence, "[a] judgment or decree among parties to a lawsuit resolves issues as among them, but it does not conclude the rights of strangers to those proceedings." Id., at 762 . . . .

Of course, these principles do not always require one to have been a party to a judgment in order to be bound by it. Most notably, there is an exception when it can be said that there is "privity" between a party to the second case and a party who is bound by an earlier judgment. For example,

---

4. "The doctrine of res judicata rests at bottom upon the ground that the party to be affected, or some other with whom he is in privity, has litigated or had an opportunity to litigate the same matter in a former action in a court of competent jurisdiction. . . . The opportunity to be heard is an essential requisite of due process of law in judicial proceedings. . . . And as a State may not, consistently with the Fourteenth Amendment, enforce a judgment against a party named in the proceedings without a hearing or an opportunity to be heard . . ., so it cannot, without disregarding the requirement of due process, give a conclusive effect to a prior judgment against one who is neither a party nor in privity with a party therein." [Postal Telegraph Cable Co. v. Newport,] 247 U.S. [464,] 476 [(1918)].

a judgment that is binding on a guardian or trustee may also bind the ward or the beneficiaries of a trust. Moreover, although there are clearly constitutional limits on the "privity" exception, the term "privity" is now used to describe various relationships between litigants that would not have come within the traditional definition of that term. See generally Restatement (Second) of Judgments, ch. 4 (1980) (Parties and Other Persons Affected by Judgments).

In addition, as we explained in *Wilks*:

> We have recognized an exception to the general rule when, in certain limited circumstances, a person, although not a party, has his interests adequately represented by someone with the same interests who is a party. See Hansberry v. Lee, 311 U.S. 32, 41-42 (1940) ('class' or 'representative' suits); Fed. Rule Civ. Proc. 23 (same); Montana v. United States, 440 U.S. 147, 154-55 (1979) (control of litigation on behalf of one of the parties in the litigation). Additionally, where a special remedial scheme exists expressly foreclosing successive litigation by nonlitigants, as for example in bankruptcy or probate, legal proceedings may terminate pre-existing rights if the scheme is otherwise consistent with due process. . . .

Here, the Alabama Supreme Court concluded that res judicata applied because petitioners were adequately represented in the *Bedingfield* action. . . . We now consider the propriety of that determination.

III

We begin by noting that the parties to the *Bedingfield* case failed to provide petitioners with any notice that a suit was pending which would conclusively resolve their legal rights. That failure is troubling because, as we explained in Mullane v. Central Hanover Bank & Trust Co., 339 U.S. 306 (1950), the right to be heard ensured by the guarantee of due process "has little reality or worth unless one is informed that the matter is pending and can choose for himself whether to appear or default, acquiesce or contest." Id., at 314 . . . . Nevertheless, respondents ask us to excuse the lack of notice on the ground that petitioners, as the Alabama Supreme Court concluded, were adequately represented in *Bedingfield*.[5]

Our answer is informed by our decision in *Hansberry v. Lee* . . . . There, certain property owners brought suit to enforce a restrictive covenant that purported to forbid the sale or lease of any property within a defined area to "any person of the colored race." Id., at 37-38. By its terms the covenant was not effective unless signed by the owners of 95 percent of frontage in the area. At trial, the defendants proved that the signers of the covenant owned

---

5. Of course, mere notice may not suffice to preserve one's right to be heard in a case such as the one before us. The general rule is that "the law does not impose upon any person absolutely entitled to a hearing the burden of voluntary intervention in a suit to which he is a stranger." Chase Nat. Bank v. Norwalk, 291 U.S. 431, 441 (1934); but cf. Penn-Central Merger and N & W Inclusion Cases, 389 U.S. 486, 505, n.4 (1968) (noting that absent parties were invited to intervene by the court).

only about 54 percent of the frontage. Nevertheless, the trial court held that the covenant was enforceable because the issue had been resolved in a prior suit in which the parties had stipulated that the owners of 95 percent had signed. . . .

Despite the fact that the stipulation was untrue, the Illinois Supreme Court held that the second action was barred by res judicata. . . . Because the plaintiff in the earlier case had alleged that she was proceeding "on behalf of herself and on behalf of all other property owners in the district," . . . the Illinois Supreme Court concluded that all members of that "class," including the defendants challenging the stipulation in the present action, were bound by the decree. We reversed.

We recognized the "familiar doctrine . . . that members of a class not present as parties to the litigation may be bound by the judgment where they are in fact adequately represented by parties who are present, or . . . the relationship between the parties present and those who are absent is such as legally to entitle the former to stand in judgment for the latter." *Hansberry*, 311 U.S., at 42-43. We concluded, however, that because the interests of those class members who had been a party to the prior litigation were in conflict with the absent members who were the defendants in the subsequent action, the doctrine of representation of absent parties in a class suit could not support the decree.

Even assuming that our opinion in *Hansberry* may be read to leave open the possibility that in some class suits adequate representation might cure a lack of notice, . . . it may not be read to permit the application of res judicata here. Our opinion explained that a prior proceeding, to have binding effect on absent parties, would at least have to be "so devised and applied as to insure that those present are of the same class as those absent and that the litigation is so conducted as to insure the full and fair consideration of the common issue." 311 U.S. at 43 . . . It is plain that the *Bedingfield* action, like the prior proceeding in *Hansberry* itself, does not fit such a description.

The Alabama Supreme Court concluded that the "*taxpayers* in the *Bedingfield* action adequately represented the interests of the taxpayers here," . . . but the three county taxpayers who were parties in *Bedingfield* did not sue on behalf of a class; their pleadings did not purport to assert any claim against or on behalf of any nonparties; and the judgment they received did not purport to bind any county taxpayers who were nonparties. That the acting director of finance for the city of Birmingham also sued in his capacity as both an individual taxpayer and a public official does not change the analysis. Even if we were to assume, as the Alabama Supreme Court did not, that by suing in his official capacity, the finance director intended to represent the pecuniary interests of all city taxpayers, and not simply the corporate interests of the city itself, he did not purport to represent the pecuniary interests of *county* taxpayers like petitioners.[6]

---

6. We need not decide here whether public officials are always constitutionally adequate representatives of all persons over whom they have jurisdiction when, as here, the underlying right is personal in nature. . . .

As a result, there is no reason to suppose that the *Bedingfield* court took care to protect the interests of petitioners in the manner suggested in *Hansberry*. Nor is there any reason to suppose that the individual taxpayers in *Bedingfield* understood their suit to be on behalf of absent county taxpayers. Thus, to contend that the plaintiffs in *Bedingfield* somehow represented petitioners, let alone represented them in a constitutionally adequate manner, would be "to attribute to them a power that it cannot be said that they had assumed to exercise." *Hansberry*, 311 U.S. at 46.

Because petitioners and the *Bedingfield* litigants are best described as mere "strangers" to one another, *Martin v. Wilks*, 490 U.S., at 762, we are unable to conclude that the *Bedingfield* plaintiffs provided representation sufficient to make up for the fact that petitioners neither participated in . . ., nor had the opportunity to participate in, the *Bedingfield* action. Accordingly, due process prevents the former from being bound by the latter's judgment.

IV

Respondents contend that, even if petitioners did not receive the kind of opportunity to make their case in court that due process would ordinarily ensure, the character of their action renders the usual constitutional protections inapplicable. They contend that invalidation of the occupation tax would have disastrous consequences on the county, which has made substantial commitments of tax revenues based on its understanding that *Bedingfield* determined the constitutionality of the tax. Respondents argue that in cases raising a public issue of this kind, the people may properly be regarded as the real party in interest and thus that petitioners received all the process they were due in the *Bedingfield* action.

Our answer requires us to distinguish between two types of actions brought by taxpayers. In one category are cases in which the taxpayer is using that status to entitle him to complain about an alleged misuse of public funds, . . . or about other public action that has only an indirect impact on his interests, *e.g.*, Stromberg v. Board of Ed. of Bratenahl, 64 Ohio St.2d 98, 413 N.E.2d 1184 (1980) . . . . As to this category of cases, we may assume that the States have wide latitude to establish procedures not only to limit the number of judicial proceedings that may be entertained but also to determine whether to accord a taxpayer any standing at all.

Because the guarantee of due process is not a mere form, however, there obviously exists another category of taxpayer cases in which the State may not deprive individual litigants of their own day in court. By virtue of presenting a federal constitutional challenge to a State's attempt to levy personal funds, petitioners clearly bring an action of this latter type. . . .

Of course, we are aware that governmental and private entities have substantial interests in the prompt and determinative resolution of challenges to important legislation. We do not agree with the Alabama Supreme Court, however, that, given the amount of money at stake, respondents were entitled to rely on the assumption that the *Bedingfield* action "authoritatively establish[ed]" the constitutionality of the tax. . . . A state court's freedom to rely on prior precedent in rejecting a litigant's claims does not afford it similar freedom to bind a litigant to a prior judgment to which he was not a party. That general rule clearly applies when a taxpayer seeks a hearing to prevent the State from subjecting him to a levy in violation of the Federal Constitution.

V

Because petitioners received neither notice of, nor sufficient representation in, the *Bedingfield* litigation, that adjudication, as a matter of federal due process, may not bind them and thus cannot bar them from challenging an allegedly unconstitutional deprivation of their property. Accordingly, the judgment of the Alabama Supreme Court is reversed, and the case is remanded to that court for further proceedings not inconsistent with this opinion.

TYUS v. SCHOEMEHL

93 F.3d 449 (8th Cir. 1996), cert. denied, — U.S. —, 117 S.Ct. 1427 (1997)

■ MAGILL, Circuit Judge. At issue in this § 2 Voting Rights Act case is whether issue preclusion bars certain plaintiffs-appellants from bringing a second suit challenging the St. Louis aldermanic district boundaries, which are drawn based on the 1990 federal decennial census. Although these appellants were not parties to the original lawsuit challenging the aldermanic boundaries, see African American Voting Rights Legal Defense Fund v. Villa, 54 F.3d 1345 (8th Cir. 1995) (the Aldermen-*AAVR* suit), cert. denied, 516 U.S. 1113 (1996), they were "virtually represented" by those plaintiffs to the Aldermen-*AAVR* suit, and therefore issue preclusion does apply. The district court held that claim preclusion, rather than issue preclusion, applies, so we affirm on alternate grounds.

I.

The city of St. Louis is governed by a Board of Aldermen consisting of twenty-eight aldermen elected from twenty-eight single-member wards. In 1991, St. Louis began to redraw the aldermanic boundaries in accordance with the 1990 census. Although the census revealed that African-Americans comprised a majority in thirteen of the twenty-eight wards, and were a plurality in one additional ward, the majority of aldermen voted to adopt an aldermanic map that provided for sixteen wards in which whites have a voting age majority and twelve wards in which African-Americans have a voting age majority.

A. *AAVR* Lawsuit

On January 16, 1992, a group of African-Americans filed the *AAVR* lawsuit, challenging the validity of the new ward boundaries. . . . Among the named plaintiffs were five African-American St. Louis aldermen — Freeman Bosley, Sr., Sharon Tyus, Bertha Mitchell, Claude Taylor, and Irving Clay, Jr. (the Aldermen plaintiffs) — and the African American Voting Rights Legal Defense Fund. Initially, several different counsel represented the plaintiffs. Eventually, these attorneys were replaced with attorney Judson Miner.

In this suit, plaintiffs contended that (1) the boundary lines were drawn in such a way as to fragment concentrations of black population, diluting black voting strength in violation of § 2 of the Voting Rights Act, 42 U.S.C.A. § 1973 (West 1994 & Supp.1996), and the First, Thirteenth, Fourteenth, and Fifteenth Amendments to the United States Constitution; (2) the boundary lines were drawn in such a way as to pack concentrations of black population into specific wards, diluting overall black voting strength in violation of the above provisions; and (3) the ward boundaries violate the Fourteenth Amendment, because they have populations with a variance in excess of ten percent.

On February 19, 1992, defendants in the Aldermen-*AAVR* suit (collectively, the City) moved for summary judgment, contending that the map had been drawn in such a way as to provide substantial proportionality. Four affidavits supporting this claim, including a statistical analysis performed by Donald L. Davidson, the City's expert, were attached. On April 27, 1992, counsel for plaintiffs opposed this motion with an affidavit from expert witness Dr. Charlene Jones. The affidavit discussed the appropriate means of measuring proportional representation and other issues surrounding both the dilution claim and the Fourteenth Amendment claim.

Meanwhile, a dispute over trial strategy had arisen between the Aldermen plaintiffs and original counsel. On April 24, 1992, the Aldermen plaintiffs hired their current attorney, Judson Miner . . . . On May 5, the Aldermen plaintiffs moved to voluntarily withdraw from the Aldermen-*AAVR* suit and have their claims dismissed without prejudice.

After having sought leave to withdraw from the Aldermen-*AAVR* suit, the Aldermen plaintiffs learned that the original counsel had responded to the City's summary judgment motion with only the Jones affidavit. On May 26, 1992, dissatisfied with this submission, the Aldermen plaintiffs sought leave to file out of time a twelve-page memorandum of law and two supporting affidavits in an attempt to bolster the Jones affidavit. This motion, made more than three months after the City's summary judgment motion, was denied by the district court without explanation.

B. *Miller* Lawsuit

On April 27, 1992, with the City's summary judgment motion pending in the Aldermen-*AAVR* suit, the Aldermen plaintiffs filed a second lawsuit against the City challenging the St. Louis map. See Sharon Tyus, et al. v. Schoemehl, No. 4:92 CV 0000801 (E.D. Mo.1992) (the *Miller* suit). In this suit, the plaintiffs raised the same claims as those raised in the Aldermen-*AAVR* suit: (1) the boundary lines as drawn fragment the black population, diluting black voting strength in violation of § 2 of the Voting Rights Act; and (2) the map was drawn with the discriminatory purpose of diluting black voting strength, in violation of the Fourteenth and Fifteenth Amendments and 42 U.S.C. § 1983. At this time, attorney Miner represented the plaintiffs in both suits. The Aldermen plaintiffs were joined in the *Miller* suit by Sterling Miller, Clarence Woodruff, and Paula Carter (an African-American Missouri state representative).

C. Subsequent Orders in the Two Suits

On June 17, 1992, the district court in the Aldermen-*AAVR* suit granted the City's motion for summary judgment. The court determined both that expert Jones's memorandum failed to refute the City's assertion that the 1991 ward map provides African-American voters with proportional representation and that the Jones memorandum raised no triable issue with respect to the one person-one vote claim. Second, the court denied as moot the Aldermen plaintiffs' motion to withdraw from the Aldermen-*AAVR* suit.

Meanwhile, on June 6, 1992, the City moved to dismiss the *Miller* suit on the grounds that the Aldermen-*AAVR* suit was still pending before the district court and the Aldermen plaintiffs were plaintiffs in both suits. On June 20, the City renewed this motion, contending now that, given the grant of summary judgment to the City in the Aldermen-*AAVR* suit, the *Miller* suit was barred by res judicata and stare decisis. [Subsequently, the *Miller* plaintiffs moved for leave to file an amended complaint that dropped the Aldermen plaintiffs from the suit; added as plaintiffs an African-American Missouri state senator, William L. Clay, Jr., and an African-American St. Louis alderman, Kenneth Jones; and expanded the factual allegations.]

The district court converted the City's June 20 motion to dismiss the *Miller* suit into a summary judgment motion, and on March 2, 1993, the court granted this motion on claim preclusion grounds. The court first noted that the Aldermen plaintiffs, who were never allowed to withdraw from the Aldermen-*AAVR* suit, were clearly barred from raising their claims by claim preclusion. Further, although plaintiffs Miller, Woodruff, and Carter were not parties to the Aldermen-*AAVR* suit, they were nevertheless in privity with the plaintiffs in the Aldermen-*AAVR* suit under a theory of "virtual representation." According to the district court, these plaintiffs had been adequately represented by the plaintiffs in the Aldermen-*AAVR* suit and thus were bound by the ruling in that suit. The court further denied as moot the motion to amend the complaint and add Jones and Clay, Jr. as plaintiffs.

Miller, Woodruff, and Carter, as well as Jones, Jr. and Clay (the Miller plaintiffs), appealed the March 2, 1993 ruling. . . .

II.

A.

Both suits raise identical dilution claims. Each contends the map boundaries violate § 2 of the Voting Rights Act by fragmenting black voters, thereby diluting black voting strength. Each also contends that the dilution of black voting strength violates the Fourteenth and Fifteenth Amendments. At issue, then, is whether the *Miller* suit is barred by issue preclusion because the claims raised in that suit were litigated and necessarily decided by the Aldermen-*AAVR* suit. We hold that it is.[6]

Under issue preclusion, once a court has decided an issue of fact or law necessary to its judgment, "the determination is conclusive in a subsequent action between the parties, whether on the same or a different claim." Restatement (Second) of Judgments § 27 (1982) . . . . Issue preclusion will also bar relitigation of an issue by one who, although not a party to the original suit, is in privity with a party to that suit. . . .

In addition to the requirement that the party in the second suit sought to be precluded was a party, or in privity with a party, to the original lawsuit, . . . there are four other prerequisites to the application of issue preclusion: (1) the issue sought to be precluded must be the same as that involved in a prior action; (2) the issue must have been actually litigated in the prior action; (3) the issue must have been determined by a valid and final judgment; and (4) the determination must have been essential to the prior judgment. . . . The parties do not contest that the last four requirements for preclusion are met in this case. The sole issue, therefore, is whether the Miller plaintiffs are in privity with the Aldermen plaintiffs, so that the Miller plaintiffs should be bound by the result in the Aldermen-*AAVR* suit.

B.

Preclusion is rooted in concerns of judicial economy. As we have noted, "[i]n this era of overcrowded dockets the courts have a positive duty to restrict needless relitigation of issues." Gerrard v. Larsen, 517 F.2d 1127, 1134 (8th Cir. 1975); see also Montana v. United States, 440 U.S. 147, 153 (1979) (preclusion doctrines "conserve[ ] judicial resources"). Additionally, the preclusion doctrines protect defendants, by relieving them of "the expense and vexation attending multiple lawsuits." . . .

However, due process concerns are present when the party sought to be precluded was not an actual party in the first lawsuit. Because preclusion based on privity is an exception to the "deep-rooted historic tradition that everyone should have his own day in court," Richards v. Jefferson County, Ala., [517 U.S. 793, 798] (1996) (citation omitted), courts must ensure that the relationship between the party to the original suit and the party sought to be precluded in the later suit is sufficiently close to justify preclusion. Thus, "the due process clauses prevent preclusion when the relationship between the party and non-party becomes too attenuated." Southwest Airlines Co. v. Texas Int'l Airlines, 546 F.2d 84, 95 (5th Cir.), cert. denied, 434 U.S. 832 (1977).

---

6. Although the district court applied claim preclusion when granting the City's motion for summary judgment, we believe that issue preclusion is the appropriate preclusion doctrine in this case. We nevertheless may affirm the district court, for "we may affirm the district court's grant of summary judgment on any ground supported by record." . . .

There are three generally recognized categories of nonparties who will be considered in privity with a party to the prior action and who will be bound by a prior adjudication: (1) a nonparty who controls the original action; (2) a successor-in-interest to a prior party; and (3) a nonparty whose interests were adequately represented by a party to the original action. . . . This case focuses on the third category.

Preclusion based on adequate representation, otherwise known as "virtual representation," was given its clearest statement in Aerojet-General Corp. v. Askew, 511 F.2d 710 (5th Cir.), cert. denied, 423 U.S. 908 (1975). In that case, the court noted that

> [u]nder the federal law of res judicata, a person may be bound by a judgment even though not a party if one of the parties to the suit is so closely aligned with his interests as to be his virtual representative.

Id. at 719. Although this principle is generally accepted, courts are sharply divided on how to implement this strand of issue preclusion.

Some courts permit a wide use of virtual representation, inquiring whether there exists a substantial relationship between the party and nonparty, such that the party adequately represented the interests of the nonparty. See, e.g., NAACP v. Hunt, 891 F.2d 1555 (11th Cir. 1990). Because of the fact-intensive nature of these inquiries, there is no clear test that can be employed to determine if virtual representation is appropriate. It is evident, however, that because virtual representation rests on the notion that it is fair to deprive a nonparty of his day in court, "virtual representation has a pronounced equitable dimension." Gonzalez v. Banco Cent. Corp., 27 F.3d 751, 761 (1st Cir. 1994). A nonparty will be barred from bringing his claim only when "the balance of the relevant equities tips in favor of preclusion." Id.

Other courts would permit a nonparty to be bound by a prior judgment under a theory of virtual representation only in very limited, technical situations. For example, in Pollard v. Cockrell, 578 F.2d 1002 (5th Cir. 1978), the court noted that "[v]irtual representation demands the existence of an express or implied legal relationship in which parties to the first suit are accountable to non-parties who file a subsequent suit raising identical issues." Id. at 1008 . . . Examples of such a relationship would be "'estate beneficiaries bound by administrators, presidents and sole stockholders by their companies, parent corporations by their subsidiaries, and a trust beneficiary by the trustee.'" Pollard, 578 F.2d at 1008-09 (quoting Southwest Airlines Co., 546 F.2d at 97). Under this view, virtual representation is little more than the doctrine of preclusion based on representation that has historically been accepted by courts.

We agree with those courts that give wider use to virtual representation. This liberal use better accommodates the competing considerations of judicial economy and due process. Although we are cognizant of the concerns underlying the Pollard decision — that broad use of this doctrine will completely eviscerate the notion that a party is entitled to his day in court — we believe that these concerns are better addressed through a careful application of the doctrine to the facts in a given case than by artificially limiting the scope of the doctrine.

This conclusion is not altered by the recent Supreme Court decision in *Richards, supra.* . . .

[In *Richards*] the Court did note one important exception to the general rule: a party to the second case will be bound by the result of an earlier case to which it was not a party "when it can be said that there is 'privity' between a party to the second case and a party who is bound by an earlier judgment." [517 U.S. at 798.] Although the Court provided some examples of what could constitute privity, it did not offer a general definition of that term. Rather, the Court acknowledged that "the term 'privity' is now used to describe various relationships between litigants that would not have come within the traditional definition of that term." Id.

Virtual representation falls squarely within this exception. A court will apply virtual representation only when it finds the existence of some special relationship between the parties justifying preclusion. In essence, this is a finding that the two parties are in privity. See *Gerrard*, 517 F.2d at 1134 ("Privity . . . is merely a word used to say that the relationship between the one who is a party on the record and another is close enough to include that other within the res judicata.") . . . When, as in *Richards*, the two parties are strangers to each other, then virtual representation would not be appropriate. However, where there is a special relationship between the parties, determined after analyzing the factors listed below, then the parties are in privity, and *Richards* is simply inapposite.

C.

Due to the equitable and fact-intensive nature of virtual representation, there is no clear test for determining the applicability of the doctrine. There are, however, several guiding principles. First, identity of interests between the two parties is necessary, though not alone sufficient. . . . Other factors to be considered "include a close relationship between the prior and present parties; participation in the prior litigation; apparent acquiescence; and whether the present party deliberately maneuvered to avoid the effects of the first action." *Petit v. City of Chicago*, 766 F. Supp. 607, 612 (N.D. Ill. 1991) . . . .

Another factor to consider is adequacy of representation, *Gonzalez*, 27 F.3d at 762, which is best viewed in terms of incentive to litigate.[7] That is,

---

7. In concluding that adequacy of representation refers to incentive to litigate rather than to actual trial strategy and possible trial errors, as some commentators have argued, . . . we are influenced by two observations. First, in applying virtual representation, courts must perform a preliminary relationship inquiry: whether one party's interests are so aligned with those of another that one party can be considered a proxy for the other party. While incentive to litigate may have some bearing on whether the two parties' interests are aligned, considerations of trial strategy and possible trial errors, because they have little bearing on the relationship between the parties, are external to this inquiry.

Second, we note that "in civil litigation, the sins of the lawyer routinely are visited upon the client." *Gonzalez*, 27 F.3d at 762 n. 12. . . . To not apply virtual representation when counsel is deficient would encourage fence-sitting: the nonparty will benefit if the party plaintiff wins, but if the party plaintiff loses due to counsel's deficient performance, the

one party "adequately represents" the interests of another when the interests of the two parties are very closely aligned and the first party had a strong incentive to protect the interests of the second party.

Finally, the nature of the issue raised — whether a public law issue or private law issue — is important. Although virtual representation may be used in the private law context, its use is particularly appropriate for public law issues. As the Supreme Court recently noted, when a case challenges a "public action that has only an indirect impact on [a party's] interests," *Richards*, [517 U.S. at 803], due process concerns are lessened. In this situation, courts have "wide latitude to establish procedures . . . to limit the number of judicial proceedings. . . ." Id.

Further, we note that in public law cases, the number of plaintiffs with standing is potentially limitless. If parties were allowed to continually raise issues already decided, public law claims "would assume immortality." Los Angeles Branch NAACP v. Los Angeles Unified Sch. Dist., 750 F.2d 731, 741 (9th Cir.1984) (applying virtual representation to preclude plaintiff from raising school desegregation claim), cert. denied, 474 U.S. 919 (1985). Concerns of judicial economy and cost to defendants, while present in every suit, are particularly important in this context. There is another important consideration: in the public law context, if the plaintiff wins, by definition everyone benefits. Holding preclusion inapplicable in this context would encourage fence-sitting, because nonparties would benefit if the plaintiffs were successful but would not be penalized if the plaintiffs lost.

D.

We conclude that issue preclusion based on virtual representation is appropriate in this case. . . .

First, both the Aldermen-*AAVR* suit and the *Miller* suit raise similar claims, and there was an overlap in plaintiffs between the two suits. Further, attorney Miner was plaintiffs' counsel in the Miller suit, and he was substituted as counsel in the Aldermen-*AAVR* suit on April 24, 1992, well before the City's summary judgment motion was granted. These factors suggest, at least partly, that a close relationship exists between the prior and present parties. . . .

We further note that plaintiff Carter, potential plaintiffs Clay Jr. and Jones, and all of the Aldermen plaintiffs were elected African-American officials. They all shared the same concern: the dilution of the African-American vote in St. Louis. This organizational commonality suggests a special commonality of interests. . . .

More importantly, . . . there is tactical maneuvering taking place in *Miller*. In an effort to circumvent trial strategy disagreements, the Aldermen plaintiffs filed the *Miller* suit, simply adding new plaintiffs. This second lawsuit directly contravenes the policies supporting the preclusion nonparty could refile suit, thereby tactically maneuvering around counsel's deficient performance. Thus, applying preclusion in this situation not only reinforces the goal of judicial economy, but it also prevents an end-run around the rule that parties are responsible for the acts of their counsel.

doctrines. A victory by the Aldermen plaintiffs in the Aldermen-*AAVR* suit would have directly benefited the Miller plaintiffs. On the other hand, without virtual representation, a loss by the Aldermen plaintiffs would cause no harm to the Miller plaintiffs. In such a situation, there is no incentive to intervene. Quite the contrary: holding preclusion inapplicable assures that a party would not intervene, for it would allow various members of a coordinated group to bring separate lawsuits in the hope that one member of the group would eventually be successful, benefiting the entire group. This entails a significant cost to the judicial system and "discourage[s] the principles and polices the doctrine of res judicata was designed to promote." [*Petit*, 766 F. Supp.] at 613.

Finally, that the *Miller* case raises an issue of public law is another factor in favor of preclusion. The Miller plaintiffs do not allege that they have been denied the individual right to vote. Rather, they allege that the strength of the black vote in general has been diluted. Because the plaintiffs do not allege that they "have a different private right not shared in common with the public," Stromberg v. Board of Educ. of Bratenahl, 64 Ohio St.2d 98, 18 O.O.3d 343, 413 N.E.2d 1184, 1186 (1980) (cited approvingly by *Richards*, [517 U.S. at 803]), the plaintiffs raise an issue of public law, and thus the due process concerns attendant with a broad application of preclusion are lessened. See *Richards*, [517 U.S. at 803]. Further, given the public nature of this case, if we held preclusion inapplicable, this case could "assume immortality," . . . and fence-sitting would be encouraged.

The Miller plaintiffs contend that preclusion is inappropriate because the Aldermen plaintiffs did not adequately represent their interests at the first trial. They note that counsel in the Aldermen-*AAVR* suit failed to file a formal motion in opposition to the summary judgment motion. Plaintiffs argue that absent an effective and diligent prosecution of the case at the first trial, virtual representation is inapplicable. We disagree.

As noted above, adequate representation is best viewed in terms of incentive to litigate. See *supra* note 7. The Aldermen plaintiffs had every incentive and opportunity to fully litigate the claims raised in the Aldermen-*AAVR* suit. No more is required. . . .

Given the factors counseling in favor of preclusion, we determine that the Aldermen plaintiffs adequately represented the interests of the Miller plaintiffs, and thus the two sets of plaintiffs are in privity. The Miller plaintiffs have vicariously had their day in court and their "one bite at the apple." As such, they are precluded from litigating those issues that were decided by the Aldermen-*AAVR* suit.

III.

We conclude that the Aldermen plaintiffs adequately represented the interests of the Miller plaintiffs and thus acted as their virtual representatives during the Aldermen-*AAVR* suit. As such, the Miller plaintiffs are precluded from relitigating those issues that were litigated in the Aldermen-*AAVR* suit. We affirm the district court's grant of summary judgment.

■ HENLEY, Senior Circuit Judge, concurring in the result. . . . [O]n balance, I agree with the panel's result: that the present case is barred by the previous litigation. Nevertheless, the case is a close one and I am uncomfortable with some of the panel's language. Accordingly, this brief statement of my reasons for concurring only in the result is tendered.

In general, I have some concern about how far we should go in extending preclusive effect to cases of so-called "virtual representation." As the panel points out, due process considerations provide an outer limit on the scope of preclusion. It is one thing to hold that a party in privity under principles of contract or property law should be bound by the results of prior litigation. It is quite another matter, however, to say that strangers to the prior litigation should be bound solely because they would raise the same issue or favor the same legal position.

More specifically, in this case, I believe it is a close question whether our result is fully consistent with the language and spirit of the Supreme Court's decision this term in Richards v. Jefferson County, Alabama, 517 U.S. 793 (1996). In *Richards*, the Court . . . said that the taxpayers in the second suit could not be bound by the decision on the merits in the first suit, because they received neither "notice of, nor sufficient representation in" the prior litigation. [517 U.S. at 804.]

The panel opinion does not directly address the issue of "notice" here and concludes that all that is necessary to satisfy the "sufficient representation" prong of *Richards* is that the plaintiffs in the first suit had the "incentive" to raise the same issues the parties in the second suit would raise. However, the Supreme Court's opinion appears to require something more than just incentive: "a prior proceeding, to have binding effect on absent parties, would at least have to be 'so devised and applied as to insure . . . that the litigation is so conducted as to insure the *full and fair consideration* of the common issue.'" *Richards*, [517 U.S. at 801], quoting, Hansberry v. Lee, 311 U.S. 32, 43 (1940) (emphasis added).

Despite these misgivings about the proposition of "virtual representation" preclusion in general and some of the language of the panel's opinion, I believe that on the facts here, the requirements of "notice" and "sufficient representation" were satisfied. In particular, the plaintiffs in the second suit clearly were on notice of the first litigation, because some of them had also been plaintiffs in the prior suit. Moreover, the same counsel represented plaintiffs in both actions. I believe that this identity of counsel and (at least some of the) plaintiffs also suggests that the "sufficient representation" requirement of due process was met. In addition, as the panel opinion points out, it appears that the principal reason for filing the second suit was to evade the judgment in the first suit.

It is noted, however, that the first suit was not filed as a class action, that the litigation was disposed of on motion for summary judgment, and that plaintiffs there filed only one affidavit and no brief opposing summary judgment. On these facts, it is not at all clear to me that under *Richards* a new plaintiff or group of plaintiffs — not on notice that their rights would be litigated in the first suit nor adequately represented there — would be barred from challenging the St. Louis districting plan even though there was a judgment on the merits in the first suit.

HARDY v. JOHNS-MANVILLE SALES CORP.

681 F.2d 334 (5th Cir. 1982)

■ GEE, Circuit Judge. [The facts in *Hardy* are described p. 194, *supra*. Briefly, the plaintiffs argued, and the district court ordered, that defendants in an asbestos product liability case were collaterally estopped from relitigating the unavoidably unsafe nature of asbestos, the absence or ineffectiveness of warnings on asbestos products, and the ability of asbestos to cause mesothelioma and asbestosis due to the adverse factual findings in a prior asbestos case, the *Borel* case. The order estopped not only the six defendants that had been parties in *Borel*, but also fourteen defendants that had not been parties in *Borel*. In this portion of the opinion, the court considered whether such issue preclusion against the fourteen nonparty defendants was permissible.]

In the wake of Parklane [Hosiery Co. v. Shore, 439 U.S. 322 91979) (p. 160, *supra*)], it is clear that a right, question, or fact distinctly put in issue and directly determined as a ground of recovery by a court of competent jurisdiction collaterally estops a party or his privy from relitigating the issue in a subsequent action. So stated, the doctrine recognizes that a person "cannot be bound by a judgment unless he has had reasonable notice of the claim against him and opportunity to be heard in opposition to that claim.["] 1B J. Moore, Moore's Federal Practice ¶ 0.411 at 1252 (2d ed. 1982) . . . The right to a full and fair opportunity to litigate an issue is, of course, protected by the due process clause of the United States Constitution. . . . Hansberry v. Lee, 311 U.S. 32 (1940). While *Parklane* made the doctrine of mutuality effectively a dead letter under federal law, the case left undisturbed the requisite of privity, *i.e.*, that collateral estoppel can only be applied against parties who have had a prior "'full and fair' opportunity to litigate their claims." 439 U.S. at 332. The requirement that a person against whom the conclusive effect of a judgment is invoked must be a party or a privy to the prior judgment retains its full vigor after *Parklane* and has been repeatedly affirmed by our court. . . .

THE NON-*BOREL* DEFENDANTS

This is the first and, in our view, insurmountable problem with the trial court's application of collateral estoppel in the case sub judice. The omnibus order under review here does not distinguish between defendants who were parties to *Borel* and those who were not; it purports to estop all defendants because all purportedly share an "identity of interests" sufficient to constitute privity. The trial court's action stretches "privity" beyond meaningful limits. While we acknowledge the manipulability of the notion of "privity," . . . this has not prevented courts from establishing guidelines on the permissibility of binding nonparties through res judicata or collateral estoppel. Without such guidelines, the due process guarantee of a full and fair opportunity to litigate disappears. Thus, we noted in *Southwest Airlines Co. v. Texas International Airlines*, 546 F.2d 84, 95 (5th Cir. 1977):

> Federal courts have deemed several types of relationships "sufficiently close" to justify preclusion. First, a nonparty who has succeeded to a party's interest in property is bound by any prior judgments against that party.... Second, a nonparty who controlled the original suit will be bound by the resulting judgment.... Third, federal courts will bind a nonparty whose interests were represented adequately by a party in the original suit.

(citations omitted). The rationale for these exceptions — all derived from Restatement (Second) of Judgments §§ 30, 31, 34, 39-41 (1982) — is obviously that in these instances the nonparty has in effect had his day in court. In this case, the exceptions elaborated in *Southwest Airlines* and in the Restatement are inapplicable. First, the *Borel* litigation did not involve any property interests. Second, none of the non-*Borel* defendants have succeeded to any property interest held by the *Borel* defendants. Finally, the plaintiffs did not show that any non-*Borel* defendant had any control whatever over the *Borel* litigation. "To have control of litigation requires that a person have effective choice as to the legal theories and proofs to be advanced in behalf of the party to the action. He must also have control over the opportunity to obtain review." Restatement (Second) of Judgments § 39, comment c (1982).... In, for example, Sea-Land Services v. Gaudet, 414 U.S. 573 (1974), the Supreme Court held that a nonparty may be collaterally estopped from relitigating issues necessarily decided in a suit by a party who acted as a fiduciary responsible for the beneficial interests of the nonparties. Even in this context, however, the Court placed the exception within strict confines: "In such cases, 'the beneficiaries are bound by the judgment with respect to the interest which was the subject of the fiduciary relationship....'" Id. at 593-94 ... Many of our circuit's cases evince a similar concern with keeping the nonparties' exceptions to res judicata and collateral estoppel within strict confines. See, *e.g.*, *Southwest Airlines Co. v. Texas International Airlines*, supra.

The fact that all the non-*Borel* defendants, like the *Borel* defendants, are engaged in the manufacture of asbestos-containing products does not evince privity among the parties. The plaintiffs did not demonstrate that any of the non-*Borel* defendants participated in any capacity in the *Borel* litigation — whether directly or even through a trade representative — or were even part of a trustee-beneficiary relationship with any *Borel* defendant. On the contrary, several of the defendants indicate on appeal that they were not even aware of the *Borel* litigation until those proceedings were over and that they were not even members of industry or trade associations composed of asbestos product manufacturers.[6]

Plaintiffs can draw little support from the doctrine of "virtual representation" of cases such as Aerojet-General Corp. v. Askew, [511 F.2d

---

6. Since *Borel* was neither designated nor approved as a class action, there can be no claim that any non-*Borel* defendant is bound as representative of a class.

710 (5th Cir.), cert. denied, 423 U.S. 908 (1975),] in which we stated that "(u)nder the federal law of res judicata, a person may be bound by a judgment even though not a party if one of the parties to the suit is so closely aligned with his interests as to be his virtual representative" and that "the question whether a party's interests in a case are virtually representative of the interests of a nonparty is one of fact for the trial court." 511 F.2d at 719. In that case we approved a district court's determination that the interests of two government entities were so closely aligned that a prior judgment against one entity bound the other. The proposition that governments may represent private interests in litigation, thereby precluding relitigation, while uncertain at the margin, appears to be an unexceptional special instance of the examples noted in Restatement (Second) of Judgments § 41(1) (1982).[7] The facts here permit no inference of virtual representation of interest. As we explained in Pollard v. Cockrell, 578 F.2d 1002, 1008-9 (5th Cir. 1978):

> Virtual representation demands the existence of an express or implied legal relationship in which parties to the first suit are accountable to nonparties who file a subsequent suit raising identical issues. . . . Representation by the same attorneys cannot furnish the requisite alignment of interest . . . .

The court's omnibus order here amounts to collateral estoppel based on similar legal positions — a proposition that has been properly rejected by at least one other district court that considered the identical issue. Mooney v. Fibreboard Corp., 485 F. Supp. 242, 249 (E.D. Tex. 1980). We agree with the Texas Supreme Court that "privity is not established by the mere fact that persons may happen to be interested in the same question or in proving the same state of facts," Benson v. Wanda Petroleum Co., 468 S.W.2d 361, 363 (Tex. 1971), and hold that the trial court's actions here transgress the bounds of due process.

Our conclusion likewise pertains to those defendants who, while originally parties to the *Borel* litigation, settled before trial. The plaintiffs here did not show that any of these defendants settled out of the *Borel* litigation after the entire trial had run its course and only the judicial act of

---

7. § 41. Person Represented by a Party

(1) A person who is not a party to an action but who is represented by a party is bound by and entitled to the benefits of a judgment as though he were a party. A person is represented by a party who is:

(a) The trustee of an estate or interest of which the person is a beneficiary; or

(b) Invested by the person with authority to represent him in an action; or

(c) The executor, administrator, guardian, conservator, or similar fiduciary manager of an interest of which the person is a beneficiary; or

(d) An official or agency invested by law with authority to represent the person's interests; or

(e) The representative of a class of persons similarly situated, designated as such with the approval of the court, of which the person is a member.

(2) A person represented by a party to an action is bound by the judgment even though the person himself does not have notice of the action, is not served with process, or is not subject to service of process.

signing a final known adverse judgment remained. Such action would suggest settlement precisely to avoid offensive collateral estoppel and, in an appropriate case, might preclude relitigation. All the indications here are, however, that the defendants in question settled out of the case early because of, for example, lack of product identification. Like the non-*Borel* defendants, these defendants have likewise been deprived of their day in court by the trial court's omnibus order.

LYNCH v. MERRELL-NATIONAL LABORATORIES

646 F. Supp. 856 (D. Mass. 1986), *aff'd* on other grounds, 830 F.2d 1190 (1st Cir. 1987)

■ MAZZONE, District Judge. This matter is before the Court on the defendant's motion for summary judgment. The case involves a claim for damages brought by the parents on behalf of a minor plaintiff, Margo Lynch, and individually as well, against the defendant Merrell-National Laboratories ("Merrell Dow"). The plaintiffs allege that Margo Lynch sustained injury in the form of the congenital absence of her right forearm as a result of the ingestion of the defendant's prescription pharmaceutical, Bendectin, by plaintiff's mother, Margaret Lynch, during her pregnancy. In support of its motion for summary judgment, the defendant has filed an extensive record, consisting of excerpts of deposition and trial testimony of nineteen expert witnesses, numerous Bendectin epidemiological studies, and an appendix containing a list of other Bendectin cases, an index of the Bendectin multi-district litigation including juror questionnaires, instructions, special questions and an exhaustive and thoughtful ruling by the trial judge in that litigation denying the plaintiffs' motions for judgment notwithstanding the verdict and for new trial. The plaintiffs have opposed the motion and have supported their opposition with a memorandum.

The two issues are: (1) whether the plaintiffs are collaterally estopped from relitigating the issue of Bendectin's role in the causation of birth defects; and (2) whether there is any factual dispute on the issue of causation. As to the first issue, the defendants claim the plaintiffs should be bound by the result of the multidistrict trial in which the jury concluded that Bendectin did not cause human birth defects. The plaintiffs say that because they did not participate in that trial, they are not bound by that result, and further, that the result is not conclusive because other cases have produced a different result favorable to them. . . .

[The Judicial Panel for Multidistrict Litigation, whose workings we shall describe in detail in Chapter Four, transferred hundreds of Bendectin cases to Judge Rubin the Southern District of Ohio. The cases were transferred for purposes of pretrial proceedings, not for trial. Among the cases transferred was *Lynch*, which had been filed in the District of Massachusetts.] Upon completion of multidistrict discovery, Judge Rubin consolidated for trial all cases originally filed in the Northern and Southern Districts of Ohio, and adopted an "opt-in" procedure, allowing plaintiffs in cases filed in other districts to participate in the proceedings upon application of plaintiffs' counsel. Approximately 1174 plaintiffs were represented at that trial. For reasons not clear in the record, the plaintiffs in the present case, although participating in the multidistrict discovery, elected not to participate in the trial. They chose instead to have their case returned to this court for a separate proceeding. . . .

The case is now before this Court for further proceedings. In a nutshell, the plaintiffs in the present case seek to relitigate the issue of whether Bendectin causes human birth defects. Plaintiffs here assert that they should not be precluded from relitigating this issue because they were not named parties in the consolidated trial, nor were they in "privity" with any parties to that proceeding. They claim that they had no financial or proprietary interest in the consolidated case, nor did they supply an attorney or in any manner exercise control over that litigation. Furthermore, plaintiffs claim that the exercise of their discretionary right not to intervene in the earlier, consolidated litigation, should not preclude the assertion of their claim here and that they would be denied their constitutional right to a trial if they were precluded. I turn, then, to the first question: whether the doctrine of collateral estoppel should be invoked under these facts to preclude plaintiffs from relitigating the issue of Bendectin's alleged responsibility for human birth defects. . . .

[After reviewing numerous cases applying issue preclusion against parties to the prior action, the court continued:] Other circuits have invoked the doctrine of collateral estoppel when, as in this case, a plaintiff has elected as a matter of litigation strategy to forego an opportunity to intervene in an action. In National Wildlife Fed'n v. Gorsuch, 744 F.2d 963 (3rd Cir. 1983), the Third Circuit held that collateral estoppel was properly invoked against plaintiffs who, though not parties to an earlier action, bypassed an opportunity to intervene in the earlier action. Like the plaintiffs in *Gorsuch*, the plaintiffs here "were not outsiders unaware of litigation in progress that would ultimately affect their interests." *Gorsuch*, 744 F.2d at 971-72. In Bronson v. Board of Educ., 525 F.2d 344 (6th Cir. 1975), the Court of Appeals for the Sixth Circuit refused to allow relitigation of racial discrimination claims by new plaintiffs following an earlier action on the same issues brought by different plaintiffs, noting that it would be inequitable to require the defendant school board to repeatedly battle the "same charge of improper conduct if it has been vindicated in an action brought by a person or group who validly and fairly represent those whose rights are alleged to have been infringed." *Bronson*, 525 F.2d at 349.

In Gerrard v. Larsen, 517 F.2d 1127, 1135 (8th Cir. 1975), the court stated that the determination of who should be bound by a prior adjudication ought to be conducted "on a case by case basis by an examination of underlying facts and circumstances rather than by reliance solely upon the formal status of persons against whom an estoppel is asserted." After examination of the underlying facts and circumstances of this case, I conclude that the plaintiffs here should be bound by the results of the consolidated trial.

The issue of causation with respect to Bendectin and birth defects was extensively litigated in the consolidated trial, and the outcome of that litigation should be accorded finality. The claims by plaintiffs in the consolidated trial were representative of all potential claims involving birth defects allegedly caused by the maternal ingestion of Bendectin, and all of the opinion witnesses designated by plaintiffs in this case testified at the consolidated trial. The plaintiffs here unconvincingly argue that their claim differs from those in the consolidated trial. They emphasize that a trial before this Court would focus on the *specific* incident of Margaret Lynch's ingestion of Bendectin. But the central issue in any proceeding involving Bendectin and its role in birth defects is that of causation, and that issue has already been fully litigated in the consolidated trial.

If this case were to be tried, there would be no reason to depart from the careful, thoughtful and fair procedure adopted by Judge Rubin in the earlier trial. Bifurcation would certainly be appropriate. Fed.R.Civ.P. 42(b). The jury's attention should be focused quickly and without distraction if both sides are to receive a fair resolution. The issue is complex; approximately 19 experts would be expected to testify, and the 4 cases tried to date lasted an average of 38 trial days. The jury would be selected in the same manner, employing the same questionnaire and voir dire procedures, and receiving essentially the same instructions. Margo Lynch would not be present in the courtroom, although she could observe the proceedings from the adjoining lobby by electronic means. The jury would be instructed at the outset that while the immediate issue was a medical-legal one, the case involved real people and birth deformity. Therefore, this would not be a mere "academic debate between the medical and scientific experts for each side," as the plaintiffs describe the consolidated trial. The plaintiffs attribute the defendant's verdict in the consolidated trial to the fact that "no individual cases were discussed" or that "confronted with the causation issue in a vacuum, the jury returned a verdict for the defendant." Not only does this argument belittle the jury's role, but it demonstrates the plaintiffs' hope that the presence of Margo Lynch in the courtroom would produce a different and favorable result. This is a case in which there would be no new medical or scientific evidence, no new expert opinion, no new studies, no new data or theories. The plaintiffs point out that a plaintiff's verdict was returned in Oxendine v. Merrell Dow Pharmaceuticals, 506 A.2d 1100 (D.C.C.A. 1986), but that state court trial did not have the full record of the consolidated trial, nor was the case tried under the same procedures. It produced the very inconsistency which the doctrine of collateral estoppel was designed to prevent.

The plaintiffs' constitutional arguments are not persuasive. A significant commonality of interest, sufficient to overcome the plaintiffs' due process objections, existed between the Lynches and the more than 1100 plaintiffs participating in the consolidated trial. The "opt-in" procedure adopted by Judge Rubin was not a commitment that every out-of-state plaintiff would receive a separate jury trial. Under the multidistrict litigation panel's orders, the case could not be transferred for trial, but only for pre-trial proceedings. The cases involving plaintiffs who chose not to participate in the consolidated trial were returned to the originating court for appropriate proceedings. As stated earlier, the record is silent as to the reasons plaintiffs elected not to participate in the consolidated trial. Were the record to reflect a worthy explanation, a lack of confidence in trial counsel, or a compelling distinction between the Lynches' claims and the others, I would have analyzed the doctrine in that light. But the plaintiffs have not provided a single sound reason for their decision. One permissible inference is that the plaintiffs elected not to participate because they felt they would not be bound by a defendants' verdict, but could take advantage of a plaintiffs' verdict by negotiating a favorable settlement or, ironically, by asserting issue preclusion or offensive collateral estoppel against the defendant. This would be the type of tactical or procedural maneuvering that should be discouraged and not rewarded. Imagine the consternation of the over 1100 plaintiffs involved in the prior litigation if the plaintiffs here were allowed to obtain an inconsistent adjudication by nothing more than a change in forum.

I am not unmindful of the harshness this ruling visits on the plaintiffs. But what it boils down to is that the plaintiffs want a second chance. Conclusiveness of adjudication is an important principle. Justice is achieved when a competent jury hears all the relevant and material evidence by competent witnesses on the issue, presented by able, competent counsel, and returns a unanimous verdict. That was achieved in the prior trial and I conclude the plaintiffs here are bound by that result.

[The court then held that, even if collateral estoppel were not appropriate, the available scientific evidence failed to demonstrate a sufficient causal link between Bendectin and human birth defects.]

The defendant's motion for summary judgment is granted and the complaint is to be dismissed.

Notes and Questions

1. Granting that *Richards* is ostensibly a case of claim preclusion and *Tyus* is ostensibly a case of issue preclusion, can you reconcile *Richards* with *Tyus*? Put differently, suppose that in *Richards* the Alabama Supreme Court had proposed to extend only issue preclusive effect to the first taxpayer action. Does the reasoning of the Eighth Circuit in *Tyus* permit the use of issue preclusion to this circumstance? Does the reasoning of the Supreme Court in *Richards* permit issue preclusion in this situation? Obviously, the effects of claim preclusion are more drastic, since claim preclusion bars the assertion of claims that should have been presented, as well as those that were presented. Should that fact make a difference?

2. In the same vein, can you reconcile *Hardy* with *Lynch*? Unlike *Richards* and *Tyus*, *Hardy* and *Lynch* involve claims for damages. Moreover, *Hardy* is different from any of the other cases; it seeks to use preclusion against nonparty defendants, while all the other cases involve preclusion against nonparty plaintiffs. Should either of these differences lead to difference in the rules that should be applied in these cases?

The First Circuit affirmed the judgment in *Lynch* on the ground that the plaintiffs had failed to prove causation. Its opinion made clear, however, that it thought that the trial court had erred in its ruling on issue preclusion:

> [W]e do not believe that either federal or state law would warrant the application of collateral estoppel in the present context. . . . [T]he Sixth

Circuit noted the teaching of *Parklane Hosiery* . . . that later plaintiffs could not invoke to their benefit a favorable result in mass tort litigation. In re Bendectin Products Liability Litigation, [749 F.2d 300, 305 (6th Cir. 1984)]. If later plaintiffs could not, why should the defendant? . . . Estoppel should not be applied unless the plaintiffs had a fair and full opportunity to litigate. . . . But the plaintiffs were allowed to think that they could withdraw from Cincinnati and lose nothing. They did not have a fair opportunity when they understood that their withdrawal would not prejudice them. If they were now bound, the multi-district litigation would in effect have been a class action leaving the Lynches no true option. We believe that their freedom to withdraw and come back to Boston was not illusory.

Lynch v. Merrell-National Laboratories, 830 F.2d 1190, 1192 (1st Cir. 1987). This pointed dicta seems consistent with the Fifth Circuit's approach in *Hardy*. Does it also call into question the Eighth Circuit's approach in *Tyus*?

3. *Richards* holds, and all of the other cases seem to agree, that nonparties to an action cannot, consistent with the due process clause, generally be precluded from re-litigating issues that were decided adversely to the party's interests in a prior similar suit. What vision or understanding of due process is suggested by this rule? Is it that a party's autonomy to present his or her own case is a fundamental historical and political right that cannot be sacrificed merely because it would be efficient or expedient to do so? Under this vision or understanding of due process, are the rules announced in *Tyus* and *Lynch* constitutional?

4. *Richards* and the other cases all recognize that there are exceptions to the rule of non-preclusion; the real debate among the cases concerns the scope of these exceptions. First, § 41 of the Restatement (Second) of Judgments, which is discussed with approval in *Richards* and quoted in footnote 7 of *Hardy*, describes the standard circumstances in which privity binds nonparties to a prior judgment involving a person representing the nonparty: a trustee or executor binding a beneficiary, an agent binding a principal, an official binding those that the official has legal authority to represent, and a class representative approved by the court binding class members. Second, immediately after citing the Restatement (Second), *Richards* also suggests that "in addition" there exists "an exception to the general rule when, in certain limited circumstances, a person, although not a party, has his interests adequately represented by someone with the same interests who is a party." The Court's citation to *Hansberry v. Lee* (a class action case) and *Montana v. United States* (a case alleging that a nonparty controlled the prior litigation) as support for this exception suggest that the exception is no broader than § 41(1)(b) and § 41(1)(e) of the Restatement (Second). Third, *Richards* suggests that a nonparty might be bound by a prior proceeding in which "a special remedial scheme exists expressly foreclosing successive litigation by nonlitigants, as for example in bankruptcy or probate." We have already described to some extent the preclusive effects of class actions (see pp. 174-94, *supra*); and we further explore the scope of class actions and bankruptcy in Chapters Five and Six. Fourth, *Richards* hints that *maybe* notice to and the nonparty's actual knowledge of the prior lawsuit is a fourth situation. We discuss this final possibility in Chapter 2.C, *infra*.

To what extent do these exceptions temper or amend the vision or understanding of due process suggested in Note 3?

5. If the Restatement (Second) and *Richards* state the constitutional limit of nonparty preclusion, preclusion against nonparties will be a rare event (except

in class actions or bankruptcy). That fact would appear to have two further consequences: first, that the success of preclusion doctrines to handle the problem of re-litigation is in some jeopardy, and, second, that an expansive view of class actions and bankruptcy becomes critical to the success of preclusion.

Note, however, that *Richards*, although it cites only *Hansberry v. Lee* and *Montana v. United States*, suggests a somewhat broader principle that preclusion might occur whenever a nonparty is adequately represented in a prior proceeding. A number of courts have seized on the idea of preclusion with adequate representation, and like *Tyus*, have developed a doctrine of "virtual representation" to bind nonparties even when none of the standard privity exceptions apply. See, *e.g.*, Aerojet-General Corp. v. Askew, 511 F.2d 710 (5th Cir.), cert. denied, 423 U.S. 908 (1975) (defendant county bound under claim preclusion to judgment entered in case against defendant state agencies); NAACP v. Hunt, 891 F.2d 1555 (11th Cir. 1990) (plaintiff civil rights organization bound under claim preclusion to judgment entered in case against plaintiff that was member of organization). But exactly how broad is the virtual representation doctrine in *Tyus*? The Eighth Circuit seems to be of two minds on the matter. On the one hand, the actual facts of the case suggest a very limited role for virtual representation — same lawyer, many of the same plaintiffs, tactical maneuvering by the plaintiffs in the second suit. Cf. Benson & Ford, Inc. v. Wanda Petroleum Co., 833 F.2d 1172, 1175 (5th Cir. 1987) (same attorneys not enough to invoke nonparty preclusion in antitrust case). On the other hand, the language of the court suggests a broader role for the doctrine; the court states that it wishes to give a "wider use to the doctrine," it takes a generous reading of the concept of adequate representation (requiring only that the first party have a "strong incentive to protect the interests of the second party"), it relaxes the limitations on the doctrine in public law litigation, it repeatedly relies on preclusion-friendly policies of efficiency and judicial economy, and it takes direct aim at "fence-sitters." This language, if transplanted from the facts of *Tyus* to the remainder of complex and complicated litigation, could be used to achieve a high degree of nonparty preclusion.

A number of courts, including *Hardy*, have rejected the application of a virtual representation theory on the facts of the case, although they have not rejected the idea of virtual representation outright. See Pollard v. Cockrell, 578 F.2d 1002 (5th Cir. 1978); *Benson & Ford*, 833 F.2d 1172; Gonzalez v. Banco Central Corp., 27 F.3d 751 (1st Cir. 1994). *Pollard*'s narrow formulation of the doctrine suggests that a claim of virtual representation will rarely succeed: "Virtual representation demands the existence of an express or implied legal relationship in which parties to the first suit are accountable to non-parties who file a subsequent suit raising identical issues." 578 F.2d at 1008. Likewise, *Gonzalez* has proposed a set of elements that effectively confine the doctrine:

> The upshot is that, today, while identity of interests remains a necessary condition for triggering virtual representation, it is not alone a sufficient condition. More is required to bring the theory to bear. . . . Many of the ensuing questions — questions like "how much more?" and "what comprises 'more'?" — seem to have no categorical answers. . . . There is no black-letter rule. . . . In the end, virtual representation is best understood as an equitable theory rather than as a crisp rule with sharp corners and clear factual predicates, . . . such that a party's status as a virtual representative of a nonparty must be determined on a case-by-case basis . . . .

Although the need for individualized analysis persists, a common thread binds these variegated cases together: virtual representation has a pronounced equitable dimension. Thus, notwithstanding identity of interests, virtual representation will not serve to bar a nonparty's claim unless the nonparty has had actual or constructive notice of the earlier litigation, and the balance of the relevant equities tips in favor of preclusion. For example, courts have applied the doctrine in situations in which a nonparty has given actual or implied consent to be bound by the results in a prior action, . . . or in which there has been "an express or implied legal relationship in which parties to the first suit are accountable to non-parties who file a subsequent suit raising identical issues," . . . or in which certain types of familial relationships link parties and nonparties, . . . or in which courts have detected tactical maneuvering designed unfairly to exploit technical nonparty status in order to obtain multiple bites of the litigatory apple . . . . Implicit in all these scenarios is the existence of actual or constructive notice.

We have considered, and rejected, another possible common characteristic. Some courts have suggested that adequacy of representation is also a condition precedent to nonparty preclusion grounded upon virtual representation. . . . Properly viewed, however, adequacy of representation is not itself a separate and inflexible requirement for engaging principles of virtual representation, although it is one of the factors that an inquiring court should weigh in attempting to balance the equities. [27 F.3d at 760-62.]

See also Southwest Airlines Co. v. Texas International Airlines, 546 F.2d 84, 97 (5th Cir.), cert. denied, 434 U.S. 832 (1977) (stating that the essential question is "the propriety of barring the private interests from relitigation" and that "[f]ederal case law requires that we direct our analysis toward answering that specific question, rather than toward identifying the doctrinal scope of virtual representation").

Finally, some cases have either rejected the theory or at least questioned its existence. For instance, in Tourangeau v Uniroyal, Inc., 101 F.3d 300, 306 (2d Cir. 1996), the court stated that some of its prior decisions holding that adequate representation in a prior lawsuit could preclude a nonparty "are of questionable continued vitality in light of more recent Supreme Court decisions" such as *Richards* and Martin v. Wilks, 490 U.S. 755 (1990) (p. 240, *infra*). Similarly, in Bittinger v. Tecumseh Products Co., 123 F.3d 877 (6th Cir. 1997), plaintiffs in a prior suit had requested that the case be certified as a class action, but the district court dismissed the case on the merits instead. When a new group of plaintiffs filed suit, defendant argued that they had been virtually represented in the prior litigation and were therefore bound by it. The trial court agreed, but the court of appeals reversed. The court of appeals began by noting that neither *Richards* nor the cases it cited — *Hansbery v. Lee* and *Montana v. United States* — "supports the broad notion of 'virtual representation' upon which the district court relied." Id. at 881. The court then proceeded to attack the theory of virtual representation more broadly:

> The "virtual representation" standard converts the traditional doctrine of res judicata from a relatively clear set of rules to a vague principle relying on balancing the equities as a result of a close inspection and analysis of the relationship between the parties in each individual case. A court attempting to apply "virtual representation" must examine the relationship

between the parties to the current suit and parties to the previous suit and look for and balance a variety of elements — including whether the facts demonstrate a close nonlitigating relationship, participation, apparent acquiescence, discussions about the first action, deliberate maneuvering to avoid the effects of the first action, and an express or implied legal relationship in which parties to the first suit are said to be "accountable" to parties to the second. . . . Gonzalez v. Banco Central Corp., 27 F.3d 751 (1st Cir.1994)[;] . . . Tyus v. Schoemehl, 93 F.3d 449, 454 (8th Cir.1996), cert. denied, 117 S.Ct. 1427 (1997) . . .

"Virtual representation" is said by some scholars to be a useful tool for broadening the finality of judgments and enhancing the efficient administration of justice. . . . Ironically, however, its expansion increases the burden on judges, who must apply its multi-factored balancing test to the facts of each case. In this area of the law that must be applied frequently, "crisp rules with sharp corners" are preferable to a round-about doctrine of opaque standards easily manipulated to reach a preferred result. Rules are more predictable and less elastic than standards and "promote economies for the legal decisionmaker by minimizing the elaborate, time-consuming, and repetitive application of background principles to facts." . . . Rules are the normal method used in a jurisprudence of judicial restraint; broad standards and balancing tests are the usual mechanism of a jurisprudence that allows individual judges to choose for themselves the preferred result in each case and to give expression to their feelings, intuition, and sense of justice. Broad standards are often useful and necessary in new areas of the law, particularly those new areas that legislative bodies direct courts to enter for the first time in order to regulate a perceived social problem, as well as in areas of law that traditionally sounded in equity.

"Virtual representation's" intense case-by-case analysis is particularly undesirable in circumstances where its application would replace settled, rule-like procedures. In cases such as the instant case, these procedures already exist in the form of Rule 23. The application of the doctrine of virtual representation in these circumstances would create an end run around the limitations of Rule 23, and would as a result both avoid its limitations (which are explicitly grounded in due process) and replace a clear rule with an unruly standard. Such a result would defeat the purposes of both res judicata and Rule 23. [Id. at 881-82.]

6. Section 41(1)(d) of the Restatement (Second) authorizes preclusion against nonparties in circumstances in which "[a]n official or agency [is] invested by law with authority to represent the person's interests." In certain public law litigation, this rule could potentially be a significant source of preclusion. For instance, although the case was generally skeptical about the doctrine of virtual representation, *Southwest Airlines* is best-known for its rather generous reading of preclusion resulting from prior representation by government authorities. In *Southwest Airlines*, the City of Dallas decided to replace its old airport (Love Field) with a new airport (Dallas-Fort Worth International). In furtherance of this plan, it passed an ordinance that shifted all passenger airline services from Love Field to the new airline. Southwest opposed the move, and the City of Dallas filed suit against Southwest Airlines in order to force Southwest to switch airports. After it lost this suit in federal court, the City passed another ordinance that levied a fine for each takeoff or landing of a passenger airline

from Love Field. Southwest successfully brought suit in federal court against the enforcement of this ordinance.

At that point, several other airlines (known as the "CAB airlines") that feared a competitive disadvantage if Southwest continued to use Love Field filed a case in state court against Southwest. The allegations were functionally identical to those of the City's first suit against Southwest. A number of the CAB airlines had appeared in the first federal suit against Southwest as amicus curiae and had also been parties in some related proceedings in the second federal suit. Southwest returned to federal court to seek an injunction against the state case. The success of its request hinged on whether the private defendants were bound by the judgments in the federal suits. The Fifth Circuit held that they were. Following the Restatement (Second), the court divided private re-litigation into three categories: cases in which the private litigants have no standing, cases in which "an agency's authority to maintain or defend litigation . . . should be construed as preempting the otherwise available opportunity of the individual or members of the public to prosecute," and cases in which "remedies that a public official is empowered to pursue may be interpreted as being supplemental to those which private persons may pursue themselves." 546 F.2d at 99 (internal quotations omitted). Only in the third category of cases could a separate suit be maintained. The court thought that the "facts here best fit the second category of the *Restatement*":

> First, the CAB carriers do not claim a breach of legal duty by Southwest, apart from the alleged violation of the general duty to obey valid ordinances. Second, the carriers request the same remedy denied the City of Dallas, namely the enforcement of the phase-out provision of the ordinance to exclude Southwest from Love Field. Third, the ordinance does not establish a statutory scheme looking toward private enforcement of its requirements. Because legal interests of the carriers do not differ from those of Dallas in [the first federal suit], we hold that they received adequate representation in the earlier litigation and should be bound by the judgment in that litigation.
>
> We have adopted the Restatement approach because it promotes the policies of res judicata in this factual setting. To allow relitigation by any private litigant with a pecuniary interest in the success of the new airport would open the door to recurrent, burdensome litigation . . . [and] would surely defeat the res judicata policies . . . . First, it would add uncertainty to the status not only of Southwest but also of the other businesses and government operations. If courts could second guess another court each time a new litigant, dissatisfied with the previous judgment, filed a new complaint, the respect of the previous parties or of the public toward the courts would inevitably decrease. Third, relitigation would continue to waste judicial resources and time, as it has already in the three post-judgment suits in this controversy. Fourth, Southwest and subsequent litigants would suffer the harassment and expense of still later lawsuits, as well as the possibility of numerous conflicting judgments. . . . We can best support the public interest by applying the *Restatement*'s approach to preclude relitigation by all persons, including the carriers, who claim nothing more than a pecuniary interest in the dispute. [Id. at 100-01.]

Aren't the interests of the *Borel* and non-*Borel* asbestos manufacturers much closer than the interests of the City of Dallas and the CAB airlines? Why is nonparty preclusion proper in the latter case, but not the former? Moreover, recall the Supreme Court's holding in *Trbovich v. United Mine Workers* (p. 144, *supra*) that the somewhat different interests of the government and a private litigant made the government an inadequate representative of the private litigant for purposes of intervention under Rule 24(a). Is *Southwest Airlines* inconsistent with *Trbovich*? If not, is the inconsistency explained by our system's goal to achieve as much preclusion as possible, so that the term "adequacy of representation" must be given whatever meaning best advances that goal in each particular context?

7. The prior discussion presumed the existence of a judgment that might operate to preclude a nonparty. Obviously, nonparty preclusion is unavailable when the parties settle voluntarily, since there is no judgment to which the nonparties can be bound. Given that many cases settle, the requirement of a judgment therefore constitutes a significant practical limitation on the concept of nonparty preclusion.

An intermediate circumstance lying somewhere between a judgment and a voluntary settlement is a consent decree, in which the parties negotiate a resolution and the court then enters a judgment that recites the essential terms of that resolution. Since there is a judgment, can nonparty preclusion principles ever apply? The answer would seem to be "no," unless the nonparty agreed to be bound by the terms of the consent decree. See *Tourangeau*, 101 F.3d at 306-07; see generally Local Number 939, International Association of Firefighters v. City of Cleveland, 478 U.S. 501, 519 (1986) ("consent decrees 'have attributes both of contracts and of judicial decrees,' a dual character that has resulted in different treatment for different purposes").

8. Appellate courts seem to disagree about the deference due a trial court's decision to preclude a nonparty. *Aerojet-General* thought that "[t]he question whether a party's interests in a case are virtually represented is one of fact for the trial court." 511 F.2d at 719. *NAACP v. Hunt* stated that "[t]he question of whether sufficient privity exists to warrant application of *res judicata* is a question of law." 891 F.2d at 1561; see also *Gonzalez*, 27 F.2d at 755 ("applicability *vel non* of the doctrine of res judicata presents a question of law").

9. As we have seen throughout this section of the chapter, an expansion of preclusion doctrine might have certain effects on the scope of joinder law. Consider, for instance, *Tyus*. It holds that two plaintiffs that were not parties to the first suit were nonetheless bound by certain issues determined in that suit. It would be difficult to imagine a clearer example of a situation in which a nonparty would as a practical — and legal — matter find his or her interests impaired or impeded. Thus, the nonparties would assuredly have been able to intervene in the prior suit under Rule 24(a), which permits intervention of right when the putative intervenor's interest "may as a practical matter [be] impair[ed] or imped[ed]." (Indeed, note how the "economy and due process" considerations in *Tyus* replicate the considerations that *Cook v. Boorstin*, p. 137, *supra* used to interpret Rule 24(a).) *Tyus*'s approach virtually requires that these nonparties intervene if they wish to protect their interests. Isn't this practical consequence of *Tyus* inconsistent with the principle, cited in footnote 5 of *Richards* (p. 210, *supra*), that "the law does not impose upon any person absolutely entitled to a hearing the burden of voluntary intervention in a suit to which he is a stranger"? Is it an answer to this argument that, even if *Tyus* is likely to lead to intervention, it does not impose the *legal* obligation of intervention? Is it also an answer that broader joinder should be encouraged, so that preclusion rules that induce broader joinder should also be favored?

But Rule 24(a) is not the only joinder rule affected by a broader use of preclusion. As *Bittinger* notes, Rule 23, the class action rule, would also seem to be affected. But *Bittinger* does not explore the full scope of this effect. Assuming that certain other criteria have also been satisfied, see p. 132-34, *supra*, one of the circumstances in which class actions can be used is when the separate adjudication of individual members' claims "would as a practical matter be dispositive of the interests of the other members not parties to the adjudications or substantially impair or impede their ability to protect their interests." F.R.Civ.P. 23(b)(1)(B). Does a broad use of preclusion in *Tyus* mean that class actions are more likely to be certified? Once a class action exists, however, an expansive use of *Tyus*'s concept of "virtual representation" becomes unnecessary, since the class members are bound to the judgment on the traditional theory of class representation. Isn't there something fishy about expanding a preclusion doctrine that in turn expands a mandatory joinder rule that in turn makes the preclusion doctrine unnecessary?

Rule 19(a) is affected by an expansive reading of preclusion as well. Recall that Rule 19 mandates the joinder, if possible, of a nonparty that "claims an interest relating to the subject matter of the action and is so situated that the disposition of the action may . . . as a practical matter impair or impede the person's ability to protect that interest." If *Lynch* is correct in precluding the Lynches' case, wouldn't the Lynches be classic necessary parties that should be joined in the Ohio litigation under Rule 19(a)? Isn't this fact inconsistent with the spirit of *Temple v. Synthes Corp.* (p. 116, *supra*)? Similarly, once we extend issue preclusion effect to their cases, the two nonparty plaintiffs in *Tyus* would also seem to fit the description of necessary parties. Does this mean that the parties should have invoked Rule 19(a) to join the two *Tyus* plaintiffs in the Aldermen-*AAVR* suit? Isn't this move subject to the same criticism as the comparable move under Rule 23: that it is circular to expand a preclusion that leads to expanded mandatory joinder that in turn destroys the need for the preclusion doctrine? What happens when the precluded plaintiffs cannot be joined — should we still preclude them? Or should we dismiss the suit for failure to join indispensable parties under Rule 19(b)? Assuming that the two plaintiffs could have been joined under Rule 19, shouldn't the City of St. Louis have moved for their joinder and permitted their participation? Is it equitable to now let the City of St. Louis try to invoke preclusion principles against people that they had the power to join in the suit? Who is sandbagging in this case — the two plaintiffs, the City of St. Louis, or both?

Do these questions, which *Tyus* and *Lynch* never address, make you less enthusiastic about the outcome in these cases?

10. Preclusion against nonparties also raises many of the autonomy-based concerns of mandatory joinder that were described in Section 2.A, *supra*. Obviously, however, the autonomy concerns are even greater here, for mandatory joinder merely prevents a plaintiff from deciding when and where to bring a suit, while preclusion prevents a party from ever bringing a suit (or at least certain critical issues in the suit).

11. Another concern with an expanded use of preclusion against nonparties is its potentially outcome-determinative effect. It is fashionable these days to distinguish "mature" from "immature" litigation. The basic sense of this distinction is that "mature" litigation has evolved, as a result of a fairly large number of individual judgments and settlements, to the point that the likely outcome and damages award for comparably situated plaintiffs can be

determined with some degree of accuracy. "Immature" litigation, by contrast, is still in the process of evolving into a mature state. Thus, individual judgments are often aberrational; the true "value" of a claim can only be developed over time. See Francis E. McGovern, *Toward a Functional Approach for Managing Complex Litigation*, 53 U. Chi. L. Rev. 440 (1986); Francis E. McGovern, *Resolving Mature Mass Tort Litigation*, 69 B.U. L. Rev. 659 (1989); Francis E. McGovern, *An Analysis of Mass Torts for Judges*, 73 Tex. L. Rev. 1821 (1995). A corollary of this idea is that the growth from immaturity to maturity often follows a predictable cycle: defendants, who often have better access to information, win many of the early cases; plaintiffs adjust and refine their litigation strategies and achieve breakthrough victories; defendants then adjust their strategies; plaintiffs adjust theirs; and eventually, in the stage of full maturity, an equilibrium is reached. See Paul Brodeur, Outrageous Misconduct (1985) (detailing cycle in asbestos litigation).

If the maturity thesis is correct, then doctrines that seek to prevent relitigation of immature claims may well be unwise, for such doctrines will have a substantive effect on the outcome of the litigation. If the corollary to the thesis is also correct, this substantive effect is most likely to be skewed in favor of defendants. Although this effect is likely to encompass both mandatory joinder and preclusion doctrines that operate on immature litigation, the effect may be especially telling in the context of preclusion doctrines; unlike mandatory joinder doctrines, which at least permit the parties to participate and provide additional perspectives on the way in which to conduct the litigation, preclusion doctrines that operate against nonparties force the nonparties to accept a judgment in a case framed by one prior perspective.

This "maturity" concern has certain limits. One is that it seems most applicable to cases seeking money damages, such as mass torts, securities fraud, or antitrust damages actions. Since both *Richards* and *Tyus* sought injunctive relief, the maturity argument may not affect our views of the proper outcomes in these cases. Nor would it necessarily affect our thinking about the use of preclusion against nonparty defendants, unless plaintiffs seek to invoke the doctrine as soon as they obtain breakthrough victories (as seems to have occurred in *Hardy*). But it would be a forceful concern in cases like *Lynch*, in which plaintiffs had not yet been successful in leveling the playing field with breakthrough victories. A second limit is that the maturity concern ends once the litigation becomes mature. At that point, continued prosecution of individual suits serves no useful purpose; rather, some method (whether joinder or preclusion) is needed both to prevent needless re-litigation and to ensure the fair and consistent treatment of all. Thus, the maturity argument is inconsistent with a strong view of litigant autonomy. Finally, once such joinder or preclusion occurs, a third limit arises: the decision not to prevent re-litigation prior to maturity means that we must tolerate a degree of inter-plaintiff inequality (some plaintiffs will have lost, some will have won a lot, and the rest will have achieved some middle equilibrium amount).

To what extent should the maturity concern affect the shape of our rules of preclusion against nonparties?

12. Should the complicated or complex nature of a case also affect the shape of these preclusion rules? In complicated litigation, the goal is to reduce inefficient re-litigation. As the materials in this section have shown, this goal would seem to suggest a fairly broad role for preclusion rules; when joined with a broadened use of offensive collateral estoppel, a broadened use of preclusion

against nonparties is one way to prevent inefficient re-litigation. Indeed, broadened preclusion may be a superior alternative to broadened rules of mandatory joinder, since joinder rules lead to messy, hydra-headed litigation that is difficult to resolve efficiently. Thus, from the viewpoint of complicated litigation, *Richards* and *Hardy* may well be wrongly decided, while *Tyus* and *Lynch* are rightly decided.

In complex litigation, the goal is to eliminate the dysfunction created by the lawyers' inability to fulfill their adversarial roles. Whether a broadened use of preclusion against nonparties can eliminate dysfunction is a difficult question. To begin with, *Richards* is probably not a complex case. Complex litigation arises when a defendant has insufficient assets, nonparties are bound to a judgment in which they did not participate, or nonparties can undo relief that other parties obtained in a prior case. *Richards* does not implicate the first concern (insufficient assets). Since the *Bedingfield* plaintiffs had obtained no relief in their litigation, and in any event the relief that the *Richards* plaintiffs sought was identical to the relief sought by the *Bedingfield* plaintiffs, *Richards* did not involve the third concern (the problem of "zero-sum" relief in which later litigants would be taking away relief that earlier litigants had obtained). The second concern (binding nonparties) would have been involved only if *Richards* had been decided the opposite way. In other words, viewed through the lens of complex litigation, *Richards* is correct precisely because it prevents a form of lawyer dysfunction from arising!

On this same analysis, *Tyus* is an unfortunate case. Like *Richards*, *Tyus* does not implicate the first and third ways in which dysfunction can arise. Unlike *Richards*, the language and analysis of *Tyus* suggest that a court can often bind nonparties to the outcome of the first litigation — a result that would create the second form of complexity because later litigants and their lawyers would have been deprived of a meaningful opportunity to shape their own proofs and arguments. Although this fact suggests that *Tyus* might well be wrongly decided, the result in *Tyus* could perhaps be salvaged by the fact that the plaintiffs' lawyer in the Aldermen-*AAVR* case and *Tyus* was the same, so that no deprivation of the opportunity to present proofs and arguments occurred in fact. But it does not seem that *Tyus* bases its holding principally on this fact. Similarly, *Tyus* might be salvaged if its effect were to force broad mandatory joinder that prevented lawyer dysfunction. See Note 9, *supra*. Again, however, it does not seem that *Tyus* intended to produce this effect, nor is it clear that it will do so. Thus, *Tyus* might well be complexity-causing, rather than complexity-reducing.

Using a comparable complexity analysis, the result in *Hardy* is probably correct, and the result in *Lynch* is probably incorrect. In the context of a claim for money damages, the complexity-causing concern is the insufficiency of assets for later parties, rather than the binding effect of an injunction on later parties. Hence, broader preclusion rules would seem to be justifiable when the issue had been fully and fairly litigated before and when broader preclusion can preserve sufficient assets to make the later-filing plaintiffs whole. *Lynch* would not appear to be a case of insufficient assets; hence, the use of broad preclusion rules was unnecessary. Furthermore, given *Lynch*'s negative effect on the plaintiffs' adversarial rights to present proofs and arguments, the case's potential to create lawyer dysfunction suggests that the First Circuit was right to disapprove it. Unlike *Lynch*, *Hardy* was a case of insufficient assets, but the amount of that insufficiency was so staggeringly large that the amount saved by not having to re-litigate the common issues would not have converted the case from one of insufficient assets to one of sufficient assets.

Hardy also presents the question of using preclusion against defendants. Under a complexity analysis, the conclusion that nonparty preclusion should be sparingly used would be the same, albeit for somewhat different reasons than the reasons mentioned above. Preclusion might be justified when the issue had been fully and fairly litigated and when preclusion would bring into the litigation enough additional defendants that the problem of insufficient assets would be overcome. There are, however, some significant limitations on this use of preclusion. First, the identity of interests between the original defendant in the first suit and the new defendant in the second suit needs to be very tight. Second, care must be taken to include in the second suit all the plaintiffs with a stake in the assets; otherwise, the problem of insufficiency of assets will not really have been removed. Thus, preclusion of defendants to prevent complexity can exist successfully only when some form of mandatory plaintiff joinder is also employed. Since the facts of *Hardy* may well fall short of satisfying the first of these conditions, and certainly fall short of the second, *Hardy* correctly refused to apply preclusion against the nonparty defendants.

13. Until now, we have seen that complexity is caused by factors external to the court, and have critiqued courts' interpretations of various joinder and preclusion doctrines for their failure to be sensitive enough to these factors. If the observations in the last Note are accurate, *Tyus* and *Lynch* present an occasion in which the courts' interpretation of a doctrine itself causes dysfunction. Is there any justification for a court adding to the problem of lawyer dysfunction? Is the stated reason in *Tyus* and *Lynch* — the promotion of judicial economy — enough of a justification?

Throughout the chapter we have suggested that our present procedural rules are best understood as being more consistent with the requirements of an adversarial procedural system and the problem of lawyer dysfunction than with the requirements of an efficient procedural system and the problem of wasteful re-litigation. With *Tyus* and *Lynch* as arguable exceptions to this statement, it would appear that the courts' generally conservative approach to nonparty preclusion continues to prove the thesis. As we have observed before, however, the thesis is descriptive rather than normative in nature, so that its present truth does not require our continued adherence to it. Is there a normative reason to adhere to adversarial process up to the point at which the process becomes dysfunctional?

14. Professor Bone would probably answer the last question with a resounding "No." In an important article that surveys the doctrine of nonparty preclusion and analyzes it against various procedural values and theories (including process-oriented participation theories and outcome-oriented participation theories like efficiency-based adjudication and rights-based adjudication), Bone concludes that the "assumption basic to the conventional account of the day in court ideal — that each person has an individual right to control her own lawsuit — is wrong on positive and normative grounds. The history of virtual representation doctrine shows the assumption to be wrong as a positive account of preclusion doctrine, and an analysis from first principles sensitive to different participation theories shows it to be wrong as a normative ideal as well." Robert G. Bone, *Rethinking the "Day in Court" Ideal and Nonparty Preclusion*, 67 N.Y.U. L. Rev. 193 (1992). According to Bone, the "day in court" ideal "is responsible for an unduly narrow and formalistic set of rules

supported by little in the way of reasoned justification," but he also contends that "[t]here is a way out of the muddle":

> It is to abandon the assumption that all individuals have a right to strategic freedom in litigation. Both history and theory suggest a more sensible starting point: the extent of an individual's right to participate in litigation should vary with the type of case. This new premise calls for a no-participation rather than a representation theory of nonparty preclusion. Instead of asking whether the absentee has actually participated through a surrogate, courts ought to ask whether the absentee has any normative claim to participate at all, and, if she does, how strong her claim is and what sort of participation opportunities it demands.
>
> The answer to this new question depends on one's theories of participation and adjudication. Within outcome-oriented theory, an efficiency-based approach calls for a different set of rules than does a rights-based approach, and each makes different demands on participation than approaches grounded in process-oriented theory. Yet, all these approaches agree on one point: current nonparty preclusion law is unjustifiably narrow. [Id. at 288-89.]

Do you agree with Bone's assessment of preclusion law and of the role of litigant autonomy? Do you agree that the level of participation to which persons are entitled should vary with the circumstance? See James R. Pielemeier, *Due Process Limitations on the Application of Collateral Estoppel Against Nonparties to Prior Litigation*, 63 B.U. L. Rev. 383 (1983).

15. Among the nonparty preclusion ideas which Bone recommends for consideration is the idea that a party who has notice of a prior case and an opportunity to participate in it should be bound by the judgment in the prior case. Id. at 270. Thus far, we have not explored this intriguing suggestion — which also surfaced in *Richards*, in Judge Henley's concurrence in *Tyus*, in *Lynch*, and in *Gonzalez*. In the final section of this chapter, we examine this cutting edge concept, which lies at the intersection of expanded rules of mandatory party joinder rules and broadened rules of preclusion.

C. MARRYING PARTY JOINDER AND PRECLUSION: THE BRAVE NEW WORLD OF PRECLUSION AFTER NOTICE AND OPPORTUNITY TO INTERVENE

By now it should be apparent that neither the rules of party joinder nor the rules of claim and issue preclusion are entirely capable of addressing the problems of lawyer dysfunction in complex cases; nor do they overcome the inefficiencies of re-litigation in complicated cases. Although numerous other factors also come into play, much of the resistance to broader joinder or preclusion rules seems grounded in the strong preference, to some extent constitutionalized in the due process clause, for a litigant's autonomy to control his or her own litigation. In turn, that preference finds voice in our traditional adversarial process.

As you studied the joinder and preclusion materials, you might have wondered whether it is possible to come to some reconciliation of our competing interests in the preservation of individual autonomy, the prevention of lawyer dysfunction, and the prevention of inefficient relitigation. You might also have wondered whether this middle path might be found through blending the best aspects of joinder and preclusion. In fact, there presently exists one such proposal. The essential idea is this: Persons with an interest in the adjudication of a particular fact or issue are given notice of an existing litigation in which that fact or issue will be decided. These persons are then extended the opportunity to intervene in the litigation as parties. Whether they intervene or not, they are bound by both favorable and unfavorable factual and legal determinations in the litigation. Since persons that intervene in a case are bound by the relevant aspects of the judgment under our present rules of joinder and preclusion, the novelty of this proposal lies particularly in two of its features: the provision of notice to nonparties and the use of issue preclusion either for or against nonparties that choose to remain on the sidelines.

In this section we examine the benefits and drawbacks of this proposal, which lies on the frontier of complex litigation.

MARTIN v. WILKS

490 U.S. 755 (1989)

■ CHIEF JUSTICE REHNQUIST delivered the opinion of the Court.

A group of white firefighters sued the city of Birmingham, Alabama (City), and the Jefferson County Personnel Board (Board) alleging that they were being denied promotions in favor of less qualified black firefighters. They claimed that the City and the Board were making promotion decisions on the basis of race in reliance on certain consent decrees, and that these decisions constituted impermissible racial discrimination in violation of the Constitution and federal statute. The District Court held that the white firefighters were precluded from challenging employment decisions taken pursuant to the decrees, even though these firefighters had not been parties to the proceedings in which the decrees were entered. We think this holding contravenes the general rule that a person cannot be deprived of his legal rights in a proceeding to which he is not a party.

The litigation in which the consent decrees were entered began in 1974, when the Ensley Branch of the National Association for the Advancement of Colored People and seven black individuals filed separate class-action complaints against the City and the Board. They alleged that both had engaged in racially discriminatory hiring and promotion practices in various public service jobs in violation of Title VII of the Civil Rights Act of 1964, 42 U.S.C. § 2000e et seq., and other federal law. After a bench trial on some issues, but before judgement, the parties entered into two consent decrees, one between the black individuals and the City and the other between them and the Board. These proposed decrees set forth an extensive remedial scheme, including long-term and interim annual goals for the hiring of blacks as firefighters. The decrees also provided for goals for promotion of blacks within the fire department.

The District Court entered an order provisionally approving the decrees and directing publication of notice of the upcoming fairness hearings. Notice of the hearings, with a reference to the general nature of the decrees, was published in two local newspapers. At that hearing, the Birmingham Firefighters Association (BFA) appeared and filed objections as *amicus curiae*. After the hearing, but before final approval of the decrees, the BFA and two of its members also moved to intervene on the ground that the decrees would adversely affect their rights. The District Count denied the motions as untimely and approved the decrees. . . . Seven white firefighters, all members of the BFA, then filed a complaint against the City and the Board seeking injunctive relief against enforcement of the decrees. The seven argued that the decrees would operate to illegally discriminate against them; the District Court denied relief.

Both the denial of intervention and the denial of injunctive relief were affirmed on appeal. . . . The District Court had not abused its discretion in refusing to let the BFA intervene, thought the Eleventh Circuit, in part because the firefighters could "institut[e] an independent Title VII suit, asserting specific violations of their rights." . . . And, for the same reason, petitioners had not adequately shown the potential for irreparable harm from the operation of the decrees necessary to obtain injunctive relief. . . .

A new group of white firefighters, the *Wilks* respondents, then brought suit against the City and the Board in District Court. They too alleged that, because of their race, they were being denied promotion in favor of less qualified blacks in violation of federal law. The Board and the City admitted to making race conscious employment decisions, but argued that the decisions were unassailable because they were made pursuant to the consent decrees. A group of black individuals, the *Martin* petitioners, were allowed to intervene in their individual capacities to defend the decrees.

The defendants moved to dismiss the reverse discrimination cases as impermissible collateral attacks on the consent decrees. The District Court denied the motions, ruling that the decrees would provide a defense to claims of discrimination for employment decisions "mandated" by the decrees, leaving the principal issue for trial whether the challenged promotions were indeed required by the decrees. After trial the District Court granted the motion to dismiss. The court concluded that "if in fact the City was required to [make promotions of blacks] by the consent decree, then they would not be guilty of [illegal] racial discrimination" and that the defendants had "establish[ed] that the promotions of the black individuals . . . were in fact required by the terms of the consent decree." . . .

On appeal, the Eleventh Circuit reversed. It held that, "because . . . [the *Wilks* respondents] were neither parties nor privies to the consent decrees, . . . their independent claims of unlawful discrimination are not precluded." . . . The court explicitly rejected the doctrine of "impermissible collateral attack" espoused by other Courts of Appeals to immunize parties to a consent decree from charges of discrimination by nonparties for actions taken pursuant to the decree. . . . Although it recognized a "strong public policy in favor of voluntary affirmative action plans," the panel acknowledged that this interest "must yield to the policy against requiring third parties to submit to bargains in which their interests were either ignored or sacrificed." . . . The court remanded the case for trial of the discrimination claims, suggesting that the operative law for judging the consent decrees was that governing voluntary affirmative-action plans. . . .

We granted certiorari, . . . and now affirm the Eleventh Circuit's judgment. All agree that "it is a principle of general application in Anglo-American jurisprudence that one is not bound by a judgment *in personam* in a litigation in which he is not designated as a party or to which he has not been made a party by service of process." Hansberry v. Lee, 311 U.S. 32, 40 (1940). See, *e.g.*, Parklane Hosiery Co. v. Shore 439 U.S. 322, 327, n. 7 (1979) . . . . This rule is part of our "deep-rooted historic tradition that everyone should have his own day in court." . . . A judgment or decree among parties to a lawsuit resolves issues to those proceeding.²

Petitioners argue that, because respondents failed to timely intervene in the initial proceedings, their current challenge to actions taken under the consent decree constitutes an impermissible "collateral attack." They argue that respondents were aware that the underlying suit might affect them, and if they chose to pass up an opportunity to intervene, they should not be permitted to later litigate the issues in a new action. The position has sufficient appeal to have commanded the approval of the great majority of the Federal Courts of Appeals, but we agree with the contrary view expressed by the Court of Appeals for the Eleventh Circuit in this case.

We begin with the words of Justice Brandeis in Chase National Bank v. Norwalk, 291 U.S. 431 (1934):

"The law does not impose upon any person absolutely entitled to a hearing the burden of voluntary intervention in a suit to which he is a stranger. . . . Unless duly summoned to appear in a legal proceeding, a person not a privy may rest assured that a judgment recovered therein will not affect his legal rights." Id. at 441.

While these words were written before the adoption of the Federal Rules of Civil Procedure, we think the Rules incorporate the same principle; a party seeking a judgment binding on another cannot obligate that person to intervene; he must be joined. . . . Against the background of permissive intervention set forth in *Chase National Bank*, the drafters cast Rule 24, governing intervention, in permissive terms. See Fed. Rule Civ. Proc. 24(a) (intervention as of right) ("Upon timely application anyone shall be permitted to intervene"); Fed. Rule Civ. Proc. 24(b) (permissive intervention) ("Upon timely application anyone may be permitted to intervene"). They

---

2. We have recognized an exception to the general rule when, in certain limited circumstances, a person, although not a party, has his interests adequately represented by someone with the same interests who is a party. See Hansberry v. Lee, 311 U.S. 32, 41-42 (1940) ("class" or "representative" suits); Fed. Rule Civ. Proc. 23 (same); Montana v. United States, 440 U.S. 147, 154-155 (1979) (control of litigation on behalf of one of the parties in the litigation). Additionally, where a special remedial scheme exists expressly foreclosing successive litigation by nonlitigants, as for example in bankruptcy or probate, legal proceedings may terminate preexisting rights if the scheme is otherwise consistent with due process. . . . Neither of these exceptions, however, applies in this case.

determined that the concern for finality and completeness of judgments would be "better [served] by mandatory joinder procedures." . . . Accordingly, Rule 19(a) provides for mandatory joinder in circumstances where a judgment rendered in the absence of a person may "leave . . . persons already parties subject to a substantial risk of incurring . . . inconsistent obligations . . . ." Rule 19(b) sets forth the factors to be considered by a court in deciding whether to allow an action to proceed in the absence of an interested party.

Joinder as a party, rather than knowledge of a lawsuit and an opportunity to intervene, is the method by which potential parties are subjected to the jurisdiction of the court and bound by a judgment or decree. The parties to a lawsuit presumably know better than anyone else the nature and scope of relief sought in the action, and at whose expense such relief might be granted. It makes sense, therefore, to place on them a burden of bringing in additional parties where such a step is indicated, rather than placing on potential additional parties a duty to intervene when they acquire knowledge of the lawsuit. The linchpin of the "impermissible collateral attack" doctrine — the attribution of preclusive effect to a failure to intervene — is therefore quite inconsistent with Rule 19 and Rule 24.

Petitioners argue that our decisions in Penn-Central Merger and N & W Inclusion Cases, 389 U.S. 486 (1968), and Provident Tradesmens Bank & Trust Co. v. Patterson, 390 U.S. 102 (1968), suggest an opposite result. The *Penn-Central* litigation took place in a special statutory framework enacted by Congress to allow reorganization of a huge railway system. Primary jurisdiction was in the Interstate Commerce Commission, with very restricted review in a statutory three-judge District Court. Review proceedings were channeled to the District Court for the Southern District of New York, and proceedings in other District Courts were stayed. The District Court upheld the decision of the Interstate Commerce Commission in both the merger and the inclusion proceedings, and the parties to that proceeding appealed to this Court. Certain Pennsylvania litigants had sued in the District Court for the Middle District of Pennsylvania to set aside the Commission's order, and this action was stayed pending the decision in the District Court for the Southern District of New York. We held that the borough of Moosic, one of the Pennsylvania litigants, could not challenge the Commission's approval of the merger and inclusion in the Pennsylvania District Court, pointing out the unusual nationwide character of the action and saying "in these circumstances, it would be senseless to permit parties seeking to challenge the merger and the inclusion orders to bring numerous suits in many different district courts." 389 U.S., at 505, n.4.

We do not think that this holding in *Penn Central*, based as it was upon the extraordinary nature of the proceedings challenging the merger of giant railroads and not even mentioning Rule 19 or Rule 24, affords a guide to the interpretation of the rules relating to joinder and intervention in ordinary civil actions in a district court.

Petitioners also rely on our decision in *Provident Bank, supra*, as authority for the view which they espouse. In that case we discussed Rule 19 shortly after parts of it had been substantially revised, but we expressly left open the question whether preclusive effect might be attributed to a failure to intervene. 390 U.S., at 114-115.

Petitioners contend that a different result should be reached because the need to join affected parties will be burdensome and ultimately discouraging to civil rights litigation. Potential adverse claimants may be numerous and difficult to identify; if they are not joined, the possibility for inconsistent judgments exists. Judicial resources will be needlessly consumed in relitigation of the same question.

Even if we were wholly persuaded by these arguments as a matter of policy, acceptance of them would require a rewriting rather than an interpretation of the relevant Rules. But we are not persuaded that their acceptance would lead to a more satisfactory method of handling cases like this one. It must be remembered that the alternatives are a duty to intervene based on knowledge, on the one hand, and some form of joinder, as the Rules presently provide, on the other. No one can seriously contend that an employer might successfully defend against a Title VII claim by one group of employees on the ground that its actions were required by an earlier decree entered in a suit brought against it by another, if the later group did not have adequate notice or knowledge of the earlier suit.

The difficulties petitioners foresee in identifying those who could be adversely affected by a decree granting broad remedial relief are undoubtedly present, but they arise from the nature of the relief sought and not because of any choice between mandatory intervention and joinder. Rule 19's provisions for joining interested parties are designed to accommodate the sort of complexities that may arise from a decree affecting numerous people in various ways. We doubt that a mandatory intervention rule would be any less awkward. As mentioned, plaintiffs who seek the aid of the courts to alter existing employment policies, or the employer who might be subject to conflicting decrees, are best able to bear the burden of designating those who would be adversely affected if plaintiffs prevail; these parties will generally have a better understanding of the scope of likely relief than employees who are not named but might be affected. Petitioners' alternative does not eliminate the need for, or difficulty of, identifying persons who, because of their interests, should be included in a lawsuit. It merely shifts that responsibility to less able shoulders.

Nor do we think that the system of joinder called for by the Rules is likely to produce more relitigation of issues than the converse rule. The breadth of a lawsuit and concomitant relief may be at least partially shaped in advance through Rule 19 to avoid needless clashes with future litigation. And even under a regime of mandatory intervention, parties who did not have adequate knowledge of the suit would relitigate issues. Additional questions about the adequacy and timeliness of knowledge would inevitably crop up. We think that the system of joinder presently contemplated by the Rules best serves the many interests involved in the run of litigated cases, including cases like the present one.

Petitioners also urge that the congressional policy favoring voluntary settlement of employment discrimination claims . . . also supports the "impermissible collateral attack" doctrine. But once again it is essential to note just what is meant by "voluntary settlement." A voluntary settlement in the form of a consent decree between one group of employees and their employer cannot possibly "settle," voluntarily or otherwise, the conflicting claims of another group of employees who do not join in the agreement. This is true even if the second group of employees is a party to the litigation . . . .

Insofar as the argument is bottomed on the idea that it may be easier to settle claims among a disparate group of affected persons if they are all before the court, joinder bids fair to accomplish that result as well as a regime of mandatory intervention.

For the foregoing reasons we affirm the decision of the Court of Appeals for the Eleventh Circuit. That court remanded the case for trial of the reverse discrimination claims. . . .

■ JUSTICE STEVENS, with whom JUSTICE BRENNAN, JUSTICE MARSHALL, and JUSTICE BLACKMUN join, dissenting. As a matter of law there is a vast difference between persons who are actual parties to litigation and persons who merely have the kind of interest that may as a practical matter be impaired by the outcome of a case. Persons in the first category have a right to participate in a trial and to appeal from an adverse judgment; depending on whether they win or lose, their legal rights may be enhanced or impaired. Persons in the latter category have a right to intervene in the action in a timely fashion, or they may be joined as parties against their will. But if they remain on the sidelines, they may be harmed as a practical matter even though their legal rights are unaffected. One of the disadvantages of sideline-sitting is that the bystander has no right to appeal from a judgment no matter how harmful it may be.

In these cases the Court quite rightly concludes that the white firefighters who brought the second series of Title VII cases could not be deprived of their legal rights in the first series of cases because they had neither intervened nor been joined as parties. . . . The consent decrees obviously could not deprive them of any contractual rights, such as seniority, . . . or accrued vacation pay, . . . or of any other legal rights, such as the right to have their employer comply with federal statutes like Title VII . . . . There is no reason, however, why the consent decrees might not produce changes in conditions at the white firefighters' place of employment that, as a practical matter, may have a serious effect on their opportunities for employment or promotion even though they are not bound by the decrees in any legal sense. The fact that one of the effects of a decree is to curtail the job opportunities of nonparties does not mean that the nonparties have been deprived of legal rights or that they have standing to appeal from that decree without becoming parties.

Persons who have no right to appeal from a final judgment — either because the time to appeal has elapsed or because they never became parties to the case — may nevertheless collaterally attack a judgment on certain narrow grounds. If the court had no jurisdiction over the subject matter, or if the judgment is the product of corruption, duress, fraud, collusion, or mistake, under limited circumstances it may be set aside in an appropriate collateral proceeding. . . . This rule not only applies to parties to the original action, but also allows interested third parties collaterally to attack judgments. In both civil and criminal cases, however, the grounds that may be invoked to support a collateral attack are much more limited than those that may be asserted as error on direct appeal. Thus, a person who can foresee that a lawsuit is likely to have a practical impact on his interests may pay a heavy price if he elects to sit on the sidelines instead of intervening and taking the risk that his legal rights will be impaired.

In these cases there is no dispute about the fact that respondents are not parties to the consent decrees. It follows as a matter of course that they are not bound by those decrees. Those judgments could not, and did not, deprive them of any legal rights. The judgments did, however, have a practical impact on respondents' opportunities for advancement in their profession. For that reason, respondents had standing to challenge the validity of the decrees, but the grounds that they may advance in support of a collateral challenge are much more limited than would be allowed if they were parties prosecuting a direct appeal.[8] . . .

The implementation of a consent decree affecting the interests of a multitude of nonparties, and the reliance on that decree as a defense to a charge of discrimination in hiring and promotion decisions, raise a legitimate concern of collusion. No such allegation, however, has been raised. Moreover, there is compelling evidence that the decrees were not collusive. . . . [I]t is evident that the decree was a product of genuine arm's-length negotiations.

Nor can it be maintained that the consent judgment is subject to reopening and further litigation because the relief it afforded was so out of line with settled legal doctrine that it "was transparently invalid or had only a frivolous pretense to validity." Walker v. Birmingham, 388 U.S. 307, 315 (1967) (suggesting that a contemner might be allowed to challenge contempt citation on ground that underlying court order was "transparently invalid"). To the contrary, the type of race-conscious relief ordered in the consent decrees is entirely consistent with this Court's approach to affirmative action. Given a sufficient predicate of racial discrimination, neither the Equal Protection Clause of the Fourteenth Amendment nor Title VII of the Civil Rights Act of 1964 erects a bar to affirmative action plans that benefit nonvictims and have some adverse effect on nonwrongdoers. . . .

Hence, there is no basis for collaterally attacking the judgment as collusive, fraudulent, or transparently invalid. Moreover, respondents do

---

8. Professors James and Hazard describe the rule as follows:

> Ordinarily, a nonparty has no legal interest in a judgment in an action between others. Such a judgment does not determine the nonparty's rights and obligations under the rules of res judicata and he may so assert if the judgment is relied upon against him. But in some situations one's interests, particularly in one's own personal legal status or claims to property, may be placed in practical jeopardy by a judgment between others. In such circumstances one may seek the aid of a court of equity, but the grounds upon which one may rely are severely limited. The general rule is that one must show either that the judgment was void for lack of jurisdiction of the subject matter or that it was the product of fraud directed at the petitioner.

James & Hazard[, Civil Procedure] § 12.15, p. 681 [(3d ed. 1985)].

not claim — nor has there been any showing of — mistake, duress, or lack of jurisdiction. Instead, respondents are left to argue that somewhat different relief would have been more appropriate than the relief that was actually granted. Although this sort of issue may provide the basis for a direct appeal, it cannot, and should not, serve to open the door to relitigation of a settled judgment....

In a case ... in which there has been no showing that the decree was collusive, fraudulent, transparently invalid, or entered without jurisdiction, it would be "unconscionable" to conclude that obedience to an order remedying a Title VII violation could subject a defendant to additional liability.... In fact, Equal Employment Opportunity Commission regulations concur in this assessment.... Any other conclusion would subject large employers who seek to comply with the law by remedying past discrimination to a never-ending stream of litigation and potential liability. It is unfathomable that either Title VII or the Equal Protection Clause demands such a counter-productive result....

The predecessor to this litigation was brought to change a pattern of hiring and promotion practices that had discriminated against black citizens in Birmingham for decades. The white respondents in this case are not responsible for that history of discrimination, but they are nevertheless beneficiaries of the discriminatory practices that the litigation was designed to correct. Any remedy that seeks to create employment conditions that would have obtained if there had been no violations of law will necessarily have an adverse impact on whites, who must now share their job and promotion opportunities with blacks. Just as white employees in the past were innocent beneficiaries of illegal discriminatory practices, so is it inevitable that some of the same white employees will be innocent victims who must share some of the burdens resulting from the redress of the past wrongs.

There is nothing unusual about the fact that litigation between adverse parties may, as a practical matter, seriously impair the interests of third persons who elect to sit on the sidelines. Indeed, in complex litigation this Court has squarely held that a sideline-sitter may be bound as firmly as an actual party if he had adequate notice and a fair opportunity to intervene and if the judicial interest in finality is sufficiently strong. See Penn-Central Merger and N & W Inclusion Cases, 389 U.S. 486, 505-506 (1968)....

There is no need, however, to go that far in order to agree with the District Court's eminently sensible view that compliance with the terms of a valid decree remedying violations of Title VII cannot itself violate that statute or the Equal Protection Clause. The city of Birmingham, in entering into and complying with this decree, has made a substantial step toward the eradication of the long history of pervasive racial discrimination that has plagued its fire department. The District Court, after conducting a trial and carefully considering respondents' arguments, concluded that this effort is lawful and should go forward. Because respondents have thus already had their day in court and have failed to carry their burden, I would vacate the judgment of the Court of Appeals and remand for further proceedings consistent with this opinion.

42 U.S.C. § 2000e-2(n)

(Enacted Nov. 21, 1991)

(n) Resolution of challenges to employment practices implementing litigated or consent judgments or orders

(1)(A) Notwithstanding any other provision of law, and except as provided in paragraph (2), an employment practice that implements and is within the scope of a litigated or consent judgment or order that resolves a claim of employment discrimination under the Constitution or Federal civil rights laws may not be challenged under the circumstances described in subparagraph (B).

(B) A practice described in subparagraph (A) may not be challenged in a claim under the Constitution or Federal civil rights laws —

(i) by a person who, prior to the entry of the judgment or order described in subparagraph (A), had —

(I) actual notice of the proposed judgment or order sufficient to apprise such person that such judgment or order might adversely affect the interests and legal rights of such person and that an opportunity was available to present objections to such judgment or order by a future date certain; and

(II) a reasonable opportunity to present objections to such judgment or order; or

(ii) by a person whose interests were adequately represented by another person who had previously challenged the judgment or order on the same legal grounds and with a similar factual situation, unless there has been an intervening change in law or fact.

(2) Nothing in this subsection shall be construed to —

(A) alter the standards for intervention under rule 24 of the Federal Rules of Civil Procedure or apply to the rights of parties who have successfully intervened pursuant to such rule in the proceeding in which the parties intervened;

(B) apply to the rights of parties to the action in which a litigated or consent judgment or order was entered, or of members of a class represented or sought to be represented in such action, or of members of a group on whose behalf relief was sought in such action by the Federal Government;

(C) prevent challenges to a litigated or consent judgment or order on the ground that such judgment or order was obtained through collusion or fraud, or is transparently invalid or was entered by a court lacking subject matter jurisdiction; or

(D) authorize or permit the denial to any person of the due process of law required by the Constitution.

(3) Any action not precluded under this subsection that challenges an employment consent judgment or order described in paragraph (1) shall be brought in the court, and if possible before the judge, that entered such judgment or order. Nothing in this subsection shall preclude a transfer of such action pursuant to section 1404 of Title 28.

American Law Institute, COMPLEX LITIGATION: STATUTORY RECOMMENDATIONS AND ANALYSIS

275-78, 282-85 (1994)

§ 5.05. Court-Ordered Notice of Intervention and Preclusion

(a) If, at the request of a party or on its own initiative, a transferee court in an action consolidated pursuant to § 3.01 or § 5.01, determines that:

(1) an existing claim or claims of nonparties involve one or more questions of fact in common with the actions pending before the transferee court and arise out of the same transaction, occurrence, or series of transactions or occurrences;

(2) intervention will advance the efficient, consistent, and final resolution of both the parties' and nonparties' claims; and

(3) intervention will not impose upon either the nonparties or parties undue prejudice, burden, or inconvenience,

it may enter an order informing the nonparties who are within the court's jurisdiction . . . that they may intervene in the action and in any event will be bound by the determinations made to the same extent as a party, unless otherwise provided by law.

(b) An order under subsection (a) shall provide both the parties and the affected nonparties with notice setting forth:

(1) the existence, status, and substance of the claims and issues to be resolved in the transferee court;

(2) the nonparties' right to intervene in the consolidated action and the time period during which intervention must be accomplished;

(3) the fact that, whether or not the nonparties exercise the opportunity to intervene, they may benefit from determinations made and will be precluded from relitigating issues adjudicated in the transferee court proceedings described in the notice; and

(4) the parties' and the nonparties' right to petition the court to show why the standards in subsection (a) have not been satisfied.

(c) Upon receipt of the notice prescribed in subsection (b), any party or nonparty may file with the transferee court within 20 days a petition setting forth reasons why the requirements of subsection (a) are not satisfied. The transferee court shall conduct a hearing at which parties and nonparties may participate and upon completion of which the transferee court shall transmit notice of its ruling either confirming, modifying, or vacating the order under subsection (a) to all parties and nonparties notified under subsection (b). That notice shall identify specifically those nonparties who may intervene and who will be bound by the determinations made in the consolidated action.

(d) The transferee court's decision under this section shall not be subject to immediate review unless it otherwise qualifies under one of the existing interlocutory appeal statutes.

Comment:

a. General Purpose and Scope. This section sets out a new procedure by which the court may issue a notice of intervention and preclusion to individuals who are not yet parties to a consolidated action but whose joinder is deemed an integral part of making a comprehensive adjudication of a complex litigation. The transfer and consolidation devices set out [elsewhere in the report] both permit and induce the gathering of existing actions .... The intervention and preclusion notice under § 5.05 is a counterpart procedure that may be used to gather the as yet unasserted claims of nonparties .... It is limited to being used with reference to existing claims and thus does not provide a mechanism for addressing the problems of duplication or inconsistency that may occur when claims mature later that involve the adjudication of some of the identical facts....

The impact of the procedure set out is not likely to be as harsh or broad-ranging as might appear at first glance. The intervention scheme is really designed to be coercive, not compulsory; the individual retains the option to join the suit or not, but is confronted with a risk of being bound to an adverse judgment should he decide to stay away. Further, it is expected that the procedure will be used only infrequently or for a small number of litigants; most parties to complex litigation are likely to have filed suit ....

Another preclusion reform proposal that is similar in many respects to the procedure in this section is to revise the rules of mandatory joinder.... The mandatory joinder approach, however, is harsher on nonparties because it forces them either to participate or default, losing their entire claim; the procedure set out in this section allows them to join or be bound. If the result is favorable to their claim, they may benefit because the judgment precludes only issues, not claims....

The failure to intervene in response to a notice under § 5.05(b) will result in issue, not claim, preclusion. By declining to enter the lawsuit, the nonparty does not forfeit his claim entirely, but merely risks losing control over the handling of issues common to the consolidated action and his individual litigation. The scheme addresses the current imbalance between nonparties and existing parties, taking away the potential advantage of nonparticipation....

b. Preclusion of nonintervening litigants. It is true that traditionally it has been held that only parties may be bound by judgments, ... and that this procedure departs from that rule. However, the Supreme Court has recognized that "where a special remedial scheme exists expressly foreclosing successive litigation by nonlitigants ... legal procedures may terminate preexisting rights if the scheme is otherwise consistent with due process." Martin v. Wilks, 490 U.S. 755, 762 n.2 (1991). Thus, the key to evaluating the constitutionality of § 5.05 lies in considering the wide range of protections and limits that are part of it and that respond to due process concerns.

Due process is satisfied in several ways. Notice requirements reasonably calculated to apprise the potential intervenor of what is involved are set out in subsection (b) and only persons who receive notice will be precluded.... The nonparty is given an opportunity to present objections to the court's order on fairness or other grounds, and if those objections are overruled, the nonparty then will have an opportunity to intervene to participate in the complex action on the merits. In this way, the nonparty is provided a fair and meaningful opportunity for a day in court.

Nonparty preclusion will advance the goals underlying transfer and consolidation in complex cases by ensuring the litigation's efficient, fair, and just resolution because, whether or not the nonparty elects to intervene, the transferee court will be able to achieve a final and binding result. If the determinations made are unfavorable to the nonparty's claim or defense, he will be precluded from relitigating them; if they are favorable, the nonparty may rely on them to preclude the losing party from relitigating the issue. In this way, the litigants realize the benefits of reduced litigation costs, finality, and repose; the judicial system advances its efficiency and decisional consistency interests; and the societal costs of multiforum, multiparty dispute resolution are reduced.

There are several limitations on the actual application of preclusion that serve to ensure that it is applied only when it is fair to do so. The most important of these is that nonparties who do not actually receive the intervention notice and thus have not had an opportunity to contest the order or to intervene will not be bound.... Although it may be useful in informing some of a right to intervene, a general notice ordinarily should not be the basis for precluding those who later assert that they never saw or received it....

The availability of preclusion is also limited by that doctrine's usual requirements. Consequently, any judgment that is entered will be binding only on those issues that were "actually" or "fully and fairly" litigated and decided in the complex case.... Nonparties also may avoid preclusion by showing that the issue was not "finally" decided, or that the determination was not "necessary" to the transferee court's judgment.... Similarly, preclusion will be applied only if a nonparty knew or should have been able to foresee that a particular issue would be litigated in the complex case.

Notes and Questions

1. In 1985 the American Law Institute commissioned a preliminary study of complex litigation. In 1994, the ALI approved the final report of its commission. Over the course of the next several chapters, we will examine various aspects of the ALI proposal. As the comments to § 5.05 state, that the ALI's preclusion proposal must be understood in conjunction with its other proposals, which essentially seek to make it easier to bring together in one forum

cases that have already been filed. Section 5.05 then proposes a means of handling cases that had not yet been filed: nonparties receive notice of the litigation, are extended an opportunity to join the litigation by means of intervention, and are precluded from re-litigating any actually litigated issues regardless of whether they become parties through intervention or remain nonparties.

2. The starting point of any evaluation of this sort of proposal is *Martin v. Wilks*. What is the exact holding in *Martin v. Wilks*? In particular, is *Martin* founded on the due process clause of the Constitution, on an interpretation of federal joinder and preclusion rules, or on the equitable ground that, in ruling on the BFA's appeal, had essentially authorized independent suits to be filed? If the ruling is based on the Constitution, then § 2000e-2(n), the ALI's proposal, and any other "notice and preclusion" proposal would seem to be unconstitutional unless they could be made to fit within the "special remedial scheme" language of footnote 2 in *Martin*.

3. In *Martin* the district court on remand held a new trial on the reverse discrimination claims of the white firefighters, but ruled in favor of the City. It found "significant evidence" of past discrimination sufficient to justify the affirmative action program which it concluded was narrowly tailored to remedy the past discrimination. Bennett v. Arrington, 806 F. Supp. 926 (N.D. Ala. 1992). A panel of the Eleventh Circuit reversed. In re Birmingham Reverse Discrimination Employment Litigation, 20 F.3d 1525 (11th Cir. 1994), cert. denied, 514 U.S. 1065 (1995). Meanwhile, the parties to the original action began discussing a plan to modify the original affirmative action decree. Although the request of the reverse discrimination plaintiffs to consolidate the original action with their suit was denied, these plaintiffs were in effect allowed to intervene in the original action for the purpose of participating in any decision to modify the original consent decree, and the district court subsequently certified separate classes consisting of all black employees and all non-black employees. The district court ultimately entered an order modifying the original affirmative action decree, but a panel of the Eleventh Circuit held that the lower court had abused its discretion by not modifying the decree further to conform to changes in the applicable law. Ensley Branch, N.A.A.C.P. v. Seibels, 31 F.3d 1548 (11th Cir. 1994).

4. As the ALI commentary shows, *Martin* has proven unpopular among many academics. See also Robert G. Bone, *Rethinking the "Day in Court" Ideal and Nonparty Preclusion*, 67 N.Y.U. L. Rev. 193, 288 (1992). *Martin* also proved immediately unpopular in Congress, which enacted § 2000e-2(n) explicitly to overrule *Martin* in the context of Title VII claims. You might have noticed that, in addition to a notice and preclusion rule in § 2000e-2(n)(1)(B)(i), Congress also passed a preclusion after adequate representation rule in § 2000e-2(n)(1)(B)(ii). We examined this issue of preclusion after representation in the last section. See pp. 207-39, *supra*.

5. Despite the criticism, however, the Court has not retreated from *Martin* in other contexts. See Richards v. Jefferson County Alabama, 517 U.S. 793 (1996) (p. 208, *supra*). If anything, *Richards* may have strengthened *Martin's* status. *Richards*, which involved claim preclusion in state court, was clearly a constitutional decision, and its invocation of *Martin* (see p. 210, *supra*) suggests that *Martin* does indeed have a constitutional component. Moreover, footnote 5 of *Richards* discusses the idea of notice and preclusion in a manner that suggests the Court remains wary of the concept (see p. 210, *supra*).

Richards was decided after passage of § 2000e-2(n) and promulgation of the ALI's proposal. Presumably, in light of the saving clause in § 2000e-2(n)(1)(D), the notice and preclusion rule and the preclusion after adequate representation rule are still constitutional in spite of *Richards*. Nonetheless, does the constitutional cloud that hangs over § 2000e-2(n) effectively neutralize the preclusion rules it develops? See Rutherford v. City of Cleveland, 137 F.3d 905 (6th Cir. 1998) (adequate representation under § 2000e-2(n) was intended to mean same thing as adequate representation under Rule 23). In light of *Martin* and *Richards*, are you satisfied with the ALI's analysis of the constitutionality of § 5.05?

6. The ALI's definition of "complex litigation," you might recall, was "multiparty, multiforum litigation . . . characterized by related claims dispersed in several forums and often involving events that occurred over long periods of time." See p. 84, *supra*. This definition is different than ours, but is consistent with the definition that we have used to describe "complicated litigation." Is there an argument that the ALI's notice and preclusion approach would be constitutional in complex litigation (as we define that term), but unconstitutional in the complicated litigation to which the ALI would also extend § 5.05?

Presumably the argument would run along these lines: An adversarial, "day in court" approach to litigation is guaranteed by the due process clause, and cannot constitutionally be overridden merely in order to achieve greater efficiency in litigation. Therefore, as applied to complicated litigation, § 5.05 is unconstitutional. On the other hand, the due process clause also guarantees a rational adjudication of each person's dispute, and this guarantee has a higher priority than the guarantee of adversarial process. Thus, when lawyer dysfunction makes it impossible for the adversarial approach to assure the rational adjudication of each interested party's dispute, the adversarial guarantee of the due process clause must give way to the rational adjudication guarantee of the due process clause. As applied to complex litigation, § 5.05 is constitutional.

This argument can be critiqued from either of two perspectives. From the perspective of a supporter of the ALI's proposal, the argument rests on debatable assumptions: that adversarial process has constitutional stature under the due process clause and that efficient adjudication does not enjoy at least a comparable constitutional stature under the due process clause. From the perspective of a person that opposes the ALI's proposal, the argument also rests on debatable assumptions: that rational adjudication occupies a higher place in the constitutional order than adversarial process and that a notice and preclusion approach is a better method of resolving the adversarialism-rationality conflict than mandatory joinder.

7. Assuming the constitutionality of the procedure, could a judge adopt without statutory authorization a notice and preclusion rule comparable to § 2000e-2(n) or § 5.05? One immediate obstacle would be the source of the judge's authority to issue a notice to nonparties. In the most analogous case, a district judge that was hearing the cases of numerous plaintiffs whose cases arose out of two airplane crashes ordered the airlines to supply the names and addresses of all the victims of the crashes. The court's reason for the request was that it wished to send a letter to the families of the victims informing them of the pendency of the litigation; the court hoped that this notice would induce other nonparties to file suit in his court and thus streamline the litigation

process. See Pan Am World Airways v. United States District Court, Central District of California, 523 F.2d 1073 (9th Cir. 1975).

The airlines refused to provide the passenger lists, and sought writs of mandamus against the judge's orders. The Ninth Circuit issued the writs. The court began by noting that the crash litigation could not be maintained as an opt-out class action, under which the court would have had both the power and the duty to provide notice to nonparty class members. See 523 F.2d at 1078; In re F.R.Civ.P. 23(c)(2). After examining the matter under Federal Rules 16, 19, 21, 42, and 83, the *Manual for Complex Litigation,* and the court's inherent equitable power, the Ninth Circuit held that there was no rule or authority that provided the judge with the power to issue a notice to nonparties. 523 F.2d at 1078-81. Judge Schackne dissented. He thought that "[t]he majority . . . reaches the wrong result because it contemplates the wrong question. The question is not whether some rule permits the action proposed, but whether any rule, statute, or logical concept forbids it." He also thought that the majority's reading of Rule 42 was "overly technical," that "[n]o right of any party is invaded" by the district court's order, and the district court "should be applauded for his initiative and innovation." Id. at 1082. See also Jackson v. Motel 6 Multipurposes, Inc., 130 F.3d 999 (11th Cir. 1997) (issuing writ of mandamus against orders permitting counsel to communicate with putative class members prior to class certification ruling).

8. Assuming that our preference for litigant autonomy must give way in at least some cases (whether complex or complicated), is it obvious that a notice and preclusion approach is the best compromise on the ideal? A mandatory joinder approach guarantees a party's participation in the shaping of proofs and arguments; a notice and preclusion approach does not. Moreover, a mandatory joinder approach avoids the problem, which plagues all preclusion approaches, that the case will settle without entry of a judgment that can be used to preclude later parties. Finally, unlike a mandatory joinder approach, a notice and preclusion approach will probably lead to collateral litigation about whether nonparties received the notice. On the other hand, a notice and preclusion approach will be administratively more convenient, since provision of notice is probably a simpler process than joining all interested plaintiffs. A notice and preclusion approach will lead to a less cluttered case, since some parties will probably decline to join the litigation. A notice and preclusion approach also avoids the problems of claim preclusion that may arise under a mandatory joinder approach, as well as the cluttering of the case with tangential issues in the event that claim preclusion would attach.

In deciding which approach is preferable, another relevant consideration would be whether mandatory joinder or notice and preclusion would do more to prevent re-litigation by nonparties. The ALI's notice and preclusion approach requires that notice actually reach a nonparty in order for preclusive effects to obtain. Notice can take one of two forms: an individual notice or a generally published notice that the nonparty happens to see or hear about. Compared to most mandatory joinder approaches, the notice and preclusion approach would cover more people; those unknown nonparties that would have seen a general notice and been precluded under the notice and preclusion approach would not be bound under a mandatory joinder approach. But there are some important exceptions to this statement. If the joinder device used is a mandatory Rule 23(b)(1) or (b)(2) class action (see pp. 133-34, *supra*), then even those class members that receive no notice of the action are barred. If the joinder device is an opt-out Rule 23(b)(3) class action (see id.), then the issue is somewhat unclear. Unlike the notice and preclusion approach, class members do not necessarily need to receive actual notice in order to be part of the class, so that preclusion is possible even when a general notice fails to reach a class member. On the other hand, in an opt-out class persons can remove themselves from the class and from the preclusive effects of a class judgment or settlement.

Do these considerations suggest that a mandatory joinder approach or a notice and preclusion approach is better? For two articles favoring a mandatory joinder approach, see John C. McCoid, *A Single Package for Multiparty Disputes*, 28 Stan. L. Rev. 707 (1976); Richard D. Freer, *Avoiding Duplicative Litigation: Rethinking Plaintiff Autonomy and the Court's Role in Defining the Litigative Units*, 50 U. Pitt. L. Rev. 809 (1989).

9. The ALI's approach rests on the assumption that a nonparty who receives actual notice will be able to intervene in the litigation. The success of the ALI approach therefore hinges on the breadth of Rule 24(a). As we have seen, Rule 24 has received a fairly generous interpretation, although some courts have been more stingy. See pp. 136-55, *supra*. But recall that Rule 24 intervention is permitted only when the nonparty seeking intervention will be inadequately represented by the existing parties. But if the existing parties do not adequately represent the nonparty, is it fair to bind the nonparty to the outcome of the case when the nonparty fails to intervene? Is it constitutional? Conversely, what happens when the existing parties do adequately represent the interests of the nonparty? Won't intervention be denied?

In order to avoid these problems, should we remove Rule 24's "inadequacy of representation" requirement in cases in which the notice and preclusion rule applies? Should we create special intervention rules just for some cases?

10. The ALI's proposal contains other significant limitations — among them the requirement of "one or more questions of fact in common" between the pending case and the nonparty's case, the requirement that the nonparty's case "arise out of the same transaction, occurrence, or series of transactions or occurrences" as the pending case, the requirement that "intervention will advance the efficient, consistent, and final resolution of both the parties' and nonparties' claims," and the requirement that "intervention will not impose upon either the nonparties or parties undue prejudice, burden, or inconvenience." Note that these requirements overlap the text and gloss of Rule 20 joinder against defendants in significant ways. See pp. 109-15, *supra*. The main difference, of course, is that the decision about who to join has been removed from the plaintiffs' hands and entrusted to the court hearing the pending case. Does this fact make you more or less disposed toward the ALI's proposal?

Another limitation of the ALI's proposal is that its notice (and hence any preclusive effect) can be extended only to "nonparties who are within the court's jurisdiction." In the next chapter we take up the issue of territorial jurisdiction and the ALI's proposal to expand that jurisdiction in order to bring nonparties within the scope of its notice and preclusion rule. See p. 288, *infra*.

A third limitation is that the ALI's proposal extends only to "claims of nonparties," which strongly implies that the only nonparties precluded under its approach are potential plaintiffs. In order to cut down on re-litigation, shouldn't potential additional defendants also be notified, provided an opportunity to intervene in the suit, and be subject to preclusion if they do not?

Does it concern you that the cases that meet the requirements of § 5.05 will receive a very different sort of procedure than those that do not? How can this inroad on the trans-substantive assumption of our present procedural system be justified?

11. In the notes to the preclusion materials in Chapter 2.B, *supra*, we suggested a range of concerns that the preclusion approach encounters: (1) the need for a final judgment that actually, necessarily, and fairly decided an identical issue, (2) the potentially outcome-determinative potential of preclusion due to the effect of immaturity on the litigation (see pp. 235-36, *supra*), (3) the infringement on litigant autonomy, and (4) the effect of preclusion on the scope of present joinder rules. To what extent is each of these concerns applicable to the notice and preclusion approach? The first concern is still the same under a notice and preclusion approach. So is the second concern, although the pro-defendant immaturity effect may be offset to some degree by the generally pro-plaintiff effect of the joinder of additional parties (see pp. 102-03, *supra*). The third concern is somewhat ameliorated in the notice and preclusion context, since it at least lays at a nonparty's feet the choice of whether (although not when or where) to participate.

The last concern is also somewhat ameliorated, since the only persons to whom Rule 19, 23, or 24 consequences might attach are those that receive actual notice of the litigation and that otherwise meet the requirements of the notice and preclusion rule. For those that meet these requirements, however, doesn't the preclusive effect of a notice and preclusion approach make them automatic candidates for mandatory joinder under Rules 19(a) and 23(b)(1), in addition to intervention of right under Rule 24(a)? Is it too much of a bootstrap argument to say that the preclusive effect under a notice and preclusion approach creates a practical impairment of interests that then requires mandatory joinder, and that mandatory joinder in turn makes notice and preclusion unnecessary? Cf. Edwards v. City of Houston, 78 F.3d 983, 1005 (5th Cir. 1996) (preclusive effect of § 2000e-2(n) creates practical impairment of interests for Rule 24(a) purposes).

Won't the effect of the bootstrap argument be that some lawsuits will be dismissed under Rule 19(b) for inability to join indispensable parties? If dismissals occur with some frequency, won't a notice and preclusion approach harm, rather than advance, the enforcement of certain rights? Could we simply avoid the entire problem by placing a proviso in Rules 19, 23, and 24 stating that they are "subject to the provisions of the notice and preclusion rule"? Cf. F.R.Civ.P. 19(c) (making Rule 19 "subject to the provisions of Rule 23"); 42 U.S.C. § 2000e-2(n)(2)(A).

12. Would some of the concerns we have raised — such as infringement on litigant autonomy and the potentially outcome-determinative effects of preclusion — make it impossible to satisfy the "undue prejudice, burden, or inconvenience" prong of § 5.05 except in cases of lawyer dysfunction? In thinking about this question, recall that Rule 23 is divided into mandatory class actions (Rules 23(b)(1) and (b)(2)) and opt-out class actions (Rule 23(b)(3)). Mandatory class actions roughly correspond to the circumstances of lawyer dysfunction that underlie complex litigation, while opt-out class actions roughly correspond to circumstances of inefficient re-litigation that underlie complicated litigation. See pp. 132-34, *supra*. The ALI's proposal acts like a mandatory class action, in the sense that a nonparty meeting § 5.05's requirements cannot opt out of the pending proceeding and commence another proceeding without a preclusion penalty. Therefore, unless the phrase "undue prejudice, burden, or

inconvenience" equates with the Rule 23(b)(1) and (b)(2) standards for mandatory class actions, the notice and preclusion approach eliminates the ability of such nonparties to make the autonomous opt-out decision that is presently guaranteed under Rule 23(b)(3) to class members in complicated litigation. Is it fair to eliminate in effect the opt-out right of nonparties in complicated litigation? Has the ALI adequately justified the change?

Conversely, viewed from the perspective of present litigants, is it fair to turn a small, two-party affair into a sprawling, multi-sided contest? Might the original plaintiff's proofs and arguments be lost sight of in the fray? Is the systemic efficiency that the ALI proposal hopes to achieve worth the loss of the sense of individual justice that the proposal might occasion? Cf. Jack H. Friedenthal, *Increased Participation by Nonparties: The Need for Conditions and Limits*, 13 U.C. Davis L. Rev. 259, 261 (1980) ("It would therefore seem appropriate as an integral part of any new statute or rule allowing broad participation of non-parties to require those who enter the case to pay the additional costs and attorneys fees reasonably necessary to deal with such new issues.").

13. It should now be obvious that a notice and preclusion rule is but one piece of a much larger response to the problem of re-litigation. For instance, a notice and preclusion rule, were it ever to be adopted, would likely entail significant revisions of our present rules regarding party joinder. To be effective, a notice and preclusion approach may also require an expansion of our present notions of jurisdiction. Moreover, the notice and preclusion approach, at least as envisioned by the ALI, operates only against nonparties; some separate mechanisms will be needed to deal with the re-litigation problems posed by multiple pending lawsuits. We have already examined a number of potential responses in this chapter, and we will examine others in the next four chapters.

It should also be obvious that any larger response might entail the sacrifice of some of our foundational procedural assumptions, such as litigant autonomy, adversarial process, and trans-substantivism. Are you convinced that the problem of inefficient re-litigation is worth the sacrifice? Are you convinced that the problem of lawyer dysfunction is worth the sacrifice? You may wish to suspend judgment on these questions, as well as on the wisdom of a notice and preclusion approach, until you have seen the full range of responses that might be employed to deal with the problem of inefficient or dysfunction-producing re-litigation.

14. Whatever the appropriate response might be, it should be evident that, at least until a proposal such as the ALI proposal is adopted, the primary vehicle through which re-litigation will be prevented is party joinder. For the remainder of Part I, we accept that fact as a given, as we explore further limitations on the ability of parties to be joined in one court, and on the methods to overcome those limitations, in Chapters Three and Four. The difficulties encountered in these chapters lead to a deeper exploration of our most powerful joinder device — the class action — in Chapter Five, and ultimately toward the most comprehensive of all joinder and preclusion devices — the bankruptcy consolidation — in Chapter Six.

CHAPTER THREE

LIMITATIONS ON THE AGGREGATION OF RELATED CASES IN A FEDERAL SYSTEM

> [W]e . . . recommend that Congress make the federal forum more readily available in certain complex cases . . . involving scattered events or parties and substantial claims by numerous plaintiffs.
>
> Report of the Federal Courts Study Committee

In an adversarial system, the plaintiff is said to be "master of the complaint" — which means that the plaintiff has the first opportunity to select the parties, the claims to be asserted, and the court to hear the case. These issues are intimately related to each other. The parties or claims that the plaintiff wishes to include in the suit may well determine the court in which the plaintiff files; conversely, the court in which the plaintiff wishes to file may determine the parties and claims that the plaintiff can include.

The last chapter examined the rules that governed plaintiff's decisions about which parties to join. We saw that the "master of the complaint" approach often permitted individual plaintiffs to make joinder decisions that caused either lawyer dysfunction or inefficiency, and often frustrated individual plaintiffs that attempted to make joinder decisions designed to avoid dysfunction or inefficiency. We also examined two possible antidotes to this problem: permitting the early-filing plaintiffs, the defendants, or the court to join nonparties on a mandatory basis, and precluding parties and nonparties from asserting certain claims or issues in later litigation. Implicit in the examination of the joinder rules and of the possible antidotes was the assumption that there existed a court system with jurisdiction over the parties that were to be joined or precluded *and* over the subject matter of the case. Also implicit was the assumption that, within that court system, there existed a single court that could hear the claims of all joined parties.

This chapter examines the first of these assumptions, and explores the limitations that doctrines of territorial and subject matter jurisdiction place on the ability of the plaintiff, the defendants, or the judge to package a complex or complicated case in a single court system. The ensuing chapter examines the second assumption, and explores the limitations that various venue and related doctrines place on the ability of the plaintiff, the defendants, or the judge to package a complex or complicated case in a single court within the court system.

Most of the limitations examined in this chapter arise from the federal nature of our government, both in the sense that jurisdiction over cases is apportioned between federal courts and state courts and in the sense that the sovereignty of the states imposes limits on how much authority a court can exercise with respect to persons not residing within that state and claims not arising in that state. Other limitations, however, are grounded more in a sense of fairness or efficiency than in a sense of federalism.

From the viewpoint of complex and complicated litigation, certain parallels exist between the questions of party joinder considered in the last chapter and "court system" questions that we consider in this chapter. First, in both instances, certain limitations prevent plaintiffs with the incentive to do so from achieving enough joinder to prevent lawyer dysfunction or needless inefficiency. In the party joinder material we considered in the last chapter, the main limitation was the notion of litigant autonomy, although issues of fairness and efficiency also played in to some extent. In the material we are about to consider, the main limitation is the concept of federalism, with issues of fairness and efficiency again playing a supporting role. Second, both the party joinder limitations from the last chapter and the "court system" limitations that we are about to study can cause either dysfunction or needless inefficiency when some plaintiffs can obtain a private advantage from separate litigation. In the last chapter, we were concerned primarily with those potential plaintiffs that sat on the sidelines, and did not focus on those that filed an individual suit to deprive others of their ability to participate equitably in the outcome of the litigation. Here the emphasis is reversed; our primary concern lies with plaintiffs that choose to file an individual suit to obtain an inequitably large share of a judgment, and the problem of sideline-sitters is downplayed.

This chapter examines the jurisdictional rules that plaintiffs must face when they attempt to avoid dysfunction or inefficiency by joining related parties and claims in one court, as well as the various devices that defendants and the judge can use to change the plaintiff's initial choice of court system. Although these rules often can be manipulated to keep related cases apart and thus to create dysfunction or inefficiency, our particular emphasis will be on those rules that can aggregate cases in a single court system. If it turns out that (1) our jurisdictional rules can be developed in a way that fosters consolidation of related cases in one court system (the subject of this chapter), (2) our venue rules can be developed in a way that fosters consolidation of related cases within that system in one courtroom (the subject of the next chapter), and (3) a method for handling sideline-sitters can be developed (the subject of the previous chapter), we will have created a full response to the problems of dysfunction and inefficiency.

The overarching label that is usually attached to such a full response is "aggregation" — all appropriately related claims (whether filed or unfiled) are aggregated (whether through joinder or through preclusion) in one forum for one adjudication. As you now study the stumbling blocks that our jurisdictional rules place in the way of aggregation, ask yourself whether plaintiffs, the defendants, and the judge should ever be entitled to override the chess match that is played out at the intersection of an adversarial system that allows parties to strive for private tactical advantage and a federal system that limits the powers of courts to adjudicate disputes. If you think that some overriding is necessary, under what circumstances should the standard rules be rejected and aggregation permitted? Is it possible to defend the creation of special jurisdictional and venue rules against the criticism that such rules violate the spirit, if not the letter, of "our Federalism"? Is it also possible to defend such aggregation rules against the criticism that they treat like cases differently, thus violating the trans-substantive aspiration of our procedural system?

A. LIMITATIONS ON AGGREGATION IMPOSED BY TERRITORIAL JURISDICTION

In a basic course on civil procedure, you may well have been exposed to the concept of territorial jurisdiction. Most likely, you focused on the problem of when a court in one jurisdiction can constitutionally exercise adjudicatory power over a defendant that the plaintiff wishes to join in a suit in that jurisdiction. This question goes to the very heart of the meaning of a federal system of government, for the scope of a court's territorial jurisdiction over persons and property simultaneously describes one of the most significant limitations on the power of one government within the federal system, establishes a critical element of the sovereignty of other governments within the federal system, and defines an important freedom enjoyed by all citizens against the power of the government. On the other hand, this question also has a very practical dimension. As the last chapter discussed (see pp. 167-68, *supra*), a party is not bound by a judgment entered in a court that cannot exercise jurisdiction over that party. Hence, in thinking about the joinder or aggregation of related cases, the rules of territorial jurisdiction are as significant as, and more foundational than, the rules of party joinder or preclusion.

As a general proposition, the question of jurisdiction can be broken into two parts: general jurisdiction and specific jurisdiction. The difference can be described using this hypothetical: Suppose that A lives in and is a citizen of Indiana. While driving through Virginia one afternoon, A gets into an accident with B, who lives in Maryland. In an entirely unrelated matter, A also breaches a contract with C, who lives in Illinois; the contract was to have been performed in Massachusetts. At an intuitive level, it should be evident that both B and C would be able to sue A in Indiana on their claims (albeit in separate suits). Also on an intuitive level, you might think that Virginia, and arguably Maryland, might be jurisdictions in which B could bring his claim; and Massachusetts, and arguably Illinois, might be jurisdictions in which C could bring her claim. Somewhat less intuitively, you might also think that neither Virginia or Maryland could exercise jurisdiction over A with respect to C's claims, since A has no connection to either state with regard to these claims. Likewise, neither Massachusetts nor Illinois could exercise jurisdiction over A with regard to B's claims. These intuitions would be accurate. Indiana can be said to have "general" jurisdiction over A, since it can entertain any kind of a claim by or against A — even a claim with no connection to Indiana. The remaining states can exercise only "specific" jurisdiction over A with regard to claims that have a connection with that state.

Generally speaking, a state can exercise general jurisdiction over a party when the party has some sustained, significant, ongoing contacts with that state; the classic example is that a party's state of domicile has general jurisdiction over the party. See Milliken v. Meyer, 311 U.S. 457 (1940); cf. Burnham v. Superior Court of California, 495 U.S. 604 (1990) (transient presence of individual in state supports jurisdiction). The problem in most multiparty litigation, however, is that there is not necessarily a single state that has general jurisdiction over everyone. Suppose, for instance, that A, a citizen of Indiana, manufactures a part and sells it to B, a citizen of Virginia. B then assembles the part into a finished product, and sells it nationwide. Plaintiffs C, D, and E are injured in New York, New Jersey, and New Mexico. Assuming that the plaintiffs were inclined to consolidate the case in one forum, there is no single forum that has general jurisdiction over the parties. Hence, the scope of specific jurisdiction is usually the critical question in complex and complicated litigation.

The last hypothetical suggests that this problem of specific jurisdiction should be subdivided into two questions: jurisdiction over defendants and jurisdiction over plaintiffs. The question of jurisdiction over defendants is obvious enough: What are the limits that our federal system places on the ability of the plaintiff to hale a defendant involuntarily into a court in a jurisdiction with which the defendant does not enjoy sustained, significant, and ongoing contacts? The issue of jurisdiction over plaintiffs raises an issue that you may not have addressed in the basic civil procedure class. The reason is that, in a standard lawsuit, there is no issue of jurisdiction over plaintiffs; assuming that the forum state selected by the plaintiff does not have any other connection with the plaintiff, the plaintiff, by filing suit in a court of that state, is deemed to have consented to the jurisdiction of that court over her. As we learned in the last chapter, however, in certain circumstances courts might be able either to join plaintiffs on a mandatory basis or to preclude their later litigation of certain claims or issues. These joined or precluded plaintiffs have no more consented to the jurisdiction of the selected forum than the defendants. Should the same limits that are applied to defendants also apply to plaintiffs? Or should the different circumstances of plaintiffs and defendants lead to different rules?

The ultimate success of any efforts to effect broader joinder or preclusion in complex and complicated litigation hinges on the answers to the questions in the last paragraph.

1. Territorial Jurisdiction over Defendants

WORLD-WIDE VOLKSWAGEN CORP. v. WOODSON

444 U.S. 286 (1980)

■ MR. JUSTICE WHITE delivered the opinion of the Court.

The issue before us is whether, consistently with the Due Process Clause of the Fourteenth Amendment, an Oklahoma court may exercise *in personam* jurisdiction over a nonresident automobile retailer and its wholesale distributor in a products-liability action, when the defendants' only connection with Oklahoma is the fact that an automobile sold in New York to New York residents became involved in an accident in Oklahoma.

I

Respondents Harry and Kay Robinson purchased a new Audi automobile from petitioner Seaway Volkswagen, Inc. (Seaway), in Massena, N. Y., in 1976. The following year the Robinson family, who resided in New York, left that State for a new home in Arizona. As they passed through the State of Oklahoma, another car struck their Audi in the rear, causing a fire which severely burned Kay Robinson and her two children.

The Robinsons subsequently brought a products-liability action in the District Court for Creek County, Okla., claiming that their injuries resulted from defective design and placement of the Audi's gas tank and fuel system. They joined as defendants the automobile's manufacturer, Audi NSU Auto Union Aktiengesellschaft (Audi); its importer, Volkswagen of America, Inc. (Volkswagen); its regional distributor, petitioner World-Wide Volkswagen Corp. (World-Wide); and its retail dealer, petitioner Seaway. Seaway and World-Wide entered special appearances, claiming that Oklahoma's exercise of jurisdiction over them would offend the limitations on the State's jurisdiction imposed by the Due Process Clause of the Fourteenth Amendment.

The facts presented to the District Court showed that World-Wide is incorporated and has its business office in New York. It distributes vehicles, parts, and accessories, under contract with Volkswagen, to retail dealers in New York, New Jersey, and Connecticut. Seaway, one of these retail dealers, is incorporated and has its place of business in New York. Insofar as the record reveals, Seaway and World-Wide are fully independent corporations whose relations with each other and with Volkswagen and Audi are contractual only. Respondents adduced no evidence that either World-Wide or Seaway does any business in Oklahoma, ships or sells any products to or in that State, has an agent to receive process there, or purchases advertisements in any media calculated to reach Oklahoma. In fact, as respondents' counsel conceded at oral argument, there was no showing that any automobile sold by World-Wide or Seaway has ever entered Oklahoma with the single exception of the vehicle involved in the present case.

Despite the apparent paucity of contacts between petitioners and Oklahoma, the District Court rejected their constitutional claim and reaffirmed that ruling in denying petitioners' motion for reconsideration. . . .

We granted certiorari . . . to consider an important constitutional question with respect to state-court jurisdiction and to resolve a conflict between the Supreme Court of Oklahoma and the highest courts of at least four other States. We reverse.

II

The Due Process Clause of the Fourteenth Amendment limits the power of a state court to render a valid personal judgment against a nonresident defendant. Kulko v. California Superior Court, 436 U.S. 84, 91 (1978). A judgment rendered in violation of due process is void in the rendering State and is not entitled to full faith and credit elsewhere. Pennoyer v. Neff, 95 U.S. 714, 732-733 (1878). Due process requires that the defendant be given adequate notice of the suit, Mullane v. Central Hanover Trust Co., 339 U.S. 306, 313-314 (1950), and be subject to the personal jurisdiction of the court, International Shoe Co. v. Washington, 326 U.S. 310 (1945). In the present case, it is not contended that notice was inadequate; the only question is whether these particular petitioners were subject to the jurisdiction of the Oklahoma courts.

As has long been settled, and as we reaffirm today, a state court may exercise personal jurisdiction over a nonresident defendant only so long as there exist "minimum contacts" between the defendant and the forum State. International Shoe Co. v. Washington, *supra*, at 316. The concept of minimum contacts, in turn, can be seen to perform two related, but distinguishable, functions. It protects the defendant against the burdens of litigating in a distant or inconvenient forum. And it acts to ensure that the States, through their courts, do not reach out beyond the limits imposed on them by their status as coequal sovereigns in a federal system.

The protection against inconvenient litigation is typically described in terms of "reasonableness" or "fairness." We have said that the defendant's contacts with the forum State must be such that maintenance of the suit "does not offend 'traditional notions of fair play and substantial justice.'" International Shoe Co. v. Washington, *supra*, at 316, quoting Milliken v. Meyer, 311 U.S. 457, 463 (1940). The relationship between the defendant and the forum must be such that it is "reasonable . . . to require the corporation to defend the particular suit which is brought there." 326 U.S., at 317. Implicit in this emphasis on reasonableness is the understanding that the burden on the defendant, while always a primary concern, will in an appropriate case be considered in light of other relevant factors, including the forum State's interest in adjudicating the dispute, see McGee v. International Life Ins. Co., 355 U.S. 220, 223 (1957); the plaintiff's interest in obtaining convenient and effective relief, see Kulko v. California Superior Court, *supra*, at 92, at least when that interest is not adequately protected by the plaintiff's power to choose the forum, cf. Shaffer v. Heitner, 433 U.S. 186, 211, n.37 (1977); the interstate judicial system's interest in obtaining the most efficient resolution of controversies; and the shared interest of the several States in furthering fundamental substantive social policies, see Kulko v. California Superior Court, *supra*, at 93, 98.

The limits imposed on state jurisdiction by the Due Process Clause, in its role as a guarantor against inconvenient litigation, have been substantially relaxed over the years. As we noted in McGee v. International Life Ins. Co., *supra*, at 222-223, this trend is largely attributable to a fundamental transformation in the American economy:

> "Today many commercial transactions touch two or more States and may involve parties separated by the full continent. With this increasing nationalization of commerce has come a great increase in the amount of business conducted by mail across state lines. At the same time modern transportation and communication have made it much less burdensome for a party sued to defend himself in a State where he engages in economic activity."

The historical developments noted in *McGee*, of course, have only accelerated in the generation since that case was decided.

Nevertheless, we have never accepted the proposition that state lines are irrelevant for jurisdictional purposes, nor could we, and remain faithful to the principles of interstate federalism embodied in the Constitution. The economic interdependence of the States was foreseen and desired by the Framers. . . . [T]he Framers also intended that the States retain many essential attributes of sovereignty, including, in particular, the sovereign power to try causes in their courts. The sovereignty of each State, in turn, implied a limitation on the sovereignty of all of its sister States — a limitation express or implicit in both the original scheme of the Constitution and the Fourteenth Amendment. . . .

Thus, the Due Process Clause "does not contemplate that a state may make binding a judgment *in personam* against an individual or corporate defendant with which the state has no contacts, ties, or relations." International Shoe Co. v. Washington, *supra*, at 319. Even if the defendant would suffer minimal or no inconvenience from being forced to litigate before the tribunals of another State; even if the forum State has a strong interest in applying its law to the controversy; even if the forum State is the most convenient location for litigation, the Due Process Clause, acting as an instrument of interstate federalism, may sometimes act to divest the State of its power to render a valid judgment. Hanson v. Denckla, [357 U.S. 235], 251, 254 [(1958)].

III

Applying these principles to the case at hand, we find in the record before us a total absence of those affiliating circumstances that are a necessary predicate to any exercise of state-court jurisdiction. Petitioners carry on no activity whatsoever in Oklahoma. They close no sales and perform no services there. They avail themselves of none of the privileges and benefits of Oklahoma law. They solicit no business there either through salespersons or through advertising reasonably calculated to reach the State. Nor does the record show that they regularly sell cars at wholesale or retail to Oklahoma customers or residents or that they indirectly, through others, serve or seek to serve the Oklahoma market. In short, respondents seek to base jurisdiction on one, isolated occurrence and whatever inferences can be drawn therefrom: the fortuitous circumstance that a single Audi automobile, sold in New York to New York residents, happened to suffer an accident while passing through Oklahoma.

It is argued, however, that because an automobile is mobile by its very design and purpose it was "foreseeable" that the Robinsons' Audi would cause injury in Oklahoma. Yet "foreseeability" alone has never been a sufficient benchmark for personal jurisdiction under the Due Process Clause. . . .

If foreseeability were the criterion, a local California tire retailer could be forced to defend in Pennsylvania when a blowout occurs there . . .; a Wisconsin seller of a defective automobile jack could be haled before a distant court for damage caused in New Jersey . . .; or a Florida soft-drink concessionaire could be summoned to Alaska to account for injuries happening there . . . . Every seller of chattels would in effect appoint the chattel his agent for service of process. His amenability to suit would travel with the chattel. . . .

This is not to say, of course, that foreseeability is wholly irrelevant. But the foreseeability that is critical to due process analysis is not the mere likelihood that a product will find its way into the forum State. Rather, it is that the defendant's conduct and connection with the forum State are such that he should reasonably anticipate being haled into court there. See Kulko v. California Superior Court, *supra*, at 97-98; Shaffer v. Heitner, 433 U.S., at 216; and see id., at 217-219 (STEVENS, J., concurring in judgment). The Due Process Clause, by ensuring the "orderly administration of the laws," International Shoe Co. v. Washington, 326 U.S., at 319, gives a degree of predictability to the legal system that allows potential defendants to structure their primary conduct with some minimum assurance as to where that conduct will and will not render them liable to suit.

When a corporation "purposefully avails itself of the privilege of conducting activities within the forum State," Hanson v. Denckla, 357 U.S., at 253, it has clear notice that it is subject to suit there, and can act to alleviate the risk of burdensome litigation by procuring insurance, passing the expected costs on to customers, or, if the risks are too great, severing its connection with the State. Hence if the sale of a product of a manufacturer or distributor such as Audi or Volkswagen is not simply an isolated occurrence, but arises from the efforts of the manufacturer or distributor to serve, directly or indirectly, the market for its product in other States, it is not unreasonable to subject it to suit in one of those States if its allegedly defective merchandise has there been the source of injury to its owner or to others. The forum State does not exceed its powers under the Due Process Clause if it asserts personal jurisdiction over a corporation that delivers its products into the stream of commerce with the expectation that they will be purchased by consumers in the forum State. Cf. Gray v. American Radiator & Standard Sanitary Corp., 22 Ill. 2d 432, 176 N. E. 2d 761 (1961).

But there is no such or similar basis for Oklahoma jurisdiction over World-Wide or Seaway in this case. . . .

Because we find that petitioners have no "contacts, ties, or relations" with the State of Oklahoma, International Shoe Co. v. Washington, *supra*, at 319, the judgment of the Supreme Court of Oklahoma is reversed.

■ MR. JUSTICE BRENNAN, dissenting. . . . The Court's opinions focus tightly on the existence of contacts between the forum and the defendant. In so doing, they accord too little weight to the strength of the forum State's interest in the case and fail to explore whether there would be any actual inconvenience to the defendant.

I would find that the forum State has an interest in permitting the litigation to go forward, the litigation is connected to the forum, the defendant is linked to the forum, and the burden of defending is not unreasonable. Accordingly, I would hold that it is neither unfair nor unreasonable to require these defendants to defend in the forum State. . . .

[T]he interest of the forum State and its connection to the litigation is strong. The automobile accident underlying the litigation occurred in Oklahoma. The plaintiffs were hospitalized in Oklahoma when they brought suit. Essential witnesses and evidence were in Oklahoma. See Shaffer v. Heitner, 433 U.S., at 208. The State has a legitimate interest in enforcing its laws designed to keep its highway system safe, and the trial can proceed at least as efficiently in Oklahoma as anywhere else.

The petitioners are not unconnected with the forum. Although both sell automobiles within limited sales territories, each sold the automobile which in fact was driven to Oklahoma where it was involved in an accident. It may be true, as the Court suggests, that each sincerely intended to limit its commercial impact to the limited territory, and that each intended to accept the benefits and protection of the laws only of those States within the territory. But obviously these were unrealistic hopes that cannot be treated as an automatic constitutional shield.

An automobile simply is not a stationary item or one designed to be used in one place. An automobile is intended to be moved around. Someone in the business of selling large numbers of automobiles can hardly plead ignorance of their mobility or pretend that the automobiles stay put after they are sold. It is not merely that a dealer in automobiles foresees that they will move. The dealer actually intends that the purchasers will use the automobiles to travel to distant States where the dealer does not directly "do business." The sale of an automobile does *purposefully* inject the vehicle into the stream of interstate commerce so that it can travel to distant States.

Furthermore, an automobile seller derives substantial benefits from States other than its own . . . The States, through their highway programs, contribute in a very direct and important way to the value of petitioners' business.

■ [The dissenting opinions of MR. JUSTICE MARSHALL and MR. JUSTICE BLACKMUN are omitted.]

ASAHI METAL INDUSTRY CO. v. SUPERIOR COURT OF CALIFORNIA

480 U.S. 102 (1987)

■ JUSTICE O'CONNOR announced the judgment of the Court and delivered the unanimous opinion of the Court with respect to Part I, the opinion of the Court with respect to Part II-B, in which THE CHIEF JUSTICE, JUSTICE BRENNAN, JUSTICE WHITE, JUSTICE MARSHALL, JUSTICE BLACKMUN, JUSTICE POWELL, and JUSTICE STEVENS join, and an opinion with respect to Parts II-A and III, in which THE CHIEF JUSTICE, JUSTICE POWELL, and JUSTICE SCALIA join.

This case presents the question whether the mere awareness on the part of a foreign defendant that the components it manufactured, sold, and delivered outside the United States would reach the forum State in the stream of commerce constitutes "minimum contacts" between the defendant and the forum State such that the exercise of jurisdiction "does not offend 'traditional notions of fair play and substantial justice.'" International Shoe Co. v. Washington, 326 U.S. 310, 316 (1945), quoting Milliken v. Meyer, 311 U.S. 457, 463 (1940).

I

On September 23, 1978, on Interstate Highway 80 in Solano County, California, Gary Zurcher lost control of his Honda motorcycle and collided with a tractor. Zurcher was severely injured, and his passenger and wife, Ruth Ann Moreno, was killed. In September 1979, Zurcher filed a product liability action in the Superior Court of the State of California in and for the County of Solano. Zurcher alleged that the 1978 accident was caused by a sudden loss of air and an explosion in the rear tire of the motorcycle, and alleged that the motorcycle tire, tube, and sealant were defective. Zurcher's complaint named, *inter alia*, Cheng Shin Rubber Industrial Co., Ltd. (Cheng Shin), the Taiwanese manufacturer of the tube. Cheng Shin in turn filed a cross-complaint seeking indemnification from its codefendants and from petitioner, Asahi Metal Industry Co., Ltd. (Asahi), the manufacturer of the tube's valve assembly. Zurcher's claims against Cheng Shin and the other defendants were eventually settled and dismissed, leaving only Cheng Shin's indemnity action against Asahi.

California's long-arm statute authorizes the exercise of jurisdiction "on any basis not inconsistent with the Constitution of this state or of the United States." Cal. Civ. Proc. Code Ann. § 410.10 (West 1973). Asahi moved to quash Cheng Shin's service of summons, arguing the State could not exert jurisdiction over it consistent with the Due Process Clause of the Fourteenth Amendment.

In relation to the motion, the following information was submitted by Asahi and Cheng Shin. Asahi is a Japanese corporation. It manufactures tire valve assemblies in Japan and sells the assemblies to Cheng Shin, and to several other tire manufacturers, for use as components in finished tire tubes. Asahi's sales to Cheng Shin took place in Taiwan. The shipments from Asahi to Cheng Shin were sent from Japan to Taiwan. Cheng Shin bought and incorporated into its tire tubes 150,000 Asahi valve assemblies in 1978; 500,000 in 1979; 500,000 in 1980; 100,000 in 1981; and 100,000 in 1982. Sales to Cheng Shin accounted for 1.24 percent of Asahi's income in 1981 and 0.44 percent in 1982. Cheng Shin alleged that approximately 20 percent of its sales in the United States are in California. Cheng Shin purchases valve assemblies from other suppliers as well, and sells finished tubes throughout the world.

In 1983 an attorney for Cheng Shin conducted an informal examination of the valve stems of the tire tubes sold in one cycle store in Solano County. The attorney declared that of the approximately 115 tire tubes in the store, 97 were purportedly manufactured in Japan or Taiwan, and of those 97, 21 valve stems were marked with the circled letter "A", apparently Asahi's trademark. Of the 21 Asahi valve stems, 12 were incorporated into Cheng Shin tire tubes. The store contained 41 other Cheng Shin tubes that incorporated the valve assemblies of other manufacturers. An affidavit of a manager of Cheng Shin whose duties included the purchasing of component parts stated: "'In discussions with Asahi regarding the purchase of valve stem assemblies the fact that my Company sells tubes throughout the world and specifically the United States has been discussed. I am informed and believe that Asahi was fully aware that valve stem assemblies sold to my Company and to others would end up throughout the United States and in California.'" . . . An affidavit of the president of Asahi, on the other hand, declared that Asahi "'has never contemplated that its limited sales of tire valves to Cheng Shin in Taiwan would subject it to lawsuits in California.'" . . . The record does not include any contract between Cheng Shin and Asahi.

Primarily on the basis of the above information, the Superior Court denied the motion to quash summons, stating: "Asahi obviously does business on an international scale. It is not unreasonable that they defend claims of defect in their product on an international scale." [The court of appeals reversed, but was in turn reversed by California's Supreme Court.]

We granted certiorari, . . . and now reverse.

II

A . . .

Applying the principle that minimum contacts must be based on an act of the defendant, the Court in World-Wide Volkswagen Corp. v. Woodson, 444 U.S. 286 (1980), rejected the assertion that a *consumer*'s unilateral act of bringing the defendant's product into the forum State was a sufficient constitutional basis for personal jurisdiction over the defendant. . . .

In *World-Wide Volkswagen* itself, the state court sought to base jurisdiction not on any act of the defendant, but on the foreseeable unilateral actions of the consumer. Since *World-Wide Volkswagen*, lower courts have been confronted with cases in which the defendant acted by placing a product in the stream of commerce, and the stream eventually swept defendant's product into the forum State, but the defendant did nothing else to purposefully avail itself of the market in the forum State. Some courts have understood the Due Process Clause, as interpreted in *World-Wide Volkswagen*, to allow an exercise of personal jurisdiction to be based on no more than the defendant's act of placing the product in the stream of commerce. Other courts have understood the Due Process Clause and the above-quoted language in *World-Wide Volkswagen* to require the action of the defendant to be more purposefully directed at the forum State than the mere act of placing a product in the stream of commerce. . . .

We now find this latter position to be consonant with the requirements of due process. The "substantial connection," Burger King [Corp. v. Rudzewicz, 471 U.S. 462, 475 (1985)]; McGee [v. International Life Insurance Co., 355 U.S. 220, 223 (1957)], between the defendant and the forum State necessary for a finding of minimum contacts must come about by *an action of the defendant purposefully directed toward the forum State*. *Burger King*, *supra*, at 476; Keeton v. Hustler Magazine, Inc., 465 U.S. 770, 774 (1984). The placement of a product into the stream of commerce, without more, is not an act of the defendant purposefully directed toward the forum State. Additional conduct of the defendant may indicate an intent or purpose to serve the market in the forum State, for example, designing the product for the market in the forum State, advertising in the forum State, establishing channels for providing regular advice to customers in the forum State, or marketing the product through a distributor who has agreed to serve as the sales agent in the forum State. But a defendant's awareness that the stream of commerce may or will sweep the product into the forum State does not convert the mere act of placing the product into the stream into an act purposefully directed toward the forum State.

Assuming, *arguendo*, that respondents have established Asahi's awareness that some of the valves sold to Cheng Shin would be incorporated into tire tubes sold in California, respondents have not demonstrated any action by Asahi to purposefully avail itself of the California market. Asahi does not do business in California. It has no office, agents, employees, or property in California. It does not advertise or otherwise solicit business in California. It did not create, control, or employ the distribution system that brought its valves to California. . . . There is no evidence that Asahi designed its product in anticipation of sales in California. . . . On the basis of these facts, the exertion of personal jurisdiction over Asahi by the Superior Court of California* exceeds the limits of due process.

B

The strictures of the Due Process Clause forbid a state court from exercising personal jurisdiction over Asahi under circumstances that would

---

* We have no occasion here to determine whether Congress could, consistent with the Due Process Clause of the Fifth Amendment, authorize federal court personal jurisdiction over alien defendants based on the aggregate of national contacts, rather than on the contacts between the defendant and the State in which the federal court sits. See Max Daetwyler Corp. v. R. Meyer, 762 F.2d 290, 293-295 (CA3 1985) . . . .

offend "'traditional notions of fair play and substantial justice.'" International Shoe Co. v. Washington, 326 U.S., at 316, quoting Milliken v. Meyer, 311 U.S., at 463.

We have previously explained that the determination of the reasonableness of the exercise of jurisdiction in each case will depend on an evaluation of several factors. A court must consider the burden on the defendant, the interests of the forum State, and the plaintiff's interest in obtaining relief. It must also weigh in its determination "the interstate judicial system's interest in obtaining the most efficient resolution of controversies; and the shared interest of the several States in furthering fundamental substantive social policies." *World-Wide Volkswagen*, 444 U.S., at 292 (citations omitted).

A consideration of these factors in the present case clearly reveals the unreasonableness of the assertion of jurisdiction over Asahi, even apart from the question of the placement of goods in the stream of commerce.

Certainly the burden on the defendant in this case is severe. Asahi has been commanded by the Supreme Court of California not only to traverse the distance between Asahi's headquarters in Japan and the Superior Court of California in and for the County of Solano, but also to submit its dispute with Cheng Shin to a foreign nation's judicial system. The unique burdens placed upon one who must defend oneself in a foreign legal system should have significant weight in assessing the reasonableness of stretching the long arm of personal jurisdiction over national borders.

When minimum contacts have been established, often the interests of the plaintiff and the forum in the exercise of jurisdiction will justify even the serious burdens placed on the alien defendant. In the present case, however, the interests of the plaintiff and the forum in California's assertion of jurisdiction over Asahi are slight. All that remains is a claim for indemnification asserted by Cheng Shin, a Tawainese corporation, against Asahi. The transaction on which the indemnification claim is based took place in Taiwan; Asahi's components were shipped from Japan to Taiwan. Cheng Shin has not demonstrated that it is more convenient for it to litigate its indemnification claim against Asahi in California rather than in Taiwan or Japan.

Because the plaintiff is not a California resident, California's legitimate interests in the dispute have considerably diminished. . . .

World-Wide Volkswagen also admonished courts to take into consideration the interests of the "several States," in addition to the forum State, in the efficient judicial resolution of the dispute and the advancement of substantive policies. In the present case, this advice calls for a court to consider the procedural and substantive policies of other *nations* whose interests are affected by the assertion of jurisdiction by the California court. The procedural and substantive interests of other nations in a state court's assertion of jurisdiction over an alien defendant will differ from case to case. In every case, however, those interests, as well as the Federal Government's interest in its foreign relations policies, will be best served by a careful inquiry into the reasonableness of the assertion of jurisdiction in the particular case, and an unwillingness to find the serious burdens on an alien defendant outweighed by minimal interests on the part of the plaintiff or the forum State. "Great care and reserve should be exercised when extending our notions of personal jurisdiction into the international field." United States v. First National City Bank, 379 U.S. 378, 404 (1965) (Harlan, J., dissenting). . . .

Considering the international context, the heavy burden on the alien defendant, and the slight interests of the plaintiff and the forum State, the exercise of personal jurisdiction by a California court over Asahi in this instance would be unreasonable and unfair.

III

Because the facts of this case do not establish minimum contacts such that the exercise of personal jurisdiction is consistent with fair play and substantial justice, the judgment of the Supreme Court of California is reversed, and the case is remanded for further proceedings not inconsistent with this opinion.

■ JUSTICE BRENNAN, with whom JUSTICE WHITE, JUSTICE MARSHALL, and JUSTICE BLACKMUN join, concurring in part and concurring in the judgment. I do not agree with the interpretation in Part II-A of the stream-of-commerce theory, nor with the conclusion that Asahi did not "purpose[ful]ly avail itself of the California market." I do agree, however, with the Court's conclusion in Part II-B that the exercise of personal jurisdiction over Asahi in this case would not comport with "fair play and substantial justice" . . . . This is one of those rare cases in which "minimum requirements inherent in the concept of 'fair play and substantial justice' . . . defeat the reasonableness of jurisdiction even [though] the defendant has purposefully engaged in forum activities." Burger King Corp. v. Rudzewicz, 471 U.S. 462, 477-478 (1985). I therefore join Parts I and II-B of the Court's opinion, and write separately to explain my disagreement with Part II-A.

Part II-A states that "a defendant's awareness that the stream of commerce may or will sweep the product into the forum State does not convert the mere act of placing the product into the stream into an act purposefully directed toward the forum State." Under this view, a plaintiff would be required to show "[a]dditional conduct" directed toward the forum before finding the exercise of jurisdiction over the defendant to be consistent with the Due Process Clause. I see no need for such a showing, however. The stream of commerce refers not to unpredictable currents or eddies, but to the regular and anticipated flow of products from manufacture to distribution to retail sale. As long as a participant in this process is aware that the final product is being marketed in the forum State, the possibility of a lawsuit there cannot come as a surprise. Nor will the litigation present a burden for which there is no corresponding benefit. . . .

■ JUSTICE STEVENS, with whom JUSTICE WHITE and JUSTICE BLACKMUN join, concurring in part and concurring in the judgment. The judgment of the Supreme Court of California should be reversed for the reasons stated in Part II-B of the Court's opinion. While I join Parts I and

II-B, I do not join Part II-A for two reasons. First, it is not necessary to the Court's decision. An examination of minimum contacts is not always necessary to determine whether a state court's assertion of personal jurisdiction is constitutional. . . . Accordingly, I see no reason in this case for the plurality to articulate "purposeful direction" or any other test as the nexus between an act of a defendant and the forum State that is necessary to establish minimum contacts.

Second, even assuming that the test ought to be formulated here, Part II-A misapplies it to the facts of this case. The plurality seems to assume that an unwavering line can be drawn between "mere awareness" that a component will find its way into the forum State and "purposeful availment" of the forum's market. Over the course of its dealings with Cheng Shin, Asahi has arguably engaged in a higher quantum of conduct than "[the] placement of a product into the stream of commerce, without more . . . ." Whether or not this conduct rises to the level of purposeful availment requires a constitutional determination that is affected by the volume, the value, and the hazardous character of the components. In most circumstances I would be inclined to conclude that a regular course of dealing that results in deliveries of over 100,000 units annually over a period of several years would constitute "purposeful availment" even though the item delivered to the forum State was a standard product marketed throughout the world.

Notes and Questions

1. Although the Supreme Court has been fairly quiet on the issue for the last decade, the question of personal jurisdiction over defendants has generated a significant number of not entirely consistent opinions from the Court. The present approach, reflected in both *World-Wide Volkswagen* and *Asahi*, involves a two-part test: first, an inquiry into whether the defendant has certain "minimum contacts" with the forum, and second, an inquiry into whether the assertion of jurisdiction would comport with "traditional notions of fair play and substantial justice." Although there continues to be some disagreement about this two-part test (see, for instance, Justice Brennan's dissents and Justice Scalia's refusal to join Part II-B of the *Asahi* opinion), the larger disagreement stems not from the test itself but from the application of the test to the facts of individual cases.

At a different level, the Court also seems to vacillate about the philosophical basis for the concept of personal jurisdiction over defendants. The standard approach, reflected in *World-Wide Volkswagen*, is to conceive of the requirement of personal jurisdiction as a limit on the sovereign power of any court within a federal system over non-citizens of that state. Just two years after *World-Wide Volkswagen*, however, Justice White, again writing for the Court, suggested a very different basis for personal jurisdiction:

> It is true that we have stated that the requirement of personal jurisdiction, as applied to state courts, reflects an element of federalism and the character of state sovereignty vis-a-vis other states. . . . The restriction on state sovereign power described in *World-Wide Volkswagen Corp.*, however, must be seen as ultimately a function of the individual liberty

interest preserved by the Due Process Clause. That clause is the only source of the personal jurisdiction requirement and the clause itself makes no mention of federalism concerns. Furthermore, if the federalism concept operated as an independent restriction on the sovereign power of the court, it would not be possible to waive the personal jurisdiction requirement. Individual actions cannot change the powers of sovereignty, although the individual can subject himself to powers from which he may otherwise be protected.

Insurance Corp. of Ireland v. Compagnie des Bauxites de Guinee, 456 U.S. 694, 702 n.10 (1982). This understanding of personal jurisdiction has been assailed as "historically, analytically, and functionally incorrect." Fleming James, Jr. et al., Civil Procedure 60 (4th ed. 1992). In which cases would a federalism-based understanding lead to different outcomes than a liberty-based understanding?

2. *World-Wide Volkswagen* and *Asahi* debate the constitutional limits that a court must face in the exercise of jurisdiction. But a court must also find some positive authority that authorizes the exercise of jurisdiction over particular defendants. In many states, this positive authority is a statute that describes the specific circumstances in which jurisdiction can be exercised. *Asahi* quoted the California statute, which is the broadest statute possible; it authorizes the assertion of jurisdiction to the constitutional maximum. The statutes in most states, however, describe more specific conduct or contacts that must exist in order for jurisdiction to be asserted.

3. Both *World-Wide Volkswagen* and *Asahi* involve attempts to subject a *person* to suit in a *state* forum. You might have wondered whether the rules are different with respect to suits against *property* or suits in a *federal* forum. With respect to cases involving property, the territorial jurisdiction rules (which encompass both in rem jurisdiction and quasi in rem jurisdiction) are somewhat different than they are in the personal jurisdiction context, especially with regard to moveable or intangible property that has no permanent physical location. Nonetheless, with the arguable exception of interpleader actions (which we study at pp. 325, 413, *infra*), few disputes in which the property itself is the defendant would be regarded as complex or complicated litigation. Therefore, we pass over this issue with the overly simplistic observation that the Court has in more recent years insisted on a somewhat close connection between the property and the forum. See Shaffer v, Heitner, 433 U.S. 186 (1977).

The issue of whether the rules of territorial jurisdiction differ between state and federal courts, however, is a matter of great significance to complex and complicated litigation. If the rules were more liberal in one of the court systems, then there would be a reason to prefer that system for the aggregation of cases that might cause dysfunction or needless inefficiency. As a theoretical matter, it would appear that the rules could be more liberal in a federal court. The United States has a relationship with all its citizens and also has contacts with a large number of foreign entities. Hence, whether using a sovereignty or a liberty approach, the federal courts could justify the assertion of jurisdiction over many more persons than could any state court. Although the matter is not entirely clear with regard to claims based on state law, arguably the federal courts' only constitutional constraints is due process clause of the Fifth Amendment, rather than the due process clause of the Fourteenth Amendment.

This theoretical possibility is bounded by the practical reality that federal courts too must find some affirmative grant of authority for the exercise of personal jurisdiction, and the most generally applicable present authority commands federal courts that sit in each state to work within the same personal jurisdiction limitations that a state court in that state must work. See F.R.Civ.P. 4(k)(1)(A) (service of a summons is "effective to establish jurisdiction over the person of a defendant . . . who could be subjected to the jurisdiction of a court of general jurisdiction in the state in which the district court is located"). There are a few exceptions to this limitation. Service is also effective in a 100-mile bubble around the federal court with regard to defendants joined under Rule 19 (see p. 116, *supra*) or Rule 14 (a rule that permits the joinder of third party defendants). F.R.Civ.P. 4(k)(1)(B). Moreover, courts can also exercise jurisdiction over anyone with requisite contacts with the United States as a whole in (1) interpleader actions, see F.R.Civ.P. 4(k)(1)(C); 28 U.S.C. § 2361; (2) other cases in which Congress authorizes such jurisdiction, see F.R.Civ.P. 4(k)(1)(D); and (3) cases based on federal law in which no state court has sufficient contacts with the defendant to exercise jurisdiction but the defendant has sufficient contacts with the nation as a whole, see F.R.Civ.P. 4(k)(2). Aside from interpleader, the number of statutes in which Congress has authorized federal courts to exercise nationwide jurisdiction in civil matters are relatively few. See 4A Charles A. Wright & Arthur R. Miller, Federal Practice & Procedure § 1125 (1987). The nationwide service of process statutes that would regularly be implicated in complex or complicated litigation include 15 U.S.C. §§ 22 (Clayton Act cases); 15 U.S.C. § 78aa (securities actions); 18 U.S.C. § 1865(d) (RICO actions); and 29 U.S.C. § 1451(d) (ERISA actions).

Can nationwide service of process also be implied from the overall structure of a federal statutory scheme? See Omni Capital International v. Rudolf Wolff & Co., 484 U.S. 97 (1987).

4. The existence of nationwide service of process for some federal claims raises an interesting question. Suppose that a plaintiff wishes to sue defendants from Iowa and Idaho on a securities case, and brings the case in a federal court in Connecticut. The plaintiff also wishes to assert related state law fraud claims against both defendants, but the requisite statutory and constitutional connection between Connecticut and the defendants is lacking with regard to the fraud claims. Would a federal court be required to apply the Connecticut and constitutional limits on territorial jurisdiction, see Fed.R.Civ.P. 4(k)(1)(A), or could it bend the limits on the theory that the defendant is already present before the court on a related federal claim? The latter argument, which would permit a federal court to exercise "pendent personal jurisdiction," has been accepted by a number of federal courts. See IUE AFL-CIO Pension Fund v. Hermann, 9 F.3d 1049, 1057 (2d Cir. 1993), cert. denied, 513 U.S. 822 (1994) (permitting pendent personal jurisdiction as long as state and federal claims arose from "a common nucleus of operative facts"); ESAB Group, Inc. v. Centricut, Inc., 126 F.3d 617 (4th Cir. 1997), cert. denied, — U.S. —, 118 S.Ct. 1364 (1998) (same); but see Wright & Miller, *supra*, § 1125 (1998 Supp.) (questioning theory). Could the concept of pendent personal jurisdiction be applied to state claims, so that as long as a court had personal jurisdiction over a defendant with regard to one claim, the court could also exercise jurisdiction over the defendant with regard to other claims for which personal jurisdiction would not otherwise attach? See Rice v. Nova Biomedical Corp., 38 F.3d 909 (7th Cir. 1994), cert. denied, 514 U.S. 1111 (1995) (permitting jurisdiction).

5. In federal court, the plaintiff bears the burden of proving that personal jurisdiction exists. See One World Botanicals Ltd. v. Gulf Coast Nutritionals, Inc., 987 F. Supp. 317 (D. N.J. 1997). If the trial judge does not hold an

evidentiary hearing on the issue of territorial jurisdiction, the plaintiff needs only to make out a prima facie case of jurisdiction, which means that the evidence, viewed in the light most favorable to the plaintiff, need be sufficient only to survive a motion for a directed verdict. See Francosteel Corp. v. M/V Charm, 19 F.3d 624 (11th Cir. 1994). On appeal the issue of territorial jurisdiction is reviewed *de novo*, see CompuServe, Inc. v. Patterson, 89 F.3d 1257 (6th Cir. 1996), although factual findings made by the trial court might be reviewed under a clearly erroneous standard, see Rano v. Sipa Press, Inc., 987 F.2d 580 (9th Cir. 1993).

6. *CompuServe* raises an interesting issue that could, perhaps, eventually spell the end of territorial jurisdiction limits: Whether a defendant is subject to jurisdiction in a state merely because its Web site can be accessed over the Internet in that state. If posting such a Web site is viewed as a sufficient minimum contact, then many defendants will be subject to jurisdiction in every state. Thus far, however, the cases have not generally held that Web page advertisements are, as such, enough contact, although they have certainly viewed Web pages as a relevant and weighty factor in deciding if minimum contacts exist. See *CompuServe*, 89 F.3d 1257; Cybersell, Inc. v. Cybersell, Inc., 130 F.3d 414 (9th Cir. 1997); see also Inset Systems, Inc. v. Instruction Set, Inc., 937 F. Supp. 161 (D. Conn. 1996) (Web page alone was sufficient contact); Maritz Inc. v. Cybergold Inc., 947 F. Supp. 1328 (E.D. Mo. 1997) (active solicitation of business over Internet sufficient contact).

7. Another potentially fruitful ground for avoiding territorial jurisdiction limitations is to allege the existence of a conspiracy, and then to hale into the forum co-conspirators over whom the court might not otherwise have had jurisdiction. Thus far, the courts have not typically been overly receptive to this theory. See Stauffacher v. Bennett, 969 F.2d 455 (7th Cir.), cert. denied, 506 U.S. 1034 (1992), Jungquist v. Sheikh Sultan Bin Khalifa al Nahyan, 115 F.3d 1020 (D.C. Cir. 1997).

8. In *World-Wide Volkswagen*, there was no doubt that Seaway and World-Wide were joined as defendants under Rule 20. Thus, rules of territorial jurisdiction can be viewed as a set of rules that exclude some of the defendants that are candidates for joinder under Rule 20. Granting this to be true, exactly why did the plaintiffs join the retail car dealer and the regional distributor when the manufacturer alone plainly bore the ultimate responsibility for the design of the car and the location of the gas tank and fuel system? The answer may be that the Robinsons wanted to sue in Oklahoma state court. Since the Robinsons, like Seaway and World-Wide, were citizens of New York at the time that the action was commenced, and since diversity jurisdiction fails when parties from the same state are both plaintiffs and defendants, the suit against Seaway and World-Wide may have been nothing more than a tactical move to defeat the diversity jurisdiction of the federal court in Oklahoma. (As we shall see in Chapter Four, a defendant can often remove a case from state to federal court when the case lies within the federal court's jurisdiction.) If this was the reasoning, the plaintiffs' lawyer may have been very savvy. After the decision in *World-Wide Volkswagen*, the remaining defendants removed the case to federal court, and a jury returned a verdict for the defendants. Their later efforts to re-open the case also proved unavailing. See Robinson v. Audi Aktiengesellschaft, 56 F.3d 1259 (10th Cir. 1995), cert. denied, 516 U.S. 1045 (1996).

This history demonstrates that the question of personal jurisdiction cannot be understood in a vacuum; it must be seen against other rules, such as joinder rules and rules of subject matter jurisdiction, that also influence a plaintiff's choice of party and court system. This history also demonstrates how rules with a significant public dimension (such as joinder rules, territorial jurisdiction rules, and subject matter jurisdiction rules) are used — indeed, manipulated — by private parties for private ends. This sort of manipulation is, perhaps, inevitable in an adversary system in which choices about the structure of the litigation are left in the hands of the parties. Does this suggest that the adversarial approach to structuring lawsuits should generally be abandoned? Does it suggest that we should develop different rules of territorial jurisdiction over defendants if a "neutral" participant (such as the judge) structured the litigation in a manner conducive to the public interest? If your answer to the last question is "Yes," could we also adopt different rules of territorial jurisdiction over defendants when the plaintiff (for whatever motivation) proposes a joinder scheme that advances the public interest?

9. This last question leads to the application of territorial jurisdiction in complex and complicated litigation. From the viewpoint of a plaintiff whose joinder strategy is consistent with the public interest in aggregating complex or complicated litigation in one forum, nationwide service of process is good, the limitation on nationwide service of process imposed by Rule 4(k)(1)(A) is bad, and pendent personal jurisdiction, while promising in some cases, is too limited to achieve aggregation in most cases. Given that the federal court's limitation on nationwide service is based on Rule 4(k)(1)(A), is there any argument that federal courts can overlook the rule in either complex or complicated litigation? One way to ground the argument would be to appeal to Rule 1, which provides that the Federal Rules "shall be construed and administered to secure the just speedy, and inexpensive determination of every action." But isn't there a difference between "construing" or "administering" a rule on the one hand, and flatly ignoring it on the other? Is the inefficiency caused by complicated litigation enough of a reason to ignore Rule 4(k)(1)(A)? Is the threat to rational adjudication caused by lawyer dysfunction enough of a reason to ignore Rule 4(k)(1)(A)? Presumably, the argument would run as follows: Rational adjudication is an essential aspect of the constitutional guarantee of due process. To the extent that lawyer dysfunction prevents rational adjudication, the adherence to Federal Rules that cause lawyer dysfunction is unconstitutional conduct; the Federal Rules must give way to the Constitution.

This argument, of course, leaves complicated litigation behind; unless the inefficiency rises to the level that it causes lawyer dysfunction, there is nothing unconstitutional about adhering to rules that produce certain inefficiencies. It also rests on at least two assumptions: first, that due process guarantees rational adjudication, and second, that the court's ability to rationally adjudicate claims not presently before the court, and not just the ability to adjudicate those pending in the court, enters the due process equation. The first assumption seems easily demonstrated; the latter is more controversial.

10. Moreover, this argument might well force a pair of constitutional conflicts. On the one hand, the claim that federal courts have an authority to override the Federal Rules through some sort of common law rulemaking creates a separation of powers tension with Congress, which has an authority to legislate in the area and which has established a process for the promulgation of federal rules of procedure. See 28 U.S.C. §§ 2071-74. In *Omni Capital*, the

Supreme Court rejected an argument by plaintiff to fill in the gaps in Rule 4 with a nationwide service of process rule that would reach a defendant that had insufficient contacts with the forum state to justify jurisdiction under the state statute authorizing jurisdiction. The Court began by noting that, "[a]t common law, a court lacked authority to issue process outside its district"; rather, "specific legislative authorization of extraterritorial service of summons was required." 484 U.S. at 108-09. After questioning whether a federal court even possesses a source of authority for creating such rules, id. at 109, the Court held that it would in any event be "unwise" to create them in the context of the case, which involved allegations of breach of the Commodity Exchange Act:

> It seems likely that Congress has been acting on the assumption that federal courts cannot add to the scope of service of summons Congress has authorized. . . . The strength of this longstanding assumption, and the network of statutory enactments and judicial decisions tied to it, argue strongly against devising common-law service of process provisions at this late date for at least two reasons. First, since Congress concededly has the power to limit service of process, circumspection is called for in going beyond what Congress has authorized. Second, as statutes and rules have always provided the measures for service, courts are inappropriate forums for deciding whether to extend them. Legislative rulemaking better ensures proper consideration of a service rule's ramifications within the pre-existing structure and is more likely to lead to consistent application. [Id. at 109-10.]

Would this logic preclude the use of nationwide service of process to overcome lawyer dysfunction?

The second constitutional conflict lies on the state-federal level. As we shall discuss in more detail shortly, federal jurisdiction typically arises from two sources: federal question and diversity. Diversity jurisdiction involves claims founded on state law. Whether a federal court, acting without congressional authorization, can override state personal jurisdiction rules for a claim based on state law has never been definitively resolved by the Supreme Court. Certainly there would be Tenth Amendment overtones to such efforts. See Erie Railroad Co. v. Tompkins, 304 U.S. 64 (1938); Guaranty Trust Co. v. York, 326 U.S. 99 (1945). On the other hand, the 100-mile bubble of Rule 4(k)(1)(B) and the concept of pendent personal jurisdiction suggest that federal courts are willing, without pangs of constitutional guilt, to make some inroads on state-based territorial jurisdiction limitations in diversity cases. Would another inroad that responds to the constitutional need for rational adjudication also be appropriate?

Assuming that such an inroad is possible, how could it be defended against the argument that any inroad would create different rules for different cases, thus creating uncertainty and violating our trans-substantive aspiration? Moreover, if left in the hands of the plaintiff, might a broader rule of territorial jurisdiction create the potential for new forms of tactical manipulation? Do the constitutional and practical concerns in this Note suggest that a broader rule of territorial jurisdiction in complex litigation is a bad idea, or only that the application of the rule must be closely supervised by the court?

11. To what extent could the concerns in the last note be alleviated if Congress enacted a statute that provided federal courts with the authority to effect nationwide service of process in all cases filed in federal court? Could Congress also enact a statute authorizing *state* courts to assert jurisdiction over defendants? Think of this question in terms of *World-Wide Volkswagen*. If it offends traditional notions of fair play and substantial justice for the Oklahoma

legislature to authorize its courts to assert jurisdiction over Seaway, would the offense be any less if Congress did so? See Roger H. Trangsrud, *The Federal Common Law of Personal Jurisdiction*, 57 Geo. Wash. L. Rev. 849, 903-904 (1989). Even if Congress could not pass legislation that generally permitted federal or state courts to assert jurisdiction over defendants like Seaway, would Congress have the authority in complex or complicated litigation? Note that the case might be easier to make in complex cases, since such a statute could presumably be enacted pursuant to the due process clauses of the Fifth and Fourteenth Amendments (as implemented by the "necessary and proper" clause and § 5 of the Fourteenth Amendment). But what would be the constitutional foundation for a statute in complicated litigation? The Commerce Clause?

12. An underlying assumption in the last two Notes was that special common law rules or statutes would be necessary to overcome the dysfunction or inefficiency in complex or complicated litigation. Would a better approach be to maintain the present regime of common law and statutory rules of territorial jurisdiction, and to interpret the Constitution in a way that would be sensitive to the needs of complex or complicated litigation? Since *World-Wide Volkswagen* and *Asahi* were both arguably complicated, a more generous interpretation of the standard constitutional line may be foreclosed in complicated litigation. But neither case was complex. Do you see any indication that the rules the cases posit would be different in complex litigation? How should the clash between two distinct due process interests (the interest in rational adjudication vs. the interests in limited sovereignty of courts and liberty) be resolved?

IN RE DES CASES

789 F. Supp. 552 (E.D.N.Y. 1992), appeal dismissed, 7 F.3d 20 (2d Cir. 1993)

■ WEINSTEIN, District Judge.

I. INTRODUCTION

This diversity case presents a classic illustration of why traditional limits on personal jurisdiction must be modified for mass torts. The torts alleged here involve numerous claims of injury from exposure in utero to diethylstilbestrol (DES). DES was developed and tested in laboratories throughout the country and the world. Permission to use it was sought and obtained from the federal Food and Drug Administration by pharmaceutical companies scattered across the nation. Some companies conducted national advertising and a national corps of salespersons hawked the drug in doctors' offices in every part of the country. . . . Even companies producing exclusively for local markets relied on the nationally developed understanding and consensus about DES and used knowledge and chemicals from all parts of the United States and the world. Thousands of persons in hamlets and cities across the country are now claiming to have been adversely affected by exposure to the drug. In short, the technology, marketing, sociology, and possible ill effects of DES knew no state boundaries. The national nature of the resulting toxic tort litigation must be reflected in the law's treatment of jurisdictional issues. . . .

II. FACTS

A. Background

DES, a synthetic estrogen, was developed in the late 1930s. . . .

In 1947 and 1948 several of the twelve DES manufacturers sought and were granted permission by the FDA to market DES to prevent miscarriage and fetal death. By 1952 the FDA considered DES proven safe. Hundreds of additional manufacturers then entered the market. Millions of pregnant women ingested DES during the 1950s and 1960s.

In 1971, doctors in Boston concluded that DES was a teratogen responsible for the appearance of adenocarcinoma, a rare form of vaginal cancer, in eight young women who had been exposed to DES in the womb. The FDA soon thereafter disapproved the continued marketing of DES for pregnancy use. . . .

Women exposed to DES in utero may develop adenosis, a pre-cancerous cell change which can be treated by cauterization or surgery. DES is said to cause a variety of other more serious disorders, including miscarriage, uterine deformities, ectopic pregnancy, and breast cancer. Male fetuses exposed to DES may be at risk of developing undescended testicles, sterility, and deformities. As persons exposed to DES in utero age, other medical problems may be linked to DES. There is also evidence that DES daughters pass on defects to their own female children. Whether permanent inheritable genetic damage will be spread more widely in future generations is uncertain.

DES was sold as a generic drug. It was produced in tablets of various dosages according to the same formula by all manufacturers and marketed nationally under a generic description. Pharmacists filled prescriptions by using DES manufactured by different companies interchangeably. Each of the many manufacturers produced and sold DES for different periods between 1949 and 1971. Some of the companies that made and sold DES no longer exist.

Litigation concerning alleged DES-related injuries has occupied courts around the country since the mid-1970s. In New York state alone, more than 500 DES cases against scores of defendants are pending in state and federal courts. . . .

B. Present Actions

In Ashley v. Abbott Laboratories, No. 91-3784, and Silveri v. Abbott Laboratories, No. 91-4986, plaintiffs claim injuries from their exposure (or their spouses' exposure) in utero to DES. Plaintiff Angela Silveri is a New York resident, as are approximately half of the *Ashley* plaintiffs. The remaining *Ashley* plaintiffs each reside in another state or a foreign country. All plaintiffs allege causes of action sounding in warranty, negligence and strict liability and seek compensatory and punitive damages. Defendants are companies that manufactured and distributed DES or are successors to such companies. Subject matter jurisdiction in each case is predicated on diversity of citizenship.

Defendant Boehringer Ingelheim Pharmaceuticals, Inc. ("Boehringer") has never produced or sold DES, but it is alleged to be responsible for Stayner Corporation, a company that did. . . . Between 1949 and 1971 Stayner obtained its supply of DES from chemical companies located in California, Tennessee and Ohio, manufactured DES tablets at a plant in California and sold the tablets in California, Oregon, Washington and Montana; undoubtedly the California, Tennessee and Ohio plants obtained some of their supplies from other states. Available figures for the years 1949-56 indicated that Stayner's DES revenues averaged a little over $5,000 per year during that period. Affidavits from senior Stayner employees indicate that the company never was licensed to do business in New York, never maintained an office or agent in New York, never solicited business in New York and never shipped DES to New York. By contrast, Boehringer, a Delaware corporation with its principal place of business in Connecticut, has been authorized to do business in New York since its inception. Boehringer markets its products (which do not include DES) in all states and is licensed to do business in several other states besides New York.

Boyle & Co. ("Boyle") is a closely held California corporation. At oral argument, counsel for Boyle indicated that the company manufactured and sold DES between 1949 and 1960 in California and other states west of the Mississippi River. Sales of DES tablets peaked in 1950, when Boyle sold about 157,000 tablets in packages of 100 and 1,000. Total revenues from all company business reached their highest point in the late 1950s and are now minimal. Boyle claims never to have shipped DES to New York or sold it here. Employee affidavits attest that the company has never been licensed to do business in New York, never maintained an office or agents in New York and never advertised in New York.

C. Motions

Boehringer has moved to dismiss the complaints under Federal Rules of Civil Procedure 12(b)(6) and 12(b)(2) for failure to state a claim and for lack of personal jurisdiction. Boyle joins in the motion to dismiss for lack of personal jurisdiction. With respect to Angela Silveri and the *Ashley* plaintiffs domiciled in New York, Boehringer's and Boyle's motions must be denied. As applied to the non-New York *Ashley* plaintiffs, defendants' motions will be addressed in a separate memorandum. Subsequent references to plaintiffs in this memorandum will refer to the New York plaintiffs unless otherwise indicated. . . .

III. NEW YORK SUBSTANTIVE LAW AND RULES AFFECTING SUBSTANTIVE RIGHTS . . .

In Hymowitz v. Eli Lilly and Co., 73 N.Y.2d 487, 539 N.E.2d 1069, cert. denied, 493 U.S. 944 (1989), the Court of Appeals frontally addressed the problem of apportioning liability. . . . *Hymowitz* followed the course charted in Sindell v. Abbott Laboratories, 26 Cal. 3d 588, 607 P.2d 924, cert. denied,

449 U.S. 912 (1980), and Brown v. Superior Court, 44 Cal. 3d 1049, 751 P.2d 470, (1988). Those cases adopted a scheme under which DES manufacturers are severally liable according to each manufacturer's share of the national market at the time of plaintiff's exposure.

California law provides exculpation, however, to any manufacturer that can prove its product did not injure a plaintiff — for example, by establishing that its product was not distributed where plaintiff's mother purchased DES or was produced in a color or shape different from that which plaintiff's mother recalls taking. See *Sindell*, 607 P.2d at 937. The *Hymowitz* court, while adopting several liability based on national market share, departed from the California approach by not allowing "exculpation of a defendant who, although a member of the market producing DES for pregnancy use, appears not to have caused a particular plaintiff's injury." *Hymowitz*, 73 N.Y.2d at 512. The court noted: "It is merely a windfall for a producer to escape liability solely because it manufactured a more identifiable pill, or sold only to certain drugstores." Id. Under the *Hymowitz* rule, only those defendants that can prove that they never participated in the marketing of DES for use by pregnant women are exculpated. Id. This rule apparently is a default rule: one-hundred percent liability will still be assessed against a single manufacturer where it can be shown that its product was the only one taken by the plaintiff's mother. . . .

V. PERSONAL JURISDICTION

Personal jurisdiction must be determined in the first instance according to the jurisdictional law of the forum — New York. . . . The application of New York law must then be measured against due process limits. See, *e.g.*, International Shoe Co. v. Washington, 326 U.S. 310 (1945). . . .

A. New York Jurisdictional Statutes

Section 302(a)(3)(ii) is the provision which applies to the activity of companies alleged not to have conducted any business in New York. It provides for jurisdiction over defendants whose out-of-state tortious acts cause injury to a person within the state, so long as the tortfeasor should have expected its act to have consequences in the state and it derives substantial revenue from interstate or international commerce. It reads:

> (a) As to a cause of action arising from any of the acts enumerated in this section, a court may exercise personal jurisdiction over any non-domiciliary . . . who in person or through an agent . . . (3) commits a tortious act without the state causing injury to person or property within the state . . . if he . . . (ii) expects or should reasonably expect the act to have consequences in the state and derives substantial revenue from interstate or international commerce. . . .

Existing case law on section 302(a)(3)(ii) . . . offers no direct guidance on the application of the "reasonable expectation" element to mass DES torts; precedent is here only a slight inhibitant against rational decisionmaking. . . . The issue must instead be resolved in a manner consistent with the court's informed prediction of what the New York Court of Appeals would do when faced with the same issue.... That court has already gone to considerable lengths to adapt state substantive law to the particular circumstances of the DES cases. Moreover, *Hymowitz* itself drew a direct link between the jurisdictional and substantive components of DES litigation by imposing several, rather than joint and several, liability.... New York law favors fully compensating plaintiffs for losses sustained.... For mass torts involving numerous defendants, this result is usually achieved by the imposition of joint and several liability.... Given the *Hymowitz* court's decision to forgo joint and several liability, a DES plaintiff's full recovery would be frustrated if all manufacturers for pregnancy use could not be brought into court....

Hymowitz and the New York Civil Practice Law and Rules as well as legislative policy must thus be read as favoring a jurisdictional reach consistent with the national market share rationale and the adoption of several liability. A consonant interpretation of C.P.L.R. § 302(a)(3)(ii) supports the conclusion that any manufacturer of DES, by its participation in the national marketing of a generic drug, should "reasonably expect" its act of selling in the national market "to have," as C.P.L.R. 302(a)(3)(ii) puts it, "consequences in the state."

Even before *Hymowitz*, all DES manufacturers knew that their acts were having forum consequences in New York. All were competing to carve out local spheres of influence within the national DES market. Since the product was a generic, perfectly fungible consumer item, each manufacturer and distributor secured its market niche knowing that, by occupying this territory, other suppliers would have cause to look elsewhere to sell the same product. Moreover, the existence of the local markets depended upon the creation of a national DES market. Defendants' engagement in the national DES industry alerted them to the fact that their conduct in marketing generic DES in one part of the country would have economic and trade flow consequences in every other part, including New York. There was here a true national market encouraged and protected by the Commerce Clause of the federal Constitution and national drug regulations, not a series of discrete inward-looking and unrelated markets. Sales in any part of the national market had a necessary impact on every other part. *Hymowitz* simply marked the Court of Appeals' recognition that these features of the DES economy were relevant to the apportionment of liability among defendants.

The fact that DES manufacturers did not anticipate *Hymowitz* or the jurisdictional consequences flowing from that decision is not significant. The parties in this suit are governed by the substantive common law and jurisdictional law in effect at the time of the suit....

B. Constitutionality of New York Statutes

C.P.L.R. §§ 301 and 302(a)(3)(ii) must be applied in a manner that does not violate the federal Constitution. The issue is whether the Constitution limits the ability of New York state to provide full compensation to residents injured by a product sold in the national DES market....

1. *Current Due Process Doctrine and Problems Raised by Its Application to Mass Torts*

There is considerable doubt about the current existence of a unitary, coherent jurisdictional due process standard. . . .

One common feature of recent Supreme Court formulations is that a defendant must reasonably expect that its activity could result in litigation in the forum state. See, *e.g.*, Burger King [Corp. v. Rudzewicz], 471 U.S. [462,] 474 [(1985)] . . . . The Court has emphasized that this standard is ultimately designed to protect the liberty interests of defendants. Insurance Corp. of Ireland, Ltd. v. Compagnie des Bauxites de Guinee, 456 U.S. 694, 702-03 n.10 (1982).

The Court has, however, acknowledged other interests besides (1) the interest of a defendant in being able to predict the location of future litigation, namely (2) the forum state's interest in providing a convenient forum to its residents, (3) the plaintiff's interest in obtaining relief, (4) the state courts' interest in efficient resolution of disputes, and (5) the shared interests of the several states. These other interests have been described as "surrogates" of defendants' underlying liberty interests. Keeton v. Hustler Magazine, Inc., 465 U.S. 770, 776 (1984). Introduction of the "surrogate" interests into due process analysis complicates matters. . . .

The Supreme Court has never had occasion to balance this multiplicity of factors in a mass tort case involving parties from across the nation. The so-called "stream of commerce" cases — *World-Wide Volkswagen* and *Asahi* — appear to prevent the assertion of jurisdiction in traditional tort cases solely on the grounds that it was foreseeable to a defendant that its product might travel through the national or international economy and therefore might surface in any given jurisdiction. See *Asahi*, 480 U.S. at 112 (plurality opinion). While some have suggested that *Asahi* is limited in applicability because it involved an indemnification action between two foreign corporations, the case has been given more general application. . . .

In any event, neither *Volkswagen* nor *Asahi*, which both involved conventional product liability claims by individual plaintiffs, are controlling in DES mass torts brought under *Hymowitz* for the same reasons that the traditional New York tort cases interpreting the "reasonable expectation" element of C.P.L.R. 302(a)(3)(ii) are unhelpful in applying that statute to mass tort cases such as this one. . . . [M]ass torts raise unique problems of substantive, quasi-substantive, and procedural law that have just begun to receive the attention they require in federal and state courts and legislatures. The wooden application of inapt precedent will not effectively resolve these cases. As both *Burger King* and *Asahi* indicate, a careful weighing of the interests of the parties, the forum states, and the interstate system is required.

In their jurisdictional cast, DES mass tort cases perhaps most resemble Keeton v. Hustler Magazine, Inc., 465 U.S. 770 (1984). Keeton, a New York resident, sued Hustler magazine for libel in New Hampshire. Jurisdiction in New Hampshire was predicated in the first instance on the defendant's distributing a small percentage of the allegedly offending publications in that state. Noting that the plaintiff had alleged injuries occurring in every state in the country, the Court focused its minimum contacts analysis on the issue of whether it would be "'fair' to compel [Hustler] to defend a multistate lawsuit in New Hampshire seeking nationwide damages . . . even though only a small portion of . . . [the allegedly libelous] copies were distributed in New Hampshire." Id. at 775. In light of New Hampshire's interest in redressing the small percentage of national injuries that occurred in its state, id. at 776, and the several states' interest in the efficient adjudication of a national claim in a single forum, id. at 777, the Court found an assertion of jurisdiction constitutional despite the fact that the defendant had *de minimis* contacts and the plaintiff no connection to the forum other than the lawsuit. Id. at 780.

Like considerations favor a finding that jurisdiction over the defendants in this case can be constitutionally asserted. *Hymowitz* . . . and the legislative modifications to New York's statutes of limitations for DES plaintiffs evince New York's intent to provide as full a recovery as is practicable to those of its residents injured by DES. New York and its residents therefore have a strong interest in the assertion of jurisdiction. Likewise, the several states share an interest in the efficient resolution of DES cases.

The fit with *Keeton* is not exact. In the present case, for example, some of the DES manufacturers cannot be said to have directly availed themselves of the forum state's market, whereas Hustler clearly did, albeit to a trivial extent. Still, by competing to establish a territorial niche within the national DES market, every manufacturer directly or indirectly benefited from the Commerce Clause of the federal Constitution and the laws of every state in the nation by participating in the national market for a generic good. In a sense, then, each DES manufacturer did "purposefully derive benefit from [its] interstate activities," such that none may be entitled to rely on the Due Process Clause "as a territorial shield to avoid interstate obligations that have been voluntarily assumed." *Burger King*, 471 U.S. at 473-74. Under the federal Commerce Clause and the substantive law of Hymowitz, the United States constitutes a common economic pond that knows no state boundaries. A substantial interjection of products at any point of the national market has ripple effects in all parts of the market.

The strain created in trying to accommodate jurisdictional issues raised by mass torts into the literal requirements of accepted formulations like "purposeful availment" suggests that modifications of jurisdictional law may be no less appropriate than modifications of substantive and quasi-substantive law already undertaken by state courts and legislatures. The standard jurisdictional formulations are, after all, the product of traditional cases which were not decided with mass litigation in mind. In this instance, at least, where substantive law has undergone significant development to accommodate socioeconomic change, it is necessary to interpret jurisdictional law so that it meets the demands of the subject matter of the litigation. . . . The need for adaptation in this case is clearly indicated by the fact that, without it, these New York plaintiffs would likely be barred from recovering from these defendants in any court. If, for example, plaintiffs sought out the defendants in the California courts, California choice-of-law rules would probably call for the application of California substantive law . . . . The defendants could then obtain a dismissal under *Sindell* by providing that they did not market DES in New York. . . .

The Supreme Court itself has suggested the need for modified jurisdictional analysis in the special context of mass litigation. . . . Phillips Petroleum Co. v. Shutts, 472 U.S. 797 (1985) (p. 294, *infra* — ED.). . . . Noting the necessity of the national class action device to provide relief where it might otherwise be unattainable, Chief Justice Rehnquist wrote that "minimum contacts" analysis was inapplicable and that, instead, a lower standard of "minimal procedural due process protection" was sufficient. . . . By this formula, the Court essentially employed the time-honored jurisdiction-stretching technique of implied consent to cope with the problem of jurisdiction in mass class actions; plaintiffs who received notice and did not opt out were deemed to have implicitly consented to jurisdiction. . . .

3. *Sovereignty and Fairness in Mass Torts*

Two aspects of the constitutional case law of personal jurisdiction must be re-emphasized.

The first is that the cases continue to rely on two distinct inquiries — sovereignty and fairness. Furthermore, both the sovereignty and fairness inquiries have required some connection between the forum state and the defendant. The Supreme Court's fairness inquiries have retained the traditional requirement of a physical, *territorial* nexus: a non-resident defendant will be constitutionally subject to state assertions of jurisdiction only if it voluntarily commits acts within the state. By contrast, the Court's sovereignty inquiry now requires only an *interest* nexus: so long as the non-resident defendant's acts give rise to a forum interest, the state has authority to assert jurisdiction.

The second feature of note is that this jurisprudence of jurisdictional due process has been developed in cases almost all of which involved one or a few parties on each side. The Supreme Court's two-pronged inquiry has never been articulated in the context of a mass tort case arising out of the national (or international) marketing of a product. Only in *Shutts* has the Court dealt with this type of case, and there it was prepared to stretch prevailing jurisdictional standards by reliance on an implied consent theory.

This pair of considerations bears directly on the Due Process Clause standard appropriate to mass torts. The issue is whether the sovereignty and fairness inquiries legitimately can be adapted to such cases.

Analysis of this issue starts from the recognition that incorporation of forum nexus concerns into the sovereignty and fairness inquiries must be regarded, at least in the first instance, as an historical accident. [The Supreme Court's] initial adoption of territorial notions of sovereignty was dubious even when enunciated. . . . Without considering the impact on the then largely unforeseen phenomenon of mass torts, the *International Shoe* Court reaffirmed the use of both of these notions. Whereas there is a plausible rationale for the continued reliance on the "forum state interest" component to the sovereignty inquiry, the territorial nexus requirement is, at least in mass tort cases, an unnecessary and debilitating element of the fairness inquiry....

The oddity of the territorial nexus requirement will only become more evident in time. In the first place, the development of transportation and particularly communications technology — which, for example, allows courts to receive voluminous briefs in minutes by facsimile machine and to conduct hearings by telephone and soon by satellite video transmissions — continues to "shrink" the country.

Second, it seems likely that the phenomenon of mass litigations will continue to grow, and it is in these cases that the irrationality of the territorial nexus requirement is arguably most evident and the need for an improved approach most urgent. Mass tort suits typically are brought against groups of corporate defendants. In these cases the intuition linking territorial and convenience concerns — that a defendant in a civil case must travel to the forum to defend him-, her- or itself — is factually least plausible. As a rule, local counsel rather than defendants appear for motion and trial practice. Discovery need not and often will not take place in the forum. In federal court, moreover, discovery is subject to Federal Rule of Civil Procedure 26(b)(1)(iii), which now requires the district courts to take account of burdens on the parties in setting discovery parameters....

The actual litigation costs per case of defendants in mass cases is also likely to be lower than the costs to defendants appearing alone. To the extent permitted by professional ethical rules, defendants often can cooperate to defray costs by effecting a division of labor. Even where defendants do not explicitly cooperate, in many mass cases some defendants will rely on the work of the defendants with the greatest potential exposure in the case and therefore the greatest interest in litigating effectively. In almost all mass torts, much of the cost of litigation is eventually paid by national insurance companies.

While the need for territorial nexus-based protections of defendants is arguably least pressing in mass torts, the continued reliance on such protections creates significant obstacles to their resolution. This is particularly evident in a case such as the instant one, where New York substantive law empowers plaintiffs to bring in all industry participants to achieve a full and economical resolution of their lawsuits, yet jurisdictional law may prevent the very result envisioned by the state's substantive, remedial and procedural laws.

4. *Due Process Standard for Mass DES Torts*

Given that New York law has evolved to promote the efficient resolution of mass DES torts, and given the problems of applying prevailing traditional jurisdictional concepts to such cases, a modification of established standards to determine the constitutionality of jurisdictional statutes that incorporates an interest nexus inquiry but not a territorial nexus inquiry is necessary in the DES context — and perhaps in other mass tort cases. The following pair of principles results from a conservative view of precedents. (Obviously, a more radical position eliminating the state interest requirement, thus allowing a neutral forum to accept jurisdiction, could be developed were the Supreme Court to revisit precedent.)

    I.   The court must first determine if the forum state has an appreciable interest in the litigation, *i.e.*, whether the litigation raises issues whose resolution would be affected by, or have a probable impact on the vindication of, policies expressed in the substantive, procedural or remedial laws of the forum. If there is an appreciable state interest, the assertion of jurisdiction is *prima facie* constitutional.

    II.   Once a *prima facie* case is made, the assertion of jurisdiction will be considered constitutional unless, given the actual circumstances of the case, the defendant is unable to mount a defense in the forum state without suffering relatively substantial hardship.

    Evidence to be considered in determining the defendant's relative hardship includes, *inter alia*, (1) the defendant's available assets; (2) whether the defendant has or is engaged in substantial interstate commerce; (3) whether the defendant is being represented by an indemnitor or is sharing the cost of the defense with an indemnitor or co-defendant; (4) the comparative hardship defendant will incur in defending the suit in another forum; and (5) the comparative hardship to the plaintiff if the case were dismissed or transferred for lack of jurisdiction.

It must be emphasized that this standard is designed only to establish the minimum due process requirements for assertions of jurisdiction absent a defendant's consent. Considerations such as parties' and witnesses' convenience, administrative practicalities, and interstate comity concerns may still counsel against exercising that jurisdiction. . . .

The mass tort standard does incorporate several factors acknowledged in Supreme Court case law and by academic commentators as relevant to the constitutional-jurisdictional inquiry. They include the size and type of litigation, the relative financial condition of the parties, other burdens on plaintiff and defendant, the forum's interest in the litigation, whether the litigation will involve only two parties or several parties or indemnitors, and whether the operation of the forum's choice-of-law rules or substantive laws impose a hardship on the defendant, favor the interests of the plaintiff, or both. . . .

Principle I incorporates the "interest" nexus requirement of cases like *Keeton*, *Burger King* and *Asahi*. By necessitating an appreciable interest, it also incorporates a proximate cause inquiry, thus imposing some limitations on the causal chain between a particular litigation and the state's interest. In keeping with current law, the burden of proving the existence of an interest is the plaintiff's. . . .

After a *prima facie* case for the constitutionality of jurisdiction is made based on the court's authority to hear the case, the court must next inquire under the second principle whether the assertion of jurisdiction will be unfair to the defendant. The factors indicated in the second principle measure, among other things, the defendant's present ability to mount a reasonable defense as compared with the hardship plaintiff may suffer in having to bring its case elsewhere....

Although the test under Principle II does not shift the burden of persuasion to defendants, the court will, as under current practice, assume fairness unless the defendant informs it of potential litigation burdens and the desirability of transfer or dismissal....

[Applying the principles to the facts of the case, the court found personal jurisdiction in New York over both defendants.]

American Law Institute, COMPLEX LITIGATION: STATUTORY RECOMMENDATIONS AND ANALYSIS

147-48, 155-57 (1994)

§ 3.08. Personal Jurisdiction in the Transferee Court

(a) Once actions have been transferred and consolidated by the Complex Litigation Panel, the transferee court may exercise jurisdiction over any parties to those actions or any parties later joined to the consolidated proceeding to the full extent of the power conferrable on a federal court under the United States Constitution....

Comment:

a. Rationale. If the unitary resolution of related elements of complex cases is to be achieved, there must be effective jurisdiction and transfer mechanisms to consolidate dispersed actions in the transferee court.... Consolidation of related cases in a single forum requires two things: a statutory transfer mechanism with which to move cases to the magnet forum, and personal jurisdiction over the litigants whose actions are before that court. There can be no effective transfer and consolidation procedure unless the transferee court has the power to bind the litigants to whatever rulings and judgments it may make.

As a practical matter these objectives cannot be achieved on a voluntary basis. Although some efficiency undoubtedly would be achieved by a voluntary system of consolidation, greater systemic efficiency — and individual fairness — will result if involuntary transfer can be accomplished in the widest range of circumstances.... This requires that the transferee court have the authority to assert power over and bind unwilling, as well as willing, parties....

e. The constitutionality of a national-contacts personal jurisdiction standard. The power of Congress to supply a federal national-contacts long-arm statute for use in complex cases seems clear. Congressional authority ... can be predicated on the Commerce Clause in Article I, as well as the Judicial Power Clause in Article III of the Constitution....

Because the proposed statute would be a creation of the federal government, it would be limited by Fifth Amendment, rather than Fourteenth Amendment, constraints. The question remains, however, how are due process limitations under the Fifth Amendment determined?

The Supreme Court never has decided a personal jurisdiction case under the Fifth Amendment, so guidance is available only by drawing analogies from the Court's Fourteenth Amendment decisions.... [J]ust as an analysis of state contacts and fairness are pertinent to the decision of whether a particular assertion of jurisdiction violates the Fourteenth Amendment, reference to national contacts and fairness appears to be proper for determining whether Fifth Amendment constraints are satisfied.

Further, there is no basis for concluding that the Fifth Amendment supports a national-contacts test for nondiversity cases, but that a more limited test must be used in diversity cases. At least in the narrow band of complex diversity cases, a national-contacts approach should withstand constitutional scrutiny because of singular need for transfer and consolidation. Complex diversity litigation has all of the characteristics that currently justify the national contacts standard: (1) the need to provide a forum for litigation to correct and control severe problems in the national economy that are likely to involve parties across the country acting in a similar fashion or being injured by similar conduct; (2) the need to provide a forum where all parties can be subjected to jurisdiction, when no single state has that power; and (3) the need to provide a convenient forum for litigation to marshal[ ] and conserve the assets of an insolvent party....

Notes and Questions

1. In *DES* Judge Weinstein ultimately dismissed the plaintiffs' complaint for want of prosecution. The defendants then attempted to appeal from the court's ruling on the personal jurisdiction question, but the Second Circuit held that, as prevailing parties, the defendants had no right to appeal. In re DES Litigation, 7 F.3d 20 (2d Cir. 1993).

2. In the last set of Notes, we suggested that two strategies for overcoming the limitations of personal jurisdiction in complex or complicated litigation were judicial re-interpretation of the statutory and constitutional limits of territorial jurisdiction or the passage of legislation authorizing a court to assert jurisdiction over defendants as long as there were minimum contacts with the nation as a whole. *DES* adopts the first approach, while the ALI proposes the second approach. Having now seen both proposals, which, if either, do you favor?

3. Thus far, there has been little favorable response to either approach. Congress has not yet accepted the ALI's invitation to enact a national minimum contacts statute. The judicial response to *DES* has been comparably cool. In Boaz v. Boyle & Co., 40 Cal. App. 4th 700, 46 Cal. Rptr. 2d 888 (Cal. App. 1995), the court refused to adopt the *DES* rationale. *Boaz* noted that the applicable law (California) was different than the law of New York, and thus made the *DES* rationale inapposite. Ultimately, however, *Boaz* refused to follow *DES* for a "more fundamental" reason: "Whatever might be said of that approach in philosophical terms, it runs counter to United States Supreme Court decisions

about the assertion of personal jurisdiction over nonresidents. . . . We have no warrant to jettison these principles in favor of an approach which recognizes no defined limits to the assertion of jurisdiction against any defendant whose national marketing somehow affects commerce in the forum state." 40 Cal. App. 4th 719-20. See also Waste Management, Inc. v. Admiral Insurance Co., 138 N.J. 106, 129, 649 A.2d 379 (1994), cert. denied, 513 U.S. 1183 (1995) (calling *DES* "a progressive jurisdictional approach" and an "unprecedented jurisdictional formulation"; distinguishing *DES* due to unique features of New York law and the lack of alternative remedy for the *DES* plaintiffs).

4. The *sui generis* nature of New York's substantive law, in which even those defendants that had never marketed a product or caused injury could nonetheless be responsible for a portion of the damages, was the occasion for the personal jurisdiction formulation used in *DES*. Indeed, given the rule in *Hymowitz*, and given the fact that plaintiffs might well have not been able to secure the application of that law had they filed suit in another state (due to choice of law concerns that we address in Chapter Seven), the outcome in *DES* was necessary if *Hymowitz* were to be given its full effect. Would a better solution be to change choice of law rules so that other states that had jurisdiction over the defendants would be required to apply *Hymowitz* to New York plaintiffs?

On the other hand, could it be argued that the rule in *Hymowitz*, although not unconstitutional on its face, was unconstitutional as applied to defendants over whom no personal jurisdiction existed? Put differently, do New York plaintiffs have a right to the application of *Hymowitz*? If not, then what is wrong with making them sue in a court that has jurisdiction over the defendants? Doesn't *DES* let plaintiffs have their cake and eat it too? Making trade-offs between forum and claims is an inveterate part of the "master of the complaint" approach to litigation. Since it does not appear that plaintiffs were attempting to avoid dysfunction or prevent inefficient re-litigation by bringing suit in New York, why change the rules of territorial jurisdiction just for them?

5. *DES* demonstrates the close relationship between procedure and substance. The jurisdictional ruling in *DES* was made necessary by the earlier substantive law change in *Hymowitz*. But *Hymowitz* itself was made possible by joinder rules that permitted the joinder of multiple defendants in one suit. This process — procedure changing substance, which in turn changes procedure, which in turn changes substance — is an ongoing one. What additional substantive law changes might you predict if *DES* becomes generally accepted? Do such changes affect your assessment of *DES*?

6. In *DES* Judge Weinstein invited the Supreme Court to revisit its precedents on territorial jurisdiction. Despite Weinstein's invitation, did you see in cases such as *World-Wide Volkswagen* and *Asahi* any indication that the Supreme Court was intending to revisit its territorial jurisdiction jurisprudence and reshape it along the lines that Weinstein suggests? Indeed, aren't the *DES* principles essentially the same as those of Justice Brennan, whose views could never command a majority of the Court?

Perhaps sensing this difficulty, *DES* adopts a pair of principles that are facially limited to mass tort cases. *DES* is certainly correct in observing that the Supreme Court had never faced the question of the territorial jurisdiction rules that should be applied in mass torts. Neither of the principles in *DES*, however, is confined to mass tort cases; the principles could as easily be applied to cases of any stripe. Wouldn't the application of these principles only to mass torts violate our trans-substantive ideal? On the other hand, would the application of the principles to other cases be necessary or appropriate?

7. One way to justify a limited use of the *DES* principles is on substantive grounds: The rule leads to greater compensation for tort plaintiffs, which is (as reflected in *Hymowitz*) an important social policy. On that rationale, procedural values such as trans-substantivity must be accorded a lesser weight. Should they be? (Note that the issues concerning the importance of procedural values, which we considered in Chapter One, are relevant in answering this question.) In any event, certain procedural rationales, such as those reflected in the rules of territorial jurisdiction, may have a constitutional status, and therefore cannot be overridden by substantive state policies.

A different way to limit the *DES* principles is to apply them only in cases in which other important procedural (as opposed to substantive) values will be harmed by the use of traditional jurisdictional rules. Two types of procedural values that we have thus far identified are the interest in efficient litigation (the concern of complicated litigation) and the interest in rational adjudication of all similarly situated claims (the concern of complex litigation). Even if it would not be appropriate to extend the two principles to all cases or just to mass tort cases, would it be appropriate to extend the two *DES* principles to all cases in which application of the principles will help to prevent inefficient re-litigation of issues? Similarly, would it be appropriate to extend the principles to cases in which application of the principles will help to prevent the lawyer dysfunction that threatens rational adjudication?

Obviously, the use of the principles in all complicated litigation would work a greater change in territorial jurisdiction rules than their use only in complex litigation. Should that fact make a difference? Moreover, do the constitutional dimensions of our present rules of territorial jurisdiction trump the concerns for efficient litigation or rational adjudication? The answer would seem to be "Yes," unless the concerns for efficient litigation or rational adjudication themselves possess a constitutional weight. The argument that the prevention of inefficient re-litigation is of a constitutional stature would hinge on the argument that the due process clause demands efficiency in litigation. Although the due process clause does concern itself to some degree with efficient process (see pp. 8-10, *supra*), the emphasis of this concern is on the circumstances in which departures from adversarial process can be tolerated for efficiency reasons; it would be a stretch to suggest that the efficiency concern of the due process clause would be of equal weight with the federalism and liberty concerns underlying the rules of territorial jurisdiction. Since the notion of rational adjudication lies at the heart of the due process clause, the argument that the interest in rational adjudication is of a constitutional stature equivalent to federalism and liberty interests is probably stronger. Is it strong enough?

Assuming that the standard rules of territorial jurisdiction should be molded to the needs of complicated or complex litigation, and further assuming that the *DES* principles are the appropriate mold, should the principles have been applied in *DES* itself? How much inefficient re-litigation was prevented by the use of the principles in *DES*? Did *DES* pose a threat to rational adjudication, either because later parties could have undone the relief obtained in the case or because nonparties would have been cheated out of a fair share of the remedy?

8. In comparison to *DES*, the ALI's proposal is directed specifically at the problem of complicated litigation (see pp. 84, 253, *supra*). Moreover, unlike *DES*, its solution does not create special exceptions to the rules of territorial

jurisdiction; instead, it replaces state-based rules of territorial jurisdiction with a nationally-based rule of territorial jurisdiction. In other words, the basic analysis (minimum contacts plus convenience) remains the same as the present rules, but the relevant entity against which the contacts and convenience are measured is changed from the state to the nation.

The ALI seems confident of the constitutionality of its proposal. To some degree this confidence is deserved. As we saw in the last set of Notes, Congress has adopted a series of nationwide service of process statutes or rules, and the Supreme Court has promulgated Rule 4(k)(2), which provides a limited form of nationwide service of process. See p. 274, *supra*. The constitutionality of these statutes or of Rule 4(k)(2) has never been definitively resolved. Nearly all of these statutes involved claims arising under federal law, so that measuring jurisdiction by the contacts with the nation as a whole makes constitutional sense. Moreover, a number of the statutes involved claims that lay within the exclusive jurisdiction of the federal courts, so that measuring jurisdiction by the contacts with the federal government is again sensible and likely constitutional.

Note, however, that the ALI's proposal pushes past this constitutional common sense in two ways. First, the congressional enactment that the ALI envisions would appear to apply in both federal and state court. Second, the enactment would apply to both federal claims and state law claims — including, perhaps, state law claims over which no federal court could have exercised jurisdiction. Although applying a nationwide service of process rule to claims that have some connection to the federal system — either because the source of the right is federal or because the court resolving the case is federal — might well be constitutional, is it constitutional to adopt a nationwide service of process rule in cases that are neither based on federal law nor amenable to jurisdiction in the federal forum? One possible argument for the constitutionality of such a rule is to invoke a notion of "pendent party personal jurisdiction," so that, as long as the non-federal case is related to other cases that either assert federal claims or are filed in federal court, the state court can exercise jurisdiction over a defendant with minimum contacts with the nation as a whole. Is this a persuasive argument? Cf. p. 274, *supra* (discussing "pendent personal jurisdiction"). Another argument would be, as the ALI suggests, that the financial impact of unnecessary re-litigation gives Congress the authority under the Commerce Clause to create nationwide service of process over defendants that have no minimum contacts (as measured by the Fourteenth Amendment) with the forum. But if the limits on the state courts' exercise of jurisdiction over such defendants derive from the Fourteenth Amendment, can Congress override those limits under its Article I powers? Wouldn't the subsequently-enacted Fourteenth Amendment limit Congress's Article I powers in this context? The ALI also suggests that the Judicial Power clause of Article III could be the constitutional basis for its proposal. But Article III describes only the powers of federal courts, not of state courts; and, like Article I, it predates the due process clause of the Fourteenth Amendment by some years.

In light of these concerns, is it as obvious as the ALI suggests that a national-contacts test can constitutionally be applied to all non-federal claims filed in state court, merely because the claims relate to other litigation filed in other forums?

9. The same constitutional problems would not necessarily infect a nationwide service of process statute that limited itself to complex litigation. In this circumstance, the harm to be prevented would be irrational adjudication,

which is a problem at which the due process clause is directed. The source of such a statute would be either the Fifth Amendment (supplemented by the necessary and proper clause) or the Fourteenth Amendment, which contains in § 5 an enabling provision authorizing Congress to "enforce this article by appropriate legislation." Whether lawyer dysfunction that threatens rational adjudication is in fact of constitutional stature is unclear, but on the assumption that it is, a statute tailored to nationwide service of process only in cases of lawyer dysfunction would seem to pass constitutional muster.

10. The ALI's proposal concerns itself with more than the exercise of jurisdiction over defendants. Section 3.08 speaks not merely of "defendants," but rather of "parties" — including plaintiffs. Likewise, as we saw in the last chapter, § 5.05 of the ALI proposal created a new "notice and preclusion" rule that prevented nonparties from re-litigating certain common issues. See pp. 249-51, *supra*. In § 5.05, the ALI stated that the rule would be applied to "nonparties within the court's jurisdiction under § 3.08." Some of the nonparties affected by § 5.05 would be defendants, but in many cases most of these nonparties would be plaintiffs. Until now, we have focused on the rules of territorial jurisdiction that affect defendants who are involuntarily joined. To what extent do the rules of territorial jurisdiction impose limitations on the joinder of plaintiffs or potential plaintiffs? The following subsection addresses this issue.

2. Territorial Jurisdiction over Plaintiffs

The issue of territorial jurisdiction over plaintiffs arises because of the existence of rules that lead to the involuntary joinder or preclusion of plaintiffs. The standard assumption of the adversarial system is that a plaintiff chooses voluntarily when to file suit. Although a plaintiff may have no minimum contacts with the forum in which she files suit, her voluntary decision to invoke that forum has always been regarded as consent to the jurisdiction of that forum. Since objections to a lack of territorial jurisdiction can be waived by a party's consent, the issue of territorial jurisdiction over the plaintiff does not arise.

As we saw in the last chapter, however, there are a series of joinder and preclusion rules that either force a plaintiff to join a lawsuit on an involuntary basis (see, *e.g.*, Rules 19 and 23) or preclude a nonparty that fails to join from re-litigating certain claims or issues. The involuntary joinder of these plaintiffs or preclusion of these nonparties raises the same concern as the involuntary joinder or preclusion of a defendant: Is it fair for a court that has no minimum contacts with the plaintiff or nonparty to adjudicate her claim? Should the territorial jurisdiction rules in this context be the same as they are in the context of defendants? Should they be more liberal? Or, on the assumption that involuntary joinder or preclusion of plaintiffs is a greater affront to the adversarial system than the involuntary joinder or preclusion of defendants, should the rules be even stricter? Whatever the precise content of the rules, should they be loosened when they threaten to create inefficient re-litigation or lawyer dysfunction? If so, how do we justify two sets of rules — one for ordinary cases and the other for complicated or complex cases?

PHILLIPS PETROLEUM CO. v. SHUTTS

472 U.S. 797 (1985)

■ JUSTICE REHNQUIST delivered the opinion of the Court.

Petitioner is a Delaware corporation which has its principal place of business in Oklahoma. During the 1970's it produced or purchased natural gas from leased land located in 11 different States, and sold most of the gas in interstate commerce. Respondents are some 28,000 of the royalty owners possessing rights to the leases from which petitioner produced the gas; they reside in all 50 States, the District of Columbia, and several foreign countries. Respondents brought a class action against petitioner in the Kansas state court, seeking to recover interest on royalty payments which had been delayed by petitioner. They recovered judgment in the trial court, and the Supreme Court of Kansas affirmed the judgment over petitioner's contentions that the Due Process Clause of the Fourteenth Amendment prevented Kansas from adjudicating the claims of all the respondents . . . . We reject petitioner's jurisdictional claim . . . .

Because petitioner sold the gas to its customers in interstate commerce, it was required to secure approval for price increases from what was then the Federal Power Commission, and is now the Federal Energy Regulatory Commission. Under its regulations the Federal Power Commission permitted petitioner to propose and collect tentative higher gas prices, subject to final approval by the Commission. If the Commission eventually denied petitioner's proposed price increase or reduced the proposed increase, petitioner would have to refund to its customers the difference between the approved price and the higher price charged, plus interest at a rate set by statute. See 18 CFR § 154.102 (1984).

Although petitioner received higher gas prices pending review by the Commission, petitioner suspended any increase in royalties paid to the royalty owners because the higher price could be subject to recoupment by petitioner's customers. Petitioner agreed to pay the higher royalty only if the royalty owners would provide petitioner with a bond or indemnity for the increase, plus interest, in case the price increase was not ultimately approved and a refund was due to the customers. Petitioner set the interest rate on the indemnity agreements at the same interest rate the Commission would have required petitioner to refund to its customers. A small percentage of the royalty owners provided this indemnity and received royalties immediately from the interim price increases; these royalty owners are unimportant to this case.

The remaining royalty owners received no royalty on the unapproved portion of the prices until the Federal Power Commission approval of those prices became final. Royalties on the unapproved portion of the gas price were suspended three times by petitioner, corresponding to its three proposed price increases in the mid-1970's. In three written opinions the Commission approved all of petitioner's tentative price increases, so petitioner paid to its royalty owners the suspended royalties of $3.7 million in 1976, $4.7 million in 1977, and $2.9 million in 1978. Petitioner paid no interest to the royalty owners although it had the use of the suspended royalty money for a number of years.

Respondents Irl Shutts, Robert Anderson, and Betty Anderson filed suit against petitioner in Kansas state court, seeking interest payments on their suspended royalties which petitioner had possessed pending the Commission's approval of the price increases. Shutts is a resident of Kansas, and the Andersons live in Oklahoma. Shutts and the Andersons own gas leases in Oklahoma and Texas. Over petitioner's objection the Kansas trial court granted respondents' motion to certify the suit as a class action under Kansas law. Kan. Stat. Ann. § 60-223 et seq. (1983). The class as certified was comprised of 33,000 royalty owners who had royalties suspended by petitioner. The average claim of each royalty owner for interest on the suspended royalties was $100.

After the class was certified respondents provided each class member with notice through first-class mail. The notice described the action and informed each class member that he could appear in person or by counsel; otherwise each member would be represented by Shutts and the Andersons, the named plaintiffs. The notices also stated that class members would be included in the class and bound by the judgment unless they "opted out" of the lawsuit by executing and returning a "request for exclusion" that was included with the notice. The final class as certified contained 28,100 members; 3,400 had "opted out" of the class by returning the request for exclusion, and notice could not be delivered to another 1,500 members, who were also excluded. Less than 1,000 of the class members resided in Kansas. Only a minuscule amount, approximately one quarter of one percent, of the gas leases involved in the lawsuit were on Kansas land.

After petitioner's mandamus petition to decertify the class was denied, . . . the case was tried to the court. The court found petitioner liable under Kansas law for interest on the suspended royalties to all class members. . . .

Petitioner . . . in its appeal to the Supreme Court of Kansas . . . asserted that the Kansas trial court did not possess personal jurisdiction over absent plaintiff class members as required by International Shoe Co. v. Washington, 326 U.S. 310 (1945), and similar cases. Related to this . . . claim was petitioner's contention that the "opt-out" notice to absent class members, which forced them to return the request for exclusion in order to avoid the suit, was insufficient to bind class members who were not residents of Kansas or who did not possess "minimum contacts" with Kansas. . . .

The Supreme Court of Kansas held that the entire cause of action was maintainable under the Kansas class-action statute, and . . . that the absent class members were plaintiffs, not defendants, and thus the traditional minimum contacts test of *International Shoe* did not apply. The court held that nonresident class-action plaintiffs were only entitled to adequate notice, an opportunity to be heard, an opportunity to opt out of the case, and adequate representation by the named plaintiffs. If these procedural due process minima were met, according to the court, Kansas could assert jurisdiction over the plaintiff class and bind each class member with a judgment on his claim. The court surveyed the course of the litigation and concluded that all of these minima had been met. . . .

I

As a threshold matter we must determine whether petitioner has standing to assert the claim that Kansas did not possess proper jurisdiction over the many plaintiffs in the class who were not Kansas residents and had no connection to Kansas. [The court found that Philips Petroleum had standing.]

II

Reduced to its essentials, petitioner's argument is that unless out-of-state plaintiffs affirmatively consent, the Kansas courts may not exert jurisdiction over their claims. Petitioner claims that failure to execute and return the "request for exclusion" provided with the class notice cannot constitute consent of the out-of-state plaintiffs; thus Kansas courts may exercise jurisdiction over these plaintiffs only if the plaintiffs possess the sufficient "minimum contacts" with Kansas as that term is used in cases involving personal jurisdiction over out-of-state defendants. *E.g.*, International Shoe Co. v. Washington, 326 U.S. 310 (1945); Shaffer v. Heitner, 433 U.S. 186 (1977); World-Wide Volkswagen Corp. v. Woodson, 444 U.S. 286 (1980). Since Kansas had no prelitigation contact with many of the plaintiffs and leases involved, petitioner claims that Kansas has exceeded its jurisdictional reach and thereby violated the due process rights of the absent plaintiffs.

In *International Shoe* we were faced with an out-of-state corporation which sought to avoid the exercise of personal jurisdiction over it as a defendant by a Washington state court. We held that the extent of the defendant's due process protection would depend "upon the quality and nature of the activity in relation to the fair and orderly administration of the laws . . . ." 326 U.S., at 319. We noted that the Due Process Clause did not permit a State to make a binding judgment against a person with whom the State had no contacts, ties, or relations. If the defendant possessed certain minimum contacts with the State, so that it was "reasonable and just, according to our traditional conception of fair play and substantial justice" for a State to exercise personal jurisdiction, the State could force the defendant to defend himself in the forum, upon pain of default, and could bind him to a judgment. Id., at 320.

The purpose of this test, of course, is to protect a defendant from the travail of defending in a distant forum, unless the defendant's contacts with the forum make it just to force him to defend there. As we explained in *Woodson, supra*, the defendant's contacts should be such that "he should reasonably anticipate being haled" into the forum. 444 U.S., at 297. In Insurance Corp. of Ireland v. Compagnie des Bauxites de Guinee, 456 U.S. 694, 702-703, and n.10 (1982), we explained that the requirement that a court have personal jurisdiction comes from the Due Process Clause's protection of the defendant's personal liberty interest, and said that the requirement "represents a restriction on judicial power not as a matter of sovereignty, but as a matter of individual liberty."

Although the cases like *Shaffer* and *Woodson* which petitioner relies on for a minimum contacts requirement all dealt with out-of-state defendants or parties in the procedural posture of a defendant, . . . petitioner claims that the same analysis must apply to absent class-action plaintiffs. In this regard petitioner correctly points out that a chose in action is a constitutionally recognized property interest possessed by each of the plaintiffs. Mullane v. Central Hanover Bank & Trust Co., 339 U.S. 306 (1950). An adverse judgment by Kansas courts in this case may extinguish the chose in action forever through res judicata. Such an adverse judgment, petitioner claims, would be every bit as onerous to an absent plaintiff as an adverse judgment on the merits would be to a defendant. Thus, the same due process protections should apply to absent plaintiffs: Kansas should not be able to exert jurisdiction over the plaintiffs' claims unless the plaintiffs have sufficient minimum contacts with Kansas.

We think petitioner's premise is in error. The burdens placed by a State upon an absent class-action plaintiff are not of the same order or magnitude as those it places upon an absent defendant. An out-of-state defendant summoned by a plaintiff is faced with the full powers of the forum State to render judgment *against* it. The defendant must generally hire counsel and travel to the forum to defend itself from the plaintiff's claim, or suffer a default judgment. The defendant may be forced to participate in extended and often costly discovery, and will be forced to respond in damages or to comply with some other form of remedy imposed by the court should it lose the suit. The defendant may also face liability for court costs and attorney's fees. These burdens are substantial, and the minimum contacts requirement of the Due Process Clause prevents the forum State from unfairly imposing them upon the defendant.

A class-action plaintiff, however, is in quite a different posture. The Court noted this difference in Hansberry v. Lee, 311 U.S. 32, 40-41 (1940), which explained that a "class" or "representative" suit was an exception to the rule that one could not be bound by judgment *in personam* unless one was made fully a party in the traditional sense. Ibid., citing Pennoyer v. Neff, 95 U.S. 714 (1878). As the Court pointed out in *Hansberry*, the class action was an invention of equity to enable it to proceed to a decree in suits where the number of those interested in the litigation was too great to permit joinder. The absent parties would be bound by the decree so long as the named parties adequately represented the absent class and the prosecution of the litigation was within the common interest.[1] 311 U.S., at 41.

Modern plaintiff class actions follow the same goals, permitting litigation of a suit involving common questions when there are too many plaintiffs for proper joinder. Class actions also may permit the plaintiffs to

---

1. The holding in *Hansberry*, of course, was that petitioners in that case had not a sufficient common interest with the parties to a prior lawsuit such that a decree against those parties in the prior suit would bind the petitioners. But in the present case there is no question that the named plaintiffs adequately represent the class, and that all members of the class have the same interest in enforcing their claims against the defendant.

pool claims which would be uneconomical to litigate individually. For example, this lawsuit involves claims averaging about $100 per plaintiff; most of the plaintiffs would have no realistic day in court if a class action were not available.

In sharp contrast to the predicament of a defendant haled into an out-of-state forum, the plaintiffs in this suit were not haled anywhere to defend themselves upon pain of a default judgment. As commentators have noted, from the plaintiffs' point of view a class action resembles a "quasi-administrative proceeding, conducted by the judge." 3B J. Moore & J. Kennedy, Moore's Federal Practice para. 23.45 [4.-5] (1984) . . . .

A plaintiff class in Kansas and numerous other jurisdictions cannot first be certified unless the judge, with the aid of the named plaintiffs and defendant, conducts an inquiry into the common nature of the named plaintiffs' and the absent plaintiffs' claims, the adequacy of representation, the jurisdiction possessed over the class, and any other matters that will bear upon proper representation of the absent plaintiffs' interest. See, *e. g.*, Kan. Stat. Ann. § 60-223 (1983); Fed. Rule Civ. Proc. 23. Unlike a defendant in a civil suit, a class-action plaintiff is not required to fend for himself. See Kan. Stat. Ann. § 60-223(d) (1983). The court and named plaintiffs protect his interests. Indeed, the class-action defendant itself has a great interest in ensuring that the absent plaintiffs' claims are properly before the forum. In this case, for example, the defendant sought to avoid class certification by alleging that the absent plaintiffs would not be adequately represented and were not amenable to jurisdiction. . . .

The concern of the typical class-action rules for the absent plaintiffs is manifested in other ways. Most jurisdictions, including Kansas, require that a class action, once certified, may not be dismissed or compromised without the approval of the court. In many jurisdictions such as Kansas the court may amend the pleadings to ensure that all sections of the class are represented adequately. Kan. Stat. Ann. § 60-223(d) (1983); see also, *e.g.*, Fed. Rule Civ. Proc. 23(d).

Besides this continuing solicitude for their rights, absent plaintiff class members are not subject to other burdens imposed upon defendants. They need not hire counsel or appear. They are almost never subject to counterclaims or cross-claims, or liability for fees or costs. Absent plaintiff class members are not subject to coercive or punitive remedies. Nor will an adverse judgment typically bind an absent plaintiff for any damages, although a valid adverse judgment may extinguish any of the plaintiff's claims which were litigated.

Unlike a defendant in a normal civil suit, an absent class-action plaintiff is not required to do anything. He may sit back and allow the litigation to run its course, content in knowing that there are safeguards provided for his protection. In most class actions an absent plaintiff is provided at least with an opportunity to "opt out" of the class, and if he takes advantage of that opportunity he is removed from the litigation entirely. This was true of the Kansas proceedings in this case. The Kansas procedure provided for the mailing of a notice to each class member by first-class mail. The notice, as we have previously indicated, described the action and informed the class member that he could appear in person or by counsel, in default of which he would be represented by the named plaintiffs and their attorneys. The notice further stated that class members would be included in the class and bound by the judgment unless they "opted out" by executing and returning a "request for exclusion" that was included in the notice.

Petitioner contends, however, that the "opt out" procedure provided by Kansas is not good enough, and that an "opt in" procedure is required to satisfy the Due Process Clause of the Fourteenth Amendment. Insofar as plaintiffs who have no minimum contacts with the forum State are concerned, an "opt in" provision would require that each class member affirmatively consent to his inclusion within the class.

Because States place fewer burdens upon absent class plaintiffs than they do upon absent defendants in nonclass suits, the Due Process Clause need not and does not afford the former as much protection from state-court jurisdiction as it does the latter. The Fourteenth Amendment does protect "persons," not "defendants," however, so absent plaintiffs as well as absent defendants are entitled to some protection from the jurisdiction of a forum State which seeks to adjudicate their claims. In this case we hold that a forum State may exercise jurisdiction over the claim of an absent class-action plaintiff, even though that plaintiff may not possess the minimum contacts with the forum which would support personal jurisdiction over a defendant. If the forum State wishes to bind an absent plaintiff concerning a claim for money damages or similar relief at law,[3] it must provide minimal procedural due process protection. The plaintiff must receive notice plus an opportunity to be heard and participate in the litigation, whether in person or through counsel. The notice must be the best practicable, "reasonably calculated, under all the circumstances, to apprise interested parties of the pendency of the action and afford them an opportunity to present their objections." *Mullane*, 339 U.S., at 314-315; cf. Eisen v. Carlisle & Jacquelin, 417 U.S. 156, 174-175 (1974). The notice should describe the action and the plaintiffs' rights in it. Additionally, we hold that due process requires at a minimum that an absent plaintiff be provided with an opportunity to remove himself from the class by executing and returning an "opt out" or "request for exclusion" form to the court. Finally, the Due Process Clause of course requires that the named plaintiff at all times adequately represent the interests of the absent class members. *Hansberry*, 311 U.S., at 42-43, 45.

We reject petitioner's contention that the Due Process Clause of the Fourteenth Amendment requires that absent plaintiffs affirmatively "opt in" to the class, rather than be deemed members of the class if they do not "opt out." We think that such a contention is supported by little, if any precedent, and that it ignores the differences between class-action plaintiffs,

---

3. Our holding today is limited to those class actions which seek to bind known plaintiffs concerning claims wholly or predominately for money judgments. We intimate no view concerning other types of class actions, such as those seeking equitable relief. Nor, of course, does our discussion of personal jurisdiction address class actions where the jurisdiction is asserted against a *defendant* class.

on the one hand, and defendants in nonclass civil suits on the other. Any plaintiff may consent to jurisdiction. . . . The essential question, then, is how stringent the requirement for a showing of consent will be.

We think that the procedure followed by Kansas, where a fully descriptive notice is sent first-class mail to each class member, with an explanation of the right to "opt out," satisfies due process. Requiring a plaintiff to affirmatively request inclusion would probably impede the prosecution of those class actions involving an aggregation of small individual claims, where a large number of claims are required to make it economical to bring suit. See, *e.g.*, *Eisen*, *supra*, at 161. The plaintiff's claim may be so small, or the plaintiff so unfamiliar with the law, that he would not file suit individually, nor would he affirmatively request inclusion in the class if such a request were required by the Constitution. If, on the other hand, the plaintiff's claim is sufficiently large or important that he wishes to litigate it on his own, he will likely have retained an attorney or have thought about filing suit, and should be fully capable of exercising his right to "opt out."

In this case over 3,400 members of the potential class did "opt out," which belies the contention that "opt out" procedures result in guaranteed jurisdiction by inertia. Another 1,500 were excluded because the notice and "opt out" form was undeliverable. We think that such results show that the "opt out" procedure provided by Kansas is by no means *pro forma*, and that the Constitution does not require more to protect what must be the somewhat rare species of class member who is unwilling to execute an "opt out" form, but whose claim is nonetheless so important that he cannot be presumed to consent to being a member of the class by his failure to do so. Petitioner's "opt in" requirement would require the invalidation of scores of state statutes and of the class-action provision of the Federal Rules of Civil Procedure, and for the reasons stated we do not think that the Constitution requires the State to sacrifice the obvious advantages in judicial efficiency resulting from the "opt out" approach for the protection of the *rara avis* portrayed by petitioner.

We therefore hold that the protection afforded the plaintiff class members by the Kansas statute satisfies the Due Process Clause. The interests of the absent plaintiffs are sufficiently protected by the forum State when those plaintiffs are provided with a request for exclusion that can be returned within a reasonable time to the court. See *Insurance Corp. of Ireland*, 456 U.S., at 702-703, and n.10. Both the Kansas trial court and the Supreme Court of Kansas held that the class received adequate representation, and no party disputes that conclusion here. We conclude that the Kansas court properly asserted personal jurisdiction over the absent plaintiffs and their claims against petitioner.

[The remainder of *Shutts*, discussing whether a Kansas court could constitutionally apply its law to the claims of the plaintiffs with no connection to Kansas is discussed at p. 797, *infra*.]

IN RE ASBESTOS LITIGATION*

90 F.3d 963 (5th Cir. 1996), vacated and remanded, 521 U.S. —, 117 S.Ct. 2503 (1997), affirmed on remand, 134 F.3d 668 (5th Cir. 1998), cert. granted, 118 S.Ct. 2339 (1998)

■ DAVIS, Circuit Judge. [An asbestos defendant, Fibreboard Corp., together with its insurers, agreed with a group of plaintiffs' lawyers to settle, on a class action basis, the claims of all potential plaintiffs that had already been injured but had not filed suit and all those that had not yet manifested an injury. The plaintiffs then filed a Rule 23(b)(1)(B) class action complaint on behalf of this "Global Health Claimant Class." Rule 23(b)(1)(B) is a mandatory class action, which means that parties cannot opt out of the class action. See pp. 133-34, *supra*.

[The district court certified the class and approved the settlement. The district court held that the limited amounts that the insurers were willing to contribute, plus Fibreboard's own limited assets, made Rule 23(b)(1)(B) treatment appropriate. Intervening objectors to the settlement appealed on numerous grounds, including the judgment's inconsistency with *Shutts*.]

The intervenors next argue that the district court cannot exercise jurisdiction over class members who do not have minimum contacts with the Eastern District of Texas and that due process requires that Global Health Claimant Class members be allowed to opt out of the class. Both of these arguments are based on language from the Supreme Court decision Phillips Petroleum Co. v. Shutts, 472 U.S. 797 (1985). In *Shutts*, the Supreme Court held that a Kansas state court could bind absent plaintiff members of the class in a "common question" class action brought under a state rule virtually identical to 23(b)(3) only if the plaintiffs were provided with "minimal procedural due process protection," including the right to opt out. Id. at 811-12. However, the Court specifically limited its holding to

> class actions which seek to bind *known* plaintiffs concerning claims *wholly or predominantly for money judgments*. We intimate no view concerning other types of class actions such as those seeking equitable relief.

Id. at 811 n.3 (emphasis added).

The limitation of *Shutts* to claims of known plaintiffs that are predominantly for money damages forecloses application of its holding to 23(b)(1)(B) actions which have always been equitable and often involve unknown plaintiffs. . . .

Class actions date back to the English common law where chancery courts used bills of peace to bind entire classes. . . . The traditional limited-fund class action is an equitable and unitary disposition of a fund too small to satisfy all claims. . . . Unitary adjudication of a limited fund is crucial because allowing plaintiffs to sue individually would make the litigation "an unseemly race to the courthouse door with monetary prizes for

---

* One of the authors of this book was a consultant to one of the insurers in this case. The other was a consultant to the Federal Judicial Center, and performed a study of this case at the request of the Center. — ED.

a few winners and worthless judgments for the rest." Coburn v. 4-R Corp., 77 F.R.D. 43, 45 (E.D. Ky.1977). Limited-fund class actions effect a pro-rata reduction of all claims in order to treat all claimants fairly. Thus, they sound in equity even though the relief they provide necessarily affects the amount of money damages that claimants can ultimately receive....

Due process standards for suits seeking equitable relief are set forth in Hansberry v. Lee, 311 U.S. 32 (1940) where the Supreme Court stated:

> this Court is justified in saying that there has been a failure of due process only in those cases where it cannot be said that the procedure adopted, fairly insures the protection of the interests of absent parties who are to be bound by it.

Id. at 42.... The rule that adequate representation is all that due process requires for the traditional mandatory class action in equity was not challenged by *Shutts*. Subsequent decisions have made it clear that, consistent with due process, absent parties can be bound by a judgment where they were adequately represented in a prior action. Martin v. Wilks, 490 U.S. 755, 762 n.2 [(1989)]....

Actions under Rule 23(b)(1)(B) are precisely the type of limited circumstances noted by *Martin* where "equitable circumstances dictate the need for a unitary adjudication regardless of the individual consent of the parties affected."... As a result, due process requires only that all parties bound by the Global Settlement Agreement were adequately represented. We have already concluded that they were.[16]

The intervenors object that some members of the class may not have minimum contacts with the Eastern District of Texas and have not otherwise consented to the district court's jurisdiction. They also claim that the Global Settlement Agreement is without authority to release future claims that have not yet accrued. These objections again ignore the equitable nature of this action.

Due process requires adequate representation in a 23(b)(1)(B) case but, as *Shutts* expressly cautioned, minimum contacts or consent to jurisdiction are not necessary in equitable class actions.... It is also well settled that a unitary adjudication of a limited fund binds future, contingent, and unknown claimants who, by definition, could not give consent to jurisdiction. Mullane v. Central Hanover Bank & Trust Co., 339 U.S. 306 (1950).

Rule 23(b)(1)(B) actions closely resemble actions for interpleader, or for the accounting of a trustee.... This is because all claimants will recover from the fund or not at all. This view of a limited-fund class action as similar to an action *in rem* makes particular sense because, although

---

16. Opt-out class actions were unheard of before the 1966 amendments to the Federal Rules of Civil Procedure created the Rule 23(b)(3) opt-out class action. The intervenors would have us read *Shutts* to mean that all class actions involving money claims under Rule 23(b)(1) or (2) are unconstitutional. If the Supreme Court had intended to so hold, it surely would have been more explicit given the ancient history of the mandatory class action, over a hundred years of precedent upholding the constitutionality of such classes, the relatively recent development of the "opt-out" class action, and the strong presumption that the Federal Rules of Civil Procedure are constitutional.

limited-fund actions often involve unknown or unavailable claimants who cannot expressly consent to jurisdiction, the court in such an action has before it for disposition all the assets in which class members could claim an interest. . . . The court can appropriately adjudicate all claims against the fund because of its jurisdiction over the fund and the fact that all potential claimants are adequately represented before it. . . .

■ SMITH, Circuit Judge, dissenting . . . . Though the Court plainly held in Phillips Petroleum Co. v. Shutts, 472 U.S. 797, 812 (1985), that class members have a right to opt out of actions (such as this) seeking primarily monetary relief, the majority refuses to recognize that right, on the ground that it was not historically available in traditional "common fund" litigation. . . . [T]his case presents anything but a traditional common fund, and the majority's attempt to analogize it to an action to settle a trust is entirely unjustified: Far from adjudicating equitable rights in a preexisting fund, the settlement *creates* a common fund by extinguishing *personal* rights of action. . . .

Following *Shutts*, a mandatory class action is viable in two cases: (1) where the court has jurisdiction over all the plaintiffs or (2) where the plaintiffs seek equitable relief. Unlike the majority, I believe that whether a class action seeks equitable relief or money damages can be determined only by focusing on the underlying remedy the plaintiffs seek. . . .

If one focuses on the plaintiffs' remedy, the *Ahearn* class cannot be characterized as one "seeking equitable relief." The complaint alleges only personal causes of action against Fibreboard for money damages. The prayer for relief seeks general and special compensatory damages, punitive damages, costs of the suit, appropriate declarations and orders, and other relief as may be deemed just and proper. These remedies represent paradigmatic legal remedies. . . .

The majority circumvents *Shutts* by calling *Ahearn* an equitable action. . . . From the historical fact that rule 23(b)(1)(B) originated in courts of equity, the majority concludes that *all* actions certified rule 23(b)(1)(B) are equitable and thus immune from *Shutts*. . . .

The exception in *Shutts* is for actions seeking "equitable relief," not for class actions that have their origins in equity. The Court explicitly recognized that class actions originated as an equitable joinder device, and *all* class actions are "equitable" in that limited sense. . . . Despite that fact, the Court classified the action in *Shutts* as one for money damages. . . .

The only possible conclusion that can be drawn from the Court's reasoning is that the distinction between damage remedies and equitable remedies turns on what remedies the plaintiff seeks, not on his choice of joinder devices. To hold otherwise, as the majority does in this case, would create an internal inconsistency in *Shutts*: If the origin of the class action is determinative of the classification of an action, then every class action, including the one in *Shutts*, would be an equitable action. . . .

Finally, the majority's reliance on the strong presumption of constitutionality that the Federal Rules of Civil Procedure receive is misplaced. The novelty in this case is not the insistence on opt-out rights but on the extension of class actions, particularly rule 23(b)(1)(B) class actions, to mass torts and the expansion of rule (b)(1)(B) to "constructive bankruptcy." Such a use of the federal rules is novel, and in particular the rise of mass torts was unforeseen by the drafters of the rule. . . .

[T]he presumption of constitutionality enjoyed by the Federal Rules of Civil Procedure disappears when the rules are applied in a way unanticipated by their drafters. . . . In short, while this action falls within the broad scope of rule 23(b)(1)(B), that fact does not immunize it from due process protections, including opt-out rights.

IN RE: GENERAL MOTORS CORP. PICK-UP TRUCK FUEL TANK PRODUCTS LIABILITY LITIGATION

134 F.3d 133 (3d Cir. 1998)

■ BECKER, Circuit Judge. [Allegedly certain General Motors pick-up trucks had improperly mounted fuel systems that created a risk of explosion during a crash. Litigation on behalf of pick-up truck owners sprouted up in various state and federal courts around the country. Eventually 277 federal cases were consolidated in the Eastern District of Pennsylvania under the multidistrict litigation statute (28 U.S.C. § 1407), which we shall examine in the next chapter. General Motors agreed to settle the claims of all pick-up truck owners on a classwide basis, and together with the federal plaintiffs moved to certify an opt-out class action of all pick-up truck owners. The district court did so, and also approved the settlement as fair and reasonable. On appeal, the Third Circuit held that the district court had erred in certifying the class. In re General Motors Corp. Pick-Up Truck Fuel Tank Products Liability Litigation, 55 F.3d 768 (3d Cir.), cert. denied, 516 U.S. 824 (1995) ("*GM I*"). This ruling had the effect of forcing the parties back to the negotiating table in the district court. It also meant the district court again had before it only the claims of the 277 plaintiffs whose cases had actually been consolidated under § 1407, rather than the claims of all 5.7 million class members.

[Meanwhile, plaintiffs in Louisiana state court action negotiated a settlement similar to the one that had been negotiated in federal court. The Louisiana plaintiffs and General Motors moved to certify the case as an opt-out class action for settlement purposes. The Louisiana trial court conditionally certified a class action. At that point, some of the persons that had successfully objected to the proposed federal settlement moved the district judge in the Eastern District of Pennsylvania to issue an injunction against the proceedings in Louisiana. The district judge refused, and the objectors then filed an appeal in the Third Circuit. While the federal case was on appeal, the Louisiana trial court finally approved the settlement.

[The Louisiana plaintiffs and General Motors raised a host of arguments in support of the district court's decision not to enjoin the Louisiana proceeding. The first was personal jurisdiction.]

At the threshold, we must examine our power over the parties. . . . Appellees assert that the district court had no jurisdiction to enjoin the Louisiana court in the first instance (had it chosen to do so), and thus we can have no jurisdiction to enjoin that court on appeal. This contention is grounded upon appellees' submission that any injunction issued by this Court would affect the nationwide group of 5.7 million people who have already settled their claims with GM through the Louisiana proceedings, and therefore, that any injunction of the Louisiana Court would necessarily enjoin those 5.7 million individual settling class members and would require this Court to exercise personal jurisdiction over them. We agree.

The minimum standards of due process require that "in order to subject a defendant to a judgment in personam, if he not be present within the territory of the forum, he must have certain minimum contacts with it such that the maintenance of the suit does not offend 'traditional notions of fair play and substantial justice.'" International Shoe Co. v. Washington, 326 U.S. 310, 316 (1945) (citations omitted). In the Rule 23(b)(3) context, the Supreme Court has held that it is possible for a court to bind an absentee class member to a judgment without abrogating minimal due process protection, even if the party did not have minimum contacts with the forum. See Phillips Petroleum Co. v. Shutts, 472 U.S. 797, 812-13, (1985). But here, in the wake of our judgment in *GM I*, there is no class pending before the [multidistrict litigation] court, and thus, virtually none of the 5.7 million class members in Louisiana are before this Court in any respect, and there is no basis upon which we can infer their consent.[2]

To be more precise, the Louisiana class members are not parties before us; they have not constructively or affirmatively consented to personal jurisdiction; and they do not, as far as has been demonstrated, have minimum contacts with Pennsylvania. Therefore, due process deprives us of personal jurisdiction and prevents us from issuing the injunction prayed for by appellants.

Notes and Questions

1. *Shutts* and *Asbestos Litigation* discuss the limitation that territorial jurisdiction imposes on plaintiffs that are involuntarily joined. *GM Pick-Up* demonstrates the way in which this limitation might act as a barrier to involuntary joinder's main rival — preclusion. *Asbestos Litigation* also proposes

2. We note that enjoining the few Louisiana class members that the MDL court does have personal jurisdiction over (the 200 named MDL plaintiffs who have successfully intervened in the Louisiana proceeding) would serve no purpose. Barring the other procedural barriers discussed infra, it is conceivable that we could direct the district court to enjoin those 200 plaintiffs from pursuing their state damage remedies in Louisiana. As the district court properly pointed out, however, since the appellants' stated goal here is to prevent the Louisiana court from further consideration of the settlement in toto, little would be accomplished by enjoining only those 200 plaintiffs, . . . and we have not been asked to do so. At all events, the limited injunction would not halt the Louisiana proceedings because the original Louisiana plaintiffs (over whom we have no jurisdiction) could simply continue with the

a way around the territorial jurisdiction limitation. Would the same escape from *Shutts* apply in the context of Rule 19 involuntary joinder? Does the answer depend on whether Rule 19 derives from historical equity practice? See 7 Charles A. Wright et al., Federal Practice & Procedure § 1601 (1986) (noting that Rule 19 originated in equity, but was also used in actions at law). Does the answer depend on the lack of procedural protections for Rule 19 plaintiffs in relation to Rule 23 plaintiffs?

2. If both *Asbestos Litigation* and *GM Pick-Up* are correct, involuntary joinder (at least with regard to mandatory class actions) enjoys a practical advantage that preclusion does not. Are they both right? Has *GM Pick-Up* taken an unduly broad reading of *Shutts*? Shouldn't a federal court be able to preclude persons that have minimum contacts with the federal system as a whole from taking legal actions that would cause irreparable harm to a case pending in federal court? Isn't the real point in *GM Pick-Up* that the actions of class members in the Louisiana litigation do not threaten such harm to the federal litigation, and not that the federal court has no jurisdiction over absent class members? Certainly the constitutional issue of jurisdiction over the person shouldn't hinge on whether irreparable harm exists, should it?

Conversely, is *Asbestos Litigation* right to so readily dismiss *Shutts* in the context of mandatory class actions, especially ones that seek monetary rather than injunctive relief? The Supreme Court has twice granted certiorari to resolve the issue of whether the due process clause requires an opt-out right in the context of mandatory class actions, but each time has dismissed the writ as improvidently granted because the issue was not properly presented for Supreme Court review. Ticor Title Insurance Co. v. Brown, 511 U.S. 117 (1994); Adams v. Robertson, 520 U.S. 83 (1997). When *Asbestos Litigation* first went up to the Supreme Court, the Court vacated and remanded the case to consider the effect of an intervening decision from the Court. That case dealt with other issues, not the *Shutts* issue. The Fifth Circuit has subsequently affirmed the original judgment, 134 F.3d 668 (5th Cir. 1998), and the Supreme Court has again granted certiorari. Unlike *Ticor Title* and *Adams*, the *Shutts* issue is clearly presented should the Court wish to address the question. Since there are numerous other grounds on which the Supreme Court could reverse *Asbestos Litigation*, it is not clear whether it will reach the *Shutts* issue in the case.

Guessing about how the Supreme Court will eventually resolve this issue is a hazardous business. In *Ticor Title*, Justice O'Connor, joined by Chief Justice Rehnquist and Justice Kennedy, dissented from the dismissal of the writ. The dissent provided virtually no indication of how it would have resolved the *Shutts* issue, but it did place an ever-so-slight emphasis on one aspect of *Shutts*, stating that its "holding was *expressly* 'limited to those class actions which seek to bind known plaintiffs concerning claims wholly or predominately for money judgments.'" 511 U.S. at 125 (emphasis added).

3. The resolution of the *Shutts-Asbestos Litigation* issue is extremely significant for the problems of lawyer dysfunction (*i.e.*, complex litigation) and inefficiency (*i.e.*, complicated litigation). Should the fact of dysfunction or inefficiency enter into the decision about the resolution of the question? Would dysfunction call for a different resolution of the issue than inefficiency? This would be the argument: The basic preference of our litigation system, to some extent constitutionalized in the due process clause, is for adversarial procedure. An aspect of adversarial procedure is the right of the plaintiff to choose when and where to bring suit. A narrow reading of the jurisdictional limitation in

Shutts (like the one that *Asbestos Litigation* developed) thwarts that adversarial right because it makes involuntary joinder easier to accomplish. When efficiency is the only gain from the thwarting of this constitutionally-derived adversarial right, *Shutts* cannot be read narrowly. Conversely, when the adversarial right creates lawyer dysfunction and thus threatens the constitutional guarantee of rational adjudication, a weightier reason to overcome the adversarial right exists. Therefore, in this situation, *Shutts* should receive a narrow reading.

Although neither *Shutts, Asbestos Litigation,* nor *GM Pick-Up* adopts this rationale, the three cases are consistent with it. Although both are complicated, neither *Shutts* nor *GM Pick-Up* is complex; thus, there is no adequate reason for the court to construe the law of territorial jurisdiction in a way that prevents re-litigation. On the other hand, *Asbestos Litigation*, in which the available assets of Fibreboard and its insurance proceeds were likely inadequate to satisfy fully the claims of all potential plaintiffs, presented a case in which the law of territorial jurisdiction needed to be bent, and standard adversarial rights suspended, in order to achieve the rational resolution of the case.

4. Courts have tried various methods of avoiding the roadblock to aggregation imposed by *Shutts*. The most notable set of efforts occurred in the antitrust action brought by professional football players against the National Football League. The various actions sought both injunctive and monetary remedies. The NFL eventually agreed to settle the case on a class action basis. The district court certified a non-opt-out class and approved the settlement. It then sought to enjoin players from commencing their own suits elsewhere. The obvious problem was that the federal court, sitting in Minnesota, had no minimum contacts with most of the 5,000 professional players involved in the case. The district court's first effort to circumvent *Shutts* was to hold that *Shutts* did not apply to mandatory class actions when claims for injunctive relief predominated over claims for monetary relief. White v. National Football League, 822 F. Supp. 1389, 1410 (D. Minn. 1993). It further held that "where sufficient alternative procedural safeguards are employed, opt-out rights are not constitutionally required." Id. at 1411. Those safeguards existed when "the objectors have been: (1) adequately represented by the named plaintiffs; (2) adequately represented by capable and experienced class counsel; (3) provided with adequate notice of the proposed settlement; (4) given an opportunity to object to the settlement; and (5) assured that the settlement will not be approved unless the court, after analyzing the facts and law of the case and considering all objections to the proposed settlement, determines it to be fair, reasonable and adequate." Id. at 1412. On appeal, the Eighth Circuit took a different tack, holding that, since the objectors had appeared in the district court to contest the merits of the settlement, and not just the court's jurisdiction, the district court had territorial jurisdiction over them. White v. National Football League, 41 F.3d 402, 407-08 (8th Cir. 1994), cert. denied, 515 U.S. 1137 (1995); compare In re Real Estate Title and Settlement Services Antitrust Litigation, 869 F.2d 760, 770-71 (3rd Cir.), cert. denied, 493 U.S. 821 (1989) (court did not have territorial jurisdiction over class member that appeared to contest only jurisdiction of court). The Eighth Circuit therefore did "not reach the issue raised by the objectors and left undecided by *Shutts*, namely whether a trial court may certify a non-opt-out plaintiff class in an action brought primarily for injunctive relief." 41 F.3d at 408.

Another tack, used in a few opinions though never really in favor, is to argue that *Shutts* is irrelevant in federal court. Under this view, *Shutts* limits state class action rules, but not Rule 23; federal courts, unlike state courts, can arguably exercise jurisdiction with respect to anyone that has minimum contacts with the nation as a whole. This rationale was used in the alternative by the district court in *Asbestos Litigation.* See Ahearn v. Fibreboard Corp., 1995 U.S. Dist. LEXIS 11523, *36-37 (E.D. Tex.); 7B Charles A. Wright et al., Federal Practice & Procedure § 1789 (1986 & 1998 Supp.) (raising issue); but see Arthur R. Miller & David Crump, *Jurisdiction and Choice of Law in Multistate Class Actions After* Phillips Petroleum v. Shutts, 96 Yale L.J. 1 (1986) (arguing that *Shutts* applies in federal court). Would there also be an argument that *Shutts* applies only to state-law claims, and not to claims based on federal law?

Still another tack, proposed by Professors Miller and Crump, is to use a four-factor test to determine whether *Shutts* should apply. The four factors are efficiency, equity, prevention of abusive use of a distant forum, and plaintiffs' interests in individual control. Id. at 55-57. The authors acknowledge that *Shutts* itself does not suggest such a test, and that "the theory is supported only by the broadest inferences from *Shutts.*" Id. at 56.

For other interesting decisions concerning the application of *Shutts*, see In re Joint Eastern and Southern District Asbestos Litigation, 78 F.3d 764 (2d Cir. 1996); In re Joint Eastern and Southern District Asbestos Litigation, 982 F.2d 721 (2d Cir. 1992), modified on other grounds, 993 F.2d 7 (2d Cir. 1993); In re Drexel Burnham Lambert Group, Inc., 960 F.2d 285 (2d Cir. 1992); Grimes v. Vitalink Communications Corp., 17 F.3d 1553 (3d Cir.), cert. denied, 513 U.S. 986 (1994); In re A.H. Robins Co., 880 F.2d 709, 745 (4th Cir.) cert. denied, 493 U.S. 959 (1989) (not following *Shutts* when a *de facto* opt-out right was provided in mandatory class action).

5. It is a slight — but only a slight — exaggeration to say that the fate of mandatory aggregation hinges on the uncertain scope of *Shutts*. If *Shutts* affects only state courts, then federal courts enjoy a significant aggregation advantage. If it affects only state-law claims, then federal question claims (and perhaps state-law claims within the court's pendent personal jurisdiction, see p. 274, *supra*) are the key to aggregation. If *Shutts* applies to claims primarily for monetary relief, then a predominance of injunctive claims is the key to aggregation. If *Shutts* is subject to a mutli-factor test, then the balance of the relevant interests determines the legitimate scope of aggregation. If *Shutts* must give way before joinder complexity, then the presence of lawyer dysfunction in one of it three forms is central. If *Shutts* requires absolutely an opt-out right be extended to all plaintiffs that are joined on a mandatory basis and that have no minimum contacts with the forum, then all mandatory joinder (and presumably all mandatory preclusion) devices contain a fatal constitutional flaw.

One way to think about the scope of *Shutts* is to focus on its holding that an opt-out right is necessary for at least some cases involving involuntary joinder. What exactly is the point of an opt-out right? Presumably, such a right is valuable because it allows an individual to exercise control over his or her personal rights — to act, in other words, in a manner consistent with basic adversarial notions. If that is so, then neither a "state court vs. federal court" nor a "state-law claim vs. federal claim" distinction is really relevant to the basic concern of *Shutts*. Nor is the four-factor balancing test, which introduces concerns (such as efficiency) that work against the opt-out right, faithful to the basic concern of *Shutts*. On the other hand, an absolute opt-out right ignores the fact that, in at least some cases, the exercise of individual control becomes inconsistent with the equal exercise of this right of control by others. Thus, an opt-out right must be extended to all plaintiffs unless that right infringes on the right of others to control their cases — in other words, when joinder complexity exists. Two of the three situations of joinder complexity — the inability of nonparties to obtain a remedy and the inability of parties to maintain their remedy in face of later lawsuits — classically involve injunctive claims. The third — the problem of insufficient assets — involves a narrow species of claims for monetary recovery. For the most part, these three circumstances are also the circumstances in which mandatory Rule 23 (b)(1) and (b)(2) class actions are maintained. See pp. 133-34, *supra*. Thus, the line suggested in some of the cases — that *Shutts* does not apply to mandatory class actions — is generally an accurate statement, although care must be taken to ensure that the mandatory class action at issue in fact presents a case of joinder complexity.

Is this analysis of the scope of *Shutts* sound?

6. *Shutts* contains another ambiguity. Note that the class members in *Shutts* to whom the opt-out right was extended were persons with whom the Kansas court had no minimum contacts. Was the Supreme Court holding only that an opt-out right needed to be extended to out-of-state residents without minimum contacts, or was it holding more broadly that an opt-out right needed to be extended to all claims involving money damages — even those with whom Kansas did have minimum contacts. Though the tenor of the opinion would seem to favor the former interpretation, there is enough loose language in the decision to support the latter view as well. See Patricia A. Solomon, Note, *Are Mandatory Class Actions Constitutional?* 72 Notre Dame L. Rev. 1627 (1997). If the latter view prevailed, mandatory class actions would be even more difficult to obtain. The "joinder complexity" analysis in the last Note would generally support the broader reading of *Shutts*, although it would not favor this reading when the problem of insufficient assets existed.

7. *Shutts* contains a final ambiguity. In *Shutts*, all class members were known and received individual notice of their right to opt out. In a case like *Asbestos Litigation*, individual notice to all class members is impossible. Does *Shutts* preclude a court from exercising jurisdiction over plaintiffs that have no minimum contacts and that did not receive actual notice of their right to opt out? See In re "Agent Orange" Product Liability Litigation MDL No. 381, 818 F.2d 145 (2d Cir. 1987), cert. denied, 484 U.S. 1004 (1988) (*Shutts* does not require individual notice); In re "Agent Orange" Product Liability Litigation, 996 F.2d 1425 (2d Cir. 1993), cert. denied, 510 U.S. 1140 (1994) (same).

In the same vein, in *Asbestos Litigation*, the class included not only persons that had been exposed to Fibreboard asbestos, but also those (such as spouses or children) with derivative claims for injury. In some cases, a class member may not yet have married, or the children of the class member may not yet have been born. Isn't it unfair for a court to exercise jurisdiction over potential plaintiffs who had no minimum contacts with the forum and who had absolutely no knowledge that they might be plaintiffs some day? Is it also unconstitutional?

8. If an individual plaintiff or a member of a plaintiff class brings an action in a state with which she has no other connection, can the defendant assert a counterclaim against the plaintiff in that forum? See Adam v. Saenger, 303 U.S. 59, 67-68 (1938).

9. Recall that the ALI's territorial jurisdiction proposal extended not only to jurisdiction over defendants, but also to jurisdiction over plaintiffs. See p. 288, *supra*. Does this proposal pass constitutional muster under *Shutts*? Would

any arguable constitutional difficulty be removed if Congress authorized such jurisdiction, as the ALI contemplated? More generally, even if it is constitutional, is it wise to replace a state minimum contacts standard for plaintiffs with a national minimum contacts standard? In which cases? How can such a standard be reconciled with the standard in other, more routine cases?

10. Courts must have jurisdiction over both the parties and the subject matter. We now turn to the question of subject matter jurisdiction.

B. LIMITATIONS ON AGGREGATION IMPOSED BY SUBJECT MATTER JURISDICTION

Although this statement is somewhat misleading, it is often said that state courts are courts of "general jurisdiction," while federal courts are courts of "limited jurisdiction." The basic point of this distinction is that state courts can hear cases involving all types of subject matter, but federal courts can hear only those cases that (1) fit within one of the nine grants of federal jurisdiction listed in Article III, § 2 of the United States Constitution, and (2) Congress has authorized the case to be filed in federal court. See Marbury v. Madison, 1 Cranch 137 (1803); Martin v. Hunter's Lessee, 1 Wheaton 304 (1816). This distinction between federal and state courts must, however, be approached with some caution: many state court systems have established courts of limited or special jurisdiction, and no state court can entertain certain claims that lie within the exclusive jurisdiction of the federal courts. Federal courts are also constrained by another requirement of Article III, § 2: there must exist a live dispute — a "case or controversy." Most state courts have a comparable jurisdictional requirement, though it is not always interpreted in the same way as the federal requirement.

This section focuses on the rules of subject matter jurisdiction in the federal courts. That focus is intentional. Although federal courts have limited jurisdiction, they also have certain advantages for resolving complex and complicated cases, including a uniform system of joinder rules, a greater actual and potential reach of territorial jurisdiction, greater resources, and (as we shall see in the next chapter) greater ability to transfer cases to a single courtroom. Most lawyers, judges, and scholars agree that, if cases are to be aggregated, the federal system is the logical place to aggregate.

Therefore, the breadth and limits of the federal jurisdictional rules are of central importance to the aggregation of complex and complicated cases. At the same time, these jurisdictional rules can frustrate aggregation. Except in the few instances in which federal claims may be heard only in federal court, the jurisdiction of the federal courts over claims is "concurrent" with that of the state courts — in other words, the claim could be filed in either federal or state court. Moreover, as master of the complaint, a plaintiff intent on obtaining a state forum can, through the artful pleading of certain claims, often use jurisdictional rules to thwart aggregation. The ability of defendants and the court to overcome the plaintiffs' dysfunction- or inefficiency-causing choice of court system is as central a question as the breadth of the rules themselves. Conversely, defendants themselves sometimes have a reason to resist aggregation in federal court even when the use of the state forum will cause dysfunction or inefficiency. The power of defendants to use the court-switching rules to frustrate aggregation is the final critical issue.

This section begins with the gauntlet of jurisdictional rules that a plaintiff who wishes to locate a case in a federal forum must run. The second subsection then examines devices that defendants and the courts can use either to switch a case from a state to a federal forum when the plaintiff chooses to file in state court or to switch a case to a state forum when the plaintiff chooses to file in federal court. As you read the materials, ask whether an adversarial approach, in which both plaintiffs and defendants manipulate jurisdictional doctrines for private advantage, should be replaced by a system in which the court takes an active role in choosing the forum. Also ask whether the usual jurisdictional doctrines should be changed to accommodate the needs of complex and complicated litigation.

1. The Basic Rules and Their Limits in Complex and Complicated Litigation

Although Article III contains nine grants of jurisdiction for the federal courts, two of those grants account for most of the cases, and nearly all of the complex or complicated cases, heard in federal district courts. The first (often called "federal question" jurisdiction) authorizes federal courts to entertain cases arising under federal law; the second (often called "diversity" jurisdiction) authorizes federal courts to entertain controversies between parties that are from different states. Sometimes, however, claims that are not within the jurisdiction of the federal court are related to claims that are. For the federal court to become the forum in which complete aggregation can occur, it must be able to entertain these "supplemental" claims. The text of Article III does not, however, clearly provide for such supplemental jurisdiction, so the existence of such jurisdiction is problematic. The text does require that there be a "case or controversy," a term that imposes its own limitations on federal jurisdiction. Finally, the meaning of Article III has been modified by the Eleventh Amendment, which limits the ability of federal courts to entertain suits against states. The following five subsections explore each of these aspects of federal jurisdiction.

Before that exploration begins, however, a few basic principles of federal jurisdiction should be noted. First, it is typically not enough for jurisdiction to exist under Article III; Congress must also enact legislation conferring jurisdiction on the federal courts. Second, the lack of federal subject matter jurisdiction may be raised at any time, even on appeal. See Louisville & Nashville R.R. v. Mottley, 211 U.S. 149 (1908); F.R.Civ.P. 12(h)(3). Third, the issue of federal jurisdiction cannot be waived by the parties or conferred by the parties' agreement. 13 Charles A. Wright et al., Federal Practice & Procedure § 3522 (1984). Fourth, under the "well-pleaded complaint" rule, federal jurisdiction is typically determined only by referring to the allegations of plaintiff's *prima facie* case; the existence of a defense arising under federal law does not confer jurisdiction. See *Mottley, supra*; but see Metropolitan Life Insurance Co. v. Taylor, 481 U.S. 58 (1987) (finding federal jurisdiction when state-law claim is entirely pre-empted by federal law and effectively arises under federal law); Bright v. Bechtel Petroleum Co., 780 F.2d 766 (9th Cir. 1986) (piercing sham state-law claim and re-characterizing it as federal claim). When combined with the "master of the complaint" rule, the well-pleaded complaint rule gives the plaintiff great power to control the forum in which the case will be ultimately be adjudicated. In order to avoid a misstep which lands her in a less desirable forum, however, the plaintiff must know the jurisdictional rules that allocate business between state and federal courts.

a. Federal Question Jurisdiction

Article III, § 2 provides, *inter alia*, that "[t]he judicial Power shall extend to all Cases, in Law and Equity, arising under this Constitution, the Laws of the United States, and Treaties made, or which shall be made, under their Authority." Despite the seemingly mandatory "shall extend" language, the Supreme Court has never held that lower federal courts must be granted the full scope of this constitutional "federal question" jurisdiction; a federal statute must also grant jurisdiction in order for a lower federal court to hear a federal question case. Cf. Sheldon v. Sill, 49 U.S. (8 How.) 441 (U.S. 1850). Today, 28 U.S.C. § 1331, which states that "[t]he district courts shall have original jurisdiction of all civil cases arising under the Constitution, laws, or treaties of the United States," contains the requisite statutory grant. The language of § 1331 tracks that of Article III. As you read the following two cases, note the different meanings which the Supreme Court attaches to "arising under" for constitutional and statutory purposes.

OSBORN v. BANK OF THE UNITED STATES

22 U.S. (9 Wheat.) 738 (U.S. 1824)

■ MR. CHIEF JUSTICE MARSHALL delivered the opinion of the Court.

[Congress granted the Bank of the United States the right to sue or be sued in federal court. In a companion case to *Osborn, Bank of the United States v. Planter's Bank of Georgia*, the federal bank had sued a state bank for breach of contract based on state law. The state bank asserted both that the federal statute did not grant jurisdiction over the case and that the case did not "arise under" federal law as required by Article III. The Supreme Court first found that the "sue and be sued" language of the statute gave the federal courts statutory jurisdiction. It then turned to the issue of whether Congress could give the lower federal courts jurisdiction over cases like *Planter's Bank*, in which state law created the plaintiff's cause of action.]

A cause may depend on several questions of fact and law. Some of these may depend on the construction of a law of the United States; others on principles unconnected with that law. If it be a sufficient foundation for jurisdiction, that the title or right set up by the party, may be defeated by one construction of the constitution or law of the United States, and sustained by the opposite construction, provided the facts necessary to support the action be made out, then all the other questions must be decided as incidental to this, which gives that jurisdiction. Those other questions cannot arrest the proceedings. Under this construction, the judicial power of the Union extends effectively and beneficially to that most important class of cases, which depend on the character of the cause. On the opposite construction, the judicial power never can be extended to a whole case, as expressed by the constitution, but to those parts of cases only which present the particular question involving the construction of the constitution or the law. We say it never can be extended to the whole case, because, if the circumstance that other points are involved in it, shall disable Congress from authorizing the Courts of the Union to take jurisdiction of the original cause, it equally disables Congress from authorizing those Courts to take jurisdiction of the whole cause, on an appeal, and thus will be restricted to a single question in that cause; and words obviously intended to secure to those who claim rights under the constitution, laws, or treaties of the United States, a trial in the federal Courts, will be restricted to the insecure remedy of an appeal upon an insulated point, after it has received that shape which may be given to it by another tribunal, into which he is forced against his will.

We think, then, that when a question to which the judicial power of the Union is extended by the constitution, forms an ingredient of the original cause, it is in the power of Congress to give the Circuit Courts jurisdiction of that cause, although other questions of fact or of law may be involved in it.

The case of the Bank is, we think, a very strong case of this description. The charter of incorporation not only creates it, but gives it every faculty which it possesses. The power to acquire rights of any description, to transact business of any description, to make contracts of any description, to sue on those contracts, is given and measured by its charter, and that charter is a law of the United States. This being can acquire no right, make no contract, bring no suit, which is not authorized by a law of the United States. It is not only itself the mere creature of a law, but all its actions and all its rights are dependent on the same law. Can a being, thus constituted, have a case which does not arise literally, as well as substantially, under the law?

Take the case of a contract, which is put as the strongest against the Bank.

When a Bank sues, the first question which presents itself, and which lies at the foundation of the cause, is, has this legal entity a right to sue? Has it a right to come, not into this Court particularly, but into any Court? This depends on a law of the United States. The next question is, has this being a right to make this particular contract? If this question be decided in the negative, the cause is determined against the plaintiff; and this question, too, depends entirely on a law of the United States. These are important questions, and they exist in every possible case. The right to sue, if decided once, is decided forever; but the power of Congress was exercised antecedently to the first decision on that right, and if it was constitutional then, it cannot cease to be so, because the particular question is decided. It may be revived at the will of the party, and most probably would be renewed, were the tribunal to be changed. But the question respecting the right to make a particular contract, or to acquire a particular property, or to sue on account of a particular injury, belongs to every particular case, and may be renewed in every case. The question forms an original ingredient in every cause. Whether it be in fact relied on or not, in the defence, it is still a part of the cause, and may be relied on. The right of the plaintiff to sue, cannot depend on the defence which the defendant may choose to set up. His right to sue is anterior to that defence, and must depend on the state of things when the action is brought. The questions which the case involves, then, must determine its character, whether those questions be made in the cause or not.

The appellants say, that the case arises on the contract; but the validity of the contract depends on a law of the United States, and the plaintiff is compelled, in every case, to show its validity. The case arises emphatically under the law. The act of Congress is its foundation. The contract could never have been made, but under the authority of that act. The act itself is the first ingredient in the case, is its origin, is that from which every other part arises. That other questions may also arise, as the execution of the contract, or its performance, cannot change the case, or give it any other origin than the charter of incorporation. The action still originates in, and is sustained by, that charter. . . .

■ MR. JUSTICE JOHNSON. . . . To me, the question appears susceptible of a very simple solution; that all depends upon the identity of the case supposed; according to which idea, a case may be such in its very existence, or it may become such in progress. An action may "live, move, and have its being," in a law of the United States . . . . In this class of cases, the occurrence of a question makes the case, and transfers it, . . . to the jurisdiction of the United States. And this appears to me to present the only sound and practical construction of the constitution on this subject; for no other case does it regard as necessary to place under the control of the general government. . . . I object to this general grant of the right to sue . . . because the principle of possible occurrence of a question is transcending the bounds of the constitution, and placing it on a ground which will admit of an *enormous accession*, if not an *unlimited assumption*, of jurisdiction.

MERRELL DOW PHARMACEUTICALS, INC. v. THOMPSON

478 U.S. 804 (1986)

■ JUSTICE STEVENS delivered the opinion of the Court.

The question presented is whether the incorporation of a federal standard in a state-law private action, when Congress has intended that there not be a federal private action for violations of that federal standard, makes the action one "arising under the Constitution, laws, or treaties of the United States," 28 U.S.C. § 1331.

I

The Thompson respondents are residents of Canada and the MacTavishes reside in Scotland. They filed virtually identical complaints against petitioner, a corporation, that manufactures and distributes the drug Bendectin. The complaints were filed in the Court of Common Pleas in Hamilton County, Ohio. Each complaint alleged that a child was born with multiple deformities as a result of the mother's ingestion of Bendectin during pregnancy. In five of the six counts, the recovery of substantial damages was requested on common-law theories of negligence, breach of warranty, strict liability, fraud, and gross negligence. In Count IV, respondents alleged that the drug Bendectin was "misbranded" in violation of the Federal Food, Drug, and Cosmetic Act (FDCA), . . ., because its labeling did not provide adequate warning that its use was potentially dangerous. Paragraph 26 alleged that the violation of the FDCA "in the promotion" of Bendectin "constitutes a rebuttable presumption of negligence." Paragraph 27 alleged that the "violation of said federal statutes directly and proximately caused the injuries suffered" by the two infants.

Petitioner filed a timely petition for removal from the state court to the Federal District Court alleging that the action was "founded, in part, on an alleged claim arising under the laws of the United States." After removal, the two cases were consolidated. Respondents filed a motion to remand to the state forum on the ground that the federal court lacked subject-matter jurisdiction. Relying on our decision in Smith v. Kansas City Title & Trust Co., 255 U.S. 180 (1921), the District Court held that Count IV of the complaint alleged a cause of action arising under federal law and denied the motion to remand. It then granted petitioner's motion to dismiss on *forum non conveniens* grounds.

The Court of Appeals for the Sixth Circuit reversed. [The court of appeals held that the district court lacked subject matter jurisdiction.]

II

Article III of the Constitution gives the federal courts power to hear cases "arising under" federal statutes. That grant of power, however, is not self-executing, and it was not until the Judiciary Act of 1875 that Congress gave the federal courts general federal-question jurisdiction. Although the constitutional meaning of "arising under" may extend to all cases in which a federal question is "an ingredient" of the action, Osborn v. Bank of the United States, 9 Wheat. 738, 823 (1824), we have long construed the statutory grant of federal-question jurisdiction as conferring a more limited power. Verlinden B. V. v. Central Bank of Nigeria, 461 U.S. 480, 494-495

(1983); Romero v. International Terminal Operating Co., 358 U.S. 354, 379 (1959).

Under our longstanding interpretation of the current statutory scheme, the question whether a claim "arises under" federal law must be determined by reference to the "well-pleaded complaint." [Franchise Tax Board v. Construction Laborers Vacation Trust, 463 U.S. 1,] 9-10 [(1983)]. A defense that raises a federal question is inadequate to confer federal jurisdiction. Louisville & Nashville R. Co. v. Mottley, 211 U.S. 149 (1908). Since a defendant may remove a case only if the claim could have been brought in federal court, 28 U.S.C. § 1441(b), moreover, the question for removal jurisdiction must also be determined by reference to the "well-pleaded complaint."

As was true in *Franchise Tax Board, supra,* the propriety of the removal in this case thus turns on whether the case falls within the original "federal question" jurisdiction of the federal courts. There is no "single, precise definition" of that concept; rather, "the phrase 'arising under' masks a welter of issues regarding the interrelation of federal and state authority and the proper management of the federal judicial system." [463 U.S.] at 8.

This much, however, is clear. The "vast majority" of cases that come within this grant of jurisdiction are covered by Justice Holmes' statement that a "'suit arises under the law that creates the cause of action.'" Id., at 8-9, quoting American Well Works Co. v. Layne & Bowler Co., 241 U.S. 257, 260 (1916). Thus, the vast majority of cases brought under the general federal-question jurisdiction of the federal courts are those in which federal law creates the cause of action.

We have, however, also noted that a case may arise under federal law "where the vindication of a right under state law necessarily turned on some construction of federal law." *Franchise Tax Board,* 463 U.S., at 9.[5] Our actual holding in *Franchise Tax Board* demonstrates that this statement must be read with caution; the central issue presented in that case turned on the meaning of the Employee Retirement Income Security Act of 1974, . . ., but we nevertheless concluded that federal jurisdiction was lacking.

This case does not pose a federal question of the first kind; respondents do not allege that federal law creates any of the causes of action that they have asserted.[6] This case thus poses what Justice Frankfurter called the

---

5. The case most frequently cited for that proposition is Smith v. Kansas City Title & Trust Co., 255 U.S. 180 (1921). . . .

The effect of this view, expressed over Justice Holmes' vigorous dissent, on his *American Well Works* formulation has been often noted. See, *e.g., Franchise Tax Board,* 463 U.S. at 9 ("[I]t is well settled that Justice Holmes' test is more useful for describing the vast majority of cases that come within the district courts' original jurisdiction than it is for describing which cases are beyond district court jurisdiction."); T.B. Harms Co. v. Eliscu, 339 F.2d 823, 827 (CA2 1964) (Friendly, J.) ("It has come to be realized that Mr. Justice Holmes' formula is more useful for inclusion than for the exclusion for which it was intended.").

6. Jurisdiction may not be sustained on a theory that the plaintiff has not advanced. See Healy v. Sea Gull Specialty Co., 237 U.S. 479, 480 (1915) ("[The] plaintiff is absolute master of what jurisdiction he will appeal to"); The Fair v. Kohler Die & Specialty Co., 228 U.S. 22, 25 (1913) ("[The] party who brings a suit is master to decide what law he will rely upon"). . . .

"litigation-provoking problem," Textile Workers v. Lincoln Mills, 353 U.S. 448, 470 (1957) (dissenting opinion) — the presence of a federal issue in a state-created cause of action.

In undertaking this inquiry into whether jurisdiction may lie for the presence of a federal issue in a nonfederal cause of action, it is, of course, appropriate to begin by referring to our understanding of the statute conferring federal-question jurisdiction. We have consistently emphasized that, in exploring the outer reaches of § 1331, determinations about federal jurisdiction require sensitive judgments about congressional intent, judicial power, and the federal system. . . .

In this case, both parties agree with the Court of Appeals' conclusion that there is no federal cause of action for FDCA violations. For purposes of our decision, we assume that this is a correct interpretation of the FDCA. Thus, as the case comes to us, it is appropriate to assume that, under the settled framework for evaluating whether a federal cause of action lies, some combination of the following factors is present: (1) the plaintiffs are not part of the class for whose special benefit the statute was passed; (2) the indicia of legislative intent reveal no congressional purpose to provide a private cause of action; (3) a federal cause of action would not further the underlying purposes of the legislative scheme; and (4) the respondents' cause of action is a subject traditionally relegated to state law. In short, Congress did not intend a private federal remedy for violations of the statute that it enacted. . . .

The significance of the necessary assumption that there is no federal private cause of action thus cannot be overstated. For the ultimate import of such a conclusion, as we have repeatedly emphasized, is that it would flout congressional intent to provide a private federal remedy for the violation of the federal statute. We think it would similarly flout, or at least undermine, congressional intent to conclude that the federal courts might nevertheless exercise federal-question jurisdiction and provide remedies for violations of that federal statute solely because the violation of the federal statute is said to be a "rebuttable presumption" or a "proximate cause" under state law, rather than a federal action under federal law. . . .

III

[P]etitioner contends that the case represents a strightforward application of the statement in *Franchise Tax Board* that federal-question jurisdiction is appropriate when "it appears that some substantial, disputed question of federal law is a necessary element of one of the well-pleaded state claims." 463 U.S., at 13. . . .

Far from creating some kind of automatic test, *Franchise Tax Board* thus candidly recognized the need for careful judgments about the exercise of federal judicial power in an area of uncertain jurisdiction. Given the significance of the assumed congressional determination to preclude federal private remedies, the presence of the federal issue as an element of the state tort is not the kind of adjudication for which jurisdiction would serve congressional purposes and the federal system. . . . We simply conclude that the congressional determination that there should be no federal remedy for the violation of this federal statute is tantamount to a congressional conclusion that the presence of a claimed violation of the statute as an element of a state cause of action is insufficiently "substantial" to confer federal-question jurisdiction.[12] . . .

IV

We conclude that a complaint alleging a violation of a federal statute as an element of a state cause of action, when Congress has determined that there should be no private, federal cause of action for the violation, does not state a claim "arising under the Constitution, laws, or treaties of the United States." 28 U.S.C. § 1331.

The judgment of the Court of Appeals is affirmed.

■ JUSTICE BRENNAN, with whom JUSTICE WHITE, JUSTICE MARSHALL, and JUSTICE BLACKMUN join, dissenting. . . . There is, to my mind, no question that there is federal jurisdiction over the respondents' fourth cause of action under the rule set forth in *Smith* and reaffirmed in *Franchise Tax Board*. Respondents pleaded that petitioner's labeling of the drug Bendectin constituted "misbranding" in violation of §§ 201 and 502(f)(2) and (j) of the Federal Food, Drug, and Cosmetic Act (FDCA), 52 Stat. 1040, as amended, 21 U.S.C. § 301 et seq. (1982 ed. and Supp. III), and that this violation "directly and proximately caused" their injuries. Respondents asserted in the complaint that this violation established petitioner's negligence *per se* and entitled them to recover damages without more. No other basis for finding petitioner negligent was asserted in connection with this claim. As pleaded, then, respondents' "right to relief [depended] upon the construction or application of the Constitution or laws of the United States." *Smith*, 255 U.S., at 199; see also *Franchise Tax Board*, 463 U.S., at 28 (there is federal jurisdiction under § 1331 where the plaintiff's right to relief "necessarily depends" upon resolution of a federal question). Furthermore, although petitioner disputes its liability under the FDCA, it concedes that respondents' claim that petitioner violated the FDCA is "colorable, and rests upon a reasonable foundation." *Smith, supra,* at 199. Of course, since petitioner must make this concession to prevail in this Court, it need not be accepted at face value. However, independent examination of respondents' claim substantiates the conclusion that it is neither frivolous nor meritless. As stated in the complaint, a drug is "misbranded" under the FDCA if "the labeling or advertising fails to reveal facts material . . . with respect to consequences which may result from the use of the article to which the labeling or advertising relates . . . ." 21 U.S.C. § 321(n). Obviously, the possibility that a mother's ingestion of Bendectin

---

12. Several commentators have suggested that our § 1331 decisions can best be understood as an evaluation of the *nature* of the federal interest at stake. . . .

The importance of the nature of the federal issue in federal-question jurisdiction is highlighted by the fact that, despite the usual reliability of the Holmes test as an inclusionary principle, this Court has sometimes found that formally federal causes of action were not properly brought under federal-question jurisdiction because of the overwhelming predominance of state-law issues. . . .

during pregnancy could produce malformed children is material. Petitioner's principal defense is that the Act does not govern the branding of drugs that are sold in foreign countries. It is certainly not immediately obvious whether this argument is correct. Thus, the statutory question is one which "discloses a need for determining the meaning or application of [the FDCA]," *T. B. Harms Co. v. Eliscu*, 339 F.2d, at 827, and the claim raised by the fourth cause of action is one "arising under" federal law within the meaning of § 1331....

The Court apparently does not disagree with any of this — except, of course, for the conclusion. According to the Court, if we assume that Congress did not intend that there be a private federal cause of action under a particular federal law (and, presumably, *a fortiori* if Congress' decision not to create a private remedy is express), we must also assume that Congress did not intend that there be federal jurisdiction over a state cause of action that is determined by that federal law. Therefore, assuming — only because the parties have made a similar assumption — that there is no private cause of action under the FDCA, the Court holds that there is no federal jurisdiction over the plaintiffs' claim....

The Court nowhere explains the basis for this conclusion. Yet it is hardly self-evident. Why should the fact that Congress chose not to create a private federal *remedy* mean that Congress would not want there to be federal *jurisdiction* to adjudicate a state claim that imposes liability for violating the federal law? Clearly, the decision not to provide a private federal remedy should not affect federal jurisdiction unless the reasons Congress withholds a federal remedy are also reasons for withholding federal jurisdiction. Thus, it is necessary to examine the reasons for Congress' decisions to grant or withhold both federal jurisdiction and private remedies, something the Court has not done....

[Section] 1331 has provided for adjudication in a forum that specializes in federal law and that is therefore more likely to apply that law correctly. Because federal question cases constitute the basic grist for federal tribunals, "the federal courts have acquired a considerable expertise in the interpretation and application of federal law." [American Law Institute, Study of the Division of Jurisdiction Between State and Federal Courts] 164-65 [(1969)]. By contrast, "it is apparent that federal question cases must form a very small part of the business of state courts." [Id. at] 165. As a result, the federal courts are comparatively more skilled at interpreting and applying federal law, and are much more likely correctly to divine Congress' intent in enacting legislation....

By making federal law an essential element of a state-law claim, the State places the federal law into a context where it will operate to shape behavior: the threat of liability will force individuals to conform their conduct to interpretations of the federal law made by courts adjudicating the state-law claim. It will not matter to an individual found liable whether the officer who arrives at his door to execute judgment is wearing a state or a federal uniform; all he cares about is the fact that a sanction is being imposed — and may be imposed again in the future — because he failed to comply with the federal law. Consequently, the possibility that the federal law will be incorrectly interpreted in the context of adjudicating the state-law claim implicates the concerns that led Congress to grant the district courts power to adjudicate cases involving federal questions in precisely the same way as if it was federal law that "created" the cause of action. It therefore follows that there is federal jurisdiction under § 1331.

Notes and Questions

1. Compare *Osborn* and *Merrell Dow*. Why has the Supreme Court given the virtually identical language in Article III, § 2 and § 1331 (actions "arising under" federal law) such vastly different interpretations? Should the concerns which the majority and the dissent in *Merrell Dow* identify as relevant to the issue of statutory construction — drafters' intent, judicial power, federalism, workload, and institutional competence — also be relevant to the proper understanding of Article III?

Given the pervasive scope of federal regulation and legislation today, the breadth of *Osborn*'s rule has been the subject of considerable discussion. There have been numerous suggestions to limit the breadth of its "potential ingredient" rule. See Textile Workers Union v. Lincoln Mills, 353 U.S. 448 (1957) (Frankfurter, J., dissenting) (rejecting *Osborn* and other broad understandings of Article III, but recognizing a reservoir of Article III jurisdiction in the event of "some substantial federal interest"). Conversely, there have been numerous efforts to ground a broad understanding of federal question jurisdiction on a more coherent intellectual footing. Many of the broader readings invoke the concept of "protective jurisdiction." One view of protective jurisdiction is that Article III permits Congress to create statutory federal question jurisdiction in any area in which Congress could have, even though it did not, legislate a substantive rule of decision. Herbert Wechsler, *Federal Jurisdiction and the Revision of the Judicial Code*, 13 Law & Contemp. Prob. 216 (1948). Another view is that Congress may legislate federal question jurisdiction "where there is an articulated and active federal policy regulating a field," even though state law actually covers the specific issue in question. Paul J. Mishkin, *The Federal "Question" in the District Courts*, 53 Colum. L. Rev. 157 (1953). Despite these efforts, the Supreme Court has in recent years continued to adhere to the *Osborn* rule. Verlinden B.V. v. Central Bank of Nigeria, 461 U.S. 480 (1983); American National Red Cross v. S.G., 505 U.S. 247 (1992).

2. The precise scope of Article III jurisdiction is of great moment to the issue of joinder complexity. If we want to join all interested parties in one forum, the federal courts are realistically better suited to the task. Assuming that Congress could be convinced that such joinder was desirable, it could use Article III's federal question grant to create statutory jurisdiction for the district courts. But the cases which could be brought in federal court would depend entirely on the scope of Article III. For instance, assume that Congress adopted a statutory grant which read: "The district courts shall have original jurisdiction of any case in which the joinder of all interested parties in any state court is infeasible." Assume further that a mass tort plaintiff cannot join all other plaintiffs and defendants in state court. Whether the federal court has jurisdiction now depends on the scope of Article III. If *Osborn* is the rule, a potential federal ingredient must be found somewhere in the mass tort; if Professor Wechsler is correct, jurisdiction depends on whether Congress could have legislated a

substantive rule of decision for the mass tort; if Professor Mishkin is correct, jurisdiction depends on whether there exists an articulated and active federal policy regarding this mass tort. Since cases of lawyer dysfunction usually involve such a significant commercial effect that Congress could invoke its Commerce Clause powers to create a rule of decision, is Professor Wechsler's view of Article III federal question jurisdiction the one which those who seek to eliminate lawyer dysfunction should advocate?

Of course, the existence of constitutional power to create a jurisdictional grant to cover lawyer dysfunction does not mean that Congress should exercise the power. Should it? Would such a grant radically shift the balance of power away from state courts, and thus threaten our present understanding of federalism? And exactly how would a statutory grant be worded to encompass only "complex" cases? Should such a grant also be extended to include "complicated" cases involving inefficient re-litigation?

3. At present, of course, there is no jurisdictional statute of the type described in the last note; instead, we have § 1331. There are also some additional, specific grants of federal question jurisdiction contained in 28 U.S.C. §§ 1334 and 1336-49 and elsewhere in the United States Code. See, e.g., 15 U.S.C. § 77v(a). Although some of these grant jurisdiction in cases that are often regarded as "complex" (such as securities, antitrust, and patent cases), none of these grants contains any language permitting federal jurisdiction to be generally exercised in complex or complicated litigation. Therefore, any general attempt to create such jurisdiction must pass through the door of § 1331.

As *Merrell Dow* says, the simplest and best way to invoke jurisdiction under §1331 is to plead a claim arising under federal law. As *Merrell Dow* also says, there is also a second, narrow method to invoke jurisdiction. This method, best represented by Smith v. Kansas City Title & Trust Co., 255 U.S. 180 (1921), permits federal jurisdiction over a state-law claim that necessarily relies upon a construction of federal law. Have *Franchise Tax Board* and *Merrell Dow* sapped the vitality of *Smith*?

In *Franchise Tax Board*, 463 U.S. at 13, the Court also stated that whether a case arises under federal law for purposes of § 1331 depends upon whether "it appears that some substantial, disputed question of federal law is a necessary element of one of the well-pleaded state claims." In *Merrell Dow* (see especially n.12), the Court also hints that the existence of a significant federal interest in a state-law matter *might* be enough to create federal jurisdiction. Is the Court suggesting that there is a third category of cases in which federal question jurisdiction exists? Is it wise to make the scope of federal jurisdiction turn on such an *ad hoc* test? Assuming that this category exists, would the prevention of lawyer dysfunction and the protection of rational adjudication be an adequate federal interest? Would the prevention of inefficient re-litigation be an adequate federal interest?

Conversely, in footnote 12 of *Merrell Dow* and in several other cases (*e.g.*, Gully v. First National Bank, 299 U.S. 109 (1936)), the Court has indicated that a careful judgment needs to be made in each case as to whether the federal ingredient in that case is of sufficient importance to warrant a finding that the case "arises under" federal law. Under this view, fitting into one of the two (or three) categories of § 1331 jurisdiction does not automatically guarantee a federal forum. In a few instances, federal courts have invoked the notion of "substantiality" to deny federal jurisdiction over a well-pleaded federal claim. See Rogers v. Platt, 814 F.2d 683, 687 (D.C. Cir. 1987) ("a formal federal cause of action that incorporates state law so as to create an 'overwhelming predominance of state-law issues' may not be brought in federal court"); Bodanner v. Graves, 828 F. Supp. 516 (W.D. Mich. 1993) (same). Would a rule of "substantiality" significantly affect a federal court's ability to hear complex or complicated cases?

4. Our present understanding of the scope of § 1331 has been supplied by court decisions; the statute itself does not define "federal question," it does not expressly state a "well pleaded complaint" rule that requires the federal question to be part of the plaintiff's *prima facie* case, and it does not suggest that a "substantial" question of federal law must exist. Indeed, some of the legislative history of the 1875 ancestor of § 1331 suggests that Congress intended statutory federal question jurisdiction to extend to the full scope of Article III jurisdiction. See Richard H. Fallon et al., Hart and Wechsler's The Federal Courts and the Federal System 909 (4th ed. 1996). Given that the most important limitations on a broader interpretation of § 1331 are judicially created, the courts could abandon those limitations without any statutory changes at all. They have never done so — probably because, on the whole, we understand that bringing every case with a potential federal ingredient into federal court would flood the federal courts, render the state courts largely superfluous, and diffuse the federal courts' expertise in, and emphasis upon, the enforcement of federal rights.

Whatever might be the justification for the narrow construction given to § 1331, should exceptions to that construction be carved out in cases of lawyer dysfunction? *Merrell Dow* can certainly be accused of insufficient sensitivity to the problem of complex and complicated litigation, since the Supreme Court must have been aware of some background facts which never made their way into the opinions themselves. During the early 1980's thousands of Bendectin cases were filed in federal and state courts around the country. 834 were filed in federal court in Ohio, and 273 in other federal courts. In addition, 73 cases initially filed in state court were removed to federal court in Ohio. All the cases in federal court were "multidistricted" for pretrial proceedings in the Southern District of Ohio. The judge then decided to hold a trial on the issue of causation. After the court gave plaintiffs the opportunity to opt out of the trial and return to the district from which their case had come, 844 cases remained for trial. A 22-day trial ended in 1985 with a defense verdict in which the jury found that no causal link existed between Bendectin and birth defects. See In re Bendectin Litigation, 857 F.2d 290 (6th Cir. 1988), cert. denied, 488 U.S. 1006 (1989).

The plaintiffs in *Merrell Dow* appeared to have gerrymandered their claims in order to avoid the federal forum in which the aggregated proceedings were taking place. As foreign citizens suing an American corporation, they could clearly have invoked federal diversity jurisdiction had they wanted to. 28 U.S.C. § 1332(a)(2). Moreover, they sued Merrell Dow, a resident of Ohio, in Ohio state court, which precluded Merrell Dow from removing to federal court under the diversity removal provision. 28 U.S.C. § 1441(b). They also declined to plead a claim under the FDCA, which would have allowed Merrell Dow to remove the case to federal court under the federal question removal provision, 28 U.S.C. § 1441(b), and then they vigorously resisted Merrell Dow's efforts to turn their negligence *per se* claim into a federal question subject to removal.

In such an aggregation-frustrating circumstance, is there any reason to allow the plaintiffs the choice of forum, and thus require another court system to resolve an issue (causation) that had already been analyzed exhaustively in federal court? Does *Merrell Dow* respect the interest of state courts in efficiently using their resources? Are there any gains in federalism from the duplicative litigation of an issue of scientific causation? Should the Supreme Court have acknowledged that lawyer dysfunction is a relevant factor in determining the scope of § 1331? Should the Supreme Court have resolved *Merrell Dow* in a different fashion if the trial judge had found a way to consolidate all of the federal cases for trial on the causation issue?

On the other hand, is *Merrell Dow* a case of lawyer dysfunction, or simply a case of inefficient re-litigation? Since Merrell Dow's assets may well have been adequate to assure payments to all claimants, it would not seem to be a case of lawyer dysfunction. Suppose that, in a case just like *Merrell Dow*, a refusal to recognize § 1331 jurisdiction meant that one set of plaintiffs (either the state or the federal plaintiffs) would receive a disproportionate share of the defendant's assets. Would a court be precluded from finding § 1331 jurisdiction because of *Merrell Dow*? Or could *Merrell Dow* be distinguished because it did not involve lawyer dysfunction? If so, we again see that complex litigation receives more favorable treatment from the courts than complicated litigation.

5. If you accept the argument that the *Merrell Dow* interpretation of § 1331 does not apply in the circumstance of lawyer dysfunction, there remains the question of how the Court could come to a different result when lawyer dysfunction exists. The narrowest approach would be to hold that state negligence *per se* claims which allege a violation of federal law "necessarily turn on some construction of federal law" for purposes of § 1331. But that approach will not work in other complex cases in which such federal violations are not alleged. The broadest, and most controversial, approach would simply be to declare that the limiting glosses on § 1331 are not operative in cases of lawyer dysfunction, so that the full scope of Article III federal question jurisdiction is available in these cases. Are the unfairness, inefficiency, and threat to rational judgment that are endemic to lawyer dysfunction sufficient to override the limiting glosses on § 1331?

6. Both the majority and the dissent in *Merrell Dow* mentioned the parties' concession that the FDCA created no private right of action. Suppose that the plaintiffs had wanted to invoke the federal forum, and therefore contended that the FDCA did create a private remedy. Would the federal courts then have subject matter jurisdiction over a state-law negligence *per se* claim, or would the plaintiff actually have to plead a claim directly under the FDCA? (As an aside, the Supreme Court's present jurisprudence concerning private rights of action makes it very doubtful that such a right of action exists, although the Court has never squarely held that it does not.) The Sixth Circuit faced this issue in the Bendectin litigation, and, in a decision subsequent to *Merrell Dow*, held that the district court had federal question jurisdiction over the cases in which Ohio plaintiffs had pleaded (either directly or by implication) a claim for recovery under the FDCA in federal court. It came to the opposite conclusion with respect to the cases filed in state court and removed by Merrell Dow:

> As the case law indicates, a substantial federal question is presented as long as the pleadings invoking federal question jurisdiction are not "so attenuated and unsubstantial as to be absolutely devoid of merit," "wholly insubstantial," "obviously frivolous," "plainly insubstantial," or "no longer open to discussion." . . . Until this court or the Supreme Court holds that there is no implied right of action under the FDCA, the opposite position cannot be deemed either frivolous or unsubstantial.

A different analysis, however, may apply to those Ohio plaintiffs who originally brought suit in state courts. Since these plaintiffs invoked the jurisdiction of state and not federal court, it is perhaps unlikely, even where the language might arguably include an implied cause of action under the FDCA, that these plaintiffs intended to plead such a cause of action.

In re Bendectin Litigation, 857 F.2d 290, 300-01 (6th Cir. 1988), cert. denied, 488 U.S. 1006 (1989). Does the different treatment of state and federal cases make sense?

7. One reason to question the Sixth Circuit's disparate treatment of state and federal plaintiffs is that, for the most part, federal question jurisdiction is shared concurrently with the state courts; in other words, both the state and the federal courts have jurisdiction to hear a federal question case. See Tafflin v. Levitt, 493 U.S. 455 (1990) (creating a presumption of concurrent jurisdiction that can be overcome by congressional intent or clear federal interest in exclusive jurisdiction). Why should a plaintiff even be given the opportunity to select a state forum for a federal claim? According to one commentary:

> If the purpose of giving the federal courts original jurisdiction is to protect the national interest in the application of federal law, it is arguable that the parties should have no choice in the matter, and that the jurisdiction of the federal courts should be exclusive in those matters thought to require a federal forum. The existing pattern of law proceeds in large part on a different premise.... Although the national government may have a strong interest in the application of national law in some cases between private litigants, the primary interest in all such cases, and the only interest in most of them, is that of the litigants themselves.

American Law Institute, Study of the Division of Jurisdiction between State and Federal Courts, Appendix C 477 (1969).

In a few circumstances of importance to complex or complicated litigation, however, the jurisdiction of the federal courts is exclusive. Thus, many securities claims, antitrust claims, core bankruptcy matters, ERISA suits, and patent cases lie exclusively within the jurisdiction of the federal courts. See generally 13 Charles A. Wright et al., Federal Practice and Procedure § 3527 (1984) (listing all areas of exclusive federal jurisdiction). For cases of exclusive federal jurisdiction, the plaintiff is put to a clear choice: state court or federal claims. In cases of concurrent jurisdiction, the plaintiff may choose both a state forum and federal claims, subject to the risk that the defendant will remove the case to federal court. See p. 373, *infra*. That risk may, of course, lead a plaintiff to avoid the federal claims for tactical reasons.

8. Since the plaintiff chooses the theories under which she wishes to bring suit, the plaintiff with substantial claims arising under § 1331 can opt into federal court by asserting those claims, and (if no other bases for removal jurisdiction occur) can avoid federal court by not asserting them. Why do we allow plaintiffs the power to decide whose court resources to consume? Why are courts reluctant to amend or "re-interpret" a plaintiff's choice of legal theories? Assuming that a violation of federal law has occurred, do we not all benefit from its enforcement? Should defendants or a federal judge be entitled to insist that a state-filed case be moved to federal court when a federal interest in the outcome is clearly present? In this vein, you might have noted that footnote 6 of *Merrell Dow* re-affirmed the "master of the complaint" rule. What might be the dangers of a breach of the "master of the complaint" rule? Are those dangers as

problematical if we breach the rule only in complex cases? Does your answer depend on exactly how we define "complex" cases?

b. Diversity Jurisdiction

Article III, § 2 of the Constitution also extends the judicial power of federal courts to controversies "between Citizens of different States . . . and between a State, or the Citizens thereof, and foreign States, Citizens or Subjects." Like the federal question grant, this constitutional grant is not self-operative; Congress must also enable lower federal courts to hear these "diversity" cases through a statutory grant. It has done so in 28 U.S.C. § 1332, which has two components. First, Congress authorizes jurisdiction when the controversy is between "citizens of different States," "citizens of a State and citizens or subjects of a foreign state," "citizens of different States and in which citizens or subjects of a foreign state are additional parties," and "a foreign state . . . as plaintiff and citizens of a State or of different States." Second, Congress limits jurisdiction only to cases "where the matter in controversy exceeds the sum or value of $75,000."

A critical difference between federal question and diversity jurisdiction is the source of law. In federal question cases, the plaintiff's *prima facie* case is grounded on federal law. In diversity cases, the prima facie case is non-federal; typically, it arises from an obligation created by state law. Therefore, cases which pose federal questions only by way of defense, as well as cases in which there are no federal elements, can be brought initially into federal court only by means of the federal courts' diversity jurisdiction.

Like federal question jurisdiction, the constitutional text and the statutory language of the diversity grant largely parallel each other. Once again, therefore, we must determine whether the language means the same thing in both contexts, how plaintiffs can use the rules of diversity jurisdiction to select the court they desire, how this use can create lawyer dysfunction or complication, and how these problems might be overcome. Since many of the controversies which create problems of lawyer dysfunction or complication are mass torts or consumer claims for which state law provides the rule of decision, the scope of diversity jurisdiction is a central question for complex civil litigation.

STATE FARM FIRE & CASUALTY CO. v. TASHIRE

386 U.S. 523 (1967)

■ MR. JUSTICE FORTAS delivered the opinion of the Court.

[The case arose out of an accident between a Greyhound bus and a pickup truck in California. Two of the passengers aboard the bus were killed; thirty-three other passengers, as well as the bus driver, the driver of the truck, and its lone passenger, were injured. One of the dead and 10 of the injured passengers were Canadians; the rest of the individuals were citizens of one of five American states. Four of the injured passengers filed suit in California state courts, seeking damages in excess of $1,000,000. Named as defendants were Greyhound Lines, Inc., a California corporation; Theron Nauta, the bus driver; Ellis Clark, who drove the truck; and Kenneth Glasgow, the passenger in the truck who was apparently its owner as well. Each individual defendant was a citizen of Oregon.

[At that point, State Farm Fire & Casualty Company, an Illinois corporation, brought an action in the nature of interpleader in the United States District Court for the District of Oregon. As we shall soon see, interpleader is a device under which a person who has possession of money or property claimed by two or more persons can join all interested persons in a single proceeding. In its complaint State Farm asserted that at the time of the collision it had in force an insurance policy with respect to Ellis Clark, driver of the truck, providing for bodily injury liability up to $20,000 per occurrence. Since the actions already filed in California and others which it anticipated would be filed far exceeded its maximum liability under the policy, State Farm paid into court the sum of $20,000 and asked the court to require all claimants to establish their claims against Clark and his insurer in the federal court proceeding.

[Joined as defendants in the interpleader action were Clark, Glasgow, Nauta, Greyhound, and each of the prospective claimants. Jurisdiction was based on 28 U.S.C. § 1335, the federal interpleader statute, which provides federal jurisdiction when there exists money, property, or a policy of insurance worth $500 or more and "[t]wo or more adverse claimants, of diverse citizenship as defined in section 1332 of this title, are claiming or may claim to be entitled to such money or property, or to any one or more of the benefits arising by virtue of any . . . policy." Jurisdiction was also based on 28 U.S.C. § 1332, because there was diversity between two or more of the claimants to the fund and between State Farm and all of the defendants.

[In interpleader practice, the district court is empowered to restrain the named defendants from filing or prosecuting any proceeding in any state or federal court affecting the property or obligation involved in the interpleader action. After the federal court in Oregon issued a stay, the California litigation halted. Several of the injured passengers then attempted to argue that interpleader was either impermissible or inappropriate in the present circumstances. The federal court in Oregon disagreed, and eventually expanded the stay to require that all suits against Clark, State Farm, Greyhound, and Nauta be prosecuted in the interpleader proceeding.

[On interlocutory appeal, the Court of Appeals reversed, holding that interpleader was impermissible under these circumstances. State Farm then obtained a writ of certiorari on the issue of the proper scope of statutory interpleader — an issue which we will explore at p. 413, *infra*.]

I.

Before considering the issues presented by the petition for certiorari, we find it necessary to dispose of a question neither raised by the parties nor passed upon by the courts below. Since the matter concerns our jurisdiction, we raise it on our own motion.... The interpleader statute, 28 U.S.C. § 1335, applies where there are "Two or more adverse claimants, of diverse citizenship...." This provision has been uniformly construed to require only "minimal diversity," that is, diversity of citizenship between two or more claimants, without regard to the circumstance that other rival claimants may be co-citizens. The language of the statute, the legislative purpose broadly to remedy the problems posed by multiple claimants to a single fund, and the consistent judicial interpretation tacitly accepted by Congress, persuade us that the statute requires no more. There remains, however, the question whether such a statutory construction is consistent with Article III of our Constitution, which extends the federal judicial power to "Controversies ... between Citizens of different States ... and between a State, or the Citizens thereof, and foreign States, Citizens or Subjects." In Strawbridge v. Curtiss, 3 Cranch 267 (1806), this Court held that the diversity of citizenship statute required "complete diversity": where co-citizens appeared on both sides of a dispute, jurisdiction was lost. But Chief Justice Marshall there purported to construe only "The words of the act of congress," not the Constitution itself.[6] And in a variety of contexts this Court and the lower courts have concluded that Article III poses no obstacle to the legislative extension of federal jurisdiction, founded on diversity, so long as any two adverse parties are not co-citizens.[7] Accordingly, we conclude that the present case is properly in the federal courts.

STRAWBRIDGE v. CURTISS

3 Cranch 267 (U.S. 1806)

This was an appeal from a decree of the circuit court, for the district of Massachusetts, which dismissed the plaintiffs' bill in chancery, for want of jurisdiction.

Some of the complainants were alleged to be citizens of the state of Massachusetts. The defendants were stated to be citizens of the same state, except Curtiss, who was averred to be a citizen of the state of Vermont....

■ MARSHALL, Ch. J. delivered the opinion of the court.

---

6. Subsequent decisions of this Court indicate that *Strawbridge* is not to be given an expansive reading....

7. See, *e.g.*, American Fire & Cas. Co. v. *Finn*, 341 U.S. 6, 10, n.3 (1951), ... construing the removal statute ...; Supreme Tribe of Ben-Hur v. *Cauble*, 255 U.S. 356, concerning class actions; Wichita R.R. & Light Co. v. Public Util. Comm., 260 U.S. 48 (1922), dealing with intervention by co-citizens. Full-dress arguments for the constitutionality of "minimal diversity" in situations like interpleader, which arguments need not be rehearsed here, are set out in ... ALI, Study of the Division of Jurisdiction Between State and Federal Courts 180-190 (Official Draft, Pt. 1, 1965).... We note that the American Law Institute's proposals to deal with the problem of multiparty, multijurisdiction litigation are predicated upon the permissibility of "minimal diversity" as a jurisdictional basis.

The court has considered this case, and is of opinion that the jurisdiction cannot be supported.

The words of the act of congress are, "where an alien is a party; or the suit is between a citizen of a state where the suit is brought, and a citizen of another state."

The court understands these expressions to mean that each distinct interest should be represented by persons, all of whom are entitled to sue, or may be sued, in the federal courts. That is, that where the interest is joint, each of the persons concerned in that interest must be competent to sue, or liable to be sued, in those courts.

But the court does not mean to give an opinion in the case where several parties represent several distinct interests, and some of those parties are, and others are not, competent to sue, or liable to be sued, in the courts of the United States.

Decree affirmed.

Notes and Questions

1. Would *Tashire* allow a plaintiff to bring one claim against a diverse defendant and join with it an entirely unrelated claim against another defendant? Or does it mean that minimal diversity is the constitutional floor only when the claims against the diverse and the non-diverse defendants are related to each other? If so, how close must that relationship be in order for a federal court to exercise jurisdiction over both claims?

2. Although the diversity statute has been amended many times since 1806, the Supreme Court has interpreted the subsequent versions in the same way that *Strawbridge* interpreted the original diversity statute: "complete" diversity between all of the plaintiffs and all of the defendants is required. See, *e.g.*, City of Indianapolis v. Chase National Bank of City of New York, 314 U.S. 63 (1941). Thus, with few exceptions, if any plaintiff has the same citizenship as any defendant, no jurisdiction exists under § 1332. Is that broad reading of the diversity statute supported by the holding in *Strawbridge*? Should the decision be limited to cases in which the interests of the several plaintiffs and defendants are "joint"?

Whatever the merits of that debate, it is clear after *Tashire*, that the Constitution requires only "minimal" diversity (*i.e.*, at least one plaintiff is of different citizenship than at least one defendant). Therefore, we have a jurisdictional situation entirely analogous to federal question jurisdiction: a broad constitutional grant of jurisdiction and a narrower statutory grant, despite the fact that the language of both are nearly identical. Is there any reason that the same language should receive such disparate treatment? Chief Justice Marshall was later said to have regretted his opinion in *Strawbridge*, thinking it wrongly decided. See Louisville, C. & C. R. Co. v. Letson, 43 U.S. (2 How.) 497, 555 (U.S. 1844).

3. One way to think about the answer to this question is to ask why we might want a broader or a narrower understanding of diversity jurisdiction. Remarkably, *Tashire* declined to provide any reasons for its constitutional

interpretation. It did, however, cite several sources that had attempted to justify minimal diversity as a constitutional matter. According to one of these sources:

> Even on a view of diversity jurisdiction as serving only to allow protection to the out-of-state citizen from a hostile local tribunal, surely Congress might at some time reasonably conclude that local tribunals could be so hostile as to discriminate against non-citizens even at the expense of hurting one of their own, and must therefore be able to extend a federal forum even where the interests are "joint." Moreover, . . . Congress must be able to act to assure that resort to an authorized federal forum not be impeded by the imposition of extra burdens, such as the necessity of double litigation with its inefficiency and expense. Certainly that would imply power to permit joinder of parties and claims at least to the degree required to achieve that objective . . . .
>
> More basically, however, . . . [t]here is substantial reason to believe that the function of the constitutional diversity provision was seen as relating to growth of the nation as a unit by helping create conditions which would facilitate persons transacting affairs beyond the boundaries of their own states. On this view, the objects sought included the giving of assurance to those who do business away from home that they would not inevitably have to rely, not only on impartiality, but on the adequacy, efficiency or, indeed, availability of state courts. . . .
>
> [T]he very notion of providing an efficient forum might well call for allowing joinder of parties in patterns inconsistent with the *Strawbridge* rule . . . . Further, to the extent that this fuller rationale of the constitutional authority for diversity jurisdiction justifies most strongly the providing of a federal forum where the state courts are entirely disabled from providing an effective or just remedy by reason of the multi-state nature of the case, it must also support the conferring of a jurisdiction based on less than complete diversity of citizenship.

American Law Institute, Study of the Division of Jurisdiction between State and Federal Courts, Proposed Final Draft No. 1, 183-86 (1965).

What are the arguments for interpreting § 1332 to require complete diversity? One is that state courts will be less prejudiced against out-of-state defendants as long as in-state defendants are also present. Whatever the merits of that argument when the liability of all defendants is joint, isn't there still a reason to believe that prejudice might exist when, more typically, liability is joint and several or several, and the state court must decide how much responsibility to allocate to out-of-state and in-state defendants? Another argument is that it reduces the number of cases within diversity jurisdiction, which frees up federal courts to deal with federal questions, lessens the number of sticky procedural and jurisdictional problems that diversity cases create, and fosters a more respectful federalism in which state courts gain more control over the shape and direction of state law. Isn't the logical endpoint of this argument that diversity jurisdiction should be abolished? Are there other arguments in favor of complete diversity as a constitutional matter?

4. Whatever the constitutional scope of diversity jurisdiction, many scholars and judges believe that diversity jurisdiction is unnecessary. They argue either that the rationales for diversity (bias, aid to the national economy, incompetent state courts) do not support the present statutory grant of diversity or that the rationales are themselves ill-founded. They point out that federal

courts are not expert in matters of state law, that diversity cases consume significant resources of the federal courts, and that diversity jurisdiction is a needless source of friction between state and federal courts. As a result, they have called either for further restriction on diversity jurisdiction or its outright abolition. See American Law Institute, Study of the Division of Jurisdiction between State and Federal Courts §§ 1301-07 (1969) ("ALI Study"); Federal Courts Study Committee 38-42 (1990) (urging congressional abolition of diversity jurisdiction in all but complex litigation); see generally Erwin Chemerinsky, Federal Jurisdiction § 5.3.2 (2d ed. 1994) (discussing arguments on both sides).

5. The point may be obvious, but it bears mention: the federal and state courts have concurrent jurisdiction over cases which fall within diversity jurisdiction. Thus, a plaintiff need not bring a case involving diverse defendants in federal court.

6. The complete diversity rule gives plaintiffs a powerful tool to locate a case in the forum of her choosing. When more than one defendant has contributed to her harm, and when some defendants are of diverse citizenship and some are not, the plaintiff can usually gain a federal forum by failing to sue the non-diverse parties. (An exception to this latter statement is that a plaintiff cannot fail to join a necessary party under Rule 19. See pp. 116-32, *supra*.) If having both the federal forum and the non-diverse parties is important, the plaintiff can try to plead federal question claims with respect to the non-diverse defendants, or else seek to invoke the court's "supplemental" jurisdiction. See pp. 348-60, *infra*.

On the other hand, if the plaintiff wants to remain in state court, she merely needs to join a non-diverse plaintiff or defendant. For instance, in Butler v. R.J. Reynolds Tobacco Co., 815 F. Supp. 982 (S.D. Miss. 1993), the plaintiff, an alleged victim of second-hand tobacco smoke, sued six cigarette manufacturers of diverse citizenship as well as four non-diverse retailers of the cigarettes. The manufacturers sought to remove the case to federal court, arguing that, under Mississippi law, the retailers were unlikely to be liable, so that the real controversy between plaintiff and manufacturers fell within the diversity grant. The court remanded the case to state court; since the possibility of recovery from the retailers under some state of the facts and law existed, complete diversity was not established.

Alternatively, if the plaintiff wants to remain in state court, she can sue only the diverse defendants, but bring the case in a court of a state in which at least one defendant resides. In that circumstance, the defendants cannot remove the case to federal court. 28 U.S.C. § 1441(b); see p. 385, *infra*.

7. A plaintiff obviously needs to know the state or states of which potential parties are citizens. For natural persons, a person is a "citizen of a State" when the person is an American citizen and has a domicile (*i.e.*, a home to which the person intends to return) in that State; a person is a "citizen of a foreign state" when a foreign country affords her that status. See Brown v. Keene, 33 U.S. (8 Pet.) 112 (U.S. 1834). The citizenship of corporations is defined by statute to their state of incorporation and their principal place of business so corporations often enjoy dual citizenship. 28 U.S.C. §1332(c). A partnership is a citizen of every state of its members whether they be general or limited partners. Carden v. Arkoma Associates, 494 U.S. 185 (1990). Similarly, an unincorporated association, such as a labor union, is a citizen of every state of its members. Steelworkers v. R.H. Bouligny, Inc., 382 U.S. 145 (1965). Viewed in light of the *Strawbridge* rule of complete diversity, do these definitions of citizenship

adequately protect out-of-state litigants from local bias? Do they restrict the scope of diversity jurisdiction excessively? To what extent are these rules dictated by Article III of the Constitution?

8. Since the complete diversity rule is a judicial gloss rather than an explicit statutory command, could we dispense with it in cases where the plaintiff's jurisdictional gerrymandering might lead to lawyer dysfunction or inefficiency? Such a result would certainly facilitate the joinder of related cases. For instance, if there were hundreds of second-hand smoking cases in the country, why should we allow the plaintiff in *Butler* to choose a state forum that will lead to duplicative litigation of similar issues? Similarly, bending the complete diversity rule in such cases would certainly make it easier to consolidate all the cases in a single (federal) forum and would reduce the burden on each state court.

Some support for a minimal diversity rule in cases of dysfunction or inefficiency already exists. First, Congress has abrogated the complete diversity rule in the instance of interpleader. Moreover, as *Tashire* noted, the Supreme Court has not always insisted on the complete diversity rule. In Supreme Tribe of Ben-Hur v. Cauble, 255 U.S. 356 (1921), the Supreme Court held that in a class action the citizenship of the class for diversity purposes is determined by the citizenship of the class representatives only; the citizenship of unnamed class members is ignored. Similarly, in Wichita R. & Light Co. v. Public Utilities Commission of Kansas, 260 U.S. 48 (1922), the Court allowed a person with an immediate commercial interest in the outcome to intervene in the case, even though there would have been a lack of complete diversity if that person had initially been joined as a plaintiff. See 7C Charles A. Wright et al., Federal Practice and Procedure § 1917 (1986); pp. 352-53, 360, *infra* (discussing effect of § 1367 on jurisdiction over non-diverse intervenor). Finally, the Court has repeatedly held that the post-filing joinder of a non-diverse party that is not indispensable under F.R.Civ.P. 19 does not defeat diversity jurisdiction; jurisdiction attaches at the outset of the case, and cannot be eliminated by subsequent events. See, *e.g.*, Freeport-McMoran Inc. v. K N Energy Inc., 498 U.S. 426 (1991).

Conversely, the Court has declined to authorize federal jurisdiction over state law cases such as most domestic relations and probate matters, even when complete diversity is present. See Ankenbrandt v. Richards, 504 U.S. 689 (1992); 13B Charles A. Wright et al., Federal Practice and Procedure §§ 3609-10 (1984).

Does the treatment of interpleader, class actions, intervention, and later-filed claims suggest a broader principle: that the complete diversity rule can be judicially suspended in instances of lawyer dysfunction? Would many of the arguments of the ALI for the existence of diversity jurisdiction — for instance, the need to assure an effective and adequate response to multi-state litigation and respect for the efficient use of state court resources — also argue for the suspension of the complete diversity rule in complex cases? Does the treatment of domestic relations and probate matters suggest that there should at least be a significant federal interest before the rule is suspended?

If you accept the premise that the complete diversity rule needs to be changed in instances of joinder complexity, should it also be eliminated in all instances of inefficient multiforum, multiparty litigation? If not, what might be the distinguishing feature between cases of joinder complexity and other cases of multiforum, multiparty litigation which permit the two circumstances to be treated differently?

9. On the other hand, would partial abrogation of the complete diversity rule turn the state courts into minor league franchises dealing with only the simplest of cases? Would federal judges spending time handling multi-party state law matters have adequate time to spend on federal question cases, on which they presumably have the greatest expertise? Would the statutory authority to join many parties from many states create insurmountable problems of interpreting joinder provisions, choosing the applicable law, and otherwise managing the pretrial, trial, and remedial phases of the case? And, once again, how do we define those cases which are so "complex" that the complete diversity rule ought not to apply to them?

10. There have been numerous proposals to adopt a minimal diversity rule for certain cases that are arguably complex. One of the earliest, and still one of the broadest, proposals was that of the ALI Study, which recommended that "[t]he district courts shall have original jurisdiction of any civil action in which the several defendants who are necessary for a just adjudication of the plaintiff's claim are not all amenable to process of any one territorial jurisdiction, and one of any two adverse parties is a citizen of a State and the other is a citizen or subject of another territorial jurisdiction." A defendant was "necessary for a just adjudication of the plaintiff's claim" when "complete relief cannot be accorded the plaintiff in his absence, or if it appears that, under federal law or relevant State law, an action on the claim would have to be dismissed if he could not be joined as a party." ALI Study, § 2371.

Recent efforts to create a federal multi-state, multi-party jurisdiction have tended to be based on the number of parties in the case. H.R. 3152, 100th Cong., 1st Sess. (1987), provided for federal diversity jurisdiction whenever 25 or more persons were injured in the amount of $50,000, at least 5 of that number suffered $10,000 in damage, minimal diversity existed among the plaintiffs and defendants, and a substantial portion of the events occurred in two or more states. H.R. 3406, 101st Cong., 1st Sess. (1989), was similar, but it limited jurisdiction to injuries which arose from "a single event or occurrence." A more recent version of this bill is H.R. 1252, 105th Cong., 1st Sess. (1997), which limits jurisdiction to situations in which 25 persons were injured in "a single accident . . . at a discrete location" and suffered more than $50,000 in damages per person; it permits jurisdiction when minimal diversity exists and either the defendant resides in a state different from the state or location in which "a substantial part of the accident took place," "any two defendants reside in different States," or "substantial parts of the accident took place in different States." This bill passed the House on April 23, 1998, and is pending in the Senate. See also Thomas D. Rowe, Jr. & Kenneth D. Sibley, *Beyond Diversity: Federal Multiparty, Multiforum Jurisdiction*, 135 U. Pa. L. Rev. 7 (1986).

11. From the inception of the diversity jurisdiction in 1789, Congress has limited it to claims which raise a certain amount in controversy. This requirement often acts as a significant barrier to aggregating factually related state law claims in the federal courts. We turn to this issue next.

ZAHN v. INTERNATIONAL PAPER CO.

414 U.S. 291 (1973)

■ MR. JUSTICE WHITE delivered the opinion of the Court.

Petitioners, asserting that they were owners of property fronting on Lake Champlain in Orwell, Vermont, brought this action in the District Court on behalf of a class consisting of themselves and 200 lakefront property owners and lessees. They sought damages from International Paper Co., a New York corporation, for allegedly having permitted discharges from its pulp and paper-making plant, located in New York, to flow into Ticonderoga Creek and to be carried by that stream into Lake Champlain, thereby polluting the waters of the lake and damaging the value and utility of the surrounding properties. The suit was brought as a diversity action, jurisdiction assertedly resting on 28 U.S.C. § 1332 (a)(1). The claim of each of the named plaintiffs was found to satisfy the $10,000 jurisdictional amount, but the District Court was convinced "to a legal certainty" that not every individual owner in the class had suffered pollution damages in excess of $10,000. Reading Snyder v. Harris, 394 U.S. 332 (1969), as precluding maintenance of the action by any member of the class whose separate and distinct claim did not individually satisfy the jurisdictional amount and concluding that it would not be feasible to define a class of property owners each of whom had more than a $10,000 claim, the District Court then refused to permit the suit to proceed as a class action. 53 F.R.D. 430 (Vt. 1971). A divided Court of Appeals affirmed, . . . principally on the authority of *Snyder v. Harris, supra.* We granted the petition for writ of certiorari . . . .

The Court of Appeals correctly held that this case is governed by the rationale of this Court's prior cases construing the statutes defining the jurisdiction of the District Court. We therefore affirm its judgment.

From the outset, Congress has provided that suits between citizens of different States are maintainable in the district courts only if the "matter in controversy" exceeds the statutory minimum, now set at $10,000. 28 U.S.C. §1332 (a).[*] The same jurisdictional-amount requirement has applied when the general federal-question jurisdiction of the district courts, 28 U.S.C. §1331 (a), is sought to be invoked.[**] A classic statement of the dichotomy that developed in construing and applying these sections is found in Troy Bank v. G. A. Whitehead & Co., 222 U.S. 39, 40-41 (1911):

> "When two or more plaintiffs, having separate and distinct demands, unite for convenience and economy in a single suit, it is essential that the demand of each be of the requisite jurisdictional amount; but when several plaintiffs unite to enforce a single title or right, in which they have a common and undivided interest, it is enough if their interests collectively equal the jurisdictional amount."

This distinction and rule that multiple plaintiffs with separate and distinct claims must each satisfy the jurisdictional-amount requirement for suit in the federal courts were firmly rooted in prior cases dating from 1832, and have continued to be the accepted construction of the controlling statutes, now §§ 1331 and 1332. The rule has been applied to forbid aggregation of claims where none of the claimants satisfies the jurisdictional

---

[*] In 1988 Congress increased the matter in controversy in diversity cases to $50,000, and in 1996 to $75,000 — ED.

[**] In 1980 Congress eliminated the matter-in-controversy requirement for § 1331 — ED.

amount, as was the case in Scott v. Frazier, 253 U.S. 243, 244 (1920), for example, where the Court stated the rule to be that "the amount in controversy must equal the jurisdictional sum as to each complainant." It also requires dismissal of those litigants whose claims do not satisfy the jurisdictional amount, even though other litigants assert claims sufficient to invoke the jurisdiction of the federal court. Clark v. Paul Gray, Inc., 306 U.S. 583 (1939) . . . .

The same rules were applied to class actions contemplated by Fed. Rule Civ. Proc. 23. The spurious class action authorized by Rule 23 (a)(3), as it stood prior to amendment in 1966, was viewed by Judge Frank, writing for himself and Judges Learned and Augustus Hand, as, "in effect, but a congeries of separate suits so that each claimant must, as to his own claim, meet the jurisdictional requirements." Steele v. Guaranty Trust Co. of N. Y., 164 F.2d 387, 388 (CA2 1947). . . . In consequence, district courts were to entertain the claims of only those class action plaintiffs whose individual cases satisfied the jurisdictional amount requirement.

The meaning of the "matter in controversy" language of § 1332 as it applied to class actions under Rule 23 reached this Court in *Snyder v. Harris, supra*, the occasion being a division of opinion in the courts of appeals as to whether the 1966 amendments to Rule 23 had changed the jurisdictional-amount requirement of § 1332 as applied to class actions involving separate and distinct claims. None of the named plaintiffs and none of the unnamed members of the class before the Court alleged claims in excess of the requisite amount. It was nevertheless urged that in class action situations, particularly in light of the 1966 amendments to the rule, aggregation of separate and distinct claims should be permitted. The Court was of a contrary view, holding that class actions involving plaintiffs with separate and distinct claims were subject to the usual rule that a federal district court can assume jurisdiction over only those plaintiffs presenting claims exceeding the $10,000 minimum specified in § 1332. Aggregation of claims was impermissible, and the federal court was without jurisdiction where none of the plaintiffs presented a claim of the requisite size. The Court unmistakably rejected the notion that the 1966 amendments to Rule 23 were intended to effect, or effected, any change in the meaning and application of the jurisdictional-amount requirement insofar as class actions are concerned. . . .

None of the plaintiffs in *Snyder v. Harris* alleged a claim exceeding $10,000, but there is no doubt that the rationale of that case controls this one. As previously indicated, *Snyder* invoked the well-established rule that each of several plaintiffs asserting separate and distinct claims must satisfy the jurisdictional-amount requirement if his claim is to survive a motion to dismiss. This rule plainly mandates not only that there may be no aggregation and that the entire case must be dismissed where none of the plaintiffs claims more than $10,000 but also requires that any plaintiff without the jurisdictional amount must be dismissed from the case, even though others allege jurisdictionally sufficient claims. . . .

We conclude, as we must, that the Court of Appeals in the case before us accurately read and applied *Snyder v. Harris*: Each plaintiff in a Rule 23 (b)(3) class action must satisfy the jurisdictional amount, and any plaintiff who does not must be dismissed from the case — "one plaintiff may not ride in on another's coattails." . . .

Affirmed.

■ MR. JUSTICE BRENNAN, with whom MR. JUSTICE DOUGLAS and MR. JUSTICE MARSHALL join, dissenting. The Court holds that, in a diversity suit, a class action under Fed. Rule Civ. Proc. 23(b)(3) is maintainable only when every member of the class, whether an appearing party or not, meets the $10,000 jurisdictional-amount requirement of 28 U.S.C. §1332 (a). It finds this ruling compelled by the "rationale of this Court's prior cases construing the statutes defining the jurisdiction of the District Court." I disagree and respectfully dissent.

The jurisdictional-amount provision of §1332 (a) tersely states that "the matter in controversy [must exceed] the sum or value of $10,000 . . . ." Those words, substantially unchanged since the passage of the Judiciary Act of 1789, apply to "civil actions," and say nothing about the requirements applicable to individual claimants and individual claims. Although Congress has several times altered the amount required, generally upward, it has left the task of defining those requirements to the judiciary. The result has been a relatively complex and sensitive set of rules designed to implement Congress' broad directive in a way that is responsive to the demands of fairness and efficiency in adjudication.

One "bright line" has emerged to control all § 1332 actions: there must be at least one plaintiff, or joint interest, seeking more than the statutory amount. Snyder v. Harris, 394 U.S. 332 (1969); Troy Bank v. G. A. Whitehead & Co., 222 U.S. 39 (1911). The "longstanding" and "well established" rule on aggregation of claims that the Court invokes was developed to determine whether a group of claims was sufficiently interrelated to constitute such a "joint" claim or "common and undivided interest."

Once jurisdiction has attached to the "action," however, the "aggregation" rule has been but one of several ways to establish jurisdiction over additional claims and parties. In this case, the claims of the named plaintiffs provided the District Court with jurisdiction over the diversity action. And petitioners make no argument inconsistent with the Court's holding that the theory of "joint" claims or interests will not support jurisdiction over the nonappearing members of their class. Their contention is rather that a second theory, ancillary jurisdiction, supports a determination that those claims may be entertained.

Ancillary jurisdiction to adjudicate claims that cannot be fitted within the aggregation rules has long been recognized by this Court, see Freeman v. Howe, 24 How. 450 (1861) . . .; Wichita R. & Light Co. v. Public Utilities Comm'n, 260 U.S. 48 (1922). But, as one commentator has pointed out, the rules developed to control the exercise of that jurisdiction cannot be explained by "any single rationalizing principle." C. Wright, Federal Courts § 9, p. 21 (2d ed. 1970). They are instead accommodations that take into account the impact of the adjudication on parties and third persons, the susceptibility of the dispute or disputes in the case to resolution in a single adjudication, and the structure of the litigation as governed by the Federal Rules of Civil Procedure.

After consideration of these factors, the Court has sustained the exercise of ancillary jurisdiction over compulsory counterclaims under Rule 13 (a) .... It has also done so where a party's intervention was held to be a matter of right, as is now provided by Rule 24 (a) .... Following this lead, the courts of appeals have sustained ancillary jurisdiction over cross-claims permitted by Rule 13 (g) ... ; over impleaded defendants under Rule 14 ...; and over defendants interpleaded under Rule 22 ....

Class actions under Rule 23 (b)(3) are equally appropriate for such treatment. There are ample assurances, in the provisions of the Rule that "the questions of law or fact common to the members of the class [must] predominate over any questions affecting only individual members," to guarantee that ancillary jurisdiction will not become a facade hiding attempts to secure federal adjudication of nondiverse parties' disputes over unrelated claims. And the practical reasons for permitting adjudication of the claims of the entire class are certainly as strong as those supporting ancillary jurisdiction over compulsory counterclaims and parties that are entitled to intervene as of right. Class actions were born of necessity. The alternatives were joinder of the entire class, or redundant litigation of the common issues. The cost to the litigants and the drain on the resources of the judiciary resulting from either alternative would have been intolerable. And this case presents precisely those difficulties: approximately 240 claimants are involved, and the issues will doubtless call for extensive use of expert testimony on difficult scientific issues.

It is, of course, true that an exercise of ancillary jurisdiction in such cases would result in some increase in the federal courts' workload, for unless the class action is permitted many of the claimants will be unable to obtain any federal determination of their rights. But that objection is applicable to every other exercise of ancillary jurisdiction. It should be a sufficient answer that denial of ancillary jurisdiction will impose a much larger burden on the state and federal judiciary as a whole, and will substantially impair the ability of the prospective class members to assert their claims.

If the State provides a class action device comparable to Rule 23 (b)(3), some of this inefficiency and unfairness may be avoided, but certainly not all. The named plaintiffs, and any other members of their class who can meet the jurisdictional-amount requirement, may choose to litigate those claims in the district courts, as these plaintiffs have shown to be their preference. Moreover, they will probably now be required separately to litigate the common issues in their cases, thus possibly enlarging the federal judiciary's burden, and ironically reversing the Court's apparent purpose.

Moreover, if the State does not provide a Rule 23 (b)(3) device, litigation of the claims of class members who either lack the jurisdictional amount or simply prefer to litigate their claims in the state courts — as they would be free to do under any construction of the jurisdictional requirement — will produce a multitude of suits. And the chief influence mitigating that flood — the fact that many of these landowners' claims are likely to be worthless because the cost of asserting them on a case-by-case basis will exceed their potential value — will do no judicial system credit.

Not only does the practical desirability of sustaining ancillary jurisdiction bring Rule 23 (b)(3) class actions within the logic of our decisions, but the Court has long since recognized that fact, and has sustained ancillary jurisdiction over the nonappearing members in a class action who do not meet the requirements of traditional rule of complete diversity laid down in Strawbridge v. Curtiss, 3 Cranch 267 (1806). In Supreme Tribe of Ben Hur v. Cauble, 255 U.S. 356 (1921), the Court not only held that only the original named plaintiffs and defendants had to satisfy the diversity requirements, but it also stated that intervention by nondiverse members of the class would not destroy the District Court's jurisdiction. . . . Particularly in view of the constitutional background on which the statutory diversity requirements are written, . . . it is difficult to understand why the practical approach the Court took in *Supreme Tribe of Ben-Hur* must be abandoned where the purely statutory "matter in controversy" requirement is concerned. . . .

It would be far more consistent . . . for the Court to rule, as it did in *Supreme Tribe of Ben-Hur*, that only the original named plaintiffs must meet the jurisdictional requirements, and that nonappearing class members and intervenors need not. Such a ruling, while going a step farther than petitioners seek, would be reasonable and pragmatically justified.

Notes and Questions

1. What is the purpose of the "amount in controversy" requirement in diversity cases? Is it intended to screen out smaller, less important cases from the federal system, thus preserving scarce federal judicial resources for larger, more important cases? In which category do cases like *Snyder* and *Zahn* fall? In which case is the federal interest greater: a car accident with $75,001 in alleged injuries, or a claim of widespread pollution?

2. Can *Zahn* be reconciled with *Ben-Hur*? Would they be reconcilable if each was decided the opposite way?

3. *Snyder* and *Zahn* are consistent with numerous earlier decisions in which the Court refused to permit the voluntary aggregation of damage claims by separate plaintiffs whose individual claims were less than the amount in controversy but whose combined claims exceeded that amount. See, *e.g.*, Pinel v. Pinel, 240 U.S. 594 (1916). Is there any reason to have a different aggregation rule in class actions than in traditional multi-party joinder cases? Cf. In re Joint Eastern and Southern Districts Asbestos Litigation, 982 F.2d 721 (2d Cir. 1992) (recognizing diversity jurisdiction over claims against bankruptcy trust fund which limited many claimants to $30,000, when the good faith full value of their claims, but for the bankruptcy limitation, exceeded $50,000), modified on other grounds, 993 F.2d 7 (2d Cir. 1993); Carlough v. Amchem Products, Inc., 834 F. Supp. 1437 (E.D. Pa. 1993) (recognizing diversity jurisdiction over claims in class action brought to settle the claims of most class members for less than $50,000, when value of claims, had they been litigated, exceeded $50,000).

4. On the other hand, the "amount in controversy" rule has been interpreted to permit a plaintiff to join together unrelated claims, each of which independently was less than the amount in controversy but which together exceeded the amount in controversy; thus, a plaintiff who coincidentally had a $30,000 tort claim and a separate $30,000 contract claim can bring both in federal court against a diverse defendant. See, *e.g.*, Edwards v. Bates County, 163 U.S. 269 (1896). Does it make sense that transactionally unrelated claims, which will likely be bifurcated for separate trial, fit within the federal diversity jurisdiction, while transactionally related claims, parts of which should logically be tried together, do not?

5. When money is at issue, the amount in controversy is measured by the stakes to each plaintiff. The usual rule is that the federal courts have jurisdiction over diversity claims alleged to involve more than $75,000 in controversy unless it appears "to a legal certainty" that the plaintiff will be unable to recover that amount. See Saint Paul Mercury Indemnity Co. v. Red Cab Co., 303 U.S. 283, 288 (1938). In cases not involving a sum certain for damages, this rule gives the plaintiff some latitude to plead for more or less than $75,000 in damages, depending upon the court system in which the plaintiff wishes to sue. A plaintiff who desires a state forum but has a claim against only diverse defendants can gain that forum by forsaking damages in excess of $75,000. See *St. Paul Mercury*, 303 U.S. at 294. Do plaintiffs need yet another tool to obtain the forum of their choosing?

6. In mass torts, several federal courts have construed *Saint Paul Mercury*'s "legal certainty" rule with some generosity, and have permitted a federal class action to be maintained when the class contains members whose claims would be quite unlikely to approach the amount in controversy threshold. See *Carlough*, 834 F. Supp. at 1458-59 (citing cases). Can persons with jurisdictionally insufficient claims nonetheless intervene in the class action to assert their own claims? Compare In re A.H. Robins, Inc., 880 F.2d 709 (1989) (suggesting that intervention is possible), cert. denied, 493 U.S. 959 (1990) with 28 U.S.C. § 1367(b), discussed at pp. 352-53, 360, *infra* (requiring that non-diverse intervenors meet all § 1332 requirements). Suppose that a plaintiff nonetheless sloppily structures a class action so that some claimants who do not meet the jurisdictional threshold are class members. Should the entire class action be dismissed, or should only those class members whose claims are insufficient be dismissed? See In re School Asbestos Litigation, 921 F.2d 1310 (3d Cir. 1990), cert. denied, 499 U.S. 976 (1991) (permitting district court to retain jurisdiction over proper claims).

7. *School Asbestos* also raises an interesting question about the timing of a court's determination about whether it has jurisdiction. As a general rule, jurisdictional questions are resolved at the outset of the case. Can a court nonetheless defer the inquiry into jurisdiction, which may require a fact-intensive investigation of each class member's claim, until later in the litigation? *School Asbestos* permitted the court to defer the jurisdictional inquiry until trial. 921 F.2d at 1315; but see Carlough v. Amchem Products, Inc., 10 F.3d 189, 201 (3d Cir. 1993) (requiring court to conduct preliminary inquiry into existence of jurisdiction early in case); Steel Co. v. Citizens for a Better Environment, — U.S. —, 118 S.Ct. 1003 (1998) (requiring court to decide jurisdictional issue of standing before deciding issues on the merits).

8. *Zahn* seemingly permits aggregation when the class plaintiffs have a "joint claim" or a "common and undivided interest." See Troy Bank v. G.A.

Whitehead & Co., 222 U.S. 39, 40-41 (1911) (allowing aggregation of claims "which neither [plaintiff] can enforce in the absence of the other"). In Allen v. R & H Oil and Gas Co., 63 F.3d 1326 (5th Cir. 1995), the Fifth Circuit held that the punitive damage claims of individual class members may be aggregated to determine whether the amount in controversy requirement is met. The court's reasoning focused on Mississippi law, under which each plaintiff was entitled to the full amount to punitive damages. Accord, Tapscott v. MS Dealer Service Corp., 77 F.3d 1353 (11th Cir. 1996) (interpreting Alabama law); but see Gilman v. BHC Securities, Inc., 104 F.3d 1418 (2d Cir. 1197) (declining to follow *Allen* and *Tapscott*). Is there also a "common and undivided interest" in the award of attorneys' fees? See Howard v. Globe Life Insurance Co., 973 F. Supp. 1412 (N.D. Fla. 1996).

Would there also exist a "common and undivided interest" if the reasonable value of the class members' claims exceeded the assets of the defendant, or if all the claims were otherwise to be paid from a single, insufficient fund? See *Tapscott*, 77 F.3d at 1359 (defining "common and undivided interest" to be "a single collective right in which . . . the failure of one plaintiff's claim will increase the share of successful plaintiffs"); Holt v. Lockheed Support Systems, Inc., 835 F. Supp. 325, 328 (W.D. La. 1993) (allowing aggregation only when "presence of each and every plaintiff is necessary and indispensable for the recovery of their common right," not when each claimant merely seeks share of common fund). Note that the set of claims involving insufficient assets or an insufficient common fund corresponds to one of the three forms of lawyer dysfunction.

9. When a plaintiff requests an injunction, how is the value of the matter in controversy to be determined? There are numerous possible rules: the harm to each plaintiff if the injunction is not granted, the cost to the defendant of complying with the injunction, the value of the injunction to whichever party desires the federal forum (the plaintiff's harm for original jurisdiction and the defendant's cost for removal jurisdiction), or the greater of plaintiff's harm or defendant's cost. The Supreme Court has never spoken definitively on the issue. See Hunt v. Washington State Apple Advertising Commission, 432 U.S. 333, 347-48 (1977) ("the amount in controversy is measured by the value of the object of the litigation"). Although there are cases to support each rule, it appears that the final rule — the value of the injunction to either party — is presently gaining ground. See Erwin Chemerinsky, Federal Jurisdiction § 5.3.4 (2d ed. 1994); 14A Charles A. Wright et al., Federal Practice & Procedure § 3703 (1985). What happens when a plaintiff requests both an injunction (worth more than $75,000 to the defendant but less than $75,000 to each plaintiff) and damages of less than $75,000 for each plaintiff? See National Organization for Women v. Mutual of Omaha Insurance Co., 612 F. Supp. 100 (D.D.C. 1985).

Note that, when the plaintiff seeks a federal forum, the first and third rules create *Zahn*-like aggregation problems. For instance, if the value to each class member of an injunction is $80, and there are 1,000 persons affected, *Zahn* would suggest that the value of the cases could not be aggregated to establish federal jurisdiction. On the other hand, the second and fourth rules (as well as the third rule if defendant seeks to remove the case from state court) permit federal jurisdiction, because the value of the injunction to the defendant is $80,000.

In light of *Zahn*, can the second, third, or fourth rule be justified? One difference between an injunctive remedy and a monetary one is that an injunctive remedy forces a defendant to act in a particular way toward all plaintiffs; a monetary remedy does not. Recall that lawyer dysfunction can arise from situations in which injunctive remedies disenfranchise nonparties or else are subject to being undone in later litigation by nonparties. See p. 88, *supra*. To what extent do the second, third, and fourth "matter in controversy" rules suggest that *Zahn* can be ignored in these instances of lawyer dysfunction? To what extent do the rules suggest that *Zahn* can also be ignored in the final instance of lawyer dysfunction — insufficient assets or funds to make all claimants whole?

10. More generally, when lawyer dysfunction exists, is it possible to distinguish *Zahn* (and perhaps *Snyder* as well) by arguing that their rules are inoperative when a single, class-wide resolution is absolutely critical to overcome lawyer dysfunction and to preserve rational adjudication? If so, what rule would we substitute in place of the *Snyder-Zahn* aggregation rules? If the Vermont state courts also had a class action rule in which all of the plaintiffs' claims could have been resolved, would it be "absolutely critical" to bend *Zahn* in order to create jurisdiction in a federal forum?

Can we extend the argument to render the *Snyder-Zahn* rules inoperative in all situations that carry a significant risk of inefficient multiforum, multiparty litigation? If not, what might justify the disparate treatment of cases involving lawyer dysfunction?

c. Supplemental Jurisdiction

The problems associated with choosing between a state and federal forum dramatically increased after the adoption of the Federal Rules of Civil Procedure in 1938. Before that time, in states which adhered to the system of common law pleading, a claimant was allowed to bring an action on only one writ (typically, one legal theory) at a time; and equitable claims were usually asserted in a different suit than common law causes of action. Thus, in many state and federal courts prior to 1938, complaints contained only one or two legal theories, and the court(s) with jurisdiction to decide the case were usually clear.

The Federal Rules, however, adopted a "transactional" approach, in which all claims associated with a particular transaction could be joined and resolved together. First, F.R.Civ.P. 2 abolished the division between legal and equitable claims. Next, the Federal Rules allowed the plaintiff to assert both legal and equitable claims in one suit, and to add in as many (related or unrelated) claims as a plaintiff had against the defendant. See F.R.Civ.P. 18(a) (permitting a claimant to "join, either as independent or alternate claims, as many claims legal, equitable, or maritime, as the party has against an opposing party"). Third, as we have seen, Rule 20 gave the plaintiff more latitude in joining plaintiffs and defendants than the common law allowed. See pp. 93-115, *supra*.

Fourth, the Federal Rules borrowed several equity rules that gave the courts the procedural ability to handle certain claims that surrounded the plaintiff's original claim. Rule 13 permits the defendant to assert counterclaims and cross-claims she has against the plaintiff in the same lawsuit. Rule 13 discusses two types of counterclaims: compulsory and permissive. The compulsory counterclaim rule, F.R.Civ.P. 13(a), generally requires the defendant to assert any claim which the defendant has against the plaintiff "if it arises out of the transaction or occurrence that is the subject matter of the opposing party's claim." The term "transaction or occurrence" is generally thought to require a logical relationship between the original claim and the counterclaim. See, *e.g.*, Revere Copper & Brass, Inc. v. Aetna Casualty & Surety Co., 426 F.2d 709 (5th Cir. 1970). The penalty for failing to assert a compulsory counterclaim is the bar of that claim. See Charles A. Wright, Estoppel by Rule: The Compulsory Counterclaim under Modern Pleading, 38 Minn. L. Rev. 423 (1954). The permissive counterclaim rule, F.R.Civ.P. 13(b), permits a defendant to assert any claim she has against the plaintiff "not arising out of the transaction or occurrence," although the failure to do so does not prejudice any future lawsuit brought on the claim. Rule 13(g) also authorizes parties to assert cross-claims, which are claims "arising out of the transaction or occurrence that is the subject matter either of the original action or of a counterclaim therein or related to any property that is the subject matter of the original action," against co-parties. The failure to assert a cross-claim does not bar a future suit on the matter. 6 Charles A. Wright et al., Federal Practice & Procedure § 1431 (1990). Rule 14 permits defendants to join as a third-party defendant "any person not a party to the action who is or may be liable to the third party plaintiff for all or part of the plaintiff's claim against the third-party plaintiff," F.R.Civ.P. 14; once again, the failure to do so is no bar to a subsequent suit. Wright, *supra*, § 1442. Finally, as we have seen, Rule 24 allows certain persons to intervene either of right or permissively into a case in order to assert their own claims. See pp. 136-55, *supra*.

Although the Federal Rules of Civil Procedure cannot expand federal jurisdiction, see 28 U.S.C. § 2072 and F.R.Civ.P. 82, the predictable effect of transactionally-oriented joinder rules was to put pressure on the federal courts to create the jurisdiction to hear all of the claims that it was now procedurally possible to join together. See Carole E. Goldberg, *The Influence of Procedural Rules on Federal Jurisdiction*, 28 Stan. L. Rev. 395 (1976). When an independent basis of federal jurisdiction existed with respect to a transactionally related claim, of course, there were no particular problems of jurisdiction. In many cases, however, there would be no independent basis of jurisdiction over some of these claims; for instance, the amount in controversy for a defendant's state-law counterclaim might be only $2,000.

In general, three separate, yet related types of jurisdictional issues were posed by this procedural power to join claims and parties not lying initially within federal jurisdiction. The first was the federal courts' ability to hear jurisdictionally insufficient claims which a plaintiff joined under Rule 18 with jurisdictionally sufficient claims. The second was the federal courts' ability to hear jurisdictionally insufficient claims asserted by way of counterclaim, cross-claim, third party claim, or intervention. The third was the federal courts' ability to hear claims asserted by or against parties who were eligible to be joined under the Federal Rules but over whom the federal courts had no independent jurisdiction.

Prior to 1990, these three issues were handled through three separate doctrines: "pendent jurisdiction," "ancillary jurisdiction," and "pendent party jurisdiction." In 1990, Congress passed the Judicial Improvements Act of 1990, which included a new provision, 28 U.S.C. § 1367. This provision was designed to unify all three branches of jurisdiction under the single rubric of "supplemental jurisdiction." In order to understand § 1367 and its limits in the context of complex or complicated litigation, we begin with short histories of pendent, ancillary, and pendent party jurisdiction.

1. Pendent Jurisdiction. To deal with the Rule 18 situation of a plaintiff's joinder of additional, jurisdictionally insufficient claims against the defendant, the federal courts borrowed from a line of older cases, especially Hurn v. Oursler, 289 U.S. 238 (1933), to develop the doctrine of pendent jurisdiction. Under pendent jurisdiction, once a federal court has the jurisdiction to dispose of one claim by a plaintiff, it also has jurisdiction to dispose of the plaintiff's factually related claims over which the court has no independent basis of jurisdiction. Although the scope of this pendent jurisdiction was initially given a stingy interpretation by the federal courts, the Supreme Court finally adopted a more generous understanding of pendent jurisdiction in United Mine Workers of America v. Gibbs, 383 U.S. 715 (1966). In *Gibbs* a plaintiff brought both a federal question and a state law claim against a non-diverse defendant. After trial, the federal claim was dismissed by the court, but a verdict on the state law claim was upheld. The defendant claimed that the federal court had no jurisdiction to entertain the state law claim. The Supreme Court held that jurisdiction was present:

> Pendent jurisdiction, in the sense of judicial *power*, exists whenever there is a claim "arising under [the] Constitution, the Laws of the United States, and Treaties made, or which shall be made, under their Authority . . .," U.S. Const., Art. III, § 2, and the relationship between that claim and the state claim permits the conclusion that the entire action before the court comprises but one constitutional "case." The federal claim must have substance sufficient to confer subject matter jurisdiction on the court. . . . The state and federal claims must derive from a common nucleus of operative fact. But if, considered without regard for their federal or state character, a plaintiff's claims are such that he would ordinarily be expected to try them in all in one judicial proceeding, then, assuming the substantiality of the federal issues, there is *power* in federal courts to hear the whole.
>
> That power need not be exercised in every case in which it is found to exist. It has consistently been recognized that pendent jurisdiction is a doctrine of discretion, not of plaintiff's right. Its justifications lie in considerations of judicial economy, convenience, and fairness to litigants; if these are not present a federal court should hesitate to exercise jurisdiction over state claims . . . . Needless decisions of state law should be avoided both as a matter of comity and to promote justice between the parties, by procuring them a surer-footed reading of applicable law. Certainly, if the federal claims are dismissed before trial, even though not insubstantial in a jurisdictional sense, the state claims should be dismissed as well. Similarly, if it appears that the state issues substantially predominate, whether in terms of proof, of the

scope of the issues raised, or of the comprehensiveness of the remedy sought, the state claims may be dismissed without prejudice and left for resolution to state tribunals. There may, on the other hand, be situations in which the state claim is so closely tied to questions of federal policy that the argument for exercise of pendent jurisdiction is particularly strong. . . . Finally, there may be reasons independent of jurisdictional considerations, such as the likelihood of jury confusion in treating divergent legal theories of relief, that would justify separating state and federal claims for trial, Fed. Rule Civ. Proc. 42(b). If so, jurisdiction should ordinarily be refused. [383 U.S. at 725-27].

Is *Gibbs* consistent with Osborn v. Bank of the United States, 22 U.S. (9 Wheat.) 738 (U.S. 1824) (p. 312, *supra*)? In *Osborn*, the Court focused on the existence of a potential federal question in the *case* as a sufficient basis for constitutional jurisdiction. In *Gibbs*, wasn't there also a federal question present in the *case*? Why did the Court focus on whether there was a federal question present in the state-law *claim*?

Gibbs left certain ambiguities in its wake. It was not clear how broadly "common nucleus of operative fact" should be interpreted, nor was it clear whether the arguably narrower "expected to be tried together" concept further defined "one constitutional case." Likewise, the scope of the federal courts' discretionary power to dismiss was uncertain; federal courts disagreed, for instance, about whether they were required to dismiss the state claims once the federal claim in a case had been dismissed.

At several levels, *Gibbs* is an extremely important case for complex and complicated litigation. First, *Gibbs* permitted the full exercise of the constitutional grant of federal jurisdiction, even though no statute had expressly authorized such a full exercise. We have already suggested that, in instances of lawyer dysfunction, federal courts might be able to ignore the statutory limits of §§ 1331 and 1332 and expand jurisdiction to the full constitutional limit; *Gibbs* provides an example of a case in which the Supreme Court took a similar approach. Second, the reasons which the Court advanced for its adoption of pendent jurisdiction — judicial economy, convenience, and fairness — are concerns particularly relevant to complex and complicated litigation, and thus suggest that federal courts might have some license to overcome complexity or complication. Third, *Gibbs* imposes an outer limit — the "common nucleus of operative fact" test — on the ability of a federal court to achieve the aggregation of related cases. Finally, although this stretches *Gibbs* a great deal, the case could be read to mean that federal jurisdiction should be shaped, at least in part, by the strength of the federal interests in the case. This reading suggests that federal judges should be imbued with more jurisdictional discretion to achieve the packaging of the case which optimally reduces joinder complexity.

At a different level, however, *Gibbs* is a precedent of limited value. It specifically deals only with the problem of the joinder by a single plaintiff of additional, jurisdictionally insufficient claims against a single defendant. This issue does not address the core concern of complex litigation, or the concern of most complicated litigation: the need to assert in one forum claims of all potential plaintiffs against all potential defendants. Should the

Gibbs approach apply in all these circumstances? Or should the Constitution and the statutory grants of jurisdiction impose a different test? Should such a different test be broader than *Gibbs*, or narrower? These questions bring into play the federal courts' jurisdiction over ancillary and pendent party claims.

    2. *Ancillary Jurisdiction.* The problem of jurisdiction over counterclaims, cross-claims, third party claims, and claims in intervention is technically distinct from the problem of pendent jurisdiction. Pendent jurisdiction involves a single party asserting claims that are both "jurisdictionally permissible" (*i.e.*, an independent basis of jurisdiction exists) and "jurisdictionally impermissible" (*i.e.*, no independent basis). With respect to counterclaims, cross-claims, third party claims, or claims in intervention, however, the plaintiff is asserting a "jurisdictionally permissible" claim and an opposing party is asserting a "jurisdictionally impermissible" claim. Obviously, the jurisdictionally permissible claim and the jurisdictionally impermissible counterclaim, cross-claim, third party claim, or claim in intervention have some relationship, but where does the federal court derive the power to hear the jurisdictionally impermissible claim?

    The concept of ancillary jurisdiction, which was developed to deal with these claims, descended from cases such as Freeman v. Howe, 65 U.S. (24 How.) 450, 460 (1861) (allowing intervention when the suit was "not an original suit, but ancillary and dependent, supplementary merely to the original suit, out of which it had arisen"), and Moore v. New York Cotton Exchange, 270 U.S. 593, 610 (1926) (allowing a counterclaim because of the "close . . . connection" between the claim and counterclaim). In its modern form, ancillary jurisdiction permits a federal court to consider jurisdictionally impermissible claims as long as they are transactionally or logically related to the plaintiff's jurisdictionally permissible claim. Using this doctrine, federal courts have declared that they have ancillary jurisdiction over compulsory counterclaims under Rule 13(a), cross-claims under Rule 13(g), third party claims under Rule 14(a), and claims of intervention of right under Rule 24(a). Traditionally excluded from the ambit of ancillary jurisdiction, however, were permissive counterclaims and claims for permissive intervention. See generally Erwin Chemerinsky, Federal Jurisdiction § 5.4 (2d ed. 1994).

    Like pendent jurisdiction, ancillary jurisdiction was not based on an express statutory grant but rather on an inherent adjudicatory authority. But the "dependent and supplementary" or "close connection" tests for ancillary jurisdiction sound considerably narrower than the "common nucleus of operative fact" test which *Gibbs* adopted for pendent jurisdiction. Since both pendent and ancillary jurisdiction involved a similar problem, there was some belief after *Gibbs* that ancillary jurisdiction should also be expanded to permit jurisdiction to be asserted over any claim that involved a common nucleus of operative fact.

    Such hopes for consistency in approach were dashed by Owen Equipment & Erection Co. v. Kroger, 437 U.S. 365 (1978). In *Kroger*, an Iowa plaintiff sued a Nebraska defendant on a state law tort theory. The

Nebraska defendant then brought a third party claim against Owen Equipment, which it believed was also a citizen of Nebraska. Subsequently, the plaintiff asserted a direct tort claim against Owen Equipment. After the original defendant settled, the plaintiff proceeded to trial only against Owen. On the third day of trial, testimony revealed that Owen Equipment was in fact a citizen of Iowa. Since complete diversity was not present, Owen Equipment moved to dismiss. The lower courts refused to do so, but the Supreme Court reversed:

> [T]he test of *Gibbs* . . . does not end the inquiry into whether a federal court has power to hear the nonfederal claims along with the federal ones. Beyond this constitutional minimum, there must be an examination of the posture in which the nonfederal claim is asserted and of the specific statute that confers jurisdiction over the federal claim . . . .
>
> If, as the Court of Appeals thought, a "common nucleus of operative fact" were the only requirement for ancillary jurisdiction in a diversity case, there would be no principled reason why the respondent in this case could not have joined her action against Owen in her original complaint as ancillary to her claim against [the original defendant]. Congress' requirement of complete diversity would thus have been completely evaded. . . .
>
> [T]he claim here arises in a setting quite different from the kinds of federal claims that have been viewed in other cases as falling within the ancillary jurisdiction of the federal courts.
>
> First, the nonfederal claim in this case was simply not ancillary to the federal one in the same sense that, for example, the impleader by a defendant of a third-party defendant always is. A third-party complaint depends at least in part upon the resolution of the primary lawsuit. Its relation to the original complaint is thus not mere factual similarity but logical dependence. . . . Far from being an ancillary and dependent one, it was a new and independent one.
>
> Second, the nonfederal claim here was asserted by the plaintiff, who voluntarily chose to bring suit upon a state-law claim in a federal court. By contrast, ancillary jurisdiction typically involves claims by a defending party haled into court against his will, or by another person whose rights may be irretrievably lost unless he can assert them in an ongoing federal action. A plaintiff cannot complain if ancillary jurisdiction does not encompass all of his possible claims in a case such as this one, since it is he who has chosen the federal rather than the state forum and must thus accept its limitations. "[T]he efficiency plaintiff seeks so avidly is available without question in the state courts." . . .
>
> It is not unreasonable to assume that, in generally requiring compete diversity, Congress did not intend to confine the jurisdiction of federal courts so inflexibly that they are unable to protect legal rights or effectively resolve an entire, logically entwined lawsuit. Those practical needs are the basis of the doctrine of ancillary jurisdiction. But neither the convenience of litigants nor considerations of judicial

economy can suffice to justify extension of the doctrine of ancillary jurisdiction to a plaintiff's cause of action against a citizen of the same State in a diversity case. [437 U.S. at 373-77].

Justice White's dissent took the majority to task for neglecting the teaching of *Gibbs* and the considerations of judicial economy, convenience, and fairness to the litigants which underlay *Gibbs*. In particular, the dissent noted that judicial economy is "certainly not served by such duplicative litigation." Id. at 382.

Kroger strongly suggested that its "logical dependence" test of ancillary jurisdiction did not represent the constitutional limit of the federal courts' Article III power to hear ancillary claims, but rather was a gloss on the federal courts' statutory grants of jurisdiction. Given that minimal diversity existed in *Kroger*, that suggestion seems correct on the facts of the case. Does the majority's argument convince you that the boundaries of ancillary jurisdiction should be drawn inside of the constitutional maximum? What is the constitutional maximum for ancillary jurisdiction. *Kroger* seems to assume that it is *Gibbs*. Is that assumption necessarily accurate?

Because the plaintiff in *Kroger* has the power to select the forum in which to bring the case, and because she could have accomplished complete joinder in state court, the Supreme Court certainly had little reason to bend § 1332's complete diversity rule. Would *Kroger* necessarily bar a similar attempt to assert a state claim against a non-diverse defendant if the plaintiff is incapable of effecting complete joinder in state court and the failure to effect joinder in state court would be lawyer dysfunction? *Kroger's* narrow "logical dependence" understanding of ancillary jurisdiction makes the sledding difficult, but it is still possible to argue that *Kroger*, which was certainly not a case of joinder complexity, should not limit a broader understanding of ancillary jurisdiction in cases of joinder complexity.

3. Pendent Party Jurisdiction. Although the doctrines of pendent and ancillary jurisdiction are somewhat relevant to mass aggregation, the doctrine of pendent party jurisdiction addresses the two critical questions in complex and complicated litigation: (1) To what extent can federal courts exercise jurisdiction over a jurisdictionally impermissible claim against one defendant, when the plaintiff asserts a jurisdictionally permissible claim against a different defendant? and (2) To what extent can federal courts exercise jurisdiction over a jurisdictionally impermissible claim of one plaintiff, when another plaintiff asserts a jurisdictionally permissible claim against the same defendant? In thinking about these questions, two paths had already been blazed: the *Gibbs* "common nucleus" approach and the *Kroger* "logical dependence" approach. Which approach, if either, is appropriate in this situation?

In Aldinger v. Howard, 427 U.S. 1 (1976), the Supreme Court denied pendent party jurisdiction when a § 1983 plaintiff attempted to append a state-law tort claim against a non-diverse county government to a civil rights claim against county employees. *Aldinger*, however, rested on an interpretation of 28 U.S.C. § 1343, the jurisdictional grant for § 1983 claims; and it was influenced by the fact that a state forum in which both claims could be asserted remained available. It did not purport to establish a general rule against pendent party jurisdiction. Indeed, it strongly implied that, if complete joinder in state court were not possible, then federal courts could assert pendent party jurisdiction.

In 1989, the Court all but shut the door on the idea of non-statutory pendent party jurisdiction. In Finley v. United States, 490 U.S. 545 (1989), the plaintiff, whose decedent had died in a one-person airplane crash, sued the United States and several private defendants on state-law negligence theories. Under the Federal Tort Claims Act (FTCA), the United States could be sued only in federal court; the private defendants, however, were citizens of the same state as the plaintiff. The plaintiff nonetheless joined all the defendants in federal court, invoking the concept of pendent party jurisdiction and distinguishing *Aldinger* on the ground that it was not possible to sue all the defendants in state court. Although the district court found that "judicial economy and efficiency" favored trying the actions together and that the cases arose "from a common nucleus of operative facts," the Supreme Court held that the claims against the joint tortfeasors should have been dismissed:

> Analytically, petitioner's case is fundamentally different from *Gibbs* in that it brings into question what has become known as pendent-party jurisdiction, that is, jurisdiction over parties not named in any claim that is independently cognizable by the federal court. We may assume, without deciding, that the constitutional criterion for pendent-party jurisdiction is analogous to the constitutional criterion for pendent-claim jurisdiction, and that petitioner's state-law claims pass that test. Our cases show, however, that with respect to the addition of parties, as opposed to the addition of only claims, we will not assume that the full constitutional power has been congressionally authorized, and will not read jurisdiction statutes broadly. . . .
>
> The most significant element . . . in the present case (as in *Zahn*, *Aldinger*, and *Kroger*) is precisely that the added claims involve added parties over whom no independent basis of jurisdiction exists. . . . As in *Kroger*, the relationship between petitioner's added claims and the original complaint is one of "mere factual similarity," which is of no consequence since "neither the convenience of the litigants nor considerations of judicial economy can suffice to justify extension of the doctrine of ancillary jurisdiction" . . . . It is true that here, unlike in *Kroger*, . . . the party seeking to bring the added claims had little choice but to be in federal court rather than state court . . . . But that alone is not enough . . . .
>
> Because the FTCA permits the Government to be sued only in federal court, our holding that parties to related claims cannot necessarily be sued there means that the efficiency and convenience of a consolidated action will sometimes have to be forgone in favor of separate actions in state and federal courts. . . .
>
> [O]ur cases do not display an entirely consistent approach with respect to the necessity that jurisdiction be explicitly conferred. The *Gibbs* line of cases was a departure from prior practice, and a departure that we have no intent to limit or impair. But *Aldinger* indicated that

the *Gibbs* approach would not be extended to the pendent-party field, and we decide today to retain that line. Whatever we say regarding the scope of jurisdiction conferred by a particular statute can of course be changed by Congress. What is of paramount importance is that Congress be able to legislate against a backdrop of clear interpretive rules, so that it may know the effect of the language it adopts. All of our cases — *Zahn*, *Aldinger*, and *Kroger* — have held that a grant of jurisdiction over claims involving particular parties does not itself confer jurisdiction over additional claims by or against different parties. Our decision today reaffirms that interpretive rule; the opposite would sow confusion. [490 U.S. at 549, 551-52, 555-56.]

There were four dissenters. Justice Blackmun observed that "[w]here, as here, Congress' preference for a federal forum for a certain category of claims makes the federal forum the *only* possible one in which a constitutional case may be heard as a whole, the sensible result is to permit the exercise of pendent-party jurisdiction." Id. at 558. Justice Stevens, joined by Justices Brennan and Marshall, argued that the majority had lost sight of the purpose of pendent jurisdiction, which "rests in part on a recognition that forcing a federal plaintiff to litigate his or her case in both federal and state courts impairs the ability of the federal court to grant full relief . . . ." Id. at 576.

Finley was not a complex case; there were no affected nonparties, nor were there insufficient assets. Moreover, the decision, which split the case into two separate suits, did not seem to place a crushing burden on the courts or the parties. Does it therefore remain possible to argue that, in instances of complex litigation, federal courts possess the inherent authority to assure that all interested parties had the opportunity to participate in a comprehensive and rational adjudication? Is the same argument available in complicated litigation? *Finley*'s unwavering "interpretive rule," as well as its reluctance to consider notions of economy, fairness, and convenience in a case which could have been jointly resolved only in federal court, gave little room for optimism about either argument's success.

4. Supplemental Jurisdiction. The congressional response to *Finley* was swift. As part of the Judicial Improvements Act of 1990, it enacted 28 U.S.C. § 1367, which was written with the express intention of overruling *Finley*. Section 1367 coined a new phrase — "supplemental jurisdiction" — that was intended to be an umbrella term that covered pendent, ancillary, and pendent party jurisdiction.

To understand § 1367, the statute must be read closely. It may be best to begin with § 1367(b), which describes the scope of supplemental jurisdiction "[i]n any civil action of which the district courts have original jurisdiction founded solely on section 1332." Then return to § 1367(a), which describes the scope of supplemental jurisdiction in all other cases of which the district courts have original jurisdiction. Next, examine § 1367(c), which, like *Gibbs*, provides certain discretionary factors that a court can consider in deciding whether to accept or decline the supplemental jurisdiction that subsections (a) and (b) otherwise give the court. Finally, note that § 1367(d) temporarily tolls the statute of limitations for certain (but not all) claims which are involuntarily or voluntarily dismissed, thus allowing a plaintiff whose dismissed claim had been timely filed in federal court to file it again in state court.

The statute is intricately interwoven, and the final word on many interpretive questions has yet to be spoken. For a range of perspectives on the statute, see Richard D. Freer, *Compounding Confusion and Hampering Diversity: Life after* Finley *and the Supplemental Jurisdiction Statute*, 40 Emory L.J. 445 (1991) (raising a host of interpretive problems with § 1367); Thomas D. Rowe, Jr. et al., *Compounding or Creating Confusion about Supplemental Jurisdiction? A Reply to Professor Freer*, 40 Emory L.J. 943 (1991) (response by the primary drafters of § 1367 to Professor Freer's criticisms); Colloquy: *Perspectives on Supplemental Jurisdiction*, 41 Emory L.J. 1 (1992) (further interpretive issues and criticisms of § 1367 explored); Denis F. McLaughlin, *The Federal Supplemental Jurisdiction Statute — A Constitutional and Statutory Analysis*, 24 Ariz. St. L. Rev. 849 (1992) (same); American Law Institute, Federal Judicial Code Revision Project, Tent. Draft No. 2 (1998).

Our particular concern is with the effect of § 1367 on complex and complicated litigation. As we saw in the last two subsections, it is already possible, though by no means easy, to interpret §§ 1331 and 1332 to provide the federal jurisdiction necessary to aggregate cases involving lawyer dysfunction. Creating similar interpretations to deal with the inefficiency of complicated litigation proved more difficult. Does § 1367 make the task of arguing for the aggregation of cases in a federal forum easier?

IN RE ABBOTT LABORATORIES

51 F.3d 524 (5th Cir. 1995)

■ HIGGINBOTHAM, Circuit Judge. This class action brought under the antitrust laws of the State of Louisiana requires that we decide whether the Judicial Improvements Act of 1990 overrules Zahn v. International Paper Co., 414 U.S. 291 (1973). We hold today that it does. We agree with the district court that the claims of the class representatives met the requisite amount in controversy and that it had diversity jurisdiction over their claims, but disagree with its decision to abstain from exercising it. We agree with the district court that it had supplemental jurisdiction over all other members of the class, but disagree with its decision not to exercise it. We vacate the order remanding to state court.

I.

Robin and Renee Free filed suit in a Louisiana state court on October 14, 1993, alleging that Abbott Laboratories, Bristol-Meyers Squibb Company, Inc., and Mead Johnson & Company had conspired to fix infant formula prices. The Frees filed for themselves and for a class of Louisiana consumers. Defendants removed to federal court, and plaintiffs moved to remand.

[Each named and unnamed plaintiff alleged $20,000 in damages, below the amount in controversy requirement of 28 U.S.C. § 1332(a). The district court, however, found diversity jurisdiction existed with respect to the named plaintiffs because of a Louisiana law that attributed all of a class's attorneys' fees to the named plaintiffs. The district court then rejected the plaintiffs' contention that attorneys' fees should be allocated pro rata among all class members, so that none would meet the matter-in-controversy requirement.]

The federal district court granted the motion to remand. The court held that it lacked federal question jurisdiction and that it had diversity jurisdiction only over the named plaintiffs' claims and not over claims of the other members of the class. The district court declined to exercise supplemental jurisdiction because the claims raised "novel issues of state law." [The district court then remanded to state court the claims of the named class members over whom it had jurisdiction, invoking abstention doctrines (see p.426, *infra*) in order to avoid piecemeal litigation and to permit Louisiana state courts to rule on the "novel and complex issues of state law" presented in the case.] Defendants both appeal and petition for mandamus, asking that we vacate the order remanding to state court.

III. DIVERSITY AND SUPPLEMENTAL JURISDICTION

[After holding that the district court had supplemental jurisdiction over the claims of the named class members, the court of appeals turned to the question of supplemental jurisdiction over the unnamed class members.]

Congress enacted § 1367 against the background of *Zahn*, in which the Supreme Court had held that the claim of each member of a class action must meet the amount-in-controversy requirement. . . . *Zahn* forbade the exercise of supplemental jurisdiction over the claims of class members who did not do so.

Defendants argue that Congress changed the jurisdictional landscape in 1990 by enacting § 1367. Section 1367(a) grants district courts supplemental jurisdiction over related claims generally, and § 1367(b) carves exceptions. Significantly, class actions are not among the exceptions.

Some commentators have interpreted this silence to mean that Congress overruled *Zahn* and granted supplemental jurisdiction over the claims of class members who individually do not demand the necessary amount in controversy. Some of § 1367's drafters disagree. No appellate court has ruled on the question yet. . . .

Perhaps, by some measure transcending its language, Congress did not intend the Judicial Improvements Act to overrule *Zahn*. The House Committee on the Judiciary considered the bill that became § 1367 to be a "noncontroversial" collection of "relatively modest proposals," not the sort of legislative action that would upset any long-established precedent like *Zahn*. . . . Plaintiffs argue that the Act was prompted not by a congressional desire for wholesale revisions of the jurisdictional rules, but by the more limited desire to restore traditional understandings of federal jurisdiction, which were upset by Finley v. United States, 490 U.S. 545 (1989). In *Finley*, the Supreme Court held that federal courts could not exercise pendent-party jurisdiction without an express legislative grant, a grant never thought necessary before. . . . In short, Congress intended the Act to "essentially restore the pre-*Finley* understandings of the authorization for and limits on other forms of supplemental jurisdiction," not, arguably, to alter *Zahn*. . . . A disclaimer in the legislative history strives to make this point clear by stating: "[T]he section is not intended to affect the jurisdictional requirements of 28 U.S.C. § 1332 in diversity-only class actions, as those requirements were interpreted prior to *Finley*." . . . The passage cites *Zahn* as a pre-*Finley* case untouched by the Act. . . .

We cannot search legislative history for congressional intent unless we find the statute unclear or ambiguous. Here, it is neither. The statute's first section vests federal courts with the power to hear supplemental claims generally, subject to limited exceptions set forth in the statute's second section. Class actions are not among the enumerated exceptions.

Omitting the class action from the exception may have been a clerical error. But the statute is the sole repository of congressional intent where the statute is clear and does not demand an absurd result. . . . Abolishing the strictures of *Zahn* is not an absurd result. Justice Brennan's dissent joined by Justices Douglas and Marshall states the counterposition. Some respected commentators would welcome *Zahn*'s demise. See, *e.g.*, [Thomas C. Arthur & Richard D. Freer, *Close Enough for Government Work: What Happens When Congress Doesn't Do Its Job*,] 40 Emory L.J. [1007,] 1008 n. 6 [(1991)] ("Abrogating Zahn would hardly be absurd" since doing so would harmonize case law and "enable federal courts to resolve complex interstate disputes in mass tort situations."). But the wisdom of the statute is not our affair beyond determining that overturning *Zahn* is not absurd. We are persuaded that under § 1367 a district court can exercise supplemental jurisdiction over members of a class, although they did not meet the amount-in- controversy requirement, as did the class representatives.

IV. ABSTENTION AND DISCRETIONARY EXERCISE OF SUPPLEMENTAL JURISDICTION

[The court determined that the district court abused its discretion in abstaining with respect to the claims of the named plaintiffs, because the "novelty or complexity of state law issues is not enough to compel abstention." It then turned to the issue of whether the district court should invoke § 1367(c) and decline to exercise supplemental jurisdiction over the unnamed plaintiffs' claims.]

The district court remanded the claims of other class members because they presented "novel issues of state law," including whether indirect purchasers could state a claim under Louisiana antitrust law and whether the antitrust claim was preempted by federal law.

Refusing to exercise supplemental jurisdiction over the unnamed plaintiffs' claims reflects respect for considerations of comity, but it assumes that the claims of the class representatives were to be remanded to state court. The court must now adjudicate claims of the class representatives —

including the same novel and complex state law issues the district court preferred to leave to Louisiana. So the interests of comity will not be served by declining to exercise supplemental jurisdiction over the class members whose claims do not meet the jurisdictional amount.

In short, the entire case should remain in federal court. The district court had diversity jurisdiction over the named plaintiffs' claims; § 1367 granted it supplemental jurisdiction over the claims of the unnamed plaintiffs; and, considering that it must try the named plaintiffs' claims, it abused its discretion on the facts here in declining supplemental jurisdiction over the unnamed plaintiffs' claims. . . . We vacate the district court's remand order, and remand to the district court for further proceedings. The petition for mandamus is denied.

Notes and Questions

1. The statutory language that *Abbott Laboratories* was focusing on was § 1367(b), which refuses to permit federal courts to exercise supplemental jurisdiction over "claims by plaintiffs against persons made parties under Rule 14, 19, 20, or 24 of the Federal Rules of Civil Procedure, or over claims by persons proposed to be joined as plaintiffs under Rule 19 of such rules, or seeking to intervene as plaintiffs under Rule 24 of such rules, when exercising jurisdiction over such claims would be inconsistent with the jurisdictional requirements of section 1332." Section 1367(b) applies only in cases in which "the district courts have original jurisdiction founded solely on section 1332."

The plain reading of § 1367(b) by *Abbott Laboratories* is defensible. Nowhere in § 1367(b) is there any mention of plaintiffs that are joined under Rule 23. This would seem to suggest that the existence of supplemental jurisdiction in the case is covered by the more generous default rule of § 1367(a), which permits a federal court to exercise supplemental jurisdiction "over all other claims that are so related to claims in the action within such original jurisdiction that they form part of the same case or controversy under Article III of the United States Constitution."

Aside from the issue of whether *Zahn* has been overruled in the class action context, § 1367(b) has presented two other interpretive difficulties of importance in complex and complicated litigation. First, note that § 1367(b) no longer permits federal courts to exercise "ancillary" jurisdiction over intervenors of right who would destroy complete diversity or who do not have the requisite amount in controversy. Conversely, § 1367(a) permits federal courts to exercise supplemental jurisdiction over state-law claims by permissive intervenors in cases not founded solely on diversity of citizenship. The limitation of "ancillary" jurisdiction in the context of intervention of right, and its expansion in the context of permissive intervention, is a significant issue. What effect might these changes have on the attempt to preclude nonparties after notice and an opportunity to intervene? See pp. 249-51, *supra*.

Second, and more significantly, § 1367(b) does not permit federal courts to exercise supplemental jurisdiction over "claims by plaintiffs *against* persons made parties under Rule 20," but it nowhere precludes the exercise of supplemental jurisdiction over claims of additional non-diverse plaintiffs that are joined pursuant to Rule 20 (as it does with regard to additional plaintiffs joined under Rules 19 and 24). Applying the same plain reading to Rule 20 plaintiffs that *Abbott Laboratories* applied to Rule 23 plaintiffs, it would seem that federal courts can also exercise supplemental jurisdiction over the claims of Rule 20 plaintiffs as long as, under § 1367(a), their claims form part of the same constitutional case or controversy.

Is this reading of § 1367(b)'s treatment of Rule 20 plaintiffs correct? In Stromberg Metal Works, Inc. and Comfort v. Press Mechanical, Inc., 77 F.3d 928 (7th Cir. 1996), two related companies brought suit for breach of contract. Both companies were of diverse citizenship from the defendants; one of the companies had a claim for $425,000 and the other a claim for $27,000. The first company filed suit in federal court, and joined the second company under Rule 20 as an additional plaintiff. The Seventh Circuit held that, as long as the lead plaintiff satisfied the diversity and matter-in-controversy requirements, supplemental jurisdiction extended to claims by additional Rule 20 plaintiffs whose claims do not satisfy § 1332:

> [A]lthough, as *Abbott Laboratories* discussed, some legislative history suggests that the responsible committees did not expect § 1367 to upset *Zahn*, the text is not limited in this way. When text and legislative history disagree, the text controls. . . .
>
> The [defendants] ask us to distinguish *Abbott Laboratories* on the ground that it, like *Zahn*, involved a class action. . . . Our case, by contrast, has just two plaintiffs. But § 1367 does not distinguish class actions from other cases; neither did *Zahn*. Indeed, the point of *Zahn* was that the class device made no difference. . . . To the extent practical considerations enter in, it is hard to avoid remarking that allowing thousands of small claims into federal court via the class device is a substantially greater expansion of jurisdiction than is allowing a single pendent party. . . .
>
> Now this does point up an apparent incongruity in § 1367(b). Claims against persons made parties under Rule 20 are forbidden, but claims by parties who join under Rule 20 are allowed. Similarly, claims by parties joined under Rule 19 because they are essential to adjudication are forbidden (if that spoils diversity), but claims by parties joined under Rule 20 for convenience are allowed. What sense can this make? Some scholars have suggested that it makes none, and they call on courts to fix the statute by inventive construction. . . . Whether § 1367(b) is a model drafting exercise may be doubted, but the language draws an important line. . . . Supplemental jurisdiction has the potential to move from complete to minimal diversity.
>
> [I]f it is possible for the principal action to be in federal court without any jurisdictional qualms then § 1367(b) does not block adding an additional plaintiff with a closely related claim against the defendants who are already in the federal forum.
>
> "Closely related" is a vital qualification. Section 1367(c)(2) provides that the district court may dismiss a supplemental claim that "substantially predominates over the claim or claims over which the district court has original jurisdiction". And § 1367(a) itself applies only if the supplemental claims are "so related to claims in the action within [the] original jurisdiction that they form part of the same case or controversy under Article III of the United States Constitution." The claims of Stromberg and Comfort Control satisfy these requirements, however. The two plaintiffs are

affiliated corporations under common control. The claims arose out of the same construction project.... This strikes us as exactly the sort of case in which pendent-party jurisdiction is appropriate. It is two for the price of one: to decide either plaintiff's claim is to decide both, and neither private interests nor judicial economy would be promoted by resolving Stromberg's claim in federal court while trundling Comfort Control off to state court to get a second opinion. [77 F.3d at 931-32.]

In *Stromberg*, the additional Rule 20 plaintiff was of diverse citizenship from the defendants, but did not have an adequate amount in controversy. Would the result be the same if the additional plaintiff had the same citizenship as one of the defendants, so that only minimal diversity was present?

2. The cases construing § 1367(b) have not been consistent. Like *Abbott Laboratories*, some cases have interpreted § 1367(b) to overrule *Zahn* in the class action context. Deep v. Manufacturuers Life Insurance Co., 944 F. Supp. 358 (D. N.J. 1996); Gilmer v. Walt Disney Co., 915 F. Supp. 1001 (W.D. Ark. 1996); see also Packard v. Provident National Bank, 994 F.2d 1039, 1045 n.9 (3d Cir.), cert. denied, 510 U.S. 964 (1993) (collecting authorites on both sides, but not resolving issue). Like *Stromberg*, some cases have interpreted § 1367(b) to permit the exercise of supplemental jurisdiction over Rule 20 plaintiffs. Patterson Enterprises, Inc. v. Bridgestone/Firestone, Inc., 812 F. Supp. 1152 (D. Kan. 1993); Garza v. National American Insurance Co., 807 F. Supp. 1256 (M.D. La. 1992). On the other side of the equation, most cases have held that *Zahn* was not overruled by § 1367. See, *e.g.*, Crosby v. America Online, Inc., 967 F. Supp. 257 (N.D. Ohio 1997); Russ v. State Farm Mutual Automobile Insurance Co., 961 F. Supp. 808 (E.D. Pa. 1997); Bernard v. Gerber Food Prods. Co., 938 F. Supp. 218 (S.D.N.Y. 1996); Mayo v. Key Financial Services, Inc., 812 F. Supp. 277 (D. Mass. 1993). *Stromberg*'s interpretation of § 1367(b) in the context of Rule 20 plaintiffs has not been litigated as frequently, although some courts have declined to follow *Stromberg*'s interpretation. See Henkel v. ITT Bowest Corp., 872 F. Supp. 872 (D. Kan. 1994); Ware v. Jolly Roger Rides, Inc., 857 F. Supp. 462 (D. Md. 1994).

3. These issues have also divided the academic literature. For a small sampling, see Denis F. McLaughlin, *The Federal Supplemental Jurisdiction Statute — A Constitutional and Statutory Analysis*, 24 Ariz. St. L. Rev. 849, 973 (1992) (*Zahn* survives); Thomas D. Rowe, Jr. et al., *Compounding or Creating Confusion about Supplemental Jurisdiction? A Reply to Professor Freer*, 40 Emory L.J. 943, 960 n.90 (1991) (legislative history probably, but not unequivocally, saves *Zahn*); Thomas C. Arthur & Richard D. Freer, *Grasping at Burnt Straws: The Disaster of the Supplemental Jurisdiction Statute*, 40 Emory L.J. 963, 981 (1991) (legislative history cannot override clear statutory language overruling *Zahn*); Karen N. Moore, *The Supplemental Jurisdiction Statute: An Important but Controversial Supplement to Federal Jurisdiction*, 41 Emory L.J. 31, 56-58 (1992) (*Zahn* might well be dead); Joan Steinman, *Section 1367 — Another Party Heard From*, 41 Emory L.J. 85, 102-04 (1992) (same); Christopher P. Simkins, Note & Comment, *Class Actions and Supplemental Jurisdiction: Will* Zahn v. International Paper Co. *Remain Viable?* 1996 B.Y.U. L. Rev. 707 (1996) (criticizing *Abbott Laboratories* and *Stromberg*); Mark C. Cawley, Note, *The Right Result for the Wrong Reasons: Permitting Aggregation of Claims under 28 U.S.C. § 1367 in Multi-Plaintiff Diversity Litigation*, 73 Notre Dame L. Rev. 1045 (1998) (defending results in *Abbott Laboratories* and *Stromberg*, though not their "plain meaning" reasoning).

The American Law Institute has recently weighed in on the issue and tentatively approved a proposed revision of § 1367. The proposed statute makes clear that *Zahn* is indeed overruled in the class action context. It also adopts the holding in *Stromberg* and permits supplemental jurisdiction to be exercised over additional plaintiffs that do not meet the amount-in-controversy requirement; it does not, however, embrace the dicta in *Stromberg* and therefore does not permit supplemental jurisdiction to be exercised over plaintiffs that were not diverse from defendants. Finally, it permits supplemental jurisdiction to be asserted over all intervenors — both intervenors of right and permissive intervenors. American Law Institute, Federal Judicial Code Revision Project, Tent. Draft No. 2 (1998).

4. Can cases like *Abbott Laboratories* and *Stromberg* be right? The reading of § 1367 in these cases is plausible, but is it so obvious that the "plain meaning" of the statute supports their result? There exists at least one other equally plausible interpretation. Note that the introductory clause to § 1367(b) requires that the district court be "founded solely on section 1332." Because complete diversity does not exist at the outset in *Abbott Laboratories* and *Stromberg*, however, couldn't it be argued that the court's jurisdiction in the cases could not be "founded solely on section 1332," so that § 1367(b) never comes into play? Isn't this alternate interpretation of § 1367(b) supported by Congress's intent that § 1367 should not be read to change the results of either *Kroger* or *Zahn*? See H.R. Rep. No. 101-734, 101st Cong. 2d Sess. 29 and n.17 (noting that "the net effect of subsection (b) is to implement the principal rationale of . . . *Kroger*" and that "[t]he section is not intended to affect the jurisdictional requirements of 28 U.S.C. § 1332 in diversity-only class actions").

This alternate interpretation also has its flaws. Consider the following:

(a) In *Abbott Laboratories* and *Stromberg*, the jurisdiction of the court *is* founded on § 1332. The alternate interpretation assumes that the introductory clause reads: "In any civil action of which the district courts have original jurisdiction *correctly* founded solely on section 1332 . . . ." Yet, in legal parlance, jurisdiction can be "founded" on a particular statutory provision even if it turns out that the statute is inapplicable; in *Zahn*, for instance, we would typically say that jurisdiction was founded (albeit incorrectly) on § 1332. Moreover, if this latter interpretation is the proper understanding, then subsection (b) is largely a tautology; it merely says that "When a court has proper jurisdiction under § 1332, it cannot exercise jurisdiction over certain claims by or against certain parties unless jurisdiction would be proper under § 1332."

(b) The manner in which § 1367(a) relates to § 1367(b) under this reading is unclear. If the gloss "correctly" is added to (b), then it would appear that a case in which § 1332 jurisdiction was *incorrectly* applied cannot be analyzed under (b). Since (b) is an exception to (a), it seems that we return to (a) to handle diversity cases which fail to come within § 1332. (Is this analysis sound?) Under (a), we encounter similar phrasing ("in any civil action of which the district courts have original jurisdiction"). Unless we are to give the benefits of § 1367(a)'s more generous supplemental jurisdiction to cases improperly pleaded as § 1332 claims but not to properly pleaded § 1332 claims — a result which would be perverse — we will need to read subsection (b)'s gloss into subsection (a), *i.e.*, "in any civil action of which the district courts *correctly* have original *statutory* jurisdiction . . . ." That gloss protects the federal courts from *Abbott Laboratories*, *Stromberg*, and other diversity cases that do not meet the requirements of § 1332. But it also jeopardizes pendent jurisdiction cases like

Gibbs and ancillary jurisdiction cases like *Freeman* and *Moore*, because the federal court did not *correctly* have *statutory* jurisdiction over the supplemental state law claims in any of those cases.

5. Even if the alternate reading is correct, another serious breach of the complete diversity rule may exist in § 1367(b). According to the drafters of § 1367, "Literally, . . . section 1367(b) does not bar an original complete diversity filing and subsequent amendment to add a nondiverse co-plaintiff under Rule 20, taking advantage of supplemental jurisdiction over the claim of the new plaintiff against the existing defendant." The drafters stated that they could "only hope that the federal courts will plug that potentially gaping hole in the complete diversity requirement — either by regarding it as an unacceptable circumvention of original diversity jurisdiction requirements, or by reference to the intent not to abandon the complete diversity rule that is clearly expressed in the legislative history of section 1367." Rowe et al., 40 Emory L.J. at 961 n.91 (1991). Are the drafters right about their interpretation of § 1367(b)? If they cannot, it seems rather silly to insist on complete diversity at the outset of a case; we might as well accept the *Abbott Laboratories-Stromberg* reading of § 1367(b). On the other hand, might the district court's discretionary power under § 1367(c) to dismiss claims "in exceptional circumstances" be sufficient to deal with this end-run around the complete diversity rule?

6. If *Zahn* has been overruled, has *Snyder* also been overruled? Here the textual argument suggests not. Even if § 1367(b) does not preserve *Snyder* explicitly, § 1367(a) still requires that at least one claim fit within federal jurisdiction. Since none of the plaintiffs' claims in a *Snyder*-like class action meets the amount in controversy requirement (barring, of course, a special rule for cases of joinder complexity, see pp. 339-40, *supra*), none of the cases lies within federal jurisdiction; thus, supplemental jurisdiction is unavailable. Should the *Snyder* and *Zahn* situations receive disparate treatment under § 1367? Is that possibility an argument against the overruling of *Zahn*?

7. Section 1367(b) applies only to actions "founded solely on section 1332." Therefore, a simple way for plaintiffs to skirt § 1367(b)'s bar against joining non-diverse defendants and its arguable bar against joining non-diverse plaintiffs is to plead at least one federal question claim in the case. As soon as at least one such claim is asserted, it appears that § 1367(b) no longer applies, and the extent of supplemental jurisdiction is measured under § 1367(a). Suppose that a plaintiff pleads both a § 1331 claim and a § 1332 claim against one defendant, and then seeks to add state law claims involving additional non-diverse defendants. Does § 1367(a) require that the claims involving non-diverse defendants be related to the § 1331 claim, or is it enough that they be related to the § 1332 claim?

Given that it is often not difficult to plead a federal question claim, why was Congress so skittish about breaching the complete diversity rule in pure diversity cases, but apparently so willing to breach it in a "nearly pure" case in which some federal claim was present? Were they relying on § 1367(c)(2) and the good sense of federal judges to keep these cases out of federal court? If so, why not make supplemental jurisdiction entirely subject to the judge's discretion to choose the optimal packaging of the case?

8. The preceding Note suggests a final interpretive problem in § 1367: When is one claim "so related to claims in the action within such original jurisdiction that they form part of the same case or controversy under Article III"? For pendent federal question jurisdiction, *Gibbs* has told us the answer:

when there exists a "common nucleus of operative fact" (and, arguably, when we would expect to try the two claims together). Does the same test apply in other circumstances? There are two separate sets of issues here. First, in *Kroger*, the Court declined to hold that the scope of Article III power to hear supplemental diversity cases was as broad as the power *Gibbs* declared in the context of a federal question claim. See *Kroger*, 437 U.S. at 371 n.10 ("The Court of Appeals in the present case believed that the 'common nucleus of operative fact' test also determines the outer boundaries of constitutionally permissible federal jurisdiction when that jurisdiction is based upon diversity of citizenship. We may assume without deciding that the Court of Appeals was correct in this regard."). Second, in *Finley*, the Court likewise refused to hold that the *Gibbs* test applied in the context of pendent party jurisdiction. See *Finley*, 490 U.S. at 549 ("We may assume, without deciding, that the constitutional criterion for pendent-party jurisdiction is analogous to the constitutional criterion for pendent-claim jurisdiction . . . ."). It is therefore possible that the scope of Article III constitutional jurisdiction could vary in each of the six circumstances represented by the following matrix:

LIMIT OF CONSTITUTIONAL POWER

Type of Supplemental Jurisdiction

Claim within Original Jurisdiction		*Pendent*	*Ancillary*	*Pendent Party*
	1331	*Gibbs*	?	?
	1332	?	?	?

Thus far, the Supreme Court has spoken definitively (in *Gibbs*) only about the constitutional limits of § 1331 pendent jurisdiction. See City of Chicago v. International College of Surgeons, — U.S. —, 118 S.Ct. 523 (1997) (re-affirming that "common nucleus of operative fact" test of *Gibbs* governed in § 1367(a) case involving federal question claims and pendent state claims). How would you go about filling in the five remaining boxes? Would you appeal to *Gibbs*'s factors of economy, convenience, and fairness? If so, do they suggest that the same line ("common nucleus of operative fact") should be drawn in each of these circumstances? With respect to cases for which § 1332 forms the basis of original jurisdiction, should notions of federalism temper the considerations of economy, convenience, and fairness, and thus restrict the power of federal courts to exercise supplemental jurisdiction more than *Gibbs* does? (It is tempting to reply that, with respect to § 1332 cases, minimal diversity is the constitutional minimum, so that the intricate problems of deciding the constitutional scope of jurisdiction are inapposite. But that reply begs the fundamental question: How much commonality must the claims of the diverse and non-diverse claimants have in order to permit a court to exercise jurisdiction over both claims?)

For the most part, it appears that the courts are ignoring these intricate constitutional issues and assuming that the *Gibbs* test is the measure of constitutional jurisdiction in all situations. In *Garza*, 807 F. Supp. 1256, an entire family was injured in a car accident. The family members sought to join their tort claims for less than the jurisdictional amount with their father's claim for more than the jurisdictional amount. The court permitted joinder:

> [T]he focus is on whether their claims are so related to the claim of Jack Garza (the claim over which the court has original jurisdiction) as to form part of the same case or controversy within the meaning of Article III.
>
> Under the seminal case of... *Gibbs*, the United States Supreme Court explained that, in the context of federal question jurisdiction, federal claims and state law claims form a single constitutional case if they 'derive from a common nucleus of operative fact'; and in... *Kroger*, the Court accepted the assumption the 'common nucleus of operative fact' test also determines the outer boundaries of constitutionally permissible jurisdiction that is based upon diversity jurisdiction. [807 F. Supp. at 1257.]

See also Rodriguez v. Pacifica of Texas, Inc., 980 F.2d 1014 (5th Cir.) (dicta to same effect), cert. denied, 508 U.S. 956 (1993); H.R. 101-734, 101st Cong., 2d Sess. 29 n.15 ([S]ubsection (a) codifies the scope of supplemental jurisdiction first articulated by the Supreme Court in... *Gibbs*"); *Finley*, 490 U.S. at 549-50 ("In *Zahn*... all of the *claims* would together have amounted to a single 'case' under *Gibbs*.")

Might the fundamental norms which we posit for any judicial system help us to decide how broadly the constitutional grant of jurisdiction should be? Remember that Article III extends only "judicial Power" to the federal courts. Presumably the federal courts could not exercise jurisdiction in a way inconsistent with the fundamental nature of the judiciary. For discussion of the potential normative limits of judicial power, see Part 1.A, *supra*.

9. The potential breadth of § 1367 makes the breadth of the judge's discretionary power under § 1367(c) a critical issue. These are a few of the interpretive issues posed by § 1367(c):

(a) The factors which the Supreme Court singled out in *Gibbs* as relevant to the decision to dismiss a pendent claim are somewhat different than the list of § 1367(c). *Gibbs* seemed to create some hard-and-fast rules requiring (or at least strongly favoring) dismissal in certain circumstances, while § 1367(c) sounds less rigid. Are these distinctions without a difference? See Executive Software North America, Inc. v. United States District Court for the Central District of California, 15 F.3d 1484 (9th Cir. 1994) (§ 1367(c)(4)'s "exceptional circumstances" permitting dismissal are narrower than *Gibbs*'s circumstances of "economy, convenience, fairness, and comity"); Brazinski v. Amoco Petroleum Additives Co., 6 F.3d 1176 (7th Cir. 1993) (§ 1367 "was intended to codify rather than to alter the judge-made principle[ ]... of pendent jurisdiction").

(b) Does § 1367(c) give the district court power to dismiss claims that traditionally fell within the court's ancillary or pendent party jurisdiction? The Supreme Court never determined whether a federal court may apply *Gibbs*-like discretion to dismiss a claim within its ancillary jurisdiction. On its face, § 1367(c) would appear to allow that result to occur.

(c) Can a federal court use § 1367(c) to dismiss an entire case, including the claims which lie within federal jurisdiction? In Bodenner v. Graves, 828 F. Supp. 516 (W.D. Mich. 1993), a plaintiff brought a 29-count complaint, of which 28 counts involved state law claims and the 29th involved violation of the federal Racketer Influenced and Corrupt Organizations (RICO) Act, 18 U.S.C. § 1961 et seq. The RICO claim was well-pleaded, and the plaintiff relied upon the "pendent claim" branch of supplemental jurisdiction for federal jurisdiction over the remainder. The court dismissed the entire case:

> [A] federal court with pendent jurisdiction should normally dismiss state claims without prejudice when it appears that the state issues "substantially predominate" over the federal issues in terms of proof, scope, or comprehensiveness of the remedy sought. . . . Plaintiffs have asserted one claim over which this Court has original jurisdiction and 28 claims over which the Court could exercise supplemental or pendent jurisdiction. I find that plaintiffs' state law claims substantially predominate over the federal claim asserted. For this reason, I dismiss counts 1-27, and count 29 without prejudice.
>
> This is not the end of my inquiry, however, as the Court has also been asked by the defendants to dismiss the RICO claim. The Court must decide whether, having dismissed the 28 of 29 claims, I may also dismiss the alleged federal claim over which the court has original jurisdiction under 28 U.S.C. § 1367. . . .
>
> [T]he Court came across several cases which address the same issue with respect to an analogous statute, 28 U.S.C. § 1441(c). These cases discuss complete dismissal in the situation where a case has been removed from state court to federal court. Section 1441(c) provides that the district court "in its discretion, may remand all matters in which State law predominates." 28 U.S.C. § 1441(c). This language closely mirrors that of § 1367(c)(2) discussed above. The Court therefore believes that reliance on the cases which address complete dismissal under § 1441(c) in the context of § 1367 is advisable. . . .
>
> Under § 1441(c), the Court found numerous cases allowing for a dismissal of the entire case when state law issues predominate. . . .
>
> Moreover, there is authority that stands for the proposition that a case with an inordinate amount of state claims should not be brought in federal court in the first place. The D.C. Circuit has said that "a formal federal cause of action that incorporates state law so as to create an 'overwhelming predominance of state-law issues' may not properly be brought in federal court." Rogers v. Platt, 814 F.2d 683 (D.C.Cir.1987). The Court is aware that this is an exception to the general rule stated by Justice Holmes that "[a] suit arises under the law that creates the cause of action", American Well Works Co. v. Layne and Bowler Co., 241 U.S. 257, 260 (1916). Nonetheless, the Court believes that this case fits the exception. When 28 of 29 causes of action arise under state law, it certainly creates an "overwhelming predominance of state-law issues." [828 F. Supp at 518-19.]

Does a plain reading of § 1367(c) permit this result? See Kabealo v. Davis, 829 F. Supp. 923, 927 (S.D. Ohio 1993) ("there is nothing in the language of § 1367(c) which suggests this authority").

10. Whatever the answer to these interpretive questions, § 1367(c) certainly entrusts judges with a measure of discretionary power to package cases. If the adversarial system is so important to us, why would we ever allow a judge to override the plaintiff's choice of forum? If we give judges the discretionary power to send cases back to state court, should we create another inroad on the "master of the complaint" rule by giving judges the converse power to pull state cases up into federal court when the federal interests are significant enough?

11. Section 1367 was written with a routine case like *Finley* in mind. What is the effect of § 1367 on the aggregation of complex and complicated cases? Probably very little. Section 1367 did nothing to change the basic understanding of § 1331 jurisdiction, and its arguable changes to § 1332 jurisdiction (other than its handling of intervention of right) were either favorable or neutral to federal aggregation. See § 1367(b) (leaving open modifications of the complete diversity rule in circumstances not "inconsistent with the jurisdictional requirements of section 1332"); Rowe et al., *supra*, at 954 ("To whatever extent the federal courts were free before to reinterpret section 1332's 'jurisdictional requirements' to abolish the complete diversity rule for alienage cases, they remain every bit as free to do so today. Section 1367 is neutral on the subject, as it should be."). The concerns of efficiency, fairness, and convenience which underlie § 1367 certainly provide some added weight to the arguments for optimal packaging in instances of lawyer dysfunction and inefficiency, as do the arguable overruling of *Zahn* and the greater discretionary powers which § 1367(c) vests in federal judges.

On the other hand, the limitation on intervention of right is not helpful to the cause of aggregation in complex or complicated cases. Moreover, § 1367 does nothing to remove such major stumbling blocks to optimal packaging as *Merrell Dow*'s gloss on § 1331, the complete diversity gloss of § 1332, and the "master of the complaint" rule. Furthermore, § 1367 could have a pernicious effect on the development of jurisdictional rules to deal with complex and complicated litigation. It could be argued that, because Congress has recently spoken about the extent to which it was willing to expand federal jurisdiction to accomplish the joinder of related cases, there should be no further judicial inroads.

Whatever view of § 1367 ultimately prevails, it should be obvious that the statute was not drafted with the problems of complex litigation in mind. If it had been, it would likely have been narrower in scope but more radical in approach.

d. The Eleventh Amendment

The Eleventh Amendment provides: "The Judicial power of the United States shall not be construed to extend to any suit in law or equity, commenced or prosecuted against one of the United States by Citizens of another State, or by Citizens or Subjects of any Foreign State." Behind these few words lies a rich, inconsistent, and still evolving history. It is not the purpose of this book to lay out, much less to resolve, the many possible meanings of the amendment. (For such a treatment, see Richard H. Fallon et al., Hart and Wechsler's The Federal Courts and the Federal System (4th ed. 1996 & 1998 Supp.).) Instead, we wish to make four basic points.

First, the Eleventh Amendment prevents the federal courts from asserting jurisdiction over some, but not all, cases filed against states. Most significantly, a federal court cannot assert jurisdiction when either (1) a citizen of another state, (2) a citizen of a foreign state, (3) a citizen of the same state, or (4) a foreign state itself sues a state. See Hans v. Louisiana, 134 U.S. 1 (1890); Principality of Monaco v. Mississippi, 292 U.S. 313 (1934). This jurisdictional bar cannot be removed by Congress pursuant to any of its constitutional powers that predate the Eleventh Amendment. Seminole Tribe of Florida v. Florida, 517 U.S. 44 (1996). When Congress authorizes jurisdiction over states pursuant to constitutional powers it received after passage of the Eleventh Amendment (most notably, its Thirteenth and Fourteenth Amendment powers), federal courts can entertain the case. See *Seminole Tribe*, 517 U.S. at 59-66; Fitzpatrick v. Bitzer, 427 U.S. 445 (1976). Congress has rarely invoked this power. See Will v. Michigan Department of State Police, 491 U.S. 58 (1989).

Second, even though suits against states are often precluded, suits against state subdivisions and state officials often are not. Subject to some important limitations, municipalities can be sued in federal court. See Owen v. City of Independence, 445 U.S. 622 (1980); Board of Commissioners of Bryan County v. Brown, 520 U.S. 397 (1997). Claims that seek an injunction or damages against a state or municipal official in his or her individual capacity are not barred. 42 U.S.C. § 1983; see generally Peter W. Low & John C. Jeffries, Jr., Civil Rights Actions 21-112 (2d ed. 1994) (discussing limitations on § 1983 individual capacity suits). Claims that seek prospective relief against such officials for violations of federal law are also, at least in most instances, authorized. Ex Parte Young, 209 U.S. 123 (1908); Edelman v. Jordan, 415 U.S. 651 (1974); *Seminole Tribe*, 517 U.S. at 73-76 (creating exception to *Ex Parte Young*); Idaho v. Coeur d'Alene Tribe of Idaho, 521 U.S. —, 117 S.Ct. 2028 (1997) (creating second exception to *Ex Parte Young*). Suits against state officials that would result in the award of monetary relief from the state as a remedy for past wrongs are not, however, generally permitted. See *Edelman*, 415 U.S. 651; but see Hutto v. Finney, 437 U.S. 678 (1978) (permitting award of monetary relief from state that was "ancillary" to prospective relief).

Third, when a federal claim against a state or state official is permitted, the Eleventh Amendment precludes a federal court from exercising pendent jurisdiction over related state law claims. See Pennhurst State School & Hospital v. Halderman, 465 U.S. 89 (1984).

Fourth, the effect of the Eleventh Amendment in complex and complicated litigation is felt most acutely in a group of cases about which this book has thus far talked very little — cases that are often called, in Professor Chayes's phrase, "public law litigation" (or, if you prefer Professor Fiss's phrase, "structural reform litigation"). The role of the federal courts in such cases is enormously controversial as a social, political, and legal matter, and the Eleventh Amendment question is but one skirmish in the larger legal battle. Because a great deal of structural reform litigation involves claims for injunctive relief, and because different groups of potential parties almost invariably have different interests in the shape of the relief, structural reform litigation raises the central concern of joinder complexity — the inability of a court to fashion a comprehensive and equitable remedy that binds parties and nonparties. See Martin v. Wilks, 490 U.S. 755 (1989) (p. 240, *supra*).

To the extent that the Eleventh Amendment makes impossible the aggregation in one forum of all relevant parties and claims, it operates as a jurisdictional barrier that appears insensitive to the concerns of complex and complicated litigation. How frequently, however, will the Eleventh Amendment have this effect? In virtually all structural reform cases, a state forum with jurisdiction over all claims and parties is available. In cases of insufficient assets, if the state can obtain a disproportionate share of the assets from state proceedings and if a single federal proceeding could have aggregated all cases and resulted in a more equitable distribution of assets, then the Eleventh Amendment has helped to create joinder complexity. But are there many such cases in fact?

In California v. Deep Sea Research, Inc., — U.S. —, 118 S.Ct. 1464 (1998), the Court held that the Eleventh Amendment does not bar a case within the federal courts' *in rem* admiralty jurisdiction when the property in dispute was not in possession of the state. Can *Deep Sea Research* be made to stand for the general principle that a "joinder complexity" exception to the Eleventh Amendment exists when a suit against a state in *federal* court is essential to the equitable distribution of assets? Can this principle then be expanded into an even more general principle that the Eleventh Amendment does not apply when joinder complexity can be avoided only by a suit in *federal* court? Cf. *Couer d'Alene Tribe*, 117 S.Ct. at 2035 (Kennedy, J.) (suggesting that *Ex Parte Young* automatically applied when only federal forum was available to vindicate federal rights). The argument would be that, in order for a federal court to adjudicate the dispute rationally, the presence of the state is necessary; and because rational adjudication is guaranteed against state interference under the Fourteenth Amendment, the federal court is not hampered by the Eleventh Amendment. Would this argument actually permit a federal court to exercise jurisdiction over the state, or merely to enjoin the state from proceeding in the state forum? Would the first solution make the Eleventh Amendment a dead letter in structural reform litigation? Would the second solution deny the federal courts an essential role in the adjudication of disputes arising under federal law?

Whatever the shape of the Eleventh Amendment in complex litigation, is there any argument that an exception to the amendment should be made merely in order to prevent the inefficiencies of complicated litigation?

e. Case or Controversy

Another limitation on federal subject matter jurisdiction is the "case or controversy" requirement of Article III. This requirement has given rise to a number of loosely related doctrines — such as standing, ripeness, mootness, and political question — whose doctrinal limits sometimes extend beyond the constitutional minimum to include a dose of prudential, policy-oriented considerations. As with the Eleventh Amendment, a full explication of these doctrines is beyond the scope of this book. (For a more detailed treatment, see Richard H. Fallon et al., Hart and Wechsler's The Federal Courts and the Federal System (4th ed. 1996 & 1998 Supp.).)

As might be expected, these doctrines receive a healthy workout in structural reform litigation seeking injunctive relief, and often operate to narrow federal court jurisdiction over these cases. The following case, however, is not a structural reform suit. It does, however, discuss many of the precedents that affect the case or controversy inquiry in structural reform cases, and it also introduces us to one of the most pressing and difficult problems facing complex and complicated litigation today

CARLOUGH v. AMCHEM PRODUCTS, INC.

834 F. Supp. 1437 (E.D. Pa. 1993)

■ REED, District Judge. This lawsuit is a class action for asbestos-related personal injuries. This memorandum opinion addresses whether this Court has subject matter jurisdiction over this case.

I. BACKGROUND

On January 15, 1993, counsel for the plaintiff class (or the "Carlough class") filed the complaint in this action along with motions for class certification and for approval of a proposed settlement agreement ("proposed settlement" or "settlement") between the plaintiff class and the defendants. The complaint alleges that the defendants, members of the Center for Claims Resolution ("the CCR defendants"), are liable to the plaintiff class under the legal theories of (1) negligent failure to warn, (2) strict liability, (3) breach of express and implied warranty, (4) negligent infliction of emotional distress, (5) enhanced risk of disease, (6) medical monitoring, and (7) civil conspiracy. In their complaint, the named plaintiffs allege that jurisdiction is based upon diversity of citizenship and that the amount in controversy for each member of the plaintiff class exceeds $100,000.

On the same day as the complaint was filed, the CCR defendants answered the complaint and joined in plaintiffs' request that the class be certified and the settlement agreement approved.

On January 29, 1993, the Honorable Charles R. Weiner of this Court conditionally certified an opt-out class [of persons exposed to asbestos made by CCR defendants, as well as their families. Included in the class were persons who, although they had been exposed to asbestos, were presently healthy. The settlement proposed to compensate these "exposure-only" class members only if they eventually developed certain asbestos-related diseases. Objecting class members raised numerous problems with the settlement, including the issue of standing for these future claimants.]

II. DISCUSSION

A. Standing

It is fundamental that a federal court lacks jurisdiction to hear any matter that is not a justiciable case or controversy under Article III of the U.S. Constitution, and that an action is not justiciable if the plaintiff does not have standing to sue.... The Supreme Court has held that a party has the requisite personal stake if s/he can demonstrate that: (1) s/he personally has suffered a concrete injury in fact, (2) the injury is fairly traceable to the challenged conduct, and (3) the injury is likely to be redressed by a favorable decision. Allen v. Wright, 468 U.S. 737, 751 (1984) (citing Valley Forge Christian College v. Americans United for Separation of Church and State, Inc., 454 U.S. 464, 472 (1982)).

The plaintiff always bears the burden of establishing the elements of standing. Lujan v. Defenders of Wildlife, [504] U.S. [555, 561](1992). . . .

First and foremost, the standing requirement preserves the separation of powers by limiting the matters that the judicial branch may address. . . .

Second, the standing requirement improves judicial decision-making because it "assures a factual setting in which the litigant asserts a claim of injury in fact[.]" *Valley Forge*, 454 U.S. at 472 . . . .

Third, the standing requirement assures that the federal courts do not become "a vehicle for the vindication of the value interests of concerned bystanders." United States v. Students Challenging Regulatory Agency Procedures (SCRAP), 412 U.S. 669, 687 [(1973)]. . . .

In this lawsuit, the objectors claim that many of the members of the *Carlough* class do not have Article III standing because they have not sustained an "injury in fact." The objectors note that the *Carlough* class includes those who have been occupationally exposed to asbestos but who do not manifest any asbestos-related condition (hereinafter "the exposure-only plaintiffs"). And, in their memoranda of law, the objectors point to several state and federal cases which have held that "subclinical injury resulting from exposure to asbestos is insufficient to constitute actual loss or damage to a plaintiff's interest required to sustain a cause of action under generally applicable principles of tort law." Schweitzer v. Consolidated Rail Corp., 758 F.2d 936, 942 (3d Cir.), cert. denied, 474 U.S. 864 (1985) . . . . The objectors argue that the lack of a cause of action under applicable state tort law mandates a finding that the exposure-only plaintiffs have alleged no injury in fact for purposes of Article III standing.[2]

In response, the settling parties argue that exposure to a toxic substance is sufficient injury in fact and that, for purposes of Article III standing, it is irrelevant whether the plaintiffs' injuries support a valid legal claim.

It is true that prior to 1970, the test for Article III standing was the so-called "legal interest" test. . . . Under that test, a plaintiff only had Article III standing "if the actions of the defendant harmed a 'legal interest' of the plaintiff." . . . In other words, plaintiffs had to show injury sufficient to sustain a valid cause of action to have standing to sue in federal court.

In Association of Data Processing Service Organizations, Inc. v. Camp, 397 U.S. 150 (1970), however, the Supreme Court jettisoned the "legal interest" test and adopted the "injury in fact" test. According to the Supreme Court in *Camp*, "[t]he 'legal interest' test goes to the merits" and is thus "quite distinct from the problem of standing." Id. at 152-53 & n. 1.

---

2. The objectors concede, and I agree, that those members of the plaintiff class who already manifest an asbestos-related condition have Article III standing to bring this lawsuit.

... In the years since the *Camp* decision, the Supreme Court has stressed that the requirement of standing "focuses on the party seeking to get his [or her] complaint before a federal court and *not on the issues [s/]he wishes to have adjudicated.*" *Valley Forge*, 454 U.S. at 484 (quoting Flast v. Cohen, 392 U.S. 83, 99 (1968) (emphasis added)). . . .

Going beyond the case law, it is easy to understand the logic behind the change from the "legal interest" test to the "injury in fact" test. If federal courts must look to whether plaintiffs in federal court under diversity jurisdiction have stated a valid cause of action in order to find that they have standing to sue in federal court, state law and not federal law would control the scope of Article III standing. Indeed, the same factual injury might be sufficient to confer standing in the federal courts of one state but not in the federal courts of another. Federal standing law, therefore, would not only depend on state law, it would vary from state to state. Because standing is a question of federal constitutional law, . . . such a lack of uniformity would be undesirable. Also, if a plaintiff had to show a valid cause of action to confer Article III jurisdiction, federal courts could never entertain diversity cases where the existence of the asserted claim under state law was unclear. This is so because standing to sue must clearly exist before a federal court is permitted to reach the merits of a case. Of course, federal courts are often called upon to decide unsettled issues of state law. . . .

Therefore, I conclude that the applicable legal precedent requires that the question of whether the exposure-only plaintiffs have standing to bring this lawsuit in federal court does not depend on whether they have stated a valid cause of action under applicable tort law. The standing analysis does not end here, however. I must still determine whether, pursuant to federal precedent, the harm alleged by the exposure-only plaintiffs, namely exposure to asbestos, constitutes injury in fact which is fairly traceable to the defendants' conduct and is likely to be redressed by a favorable decision.

1. *Injury in Fact*

To satisfy the first requirement of standing, the exposure-only plaintiffs must demonstrate that they have suffered an injury in fact which is concrete and particularized, and actual or imminent rather than merely conjectural or hypothetical. . . . By this the Supreme Court means "that the injury must affect the plaintiff in a personal and individual way." *Lujan*, [504] U.S. at [560] n.1. Put another way, "an interest need only be expressible in terms of the individual[ ]'s satisfaction or experiences; but such satisfaction or experiences need not be unique to the litigant." L. Tribe, American Constitutional Law § 3-16, at 117 (2d ed. 1988) (emphasis omitted).

The severity of the injury is immaterial. The Supreme Court and the Court of Appeals for the Third Circuit have explained that "[t]hese injuries need not be large, an 'identifiable trifle' will suffice." Public Interest Research Group, Inc. v. Powell Duffryn Terminals Inc., 913 F.2d 64, 71 (3d Cir. 1990) (quoting [*SCRAP*, 412 U.S. at 689 n.14]), cert. denied, 498 U.S. 1109 (1991). Indeed, other kinds of non-economic harm have been accepted as Article III injury in fact, including aesthetic harm and emotional distress. Sierra Club v. Morton, 405 U.S. 727, 734-41 (1972) . . . .

In Duke Power [Co. v. Carolina Environmental Study Group, Inc., 438 U.S. 59 (1978)], the Supreme Court addressed the issue of whether exposure to a toxin is sufficient to confer Article III standing. In that case, the plaintiffs claimed that the future exposure to radiation from two nuclear power plants under construction constituted injury in fact entitling them to challenge the constitutionality of a statute which limited the liability for accidents at nuclear power plants. At the time the suit was brought, the plants were still under construction, and, therefore, plaintiffs had sustained no radiation-related diseases as a result of future emissions. The district court found "immediate" injury to the plaintiffs in "the production of small quantities of non-natural radiation which would invade the air and water" and "a 'sharp increase' in the temperature of two lakes presently used for recreational purposes. . . ." *Duke Power*, 438 U.S. at 73-74. The Supreme Court agreed that each of these effects constituted injury in fact for purposes of Article III standing analysis: It is enough that several of the "immediate" adverse effects were found to harm appellees. Certainly the environmental and aesthetic consequences of the thermal pollution of the two lakes in the vicinity of the disputed power plants is the type of harmful effect which has been deemed adequate in prior cases to satisfy the "injury in fact" standard. . . .

[E]xposure to a toxic substance constitutes sufficient injury in fact to give a plaintiff standing to sue in federal court. The objectors do not dispute, nor could they, that asbestos is a toxin. . . . In this case, the class consists of persons who have been exposed to asbestos either occupationally or through the occupational exposure of a spouse or household member. Accordingly, by definition, each class member sues on the basis of actual exposure and not future exposure to asbestos. Without more, the exposure-only plaintiffs have alleged sufficient injury in fact.

Apart from the authority dealing with exposure to a toxin as Article III injury in fact, I conclude that the available medical data on the health consequences of exposure to asbestos also require a conclusion that the exposure-only plaintiffs have alleged a demonstrable physical injury which satisfies the Article III injury in fact requirement. . . .

[T]he weight of recognized medical research on asbestos-related diseases shows that exposure to asbestos causes immediate cellular changes. And, only those who have been exposed to asbestos are members of the plaintiff class. They have been personally affected by defendants' conduct in a concrete and particular way whether or not they ever develop a serious medical condition. This is exactly the type of personal stake the Article III injury-in-fact requirement demands. Therefore, I conclude that the exposure-only plaintiffs have alleged Article III injury in fact.

2. *Traceability*

The second requirement of standing is that the plaintiff show that there is some causal connection between the injury and the conduct complained of, *i.e.*, the injury has to be fairly traceable to the challenged action of the defendants and not the result of the independent action of some third party. *Lujan*, [504] U.S. at [560-61].

In their complaint, plaintiffs allege that their injuries are the proximate result of exposure to the CCR defendants' asbestos products. It is clear that they have been exposed to asbestos, and it is clear that the CCR defendants manufactured asbestos and asbestos-containing products. Therefore, I conclude that plaintiffs have shown, for purposes of Article III standing, that their injuries are fairly traceable to the defendants' conduct.

3. *Redressability*

To satisfy the final requirement of standing, a federal plaintiff must show that his or her injury is likely to be redressed by a favorable decision. Lujan, [504] U.S. at [561]. Because of this requirement, "the form of relief sought is often critical in determining whether the plaintiff has standing." Brown v. Fauver, 819 F.2d 395, 400 (3d Cir. 1987).

The redressability requirement has been problematic only in cases requesting declaratory or injunctive relief. . . .

[I]n Warth v. Seldin, 422 U.S. 490 (1975), several plaintiffs challenged the constitutionality of a suburb's exclusionary zoning practices. They claimed that the zoning practices prevented construction of multifamily dwellings and low-income housing and, therefore, effectively excluded them from the neighborhood. The Supreme Court held that these plaintiffs lacked standing because they could not demonstrate that appropriate housing would be constructed without the exclusionary zoning ordinances. The Court felt that overturning the zoning ordinances would not guarantee that builders would choose to construct new housing in the area, or that low-income residents would be able to afford to live there. . . .

In this case, it is self-evident that the very conventional remedy sought by the plaintiffs — money damages — would do much to redress their injuries. Unlike claims for injunctive or declaratory relief, as in the above-cited cases, "[a] damage claim, by definition, presents a means to redress an injury." Cardenas v. Smith, 733 F.2d 909, 914 (D.C.Cir. 1984). Therefore, I conclude that the exposure-only plaintiffs have shown that their injuries are likely to be redressed by the relief requested in their complaint.

4. *Conclusion*

The exposure-only plaintiffs have satisfied the three requirements of Article III standing. Beyond that, a reexamination of the policies served by the standing requirement convinces me of the propriety of this finding. . . . First, this is not a case where the courts are being "called upon to decide abstract questions of wide public significance . . . [.]" *Warth*, 422 U.S. at 500. Here, the plaintiffs have particular, concrete and individual claims of injury. That there are many victims of asbestos does not change the individual and personal stake each plaintiff has in the outcome of this litigation. Judicial intervention is, therefore, appropriate and necessary.

Second, this case provides the type of factual setting which is necessary for judicial review to be effective. Because the claims of the exposure-only plaintiffs are based on their personal experiences and involve particularized concrete injuries, there is no risk of ruling on an ill-defined or abstract controversy.

Finally, the exposure-only plaintiffs have been directly affected by the CCR defendants' conduct. They are not merely concerned bystanders. Therefore, this case serves the Article III policy of reserving the federal courts for parties whose lives will be directly affected by the outcome of specific litigation. . . .

I conclude, therefore, that the exposure-only plaintiffs have Article III standing to bring this suit. . . .

C. Collusion

Because of the "case or controversy" requirement in Article III, "federal courts will not entertain friendly suits, or those which are feigned or collusive in nature." *Flast*, 392 U.S. at 100. The Constitution demands a "honest and actual antagonistic assertion of rights." United States v. Johnson, 319 U.S. 302, 305 (1943) . . . . "[I]f two litigants commence a suit with the same goals in mind, no controversy exists to give the district court jurisdiction[.]" Pennsylvania Ass'n for Retarded Children v. Pennsylvania, 343 F. Supp. 279, 290 (E.D. Pa. 1972).

The objectors argue that this class action is collusive, or "friendly," because (1) the complaint and the proposed settlement were filed simultaneously, and (2) a provision of the proposed settlement provides that the CCR defendants will pay class counsel's fees. . . .

The settling parties do not dispute that this class action was settled before the complaint was filed. They claim, however, that the CCR defendants, as asbestos manufacturers, and the plaintiffs, as asbestos victims, have diametrically opposed legal interests in this lawsuit just as they have throughout the twenty-year history of asbestos litigation. The settling parties claim, and the objectors do not dispute, that the negotiations leading to the proposed settlement were long, arduous, complex and arms-length. This type of controversy, the settling parties argue, is the opposite of the type banned from the federal courts for lack of a genuine dispute. . . .

Looking to the nature of the controversy, and not the timing of the settlement agreement, it is clear that the plaintiffs and the CCR defendants are true adversaries. The proposed settlement simply represents a compromise of a genuine dispute. . . . [T]he settlement[ ] [was] reached only after long negotiations.

I conclude that this case is one involving genuinely adverse interests, but, because of the settlement, it lacks a dispute as to the remedy. I conclude, therefore, that the simultaneous filing of the complaint and the proposed settlement does not require a conclusion that the case is collusive or lacks a genuine dispute. A contrary rule would unwisely discourage pre-litigation negotiations and, by encouraging parties to wait an "appropriate" period of time after filing suit to file a proposed settlement, elevate form over substance.

The objectors' second collusion argument is that the CCR defendants' agreement in the settlement to pay class counsel's fees is evidence that this lawsuit is "friendly." A review of class action cases, however, quickly reveals that such agreements are standard practice. . . . Because in those cases, as in this case, the amount of class counsel's fees is to be fixed by the court, the fee agreements do not support an allegation of collusion. . . .

D. Mootness

To satisfy the Article III case or controversy requirement, the parties must not only present a "honest and actual antagonistic assertion of rights," *Johnson*, 319 U.S. at 305 but the controversy must continue to exist at all stages of the federal proceedings. If events subsequent to the filing of the complaint resolve the dispute, the case should be dismissed as moot. United States Parole Com. v. Geraghty, 445 U.S. 388, 397 (1980). Generally, if the parties reach a settlement, the case is no longer justiciable as an Article III controversy. There is, however, an exception to this rule: a case does not become moot when the parties reach a *proposed* settlement that is contingent on the approval of the court. Havens Realty Corp. v. Coleman, 455 U.S. 363, 371 n.10 (1982)]; Coopers & Lybrand v. Livesay, 437 U.S. 463, 465 n.3 (1978). And, as discussed above in the context of collusion, a class action settlement requires judicial approval pursuant to Rule 23 to be binding on the class members. Thus, the objectors' first argument, that the proposed settlement moots the case, is without merit.

The objectors also argue, however, that certain "side agreements" between class counsel and the CCR defendants effectively settle the claims of the named or representative plaintiffs. The objectors claim that because of these side agreements, the individual claims of the named plaintiffs and the entire class action are moot.

The objectors point to the existence of certain side agreements between the CCR defendants and various law firms who represent asbestos victims, including class counsel, as requiring a finding that this lawsuit is moot. . . . The agreements are an attempt by the CCR defendants to provide an alternative dispute resolution ("ADR") procedure with respect to future asbestos claims in the event that the proposed settlement in this case fails to be approved and implemented. Under the terms of the side agreements, the signatory law firms will recommend to their future asbestos clients that they defer filing suit against the CCR defendants until any asbestos-related disease is manifested. By deferring their claims, these clients would be accepting the criteria in the CCR defendants' ADR procedure which is virtually identical to the criteria in the proposed settlement. The clients are free to reject the recommendation of counsel, however, and sue the CCR defendants at any time. . . .

The objectors claim that these side agreements require dismissal of this class action as moot under the recent Third Circuit case of Lusardi v. Xerox Corp., 975 F.2d 964, 983 (3d Cir.1992). In *Lusardi*, former employees brought an age discrimination class action case against their employer. After the case was filed and while no class certification motion was yet pending, the named plaintiffs fully and unconditionally settled their own claims against their employer. The claims of the rest of the putative class remained unsettled, and the named plaintiffs wished to reserve their right to act as class representatives. The Third Circuit held that because the named plaintiffs settled their claims before class certification, the class action was moot. . . .

The objectors claim that, as in *Lusardi*, the named plaintiffs in this case have, through the existence of the side agreements, effectively settled their claims against the CCR defendants whether or not the proposed settlement is approved. This statement is factually untrue. The side agreements do not settle any claims with any asbestos victims. The side agreements only bind the signatory law firms, not their individual clients. Thus, in the event that the proposed settlement is not approved, the claims of the named plaintiffs are not settled. They, and all future asbestos claimants, remain free to sue the CCR defendants, and the various signatory law firms can still represent them in their suit. Therefore, *Lusardi* is inapplicable here because, unlike the named plaintiffs in that case, the named plaintiffs in this class action have not definitively settled their claims.

I conclude, therefore, that this class action is not moot.

Notes and Questions

1. *Carlough* was filed as a settlement class action; the parties never intended to litigate the case. The CCR defendants were interested in the settlement only if they could buy total peace from both present and future claims; a settlement that resolved present claims but left them exposed to future claims was not especially useful. The real issue in *Carlough*, therefore, was whether the various case or controversy doctrines would get in the way of the parties' efforts to settle. At one level, it is tempting to say that, since the parties had agreed to settle a large number of cases that would otherwise clog the docket, these doctrines should get a light review. At another level, however, the case was being settled on a class action basis, and resolved the claims of healthy people who had no present compelling reason to give serious consideration to their legal rights. To the extent that this fact should make us cautious about this type of settlement, standing and other doctrines were gatekeepers that limited the settlement class action. Once again, we see that a doctrine created with a very different type of case in mind is being used by parties to accomplish litigation or policy objectives that bear little relation to the reasons that the doctrine exists.

2. The district court in *Carlough* eventually certified the class action and approved the settlement. Georgine v. Amchem Products, Inc., 157 F.R.D. 246 (E.D. Pa. 1994). The Third Circuit reversed the order of class certification, Georgine v. Amchem Products, Inc., 83 F.3d 610 (3d Cir. 1996), and, in a decision we will encounter later, the Supreme Court affirmed that reversal. See Amchem Products, Inc., v. Windsor, — U.S. —, 117 S.Ct. 2231 (1997) (p. 670, *infra*). In both the court of appeals and the Supreme Court, the objectors continued to press their case or controversy arguments, and in the Supreme Court they

explicitly added a ripeness argument — that the claims of future plaintiffs were not yet ripe for judicial action. *Amchem*, 117 S.Ct. at 2244. Neither the court of appeals nor the Supreme Court ruled on the case or controversy issues, although both were troubled by them. The Third Circuit thought that the case or controversy issue "was not free from doubt." *Georgine*, 83 F.3d at 623. The Supreme Court noted the Third Circuit's reservations, and also stated that, in its own decision on the class certification issue, it was "mindful that Rule 23's requirements must be interpreted in keeping with Article III constraints." *Amchem*, 117 S.Ct. at 2242, 2244.

3. Standing, ripeness, and mootness address somewhat different constitutional concerns. Ripeness requires that the case or controversy have sufficiently matured to justify judicial review. Mootness presents the opposite problem: The case or controversy have so far matured that no live dispute exists any longer. Standing presumes that the case or controversy is neither too young nor too old; rather, it concerns the question about whether a particular person has a sufficient interest in the outcome to justify allowing that specific person to be a party in the case.

Another case or controversy doctrine — the political question doctrine — requires that courts not assert jurisdiction over certain subject areas that are deemed not to be appropriate for judicial review. Collusion, which *Carlough* also discusses, is the least invoked of the case or controversy requirements; it insists upon a live dispute between the plaintiff and the defendant involved in the case. In all but the rarest cases, collusion is not an issue.

As a general matter, the Supreme Court loosened the case or controversy doctrines (especially standing, ripeness, and mootness) during the 1960's and 1970's, and has been tightening them up in more recent years. See generally Erwin Chemerinsky, Federal Jurisdiction 53-166 (2d ed. 1994). For some recent cases, see Federal Election Commission v. Akins, — U.S. —, 118 S.Ct. 1777 (1998) (standing); Ohio Forestry Association, Inc., v. Sierra Club, — U.S. —, 118 S.Ct. 1665 (1998) (ripeness); Steel Co. v. Citizens for a Better Environment, — U.S. —, 118 S.Ct. 1003 (1998) (standing); Spencer v. Kemna, — U.S. —, 118 S.Ct. 978 (1998) (mootness); Raines v. Byrd, — U.S. —, 117 S.Ct. 2312 (1997) (standing). In *Steel Co.*, the Court held that questions of Article III jurisdiction must be decided before a court proceeds to the merits; a court cannot avoid a difficult case or controversy question by ruling on a matter of substantive law.

There is, however, one exception to the general tightening up of case or controversy doctrines. The Supreme Court has maintained its earlier rulings that a class action (whether or not certified) does not become moot when the cases of the class representatives settle or are dismissed. See Sosna v. Iowa, 419 U.S. 393 (1975); Franks v. Bowman Transportation Co., 424 U.S. 747 (1976); United States Parole Commission v. Geraghty, 445 U.S. 388 (1980).

4. In a general way, all the justiciability doctrines reflect an effort to assure the existence of a dispute that is capable of judicial resolution. The standing and collusion doctrines support this effort by assuring that the parties in the litigation have a strong adversary relationship and will therefore present the court with the proofs and arguments upon which to base a decision. If we did not have an adversary system, would we have standing and collusion doctrines, and if so, what would they look like? Indeed, throughout this book we have seen (and will continue to see) that, in the subset of cases we call "complex," an unfettered adversary system cannot guarantee for all persons the sort of rational adjudication upon which our judicial system is grounded. In the subset of cases

we call "complicated," an unfettered adversary system can guarantee rational adjudication, but only at the high price of wasteful re-litigation. If standing and collusion doctrines are indeed premised on a well-functioning adversarial system, should those doctrines change to account for complex cases? For complicated cases? How? Can the outcome in *Carlough* be defended on the theory that the insufficiency of the CCR defendants' assets made the case complex, and the ordinary doctrines of standing, collusion, ripeness, and mootness needed to be loosened in order to accommodate a settlement that treated all plaintiffs equitably?

Note that this rationale makes the justiciability doctrines work together with the concerns of complex litigation, rather than at cross purposes to them. Note as well that this rationale depends on the settlement's equitable treatment of all parties and nonparties. Whether that in fact occurred in the *Carlough* settlement is debatable. See p. 670, *infra*; Jay Tidmarsh, Mass Tort Settlement Class Actions 47-58 (1998). If the settlement was not equitable, then the district court may have decided the standing, collusion, and mootness issues incorrectly. Should the constitutional issue of "case or controversy" hinge on the way in which the parties are treated?

One response to the argument that case or controversy doctrines should be interpreted with complexity in mind is that the meaning of foundational constitutional doctrines should not depend on such subtleties. Given the plethora of constitutional balancing tests, it may be difficult to press this point too hard; in any event, the due process overtones of lawyer dysfunction may provide the constitutional counterweight that forces a nuanced look at the meaning of the case or controversy requirement in complex litigation. A second response is that the Court's recent retreat from a broad understanding of case or controversy has occurred in cases that would typically be regarded as structural reform or public law litigation. Injunctive claims present a classic circumstance of lawyer dysfunction, and the Court's willingness to cut back on the case or controversy requirement in these cases might suggest that complexity is not a relevant variable in the Court's mind. Indeed, it is difficult, in reading the Court's recent decisions, to see a role for complexity in the case or controversy analysis. On the other hand, none of these cases really presented the Court with the opportunity to consider the issue. Unlike *Carlough*, the "typical" public law plaintiff does not seek to join all nonparties that might be affected adversely by the remedy the plaintiff seeks. When complete joinder is not achieved, there is little reason to stretch the case or controversy doctrines merely to permit one adversary a tactical advantage in relation to nonparties.

2. Overcoming the Basic Rules to Aggregate Cases in a Single Court System

Although plaintiffs, as masters of the complaint, have great power to tailor the claims and parties to obtain the court system of their choice, their choice of forum has never been sacrosanct. Certain rules permit defendants (or, more rarely, the court) to change the plaintiffs' chosen court system. As a practical matter, forum-changing rules can be divided into two types. First, there are rules which effect the transfer of a case from one court system to another. Second, there are rules that require one court system (whether state or federal) to stay its hand in favor of a case filed in the other system (whether federal or state). This second category of doctrines can be further subdivided into two types of stays: stays in which one court orders that persons not proceed with a case in the other system, and stays in which the court decides to stay itself in favor of a proceeding in the other system.

In this section of the materials, we examine each type of structural rule in turn. We explore the circumstances under which changes of court system are presently possible, as well as the limitations of these rules. In particular, we focus on the ways in which these rules can be used either to overcome non-optimal, dysfunction- or inefficiency-causing forum choices of plaintiffs or, conversely, to undo the optimal, dysfunction- or inefficiency-eliminating choices of plaintiffs.

For the most part, these rules will be invoked by defendants. Since our present jurisdictional and venue rules can create dysfunction or inefficiency when plaintiffs are entrusted with the forum choice, you might think that rules that permit defendants to change the plaintiffs' initial choice are a good solution to the problem. But defendants are no more altruistic than plaintiffs; forums which are desirable to plaintiffs are typically undesirable to defendants, and defendants' interests are primarily in changing the forum to another forum in which the tactical advantages for plaintiffs are smaller. Thus, defendants will try to eliminate lawyer dysfunction or inefficiency when it suits their interests, and they will suffer the consequences of lawyer dysfunction or inefficiency when it does not.

As you study the following materials, consider whether the rules which allow changes to plaintiffs' forum choices are adequately sensitive to the needs of complex or complicated litigation, whether further changes might be necessary to make them more sensitive, and whether judges, acting *sua sponte*, should be permitted to manipulate these rules in order to reduce or avoid joinder complexity. Consider as well whether an adversarial system, when joined with jurisdictional and venue rules that permit each side to jockey for tactical advantage, is ever capable of resolving the problems of complex and complicated litigation; what advantages attach to giving judges more power to override the parties' jurisdictional chess match; whether those advantages outweigh the reasons that we have an adversarial system in the first place; and whether we should maintain a different, less adversarial system just for complex and complicated cases.

a. Removal Jurisdiction

Since state and federal courts have concurrent jurisdiction in many diversity and federal question cases, a plaintiff typically can file in state court a case that also lies within the subject matter jurisdiction of the federal courts. Under certain circumstances, Congress has authorized defendants to remove such cases to federal court. The basic rules of removal jurisdiction can be found in 28 U.S.C. §§ 1441-52; other, more specialized rules authorizing or withdrawing the right of removal can be found throughout the United States Code. See American Law Institute, Study of the Division of Jurisdiction between State and Federal Courts, Appendix C, 479-81 (1969) (discussing specific removal provisions). Although removal jurisdiction is not specifically mentioned in Article III, its constitutionality seems beyond doubt. See Tennessee v. Davis, 100 U.S. (10 Otto) 257 (1880).

As a general matter, federal courts have only the jurisdiction on removal which they would have had if the case had initially been filed in federal court. Thus, removal jurisdiction is determined by the allegations of the plaintiffs' well-pleaded complaint, not by the ancillary claims involved in the case. See 14A Charles A. Wright et al., Federal Practice & Procedure § 3731 (1985). It is fairly well settled that only defendants can remove an action to federal court; unless special statutory authority exists, neither third party defendants nor plaintiffs (even plaintiffs who become counterclaim defendants) may remove a case. Shamrock Oil & Gas Corp. v. Sheets, 313 U.S. 100 (1941). In terms of "removability," an important difference exists between federal question and diversity cases. A federal question case can be removed "without regard to the citizenship or residence of the parties." 28 U.S.C. § 1441(b). "Any other action" — in particular, a diversity claim — is removable only if none of the proper defendants "is a citizen of the State in which such action is brought." Id.

The process of removal begins when the defendant(s) file a petition for removal in the federal district court which "embraces the place where such action is pending." 28 U.S.C. § 1441(a). Unless special statutory authority exists, the petition must be signed by all defendants in a multiple defendant case. The petition for removal must be filed within 30 days of the date on which the defendant(s) first receive a pleading demonstrating that the action is removable; moreover, in a case removed under § 1332, no removal petition may be filed more than one year after the action is commenced. 28 U.S.C. § 1446(b). Upon the filing of the petition, the case is automatically transferred, and no further state proceedings are valid.

Plaintiffs who believe that the case was improperly removed have 30 days within which to file a petition for remand. 28 U.S.C. § 1447(c). Should the federal court determine that the case was improperly removed, it must remand the entire action to state court; an exception to that rule is § 1441(c), which allows a judge to remand just those portions of the case in which "State law predominates."

The following materials explore some of the specific issues that surround the process of removal and remand in complex and complicated litigation.

IN RE GENERAL MOTORS CORP. PICKUP TRUCK FUEL TANK PRODUCTS LIABILITY LITIGATION

1993 WL 147245 (E.D.Pa.)

■ YOHN, District Judge. This purported class action suit was transferred to this court from the United States District Court for the Eastern District of Tennessee as part of the multidistrict litigation involving General Motor's ("GM") side-mounted fuel tank designs on its 1973 to 1987 model year full size pickup trucks. . . .

BACKGROUND

The plaintiff commenced this action by filing a class action complaint in the Circuit Court of Cocke County, Tennessee on January 21, 1993. The plaintiff, who allegedly purchased a 1987 Chevrolet pickup truck, asserts that GM's side-mounted fuel tank designs on its 1973 to 1987 full size pickup trucks are defective. This complaint stated several causes of action under Tennessee state contract and consumer law. The plaintiff's complaint sought both compensatory and punitive damages.

The defendant removed this action to Eastern District of Tennessee on January 28, 1993 pursuant to 28 U.S.C. § 1441. The basis of removal was diversity jurisdiction. Diversity jurisdiction existed since the plaintiff and the defendant were diverse citizens and the amount in controversy exceeded $50,000.[1]

On March 5, 1993, the plaintiff filed an amended complaint in the Eastern District of Tennessee. This amended complaint deleted the request for punitive damages. The amended complaint also specifically limited each plaintiff's demand for damages to less than $5,000.

On March 25, 1993, this action was transferred to this court by an order from the judicial panel on multidistrict litigation. The plaintiff now seeks to have this court remand this case to the Tennessee state court where the action was initially filed.

DISCUSSION

When ruling on whether an action should be remanded from federal court to the state court from which it was removed, the federal district court must focus on the plaintiff's complaint as it existed at the time the removal petition was filed. . . . In this instance, the plaintiff does not dispute that punitive damages were part of the complaint when the removal petition was filed. The plaintiff also does not dispute that the defendant properly removed this action to federal court because of diversity jurisdiction.

---

1. In a class action suit, diversity of citizenship is determined only by the citizenship of the named representatives. Snyder v. Harris, 394 U.S. 332, 340 (1969). In the present action, the plaintiff does not dispute that diversity of citizenship exists among the parties. As for the jurisdictional amount, the plaintiff's complaint controls if the amount claimed is made in good faith. St. Paul Mercury Indemnity Co. v. Red Cab Co., 303 U.S. 283, 288 (1938). To justify dismissal or remand, it must appear to a legal certainty that the claim is really for less than the jurisdictional amount. Id. at 592. In this instance, the court cannot say to a legal certainty that the total award will not yield more than $50,000 to each successful claimant. Also, this claim for punitive damages could possibly be aggregated to arrive at the jurisdictional amount in that the multiple parties have united to vindicate a common interest against the defendant. Pinel v. Pinel, 240 U.S. 594 (1916); Berman v. Narragansett Racing Association, 414 F.2d 311 (1st Cir.1969).

When a suit is properly removed because of diversity jurisdiction, "events occurring subsequent to removal which reduce the amount recoverable, whether beyond the plaintiff's control or the result of his volition, do not oust the district court's jurisdiction once it has attached." St. Paul Mercury Indemnity Co. v. Red Cab Co., 303 U.S. 283, 293 (1938). In *St. Paul*, the defendant removed a diversity case to federal court. The plaintiff later reduced the amount of damages claimed to a figure below the jurisdictional amount. The *St. Paul* court held that the district court continued to have diversity jurisdiction over the case and that the court could not relinquish control over the case either through dismissal or remand. *St. Paul*, 303 U.S. at 296. The rationale for this opinion was that "[I]f the plaintiff could, no matter how bona fide his original claim in the state court reduce the amount of his demand to defeat federal jurisdiction the defendant's supposed statutory right of removal would be subject to the plaintiff's caprice." *St. Paul*, 303 U.S. at 294.

In this instance, the plaintiffs filed their amended complaint deleting the request for punitive damages after the removal petition was filed. Thus, this court concludes that the plaintiff's amended complaint does not defeat diversity jurisdiction.

The plaintiff asserts that even though the defendant's removal was proper, the court can exercise its discretion and remand the action because the amended complaint reduced the dollar amount below that required for diversity jurisdiction. The plaintiff primarily relies on Carnegie-Mellon University v. Cohill, 484 U.S. 343 (1988) to support his position. The court finds that *Cohill* does not support the plaintiff's position.

Cohill involved an action initially instituted in state court that contained both federal and state law claims. The defendant removed the action to federal court based on federal question jurisdiction. The federal court exercised the doctrine of pendent jurisdiction over the state law claims. Sometime after the proper removal of this action to federal court, the plaintiffs dropped all of the federal claims from the lawsuit. The district court then remanded the action to state court. The *Cohill* court upheld the remand.

The *Cohill* decision limited its inquiry to actions removed pursuant to federal question jurisdiction that also involved pendent state law claims. As the *Cohill* court stated, it granted certiorari "to resolve the split among the Circuits as to whether a district court has discretion to remand a removed case to state court when all federal-law claims have dropped out of the action and only pendent state-law claims remain." *Cohill*, 484 U.S. at 348. *Cohill* found that pendent jurisdiction, unlike diversity jurisdiction, is a doctrine of discretion. Id. at 350. Thus, the *Cohill* court held that a district court could exercise its discretion and remand the case to state court even though not specified in the federal statutes authorizing remand.

The *Cohill* court also showed that its holding was limited to federal question removal cases that included pendent state law claims by distinguishing its earlier decisions in Thermtron Products, Inc. v. Hermansdorfer, 423 U.S. 336 (1976), and St. Paul Mercury Indemnity Co. v. Red Cab Co., *supra*. Both of these cases involved attempts to remand cases that were removed based on diversity jurisdiction. *Cohill* stated that those two cases were correct in not being remanded since diversity jurisdiction "is not discretionary" and thus remand would have been impermissible. *Cohill*, 484 U.S. at 356-57. Therefore, since the basis for removing this action was diversity jurisdiction, which is not discretionary, the court will not and cannot exercise its discretion and remand this action to state court.

PEOPLE OF THE STATE OF CALIFORNIA v. KEATING

986 F.2d 346 (9th Cir. 1993)

■ O'SCANNLAIN, Circuit Judge. We consider whether impleading the Resolution Trust Corporation ("RTC") in a state court proceeding gives defendants the right to remove a complaint containing only state law claims to federal court.

I

On July 30, 1990, the California Attorney General filed a consumer fraud action in California state court against various former officers and directors of American Continental Corporation ("ACC") (collectively, "the Keating defendants"), the accounting firm of Arthur Young and Associates ("AY") and several former AY partners (now partners of Ernst and Young) (collectively, "the AY defendants"). The first amended complaint stated five causes of action, alleging that the Keating defendants and the AY defendants had engaged in unfair and fraudulent business practices in violation of the Unfair Business Practices Act, Cal.Bus. & Prof.Code § 17200, had produced and disseminated false and misleading financial statements to buyers of ACC's subordinate debentures in violation of section 17500, and had conspired to engage in unlawful business practices.

On November 28, 1990, defendant AY partner Frank O'Brien filed a third-party complaint in the state court action for equitable indemnity against the RTC, the successor in interest to Lincoln Savings and Loan. On November 29, 1990, all of the defendants filed a Notice of Removal, and the matter was removed to the U.S. District Court for the Central District of California. The matter was then transferred to the District of Arizona whereupon the Attorney General filed a motion to remand, and in the alternative, a motion to sever and to remand. The Attorney General also filed a motion to dismiss the third-party complaint against the RTC. The AY defendants filed a motion to dismiss the Attorney General's complaint for failure to state a claim.

The district court exercised removal jurisdiction over the entire case, denying all of the Attorney General's motions. The court then granted the AY defendants' Rule 12(b)(6) motion and dismissed the complaint against all defendants. . . .

II . . .

Here, when the complaint was originally filed, there was no federal jurisdiction. All claims in the complaint were brought under state law; federal law is not a component of any of them. Thus, under the well-pleaded complaint rule, the Attorney General could not have brought the complaint in federal court. See Franchise Tax Bd. v. Construction Laborers Vacation Trust, 463 U.S. 1, 9-11 (1983).

Nevertheless, the addition of the RTC as a party transforms the entire action into one that "arises under" the laws of the United States. The jurisdictional provision of Financial Institutions Reform, Recovery and Enforcement Act of 1989 ("FIRREA"), 12 U.S.C. § 1441a(*l*)(1) provides:

> Notwithstanding any other provision of law, any civil action, suit, or proceeding to which the [RTC] is a party shall be deemed to arise under the laws of the United States, and the United States district courts shall have original jurisdiction over such action, suit, or proceeding.

The words "action, suit, or proceeding" are not limited to specific claims, but are synonymous with the term "case" in the constitutional sense. . . . Here, the Attorney General's claims and the third-party complaint for indemnification are part of the same case, and the RTC is a party to the action. Thus, once the RTC was added, the entire suit was transformed into one that "arose under" federal law. . . .

Not surprisingly, the appellees argue that because the entire suit "arose under" federal law once the RTC was impleaded, they, as defendants, have the right to remove. However, when an event occurring after the filing of a complaint gives rise to federal jurisdiction, the ability of a defendant to remove is not automatic; instead, removability is governed by the "voluntary/involuntary rule." See Self v. General Motors, 588 F.2d 655, 657-60 (9th Cir.1978) . . . . The rule provides that a suit which, at the time of filing, could not have been brought in federal court must "remain in state court unless a 'voluntary' act of the plaintiff brings about a change that renders the case removable." *Self*, 588 F.2d at 657. As the Supreme Court has stated:

> The obvious principle of [the decisions developing the voluntary/involuntary rule] is that, in the absence of a fraudulent purpose to defeat removal, the plaintiff may by the allegations of his complaint determine the status with respect to removability of a case . . . and that this power to determine the removability of his case continues with the plaintiff throughout the litigation, so that whether such a case nonremovable when commenced shall afterwards become removable depends not upon what the defendant may allege or prove or what the court may, after hearing upon the merits, *in invitum*, order, but solely upon the form which the plaintiff by his voluntary action shall give to the pleadings in the case as it progresses towards a conclusion.

Great Northern Ry. v. Alexander, 246 U.S. 276, 282 (1918) . . . .[1] Here, this

---

1. Although the rule typically arises in diversity cases, we see no reason to *limit* its application to the diversity context.

case was transformed into an action "arising under" federal law not by the voluntary action of the plaintiff, but instead by action of a defendant. Since a voluntary act by the plaintiff has not rendered the case removable, it must remain in state court. Thus, the district court improperly exercised removal jurisdiction over the case.

The voluntary/involuntary rule does not affect the right of the *RTC* to remove. Congress, which has the absolute right to confer removal jurisdiction as long as federal jurisdiction is within constitutional limits, has specifically exempted the RTC from the ordinary removal scheme. FIRREA, 12 U.S.C. § 1441a(*l*)(3) provides, in relevant part:

> The Corporation [RTC] may . . . remove any such action or proceeding from a State court to the United States District Court for the District of Columbia, or if the action, suit or proceeding arises out of the actions of the [RTC] with respect to an institution for which a conservator or a receiver has been appointed, the United States district court for the district where the institution's principal business is located.

Thus, once the RTC is a party to an action, it may remove at any time. Here, however, the RTC has not attempted to remove; it is the third-party plaintiff, joined by other defendants, that has attempted removal. The removal provisions of FIRREA do not confer the right to remove on any parties *other than* the RTC.

We conclude that the district court lacked jurisdiction in this case and thus do not consider appellants' other arguments. We remand to the district court with instructions to remand this action to state court.

American Law Institute, COMPLEX LITIGATION: STATUTORY RECOMMENDATIONS AND ANALYSIS

177-78, 220-22 (1994)

§ 4.01 Designating a State Court as Transferee Forum for Federal Actions

(a) Subject to the exceptions in subsection (c), when determining under § 3.04 where to transfer and consolidate actions, the Complex Litigation Panel may designate a state court as the transferee court if the Panel determines

> (1) that the events giving rise to the controversy are centered in a single state and a significant portion of the existing litigation is lodged in the courts of that state;
>
> (2) that fairness to the parties and the interests of justice will be materially advanced by transfer and consolidation of the federal actions with other suits pending in the state court; and
>
> (3) that the state court is more appropriate than other possible transferee courts.

The Complex Litigation Panel may designate a state court as the transferee court solely for pretrial proceedings, including discovery and motion practice, or for the full or partial adjudication of the controversy. . . .

(c) The Complex Litigation Panel shall not transfer to a state court any action that is within the exclusive jurisdiction of the federal courts, or any action that has been removed to a federal court . . ., or brought in federal court under the provisions of 42 U.S.C. § 1983. . . .

§ 5.01. Removal Jurisdiction

(a) Except as otherwise provided by Act of Congress, the Complex Litigation Panel may order the removal to federal court and consolidation of one or more civil actions pending in one or more state courts, if the removed actions arise from the same transaction, occurrence, or series of transactions or occurrences as an action pending in the federal court, and share a common question of fact with that action. The Complex Litigation Panel shall evaluate whether to order removal and consolidation by reference to (1) the criteria set forth in § 3.01 to determine whether the transfer and consolidation of the cases is warranted and (2) consideration of whether removal will unduly disrupt or impinge upon state court or regulatory proceedings or impose an undue burden on the federal courts. When making its determination under subsections (a)(1)and (a)(2), the Complex Litigation Panel should consider factors such as

   a. the amount in controversy for the claims to be removed;
   b. the number and size of the actions involved;
   c. the number of jurisdictions in which the state cases are lodged;
   d. any special reasons to avoid inconsistency;
   e. the presence of any special local community or state regulatory interests;
   f. whether removal and consolidation will result in a change in the applicable law that will cause undue unfairness to the parties; and
   g. the possibility of facilitating informal cooperation or coordination with the state courts in which the cases are lodged.

If the standard is met, the Panel may order the cases removed, consolidated, and transferred pursuant to § 3.04.

(b) If all of the parties as well as the appropriate state judge object to removal of a particular action, that action shall not be removed, although the remaining cases may be removed and consolidated.

(c) In exercising its discretion under subsection (a), the Complex Litigation Panel shall have the authority to remove common issues, related claims, or entire actions.

(d) Claims to which any state is a party may not be removed under subsection (a) unless the state itself requests or consents to removal.

(e) Removal under subsection (a) may be initiated upon

   (1) the request of any party to any one of the state actions; or

(2) the certification of any state judge presiding over one or more of the actions.

Notes and Questions

1. *Pickup Truck* shows the way in which removal can be used, in conjunction with venue-changing devices, to accomplish the joinder of related claims in a single forum. The first step is to remove the case from state to federal court — here, from a Tennessee state court to the federal court in Tennessee. The second step is to switch the venue of the case from the Tennessee federal court to the Pennsylvania federal court, in which other similar cases had already been aggregated under the multidistrict transfer statute. We will examine the multidistrict statute in the next chapter. See p. 494, *infra*. For now it is important to know only that this statute does not permit parties or the court to transfer cases from state to federal court, but only to aggregate cases already in the federal system. Hence, removal jurisdiction is an important tool in complex and complicated litigation, and a proper appreciation of its scope and its limitations is vital.

Keating demonstrates that removal is not entirely sympathetic to the problems of complex and complicated litigation. *Keating* involved the same two-step "removal-venue switch" as *Pickup Truck*. The case brought by the California Attorney General was merely one of many filed in the wake of the collapse of the Lincoln Savings and Loan, which had been run by the infamous Charles Keating, Jr. The Ninth Circuit did not mention that most of the cases against Keating had already been consolidated in the District of Arizona, and the judge there had a great deal of familiarity with the substantive factual and legal issues in the matter. Moreover, unlike *Pickup Truck*, *Keating* seems to have involved a true instance of lawyer dysfunction; in *Pickup Truck*, General Motors was large enough a corporation that there were unlikely to be any remediless, "end-of-the-queue" plaintiffs, while in *Keating*, a quick trial and recovery for California plaintiffs would have left non-California plaintiffs with less than their equitable share of the available assets. Does *Keating*'s result suggest that our removal rules are not concerned with the problem of complex litigation, or only that *Keating* itself was unconcerned? If the answer is the former, should the removal rules be made more sensitive to complex litigation? Here, one of the standard arguments against special rules for complex cases — that they interfere with plaintiffs' adversarial right to control the case — is rather weak, for in passing § 1441 Congress has already authorized defendants to tamper with plaintiffs' forum choices in at least some cases.

2. As *Pickup Truck* and *Keating* suggest, a major problem of removal jurisdiction is that its availability depends on the pleading of at least one claim which lies within federal jurisdiction; if the plaintiff can successfully avoid any such claims, the federal courts do not have authority to entertain a case on removal despite its relation to other cases within federal jurisdiction. To a certain degree, the result in *General Motors Pickup Truck* was the result of plaintiffs' greed. Had plaintiffs stated clearly on the face of their complaint that each plaintiff sought only $5,000, and had they not asked for punitive damages they could *probably* have maintained their state forum. We say "probably" because the amount in controversy rule of § 1332 could arguably be interpreted not to apply in cases of lawyer dysfunction (which *Pickup Truck* may or may not

be), and because *Snyder v. Harris* has arguably been overruled by § 1367. See pp. 339-40, 349, *supra*.

Indeed, a proper understanding of §§ 1331, 1332, and 1367 is essential to a proper understanding of § 1441. If §§ 1331, 1332, and 1367 can be stretched to accommodate the problems of complex or complicated litigation, then removal can be an effective tool in reducing dysfunction or inefficiency. In *Keating*, for instance, should the court have considered abandoning the complete diversity rule in order to avoid the threat of unfair treatment for non-California residents? If so, then the case would have been removable independently of the RTC's presence in the case.

3. Section 1367 has had a somewhat liberalizing effect on removal jurisdiction. Assuming that a plaintiff sues one defendant on a federal question claim and another, non-diverse defendant on a state law claim, the pre-§ 1367 world of *Finley* would have suggested that the case was not removable unless the federal question claim was "separate and independent" under § 1441(c). Since passage of § 1367, federal courts have had little trouble concluding that the entire case is removable by defendants as long as all claims amount to a single constitutional case. See, *e.g.*, Rodriguez v. Pacificare of Texas, Inc., 980 F.2d 1014 (5th Cir.), cert. denied, 508 U.S. 956 (1993); cf. City of Chicago v. International College of Surgeons, — U.S. —, 118 S.Ct. 523, 530 (1997) ("[O]nce the case was removed, the District Court had original jurisdiction over [plaintiff's] claims arising under federal law, and thus could exercise supplemental jurisdiction over the accompanying state law claims so long as those claims constitute 'other claims that . . . form part of the same case or controversy.'"). See generally Joan Steinman, *Supplemental Jurisdiction in § 1441 Removed Cases: An Unsurveyed Frontier of Congress' Handiwork*, 35 Ariz. L. Rev. 305 (1993).

Suppose, however, that the plaintiffs file two separate cases for the same injuries: one alleging federal violations in federal court, and one alleging state law violations in state court. Had all of the claims been brought one case in state court, supplemental jurisdiction would seemingly authorize removal. Can the state defendants successfully remove the state case on the theory that it lies with the court's § 1367 jurisdiction? See Holt v. Lockheed Support Systems, Inc., 835 F.Supp. 325, 329 (W.D. La. 1993) (removal not permitted); Joico Laboratories, Inc. v. Fuencarral, 1993 WL 332563 (C.D. Cal. 1993) (same). Was not § 1367 intended to reduce duplicative litigation by providing a federal forum for state-law claims related to federal claims?

4. In some circumstances, federal law may so pre-empt a particular field that a purported state-law claim is a federal claim. The state-law case can then be removed to federal court. See Metropolitan Life Insurance Co. v. Taylor, 481 U.S. 58 (1987); Caterpillar Inc. v. Williams, 482 U.S. 386 (1987). This doctrine of "complete pre-emption" has been narrowly confined. For the most part, claims of pre-emption are treated as a defense; because they are not part of the well-pleaded complaint, removal is impermissible.

Based on a rather cryptic footnote in Federated Department Stores v. Moitie, 452 U.S. 394, 397 n.2 (1981) (p. 157, *supra*), some courts also thought that removal jurisdiction existed when a plaintiff attempted to re-litigate in state court a state-law claim that was effectively identical to a federal question claim previously litigated in federal court. See, *e.g.*, Travelers Indemnity Co. v. Sarkasian, 794 F.2d 754 (2d Cir.), cert. denied, 479 U.S. 885 (1986). Subsequently, the Supreme Court essentially disowned "*Moitie*'s enigmatic footnote 2," and held that "claim preclusion by reason of a prior federal judgment is a defensive plea that provides no basis for removal under § 1441(b)." Rivet v. Regions Bank of Louisiana, — U.S. —, 118 S.Ct. 921, 926 (1998). *Rivet* did not, however, expressly overrule *Moitie*, so the possibility that removal of certain state-law claims might be possible in extraordinary circumstances is arguably still alive.

Should an exception be created to allow removal to the constitutional limit when aggregation in a federal forum can prevent lawyer dysfunction? Why should we respect the plaintiffs' efforts to plead only non-federal claims when that choice threatens the ability of certain persons to obtain an appropriate remedy? Is the federal interest in complex cases stronger than the federal interest represented by the complete pre-emption doctrine?

5. Needing to rely on plaintiffs' pleading of claims within federal jurisdiction is a major problem with using removal jurisdiction as a panacea for the problems of lawyer dysfunction or inefficiency, but there are other obstacles as well. One hitch is that § 1446 has been interpreted to require that all defendants must join the petition for removal; if some do not, the case remains in state court. See, *e.g.*, Bradley v. Maryland Casualty Co., 382 F.2d 415 (8th Cir. 1967); 14A Charles A. Wright et al., Federal Practice & Procedure § 3731 (1985). In rare circumstances, however, fewer than all of the properly served defendants can remove a case to federal court. The most typical situation involves an argument by diverse defendants that other, non-diverse defendants were fraudulently or collusively joined in order to prevent removal. See Rose v. Giamatti, 721 F. Supp. 906 (S.D. Ohio 1989). In most contexts, however, fraud or collusion is difficult to prove. See, *e.g.*, Batoff v. State Farm Insurance Co., 977 F.2d 848 (3d Cir. 1992) (ordering remand even though claim against non-diverse defendant might not withstand a motion to dismiss).

A second situation in which fewer than all defendants can remove a case occurs when a particular defendant (or third party defendant) that enjoys a special statutory right of removal. As *Keating* says, for instance, Congress gave the RTC its own right of removal — one which could be exercised even if it first became a party while the case was on appeal in state court. See FDIC v. Kahlil Zoom-In Markets, Inc., 978 F.2d 183 (5th Cir. 1992). Similarly, foreign states are given the right to remove an entire action from state court. 28 U.S.C. § 1441(d), see In re Surinam Airways Holding Co., 974 F.2d 1255 (11th Cir. 1992). Federal officers, federal agencies, and persons "acting under" federal officers are also entitled to remove cases brought in state court which challenge their actions under color of federal authority and for which they have at least a colorable defense under federal law. See generally International Primate Protection League v. Administrators of Tulane Educational Fund, 500 U.S. 72 (1991); Mesa v. California, 489 U.S. 121 (1989). This rule has gotten a recent workout in mass toxic tort claims brought against government contractors, albeit with little success for the contractors. Compare Bahrs v. Hughes Aircraft Co., 795 F. Supp. 965 (D. Ariz. 1992) (removal not available unless military officers directed waste disposal) and Ryan v. Dow Chemical Co., 781 F. Supp. 934 (E.D.N.Y. 1992) (removal not available when government ordered production of herbicide that was combination of commercially available ingredients) with Winters v. Diamond Shamrock Chemical Co., 901 F. Supp. 1195 (E.D. Tex. 1995) (disagreeing with *Ryan* and permitting removal).

Third, an entity to whom Congress extends a "sue and be sued" clause in federal courts may be able to remove a case without the consent of other defendants. Compare Roe v. Little Company of Mary Hospital, 815 F. Supp. 241 (N.D. Ill. 1992) (removal permitted without consent of other defendants) with Doe v. Kerwood, 969 F.2d 165 (5th Cir. 1992) (removal not permitted unless co-defendants unanimously consent).

A final exception to the requirement that all defendants join in a removal petition is contained in § 1441(c), which permits removal by those defendants sued on "a separate and independent claim or cause of action within the jurisdiction conferred by section 1331 . . . [which] is joined with one or more otherwise non-removable claims or causes of action." The scope of § 1441(c) — in particular, what constitutes "a separate and independent claim or cause of action" — has long been the subject of interpretive and constitutional debate. See American Fire & Casualty Insurance Co. v. Finn, 341 U.S. 6 (1951). Might a defendant or court be able to make § 1441(c) work in complex and complicated cases by arguing that the plaintiffs' dysfunction- or inefficiency-causing packaging of a case in state court creates "separate and independent claims or causes of action"? Or does that argument stretch the meaning of the phrase too much?

More generally, do these specific exceptions convince you that a new gloss should be read into § 1446: that any defendant may successfully petition for removal when lawyer dysfunction may be avoided through aggregation in federal court? Would you extend such a gloss to cases in which federal aggregation would prevent inefficient re-litigation?

6. Another problem of removal jurisdiction is that entire cases, rather than particular claims, must be removed. For instance, in a case like *Pickup Truck*, some plaintiffs sued retailers of GM pickups in addition to suing General Motors itself. Obviously the retailers had little interest in most of the other consolidated cases. To bring all of the retailers into federal court may very well create more complexity than it solves; using removal to deal with complex litigation is a bit like using an ax to do open heart surgery.

In some situations, the court has the power to shave off some claims and hold onto the remainder. The leading case is Carnegie-Mellon University v. Cohill, 484 U.S. 343 (1988), in which the Supreme Court held that a district court had discretion to remand pendent state claims once the claims within federal jurisdiction had been decided. *Cohill* does not squarely hold that federal courts have the power to remand the state claims prior to elimination of the federal issues, although it strongly implies that the discretion exists to do so. Since the passage of the supplemental jurisdiction statute, some courts have used § 1367(c) to fill this gap. See *Roe*, 815 F. Supp. 241; Doe v. Abbott Laboratories, 1993 WL 278458 (N.D. Ill. 1993). Does § 1367(c) give the court the power to remand these claims, or just to dismiss them? See § 1367(d).

Portions of a case can also be remanded under § 1441(c), which allows a court to remand independently non-removable claims when "State law predominates." A third power to retain a part of a case occurs when a state-court suit names the state or a state official in an official capacity, and the defendants then remove the case to federal court. The Supreme Court has held that the Eleventh Amendment does not bar removal, but that the federal court must dismiss the state from the suit after removal. Wisconsin Department of Corrections v. Schacht, — U.S. —, 118 S.Ct. 2047 (1998).

But the power to remove and hear only the complex issues in a case is limited. In the first instance, discretionary powers of dismissal or remand are not specifically geared to the problem of complex or complicated litigation. Second, there may be limits on the power to remand certain types of claims or issues. See *In re Surinam Airways*, 974 F.2d 1255 (federal court must retain jurisdiction over entire case in which instrumentality of foreign government was a third party defendant). Third, as *Pickup Truck* states, when all of the removed claims lie within federal jurisdiction, the court cannot use § 1367-like discretion to remand some of the federal claims. Cf. Thermtron Products, Inc. v. Hermansdorfer, 423 U.S. 336, 340, 344 (1976) (even though federal docket was so clogged that "plaintiffs' right of redress [was] being severely impaired," "an otherwise properly removed action may no more be remanded because the district court considers itself too busy to try it than an action properly filed in the federal court in the first instance may be dismissed or referred to state courts for such reason").

7. Several specific removal problems arise in diversity cases. First, a plaintiff can prevent removal of a diversity case simply by adding a non-diverse party or by suing in a state court in which one defendant resides. 28 U.S.C. § 1441(b). Second, diversity cases which become removable more than one year after they are first filed lose the privilege of removal. 28 U.S.C. § 1446(b). There is very little play in these rules. Compare Wind v. Eli Lilly & Co., 814 F. Supp. 305 (E.D.N.Y. 1993) (applying the one-year limit to case in which defendants tried to remove six-year-old DES case after non-diverse defendant settled on the eve of trial) with Caterpillar, Inc. v. Lewis, 519 U.S. 61 (1996) (lack of complete diversity at outset of case can be cured if non-diverse party is no longer present at time judgment entered) and Newman-Green, Inc. v. Alfonzo-Larrain, 490 U.S. 826 (1989) (district and appellate courts can dismiss dispensable non-diverse party in order to maintain diversity jurisdiction).

8. Removal jurisdiction is also limited by the "voluntary/involuntary" rule discussed in *Keating*. The rule was designed to prevent removal in situations in which a court during trial involuntarily dismissed the claims or parties that had made the case non-removable; in this situation, there was an understandable desire not to permit defendants to switch court systems. Although it has never been clearly established that the rule survived the 1949 amendments to § 1446, *Keating* shows that some courts continue to adhere to it. Should an exception to this rule be made in complex or complicated litigation?

9. Yet another problem with removal is that the federal forum is never completely secure; plaintiffs can sometimes fiddle with their claims to secure a remand. *Pickup Truck* is a straight-forward application of one of the standard interpretive rules of § 1441: that removal jurisdiction is based on the complaint as it exists on the day of removal, and subsequent steps taken by the plaintiff to eliminate federal jurisdiction — such as proposing to lower the amount in controversy, drop the claims which lie within federal jurisdiction, or add non-diverse parties to destroy diversity jurisdiction — do not automatically entitle a plaintiff to a remand to state court. For instance, post-removal efforts to reduce the amount in controversy have no effect on federal jurisdiction. See, *e.g.*, St Paul Mercury Indemnity Co. v. Re Cab Co., 303 U.S. 283 (1938); Angus v. Shiley, Inc., 989 F.2d 142 (3d Cir. 1993). On the other hand, when the claims within federal jurisdiction are dropped or eliminated from the case, the federal courts appear to have discretion to hear the remaining claims or to remand to state court. See FSLIC v. Griffin, 935 F.2d 691 (5th Cir. 1991), cert. denied, 502 U.S. 1092 (1992); Harrell v. 20th Century Insurance Co., 934 F.2d 203 (9th Cir. 1991).

The attempted addition of non-diverse parties has resulted in varying treatment. When the party sought to be joined is necessary and indispensable under Rule 19 (see pp. 116-32, *supra*), most courts hold that the case must be dismissed, although some courts have read § 1447(e) to permit the court to retain the case. Compare Yniques v. Cabral, 985 F.2d 1031 (9th Cir. 1993) (dismissal required) with DiNardi v. Ethicon, Inc., 145 F.R.D. 294 (N.D.N.Y. 1993) (retaining case is appropriate; factors used to decide whether to retain include delay in request for joinder, prejudice to defendant, likelihood of multiple litigation, and plaintiff's motivation). When the party sought to be joined is not indispensable, the court can deny joinder and proceed to hear the case against those already joined. See Stransky v. American Isuzu Motors, Inc., 829 F. Supp. 788 (E.D. Pa. 1993). The court can also permit joinder. According to § 1447(e), when that joinder is of "additional defendants," the court must remand the entire case to state court. There is no statutory rule regarding the consequences of permitting joinder of additional plaintiffs; here, most courts seem to remand the entire case to state court, but a few either have dismissed the case or, in a result that appears to be another judicially created exception to the complete diversity rule, have retained jurisdiction of the entire case under the court's supplemental jurisdiction. See *Yniques*, 985 F.2d 1031; Wright et al., *supra*, §§ 3723, 3739. Why not adopt the *St. Paul Mercury* rule for all subsequent attempts by plaintiffs to defeat removal jurisdiction, at least in instances in which the attempt will frustrate the joinder of complex cases? Should the same rule be applied in complicated cases?

10. Another problem with removal is that it requires that a case already exist in state court. Unless that case is a class action, removal does nothing to draw "sideline-sitting" nonparties into the litigation.

11. Another difficulty with removal is that it is a one-way ratchet; cases cannot be "removed" from federal to state court even when it might make more sense to aggregate a case in state court. The existence of a one-way removal power could defeat, in some cases, the appropriate aggregation of complex or complicated cases. It also is one of the primary reasons why federal courts are regarded as superior to state courts with respect to resolving the aggregation problems in complex and complicated litigation.

12. A final problem with the present removal statute is the difficulty of obtaining appellate review of an erroneous district court decision concerning remand. A decision not to remand is appealable, although typically not until the conclusion of the case — at which point the pressure not to undo the district court's work is often irresistible. Wright et al., *supra*, § 3740. With respect to decisions to remand, § 1447(d) provides that, except in certain civil rights cases, "[a]n order remanding a case to the State court from which it was removed is not reviewable on appeal or otherwise." Despite the apparent finality of this rule, *Thermtron* held that only those remand orders which were premised on the belief either that there were defects in the removal petition or that the federal court did not have jurisdiction over the remanded case are not reviewable. When a federal judge bases a remand order on other considerations, the decision can be reviewed, most typically by mandamus. *Thermtron*, 423 U.S. at 345-53. On the other hand, if the stated basis of the remand order is a defect in the removal petition or a lack of subject matter jurisdiction, appellate review is precluded even when the district court is clearly wrong. In re Decorator Industries, Inc., 980 F.2d 1371 (11th Cir. 1992). Recently, some district courts that did not believe they had jurisdiction nonetheless have turned to using interlocutory

appeals under 28 U.S.C. § 1292(b) as a means to obtain an appellate court's opinion about whether they in fact had jurisdiction. See In re TMI Litigation Cases Consolidated II, 940 F.2d 832 (3d Cir. 1991), cert. denied, 503 U.S. 906 (1992); *Ryan*, 781 F. Supp. at 952-53. Does this approach flaunt § 1447(d)?

Appeal of a remand order is also not precluded when remand is ordered pursuant to the court's discretionary power under § 1367 or § 1441(c), see *Cohill*, 484 U.S. 343; when a party has a statutory right of appeal, see, *e.g.*, 12 U.S.C. § 1819(b)(2)(C) (granting FDIC right of appeal from remand orders); or when a court remands a case because of a technical defect in the removal petition not noticed within the thirty days for filing requests for remand, see Williams v. AC Spark Plugs, 985 F.2d 783 (5th Cir. 1993).

13. The removal proposal of the American Law Institute avoids many of the present pitfalls with removal. Note that removal is keyed to "the criteria set forth in § 3.01," which we will study in the next chapter. See p. 525, *infra*. In brief, however, § 3.01 permits federal courts to transfer cases that "involve one or more common questions of fact" to a single federal forum when "transfer and consolidation will promote the just, efficient, and fair conduct of the actions." The removal provision in § 5.01 extends that power to order removal of cases in state court.

The ALI proposes to overcome the difficulties mentioned in the prior Notes as follows:

- The ALI's proposal accomplishes both removal and venue-switching in a single step. To accomplish this result, the ALI proposes the creation of a single Complex Litigation Panel to make the removal and venue-switch decisions.

- The ALI's proposal does not require that plaintiffs necessarily have pleaded claims within federal jurisdiction as long as it raises common issues of fact with those that are.

- Any party in the state action or the state judge can request removal; all defendants do not have to join in the request, nor are plaintiffs precluded from requesting removal.

- The ALI's proposal permits the removal of certain issues, in addition to the removal of entire claims or actions.

- Neither a "defendant's home forum" nor a "one-year limit" exist with regard to removal of diversity cases.

- The "voluntary/involuntary" rule seems to have been abandoned.

- Other provisions of the ALI proposal (in particular, § 5.05 (see p. 249, *supra*)) handle the problem of sideline-sitters.

- Under § 4.01 of the ALI's proposal, state courts can often (though not always) be used as the system for aggregation of cases.

One problem that the ALI's proposal changes, albeit not in a particularly helpful way, is appealability. Under § 3.07 of the ALI's proposal, transfer and consolidation decisions of the Complex Litigation Panel "will not be subject to review by any court, except by extraordinary writ." With respect to a decision denying transfer and consolidation, however, § 3.07 provides that "[t]here shall be no review by appeal or otherwise."

The ALI's proposal is tailored to the problem of inefficient re-litigation (see p. 84, *supra*), but would appear to include within its sweep cases of lawyer dysfunction. Having now seen the ALI's proposal for removal and aggregation, do you favor it over the present rules of removal? Is the ALI's proposal is too broad, in that it overrides the adversarial system's master of the complaint rule in cases in which inefficiency is the primary concern?

14. One of the concerns of present removal law is that the decision to seek removal is usually entrusted to the defendant, who may not wish to see related cases aggregated. The ALI's proposal gives judges the *sua sponte* power to request the Complex Litigation Panel to remove a case filed in state court. Is a comparable authority available under existing law? Judges traditionally have had the power to dismiss removed cases when they notice a defect in the removal petition or when a lack of jurisdiction is obvious. See Maniar v. Federal Deposit Insurance Corp., 979 F.2d 782 (9th Cir. 1992) (limiting power to order remand for technical defects to the same 30-day period parties possess). But do judges possess the converse power to order cases removed to federal court? The first issue, of course, is what the source of power would be for such an exercise of judicial power. It seems fairly plain that the Federal Rules do not provide the power. See F.R.Civ.P. 82 (Federal Rules do not expand jurisdiction of the federal courts); *DiNardi*, 145 F.R.D. 294 (Rule 42 power to consolidate cases does not permit the court to consolidate related state and federal cases). Nor do the federal courts' general equitable powers seemingly authorize courts to remove cases merely to prevent re-litigation of claims. Cf. In re Sugar Antitrust Litigation, MDL 201, 588 F.2d 1270, 1273-74 (9th Cir. 1978) (defendants that sought to remove state law antitrust claims and join them with federal antitrust claims could not use removal "as a bill of peace, designed simply to put together in one forum all claims based upon the same cause of action").

Some judicial power to remove *sua sponte* might nonetheless exist. After settlement of the Agent Orange class action had been approved by Judge Weinstein, several disgruntled members of the class filed new suits against the defendants in Texas state court. The defendants removed the case to federal court in Texas, and the Judicial Panel on Multidistrict Litigation transferred the case to Weinstein. Because complete diversity was not present in the Texas state cases, however, the authority for removal was uncertain. Weinstein found the authority in the All-Writs Act, 28 U.S.C. § 1651(a), which authorizes federal courts to "issue all writs necessary or appropriate in aid of their respective jurisdictions." He suggested in dicta that this power could be exercised by the court *sua sponte*:

> The Act . . . authorizes federal courts to exercise jurisdiction over persons "'who . . . are in a position to frustrate the implementation of a court order or the proper administration of justice.'" Yonkers Racing Corp. v. City of Yonkers, 858 F.2d 855, 863 (2d Cir. 1988) . . . . The Act even permits a federal court to remove state court actions to federal court in situations where a specific statutory removal authority is absent. . . .
>
> By bringing new suits in state court, the plaintiffs challenge the binding effect of the Settlement Agreement and the order of this court prohibiting new suits by class members. The new suits are a direct threat to the continuing viability of the judgment settling the class action. The suits will also consume the $10 million set aside to indemnify the settling defendants and reduce the recovery of the remaining class members.
>
> If the cases had remained in state court, the court would have had the authority to order their removal.

Ryan v. Dow Chemical Co., 781 F. Supp. 902, 918 (E.D.N.Y. 1991). The Second Circuit affirmed this All-Writs power in the context of a class action settlement in which the district court "was enforcing an explicit, ongoing order against relitigation of matters it already had decided, and guarding the integrity of its rulings in complex multidistrict litigation over which it had retained jurisdiction," but warned that "the All Writs Act is not a jurisdictional blank check which district courts may use whenever they deem it advisable" to avoid compliance with statutory procedures. In re "Agent Orange" Product Liability Litigation, 996 F.2d 1425, 1431 (2d Cir. 1993), cert. denied, 510 U.S. 1140 (1994); accord, In the Matter of VMS Securities Litigation, 103 F.3d 1317 (7th Cir. 1996); contra, Hillman v. Webley, 115 F.3d 1461 (10th Cir. 1997).

How broadly should a *sua sponte* removal power be construed? Should it be limited just to instances in which a new suit constitutes a threat to an existing judgment? Or can it reach cases such as *Keating*, in which a state suit threatens to inequitably diminish the recovery of federal plaintiffs?

b. Injunctions and Stays that Preclude One Court System from Hearing Claims

At the present time, the limitations of removal jurisdiction often make it an unattractive device for aggregating related cases in a single forum. The other traditional method by which aggregation could be accomplished is through judicial orders that stay the prosecution or defense of related cases in forums other than a designated forum. The use of such injunctions or stays descends from the power of equity to issue bills of peace that protected parties from the inconvenience of multiple lawsuits on the same matter through the means of a single equitable proceeding that resolved the litigation-provoking questions once and for all. See Dan B. Dobbs, Law of Remedies § 2.9(4) (2d ed. 1993); Zechariah Chafee, Jr., *Bills of Peace with Multiple Parties*, 45 Harv. L. Rev. 1297 (1932); p. 423, *infra.*. Unlike a bill of peace, a stay results only indirectly in the aggregation of claims; the party under the stay order has no obligation to join the other proceeding. In those complex cases in which assets are insufficient to cover all claims, however, a stay in one forum typically has the desired effect. In other complex cases and in complicated litigation, a stay is relatively powerless against a party with the patience (and the statute of limitations) to outlast the case in which the stay was entered — unless the court can make the stay permanent.

Stays can come in one of two forms: orders by one court preventing litigation in another court, and orders by one court staying its own jurisdiction in favor of another court. Stays can be sought by either party; a defendant can seek a stay against a plaintiff who is prosecuting a case in another forum, and a plaintiff can seek a stay against an effort by the defendant to prosecute a related claim in a different forum.

Obviously, when the stay involves a federal court on one side and a state court on the other, stays become devices through which the plaintiffs' initial choice of forum can be changed. In this section, we primarily examine two types of stays that can have this effect: those issued by a federal court against a state court which preclude the exercise by the state court of jurisdiction over the claims, and those issued by a federal court staying its own jurisdiction in favor of a state court.

Before we begin, two caveats are in order. First, we do not examine here the stay in bankruptcy, which is one of the most powerful devices to enjoin state proceedings; instead, we devote Chapter Six to its uses and problems. Second, we do not consider here the utility of the stay as a means of preventing one court in a judicial system from hearing a case related to a case pending in another court of the same system; those stays, which raise somewhat different issues, are addressed in Chapter Four.

Federal-state stays raise difficult issues of federalism, as well as the usual concerns about allowing defendants and courts to override the plaintiffs' control of their own litigation. Pay attention to the circumstances in which stays seem to be granted most readily. Do these circumstances reflect the particular needs of complex litigation? Of complicated litigation? Can they be abused in ways that create dysfunction or inefficiency?

i. Injunctions against Suits in Other Courts

The problem of a federal court injunction against proceedings in a state court and the problem of a state court injunction against proceedings in a federal court are mirror images of each other. You might think, therefore, that they should receive equivalent treatment. To some extent, it does turn out that the powers of each court system to enjoin the other are identical. For the most part, however, federal courts enjoy far greater power to enjoin related state proceedings than do their state court counterparts.

The starting point for appreciating the similarities and differences among state court and federal court injunctions is the distinction among *in rem*, *quasi in rem*, and *in personam* proceedings. *In rem* actions involve a dispute regarding a piece of property, in which all persons with a possible claim to the property are notified and the various interests in the property are definitively settled. *Quasi in rem* actions also determine the interests in a piece of property, but do so only with respect to those claimants that are joined in the case. *In personam* actions include virtually all other types of actions; they may or may not involve a dispute regarding property, and they determine only the relative rights of the parties to the case. See Fleming James, Jr. et al., Civil Procedure § 2.4 (4th ed. 1992).

1. Injunctions Issued in In Rem *or* Quasi in Rem *Proceedings*. When federal and state courts both assert jurisdiction over a case *in rem* or *quasi in rem*, there is the possibility that one court will decide that person A owns the property, while the other court will decide that person B owns the property. Since only A or B can possess the property, this situation is fraught with danger. This situation is also a classic, though very simple, example of the type of lawyer dysfunction that creates complex litigation.

Since the early days of our federal court system, we have maintained a rule that the court which first secures jurisdiction over a proceeding *in rem* has exclusive jurisdiction to hear the case as against any other court, state or federal. See Hagan v. Lucas, 35 U.S. (10 Pet.) 400 (U.S. 1836); Harkin v. Brundage, 276 U.S. 36 (1928); 14 Charles A. Wright et al., Federal Practice & Procedure § 3631 (1985) (discussing rule and some limited exceptions). A corollary of this rule is that the court which obtains jurisdiction over the *res* has the power to enjoin any other proceedings which seek to determine the interests in that property. Thus, a federal court which obtains *in rem* jurisdiction can enjoin state court proceedings which relate to the property. Kline v. Burke Construction Co., 260 U.S. 226 (1922). Conversely, a state court which first obtains *in rem* jurisdiction can enjoin federal proceedings. Princess Lida of Thurn & Taxis v. Thompson, 305 U.S. 456 (1939).

The same jurisdictional rule and power to enjoin related cases has been extended to *quasi in rem* proceedings. See Donovan v. City of Dallas, 377 U.S. 408, 412 (1964). See generally Richard S. Arnold, *State Court Power to Enjoin Federal Court Proceedings*, 51 Va. L. Rev. 59 (1965).

Other than bankruptcy or state receivership matters, however, few complex cases are *in rem* or *quasi in rem* proceedings. The fairly simple, aggregation-friendly, and complexity-reducing rules for *in rem* and *quasi in rem* proceedings have never carried over to *in personam* actions.

2. Injunctions Issued in In Personam *Proceedings*. In discussing the powers of federal and state courts to enjoin *in personam* actions in each other's courtrooms, it is easiest to begin with the power of the state courts to enjoin federal proceedings. Simply put, the power is non-existent. Although there is no statute specifically precluding state injunctions of federal proceedings, the Supreme Court has long followed the opinion of Justice Story in his famous treatise on equity that "the State Courts cannot injoin proceedings in the Courts of the United States." 2 Joseph Story, Equity Jurisprudence 186 (1st ed. 1836); see Farr v. Thompson, 78 U.S. (11 Wall.) 139 (1871). In spite of a passing post-*Erie* suggestion that states might have such power, see Baltimore & Ohio R. Co. v. Kepner, 314 U.S. 44, 51-52 (1941), the Supreme Court strongly reaffirmed the lack of state power to enjoin federal *in personam* proceedings in *Donovan*, 377 U.S. 408.

It would be difficult to imagine a more compelling case for an injunction than *Donovan*. Plaintiffs commenced a class action in state court and lost. More than one hundred plaintiffs, some of whom were also plaintiffs in the state action, then brought suit in federal court on the same claims. In order to protect its own judgment, the state court issued an injunction preventing the plaintiffs from prosecuting the federal claim and requiring them to dismiss the federal case. They refused. On certiorari from the state court's order of contempt, the Supreme Court held that the state injunction was invalid: "While Congress has seen fit to authorize courts of the United States to restrain state-court proceedings in some special circumstances, it has in no way relaxed the old and well-established judicially declared rule that state courts are completely without power to restrain federal-court proceedings, in *in personam* actions like the one here." 377 U.S. at 412-13.

The *Donovan* rule was re-affirmed and even strengthened in General Atomic Co. v. Felter, 434 U.S. 12 (1977). *Felter* arose out of a dispute over the supply of uranium, and had spawned litigation all around the country.

A New Mexico state court finally enjoined one of the principal parties (GAC) "from filing or prosecuting any original, third-party, or arbitration actions relating to the subject matter of the Santa Fe lawsuit . . . ." Since GAC was about to implead the plaintiff in the New Mexico case in another case filed in federal court, the effect of the order was to prevent the filing in federal court of a claim already pending in state court. Although the case was distinguishable from *Donovan* — in *Felter*, the federal court had not yet obtained jurisdiction over the enjoined claims — the Supreme Court held that the injunction was invalid:

> It is . . . clear from *Donovan* that the rights conferred by Congress to bring *in personam* actions in federal courts are not subject to abridgement by state-court injunctions, regardless of whether the federal litigation is pending or prospective. . . .
>
> There is even less basis for the injunction in this case [than in *Donovan*]. Here there is no final state-court judgment . . . . In addition, GAC's opportunity to fairly litigate the various claims arising from this complex action would be substantially prejudiced if the injunction were allowed to stand. What the New Mexico Supreme Court has described as "harassment" is principally GAC's desire to defend itself by impleading [another party] in the federal lawsuits and federal arbitration proceedings brought against it by the utilities. This, of course, is something which GAC has every right to do under Fed. Rule Civ. Proc. 14 and the Federal Arbitration Act. . . . Federal courts are fully capable of preventing their misuse for purposes of harassment. [434 U.S. at 17-18.]

Justice Rehnquist dissented, arguing that, because federal courts have power to enjoin state proceedings when necessary to protect their jurisdiction or judgments (we shall see why in a couple of paragraphs), "a state court must have a similar power to forbid the initiation of vexatious litigation in federal court." Id. at 20.

Donovan and *Felter* make it difficult, if not impossible, to argue that state courts can enjoin federal proceedings merely to prevent inefficient relitigation of claims. If, as appears to be the case, the *Donovan-Felter* rule is not of constitutional dimension, could it still be argued that the rule has no application in complex cases in which a state injunction is necessary to preserve rational adjudication? Cf. American Law Institute, Study of the Division of Jurisdiction between State and Federal Courts §§ 1373 (1969) (recommending congressional authorization for state-court injunctions of *in personam* federal actions when they are "otherwise warranted" by equitable principles and "the injunction is necessary to protect against vexatious and harassing relitigation of matters determined by an existing judgment of the State court in a civil action"). In how many cases would it be true that a state-court injunction against federal litigation would prevent lawyer dysfunction and promote the rational adjudication of all claimants' disputes?

In contrast to the problems of state-court injunctions against federal proceedings, the federal courts have always had some power to enjoin ongoing state *in personam* proceedings. Like the power of removal, the existence of this injunctive power (and the lack of a comparable power in the state courts) is an important reason that federal courts are viewed as the only court system which can deal adequately with the aggregation of related cases. As you read the following materials, consider whether this power is adequate to deal with the peculiar problems of complex and complicated litigation.

IN RE CORRUGATED CONTAINER ANTITRUST LITIGATION

659 F.2d 1332 (5th Cir. 1981), cert. denied, 456 U.S. 936 (1982)

■ CLARK, Circuit Judge. This is an appeal from an order of the United States District Court for the Southern District of Texas enjoining certain of the plaintiffs in this class action from pursuing a lawsuit pending in a South Carolina state court in which these same persons are also plaintiffs and from pursuing any claims relating to this class action in any court other than the United States District Court in Texas. For the reasons stated herein, we affirm.

The litigation that is the basis of this appeal is an enormous class action in which more than fifty private treble damage actions brought on behalf of all purchasers of corrugated containers and sheets against thirty-seven manufacturers, alleging an antitrust conspiracy, were consolidated by the Judicial Panel on Multidistrict Litigation and transferred to the United States District Court for the Southern District of Texas (the multidistrict court). . . .

The South Carolina state court plaintiffs (South Carolina Plaintiffs) against whom the injunction was issued are also members of the plaintiff class in the case still pending in the multidistrict court. On June 30, 1978, Three J Farms, Inc., and three other corporations filed a complaint in the Court of Common Pleas for Spartanburg County, South Carolina, (South Carolina Complaint) purporting to represent the class of all persons injured during the alleged conspiracy in the corrugated industry by actions that violated the antitrust laws of South Carolina, S.C. Code § 39-3-10, et seq. (1976). The same attorneys who represented the named plaintiffs in filing the South Carolina Complaint represent these parties in the multidistrict court. That complaint is similar to the Unified Complaint filed in the multidistrict case. Indeed, some of the paragraphs in the two complaints are identical. The South Carolina Complaint, however, contains no allegations of violations of federal antitrust laws. On July 31, 1978, the defendants in the South Carolina action removed it to the United States District Court for the District of South Carolina. On October 13, 1978, that court remanded the action to the Court of Common Pleas. Two weeks later, the United States district judge stated that his remand order had been entered inadvertently, and held that it was null and void. The court of appeals reversed, holding that the district judge lacked power under 28 U.S.C. § 1447(d) to vacate his order of remand. Three J Farms, Inc. v. Alton Box Board, 609 F.2d 112 (4th Cir. 1979), cert. denied, 445 U.S. 911 (1980).

The South Carolina litigation has been stayed by agreement of the parties pending the outcome of the instant appeal.

The South Carolina Plaintiffs advance four objections to the injunction order of the multidistrict court. They argue that the injunction violates the federal Anti-Injunction Act, that it violates the fifth and tenth amendments to the United States Constitution, that the South Carolina claims were not before the multidistrict court, and that the multidistrict court would have had no jurisdiction over those claims even had they been asserted there.

The Anti-Injunction Act, 28 U.S.C. § 2283, provides: "A court of the United States may not grant an injunction to stay proceedings in a State court except as expressly authorized by Act of Congress, or where necessary in aid of its jurisdiction, or to protect or effectuate its judgments." This statute does not apply to those parts of the multidistrict court order that relate to state court actions that have not yet been filed. Dombrowski v. Pfister, 380 U.S. 479, 484 n.2 (1965); [c]f. Younger v. Harris, 401 U.S. 37, 41 (1971). The only question is whether section 2283 precludes the multidistrict court from entering its injunction against prosecution of the *Three J Farms* case presently pending in South Carolina.

The Anti-Injunction Act embodies important principles of federalism. The Supreme Court has instructed:

> Any doubts as to the propriety of a federal injunction against state court proceedings should be resolved in favor of permitting the state courts to proceed in an orderly fashion to finally determine the controversy. The explicit wording of § 2283 itself implies as much, and the fundamental principle of a dual system of courts leads inevitably to that conclusion.

Atlantic Coastline R.R. v. Brotherhood of Locomotive Engineers, 398 U.S. 281, 297 (1970). Likewise, this court has held that the "complainant must make a strong and unequivocal showing of relitigation of the same issue in order to overcome the federal courts' proper disinclination to intermeddle in state court proceedings." . . .

The statute excepts from its interdict injunctions necessary (1) to aid the court's jurisdiction and (2) to protect or effectuate its judgments. It is undisputed that the multidistrict court has jurisdiction of the class action before it. The multidistrict court perceived that the actions of the appellants in pursuing substantially similar state law claims in the South Carolina court would be a challenge to that jurisdiction. We agree. As the Supreme Court has explained, this exception to the Anti-Injunction Act means that injunctions may be issued where "necessary to prevent a state court from so interfering with a federal court's consideration or disposition of a case as to seriously impair the federal court's flexibility and authority to decide that case." Atlantic Coastline R.R. v. Brotherhood of Locomotive Engineers, 398 U.S. 281, 295 (1970) (dicta). This complicated antitrust action has required a great deal of the district court's time and has necessitated that it maintain a flexible approach in resolving the various claims of the many parties. Further, the presiding judge of the Seventh Judicial Circuit, Court of Common Pleas of Spartanburg County, South Carolina, entered a temporary restraining order on October 23, 1978, enjoining the defendants in the *Three*

J Farms suit, many of whom are also defendants in the federal multidistrict action, from "preparing, disseminating or utilizing any settlement document in connection with any action pending in any Court wherein such settlement document contains any release of any antitrust claims under the laws of the State of South Carolina without the prior approval of this Court." Such a limitation on the terms of settlement would clearly interfere with the multidistrict court's ability to dispose of the broader action pending before it.

The entry of an appealable order is generally considered a prerequisite to invocation of the relitigation or "protection of judgment" exception.... The judgments involved in the multidistrict action which are sought to be protected are those approving settlements executed between the class plaintiffs and most of the defendants. They are appealable. These judgments were entered shortly after the order appealed from here. However, when the injunction order was issued, the multidistrict court had approved the settlements and the final judgments were predictable if not assured. Since such an objection would most probably be moot, the state court plaintiffs do not complain that the injunction preceded final judgment.

An exception to the general rule that a federal forum may not enjoin the prosecution of a simultaneous *in personam* action on the same cause of action in state court comes into play once judgment is entered. Unless the judgment is set aside on appeal, state proceedings seeking to relitigate issues covered by the federal judgment may be enjoined under the "protection" exception. Woods Exploration & Producing Co. v. Aluminum Co. of America, 438 F.2d 1286, 1311-1316 (5th Cir. 1971), cert. denied, 404 U.S. 1047 (1972).... As this court explained in *Woods Exploration*, the exception applies where the state proceeding would be precluded by res judicata. *Woods Exploration* explained that although the state and federal cases asserted different theories, the causes of action based on the same asserted right of the plaintiff and the same alleged acts of the defendant were identical. The same is true in this case. Res judicata would bar the South Carolina litigation. Since there are federal judgments that approve some of the settlements and that control the further litigation of the appellants' cause of action, ... the injunction was and is not precluded by 28 U.S.C. § 2283.

Moreover, the policies of federalism are not flouted by this injunction. In this case, the multidistrict court found that attorneys I. Walton Bader, Robert L. Stoddard, and Wesley A. Stoddard "have taken, and manifested an intention to continue to take, actions threatening this court's exercise of its proper jurisdiction and the effectuation of its judgments, by filing and threatening to file duplicative and harassing litigation in the courts of various states and by seeking therein orders disrupting the proceedings in M.D.L. 310." The appellants have not attacked the multidistrict court's characterization of the motivation behind the actions taken by these attorneys. Under these circumstances, the South Carolina court could not be offended by losing the opportunity to entertain an harassing lawsuit.

The second argument raised is that the injunction violates the fifth and tenth amendments to the United States Constitution.... There is "nothing in the tenth amendment or its accompanying case law" that prevents the entry of this injunction under the circumstances. . . . [T]he parties to the multidistrict litigation could protect their state law claims by asserting them as pendent claims in the federal forum. Thus, there is no deprivation of property. . . .

In their third point, the South Carolina plaintiffs complain that the multidistrict court's injunction precludes indirect purchasers from bringing suits in state court. They urge that this is particularly egregious since indirect purchasers have no cause of action under federal antitrust laws. The multidistrict court order does not address this issue. The transcript of the hearing on the motion for injunction reveals that the court considered it impractical to enjoin the suit in the South Carolina state court only as to the direct purchasers and to allow it to continue in favor of indirect purchasers. The complaint filed in the South Carolina state court action contains no allegations of an indirect purchaser cause of action. Thus, this argument concerns actions not yet filed, as to which the Anti-Injunction Act does not apply. The arguments of the South Carolina state court plaintiffs that these claims were not before the multidistrict court is similar to their final argument, that since the state claims were not pleaded, the multidistrict court lacked jurisdiction over those claims. These arguments, made without citation, ignore the district court's pendent jurisdiction under United Mine Workers v. Gibbs, 383 U.S. 715 (1966), and the holding of *Woods Exploration*, 438 F.2d at 1315, that "res judicata would be applicable if plaintiffs were afforded an opportunity to allege the state grounds which constituted the same cause of action in the federal proceedings."

The order of the district court is affirmed.

Notes and Questions

1. Granted that the Anti-Injunction Act did not *preclude* the entry of the order in *Corrugated Container*, what source affirmatively *gave* the court the power to enjoin the plaintiffs from filing a state court suit?

2. An injunction was not the only way in which the defendants could have prevented dual litigation of related issues. As the court mentions, the defendants in *Corrugated Container* first tried to remove the South Carolina case to federal court, undoubtedly as the first step in the "removal-venue switch" tactic which we have already seen in *General Motors Pickup Truck* and *Keating*. Unfortunately, their plan was derailed when the federal court in South Carolina inadvertently remanded the case. Thus, the defendants scrambled to find "Plan B," and they successfully hit on the idea of an injunction against the state court proceeding. From the viewpoint of complex and complicated litigation, the injunction is a second-best remedy from the viewpoint of joinder complexity, for it does not actually join the related cases together. From the defendant's viewpoint, however, an injunction may be superior; while the "removal-venue switch" method creates additional claims against which the defendant must defend, the injunctive method puts the burden on the plaintiff to file her claims in the other forum. Some plaintiffs may decide not to do so, thus reducing the number of claims against the defendant.

Should the federal court consider this fact in deciding whether to issue an injunction against state proceedings? Should it withhold an injunction until the "removal-venue switch" approach fails, on the theory that an injunction is unnecessary when there is an "adequate remedy at law"?

3. Related to this question is the question of whether the federal district court in Texas could have removed the South Carolina case pursuant to its inherent power. Remember that, in some situations, federal courts may possess such power, and that this power seemingly exists in the same circumstances in which *Corrugated Container* said the injunctive power exists: when it is necessary either in aid of jurisdiction or to protect a federal judgment from challenge by parties to the original suit. See pp. 388-89, *supra*. Is the power of the federal court to remove state proceedings identical to the power of a federal court to stay state proceedings? If so, why do we need the injunctive power in situations such as *Corrugated Container*, in which the same parties are involved in both state and federal cases? Could it be that the injunctive power is broader than the removal power? How much broader?

4. Whatever the proper scope of the injunctive power, *Corrugated Container* demonstrates that this power will be affected by the terms of the Anti-Injunction Act, which is a cornerstone of our present federal structure.

Parse the statute closely. First, note that it applies only to "proceedings in a State court." When there are no present proceedings in state court at the time the federal complaint is filed, the Supreme Court has said that § 2283 is inapplicable. Ex Parte Young, 209 U.S. 123 (1908); Dombrowski v. Pfister, 380 U.S. 479 (1965). (Of course, if no proceedings are pending, ripeness problems may exist, and the federal court may therefore be unwilling to issue the injunction.) Even when no state proceedings exist, however, the inapplicability of § 2283 does not automatically authorize an injunction. There may be equitable reasons not to issue the injunction, and the federal court must also consider whether it should abstain from interfering with state court jurisdiction. See Younger v. Harris, 401 U.S. 37 (1971); see also pp. 426-37, *infra* (discussing abstention); cf. Owen M. Fiss, Dombrowski, 86 Yale L.J. 1103, 1107 (1977) (arguing that it is wrong to use "doctrines of equity — doctrines forged in the battles of English Chancery — to further views of federalism, a political principle central to American Government").

Second, note that § 2283 contains three exceptions which permit federal courts to issue injunctions against state proceedings in some cases:

(a) *"Expressly Authorized by Act of Congress."* In some instances, Congress has expressly authorized federal courts to enjoin ongoing state court proceedings. Primary among them are some cases removed from state court (see 28 U.S.C. § 1446(e)); bankruptcy proceedings (11 U.S.C. §§ 105, 362) (see pp. 706-07, *infra*); statutory interpleader cases (28 U.S.C. § 2361) (see p. 413, *infra*); habeas corpus proceedings (28 U.S.C. § 2251); and certain actions involving shipowners and farm mortgages (see 46 U.S.C. § 185 and 11 U.S.C. § 203(s)(2)). The All-Writs Act — which gives federal courts the authority to "issue all writs necessary or appropriate in aid of their respective jurisdictions and agreeable to the usages and principles of law" — has also long been viewed as an express authority to enjoin state proceedings. 28 U.S.C. § 1651(a); In re Baldwin-United Corp., 770 F.2d 328 (2d Cir. 1985) (p. 401, *infra*).

When Congress does not expressly authorize the stay of state court proceedings in a particular statutory scheme, can the power nonetheless be implied from the statute in a way which satisfies the "expressly authorized" clause of § 2283? In Mitchum v. Foster, 407 U.S. 225 (1972), the Supreme Court held that 42 U.S.C. § 1983 was such an "implied" express authorization. According to *Mitchum*, the test to determine whether a stay is expressly authorized is "whether an Act of Congress, clearly creating a federal right or remedy enforceable in a federal court of equity, could be given its intended scope only by the stay of a state court proceeding." 407 U.S. at 238.

Do any other statutes reflect a similar congressional intent? See Vendo Co. v. Lektro-Vend Corp., 433 U.S. 623 (1977) (plurality opinion) (no express authorization under Clayton Act); General Motors Corp. v. Buha, 623 F.2d 455 (6th Cir. 1980) (express authorization under ERISA); Dilworth v. Riner, 343 F.2d 226 (5th Cir. 1965) (express authority under 1964 Civil Rights Act); International Controls Corp. v. Vesco, 490 F.2d 1334 (2d Cir. 1974) (no express authorization under § 21(e) of the Securities Exchange Act). Cf. Moses H. Cone Memorial Hospital v. Mercury Construction Corp., 460 U.S. 1, 25 n.32 (1983) (reserving issue under the Arbitration Act, 9 U.S.C. §4).

Can the Federal Rules of Civil Procedure ever constitute an express authorization which permits federal courts to enjoin state courts from proceeding with a case? For an argument (ultimately rejected) that the class action rule, F.R.Civ.P. 23, constituted such an authorization, see In re Glenn W. Turner Enterprises Litigation, 521 F.2d 775, 781 (3d Cir. 1975); cf. In re Federal Skywalk Cases, 680 F.2d 1175 (8th Cir.), cert. denied, 459 U.S. 988 (1982) (p. 614, *infra*). See also Edward F. Sherman, *Class Actions and Duplicative Litigation*, 62 Ind. L.J. 507, 528-36 (1987) (discussing relationship between Rule 23 and § 2283).

(b) *"Where Necessary in Aid of Jurisdiction."* Corrugated Container quotes the passage from Atlantic Coastline R.R. v. Brotherhood of Locomotive Engineers, 398 U.S. 281 (1970), that describes our present understanding of the scope of this exception to § 2283. Given this language, is *Corrugated Container* correct in its claim that the stay of the South Carolina case was "necessary in aid of its jurisdiction"? Note that *Corrugated Container* does not ultimately stake the court's injunctive power on this exception. In *Vendo Co.*, a plurality of the Supreme Court stated that "[w]e have never viewed parallel *in personam* actions as interfering with the jurisdiction of either court." 433 U.S. at 642. Is *Vendo* or the contrary dicta in *Corrugated Container* more consistent with *Atlantic Coastline*'s admonition that § 2283's exceptions are "not [to] be enlarged by loose statutory construction"? 398 U.S. at 287. Which is more consistent with economy and fairness in complex and complicated litigation?

Does this exception authorize federal courts to enjoin state proceedings in which the plaintiff has made claims that lie within exclusive federal jurisdiction, such as many antitrust and securities claims? Compare Bowles v. Willingham, 321 U.S. 503, 510-11 (1944) (suggesting injunction is permissible when there also exists statutory power to enjoin substantive violations) with *Atlantic Coastline*, 398 U.S. at 294 (stating that § 2283 cannot be avoided merely because the state proceeding "interfere[s] with a protected federal right or invade[s] an area preempted by federal law").

More generally, when a federal court is the only forum in which the problems of lawyer dysfunction or inefficient re-litigation can be adequately avoided, can this second exception be invoked? Much depends on how broadly we understand the term "jurisdiction." The presence of similar state suits, even in complex or complicated litigation, typically constitutes no threat to the federal court's *power* to hear the cases before it; in this narrow sense, the state cases do not affect the court's *jurisdiction*. But the possibility that the judgments in the state cases might deprive the federal court of the ability to assure that the federal litigants are treated fairly does threaten the adversarial right of the federal litigants to participate through proofs and reasoned arguments and the adjudicatory demand of rational adjudication. If these normative concerns can be read into the term "jurisdiction," perhaps § 2283 stands as no barrier in complex cases. Cf. Martin H. Redish, *The Anti-Injunction Statute Reconsidered*, 44 U. Chi. L. Rev. 717, 754 (1977) (arguing that second exception should be construed "to empower the federal court to enjoin a concurrent state proceeding that might render the exercise of the federal court's jurisdiction nugatory"). This theory would not, of course, create an exception to § 2283 in complicated cases.

In at least three situations arguably involving lawyer dysfunction, courts have relied upon the "necessary in aid of jurisdiction" exception to enjoin related state proceedings. First, federal courts have enjoined a state case that threatened to interfere with a federal desegregation remedy. Swann v. Charlotte-Mecklenburg Board of Education, 501 F.2d 383 (4th Cir. 1974); see 17 Charles A. Wright et al., Federal Practice & Procedure § 4225 (1988) (collecting cases). Second, federal courts have enjoined state proceedings in the context of Rule 22 interpleader actions, a subject which we address shortly. See p. 419, *infra*. Third, a district court sitting in bankruptcy has enjoined all state asbestos suits brought against the trust fund established by a debtor when the suits threatened to deplete the fund. In re Joint Eastern and Southern Districts Asbestos Litigation, 120 B.R. 648 (E.&S.D.N.Y. 1990). Do these cases suggest a flexible attitude toward § 2283 which would be beneficial in other complex cases?

(c) *"To Protect and Effectuate Its Judgments."* The final clause of § 2283, which is referred to as the "re-litigation exception," "was designed to permit a federal court to prevent state litigation of an issue that previously was presented to and decided by the federal court. It is founded on the well-recognized concepts of res judicata and collateral estoppel." Chick Kam Choo v. Exxon Corp., 486 U.S. 140, 147 (1988). In *Chick Kam Choo*, a seaman injured in Singapore brought an action in federal court under the Jones Act. The federal court concluded that Singapore law applied, and dismissed on *forum non conveniens* grounds. The plaintiff then re-filed in Texas state court, which had more favorable rules on venue. The district court enjoined the state action. The Supreme Court found that this injunction violated § 2283, but noted that a narrower injunction that would prevent the state court from applying Texas law would have been permissible. Cf. Parsons Steel, Inc. v. First Alabama Bank, 474 U.S. 518 (1986) (§ 2283 barred federal court from enjoining state judgment inconsistent with prior federal judgment once state proceedings terminated).

In theory, the re-litigation exception holds some promise in complex cases: In order to assure that its judgment will not as a practical matter be far less meaningful to the federal litigants than the state judgment will be to the related state litigants, the federal court should not be restrained by § 2283 from issuing a stay against state proceedings which threaten to make its judgment a practical nullity. Thus far, however, the "relitigation" exception has not been read so broadly; as *Corrugated Container* and *Chick Kam Choo* demonstrate, the usual thinking is that this exception does not permit federal courts to enjoin state proceedings until a judgment (or, at least, very nearly a judgment) has been rendered. See also Battle v. Liberty National Life Insurance Co., 877 F.2d 877

(11th Cir. 1989); In re Agent Orange Product Liability Litigation, 996 F.2d 1425 (2d Cir. 1993), cert. denied, 510 U.S. 1140 (1994); Carlough v. Amchem Products, Inc., 10 F.3d 189 (3d Cir. 1993); cf. J.R. Clearwater Inc. v. Ashland Chemical Co., 93 F.3d 176 (5th Cir. 1996) (Anti-Injunction Act precludes federal court from enjoining plaintiffs that failed to obtain class certification in federal court from commencing state court action seeking class certification; federal order was not final enough under re-litigation exception). Thus, in most circumstances, the federal injunction will come very late in the day — perhaps after the conclusion of the state proceedings, or at least so close to the conclusion of those proceedings that the economies of a single resolution will have been lost.

In some circumstances, plaintiffs and defendants might agree to a global settlement of all claims early in the case, thus giving the federal court an early power to enjoin state proceedings. For instance, in *Carlough*, certain defendants agreed, prior to filing the lawsuit, to a global class action settlement of all asbestos claims against them. Some putative class members that opposed the settlement then filed a class action complaint in West Virginia state court. Even though it had not yet determined whether it had territorial jurisdiction over the plaintiffs or subject matter jurisdiction over the case, the federal court enjoined putative class members from prosecuting further proceedings in state court. About six months after the injunction was issued, the federal court found that territorial and subject matter jurisdiction existed, preliminarily certified the class, and preliminarily approved the settlement.

On appeal, the Third Circuit upheld the injunction, but was troubled by the celerity of the district court's actions:

> [N]either the Anti-Injunction Act . . . nor the All-Writs Act . . . dispels the federal court's jurisdictional requisite or divests the West Virginia court of its jurisdiction . . . . Thus the application of the Anti-Injunction and All-Writs Acts should have been *preceded* by the satisfaction of jurisdictional prerequisites. . . . Strictly and narrowly enforcing the requisite opportunity to opt out for Rule 23 class plaintiffs before exercising personal jurisdiction comports with the overall class action mechanism and is derived from policy considerations bearing upon comity and federalism. . . . As with personal jurisdiction, the district court was obliged to ascertain, at least in a preliminary fashion, its own subject matter jurisdiction over the *Carlough* case before issuing an injunction in aid of that jurisdiction. [10 F.3d at 198, 201.]

Nevertheless, the court upheld the injunction, finding that the subsequent decisions by the district court which permitted an opt out period and which found subject matter jurisdiction to exist cured "the initial jurisdictional overreach." Id. at 201. Does this last holding take all the bite out of the initial admonition not to enjoin the state proceedings? See Georgine v. Amchem Products, Inc., 878 F. Supp. 716 (E.D. Pa. 1994) (entering preliminary injunction against further state suits after entry of final judgment certifying class and approving *Carlough* settlement), *rev'd* on other grounds, 83 F.3d 610 (3d Cir. 1996), *aff'd*, — U.S. —, 117 S.Ct. 2231 (1997).

5. Since the express statutory exceptions to the Anti-Injunction Act may not always be sensitive to the problems of complex and complicated litigation, could an argument for a judicial exception to its terms be made in these cases? There already exist a few judicial glosses on § 2283. First, § 2283 has been held not to apply to injunctions sought by the United States. Leiter Minerals v. United States, 352 U.S. 220 (1957). Second, the power to enjoin state

enforcement of a fraudulently obtained state court judgment has long been recognized, and arguably survives today. See Simon v. Southern Ry., 236 U.S. 115 (1915); Hill v. Martin, 296 U.S. 393 (1935). Third, the power to enjoin state courts from proceeding against a *res* within federal control is arguably a judicially created gloss, although some courts and commentators have suggested that this power is grounded in the "necessary in aid of jurisdiction" exception to § 2283. See, *e.g.*, Standard Microsystems Corp. v. Texas Instruments, Inc., 916 F.2d 58 (2d Cir. 1990). It is admittedly difficult to distill from these three exceptions a more general exception for complex and complicated litigation. Moreover, any such effort must deal with *Atlantic Coastline*'s well-known caveat that "any injunction against state court proceedings . . . must be based on one of the specific statutory exceptions to § 2283 . . . . [T]he exceptions should not be enlarged by loose statutory construction." 398 U.S. at 287.

6. In County of Imperial v. Munoz, 449 U.S. 54 (1980), a county obtained a state court injunction prohibiting the defendant from selling water outside of the county. Three Mexican citizens then sued the county in federal court, alleging that the injunction was in violation of the Commerce Clause. The federal district court granted injunctive relief against enforcement of the state injunction. The Supreme Court held that, if the federal plaintiffs were indeed strangers to the state suit, § 2283 did not bar the injunction. Might *Munoz* be read to permit federal courts to enter injunctions whenever the state proceeding threatens the ability of nonparties to the state suit to secure adequate relief in federal court? Although it would not seem to permit injunctions to prevent inefficient re-litigation in state and federal court, wouldn't this reading make § 2283 largely irrelevant in complex cases?

7. Assuming that complex or complicated cases can navigate the troubled waters around § 2283, an injunction is still not a certainty. In some circumstances, the Supreme Court has suggested that "the principles of equity, comity, and federalism" might require a federal court to abstain from hearing a particular case. *Mitchum*, 407 U.S. at 243. Likewise, in *Chick Kam Choo*, the Court concluded by noting that "the fact an injunction *may* issue does not mean that it *must* issue." 486 U.S. at 151.

8. When all else fails, the party seeking the federal injunction can always resort to "Plan C": Ask the state court to abstain in favor of the federal court. The general principles of such abstention, as well as the limits on the state court's ability to do so, are considered at p. 437, *infra*.

9. A final question that leads us back to where we began these Notes: Was *Corrugated Container* "complex" in the sense that lawyer dysfunction threatened to create an unfair allocation of remedies among state and federal plaintiffs? If not, was it an appropriate case for an injunction? Consider this question in light of the next case.

IN RE BALDWIN-UNITED CORP.

770 F.2d 328 (2d Cir. 1985)

■ MANSFIELD, Circuit Judge. Thirty-one states appeal a preliminary injunction issued in the Southern District of New York by Judge Charles L. Brieant, Jr., in the course of a consolidated multi-district, class action against various broker-dealers who sold securities of the now-bankrupt Baldwin-United Corporation and its insurance subsidiaries. Appellants, with the exception of the State of Maine, were neither parties to nor intervenors in the district court proceedings below. They object on procedural and constitutional grounds to the injunction, which enjoins them as "persons having actual knowledge of this Order," from "commencing any action or proceeding" against any defendants in the multi-district litigation (MDL 581) that "may in any way affect the right of any plaintiff or purported class member in any proceeding under" MDL 581. Appellees include both the plaintiffs and the defendants in the federal class action. Because we find that the issuance of the injunction was within the scope of the district court's power and was not an abuse of its discretion, we affirm.

MDL 581, pending before Judge Brieant, represents the consolidated proceedings of more than 100 federal securities lawsuits. Plaintiffs, some 100,000 holders of Baldwin single-premium deferred annuities (SPDAs), have asserted claims under the Securities Act of 1933 and the Securities Exchange Act of 1934 against 26 broker-dealers and related individuals who sold the SPDAs by representing them to be safe and desirable investments. Many of the plaintiffs have also raised pendent state law claims, such as consumer protection actions under statutes providing private rights of recovery. All these claims are designed to obtain additional recoveries beyond the amounts that plaintiffs will eventually receive under a rehabilitation plan for Baldwin's insurance subsidiaries that took effect in May 1984. Of the 100,000 or so in the plaintiff class less than 400 chose to opt out of the action.

During the past two years the district court has coordinated settlement talks between the parties. Negotiations proved successful as to 18 of the 26 broker-dealer defendants and stipulations of settlement were signed in September 1984 providing for payment of approximately $140 million to the plaintiffs in exchange for a release of all the plaintiffs' federal claims against the settling defendants as well as any claims available to each plaintiff under relevant state laws. This money is to be used in a Global Enhancement Plan, the terms of which are being separately negotiated by the parties. The Plan would provide the SPDA holders with a replacement investment property that would supplement their recovery under a rehabilitation plan. If no such agreement should be reached, the settlement money would be distributed as a lump sum to SPDA holders. Only about 50 individual plaintiffs objected to this settlement. For the purposes of ruling on these settlements, the district court provisionally approved class status.

On hearing of the proposed settlements the representatives of 40 states in the National Association of Attorneys General (NAAG), concluded that the proposal did not adequately compensate plaintiffs for their federal and state law claims. The states were also concerned about violations by the Baldwin companies of various state regulatory and criminal laws enforced by each state's attorney general. Following a meeting of the concerned NAAG members, the Maine Attorney General petitioned on behalf of the relevant NAAG subcommittee to be added to the service list in the suit. One month later, the district court preliminarily approved the settlement and scheduled a hearing on its fairness.

Meanwhile, between the time when the stipulations of settlement were signed and the year's end, some 10 states had issued subpoenas or other requests for information from various defendants. The states' objective, as revealed in some draft complaints and conceded by them upon oral argument of this appeal, is to enforce state laws authorizing them in their representative capacities to seek restitution and monetary recovery from the defendants to be paid over to those of the states' citizens who are plaintiffs in the consolidated class actions before Judge Brieant. In addition, some states may wish to pursue other state remedies, including prospective injunctive relief and enforcement of state criminal and regulatory laws designed to guard against repetition of the conduct forming the basis of the consolidated federal actions.

After an unsuccessful meeting in late January 1985 between certain state representatives and the defendants in which the states sought a higher settlement figure in exchange for the termination of all proposed state administrative proceedings and civil litigation against the defendants, 22 states, including about half of the appellant states, submitted an amicus brief opposing the settlements as inadequate. No state intervened except Maine, which did so for the purpose of commenting on the fairness of the settlement. In mid-February, several defendants received from the State of New York notices of its intent to bring a suit seeking restitution for New York citizens who held Baldwin SPDAs. These defendants moved the district court to enjoin the imminent New York actions.

Following the grant of a temporary restraining order and a hearing on the need for injunctive relief, the district court on February 26, 1985, orally approved an injunction. The judge stated that the injunction was necessary "in aid of preserving [the court's] jurisdiction" pursuant to the All-Writs Act, 28 U.S.C. § 1651 (1982) and Fed. R. Civ. P. 23(d). . . .

Recognizing the states' interests in enforcing their laws, Judge Brieant stated that it was to be "absolutely clear that the injunction will not extend to the enforcement of the criminal law against anybody who may be deemed to have violated it, and it will not extend to a request of a state court for prospective injunctive relief as to any business practice on the part of any defendant." The court provided that it is eventually denied class action status, it would modify the injunction so that the states would be free to bring actions representing non-party class members.

A proposed order was drawn up by defendants and served on the New York Attorney General, as representative of the amici states, on the Maine Attorney General as the NAAG representative, and on various state insurance officials. At the hearing about the form of the order, the defendants sought to bind all persons with notice of the order, while the State of Maine submitted language that would only have enjoined those acting "in concert" with New York.

Judge Brieant issued the injunction on March 19, 1985. The order enjoins the New York Attorney General and "all other persons having actual knowledge of th[e] Order" from

> commencing any action or proceeding of any kind against any defendant . . . on behalf of or derivative of the rights of any plaintiff or purported

class member . . . or which action or proceeding may in any way affect the rights of any plaintiff . . . or which action or proceeding seeks money damages arising out of the sale to any plaintiff . . . [of the Baldwin annuities] . . . or which action or proceeding seeks any declaratory relief with respect to any of the above. . . .

The injunction was to continue in effect until the entry of final judgment in all of the multidistrict proceedings.

The defendants served a copy of the injunction on every state attorney general. . . .

Thirty states then filed the present appeal and sought a stay from this court . . . . Meanwhile, on May 1, 1985, the district court approved the proposed settlements as fair, reasonable and adequate, and entered final judgments in 18 of the 26 consolidated class actions.

DISCUSSION

A preliminary injunction will be overturned only when the district court abuses its discretion. . . . An abuse of discretion may be found when the district court relies on clearly erroneous findings of fact or on an error of law in issuing the injunction. . . .

Authority for the Issuance of the Injunction

Federal courts have authority under the All-Writs Act, 28 U.S.C. § 1651 (1982), to "issue all writs necessary or appropriate in aid of their respective jurisdictions and agreeable to the usages and principles of law." In determining whether the injunction was a permissible exercise of Judge Brieant's authority under the All-Writs Act, we look both to cases interpreting this Act and also to cases interpreting similar language appearing in the Anti-Injunction Act, 28 U.S.C. § 2283 (1982). The latter statute bans injunctions against actions pending in state court, subject to specified exceptions, including an exception for injunctions "necessary in aid of the federal court's jurisdiction." While the parties agree that the Anti-Injunction Act is inapplicable here since the injunction below issued before any suits were commenced in state court, see Dombrowski v. Pfister, 380 U.S. 479, 484 n.2 (1965), cases interpreting this clause of the Anti-Injunction Act have been helpful in understanding the meaning of the All-Writs Act. . . .

We do not find independent authority for the issuance of the injunction in the Fed. R. Civ. P. 23(d) provision empowering the district judge to issue orders appropriate "for the protection of the members of the class or otherwise for the fair conduct of the action"; that rule is a rule of procedure and creates no substantive rights or remedies enforceable in federal court. . . .

When a federal court has jurisdiction over its case in chief, as did the district court here, the All-Writs Act grants it ancillary jurisdiction to issue writs "necessary or appropriate in aid of" that jurisdiction. This provision permits a district court to enjoin actions in state court where necessary to prevent relitigation of an existing federal judgment, see United States v. New York Telephone, 434 U.S. 159, 172 (1977) . . ., notwithstanding the fact that the parties to the original action could invoke res judicata in state courts against any subsequent suit brought on the same matters. . . . Even before a federal judgment is reached, however, the preservation of the federal court's jurisdiction or authority over an ongoing matter may justify an injunction against actions in state court. Such "federal injunctive relief may be necessary to prevent a state court from so interfering with a federal court's consideration or disposition of a case as to seriously impair the federal court's flexibility and authority to decide that case." Atlantic Coast Line R.R. Co. v. Brotherhood of Locomotive Engineers, 398 U.S. 281, 295 (1970) (dicta) (Anti-Injunction Act); see In re: Corrugated Container Antitrust Litigation, 659 F.2d 1332, 1334-35 (5th Cir. 1981) (Anti-Injunction Act) . . . .

On the other hand, the mere existence of a parallel lawsuit in state court that seeks to adjudicate the same *in personam* cause of action does not in itself provide sufficient grounds for an injunction against a state action in favor of a pending federal action. See Vendo Co. v. Lektro-Vend Corp., 433 U.S. 623, 642 (1977) ("We have never viewed parallel *in personam* actions as interfering with the jurisdiction of either court.") . . . This principle does not apply when federal courts have jurisdiction over a res in an *in rem* action; in such a case, because the "exercise by the state court of jurisdiction over the same res necessarily impairs, and may defect, the jurisdiction of the federal court already attached," the federal court is empowered to enjoin any state court proceeding affecting that res. Kline v. Burke Construction Co., 260 U.S. [226,] 229 [(1922)].

Here the findings of the district court that the injunction was necessary to preserve its jurisdiction and protect its judgments, if sustainable, would be sufficient to justify the issuance of the injunction under the All-Writs Act. We must therefore examine whether the district court's finding that the maintenance of actions in state court would impair its jurisdiction and authority over the consolidated federal multidistrict actions was clearly erroneous.

At the time when the injunction issued the parties in 18 of the 26 class actions had reached stipulated settlements that had been provisionally approved by the court and were awaiting final court approval, and the parties in the remaining 8 suits were continuing settlement negotiations. Final judgments in the 18 settling actions were entered shortly after the injunction issued. As for the defendants participating in the stipulated settlements, we conclude that the injunction was "necessary or appropriate in aid of" the court's jurisdiction. There is no question that an injunction could have been appropriately ordered after the 18 final federal judgments were entered, since it would properly have forestalled relitigation of those judgments. Because, as a condition of the settlement, the plaintiffs agreed to release all claims arising under federal and state law on account of the purchase of the Baldwin SPDAs from the settling defendants, such as post-settlement injunctions would have barred the states from bringing state law claims derivative of the plaintiffs' rights. . . . Were this not the case, the finality of virtually any class action involving pendent state claims could be defeated by subsequent suits brought by the states asserting rights derivative of those released by the class members. For instance, as a practical matter no defendant in the consolidated federal actions in the present case could reasonably be expected to consummate a settlement of those claims if their claims could be reasserted under state laws, whether by states on behalf of the plaintiffs or by anyone else, seeking recovery of money to be paid to the plaintiffs. Whether a state represented itself to be acting as a "sovereign" in such a suit or described its prayer as one for "restitution" or a "penalty" would make no difference if the recovery sought by the state was to be paid over to the plaintiffs. The effect would be to threaten to reopen the settlement unless and until it had been reduced to a judgment that would have res judicata consequences.

We recognize that under the line of cases typified by *Kline v. Burke Construction Co.*, *supra*, until the issuance of a final federal judgment the pendency of duplicative *in personam* actions in state court — even those actions derivative of the rights of parties of the federal action — would not ordinarily justify enjoining the state court actions. Here, however, the potential for an onslaught of state actions posed more than a risk of inconvenience or duplicative litigation; rather, such a development threatened to "seriously impair the federal court's flexibility and authority" to approve settlements in the multi-district litigation.... The circumstances faced by Judge Brieant threatened to frustrate proceedings in a federal action of substantial scope, which had already consumed vast amounts of judicial time and was nearing completion. Some 100,000 plaintiffs participated as parties in the action, compared to a mere 50 who chose to opt out. Settlement negotiations in the federal court had been under way for many months, agreement had been reached, and all that remained was approval of the settlement by the district court. Several evidentiary hearings on the settlement had been held, featuring testimony by representatives of the plaintiffs, the defendants, and various state agencies. The district court had before it thousands of pages of materials regarding the rehabilitation proceedings in courts in Arkansas and Indiana. In contrast, although the Baldwin bankruptcy occurred in 1983, the states waited until the eve of settlement approval to take any significant actions against the broker-dealers.

The existence of multiple and harassing actions by the states could only serve to frustrate the district court's efforts to craft a settlement in the multidistrict litigation before it. The success of any federal settlement was dependent on the parties' ability to agree to the release of any and all related civil claims the plaintiffs had against the settling defendants based on the same facts. If states or others could derivatively assert the same claims on behalf of the same class or members of it, there could be no certainty about the finality of any federal settlement. Any substantial risk of this prospect would threaten all of the settlement efforts by the district court and destroy the utility of the multidistrict forum otherwise ideally suited to resolving such broad claims. To the extent that the impending state court suits were vexatious and harassing, our interest in preserving federalism and comity with the state courts is not significantly disturbed by the issuance of injunctive relief. See *In re: Corrugated Container Antitrust Litigation, supra,* 659 F.2d at 1335. . . .

In effect, unlike the situation in the *Kline v. Burke Construction Co.* line of cases, the district court had before it a class action proceeding so far advanced that it was the virtual equivalent of a res over which the district judge required full control. Similar authority for the injunction comes from the court's power to protect and effectuate its order provisionally approving the 18 settlements. See . . . *In re: Corrugated Container Antitrust Litigation, supra,* 659 F.2d at 1334-35.

Under the circumstances we conclude that the injunction protecting the settling defendants was unquestionably "necessary or appropriate in aid of" the federal court's jurisdiction. Although the question is closer as to the application of the injunction to the 8 defendants who have not yet settled, we cannot find that the injunction was erroneous as to them. Given the extensive involvement of the district court in settlement negotiations to date and in the management of this substantial class action, we perceive a major threat to the federal court's ability to manage and resolve the actions against the remaining defendants should the states be free to harass the defendants through state court actions designed to influence the defendants' choices in the federal litigation. So long as there is a substantially significant prospect that these 8 defendants will settle in the reasonably near future, we conclude that the injunction entered by the district court is not improper. If, however, at some point in the continued progress of the actions against the remaining 8 defendants it should appear that prompt settlement was no longer likely, we anticipate that upon application the injunction against parallel actions by the states might be lifted; in that event the situation would fall within the [*Kline v. Burke*] *Construction Co.* rule that *in personam* proceedings in state court cannot be enjoined merely because they are duplicative of actions being heard in federal court. That situation, however, does not presently exist.

Having found the injunction necessary and appropriate in aid of the district court's jurisdiction we conclude that it is no less valid because it applies to states other than New York. An important feature of the All-Writs Act is its grant of authority to enjoin and bind non-parties to an action when needed to preserve the court's ability to reach or enforce its decision in a case over which it has proper jurisdiction. See, *e.g., United States v. New York Telephone Co., supra,* 434 U.S. at 174 ("The power conferred by the Act, extends, under appropriate circumstances, to persons who, though not parties to the original action or engaged in wrongdoing, are in a position to frustrate the implementation of a court order or the proper administration of justice, [citations omitted], and encompasses even those who have not taken any affirmative action to hinder justice."); . . . *United States v. Hall,* 472 F.2d 261, 265 (5th Cir. 1972) (upholding a contempt citation based on an injunction enjoining a non-party in a school desegregation case from causing disruption on the school campus because the "integrity of the court's power to render a binding judgment in an action over which it has jurisdiction [was] at stake"). The power to bind non-parties distinguishes injunctions issued under the Act from injunctions issued in situations in which the activities of the third parties do not interfere with the very conduct of the proceeding before the court. . . .

As for notice the requirements of the All-Writs Act are satisfied if the parties whose conduct is enjoined have actual notice of the injunction and an opportunity to seek relief from it in the district court. Cf. *United States v. Hall, supra,* 472 F.2d at 266-67. These requirements were met here, since each state's attorney general was served with the injunction and since each had the opportunity to present arguments against it to the district court. None sought to introduce evidence. Although it would under many circumstances be desirable for service to be made in advance of any proposed injunction on all non-parties whose conduct would thereby be restricted, we cannot impose such a condition on use of the All-Writs Act. In exercising its powers under that Act, the district court may face circumstances in which such notice is impractical or even impossible. . . . So long as the injunction is limited to those engaged in such conduct with actual notice of the terms of the injunction, as is the injunction here, we cannot say that it must fail for lack of notice, even though it appears that not all of the appellant states were aware in advance that an order of injunction was being entered that would limit their conduct as well as the conduct of the State of New York.

[The Second Circuit then rejected the argument that the injunction violated the Eleventh Amendment.]

Having rejected the state's objections to the district court's injunction, we affirm.

American Law Institute, COMPLEX LITIGATION: STATUTORY RECOMMENDATIONS AND ANALYSIS

263 (1994)

§ 5.04 Antisuit Injunctions

(a) When actions are transferred and consolidated pursuant to § 3.01 or § 5.01, the transferee court may enjoin transactionally related proceedings, or portions thereof, pending in any state or federal court whenever it determines that the continuation of those actions substantially impairs or interferes with the consolidated actions and that an injunction would promote the just, efficient, and fair resolution of the actions before it.

(b) Factors to be considered in deciding whether an injunction should issue under subsection (a) include

> (1) how far the actions to be enjoined have progressed;
>
> (2) the degree to which the actions to be enjoined share common questions with and are duplicative of the consolidated actions;
>
> (3) the extent to which the actions to be enjoined involve issues or claims of federal law; and

(4) whether parties to the action to be enjoined were permitted to exclude themselves from the consolidated proceeding....

Notes and Questions

1. *Baldwin-United* is an important complement to and extension of *Corrugated Container*. it complements *Corrugated Container* by clearly locating the source of the power to enjoin state proceedings in the All-Writs Act. It extends *Corrugated Container* by authorizing an injunction with the potential to be considerably broader than the one authorized in *Corrugated Container*. Like *Corrugated Container*, *Baldwin-United* permitted a federal court to enjoin state proceedings that threatened a settlement reached with eighteen defendants in the federal class action. Unlike *Corrugated Container*, however, it extended the injunctive power to protect the eight defendants who had not yet agreed to settle from duplicative litigation in other forums. It further broadened the boundaries of *Corrugated Container* by permitting a federal court to enjoin cases brought by potential plaintiffs who were not themselves parties to the federal litigation. Each of these extensions is significant.

(a) *Enjoining Suits Against Defendants That Have Not Yet Settled*. One of the apparent limits of *Corrugated Container* is that its power to enjoin state proceedings does not arise until a settlement or judgment fund has been, or is imminently about to be, created. From the viewpoint of efficiency and justice, waiting until the time of settlement or judgment to issue an injunction against state proceedings is undesirable; because settlement or judgment funds typically are created late in the litigative day, a great deal of the duplication and expense that an injunction might have prevented has already occurred. As this power to enjoin duplicative litigation is extended back toward the start of the litigation, it becomes (indirectly) the state-federal consolidation device for which complex and complicated litigation is searching. To extend the All-Writs power further back toward the start of the litigation, however, requires that we abandon the existence of the settlement fund as the touchstone of the injunction. *Baldwin-United*'s admonition that the injunctive power against a non-settling defendant would end once it became clear that settlement with that defendant was not possible shows that the Second Circuit was unwilling to depart too far from that touchstone. But it at least sets the table for bolder efforts, such as the ALI's proposal, to enjoy related litigation before the settlement occurs.

(b) *Enjoining Suits By Nonparties Against Defendants*. The second extension of *Corrugated Container* in *Baldwin-United* involves the issuance of an injunction against persons who are not parties to the suit. This extension, of course, raises a host of difficulties. One, of course, is federalism, but there are also the problems of depriving a nonparty of the opportunity to be heard and the adversarial ability to control the terms and the forum of her litigation. We have already examined this latter difficulty in Chapter Two, when we explored joinder and preclusion mechanisms for dealing with nonparties to a litigation. An injunction mechanism, which bears a certain resemblance to the preclusion mechanism, is still a third way to deal with the problem of "sideline sitters."

Obviously, the power to deal with sideline sitters suggested in *Baldwin-United* is far less comprehensive than the joinder or preclusion alternatives we examined before. First, if the settlement either falls apart or the case otherwise terminates without a settlement distribution, the injunction against the nonparties also ends, and there is no binding or preclusive effect that attaches to their claims. Second, the All-Writs power to enjoin nonparties arises only because of the threat that the nonparties pose to the potential settlement fund.

Although injunctions are limited, they are vitally important. The real utility of an injunction is not its ability to bind or permanently preclude nonparties; its utility is to prevent nonparties from pursuing litigation prior to the entry of a judgment. In this regard, an injunction is important even with respect to parties, for it is not uncommon for plaintiffs in large-scale litigation to file the same case in state and federal court. The power of one court (typically the federal court, because state courts have no power to enjoin federal *in personam* actions) is, at least in some cases, essential.

The second issue, of course, is to discern the cases in which the power is essential. *Baldwin-United* hinges the power on the existence of a settlement. The ALI's proposal hinges the power on the need to prevent wasteful re-litigation in complicated cases. A third, intermediate possibility is to limit the power to cases in which lawyer dysfunction can be avoided (*i.e.*, cases in which state suits threaten to disrupt the federal courts' ability to provide a fair remedy to all affected persons). The alternative that is most palatable to you may be determined by the amount of joinder or preclusion that you feel is appropriate.

2. In Alton Box Board Co. v. Esprit de Corp., 682 F.2d 1267 (9th Cir. 1982), the Ninth Circuit resolved an issue left open in *Corrugated Container*: whether a federal court had the power to enjoin state law antitrust claims by indirect purchasers who had no claim against the *Corrugated Container* defendants under federal antitrust law. Since they had no viable federal claims, these indirect purchasers were not members of the *Corrugated Container* class action, but their independent suits, filed in California state court, threatened the federal settlement; obviously the *Corrugated Container* defendants had far less incentive to settle one set of claims when they were faced with a set of state-law claims seeking further compensation for precisely the same conduct and injuries. The defendants attempted the "removal-venue switch" tactic of first removing the state case to federal court in California, with the hope of then transferring the case to the multidistrict court in Texas. But the effort got hung up on the first step, when Judge Schwarzer remanded the case to state court and refused to enjoin the state proceeding. Scwarzer's decision was affirmed on appeal:

> The district court held that injunctive relief was "unequivocally" barred by the [Anti-Injunction] Act because the manufacturers' action fell within none of the Act's exceptions. We agree. The first exception does not apply . . . . Nor does the second exception apply: an injunction is not necessary to aid the district court's jurisdiction. . . .
>
> Esprit is not a direct purchaser, has never been and cannot be a member of the federal class, and has never been subject to the jurisdiction of the multidistrict litigation court. See In re Corrugated Container Antitrust Litigation, [659 F.2d 1332, 1336 (5th Cir. 1981)] (multidistrict litigation court's injunction would not bar indirect purchaser suit brought under state antitrust law). Therefore, the district court correctly concluded that an injunction was not "necessary in aid of its jurisdiction."
>
> The manufacturers argue creatively that an injunction is necessary to aid the district court's jurisdiction because Esprit's state [antitrust] class action involves a claim to the same "common fund -- the amount of the alleged overcharge" . . . . over which the multidistrict litigation court is

charged with determining the rights and liabilities of the parties thereto. This argument is persuasive. It highlights the risk that Esprit's state suit may result in the "duplicative recoveries" condemned by the Supreme Court. Its defect is that it runs to the merits. With respect to the issue of whether the district court had jurisdiction under the Anti-Injunction Act, it is not on point. . . .

Even if the "fund" of overcharges may be considered sufficiently analogous to a res to invoke this rule, however, the plea of the manufacturers is to the wrong court. The court with jurisdiction over the res is the multidistrict litigation court. . . . Having been instructed that the exceptions to the Anti-Injunction Act should be narrowly construed, we refuse to construe the Act to allow one federal district court to enjoin a pending state lawsuit "in aid of" the jurisdiction of another federal district court.

These same considerations establish that an injunction is not necessary under the third exception: to "protect or effectuate" the judgment entered by the multidistrict litigation court. . . . Esprit cannot be a class member in that action since it is an indirect purchaser; therefore, Esprit's state [antitrust] suit does not interfere with the judgment entered by the multidistrict litigation court. Further, as we decided with respect to the second exception, the district court in this case is not authorized by the third exception to enjoin Esprit's state action in order to protect the judgment of the multidistrict litigation court. As we pointed out earlier, the Act's language allows a federal court to issue an injunction only if "necessary in aid of its jurisdiction, or to protect or effectuate its judgments," 28 U.S.C. § 2283, and thus it would impermissibly enlarge the exceptions "by loose statutory construction," [*Atlantic Coastline*], 398 U.S. at 287, to allow one federal court to issue an injunction in order to aid the jurisdiction or protect the judgment of another federal district court. If an injunction is necessary to protect the judgment of the multidistrict litigation court, it must issue from that court. [682 F.2d at 1272-73.]

Unlike *Baldwin-United*, the settlement in *Corrugated Container* did not involve an insolvent defendant. Does *Alton Box* demonstrate that concerns for duplicative litigation or threats to a settlement fund are not, in and of themselves, a sufficient reason for a federal court to invoke its All-Writs power to enjoin the cases of nonparties? Does the different result in *Baldwin-United* demonstrate that the prospect of lawyer dysfunction is a sufficient reason for a federal court to invoke its All-Writs power to enjoin the cases of nonparties? If this suggestion is accurate, two further questions follow. First, is the ALI's proposal overkill? Second, is *Corrugated Container*, which never indicated the source of its power to enjoin state cases, wrongly decided?

3. You might wish to test these questions in the context of a specific case. Take the *Keating* litigation described at p. 377, *supra*. Having failed to secure removal of the Attorney General's claims on behalf of California residents, could the defendants have asked the multidistrict judge in Arizona to enjoin the prosecution of the action in California state court? Would your answer depend on whether the California residents represented by the Attorney General were already parties in the Arizona case? On whether the Arizona case was close to settlement? On whether an injunction would prevent duplicative litigation? On whether the *Keating* defendants have insufficient assets to make both California and non-California plaintiffs whole? Cf. Safeco Insurance Co. of America v.

Norris & Hirshberg, Inc., 640 F. Supp. 712 (N.D. Ga. 1986) (refusing to enjoin state case that was related to federal case but involved different plaintiffs).

4. Suppose that the parties in a state court class action had either settled or were close to settling the case, and related litigation was pending in federal court. Could the state court enjoin the federal proceeding, using the reasoning of *Corrugated Container* and *Baldwin* that the settlement fund is a *res* and the holding of *Princess Lida* (p. 391, *supra*) that state courts which first obtain jurisdiction of a *res* may enjoin related federal proceedings? Could the injunction extend to preclude prosecution of federal actions against non-settling defendants who might possibly settle in state court? To non-parties to the state proceeding who threaten to undo the state settlement in the federal proceedings? Since state courts can be transferee courts under the ALI's proposal, the ALI would apparently give the power to state courts to enjoin related federal proceedings whenever it is necessary to prevent wasteful re-litigation. If you are uncomfortable with giving the state courts this power, should federal courts enjoy it? If so, why? Is it because federal courts are more competent to handle the problems of complex and complicated litigation? More competent generally?

A related set of issues arose in Romstadt v. Apple Computer, Inc., 948 F. Supp. 701 (N.D. Ohio 1996), in which an alleged deceptive practice by the defendant resulted in the sale of thousands of personal computers that were less powerful than advertised. After the federal court awarded summary judgment in favor of an individual plaintiff, the court prepared to turn to the issue of class certification for other injured consumers. During this time period, the defendant had settlement discussions with the plaintiff, and proposed a class settlement that the plaintiff rejected. The defendant then commenced negotiations with another plaintiff in a case in Texas state court, who agreed to accept the class settlement (which included $2 million in attorneys' fees). The parties in the Texas case presented the state judge with a stipulation of settlement, and requested that the judge certify a settlement class and approve the settlement. That day, after a short hearing, the state court signed an order certifying the class and preliminarily approving the settlement. The plaintiff in the federal case was never notified of the settlement, nor given an opportunity to appear and present objections. Nor was the state judge told about the federal proceedings.

The defendant then asked the federal judge to stay the federal case in deference to the state case. (We will examine the idea of a stay in more detail shortly. See p. 426, *infra*.) The plaintiff responded by requesting a preliminary injunction against the further proceedings in state court. The federal judge declined to grant either motion. Nonetheless, the court found that the failure to permit the plaintiff to appear and present objections in the Texas proceeding amounted to a violation of his due process rights. As a remedy, it conditionally certified a class of consumers in federal court, and held that, with respect to members of the federal class action, the judgment in the Texas case would have preclusive effect only for those class member who affirmatively agreed to take advantage of the Texas settlement. The federal court held that it would vacate its order if the state court vacated its own prior orders and held a hearing on the settlement at which the plaintiff could participate. Could the defendant and the Texas plaintiff have asked the state court to enjoin the federal proceeding when it preliminarily approved the settlement? On the facts of the case, should the federal court have obeyed such an injunction? Suppose that the plaintiff in the federal case had not yet obtained summary judgment — should the federal court have obeyed the injunction then?

STATE FARM FIRE & CASUALTY CO. v. TASHIRE

386 U.S. 523 (1967)

■ MR. JUSTICE FORTAS delivered the opinion of the Court.

[A fuller description of the facts of the case can be found at p. 325, *supra*. Briefly, a Greyhound bus collided with a pickup truck driven by Ellis Clark. Two passengers were killed and 33 were injured; most were American citizens, and 11 were Canadians. The accident occurred in Shasta County, California. Greyhound was a California corporation. Clark, his passenger, and the bus driver were all residents of Oregon. Clark had in force a $20,000 insurance policy, issued by State Farm, an Illinois corporation, which covered automobile accidents.

[Four passengers filed suit in California state court against Greyhound, Clark, the bus driver, and the pickup's passenger. After paying into the court the $20,000 proceeds of the policy, State Farm filed an action in the nature of interpleader in the United States District Court for the District of Oregon, joining as defendants in the case Clark, Greyhound all of the bus passengers, the bus driver, and the pickup's passenger

[In conjunction with the interpleader action, the district court exercised its powers under 28 U.S.C. § 2361 and enjoined prosecution of any further proceedings against Clark and State Farm. During the same time, Greyhound moved that the injunction be broadened to include any actions brought against it or its driver. The court granted the requested injunction, although it permitted the filing — although not the prosecution — of suits in other courts. In effect, the injunction forced all suits against Clark, State Farm, Greyhound, and Greyhound's driver to be prosecuted as part of the interpleader proceeding.]

On interlocutory appeal, the Court of Appeals for the Ninth Circuit reversed. The court found it unnecessary to reach respondents' contentions relating to service of process and the scope of the injunction, for it concluded that interpleader was not available in the circumstances of this case. It held that in States like Oregon which do not permit "direct action" suits against insurance companies until judgments are obtained against the insured, the insurance companies may not invoke federal interpleader until the claims against the insured, the alleged tortfeasor, have been reduced to judgment. Until that is done, said the court, claimants with unliquidated tort claims are not "claimants" within the meaning of § 1335, nor are they "persons having claims against the plaintiff" within the meaning of Rule 22 of the Federal Rules of Civil Procedure.[3] In accord with that view, it directed

---

3. We need not pass upon the Court of Appeals' conclusions with respect to the interpretation of interpleader under Rule 22, which provides that "(1) Persons having claims against the plaintiff may be joined as defendants and required to interplead when their claims are such that the plaintiff is or may be exposed to double or multiple liability. . . ." First, as we indicate today, this action was properly brought under § 1335. Second, State Farm did not purport to invoke Rule 22. Third, State Farm could not have invoked it in light of venue and service of process limitations. Whereas statutory interpleader may be brought in the district where any claimant resides (28 U.S.C. § 1397), Rule interpleader based upon diversity of citizenship

dissolution of the temporary injunction and dismissal of the action. Because the Court of Appeals' decision on this point conflicts with those of other federal courts, and concerns a matter of significance to the administration of federal interpleader, we granted certiorari. Although we reverse the decision of the Court of Appeals upon the [§ 1335] question, we direct a substantial modification of the District Court's injunction for reasons which will appear.

I.

[The Court's held that 28 U.S.C. § 1335, which requires only minimal diversity in statutory interpleader actions, was constitutional. See p. 325, *supra*.]

II.

We do not agree with the Court of Appeals that, in the absence of a state law or contractual provision for "direct action" suits against the insurance company, the company must wait until persons asserting claims against its insured have reduced those claims to judgment before seeking to invoke the benefits of federal interpleader. That may have been a tenable position under the 1926 and 1936 interpleader statutes. These statutes did not carry forward the language in the 1917 Act authorizing interpleader where adverse claimants "may claim" benefits as well as where they "are claiming" them. In 1948, however, in the revision of the Judicial Code, the "may claim" language was restored. Until the decision below, every court confronted by the question has concluded that the 1948 revision removed whatever requirement there might previously have been that the insurance company wait until at least two claimants reduced their claims to judgments. The commentators are in accord.

Considerations of judicial administration demonstrate the soundness of this view which, in any event, seems compelled by the language of the present statute, which is remedial and to be liberally construed. Were an insurance company required to await reduction of claims to judgment, the first claimant to obtain such a judgment or to negotiate a settlement might appropriate all or a disproportionate slice of the fund before his fellow claimants were able to establish their claims. The difficulties such a race to judgment pose for the insurer, and the unfairness which may result to some claimants, were among the principal evils the interpleader device was intended to remedy.[15]

---

may be brought only in the district where all plaintiffs or all defendants reside (28 U.S.C. § 1391 (a)). And whereas statutory interpleader enables a plaintiff to employ nationwide service of process (28 U.S.C. § 2361), service of process under Rule 22 is confined to that provided in Rule 4. . . .

15. The insurance problem envisioned at the time was that of an insurer faced with conflicting but mutually exclusive claims to a policy, rather than an insurer confronted with the problem of allocating a fund among various claimants whose independent claims may exceed the amount of the fund. . . .

III.

The fact that State Farm had properly invoked the interpleader jurisdiction under § 1335 did not, however, entitle it to an order both enjoining prosecution of suits against it outside the confines of the interpleader proceeding and also extending such protection to its insured, the alleged tortfeasor. Still less was Greyhound Lines entitled to have that order expanded so as to protect itself and its driver, also alleged to be tortfeasors, from suits brought by its passengers in various state or federal courts. Here, the scope of the litigation, in terms of parties and claims, was vastly more extensive than the confines of the "fund," the deposited proceeds of the insurance policy. In these circumstances, the mere existence of such a fund cannot, by use of interpleader, be employed to accomplish purposes that exceed the needs of orderly contest with respect to the fund.

There are situations, of a type not present here, where the effect of interpleader is to confine the total litigation to a single forum and proceeding. One such case is where a stakeholder, faced with rival claims to the fund itself, acknowledges — or denies — his liability to one or the other of the claimants. In this situation, the fund itself is the target of the claimants. It marks the outer limits of the controversy. It is, therefore, reasonable and sensible that interpleader, in discharge of its office to protect the fund, should also protect the stakeholder from vexatious and multiple litigation. In this context, the suits sought to be enjoined are squarely within the language of 28 U.S.C. § 2361, which provides in part:

> "In any civil action of interpleader or in the nature of interpleader under section 1335 of this title, a district court may issue its process for all claimants and enter its order restraining them from instituting or prosecuting *any proceeding* in any State or United States court *affecting the property, instrument or obligation involved in the interpleader action* . . . ." (Emphasis added.)

But the present case is another matter. Here, an accident has happened. Thirty-five passengers or their representatives have claims which they wish to press against a variety of defendants: the bus company, its driver, the owner of the truck, and the truck driver. The circumstance that one of the prospective defendants happens to have an insurance policy is a fortuitous event which should not of itself shape the nature of the ensuing litigation. For example, a resident of California, injured in California aboard a bus owned by a California corporation should not be forced to sue that corporation anywhere but in California simply because another prospective defendant carried an insurance policy. And an insurance company whose maximum interest in the case cannot exceed $20,000 and who in fact asserts that it has no interest at all, should not be allowed to determine that dozens of tort plaintiffs must be compelled to press their claims — even those claims which are not against the insured and which in no event could be satisfied out of the meager insurance fund — in a single forum of the insurance company's choosing. There is nothing in the statutory scheme, and very little in the judicial and academic commentary upon that scheme, which requires that the tail be allowed to wag the dog in this fashion.

State Farm's interest in this case, which is the fulcrum of the interpleader procedure, is confined to its $20,000 fund. That interest receives full vindication when the court restrains claimants from seeking to enforce against the insurance company any judgment obtained against its insured, except in the interpleader proceeding itself. To the extent that the District Court sought to control claimants' lawsuits against the insured and other alleged tortfeasors, it exceeded the powers granted to it by the statutory scheme.

We recognize, of course, that our view of interpleader means that it cannot be used to solve all the vexing problems of multiparty litigation arising out of a mass tort. But interpleader was never intended to perform such a function, to be an all-purpose "bill of peace."[17] Had it been so intended, careful provision would necessarily have been made to insure that a party with little or no interest in the outcome of a complex controversy should not strip truly interested parties of substantial rights — such as the right to choose the forum in which to establish their claims, subject to generally applicable rules of jurisdiction, venue, service of process, removal, and change of venue. None of the legislative and academic sponsors of a modern federal interpleader device viewed their accomplishment as a "bill of peace," capable of sweeping dozens of lawsuits out of the various state and federal courts in which they were brought and into a single interpleader proceeding....

In light of the evidence that federal interpleader was not intended to serve the function of a "bill of peace" in the context of multiparty litigation arising out of a mass tort, of the anomalous power which such a construction of the statute would give the stakeholder, and of the thrust of the statute and the purpose it was intended to serve, we hold that the interpleader statute did not authorize the injunction entered in the present case. Upon remand, the injunction is to be modified consistently with this opinion.

IV.

The judgment of the Court of Appeals is reversed, and the case is remanded to the United States District Court for proceedings consistent with this opinion.

Notes and Questions

1. The § 1335 interpleader remedy combines a number of different concepts that we have explored over the last two chapters. First, it is a joinder device that permits a person holding a stake to join on an involuntary basis all parties that might have a claim to the stake. Second, it provides for an injunction, so that claimants cannot continue to prosecute cases in other courts. Third, § 1335 interpleader overcomes many of the limitations of territorial jurisdiction by authorizing nationwide service of process. See 28 U.S.C. 2361; p. 274, *supra*. Fourth, interpleader provides a remedy in a single court as long as minimal

---

17. There is not a word in the legislative history suggesting such a purpose. See S. Rep. No. 558, 74th Cong., 1st Sess. (1935)...

diversity and a matter in controversy of $500 exist. See 28 U.S.C. § 1335, p. 325, *supra*. Indeed, interpleader is by far the most potent aggregation device that we have thus far encountered.

2. As powerful a device as it is, however, § 1335 interpleader operates only in cases in which insurance proceeds, bonds, money, or other property are at stake. Unless this requirement receives a very generous reading, interpleader will prove to be a very narrow remedy as well. In this regard, the result in *Tashire* is a classic "good news-bad news" situation. The good news is that interpleader is authorized, and related litigation in other forums can be enjoined, even when (a) the claimants' entitlement to the insurance proceeds have not been established and (b) some or all of the claimants have not yet filed suit. Thus, interpleader avoids one of the principal problems of the *Corrugated Container* and *Baldwin-United* injunctions: The interpleader stay can be used early in the litigative day, rather than at the moment of settlement.

The bad news is that the Supreme Court does not permit an expansive use of interpleader to prevent the re-litigation of claims which are related to, but distinct from, the claims against the insurance proceeds. As in *Corrugated Container* and *Baldwin-United*, therefore, we are left with an injunctive authority which is closely tied to the existence of a *res*: a settlement or insurance fund from which the plaintiffs' claims will be satisfied. To the extent that plaintiffs' recovery is not dependent on this res, there is no authority to enjoin their claims. Why should an important question like the power of a federal court to enjoin wasteful litigation hinge on the existence (some might even say, the fetish) of a res? Is the focus on the existence, or the imminent creation, of a piece of property merely a throwback to a bygone era in which property rights often received favored treatment from the law? Is there any reason to perpetuate that treatment in modern complex and complicated litigation? Isn't it odd that the federal court in *Tashire* can decide the entitlement to a $20,000 insurance policy, but is powerless to prevent inefficient re-litigation whose preventable excess costs might well exceed $20,000 by a substantial margin?

3. *Tashire* was not necessarily a complex case. Although the insurance proceeds were limited, the assets of the remaining defendants were undoubtedly enough to make every plaintiff whole. (This assumes that the claims against Greyhound were at least colorable.) Hence, there was no risk that early and late filers would be treated disparately.

Suppose that the combined assets of all of the tort defendants were inadequate to satisfy the plaintiffs' claims. Would the "bad news" half of *Tashire* still apply in such complex, as opposed to complicated, litigation? Or would *Tashire*'s concern for the adversarial right of each tort plaintiff to be master of her own complaint outweigh the need to prevent inter-plaintiff inequity? If *Tashire*'s "bad news" did not apply in complex cases, we would again be presented with a situation in which the rules for complex litigation differed from that of complicated and routine litigation. What justifies this disparate (*i.e.*, non-transsubstantive) outcome?

4. In considering the use of interpleader to avoid joinder complexity or wasteful re-litigation, you should know that there are actually two forms of interpleader: statutory interpleader (§ 1335) and rule interpleader (Rule 22). *Tashire* involves § 1335, or statutory, interpleader. As Rule 22(2) makes clear, rule interpleader is an independent form of joinder. It is important to

understand the differences between the two types of interpleader and to see when each might be used most effectively.

There are at least six differences between statutory and rule interpleader. The first is the standard under which the interpleader is permissible. Statutory interpleader can be invoked when there are two or more adverse claims to money, property a bond, a certificate, a policy of insurance, "or other instrument of value or amount of $500 or more." Rule interpleader is permissible when there is a risk of "double or multiple liability." Although the latter standard in theory could be expanded to include non-res situations (such as claims by multiple plaintiffs arising from a mass tort or punitive damages claims in which each plaintiff seeks to punish a defendant for the same conduct), in practice the two terms have been identically construed: they apply to circumstances in which two or more claims are made against the same *res* or limited fund. See 7 Charles A. Wright et al., Federal Practice & Procedure § 1704 (1986).

Second, the rules of subject matter jurisdiction differ. Statutory interpleader contains its own grant of jurisdiction (§ 1335), and requires only minimal diversity between two or more adverse claimants. Rule interpleader has no independent grant of jurisdiction; jurisdiction must be found elsewhere in the United States Code (most typically in 28 U.S.C. §§ 1331 or 1332). For interpleader claims based on state law, § 1332 requires that there be complete diversity between the interpleader plaintiff(s) and the interpleader defendant(s), and also that more than $75,000 be at stake. For the most part, this difference means that statutory interpleader will be more useful, but there are two situations in which rule interpleader might be available when statutory interpleader is not: (1) when all of the adverse claimants to the property are of the same citizenship but interpleader plaintiff who has no claim to the proceeds is of diverse citizenship; and (2) when the claims to the property are based on a federal question, so that § 1331 jurisdiction exists. See Morongo Band of Mission Indians v. California State Board of Equalization, 858 F.2d 1376 (9th Cir. 1988), cert. denied, 488 U.S. 1006 (1989); Wright et al., *supra*, §§ 1703, 1710. Is it possible to argue, in the context of a case of joinder complexity, that only minimal diversity is required for rule interpleader? See pp. 331-32, *supra*.

Third, statutory and rule interpleader have different rules of personal jurisdiction. Although 28 U.S.C. § 2361 permits a federal court to exercise nationwide service of process in a case of statutory interpleader, courts in rule interpleader cases are limited to the traditional, more restrictive rules of service of process for *in personam* actions in federal court. See New York Life Insurance Co. v. Dunlevy, 241 U.S. 518 (1916); pp. 260-78, *supra*. On the other hand, it might be possible in cases of rule interpleader to invoke 28 U.S.C. § 1655, which permits a court to order a defendant not amenable to jurisdiction in the forum state to appear in the court in any action "to enforce any lien or claim to, or to remove any incumbrance or lien or cloud upon the title to, real or personal property within the district." Section 1655 is arguably even broader than § 2361, in that it authorizes substituted service (usually by notice) when a defendant cannot be found and personally served or is absent from the United States. For a discussion of the merits and demerits of interpreting § 1655 to cover interpleader and a description of interpleader cases (both rule and statutory) invoking § 1655, see Wright et al., *supra*, § 1711.

Fourth, venue rules, which we study in Chapter Four, differ for statutory and rule interpleader. Rule interpleader relies on the same venue rules as other federal cases. See pp. 450-56, *infra*. Statutory interpleader has its own, more generous venue provision which allows a case to be brought in any district in which "one or more of the claimants resides." 28 U.S.C. § 1397.

Fifth, statutory interpleader requires the deposit of the disputed property or else the posting of a bond. Rule interpleader does not, although a court can order one in its discretion.

Finally, § 2361 expressly authorizes a district court to issue an injunction against related proceedings in a statutory interpleader case. There is no similar express power in rule interpleader cases, although it is widely understood that such a power exists. See Wright et al., *supra*, § 1717. For statutory interpleader, the Anti-Injunction Act, 28 U.S.C. § 2283, presents no problem, since § 2361 is an express congressional authorization to enjoin state suits. But rule interpleader injunctions are not expressly authorized, the Anti-Injunction Act does have a potential effect on rule interpleader. Nonetheless, the better present thought is that rule interpleader injunctions escape the prohibition of § 2283. First, § 2283 does not affect the power of a federal court to enjoin actual or threatened proceedings in another federal court, nor does it affect the power to enjoin threatened proceedings in state court. Second, with respect to existing proceedings in state court, the "necessary in aid of jurisdiction" exception to § 2283 has been interpreted to permit injunctions against state cases that affect a *res* within the federal court's jurisdiction; and interpleader involves a *res* brought within the federal court's jurisdiction. See United States v. Major Oil Corp., 583 F.2d 1152 (10th Cir. 1978); Pan American Fire & Casualty Co. v. Revere, 188 F. Supp. 474 (W.D. La. 1960). If we move away from using interpleader only to deal with multiple claims to a res, however, the Anti-Injunction Act problems of rule interpleader might become disabling.

5. Whether statutory or rule interpleader is used, there exist several practical hurdles to the creation of a "complex-friendly" interpleader regime. First, under § 1335(a)(2), an interpleader plaintiff must either deposit the disputed assets in dispute into court or post a bond for their value. Since this requirement is a part of the jurisdictional statute, courts have held that the deposit or bond requirement cannot be waived. See Wright et al., *supra*, § 1716. In many cases, it is impossible to pay in all of the assets of the corporation; even if it were, payment of all assets would effectively be equivalent to a bankruptcy liquidation without the protections of the bankruptcy code. Likewise, a bond might be very costly to post.

This problem does not necessarily infect Rule 22 interpleader, which has no comparable pay-in provision; the court has the equitable discretion to decide whether deposit or a bond is appropriate. Id. Nevertheless, a second, equally thorny problem exists for rule interpleader: it is not clear that Rule 22's standard — exposure to "double or multiple liability" — can be met. Because the mass tortfeasor's liability is limited to its available assets, and because the inequitable distribution of those assets in no way results in double or multiple liability, rule interpleader may be unavailable in the mass tort context.

A third problem, equally an issue in statutory and rule interpleader, is the occasionally invoked rule that interpleader is unavailable to one who seeks protection from his own wrong. For instance, in Farmers Irrigating Ditch & Reservoir Co. v. Kane, 845 F.2d 229 (10th Cir. 1988), an impecunious tortfeasor whose conduct caused severe flooding to numerous individuals attempted to pay into the court what it claimed to be virtually all its assets. The court declined to authorize interpleader:

> Our attention has not been directed to any case where a tortfeasor in a multi-claim tort can admit liability, tender into court a minimal amount of money with the representation that such is all he has, force the claimants to prorate the amount deposited, and then obtain an order discharging him from any further liability for his tort. . . . . It is the general rule that a party seeking interpleader must be free from blame in causing the controversy, and where he stands as a wrongdoer with respect to the subject matter of the suit or any of the claimants, he cannot have relief by interpleader. [845 F.2d at 232.]

See also *Pan American Fire & Casualty*, 188 F. Supp. 474; Paula J. McDermott, Note, *Can Statutory Interpleader Be Used as a Remedy by the Tortfeasor in Mass Tort Litigation*, 90 Dick. L. Rev. 439 (1985). Some courts have apparently overlooked this equity-based rule in particular cases. Cf. Holcomb v. Aetna Life Insurance Co., 228 F.2d 75 (10th Cir. 1955) (refusing to deny interpleader until allegations of bad faith had been established at trial), cert. denied, 350 U.S. 986 (1956); Aetna Casualty and Insurance Co. v. Ahrens, 414 F. Supp. 1235 (S.D. Tex. 1975) (allowing interpleader by insolvent tortfeasor without reference to tortfeasor's wrongful conduct).

Fourth, in many mass torts it may be impossible to identify all, or even very many, of the potential claimants; and, unless an insolvent wrongdoer is going to go to the trouble of providing widespread notice, many of the potential claimants will probably remain unaware of the case. Since the real reason to interpret interpleader liberally in the case of mass wrongdoing is to assure that the wrongdoer's assets will be fairly distributed, the inability to join all victims undercuts the need for interpleader.

Finally, the use of statutory or rule interpleader in the context of arguably insufficient assets raises interpretive problems equivalent to the similar effort to use one of the class action rules, F.R.Civ.P. 23(b)(1)(B), to join all potential claimants to a limited fund. We will examine these problems in greater detail later, but two critical ones are the level of the showing required the available assets are in fact insufficient and the fear that the Federal Rules should not be construed to provide bankruptcy-like remedies without any of the protections built into the Bankruptcy Act. See pp. 593-98, 778-87, *infra*.

6. Perhaps as a result of these practical problems, statutory and rule interpleader have received very limited workouts in mass torts in which funds are inadequate to cover all claims. The high water mark may well be *Ahrens, supra*, in which a court used statutory interpleader to effect joinder of more than 300 potential claimants who had received food poisoning at an insolvent (or marginally solvent) defendant's restaurant. The claims greatly exceeded the combined assets of the defendants and their insurance carriers. The federal plaintiffs and the insurers, who desired consolidation of all claims against the insurance policies and the insureds' other assets in a single forum, seized upon the language in *Tashire* that a fund which is the target of the claimants marks the outer boundaries of interpleader, and argued that the avaialble assets were such a targeted fund. The court was sympathetic, but unwilling to embrace the argument entirely:

> [A] probing of the depths of this "solvency" standard fails to reveal that it is as controlling a factor as plaintiffs would indicate. This Court does not discredit the insureds' assertions of marginal solvency. However, the possibility of improvement in financial condition, viewed together with the recognition that many tortfeasors face comprehensive insolvency whenever

their assets are levied against with substantial adverse judgments, causes this Court to conclude that solvency alone, or its absence, cannot justify expanding interpleader jurisdiction. [414 F. Supp. at 1246.]

The court went on, however, to hold that insolvency "remains as a factor to be considered." Id. After considering all of the other factors it thought relevant — including the fact that, unlike *Tashire*, the insurance funds were the bulk of the available assets; the desire of all the insureds for interpleader; the duplication and expense of multiple state and federal trials; the possibility that state actions would frustrate the "orderly, uniform manner" of contesting liability in the federal interpleader proceeding; the possibility that early judgments in state court could interfere with an orderly distribution of assets; and the degree to which interpleader would frustrate the plaintiffs' choice of forum — the court preliminarily enjoined the state proceedings pending further evidence on the issues of insolvency and frustration of plaintiffs' chosen forum. Id. at 1247-49. Since all but the last factor strongly counsel the use of interpleader in cases of potential insolvency, how serious is the court's claim that insolvency is not dispositive on the issue of using interpleader in a mass tort?

7. Even if interpleader could be used to prevent joinder complexity in the case of insufficient assets, it is still not effective in preventing other types of joinder complexity. For instance, when a plaintiff seeks an injunctive remedy and other plaintiffs who might desire a different injunctive remedy refuse to participate in the lawsuit, statutory interpleader will often be unavailing because no specific property or insurance policy is at stake. See Murphy v. Travelers Insurance Co., 534 F.2d 1155, 1159 (5th Cir. 1976) ("Federal interpleader jurisdiction depends on identifiable property or a limited fund or pecuniary obligation . . . ."). Rule interpleader, which is designed to operate whenever there might be "double or multiple liability," likewise is not geared to the problem of inconsistent equitable obligations not related to property or some other identifiable fund. See Wright et al., *supra*, §§ 1702-04; cf. F.R.Civ.P. 19(a)(2)(ii) (permitting joinder as necessary party whenever a party is subject to "a substantial risk of incurring double, multiple, *or otherwise inconsistent* obligations) (emphasis added), and F.R.Civ.P. 23(b)(1)(A) (permitting a class action when, *inter alia*, there is a risk of "inconsistent or varying adjudications with respect to members of the class which would establish incompatible standards of conduct for the party opposing the class").

8. Suppose that in *Tashire* all of the interpleaded victims filed Rule 13(g) cross-claims for their injuries against the tortfeasor co-defendants. Wouldn't the interpleader proceeding then become the vehicle for the aggregation of all claims? An obvious problem of this approach is that it requires voluntary action by the victims to file a cross-claim; it cannot be forced on unwilling interpleader defendants. (Defendants are not required under our present rules of res judicata to file cross-claims, even when they arise from the same transaction or occurrence. 6 Charles A. Wright et al., Federal Practice & Procedure § 1431 (1990).) Furthermore, this approach creates several thorny jurisdictional problems. First, there is at least some question whether the interpleader claim and the underlying claims of wrongdoing "aris[e] out of the [same] transaction or occurrence," as required by Rule 13(g) and presumably by Article III as well. Compare Wayzata Bank & Trust Co. v. A & B Farms, 855 F.2d 590 (8th Cir. 1988) (compulsory counterclaim against interpleader plaintiff lay within supplemental jurisdiction) and Dean Witter Reynolds Inc. v. Fernandez, 489 F. Supp. 434 (S.D. Fla. 1979) (cross-claims lay within supplemental jurisdiction)

with American Security Bank v. Bank of Honolulu, 646 F. Supp. 1063 (D. Haw. 1986) (cross-claims did not lie within supplemental jurisdiction).

A second problem is whether *Tashire*'s language that interpleader "was never intended . . . to be an all-purpose 'bill of peace'" means that these efforts to use counterclaims and cross-claims are prohibited. In the context of a fraud claim in which a portion of the misappropriated amount was paid into the court and the victims asserted Rule 13(g) and 13(h) claims against the alleged defrauder and three additional defendants, one court has held that the liberal joinder provisions of the Federal Rules overrode *Tashire*'s concern. *Fernandez*, 489 F. Supp. 434. The court stated that *Tashire*'s language should be read "[a]t most" as a limit on using "cross-claims seeking to establish liability in the context of a mass tort rather than as an across-the-board proscription against cross-claims in interpleader actions." Id. at 439 (quoting Wright et al., *supra*, § 1715); but see Allstate Insurance Co. v. McNeill, 382 F.2d 84 (4th Cir. 1967), cert. denied, 392 U.S. 931 (1968) (*Tashire* eliminated availability of cross-claims in interpleader cases). In the non-mass tort context, *Fernandez* held that cross-claims were permitted to the full extent of the court's supplemental jurisdiction; it bolstered its conclusion with such equitable considerations as "manageability," "fairness to litigants," and "judicial economy." Id. at 440-42.

A third problem involves territorial jurisdiction. Statutory interpleader cases permit the plaintiff to invoke the nationwide service of process provisions of 28 U.S.C. § 2361. Some of the interpleader defendants, however, might not otherwise be subject to jurisdiction in the interpleader forum. When a cross-claim is asserted against such a defendant, and when the defendant could have successfully argued lack of territorial jurisdiction if that claim had been sued on independently in the forum, some courts have intimated that the cross-claim can be asserted only if the defendant voluntarily waives the personal jurisdiction objection. *Fernandez*, 489 F. Supp. at 438-39; Irving Trust Co. v. Nationwide Leisure Corp., 562 F. Supp. 960 (S.D.N.Y. 1982). Wouldn't actual presence in the forum or pendent personal jurisdiction create the necessary contact? See pp. 261, 274, *supra*; Wright et al., *supra*, § 1715.

Finally, even if counterclaims and cross-claims are permitted in the interpleader action, *Tashire* strongly suggests that the interpleader court cannot enjoin the simultaneous prosecution of state or federal actions that raise the same issues as the counterclaim or cross-claim. Thus, a plaintiff might proceed in both forums, racing to the first judgment she can get. Unless the state forum voluntarily stays its hand (see p. 437, *infra*), this tactic will cause unnecessary duplication and expense. Should we create an exception to *Tashire*, and permit an injunction when claims that exceed the scope of the interpleader proceeding are asserted by way of counterclaim or cross-claim in the interpleader proceeding?

9. Interpleader began as a common law remedy six centuries ago, but quickly became available only in equity. By 1791, when the Seventh Amendment was enacted, interpleader was exclusively an equitable remedy. Does the Seventh Amendment right to trial by jury, which applies to "Suits at common law" but not to equitable claims apply in interpleader proceedings? On the issue of whether interpleader is appropriate (sometimes referred to as "the first stage of interpleader"), the answer seems to be no; this is an issue for the court. On the issue of whether particular claimants are entitled to the interpleaded proceeds (sometimes referred to as "the second stage of interpleader"), the answer depends on whether the claimants' claims to the

proceeds are based on legal or equitable principles. If the claims are legal, a right to jury trial attaches; if equitable, no jury right exists. When some claims are equitable and some legal, common factual issues are first decided by the jury. See pp. 1211-12, *infra*; Wright et al., *supra*, § 1718.

As an equitable device, the interpleader injunction is subject to the discretion of the court. Thus, wrongdoing by the interpleader plaintiff as well as laches and all other defenses that might limit an equitable remedy might defeat a request for an interpleader injunction. Of particular importance is the rule that interpleader is unnecessary when an action pending before another court is capable of resolving completely the rights to the property or fund. See Wright et al., *supra*, § 1709.

10. An excellent historical survey of the interpleader remedy, as well as an attempt to describe why interpleader should stop short of authorizing joinder whenever a wrongdoer is potentially subject to inconsistent rulings in "big lawsuits," can be found in Geoffrey C. Hazard, Jr. and Myron Moskovitz, *An Historical and Critical Analysis of Interpleader*, 52 Cal. L. Rev. 706 (1964). The authors do recommend that interpleader be available when "the claims may exhaust a limited fund to which the claimants look for recovery," id. at 763, but they do not apply that rule in the context of the potentially insolvent mass wrongdoer.

11. We have not specifically mentioned the problem of polycentrism for some time, but it becomes important in interpleader cases. Although the first stage of interpleader rarely raises problems of polycentrism, the second stage might. Interpleader is designed to join each individual claimant to a fund or piece of property, and each individual therefore is entitled to be represented. Because the dispute — who is entitled to this property? — is often discrete, interpleader does not usually raise the "many-centered" problem that Professor Fuller described at pp. 16-17, *supra*. When the numbers of potential claimants multiply, or when the "fund" involves the assets of a potentially insolvent major corporation, however, it becomes quite difficult to guarantee that each claimant or other person with an interest in the outcome of the case will be able to participate individually through proofs and reasoned arguments. In this circumstance, interpleader can create polycentrism.

It is tempting in these cases to marry the class action to the interpleader remedy, and to assign class representatives the function of pressing claims on behalf of other, similarly situated interpleader defendants. Thus far, the interrelationship of class actions and interpleader proceedings remains largely unexplored. On the other hand, because courts in class actions rarely have power to enjoin related litigation until a settlement is imminent, there are tactical advantages to grafting the class action onto interpleader. Would the combination of interpleader and class action move the remedy to close to the proscribed bill of peace?

NOTE ON THE BILL OF PEACE

Tashire's observation that interpleader is not a "bill of peace" raises the issues of what a bill of peace is and whether it might be the elusive device to eliminate the litigation of related claims in multiple forums. Like interpleader, the bill of peace was a device used in equity. Unlike interpleader, however, the bill of peace did not rely on the existence of a *res* of disputed ownership; rather, a court sitting in equity was authorized to enjoin related proceedings either when (1) "[e]ach member of [a large group] threatens litigation or is engaged in pending litigation with the adversary, and these parallel actions involve one or more common questions of law or fact, or both"; or (2) "there are only two parties with numerous parallel litigations between them." Zechariah Chafee, Jr., *Bills of Peace with Multiple Parties*, 45 Harv. L. Rev. 1297, 1297 (1932). The basic issue was whether the multiple litigations subjected the parties to harassment or vexation; if so, equity sometimes claimed the power to consolidate the cases in a single forum. The exact scope of the power was much debated. Some courts, following Pomeroy's suggestion in his *Treatise on Equity Jurisprudence*, allowed equity to enjoin the separate prosecution of both multiple suits in equity and actions at law whenever there were common questions in the cases; other courts, following Tribette v. Illinois Central R.R., 70 Miss. 182, 12 So. 32 (1892), held that a common interest which each claimant was entitled to protect through equity was required to invoke equity jurisdiction. See generally Stephen Yeazell, From Medieval Group Litigation to the Modern Class Action (1987) (describing bills of peace and other joinder devices in equity).

The bill of peace was created to ease some of the strictures of common law procedure, which was notoriously stingy in allowing the joinder of related cases. See p. 39, *supra*. In the twentieth century, however, the focus on transactional litigation led the drafters of the Federal Rules of Civil Procedure, and of most state procedural codes, to liberalize considerably the rules of party joinder. The need for the bill of peace consequently declined. In some states the bill of peace remains an available, albeit rarely used, means of preventing multiple litigation. See, *e.g.*, State of New Jersey v. Interstate Recycling, Inc., 267 N.J.Super. 574, 632 A.2d 526 (1993); Allstate Insurance Co. v. Hill, 218 Ga. 430, 128 S.E.2d 321 (1962) (bill of peace specifically authorized by code); Nowell v. Neal, 249 N.C. 516, 107 S.E.2d 107 (1959); cf. Walter E. Heller & Co. v. Cox, 379 F. Supp. 299 (S.D.N.Y. 1974) (suggesting that the All-Writs Act gives federal courts the power to issue bills of peace); In re Sugar Antitrust Litigation, MDL 201, 588 F.2d 1270, 1273-74 (9th Cir. 1978) (refusing to authorize removal as a form of bill of peace when the removed claims were not identical to the claims of other plaintiffs already in federal court). In other states, however, modern joinder devices (such as liberalized interpleader, rules that permit the voluntary joinder of factually and legally related claims, the consolidation of related cases, and class actions) and the merger of law and equity have combined to doom the bill of peace. Typical of this trend is Baughman v. American Telephone & Telegraph Co., 298 S.C. 127, 378 S.E.2d 599, 601 (1989):

> [W]e hold the bill of peace is no longer an available procedure in view of the enactment of the South Carolina Rules of Civil Procedure (SCRCP). . . . Under the SCRCP, Rules 23 and 42 regarding class action and consolidation accomplish the same effect as a bill of peace and therefore supplant it. Moreover, Rule 16 allowing pre-trial case management provides a vehicle for processing complex litigation without depriving a

party of its right to a jury trial. For these reasons we reverse the circuit court's order imposing a bill of peace.

Among the states that retain the bill of peace, some take a narrow view of its scope, while others are more liberal. Compare Georgia Education Authority (Schools) v. Davis, 227 Ga. 36, 40, 178 S.E.2d 853, 856 (1970) ("[A] bill of peace is a very rigorous and extreme remedy, and [e]very reasonable doubt of its being the more appropriate remedy should be given against it.") and Hooker Chemicals & Plastic Corp. v. Attorney General, 100 Mich. App. 203, 207-08, 298 N.W.2d 710, 712 (1980) ("A bill of peace 'will lie, after repeated trials at law and satisfactory verdicts, to have an injunction against further litigation.' . . . However, in the instant case, there is no showing of vexatious litigation. . . . Res judicata provides adequate protection to Hooker's right . . . .") with Shaid v. Consolidated Edison Co. of New York, 95 A.D. 610, 622, 467 N.Y.S.2d 843, 851 (1983) ("[A] court of record has power 'to devise and make new process and forms of proceedings, necessary to carry into effect the powers and jurisdiction possessed by it.' Pursuant to its equity powers, a court may entertain a plenary action to enjoin all pending and prospective claimants from proceeding to trial and to direct a joint trial of such claims under a liberal interpretation of the process known as a bill of peace . . . .").

Moreover, even in states which retain a bill of peace, the bill turns out to suffer from predictable problems. First, the court cannot enjoin parties over whom it has no personal jurisdiction. Second, the court must worry whether the bill of peace in some instances might run afoul of bankruptcy provisions or the more specific joinder devices of the relevant procedural codes. Third, a state court does not have power to enjoin the prosecution of claims lying within the federal court's exclusive jurisdiction, or the power to enjoin most cases already pending in federal court. Fourth, a federal court might not have subject matter jurisdiction over the case if there is no federal question, a lack of complete diversity, or $75,000 or less at stake. Venue restrictions might make it difficult to find a federal forum in which all of the multiple parties can be joined. Cf. Summit Insurance Co. of New York v. Mulherin, 233 Ga. 606, 212 S.E.2d 788 (1975) (refusing to entertain bill of peace which effectively overrode usual venue rules for state actions). Finally, federal courts might not be able to overcome the obstacle of the Anti-Injunction Act (see pp. 393-401, *supra*) with respect to claims already pending in state court.

Equity sprang up when the common law's procedural rules were perceived to create unfairness in certain unique circumstances. See pp. 36-47, *supra*. Do the failures of the present rules of removal, anti-suit injunction, and party joinder suggest that we should re-invigorate and expand the bill of peace to deal with the unique problem of multiple litigation in cases involving joinder complexity? Would that approach be consistent with the views of Pound and other procedural reformers that procedural rules must be saved from ossification by the constant infusion of equitable principles? Again we face, in a modern context, the relative merits of equitable discretion and common law certainty.

ii. Stays of Federal (or State) Proceedings in Favor of State (or Federal) Proceedings: Herein of Abstention

Our task in this chapter has been to determine whether it is possible to consolidate related cases (especially those involving lawyer dysfunction) in a single federal or state forum. The last subsection examined the possibility of giving one forum the power to enjoin cases from proceeding in the other forum. This subsection examines the flip-side of that issue: the possibility of the courts of one forum declining to exercise jurisdiction in favor of the other forum. The effect of both approaches is the same: One court system exercises jurisdiction over the case, and one court system does not. But the manner of the two approaches are quite different: In the former approach, a court system is ordered by another system not to proceed, while in the latter approach, a court system merely "orders" itself not to proceed. On the surface, therefore, it might seem that this latter approach, which is generally known as "abstention," would be widely used in complex cases.

As it turns out, however, abstention doctrines have not been tailored specifically to meet the problems of complex and complicated litigation. Rather, abstention rules have been designed to cover quite different circumstances, with the result that the fit between the needs of complex and complicated cases and the actual abstention doctrines is uneasy. The following materials, which look first at abstention rules in federal courts and then at abstention rules in state courts, explore the relationship among abstention, dysfunction, and inefficiency from two perspectives. First, they describe the abstention rules presently at work, and show how those rules can alternatively be used to overcome or to create dysfunction or inefficiency. Second, they ask us to consider whether we should use some of the principles and arguments from traditional abstention doctrines to create a form of abstention specifically geared to the problem of dysfunction or inefficient re-litigation.

a) Abstention by Federal Courts in Favor of State Proceedings

Abstention by the federal courts is one of the most discussed and controversial aspects of federal jurisdiction. These materials sail quickly over deep waters, describing the basics of abstention and its relationship to complex and complicated litigation. For those interested in more detailed treatments of the topic, a small but representative slice of the commentary can be found in Richard H. Fallon et al., Hart & Wechsler's The Federal Courts and the Federal System 1222-1336 (4th ed. 1996); Martin H. Redish, Federal Jurisdiction 281-308 (2d ed. 1990); Michael Wells, *Why Professor Redish is Wrong about Abstention*, 19 Ga. L. Rev. 1097 (1985); David L. Shapiro, *Jurisdiction and Discretion*, 60 N.Y.U. L. Rev. 543 (1985); Owen M.

Fiss, Dombrowski, 86 Yale L.J. 1103 (1977); Martha A. Field, *Abstention in Constitutional Cases: The Scope of the* Pullman *Abstention Doctrine*, 122 U. Pa. L. Rev. 1071 (1974); David P. Currie, *The Federal Courts and the American Law Institute, Part II*, 36 U. Chi. L. Rev. 268 (1969). Detailed bibliographies on abstention can be found in 17A Charles A. Wright et al., Federal Practice & Procedure §§ 4241 n.1, 4252 n.1 (1988).

There are at least three (and some would say four or five or six) forms of federal abstention which permit a federal court to stay a case within its jurisdiction in favor of state proceedings. The three "card-carrying" forms of abstention are *Pullman* abstention, *Burford* abstention, and *Younger* abstention. In addition, there are several other doctrines that are rarely labeled abstention doctrines by the Supreme Court, but nonetheless act, look, and sound just like the classic forms of abstention. These are *Colorado River* abstention, *Thibodaux* abstention, and certification of state law issues to the highest court of a state.

(1) Pullman *Abstention. Pullman* abstention takes its name from Railroad Commission of Texas v. Pullman Co., 312 U.S. 496 (1941), in which railroads operating in Texas sought to enjoin, on constitutional grounds, enforcement of a ruling of the Texas Railroad Commission which effectively required a white conductor to be present in each Pullman car. The statutory authority of the Railroad Commission to issue such an order was uncertain, and a three-judge federal court held that the Commission did not in fact have this power. The Supreme Court nonetheless held that the federal court should have abstained until the legality of the Commission's order was decided in the Texas courts. In its reasoning, the Court invoked three arguments: that federal courts should avoid reaching constitutional questions which may be obviated by an interpretation of state law, that issuance of an injunction is an extraordinary remedy available only when other remedies (here, the state court challenge) are unavailable, and that the use of equitable restraint would foster more harmonious relations between state and federal courts.

The zeal with which the Supreme Court has required *Pullman* abstention has varied over the years. So has the Supreme Court's view on how unclear the state issue must be, on whether *Pullman* abstention applies when the unclear issue is one of state constitutional law, and on whether *Pullman* abstention is mandatory or discretionary. See Fallon et al., *supra*, at 1232-42. For present purposes, the basic point which can be taken from *Pullman* and the cases following it is that abstention is appropriate when there is an unclear question of state law, the answer to which might obviate the need for a constitutional decision, and there is a state court both able and likely to resolve the unclear question.

Aside from complex civil rights and institutional reform litigation, *Pullman* abstention has only a small application to complex civil litigation. Whatever the scope of the effect, however, it is hardly salutary. In the first instance, *Pullman* abstention is not keyed to the existence of other related litigation in state court. Second, even when related litigation is pending, the federal court simply splits off the state issues in the federal case; it does not necessarily assure itself that the federal parties will consolidate their case with whatever other state proceedings are pending. Third, unless the answer to the state law issue effectively terminates both the state and federal litigation, the federal court will need to resolve the federal constitutional questions independently of the state courts, which may well be facing the same constitutional issues in the cases already pending in state court. In short, although *Pullman* abstention can in theory be used creatively by state and federal judges to handle cooperatively cases which otherwise cannot be joined in a single forum, it cannot be used to achieve the joinder of all the claims of all the related parties in a single forum.

(2) Burford *Abstention*. The second form of abstention, *Burford* abstention, concerns deference to state courts when certain important state policies are at issue. In Burford v. Sun Oil Co., 319 U.S. 315 (1943), the Supreme Court faced a challenge to a different type of order of the Texas Railroad Commission, which, along with the state courts in one county in Texas, had been given the responsibility of regulating the oil industry. The Supreme Court thought that federal review of the Commission's oil-related orders would lead to "[d]elay, misunderstanding of local law, and needless federal conflict with the State policy. . . . These questions of regulation of the industry by the State administrative agency . . . so clearly involve[ ] basic problems of Texas policy that equitable discretion should be exercised to give the Texas courts the first opportunity to consider them." 319 U.S. at 327, 332. Thus, *Burford* seemed to insist on both an uncertain, complex, and important issue of state law and a comprehensive administrative scheme designed to centralize the resolution of such issues.

The precise scope of *Burford* abstention was unclear for many years. In New Orleans Public Service, Inc. v. Council of City of New Orleans, 491 U.S. 350 (1989) (*NOPSI*), the Court clarified that there were only two circumstances under which *Burford* abstention was appropriate: when state administrative orders or proceedings involved "'difficult issues of state law bearing on policy problems of substantial public import whose importance transcends the case at bar,'" or when federal review of such orders or proceedings "'would be disruptive of state efforts to establish a coherent policy with respect to a matter of substantial public concern.'" 491 U.S. at 361 (quoting Colorado River Water Conservation District v. United States, 424 U.S. 1236, 1244 (1976)); see Quackenbush v. Allstate Insurance Co., 517 U.S. 706 (1996). Although these standards are vague, their application in *NOPSI* suggested that *Burford* abstention should not be given a broad reading. In finding that abstention was inappropriate in the context of a utility ratemaking procedure, the Court observed that "*Burford* . . . does not require abstention whenever there exists [a complex state administrative] process, or even in all cases where there is a 'potential for conflict' with state regulatory law or policy," nor is there any "doctrine requiring abstention merely because resolution of a federal question may result in the overturning of a state policy." Id. at 362-63.

Burford abstention requires that the federal case be dismissed outright; the federal court does not retain jurisdiction over the case, nor does the case return to federal district court. Hence, *Burford* abstention is potentially a useful device for complex or complicated litigation in which ongoing state proceedings related to the federal case can resolve the entire controversy.

Burford abstention has been invoked with some frequency in circumstances in which an insolvent entity is going through state receivership or rehabilitation proceedings, and federal plaintiffs seek to avoid those proceedings by bringing claims against the entity or its directors and officers in federal court. See Brandenburg v. Seidel, 859 F.2d 1179 (4th Cir. 1988); Gonzales v. Media Elements, Inc., 946 F.2d 157 (1st Cir. 1991); Corcoran v. Universal Reinsurance Corp., 713 F. Supp. 77 (S.D.N.Y. 1989); Riley v. Simmons, 839 F. Supp. 1113 (D.N.J. 1993) (discussing abstention against both insolvent insurer and its past and present directors and officers). But it has received some use in other contexts as well. See, *e.g.*, Berman Enterprises, Inc. v. Jorling, 6 F.3d 602 (2d Cir. 1993) (given local interest in and creation of administrative scheme to deal with local pollution, abstention to regulatory process on claim that state environmental regulators were motivated by malice was appropriate), cert. denied, 510 U.S. 1073 (1994); cf. In re Eastern and Southern District Asbestos Litigation, 78 F.3d 764 (2d Cir. 1996) (*Burford* abstention inappropriate to permit state courts to calculate certain set-off rights under settlement involving trust of insolvent debtor).

The critical abstention questions in the insolvency context are whether the federal case threatens to cause an inequitable distribution of the insolvent entity's assets, and whether an adequate and comprehensive state remedial scheme exists. For instance, in University of Maryland at Baltimore v. Peat Marwick Main & Co., 923 F.2d 265 (3d Cir. 1991), the court of appeals refused to permit *Burford* abstention when a federal suit against unrelated third parties did not threaten to create difficulties for a state insolvency proceeding; on the contrary, the federal plaintiffs' successful recovery from a separate source was likely to increase the assets available to the remaining state law plaintiffs. Similarly, in Grode v. Mutual Fire, Marine & Inland Insurance Co., 8 F.3d 953 (3d Cir. 1993), the court found no reason to abstain in a case brought by an insurer undergoing insolvency proceedings; this claim did not run the risk of dissipating the insurer's fund by defending multiple actions, but was rather an effort to augment the funds available to creditors. See id. at 960 (noting that the case was not one in which "a single forum [was] necessary to dispose of the company's limited assets so as to avoid a race to the courthouse").

Perhaps the most interesting decision regarding the adequacy of the state remedial scheme is *Riley*, in which the federal plaintiffs brought securities claims that lay within the exclusive jurisdiction of the federal courts. In the state rehabilitation proceedings, the Rehabilitator had brought similar claims, but relied on a theory of common law fraud. *Riley* found that the facts alleged in support of the federal securities claims were the same as those alleged in state court; that the Rehabilitator had statutory standing to assert any claim available to any creditor of the insurer; and that the remedies under state and federal law were identical. As a result, it held the state process adequate, and abstained from hearing claims within its exclusive jurisdiction. 839 F. Supp. at 1126-27. *Riley*'s holding on this point is debatable. See Key v. Wise, 629 F.2d 1049 (5th Cir. 1980), cert. denied, 454 U.S. 1103 (1981) (Brennan, J., dissenting from the denial of certiorari) (federal courts cannot abstain on claims that lie within exclusive federal jurisdiction); Note, *Judicial Abstention and Exclusive Federal Jurisdiction: A Reconciliation*, 67 Corn. L. Rev. 219 (1981).

Should *Burford* abstention be extended to permit abstention whenever the total of state and federal claims exceeds the defendant's available assets, so that the continued prosecution of the federal claims threatens lawyer dysfunction? At present, the ability to use *Burford* abstention in this context is hampered by three facts: Abstention does not guarantee that the two groups of cases will in fact be consolidated; a comprehensive administrative scheme and an unclear matter of important local policy requiring uniform treatment are both required before abstention can occur; and abstention may be inappropriate for claims, such as many antitrust and securities claims, lying within the exclusive federal jurisdiction. Hence, *Burford* abstention stops far short of the type of device needed to assure the single state-court treatment of related state and federal proceedings.

(3) Younger *Abstention*. In Younger v. Harris, 401 U.S. 37 (1971), the Supreme Court announced that, absent certain extenuating circumstances, "Our Federalism" required a federal court to abstain from hearing a constitutional challenge to an ongoing criminal prosecution. *Younger* abstention, which was grounded in notions of state-federal comity, avoidance of constitutional issues, and equitable restraint, immediately became a lightning rod for discussion about the relationship between state and federal courts. Because it involved abstention only in the criminal context, however, its direct effect on civil litigation, and on complex civil litigation in particular, was not immediately apparent.

Within a few years, however, the Supreme Court had extended *Younger* to the civil context, first to require abstention in civil proceedings in aid of criminal statutes, see Huffman v. Pursue, Ltd., 420 U.S. 592 (1975), then more generally to federal cases which challenged other civil proceedings such as contempt and attorney disciplinary proceedings which were "judicial in nature," see Juidice v. Vail, 430 U.S. 327 (1977), and Middlesex Ethics Commission v. Garden State Bar Association, 457 U.S. 423, 434 (1982), and finally to federal cases which sought to litigate in federal court certain constitutional issues regarding enforcement of the judgment which were then on appeal between the same parties in state court, Pennzoil Co. v. Texaco, Inc., 481 U.S. 1 (1987). More recent cases, however, have stopped the expansion of *Younger* in the civil arena. *NOPSI*, 491 U.S. at 364-73; Ankenbrandt v. Richards, 504 U.S. 689 (1992).

Is the desire to assure the like treatment of like people a sufficiently "important state interest" to justify *Younger* abstention? How about the reduction of multiforum, multiparty litigation? *Pennzoil* itself stressed that *Younger* abstention was appropriate when the federal constitutional claim challenged "important interests in administering certain aspects of their judicial systems." 481 U.S. at 12-13; *NOPSI*, 491 U.S. at 368 (*Younger* principles applied only to civil enforcement proceedings and "civil proceedings involving certain orders that are uniquely in furtherance of the state courts' ability to perform their judicial functions"). If *Pennzoil* is read to mean that no federal suit can be filed to vindicate the federal interests in a case as long as state courts hearing related claims are adequate to hear the federal issues and have a significant interest in providing complete relief to all parties, then *Younger* could have far-reaching consequences in complex (and possibly complicated) litigation. Indeed, although this idea stretches the *Younger-Pennzoil* principle far beyond the facts of the extant cases, it is possible that *Younger* could be read to require abstention when Party A is litigating a federal issue against Party B in state court, and then Party C brings a substantially similar claim against Party B (or even Party D!) in federal court. Cf. Laurence H. Tribe, American Constitutional Law § 3-30 (2d ed. 1988) ("there now appears to be no principled way to prevent the application of the *Younger* doctrine to preclude litigation of any threatened federal interest where the litigant is involved in a pending state judicial proceeding that is adequate to ventilate the federal claim"). If extended this far, *Younger* abstention would be a tremendous tool to force a single state-forum treatment of related cases presently pending in both state and federal forums.

It presently seems unlikely that *Younger* and *Pennzoil* will receive a reading remotely approaching this possibility. See Schall v. Joyce, 885 F.2d 101, 109 (3d Cir. 1989) ("*Pennzoil*'s limiting principle is its focus on the special interest that a state has in enforcing the orders and judgments of its courts"). Moreover, it may well be that *federal*, rather than *state*, court is the appropriate forum for resolution of the entire case, and *Younger* abstention could actually create dysfunction or inefficiency. For instance, in *Agent Orange*, several members of the class that were dissatisfied with the settlement commenced suits in state court. The defendants removed, and the district court dismissed the cases because they were precluded by the settlement. On appeal, the Second Circuit had little trouble rejecting the plaintiffs' *Younger* argument that state court procedures were adequate to determine the proper effect to be given to the federal settlement:

> This argument stands *Younger* on its head. *Younger* teaches us to recognize the interest of the states in protecting the authority of their judicial system so that their orders and judgments are not rendered nugatory.... The application of *Younger*, as advocated by [plaintiffs], would threaten the authority of the federal judicial system and potentially nullify the federal courts' orders and judgments. This result is not the sort of federal-state comity envisioned in *Younger* and *Pennzoil*.

In re Agent Orange Product Liability Litigation, 996 F.2d 1425, 1432 (2d Cir. 1993), cert. denied, 510 U.S. 1140 (1994). Suppose, though, that the federal class action had not yet settled. Should the federal court have abstained in favor of the related state cases involving Agent Orange?

Whatever its precise breadth, *Younger* presently requires that there be a federal question involved in the federal proceeding, and that the federal litigation involve the same parties as those in state court. As long as these two facts continue to obtain, *Younger* and its penumbra of "Our Federalism" will be far more important as a complexity-causing limit on the federal courts' power to consolidate cases through a federal injunction against state proceedings (see pp. 393-412, *supra*) than as a complexity-reducing means of ensuring consolidated state handling.

(4) Colorado River *Abstention*. Although the Supreme Court has never called the *Colorado River* doctrine a form of abstention, commentators and lower courts have had little trouble recognizing it for what it is. The basic notion of the *Colorado River* doctrine is that, as a matter of "wise judicial administration," a federal court should abstain in favor of a parallel state proceeding. *Colorado River*, 424 U.S. at 817. *Colorado River* abstention therefore has the potential to be a workhorse in complex and complicated litigation, for it grants federal courts an explicit power to stay its hand in favor of state litigation involving the same subject matter.

The important issue is to determine the circumstances under which deference to state proceedings is proper. The Supreme Court has analyzed this issue on three occasions — *Colorado River*, Will v. Calvert Fire Insurance Co., 437 U.S. 655 (1978), and Moses H. Cone Memorial Hospital v. Mercury Construction Co., 460 U.S. 1 (1983). After *Moses H. Cone*, three factors seem to determine the success of *Colorado River* abstention requests.

First, the Supreme Court has made clear that a strong presumption against *Colorado River* abstention exists. According to *Colorado River*:

> [Federal courts have] the virtually unflagging obligation . . . to exercise the jurisdiction given them. . . . Given this obligation, and the absence of weightier considerations of constitutional adjudication and state-federal relations, the circumstances permitting the dismissal of a federal suit due to the presence of a concurrent state proceeding for reasons of wise judicial administration are considerably more limited than the circumstances appropriate for abstention. . . . Only the clearest of justifications will warrant dismissal. [424 U.S. at 817-19.]

Second, some "exceptional" circumstances do allow abstention. *Colorado River* had identified four factors relevant to deciding whether these circumstances were present, and *Moses H. Cone* added two more. They are: (1) the court first assuming jurisdiction over property may exercise that jurisdiction to the exclusion of other courts; (2) the inconvenience of the federal forum; (3) the desirability of avoiding piecemeal litigation; (4) the order in which jurisdiction was obtained by the concurrent forums; (5) the source of governing law, whether state or federal; and (6) the possible inadequacy of the state-court proceeding to protect the litigants' rights. See *Moses H. Cone*, 460 U.S. at 15-16, 23, 26. That list is not exhaustive. See Caminiti & Iatorola v. Behnke Warehousing, Inc., 962 F.2d 698 (7th Cir. 1992) (also adding in the relative progress of state and federal proceedings, the presence or absence of concurrent jurisdiction, the availability of removal, and the strength of the federal claim as relevant factors). No single factor is determinative, but in weighing the relevant factors, "the balance [is] heavily weighted in favor of the exercise of jurisdiction." *Moses H. Cone*, 460 U.S. at 16.

Third, the two critical variables in deciding whether *Colorado River* abstention is appropriate may well be the existence of a congressional intent to avoid duplicative litigation and a state proceeding which is a superior mechanism for resolution of the dispute between the parties. For instance, in *Colorado River*, which involved a dispute among the United States and more than 1,000 other persons regarding water rights, the driving forces behind the Court's decision to abstain were a statute that contained a "clear federal policy" to avoid piecemeal adjudication of water rights and the fact that adjudication of water rights was "appropriate for comprehensive treatment in the forums having the greatest experience and expertise, assisted by state administrative officers acting under the state courts." See *Moses H. Cone*, 460 U.S. at 16. In contrast, *Moses H. Cone*, in which the Supreme Court found that abstention was inappropriate, no statutory policy of avoiding piecemeal litigation was present, the state court had no institutional superiority in deciding the contractual and statutory issues in the case, and serious doubts existed about whether the state court could provide relief equivalent to the relief available in federal court.

In applying *Colorado River*, lower courts have often tended not to examine whether state courts have some *de jure* advantage over federal courts (such as specialized courts or administrative mechanisms), but rather whether the state court is better suited to hear the case *de facto*. For instance, *Colorado River* abstention has received frequent use in the insurance coverage litigation often associated with complex and complicated litigation; the fact that, in a particular case, the state court had already succeeded in obtaining an inclusive joinder of parties has been regarded as a proper reason for *Colorado River* abstention. See, *e.g.*, Lumbermens Mutual Casualty Co. v. Connecticut Bank & Trust Co., 806 F.2d 411, 414-15 (2d Cir. 1986) ("The critical factor . . . is the desirability of avoiding piecemeal litigation and the possibility of two interpretations of the same policy language in different courts, leaving the insured possibly with insufficient coverage from the insurers . . . ."); Insurance Co. of the State of Pennsylvania v. Syntex Corp., 964 F.2d 829 (8th Cir. 1992) (dismissing federal declaratory judgment action by insurer in favor of more comprehensive state court coverage litigation of insured against all its insurers). *Colorado River* has also been used to dismiss a case in favor of a state class action that was capable of resolving all the issues in the federal suit. Allison v. Security Benefit Life Insurance Co., 980 F.2d 1213 (8th Cir. 1992) (alternate holding). Obviously, from the vantage point of assuring the consolidation of the greatest number of parties in one forum, the results in these cases are appropriate. But are they consistent with *Colorado River*?

It is generally believed that the state court must be capable of hearing the claims raised in the federal litigation before *Colorado River* abstention is appropriate. Therefore, a case involving claims lying exclusively within federal jurisdiction should not be stayed in favor of related state litigation. See Wright et al., *supra*, § 4247, especially n.57. Moreover, *Colorado River* abstention is not generally thought to be available unless the parties and claims in the federal litigation are included among the parties and claims in the state litigation. See *University of Maryland*, 923 F.2d at 276; Erwin Chemerinsky, Federal Jurisdiction § 14.3 (2d ed. 1994). This fact dramatically reduces the utility of *Colorado River* in complex litigation in two ways. First, assume either that Party A sues Party B in federal court, while Parties C through Z sue Party B in state court; or Party A sues Party B in state court and Party C in federal court for the same injuries. Here *Colorado River* abstention is inappropriate, even though consolidation might well be necessary to avoid joinder complexity or reduce multiforum, multiparty litigation. But see In re Chicago Flood Litigation, 819 F. Supp. 762, 764 (N.D. Ill. 1993) (stating in dicta that *Colorado River* abstention can be appropriate when defendants in state and federal court are the same and both state and federal plaintiffs "share equivalent litigation interests"; abstention nonetheless denied because federal actions could be expeditiously resolved and tort issues were neither novel nor complex).

Because of the high degree of parallelism that must exist between the state and federal cases, *Colorado River* abstention is a limited tool in the typical situation of complex or complicated litigation. The "virtually unflagging obligation" of the federal courts to exercise the jurisdiction given to them, as well as the presumption of equal competence of state and federal courts to adjudicate complex and complicated controversies, make it even more difficult to use *Colorado River* abstention to consolidate related state and federal cases in a single state forum.

(5) Thibodaux *Abstention.* A fifth form of abstention, *Thibodaux* abstention, takes its name from Louisiana Power and Light Co. v. City of Thibodaux, 360 U.S. 25 (1959). In *Thibodaux*, the Supreme Court held that a federal court properly abstained from hearing an eminent domain proceeding which had been removed to federal court because of the "special and peculiar nature" of eminent domain proceedings, which was "intimately involved with sovereign prerogative." 360 U.S. at 27-28. In a similar case decided the same day, however, the Court did not permit abstention. Allegheny County v. Frank Mashuda Co., 360 U.S. 185 (1959). The only difference between the cases was that, in *Mashuda*, the state law on eminent domain was clear. But *Thibodaux* and *Mashuda* were both 5-4 decisions, and only one Justice definitively stated that the clearness or lack of clearness of state law was a relevant distinction. Hence, *Thibodaux* abstention seems clearly appropriate when an important state interest intimately involved with a sovereign state prerogative is involved, and when the state law surrounding that prerogative is unclear. Beyond that, the scope of *Thibodaux* abstention is uncertain, and unlikely to be invoked in complex or complicated litigation. See *Quackenbush*, 517 U.S. at 720-22 (discussing *Thibodaux*).

(6) *Certification.* A final form of "abstention" is certification of an issue of law to a state's highest court. Once the state court decides the certified question, the case returns to federal court and proceeds to an appropriate conclusion. See Lehman Brothers v. Schein, 416 U.S. 386 (1974). Thirty-seven states and the District of Columbia have adopted certification statutes or rules, although some state courts do not accept certified questions from district courts, and all state courts retain the discretion to refuse to answer the certified question. See Wright et al., *supra*, § 4248 n.30.

Certification is useful as a means of clarifying the relevant state law prior to setting out on a course of pretrial discovery which may otherwise prove needless. Hence, it is primarily a pretrial management tool; it does nothing to foster the joinder of related cases or eliminate the problems of joinder complexity or multiforum, multiparty litigation. At best, it makes the coordinated management of state and federal cases that cannot otherwise be joined in one forum somewhat simpler.

Notes and Questions

1. In *Quackenbush*, the Court held "federal courts have the power to dismiss or remand cases based on abstention principles only where the relief being sought is equitable or otherwise discretionary." 517 U.S. at 731. Although this statement was made in the specific context of a claim for *Burford* abstention, the Court's general survey of other abstention doctrines in the opinion suggests that it intended this principle to apply more generally. On the other hand, the Court did recognize that, in cases seeking money damages, it might be appropriate for the federal court to stay its proceedings in favor of state proceedings for at least some period of time. In *Quackenbush*, the same issue "was being decided by the state courts at the time the District Court ruled, . . . and in the interest of avoiding inconsistent adjudications on that point, the District Court might have been justified in entering a stay to await the outcome of the state court litigation." Id. Do these statements provide any impetus for the creation of a special abstention doctrine for complex litigation? For complicated litigation?

2. At present, none of the forms of abstention specifically permits a federal court to abstain when the state court is the only court in which the entire controversy can be rationally or efficiently packaged. At the same time, *Burford* abstention and, in particular, *Colorado River* abstention have the potential to be useful in the packaging of at least some complex and complicated cases. Could a federal court combine the basic wisdom of these two forms of abstention, mix in some concepts from *Younger* abstention, and create "joinder complexity" abstention. Under this form of abstention, when the separate handling of cases in state and federal court threatens to cause disparate remedial treatment for identically situated persons, and the state court is the only court in which all of the parties can be joined, then the federal court should abstain in favor of the state court.

Is this a good rule? How would you argue for its adoption by a federal court in light of the limited willingness of federal courts to abstain? In *Brandenburg*, 859 F.2d 1179, and *Riley*, 839 F. Supp. 1113, state receivership suits had been filed in order to take over the affairs of insolvent or corrupt entities. Some plaintiffs sought to obtain the lion's share of assets by filing cases in federal court. In both cases, the federal courts dismissed the federal actions on *Burford* grounds. (After *Quackenbush*, the better approach would be to stay the federal cases.) Were these abstention orders a proper use of *Burford*? Or were they really a form of "joinder complexity" abstention? Would you also create a form of abstention for complicated cases?

3. The standard of appellate review for an abstention decision is abuse of discretion, although some courts have stated that this standard is applied "somewhat rigorous[ly]" in this context. See In re Joint Eastern and Southern District Asbestos Litigation, 78 F.3d 764, 775 (2d Cir. 1996).

4. Another abstention-like concept is the doctrine of primary jurisdiction. Primary jurisdiction is essentially a doctrine of comity between the executive and judicial branches, and is invoked in circumstances in which *both* a court *and* an administrative agency have concurrent jurisdiction over a particular controversy. Even though the controversy lies within the state or federal court's original jurisdiction, the court will defer to the "primary jurisdiction" of the agency and stay its own hand "whenever enforcement of the claim requires resolution of issues which, under a regulatory scheme, have been placed within

the special competence of an administrative body . . . ." United States v. Western Pacific Railroad Co., 352 U.S. 59, 63-64 (1956); see also Far East Conference v. United States, 342 U.S. 570, 574 (1952) (primary jurisdiction appropriate for "cases raising issues of fact not within the conventional experience of judges or cases requiring the exercise of administrative discretion"). Judicial review is thus limited to review of the agency's actions, rather than a *de novo* examination of the controversy. The doctrine contains numerous exceptions, perhaps the most significant of which is that it does not apply to pure questions of law on which agency expertise has no bearing. See Great Northern Railway v. Merchants Elevator Co., 259 U.S. 285 (1922); see generally Bernard Schwartz, Administrative Law §§ 8.26-.28 (3d ed. 1991).

Although the relationship of primary jurisdiction to *Pullman* and *Burford* abstention is obvious, the significant difference is that primary jurisdiction requires deference to another branch of the same sovereign, rather than deference to the sovereignty of the state. Should a federal court invoke the doctrine of primary jurisdiction when some of the issues in litigation have been primarily entrusted to a state administrative agency? Compare County of Suffolk v. Long Island Lighting Co., 907 F.2d 1295 (2d Cir. 1990) (use of primary jurisdiction, which is designed to deal with executive-judicial branch problems of comity, is inapplicable in federal court-state agency context) with Penny v. Southwestern Bell Telephone Co., 906 F.2d 183 (5th Cir. 1990) (applying primary jurisdiction to require federal court deference to state agency).

Primary jurisdiction is related to complex litigation in two important ways. First, and most obviously, some types of controversies involving many parties could fit concurrently within administrative and judicial processes; here, the doctrine may keep parts or all of these cases out of the court system. Perhaps the most common area of overlap is in the area of antitrust regulation, in which there is a rich body of law regarding the limits of the primary jurisdiction concept. See Schwartz, *supra*, § 8.31; 4 Kenneth C. Davis, Administrative Law Treatise, § 22:6-:10. But other areas of overlap, such as labor law and rate-setting controversies, also can invoke the concerns of primary jurisdiction. See Davis, *supra*, §§ 22:4-:5.

Second, the concept of primary jurisdiction often has the unfortunate consequence of fractionalizing litigation and creating the types of dysfunction and inefficiency we have seen in other contexts. One problem is that the doctrine has been interpreted to apply to issues rather than to entire cases. As a result, primary jurisdiction divides the controversy between two different entities — one judicial and one administrative. As you might imagine, this consequence of primary jurisdiction has not escaped criticism. See Schwartz, *supra*, § 8.30 ("To require preliminary resort to a forum that cannot give plaintiffs the full relief to which they are entitled is to revert to artificial dichotomization of remedial justice, such as that prevailing when law and equity were separate and competing systems.").

There have been numerous proposals to remove various types of complex and complicated litigation from the courts and place them into an administrative system. See, *e.g.*, Report of the Judicial Conference Ad Hoc Committee on Asbestos Litigation 27-35 (1991); Kenneth R. Feinberg, *Do Mass Torts Belong in the Courtroom?*, 74 Judicature 237 (1991); Jack B. Weinstein, *Preliminary Reflections on the Law's Reaction to Disasters*, 11 Colum. J. Envtl. L. 1, 32-36 (1991). Based on what you have seen so far of the joinder problems of complex and complicated litigation, would you prefer an administrative solution?

5. Whether or not you think that federal abstention in cases of joinder complexity or multiforum, multiparty litigation is a good idea, abstention is extremely important thematically in complex litigation. Throughout this chapter we have asked whether the "master of the complaint" rule, which puts plaintiffs (and, to a much lesser extent, defendants) in charge of selecting the court, is preferable to a system in which judges are given greater discretion to select the appropriate forum. Abstention is an example of a situation in which the plaintiff selects a court system in which there is jurisdiction, but the court has the discretion not to honor that selection. If you want to see the judicial power to ignore the adversaries' choices broadened in complex or complicated litigation (whether through broader powers of removal, injunction, or stay), abstention remains one of your strongest analogies and one of your strongest replies to the argument that we must honor the parties' adversarial right to select the forum.

6. If we recognize some form of "joinder complexity" abstention, would we also need to recognize the converse rule: that state courts abstain when only the federal court can handle the entire case? In order to answer this question, we now turn to the circumstances under which state courts have traditionally stayed their hand in favor of federal courts.

b) Abstention by State Courts in Favor of Federal Proceedings

A state court can abstain in favor of a federal court with respect to either a federal question claim or a claim founded on state law. On one level, state abstention in federal question cases makes more sense than state abstention in state-law cases; federal courts arguably have a steadier diet of, and thus are more expert in, issues of federal law, while the converse is true on issues of state law. On another level, however, concerns of federalism, separation of powers, and the Supremacy Clause make the notion of state abstention on issues of federal right problematic: State courts may claim equal competence in matters of federal law; we may not wish state courts to be shut out of the discussion about the meaning of federal rights; and the congressional decision not to create exclusive federal jurisdiction for most federal question cases implies the command that state courts exercise jurisdiction over federal question cases. See generally Martin H. Redish, Federal Jurisdiction 165-78 (2d ed. 1990).

As a result of these concerns, state abstention in favor of federal adjudication of federal rights is rarely available. In Howlett v. Rose, 496 U.S. 356 (1990), a Florida state court dismissed a civil rights action brought under 42 U.S.C. § 1983 because the defendants were protected from suit in Florida courts by sovereign immunity, which had never been abrogated for § 1983 claims. The Supreme Court reversed, holding that the case met none of the narrow exceptions for such refusals:

> Federal law is enforceable in state courts not because Congress has determined that federal courts would otherwise be burdened or that state courts might provide a more convenient forum — although both might well be true — but because the Constitution and laws passed

pursuant to it are as much laws in the States as laws passed by the state legislature. The Supremacy Clause makes those laws "the supreme Law of the Land," and charges state courts with a coordinate responsibility to enforce that law according to their regular modes of procedure. . . .

Three corollaries follow from the proposition that "federal" law is part of the Law of the Land in the State:

1. A state court may not deny a federal right, when the parties and controversy are properly before it, in the absence of "valid excuse." Douglas v. New York, N. H. & H. R. Co., 279 U.S. 377, 387-388 (1929) (Holmes, J.). "The existence of the jurisdiction creates an implication of duty to exercise it." Mondou v. New York, N. H. & H. R. Co., 223 U.S. 1, 58 (1912); see Testa v. Katt, 330 U.S. 386 (1947) . . . .

2. An excuse that is inconsistent with or violates federal law is not a valid excuse: The Supremacy Clause forbids state courts to dissociate themselves from federal law because of disagreement with its content or a refusal to recognize the superior authority of its source. . . .

3. When a state court refuses jurisdiction because of a neutral state rule regarding the administration of the courts, we must act with utmost caution before deciding that it is obligated to entertain the claim. See Missouri ex rel. Southern R. Co. v. Mayfield, 340 U.S. 1 (1950); . . . Herb v. Pitcairn, 324 U.S. 117 (1945); Douglas v. New York, N. H. & H. R. Co., 279 U.S. 377 (1929). The requirement that a state court of competent jurisdiction treat federal law as the law of the land does not necessarily include within it a requirement that the State create a court competent to hear the case in which the federal claim is presented. The general rule "bottomed deeply in belief in the importance of state control of state judicial procedure, is that federal law takes the state courts as it finds them." . . . The States thus have great latitude to establish the structure and jurisdiction of their own courts. . . . In addition, States may apply their own neutral procedural rules to federal claims, unless those rules are pre-empted by federal law. . . .

On only three occasions have we found a valid excuse for a state court's refusal to entertain a federal cause of action. Each of them involved a neutral rule of judicial administration. In Douglas v. New York, N. H. & H. R. Co., 279 U.S. 377 (1929), the state statute permitted discretionary dismissal of both federal and state claims where neither the plaintiff nor the defendant was a resident of the forum state. In *Herb*, the city court denied jurisdiction over a FELA action on the grounds that the cause of action arose outside its territorial jurisdiction. Although the state court was not free to dismiss the federal claim "because it is a federal one," we found no evidence that the state court "construed the state jurisdiction and venue laws in a discriminatory fashion." Finally, in *Mayfield*, we held that a state court could apply the doctrine of forum non conveniens to bar adjudication of a FELA case if the State "enforces its policy impartially so as not to involve a discrimination against Employers' Liability Act suits." [496 U.S. at 367, 369-72, 374-75.]

Prior to *Howlett*, some state courts appeared to adopt reverse-*Pullman* or reverse-*Burford* abstention doctrines either when a decision on a federal issue might obviate the need to decide a difficult issue of state constitutional law or when state court review of a difficult issue of federal law threatened coherent federal policy. See Gnutti v. Heintz, 539 A.2d 118 (Conn. 1988) (requiring state courts to abstain from considering Medicaid disability claims until federal administrative and judicial avenues are exhausted); Delaware Tire Center, Inc. v. State of Delaware, 508 A.2d 470 (Table), 1986 WL 16794, *1 (Del. 1986) (refusing interlocutory appeal of state action which allegedly violated federal regulations, when "principles of comity and abstention would seem to dictate that a federal court is the more appropriate forum to litigate such issues"). Does *Howlett* eliminate any possibility of "reverse abstention" doctrines in federal question cases?

Obviously the federalism and separation of powers concerns which gave rise to *Howlett* do not speak to state court abstention in favor of federal courts on matters of state law. But such abstention usually has little logic and therefore is exceedingly rare. There are, however, a few exceptions, notably in the bankruptcy area. See, *e.g.*, Eways v. Governor's Island, 326 N.C. 552, 391 S.E.2d 182 (1990).

Another form of state abstention is reverse-*Colorado River* abstention. Like *Colorado River* abstention, this abstention is potentially important in complex cases. Many states have a general rule of comity that a state court will stay its hand when a similar case is already pending in federal court. See, *e.g.*, Farmland Irrigation Co. v. Dopplmaier, 48 Cal.2d 208, 308 P.2d 732 (1957); Consumers Power Co. v. Public Utilities Commission, 270 Mich. 213, 258 N.W. 250 (1935). This rule of comity applies to actions *in personam* and to actions *in rem*; thus, a state court may stay itself in circumstances in which the federal court could not have enjoined the state action. Moreover, the stay applies both to claims brought under both state and federal law. See, *e.g.*, *Consumers Power, supra* (suspending suit on issue of state ratemaking while same issue pends in federal court); Barnes v. Peat, Marwick, Mitchell & Co., 42 A.D.2d 15, 344 N.Y.S.2d 645 (1973) (stay issued when case alleged violations of federal securities law). Is such a stay of a federal question claim a "neutral state rule regarding the administration of the courts" and thus a "valid excuse" under *Howlett*?

Behind this question lie a host of interpretive issues for reverse-*Colorado River* abstention. One disagreement among the states concerns the precise circumstances under which there should be abstention in favor of an earlier-filed federal case. California, for instance, considers six factors: the importance of discouraging multiple litigation designed solely to harass an adverse party, the avoidance of unseemly conflicts with the federal court, whether the rights of the parties can best be determined by the California state court or the federal court given the nature of the subject matter, the availability of witnesses, the stage to which the proceedings in federal court have already advanced, and whether the federal action is pending in California federal court as opposed to another federal court. See *Farmland Irrigation*, 48 Cal.2d 208; Thomson v. Continental Ins. Co., 66 Cal.2d 738, 59 Cal.Rptr. 101, 427 P.2d 765 (1967); Caiafa Professional Law Corp. v.

State Farm Fire & Casualty Co., 15 Cal.App.4th 800, 19 Cal.Rptr.2d 138 (1993). North Carolina considers eight factors: the nature of the case; the convenience of witnesses; the availability of compulsory process to produce witnesses; the relative ease of access to sources of proof; the applicable law; the burden of litigating matters not of local concern; the desirability of litigating matters of local concern in local courts; and convenience and access to another forum. See Home Indemnity Co. v. Hoechst-Celanese Corp., 99 N.C.App. 322, 393 S.E.2d 118 (1990). New York used to consider whether the state or federal forum provided a more complete disposition of the issues, which court had more expertise in the trial of the issues, and the extent of duplication in proceedings. See *Barnes*, 344 N.Y.S.2d 645; Grand Central Building, Inc. v. New York and Harlem Railroad Co., 59 A.D.2d 207, 398 N.Y.S.2d 888 (1977). In recent years, however, New York seems to have adopted a more stringent rule permitting abstention only when the parties, the causes of action, and the requested relief are identical, or when the first-filed federal action will necessarily determine the issues in the state case. See Guilden v. Baldwin Securities Corp., 189 A.D.2d 716, 592 N.Y.S.2d 725 (1993); Congress Factors Corp. v. Meinhard Commercial Corp., 129 Misc.2d 726, 493 N.Y.S.2d 917 (1985). Florida too seems to require an identity of parties and issues, and will further refuse a stay if the federal docket is too congested. See City of Miami Beach v. Miami Beach Fraternal Order of Police, 619 So.2d 447 (Fla. App. 1993); Koehlke Components, Inc. v. South East Connectors, Inc., 456 So.2d 554 (Fla. App. 1984). Texas requires a stay in cases between the same parties unless the plaintiff or the court in the first-filed federal suit is guilty of fraud, sinister motive, inattention, or delay in the filing and prosecution of the federal suit. See Alpine Gulf, Inc. v. Valentino, 563 S.W.2d 358 (Tex.App. 1978).

There are other sources of disagreement as well. State courts differ on whether issuance of a stay is a matter of discretion or duty, compare Sumitomo Bank of California v. Davis, 4 Cal.App.4th 1306, 6 Cal.Rptr.2d 381 (1992) (discretion) and Greenhouse v. Hargrave, 509 P.2d 1360 (Okla. 1973) (discretion) with *Alpine Gulf*, 563 S.W.2d 358 (nearly unflagging duty) and *Koehlke Components*, 456 So.2d 554 (same); whether a stay should be issued in favor of a case in a federal court of another state, compare *Caiafa*, 19 Cal.Rptr.2d 138 (no) with Reliance Insurance Co. v. Tiger International, Inc., 91 A.D.2d 925, 457 N.Y.S.2d 813 (1983) (staying New York action in favor of California suit) and *Alpine Gulf, supra* (staying Texas action in favor of District of Columbia suit); whether the proper remedy is a stay or a dismissal, compare *Koehlke Components*, 456 So.2d 554 (stay) with Terracorn Development Group, Inc. v. Village of Westhaven, 209 Ill.App.3d 758, 568 N.E.2d 376 (1991) (dismissal); and whether the source of the law underlying the case should influence a decision to stay, compare Polaris Public Income Funds v. Einhorn, 625 So.2d 128 (Fla.App. 1993) (staying state case brought under Florida law in favor of federal action brought under federal and New York common law) with CBS, Inc. v. Fitchelberg, 88 A.D.2d 881, 452 N.Y.S.2d 596 (1982) (refusing a stay in favor of *later*-filed federal action in part because state law issues were more properly interpreted by state rather than federal judiciary) and *Home Indemnity*, 393 S.E.2d 118 (stating that applicable law is a relevant consideration).

From the standpoint of complex and complicated litigation, three other issues regarding a reverse-*Colorado River* stay are significant. The first is the extent to which a state court has the power to issue a stay when the parties and issues in the state case are related to, but not identical to, the parties in the federal case. Thus far, this issue has received its most thorough, albeit inconsistent, treatment in the New York state courts. Some New York cases have held that a stay of a state case in favor of a related federal case is inappropriate unless the parties and issues in the cases are identical. See *Guilden*, 592 N.Y.S.2d 725; *Grand Central Building*, 398 N.Y.S.2d 888 (refusing a stay when certain issues and parties were not before federal bankruptcy court, and New York action had joined all entities having an interest in the case); Mackay Construction Corp. v. Brooklyn Union Gas Co., 39 A.D.2d 687, 332 N.Y.S.2d 486 (1972) (refusing a stay of state law contract claim even though contract claim was arguably a compulsory counterclaim in federal action); cf. Cannon v. Equitable Life Assurance Society of the United States, 106 Misc.2d 1060, 433 N.Y.S.2d 378 (1980) (certifying state class action that contained parties not included in federal suit, in part because the parties were not identical and because plaintiffs' choice of forum should rarely be disturbed). Other New York cases have allowed a stay even when the party and issue structure in federal court was different. In *Barnes*, 31 state plaintiffs alleged violations of § 17(a) of the Securities Act of 1933 and of New York state law. At the same time three private actions from the Southern District of New York, four private actions from other federal courts, and an SEC action had been consolidated in the Southern District of New York for pretrial purposes. Some of the federal cases were class actions, of which the state plaintiffs were members. The state court stayed the state case:

> It would appear that the action taken in the United States courts is the most efficient way of handling the large number of cases that have arisen or may arise out of this stock offering. The Federal Court has before it all of the defendants and all of the issues here asserted. The prosecution of this action and others that may conceivably be brought in state courts would necessarily involve going over the same grounds covered in the Federal actions and result in a duplication of effort and a consequent waste of court time. [344 N.Y.S.2d at 646-47.]

Accord, Barron v. Bludhorn, 68 A.D.2d 809, 414 N.Y.S.2d 15 (1979); see also *Polaris, supra* (staying Florida class action when New York class action raised most of the same issues and Florida plaintiffs were members of the New York class). Is it possible to argue that the holdings in *Grand Central Building* and *Cannon* are consistent with *Barron*, *Barnes*, and *Polaris*, in that the grant or denial of a stay turned on whether the state or federal court system had the greater ability to package related claims and parties?

Second, the use of a stay in state court may be in some circumstances a useful alternative to a request for an injunction in federal court. Indeed, a few state cases have stayed their hand in situations in which a federal court had the arguable power to enjoin the state proceedings. For instance, in Wolgin v. State Mutual Investors, 265 Pa.Super. 525, 402 A.2d 669 (1979), the plaintiffs in the state suit requested that the state court enjoin defendants from effecting a settlement then on appeal in federal court, appoint a receiver to monitor defendant's operations, and award $125,000,000 in damages. The Pennsylvania state court dismissed the case. Relying on Donovan v. City of Dallas, 377 U.S. 408 (1964) (p. 391, *supra*), it held that it had no power to enjoin a federal *in personam* proceeding, and thus could not prevent the settlement from taking effect. With respect to the other requested relief, it found that the federal court was capable of deciding whether the plaintiff class was not properly compensated by the federal settlement, that the federal action was nearly finalized, and that any state court relief would have severely interfered with the ongoing federal action. 265 Pa.Super. at 532-34, 402 A.2d at 673. Would the federal court have had the power to enjoin the Pennsylvania proceeding? If so, is there a tactical reason to ask the state court to stay itself rather than to ask the federal court to enjoin the state court?

Third, there is general agreement that the federal suit must be filed first in order for the state court to consider a stay. See Department of Game of State of Washington v. Puyallup Tribe, Inc., 86 Wash.2d 664, 548 P.2d 1058 (1976), vacated, 433 U.S. 165 (1977); Goldblum v. Boyd, 267 So.2d 610 (La.App. 1972) (no stay when state and federal cases filed on same day). In this respect, reverse-*Colorado River* abstention varies from *Colorado River* abstention, in which the order of filing is a relevant but not dispositive factor. Should a complex case that is better packaged in federal court be forced to proceed in state court because of the fortuity that the state case was filed first? Would your answer be the same for complicated cases?

c. Cooperation between State and Federal Courts

The combination of the "master of the complaint" rule and the present patchwork of jurisdictional doctrines often guarantees that related cases will proceed simultaneously in state and federal forums. When intersystem aggregation is ultimately impossible or impractical, only one avenue remains open: cooperation and co-ordination by the state and federal judges. See, *e.g.*, Union Light, Heat and Power Co. v. United States District Court, 588 F.2d 543 (6th Cir. 1978), cert. dismissed, 443 U.S. 913 (1979). The following article explores some of the benefits and drawbacks of intersystem cooperation as a means of overcoming the problems of joinder complexity and multiforum, multiparty litigation.

William W Schwarzer et al., JUDICIAL FEDERALISM IN ACTION: COORDINATION OF LITIGATION IN STATE AND FEDERAL COURTS

78 Va. L. Rev. 1689, 1670, 1733-49 (1992)

[I]nsufficient attention has been given to the extensive coordination between state and federal courts that can be achieved without new legislation or rules, and without subordinating one system to the other. [The authors then studied eleven cases, mostly mass tort, in which the state and federal courts engaged in some form of intersystem cooperation. They then synthesized their results.]

IV. Effective Coordination: An Overview

This Section discusses a wide range of issues relevant to the achievement of effective intersystem coordination: how judges might initiate and maintain contact with one another; the necessity of establishing a strong working relationship; the role attorneys can play; the kinds of situations most conducive to coordination; and the federalism concerns implicated by state-federal coordination.

A. Initiation of Contact . . .

Coordination obviously cannot take place until a judge contacts his or her counterpart in the other judicial system. Some judges prefer not to initiate contact until they have systems in place and can offer tangible resources to the other court. . . . The majority of judges interviewed, however, preferred early contact so that the state and federal judges could coordinate their schedules, consider joint discovery, and begin thinking about greater cooperation. . . .

B. Maintaining Contact

The judges' initial conversations tend to focus on general perspectives of the litigation, case management strategies, and areas appropriate for state-federal cooperation. As the cases progress, the judges need to maintain contact on a range of matters including scheduling, simply keeping abreast of cases in the other system, preparing for joint hearings, making joint rulings, or consulting on matters of procedure or substantive law. . . .

C. The Working Relationship

Those who have engaged in intersystem coordination tend to agree that the strength of the personal and working relationship developed between the judges influences the success of the enterprise more than any other factor. As Judge Weinstein puts it: "Coordination has nothing to do with procedures; it has to do with personality." A number of important dimensions of this relationship can be highlighted. Successful coordination requires flexibility and willingness to compromise in order to develop arrangements acceptable to both courts. Judge Zampano explains that an "exchange of communication, discussion, and camaraderie is very important. . . . There can't be egos here." His collaborator Judge Meadow agrees, adding that coordination requires "two judges that are not going to in any way let their personalities get in the way of their objectives." Judge Bechtle suggests that state and federal judges trying to develop a supportive relationship need to take into account "[s]ome degree of informality" as well as "more diplomacy and more consideration and more public relations and courtesy." Judge Rubin also stresses the need for informality. A true partnership cannot emerge unless the judges feel comfortable with one another and let down barriers. . . .

D. The Role of Attorneys . . .

The role of attorneys in state-federal coordination extends beyond getting it started. Their active participation is vital at every stage of coordination. Attorneys may be more knowledgeable than the court about numerous matters relevant to coordination, such as relationships among counsel, parties' different priorities and stages of preparation, or ongoing settlement talks. Furthermore, because the judiciary has limited experience with intersystem coordination, attorneys are a welcome source of ideas. . . .

Coordination requires not only that attorneys communicate with the court, but also cooperate with one another. This is partly because "[a] bar that is collegial and cooperative will foster joint activity by judges," but also because the actual state-federal arrangements often involve committees of attorneys taking the lead in achieving intersystem coordination. . . .

Yet, cooperation among attorneys has limits. In the Hyatt Skywalk litigation, the attorneys in federal court preferred a class action while the attorneys in the state cases wanted to handle their cases individually, and considerable tension resulted. In general, lawyers favor state-federal coordination of discovery and settlement, but are sometimes reluctant to proceed further because they have consciously chosen to proceed in one forum, and do not want to see the significance of that decision diminished. Courts should be sensitive to their interests and seek the lawyers' approval (not merely their grudging acceptance) of such intersystem coordination as seems desirable. This may involve assuring counsel that even when matters are jointly briefed, argued, and even decided, the judge in whose court the case is brought will not abdicate his or her responsibility to give the matter independent consideration.

E. Situations Most Conducive to Effective Coordination

Most coordination has occurred in litigation arising out of a single, discrete event. Although such cases are typically the best candidates for coordination, they are not the only ones. . . . Whenever there are closely related cases in the state and federal courts, intersystem coordination is a possibility worth exploring. There are, however, certain circumstances under which coordination has proven most feasible. . . .

Not surprisingly, judges have found that coordination works best when the state and federal courts are in close proximity. . . .

The possibility of intersystem coordination is enhanced when the cases within each system are aggregated. When one judge is in charge of all the cases in a system, that judge can structure the litigation and ensure uniform treatment of the cases. This, in turn, makes it possible to develop a coherent plan for coordinating related cases with another court. . . . Such things as coordinated scheduling, a common case management plan, and joint hearings require extensive effort and communication between two judges and become far more difficult as the number of judges increases. Moreover, when only a few judges manage all of the related cases, these judges have access to all of the parties and thus an opportunity to encourage a global settlement, which would be far less likely if the cases were scattered among many courts. In all of the cases studied, some form of aggregation was achieved within both the state and federal systems. . . .

Although the actual state-federal coordination usually involves the work of a few individual judges, the appropriate judicial environment throughout a jurisdiction can facilitate coordination. For example, Judge Shortell describes the Alaska court systems as "more relaxed" than those in larger jurisdictions such that "[t]here is not so much formality" and certainly no "friction" between the state and federal courts. Because of this, he says, "there is no impediment . . . even to [judges] who don't know each other, getting together and talking [about their cases]." Similarly, Judge Zampano believes that his coordination with Judge Meadow was aided by the nature of Connecticut's judicial community in which the courts "have comity beyond the everyday business." . . .

F. Federalism Concerns

The potential benefits of intersystem coordination should be clear. There are, however, potential drawbacks as well, mostly stemming from the fact that intersystem coordination invites tampering with the traditional jurisdictional boundaries of the state and federal court systems. The United States Constitution envisions two separate judiciaries. For the country at large, this division provides varied laboratories in which to test different approaches. For individual litigants dual judiciaries can offer a choice of where to pursue or defend against a claim. Judges must be sensitive to the possibility that state-federal coordination can undermine these interests. . . .

Coordination requires judges to make joint decisions involving both case management and legal interpretation. Certain risks inhere in any joint decisionmaking situation. First, the necessary compromises will, in the perception of an individual judge, sometimes come at the expense of excellence. . . .

Another potential problem with any power-sharing arrangement is that one party may exert too much influence. As a result, the methods and interpretations of the subordinate partner are lost. . . . In addition, judges risk diminishing the integrity of their court's decisionmaking process if they become a rubber stamp for another court. In several of the cases under study, one judge essentially controlled the litigation in both systems. It was not uncommon for the federal court to play this role. In light of federal courts' greater resources, this tendency is understandable, but judges should take care that dominance be avoided if possible. In addition to the risks described, federal courts should be wary of overstepping their Article III function by making decisions affecting persons over whom they have no jurisdiction. . . .

Perhaps the greatest concern is that intersystem coordination can diminish the litigants' benefits of their choice of forum. They might have had good reason for selecting one court system over the other, and when judges work together and influence one another, or mold their rules to conform to those of another system, or decide matters jointly, litigants may lose the advantages of their chosen forum. . . .

Although state-federal coordination may deprive some parties of the benefits of their chosen forum, that price may be worth the gains to the entire judicial system. Nevertheless, there is a trade-off, and courts should keep sight of the costs.

[A] middle path offers a fruitful possibility to federal and state courts coordinating their companion cases: although the state court should not automatically follow the federal court's determinations on federal law, it may accord them great weight, perhaps even a rebuttable presumption of correctness. This policy of deference would seem especially justified in light of the value of producing consistent results in related cases. As long as the deference is not blind, the state court arguably fulfills its responsibility. . . .

[With respect to issues of state law,] it is settled doctrine that the decisions of lower state courts on matters of state law, although not binding on federal courts, carry significant weight. In the context of companion state-federal cases, the value of consistency arguably justifies the federal court giving the state court's interpretation of state law even more weight than it otherwise might — albeit still making sure that it regards the state court's interpretation as reasonable. This also ensures that the federal court does not excessively interfere with the development of state law.

Notes and Questions

1. Intersystem cooperation and co-ordination have certain advantages over mechanisms that seek mandatory consolidation in one (usually federal) forum. In addition to the benefits described by Judge Schwarzer and his co-authors, there are the advantages that cooperation and co-ordination are that they are more respectful of the interests of both state and federal courts to adjudicate cases within their jurisdiction, that two judicial heads are often better than one, and that the presence of a second judge may dilute some of the concerns we have seen about vesting too much power in a single judicial officer. On the other hand, cooperation and co-ordination possess the limitations and drawbacks identified by Judge Schwarzer and his co-authors. On balance, does co-ordination or lack of co-ordination seem the greater evil? If you like the idea of co-ordination, does consolidation in one forum seem an even better alternative? If you do not like the idea of co-ordination, is it because you think that it is too weak a remedy or too strong?

2. We have suggested that the responses of the court system to instances of joinder complexity and to instances of multiforum, multiparty litigation should be different; with joinder complexity, the demand for like treatment of like parties may require changes in adversarial process, while with complicated litigation, the efficiency of aggregation may not outweigh the importance of individual control of litigation. If this is so, might it be argued that intersystem

cooperation and co-ordination is an adequate remedy to deal with the problem of complicated litigation; but it is inadequate to deal with the narrower problem of joinder complexity?

3. Is it appropriate for a federal judge to defer to a state judge's view on state law? Doesn't this deference create a form of "abstention" much broader than *Pullman*, *Burford*, and *Thibodaux* abstention, which among them have worked out the parameters of federal court deference on matters of unclear state law? In states with certification statutes, isn't certification the proper mechanism for a federal judge to use when confronted with uncertain state law? Under Howlett v. Rose, 496 U.S. 356 (1990) (p. 437, *supra*), can a state judge legitimately defer to a federal judge's views on federal law? As a policy matter, doesn't our federal system value the views of state judges on federal questions as much as it values the views of federal district judges? Suppose that the federal (or state) judge sincerely believes that the state (or federal) judge is making a mistake on a matter for which the other judge is taking lead responsibility. Is it ethical for the judge to communicate this belief *ex parte*?

4. Whatever your views about the academic merits of intersystem cooperation and co-ordination, you should realize that cooperation and co-ordination are presently the order of the day in complex and complicated litigation. State and federal judges faced with restrictive jurisdictional rules are not sitting idly by and letting the state and federal cases meander to their separate conclusions; they are actively co-ordinating their caseloads. For instance, in the silicone gel breast implant litigation, the federal judge before whom all federal cases had been aggregated had regular meetings and conversations with state judges handling similar cases, and he kept them regularly informed about the status of settlement negotiations.

5. Neither the 1960 precursor to the present *Manual for Complex Litigation* nor the original 1970 edition of the *Manual* contained any references to intersystem cooperation and co-ordination. The 1985 second edition of the *Manual* contained only two pages describing and weakly recommending cooperation and co-ordination. See Manual for Complex Litigation (Second) § 31.31 (1985). The 1995 edition of the *Manual* takes a more enthusiastic and aggressive attitude toward cooperation and co-ordination. See Manual for Complex Litigation, Third § 31.31 (1995). In 1997, the Federal Judicial Center (which also publishes the *Manual for Complex Litigation*), the National Center for State Courts, and the State Justice Institute jointly authored a 248-page manual specifically on the subject of cooperation and co-ordination. James G. Apple et al., Manual for Cooperation between State and Federal Courts (1997). Although some parts of this *Manual* relate to other matters, many parts are targeted to the problems of complex and complicated litigation.

6. Cooperation and co-ordination occurs not only among judges, but also among lawyers. In many types of complex and complicated litigation, lawyers create networks and share information. In many cases, most of the litigation is ultimately controlled by a few firms that associate with other firms around the country, further aiding the co-ordination process. Moreover, in some areas, specialized newsletters or media develop to keep everyone abreast of recent developments in the field. The classic article describing successful cooperation and co-ordination by plaintiffs' lawyers is Paul D. Rheingold, *The MER/29 Story — An Instance of Successful Mass Disaster Litigation*, 56 Cal. L. Rev. 116 (1968).

7. Judge Schwarzer and his co-authors noted that the chance of successful intersystem cooperation and co-ordination is improved when all of the cases

within the state and system are aggregated in a single state forum and all of the cases within the federal system are aggregated in a single federal forum. Aggregation of cases within a single system is the issue to which we now turn.

CHAPTER FOUR

LIMITATIONS ON THE AGGREGATION OF RELATED CASES PENDING IN A SINGLE COURT SYSTEM

> [T]ransferee judges have contributed immeasurably to the public welfare and to the capacity of the federal judiciary to carry its ever increasing burden of litigation.
>
> Stanley A. Weigel

The rules of subject matter and territorial jurisdiction are not the only structural rules that affect the location of a case. In general, rules of subject matter jurisdiction define the court system(s) with the power to hear a case. Rules of territorial jurisdiction determine the parties that this court system may bring before it. But a final set of structural rules must be considered by plaintiffs deciding where to locate a case: the rules of venue. These rules determine the courts within a court system that may entertain a case.

Venue rules are necessary because, even within a single court system, there may exist many different districts or divisions that have no connection to a particular case. To take an extreme example, it makes little sense for the United States District Court for the District of Hawaii to try a case involving a car crash in Vermont when the plaintiff is a citizen of Maine and the defendant is a citizen of Massachusetts. Since the federal court in Hawaii has diversity jurisdiction, and since in at least some situations Hawaii may be able to exercise territorial jurisdiction over the defendant, venue rules are required to assure both that one party does not significantly inconvenience other parties and that lawsuits are tried in a court with a sensible relationship to the claims and the parties.

In general terms, venue rules permit only those courts with some connection to one or more of the parties or to one or more of the events creating liability to entertain a claim. Both state and federal courts have venue rules for cases brought within their system. In the federal system, venue rules are based entirely on statute and common law; the Supreme Court has never imposed any constitutional limitations on venue. The venue rules are located, for the most part, in 28 U.S.C. §§ 1391-1407, although hundreds of special venue provisions are scattered throughout the United States Code. See American Law Institute, Study of the Division of Jurisdiction between State and Federal Courts, Appendix F (1969). Since venue is a matter of convenience rather than judicial power, defendants are generally able to waive defects in venue and to proceed in an inconvenient forum. See F.R.Civ.P. 12 (b)(3), (h).

As with the rules of joinder and the rules of subject matter and territorial jurisdiction, the plaintiff, as the master of the complaint, has the first and most important say in choosing the proper venue. See generally 15 Charles A. Wright et al., Federal Practice & Procedure § 3848 (1986) ("The courts have developed a bewildering variety of formulations on how much weight is to be given to plaintiff's choice of forum."). As you might expect with a doctrine grounded in convenience, however, that say is not absolute. In the first section, we examine the rules that initially guide the plaintiffs' choice of venue. In the second section, we turn to a series of devices by which the parties — in particular, the defendants and the court, but also in some cases the plaintiffs — can switch the venue. In the third section, we examine the American Law Institute's proposal to change present venue rules in order to overcome some of the remaining deficiencies in aggregation.

This chapter focuses primarily, although not exclusively, on the federal courts. As we shall see, one of the most significant advantages that federal courts enjoy over state courts in the aggregation of related cases is in the area of venue. The reason is simple. A state court in Mississippi has no present power to transfer a case to a state court in Texas in which related cases may be pending. A federal court in Mississippi, however, does enjoy various powers to transfer a case to a federal court in Texas in order to achieve aggregation of related litigation. If aggregation is the goal, therefore, knowledge of the basic rules of federal venue, as well as of the various aggregation powers of the federal courts, is key.

A. LIMITATIONS ON AGGREGATION IMPOSED BY VENUE RULES

1. *The Basic Venue Rule: 28 U.S.C. § 1391.* 28 U.S.C. § 1391, which is the default venue provision for federal courts, is the product of a series of congressional amendments in 1988, 1990, 1992, and 1995 to earlier versions of § 1391. Note that § 1391 distinguishes between proper venues in diversity cases (§ 1391(a)) and proper venues in cases "not founded solely on diversity of citizenship" (§ 1391(b)). Note further that subsections (a)(1) and (a)(2) are identical to subsections (b)(1) and (b)(2). Subsections (a)(1) and (b)(1) both allow a case to be brought in any judicial district in which "any defendant

resides, if all defendants reside in the same State." (Subsection (c) states that, for purposes of subsections (a)(1) and (b)(1), a corporation resides in any judicial district in which it is subject to personal jurisdiction, or, in the event that there are insufficient contacts with any district but sufficient contacts with the entire state for personal jurisdiction purposes, in the district with the most significant contacts.) Subsections (a)(2) and (b)(2) both authorize venue in any judicial district in which "a substantial part of the events or omissions giving rise to the claim occurred, or a substantial part of property that is the subject of the action is situated." Subsection (a)(3), however, differs from subsection (b)(3); in diversity cases, venue is also proper in "a judicial district in which any defendant is subject to personal jurisdiction at the time the action is commenced, if there is no district in which the action may otherwise be brought," while in federal question cases, venue is proper in "a judicial district in which any defendant may be found, if there is no district in which the action may otherwise be brought."

Is there any practical difference between subsection (a)(3) and subsection (b)(3)? In particular, does "subject to personal jurisdiction" under subsection (a)(3) mean anything different than "may be found" under subsection (b)(3)? If it does, what is the point of creating (b)(3) venue in a forum that cannot exercise territorial jurisdiction over a defendant? Why does subsection (a)(3) require that the defendants be subject to personal jurisdiction "at the time the action is commenced," while (b)(3) is silent about any similar requirement? It is tempting to say that these differences are semantic rather than substantive. But if subsections (a)(3) and (b)(3) are the same, why did Congress not combine § 1391(a) and § 1391(b)? More generally, why did Congress repeat identical language in (a)(1) and (b)(1), and in (a)(2) and (b)(2)? Could it be that, although Congress used the same words in both sections, it intended courts to construe those words more generously in federal question cases than in diversity cases? For a good review of some of the interpretive difficulties of § 1391, see David D. Siegel, *Commentary on 1988 and 1990 Revisions of Section 1391*, reprinted after 28 U.S.C.A. § 1391 (1993), and David D. Siegel, *Commentary on 1995 Revision of Subdivision (a), Clause (3)*, reprinted after 28 U.S.C.A. § 1391 (Supp. 1998).

The basic venue rule, which was not written with complex and complicated litigation in mind, creates two distinct problems in complex and complicated litigation. The first is the power that the rule places in the hand of a plaintiff that wishes to litigate her case separately to avoid aggregation. For instance, if a plaintiff really wants the case to be heard in the Southern District of Florida, she will need to be sure either to (1) join only Florida defendants (to invoke venue under (a)(1) or (b)(1)); (2) add or delete certain claims in order to ensure that a substantial part of the conduct occurred in the district (to invoke either (a)(2) or (b)(2)); or (3) shape the claims and the parties in order to ensure that defendants have different residence, that no substantial part of the allegations in the case occurred in any other district, and that territorial jurisdiction over (or presence of) the defendants exists in the Southern District of Florida (to invoke the catch-all (a)(3) or (b)(3)).

Whether this manipulation is tolerable in ordinary litigation in which a plaintiff is merely seeking the tactical advantages of a particular venue, giving plaintiffs the "venue privilege" in complex or complicated litigation can lead to problems of dysfunction (*i.e.*, inequitable distribution of assets) or inefficiency (*i.e.*, related litigation occurring simultaneously in multiple forums) when other related cases are pending in the District of Wyoming. Indeed, adherence to the adversarial process would seem to achieve the socially optimal selection of venue only fitfully and coincidentally. In these cases, should we respect plaintiffs' choice of courtroom less than her choice of court system? Granting that the individual autonomy that underlies the adversarial process is important, should the doctrine of venue, which is grounded in notions of fairness and convenience to the parties, be treated more malleably than doctrines of territorial and subject matter jurisdiction, which are grounded in notions of power, authority, and constitutional liberty? Or does the fact that § 1391 is a statute (and one that Congress has changed four times in the last 10 years) make judicial innovation under § 1391 impossible?

Second, and conversely, even if a plaintiff wishes to aggregate, § 1391 may frustrate that desire. In a large-scale case involving nationwide injuries due to patterns of conduct by various defendants who resided and acted in different states, it may be impossible to find a single venue in which all defendants reside, in which a substantial part of the claims of all plaintiffs occurred, or in which there is personal jurisdiction over or presence of all defendants. In complex cases, therefore, we need first to determine how pliable § 1391 is, and then to determine the point at which § 1391 will finally break. The critical issue is how little of a connection we are willing to accept for venue purposes. If we insist on a strong connection between a forum and a party, a case may need to be broken up into smaller cases heard in various forums; if we allow a loose connection of some parties or some activities to a particular forum to suffice, we risk the inconvenience and unfairness to litigants that venue rules are intended to prevent.

The first issue — whether the defendants or courts can overcome a venue choice made by plaintiffs seeking a tactical advantage — will be the focus of the following section of this chapter. The second issue — how pliable § 1391 or other venue provisions are when a plaintiff wishes to achieve socially optimal aggregation in complex or complicated litigation — is the subject of the remainder of this section.

(a) *Subsections 1391(a)(1) and (b)(1)*. Suppose that there is a mass tort in which several corporate manufacturers sell a chemical that causes thousands of injuries nationwide. The chemical formula is identical. Manufacturer 1, with 40% of the market, makes its product in Massachusetts; Manufacturer 2, with 35% of the market, makes its product in Missouri; and Manufacturer 3, with 25% of the market, makes its product in Hawaii. Each defendant aggressively solicits business and sells products in many federal judicial districts, and all do so in the federal districts which comprise the states of New York, Illinois, Texas, and California. Further assume that, if complete joinder of all affected parties is not accomplished, later-filing parties stand to recover nothing; hence, in order to avoid dysfunction, a single resolution is necessary. Finally, assume that the plaintiffs desire aggregation of their claims.

In this situation, regardless of whether they plead a diversity or federal question theory, a significant number of venues are likely to be available to the plaintiffs. Venue is proper in any judicial district in which the defendants reside (§ 1391(a)(1) or (b)(1)); as corporate defendants, they reside wherever they are subject to personal jurisdiction when the action is commenced (§ 1391(c)); and personal jurisdiction can be obtained over a defendant who "does business" in a judicial district. Thus, under either (a)(1) or (b)(1), venue is proper over all three manufacturers in any federal judicial district in New York, Illinois, Texas, and California. Aggregation-minded plaintiffs should have no difficulty finding a single venue for all the cases.

(b) *Subsections (a)(2) and (b)(2).* Now suppose that Manufacturer 1 manufactures its product in Massachusetts and sells and does business only in Massachusetts and Wyoming; Manufacturer 2 manufactures, sells, and does business only in Massachusetts; and Manufacturer 3 manufactures in California, and sells and does business in every federal judicial district west of the Mississippi River. In this scenario, subsections (a)(1) and (b)(1) are no longer helpful. Thus, the scope of subsections (a)(2) and (b)(2) becomes important. If both Manufacturer 1 and Manufacturer 2, who occupy 75% of the total market, sold products that caused injuries in the District of Massachusetts, is the District of Massachusetts a proper forum for the claims against Manufacturer 3? Obviously, much hinges on how broadly we construe the phrase "substantial part of the of the events or omissions giving rise to the claim that occurred."

In deciding on a proper construction, a bit of history may be useful. The predecessor to the present subsections (a) and (b) created venue in any judicial district "in which the claim arose." In Leroy v. Great Western United Corp., 443 U.S. 173 (1979), the Supreme Court held that this phrase was to be read narrowly, and only in rare cases would there be more than one district in which a claim "arose." Id. at 184-85. The Court also suggested a number of other interpretive guides to the phrase "in which the claim arose": "(1) the purpose of the 1966 statute was to close venue gaps and should not be read more broadly than necessary to close those gaps, id. at 184; (2) the general purpose of the venue statute was to protect defendants against an unfair or inconvenient trial location, id. at 183-84; (3) location of evidence and witnesses was a relevant factor, id. at 186; (4) familiarity of the Idaho federal judges with the Idaho anti-takeover statute was a relevant factor, id. at 186; [and] (5) plaintiff's convenience was not a relevant factor, id. at 183." Bates v. C & S Adjusters, Inc., 980 F.2d 865, 867 (2d Cir. 1992).

In enacting the present (a)(2) and (b)(2), Congress intended to overrule that part of *Leroy* which suggested that a claim typically could arise in only one venue. H.R. Rep. 734, 101st Cong., 2d Sess. 23, reprinted in 1990 U.S.C.C.A.N. 6860, 6869 ("The great advantage of referring to the place where things happened . . . is that it avoids the litigation breeding phrase 'in which the claim arose.' It also avoids the problem created by the frequent cases in which substantial parts of the underlying events have occurred in several districts."). Whether it also intended to overrule the remaining interpretive guides from *Leroy* — especially guides (1), (2), and (5), which portend a narrow interpretation of (a)(2) and (b)(2) — is unclear. See *Bates*, 980 F.2d at 867 ("*Leroy* remain[s] important source[ ] of guidance").

Should we add another factor to the surviving *Leroy* factors in complex litigation: the unfairness and disparate treatment of plaintiffs? Should we add another factor to the *Leroy* factors in complicated litigation: the inefficiency of repeated re-litigation of related issues?

(c) *Subsections (a)(3) and (b)(3)*. Before answering these questions, you might wish to consider the effect of subsections (a)(3) and (b)(3), which can be used when none of the prior sections is applicable. These default provisions apply when neither (a)(1) nor (a)(2) is applicable in a diversity case, or when neither (b)(1) nor (b)(2) is applicable in a case not founded solely on diversity. Let us assume, for purposes of the hypothetical in the last section, that "may be found" is not a more stringent test than "subject to personal jurisdiction." Let us also assume that neither (a)(2) nor (b)(2) can be construed to provide a single venue for the cases against all the manufacturers. Finally, let us assume that the manufacturers are subject to personal jurisdiction (or may be found) only in the districts in which they manufacture, sell, or do business.

On these assumptions, venue would be proper in multiple judicial districts — Massachusetts and every judicial district west of the Mississippi River. In a case such as this, a broad construction of subsections (a)(2) and (b)(2) would actually make more difficult the finding of a number of hospitable venues for aggregation-minded plaintiffs. Moreover, a broad construction of subsections (a)(2) and (b)(2) may be unnecessary if we relax our rules of territorial jurisdiction in complex and complicated cases in a way that permits the federal court in Massachusetts to exercise jurisdiction over Manufacturer 3. See pp. 268-310, *supra*. Indeed, if we do not do so, securing venue under § 1391(a)(3) or (b)(3) will be a phyrric victory, for venue will exist in Massachusetts but Manufacturer 3 will still be able to avoid suit by arguing that Massachusetts courts lack territorial jurisdiction. Should the venue implications of territorial jurisdiction affect our understanding of the scope of territorial jurisdiction?

(d) *Conclusion*. A generous interpretation of § 1391 also becomes unnecessary if there are other devices by which a separate case against Manufacturer 3 (filed in some court in which jurisdiction over Manufacturer 3 can be obtained) can be consolidated with the Massachusetts case. As we shall see in the next section, such devices exist, although their present limitations suggest that a generous understanding of § 1391 is still useful. Before we turn to those devices, however, a brief review of other aspects of venue might be helpful.

2. *Special Venue Rules*. Of the hundreds of specific venue provisions, several have particular importance in complex and complicated litigation: 28 U.S.C. § 1397, which authorizes venue in a § 1335 interpleader case in any judicial district "in which one or more of the defendants reside"; 28 U.S.C. § 1400(b), which authorizes venue for patent infringement cases in any district in which the defendant resides, or in which acts of infringement have occurred and "the defendant has a regular and established place of

business"; 28 U.S.C. § 1401, which allows stockholders to prosecute derivative actions in the same venues in which the corporation could have done so; 28 U.S.C. § 1409, which permits venue of bankruptcy proceedings or cases related to bankruptcy proceedings to be "commenced in the district court in which such case is pending"; 28 U.S.C. § 1441(a) states that the proper venue for a removed case is the "district and division embracing the place where the [state] action is pending"; 15 U.S.C. § 15, which allows venue in any district in which the antitrust defendant resides; 15 U.S.C. § 78aa, which provides venue in any district in which the defendant is an inhabitant or "may be found" for certain securities cases; and 18 U.S.C. § 1964(c), which allows "any appropriate district court" to entertain a civil RICO claim. Examine 28 U.S.C. §§ 1397 and 18 U.S.C. § 1964(c) again. Assuming that creative interpretation of § 1391 is unavailing, should there be a similar special venue rule for complex cases: Venue should be available in any judicial district in which any defendant or agent of the defendant resides, or which is otherwise appropriate? Would a similar rule be appropriate for complicated cases? How would such a statute be worded?

3. *Ancillary Venue.* What should happen when a party brings a counterclaim, cross-claim, third party claim, or claim in intervention, but venue for such a claim does not lie in the original forum? The general rule was that, as long as the new claim lay within the ancillary jurisdiction of the court, an independent basis for venue were unnecessary. With respect to permissive counterclaims and permissive claims in intervention, which fell outside the ancillary jurisdiction of the federal court, an independent basis for venue was necessary. See 15 Charles A. Wright et al., Federal Practice & Procedure § 3808 (1986). How does the passage of § 1367 affect the concept of "ancillary venue"?

Similarly, suppose that a plaintiff adds new claims or new parties after the suit was filed in a proper forum. If the venue would have been improper for such claims or parties at the outset, can the court ignore the lack of independent venue when they are added later? The answer appears to be "No." See id., §§ 3807-08. In Texas state courts, however, the rule is apparently the opposite: Once venue attaches, it cannot be defeated by any changes subsequent to the initial pleading. See John MacCormick, *Remote Venue: Plaintiff's Pick*, 16 National Law Journal No. 22, p.1 (Jan. 31, 1994).

4. *The "Local Action" Exception.* There is an often-overlooked but well-entrenched exception to the federal venue rules: The venue rules apply only to "transitory" as opposed to "local" actions. See Livingston v. Jefferson, 15 Fed. Cas. 660 (No. 8411) (C.C.D. Va. 1811) (Marshall, C.J.). According to Chief Justice Marshall, "actions are deemed transitory, where transactions on which they are founded might have taken place anywhere; but are local where their cause is in its nature essentially local." Id. at 664. Subsequent efforts at definition shed little additional light on the distinction, although it is generally fair to say that local actions usually involve disputes regarding ownership of, trespass on, and injury to land or other forms of property. See Wright et al., *supra*, § 3822; cf. 28 U.S.C. § 1392 (providing that "[a]ny civil action, of a local nature, involving property located in different districts in the same State, may be brought in any of such districts").

There is some dispute about whether the "local action" doctrine is a question of subject matter jurisdiction, so that courts other than the court in which the property is located have no power to hear a "local" action, or rather is a matter of venue that can be waived. Compare Hayes v. Gulf Oil Corp., 821 F.2d 285 (5th Cir. 1987) (subject matter jurisdiction) with Wheatley v. Phillips, 228 F. Supp. 439 (D.N.C. 1964) (venue).

For the most part, the "local action" rule plays little part in complex litigation. In environmental claims seeking an abatement of interstate pollution or in mass tort cases involving injury to property, however, the rule threatens to divide essentially similar claims into many separate lawsuits. In In re School Asbestos Litigation, 921 F.2d 1310 (3d Cir. 1990), cert. denied, 499 U.S. 976 (1991), the Third Circuit rejected an argument that class action claims for property damage to school buildings across the country should be dismissed due to improper venue:

> Petitioner Kaiser Gypsum Company also contends that because the "local action" doctrine applies to any action directly affecting land and real property, the district court's subject matter jurisdiction is limited by the doctrine to claims related to property located in Pennsylvania. . . .
>
> The district court in this case conceded in its order that questions relating to the ownership of some of the school buildings may arise later in the litigation. As an alternative to dismissing the complaints now, the district court determined that it could dismiss those school districts for lack of subject matter jurisdiction once the local action doctrine is shown to apply.
>
> We agree that it is premature to invoke the local action doctrine at this time. Because the alleged claims appear transitory and are not bound to any issues of title or possession of real property, we reject Kaiser Gypsum's local action argument. [921 F.2d at 1318-19.]

Does § 1391 effectively overrule a significant portion of the local action doctrine by providing venue in any judicial district in which "a substantial part of property that is the subject of the action is situated." 28 U.S.C. §§ 1391 (a)(2), (b)(2). Does the answer depend on whether the "local action" doctrine is one of subject matter jurisdiction or venue? In complex and complicated cases, can you think of any argument for retention of the "local action" rule?

5. *Procedure.* The traditional remedy for filing a case in an improper venue was dismissal. See F.R.Civ.P. 12(b)(3). In the federal system and in some state systems, however, a case can be transferred, "if it be in the interest of justice," to "any district or division in which it could have been brought." 28 U.S.C. § 1406(a). Today, "[t]he usual procedure should be transfer rather than dismissal." See Wright et al., *supra*, § 3827; Goldlawr, Inc. v. Heiman, 369 U.S. 463 (1962) (authorizing § 1406(a) transfer even though transferring court had no personal jurisdiction over defendant).

The power of the court to transfer a case filed in a proper venue to another venue is considered in the following section.

B. OVERCOMING VENUE LIMITATIONS TO ACHIEVE AGGREGATION IN A SINGLE FORUM

Venue rules pose some challenges to plaintiffs that seek to aggregate cases in a single forum. When the rules preclude such aggregation, or when plaintiffs consciously choose not to file their cases in the same venue as related litigation, the issue becomes whether there exist devices by which the defendants or the court can achieve aggregation. This issue is akin to the issue that we studied in Chapter Three: the ability of the defendants or the court to change the plaintiffs' initial choice of court system.

Since changing courthouses within a single system does not raise the same issues of federalism as intersystem changes, you might expect that intrasystem changes are a relatively simpler thing to accomplish. For the most part, that expectation is correct, but it must be qualified. When a defendant or judge wishes to change the forum of a case from one state court (say in Minnesota) to another state court (say in Montana), the separate sovereignty of the two court systems creates tensions and problems reminiscent of the state-federal relationship. Within the courts of a single sovereign (say among Minnesota state courts or among the federal district courts), however, moving cases is easier, albeit not easy.

In Chapter Three we saw that the two main devices for changing plaintiffs' initial forum choice were removal, which affirmatively brought cases together in one system, and injunctions and stays, which indirectly achieved aggregation. That same pattern of affirmative and indirect devices is replicated with venue changes. So too is the reality that these devices can sometimes be used by defendants seeking to thwart aggregation.

1. Injunctions and Stays that Permit a Case to Proceed Only in a Designated Venue

Injunctions against the prosecution of related cases in other venues and stays of a case in favor of a proceeding in another venue are mirror-image methods by which the consolidation of related cases in a single venue can be accomplished. As Chapter Three's examination of anti-suit injunctions and abstention shows, however, injunctions and stays are a relatively weak method of obtaining consolidation; they do not affirmatively achieve consolidation but only make the parties in the enjoined or stayed proceeding prosecute the action elsewhere if that is what the parties choose to do. Nonetheless, injunctions and stays are extremely important: They are the only presently viable way by which a state-court-to-state-court transfer can be accomplished, they form the historical basis for the modern transfer mechanisms in the federal courts, and they remain a residual source of power in the federal system when other transfer mechanisms fail.

In this section we examine the most important injunctions and stays designed to change venue among courts of coordinate jurisdiction: the *forum non conveniens* dismissal, the federal-court-to-federal-court *Kerotest* injunction or stay, and the related state-court-to-state-court injunction or stay.

a. The *Forum Non Conveniens* Dismissal

KEMPE v. OCEAN DRILLING & EXPLORATION CO.

876 F.2d 1138 (5th Cir. 1989)

■ ALDISERT, Circuit Judge. The major question for decision is whether a count alleging a violation of the Racketeer Influenced and Corrupt Organizations Act, 18 U.S.C. §§ 1961-1968, (RICO) immunizes a civil complaint from the doctrine of *forum non conveniens*. Should we decide there is no immunity, we are then required to determine whether the district court abused its discretion in concluding that Bermuda was the proper forum for this case after analyzing the private interest factors affecting the litigants' convenience and the public interest factors affecting the forum's convenience as set forth in Gulf Oil Corp. v. Gilbert, 330 U.S. 501 (1947), and re-affirmed in Piper Aircraft Co. v. Reyno, 454 U.S. 235 (1981). We conclude that the civil RICO complaint at issue here is not immune from the application of the doctrine and that the district court did not abuse its discretion in applying the doctrine.

I.

Charles W. Kempe, Jr., and Michael J. Arnold, plaintiffs below, prosecute this appeal as joint liquidators appointed by the Bermuda Supreme Court to wind up the affairs of bankrupt Mentor Insurance Limited (Mentor), a company organized by special act of the Bermuda Parliament and located throughout its existence in Bermuda. Kempe is a Bermudian and a principal partner in one of Bermuda's largest accounting firms. Arnold is an accountant-liquidator, resident in England. Mentor's parent organization is Mentor Holding Corporation (MHC) which, in turn, is owned by Ocean Drilling & Exploration Co. (ODECO). MHC is a Delaware corporation with its principal place of business in New Orleans, Louisiana. ODECO is also a Delaware corporation with its principal place of business in New Orleans. Pinnacle Reinsurance Co., Ltd., is a reinsurance corporation having contractual relations with insurance company clients, including Mentor. Pinnacle is organized under the laws of Bermuda and has its principal place of business in Bermuda.

Mentor was formed in Bermuda by ODECO as a captive insurer to insure ODECO's oil drilling rigs. Mentor's business later expanded to insurance areas unrelated to ODECO or the oil business. By the 1980's, over 90% of Mentor's business was unrelated to ODECO.

In 1982, 1983, and 1984, Mentor entered into reinsurance agreements with Pinnacle. Reinsurance typically allows an insurance writing company to assign its risk to a reinsurance company in whole or in part. This has the effect of reducing its reportable loss reserves, thereby increasing its reported net worth. Once insurance risks are assumed by the reinsurer, the reinsured need not report these risks as liabilities on its balance sheet. However, certain accounting standards must be met in order for there to be a *bona fide* transfer of risk.

The liquidators allege that Mentor's agreements with Pinnacle, its reinsurance company, did not meet these standards. They contend that for each of the years in question, a secret side letter agreement provided that, notwithstanding the ostensible reinsurance agreement, Pinnacle's obligations would be limited to one fixed amount, unrelated to actual insurance losses, and payable only at the end of ten years. These secret side agreements, the liquidators allege, turned the agreements into financing arrangements ineligible to justify the balance sheet relief that Mentor claimed. The liquidators also allege that Mentor's financial statements were intentionally falsified by ODECO and its management from at least 1982 to March 1985. They contend that the financial reports materially overstated Mentor's financial health and concealed its dire financial condition by, *inter alia*, failing to disclose and properly account for the true nature of purported reinsurance agreements between Mentor and Pinnacle.

Although ODECO asserts that it did not discover these agreements until 1985, the liquidators allege that ODECO was a party to them all along. In its defense, ODECO contends that there was no falsification, that it relied on the work of Mentor's Bermudian accountants and auditors, and that the agreements were in accordance with generally accepted accounting principles in Bermuda.

Mentor went into involuntary liquidation in June 1985. The majority of Mentor's creditors are in the United States. On March 3, 1986, the liquidators brought this action in federal district court against ODECO, MHC, Pinnacle, and eight individual officer/directors of Mentor and/or MHC and ODECO. The complaint alleged violations of federal mail and wire fraud statutes comprising elements of RICO violations. In addition, plaintiffs asserted pendent state law claims for breach of fiduciary duty, fraudulent trading, and negligent misrepresentation. The merits of these arguments are not before us. The nature of appellants contentions, however, is relevant to the issue of the degree of relief available in Bermuda courts.

In granting appellees' motion to dismiss the complaint on the grounds of *forum non conveniens*, the district court found that Bermuda was an available and adequate forum, and that both private and public interest factors favored litigation in Bermuda.... The liquidator plaintiffs appeal the court's dismissal of the case on *forum non conveniens* grounds....

II....

The trial court's decision on the application of the *forum non conveniens* doctrine may be reversed only where there has been a clear abuse of discretion. Piper Aircraft v. Reyno, 454 U.S. 235, 257 (1981)....

III.

Our analysis begins with the balancing test set forth in Gulf Oil Corp. v. Gilbert, 330 U.S. 501 (1947), and its companion case, Koster v. Lumbermens Mutual Casualty Co., 330 U.S. 518 (1947). Although "a plaintiff's choice of forum should rarely be disturbed," Piper Aircraft Co. v. Reyno, 454 U.S. 235, 241 (1981), a federal court may resist imposition upon its jurisdiction even when jurisdiction is authorized by the letter of a general venue statute. *Gulf Oil*, 330 U.S. at 507. When an alternative forum has jurisdiction to hear the case, and when trial in the plaintiff's chosen forum would "establish . . . oppressiveness and vexation to a defendant . . . out of all proportion to plaintiff's convenience," or when the "chosen considerations affecting the court's own administrative and legal problems," the court may, in the exercise of its sound discretion, dismiss the case. *Koster*, 330 U.S. at 524. To guide trial court discretion, the Court has suggested a balancing of "private interest factors" affecting the convenience of the litigants, and "public interest factors" affecting the convenience of the forum. See *Gulf Oil*, 330 U.S. at 508-09.

Factors pertaining to the private interests of the litigants include the "relative [e]ase of access to sources of proof; availability of compulsory process for attendance of unwilling, and the cost of obtaining attendance of willing, witnesses; possibility of view of premises, if view would be appropriate to the action; and all other practical problems that make trial of a case easy, expeditious and inexpensive." Id. at 508. Public interest factors bearing on the question include administrative difficulties flowing from court congestion, the "local interest in having localized controversies decided at home," the interest in "having the trial of a diversity case in a forum that is at home with the state law that must govern the case," the avoidance of unnecessary problems in conflict of laws, or in the application of foreign law, and the unfairness of burdening citizens in an unrelated forum with jury duty. Id. at 508-09.

The teachings of *Gulf Oil* and *Koster* were reaffirmed in Piper Aircraft Co. v. Reyno, 454 U.S. 235 (1981). But *Reyno* added still another dimension to the test. We emphasize this dimension now because it is extremely important in light of the major argument posed by the appellants here. *Reyno* specifically held that plaintiffs may not defend a motion to dismiss on the ground of *forum non conveniens* merely by showing that the substantive law that would be applied in the alternative forum is less favorable to the plaintiffs than that of the chosen forum. . . . In *Reyno*, the Court ruled that the possibility of an unfavorable change in the law is merely a factor to be considered, but that ordinarily this factor should not be given conclusive or even substantial weight in the forum inquiry. The Court carefully explained that giving such a consideration inordinate weight "is not only inconsistent with the purpose of the *forum non conveniens* doctrine, but also poses substantial practical problems." Id. at 251.

In *Reyno*, a small commercial aircraft crashed in the Scottish highlands. The plaintiffs sued the aircraft manufacturer and the company that made the propellers in a United States federal district court claiming negligence and strict liability. . . .

The Court was careful to indicate that in certain cases — where the alternative forum could not provide any remedy whatsoever — the unfavorable change in the law could be given substantial weight:

> We do not hold that the possibility of an unfavorable change in law should never be a relevant consideration in a *forum non conveniens* inquiry. Of course, if the remedy provided by the alternative forum is so clearly inadequate or unsatisfactory that it is no remedy at all, the unfavorable change in law may be given substantial weight; the district court may conclude that dismissal would not be in the interests of justice. In these cases, however, the remedies that would be provided by the Scottish courts do not fall within this category. Although the relatives of the decedents may not be able to rely on a strict liability theory, and although their potential damages award may be smaller, there is no danger that they will be deprived of any remedy or treated unfairly.

This court has found a similar exception to the general rule to be appropriate in cases involving alleged violations of United States antitrust laws. In Industrial Development Corp. v. Mitsui & Co., 671 F.2d 876 (5th Cir. 1982), vacated and remanded on other grounds, 460 U.S. 1007 (1983), we held that a complaint seeking relief solely under the federal antitrust laws, sections 1 and 2 of the Sherman Act, could not be dismissed under the doctrine of *forum non conveniens*. We stated there that to determine Indonesia to be the proper forum for that case would, in effect, "deprive[ ] [plaintiffs] of any remedy." *Reyno*, 454 U.S. at 255. . . .

The crucial point succinctly stated in *Mitsui* was later amplified in Laker Airways Ltd. v. Pan American World Airways, 568 F. Supp. 811, 818 (D.D.C. 1983):

> Antitrust cases are unlike litigation involving contracts, torts, or other matters recognized in some form in every nation. A plaintiff who seeks relief by means of one of these types of actions may appropriately be sent to the courts of another nation where presumably he will be granted, at least approximately, what he is due. But the antitrust laws of the United States embody a specific congressional purpose to encourage the bringing of private claims in the American courts in order that the national policy against monopoly may be vindicated. To relegate a plaintiff to the courts of a nation which does not recognize these antitrust principles would be to defeat this congressional direction by means of a wholly inappropriate procedural device.

The foregoing relevant legal precepts having been stated, we now turn to the appellants' specific contentions before us.

IV.

It seems to be conceded that Bermuda would not recognize a civil RICO claim. From this basic premise, appellants argue that dismissal in favor of Bermuda would deprive them of a private suit which was conceived by

Congress as part of a national scheme of enforcement to protect United States commerce.... Appellants argue that to apply the doctrine of *forum non conveniens* to a RICO action would frustrate Congress' intent to give RICO plaintiffs a right of access to a federal forum to seek redress....

We are satisfied that appellants' legislative history argument proves too much. It has not persuaded us that Congress intended that *forum non conveniens* would not apply to civil RICO actions. Our independent review of the legislative history does not disclose that Congress intended directly or by fair inference to suggest that RICO would be immune from the doctrine's operation....

Accordingly, we must now turn to what we believe to be the critical issue in this case: Without the RICO claim, will the plaintiffs "be deprived of any remedy" on the basis of the factual predicate of their complaint? The important inquiry here is whether the facts more resemble the products liability facts of *Reyno* or the antitrust facts of *Mitsui*. If they come within the rule of *Reyno*, appellants attempt to prove RICO immunity must fail; if they come within the rule of *Mitsui*, they will prevail.

To ask this question is to answer it. The district court specifically found that even without the RICO count, Bermuda permits litigation in its courts of the fraud, negligent misrepresentation, breach of fiduciary duty, and piercing the corporate veil counts of the liquidators' complaint. Bermuda courts are totally competent to adjudge the claims that defendants falsified Mentor's financial statements, that the statements materially overstated Mentor's financial health and concealed its dire financial condition, and that they failed to disclose and properly account for the true nature of the purported reinsurance agreements between Mentor and Pinnacles.

Moreover, the district court found that the Bermuda trial courts have the power to "see to it that defendants make good whatever harm they did." Accordingly, we conclude that "although [the liquidators'] potential damage award may be smaller, there is no danger they will be deprived of any remedy or treated unfairly." *Reyno*, 454 U.S. at 255. This case is a far cry from *Mitsui*, where the complaint was solely bottomed on Sections 1 and 2 of the Sherman Act. In that case, dismissal in favor of a forum in Indonesia would have been the functional equivalent of denying the plaintiffs any remedy whatsoever.

We conclude, therefore, that the material facts here more closely resemble the facts in *Reyno* and should be subject to the same analysis employed there.

V.

We are satisfied that the district court correctly utilized the *forum non conveniens* analysis set out by the Supreme Court in Gulf Oil Corp. v. Gilbert and Piper v. Reyno, and by this court in In re Air Crash Disaster Near New Orleans, Louisiana, 821 F.2d 1147 (5th Cir. 1987), vacated and remanded on other grounds sub nom. Pan American World Airways, Inc. v. Lopez, 490 U.S. 1032 (1989). This analysis requires a district court to first decide whether an available and adequate forum exists. "A foreign forum is available when the entire case and all parties can come within the jurisdiction of that forum.... A foreign forum is adequate when the parties will not be deprived of all remedies or treated unfairly ... even though they may not enjoy the same benefits as they might receive in an American court." *Air Crash Disaster*, 821 F.2d at 1165. If the court decides that the foreign forum is both available and adequate, it must then consider the parties' private interests, allowing for the relevant deference given the plaintiff's choice of forum, and factors of the public interest, such as burdens upon the court, public interest in the dispute, and questions of foreign law. The court should consider the specific factors set forth in part II of this opinion and enumerated in *Gulf Oil* and *Koster*.

The district court correctly determined that Bermuda is both an available and adequate forum. Although the RICO cause of action is not available in Bermuda, a forum is inadequate only where it would afford a plaintiff no remedy at all. *Air Crash Disaster*, 821 F.2d at 1165. The district court found that plaintiffs would be able to bring all their other causes of action before the courts in Bermuda. The court then carefully examined the private interests of the litigants. All defendants have agreed to stipulate to jurisdiction in Bermuda. Mentor is a Bermuda corporation heavily regulated by Bermuda law. The agreements at issue were between Mentor and Pinnacle, also a Bermuda company with offices located only in Bermuda. The agreements provide that disputes are to be arbitrated in Bermuda, and provide for the application of the laws of Bermuda to the agreements.

Both plaintiffs and defendants have identified numerous individuals and corporations residing in Bermuda whose testimony at trial will be significant. The district court pointed out that plaintiffs have identified as potential witnesses only three non-party individuals within the Louisiana court's subpoena power. The court also made dismissal subject to a six-month stay to permit discovery in the United States.

Finally, plaintiffs in this care are a Bermudian and an Englishman, representing a Bermuda corporation. Both this court and the Supreme Court have recognized that a foreign plaintiff's choice of an American forum deserves less deference than an American citizen's selection of his home forum. *Reyno*, 454 U.S. at 255-56; *Air Crash Disaster*, 821 F.2d at 1164.

The district court also analyzed the public interest factors here, including the "drain on the court's time and energy which trial in New Orleans will entail." With regard to the local interest in having localized controversies resolved at home, the court explained that Bermuda is an international insurance center and has a strong interest in regulating its industry so as to retain credibility abroad. In contrast, the defendants' residence in Louisiana does not represent any broader interests of the state in this action. Finally, the court found that trial of this matter will entail the application of Bermudian law to at least two of the causes of action.

We conclude that the district court did not abuse its discretion in deciding that both private interest factors affecting the convenience of the litigants and the public interest factors affecting the convenience of the forum favor resolution of this lawsuit in Bermuda rather than in Louisiana.

. . .

The judgment of the district court is affirmed.

Notes and Questions

1. Once upon a time, a *forum non conveniens* dismissal was the only way in which to handle the problem of an inconvenient forum. Obviously a dismissal is overkill. The basic premise of *forum non conveniens* is that the plaintiff's chosen forum is a legally permissible one (in terms of subject matter jurisdiction, territorial jurisdiction, and venue), but it is less convenient than some other available forum. Although it would be simpler, easier, and fairer if the court could transfer the case to the more appropriate forum, an outright dismissal of the case is a drastic remedy, especially in cases in which the statute of limitations may have already run. See Piper Aircraft Co. v. Reyno, 454 U.S. 235, 255 (1981) ("[T]here is ordinarily a strong presumption in favor of the plaintiff's choice of forum, which may be overcome only when the private and public interest factors clearly point towards trial in the alternative forum.").

The problem for many years, however, was that no transfer mechanism existed. Hence, the doctrine of *forum non conveniens* developed, but was used sparingly. As we shall see shortly, there now exists a transfer mechanism — 28 U.S.C. § 1404(a) — that permits a case to be transferred from a less convenient to a more convenient federal court. A respectable line of thinking holds that § 1404(a) has abolished the *forum non conveniens* doctrine in federal court, at least with regard to transfers that can be made to another federal court. See 15 Charles A. Wright et al., Federal Practice & Procedure § 3828 (1986). As a result, *forum non conveniens* continues to have vitality in only three situations: cases in federal court in which, like *Kempe*, a foreign tribunal is the more convenient forum; cases in federal court in which a state court is the more convenient forum; and cases in state court in which a court in another state, a federal court, or a foreign tribunal is the more convenient forum. Of these three situations, the first and third are the most common; the second is rarely invoked. See id., especially n.7.

2. The first situation most typically arises with regard to foreign plaintiffs that wish to take advantage of more favorable American substantive and procedural law. For instance, in *Reyno*, 454 U.S. 235, Scottish plaintiffs whose decedents were killed in a Scottish airplane crash sued the American manufacturers of the plane and propeller in federal court. Under the applicable American law, plaintiffs would have been entitled to have strict products liability applied to the claim; in Scotland, negligence was the standard of liability. The Supreme Court rejected the plaintiffs' argument that the *forum non conveniens* doctrine was *per se* inapplicable when the alternate forum would apply less favorable law, noting that if "central emphasis were placed on any one factor, the *forum non conveniens* doctrine would lose much of the very flexibility that makes it so valuable." 454 U.S. at 249-50.

Unlike *Kempe*, *Reyno* involved a case in which the legal theory under which the plaintiffs were proceeding was at least recognized. Does *Kempe* convince you that this factor should be overlooked — especially when the remedy for the discarded legal theory is treble damages? An even more dramatic example of a *forum non conveniens* dismissal entered in spite of the inadequate damages available in the alternate forum (at least by American standards) is the Bhopal disaster, in which 2,000 Indian citizens were killed and 200,000 injured. In re

Union Carbide Corp. Gas Plant Disaster, 809 F.2d 195 (2d Cir. 1987); see William L. Reynolds, *The Proper Forum for a Suit: Transnational Forum Non Conveniens and Counter-Suit Injunctions in the Federal Courts*, 70 Tex. L. Rev. 1663 (1992); Stephen L. Cummings, Note, *International Mass Tort Litigation:* Forum Non Conveniens *and the Adequate Alternative Forum*, 16 G. J. Intl. L. 109 (1986).

3. A far different approach to the *forum non conveniens* issue was taken by the Texas Supreme Court in Dow Chemical Co. v. Castro Alfaro, 786 S.W.2d 674 (Tex. 1990), cert. denied, 498 U.S. 1024 (1991). In that case eighty-two Costa Rican residents exposed to a pesticide while working in Costa Rica sued the manufactures in Texas state court. One of the defendants, Shell Oil Company, had its headquarters in Texas, and it allegedly made its decisions regarding the pesticide in Texas.

After an unsuccessful attempt to remove the case to federal court, the defendants persuaded the Texas trial court to dismiss on *forum non conveniens* grounds. The Texas Supreme Court reversed on the basis of a Texas statute which provided that an "action for personal damages for the death or injury of a citizen of . . . the United States, or of a foreign country may be enforced in this state, although the wrongful act, neglect, or default takes place in a foreign state or country" when certain prerequisites were satisfied. Tex. Civ. Proc. & Rem. Code. Ann. § 71.031. Over several vigorous dissents, the court held that this statute abolished the doctrine of *forum non conveniens* and required Texas state courts to entertain the claim. Subsequently the Texas legislature enacted a specific *forum non conveniens* statute. Tex. Civ. Proc. & Rem. Code § 71.051. The statute specifically precludes a *forum non conveniens* dismissal or stay if a plaintiff is a Texas resident, if a tortious act occurred in Texas, or if the "harm was caused by exposure to asbestos fibers." Id., § 71.051(f)(1), (2), (5).

Are there any due process limitations on *Castro Alfaro*? Why did the defendants want to remove the case to federal court, other than (presumably) to obtain the benefit of federal *forum non conveniens* law? Did they have any basis for doing so, other than the arguable due process violation of being subject to jurisdiction in a state court that had, at the time, no *forum non conveniens* rule? Cf. Chick Kam Choo v. Exxon Corp., 486 U.S. 140 (1988) (federal case dismissed on *forum non conveniens* grounds; Anti-Injunction Act prevented federal court from enjoining same case when it was re-filed in Texas state court).

4. *Castro Alfaro* was a state, rather than a federal, case. It does, however, raise several instructive points. First, with respect to *forum non conveniens* concerns, both state and federal courts must deal with the problem of *forum non conveniens* dismissals in favor of foreign tribunals. Second, as *Chick Kam Choo* implies, there is no requirement that state and federal courts use the same rules of *forum non conveniens* to deal with this situation or, for that matter, any other situation calling for application of the doctrine. These two facts lead to a third question: What are the *Erie* implications of the *forum non conveniens* doctrine?

The Supreme Court has never held that federal courts in diversity cases must apply the *forum non conveniens* rules of the state in which they sit. See, e.g., *Reyno*, 454 U.S. at 248 & n.13. Lower federal courts have held *Erie* does not compel the use of state *forum non conveniens* rules. See Seguros Comercial America S.A. de C.V. v. American President Lines, Ltd., 105 F.3d 198 (5th Cir. 1996); Wright et al., *supra*, § 3828 (suggesting that *forum non conveniens* rules are matters of administration, so that state rules are not binding); but see Allen R. Stein, Erie *and Court Access*, 100 Yale L.J. 1935 (1991) (state *forum non conveniens* rules should control in diversity cases). Conversely, the Supreme

Court has held that state courts are not required to apply federal *forum non conveniens* rules when a federal question is presented in state court. American Dredging Co. v. Miller, 510 U.S. 443 (1994).

5. Often a defendant will attempt to use *forum non conveniens* for private tactical advantage rather than for the public good of aggregation in a single venue. To lessen some of the incentive to obtain private gain, a *forum non conveniens* dismissal can be accompanied by conditions. For instance, in *Union Carbide, supra,* the district court dismissed an action brought in the United States by Indian citizens, but required the defendants (1) to consent to jurisdiction of Indian courts and to waive any statute of limitations defense, (2) to consent to enforcement in the United States of any Indian judgment which comported with minimal due process requirements, and (3) to consent to discovery under the Federal Rules of Civil Procedure. The Second Circuit overturned the second condition, and found that principles of equal treatment required the plaintiffs also to be subject to discovery under the Federal Rules. *Union Carbide,* 809 F.2d at 202-06; see also Tex. Civ. Proc. & Rem. Code § 71.051(c) (requiring waiver of territorial jurisdiction and statute of limitations defenses as condition of dismissal or stay).

6. With plaintiffs manipulating venue rules and defendants manipulating the *forum non conveniens* rule, is there any chance that the optimal level of single-venue aggregation will occur? In terms of its ability to achieve this optimal level, *forum non conveniens* is rather limited. In the first place, the doctrine applies, if at all, only to cases that have already been filed; it does nothing to achieve the aggregation of the claims of "sideline-sitters" or others whose claims have not matured. Second, the dismissal of a case in one forum does not guarantee that the case will be filed in the forum in which other cases are being aggregated. Third, the harshness of the doctrine makes it difficult to obtain. Fourth, the doctrine has limited application in federal court, in which other transfer doctrines have for the most part replaced it. Finally, the doctrine requires that the party seeking aggregation go into each court in which a related case pops up and make a *forum non conveniens* motion. Not only is it likely that some courts will decline to grant the motion, but the inefficiency of making the argument in many decentralized forums is also significant. To be truly effective, some centralized authority that can aggregate cases in one forum is needed.

Nonetheless, because it is one of the few doctrines that deals with the problem of cases in state court and the problem of international litigation, *forum non conveniens* remains important in complex and complicated litigation. Should there be an automatic ability to obtain a *forum non conveniens* dismissal when it can be shown that the maintenance of a separate suit in a particular forum will lead to lawyer dysfunction? Isn't there a compelling "public interest" in the prevention of lawyer dysfunction? (Note that Gulf Oil Corp. Gilbert, 330 U.S. 501 (1947), which suggested a list of such "public interest" factors, was not a complex case.) Indeed, isn't there an argument that the failure to provide such a dismissal violates the due process rights of those that stand to be foreclosed from an effective remedy because of the separate suit?

Even if such an argument for an automatic *forum non conveniens* can be made, can it be extended to complicated litigation, in which the primary problem is the inefficient re-litigation of issues? Or does the presumption in favor of the plaintiffs' venue privilege require that the remaining public and private factors still be balanced against the efficiencies and the other public and private interests in the case?

To some extent, the answers to these questions may depend on the scope of other stay or injunctive doctrines that permit aggregation in a single venue. These doctrines are the subject of the following subsection.

b. The *Kerotest* Stay and Related Doctrines

In Kerotest Manufacturing Co. v. C-O-Two Fire Equipment Co., 342 U.S. 180 (1952), the Court held that a federal court had the authority to enjoin the prosecution of a related lawsuit in another venue. The facts in *Kerotest* involved two lawsuits: first, a lawsuit by a patent owner against a company that bought component parts alleged to infringe the patent; and second, a lawsuit by the company that made the component part against the patent owner seeking a declaration that the patent was invalid and an injunction against the further prosecution of the first lawsuit. The first suit was brought in the United States District Court for the Northern District of Illinois; the second was brought in the United States District Court for the District of Delaware. The manufacturer was subsequently joined in the Illinois proceeding, and the Delaware court temporarily stayed its proceeding while it obtained information about the Illinois proceeding. The Delaware court eventually refused to continue the stay, and even issued an injunction against the further prosecution by the manufacturer of the Illinois lawsuit. The court of appeals reversed this injunction, and ordered the Delaware court to stay its hand until the completion of the Illinois case. The Supreme Court affirmed the decision of the court of appeals.

Kerotest demonstrates two possible approaches to the problem of preventing re-litigation of related cases in different venues — the injunctive approach under which a court issues an injunction against proceedings elsewhere, and a stay approach under which a court stays its own hand in favor of related litigation elsewhere. Both doctrines, of course, have a comparable effect; neither can force a party to litigate elsewhere, but may induce the party to do so when a party might sacrifice valuable rights by failing to join the related case.

Kerotest favored the stay approach. On its facts, that seems the right result — once you grant the assumption that something needs to be done about re-litigation. The Illinois litigation had been filed first, the Illinois forum had all the relevant parties already before it, the Illinois forum could provide complete relief, and the Delaware declaratory judgment proceeding by a defendant in the underlying case smacked of forum shopping. The only contrary arguments, which the Court rejected, were that the patent owner's suit against the manufacturer's customer in Illinois was an indirect way of attacking the manufacturer and that the Illinois suit was itself a forum-shopping venture designed to inconvenience the manufacturer.

In the patent infringement area, a nice body of law, replete with a rule (the first-filed case wins) and exceptions, has sprung up around the *Kerotest* stay. See, *e.g.*, William Gluckin & Co. v. International Playtex Corp., 407 F.2d 177 (2d Cir. 1969); Kahn v. General Motors Corp., 889 F.2d 1078 (Fed.

Cir. 1989). The interesting question, however, is whether the concept of the *Kerotest* stay has a broader application in complex or complicated litigation.

As a broader doctrine, two obvious difficulties with the *Kerotest* stay leap to mind. The first is that *Kerotest* involved essentially the same parties and claims in both proceedings, while most complex and complicated litigation involves different parties and often different claims. The second is that a stay obtained from each of the later-filed forums is less effective than a single injunction against related lawsuits issued by a single court. If the *Kerotest* concept is to be useful, both problems must be overcome.

Although there is a fair amount of caselaw on injunctions or stays of related proceedings pending in another venue of the federal court system (or the court of another state when one state court has a case), little of it has been devoted to these issues. One of the more interesting cases is Asset Allocation and Management Co. v. Western Employers Insurance Co., 892 F.2d 566 (7th Cir. 1989), in which a federal court in Illinois enjoined a defendant (Western) from proceeding with a lawsuit against the plaintiff in federal court in California. The reason was that the California claims were compulsory counterclaims in the Illinois lawsuit, and the Illinois defendant had recently moved to plead the claims in the Illinois case. The Illinois plaintiff (Asset) moved for both a stay in the California case and an injunction against the California case in the Illinois case. Judge Conlon in Illinois granted the injunction, which Judge Posner questioned in dicta:

> [Judge Conlon's] ground was that if a claim is a compulsory counterclaim, the plaintiff is entitled to enjoin the defendant from litigating it other than as a counterclaim in the plaintiff's suit, provided that that suit was filed before the defendant brought his own suit to enforce his claim. The district judge found the source of this rule in the language and purpose of the compulsory counterclaim rule . . . . That rule says nothing about injunctions, however, and the usual method by which it is enforced is simply by the plaintiff's pleading the judgment as res judicata in the defendant's suit. . . .
>
> If not Rule 13(a), what could be the basis for the district court's assertion of power to enjoin Western from proceeding with its suit in California? One possibility is the equitable doctrine mentioned earlier that entitles a litigant to enjoin his adversary from tormenting him with a multiplicity of identical suits. That ground might be available here if Western's motive for suing in California had been to make it prohibitively costly for Asset to recover its unpaid advisory fees — a modest $18,500 . . . . [But what] Western wants is to recover more than $3.5 million in trading losses sustained as a result of its contract with Asset. . . .
>
> Despite the absence of a clear source of authority for enjoining a second, nonharassing lawsuit (albeit one identical to the first), there is overwhelming case authority that the first court has power, independently of the equitable doctrine that bars vexatious litigation, to enjoin the defendant from bringing a separate suit against the plaintiff in another court, thereby forcing the defendant either to litigate his claim as a counterclaim or to abandon it. The power is assumed in

Kerotest Mfg. Co. v. C-O-Two Fire Equipment Co., 342 U.S. 180 (1952), and asserted and exercised in a host of lower-court decisions....

The real basis for the power, it seems to us, is practical. A court — some court — should have the power to prevent the duplication of litigation even though neither party is acting abusively; this is implicit in the very concept of a compulsory counterclaim. It might as well be the first court. It is not a traditional equitable power that the courts are exercising in these cases but a new power asserted in order to facilitate the economical management of complex litigation.

But it is a power, not a duty.... It is to be exercised with due regard for the balance of convenience in litigating the parties' disputes in one forum rather than another.... There is, no doubt, a presumption that subject to the principles that govern requests for transfer to a more convenient forum, the first case should be allowed to proceed and the second should be abated; and certainly Judge Conlon was right not to countenance the simultaneous litigation of identical claims in two federal courts. But the presumption is rebuttable.... It may — no stronger statement is possible — have been rebutted here.... Western may not be able to obtain jurisdiction in Illinois over one of the defendants in its California suit. More important, Asset's suit in Illinois appears to be a sideshow to the real dispute between the parties, which is over liability for Western's trading losses. In these circumstances, we are puzzled by Judge Conlon's action in enjoining the California suit — especially when Asset had filed a motion with the district judge in California to stay that suit. Judge Conlon could have waited until that motion was decided before issuing an injunction.... [892 F.2d at 571-73.]

In *Asset Allocation*, the same parties were involved in both suits, and all the claims were present before the court in Illinois. Would it be even more difficult to convince a federal court to issue an injunction against other federal proceedings in which different parties or claims were involved? On the other hand, isn't Judge Posner right — we need some injunctive device by which to prevent multiforum re-litigation? In *Asset Allocation*, the threat of preclusion in the Illinois case ultimately induced Western to file its claims in the Illinois proceeding. As we saw in Chapter Two, however, preclusion often does not run against nonparties to a particular litigation. If preclusion does not exist, can the reluctance expressed by Judge Posner be overcome? Might the All-Writs Act be a source of the power to enjoin related federal proceedings for which Judge Posner was searching? Cf. In re Winslow, 17 F.3d 314 (10th Cir. 1994) (using All-Writs Act to enjoin future filings by party whose past filings were abusive and repetitive). Should that power be exercised only in complex cases? In complicated cases? In all cases? Or should we respect the right of each plaintiff to secure the most advantageous venue in all cases?

Federal anti-suit injunctions have been used against other federal proceedings in at least some complex cases. For instance, in Schauss v. Metals Depository Corp., 757 F.2d 649 (5th Cir. 1985), a receiver was appointed in federal court in New York to handle the affairs of an insolvent entity. An injunction was issued against further proceedings in any other federal or state court. Subsequently, a plaintiff filed a garnishment action in Texas federal court against the entity's bank and the entity itself, and the bank filed an interpleader action that included the receiver in the Texas case. Obviously, the Texas case was an attempt by one plaintiff to obtain a disproportionate share of the available assets. After a judgment for the plaintiff in the Texas case, the court of appeals held (correctly from the viewpoint of complex litigation) that the New York injunction precluded entry of the Texas judgment. What was the precise source of the authority for the New York court's injunction? Cf. 28 U.S.C. § 754 (giving receivers "complete jurisdiction and control" of property within a district). Would it be wise in complex cases involving insufficient assets to ask automatically for such an injunction? By the way, *Schauss* tantalizingly suggested that the power to enjoin related litigation extended to nonparties as well. Id. at 654. See also West Gulf Maritime Association v. ILA Deep Sea Local 24, 751 F.2d 721 (5th Cir. 1985) (excellent review of cases and arguments that later-filed cases should issue stay, dismiss, or transfer case to venue of first-filed case; second-filed case's injunction in nationwide labor dispute vacated, and entry of stay, dismissal, or transfer to venue of first-filed case ordered).

As a general matter, however, the use of injunctions or stays, although significant in certain circumstances, are not a pressing issue in the federal system. We will see shortly that related cases can often be transferred to another federal forum for trial; moreover, when enough related suits are pending, related cases can be consolidated for pretrial purposes as well. If the problem of related litigation is confined to two- or three-party suits like *Kerotest* and *Asset Allocation*, it is not a problem with which we typically need to be concerned. See Hemmings v. United States, 842 F. Supp. 935, 937 (S.D. Tex. 1993) ("This Court has the authority, inherent in the p[a]st, to exercise its discretion to avoid duplication of proceedings where related claims are being litigated in other districts.").

The problem does remain very alive, however, in the contexts of litigation proceeding in multiple state forums and transnational litigation. In state litigation, many states have a rule equivalent to *Kerotest* that permits one district of a state court to issue an anti-suit injunction against another district or else stay its own hand in favor of another district. See, *e.g.*, Atkinson v. Arnold, 893 S.W.2d 294 (Tex. App. 1995). With respect to stays in favor of proceedings elsewhere, the question is essentially the same as the issuance of state stays in favor of a federal forum (see p. 437, *supra*). Some states also treat the question of a stay under its *forum non conveniens* doctrine. See Tex. Civ. Proc. & Rem. Code § 71.051. The difficult question is whether one state court can enjoin parties from proceeding with related litigation in other state courts — in other words, whether one centralized authority can prevent the problems of non-aggregation.

In Gannon v. Payne, 706 S.W.2d 304 (Tex. 1986), the Supreme Court of Texas stated that it had the power to issue an injunction against proceedings in other state courts:

> [W]hen a suit is filed in a court of competent jurisdiction, that court is entitled to proceed to judgment and may protect its jurisdiction by

enjoining the parties to a suit subsequently filed in another court of this state. This same rule applies to suits subsequently filed in the courts of sister states.... Obviously, anti-suit injunctions prohibiting litigants from proceeding in out-of-state courts necessarily involve two sovereigns with concurrent jurisdiction to decide the controversy. For this reason, the courts of this state have consistently recognized that the power to enjoin proceedings pending in a foreign jurisdiction should be exercised sparingly and only by reason of very special circumstances. [Id. at 305-06.]

In Golden Rule Insurance Co. v. Harper, 925 S.W.2d 649 (Tex. 1996), the Texas Supreme Court fleshed out these sparing and special circumstances:

> An anti-suit injunction is appropriate in four instances: 1) to address a threat to the court's jurisdiction; 2) to prevent the evasion of important public policy; 3) to prevent a multiplicity of suits; or 4) to protect a party from vexatious or harassing litigation.... The party seeking the injunction must show that "a clear equity demands" the injunction.... "A single parallel proceeding in a foreign forum, however, does not constitute a multiplicity nor does it, in itself create a clear equity justifying an anti-suit injunction." [925 S.W.2d at 651.]

Other courts have agreed, both with the existence of an anti-suit injunctive power and with the infrequency of its use. See Ackerman v. Ackerman, 219 A.D.2d 515, 631 N.Y.S.2d 657, 657 (1995) ("The rule of comity forbids our courts from enjoining an action in a sister State unless it is clearly shown that the suit sought to be enjoined was brought in bad faith, motivated by fraud or an intent to harass the party seeking an injunction, or if its purpose was to evade the law of the domicile of the parties.") (quotations omitted); Halmos v. Safecard Services, Inc., 272 Ill.App.3d 532, 650 N.E.2d 555, 557 (1995) ("court maintains the authority to 'restrain the prosecution of a foreign action which will result in fraud or gross wrong or oppression...'"). Should the existence of joinder complexity be a ground for an anti-suit injunction?

As might be expected, such injunctions are not always heeded in other forums, often on the argument that the enjoining court had no jurisdiction over the persons enjoined. See Mahan v. Gunther, 278 Ill.App.3d 1108, 663 N.E.2d 1139 (1996). If the suit runs against other possible plaintiffs, which rule of personal jurisdiction should pertain — the "minimum contacts" rule for defendants or the "opt-out" rule suggested for plaintiffs in Phillips Petroleum Co. v. Shutts, 472 U.S. 797 (1985)? Under either rule, the requirement of territorial jurisdiction already makes the possibility of a state-to-state anti-suit injunction a less than ideal aggregation remedy.

Even if jurisdiction exists, most courts believe that they do not need to give full faith and credit to the injunctions of other states, and will do so only when comity so dictates. *Mahan*, 663 N.E.2d at 1144; Albrecht v. Zwaanshoek Holding en Financiering, B.V., 762 P.2d 1174 (Wyo. 1988); Geoffrey P. Miller, *Class Actions and Jurisdictional Boundaries: Overlapping Class Actions*, 71 N.Y.U. L. Rev. 514 (1996); see also Great Global Assurance Co. v. McFarlin, 728 S.W.2d 401 (Tex. App. 1987) (out-of-state injunction in receivership proceeding not binding on Texas court that had no notice or knowledge of injunction). What happens when one state issues the injunction and the other state refuses to abide by it? See James v. Grand Trunk Western Railroad Co., 14 Ill.2d 356, 152 N.E.2d 858, (injunctions issued in both states against further proceedings in other states), cert. denied, 358 U.S. 915 (1958).

The dueling-injunction issue in *James* has also arisen in transnational litigation, in which an American court has sought to enjoin parties from prosecuting actions in a foreign tribunal, and the foreign tribunal has enjoined the parties from proceeding in an American tribunal. The most famous case is Laker Airways Ltd. v. Sabena, Belgian World Airlines, 731 F.2d 909 (D.C. Cir. 1984), in which Laker brought an antitrust suit in federal court against foreign airlines. The airlines then filed claims, which would have been counterclaims in the American suit, against Laker in a British court. The real purpose of the British lawsuit was to obtain an injunction barring Laker from prosecuting its American suit. The British trial court issued the injunction. Laker then obtained an injunction from the American court against prosecution of foreign suits by the remaining defendants. The British injunction and American counter-injunction created an international dilemma that subsided when the House of Lords vacated the British injunction. British Airways v. Laker Airways Ltd., 1985 App. Cas. 58, 96.

Laker affirmed the entry of the injunction, but indicated that an anti-suit injunction should be issued only (1) when the conduct by the parties against whom the injunction is sought amounted to harassment or a war of attrition, (2) to protect the court's ability to provide a full and fair adjudication, or (3) to protect an important policy of the forum. Id. at 928-33. Significantly, *Laker* thought that "duplication of parties and issues alone is not sufficient to justify issuance of an anti-suit injunction," id. at 928, nor was the possibility of a race to judgment, id. at 928-29. See also China Trade and Development Corp. v. M.V. Choony Yong, 837 F.2d 33 (2d Cir. 1987) (injunction against foreign suits is proper either in *in rem* and *quasi in rem* proceedings, or when foreign court seeks to obtain exclusive jurisdiction over controversy). Should the existence of joinder complexity also provide a ground for an anti-suit injunction in the transnational context, or do the due process implications of complex litigation stop at the American border?

State courts too become embroiled in cases involving foreign claims, and generally express a comparable reluctance to enjoin foreign proceedings. See *Gannon*, 706 S.W.2d 304; but see Owens-Corning Fiberglas Corp. v. Baker, 838 S.W.2d 838 (Tex. App. 1992) (affirming issuance of "anti-anti-suit injunction" against defendants that had requested Canadian courts to enjoin Canadian plaintiffs from filing asbestos cases in Texas courts).

Aside from some "world court" or international treaty, there is little that can presently be done with respect to complex or complicated litigation that spills over American borders. But dismissals, stays, and injunctions also prove a very fitful way to achieve single-venue aggregation even in domestic litigation. Since the doctrines were not designed with complex or complicated litigation in mind, this is not surprising. Whether more can be achieved through transfer devices is the next issue to consider.

2. Transfer Devices that Aggregate Cases in a Single Venue

The most direct method of achieving single-venue aggregation is to allow the court to transfer cases to a single forum. Although no such devices generally exist in the state-to-state context, transfer devices do exist in federal court. In this subsection we examine three such devices: Rule 42 consolidation, § 1404(a) transfers, and § 1407 transfers. As we examine each device, analyze whether it overcomes the problems associated with *forum non conveniens* dismissals and inter-venue stays and injunctions — in particular, the inability to include nonparties, the inability to aggregate all cases in a single forum, and the lack of a centralized transfer authority.

a. Consolidation

Of the transfer devices, Rule 42 consolidation is, in a sense, the odd one out; it permits only the consolidation of two or more cases that are already pending in the same venue. Rule 42 is, nonetheless, the significant first piece in the transfer puzzle. All federal districts have multiple sitting judges. It does little good to transfer related cases to a single district if the cases will end up being heard by different judges in that district. Hence, it is crucial that there exist some mechanism by which all cases can be brought before, and handled by, one judge in a particular venue. The desirability of consolidation seems so obvious that it may be hard to imagine any reasons to oppose it. Reconsider that view after you read the following three cases.

JOHNSON v. CELOTEX CORP.

899 F.2d 1281 (2d Cir.), cert. denied, 498 U.S. 920 (1990)

■ CARMAN, Judge. Defendant-appellant The Celotex Corporation (Celotex or appellant) appeals from a judgment entered in the Southern District of New York after a jury trial before Charles P. Sifton, J. . . . awarding compensatory and punitive damages and damages for loss of consortium in an asbestos products liability personal injury case. Celotex appeals from orders denying its motion for judgment notwithstanding the verdict, or in the alternative, a new trial and for a mistrial. Defendant-appellant, Owens-Illinois, Inc. (Owens-Illinois or appellant) appeals from the same judgment and orders . . . .

BACKGROUND

This appeal is one of many which arises from thousands of cases filed against manufacturers and producers of asbestos, resulting in unparalleled litigation in American tort law. . . . To manage the litigation, all of the cases in the Southern and Eastern Districts were assigned for pre-trial purposes to Judge Sifton....

At a pretrial conference on November 4, 1988, the court proposed that another asbestos tort case, Higgins v. Raymark Industries, Inc., CV-87-0537 (S.D.N.Y.), be consolidated with Johnson which was scheduled for trial on November 7, 1988. The trial court ordered on November 7, 1988 that *Higgins* and *Johnson* be consolidated for trial. Plaintiff Higgins, a chipper and caulker, whose work included chipping off welded sections to prepare for repair work of others, was alleged to have died because of exposure to asbestos while at the Brooklyn Navy Yard from approximately 1946 to 1966. Appellee-plaintiff, John Johnson (plaintiff), an electrician's helper, alleged that he had contracted lung disease while working at the Brooklyn Navy Yard from 1942 to 1945 by inhaling asbestos fibers during this employment. [Plaintiff Johnson was unable to identify which asbestos products he had been exposed to, nor had he been exposed to asbestos or any other asbestos containing products after he left the shipyard in 1945. In 1985 he was diagnosed as suffering from an asbestos-related lung condition.]

In *Johnson* and *Higgins* compensatory and punitive damages were sought for claims sounding in negligence and strict liability for defendants' failure to warn of the health risks of their asbestos-containing products.

The Court declined to trifurcate or bifurcate the trial to separate issues of causation and compensatory damages from issues of liability and punitive damages. Appellants' motions to have separate juries consider claims of liability and punitive damages in *Johnson*, apart from claims in *Higgins*, were denied.... Eight defendants settled and one filed a petition in bankruptcy prior to trial. The *Higgins* and *Johnson* cases proceeded to trial against defendants Celotex, Owens-Illinois and Raymark Industries, Inc. (Raymark). The jury rendered a verdict for the plaintiffs in both cases. In *Higgins*, plaintiff was awarded $1 million in compensatory damages and $3 million in punitive damages, divided equally among Celotex, Raymark and Owens-Illinois. In *Johnson* compensatory damages were $350,000 (Celotex 12.5%, Raymark 12.5%, Owens-Illinois 5.0%, seven settling co-defendants 10% each), and punitive damages were assessed as follows: Celotex $1 million, Raymark $1 million and Owens-Illinois $800,000. Plaintiff Ann Marie Johnson was awarded $30,000 for loss of services....

Appellants contend the trial court abused its discretion in consolidating the *Johnson* and *Higgins* cases....

DISCUSSION

Consolidation

Rule 42(a) of the Federal Rules of Civil Procedure empowers a trial judge to consolidate actions for trial when there are common questions of law or fact to avoid unnecessary costs or delay....

Consolidation of tort actions sharing common questions of law and fact is commonplace.... This is true of asbestos-related personal injury cases as well. See, *e.g.*, Hendrix v. Raybestos-Manhattan, Inc., 776 F.2d 1492 (11th Cir. 1985) . . . .

The trial court has broad discretion to determine whether consolidation is appropriate. . . . In the exercise of discretion, courts have taken the view that considerations of judicial economy favor consolidation. . . . However, the discretion to consolidate is not unfettered. . . . Considerations of convenience and economy must yield to a paramount concern for a fair and impartial trial. . . . When exercising its discretion, the court must consider:

> [W]hether the specific risks of prejudice and possible confusion [are] overborne by the risk of inconsistent adjudications of common factual and legal issues, the burden on parties, witnesses and available judicial resources posed by multiple lawsuits, the length of time required to conclude multiple suits as against a single one, and the relative expense to all concerned of the single-trial, multiple-trial alternatives.

Hendrix, 776 F.2d at 1495 . . . . When considering consolidation, a court should also note that the risks of prejudice and confusion may be reduced by the use of cautionary instructions to the jury and verdict sheets outlining the claims of each plaintiff. Id.

In the instant case, the court properly exercised its discretion in consolidating these two cases for trial. Courts in the Southern and Eastern Districts of New York have used the criteria outlined in an unreported Maryland district court case, In re All Asbestos Cases Pending in the United States District Court for the District of Maryland, (D. Md. Dec. 16, 1983) (en banc) (hereinafter *In re Maryland Asbestos Cases*) as a guideline in determining whether to consolidate asbestos exposure cases. . . . In *In re Maryland Asbestos Cases*, the criteria included: "(1) common worksite; (2) similar occupation; (3) similar time of exposure; (4) type of disease; (5) whether plaintiffs were living or deceased; (6) status of discovery in each case; (7) whether all plaintiffs were represented by the same counsel; and (8) type of cancer alleged." *In re Maryland Asbestos Cases* at 3. *Johnson* and *Higgins* had the following characteristics: (1) common worksite; (2) similar occupation to the extent that both workers were exposed to asbestos in a bystander capacity (they worked in trades that did not involve direct handling of asbestos products); (3) Johnson's period of exposure was from 1942 to 1945 while Higgins' exposure was from approximately 1946 to 1966; (4) Johnson contended that he suffered from asbestosis and asbestosis-related pleural disease while it was alleged that Higgins died as a result of asbestosis and lung disease; (5) Johnson was living and Higgins was deceased; (6) *Johnson* and *Higgins* were both ready for trial; and (7) all plaintiffs were represented by the same counsel. Instructions were given throughout the trial and in the charge to caution the jury to consider each plaintiff's claims individually. Two separate verdict forms were provided to the jury, one for *Johnson*, the other for *Higgins*.

An appellate court will not disturb a trial court's decision to consolidate unless a clear abuse of discretion is shown. *Hendrix*, 776 F.2d at 1495. In the instant case, the trial court was well within its discretion to consolidate the two cases and the court acted throughout in a manner which ensured that each plaintiff's claim was considered separately.

MALCOLM v. NATIONAL GYPSUM CO.

995 F.2d 346 (2d Cir. 1993)

■ McLAUGHLIN, Circuit Judge. Keene Corporation appeals from a final judgment of the United States District Courts for the Eastern and Southern Districts of New York (Charles P. Sifton, Judge) awarding plaintiff Roberta Kranz, as the executrix of the estate of Lee Lewis, $226,038.49 for personal injury, wrongful death, and loss of consortium.... The claims arose from Lewis's exposure to asbestos products manufactured by Keene's subsidiary, the Baldwin-Ehret-Hill Company ("BEH"). For the reasons stated below, we reverse and remand for a new trial.

BACKGROUND

The Explosion Of Asbestos Litigation

One of the greatest challenges facing both state and federal courts is the crush of tort suits arising from the extensive use of asbestos as flame-retardant insulation throughout much of this century. Asbestos litigation today constitutes the largest mass toxic tort in the United States. See In re Joint E. & S. Dists. Asbestos Litig., 125 F.R.D. 60, 63 (E.D.N.Y. 1989) (hereinafter "*Drago*"). To date, more than 200,000 asbestos cases have been filed by injured persons and their heirs, and as many as 250,000 additional cases may be filed in years to come....

[B]oth the state and federal courts were swamped with asbestos suits. In response, the federal courts tried several innovative procedures. For example, recognizing that "[t]he heyday of individual adjudication of asbestos mass tort lawsuits has long passed," the Judicial Panel on Multidistrict Litigation ordered the pre-trial consolidation of 26,639 pending asbestos cases in July 1991. In re Asbestos Prods. Liab. Litig. (No. VI), 771 F. Supp. 415, 419 (J.P.M.L.1991).

In New York, the Chief Judges of the Second Circuit, the Southern District, and the Eastern District transferred all cases filed in either district to the district judge in this action for purposes of discovery.... We commend Judge Sifton for his masterful stewardship of these cases. Eventually, the cases approached the Rubicon of either settling or going to trial. To facilitate settlements and provide for manageable trials, the cases were "subdivided by the location in which the plaintiff suffered primary exposure."

The Consolidation Here

In the instant action, 600 cases were consolidated. The thread upon which all 600 cases hung was that each plaintiff had been exposed to asbestos in one or more of over 40 power-generating stations, or "powerhouses" as they are called, in New York State.

Forty-eight were selected from the 600 cases for trial on a reverse-bifurcated basis, *i.e.* damages to be tried first and then liability. The damages trial began on April 1, 1991. Each of the 48 plaintiffs had named as defendants between 14 and 42 manufacturers or distributors of asbestos-containing products. Of these, 25 appeared at trial as direct defendants. Several of the defendants impleaded third-party defendants. For example, on March 18, 1991, 13 days before the trial began, Judge Sifton allowed defendant Owens-Corning Fiberglas Corporation to implead over 200 companies. Some of the third-party defendants, in turn, impleaded fourth-party defendants.

During the four-month damages trial, evidence of the debilitating diseases and/or deaths of all 48 plaintiffs was presented to the jury. Often, the plaintiffs themselves would testify.... Where, as in Kranz-Lewis's case, a particular victim had died prior to trial, evidence regarding his disease and death was presented by family members. A parade of medical doctors testified on the etiologies and pathologies of the asbestos-related diseases suffered by each of the plaintiffs. Economists testified concerning the present value of past and future income streams, and the dollar value of ordinary household services.

In addition, detailed testimony for each victim was necessary concerning his degree of impairment, specific medical history, emotional state, and medical prognosis. Further complicating matters, the jury had to sift through each victim's medical history to determine whether factors other than asbestos, such as smoking, were responsible, in whole or part, for his physical complaints.... Claims by spouses and children presented extensive plaintiff-specific evidence.

After four months of such evidence, the jury returned verdicts for 45 of the plaintiffs for an aggregate of over $94 million. Kranz-Lewis's damages were calculated as $1,682,795, including $1,250,000 for "Pain, Suffering and Other Non-Economic Losses to Decedent."

The liability portion of the trial began on September 11, 1991. During this phase, the jury was presented with a dizzying amount of evidence regarding each victim's work history. Where a victim, like Lewis, had died before trial, the sites where he had worked during his career, the types of asbestos-containing products with which he had been involved, and the identity of the manufacturers or distributors of the asbestos products to which he may have been exposed were reconstructed through the testimony of family members and co-workers.

The testimony of just one plaintiff illustrates the cosmic sweep of the factual data that the jury had to absorb. That plaintiff, Hubert Feeley, testified that from 1953 until 1974, he worked in "hundreds of" buildings; "could not keep track of all of them;" used "[p]ipe covering, block cement, asbestos cloth, all different sorts of cement;" worked for "[t]wenty-five or so" employers; travelled as an asbestos worker to Alaska, Egypt, Wyoming, Minnesota, West Virginia, Connecticut, White Plains and New Jersey; worked in "[o]ffice buildings, high-rises, shopping centers, [and] state office buildings" including the Chase Manhattan Building, the Exxon Building and the Holiday Inn; and worked in at least seven powerhouses throughout the greater New York area. He also testified that he used at least ten different products while working for one of his many employers. He candidly testified on direct examination that "of the hundreds of buildings [he had] worked on," "[m]aybe eight or nine were powerhouses." Finally, the longest period that he could recall working at any one powerhouse was "about six months." (It should be remembered that the common thread supporting consolidation of all these cases was asbestos-exposure in a powerhouse.)[ ]

After three months, plaintiffs rested on December 4, 1991. For the next three months, the defendants presented their case. The district court and the lawyers valiantly attempted to maintain the identity of each claim throughout the trial. The jury was instructed on several occasions to consider each case separately and each juror was given a notebook for this purpose. Thanks to the effective settlement techniques of the district judge and a special master, only two plaintiffs remained by the time the jury rendered its liability verdict. It concluded that appellant Keene Corporation was 9% liable for the Kranz-Lewis damages.

Following the verdict, Keene moved for judgment as a matter of law, a new trial, or other post-verdict relief, contending, *inter alia*, that the district court's decision to consolidate the 48 cases for trial constituted prejudicial error. The district judge rejected this argument without extended discussion; and, after molding the verdict in accordance with various New York statutes to add interest and to reflect different degrees of fault among defendants, entered a judgment for Kranz against Keene for $226,038.29.

DISCUSSION

Addressing the complaints of hundreds of thousands of severely injured asbestos plaintiffs, while safeguarding the rights of the defendants, all the while searching for equitable resolutions in each case, is a herculean task. Many of the asbestos victims suffered exposure for decades and at many different worksites. Finding an appropriate forum to resolve all these claims with minimal delay is the goal. Faced with this challenge, district judges throughout the country have reacted with commendable ingenuity. Pre-trial consolidation for the purposes of discovery, the appointment of special masters to expedite settlement, and, especially, the liberal use of consolidated trials have ameliorated what might otherwise be a sclerotic backlog of cases. . . .

[The court discussed Rule 42 and *Johnson v. Celotex Corp.* (p. 473, *supra*), and then continued:]

The benefits of efficiency can never be purchased at the cost of fairness. As we recently stated:

> [W]e are mindful of the dangers of a streamlined trial process in which testimony must be curtailed and jurors must assimilate vast amounts of information. The systemic urge to aggregate litigation must not be allowed to trump our dedication to individual justice, and we must take care that each individual plaintiff's — and defendant's — cause not be lost in the shadow of a towering mass litigation.

In re Brooklyn Navy Yard Asbestos Litig., 971 F.2d 831, 853 (2d Cir. 1992); see also Arnold v. Eastern Air Lines, Inc., 712 F.2d 899, 906 (4th Cir. 1983) (en banc) ("considerations of convenience may not prevail where the inevitable consequence to another party is harmful and serious prejudice"), cert. denied, 464 U.S. 1040 (1984); Baker v. Waterman S.S. Corp., 11 F.R.D. 440, 441 (S.D.N.Y. 1951) ("a fair and impartial trial to all litigants" is the foremost concern when considering consolidation); Cain v. Armstrong World Indus., 785 F. Supp. 1448, 1457 (S.D. Ala. 1992) (new trial warranted where "[a]s the evidence unfolded . . . it became more and more obvious . . . that a process had been unleashed that left the jury the impossible task of being able to carefully sort out and distinguish the facts and law of thirteen plaintiffs' cases that varied greatly in so many critical aspects").

To strike the appropriate balance as to consolidation *vel non*, "[c]ourts in the Southern and Eastern Districts of New York have used [a standard set of] criteria . . . as a guideline in determining whether to consolidate asbestos exposure cases." *Johnson*, 899 F.2d at 1285. These criteria include: "'(1) common worksite; (2) similar occupation; (3) similar time of exposure; (4) type of disease; (5) whether plaintiffs were living or deceased; (6) status of discovery in each case; (7) whether all plaintiffs were represented by the same counsel; and (8) type of cancer alleged. . . .'" . . . As in *Johnson*, we again conclude that the test furnishes a useful guideline to evaluate consolidation of asbestos cases.

(1) *Worksite*

Plaintiffs did not all work at the same worksite. Rather, their only worksite similarity was that each was alleged to have suffered some part of his asbestos exposure at one or more of over 40 power-generating plants throughout New York State. Judge Sifton apparently selected the 48 cases based on his conclusion that, in each case, the plaintiff had suffered "primary" exposure in such powerhouses. . . .

The work history evidence of [plaintiffs] dispels the notion that they shared primary exposure at the 40-odd power plants. Indeed, the record contains evidence of over 250 worksites. Thus, not only was there no common worksite in this case, but any contention that there was a common type of worksite must be viewed with a skeptical eye.

(2) *Similar Occupation*

This inquiry is significant because a worker's exposure to asbestos must depend mainly on his occupation. . . . The occupations of the plaintiffs in this case ranged from plumbers to machinists to carpenters to boilermakers to sheet-metal workers.

(3) *Times of Exposure*

The third factor similarly does not support a finding of commonality. The time frame that the jury was required to consider was enormous: a period involving exposures in intervals that began as early as the 1940's and ended as late as the 1970's. While some plaintiffs suffered asbestos exposure over periods of up to 30 years, others had much shorter periods of exposure, undercutting the benefit of efficiency, and increasing the likelihood of prejudice . . . .

(4) *Disease Type*

Not all plaintiffs alleged the same type of disease. Rather, of the 48 plaintiffs, 28 suffered from asbestosis, 10 suffered from lung cancer, and 10 from mesothelioma. The significance of this disparity is obvious. When the plaintiffs suffer from the same disease, the economy derived by not rehashing the etiology and pathology of the particular disease will be great, while the concomitant prejudice will be minimal. Here, by contrast, the jury was required to hear testimony about three different diseases. The opportunity for prejudice is particularly troubling where, as here, asbestosis sufferers, who may under certain circumstances expect close to normal life spans, are paired for trial with those suffering from terminal cancers, such as mesothelioma and lung cancer.

(5) *The Living & The Dead*

Some victims in this case were still living during trial. Others had already died.... The significance of this factor is evident. *Drago*, 125 F.R.D. at 65-66 ("[T]he presence of wrongful death claims and personal injury actions in a consolidated trial is somewhat troublesome.... [T]he dead plaintiffs may present the jury with a powerful demonstration of the fate that awaits those claimants who are still living.").

(6) *Discovery Status*

Keene does not argue that any of the 48 cases was not ready for trial. We note however, the absence of any express finding of readiness in the district court's decision rejecting a challenge to consolidation. Query: were the 200 third-party defendants that were impleaded two weeks before the trial ready for the trial?

(7) *Counsel*

Plaintiffs were represented by five law firms, each of which played an active role throughout the trial.

(8) *Cancer*

Two different types of cancer were alleged: lung cancer, and mesothelioma, a cancer of the lining of the wall of the chest. Each required distinct testimony regarding its etiology, pathology, and consequences.

In addition to the foregoing eight factors, courts contemplating consolidation must also take into account the number of cases affected. In re New York Asbestos Litig., 145 F.R.D. 644, 653 (S.D.N.Y. 1993) (consolidating twelve cases). Here, the maelstrom of facts, figures, and witnesses, with 48 plaintiffs, 25 direct defendants, numerous third-and-fourth party defendants, and evidence regarding culpable non-parties and over 250 worksites throughout the world was likely to lead to jury confusion. Kranz quite properly emphasizes the number of precautions the district court took to assure that each case maintained its identity.... We conclude, however, that the sheer breadth of the evidence made these precautions feckless in preventing jury confusion.

Plaintiff contends that even if the consolidation was not warranted, the decision below should nevertheless be affirmed because Keene can show no prejudice arising from it. We disagree. At trial, Keene did not dispute that Lewis was exposed to a wide array of asbestos-containing products; rather, Keene disputed exposure to *its* products. Also, Keene readily conceded that it was known early on that massive, prolonged, and *direct* exposure to pure asbestos dust was dangerous; but Keene vehemently disputed that *bystander* exposure, such as that suffered by Mr. Lewis, was known to be dangerous when Lewis was allegedly exposed to Keene's products.

We are concerned that the jury's ability to focus on this distinction may have been compromised in this case. While the evidence regarding Lewis's exposure to Keene's products was vague, minimal, and heavily circumstantial when compared to the extensive evidence regarding the products of defendant Owens-Corning Fiberglas, the jury apportioned an equal 9% liability to each defendant. This is hard to explain. We conclude that under the unique circumstances of this case, there is an unacceptably strong chance that the equal apportionment of liability amounted to the jury throwing up its hands in the face of a torrent of evidence....

While district courts need not perform any specific rituals or recite any incantations before ordering cases to be consolidated, they must in every instance consider whether the "actions involv[e] a common question of law or fact." Only then can all be assured that innovative and creative efforts to provide compensation to deserving plaintiffs do not violate Federal Rule of Civil Procedure 42(a), which is designed to achieve efficiency without compromising a litigant's right under the Seventh Amendment to a jury trial.

We do not wish to be understood as condemning all consolidations of asbestos cases. Our holding today is narrow and amounts to little more than a caution that it is possible to go too far in the interests of expediency and to sacrifice basic fairness in the process. In ordering consolidation we repeat the counsel of Talleyrand, "Pas trop de zele" — not too much zeal.

Accordingly, the judgment of the district court is reversed, and the matter remanded for a new trial.

■ WALKER, Circuit Judge, dissenting.... Consolidated trials are an indispensable means of resolving the thousands of asbestos claims flooding our state and federal courts, as well as claims arising from other types of mass torts. I agree that trial courts should not employ consolidated trials where they pose substantial risks of prejudice, and that to do so when the risks are manifest and prejudice results amounts to an abuse of the considerable discretion the law accords to trial courts in deciding whether to consolidate. However, by overturning the consolidated trial here, where indisputably substantial common issues of fact and law prevailed, without a substantial showing of prejudice, I think the majority errs, while sending the wrong message to courts faced with the difficult task of administering such claims in a manner that is fair to all parties involved.

IN RE: REPETITIVE STRESS INJURY LITIGATION

11 F.3d 368 (2d Cir. 1993)

■ WINTER, Circuit Judge. Defendants-appellants International Business Machines Corporation ("IBM") and Wang Laboratories, Inc. ("Wang") appeal from Judge Weinstein's order . . . granting the plaintiffs-appellees' motion to consolidate the forty-four cases in the Eastern District of New York that assert a claim for damages for "repetitive stress injuries." [Other defendants] appeal from Judge Hurley's subsequent order . . . that extended the Weinstein Order to include all actions filed thereafter in the Eastern District claiming "repetitive stress injuries."

[W]e treat the attempted appeals as petitions for writs of mandamus and grant the petitions. We vacate the consolidation orders and remand to the district court for further proceedings consistent with this decision. . . .

Plaintiffs are individuals who have brought actions alleging injuries resulting from "repetitive stress" encountered in the use of equipment manufactured or distributed by various defendants. These so-called "repetitive stress injuries" ("RSI") include "carpal tunnel" syndrome, a malady of the hands and wrists, and a diverse array of other ailments . . . . The claimed afflictions do not have a single cause and, defendants argue, may result, *inter alia*, from hereditary factors, vascular disorders, obesity, metabolic disorders, high blood cholesterol levels, connective tissue disorders, primary pulmonary hypertension, and prior trauma.

Defendants are companies that manufacture, and in some cases distribute, various types of equipment, including keyboards, keypunches, alphanumeric machines, video display terminals, cash registers, supermarket workstations, stenographic machines, and computer "mouse" devices. . . .

On June 2, 1992, Judge Weinstein consolidated the forty-four pending "RSI" cases before Judge Hurley as the judge with the earliest-filed RSI case on his docket, pursuant to the usual practice of the district court. . . . Although Judge Weinstein's opinion seemed at times to recognize that the factual or legal issues of the various cases were not identical and might subsequently lead to the subdividing of proceedings by classes of issues, he ordered full consolidation with the result that, as matters presently stand, all counsel must attend all discovery and all court proceedings.

On July 14, 1992, Judge Hurley established preliminary discovery procedures and solicited from the parties their suggestions for composing relevant "subgroups" for purposes of discovery, as suggested by Judge Weinstein. . . .

Pursuant to 28 U.S.C. § 1407, appellees have also moved before the Judicial Panel on Multidistrict Litigation ("MDL") for an order consolidating all RSI cases pending nationwide in the Eastern District of New York. The MDL Panel denied appellees' motion because it was not persuaded that "the degree of common questions of fact among these actions rises to the level that transfer under Section 1407 would best serve the overall convenience of the parties and witnesses and promote the just and efficient conduct of this entire litigation." In re: Repetitive Stress Injury Products Liability Litig., 1992 WL 403023 (J.P.M.L. 1992). . . .

The granting of a writ of mandamus is an extraordinary measure and should be done sparingly, to redress a "clear abuse of discretion," or "to confine an inferior court to a lawful exercise of its prescribed authority . . . ."

A party moving for consolidation must bear the burden of showing the commonality of factual and legal issues in different actions, . . . and a district court must examine "the special underlying facts" with "close attention" before ordering a consolidation. . . . The allegations of the complaints afford no support to the district courts' conclusion that these cases are sufficiently related to warrant consolidation. Indeed, the district court substituted a discussion of so-called mass torts for precise findings as to what are the "common questions of law or fact" justifying consolidation pursuant to Fed. R. Civ. P. 42.

We believe that consolidation here was a sufficiently clear abuse of discretion to warrant mandamus relief. At this stage of the litigation, the sole common fact among these cases is a claim of injury of such generality that it covers a number of different ailments for each of which there are numerous possible causes other than the tortious conduct of one of the defendants. As a class, the plaintiffs presumably have the usual wide variety of individual health conditions and problems that are found in any similar sample of persons and that might be relevant to the claimed injuries. The defendants manufacture or distribute a variety of mechanical devices with differing propensities, if any, to cause the harm alleged. With regard to issues of law, the plaintiffs come from a variety of jurisdictions and rely for their claims on the laws of different states. An order that merges all discovery and court proceedings and requires the participation of all counsel simply has no basis in Rule 42.

Although consolidation may enhance judicial efficiency, "[c]onsiderations of convenience and economy must yield to a paramount concern for a fair and impartial trial." Johnson v. Celotex Corp., 899 F.2d 1281, 1285 (2d Cir.), cert. denied, 498 U.S. 920 (1990). As we have recently cautioned, "The systemic urge to aggregate litigation must not be allowed to trump our dedication to individual justice, and we must take care that each individual plaintiff's — and defendant's — cause not be lost in the shadow of a towering mass litigation." In re: Brooklyn Navy Yard Asbestos Litig., 971 F.2d 831, 853 (2d Cir. 1992).

In *Johnson*, we enumerated the factors to consider in ordering consolidation in the context of analogous claims involving asbestos. They are, in relevant part: "'(1) common worksite; (2) similar occupation; (3) similar time of exposure; (4) type of disease . . .; (6) status of discovery in each case; (7) whether all plaintiffs were represented by the same counsel. . . .'" . . . Although the majority of the plaintiffs are represented by the same counsel and discovery had not yet begun in any of the cases, the other factors strongly militate against consolidation. The plaintiffs are employed at different worksites and in different occupations, ranging from word processor, to key puncher, to stenographer. They report different conditions relating to the alleged ailments and disparate ailments themselves. Moreover, each of the ailments alleged may have a cause other than the tortious conduct of an individual defendant much less all the defendants. Finally, factors 1-4 are far more important than identity of counsel and progress of discovery. *Johnson* factors 1-4 go to the central issue of commonality, while factors 6-7 go solely to convenience, and here the convenience of only one side. As we recently stated, "it is possible to go too far in the interests of expediency and to sacrifice basic fairness in the process." Malcolm v. National Gypsum Co., 995 F.2d 346, 353 (2d Cir. 1993).

When entering the consolidation orders, the district court contemplated the subdividing of discovery or other proceedings and even the severance of some cases as the litigation proceeds. Because the question of whether there are common issues of law or fact in these cases is open, there is no doubt some discovery that is applicable to a group of, or all, cases. The district judges' approach, however, reverses the proper process. The burden is on the party seeking aggregation to show common issues of law or fact; the burden is not on the party opposing aggregation to show divergences. This is so even in the case of the so-called mass tort, where a shifting of this burden is likely to render the label mass tort into a self-fulfilling prophecy.

We emphasize, however, that we see nothing wrong with assigning all RSI cases in a district to a single district judge who may order that particular proceedings or certain discovery requests relate to defined groups of RSI cases or, when appropriate, all the RSI cases in the district. Our differences with the district court are more than philosophical. The burden is on the party seeking aggregation of discovery or other proceedings to show common factual or legal issues warranting it. A party may not use aggregation as a method of increasing the costs of its adversaries — whether plaintiffs or defendants — by forcing them to participate in discovery or other proceedings that are irrelevant to their case. It may be that such increased costs would make settlement easier to achieve, but that would occur only at the cost of elemental fairness.

Notes and Questions

1. What are the proper limits of a trial court's discretion to order consolidation under Rule 42? The progression from *Johnson* to *Malcolm* to *RSI* presents three cases, each applying the same test, that take increasingly narrow views of consolidation. *Johnson* permits two cases with a fairly minimal factual relation to be consolidated for trial. *Malcolm* refuses to permit consolidation of 48 cases with an even more minimal factual relation to proceed to trial, although it does not seem to believe that consolidated pretrial handling was improper. *RSI* rejects — indeed, issues a writ of mandamus against — the pretrial consolidation of 44 cases whose factual relation is (although this point is debatable) more minimal than *Malcolm*.

2. There are different ways in which to analyze the cases. One is to say that the main distinction lies in the number of cases aggregated. If that is the distinction, however, consolidation is unlikely to be helpful in complicated and most complex cases. Another method of analysis is to say that the critical

variable is that consolidation should not occur until the litigation is sufficiently mature, although this distinction does not explain refusal to permit the consolidation in *Malcolm*. A third way to analyze the cases is to consider the purpose of the consolidation: pretrial or trial. Trial consolidation presents the more difficult issue, because improper trial consolidation can significantly prejudice defendants. See Irwin A. Horowitz & Kenneth S. Bordens, *The Effects of Outlier Presence, Plaintiff Population Size, and Aggregation of Plaintiffs on Simulated Civil Jury Decisions*, 12 L. & Hum. Behav. 209 (1988) (pp. 102-03, *supra*). Under this approach, consolidation for pretrial purposes is generally not problematic, at least when pretrial transfer under § 1407 would be appropriate. (We study § 1407 in detail shortly. In brief, however, § 1407 permits transfers of related cases involving common questions of fact for pretrial purposes only. Note that a (critical?) distinction between *Malcolm* and *RSI* was that a § 1407 transfer had been authorized in asbestos cases, but not in RSI cases.)

A fourth way of considering the cases is to apply an efficiency analysis; the efficiencies of a joint trial of two minimally related cases in *Johnson* may well have outweighed the inefficiencies, while the inefficiencies of trying the 48 minimally related cases in *Malcolm*, or conducting pretrial proceedings of the 44 minimally related cases in *RSI*, strongly outweighed any arguable efficiencies. A fifth way to consider the cases is in terms of unfairness to the defendant. In *Johnson* and *Malcolm*, the unfairness was the possibility of jury confusion — a possibility that increases as the factual dissimilarity of the cases increases. Under this analysis, what is the unfairness of consolidation in *RSI*? Is *RSI* wrong?

A sixth way of analyzing the cases is a textual approach. Rule 42(a) permits consolidation when "actions involving a common question of law or fact are pending before the court." Certainly all of the cases in *Malcolm* and *RSI* literally fulfill the requirement of at least one "common question of law or fact." Should the literal satisfaction be the end of the inquiry? In Chapter Two, we encountered similar "common question of law or fact" language in some of the joinder rules, especially in Rule 20. There we saw a seventh, contextual approach, in which the "common question" language was read against concerns of both efficiency and fairness; that the meaning of the phrase varied according to the voluntary or involuntary nature of joinder (*i.e.*, the concerns for plaintiffs' adversarial right to be master of the complaint and defendants' right to a hearing whose outcome is not unduly skewed by the joinder of outlier plaintiffs); and that the court's interest in efficient packaging was a much weaker variable. Should the same contextual approach inform the understanding of Rule 42? Is this approach the best way to explain the statement in *RSI* that the first four factors (which emphasized commonality) were more important than the last group of factors (which emphasized convenience)? Is there any way to create clear guidelines from such imponderable variables as efficiency, fairness, adversarialism, right to jury trial, and effective judicial administration? Is there a risk that judges, who are most directly affected by the last variable, will unduly emphasize that variable in a multi-factor analysis?

Which method of analysis best explains the three cases? Which seems the best construction of Rule 42? Which seems the most desirable policy for consolidation of related cases?

3. Under several of the methods of analyzing Rule 42, as well as in the three cases, a critical issue is whether the consolidation makes it impossible for the factfinder to distinguish clearly among numerous plaintiffs, defendants,

evidence, and claims put forward. How can a jury be instructed to avoid bias or confusion? How can it rationally determine the facts in a lengthy and confusing trial? We examine some devices to reduce confusion and increase comprehension in Chapter Eleven. The probable success of those devices might well determine the success of a motion for consolidation. Once again, we see that procedure is a seamless web, in which late-in-the-game issues such as trial procedure affects early-in-the-day decisions on aggregation. Since most cases settle during pretrial, however, should possible difficulties at trial determine whether consolidation for pretrial purposes is appropriate?

4. For other interesting cases concerning consolidation, see In re Asbestos Litigation, 1998 WL 230950 (S.D.N.Y.) (consolidating 7 asbestos cases for trial; distinguishing *Malcolm*); In re Asbestos Litigation, 173 F.R.D. 81 (S.D.N.Y. 1997) (permitting consolidation of 5 plaintiffs against 6 defendants); Consorti v. Armstrong World Industries, Inc., 72 F.3d 1003 (2d Cir. 1995) (consolidation of 6 asbestos cases for trial against 12 defendants proper, when judge took precautions to prevent jury confusion), vacated on other grounds, 518 U.S. 1031 (1996); ACandS, Inc. v. Godwin, 340 Md. 334, 667 A.2d 116 (1995) (consolidation of 6 asbestos cases against 6 defendants proper). *Godwin* arose out of one of the largest consolidations in history; the Circuit Court for Baltimore City consolidated 8,555 separate asbestos cases against 150 manufacturers for pretrial handling. For trial, however, the Circuit Court consolidated only groups of five to ten cases. 667 A.2d at 119-20. *Godwin* affirmed one of those trial consolidations.

5. To the extent that cases such as *Johnson, Malcolm, RSI, Asbestos Litigation, Consorti,* and *Godwin* suggest that it is easier to consolidate a small number of cases rather than a great number of cases, how much does consolidation help to resolve the aggregation problems in complex and complicated litigation? Indeed, doesn't consolidation actually help to create lawyer dysfunction in cases with insufficient assets? The reason is that the few plaintiffs (for instance, two plaintiffs in *Johnson* or six plaintiffs in *Godwin*) who are consolidated for early trials collect the full value of their judgments, thus leaving less money for other plaintiffs further back in queue. Granting that courts cannot always prevent lawyer dysfunction, is a court ever justified in interpreting a procedural rule in a way that might create lawyer dysfunction? Should the prevention of lawyer dysfunction also be a factor in determining the scope of consolidation? Can *Malcolm*'s outcome be justified because the consolidation had permitted one subset of one group of asbestos victims to skip impermissibly to the front of the line? Can *RSI*'s outcome be justified, at least in part, by the fact that the cases did not appear to be complex (the assets of the defendants appeared more than adequate to satisfy the expected value of all claims), so that the strongest reason to support consolidation was lacking?

Note that, under this analysis, the critical question is whether consolidation can prevent lawyer dysfunction. Until now, we have examined lawyer dysfunction only in the context of joinder and aggregation. As we shall see in later parts of the book, lawyer dysfunction can also arise in pretrial, trial, or post-trial proceedings. Hence, in some cases consolidation may be necessary not to prevent joinder complexity, but to prevent pretrial, trial, or remedial complexity. The web is indeed seamless.

6. When cases are consolidated, they do not lose their individual procedural identity; thus, separate orders and judgments must still be entered in each of the cases. See Johnson v. Manhattan Railway Co., 289 U.S. 479, 496-97 (1933)

("consolidation is permitted as a matter of convenience and economy in administration, but does not merge the suits into a single cause, or change the rights of the parties, or make those who are parties in one suit parties in another"). For a detailed two-part analysis of other jurisdictional and procedural consequences of consolidated litigation, see Joan Steinman, *The Effects of Case Consolidation on the Procedural Rights of Litigants: What They Are, What They Might Be Part 1: Justiciability and Jurisdiction (Original and Appellate)*, 42 UCLA L. Rev. 717 (1995), and *Part 2: Non-Jurisdictional Matters*, 42 UCLA L. Rev. 967 (1995).

7. Courts enjoy a *sua sponte* power to order consolidation; the parties do not need to consent. See 9 Charles A. Wright & Arthur R. Miller, Federal Practice & Procedure § 2382 (1995). Consolidation can also usually be effected by the order of a single judge; it does not require the action of each judge before whom a case is pending. Because, even in an adversarial system, the plaintiffs do not usually have the right to choose the judge before whom the case will be heard, providing this power does not constitute a breach of the adversarial ideal. At the same time, a *sua sponte* power of the judge avoids one of the concerns that we saw with *forum non conveniens* and *Kerotest*-type stays: A centralized decisionmaker can order the necessary aggregation.

In other ways, however, consolidation falls well short of the mark as an aggregation device. It does not force nonparties into the consolidated litigation. Nor is it generally thought to permit consolidation of cases pending in different venues. Wright & Miller, *supra*, § 2382. Whether other transfer devices can retain the *sua sponte*, single-judge benefits of consolidation, while overcoming the nonparty and inter-district limitations of consolidation and the outcome-determinative dangers of aggregation, now becomes our focus.

b. Venue Transfers under §1404

Section 1404(a) states in full: "For the convenience of parties and witnesses, in the interest of justice, a district court may transfer any civil action to any other district or division where it might have been brought." Is this the aggregation device for which we have been searching?

IN RE JOINT EASTERN AND SOUTHERN DISTRICTS ASBESTOS LITIGATION

769 F. Supp. 85 (E. & S.D.N.Y. 1991)

■ WEINSTEIN, District Judge. Some 700 asbestos cases in which workers were allegedly exposed to asbestos while working in New York state powerhouses were consolidated for trial and settlement by Judge Charles P. Sifton. Some of these cases were pending in the Southern District of New York and others were pending in the Eastern District of New York. After Judge Sifton, a judge of the Eastern District of New York, was designated by the Chief Judge of the Court of Appeals to sit in the Southern District of New York, he was designated by the Chief Judges of the Eastern and Southern

District courts of New York to supervise all asbestos cases in the districts. The first forty-eight of these cases are on trial before Judge Sifton. Judge Sifton's designation to serve as a judge in the Southern District has temporarily lapsed as a result of clerical error.

All 700 cases are before Judge Jack B. Weinstein for purposes of settlement. He has been designated by the Chief Judge of the Court of Appeals to sit in the Eastern and Southern Districts to hear asbestos cases.

Several third-party defendants have moved to dismiss defendant Owens Corning Fiberglas' (OCF) third-party contribution claims against them on the ground that . . . the order of consolidation previously entered must be vacated because actions pending in different districts cannot be consolidated. . . .

Consolidations have become increasingly common as the courts struggle to meet the challenges posed by the asbestos litigation crises. . . . Presently, over 30,000 asbestos personal injury cases are pending in federal courts nationwide. Extraordinary steps, such as this large consolidation, are necessary to cope with the current judicial asbestos emergency. . . .

Rule 42 of the Federal Rules of Civil Procedure permits a court to order consolidation of actions pending before the court involving a "common question of law or fact." Fed. R. Civ. P. 42(a). The powerhouse cases all involve common questions of law and fact.

Nevertheless, it is asserted that prior cases deny power to consolidate cases pending in different districts. See, *e.g.*, Town of Warwick v. New Jersey DEP, 647 F. Supp. 1322, 1324-25 (S.D.N.Y. 1986); Facen v. Royal Rotterdam Lloyd S.S. Co., 12 F.R.D. 443, 443 (S.D.N.Y. 1952). . . .

We do not need to decide whether these precedents apply to consolidation of related mega-mass tort cases pending before the courts in different districts in the same circuit. Nor need we decide whether Section 1407 of Title 28, empowering the Multidistrict Panel to transfer cases, exhausts the power of the courts within the same circuit to consolidate cases pending in different districts for trial. The matter is easily resolved by applying Section 1404 of Title 28 to transfer all the related cases to a single district within the circuit.

Transfer is appropriate "for the convenience of the parties and witnesses, in the interest of justice" to any district where the action might have been brought originally. 28 U.S.C. § 1404(a). Factors relevant to a transfer determination include convenience of parties and witnesses, the relative ease of access to the sources of proof, the availability of process to subpoena witnesses if necessary, considerations of trial efficiency and the interests of the law in the "just, speedy and inexpensive determination" of actions. Fed. R. Civ. P. 1; see also *Town of Warwick*, 647 F. Supp. at 1323 . . .

In view of the context of asbestos cases, in particular the enormous burden they place on the courts, the plaintiffs' need for prompt relief, and defendants' need to reduce transaction costs, transfer of the Southern District cases to the Eastern District will serve the interests of justice. Consolidation of these legally and factually similar asbestos claims will afford litigants an opportunity to prosecute the cases efficiently and expeditiously. It will avoid needless duplication in proof and decrease wasteful expenditures of time, energy and money. Availability of evidence, process, witnesses and other aspects of convenience weigh heavily in favor of the transfer.

Venue is proper in the Eastern District because each third-party defendant conducts business in the district sufficient to support a finding of residency and because a "substantial part of the events or omissions giving rise to the claim" occurred in the district. 28 U.S.C. § 1391(a). . . .

A judge sitting by designation in a district has authority to transfer cases from that district. This general power is particularly useful in the instant litigation. The pool of attorneys and witnesses is exactly the same in the Eastern and Southern Districts, and their main courthouses are in the City of New York within semaphore flag distance of each other. Consolidation is appropriate and necessary both for judicially efficiency and to provide effective justice to the litigants. Breaking up the consolidated powerhouse cases at this point in the litigation would be wasteful of both court and litigant resources. Cf. 28 U.S.C. § 1406 (transfer from "wrong" district to proper district "in the interests of justice").

All consolidated powerhouse cases pending in the Southern District are transferred to the Eastern District.

HOFFMAN v. BLASKI

363 U.S. 335 (1960)

■ MR. JUSTICE WHITTAKER delivered the opinion of the Court.

To relieve against what was apparently thought to be the harshness of dismissal, under the doctrine of *forum non conveniens*, of an action brought in an inconvenient one of two or more legally available forums, . . . Congress, in 1948, enacted 28 U.S.C. § 1404(a) . . .

The instant cases present the question whether a District Court, in which a civil action has been properly brought, is empowered by § 1404 (a) to transfer the action, on the motion of the defendant, to a district in which the plaintiff did not have a *right* to bring it. . . .

Respondents, Blaski and others, residents of Illinois, brought this patent infringement action in the United States District Court for the Northern District of Texas against one Howell and a Texas corporation controlled by him, alleging that the defendants are residents of, and maintain their only place of business in, the City of Dallas, in the Northern District of Texas, where they are infringing respondents' patents. After being served with process and filing their answer, the defendants moved, under § 1404 (a), to transfer the action to the United States District Court for the Northern District of Illinois. Respondents objected to the transfer on the ground that, inasmuch as the defendants did not reside, maintain a place of business, or infringe the patents in, and could not have been served with process in, the Illinois district, the courts of that district lacked venue over the action and ability to command jurisdiction over the defendants; that therefore that district was not a forum in which the respondents had a right to bring the action, and, hence, the court was without power to transfer it to that district. Without mentioning that objection or the question it raised, the District Court found that "the motion should be granted for the convenience of the parties and witnesses in the interest of justice," and ordered the case transferred to the Illinois district. . . .

Petitioners' "thesis" and sole claim is that § 1404 (a), being remedial, Ex parte Collett, 337 U.S. 55, 71, should be broadly construed, and, when so construed, the phrase "where it might have been brought" should be held to relate not only to the time of the bringing of the action, but also to the time of the transfer; and that "if at such time the transferee forum has the power to adjudicate the issues of the action, it is a forum in which the action might *then* have been brought." (Emphasis added.) They argue that in the interim between the bringing of the action and the filing of a motion to transfer it, the defendants may move their residence to, or, if corporations, may begin the transaction of business in, some other district, and, if such is done, the phrase "where it might have been brought" should be construed to empower the District Court to transfer the action, on motion of the defendants, to such other district; and that, similarly, if, as here, the defendants move to transfer the action to some other district and consent to submit to the jurisdiction of such other district, the latter district should be held one "in which the action might *then* have been brought." (Emphasis added.) . . .

It is not to be doubted that the transferee courts, like every District Court, had jurisdiction to entertain actions of the character involved, but it is obvious that they did not acquire jurisdiction over these particular actions when they were brought in the transferor courts. The transferee courts could have acquired jurisdiction over these actions only if properly brought in those courts, or if validly transferred thereto under § 1404 (a). Of course, venue, like jurisdiction over the person, may be waived. A defendant, properly served with process by a court having subject matter jurisdiction, waives venue by failing seasonably to assert it, or even simply by making default. . . . But the power of a District Court under § 1404 (a) to transfer an action to another district is made to depend not upon the wish or waiver of the defendant but, rather, upon whether the transferee district was one in which the action "might have been brought" by the plaintiff.

The thesis urged by petitioners would not only do violence to the plain words of § 1404 (a), but would also inject gross discrimination. That thesis, if adopted, would empower a District Court, upon a finding of convenience, to transfer an action to any district desired by the defendants and in which they were willing to waive their statutory defenses as to venue and jurisdiction over their persons, regardless of the fact that such transferee district was not one in which the action "might have been brought" by the plaintiff. Conversely, that thesis would not permit the court, upon motion of the plaintiffs and a like showing of convenience, to transfer the action to the same district, without the consent and waiver of venue and personal jurisdiction defenses by the defendants. Nothing in § 1404 (a), or in its legislative history, suggests such a unilateral objective and we should not, under the guise of interpretation, ascribe to Congress any such discriminatory purpose. . . .

Inasmuch as the respondents (plaintiffs) did not have a right to bring these actions in the respective transferee districts, it follows that the judgments of the Court of Appeals were correct and must be

Affirmed.

■ [A concurring opinion by MR. JUSTICE STEWART has been omitted.]

■ MR. JUSTICE FRANKFURTER, whom MR. JUSTICE HARLAN and MR. JUSTICE BRENNAN join, dissenting. . . . At the crux of the business, as I see it, is the realization that we are concerned here not with a question of a limitation upon the power of a federal court but with the place in which that court may exercise its power. We are dealing, that is, not with the jurisdiction of the federal courts, which is beyond the power of litigants to confer, but with the locality of a lawsuit, the rules regulating which are designed mainly for the convenience of the litigants. . . .

The transferee court in this case plainly had and has jurisdiction to adjudicate this action with the defendant's acquiescence. As the defendant, whose privilege it is to object to the place of trial, has moved for transfer, and has acquiesced to going forward with the litigation in the transferee court, it would appear presumptively, unless there are strong considerations otherwise, that there is no impediment to effecting the transfer so long as "convenience" and "justice" dictate that it be made. . . . A transfer can be made under § 1404 (a) to a place where the action "might have been brought" only when "convenience" and "justice" so dictate, not whenever the defendant so moves. A legitimate objection by the plaintiff to proceeding in the transferee forum will presumably be reflected in a decision that the interest of justice does not require the transfer, and so it becomes irrelevant that the proposed place of transfer is deemed one where the action "might have been brought." If the plaintiff's objection to proceedings in the transferee court is not consonant with the interests of justice, a good reason is wanting why the transfer should not be made.

On the other hand, the Court's view restricts transfer, when concededly warranted in the interest of justice, to protect no legitimate interest on the part of the plaintiff.

Notes and Questions

1. To start with a bit of nomenclature, the court that enters the transfer order is called the "transferor court." The court to which the case is transferred is called the "transferee court."

2. In *Eastern and Southern Districts*, Judge Weinstein hints that § 1404 is not the only power that a transferor court can use to effect inter-district transfers. He first suggests that such a power might exist in Rule 42, which has generally been held not to contain such a power. See Note 7, p. 487, *supra*. Next, he alludes to the possibility that courts may enjoy some (inherent?) power to transfer cases even if transfer is not authorized under §§ 1404 and 1407. He ultimately avoids the question of power, however, by resolving the case under § 1404. You might wish to keep Weinstein's idea of alternative sources in mind as you examine the limits of §§ 1404 and 1407.

3. In *Eastern and Southern Districts*, was § 1404 transfer appropriate? In what ways was the case *after* transfer more convenient for the witnesses or the parties than *before* transfer? Was proof more accessible in Brooklyn than in Manhattan? Was testimony easier or cheaper to obtain? Was the availability of process different? See 15 Charles A. Wright et al., Federal Practice & Procedure § 3854 (1986) (transfers from transferor forum to nearby transferee forum are not usually "in the interest of justice"). Does *Eastern and Southern Districts* reduce to the claim that a case can be transferred whenever it can be packaged more efficiently elsewhere? Is this the standard of § 1404(a)? Should it be? If it were, then has a plaintiff's right of forum selection been effectively abolished? Or is *Eastern and Southern Districts* limited to its facts, including the lawyer dysfunction caused by insufficient assets? Did the transfer of some, but not all, asbestos victims to a new forum overcome the insufficient asset problem?

Courts have mentioned a number of factors that go into the transfer decision, among them the plaintiff's right to choose a forum, the convenience of parties and witnesses, the location of counsel, and the location of documents and other evidence, and the interest of justice. See Wright et al., *supra*, §§ 3847-54. How many of these factors are mentioned in the statute? According to the statute, isn't "the interest of justice" subordinated to "convenience," rather than a factor of equal weight? See New York Central Railroad Co. v. United States, 200 F. Supp. 944 (S.D.N.Y. 1961) (Friendly, J.) (raising issue); Heller Financial, Inc. v. Midwhey Powder Co., 883 F.2d 1286, 1293 (7th Cir. 1989) ("interest of justice" factor has independent status; "[t]he 'interest[s] of justice' include such concerns as ensuring speedy trials, trying related litigation together, and having a judge who is familiar with the applicable law try the case"); cf. Continental Grain Co. v. The Barge FBL—585, 364 U.S. 19 (1960) (failing to aggregate cases involving "precisely the same issues . . leads to the wastefulness of time, energy and money that § 1404(a) was designed to prevent").

To what extent does the inroad made by Congress on plaintiffs' venue privilege under § 1404 give license to courts to make inroads on the venue privilege in other areas, such as the construction of joinder or preclusion rules? Cf. Norwood v. Kirkpatrick, 349 U.S. 29, 32 (1955) (under § 1404, "plaintiff's choice of forum is . . . to be considered," but is not dispositive).

4. Transfer orders under § 1404 are appealable after entry of final judgment, although, since these orders are often discretionary, the chance of success on appeal is slight. There are some interesting questions of appellate jurisdiction raised when the transferor and transferee forums are located in different circuits, and the circumstances under which interlocutory review or mandamus is available to review a decision on § 1404 transfer varies somewhat among the circuits. See Wright et al., *supra*, § 3855.

5. In *Hoffman*, the defendants sought a § 1404 transfer, while in *Eastern and Southern Districts* the court itself ordered transfer. Plaintiffs can also request transfer. See Ferens v. John Deere Co., 494 U.S. 516 (1990) (p. 809, *infra*). So can additional parties. Wright et al., *supra*, § 3844. Thus, § 1404 contains one of the necessary components of any effective single-venue aggregation device — the ability of the court to act *sua sponte*. Similarly, when a case is transferred under § 1404, the transfer is effective for all purposes — pretrial, trial, and post-trial. After transfer, the case quite literally behaves as if it had been filed in the transferee forum.

In other ways, however, § 1404 is still not the ideal single-venue aggregation device in complex and complicated litigation. First, the order of transfer must be entered in the transferor court; a party seeking transfer of numerous related cases bears the burden of obtaining consolidation orders from each forum. There is, of course, no guarantee that each transferor judge will grant the motion. Second, § 1404 does nothing to draw into the venue the claims of parties that have filed suit in state court and nonparties that have not yet filed suit in any court. Third, § 1404 transfers move an entire "action" from one venue to another, rather than just the claims that are related to cases in another forum. See In the Matter of Orthopedic Bone Screw Products Liability Litigation (MDL No. 1014), 79 F.3d 46, 47 (7th Cir. 1996). In some cases, however, it makes little sense for the entire action to be transferred; for instance, in medical product liability cases, it is common for a plaintiff to join both the manufacturer and the physician. It may be convenient for the cases against the manufacturer to be aggregated in one forum, but extremely inconvenient for the doctor to find the case shipped off to some other part of the country. Yet § 1404 does not permit the transferor court to carve out only some aspects of the case for transfer. Might it be possible to overcome this defect by severing the transferable portion of the action under Rule 42(b), and transferring only that portion? See Sunbelt Corp. v. Noble, Denton & Associates, Inc., 5 F.3d 28 (3d Cir. 1993) (raising possibility of severance).

A fourth, very significant limitation on § 1404 transfers is the rule in *Hoffman v. Blaski* — a transfer can be made only to a forum in which the case could have originally been filed. The recent amendments to 28 U.S.C. § 1391 have, to some extent, tempered the effect of *Hoffman v. Blaski*, since they opened up more forums in which a case could have initially been filed. As we saw when we examined § 1391, however, sometimes there is no single venue in which all aspects of a multiparty complex or complicated controversy could have been filed. See pp. 450-54, *supra*. In these cases, *Hoffman v. Blaski* works to prevent the aggregation of cases in a single forum. Moreover, note that the liberalization of § 1391 also has a downside in complex and complicated litigation: It provides more forums to which defendants that want to frustrate single-venue aggregation can seek to have the case transferred. Does giving the plaintiffs the venue privilege, giving the defendants the right to seek transfer, and giving the courts great discretion to referee the parties' efforts to manipulate the forum seem like the correct formula for securing the best forum in complex or complicated litigation? Note that *Hoffman v. Blaski* was neither complex nor complicated. Is it possible to create an exception to its rule in complex cases? In complicated cases? Cf. In re Fine Paper Antitrust Litigation, 685 F.2d 810 (3d Cir. 1982) (court could transfer action to venue in which case could not originally have been brought after parties that had made venue transfer impossible settled and venue in transferee forum existed with respect to remaining parties).

A fifth limitation on § 1404 transfers is that transfers cannot be made to a district that would not have territorial jurisdiction over the parties. See *Sunbelt*, 5 F.3d 28; Wright et al., *supra*, § 3845. Once again, the scope of territorial jurisdiction affects the scope of aggregation.

A sixth possible limitation on § 1404 transfers is the timing of transfer. How is a transferor court to determine whether the facts dictate transfer until some discovery has occurred? But if discovery on the issues must occur in each transferor forum in order to determine whether the standards of § 1404 have been met, won't much of the efficiency of consolidated treatment have been lost? Indeed, it is not at all uncommon for cases to be transferred for trial to a transferee district only after discovery has been completed. See Winbourne v. Eastern Air Lines, Inc., 632 F.2d 219 (2d Cir. 1980); see also Apache Products Co.

v. Employers Insurance of Wausau, 154 F.R.D. 650 (S.D. Miss. 1994) (ordering severance of case against one defendant in order to permit transfer to other forum for trial, but delaying effect of order in order to permit plaintiff to conduct discovery against both defendants in transferee forum); but see Wood v. Zapata Corp., 484 F.2d 350 (3d Cir. 1973) (discovery in transferor forum not required prior to granting § 1404 motion). Should courts in potentially complex and complicated cases dispense with discovery on the § 1404 motion, and decide the case on general principles and minimal information?

A seventh limitation is that § 1404 does not permit transfers from one state court to another state court, or between state and federal courts. In 1991 the National Conference of Commissioners on Uniform State Laws proposed a Uniform Transfer of Litigation Act to allow participating states to transfer cases between them "to serve the fair, effective, and efficient administration of justice and the convenience of the parties and witnesses." This transfer was to be made after considering "all relevant factors." The two specific factors mentioned in the Act were "the interest of each plaintiff in selecting a forum and the public interest in securing a single litigation and disposition of related matters." Uniform Transfer of Litigation Act, § 104, reprinted in 14 U.L.A. (Supp. 1998). So far, no state has enacted the Act. See also American Law Institute, Complex Litigation § 4.02 (recommending passage of Uniform Complex Litigation Act).

6. There are also three specific problems that may make the single-venue § 1404 transfers in most complex and complicated litigation unlikely. To consider these problems, return for a minute to *Eastern and Southern Districts*. Assuming that venue and territorial jurisdiction was proper in the Eastern District of New York, could the chief judges of all 94 federal districts have gotten together and agreed to consolidate their pending asbestos cases in a single forum? The first problem with such a wide-scale use of § 1404 problem is that the transferee judge may not be able to consolidate the cases under Rule 42 after she receives all the cases on her docket. See p. 473, *supra*. The second problem with such a move is that, for reasons that we will see in Chapter Seven, the transferee court would likely need to resolve the cases under the laws of numerous states. The difficulty of having a judge unfamiliar with the relevant state law decide the case has sometimes been cited as a factor in § 1404 decisions, see Wright et al., *supra*, § 3854, and might make the chief judges less willing to order transfer. Third, although this move effects a single-venue consolidation, it is also a blatant end-run around § 1407, which, as we are about to see, limits mass transfers to pretrial matters only. Does § 1407 effectively eliminate the ability to use § 1404 to achieve mass aggregation of complex or complicated litigation? *Eastern and Southern Districts* suggests that § 1407 does not have such a pre-emptive effect. As you now read about the possibilities and the limits § 1407 in complex and complicated litigation, ask whether the court was correct in its belief.

c. Mass Multidistrict Transfers under § 1407

Enacted in 1968, 28 U.S.C. § 1407 created an entity called the Judicial Panel on Multidistrict Litigation, which is comprised of seven federal circuit and district judges. The Panel has the power to order the transfer of cases for "coordinated or consolidated pretrial proceedings" to a single transferee forum that is chosen by the Panel. (The Panel does not itself handle the transferred cases.) A close reading of § 1407(a) reveals four requirements that must be established in order for a transfer to occur: (1) "civil actions involving one or more common questions of fact are pending in different districts"; (2) transfer "will be for the convenience of the parties"; (3) transfer "will be for the convenience of the . . . witnesses"; and (4) transfer will be in the interests of justice." After completion of the coordinated pretrial proceedings, the Panel is then to remand the transferred cases from the transferee court back to their original transferor forums for trial. Moreover, the panel can also "separate any claim, cross-claim, counterclaim, or third-party claim and remand any of such claims before the remainder of the action is filed." 28 U.S.C. § 1407(a). Although the statute does not clearly provide for this event, the Panel also has the authority to transfer related cases (often called "tag-along action") that are filed in districts other than the transferee district after the initial consolidation order is entered. See Rules of Procedure for the Judicial Panel on Multidistrict Litigation 1, 12-13. The Panel also has the power to transfer cases on its own initiative, or on the motion of any party in any of the related cases.

Obviously, multidistrict transfer does not overcome all of the problems of a single-venue aggregation device; for instance, it applies only to actions pending in federal court (thus allowing nonparties to federal actions to escape its reach), it does not appear to permit consolidation for trial. In other ways, however, it appears at first blush to be the most useful device we have seen. A centralized decisionmaker chooses whether to aggregate cases; the device reaches every federal case; although the Panel has no power to stay related litigation, its power to deal with tag-along cases is actually better; it can aggregate just those claims deserving of consolidated treatment; and there appear to be no requirements that the district to which the case is transferred be either a venue in which the case might originally have been brought or a venue in which territorial jurisdiction over the parties exists.

Have we found at last the single-venue transfer device for which we have been seeking? Should it be expanded to overcome its present limitations? Or does it already go too far to destroy the plaintiffs' adversarial right to choose the forum? How do we justify the different treatment accorded to plaintiffs' venue privilege in cases in which § 1407 applies?

IN RE "EAST OF THE ROCKIES" CONCRETE PIPE ANTITRUST CASES

302 F. Supp. 244 (J.P.M.L. 1969)

[In one of the earliest cases to come before the Judicial Panel on Multidistrict Litigation, treble damage antitrust actions sprouted up in numerous federal districts after defendants pleaded *nolo contendere* to criminal antitrust indictments. The civil complaints alleged that the defendants engaged in price fixing and other anti-competitive behavior in every state east of the Rocky Mountains except Texas, Louisiana, and Mississippi (hence the caption "East of the Rockies").

[The Panel, on its own initiative, issued an order to show cause why the cases should not be transferred under § 1407. The Panel ordered the cases consolidated for pretrial purposes in the Eastern District of Pennsylvania. In the following concurrence, which remains today one of the most detailed descriptions of its kind, one of the members of the Panel discussed some of the considerations that enter into a decision to order a transfer under § 1407.]

■ WEIGEL, Judge of the Panel (concurring). The record in this matter makes it clear that a very substantial amount of discovery in each case will be pertinent only to those cases brought in the same district. This accentuates the question as to whether transfer for coordinated or consolidated pretrial proceedings will, in fact, "be for the convenience of parties and witnesses and will promote the just and efficient conduct of such actions." 28 U.S.C. 1407. If we are to order transfer, the statute requires us to determine that the answer to that question, including each of its four elements, is in the affirmative.

The cases here involve non-pressure pipe for sewers and culverts. Because of the difficulty of transporting such pipe and because of the ease of entry into the industry, non-pressure pipe is sold in distinctly local markets by competitors with plants in those areas. Only two defendants, Interpace and Martin Marietta, sold such pipe throughout the area "East of the Rockies." Martin Marietta had 67 plants in the area; Interpace, 36 permanent plants and 16 temporary ones. All the plaintiffs allege that these two defendants conspired to fix prices and to allocate markets throughout the region, and implemented their scheme through various local conspiracies.

Plainly, then, the cases do present some common questions of fact, *i.e.*, those concerning region-wide industry conditions as well as concerning the existence and local effect of the alleged broad conspiracy between Interpace and Martin Marietta. Even so, much — probably most — of the pretrial discovery and proceedings will concern local witnesses, local records and local aspects of the alleged conspiracies. Such matters are best handled by the local United States District Courts.

If the statute required all pretrial proceedings to be conducted by the transferee court, then the case against ordering transfer would be compelling. However, it is manifest from the statute and its legislative history that the Panel may order remand to the transferor courts for local discovery. Subsection (a) of 28 U.S.C. 1407 provides, in part, that "each action so transferred shall be remanded by the panel at *or before* the conclusion of such [joint] pretrial proceedings to the district from which it was transferred . . . ." . . .

This is not to say that the provisions for remand justify anything less than the most careful assessment of the pros and cons of transfer. The statutory objectives are not necessarily served by requiring joint pretrial whenever some — even many — questions of fact are common to a large number of cases. In some such cases, if not in these at hand, coordination and consolidation may impair, not further, convenience, justice and efficiency. To put it in other words, neither the convenience of witnesses and parties nor the just and efficient conduct of actions are served, *ipso facto*, by transfer just because there are common questions of fact in the civil actions involved.

There are a number of inherent inconveniences in transfers for coordinated or consolidated pretrial. Some plaintiffs are temporarily deprived of their choices of forum and some defendants may be forced to litigate in districts where they could not have been sued. Considerable time and trouble are involved in the sheer mechanics of transferring and remanding. After transfer, the process of segregating the pretrial matters which should be remanded for handling by the transferor courts may be time-consuming as well as subject to reasonable disagreement. Since remand must be by order of the Panel, the Panel may have to hold further hearings to resolve disagreements among the parties.

The basic question before the Panel in each proceeding looking to coordinated or consolidated pretrial is, then, whether the objectives of the statute are sufficiently served to justify the necessary inconveniences of transfer and remand. Many factors are relevant to the answer. Some will be applicable to all proceedings under the statute; some will not. Some will count heavily in some proceedings; lightly in others. It will be useful — for illustration, if nothing more — to articulate some of these considerations.

How many common questions of fact are there? What is their nature? How many cases are presently and prospectively involved? What is the geographical location of the districts in which the cases pend? If it is anticipated that further cases will be filed, in what districts? Who are the principal witnesses in the cases and where do they reside? What detriment, financial or otherwise, will be imposed upon any of the parties by ordering transfer? Will transfer result in a substantial saving of duplicative work? Will transfer usefully avoid conflicting rulings in the pretrial proceedings of the cases involved? Can many of the advantages of transfer be worked out by cooperation among counsel *without* transfer? Are pretrial proceedings already far along in any one or more of the cases? Will transfer hasten or delay progress in the cases? What is the availability of a judge or judges in the proposed transferee court or courts? Will the advantages of transfer overcome the normal desirability of having the same judge who conducts the trial also conduct pretrial proceedings? Will transfer impede or promote the prospect of settlements? Will transfer serve any ulterior motive of any party or parties, such as forum-shopping? If class actions are involved, will transfer make for complexity or for simplification? Will transfer unjustly delay or deny any party's right to provisional remedies such as injunctive relief? What is the status and possible effect of any appeals pending in any of the cases? Will transfer operate to eliminate or avoid an undesirable multiplicity of appeals on similar issues?

In evaluating such of the foregoing considerations as are relevant to this proceeding, the balance does seem very close to me. Notwithstanding the conceded common questions of fact and the anticipated advantages of joint pretrial, the countervailing considerations here are fairly strong. To begin with, there are the inherent inconveniences referred to above. In addition, the indications are that there will be genuine financial hardship upon a number of small defendants, that much of the saving of judicial time through transfer will be offset by the time required for segregation of local from common issues, and that the advantage of having all pretrial proceedings conducted by the trial judge will be lost in all transferred cases. Moreover, since a great number of the plaintiffs are represented by the same counsel, the opportunity exists for gaining many of the advantages of transfer through informal cooperation. However, I am not convinced that these factors weighing against consolidated or coordinated pretrial sufficiently tip the scale to require dissent from the decision of the Panel.

IN RE ASBESTOS AND ASBESTOS INSULATION MATERIAL PRODUCTS LIABILITY LITIGATION

431 F. Supp. 906 (J.P.M.L. 1977)

■ PER CURIAM. This litigation consists of 103 actions pending in nineteen districts. . . .

The 103 actions have been brought by workers who were exposed to asbestos dust in the course of their employment, or by persons associated with those workers, either as co-workers or as members of the family. Many diverse types of vocational exposure are involved in these actions.

Plaintiffs in most of the actions are or were workers at plants which produce asbestos products (the factory worker actions), or tradesmen who work with a variety of asbestos products (the tradesman actions). A majority of the tradesmen are installers of insulation products containing asbestos. Ninety-four of the actions are tradesman actions and nine of the actions are factory worker actions.

Six of the actions were brought as class actions on behalf of employees at three different plants that manufacture or once manufactured asbestos products. Three of the actions in the Eastern District of Texas were brought as class actions on behalf of employees at a PPG Industries plant in Tyler, Texas. Class certification has been denied in these three actions. The other three purported class actions are pending in the District of New Jersey. Two are brought on behalf of employees of Raybestos Manhattan, Inc. at a now defunct plant in Passaic, New Jersey. The other action is brought on behalf of employees at a Johns-Manville, Inc. plant in Manville, New Jersey. Class certification is still pending in the New Jersey actions.

There are a total of 80 defendants in the 103 actions. The majority of the defendants are manufacturers or distributors of various asbestos products. Johns-Manville is a defendant in 91 of the actions. Seven other defendant corporations are named in more than 50 actions, seven others are named in more than 30 actions, and ten others are named in ten or more actions.

The complaints in the actions generally allege that the defendants wrongfully caused the plaintiffs to be exposed to asbestos dust and asbestos fibers over a period of time, as a result of which the plaintiffs have contracted or are in danger of contracting asbestosis, mesothelioma, or other disorders. Alleged liability is based on the principles of strict liability, negligence, and/or breach of warranties of merchantability and/or fitness. It is also alleged that the defendants knew or should have known of the dangers to persons exposed to asbestos products, but that defendants failed to warn the plaintiffs of these dangers; failed to provide adequate precautions, safety devices, or wearing apparel to prevent exposure; and/or failed to establish reasonable standards for exposure.

Pursuant to 28 U.S.C. § 1407(c)(i) and Rule 8, R.P.J.P.M.L., 65 F.R.D. 253, 258-59 (1975), the Panel issued an order to show cause why all these actions should not be transferred to a single district for coordinated or consolidated pretrial proceedings. All except one of the 55 respondents to the Panel's order to show cause oppose transfer in this litigation. The primary arguments presented by the parties in opposition to transfer are the following:

(1) Many of the actions have been pending for several years and are well advanced in discovery. In several actions a discovery cutoff date or a trial date has been set. Transfer would merely delay the progress of discovery or the trial of those actions.

(2) In several districts, arrangements for voluntarily sharing the common aspects of discovery have been made among the parties to the actions pending within those districts. Transfer would cause unnecessary additional expenses which can be avoided by voluntary coordination of efforts among the parties.

(3) There is a lack of commonality among the parties in these actions.

(a) There is considerable variation in named defendants from action to action. No defendant or category of defendants is a party to all actions. Defendants include manufacturers of asbestos products, distributors of asbestos products, insurance companies, doctors, suppliers of raw asbestos fibers, trade associations, trade unions, and the United States of America.

(b) The plaintiffs are not a homogeneous group. They include insulation workers involved in the installation or removal of insulation products, workers in factories manufacturing asbestos products, co-workers, members of workers' families, and persons living in the proximity of asbestos manufacturing facilities.

(4) Although a common thread among these actions is exposure to some type of asbestos or asbestos product, the circumstances of exposure are predominantly individual to each action. The variables include the following:

(a) type of vocational exposure (*e.g.* — miner, transporter, factory worker, or tradesman);

(b) products to which exposed;

(c) conditions of exposure;

(d) duration and intensity of exposure;

(e) safety precautions taken by the worker;

(f) medical, personal, employment, and family history of the worker over the long periods of exposure involved (up to 50 years).

Regarding the factory workers and tradesmen, the two basic types of vocational exposure involved, the exposure of factory workers was to 100% raw asbestos, while the exposure of tradesmen was to products which generally contain about 15% asbestos.

(5) The question of causation is an individual issue. Several different types of disorders are alleged, including asbestosis, lung cancer, peritoneal mesothelioma, mesothelioma of the lining of the stomach or gastric organs, cancer of the esophagus, cancer of the colon, and cancer of the rectum. The question of whether particular disorders may be attributable to exposure to a particular type of asbestos is a matter of dispute among medical authorities. Causation of an individual's disability by asbestos exposure will necessarily be related to the individual factors of length, intensity, and type of vocational exposure, and to the physical characteristics of the person. A considerable amount of technical medical evidence such as diagnoses, x-rays and tissue microscopies will be involved in each action. This evidence is of an individual nature.

Significant differences in causation will exist between the factory worker actions and the tradesman actions. Medical and scientific knowledge concerning the two types of exposure is different. The tradesmen will have been exposed to a wider variety of asbestos products, and will need to prove which products caused their disabilities.

(6) The liability of each defendant in each action is predominantly an individual question. The variables will include the defendants' knowledge at a particular time of the health risks involved in exposure to asbestos, the adequacy of any product testing by the defendant manufacturers, the sufficiency of any warnings or directions for use of products, and the issue of assumption of risk by the plaintiffs. Other variables will include the materials used, the method of manufacture, and the period of production.

(7) Although a common aspect among these actions is the state of medical and scientific knowledge at a particular time regarding the health hazards posed by exposure to asbestos, this knowledge can be readily discerned from literature which is easily available in most medical libraries. The common need for this literature is therefore not a significant justification for transfer.

(8) Local issues will predominate in the discovery process. The medical, personnel, and product use records of each individual will be found locally. Liability in these actions will be based on state substantive law. As a result, transfer would not promote the parties' and witnesses' convenience regarding discovery.

(9) There is not a significant possibility of inconsistent or overlapping class action determinations since any certifiable class could include only those persons who were exposed to asbestos in a specific plant or in the service of a particular employer. The classes alleged to date are properly restricted, and do not overlap in any respect.

Although we recognize the existence of some common questions of fact among these actions, we find that transfer under Section 1407 would not necessarily serve the convenience of the parties and witnesses or promote the just and efficient conduct of the litigation. Accordingly, the order to show cause is vacated.

The virtually unanimous opposition of the parties to transfer, though a very persuasive factor in our decision to deny transfer in this litigation, is not by itself determinative of the question of transfer under Section 1407. In an appropriate situation, the Panel has the power to order transfer in multidistrict litigation even if all parties are opposed to transfer.

We are, however, persuaded by the parties' arguments in this particular litigation. On the basis of the record before us, the only questions of fact common to all actions relate to the state of scientific and medical knowledge at different points in time concerning the risks of exposure to asbestos. The pertinent literature on this subject is readily available. . . . Many factual questions unique to each action or to a group of actions already pending in a single district clearly predominate, and therefore transfer is unwarranted. . . . Furthermore, many of these actions already are well advanced. Some of the actions have been pending for up to four years, and trial dates or discovery cutoff dates have been set in several actions. Under these circumstances, transfer would not further the purposes of Section 1407. . . .

It is therefore ordered that the order to show cause regarding the actions listed on the following Schedule A be, and the same hereby is, vacated.

[Schedule A is omitted.]

IN RE ASBESTOS PRODUCTS LIABILITY LITIGATION (NO. VI)

771 F. Supp. 415 (J.P.M.L. 1991)

■ Judge NANGLE, Chairman, Delivered the Opinion of the Panel, in which Judges POLLAK, WOODWARD, MERHIGE and ENRIGHT joined.*

On January 17, 1991, the Panel issued an order to show cause why all pending federal district court actions not then in trial involving allegations of personal injury or wrongful death caused by asbestos should not be centralized in a single forum under 28 U.S.C. § 1407. Because of the difficulty in serving this order on the enormous number of parties in this docket, the Panel relied on the clerks of all district courts to serve the parties to actions in their respective districts. As a result, the parties to the 26,639 actions pending in 87 federal districts and listed on the following Schedule A are subject to the Panel's order.[2] More than 180 pleadings have been filed in response to the Panel's order, and a four hour hearing on the question of

---

* Judges Dillin and Pollack did not participate in the decision of this matter.

2. The Statistical Division of the Administrative Office of the United States Courts reports that as of March 31, 1991, nearly 31,000 actions were pending in federal districts. Based on Panel communications with courts throughout the country, the approximately 4,000 pending actions not embraced by the present order likely include actions that, as of January 17, 1991, were overlooked, in trial or already at least partially tried but not yet statistically closed because, *inter alia*, claims against one or more defendants were stayed under the Bankruptcy Code.

transfer was held on May 30, 1991 in New York City, at which time 37 counsel presented oral argument. In many instances the attorneys filing these pleadings or participating in oral argument were representing the views of large groups of parties.

Supporting transfer are plaintiffs in approximately 17,000 actions (including a core group of more than 14,000 plaintiffs represented by over 50 law firms) and 30 defendants (24 of which are named in more than 20,000 actions). Opposing transfer are plaintiffs in at least 5,200 actions and 454 defendants. The positions of those parties that have expressed a preference with respect to transferee district are varied. Many parties suggest centralization in what amounts to their home forum. The Eastern District of Pennsylvania is the district either expressly favored or not objected to in the greatest number of pleadings. The Eastern District of Texas, which is the choice of the aforementioned core group of 14,000 plaintiffs, is also the district that has generated the most opposition from defendants. Other suggested districts that go beyond the home forum approach are the District of the District of Columbia, the Eastern District of Louisiana, the Northern District of Ohio, and the Eastern District of New York. Some parties' forum recommendations are expressed in the forum of a suggested individual transferee judge or transferee judge structure.

On the basis of the papers filed and the hearing held, the Panel finds that the actions in this litigation involve common questions of fact relating to injuries or wrongful death allegedly caused by exposure to asbestos or asbestos containing products, and that centralization under § 1407 in the Eastern District of Pennsylvania will best serve the convenience of the parties and witnesses and promote the just and efficient conduct of this litigation.

DISCUSSION

Any discussion of § 1407 transfer in this docket must begin with the recognition that the question does not arise in a vacuum. Indeed, the impetus for the Panel's order to show cause was a November 21, 1990 letter signed by eight federal district judges responsible for many asbestos actions in their respective districts. These judges, citing the serious problem that asbestos personal injury litigation continues to be for the federal judiciary, requested that the Panel act on its own initiative to address the question of § 1407 transfer. Furthermore, as the title of this docket suggests, this is the sixth time that the Panel has considered transfer of asbestos litigation. On the five previous occasions (1977, 1980, 1985, 1986 and 1987) that the Panel considered the question, it denied transfer in each instance.

The Panel's constancy is not as dramatic as a mere recitation of the denials might suggest, however. The 1986 and 1987 dockets considered by the Panel involved only five and two actions, respectively. The 1985 Panel decision pertained not to personal injury/wrongful death asbestos actions but rather to property damage claims of school districts that incurred significant costs in removing asbestos products from school buildings. The denial in the 1980 Panel docket was based almost exclusively on the movants' failure to offer any distinctions that would warrant a disposition different from the Panel's first asbestos decision in 1977.

It is only in the 1977 decision, pertaining to 103 actions in nineteen districts, that the Panel offered any detailed analysis of its asbestos litigation reasoning with respect to asbestos personal injury/wrongful death actions....

Many of the parties presently opposing transfer in this docket rely on the facts and reasoning of the Panel's 1977 transfer decision. They insist that the situation that warranted denial then not only still prevails but has been magnified by the greatly increased number of actions and parties in federal asbestos personal injury/wrongful death litigation — more than 30,000 pending federal actions now, as opposed to the 103 actions subject to the Panel's 1977 decision. In our view, it is precisely this change that now leads us to conclude that centralization of all federal asbestos personal injury/wrongful death actions, in the words of 28 U.S.C. § 1407(a), "will be for the convenience of parties and witnesses and will promote the just and efficient conduct of such actions." In short, we are persuaded that this litigation has reached a magnitude, not contemplated in the record before us in 1977, that threatens the administration of justice and that requires a new, streamlined approach.

The Panel is not the first to reach such a conclusion. Just this past March 1991, the Judicial Conference Ad Hoc Committee on Asbestos Litigation ... stated as follows:

> The committee has struggled with the problems confronting the courts of this nation arising from death and disease attributable to airborne asbestos industrial materials and products. The committee has concluded that the situation has reached critical dimensions and is getting worse. What has been a frustrating problem is becoming a disaster of major proportions to both the victims and the producers of asbestos products, which the courts are ill-equipped to meet effectively.
> ...
> It is a tale of danger known in the 1930s, exposure inflicted upon millions of Americans in the 1940s and 1950s, injuries that began to take their toll in the 1960s, and a flood of lawsuits beginning in the 1970s. On the basis of past and current filing data, and because of a latency period that may last as long as 40 years for some asbestos related diseases, a continuing stream of claims can be expected. The final toll of asbestos related injuries is unknown. Predictions have been made of 200,000 asbestos disease deaths before the year 2000 and as many as 265,000 by the year 2015.
>
> The most objectionable aspects of asbestos litigation can be briefly summarized: dockets in both federal and state courts continue to grow; long delays are routine; trials are too long; the same issues are litigated over and over; transaction costs exceed the victims' recovery by nearly two to one; exhaustion of assets threatens and distorts the process; and future claimants may lose altogether.

Report of The Judicial Conference Ad Hoc Committee on Asbestos Litigation, 1-3 (1991) (footnote omitted).... The Committee pointed out that presently in the federal system nearly two new asbestos actions are being filed for every action terminated, and that at the current rate, there will be more than 48,000 actions pending in the federal courts at the end of three years. ...

Conclusions similar to those of the Judicial Conference Asbestos Committee have also been reached by judges actively involved in asbestos litigation. In perhaps the most recent comprehensive review of asbestos litigation, Judge Jack B. Weinstein (E.D.N.Y.) observed:

> The large number of asbestos lawsuits pending throughout the country threatens to overwhelm the courts and deprive all litigants, in asbestos suits as well as other civil cases, of meaningful resolution of their claims. ...
>
> The heyday of individual adjudication of asbestos mass tort lawsuits has long passed.... The reasons are obvious: the complexity of asbestos cases makes them expensive to litigate; costs are exacerbated when each individual has to prove his or her claim *de novo*; high transaction costs reduce the recovery available to successful plaintiffs; and the sheer number of asbestos cases pending nationwide threatens to deny justice and compensation to many deserving claimants if each claim is handled individually. The backlog is eroding a fundamental aspiration of our judicial system to provide equality of treatment for similarly situated persons. ...
>
> Overhanging this massive failure of the present system is the reality that there is not enough available from traditional defendants to pay for current and future claims. Even the most conservative estimates of future claims, if realistically estimated on the books of many present defendants, would lead to a declaration of insolvency — as in the case of some dozen manufacturers already in bankruptcy. ...

In re Johns-Manville Corporation, et al., No. 90-3973, slip op. at 61-63, 1991 WL 86304 (E.D.N.Y. May 16, 1991).

Given the dimensions of the perceived problem in federal asbestos litigation, it is not surprising that no ready solution has emerged. The Judicial Conference Asbestos Committee concluded that the only true solution lies in Congressional legislation. Nevertheless, it stressed that "at the same time, or failing congressional action, the federal judiciary must itself act now to achieve the best performance possible from system under current law." The Committee also noted that the Panel's order to show cause was pending at the time of the issuance of the Committee's report. The Committee observed that "this committee, by its recommendations, does not intend to affect or restrict in any way the actions of the Panel under 28 U.S.C. § 1407 or reduce the Panel's jurisdiction or authority." ...[5]

---

[5] The Committee also observed that, in the interest of centralizing asbestos claims to the greatest extent possible, the Panel's authority "could be expanded to allow the Panel to transfer actions for trial as well as for pretrial proceedings."

It is against this backdrop that the Panel's decision and role in this litigation must be understood. First of all, our decision to order transfer is not unmindful of the fact that the impact of asbestos litigation varies from district to district, and that in some courts asbestos personal injury actions are being resolved in a fashion indistinguishable from other civil actions. It is not surprising, therefore, that parties and courts involved in such actions might urge that inclusion of their actions in multidistrict proceedings is inappropriate. The Panel, however, must weigh the interests of all the plaintiffs and all the defendants, and must consider multiple litigation as a whole in the light of the purposes of the law. . . . It is this perspective that leads us to conclude that centralization in a single district of all pending federal personal injury and wrongful death asbestos actions is necessary.

Much of the argument presented to the Panel in response to its order to show cause is devoted to parties' differing (and often inconsistent) visions of § 1407 proceedings: 1) some plaintiffs see centralized pretrial proceedings as a vehicle leading to a single national class action trial or other types of consolidated trials on product defect, state of the art and punitive damages, while many defendants staunchly oppose such a trial, favor a reverse bifurcation procedure where actual damages and individual causation are tried before liability, and hope to use § 1407 proceedings to effect the severance of claims for punitive damages through a transferee court order directing that, upon the return of any case to its transferor district, such claims not be tried until claims for compensatory damages have been resolved in all federal cases; 2) some parties hope to persuade the transferee court to establish case deferral programs for plaintiffs who are not critically ill, or who have been exposed to asbestos but do not presently show any signs of impairment (i.e., pleural registries), while many plaintiffs assert that such procedures are unfair or unconstitutional; 3) in response to the pressing concern about transaction costs in this litigation, some defendants consider § 1407 transfer necessary in order to provide a single federal forum in which limits on plaintiffs' contingent fees can be addressed, while some plaintiffs maintain that transfer is necessary to prevent the depletion of defendants' limited insurance coverage by defense costs incurred in multiple districts; 4) some plaintiffs and defendants urge that transfer is necessary in order to develop through discovery proceedings nationwide product data bases on all asbestos products and corporate histories of all asbestos defendants, while other plaintiffs and defendants contend that such efforts would be of no utility and are simply designed to shift liability; 5) some plaintiffs are suggesting that defendants' finances are so fragile as to require limited fund class action determinations pursuant to Fed.R.Civ.P. 23(b)(1)(B), while other plaintiffs resist any attempt to restrict their right to pursue punitive damages; 6) some parties anticipate that a single transferee court would speed up case disposition and purge meritless claims, while others expect a system of spacing out claims so as not to overwhelm currently solvent defendants' cash flow and drive them into bankruptcy; and 7) some parties contend that single transferee court is necessary for the purpose of exploring the opportunities for global settlements or alternative dispute resolution mechanisms, while other parties assert that such hopes are utopian at best as long as i) more than twice as many asbestos cases remain pending in state courts as in federal courts, and ii) currently stayed claims against bankrupt defendants cannot be addressed by the transferee court.[6]

We enumerate these issues not for the purpose, as some parties seemingly misunderstand, of passing on their merits. The language of the first sentence of paragraph (b) of § 1407 is quite clear about the proper forum for resolution of such issues — "coordinated or consolidated pretrial proceedings shall be conducted by a judge or judges to whom such actions are assigned" by the Panel. The Panel has neither the power nor the disposition to direct the transferee court in the exercise of its powers and discretion in pretrial proceedings. In re Plumbing Fixture Cases, 298 F. Supp. 484, 489 (J.P.M.L. 1968).

We cite these issues only as illustrations of 1) the types of pretrial matters that need to be addressed by a single transferee court in order to avoid duplication of effort (with concomitant unnecessary expenses) by the parties and witnesses, their counsel, and the judiciary, and in order to prevent inconsistent decisions; and 2) why, at least initially, all pending federal personal injury or wrongful death asbestos actions not yet in trial must be included in § 1407 proceedings. For example, if, as some courts, parties and commentators have suggested, there are insufficient funds to fairly compensate all deserving claimants, this should be determined before plaintiffs in lightly impacted districts go to trial and secure recoveries (often including punitive damages) at the possible expense of deserving plaintiffs

---

6. There appears to be some confusion among the parties concerning the interaction of the provisions of the Bankruptcy Code and § 1407. Transfer under § 1407 of an action containing claims against a defendant in bankruptcy has no effect on the automatic stay provisions of the Bankruptcy Code (11 U.S.C. § 362). Claims that have been stayed in the transferor court remain stayed in the transferee court. The Panel, however, has never considered the pendency of such stayed claims in an action to be an impediment to transfer of the action. 28 U.S.C. § 1407(a) authorizes the Panel to transfer only "civil actions" and not claims. The complex multidistrict litigations before the Panel have often included actions brought against multiple defendants, the claims against one or more of which have been stayed as a result of bankruptcy. To have allowed the pendency of claims against a single bankrupt defendant to preclude the transfer of actions containing claims actively being litigated against common nonbankrupt defendants would have frustrated the essential purpose of § 1407.

Some parties have urged the Panel to treat the bankruptcy reorganizations themselves as "civil actions" appropriate for transfer under § 1407 to the transferee district. The reorganization proceedings are not subject to our order to show cause, and this question is therefore not ripe for a Panel decision. We have not addressed this question before and would be reluctant to do so until: 1) the transferee court determines that other alternatives, such as coordination with the concerned bankruptcy courts, are insufficient to accomplish the goals of § 1407; and 2) other suggested means of transferring the bankruptcy reorganizations or relevant portions thereof have been fully explored by the transferee court and the concerned bankruptcy courts.

Finally, we note that to the extent that state court actions and bankruptcy proceedings are excluded from the ambit of the Panel's transfer decision, transfer will nonetheless have the salutary effect of creating one federal court with which such proceedings can be coordinated, to the extent deemed desirable by the concerned courts. Indeed, state court judges have communicated to the Panel that coordination among state courts and a single transferee court for the federal actions is an objective worthy of pursuit.

litigating in districts where speedy trial dates have not been available. Similarly, if there are economies to be achieved with respect to remaining national discovery, pretrial rulings or efforts at settlement, these should be secured before claims against distinct types or groups of defendants are separated out of the litigation. Finally, because many of the arguments of parties seeking exclusion from transfer are intertwined with the merits of their claims or defenses and affect the overall management of this litigation, we are unwilling, on the basis of the record presently before us, to carve out exceptions to transfer. We prefer instead to give the transferee court the opportunity to conduct a substantive review of such contentions and how they affect the whole proceedings.

It may well be that on further refinement of the issues and close scrutiny by the transferee court, some claims or actions can be remanded in advance of the other actions in the transferee district. Should the transferee court deem remand of any claims or actions appropriate, the transferee court can communicate this to the Panel, and the Panel will accomplish remand with a minimum of delay. See Rule 14, R.P.J.P.M.L., 120 F.R.D. 251, 259-61 (1988).[8] We add that for those parties urging that resolution of this litigation lies primarily in the setting of firm, credible trial dates, § 1407 transfer may serve as a mechanism enabling the transferee court to develop a nationwide roster of senior district and other judges available to follow actions remanded back to heavily impacted districts, for trials in advance of when such districts' overburdened judges may have otherwise been able to schedule them.

We remain sensitive to the concerns of some parties that § 1407 transfer will be burdensome or inconvenient. We note that since § 1407 transfer is primarily for pretrial, there is usually no need for the parties and witnesses to travel to the transferee district for depositions or otherwise. . . . Furthermore, the judicious use of liaison counsel, lead counsel and steering committees will eliminate the need for most counsel ever to travel to the transferee district. . . . And it is most logical to assume that prudent counsel will combine their forces and apportion their workload in order to streamline the efforts of the parties and witnesses, their counsel, and the judiciary, thereby effectuating an overall savings of cost and a reduction of inconvenience to all concerned. . . . Hopefully, combining such practices with a uniform case management approach will, in fact, lead to sizeable reductions in transaction costs (and especially in attorneys' fees).

In a docket of this size and scope, no district emerges as the clear nexus where centralized pretrial proceedings should be conducted. The Panel has decided to centralize this litigation in the Eastern District of Pennsylvania before Judge Charles R. Weiner. We note that: 1) more asbestos personal injury or wrongful death actions are pending in that district than any other; 2) the court there has extensive experience in complex litigation in general and asbestos litigation in particular; and 3) the court has graciously

---

8. Those parties who may seek early remand of their actions or claims are reminded of i) Panel Rule 14(d)'s expression of the Panel's reluctance to order remand absent a suggestion of remand from the transferee judge, and ii) the special affidavit requirement of that Rule. . . .

expressed its willingness to assume the responsibility for this massive undertaking. Furthermore, in the person of Judge Weiner the Panel finds a judge thoroughly familiar with the issues in asbestos litigation, a track record of accomplishment and successful innovation,[10] and, on the basis of pleadings before the Panel in which an opinion was expressed, a selection to which the majority of responding plaintiffs and defendants either expressly agree or are not opposed.

Many parties have suggested that the dynamics of this litigation make it impractical, if not impossible, for one single judge to discharge the responsibilities of transferee judge, while other parties have emphasized that more than a single transferee judge would dilute the judicial control needed to effectively manage the litigation. Varying suggestions have been made that the Panel appoint additional transferee judges to handle specific issues (*e.g.*, class or limited fund determinations, discovery, settlement, claims administration, etc.), to deal with separate types of claims or defendants (*e.g.*, maritime asbestos actions, railroad worker actions, friction materials actions, tire workers actions, etc.), or to divide the litigation along regional or circuit lines (helping to insure uniformity of decisions within each circuit pertaining, inter alia, to state law questions involved in the actions). Each of these suggestions has merit, as long as one judge has the opportunity to maintain overall control.

Section 1407(b) contemplates that multidistrict litigation may be conducted by "a judge or judges." It further expressly provides that "upon request of the panel, a circuit judge or a district judge may be designated and assigned temporarily for service in the transferee district by the Chief Justice of the United States of the United States or the chief judge of the circuit, as may be required, in accordance with the provisions of chapter 13 of this title." And the Panel has long expressed its willingness to appoint additional transferee judges in litigants whose size and complexity make it difficulty for the original transferee judge to handle § 1407 proceedings alone. . . . We emphasize our intention to do everything within our power to provide such assistance in this docket. Before making any specific appointments, however, we deem it advisable to allow the transferee judge

---

10. The Asbestos Committee Report, *supra*, noted:

> Judge Charles Weiner, the asbestos case manager in the Eastern District of Pennsylvania, is able to call upon over 20 active and senior judges in the district to handle asbestos cases on a priority basis. In addition to mandating standard, abbreviated pleadings, such as complaint, answer, and discovery requests, Judge Weiner meets regularly with counsel and handles on a regular basis all motions and discovery requests. Applying these sophisticated case management techniques, Judge Weiner and his colleagues have disposed of more than 2,000 cases through 1990. . . .

Our reference to these passages is not meant to be an endorsement of any pretrial techniques to the exclusion of others, and in no way should be viewed as limiting Judge Weiner in his assessment of the appropriate tools to be used now that all federal personal injury/wrongful death asbestos actions will be before him for pretrial proceedings. We do consider such passages to be helpful, however, in allaying the fears of parties not familiar with Judge Weiner that § 1407 transfer will result in their actions entering some black hole, never to be seen again.

to make his own assessment of the needs of this docket and communicate his preferences to us.

The Panel is under no illusion that centralization will, of itself, markedly relieve the critical asbestos situation. It offers no panacea. Only through the combined and determined efforts of the transferee judge and his judicial colleagues, of the many attorneys involved in asbestos matters, and of the parties, can true progress be made toward solving the "asbestos mess." This order does offer a great opportunity to all participants who sincerely wish to resolve these asbestos matters fairly and with as little unnecessary expense as possible.

Finally, in light of the Panel's disposition in this docket, it is necessary to remind parties and counsel of their continuing responsibility with respect to transfer of potential tag-along actions, including those either inadvertently overlooked at the time of the January 17, 1991 filing of the Panel's order to show cause or filed subsequent to the issuance of the Panel's order to show cause. We note that Panel Rule 13(e) provides as follows:

> Any party or counsel in actions previously transferred under Section 1407 or under consideration by the Panel for transfer under Section 1407 shall notify the Clerk of the Panel of any potential "tag-along actions" in which that party is also named or in which that counsel appears.

It is therefore ordered that, pursuant to 28 U.S.C. § 1407, the actions listed on the following Schedule A that are pending as of the date of this order, are not in trial, and are pending outside the Eastern District of Pennsylvania, be, and the same hereby are, transferred to the Eastern District of Pennsylvania and, with the consent of that court, assigned to the Honorable Charles R. Weiner for coordinated or consolidated pretrial proceedings with the actions on Schedule A that remain pending in that district and are not in trial.

[Schedule A is omitted.]

Notes and Questions

1. Between its inception and this writing, the Judicial Panel on Multidistrict Litigation has considered the § 1407 consolidation of slightly more than 1,200 sets of related proceedings (or, on average, about 40 per year). The *Asbestos Products* consolidation of 26,000 cases (which has since blossomed to more than 62,000 cases, see In re Asbestos Products Liability Litigation (No. VI), 1996 WL 539589 (E.D. Pa.)) was by far the largest number of individual actions actually transferred into one consolidated proceeding. The fewest number of individual actions was two. In re CBS Licensing Antitrust Litigation, 328 F. Supp. 511 (J.P.M.L. 1971).

For the most part, the Panel's decisions are unpublished. They are also notoriously short, rarely running for more than two to three pages. Usually the opinions recite the facts of the case; the positions of the parties; conclusory and formulaic statements that "the actions in this litigation involve common questions of fact, and that centralization under Section 1407 . . . will best serve the convenience of the parties and witnesses and promote the just and efficient conduct of this litigation," see In re Phonometrics, Inc., Electronic Long Distance Call Cost Computer and Recorder Patent Litigation, 1997 WL 83673 (J.P.M.L.); and a brief discussion of the appropriate forum to which the case should be transferred. The first and last parts of a Panel opinion are typically the longest. On the question of whether the statutory criteria for transfer have been met, the *East of the Rockies* concurrence and the two *Asbestos Products* decisions are certainly among the most detailed and thoughtful. As a contrast to these cases, consider the following order of the Panel, which is, in comparison to most of its opinions, contains a "lengthy" discussion of the appropriateness of consolidation under the statute:

> On the basis of the papers filed and the hearing held, the Panel finds that the actions in this litigation involve common questions of fact and that centralization under Section 1407 in the Eastern District of Pennsylvania will serve the convenience of the parties and witnesses and promote the just and efficient conduct of this litigation. Common factual questions arise because the more than 200 federal court actions in this litigation focus on alleged defects in three prescription drugs — known by the chemical names fenfluramine, dexfenfluramine and phentermine — used in the treatment of obesity. In addition, approximately half of those actions are brought on behalf of alleged nationwide or statewide classes of users of these diet drugs. Centralization under Section 1407 is thus necessary in order to eliminate duplicative discovery, prevent inconsistent or repetitive pretrial rulings (especially with respect to class certification), and conserve the resources of the parties, their counsel and the judiciary.
>
> Opponents of transfer principally argue that non-common questions of fact relating to individual causation and damages will predominate in this litigation. We do not agree. On the basis of the record now before us, the core issues presented in the litigation involve the causal connection between use of the three diet drugs (singly or in combination) and the alleged incidence of serious side effects such as valvular heart disease and primary pulmonary hypertension. Moreover, the sheer size of the litigation, coupled with its rapid growth rate at the present time, serve to underscore the economies of scale that centralized pretrial management of the federal court actions will provide.

In re Diet Drugs (Phentermine, Fenfluramine, Dexfenfluramine) Products Liability Litigation, 990 F. Supp. 834, 835-36 (J.P.M.L. 1998).

2. Given the terse nature of the Panel's decisions, it is not easy to analyze the exact circumstances under which transfer will occur. Let us start, however, with the requirement of "common questions of fact." The Panel has been criticized for finding common questions of fact too readily. See Blake M. Rhodes, Comment, *The Judicial Panel on Multidistrict Litigation: Time for Rethinking*, 140 U. Pa. L. Rev. 711 (1991). Whether or not that criticism is fair, the Panel has made it clear that common questions of law — as opposed to common questions of fact — are not a ground for transfer, although the common questions of fact are not always significant in relation to the common questions of law. See In re Air Fare Litigation, 322 F. Supp. 1013 (J.P.M.L. 1971).

An interesting issue, on which the Panel has taken a somewhat wavering position, is whether common questions of fact must predominate over individual questions. Suppose, for instance, that ten entirely unrelated personal injury cases were filed in different courts, and the only common issue of fact between them was the discount rate to apply to damage calculations. Certainly, there would be insufficient commonality to justify transfer. But how much commonality among actions is required? Must the common questions predominate? In *Diet Drugs, supra,* note how the Panel rejects the argument that common questions failed to predominate, yet it does not hold that such questions must predominate. Likewise, in the first *Asbestos Products* decision, the Panel repeatedly points out that individual issues predominate, but do not squarely make predomination a requirement. The clearest statement that there was a predomination requirement was In re Asbestos School Products Liability Litigation, 606 F. Supp. 713, 714 (J.P.M.L. 1985), in which the Panel declined to order transfer with this observation: "Although we recognize that the actions in this litigation involve some common questions of fact, we are not persuaded that these common questions of fact will predominate over individual questions of fact present in each action." See also In re Westinghouse Electric Corp. Uranium Contract Litigation, 436 F. Supp. 990, 996 (J.P.M.L. 1977) (Panel refused to order transfer when it was "persuaded that any common factual issues do not predominate"). On the other hand, in *Asbestos Products (No. VI),* in which the Panel finally ordered consolidation, the common questions were no more predominant than they had been in the first *Asbestos Litigation* or in *Asbestos School Litigation,* yet the Panel ordered transfer.

Perhaps the most balanced — and accurate — way to think about the issue is to see commonality on a sliding scale: As more convenience and fairness is achieved through transfer, less commonality is required; as less convenience and fairness is achieved, more commonality is required. See In re Westinghouse Electric Corp. Uranium Contracts Litigation, 405 F. Supp. 316, 319 (J.P.M.L. 1975) ("we are persuaded that sufficient commonality of factual issues exists to warrant transfer and that the most just and efficient conduct of these actions can best be achieved through centralized management"); cf. In re Air Crash off Long Island, New York, on July 17, 1996, 965 F. Supp. 5, 8 (S.D.N.Y. 1997) ("a practical application of the policies behind and limitations of consolidated multidistrict litigation should minimize the difficulty of resolving" issue of commonality).

Turning then to the second and third criteria — convenience to parties and witnesses — the Panel does not often discuss the convenience issues in detail. For instance, in *Asbestos Products (No. VI),* does the Panel ever describe the conveniences that consolidation would achieve? As the excerpt from *Diet Drugs* shows, convenience factors that the Panel most often mentions in its formulaic transfer orders are the elimination of duplicative litigation, the reduction of discovery costs, and the conservation of the parties' resources. One of the striking features about these assertions is that the Panel never engages in factfinding to determine whether the convenience factors in fact exist; indeed, little to no discovery of any kind is ever attempted in the proceedings before the Panel. Moreover, the Panel is quite clear that inconvenience to individual litigants is irrelevant as long as, on balance, more convenience is achieved from consolidation. See, *e.g.,* In re West of the Rockies Concrete Pipe Antitrust Cases, 303 F. Supp. 507, 509 (J.P.M.L. 1969) (burdens to local defendants of litigating in distant forum "will be offset by the savings from and convenience of coordinated or consolidated pretrial proceedings directed by the transferee judge"). Does the combination of these two facts essentially let the Panel make unsupportable assertions about convenience? See Wilson W. Herndon & Ernest R. Higginbotham, *Complex Multidistrict Litigation — An Overview of 28 U.S.C.A. § 1407,* 31 Baylor L. Rev. 33, 43 (1979) ("the Panel has largely eliminated this guideline as a determinative standard"). Does the focus on overall efficiency mean that, in most cases, defendants (who often have the most to save from consolidated litigation) will receive the lion's share of the benefit of multidistricting?

If the first requirement of § 1407 is loose and the second and third unhelpful, then the critical question would seem to be the last — "the just and efficient conduct of such actions." Again, *Diet Drug* describes the kinds of factors that the Panel regards as relevant to this inquiry: the prevention of inconsistent rulings, the desire to resolve the issue of class certification in a single proceeding, and the conservation of judicial resources. See Herndon & Higginbotham, *supra*, at 45 (listing 6 factors that boil down into these three categories). Another fairness factor that the Panel frequently mentions is the parties' consent to transfer; as the first *Asbestos Products* case says, consent is not determinative, but it is often influential, especially when all parties consent to transfer.

Look again at Judge Weigel's richer effort to describe the types of factors that should enter the "fair and efficient" equation. Isn't he correct that a possible § 1407 transfer might often be unfair and inefficient? Should the Panel use his list of factors to determine whether a particular transfer is in fact fair and efficient? The Panel does not engage in factfinding to determine whether transfer will, in the context of a particular case, create more inefficiencies than efficiency. Is it possible to test in an empirical way whether a transfer is fair? What factors should enter into the fairness inquiry? Certainly the prevention of inconsistent rulings and consent are not the only relevant "fairness" factors, yet they are often the only ones mentioned in a transfer order. What about the plaintiffs' interest in litigating in their own forum? What about the possibility that the litigation will slow down to a snail's pace? What about the possibility that consolidated litigation will skew the outcome of individual cases in relation to separate litigation?

Look again at the two *Asbestos Products* opinions. Certainly, in terms of the fair and efficient adjudication of the controversy, it made more sense to consolidate the cases early in the litigative day. By 1991, the script for asbestos trials had essentially been written, and the important legal issues had been resolved. Very little new discovery, and very few new pretrial motions, needed to be attempted. Was transfer "for pretrial proceedings" necessary? One factual difference between the first and sixth *Asbestos Products* decisions was that, by 1991, many of the parties now consented to transfer. Does that fact alone make the multidistrict proceeding fair and efficient? A second factual difference was that, by 1991, several asbestos manufacturers had declared bankruptcy, and it was obvious that there were insufficient assets to meet all the possible claims that could be asserted against the defendants. Should the fact of lawyer dysfunction enter the Panel's equation? Was the Panel really trying to consolidate the cases for pretrial proceedings, or merely aggregating them in the hope that some global solution could be achieved? What about the state asbestos cases and the cases of those not yet injured by asbestos — wouldn't the aggregation and resolution of the pending federal cases potentially leave these claimants worse off? Should the Panel aggregate some cases when doing so does not eliminate the problem of lawyer dysfunction?

3. In thinking about these last questions, you might be interested to know that, after consolidation of the asbestos cases, there have been virtually no trials of asbestos cases in the federal system. As of 1996, the multidistrict proceeding had resulted in 40,000 cases being closed (often through settlement); only 22,000

remained open. The number of asbestos cases disposed of each year finally exceeded the number of new federal asbestos filings per year. The most seriously injured plaintiffs were being processed and resolved first. *Asbestos Products*, 1996 WL 539589. In addition, two class actions designed to settle the cases of hundreds of thousands of victims of asbestos exposure arose out of the multidistrict proceedings, although one subsequently fell apart on appeal and, as of this writing, the other is still pending on appeal. (We study both settlements at pp. 658-89, *infra*.) Finally, Judge Weiner has declined to request the Panel to remand unresolved actions for trial, even when the plaintiffs' lawyer represented that he would not settle the cases. Judge Weiner's stated reason was that the MDL proceedings had helped plaintiffs make "great strides toward settlement of their cases." He also noted that the loss of any defendant to bankruptcy (which might occur if trials commenced again) would hurt most other plaintiffs. *Asbestos Products*, 1996 WL 539589.

Do these facts suggest that the decision to multidistrict the asbestos litigation was the correct one? Does it concern you that one judge has the power and discretion to determine the fate of thousands of cases — including the power to hold up trial in the forum of their choice? Does Judge Weiner's observation about the deleterious effect that separate proceedings would have other cases in the queue assuage that concern?

4. Would a multidistrict approach in a case like *Asbestos Products (No. VI)* have been necessary if we had an effective system of preclusion? If we had an effective system of involuntary joinder of parties? If a preclusion or involuntary joinder system could be created for complex cases, is the multidistrict transfer an adequate response to the problem of complicated cases? If preclusion and joinder doctrines are not created to overcome the problem of lawyer dysfunction, should the Panel explicitly recognize that the problem of lawyer dysfunction is a reason to order multidistrict consolidation? On the other hand, unless all of the cases creating dysfunction have already been filed in the federal system, will multidistrict transfer really overcome the problem of lawyer dysfunction?

5. Perhaps we are being too hard on the multidistrict proceeding. As the history of the multidistricted asbestos cases shows, maybe the relevant question is not whether the multidistrict transfer can itself overcome dysfunction, but whether it can be the catalyst for other procedures that will do so. Once the cases are consolidated, for instance, it may be possible to use other devices (such as class actions, interpleader, or collateral estoppel) to take care of what multidistrict consolidation cannot. Was this the real reason that the Panel agreed to consolidate the asbestos cases in 1991?

6. One of the things that the Panel presumes when it orders consolidation is that it is possible to manage in a single proceeding the many individual actions involved. In a case arising out of a single event (such as an airplane crash), the management difficulties of a single case and of a consolidated proceeding are pretty much the same, at least on the question of liability. See In re Air Crash Disaster at Detroit Metropolitan Airport on August 16, 1987, 737 F. Supp. 391, 395 (E.D. Mich. 1989) (suggesting that remand to transferor forums for damage determinations would be appropriate after conclusion of common determination of liability in air crash). The efficiency of a single handling of such liability issues is evident. In dispersed-event cases (like asbestos exposure), however, the aggregation of related claims often creates new case management difficulties, even on the liability issue. We examine possible pretrial case management options that the transferee court can employ in Part Two of the book. Thus, a

§ 1407 transfer does not merely aggregate cases in a single venue; it also often ushers the case into a different procedural world. Moreover, as we will see, the outcomes of cases might well hinge on the management techniques that the court chooses. After studying these techniques and their difficulties, you might wish to revisit the question whether § 1407 transfers do indeed lead to the fair and efficient resolution of consolidated actions.

7. Often the parties do not contest the multidistrict transfer, but they do contest vigorously the forum to which the case should be transferred. You see a bit of that angling in *Asbestos Products (No. VI)*, in which there were several well-known judges (such as Judges Lambros, Parker, Weiner, and Weinstein) who had significant experience in asbestos or other mass tort litigation, who would have gladly taken on the assignment, and who were championed by one or more groups of litigants. Each of these judges, however, had different attitudes about the litigation, and would likely have used different case management techniques to resolve the cases. Is it appropriate to let so much ride on the choice of judge? Should the transferee judge's discretion about how to manage the case be guided by specific rules? Cf. In re Data General Corp. Antitrust Litigation, 510 F. Supp. 1220, 1226-27 (J.P.M.L. 1979) ("The Panel has neither the statutory authority nor the inclination to review decisions of . . . transferee courts.").

In choosing the transferee judge, the Panel is not constrained by the holding of Hoffman v. Blaski, 363 U.S. 335 (1960) (p. 489, *supra*), that § 1404 transfers can be made only to venues in which the case could originally have been brought. See In re FMC Corp. Patent Litigation, 422 F. Supp. 1163 (J.P.M.L. 1976). A number of factors influence the Panel's decision, including the experience of the potential transferee judges, the centrality of a forum and its convenience for the parties, the desires of the parties, the burden on the dockets of potential transferee forums, and the number of cases pending in various forums. The transferee judge need not have any multidistrict cases pending on her docket. See Charles A. Wright et al., Federal Practice & Procedure § 3864 (1986).

Often a single forum emerges as the clear choice, but not always. One of the more interesting forum selections that the Panel has made in recent years arose in the *Silicone Gel Breast Implants Products Liability Litigation*. The plaintiffs' bar in the case was divided between "class action" lawyers who wanted to achieve an early, global resolution of the case and "individual plaintiff" lawyers who wanted to conduct consolidated discovery and then return the cases for individual damage suits. Prior to the Panel's decision to consolidate, Judge Rubin of the Southern District of Ohio had already certified a class action, which was exactly what the "individual plaintiff" lawyers feared. They preferred Judges Henderson or Patel of the Northen District of California or Judge Kelly of the District of Kansas. The defendants were nervous about the California forum because two large verdicts had been entered against them in California. Instead, the Panel chose Judge Pointer, who had no breast implant cases pending before him:

> Selection of the transferee court and judge for this litigation has been a challenging task. The parties' arguments in their briefs and at the Panel hearing in this matter have focused primarily on the relative merits of the suggested California and Ohio forums. Proponents of the California forum stress that i) both Judge Henderson and Judge Patel have tried breast implant actions and are thus very familiar with the issues raised in this docket, ii) several implant manufacturers . . . have their principal places of business in California, and iii) California is presumptively the state with the largest number of actual and potential claimants in the breast implant

litigation. Meanwhile, proponents of the Ohio forum emphasize Judge Rubin's familiarity with the litigation, gained by presiding over the consolidated breast implant action . . . in his district since January 1992. During that time, Judge Rubin has conditionally certified a nationwide, opt-out class of breast implant recipients; established a document depository; appointed a Plaintiffs' Lead Counsel Committee consisting of seven members; scheduled trial on common issues for June 1993; and initiated the dissemination of notice to class members.

We observe that either the Northern District of California or the Southern District of Ohio could be an appropriate forum for this docket and certainly the judges referred to are experienced and well-qualified to handle this litigation. We are troubled, however, by the volume and tone of the negative arguments with which opposing counsel have sought to denigrate each other's forum choices, litigation strategies and underlying motives. . . .

Essentially, these arguments are fueled by an acrimonious dispute among counsel, relating to control of the litigation as well as to how it should proceed (class versus individual treatment). It is neither our function nor our inclination to take sides in this dispute. But we are indeed persuaded that the level of acrimony has caused the parties and counsel on each side to harbor a perception that they would be unfairly affected by selection of any of the suggested forums. This perception of "unfairness" is unwarranted, because this Panel believes that all of the federal judges involved in these 78 actions would conduct these proceedings in a fair and impartial manner. Nevertheless, we recognize that in a mega-tort docket of this nature, involving claimants who may be experiencing litigation for the first time, such a perception could become a dark cloud over these proceedings and threaten their just and efficient conduct.

In light of these considerations, we have determined to look beyond the preferences of the parties in our search for a transferee judge with the ability and temperament to steer this complex litigation on a steady course that will be sensitive to the concerns of all parties. Because no single location stands out as the geographic focal point for this nationwide docket, the scope of our search embraced the universe of federal district judges. By selecting Chief Judge Pointer, a former member of our Panel, Chairman of the Board of Editors of the Manual for Complex Litigation, Chairman of the Judicial Conference's Advisory Committee on Civil Rules, and an experienced multidistrict transferee judge, we are confident that we are entrusting this important and challenging assignment to a distinguished jurist.

In re Silicone Gel Breast Implants Products Liability Litigation, 793 F. Supp. 1098, 1100-01 (J.P.M.L. 1992). The *Breast Implants* litigation eventually involved about 450,000 claimants. Should the fate of so many persons hang in the balance of the decision about a transferee judge? Even the mighty Chancellors (see pp. 36-47, *supra*) did not have this much influence and discretion over this many cases.

8. The moving party has the burden of proving that a § 1407 consolidation is appropriate. In re Chiropractic Antitrust Litigation, 483 F. Supp. 811 (J.P.M.L. 1980). There is no appellate review of the Panel's orders; review may be had only by extraordinary writ in the circuit encompassing the place in which the Panel's hearing on a transfer order takes place. 28 U.S.C. § 1407(e). Predictably, such writs are nearly impossible to obtain. See In re Ivy, 901 F.2d 7 (2d Cir. 1990).

9. Until a case is transferred by the Panel, the transferor court can continue to handle the case. It is common, however, for the transferor court to stay its hand until the Panel makes its decision. See Good v. Prudential Insurance Co. of America, — F. Supp. —, 1998 WL 244597 (N.D. Cal.).

10. The multidistrict statute authorizes the Panel to establish rules of procedure for its operation. 28 U.S.C. § 1407(f). The Panel has established 25 rules, the most significant of which (for our purposes) are Rules 11-14, which govern the issuance of show cause orders to determine if cases should be consolidated, the handling of tag-along actions, and the procedures for termination of the multidistrict proceeding and remand to the transferor forums.

11. The Panel will rarely order remand until the transferee judge enters a suggestion that remand is appropriate. *Data General*, 510 F. Supp. at 1226. After a case is remanded to the transferor forum, the rulings of the transferee court travel with the case, and any appeals of the transferee court's rulings are taken to the transferor court's circuit. See Wright et al., *supra*, §§ 3862, 3866-67; but see In re Food Lion, Inc., Fair Labor Standards Act "Effective Scheduling" Litigation, 73 F.3d 528 (4th Cir. 1996) (ordering Panel to transfer case back to transferee forum to permit appeal of transferee court's ruling in transferee circuit); cf. In the Matter of Rhone-Poulenc Rorer Pharmaceuticals, Inc., 138 F.3d 695 (7th Cir. 1998) (refusing to issue mandamus against transferee judge's order limiting expert witnesses in trials in transferor forums). As with the transferee judge, the Panel "is neither empowered nor inclined to direct, or to suggest to, a transferor judge how he or she should conduct further proceedings in actions after remand." In re A.H. Robins Co. "Dalkon Shield" IUD Products Liability Litigation, 453 F. Supp. 108, 110 (J.P.M.L. 1978).

Most cases, however, are never remanded to the transferor forum; they are resolved (whether by settlement, dispositive motion, or trial) in the transferee forum. The authority of the transferee court to settle a case or to decide dispositive motions is beyond cavil. See In re "Agent Orange" Product Liability Litigation, 996 F.2d 1425 (2d Cir. 1993), cert. denied, 510 U.S. 1140 (1994). Since a § 1407 transfer is for pretrial purposes only, you might wonder how the transferee court could try the case. The device employed by transferee courts was to transfer the cases to itself for all purposes under § 1404. (Under *Hoffman v. Blaski*, this self-transfer move worked only when the transferee court was a forum in which the case could have originally been brought.) As we see in the next case, however, the transferee court may no longer enjoy the power to self-transfer. After examining this case, we conclude our look at the benefits and drawbacks of multidistrict transfer.

LEXECON INC. v. MILBERG WEISS BERSHAD HYNES & LERACH

— U.S. —, 118 S.Ct. 956 (1998)

■ JUSTICE SOUTER delivered the opinion of the Court.[*]

28 U.S.C. § 1407(a) authorizes the Judicial Panel on Multidistrict Litigation to transfer civil actions with common issues of fact "to any district

---

[*] JUSTICE SCALIA joins this opinion, except as to Part II-C.

for coordinated or consolidated pretrial proceedings," but imposes a duty on the Panel to remand any such action to the original district "at or before the conclusion of such pretrial proceedings." The issue here is whether a district court conducting such "pretrial proceedings" may invoke § 1404(a) to assign a transferred case to itself for trial. We hold it has no such authority.

I

In 1992, petitioners, Lexecon Inc., a law and economics consulting firm, and one of its principals (collectively, Lexecon), brought this diversity action in the Northern District of Illinois against respondents, the law firms of Milberg Weiss Bershad Hynes & Lerach (Milberg) and Cotchett, Illston & Pitre (Cotchett), claiming malicious prosecution, abuse of process, tortious interference, commercial disparagement and defamation. The suit arose out of the firms' conduct as counsel in a prior class action brought against Charles Keating and the American Continental Corporation for violations of the securities and racketeering laws. Lexecon also was a defendant, charged with giving federal and state banking regulators inaccurate and misleading reports about the financial condition of the American Continental Corporation and its subsidiary Lincoln Savings and Loan. Along with other actions arising out of the failure of Lincoln Savings, the case against Lexecon was transferred under § 1407(a) for pretrial proceedings before Judge Bilby in the District of Arizona, where the matters so consolidated were known as the Lincoln Savings litigation. Before those proceedings were over, the class action plaintiffs and Lexecon reached what they termed a "resolution," under which the claims against Lexecon were dismissed in August of 1992.

Lexecon then filed this case in the Northern District of Illinois charging that the prior class action terminated in its favor when the respondent law firms' clients voluntarily dismissed their claims against Lexecon as meritless, amounting to nothing more, according to Lexecon, than a vendetta. When these allegations came to the attention of Judge Bilby, he issued an order stating his understanding of the terms of the resolution agreement between Lexecon and the class action plaintiffs. . . . Judge Bilby's characterization of the agreement being markedly at odds with the allegations in the instant action, Lexecon appealed his order to the Ninth Circuit.

Milberg joined by Cotchett then filed a motion under§ 1407(a) with the Judicial Panel on Multidistrict Litigation seeking transfer of this case to Judge Bilby for consolidation with the Lincoln Savings litigation. Although the judge entered a recusal because of the order he had taken it upon himself to issue, the law firms nonetheless renewed their motion for a § 1407(a) transfer.

The Panel ordered a transfer in early June of 1993 and assigned the case to Judge Roll, noting that Lexecon's claims "share questions of fact with an as yet unapproved settlement involving Touche Ross, Lexecon, Inc. and the investor plaintiffs in the Lincoln Savings investor class actions in MDL-834." The Panel observed that "i) a massive document depository is located in the District of Arizona and ii) the Ninth Circuit has before it an appeal of an order [describing the terms of Lexecon's dismissal from the Lincoln Savings litigation] in MDL-834 which may be relevant to the Lexecon claims." Prior to any dispositive action on Lexecon's instant claims in the District of Arizona, the Ninth Circuit appeal mentioned by the Panel was dismissed, and the document depository was closed down.

In November 1993, Judge Roll dismissed Lexecon's state law malicious prosecution and abuse of process claims, applying a "heightened pleading standard".... Although the law firms then moved for summary judgment on the claims remaining, the judge deferred action pending completion of discovery, during which time the remaining parties to the Lincoln Savings litigation reached a final settlement, on which judgment was entered in March 1994.

In August 1994, Lexecon moved that the district court refer the case back to the Panel for remand to the Northern District of Illinois, thus heeding the point of Multidistrict Litigation Rule 14(d), which provides that "[t]he Panel is reluctant to order remand absent a suggestion of remand from the transferee district court." The law firms opposed a remand because discovery was still incomplete and filed a countermotion under § 1404(a) requesting the District of Arizona to "transfer" the case to itself for trial. Judge Roll deferred decision on these motions as well.

In November 1994, Lexecon again asked the District Court to request the Panel to remand the case to the Northern District of Illinois. Again the law firms objected and requested a § 1404 transfer, and Judge Roll deferred ruling once more. On April 24, 1995, however, he granted summary judgment in favor of the law firms on all remaining claims except one in defamation brought against Milberg, and at the same time he dismissed the law firms' counterclaims....

In the meantime, the Arizona court had granted the law firms' § 1404(a) motions to assign the case to itself for trial, and simultaneously had denied Lexecon's motions to request the Panel to remand under § 1407(a). Lexecon sought immediate review of these last two rulings by filing a petition for mandamus in the Ninth Circuit. After argument, a majority of the Circuit panel, over the dissent of Judge Kozinski, denied Lexecon's requests to vacate the self-assignment order and require remand to the Northern District of Illinois....

Trial on the surviving defamation claim then went forward in the District of Arizona, ending in judgment for Milberg, from which Lexecon appealed to the Ninth Circuit. It again appealed the denial of its motion for a suggestion that the Panel remand the matter to the Northern District of Illinois, and it challenged the dismissal of its claims for malicious prosecution and abuse of process, and the entry of final judgment in favor of Cotchett. Lexecon took no exception to the Arizona court's jurisdiction (as distinct from venue) and pursued no claim of error in the conduct of the trial.

A divided panel of the Ninth Circuit affirmed, relying on the Panel's Rule 14 and appellate and district court decisions in support of the District Court's refusal to support remand under § 1407(a) and its decision to assign the case to itself under § 1404(a)..... While the majority indicated that permitting the transferee court to assign a case to itself upon completion of its pretrial work was not only consistent with the statutory language but conducive to efficiency, Judge Kozinski . . . dissented, relying on the texts of §§ 1407(a) and 1404(a) and a presumption in favor of a plaintiff's choice of forum. We granted certiorari to decide whether § 1407(a) does permit a transferee court to entertain a § 1404(a) transfer motion to keep the case for trial.

II

A

In defending the Ninth Circuit majority, Milberg may claim ostensible support from two quarters. First, the Panel has itself sanctioned such assignments in a rule issued in reliance on its rulemaking authority under 28 U.S.C. § 1407(f). The Panel's Rule 14(b) provides that "[e]ach transferred action that has not been terminated in the transferee district court shall be remanded by the Panel to the transferor district for trial, unless ordered transferred by the transferee judge to the transferee or other district under 28 U.S.C. § 1404(a) or 28 U.S.C. § 1406." Thus, out of the 39,228 cases transferred under § 1407 and terminated as of September 30, 1995, 279 of the 3,787 ultimately requiring trial were retained by the courts to which the Panel had transferred them. . . . Although the Panel's rule and the practice of self-assignment have not gone without challenge, see, *e.g.*, . . . Trangsrud, Joinder Alternatives in Mass Tort Litigation, 70 Cornell L.Rev. 779, 809 (1985) . . ., federal courts have treated such transfers with approval, beginning with the Second Circuit's decision in Pfizer, Inc. v. Lord, 447 F.2d 122, 124-125 (C.A.2 1971) (per curiam) . . . .

The second source of ostensible authority for Milberg's espousal of the self-assignment power here is a portion of text of the multidistrict litigation statute itself:

> "When civil actions involving one or more common questions of fact are pending in different districts, such actions may be transferred to any district for coordinated or consolidated pretrial proceedings." 28 U.S.C. § 1407(a).

Although the statute limits a transferee court's authority to the conduct of "coordinated or consolidated" proceedings and to those that are "pretrial," these limitations alone raise no obvious bar to a transferee's retention of a case under § 1404. If "consolidated" proceedings alone were authorized, there would be an argument that self-assignment of one or some cases out of many was not contemplated, but because the proceedings need only be "coordinated," no such narrow limitation is apparent. While it is certainly true that the instant case was not "consolidated" with any other for the purpose literally of litigating identical issues on common evidence, it is fair to say that proceedings to resolve pretrial matters were "coordinated" with the conduct of earlier cases sharing the common core of the Lincoln Savings debacle, if only by being brought before judges in a district where much of the evidence was to be found and overlapping issues had been considered. Judge Bilby's recusal following his decision to respond to Lexecon's Illinois pleadings may have limited the prospects for coordination, but it surely did not eliminate them. Hence, the requirement that a transferee court conduct "coordinated or consolidated" proceedings did not preclude the transferee Arizona court from ruling on a motion (like the § 1404 request) that affects only one of the cases before it.

Likewise, at first blush, the statutory limitation to "pretrial" proceedings suggests no reason that a § 1407 transferor court could not entertain a § 1404(a) motion. Section 1404(a) authorizes a district court to transfer a case in the interest of justice and for the convenience of the parties and witnesses. See § 1404(a). Such transfer requests are typically resolved prior to discovery, . . . and thus are classic "pretrial" motions.

Beyond this point, however, the textual pointers reverse direction, for § 1407 not only authorizes the Panel to transfer for coordinated or consolidated pretrial proceedings, but obligates the Panel to remand any pending case to its originating court when, at the latest, those pretrial proceedings have run their course.

"Each action so transferred shall be remanded by the panel at or before the conclusion of such pretrial proceedings to the district from which it was transferred unless it shall have been previously terminated." § 1407(a) (proviso without application here omitted).

The Panel's instruction comes in terms of the mandatory "shall," which normally creates an obligation impervious to judicial discretion. . . . In the absence of any indication that there might be circumstances in which a transferred case would be neither "terminated" nor subject to the remand obligation, then, the statutory instruction stands flatly at odds with reading the phrase "coordinated or consolidated pretrial proceedings" so broadly as to reach its literal limits, allowing a transferee court's self-assignment to trump the provision imposing the Panel's remand duty. If we do our job of reading the statute whole, we have to give effect to this plain command, . . . even if doing that will reverse the longstanding practice under the statute and the rule . . . .

As the Ninth Circuit panel majority saw it, however, the inconsistency between an expansive view of "coordinated or consolidated pretrial" proceedings and the uncompromising terms of the Panel's remand obligation disappeared as merely an apparent conflict, not a real one. The "focus" of § 1407 was said to be constituting the Panel and defining its authority, not circumscribing the powers of district courts under § 1404(a). 102 F.3d, at 1533. Milberg presses this point in observing that § 1407(a) does not, indeed, even apply to transferee courts, being concerned solely with the Panel's duties, whereas § 1407(b), addressed to the transferee courts, says nothing about the Panel's obligation to remand. But this analysis fails to persuade, for the very reason that it rejects that central tenet of interpretation, that a statute is to be considered in all its parts when construing any one of them. To emphasize that § 1407(b) says nothing about the Panel's obligation when addressing a transferee court's powers is simply to ignore the necessary consequence of self-assignment by a transferee court: it conclusively thwarts the Panel's capacity to obey the unconditional command of § 1407(a).

A like use of blinders underlies the Circuit majority's conclusion that the Panel was not even authorized to remand the case under its Rule 14(c), the terms of which condition the remand responsibility on a suggestion of the transferee court, a motion filed directly with the Panel, or the Panel's *sua sponte* decision to remand. None of these conditions was fulfilled, according to the Court of Appeals, which particularly faulted Lexecon for failing to file a remand motion directly with the Panel, as distinct from the transferee court.[1] This analysis, too, is unpersuasive; it just ignores the fact that the statute places an obligation on the Panel to remand no later than the conclusion of pretrial proceedings in the transferee court, and no exercise in rulemaking can read that obligation out of the statute. See 28 U.S.C. § 1407(f) (express requirement that rules be consistent with statute).

B . . .

Milberg tries to draw an inference in its favor from the one subsection of § 1407 that does authorize the Panel to transfer a case for trial as well as pretrial proceedings. Subsection (h) provides that,

> "[n]otwithstanding the provisions of section 1404 or subsection (f) of this section, the judicial panel on multidistrict litigation may consolidate and transfer with or without the consent of the parties, for both pretrial purposes and for trial, any action brought under section 4C of the Clayton Act."

Milberg [argues that the introductory language, in failing to mention transfers under § 1407(a), impliedly authorized § 1404 self-assignments in cases transferred under § 1407(a).] This reasoning is fallacious, however. Subsections (a) and (h) are independent sources of transfer authority in the Panel; each is apparently written to stand on its own feet. Subsection (h) need not exclude the application of subsection (a), because nothing in (a) would by its terms limit any provision of (h).

Subsection (h) is not merely valueless to Milberg, however; it is ammunition for Lexecon. For the one point that subsection (h) does demonstrate is that Congress knew how to distinguish between trial assignments and pretrial proceedings in cases subject to § 1407. Although the enactment of subsection (a), Act of Apr. 29, 1968, 82 Stat. 109, preceded the enactment of subsection (h), Act of Sept. 30, 1976, § 303, 90 Stat. 1394, 1396, the fact that the later section distinguishes trial assignments from pretrial proceedings generally is certainly some confirmation for our conclusion, on independent grounds, that the subjects of pretrial proceedings in subsections (a) and (b) do not include self-assignment orders.

C

There is, finally, nothing left of Milberg's position beyond an appeal to

---

1. The Ninth Circuit stopped short of expressly inferring a waiver from Lexecon's failure to file a motion for remand directly with the Panel, and any inference of waiver would surely have been unsound. . . . [E]ven if a party may waive the § 1407 remand requirement by failing to request remand from the transferor court, see 28 U.S.C. § 1406(b), Rule 14(d) precludes an inference of waiver from mere failure to request remand from the Panel. . . .

legislative history, some of which turns out to ignore the question before us, and some of which may support Lexecon. Milberg cites a House Report on the bill that became § 1407, which addresses the question of trial transfer in multidistrict litigation cases by saying that "[o]f course, 28 U.S.C. 1404, providing for changes of venue generally, is available in those instances where transfer of a case for all purposes is desirable." H.R. Rep. No. 1130, 90th Cong., 2d Sess., p. 4 (1968) (hereinafter H.R. Rep.). But the question is not whether a change of venue may be ordered in a case consolidated under § 1407(a); on any view of § 1407(a), if an order may be made under § 1404(a), it may be made after remand of the case to the originating district court. The relevant question for our purposes is whether a transferee court, and not a transferor court, may grant such a motion, and on this point, the language cited by Milberg provides no guidance.

If it has anything to say to us here, the legislative history tends to confirm that self-assignment is beyond the scope of the transferee court's authority. The same House Report that spoke of the continued vitality of § 1404 in § 1407 cases also said this:

> "The proposed statute affects only the pretrial stages in multidistrict litigation. It would not affect the place of trial in any case or exclude the possibility of transfer under other Federal statutes. . . .
>
> The subsection requires that transferred cases be remanded to the originating district at the close of coordinated pretrial proceedings. The bill does not, therefore, include the trial of cases in the consolidated proceedings." H.R. Rep., at 3-4.

The comments of the bill's sponsors further suggest that application of § 1407 (before the addition of subsection h) would not affect the place of trial. See, *e.g.*, Multidistrict Litigation: Hearings on S. 3815 and S. 159 before the Subcommittee on Improvements in Judicial Machinery of the Senate Comm. on the Judiciary, 90th Cong., 1st Sess. pt. 2, p. 110 (1967) (Sen. Tydings) . . . . Both the House and the Senate Reports stated that Congress would have to amend the statute if it determined that multidistrict litigation cases should be consolidated for trial. S. Rep. No. 454, 90th Cong., 1st Sess., p. 5 (1967).

D

In sum, none of the arguments raised can unsettle the straightforward language imposing the Panel's responsibility to remand, which bars recognizing any self-assignment power in a transferee court and consequently entails the invalidity of the Panel's Rule 14(b). See 28 U.S.C. § 1407(f). Milberg may or may not be correct that permitting transferee courts to make self-assignments would be more desirable than preserving a plaintiff's choice of venue (to the degree that § 1407(a) does so), but the proper venue for resolving that issue remains the floor of Congress. . . .

III

The remaining question goes to the remedy, which Milberg argues may be omitted under the harmless error doctrine. Milberg posits a distinction between a first category of cases erroneously litigated in a district in which (absent waiver) venue may never be laid under the governing statute, . . . and a second category, in which the plaintiff might originally have chosen to litigate in the trial forum to which it was unwillingly and erroneously carried, as by a transfer under § 1404. In the first, reversal is necessary; in the second affirmance is possible if no independent and substantial right was violated in a trial whose venue was determined by a discretionary decision. Since Lexecon could have brought suit in the Arizona district consistently with the general venue requirements of 28 U.S.C. § 1391, and since the transfer for trial was made on the authority of § 1404(a), Milberg argues, this case falls within the second category and should escape reversal because none of Lexecon's substantial rights was prejudicially affected, see § 2111. Assuming the distinction may be drawn, however, we think this case bears closer analogy to those in the first category, in which reversal with new trial is required because venue is precluded by the governing statute.

Milberg's argument assumes the only kind of statute entitled to respect in accordance with its uncompromising terms is a statute that categorically limits a plaintiff's initial choice of forum. But there is no apparent reason why courts should not be equally bound by a venue statute that just as categorically limits the authority of courts (and special panels) to override a plaintiff's choice. If the former statute creates interests too substantial to be denied without a remedy, the latter statute ought to be recognized as creating interests equally substantial. In each instance the substantiality of the protected interest is attested by a congressional judgment that in the circumstances described in the statute no discretion is to be left to a court faced with an objection to a statutory violation. . . . [The] strict remand requirement contained in § 1407 should suffice to establish the substantial significance of any denial of a plaintiff's right to a remand once the pretrial stage has been completed. . . .

Accordingly, the judgment of the Court of Appeals is reversed, and the case is remanded for further proceedings consistent with this opinion.

Notes and Questions

1. It would be difficult to imagine a less compelling case for § 1404 self-transfer than *Lexecon* — the transferred case had little to do with the multidistrict proceedings, the multidistrict proceeding had already wound down, and the multidistrict transferee judge, who was familiar with the litigation, recused himself. Is there any room in *Lexecon*'s analysis to suggest that it should be limited by these facts?

2. In the three months between *Lexecon* and this writing, the decision has already been criticized for undoing nearly thirty years of settled practice — a practice that was generally thought to enhance the powers of the transferee judge to deal with multidistrict litigation in a fruitful way. There have been numerous calls for Congress to overrule its result, and to permit multidistrict cases transferred for pretrial purposes also to be transferred for trial purposes. The ultimate fate of such a bill, should one be introduced in Congress, is uncertain.

3. *Lexecon* can be critiqued at two levels: its result and its method of analysis. Beginning with its result — that multidistrict transferee courts cannot use § 1404 to self-transfer — is this holding really as bad as its early critics have suggested? Section 1407 transfer constitutes a significant inroad on plaintiffs' venue privilege; self-transfer for trial makes that inroad even more severe, infringes on Congress' judgment that plaintiffs should continue to enjoy that privilege at trial, expands the power of a single transferee judge, and treats cases that fall within § 1407 under a different set of rules than cases that do not. We have seen in prior chapters that consolidation for trial may well affect the outcome at trial. We have also seen that the timing of the consolidation — especially consolidation when a case is still immature — may affect the outcome of the litigation. We will see in Part Three that consolidated trials often create significant problems of management, and some of the solutions to those problems also influence the outcome of the litigation. Is *Lexecon* therefore correct to end a practice laden with policy implications, and to force the legislative branch to consider the appropriate degree of consolidation?

If the answer to this question is, as a general matter, "Yes," should the answer be the same in complex litigation? Although the *Keating* case, out of which *Lexecon* arose, was a classic instance of joinder complexity (the assets were insufficient to cover all the claims), a consolidated trial in *Lexecon* itself would have done nothing to reduce or eliminate that complexity — the trial of the *Lexecon* case would not have placed any more assets into the kitty for distribution to plaintiffs. If *Lexecon* is read to prevent the self-transfer of litigation that might result in a greater pot of assets being made available to victims in the multidistrict proceeding, then there is a real problem with the *Lexecon* result. Is there still room to argue that *Lexecon*'s rule does not pertain in instances of lawyer dysfunction? The argument would presumably run as follows: The denial of a right of self-transfer results in the disparate award of remedies to similarly situated people and possibly the denial of any remedy to some, and thus violates the due process norm in adjudication. Note that this argument assumes that one victim has a due process interest in the award given to another victim. If she does, would it be better to argue that *Lexecon* is inapplicable on the issue of § 1404 self-transfer, or rather to argue that *Lexecon* correctly decides the § 1404 issue but the transferee judge's self-transfer power in complex cases derives from some source other than § 1404? What might the source be? Recall Judge Weinstein's suggestion that § 1404 might not be the sole source of power for all-purpose transfers. See p. 488, *supra*. It now appears that finding such an alternate source might be important. How about the All-Writs Act, 28 U.S.C. § 1651? Cf. pp. 388-89, *supra* (All-Writs Act gives *sua sponte* power to judges to remove certain cases from state court).

4. *Lexecon*'s analysis can also be critiqued. The opinion is essentially an attempt to read the tea leaves of the statutory language, with a bit of help from the legislative history. The opinion is nearly devoid of any discussion of the policy implications of § 1407 transfers. Does that mean that such policy implications are not relevant to the interpretation of § 1407? What does this method of analysis portend for the proper interpretation of other statutory terms, such as "common questions of fact," "convenience of parties and witnesses," and "promot[ing] the just and efficient conduct of such actions"? Will the Panel need to pay closer attention to these criteria? Will it need to engage in factfinding to determine if the criteria have been met? Should the concern for plaintiffs' venue privilege continue to be relevant in interpreting § 1407? Should the single-accident vs. dispersed nature of the injuries be relevant? Is there room to

consider how multidistrict transfer affects the problems of wasteful re-litigation or lawyer dysfunction, except to the limited extent that these concerns find specific expression in the legislative history? The legacy of *Lexecon* may lie in the answers to these questions, rather than in its specific holding on self-transfer.

5. *Lexecon*'s holding on self-transfer diminishes the utility of § 1407 as a single-venue aggregation device. If *Lexecon* makes the issues of complexity or complication irrelevant to the more general interpretation of § 1407, then the utility of § 1407 as a single-venue aggregation device in complex or complicated litigation will be diminished even more. As we come to the end of our examination of existing devices to achieve single-venue aggregation, then, we find a rather mixed bag. We do not have a device that permits a single decisionmaker to transfer related issues or cases for all purposes to a single venue. The best device we do have — § 1407 — provides a single decisionmaker, and permits the aggregation in a single venue of related issues or cases only for pretrial purposes. When joined with § 1404 motions in each transferor forum, some measure of all-purpose consolidation may yet be achieved through § 1407 — although *Hoffman v. Blaski* looms over the entire enterprise. Neither § 1404 nor § 1407 is capable of dealing with the problem of nonparties. Neither permits the consolidation of cases filed in state court.

Therefore, our present quilt of jurisdictional and venue doctrines stops short of simple, efficient single-venue aggregation in complex and complicated litigation. If a solution to this problem is considered necessary or desirable — either for complex cases or for complicated ones — it must be found beyond the bounds of our present rules of jurisdiction and venue.

C. BEYOND THE PRESENT DOCTRINE

Throughout the last three chapters, we have studied the American Law Institute's proposal to deal with the problem of multiparty, multiforum litigation. There is only one piece of the proposal, which is in many ways its linchpin, left to consider.

American Law Institute, COMPLEX LITIGATION: STATUTORY RECOMMENDATIONS AND ANALYSIS

37-38, 85, 94-95, 106-07 (1994)

§ 3.01. Standard for Consolidation

(a) Actions commenced in two or more United States District Courts may be transferred and consolidated if:

    (1) they involve one or more common questions of fact, and

    (2) transfer and consolidation will promote the just, efficient, and fair conduct of the actions.

(b) Factors to be considered in deciding whether the standard set forth in subsection (a) is met include

    (1) the extent to which transfer and consolidation will reduce duplicative litigation, the relative costs of individual and consolidated litigation, the likelihood of inconsistent adjudications, and the comparative burdens on the judiciary, and

    (2) whether transfer and consolidation can be accomplished in a way that is fair to the parties and does not result in undue inconvenience to them and the witnesses.

In considering those factors, account may be taken of matters such as

    a. the number of parties and actions involved;
    b. the geographic dispersion of the actions;
    c. the existence and significance of local concerns;
    d. the subject matter of the dispute;
    e. the amount in controversy;
    f. the significance and number of common issues involved, including whether multiple laws will have to be applied to those issues;
    g. the likelihood of additional related actions being commenced in the future;
    h. the wishes of the parties; and
    i. the stages to which the actions already commenced have progressed.

. . .

(d) Transfer and consolidation need not be denied simply because one or more of the issues are not common so that consolidated treatment of all parts of the dispersed actions cannot be achieved. The interests of particular individual litigants can be considered when determining whether they have shown cause to be excluded from the consolidated proceeding, as provided in § 3.05(a). . . .

§ 3.04. Standard for Determining Where to Transfer Consolidated Actions

(a) Cases may be transferred to and consolidated in any district court in which the just and efficient resolution of the actions will be promoted and fairness to the individual litigants can be facilitated.

(b) When the just, efficient, and fair resolution of the actions will be promoted, the Complex Litigation Panel may designate more than one transferee court. The Panel should give great weight to the convenience to the litigants in assigning individual actions among multiple transferee courts.

§ 3.05. Panel Procedure . . .

(d) . . . A lawsuit not identified or commenced at the time of the Complex Litigation Panel's original decision may be joined with those that have been transferred and consolidated pursuant to a tag-along procedure comparable to that under 28 U.S.C. § 1407.

§ 3.06. Powers of the Transferee Court

(a) Unless the Complex Litigation Panel otherwise provides, transfer and consolidation shall be for all purposes, and the transferee judge shall have the full power to manage and organize the consolidated proceeding so as to promote its just, efficient, and fair resolution. Among the things that the transferee court may consider are the organization of the parties into groups with like interests and the structuring of the litigation by separating the issues into those common questions that should be treated on a consolidated basis and those individual questions that should not. The transferee court also may certify classes either encompassing the entire litigation or for particular issues. Discovery and trial preparation on issues not consolidated by the transferee court may be stayed until the close of the consolidated proceeding.

(b) The transferee court shall prepare a preliminary plan and order for the disposition of the litigation. The plan shall specify whether the entire action or only specified issues shall be determined in the transferee district and also shall provide for the disposition of the issues not to be determined in the transferee court. This plan is conditional and may be altered or amended should it be appropriate to do so.

(c) When the transferee court severs issues, it shall have broad discretion to order the separated issues to be transferred for consolidated treatment in one or more transferee districts; to return individual issues to the districts in which they originated; to retain those issues for trial; or to order any other appropriate resolution. The transferee court may order the immediate transfer of those issues not to be determined by it, or it may postpone transfer until a later stage of the proceedings. When damage issues are severed, the discretion of the transferee court includes the transfer of those issues either prior to or after the trial of liability for a consolidated damages trial in one or more transferee districts.

Notes and Questions

1. With § 3.01 and its accompanying provisions, we finish our study of the ALI's proposal to deal with the aggregation of multiparty, multiforum litigation. Previously, we had seen that the ALI's Complex Litigation Panel, which is modeled after the Judicial Panel of Multidistrict Litigation, was given the authority to consolidate in a single forum nearly all cases pending in both state and federal forums (see p. 379, *supra*); and the transferee court had been given the power to stay related litigation (see p. 408, *supra*), to exercise territorial jurisdiction over persons that had minimum contacts with the nation as a whole (see p. 288, *supra*), and to preclude nonparties that failed to intervene after notice (see p. 249, *supra*). With the ability to consolidate cases pending in various federal forums, the task of consolidating related cases and nonparty claims is complete.

2. Note that §§ 3.01, 3.04, and 3.06 are built on 28 U.S.C. § 1407. Indeed, many of the factors that the Complex Litigation Panel is to consider in making decisions about whether and where to transfer cases sound rather like the factors that the Judicial Panel on Multidistrict Litigation already considers. Like § 1407, issues, rather than entire cases, can be consolidated.

But notice that there are important differences as well. Consolidation for trial purposes is clearly authorized. Gone as a prerequisite for transfer is the convenience of parties and witnesses; common issues of fact and the just, efficient, and fair conduct of litigation are the only two elements, and convenience comes in only as a back door limitation when transfer is too inconvenient. The layered sets of factors — in which the two basic elements are further defined by two more factors, which in turn are fleshed out by nine more factors — are also different, although this difference may be more a matter of style than substance.

3. The ALI designed its proposal to apply to all cases that involved wasteful re-litigation of common issues — in other words, to all complicated litigation. Based on what you have seen, do you favor the comprehensive proposal of the ALI in complicated litigation? What would be left of the adversarial system's master of the complaint rule? Should the Complex Litigation Panel and the transferee judge be able to exercise this much power over the cases of thousands of people? Will consolidation favor defendants or plaintiffs? Would the proposal make more sense if it were limited just to single-accident cases, rather than cases of dispersed harm? Would it make more sense if it were limited just to mature cases? How do we justify the creation of a new set of procedural rules — and the violation of our trans-substantive procedural ideal — just in some cases?

Would the proposal be less objectionable if it were limited just to complex litigation?

4. To answer these questions, you need more information than you now have. In the first place, you need to know whether the consolidation of litigation will make it impossible for the judge to manage the litigation during pretrial, to try the case, or to implement a remedy. We explore these issues in Parts Two through Four of the book. Second, you need to know if there are alternatives to the ALI's method of attempting a single consolidation. In fact, there are two methods, to which we have alluded throughout the last three chapters. The first method is to use the class action to achieve the appropriate joinder of parties in one forum. The second is to use bankruptcy as a means of aggregating litigation. We look at these issues in, respectively, Chapters Five and Six. If either of these seems more attractive as a means of handling complex and complicated litigation, then the ALI's proposal would not be as appealing. On the other hand, if these options raise concerns that are more significant than those raised by the ALI's proposal, the issue then becomes whether the concerns raised by the ALI's proposal outweigh its benefits in complex or complicated litigation.

The ALI was aware of the use of other devices when it made its proposal. It specifically rejected the idea that class actions were better than its proposal with this observation: "[I]t may not always be desirable as a matter of policy to force litigants to sacrifice control of their own actions, possibly depriving them of a meaningful day in court. In sum, merely altering the current class action rule, although it would ensure some improvements, falls short of achieving the maximum consolidation and coordination that is possible and desirable." *Complex Litigation, supra*, at 29. Aren't these two sentences internally inconsistent?

We now turn to class actions, and examine whether the ALI's concerns are correct.

CHAPTER FIVE

CLASS ACTIONS

> The appropriate action for this Court is to . . . put an end to this Frankenstein monster posing as a class action.
>
> J. Edward Lumbard

Until now we have studied numerous devices — joinder, preclusion, anti-suit injunctions, and consolidation — designed to resolve in one forum the claims of similarly situated persons. To locate the class action in the context of these devices, it is an involuntary joinder device that permits a representative person (or group of persons) to bring a claim on behalf of all persons similarly situated. Once a judgment in a class action is entered, the members of the class receive the same benefits and suffer the same consequences of claim and issue preclusion as individually joined parties.

The class action is not, however, precisely akin to any other joinder device. Unlike Rule 20 joinder, plaintiffs can be forced into a lawsuit without their consent, and unlike Rule 19, this forced joinder occurs on a group basis using far different criteria than Rule 19(a). Indeed, the closest analogy to class action in the joinder rules might be interpleader, but Rule 23 does not necessarily require that the person opposing the class be subject to the risk of competing claims for the same fund or obligation, nor does individual joinder occur.

Class actions are virtually unknown in civil law and socialist systems. They are the creature of Anglo-American equity practice. Predictably, the decision whether or not to certify a class action has enormous practical importance. In many cases — such as antitrust, securities fraud, employment discrimination, and toxic and other mass tort cases — the certification decision is often the decisive ruling in the case. Even though the decision is not directly related to the merits of the plaintiffs' claims, it can determine the relevant settlement leverage of the parties, the size of the fees which may earned by both plaintiff and defense counsel, the likely costs of discovery and trial, and the publicity which will or will not attend the litigation. Moreover, the potential for class treatment exerts an influence on the very nature of the case; lawyers sometimes choose to sue on certain substantive grounds, and forgo others, in an effort to qualify for or avoid class action certification. Considerations of procedure sometimes still trump substantive law.

No other federal rule of civil procedure has generated as much debate, or as much division, as Rule 23. The class action device has alternately been viewed as the cure-all for or the cause of complex civil litigation. See Arthur R. Miller, *Of Frankenstein Monsters and Shining Knights: Myth, Reality, and the "Class Action Problem,"* 92 Harv. L. Rev. 664 (1979). This chapter enters this debate from the perspective of the needs of complex and complicated litigation. The first section examines some of the benefits and drawbacks of class actions as an aggregation device. The second section then examines the "law" of class actions, and seeks to show how some of the benefits and drawbacks of Rule 23 influence the basic elements that must be established in order to maintain a class action. The final section locates the debate about Rule 23 within a larger context, looking both at proposals to reform Rule 23 and at state class actions.

Until this last section, the focus of this chapter is on Rule 23, the class action rule for federal courts. Rule 23 led the way into the modern class action world, and its interpretation exerts enormous influence over the interpretations of most state class action rules. Moreover, because of the advantages of federal court as a forum for the aggregation of related litigation, it is still the most significant of the various state and federal class action rules. Yet there is some emphasis that its influence is on the wane. As it has becomes more difficult, cumbersome, or tactically undesirable to maintain class actions in federal court, aggregation-minded parties have looked increasingly to state courts with more generous class action rules as the best forum for aggregation. If this trend continues, the view that the federal courts are best-suited to the aggregation of complex and complicated litigation may no longer hold true.

Before you begin this chapter, you should read both Rule 23 and the summary of Rule 23 found at pp. 132-34, *supra*. Basic familiarity with the rule is presumed in the following sections. In particular, be sure you understand the distinction between mandatory and opt-out class actions.

A. THE ADVANTAGES AND DISADVANTAGES OF THE CLASS ACTION AS AN AGGREGATION DEVICE

1. Doctrinal Advantages and Disadvantages

Over the last three chapters we have seen various doctrinal difficulties with joinder, preclusion, and consolidation devices. In this section we recap some of those concerns, examine the possible advantages of the class action in overcoming those concerns, and further describe the disadvantages of the class action as an aggregation device.

Subject Matter Jurisdiction. In federal court, the aggregation of related cases through individual joinder is often thwarted in diversity cases because of the rule of complete diversity and the amount-in-controversy requirement. As we have seen, class actions can often be structured to avoid the complete diversity rule; as long as the named class representatives are of diverse citizenship from the defendants, complete diversity is satisfied. See p. 331, *supra*. Avoidance of the matter-in-controversy requirement has proven more difficult, see p. 332, *supra*, although it is possible that 28 U.S.C. § 1367 abrogates the matter-in-controversy rule, see p. 349, *supra*. Section 1367 also makes it easier to exercise supplemental jurisdiction over state-law claims of class members that are related to a federal question claim, which can often be pleaded by aggregation-minded plaintiffs.

On the other hand, it is not presently clear whether the matter-in-controversy limit has been abolished in diversity cases. If it has not, class actions cannot be used to package small-stakes state-law claims in federal court; and, as we shall see later in the chapter, large-stakes state-law claims are often difficult to certify for other reasons. Thus, class actions may not be a panacea for the federal aggregation of state-law claims. Moreover, in federal question cases, the class action has no special jurisdictional advantage over other methods of joinder. Finally, the present jurisdictional rules still leave in the hands of the plaintiff seeking class certification the decision about whether to plead claims that invoke federal jurisdiction. In most situations, a plaintiff that wishes to avoid federal court can easily do so by pleading no federal claims and adding as a class representative or defendant one person that destroys complete diversity.

More generally, in prior chapters we saw that the Supreme Court seems to interpret the rules of subject matter jurisdiction with an eye toward the concerns of federalism. To what extent does the mass aggregation of claims that, but for their association with those of a diverse class representative, would never see a federal courthouse offend these concerns for federalism? Does class aggregation threaten to turn state courts into backwaters of routine litigation? Is this the appropriate role for our state courts?

Territorial Jurisdiction. With respect to defendants sued by a class of plaintiffs, class actions seem to have no particular advantage over individual litigation; in both situations, the forum court must have jurisdiction over the defendants. With respect to plaintiffs in a class action, the class action is in some ways inferior to voluntary joinder under Rule 20. When a plaintiff voluntarily brings suit against a defendant in a forum with which the plaintiff otherwise had no connection, the plaintiff can be deemed to consent to the jurisdiction of the forum. When the plaintiff is an involuntary plaintiff under Rule 23, however, the court typically must either have minimum contacts with the forum or the plaintiff must be extended an opportunity to opt out of the class action. We examine the limits of this concept, which might make the mandatory aggregation of plaintiffs in one federal court impossible, at p. 614, *infra*. There are also a number of older cases holding that, when a claim is brought against a defendant class, the court needs to have jurisdiction only over the representative defendant, not over every member of the class. It is unlikely that this rule continues to survive. See 7A Charles A. Wright et al., Federal Practice & Procedure

§ 1757 (1986). Thus, class actions present no advantages with respect to territorial jurisdiction.

Venue and Venue Transfers. As we have also seen, the venue statutes pose certain difficulties for efforts to aggregate in one federal forum the cases of individually joined plaintiffs and defendants. Although the Supreme Court has never passed on the issue, it is generally believed that, for class actions, residence-based venue rules (such as §§ 1391(a)(1) and (b)(1)) can be satisfied as long as the named class representatives all enjoy the same residence; the fact that other class members have residences in different states does not defeat venue. See Wright et al., *supra*, § 1757; but see Sperberg v. Firestone Tire & Rubber Co., 61 F.R.D. 70 (N.D. Ohio 1973). As with the complete diversity rule, therefore, a careful selection of class representatives can usually provide access to a single federal venue.

Moreover, because all the claims are aggregated in one suit, there is often no need to engage in transfers among districts. This is not, however, always the case; in some situations, different groups of plaintiffs file separate class action lawsuits in different federal courts, or else class members file individual lawsuits in different federal forums. In these cases, the use of transfer devices to locate all the cases to a single federal forum is still necessary.

Avoidance of Dual State-Federal Litigation. In Chapter Three we saw that a common problem is the maintenance of related lawsuits in both state and federal forums. Rule 23 has only a limited ability to deal with this problem. In the first place, in an opt-out class action, class members are always free to opt out and pursue their litigation independently, whether in another federal court or in a state court. Second, Rule 23 does not on its face prevent a class member from simultaneously maintaining a case in state court and participating as a class member in the federal litigation. As we shall see, some courts have held that the certification of a mandatory class action acts as a stay that prevents class members from commencing litigation in state court, but the effort to enforce such a stay against class members with already extant state suits violates the Anti-Injunction Act. See p. 614, *infra*. Moreover, as we saw in Chapter Three, state courts will sometimes issue a stay in favor of federal cases, including class actions. See p. 437, *supra*. But such stays are not automatically granted. Thus, the certification of a federal class action does not, of its own force, prevent the existence of dual state-federal litigation.

Obviously, the knowledge that a class action has already been filed may deter some class members from filing state lawsuits that they would otherwise have brought. Furthermore, once the class action is reduced to a judgment, all class members are bound by the outcome, and the federal court has the ability to enjoin state suits that seek to raise the same issues. See pp. 393-412, *supra*. But this preclusive effect extends only to claims that were encompassed within the class action, and may be defeated by a showing that the class representative failed to represent the class member adequately. See pp. 174-94, *supra*. On balance, therefore, class actions are unlikely to prevent all dual state-federal litigation.

Preclusion of Nonparties. As we have seen, one of the great problems of most joinder rules, as well as of multidistrict and other forms of venue transfer, is that these devices cannot force the "sideline-sitter" (the person that files no suit) into a case that resolves the issues for all. One of the class action's potential strengths is it ability to overcome this difficulty, for it involuntarily joins all persons that meet the class definition — including those that have not yet filed suit. (Technically class members are parties, but since they do not typically appear individually, they act as if they were nonparties.) As with parties in state court, however, nonparties can avoid the preclusive effect of the class judgment by demonstrating that they were inadequately represented in the class action.

Consolidation. In Chapter Four we also discovered that it is not always possible to consolidate related cases that are pending in a single federal forum. See pp. 473-87, *supra*. The class action, however, is a single proceeding, rather than a conglomeration of related cases. Hence, the concerns that lead some courts not to consolidate related cases, though relevant to the court's decision whether to certify a class in the first instance, do not affect the lawsuit once the class has been certified.

Single Decisionmaker. One of the problem of many aggregation devices is that they required multiple decisionmakers to agree to aggregate the cases in one forum. The class action avoids diffuse decisionmaking. A single judge makes the determination whether to certify the class.

Sua Sponte *Power.* Another defect in some aggregation devices is the inability of the judge to initiate aggregation on her own; instead, she needed to wait for an aggregation request to be presented by the parties, who might have private tactical reasons for not making the request. Although the power exists in theory, the issue of the court's *sua sponte* power to certify a class action rarely arises; if there are no willing parties and lawyers willing to serve as class representatives and counsel, the class is unlikely to pass muster under Rule 23(a). See 7B Charles A. Wright et al., Federal Practice & Procedure § 1785 91986); cf. In re Northern District of California Dalkon Shield IUD Products Liability Litigation, 693 F.2d 847 (9th Cir. 1982), cert. denied, 459 U.S. 1171 (1983) (defendants moved for certification of plaintiff class; class could not be certified in part because no plaintiffs' attorney already involved in litigation was willing to serve as class counsel). Hence, as a practical matter, judges have little *sua sponte* to overcome the parties' adversarial decisions to litigate on an individual basis.

Issue-Specific Rulings. Another problem with some aggregation devices that we have examined is that they force the aggregation of entire cases, even when some of the parties or claims in the case need not be aggregated. It is possible, though not particularly common, to create class actions to resolve only certain specific issues. See F.R.Civ.P. 23(c)(4)(A). It is also possible, although again uncommon, for subclasses with particular interests to be created (see F.R.Civ.P. 23(c)(4)(B)). Whichever device is employed, class actions can be better tailored to resolve only the truly common issues than other devices we have studied. But see Thomas E. Willging et al., Empirical Study of Class Actions in Four Federal District Courts 41-44 (1996) (finding no use of issue classes and little use of subclasses).

2. Policy Concerns of Class Actions

The prior subsection focused on some of the doctrinal ways in which class actions may be superior or inferior to other methods of aggregation. As we saw when we examined these other methods, however, aggregation devices also raise a host of policy concerns. We now examine whether the class action device heightens or reduces these concerns, and whether it adds in new concerns.

Autonomy to Control Litigation, Adequacy of Representation, and Collective Power. One of the concerns that aggregation devices pose is the loss of control over plaintiffs' decision about whether, when, and where to file suit. Class actions raise this concern in a far more significant way than any of the other aggregation devices that we have examined. Until now, every other aggregation device has affected at least one of the "whether, where, and when" decisions, but has presumed that a party who was brought into the litigation, or whose case was transferred to a different forum, would at least retain the lawyer of his or her choosing and thus would control major litigation decisions. (We examine important limitations on this presumption in Chapter Eight. See p. 879, *infra*). Class actions affect the "whether to file" decision by involuntarily joining nonparties. They affect the "where to file" decision by locating a class member's suit in a forum of the class representative's choosing. They affect the "when to file" decision by again placing the timing decision in the hands of the class representative. Perhaps most significantly, though, class actions place a lawyer not of the class member's choosing in charge of the litigation, and a class representative in charge of controlling (at least in theory) the lawyer's decisions concerning the prosecution or defense of the class member's case.

These factors mean that class actions are a significant inroad on the traditional adversarial approach to litigation. In order to assure that class actions protect the interests of individual litigants, the Supreme Court has insisted that the class representative be an "adequate" representative of each class member's claim; if the class representative is inadequate, then the class member is not bound by the class judgment and may prosecute or defend his or her own suit. The classic statement of the "adequacy of representation" requirement is contained in *Hansberry v. Lee*, to which a number of the earlier cases in this book have referred.

HANSBERRY v. LEE

311 U.S. 32 (1940)

■ MR. JUSTICE STONE delivered the opinion of the Court.

[Property in a Chicago neighborhood contained a racially restrictive covenant. The covenant became effective when it was signed by 95% of all property owners. Although the covenant had been signed by about only 54% of the owners, some of the owners brought suit in Illinois state court when one of the property owners leased to an African-American. The state case was brought "on behalf of" all property owners in the neighborhood. One of these owners was the grantor of the Hansberrys. The parties stipulated in the state proceeding that the racially restrictive covenant had been signed by the requisite 95%, and the property owners ultimately prevailed.

[The Hansberrys, who were African-American, later bought a property allegedly subject to the covenant. Other owners sued to rescind the sale. When the Hansberrys tried to defend by claiming that the requisite 95% of the signatures had never been obtained, the Illinois Supreme Court found that the issue had been determined in the prior lawsuit, that the 95% determination was not the product of collusion or fraud, that the prior suit had been a class or representative suit, and that the 95% determination was binding on the Hansberrys' grantor and the Hansberrys as res judicata.

[The Hansberrys claimed that this outcome violated the due process clause of the Fourteenth Amendment.]

It is a principle of general application in Anglo-American jurisprudence that one is not bound by a judgment *in personam* in a litigation in which he is not designated as a party or to which he has not been made a party by service of process. . . . A judgment rendered in such circumstances is not entitled to the full faith and credit which the Constitution and statute of the United States . . . prescribe, . . . and judicial action enforcing it against the person or property of the absent party is not that due process which the Fifth and Fourteenth Amendments requires. . . .

To these general rules there is a recognized exception that, to an extent not precisely defined by judicial opinion, the judgment in a "class" or "representative" suit, to which some members of the class are parties, may bind members of the class or those represented who were not made parties to it. . . .

The class suit was an invention of equity to enable it to proceed to a decree in suits where the number of those interested in the subject of the litigation is so great that their joinder as parties in conformity to the usual rules of procedure is impracticable. Courts are not infrequently called upon to proceed with causes in which the number of those interested in the litigation is so great as to make difficult or impossible the joinder of all because some are not within the jurisdiction or because their whereabouts is unknown or where if all were made parties to the suit its continued abatement by the death of some would prevent or unduly delay a decree. In such cases where the interests of those not joined are of the same class as the interests of those who are, and where it is considered that the latter fairly represent the former in the prosecution of the litigation of the issues in which all have a common interest, the court will proceed to a decree. . . .

Here, as elsewhere, the Fourteenth Amendment does not compel state courts or legislatures to adopt any particular rule for establishing the conclusiveness of judgments in class suits; . . . nor does it compel the adoption of the particular rules thought by this court to be appropriate for the federal courts. With a proper regard for divergent local institutions and interests, . . . this Court is justified in saying that there has been a failure of due process only in those cases where it cannot be said that the procedure adopted, fairly insures the protection of the interests of absent parties who are to be bound by it. . . .

It is familiar doctrine of the federal courts that members of a class not present as parties to the litigation may be bound by the judgment where they are in fact adequately represented by parties who are present, or where they actually participate in the conduct of the litigation in which members of the class are present as parties, . . . or where the interest of the members of the class, some of whom are present as parties, is joint, or where for any other reason the relationship between the parties present and those who are absent is such as legally to entitle the former to stand in judgment for the latter. . . .

In all such cases, so far as it can be said that the members of the class who are present are, by generally recognized rules of law, entitled to stand in judgment for those who are not, we may assume for present purposes that such procedure affords a protection to the parties who are represented though absent, which would satisfy the requirements of due process and full faith and credit. . . . We decide only that the procedure and the course of litigation sustained here by the plea of res judicata do not satisfy these requirements.

The restrictive agreement did not purport to create a joint obligation or liability. If valid and effective its promises were the several obligations of the signers and those claiming under them. The promises ran severally to every other signer. It is plain that in such circumstances all those alleged to be bound by the agreement would not constitute a single class in any litigation brought to enforce it. Those who sought to secure its benefits by enforcing it could not be said to be in the same class with or represent those whose interest was in resisting performance, for the agreement by its terms imposes obligations and confers rights on the owner of each plot of land who signs it. If those who thus seek to secure the benefits of the agreement were rightly regarded by the state Supreme Court as constituting a class, it is evident that those signers or their successors who are interested in challenging the validity of the agreement and resisting its performance are not of the same class in the sense that their interests are identical so that any group who had elected to enforce rights conferred by the agreement could be said to be acting in the interest of any others who were free to deny its obligation.

Because of the dual and potentially conflicting interests of those who are putative parties to the agreement in compelling or resisting its performance, it is impossible to say, solely because they are parties to it, that any two of them are of the same class. Nor without more, and with the due regard for the protection of the rights of absent parties which due process exacts, can some be permitted to stand in judgment for all.

It is one thing to say that some members of a class may represent other members in a litigation where the sole and common interest of the class in the litigation, is either to assert a common right or to challenge an asserted obligation. . . . It is quite another to hold that all those who are free alternatively either to assert rights or to challenge them are of a single class, so that any group merely because it is of the class so constituted, may be deemed adequately to represent any others of the class in litigating their interests in either alternative. Such a selection of representatives for purposes of litigation, whose substantial interests are not necessarily or even probably the same as those whom they are deemed to represent, does not afford that protection to absent parties which due process requires. The doctrine of representation of absent parties in a class suit has not hitherto been thought to go so far.... Apart from the opportunities it would afford for the fraudulent and collusive sacrifice of the rights of absent parties, we think that the representation in this case no more satisfies the requirements of due process than a trial by a judicial officer who is in such situation that he may have an interest in the outcome of the litigation in conflict with that of the litigants....

The plaintiffs in the [prior state] case sought to compel performance of the agreement in behalf of themselves and all others similarly situated. They did not designate the defendants in the suit as a class or seek any injunction or other relief against others than the named defendants, and the decree which was entered did not purport to bind others. In seeking to enforce the agreement the plaintiffs in that suit were not representing the petitioners here whose substantial interest is in resisting performance. The defendants in the first suit were not treated by the pleadings or decree as representing others or as foreclosing by their defense the rights of others, and even though nominal defendants, it does not appear that their interest in defeating the contract outweighed their interest in establishing its validity. For a court in this situation to ascribe to either the plaintiffs or defendants the performance of such functions on behalf of petitioners here, is to attribute to them a power that it cannot be said that they had assumed to exercise, and a responsibility which, in view of their dual interests it does not appear that they could rightly discharge.

■ MR. JUSTICE McREYNOLDS, MR. JUSTICE ROBERTS and MR. JUSTICE REED concur in the result.

Notes and Questions

1. Granting that adequacy of representation can substitute for party control of litigation, does the Supreme Court in *Hansberry* explain *why* adequacy is a surrogate for autonomy? Is it purely a matter of utility — that there are too many parties, or the parties are not known to or within the reach of the court, or the joinder of parties might delay litigation? Does *Hansberry* mean that all class members must have precisely the same interests in order for a class action to be certified? If not, how many conflicts of interest can be tolerated? Is the entire discussion of adequacy of representation in *Hansberry* dicta?

2. Under Rule 23, there are two ways in which individual autonomy can be preserved in a class action. First, certain class actions (Rule 23(b)(3) actions) permit class members to opt out of the suit and maintain control of their litigation. But other class actions are mandatory, and do not provide an opt-out right. Moreover, unlike the traditional adversarial approach, the onus in a (b)(3) class action is on the class member to opt out, rather than on the class representative to ask the member to opt in. The distinction is critical, because

in many class actions, some class members may never know about the litigation or the right to opt out. (Indeed, prior to 1966, the ancestor of Rule 23(b)(3) was, in effect, an opt-in rule.)

Second, a class member that does not or cannot opt out can move to intervene in the case. F.R.Civ.P. 23(d)(2). But such a motion is not granted automatically, and can be made subject to certain conditions. F.R.Civ.P. 23(d)(3); 7B Charles A. Wright et al., Federal Practice & Procedure §§ 1794, 1799 (1986).

3. One response to the problem of loss of individual control is to concede the loss but to argue that it has been replaced by something better — the collective power that a class action might bring to bear on individual claims. Whether a party opposing the would look on this collective power in quite the same light is another matter.

Total Peace, Optimal Deterrence, and Legalized Blackmail. Concern for individual autonomy and adequacy of representation are the primary focus for class members. The persons opposing the class — typically defendants — see other advantages and drawbacks in a class action. From the perspective of many defendants, a major advantage of the class action is its ability to bring a measure of total peace to a controversy; indeed, no other present aggregation device is capable of achieving the same degree of joinder or preclusion, and thus the same amount of finality. But this sense of finality is tempered by a series of other concerns. First, in opt-out class actions, the class action does not end all litigation; indeed, by making class members aware of the wrongdoing, it may increase the amount of litigation that the defendant faces. Second, the presence of significant numbers of claimants might increase the likelihood that the factfinder will hold the defendant responsible. See pp. 102-03, *supra.*

Third, the finality of a class action may be purchased at a dear price. For instance, suppose that a defendant engages in a course of conduct that harms 1,000,000 people, but the harm suffered is only $10 apiece. It is unlikely that any people will bring individual lawsuits; the defendant has a practical, even if not a legal, sense of finality. The class action now makes it economically viable for individuals to bring suit. An obvious response to this concern is that defendants should not be permitted to get away with any wrongdoing; indeed, a positive advantage of class actions is that it has the potential to achieve a full measure of deterrence unavailable under any other aggregation device. See, *e.g.,* David Rosenberg, *Class Actions for Mass Torts: Doing Individual Justice by Collective Means,* 62 Ind. L.J. 561 (1987). But a counterargument to this response is that, at least in some situations, the law does not intend full internalization of wrongful behavior, so that the class action in fact threatens to create an excessive level of deterrence. See Ratner v. Chemical Bank New York Trust Co., 54 F.R.D. 412 (S.D.N.Y. 1972); Kenneth W. Dam, *Class Actions: Efficiency, Compensation, Deterrence, and Conflict of Interest,* 4 J. Leg. Stud. 47 (1975). Moreover, by aggregating all claims against the defendant at one time, a single massive judgment may create financial difficulties that a series of judgments spread out over numerous earning periods would not have created.

This last counterargument raises a fourth concern for those opposing the class — the plaintiffs will use defendants' fear of a crippling class judgment to extort an unreasonably large settlement from the defendant. See Milton Handler, *The Shift from Substantive to Procedural Innovations in Antitrust Suits — The Twenty-Third Annual Antitrust Review*, 71 Colum. L. Rev. 1, 9 (1971) ("Any device which is workable only because it utilizes the threat of unmanageable and expensive litigation to compel settlement is not a rule of procedure — it is a form of legalized blackmail."). This tactical use of the class action has created concern in some courts.

IN THE MATTER OF RHONE-POULENC RORER INC.

51 F.3d 1293 (7th Cir.), cert. denied, 516 U.S. 867 (1995)

■ POSNER, Chief Judge. [Defendants petitioned for mandumus relief from an order of the district court allowing class certification. Although noting that mandamus is granted sparingly and requires a showing of irreparable harm from lack of immediate review and abuse of discretion, the court thought that the writ was appropriate in this case for three reasons. The facts of the case, as well as the first of the three reasons, follows here.]

The suit to which the petition for mandamus relates, Wadleigh v. Rhone-Poulenc Rorer Inc., 157 F.R.D. 410 [(N.D. Ill. 1994),] arises out of the infection of a substantial fraction of the hemophiliac population of this country by the AIDS virus because the blood supply was contaminated by the virus before the nature of the disease was well understood or adequate methods of screening the blood supply existed. The AIDS virus (HIV — human immunodeficiency virus) is transmitted by the exchange of bodily fluids, primarily semen and blood. Hemophiliacs depend on blood solids that contain the clotting factors whose absence defines their disease. These blood solids are concentrated from blood obtained from many donors. If just one of the donors is infected with the AIDS virus the probability that the blood solids manufactured in part from his blood will be infected is very high unless the blood is treated with heat to kill the virus. . . .

First identified in 1981, AIDS was diagnosed in hemophiliacs beginning in 1982, and by 1984 the medical community agreed that the virus was transmitted by blood as well as by semen. That year it was demonstrated that treatment with heat could kill the virus in the blood supply and in the following year a reliable test for the presence of the virus in blood was developed. By this time, however, a large number of hemophiliacs had become infected. Since 1984 physicians have been advised to place hemophiliacs on heat-treated blood solids, and since 1985 all blood donated for the manufacture of blood solids has been screened and supplies discovered to be HIV-positive have been discarded. Supplies that test negative still are heat-treated, because the test is not infallible and in particular may fail to detect the virus in persons who became infected within six months before taking the test.

The plaintiffs have presented evidence that 2,000 hemophiliacs have died of AIDS and that half or more of the remaining U.S. hemophiliac population of 20,000 may be HIV-positive. Unless there are dramatic breakthroughs in the treatment of HIV or AIDS, all infected persons will die from the disease. The reason so many are infected even though the supply of blood for the manufacture of blood solids (as for transfusions) has been safe since the mid-80s is that the disease has a very long incubation period; the median period for hemophiliacs may be as long as 11 years. Probably most of the hemophiliacs who are now HIV-positive, or have AIDS, or have died of AIDS were infected in the early 1980s, when the blood supply was contaminated.

Some 300 lawsuits, involving some 400 plaintiffs, have been filed, 60 percent of them in state courts, 40 percent in federal district courts under the diversity jurisdiction, seeking to impose tort liability on the defendants for the transmission of HIV to hemophiliacs in blood solids manufactured by the defendants. Obviously these 400 plaintiffs represent only a small fraction of the hemophiliacs (or their next of kin, in cases in which the hemophiliac has died) who are infected by HIV or have died of AIDS. One of the 300 cases is *Wadleigh*, filed in September 1993, the case that the district judge certified as a class action. Thirteen other cases have been tried already in various courts around the country, and the defendants have won twelve of them. All the cases brought in federal court (like *Wadleigh*) — cases brought under the diversity jurisdiction — have been consolidated for pretrial discovery in the Northern District of Illinois by the panel on multidistrict litigation. . . .

The district judge did not think it feasible to certify *Wadleigh* as a class action for the adjudication of the entire controversy between the plaintiffs and the defendants. Fed.R.Civ.P. 23(b)(3). The differences in the date of infection alone of the thousands of potential class members would make such a procedure infeasible. . . . Instead the judge certified the suit "as a class action with respect to particular issues" only. Fed.R.Civ.P. 23(c)(4)(A). He explained this decision in an opinion which implied that he did not envisage the entry of a final judgment but rather the rendition by a jury of a special verdict that would answer a number of questions bearing, perhaps decisively, on whether the defendants are negligent . . . . If the special verdict found no negligence . . ., that presumably would be the end of all the cases unless other theories of liability proved viable. If the special verdict found negligence, individual members of the class would then file individual tort suits in state and federal district courts around the nation and would use the special verdict, in conjunction with the doctrine of collateral estoppel, to block relitigation of the issue of negligence.

With all due respect for the district judge's commendable desire to experiment with an innovative procedure for streamlining the adjudication of this "mass tort," we believe that his plan so far exceeds the permissible bounds of discretion in the management of federal litigation as to compel us to intervene and order decertification. The plaintiffs' able counsel argues that we need not intervene now, that it will be time enough to intervene if and when a special verdict adverse to the defendants is entered and an appeal taken to us. But of course a verdict as such is not an appealable order. Only when a final judgment is entered, determining liability and assessing damages, will the case, including interim rulings such as the certification of certain issues in the case for determination in a class action, be appealable to us. . . .

[W]e shall assume . . . that eventually there will be a final judgment to review. Only it will come too late to provide effective relief to the defendants; and this is an important consideration in relation to the first condition for mandamus, that the challenged ruling of the district court have inflicted irreparable harm, which is to say harm that cannot be rectified by an appeal from the final judgment in the lawsuit. The reason that an appeal will come too late to provide effective relief for these defendants is the sheer *magnitude* of the risk to which the class action, in contrast to the individual actions pending or likely, exposes them. Consider the situation that would obtain if the class had not been certified. The defendants would be facing 300 suits. More might be filed, but probably only a few more, because the statutes of limitations in the various states are rapidly expiring for potential plaintiffs. The blood supply has been safe since 1985. That is ten years ago. The risk to hemophiliacs of having become infected with HIV has been widely publicized; it is unlikely that many hemophiliacs are unaware of it. Under the usual discovery statute of limitations, they would have to have taken steps years ago to determine their infection status, and having found out file suit within the limitations period running from the date of discovery, in order to preserve their rights.

Three hundred is not a trivial number of lawsuits. The potential damages in each one are great. But the defendants have won twelve of the first thirteen, and, if this is a representative sample, they are likely to win most of the remaining ones as well. Perhaps in the end, if class-action treatment is denied (it has been denied in all the other hemophiliac HIV suits in which class certification has been sought), they will be compelled to pay damages in only 25 cases, involving a potential liability of perhaps no more than $125 million altogether. These are guesses, of course, but they are at once conservative and usable for the limited purpose of comparing the situation that will face the defendants if the class certification stands. All of a sudden they will face thousands of plaintiffs. Many may already be barred by the statute of limitations, as we have suggested, though its further running was tolled by the filing of *Wadleigh* as a class action. . . .

Suppose that 5,000 of the potential class members are not yet barred by the statute of limitations. And suppose the named plaintiffs in *Wadleigh* win the class portion of this case to the extent of establishing the defendants' liability . . . . It is true that this would only be prima facie liability, that the defendants would have various defenses. But they could not be confident that the defenses would prevail. They might, therefore, easily be facing $25 billion in potential liability (conceivably more), and with it bankruptcy. They may not wish to roll these dice. That is putting it mildly. They will be under intense pressure to settle. . . . If they settle, the class certification — the ruling that will have forced them to settle — will never be reviewed. . . . Judge Friendly, who was not given to hyperbole, called settlements induced by a small probability of an immense judgment in a class action "blackmail settlements." Henry J. Friendly, Federal Jurisdiction: A General View 120 (1973). Judicial concern about them is legitimate, not "sociological," as it was derisively termed in In re Sugar Antitrust Litigation, 559 F.2d 481, 483 n.1 (9th Cir.1977)....

We do not want to be misunderstood as saying that class actions are bad because they place pressure on defendants to settle. That pressure is a reality, but it must be balanced against the undoubted benefits of the class action that have made it an authorized procedure for employment by federal courts. We have yet to consider the balance. All that our discussion to this point has shown is that the first condition for the grant of mandamus — that the challenged ruling not be effectively reviewable at the end of the case — is fulfilled. The ruling will inflict irreparable harm; the next question is whether the ruling can fairly be described as usurpative.... Three concerns, none of them necessarily sufficient in itself but cumulatively compelling, persuade us to this conclusion.

The first is a concern with forcing these defendants to stake their companies on the outcome of a single jury trial, or be forced by fear of the risk of bankruptcy to settle even if they have no legal liability, when it is entirely feasible to allow a final, authoritative determination of their liability for the colossal misfortune that has befallen the hemophiliac population to emerge from a decentralized process of multiple trials, involving different juries, and different standards of liability, in different jurisdictions; and when, in addition, the preliminary indications are that the defendants are not liable for the grievous harm that has befallen the members of the class. These qualifications are important. In most class actions — and those the ones in which the rationale for the procedure is most compelling — individual suits are infeasible because the claim of each class member is tiny relative to the expense of litigation. That plainly is not the situation here. A notable feature of this case, and one that has not been remarked upon or encountered, so far as we are aware, in previous cases, is the demonstrated great likelihood that the plaintiffs' claims, despite their human appeal, lack legal merit. This is the inference from the defendants' having won 92.3 percent (12/13) of the cases to have gone to judgment. Granted, thirteen is a small sample and further trials, if they are held, may alter the pattern that the sample reveals. But whether they do or not, the result will be robust if these further trials are permitted to go forward, because the pattern that results will reflect a consensus, or at least a pooling of judgment, of many different tribunals.

For this consensus or maturing of judgment the district judge proposes to substitute a single trial before a single jury instructed in accordance with no actual law of any jurisdiction — a jury that will receive a kind of Esperanto instruction, merging the negligence standards of the 50 states and the District of Columbia. One jury, consisting of six persons (the standard federal civil jury nowadays consists of six regular jurors and two alternates), will hold the fate of an industry in the palm of its hand. This jury, jury number fourteen, may disagree with twelve of the previous thirteen juries — and hurl the industry into bankruptcy. That kind of thing can happen in our system of civil justice (it is not likely to happen, because the industry is likely to settle — whether or not it really is liable) without violating anyone's legal rights. But it need not be tolerated when the alternative exists of submitting an issue to multiple juries constituting in the aggregate a much larger and more diverse sample of decision-makers. That would not be a feasible option if the stakes to each class member were too slight to repay the cost of suit, even though the aggregate stakes were very large and would repay the costs of a consolidated proceeding. But this is not the case with regard to the HIV-hemophilia litigation. Each plaintiff if successful is apt to receive a judgment in the millions. With the aggregate stakes in the tens or hundreds of millions of dollars, or even in the billions, it is not a waste of judicial resources to conduct more than one trial, before more than six jurors, to determine whether a major segment of the international pharmaceutical industry is to follow the asbestos manufacturers into Chapter 11....

[The court's latter two reasons for ordering decertification of the class are found at pp. 860, 1283, *infra*.]

■ ROVNER, Circuit Judge, dissenting.... [E]ven if the possibility of a settlement were relevant to the first mandamus requirement, ... I still cannot agree with the majority's premise that Judge Grady's order in fact will prompt a settlement. Contrary to the clear implication of the majority's opinion, the class portion of the anticipated trial in this case would not go so far as to establish defendants' liability to a class of plaintiffs; it would instead resolve only the question of whether defendants were negligent in distributing tainted clotting factor at any particular point in time. Even if defendants were faced with an adverse class verdict, then, a plaintiff still would be required to clear a number of hurdles before he would be entitled to a judgment. For example, defendants no doubt would contest at that stage whether a particular plaintiff could establish proximate causation or whether his or her claim is in any event barred by the statute of limitations. Thus, contrary to the majority's implication, a class verdict in favor of plaintiffs would not automatically entitle each member of the class to a seven-figure judgment.... The defendants will thus have ample opportunity to settle should they lose the class trial. And that would seem to me an advisable strategy in light of the success they have had in earlier cases. That factor distinguishes this case from a more standard class action, where a non-bifurcated trial would resolve all relevant issues and conclusively establish liability to the class. Perhaps that explains why defendants' own arguments in support of their petition are based on the assumption that a class trial would ensue, rather than on the proposition that a settlement would follow inevitably from Judge Grady's order.

Finally, ... the majority's arguments addressed to the propriety of forcing "defendants to stake their companies on the outcome of a single jury trial" or of allowing a single jury to "hold the fate of an industry in the palm of its hand" seem to me at odds with Fed.R.Civ.P. 23 itself. That rule expressly permits class treatment of such claims when its requirements are met, regardless of the magnitude of potential liability. And I see nothing in Rule 23, or in any of the relevant cases, that would make likelihood of success on the merits a prerequisite for class certification. The majority's preference for avoiding a class trial and for submitting the negligence issue "to multiple juries constituting in the aggregate a much larger and more diverse sample of decision-makers" is a rationale for amending the rule, not for avoiding its application in a specific case.

Notes and Questions

1. This portion of *Rhone-Poulenc* was rejected in In re Copley Pharmaceutical, Inc., 161 F.R.D. 456 (D. Wyo. 1995), in which the trial court certified a nationwide class action against a drug manufacturer. The court thought that "consideration of the merits of the plaintiffs' claims is expressly prohibited when deciding whether to certify a class" and that apprehension about a single jury "simply is not a legal basis to deny class certification. Such economic reasoning may carry substantial weight in the Seventh Circuit, but this Court must look to Fed.R.Civ.P. 23 and its interpretation by courts to determine the appropriateness of class certification." Id at 460.

2. Assuming that Judge Posner is correct, the threat of legalized blackmail is a detriment to defendants facing a class action, but it is a real boon to plaintiffs that bring class actions. Does this suggest that Rule 23 has created a significant shift in power from defendants to plaintiffs? Does this mean that Rule 23 violates the Rules Enabling Act, which precludes the promulgation of rules that "abridge, enlarge or modify any substantive right"? 28 U.S.C. § 2072(b). Given that Rule 23 is on the books, how is a court to choose between a plaintiff-favoring class certification and a defendant-favoring denial of certification? Should it just close its eyes entirely to the substantive effects of the certification order, or make them explicit, as Posner does?

3. There are some pro-defendant effects to a class action that Posner does not mention. As we have seen, although mass aggregation may make a jury more inclined to find for plaintiffs, it also reduces the likely compensation that any given plaintiff will receive. See pp. 102-03, *supra*. Second, as we have also seen, and as the history of the hemophilia cases bears out, aggregation in immature litigation may favor defendants, who usually win early lawsuits. See pp. 235-36, *supra*. Do these additional potential effects of aggregation balance out Posner's concern? Do they further convince you that Rule 23 is really a substantive rule that lies beyond the bounds of the Rules Enabling Act?

4. The hemophilia litigation continued to be prosecuted in the transferee court. Within seventeen months of the decision in *Rhone-Poulenc*, the manufacturers agreed to settle the case for approximately $640 million, on the condition that the case was settled as a class action. The district court certified the class on an opt-out basis and approved the settlement. See Jay Tidmarsh, Mass Tort Settlement Class Actions 91-100 (1998). Note that the settlement amount is significantly more that Posner set as the outside limit of the likely value of the individual cases, suggesting that the manufacturers were willing to spend a considerable sum to obtain near-total peace. Obviously, since the defendants had become willing partners in the class certification motion, the blackmail concern no longer existed. We examine other ways in which class actions that are used to settle cases affect policy concerns later in this chapter.

Efficiency vs. Unmanageability. The prior two policy concerns have focused primarily on the interests and concerns of class members and persons opposing the class. The court too is an interested player, and has its own interests and concerns in the use of class actions.

From the judicial viewpoint, one of the main reasons to seek aggregation is the efficiency that a single handling of related litigation creates. Whether that efficiency outweighs the inefficiencies of any large-scale aggregation is an open question that we have been exploring throughout this part of the book. Among aggregation devices, however, there are some reasons to think that class actions may be the most likely to achieve a significant measure of efficiency. First, there will typically be only one set of lawyers that represent the class, and a single consistent view of the litigation will streamline the pretrial and trial proceedings. Second, there is no need (as in § 1404 transfers) to file transfer motions in multiple forums, nor (as in § 1407 transfers) to remand cases for separate trials. Third, there will be a single set of pleadings and a single set of claims, rather than myriad overlapping claims that sometimes infect separately filed cases that are aggregated. Putting a single set of class representatives and lawyers in charge of the litigation simplifies matters considerably.

On the other side of the ledger, however, is the concern that the class action will become an unwieldy beast that will be expensive to litigate, cannot be easily managed or tried, and will result in inordinate problems of declaring and implementing remedies. The extent to which these concerns can be alleviated will be the subjects of Parts Two, Three, and Four of this book. In general, techniques to reduce some of the difficulties of class actions exist, but they are not costless in terms of procedural values such as adversarial process, trans-substantivity, and constrained judicial power. When you study these materials, realize that they have a direct effect on the likelihood of class certification in particular cases.

Let us, however, mention one concern now. A defendant faced with an all-or-nothing case is likely to invest considerable resources to fight the case. This requires class counsel to spend considerable time and money in return. Often class counsel fronts this money, and may be unable to collect it if the case is lost; indeed, class counsel may well have more financially at risk in the case than any class member. This fact puts enormous pressure on class counsel to seek a settlement that permits him to recover his fees and costs — even if the best interests of the class dictate otherwise. The wedge that is created between counsel and class is not unique to class litigation; but it is magnified in such litigation, and raises a constant concern about collusion between class counsel and the party opposing the class. These are only some of the ethical problems that class actions pose.

Ethical Concerns. Class actions not only have advantages and disadvantages for the plaintiffs, defendants, and the court, but they also have advantages and disadvantages for class counsel. As we examine in more detail in Chapter Eight, the ethical rules under which lawyers today operate were designed with traditional, adversarial, bi-polar litigation in mind. An early, and unflattering, recognition of the pressures that class litigation places on counsel was a concurring opinion by Judge Duniway in Kline v. Coldwell, Banker & Co., 508 F.2d 226 (9th Cir. 1974), cert. denied 421 U.S. 963 (1975). In *Kline*, a plaintiff claimed that the real estate commissions that brokers in Los Angeles County charged to home sellers violated the antitrust laws. The plaintiff had sold only one house through one agent — hardly a transaction worth a lawsuit — and so brought the case as a plaintiff class action on behalf of all sellers of real estate against a defendant class action of all real estate brokers. The court of appeals refused to certify the case on two now-familiar grounds: the crushing effect that a $750 million judgment could have on individual brokers that would be jointly and severally liable, and a trial of thousands of plaintiffs against 2,000 defendants was unmanageable. The concurrence focused as well on the ethical issues that such a class action raised:

> I cannot believe that Rule 23, as amended, was intended or should be construed to authorize the kind of judicial juggernaut that plaintiffs and their counsel seek to create here. The plaintiffs Kline have been designated as the representatives of an estimated 400,000 sellers of real property in Los Angeles County, sellers of residential dwellings containing up to twelve units. The Klines sold one residence, in 1970, for $42,500. They paid a commission to one broker, Lelah Pierson, of 6%, or $2,550. . . . Yet the plaintiffs seek to parlay their claim into a lawsuit on behalf of 400,000 sellers, not one of whom, so far as we are advised, except the Sherman plaintiffs, has indicated the slightest interest in suing anyone. . . .
>
> [N]otice will be sent to each of the 400,000 represented plaintiffs. I would expect that the Rule 23 notice to each "represented" plaintiff, as prepared by plaintiffs' counsel, would give him a brief description of the nature of the case, and then would tell him (Rule 23(c)(2)(A)) that he can "opt out," but would also tell him that, if he does not opt out, he will incur no financial obligation, while, if the suit is won, he will share in the loot. I wonder if this is proper. Why shouldn't a "represented" plaintiff be told that if he elects to participate in the alleged bonanza, he may, by so electing, subject himself to liability for his share of the costs of suit if the bonanza is not forthcoming? Why should the court offer him a free ride in a case in which the defendants' costs, if they win, may be very large, and will probably not be collectible from the named plaintiffs? Why shouldn't what I have said also apply to plaintiffs' attorneys' fees, unless there is an ironclad agreement by the attorneys that they will collect no fees from anyone if the suit is lost? . . . The real bonanza in a case like this, if it is won, will go to counsel. Perhaps the class action order could be conditioned upon an agreement by counsel that they will pay all costs of all defendants if the suit is lost.
>
> I venture to suggest that none of the class action features of this case was dreamed up by the named plaintiffs, but that all of them are the brain children of their attorneys. In California, barratry is a crime (Cal.Pen.C. § 158). The Rules of Professional Conduct of the State Bar, authorized by Cal. Bus. and Prof. Code § 6076, provide (Rule 2 § a): "a member of the State Bar shall not solicit professional employment by advertisement or otherwise." Does solicitation cease to be solicitation when done under the aegis of a judge? If so, what has become of the centuries old policy of the law against stirring up litigation? Did the Supreme Court, when it adopted Rule 23, as amended, intend to

abrogate that policy for a case like this? I am loath to believe that it did. I also have grave doubt whether such a change in the law, if intended, can properly be called a matter of procedure. In other words, I doubt that the Supreme Court has power, by a procedural rule, to abrogate the policy to which I have referred, assuming that that is what the Court intended.

I do not say that the Rule 23(b)(3) class action is always unethical and improperly coercive. Doubtless there are circumstances in which it is the only viable means of obtaining relief for classes of truly and actively aggrieved plaintiffs. But courts should not be in the business of encouraging the creation of lawsuits like this one. [508 F.2d at 236-39.]

Leaving the hyperbole to the side, it should be evident that class counsel is often in a difficult position. Economically, in a case like *Kline*, the only way to make a go of the litigation is to bring it on a classwide basis. But that very same class action creates certain tensions between counsel and the class. Moreover, when the adequacy of representation requirement permits some tensions or conflicts to exist within the class, class counsel finds himself somewhat at sea in trying to figure out exactly who the client is. Is it the class representative? Is it some fictional amalgam of the hypothetical "ordinary" class member? Is it the lawyer's own view about the best interests of the class? See David L. Shapiro, *Class Actions: The Class as Party and Client*, 73 Notre Dame L. Rev. 913 (1998). These are difficult questions that standard bi-polar litigation does not raise.

There are comparable concerns for the proper ethical responsibilities of judges. Like attorney rules of ethics, judicial codes of ethics are premised on the traditional adversarial model, in which the judge is a neutral, passive figure. But class actions create the potential for conflicts among class members and between class counsel and class members. To some extent, the judge needs to moderate these conflicts in deciding who should act as class representative and counsel. But this moderator's role must continue throughout the litigation in order to ensure that the rights of absent class members are being adequately protected. Does the solicitude that the judge must show for the class create a risk that the judge will ultimately empathize with the class and lose her neutrality?

Similarly, class actions that result in widespread relief force judges to act in a more legislative, and less judicial, capacity. In La Mar v. H & B Novelty & Loan Co., 489 F.2d 461 (9th Cir. 1973), another dual plaintiff-defendant class action that alleged the violation of federal consumer statutes, the court declined to certify either class. Its specific ruling on the meaning of Rule 23 was influenced by the following concerns:

> The emergence of the class action inescapably forces consideration of the characteristics of the judicial and administrative processes because its features in many instances are derived from both. In a broad sense, fixing the outer limits of permissible class actions involves the determination of the extent to which proceedings within the judiciary will be permitted to resemble in function the administrative process.

It is obvious to even the casual observer that the two processes have features in common and that there is no bright line between them. Judges, for example, bring to their tasks the same informed judgment about the society within which their rulings operate as do administrators. Also those in executive positions frequently find themselves involved, either in a formal or informal setting, in passing judgment on particular claims presented on the basis of a substantially circumscribed record.

Nonetheless, the archetypes are distinguishable and it is in the interest of the judiciary, as well as the executive, to recognize and maintain these distinctions. There is no need to dwell on them at great length. It is enough to observe that the judicial process generally is concerned with discrete complaints of injury by one or a very small number of alleged wrong-doers. Those invoking the aid of the courts generally have in mind particular relief which can be provided by the court in a relatively easy and expeditious manner. The passivity of the judiciary is underscored by its dependence on the evidence provided by the parties and the relatively narrow scope of possible resolutions of the controversy imposed by the applicable rules of law which it must observe. The attorneys for the parties function in a manner compatible with this structure. The method by which evidence is introduced and the type of evidence that is permissible are rigidly controlled. The forums within which persuasion may be attempted are fixed and the methods of persuasion limited and to a degree quite formal. Finally, and of particular importance to class actions, the attorneys are restrained in their pursuit of clients. While the limits of these restraints continue to perplex the profession, which must function in a world in which advertising and salesmanship are omnipresent, no one will deny that restraints do and should exist. All perceive that they are congruent with the fundamentally passive role of the judiciary.

The administrative process, on the other hand, frequently need not await the specific complaint. It can initiate, *sua sponte*, steps designed to correct perceived evils in accordance with the authority provided it by legislative action or delegation from higher executive authority. Traditionally it represents large and imprecise interests which, at the highest level of abstraction, are designated "the public interest." Continuous oversight, as opposed to intervention by invitation as in the judiciary's case, is a normal administrative function. And, not surprisingly, lawyers function quite differently in the administrative setting. Procedures and forms of persuasion are less hampered, and representation of large groups having broad common interests is quite common.

These observations set the stage for an examination of the issues [in this case]. Class actions, we believe, must be structured so as to conform in the essential respects to the judicial process. This is the principle by which we are guided. [489 F.2d at 463-64.]

The Concern for Trans-Substantive Rules. Taken as a whole, the various concerns described above might suggest that cases that qualify for class treatment might well result in different outcomes for class members than individual litigation. If this is indeed true, how can the use of an outcome-determinative rule be justified?

Conclusion. Obviously, class actions hold both great promise as an aggregation device and raise great concerns. We turn now to the circumstances under which class actions can in fact be maintained.

B. BALANCING THE BENEFITS AND RISKS OF CLASS ACTIONS: THE PRESENT LIMITS OF RULE 23

Rule 23 explicitly requires all federal class actions to satisfy the four criteria set out in Rule 23(a), as well as one of the four criteria in Rule 23(b). Most of the criteria are rather general, and therefore capable of being molded to the context of particular cases. In this section, we explore the interpretation that Rule 23 has been given over a range of substantive areas and possible uses of Rule 23.

The basic structural division that we use to explore the interpretations that Rule 23 might receive in different contexts is the division between litigation class actions and settlement class actions. Fifteen years ago, this division in class actions was essentially unknown; all class actions were brought, at least ostensibly, to litigate the claims of class members against a defendant or group of defendants, and defendants typically resisted class certification vigorously. Today, however, as defendants have grown to appreciate the benefits of total peace that a class action can provide, Rule 23 is increasingly being used as a vehicle not to litigate contested issues but rather to implement a settlement that individual plaintiffs and the defendants have earlier agreed upon; plaintiffs and defendants find themselves mutually arguing for class certification. Indeed, according to one recent estimate, as many as one-quarter of all class actions filed today may be settlement class actions. See Thomas E. Willging, Empirical Study of Class Actions in Four Federal District Courts 61-61 (1996). A critical issue is whether the requirements of Rule 23 should change in these two settings.

Before we study these basic divisions, however, we stop to examine some of the mechanics of class certification that are the backdrop against which the arguments concerning the Rule 23(a) and 23(b) prerequisites occur.

1. The Mechanics of Certification Practice

The Process of Obtaining Class Certification. The process of certifying a class usually begins with the filing of a pleading that alleges that the essential elements of a class action exist and ask that a class action be certified. The pleading may be filed by either the plaintiff or the defendant. The Federal Rules do not require that the request be made in an original pleading; often, the pleading requesting class certification is filed in an amendment. Once the allegations are made, Rule 23(c)(1) directs the court to determine whether the case may be maintained as a class action "[a]s soon as practicable after the commencement of the action." Some courts by local rule require that the parties present arguments on the appropriateness of class certification within a definite time period (say, 90 days), although they do not necessarily impose a similar deadline on the court's own ruling.

The usual process by which the determination is made commences with a period of discovery in which the allegations of the pleading may be tested. Parties sometimes engage in little or no discovery, but when discovery does occur, it commonly focuses on two things. The first is the legal theory or theories that the class representative is pursuing, with the party opposing class certification seeking to demonstrate that the claims of the class raise a host of individual, case-specific issues or that the putative representative's claims raise unique issues not shared by other members of the class. The second is a factual examination of the class representative and class counsel to determine if they have the financial and/or emotional stability to ensure adequate representation.

After discovery is finished, one party then moves formally for class certification. Usually briefs are submitted in support of and in opposition to the motion, and arguments are held. The court then renders a decision. The Supreme Court has held that, in deciding whether to certify a class, the district court should not conduct an inquiry into the merits of the case. Eisen v. Carlisle & Jacquelin, 417 U.S. 156, 177-78 (1974).

If the case is certified as an opt-out class action, the court will then order that notice be given to class members advising them of their right to opt out. In many cases this is the first time that class members will discover that they are now part of a lawsuit, and they must make their decision to remain in or opt out of the case within the time period ordered by the court. In mandatory class actions, in which notice is not necessary even at this stage, class members may not know about their class membership even after certification. See Manual for Complex Litigation, Third § 30.211 (recommending that notice of class certification be given in mandatory class actions). Unless a class member (or more likely his or her lawyer) finds out about the case, the class member may never participate in the class certification process. If the class member does wish to participate, however, he or she can seek to intervene in the case.

This process described above is common, but not inevitable. Some courts will conditionally certify a class on the basis of the pleadings (and perhaps affidavits), and then delay a final decision on class certification until a later date. See F.R.Civ.P. 23(c)(1). Often the preliminary certification is regarded as an adequate ground to send notice to class members. In an opt-out class action, class members will typically be required to decide whether to opt out at this point, rather than after final certification. See *Manual supra* § 30.11.

When the court certifies the class, it usually designates class counsel at the same time.

A court that has certified a class always reserves the right to either decertify the class or amend the class at a later date. F.R.Civ.P. 23(c)(1).

The Requirement of Notice. In many ways, the matter of notice is central to the entire class action mechanism. Rule 23 expressly requires that notice should be given to class members in two situations: (1) when an opt-out class has been certified, and class members must be told about their right to opt out (which they do by means of writing the court and requesting exclusion); and (2) when the court is considering the settlement or dismissal of the case. See F.R.Civ.P. 23(c)(2), (e). In addition, the court can order notice in other appropriate circumstances. F.R.Civ.P. 23(d)(2). Thus, notice is required in all opt-out class actions; it is not necessarily required in mandatory class actions. In opt-out class actions, it is standard practice for the moving party to submit with the motion for class certification a plan for notifying class members, and for the court to order, at the time that the class is certified, that a notice plan be implemented immediately.

This fact is especially significant because of the Supreme Court's holding in Eisen v. Carlisle & Jacquelin, 417 U.S. 156 (1974). *Eisen*, which was a opt-out securities class action, held that the explicit language of Rule 23(c)(2) required individual notice to be sent to all class members who could be identified by reasonable effort. According to the Court, individual notice meant, at a minimum, notice by first-class mail; the Court rejected the argument that various forms of substituted notice (such as newspaper advertising, TV advertising, pamphlets, and the like) was adequate notice for those who could be identified by reasonable efforts. The Court further held that the cost of notice was to be borne by the class representative, not by the defendant. Nor did *Eisen* excuse the separate requirement of a campaign of substituted notice for those members that were not reasonably identifiable.

In *Eisen*, the number of identifiable class members allegedly exceeded two million. The claim of the class representative was about $70. Therefore, the practical result of *Eisen* was the "death knell" of the class action; no rational plaintiff would incur a $315,000 expense (using the then-extant postal rate) for individual notice, plus the additional expense of a substituted notice campaign (which can also run into the hundreds of thousands to millions of dollars), on the chance that the expense might be recovered after successful litigation of a $70 claim. Obviously, the way that this problem is avoided in many cases is that class counsel fronts the money for notice. But this fact creates problems as well, for it means that only very well-off firms can even hope to be appointed class counsel, and it creates an enormous financial incentive for class counsel to settle the case in order to recoup the expense. Does it make sense to preclude class certification, or to create a wedge between class counsel and class members with small-stake claims, on the ground that notice must be given to the entire class to protect it? Protected from what — the loss of a claim that it is not economically viable to bring in an individual suit? Should Rule 23 be amended to dispense with the requirement for notice when the cost of providing notice forecloses any chance for the plaintiff class to obtain a recovery?

Obviously, given the practical difficulties of notice, class representatives often prefer, if possible, to obtain class certification under the mandatory provisions of (b)(1) or (b)(2). See George Rutherglen, *Better Late Than*

Never: Notice and Opt Out At the Settlement Stage of Class Actions, 71 N.Y.U. L. Rev. 258, 271 (1996).

The Statute of Limitations. One of the central practical advantages of a class action is that the statute of limitations is tolled between the time that the request for class certification is first made and the time that the class certification motion is denied or a certified class action is ultimately decertified. American Pipe & Construction Co. v. Utah, 414 U.S. 538 (1974); Glidden v Chromalloy American Corp., 808 F.2d 621 (7th Cir. 1986).

The Dismissal or Settlement of Class Actions. Like any lawsuit, class actions can be dismissed or settled. Unlike ordinary lawsuits, however, Rule 23(e) requires that any dismissal or settlement must receive "the approval of the court," and cannot occur until a court-approved notice of the dismissal or settlement has been given to class members. Class members that oppose a settlement or dismissal have an ability to file objections with the court, although in some circuits they need to have attempted to intervene in the case in order to preserve their right to appeal the approval or dismissal. Loran v. Furr's/Bishop's Inc., 988 F.2d 554 (5th Cir. 1993). Typically the court will hold a hearing on the issue of settlement or dismissal. The hearing does not need to be adversarial, nor are objecting class members guaranteed the right to discover information concerning the settlement or dismissal. See p. 656, *infra*.

Rule 23(e) does not describe the factors that a court should use in deciding whether to approve a dismissal or settlement. The most common formulation of the test for determining whether a settlement should be approved is whether a settlement is "fair, reasonable, and adequate." See Jay Tidmarsh, Mass Tort Settlement Class Actions 6 (1998). This formulation is hardly self-executing, and courts have often developed more detailed lists of factors to determine fairness, reasonableness, and adequacy. The Third Circuit uses nine factors: "(1) the complexity and duration of the litigation; (2) the reaction of the class to the settlement; (3) the stage of the proceedings; (4) the risks of establishing liability; (5) the risks of establishing damages; (6) the risks of maintaining a class action; (7) the ability of the defendants to withstand a greater judgment; (8) the range of reasonableness of the settlement in light of the best recovery; and (9) the range of reasonableness of the settlement in light of all the attendant risks of litigation." See In re General Motors Corp. Pick-Up Truck Fuel Tank Products Liability Litigation, 55 F.3d 768, 785 (3rd Cir.), cert. denied, 516 U.S. 824 (1995). The Seventh Circuit uses six: "(1) the strength of the case for plaintiffs on the merits, balanced against the extent of settlement offer; (2) the complexity, length, and expense of further litigation; (3) the amount of opposition to the settlement; (4) the reaction of members of the class to the settlement; (5) the opinion of competent counsel; and (6) stage of the proceedings and the amount of discovery completed." Gautreaux v. Pierce, 690 F.2d 616, 631 (7th Cir. 1982). See also Wright et al., *supra*, § 1797.1 (describing factors used by various courts).

Appeal from an Order Granting or Denying Class Certification. Presently, an order granting or denying class certification is not immediately appealable of right, even when the refusal to certify the class occurs in a small-stakes case and the refusal amounts to the "death knell" of the litigation. Coopers & Lybrand v. Livesay, 437 U.S. 463 (1978). As you will see in this chapter, appellate courts have increasingly been finding ways around this rule, and will sometimes review class certification orders through a writ of mandamus under 28 U.S.C. § 1651, sometimes on interlocutory appeal under 28 U.S.C. § 1292(b), and sometimes on the theory that the class certification amounts to a preliminary injunction that is immediately appealable under 28 U.S.C. § 1292(a)(1). In May, 1998, the Supreme Court forwarded to Congress a new Rule 23(f), which would permit appeals of class certification orders on a discretionary basis. See p. 696, *infra*.

The standard of review on appeal is generally said to be abuse of discretion, although we will see in some of the cases in this chapter that appellate courts give less rein to district courts than this standard implies.

Attorneys' Fees. In many ways, attorneys' fees lie at the very heart of class action practice, and the entire device cannot be understood apart from the economic incentives that attorneys' fees create. Unfortunately, we can touch on the issue only briefly. Rule 23 does not itself permit the court to award attorneys' fees or expenses. Nonetheless, based on the equitable notions of unjust enrichment and compensation for the creation of a common benefit, courts have routinely claimed, and used, the power to award fees and expenses. Unless there is statutory authority for the separate award of attorneys' fees, attorneys will be paid from any recovery that the attorney obtains on behalf of the class. The fee agreement that the attorney enters into with the class representative does not necessarily determine the fee that counsel receives, and an attorney may not bill the class for his services; rather, the court determines what a reasonable fee should be. See In re Combustion, Inc., 968 F. Supp. 1116, 1132 (W.D. La. 1997). In determining fees, courts use either a percentage approach or an hourly ("lodestar") approach, and consider a wide range of factors in setting the appropriate fee. See Wright et al., *supra*, § 1803.

The entire issue of attorneys' fees has something of a mythic quality to it. There are a few well-known cases in which class members received next-to-nothing, and class counsel walked away with millions of dollars in fees. There are a few well-known cases in which district courts have exercised their fee-setting authority with some vengeance, and have sliced the fee requests of class counsel drastically because the court thought that the fee request was exorbitant in relation to the quality of the work performed or the risks assumed, the work was duplicative of the work of others, or the work did not benefit the class as a whole; the most famous of these was probably the *Agent Orange* litigation, in which Judge Weinstein whittled requests for fees and expenses down to $10.7 million (out of a settlement fund of $180 million), even though counsel had requested several times that amount. In re "Agent Orange" Product Liability Litigation, 611 F. Supp. 1296 (E.D.N.Y. 1985), *aff'd* in part, *rev'd* in part, 818 F.2d 226 (2d Cir. 1987). Despite these stories, an empirical study of federal class actions has found that awards for fees and expenses are not excessive; median fees in class actions ranged from 27% to 30% of total recovery, less than a standard 33% contingency fee in individual litigation. Thomas E. Willging et al., Empirical

Study of Class Actions in Four Federal District Courts 68-69 (1996). The study also found that the problem of trivial relief — in which class members receive little and class counsel receive huge fees — was a rare phenomenon; the fee-to-recovery ratio exceeded 40% in only 5 out of 68 cases that were studied. Id. at 77.

Even if the "rich lawyer-poor class member" myth is false, there can be no doubt that the existence of enormous potential fees (in absolute dollars) creates numerous difficulties for class actions. In the first place, the existence of attorneys' fees may set off a competition among lawyers to be the first to certify a class, in order to be appointed class counsel; and it may also create hostilities between lawyers who prefer to litigate cases individually and those who prefer to move in quickly, certify a class, strike a deal, and move on to the next case. Second, the possibility of large fees creates a situation in which collusion is always possible, and thus requires the court to be constantly vigilant. Third, even without collusion, the possibility of enormous fees often creates very different incentives for class counsel and class members, and thus creates an inevitable tension between class counsel and class members. When these tensions become great enough, of course, the adequacy of class representation is called into question, and the ability to certify a class is jeopardized.

It is to this issue — the circumstances under which class certification is appropriate — that we now turn.

2. Litigation Class Actions

In this subsection we examine the requirements of Rules 23(a) and (b) that pertain to litigation class actions. In order to be certified as a class action, the person seeking class treatment must meet the burden of establishing each element of Rule 23(a), and at least one of the elements of Rule 23(b). See, *e.g.*, In re American Medical Systems, Inc., 75 F.3d 1069, 1079 (6th Cir. 1996). The plain language of Rule 23(a) seems to create four elements, which are generally referred to as numerosity, commonality, typicality and adequacy of representation. But federal courts have long held that two additional requirements must also be established in order to pass over the bar of Rule 23(a): The class must be adequately defined, and the class representative must be a member of the class. See, *e.g.*, Roman v. ESB, Inc., 550 F.2d 1343, 1348 (4th Cir. 1976) (definition of the class is essential prerequisite to maintaining a class action); Long v. District of Columbia, 469 F.2d 927, 930 (D.C. Cir. 1972) ("A person simply cannot represent a class of which he is not a member.").

As you read the following materials on the requirements of Rules 23(a) and (b), ask yourself what purposes are served by the prerequisites to class action certification, whether these purposes adequately address the reasons for and concerns of class actions, and whether these same policies could be better served by a substantially revised Rule 23. Ask as well whether the prerequisites are, or should be, given the same interpretation in complex and in complicated litigation.

a. The Existence and Definition of a Class

The implied requirement that the class be adequately defined and identified derives from the language of Rule 23, which speaks of "members of a class" suing or being sued. A proper class definition is critical for many reasons. First, it is impossible to know whether the Rule 23 criteria have been met until the class is defined; for instance, how can a court determine if the class representatives adequately represent the class when it is not clear who is in the class? A proper class definition can also be important for other reasons, such as determining the proper scope of discovery, the applicable law, the proper scope of the remedy, the notice that might need to be given to class members, the preclusive effect of any judgment, and the true interests of the class in any settlement.

RICE v. CITY OF PHILADELPHIA

66 F.R.D. 17 (E.D. Pa. 1974)

■ FULLAM, District Judge. [The plaintiffs alleged "the existence of a pattern or practice which results in illegal detention of persons charged with crime, because of delays in holding preliminary arraignments, and sought declaratory, injunctive, and compensatory relief against the City of Philadelphia, its Police Commissioner, its District Attorney, and its Municipal Court judges. The plaintiffs sought to certify the case as a class action on behalf of "all persons who are, who have been, or who will be illegally detained by the Police Department of the City of Philadelphia between arrest and preliminary arraignment, and who are denied a prompt preliminary arraignment by defendants." The plaintiffs also proposed to certify a defendant class consisting of the 22 judges of the Philadelphia Municipal Court, represented by the President Judge of that Court.

[The court declined to certify the defendant class. It also addressed the request for certification of a Rule 23(b)(3) plaintiff class with respect to the claims for monetary relief and a Rule 23(b)(2) plaintiff class with respect to the injunctive and declaratory claims.]

This case brings into sharp focus the relationship between class actions under Rule 23(b)(2), and class actions under Rule 23(b)(3). The provisions of Rule 23(b)(2) are designed to cover cases in which the primary concern is the grant of injunctive or declaratory relief. In such cases, there is no requirement that notice be given to all of the class members, and there is no opportunity for putative class members to "opt out." Moreover, the precise definition of the class is relatively unimportant. If relief is granted to the plaintiff class, the defendants are legally obligated to comply, and it is usually unnecessary to define with precision the persons entitled to enforce compliance, since presumably at least the representative plaintiffs would be available to seek, and interested in obtaining, follow-up relief if necessary.

In a (b)(3) action, on the other hand, because of the notice and "opt out" features, greater precision in class definition is required. Moreover, most such actions involve claims for damages, and it is usually necessary, at some point, to identify individual members of the class.

In the present case, plaintiffs argue that the primary thrust of their action is for injunctive and declaratory relief, and that the case should therefore be permitted to proceed as a (b)(2) class action. Plaintiffs appear to concede that their proposed definition of the class would be unsatisfactory for a (b)(3) action. However, plaintiffs also are seeking damages, contending that this is merely incidental to the basic purpose of the action; and it is this feature which causes difficulties.

Defining a class as consisting of all persons who have been or will be affected by the conduct charged to the defendants is entirely appropriate where only injunctive or declaratory relief is sought. Indeed, the principal beneficiaries of an injunctive decree would seem likely to be those class members whose rights have not yet been violated. But the proposed class definition is clearly unsatisfactory where damage claims are asserted. Persons whose rights have not yet been violated cannot very well obtain damages. Moreover, the definition is too broad, since it purports to include all persons whose rights have ever been violated in the past, in the respects complained of. If for no other reason than the statute of limitations, this definition would be unacceptable....

In the present case, not only would the calculation of the amount of damages depend upon the individual facts of each claimant's case, but virtually all of the issues would have to be litigated individually in order to determine whether a particular alleged class member was entitled to any damages at all. Each claimant, in order to obtain the benefits of the class suit, would have to establish his membership in the class (*i.e.*, that his rights were violated).

Of perhaps greater significance, the issues involved in determining whether the plaintiff class is entitled to injunctive or declaratory relief are simply not the same issues involved in determining whether individual members of the class may be entitled to damages. There could be many reasons for denying injunctive or declaratory relief which ought not to have the effect of precluding particular class members from obtaining damages. . . .

Plaintiffs appear to concede the impracticability of giving notice to the proposed class. And, as mentioned above, there is no right to opt out in a (b)(2) action. I find particularly troublesome the notion that individuals who may never learn of the pendency of this case might encounter difficulty in pursuing meritorious individual litigation in the future, on the basis of lis pendens, res judicata, or collateral estoppel. In short, I believe this is the kind of case in which notice should be required before permitting a class action for damages, even incidentally. Since notice is not feasible, class action treatment on issues of liability for damages should not be permitted.

Notes and Questions

1. If a court finds that a proposed class action has been inadequately defined, it can either dismiss the class action or redefine the class in some manner that satisfies Rule 23. See 7A Charles A. Wright et al., Federal Practice & Procedure § 1760 (1986). Courts sometimes express an unwillingness to dismiss a case when a change in class definition can fix the problem. See Smith v. Brown & Williamson Tobacco Corp., 174 F.R.D. 90, 92 n.1 (W.D. Mo. 1997); but see Heaven v. Trust Co. Bank, 118 F.3d 735 (11th Cir. 1997) ("The district court has no *sua sponte* obligation to subclassify; it is the plaintiff's burden to designate an appropriate class."); cf. In re Silicone Gel Breast Implant Products Liability Litigation, 1994 WL 578353, *17 (N.D. Ala.) (re-defining class to exclude persons living in Australia, Ontario, and Quebec because most objections to settlement came from these areas).

2. Given the many purposes that a proper class definition is designed to serve, was *Rice* correct to focus solely on the nature of the remedy the class is pursuing? Was *Rice* actually holding that the class was inadequately defined, that the class representatives' claims for damages were not typical of the claims of other class members (see Rule 23(a)(3)), that the class representatives did not adequately represent the damages claims of class members (see Rule 23(a)(4)), or that the individual damages issues of class members predominated over common issues (see Rule 23(b)(3))? Should these other requirements of Rule 23 influence the issue of the class definition? Cf. Carpenter v. Davis, 424 F.2d 257, 260 (5th Cir. 1970) (finding that "[i]t is not necessary that the members of the class be so clearly identified that any member can be presently ascertained" when other elements of Rule 23(a) and (b) are established).

3. *Rice* was brought under 42 U.S.C. § 1983. When the courts wish to enforce civil rights vigorously, should courts be more willing to accept some indefiniteness in the class definition? When civil rights are not favored, should any looseness in the class definition be grounds for denial of certification? How can such a breach of our trans-substantive aspiration be justified?

4. Should the complexity of the case influence the class definition issue? *Rice* was not a complex case. With respect to monetary claims, there were sufficient assets to compensate all victims, and with respect to injunctive claims, all class members had an essentially unitary interest in prompt arraignments — there was no antagonism between early- and late-filing claimants. Suppose, however, that the defendants were teetering on the verge of bankruptcy, and the failure to certify a class action would have meant that the early-filing plaintiffs would have received all of their assets. Should the court tolerate more indefiniteness in the class definition in this situation? How can such a breach of our trans-substantive aspiration be justified?

5. Federal courts have taken widely different views on how specifically a proposed class must be defined. Usually courts do not insist that every class member be identified at the beginning of the litigation, but they may require that the general size of the class be known and that the identity of particular class members be ascertainable in the future with reasonable effort. See generally Wright et al., *supra*, § 1760.

6. Courts have traditionally been very reluctant to certify classes whose membership depends upon the "state of mind" of the class member. See DeBremaecker v. Short, 433 F.2d 733 (5th Cir. 1970); Simer v. Rios, 661 F.2d 655 (7th Cir. 1981).

7. As *Rice* says, one reason that it has usually been thought essential that the identity of the class members be known as exactly as possible is the need to provide both notice and an opportunity to opt out must be given to class members in Rule 23(b)(3) class actions. Another reason is the need to provide notice to class members in any Rule 23(b) class action in the event that the class representatives propose to dismiss or settle the case. With regard to the latter concern, is it ever possible to define a class action that includes persons that have not yet suffered an identifiable injury? *Rice* seems not to think so. If *Rice* is correct, the utility of the class action as a device either to litigate the claims of future victims under Rule 23(b)(3) or to settle claims on a truly global basis under any provision of Rule 23(b) is in jeopardy. See pp. 658-89, *infra* (discussing the use of settlement class actions to resolve future claims).

A third reason for a well-defined class under Rule 23(b)(3) is that the damages typically sought in such actions normally must be distributed to an identifiable group. Could a class be more loosely defined if some other method of distributing damages were found? See pp. 1410-19, *infra* (discussing use of fluid damage recoveries in some types of class actions).

b. Membership in a Class

A second implied requirement for all class actions is that the class representative be a member of the class. This requirement has its roots in the language of Rule 23 itself ("one or more members of a class may sue"), in the Article III requirement of standing, and in the real party in interest requirement of Rule 17(a). The most frequent and difficult situation created by the class membership prerequisite arises in the context of a class action brought by or against an association seeking to represent its members. A number of courts have held that, even though the union or cooperative association may seem to be the most appropriate entity to represent the class, the association's failure to request any remedy for itself prevents it from being a member and representative of the class. See, *e.g.*, Farmers Co-op Oil Co. v. Socony-Vacuum Oil Co., 133 F.2d 101 (8th Cir. 1942) (co-op cannot represent individual farmers in antitrust suit); Wilhite v. South Central Bell Tel. & Tel. Co., 426 F. Supp. 61 (E.D. La. 1976) (union can represent its members in seeking injunctive relief for discrimination in employment, but cannot represent them for monetary relief). Some of the problems the class membership requirement creates in suits by or against unincorporated associations have been ameliorated by Rule 23.2. See 7C Charles A. Wright et al., Federal Practice & Procedure § 1861 (1986).

c. Numerosity

Rule 23(a)(1) provides that a class action may be certified only if "the class is so numerous that joinder of all members is impracticable." On its face, this requirement seems an unequivocal expression of the adversary system's historical preference for individual rather than representational litigation. But that preference obviously ends at some point, and the question is exactly when. When some definite number of persons (say 100 or more) are members of the class? When a single class resolution is more efficient than individual litigation? When individual litigation is unlikely because of the small stakes involved? When a single class resolution is necessary to prevent lawyer dysfunction? Determining how many parties are "too many" for traditional joinder also requires the trial court to be intimately familiar with other joinder rules, and to consider carefully the practical problems likely to attend the litigation of claims under those rules.

ROUBIDOUX v. CELANI

987 F.2d 931 (2d Cir. 1993)

■ PECKHAM, Senior District Judge. This is an action by three recipients of public assistance in Vermont seeking to represent a class of persons whose applications for public assistance have been delayed unlawfully by the Vermont Department of Social Welfare (Department). Appellants Julie Robidoux, Kathleen Rock and Margaret Bevins appeal from a judgment . . . dismissing their lawsuit brought under 42 U.S.C. section 1983. Appellants challenge the district court's refusal to certify their suit as a class action and the district court's subsequent dismissal of the suit as moot. For the reasons stated below, we vacate the judgment of the district court and remand for further proceedings consistent with this opinion.

I. BACKGROUND AND PROCEEDINGS BELOW

The Vermont Department of Social Welfare administers several public assistance programs, including the Food Stamp Program [and] the Aid to Needy Families with Children Program (ANFC) (known as Aid to Families with Dependent Children, or AFDC, in the federal lexicon) . . . . [Federal and state regulations required that state social welfare agencies determine applicants' eligibility for these programs within 30 days of the date of application.]

In spring 1991, finding their resources inadequate to support their families, Robidoux, Rock, and Bevins applied for Food Stamp and/or ANFC benefits to supplement their incomes. The Department did not process any of these applications within the 30-day deadlines. . . .

The plaintiff[s] . . . moved, pursuant to Fed. R. Civ. P. 23(b)(2), to certify as a class "all current and future Vermont applicants for assistance from the Food Stamp [and] ANFC . . . Programs." In support of their motion for class certification, Appellants submitted two documents. One was a letter from the Department's Commissioner to the U.S. Department of Agriculture which indicated that from July to September 1990, 8 percent of the approximately 800 monthly Vermont Food Stamp applications, or about 65 applications per month, had taken more than 30 days to process. The second document was a monitoring record by the U.S. Department of Health and Human Services, which indicated that 71 of 4017, or nearly 2 percent, of quarterly ANFC applications had taken the Department more than 45 days to process during that same period.

The district court denied the motion for class certification. The district court concluded that Appellants had not shown sufficient evidence of numerosity, because

> [p]laintiff has the burden to show that the class is so large that joinder is impossible. Plaintiff has only shown three people who may be affected, and speculatively an undetermined number of future class members....

In support of their motion for reconsideration of the denial of class certification, Appellants submitted a Department report showing overdue applications for May 1990, December 1990, and February 1991. This document indicated that decisions in ANFC were overdue in 22 cases (6% of 365 cases) in May 1990, 74 cases (14% of 528) in December 1990, and 68 cases (13% of 522) in February 1991. Overdue Food Stamp decisions totalled 52 cases (10% of 518) in May 1990, 133 cases (15% of 884) in December 1990, and 113 cases (13% of 867) in February 1991. The study indicated that an increase in applications caused the increase in overdue cases. The district court denied the motion for reconsideration on the same basis as its earlier order.

[The district court then granted summary judgment for the defendant, ruling that Appellants' claims were moot.]

II. DISCUSSION ...

If the district court has applied the proper legal standards in deciding whether to certify a class, its decision may be overturned only if it has abused its discretion.... At the same time, however, abuse of discretion can be found more readily on appeals from the denial of class status than in other areas, for the courts have built a body of case law with respect to class action status....

Appellants first argue that the district court applied an incorrect legal standard in requiring plaintiffs to show the existence of a class so numerous that "joinder is impossible," while Rule 23(a) requires a finding that the numerosity makes joinder of all class members "impracticable."

Impracticable does not mean impossible.... Thus, the district court in the present case, in concluding that numerosity was lacking because plaintiffs had not shown the class to be so large that joinder was "impossible," applied the wrong standard.

Appellants further contend that, under the proper standard, they met the burden of showing numerosity. We agree. Courts have not required evidence of exact class size or identity of class members to satisfy the numerosity requirement....

Appellants presented documentary evidence of delays in 22 to 133 cases per month, depending on the month and whether the assistance sought was Food Stamps or ANFC. Other government benefits cases have held that class representatives who presented similar numbers of potential class members satisfied the numerosity requirement. See, *e.g.*, Grant v. Sullivan, 131 F.R.D. 436, 446 (M.D. Pa. 1990) (a court "may certify a class even if it is composed of as few as 14 members").... A leading treatise concludes, based on prevailing precedent, that the difficulty in joining as few as 40 class members should raise a presumption that joinder is impracticable. 1 [Herbert B. Newberg, Newberg on Class Actions,], § 3.05, at 141-42 [(2d ed. 1985)]....

The district court also failed to address other factors relevant to the practicability of joinder. Determination of practicability depends on all the circumstances surrounding a case, not on mere numbers. Relevant considerations include judicial economy arising from the avoidance of a multiplicity of actions, geographic dispersion of class members, financial resources of class members, the ability of claimants to institute individual suits, and requests for prospective injunctive relief which would involve future class members....

Many of these additional factors are present in this case. Consolidating in a class action what could be over 100 individual suits serves judicial economy. Moreover, the potential class members are distributed over the entire area of Vermont. They are also economically disadvantaged, making individual suits difficult to pursue. An injunction requiring the Department to comply with the statutory deadlines would affect all potential class members, and individual suits could lead to potentially inconsistent results.

Thus, the district court abused its discretion in determining that the class was not so numerous that joinder of all members would be impracticable....

[After rejecting in whole or in part various arguments raised by the defendants concerning the typicality of the claims of the class, standing, and mootness, the court of appeals vacated the district court's judgment remanded the case for further proceedings, including] certification of a class comprising at least "all current and future Vermont applicants for assistance from the Food Stamp and ANFC programs"....

Notes and Questions

1. In common parlance, "impracticable" means "Not practicable; that cannot be carried out, effected, accomplished, or done; practically impossible." VII Oxford English Dictionary 736 (2d ed. 1989). If a class action could be used only when it was practically impossible to join all plaintiffs under Rule 20, it would be a far less useful device for the aggregation of related claims. Instead of engaging in a literalist interpretation of the numerosity requirement, however, most courts engage in a multi-factor inquiry like the one used in *Roubidoux.* See 7A Charles A. Wright et al., Federal Practice & Procedure § 1762 (1986). Some develop basic presumptions that the numerosity requirement has been satisfied. See In re Amerifirst Securities Litigation, 139 F.R.D. 423 (S.D. Fla. 1991) ("the numerosity requirement . . . is generally assumed to have been met in class action suits . . . involving nationally traded securities"). Other cases suggest that, when the number of class members reaches a certain threshold, "the impracticability requirement is usually

satisfied by the numbers alone." In re American Medical Systems, Inc., 75 F.3d 1069, 1079 (6th Cir. 1996). Still others explicitly compare the manageability issues of traditional joinder and class certification to determine which approach is the most practical way of organizing the litigation. See Boggs v. Divested Atomic Corp., 141 F.R.D. 59, 63 (S.D. Ohio 1991) ("Satisfaction of the numerosity requirement does not require that joinder is impossible, but only that plaintiff will suffer a strong litigational hardship or inconvenience if joinder is required."). There seems to be no magic number above which the numerosity requirement is automatically satisfied and below which it is automatically not. See General Telephone Co. of the Northwest v. Equal Employment Opportunity Commission, 446 U.S. 318, 330 (1980) (noting that the "numerosity requirement requires examination of the specific facts of each case and imposes no absolute limitations," but suggesting that 15 putative plaintiffs would be too few).

2. Assume a court concludes that it would be marginally more efficient to proceed as a class action, but that it would also be feasible to adjudicate the claims of the fifty putative class members via traditional joinder. How much weight should the court give to the preference for traditional joinder and party autonomy and how much weight to the interests of efficiency? Should the possibility of excessive deterrence through a class action influence the decision on numerosity? What if the case seems unmanageable? What if the case involves a substantive theory that has fallen out of favor? What if the case involves lawyer dysfunction? In In re Drexel Burnham Lambert Group, Inc., 960 F.2d 285 (2d Cir. 1992), cert. denied, 506 U.S. 1088 (1993), two subclasses of disappointed investors (one numbering about 800 persons and the other 160) agreed to settle their claims on a classwide basis. In holding that both subclasses satisfied the numerosity requirement, the Second Circuit observed that the failure to certify a class might well consume the defendant's assets and that "[i]ndividual adjudication of each claim would take many years, and would drastically increase the legal expenses for all of the parties." Id. at 290.

Suppose that, in *Drexel Burnham*, the defendant had not been insolvent. Should the same considerations have played as large a role in determining whether the numerosity requirement had been established? Or should party autonomy have weighed more heavily?

3. A specific example against which you can test your answers to some of these questions arises when the size of the plaintiff class is unknown or unknowable. In Doe v. Charleston Area Medical Center, Inc., 529 F.2d 638 (4th Cir. 1975) the court certified a class action under 23(b)(2) against enforcement of an anti-abortion policy in a government hospital even though the number of local women who were obliged to go outside the state for abortion services was impossible to assess accurately. But in Male v. Crossroads Associates, 320 F. Supp. 141 (S.D.N.Y. 1970), the court refused certification of a 23(b)(2) suit against an apartment owner because the number of welfare recipients who had allegedly been denied the opportunity to rent apartments from the defendant or deterred from applying had not been established and was speculative.

4. When we examined the requirement of class definition, we saw that the policy issues that swirl around class actions influenced the scope of the doctrine. Now we see that the same policy issues influence the issue of numerosity. Do you like the idea that policy questions shape doctrines that, in theory, could be answered objectively (by saying, for instance, that "numerosity means 100 people")? Doesn't a policy-oriented approach guarantee that there will be many different "laws" of class action, depending on the extent to which a particular

case advances certain objectives? Continue to consider this question as we turn to the last three, highly malleable criteria of Rule 23(a).

d. The Critical Elements of Rule 23(a): Commonality, Typicality, and Adequacy of Representation

The remaining three Rule 23(a) prerequisites for all class actions are closely related. Rule 23(a)(2) requires that there be "questions of law or fact common to the class"; Rule 23(a)(3) requires "the claims or defenses of the representative parties [be] typical of the claims or defenses of the class"; and Rule 23 (a)(4) requires that "the representative parties . . . fairly and adequately protect the interests of the class." Individually and in combination, these criteria seek to assure that the class has proper legal representation, is free of substantial internal antagonisms or tensions, and is suitable for management as a litigation package. They establish, in other words, the irreducible criteria on which our legal system insists in return for a person's sacrifice of their autonomy interest to control their own litigation. At the same time, none of these criteria is self-defining. Do the inherent ambiguities in the three phrases make a party's autonomy interest subject to the vagaries of policy-oriented balancing tests?

GENERAL TELEPHONE COMPANY OF THE SOUTHWEST v. FALCON

457 U.S. 147 (1982)

■ JUSTICE STEVENS delivered the opinion of the Court.

The question presented is whether respondent Falcon, who complained that petitioner did not promote him because he is a Mexican-American, was properly permitted to maintain a class action on behalf of Mexican-American applicants for employment whom petitioner did not hire.

I

In 1969 petitioner initiated a special recruitment and training program for minorities. Through that program, respondent Falcon was hired in July 1969 as a groundman, and within a year he was twice promoted, first to lineman and then to lineman-in-charge. He subsequently refused a promotion to installer-repairman. In October 1972 he applied for the job of field inspector; his application was denied even though the promotion was granted several white employees with less seniority.

Falcon thereupon filed a charge with the Equal Employment Opportunity Commission stating his belief that he had been passed over for promotion because of his national origin and that petitioner's promotion policy operated against Mexican-Americans as a class. In due course he received a right-to-sue letter from the Commission and, in April 1975, he commenced this action under Title VII of the Civil Rights Act of 1964, 42 U.S.C § 2000e et seq. (1976 ed. and Supp. IV), in the United States District Court for the Northern District of Texas. His complaint alleged that petitioner maintained "a policy, practice, custom, or usage of: (a) discriminating against [Mexican-Americans] because of national origin and with respect to compensation, terms, conditions, and privileges of employment, and (b) . . . subjecting [Mexican-Americans] to continuous employment discrimination." Respondent claimed that as a result of this policy whites with less qualification and experience and lower evaluation scores than respondent had been promoted more rapidly. The complaint contained no factual allegations concerning petitioner's hiring practices.

Respondent brought the action "on his own behalf and on behalf of other persons similarly situated, pursuant to Rule 23(b)(2) of the Federal Rules of Civil Procedure." The class identified in the complaint was "composed of Mexican-American persons who are employed, or who might be employed, by General Telephone Company at its place of business located in Irving, Texas, who have been and who continue to be or might be adversely affected by the practices complained of herein."

After responding to petitioner's written interrogatories, respondent filed a memorandum in favor of certification of "the class of all hourly Mexican American employees who have been employed, are employed, or may in the future be employed and all those Mexican Americans who have applied or would have applied for employment had the Defendant not practiced racial discrimination in its employment practices." His position was supported by the ruling of the United States Court of Appeals for the Fifth Circuit in Johnson v. Georgia Highway Express, Inc., 417 F.2d 1122 (1969), that any victim of racial discrimination in employment may maintain an "across the board" attack on all unequal employment practices alleged to have been committed by the employer pursuant to a policy of racial discrimination. Without conducting an evidentiary hearing, the District Court certified a class including Mexican-American employees and Mexican-American applicants for employment who had not been hired.

Following trial of the liability issues, the District Court entered separate findings of fact and conclusions of law with respect first to respondent and then to the class. The District Court found that petitioner had not discriminated against respondent in hiring, but that it did discriminate against him in its promotion practices. The court reached converse conclusions about the class, finding no discrimination in promotion practices, but concluding that petitioner had discriminated against Mexican-Americans at its Irving facility in its hiring practices.

After various post-trial proceedings, the District Court ordered petitioner to furnish respondent with a list of all Mexican-Americans who had applied for employment at the Irving facility during the period between January 1, 1973, and October 18, 1976. Respondent was then ordered to give notice to those persons advising them that they might be entitled to some form of recovery. Evidence was taken concerning the applicants who responded to the notice, and backpay was ultimately awarded to 13 persons, in addition to respondent Falcon. The total recovery by respondent and the entire class amounted to $67,925.49, plus costs and interest.[7]

Both parties appealed. The Court of Appeals rejected . . . petitioner's argument that the class had been defined too broadly. For, under the Fifth Circuit's across-the-board rule, it is permissible for "an employee complaining of one employment practice to represent another complaining of another practice, if the plaintiff and the members of the class suffer from essentially the same injury. In this case, all of the claims are based on discrimination because of national origin." . . .

On the merits, the Court of Appeals [remanded to the district court for further consideration both of the disparate treatment in promotion claims and the disparate impact in hiring claims. The Supreme Court] granted certiorari to decide whether the class action was properly maintained on behalf of both employees who were denied promotion and applicants who were denied employment.

II

The class-action device was designed as "an exception to the usual rule that litigation is conducted by and on behalf of the individual named parties only." . . . Class relief is "peculiarly appropriate" when the "issues involved are common to the class as a whole" and when they "turn on questions of law applicable in the same manner to each member of the class." . . . For in such cases, "the class-action device saves the resources of both the courts and the parties by permitting an issue potentially affecting every [class member] to be litigated in an economical fashion under Rule 23." . . .

Title VII of the Civil Rights Act of 1964, as amended, authorizes the Equal Employment Opportunity Commission to sue in its own name to secure relief for individuals aggrieved by discriminatory practices forbidden by the Act. In exercising this enforcement power, the Commission may seek relief for groups of employees or applicants for employment without complying with the strictures of Rule 23. Title VII, however, contains no special authorization for class suits maintained by private parties. An individual litigant seeking to maintain a class action under Title VII must meet "the prerequisites of numerosity, commonality, typicality, and adequacy of representation" specified in Rule 23(a). . . . These requirements effectively "limit the class claims to those fairly encompassed by the named plaintiff's claims." . . .

We have repeatedly held that "a class representative must be part of the class and 'possess the same interest and suffer the same injury' as the class members." East Texas Motor Freight System, Inc. v. Rodriguez, 431 U.S.

---

7. Respondent's individual recovery amounted to $1,040.33. A large share of the class award, $28,827.50, represented attorney's fees. Most of the remainder resulted from petitioner's practice of keeping all applications active for only 90 days; the District Court found that most of the applications had been properly rejected at the time they were considered, but that petitioner could not justify the refusal to extend employment to disappointed applicants after an interval of 90 days.

395, 403 [(1977)].... In *East Texas Motor Freight*, a Title VII action brought by three Mexican-American city drivers, the Fifth Circuit certified a class consisting of the trucking company's black and Mexican-American city drivers allegedly denied on racial or ethnic grounds transfers to more desirable line-driver jobs. We held that the Court of Appeals had "plainly erred in declaring a class action." Because at the time the class was certified it was clear that the named plaintiffs were not qualified for line-driver positions, "they could have suffered no injury as a result of the allegedly discriminatory practices, and they were, therefore, simply not eligible to represent a class of persons who did allegedly suffer injury."

Our holding in *East Texas Motor Freight* was limited; we noted that "a different case would be presented if the District Court had certified a class and only later had it appeared that the named plaintiffs were not class members or were otherwise inappropriate class representatives." We also recognized the theory behind the Fifth Circuit's across-the-Board rule, noting our awareness "that suits alleging racial or ethnic discrimination and often by their very nature class suits, involving classwide wrongs," and that "[c]ommon questions of law or fact are typically present." In the same breath, however, we reiterated that "careful attention to the requirements of Fed. Rule Civ. Proc. 23 remains nonetheless indispensable" and that the "mere fact that a complaint alleges racial or ethnic discrimination does not in itself ensure that the party who has brought the lawsuit will be an adequate representative of those who many have been the real victims of that discrimination."

We cannot disagree with the proposition underlying the across-the-board rule — that racial discrimination is by definition class discrimination. But the allegation that such discrimination has occurred neither determines whether a class action may be maintained in accordance with Rule 23 nor defines the class that may be certified. Conceptually, there is a wide gap between (a) an individual's claim that he has been denied a promotion on discriminatory grounds, and his otherwise unsupported allegation that the company has a policy of discrimination, and (b) the existence of a class of persons who have suffered the same injury as that individual, such that the individual's claim and the class claims will share common questions of law or fact and that the individual's claim will be typical of the class claims.[13]

13. The commonality and typicality requirements of Rule 23(a) tend to merge. Both serve as guideposts for determining whether under the particular circumstances maintenance of a class action is economical and whether the named plaintiff's claim and the class claims are so interrelated that the interests of the class members will be fairly and adequately protected in their absence. Those requirements therefore also tend to merge with the adequacy-of-representation requirement, although the latter requirement also raises concerns about the competency of class counsel and conflicts of interest. In this case, we need not address petitioner's argument that there is a conflict of interest between respondent and the class of rejected applicants because an enlargement of the pool of Mexican-American employees will decrease respondent's chances for promotion. See General Telephone Co. of Northwest v. EEOC, 446 U.S. 318, 331 [(1980)] ("In employment discrimination litigation, conflicts might arise, for example, between employees and applicants who were denied employment and who will, if granted relief, compete with employees for fringe benefits or seniority. Under Rule 23, the same plaintiff could not

For respondent to bridge that gap, he must prove much more than the validity of his own claim. Even though evidence that he was passed over for promotion when several less deserving whites were advanced may support the conclusion that respondent was denied the promotion because of his national origin, such evidence would not necessarily justify the additional inferences (1) that this discriminatory treatment is typical of petitioner's promotion practices, (2) that petitioner's promotion practices are motivated by a policy of ethnic discrimination that pervades petitioner's Irving division, or (3) that this policy of ethnic discrimination is reflected in petitioner's other employment practices, such as hiring, in the same way it is manifested in the promotion practices. There additional inferences demonstrate the tenuous character of any presumption that the class claims are "fairly encompassed" within respondent's claim.

Respondent's complaint provided an insufficient basis for concluding that the adjudication of his claim of discrimination in promotion would require the decision of any common question concerning the failure of petitioner to hire more Mexican-Americans. Without any specific presentation identifying the questions of law or fact that were common to the claims of respondent and of the members of the class he sought to represent, it was error for the District Court to presume that respondent's claim was typical of other claims against petitioner by Mexican-American employees and applicants. If one allegation of specific discriminatory treatment were sufficient to support an across-the-board attack, every Title VII case would be a potential companywide class action. We find nothing in the statute to indicate that Congress intended to authorize such a wholesale expansion of class-action litigation.[15]

The trial of this class action followed a predictable course. Instead of raising common questions of law or fact, respondent's evidentiary approaches to the individual and class claims were entirely different. He attempted to sustain his individual claim by proving intentional discrimination. He tried to prove the class claims through statistical evidence of disparate impact. Ironically, the District Court rejected the class claim of promotion discrimination, which conceptually might have borne a closer typicality and commonality relationship with respondent's individual claim, but sustained the class claim of hiring discrimination. As the District Court's bifurcated findings on liability demonstrate, the individual and class claims might as well have been tried separately. It is clear that the

represent these classes") . . . .

15. If petitioner used a biased testing procedure to evaluate both applicants for employment and incumbent employees, a class action on behalf of every applicant or employee who might have been prejudiced by the test clearly would satisfy the commonality and typicality requirements of Rule 23(a). Significant proof that an employer operated under a general policy of discrimination conceivably could justify a class of both applicants and employees if the discrimination manifested itself in hiring and promotion practices in the same general fashion, such as through entirely subjective decisionmaking processes. In this regard it is noteworthy that Title VII prohibits discriminatory employment practices, not an abstract policy of discrimination. The mere fact that an aggrieved private plaintiff is a member of an identifiable class of persons of the same race or national origin is insufficient to establish his standing to litigate on their behalf all possible claims of discrimination against a common employer.

maintenance of respondent's action as a class action did not advance "the efficiency and economy of litigation which is a principal purpose of the procedure." American Pipe & Construction Co. v. Utah, 414 U.S. 538, 553 [(1974)].

We do not, of course, judge the propriety of a class certification by hindsight. The District Court's error in this case, and the error inherent in the across-the-board rule, is the failure to evaluate carefully the legitimacy of the named plaintiff's plea that he is a proper class representative under Rule 23(a). As we noted in Coopers & Lybrand v. Livesay, 437 U.S. 463 [(1978)], "the class determination generally involves considerations that are 'enmeshed in the factual and legal issues comprising the plaintiff's cause of action.'" . . . Sometimes the issues are plain enough from the pleadings to determine whether the interests of the absent parties are fairly encompassed within the named plaintiff's claim, and sometimes it may be necessary for the court to probe behind the pleadings before coming to rest on the certification question. Even after a certification order is entered, the judge remains free to modify it in the light of subsequent developments in the litigation. For such an order, particularly during the period before any notice is sent to members of the class, "is inherently tentative." . . . This flexibility enhances the usefulness of the class-action device; actual, not presumed, conformance with Rule 23(a) remains, however, indispensable.

III

The need to carefully apply the requirements of Rule 23(a) to Title VII class actions was noticed by a member of the Fifth Circuit panel that announced the across-the-board rule. In a specially concurring opinion in *Johnson v. Georgia Highway Express, Inc.*, 417 F.2d, at 1125-1127, Judge Godbold emphasized the need for "more precise pleadings," for "without reasonable specificity the court cannot define the class, cannot determine whether the representation is adequate, and the employer does not know how to defend." He termed as "most significant" the potential unfairness to the class members bound by the judgment if the framing of the class is overbroad. And he pointed out the error of the "tacit assumption" underlying the across-the-board rule that "all will be well for surely the plaintiff will win and manna will fall on all members of the class." With the same concerns in mind, we reiterate today that a Title VII class action, like any other class action, may only by certified if the trial court is satisfied, after a rigorous analysis, that the prerequisites of Rule 23(a) have been satisfied.

The judgment of the Court of Appeals affirming the certification order is reversed, and the case is remanded for further proceedings consistent with this opinion.

■ CHIEF JUSTICE BURGER, concurring in part and dissenting in part. I agree with the Court's decision insofar as it states the general principles which apply in determining whether a class should be certified in this case under Rule 23. However, in my view it is not necessary to remand for further proceedings since it is entirely clear on this record that no class should have been certified in this case. . . .

As the Court notes, the purpose of Rule 23 is to promote judicial economy by allowing for litigation of common questions of law and fact at one time. We have stressed that strict attention to the requirements of Rule 23 is indispensable in employment discrimination cases. . . .

The record in this case clearly shows that there are no common questions of law or fact between respondent's claim and the class claim; the only commonality is that respondent is a Mexican-American and he seeks to represent a class of Mexican-Americans. . . .

Like so many Title VII cases, this case has already gone on for years, draining judicial resources as well as resources of the litigants. Rather than promoting judicial economy, the "across-the-board" class action has promoted multiplication of claims and endless litigation. Since it is clear that the class claim brought on behalf of unsuccessful applicants for jobs with petitioner cannot succeed, I would simply reverse and remand with instructions to dismiss the class claim.

DOLGOW v. ANDERSON

43 F.R.D. 472 (E.D.N.Y. 1968)

■ WEINSTEIN, District Judge. Four purchasers of Monsanto Company common stock sue that corporation and its principal officers and directors. Defendants are charged with engaging in a scheme to manipulate the price of Monsanto stock so that the individual defendants could sell their own stock in the corporation at an artificially inflated price.

Cross-motions have been made by the corporate defendant and the plaintiffs under Rule 23(c) (1) of the Federal Rules of Civil Procedure to determine whether this litigation should be maintained as a class action. . . .

Monsanto is one of the world's largest producers of chemical synthetic fibres, with assets and sales of hundreds of millions of dollars. The company's securities are widely held; it has almost one hundred thousand shareholders and its more than thirty million shares of common stock are traded on the New York Stock Exchange. During the period in which the plaintiffs seek to represent all purchasers of Monsanto securities, there were approximately one hundred thousand purchasers and more than twice that many traders in Monsanto stock. . . .

Recently, Monsanto — like most other concerns in the chemical fibre industry — has faced serious economic problems. Its earnings declined from three dollars and eighty-nine cents per share in 1965 to three dollars and forty-eight cents per share in 1966. Correspondingly, the price of its common stock has declined, from a high of above ninety dollars per share during 1965 to a current price in the mid forty's.

Three of the plaintiffs are presently Monsanto stockholders: Mildred and Benjamin Dolgow (Dolgows) own twenty-three shares as joint tenants; Sarah Fischer (Mrs. Fischer) owns seventy-two shares. The fourth plaintiff, Reuben Isaacson, purchased three hundred shares on April 9, 1965 at a total cost of approximately twenty-seven thousand dollars and sold them (along with six additional shares he acquired as a stock dividend) on October 5, 1966 at a loss of fourteen thousand seventy-six dollars and eighty-eight cents. . . .

Plaintiffs purchased their Monsanto stock at prices approximately twice its market price when this suit was commenced. They claim they did so in reliance upon the false statements and reports issued by the defendants and without knowledge of the company's actual financial condition, and that the prices they paid had not been determined by supply and demand, but had been manipulated to an artificially high level by the defendants. In addition, Mrs. Fischer claims to have purchased one share of Monsanto stock in December, 1965, in reliance upon the false statement filed in September, 1965 by Edgar Monsanto Queeny, then chairman of Monsanto's Board of Directors, in which he stated he had not disposed of any of his holdings in Monsanto.

The Dolgows and Mrs. Fischer seek individual damages of one hundred and sixty dollars and Isaacson seeks damages of fourteen thousand seven hundred and sixty dollars. They also request rescission and punitive damages. In addition, they each seek similar relief on behalf of all purchasers of all Monsanto securities since December, 1964 "similarly situated."

[The plaintiffs' complaint alleged common law fraud and violations of the Securities Act of 1933. After rejecting various objections to the proposed class action and finding that it qualified for certification under Rule 23(b)(3), the court turned to the defendant's argument that the four named plaintiffs and their counsel did not meet the requirement of Rule 23(a)(4).]

Two requirements need to be met in order for the court to be satisfied that the representative parties will adequately protect the interests of the class they seek to represent. First, "the interests of the unnamed persons . . . must be closely identified with the interests of the representatives" — *i.e.*, they must be members of the class sharing common issues and interests. . . . See, *e.g.*, Hansberry v. Lee, 311 U.S. 32 (1940) . . . . Second, the court must be assured that "the representatives will put up a real fight." . . .

Both these requirements have been met in the present action. No conflict of interest between the representatives and the represented has been suggested. There is nothing to indicate that the plaintiffs do not intend to prosecute this action vigorously or that plaintiffs' attorney is not competent to do so.

Nevertheless, defendants forcefully contend that representation requirements have not been met. They rely upon: (1) the miniscule holdings of plaintiffs; (2) the numerical disparity between those before the Court and those they seek to represent; and (3) the inability of plaintiffs' attorney to represent such large classes.

A. *Miniscule Holdings of Plaintiffs.*

In contending that the size of the claims of the parties before the court should be given great weight in determining the question of adequacy of representation, the defendants assume that the plaintiffs' force in prosecuting the action is proportionate to the amount they hope to recover. This equation is based on the assumption that the plaintiffs bring this action solely to recover their individual damages. The realities of the situation here and in the vast majority of class actions suggest that the amount of possible recovery by the class rather than by the individual plaintiffs furnishes the motivating force behind prosecution....

In some areas of the law, society is dependent upon "the initiative of lawyers ... for the assertion of rights" ... and the maintenance of desired standards of conduct. The prospect of handsome compensation is held out as an inducement to encourage lawyers to bring such suits.... The instant case presents a classic example of such a lawsuit. Quite obviously, a major incentive to forceful prosecution is the substantial counsel fee plaintiffs' attorney believes he may be awarded if he is successful.

To assert that the minute interests of the parties before the court is a factor which militates against allowing a class action is to ignore the spirit of Rule 23.... Since, as we have seen, if the plaintiff's claim is very large a class action is rendered unnecessary, the main purpose of the class action is to provide a means of vindicating small claims. It would be anomalous to hold that only major financial interests can make use of it.

Large publicly owned corporations tend to be highly capitalized with large amounts of stock outstanding. Most shareholders own comparatively few shares of stock. The few persons who do own a substantial bloc of stock in a corporation are usually either officers, directors, or other "insiders" — in a word, the very people whose conduct the securities laws are designed to regulate. Therefore, to restrict the use of the class action to those persons would virtually preclude its application in the area of securities regulation.
...

Finally, we need no longer be unduly concerned that small shareholders will misuse the class action device by bringing strike suits.... As we have seen, Rule 23 contains sufficient protective provisions to adequately guard against such abuse.

B. *Numerical Disparity Between Those Before the Court and Those They Seek to Represent.*

There is, of course, "no magic in numbers.... The quality of representation is more important than numbers."... Were it otherwise, a premium would be put on injuring large groups of people. In the present case, even if there were one hundred parties of record, there would still be only an exceedingly small percentage of the classes before the court....

The fact that in this case there are only four plaintiffs — all of whom are related to each other or are close friends — before the Court at the present time, while the classes they seek to represent have a total of over two hundred thousand members, is troublesome. There are two possible explanations for this situation other than acquiescence in defendants' activities by other members of the class. First, the action has received virtually no publicity and thus it is possible that most members are not aware of it. Second, under the new Rule every member of the class is assured of sharing in a favorable verdict without having to intervene; their failure to come forward is as consistent with the view that they are sitting back watching the action proceed, content with the job their representatives are doing, as it is with the view that they disapprove of the bringing of the action.... Thus, at this early stage of the proceedings, when the court has yet to determine whether there is any merit to plaintiffs' claim, the lack of participation by other members of the class would not justify the drastic step of ruling that this litigation could not proceed as a class action.

C. *Ability of Plaintiffs' Attorney to Adequately Represent Large Class.*

Defendants' final argument on the question of adequacy of representation goes to the qualifications of plaintiffs' attorney and his ability to represent such large classes. The representation might be so poor that the judgment would not have any res judicata effect. See Hansberry v. Lee, 311 U.S. 32 (1940). The defendants would then be in the position of having gone through a contested litigation only to be forced to relitigate the entire controversy. While it seems doubtful that this threat is serious in view of the running of applicable statutes of limitation, we assume that this is a matter of legitimate concern.

Defendants point out that plaintiffs' counsel graduated from law school only seven years ago and is handling the case by himself. They suggest that he was only retained by these plaintiffs because he is closely related to them.

This argument is untenable. Plaintiffs' counsel is admitted to practice in both state and federal courts. Until the contrary is demonstrated, courts will assume that members of the bar are skilled in their profession. Moreover, in a case such as a stockholder's class action which is pregnant with public interest, defendants may be "underestimating the ability of a court to safeguard the interests of all parties." ... Subdivision (d)(2) of Rule 23 gives the courts express authority to give those not before the court "the opportunity ... to signify whether they consider the representation fair and adequate, to intervene and present claims or defenses, or otherwise to come into the action." In addition, under subdivision (d)(3) the court may impose "conditions on the representative parties." It has a broad range of discretion to assure adequacy of representation according to the individual circumstances of every case.

Defendants also maintain that, in view of the nature and size of the classes involved here, no lawyer — no matter how large his office, no matter how vast his experience — could adequately represent the interests of those not before the court. If this argument were accepted, resort to the class action would be automatically precluded in cases where large numbers of investors had been defrauded through complex schemes and the perpetrators of such schemes would be assured of virtual immunity from many of the penalties provided by the securities laws — a patently absurd result.

The lawyer's task with respect to common questions of law and fact is not more difficult whether he is representing one person or a class of a million. In either case he will have to prove the same allegations if he is to prevail.

IN RE AMERICAN MEDICAL SYSTEMS, INC.

75 F.3d 1069 (6th Cir. 1996)

■ SUHRHEINRICH, Circuit Judge. Petitioners American Medical Systems ("AMS") and Pfizer, Inc., defendants below, both seek a writ of mandamus directing the district court to vacate orders conditionally certifying a class in a products liability suit involving penile prostheses. This court has held that class certification is generally not the kind of subject matter for which mandamus relief is available on the grounds that class certification decisions are reviewable on direct appeal. However, on the extraordinary facts of this case we find that the district judge's disregard of class action procedures was of such severity and frequency so as to warrant its issuance here.

I.

Since 1973, AMS, a wholly-owned subsidiary of Pfizer, has manufactured and marketed penile prostheses, which are used to treat impotence. The plaintiffs, respondents in this proceeding, all use or have used AMS' products.

Plaintiff Paul Vorhis was implanted with an AMS penile prosthesis on April 25, 1989. It failed to function in January of 1993, and Vorhis had the prosthesis replaced with an AMS 700 Ultrex prosthesis in May 1993. This second prosthesis caused him pain and discomfort, and plaintiff had it removed in August of 1993 and replaced with a third AMS prosthesis, with which he is presently satisfied. Vorhis filed this action against defendant AMS in the Southern District of Ohio on December 5, 1994, individually and on behalf of others similarly situated who suffered damages as a result of the implantation of penile prostheses manufactured by AMS. The complaint alleges strict product liability, negligence, breach of implied and express warranties, fraud and punitive damages, and seeks a declaratory judgment for medical monitoring. . . .

At the class certification hearing, the district judge indicated that he was concerned principally with the question of whether Vorhis was an appropriate class representative, and directed AMS to proceed first. AMS challenged Vorhis' suitability as a class representative on several grounds. First, AMS pointed out that Vorhis had a history of psychiatric problems, for which he received total and permanent disability benefits from the State of Ohio. AMS introduced reports prepared by Vorhis' psychiatrist and psychologist showing that Vorhis suffered from memory loss, impaired concentration, and a lack of common sense, all factors which AMS maintained would interfere with plaintiff's ability to make rational decisions on behalf of other members of the purported class. AMS also contended that Vorhis was an unsuitable representative because his need for the prosthesis stemmed from a unique condition, Peyronie's disease, or curvature of the penis. Third, AMS argued that because Vorhis had a problem with only one of the ten types of prostheses AMS manufactured, he could not represent those who had problems with the other kinds of devices.

In response to AMS' first argument, plaintiff offered the deposition testimony of his treating psychiatrist, Dr. Edelstein, who opined that Vorhis was competent to withstand the rigors of trial. As to defendant's third argument, plaintiff countered that the basic design of all ten devices was the same.... Vorhis did not directly respond to AMS' second argument.

On February 28, 1995, the district judge issued a two-page order stating, "based upon the information currently available to it, that class certification appears to be the most efficient and appropriate manner in which to handle this matter," and promised a "further order outlining the reasoning supporting that conclusion" to follow. The order was conditional, subject to decertification at any time, and conditioned further "upon class counsel acting to amend the complaint within thirty (30) days ... in order to add additional plaintiffs who qualify as appropriate class representatives and who are free of the alleged infirmities on which Defendant's objections to the suitability of the current Plaintiff/class representative are premised."...

On March 10, 1995, Vorhis filed an amended complaint, adding three additional plaintiffs as class representatives and Pfizer as an additional defendant. AMS and Pfizer were both served with the amended complaint on March 13, 1995....

Without any further discovery, briefing, or argument, the district judge issued an amended order of class certification on March 16, 1995. The judge found that all the prerequisites of Fed.R.Civ.P. 23(a) had been met, and that the class was maintainable under Fed.R.Civ.P. 23(b)(3) because common questions of law or fact predominated....

On March 13, 1995, AMS filed a petition for writ of mandamus pursuant to 28 U.S.C. § 1651 and Fed.R.App.P. 21 asking this Court to set aside the district court's order of February 28. AMS filed a supplemental petition on March 21, 1995, in response to the amended order certifying the class....

II.

The All Writs Statute creates an exception to the final judgment rule, which rule is the "dominant principle" of federal appellate jurisdiction.... The writ provides some flexibility in instances where rigid enforcement of the final judgment rule would result in injustice....

III....

We begin our analysis by considering whether the lower court committed patent error.... We address in tandem petitioners' contentions that the lower court disregarded the standards for class certification and certified a class despite the absence of an adequate factual record establishing the elements of Rule 23.

The Supreme Court has required district courts to conduct a "rigorous analysis" into whether the prerequisites of Rule 23 are met before certifying a class. General Tel. Co. v. Falcon, 457 U.S. 147, 161 (1982). The trial court has broad discretion in deciding whether to certify a class, but that discretion must be exercised within the framework of Rule 23. . . .

1.

[After finding that 15,000 to 120,000 class members existed, the court of appeals held the numerosity requirement was satisfied.]

2.

Rule 23(a)(2) requires that for certification there must be "questions of law or fact common to the class." The commonality requirement is interdependent with the impracticability of joinder requirement, and the "tests together form the underlying conceptual basis supporting class actions." 1 [Herbert B Newberg & Alba Conte, Newberg on Class Actions,] § 3.10, at 3-47 [(3d ed. 1992)]. . . .

Plaintiffs' complaint and class certification motion simply allege in general terms that there are common issues without identifying any particular defect common to all plaintiffs. Yet AMS introduced uncontradicted evidence that since 1973 AMS has produced at least ten different models, and that these models have been modified over the years. Plaintiffs' claims of strict liability, fraudulent misrepresentation to both the FDA and the medical community, negligent testing, design and manufacture, and failure to warn will differ depending upon the model and the year it was issued.

Proofs as to strict liability, negligence, failure to warn, breach of express and implied warranties will also vary from plaintiff to plaintiff because complications with an AMS device may be due to a variety of factors, including surgical error, improper use of the device, anatomical incompatibility, infection, device malfunction, or psychological problems. Furthermore, each plaintiff's urologist would also be required to testify to determine what oral and written statements were made to the physician, and what he in turn told the patient, as well as to issues of reliance, causation and damages. . . .

The amended complaint reflects that the plaintiffs received different models and have different complaints regarding each of those models. In the absence of more specific allegations and/or proof of commonality of any factual or legal claims, plaintiffs have failed to meet their burden of proof on Rule 23(a)(2).

This failure of proof highlights the error of the district judge. Despite evidence in the record presented by the nonmoving party that at least ten different models existed, testimony from a urologist that there is no "common cause" of prostheses malfunction, and conclusory allegations by the party with the burden of proof on certification, we find not even the hint of any serious consideration by the judge of commonality. Moreover, although not dispositive, it is noteworthy that a Judicial Panel on Multidistrict Litigation denied consolidation of all federal AMS penile prostheses case pursuant to 28 U.S.C. § 1407, concluding that "the degree of factual commonality among the actions in this litigation [does not] rise[ ] to a level that warrants Section 1407 transfer." In re Penile Implants Prod. Liab. Litig., MDL No. 1020 (J.P.M.L. Sept. 30, 1994). The district judge was made aware of this ruling, and still did not give the question of commonality any discernible degree of scrutiny.

3.

Rule 23(a)(3) requires that "claims or defenses of the representative parties [be] typical of the claims or defenses of the class."

> Typicality determines whether a sufficient relationship exists between the injury to the named plaintiff and the conduct affecting the class, so that the court may properly attribute a collective nature to the challenged conduct. In other words, when such a relationship is shown, a plaintiff's injury arises from or is directly related to a wrong to a class, and that wrong includes the wrong to the plaintiff. Thus, a plaintiff's claim is typical if it arises from the same event or practice or course of conduct that gives rise to the claims of other class members, and if his or her claims are based on the same legal theory.

1 Newberg, *supra*, § 3-13, at 3-76 (footnote omitted). See also General Tel. Co. v. EEOC, 446 U.S. [318,] 330 [(1980)] ("typicality requirement is said to limit the class claims to those fairly encompassed by the named plaintiffs' claims"); Senter [v. General Motors Corp., 532 F.2d 511,] 525 n.31 [(6th Cir.)] ("[t]o be typical, a representative's claim need not always involve the same facts or law, provided there is a common element of fact or law")[, cert. denied, 429 U.S. 870 (1976)]. A necessary consequence of the typicality requirement is that the representative's interests will be aligned with those of the represented group, and in pursuing his own claims, the named plaintiff will also advance the interests of the class members. . . .

Vorhis' claim relates to a previous AMS penile prosthesis which, several years after insertion, allegedly could not be inflated due to a possible leak in the input tube of a CX device. This in turn may have been caused by rear-tip extender surgery Vorhis had in 1990, in an attempt to increase penile length that was lost through surgery to correct a curvature of his penis. Based on what little we have to go on, it is hard to imagine that Vorhis' claim is typical of the class certified in this case.

Because the district judge issued its amended order of certification before discovery of the plaintiffs other than Vorhis, we have less information about them. However, we know from the amended complaint that each plaintiff used a different model, and each experienced a distinct difficulty. York claims that his 700 inflatable penile prosthesis fails to fully inflate. Kennedy alleges that his Ultrex inflatable penile prosthesis malfunctioned because the cylinders and pump leaked. Finally, Gordy maintains that his Hyrdoflex failed, and that his current implant, the Dynaflex prosthesis, inflates on one side only. These allegations fail to establish a claim typical to each other, let alone a class.

Once again, it should have been obvious to the district judge that it needed to "probe behind the pleadings" before concluding that the typicality requirement was met. See *Falcon,* 457 U.S. at 160. Instead, the district judge gave no serious consideration to this factor, but simply mimicked the language of the rule. This was error. . . .

4.

Rule 23(a)(4) allows certification only if "the representative parties will fairly and adequately protect the interests of the class." Fed.R.Civ.P. 23(a). This prerequisite is essential to due process, because a final judgment in a class action is binding on all class members. Hansberry v. Lee, 311 U.S. 32 (1940); 1 Newberg, *supra,* § 3.21, at 3-125. . . .

In *Senter,* we articulated two criteria for determining adequacy of representation: "1) the representative must have common interests with unnamed members of the class, and 2) it must appear that the representatives will vigorously prosecute the interests of the class through qualified counsel." . . . The adequate representation requirement overlaps with the typicality requirement because in the absence of typical claims, the class representative has no incentives to pursue the claims of the other class members.

Although the district judge considered the qualifications of plaintiff's counsel, he made no finding on the first *Senter* criterion, and did not consider whether Vorhis or the other plaintiffs would "vigorously prosecute the interests of the class." AMS raised a serious question as to Vorhis' suitability to serve as a class representative given his history of psychological problems. . . . At the hearing, the judge made no finding regarding plaintiff, but remarked that:

> I don't think he is going to control anything. I don't think a client in a class action ever controls anything. And if you want my feeling on it, he is a name. He's a symbol. I just want to make sure there aren't defenses against that symbol that would then be transmitted against the class.

This statement is clearly contrary to our holding in *Senter.*

The district judge's February 28 and March 16 orders compound the problem. In the first order the judge again deferred making a finding, referring to plaintiff's "alleged infirmities," and allowing the addition of other class representatives. In the March 16 order the judge not only again failed to make an explicit decision regarding Vorhis, but added three additional class representatives without a record and without any meaningful findings of fact.

As amply illustrated, plaintiffs' complaint and class certification motion simply allege the elements of Rule 23(a) in conclusory terms without submitting any persuasive evidence to show that these factors are met. Because the plaintiffs did not create a factual record, and petitioners have demonstrated that the products at issue are very different and that each plaintiff's claim is unique, class certification was inappropriate.

[The court went on to hold that the requirements of Rule 23(b)(3) had also not been established, and that the other factors necessary to obtain mandamus relief were present.]

IV.

For all the foregoing reasons, the petitions for writ of mandamus are granted, and the district judge is directed to decertify the plaintiff class.

Notes and Questions

1. According to *Medical Systems*, numerosity is related to commonality; according to *Falcon*, commonality is related to typicality, and typicality to adequacy. If this is so, why aren't the subparts of Rule 23(a) re-written into a single rule: A class action is permissible when a large number of people have interests closely enough aligned to justify extending preclusive effect to a judgment obtained by a class representative. Indeed, aren't the four subparts of (a) merely specific aspects of this inquiry? If so, are the subparts of (a) really a sliding scale, so that a person seeking certification can make up a weak showing on one subpart with a strong showing elsewhere? Is it also fair to say that, in terms of relative weight, the factors in (a) get more important as they move from (1) to (4)?

2. If this observation about the relationship among numerosity, commonality, typicality, and adequacy is accurate, then lawyers attempting to certify a class should tactically train their arguments on the issue of adequacy. Although commonality and typicality cannot be ignored, a strong showing of adequacy of representation should counterbalance weaker showings on the other two elements.

On the other hand, a lawyer opposing a class action may want to put the court into the mindset that each of the three elements of commonality, typicality, and adequacy must be independently satisfied, so that a weak showing on any element is fatal to the case. In order to do so, however, you might need to convince the court that more fundamental issues are at stake than mere commonality or typicality. For instance, *American Medical* is instructive. Is it really true, as the court suggested, that the class members' cases lacked common questions of fact? If not, why did the court of appeals chastise the district court for failing to scrutinize the issue more closely? Is it because the court had decided, for other reasons, not to certify the class action, and narrowly interpreted the commonality requirement to bolster its result?

3. Indeed, to what extent are *Falcon, Dolgow,* and *American Medical* the result of a particular view (whether articulated or not) of the role of the courts and the role of adjudication? To the extent that judges are influenced by these considerations, the theoretical material in Chapter One and at the outset of this chapter is highly relevant to the advocate's task in filing or resisting class certification motions. Understanding and articulating the deeper theory of procedure might well be vital to the success of a novel procedural argument you are asked to make.

4. To demonstrate the interwoven nature of the Rule 23(a) inquiry, ask yourself whether *Falcon* is a commonality decision, a typicality decision, or an adequacy decision. Does the Court say? Does it seem to care?

5. Despite *Falcon*, courts typically analyze the requirements of (a)(2), (a)(3), and (a)(4) separately. Far and away the *least* important of these three constraints is the (a)(2) requirement of a common question. Because a single shared question is usually viewed as being sufficient to satisfy this test, rarely, if ever, will a proposed class action falter on this ground alone. This fact had led several courts to conclude that the (a)(2) commonality test is, for all practical purposes, superfluous. See, *e.g.*, Edgington v. R.G. Dickinson & Co., 139 F.R.D. 183, 189 (D. Kan. 1991); Smith v. MCI Telecommunications Corp., 124 F.R.D. 665, 675 (D. Kan. 1989).

6. What is the precise purpose of the typicality requirement? Don't both the (a)(3) typicality and the (a)(4) adequacy requirements focus on whether the proposed representative is suitable to act as a fiduciary for the interests of the class? Some courts and commentators have suggested that the typicality requirement serves no independent purpose, but the Supreme Court in *Falcon* and numerous lower federal courts have asserted or assumed that the two requirements are complementary and separate without explaining exactly how. *See, e.g.*, Rosado v. Wyman, 322 F. Supp. 1173 (E.D.N.Y. 1970), *aff'd* on other grounds, 437 F.2d 619 (2d Cir. 1970). See generally Howard M. Downs, *Federal Class Actions: Due Process by Adequacy of Representation (Identity of Claims) and the Impact of* General Telephone v. Falcon, 54 Ohio St. L.J. 607 (1993).

7. The Supreme Court has made it clear that due process requires that a class be adequately represented if the members of the class are to be bound by the resulting judgment. Hansberry v. Lee, 311 U.S. 32 (1940). Rule 23(a)(4) is intended to assure adequate representation through a pre-certification inquiry into the qualities and abilities of the class representative and class counsel. See generally Note, *Collateral Attack on the Binding Effect of Class Action Judgments*, 87 Harv. L. Rev. 589 (1978).

8. Do the (a)(2) through (a)(4) requirements depend at all on whether the plaintiff is seeking injunctive or monetary recovery? On whether the plaintiff is pleading a favored or disfavored legal theory? *Dolgow* uses the policies underlying substantive securities law to help interpret Rule 23(a). Neither *Falcon* nor *American Medical* does. Is *Dolgow* being more honest about the substantive influences on procedure, or did *Falcon* and *American Medical* actually close their eyes to the substantive effect of their decision? If substance is permitted to influence procedure, as *Dolgow* suggests, is it possible to maintain a trans-substantive procedural code?

9. Why is Falcon suitable to represent the class of Mexican-American employees seeking promotion, but unsuitable to represent the class of Mexican-American applicants? The Court emphasizes that in applying the typicality requirement it is imperative to consider carefully the kind of evidence to be proffered by the class representative on behalf of the class. If Falcon and his counsel are competent to present statistical evidence of discrimination on behalf of Falcon's co-employees, why can't they do the same on behalf of the applicants? What genuine differences divide the applicant class from the promotion class such that it is not appropriate for Falcon to represent both?

In footnote 15, *Falcon* observes that an actual or potential conflict of interest may exist between the applicant and employee classes because enlargement of the pool of Mexican-American employees will decrease an individual employee's chances for promotion. The Court expressly notes, however, that its decision does not rest on this ground. Isn't this potential antagonism more troubling than the differences in proof relied on by the Court?

10. Compare *Falcon* with Cooper v. Federal Reserve Bank of Richmond, 467 U.S. 867 (1984) (p. 174, *supra*). If an employee in Grade 4 alleging race discrimination in promotion can represent a different employee in Grade 8 on a discrimination claim, as the Court seems to suggest, why can't Falcon represent the applicant class? Also compare *Falcon* to Mosley v. General Motors Corp., 497 F.2d 1330 (8th Cir. 1974) (p. 93, *supra*). If across-the-board discriminatory practices generally create insufficient commonality for Rule 23(a) purposes, how can they create common questions for Rule 20(a) purposes? Does this anomaly suggest that *Falcon* is really a typicality or adequacy decision? Or can *Mosley* be explained because it involves voluntary joinder, in which plaintiffs are presumed to waive any potential conflicts? Do you believe that plaintiffs who voluntarily join cases appreciate either the potential conflicts they have with other plaintiffs or the resulting problems of inadequate representation?

11. What assurance do we really have in *Dolgow* that four seemingly unsophisticated small-time investors adequately represent the hundreds of thousands of other investors in the class — many of whom may be much more knowledgeable and have much more money at stake? Is the court suggesting that the attorneys for the class are the real parties in interest in this action, that they have substantial economic incentives to represent the class successfully, and they are the real fiduciaries for the absent class members? *See* Jean W. Burns, *Decorative Figureheads: Eliminating Class Representatives in Class Actions*, 42 Hastings L. J. 165, 167-86 (1990) (contending that named class plaintiffs have no legal authority and serve no useful purpose); Jonathan R. Macey & Geoffrey P. Miller, *The Plaintiffs' Attorney's Role in Class Action and Derivative Litigation: Economic Analysis and Recommendation for Reform*, 58 U. Chi. L. Rev. 1, 93-94 (1991) (arguing that discovery into the private characteristics of the named plaintiffs should be prohibited since they are merely figureheads). Or is Judge Weinstein saying that he will attend to the matter and assure that the class will be properly represented? From whence would the authority for this alteration of the judge's traditional adversarial role emanate?

12. Were you puzzled by the fact that the defendant — Monsanto — was contending that the absent class members were not adequately represented? Is it reasonable to rely primarily on the defendant to argue the matter? Don't defendants want representatives and counsel opposing them that are just a hair's breadth above the *Hansberry* floor? Doesn't this dynamic assure that, in many cases, class members will not receive the very best representation? But if the defendant does not uncover and establish the reasons why the named representative may not be adequate to represent the class, who will?

13. One way to avoid some of these problems is to have the court open up the process of obtaining class counsel to various bidders for the job, and then to choose the best responsible bidder. We examine this idea at pp. 887-88, *infra*.

14. In fact, defendants' incentive to argue inadequacy may depend on the stakes that are involved in the case. In small-scale litigation, defendants know that, if they can defeat the class certification motion, the entire litigation might well go away; few if any plaintiffs have the wherewithal or incentive to prosecute the case on an individual basis. Hence, defendants have a strong incentive to raise the inadequacy point. In large-scale litigation, however, the litigation is

not going to go away; the cases are worth being brought on an individual basis. In these cases, defendants have far less of an incentive to argue inadequacy when the class representatives and counsel are marginally qualified.

15. Some of the concerns with adequacy that *Dolgow* faced have been superseded — in the securities fraud context — by the Private Securities Litigation Reform Act of 1995. Under the Act, when a securities fraud case is brought as a class action, a plaintiff must place a notice of the suit in a widely circulating business-oriented newspaper or news service, and invite others to seek the position of lead plaintiff. From among the persons that apply for the position, the court is then to choose the "most adequate plaintiff." The Act establishes a presumption that the "most adequate plaintiff" will be the person that "has the largest financial interest in the relief sought by the class" and that has "otherwise satisfied the requirements of Rule 23." The presumption can be rebutted only by showing either that the presumptive lead plaintiff "will not fairly and adequately protect the interests of the class" or "is subject to unique defenses that render such plaintiff incapable of adequately representing the class." See 15 U.S.C. § 78u-4. Once the "most adequate plaintiff" is selected, then that plaintiff chooses the counsel for the class. Id. The Act also places a prohibition on so-called "professional plaintiffs" who own small numbers of shares in many corporations and who are often affiliated with certain plaintiffs' firms. Cf. In re Gibson Greetings Securities Litigation, 159 F.R.D. 499 (S.D. Ohio 1994) (rejecting as class representative a plaintiff who had filed 182 class actions in the prior twelve years). The Act permits a person to be "a lead plaintiff, or an officer, director, or fiduciary of a lead plaintiff, in no more than 5 securities class actions brought as plaintiff class actions pursuant to the Federal Rules of Civil Procedure during any 3-year period." 15 U.S.C. § 78u-4.

On the one hand, it is difficult to argue with the intent of the Act to ensure more vigorous representation by the class representative and class counsel. On the other hand, the Act has a chilling effect on securities litigation, for the parties and lawyers that bring the case have no guarantee that they will control it. Should rules similar to those in the Act be adopted for all class actions under Rule 23? Should the rules be adopted only in small-stakes cases? Does the substantive effect of such rules make you wary of this proposal?

16. Claims that class representatives or class counsel are flatly incompetent or inadequate are relatively rare. More typical are claims that the class representatives or class counsel have a conflict of interest that makes them unable to protect the interests of the class adequately. See, *e.g.*, Amchem Products, Inc. v. Windsor, — U.S. —, 117 S.Ct. 2231 (1997) (p. 670, *infra*) (discussing conflicts of interest in settlement class action); Gary Plastic Packaging Corp. v. Merrill Lynch, Pierce, Fenner & Smith, Inc., 903 F.3d 176 (2d Cir. 1990) (person subject to unique defenses is inadequate class representative), cert. denied 498 U.S. 1025 (1991). Obviously, this question brings to the fore the ethical expectations that we have in class litigation. Given that class litigation is different than individual litigation, should we transplant our norms of adversarial, individual-litigation ethics into the class context? If not, with what set of ethical norms shall we replace our traditional norms? Is it possible to answer the Rule 23(a)(4) question without first establishing the ethical principles under which we expect class members and their lawyers to operate?

In answering this question, should we begin by asking what effect class actions in fact have on the traditional lawyer-client relationship? Would you expect to find that the class representatives in *Dolgow* exercised effective control over the progress of the litigation? That the class representatives were kept apprised of the progress of the litigation? That the court advised them of the duties and possible liabilities they are exposing themselves to by agreeing to serve as the class representative?

17. Another way to test the ethical system under which you believe class actions should operate is to ask whether class counsel should advise the class representative that, by proceeding in a class action, the class representative may be foregoing a larger remedy available in traditional bi-polar litigation, while the lawyer will receive a larger fee in the class action. Cf. Rivera v. Fair Chevrolet Geo Partnership, 165 F.R.D. 361 (D. Conn. 1996) (approving class certification in Truth in Lending Act suit even though named plaintiff could recover $1000 in individual action, but only $200 in class action).

18. Is there any limit on the prior relationship between the class representative and the lawyers for the class? Compare Cotchett v. Avis Rent A Car, 56 F.R.D. 549 (S.D.N.Y. 1972) (class representative may not be law partner of class counsel) with Lewis v. Goldsmith, 95 F.R.D. 15 (D.N.J. 1982) (uncle of class counsel may be class representative).

19. Because of the requirement of a pre-certification finding of adequate representation, it is difficult for an absent class member to later attack the judgment resulting from the class action as not binding due to inadequate representation of the class. On rare occasions, however, such collateral attacks do succeed. In Gonzales v. Cassidy, 474 F.2d 67 (5th Cir. 1973), the trial court granted retroactive relief to the class representative, but only prospective relief to all other class members. No appeal was taken. In a later lawsuit, the Fifth Circuit held that the failure of the class representative to appeal the denial of retroactive relief to the class rendered the representative inadequate, so that the absent class members were not bound by the first law suit. See also Epstein v. MCA, Inc, 126 F.3d 1235 (9th Cir. 1997) (p. 179, *supra*).

20. Recall the fear, expressed in *Rhone-Poulenc* (pp. 542-44, *supra*), that class actions expose defendants to enormous liability and coerced settlements. Given this fear, what outcome would you have expected in *Dolgow*? Judge Weinstein ultimately entered summary judgment for the defendants on the merits. Before he did so, however, he also granted defendants' renewed motion to decertify the class, thus depriving the defendants of the classwide preclusive effect of the judgment. See Dolgow v. Anderson, 438 F.2d 825 (2d Cir. 1970).

e. The Final Requirement: Qualifying under Rule 23(b)

In addition to satisfying all of the express and implied requirements of Rule 23(a), a class action must qualify for certification under one or more of the categories of Rule 23(b). Rule 23(b) permits three types of mandatory class actions — (b)(1)(A), (b)(1)(B), and (b)(2); in these class actions, no opt-out right is provided. Rule 23(b) also provides one type of "voluntary" class action — (b)(3); in this class action, class members must be extended the opportunity to opt out of the class. As an aggregation device in complex and complicated litigation, a mandatory class action is obviously preferable. As a device that respects the autonomous interest of each plaintiff to control the course of his or her own litigation, an opt-out class action, while not as good as an opt-in class action, is far better than a mandatory class action.

In earlier chapters, we saw that concerns such as the interest in party control and the proper scope of state-federal relations made it difficult to join, consolidate, enjoin, or preclude related cases merely because separate litigation was inefficient; when lawyer dysfunction existed, however, the chances for successful aggregation were greater. Should a comparable dynamic work in the Rule 23(b) area, so that mandatory class actions will be available in order to overcome lawyer dysfunction in complex cases, while only opt-out class actions will be available to deal with inefficient re-litigation in complicated cases? If so, how much inefficiency must exist in order to overcome the adversarial system's preference for individual control? Are there jurisdictional limits on the ability of federal courts to achieve mandatory class joinder even in complex cases? If so, should it be easier to obtain an opt-out class action in complex cases than in complicated cases?

i. Class Actions with No Opt-out Right

For years mandatory class actions under either (b)(1)(A) or (b)(1)(B) were rare. Mandatory class actions under (b)(2) were more common, but principally in civil rights actions. In recent years, imaginative lawyers have begun to seek certification of mandatory class actions in environmental, mass tort, securities, and other kinds of cases that lie far beyond the originally contemplated scope of Rules 23(b)(1) and (b)(2). In many situations, it is not difficult to see why. From the plaintiffs' viewpoint, aggregation without an opt-out right both saves the sometimes considerable expense of providing notice of opt-out rights and provides additional leverage in the litigation and settlement of the case. From the defendants' viewpoint, non-opt-out class actions can bring finality. From the court's viewpoint, a mandatory class action conserves judicial resources and provides an identical procedure for all similar victims.

At the same time, the totality of mandatory class actions raises significant issues of the right to individual control of litigation, state-federal relations, limits of judicial power, and outcome-determinative procedural shifts. Do the benefits or drawbacks of these class actions seem greater? Consider this question against the likelihood that experimentation with mandatory class actions will continue as lawyers and judges search for ways to find aggregation solutions for complex and complicated cases.

a) Incompatible Standards and Limited Fund Class Actions

The original, paradigmatic cases certified as (b)(1)(A) class actions involved situations where a large group of taxpayers, bondholders, insureds, alleged patent infringers, or entitlement recipients sought or required equitable or declaratory relief with respect to other parties. See generally 7A Charles A. Wright et al., Federal Practice & Procedure § 1773 (1986). Absent a unitary adjudication of the rights of the class members against the party opposing the class, there was a real risk that the opposing party would be subject to conflicting judgments regarding its future conduct toward individual members of the class. Class actions under (b)(1)(A) thus bear a relationship to the involuntary joinder permitted under Rule 19(a)(2)(ii), Rule 22(1), and 28 U.S.C. § 1335; each of these rules attempts to protect a party from multiple, inconsistent, or otherwise unfair judgments, and also protects the early-filing plaintiffs from the destruction of their remedy through later lawsuits.

The paradigmatic cases certified under (b)(1)(B) involved situations in which the rights of members of the class would be effectively determined by individual litigation to which they were not parties. See Wright et al., *supra*, § 1774. For example, there might be a dispute as to the beneficial ownership of a trust in which many persons claimed an interest; a successful suit by one putative beneficiary of the trust might effectively bar relief in favor of other members of the trust. The same result would occur in situations in which a defendant had insufficient assets to satisfy all claims. Class actions under (b)(1)(B) thus bear a relationship to involuntary joinder under Rule 19(a)(2)(i), Rule 22(1), and 28 U.S.C. § 1335, and to intervention under Rule 24(a)(2); each of these rules attempts to protect nonparties from the lack of any effective remedy.

Note that a feature of (b)(1)(A) and (b)(1)(B) class actions is an almost inevitable conflict of interest among class members. Is it possible for any class representative to represent the interests of all class members when different class members are interested in maximizing relief for themselves? Who should mediate these conflicts — class counsel or the court?

IN RE DENNIS GREENMAN SECURITIES LITIGATION

829 F.2d 1539 (11th Cir. 1987)

■ HENLEY, Senior Circuit Judge. This is an appeal from a final district court judgment certifying a class action and approving a settlement in a complex securities fraud case. The plaintiffs are victims of a fraud perpetrated by Dennis Greenman, a securities seller. The defendants are brokerage firms that employed Greenman while he was conducting the fraud as well as others who might be liable for Greenman's actions. Appellants, some alleged victims of Greenman, contend that the district court erred in certifying the class for settlement purposes pursuant to Fed.R.Civ.P. 23(b)(1). For reasons to be stated, we reverse.

Greenman conducted the fraud over a period of almost four years beginning in mid-1977 as a broker for or associate of three different brokerage firms: Merrill Lynch, Pierce, Fenner & Smith Incorporated

(Merrill Lynch), Paine Webber Jackson & Curtis, Inc. (Paine Webber), and Barclay Financial Corp. (Barclay). Greenman represented himself as operating a riskless, highly profitable computer-driven arbitrage system. In actuality, he was investing the funds in high risk options trading and lost substantial sums of money. Greenman also converted funds to his own use. He concealed the fraud by diverting the genuine account statements to false post office box addresses and forwarding fictitious account statements. Investors who sought to withdraw funds from their accounts were paid with other investors' funds in a "Ponzi" type scheme. Over 600 people participated in the scheme either dealing directly with Greenman or investing through other participants. They invested approximately $86 million, of which they lost over $50 million.

In April of 1981, the Securities and Exchange Commission filed a complaint against Greenman, Barclay, and its principals seeking injunctive relief and the appointment of a receiver to collect and distribute the investors' assets under the custody of control of Greenman, Barclay, or A.G. Becker. The receiver found that the investors' funds were commingled to the extent that specific ownership could not be traced.... The total amount distributed [to investors] from the receivership fund was $17,280,681.76, which represented a 35% return of net investments to investors with net losses.

Subsequent to the SEC's disclosure of the fraud, numerous suits were filed on behalf of investors. Among the suits, a complaint was filed on behalf of all people and entities who lost investments. The class action complaint named as defendants: Greenman, Paine Webber, Barclay, A.G. Becker, Inc., and various officers of Paine Webber and Barclay. The plaintiffs alleged violations of the Security Exchange Acts of 1933 and 1934, the Investment Company Act of 1940, the R.I.C.O. Act, various Florida statutes, the rules of the New York Stock Exchange and the National Association of Securities Dealers. In addition, plaintiffs alleged common law causes of action of fraudulent misrepresentation, concealment, nondisclosure, breach of fiduciary duty, conversion, and negligence. As relief, the plaintiffs sought their lost investments, the three-fold damage award provided for in the R.I.C.O. Act, punitive damages, interest, costs, and attorney fees.

After receiving advice from counsel and conducting hearings, the district court consolidated and stayed the individual suits and certified a class action pursuant to Fed.R.Civ.P. 23(b)(1).... The district court ruled that the general class action prerequisites of Rule 23(a) were satisfied because of the large number of investors and the similarity of their claims. In reaching its decision to certify the class pursuant to Rule 23(b)(1), the district court reasoned that the case's unique facts made the possibility of individual actions, as would be allowed under Rule 23(b)(3), undesirable. The district court observed that: (1) all investors were involved in the same fraud scheme and shared causes of action; (2) individual actions may cause both defendants and plaintiffs to develop inconsistent claims and defenses; (3) class members' interests would best be protected by insuring that the receivership fund was used and distributed equitably; and (4) individual actions would result in huge attorney fees and burden the judicial system.

After a year and a half of discovery, the parties began to seek a settlement.... The parties reached an agreement. Adherence to the agreement was conditioned upon the district court certifying a class action pursuant to Rule 23(b)(1). The district court certified a class for settlement purposes pursuant to Rule 23(b)(1) and approved the settlement....

In certifying the class, the district court again emphasized the special circumstances of the case. The court reasoned that the cohesion among the plaintiffs' claims caused each plaintiff's ability to recover to be intertwined with that of other plaintiffs. Specifically, the court expressed concern that plaintiffs, who brought their actions first, might bankrupt potential sources of recovery and, thereby, preclude recovery for those plaintiffs who brought later actions. In addition, the district court feared that individual actions would cause the defendants to face incompatible standards of conduct or create for them inconsistent adjudications. The court also noted that Rule 23(b)(1) certification would aid in equitably distributing the receivership fund. The court further recited several negative consequences that would result if the class was not certified pursuant to Rule 23(b)(1). Individual defendants would lose the ability to set off, against their investors' claims, the money they paid through the receivership fund to those who invested at other brokerage firms. Individual actions would also create both burdens for the court and the prospect of enormous attorneys' fees. The court also expressed concern that by not certifying the class pursuant to Rule 23(b)(1), most plaintiffs would be deprived of the settlement they desire.

A group of plaintiffs, named the Baer plaintiffs, brought this appeal challenging the district court's class certification under Rule 23(b)(1). Appellants contend that the class should have been certified pursuant to Rule 23(b)(3) to allow class members to opt out.

Determination of the question whether a lawsuit may proceed as a class action is committed to the sound discretion of the district court, and its determination will not be overturned absent a showing that it has abused its discretion.... Nonetheless, the district court erred by certifying the class pursuant to Rule 23(b)(1).

A class must satisfy the requirements of one of the subsections to Rule 23(b). We note that the propriety of certification under the various subsections is quite controversial and not well defined. At stake are the nature of the notice to be given to class members and their right to opt out from or refuse to be part of the class.... These practical differences affect the ability of plaintiffs to bring class actions as well as their attractiveness to defendants. Applying the various subsections of Rule 23(b) requires a balance between an individual's due process rights and the judiciary's need to expedite the orderly resolution of conflict....

The district court certified the class both under subpart (A) and (B) of Rule 23(b)(1)....

As a threshold consideration to certification under sub-part A, it must be ascertained that separate actions would result if the class was not certified pursuant to Rule 23(b)(1). It is clear in this case that separate actions would be filed if the class was not certified pursuant to Rule 23(b)(1). At the time the district court first certified the class, twenty-five separate actions were pending. Indeed, the appellants bring this appeal for the purpose of prosecuting or being able to prosecute their own actions. Consequently, this threshold concern is satisfied.

The identity of judicial action that creates "inconsistent or varying adjudications" is not clear. Many courts confronting the issue have held that Rule 23(b)(1)(A) does not apply to actions seeking compensatory damages. . . . These courts reason that inconsistent standards for future conduct are not created because a defendant might be found liable to some plaintiffs and not to others. . . . Implicit in these decisions is the view that only actions seeking declaratory or injunctive relief can be certified under this section. . . . Underlying is the concern that if compensatory damage actions can be certified under Rule 23(b)(1)(A), then all actions could be certified under the section, thereby making the other sub-sections of Rule 23 meaningless, particularly Rule 23(b)(3). . . .

Albeit reluctantly, we must agree. Although sound criticism exists for this interpretation, the Advisory Committee Notes support the proposition that (b)(1)(A) certification is for cases seeking injunctive and declaratory relief. The relevant Note states that the section is proper in suits to invalidate a bond issue, to declare the rights and duties of riparian owners or landowners, or to abate a common nuisance. . . . Since the plaintiffs sought compensatory damages, the district court erred by certifying the class pursuant to (b)(1)(A).

[The court then turned to certification under Rule 23(b)(1)(B).]

The district court found that if separate cases were litigated "determination in the prior action would as a practical matter create a predisposition to a similar determination in a subsequent action."

It is settled that the possibility that an action will have either precedential or stare decisis effect on later cases is not sufficient to satisfy Rule 23(b)(1)(B). . . . A contrary rule would enable any action, with the possibility that it might be one of multiple actions, to be certified pursuant to Rule 23(b)(1)(B). Consequently, the district court's finding that earlier decisions would create a "predisposition" for the determination of later actions standing alone is clearly not a sufficient basis for certification.

The district court also certified the settlement class pursuant to Rule 23(b)(1)(B) because a limited fund existed. Limited fund cases exist where a fund is insufficient to satisfy all of the claims against it. . . . The district court found two bases for certification based on this theory. First, the district court relied on the existence of the receivership fund. The court indicated that the fund has been and would be protected throughout the litigation and "that certification under Rule 23(b)(1) will aid in protecting, managing and equitably distributing this fund." We do not find this to be an adequate basis for certification. The district court doubtless stated correctly that the fund would be protected but that protection does not depend upon Rule 23(b)(1) certification. In addition, the district court did not indicate that the receivership fund initially was intended to be the sole source of recovery for plaintiffs. It is of no consequence that the receivership fund now contains settlement contributions. Consequently, the receivership fund is not a limited fund for purposes of Rule 23(b)(1).

The district court also found a limited fund on the basis that some investors may bankrupt potential sources of recovery. The court made no specific findings of the defendants' financial status. Absent such findings the district court could not properly rely on this ground for certification. . . .

Accordingly, we reverse the district court's judgment now under attack and remand for further proceedings consistent with this opinion.

IN RE TELECTRONICS PACING SYSTEMS, INC., ACCUFIX ATRIAL "J" LEADS PRODUCTS LIABILITY LITIGATION

172 F.R.D. 271 (S.D. Ohio 1997)

■ SPIEGEL, Senior District Judge. . . . There has been much discussion regarding the need to reform or improve how federal courts deal with mass tort litigation. While we agree changes might be appropriate, the district courts are left to fight the battles and resolve the Parties disputes' with the tools provided by Congress and our appellate courts. Thus, we must grant or deny certification on the basis of the federal rules as written today and interpreted by the Sixth Circuit and the Supreme Court.

In deciding this question, the Court is mindful of the applicable law and rules, the procedural and substantive legal rights of the Parties and the ethical concerns raised by adjudication of mass tort claims. Recently, several Circuit Court[s] have been highly critical of the use of class actions in mass tort and product liability cases. While we recognize the difficulties inherent in diversity based-class actions as outlined by the Circuit Courts, we continue to believe that class action provides the fairest, most efficient and economical means of dealing with these types of cases. We believe courts must play an important role in the efficient resolution of mass tort action. This is especially so where, as here, there is a danger that the expense of litigation and potential for large damage awards threaten to bankrupt the defendant and leave some class members without a remedy. . . .

We also strongly disagree with those Circuit Courts which have allowed their apparent economic biases to influence their interpretation of the requirements of Rule 23. For example, in Castano v. American Tobacco Co., 84 F.3d 734 (5th Cir. 1996), the Fifth [C]ircuit found that class certification of all nicotine dependent individuals was not superior under Rule 23(b)(3) because of the strategic effect class certification has upon the defendants' chances.

> In the context of mass tort class actions, certification dramatically affects the stakes for defendants. Class certification magnifies and strengthens the number of unmeritorious claims. Aggregation of claims also makes it more likely that a defendant will be found liable and results in significantly higher damage awards.

Id. at 746 (citations omitted); [s]ee also Matter of Rhone-Poulenc Rorer Inc., 51 F.3d 1293 (7th Cir. 1995). To credit the Fifth Circuit's statement is to also state that its converse — denying class certification makes it less likely defendants will be found liable or responsible for lower damage awards — is true. Plaintiffs in individual actions will have to bear a greater share of the cost and risk for maintaining their action as compared to plaintiffs in a class action. Often an individual action pits a single plaintiff relying on his or her own resources to fund the litigation against the vast resources of a large manufacturer and the large law firms which represents it.

Obviously, the procedural rules affect the outcome of litigation. These Circuit Courts seemed to ignore the essence of Rule 23 because of their philosophical disagreement with the effects of Rule 23.

[The case involved pacemakers that had an allegedly defective J-shaped retention wire that fractured and caused serious injury to the heart or surrounding blood vessels. The pacemakers were made by TPLC, Inc., a wholly owned subsidiary of TPSI, Inc. Both companies were in turn owned by an Australian holding company, Nucleus, which was later purchased by another Australian company, Pacific Dunlop Limited (PDL). PDL had more than 225 corporate affiliates, and annual sales of $5.5 billion.

[Approximately 25,000 of the defective pacemakers were implanted in American citizens prior to 1994, when 7 fracture-related injuries were reported. In response to the fracture problem, TPLC created an institute to manage the recall of the defective wires. It also formed a Physicians' Advisory Committee to provide advice to physicians concerning the clinical management of patients. It also agreed to reimburse reasonable, unreimbursed expenses for screening patients and extracting pacemakers.

[After numerous actions were filed in various federal courts, the Judicial Panel on Multidistrict Litigation consolidated the cases in the Southern District of Ohio. The consolidated complaint alleged negligence, strict liability, breach of warranty, fraud, misrepresentation, fear of product failure, and infliction of emotional distress. Compensatory and punitive damages were sought. Also included was a claim for medical monitoring.

[The transferee court certified a worldwide class of pacemaker recipients, but later amended the order to a nationwide class. In light of In re American Medical Systems, Inc., 75 F.3d 1069 (6th Cir. 1996) (p. 574, supra), the court then decertified the class in its entirety. Among the court's concerns was that a single nationwide class would involve the application of numerous state laws, and would therefore run afoul of the requirements of Rule 23(a). The plaintiffs responded by restructuring the class and renewing their motions for class certification. The plaintiffs proposed ten separate subclasses: a single nationwide subclass on the medical monitoring claim, two subclasses to account for state-law variations on negligence, four subclasses to account for state-law variations on strict liability, and three subclasses to account for state-law variations on punitive damages. The transferee court found that all of the Rule 23(a) requirements were satisfied for all ten subclasses. The court then held that the medical monitoring subclass could be certified under both Rule 23(b)(1)(A) and Rule 23(b)(3), that the negligence and strict liability class actions could be certified under

Rule 23(b)(3), and the punitive damages subclasses could not be certified under any provision of Rule 23(b). The following excerpt is the court's ruling on the Rule 23(b)(1) certification of the medical monitoring subclass.]

"Certification under Rule 23(b)(1) is appropriate when a unitary decision is essential." In re Joint E[.] & S[.] Dist. Asbestos Lit., 129 B.R. 710, 824 (E. & S.D.N.Y. 1991), vacated on other grounds, 982 F.2d 721 (2d. Cir. 1992). "Rule 23(b)(1) classes are designed to avoid prejudice to the defendant or absent class members if individual actions were prosecuted in contrast to a class suit yielding a unitary adjudication." [1 Herbert Newberg & Alba Conte, Newberg on Class Actions,] § 4.01 [(3d ed. 1992)]. However, the possibility that some plaintiffs might recover and others might not does not justify class certification under Rule 23(b)(1)(A). In re Bendectin Prod. Liability Lit., 749 F.2d 300, 305 (6th Cir. 1984).

A. Class Certification of Medical Monitoring pursuant to Rule 23(b)(1)(A).

Rule 23(b)(1)(A) states that class certification is proper if separate actions "would create a risk of inconsistent or varying adjudications with respect to individual members of the class which would establish incompatible standards of conduct for the party opposing the class. . . ." Fed.R.Civ.P. 23(b)(1)(A). "The phrase 'incompatible standards of conduct' is thought to refer to the situation where different results in separate actions would impair the opposing party's ability to pursue a uniform continuing course of conduct." Charles A. Wright, et al., 7A Federal Practice & Procedure, § 1773 at 431 (2d ed.1986) (citing cases). "[S]ubdivision (b)(1)(A) is applicable when practical necessity forces the opposing party to act in the same manner toward the individual class members and thereby makes inconsistent adjudications in separate actions unworkable or intolerable." Id. at 434.

The medical monitoring claim here is an ideal candidate for class certification pursuant to Rule 23(b)(1)(A) because separate adjudications would impair TPLC's ability to pursue a single uniform medical monitoring program. . . . TPLC asserts that medical monitoring beyond that recommended by TPLC's Physicians' Advisory Committee is not warranted. TPLC's research program is a uniform benefit to the class of "J" lead implantees as a whole. Any judicially-imposed modification of this program would then, by necessity, affect all of the "J" lead implantees. Furthermore, separate judicial orders pertaining to medical monitoring could require TPLC to institute differing types of monitoring programs which TPLC would have to reconcile.

TPLC argues that the recommendations of the Physicians' Advisory Committee are subject to approval by the FDA. TPLC insists that "the Court [will] have to reconcile its involvement in a medical monitoring program with FDA's statutorily mandated oversight function. . . . The potential for unnecessary conflict and expense with no patient benefit is readily apparent, with TPLC caught in an impossible position between the judicial and executive branches of government." Whether FDA regulations preempt or otherwise limit state law tort claims for medical monitoring goes to the merits of the class claims and must be determined at a later date.

However, individual adjudication of implantees claims for medical monitoring would not alleviate TPLC's fear of conflicting standards of medical monitoring imposed by the judicial branch and executive branch. In fact, the danger of courts imposing conflicting duties upon Telectronics would only be compounded if the question of medical monitoring is not certified as a class action pursuant to Rule 23(b)(1)(A). Presently, there are over 400 individual actions consolidated before this Court by the Judicial Panel for Multidistrict Litigation. Certainly, a large number of similar cases are pending in state courts across the country. Thus, TPLC could still face multiple and conflicting orders rendered from different courts regarding the scope and necessity of a medical monitoring program which may also conflict with FDA imposed requirements. Accordingly, the Court certifies the medical monitoring subclass under Rule 23(b)(1)(A).

In addition to the danger of various courts mandating differing standards of conduct concerning monitoring, there are also significant policy reasons for requiring one medical monitoring class. Any research component should be coordinated in order to maximize resources and avoid duplication. To promote consistency in treatment, doctors should also be given one set of advice in terms of treatment options for their "J" lead patients.

B. Class Certification of Medical Monitoring pursuant to Rule 23(b)(1)(B).

The argument for certification of a medical monitoring subclass is bolstered by the fact that separate adjudications may adversely affect other implantees' ability to recover anything. . . . The most common use of subsection (b)(1)(B) is in limited fund cases. 1 Newberg, *supra*[,] § 4.09. "A limited fund exists when a fixed asset or piece of property exists in which all class members have a preexisting interest, and an apportionment or determination of the interests of one class member cannot be made without affecting the proportionate interests of other class members similarly situated." Id. In the same limited circumstances, the potential or probable insolvency of the defendant due to a large number of pending tort actions can create a limited fund appropriate for adjudication under Rule 23(b)(1)(B). . . .

According to previous pleadings and the representations of counsel for both sides, TPLC has recently sold all of its assets to another corporation. Thus, TPLC is no longer an operating corporation. TPLC received approximately $105 million for all of its assets. TPLC also has a $25 million liability policy. This policy is a diminishing policy; that is defense costs are deducted from the total coverage. TPLC has depleted approximately $9 million of their insurance coverage to cover legal fees and medical monitoring expenses. Thus, TPLC currently has approximately $120 million in assets and insurance to cover its liabilities related to the "J" lead litigation.[10]

10. Plaintiffs have also sued TPLC's parent companies, Pacific Dunlop Limited and Nucleus Limited. Plaintiffs have not moved to certify a class action against these defendants. Furthermore, there is a substantial question whether Pacific Dunlop or Nucleus can be held liable for the activities of their subsidiary, TPLC.

In the United States, an estimated 25,000 individuals have had the "J" Lead implanted. Dividing $120 million by the number of implantees, TPLC has about $4800 to spend on each of the implantees for medical monitoring and any potential damage awards. TPLC has spent over $2.5 million on medical monitoring since it agreed to pay for the reasonable unreimbursed expenses of fluoroscopy and explantation. Because the Parties did not submit evidence regarding the potential cost of the medical monitoring program, the Court cannot determine whether TPLC faces insolvency as a result its expenses arising out of the "J" lead controversy. The possibility of the existence of a limited fund, however, lends further support to a conclusion that medical monitoring class should be certified under Rule 23(b)(1).

IN RE "AGENT ORANGE" PRODUCT LIABILITY LITIGATION

100 F.R.D. 718 (E.D.N.Y. 1983), mandamus denied, 725 F.2d 858 (2d Cir. 1984)

■ WEINSTEIN, Chief Judge. [This mass tort involved claims by Vietnam veterans that they had suffered injuries due to exposure to herbicides used during the war. As many as 2.4 million service personnel were estimated to have been exposed. The defendants in the case were the government contractors that had made the herbicides. The court certified a (b)(3) class. It then considered whether the class should also be certified under (b)(1).]

Rule 23(b)(1)(A) . . .

The court has already stated that "Rule 23(b)(1)(A) is not meant to apply . . . where the risk of inconsistent results in individual actions is merely the possibility that the defendants will prevail in some cases and not in others, thereby paying damages to some claimants and not others." [In re "Agent Orange" Product Liability Litigation,] 506 F. Supp. [762,] 789 [(E.D.N.Y. 1980)] (citations omitted). If the risk of paying money damages to some and not others were sufficient for (b)(1)(A) certification, almost every class action could be certified under (b)(1)(A). . . .

Plaintiffs attempt to distinguish the current litigation by expressing concern that if different courts decide differently future contractors will not know the possible extent of their responsibility and whether they should bid on government defense or war contracts. Their concern is commendable, but misplaced. Any inconsistent or erroneous theories of law applied by trial courts in Agent Orange cases will certainly be rectified in the highest courts. It is unlikely that the Supreme Court would avoid clarifying the law on the subject. Rule 23(b)(1)(A) is not applicable.

Rule 23(b)(1)(B) . . .

The rationale for using (b)(1)(B) in mass tort litigation is that of the "limited fund." . . .

As applied to mass tort litigation, the "limited fund" is generally construed to be the assets of the defendants as extended by insurance coverage and the assets of the insurers. The "fund" may also have a more limited bearing, as where the first judgments may take all of a limited punitive damage award. If earlier claimants proceed on an individual basis, it is urged, they will deplete the defendants' assets and leave nothing for later claimants. . . .

Before determining whether to certify the plaintiffs' class under (b)(1)(B), two threshold questions must be addressed. The first is whether (b)(1)(B) should ever be applied in mass tort litigation. The second, assuming that it should, is what standard to use in determining whether there is a risk that earlier litigants will deplete the fund and leave nothing for latecomers.

Although the matter is not free from doubt, most courts that have considered the issue have concluded that, in the proper circumstances, Rule (b)(1)(B) may be used in mass tort cases. . . .

Courts that have considered the issue disagree over how to determine when the danger of fund exhaustion is great enough to justify certification. All conclude that "without more, numerous plaintiffs and a large ad damnum clause should not guarantee (b)(1)(B) certification." Payton v. Abbott Labs, 83 F.R.D. 382, 389 (D. Mass. 1979). The Ninth Circuit has held that (b)(1)(B) certification is proper only when "separate punitive damage claims necessarily will affect later claims." [In re Northern District of California "Dalkon Shield" IUD Product Liability Litigation,] 693 F.2d [847,] 852 [(9th Cir. 1982), cert. denied, 459 U.S. 1171 (1983)]. Strict adherence to the Ninth Circuit certainty standard would mean either the elimination of (b)(1)(B) certification in mass tort actions . . ., or require a pretrial determination on the merits, which the Supreme Court has frowned on in another class action context. See Eisen v. Carlisle & Jacquelin, 417 U.S. 156, 177-78 (1974) . . . . This strict Ninth Circuit standard flies in the face of the language of Rule 23, which requires only that there be a "risk" of impairment, not that there be a conclusive determination of impairment. . . .

Given the speculative nature of many of the rulings that must be made at the time of a class certification when the facts have not been fully developed, such as typicality of representative claims and adequacy of representation, the probable risk standard appears most useful.

How high the probability needs to be requires an evaluation of the advantages and disadvantages of class certification to the actual and prospective parties. We must, for example, remember that the court is in the position of protecting a large group of war veterans against the possibility that after possibly winning a long-sought after victory in the courts, they will not be able to collect on a judgment in their favor. Without now rehearsing all those effects, it is enough to say that considering the particular facts of the instant litigation, the proper standard is whether there is substantial probability — that is less than a preponderance but more than a mere possibility — that if damages are awarded, the claims of earlier litigants would exhaust the defendants' assets. . . .

To determine whether that substantial probability exists in this case, the Special Master, Sol Schreiber, was directed to conduct a limited evidentiary hearing. At the hearing, defendants' counsel submitted certified copies of their most recent balance sheets. The plaintiffs' counsel selected a cross-section of their cases and made a brief presentation as to the nature of the damage alleged. The Master found that the combined net assets of the defendants, including insurance, total approximately $9 to $16 billion. Collection of judgments, if any, would be spread over a number of years and payment could probably be handled from year-to-year and paid out of earnings. The Master also found that, based on the information presently available, his best estimate is that the number of claims may total 40,000 to 50,000. He concluded that the evidence now before the court does not support the view that provable claims will exhaust the defendants' assets.

. . .

[T]he information elicited at the hearing and in appearance before this court indicates that sufficient assets are and will be available to respond to any probable judgments. Without the aid of a full trial, on the basis of facts presently available, it cannot be said that there is a substantial probability that if plaintiffs' claims are successful, the compensatory recovery will exceed defendants' assets.

Based on information thus far supplied to the court, it also cannot be found, as a preliminary matter, that there is a substantial probability that punitive damages, if allowed[,] will, when added to compensatory damages, exceed defendants' assets. . . .

Nevertheless, there is a substantial probability that limited punitive damages may be allowed. If they are, it would be equitable to share this portion of the possible award among all plaintiffs who ultimately recover compensatory damages. Yet, if no class is certified under Rule (b)(1)(B), non-class members who opt out under Rule 23(b)(3) would conceivably receive all of the punitive damages or, if their cases are not completed first, none at all.

It is axiomatic that the purpose of punitive damages is not to compensate plaintiffs for their injury, but to punish defendants for their wrongdoing. In theory, therefore, when a plaintiff recovers punitive damages against a defendant, that represents a finding by the jury that the defendant was sufficiently punished for the wrongful conduct. There must, therefore, be some limit, either as a matter of policy or as a matter of due process, to the amount of times defendants may be punished for a single transaction. . . . There is, therefore, a substantial probability that "adjudication with respect to individual members of the class . . . would as a practical matter be dispositive of the interests of the other members not parties to the adjudication." Accordingly, a class of all those described as members of the (b)(3) class are also certified under (b)(1)(B). The (b)(1)(B) certification is for the award of punitive damages.

How this decision under (b)(1)(B) affects plaintiffs' rights to opt out under Rule (b)(3) need not be decided now. In the first place, it is not clear that any appreciable number of plaintiffs will exercise their right to opt out under (b)(3). Nor is it clear that punitive damages will be awarded.

Notes and Questions

1. *Agent Orange* and *Telectronics* demonstrate that it is possible to certify a class under different provisions of Rule 23(b) with respect to different issues. Class actions that mix opt-out rights on some claims and mandatory joinder on others are sometimes called "hybrid" class actions. It is also possible that the same class might be eligible for certification under both Rule 23(b)(3) and one of the mandatory provisions. When this occurs, some courts state a "preference" that the class should be certified under the relevant mandatory class rule. See Bing v. Roadway Express, Inc., 485 F.2d 441, 447 (5th Cir. 1973). This preference dispenses with the requirement of an opt-out notice, and assures that all class members will be bound. See 7A Charles A. Wright et al., Federal Practice & Procedure § 175 (1986). Unless the court involves lawyer dysfunction, in which individual opt-out adjudication threatens rational adjudication, is this the right presumption?

2. La Mar v. H & B Novelty & Loan Co., 489 F.2d 461, 467 (9th Cir. 1973) explained the relationship between (b)(1)(A) and (b)(1)(B) as follows:

> In essence, (b)(1)(A) and (b)(1)(B) of Rule 23 are opposite sides of the same coin — a coin which determines suitability for class action by reference to either the awkwardness, irrationality, or the probability of severe prejudice of separate actions. Depriving the plaintiffs in these proceedings of their representative status with respect to defendants whose conduct caused the plaintiffs no injury does not contravene these purposes of Rule 23(b)(1).

Does this understanding suggest that the motivating idea behind (b)(1)(A) and (b)(1)(B) is the prevention of lawyer dysfunction — (b)(1)(A) to deal with the problems that suits by later-filing nonparties might cause to the remedy obtained by the present parties, and (b)(1)(B) to deal with the problem that the present lawsuit might pose to the ability of later-filing nonparties to obtain a meaningful remedy? Should (b)(1)(A) be amended to refer expressly to the problems that a later lawsuit might create for those present parties (typically plaintiffs) that would fit within the class, rather than focusing entirely on the problems that later lawsuits create for the present parties (typically defendants) that oppose the class?

3. Both *Greenman* and *Agent Orange* reflect the standard thinking that the likelihood of different damage awards is not an adequate reason to certify a (b)(1)(A) class. This rule is entirely consistent with the view of Rule 23(b)(1) as a rule concerned with preventing lawyer dysfunction. The reason is that the only persons harmed by the distribution of differing levels of awards are persons that are not involved in the litigation; the present plaintiffs prefer to obtain large damage awards (and thus the lion's share of the available assets), and the present defendants are generally indifferent about which plaintiffs receive the available assets. Hence, as a general matter, (b)(1)(A), which focuses on harm to present litigants, does not apply in the context of claims for money damage.

4. In Arch v. American Tobacco Co., 175 F.R.D. 469 (E.D. Pa. 1997), the district court refused to certify a class of Pennsylvania residents that sought to establish a medical monitoring program. In *Arch*, the plaintiffs claimed that certification was appropriate under (b)(2), which we study shortly, rather than (b)(1)(A). Would they have had more success had they tried (b)(1)(A)? We would argue not. An important difference between *Telectronics* and *Arch* is that, in *Telectronics*, a nationwide class was involved, while in *Arch*, only a single-state

class was involved. Not all states recognize a medical monitoring theory, and among those that do, the requirements for medical monitoring might well differ. To expect the defendants in *Telectronics* to design monitoring programs pursuant to individual litigation for each of fifty states might indeed lead either to an impossible remedial situation for the defendants, and might threaten the monitoring program established in early litigation. In *Arch*, however, only one state was involved, and all plaintiffs had an identical interest under state law in the same monitoring program. Hence, certification of a monitoring class in *Arch* would have done nothing to prevent dysfunction; indeed, by leaping one class to the front of the medical monitoring line, class certification in *Arch* might have created dysfunction. Is this the best explanation of the different outcomes in *Telectronics* and *Arch*? Should *Arch* have certified a (b)(1)(A) class if nationwide class action had been requested?

5. Of course, this analysis of the difference in the two cases highlights an important problem in (b)(1)(A) class actions. If the reason to certify a class in *Telectronics* is the difference in state law — and thus difference in remedy — how can any class representative be regarded as an adequate class representative of an entire class? Won't those persons in states with generous rights of medical monitoring inevitably be in conflict with those in states with more conservative rights (or those in states with no right of monitoring), who would probably trade monitoring claims for a larger cash settlement more willingly? More generally, isn't there an inevitable conflict of interest among class members whenever there is a risk that the defendant will be subject to "incompatible standards of conduct"? Does this mean that Rule 23(b)(1)(A) is a cruel hoax, so that any class that might be certified under it is automatically disqualified under Rule 23(a)(4)? If not, then how is the court to manage the potential conflicts within the class? By picking representatives from the jurisdiction with the most stringent law? By using subclasses for different states' laws (as *Telectronics* did with respect to damages actions)? By reconceiving the divergent individual interests involved as a single group interest? By becoming a super-guardian of the interests of all?

6. Rule 23(b)(1)(B) creates a mandatory class action to deal with a common form of dysfunction that we have repeatedly encountered: the problem of insufficient assets. *Greenman*, *Telectronics*, and *Agent Orange* force us to consider an issue that we have not discussed in detail before now: Exactly how clear must the insufficiency of assets be in order to regard a case as "complex"? For instance, isn't it unclear in *Greenman* whether the plaintiffs will be able to sue successfully enough defendants with collectable assets in order to be made whole for this fraud? Given this uncertainty, why doesn't the court find a limited fund to exist? *Agent Orange* stakes out the possible positions on this matter, and ultimately suggests the most aggregation-favoring approach. Knowing that the right to individual, adversarial adjudication hinges on your answer, how much certainty would you require?

Courts typically require a strong evidentiary showing that the provable damage claims of the class will exceed the insurance and other assets of the defendant. Speculative allegations to that effect will not suffice. See In re Bendectin Products Liability Litigation, 749 F.2d 300 (6th Cir. 1984). How can a trial court responsibly and successfully undertake such an analysis early in the litigation? Should the available assets of the all of the defendants be compared to the aggregate value of the damages sought by the class? What difference does it make, if any, that the plaintiff class is also suing other defendants whose assets are adequate to pay the claims of the class? In this regard, note the plaintiffs' move in *Telectronics*: They did not join other possible defendants that might well have been responsible and whose assets might well have converted an insufficient asset case into one with ample assets. Should the plaintiffs' voluntary pleading choices be allowed to create a limited fund? Should the court deny certification under (b)(1)(B) unless all potential defendants are joined?

7. Even under a generous standard of insufficiency of assets, Judge Weinstein did not certify a mandatory class for either compensatory or punitive damages. In order to establish a limited fund, Weinstein instead suggested that there was an absolute limit on the amount of punitive damages defendants could be expected to pay, and that difficult issues that could arise over the equitable allocation of those awards among plaintiffs. The Third Circuit has rejected the use of a (b)(1)(B) class action to address this problem. In re School Asbestos Litigation, 789 F.2d 996 (3rd Cir. 1986).

8. Assuming that a genuine limited fund exists, what should be the proper relationship between the federal bankruptcy laws and limited fund class actions under (b)(1)(b)? How can the claims of non-class members against the defendant (such as trade creditors of the manufacturers in *Agent Orange*) be equitably managed by the court when such claims are not before it? Should the defendant automatically be treated as insolvent, thereby giving one federal court bankruptcy jurisdiction over all claims against the defendant? See p. 778, *infra*; Richard L. Epling, *Are Rule 23 Class Actions a Viable Alternative to the Bankruptcy Code?*, 23 Seton Hall L. Rev. 1555 (1993).

b) Equitable Class Actions: Rule 23(b)(2)

The modern class action rule was promulgated in 1966, just two years after passage of the landmark 1964 Civil Rights Act. Rule 23(b)(2) was explicitly drafted to ensure that the class action would be available to remedy the effects of race and other forms of discrimination. Often called the "Equitable Class Action Rule," Rule 23(b)(2) requires that the party opposing the class have acted in a way that justifies injunctive or declaratory relief with respect to the class as a whole. While the Advisory Committee Notes make clear that Rule 23(b)(2) was not limited to civil rights cases, for many years the vast majority of class actions certified under this section were of that type.

How is the (b)(2) class action different from the (b)(1)(A) class action? One line of thinking is that there really is no difference; (b)(2) is nothing more than a specific application of (b)(1)(A). But that may not always be true. Think, for instance, of *Rice v. City of Philadelphia* (p. 556, *supra*), in which all class members had an essentially united interest in an injunction that required arraignments within the constitutional time period. Although there might have been some disagreement about exactly what that time period should be as a factual matter, there were no intra-class conflicts with respect to the issue of entitlement to an appropriate remedy. Moreover, the factual disagreement could eventually be cleared up by an authoritative decision from the Supreme Court. Hence, it is not clear that (b)(1)(A) would really pertain in *Rice*, while it is quite clear that, insofar as the *Rice* plaintiffs sought only an injunctive remedy, (b)(2) does.

If this suggested distinction between (b)(1)(A) and (b)(2) is accurate, then should it be easier to obtain a certification under (b)(2), in which the interests of all class members are united, than it is under (b)(1)(A)? Perhaps not. The distinction also suggests that (b)(2) class actions with united interests do not involve lawyer dysfunction and are therefore not complex. Moreover, in an affirmative action case, there may be several subgroups with distinct and opposing interests in a particular remedy. Doesn't (b)(2) permit the court to certify a class action of just one subgroup with a united interest, thereby actually creating lawyer dysfunction? Should these facts make courts more reluctant to certify a (b)(2) united-interest equitable class action than a (b)(1)(A) conflicting-interests class action?

ALLISON v. CITGO PETROLEUM CORP.

___ F.3d ___, 1998 WL 244989 (5th Cir. 1998)

■ JOLLY, Circuit Judge. This interlocutory appeal presents the question whether the district court properly refused to certify a class action challenging employment practices by the Citgo Petroleum Corporation ("Citgo") under Title VII (as amended in 1991) and the Civil Rights Act of 1866, 42 U.S.C. § 1981. . . . [We] affirm and hold that the district court did not abuse its discretion in denying class certification.

I

This race discrimination case involves a potentially huge and wide-ranging class action lawsuit concerning employment practices at Citgo's Lake Charles manufacturing complex. Specifically, the plaintiffs identified the following employment practices as resulting in unlawful race discrimination: (1) failure to post or announce job vacancies; (2) use of an informal word-of-mouth announcement process for filling job vacancies; (3) use of racially biased tests to evaluate candidates for hire or promotion; and (4) use of a subjective decision-making process by a predominantly white supervisory staff in reviewing applicants for hire and employees for promotion. The plaintiffs challenged each of these policies under both the disparate impact and systemic disparate treatment theories of Title VII.

In September 1993, the plaintiffs filed a motion for the certification of a class estimated to contain more than 1000 potential members. The class was identified as "all African-American employees and applicants of Citgo Petroleum Corporation (Citgo) from April 11, 1979 until the present." Its members are current and former employees and unsuccessful applicants for employment in "hourly" positions at Citgo's Lake Charles complex. They are spread across two separate facilities. They are represented by six different unions, come from five different skill groups, and work in seven different functional areas at the complex. Nevertheless, the plaintiffs maintain that a class action is appropriate because they are challenging general hiring, training, and promotional policies applied uniformly throughout the complex.

To remedy the alleged discrimination, the plaintiffs seek every available form of injunctive, declaratory, and monetary relief. In terms of affirmative injunctive relief, the plaintiffs seek restructuring of offending policies, instatement into existing jobs, and retroactive seniority and benefits. As for monetary relief traditionally available under Title VII, the plaintiffs request back pay, front pay, pre-judgment interest, and attorneys' fees. Furthermore, invoking the provisions added to Title VII by the Civil Rights Act of 1991, the plaintiffs seek compensatory and punitive damages to the maximum amount permissible under the law. Finally, the plaintiffs demand a jury trial on their claims of intentional discrimination, to which they are now also entitled under the 1991 amendments.

The district court referred the plaintiffs' motion for class certification to a magistrate judge, who conducted an evidentiary hearing and subsequently entered a report and recommendation denying class certification. The magistrate judge determined that, although the proposed class met the requirements of Rule 23(a) of the Federal Rules of Civil Procedure, it could not be certified under any of the alternatives provided in 23(b). . . .

The district court adopted the report and recommendation in its entirety and denied class certification. On petition by the plaintiffs, the court certified the question for interlocutory appeal under 28 U.S.C. § 1292(b), which we granted in May 1996. This appeal followed.

II

We note at the outset that the district court maintains substantial discretion in determining whether to certify a class action, a decision we review only for abuse. See Jenkins v. Raymark Indus., 782 F.2d 468, 471-72 (5th Cir. 1986). Implicit in this deferential standard is a recognition of the essentially factual basis of the certification inquiry and of the district court's inherent power to manage and control pending litigation. . . . Whether the district court applied the correct legal standard in reaching its decision on class certification, however, is a legal question that we review *de novo*. . . .

IV

Class actions brought under Title VII typically proceed under two theories, disparate impact and systemic disparate treatment, both of which are advanced in this case. The disparate impact theory is used to challenge a facially neutral employment policy that falls more harshly on a protected class of employees. . . . The systemic disparate treatment theory focuses on whether the employer engaged in a "pattern or practice" of intentional discrimination, that is, whether discrimination was the employer's standard operating procedure rather than a sporadic occurrence. . . . In years past, we have routinely upheld certification of class actions to resolve Title VII cases involving disparate impact and pattern or practice claims of discrimination. . . .

In doing so, we have recognized that the class action device could be implemented effectively to eradicate widespread or institutional-scale discrimination. . . . Disparate impact cases in particular, which challenge specific, facially-neutral policies with proof of statistical disparities resulting from their uniform application to an employer's workforce, by their very nature implicate class-based claims. We also have molded class actions to accommodate claims that an employer engaged in a pattern or practice of intentional discrimination. . . .

The Civil Rights Act of 1991, however, made fundamental changes in both the procedures and remedies available to Title VII litigants. Among other things, the Act now permits plaintiffs to recover compensatory and punitive damages from an employer who engaged in unlawful intentional discrimination (to include individual disparate treatment and pattern or practice cases). See 42 U.S.C. § 1981a(a)(1). Compensatory damages include relief for "future pecuniary losses, emotional pain, suffering, inconvenience, mental anguish, loss of enjoyment of life, and other nonpecuniary losses." § 1981a(b)(3). The Act also allows punitive damages if the employer discriminated "with malice or with reckless indifference to the federally protected rights of an aggrieved individual," § 1981a(b)(1)(2), with the total recovery of compensatory and punitive damages capped at a maximum of $300,000 per plaintiff, see § 1981a(b)(3). Finally, in all cases where the plaintiff seeks compensatory and punitive damages, either party is entitled to demand a trial by jury. See § 1981a(c).

In the class action context, the changes to Title VII are not inconsequential. It is important to remember that the class action device exists primarily, if not solely, to achieve a measure of judicial economy, which benefits the parties as well as the entire judicial system. It preserves the resources of both the courts and the parties by permitting issues affecting all class members to be litigated in an efficient, expedited, and manageable fashion. . . . Before passage of the Civil Rights Act of 1991, liability and the appropriate remedies in all Title VII cases were determined in bench trials. Monetary relief was limited to back pay and other equitable remedies. By bringing additional monetary claims within the scope of intentional discrimination cases, the Civil Rights Act of 1991 added to the complexity and diversity of the issues to be tried and decided. By injecting jury trials into the Title VII mix, the 1991 Act introduced, in the context of class actions, potential manageability problems with both practical and legal, indeed constitutional, implications. The broad question we consider here is whether and to what extent these factors affect a class action in this case.

V

The plaintiffs' principal argument is that the district court erred in refusing to certify the entire case as a class action under Rule 23(b)(2). . . .

A

We consider first whether the district court erred in determining that the primary limitation on a Rule 23(b)(2) class action is the requirement that injunctive or declaratory relief be the predominant relief sought for the class. Naturally, we begin by looking at the plain language of the rule. . . .

The rule is clear that claims seeking injunctive or declaratory relief are appropriate for (b)(2) class certification. Thus, if the plaintiffs sought only injunctive and declaratory relief, this case could readily be certified as a class action under Rule 23(b)(2).

The plaintiffs, however, also seek monetary relief. Rule 23(b)(2) is silent as to whether monetary remedies may be sought in conjunction with injunctive or declaratory relief. The Advisory Committee Notes on Rule 23 state that class certification under (b)(2) "does not extend to cases in which the appropriate final relief relates exclusively or predominantly to money damages." . . . This commentary implies that the drafters of Rule 23 believed that at least some form or amount of monetary relief would be permissible in a (b)(2) class action. . . .

In addressing what monetary relief is permissible in a (b)(2) class action, this circuit has chosen an intermediate approach, neither allowing certification without regard to the monetary remedies being sought, nor restricting certification to classes seeking exclusively injunctive or declaratory relief. . . . We, like nearly all other circuits, have adopted the position taken by the advisory committee that monetary relief may be obtained in a (b)(2) class action so long as the predominant relief sought is injunctive or declaratory.[3] . . . The district court's decision to impose a predomination requirement for (b)(2) class certification is fully consistent with these cases and, therefore, was not error.

B

We consider next the substantially more difficult question whether the district court's formulation of (b)(2)'s predomination requirement was correct. As the district court noted, there is little discussion by appellate courts as to what it means for a particular form of relief to be "predominant." . . . We must determine, therefore, what the concept of predomination means in the context of Rule 23(b)(2).

(1)

In the absence of clear guidance from the Rule or our cases, we turn to the principles and assumptions underlying the (b)(2) class and class actions in general to ascertain whether they add substance to the concept of predomination under Rule 23(b)(2). . . .

(a)

Under Rule 23, the different categories of class actions, with their different requirements, represent a balance struck in each case between the need and efficiency of a class action and the interests of class members to

---

3. We recognize that the Supreme Court's decision in Ticor Title Ins. Co. v. Brown, 511 U.S. 117 (1994), casts doubt on the proposition that class actions seeking money damages can be certified under Rule 23(b)(2). . . . However, in the absence of a clearer statement by the Supreme Court or en banc reconsideration of the issue, this panel is bound by circuit precedent. . . .

pursue their claims separately or not at all.... The different types of class actions are categorized according to the nature or effect of the relief being sought. The (b)(1) class action encompasses cases in which the defendant is obliged to treat class members alike or where class members are making claims against a fund insufficient to satisfy all of the claims.... The (b)(2) class action, on the other hand, was intended to focus on cases where broad, class-wide injunctive or declaratory relief is necessary.... Finally, the (b)(3) class action was intended to dispose of all other cases in which a class action would be "convenient and desirable," including those involving large-scale, complex litigation for money damages.... Limiting the different categories of class actions to specific kinds of relief clearly reflects a concern for how the interests of class members will vary, depending upon the nature of the class injury alleged and the nature of the relief sought.

First, different presumptions with respect to the cohesiveness and homogeneity of interests among members of (b)(1), (b)(2), and (b)(3) classes are reflected in the different procedural safeguards provided for each potential class.... For example, the drafters of Rule 23 found it unnecessary to provide (b)(1) and (b)(2) class members with the absolute right to notice or to opt-out of the class — procedural safeguards made mandatory under (b)(3) for class members who might wish to pursue their claims for money damages in individual lawsuits and to not be bound by membership in a class action. . . . Providing these rights exclusively to (b)(3) classes demonstrates concern for the effect of monetary claims on class cohesiveness.... Monetary remedies are more often related directly to the disparate merits of individual claims.... As a result, a class seeking substantial monetary remedies will more likely consist of members with divergent interests. In contrast, because of the group nature of the harm alleged and the broad character of the relief sought, the (b)(2) class is, by its very nature, assumed to be a homogenous and cohesive group with few conflicting interests among its members.... The underlying premise of the (b)(2) class — that its members suffer from a common injury properly addressed by class-wide relief — "begins to break down when the class seeks to recover back pay or other forms of monetary relief to be allocated based on individual injuries." Eubanks v. Billington, 110 F.3d 87, 95 (D.C. Cir. 1997). Thus, as claims for individually based money damages begin to predominate, the presumption of cohesiveness decreases while the need for enhanced procedural safeguards to protect the individual rights of class members increases, ... thereby making class certification under (b)(2) less appropriate.

We know, then, that monetary relief "predominates" under Rule 23(b)(2) when its presence in the litigation suggests that the procedural safeguards of notice and opt-out are necessary, that is, when the monetary relief being sought is less of a group remedy and instead depends more on the varying circumstances and merits of each potential class member's case.... Because it automatically provides the right of notice and opt-out to individuals who do not want their monetary claims decided in a class action, Rule 23(b)(3) is the appropriate means of class certification when monetary relief is the predominant form of relief sought and the monetary interests of class members require enhanced procedural safeguards.

(b)

The fact that the predomination requirement serves to protect the rights of class members regarding their monetary interests does not imply, however, that the availability of monetary relief in a (b)(2) class action depends solely or directly on whether class members are entitled to notice or opt-out rights. Such a narrow focus would ignore the other half of the balance struck by the different categories of Rule 23 — the need and efficiency of a class action. As we have earlier observed, the chief purpose behind the class action device is to achieve a significant measure of judicial economy, . . . an interest for which (b)(2)'s predomination requirement must also account. By requiring the predomination of injunctive or declaratory remedies, (b)(2) was intended to serve this purpose by inherently concentrating the litigation on common questions of law and fact. . . .

Actions for class-wide injunctive or declaratory relief are intended for (b)(2) certification precisely because they involve uniform group remedies. Such relief may often be awarded without requiring a specific or time-consuming inquiry into the varying circumstances and merits of each class member's individual case. When it does, the relatively complex calculations typically required in class actions for money damages are unnecessary. For these reasons, proposed (b)(2) classes need not withstand a court's independent probe into the superiority of the class action over other available methods of adjudication or the degree to which common issues predominate over those affecting only individual class members, as (b)(3) classes must. . . .

(c)

In sum, the predomination requirement of Rule 23(b)(2) serves essentially the same functions as the procedural safeguards and efficiency and manageability standards mandated in (b)(3) class actions. In balancing the competing interests underlying the class action device, (b)(2)'s predomination requirement serves two basic purposes: first, it protects the legitimate interests of potential class members who might wish to pursue their monetary claims individually; and, second, it preserves the legal system's interest in judicial economy.

(2)

Consistent with this analysis, we reach the following holding: monetary relief predominates in (b)(2) class actions unless it is incidental to requested injunctive or declaratory relief. . . . By incidental, we mean damages that flow directly from liability to the class as a whole on the claims forming the basis of the injunctive or declaratory relief. See Fed. R. Civ. P. 23(b)(2) (referring only to relief appropriate "with respect to the class as a whole"). Ideally, incidental damages should be only those to which class members automatically would be entitled once liability to the class (or subclass) as a whole is established. See . . . Arnold v. United Artists Theatre Circuit, Inc., 158 F.R.D. 439 (N.D. Cal. 1994) (defendant's liability entitled class to a statutorily mandated damage award). That is, the recovery of incidental damages should typically be concomitant with, not merely consequential to, the injunctive or declaratory relief. Moreover, such damages should at least be capable of computation by means of objective standards and not dependent in any significant way on the intangible, subjective differences of each class member's circumstances. Incidental damages should not require additional hearings to resolve the disparate merits of each individual's case; they should neither introduce new and substantial legal or factual issues, nor entail complex individualized determinations. Thus, incidental damages will, by definition, be more in the nature of a group remedy, consistent with the forms of relief intended for (b)(2) class actions. . . .

C

Having determined that the district court adopted the correct legal standard in assessing the plaintiffs' monetary claims, we must now resolve whether it abused its discretion in applying that standard to deny certification of a class action under Rule 23(b)(2). The plaintiffs' claims for monetary relief include back pay, front pay, compensatory damages, punitive damages, prejudgment interest, attorneys' fees, and retroactive benefits. . . .

We have little trouble affirming the district court's finding that the plaintiffs' claims for compensatory and punitive damages are not sufficiently incidental to the injunctive and declaratory relief being sought to permit them in a (b)(2) class action. We start with the premise that, in this circuit, compensatory damages for emotional distress and other forms of intangible injury will not be presumed from mere violation of constitutional or statutory rights. . . . Specific individualized proof is necessary, and testimony from the plaintiff alone is not ordinarily sufficient. . . . The very nature of these damages, compensating plaintiffs for emotional and other intangible injuries, necessarily implicates the subjective differences of each plaintiff's circumstances; they are an individual, not class-wide, remedy. The amount of compensatory damages to which any individual class member might be entitled cannot be calculated by objective standards. Furthermore, by requiring individualized proof of discrimination and actual injury to each class member, compensatory damages introduce new and substantial legal and factual issues. Clearly, . . . compensatory damages under Title VII and 42 U.S.C. § 1981 are not incidental to class-wide injunctive or declaratory relief for discrimination.

The plaintiffs' claims for punitive damages are similarly non-incidental. . . . Assuming punitive damages may be awarded on a class-wide basis, without individualized proof of injury, where the entire class or subclass is subjected to the same discriminatory act or series of acts, no such discrimination is alleged in this case. The plaintiffs challenge broad policies and practices, but they do not contend that each plaintiff was affected by these policies and practices in the same way. Indeed, the plaintiffs seek to certify a class of a thousand potential plaintiffs spread across two separate facilities, represented by six different unions, working in seven different departments, challenging various policies and practices over a period of nearly twenty years. Some plaintiffs may have been subjected to more virile discrimination than others: with greater public humiliation, for a longer periods of time, or based on more unjustifiable practices, for example. Particular discriminatory practices may have been gradually ameliorated year by year over the twenty-year period. Some discriminatory policies may have been implemented more, or less, harshly depending on the department or facility involved. . . .

Given the degree to which recovery of compensatory and punitive damages requires individualized proof and determinations, they clearly do not qualify as incidental damages in this case. Such damages, awarded on the basis of intangible injuries and interests, are uniquely dependent on the subjective and intangible differences of each class member's individual circumstances. We cannot, therefore, detect an abuse of discretion in the district court's finding that the plaintiffs' claims for compensatory and punitive damages were inappropriate for (b)(2) certification.

[The court went on to hold that the claims for damages could not be certified as a class action under Rule 23(b)(3), and then held, in a portion of the opinion that reproduced at p. 617, *infra*, that the right-to-jury-trial implications of individual damages trials required that the case not be certified under (b)(2) even for the injunctive claims.]

Affirmed.

■ DENNIS, Circuit Judge, dissenting. . . . The majority's decision rests on a conception of Rule 23(b)(2) that is irreconcilable with the basic purposes of Rule 23, the text of Rule 23(b)(2), the Advisory Committee Notes on Rule 23(b)(2), the exercise of informed and sound discretion by the district court in deciding whether to certify a class, and Rule 23(b)(2)'s proven effectiveness and unique appropriateness in civil rights cases, especially Title VII actions. Rule 23 plainly limits this court's judicial inventiveness; we have no authority to require a district court to automatically disallow (b)(2) certification simply because a member of the class seeks compensatory or punitive damages in addition to final injunctive relief.

COOK v. ROCKWELL INTERNATIONAL CORP.

151 F.R.D. 378 (D. Colo. 1993)

■ KANE, Senior District Judge. [Property owners near the Rocky Flats weapons production facility brought a class action against the various owners of that facility (the Department of Energy, Dow Chemical Co., and Rockwell International Corp.). Their complaint asserted claims under Colorado common law; the Price Anderson Act (which incorporates common law); and the Comprehensive Environmental Response, Compensation, and Liability Act (CERCLA). They sought compensatory damage for property and other economic harm, and for mental and emotional distress. They also sought punitive damages and response costs under CERCLA. In addition, they asked the court to establish a medical monitoring program. They then sought certification of two classes — one a medical monitoring class under

Rule 23(b)(2) and the other a property damage class under Rule 23(b)(3). The court certified both classes. The following portion of the opinion concerns the Rule 23(b)(2) medical monitoring class.]

Courts have differed in their responses to requests for certification of medical monitoring claims in the form of injunctive relief. As Dow has noted, many decisions classify medical monitoring costs as an item of damage, the traditional remedy at law.... Such classification appears more appropriate where plaintiffs merely seek the costs of medical monitoring from plaintiffs. Here, however, the plaintiffs seek relief similar to that sought in Day v. NLO, Inc.[, 144 F.R.D. 330 (S.D. Ohio 1992)]. Plaintiffs in *Day* requested the court to "establish an elaborate medical monitoring program of its own, managed by court-appointed court supervised trustees, pursuant to which a plaintiff is monitored by particular physicians and the medical data utilized for group studies." 144 F.R.D. at 335. The district court in *Day* . . . held that, in such circumstances, the relief constitutes injunctive relief as required by Rule 23(b)(2)....

Dow argues that Rule 23(b)(2) requires that the ongoing conduct of the defendant be the subject of the relief that is being sought and that, since neither Dow nor Rockwell now conduct operations at Rocky Flats and plaintiffs do not seek to enjoin any conduct by Dow or Rockwell, the action should not be classified under Rule 23(b)(2). To the contrary, injunctive relief embraces all forms of judicial orders, whether they be mandatory or prohibitory....

Dow further argues that any injunctive relief will not apply to the class as a whole because of the individualized nature of each individual's claim. However, common evidence would be required to establish the level and nature of injury or disease by substances released from Rocky Flats and the causal connection, if any, between the release of the substances and any injuries or disease allegedly sustained. Therefore, despite the fact that there would be some issues of individual proof, injunctive relief in the form of medical monitoring would seem appropriate to the class as a whole.

Class members in an action where a class has been certified under (b)(2) do not have the option of opting out of the class and a judgment will be binding and will have a res judicata effect as to the whole class. However, where a class has been certified under (b)(3), class members may opt out of the class and, a judgment will not have a res judicata effect on those who elect to do so. When class certification is validly sought in the alternative under Rule 23(b)(2) and (b)(3), a mandatory (b)(2) class is preferred. . . . Therefore, I find that plaintiffs have satisfied the requirements of Rule 23(b)(2) and that the medical monitoring class be certified under that rule.

Notes and Questions

1. The case that popularized the "predominance" idea discussed in *Allison* was Wetzel v. Liberty Mutual Insurance Co., 508 F.2d 239 (3d Cir.), cert. denied, 421 U.S. 1011 (1975). What basis is there in the text of Rule 23(b)(2) for permitting damages actions to be asserted at all?

2. Is *Allison* right for the wrong reasons? As is typical in employment discrimination litigation, the plaintiffs in *Allison* failed to include in the case non-African-American employees. As should be apparent after Martin v. Wilks, 490 U.S. 755 (1989) (p. 240, *supra*), these non-African-American employees also had legal relationships with the employer and thus had a cognizable stake in the outcome of the litigation. Thus, the class in *Allison* was artificially homogenous. We raised the same concern in Notes 4 and 6 in the last subsection (pp. 596-98, *supra*), in which we noted that the plaintiffs' pleading choice in Arch v. American Tobacco Co., 175 F.R.D. 469 (E.D. Pa. 1997), created the possibility that the judgment in a homogenous Pennsylvania-only lawsuit might be undone by a later lawsuit invoking the law of other jurisdictions, and the plaintiffs' pleading choices in In re Telectronics Pacing Systems, Inc., Accufix Atrial "J" Leads Products Liability Litigation, 172 F.R.D. 271 (S.D. Ohio 1997), intentionally failed to avoid dysfunction. (Recall Professor Fuller's observation that such efforts to turn many-sided disputes into two-sided affairs are inevitable when a polycentric problem is shoehorned into adjudication. See p. 108, *supra*.)

How should the courts respond to this problem? Consider the following suggestions:

(a) If other interest groups in fact exist, so that an injunctive award to one group would cause dysfunction, then the attempt to single out one of those groups with a common interest in a single injunctive remedy should be rejected, and certification of such a class under Rule 23(b)(2) should be denied. *All interested groups should be joined under Rule 23(b)(1)(A), which is designed to prevent lawyer dysfunction, or not at all.*

(b) If no other groups with a contrary, legally cognizable interest in the remedy exist, so that all putative class members really do have a common interest in the injunctive remedy, then the issue becomes a matter of balancing the interests of individuals in maintaining control of their own claim against the efficiency of a single resolution. But how valuable is the right of individual control when exactly the same relief will be awarded in a person's favor regardless of whether they litigate separately, sit out, or become part of the class? Indeed, individual control in this situation is valuable only if the first plaintiff loses, thereby preserving the rights of other putative class members to bring their own suits. As long as the requirements of Rule 23(a) have been met, however, this ability to subject the defendants to multiple lawsuits would seem to be an inadequate reason to refuse to certify a (b)(2) class and preclude future litigation. A Rule 23(b)(2) class should be certified.

(c) Once it is acknowledged that a Rule 23(b)(2) suit can be certified in some cases, the next issue is how to handle related claims on which the class members might have differing interests. Unlike category (b), there is now a reason — the existence of separate and distinct claims — to suggest that individual control of litigation is important. The central issue, which *Allison* addresses, is how much divergence in related claims can be tolerated under Rule 23(b)(2), when the rationale for a (b)(2) suit is common and undivided interests. *Allison*'s analysis on this point is provocative, and may prove to be influential. But *Allison*'s analysis, while relevant in cases like *Cook*, is irrelevant in *Allison* itself, in which class certification should have been denied under category (a) because of the plaintiffs' dysfunction-causing pleading choices.

Are you persuaded by the analysis in this Note? Does it adequately preserve some role for Rule 23(b)(2) while avoiding an interpretation of the rule that would create lawyer dysfunction?

3. Might the analysis in the last Note also explain the difference between *Cook*, which used a (b)(2) class, and *Telectronics*, which used a (b)(1)(A) and (b)(1)(B) class? The reason that no (b)(2) class could be used in *Telectronics* was that the members of the putative nationwide class did not have a common and undivided interest in the same form of relief. (In other words, the plaintiffs in *Telectronics* fell into category (a), rather than category (b).) In *Cook*, however, only one state was involved; unlike *Arch* (another category (a) case), there were no other states with an interest in the controversy that might force the defendant to act in a different way. Since the plaintiffs also did not seek individualized damages incidentally to the (b)(2) class (they instead obtained a separate (b)(3) certification for those damages), the concerns of category (c) also never came into play. Thus, once you accept the notion that medical monitoring is a form of injunctive relief, *Cook* is a straight-forward case for the application of Rule 23(b)(2) — albeit in a new context.

Consider as well the following two cases. In Haley v. Medtronic, Inc., 169 F.R.D. 643 (C.D. Cal. 1996), a case involving the same pacemakers as *Telectronics*, the plaintiffs sought to certify a nationwide damages class under Rule 23(b)(3) and a medical monitoring class under Rule 23(b)(2). After first declining to certify the damage class, the court then declined to certify the medical monitoring class. Like *Allison*, the court argued that individual damage actions predominated over the class interest in medical monitoring, thus requiring denial of (b)(2) class certification. Isn't *Haley*, like *Allison*, really a category (a) case, not a category (c) case, as *Haley* suggested? Likewise, in Barnes v. American Tobacco Co., 176 F.R.D. 479 (E.D. Pa. 1997), the plaintiffs in the *Arch* litigation significantly amended their complaint to remove all claims for individual damages, and sought only medical monitoring. Again they moved to certify a Rule 23(b)(2) class only of Pennsylvania citizens. Again, the district court rebuffed their effort, on the theory that individual issues concerning the need for medical monitoring meant that relief to the class as a whole was inappropriate. Should the court simply have refused certification because the complaint did not remove the central defect in *Arch*: that the case still fit into category (a)?

Although cases such as *Cook*, *Haley*, and *Barnes* are consistent with the analysis in the last Note, you should know that they do not adopt the analysis, either. The interpretation is ours.

4. In the category (c) cases, in which the issue is whether the individual relief predominates over the common relief, *Allison* takes an extremely narrow, albeit interesting, view of predominance. Although *Allison* seeks to fit it within its own analysis, a different, and more mainstream, analysis of the issue is found in Arnold v. United Artists Theatre Circuit, Inc., 158 F.R.D. 439 (N.D. Cal. 1994). In *Arnold*, persons who used wheelchairs or were semi-ambulatory sued the defendant movie theater chain for their failure to provide adequate accommodations. They sought injunctive relief under the Americans with Disabilities Act and California law, and damages under California law. The court held that the entire case could be certified under (b)(2):

> Defendant contended at oral argument that claims for monetary relief may be included as part of subpart (b)(2) class actions only where such claims are classified as equitable relief, as in claims for back pay in employment discrimination actions under Title VII of the 1964 Civil Rights Act. This contention is, however, false, as demonstrated by the numerous cases in which claims seeking the legal — as opposed to equitable — remedy

of money damages have been approved for certification as part of (b)(2) class actions. . . .

Rather, whether plaintiffs' damage claims may be certified as part of a (b)(2) class action depends on whether inclusion of those claims with plaintiffs' claims for injunctive relief would render the suit one "relat[ing] . . . *predominantly* to money damages" (emphasis added). Most of the reported cases applying this "predominance" standard are rather conclusory and do not enunciate clear rules for applying the test. . . . Addressing this issue, this Court has written:

> . . . The hallmark of the (b)(2) action is homogeneity. It is this characteristic that allows the court to dispense with notice to the class and bind all members to any judgment on the merits without an opportunity to opt out. In class actions alleging employment discrimination, homogeneity is usually ensured because, the class "by sharing a common characteristic subjected to discrimination becomes cohesive." In short, the defendant's allegedly discriminatory conduct affects the class as a whole, and makes final injunctive relief appropriate. . . .

Other courts have concurred in this analysis, identifying the cohesiveness of the class and the homogeneity of the members' interests as the salient factors on which the availability of the (b)(2) class action form hinges . . . .

Analyzing the proposed class in terms of this criterion, it is clear that the claims of the class members are remarkably homogenous. . . . In this case the class members, rather than challenging individual actions taken by the defendant against each of them separately, all challenge the same actions: defendant's failure to change certain architectural features found at its various theaters. The challenged design features affect all class members in almost precisely the same way because of common distinguishing characteristics shared by all the class members: their status as wheelchair-using or semi-ambulatory disabled persons. This fact lends the proposed class an extraordinary degree of homogeneity, far greater than that of even the average Title VII disparate treatment suit in which plaintiffs allege that many separate actions against individuals manifest a common pattern and practice of discrimination. In view of this high degree of homogeneity, it is clear that this suit is a paradigm of the type of action for which the (b)(2) form was created.

Defendant cites a variety of cases for the proposition that where large amounts of damages or statutory penalties are sought, an action may not be certified as a (b)(2) class action. . . . However, nearly all such cases cited by defendant involve claims under the federal antitrust laws or other business regulatory statutes. Those cases are distinguishable on the grounds that, first, they were not civil rights suits — the type of action for which the (b)(2) form was specifically designed — and, second, they all included damage claims in which the quantum of damages suffered involved a complicated, individual-specific calculus. While the presence of damage claims of that sort undermines class homogeneity, sometimes to the point of precluding (b)(2) certification, . . . this case is not complicated in that way by the presence of such claims. [158 F.R.D. at 451-52.]

See also Eubanks v. Billington, 110 F.3d 87 (D.C. Cir. 1997) (authorizing use of (b)(2) class action in Title VII case involving claims for individual damages).

5. As *Cook* shows, the failure to obtain class certification under (b)(2) is not necessarily the end of the line; a hybrid (b)(2)-(b)(3) class action might still be possible. Although *Allison* refused to certify a (b)(3) class for the claims of individual damages, other Title VII suits have used (b)(3) to deal with monetary claims. See Diaz v. Hillsborough County Hosp. Authority, 165 F.R.D. 689 (M.D. Fla. 1996) ((b)(2) class action for injunctive relief certified on behalf of class of pregnant women allegedly subjected to experimentation by medical researchers without informed consent and (b)(3) class certified for related damage claims). Should resort to (b)(3) be automatic in these cases? See George Rutherglen, *Notice, Scope, and Preclusion in Title VII Class Actions*, 69 Va. L. Rev. 11, 27-28 (1983) (arguing that civil rights actions should be bifurcated into (b)(2) and (b)(3) class actions). If not, and we continue to allow some mandatory class actions seeking for monetary relief under (b)(2), should we amend (b)(3) to provide that the opt-out right exists only in those cases where the trial court concludes it is necessary or appropriate? *See* Air Line Stewards and Stewardesses Association, Local 550 v. American Airlines, Inc., 490 F.2d 636 (7th Cir. 1973) (employees in a Title VII sex discrimination case were afforded the right to opt out if they disagreed with the type of relief granted), cert. denied, 416 U.S. 993 (1974).

6. More generally, should the due process clause be construed to require notice before the monetary claim of an absent class member is adjudicated in a way which will preclude her later asserting it in a suit of her own? See Laskey v. UAW, 638 F.2d 954, 956-57 (6th Cir. 1981) ("[F]ailure to notify [(b)(2) class members of the right to opt out of the class is not a violation of due process."); DeBoer v. Mellon Mortgage Co., 64 F.3d 1171 (8th Cir. 1995) (approving certification of (b)(2) class action on behalf of borrowers seeking to require mortgagors to alter their practices for managing escrow accounts and seeking damages; some class members objected that class should be certified under (b)(3) so they could opt out); cf. Holmes v. Continental Can Co., 706 F.2d 1144, 1160 (11th Cir. 1983) (holding that district court abused its discretion in refusing to provide opt-out procedure in (b)(2) class action). One reason to provide notice is to permit class members to intervene in the litigation to protect their own interests. See F.R.Civ.P. 23(d)(2). If a notice were given and intervention allowed, should *Allison*'s strict view of predominance be rejected?

In Johnson v. General Motors Corp., 598 F.2d 432 (5th Cir. 1979), an earlier (b)(2) class action alleging race discrimination had resulted in an injunction and monetary relief to the class representatives, but not to the absent class members. When one of the absent class members, Johnson, later brought his own action for damages the court said: "Before an absent class member may be forever barred from pursuing an individual damage claim . . . due process requires that he receive some form of notice that the class action is pending and that his damage claims may be adjudicated as part of it." Id. at 438. A similar conclusion was reached by the Ninth Circuit in Brown v. Ticor Title Ins. Co., 982 F.2d 386 (9th Cir. 1992), in which the court held that absent class members were free to file a suit for damages for price-fixing even though in an earlier lawsuit the court had certified a mandatory settlement class action under both (b)(1) and (b)(2) and approved a settlement for injunctive relief, but not damages. Because they had not been given notice and an opportunity to opt out of the settlement, the absent class members were not precluded by the earlier judgment from suing again. The Supreme Court initially granted certiorari in *Brown*, but then dismissed the writ as improvidently granted. Ticor Title Insurance Co. v. Brown, 511 U.S. 117 (1994). Thus, as *Allison* notes, the Supreme Court has left open the question whether monetary claims can ever be asserted in mandatory class actions. Some state courts have held, however, that such class actions are proper. See, *e.g.*, Nottingham Partners v. Dana, 564 A.2d 1089 (Del. Supr. 1989) (certification of mandatory class action and resulting settlement precluded class members from later asserting either equitable or monetary claims).

7. Civil rights actions seeking only injunctive relief are routinely filed by individual plaintiffs on behalf of proposed classes of applicants, employees, tenants, and so on. What advantage is there in such cases in suing as a class? If the individual plaintiff obtains an injunction forbidding, for example, sex discrimination in hiring by the defendant in the future, won't others be able to rely upon this injunction? On occasion, courts have held that it is not necessary to certify a (b)(2) class action because the injunction sought by the individual plaintiff will inure to the benefit of the entire putative class anyway. See, *e.g.*, Galvan v. Levine, 490 F.2d 1255 (2d Cir. 1973). The majority of courts, however, have held that, unless a class action is certified, an injunction against future discrimination or other illegal conduct can only protect the individual named plaintiffs. See McKinnon v. Patterson, 568 F.2d 930 (2d Cir. 1977); Zepeda v. INS, 753 F.2d 719 (9th Cir. 1985). Moreover, certification of a (b)(2) class can also avoid dismissal of the case when the named plaintiff's claim becomes moot or the named plaintiff is found to be an unsatisfactory class representative for some other reason. See East Motor Freight System v. Rodriguez, 431 U.S. 395 (1977); Pasadena City Board of Education v. Spangler, 427 U.S. 424 (1976).

8. Assuming *Allison* is correct, it would seem plaintiffs and their counsel may be faced with a difficult tactical decision. Do they forgo the new remedies and jury trial rights available under the statute and seek only an injunction and equitable remedies like backpay in order to maximize their chances for certification of a class under Rule 23(b)(2)? Or do they seek these new remedies and demand a jury trial which may be fatal to their request for class action certification? *See* Phyllis T. Baumann, et al., *Substance in the Shadow of Procedure: The Integration of Substantive and Procedural Law in Title VII Cases*, 33 B.C. L. Rev. 211, 257 (1992) (asserting that certain Supreme Court decisions have crippled class actions as a workable device for seeking collective relief in Title VII cases).

Similarly, in Fried v. Sungard Recovery Services, Inc., 925 F. Supp. 372 (E.D. Pa. 1996), citizens sued a contractor for violations of various federal laws regulating the removal of asbestos seeking, in part, damages for medical monitoring. The contractor moved to strike the plaintiffs' demand for a jury, but the trial court ruled that the medical monitoring claim was a jury-triable claim for compensatory damages. The court indicated its holding would have been different if plaintiffs had sought creation of a medical monitoring fund, but also added that it reserved the right to structure any remedy as it thought best. Assuming that the only request for relief is medical monitoring, does the plaintiff class necessarily forgo its right to a jury by seeking certification under (b)(2)? Or might a monitoring claim be "equitable" for purposes of Rule 23(b)(2) but "legal" for purposes of the Seventh Amendment's right to jury trial? See pp. 1209-19, *infra* (discussing meaning of Seventh Amendment).

9. *Cook* shows how far the (b)(2) class action has come from its civil rights roots. For another example of the successful use of a (b)(2) class action to pursue a variety of legal and equitable claims in a toxic torts case, see Yslava v. Hughes Aircraft Co., 845 F. Supp. 705 (D. Ariz. 1993), where the court certified a mandatory (b)(2) class action for costs incurred by the plaintiff class in

determining to what extent they had been exposed to contaminated water from a hazardous waste site and for future medical monitoring costs as "costs of response" under § 107(a) of the Comprehensive Environmental Response, Compensation, and Liability Act, 42 U.S.C. § 9601 et seq. As in *Cook*, the court reasoned that the plaintiffs were not seeking money damages, but rather requesting a court-supervised medical monitoring remedy and that certification under (b)(2) was to be preferred over (b)(3). Accord Day v. NLO, 851 F. Supp. 869 (S.D. Ohio 1994) ((b)(2) class action by employees and "frequenters" of nuclear weapons plant approved over objections that claims were for monetary damages).

c) Constitutional and Jurisdictional Limits on Mandatory Class Actions

Thus far, we have looked at the appropriateness of mandatory class actions from the viewpoint of the language of Rule 23(b) and the policy concerns that such class actions might raise. Some of these policy concerns, however, are of arguable constitutional and jurisdictional stature. In this subsection, we consider three such concerns — territorial jurisdiction, the Anti-Injunction Act, and the right to jury trial. To the extent that these doctrines make it impossible for courts to entertain certain mandatory class actions, the aggregative finality of a mandatory class action is lost.

PHILLIPS PETROLEUM CO. v. SHUTTS

472 U.S. 797 (1985)

See p. 294, *supra*.

IN RE ASBESTOS LITIGATION

90 F.3d 963 (5th Cir. 1996), vacated and remanded, 521 U.S. —, 117 S.Ct. 2503 (1997), affirmed on remand, 134 F.3d 668 (5th Cir. 1998), cert. granted, 118 S.Ct. 2339 (1998)

See p. 301, *supra*.

Notes and Questions

1. The issue concerning the scope of territorial jurisdiction over absent class members has been explored in the preceding two cases, in the Notes following the cases, and in Note 6, p. 611, *supra*. Obviously, the issue about whether absent class members must be extended a right to opt out, and if so under what circumstances (for instance, must all absent members be extended the right to opt out, or merely those with whom the forum has no minimum contacts), is vitally important to the future of mandatory class actions. If an opt-out right is ultimately found to be required as a matter of constitutional law —

which is one of the grounds on which the Supreme Court might decide *In re Asbestos Litigation* — then there might no longer be such a thing as a mandatory class action. See Stephen T.O. Cottreau, Note, *The Due Process Right to Opt Out of Class Actions*, 73 N.Y.U. L. Rev. 480 (1998) (applying *Mathews v. Eldridge* due process analysis to determine when opt-out rights are required).

2. Would it be possible to argue that an opt-out right is required in cases not involving lawyer dysfunction, but that no opt-out right is necessary in cases in which opt-outs might create lawyer dysfunction? We have already made the argument that such a result is appropriate in earlier notes. See Notes 3-7, pp. 306-09, *supra*. Let us make only one additional point here. Using the analysis that we developed in Note 2, p. 608, *supra*, it would appear that notice and an opportunity to opt out could legitimately be extended to Rule 23(b)(2) class actions that fell into categories (b) and (c) — *i.e.*, cases in which all persons with a legally cognizable interest in an injunctive remedy have a common interest in the shape of that remedy. Permitting an opt-out right in these cases is inefficient, and does not vindicate any strong interest in individual control of litigation, but worse things have happened. The real concern would be if *Shutts* were applied in cases of lawyer dysfunction, so that some opt-outs were able to disrupt a fair remedy for the remainder of the class — in other words, in the (b)(1)(A) and (b)(1)(B) situations. This logic does not, however, automatically save *In re Asbestos Litigation*, for it is not clear that the case involved insufficient assets or that it was properly certified under Rule 23(b)(1)(B). See pp. 687-88, *infra*. But the answer to the question of whether the case was properly certified under (b)(1)(B) should, under this analysis, also answer the question of whether an opt-out right was constitutionally required.

3. The converse of the *Shutts* issue — whether courts have the discretion to permit class members to opt out of a mandatory class action in some situations — has received a fair degree of attention in the last ten years. Nothing in the text of Rule 23(b)(1), (b)(2), or (c) suggests a discretionary power to permit opt-outs. Nonetheless, appellate courts have begun to recognize the existence of an opt-out right in mandatory class actions. See Holmes v. Continental Can Co., 706 F.2d 1144, 1160 (11th Cir. 1983); County of Suffolk v. Long Island Lighting Co., 907 F.2d 1295 (2d Cir. 1990); Eubanks v. Billington, 110 F.3d 87 (D.C. Cir. 1997); but see Thomas v. Albright, 139 F.3d 227 (D.C. Cir. 1998) (district court abused discretion in permitting plaintiffs to opt out). In *Eubanks*, the court noted that opt-outs should not be permitted "when doing so would undermine the policies behind (b)(1) or (b)(2) certification." 110 F.3d at 94-95. It also noted that *County of Suffolk* was a case in which the opt-out right "did not undermine the fundamental basis for certification of a (b)(1)(B) class action: that recovery by some class members might effectively preclude other class members from recovery." Id. at 94. Thus, opt-out rights that create lawyer dysfunction would not generally seem to be permitted.

IN RE FEDERAL SKYWALK CASES

680 F.2d 1175 (8th Cir. 1982)

■ McMILLIAN, Circuit Judge. [The collapse of two skywalks at the Hyatt Regency Hotel in Kansas City, Missouri in July, 1981 gave rise to numerous lawsuits in state and federal court. Eventually, the federal district judge, invoking both (b)(1)(A) and (b)(1)(B), certified a class on the issues of liability for compensatory and punitive damages and on the amount of punitive damages.

[The Eighth Circuit first determined that the certification order was appealable under 28 U.S.C. § 1292(a)(1), which permits an immediate appeal of preliminary injunctions. In order to invoke § 1292, however, the court of appeals needed to demonstrate that the certification order was in effect an injunction. That inquiry then led to concerns for the applicability of the Anti-Injunction Act to (b)(1) certifications.]

In the present case, contrary to the class's assertion, the district court expressly prohibited class members from settling their punitive damage claims.... In addition, the substantial effect of the order also enjoined the state plaintiffs from pursuing their pending state court actions on the issues of liability for compensatory and punitive damages and the amount of punitive damages....

It is true that parties to a mandatory class are not free to initiate actions in other courts to litigate class certified issues. However, in the present case the objectors had commenced their state court actions before the motion for class certification had been filed in district court. The state court cases had been filed, consolidated, and discovery had begun. It is this injunction against pending state court actions that gives us jurisdiction under 28 U.S.C. § 1292(a)....

Our conclusion that the order enjoins pending state proceedings necessitates an inquiry as to the propriety of that order under the Anti-Injunction Act, 28 U.S.C. § 2283. The Act provides that "[a] court of the United States may not grant an injunction to stay proceedings in a state court except as expressly authorized by Act of Congress, or where necessary in aid of its jurisdiction, or to protect or effectuate its judgment."

In Atlantic Coast Line R.R. v. Locomotive Engineers, 398 U.S. 281, 286-87 (1970), the Supreme Court recognized that the Act imposes a flat and positive prohibition:

> On its face the present Act is an absolute prohibition against enjoining state court proceedings, unless the injunction falls within one of three specifically defined exceptions. The respondents here have intimated that the Act only establishes a "principle of comity," not a binding rule on the power of the federal courts. The argument implies that in certain circumstances a federal court may enjoin state court proceedings even if that action cannot be justified by any of the three exceptions. We cannot accept any such contention....

Therefore, if the injunction is to be upheld, it must be on the basis that the district court's authority derives from one of the three exceptions. On appeal the class relies on the "necessary in aid of its jurisdiction" exception. In support it first draws an analogy between the order and a Rule 22 interpleader under which a federal court can enjoin claimants from prosecuting claims in state court. The class reasons that here, as in the interpleader situation, there is a limited fund and that the class action is necessary to protect all claimants. We disagree.

The analogy is based on the premise that the possibility of defendants being required to pay only one punitive damage award is comparable to the limited fund concept underlying federal interpleader. That premise is erroneous. "Federal interpleader jurisdiction depends on identifiable property or a limited fund or pecuniary obligation, and it is not proper to predicate jurisdiction on the mere potential to recover damages for pecuniary injury." Murphy v. Travelers Insurance Co., 534 F.2d 1155, 1159 (5th Cir. 1976) . . . .

In the present case the class has an uncertain claim for punitive damages against defendants who have not conceded liability. The claim does not qualify as a limited fund which is a jurisdictional prerequisite for federal interpleader. Without the limited fund there is no analogy to an interpleader and no reason to treat the class action as an interpleader for purposes of the Anti-Injunction Act. . . .

Next the class argues that allowing individual actions in state court will nullify the purpose of the class. The Supreme Court has narrowly interpreted the "necessary in aid of jurisdiction" exception, and a pending state suit must truly interfere with the federal court's jurisdiction. As the objectors correctly point out, a plurality of the Supreme Court reaffirmed in [in Vendo Co. v. Lektro-Vend Corp., 433 U.S. 623 (1977)] its earlier holdings that a simultaneous *in personam* state action does not interfere with the jurisdiction of a federal court in a suit involving the same subject matter. . . .

In the present case the federal and state actions are *in personam* claims for compensatory and punitive damages. Therefore, based on the foregoing principles, we are compelled to hold that despite Judge Wright's legitimate concern for the efficient management of mass tort litigation, the class certification order must be vacated. . . .

■ HEANEY, Circuit Judge, dissenting. . . . Admittedly, the relationship between mandatory class actions and the Anti-Injunction Act appears to present an open question. The approach adopted by the majority, however, broadly forecloses mandatory class actions whenever a class member has commenced state court proceedings. I would agree that class actions should not become a vehicle for circumventing the ordinary relations between state and federal courts. The requirements for a mandatory class action, however, are quite rigorous and, by their nature, will prevent any such trend from developing. Moreover, there are unusually strong reasons for certifying the mandatory class here, a procedure which the district court found was essential to fair adjudication of all claims. Such circumstances will not often arise; yet in face of them, the majority has adopted a rule which broadly defeats the purpose of mandatory class action jurisdiction. I do not agree that such a rule is required by the Anti-Injunction Act, nor by any sensible view of the relations between state and federal courts.

Notes and Questions

1. As we learned in Chapter Three, the Anti-Injunction Act does not pertain to cases that are not pending at the time that the federal injunction is

issued. See p. 397, *supra*. The real issue, therefore, is whether the Act bars the use of mandatory class actions when some of the class members have filed actions in state court. On this point, several courts have agreed with the majority in the *Federal Skywalk Cases* that the Anti-Injunction Act precludes the certification of a federal limited fund class action. See, *e.g.*, Waldron v. Raymark Industries, 124 F.R.D. 235 (N.D. Ga. 1989); In re Glenn W. Turner Enterprises Litigation, 521 F.2d 775 (3d Cir. 1975); cf. In re School Asbestos Litigation, 789 F.2d 996 (3rd Cir. 1986) (Anti-Injunction Act concern gave appellate jurisdiction over Rule 23(b)(1)(B) certification order, though court did not state whether (b)(1)(B) order in fact acted as an injunction). In In re Temple, 851 F.2d 1269 (11th Cir. 1988) and In re Dennis Greenman Securities Litigation, 829 F.2d 1539 (11th Cir. 1987), the Eleventh Circuit intimated, without deciding, that the Anti-Injunction Act forbids a mandatory class action that would have the effect of enjoining pending state actions.

2. On the other hand, other courts have allowed federal judges to enjoin pending state litigation while a class action settlement in federal court was under consideration. See In re Corrugated Container Antitrust Litigation, 659 F.2d 1332 (5th Cir. 1981), cert. denied, 456 U.S. 936 (1982) (p. 393, *supra*); In re Baldwin-United Corp., 770 F.2d 328 (2d. Cir. 1985) (p. 401, *supra*); In re Joint Eastern & Southern District Asbestos Litigation, 134 F.R.D. 32 (E. & S.D.N.Y. 1990). Injunctions against the filing of state proceedings have also been granted to facilitate the use of federal settlement class actions. *See* Carlough v. Amchem Products, Inc., 10 F.3d 189, 203 (3d Cir. 1993).

3. Once you grant the premise that certification of a mandatory class action precludes class members from maintaining a previously filed state case, the outcome in *Skywalk* and similar cases seems required under the Anti-Injunction Act. But isn't the premise flawed? Plaintiffs have always been able to file contemporaneous lawsuits in both state and federal court, and in complex and complicated litigation they often do. The fact that the plaintiff is an involuntary plaintiff in the federal suit shouldn't change the general practice permitting dual filings, should it? Moreover, how can a (b)(1)(B) limited fund to be equitably distributed by the federal court if, using the *Skywalk* rationale, the fund can be depleted by earlier state judgments? *See* Bryan J. Schillinger, *Preventing Duplicative Mass Tort Litigation Through the Limited Resources Doctrine*, 14 Rev. Litig. 465 (1995). On the other hand, how can Rule 23, which was promulgated by the Supreme Court, be considered an exception to the statutory command of the Anti-Injunction Act? See pp. 400-01, *supra* (considering whether the Anti-Injunction Act contains a "joinder complexity" exception).

4. One exception to the Anti-Injunction Act is the stay in bankruptcy. See pp. 397, *supra*; 706-07, *infra*. Does the ruling in *Skywalk*, if correct, mean that the only way to obtain a truly mandatory limited fund class action is to throw the defendant into bankruptcy? Does that result make sense?

ALLISON v. CITGO PETROLEUM CORP.

__ F.3d __, 1998 WL 244989 (5th Cir. 1998)

■ JOLLY, Circuit Judge. [The basic facts of this lawsuit are set out at p. 599, *supra*. Briefly, the plaintiffs sought certification of a Rule 23(b)(2) class of approximately 1000 African-American employees who were allegedly victims of both the company's pattern and practice of racial discrimination and the disparate impact that the company's policies had on African-American employees. The plaintiffs sought both injunctive relief and individual monetary recovery. The district court denied certification. The court of appeals first held that the claims for monetary damages could not be certified under Rule 23(b)(2). It then held that the claims for compensatory or punitive damages could not be certified under Rule 23(b)(3). The plaintiffs still argued, however, that the district court should have certified its claims for injunctive relief under (b)(2).]

We will therefore consider whether the district court abused its discretion in refusing to certify the plaintiffs' claims for equitable relief in a (b)(2) class action. As noted previously, injunctive, declaratory, and other forms of equitable relief such as back pay are ordinarily available in class actions certified under Rule 23(b)(2). Indeed, our cases have held that failure to certify a class action on such claims may amount to an abuse of discretion. . . . The standards of Rule 23, however, are not the only limitations on the availability of a class action in this case. As the district court recognized, the right to a jury trial provided by the Civil Rights Act of 1991, and demanded by the plaintiffs, implicates the Seventh Amendment. Thus, we consider whether Seventh Amendment concerns preclude a class action on the plaintiffs' claims for equitable relief, severed from those for compensatory and punitive damages.

The Seventh Amendment preserves the right to a jury trial "in Suits at common law." . . . This right encompasses all actions in which legal rights are to be determined, as opposed to those in which only equitable rights and remedies are involved. . . . Of course, application of the Seventh Amendment is not limited to actions at common law. Legal rights, to which the right to a jury trial attaches, may be statutorily created as well. . . . Section 1981a of the Civil Rights Act of 1991 is such a statute. It grants both parties the right to demand a jury trial when compensatory and punitive damages are sought in intentional discrimination claims under Title VII. . . .

When claims involving both legal and equitable rights are properly joined in a single case, the Seventh Amendment requires that all factual issues common to these claims be submitted to a jury for decision on the legal claims before final court determination of the equitable claims. . . .

The plaintiffs' disparate impact claim is the only claim in this case that could be tried in a (b)(2) class action because it is the only claim limited to equitable relief. In deciding whether the district court should have severed the disparate impact claim for class treatment, we must ascertain, therefore, whether this claim shares any factual issues with the pattern or practice claim, which both parties are entitled to have decided first by a jury.

Because the same employment policies and practices are challenged under both claims, it is clear that there are over-lapping issues. First and foremost, an essential factual element of both claims is a finding that the challenged employment practice caused class members to suffer an adverse employment action (*e.g.*, whether class members failed a challenged employment test and were not hired because of that failure). Indeed, in resolving either claim, the trier of fact must determine whether class members were even in a position to be affected by the challenged employment practice (*e.g.*, whether class members applied for an open job). . . .

Similarly, the business necessity defense to disparate impact claims and the legitimate nondiscriminatory reason defense to disparate treatment claims are not "so distinct and separable" from one another that they may be considered separately by multiple factfinders without violating the Seventh Amendment. . . . To rebut the plaintiffs' claim that any one of Citgo's challenged employment practices resulted in a disparate impact, Citgo would have to establish that the "challenged practice is job-related for the position in question and consistent with business necessity." 42 U.S.C. § 2000e-2(k)(1)(A)(I). It is the rare case indeed in which a challenged practice is job-related and a business necessity, yet not a legitimate nondiscriminatory reason to an adverse employment action taken pursuant to that practice. Thus, a finding that a challenged practice is job related and a business necessity in response to a disparate impact claim strongly, if not wholly, implicates a finding that the same practice is a legitimate nondiscriminatory reason for the employer's actions in a pattern or practice claim. These issues are questions of fact . . . common to the plaintiffs' disparate impact and pattern or practice claims.

In sum, the existence of factual issues common between the plaintiffs' disparate impact and pattern or practice claims precludes trial of the equitable aspects of those claims as a class action severed from the remaining non-class claims in the case. The claims for injunctive relief, declaratory relief, and any equitable or incidental monetary relief cannot be litigated in a class action bench trial (in the same case) without running afoul of the Seventh Amendment. . . . Nor may they be advanced in a subsequent class action without being barred by res judicata and collateral estoppel, . . . because all of the common factual issues will already have been decided, or could have been decided, in the prior litigation. The district court, therefore, did not err in denying class certification on any and all aspects of this case.

Notes and Questions

1. We will examine the meaning of the Seventh Amendment and its effect on the trials of complex and complicated cases in Chapters Ten and Eleven. See pp. 1209-40, 1283-84, *infra*. For now, it is enough to realize that the right to jury trial, which generally attaches to claims for damages but not to claims for injunctive relief, may influence the ability of the parties to obtain certification of a mandatory class.

2. Doesn't the majority in *Allison* oversell the right to jury trial argument? In the "old days" (*i.e.*, before 1938 in the federal system), a party could first bring a claim in equity, and then a claim in law. Aside from potential collateral estoppel consequences, no penalties attached to the filing of two consecutive suits, because the claims in law and equity could not both be brought in one case. Cf. American Life Insurance Co. v. Stewart, 300 U.S. 203 (1937). There was never thought to be any Seventh Amendment bar to such a procedure. Today,

after the merger of law and equity and the expansion of res judicata, a plaintiff that first brings an equitable claim will find that a subsequent legal claim is likely to be precluded under res judicata. In *Allison*, however, the subsequent legal claims of class members would not be precluded because of the limitations of res judicata in the class action context. Cooper v. Federal Reserve Bank of Richmond, 467 U.S. 867 (1984) (p. 174, *supra*). In this situation, wouldn't the rules from the "old days" still apply (*i.e.*, the subsequent legal claim is not precluded, although collateral estoppel consequences might attach)? If there wasn't a Seventh Amendment problem in the old days, why is there one now?

Moreover, assuming that it has some validity, isn't the Seventh Amendment issue the creation of the majority's stingy interpretation of Rule 23(b)(3)? Rather than creating a constitutional difficulty with such an interpretation, isn't it consistent with general principles of jurisprudence to try to construe Rule 23(b)(3) in a way that avoids the constitutional issue?

Finally, as we shall see, some courts have used the Seventh Amendment as a reason to deny class certification under Rule 23(b)(3). See pp. 642-43, 1283-84, *infra*. If the Seventh Amendment makes it hard to obtain certification under Rule 23(b)(3), and then the inability to obtain a (b)(3) certification creates Seventh Amendment problems for certification under (b)(2), isn't the Seventh Amendment argument bootstrapping itself? Is the endpoint of this argument that the Seventh Amendment bars any class action in which damages might be available? That can't be what the Seventh Amendment means, can it?

ii. Class Actions with an Opt-Out Right: Rule 23(b)(3)

Rule 23(b)(3) authorizes class actions upon a finding that common questions predominate and that the class action would be superior to other available devices for managing factually related claims. Rule 23(b)(3) represents a potentially powerful tool for aggregating many claims: tort, environmental, antitrust, securities fraud, consumer, and the like. Not surprisingly, it has also been the most controversial form of class action ever since its creation in 1966.

After some skirmishes in the early years, the basic principle that opt-out class actions should be certified for damages claims arising under various federal statutes regulating commercial activity (*e.g.*, Sherman Act, Clayton Act, Securities Act of 1933, Securities Exchange Act of 1934, and various consumer credit statutes) has won fairly broad acceptance. Such class actions are frequently certified — although of late new questions have been raised about their utility in some cases. For the last fifteen years, however, the real battleground has been the use of the (b)(3) class action to deal with the problem of the mass tort. Before that time, the federal courts were decidedly opposed to certification of any mass tort, even when all of the plaintiffs' injuries arose out a single event and the only individual issues in the case concerned the amount of damages. See, *e.g.*, Hobbs v. Northeast Airlines, 50 F.R.D. 76 (E.D. Pa. 1976). Beginning in the early 1980's, however, that attitude began to change. Nonetheless, the precise circumstances under which mass torts can be certified under Rule 23(b)(3) remains one of the most hotly contested issues in class action practice.

Two of the primary differences between most commercial class actions and most mass tort class actions are that commercial class actions typically arise primarily under federal law and involve relatively small individual stakes. For instance, most victims of a securities fraud may have suffered only a few hundred dollars worth of damage. Plainly, it is not worth the trouble to file an individual lawsuit in such cases; if the defendant's conduct is to be sanctioned and the plaintiffs to receive compensation, the class action is an essential tool. On the other hand, if the class action did not exist, virtually none of these cases would be filed, and the court would be saved the management headaches of a difficult piece of litigation.

In contrast, the mass tort often arise under state law and involves significant claims for injury. It is often worthwhile for individuals to litigate these cases. Given the preference for party autonomy that underlies the adversary system, what reason is there to aggregate these cases in a single forum? Given that most mass torts involve issues of state law, what reason is there to aggregate these cases in a federal forum? Given that both the fact of aggregation and the timing of aggregation can influence the outcome of the litigation, what reason is there to depart from the standard trial procedures used in more routine litigation?

There are two standard replies to these questions from those who favor certification. First, those who wish to not to participate in the class action are always free to opt out. Second, these concerns are outweighed by the efficiency that the class action generates — after all, a (b)(3) class can be certified only when common issues predominate and the class action is a superior means to handle the litigation. Are these adequate reasons? Is it also a reason that the substantive theory of the lawsuit (whether securities or tort) should not determine the scope of a person's procedural rights? (Another possible reason that we have suggested throughout this book — that aggregation is necessary to protect the interests of similarly situated persons in a fair share of the remedy — is only weakly available, since this problem is dealt with through mandatory (b)(1) and (b)(2) class actions.)

These are the issues that swirl around the Rule 23(b)(3) class action, which forces us to focus squarely on the question of how much we value efficiency in relation to other procedural values.

a) Commercial Common Question Class Actions

We ordinarily think of procedure as the servant of substance; procedure is simply the process by which the substantive law is implemented. In fact, the relationship of procedure and substance in our law is often far more dynamic. Nowhere is this interaction more evident than in the history of class action litigation under the federal securities laws, which we use as the vehicle to explore the issue of the commercial common question class action.

Beginning in the 1960s, and continuing apace thereafter, large numbers of (b)(3) class actions asserted Rule 10b-5 claims against corporations, their officers and directors, and others for misrepresentations or omissions of material fact in public statements related to their securities. See 15 U.S.C. § 78j(b); 17 C.F.R. § 240.10(b)-5. A plaintiff needed to prove six elements to establish a 10b-5 claim: a misstatement or omission, materiality, scienter, reliance, proximate causation and damages. The first three elements (misstatement/omission, materiality, and scienter) were readily provable on a classwide basis. The remaining three elements (actual reliance, proximate causation, damages), however, raised factual questions that seemingly required individual proof peculiar to each plaintiff. Since Rule 23(b)(3) class actions require a finding that common questions *predominate* over non-common questions and that the class is *superior* to alternative devices for managing the litigation, non-common questions threatened to turn the class action into a morass of hundreds of individual trials. Despite this vexing problem, most federal district courts certified 10b-5 class actions — largely based on the conviction that not to do so would cripple the private enforcement of the federal securities laws and often deny individual investors a day in court. See, *e.g.*, Green v. Wolf, 406 F.2d 291, 301 (2d Cir. 1968). They dismissed objections to certification with vague references to the possibility of subclasses and the use of bifurcated trials.

In 1972 the Supreme Court interpreted the substantive law in a way that reduced these procedural difficulties in some cases. It held that a plaintiff bringing a 10b-5 "omissions" case (as opposed to a misrepresentation case) did not need to prove actual reliance by each class member on the omission; reliance was presumed if the omission was material. Affiliated Ute Citizens of Utah v. United States, 406 U.S. 128 (1972). This theory did not apply to "misrepresentation" cases, and plaintiffs continued to struggle with the task of how to prove the three non-common questions in such a class action.

The response of the federal courts to these procedural difficulties was again to revise the substantive law.

KIRKPATRICK v. J.C. BRADFORD & CO.

827 F.2d 718 (11th Cir. 1987), cert. denied, 485 U.S. 959 (1988)

■ KRAVITCH, Circuit Judge. Plaintiffs in these companion cases filed certified interlocutory appeals pursuant to 28 U.S.C. § 1292(b) challenging the district court's denial of class certification under Rule 23 of the Federal Rules of Civil Procedure. . . . Concluding that the district court applied erroneous legal standards, we reverse and remand for further consideration.

I. BACKGROUND

These are a few of the many cases arising out of the virtual collapse in 1984 of the Petro-Lewis oil and natural gas investment funds. From 1970 to 1984, about 180,000 people purchased more than $3 billion worth of

Petro-Lewis securities and limited partnerships. When the price of oil and gas declined in 1981 and 1982, Petro-Lewis began borrowing funds to pay partnership distributions, to service its debt, and to promote the sale of additional programs. In February 1984, revealing for the first time that it was in dire financial straits, Petro-Lewis announced that it would implement a series of drastic economy measures, including cutting partnership distributions by as much as 50 per cent and selling between one quarter and one third of its reserves. Numerous lawsuits followed.

[A federal district court in Colorado ultimately approved a settlement of 11 consolidated class suits brought under the federal securities laws against the directors and certain corporate entities of the Petro-Lewis organization. The settlement established a royalty trust and paid plaintiffs $23.5 million. Subsequently, the plaintiffs in this litigation filed suit against broker-dealers of Petro-Lewis securities and limited partnerships.]

[P]laintiffs allege that the actions of the defendant brokerage firms and individuals in selling and promoting interests in Petro-Lewis violated sections 11 and 12(2) of the Securities Act of 1933, 15 U.S.C. §§ 77k, 77l (2), section 10 of the Securities Exchange Act of 1934, 15 U.S.C. § 78j, Rule 10b-5 promulgated thereunder, 17 C.F.R. § 240.10b-5, and various common law and statutory obligations under state law. Claiming to represent classes of plaintiffs who, between January 1, 1981 to February 6, 1984, purchased, reinvested in, or otherwise acquired Petro-Lewis limited partnership interests from the defendant firms, the plaintiffs alleged that the defendants knowingly or recklessly participated with Petro-Lewis in disseminating materially misleading information regarding Petro-Lewis' financial condition and failed to provide other information that would have made the statements not misleading.

After discovery and hearings, the district court issued an order and an amended order denying certification of the classes under Rule 23 of the Federal Rules of Civil Procedure. Although the court determined that each suit satisfied the class action prerequisites of Rule 23(a)(1), (2), and (3), the court denied certification on the ground that the named plaintiffs were not adequate class representatives as required by Rule 23(a)(4). The basis for this determination was that the named plaintiffs did not demonstrate that they would pursue the litigation with sufficient vigor to protect the interests of the class. As an alternative ground of decision, the court held that individual questions of law and fact outweighed common questions and thus that the actions did not satisfy the standards of Rule 23(b)(3). . . . [T]he court certified its order for an interlocutory appeal pursuant to 28 U.S.C. § 1292(b). We accepted jurisdiction.

II. RULE 23(b)(3): PREDOMINANCE OF COMMON OR INDIVIDUAL QUESTIONS

The district court's conclusion that individual questions predominate over common questions is based directly on the court's interpretation of the substance of the plaintiffs' claims. Consequently, we will consider first that aspect of the court's denial of class certification.

In holding that certification was improper under Rule 23(b)(3), the court concluded that common questions of law and fact in the 10(b) and 10b-5 claims were dominated by individual questions of reliance on the part of the particular purchasers, statutes of limitations in each state in which there may be class members, and arbitration agreements in many of the purchase contracts. The court viewed the state law claims to be inappropriate for class action treatment because liability would depend upon the substantive law of the different states. Finally, the court refused to consider certifying classes limited to the section 11 and 12(2) claims after concluding that the 10(b) and state law claims were the dominant claims asserted in the complaints.

A. Section 10(b) and Rule 10b-5

The complaints allege that the defendants violated section 10(b) and Rule 10b-5 by engaging in two related but different courses of conduct. First, the complaints contend that the defendants participated with Petro-Lewis in disseminating misleading prospectuses and in engaging in a standardized promotion by the individual brokers. Second, the plaintiffs claim that the firms continued to sell and promote Petro-Lewis shares despite the firms' awareness or reckless disregard of Petro-Lewis' severe financial difficulties. Based on these allegations, the plaintiffs assert three theories of liability under which common issues of law and fact necessarily would outweigh individual issues. They first contend that their claims concern primarily acts of omission and thus that reliance on the part of individual purchasers should be presumed under the rule of Affiliated Ute Citizens v. United States, 406 U.S. 128 (1975). Second, they argue that the claims fall under the fraud-on-the-market theory adopted by our predecessor court in Shores v. Sklar, 647 F.2d 462 (5th Cir. 1981) (en banc), cert. denied, 459 U.S. 1102 (1983). Finally, they argue that the allegations involve a common course of conduct toward all defendants, and thus that any issues of individual reliance could not predominate over common questions of facts. Kennedy v. Tallant, 710 F.2d 711 (11th Cir. 1983). . . .

We agree with the district court that under the precedent of this circuit the plaintiffs' complaints cannot be properly characterized as omissions cases under the standards of *Affiliated Ute*. . . .

We cannot agree, however, with the court's rejection of the fraud-on-the-market theory as a basis for class action treatment. In *Shores v. Sklar, supra*, the former Fifth Circuit sitting en banc held that, in fraud claims asserted under Rules 10b-5(1) and (3), the reliance element of Rule 10b-5 may be satisfied by proof that the plaintiff relied on the integrity of the market rather than on specific misrepresentations by the defendants. Under *Shores*, reliance may be established by proof that securities not traded on the open market could not have been issued but for a fraudulent scheme by the defendants. . . . Here, consistent with *Shores*, plaintiffs alleged that the Petro-Lewis shares, which were not traded on the open market, could not have been marketed but for the defendants' fraud.

In rejecting this claim as improper for class treatment, the court relied solely on its conclusion that the plaintiffs' allegations lacked evidentiary support. Despite the court's assertions to the contrary, this determination was an inappropriate inquiry into the merits of the plaintiffs' claims. Certainly, as the court noted in its order, a court may look beyond the allegations of the complaint in determining whether a motion for class certification should be granted. General Telephone Co. of Southwest v. Falcon, 457 U.S. 147, 160 (1982) . . . . Here, however, the court's rejection of the fraud-on-the-market theory was based upon nothing other than the court's assessment of the plaintiffs' likelihood of success on the claims. This is an improper basis for deciding the propriety of a class action. *E.g.*, Eisen v. Carlisle & Jacquelin, 417 U.S. 156, 177-78 (1974) . . . .

Nor can the court's rejection of the fraud-on-the-market theory be upheld under the rationale that fraud-on-the-market claims are improper for class treatment where, as here, the evidence indicates that the named plaintiffs relied on the advice of their brokers rather than solely on the integrity of the market. As the defendants note, several district courts have denied class certification for fraud-on-the-market claims where evidence indicates that the named plaintiffs may in fact have relied on factors other than the market's integrity. These cases, however, generally have concerned fraud-on-the-market claims involving securities traded in an open market. . . . . That version of the fraud-on-the-market theory focuses on the plaintiffs' reliance on the integrity of an open and developed market to set a price accurately reflecting the security's value. . . . The issue of reliance on an open market thus turns on a matter of degree — the price of the security — and not, as in *Shores*, the absolute question of whether the security was worthy of being issued.

Because the Petro-Lewis shares were not traded on the open market, we need not now consider the appropriateness of class certification of traditional fraud- on-the-market claims involving securities that are openly traded. We conclude, however, that where as here, a complaint alleges that a security not traded on the open market could not have been issued but for the fraud of the defendants, class action treatment is not precluded by the possibility that some purchasers, including the named plaintiffs, might have relied on factors other than the integrity of the market. . . .

We conclude for similar reasons that the district court also improperly found that the plaintiffs' 10b-5(2) misrepresentation claims were not suited for class treatment. The basis for the court's denial of class certification of the misrepresentation claims was the court's conclusion that the claims involved primarily oral representations and thus would present individual issues of reliance. To arrive at this conclusion, the court focused on deposition evidence indicating that the named plaintiffs relied not so much on prospectuses and other written materials as on the recommendations of their individual brokers. The court further found that the plaintiffs had uncovered no evidence to show that their particular brokers had attended the Petro-Lewis sales sessions or explicitly followed the standardized sales pitch.

Contrary to the court's construction of the claims, however, the complaints alleged that the defendant brokerage firms and individual officers engaged in a common course of conduct to misrepresent, by affirmative acts and by omission, the financial condition of Petro-Lewis. . . . Neither the complaints nor the deposition testimony relied upon by the district court indicate that any oral representations to the named plaintiffs varied materially from the misleading information alleged to have been disseminated generally as a result of the defendants' common schemes. . . . Consequently, the possibility that the named plaintiffs or other potential class members may have obtained the allegedly misleading information via their individual brokers rather than through widely distributed written information cannot transform the allegations of the complaints into claims concerning primarily questions of individual reliance. The claims essentially involve allegations that the defendants "committed the same unlawful acts in the same method against the entire class." . . .

As in any 10b-5(2) misrepresentation claim, each potential class member must prove reliance on some form of the allegedly misleading information in order to recover. . . . In view of the overwhelming number of common factual and legal issues presented by plaintiffs' misrepresentation claims, however, the mere presence of the factual issue of individual reliance could not render the claims unsuitable for class treatment. Here, . . . each of the complaints alleges "a single conspiracy and fraudulent scheme against a large number of individuals" and thus is "particularly appropriate for class action." . . . Moreover, given the numerous and substantial common issues presented by both the fraud-on-the-market and the misrepresentation claims, the common questions in these cases cannot legitimately be considered subordinate to the individual questions presented by the different state statutes of limitations that may be applicable or by the arbitration agreements contained in some of the purchasers' contracts. "Rule 23 does not require that all the questions of law and fact raised by the dispute be common." Cox v. American Cast Iron Pipe Co., 784 F.2d 1546, 1557 (11th Cir.), cert. denied, [479 U.S. 883] (1986).

In sum, we conclude that as a result of the district court's erroneous analysis of the fraud-on-the-market claims and its mischaracterization of the misrepresentations claims, the court incorrectly determined that individual issues predominated over common issues. Contrary to the court's conclusions, these claims involve common issues that clearly overwhelm the individual issues that may be present. Consequently, "[s]eparate actions by each of the class members would be repetitive, wasteful, and an extraordinary burden on the courts." *Kennedy v. Tallant*, 710 F.2d at 718. The district court thus abused its discretion in ruling that the requirements of Rule 23(b)(3) were not satisfied in this case. . . .

B. State Law Claims

In concluding that the state law claims failed to satisfy the requirements of Rule 23(b)(3), the district court reasoned that the differing standards of liability required by the laws of the various states would render class action treatment unmanageable. We agree with the district court that the state law claims would require application of the standards of liability of the state in which each purchase was transacted. The district court thus did not abuse its discretion in denying class certification on these claims. . . .

C. Section 11 and 12(2) Claims

In explaining its denial of class certification of the section 11 and 12(2) claims, the district court stated that it "did not address" these claims individually because to separate these claims from the Rule 10b-5 and state law claims would be "unduly burdensome" on the court. The court consequently denied class certification of the Rule 11 and 12(2) claims based upon its conclusion that the 10b-5 and the state law claims did not meet the requirements of Rule 23(b)(3). In view of our determination that the court erroneously ruled that the 10b-5 claims did not meet the requirements of Rule 23(b)(3), the court must of course reconsider its decision regarding the section 11 and 12(2) claims.

Independent of our decision on the 10b-5 claims, however, we conclude that the court erred in failing to consider separately the appropriateness of the class action treatment of the section 11 and 12(2) claims. Although there is some overlap between section 10(b) and sections 11 and 12(2), the provisions "involve distinct causes of action and were intended to address different types of wrongdoing." . . . The failure of the district court to give separate consideration to class action certification of these distinct claims thus could serve neither the securities laws' purpose of protecting investors, . . . nor Rule 23's purpose of protecting the courts from needlessly repetitious litigation . . . . By failing to consider these claims separately, the court abused its discretion.

[The court then held that the district court used an erroneous standard to determine whether the named plaintiffs were adequate representatives, and remanded for the district court to apply the correct standard.]

For the foregoing reasons, the order of the district court is reversed in part, affirmed in part, and remanded with instructions.

Notes and Questions

1. The essence of the fraud-on-the-market theory is that a section 10b-5 plaintiff, alleging material misrepresentations by a corporation or its officers, does not need to prove his own personal reliance on the particular misrepresentation; instead, reliance will be presumed because the plaintiff is deemed to have relied on the actual market price which was distorted by the material misrepresentation. The fraud-on-the-market theory of liability in section 10b-5 cases was first articulated in Blackie v. Barrack, 524 F.2d 891 (9th Cir. 1975), cert. denied, 429 U.S. 816 (1976). *Blackie* was followed by many other circuits. Shortly after *Kirkpatrick*, a plurality of the Supreme Court at last embraced this theory in Basic, Inc. v. Levinson, 485 U.S. 224 (1988). As a practical matter, defendants find the presumption of reliance virtually irrebuttable. See *Basic*, 485 U.S. at 256 n.7 (White, J., dissenting).

2. In *Kirkpatrick*, the plaintiffs had to plead a less-than-likely theory of conspiracy in order to jump over the class certification hurdle. Does this sort of pleading do a disservice to class members, who might have legitimate non-conspiracy theories of recovery against some brokers? Does you answer depend on the preclusive effect that a negative judgment on the conspiracy theory might

have on the individual claims? See Cooper v. Federal Reserve Bank of Richmond, 467 U.S. 867 (1984) (p. 174, *supra*). Does your answer depend on whether the individual claims are worth enough money to bring as a separate lawsuit, or instead have a "negative net worth"? Does the fact that the class action might exert some pressure on the defendants to settle — thus obtaining at least a surrogate measure of recovery for individual "negative net worth" claims — influence your judgment?

3. Some courts have recently come to question whether section 10b-5 class actions, relying on the fraud-on-the-market approach, should be routinely certified. The argument is that in many fraud-on-the-market cases, class plaintiffs that purchased securities at different points during the allegedly fraudulent course of behavior have inherent conflicts of interest on matters of proof and damages. This fact is especially true when the corporation makes a series of partially curative disclosures before the misrepresentation is fully disclosed. An important and controversial development of these conflicts of interest can be found in In re Seagate Technology II Securities Litigation, 843 F. Supp. 1341 (N.D. Cal. 1994), in which the court demonstrated that conflicts of interest existed among "those in/out traders who sold securities on a particular day, and those plaintiffs who purchased on that same day," and among "those persons who still hold some of the relevant securities on the date of suit, and those who have divested themselves of all such holdings. And as a variant of this latter conflict, antagonism may even surface amongst those holding securities on the date of suit." Id. at 1359. *Seagate* also purported to show that subclasses were unable to resolve this problem. The result, the court stated, was that there were severe Rule 23(a)(4) adequacy-of-representation problems. As a result, the court ordered an evidentiary hearing to determine the extent of the conflict. Id. at 1367.

The evidentiary hearing was never held. In response to this opinion, the plaintiffs modified the definition of the class so that it consisted only of one subclass of purchasers that retained their stock throughout the entire class period. The district court then certified the class. In re Seagate Technology II Securities Litigation, 156 F.R.D. 229 (N.D. Cal. 1994).

4. *Seagate*, which explains in detail how different plaintiffs in a 10b-5 class action have different interests in "shaping the pertinent evidence" about the effect of the alleged fraud-on-the-market price of the stock at different times during the relevant period for which damages are sought, assumes that named class representatives and even absent class members influence or control the evidence that is presented to the court. Is this at all realistic? Even in simple bi-polar cases, the attorney, and not the client, typically decides what evidence to use and oversees its preparation and presentation. In class actions, the class has no internal mechanism for monitoring or directing the lawyer (meetings aren't held; votes aren't taken), so it is even more likely that the evidence proffered on behalf of the class will be decided by counsel and not by class members.

5. In view of the problems of proof and conflicts within the plaintiff class identified in *Seagate*, should federal district courts routinely continue to certify section 10b-5 class actions? Some courts have followed the logic of *Seagate II* and declined to certify 10b-5 class actions due to class conflicts. See, *e.g.*, Ballan v. Upjohn Co., 159 F.R.D. 473 (W.D. Mich. 1994). Other courts have deemed *Seagate* aberrational and have continued to certify section 10b-5 class actions. See, *e.g.*, Welling v. Alexy, 155 F.R.D. 654 (N.D. Cal. 1994); In re Proxima Corp.

Securities Litigation, 1994 WL 374306 (S.D. Cal.); Picard Chemical Inc. Profit Sharing Plan v. Perrigo Co., 1996 WL 739170 (W.D. Mich) (collecting cases on both sides).

6. In light of the internal class conflicts identified in *Seagate*, how can counsel for the class determine fairly what approach to take to the evidence? For instance, an argument that early curative disclosures by the corporation were inadequate and ineffective will benefit some members of the class (*i.e.*, new purchasers during this period), but disadvantage others (*i.e.*, earlier purchasers who sold during this period). Should counsel for the class proffer whatever evidence and expert witness testimony will maximize the total possible damage recovery of the class? If individual class members have the right to opt out of the class, and choose to remain in, do they have any basis for objecting if their damage recovery is reduced in order to secure a larger recovery for the class? Is the problem that they are unlikely to understand what is at stake when they make their opt-out decision?

7. *Blackie* acknowledged the conflicts of interest that partial curative disclosures created within a section 10b-5 class, but asserted that, if the conflicts proved too troublesome under the out-of-pocket loss measure of damages in such cases, the court could adopt a different measure of damages, such as recission or compensatory damages. 524 F.2d at 908-11. Can it ever be proper to skirt a problem with a proposed joinder device (*i.e.*, the class action) by changing the proper remedy due the plaintiffs? Since different remedial theories will inevitably increase or decrease what the defendant must pay and how much each class member will recover, isn't the norm of trans-substantivism violated by such an approach?

8. More generally, the common theme running through many of these cases is the need to modify the relevant substantive and remedial law in order to facilitate the use of Rule 23(b)(3) class actions by investors pleading securities claims. When is it proper and improper for procedural considerations to override substantive ones? Or is the decision to use a class action a substantive one?

9. *Seagate* aside, the dominant attitude of the federal courts since the mid-1960's has been to find ways to certify securities class actions in order to buttress private enforcement of the federal securities laws and to allow small investors a day in court. Of late, however, Congress has viewed these cases quite differently, and in 1995 passed, over the President's veto, the Private Securities Litigation Reform Act ("PSLRA"). Pub. L. No. 104-67, 109 Stat. 737. The PSLRA was intended to curb the number of securities fraud class actions and the behavior of the entrepreneurial lawyers who had often initiated such suits. We examined some of the PSLRA's specific changes to class action practice at p. 582, *supra*. Should this legislation influence how Rule 23(b)(3) is interpreted in securities class actions on matters that the PSLRA does not directly address?

10. Other types of commercial common question class actions remain popular. For example, antitrust price-fixing claims are frequently certifed under (b)(3) as class actions. See, *e.g.*, In re Industrial Diamonds Antitrust Litigation, 167 F.R.D. 374 (S.D.N.Y. 1996) (finding class action superior to consolidation as a device for managing price-fixing claims against industrial diamond producers). Consumer class actions have not, however, always been received as warmly. See, *e.g.*, Andrews v. American Telephone & Telegraph Co., 95 F.3d 1014 (11th Cir. 1996) (class action by callers of "900" numbers against long distance telephone companies alleging racketeering, mail fraud, and wire fraud claims reversed because common questions did not predominate and class action was

not manageable); Heaven v. Trust Co. Bank, 118 F.3d 735 (11th Cir. 1997) (failure to certify class under Consumer Leasing Act not an abuse of discretion); Ratner v. Chemical Bank New York Trust Co., 54 F.R.D. 412 (S.D.N.Y. 1972) (refusing to certify class in Truth-in-Lending Act case).

11. Many commercial class actions arise under federal law, or at least the law of a single state. Note that *Kirkpatrick* refused to certify certain state law claims because the nationwide class implicated the securities laws of many states. Is certification of a federal (b)(3) class action asserting violations of the laws of numerous states ever possible? To answer this question, we turn to the use of (b)(3) class actions in mass tort cases.

b) Mass Tort Common Question Class Actions

While the authors of Rule 23(b)(3) expected the common question class action to be used to recover damages in the commercial setting, they did not think Rule 23(b)(3) to be generally suitable for mass tort cases. See Advisory Committee Note to the 1966 Amendment to Rule 23, 39 F.R.D. 98, 103 (1966). They feared that such cases would degenerate into multiple lawsuits whose non-common issues of liability and damages would need to be tried separately. Most federal courts who faced this issue in the 1960's and in the 1970s concurred in this view. During the 1980's, the view began to retreat, although during the 1990's, reluctance continues to be shown, especially at the appellate level, toward the use of litigation class actions that involve widely dispersed mass torts. If aggregation of at least some of these claims would be fair and efficient, why not certify the class and allow class members to opt out if they wish to pursue their claims in a different venue? If Rule 23(b)(3) cannot aggregate most of these cases in a single venue, aren't we are left to other aggregation devices — none of which, we have seen, holds great promise to prevent the re-litigation of related issues? On the other hand, is it worth aggregating some, but not all, related cases? Moreover, might individual adjudication of these claims be desirable?

Roger H. Trangsrud, JOINDER ALTERNATIVES IN MASS TORT LITIGATION

70 Corn. L. Rev. 779, 820-822 (1985)

The Federal Rules of Civil Procedure recognize an individual litigant's interest in controlling the prosecution of his own tort claim as an important consideration limiting the desirability of the common question class action. The individual's interest in personal control directly relates to the nature and size of his tort claim. Recently courts have certified class actions where the plaintiffs have suffered only property damage or relatively minor personal injuries. They have been extremely reluctant, however, to do so in serious personal injury or wrongful death cases because the nature of the claim indicates a strong interest in personal control over its management. As the severity of the plaintiff's injury increases, the psychological and emotional importance of individually vindicating his rights against the responsible parties also increases. The importance of a family's control over its claim for the wrongful death of its sole provider, for example, cannot be gainsaid.

In a mass tort case several factors affect the plaintiff's interest in individual control over his personal injury or wrongful death claim. First, the individual plaintiff may perceive a number of tactical advantages in proceeding alone. Because significant differences in likely jury awards for particular injuries are perceived to exist between judicial districts, an individual plaintiff will probably file his case in the most convenient, high-award district that the applicable venue and jurisdictional rules permit. Defendants have a very heavy burden to overcome when trying to disturb the plaintiff's choice of forum in individual cases. In a mass tort case, however, if a class action is requested, or the transfer of the related claims to a single forum proposed, the deciding court is much less likely to defer to the forum preferences of individual litigants. The court will more likely site the litigation in the forum most convenient to witnesses or where most or all of the injuries occurred. The individual plaintiff may thus find himself before an unfamiliar jury in a district where jury awards tend to be less generous than those generally granted in the original forum. A plaintiff's right to have his damages evaluated by a jury familiar with his actual costs and economic situation is a substantial interest worthy of protection in most mass tort cases.

Second, if a class action is certified, the individual plaintiff may find that the state law applied by the forum court is not as favorable as the law which would have been applied had he been able to choose his own forum. The individual plaintiff also runs the risk that the representative plaintiffs in a class action will elect to proceed on liability theories better suited for class treatment at the expense of theories especially favorable to the individual plaintiff. These important considerations may not be highlighted during the certification process because named representatives and attorneys for the putative class have strong personal or financial interests in securing certification and will down-play possible conflicts of interest within the class.

Third, class members lack the direct control that an individual tort litigant can exercise over his own personal lawyer. The class action plaintiff cannot easily influence or control the handling of his claim. Even named plaintiffs exercise little control over class counsel. Class counsel proceeds based upon his estimation of what the interests of the class as a whole are, rather than those of individual plaintiffs, because no internal procedures exist by which a class can make decisions. Class counsel can thus easily ignore or poorly serve the interests of individual class members. Moreover, some courts exacerbate this problem by placing restrictions on the freedom of class counsel to communicate with absent class members without court approval.

In summary, given the traditional respect afforded an individual tort litigant's right to control the prosecution of a substantial personal injury or wrongful death claim, and that the plaintiff loses much of this individual control when the court certifies a class action, courts should avoid using this joinder device to try these cases.

JENKINS v. RAYMARK INDUSTRIES, INC.

782 F.2d 468 (5th Cir. 1986)

■ REAVLEY, Circuit Judge. In this interlocutory appeal, the thirteen defendants challenge the decision of District Judge Robert M. Parker to certify a class of plaintiffs with asbestos-related claims. We affirm.

I. Background to Judge Parker's Plan

Experts estimate that at least 21 million American workers have been exposed to "significant" amounts of asbestos at the workplace since 1940; other millions have been exposed through environmental contact or contact with relatives who have worked with the products.... Because of its injurious propensities, such exposure, in human terms, has meant that literally tens of thousands of people fall ill or die from asbestos-related diseases every year.... In legal terms, it has translated into thousands of lawsuits, over 20,000 as of 1983, centered mainly in industrialized areas along the country's coasts....

Courts, including those in our own circuit, have been ill-equipped to handle this "avalanche of litigation."... Our numerous opinions in asbestos-related cases have repeatedly recognized the dilemma confronting our trial courts, and expressed concern about the mounting backlog of cases and inevitable, lengthy trial delays....

About 5,000 asbestos-related cases are pending in this circuit. Much, though by no means all, of the litigation has centered in the Eastern District of Texas. Nearly nine hundred asbestos-related personal injury cases, involving over one thousand plaintiffs, were pending there in December of 1984. Despite innovative streamlined pretrial procedures and large-scale consolidated trials of multiple plaintiffs, the dockets of that district's courts remained alarmingly backlogged. Plaintiffs had waited years for trial, some since 1979 — and new cases were (and still are) being filed every day. It is predicted that, because asbestos-related diseases will continue to manifest themselves for the next 15 years, filings will continue at a steady rate until the year 2000.

In early 1985, ten of these plaintiffs responded by moving to certify a class of all plaintiffs with asbestos-related personal injury actions pending in the Eastern District on December 31, 1984.[2] These plaintiffs hoped to determine in the class action one overarching issue — the viability of the "state of the art" defense. Because the trial of that issue consistently

---

2. Three additional plaintiffs later moved to intervene. Proposed class counsel already represented about 80% of all member plaintiffs in their individual cases, and has tried numerous large and small asbestos cases.

consumed substantial resources in every asbestos trial, and the evidence in each case was either identical or virtually so, they argued, a class determination would accelerate their cases.

II. The Plan

Following copious briefing and several hearings, the district court granted the motion. In his order of October 16, 1985, Judge Parker carefully considered the request under Rule 23(a), (b)(1) and (b)(3) of the Federal Rules of Civil Procedure. Finding a "limited fund" theory too speculative, he refused to certify the class under Rule 23(b)(1); by contrast, he found all of the elements for a 23(b)(3) action present. Drawing on his past experience, the judge concluded that evidence concerning the "state of the art" defense would vary little as to individual plaintiffs while consuming a major part of the time required for their trials. Considerable savings, both for the litigants and for the court, could thus be gained by resolving this and other defense and defense-related questions, including product identification, product defectiveness, gross negligence and punitive damages, in one class trial. The court further found that the named representatives had "typical" claims, and that they and their attorneys would adequately represent the other class members. Accordingly, it certified the class as to the common questions, ordering them resolved for the class by a class action jury. The class jury would also decide all the individual issues of the unnamed members which would be resolved later in "mini-trials" of seven to ten plaintiffs. Although the class action jury would evaluate the culpability of defendants' conduct for a possible punitive damage award, any such damages would be awarded only after class members had won or settled their individual cases. The court subsequently appointed a special master to survey the class and prepare a report, detailing the class members and their claims, to apprise the jury of the gravity and extent of the absent members' claims and the typicality of the representatives' claims.

Defendants moved for reconsideration or, in the alternative, certification of the decision for interlocutory appeal. The court granted defendants' alternate motion.

On appeal, defendants challenge the court's decision on three grounds: (1) the class fails to meet the requirements of Rule 23; (2) Texas law proscribes a bifurcated determination of punitive damages and actual damages; and (3) the contemplated class format is unconstitutional.

III. Discussion

The purpose of class actions is to conserve "the resources of both the courts and the parties by permitting an issue potentially affecting every [class member] to be litigated in an economical fashion." General Telephone Co. of Southwest v. Falcon, 457 U.S. 147, 155 (1982) . . . . To ensure that this purpose is served, Rule 23 demands that all class actions certified under Rule 23(b)(3) meet the requirements of both 23(a); numerosity, commonality, typicality, and adequacy of representation; and 23(b)(3): predominance and superiority. The district court has wide discretion in deciding whether or not to certify a proposed class. Assuming the court considers the Rule 23 criteria, we may reverse its decision only for abuse of discretion. . . .

IV. Rule 23

Defendants argue that this class meets none of the Rule 23 requirements, except "numerosity." There is no merit to this argument.

The threshold of "commonality" is not high. Aimed in part at "determining whether there is a need for combined treatment and a benefit to be derived therefrom," In re Agent Orange Product Liability Litigation, 506 F. Supp. 762, 787 (E.D.N.Y.1980), modified, 100 F.R.D. 718 (1983), mandamus denied sub nom. In re Diamond Shamrock Chemicals Co., 725 F.2d 858 (2d Cir.), cert. denied, 465 U.S. 1067 (1984), the rule requires only that resolution of the common questions affect all or a substantial number of the class members . . . . Defendants do not claim that they intend to raise a "state of the art" defense in only a few cases; the related issues are common to all class members.

The "typicality" requirement focuses less on the relative strengths of the named and unnamed plaintiffs' cases than on the similarity of the legal and remedial theories behind their claims. *E.g.*, In re School Asbestos Litigation, 104 F.R.D. 422, 429 (E.D. Pa. 1984) . . . . Defendants do not contend that the named plaintiffs' claims rest on theories different from those of the other class members.

The "adequacy" requirement looks at both the class representatives and their counsel. Defendants have not shown that the representatives are "inadequate" due to an insufficient stake in the outcome or interests antagonistic to the unnamed members. . . . Neither do they give us reason to question the district court's finding that class counsel is "adequate" in light of counsel's past experience in asbestos cases, including trials involving multiple plaintiffs.

We similarly find no abuse in the court's determination that the certified questions "predominate," under Rule 23(b)(3). In order to "predominate," common issues must constitute a significant part of the individual cases. . . . It is difficult to imagine that class jury findings on the class questions will not significantly advance the resolution of the underlying hundreds of cases.

Defendants also argue that a class action is not "superior"; they say that better mechanisms, such as the Wellington Facility[7] and "reverse bifurcation,"[8] exist for resolving these claims. Again, however, they have failed to show that the district court abused its discretion by reaching the

---

7. The Wellington Facility, funded by major asbestos producers, is a newly-operational center designed to resolve asbestos-related claims. The center is named for Dean Wellington of the Yale University Law School, who assisted in its organization.

8. "Reverse bifurcation" originated in the Third Circuit as a means of processing that circuit's backlog of asbestos-related cases. As its name suggests, it is a modified bifurcated trial format whereby plaintiffs in a first trial prove only that exposure to some asbestos product has caused their damages. Thereafter, either the cases are settled or remaining issues are resolved in second or third trials.

contrary conclusion. We cannot find that the Wellington Facility, whose merits we do not question, is so superior that it must be used to the exclusion of other forums. Similarly, even if we were prepared to weigh the merits of other procedural mechanisms, we see no basis to conclude that this class action plan is an abuse of discretion.

Courts have usually avoided class actions in the mass accident or tort setting. Because of differences between individual plaintiffs on issues of liability and defenses of liability, as well as damages, it has been feared that separate trials would overshadow the common disposition for the class. See Advisory Committee Notes to 1966 Amendment to Fed. R. Civ. P. 23(b)(3). The courts are now being forced to rethink the alternatives and priorities by the current volume of litigation and more frequent mass disasters. . . . If Congress leaves us to our own devices, we may be forced to abandon repetitive hearings and arguments for each claimant's attorney to the extent enjoyed by the profession in the past. Be that as time will tell, the decision at hand is driven in one direction by all the circumstances. Judge Parker's plan is clearly superior to the alternative of repeating, hundreds of times over, the litigation of the state of the art issues with, as that experienced judge says, "days of the same witnesses, exhibits and issues from trial to trial."

This assumes plaintiffs win on the critical issues of the class trial. To the extent defendants win, the elimination of issues and docket will mean a far greater saving of judicial resources. Furthermore, attorneys' fees for all parties will be greatly reduced under this plan, not only because of the elimination of so much trial time but also because the fees collected from all members of the plaintiff class will be controlled by the judge. From our view it seems that the defendants enjoy all of the advantages, and the plaintiffs incur the disadvantages, of the class action — with one exception: the cases are brought to trial. That counsel for plaintiffs would urge the class action under these circumstances is significant support for the district judge's decision.

Necessity moves us to change and invent. Both the *Agent Orange* and the *Asbestos School* courts found that specific issues could be decided in a class "mass tort" action — even on a nationwide basis. We approve of the district court's decision in finding that this "mass tort" class could be certified.

V. Other Contentions

Defendants' remaining arguments challenge the bifurcated trials under Texas law and the United States Constitution. Defendants contend that, under Texas law, punitive damages cannot be determined separately from actual damages because the culpability of their conduct must be evaluated relative to each plaintiff. We disagree. . . .

The format in this case allows for the district court's review of the reasonableness of each plaintiff's punitive damage award and for our review of the standards which the court has applied. Texas law does not require more.

Defendants' constitutional challenges to bifurcation are equally unavailing. Like their other claims, these arguments only recast in constitutional terms their concern that, because the representatives' cases are "better" than the unnamed plaintiffs', the jury's view of the class claims will be skewed.

Although it fails to raise an issue of constitutional magnitude, this concern is nevertheless legitimate. Care must, of course, be taken to ensure fairness. Whatever the jury is told about the claims of the unnamed plaintiffs, it must be made aware that none of those claims have been proved; even after the class trial, they will still be mere allegations. The jury must not assume that all class members have equivalent claims: whatever injuries the unnamed plaintiffs have suffered may differ from the class representatives' as well as from one another's. Should the jury be allowed to award in the aggregate any punitive damages it finds appropriate, it must be instructed to factor in the possibility that none of the unnamed plaintiffs may have suffered any damages. Alternatively, the jury could be allowed to award an amount of money that each class member should receive for each dollar of actual damages awarded. Either way, the jury should understand that it must differentiate between proven and still-unproved claims, and that all class members, who recover actual damages from a defendant held liable for punitive damages, will share in the punitive award.

Furthermore, fairness as well as necessity dictates that both the parties and the court ensure that all of the necessary findings can be and are made in the class action trial. Sufficient evidence must be adduced for every one of each defendant's products to which a class member claims exposure so that the class jury can make the requisite findings as to each product and each defendant for such questions as periods of manufacture; areas and dates of distribution; "state of the art" knowledge for each relevant kind of product, use and user; when, if ever, conduct was grossly negligent; and dates and types of warnings if marketing defect is alleged.

The task will not be easy. Nevertheless, particularly in light of the magnitude of the problem and the need for innovative approaches, we find no abuse of discretion in this court's decision to try these cases by means of a Rule 23(b)(3) class suit.

CASTANO v. AMERICAN TOBACCO CO.

84 F.3d 734 (5th Cir. 1996)

■ SMITH, Circuit Judge. In what may be the largest class action ever attempted in federal court, the district court in this case embarked "on a road certainly less traveled, if ever taken at all," . . . and entered a class certification order. The court defined the class as:

(a) All nicotine-dependent persons in the United States . . . who have purchased and smoked cigarettes manufactured by the defendants;

(b) the estates, representatives, and administrators of these nicotine-dependent cigarette smokers; and

(c) the spouses, children, relatives and "significant others" of these nicotine-dependent cigarette smokers as their heirs or survivors.

The plaintiffs limit the claims to years since 1943.

This matter comes before us on interlocutory appeal, under 28 U.S.C. § 1292(b), of the class certification order. Concluding that the district court abused its discretion in certifying the class, we reverse.

I.

A. The Class Complaint

The plaintiffs filed this class complaint against the defendant tobacco companies and the Tobacco Institute, Inc., seeking compensation solely for the injury of nicotine addiction. The gravamen of their complaint is the novel and wholly untested theory that the defendants fraudulently failed to inform consumers that nicotine is addictive and manipulated the level of nicotine in cigarettes to sustain their addictive nature. The class complaint alleges nine causes of action: fraud and deceit, negligent misrepresentation, intentional infliction of emotional distress, negligence and negligent infliction of emotional distress, violation of state consumer protection statutes, breach of express warranty, breach of implied warranty, strict product liability, and redhibition pursuant to the Louisiana Civil Code.

The plaintiffs seek compensatory and punitive damages and attorneys' fees. In addition, the plaintiffs seek equitable relief for fraud and deceit, negligent misrepresentation, violation of consumer protection statutes, and breach of express and implied warranty. The equitable remedies include a declaration that defendants are financially responsible for notifying all class members of nicotine's addictive nature, a declaration that the defendants manipulated nicotine levels with the intent to sustain the addiction of plaintiffs and the class members, an order that the defendants disgorge any profits made from the sale of cigarettes, restitution for sums paid for cigarettes, and the establishment of a medical monitoring fund.

The plaintiffs initially defined the class as "all nicotine dependent persons in the United States," including current, former and deceased smokers since 1943. Plaintiffs conceded that addiction would have to be proven by each class member; the defendants argued that proving class membership will require individual mini-trials to determine whether addiction actually exists.

In response to the district court's inquiry, the plaintiffs proposed a four-phase trial plan. In phase 1, a jury would determine common issues of "core liability." Phase 1 issues would include (1) issues of law and fact relating to defendants' course of conduct, fraud, and negligence liability (including duty, standard of care, misrepresentation and concealment, knowledge, intent); (2) issues of law and fact relating to defendants' alleged conspiracy and concert of action; (3) issues of fact relating to the addictive nature/dependency creating characteristics and properties of nicotine; (4)

issues of fact relating to nicotine cigarettes as defective products; (5) issues of fact relating to whether defendants' wrongful conduct was intentional, reckless or negligent; (6) identifying which defendants specifically targeted their advertising and promotional efforts to particular groups (*e.g.* youths, minorities, etc.); (7) availability of a presumption of reliance; (8) whether defendants' misrepresentations/suppression of fact and/or of addictive properties of nicotine preclude availability of a "personal choice" defense; (9) defendants' liability for actual damages, and the categories of such damages; (10) defendants' liability for emotional distress damages; and (11) defendants' liability for punitive damages.

Phase 1 would be followed by notice of the trial verdict and claim forms to class members. In phase 2, the jury would determine compensatory damages in sample plaintiff cases. The jury then would establish a ratio of punitive damages to compensatory damages, which ratio thereafter would apply to each class member. Phase 3 would entail a complicated procedure to determine compensatory damages for individual class members. The trial plan envisions determination of absent class members' compensatory economic and emotional distress damages on the basis of claim forms, "subject to verification techniques and assertion of defendants' affirmative defenses under grouping, sampling, or representative procedures to be determined by the Court."

The trial plan left open how jury trials on class members' personal injury/wrongful death claims would be handled, but the trial plan discussed the possibility of bifurcation. In phase 4, the court would apply the punitive damage ratio based on individual damage awards and would conduct a review of the reasonableness of the award.

B. The Class Certification Order

Following extensive briefing, the district court granted, in part, plaintiffs' motion for class certification, concluding that the prerequisites of Fed. R. Civ. P. 23(a) had been met. The court rejected certification, under Fed. R. Civ. P. 23(b)(2), of the plaintiffs' claim for equitable relief, including the claim for medical monitoring. . . .

The court did grant the plaintiffs' motion to certify the class under Fed. R. Civ. P. 23(b)(3), organizing the class action issues into four categories: (1) core liability; (2) injury-in-fact, proximate cause, reliance and affirmative defenses; (3) compensatory damages; and (4) punitive damages. It then analyzed each category to determine whether it met the predominance and superiority requirements of rule 23(b)(3). [The district court thought that class action was appropriate for "core liability" issues and the issue of punitive damages. It did not certify a class on the issues of injury-in-fact, proximate cause, reliance, affirmative defenses, and compensatory damages.] Using its power to sever issues for certification under Fed. R. Civ. P. 23(c)(4), the court certified the class on core liability and punitive damages, and certified the class conditionally pursuant to Fed. R. Civ. P. 23(c)(1). . . .

II. . . .

The district court erred in its analysis in two distinct ways. First, it failed to consider how variations in state law affect predominance and superiority. Second, its predominance inquiry did not include consideration of how a trial on the merits would be conducted.

Each of these defects mandates reversal. Moreover, at this time, while the tort is immature, the class complaint must be dismissed, as class certification cannot be found to be a superior method of adjudication.

A. Variations in State Law . . .

In a multi-state class action, variations in state law may swamp any common issues and defeat predominance. . . .

A district court's duty to determine whether the plaintiff has borne its burden on class certification requires that a court consider variations in state law when a class action involves multiple jurisdictions. "In order to make the findings required to certify a class action under Rule 23(b)(3) . . . one must initially identify the substantive law issues which will control the outcome of the litigation." Alabama v. Blue Bird Body Co., 573 F.2d 309, 316 (5th Cir. 1978).

A requirement that a court know which law will apply before making a predominance determination is especially important when there may be differences in state law. . . .

In response to the defendants' extensive analysis of how state law varied on fraud, products liability, affirmative defenses, negligent infliction of emotional distress, consumer protection statutes, and punitive damages,[15]

---

15. We find it difficult to fathom how common issues could predominate in this case when variations in state law are thoroughly considered. . . The class members were exposed to nicotine through different products, for different amounts of time, and over different time periods. Each class member's knowledge about the effects of smoking differs, and each plaintiff began smoking for different reasons. Each of these factual differences impacts the application of legal rules such as causation, reliance, comparative fault, and other affirmative defenses.

Variations in state law magnify the differences. In a fraud claim, some states require justifiable reliance on a misrepresentation, . . . while others require reasonable reliance . . . . States impose varying standards to determine when there is a duty to disclose facts. . . .

Products liability law also differs among states. Some states do not recognize strict liability. . . . Among the states that have adopted the Restatement, there are variations. . . .

Differences in affirmative defenses also exist. Assumption of risk is a complete defense to a products claim in some states. . . . In others, it is a part of comparative fault analysis. . . . Some states utilize "pure" comparative fault . . .; others follow a "greater fault bar" . . .; and still others use an "equal fault bar" . . . .

Negligent infliction of emotional distress also involves wide variations. . . . Some states do not recognize the cause of action at all. . . . Some require a physical impact. . . .

Despite these overwhelming individual issues, common issues might predominate. We are, however, left to speculate. The point of detailing the alleged differences is to demonstrate the inquiry the district court failed to make.

the court examined a sample phase 1 jury interrogatory and verdict form, a survey of medical monitoring decisions, a survey of consumer fraud class actions, and a survey of punitive damages law in the defendants' home states. The court also relied on two district court opinions granting certification in multi-state class actions.

The district court's consideration of state law variations was inadequate. . . .

The court also failed to perform its duty to determine whether the class action would be manageable in light of state law variations. The court's only discussion of manageability is a citation to [Jenkins v. Raymark Industries, Inc., 782 F.2d 468 (5th Cir. 1986)] and the claim that "while manageability of the liability issues in this case may well prove to be difficult, the Court finds that any such difficulties pale in comparison to the specter of thousands, if not millions, of similar trials of liability proceeding in thousands of courtrooms around the nation."

The problem with this approach is that it substitutes case-specific analysis with a generalized reference to *Jenkins*. The *Jenkins* court, however, was not faced with managing a novel claim involving eight causes of action, multiple jurisdictions, millions of plaintiffs, eight defendants, and over fifty years of alleged wrongful conduct. Instead, *Jenkins* involved only 893 personal injury asbestos cases, the law of only one state, and the prospect of trial occurring in only one district. Accordingly, for purposes of the instant case, *Jenkins* is largely inapposite.

In summary, whether the specter of millions of cases outweighs any manageability problems in this class is uncertain when the scope of any manageability problems is unknown. Absent considered judgment on the manageability of the class, a comparison to millions of individual trials is meaningless.

B. Predominance

The district court's second error was that it failed to consider how the plaintiffs' addiction claims would be tried, individually or on a class basis. The district court, based on Eisen v. Carlisle & Jacquelin, 417 U.S. 156, 177-78 (1974), . . . believed that it could not go past the pleadings for the certification decision. The result was an incomplete and inadequate predominance inquiry. . . .

A district court certainly may look past the pleadings to determine whether the requirements of rule 23 have been met. Going beyond the pleadings is necessary, as a court must understand the claims, defenses, relevant facts, and applicable substantive law in order to make a meaningful determination of the certification issues.

The district court's predominance inquiry demonstrates why such an understanding is necessary. The premise of the court's opinion is a citation to *Jenkins* and a conclusion that class treatment of common issues would significantly advance the individual trials. Absent knowledge of how addiction-as-injury cases would actually be tried, however, it was impossible for the court to know whether the common issues would be a "significant" portion of the individual trials. The court just assumed that because the common issues would play a part in every trial, they must be significant. The court's synthesis of *Jenkins* and *Eisen* would write the predominance requirement out of the rule, and any common issue would predominate if it were common to all the individual trials. . . .

III.

In addition to the reasons given above, regarding the district court's procedural errors, this class must be decertified because it independently fails the superiority requirement of rule 23(b)(3). In the context of mass tort class actions, certification dramatically affects the stakes for defendants. Class certification magnifies and strengthens the number of unmeritorious claims. . . . Aggregation of claims also makes it more likely that a defendant will be found liable and results in significantly higher damage awards. . . .

In addition to skewing trial outcomes, class certification creates insurmountable pressure on defendants to settle, whereas individual trials would not. . . . The risk of facing an all-or-nothing verdict presents too high a risk, even when the probability of an adverse judgment is low. [In the Matter of Rhone-Poulenc Rorer, Inc.,] 51 F.3d [1293,] 1298 [(7th Cir.), cert. denied, 516 U.S. 867 (1995)]. These settlements have been referred to as judicial blackmail.

It is no surprise then, that historically, certification of mass tort litigation classes has been disfavored. The traditional concern over the rights of defendants in mass tort class actions is magnified in the instant case. Our specific concern is that a mass tort cannot be properly certified without a prior track record of trials from which the district court can draw the information necessary to make the predominance and superiority requirements required by rule 23. This is because certification of an immature tort results in a higher than normal risk that the class action may not be superior to individual adjudication.

We first address the district court's superiority analysis. The court acknowledged the extensive manageability problems with this class. Such problems include difficult choice of law determinations, subclassing of eight claims with variations in state law, *Erie* guesses, notice to millions of class members, further subclassing to take account of transient plaintiffs, and the difficult procedure for determining who is nicotine-dependent. . . .

The district court's rationale for certification in spite of such problems — *i.e.*, that a class trial would preserve judicial resources in the millions of inevitable individual trials — is based on pure speculation. Not every mass tort is asbestos, and not every mass tort will result in the same judicial crises. . . .

Severe manageability problems and the lack of a judicial crisis are not the only reasons why superiority is lacking. The most compelling rationale for finding superiority in a class action — the existence of a negative value suit — is missing in this case. Accord Phillips Petroleum Co. v. Shutts, 472 U.S. 797, 809 (1985); *Rhone-Poulenc*, 51 F.3d at 1299.

As he stated in the record, plaintiffs' counsel in this case has promised to inundate the courts with individual claims if class certification is denied. Independently of the reliability of this self-serving promise, there is reason to believe that individual suits are feasible. First, individual damage claims are high, and punitive damages are available in most states. The expense of litigation does not necessarily turn this case into a negative value suit, in part because the prevailing party may recover attorneys' fees under many consumer protection statutes. . . . [W]e cannot say that it would be a waste to allow individual trials to proceed, before a district court engages in the complicated predominance and superiority analysis necessary to certify a class.

The remaining rationale for superiority — judicial efficiency — also lacking. In the context of an immature tort, any savings in judicial resources is speculative, and any imagined savings would be overwhelmed by the procedural problems that certification of a *sui generis* cause of action brings with it. . . .

The district court's predominance inquiry, or lack of it, squarely presents the problems associated with certification of immature torts. Determining whether the common issues are a "significant" part of each individual case has an abstract quality to it when no court in this country has ever tried an injury-as-addiction claim. As the plaintiffs admitted to the district court, "we don't have the learning curb [sic] that is necessary to say to Your Honor 'this is precisely how this case can be tried and that will not run afoul of the teachings of the 5th Circuit.'"

Yet, an accurate finding on predominance is necessary before the court can certify a class. It may turn out that the defendant's conduct, while common, is a minor part of each trial. Premature certification deprives the defendant of the opportunity to present that argument to any court and risks decertification after considerable resources have been expended. . . .

Through individual adjudication, the plaintiffs can winnow their claims to the strongest causes of action. The result will be an easier choice of law inquiry and a less complicated predominance inquiry. State courts can address the more novel of the plaintiffs' claims, making the federal court's *Erie* guesses less complicated. It is far more desirable to allow state courts to apply and develop their own law than to have a federal court apply "a kind of Esperanto [jury] instruction." *Rhone-Poulenc*, 51 F.3d at 1300 . . . .

The full development of trials in every state will make subclassing an easier process. . . .

Another factor weighing heavily in favor of individual trials is the risk that in order to make this class action manageable, the court will be forced to bifurcate issues in violation of the Seventh Amendment. This class action is permeated with individual issues, such as proximate causation, comparative negligence, reliance, and compensatory damages. In order to manage so many individual issues, the district court proposed to empanel a class jury to adjudicate common issues. A second jury, or a number of "second" juries, will pass on the individual issues, either on a case-by-case basis or through group trials of individual plaintiffs.

The Seventh Amendment entitles parties to have fact issues decided by one jury, and prohibits a second jury from reexamining those facts and issues.... Alabama v. Blue Bird Body Co., 573 F.2d 309, 318 (5th Cir. 1978) (citations and footnotes omitted)....

Severing a defendant's conduct from comparative negligence results in the type of risk that our court forbade in *Blue Bird*. Comparative negligence, by definition, requires a comparison between the defendant's and the plaintiff's conduct. *Rhone-Poulenc*, 51 F.3d at 1303.... At a bare minimum, a second jury will rehear evidence of the defendant's conduct. There is a risk that in apportioning fault, the second jury could reevaluate the defendant's fault, determine that the defendant was not at fault, and apportion 100% of the fault to the plaintiff. In such a situation, the second jury would be impermissibly reconsidering the findings of a first jury. The risk of such reevaluation is so great that class treatment can hardly be said to be superior to individual adjudication....

IV.

The district court abused its discretion by ignoring variations in state law and how a trial on the alleged causes of action would be tried. Those errors cannot be corrected on remand because of the novelty of the plaintiffs' claims. Accordingly, class treatment is not superior to individual adjudication.

We have once before stated that "traditional ways of proceeding reflect far more than habit. They reflect the very culture of the jury trial...." In re Fibreboard Corp., 893 F.2d 706, 711 (5th Cir. 1990). The collective wisdom of individual juries is necessary before this court commits the fate of an entire industry or, indeed, the fate of a class of millions, to a single jury. For the forgoing reasons, we reverse and remand with instructions that the district court dismiss the class complaint.

Notes and Questions

1. What do *Jenkins* and *Castano* tell us about how Rule 23(b)(3) should be interpreted? What does it really mean to say that common questions "predominate"? If it intended to be a quantitative test, then aren't there more non-common than common questions in *Jenkins*? If it is not a quantitative test and instead a test of desirability, then how is it distinct from the superiority test?

2. How should the superiority test be applied? Must the court consider all available devices for the aggregation of the relevant claims as well as the alternative of individualized adjudication of the claims? If the claims are not viable except in the form of a class action, should the class be certified despite enormous management difficulties? Or should the plaintiffs be denied access to any judicial remedy at all?

3. Rule 23(b)(3) lists four factors "pertinent" to the issues of predominance and superiority:

"(A) the interest of members of the class in individually controlling the prosecution or defense of separate actions; (B) the extent and nature of any litigation concerning the controversy already commenced by or against members of the class; (C) the desirability or undesirability of concentrating the litigation of the claims in the particular forum; (D) the difficulties likely to be encountered in the management of a class action."

All four factors seem obviously relevant to the superiority test, but what does any of the factors have to do with the question of whether common questions predominate over non-common questions? Cf. Haley v. Medtronic, Inc., 169 F.R.D. 643 (C.D. Cal. 1996) (finding that common questions predominated, but class action was not superior; four factors applied only to superiority inquiry).

Rule 23(b)(3) offers no explanation of how such different factors are to be weighed against one another. Factor A reflects the preference for traditional litigation. But how is this normative preference for individual autonomy to be balanced against the efficiency benefits of class litigation? Why is Factor B relevant, and which way does the existence of pending litigation cut? How much has Factor C been undercut by the subsequent enactment of 28 U.S.C. § 1407? Since most class actions pose substantial management difficulties compared to traditional bi-polar litigation, does Factor D mean the class should be certified unless it is entirely unmanageable?

Note that neither *Jenkins* not *Castano* directly addresses the four factors, focusing instead on the central questions of predominance and superiority. The same focus is also true of other recent appellate decisions on Rule 23(b)(3). See, *e.g.*, In the Matter of Rhone-Poulenc Rorer, Inc., 51 F.3d 1293 (7th Cir.), cert. denied, 516 U.S. 867 (1995); In re American Medical Systems, Inc., 75 F.3d 1069 (6th Cir. 1996); Valentino v. Carter-Wallace, Inc., 97 F.3d 1227 (9th Cir. 1996). It is more common for decisions in the district court to rely on the four factors. See, *e.g.*, *Haley*, 169 F.R.D. 643.

4. How could one jury in *Jenkins* be expected to resolve more than 1,000 asbestos claims when the jury must both make classwide findings and then decide all individual issues in "mini-trials" of seven to ten plaintiffs? Would this process run afoul of the Seventh Amendment as interpreted in *Castano*, or would the fact that it was the same jury avoid the problem? Wouldn't such a plan turn a few individuals into a professional jury for the rest of their lives?

The trial process in *Jenkins* turned out to be far more cumbersome and difficult than *Jenkins* envisioned. For the later developments in the case, see pp. 1306-10, *infra*.

5. How relevant was it in *Jenkins* that one plaintiffs' lawyer controlled about 80% of the individual cases? That the class consisted only of plaintiffs that had already *filed* their cases in the Eastern District of Texas? Would consolidation under Rule 42(a) have been a superior method for handling the cases? See p. 473, *supra*. What benefits did the class action create that consolidation could not? Do those benefits outweigh the deprivation for 20% of the class of the lawyer of their choice?

6. To what extent should objections to certifying voluntary class actions be ignored because, under Rule 23(c)(2), the members of a (b)(3) class are entitled to notice and the opportunity to opt-out? Does your answer depend on whether, before they make their decision, class members have the benefit of advice of counsel and truly understand the advantages and disadvantages of opting out?

7. Apart from a few cases, like *Jenkins*, appellate courts remain largely hostile to mass tort class actions in product liability cases. *Castano* is an influential exemplar of this trend, but there are others. We have already examined *Rhone-Poulenc* (p. 540, *supra*); and *American Medical Systems* (p. 574, *supra*), in which the Sixth Circuit found not only that the requirements of Rule 23(a) had not been established, but also found that neither the predominance nor the superiority test of Rule 23(b)(3) had been established. Likewise, in *Valentino*, the Ninth Circuit refused to create an absolute bar against multi-state plaintiff class actions for medical products liability, but nonetheless overturned certification of a nationwide class against a drug manufacturer because the trial court had not conducted a "rigorous analysis" of the requirements of Rule 23 and had not made the detailed findings of predominance and superiority necessary for certification of a (b)(3) mass tort. Some of that hostility has filtered down to the level of the district courts. See, *e.g.*, *Haley*, 169 F.R.D. 643; Arch v. American Tobacco Co., 175 F.R.D. 469 (E.D. Pa. 1997). *Arch* is a particularly interesting case, for it represented the next wave of tobacco class action litigation after the plaintiffs' defeat in *Castano* — a single-state class action designed to avoid the multistate predominance and superiority problems identified in *Castano*. *Arch* held that a class of Pennsylvania smokers satisfied the requirements of Rule 23(a), but, as in *Castano*, failed to meet the predominance and superiority requirements of Rule 23(b)(3). In a noteworthy aspect of the decision, the district court held that, although the use of classes to decide certain issues was appropriate, "the court must first find that a cause of action, as whole, satisfies the predominance requirement of (b)(3)." Id. at 496.

On the other hand, some courts still demonstrate a willingness to certify classes or subclasses that are tailored to avoid the multistate problems that put such pressure on the predominance and superiority tests. See In re Telectronics Pacing Systems, Inc., Accufix Atrial "J" Leads Products Liability Litigation, 172 F.R.D. 271 (S.D. Ohio 1997).

8. Class actions under (b)(3) have been approved as a device for aggregating the claims of large numbers of landowners and others allegedly injured by environmental pollution from a single site. See, *e.g.*, Ouellette v. International Paper Co., 86 F.R.D. 476 (D. Vt. 1980) (pulp mill on lake); Sterling v. Velsicol Chemical Corp., 855 F.2d 1188 (6th Cir. 1988) (chemical waste burial site); Boggs v. Divested Atomic Corp., 141 F.R.D. 58 (S.D. Ohio 1991) (plant handling radioactive materials). Should the courts be more generous in certifying environmental class actions in which there is a common interest in cleaning up the environment than product liability cases in which the dominant remedy is money damages? See In re Three Mile Island Litigation, 87 F.R.D. 433 (M.D. Pa. 1980) (certifying class action for persons suffering economic harm from release of radioactive material and for purposes of medical monitoring of nearby residents, but refusing to certify class of persons claiming physical injuries).

9. Likewise, courts have usually been more willing to certify classes in cases seeking to recover for damages to property. See, *e.g.*, Central Wesleyan College v. W.R. Grace & Co., 6 F.3d 177 (4th Cir. 1993) (colleges and universities seeking damages for friable asbestos); but see In re Stucco Litigation, 175 F.R.D. 210 (E.D.N.C. 1997) (non-common questions predominated in cases alleging defects in insulation materials). Difficult management problems have plagued this kind of litigation, however, and in one case ten years elapsed with no trial

having been held. See In re School Asbestos Litigation, 977 F.2d 764 (3d. Cir. 1992).

10. One part of the omnibus tobacco bill that failed to pass the Senate in 1998 was a provision that terminated all pending class action suits against tobacco companies, and precluded any future class actions from being certified. See S. 1415, 105th Cong. 2d Sess., § 701(b)(1) (1998). Does this fact suggest to you that *Castano* was right? That the entire issue of class actions in mass torts should be left to Congress?

11. To what extent is the difficulty seen in the certification of (b)(3) mass tort actions a reflection of the distinction between complex and complicated cases? Most complex cases — cases in which the inability to adjudicate all claims in a single proceeding jeopardizes the ability of early- or late-filing claimants to obtain a meaningful remedy — can be fit within Rule 23(b)(1) or (b)(2); for the most part, the only cases that fit within Rule 23(b)(3) are the complicated cases which would be arguably efficient, but not essential from the viewpoint of fundamental remedial fairness, to handle in a single proceeding. When each plaintiff can be assured of obtaining a completely adequate remedy in an individual proceeding, and when the stakes are sufficiently large that the plaintiff has an incentive to bring the suit if she chooses, efficiency gains are an insufficient reason to force a plaintiff to sacrifice the adversarial right to be master of her own complaint — unless, perhaps, those efficiency gains are utterly overwhelming (which they were certainly not in *Castano*).

This view of Rule 23(b)(3) makes certification in mass tort cases difficult, though not impossible. When there is reason to doubt the ability to obtain a complete remedy (yet that doubt does not rise to the level of permitting a mandatory class), when the stakes are too small to justify individual litigation, or, arguably, when the efficiency gains are overwhelming, (b)(3) can still be used. *Jenkins*, which arose just as asbestos manufacturers were starting to file bankruptcy and everyone was just beginning to realize that the assets of asbestos companies were inadequate, would seemingly fall into the first exception. If tobacco litigation ultimately goes the route of asbestos litigation, and if it begins to appear that the assets of tobacco companies are inadequate, *Castano*, which seems correctly decided under the standards suggested in this Note, would need to be revisited. (Note that these standards make use of *Castano*'s concern that tobacco litigation is insufficiently mature, but the test for determining the litigation's maturity is rather different than the one *Castano* suggests.)

Should this be test used for (b)(3) certifications of mass torts?

12. Mass tort class actions for damages are largely unknown in other countries. In recent years, however, certain courts in Canada and Australia have begun to permit them. See Jon G. Fleming, *Mass Torts*, 42 Am. J. Comp. L. 507, 521 (1994).

13. There is a large literature exploring the advantages and disadvantages of aggregation in mass tort cases. See, *e.g.*, David Rosenberg, *Individual Justice and Collectivizing Risk-Based Claims in Mass-Exposure Cases*, 71 N.Y.U. L. Rev. 210 (1996); David Rosenberg, *Class Actions for Mass Torts: Doing Individual Justice by Collective Means*, 62 Ind. L.J. 561 (1987); Linda S. Mullenix, *Beyond Consolidation: Post-Aggregative Procedure in Asbestos Mass Tort Litigation*, 32 Wm. & Mary L. Rev. 475 (1991); Francis E. McGovern, *An Analysis of Mass Torts*

for Judges, 73 Tex. L. Rev. 1821 (1995); Francis E. McGovern, *Resolving Mature Mass Tort Litigation*, 69 B.U. L. Rev. 659 (1989).

3. Settlement Class Actions

Class actions, like most lawsuits, are settled more often than they are tried. Given the enormous consequences to both sides should they lose, this fact is hardly surprising. In recent years, however, the parties have found a new, and rather different, use for class actions — the settlement class action. Unlike the litigation class action that happens to settle, the settlement class action is designed at the outset to settle the contested issues between class members and the defendants. The negotiations over the terms of the settlement typically occur before the class is certified, and the defendants agree to settle the case only if the case is settled on a classwide basis. Therefore, rather than fighting class certification, the defendants actively support certification. The reason that they do so is simple: The class action promises to bring the defendant total peace from further litigation; the defendants have substituted a fixed cost for the uncertainties of litigation, and can go on about their business.

As a theoretical matter, settlement class actions raise the same policy concerns as litigation class actions, but the emphasis of those issues is somewhat different. For instance, the concern for excessive deterrence is essentially gone, since defendants have agreed to the settlement terms. Likewise, the court's manageability concerns are downplayed, since the case will never be litigated. On the other hand, concerns for collusion increase, since the defendants might shop for lawyers who are likely to give them the best deal. Concerns for adequacy also rise, because the negotiations often take place before a certification order has determined that the counsel and class representatives are effective representatives of the class. Concerns that the parties are using the courts as a quasi-administrative agency to distribute proceeds are significant. The inability of class members to contest the certification effectively, and thus to decide whether to give up their right to litigate their own cases, creates additional concerns.

One of the great advantages of the settlement class action — at least to those who wish to resolve all cases in a single forum — is that the settlement class action can in theory be used to settle not only the cases of those with present claims, but also those with claims that will not mature until some point in the future. We encountered the issue of these "future plaintiffs" briefly in Chapter Three. (See p. 363, *supra*.) In many types of class action litigation, there are no future plaintiffs; for instance, in a typical securities case, a past misrepresentation has already caused all the legally cognizable financial harm that it can before the lawsuit commences. On the other hand, in a race discrimination class action seeking injunctive relief, every class member is a "future plaintiff," in the sense that the threatened conduct, and thus the threatened harm, has not yet occurred. The type of "future plaintiffs" that we describe here, however, are a hybrid; they are victims of wrongful conduct that occurred in the past (and are thus unlike class members seeking only injunctive relief), but their injuries have not yet manifested themselves (and are thus unlike class members who seek compensation for past harms). The classic "future plaintiffs" are those that have been exposed to a toxic substance in the past (thus, the wrongful conduct has occurred), but due to the latency period before injury develops have no present injury (thus the harm has not yet occurred). Since these future plaintiffs do not, by definition, have present injuries, it is impossible to bring them within the confines of a litigation class action. But a settlement class action is not necessarily so constrained. Defendants have always been able to settle — on an individual basis — the claims of future plaintiffs even if these plaintiffs cannot yet litigate the cases. The only issue is whether they can use the class action to settle with everyone.

Obviously, the settlement class action portends to be the most powerful aggregation device we have seen, at least with settlement-minded defendants. But the express language of Rule 23 does not contemplate settlement class actions. Thus, the text of the rule leaves unanswered a host of important questions: Can the class representatives and class counsel negotiate a settlement on behalf of the class before the class has been certified? When must notice of the settlement be given to the class and what should the contents of that notice be? How is a trial judge to determine whether a proposed settlement is fair and reasonable or the product of collusion and conflicts of interest between the parties and their counsel? Is it permissible to certify a class action for settlement purposes when it is apparent that the case would not meet the Rule 23 criteria as a litigation class action? Can settlement class actions include the claims of future plaintiffs? Should the complexity or complication of the case make a difference in the use of settlement class actions? In short, is the settlement class action the Holy Grail of aggregation devices, or another occasionally useful dead-end?

IN RE BALDWIN-UNITED CORP.

105 F.R.D. 475 (S.D.N.Y. 1984)

■ BRIEANT, District Judge. These consolidated cases, transferred to the Southern District of New York by the Judicial Panel on Multidistrict Litigation on February 27, 1984, arise out of the sale by insurance company subsidiaries of Baldwin-United Corporation of certain contracts known to the Court as single premium deferred annuities ("SPDAs"). These SPDAs were issued principally between 1979 and May 1983 by National Investors Life Insurance Company, an Arkansas insurance corporation, and University Life Insurance Company of America, an Indiana insurance corporation. The annuities were sold to the public on a nation-wide basis through various broker-dealers and other entities.

In July 1983, the two issuing insurance companies, as well as four companies which reinsured the SPDAs in part, were placed in rehabilitation. The ultimate corporate parent of these six companies, Baldwin-United Corporation, entered bankruptcy proceedings pursuant to voluntary and involuntary petitions for reorganization filed on September 26, 1983. During 1983 and 1984 SPDA purchasers filed more than 90 federal civil actions alleging fraud and/or violations of the federal and state securities laws and other pendent state law claims. Finding that the initial forty actions before it involved common questions of fact, the MDL Panel ordered that they be transferred to this district court for coordinated or consolidated pre-trial proceedings pursuant to 28 U.S.C. § 1407. . . .

This Court held a pre-trial conference on April 3, 1984 and thereafter entered pre-trial orders approving the creation of a plaintiff's steering committee and providing, among other things, for the filing of separate consolidated class complaints with respect to each of the unrelated broker-dealer defendants. . . .

A recent significant event with which the within motion is concerned is the filing beginning on September 21, 1984 of fourteen stipulations of settlement between plaintiffs and the defendants in fourteen of the actions (the "settling actions"). The parties to the proposed settlements now request the Court (1) to certify tentative or conditional classes solely for the purpose of considering the proposed settlement; (2) to conduct a fairness hearing on whether the proposed settlements should be approved; and (3) to order that notice of the hearing be sent to members of the proposed class and to resolve issues affecting the content of such notice. . . .

Whether this Court should certify a conditional settlement class solely for purposes of approving or disapproving a settlement already formulated by the parties is a controversial issue. On one hand, the current edition of the Manual for Complex Litigation, § 1.46 (5th ed. 1982) ("Manual"), concludes that tentative classes for the purpose of settlement ordinarily should not be formed. . . . Similarly there is an apparent inconsistency between the language of Rule 23, F.R.Civ.P., and a mechanism whereby formal class certification would be bypassed until a date when first notice of the pendency of a class action and notice of a proposed settlement are sent simultaneously to prospective class members. . . . On the other hand, many courts have employed this practice in the name of judicial efficiency in order to facilitate apparently beneficial settlement proposals.

For the reasons set forth below, this Court finds that under the circumstances of the cases at bar, tentative class certification for settlement purposes only is appropriate at this time and is in the interests of Justice. . . .

Among the policy reasons advanced by the Manual is the concern that class members will not have been represented adequately during settlement negotiations due to the fact that the negotiations precede judicial findings as to the prerequisites to class formation under Rule 23(a). . . . The Court agrees that arguments in opposition to settlement classes have merit when they are addressed to the problem of inadequate representation or possible collusion among the named plaintiffs and some or all defendants. Rule 23(a)(4), F.R.Civ.P. However, in the case at bar, there is no danger of inadequate representation because all of the named plaintiffs have virtually identical claims for recovery which have been pursued by a steering committee and liaison counsel exclusively authorized to negotiate on behalf of the class by Pretrial Order No. 1 entered by this Court on April 11, 1984. The settlement class representatives have the same class interests as would a typical conditional class representative selected after a Rule 23 evidentiary hearing, and have no incentive to engage in collusion or recommend an improvident settlement in order to serve some unrelated purpose of their own.

This is not a case where several different counsel were competing for designation as class representatives; nor is this a case where defendants had the opportunity during negotiations to play one plaintiff's attorney off against another.... These dangers were prevented by the early designation of a plaintiffs' steering committee in Pretrial Order No. 1, and the enumeration therein of the committee's powers and duties. No plaintiffs' counsel in this multidistrict action other than members of the steering committee have had the authority to negotiate for settlements on behalf of the proposed classes in the settling actions. Thus plaintiffs have spoken with one consistent voice during settlement discussions and one of the Manual's major concerns is absent....

Another of the policy reasons supporting the Manual's rationale against the tentative settlement class mechanism is that there can be no assurance that the membership of the class will be delineated appropriately or that the tentative class will not be composed of plaintiffs with conflicting interests. Again, this important concern is not implicated in the case at bar, because the facts show that all SPDA purchasers from the settling defendants are readily identifiable through the books and records of the issuing insurance companies, and all are treated alike by the settlements. The tentative class members thus have no conflicts among themselves; they all stand to gain the exact same relief through the proportionate formula of recovery contained in the stipulations of settlement. Here, there is no danger comparable to that perceived in Plummer v. Chemical Bank, 668 F.2d 654 (2d Cir. 1982), where the court expressed its concern over preferential treatment afforded the named plaintiffs by the proposed settlement.

Yet another policy reason expressed in the Manual is that formation of a settlement class preempts determination of whether plaintiffs should continue to litigate their claims for relief with an eye towards a better settlement agreement or even a trial on the merits. In the stipulations of settlement filed herein, the class members have been provided with a full opportunity to object to the terms of the settlement while remaining a member of the class.... As an alternative, plaintiffs can opt out of a settlement class and pursue their litigation goals either individually or as another putative class. This procedure ... safeguards the individual freedom of choice of each SPDA purchaser from a settling defendant. Also it appears more sensible under the circumstances of this case to provide SPDA purchasers with the financial information contained in the settlement agreements now, so that they will have a more concrete basis for deciding whether to opt out of a plaintiffs' class, than to expect opt-out decisions to precede advisement of the possibility of settlement, as they typically must do under the policy of the Manual. ...

The Court of Appeals for the Second Circuit has ruled that it "refuse[s] to adopt a *per se* rule prohibiting approval when a class action settlement has been reached by means of settlement classes certified after the settlement, with notice simultaneous with that of the settlement . . . ." Weinberger v. Kendrick, 698 F.2d [61,] 73 [(2d Cir. 1982), cert. denied, 464 U.S. 818 (1983)]. In so holding, the Court stressed that the trial courts "are bound to scrutinize the fairness of the settlement agreement with even more than the usual care . . . in order to meet the concerns noted in the Manual." Id. at 73. If the settlement agreement is found to be fair, reasonable and adequate — both in its substantive provisions and in the process of its creation — then the policy reasons behind the Manual's admonition become inapplicable. . . .

[One objector has] contended that, as a practical matter, SPDA purchasers will not exercise their opt-out rights. This contention is speculative. . . .

The better solution for this perceived problem would be to make certain that the form of notice approved by the Court is sufficiently clear and informative in its content and directions . . . .

Similarly, objections voiced by [other objectors] do not persuade the Court that a tentative class for settlement purposes should not be certified. The only objectors who have argued to the Court in opposition to the within motion are plaintiffs Shay, Bernard and Anna Shipman, and the Intervening guaranty associations. This small amount of opposition, in view of the relatively widespread publicity and the circulation of the settlement stipulations among plaintiffs' counsel, is another factor which supports approval of tentative class certification and the scheduling of a fairness hearing.

Upon consideration of the proposed settlement presented to this Court for preliminary approval, the Court finds that it is at least sufficiently fair, reasonable and adequate to justify notice to those affected and an opportunity to be heard. The substantive terms of the proposed agreement call for a cash payment of approximately $138,000,000 to the members of the classes in the fourteen settling actions. According to the affidavit of plaintiffs' liaison counsel, . . . this fund "represents a payment of approximately 30% of the damages sustained by members of the class when measured by the difference between the tangible assets in the hands of the rehabilitators and the liabilities of the rehabilitators to the members of the classes." In comparing the advantages of an immediate cash payment with the risks involved in long and uncertain litigation, it appears that the settlement is sufficiently substantial at this stage to present it to the SPDA purchasers and conduct a fairness hearing on notice.

The terms of the settlement also appear fair because they do not differentiate among the broker-dealer defendants in any way that would suggest collusion or abuse. Each of the defendants is to pay in the same ratio and each class member is to obtain the same proportionate settlement regardless of which broker-dealer sold the SPDA. In addition, the fact that there are several broker-defendants who were presented with the opportunity to join these settlement stipulations and declined to do so implies that the settlement terms are favorable to the plaintiffs and that the negotiations preceding settlement operated in the required adversarial posture free of any possible collusion.

In order to supplement judicial examination of the substance of a compromise agreement, and because a court cannot conduct a trial in order to avoid a trial, attention must be paid to the process by which a settlement has been reached. . . . The negotiations in these settling actions were conducted on behalf of plaintiffs by experienced attorneys who are familiar with this type of litigation. As a consequence, their judgment is entitled to some weight. . . . The Court finds that the negotiating parties considered [the relevant] legal issues during the course of negotiations and, at least based on information presently available to the Court, they have been able to assess fairly the value of the claims asserted in the class complaints against the settling broker-dealer defendants.

Both the Intervenor-Plaintiffs (six state guaranty associations) and a California plaintiff . . . object that the settlements are not within the range of reasonableness because formal discovery has not occurred. While it is true that full-fledged discovery has not been had, this is not always a bar to class certification or even to approving a settlement. . . .

In addition to discussions with defense counsel over a three-month period, plaintiffs' steering committee has had access to the expert testimony and other evidence received by the Arkansas and Indiana state courts supervising the development of rehabilitation plans. Plaintiffs' steering committee has had available for its review various documents produced by some of the settling defendants in response to plaintiffs' initial discovery requests. The Stipulations of Settlement . . . provide that this production will continue during the notice period. Finally, a vast amount of relevant discoverable information was available through public documents concerning the financial condition of Baldwin-United Corporation and its subsidiaries. We believe that counsel availed themselves of all of these sources of information and conducted full adversarial negotiations, as they were authorized to do by Pretrial Order No. 1.

In light of the foregoing, the Court finds that a conditional class should be certified for the purpose of considering the proposed settlements. The requirements of numerosity, typicality, common questions of law or fact, and adequacy of representation have been met and the Court finds that, under Rule 23(b)(3), the tentative class procedure presents the most efficient method for adjudication of the immediate issues presented by the parties to the settling actions. . . .

[The court turned to the notice that needed to be sent to the members of the class.] The approved class notice fairly apprises "prospective class members of the class action's pendency, the relevant terms of the proposed settlement[s], and their options in connection with [this] case." *Weinberger*, 698 F.2d at 70. The notice adequately describes, among other things, the status of the rehabilitation proceedings, the litigation posture of the plaintiffs and the settling defendants, the settlement fund, and the application for attorneys' fees and expenses. In addition the notice advises the class members as to what effect the settlements will have on the future legal rights of class members.

As to the "opt-out" provisions contained in the notice, the Court finds that these instructions and explanations are clear and easy to follow. They inform class members that if requests for exclusion are not received in the manner specified, then the class member shall be bound by any judgments rendered by the Court pursuant to the settlement of the settling actions. The notice also provides that a settling class member who has not opted out may file objections and appear at the fairness hearing. It is proper for the notice to require opt-outs to be filed prior to the fairness hearing since this procedure "places potential objectors in no worse position than occurs when formal class certification precedes settlement...." *Weinberger*, 698 F.2d at 72....

All of the foregoing is without prejudice to the findings the Court will make after conducting the fairness hearing, at which time all objections or arguments in opposition to the proposed settlements will be heard and considered and proponents must discharge their burden to prove that the proposed settlement agreements are fair and reasonable.

Notes and Questions

1. Unlike the version discussed in *Baldwin-United*, the most recent edition of the *Manual for Complex Litigation* endorses the concept of settlement class actions even in cases where a litigation class action might not be certifiable. Manual for Complex Litigation, Third § 30.4 (1995).

2. When a trial judge reviews a class action settlement to determine if it is fair to the class, is the trial judge to act as a backup, surrogate lawyer for the class? How is this role consistent with the traditional role of the trial judge as neutral umpire? Can the judge rely on the fact that there may have been adversarial individual litigation before the settlement was entered?

3. How effective can a trial judge be in assessing the fairness of a settlement in cases like *Baldwin-United* when: (1) most of the information about the merits of the plaintiffs' case and the strength of possible defenses is in the possession of the lawyers who concocted the settlement and now seek its approval; (2) when little or no discovery about the merits of the case has yet occurred; and (3) when any collusion between counsel regarding fees or kickbacks is unlikely to be documented or readily discoverable by dissenting class members?

4. How likely is it that a trial judge will extensively and vigorously investigate the fairness of a settlement when she has a powerful incentive to approve the settlement in order to remove from an already overcrowded docket a particularly difficult case? See In re Ford Motor Co. Bronco II Products Liability Litigation, 1995 WL 222177 (E.D. La.) (trial judge rejected class action settlement that gave class members a safety videotape, a sun-visor warning sticker, a road map, and a free truck inspection, but awarded $4 million in fees to counsel for the class).

5. Should the judge worry about possible conflicts of interest within a class between the class and class counsel if the terms of the settlement itself appear

to be fair and reasonable? Should the judge worry about collusion between class representatives and/or class counsel and the defendant if the settlement appears to be fair and reasonable? In other words, should an apparently fair substantive bargain ever be rejected because of perceived defects in the bargaining process leading to it? How much is procedural fairness worth? See Mars Steel Corp. v. Illinois National Bank and Trust Co. of Chicago, 834 F.2d 677 (7th Cir. 1987) (district court should focus on the substantive terms of the settlement because the "proof of the pudding was indeed in the eating"); cf. Pettway v. American Cast Iron Pipe Co., 576 F.2d 1157 (5th Cir. 1978), cert. denied, 439 U.S. 1115 (1979) (permitting appeal of final relief in litigation class action even though class counsel refused to appeal); John C. Coffee, Jr., *Class Wars: The Dilemma of Mass Tort Class Actions*, 95 Colum. L. Rev. 1343, 1346 (1995) (asserting that "individual plaintiffs have weak to nonexistent control over their attorneys across the mass tort context for reasons that are inherent to the economics of mass tort litigation.").

Assuming that conflicts of interest or collusion are a concern, how should trial judges manage and evaluate settlement class actions to assure that the interests of some absent class members are not being sacrificed for the benefit of other class members or counsel? How should lawyers representing a class determine what is an appropriate negotiation strategy on behalf of the class? See Nancy Morawetz, *Bargaining, Class Representation, and Fairness*, 54 Ohio St. L.J. 1 (1993) (arguing that class counsel will often face stark distributional choices between class members when negotiating a settlement and must develop a coherent theory of fairness to arbitrate these differences).

6. How many of the foregoing problems exist because Rule 23 contains no provisions governing how a class is supposed to make decisions about, for example, whether to settle on certain terms, whether to forgo certain claims or types of discovery in order to expedite getting to trial, or whether to retain one set of lawyers or another to represent the class in negotiations? In light of the practical importance to absent class members of such questions, should Rule 23 articulate a scheme for decisionmaking by the class as a whole? *See* Judith Resnik et al., *Individuals Within the Aggregrate: Relationships, Representation, and Fees*, 71 N.Y.U. L. Rev. 296, 300 (1996) (noting that at present "[l]ittle by way of rules or case law guides courts in sorting out the relationships among clients and the many lawyers within group litigation."). Litigants and their lawyers in ordinary litigation often have conflicts of interest, but they have the opportunity for direct and frequent contact as the case progresses. Little to no contact occurs in class actions. See Howard M. Downs, *Federal Class Actions: Diminished Protection for the Class and the Case for Reform*, 73 Neb. L. Rev. 646 (1994) (arguing that the Rule 23 requirements have not been effective in protecting the interest of absent class members whose interests are often compromised by conflicts with that of class counsel or the class representative).

7. In (b)(3) settlement class actions like *Baldwin-United*, individual class members have the right to opt out of the settlement and litigate their claims individually. Why should the trial judge pass on the fairness of the settlement when each class member is free to do so? In ordinary litigation, trial judges do not check on the fairness of the terms of settlement before dismissing the case. Is the concern that class members will be uninformed and unsophisticated? That class notice will be one-sided? In mandatory settlement class actions, class members have the right to voice objections to the terms of the settlement, but if the trial judge approves the settlement over the objection, the dissenting class

member has no opportunity to opt out and is bound by the settlement. Does this fact mean that a higher standard of fairness and greater scrutiny of settlement should be required in mandatory settlement class actions? How much higher? See Jay Tidmarsh, Mass Tort Settlement Class Actions: Five Case Studies and Their Implications for the Reform of Rule 23 (unpublished paper 1998) (analyzing both process of giving notice and content of notice in mandatory and opt-out mass tort settlement class actions).

8. Since *Baldwin-United* was a settlement class action, members of the class had the opportunity to consider the terms of the settlement before making their opt-out decision. In litigation class actions that are later settled, class members who did not opt out following the earlier certification order are ordinarily not given the chance to opt out of the settlement. They may object to its terms, but if the trial judge finds the settlement fair and reasonable, they are bound. Is this fair? For an argument that in such cases class members should be given a second chance to opt out of (b)(3) class actions if they dislike the terms of the settlement, see George Rutherglen, *Better Late Than Never: Notice and Opt Out at the Settlement Stage of Class Actions*, 71 N.Y.U. L. Rev. 258 (1996).

9. Sometimes the plaintiff class may not learn of the true character of a collusive class action settlement until it is too late to opt out or object to the settlement. In Hoffman v. BancBoston Mortgage Corp., No. CV-91-1880 (Mobile Cty. Cir. Ct. Ala. 1994), the state court granted partial summary judgment to the class finding that the defendant-bank had managed the mortgage escrow accounts in a manner inconsistent with mortgage contract and that, in effect, a small sum of money was owed to each member of the class. Thereafter, the bank agreed to a proposed class action settlement. The notice sent to the class said only that the terms of the settlement were reasonable, and that the attorneys fees sought were also reasonable. There were few objections or opt-outs, and the settlement was approved by the state court. The bank credited all money due under the settlement to class members' individual accounts, but numerous class members discovered to their surprise that their share of the attorneys fees, which was automatically deducted from their account, exceeded the credit they had received via the settlement. Outraged, they brought a federal suit against the lawyers for the class, alleging malpractice, fraud, conversion, and RICO claims. They also sued the bank and its lawyers. The district court dismissed their suit. The Seventh Circuit affirmed on the ground that the federal suit was barred by the *Rooker-Feldman* doctrine, which holds that only the United States Supreme Court may review the validity of a state judgment and the time for such review had elapsed. Kamilewicz v. Bank of Boston, 92 F.3d 506 (7th Cir. 1996). Five judges on the Seventh Circuit dissented from the refusal of the circuit to grant rehearing en banc. 100 F.3d 1348 (7th Cir. 1996). The Supreme Court denied certiorari. — U.S. —, 117 S.Ct. 1569 (1997).

10. If a state court approves a settlement class action which purports to release and extinguish not only the state law claims of the class, but also unstated federal claims which may only be asserted in federal court, does that state judgment preclude the later assertion of those federal claims by class members in federal court? In Matsushita Electric Industrial Co. v. Epstein, 516 U.S. 367 (1996), the Supreme Court held the effect of state judgments in this setting was governed by state law and, if state preclusion law permitted the release of exclusive federal claims in this setting — as Delaware law did, then no federal law or policy required otherwise. On remand, the Ninth Circuit found a due process escape to the preclusive effect of the state judgment. See Epstein

v. MCA, Inc., 126 F.3d 1235 (9th Cir. 1997) (p. 179, *supra*). In a provocative article responding to the *Matsushita* decision, Professors Kahan and Silberman argue that state class action settlements encompassing exclusive federal claims present special risks of unfairness, collusion, and the like, and should be approved by state courts only after they adopt special precautions to assure the fairness of the settlement. Marcel Kahan & Linda Silberman, Matsushita *and Beyond: The Role of State Courts in Class Actions Involving Exclusive Federal Claims*, 1996 Sup. Ct. Rev. 219. They have also written a follow-up article critiquing the Ninth Circuit's effort to avoid *Matsushita*. Marcel Kahan & Linda Silberman, *The Inadequate Search for "Adequacy" in Class Actions: A Critique of* Epstein v. MCA, Inc., 73 N.Y.U. L. Rev. 765 (1998). See also Stephen E. Morrissey, Note, *State Settlement Class Actions That Release Exclusive Federal Claims: Developing a Framework for Multijurisdictional Management of Shareholder Litigation*, 95 Colum. L. Rev. 1765 (1995).

11. *Baldwin-United* preliminarily certifies the class, and then orders that a hearing be held to determine if the settlement itself should be approved. What sort of a hearing is appropriate in a settlement class action — an adversarial hearing, an inquisitorial hearing, or an informal hearing in which parties, objectors, and lawyers make presentations? How much discovery should the parties and objectors be entitled to before the hearing — no discovery, informal exchanges of information, or full rights to engage in written discovery and depositions? Can the lawyers that settled the case be deposed? Can their fee arrangements or other possible evidence of collusion be discovered without a colorable showing of collusion? Rule 23(e), which states that class actions can be settled only after court approval, does not answer any of these questions. As a result, courts have used a wide variety of procedures to handle the fairness hearings and pre-hearing discovery. See Jay Tidmarsh, Mass Tort Settlement Class Actions (1998) (describing variety of procedures used in five mass tort settlement class actions). Should Rule 23(e) be amended to provide a single, consistent approach to fairness hearings? In order to guard against some of the concerns regarding settlement class actions, should that approach tend toward an adversarial hearing with full rights of discovery and a full and fair opportunity to explore the issue of collusion?

12. We have already examined the general standards that courts use to determine whether to approve a settlement in a class action. See p. 553, *supra*. Should the standards be the same in settlement class actions, or should the unique circumstance of settlement class actions change the usual factors in some way? See In re General Motors Corp. Pick-Up Truck Fuel Tank Products Liability Litigation, 55 F.3d 768 (3rd Cir.), cert. denied, 516 U.S. 824 (1995) (using same factors); Tidmarsh, *supra* Note 9, at 12 (analyzing factors in five mass tort settlements; factors used were the same as those used in litigation class actions that settled); Tidmarsh, *supra* Note 5, at 235-38 (proposing specific standards for settlement class actions). Cf. Note, *In-Kind Class Action Settlements*, 109 Harv. L. Rev. 810, 812 (1996) (discussing the special difficulties which attend evaluating the reasonableness and adequacy of in-kind settlements).

13. Once a federal court has approved a settlement class action, however, those courts have held that they have the power to enjoin new or ongoing litigation by class members in state court raising the same claims settled in the federal action. See Gross v. Barnett Banks, Inc., 934 F. Supp. 1340 (M.D. Fla. 1995) (even class member who did not receive actual notice of the federal class

action settlement may be enjoined from continuing to litigate his ongoing claim in state court).

14. In many ways, *Baldwin-United* presents a very strong case for settlement. The case had been vigorously litigated (albeit not on a class action basis) for some time. The stakes of most individual investors were small — far too small to justify individual suits. Baldwin-United was in bankruptcy proceedings, thus raising the specter of insufficient assets and the concomitant problem of lawyer dysfunction if a global settlement were not achieved. All the claimants had a present claim; there were no future claimants involved.

In some ways, however, the case was not ideal. The litigation was not fully mature, so it was somewhat difficult to know whether the settlement represented a fair adjustment of the parties' likely chances of success. Class members were allowed to opt out, which potentially created problems if the defendants assets were indeed insufficient. The latter problem was unlikely to arise, for if the assets of the defendants were truly insufficient, few people would opt out of the settlement just for the privilege of ending up with less money. Should the court have addressed the maturity problem by letting some cases proceed to trial? (Recall that numerous state attorneys general had brought suit on behalf of citizens in their states (see p. 402, *supra*), so there were some entities with the incentive to prosecute the cases to trial vigorously.) Or would that tactic have killed the parties' incentive to settle, and doomed the case to a long future course in which the available assets would be consumed in transaction costs? How is a court, sitting *ex ante*, to know whether greater maturity will lead to a better or a worse settlement? Should a hard-and-fast rule on the amount of maturity needed for a settlement class action be established?

15. Beginning in the late 1970s, settlement class actions have been used with some frequency in a range of commercial contexts. See, *e.g.*, In re Beef Industry Antitrust Litigation, 607 F.2d 167 (5th Cir. 1979) (antitrust case), cert. denied, 452 U.S. 905 (1981); Weinberger v. Kendrick, 698 F.2d 61 (2d Cir. 1982) (securities case), cert. denied, 464 U.S. 818 (1983); *Mars Steel*, 834 F.2d 677 (consumer rights). The most famous refusal to approve a settlement class action is probably *GM Pick-Up Truck*, in which GM agreed to settle on a class basis the claims of purchasers of pick-ups that allegedly had a defective fuel tank design that made the trucks susceptible to explosion. The settlement, which did not deal with any claims for personal injury, entitled each pick-up truck owner to a $1,000 coupon toward the purchase of certain other GM trucks or $500 toward the purchase of certain other GM trucks. The total value of the settlement was valued by the district court at about $2 billion. Class counsel received a $9.5 million fee. On appeal, the Third Circuit held both that the class action should not have been certified because of its failure to meet the adequacy of representation requirement of Rule 23(a)(4) and because the settlement itself was not fair, reasonable, and adequate. 55 F.3d 765.

16. The first holding in *GM Pick-Up Truck* — especially the court's observation that the Rule 23(a) and (b) requirements in a settlement class action needed to be interpreted exactly as they would be interpreted for a litigation class action — sent something of a shock wave through the federal courts. The view that was increasingly coming to dominate the jurisprudence of settlement class actions was that, as long as the settlement was substantively fair, some of the Rule 23(a) and (b) requirements could be relaxed; in particular, class members' common interest in a substantively fair settlement served to satisfy the commonality, typicality, adequacy, and predominance prongs of Rules 23 (a)

and (b). See, *e.g.*, Bowling v. Pfizer, 143 F.R.D. 141 (S.D. Ohio 1992). Does it seem intuitively correct that the posture of the case — litigation vs. settlement — should influence the interpretation of Rule 23(a) and (b)? Should the answer to this question depend on whether the case is mature? On whether the injury arises from a single event or a dispersed course of events? On whether future claims are involved? On whether the case is small-stakes litigation in which individual plaintiffs have little incentive to bring individual suits, or large-stakes litigation in which individual suits are viable? On whether the settlement creates ethical difficulties for settling counsel? On whether the settlement prevents lawyer dysfunction that continued litigation would not? The two following cases, including the Supreme Court's first foray into the world of settlement class actions, pursue these questions and provide further guidance.

IN RE ASBESTOS LITIGATION*

90 F.3d 963 (5th Cir. 1996), vacated and remanded, 521 U.S. —, 117 S.Ct. 2503 (1997), affirmed on remand, 134 F.3d 668 (5th Cir. 1998), cert. granted, 118 S.Ct. 2339 (1998)

■ DAVIS, Circuit Judge. In this consolidated appeal, we consider a number of challenges to the district court's approval of a class settlement of future asbestos victims with Fibreboard along with several related settlements. For the reasons that follow, we affirm the district court's judgment.

I. BACKGROUND

[Fibreboard, a manufacturer of asbestos products, faced thousands of asbestos-related tort claims, and the prospect of thousands of additional claims in the future. Fibreboard had approximately $235 million in corporate assets and about $100 million in insurance to pay these claims. It also contended, however, that it had additional insurance coverage under the policies of two of its carriers, Pacific Indemnity and Continental Casualty. The Pacific and Continental policies had been issued in the 1950's, and covered personal injury claims for exposures to Fibreboard's asbestos that occurred before 1957 and 1959, respectively. The policies had a $500,000 per injury cap, but no aggregate cap. Both insurers denied that they were liable in unlimited amounts. Since the two insurers had between them billions of dollars in assets, both Fibreboard and asbestos plaintiffs had a mutual interest in access to these insurance proceeds, while the insurers faced the possibility of crushing liability.

[Fibreboard sued the insurers in California state court, and essentially won on its claim of unlimited coverage. Pacific and Continental appealed. While the case was on appeal, Fibreboard settled its case against Pacific for an amount that was contingent on the outcome of the appeal. Fibreboard also agreed with the Ness, Motley law firm to settle 22,000 of its asbestos

---

* One of the authors of this book was a consultant to one of the insurers in this case. The other was a consultant to the Federal Judicial Center, and performed a study of this case at the request of the Center. — ED.

claims against Fibreboard by assigning Fibreboard's rights under the Continental policy to the plaintiffs. Fibreboard thereafter filed an action in federal court in the Eastern District of Texas, seeking a declaration that this assignment did not violate the Continental policy. At about the same time, the Judicial Panel on Multidistrict Litigation, on the suggestion of the transferee judge in the multidistrict asbestos proceedings, transferred certain asbestos cases against Fibreboard back to the Eastern District of Texas. All of these developments placed great pressure on Continental to seek a settlement.

[With the approval of the parties, Chief Judge Parker of the Eastern District of Texas named Judge Higginbotham of the Fifth Circuit to serve as a settlement facilitator. At Higgonbotham's suggestion the parties negotiated a revised agreement (called the "Substitute Ness Motley Agreement") that resolved all 45,000 asbestos claims that the Ness, Motley firm had filed against Fibreboard. That settlement, which was estimated to exceed $1 billion in value, was funded largely by Continental. Under the terms of the settlement, Ness, Motley agreed to recommend to all future clients the settlement of their claims on the same terms. Judge Parker approved the settlement as fair and reasonable on August 9, 1993.

[Immediately thereafter, at Higginbotham's suggestion, Parker appointed two lawyers from Ness, Motley, plus two other lawyers, as negotiating counsel to attempt to negotiate a global resolution of all future claims against Fibreboard. The impetus for this settlement was the appellate argument in the California coverage case, which was slated to occur on August 27, 1993. After a flurry of intense negotiations among plaintiffs' counsel, Fibreboard, and its insurer — during which the insurers insisted that they would settle only if the settlement brought them total peace from any future claims — the parties agreed to a global settlement. First, the insurers agreed to pay Fibreboard $475 million to defend and settle all filed claims not covered by the Substitute Ness Motley Agreement. Second, the parties agreed to a global $1.535 billion settlement of unfiled claims. The insurers paid nearly the entire $1.535 billion; Fibreboard contributed only $10 million to the settlement, which was called the "Global Settlement Agreement." Third, Fibreboard and its insurers also negotiated a separate backup agreement (called the "Trilateral Settlement Agreement") of their coverage disputes in case Judge Parker declined to approve the Global Settlement Agreement with the plaintiffs. Under the Trilateral Settlement Agreement, Fibreboard received $1.525 billion to pay all costs of defense, judgment, and settlement for all unfiled claims; when joined with the $475 million to defend and pay present claims, this settlement gave Fibreboard a total of $2 billion to deal with all asbestos claims against it. Under either the Global Settlement Agreement or the Trilateral Settlement Agreement, the insurers were essentially able to walk away without further exposure.

[The Global Settlement Agreement called for the creation of a trust, funded with the $1.535 billion, which was to administer and pay all future asbestos personal injury and death claims. The amount of any settlement was to be determined by the historical value of settlements for comparable injuries, reduced to Fibreboard's pro rata share of the injury. The settlement restricted the amount of trust funds that could be paid out in any one year in order to assure that funds would be available for all class members. Under the agreement, a class member was required first to try to settle his claim with the trust. If no agreement was reached, the claimant would then proceed to mediation, arbitration, and finally tort litigation before a jury or judge. (This ultimate right to re-enter the tort system is usually called a "back-end opt-out right.") In the tort system, however, the claimant could recover no more than $500,000 per claim in compensatory damages, and punitive damages were barred.

[Once the Global Settlement Agreement had been reached in principle, plaintiffs' counsel filed *Ahearn v. Fibreboard Corp. Ahearn* sought certification of a mandatory class under Rule 23(b) and requested approval of the settlement. Parker promptly granted provisional class certification and enjoined any separate litigation against Fibreboard by class members. Fibreboard's insurers also filed a mandatory defendant class action against Fibreboard's major co-defendants to settle and extinguish any claims for contribution and indemnity. In this suit, Fibreboard's insurers also sought judicial approval of the backup Trilateral Settlement Agreement in the event the Global Settlement Agreement was not approved. This action was called *Rudd*.

[Notice was given to members of the classes affected by the proposed settlements. A law professor was appointed to serve as guardian ad litem for the *Ahearn* class. Several counsel intervened to object to the Global Settlement Agreement at issue in *Ahearn*, and separate objections were also lodged against the Trilateral Settlement Agreement in *Rudd*. Discovery ensued and two separate fairness hearings were held. Judge Parker made extensive findings and concluded that the proposed settlements were fair and reasonable and that the requirements for class certification under Rule 23(b)(1)(B) were satisfied. The intervenors appealed.]

II. AHEARN ...

A. Rule 23(a)

Rule 23(a) lists four prerequisites to a class action: (1) numerosity, (2) commonality, (3) typicality and (4) adequacy of representation. The district court found that all four of these prerequisites were satisfied. The intervenors do not dispute the district court's finding of numerosity, but argue that the Global Health Claimant Class meets none of the other prerequisites to a class action.

The intervenors argue that the district court erred by considering the circumstances surrounding the settlement and the evidence adduced at the fairness hearing in making findings under Rule 23(a). This argument is contrary to Fifth Circuit precedent and would require a court to ignore important and relevant information that sits squarely in front of it when deciding whether to certify a settlement class. In *In re Corrugated Container Antitrust Litigation (Container I)*, we held that the district court should consider the settlement in deciding whether the settlement class satisfied the prerequisites of Rule 23. 643 F.2d 195, 211 (5th Cir.), *aff'd*, 659 F.2d 1322 (5th Cir. 1981), cert. denied, 456 U.S. 998 (1982)....

Most circuits to decide the issue have held that courts should consider the settlement in determining whether Rule 23 prerequisites are satisfied. ... Only the Third Circuit has refused to look at settlements before it when deciding class certification issues and even that court admits that taking the settlement into account may be "the better policy." Georgine v. Amchem Products, Inc., 83 F.3d 610, 617-18 (3d Cir. 1996).* The rule that a court should consider a proposed settlement, if one is before it, when deciding certification issues makes good sense. Settlements and the events leading up to them add a great deal of information to the court's inquiry and will often expose diverging interests or common issues that were not evident or clear from the complaint. ...

We are bound to follow *Container I*'s holding that the district court can and should look at the terms of a settlement in front of it as part of its certification inquiry. We would adopt this rule even if we were not bound by precedent because it enhances the ability of district courts to make informed certification decisions.

1. Commonality and typicality

The district court, in its findings of fact, found that the entire Global Health Claimant Class had the following issues in common:

> (i) avoiding the potentially disastrous results of a loss by Fibreboard in the Coverage Case appeal; (ii) maximizing the total settlement contribution from Fibreboard and the Insurers; (iii) streamlining the procedures for the filing, processing and resolution of claims, and thereby reducing transactions costs and delays in compensation; (iv) minimizing the percentage of their compensation diverted from them to pay attorneys' fees; and (v) adopting procedures that provide for payments to claimants in an equitable manner....

Because the evidence is overwhelming that the class holds the above issues in common under the settlement . . ., we agree with the district court that the *Ahearn* action and the Global Settlement Agreement presented it with questions of law and fact common to the entire Global Health Claimant Class.

Typicality focuses on the similarity between the named plaintiffs' legal and remedial theories and the legal and remedial theories of those whom they purport to represent. Jenkins v. Raymark Industries, Inc., 782 F.2d 468, 472 (5th Cir. 1986). The district court found that the legal and remedial theories of the representative plaintiffs were typical of the class because all members of the Global Health Claimant Class presented claims based on exposure to Fibreboard asbestos. The district court also found that the named plaintiffs' interests in maximizing recovery for the class and

---

* After *In re Asbestos Litigation* was decided, the Supreme Court granted certiorari in *Georgine*. We study the Court's opinion, *Amchem Products, Inc. v. Windsor*, at p. 670, *infra*. — ED.

eliminating the risk posed by the insurance coverage litigation were identical to interests held by all members of the class.

The intervenors do not argue that the named plaintiffs' claims rest on theories different from those of the other class members. Instead, in their attempt to show that the class is too diverse to meet the typicality requirement, they point to individual issues such as varying family situations, separate histories of cigarette smoking, differences in medical expenses and differences in state law. These differences will certainly result in significant differences in the amount of damages that each claimant recovers but do not affect the settlement in the least. The Global Settlement Agreement does not award damages to individual victims:[7] it provides money and an equitable distribution process to pay victims.[8]

The central remedial and legal theory of each of the named plaintiffs, that Fibreboard is liable in tort for damages incurred due to exposure to Fibreboard asbestos, is typical of the entire class.... Further, the issues that brought the named plaintiffs to settle *Ahearn* are the same issues that the district court found common to the entire class. The named plaintiffs settled *Ahearn* because of their desire to avoid the risks of insurance coverage litigation and to insure that money remains available to pay their claims when they make it through the settlement and/or trial process to final judgment. These same concerns affect each member of the Global Health Claimant Class. We are satisfied that the district court did not abuse its discretion by finding that the issues of law and fact faced by the named plaintiffs were typical of the Global Health Claimant Class.

2. Adequacy of representation

The intervenors argue that the district court should not have certified the Global Health Claimant Class because of impermissible conflicts of interests by class counsel.[10] ...

The intervenors do not question the skill, competence or experience of class counsel, but instead argue the existence of impermissible conflicts that prevented them from adequately representing the class. Both sides agree

7. Determinations of individual damage awards will be made by the trust and the plaintiff's attorney in settlement negotiations or in a full trial on the merits. The back-end opt out provision will force the trust and plaintiffs to consider state law and individual circumstances, such as smoking history, when negotiating damages because the alternative to agreement is a full trial by jury under relevant state law.

8. This is in stark contrast to the *Georgine* case where the settlement attempted to award damages to class members based on the severity of their injuries alone.... We would likely agree with the Third Circuit that a class action requesting individual damages for members of a global class of asbestos claimants would not satisfy the typicality requirements due to the huge number of individuals and their varying medical expenses, smoking histories, and family situations. In *Ahearn*, only commonly held questions regarding insurance coverage for the class' injuries and establishment of an equitable distribution process to insure that all class members receive compensation were decided. As a result, this settlement is unaffected by the typicality and commonality problems cited in *Georgine*.

10. Intervenors do not challenge the adequacy of representation of class representatives so we do not consider this issue.

that in determining the existence of a conflict, we look to the ABA Model Rules of Professional Conduct for guidance. Rule 1.7 states:

> (b) A lawyer shall not represent a client if the representation of that client may be materially limited by the lawyer's responsibilities to another client or to a third person, or by the lawyer's own interests, unless:
>
> > (1) the lawyer reasonably believes the representation will not be adversely affected; and
> >
> > (2) the client consents after consultation. When representation of multiple clients in a single matter is undertaken, the consultation shall include explanation of the implications of the common representation and the advantages and risks involved....

The intervenors argue that class counsel for the Global Health Claimant Class had impermissible conflicts due to concurrent representation both (1) of present asbestos claimants and the Class of future claimants and (2) of purported conflicting subgroups within the class.

a. Alleged conflict between present claimants and the class

The intervenors contend that class counsel by simultaneously representing both present claimants and the class of future claimants represented clients who were directly competing for Fibreboard's limited resources. The district court found that during the negotiations no conflict existed that materially limited counsel's responsibilities to the future claimant class....

[In particular, the] intervenors argue that an impermissible conflict existed [during the negotiations between April, 1993 and August 9, 1993] because the Ness Motley counsel were simultaneously negotiating for both present claimants (the inventory claims) and the class of future claimants. Professor Hazard testified that the present and future claimants were not competing for the same funds. At this stage of the negotiations, counsel were concentrating on the settlement of their inventory of present claims. It is true that they were also discussing a global settlement, but these discussions were in the preliminary exploratory stage.... Counsel certainly knew in a general way that there was a sum beyond which Continental would not pay. But because they did not know that limit, they did not know that this limit would be less than an amount they were willing to accept in settlement for both classes of claimants. As the district court found, the Substitute Ness Motley Agreement likely aided the global settlement by increasing the average value per claim. We are persuaded that the record supports the district court's conclusion that class counsel vigorously represented both the present claimants and their future claimant clients against the same defendant....

[Similarly, during the August 9-27, 1993 period, the] district court found that all negotiations during this time were vigorous, contentious, and at arm's length. Professors Hazard and Green both testified that the future claimants were not impaired by counsel's representation of present claimants during this period. Indeed, they found that the present claimants had a substantial interest in a global settlement because such a settlement would secure their contingent back-end payments under the Substitute Ness Motley Agreement. Class counsel were also aware that any class settlement must be approved by the court and would face meticulous scrutiny. Thus, the present and future claimants had two common interests in reaching a settlement. First, they both wanted to avoid the risk of Fibreboard losing the coverage case. Second, they both wanted a diligently negotiated settlement: the future claimants wanted the settlement that yielded them maximum dollar recovery; the present claimants wanted a settlement that would withstand intense judicial scrutiny. . . .

b. The alleged intraclass conflicts . . .

Whether [an intraclass] conflict exists is governed by Rule 1.7(b) as discussed above. Not every intraclass conflict, however, will preclude approval of the settlement for inadequate representation. . . .

The district court found that neither subclasses nor separate negotiating attorneys were required because no material intraclass conflict existed. The court found the common interests far outweighed any divergent interests the intraclass groups might have. The court enumerated those common interests as follows: avoiding the catastrophic results of a loss by Fibreboard in the coverage case appeal; maximizing the total settlement contribution from Fibreboard and the Insurers; streamlining the procedures for the filing, processing, and resolution of claims, thereby reducing transaction costs and delays in compensation; minimizing the percentage of their compensation diverted from the fund to pay attorney's fees; and adopting procedures that provide for payments to claimants in an equitable manner.

Intervenors suggest two intraclass conflicts. First, they argue that the "near" futures would prefer a settlement agreement that places no limits on the amount an individual may recover because these claimants do not anticipate that Fibreboard's assets will be depleted before their claims mature. The "far" futures, on the other hand, would prefer to limit individual claims to conserve funds so that resources will be available to pay for their future illnesses.

Professors Hazard and Green found no conflict between these two groups that would materially impair the performance of class counsel. Specifically, each found that the common interest in avoiding a lack of coverage vastly overwhelmed any differences between these groups. The "near" futures have no assurance that they would fare better in the absence of the Global Settlement Agreement. These claimants would face the risk that Fibreboard would live up to its pledge to actively defend any claims and delay any recovery. These claimants would also face the risk of attrition of available funds from increased legal fees. Under the Global Settlement Agreement the entire class is benefited by the greater likelihood that funds will be available to compensate both "near" and "far" future claimants under a less complicated system. . . .

Next, intervenors argue that counsel could not represent claimants who were exposed before 1959 and after 1959 in negotiating a global settlement. They contend that this conflict exists because a pre-1959 exposure claimant's case has a higher settlement value than a post-1959 exposure claimant's. This is premised on the argument that pre-1959 claimants have a greater likelihood of available insurance coverage because both Continental and Pacific insurance policies covered only pre-1959 asbestos exposure. . . .

Professors Hazard and Green both found no substantial conflict between pre- and post-1959 claimants. Both pre- and post-1959 claimants share the common class interests recited above. Neither the Substitute Ness Motley Agreement, the Trilateral Settlement Agreement, nor the Global Settlement Agreement distinguish between these two groups of claimants in any way. To distinguish between the two groups in the Global Settlement Agreement was impractical because the class had no chance of persuading Fibreboard to agree to a settlement that did not address the claims by both groups. Also, to maintain the distinction in the Global Settlement Agreement would have undermined the attempts to provide maximum compensation and an efficient, streamlined process to claimants.

The district court made the following findings of fact: (1) all negotiations were vigorous and at arm's length, often conducted under the auspices of Judge Higginbotham; (2) common interests within the class overwhelmed minimal conflicts; (3) the settlement treated all class members the same; and (4) the Global Settlement Agreement was fair and reasonable, a finding that the intervenors have not appealed. The independent guardian ad litem also found that class counsel had no conflicts and that the Global Settlement Agreement was fair and reasonable and was the best alternative available. The district court did not abuse its discretion in finding that the class was adequately represented and that subclasses were not required.

B. Certification Under 23(b)(1)(B)

We turn next to the intervenors' challenge to class certification under 23(b)(1)(B). . . .

The district court found that the prosecution of separate actions by members of the Global Health Claimant Class would substantially impair or impede the ability of other members of the class to receive full payment for their injuries from Fibreboard's limited assets. This finding has strong support in the record and is not clearly erroneous. The district court heard expert testimony on the probable number, mix and timing of future asbestos personal injury claims against Fibreboard, the anticipated costs of defense relating to such claims, and the present value of Fibreboard's non-insurance assets. The experts agreed that Fibreboard faced enormous liability and defense costs that would likely equal or exceed the amount of damages paid out. More importantly, these experts testified that even under the Trilateral Settlement Agreement where Fibreboard is given $2 billion in insurance money to add to its own value of approximately $235 million, Fibreboard would be unable to pay all the valid claims against it within five to nine years. The district court credited the testimony of these experts and found that Fibreboard is a limited fund.

1. Rule 23(b)(1)(B) and the Bankruptcy Code

[For this portion of the opinion, see p. 780, *infra*.]

2. Jurisdictional and due process considerations in 23(b)(1)(b) class actions

[For the portion of the opinion discussing whether class members had a constitutional right to opt out of the suit, see p. 301, *supra*.]

Finally, the intervenors complain that the Global Settlement Agreement purports to release claims which do not present "a case or controversy." This misconstrues the nature of the settlement which does not purport to make any determination of the validity or amount of individual personal injury claims against Fibreboard. What the settlement does is address the immediate and important controversy of whether future claimants will be able to receive compensation for their injuries before Fibreboard runs out of money. It resolves this controversy by settling the insurance coverage litigation, capping the amount recovered by individual plaintiffs at $500,000, prohibiting punitive damage awards, and limiting the amount that the Global Trust can pay out in any given year. These provisions are designed to ensure that latecomers do not find their claims impaired because the winners of the race to the courthouse have claimed all of Fiberboard's assets in the early rounds of individual litigation. The argument that plaintiffs who have already been exposed to asbestos have no justiciable interest in ensuring that funds remain available to compensate them when they contract asbestos-related diseases is not supportable and has been widely rejected. . . . The intervenors' objection is meritless. . . .

III. *RUDD*

[The court rejected the contentions that the *Rudd* action had to be dismissed because of the absence of an indispensable party (*i.e.*, Fibreboard) and that the *Rudd* settlement is not ripe for judicial review because it is contingent upon the failure of the *Ahearn* settlement.]

CONCLUSION

Although appellants' arguments challenging the approval of the global settlement are not insubstantial, on the unique facts presented here they do not carry the day. The global settlement was driven by insurance coverage litigation between Fibreboard and the Insurers which would have been catastrophic for whomever was on the losing side. None of the parties was prepared to take the enormous risk inherent in that litigation. The global settlement offers all sides the best solution possible by eliminating costly disputes between Fibreboard, its insurers, and asbestos claimants and ensuring an equitable distribution to asbestos claimants. The $1.5 billion global settlement was a major accomplishment by all parties concerned and no one seriously challenges its adequacy or the desirability of avoiding another bankruptcy of a vigorous American company.

For the reasons stated above, we conclude that in this case none of the legal impediments argued by appellants precluded the district court from approving the global or trilateral settlements. Both settlements were legally sound resolutions of serious disagreements. The judgment of the district court is affirmed.

■ SMITH, Circuit Judge, dissenting. . . . The district court and the majority undoubtedly are driven by a commendable desire to resolve voluminous personal injury claims against an otherwise strong American company and to ensure an orderly transfer of funds from the company's insurers to its victims. In order to accomplish this result, however, they have extinguished claims over which they have no jurisdiction and deprived thousands of asbestos victims of basic constitutional rights. The result is the first no-opt-out, mass-tort, settlement-only, futures-only class action ever attempted or approved.

Ironically, the willingness to jettison centuries-old legal precepts hurts the very victims they intend to help: The settlement forces asbestos victims to surrender their claims in exchange for a meager $10 million of Fibreboard's $225-250 million net worth. They also benefit from Fibreboard's settlement with its insurers, but Fibreboard and the insurers had powerful incentives to settle that dispute by themselves; in fact, they did so for $2 billion.

On the other hand, the district court and the majority have bailed Fibreboard's shareholders out of a mammoth liability and awarded $43.7 million to class counsel. This suit was supposedly brought on behalf of Fibreboard's victims, but of the four entities directly affected by the settlement Fibreboard, class attorneys, courts, and asbestos victims the victims were the only entity absent from the bargaining table. Perhaps for that reason, they also were the only losers. . . .

We must keep in mind that it was the *defendant* — Fibreboard — who selected the class that was to "sue" it and the class action lawyers who were to do the dirty work. Fibreboard hand-picked a class that was uniquely vulnerable to exploitation, class counsel who were widely reported to have sold out a similar class [in *Georgine*], and a court with a reputation for favoring a global settlement. Class counsel then cut a side deal with Fibreboard before agreeing to the class settlement, and the district judge presided at the fairness hearing on the very settlement he had helped to craft. . . .

We must not confuse rule 23(a)(4) with rule 23(e), which scrutinizes only the substantive fairness of a settlement. Rule 23(a)(4) guarantees due process, and a substantively adequate result cannot cure procedural injustice.

More importantly, substantive adequacy does not necessarily mean that a settlement is truly fair; an attorney who negotiated an adequate settlement might have negotiated a better one but for a conflict of interest.

. . . Rules 23(a)(4) and 23(e) are complements, not substitutes; a court applies rule 23(a)(4) before certification to insure procedural fairness and rule 23(e) after settlement to guarantee substantive adequacy. . . .

Ness Motley represented the class during settlement negotiations despite a financial interest in reaching a settlement that diverged from the class's interest. A divergent financial interest is a paradigmatic conflict of interest, yet the majority refuses to concede that this conflict may have denied the class adequate representation.

The conflict stemmed from Ness Motley's simultaneous representation of both the class and individual plaintiffs who were also suing Fibreboard. While the class settlement negotiations were proceeding, Fibreboard and Ness Motley agreed to settle all of Ness Motley's pre-existing individual lawsuits for a higher-than-average amount. That settlement was partly contingent, however, on Ness Motley and Fibreboard's settling the class claims.

If the class did not settle its claims, Fibreboard would still pay half of the individual plaintiffs' settlement, but they would receive the entire settlement if the class settled. Because Ness Motley represented the individual plaintiffs, but not the class, on a contingency basis, it had a financial interest in settling the class claims on any terms whatsoever, even if those terms were unfavorable to the class. . . .

In contrast, the class desired a settlement only if it was more lucrative than the alternative awaiting the outcome of the coverage case. The expected value of that alternative was significant. If the California Supreme Court affirmed the two lower courts that had ruled favorably for the class, the class would enjoy a practically unlimited compensation fund. Accordingly, it is easy to imagine a proposed settlement beneficial to Ness Motley and the individual plaintiffs but unfavorable to the class.

The conflict of interest in this case was direct and egregious. But I would go a step further and prohibit class counsel from ever simultaneously representing individual plaintiffs in cases such as this, as there is too great an opportunity for corruption. . . .

Another conflict of interest arose from the class attorneys' simultaneous representation of both class members with extant claims and those with latent claims. Because they may seek recovery from the settlement fund immediately, extant claimants would profit from high ceilings on recovery or none at all, as there was little danger that the fund would be depleted before it paid their claims. Latent claimants, on the other hand, cannot seek recovery until some triggering event occurs. Because they may be unable to file a claim for a number of years, they would benefit from damage caps low enough to ensure that the settlement fund will not dry up before it pays their claim.

Even if there was no conflict between extant and latent claimants as to whether a settlement was a good idea, there was undeniably a conflict between the two groups over the terms of the settlement. It may well have been appropriate for the same attorneys to represent extant and latent claimants when negotiating with the defendants over the total amount of the settlement. Once the parties agreed to an amount, however, the interests of extant and latent claimants diverged, and they should have been represented by different attorneys for determination of the terms under which the settlement would be distributed to the class....

[Furthermore, because] the settlement deprived pre-1959 claimants of a substantial right, they were entitled to separate representation. The majority contends that the class as a whole benefited by sacrificing the special rights of pre-1959 claimants, and I emphatically agree. That is precisely the problem: It was in the best interest of one part of the class to give up something that belonged to another part of the class, and that created a conflict of interest.

The only protection accorded the class was a rule 23(e) fairness hearing. The district court also appointed a guardian ad litem to represent absent class members, but he did so only after class and defense counsel had completed the settlement. Thus, class members received absolutely no structural or procedural protections; instead, they had to rely on an after-the-fact review of the settlement's substance.

The district court and the guardian ad litem undertook that task diligently, but an after-the-fact substantive review is far too little, far too late. The court cannot conduct a trial in order to avoid one; nor can it turn back the clock and appoint different counsel to renegotiate the settlement fairly. Thus, the extent to which class counsel's numerous conflicts and Fibreboard's stacking of the deck actually affected the final settlement is unknowable. As Fibreboard entered the negotiations in constructive bankruptcy and left with more than ninety-five percent of its assets intact, however, there is reason to be skeptical.

The effect of replacing the tort system with an administrative processing center is equally hard to ascertain, for judges lack legislative fact-finding and investigative capabilities. If the trust proves to be funded adequately and managed fairly, it might process claims more efficiently than the courts, reducing transaction costs and providing plaintiffs with faster and more reliable recovery. As such a reduction in transaction costs would generate a surplus for Fibreboard and the class, Fibreboard might deserve to walk away with over $200 million in remaining assets.

On the other hand, the trust might attempt to impose arbitrary limits ... and stonewall plaintiffs' counsel who protest, forcing them to endure a tedious series of procedural delays before their clients finally receive a day in court. The trust might also be inadequately funded, ... leaving plaintiffs scraping for what little they can get while bureaucrats struggle to hold on to their jobs.

In short, we simply do not know what the courts have wrought. What we do know is that this "reform" involves denial of established constitutional rights; relaxation of already lax ethical rules; extinguishing of claims that we have no power to adjudicate, much less abolish; and a significant likelihood of collusion between the defendant and the class counsel.

AMCHEM PRODUCTS, INC. v. WINDSOR*

— U.S. —, 117 S.Ct. 2231 (1997)

■ JUSTICE GINSBURG delivered the opinion of the Court.

This case concerns the legitimacy under Rule 23 of the Federal Rules of Civil Procedure of a class-action certification sought to achieve global settlement of current and future asbestos-related claims. The class proposed for certification potentially encompasses hundreds of thousands, perhaps millions, of individuals tied together by this commonality: each was, or some day may be, adversely affected by past exposure to asbestos products manufactured by one or more of 20 companies. Those companies, defendants in the lower courts, are petitioners here.

The United States District Court for the Eastern District of Pennsylvania certified the class for settlement only, finding that the proposed settlement was fair and that representation and notice had been adequate. That court enjoined class members from separately pursuing asbestos-related personal-injury suits in any court, federal or state, pending the issuance of a final order. The Court of Appeals for the Third Circuit vacated the District Court's orders, holding that the class certification failed to satisfy Rule 23's requirements in several critical respects. We affirm the Court of Appeals' judgment.

I

A

The settlement-class certification we confront evolved in response to an asbestos-litigation crisis. . . . A United States Judicial Conference Ad Hoc Committee on Asbestos Litigation, appointed by the Chief Justice in September 1990, described facets of the problem in a 1991 report:

". . . The most objectionable aspects of asbestos litigation can be briefly summarized: dockets in both federal and state courts continue to grow; long delays are routine; trials are too long; the same issues are litigated over and over; transaction costs exceed the victims' recovery by nearly two to one; exhaustion of assets threatens and distorts the process; and future claimants may lose altogether." . . .

Real reform, the report concluded, required federal legislation creating a national asbestos dispute-resolution scheme. . . . To this date, no congressional response has emerged.

In the face of legislative inaction, the federal courts — lacking authority to replace state tort systems with a national toxic tort compensation regime — endeavored to work with the procedural tools available to improve management of federal asbestos litigation. . . . [T]he Judicial Panel on Multidistrict Litigation (MDL Panel) . . . transferred all asbestos cases then

---

* One of the authors of this book was a consultant to the Federal Judicial Center, and performed a study of this case at the request of the Center. — ED.

filed, but not yet on trial in federal courts to a single district, the United States District Court for the Eastern District of Pennsylvania .... See In re Asbestos Products Liability Litigation (No. VI), 771 F. Supp. 415, 422-424 (Jud.Pan.Mult.Lit. 1991). The order aggregated pending cases only; no authority resides in the MDL Panel to license for consolidated proceedings claims not yet filed.

B

After the consolidation, attorneys for plaintiffs and defendants formed separate steering committees and began settlement negotiations. Ronald L. Motley and Gene Locks — later appointed, along with Motley's law partner Joseph F. Rice, to represent the plaintiff class in this action — co-chaired the Plaintiffs' Steering Committee. Counsel for the Center for Claims Resolution (CCR), the consortium of 20 former asbestos manufacturers now before us as petitioners, participated in the Defendants' Steering Committee. Although the MDL order collected, transferred, and consolidated only cases already commenced in federal courts, settlement negotiations included efforts to find a "means of resolving ... future cases." ...

[After an initial round of negotiations fell apart,] CCR counsel approached the lawyers who had headed the Plaintiffs' Steering Committee in the unsuccessful negotiations, and a new round of negotiations began; that round yielded the mass settlement agreement now in controversy. At the time, the former heads of the Plaintiffs' Steering Committee represented thousands of plaintiffs with then-pending asbestos-related claims — claimants the parties to this suit call "inventory" plaintiffs. CCR indicated in these discussions that it would resist settlement of inventory cases absent "some kind of protection for the future." ...

Settlement talks thus concentrated on devising an administrative scheme for disposition of asbestos claims not yet in litigation. In these negotiations, counsel for masses of inventory plaintiffs endeavored to represent the interests of the anticipated future claimants, although those lawyers then had no attorney-client relationship with such claimants.

Once negotiations seemed likely to produce an agreement purporting to bind potential plaintiffs, CCR agreed to settle, through separate agreements, the claims of plaintiffs who had already filed asbestos-related lawsuits. In one such agreement, CCR defendants promised to pay more than $200 million to gain release of the claims of numerous inventory plaintiffs. After settling the inventory claims, CCR, together with the plaintiffs' lawyers CCR had approached, launched this case, exclusively involving persons outside the MDL Panel's province — plaintiffs without already pending lawsuits.

C

The class action thus instituted was not intended to be litigated. Rather, within the space of a single day, January 15, 1993, the settling parties — CCR defendants and the representatives of the plaintiff class described below — presented to the District Court a complaint, an answer, a proposed settlement agreement, and a joint motion for conditional class certification.

The complaint identified nine lead plaintiffs, designating them and members of their families as representatives of a class comprising all persons who had not filed an asbestos-related lawsuit against a CCR defendant as of the date the class action commenced, but who (1) had been exposed — occupationally or through the occupational exposure of a spouse or household member — to asbestos or products containing asbestos attributable to a CCR defendant, or (2) whose spouse or family member had been so exposed. Untold numbers of individuals may fall within this description. All named plaintiffs alleged that they or a member of their family had been exposed to asbestos-containing products of CCR defendants. More than half of the named plaintiffs alleged that they or their family members had already suffered various physical injuries as a result of the exposure. The others alleged that they had not yet manifested any asbestos-related condition. The complaint delineated no subclasses; all named plaintiffs were designated as representatives of the class as a whole. . . .

A stipulation of settlement accompanied the pleadings; it proposed to settle, and to preclude nearly all class members from litigating against CCR companies, all claims not filed before January 15, 1993, involving compensation for present and future asbestos-related personal injury or death. An exhaustive document exceeding 100 pages, the stipulation presents in detail an administrative mechanism and a schedule of payments to compensate class members who meet defined asbestos-exposure and medical requirements. The stipulation describes four categories of compensable disease: mesothelioma; lung cancer; certain "other cancers" (colon-rectal, laryngeal, esophageal, and stomach cancer); and "non-malignant conditions" (asbestosis and bilateral pleural thickening). Persons with "exceptional" medical claims — claims that do not fall within the four described diagnostic categories — may in some instances qualify for compensation, but the settlement caps the number of "exceptional" claims CCR must cover.

For each qualifying disease category, the stipulation specifies the range of damages CCR will pay to qualifying claimants. Payments under the settlement are not adjustable for inflation. Mesothelioma claimants — the most highly compensated category — are scheduled to receive between $20,000 and $200,000. The stipulation provides that CCR is to propose the level of compensation within the prescribed ranges; it also establishes procedures to resolve disputes over medical diagnoses and levels of compensation.

Compensation above the fixed ranges may be obtained for "extraordinary" claims. But the settlement places both numerical caps and dollar limits on such claims. The settlement also imposes "case flow maximums," which cap the number of claims payable for each disease in a given year.

Class members are to receive no compensation for certain kinds of claims, even if otherwise applicable state law recognizes such claims.

Claims that garner no compensation under the settlement include claims by family members of asbestos-exposed individuals for loss of consortium, and claims by so-called "exposure-only" plaintiffs for increased risk of cancer, fear of future asbestos-related injury, and medical monitoring. "Pleural" claims, which might be asserted by persons with asbestos-related plaques on their lungs but no accompanying physical impairment, are also excluded. Although not entitled to present compensation, exposure-only claimants and pleural claimants may qualify for benefits when and if they develop a compensable disease and meet the relevant exposure and medical criteria. Defendants forgo defenses to liability, including statute of limitations pleas.

Class members, in the main, are bound by the settlement in perpetuity, while CCR defendants may choose to withdraw from the settlement after ten years. A small number of class members — only a few per year — may reject the settlement and pursue their claims in court. Those permitted to exercise this option, however, may not assert any punitive damages claim or any claim for increased risk of cancer. Aspects of the administration of the settlement are to be monitored by the AFL-CIO and class counsel. Class counsel are to receive attorneys' fees in an amount to be approved by the District Court.

D

On January 29, 1993, as requested by the settling parties, the District Court conditionally certified, under Federal Rule of Civil Procedure 23(b)(3), an encompassing opt-out class. . . . Judge Weiner appointed Locks, Motley, and Rice as class counsel, noting that "[t]he Court may in the future appoint additional counsel if it is deemed necessary and advisable." . . . At no stage of the proceedings, however, were additional counsel in fact appointed. Nor was the class ever divided into subclasses. In a separate order, Judge Weiner assigned to Judge Reed, also of the Eastern District of Pennsylvania, "the task of conducting fairness proceedings and of determining whether the proposed settlement is fair to the class." Various class members raised objections to the settlement stipulation, and Judge Weiner granted the objectors full rights to participate in the subsequent proceedings.

In preliminary rulings, Judge Reed held that the District Court had subject-matter jurisdiction, . . . and he approved the settling parties' elaborate plan for giving notice to the class . . . . The court-approved notice informed recipients that they could exclude themselves from the class, if they so chose, within a three-month opt-out period.

Objectors raised numerous challenges to the settlement. They urged that the settlement unfairly disadvantaged those without currently compensable conditions in that it failed to adjust for inflation or to account for changes, over time, in medical understanding. They maintained that compensation levels were intolerably low in comparison to awards available in tort litigation or payments received by the inventory plaintiffs. And they objected to the absence of any compensation for certain claims, for example, medical monitoring, compensable under the tort law of several States. Rejecting these and all other objections, Judge Reed concluded that the settlement terms were fair and had been negotiated without collusion. He also found that adequate notice had been given to class members, and that final class certification under Rule 23(b)(3) was appropriate....

Strenuous objections had been asserted regarding the adequacy of representation, a Rule 23(a)(4) requirement. Objectors maintained that class counsel and class representatives had disqualifying conflicts of interests. In particular, objectors urged, claimants whose injuries had become manifest and claimants without manifest injuries should not have common counsel and should not be aggregated in a single class. Furthermore, objectors argued, lawyers representing inventory plaintiffs should not represent the newly-formed class.

Satisfied that class counsel had ably negotiated the settlement in the best interests of all concerned, and that the named parties served as adequate representatives, the District Court rejected these objections. Subclasses were unnecessary, the District Court held, bearing in mind the added cost and confusion they would entail and the ability of class members to exclude themselves from the class during the three-month opt-out period. Reasoning that the representative plaintiffs "have a strong interest that recovery for *all* of the medical categories be maximized because they may have claims in *any*, or several categories," the District Court found "no antagonism of interest between class members with various medical conditions, or between persons with and without currently manifest asbestos impairment." Declaring class certification appropriate and the settlement fair, the District Court preliminarily enjoined all class members from commencing any asbestos-related suit against the CCR defendants in any state or federal court....

The objectors appealed. The United States Court of Appeals for the Third Circuit vacated the certification, holding that the requirements of Rule 23 had not been satisfied.

E

The Court of Appeals, in a long, heavily detailed opinion by Judge Becker, first noted several challenges by objectors to justiciability, subject-matter jurisdiction, and adequacy of notice. These challenges, the court said, raised "serious concerns." However, the court observed, "the jurisdictional issues in this case would not exist but for the [class action] certification." Turning to the class-certification issues and finding them dispositive, the Third Circuit declined to decide other questions.

On class-action prerequisites, the Court of Appeals referred to an earlier Third Circuit decision, In re General Motors Corp. Pick-Up Truck Fuel Tank Products Liability Litigation, 55 F.3d 768 (C.A.3), cert. denied, 516 U.S. [824] (1995) (hereinafter *GM Trucks*), which held that although a class action may be certified for settlement purposes only, Rule 23(a)'s requirements must be satisfied as if the case were going to be litigated. The same rule should apply, the Third Circuit said, to class certification under Rule 23(b)(3). But cf. In re Asbestos Litigation, 90 F.3d 963, 975-976, and n.8 (C.A.5 1996), cert. pending, Nos. 96-1379, 96-1394. While stating that the requirements of Rule 23(a) and (b)(3) must be met "without taking into account the settlement," the Court of Appeals in fact closely considered the terms of the settlement as it examined aspects of the case under Rule 23 criteria. . . .

II

Objectors assert in this Court, as they did in the District Court and Court of Appeals, an array of jurisdictional barriers. Most fundamentally, they maintain that the settlement proceeding instituted by class counsel and CCR is not a justiciable case or controversy within the confines of Article III of the Federal Constitution. In the main, they say, the proceeding is a nonadversarial endeavor to impose on countless individuals without currently ripe claims an administrative compensation regime binding on those individuals if and when they manifest injuries.

Furthermore, objectors urge that exposure-only claimants lack standing to sue . . . . Objectors also argue that exposure-only claimants did not meet the then-current amount-in-controversy requirement (in excess of $50,000) specified for federal-court jurisdiction based upon diversity of citizenship. See 28 U.S.C. § 1332(a).

As earlier recounted, the Third Circuit declined to reach these issues because they "would not exist but for the [class action] certification." We agree that "[t]he class certification issues are dispositive"; because their resolution here is logically antecedent to the existence of any Article III issues, it is appropriate to reach them first . . . . We therefore follow the path taken by the Court of Appeals, mindful that Rule 23's requirements must be interpreted in keeping with Article III constraints, and with the Rules Enabling Act, which instructs that rules of procedure "shall not abridge, enlarge or modify any substantive right," 28 U.S.C. § 2072(b). See also Fed. Rule Civ. Proc. 82 ("rules shall not be construed to extend . . . the [subject matter] jurisdiction of the United States district courts").

III

To place this controversy in context, we briefly describe the characteristics of class actions for which the Federal Rules provide. Rule 23, governing federal-court class actions, stems from equity practice and gained its current shape in an innovative 1966 revision. . . . Rule 23(a) states four threshold requirements applicable to all class actions: (1) numerosity . . .; (2) commonality . . .; (3) typicality . . .; and (4) adequacy of representation . . . .

In addition to satisfying Rule 23(a)'s prerequisites, parties seeking class certification must show that the action is maintainable under Rule 23(b)(1), (2), or (3). Rule 23(b)(1) covers cases in which separate actions by or against individual class members would risk establishing "incompatible standards of conduct for the party opposing the class," Fed. Rule Civ. Proc. 23(b)(1)(A), or would "as a practical matter be dispositive of the interests" of nonparty class members "or substantially impair or impede their ability to protect their interests," Fed. Rule Civ. Proc. 23(b)(1)(B). Rule 23(b)(1)(A) "takes in cases where the party is obliged by law to treat the members of the class alike (a utility acting toward customers; a government imposing a tax), or where the party must treat all alike as a matter of practical necessity (a riparian owner using water as against downriver owners)." . . . Rule 23(b)(1)(B) includes, for example, "limited fund" cases, instances in which numerous persons make claims against a fund insufficient to satisfy all claims. See Advisory Committee's Notes on Fed. Rules Civ. Proc. 23, 28 U.S.C.App., pp. 696-697 (hereinafter Adv. Comm. Notes).

Rule 23(b)(2) permits class actions for declaratory or injunctive relief where "the party opposing the class has acted or refused to act on grounds generally applicable to the class." Civil rights cases against parties charged with unlawful, class-based discrimination are prime examples. . . .

In the 1966 class-action amendments, Rule 23(b)(3), the category at issue here, was "the most adventuresome" innovation. See Kaplan, A Prefatory Note, 10 B.C. Ind. & Com. L. Rev. 497, 497 (1969) (hereinafter Kaplan, Prefatory Note). Rule 23(b)(3) added to the complex-litigation arsenal class actions for damages designed to secure judgments binding all class members save those who affirmatively elected to be excluded. . . .

Framed for situations in which "class-action treatment is not as clearly called for" as it is in Rule 23(b)(1) and (b)(2) situations, Rule 23(b)(3) permits certification where class suit "may nevertheless be convenient and desirable." Adv. Comm. Notes, 28 U.S.C.App., p. 697. To qualify for certification under Rule 23(b)(3), a class must meet two requirements beyond the Rule 23(a) prerequisites: Common questions must "predominate over any questions affecting only individual members"; and class resolution must be "superior to other available methods for the fair and efficient adjudication of the controversy." In adding "predominance" and "superiority" to the qualification-for-certification list, the Advisory Committee sought to cover cases "in which a class action would achieve economies of time, effort, and expense, and promote . . . uniformity of decision as to persons similarly situated, without sacrificing procedural fairness or bringing about other undesirable results." Ibid. Sensitive to the competing tugs of individual autonomy for those who might prefer to go it alone or in a smaller unit, on the one hand, and systemic efficiency on the other, the Reporter for the 1966 amendments cautioned: "The new provision invites a close look at the case before it is accepted as a class action. . . ." . . .

Rule 23(b)(3) includes a nonexhaustive list of factors pertinent to a court's "close look" at the predominance and superiority criteria:

"(A) the interest of members of the class in individually controlling the prosecution or defense of separate actions; (B) the extent and nature of any litigation concerning the controversy already commenced by or against members of the class; (C) the desirability or undesirability of concentrating the litigation of the claims in the particular forum; (D) the difficulties likely to be encountered in the management of a class action."

In setting out these factors, the Advisory Committee for the 1966 reform anticipated that in each case, courts would "consider the interests of individual members of the class in controlling their own litigations and carrying them on as they see fit." Adv. Comm. Notes, 28 U.S.C.App., p. 698. They elaborated:

> "The interests of individuals in conducting separate lawsuits may be so strong as to call for denial of a class action. On the other hand, these interests may be theoretic rather than practical; the class may have a high degree of cohesion and prosecution of the action through representatives would be quite unobjectionable, or the amounts at stake for individuals may be so small that separate suits would be impracticable." Ibid. . . .

As the Third Circuit observed in the instant case: "Each plaintiff [in an action involving claims for personal injury and death] has a significant interest in individually controlling the prosecution of [his case]"; each "ha[s] a substantial stake in making individual decisions on whether and when to settle."

While the text of Rule 23(b)(3) does not exclude from certification cases in which individual damages run high, the Advisory Committee had dominantly in mind vindication of "the rights of groups of people who individually would be without effective strength to bring their opponents into court at all." Kaplan, Prefatory Note 497. As concisely recalled in a recent Seventh Circuit opinion:

> "The policy at the very core of the class action mechanism is to overcome the problem that small recoveries do not provide the incentive for any individual to bring a solo action prosecuting his or her rights. A class action solves this problem by aggregating the relatively paltry potential recoveries into something worth someone's (usually an attorney's) labor." Mace v. Van Ru Credit Corp., 109 F.3d 338, 344 (1997).

To alert class members to their right to "opt out" of a (b)(3) class, Rule 23 instructs the court to "direct to the members of the class the best notice practicable under the circumstances, including individual notice to all members who can be identified through reasonable effort." Fed. Rule Civ. Proc. 23(c)(2) . . . .

In the decades since the 1966 revision of Rule 23, class action practice has become ever more "adventuresome" as a means of coping with claims too numerous to secure their "just, speedy, and inexpensive determination" one by one. See Fed. Rule Civ. Proc. 1. The development reflects concerns about the efficient use of court resources and the conservation of funds to compensate claimants who do not line up early in a litigation queue. . . .

Among current applications of Rule 23(b)(3), the "settlement only" class has become a stock device. . . . Although all Federal Circuits recognize the utility of Rule 23(b)(3) settlement classes, courts have divided on the extent to which a proffered settlement affects court surveillance under Rule 23's certification criteria.

In *GM Trucks*, 55 F.3d, at 799-800, and in the instant case, the Third Circuit held that a class cannot be certified for settlement when certification for trial would be unwarranted. Other courts have held that settlement obviates or reduces the need to measure a proposed class against the enumerated Rule 23 requirements. See, *e.g., In re Asbestos Litigation*, 90 F.3d, at 975 (C.A.5) . . . .

A proposed amendment to Rule 23 would expressly authorize settlement class certification, in conjunction with a motion by the settling parties for Rule 23(b)(3) certification, "even though the requirements of subdivision (b)(3) might not be met for purposes of trial." . . . In response to the publication of this proposal, voluminous public comments — many of them opposed to, or skeptical of, the amendment — were received by the Judicial Conference Standing Committee on Rules of Practice and Procedure. . . . The Committee has not yet acted on the matter. We consider the certification at issue under the rule as it is currently framed.

IV

We granted review to decide the role settlement may play, under existing Rule 23, in determining the propriety of class certification. The Third Circuit's opinion stated that each of the requirements of Rule 23(a) and (b)(3) "must be satisfied without taking into account the settlement." That statement, petitioners urge, is incorrect.

We agree with petitioners to this limited extent: settlement is relevant to a class certification. The Third Circuit's opinion bears modification in that respect. But, as we earlier observed, the Court of Appeals in fact did not ignore the settlement; instead, that court homed in on settlement terms in explaining why it found the absentees' interests inadequately represented. The Third Circuit's close inspection of the settlement in that regard was altogether proper.

Confronted with a request for settlement-only class certification, a district court need not inquire whether the case, if tried, would present intractable management problems, see Fed. Rule Civ. Proc. 23(b)(3)(D), for the proposal is that there be no trial. But other specifications of the rule — those designed to protect absentees by blocking unwarranted or overbroad class definitions — demand undiluted, even heightened, attention in the settlement context. Such attention is of vital importance, for a court asked to certify a settlement class will lack the opportunity, present when a case is litigated, to adjust the class, informed by the proceedings as they unfold. See Fed. Rule Civ. Proc. 23(c), (d).

And, of overriding importance, courts must be mindful that the rule as now composed sets the requirements they are bound to enforce. Federal Rules take effect after an extensive deliberative process involving many reviewers: a Rules Advisory Committee, public commenters, the Judicial Conference, this Court, the Congress. See 28 U.S.C. §§ 2073, 2074. The text of a rule thus proposed and reviewed limits judicial inventiveness. Courts are not free to amend a rule outside the process Congress ordered, a process properly tuned to the instruction that rules of procedure "shall not abridge . . . any substantive right." § 2072(b).

Rule 23(e), on settlement of class actions, reads in its entirety: "A class action shall not be dismissed or compromised without the approval of the court, and notice of the proposed dismissal or compromise shall be given to all members of the class in such manner as the court directs." This prescription was designed to function as an additional requirement, not a superseding direction, for the "class action" to which Rule 23(e) refers is one qualified for certification under Rule 23(a) and (b). . . . Subdivisions (a) and (b) focus court attention on whether a proposed class has sufficient unity so that absent members can fairly be bound by decisions of class representatives. That dominant concern persists when settlement, rather than trial, is proposed.

The safeguards provided by the Rule 23(a) and (b) class-qualifying criteria, we emphasize, are not impractical impediments — checks shorn of utility — in the settlement class context. First, the standards set for the protection of absent class members serve to inhibit appraisals of the chancellor's foot kind — class certifications dependent upon the court's gestalt judgment or overarching impression of the settlement's fairness.

Second, if a fairness inquiry under Rule 23(e) controlled certification, eclipsing Rule 23(a) and (b), and permitting class designation despite the impossibility of litigation, both class counsel and court would be disarmed. Class counsel confined to settlement negotiations could not use the threat of litigation to press for a better offer, . . . and the court would face a bargain proffered for its approval without benefit of adversarial investigation . . . .

Federal courts, in any case, lack authority to substitute for Rule 23's certification criteria a standard never adopted — that if a settlement is "fair," then certification is proper. Applying to this case criteria the rulemakers set, we conclude that the Third Circuit's appraisal is essentially correct. Although that court should have acknowledged that settlement is a factor in the calculus, a remand is not warranted on that account. The Court of Appeals' opinion amply demonstrates why — with or without a settlement on the table — the sprawling class the District Court certified does not satisfy Rule 23's requirements.

A

We address first the requirement of Rule 23(b)(3) that "[common] questions of law or fact . . . predominate over any questions affecting only individual members." The District Court concluded that predominance was satisfied based on two factors: class members' shared experience of asbestos exposure and their common "interest in receiving prompt and fair compensation for their claims, while minimizing the risks and transaction costs inherent in the asbestos litigation process as it occurs presently in the tort system." The settling parties also contend that the settlement's fairness is a common question, predominating over disparate legal issues that might be pivotal in litigation but become irrelevant under the settlement.

The predominance requirement stated in Rule 23(b)(3), we hold, is not met by the factors on which the District Court relied. The benefits asbestos-exposed persons might gain from the establishment of a grand-scale compensation scheme is a matter fit for legislative consideration, but it is not pertinent to the predominance inquiry. That inquiry trains on the legal or factual questions that qualify each class member's case as a genuine controversy, questions that preexist any settlement.[18]

The Rule 23(b)(3) predominance inquiry tests whether proposed classes are sufficiently cohesive to warrant adjudication by representation. . . .[19] The inquiry appropriate under Rule 23(e), on the other hand, protects unnamed class members "from unjust or unfair settlements affecting their rights when the representatives become fainthearted before the action is adjudicated or are able to secure satisfaction of their individual claims by a compromise." . . . But it is not the mission of Rule 23(e) to assure the class cohesion that legitimizes representative action in the first place. If a common interest in a fair compromise could satisfy the predominance requirement of Rule 23(b)(3), that vital prescription would be stripped of any meaning in the settlement context.

The District Court also relied upon this commonality: "The members of the class have all been exposed to asbestos products supplied by the defendants. . . ." Even if Rule 23(a)'s commonality requirement may be satisfied by that shared experience, the predominance criterion is far more demanding. Given the greater number of questions peculiar to the several categories of class members, and to individuals within each category, and the significance of those uncommon questions, any overarching dispute about the health consequences of asbestos exposure cannot satisfy the Rule 23(b)(3) predominance standard.

The Third Circuit highlighted the disparate questions undermining class cohesion in this case:

> "Class members were exposed to different asbestos-containing products, for different amounts of time, in different ways, and over different periods. Some class members suffer no physical injury or have only asymptomatic pleural changes, while others suffer from lung cancer, disabling asbestosis, or from mesothelioma. . . . Each has a different history of cigarette smoking, a factor that complicates the causation inquiry.
>
> "The [exposure-only] plaintiffs especially share little in common, either with each other or with the presently injured class members. It is unclear whether they will contract asbestos-related disease and, if so, what disease each will suffer. They will also incur different medical expenses because their monitoring and treatment will depend on singular circumstances and individual medical histories." [83 F.2d] at 626.

Differences in state law, the Court of Appeals observed, compound these

---

18. In this respect, the predominance requirement of Rule 23(b)(3) is similar to the requirement of Rule 23(a)(3) that "claims or defenses" of the named representatives must be "typical of the claims or defenses of the class." The words "claims or defenses" in this context — just as in the context of Rule 24(b)(2) governing permissive intervention — "manifestly refer to the kinds of claims or defenses that can be raised in courts of law as part of an actual or impending law suit." . . .

19. This case, we note, involves no "limited fund" capable of supporting class treatment under Rule 23(b)(1)(B), which does not have a predominance requirement. . . . The settling parties sought to proceed exclusively under Rule 23(b)(3).

disparities. See id., at 627 (citing Phillips Petroleum Co. v. Shutts, 472 U.S. 797, 823 (1985)).

No settlement class called to our attention is as sprawling as this one. Cf. *In re Asbestos Litigation*, 90 F.3d, at 976, n.8 ("We would likely agree with the Third Circuit that a class action requesting individual damages for members of a global class of asbestos claimants would not satisfy [Rule 23] requirements due to the huge number of individuals and their varying medical expenses, smoking histories, and family situations."). Predominance is a test readily met in certain cases alleging consumer or securities fraud or violations of the antitrust laws. See Adv. Comm. Notes, 28 U.S.C.App., p. 697. Even mass tort cases arising from a common cause or disaster may, depending upon the circumstances, satisfy the predominance requirement. The Advisory Committee for the 1966 revision of Rule 23, it is true, noted that "mass accident" cases are likely to present "significant questions, not only of damages but of liability and defenses of liability, . . . affecting the individuals in different ways." Ibid. And the Committee advised that such cases are "ordinarily not appropriate" for class treatment. Ibid. But the text of the rule does not categorically exclude mass tort cases from class certification, and district courts, since the late 1970s, have been certifying such cases in increasing number. . . . The Committee's warning, however, continues to call for caution when individual stakes are high and disparities among class members great. As the Third Circuit's opinion makes plain, the certification in this case does not follow the counsel of caution. That certification cannot be upheld, for it rests on a conception of Rule 23(b)(3)'s predominance requirement irreconcilable with the rule's design.

B

Nor can the class approved by the District Court satisfy Rule 23(a)(4)'s requirement that the named parties "will fairly and adequately protect the interests of the class." The adequacy inquiry under Rule 23(a)(4) serves to uncover conflicts of interest between named parties and the class they seek to represent. See General Telephone Co. of Southwest v. Falcon, 457 U.S. 147, 157-158, n.13 (1982). "[A] class representative must be part of the class and 'possess the same interest and suffer the same injury' as the class members." East Tex. Motor Freight System, Inc. v. Rodriguez, 431 U.S. 395, 403 (1977) . . . .[20]

As the Third Circuit pointed out, named parties with diverse medical conditions sought to act on behalf of a single giant class rather than on behalf of discrete subclasses. In significant respects, the interests of those

---

20. The adequacy-of-representation requirement "tend[s] to merge" with the commonality and typicality criteria of Rule 23(a) . . . . General Telephone Co. of Southwest v. Falcon, 457 U.S. 147, 157, n.13 (1982). The adequacy heading also factors in competency and conflicts of class counsel. See id., at 157-158, n.13. Like the Third Circuit, we decline to address adequacy-of-counsel issues discretely in light of our conclusions that common questions of law or fact do not predominate and that the named plaintiffs cannot adequately represent the interests of this enormous class.

within the single class are not aligned. Most saliently, for the currently injured, the critical goal is generous immediate payments. That goal tugs against the interest of exposure-only plaintiffs in ensuring an ample, inflation-protected fund for the future....

The disparity between the currently injured and [exposure]-only categories of plaintiffs, and the diversity within each category are not made insignificant by the District Court's finding that petitioners' assets suffice to pay claims under the settlement. Although this is not a "limited fund" case certified under Rule 23(b)(1)(B), the terms of the settlement reflect essential allocation decisions designed to confine compensation and to limit defendants' liability. For example, as earlier described, the settlement includes no adjustment for inflation; only a few claimants per year can opt out at the back end; and loss-of-consortium claims are extinguished with no compensation.

The settling parties, in sum, achieved a global compromise with no structural assurance of fair and adequate representation for the diverse groups and individuals affected. Although the named parties alleged a range of complaints, each served generally as representative for the whole, not for a separate constituency. In another asbestos class action, the Second Circuit spoke precisely to this point:

> "[W]here differences among members of a class are such that subclasses must be established, we know of no authority that permits a court to approve a settlement without creating subclasses on the basis of consents by members of a unitary class, some of whom happen to be members of the distinct subgroups. The class representatives may well have thought that the Settlement serves the aggregate interests of the entire class. But the adversity among subgroups requires that the members of each subgroup cannot be bound to a settlement except by consents given by those who understand that their role is to represent solely the members of their respective subgroups." In re Joint Eastern and Southern Dist. Asbestos Litigation, 982 F.2d 721, 742-743 (C.A.2 1992), modified on reh'g sub nom. In re Findley, 993 F.2d 7 (C.A.2 1993).

The Third Circuit found no assurance here — either in the terms of the settlement or in the structure of the negotiations — that the named plaintiffs operated under a proper understanding of their representational responsibilities. That assessment, we conclude, is on the mark.

C

Impediments to the provision of adequate notice, the Third Circuit emphasized, rendered highly problematic any endeavor to tie to a settlement class persons with no perceptible asbestos-related disease at the time of the settlement. [83 F.2d] at 633; cf. *In re Asbestos Litigation*, 90 F.3d, at 999-1000 (Smith, J., dissenting). Many persons in the exposure-only category, the Court of Appeals stressed, may not even know of their exposure, or realize the extent of the harm they may incur. Even if they fully appreciate the significance of class notice, those without current afflictions may not have the information or foresight needed to decide, intelligently, whether to stay in or opt out.

Family members of asbestos-exposed individuals may themselves fall prey to disease or may ultimately have ripe claims for loss of consortium. Yet large numbers of people in this category — future spouses and children of asbestos victims — could not be alerted to their class membership. And current spouses and children of the occupationally exposed may know nothing of that exposure.

Because we have concluded that the class in this case cannot satisfy the requirements of common issue predominance and adequacy of representation, we need not rule, definitively, on the notice given here. In accord with the Third Circuit, however, we recognize the gravity of the question whether class action notice sufficient under the Constitution and Rule 23 could ever be given to legions so unselfconscious and amorphous.

V

The argument is sensibly made that a nationwide administrative claims processing regime would provide the most secure, fair, and efficient means of compensating victims of asbestos exposure. Congress, however, has not adopted such a solution. And Rule 23, which must be interpreted with fidelity to the Rules Enabling Act and applied with the interests of absent class members in close view, cannot carry the large load CCR, class counsel, and the District Court heaped upon it. As this case exemplifies, the rulemakers' prescriptions for class actions may be endangered by "those who embrace [Rule 23] too enthusiastically just as [they are by] those who approach [the rule] with distaste." . . .

For the reasons stated, the judgment of the Court of Appeals for the Third Circuit is

Affirmed.

■ JUSTICE O'CONNOR took no part in the consideration or decision of this case.

■ JUSTICE BREYER, with whom JUSTICE STEVENS joins, concurring in part and dissenting in part. Although I agree with the Court's basic holding that "settlement is relevant to a class certification," I find several problems in its approach that lead me to a different conclusion. First, I believe that the need for settlement in this mass tort case, with hundreds of thousands of lawsuits, is greater than the Court's opinion suggests. Second, I would give more weight than would the majority to settlement-related issues for purposes of determining whether common issues predominate. Third, I am uncertain about the Court's determination of adequacy of representation, and do not believe it appropriate for this Court to second-guess the District Court on the matter without first having the Court of Appeals consider it. Fourth, I am uncertain about the tenor of an opinion that seems to suggest the settlement is unfair. And fifth, in the absence of further review by the Court of Appeals, I cannot accept the majority's suggestions that "notice" is inadequate. . . .

The issues in this case are complicated and difficult. The District Court might have been correct. Or not. Subclasses might be appropriate. Or not. I cannot tell. And I do not believe that this Court should be in the business of trying to make these fact-based determinations. That is a job suited to the district courts in the first instance, and the courts of appeal on review. But there is no reason in this case to believe that the Court of Appeals conducted its prior review with an understanding that the settlement could have constituted a reasonably strong factor in favor of class certification. For this reason, I would provide the courts below with an opportunity to analyze the factual questions involved in certification by vacating the judgment, and remanding the case for further proceedings.

Notes and Questions

1. Is *Asbestos Litigation* consistent with *Amchem*? Immediately after deciding *Amchem*, the Supreme Court granted certiorari in *Asbestos Litigation*, vacated the judgment, and remanded for further consideration in light of *Amchem*. In a five-paragraph decision, the Fifth Circuit affirmed its original decision:

> After oral argument and reconsideration, we can find nothing in the *Amchem* opinion that changes our prior decision. . . .
>
> There are two controlling differences between this case and *Amchem*. First, this class action proceeded under Rule 23(b)(1); *Amchem* was a Rule 23(b)(3) case. Second, there was no allocation or difference in award, according to nature or severity of injury, in the present case as there was in *Amchem*; in the case here all members of the future claimant class are treated alike. Individual damage awards will subsequently be decided according to individual damages.
>
> The district court made extensive findings and found, specifically, that separate actions by members of the class would create a risk of adjudications with respect to individual members of the class which would as a practical matter be dispositive of the interests of the other members not parties to the adjudications or substantially impair or impede their ability to protect their interests. The language of the district court matches the language of Rule 23(b)(1)(B). No one has contested that finding of the district court, probably because it is incontestable.
>
> The Supreme Court stated in *Amchem* that a settlement class action, like all federal class actions, cannot proceed unless the requirements of Rule 23(a) are met, irrespective of whether the proposed settlement is deemed fair under Rule 23(e). We detailed in our prior opinion our agreement with the thorough study and conclusions by the district court, satisfying the requirements of class certification under Rule 23(a). All members of the class, and all class representatives, share the common interests: suffering harm from asbestos exposure and seeking equitable distribution of compensation from limited funds. None of the uncommon questions, abounding in *Amchem*, exist in the present case.
>
> The only conflict between members of the future claimant class could be competition for larger and earlier shares of available money, but that is precisely the reason for Rule 23(b)(1)(B) and the problem it is designed to

solve where the money is limited. That conflict or competition is controlled for the benefit of all members of the class. It follows that the lawyer representing the class serves only common interests of the class. [134 F.2d at 669-70.]

Judge Smith filed a lengthy dissent arguing that *Amchem* mandated reversal. Does the majority opinion convince you that *Amchem* is inapplicable? The Supreme Court has again granted certiorari in *Asbestos Litigation*. Because the case presents other issues — including the Rules Enabling Act issue hinted at in *Amchem*, the conflict with the Bankruptcy Code, the lack of jurisdiction over (and consequent failure to provide an opt-out right for) the absent *Asbestos Litigation* class members, and the lack of a "case or controversy" with respect to future claimants — it is not certain whether the Court will answer the question, though it is likely to do so.

2. In many ways, *Amchem* is as interesting for its dicta as for its holdings. It contains the Court's most extended discussion of the relationship among all of the Rule 23(b) provisions, even though the case itself was clearly a (b)(3) class action. It goes out of its way to state that class actions can be used in mass tort cases and to disown any contrary implications in the 1966 Advisory Committee Notes. Indeed, the Court seems to bless the modern trend of mass tort litigation class actions in appropriate "circumstances," although the Court refused to describe exactly what those "circumstances" might be. But the Court's blessing arose in the context of its discussion of the predominance requirement of Rule 23(b)(3), and did not indicate whether a similar attitude should carry over to other Rule 23 requirements.

The Court holds that settlement class actions are sometimes appropriate, and that they do not necessarily need to meet all of the requirements that a litigation class action would need to meet. The Court also holds that the fact of settlement is at least relevant to determining whether the requirements of a class action have been established, but that the settlement context of the class certification requires heightened attention to other elements of Rule 23 — especially the Rule 23(a)(4) requirement of adequacy of representation and, perhaps, the specific requirements of Rule 23(b). It also holds that the substantive fairness of the settlement cannot act as a surrogate for these requirements, nor can the common interests in the settlement be used to satisfy the common interest requirements of Rule 23(a) and (b)(3).

Aside from these statements, and the Court's observation that *Amchem* was simply too "sprawling," do you have any sense about when a settlement class action is appropriate and when it is not? How much influence should *Amchem* exercise over cases involving smaller stakes in which individual suits are not economically viable? What if the same conflicts of interest are not present? Does it signal that settlements in cases that are less mature than the asbestos litigation are automatically in trouble, or is maturity simply not a relevant factor in settlement class certification? Does *Amchem* mean that the efficient resolution of widespread controversies is irrelevant to the certification decision in a settlement class action? Does *Amchem* mean that no future claims can be settled through the class action device? How relevant is *Amchem* when the class action settles only present claims? How relevant is *Amchem* when a case can be certified as a mandatory class action? Does it affect the ability to use settlement class actions in non-tort cases?

3. The early returns on the meaning of *Amchem* are mixed. In addition to the Fifth Circuit's decision on remand in *Asbestos Litigation*, another federal

district court has certified a (b)(1)(B) limited fund mass tort settlement class action in In re Orthopedic Bone Screw Products Liability Litigation, 176 F.R.D. 158 (E.D. Pa. 1997). Settlement class actions in non-tort areas have also been approved. See Hanlon v. Chrysler Corp., — F.3d —, 1998 WL 296890 (9th Cir.) ((b)(3) settlement of consumer claims arising from defective minivans); In re Foundation for New Era Philanthropy Litigation, 175 F.R.D. 202, 205 (E.D. Pa. 1997) ((b)(1)(B) securities class action against insolvent debtor; distinguishing *Amchem* in part because claims were "exclusively for economic injury" and in part because *Amchem* approved class actions in securities cases). On the other hand, another district court refused to certify a nationwide settlement class action comprised of plaintiffs that smoked one tobacco company's cigarettes. Walker v. Liggett Group, Inc., 175 F.R.D. 226 (S.D. W.Va. 1997).

4. *Amchem* makes clear that the conflicts of interest within a class cannot be smoothed over by the common interests of a class in a settlement. Does *Amchem* suggest that class actions must be viewed as the aggregation of individual persons with individual interests, rather than as a collective entity with group interests? If so, does any conflict between two individual class members mean that a single class cannot be certified? If not, how much variation in interests is permissible before we say that a single class can no longer be used? Do the conflicts of interest among class members also doom *Asbestos Litigation*? Is the conflict-of-interest analysis of Judge Davis or Judge Smith more convincing?

Note *Amchem*'s suggestion that some of the conflicts of interest could be avoided by subclassing members with different interests. How would such a system work? Would separate counsel need to be appointed for each subclass? Would the subclasses need to be changed every time there was a change in the terms of the settlement? Isn't there a risk that one subclass will engage in strategic behavior in order to obtain a disproportionate share of the settlement? Whether strategic or not, what happens when one subclass declines to go along with the settlement, and jeopardizes the interests of all class members in the settlement?

5. In *Amchem*, the Court did not examine the issues of the potential conflicts of interest between class counsel and the class or of the alleged collusion between class counsel and the defendants. Both of these claims had been main attacks that objectors launched against the settlement in the trial court. See Georgine v. Amchem Products, Inc., 157 F.R.D. 246, 294-311 (E.D. Pa. 1994) (finding as a matter of fact that neither conflicts of interest nor collusion existed). For a passionate statement of the existence of such conflicts, written by a professor that was an expert witness on legal ethics for the objectors in the trial court, see Susan P. Koniak, *Feasting While the Widow Weeps:* Georgine v. Amchem Products, Inc., 80 Corn. L. Rev. 1045 (1995). Koniak argued that the future class members in *Amchem* were treated worse than class counsel's "inventory" plaintiffs, with whom the CCR defendants settled in a separate deal, and that class counsel sold out the interests of future claimants in order to obtain higher fees on their inventory cases. Judge Smith raises a variant of that same argument in *Asbestos Litigation*. For another view of the ethical conflicts that *Amchem* presented, see Carrie J. Menkel-Meadow, *Ethics and the Settlement of Mass Torts: Where the Rules Meet the Road*, 80 Corn. L. Rev. 1159 (1995).

The potential for conflicts, either within the class or between class counsel and class members, invariably exists in any settlement of class action claims.

Some groups of claimants always stand to do better in individual litigation rather than in the settlement, and others worse. If class counsel is adequate, he or she is likely to have numerous individual clients, not all of whom will necessarily be members of the class. On the other hand, the class definitions in both *Amchem* and *Asbestos Litigation*, which defined the class to include only those persons that had not yet filed a claim as of a certain date, guaranteed that class counsel would be representing claimants in the class and claimants not in the class simultaneously. In this situation, any differential treatment of the counsel's non-class plaintiffs raises a concern for conflict of interest and collusion. Should the problem be dealt with by insisting that, in order to meet the Rule 23(a)(4) adequacy requirement, class counsel define the class in a way that all of counsel's clients fit within the class? Should it be dealt with by requiring that counsel representing future claimants not represent any present claimants? Will this latter alternative lead to the appointment of class counsel that is less able than individual counsel are?

More generally, cases such as *Amchem* and *Asbestos Litigation* force us to consider the ethical responsibilities of lawyers in class actions. We examine the ethical concerns of representing groups in greater detail at pp. 898-925, *infra*. As a general proposition, however, our ethical rules are premised on traditional, adversarial, bi-polar litigation. Class actions, and especially settlement class actions, lie far afield from this model. Is it ultimately possible to determine the circumstances under which settlement class actions are appropriate without first determining the ethical responsibilities of counsel?

6. Should notions of dysfunction play into the decision about whether settlement class actions are appropriate? In *Amchem*, the risk of insolvency, and thus of insufficient assets, certainly existed, but the CCR defendants sought a settlement in which fewer than all their assets were committed to the settlement. In *Asbestos Litigation*, Fibreboard's own assets were clearly insufficient to satisfy all claims, but it had a contingent asset — the chance at unlimited insurance coverage — that was possibly worth billions. Fibreboard's settlement with its insurers reduced that contingent asset to a sum certain. Thus, Fibreboard's limited assets, plus its insurance proceeds, seemed to present a more classic circumstance of insufficient assets than the situation in *Amchem*.

In the Fibreboard situation, is a Rule 23(b)(1)(B) class therefore appropriate? Or would Fibreboard need to pay in all of its assets in order to make the limited fund argument? What incentive would there be for Fibreboard to settle the case if it had to give away the entire company in order to obtain class certification? Isn't Fibreboard entitled to some discount for the possibility that it might prevail in some cases, that its assets might not be consumed in litigation, and that it is saving plaintiffs the transaction costs of litigation? How much of a discount? Specifically, is the preservation of virtually all of its corporate assets for other creditors and stockholders too much of a discount? Suppose that Fibreboard had settled the insurance coverage case for $10 — could it still make the argument that it was entitled to (b)(1)(B) treatment? In other words, to what extent should the fairness of the insurance settlement that created the limited fund influence the question of whether (b)(1)(B) treatment is appropriate? How is a court to determine the fairness of the insurance settlement?

Using a dysfunction analysis, would the appropriate way to think about these questions be: (a) Is the settlement with the insurers a fair settlement of the dispute between them, given the risks to both Fibreboard and the insurers if they lost the coverage litigation? If the answer is no, then class certification under (b)(1)(B) is inappropriate, on the principle that a party hoping to benefit from a class action cannot voluntarily act in a way that creates dysfunction (see pp. 596-98, 608, *supra*); (b) If the answer is yes, then is there a likelihood that, without the class settlement, there would be insufficient assets available to satisfy all potential claimants? If the answer is no, then certification under (b)(1)(B) is inappropriate; and (c) If the answer is yes, then does the settlement equitably distribute the assets among claimants, treating claimants with similar legal claims similarly and dissimilar claimants in an appropriately dissimilar way? If the answer is no, then the settlement should not be approved. If the answer is yes, then the settlement has appropriately overcome the problem of lawyer dysfunction, and should be approved. In answering this last question, the court would need to consider the possibility of collusion and the creation of appropriate mechanisms to ensure that relevant differences in groups are accounted for, that adequate information is provided to class members about the settlement, and that inflation is accounted for in a way that the real value of future claims equates with the value of present claims.

It is not certain whether *Asbestos Litigation* would survive under this analysis. One of the great concerns would be that the class excluded the inventory claims of class counsel, so that the settlement might have treated some similar claims (those under the inventory settlements and those under the class settlement) differently and might have created an incentive for class counsel to agree to the class settlement in order to protect their present clients. Another would be the potential that post-1959 claims were treated too generously under the settlement.

7. The dysfunction analysis in the last Note would not have saved *Amchem*. Does this mean that settlement class actions of future claims are never permissible unless dysfunction can be avoided? Not necessarily. If a primary concern with (b)(3) class actions is the loss of individual control, couldn't the problems in a case like *Amchem*, in which assets are presumably sufficient to satisfy all claims, be handled by the simple device of an automatic and unlimited opt-out right at the time that the injury manifests itself? The CCR was unwilling to provide such a right in *Amchem*; instead, by limiting the number of claimants that could use the back-end opt-out right, they sought to make it difficult to exercise the right in practice. Other cases, however, have provided an unlimited back-end opt-out right. See Bowling v. Pfizer, Inc., 143 F.R.D. 141 (S.D. Ohio 1992). Thus, assuming that the Rule 23(a) requirements are satisfied (a condition which admittedly may occur more readily in the limited asset context), settlement class actions could occur whenever they would prevent dysfunction or when a back-end opt-out right is provided.

Alternatively, would settlements such as *Amchem* be more palatable if judges had the authority to modify the settlement in the event that it turned out to be inequitable for later claimants? See Jack B. Weinstein & Karin S. Schwartz, *Notes from the Cave: Some Problems of Judges in Dealing with Class Action Settlements*, 163 F.R.D. 369 (1995).

Would either of these proposals make settlement class actions in cases not involving dysfunction so unpalatable that they would rarely be used? Would that be such a bad result?

8. The answer to this last question may depend on what the alternatives are. As a practical matter, if we assume that *Amchem* signals a cutback in the ability to use mass tort settlement class actions, plaintiffs, defendants, and courts will simply find other ways to aggregate and resolve these cases. Will the

likely ultimate effect of *Amchem* be the use of more large-scale inventory settlements like the Substitute Ness Motley Agreement? Given that such settlements can occur without court approval, don't these types of agreements provide less protection to individual plaintiffs than a class settlement? Will the likely effect be that plaintiffs and defendants will simply file settlement class actions in more hospitable state courts? If so, are any of *Amchem*'s holdings of constitutional stature, and thus binding on state courts? Will the likely effect be the greater use of bankruptcy by defendants like Fibreboard and the CCR companies? If so, will the class members and other creditors of Fibreboard and the CCR defendants fare better or worse in bankruptcy? Should the Court have considered these questions in deciding *Amchem,* or are such consequences irrelevant to a proper understanding of Rule 23 in the settlement context?

4. Defendant Class Actions

Rule 23(a) states that a class "may sue or be sued." This language suggests that there can be defendant class actions as well as plaintiff class actions. Although we have focused until now on plaintiff class actions, it is in fact true that some courts have certified classes of defendants. Defendant class actions are, however, uncommon. Voluntary defendant class actions have rarely been widely sought under Rule 23(b)(3), presumably because, in most cases, most defendants that received notice of the action would opt out. This has been the common result, even when plaintiffs have threatened to sue individually any defendant who opted out. See In re Activision Securities Litigation, 621 F. Supp. 415 (N.D. Cal. 1985); Thillens, Inc. v. Community Currency Exchange Association of Illinois, Inc., 97 F.R.D. 668 (N.D. Ill. 1983). When class members opt out in large numbers, the usefulness of the defendant class action is largely lost. Compare In re Gap Stores Securities Litigation, 79 F.R.D. 283 (N.D. Cal. 1978) with Appleton Electric Co. v. Advance-United Expressways, 494 F.2d 126 (7th Cir. 1974).

Because mandatory defendant class actions certified under a Rule 23(b)(1) or (2) do not permit opt out by members of the class, they are a potential weapon in the aggregation of claims and parties in a common venue. Only a few defendant class actions have been certified under (b)(1). See, *e.g.,* In re Itel Securities Litigation, 89 F.R.D. 104, 126 (N.D. Cal. 1981); Technograph Printed Circuits, Ltd. v. Methode Electronics, Inc., 285 F. Supp. 714 (N.D. Ill. 1968). As a result, most defendant class actions have been certified under (b)(2). Note, though, that the language of (b)(2) is ambiguous about the possibility of defendant classes. Rule 23(b)(2) states such class actions are proper only when "the party opposing the class has acted or refused to act" in such a way as to justify injunctive or declaratory judgment relief." Some courts have thought it anomalous that a *plaintiff's* actions or inactions could be the predicate for a *defendant* class action and have refused to certify (b)(2) defendant class actions on that basis. See, *e.g.,* Paxman v. Campbell, 612 F.2d 848, 854 (4th Cir. 1980), cert.denied, 449 U.S. 1129 (1981); Henson v. East Lincoln Township, 814 F.2d 410 (7th Cir.), cert. granted, 484 U.S. 923 (1987). The Supreme Court has never spoken on the issue of defendant class actions. It granted certiorari in *Henson*, in which the Seventh Circuit had held that (b)(2) defendant class actions were impermissible, but deferred further proceedings for more than five years until the writ was finally dismissed. See 484 U.S. 1001 (1988); 506 U.S. 1042 (1993).

Assuming mandatory defendant class actions are permissible under either (b)(1) or (b)(2), they raise a number of difficult issues. Is it fair to bind an absent defendant class member to a judgment entered against the class when: (1) the member may not have even been given notice of the defendant class action (recall that no notice is required in a (b)(1) or (b)(2) class action); (2) the *plaintiff*, and not the defendant class, picked the defendant class representative; (3) the defendant class representative may have been an unwilling litigant and class representative; (4) absent class members may or may not be allowed to intervene; and (5) the absent class members may have objections to the jurisdiction, venue, or choice of law rules of the forum court which will not be available to the defendant class representative. See Elizabeth B. Brandt, *Fairness to the Absent Members of a Defendant Class: A Proposed Revision of Rule 23*, 1990 B.Y.U. L. Rev. 909.

One of the leading cases authorizing certification of a defendant class is Marcera v. Chinlund, 595 F.2d 1231 (2d Cir.), vacated on other grounds, 442 U.S. 915 (1979). Prior to *Marcera*, the Second Circuit had held that due process requires that pretrial detainees be permitted to have contact visits with family members. County jails in New York resisted this holding, thus forcing detainees in each county to sue to enforce the right. At the time of *Marcera*, 47 of 62 county jails still refused detainees this right. Then the lawyers representing the detainees hit upon the idea using both a plaintiff class of detainees and a defendant class, in which a single sheriff was sued as the representative of all 42 sheriffs in counties in which litigation over the issue had not yet commenced. The district court and Second Circuit both approved this tactic. The Supreme Court vacated the Second Circuit's decision and remanded for further consideration in view of Bell v. Wolfish, 441 U.S. 520 (1979), which had had overturned an earlier Second Circuit case defining the rights of pretrial detainees. The Supreme Court did not address the class action issues in its opinion, however, and on remand the trial court again certified a defendant class under Rule 23(b)(2). *Marcera v. Chinlund*, 91 F.R.D. 579 (W.D.N.Y. 1981).

The use of a dual plaintiff-defendant class in *Marcera* raised significant questions, including issues of numerosity (Were 42 sheriffs numerous enough, and how impracticable was joinder when all 42 were known and easily served?); typicality (Might different sheriffs have different security concerns, different jail architectures, and different levels of staffing?); and adequacy (How much could one sheriff be counted on to represent the interests of others?). The court nonetheless certified the class. Should the court have also considered the question of whether a suit in which the plaintiff class members had no dispute with 41 of the 42 defendants created a constitutional "case or controversy"? See Turpeau v. Fidelity Financial Services, Inc., 936 F. Supp. 975, 978 (N.D. Ga. 1996) (noting "the general rule that each named plaintiff must have a colorable claim against each defendant class member"; only exceptions involve conspiracy cases and cases in which defendants share a "juridical link . . . which sufficiently relates all the defendants so that a single action is preferable"), *aff'd*, 112 F.3d 1173 (11th Cir. 1997). Moreover, of what practical use was the defendant class in *Marcera*? Presumably the court could order all 42 sheriffs to obey the law, but they already knew that. The real fight would be over the implementation of the due process guarantee in each of the 42 different jails, and that would still require 42 essentially separate lawsuits.

Similar, but even larger, efforts to maintain a defendant class action failed in La Mar v. H & B Novelty Co., 489 F.2d 461 (9th Cir. 1973), and Kline v. Coldwell, Banker & Co., 508 F.2d 226 (9th Cir. 1974), cert. denied, 421 U.S. 963 (1975). In *La Mar*, a plaintiff who alleged that pawn brokers in Oregon violated the Truth in Lending Act brought a dual plaintiff-defendant (b)(3) class action, in which the plaintiff was the named representative for the plaintiff class and the pawn shop with which he dealt was the representative for the defendant class. The Ninth Circuit noted the significant standing issues presented in the case, but ultimately held that neither the typicality nor the adequacy requirements of Rule 23(a) could be met by a plaintiff who had no claim against most of the defendants in the case. In *Kline*, a plaintiff who alleged that real estate agents had conspired to fixed artificially high commissions for the sale of property in Los Angeles County also brought a dual plaintiff-defendant (b)(3) class of 400,000 sellers against 2,000 brokers. Focusing on the jury trial and other manageability problems that such a suit would cause even against one defendant, much less 2,000, the court held that no class could be certified.

In re Asbestos Litigation (p. 658, *supra*) employed a defendant class action successfully in the settlement class context. In order to obtain total peace, Fibreboard and its insurers needed to be certain that they would not be exposed to third-party claims for indemnity or contribution from other asbestos manufacturers. Fibreboard and the insurers agreed with one of the manufacturers agreed to give up all indemnity or contribution claims in return for Fibreboard and its insurers giving up their claims for indemnity and contribution. In order to give effect to this agreement, the insurers sued a defendant (b)(1) class, represented by the one asbestos manufacturer, for a determination that the proposed settlement was fair and reasonable. The district court held that it was. See Ahearn v. Fibreboard Corp., 162 F.R.D. 505 (E.D. Tex. 1995). The reason that the settlement went through without complaint from other manufacturers was that all manufacturers were interested in the infusion of $2 billion into the overall asbestos settlement pot, and had no reason to challenge the settlement.

Assuming that a defendant class representative does in fact litigate on behalf of the class as a whole, how does the representative recover the costs of this representation from the absent class members? No established rule exists today regarding the equitable apportionment of these fees and expenses. Unless this issue is resolved, isn't there also a serious potential conflict of interest present between the class representative and absent class members when the potential liability of the defendant class representative varies from that of the absent class members? Compare Richardson v. Kelly, 144 Tex. 497, 191 S.W.2d 857 (1945) (potential liability of class members ranged from $18 to $16,000) with *Gap Stores Securities Litigation*, 79 F.R.D. 283 (potential liability ranged from $42,000 to over $1 million).

For some of the literature concerning the proper scope of defendant class actions, see Brandt, *supra*; Scott D. Miller, Note, *Certification of Defendant Classes Under Rule 23(b)(2)*, 84 Colum. L. Rev. 1371 (1984); Note, *Defendant Class Actions*, 91 Harv. L. Rev. 630 (1978); A. Peter Parsons & Kenneth W. Starr, *Environmental Litigation and Defendant Class Actions: The Unrealized Viability of Rule 23*, 4 Ecology L.Q. 881 (1975); Angelo N. Ancheta, Comment, *Defendant Class Actions and Federal Civil Rights Litigation*, 33 UCLA L. Rev. 283 (1985); John M. Rogers, Comment, *Personal Jurisdiction and Defendant Class Actions*, 53 Ind. L.J. 841 (1978).

C. THE FUTURE OF CLASS ACTIONS

One thing should be apparent from our study of class actions: The federal class action today is being used in ways that the drafters would never have imagined in 1966. Whether you regard that fact as a good or a bad development, you might think that the time has come for a thoroughgoing revision of the rule — if for no other reason than to clarify so many of the loose ends left dangling in the bevy of inconsistent interpretations of the rule itself and of the policies that undergird the rule. Yet, aside from the likely adoption of Rule 23(f) later in 1998 and some specific legislation with respect to certain types of cases, Rule 23 has never received even a cosmetic facelift. Should the rule be revised? If so, how? Given the political winds that swirl around the rule, who should reform the rule — Congress or the Supreme Court?

The answers to these questions, as difficult as they are, must also account for a recent development in class action practice: the rise of the state class action. We previously studied one such class action in Phillips Petroleum Co. v. Shutts, 472 U.S. 797 (1985) (p. 294, *supra*), in which the Kansas class action was identical to Rule 23. As plaintiffs have perceived that federal courts are becoming more hostile to Rule 23, they are filing cases in state courts that either have more liberal class action rules, or at least more liberal interpretations of class action rules identical in language to Rule 23. Any efforts to tighten up Rule 23 to make it more difficult to obtain class certification in federal court will accelerate the trend toward state class actions; any efforts to liberalize federal class actions will likely slow down or reverse the trend. Should we tolerate two procedural systems in which the choice of court system can have such a dramatic effect on parties' ability to control their own litigation? Is the ultimate solution to make all class actions removable to federal court? Does this idea show insufficient respect for the role of state courts as laboratories of procedural experimentation and innovation?

We explore some of these issues by first examining some recent proposals for the reform of Rule 23, and then examining one mass tort case certified under the somewhat different standards of one state court.

1. The Reform of Rule 23

If you were asked to re-write Rule 23, how would you do it? Would you seek a dramatic overhaul — perhaps by requiring opt-in class actions to replace opt-out class actions, or by making all class actions mandatory? Or would you tinker with the rule to address a few of the more troubling aspects of present class action practice? Would you make the criteria for class certification more definite, or would you make them more discretionary? Would you entirely revamp the elements of Rule 23(a)? Would you also revamp Rule 23(b)? In the following two selections, we see two recent proposals for amending Rule 23 that were considered by the Advisory Committee on the Federal Rules of Civil Procedure. The second is more modest than the first.

PROPOSED REVISION TO RULE 23

February, 1995 Draft

Rule 23 . . .

(a) Prerequisites. One or more members of a class may sue or be sued as representative parties on behalf of all if — with respect to the claims, defenses, or issues certified for class action treatment —

    (1) the members are so numerous that joinder of all is impracticable,

    (2) legal or factual questions are common to the class,

    (3) the representative parties' positions typify those of the class,

    (4) the representative parties and their attorneys are willing and able to fairly and adequately protect the interests of all persons while members of the class until relieved by the court from that fiduciary duty; and

    (5) a class action is superior to other available methods for fair and efficient adjudication of the controversy.

(b) Whether a Class Action is Superior. The matters pertinent in deciding under (a)(5) whether a class action is superior to other available methods include:

    (1) the extent to which separate actions by or against individual members might result in

        (A) inconsistent or varying adjudications that would establish incompatible standards of conduct for the party opposing the class, or

        (B) adjudications that, as a practical matter, would dispose of the nonparty members' interests or reduce their ability to protect their interests;

(2) the extent to which the relief may take the form of an injunction or declaratory judgment respecting the class as a whole;

(3) the extent to which common questions of law or fact predominate over any questions affecting only individual members;

(4) the class members' interests in individually controlling the prosecution or defense of separate actions;

(5) the extent and nature of any related litigation already begun by or against members of the class;

(6) the desirability or undesirability of concentrating the litigation in the particular forum; and

(7) the likely difficulties in managing a class action which will be eliminated or significantly reduced if the controversy is adjudicated by other available means.

(c) Determination by Order Whether Class Action to Be Certified; Notice and Membership in Class; Judgment; Multiple Classes and Subclasses.

(1) As soon as practicable after persons sue or are sued as representatives of a class, the court must determine by order whether and with respect to what claims, defenses, or issues the action should be certified as a class action.

(A) An order certifying a class action must describe the class and determine whether, when, how, and under what conditions putative members may elect to be excluded from, or included in, the class. The matters pertinent to this determination will ordinarily include:

(i) the nature of the controversy and the relief sought;

(ii) the extent and nature of the members' injuries or liability;

(iii) potential conflicts of interest among members;

(iv) the interest of the party opposing the class in securing a final and consistent resolution of the matters in controversy; and

(v) the inefficiency or impracticality of separate actions to resolve the controversy.

When appropriate, a putative member's election to be excluded may be conditioned upon a prohibition against its maintaining a separate action on some or all of the matters in controversy in the class action or a prohibition against its relying in a separate action upon any judgment rendered or factual finding in favor of the class, and a putative member's election to be included in a class may be conditioned upon its bearing a fair share of litigation expenses incurred by the representative parties.

(B) An order under this subdivision may be conditional, and may be altered or amended before final judgment.

(2) When ordering that an action be certified as a class action under this rule, the court must direct that appropriate notice be given to the class under subdivision (d)(1)(C). The notice must concisely and clearly describe the nature of the action; the claims, defenses, or issues with respect to which the class has been certified; the persons who are members of the class; any conditions affecting exclusion from or inclusion in the class; and the potential consequences of class membership. In determining how, and to whom, notice will be given, the court may consider the matters listed in (b) and (c)(1)(A), the expense and difficulties of providing actual notice to all class members, and the nature and extent of any adverse consequences that class members may suffer from a failure to receive actual notice. . . .

(4) When appropriate, an action may be certified as a class action with respect to particular claims, defenses, or issues by or against multiple classes or subclasses. Subclasses need not separately satisfy the requirements of subdivision (a)(1). . . .

(e) Dismissal or Compromise. An action in which persons sue or are sued as representatives of a class must not, before the court's ruling under subdivision (c)(1), be dismissed, be amended to delete the request for certification as a class action, or be compromised without approval of the court. An action certified as a class action must not be dismissed or compromised without approval of the court, and notice of a proposed voluntary dismissal or compromise must be given to some or all members of the class in such manner as the court directs. A proposal to dismiss or compromise an action certified as a class action may be referred to a magistrate judge or other special master under Rule 53 without regard to the provisions of Rule 53(b).

(f) Appeals. A court of appeals may permit an appeal from an order granting or denying a request for class action certification under this rule upon application to it within ten days after entry of the order. An appeal does not stay proceedings in the district court unless the district judge or the court of appeals so orders.

PROPOSED REVISION TO RULE 23

August, 1996 Draft

Rule 23 . . .

(b) **Class Actions Maintainable.** An action may be maintained as a class action if the prerequisites of subdivision (a) are satisfied, and in addition: . . .

(3) the court finds that the questions of law or fact common to the members of the class predominate over any questions affecting only individual members, and that a class action is superior to other available methods for the fair and efficient adjudication of the controversy. The matters pertinent to the findings include:

(A) the practical ability of individual class members to pursue their claims without class certification;

(B) class members' interests in maintaining or defending separate actions;

(C) the extent, nature, and maturity of any related litigation involving class members;

(D) the desirability or undesirability of concentrating the litigation of the claims in the particular form;

(E) the difficulties likely to be encountered in the management of a class action; and

(F) whether the probable relief to individual class members justifies the costs and burdens of class litigation; or

(4) the parties to a settlement request certification under subdivision (b)(3) for purposes of settlement, even though the requirements of subdivision (b)(3) might not be met for purposes of trial.

(c) **Determination by Order Whether Class Action to be Maintained; Notice; Judgment; Actions Conducted Partially as Class Actions**

(1) When practicable after the commencement of an action brought as a class action, the court shall determine by order whether it is to be so maintained. . . .

(e) **Dismissal or Compromise.** A class action shall not be dismissed or compromised without hearing and the approval of the court, after notice of the proposed dismissal or compromise has been given to all members of the class in such manner as the court directs.

(f) **Appeals.** A court of appeals may in its discretion permit an appeal from an order of a district court granting or denying class action certification under this rule if application is made to it within ten days after entry of the order. An appeal does not stay proceedings in the district court unless the district judge or the court of appeals so orders.

Notes and Questions

1. Of the changes proposed in the August, 1996 draft, only the amendment to subsection (f) was sent forward by the Standing Committee to the Supreme Court, and by the Supreme Court to Congress. Barring congressional action disapproving the amendment, the amendment, which significantly changes the rule of appealability for class actions (see p. 553-54, *supra*) will go into effect in December, 1998. See 118 S.Ct., No.14, at Ct.R.-1 (May 15, 1998).

2. There is some chance that Congress will act. There are presently several bills pending in Congress to reform aspects of federal class action practice. One of the proposals is to permit the appeal of class actions on somewhat different terms than the terms stated in the amendment to subsection (f). See H.R. 1252, 105th Cong., 2d Sess., § 3 (1998).

3. After having spent the last chapter examining the present structure of Rule 23 and its constitutional, jurisdictional, political, economic, and social implications, who would you trust with the task of reforming Rule 23?

4. Between the January, 1995 and August, 1996 drafts presented above, another draft was circulated to the Advisory Committee. This draft looked something like the earlier draft, but it also included the provision for settlement class actions found in the later draft. It also proposed the creation of an opt-in class action when the action met the requirements of Rule 23(a) and when, in addition:

> "the court finds that permissive joinder should be accomplished by allowing putative members to elect to be included in a class. The matters pertinent to this finding include:
>
> "(A)   the nature of the controversy and the relief sought;
>
> "(B)   the extent and nature of the members' injuries or liability;
>
> "(C)   potential conflicts of interest among members;
>
> "(D)   the interest of the party opposing the class in securing a final and consistent resolution of the matters in controversy; and
>
> "(E)   the inefficiency or impracticality of separate actions to resolve the controversy."

See Edward H. Cooper, *Rule 23: Challenges to the Rulemaking Process*, 71 N.Y.U. L. Rev. 13, 68 (1996).

5. The Advisory Committee's February, 1995 proposal ignited a firestorm of opposition from virtually every quarter — including consumer groups, defense counsel, and academics. Does the history of the efforts of the Advisory Committee, which thus far have resulted only in a modest change to the appealability of class actions, suggest that the present rulemaking process for the Federal Rules of Civil Procedure is not the best vehicle for reform efforts? Does it suggest that we will be stuck with the present Rule 23 for a very long time?

6. The Advisory Committee's proposals retained the rather loosely textured wording and the basic structure of the present rule. Would it be better if the rule were less ambiguous? If it were even more general? How much discretion should the trial judge have?

7. The first Advisory Committee proposal was rather ambiguous about exactly when a class action would be mandatory, and when it would be an opt-out. Why the ambiguity? Was the Committee anticipating that the Supreme Court might require that absent class members be able to opt out in all cases? Did it wish to give the trial court the discretion to permit opt-outs even in presently mandatory class actions? Did it wish to withdraw the right to opt out in (b)(3) cases? Would such a proposal make it more difficult to obtain the aggregation in a single forum of truly complex litigation? Would it override plaintiffs' adversarial right to bring individual litigation in complicated cases?

8. The last Advisory Committee proposal attempts to authorize the use of settlement class actions. Would the outcome of *Amchem* have been any different, however, if the proposed (b)(4) had been in place? If not, in which cases would (b)(4) make a difference?

9. Proposals to amend the federal class action rule have spawned a rich literature. For a sampling, see American Bar Association, Report and

Recommendations of the Special Committee on Class Action Improvements, 110 F.R.D. 195 (1986); Bruce H. Nielson, *Was the Advisory Committee Right?: Suggested Revisions of Rule 23 to Allow More Frequent Use of Class Actions in Mass Tort Litigation*, 25 Harv. J. Leg. 461 (1988); William W Schwarzer, *Structuring Multiclaim Litigation: Should Rule 23 Be Revised?*, 94 Mich. L. Rev. 1250 (1996); Robert G. Bone, *Rule 23 Redux: Empowering the Federal Class Action*, 14 Rev. Litig. 79 (1994); Linda S. Mullenix, *Class Resolution of the Mass-Tort Case: A Proposed Federal Procedure Act*, 64 Tex. L. Rev. 1039 (1986); Thomas D. Rowe, Jr., *Beyond the Class Action Rule: An Inventory of Statutory Possibilities To Improve the Federal Class Action*, 71 N.Y.U. L. Rev. 186 (1996); Thomas E. Willging et al., *An Empirical Analysis of Rule 23 to Address the Rulemaking Challenges*, 71 N.Y.U. L. Rev. 74 (1996).

2. State Court Class Actions

SPITZFADEN v. DOW CORNING CORP.

619 So.2d 795 (La. App. 1993)

■ BARRY, Judge. This is an appeal from an order which certifies a class action. We affirm.

On February 12, 1992 Mary Spitzfaden filed a petition which alleges that she represents a class of residents and domiciliaries of Louisiana, and victims' spouses and children, who have suffered as a result of silicone breast implants. Defendants are Dow Corning Corporation, Dow Corning Wright Corporation, and Southern Baptist Hospital. Suit was filed under products liability, negligence, fraudulent misrepresentation and/or redhibition, breach of implied and express warranty, and intentional and negligent infliction of emotional distress. [Baptist Hospital was dismissed, and eight more plaintiffs and nine more defendants were added.]

On February 19, 1992 plaintiffs filed a motion to maintain and certify the class. A second supplemental and amending petition added two non-resident females based on breast implant surgery in Louisiana. Several defendants filed an objection to class certification.

On March 4, 1992 the trial court *ex parte* signed an order conditionally certifying the class and a hearing was scheduled. Several defendants filed for a continuance based on their need to investigate the claims. The court stated that certification, if granted, could be recalled. The court denied the motion and informed defense counsel that a hearing on the issue of certification would be held April 3, 1992.

On April 3, 1992 defense counsel argued that a continuance should be granted to permit discovery. No testimony was taken. Plaintiffs introduced documents from a federal lawsuit that related to silicone implants, and submitted an FDA pamphlet (which states that 2,000,000 American women have breast implants) and an DHHR update on silicone gel-filled implants. On April 14, 1992 the trial court signed an order certifying the class "in accordance with" an Ohio federal judge's certification of a similar class. The defendants appeal the certification. . . .

THE LAW

La.C.C.P. art. 591 et seq. set forth criteria for a class action:

(1) A class so numerous that joinder is impractical;

(2) The joinder as a party of at least one member of the class who is able to provide adequate representation for the absent members; and

(3) A "common character" among the rights of the representative(s) and the absent members of the class. . . .

The burden of proof as to the criteria is on the plaintiffs. . . . Certification will not be denied because of individual questions of [damages] when predominant liability issues are common to the class. . . .

If the superiority of a class action is disputed, the trial court must decide whether the intertwined goals of effectuating substantial law, judicial efficiency and individual fairness would be better served by another procedural device. . . .

The "common character" requirement encompasses more than the existence of questions of law and fact as to each member or class. The requirement restricts the class action to those cases in which it would achieve economy of time, effort, expense, and promote uniformity of decision as to the plaintiffs similarly situated without sacrificing fairness or bringing about undesirable results. . . .

A trial court has great discretion to certify a class. The court has wide latitude when considering policy matters and applying an analysis of the facts. The decision will not be overturned absent manifest error. . . .

ANALYSIS

In the April 14, 1992 order certifying the class the trial court defined the class to be:

> All residents and domiciliaries of Louisiana who have had silicone gel breast implants placed in their bodies, and spouses and children of such persons, whose implants were manufactured, developed, designed, fabricated, sold, distributed or otherwise placed into the stream of commerce by defendants, and who have sustained any adverse medical condition thereby, or who are likely to suffer such adverse medical condition as a result thereof in the future; and all persons who had such silicone gel breast implants placed in their bodies within the state of Louisiana, and spouses and children of such persons, whose implants were manufactured, developed, designed, fabricated, sold, distributed, or otherwise placed into the stream of commerce by defendants.

The trial court noted that a federal court in Ohio recently certified a class in a similar silicone gel breast implant lawsuit. The trial court said the class would "protect Louisiana litigants" against "the possibility of other litigants in other jurisdictions rushing to judgment." The trial court declared that suits of this potential magnitude should be managed efficiently and economically from the outset.

The trial court determined that the persons constituting the class are so numerous that it would be impractical for all to join or be joined. The court found that the number of claimants would amount to thousands. The court noted Dow Corning's statistics that at least 1,000,000 women in the United States have silicone gel breast implants, or about 20,000 females in Louisiana with a potential claim. The element of numerosity was met.

The court found a common character because all members of the class had surgery and have a potential common right against the defendants. The trial court felt that the named representatives of the class and the class' counsel would fairly represent the other members of the class. The claims as to liability are claims of every member of the class.

Common issues of law and fact predominate over any individual issues and the class action is the superior procedural vehicle. The cost of individual litigation would be prohibitive. It is in the interest of Louisiana courts to maintain the class because it would prevent a multitude of lawsuits which would inundate the court system.

The trial court did not abuse its . . . discretion. We find no manifest error in the court's judgment. The judgment is affirmed.

Notes and Questions

1. The requirements of the Louisiana class action rule overlap those of Rule 23 to a significant extent, but the Louisiana rule is more explicit than the federal rule about the desire to achieve economy, fairness, and similar treatment of similar persons. It is also simpler, although beneath its simplicity lies a great deal of interpretation and the constitutional limitations of all class actions. Overall, is the Louisiana approach better than Rule 23?

2. As it has become more difficult to achieve class certifications in federal court, the use of state court class actions (especially in certain "class-action-friendly" states) has been on the rise. If the parties can accomplish in state court that which they cannot accomplish in federal court, then the role of Rule 23 will diminish in importance and influence. Constrained only by the federal and state constitutions, state court may well lead the way into the next round of procedural reform. Since the national government led the way into the last round, perhaps this is as it should be.

3. There are different ways to deal with increasing divergence between state and federal class action practice. One way, which we suggested in the last Note, is to accept it and learn from it. A second way is to federalize state class actions. After passage of the Private Securities Litigation Reform Act in 1995, many plaintiffs, faced with unfavorable law in federal court, abandoned their federal securities claims, and, being careful to avoid complete diversity, have started to bring class actions in state court in which they plead only state-law fraud claims. This tactic has not escaped the attention of Congress, which presently has pending before it legislation that would permit the automatic removal of state-law securities cases to federal court. See H.R. 1689, 105th Cong., 1st Sess. (1997). More generally, there are also proposals to make any

state class action involving parties from different states removable to federal court. See, *e.g.*, H.R. 3789, 105th Cong., 2d Sess. (1998). Are these proposals wise?

4. A third response to state class actions is to make state class action practice uniform. In 1986, the American Bar Association proposed a uniform class action act that could be adopted at both the state and the federal level. It was quite similar to the February, 1995 Advisory Committee draft that we examined at p. 693, *supra*. See American Bar Association, Report and Recommendations of the Special Committee on Class Action Improvements, 110 F.R.D. 195 (1986). But the idea of a unified standard for all class actions predated the ABA Proposal. See Uniform Law Commissioners' Model Class Actions [Act][Rule] §§ 1-3, in 12 Uniform Laws Annotated 27, 28-32 (Supp. 1994); see also Allen D. Vestal, *Uniform Class Actions*, 63 A.B.A. J. 837 (1977). At least four different states have state class action rules more or less patterned on this approach. See Iowa R. Civ. P. 42.1-42.20; N.D. R. Civ. P. 23; Mich. Ct. R. 3.501; Or. R. Civ. P. 32.

5. A final response to the rise of state class actions is to find other ways to aggregate cases. In the context of complex litigation, one of the dangers of state class actions is the attitude expressed in *Spitzfaden* — the desire to certify a class to "protect" local citizens against a potentially global resolution elsewhere. When that protection permits local plaintiffs to obtain an disproportionately large share of limited relief, however, state class actions can create dysfunction. Is there anything that can prevent this problem from occurring? We turn now to the last aggregation device available — the proceeding in bankruptcy.

CHAPTER SIX

COMPULSORY CONSOLIDATION IN BANKRUPTCY

> When they came, the cupboard was bare.
>
> Jack B. Weinstein

Our search for the Holy Grail — the procedural tool that permits the consolidation of all the claims of all the parties as a means of preventing joinder complexity — has foundered. We have seen that traditional joinder tools are unable to bring in bystanders who do not wish to join the fray. Class actions can accomplish this task, but they too are limited. First, except in limited circumstances, they cannot force the joinder of claimants who wish to opt out and proceed separately. Second, state (and arguably federal) mandatory class actions must allow class members who do not have sufficient contacts with the forum to opt out of the class. Third, at least until a settlement appears imminent, a federal judge has no power to prevent class members from proceeding in state or federal court with suits identical to the class action. Fourth, the size of class actions are necessarily limited by concerns for manageability and adequate representation; it is unlikely that, in cases involving diffuse harms allegedly caused by many defendants, all of the claims of all of the potentially interested parties can be brought together in one action. Finally, class members need to possess a claim against their opponents. Class actions may not be able to include future claimants whose claims against an opponent have not yet matured; thus, even if all the other hurdles can be overcome, class actions can buy peace only for a time in situations in which injuries are ongoing and new claims are arising daily.

Sixteen years ago, this was how far our joinder and consolidation rules had come. For most cases it was far enough, but for the truly massive case, it was not. In 1982, however, everything changed. Johns-Manville, the world's largest manufacturer of asbestos, filed for Chapter 11 bankruptcy. The filing sent shock waves through the legal community. Part of the shock resulted from the fact that Johns-Manville was still solvent. The other part resulted from the way in which Johns-Manville proposed to use bankruptcy: to consolidate both present and future asbestos claims in one forum, to create a mechanism to pay all present and future claims within this proceeding, and to emerge from the Chapter 11 reorganization intact, healthy, and claim-free.

In this chapter we examine whether bankruptcy can in fact accomplish what Johns-Manville set out to do. In Section A we examine, very briefly, some of the basic jurisdictional, procedural, and substantive principles of bankruptcy. In Section B, we examine the use of bankruptcy as a means of consolidating related cases in one forum; here we explore the ability of a bankruptcy court to consolidate claims against parties other than the entity filing for bankruptcy and the ways in which a bankruptcy court can consolidate the claims of those whose injuries will occur in the future. Fn Section C, we look at the bankruptcy court's ability to modify its orders when unforeseen circumstances occur. In Section D, we compare the bankruptcy solution with class action aggregation.

A. A PRIMER ON BANKRUPTCY

Because we cannot fully explain bankruptcy jurisdiction, procedure, and substance in a few pages, our more modest goal is to provide enough information for you to appreciate the benefits and drawbacks of using bankruptcy as a consolidation device in complex litigation. Consequently, we begin our explanation of bankruptcy law not with the substance of bankruptcy, but rather with its jurisdictional and procedural provisions — provisions that create the most powerful, comprehensive consolidation device we have thus far studied. Then we can turn to a discussion of the substance of bankruptcy in order to see when a party can use bankruptcy to effectuate joinder.

1. Jurisdiction and Procedure

In the prior chapters, we have seen that, in order for a consolidation technique to be completely effective, it must possess certain features: (1) A single court system must have subject matter jurisdiction over all the claims asserted by and against all the relevant parties and bystanders; (2) If jurisdiction is not exclusive, some mechanism for removal of claims from parallel courts must exist; (3) Once related cases are consolidated in one court system, some transfer mechanism must allow all of the cases to be consolidated, for both pretrial and trial purposes, in one venue; (4) The transferee court must be able to assert personal jurisdiction over all parties and bystanders; (5) The transferee court must possess the power to stay proceedings in other courts; and (6) The transferee court must possess some mechanism for drawing in (or precluding) the claims of bystanders who do not wish to assert their claims at the present time. Despite proposals to create such a device, we have seen that no present joinder device meets each of these criteria. Let's examine how bankruptcy fares.

Need for a Court with Subject Matter Jurisdiction over All Claims. 28 U.S.C. § 1334(a) grants to the federal district courts "original and exclusive jurisdiction of all cases under title 11." (Title 11 is the title that contains the entire Bankruptcy Code, and should not be confused with Chapter 11, which is one set of provisions within the Bankruptcy Code.) In addition, 28 U.S.C. § 1334(b) grants "original but not exclusive jurisdiction of all civil proceedings arising under title 11, or arising in or related to cases under title 11." This promising language makes a distinction among (1) a "case," which is the process triggered when the plaintiff (usually called the debtor) files a bankruptcy petition that seeks to release the debtor from his or her debts, (2) a "civil proceeding," which is a controversy that is resolved in the context of settling the debtor's affairs, and (3) a "related to" case, which (in general terms) is a case that might have an effect on the debtor's estate. See Douglas G. Baird, The Elements of Bankruptcy 22 (rev. ed. 1993). Although the court has exclusive jurisdiction only with respect to the "case" itself, the concurrent jurisdiction over "civil proceedings" and "related to" cases provides one court that can in theory hear all the claims by or against all the parties. But see Richard H. Fallon et al., Hart Wechsler's Federal Courts and Federal System 901-02 (4th ed. 1996) (describing potential constitutional defects with "related to" jurisdiction).

There is, however, a fly in the jurisdictional ointment. Under 28 U.S.C. § 1334(c)(1), a district court *may*, "in the interest of justice, or in the interest of comity with State courts or respect for State law, . . . abstain[ ] from hearing a particular proceeding arising under title 11 or arising in or related to a case under title 11." See In re Franklin, 179 B.R. 913 (Bankr. E.D. Cal. 1995) (listing 12 factors to consider in deciding whether to invoke discretionary abstention). Moreover, under § 1334(c)(2), a district court *must* abstain, upon timely motion, in "a proceeding based upon a State law claim or State law cause of action, related to a case under title 11 but not arising under title 11, with respect to which an action could not have been commenced in a court of the United States absent jurisdiction under [§ 1334]" as long as the "action is commenced, and can be timely adjudicated, in a State forum of appropriate jurisdiction." There is one important limitation on mandatory abstention: The liquidation or estimation of personal injury and wrongful death cases "shall not be subject to the mandatory abstention provisions of section 1334(c)(2)." 28 U.S.C. § 157(b)(4).

Need for Power to Remove Cases from State to Federal Court. Because federal jurisdiction is not exclusive for civil proceedings and "related to" cases, some mechanism for removal of these cases is required if global consolidation is to be achieved. 28 U.S.C. § 1452(a) gives a "party" the right to remove "any claim or cause of action in a civil action other than a proceeding before the United States Tax Court or a civil action by a governmental unit to enforce such governmental unit's police or regulatory power, to the district court for the district where such civil action is pending, if such district court has jurisdiction of such claim or cause of action under section 1334 of [Title 28]." Under this broad removal power, civil proceedings and "related to" cases can be removed without the restrictions that we saw in other removal statutes. See 1 Collier on Bankruptcy ¶ 3.01[4][c] (Lawrence P. King ed., 15th ed. 1996) (comparing § 1452 with § 1441). Moreover, since the removal provisions are separate from § 1334, some courts have held that the mandatory abstention provisions of § 1334(c)(2) do not apply to removed actions. See In re Duval County Ranch Co., 167 B.R. 848 (Bankr. S.D. Tex. 1994); In re Branded Products, Inc., 154 B.R. 936 (Bankr. W.D. Tex. 1993); but see In re Fulfer, 159 B.R. 921 (Bankr. D. Id. 1993) (mandatory abstention applies to removed action).

Bankruptcy courts are not, however, required to hear all removed claims. Under § 1452(b), the district court "may remand such [removed] claim or cause of action on any equitable ground." Among the factors usually considered are the possibility that remand will avoid duplication or uneconomical use of judicial resources, the degree of relatedness of the removed case and the underlying bankruptcy case, the effect that remand will have on the bankruptcy estate, whether the removed claim or cause of action involves state law issues (particularly unsettled or difficult state law issues), comity, prejudice to involuntarily removed parties, the possibility of inconsistent results, and concerns of forum non conveniens. See River Cement Co. v. Bangert Bros. Construction Co., 852 F. Supp. 25 (D. Colo. 1994); *Branded Products*, 154 B.R. at 947; In re Riverside Nursing Home, 144 B.R. 951 (S.D.N.Y. 1992).

Another hitch in removal jurisdiction is that removal occurs to the federal district encompassing the state court from which the case was removed; some venue-transfer mechanism for aggregating all the related proceedings in one federal forum is still required. Cf. In re National Developers, Inc., 803 F.2d 616 (11th Cir. 1986) (district court lacked jurisdiction over case removed to district court in which bankruptcy case was filed); In re Trafficwatch, 138 B.R. 841 (Bankr. E.D. Tex. 1992) (although removal should occur to district court embracing state court, removal directly to district court in which bankruptcy case was filed is not a jurisdictional defect).

Need for a Transfer Mechanism to Place All Cases in One Venue for All Purposes. 28 U.S.C. § 1408, the basic venue provision, locates the bankruptcy case either in the district of the debtor's domicile, residence, principal place of business, or principal location of assets, or in the district in which certain related bankruptcy proceedings are pending. With minor exceptions, proceedings and "related to" cases also "may be commenced" in the district court in which the underlying bankruptcy case has been filed. 28 U.S.C. § 1409(a). So far, so good: The bankruptcy case, as well as civil proceedings and "related to" cases, can be venued in a single forum.

There are, however, two problems. First, we need a mechanism to transfer removed cases from the district to which they have been removed to the district in which the bankruptcy case is pending. Second, § 1409 says "may," not "shall." There is some case authority for the proposition that, despite the use of the word "may," § 1409(a) requires that proceedings and "related to" cases be filed in the district in which the bankruptcy case is pending. See Jeffrey T. Ferriell, *The Perils of Nationwide Service of Process in a Bankruptcy Context*, 48 Wash. & Lee L. Rev. 1199, 1207 n.43 (1991). The better reading of § 1409 and related provisions, however, is that proceedings and "related to" cases can be commenced in any federal district in which venue exists. See 1 Collier on Bankruptcy, *supra*, ¶ 3.02[2][a]; Brock v. American Messenger Service, Inc., 65 B.R. 670 (D.N.H. 1986).

To solve these problems, the bankruptcy statutes have two distinct transfer provisions. First, 28 U.S.C. § 1412 provides that "[a] district court may transfer a case or proceeding under title 11 to a district court for another district, in the interest of justice or for the convenience of the parties." See *National Developers*, 803 F.2d at 844. Second, 28 U.S.C. § 157(b)(5) requires "personal injury tort and wrongful death claims" to be tried either "in the district court in which the bankruptcy case is pending, or in the district court in the district in which the claim arose, as determined by the district court in which the bankruptcy case is pending." While judges typically use § 157(b)(5) to transfer tort cases to forums other than the forum in which the bankruptcy case is pending, it also can be used as a means to consolidate tort cases in a single forum.

Like § 1404, the bankruptcy provisions allow the transfer of a case for all purposes, including trial; moreover, unlike § 1404, neither § 1412 nor § 157(b)(5) limits transfer just to those federal courts in which the case might initially have been brought. But some negatives of § 1404 still remain. Proceedings and "related to" cases can often be brought in multiple venues. Aside from tort claims, there is no mechanism, akin to § 1407, for consolidating all cases and proceedings in a single forum. To achieve global consolidation, reliance on other venue transfer mechanisms is required. The venue transfer provisions are a weak link if bankruptcy is to be used as a means of consolidating related cases.

Need for a Court with Jurisdiction over the Person and Property of Those Individuals with an Interest in the Litigation. Bankruptcy courts have their own rules of procedure, which often mimic the Federal Rules of Civil Procedure. One rule that is significantly different, however, is Bankruptcy Rule 7004(d), which states in full: "The summons and complaint and all other process except a subpoena may be served anywhere in the United States." See also § 1334(e) (granting exclusive jurisdiction over "all of the property, wherever located, of the debtor as of the commencement of such case, and of property of the estate"). Thus, district courts sitting in bankruptcy need not worry about territorial limitations; nationwide service of process exists. But see Ferriell, *supra* (suggesting use of minimum contacts standard in order to avoid constitutional difficulties, unfairness, and forum shopping); cf. Edward S. Adams & Rachel E. Iverson, *Personal Jurisdiction in the Bankruptcy Context: A Need for Reform*, 44 Cath. U. L. Rev. 1081 (1995) (suggesting need for broader personal jurisdiction over foreign defendants).

Need for a Power to Stay Related Litigation as a Means of Forcing Litigation into a Single Forum. Some of the deficiencies in subject matter jurisdiction, removal, and venue could be cured if the court sitting in bankruptcy had the power to stay cases in other forums. The primary source for a stay in bankruptcy is 11 U.S.C. § 362. Section 362 is long and intricate; here we can highlight only some basic notions. The fundamental point of § 362 is that the filing of a petition automatically "operates as a stay, applicable to all entities, of . . . the commencement or continuation . . . of a judicial, administrative, or other action or proceeding against the debtor that was or could have been commenced before the commencement of the case under this title, or to recover a claim against the debtor that arose before the commencement of the case under this title"; it also stays various other actions that are designed to jump a particular creditor ahead of the queue and thereby disadvantage other creditors and the bankruptcy estate. Note that the stay does not make distinctions as such among the bankruptcy case, civil proceedings, and "related to" cases; *any* actions and proceedings that might affect the debtor's estate must come to a halt.

Nonetheless, the stay has significant limits. Some claims, which can loosely be described as governmental enforcement actions that affect the debtor's estate, are not stayed. § 362(b). Moreover, under § 362(d), a party can petition the bankruptcy court for relief from the automatic stay. The standard ground for requesting, and for granting, such relief is that a party in interest in the bankruptcy case lacks "adequate protection," see § 362(d)(1), which means in essence that the party's interest in specific property is likely to become less valuable during the pendency of the bankruptcy case, see § 361. Since litigants typically have unsecured claims, they cannot take advantage of § 362(d).

Another way in which the stay is limited is that it stays only those proceedings that affect the debtor's estate. Thus, actions against third parties do not typically come within the stay. Even should a stay run to third parties, the stay is not permanent; it expires, at the latest, at the end of the bankruptcy case. At that point, the case against the debtor having ended, the case against the second manufacturer can proceed — unless a global settlement of all claims is achieved in the bankruptcy proceeding.

Furthermore, the stay is usually operative only against those claims which were or could have been brought on the date of the filing of the bankruptcy petition. It does not affect proceedings or cases that first arose after the bankruptcy petition was filed. With post-petition cases, the stay is important only in the sense that it prevents any effort to enforce a judgment against the debtor.

A second source of power to enter a stay is § 105, which empowers a court to "issue any order, process, or judgment that is necessary or appropriate to carry out the provisions of this title." This grant suggests a quasi-All Writs Act power that can smooth over the limitations of § 362, but it is not quite as broad as it sounds: A § 105 stay is available only when "a policy embraced in some other part of the Bankruptcy Code justifies it." See Baird, *supra*, at 9.

Need for Power to Draw in (or Preclude) Claims of Bystanders. The automatic stay prevents prosecution of claims or causes of action not only of present litigants, but also of those who could have brought claims prior to the filing of the petition. Thus, the stay solves a part of the bystander problem. But other parts of the problem still remain. The stay cannot affect those bystanders who do not yet have a claim. Furthermore, a stay of a claim is a pretty small stick to force bystanders into litigation; barring statute of limitations issues, they could simply wait out the bankruptcy case and file after the stay has dissolved. What is really needed is a way either to force parties and bystanders into the bankruptcy case (the Rules 19, 22, and 23 approaches), or else to preclude their claims forever as a consequence of their failure to do so (the ALI approach).

The Bankruptcy Code adopts the latter, preclusive method. The end result of a successful bankruptcy is a discharge of the debtor's debts. (There are some important types of debts that cannot be discharged in bankruptcy, but we do not explore them here. See 11 U.S.C. § 523; Cohen v. De La Cruz, — U.S. —, 118 S.Ct. 1212 (1998).) This discharge "voids any judgment . . . to the extent that such judgment is a determination of the personal liability of the debtor with respect to any debt discharged," and it also "operates as an injunction against the commencement or continuation of an action, the employment of process, or an act, to collect, recover, or offset any such act as a personal liability of the debtor." §§ 524(a)(1), (a)(2). Therefore, a person who, as of the date of the filing of the petition for bankruptcy, has a claim against the debtor must assert the claim within the bankruptcy proceeding — or else the claim is forever barred.

This preclusion method has one qualification and two important limitations. The qualification is simply that a particular debt cannot be discharged (and thus the claimant precluded from further suit) unless the debt was listed or placed on a schedule of liabilities in such a way that the creditor had an opportunity to file a timely proof of claim. § 523(a)(3).

The first significant limitation of the bankruptcy discharge is that it discharges only those debts accrued up to a specified time during the bankruptcy proceedings. (For some of the provisions establishing appropriate cut-off dates, see §§ 502(f), 727(b), 1141(d).) Since the later-accruing claims will typically be unrelated to the earlier, this limitation usually poses no real issue for consolidation of related cases. In some cases, however, it does. Take, for example, the Johns-Manville situation. Due to the long latency period involved with asbestos exposure, there were some persons who had not yet manifested an injury from their exposure to Johns-Manville asbestos products. Since their claims had not yet accrued, it was problematic at best to argue that they had a "claim" to assert in the bankruptcy proceedings in the same way that those who had existing injuries had a claim. Without a claim, however, the court could not discharge Johns-Manville's obligations to future claimants, and there would be no way that a global resolution of the asbestos controversy could occur.

Second, and obviously, the bankruptcy discharge is effective only against the debtor, not against other defendants (unless they too file for bankruptcy). Therefore, discharge cannot force a single resolution of all aspects of a multi-defendant controversy.

Other Provisions. Two other procedural provisions are relevant. First, our description thus far has proceeded as if the district judges personally handle bankruptcy cases. In fact most activity in bankruptcy cases occurs before bankruptcy judges, who are Article I appointees. The requirement that cases be adjudicated by Article III judges puts certain limits on the powers of bankruptcy judges, and has led to a curious division of responsibility in which district judges are authorized to (and almost always do) refer to bankruptcy judges most matters known as "core proceedings," but cannot refer to bankruptcy judges "non-core proceedings" and tort actions that are core proceedings. See 28 U.S.C. § 157. We do not wish to wade into the swampy distinctions between "core" and "non-core" proceedings or about the constitutionality of this division of responsibility, except to note that many important issues remain unresolved. Our point is a simple one: The notion that bankruptcy consolidates cases in a single forum is a bit disingenuous. In fact, some of the proceedings are likely to be conducted by the district judge and some proceedings are likely to be conducted by the bankruptcy judge, with the district judge acting in effect as an appellate court over the bankruptcy judge's decisions. See 28 U.S.C. §§ 157, 158. A district judge can avoid this split by declining to refer a case to the bankruptcy court or by withdrawing an order of reference. See §§ 157(a), (d). Given the intricacies of bankruptcy law, however, district judges are loathe to exercise this power in even the most complex cases.

Second, the Seventh Amendment, which guarantees the right to jury trial in certain civil actions, casts a large shadow over bankruptcy law. Bankruptcy itself was an equitable device, and jury trials did not obtain in equitable cases. Therefore, the essential functions of the bankruptcy court in collecting the debtor's assets, passing on asserted claims, and distributing the assets, do not involve jury trial. But many of the civil proceedings and "related to" cases over which the district court has jurisdiction carry a right to jury trial. Presently, there is considerable debate about how far the jury trial right carries into bankruptcy proceedings and whether Article I bankruptcy judges can conduct jury trials. See Granfinanciera, S.A. v. Nordberg, 492 U.S. 33 (1989); Baird, *supra*, at 20-22. The fact that many bankruptcy proceedings are jury-triable, and the likelihood that only the district court can try these proceedings means that a bankruptcy case is likely to be divided between the district and bankruptcy courts; once again, a global resolution in a single courtroom is problematic.

Conclusion. Bankruptcy is the most comprehensive device for the aggregation of related cases in a single forum. But as an aggregation device, it has important limitations. In Section B, we explore some creative efforts to overcome these limitations. Before we do, however, we need to sketch some substantive bankruptcy law

2. Substance

Until now we have been talking about bankruptcy as if it were a fabulous procedural device for complex cases. There is, however, an obvious problem with bankruptcy: Someone has to go bankrupt. This is not an event that most people, or most businesses, relish. It is also not easy to do.

While you do not technically have to be insolvent to enter bankruptcy, you will need to demonstrate some cash flow problem that makes it unlikely that you will be able to meet your present or future debt responsibilities.

In this subsection we examine a few key substantive aspects of bankruptcy. Our goal is not to teach you bankruptcy law; it is rather to tell you enough so that you can appreciate the substantive backdrop against which consolidation in bankruptcy must occur.

Douglas G. Baird, THE ELEMENTS OF BANKRUPTCY

5, 7-9, 12-18 (rev. ed. 1993)

Like other titles of the United States Code, Title 11 is divided into chapters. Chapters 1, 3, and 5 contain provisions that are generally applicable to all bankruptcy cases. The remaining chapters set out different procedures for each distinct kind of bankruptcy case. . . .

Chapter 1 provides definitions (§ 101) . . . [and, *inter alia*,] contains what appears to be a broad grant of power to the bankruptcy judge [(§ 105)]. . . .

Chapter 3 of the Bankruptcy Code deals with case administration. Sections 301 through 307 tell us how a bankruptcy case begins. Sections 321 through 331 set out the rules governing those who administer the bankruptcy estate. . . . Sections 341 through 350 set out a number of basic procedures. . . .

Because even the simplest bankruptcy cases take time, we need to have rules that allow the trustee (and the debtor in possession) to act and that keep the creditors from taking matters into their own hands. These rules are largely the province of § 361 through § 366. By far the most important of these sections is § 362. Section 362 imposes an "automatic stay" upon all creditors. . . .

A crucial part of any bankruptcy case is identifying the claims that exist against the debtor and the assets the debtor has. Chapter 5 of the Bankruptcy Code tells us how to go about doing this. Sections 501 through 510 focus on claims against the estate.

Sections 541 through 560 tell us what assets the estate has. . . . The trustee (or the debtor in possession) is charged with assembling the assets that are available to meet the creditors' claims and then distributing them. These assets are called "property of the estate" and form the "bankruptcy estate." Section 541 also draws a sharp distinction between individuals and corporations. The future income of individuals does not become property of the estate, while the future income of a corporation does. . . .

In many cases, property to which the creditors of a debtor are entitled is property to which a third party lays claim. In these cases, the trustee may have to bring an action to vindicate the creditors' right to the property. If the debtor itself could have brought the cause of action, it is property of the estate under § 541. In other cases, the trustee must exercise one of the so-called "avoiding" powers. . . . The avoiding powers . . . allow the trustee to set aside fraudulent conveyances. . . . Another provision allows the trustee to set aside transfers that were made to a creditor on the eve of bankruptcy. . . .

The remaining chapters in Title 11 set out different kinds of bankruptcy cases. For example, Chapter 9 is reserved for municipalities. . . .

Individuals and corporations typically can choose from several different chapters. An individual debtor will most often be in either Chapter 7 or Chapter 13. An ordinary corporation can file either a Chapter 7 petition or a Chapter 11 petition. The kind of bankruptcy petition that is brought turns on the goals of the person filing the petition. The court, however, enjoys a broad power to convert a case brought under one chapter into a case brought under another. . . .

An individual who is hopelessly in debt can file a Chapter 7 bankruptcy petition, give up all nonexempt assets, and walk away from nearly all prebankruptcy obligations. Section 727 gives this debtor a "discharge." Because future income of an individual does not become property of the estate under § 541, the effect of § 727 is to give the individual debtor the right to enjoy future income free from the claims of creditors. This right, coupled with other bankruptcy doctrines that apply in cases involving individuals, provides the debtor with a "fresh start." . . .

Like individuals, corporations may file under Chapter 7. These cases, however, have nothing to do with giving someone a fresh start. Chapter 7 offers no discharge to a corporation. In the typical Chapter 7 case, the firm has ceased its operations or will cease them in short order. . . . Chapter 7 gives the managers of a corporation a way of surrendering. . . .

Chapter 11 serves principally as a vehicle for restructuring corporations. . . . Although individuals are eligible for Chapter 11, only those with substantial business ventures are likely to find it in their interest to use it. . . . [T]he debtor in possession rather than the trustee ordinarily continues to run the firm. In Chapter 11, however, enough may be at stake so that creditors themselves play a role. A committee of creditors is chosen by the United States trustee at the start of the case. . . . In practice, . . . the United States trustee often attempts to find a "representative" creditors' committee. . . . In the largest cases, there may be multiple creditors' committees as well as a committee of the equityholders. . . .

David L. Buchbinder, FUNDAMENTALS OF BANKRUPTCY

457-58, 461-63, 468-69, 479, 482-90 (1991)

The goal of a Chapter 11 proceeding is to obtain confirmation of a Chapter 11 reorganization plan that will satisfy creditors while retaining assets or continuing the debtor's business. . . .

The first step is to file a reorganization plan. Along with the plan, the *plan proponent* (entity filing the plan) must also file a *disclosure statement*.

... The purpose of a disclosure statement is to tell the creditors anything about the plan and debtor that may affect the creditors' decision to vote for or against the plan....

Once the court approves the disclosure statement, the plan proponent may solicit acceptances or rejections of the plan in attempting to seek confirmation.... Creditors return their ballots to the plan proponent, who must file a report with the court summarizing the results of the balloting. This report, along with all original ballots, is filed before the hearing....

Section 1122 concerns the classification of claims within a plan. All creditors must be placed within classes. All creditors in a given class must have claims that are substantially similar. For example, a secured creditor and an unsecured creditor may not be included in the same class because these claims are not substantially similar.... More than one secured claim may also be included in the same class, but it is a better and recommended practice to separately classify each secured claim....

Section 1122 does not require that all creditors of the same type be placed within the same class. Thus, it is possible to divide substantially similar claims into separate classes....

Section 1124 creates a distinction between impaired and unimpaired claims or interests. This concept is peculiar to Chapter 11. Generally, an unimpaired claim is a claim that is being paid according to its terms on the effective date of the plan. Otherwise, the claim is impaired. For example, when a class of unsecured claims is scheduled to be paid in full upon the effective date of a plan, the class is unimpaired....

There is an important difference in treatment accorded to unimpaired versus impaired classes of claims. An unimpaired class of claims is deemed to have accepted a plan whether or not the class votes to accept or reject the plan. ... Only impaired creditors are entitled to vote for or against confirmation of the plan....

A class of claims accepts a plan if, among those voting, a majority of creditors in number and two-thirds in dollar amount vote to accept the plan. This is a dual requirement. If either less than a majority of creditors in number or less than two-thirds in dollar amount, among those voting, vote to accept a plan, then the class has rejected the plan and a cramdown procedure will be necessary to confirm the plan over the class rejection....

A class of interests, such as shareholders, will accept a plan if two-thirds in dollar amount of the class of interests accepts the plan....

At the confirmation hearing, the court will confirm the plan only if it finds that the plan meets each and every requirement of Section 1129(a).... Under Section 1129(a), the court must make twelve findings.... Many of the findings that the court must make will not be problematic in most proceedings.

First, the court must find that the plan complies with all provisions of the Bankruptcy Code.... Second, the proponent of the plan must comply with any applicable provisions of the Bankruptcy Code.... Third, the plan must be proposed in good faith and not by any means forbidden by law.... Fourth, any fees to be paid to an issuer of securities or for acquiring property under the plan must be approved by the court as reasonable. Fifth, the court must approve the debtor's postconfirmation management. . . . Sixth, if the debtor's rates are subject to governmental regulation, the Bankruptcy Court must find that any applicable regulatory agency has approved any rate changes provided for in the Chapter 11 plan. . . . Disputes regarding any of the six foregoing confirmation requirements arise infrequently. The final [six] elements present a somewhat different state of affairs.

Seventh, the court must find that as to each impaired class of claims, the individual claimholders have either accepted the plan or will be receiving, on the effective date of the plan, an amount not less than the class would receive in the event the debtor were liquidated under Chapter 7. . . . The mere fact that creditors are assured a minimum dividend, however, does not act to approve the plan over rejection of the plan by the class. Approval of a plan over class rejection will require use of the Chapter 11 cramdown procedures. . . .

Eighth, the court must find that each class either accepts the plan or is unimpaired. . . . If an impaired class of claims or interests does not accept a plan, the plan will only be confirmable if the debtor can successfully comply with the Chapter 11 cramdown procedures. . . .

Ninth, the court must find that the plan will pay all administrative expenses in full on the effective date of the plan and all other nontax priority claims in cash on the effective date of the plan, unless any affected class of priority claim agrees to deferred payments. . . .

Tenth, the court must find that at least one impaired noninsider class has accepted the plan. . . .

Eleventh, the court must find that the reorganization is not likely to be followed by further reorganization or liquidation unless the plan so provides. This is commonly known as a *feasibility requirement*. . . .

Twelfth, the court must find that any fees due the court will be paid in full on the effective date of the plan. . . .

Any good Chapter 11 plan will be constructed so as to be able to achieve a successful cramdown upon dissenting classes. . . . Cramdown litigation is among the most intense in the bankruptcy system. . . .

For the court to proceed with a cramdown, it must first find that all other elements of Section 1129(a) have been complied with except . . . the plan's acceptance by one or more impaired classes . . . . To achieve a successful cramdown, the court must find that the plan does not discriminate unfairly and that the plan is fair and equitable with regard to each class of rejecting impaired claims or interests against whom cramdown is sought. The issue of unfair discrimination is often raised but is rarely found. More frequently, it is the "fair and equitable" standard that creates dispute. Fortunately, Section 1129(b)(2) defines the meaning of "fair and equitable" depending upon whether the class of claim to be crammed down is secured, unsecured, or is a class of interest holders. . . .

[T]he concept of cramdown with regard to a class of secured claims is simple. If the class is going to be paid the full value of its claims in some manner, the plan will be confirmable over the claimant's objection. . . .

There are two methods of obtaining confirmation over rejection of a plan by a class of unsecured claims. The first method is very simple. If the plan proposes to pay an affected unsecured class in full on either the effective date of the plan or over time, the plan will be confirmable. Once again, a class that receives all that it is entitled to will not be heard to complain. Second, if a class of unsecured claims is not going to be paid in full, the court must find that no junior class of claims or interests will retain any interest in any property of the estate. This is commonly known as the absolute priority rule. . . .

A plan may be confirmed over the objection of a class of interest holders under two circumstances. First, if the affected interest holders are paid any redemption prices to which they be entitled, the plan may be confirmed over their objection. Second, if no junior interest holder retains any interest in the estate, the plan may be confirmed over rejection by a dissenting class. . . .

A confirmed Chapter 11 plan acts as a new contract between the debtor and *all* of its creditors. . . . Confirmation also revests the debtor with all property of the estate free and clear of all liens and interests except as provided for by the plan. Confirmation of a plan also acts to discharge all debts that arose before the date of confirmation except as provided in the plan.

Notes and Questions

1. Bankruptcy proceedings can begin in either of two ways: with a petition from the debtor (this is called a voluntary proceeding) or with a petition filed by a certain number of creditors (an involuntary proceeding). 11 U.S.C. §§ 301, 303.

2. Collecting assets, voiding preferences, allowing claims, creating classes of claims and interests, establishing and negotiating with creditors' committees, developing and confirming plans, balloting, using the cramdown procedure, distributing assets — bankruptcy litigation sounds very complex all by itself. But we are talking about using bankruptcy as a means of aggregating cases that affect the debtor. So now we have two complex matters going on in one forum: resolution of a bunch of cases that were causing joinder complexity and resolution of a bankruptcy case. Might the joinder of these two different types of cases cause other problems, such as pretrial, trial, or remedial complexity? If so, will the cure for joinder complexity be worse than the disease?

3. On the other hand, one of the benefits of aggregation in bankruptcy is similarity in treatment: Similar classes of claimants seem to receive roughly comparable remedies. In this book we have especially stressed the importance of the like procedural treatment of like cases. Is the like substantive treatment of like cases equally or more important? Does substantively equal treatment make pretrial, trial, or remedial problems worthwhile?

4. You might have noticed a huge problem with using bankruptcy to aggregate and resolve large numbers of cases. In order to know how to distribute assets equitably in a liquidation, or in deciding whether holders of two-thirds of the value of a particular class of claims approves the plan, the court needs to have some sense of how much each claim is worth. This process, which includes

the collection of possible claims, the allowance of proper claims, the estimation of their value, and the ranking of their priority for payout, is described in §§ 501-10 of the Bankruptcy Code. When only a few of the claims — say, tort suits — are for uncertain amounts and uncertain liability, it is usually easiest to try these claims as a part of the bankruptcy proceedings; then their value is established to a certainty. In complex mass torts, however, trying each case to establish a precise value for each tort claim would take decades, would deprive everyone of a remedy until the last case was tried, and might consume all of the resources of the debtor. Hence, the standard allowance process is an obstacle to the use of bankruptcy to resolve related cases in a single proceeding. It becomes an even higher hurdle when a bankruptcy court tries to figure out how to deal with the future claims of people who have not yet manifested an injury.

5. Throughout this primer we have focused on obstacles to using bankruptcy as a consolidation tool. Therefore, the successful use of bankruptcy depends on whether all, or at least most, of these obstacles can be overcome in complex litigation. Potential solutions are the subject of the ensuing section.

B. STRETCHING BANKRUPTCY TO MEET THE NEEDS OF COMPLEX LITIGATION

The types of problems that complex litigation poses for bankruptcy as a consolidation device can be loosely grouped into three categories. First, assume the simplest situation: that the cases causing joinder complexity involve (a) only one defendant, and (b) only claimants who have already been injured by the defendant's conduct. Second, now assume that the cases creating joinder complexity involve more than one defendant. Third, assume that some of the claimants do not yet have matured claims. In a truly complex case, all three scenarios may be involved.

The success of bankruptcy as a consolidation tool hinges entirely on bankruptcy's ability to solve the problems posed by these three scenarios. In this section we examine each set of problems in turn. As you read the progression from the first scenario to the third, ask whether, at some point, the usefulness of bankruptcy as an aggregation tool breaks down. If so, at what point, and what can we do with cases that lie beyond that point?

1. Consolidating Present Cases and Claims against a Debtor in a Single Forum

A.H. ROBINS CO. v. PICCININ

788 F.2d 994 (4th Cir.), cert. denied, 479 U.S. 876 (1986)

■ RUSSELL, Circuit Judge. Confronted, if not overwhelmed, with an avalanche of actions filed in various state and federal courts throughout the United States by citizens of this country as well as of foreign countries seeking damages for injuries allegedly sustained by the use of an intrauterine contraceptive device known as a Dalkon Shield, the manufacturer of the device, A.H. Robins Company, Incorporated (Robins) filed its petition under Chapter 11 of the Bankruptcy Code, 11 U.S.C. §§ 101 et. seq., in August, 1985.

Background

The device, which is the subject of these suits, had been developed in the 1960's by Dr. Hugh Davis at the Johns Hopkins Hospital in Baltimore, Maryland. In mid-1970 Robins acquired all patent and marketing rights to the Dalkon Shield and engaged in the manufacture and marketing of the device from early 1971 until 1974, when it discontinued manufacture and sale of the device because of complaints and suits charging injuries arising allegedly out of the use of the device. The institution of Dalkon Shield suits did not, however, moderate with the discontinuance of manufacture of the device, since Robins did not actually recall the device until 1984. By the middle of 1985, when the Chapter 11 petition was filed the number of such suits arising out of the continued sale and use of the Dalkon Shield device earlier put into the stream of commerce by Robins had grown to 5,000. More than half of these pending cases named Robins as the sole defendant; a codefendant or codefendants were named in the others. Prior to the filing, a number of suits had been tried and, while Robins had prevailed in some of the actions, judgments in large and burdensome amounts had been recovered in others. Many more had been settled.[4] Moreover, the costs of defending these suits both to Robins and to its insurance carrier had risen into the millions. A large amount of the time and energies of Robins' officers and executives was also being absorbed in preparing material for trial and in attending and testifying at depositions and trials. The problems arising out of this mounting tide of claims and suits precipitated this Chapter 11 proceeding.

The filing of the Chapter 11 petition automatically stayed all suits against Robins itself under section 362(a) of the Bankruptcy Code, even though no formal order of stay was immediately entered. . . .

[After discussing whether the stay could be extended to include claims against Robins' co-defendants, see p. 742, *infra*, the court continued:]

The second appeal questions the validity of the district court's order of November 9, 1985, fixing the venue for the trial of all Dalkon Shield cases and providing for the transfer of such cases to the District Court of the Eastern District of Virginia at Richmond. . . .

Turning to the merits of the appeal on this part of the case, we address first the power of the district court, sitting in bankruptcy, to enter an order fixing the venue for the trial of tort personal injury claims against the debtor and for transferring all such cases to the bankruptcy court for trial and disposition. . . . We do not understand the appellants to contend that under

---

4. . . . A recent article in the Nat. L.J. . . . states that by mid 1985, Robins, along with its insurer, Aetna Casualty & Surety Company, "had paid roughly $517 million for 25 trial judgments and 9,300 settlements since the first verdict in 1975."

[28 U.S.C. § 157(b)(5)] the district court did not have authority . . . to issue an order fixing the venue for trial of cases against a Chapter 11 debtor. They do argue, however, that the sense of the section, if not its precise language, was to decentralize the trial of these tort claims and to permit their continuance for trial in the court in which the complaints were filed and that the ruling of the district judge in this case fixing venue in the district court in which the bankruptcy petition was filed flies in the face of this congressional purpose.

[After reviewing the legislative history of this section, the court of appeals disagreed.] Unquestionably the district court in this case had the power under the statute to fix the trial venue in its district for all the Dalkon Shield cases. . . .

And there are very real considerations that support a centralization of all the Dalkon Shield claims, *at least at first*, in the district court having jurisdiction of the bankruptcy. The "single focal point" of this proceeding is the development of a reasonable plan of reorganization for the debtor, one which will work a rehabilitation of the debtor and at the same time assure fair and non-preferential resolution of the Dalkon Shield claims. These Dalkon Shield claims, asserted by thousands of individuals in courts throughout the United States on behalf of both citizens of this country and citizens or residents of other countries, represent what are characterized in the Act as "contingent or unliquidated claims." 11 U.S.C. § 502. Ordinarily such claims would be "estimated" by the bankruptcy court as a "core proceeding," 28 U.S.C. § 157(b)(2), for purpose of allowance if failure to do so "would unduly delay the administration of the case." 11 U.S.C. § 502(c); 3 Collier on Bankruptcy, § 502.03 (15 ed. 1982). That duty of estimation in a proper case under section 502(c) is not a permissive one; it is a mandatory obligation of the bankruptcy court. This customary process of estimation of contingent claims is, however, different where the unliquidated, contingent claims are personal injury tort claims.

Section 157(b)(2)(B) excepts from the definition of "core proceedings" personal tort claims against the debtor. The bankruptcy court thus is without authority under the Act over "the liquidation or estimation of contingent or unliquidated personal injury or wrongful death claims against the estate for purposes of *distribution* under Title 11[.]" 28 U.S.C. § 157(b)(2)(B) [(italics added)]. It will be observed, however, that the statute denies authority to the bankruptcy court to "estimate" contingent claims only if the purpose is to make a "distribution" of the assets of the debtor; the statute does not in express terms deny to the bankruptcy court the authority, or relieve it of the duty, to "estimate" the contingent "personal injury" claims for purposes of determining the feasibility of a reorganization. And such has been the construction of statute which has been adopted by the courts which have had to face the issue, the two leading cases being proceedings arising out of the asbestos litigation. Roberts v. Johns-Manville Corp., 45 B.R. 823, 825-26 (S.D.N.Y. 1984); In re UNR Industries, Inc., 45 B.R. 322, 326-27 (N.D. Ill. 1984). Both of these cases hold that estimation of the debtors' potential personal injury tort liabilities as an incident of the development of a plan of reorganization are core proceedings within the bankruptcy court's jurisdiction and that such estimations are not foreclosed by Section 157 (b)(5) of the [Bankruptcy] Act.

This is not to say the personal injury claimants in this proceeding will not be ultimately entitled, if they elect to do so, to have a jury trial of their claim in the district court. Section 157(b)(5) gives them that right. But, even though the tort claimants may be entitled to their jury trials, the bankruptcy court is not relieved of its duty in a Chapter 11 proceeding to estimate those contingent claims. The real question thus arises as to which proceedings take precedence, whether the estimation by the bankruptcy court of the claims or the jury trials in the district court of the claims. The authorities which have considered this question in connection with a complicated products liability situation such as this are all unanimous. The estimations of the potential and pending claims by the bankruptcy courts should precede any trials of the claims.... After all, the first and primary purpose of the proceedings ... is to ascertain whether a fair reorganization of the debtor can be achieved. This purpose may well be thwarted if the energies of the debtor's executives and officers are initially diverted by, and the resources of the debtor dissipated in the expenses of litigating, the trial of thousands of personal injury suits in courts throughout the land spread over an interminable period of time....

There are 5,000 suits pending against the debtors in this proceeding. There are perhaps an equal number not filed. If all these claims were to be tried, the expense of discovery proceedings and trial would likely consume all the assets of the debtor and exhaust all the resources of its executives and employees.... Since the Dalkon Shield litigation began, forty claims have actually been tried but over $517,000,000 have been expended in defending or settling Dalkon Shield suits or claims. It is impossible to anticipate the stupendous costs that would be involved if all the claims here had to be tried. If the claimants as a whole are to realize reasonable compensation for their claims, it is obviously in the interest of the class of claimants as a whole to obviate the tremendous expense of trying these cases separately. If the bankruptcy court could arrive at a fair estimation of the value of all the claims and submit a fair plan of reorganization based on such estimation, with some mechanism for dispute resolution and acceptable to all interested parties, great benefit to all the claimants could be achieved and the excessive expense of innumerable trials, stretching over an interminable time, could be avoided. In addition, the real purpose of the proceeding (*i.e.*, a reorganization of the debtor and its continuance as a going business) could be attained....

No progress along estimating these contingent claims, however, can be made until all Dalkon Shield claims and suits are centralized before a single forum where all interests can be heard and in which the interests of all claimants with one another may be harmonized.... We approve of the idea and find it conducive of the interests of all concerned.

However persuasive may be the reasons for fixing temporarily at least venue of all the pending suits against the debtor in the district court sitting in bankruptcy where all the other Dalkon Shield claims not in suit may be handled together, the question remains as to what procedure must be followed in effecting such change of venue in order to satisfy the requirements of due process. It is the position of the appellants that a right of action in tort is "property" which may not under due process be adversely affected by an involuntary change of venue in the absence of a full hearing after reasonable notice....

"Due process" does not establish an inflexible standard to be rigorously applied in all cases.... We conclude, therefore, that due process requires some form of notice and opportunity for a hearing before there can be a change of venue and before trial of a personal injury tort cause of action against a debtor may be transferred *finally* from the court in which the cause was initially filed to the district where the bankruptcy proceedings are pending.

We reach this conclusion not only under due process analysis, but also under the language and Rules issued under the Bankruptcy Act....

[Since no notice was given to the individual Dalkon Shield claimants, but was instead given only to a committee created in the bankruptcy proceeding (the Committee of Representatives of Dalkon Shield Claimants), the court of appeals concluded that the notice of the hearing on the transfer motion] did not represent compliance with Bankruptcy Rule 9014 or with due process.

Conceding that notice to the Committee did not qualify as service on the individual claimants, it does not follow that the absence of such notice may be fatal to due process in this proceeding. The notice to the Committee may have been sufficient . . . to permit the issuance of a provisional order providing for a fixing of venue in the district court sitting in bankruptcy for all the pending Dalkon Shield cases against the debtor *but giving the claimants individual notice and an opportunity to object and to be heard before the order became final in any case where the plaintiff has filed an objection.* That procedure would satisfy due process.... And, as we read the record as well as the formal order of the district court, this is precisely what the district court intended, though the language of its order may be obscure on the point....

We are of the opinion, because of this possible want of clarity in the order assailed, that such order must be modified to make it crystal clear that the determination of venue therein is, as we have said, conditional, dependent finally and ultimately on a ruling to be made only after notice to all claimants advising them of their right to enter any objections they may have to such a tentative ruling and to submit a motion for abstention in their particular case. The notice to be given all claimants could be in the form of a letter both to the claimant and to his or her attorney stating the conditional ruling made subject to a final hearing, to become final only after reasonable opportunity given all claimants to object and/or to seek abstention.... In order to achieve this modification in the order of the district judge, this phase of the appeal is remanded to the district court for further proceedings in accordance with the opinion herein.

We do not presume to suggest rigid guidelines for the district judge to follow when considering objections to the transfer. We believe it important, however, to observe that although there may be distinct advantages of the tort claims being transferred to Richmond, those advantages should be balanced against the disadvantages that may be advanced at the hearing. In that regard, some cases may be fully prepared and ready for state trial. Some cases may require substantial numbers of local witnesses. Claimants may be receiving critical medical, physical or psychological care in a local area which would have to be halted or transferred to Richmond. All of these factors are relevant. Moreover, there are issues of state law that may substantially affect the results in individual cases.

IN RE A.H. ROBINS CO.

880 F.2d 694 (4th Cir.), cert. denied, 493 U.S. 959 (1989)

■ WIDENER, Circuit Judge. On July 26, 1988, the bankruptcy court and the district court jointly confirmed the "Sixth Amended and Restated Plan of Reorganization" (the Plan) submitted by A.H. Robins Company, Inc. (Robins). In Re A.H. Robins Co. Inc., 88 B.R. 742 (E.D. Va. 1988). Rosemary Menard-Sanford and certain other personal injury claimants, who voted against the Plan, appeal. They challenge the district court's approval of the disclosure statement, the district court's use of a one claimant one vote voting procedure, [and] the district court's feasibility finding . . . . We affirm.

On April 1, 1988, the district court approved the "Sixth Amended and Restated Disclosure Statement". The appellants argue that the disclosure statement does not contain adequate information. 11 U.S.C. § 1125(b) requires that before solicitation of approval or disagreement of a plan of reorganization the disclosure statement must contain "adequate information" and be approved by the court. 11 U.S.C. § 1125(a)(1) defines "adequate information" as "information of a kind, and in sufficient detail, as far as is reasonably practicable in light of the nature and history of the debtor and the condition of the debtor's books and records, that would enable a hypothetical reasonable investor typical of holders of claims or interests of the relevant class to make an informed judgment about the plan." The determination of whether the disclosure statement has adequate information is made on a case by case basis and is largely within the discretion of the bankruptcy court. . . . The challenged disclosure statement began its 261 pages of information with a thorough summary of the complex plan in terms that almost anyone could understand. It explained, among much more, the amount to be put into trust and made available for the payment of claims, the various estimates of how much money was required, a warning that the funds furnished to pay the estimates might not be enough to pay all claims in full, the sources of funding, an explanation of the various funding provisions which depended on the outcome of various appeals, how claims would be handled, the four options for processing claims and the background of the case. The disclosure statement continued with a discussion of the Robins company, the Dalkon Shield, various litigation regarding the Dalkon Shield, the reorganization, the proposed merger with American Home Products Corporation (AHP), the historical stock values of both AHP and Robins, and federal income tax consequences. The final part of the disclosure statement contains actual copies of the Plan, the Claimants Trust Agreement, the Other Claimants Trust Agreement, the Claims Resolution Facility, the Merger Agreement, Aetna's additional insurance policy, AHP's Annual Report, the Liquidation Analysis and biographies of the proposed Trustees.

The appellants contend that the disclosure statement is misleading because it contains a statement that in order to approve the Plan the district court must make a finding that the Plan contains enough money to satisfy all claims in full. They point out that in reality there may not be enough money to cover all claims. The disclosure statement, however, makes that clear to the claimants. . . .

The appellants' principal challenge to the disclosure statement, however, is that it is inadequate because it does not contain ranges of recovery for claimants with specified injuries. . . . There is no requirement in case law or statute that a disclosure statement estimate the value of specific unliquidated tort claims. In fact, with so many various unliquidated personal injury claims which vary so much in the extent and nature of injury, medical evidence and causation factors, any specific estimates may well have been more confusing than helpful and certainly would be more calculated to mislead. Given the quantity and quality of the information in the disclosure statement we can not say that the district court abused its discretion in finding that it contained "adequate information."

The appellants next challenge the legality of the voting procedure used to confirm the Plan. The difficulty surrounding the voting procedure resulted from the 195,000 unliquidated claims for personal injuries (Dalkon Shield Claims). The controlling legal provisions for the reorganization include 11 U.S.C. § 1126(a) which provides that a "holder of a claim or interest allowed under section 502 of this title" is entitled to vote on the acceptance of a plan. 11 U.S.C. § 502(a) provides that a claim filed "is deemed allowed unless a party in interest" objects. Robins objected to all the Dalkon Shield Claims. [Bankruptcy Rule] 3018(a) provides that "[n]otwithstanding objection to a claim or interest, the court after notice and hearing may temporarily allow the claim or interest in an amount which the court deems proper for the purpose of accepting or rejecting a plan." The district court, after notice and a hearing, ordered that, for purposes of voting, each Dalkon Shield Claim was estimated and allowed to be equal. It found, fully supported by the record, that any attempt to evaluate each of the 195,000 individual claims for voting purposes would cause intolerable delay. The challenge to the voting procedure relies on 11 U.S.C. § 1126(c) which requires that for a plan to be approved by a class the creditors "that hold at least two-thirds in amount and more than one-half in number" accept the plan. The argument is that § 1126(c) requires use of a weighted voting method which estimates the value of the claims and gives larger claims more votes.

We do not decide whether the district court's voting procedure violated § 1126(c) because, in view of the outcome of the vote, the challenged procedure was at most harmless error. 139,605 claimants voted. Of that 131,761 (94.38%) voted in favor of the Plan. In Kane v. Johns-Manville

Corp., 843 F.2d 636, 641-647 (2d Cir. 1988), the district court, faced with 52,440 unliquidated personal injury claims, assigned each claim the value of one dollar for voting purposes. 95.8% of those claims voted to approve the plan. The Second Circuit in reviewing the decision did not decide whether the equal voting plan was error and decided instead that the alleged irregularities were at most harmless error. Given that 94.38% of the Dalkon Shield Claimants voted for the Plan, we hold that, at most, harmless error was committed.[3]

Appellants' next point on appeal is that the district court erred in finding that the Plan complied with 11 U.S.C. § 1129(a)(7)(A)(ii) which requires that an impaired class of claims such as the Dalkon Shield claimants must "receive . . . under the Plan . . . property of a value . . . that is not less than the amount that . . . [they would] receive . . . if the debtor were liquidated under Chapter 7" and § 1129(a)(11) which requires that confirmation is not likely to be followed by liquidation or the need for further reorganization. This latter is called the feasibility requirement.

Both such complaints are based on the "same source: the failure of the district court to break out the components of the $2.475 billion figure."[*] The argument is that since the figure was not broken down, if it turned out to be too low, then the Plan would not be feasible because it could not pay all the claimants in full, which, as the appellants note, is an assumption of the Plan and the disclosure statement. The appellants thus complain about the same fact again, except in slightly different context. In all events, we think there is no merit to the claim, but that the care the district court took in arriving at its estimate deserves mention.

The challenged findings are based on an estimation process that the district court undertook as a result of our decision in A.H. Robins Co., Inc. v. Piccinin, 788 F.2d 994, 1013 (4th Cir. 1986), cert. denied, 479 U.S. 876 (1986). . . . To assist in the estimation process, the district court appointed Professor Francis E. McGovern, who was familiar with such matters, as the court's expert to develop a data base regarding Dalkon Shield Claims. The Dalkon Shield Claimant's Committee, the Unsecured Creditor's Committee, the Future Claimant's Representative, the Equity Security Holder's Committee, Robins and Aetna all had experts to assist Professor McGovern. The data base included the results of a two page "Dalkon Shield Questionnaire and Claim Form" from more than 195,000 claimants. It also contained roughly 6,000 responses to a fifty page, "McGovern Survey Questionnaire" and medical records from a random sample of 7,500 claimants. The data collection process lasted more than a year and a half.

---

3. We are not persuaded by the argument that the 5.62% NO votes were from the claimants with the largest claims, that being necessary of course to make up more than one-third of the claims in amount. The argument goes that such claimants have the most to gain from a rejection of the Plan, but that proposition, we think, is not only supported by no evidence, it is not supported by logic, and is no more likely than the fact that the largest claimants have the most to lose by a rejection of the Plan. . . . [W]ith a rejection of the Plan which resulted in liquidation, the largest claimants would be the biggest losers.

* This figure was the district court's estimate of the total value of all the Dalkon Shield claims — ED.

Each of the experts hired by the various parties used the basic data in various ways to arrive at an estimation.

The district court conducted an estimation hearing from November 5, 1987 to November 11, 1987. At the hearing the parties' various experts testified. The district court considered that the testimony of the various experts estimated the claims as follows: Robins' — .8 to 1.3 billion, Equity Security Holders' — 1.03 billion, Unsecured Creditors' — 1.54 billion, Aetna's' — 2.2 to 2.5 billion, and the Dalkon Shield Claimants' — 4.2 to 7 billion. The district court decided that the proper estimate was 2.475 billion.

. . .

[T]he district court entered a bar date on claims and prescribed a very informal method of advising the court that a claim was being filed. The bar date of course limited the potential claimants. From these potential claimants, there were eliminated, by standard statistical and analytical methods, about one-third of the initial claims which had been filed. A detailed analysis of those claims not eliminated was performed by sending the detailed questionnaire previously mentioned to a randomly selected sample of several thousand of the claims remaining. The questionnaire asked for information, which, in the most general sense, was received back, concerning the insertion of the Dalkon Shield in the claimant and the nature of the claimant's injuries, including verification by way of medical records where possible.

A detailed analysis of all of the responses was then performed by the expert witnesses who testified in the case. A good example of competent testimony was that of Dr. Francine F. Rabinovitz, who testified on behalf of Aetna. [Dr. Rabinovitz' methods led her to conclude that the proper range lay between 2.0 and 2.5 billion dollars, with a 2.2 billion to 2.3 billion dollar range as most likely.]

From our brief recital of a small part of the evidence before the district court, we see that its finding of 2.475 billion dollars as the estimate to include all Dalkon Shield claims is not clearly erroneous under Rule 8013. Indeed, we think the district court would have been quite justified in accepting Dr. Rabinovitz' testimony, so appellants may not complain about the district court's arrival at a somewhat higher figure. . . .

The orders of the district court appealed from are accordingly affirmed.

Notes and Questions

1. Between the two *Robins* cases, you can see the types of problems that a court must consider in aggregating and then resolving related cases against a debtor. First, the cases must be brought together in one forum. The first step of this process is to bring all the related cases into a single court system. As long as the debtor wants consolidation to occur, this is not difficult; it need only file removal petitions under 28 U.S.C. § 1452. But filing thousands of these petitions will be costly, and pragmatically the debtor may prefer other forums to the bankruptcy forum for resolving some cases. Should other parties be entitled to remove? See § 1452(a) (any "party" may remove); 1 Collier on Bankruptcy

¶ 3.02[4][c] & n.233 (Lawrence P. King ed., 15th ed. 1996) (suggesting that plaintiffs will rarely remove). Should a court be entitled to order removal, using either the general power of 11 U.S.C. § 105 or the All Writs power of 28 U.S.C. § 1651? Cf. Fraidin v. Stutz, 68 Md. App. 693, 515 A.2d 775 (1987) (state judge could not order transfer of case to bankruptcy court).

2. The second stage of bringing the cases together is venue transfer, which is the problem addressed in *Piccinin*. The arguments of the Dalkon Shield plaintiffs notwithstanding, it seems fairly obvious that § 157(b)(5) gives district judges sitting in bankruptcy the power to consolidate related tort cases in the bankruptcy forum. See also In re Dow Corning Corp., 86 F.3d 482 (6th Cir. 1996), cert. denied, — U.S. —, 117 S.Ct. 718 (1997) (p. 730, *infra*) (adopting *Piccinin*'s analysis). Is there a reason that district judges should have this power only for tort cases? Why must a party with a non-tort case rely on the district judge in which the case is venued to transfer the case to the bankruptcy forum (see 28 U.S.C. § 1412)? Shouldn't the court sitting in bankruptcy be able to bring these cases into the bankruptcy forum without having to rely on district judges around the country to transfer the cases to it?

One argument for treating tort cases differently is that district judges have other tools to handle other litigation. For instance, unlike mass tort class actions, class actions in securities cases are routinely permitted; once the class action is certified, there is less need of bankruptcy to force consolidation. This argument, however, is inadequate. There is no guarantee that the court which certifies the class action will be the court that is handling the bankruptcy proceedings. Moreover, it is difficult to believe that Congress intended to create a "quasi-class-action" bankruptcy procedure only for tort cases. Cf. Richard B. Sobol, Bending the Law: The Story of the Dalkon Shield Bankruptcy 326 (1991) (criticizing use of bankruptcy as substitute for mandatory class actions).

A final problem with the different treatment accorded tort and non-tort cases is that, in any mass product liability case like the Dalkon Shield, some of the causes of action will be for breach of implied or express warranty. Usually such claims are regarded as sounding in contract rather than tort. Because § 157(b)(5) gives the district judge the power to consolidate only "personal injury tort and wrongful death claims," do these warranty claims remain in the transferor districts? Could plaintiffs, as masters of their complaints, make a single resolution too difficult simply by pleading these contract claims?

Even if § 157(b)(5) doesn't give district judges the power to consolidate non-tort cases in the bankruptcy forum, might the power exist in the residual authority of 11 U.S.C. § 105 or 28 U.S.C. § 1651? Would such power trample on the rights of a plaintiff to be master of her complaint?

3. *Piccinin* also shows that a § 157(b)(5) transfer is fragile. Although the related cases can be preliminarily consolidated for purposes of trying to work out a reorganization plan, individual claimants must be given a post-transfer right to return to the original forum. Moreover, should trials need to be held in some of the cases, the court implies that transfers back to the original forum would be wise. Doesn't § 157(b)(5) limit the district court's choice just to two forums — the bankruptcy forum and the forum in which the claim arose? Moreover, if transfers to the forum in which the claim arose will cause joinder complexity, wouldn't such transfers be a bad idea?

4. *Piccinin* argues that one reason for consolidating cases is to assist the court in the process of estimating exactly how much the plaintiffs' claims are

worth. Obviously the estimation process is critical to a bankruptcy proceeding; until the parties and the court have a sense of the magnitude and value of unliquidated, contingent claims such as tort claims, it is impossible to prepare an adequate disclosure to voting classes, to see whether a class of creditors has voted to accept the plan, to see if a plan is fair and adequate, or to distribute assets. In a standard bankruptcy case, the court does not estimate the claim. Rather, the appropriate court tries the claim, and thereby reduces the claim to a value certain. But in a mass tort bankruptcy a trial of each claim against the debtor would take incredibly long and would be tremendously costly. In many ways, therefore, the real victory for Robins in *Piccinin* was the Fourth Circuit's endorsement of the ideas that (1) these claims could be estimated in the bankruptcy proceeding without individual trials and (2) the trial process could be put on hold while the estimation process went forward. Stopping all individual trials while the parties and court sought to find a way of treating all similar cases alike is a great advantage of bankruptcy.

The practical problem is to find a way of estimating the claims. If a way cannot be found, then it is impractical to reorganize a debtor under Chapter 11, and the usefulness of bankruptcy as a device to consolidate and resolve large numbers of related cases will be virtually destroyed. If you were the judge, how would you go about estimating the value of the compensatory and punitive damage claims of the thousands of Dalkon Shield claimants?

The method ultimately adopted in the Dalkon Shield case is outlined in the second *Robins* decision, and described more fully in Francis E. McGovern, *Resolving Mature Mass Torts*, 69 B.U. L. Rev. 659 (1989). In brief, Professor McGovern accumulated a database of 9,500 prior Dalkon Shield judgments and settlements. From this lot he selected the cases of 1600 women, and sent them a 150-page questionnaire soliciting pertinent information concerning their age, use, medical history, pregnancies, and so forth. He also collected their medical records and litigation materials. After throwing out the highest and lowest 100 cases, he then developed a model that suggested what the likely verdict for a Dalkon Shield user with certain characteristics would be. Next, he surveyed the population of Dalkon Shield claimants involved in the bankruptcy proceeding by sending a 50-page form to 6,340 of the claimants, and collected from this sample any pertinent medical records. By correlating this database with the one for past Dalkon Shield users, and then extrapolating the results to the universe of Dalkon Shield claimants, the experts for each party were then able to estimate a value for the tort claims as a whole. After hearing the estimates, the judge was able to make his estimation of $2.475 billion.

This approach to estimation required, to use McGovern's phrase, a "mature mass tort," in which good data on a large number of past judgments and settlements exists. What happens when the absolute numbers are inadequate or the quality of the data is too poor to make the necessary statistical inferences?

5. In *Robins*, the Fourth Circuit applauded the McGovern approach to estimation. Let us, however, raise some problems. First, note that the range of estimates varied by a factor of ten, which suggests that the process is far less precise than the use of actual trials and that there is considerable room for the judge sitting in bankruptcy to impose her own view of a fair figure. Second, the estimation process was hardly free of flaws. Of the 6,340 claimants surveyed, 2,000 were not eligible to participate in the fund, and the survey garnered only a 65% response rate — facts that gave the statisticians room to maneuver. See Sobol, *supra*, at 176, 184. Similarly, the McGovern method did not address the

actual number of Dalkon Shield claimants that could prevail against Robins, and the experts varied widely in their opinions about this number. See id. at 183; Ronald J. Bacigal, The Limits of Litigation 99-102 (1990). Third, statistics are not people, and the statistical experts did not always inspire confidence. For instance, one expert stated that a particular hypothetical claimant with certain characteristics should receive $5000 based on the proposed settlement formula. The actual plaintiff after whom the hypothetical claimant was modeled had in fact received $710,000. Bacigal, *supra*, at 102. Fourth, Judge Merhige, who presided over the estimation hearing, adamantly refused to allow actual Dalkon Shield victims, who might have put a human face on the statistics, to testify. In fact, he did not even want them in the courtroom. Sobol, *supra*, at 179-80.

Finally, when we come to the issue of trial complexity, we will see that courts have not been receptive to using a comparable "trial by statistics" method for resolving mass tort controversies that are not in bankruptcy. See p. 1294, *infra*. Among the reasons for this hostility are the nature of the substantive law, the effect on the right to jury trial, and the damage that this method causes to the adversarial right to present individualized proofs and arguments. Does the availability of the "trial by statistics" method make bankruptcy a better or a worse alternative than non-bankruptcy resolution of mass controversies? What might justify a procedural difference that gives one set of claimants a right to individual trial and damage assessment and treats another set collectively? Is the reorganization of the debtor an adequate reason? Has bankruptcy focused myopically on its substantive goals, and ignored procedural values such as adversarialism and trans-substantivism?

6. One response to these criticisms is to say that the claimants in bankruptcy are free to give up their rights to adversarial and trans-substantive procedure if they so desire. If the Dalkon Shield claimants wanted individual trials, they could have voted the plan down. But this response is somewhat disingenuous. The claimants had no choice about their collectivization for purposes of estimation. Once the estimation had occurred, and a reorganization plan proposed, all the momentum had shifted toward acceptance of the plan. Furthermore, even the claimants' vote was collective; individual women could not opt for trial if the Dalkon Shield class as a whole voted to approve the plan.

Moreover, this response can only be as valid as the legitimacy and accuracy of the voting procedures. As *Robins* shows, the voting process is itself an enormous hurdle in bankruptcy procedure — one that must be overcome if bankruptcy is to have a chance of resolving all the cases. The basic problem with voting is the requirement of 11 U.S.C. § 1126(c) that creditors who hold "at least two-thirds in amount" of the allowed claims for a particular class must accept the plan in order for the class as a whole to accept the plan. But how could the judge know whether "two-thirds in amount" of the Dalkon Shield claimants had accepted the plan without individual trials through which the value of each claimant's claim would be established? The Fourth Circuit had two arguments, neither entirely adequate. First, the court suggested that the district court could set any "proper" amount as the value of their claims because Robins had objected to them. See Bankruptcy Rule 3018(a). But this argument begs the question about what is a "proper" amount. Typically, when there is an objection, § 502(b) says that the court, "after notice and a hearing, shall determine the amount of such claim . . . and shall allow such claim in such amount except to the extent . . . such claim is unenforceable against the debtor and property of the debtor." The only alternative to § 502(b) is § 502(c), which allows a court sitting in bankruptcy to "estimate[ ] for purpose of allowance" contingent claims (such as tort claims) whose precise allowance "would unduly delay administration of the case." Nothing in Rule 3018(a), § 502(b), or § 502(c) allows the court to make up a value for a claim out of thin air; the $1 value must have some reasonable basis. Hence, we are back to square one: How do we establish a proper value?

Second, the Fourth Circuit upheld the district court's decision to treat each claim as having an equal value; since 94% of the votes favored reorganization, this assumption meant that the court could say that 94% of the value of the class also supported the reorganization. Doesn't this assumption, which equates voting right with value, fly in the face of Congress' decision to distinguish these two facts by requiring half of the votes and two-thirds of the value to approve a plan? As a practical matter, this solution also had problems:

> The vast majority of the women eligible to vote within the class of Dalkon Shield claimants — some 94 percent according to a study performed for Robins — had not and would not have made a claim against the company outside of bankruptcy. Many had only minor or insupportable claims, and would be glad to accept a plan that offered them a quick, albeit small, payment without proof of Dalkon Shield use or injury. An estimated 35,000 of the eligible voters — potential future claimants who responded to the notice — did not even claim to have suffered an injury. At the same time, other women, mostly those with cases pending when Robins entered bankruptcy, had suffered serious injuries and had claims of great value. [Sobol, *supra*, at 228.]

There is an amazing correspondence between the 94% figure of claimants unlikely to sue and the 94% figure of class members who voted to accept the plan. Was it the same 94%? Shouldn't the court have checked? At a minimum, shouldn't the court have used the data gathered from the McGovern process to get a rough sense of the value of the claims that were voting both for and against the plan? If such checks were too difficult, could the court then alter the "two-thirds in amount" requirement? See Sobol, *supra*, at 329 ("If it is too difficult or too burdensome to conduct a vote that accords claimants a voice in that decision in proportion to the size of their claims, as required by the Bankruptcy Code, the appropriate conclusion is that there can be no effective waiver of the right to absolute priority, not that it can be waived under some lesser standard."). See also Douglas G. Baird, The Elements of Bankruptcy 87-89 (rev. ed. 1993) (for purposes of reorganization, claimants whose lawsuits are unlikely to succeed should have their claims valued at $0).

The voting procedure had other serious flaws. Sobol explains:

> [T]he disclosure statement failed by a wide margin to provide the information necessary for the "informed suffrage which is at the heart of Chapter 11." The Dalkon Shield claimants were told that the proposed trust fund exceeded Judge Merhige's estimate of the value of their claims, but they were denied any information that would provide a basis on which to make their own judgments on the adequacy of the trust fund to pay their claims. In the absence of explanatory information, the statement of the total amount of the fund had no meaning whatsoever.

> [Furthermore,] Judge Merhige prevented the dissemination of any information or opinion in opposition to Robins's plan of reorganization. He accomplished this by refusing to make the names and addresses of the claimants available to independent voices on reasonable terms and by

refusing to allow opponents of the plan to include a dissenting statement with the statements in support of the plan that were distributed to the claimants. As a result, the claimants heard nothing other than endorsements of the plan. [Sobol, *supra*, at 329.]

Of course, the "vote equals value" approach does make it easier to dispose of related cases in a single forum, and is consistent in spirit, if not in precise language, with the Bankruptcy Code's "strong preference for facilitating reorganizations." See Kane v. Johns-Manville Corp., 843 F.2d 636, 646 (2d Cir. 1988) (finding that use of "vote equals value" rule was "harmless error" when 95.8% of class claimants voted to approve reorganization plan).

7. A judge can establish as many or as few classes of creditors and interests as she deems expedient, as long as a single class contains claims that are "substantially similar" to each other. 11 U.S.C. § 1122(a). The way in which these classes are established will have a significant effect on the chances for a plan's confirmation. For instance, in *Robins* Judge Merhige put all the Dalkon Shield claimants into one class. Had he broken them into two classes — dividing the more seriously injured women from the less seriously injured — it is possible that the former class would have voted down the reorganization plan; and, because the plan did not satisfy the absolute priority rule, Judge Merhige could never have crammed the plan down. In a very real sense, the organization of voting classes determined the outcome of the *Robins* proceeding.

Should Judge Merhige have put all the Dalkon Shield victims in a single class? If this had been a class action, it is likely that, in order to assure adequacy of representation, both types of claimants would have needed separate representation. Cf. In re Joint Eastern and Southern Districts Asbestos Litigation, 982 F.2d 721 (2d Cir. 1992), modified, 993 F.2d 7 (2d Cir. 1993) (p. 771, *infra*). Shouldn't the judge be equally concerned with adequate representation in the bankruptcy context? Since adequacy of representation has a grounding in due process, might there be some due process constraints on a judge's ability to organize classes of claims and interests for purposes of voting? Did Judge Merhige exceed those constraints in *Robins*? Does it concern you that judges in bankruptcy have this type of discretion to organize interests to facilitate or hinder reorganization plans? Ought the judge at least have this discretion when bankruptcy is being used as a tool to overcome joinder complexity?

8. The reorganization plan in *Robins* created a series of payment options for Dalkon Shield claimants. Under Option One claimants were able to receive $725 quickly merely by submitting an affidavit that they had used the Dalkon Shield and suffered an injury that had been associated with its use. Under Option Two claimants quickly received a larger sum, from $850 to $5,500 according to a schedule of injuries, upon submission of medical records verifying Dalkon Shield use and the presence of the designated injury. Under Option Three a claimant needed to submit medical records and other evidence establishing a causal link between use of the Dalkon Shield and a particular injury, as well as the actual damages resulting from that injury. The Trust was then to undertake a full review and make a settlement offer. (In practice the Trust has been slow in making such offers and has ordinarily refused to negotiate further with the claimant.) If the claimant accepted the offer, she was promptly paid. If the claimant rejected the offer, however, her claim proceeded to arbitration or trial. The trial was to occur in the original venue of the case.

Does this ultimate option of trial save the Robins reorganization plan from the criticisms developed above? Does it adequately protect a tort claimant's right to liquidate her claim through a jury trial (see 28 U.S.C. §§ 157(b)(2), 157(b)(5), 1411)? As of January 1991, 19,367 women (out of a total of 127,035 submitting claims) had opted for Option Three. Does the reservation of a trial option threaten to thwart the very reason that bankruptcy is an appealing concept — the aggregation of related cases in one forum under one set of procedures?

9. The final (?) chapter of the Dalkon Shield case was written in In re A.H. Robins Co., 86 F.3d 364 (4th Cir.), cert. denied, — U.S. —, 117 S.Ct. 483 (1996). Apparently 84% of all claimants who chose Option Three accepted the Trust's offer (a figure that was partly due to certain strong-arm tactics by the Trust, see Sobol, *supra*, at 315-17). The Dalkon Shield Trust, which had kept administrative expenses low, ended up with a $1 billion excess. The district court ordered this money distributed on a pro rata basis to all Option Two and Option Three claimants. This distribution resulted in additional payments estimated to be about 75% of the original payments. As part of the order, the district court limited the amount that a claimant's attorney could recover from the additional payment to 10%. In a "wonderful example[ ] of chutzpah," a few attorneys challenged this limit, and were unceremoniously told that 10% was plenty. See 86 F.3d at 377. Does the ultimate outcome of *Dalkon Shield* convince you that the bankruptcy solution was a good one? That Judge Merhige badly overestimated? That Dalkon Shield victims were still undercompensated?

10. Thus far, we have said little about the role of the district judge. Judge Merhige declined to refer most aspects of the Robins reorganization to the bankruptcy court, a decision which guaranteed a single forum for resolution of the issues. He also committed early in the process to the key elements of Robins' bankruptcy plan: (1) the concept of a limited trust fund from which Dalkon Shield claimants would need to seek compensation, and (2) the notion that stockholders of Robins would be entitled to any excess value (an amount which turned out to be about $900 million). Id. at 327-28. These elements, of course, violated the absolute priority rule of Chapter 11, making it impossible for Judge Merhige to cram the reorganization down if any class of creditors or interests opposed the plan. We have explored some of the tactics Merhige used to ensure that the concept of the plan was favorably received. Other tactics are described, not entirely favorably, in Sobol, *supra*, and Bacigal, *supra*. This was Bacigal's final assessment of Judge Merhige:

> While eschewing the activist label, Judge Merhige concedes that he "actively" adjusted the exercise of his judicial power to meet the conflicting demands of the litigants. At various stages of the proceedings the judge played the part of coercive mediator, courtroom tyrant, guardian of the victims, social conscience of corporate America, and practical businessman. The judge's role in the litigation is far removed from the classic image of trial judges as umpires or arbiters who merely react to the issues as framed by the litigants. Nonetheless, Judge Merhige insists that the propriety of his role in the case must be measured by the ultimate success or failure of the settlement trust fund in bringing the maximum equitable compensation to the maximum number of victims. [Bacigal, *supra*, at 126.]

Do you agree with Judge Merhige's criteria for assessing his role? If an activist judge is what it takes to bring about the successful consolidation and resolution of a mass tort, is the game worth the candle?

11. That, ultimately, is the question you must face. We have not been able, in these few pages, to give you all of the procedural and substantive impediments that consolidation in bankruptcy faces, but we have tried to select some significant ones, and to show how it is possible to work around them. You now need to decide whether we should.

2. Using the Bankruptcy Forum to Consolidate Cases and Claims against Other Defendants

Most complex litigation involves more than one defendant. If bankruptcy is able just to consolidate the cases and claims against the debtor, we would not have accomplished the task of consolidating the entire litigation; all we would have accomplished would be the removal of one defendant from cases that remain dispersed throughout the country. While the removal of one defendant may reduce the complexity of subsequent pretrial and trial proceedings, it does little to avoid the problem of joinder complexity. Indeed, it creates disparate treatment among defendants, and it means that plaintiffs may now need to bear the cost of two sets of proceedings for the same injury.

Unless bankruptcy is capable of solving these latter problems, it becomes a tool that can cause more inequity and joinder complexity than it solves. A bankruptcy lawyer, who cares more about bankruptcy's policy of debt forgiveness than procedural concerns for efficiency and interpersonal fairness, might not be deeply concerned with these problems. Might it be possible, though, to have our cake and eat it too? Yes — if we could somehow find within bankruptcy law the power to bring into the bankruptcy forum the cases and claims involving other defendants. We would, however, find ourselves embroiled in a Janus-faced proceeding, in which the debtor's bankruptcy might become the sideshow to the consolidated actions and the juggling of two sets of complicated proceedings might substitute pretrial, trial, or remedial complexity for joinder complexity.

Would this power to consolidate related proceedings in the bankruptcy case be a blessing or a curse for complex litigation? How about for bankruptcy law? These are the central questions of this subsection, which examines whether a judge sitting in bankruptcy has jurisdiction over cases against co-defendants, whether the judge can transfer these related cases to herself, and whether she can stay other courts from proceeding with the related cases, both during the bankruptcy proceedings and afterwards.

IN RE DOW CORNING CORP.

86 F.3d 482 (6th Cir. 1996), cert. denied, — U.S. —, 117 S.Ct. 718 (1997)

■ MARTIN, Circuit Judge. This is an appeal to determine the subject matter jurisdiction of federal district courts, sitting as bankruptcy courts, over proceedings "related to" a case filed under Chapter 11 of the

Bankruptcy Code, and the ability of federal district courts to transfer such proceedings to the district court in which the bankruptcy case is pending.... The district court held that it did not have "related to" jurisdiction over those claims pursuant to 28 U.S.C. § 1334(b) and concluded that they could not be transferred to it pursuant to 28 U.S.C. § 157(b)(5). For the following reasons, we reverse and remand for further proceedings consistent with this opinion.

I.

Until it ceased their manufacture in 1992, Dow Corning was the predominant producer of silicone gel breast implants, accounting for nearly 50% of the entire market. In addition, Dow Corning supplied silicone raw materials to other manufacturers of silicone gel breast implants. In recent years, tens of thousands of implant recipients have sued Dow Corning, claiming to have been injured by autoimmune reactions to the silicone in their implants. Dow Chemical Company, Corning Incorporated, Minnesota Mining and Manufacturing Company, Baxter Healthcare Corporation and Baxter International Incorporated, and Bristol-Myers Squibb Company and Medical Engineering Corporation are other manufacturers and suppliers of silicone gel-filled implants, and are codefendants with Dow Corning in a large number of personal injury actions.

On June 25, 1992, prior to Dow Corning's filing of its Chapter 11 petition, the Federal Judicial Panel on Multidistrict Litigation ordered the consolidation of all breast implant actions pending in federal courts for coordinated pretrial proceedings, and transferred those actions to Chief Judge Pointer of the Northern District of Alabama. On September 1, 1994, Chief Judge Pointer certified a class for settlement purposes only, and approved a complex agreement between members of the class and certain defendants that contemplated the creation of a $4.25 billion fund to cover, among other things, the costs of treatment and other expenses incurred by breast implant recipients. Each class member was given the opportunity to opt out of the class and to pursue her individual claims separately. Several thousand plaintiffs opted out of the settlement class, while approximately 440,000 elected to register for inclusion in the Global Settlement.

Due to the litigation burden imposed by what is one of the world's largest mass tort litigations, and the threatened consequences of the thousands of product liability claims arising from its manufacture and sale of silicone breast implants and silicone gel, Dow Corning filed a petition for reorganization under Chapter 11 of the Bankruptcy Code on May 15, 1995, in the United States District Court for the Eastern District of Michigan. The district court had jurisdiction over that proceeding pursuant to 28 U.S.C. § 1334(a). As a result of Dow Corning's Chapter 11 filing, all breast implant claims against it were automatically stayed pursuant to 11 U.S.C. § 362(a). Claims against Dow Corning's two shareholders, Dow Chemical and Corning Incorporated, and the other nondebtor defendants were not stayed. Dow Chemical, Corning Incorporated, Minnesota Mining, Baxter and Bristol-Myers Squibb subsequently removed many opt-out claims in which those companies were named defendants with Dow Corning from state to federal court pursuant to 28 U.S.C. § 1452(a).

On June 12, 1995, Dow Corning filed a motion pursuant to 28 U.S.C. § 157(b)(5) to transfer to the Eastern District of Michigan opt-out breast implant claims pending against it and its shareholders, Dow Chemical and Corning Incorporated. Dow Corning's motion covered claims that had been removed to federal court and were pending in the multidistrict forum, as well as claims pending in state courts which were in the process of being removed to federal courts pursuant to 28 U.S.C. § 1452(a). Dow Corning envisioned its transfer motion as the first step in ensuring a feasible plan of reorganization, and indicated that it would seek to have the transferred actions consolidated for a threshold jury trial on the issue of whether silicone gel breast implants cause the diseases claimed. Dow Chemical and Corning Incorporated joined in Dow Corning's motion.

On June 14, 1995, Minnesota Mining, Baxter, and Bristol-Myers Squibb also moved, pursuant to Section 157(b)(5), to transfer to the Eastern District of Michigan the opt-out cases in which those manufacturers were named as defendants with Dow Corning. In their Section 157(b)(5) motions, Minnesota Mining, Baxter, and Bristol-Myers Squibb also asked the district court to order that the claims at issue be transferred to the district court in which the bankruptcy case is pending so that the court could conduct a consolidated trial on the issue of causation.

On September 12, 1995, the district court issued two opinions and companion orders regarding the Section 157(b)(5) transfer motions. With respect to opt-out breast implant cases pending against Dow Corning, the district court asserted jurisdiction under Section 1334(b) and permitted transfer pursuant to Section 157(b)(5). The district court, however, denied the remainder of the transfer motions on the ground that, as a matter of law, it lacked subject matter jurisdiction over the claims sought to be transferred because they were not "related to" Dow Corning's bankruptcy proceeding pursuant to 28 U.S.C. § 1334(b). In denying the transfer motions, the district court also directed that individual federal courts nationwide dismiss or sever Dow Corning and/or remand the combined opt-out actions to state court, and enjoined the nondebtor codefendants from removing any other cases from state to federal court pursuant to 28 U.S.C. § 1452 if the only basis for such removal was 28 U.S.C. § 1334(b) or 28 U.S.C. § 1367(a). In a September 14, 1995 order, the district court extended its rulings to include opt-in breast implant claims.

Dow Corning, Dow Chemical, Corning Incorporated, Minnesota Mining, Baxter, and Bristol-Myers Squibb subsequently filed appeals . . . . [W]e are now faced with a complex set of questions pertaining to the scope of a district court's jurisdiction when it sits in bankruptcy, and its power to fix venue for the trial of wrongful death and personal injury tort claims that are "related to" a bankruptcy proceeding. In addressing these issues, we begin, as we do in any case involving a question of statutory construction, with the express language of the statute at issue and an examination of Congressional intent. In addition, we recognize that our decision will significantly impact the future course of this massive litigation. Realizing that we cannot satisfy all competing interests perfectly, our primary goal is to establish a mechanism for resolving the claims at issue in the most fair and equitable manner possible. In seeking to achieve that goal, we are called upon to balance four different, and frequently competing, interests: those of the individuals who have brought and will bring breast implant claims; Dow Corning's interests with regard to its attempt to formulate a successful reorganization plan; Dow Chemical and Corning Incorporated's interests as shareholders of Dow Corning; and the judicial system's interest in allocating its limited resources effectively and efficiently.

II.

[The court of appeals held that the district court's partial denial of the motions to transfer was immediately appealable.]

III.

The first issue to be resolved is whether the district court has subject matter jurisdiction over breast implant claims pending not only against the debtor, Dow Corning, but also over certain claims pending against the nondebtor defendants. The nondebtor defendants argue that such jurisdiction exists pursuant to 28 U.S.C. § 1334(b) or, alternatively, 28 U.S.C. § 1367(a). We review the district court's jurisdictional ruling *de novo*.
. . .

In addressing the extent of a district court's bankruptcy jurisdiction under Section 1334(b) over civil proceedings "related to" cases under title 11, we start with the premise that the "emphatic terms in which the jurisdictional grant is described in the legislative history, and the extraordinarily broad wording of the grant itself, leave us with no doubt that Congress intended to grant to the district courts broad jurisdiction in bankruptcy cases." In re Salem [Mortgage Co.], 783 F.2d [626, 634 (6th Cir. 1986)]. Although "situations may arise where an extremely tenuous connection to the estate would not satisfy the jurisdictional requirement" of Section 1334(b), Robinson v. Mich. Consol. Gas Co., Inc., 918 F.2d 579, 584 (6th Cir. 1990), Congressional intent was "to grant comprehensive jurisdiction to the bankruptcy courts so that they might deal efficiently and expeditiously with all matters connected with the bankruptcy estate." Celotex Corp. v. Edwards, [514 U.S. 300, 308] (1995) (citations omitted).

The definition of a "related" proceeding under Section 1334(b) was first articulated by the Third Circuit in [Pacor, Inc. v. Higgins, 743 F.2d 984 (3d Cir. 1984)]. As stated in that case, the "usual articulation of the test for determining whether a civil proceeding is related to bankruptcy is whether the outcome of that proceeding could conceivably have any effect on the estate being administered in bankruptcy." *Pacor*, 743 F.2d at 994. An action is "related to bankruptcy if the outcome could alter the debtor's rights, liabilities, options, or freedom of action (either positively or negatively) and which in any way impacts upon the handling and administration of the bankrupt estate." Id. A proceeding "need not necessarily be against the debtor or against the debtor's property" to satisfy the requirements for "related to" jurisdiction. Id. However, "the mere fact that there may be common issues of fact between a civil proceeding and a controversy involving the bankruptcy estate does not bring the matter within the scope of section [1334(b)]." Id. (stating also that "[j]udicial economy itself does not justify federal jurisdiction"). Instead, "there must be some nexus between the 'related' civil proceeding and the title 11 case." Id.

Our Circuit adopted the *Pacor* test for determining whether a civil proceeding is "related to" a bankruptcy proceeding under Section 1334(b) in *Robinson*, 918 F.2d at 583 . . . . The majority of our sister circuits have likewise adopted the Pacor test for "related to" jurisdiction. . . . According to the Supreme Court, the Second and Seventh Circuits have adopted slightly different tests for determining whether Section 1334(b) jurisdiction exists. *Celotex*, [514 U.S. at 308] n.6 . . . .

In addition, the Supreme Court recently cited *Pacor* with approval in addressing the broad scope of the jurisdictional grant in Section 1334(b). . . . *Celotex*, [514 U.S. at 307-08] (recognizing at the same time that a bankruptcy court's jurisdiction cannot be limitless). The Court also stated that proceedings "related to" a bankruptcy proceeding include "suits between third parties which have an effect on the bankruptcy estate." Id. at 1499 n.5 (citing 1 Collier on Bankruptcy ¶ 3.01[1][c][iv], pp. 3-28 (15th ed. 1994)). With these standards in mind, we turn to an examination of whether subject matter jurisdiction exists pursuant to Section 1334(b) over joint claims pending against Dow Corning and the various nondebtor defendants.

In their briefs and at oral argument, . . . the defendants argued that contingent claims for contribution and indemnification, jointly-held insurance policies,[8] the possibility of collateral estoppel with a corresponding increased exposure to liability, and the burden of defending against the overwhelming number of breast implant claims all give rise to the possibility that the Dow Corning estate will be seriously impacted if the claims at issue, all of which to some degree affect the reorganization of Dow Corning under Chapter 11, are permitted to proceed in separate forums nationwide. We believe two of these theories support a finding that the district court has "related to" jurisdiction over the claims at issue, and address them in turn.

1. Claims for Contribution and Indemnification

Dow Corning, Dow Chemical and Corning Incorporated argue that . . ., in addition to the claims asserted by the personal injury claimants, Dow Chemical and Corning Incorporated have asserted cross-claims against each other and Dow Corning in the underlying litigation, which will have an effect on the bankruptcy estate. Minnesota Mining, Baxter, and Bristol-Myers Squibb argue that, despite the fact that they have not yet filed contribution and indemnification claims or proofs of claim relating to

---

8. The joint insurance argument is only applicable to Dow Chemical and Corning Incorporated because they are the only defendants who are co-insured with Dow Corning under various liability policies.

implant litigation in Dow Corning's bankruptcy case, they have contingent claims for contribution and indemnification that will have a conceivable effect on the bankruptcy proceedings. Minnesota Mining, Baxter, and Bristol-Myers Squibb therefore argue that the breast implant claims covered by their Section 157(b)(5) motions will give rise to thousands of claims against Dow Corning for indemnification and contribution. In addition, the nondebtor defendants claim that Dow Corning may itself have claims against them for contribution and indemnification under theories of joint and several liability. The companies argue that these claims need to be resolved as part of Dow Corning's bankruptcy proceedings and reorganization plan, and certainly will affect the debtor's rights, liabilities, options, and freedom of action in the administration of its estate.

Relying on *Pacor*, the district court rejected this basis for "related to" jurisdiction and held that the possibility of contribution or indemnification should only be regarded as relevant if and when judgments are actually entered against the nondebtors. . . . [T]he court in *Pacor* viewed the absence of "automatic" liability on the part of the debtor as dispositive in determining that Section 1334(b) "related to" jurisdiction did not exist.

It has become clear following *Pacor* that "automatic" liability is not necessarily a prerequisite for a finding of "related to" jurisdiction. . . .

Our Circuit has held that Section 1334(b) "does not require a finding of definite liability of [an] estate as a condition precedent to holding an action related to a bankruptcy proceeding." *In re Salem*, 783 F.2d at 635. . . .

This Court's decision in *In re Salem* has been cited for the proposition that "when [a] plaintiff alleges liability resulting from the joint conduct of the debtor and non-debtor defendants, bankruptcy jurisdiction exists over all claims under section 1334." In re Wood, 825 F.2d [90, 94 (5th Cir. 1987)].

. . .

We find that it is not necessary for the appellees first to prevail on their claims against the nondebtor defendants, and for those companies to establish joint and several liability on Dow Corning's part, before the civil actions pending against the nondebtors may be viewed as conceivably impacting Dow Corning's bankruptcy proceedings. The claims currently pending against the nondebtors give rise to contingent claims against Dow Corning which unquestionably could ripen into fixed claims. The potential for Dow Corning's being held liable to the nondebtors in claims for contribution and indemnification, or vice versa, suffices to establish a conceivable impact on the estate in bankruptcy. Claims for indemnification and contribution, whether asserted against or by Dow Corning, obviously would affect the size of the estate and the length of time the bankruptcy proceedings will be pending, as well as Dow Corning's ability to resolve its liabilities and proceed with reorganization. In addition, we believe there is a qualitative difference between the single suit involved in *Pacor* and the overwhelming number of cases asserted against Dow Corning and the nondebtor defendants in this case. A single possible claim for indemnification or contribution simply does not represent the same kind of threat to a debtor's reorganization plan as that posed by the thousands of potential indemnification claims at issue here.

Cognizant of the fact that "related to" jurisdiction cannot be limitless and concerned about granting benefits of the automatic stay in bankruptcy to solvent codefendants, we nevertheless believe the possibility of contribution or indemnification liability in this case is far from attenuated. We conclude that Section 1334(b) jurisdiction exists over the actions pending against Dow Chemical, Corning Incorporated, Minnesota Mining, Baxter, and Bristol-Myers Squibb that are the subject of the companies' Section 157(b)(5) motions.

2. Joint Insurance

Dow Corning, Dow Chemical and Corning Incorporated also argue that "related to" jurisdiction exists as to claims pending against the shareholders because the three companies share joint insurance. We believe this argument provides additional support for the existence of "related to" jurisdiction under the unique facts of this case, but address it only briefly because we have already concluded that Section 1334(b) jurisdiction exists over breast implant claims pending against Dow Corning and one or both of its parents.

Dow Corning, Dow Chemical and Corning Incorporated are co-insured under various insurance policies, which together provide over $1 billion in coverage. Dow Corning's interest in the policies is one of the largest assets of its bankruptcy estate. In addition, Dow Corning recently entered into ten new insurance settlements under which the estate will receive, if approved by the bankruptcy court, approximately $350 to $450 million in cash. Most of these settlements involve policies under which Dow Chemical or Corning Incorporated is a co-insured. . . .

Dow Corning's interest in the insurance policies at issue is property of its estate under the expansive definition set forth in 11 U.S.C. § 541(a)(1). The threat posed to those insurance policies if claims pending against Dow Chemical and Corning Incorporated are permitted to go forward in a separate manner supports a finding of "related to" jurisdiction under Section 1334(b). The prospect of Dow Chemical and Corning Incorporated being able to assert mature, liquidated claims against the insurance proceeds if litigation pending against them is permitted to go forward demonstrates a conceivable impact on the bankruptcy proceedings. If it is determined that Dow Chemical or Corning Incorporated has a priority to the insurance proceeds, even if the bankruptcy court has the power to prevent payments of the proceeds while Dow Corning is in bankruptcy, the risk remains that the insurance coverage may be eviscerated when the proceeds are eventually distributed. In addition, certain of the policies cover defense expenses, and those costs alone may significantly reduce the pool of coverage available to Dow Corning if the claims pending against Dow Chemical and Corning Incorporated are allowed to proceed separately. In addition, the bankruptcy court has yet to determine whether it has the power to prevent Dow Corning's co-insureds from receiving proceeds of the jointly-held policies while Dow Corning is in bankruptcy. Resolution of the dispute over the right to proceeds alone will have a conceivable effect on Dow Corning's bankruptcy proceedings.

IV.

We next address the power of the district court, sitting in bankruptcy, to fix the venue for the trial of personal injury tort and wrongful death claims asserted in non-bankruptcy forums pursuant to 28 U.S.C. § 157(b)(5). . . .

The purpose of Section 157(b)(5) is "to centralize the administration of the estate and to eliminate the 'multiplicity of forums for the adjudication of parts of a bankruptcy case.'" A.H. Robins Co. [v. Piccinin, 788 F.2d 994, 1011 (4th Cir.), cert. denied, 479 U.S. 876 (1986)] (citation omitted). Centralization of claims increases the debtor's odds of developing a reasonable plan of reorganization which will "work a rehabilitation of the debtor and at the same time assure fair and non-preferential resolution of the . . . claims." Id.

It has been established that a "bankrupt debtor who is a defendant in a personal injury action may move under section 157(b)(5) to transfer the case to one of two venues: (1) the district where the bankruptcy is proceeding; or (2) the district where the claim arose." In re Pan Am Corp., [16 F.3d 513, 516 (2d Cir. 1994)]. The question for our consideration is whether Section 157(b)(5) allows for the transfer of personal injury and wrongful death claims pending against nondebtor defendants who have been sued with a debtor under claims of joint and several liability.

The Fourth Circuit has construed Section 157(b)(5) as permitting the transfer of such cases, and we follow that Circuit's approach. . . .

We agree with the Fourth Circuit that Section 157(b)(5) should be read to allow a district court to fix venue for cases pending against nondebtor defendants which are "related to" a debtor's bankruptcy proceedings pursuant to Section 1334(b).[12] This approach will further the prompt, fair, and complete resolution of all claims "related to" bankruptcy proceedings, and harmonize Section 1334(b)'s broad jurisdictional grant with the oft-stated goal of centralizing the administration of a bankruptcy estate.

V.

Finally, a Section 157(b)(5) motion "requires an abstention analysis." . . . The abstention provisions of 28 U.S.C. § 1334(c) qualify Section 1334(b)'s broad grant of jurisdiction. . . . It is for the district court to "determine in each individual case whether hearing it would promote or impair efficient and fair adjudication of bankruptcy cases." . . .

Section 1334 provides for two types of abstention: discretionary abstention under 28 U.S.C. § 1334(c)(1) and mandatory abstention under 28 U.S.C. § 1334(c)(2). . . .

For mandatory abstention to apply, a proceeding must: (1) be based on a state law claim or cause of action; (2) lack a federal jurisdictional basis

---

12. We note that our holding here is limited to the district court's ability to consider motions under 28 U.S.C. § 157(b)(5) with respect to the trial venue of the breast implant claims at issue.

absent the bankruptcy; (3) be commenced in a state forum of appropriate jurisdiction; (4) be capable of timely adjudication; and (5) be a non-core proceeding. Non-core proceedings under Section 157(b)(2)(B) (*i.e.* liquidation of personal injury tort or wrongful death case) are not subject to Section 1334(c)(2)'s mandatory abstention provisions pursuant to 28 U.S.C. § 157(b)(4).

The district court in this case determined that Section 157(b)(4) rendered exempt from the mandatory abstention requirement all personal injury tort claims pending solely against Dow Corning, and decided not to abstain discretionarily with regard to those claims at this time. Because the district court found that it did not have subject matter jurisdiction over the claims pending against the nondebtor defendants, it did not address the abstention issue in detail and merely incorporated by reference its analysis of the abstention issue pertaining to claims pending solely against Dow Corning. It also remains to be fully determined whether the abstention exception in Section 157(b)(4) applies to claims pending against nondebtor defendants and, if not, whether the factors calling for mandatory exemption under Section 1334(c)(2) have been met. The district court did not directly address these matters, and we refrain from addressing them in the first instance. Because we believe the district court is in a better position to make the necessary abstention determinations, as to both mandatory and discretionary abstention, we remand the case to the district court for further proceedings on this issue.

Notes and Questions

1. *Dow Corning* must be understood against the backdrop of the multidistrict proceedings referred to in the opinion. It appeared in 1994 that the parties in the multidistrict case would settle for $4.23 billion. It turned out, however, that too many plaintiffs filed claims against the defendants and too many plaintiffs opted out of the settlement, thus frustrating the objective of Dow Corning to resolve the case "cheaply" and finally. As a result, it filed a bankruptcy petition, apparently with the idea of trying to keep the global settlement together while eliminating opt-out claims against it. See John C. Coffee, Jr., *Class Wars: The Dilemma of the Mass Tort Class Action*, 95 Colum. L. Rev. 1343, 1409-10 (1995). The other defendants, apparently, were not so desirous of a single resolution that they wanted to follow down the Chapter 11 path. But they did want a way of consolidating all of the opt-out suits, so that at most they would need to proceed in fewer forums.

2. Note how these defendants accomplished their objective. First, they removed the state court cases to federal court pursuant to 28 U.S.C. § 1452. In order for removal to be successful, the defendants needed to demonstrate that the claims against them fell within the subject matter jurisdiction of the federal courts; specifically, they needed to demonstrate that the district court had "related to" jurisdiction over their cases. In Celotex Corp. v. Edwards, 514 U.S. 300 (1995), which is discussed in *Dow Corning*, the Supreme Court held that "related to" jurisdiction can exist in a case between nondebtors. In *Celotex*, plaintiffs sought to execute on a supersedeas bond that Celotex procured in order to file an ultimately unsuccessful appeal from an asbestos judgment entered in

a Texas federal court. Celotex later went into Chapter 11 reorganization in Florida, and the bankruptcy court issued a § 105 stay against execution on the bond. Although the plaintiffs' suit was against the surety, not Celotex, the Court held that, because the surety had taken collateral from Celotex when it issued the bond, any effort to collect on the bond would trigger the surety's effort to obtain the collateral. Therefore, the execution on the bond did have an effect on the bankrupt's estate, and the bankruptcy court had the authority to issue the injunction. *Celotex* did not, however, attempt to state a general test for "related to" jurisdiction; it stated that Congress' "choice of words [in § 105] suggests a grant of some breadth," but it also acknowledged that "a bankruptcy court's 'related to' jurisdiction cannot be limitless." It specifically refused to resolve an apparent conflict among the circuits over the precise extent of § 105. Id. at 307-08 & n.6. Moreover, the Court was concerned primarily with whether the plaintiff could avoid the jurisdiction of the bankruptcy court by filing a collateral proceeding, not whether the bankruptcy court had properly issued the stay; it analyzed the § 105 issue just enough to assure itself that the bankruptcy court's order was not so far beyond its jurisdiction that the plaintiff was free to attack it collaterally.

Do you agree with *Dow Corning* that "related to" jurisdiction exists on the facts of the breast implant litigation? *Dow Corning*'s distinction of *Pacor* suggests that the nature and quantity of suits influence whether jurisdiction exists. Should federal jurisdiction hinge on such a "squishy" test? Should the fact that other avenues of federal jurisdiction (here, the diversity-based class action) failed to prevent joinder complexity also be a factor? Since the other defendants were not yet insolvent, however, what was the exact source of joinder complexity in this case? Whether or not joinder complexity existed here, what do you think about the general proposition that "related to" bankruptcy jurisdiction exists when other avenues of federal jurisdiction fail to overcome joinder complexity?

3. Once federal jurisdiction was established and the cases were subject to removal, the defendants' strategy entered a second phase. The removed cases were still spread among district courts all over the country. The nondebtor defendants could have asked each district judge to transfer the cases to the bankruptcy forum under 28 U.S.C. § 1412, but that was both legally and practically dubious. Cf. Calumet National Bank v. Levine, 179 B.R. 117 (N.D. Ind. 1995) (court in which tort claim was filed had no authority to transfer case to bankruptcy forum; specific provisions of § 157(b)(5), not provisions of more general § 1412, control transfer of tort claims); Spitzfaden v. Dow Corning Corp., 1995 WL 662663 (E.D. La.) (ordering remand of claims against nondebtor breast implant defendants on abstention and equitable grounds). Fortunately, the cases against the defendants sounded in tort, so they were able to invoke 28 U.S.C. § 157(b)(5), under which the district judge handling the Dow Corning bankruptcy decided whether to consolidate the cases. In *Dow Corning* the court of appeals again came to the rescue, suggesting strongly that the judge transfer the cases to her district.

Nonetheless, *Dow Corning* seems to stop short of ordering that the cases be transferred to the Eastern District of Michigan. As district judge, would you order their transfer? What factors would you consider? See A.H. Robins Co. v. Piccinin, 788 F.2d 994, 1016 (4th Cir.), cert. denied, 479 U.S. 876 (1986) (pp. 719-20, *supra*). Can you think of any reason that the judge sitting in bankruptcy has the power to consolidate tort cases, but not securities or antitrust cases?

4. Finally, even if the nondebtors can convince the district judge to change the venue, the game is still not won. Abstention issues still loom large. As we learned in Chapter Three, abstention is a double-edged sword that can both facilitate consolidation and frustrate it. In *Dow Corning*, the district judge issued a blanket abstention order against all the nondebtor defendants, including Dow Corning's two shareholders (Dow Chemical and Corning); the judge thought that abstention was appropriate on both mandatory and discretionary grounds. In re Dow Corning Corp., 1996 WL 511646 (E.D. Mich.). The judge also found herself facing a writ of mandamus from the court of appeals, which held that the judge needed to perform a more individualized abstention analysis and strongly suggested that abstention was inappropriate for the cases against the shareholders. In re Dow Corning Corp., 113 F.3d 565 (6th Cir.), cert. denied, — U.S. —, 118 S.Ct. 435 (1997). Undeterred, the district judge performed the individualized analysis and abstained, at least with respect to liability issues, in favor of the *Spitzfaden* class action being tried in state court in Louisiana after the unsuccessful efforts to remove to federal court. See Mealey's Litigation Reports: Drugs & Medical Devices (June 13, 1997).

In In re Apex Oil Co, 980 F.2d 1150 (8th Cir. 1992), abstention had the opposite effect. In *Apex Oil*, a group of shipbuilding enterprises, who were facing the cases of 232 mariners who had sued the debtors for asbestos exposure and the unfiled claims of 21 other mariners, filed a voluntary petition for bankruptcy in the Eastern District of Missouri. The debtor then moved to consolidate the trials in the bankruptcy forum under § 157(b)(5). Instead, the district court abstained under 28 U.S.C. § 1334(c)(1), reasoning that the cases had been transferred by the Judicial Panel on Multidistrict Litigation to the Eastern District of Pennsylvania (see p. 501, *supra*) and that it was therefore in the interests of justice to abstain. (The judge also lifted the automatic stay to allow claimants to proceed against the debtor in the multidistrict proceedings.) The court of appeals intimated that the Judicial Panel did not have the authority to order the transfer of the bankruptcy claims, but nonetheless held that the district court had the authority to abstain: "The district court should [not] be obliged to conduct duplicative proceedings, thus squandering the very economies which are the purpose of multidistrict transfer." 980 F.2d at 1153.

5. Assuming that the Sixth Circuit's view of jurisdiction holds up and the district court's views on venue and abstention do not interfere, bankruptcy might still turn out to be a better aggregation solution in *Dow Corning* than multidistricting and class action. At a minimum, bankruptcy is a tool to use in conjunction with such other consolidation devices: Consolidate what you can using one method, and consolidate the rest using others. That tactic was used in the Robins reorganization proceedings, in which a number of plaintiffs, in order to get around the stay against Robins, started filing suits against Aetna on the theory that Aetna's conduct in insuring the Dalkon Shield made it a joint tortfeasor with Robins. Judge Merhige, who was handling the Robins reorganization, then certified a mandatory Rule 23(b)(1)(b) class against Aetna, and approved a settlement of the class action. The settlement simply shunted the plaintiffs into the compensation scheme established as part of the Robins reorganization. Merhige found that this scheme, to which Aetna made a large financial contribution, was fair and adequate. See In re A.H. Robins Co., 880 F.2d 709 (4th Cir.), cert. denied, 493 U.S. 959 (1989) (affirming settlement); but see In re Eastern and Southern District Asbestos Litigation, 14 F.3d 726 (2d Cir. 1993) (p. 778, *infra*) (use of class action to accomplish quasi-bankruptcy distribution of assets inappropriate).

In *Robins* one judge handled both the bankruptcy proceedings and the class action. In *Dow Corning*, however, at least two judges (three, if a bankruptcy judge enters the picture) were involved. Is there a way to reduce these forums to one? In In re Natural Resources Fund, Inc., Securities Litigation, 372 F. Supp. 1403 (J.P.M.L. 1974), the Judicial Panel on Multidistrict Litigation ordered cases related to an ongoing bankruptcy case transferred under § 1407 to the court entertaining the bankruptcy case; see also *Apex Oil*, 980 F.2d 1150. On the other hand, in In re Asbestos Bankruptcy Litigation, 1992 WL 423943 (J.P.M.L.), the Judicial Panel on Multidistrict Litigation declined to order the transfer of bankruptcy cases of asbestos manufacturers pending in 8 different districts to the multidistrict forum. It did, however, invite the judges sitting in bankruptcy forums to consult and coordinate with the multidistrict judge. Should the district court transfer the tort aspects of the Dow Corning bankruptcy to the multidistrict proceedings (at least for pretrial purposes)? Could the Judicial Panel have re-transferred the multidistrict proceedings to the Eastern District of Michigan? See *Calumet National Bank*, 179 B.R. 117. Under the Sixth Circuit's broad view of § 157(b)(5), could the district judge in the *Dow Corning* proceedings order the transfer of the multidistricted cases to the bankruptcy forum? In *Dow Corning* itself, the matter was resolved in June, 1997, when Chief Justice Rehnquist appointed Judge Pointer, who was handling the MDL proceedings in Alabama, as the judge in charge of the bankruptcy proceedings.

Not so fast, you might say: These two very different proceedings — a reorganization proceeding involving a debtor and a multidistricted class action proceeding involving nondebtors — would be better handled separately. If so, would the judge in the Dow Corning bankruptcy at least have the authority to consolidate the nondebtor cases under § 157(b)(5), and then transfer the cases to the multidistrict proceeding under § 1334(c)(1) or abstain under § 1412? This tactic puts all the debtor cases in one forum and all the non-debtor cases in another. Is it an abuse of the bankruptcy consolidation and transfer powers?

6. The last Note raises interesting issues of adversarial theory. The nondebtors in *Dow Corning* apparently wanted to consolidate only the opt-out cases; they did not want to consolidate the multidistrict cases as well. Should a court accede to that adversarial decision, and do only as much consolidation as the requesting parties want? Should it use the non-debtors' unwillingness to achieve a global consolidation as a reason not to do any consolidation at all? Or should the judge have the power to override the parties' wishes, and order the degree of consolidation that seems most appropriate for the case?

7. *Dow Corning* needed to take a broad view of jurisdiction, venue, and abstention in order to keep prospects for a global consolidation alive. So would the consolidation proposals we considered in Note 5, *supra*. Thus, the bankruptcy solution still requires consolidation-oriented judges willing to manipulate somewhat pliable doctrine. It also requires willing parties to file removal petitions and ask for § 1412 or § 157(b)(5) transfers. Would the judge sitting in bankruptcy have power under the All Writs Act, 28 U.S.C. § 1651, to order removal and transfer in the event the parties did not wish to do so? Could she accomplish the same thing by ordering the "related to" litigation stayed under 11 U.S.C. § 105?

8. Bringing the cases against nondebtors together with the cases against the debtor is a necessary step in the global resolution of related claims in a single forum. But it is not sufficient. The following cases explore the power of

the bankruptcy forum to ban further litigation against the nondebtors in nonbankruptcy forums both during the bankruptcy proceeding and thereafter.

A.H. ROBINS CO. v. PICCININ

788 F.2d 994 (4th Cir.), cert. denied, 479 U.S. 876 (1986)

■ RUSSELL, Circuit Judge. [The facts of this case are set out on p.715, *supra*. Briefly, A.H. Robins Co., manufacturer of the Dalkon Shield, filed a Chapter 11 reorganization petition in the Eastern District of Virginia. Some of the cases named officers, members of the board of directors, and Robins' insurer, Aetna Casualty and Insurance Co., as co-defendants.]

The filing of the Chapter 11 petition automatically stayed all suits against Robins itself under section 362(a) of the Bankruptcy Code, even though no formal order of stay was immediately entered.... But a number of plaintiffs in suits where there were defendants other than Robins, sought to sever their actions against Robins and to proceed with their claims against the codefendant or codefendants. Robins responded to the move by filing an adversary proceeding in which it named as defendants the plaintiffs in eight such suits pending in various state and federal courts. In that proceeding, the debtor sought (1) declaratory relief adjudging that the debtor's products liability policy with Aetna ... was an asset of the estate in which all the Dalkon Shield plaintiffs and claimants had an interest and (2) injunctive relief restraining the prosecution of the actions against its codefendants....

[The district judge granted a preliminary injunction pursuant to 11 U.S.C. § 362(a)(1) and (a)(3), as supplemented by 11 U.S.C. § 105. Three weeks later] Robins filed a motion for (1) a determination of trial venue of all Dalkon Shield suits, (2) identification of such Dalkon Shield cases as were "related to" the Chapter 11 case, and (3) transfer of such cases to the Eastern District of Virginia for trial....

After a hearing on the motions, the district judge entered an order holding that (1) pursuant to 28 U.S.C. § 1334(b), all actions based upon personal injury tort or wrongful death claims arising from the use of the Dalkon Shield were proceedings related to this Chapter 11 case over which this court had jurisdiction; (2) pursuant to 28 U.S.C. §§ 157(b)(5) and 1334(b), all such actions, wherever pending, were to be tried in the Richmond Division of the United States District Court for the Eastern District of Virginia, (3) all actions related to the Robins' Chapter 11 case now pending in any federal district court or subsequently removed to any federal district court, during the pendency of this Chapter 11 case, were to be transferred to [the Eastern District of Virginia]; and (4) nothing in the order limited the power of [the court] later to abstain from hearing any proceeding under section 1334(c)(1) or remanding under section 1452(b), 28 U.S.C....

The initial question in the appeal of the first issue relates to the court's jurisdiction to grant a stay or injunction of suits in other courts against codefendants of the debtor or of third parties; none of the parties herein contest the jurisdiction of the bankruptcy court to stay actions against the debtor itself in any court. Jurisdiction over suits involving codefendants or third-parties may be bottomed on two statutory provisions of the Bankruptcy Act itself as well as on the general equitable powers of the court. The first of these statutory grants of jurisdiction is found in section 362, 11 U.S.C. The purpose of this section by its various subsections is to protect the debtor from an uncontrollable scramble for its assets in a number of uncoordinated proceedings in different courts, to preclude one creditor from pursuing a remedy to the disadvantage of other creditors, and to provide the debtor and its executives with a reasonable respite from protracted litigation, during which they may have an opportunity to formulate a plan of reorganization for the debtor....

Section 362 is broken down into several subsections, only two of which are relevant on this appeal. The first of such subsections is (a)(1), which imposes an automatic stay of any proceeding "commenced or [that] could have been commenced against the debtor" at the time of the filing of the Chapter 11 proceeding; the second is (a)(3), which provides similar relief against suits involving the possession or custody of property of the debtor, irrespective of whether the suits are against the debtor alone or others....

(a)

Subsection (a)(1) is generally said to be available only to the debtor, not third party defendants or codefendants.... [I]n order for relief for such non-bankrupt defendants to be available under (a)(1), there must be "unusual circumstances" and certainly "'something more than the mere fact that one of the parties to the lawsuit has filed a Chapter 11 bankruptcy must be shown in order that proceedings be stayed against non-bankrupt parties.'" ... This "unusual situation," it would seem, arises when there is such identity between the debtor and the third-party defendant that the debtor may be said to be the real party defendant and that a judgment against the third-party defendant will in effect be a judgment or finding against the debtor. An illustration of such a situation would be a suit against a third-party who is entitled to absolute indemnity by the debtor on account of any judgment that might result against them in the case. To refuse application of the statutory stay in that case would defeat the very purpose and intent of the statute....

(b) ...

Subsection (a)(3) directs stays of any action, *whether against the debtor or third-parties*, to obtain possession or to exercise control over property of the debtor. A key phrase in the construction and application of this section is, of course, "property" as that term is used in the Act. Section 541(a)(1) of the Bankruptcy Act defines "property" in the bankruptcy context....

Under the weight of authority, insurance contracts have been said to be embraced in this statutory definition of "property." ... [I]t is a valuable property of a debtor, particularly if the debtor is confronted with substantial liability claims within the coverage of the policy in which case the policy may well be, as one court has remarked in a case like the one under review, "the most important asset of [*i.e.*, the debtor's] estate," In re Johns Manville Corp., 40 Bankr. 219, 229 (S.D.N.Y. 1984). Any action in which the judgment may diminish this "important asset" is unquestionably subject to a stay under this subsection. In re Johns Manville Corp., 33 Bankr. 254, 261 (S.D.N.Y. 1983). Accordingly actions "related to" the bankruptcy proceedings against the insurer or against officers or employees of the debtor who may be entitled to indemnification under such policy or who qualify as additional insureds under the policy are to be stayed under section 362 (a)(3). Ibid.

(c)

The statutory power of the bankruptcy court to stay actions involving the debtor or its property is not, however, limited to section 362(a)(1) and (a)(3). It has been repeatedly held that 11 U.S.C. § 105 which provides that the bankruptcy court "may issue any order, process, or judgment that is necessary or appropriate to carry out the provisions of this title," "empowers the bankruptcy court to enjoin parties other than the bankrupt" from commencing or continuing litigation. In re Otero Mills, Inc., 25 B.R. 1018, 1020 (D.N.M. 1982). . . .

Accepting that section 105 confers on the bankruptcy court power . . . to enjoin suits against parties in other courts, whether state or federal, it is necessary to mark out the circumstances under which the power or jurisdiction may be exercised. In *Otero Mills, supra*, the Court approved a ruling that "[t]o so enjoin a creditor's action against a third party, the court must find that failure to enjoin would effect [sic] the bankruptcy estate and would adversely or detrimentally influence and pressure the debtor through the third party." 25 B.R. at 1020. In *Johns-Manville*, the Court phrased somewhat fuller the circumstances when section 105 may support a stay:

> In the exercise of its authority under § 105, the Bankruptcy Court may use its injunctive authority to "protect the integrity of a bankrupt's estate and the Bankruptcy Court's custody thereof and to preserve to that Court the ability to exercise the authority delegated to it by Congress" [citing authority]. Pursuant to the exercise of that authority the Court may issue or extend stays to enjoin a variety of proceedings . . . which will have an adverse impact on the Debtor's ability to formulate a Chapter 11 plan. 40 B.R. at 226.

(d)

Beyond these statutory powers under section 362 and section 105 to enjoin other actions whether against the debtor or third-parties and in whatsoever court, the bankruptcy court under its comprehensive jurisdiction as conferred by section 1334, 28 U.S.C., has the "inherent power of courts under their general equity powers and in the efficient management of the dockets to grant relief" to grant a stay. Williford v. Armstrong World Industries, Inc., [715 F.2d 124, 127 (4th Cir. 1983)]; Austin v. Unarco

Industries, Inc., 705 F.2d 1, 5 (1st Cir. 1983). In exercising such power the court, however, must "weigh competing interests and maintain an even balance" and must justify the stay "by clear and convincing circumstances outweighing potential harm to the party against whom it is operative.". . .

(e)

There are thus four grounds on which the bankruptcy court may enjoin suits against the bankrupt or its assets and property. In some instances only one of these grounds may be relevant; in an involved and complex case, several or even all of the grounds may require consideration. The present case is such an involved and complex case. It has a striking similarity to a Chapter 11 proceeding[ ], initially begun in the bankruptcy court of the Southern District of New York, concerning the reorganization of the Johns-Manville Corporation. . . .

(g) . . .

In the three situations in which the defendants have challenged the injunction granted by the district judge . . ., the only defendants other than the debtor, are the two Robins [E. Claiborne Robins, Sr. and E. Claiborne Robins, Jr.], Dr. Frederick A. Clark, Jr., Dr. Hugh J. Davis, and the debtor's insurer Aetna. So far as the suits against the two Robins and Dr. Clark, those defendants were entitled to indemnification by the debtor under the corporate by-laws and the statutes of Virginia, the State of debtor's incorporation, and were, in addition, additional insureds under the debtor's insurance policy. Dr. Davis was the beneficiary of an express contract of indemnification on the part of Robins and was, under a compromise agreement with Robins and Aetna, an additional insured under Robins' insurance policy. The Manville court had granted a preliminary injunction in favor of defendants in the same position as these defendants . . . on facts similar to those here, finding that the requirements of possible irreparable harm "had been satisfied by the showing . . . [that the suits against the defendant would represent] an immediate and irreparable impact on the pool of insurance assets, of the existence of sufficiently serious question going to the merits," and of the tipping in the defendants' favor [of] the hardships . . . . 33 B.R. at 262-63. That court had previously disposed of the public interest being weighted in the debtor's favor: "Indeed, this Court finds the goal of removing all obstacles to plan formulation eminently praiseworthy and supports every lawful error to foster this goal while protecting the due process rights of all constituencies." 26 B.R. at 428. . . .

The record is not extensive but it includes every fact considered by the courts in the *Manville* cases to be necessary for their decision. . . . It is obvious from the record that if suits are permitted to proceed against indemnitees on claims on which the indemnitees are entitled to indemnity by Robins, either a binding judgment against the debtor will result or . . . inconsistent judgments will result, calling for the exercise of the court's equitable powers. In our opinion, the record was thus more than adequate to support the district court's grant of injunctive relief. Certainly, the district court did not commit an abuse of discretion in granting the injunction herein. . . .

We are sustained in this conclusion by the fact, recognized by the district judge on the record, that any Dalkon Shield plaintiff may at any time petition for the vacation of the stay as it affects his or her suit and he or she is entitled to a hearing on such a petition.

[The court then found that the district court could properly transfer all Dalkon Shield cases, including the claims against co-defendants, to the Eastern District of Virginia. See p. 715, *supra*.]

IN RE A.H. ROBINS CO.

880 F.2d 694 (4th Cir. 1988), cert. denied, 493 U.S. 959 (1989)

■ WIDENER, Circuit Judge. [The facts of this case are set out on p. 720, *supra*. Briefly, after remand of the Dalkon Shield bankruptcy case to the trial court, the trial court confirmed a reorganization plan. The plan created a mandatory, non-opt-out class action for Dalkon Shield claimants (known as the "Class A" claimants) who met the filing deadline requirements, and established a claims resolution system for these claims. For claimants who did not meet these requirements (known as the "Class B" claimants), a separate opt-out class was created. Unless a Class B claimant opted out, she received the same claims resolution process as Class A claimants, except that no jury trial would be available under one of the claims resolution options. If a Class B claimant did opt out, however, she was barred from suing both Robins *and* all third parties, except that she could still bring claims against insurers and claims based exclusively on medical malpractice. Specifically, Dalkon Shield claimants were permanently enjoined from suing Robins' directors and the law firms that represented Robins and Aetna. Most claims against Aetna were also enjoined, but not the claims that were the subject of this appeal. After upholding the confirmation plan, the court of appeals turned to the propriety of the permanent injunction.]

Robins argues that the injunction is a proper exercise of the district court's power to channel claims to a specific *res* or alternately that the injunction is proper because 94.38% of the claimants voted for the Plan and thereby consented to the injunction. We affirm, but our reasoning differs somewhat from that of Robins, although its position, of course, should enter into consideration. . . .

The Plan's injunction . . . only has real impact upon members of Class B who have elected to opt-out of the . . . settlement. . . . The class B members who have elected to opt-out, it is remembered, claim to have causes of action as joint tortfeasors with Robins against Robins' directors, Aetna, and law firms who represented both Robins and Aetna. A suit against any of the parties mentioned by the class B opt-out members would affect the bankruptcy reorganization in one way or another such as by way of indemnity or contribution. See A.H. Robins Co. Inc. v. Piccinin, 788 F.2d

994 (4th Cir. 1986), cert. denied, 479 U.S. 876 (1986). And, in all events, provision for payment in full of all class B claimants has been made.

Bankruptcy courts are courts of equity. See NLRB v. Bildisco & Bildisco, 465 U.S. 513, 527 (1984). 11 U.S.C. § 105(a) gives a bankruptcy court the power to issue "any order, process or judgment that is necessary or appropriate to carry out the provisions of this title," and confers equitable powers upon the bankruptcy courts. . . . Given the impact of the proposed suits on the bankruptcy reorganization and the fact that the class B members who chose to opt-out could have had their claims fully satisfied by staying within the settlement, the bankruptcy court's equitable powers support the questioned injunction. We think the ancient but very much alive doctrine of marshalling of assets is analogous here. A creditor has no right to choose which of two funds will pay his claim. The bankruptcy court has the power to order a creditor who has two funds to satisfy his debt to resort to the fund that will not defeat other creditors. . . . Here, the carefully designed reorganization of Robins, in conjunction with the settlement in *Breland*,* provided for satisfaction of the class B claimants. However, some chose to opt-out of the settlement in order to pursue recovery for their injuries from Aetna or from medical providers for malpractice. It is essential to the reorganization that these opt-out plaintiffs either resort to the source of funds provided for them in the Plan and *Breland* settlement or not be permitted to interfere with the reorganization and thus with all the other creditors. Since they have chosen opt-out rather than payment in full, they may have no complaint about a restriction placed on their ability to sue others. Permitting a suit by them in violation of the Plan is a defeat of the Plan and a resulting defeat of the other creditors. "Particularly since the insurance settlement/injunction arrangement was essential in this case to a workable reorganization, it falls within the bankruptcy court's equitable powers 'which traditionally have been invoked to the end that . . . substance will not give way to form, that technical considerations will not prevent substantial justice.'" . . .

The appellants finally contend that 11 U.S.C. § 524(e) prohibits the injunction. Section 524(e) states that "[e]xcept as provided in subsection (a)(3) of this section, discharge of a debt of the debtor does not affect the liability of any other entity on, or the property of any other entity for, such debt." Some courts have held that § 524(e) and its predecessor, § 16 of the 1898 Bankruptcy Act, result[ ] in the bankruptcy court having no power to discharge liabilities of a nondebtor pursuant to the consent of creditors as a part of a reorganization plan. . . . However, the Fifth Circuit has stated that "[a]lthough section 524 has generally been interpreted to preclude release of guarantors by a bankruptcy court, the statute does not by its specific words preclude the discharge of a guaranty when it has been accepted and confirmed as an integral part of reorganization." Republic Supply Co. v. Shoaf, 815 F.2d 1046, 1050 (5th Cir. 1987).

We find the language used by the Fifth Circuit persuasive. Whatever the result might be as to the application of § 524(e) in other cases, we do not

---

* The *Breland* case settled all Class A and Class B non-opt-out claims against Aetna by means of a mandatory Rule 23(b)(1)(B) class action. — ED.

think that section must be literally applied in every case as a prohibition on the power of the bankruptcy courts, as appellants would have us apply it here. In this situation where the Plan was overwhelmingly approved, where the Plan in conjunction with insurance policies provided as a part of a plan of reorganization gives a second chance for even late claimants to recover[,] where, nevertheless, some have chosen not to take part in the settlement in order to retain rights to sue certain other parties, and where the entire reorganization hinges on the debtor being free from indirect claims such as suits against parties who would have indemnity or contribution claims against the debtor, we do not construe § 524(e) so that it limits the equitable power of the bankruptcy court to enjoin the questioned suits. We leave questions concerning cases in which § 524(e) does apply for another day.

Notes and Questions

1. Both of the stay powers in *Piccinin* and *Robins* are important. The former stay, which bars litigation against nondebtors during the bankruptcy proceedings, is a valuable tool that usually forces plaintiffs into the bankruptcy forum, in which a global settlement or resolution of all claims might be achieved. But it is effective only in cases filed against the nondebtors during the period of the bankruptcy proceedings. The latter stay, which prevents litigation against nondebtors after the bankruptcy proceedings have closed, is even more important. It binds both claimants and bystanders to whatever resolution is achieved against the nondebtors in the bankruptcy proceedings.

In Chapters Two, Three, and Four, we explored both stay and preclusion powers, and found that the power of preclusion was, as a general matter, the more effective and more permanent device for enforcing a global resolution of related claims. Indeed, its very effectiveness and permanence generated concern that the rights of persons would be adjudged without an opportunity for them to present individual proofs and arguments in a forum and at a time of their choosing. We are now faced with the same concerns in the context of a bankruptcy injunction. Should a court sitting in bankruptcy be more willing to enjoin suits for the duration of the bankruptcy proceedings than to enter a permanent injunction? Cf. In re American Hardwoods, Inc., 885 F.2d 621 (9th Cir. 1989) (bankruptcy court preliminarily enjoined suit against nondebtors during reorganization period, but found that permanent injunction against suit was beyond its powers).

2. Traditionally courts have taken a dim view of the existence of a power permanently to enjoin suits against nondebtors. For instance, in *American Hardwoods*, 885 F.2d 621, the president and vice-president of the debtor guaranteed a loan issued to the debtor. The debtor then asked for a permanent injunction against a state court suit that sought to collect on the guarantee. The Ninth Circuit affirmed the bankruptcy court's refusal to do so, holding that such an injunction was in effect a discharge under 11 U.S.C. § 524 and that the court had no power to discharge nondebtors. Likewise, in In re United States Brass Corp., 194 B.R. 420 (Bankr. E.D. Tex. 1994), a debtor that had manufactured defective polybutylene plumbing proposed a reorganization plan under which the claims against it and against other manufacturers of polybutylene and polybutylene components would be permanently enjoined. The Bankruptcy Court refused to submit the plan for a vote, since the proposed injunction against

suits brought against nondebtors made the plan non-confirmable on its face. Subsequently, the debtor submitted a new plan, under which the nondebtor defendants agreed to contribute $200 million to a trust fund for persons with polybutylene plumbing in return for an injunction. In the event that the court did not approve the settlement, the nondebtor defendant then reserved the right to withdraw its $200 million and to re-assert its contribution and indemnity claims. The court found that this second proposal could be confirmable, since the nondebtor defendant could simply withdraw. The opinion clearly implied, however, that the court still had no power to enjoin claims against the nondebtor joint tortfeasors. 194 B.R. at 423.

On the other hand, there are a few cases, notably *Robins* and some others in the asbestos context, in which permanent injunctions against nondebtors were upheld. In *Robins* the Fourth Circuit found that a number of factors, when taken together, justified the permanent injunction. How critical to the decision was each factor? For instance, suppose that the confirmation plan had been supported by only 70% of the Dalkon Shield claimants. Suppose that the Class B plaintiffs had no right to seek recovery from the Dalkon Shield trust fund. Suppose Aetna had contributed no money to the reorganization plan, but still sought an injunction. Or suppose that, like *Robins*, the nondebtors who sought the injunction were joint tortfeasors rather than insiders or agents of the debtor. (Aetna was a non-insider tortfeasor, but the injunction in favor of Aetna ran only to claimants (Class A and Class B non-opt-outs) with whom Aetna had settled.)

Other than *Robins*, the best-known case involving an injunction in favor of a nondebtor is MacArthur Co. v. Johns-Manville Corp., 837 F.2d 89 (2d Cir.), cert. denied, 488 U.S. 868 (1988). In *MacArthur*, a distributor of Johns-Manville products was co-insured under some of Johns-Manville's insurance policies. As part of the Manville reorganization, the insurers contributed certain funds to the Manville Trust and received, in exchange, an injunction against further suits. The distributor, which stood to lose valuable insurance protection and to become just another claimant against the Manville Trust, argued that the bankruptcy court had no power to issue the injunction. The Second Circuit disagreed:

> MacArthur insists that its interests in the vendor endorsements is a contractual right solely between it and the non-debtor insurance companies and is therefore beyond the reach of the Bankruptcy Court. The flaw in MacArthur's reasoning is that the injunctive orders do not offer the umbrella protection of a discharge in bankruptcy. Rather, they preclude only those suits against the settling insurers that arise out of or relate to Manville's insurance policies. Moreover, claims against the insurers based on Manville's policies are not extinguished; they are simply channeled away from the insurers and redirected at the proceeds of the settlement. The Bankruptcy Court properly issued the orders pursuant to its equitable and statutory powers to dispose of the debtor's property free and clear of third-party interests and to channel those interests to the proceeds thereby created. [837 F.2d at 91.]

Isn't a permanent injunction, as *American Hardwoods* said, effectively a discharge?

Courts have sought to distinguish cases like *Robins* and *MacArthur*, or at least to limit their application. *United States Brass* distinguished the cases with the observation that "the claims enjoined in those cases were claims for vicarious liability, based on the debtor's action." 194 B.R. at 423. In re Forty-Eight Insulations, Inc., 149 B.R. 860 (N.D. Ill. 1992) upheld a bankruptcy judge's refusal to enjoin a suit by the parent corporation of an asbestos debtor against the debtor's insurer when the parent had paid a premium for co-insurance; the court distinguished *MacArthur* by saying that the insurance provided to the parent was not property of the estate and that *MacArthur* involved a reorganization while *Forty-Eight* involved a liquidation. *American Hardwoods*, which made a point of saying that the guarantors in the case had not contributed any money to the bankruptcy estate, thought that the facts in *Robins* were unique:

> [*Robins*] expressly limited its holding to the unusual facts before it: (1) the reorganization plan, which included the injunction, was approved by over 94% of the claimants; (2) the plan provided for full payment of creditors' claims; (3) the injunction affected only about 1.5% of the claimants; (4) it was "essential" to the plan that claimants "either resort to the source of funds for them in the Plan . . . or not be permitted to interfere with the reorganization and thus with all other creditors"; and (5) "the entire reorganization [hinged] on the debtor being free from indirect claims such as suits against parties who would have indemnity or contribution claims against the debtor." [885 F.2d at 626.]

Which reading of *Robins* and *MacArthur* is most sensible? Ought the court sitting in bankruptcy have a broad power to bar suits against nondebtors in appropriate circumstances? What might those circumstances be? Must joinder complexity exist? Or should we disavow *Robins* and *MacArthur* because their injunctive power removes the court too far from its central task of rehabilitating or liquidating the debtor? Interestingly, in Celotex Corp. v. Edwards, 514 U.S. 300, 310-11 (1995), the Supreme Court cited *American Hardwoods*, *Robins*, and *MacArthur* in a favorable way.

3. Richard Sobol, a staunch critic of the Robins reorganization, has raised certain fairness concerns with the permanent injunction in *Robins*. The Robins reorganization plan called for the shareholders to retain $900 million in value in the reorganized Robins. Of that amount, nearly $385 million was paid to two potential individual defendants, E. Claiborne Robins, Sr. and E. Claiborne Robins, Jr. As a result of the injunction, Dalkon Shield claimants who received incomplete compensation through the reorganization plan were unable to obtain additional compensation from the joint tortfeasors:

> [T]he very purpose of the prevailing doctrine of "joint and several liability" . . . is to increase the likelihood that the victim will receive full recovery notwithstanding an inability to recover from one of the wrongdoers. Unless a plan of reorganization guarantees full payment of all claims, the abrogation of the liability of other wrongdoers because one is in bankruptcy denies this protection just when it is needed the most.

Richard B. Sobol, Bending the Law: The Story of the Dalkon Shield Bankruptcy 333-34 (1991). Should these substantive concerns factor into a decision to issue a permanent injunction in favor of nondebtor defendants? Were the courts handling the Dalkon Shield bankruptcy so intent on crafting a workable plan of reorganization that they overlooked the concerns, or are they simply unimportant?

4. A permanent injunction against a nondebtor is permanent only in the sense that it remains in effect until the court modifies it. In the context of a Chapter 11 reorganization, the court's power to lift an injunction against a nondebtor is largely untested. Cf. p. 769, *infra* (discussing court's power to

modify confirmed reorganization plan). In other bankruptcy cases, a modification should in theory be available on the same terms as the modification of any permanent injunction. For instance, in In the Matter of Hendrix, 986 F.2d 195 (7th Cir. 1993), a Chapter 7 discharge included an injunction against suits brought against the debtor's insurer. Under Indiana law, however, the discharge of a debtor did not release the insurer from liability to third parties. On motion of a plaintiff who was injured in a car accident with the debtor, the bankruptcy court modified the injunction to permit a suit against the insurer. The Seventh Circuit affirmed.

A number of states have statutes similar to the Indiana statute. Should such statutes affect a court's willingness to enjoin suits against a debtor's insurer?

5. Although stays against nondebtors during the pendency of a bankruptcy proceeding may be easier to obtain than a permanent injunction, they are hardly automatic. For instance, in Wedgeworth v. Fibreboard Corp., 706 F.2d 541 (5th Cir. 1983), co-defendants of Johns-Manville asked for a stay of proceedings in asbestos cases in the Western District of Louisiana, arguing that the bankruptcy proceedings in the Manville case would significantly affect the future course of the cases. After acknowledging that Johns-Manville itself was entitled to the stay, the Fifth Circuit declined to extend the benefit of § 362 to co-defendants. See also In the Matter of Johns-Manville Corp., 26 B.R. 405 (Bankr. S.D.N.Y. 1983) (automatic stay of § 362 did not cover co-defendants). The Fifth Circuit also held that the district court properly refused to stay its proceedings under other discretionary stay doctrines that we studied in Chapter Four. Finally, the court ordered the district court to lift its stay against cases that named Johns-Manville's insurers as a direct defendant (a procedure allowed in Louisiana). When the bankruptcy court handling the Manville reorganization subsequently issued a stay against suits against Johns-Manville's insurers and executives, however, the Fifth Circuit refused to issue a writ of mandamus or prohibition to allow such suits to proceed. In re Davis, 730 F.2d 176 (5th Cir. 1984). See generally Willis v. Celotex Corp., 978 F.2d 146 (4th Cir. 1992) (upholding stay against surety on supersedeas bond during pendency of reorganization proceedings, even though surety's obligation was independent of debtor's obligation; power to stay did not exist under 11 U.S.C. § 362, but did exist under § 105), cert. denied, 507 U.S. 1030 (1993).

6. If co-defendants cannot obtain a preliminary stay, all is not lost. As *Dow Corning* showed, they can still remove cases and transfer them to the bankruptcy forum through 28 U.S.C. §§ 157(b)(5) or 1412. In some ways, such an approach is preferable, since transfer actually consolidates the cases while a stay does not. Ought a court consider this alternate approach in deciding whether to issue a stay? When there exists the prospect of a § 157(b)(5) transfer, a court should probably be reluctant to adopt an inferior aggregation method like a stay. When the only option is a § 1412 transfer, under which the co-defendant must move in each district court for transfer, a stay issued in the bankruptcy forum may be the preferable option.

7. For an article examining the history and present status of nondebtor releases in bankruptcy, which concludes that "the bankruptcy courts' practice of discharging creditor actions against non-debtors is an abusive one, with no redeeming theoretical merit," see Ralph Brubaker, *Bankruptcy Injunctions and Complex Litigation: A Critical Reappraisal of Non-Debtor Releases in Chapter 11 Reorganizations*, 1997 U. Ill. L. Rev. 959, 1080.

8. The bottom line seems to be that bankruptcy has some ability to consolidate, stay, and preclude related claims. The available powers, however, are not adequate — at least if the conventional wisdom about the scope of these powers is accurate. Should we seek to change the conventional wisdom, as cases such as *Dow Corning, Piccinin,* and *Robins* try to do? Should we instead amend the bankruptcy statute? Or should we affirm the traditional limits of bankruptcy? Would your answer depend on whether we are faced with joinder complexity?

3. Using Bankruptcy to Aggregate the Claims of Future Plaintiffs in a Single Forum

In order to be a completely effective aggregation device, bankruptcy must be able to aggregate the claims of all potential plaintiffs. When the debtor's conduct has already caused harm to a group of potential plaintiffs, bankruptcy works well as an aggregation device; the bankruptcy discharge forces claimants with notice of the bankruptcy proceedings either to file a claim against the estate or forfeit any chance for recovery. In latent-injury toxic tort cases, however, some persons may not yet have received an injury at the time of the filing of the bankruptcy petition. The bankruptcy statute was not drafted with persons holding later-occurring debts in mind, and there is no easy textual way for the court sitting in bankruptcy to bring these persons into the proceeding or to discharge these later-occurring debts. On the other hand, there is also no easy way to aggregate potential claimants under any other consolidation or preclusion device. If we can find a way to accomplish this result in bankruptcy, bankruptcy becomes a very powerful aggregation tool in latent-injury litigation.

GRADY v. A.H. ROBINS CO.

839 F.2d 198 (4th Cir.), cert. dismissed, 487 U.S. 1260 (1988)

■ WIDENER, Circuit Judge. Rebecca Grady and the Legal Representative of the Future Claimants appeal an order of the district court deciding that Mrs. Grady's claim against A.H. Robins Co., Inc. (Robins) arose prior to the date Robins sought protection under the Bankruptcy Code and therefore was subject to the automatic stay provision of 11 U.S.C. § 362(a)(1). . . . We affirm. . . .

Mrs. Grady had had inserted a Dalkon Shield some years before [the bankruptcy petition was filed on August 21, 1985] but thought that the device had fallen out. On August 21, 1985, she was admitted to Salinas Valley Memorial Hospital, Salinas, California, complaining of abdominal pain, fever and chills. X-rays and sonograms revealed the presence of the Dalkon Shield. On August 28, 1985, the Dalkon Shield was surgically removed. Mrs. Grady was discharged from the hospital but not long after returned to her physician, complaining of persistent pain, fever and chills.

She was again admitted to the hospital on November 14, 1985, on which admission she was diagnosed as having pelvic inflammatory disease, and underwent a hysterectomy. She blames the Dalkon Shield for those injuries.

On October 15, 1985 (almost two months after Robins filed its petition for reorganization), Mrs. Grady filed a civil action against Robins in the United States District Court for the Northern District of California.... The case was subsequently transferred to the Eastern District of Virginia....

Mrs. Grady then filed a motion in the bankruptcy court, seeking a decision that her claim did not arise before the filing of the petition so that it would not be stayed by the automatic stay provision of the Code. If the claim arose when the Dalkon Shield was inserted into her, the district court reasoned, then it would be considered a claim under the Bankruptcy Code and its prosecution would be stayed by the provisions of 11 U.S.C. § 362(a)(1). If, however, the claim was found to arise when the injuries became apparent, then it might not be a claim for bankruptcy purposes and the automatic stay provision would be inapplicable.

The bankruptcy court ... held that the right to payment under 11 U.S.C. § 101(4)(A) of Mrs. Grady's claim arose when the acts giving rise to the liability were performed and thus the claim was pre-petition under 11 U.S.C. § 362(a)(1).

We emphasize the narrowness of the district court's holding. It held only that the automatic stay provision of 11 U.S.C. § 362 applied, and we have recited its reasoning to arrive at that conclusion. It did not decide whether or not Mrs. Grady's claim would constitute an administrative expense under 11 U.S.C. § 503(b)(1)(A), and it also did not decide whether or not the Future Tort Claimants would have a dischargeable claim within the reorganization case....

The district court correctly noted that the automatic stay is particularly critical to a debtor seeking to reorganize under Chapter 11 because he needs breathing room to restructure his affairs.... While the importance of § 362 cannot be over-emphasized, its coverage extends only to claims against the debtor that arose prior to the filing of its petition....

Mrs. Grady argues that her cause of action against Robins did not accrue until after Robins had filed its reorganization petition and therefore the stay provision is inapplicable. Under California law, she argues that she could not have sued Robins until she knew the nature of her injuries. The argument goes that because she had no right to payment from Robins under state law until she was injured, and since that injury occurred after the reorganization petition was filed, the stay provision of § 362 should not bar her case from its prosecution....

We commence with the proposition that "... except where federal law, fully apart from bankruptcy, has created obligations by the exercise of power granted to the federal government, a claim implies the existence of an obligation created by State law." Vanston Committee v. Green, 329 U.S. 156, 167, 170 (1946) (Justice Frankfurter concurring), and further, from that concurring opinion, that "[b]ankruptcy legislation is superimposed upon rights and obligations created by the laws of the States." 329 U.S. at 171.

The opinion of the court in *Vanston* further stands for the proposition that "In determining what claims are allowable and how a debtor's assets are to be distributed, a bankruptcy court does not apply the law of the State where it sits." 329 U.S. at 162. . . . The Code contemplates the broadest possible relief in the bankruptcy court. Also, that history tells us that the automatic stay is one of the fundamental debtor protections provided by the bankruptcy laws. . . .

With those thoughts in mind, we turn to the pertinent parts of the statutes at hand. Section 362(a)(1) provides for an automatic stay of, among other things, judicial action against the debtor ". . . to recover a claim against the debtor that arose before the commencement of the case under this title." Section 101(4)(A) defines a claim to be a "right to payment whether or not such right is reduced to judgment, liquidated, unliquidated, fixed, contingent, matured, unmatured, disputed, undisputed, legal, equitable, secured or unsecured." . . .

Mrs. Grady's claim, as well as whatever rights the other Future Tort Claimants have, is undoubtedly "contingent." It depends upon a future uncertain event, that event being the manifestation of injury from use of the Dalkon Shield. We do not believe that there must be a right to the immediate payment of money in the case of a tort or allied breach of warranty or like claim, as present here, when the acts constituting the tort or breach of warranty have occurred prior to the filing of the petition, to constitute a claim under § 362(a)(1). . . .

Not only do we think that a literal reading of the statute requires the result we have reached, our reading is fortified by other considerations. The broad reading of the word "claim" required by the legislative history and the cases . . . is considerable support. That the legislative history contemplates "the broadest possible relief in the bankruptcy court" also enters our reasoning. If Mrs. Grady and the Future Tort Claimants, who had no right to the immediate payment of money at the time of the filing of the petition, were participants in a Chapter 7 proceeding, the chances are that they would receive nothing, for no compensable result had manifested itself prior to the filing of the petition.

We also find persuasive the fact that the district court probably had authority to achieve the same result by staying Mrs. Grady's suit under 11 U.S.C. § 105(a) in the use of its equitable powers to assure the orderly conduct of reorganization proceedings. . . .

We emphasize, as did the district court, that we do not decide whether or not Mrs. Grady's claim or those of the Future Tort Claimants are dischargeable in this case. Neither do we decide whether or not post-petition claims constitute an administrative expense. We hold only that the Dalkon Shield claim in the case before us, when the Dalkon Shield was inserted in the claimant prior to the time of filing of the petition, constitutes a "claim" "that arose before the commencement of the case" within the meaning of 11 U.S.C. § 362(a)(1).

IN RE JOHNS-MANVILLE CORP.

52 B.R. 940 (S.D.N.Y. 1985)

■ LEVAL, District Judge. . . . This bankruptcy appeal arises out of a reorganization proceeding initiated by Johns-Manville Corp. and its affiliated companies ("Manville"). On August 26, 1982, Manville filed a petition for relief under Chapter 11 of the Bankruptcy Reform Act of 1978, 11 U.S.C. § 1101 et seq. (1982). At that time, thousands of claims for illnesses caused by asbestos had already been filed against the debtor. A committee was appointed to represent the approximately 17,000 asbestos victims who had filed actions against Manville before the commencement of the bankruptcy proceedings. In October, 1983, Keene Corp., one of Manville's codefendants in the asbestos actions and a putative creditor, filed a motion for appointment of a legal representative for "future asbestos claimants." This group consists of an uncertain but large number of individuals exposed by Manville to asbestos in the past and whose disease had not yet manifested itself as of the date of the petition.[1]

On January 23, 1984, Bankruptcy Judge Lifland held that the future claimants were "parties in interest" under § 1109 and ruled, relying in part on its equitable powers under the then-existing provisions in 28 U.S.C. § 1481, 11 U.S.C. § 105(a), that a representative should be appointed, but reserved decision on the representative's precise form and function until after a hearing. 11 U.S.C. § 1109(b). In re Johns-Manville Corp., 36 B.R. 743 (Bankr. S.D.N.Y. 1984). In dicta Bankruptcy Judge Lifland suggested that these future interests may constitute "claims" under § 101(4) of the Code and may therefore be subject to discharge. Id. at 754-56 n. 5. . . .

On August 14, 1984, Judge Lifland ordered the appointment of Leon Silverman, Esq. as a representative for the future claimants. The order defined "future claimants" as those persons who "have been exposed to asbestos or asbestos products mined, manufactured or supplied by Manville [before the August 26, 1983 Chapter 11 petition] and have manifested or will manifest disease post-petition and who are not otherwise represented in these proceedings." It provided that the legal representative was authorized "to exercise the powers and perform the duties of a Committee under Section 1103 of the Bankruptcy Code subject to the reduction or enlargement of such powers and duties by order of this court."

Appeal was taken from this order [by various committees of creditors and by a potential future claimant]. . . .

Initially the briefs of the appellants objected to the finding that the future claimants were parties-in-interest, as well as to the appointment of the representative.

At that time, two other courts in similar proceedings had denied applications to appoint representatives for future claimants, holding that

---

1. At the time it filed its petition, Manville estimated that millions of people had been exposed to asbestos before the filing of the petition. Because of the long latency period for asbestos-related diseases, hundreds of thousands of these people may contract asbestos-related diseases in the next twenty to thirty years.

these individuals had no cognizable claims and were not creditors whose claims could be discharged or affected in a reorganization plan. See In re UNR Industries, Inc., 29 B.R. 741 (N.D. Ill. 1983), appeal dismissed, 725 F.2d 111 (7th Cir. 1984); In re Amatex Corp., 30 B.R. 309 (Bankr. E.D.Pa. 1983), aff'd, 37 B.R. 613 (E.D. [Pa.] 1983). Appellants relied heavily on these cases in their briefs. However, shortly prior to the oral argument in this case, both decisions were reversed. See UNR, 46 B.R. 671 (Bankr. N.D. Ill. 1985); Amatex, 755 F.2d 1034 (3d Cir. 1985). Both the Third Circuit in Amatex and the bankruptcy court in UNR held that future claimants are "parties in interest" who deserve to be heard in the reorganization process regardless of whether they are creditors with dischargeable claims.

At the oral argument, appellants generally conceded that future claimants could appropriately be considered "parties in interest" under the Code as long as their rights are not subject to discharge. Nor were appellants particularly troubled [by] the mere appointment of a representative. The appellants contended, however, that the provision of the August 14, 1984 order authorizing the representative to exercise the § 1103 powers of a committee, implicitly conferred creditor status on the future claimants. . . . They contended that this order . . . implies dischargeability of these future claims. . . .

I find no implication in the bankruptcy court's August 14, 1984 order that the future claimants are "creditors" whose interests are dischargeable in bankruptcy. The reference to § 1103 in the order is simply a convenient, short-hand description of the responsibilities of the representative. . . .

The appointment of such a representative for future claimants is in my view a wise decision. The future claimants have an important stake in the outcome of the Manville reorganization. Even though they may not have cognizable claims against Manville at present, they have a right to be heard as "parties in interest" under § 1109(b) of the Code. Accord Amatex, 755 F.2d at 1042. Their interests may be substantially affected by the terms of a plan.

It is entirely appropriate, furthermore, that their representative be authorized to exercise such powers and duties as are listed in § 1103. These include consulting with the trustee, investigating the debtor, participating in the formulation of a plan and requesting the appointment of a trustee. Other sections of the Code explicitly grant a party in interest similar powers. For example, a party in interest has a right to be heard (§ 1109) and to file a plan (§ 1121(c)) and request an examiner be appointed to investigate the debtor (§ 1104) with certain limitations. It should also be noted that the powers described in § 1103 are nonbinding. Authorizing the representative to exercise the powers listed in § 1103 simply assures that these future claimants will have a meaningful opportunity to be heard and to participate.

At argument, all appellees acknowledged that they did not and would not contend that the order appointing the representative carried any implications as to the status or dischargeability of the claims of the future claimants. It is with that understanding that the order is affirmed.

Thomas A. Smith, A CAPITAL MARKETS APPROACH TO MASS TORT BANKRUPTCY

104 Yale L.J. 367, 371-72, 383-87, 389-91 (1994)

While still somewhat controversial, several leading bankruptcy courts have suggested that present and future claimants in mass tort bankruptcy should be treated equally in the bankruptcy reorganization process. This principle of equality, however, is easier to state than to implement. Strong forces militate against equal treatment of present and future claimants, causing what I call the "fair distribution problem." . . .

1. *Psychological Factors*

Present claimants have powerful psychological advantages over future claimants in their battle to maximize their share of the debtor's estate. Present claimants in mass tort bankruptcies are identifiable persons with urgent medical and financial needs, while future claimants are only statistical probabilities. Empirical psychology suggests that decisionmakers give excessive weight to concrete and vivid information before them at the expense of more abstract information that should be given equal weight in a rational decisionmaking process. This phenomenon is called the "vividness effect." The vividness effect makes it difficult for the legal representative of abstract future claimants to persuade the court to leave unsatisfied the needs of present claimants so that future claimants may be treated equally. This psychological factor also disposes a bankruptcy court to underestimate the number and size of future claims so that the bankruptcy plan can award present claimants something closer to adequate compensation.

2. *Judicial and Attorney Incentives*

Empirical evidence suggests that bankruptcy courts tend to overvalue reorganized firms, resulting in at least the temporary illusion that the reorganization gives all creditors and interested parties some reasonable value for their claims. Underestimating the value of future claims creates the appearance that all claimants will be reasonably if not fully compensated, an illusion that may last long enough to support judicial confirmation of the plan and the clearing of the court's docket.

Present claimants typically have claims that juries or settlement agreements have already liquidated or will liquidate in the foreseeable future. Future claims, by contrast, are often highly uncertain and likely to remain so for extended periods. To estimate future claims, administrative processes must consider many factors that bear on the ultimate magnitude of future claims. To estimate future mass tort liability, an administrative process must determine, for example, how many future claimants there will be, what diseases they will suffer, what medical treatments they will require, and so on. Each of these decisions offers a point of entry for present claimants to argue their position: Respecting the issues above, for example, they would argue "not very many," "mild diseases," and "inexpensive treatments." The more complex the methodology of estimation, the more opportunities interested parties have to influence the outcome. Estimating future mass tort liability involves an extremely complex methodology and accords present claimants many opportunities to advance their interests. . . .

The attorneys who represent present claimants receive a substantial percentage of the settlements they reach with, or the verdicts they obtain against, the debtor. Future claimants, however, are typically represented by a guardian appointed by the bankruptcy court. Wanting their dockets cleared, courts may tend to appoint guardians who are excessively accommodating. These guardians are not compensated by a percentage of the debtor's assets that they secure for their clients. They thus lack the economic incentive that plaintiffs' attorneys have to seek the maximum attainable settlement.

3. *Strategic Bargaining in the Bankruptcy Process*

Perhaps most important, future claimants are at a strategic disadvantage in the bargaining that characterizes the bankruptcy process. The only monitor of the performance of the future claimants' representative is the court itself, whose incentive is less to ensure that future claimants receive the maximum possible or even a fair share, than it is to ensure that the parties reach some agreement. Both present claimants and equity holders of the debtor have a common interest in a reorganization or liquidation plan that undervalues future claims. . . . A mass tort reorganization that treated present and future claimants equally and observed absolute priority would place the entire value of the debtor's assets in trust for all tort claimants. Equity holders would oppose such a plan, however, and would not hesitate to use the weapon of delay to prevent its creation.

Equity holders have a strong incentive to employ dilatory tactics because of the fundamental nature of their financial claim on the firm's assets. Because of its low priority, equity in a bankrupt firm would usually be worthless if the firm were liquidated promptly upon its bankruptcy in order to satisfy creditors. . . . The longer the period of time during which equity holders can wait to see whether the firm's value increases, the more equity is worth. When a firm is bankrupt, therefore, equity holders have everything to gain and nothing to lose from delaying the completion of bankruptcy and the paying off of creditors. . . .

To present tort claimants, by contrast, delay is especially damaging. They typically have pressing medical and financial needs. In addition, they have positive discount rates, preferring to have their money sooner rather than later. Tort claimants are, therefore, in a difficult position. Equity holders, if they choose, can delay bankruptcy proceedings by using a number of tactics. To avoid delay, tort creditors must deal with equity holders in the reorganization process. . . .

To induce equity holders to consent to a plan, present claimants can offer to agree on a reorganization plan that divides the value of the firm between present claimants and equity holders, but leaves little or nothing for future claimants.... Thus present tort claimants can forgo their absolute priority over equity holders in exchange for an agreement by equity holders not to obstruct the bankruptcy process....

Essentially, present claimants and equity holders can agree to split among themselves the share that belongs to future claimants under the equal-treatment norms. All that stands in the way of this split is the future claims representative, who is accountable not to the anonymous future claimants, but to the court, an institution with incentives that incline it less to fair allocation than to final agreement on a plan.

4. *Strategic Behavior by Equity in the Manville Reorganization* ...

The Manville reorganization is a more complex story, but it has a similar conclusion. Although negotiations among the debtor, creditors, and equity holders in the Manville reorganization were strained from the beginning, relations between the Equity Committee and the debtor (Manville management) worsened in the summer of 1984....

In August 1984, the court fatefully decided to appoint a legal representative (LR) of future claimants. Before the appointment of the LR, negotiations were multiparty and very slow and acrimonious. The LR adopted the role of shuttle diplomat, selling his proposed plan to the various parties separately. He apparently saw his role not as the intransigent defender of future claimants, but as the honest broker among constituencies. That the LR adopted the role of broker was not an accident, as the LR was the only claimant representative whose constituency was entirely unable to monitor his performance. In truth he was as he behaved, less a representative than a go-between among representatives....

Liberated from any concrete constituency, the LR brokered a deal that gave tort claimants 80% of the firm's value, and equity holders the remaining 20%. Present claimants objected not that the plan awarded future claimants too much of the firm's value, but that the plan inadequately funded the trust (a fear that later proved justified) even for present claimants. The ultimate result, whatever the LR's intentions may have been, was a division of the debtor's value between present claimants and equity holders that left future claimants almost entirely unprovided for, as the protections of future claimants in the plan proved completely ineffective.... Strategic behavior of present claimants and equity holders left future claimants without remedy.

EPSTEIN v. OFFICIAL COMMITTEE OF UNSECURED CREDITORS, OF THE ESTATE OF PIPER AIRCRAFT CORP.

58 F.3d 1573 (11th Cir. 1995)

■ BLACK, Circuit Judge. This is an appeal by David G. Epstein, as the Legal Representative for the Piper future claimants (Future Claimants), from the district court's order of June 6, 1994, affirming the order of the bankruptcy court entered on December 6, 1993. The sole issue on appeal is whether the class of Future Claimants, as defined by the bankruptcy court, holds claims against the estate of Piper Aircraft Corporation (Piper), within the meaning of § 101(5) of the Bankruptcy Code. After review of the relevant provisions, policies and goals of the Bankruptcy Code and the applicable case law, we hold that the Future Claimants do not have claims as defined by § 101(5) and thus affirm the opinion of the district court.

I. FACTUAL AND PROCEDURAL BACKGROUND . . .

Piper has been manufacturing and distributing general aviation aircraft and spare parts throughout the United States and abroad since 1937. Approximately 50,000 to 60,000 Piper aircraft still are operational in the United States. Although Piper has been a named defendant in several lawsuits based on its manufacture, design, sale, distribution and support of its aircraft and parts, it has never acknowledged that its products are harmful or defective.

On July 1, 1991, Piper filed a voluntary petition under Chapter 11 of Bankruptcy Code in the United States Bankruptcy Court for the Southern District of Florida. Piper's plan of reorganization contemplated finding a purchaser of substantially all of its assets or obtaining investments from outside sources, with the proceeds of such transactions serving to fund distributions to creditors. On April 8, 1993, Piper and Pilatus Aircraft Limited signed a letter of intent pursuant to which Pilatus would purchase Piper's assets. The letter of intent required Piper to seek the appointment of a legal representative to represent the interests of future claimants by arranging a set-aside of monies generated by the sale to pay off future product liability claims.

On May 19, 1993, the bankruptcy court appointed Appellant Epstein as the legal representative for the Future Claimants. The Court defined the class of Future Claimants to include:

> All persons, whether known or unknown, born or unborn, who may, after the date of confirmation of Piper's Chapter 11 plan of reorganization, assert a claim or claims for personal injury, property damages, wrongful death, damages, contribution and/or indemnification, based in whole or in part upon events occurring or arising after the Confirmation Date, including claims based on the law of product liability, against Piper or its successor arising out of or relating to aircraft or parts manufactured and sold, designed, distributed or supported by Piper prior to the Confirmation Date.

This Order expressly stated that the court was making no finding on whether the Future Claimants could hold claims against Piper under § 101(5) of the Code.

On July 12, 1993, Epstein filed a proof of claim on behalf of the Future Claimants in the approximate amount of $100,000,000. The claim was based on statistical assumptions regarding the number of persons likely to suffer, after the confirmation of a reorganization plan, personal injury or property damage caused by Piper's pre-confirmation manufacture, sale, design, distribution or support of aircraft and spare parts. The Official Committee of Unsecured Creditors (Official Committee), and later Piper, objected to the claim on the ground that the Future Claimants do not hold § 101(5) claims against Piper. After a hearing on the objection, the bankruptcy court agreed that the Future Claimants did not hold § 101(5) claims.... On June 6, 1994, the district court affirmed and accepted the decision of the bankruptcy court. Epstein now appeals from the district court's order, challenging in particular its use of the prepetition relationship test to define the scope of a claim under § 101(5).

II. DISCUSSION

The sole issue on appeal, whether any of the Future Claimants hold claims against Piper as defined in § 101(5) of the Bankruptcy Code, is one of first impression in this Circuit. Interpretation and application of the Bankruptcy Code is a question of law, to which this Court will apply a *de novo* standard of review....

A. *Statute*

Under the Bankruptcy Code, only parties that hold preconfirmation claims have a legal right to participate in a Chapter 11 bankruptcy case and share in payments pursuant to a Chapter 11 plan. 11 U.S.C.A. §§ 101(10), 501, 502 (West 1993). In order to determine if the Future Claimants have such a right to participate, we first must address the statutory definition of the term "claim." The Bankruptcy Code defines claim as:

> (A) right to payment, whether or not such right is reduced to judgment, liquidated, unliquidated, fixed, contingent, matured, unmatured, disputed, undisputed, legal, equitable, secured, or unsecured;* or
>
> (B) right to an equitable remedy for breach of performance if such breach gives rise to a right to payment, whether or not such right to an equitable remedy is reduced to judgment, fixed, contingent, matured, unmatured, disputed, undisputed, secured, or unsecured.

11 U.S.C.A. § 101(5). The legislative history of the Code suggests that Congress intended to define the term claim very broadly under § 101(5), so that "all legal obligations of the debtor, no matter how remote or contingent, will be able to be dealt with in the bankruptcy case." H.R.Rep. No. 595, 95th Cong., 2d Sess. 309 (1978)....

B. *Case Law*

Since the enactment of § 101(5), courts have developed several tests to determine whether certain parties hold claims pursuant to that section: the

---

* Due to an intervening amendment to 11 U.S.C. § 101, present § 101(5)(A) is the same as the former § 101(4)(A) that was considered in *Grady*, p. 752, *supra*. — ED.

accrued state law claim test,[2] the conduct test, and the prepetition relationship test. The bankruptcy court and district court adopted the prepetition relationship test in determining that the Future Claimants did not hold claims pursuant to § 101(5).

Epstein primarily challenges the district court's application of the prepetition relationship test. He argues that the conduct test, which some courts have adopted in mass tort cases,[3] is more consistent with the text, history, and policies of the Code. Under the conduct test, a right to payment arises when the conduct giving rise to the alleged liability occurred. See *A.H. Robins*, 839 F.2d at 199; *Waterman*, 141 B.R. at 556. Epstein's position is that any right to payment arising out of the prepetition conduct of Piper, no matter how remote, should be deemed a claim and provided for, pursuant to § 101(5), in this case. He argues that the relevant conduct giving rise to the alleged liability was Piper's prepetition manufacture, design, sale and distribution of allegedly defective aircraft. Specifically, he contends that, because Piper performed these acts prepetition, the potential victims, although not yet identifiable, hold claims under § 101(5) of the Code.

The Official Committee and Piper dispute the breadth of the definition of claim asserted by Epstein, arguing that the scope of claim cannot extend so far as to include unidentified, and presently unidentifiable, individuals with no discernible prepetition relationship to Piper. Recognizing, as Appellees do, that the conduct test may define claim too broadly in certain circumstances, several courts have recognized "claims" only for those individuals with some type of prepetition relationship with the debtor. See In re: Jensen, 995 F.2d 925, 929-31 (9th Cir. 1993); In re: Chateaugay Corp., 944 F.2d 997, 1003-04 (2d Cir. 1991); In re: Correct Mfg. Corp., 167 B.R. 458, 459 (Bankr. S.D.Ohio 1994). The prepetition relationship test, as adopted by the bankruptcy court and district court, requires "some prepetition relationship, such as contact, exposure, impact, or privity, between the debtor's prepetition conduct and the claimant" in order for the claimant to hold a § 101(5) claim. . . .

Upon examination of the various theories, we agree with Appellees that the district court utilized the proper test in deciding that the Future Claimants did not hold a claim under § 101(5). Epstein's interpretation of "claim" and application of the conduct test would enable anyone to hold a claim against Piper by virtue of their potential future exposure to any aircraft in the existing fleet. Even the conduct test cases, on which Epstein relies, do not compel the result he seeks. In fact, the conduct test cases recognize that focusing solely on prepetition conduct, as Epstein espouses,

---

2. The accrued state law claim theory states that there is no claim for bankruptcy purposes until a claim has accrued under state law. . . . This test since has been rejected by a majority of courts as imposing too narrow an interpretation on the term claim. See, *e.g.*, Grady v. A.H. Robins Co., 839 F.2d 198, 201 (4th Cir.), cert. denied, 487 U.S. 1260 (1988) . . . . We agree with these courts and decline to employ the state law claim theory.

3. See, *e.g.*, *A.H. Robins Co.*, 839 F.2d at 203 (Dalkon Shield); In re: Waterman Steamship Corp., 141 B.R. 552, 556 (Bankr. S.D.N.Y. 1992) (asbestos), vacated on other grounds, 157 B.R. 220 (Bankr. S.D.N.Y. 1993); In re: Johns-Manville Corp., 36 B.R. 743, 750 (Bankr. S.D.N.Y. 1984) (asbestos).

would stretch the scope of § 101(5). Accordingly, the courts applying the conduct test also presume some prepetition relationship between the debtor's conduct and the claimant. See *A.H. Robins*, 839 F.2d at 203; *Waterman*, 141 B.R. at 556.

While acknowledging that the district court's test is more consistent with the purposes of the Bankruptcy Code than is the conduct test supported by Epstein, we find that the test as set forth by the district court unnecessarily restricts the class of claimants to those who could be identified prior to the filing of the petition. Those claimants having contact with the debtor's product post-petition but prior to confirmation also could be identified, during the course of the bankruptcy proceeding, as potential victims, who might have claims arising out of debtor's prepetition conduct.

We therefore modify the test used by the district court and adopt what we will call the "Piper test" in determining the scope of the term claim under § 101(5): an individual has a § 101(5) claim against a debtor manufacturer if (i) events occurring before confirmation create a relationship, such as contact, exposure, impact, or privity, between the claimant and the debtor's product; and (ii) the basis for liability is the debtor's prepetition conduct in designing, manufacturing and selling the allegedly defective or dangerous product. The debtor's prepetition conduct gives rise to a claim to be administered in a case only if there is a relationship established before confirmation between an identifiable claimant or group of claimants and that prepetition conduct.

In the instant case, it is clear that the Future Claimants fail the minimum requirements of the Piper test. There is no preconfirmation exposure to a specific identifiable defective product or any other preconfirmation relationship between Piper and the broadly defined class of Future Claimants. As there is no preconfirmation connection established between Piper and the Future Claimants, the Future Claimants do not hold a § 101(5) claim arising out of Piper's prepetition design, manufacture, sale, and distribution of allegedly defective aircraft.

Notes and Questions

1. Unlike *Grady* or *Johns-Manville*, *Epstein* acknowledges that some claimants with no present injuries actually hold "claims" within the meaning of the Bankruptcy Code. See also In the Matter of UNR Industries, Inc., 20 F.3d 766, 770 (7th Cir. 1994) (strongly implying that future asbestos lawsuits were "claims" under 11 U.S.C. § 101(5)(A)), cert. denied, 513 U.S. 999 (1994). The consequences of calling a future lawsuit a "claim" are significant. "Claims" can be discharged in bankruptcy, meaning that the claim holder cannot successfully sue the reorganized entity on the claim. From the viewpoint of the debtor, this discharge is critical, for it allows the debtor to begin a new life without fear of continued litigation over past conduct. From the viewpoint of the court sitting in bankruptcy, the discharge is also important, for it makes it easier to find that a reorganization plan is feasible. From the social viewpoint of fairness, the discharge is also desirable, for it seems to guarantee that similarly situated persons are not treated disparately merely because their injuries fall on one side

or the other of some fortuitous date. See Smith, p. 757, *supra*, 104 Yale L.J. at 382 (Rawlsian "[h]ypothetical contract analysis indicates that, for mass tort bankruptcies that involve serious injury to at least some claimants, fairness requires equal treatment of claimants regardless of the timing of their claims. This result, I believe, is consistent with the moral intuitions of most people who have reflected on the issue.")

2. Although *Epstein* is the first appellate decision squarely to state that some future claims are dischargable in bankruptcy, it is easy to overstate the importance of the case. The Manville reorganization plan, for instance, contained the following provisions:

> [T]he parties agreed that as a condition precedent to confirmation of the Plan, the Bankruptcy Court would issue an injunction channeling all asbestos-related personal injury claims to the Trust (the "Injunction"). The Injunction provides that asbestos health claimants may proceed only against the Trust to satisfy their claims and may not sue Manville, its other operating entities, and certain other specified parties, including Manville's insurers. Significantly, the Injunction applies to all health claimants, both present and future, regardless of whether they technically have dischargeable "claims" under the Code. The Injunction applies to any suit to recover "on or with respect to any Claim, Interest or Other Asbestos Obligation." "Claim" covers the present claimants, who are categorized as Class-4 unsecured creditors under the Plan and who have dischargeable "claims" within the meaning of 11 U.S.C. § 101(4). The future claimants are subject to the Injunction under the rubric of "Other Asbestos Obligation," which is defined by the Plan as asbestos-related health liability caused by pre-petition exposure to Manville asbestos, regardless of when the individual develops clinically observable symptoms. Thus, while the future claimants are not given creditor status under the Plan, they are nevertheless treated identically to the present claimants by virtue of the Injunction, which channels all claims to the Trust.

Kane v. Johns-Manville Corp., 843 F.2d 636, 640 (2d Cir. 1988). In *Kane* a present asbestos claimant challenged the inclusion of future claimants in the Manville Trust. The Second Circuit punted on the issue of whether a court had the power to address future claims. Rather, it held that present claimants had no standing to assert the rights of the future claimants. Although expressing "no opinion" about whether such a challenge would be successful, the court left open the possibility that "future claimants may at some later point attempt to challenge the Injunction," that they might be "permitted to advance a position contrary to that taken by the Legal Representative," and that "the future claimants' objections to the Injunction [might be] upheld." Id. at 645.

When cases like *Grady* are combined with cases like *Johns-Manville* and *Kane*, how important is it that a future claimant actually have a "claim"? By asserting the powers (1) to stay future claims during the reorganization proceedings and (2) to appoint a Legal Representative for such claims with the power to agree to permanent injunctions against the assertion of future claimants, and then by refusing (3) to review these assertions of power, haven't we functionally arrived at a point at which future claims can be discharged in bankruptcy? See Smith, 104 Yale L.J. at 375 ("Mass tort bankruptcy thus has occasioned a practical revision of bankruptcy law, allowing future claims to be addressed in reorganization plans."). Could the Legal Representative in *Epstein* rely on the "Manville solution" to achieve indirectly what he could not achieve directly? Or is the "Manville solution" limited just to those types of future claims that *Epstein* now recognizes as dischargeable in bankruptcy?

3. One criticism of *Epstein*'s test is that it may ignore congressional intent. Congress, as a part of the Bankruptcy Reform Act of 1994, amended 11 U.S.C. § 524 (the general discharge statute) by adding new sections (g) and (h). As summarized by Judge Weinstein:

> The Act authorizes issuance of an injunction immunizing an asbestos debtor from future claims where the debtor, as part of a bankruptcy proceeding, establishes a qualifying trust to compensate asbestos claimants. The law is expressly written "so that Johns-Manville and UNR, both of which have met and surpassed the standards imposed in this section, will be able to take advantage of the certainty it provides without having to reopen their cases." . . .
>
> To qualify for the injunction, the trust established under the reorganization must (1) assume the debtor's wrongful death, personal injury and property damage liabilities for exposure to asbestos products; (2) be funded by the debtor, with an obligation by the debtor to make future payments; (3) own, or be entitled to, a majority of the voting shares of the debtor, the debtor's parent corporation or the debtor's subsidiaries who are also debtors; and (4) "use its assets or income to satisfy claims and demands." [11 U.S.C.] §§ 524(g)(2)(B)(i)(I)-(IV). In addition, the court must determine that the debtor is likely to be subject to "substantial future demands," id. § 524(g)(2)(B)(ii)(I), "the actual amounts, numbers and timing [of which] cannot be determined," id. § 524(g)(2)(B)(ii)(II), and the pursuit of which in separate proceedings would "threaten the plan's purpose to deal equitably with claims and future demands." Id. § 524(g)(2)(B)(ii)(III). The court must ensure that the terms of any proposed injunction are set out in the reorganization plan and any required disclosure statement, and that 75% of the class of claimants vote to approve the plan. Id. § 524(g)(2)(B)(ii)(IV). Methods for operating the trust must be established, "such as structured, periodic, or supplemental payments, pro rata distributions, matrices, or periodic review of estimates of numbers and values of present claims and future demands . . . that provide reasonable assurance that the trust will value, and be in a financial position to pay, present claims and future demands that involve similar claims in substantially the same manner." Id. § 524(g)(2)(B)(ii)(V). . . .
>
> An injunction issued pursuant to the statute will only be valid and enforceable as to future claimants if a legal representative was appointed to protect future claimants' rights in the proceedings, and if the court determines that applying the injunction to them is "fair and equitable, in light of the benefits the trust will confer on the future demanders." Id. §§ 524(g)(4)(B)(i)-(ii). . . .
>
> Moreover, Bankruptcy Reform Act § 111(a) contains a provision that recognizes "existing injunctions" and provides for their continuation in harmony with the Act. See 11 U.S.C. § 524(h).

In re Joint Eastern and Southern Districts Asbestos Litigation, 878 F. Supp. 473, 570-72 (E. & S.D.N.Y. 1995), affirmed in part, dismissed in part, and vacated in part, 78 F.3d 764 (2d Cir. 1996).

Sections 524(g) and (h) are explicitly limited to future claims in *asbestos* cases that are compensated through a trust mechanism. *Epstein* involved neither an asbestos case nor a trust. Does its discussion of the types of future claims that can be discharged ignore Congress's intent? Is it an adequate response that *Epstein*'s interpretation of the word "claim" is merely dicta? See National Bankruptcy Review Commission, Treatment of Mass Future Claims in Bankruptcy 315-350 (1997) (proposing that § 524(g) be expanded to non-asbestos mass torts and that liabilities of future plaintiffs be treated as "claims").

4. If present creditors had no standing to contest the inclusion of future claimants in the Manville trust mechanism, did they even have standing to request the appointment of a legal representative? In Locks v. United States Trustee, 157 B.R. 89 (W.D. Pa. 1993), the district upheld a bankruptcy judge's refusal to appoint a representative for future claimants, holding in part that a lawyer for present plaintiffs was not a proper person to request such an appointment. The question of who can request an appointment is hardly academic. Unless a representative for future claimants is appointed, our notions of due process would not allow a court to dispose of their claims. If neither the debtor, the present plaintiffs, nor the court have the authority to appoint a representative, then a court's hands are tied unless and until a future claimant steps forward to request an appointment. But future claimants will typically have an incentive to step forward only in liquidation cases, not in reorganization cases:

> First [consider] the mass tort case in which a firm is liquidating in Chapter 7. If the tort victims who do not yet know about their injury do not have prepetition claims within the meaning of the Bankruptcy Code, they will receive nothing in Chapter 7 . . . . On the other hand, if the firm is in Chapter 11, the firm will have a postbankruptcy life. In such cases, tort victims may be better off if they do not have a prepetition claim. . . . The discharge a corporation receives under § 1141 extinguishes only the rights of those who hold claims that have already arisen.

Douglas G. Baird, The Elements of Bankruptcy 90 (rev. ed. 1993). Conversely, in a liquidation context, present creditors would be hostile to the appointment of a representative (since it dilutes their shares), while the judge and the debtor are at most indifferent and likely hostile. See *Locks*, 157 B.R. at 98-99 (cost and burden of maintaining claims facility for future claimants in liquidation case used as grounds for refusing to appoint legal representative). In the reorganization context, however, the debtor usually wants a representative, and present creditors and the judge can be persuaded to support the idea if it will have a positive effect on the reorganization plan or future health of the debtor.

Whose interests are being served by the appointment of a legal representative — those of the victims or those of the court and the other parties? Once again, we face the fundamental question: Under exactly what circumstances can the interests of the court and other parties take precedence over the interests of potential plaintiffs in deciding when, where, and against whom to file suit?

5. Professor Smith's observations might make you uneasy about how vigorously a legal representative is going to represent the interests of his or her constituency. If you were the legal representative for the Manville future claimants, wouldn't you have argued long and loud that your "clients" ought not be part of the reorganization proceedings? Wouldn't you have objected vigorously to a reorganization plan that shunted your clients' claims into a trust that was probably underfunded? Maybe not, if you were convinced that the reorganization would crumble without the future claims and that the present claimants would

devour Johns-Manville's assets before your clients could get anything. But Johns-Manville was far from insolvent when it entered bankruptcy, and the Manville trust was functionally bankrupt within eighteen months of opening its doors. See *Eastern and Southern Districts*, 878 F. Supp. at 485-87. Either the legal representative in *Manvilee* guessed badly, or he didn't represent his interests vigorously.

Moreover, the legal representative in *Manville* was not himself a person with a future claim; he was a lawyer. In the class action context, the legal representative could never have served as a class representative (for commonality, typicality, *and* adequacy reasons), and class members would never have been bound to a judgment or settlement he obtained or consented to. Why should the legal representative have the power to speak for future claimants in the bankruptcy context? Should a legal representative be subject to the same selection process as a class representative? Should future claimants be given the right to opt out of the compensation process proposed as part of the reorganization plan? (If not, isn't the use of the legal representative equivalent to a mandatory class action, only with none of the class action protections?) Wouldn't most of the claimants opt out of the plan and retain their rights against the healthy and wealthy Manville that emerged from Chapter 11? How can adequate notice be given to claimants who are by definition unknown? Can we avoid these problems by giving future claimants a back-end right to opt out of the compensation scheme at the point when their diseases manifest themselves?

Does the lack of adequate representation and notice suggest that the use of legal representatives, and maybe even the attempt to discharge future claims, are unconstitutional? See *UNR Industries*, 20 F.3d at 770 (dismissing constitutional concerns); Ralph R. Mabey & Jamie A. Gavrin, *Constitutional Limitations on the Discharge of Future Claims in Bankruptcy*, 44 S.Car. L. Rev. 745 (1993) (same); but see John C. Coffee, Jr., *Class Wars: The Dilemma of the Mass Tort Class Action*, 95 Colum. L. Rev. 1343, 1422-33 (1995) (questioning whether standing exists with regard to future claimants for bankruptcy purposes). Compare In re Asbestos Litigation, 90 F.3d 963 (5th Cir. 1996) (suggesting that uncertain and second-class status of legal representative makes Rule 23(b)(1)(B) class action a superior method for addressing future claims), vacated and remanded, 521 U.S. —, 117 S.Ct 2503 (1997), *aff'd* on remand, 134 F.3d 668 (5th Cir. 1998), cert. granted, 118 S.Ct. 2339 (1998), with id. at 1015-26, esp. n.76 (Smith, J., dissenting) (suggesting that future cases are not justiciable under Article III and cannot be discharged if Article III applies to bankruptcy courts).

6. Another problem with the use of a legal representative in a Chapter 11 case is voting. Voting for a reorganization plan is limited to persons who hold "claims" and "interests." "Interests" are usually thought to include only the interests of the shareholders. See 11 U.S.C. § 501(a). If future claims are neither "claims" nor "interests," then future claimants might well be stuck with a compensation plan that they never voted on; the legal representative would be their only voice, and it is not even a voice that the Bankruptcy Code tells the judge to consider when deciding whether to confirm the plan. See §§ 1128-29. On the other hand, if future claims are considered either "claims" or "interests," then the claimants must be entitled to vote on the reorganization plan if their claims or interests are allowed. § 1126. When the claimants are unknown, how can a vote be taken?

7. Still another practical problem of including future claims in a bankruptcy proceeding is calculating both the number and the value of the future claims. We saw the difficulties that the *Robins* court faced in estimating the number and value of present claimants, who in theory are known. See p. 720, *supra*. The problems of calculating unknown claims would obviously be even greater. See *Eastern and Southern Districts*, 878 F. Supp. at 485-86 (reporting how Manville's reorganization plan estimated that a total of 83,000 to 100,000 claims would be filed during 25-year life of Manville Trust, and how 240,000 claims had already been received in first 5 years).

8. So far we have had little favorable to say about the inclusion or discharge of future claims in a bankruptcy proceeding. Favorable things can, however, be said:

> Bankruptcy separates the past and future of an enterprise, satisfying claims attributable to yesterday's activities out of existing assets and thereby enabling business operations that have positive value to carry on, unburdened by the sunk costs of blunders that are beyond recall. . . . By letting bygones be bygone, from the firm's perspective, while assuring some compensation to those who learn in the future that these bygones caused them injury, a plan of reorganization . . . promotes both productivity and compensation. Failing to satisfy, out of assets available at the time of the petition, the claims of persons whose injury becomes manifest after the filing of the petition, would simultaneously provide (other) creditors with excessively large shares of the estate, and create a drag on ongoing operations that could cause the dissolution of business ventures with positive cash flow (and thus potentially substantial social and private value). . . . We observed in an earlier appeal . . . that making provision for future claimants would pose formidable logistical problems, but these have been overcome. We were concerned that the effort might be "a quixotic undertaking far beyond the realistic boundaries of judicial competence". . . . Things have turned out better than we feared in 1984. By 1992 we could declare the outcome a "notable success". . . . So there is no absolute bar to the [inclusion of future claims] adopted in UNR's plan of reorganization.

UNR Industries, 20 F.3d at 771 (Easterbrook, J.). Are you persuaded?

9. Future claims are a problem in cases other than mass torts. See In the Matter of Chicago, St. Paul & Pacific Railroad Co., 974 F.2d 775 (7th Cir. 1992) (future response costs under CERCLA); In re Chateaugay Corp., 944 F.2d 997 (2d Cir. 1991) (same); In re National Gypsum Co., 139 B.R. 397 (N.D. Tex. 1992) (same). One aspect of the problem concerns the liability of successor corporations sued on a claim for which the debtor received a discharge. Compare Zerand-Bernal Group, Inc. v. Cox, 23 F.3d 159 (7th Cir. 1994) (discharge did not run to successor; asbestos cases distinguished) with In re Paris Industries Corp., 132 B.R. 504 (D. Me. 1991) (injunction against state court suit against successor upheld). For recent scholarly commentary, see, *e.g.*, National Bankruptcy Conference, Reforming the Bankruptcy Code 281-87 (1994); Michelle M. Morgan, *The Denial of Future Tort Claims in* In re Piper Aircraft: *Will the Court's Quick-Fix Solution Keep the Debtor Flying High or Bring It Crashing Down?* 27 Loy. U. Chi. L. Rev. 27 (1995).

10. The reasons for including future claims within the bankruptcy proceeding were to achieve a single forum for the resolution of all related claims and to assure equal treatment of all claimants. Undoubtedly you noticed that *Manville* fell short of these objectives. The only future claims included within

the reorganization plan were those in which the exposure to Manville asbestos had occurred prior to the filing of the bankruptcy petition. Since Manville asbestos remained in place even after the filing of the petition, it is likely that some persons received their first exposure to Manville asbestos after the cut-off date. These future claimants presumably retain the right to sue the reorganized Manville for full damages — simply because of the fortuity of the timing of their exposure. Only some sort of conduct test, which *Epstein* rejects, would be capable of bringing these claims into the bankruptcy proceeding. Is there some way to modify the conduct test to allow joinder of these types of claims, but not the claims with which *Epstein* was concerned?

And so, like modern-day Galahads, our five-chapter search for the Holy Grail of aggregation is at an end. Bankruptcy takes us well along the way, but not far enough — not nearly far enough. Whether that fact is an event to mourn or to celebrate, we leave to your judgment.

C. MODIFYING A REORGANIZATION PLAN

In Section B we saw that one concept that bankruptcy has developed to deal with mass injuries is a trust, established from the assets and future profits of the debtor, whose function is to compensate present claimants, future claimants, and co-defendants. Once the trust is established, the debtor walks away from its obligations to present and future claimants. Nonetheless, if the trust is underfunded, or if its measures for distributing its funds turns out to treat claimants inequitably, the reorganization plan stops being a workable solution and starts becoming an instrument of injustice. Calls for the reformation of the trust, and perhaps even for the reopening of proceedings against the debtor, can be expected.

Indeed, this is exactly what happened to the Manville Trust, which ran out of money within eighteen months of beginning operation. In retrospect, part of the problem of the Manville Trust was its policy of paying off each asbestos claim in full — including attorneys' fees — after a judgment had been reached, and in paying each claim in the order in which it was submitted. It should not have taken a rocket scientist to figure out that, with such a payout system, the assets of the Trust would soon be spent; but the bankruptcy court and the various creditors deluded themselves into thinking that judgments would be smaller and that fewer claims would be filed than turned out to be the case. The result was a budding catastrophe. The lucky claimants that were first to judgment or settlement received 100 cents on the dollar. As for the rest, there would be nothing. Not only would there be no money available for future claimants, but there would also be no money available to pay off all of the claims of present claimants, many of whom had voted to accept the reorganization plan in the belief that they would receive compensation for their injuries.

Obviously, the Trust needed to be changed, in order to limit awards and attorneys' fees and to preserve assets for all claimants. Whether the courts had the legal power to do so, however, was problematic.

In a series of lengthy decisions that constitute a fascinating dialogue between the district court and the Second Circuit over a range of complex issues, both courts agreed that a power of modification exists. In 1990 Judge Weinstein was granted supervisory responsibility over the Manville reorganization plan by the Second Circuit. Weinstein appointed Marvin E. Frankel as a special master; Judge Frankel's investigation led him to conclude that the Trust's assets had a value between $2.1 and $2.7 billion, that current and future claims were estimated at $6.5 billion, and that the Trust currently lacked the cash to pay the then liquidated total of $448.5 million in claims — in other words, the Trust was "deeply insolvent."

There ensued negotiations among lawyers representing present claimants, future claimants, the Trust, asbestos manufacturers who were co-defendants of the Trust in pending lawsuits, and Manville. The negotiations resulted in a proposal, agreed to by lawyers representing many of the interested parties but not all of the claimants, for paying present and future claimants. The proposal called for a revised Trust Distribution Process ("TDP"). The problem for Judge Weinstein, of course, was whether he could approve the restructuring when the revisions were not universally accepted.

Weinstein's task was considerably eased when five plaintiffs who had claims against the Trust filed a class action complaint. The complaint invoked both diversity jurisdiction (§ 1332) and bankruptcy jurisdiction (§ 1334), and alleged a single count that sought to establish an equitable distribution of the Trust *res*. As relief, the complaint sought a judgment determining an equitable, efficient, and inexpensive method of allocating the *res* among all beneficiaries and a permanent injunction against "all pending and future proceedings by Beneficiaries against the Trust in all state and federal courts except in accordance with the procedures determined hereby."

Weinstein put the case on a lightning track. Four days after it was filed, he held hearings, conditionally certified the class, and stayed payments by the Trust to asbestos claimants. In less than three months he certified the case as a mandatory Rule 23(b)(1)(B) class action, containing a single class of all present or future plaintiffs and co-defendants with claims against the Manville Trust resulting from pre-confirmation exposure to Manville asbestos. Within seven months he approved the settlement, made permanent the prior stay of proceedings against the Trust, and reaffirmed the prior injunction, issued in the Chapter 11 proceeding, restricting suits against the reorganized Manville.

The objective of the revised TDP was stated to be "to treat all claimants alike by paying all claimants an equal percentage of their claims' values over time." The TDP divided all asbestos disease claims into two levels. The most serious claims (deaths, cancers, and other severe injuries) were placed in Level One. All other claims were placed in Level Two.

The TDP made three distinctions in the payment of Level One and Level Two claims. First, the TDP established a schedule of maximum payments for various diseases, with maximums for Level One claims set substantially higher than maximums for Level Two claims. Second, the TDP provided for faster payment for Level One claims. Level One claims were to begin receiving payments in the first two years of the TDP. Level Two claims were to begin receiving payments in the third year of the TDP. Claimants in Level One were initially to be paid up to 45 percent of their claims. They then stopped receiving payment until all other claimants had received 45 percent of their claims. Thereafter, payments were to be made to all claimants on a pro rata basis, as funds were available, until all claims had been fully paid. Third, the combination of the delayed payment schedule for Level Two claims and the possibility that the present and future assets available to pay claims would be insufficient to pay all claims in full created a risk that the Level Two claimants would receive a smaller share of their damages than Level One claimants, and early Level Two claimants would receive substantially less than under the existing payment plans.

The Settlement also included a Master Agreement between the Trust and Manville, under which Manville agreed to pay the Trust an additional $280 million during the first four years and up to an additional $240 million through the seventh year. It limited the fees of lawyers for health claimants to the lesser of their contracted fees or 25 percent of any recovery. It sought to reduce the Trust's expenses by preventing all Trust beneficiaries from litigating their claims in state or federal court, and further purported to make procedural changes that effectively left Manville's co-defendants responsible for a larger share of asbestos judgments and settlements.

Most of the foregoing history is taken from Judge Weinstein's opinion approving the settlement, see In re Joint Eastern and Southern Districts Asbestos Litigation, 129 B.R. 710 (E. & S.D.N.Y. 1991), and from the ensuing appeal (excerpted below). In essence, Weinstein's restructuring changed the Manville Trust into something analogous to a worker's compensation system. It did so in a way that introduced divisions among those more severely injured and those less severely injured, and among health claimants and co-defendants — divisions that had not inhabited the original reorganization plan. But enough about what it did. The real issue is where Judge Weinstein got the power to do anything at all.

IN RE JOINT EASTERN AND SOUTHERN DISTRICT ASBESTOS LITIGATION

982 F.2d 721 (2d Cir. 1992), modified, 993 F.2d 7 (2d Cir. 1993)

■ NEWMAN, Circuit Judge. . . . Though the appellants challenge the exercise of both diversity and bankruptcy jurisdiction, they appear, at times, to argue that only bankruptcy jurisdiction is available to deal in any way with the Manville Trust because it is an integral component of a confirmed plan of reorganization. If that is their contention, it is not correct. . . . [I]f a lawsuit is filed asserting a valid state law cause of action against an entity that has emerged from a reorganization plan, that suit may be settled, and any state law rights may be voluntarily modified so long as the settlement is within the subject matter jurisdiction of the court approving it and the settlement is accomplished in observance of all applicable procedural requirements. That is what the appellees contend has occurred in this case

— the filing of a state law cause of action to restructure the Trust in a diversity court with subject matter jurisdiction and the settlement of that suit in observance of the procedural requirements of Rule 23. We therefore turn first to the objections to the exercise of the Trial Courts' diversity jurisdiction and then proceed, in the event deficiencies are encountered, to consider whether the changes wrought by the Settlement may be accomplished in the exercise of bankruptcy jurisdiction.

III. EXERCISE OF DIVERSITY JURISDICTION

[The court held that subject matter and personal jurisdiction existed. It then turned to the class action issues.]

C. Rule 23 requirements — the (b)(1)(B) non-opt-out class . . .

The Trial Courts certified a class under Rule 23(b)(1)(B) . . . . In their view, this case presented the sort of "limited fund" for which the Advisory Committee's note to the 1966 amendment of Rule 23 makes a (b)(1)(B) class "plainly" available — "when claims are made by numerous persons against a fund insufficient to satisfy all claims." . . .

Plainly, insolvency does not present the classic instance of a "limited fund," such as would be involved if a group of claimants asserted claims of an aggregate amount that would deplete a fixed sum of money. Whether, and for what purposes, (b)(1)(B) may be used with respect to an insolvent entity are perplexing issues that we would have expected to have received more extended consideration than is apparent in the cases thus far decided.

With respect to aggregate claims in excess of a fixed sum of money, a (b)(1)(B) class action is appropriate to avoid an unfair preference for the early claimants at the expense of later claimants. With respect to an insolvent entity, however, bankruptcy law is normally the source of protection to assure a fair and orderly distribution of assets insufficient to meet claims. Insolvency exerts powerful pressures upon contending creditors to compromise their positions so that a fair distribution of assets is achieved — through a reorganization that contemplates the continuation of the debtor where feasible, and otherwise through liquidation. To lessen the risk that these pressures will lead to unfair compromises, bankruptcy law provides numerous safeguards not contained in class action procedures. For example, for a plan of reorganization to be approved, the plan must be put to a vote of all members of impaired classes of creditors, 11 U.S.C. § 1126, the vote is taken only after a solicitation based on a detailed description of the plan, id. § 1125, the plan can be "crammed down" over the objection of a dissenting class of creditors only if strict fairness standards are met, id. § 1129(b)(1), and the plan may not be imposed against the wishes of an impaired class that would fare better under liquidation, id. § 1129(a)(7).

By contrast, Rule 23 is less elaborate in its protections, for example, permitting named representatives of a class, or subclass, to consent to a settlement that binds all the members of the class, or subclass, without a vote of the class or subclass members. And there is no option for those who would fare better under liquidation than under settlement of the class action followed by reorganization to insist on liquidation.

These differences raise a substantial question whether a class action may be used to adjust claims against an insolvent entity that is eligible for bankruptcy protection. And, even if, in the context of insolvency, a "limited fund" class action may be used for its traditional purpose of effecting a pro rata reduction of all claims, ... an even more substantial question is raised as to whether a class action may be used against an insolvent entity to adjust the claims of creditors vis-a-vis each other, without observing the protections that would be available under bankruptcy law. . . .

However, respect for the binding force of precedent within this Circuit obliges us to take careful note of the recent decision in In re Drexel Burnham Lambert Group, Inc., 960 F.2d 285 (2d Cir. [1992]), [cert. dismissed, 506 U.S. 1088 (1993)], which approved a more adventuresome use of a class action settlement to make a non-uniform adjustment of creditors' rights against an insolvent entity. . . .

Drexel acknowledges that class actions are not normally to be used in the context of bankruptcy. . . . But, though the question is close, we are not persuaded that the need to insist on bankruptcy law protections is greater in this case than it was in *Drexel*, and the reasonableness of using a (b)(1)(B) non-opt-out class is at least as compelling in this case as in *Drexel*.

We are therefore willing to permit the use of such a class action in the pending case, so long as there exists, as occurred in *Drexel*, appropriate designation of subclasses to provide assurance that the consent of groups of claimants who are being treated differently by the settlement is being given by those who fairly and adequately represent only the members of each group. The inevitable tension between the limited protections of Rule 23 and the more complete protections of the Bankruptcy Code is strained by any use of a mandatory non-opt-out class to settle claims against an insolvent entity that is subject to bankruptcy jurisdiction. But that tension reaches the breaking point when, instead of the traditional limited fund settlement that achieves a pro rata reduction of the claims of all members of the plaintiff class, the rights of the plaintiff class are revised vis-a-vis each other and consent to the resulting settlement is given by representatives who purport to represent the undifferentiated class of plaintiffs as a whole, rather than the interests of each of the subclasses whose rights are being altered. We therefore proceed to an examination of the appellants' contentions regarding the lack of subclasses, mindful that these contentions require careful scrutiny in the unusual context where settlement of a class action is used to readjust creditors' claims against an insolvent entity, without observance of the protections that would otherwise be available under the Bankruptcy Code.

D. Rule 23 requirements — the class definition

1. *Objection of the co-defendant manufacturers.* The co-defendant manufacturers object to the class definition on the ground that it improperly places them within the same class as the health claimants, a grouping that

they contend violates the typicality and adequacy of representation requirements of Rule 23(a)(3) and (4). We agree with their objection. The health claimants and the co-defendant manufacturers have been adversaries for many years in thousands of lawsuits in courts throughout the country. Their interests are profoundly adverse to each other. The health claimants wish to receive as much as possible from the co-defendant manufacturers, and the latter wish to hold their payment obligations to a minimum. More significantly, this adversity was at the heart of one important aspect of the proposed restructuring of the Trust — the provisions of Section H of the Settlement adjusting the co-defendant manufacturers' rights to contribution and setoff. The co-defendant manufacturers assert that the effect of Section H is to shift hundreds of millions of dollars of Manville asbestos liability to the co-defendants. Whether or not that adjustment is "fair" and whether or not it can be made in disregard of applicable state law, it surely cannot be made in a settlement on behalf of a single class that includes both the health claimants and the co-defendant manufacturers. The conflict is overwhelming....

2. *Objection of the health claimants.* Within the category of health claimants, marked differences exist between identifiable subgroups that require division of the health claimants themselves into appropriate subclasses. The first difference results from a combination of the payment procedures of the Manville Trust, as originally established, and the insolvency of the Trust. [The original payment procedures] established a strict order-of-filing priority to govern payment of all health claims. Once the Trust became insolvent, the effect of the payment priority was to divide the health claimants into two subgroups. The first subgroup comprises those claimants with sufficiently early filing dates to assure the full payment of their claims before the Trust runs out of money. The second subgroup comprises those with later filing dates who will receive no payments at all: the Trust will run out of cash by the time their payment priority is reached. Plainly, the members of each of these subgroups have sharply conflicting interests with respect to the maintenance of the order-of-filing priority....

Once the health claimants have been divided into two priority-of-payment subclasses, a further sub-division of each subclass is required to reflect the Settlement's division of health claimants between Level One and Level Two. The interests of the health claimants within each priority subclass diverge sharply with respect to payment formulas, once payment priority has been abandoned.... Thus, before any settlement can be approved, the health claimants must be divided into at least two subclasses — the high priority claimants and the low priority claimants, reflecting the initial adversity among the entire group of health claimants once the Trust became insolvent. If a settlement purports to make significant distinctions among the rights of health claimants, then these initial subclasses must be further divided to reflect whatever adversity results from the settlement. For valid approval of the current Settlement, for example, there would have to be four subclasses — the high priority claimants in Level One, the high priority claimants in Level Two, the low priority claimants in Level One, and the low priority claimants in Level Two.

Observance of subclass requirements before any settlement is involuntarily imposed upon all the health claimant beneficiaries of the Trust through the consent of "representatives" is especially important in this case .... [T]he use of a class action settlement, imposed upon all members of a mandatory non-opt-out class, in the context of an insolvent defendant, creates a risk that the protections of bankruptcy law will be circumvented. *Drexel* committed this Circuit to the acceptance of that risk, and we are obliged to follow the force of that precedent. But *Drexel* took that step only where the significant differences among the class members were recognized by the creation of appropriate subclasses. If a class action settlement is to be permitted in the insolvency context, in which adjustment of creditors' rights would normally be accomplished pursuant to the Bankruptcy Code, there must be careful observance of subclass requirements. No members of a significant subclass can be mandatorily bound by the consent of "representatives" in the context of this litigation unless those representatives have undivided loyalty only to subclass members. . . .

IV. EXERCISE OF BANKRUPTCY JURISDICTION

Though the Trial Courts relied primarily on the exercise of diversity jurisdiction and the application of Rule 23(b)(1)(B) as authority to approve the Settlement restructuring the Trust, they also invoked their bankruptcy jurisdiction to some unspecified extent. We therefore proceed to inquire whether approval of the Settlement is valid in the exercise of the Trial Courts' bankruptcy jurisdiction. The objecting health claimants contend that the modification of their rights as Class-4 creditors is not authorized by the Plan or its attached documents and, in any event, violates section 1127 of the Code. We consider first the amending authority within the Plan.

A. Amending authority within the Plan

[The court examined the various provisions of the original bankruptcy plan which permitted modification of the plan.] We conclude that the restructuring of the Trust was not permitted pursuant to any of the specific amending powers reserved to the various parties identified in the Plan and the Plan-related documents. We therefore consider whether the changes were authorized by the more general reserved power of the Bankruptcy Court to modify the Plan "to the full extent permitted by the Code." Plan § 10.1(H).

B. Conflict with the Code

The extent to which a bankruptcy court may make changes in a confirmed reorganization plan is largely uncharted terrain. . . . Appellants contend that the restructuring violates the Code in two respects. First, they contend, it violates the fundamental bar of section 1127(b), which prohibits modifications of a confirmed and substantially consummated plan of reorganization. Second, they contend, it violates section 1123(a)(4), which requires that a plan "provide the same treatment for each claim or interest of a particular class."

1. *Section 1127(b)*. The Trial Courts sought to avoid the bar of section 1127(b) by maintaining that the restructuring of the Trust was not a "modification." We cannot agree. Even if the concept of "modification" implies some distinction between significant changes of substance, which are prohibited, and minor changes of procedure, which might be allowed, the alterations accomplished by the Settlement are both substantive and significant. Health claimants who formerly stood on an equal footing, entitled to payment in the order their claims were filed, and with jury trial rights unimpaired, emerged divided into two groups, with differing rights as to maximum amounts recoverable and as to timing and rate of payments. The FIFO [first-in, first-out] ordering of payments was scrapped. For all claimants, the opportunity to have a jury determine the amount of their damages was drastically curtailed by the disincentive created by the payment of jury verdicts in excess of offers or arbitration awards only out of a secondary pool of money, unlikely to have sufficient resources to meet its obligations. . . .

2. *Section 1123(a)(4)*. Since the purported exercise of bankruptcy jurisdiction violates the bar of section 1127(b), we need not decide whether the Settlement also violates section 1123(a)(4) by failing to accord the "same treatment" to the health claimant members of Class-4. We have summarized the extensive changes that the Settlement makes in the rights of the Class-4 claimants in pointing out why those changes qualify as "modifications" for purposes of section 1127(b).

The Trial Courts sought to justify the acknowledged distinction between Level One and Level Two claimants on the ground that "the distinction between claimants reflects underlying differences in the nature and strength of the claims." Without question, the "same treatment" standard of section 1123(a)(4) does not require that all claimants within a class receive the same amount of money. Asbestos health claimants would receive the "same treatment" if they all were permitted to present their claims to a jury and were all paid whatever amounts the jury awarded, until funds were no longer available. But some classification of claimants within a class is permissible. See In re AOV Industries, Inc., 792 F.2d 1140, 1154 (D.C. Cir. 1986). Whether the Settlement permissibly classifies according to seriousness of injury or impermissibly denies health claimant creditors the "same treatment" need not be resolved, since any effort to use bankruptcy authority to accomplish the objectives of the Settlement would in any event require a second reorganization. . . .

CONCLUSION

With considerable regret, we hold that the Settlement must be set aside, and we vacate the judgment of the Trial Courts. Our regret arises from two sources: both the extraordinary efforts that have been made by all concerned with this litigation — judges, lawyers, and court-appointed experts — in crafting an ingenious set of arrangements to resolve an extremely difficult set of problems, and the obvious benefits that the result of their combined labors would have brought to most of those with interests in this litigation. But we cannot uphold as "sensible" or "useful" or "fair" or even "achieving the most good for the most people" an impairment of rights accomplished in violation of applicable legal rules.

Notes and Questions

1. In a subsequent opinion the Second Circuit held that Rule 23(a) did not require the creation of separate subclasses for early-filing and late-filing claimants. In re Joint Eastern and Southern District Asbestos Litigation, 993 F.2d 7 (2d Cir. 1993). On remand, Judge Weinstein then went back to work. Although he had been shut out on the bankruptcy jurisdiction theory, he still had the state law theory, if he could create the appropriate subclasses and then find that the settlement was fair, reasonable, and adequate. The first task was not difficult, but it took about two years before he was able to complete the second task of approving the settlement. In re Eastern and Southern Districts Asbestos Litigation, 878 F. Supp. 473 (E. & S.D.N.Y 1995). The Second Circuit substantially affirmed, but vacated a small piece, 78 F.3d 764 (2d Cir. 1996). On remand Judge Weinstein fixed the problem, 929 F. Supp. 1 (E. & S.D.N.Y 1996).

2. The opinions in this case cover hundreds of pages. In our editing, we have left out much of the creative energy and uncertainty that underlay the modification of the Manville Trust. The issue of modification, both factually and legally, is enormously complicated. But its essence seems to be this: Shy of a second bankruptcy proceeding with a second reorganization plan, a court does not have the power under the Bankruptcy Code to revise a reorganization plan after the "substantial confirmation" of the plan. 11 U.S.C. § 1127. If the plan creates a trust or other similar entity, however, the judge has the power under the relevant state or federal law to reform that entity. In order to make the reformation binding, the judge must have the power to bring before her all the parties with an interest in the preservation or reformation of the plan. Whether the judge can use mandatory joinder devices to aggregate the parties remains an open issue, one that the Second Circuit resolved affirmatively with greatest reluctance in the most pressing circumstance imaginable.

There is a nice logic in this solution: If state law creates an equitable entity like the Manville Trust, then state law ought to be the source of the grounds for the entity's reform. But at a different level, it is not so simple. The health claimants and the co-defendants voted to support a reorganization plan in which they were assured that they would receive full compensation from the Manville Trust. Most of them did not. Now they found themselves thrown into a state-law proceeding that left them, at most, with 45% of their damages compensated. They had no vote on this plan, and they had no right to opt out; rather, they had only a class representative and an opportunity to speak at a fairness hearing. How many Manville claimants, had they known how things turned out, would have voted for the reorganization plan in the first instance? Doesn't the state-law proceeding act just like a cramdown procedure, with the difference being that the shareholders of Manville were able to escape the absolute priority rule and retain much of the company's value? Why impose the entire burden of an underfunded trust on the claimants caught in the middle between the early claimants who got 100 cents on the dollar and the claimants not yet exposed to Manville's asbestos who retain the right to sue for full damages? Should we amend the Bankruptcy Code to permit early payments to be recaptured, later claimants to be aggregated, and proceedings against the debtor to be reopened? Can the courts do these things under their inherent powers? Cf. In re Vecchio, 20 F.3d 555 (2d Cir. 1994) (in Chapter 7 case court has discretion to order disgorgement of excess funds paid to one creditor).

By the way, how did Judge Weinstein convince Manville to contribute an additional $250-500 million to the reformed Trust? Perhaps Manville feared that Weinstein was going to reopen the reorganization proceeding, and it bought its peace. Would this possibility suggest that giving a judge the power to reopen confirmed plans is a bad idea? After the Second Circuit's ruling that Weinstein had no power in bankruptcy to modify the plan, could another reorganized entity in Manville's position be "convinced" to contribute additional money?

3. Was the modification of the Manville Trust a victory for the non-adversarial use of judicial power to achieve fair treatment of claimants? Or did its payment scheduling effectively cheat claimants out of their right to present individual proofs and arguments? Would the modification have been necessary if the judges in the original Manville reorganization proceedings had acted in keeping with their adversarial roles?

4. Other cases have also discussed the modification of a confirmed plan. These cases usually involve the court's ability to modify a plan that has not been stayed pending appeal; none analyzes the modification issue with the level of sophistication of the *Eastern and Southern District* opinions. See In the Matter of Manges, 29 F.3d 1034 (5th Cir. 1994), cert. denied, 513 U.S. 999 (1995); In the Matter of UNR Industries, Inc., 20 F.3d 766 (7th Cir. 1994); In re Chateaugay Corp., 10 F.3d 944 (2d Cir. 1993). See also In re A.H. Robins Co., 86 F.3d 364 (4th Cir.), cert. denied, — U.S. —, 117 S.Ct. 483 (1996) (order limiting attorneys' fees on supplemental bankruptcy distribution to 10% not impermissible modification of reorganization plan; order further authorized by 11 U.S.C. § 105).

5. Earlier in the chapter we encountered the argument that bankruptcy ought not be used as a substitute for Rule 23(b)(1)(B) mandatory aggregation because of the special protections accorded class members. In *Eastern and Southern District*, the Second Circuit used the opposite argument: that Rule 23(b)(1)(B) class actions ought not be used as a substitute for bankruptcy because of the special protections accorded bankruptcy creditors. Can both propositions be right? Can a judge or party use whichever device is best suited to the situation? What is the proper relationship between our most powerful aggregation devices — the class action and the bankruptcy proceeding?

D. CLASS ACTION OR BANKRUPTCY?

IN RE JOINT EASTERN AND SOUTHERN DISTRICT ASBESTOS LITIGATION

14 F.3d 726 (2d Cir. 1993)

■ WINTER, Circuit Judge. [Keene Corp., an asbestos defendant, filed a mandatory Rule 23(b)(1)(B) class action. The suit, in essence, sought an injunction against all asbestos suits against it while it tried to complete a global settlement of present and future asbestos claims. Specifically, the complaint alleged: "This is a settlement class action. Keene seeks court assistance, as provided by Rule 23(b)(1)(B), to negotiate and eventually approve a settlement that fairly resolves the claims with the limited funds Keene has available. . . . The Settlement Agreement will be designed to ensure that Keene complies with its obligations to the Class, but at the same time will preserve a portion of its assets for continued operations, in order that Keene may achieve an adequate balance for the protection of its shareholders. . . . Certification of the Class for settlement purposes can avoid a potential bankruptcy of Keene by allowing the asbestos-related personal injury, wrongful death, property damage and contribution litigations against Keene to come to a successful and final resolution in an expeditious and fair manner with a minimum of transaction costs."

[Judge Weinstein appointed a special master to investigate Keene's claim of a limited fund. The master discovered that Keene's present assets exceeded liabilities by $51 million, and found that these assets were probably inadequate to guarantee payments to all present and future claimants. Weinstein then certified a limited-fund class action, pursuant to Rule 23(b)(1)(B), that contained five subclasses. He also appointed a Special Settlement Master "to facilitate discussions among the parties," and directed that "settlement discussions should begin immediately." Finally, the order enjoined Keene and all class members from continuing or commencing asbestos-related litigation, except for trials already underway; enjoined class members from attempting to collect judgments against Keene or its assets; and forbade Keene to make any payments other than reasonable expenses in operating its business.

[Some asbestos victims appealed from the preliminary injunction order. The Second Circuit held that Keene's claim was "not a case or controversy within the meaning of Article III" because it presented no "legal claim to adjudicate." Prior to vacating the preliminary injunction and ordering the complaint dismissed, the Second Circuit made the following observations.]

[I]t is clear that the complaint is an attempt to compel an adjustment of Keene's creditors' rights outside the Bankruptcy Code and is defended almost entirely by the argument that a mandatory class settlement of present or future asbestos claims would be better for all parties than a bankruptcy proceeding. Indeed, the process contemplated by Keene mirrors a bankruptcy proceeding. The finding of a limited fund corresponds to a finding of insolvency. The preliminary injunction serves much the same function as the automatic stay under Section 362(a) of the Bankruptcy Code. 11 U.S.C. § 362(a) (1988). The class representatives correspond to creditors' committees in Chapter 11 proceedings. See 11 U.S.C. § 1102 (1988). The proposed mandatory class settlement mirrors a reorganization plan and "cram-down," see 11 U.S.C. § 1123, 1129(b); In re Johns-Manville, 982 F.2d 721, 736 (2d Cir. 1992), modified on different grounds, 993 F.2d 7 (2d Cir. 1993), followed by a discharge, 11 U.S.C. § 1141(d).

Keene's argument is self-defeating, however, because it is a self-evident evasion of the exclusive legal system established by Congress for debtors to seek relief. See *In re Johns-Manville*, 982 F.2d at 735. The adoption of

Keene's position would surely lead to further evasion of the Bankruptcy Code as other debtors sought relief in mandatory class actions. Keene argues that such a precedent would be limited to situations, like Keene's, of mass torts in which some plaintiffs are not known at the time of the accident. We are dubious that a limit to unknown plaintiffs is feasible. Under the limited fund theory espoused here, a class representative for a large number of trade creditors might be appointed to seek a settlement on their behalf where a company was deemed to be a limited fund because of insolvency. The argument that the company and its creditors would all be better off in such an action than in bankruptcy would be as plausible in a case involving a large number of contract creditors as it is here. Breach of warranty cases involving numerous purchasers might also fall within the theory.

Moreover, even if limited to so-called mass torts with yet unknown plaintiffs, Keene's theory would cover a large number of cases. The use of aggregative techniques and inventive legal theories are causing mass torts to become rather routine. Certainly the theory pressed here would apply to many products liability cases, . . . environmental torts, . . . and even physical disasters. . . .

Evasion of bankruptcy is also not without costs or other perils. The injunction in the instant matter has already prevented execution of final judgments on supersedeas bonds and funds in escrow that are not Keene's assets. Moreover, class members in cases such as this would have no say in the conduct of the court-appointed class representatives and, unlike creditors in bankruptcy, are not able to vote on a settlement. See 11 U.S.C. § 1126. For them, it would be "cram-down" from start to finish. Finally, unlike a lawyer for a creditors' committee, the class representatives in matters like the present one may not be compensated unless a settlement is reached, a situation fraught with danger to the rights of plaintiffs. . . .

Keene argues passionately that bankruptcy will be a more costly route for the defendant class than this mandatory class action. It may be that the amount distributed to the class in a Keene bankruptcy will be less than in a settlement in the instant class action. Indeed, Keene has suggested that a trial be held on that issue. However, the function of federal courts is not to conduct trials over whether a statutory scheme should be ignored because a more efficient mechanism can be fashioned by judges.

IN RE ASBESTOS LITIGATION*

90 F.3d 963 (5th Cir. 1996), vacated and remanded, 521 U.S. —, 117 S.Ct. 2503 (1997), affirmed on remand, 134 F.3d 668 (5th Cir. 1998), cert. granted, 118 S.Ct. 2339 (1998)

■ DAVIS, Circuit Judge. [The facts of this complex set of asbestos cases are set out on p. 658, *supra*. Briefly, Fibreboard and its insurers proposed to settle all claims against Fibreboard by future asbestos claimants or future

---

* One of the authors of this book was a consultant to one of the insurers in this case. The other was a consultant to the Federal Judicial Center, and performed a study of this case at the request of the Center. — ED.

third-party claims of co-defendants by means of a $1.535 billion global settlement. The global settlement was to be achieved by use of a Rule 23(b)(1)(B) class action. At the time of the settlement, Fibreboard's claims against its insurers were the subject of litigation on appeal in California; Fibreboard claimed that the insurance companies had a nearly unlimited responsibility to indemnify Fibreboard, while the insurers claimed that their policy limits had already been exhausted. Depending on which view prevailed (Fibreboard had prevailed at the trial level), Fibreboard would have had either a large pot of insurance money to pay future judgments or only its own corporate assets, which were worth between $200 and $300 million. In the event that the $1.535 billion global settlement fell apart, Fibreboard and its insurers had also negotiated a Trilateral Settlement Agreement, under which Fibreboard agreed to drop any further indemnity claims against the insurers in return for $2 billion. The $2 billion was to be used for legal expenses, as well as to pay for all present *and* future personal injury *and* property damage claims. Any additional amounts would need to be paid from Fibreboard's assets. Under the $1.535 billion global settlement, Fibreboard agreed to contribute only $10 million, thus preserving the bulk of its assets for its shareholders.

[In the course of ruling that class certification was appropriate for future claimants and that the settlement was fair, the court addressed the argument of the two intervening objectors that the $1.535 billion settlement was an impermissible end-run around the Bankruptcy Code.]

The district court found that the prosecution of separate actions by members of the Global Health Claimant Class would substantially impair or impede the ability of other members of the class to receive full payment for their injuries from Fibreboard's limited assets. This finding has strong support in the record and is not clearly erroneous. The district court heard expert testimony on the probable number, mix and timing of future asbestos personal injury claims against Fibreboard, the anticipated costs of defense relating to such claims, and the present value of Fibreboard's non-insurance assets. The experts agreed that Fibreboard faced enormous liability and defense costs that would likely equal or exceed the amount of damages paid out. More importantly, these experts testified that even under the Trilateral Settlement Agreement where Fibreboard is given $2 billion in insurance money to add to its own value of approximately $235 million, Fibreboard would be unable to pay all the valid claims against it within five to nine years. The district court credited the testimony of these experts and found that Fibreboard is a limited fund. . . .

The intervenors argue that if the reason Fibreboard is a limited fund is because it will become insolvent before it pays all claims, then the Global Settlement Agreement is an impermissible attempt to circumvent bankruptcy proceedings and bankruptcy's absolute priority rule. This argument fails to consider (1) decisions of other courts which have certified 23(b)(1)(B) classes because the claims of the class would bankrupt the defendant, (2) the significance of Fibreboard's settlement with its insurers in driving the Global Settlement Agreement, (3) the plain meaning of Rule 23, and (4) the nonexclusivity of the Bankruptcy Code and its inferiority to a 23(b)(1)(B) class action in the instant case.

Other courts have uniformly found that, in appropriate and limited circumstances, potential or probable insolvency of a defendant can create a limited fund appropriate for adjudication under Rule 23(b)(1)(B). The Second Circuit, in In re Joint Eastern and Southern District Asbestos Litigation (*Findley*), upheld the district court's conclusion that the likely insolvency of the Manville Trust rendered it a limited fund and qualified it for treatment under Rule 23(b)(1)(B). 982 F.2d 721, 739 (2d Cir. 1992) . . . . In In re the Drexel Burnham Lambert Group, Inc., 960 F.2d 285 (2d. Cir. 1992), the Second Circuit approved a 23(b)(1)(B) class action on the ground that individual litigation would reduce the recovery for all plaintiffs from Drexel's limited assets. Id. at 292. See also, In re Joint Eastern and Southern District Asbestos Litigation (Eagle-Picher Industries), 134 F.R.D. 32, 34 (E. & S.D. N.Y. 1990); Coburn v. 4-R Corporation, 77 F.R.D. 43 (E.D. Ky. 1977).

In fact, even courts that have refused to certify 23(b)(1)(B) classes have done so on the ground that the parties seeking class certification have failed to present sufficient evidence that the assets of the defendant are insufficient to pay the claims against it. . . .

In support of their claim that *any* 23(b)(1)(B) limited-fund action based on a defendant's insolvency is an improper circumvention of the Bankruptcy Code, the intervenors can rely only on dicta from In re Joint Eastern and Southern District Asbestos Litigation (*Keene*), 14 F.3d 726 (2d Cir. 1993).[14] The intervenors' conclusion is contrary to the overwhelming majority of court decisions on this issue, ignores crucial facts in both *Ahearn* and *Keene* and reads *Keene* in a way that creates an intra-circuit split in the Second Circuit.

Ahearn's Global Settlement Agreement was undisputedly driven by insurance coverage litigation between Fibreboard and its insurers which created a serious risk for all parties to the agreement. The Global Health Claimant Class and Fibreboard faced the real possibility that Fibreboard would be insolvent simply on the basis of claims already settled. The Insurers, on the other hand, faced the possibility of virtually unlimited liability for damage caused by Fibreboard asbestos. This pressure, felt by all parties to the global settlement, is what finally brought them together on the eve of the coverage case appeal. The unique risks posed by the coverage cases distinguish *Ahearn* from a blatant attempt to circumvent the Bankruptcy Code such as occurred in *Keene*.

The facts of *Keene* further distinguish it from our case. First, an already weak Keene attempted to avoid impending bankruptcy by asking the court to coerce its tort victims to settle claims in a court where no claims were filed against Keene. Second, Keene attempted to utilize the 23(b)(1)(B) injunction to halt pending actions in other courts. Third, and most importantly, Keene's complaint was dismissed on the ground that it failed to present the court with any case or controversy because it requested only

---

14. Notwithstanding the *Keene* court's gratuitous discussion of its concerns about use of a class action to circumvent bankruptcy laws, the court's *holding* is that the case was properly dismissed because the plaintiff-manufacturer had no cognizable claim against the defendant class members. *Keene*, 14 F.3d at 733.

that the court compel all plaintiffs in suits against Keene to appear and negotiate.

Ahearn by comparison, presents us with claims against a healthy company for personal injuries and a proposed settlement of those claims. *Ahearn* presents no danger that Fibreboard may simply be abusing this proceeding to delay other actions or to improve its negotiating position with present claimants because it only enjoins future proceedings, not those already pending. We agree with the *Keene* court that under the facts presented to it, a 23(b)(1)(B) action was not appropriate. We also agree that, in the vast majority of cases, the Bankruptcy Code should govern the as the risk of an adverse judgment in the coverage litigation support an early resolution of the claims against an entity and all parties can benefit from a settlement under Rule 23(b)(1)(B), we see no legal or policy reason to deny the parties this benefit. The essential basis of any settlement is to avoid the uncertainty, risks, and expense of ongoing litigation. In our case, the risks facing Fibreboard, the Insurers, and the health claimants as a result of the California coverage litigation were real and enormous. Holding that the bankruptcy laws require the parties to wait until catastrophe befalls one or more of them as a result of the California litigation would be a denial of justice to the parties before us and unwarranted by the law.

The intervenors' argument that all 23(b)(1)(B) limited-fund actions based on the insolvency of the defendant are improper ignores the special circumstances presented by Ahearn and certifications by other courts. In light of the *Findley* and *Drexel* decisions, also from the Second Circuit, which allow 23(b)(1)(B) actions where the defendant's insolvency creates a limited fund, we decline to read *Keene* so broadly as to bar all such 23(b)(1)(B) settlements.

The plain meaning of Rule 23 also supports a finding that the insolvency of a defendant can support a 23(b)(1)(B) class action. The rule clearly does not distinguish between limited funds which assume insolvency of the defendant and limited funds such as proceeds of an insurance policy which constitute the entire fund from which plaintiffs may recover.... In its Note to the 1966 Amendment to Rule 23, the Advisory Committee concludes that a limited-fund class action is appropriate in actions by creditors "when the debtor's assets are insufficient to pay all creditors' claims." Fed.R.Civ.P. advisory committee's note. This explicit reference to use of a 23(b)(1)(B) action when the debtor is insolvent offers further support for the proposition that insolvency is an appropriate basis for a limited-fund class action.

Further, the express language of the Rule compels a flexible construction. Rule 23(b)(1)(B) authorizes class certification where there is a "risk" that separate adjudications "as a practical matter" would "substantially impair or impede" the interests of the class. The rule does not require proof to a certainty that the defendant faces insolvency.

The Bankruptcy Code allows courts to dismiss or suspend bankruptcy proceedings where superior alternatives to the code are available. See 11 U.S.C. § 305(a)(1). This concession to the possibility of other proceedings to distribute an insolvent debtor's assets reveals that Congress understood that, at least some of the time, the terms and principles of the Bankruptcy

Code would be circumvented by debtors and creditors who found superior methods of asset distribution. . . .

Ahearn presented the district court with a superior alternative to the Bankruptcy Code and did so long before any bankruptcy court would have had jurisdiction over Fibreboard's assets. Indeed, one of the most important facts of this case is that, in spite of the threat posed by future personal injury litigation, Fibreboard is currently solvent and healthy. In the short term, no trade or tort creditor has the ability or the incentive to force Fibreboard into a Chapter 11 reorganization. It is also clear that shareholders and management, who stand to lose equity and/or employment if Fibreboard enters bankruptcy proceedings, will refuse to file a voluntary petition at least until the coverage dispute is resolved against it. That, of course, would be too late for the Global Health Claimant Class.

Even in the unlikely event that Fibreboard could be persuaded to file a voluntary bankruptcy petition, the Global Health Claimant Class would be worse off than it is under the Global Settlement Agreement. Under the Bankruptcy Code, representation for the class may not be available at all and courts that have allowed representation of future tort claimants have left them in an uncertain position that falls short of full "creditor" status. Additionally, full-blown bankruptcy proceedings would bring in all of Fibreboard's other creditors and impose large transaction[ ] costs on Fibreboard that, ultimately, would come out of any distribution. . . . In stark contrast to the uncertain and weak position afforded future tort claimants under the Bankruptcy Code, the plaintiff class and its representatives in *Ahearn* had center stage and ran no risk of encountering a cram-down reorganization approved only by trade creditors and rammed through over the objections of class representatives.

To the extent intervenors are arguing that certification is improper because Fibreboard fares better under the class action settlement than under a bankruptcy proceeding, we find their focus misplaced. The inquiry instead should be whether the class is better served by avoiding impairment of their interests. . . . Early settlement allows the class to recover far more as a group than it could if it was forced to wait until Fibreboard enters bankruptcy on its own and encounters the high transaction costs of insolvency. See Mark J. Roe, *Bankruptcy and Mass Tort*, 84 Colum. L. Rev. 846, 851-64, 905-17 (1984) (advocating early reorganizations because they avoid the waste of insolvency and distribute more to victims, but noting that no one with the ability to push the mass tortfeasor into an early reorganization has the incentive to do so). Precisely because it avoids the enormous transactions costs of litigation and insolvency, the Global Settlement Agreement can offer a deal from which all parties gain. Members of the Global Health Claimant Class receive more money in payment for their injuries and Fibreboard's shareholders keep their stake in a viable entity. The only loser under the Global Settlement Agreement is the asbestos litigation industry.

For all of these reasons, we find that the district court's decision to certify *Ahearn* as a 23(b)(1)(B) class action is an appropriate interpretation of Rule 23 that does not conflict with the Bankruptcy Code and upholds the principles of equity and fairness.

■ SMITH, Circuit Judge, dissenting.... In bankruptcy, the claims of *all* of Fibreboard's creditors, not just its "future" personal injury victims would be crammed down. Permitting Fibreboard to effect a reorganization bankruptcy proceeding in the guise of a futures-only class action circumvents the detailed protections of the Bankruptcy Code for the express *purpose* of imposing the entire cost of the bailout on Fibreboard's most vulnerable creditors, to the betterment of its shareholders....

The novelty in this case is not the insistence on opt-out rights but on the extension of class actions, particularly rule 23(b)(1)(B) class actions, to mass torts and the expansion of rule 23(b)(1)(B) to "constructive bankruptcy."... [T]he presumption of constitutionality enjoyed by the Federal Rules of Civil Procedure disappears when the rules are applied in a way unanticipated by their drafters....

The *only* protection accorded the class was a rule 23(e) fairness hearing. The district court also appointed a guardian *ad litem* to represent absent class members, but he did so only after class and defense counsel completed the settlement. Thus, class members received absolutely *no* structural or procedural protections; instead, they had to rely on an after-the-fact review of the settlement's substance.

Notes and Questions

1. *Asbestos Litigation* is correct that *Keene* is factually distinguishable. But *Asbestos Litigation* is also factually distinguishable from *Eastern and Southern District*, p. 771, *supra*, on which it relies heavily. Aside from the factual distinctions, isn't it true that both *Keene* and *Eastern and Southern District* evince an attitude about the relationship between Rule 23 and the Bankruptcy Code that is contrary to the attitude in *Asbestos Litigation*?

2. We have seen in this chapter some of the protections, as well as some of the limits of those protections, accorded to bankruptcy claimants. In the last chapter we saw the protections, and the limits of those protections, accorded to absent class members. Which set of protections is greater? Should the proper relationship between class actions and bankruptcy proceedings be determined which one provides more protection to present and future plaintiffs? Does either a class action or a bankruptcy proceeding provide adequate protection to the average victim? Should other factors also be added into the balance in deciding which is the better solution for the aggregation of related claims?

3. *Asbestos Litigation* begins by asserting that there is a limited fund for purposes of Rule 23(b)(1)(B), because the $2.235 billion fund ($2 billion in insurance plus $235 million in company assets) was inadequate to compensate all victims. Note, however, that the $2 billion fund was created by the voluntary agreement of Fibreboard with its insurers; had Fibreboard prevailed in its California action, it would have had considerably more money at its disposal. Should we let the party who will benefit from a mandatory class action create the limited fund through its voluntary actions? What if it had settled the insurance suit for $2? Wouldn't it be better for a bankruptcy trustee to review the

transaction and to void the contract as a preference if appropriate? Cf. John C. Coffee, Jr., *Class Wars: The Dilemma of the Mass Tort Class Action*, 95 Colum. L. Rev. 1343, 1403-04 (*Ahearn*'s rule may give companies an incentive to underinsure and "reverse[s] the historic relationship between debt and equity — perversely shifting risk from diversified and logically risk neutral shareholders to non-diversified and normally risk averse tort creditors").

Once the court says that a limited fund exists for Rule 23 purposes, it turns around and says that, unlike Keene, Fibreboard was a financially healthy, solvent company for which bankruptcy treatment was inappropriate. Can you reconcile this shift — being insolvent for Rule 23 purposes but not for Chapter 11 purposes? Would the Fifth Circuit's attitude have doomed the Manville reorganization (recall that Manville too was financially healthy when it filed its bankruptcy petition)? See In re Johns-Manville Corp., 36 B.R. 727, 730 (Bankr. S.D.N.Y. 1984) (rebuffing efforts to dismiss Manville's bankruptcy petition; noting that "there is no insolvency requirement for Chapter 11 debtor status"). Or is the Fifth Circuit merely saying that federal courts ought to have the discretion to use whichever approach makes the most sense in the particular case?

If that is how *Asbestos Litigation* is to be read, what is it about the case that makes class action treatment superior to bankruptcy? Is it that everyone — shareholders, creditors, insurers, and plaintiffs — stood to lose in the California coverage litigation, and therefore everyone was better off with a piece of the pie rather than some people ending up with nearly the whole pie and others with virtually nothing? If so, then class action treatment will be superior to bankruptcy only in rare cases in which there exists serious doubt about the entitlement to a significant potential asset of the putative debtor. Is the class action superior because the payments to the plaintiff class exceeded the likely payments that they would receive in a bankruptcy distribution? If so, then the superiority of class action treatment will be available in a somewhat greater range of cases. Is the class action superior because Fibreboard was still financially healthy? If so, class action treatment will also be superior in a greater range of cases. Is it superior because the transaction costs of the class action are less than the transaction costs of a bankruptcy proceeding? If so, class action treatment will nearly always be superior (at least as long as the costs of the class action are less than the costs of the bankruptcy proceeding).

4. One of the reasons that the Fifth Circuit thought that the future claimants stood better under the present settlement than under a bankruptcy proceeding was that the trade creditors could cram down a reorganization over the future claimants' objections. Did the Fifth Circuit misunderstand Chapter 11? Can future claimants vote on a reorganization plan? If they could, and if the claimants objected as a class to a reorganization plan for Fibreboard, then the court could not have approved the plan unless the absolute priority rule were satisfied — meaning that the shareholders, and not the claimants, would be the most disadvantaged. Moreover, given that only two intervenors objected to the *Ahearn* settlement, and given the way in which courts have handled the voting issues for tort claimants (see pp. 726-28, *supra*), was it realistic to think that anything would have been crammed down the claimants' throats?

5. How does the Fifth Circuit know that the future claimants are better off with this settlement than with a bankruptcy distribution? Even if they are, we are talking about a zero sum game — Fibreboard has only so many assets, and the more the future claimants win, the more the others lose. Should the court

have considered the effect of the settlement on present claimants and other creditors before finding the class action a superior mechanism to a bankruptcy proceeding? Put differently, is the court asking the wrong question when it asks only whether the future claimants are better off under this settlement? Wouldn't the court be forced to take a broader view in a bankruptcy proceeding?

6. In Section B we discovered that, in 1994, Congress established a specific bankruptcy mechanism to deal with future asbestos claims. See 11 U.S.C. § 524(g), (h); p. 765, *supra*. This settlement was consummated in 1993, but not decided on appeal until 1996. The Fifth Circuit never cited § 524. Should the amendments to § 524 have influenced the court's decision about whether the class action mechanism is superior? In a similar case settled after the effective date of § 524, should a court decline to certify a class action because of this statutory mechanism? Should it at least refuse to approve a class settlement in which the protections and outcome are less than would be obtained under a § 524 qualifying trust?

7. Article I, § 8, clause 4 of the United States Constitution extends to Congress the exclusive power "To establish . . . uniform Laws on the subject of Bankruptcies throughout the United States." Is the use of the Rule 23(b)(1)(B) class action to handle the problem of insolvent debtors therefore unconstitutional? Perhaps the Supreme Court, which has now granted certiorari for a second time in *Asbestos Litigation*, will resolve this issue. As we have seen in earlier chapters, however, there are also other grounds on which the case could be resolved. See pp. 301, 658, 685, *supra*.

8. Until now, we have asked whether the class action or the bankruptcy proceeding is better. Is either good enough?

E. CONCLUDING THOUGHTS

Bankruptcy law, rightfully perhaps, focuses primarily on the situation of the debtor, not on the larger controversy of which the debtor is a part. The consequence of this focus, however, is that the most useful consolidation tool in existence still falls far short of being adequate enough to solve the problem of joinder complexity. Nonetheless, bankruptcy is vitally important to the study of complex litigation for several reasons.

First, however inadequate bankruptcy might be, it is the best that we have. In many cases, a patchwork of other doctrines — perhaps joining supplemental jurisdiction to interpleader to class action — can achieve comparable results. But in many cases nothing else will do. In terms of our present situation, bankruptcy is an essential piece of the puzzle.

Second, bankruptcy may act as a limit on our ability to effect complete joinder through other devices. This point was made directly in our last two sections, in which various courts strongly suggested that, at least in many circumstances, Rule 23(b)(1)(B) mandatory class actions are inappropriate when a debtor's insolvency creates the "limited fund." The same argument might be made in other contexts as well: We cannot use this or that aggregation doctrine because to do so would override the specific protections of bankruptcy. This argument is likely to be important in a significant number of complex cases, since the insufficiency of a defendant's assets to satisfy all claims is a major cause of joinder complexity. Indirectly, the explicit jurisdictional and procedural powers in bankruptcy might make a judge cautious to imply such powers in non-bankruptcy settings.

Third, bankruptcy acts as a laboratory for consolidation proposals such as the ALI's proposals for a national Complex Litigation Panel and issue preclusion for bystanders. We have considered aspects of such proposals in earlier chapters. Now we see a system — the bankruptcy system — that has most of the features that such proposals advocate. We can, in a limited way, empirically check these proposals by seeing how well bankruptcy functions in these types of cases. From what you have seen of bankruptcy, are you pessimistic or optimistic about broader consolidation proposals? Is joinder complexity an inveterate feature of the procedural landscape, or can we some day look forward to its end?

CHAPTER SEVEN

THE IMPACT OF CHOICE OF LAW ON THE JOINDER OF RELATED CASES

> I fly a good deal, and my wife has instructions that if I go down, she is to get in touch with a particular New York attorney who is skilled in discovery, working juries, and *conflicts* law.
>
> Andreas Lowenfeld

Throughout this book we have talked about the adversarial cornerstone known as the "master of the complaint" rule, which entrusts to the plaintiff the decision about which parties to sue, which court to sue in, and which claims to sue on. Until now, we have assumed that the main factors guiding a plaintiff's decision — as well as the main factors that might motivate a defendant or a court to upset that decision — were procedural in nature. In other words, we have assumed that the substantive law that will apply to the case is the same in any court that might serve as a trial venue.

Now is the time to tell the truth (and it should not surprise you): Different forums are likely to apply different principles of substantive law. This is obvious for claims founded on state law. It is less obvious, but equally true, for claims based on federal law; often different districts or circuits have different interpretations of federal law. Both the plaintiff and the defendant will want to locate a case in a forum that, other procedural and pragmatic factors being equal, provides the best substantive rules.

Figuring out which forum has the best substantive rules, however, is a tricky business. For instance, suppose that Connecticut law provided the most favorable rule in a particular case. You might think that the plaintiff ought to file her case in Connecticut. If you have taken a course in choice of law, however, you know that things are not so easy. Part of the law of every tribunal — whether federal, state, or international — are choice of law rules. These rules tell the tribunal the substantive and procedural law to apply to a controversy. It might well be that, if the case were filed in Connecticut, Connecticut's choice of law rules would dictate the use of another state's law. If a plaintiff really wants Connecticut law to apply, she needs to find some other state whose choice of law rules require the use of Connecticut law, and then hope that this state has personal jurisdiction over the defendants, has subject matter jurisdiction over the controversy, and is a convenient venue.

Forum manipulation to take advantage of choice of law rules is hardly fanciful; the best lawyers do it all the time. Professor Lowenfeld tells the story of a couple killed in an airplane crash in Texas. The couple had three adult daughters. The husband had recently moved from Florida to Connecticut in order to take a job in New York. Connecticut law was most favorable to the daughters on the issue of damages. Had the case been filed in Connecticut, however, the state's choice of law rule would have required the use of Texas damage law. Hence, the daughters' attorney brought the case in New York, whose choice of law rule required that damages be determined under the law of the decedent's domicile. A New York jury awarded nearly $8 million. Andreas F. Lowenfeld, *Mass Torts and the Conflict of Laws: The Airline Disaster*, 1989 U. Ill. L. Rev. 157, 158 n.12.

The existence of choice of law rules creates complexity in two distinct ways. First, choice of law rules often lead different plaintiffs to file cases in different forums. Ideally, all of the cases arising from a plane crash in Texas would be filed in Texas. When some choice of law rules make it desirable for some plaintiffs to file in New York and others in Alaska, and when plaintiffs get to choose the forum in which to file their cases, choice of law rules scatter related cases across the country. While other factors may counteract this effect, choice of law rules are a significant cause of the multiforum litigation that can cause complexity or complication.

Second, choice of law rules can make it impractical or impossible to aggregate cases in a single forum. Assume that a mass tort has injured persons in every state, that each state's law differs in some regards, and that each state's choice of law rule would lead to the application of its own law. If cases are filed in each state, and if the law of each transferor court must be applied in an aggregated proceeding, the aggregated case would require the application of the law of fifty different jurisdictions. In turn, different laws would require as many as fifty different sets of discovery, pretrial rulings, jury instructions, and remedial provisions. In short, the application of different laws brought about by choice of law rules might create such pretrial, trial, or remedial complexity that an aggregated case becomes unmanageable.

Obviously, we could avoid the complexity-causing problems of choice of law rules if we could: (1) dictate a choice of law rule that would make every court choose the same law; (2) dictate the substantive law that every court must use to resolve the related cases; or (3) find a procedural device that forced all cases into one forum and resulted in the application of a single law to all claims. Some of these solutions could have the effect of treating different cases alike — a "procedure defining substance" move that seems out of step with modern procedural theory. Moreover, these solutions threaten to treat groups of tort claimants (those in the complex case and those in routine cases) differently, and also threaten to eliminate at least some of a plaintiff's adversarial ability to choose the most favorable forum. To the extent that the solutions make aggregation more attractive, they also indirectly bring about harm to adversarial and trans-substantive values.

In Section A we examine the choice of law rules that presently create joinder and other forms of complexity, or else make litigation more complicated. In Section B we consider a number of specific forms that the solutions for overcoming the choice of law conundrum might take.

A. CHOICE OF LAW ISSUES IN A FEDERAL SYSTEM

A federal system presents a number of distinct choice of law problems. For our purposes, three are important. The first is to create a set of choice of law principles to deal with situations in which two or more states claim an interest in the application of their law. The second is to create a set of principles to deal with situations in which federal courts decide cases based on state law, and state courts on federal law. The final issue is whether the federal court to which a case is transferred must accept the law that would have been chosen in the federal court from which the case was transferred.

This last problem is particularly critical in complex cases. The inability to choose new law burdens the transferee court with multiple laws that could result in a legal Tower of Babel. But this last problem cannot be understood in isolation from the prior two.

1. Choice of Law: Basic Principles and Limitations

Friedrich K. Juenger, MASS DISASTERS AND THE CONFLICT OF LAWS

1989 U. Ill. L. Rev. 105, 109-17

Choice-of-law approaches that subject the victims' claims to different substantive laws are not merely unfair: by necessitating separate trials they further complicate complex litigation. How, then, do the various approaches proffered for application to mass disasters meet the twin goals of fairness and efficiency?

III. POSSIBLE APPROACHES

A. *The Lex Loci Delicti*

In air crash cases, some federal courts have applied, on differing rationales, the law of the place of the accident. In addition, a bill introduced in Congress adopts this principle to govern products liability actions brought by aliens in United States courts. At first blush, the old rule has much to commend itself. Courts are currently "saddled with a cumbersome and unwieldy body of conflicts law that creates confusion, uncertainty and inconsistency...." Judicial opinions that purport to apply that law to mass disasters are, in Willis Reese's words, "opaque" and "make for dreary reading." After plowing through some of these judicial efforts ... one begins to wonder whether reverting to a hard and fast rule would not be preferable. Clearly, the courts' quixotic attempts to divine interests or weigh contacts inspire little confidence in contemporary choice-of-law techniques. Apart from ease of application, the lex loci delicti rule also assures equal treatment of victims who perish in a common disaster.

Yet, simple and evenhanded as it may be, the traditional approach is an unlikely candidate for congressional or judicial adoption. Denounced by generations of scholars and tainted by its association with the vested rights theory, lex loci delicti has become altogether unpalatable. Moreover, the rule works well only in the limited group of mass disasters that, like plane crashes, happen in one particular place. Applying the law of the tortious impact does not produce uniformity in cases such as *Agent Orange*, where the injuries occurred in several different Indochinese locations. It would be patently absurd to relegate American service personnel to whatever remedies Vietnamese or Cambodian law may provide. Even where the injuries are suffered in one particular state, exclusive reliance on the lex loci delicti rule can be problematic. A plane, for instance, may crash in a state where it was not destined to go....

Moreover, the place-of-the-wrong rule's seeming simplicity is deceptive. The traditional choice-of-law approach engendered a number of conceptual problems for which no solution has ever been found.... Should the plaintiffs, in addition to their tort claims, be able to sue in contract against the airline and to assert warranty cause of action against the aircraft's manufacturer? Can ceilings on wrongful death recovery be characterized as "procedural"? To what extent may the forum's public policy justify the disregard of the accident state's unreasonable rules? As this brief list shows, far from operating predictably and evenhandedly, the traditional rule poses more questions than it answers.

B. The Most Significant Relationship

The Second Restatement's "most-significant-relationship" formula is equally unhelpful. By now it should be apparent that this impressionistic phrase "means nothing except, perhaps, that the answer is not ready at hand." Such a nonrule approach does not work well even in fairly simple situations; much less can it resolve the choice-of-law problems posed by complex litigation such as the Dalkon Shield or asbestos cases, which, being truly multistate in nature, of necessity lack a center of gravity. As the *Second Restatement*'s reporter acknowledges, "it would be desirable to avoid such vague criteria as application of the law of the state with the most significant relationship.... Formulations of this sort are hard for the courts to apply and afford little predictability of result...."

C. Interest Analysis

A recent article by Seidelson claims that interest analysis is a "viable method" for resolving choice-of-law problems presented by products liability cases and attempts to outline how that approach would work in practice. The article does not, however, deal with mass disasters; it merely discusses two-state hypotheticals. As applied to truly multistate situations, Currie's approach, quite apart from its questionable assumption that private litigation serves the purpose of vindicating governmental interests, is fundamentally unsatisfactory.

In practice, interest analysis amounts to little more than a long-winded pretext for the refusal to apply foreign law. An action will rarely be brought in a "disinterested" forum, because such a forum usually lacks the minimum contacts required for jurisdiction. An "interested forum," however, will usually apply its own law, even though judges may hesitate to endorse Currie's prescription to cut the Gordian knot of a "true conflict" in this parodical manner. The approach's forum bias produces desirable results only because it allows those plaintiffs who know how to forum shop to select the most favorable law. By permitting the parties to evade whatever interests other states may have, interest analysis enhances the protection of interstate accident victims.

In mass disaster cases, however, applying the law of the state where each action is brought makes little sense, especially if suits initially filed in various jurisdictions are later consolidated by the Panel on Multidistrict Litigation. In such cases, a court following the governmental interest approach would have to try the same set of facts under several different laws. It seems inconsistent on the one hand to offer a procedure that facilitates consolidation and, on the other, to countenance the kind of fragmentation that interest analysis inevitably entails.

D. "Comparative Impairment"

Twenty-five years ago, Baxter wrote an article that, while accepting the proposition that state interests matter in choice of law, would accord federal courts a role in resolving multistate cases. He . . . urged the adoption of a "comparative-impairment" principle to resolve the "true conflicts" that governmental interest analysis creates. That principle was designed to allocate to the states spheres of law-making control by sacrificing, "in the particular case, the external objective of the state whose internal objective will be least impaired in general scope and impact by subordination in cases like the one at hand."

Baxter's proposal assumes that it is possible to measure the impairment of policies, a proposition that would be open to doubt even if governmental interests had more substance than they do have. In any event, Baxter's examples, which are simple two-state hypotheticals, shed no light on how his principle could be made to work in cases implicating the interests of numerous states. . . . [B]ecause the comparative impairment only applies to true conflicts, Baxter's approach has the effect of grouping victims into two categories: those who share the defendant's domicile and all others.

Accordingly, it subjects victims of a common disaster to unequal treatment and, at the same time, complicates the disposition of mass disaster cases.

E. *"Comparative Impairment" California-Style*

Seidelson's article also propounds the adoption of a comparative impairment principle, but one quite different from that which Baxter advocated.... Seidelson introduces a teleological component by according a higher rank to state interests in safeguarding health and human life than to interests in the defendants' economic integrity. This California variant of "comparative impairment" is, of course, at odds with Baxter's principle. Baxter... explicitly rejected "super-value judgments" about the quality of conflicting rules of decision.

Thus Seidelson, although ostensibly committed to interest analysis, in effect proposes a result-oriented approach premised on assumed differences in the intensity of various kinds of policies. The evaluation of conflicting policies is of course at loggerheads with Currie's teachings. This inconsistency notwithstanding, Seidelson's emphasis on teleology is commendable, for teleology indeed ought to play a role in the resolution of choice-of-law problems posed by mass disaster cases. His article, however, does not deal with such cases.... He therefore fails to come to grips with an aspect of complex litigation that ought to attract the interest analysts' attention: whenever there are multiple plaintiffs and defendants, the emphasis on the parties' domiciliary nexus is bound to generate a large number of "true conflicts." That propensity is further enhanced if one recognizes, as Seidelson does, territorial deterrent interests.

How courts should deal with such a proliferation of "true conflicts" is not apparent from Seidelson's article. Presumably, however, he, like Baxter, would single out for separate treatment those plaintiffs who share the defendant's residence.... Such differential treatment seems inequitable and would complicate the disposition of mass disaster cases. Even in simple two-state situations, Seidelson's methodology requires complex analyses, and his belief in counsel's ability to unravel these complexities is probably unfounded.

RESTATEMENT (SECOND) OF CONFLICT OF LAWS

350 (1971)

§ 122. Issues Relating to Judicial Administration

A court usually applies its own local law rules prescribing how litigation shall be conducted even when it applies the local law of another state to resolve other issues in the case.

Notes and Questions

1. Professor Juenger's article describes some of the possible approaches that could be used to decide which jurisdiction's *substantive* law should apply to a particular case. The excerpt from the *Restatement (Second)* describe the approaches used in most courts to decide which jurisdiction's *procedural* law should apply. Substantive choice of law principles will often lead to the application of non-forum substantive law, while the procedural principles will almost always lead to the application of forum procedural law. Does this make sense? Can't procedural rules influence outcomes as much as substantive rules? Aren't substantive rules often promulgated against a particular procedural backdrop, so that their use in conjunction with another set of procedural rules might distort their intent? Would a rule that required a court to choose the procedural and substantive law of the same state reduce forum shopping? On the other hand, if a transferee court must apply the substantive *and* procedural law of each of the transferor forums, pretrial, trial, and remedial complexity will be enormously increased. How about a principle that says a case must use the procedural rules of the forum that provides the substantive law, but upon aggregation of related cases in one forum, the procedural law of one forum will apply?

Choice of law scholars often overlook the favored treatment that choice of law principles give to the forum's procedural rules, focusing instead on the second-tier "characterization" problem of whether a particular rule is procedural or substantive. See, *e.g., Restatement (Second)*, § 7; Eugene F. Scoles & Peter Hay, Conflict of Laws 57-67 (2d ed. 1992).

2. The fact that a court might apply its own law to procedural matters but another jurisdiction's law to substantive matters recognizes that choice of law principles must be applied issue-by-issue. You might have wondered whether the same is true of issues of substantive law, so that one state's law might apply on issues of liability and another state's law on issues of damage. This approach makes sure that the most relevant law is applied to each aspect of a case, but it also takes time, creates uncertainty, increases the incentives to forum shop, and makes the management of aggregated cases more difficult. Most of the modern approaches to choice of law accept the idea that different laws might apply to different aspects of a case or claim. See, *e.g., Restatement (Second)*, §§ 145(2), 188(2). This concept usually travels under the name *dépeçage*.

3. Another foreign phrase of some importance to choice of law analysis is *renvoi*. Typically the forum court applies the forum's own choice of law rules to determine whose law applies. When the choice of law principles of State A require a court in State A to choose the law of State B, the issue arises whether the court should choose the substantive law of State B or the "whole law" of State B, including State B's choice of law principles. If the whole law of State B is adopted, then it might well be that the substantive law of State A (or even State C) will apply. This acceptance of the whole law, which is known as *renvoi*, is not usually invoked, but there are important exceptions to this rule. See, *e.g., Restatement (Second)*, § 8; Scoles & Hay, *supra*, at 67-72.

4. Traditionally, American choice of law rules were "*lex loci*," which means that the substantive law of the place of a specified event (in torts the place of the wrong, in contracts the place of the contract's signing) governed the litigation. See Restatement of Conflict of Laws (1934). According to a recent survey, 13 states still adhere to the old *lex loci delicti* rule in tort cases, 22 follow the

Restatement (Second)'s "most significant relationship" approach, 2 (plus the District of Columbia) use interest analysis (one of them — California — uses comparative impairment), 2 use a home-favoring *lex fori* approach, 5 use an approach pioneered by Professor Leflar to apply the "better law," and the rest follow other eclectic approaches. The numbers are comparable for contract claims. States continue to migrate away from the old *lex loci* rules, and toward one of the modern approaches. See Symeon C. Symeonides, *Choice of Law in the American Courts in 1993 (and in the Six Previous Years)*, 42 Am. J. Comp. Law 599 (1994); see also Gregory E. Smith, *Choice of Law in the United States Courts*, 38 Hastings L.J. 1041 (1987) (analyzing rules in each state in 1986).

The beauty of the old *lex loci* approach was that, for catastrophic-event mass torts that caused injury in a single state (such as airplane crashes), the same state law would be applied regardless of the forum in which the case was filed. Plaintiffs therefore had less incentive to file in separate forums in order to obtain more favorable substantive law. Moreover, upon consolidation of cases from multiple forums, a court would not need to worry about managing a case with multiple substantive laws. The *lex loci* approach therefore avoided both of the ways in which choice of law can cause joinder complexity. None of the more modern approaches performs these tasks as well; they either do not point unequivocally to a particular state's law, they do not avoid the manageability problems when cases from multiple forums are consolidated, or both. Of course, the fact that individual states have adopted different choice of law principles compounds both problems.

These observations should not be construed as an unadulterated sales pitch for a return to *lex loci* principles. There were reasons, largely grounded in fairness and policy, that most courts abandoned *lex loci* rules in the latter half of this century. See generally Scoles & Hay, *supra*, at 11-44 (tracing history). Moreover, as Professor Juenger explains, *lex loci* principles are often inadequate or unfair. What happens when there is a dispersed mass tort, in which injuries occur in many jurisdictions? Doesn't a *lex loci* rule ignore the interests of the victims' states in ensuring the safety and compensation of its citizens? If a state generally adopts a more modern approach to choice of law issues, why should victims of mass disasters be given a different, old-fashioned set of rules to play by?

5. Legislatures can, and sometimes do, create choice of law rules. See Symeonides, *supra* at 604-05 (describing recent legislative developments); *Restatement (Second)* § 6(1) (requiring court to follow choice of law legislation). But the choice of law field is almost entirely judge-made law, which means that judges have the ability to create new or different choice of law rules to deal with particular types of cases. Unlike the prior chapters of this book, in which judges needed to work around jurisdictional or procedural rules to overcome joinder complexity, here judges need only get past their own predilection for stare decisis to overcome joinder and other forms of complexity. Should they create special choice of law rules when rational adjudication is at stake? Exactly what should the content of these rules be?

6. We return to these questions later in the chapter. For now, let us suggest that the nature of choice of law is to create one winner (the state whose law is adopted) and one or more losers (the state(s) whose law is not adopted). But choice of law issues arise because the controversy at hand is larger than the law of any particular jurisdiction. Does it make sense to pick one law to the exclusion of others? Isn't it particularly senseless in complex litigation, where

values such as rational adjudication are at stake? Does it make more sense to create some overarching law, which would act as a synthesis or compromise of the laws of the interested states? Or does such a solution give too much power to judges (federal judges in particular) to override the policy choices of individual legislatures and courts? See generally Friedrich K. Juenger, Choice of Law and Multistate Justice (1993) (arguing that judges should be able to create law that transcends state boundaries); Stanley E. Cox, *Back to Conflicts Basics*, 44 Cath. U. L. Rev. 525 (1995) (book review strongly critiquing Juenger's theory).

Until "transcendent law" is adopted to replace our standard choice of law analysis, however, we are faced with the reality that one state's law will win and others will lose. The following case explores the outer constitutional limits on the ability of a court to apply a state's substantive law to a particular claim or person.

PHILLIPS PETROLEUM CO. v. SHUTTS

472 U.S. 797 (1985)

■ JUSTICE REHNQUIST delivered the opinion of the Court. [The basic facts of the case are set out at p. 294, *supra*. In addition to the issue of whether a state had personal jurisdiction over a plaintiff class member who did not have minimum contacts with the state, *Shutts* also involved the issue of whether a Kansas court could apply Kansas law to the royalty claims involved in the class action.]

The trial court relied heavily on an earlier, unrelated class action involving the same nominal plaintiff and the same defendant, Shutts, Executor v. Phillips Petroleum Co., 222 Kan. 527, 567 P. 2d 1292 (1977), cert. denied, 434 U.S. 1068 (1978). The Kansas Supreme Court had held in *Shutts, Executor* that a gas company owed interest to royalty owners for royalties suspended pending final Commission approval of a price increase. No federal statutes touched on the liability for suspended royalties, and the court in *Shutts, Executor* held as a matter of Kansas equity law that the applicable interest rates for computation of interest on suspended royalties were the interest rates at which the gas company would have had to reimburse its customers had its interim price increase been rejected by the Commission. The court in *Shutts, Executor* viewed these as the fairest interest rates because they were also the rates that petitioner required the royalty owners to meet in their indemnity agreements in order to avoid suspended royalties. The trial court in the present case applied the rule from *Shutts, Executor*, and held petitioner liable for prejudgment and postjudgment interest on the suspended royalties, computed at the Commission rates governing petitioner's three price increases. The applicable interest rates were: 7% for royalties retained until October 1974; 9% for royalties retained between October 1974 and September 1979; and thereafter at the average prime rate. The trial court did not determine whether any difference existed between the laws of Kansas and other States, or whether another State's laws should be applied to non-Kansas plaintiffs or to royalties from leases in States other than Kansas....

The court stated that generally the law of the forum controlled all claims unless "compelling reasons" existed to apply a different law. The court found no compelling reasons, and noted that "[the] plaintiff class members have indicated their desire to have this action determined under the laws of Kansas." The court affirmed as a matter of Kansas equity law the award of interest on the suspended royalties, at the rates imposed by the trial court. The court set the postjudgment interest rate on all claims at the Kansas statutory rate of 15%. . . .

III

The Kansas courts applied Kansas contract and Kansas equity law to every claim in this case, notwithstanding that over 99% of the gas leases and some 97% of the plaintiffs in the case had no apparent connection to the State of Kansas except for this lawsuit. Petitioner protested that the Kansas courts should apply the laws of the States where the leases were located, or at least apply Texas and Oklahoma law because so many of the leases came from those States. . . .

Petitioner contends that total application of Kansas substantive law violated the constitutional limitations on choice of law mandated by the Due Process Clause of the Fourteenth Amendment and the Full Faith and Credit Clause of Article IV, § 1. We must first determine whether Kansas law conflicts in any material way with any other law which could apply. There can be no injury in applying Kansas law if it is not in conflict with that of any other jurisdiction connected to this suit.

Petitioner claims that Kansas law conflicts with that of a number of States connected to this litigation, especially Texas and Oklahoma. These putative conflicts range from the direct to the tangential, and may be addressed by the Supreme Court of Kansas on remand under the correct constitutional standard. For example, there is no recorded Oklahoma decision dealing with interest liability for suspended royalties: whether Oklahoma is likely to impose liability would require a survey of Oklahoma oil and gas law. Even if Oklahoma found such liability, petitioner shows that Oklahoma would most likely apply its constitutional and statutory 6% interest rate rather than the much higher Kansas rates applied in this litigation. . . .

Petitioner also points out several conflicts between Kansas and Texas law. Although Texas recognizes interest liability for suspended royalties, Texas has never awarded any such interest at a rate greater than 6%, which corresponds with the Texas constitutional and statutory rate. [7] . . . Moreover, at least one court interpreting Texas law appears to have held that Texas excuses interest liability once the gas company offers to take an indemnity from the royalty owner and pay him the suspended royalty while the price increase is still tentative. . . . Such a rule is contrary to Kansas law as applied below, but if applied to the Texas plaintiffs or leases in this case, would vastly reduce petitioner's liability.

---

7. The Kansas interest rate also conflicts with the rate which is applicable in Louisiana. At the time this suit was filed that rate was 7%. . . .

The conflicts on the applicable interest rates, alone — which we do not think can be labeled "false conflicts" without a more thoroughgoing treatment than was accorded them by the Supreme Court of Kansas — certainly amounted to millions of dollars in liability. We think that the Supreme Court of Kansas erred in deciding on the basis that it did that the application of its laws to all claims would be constitutional.

Four Terms ago we addressed a similar situation in Allstate Ins. Co. v. Hague, 449 U.S. 302 (1981)....

The plurality in *Allstate* affirmed the application of Minnesota law because of the forum's significant contacts to the litigation which supported the State's interest in applying its law. . . . Kansas' contacts to this litigation, as explained by the Kansas Supreme Court, can be gleaned from the opinion below.

Petitioner owns property and conducts substantial business in the State, so Kansas certainly has an interest in regulating petitioner's conduct in Kansas. . . . Moreover, oil and gas extraction is an important business to Kansas, and although only a few leases in issue are located in Kansas, hundreds of Kansas plaintiffs were affected by petitioner's suspension of royalties; thus the court held that the State has a real interest in protecting "the rights of these royalty owners both as individual residents of [Kansas] and as members of this particular class of plaintiffs." . . . The Kansas Supreme Court pointed out that Kansas courts are quite familiar with this type of lawsuit, and "[the] plaintiff class members have indicated their desire to have this action determined under the laws of Kansas." . . . Finally, the Kansas court buttressed its use of Kansas law by stating that this lawsuit was analogous to a suit against a "common fund" located in Kansas.

We do not lightly discount this description of Kansas' contacts with this litigation and its interest in applying its law. There is, however, no "common fund" located in Kansas that would require or support the application of only Kansas law to all these claims. . . . As the Kansas court noted, petitioner commingled the suspended royalties with its general corporate accounts. . . . There is no specific identifiable res in Kansas, nor is there any limited amount which may be depleted before every plaintiff is compensated. Only by somehow aggregating all the separate claims in this case could a "common fund" in any sense be created, and the term becomes all but meaningless when used in such an expansive sense.

We also give little credence to the idea that Kansas law should apply to all claims because the plaintiffs, by failing to opt out, evinced their desire to be bound by Kansas law. Even if one could say that the plaintiffs "consented" to the application of Kansas law by not opting out, plaintiff's desire for forum law is rarely, if ever controlling. . . . Even if a plaintiff evidences his desire for forum law by moving to the forum, we have generally accorded such a move little or no significance. . . . In *Allstate* the plaintiff's move to the forum was only relevant because it was unrelated and prior to the litigation. . . . Thus the plaintiffs' desire for Kansas law, manifested by their participation in this Kansas lawsuit, bears little relevance.

The Supreme Court of Kansas in its opinion in this case expressed the view that by reason of the fact that it was adjudicating a nationwide class action, it had much greater latitude in applying its own law to the transactions in question than might otherwise be the case:

> "... Where a state court determines it has jurisdiction over a nationwide class action and procedural due process guarantees of notice and adequate representation are present, we believe the law of the forum should be applied unless compelling reasons exist for applying a different law.... Compelling reasons do not exist to require this court to look to other state laws to determine the rights of the parties involved in this lawsuit." 235 Kan., at 221-222, 679 P.2d, at 1181.

We think that this is something of a "bootstrap" argument. The Kansas class-action statute, like those of most other jurisdictions, requires that there be "common issues of law or fact." But while a State may, for the reasons we have previously stated, assume jurisdiction over the claims of plaintiffs whose principal contacts are with other States, it may not use this assumption of jurisdiction as an added weight in the scale when considering the permissible constitutional limits on choice of substantive law. It may not take a transaction with little or no relationship to the forum and apply the law of the forum in order to satisfy the procedural requirement that there be a "common question of law." The issue of personal jurisdiction over plaintiffs in a class action is entirely distinct from the question of the constitutional limitations on choice of law; the latter calculus is not altered by the fact that it may be more difficult or more burdensome to comply with the constitutional limitations because of the large number of transactions which the State proposes to adjudicate and which have little connection with the forum.

Kansas must have a "significant contact or significant aggregation of contacts" to the claims asserted by each member of the plaintiff class, contacts "creating state interests," in order to ensure that the choice of Kansas law is not arbitrary or unfair.... Given Kansas' lack of "interest" in claims unrelated to that State, and the substantive conflict with jurisdictions such as Texas, we conclude that application of Kansas law to every claim in this case is sufficiently arbitrary and unfair as to exceed constitutional limits.

When considering fairness in this context, an important element is the expectation of the parties.... There is no indication that when the leases involving land and royalty owners outside of Kansas were executed, the parties had any idea that Kansas law would control....

Here the Supreme Court of Kansas took the view that in a nationwide class action where procedural due process guarantees of notice and adequate representation were met, "the law of the forum should be applied unless compelling reasons exist for applying a different law." ... Whatever practical reasons may have commended this rule to the Supreme Court of Kansas, for the reasons already stated we do not believe that it is consistent with the decisions of this Court. We make no effort to determine for ourselves which law must apply to the various transactions involved in this lawsuit, and we reaffirm our observation in *Allstate* that in many situations a state court may be free to apply one of several choices of law. But the constitutional limitations laid down in cases such as *Allstate* . . . must be respected even in a nationwide class action.

We therefore [reverse] the judgment of the Supreme Court of Kansas . . . insofar as it held that Kansas law was applicable to all of the transactions which it sought to adjudicate. We remand the case to that court for further proceedings not inconsistent with this opinion.

■ STEVENS, J., . . . dissenting in part. . . . A fair reading of the Kansas Supreme Court's opinion in light of its earlier opinion . . . reveals that the Kansas court has examined the laws of connected jurisdictions and has correctly concluded that there is no "direct" or "substantive" conflict between the law applied by Kansas and the laws of those other States. Kansas has merely developed general common-law principles to accommodate the novel facts of this litigation — other state courts either agree with Kansas or have not yet addressed precisely similar claims. Consequently, I conclude that the Full Faith and Credit Clause of the Constitution did not require Kansas to apply the law of any other State, and the Fourteenth Amendment's Due Process Clause did not prevent Kansas from applying its own law in this case. . . .

[I]t has long been settled that "a mere misconstruction by the forum of the laws of a sister State is not a violation of the Full Faith and Credit Clause." . . . That Clause requires only that States accord "full faith and credit" to other States' laws — that is, acknowledge the validity and finality of such laws and attempt in good faith to apply them when necessary as they would be applied by home state courts. . . .

Merely to state these general principles is to refute any argument that Kansas' decision below violated the Full Faith and Credit Clause. . . . [T]he Kansas court made a careful survey of the relevant laws of Oklahoma and Texas. . . .

In final analysis, the Court today may merely be expressing its disagreement with the Kansas Supreme Court's statement that in a "nationwide class action . . . the law of the forum should be applied unless compelling reasons exist for applying a different law."

Notes and Questions

1. *Shutts* holds that Kansas law may not apply to the claims of class members that have no contacts with Kansas, but it does not say whose law should apply. Since its own choice of law rule led to an unconstitutional result, what choice of law rule should Kansas adopt? On remand, the Kansas Supreme Court avoided the question by holding that, even though there was no explicit agreement to this effect, the parties had implicitly agreed to an interest rate established by Federal Power Commission regulations, rather than the lower rates of interest generally applicable in Oklahoma, Texas, and Louisiana. Despite the lack of authority that the courts of these states would apply such an "implicit agreement" test and despite the general adoption in these states of lower rates of interest, no case had squarely rejected the approach. See Shutts v. Phillips Petroleum Co., 240 Kan. 764, 732 P.2d 1286 (1987), cert. denied, 487

U.S. 1223 (1988). It applied this ruling in a similar class action against a different oil company. Wortman v. Sun Oil Co., 241 Kan. 226, 755 P.2d 488 (1987).

The United States Supreme Court granted certiorari in *Wortman*, and upheld the Kansas courts' interpretation of Oklahoma, Texas, and Louisiana law against Full Faith and Credit and due process challenges:

> [*Shutts*] held that Kansas could not apply its own law to claims for interest by nonresidents concerning royalties from property located in other States. The Kansas Supreme Court has complied with that ruling, but petitioner claims that it has unconstitutionally distorted Texas, Oklahoma, and Louisiana law in its determination of that law....
>
> To constitute a violation of the Full Faith and Credit Clause or the Due Process Clause, it is not enough that a state court misconstrue the law of another State. Rather, our cases make plain that the misconstruction must contradict law of the other State that is clearly established and that has been brought to the court's attention.... We cannot conclude that any of the interpretations at issue here runs afoul of this standard.

Sun Oil Co. v. Wortman, 486 U.S. 717, 730-31 (1988). The decision evoked a strong dissent from Justice O'Connor, joined by Chief Justice Rehnquist:

> Today's decision discards important parts of [*Shutts*] and of the Full Faith and Credit Clause. Faced with the constitutional obligation to apply the substantive law of another State, a court that does not like that law apparently need take only two steps in order to avoid applying it. First, invent a legal theory so novel or strange that the other State has never had an opportunity to reject it; then, on the basis of nothing but unsupported speculation, "predict" that the other State would adopt that theory if it had the chance. To call this giving full faith and credit to the law of another State ignores the language of the Constitution and leaves it without the capacity to fulfill its purpose. Rather than take such a step, I would remand this case to the Supreme Court of Kansas with instructions to give effect to the interest rates established by law in Texas, Oklahoma, and Louisiana. [486 U.S. at 749.]

How clearly established does the law of a state have to be before another state court's failure to apply it violates the Constitution? If Justice O'Connor is correct, how serious an impediment is the Full Faith and Credit clause in aggregated complex or complicated cases? Many such cases are, in a sense, *sui generis*, so it would be easy for a court to create uniform law by adopting a theory that no state had squarely rejected. Do you worry that judges operating under a loose constitutional standard will have too much power to affect the outcome of the litigation? Do you worry that judges have too much power to create different rules of law for parties in large cases? Since aggregation will usually occur in federal court, do you worry that a loose constitutional standard shifts too much law-making power over state-law claims from individual states to a single federal judge? Or should the constitutional standard remain as loose as it is, in order to give judges the ability to work around complexity-causing choice of law problems?

2. *Wortman* was also significant for a second holding. The Kansas Supreme Court applied a 5-year Kansas statute of limitations to the classes' claims. The statutes of limitations in Oklahoma, Texas, and Louisiana were all shorter, and, if applicable, would have required the dismissal of most of the

claims brought by class members from those states. The Court upheld the application of the Kansas statute of limitations to the out-of-state claims against Full Faith and Credit and due process challenges:

> The Full Faith and Credit Clause does not compel "a state to substitute the statutes of other states for its own statutes dealing with a subject matter concerning which it is competent to legislate." . . . Since the procedural rules of its courts are surely matters on which a State is competent to legislate, it follows that a State may apply its own procedural rules to actions litigated in its courts. The issue here, then, can be characterized as whether a statute of limitations may be considered as a procedural matter for purposes of the Full Faith and Credit Clause.
>
> [The Court then held that, even though a statute of limitation might be regarded as substantive for other purposes such as *Erie*, it was a procedural rule for Full Faith and Credit purposes. It also rejected the idea that modern choice of law scholarship, which tends to characterize statutes of limitation as substantive, should affect this analysis.] [L]ong established and still subsisting choice-of-law practices that come to be thought, by modern scholars, unwise, do not thereby become unconstitutional. If current conditions render it desirable that forum States no longer treat a particular issue as procedural for conflict of laws purposes, those States can themselves adopt a rule to that effect, . . . or it can be proposed that Congress legislate to that effect under the second sentence of the Full Faith and Credit Clause. . . .
>
> A State's interest in regulating the workload of its courts and determining when a claim is too stale to be adjudicated certainly suffices to give it legislative jurisdiction to control the remedies available in its courts by imposing statutes of limitations. Moreover, petitioner could in no way have been unfairly surprised by the application to it of a rule that is as old as the Republic. There is, in short, nothing in Kansas' action here that is "arbitrary or unfair," [*Shutts*,] 472 U.S., at 821-822, and the due process challenge is entirely without substance. [486 U.S. at 722-23, 728-30.]

Note that *Wortman* seems to accept, without significant discussion, the proposition that a state can constitutionally choose its own procedural rules to adjudicate a case, even when another state's substantive law applies; the Court spends its time on the "characterization" issue of whether a statute of limitations is procedural or substantive in the particular constitutional context. Note as well that there may be constitutional defects in the procedures themselves. As *Shutts* itself shows (see p. 294, *supra*), the Court is not foreclosing those sorts of constitutional challenges.

3. *Shutts* seems to rule out a *lex fori* approach (at least on issues of substantive law) to claims that have no connection to the forum. Cf. Allstate Insurance Co. v. Hague, 449 U.S. 302 (1981) (plurality decision) (state court can adopt "better law" approach on issues of substantive law to claims that have minimal connection to the forum).

4. One of the beauties of the *lex fori* approach is that, like the *lex loci* approach, it can lead to the application of a single law to all cases that are joined together; indeed, it is even better at achieving the application of a single law in dispersed-injury contexts. Assuming that one state's law really is superior for plaintiffs than others, a *lex fori* approach is likely to reduce drastically, if not altogether eliminate, the multistate forum shopping that present choice of law

rules engender, and thus might facilitate the joinder or consolidation of related cases in one forum.

Note that *Shutts* itself was not a complex case, at least in the sense that we are discussing in this chapter. The application of four different interest rates, as opposed to just one rate, was not likely to create joinder, pretrial, trial, or remedial complexity. Does *Shutts* leave open the possibility that the choice of a single law (or perhaps a limited number of laws) is still constitutionally permissible when the use of multiple laws would create some form of complexity? The argument would run, presumably, that the inability to use a single law threatens the rational adjudication that lies at the heart of due process, and that this threat outweighs the countervailing due process and Full Faith and Credit considerations that animated *Shutts*.

One practical problem with this analysis is that it cannot dictate which approach should be used to choose the single law. A *lex fori* approach strongly favors plaintiffs as long as they retain their adversarial right to choose the forum under the "master of the complaint" rule. A "better law" approach inevitably forces the court to consider the question "Better for whom?" — and thus imbues the judge with great discretion to influence the outcome. A *lex loci* approach still cannot handle most dispersed-injury mass torts. In addition, even if this practical problem can be overcome, we must address the potential damage to adversarial and trans-substantive concerns that a "complexity-only" choice of law rule would generate.

5. Our brief survey of choice of law has disclosed the difficulty that traditional choice of law analysis poses for multistate controversies in which state law provides the rule of decision. We have also discovered some constitutional, theoretical, and practical problems with the apparent solution to this difficulty — the use of a single law. Before we turn to some possible ways through the horns of this dilemma, we need to add one more layer of facts for your consideration: the role of the federal courts.

2. Federal Courts and Choice of Law: Further Confusion or Possible Solution?

When federal courts hear claims grounded in state law, the issue arises whether they must adopt the same choice of law rules that a state court in the same jurisdiction would adopt, or whether they have the power to develop their own choice of law rules. If they must act just as a state court, then the federal forum provides no solution to the complexity-causing problems of the choice of law analysis. If they can make an independent choice of state law, and choose a single or limited number of those laws, then the federal forum has advantages (from the viewpoint of reducing complexity) that no state forum enjoys.

There also arises a second, related problem in federal cases premised on state law. As we learned in Chapter Four, federal courts enjoy some power to transfer cases from one district to another within the federal system. Suppose that a federal court in State A would apply the law of State A to a case. The case is now transferred to a federal court in State B.

Must the federal court in State B use the law of State A, or is it free to make a new choice of law decision? If it must accept the choice-of-law rule of the federal court in State A, and if the federal court in State A must adopt the same choice-of-law rule as a state court in State A, then the transfer of federal cases cannot solve the complexities created by choice-of-law rules. On the other hand, if the transfer of cases allows the federal court in the transferee forum to make a new choice of law decision, then the interdistrict consolidation techniques available in federal court can ease, if not eliminate, the dysfunction or inefficiency of complex or complicated litigation. The potential availability of new choice of law rules would also create a positive reason to attempt to aggregate cases in a federal forum.

When federal courts hear claims based on federal law, a third, somewhat different set of issues is presented. Unlike the prior two situations, in which it is not clear which state's law will apply, the federal court in this circumstance will clearly choose federal law. In the event that different circuits or districts have developed different interpretations of the applicable law, however, the court needs to decide which interpretation to adopt. For the most part, the answer to this question is simple enough: The court adopts the law (if any) of its own circuit or district. The catch comes when cases are transferred — again through one of the transfer devices we explored in Chapter Four — from a circuit or district with one interpretation to another circuit or district with another interpretation. Do the parties bring the "old" law into the "new" forum, or is the new forum free to choose its own law? If the "old" law applies, then transfer for consolidation purposes may create the same problems of complexity that the consolidation of multiple cases involving different state laws presents. If the new forum can choose its own law, then a single law will apply, and the complexities generated by choice of law concerns will evaporate.

The following two sections examine these issues, first in the state law context and then in the federal law context. Note how federal courts have developed different approaches in the two contexts, and ask yourself which approach, if either, strikes the best balance among concerns such as the reduction of complexity, the adversarial right to choose the best forum, and the like treatment of like claimants.

a. The Approach in Diversity Cases: The Confusion?

DAY & ZIMMERMANN, INC. v. CHALLONER

423 U.S. 3 (1975)

■ PER CURIAM.

Respondents sued petitioner in the United States District Court for the Eastern District of Texas seeking to recover damages for death and personal injury resulting from the premature explosion of a 105-mm. howitzer round in Cambodia. Federal jurisdiction was based on diversity of citizenship. The District Court held that the Texas law of strict liability in tort governed and submitted the case to the jury on that theory. The Court of Appeals for the Fifth Circuit affirmed a judgment in favor of respondents.

The Court of Appeals stated that were it to apply Texas choice-of-law rules, the substantive law of Cambodia, the place of injury, would certainly control as to the wrongful death, and perhaps as to the claim for personal injury. It declined nevertheless to apply Texas choice-of-law rules, based in part on an earlier decision . . ., which it summarized as holding that "[w]e refused to look to the Louisiana conflict of law rule, deciding that as a matter of federal choice of law, we could not apply the law of a jurisdiction that had no interest in the case, no policy at stake." The Court of Appeals further supported its decision on the grounds that the rationale for applying the traditional conflicts rule applied by Texas "is not operative under the present facts"; and that it was "a Court of the United States, an instrumentality created to effectuate the laws and polices of the United States."

We believe that the Court of Appeals either misinterpreted our longstanding decision in Klaxon Co. v. Stentor Electric Mfg. Co., 313 U.S. 487 (1941), or else determined for itself that it was no longer of controlling force in a case such as this. We are of the opinion that *Klaxon* is by its terms applicable here and should have been adhered to by the Court of Appeals. In *Klaxon, supra*, this Court said:

> The conflict of laws rules to be applied by the federal court in Delaware must conform to those prevailing in Delaware's state courts. Otherwise, the accident of diversity of citizenship would constantly disturb equal administration of justice in coordinate state and federal courts sitting side by side. See Erie R. Co. v. Tompkins, [304 U.S. 64, 74-77 (1938)].
> . . .

By parity of reasoning, the conflict-of-laws rules to be applied by a federal court in Texas must conform to those prevailing in the Texas state courts. A federal court in a diversity case is not free to engraft onto those state rules exceptions or modifications which may commend themselves to the federal court, but which have not commended themselves to the State in which the federal court sits. The Court of Appeals in this case should identify and follow the Texas conflicts rule. What substantive law will govern when Texas' rule is applied is a matter to be determined by the Court of Appeals.

The petition for certiorari is granted, the judgment of the Court of Appeals is vacated, and the case is remanded for further proceedings in conformity with this opinion.

■ JUSTICE BLACKMUN, concurring. . . . [A]s I read the Court's per curiam opinion, the Court of Appeals on remand is to determine and flatly to apply the conflict of laws rules that govern the state courts of Texas. This means to me that the Court of Appeals is not foreclosed from concluding, if it finds it proper so to do under the circumstances of this case, that the Texas state courts themselves would apply the Texas rule of strict liability. . . . I make this observation to assure the Court of Appeals that, at least in my view, today's per curiam opinion does not necessarily compel the determination that it is only the law of Cambodia that is applicable.

Notes and Questions

1. *Day & Zimmerman* is a re-affirmation of Klaxon Co. v. Stentor Electric Manufacturing Co, 313 U.S. 487 (1941), in which the Court, just three years after its decision in Erie Railroad Co. v. Tompkins, 304 U.S. 64 (1938), held that a federal court must apply the choice of law rule that a court of the forum state would apply. *Erie* itself held that a federal court cannot create "federal general common law" when a state court would apply state law to an identical claim; the federal and state courts must both apply state law. *Erie* relied on numerous rationales, including the less-than-pellucid text of the Rules of Decision Act, which directed federal courts to apply "[t]he laws of the several States, except where the Constitution, treaties, or statutes of the United States otherwise require or provide, shall be regarded as rules of decision in trials at common law, in the courts of the United States, in cases where they apply"; the evils that the application of different rules in state and federal court would create — in particular, the evils of forum shopping and non-uniform, inequitable administration of law; and the need to avoid a conflict with Tenth Amendment, which reserves to the states those powers not specifically provided to the federal government.

The result in *Klaxon* might seem dictated by *Erie*. If the federal court applies a different choice of law rule than the state court across the street, different substantive law may (not must, but may) apply. Likewise, the evils of forum shopping and inequitable administration of law that *Erie* sought to eradicate would exist if the choice of federal court resulted in application of different law. In fact, the case for *Klaxon* is not nearly as strong as the case for *Erie*. First, whether the term "laws" in the Rules of Decision Act includes choice of law rules is far from clear. Moreover, the Tenth Amendment overlays in *Klaxon* are much weaker. Unlike *Erie*, in which the constitutional authority of federal courts to ignore state substantive law is uncertain, the constitutional authority of federal courts to choose their own choice of law principles is fairly clear. By definition, in the conflicts situation, more than one state has an interest in the application of its law to the controversy, and "the choice of *which* state's law applies in a federal court is clearly a matter of federal concern." Richard H. Fallon et al., Hart & Wechsler's The Federal Courts and the Federal System 697 (4th ed. 1996). Congress would seem to possess the authority to enact such choice of law rules under any of a number of constitutional grants: the Commerce Clause (Art. I, § 8), the Full Faith and Credit Clause (Art. IV, § 1), and the Judicial Power Clause (Art. III, § 2). See Henry J. Friendly, *In Praise of* Erie — *and of the New Federal Common Law*, 39 N.Y.U. L. Rev. 383 (1964); American Law Institute, Study of the Division of Jurisdiction between State and Federal Courts 442-48 (1969); American Law Institute, Complex Litigation 310-13 (1994).

To say that Congress can create choice of law rules is not, however, to say that federal courts can do so without congressional direction. Perhaps separation of powers concerns, when joined with the evils that *Erie* sought to prevent, are adequate justification for *Klaxon*. Unless those separation of powers concerns are of constitutional stature, however, the issue is not whether federal courts can create their own choice of law rules; the issue is whether they should. A corollary issue is whether the authority of federal courts to create choice of law rules should vary with the situation and with the strength of the reasons to create such rules.

2. That corollary leads to the question whether *Klaxon* should be applied in the circumstances of complex or complicated litigation. Neither *Klaxon* nor *Day & Zimmerman* was complex or complicated. Adoption of state choice of law rules in diversity cases prevented plaintiffs from doing vertical forum shopping — in other words, shopping between state and federal courts. On the other hand, adoption of state choice of law rules created an incentive to engage in horizontal forum shopping among various federal (or state) courts. As long as only one lawsuit was to be filed, as in *Klaxon* or *Day & Zimmerman*, the system as a whole could be indifferent to the horizontal forum shopping problem, and entrust to the plaintiff, as master of the complaint, the decision about the forum in which the case would be lodged. In complex or complicated litigation, however, the effect of horizontal forum shopping is to allow multiple lawsuits to be filed in different federal and state forums — and the effect of these filings is to create lawyer dysfunction or needless inefficiency.

Is either dysfunction or inefficiency an adequate ground to change the *Klaxon* rule? Start with inefficiency. Is the expense of re-litigating comparable issues in multiple forums an adequate counterweight to the federalism and separation of powers concerns that underpin *Klaxon*? Is inefficiency an adequate ground to justify the breach of trans-substantivism that occurs when *Klaxon* mandates the application of one set of substantive rules in routine cases and a non-*Klaxon* rule mandates in complicated cases?

How would you answer the same questions in the context of lawyer dysfunction? The answer to this question is not obvious. Unlike many procedural rules, choice of law rules directly determine the substantive law that applies. See Larry Kramer, *Choice of Law in Complex Litigation*, 71 N.Y.U. L. Rev. 547, 569-74 (1996). Until now, our discussion of complex litigation has generally presupposed that the applicable substantive law was known; the problem has been that early-filing or late-filing claimants will be unable to obtain the remedy that this substantive law provides. Under what circumstances, therefore, will a rule that permits a federal court to depart from *Klaxon* reduce or eliminate dysfunction?

Four such circumstances seem to exist. First, the substantive rule(s) that *Klaxon* would require to be applied might lead either to so many more findings of liability or to such a greater remedy for some that the ability of others to obtain an equitable remedy is threatened, while the rule(s) that a court freed of *Klaxon* would apply would avoid the problems of inequitable distribution of the remedy. Second, the expense of the litigation that the defendant incurs to litigate choice of law issues in individual cases might consume the defendants' resources and the simplification of the choice of law inquiry saves enough money to guarantee an effective remedy for all plaintiffs. Third, if a federal court's power to select a choice of law rule reduces the incentive to file cases in numerous forums, and that reduction in disparate filings in turn permits a court to render a more equitable remedy for similarly situated plaintiffs, there would be a reason to change *Klaxon*'s rule in complex cases. Fourth, the reduction in the number of applicable laws might eliminate dysfunction during the pretrial or trial phases examined in Parts Two and Three of the book.

How many such cases fit into these categories? There are certainly cases that fit into the first category, but only when a non-*Klaxon* rule would reduce the plaintiffs' remedy — hardly an outcome-neutral ground on which to base choice of law rules. The second category may well be an empty set. In the third category, it is not clear that abandoning *Klaxon* will reduce significantly plaintiffs' existing incentives to file in different forums. Moreover, any such reduction would have to be counterbalanced against the fact that a departure from *Klaxon* would likely drive a number of cases into the state courts, in which horizontal forum shopping is still possible. As we have seen, once a case is driven into the state court system, it is much more difficult to aggregate than a case in the federal system. (Note that this last concern would also apply in complicated litigation.) Finally, the fourth category may be significant, since the reduction in the number of applicable laws can reduce the number of issues to be litigated during pretrial and trial. Again this reduction must be balanced against the number of cases that a non-*Klaxon* rule will drive into state court, and must also be viewed against other issue-narrowing techniques that, as we shall see in the ensuing four chapters, might accomplish a similar goal without raising the same federalism, separation of powers, and trans-substantive concerns that abandoning *Klaxon* would.

Therefore, from the viewpoint of complex litigation, the departure from *Klaxon* would not appear to be a panacea. More fruitful endeavors might be to eliminate the plethora of state laws and state choice of law rules that permit horizontal forum shopping to occur, or to overrule *Klaxon* in all cases.

3. One problem that we assumed away in the last Note was that, were *Klaxon* to be abandoned in complex or complicated litigation, a federal court could readily determine the content of the choice of law rule. Later in the chapter we return to the problem of choosing a choice of law rule when we examine various proposals to authorize federal courts to establish choice of law rule in complex or complicated litigation. See p. 869, *infra*. For now, however, it is enough to note that our present choice of law regime does not appear to authorize federal courts to avoid the incentives to fracture related litigation that the plethora of state choice of law rules presently creates. The remaining issue, therefore, is whether federal courts can limit these incentives indirectly, by applying a single choice of law rule to related cases that are transferred to a single forum pursuant to federal venue transfer provisions.

FERENS v. JOHN DEERE CO.

494 U.S. 516 (1990)

■ JUSTICE KENNEDY delivered the opinion of the Court.

Section 1404(a) of Title 28 states: "For the convenience of parties and witnesses, in the interest of justice, a district court may transfer any civil action to any other district or division where it might have been brought." 28 U.S.C. § 1404(a) (1982 ed.). In Van Dusen v. Barrack, 376 U.S. 612 (1964), we held that, following a transfer under § 1404(a) initiated by a defendant, the transferee court must follow the choice of law rules that prevailed in the transferor court. We now decide that, when a plaintiff moves for the transfer, the same rule applies.

I

Albert Ferens lost his right hand when, the allegation is, it became caught in his combine harvester, manufactured by Deere & Company. The accident occurred while Ferens was working with the combine on his farm in Pennsylvania. For reasons not explained in the record, Ferens delayed filing a tort suit and Pennsylvania's 2-year limitations period expired. In the third year, he and his wife sued Deere in the United States District Court for the Western District of Pennsylvania, raising contract and warranty claims as to which the Pennsylvania limitations period had not yet run. The District Court had diversity jurisdiction, as Ferens and his wife are Pennsylvania residents, and Deere is incorporated in Delaware with its principal place of business in Illinois.

Not to be deprived of a tort action, the Ferenses in the same year filed a second diversity suit against Deere in the United States District Court for the Southern District of Mississippi, alleging negligence and products liability. Diversity jurisdiction and venue were proper. The Ferenses sued Deere in the District Court in Mississippi because they knew that, under Klaxon Co. v. Stentor Electric Mfg. Co., 313 U.S. 487, 496 (1941), the federal court in the exercise of diversity jurisdiction must apply the same choice of law rules that Mississippi state courts would apply if they were deciding the case. A Mississippi court would rule that Pennsylvania substantive law controls the personal injury claim but that Mississippi's own law governs the limitation period. . . .

The issue now before us arose when the Ferenses took their forum shopping a step further: having chosen the federal court in Mississippi to take advantage of the State's limitations period, they next moved, under § 1404(a), to transfer the action to the federal court in Pennsylvania on the ground that Pennsylvania was a more convenient forum. The Ferenses acted on the assumption that, after the transfer, the choice of law rules in the Mississippi forum, including a rule requiring application of the Mississippi statute of limitations, would continue to govern the suit.

Deere put up no opposition, and the District Court in Mississippi granted the § 1404(a) motion. The Court accepted the Ferenses' arguments that they resided in Pennsylvania; that the accident occurred there; that the claim had no connection to Mississippi; that a substantial number of witnesses resided in the Western District of Pennsylvania but none resided in Mississippi; that most of documentary evidence was located in the Western District of Pennsylvania but none was located in Mississippi; and that the warranty action pending in the Western District of Pennsylvania presented common questions of law and fact.

The District Court in Pennsylvania consolidated the transferred tort action with the Ferenses' pending warranty action but declined to honor the Mississippi statute of limitations as the District Court in Mississippi would have done. It ruled instead that, because the Ferenses had moved for transfer as plaintiffs, the rule in *Van Dusen* did not apply. Invoking the 2-year limitations period set by Pennsylvania law, the District Court dismissed their tort action. . . .

The Court of Appeals for the Third Circuit affirmed.... The Court of Appeals relied at the outset on the separate theory that applying Mississippi's statute of limitations would violate due process because Mississippi had no legitimate interest in the case. We vacated this decision and remanded in light of Sun Oil Co. v. Wortman, 486 U.S. 717 (1988), in which we held that a State may choose to apply its own statute of limitations to claims governed by the substantive laws of another State without violating either the Full Faith and Credit Clause or the Due Process Clause.... On remand, the Court of Appeals again affirmed, this time confronting the *Van Dusen* question and ruling that a transferor court's choice of law rules do not apply after a transfer under § 1404(a) on a motion by a plaintiff....

II

Section 1404(a) states only that a district court may transfer venue for the convenience of the parties and witnesses when in the interest of justice. It says nothing about choice of law, and nothing about affording plaintiffs different treatment from defendants. We touched upon these issues in *Van Dusen*, but left open the question presented in this case.... In *Van Dusen*, an airplane flying from Boston to Philadelphia crashed into Boston Harbor soon after take-off. The personal representatives of the accident victims brought more than 100 actions in the District Court for the District of Massachusetts and more than 40 actions in the District Court for the Eastern District of Pennsylvania. When the defendants moved to transfer the actions brought in Pennsylvania to the federal court in Massachusetts, a number of the Pennsylvania plaintiffs objected because they lacked capacity under Massachusetts law to sue as representatives of the decedents. The plaintiffs also averred that the transfer would deprive them of the benefits of Pennsylvania's choice of law rules because the transferee forum would apply to their wrongful death claims a different substantive rule. The plaintiffs obtained from the Court of Appeals a writ of mandamus ordering the District Court to vacate the transfer....

We reversed. After considering issues not related to the present dispute, we held that the Court of Appeals erred in its assumption that Massachusetts law would govern the action following transfer.... We said:

"This legislative background supports the view that § 1404(a) was not designed to narrow the plaintiff's venue privilege or to defeat the state-law advantages that might accrue from the exercise of this venue privilege but rather the provision was simply to counteract the inconveniences that flowed from the venue statutes by permitting transfer to a convenient federal court. The legislative history of § 1404(a) certainly does not justify the rather startling conclusion that one might 'get a change of a law as a bonus for a change of venue.' Indeed, an interpretation accepting such a rule would go far to frustrate the remedial purposes of § 1404(a). If a change in the law were in the offing, the parties might well regard the section primarily as a forum-shopping instrument. And, more importantly, courts would at least be reluctant to grant transfers, despite considerations of convenience, if to do so might conceivably prejudice the claim of a plaintiff who initially selected a permissible forum. We believe, therefore, that both the history and purposes of § 1404(a) indicate that it should be regarded as a federal judicial housekeeping measure, dealing with the placement of litigation in the federal courts and generally intended, on the basis of convenience and fairness, simply to authorize a change of courtrooms." [376 U.S.] at 635-37 (footnotes omitted).

We thus held that the law applicable to a diversity case does not change upon a transfer initiated by a defendant.

III

The quoted part of *Van Dusen* reveals three independent reasons for our decision. First, § 1404(a) should not deprive parties of state law advantages that exist absent diversity jurisdiction. Second, § 1404(a) should not create or multiply opportunities for forum shopping. Third, the decision to transfer venue under § 1404(a) should turn on considerations of convenience and the interest of justice rather than on the possible prejudice resulting from a change of law. Although commentators have questioned whether the scant legislative history of § 1404(a) compels reliance on these three policies, . . . we find it prudent to consider them in deciding whether the rule in *Van Dusen* applies to transfers initiated by plaintiffs. We decide that, in addition to other considerations, these policies require a transferee forum to apply the law of the transferor court, regardless of who initiates the transfer. A transfer under § 1404(a), in other words, does not change the law applicable to a diversity case.

A

The policy that § 1404(a) should not deprive parties of state law advantages, although perhaps discernible in the legislative history, has its real foundation in Erie R. Co. v. Tompkins, 304 U.S. 64 (1938). . . . The *Erie* rule remains a vital expression of the federal system and the concomitant integrity of the separate States. We explained *Erie* in Guaranty Trust Co. v. York, 326 U.S. 99, 109 (1945), as follows:

"In essence, the intent of [the *Erie*] decision was to insure that, in all cases where a federal court is exercising jurisdiction solely because of the diversity of citizenship of the parties, the outcome of the litigation in the federal court should be substantially the same, so far as legal rules determine the outcome of a litigation, as it would be if tried in a State court. The nub of the policy that underlies Erie R. Co. v. Tompkins is that for the same transaction the accident of a suit by a non-resident litigant in a federal court instead of in a State court a block away should not lead to a substantially different result." . . .

The *Erie* policy had a clear implication for *Van Dusen*. The existence of diversity jurisdiction gave the defendants the opportunity to make a motion to transfer venue under § 1404(a), and if the applicable law were to change after transfer, the plaintiff's venue privilege and resulting state-law advantages could be defeated at the defendant's option.... To allow the transfer and at the same time preserve the plaintiff's state-law advantages, we held that the choice of law rules should not change following a transfer initiated by a defendant....

Transfers initiated by a plaintiff involve some different considerations, but lead to the same result. Applying the transferor law, of course, will not deprive the plaintiff of any state law advantages. A defendant, in one sense, also will lose no legal advantage if the transferor law controls after a transfer initiated by the plaintiff; the same law, after all, would have applied if the plaintiff had not made the motion. In another sense, however, a defendant may lose a nonlegal advantage. Deere, for example, would lose whatever advantage inheres in not having to litigate in Pennsylvania, or, put another way, in forcing the Fereses to litigate in Mississippi or not at all.

We, nonetheless, find the advantage that the defendant loses slight.... By asking for application of the Mississippi statute of limitations following a transfer to Pennsylvania on grounds of convenience, the Fereses are seeking to deprive Deere only of the advantage of using against them the inconvenience of litigating in Mississippi.... [Section 1404(a)] exists to eliminate inconvenience without altering permissible choices under the venue statutes.... By creating an opportunity to have venue transferred between courts in different States on the basis of convenience, an option that does not exist absent federal jurisdiction, Congress, with respect to diversity, retained the *Erie* policy while diminishing the incidents of inconvenience.

Applying the transferee law, by contrast, would undermine the *Erie* rule in a serious way. It would mean that initiating a transfer under § 1404(a) changes the state law applicable to a diversity case.... In general, however, we have seen § 1404(a) as a housekeeping measure that should not alter the state law governing a case under *Erie*.... The Mississippi statute of limitations, which everyone agrees would have applied if the Fereses had not moved for a transfer, should continue to apply in this case....

B

Van Dusen also sought to fashion a rule that would not create opportunities for forum shopping. Some commentators have seen this policy as the most important rationale of *Van Dusen*, ... but few attempt to explain the harm of forum shopping when the plaintiff initiates a transfer. An opportunity for forum shopping exists whenever a party has a choice of forums that will apply different laws. The *Van Dusen* policy against forum shopping simply requires us to interpret § 1404(a) in a way that does not create an opportunity for obtaining a more favorable law by selecting a forum through a transfer of venue. In the *Van Dusen* case itself, this meant that we could not allow defendants to use a transfer to change the law....

No interpretation of § 1404(a), however, will create comparable opportunities for forum shopping by a plaintiff because, even without § 1404(a), a plaintiff already has the option of shopping for a forum with the most favorable law.... Diversity jurisdiction did not eliminate these forum shopping opportunities; instead, under *Erie*, the federal courts had to replicate them. . . .

C

Van Dusen also made clear that the decision to transfer venue under § 1404(a) should turn on considerations of convenience rather than on the possibility of prejudice resulting from a change in the applicable law. . . . We reasoned in *Van Dusen* that, if the law changed following a transfer initiated by the defendant, a district court "would at least be reluctant to grant transfers, despite considerations of convenience, if to do so might conceivably prejudice the claim of a plaintiff." . . . . This same policy requires application of the transferor law when a plaintiff initiates a transfer. . . .

The desire to take a punitive view of the plaintiff's actions should not obscure the systemic costs of litigating in an inconvenient place.

D

This case involves some considerations to which we perhaps did not give sufficient attention in *Van Dusen*. Foresight and judicial economy now seem to favor the simple rule that the law does not change following a transfer of venue under § 1404(a). Affording transfers initiated by plaintiffs different treatment from transfers initiated by defendants may seem quite workable in this case, but the simplicity is an illusion. If we were to hold that the transferee law applies following a § 1404(a) motion by a plaintiff, cases such as this would not arise in the future. Although applying the transferee law, no doubt, would catch the Ferenses by surprise, in the future no plaintiffs in their position would move for a change of venue.

Other cases, however, would produce undesirable complications. The rule would leave unclear which law should apply when both a defendant and a plaintiff move for a transfer of venue or when the court transfers venue on its own motion. . . . The rule also might require variation in certain situations, such as when the plaintiff moves for a transfer following a removal from state court by the defendant, or when only one of several plaintiffs requests the transfer, or when circumstances change through no fault of the plaintiff making a once convenient forum inconvenient. True, we could reserve any consideration of these questions for a later day. But we have a duty, in deciding this case, to consider whether our decision will create litigation and uncertainty. On the basis of these considerations, we again conclude that the transferor law should apply regardless who makes the § 1404(a) motion.

IV . . .

Our rule may seem too generous because it allows the Ferenses to have both their choice of law and their choice of forum, or even to reward the Ferenses for conduct that seems manipulative. We nonetheless see no alternative rule that would produce a more acceptable result. . . .

For the foregoing reasons, we conclude that Mississippi's statute of limitations should govern the Fereneses' action. We reverse and remand for proceedings consistent with this opinion.

■ JUSTICE SCALIA, with whom JUSTICE BRENNAN, JUSTICE MARSHALL, and JUSTICE BLACKMUN join, dissenting.... The question we must answer today is whether 28 U.S.C. § 1404(a) (1982 ed.) and the policies underlying *Klaxon* — namely, uniformity within a State and the avoidance of forum shopping — produce a result different from *Klaxon* when the suit in question was not filed in the federal court initially, but was transferred there under § 1404(a) on plaintiff's motion. In Van Dusen v. Barrack, 376 U.S. 612 (1964), we held that a result different from *Klaxon* is produced when a suit has been transferred under § 1404(a) on defendant's motion....

We left open in *Van Dusen* the question presented today, viz., whether "the same [venue privilege and *Erie*] considerations [that motivated *Van Dusen*] would govern" if a plaintiff sought a § 1404(a) transfer.... In my view, neither of those considerations is served — and indeed both are positively defeated — by a departure from *Klaxon* in that context. First, just as it is unlikely that Congress, in enacting § 1404(a), meant to provide the defendant with a vehicle by which to manipulate in his favor the substantive law to be applied in a diversity case, so too is it unlikely that Congress meant to provide the plaintiff with a vehicle by which to appropriate the law of a distant and inconvenient forum in which he does not intend to litigate, and to carry that prize back to the State in which he wishes to try the case. Second, application of the transferor court's law in this context would encourage forum-shopping between federal and state courts in the same jurisdiction on the basis of differential substantive law. It is true, of course, that the plaintiffs here did not select the *Mississippi* federal court in preference to the Mississippi state courts because of any differential substantive law; the former, like the latter, would have applied Mississippi choice-of-law rules, and thus the Mississippi statute of limitations. But one must be blind to realty to say that it is the *Mississippi* federal court in which these plaintiffs have chose to sue. That was merely a way station en route to suit in the *Pennsylvania* federal court. The plaintiffs were seeking to achieve exactly what *Klaxon* was designed to prevent: the use of a Pennsylvania federal court instead of a Pennsylvania state court in order to obtain application of a different substantive law.... The significant federal judicial policy expressed in *Erie* and *Klaxon* is reduced to a laughingstock if it can so readily be evaded through filing-and-transfer....

Saved by the Court's rule will be the incremental cost of trying in forums that are inconvenient (but not so inconvenient as to prompt the court's *sua sponte* transfer) those suits that are now filed in such forums for choice-of-law purposes. But incurred by the Court's rule will be the costs of considering and effecting transfer, not only in those suits but in the indeterminate number of additional suits that will be filed in inconvenient forums now that filing-and-transfer is an approved form of shopping for law; plus the costs attending the necessity for transferee courts to figure out the choice-of-law rules (and probably the substantive law) of distant States much more often than our *Van Dusen* decision would require. It should be noted that the file-and-transfer ploy sanctioned by the Court today will be available not merely to achieve the relatively rare (and generally unneeded) benefit of a longer statute of limitations, but also to bring home to the desired state of litigation all sorts of favorable choice-of-law rules regarding substantive liability — in an era when the diversity among the States in choice-of-law principles has become kaleidoscopic. . . .

For the Court, this case involves an "interpretation of § 1404(a)," and the central issue is whether *Klaxon* stands in the way of the policies of that statute. For me, the case involves an interpretation of the Rules of Decision Act,* and the central issue is whether § 1404(a) alters the "principle of uniformity within a state" which *Klaxon* says that Act embodies. I think my approach preferable, not only because the Rules of Decision Act does, and § 1404(a) does not, address the specific subject of which law to apply, but also because, as the Court acknowledges, our jurisprudence under that statute is "a vital expression of the federal system and the concomitant integrity of the separate States." To ask, as in effect the Court does, whether *Erie* gets in the way of § 1404(a), rather than whether § 1404(a) requires adjustment of *Erie*, seems to me the expression of a mistaken sense of priorities.

Notes and Questions

1. The majority seems to be most concerned with the defendant's forum shopping argument. It never mentions the damage that its ruling does to a fundamental assumption underlying the Federal Rules of Civil Procedure: the joinder of all transactionally related claims in a single suit. Do we want to encourage plaintiffs initially to parse their cases up into legal theories and lodge each theory in the court most hospitable to it? Is *Ferens* the point at which the Court should have refused to bow further to plaintiffs' admittedly primary right to shape the litigation?

2. Could John Deere have taken other measures to prevent the assertion of the Mississippi claim? Would it have been entitled to ask the Pennsylvania federal court hearing the warranty claim to stay the Mississippi tort case? Would it be able to move for dismissal on *forum non conveniens* grounds in Mississippi federal court?

The first strategy might work. As we saw in Chapter Four, one ground for a stay of related proceedings in another federal court is the prevention of forum shopping. See pp. 467-70, *supra*. While the argument that the two cases involve different legal theories might well preclude issuance of the stay, the distaste for forum shopping at least makes the argument worth trying. Could the plaintiff avoid the stay by *first* filing the tort action in Mississippi and *then* filing the warranty claim in Pennsylvania? The further litigation which will surround

---

* The present version of the Rules of Decision Act reads in full: "The laws of the several states, except where the Constitution or treaties of the United States or Acts of Congress otherwise require or provide, shall be regarded as rules of decision in civil actions in the courts of the United States, in cases where they apply." 28 U.S.C. § 1652. —

these issues calls into question the majority's belief that its decision will create less "litigation and uncertainty" than the dissent's interpretation of § 1404(a).

The second strategy — a dismissal on *forum non conveniens* grounds — is unlikely to succeed. 28 U.S.C. § 1404(a) has been thought to abrogate the doctrine when there is a convenient federal forum to which an inconveniently venued federal case can be transferred. Vanity Fair Mills, Inc. v. T. Eaton Co., 234 F.2d 633 (2d Cir.), cert. denied, 352 U.S. 871 (1956); Harbolt v. Carpenter, 536 F.2d 791 (8th Cir. 1976).

3. As the majority suggests, the defendant could also try a third tactic: opposing the transfer because it would not be "in the interest of justice" to permit forum shopping. Should this factor be given controlling weight? If so, the only persons who would ever be able to take advantage of *Ferens* are the Ferenses. If not, will *Ferens* generate "litigation and uncertainty" until the relative weight given to the forum shopping factor is decided?

Along these lines, note that John Deere did not oppose the plaintiffs' motion to transfer. Why? Probably because it was also engaged in a bit of forum shopping; it hoped to make the argument for dismissal of the tort claim after the transfer to Pennsylvania, where the court was unlikely to be pleased with the plaintiffs' tactics. While we might feel some sympathy for the defendant if it had opposed the transfer at the outset, is there any reason to feel sorry for it when it made a calculated tactical gamble and lost?

4. *Van Dusen* and *Ferens* involve transfers under § 1404. Would the same rule apply in transfers under other federal statutes? In particular, would the same rule apply under § 1407? The answer would seem to be "Yes." Given that § 1407 transfers are for pretrial purposes only, that the original state's law will be applied on remand, and that choice of law considerations are not relevant in making a § 1407 transfer decision, see pp. 494-525, *supra*; In re General Motors Class E Stock Buyout Securities Litigation, 696 F. Supp. 1546 (J.P.M.L. 1988), it would be difficult to imagine that the transferee judge could change the applicable choice of law rules just during the pendency of the case in the transferee forum. See In re Temporomandibular Joint (TMJ) Implants Products Liability Litigation, 97 F.3d 1050 (8th Cir. 1996).

5. Are there any exceptions to the *Van Dusen-Ferens* rule? Assume that you represent the plaintiff, a citizen of California, in a diversity case in which the choice of law rules of California will lead the court to apply favorable California substantive law. If you sued the defendant in North Carolina, of which the defendant is a citizen, North Carolina choice of law rules would lead to application of less favorable North Carolina substantive law. Also assume you prefer federal court. Obviously, given these assumptions, you will sue in California federal court.

Now further assume that you cannot obtain service of process on the defendant in California. Can you file in California, where subject matter jurisdiction and venue exist, and then request a § 1404(a) transfer to North Carolina to effect service? If there were no exception to *Van Dusen* in this situation, this tactic would give the plaintiff the benefit of California law when a properly filed case would not have. See Nelson v. International Paint Co., 716 F.2d 640 (9th Cir. 1983) (creating an exception to *Van Dusen* on comparable facts). How does the reasoning of *Ferens* affect this problem?

6. Granting that there might be an exception to *Van Dusen* and *Ferens* on facts such as *Nelson*, would it also be possible to create exceptions in the cases

of complex or complicated litigation? Obviously, the basic rule of these cases means that, when a complex or complicated case is aggregated in one federal forum, the transferee court will need to determine the choice of law rules that apply to each of the transferred cases and, depending on the content of those rules, might end up applying many different laws to those cases. On the other hand, if *Van Dusen* and *Ferens* could be "overlooked" in these cases, the transferee court would be able to apply a single choice of law rule (according to *Klaxon*, the law of the forum state). Then the step of analyzing the case under different choice of law rules will be avoided.

The elimination of this step will not necessarily lead to the application of fewer substantive rules. In some cases different choice of law rules might all point in the direction of using one substantive law (see p. 833, *infra*), while the application of the choice of law rule from the transferee forum's state might lead to the use of multiple substantive laws. Typically, more dysfunction or inefficiency is generated by a transferee court having to use multiple substantive laws than by a transferee court having to sort out the choice of law consequences of multiple states. This is not, however, invariably the case; the multiple substantive laws might be so unfavorable to one side that, in reality, the use of multiple laws creates fewer difficulties than the use of a smaller number of substantive laws that provide incentives for both sides to litigate. Therefore, should an exception to *Van Dusen* and *Ferens* should be created only when (1) an exception will in fact reduce the number of substantive laws that will apply to the transferred cases, and (2) the substantive laws that remain will make the litigation simpler? In order to figure out whether the first part of the exception applies, wouldn't a court have to analyze the choice of law outcome both under *Van Dusen* and *Ferens* and under the exception to *Van Dusen* and *Ferens*? In order to figure out whether the second part of the exception applies, wouldn't the judge have to make some initial determinations about the likely outcome of the case?

7. Another problem with creating an exception to *Van Dusen* and *Ferens* also exists: Such an exception may actually create more litigation than it saves. Assuming that the dissent had prevailed in *Ferens*, future plaintiffs in the Ferenses' position would have four choices — forgo suit on the tort claim, file in Mississippi federal court and fight any efforts to transfer, file in Mississippi state court and fight John Deere's efforts to remove and transfer, or (assuming that this state also has more desirable substantive law) file in the state(s) in which John Deere is a citizen and frustrate removal entirely. To the extent that any of these tactics is successful, the hypothetical exception to *Van Dusen* and *Ferens* will keep litigation separated when it could have been handled together. As troubling as that fact may be in a case like *Ferens*, it is more troubling when the effect of the exception would be to induce plaintiffs in large-scale litigation to file cases in state courts, from which, we have seen, aggregation becomes far more difficult.

8. The last two Notes should not be read as an unadulterated endorsement of the results in *Van Dusen* and *Ferens*. Often the application of these rules will require the selection of multiple laws that will cause more dysfunction or inefficiency than would the laws selected under an anti-*Van Dusen-Ferens* approach. Rather, the point of these Notes is to suggest that, despite the intuitively appealing idea of creating an exception to *Van Dusen* and *Ferens* in complex or complicated litigation, it is not necessarily true that such an exception will reduce dysfunction or inefficiency. The rules are designed with

other purposes in mind, and there is no *a priori* way to know whether the *Van Dusen-Ferens* rules or their opposite will lead to a "better" outcome from the viewpoint of complex or complicated litigation.

The *Van Dusen-Ferens* problem is, frankly, more a symptom of other difficulties — varying state laws, varying state choice of law rules, and *Klaxon* — than a primary disease that can be treated and cured on its own. As we saw in the last set of Notes, even *Klaxon* is hardly a primary disease. If the dysfunction- or inefficiency-causing problems of multiple applicable laws are to be avoided, the focus of the attack should be on the existence of multiple state laws and/or multiple choice of law rules. In Section B, we examine some of the possible avenues of attack in cases grounded on state law. Before we explore those avenues, we stop to examine the comparable choice of law issues in cases arising under federal law — both because complex and complicated litigation often involve claims arising under federal law and because the federal law approach might provide useful information about the proper approach to the state-law problem.

b. The Approach in Federal Question Cases: The Solution?

The primary problems posed by choice of law in the state law context are multiple state laws and multiple state choice of law rules — problems that, due to the combination of *Klaxon*, *Van Dusen*, and *Ferens*, are not alleviated when state claims are filed in federal court. To what extent are these problems replicated for claims based on federal law? Since federal law is in theory uniform in every state and federal court, you might think that neither the problem of multiple laws nor, consequently, the problem of multiple choice of law rules exists; therefore, there is also no reason to worry about the federal court overlays of *Klaxon*, *Van Dusen*, and *Ferens*.

Theory and practice are two different things. Federal law is not, in fact, uniform; different circuits and districts develop different interpretations. Federal courts are not bound to follow the interpretation of other circuits or districts. Likewise, although they sometimes defer to the interpretation of the federal circuit that encompasses them, state courts are not required to follow any circuit's interpretation of federal law. See, *e.g.*, Dewey v. R.J. Reynolds Tobacco Co., 121 N.J. 69, 577 A.2d 1239 (1990). Although all courts must follow the decisions of the United States Supreme Court on matters of federal law, the Supreme Court resolves only a tiny fraction of the interpretive differences, and its resolutions often touch off a further round of interpretive difficulties.

Therefore, the picture that federal law presents is not, as a practical matter, that different than the picture that multiple state laws present. The way in which the courts respond to the problem of multiple federal interpretations is.

IN RE KOREAN AIR LINES DISASTER OF SEPTEMBER 1, 1983

829 F.2d 1171 (D.C. Cir. 1987), affirmed on other grounds
sub nom. Chan v. Korean Air Lines, 490 U.S. 122 (1989)

■ GINSBURG, RUTH BADER, Circuit Judge. This case arises out of an air disaster and raises turbulent federal questions. On September 1, 1983, Korean Air Lines (KAL) Flight 007, a commercial craft departing from Kennedy Airport in New York and bound for Seoul, South Korea, was destroyed over the Sea of Japan by Soviet Union military aircraft. Wrongful death actions were filed against KAL in several federal district courts; the Judicial Panel on Multidistrict Litigation transferred these actions to the District Court for the District of Columbia for pretrial proceedings pursuant to 28 U.S.C. § 1407 . . . .

The nub of the controversy relates to the per passenger damage limitation of the Warsaw Convention, raised to $75,000 by an accord among airlines known as the Montreal Agreement. By motion for partial summary judgment, plaintiffs sought a declaration "that [KAL] is liable without fault for compensatory damages without any limitation of $75,000." . . . Denying plaintiffs' motion, the district court, on July 25, 1985, held that KAL could avail itself of the $75,000 per passenger limitation. . . . In so ruling, the district court considered and rejected contrary Second Circuit precedent . . . .

[The MDL proceeding involved cases from the Eastern District of Michigan, the District of Massachusetts, the District of Columbia, and most significantly, the Southern and Eastern Districts of New York. The district court held in a subsequent order that its decision denying plaintiffs' motion applied to the cases transferred from all the districts.]

We now affirm the district court's dispositions. On the Warsaw Convention/Montreal Agreement $75,000 per passenger damage limitation issue, we adopt as our opinion the comprehensive July 25, 1985 decision of the district court . . . . We set out below our reasons for concluding that the district court properly adhered to its own interpretation of the Warsaw Convention/Montreal Agreement in all actions, including those transferred from district courts within the Second Circuit. . . .

The Supreme Court, in Van Dusen v. Barrack, 376 U.S. 612 (1964), addressed and resolved this question: when a defendant in a diversity action moves for a venue transfer under 28 U.S.C. § 1404(a), which state's law applies post-transfer? The state law that would have applied in the transferor court adheres to the case, the Supreme Court held; in the Court's words, "with respect to state law," the venue change will accomplish "but a change of courtrooms." . . .

The *Van Dusen* interpretation of 28 U.S.C. § 1404(a), as the latter applies in diversity actions, rests on principles advanced in Erie R.R. v. Tompkins, 304 U.S. 64 (1938), and cases in the *Erie* line. Van Dusen, 376 U.S. at 637-40; see particularly Klaxon Co. v. Stentor Elec. Mfg. Co., 313 U.S. 387 (1941) . . . .

The question before us is whether the *Van Dusen* rule — that the law applicable in the transferor forum attends the transfer — should apply to transferred federal claims. It is a question meriting attention from Higher Authority. Congress, it appears, has not focused on the issue, nor has the Supreme Court addressed it. The Judicial Panel on Multidistrict Litigation assumed, on at least one occasion, that the *Van Dusen* rule would apply to transferred federal claims, see In re Plumbing Fixtures Litigation, 342 F. Supp. 756, 758 (J.P.M.L. 1972), but the Panel, from what we can glean, has given the matter only fleeting consideration. Recognizing that the question is perplexing, particularly in the context of 28 U.S.C. § 1407, a statute authorizing transfers only for pretrial purposes, we are persuaded by thoughtful commentary that "the transferee court [should] be free to decide a federal claim in the manner it views as correct without deferring to the interpretation of the transferor circuit." Marcus, Conflict Among Circuits and Transfers Within the Federal Judicial System, 93 Yale L.J. 677, 721 (1984) . . . .

[T]he *Erie* policies served by the *Van Dusen* decision do not figure in the calculus when the law to be applied is federal, not state. Given the reality of conflict among the circuits on the proper interpretation of federal law, however, why deny to a plaintiff with a federal claim the "venue privilege" a diversity claimant enjoys? Plaintiffs in the *Van Dusen* situation could effectively pick Pennsylvania rather than Massachusetts law and retain the benefit of that choice after transfer. Why deny a similar right of selection and retention to plaintiffs who would fare better under the Second Circuit's interpretation of federal law than under the D.C. Circuit's interpretation?

The point has been cogently made that venue provisions are designed with geographical convenience in mind, and not to "guarantee that the plaintiff will be able to select the law that will govern the case." Piper Aircraft Co. v. Reyno, 454 U.S. 235, 257 n.24 (1981) . . . In diversity cases, however, federal courts are governed by *Klaxon* and therefore may not compose federal choice-of-law principles; instead, they must look to state prescriptions in determining which state's law applies. With "no federal choice-of-law principles that favor the application of the law of one state over the law of another," the diversity plaintiff's opening move or "venue privilege" ordinarily fills the gap — it "prevails by default." Marcus, *supra*, 93 Yale L.J. at 700-01. For the adjudication of federal claims, on the other hand, "the federal courts comprise a single system [in which each tribunal endeavors to apply] a single body of law," H.L. Green Co. v. MacMahon, 312 F.2d 650, 652 (2d Cir. 1962), cert. denied, 372 U.S. 928 (1963); there is no compelling reason to allow plaintiff to capture the most favorable interpretation of that law simply and solely by virtue of his or her right to choose the place to open the fray.

As summarized in the commentary we find persuasive:

> . . . For federal courts, the most significant choice-of-law difference between issues of state law and issues of federal law is that they lack competence to [develop rules of decision for] the former and are presumptively competent to decide the latter . . . . [T]he federal courts have not only the power but the duty to decide [issues of federal law]

correctly. There is no room in the federal system of review for rote acceptance of the decision of a court outside the chain of direct review. If a federal court simply accepts the interpretation of another circuit without [independently] addressing the merits, it is not doing its job.

Marcus, *supra*, 93 Yale L.J. at 679, 702; see also Friendly, The "Law of the Circuit" and All That, 46 St. John's L. Rev. 406, 412 (1972) ("I take [*Van Dusen*] to be limited to choices of *state* law.") (emphasis in original).

Application of *Van Dusen* in the matter before us, we emphasize, would not produce uniformity. There would be one interpretation of federal law for the cases initially filed in districts within the Second Circuit, and an opposing interpretation for cases filed elsewhere. Applying divergent interpretations of the governing federal law to plaintiffs, depending solely upon where they initially filed suit, would surely reduce the efficiencies achievable through consolidated preparatory proceedings. Indeed, because there is ultimately a single proper interpretation of federal law, the attempt to ascertain and apply diverse circuit interpretations simultaneously is inherently self-contradictory. Our system contemplates differences between different states' laws; thus a multidistrict judge asked to apply divergent state positions on a point of law would face a coherent, if sometimes difficult, task. But it is logically inconsistent to require one judge to apply simultaneously different and conflicting interpretations of what is supposed to be a unitary federal law.

The district judge in the instant case observed that

[i]f ... more than one interpretation of federal law exists, the Supreme Court of the United States can finally determine the issue and restore uniformity in the federal system. The uniformity achieved in this [way] is an "informed uniformity" unlike the "blind uniformity" which would result from one court applying the interpretation of another by rote....

We agree. The federal courts spread across the country owe respect to each other's efforts and should strive to avoid conflicts, but each has an obligation to engage independently in reasoned analysis. Binding precedent for all is set only by the Supreme Court, and for the district courts within a circuit, only by the court of appeals for that circuit.

We return, finally, to the most anomalous feature of this case. As earlier observed, we deal here not with an "all-purpose" transfer under 28 U.S.C. § 1404(a), but with a transfer under 28 U.S.C. § 1407 "for coordinated or consolidated pretrial proceedings." We have held, in accord with the district court, that the law of a transferor forum — here, the law of the Second Circuit — merits close consideration, but does not have stare decisis effect in a transferee forum situated in another circuit. Should the several cases consolidated for pretrial preparation in the instant proceeding eventually return to transferor courts outside this circuit, would our district court's Warsaw Convention/Montreal Agreement ruling, which we have affirmed, have binding force? We believe it should, as "law of the case," for if it did not, transfers under 28 U.S.C. § 1407 could be counterproductive, *i.e.*, capable of generating rather than reducing the duplication and protraction Congress sought to check.... On this issue in the case at hand, however, our circuit is not positioned to speak the last word....

We affirm the order of the district court that KAL is entitled to avail itself of the limitation on damages provided by the Warsaw Convention and raised to $75,000 by the Montreal Agreement; and we note again that the proper interpretation of the Convention and Agreement, as well as the scope of the transferee court's interpretive authority in a cause such as this one, are matters in need of definitive resolution for our national court system.

■ D. H. GINSBURG, Circuit Judge, concurring, in which WILLIAMS, Circuit Judge, joins. . . . [T]he New York plaintiffs' suggestion that transfer under section 1407(a) presents the type of exceptional circumstance that justifies imposing upon a federal court the duty to accept as binding another circuit's interpretation of federal law would constitute a novel departure from the norm of independent judgment. . . .

The conduct of multidistrict litigation, which is invariably time consuming as it is, will grind to a standstill while transferee judges read separate briefs, each based on the case law of a transferor circuit, on a single issue of federal law. Much of the advantage that transfer was intended to produce, and particularly the desiderata of furthering efficiency and preventing inconsistent rulings, will be lost by requiring transferee judges a wear a number of judicial hats. It is the prospect of this kind of quagmire that is likely to yield the result feared by the Court in *Van Dusen* — that courts would be "reluctant to grant transfers" and thereby "frustrate the remedial purposes of [section 1407]." It may well be preferable to have multidistrict litigation remain dispersed in the courts of origin than to have transferee judges burdened with the hopelessly complex task of sitting as several federal judges at once. Consequently, even though having transferee judges exercise independent judgment may in isolated instances result in an unraveling of a transferred case, I believe that this approach, although not a perfect solution, is by far the less problematic and the more consistent with the intent of Congress in enacting section 1407. . . .

In order for cases to be transferred from one circuit to another with a minimum loss of efficiency and consistency, the only solution is for Congress to amend section 1407(a), as well as section 1404(a), to provide that rulings by a court in one circuit will not be reviewed under the case law of another circuit. In this respect, the options seem to be: (1) adopt the New York plaintiffs' position, and have the law of the transferor court govern a transferred case throughout its disposition; (2) provide that a ruling in a transferred case is to be reviewed, by whatever circuit court, under the case law of the circuit in which the ruling was made; and (3) make transfer comprehensive, extending through trial and appeal in the transferee circuit (applying its transfer circuit precedents, of course). For the reasons I have given, the first option involves considerable costs. . . .

The second option appears to be far more advantageous. . . .

The third option entails all of the benefits of efficiency and consistency and none of the drawbacks of the second option. Insofar as transfer is burdensome for plaintiffs, however, it would tend to magnify their hardship, especially if they are to testify at trial. This detriment may be more or less offset by the reciprocal advantage accruing to a defendant that does not have to defend multiple trials at different places. . . . As between the second and third options, therefore, considerable study would be needed in order to make an informed judgment, one that balances the goals of judicial economy and consistency against the distribution of costs imposed on plaintiffs and defendants in the course of realizing those goals.

American Law Institute, COMPLEX LITIGATION: STATUTORY RECOMMENDATIONS AND ANALYSIS

430 (1994)

§ 6.08. Intercircuit Conflicts

In actions consolidated under § 3.01 or removed under § 5.01, the transferee court shall not be bound by the federal law as interpreted in the circuits in which the actions were filed, but may determine for itself the federal law to be applied to the federal claims and defenses in the litigation.

Robert A. Ragazzo, TRANSFER AND CHOICE OF FEDERAL LAW: THE APPELLATE MODEL

93 Mich. L. Rev. 703, 732, 744-747, 755-757 (1995)

Van Dusen, as viewed through the lens of *Ferens*, expresses three concerns that are potentially applicable to [§ 1404(a)] transfers in cases with federal issues. Transfers should not (i) disturb preexisting choice of law advantages accruing to the plaintiff, (ii) give the defendant an incentive to seek transfer for the purpose of obtaining more favorable law, or (iii) introduce choice of law considerations into transfer decisions. . . .

By contrast to the state law context, the plaintiff has no choice of law privilege with respect to federal law. . . . Congress . . . created section 1404(a) as a limitation on [the basic] venue provisions. As a consequence, the plaintiff has no legitimate cause for complaint if transfer changes applicable federal law.

The rule that transferee federal law should apply does not violate the concern of *Van Dusen* and *Ferens* that transfer decisions should be determined by efficiency rather than choice of law considerations. Because the uniformity of federal law is accepted as a given, applicable federal law is deemed to remain unchanged after transfer. As a consequence, any detriment to the plaintiff receives no weight in the transfer calculus because, by hypothesis, no detriment exists.

Nor is this result unfair. The absence of choice of law rules with respect to federal issues gives the plaintiff a significant litigation advantage. The plaintiff is often presented with a wide range of venue options, and the plaintiff's initial choice of forum is entitled to respect. The defendant has the burden of overcoming the presumption in favor of the plaintiff's choice of venue. Because the plaintiff is the first actor in the venue process, the plaintiff has a greater ability than the defendant to influence venue and, as a consequence, choice of law. Any detriment to plaintiffs in transferred cases would seem at least offset by the plaintiff's ability to choose the applicable federal law in cases that are not transferred.

The last of the *Van Dusen-Ferens* concerns presents a greater obstacle to the application of transferee federal law. Applying transferee federal law presents defendants with the prospect of obtaining a better law in some cases as a result of transfer. As a consequence, defendants will have an incentive to seek transfer for reasons not related to trial efficiencies. Although the trial court has the power to deny transfer motions that are not founded on efficiency considerations, the system wastes resources in disposing of transfer motions that originate from choice of law concerns.

Nevertheless, the fundamental assumptions of the federal system require the application of transferee federal law. There is no choice of law with respect to federal law because federal law is theoretically uniform. Although this result does not obtain in practice, the lack of practical uniformity is a fact that federal courts are not permitted to consider. Were they allowed to admit the existence of variations in federal law, the creation of federal choice of law rules would be a necessity. Just as the theoretical uniformity of federal law outweighs choice of law considerations, it outweighs any efficiency concern related to forum shopping by defendants.

Perhaps the better practice would be to recognize the lack of uniformity of federal law with all its attendant implications. Federal courts might then create choice of law rules to determine applicable circuit law. The plaintiff might receive a choice of law privilege that courts should protect in the transfer process, and federal choice of law rules might discourage defendants from forum shopping. Until the fundamental assumptions of the system change, however, courts should treat transfers in accordance with the same assumptions that govern cases that are not transferred, including the assumptions that a single federal law governs all federal issues and that the venue of appeal determines which circuit's law applies in district court. It is not so much that *Van Dusen*'s policies are inapplicable in the federal issue context as that the federal courts are disabled from considering them.

. . .

[Nonetheless,] contrary to the emerging consensus view, . . . MDL courts should apply the law of the transferor court after the conclusion of pretrial proceedings. This result flows from the structure and purposes of the MDL Act. The MDL Act contemplates a remand to the transferor court after the conclusion of pretrial proceedings. As a consequence, the transferor circuit is the ultimate appellate forum, and its law should apply during all phases of the case. Moreover, although there is little direct legislative history, the limited purposes of MDL transfers suggest that Congress did not desire MDL transfers to have outcome-determinative effects. . . .

This result is consistent with the rule that, due to the absence of federal choice of law principles, the venue of appeal determines applicable circuit law. The application of transferor federal law in MDL cases is justified by the same efficiency considerations that require district courts to apply the precedents of their own circuits in cases that are not transferred and in cases that are permanently transferred under section 1404(a). Were an MDL court in Ohio to hold, in accordance with the Sixth Circuit's law, that section 14(a) of the Securities Exchange Act requires proof of scienter, the Second Circuit would overturn this result on ultimate appeal. As a consequence, after remand the federal district court in New York would probably vacate the MDL judge's ruling to save the Second Circuit the trouble and allow the trial to proceed . . . .

[Moreover,] if transferee federal law applies in the MDL context, some cases will be dismissed that would not have been dismissed in the original forum. Thus, applying transferee law will affect settlement value. Because the MDL scheme adopted by Congress suggests that Congress did not intend MDL transfers to have outcome-determinative effects, the *Korean Air Lines* rule is subject to challenge on more than just efficiency grounds. . . .

[A]pplying transferee circuit law in this context poses its own problems. . . . If the MDL circuit court affirms the judgment of dismissal, it is the ultimate appellate venue and the case is never remanded. But if the MDL circuit court reverses the judgment and holds that the MDL district court erred in dismissing the complaint, the case will be remanded to the original forum for trial and an appeal to the transferor circuit. Choice of federal law cannot be made to depend on the substantive result in the transferee circuit court.

Applying transferee law also distinguishes irrationally between final and interlocutory judgments. In our hypothetical, if the plaintiff asserts a section 14(a) claim based solely on allegations of negligence, MDL courts applying the Sixth Circuit's scienter requirement would dismiss this claim, and no remand would be required. If the complaint alleges both negligence and scienter, however, dismissing the negligence count does not prevent the case from being remanded for trial, with any appeal following trial occurring in the Second Circuit.

Applying transferee federal law when the MDL circuit court is the final appellate venue also unfairly favors defendants. If the defendant succeeds in getting an entire complaint dismissed in the courts of the MDL circuit, this result is final and not subject to reexamination. If the MDL courts permit the plaintiff to proceed, however, the defendant gets a second bite at the apple after remand. Thus, the defendant wins if the courts in either circuit are convinced to dismiss the case. The plaintiff must win in both circuits to be allowed to try the case.

Consistency with the rest of the MDL scheme requires that the MDL district and circuit courts apply transferor federal law even in cases that will not be remanded. Congress would do well to remedy this glitch in the legislative scheme.

Notes and Questions

1. At nearly every level, the *Korean Air Lines*-ALI approach to the federal choice of law problem is different than the choice of law approach that is used in the context of state law. Here are the highlights:

(a) For claims based on state law, there may be multiple rules of substantive law, and those differences are honored in making the choice of law analysis. For claims based on federal law, there is in theory only one law. Though in practice there are multiple interpretations of that law, those differences are not, as Professor Ragazzo says, honored.

(b) For claims based on state law, there are well-developed choice of law principles to determine whose law applies. For claims based on federal law, there are no stated choice of law principles; courts are required to follow the law of their own circuit. In the transfer context, however, choice of law principles of some sort must be created. Doesn't the *Korean Air Lines*-ALI approach *sub silentio* adopt a *lex fori* ("law of the forum") principle? In the context of state choice of law rules, a blatant *lex fori* approach, at least on matters of substantive law, would likely be held unconstitutional. See Note 3, p. 803, *supra*. Does the use of that approach here raise any constitutional concerns? Wouldn't any constitutional argument hinge on the dubious proposition that federal courts have a constitutional right to render their own interpretation of federal law? Even if no constitutional concerns are present, does the fact that a *lex fori* approach was never widely adopted by state courts (even before its unconstitutionality became apparent) argue against its use in the federal law context?

(c) For claims based on state law, the federal forum is required to adopt the choice of law rules used by the state courts in the jurisdiction in which they sit. In the federal law context, state courts are not required to use the *lex fori* approach of *Korean Air Lines* or any other principle that the federal courts in the same jurisdiction might use, although the ALI's proposal encourages the use of a *lex fori* approach even if the federal court did not use this approach.

(d) For claims based on state law, a transferee federal forum is required to adopt the choice of law rules that the transferor federal forum would adopt. For claims based on federal law, the transferee forum is free to adopt its own choice of law principle (*lex fori* of the transferee forum) rather than accept the choice of law principle of the transferor forum (*lex fori* of the transferor forum).

2. After *Korean Air Lines*, the federal courts that have considered the question have generally agreed with its holding that the law of the transferee circuit applies to both §1407 transfers. The same rule has also been applied to § 1404 transfers. See, *e.g.*, Campos v. Ticketmaster Corp., 140 F.3d 1166, 1171 n.4 (8th Cir. 1998); Menowitz v. Brown, 991 F.2d 36 (2d Cir. 1993); In re Air Disaster, 819 F. Supp. 1352 (E.D. Mich. 1993); In re Air Crash at Detroit Metropolitan Airport, Detroit, Michigan, on August 16, 1987, 791 F. Supp. 1204, 1212-1213 (E.D. Mich.1992) (transferee circuit law determines whether state or federal preclusion law governs effect of prior judgment), *aff'd*, 86 F.3d 498 (6th Cir. 1996); but see In re The Dow Company "Sarabond" Products Liability Litigation, 666 F. Supp. 1466 (D. Colo. 1987) (transferor circuit law applies to questions of federal law; case decided two months before *Korean Air Lines*).

One narrow exception to *Korean Air Lines* has developed in some courts, and involves a situation in which the relevant federal law incorporated state law as the rule of decision. In this circumstance, "[w]hen the law of the United States is geographically non-uniform, a transferee court should use the rule of the transferor forum in order to implement the central conclusion of *Van Dusen* and *Ferens*: that a transfer under § 1404(a) accomplishes 'but a change of courtrooms'." Eckstein v. Balcor Film Investors, 8 F.3d 1121, 1127 (7th Cir. 1993), cert. denied, 510 U.S. 1073 (1994) (§1404 transfer); accord, Olcott v.

Delaware Flood Co., 76 F.3d 1538 (10th Cir. 1996) (§ 1404 transfer); In re United Mine Workers of America Employee Benefit Plans Litigation, 854 F. Supp. 914 (D.D.C. 1994) (§1407 transfer). *Menowitz* has rejected this exception. 991 F.2d at 39-41.

Isn't there a delicious irony that the circuits have developed different interpretations of the law to be applied to determine the law to be applied when circuits have different interpretations of federal law?

3. That irony also finds voice in the opinions of the Judicial Panel on Multidistrict Litigation. Prior to *Korean Air Lines*, the MDL Panel had intimated that transferor circuit law applied in the transferee court after a §1407 transfer. See In re Plumbing Fixtures Litigation, 342 F. Supp. 756 (J.P.M.L. 1972). After *Korean Air Lines*, the Panel has stated that "[w]hen determining whether to transfer an action under Section 1407 . . . it is not the business of the Panel to consider what law the transferee court might apply" and "[a]ny suggestion to the contrary in [*Plumbing Fixtures*] is withdrawn." In re General Motors Class E Stock Buyout Securities Litigation, 696 F. Supp. 1546, 1547 & n.1 (J.P.M.L. 1988). The Panel further suggested that *Van Dusen* was irrelevant to the issue of which circuit's interpretation of federal law should apply because *Van Dusen* was a diversity case. Id. at 1547 n.1. But see *United Mine Workers*, 854 F. Supp. at 918-19 (rejecting *General Motors* to extent that it suggested that *Van Dusen* was irrelevant to transfer of federal claims that incorporated state law).

Why isn't the law that is to be applied to a federal claim a relevant question in determining whether a multidistrict transfer "will promote the just . . . conduct" of the actions? See 28 U.S.C. § 1407(a). Isn't the Panel burying its head in the sand, and simply refusing to deal with one of the primary reasons that parties located in forums with unfavorable law will want an MDL transfer and one of the primary factors that motivates both sides to argue for a transfer to one forum or another?

4. The D.C. Circuit's choice-of-law holding in *Korean Air Lines*, though widely influential, could ultimately be regarded as dictum. In *Korean Air Lines* the Supreme Court granted certiorari to resolve the differences between the Second and D.C. Circuits on the applicability of the Warsaw Convention. It agreed with the D.C. Circuit that the $75,000 limitation was enforceable. Chan v. Korean Air Lines, 490 U.S. 122 (1989). (Parenthetically, plaintiffs were later able to prove at trial that the limitation was inapplicable because of Korean Air Line's wilful behavior.) One of the most common reasons for the Supreme Court to grant certiorari is that "a United States court of appeals has entered a decision in conflict with the decision of another United States court of appeals on the same important matter." Sup.Ct.R. 10(a). Does this rule, when joined with the Supreme Court's response in *Chan*, demonstrate that the problem of whose interpretation to apply is not especially important? Even though the issue of whose interpretation to apply has arisen in later federal litigation involving § 1404 or § 1407 transfers (see, *e.g.*, cases cited in Note 1, *supra*), only one of those cases has sought Supreme Court review. Review was denied, although the only circuit conflict that the case posed was not on the substantive rule to be applied but on the procedural question of whether there might be an exception to *Korean Air Lines* for some federal claims. See *Eckstein*, 8 F.3d 1121, cert. denied, 510 U.S. 1073.

5. The *Korean Air Lines* approach raises some interesting questions of practical administration. For instance, in *Korean Air Lines*, the determination

of the Warsaw Convention issue did not end the litigation. Unless the cases settled during the MDL proceedings, they would eventually have been remanded to the original forums and tried there. (Indeed, after Lexecon Inc. v. Milberg Weiss Bershad Hynes & Lerach, — U.S. —, 118 S.Ct. 956 (1998) (p. 516, *supra*), a remand will be required.) Once remanded, is a district court in the Second Circuit to apply the law of the Second Circuit or the law of the D.C. Circuit on the Warsaw Convention issue?

Korean Air Lines assumed that, under the "law of the case" doctrine, the D.C. Circuit's ruling would carry back to the original forum and continue to control. Unfortunately, this book does not explore in any detail the "law of the case" doctrine, which as a practical matter is often important in complex and complicated litigation. The sense of the doctrine, however, is that, "in the absence of extraordinary circumstances such as where a prior decision was 'clearly erroneous and would work a manifest injustice,'" a matter previously determined in a case cannot be challenged or re-litigated during later stages of the same case. See Christianson v. Colt Industries Operating Co., 486 U.S. 800, 817 (1988); Public Interest Research Group of New Jersey, Inc. v. Magnesium Elektron, Inc., 123 F.3d 111 (3d Cir. 1997); Joan Steinman, *Law of the Case: A Judicial Puzzle in Consolidated and Transferred Cases and in Multidistrict Litigation*, 135 U. Pa. L. Rev. 595 (1987). *Christianson* also holds that "the doctrine applies as much to the decisions of a coordinate court in the same case as to a court's own decisions." 486. U.S. at 816.

On one level the invocation of the "law of the case" doctrine to handle the remand problem in *Korean Air Lines* seems the proper result: the disparate treatment of parties that are similarly situated under the relevant federal law and that are actually placed together in the same proceeding should be disfavored; revisiting issues decided in the MDL proceeding would undermine some of the efficiencies that the proceeding was designed to create; and a refusal to accept the D.C. Circuit's ruling would create an incentive for the plaintiffs whose cases arose in the Second Circuit to refuse to settle during the MDL proceedings. See generally Stanley A. Wiegel, *The Judicial Panel on Multidistrict Litigation, Transferor Courts and Transferee Courts*, 78 F.R.D. 575 (1977). On another level, though, the invocation of the "law of the case" doctrine raises certain problems. The first is whose "law of the case" doctrine should apply: the doctrine of the transferor circuit or that of the transferee circuit? See Steinman, 135 U. Pa. L. Rev. at 683 ("law of the case" doctrine of transferee forum usually applied, but arguing for opposite result). Second, the purpose of multidistrict proceedings is to streamline pretrial proceedings, not to resolve issues that could be seriously disputed at trial in the transferor court. Third, the transferee court in MDL proceedings often does not grant "law of the case" status to prior rulings of the transferor court, on the theory that a power to revisit prior rulings is necessary to make the MDL proceedings work effectively. See id. at 672-84. There is a certain inequality in allowing the MDL transferee court to discard prior rulings of the transferor court, but not to permit the transferor court to revisit the rulings of the MDL transferee court. Finally, wouldn't the same inefficiency that occurs when a transferee court must determine the law of a transferor court — an inefficiency that was one of the arguments used in *Korean Air Lines* — exist when the transferor court is forced to apply the law of the transferee court on remand?

In contrast to the *Korean Air Lines* dicta, some courts have assumed that a transferor court will apply its own law on remand. For instance, in In re Food

Lion, Inc., Fair Labor Standards Act "Effective Scheduling" Litigation, 73 F.3d 528 (4th Cir. 1996), the MDL court issued orders that dismissed of certain claims of certain plaintiffs, but other claims of those plaintiffs remained alive. Because the MDL orders dismissed fewer than all of the claims of the plaintiffs, plaintiffs could not immediately appeal from the dismissal. The MDL court then remanded the cases to their original forums, and some of the plaintiffs sought to appeal from the MDL orders under Rule 54(b), which allows a final (and therefore appealable) judgment to be entered on a distinct claim in a case. The Fourth Circuit, which was the circuit that encompassed the MDL transferee court, ordered the Judicial Panel on Multidistrict Litigation to re-transfer the dismissed claims to the MDL transferee court, and then ordered the transferee court to enter Rule 54(b) judgments in the cases in order to allow them to appeal the cases to the Fourth Circuit. The reasoning of the Fourth Circuit was that "[a] consolidated appeal, heard by the appellate court having jurisdiction over the transferee district court that entered the orders, is the best means of achieving the goals of efficient and uniform adjudication of numerous actions." Id. at 533. The Fourth Circuit also suggested that the "better practice" would have been for the transferee court to have entered a Rule 54(b) judgment before remand of the cases occurred. See also In re American Honda Motor Co. Dealerships Relations Litigation, 958 F. Supp. 1045 (D. Md. 1997) (entering order permitting interlocutory appeal from order refusing to dismiss certain claims in MDL case.)

Do some of these practical difficulties call the wisdom of *Korean Air Lines* into question? Or does the *Food Lion* solution adequately address and avoid the difficulties?

6. The ALI's proposal essentially adopts the *Korean Air Lines* rule. But it takes no position on many of the issues that the prior Notes have raised. Since the ALI's proposal would permit transfer for all purposes, rather than just for pretrial purposes, some of these issues will no longer be relevant. Recall as well that the ALI's proposal permits transfer to a state court, and encourages state courts to make an independent determination of federal law. Such a determination would be subject to Supreme Court review. 28 U.S.C. § 1257. As a practical matter, however, does the ALI's proposal encourage further fracturing in the interpretation of federal law? Is there anything unfair about forcing a plaintiff that located a case in federal court because of its favorable interpretation of federal law to accept a less expansive determination of federal law from a state court?

7. The issue of whose interpretation of federal law should control in § 1404 and § 1407 transfers has received a fair amount of scholarly attention. The seminal article is Richard L. Marcus, *Conflicts among the Circuits and Transfers within the Federal Judicial System*, 93 Yale L.J. 679 (1984). In addition to Professor Ragazzo's contribution, other recent articles include Kimberly J. Norwood, *Double Forum Shopping and the Extension of* Ferens *to Federal Claims that Borrow State Limitations Periods*, 44 Emory L.J. 501 (1995); Ross D. Cooper, *Civil Procedure: The* Korean Air *Disaster: Choice of Law in Federal Multidistrict Litigation*, 57 Geo. Wash. L. Rev. 1145 (1989).

8. The *Korean Air Lines*-ALI approach partially deprives the plaintiff of her venue privilege; she can no longer control, through selection of the forum, the law that will apply to her claim. Of course, since a court's ruling on the choice of law question is never certain, she does not always control the law even when she does pick the forum. Nor is she entirely powerless to affect the choice under the *Korean Air Lines*-ALI approach; she can still argue either against transfer

or for transfer to a favorable forum. Granting these factors, however, the approach on issues of federal law represents a marked paradigm shift from the standard "master of the complaint" approach of adversarial litigation.

What justifies this shift? *Korean Air Lines* was not a complex case. While it was a complicated case, the Warsaw Convention issue was not the matter that made the case complicated, nor did the resolution of that issue reduce the complications that the case presented. (Indeed, the ruling actually increased the complication, for now plaintiffs needed to pursue another, fact-intensive way of overcoming the Warsaw Convention.) Is *Korean Air Lines* best understood as a case in which it seemed inequitable to permit two plaintiffs, both injured in the same accident and both present in the same courtroom, to receive different treatment under a law that is, in theory, uniform for both of them? But suppose that the cases of the two plaintiffs raised both state law and federal law issues (as *Korean Air Lines* did). Isn't it unfair to use one principle (the law of the transferor forum) for some issues and a different principle (law of the transferee forum) for other issues? How can that be explained to the plaintiff?

If inequitable treatment is the concern that drives *Korean Air Lines*, note how it is the reverse of the trans-substantive concern that we have raised through this book. The trans-substantive concern comes into play when differing procedures that are used to resolve like cases result in different outcomes. Here the concern is that the same procedure (use of a *lex fori* principle) applied in like cases will result in different outcomes; or, put differently, that a different procedural rule (contrary to the one used to resolve state law claims) must be adopted to guarantee the same substantive outcome for like cases. Which, ultimately, is more important: like procedural treatment even when it results in disparate substantive outcomes, or like substantive outcomes even when it requires disparate procedural treatment to obtain the outcomes? Isn't this a variant of the question with which we began the book: Whether procedure is substance's servant or its equal?

Some of the problems raised in this Note could be avoided in either of two ways. One way would be to reject *Korean Air Lines* and apply the law of the transferor forum to federal claims. The opposing way would be to reject *Van Dusen* and *Ferens* and apply the law of the transferee forum to state law claims. Which approach is preferable? As the analysis of *Van Dusen* and *Ferens* suggested (see pp. 817-19, *supra*) notions of efficiency indicate that *Van Dusen* and *Ferens* should be abandoned, although the question was not entirely clear. An analysis based on overcoming dysfunction also did not clearly favor one approach over another. In terms of unequal treatment, both approaches will result in unequal treatment of state law claims, since neither the choice of law principle of the transferor forum nor the choice of law principle of the transferee forum will necessarily guarantee equal substantive treatment of both plaintiffs. But only the latter approach — the application of transferee law to all claims — will prevent unequal treatment of federal claims. So, perhaps, the *Korean Air Lines* approach should be used, at least presumptively, for claims based both on state law and on federal law. *Van Dusen* and *Ferens* should be overruled, not because they themselves create more inefficiency or dysfunction, but because our trans-substantive ideal prefers that the federal and state choice of law principles be the same, and only the *Korean Air Lines*-ALI approach also assures like substantive treatment of like parties on their federal claims.

Is this analysis sound? Does it adequately address the question with which this Note began: Why change the "master of the complaint" rule? Indeed, doesn't this analysis, if accepted, create an even bigger hole in this adversarial cornerstone? Should that cornerstone remain in place unless it becomes a cause of dysfunction?

9. A different response to the analysis in the last Note is that it focuses on second stage manifestations of the problem, rather than the root cause. As we have observed before, the real problem may be the plethora of state laws and state choice of law rules; resolving the *Van Dusen-Ferens-Korean Air Lines* issue does nothing to address this larger concern. As the analysis in Note 1, *supra*, suggests, however, the manner in which the courts have resolved federal claims provides some useful insights into how this larger concern might be addressed. With respect to section (a) of Note 1,, the federal approach provides two possible responses to the "plethora of state laws" problem: either replace the non-uniformity of state law with a nationally uniform standard, or shut our eyes to the existence of non-uniformity and pretend that all state law is of one piece. With respect to section (b) of Note 1, the federal approach would suggest the choice of law principles for state law claims be made simpler, more uniform, and lead more clearly to the application of a limited number of state laws.

Obviously, these various solutions to the state choice of law problem are not all consistent with each other, and some of them would require re-interpretation or change in constitutional law. See pp. 797-804, *supra*. In the following section, we discover that, under various guises, different courts and commentators faced with the state choice of law conundrum have adopted or recommended the adoption of each of these approaches.

B. EXPANDING THE SOLUTION TO CLAIMS BASED ON STATE LAW: ALTERNATIVES AND THEIR LIMITS

The last section suggested that one solution to choice of law problems in complex cases is to have the court in which the case is filed (or, in the event of transfer, to which the case is transferred) apply a single, consistent substantive law for all claimants. That solution, which creates problems enough in the context of theoretically uniform federal law, creates enormous problems in the context of state law, which is not uniform in theory or practice. In light of the Full Faith and Credit clause, the due process clause, and *Erie*, where would a state or federal judge get the authority to declare a single substantive law for claims arising under the laws of various states?

Declaration of a single substantive law is not, however, the only possible way to avoid the complications of the choice of law inquiry. A second option would be to create a single choice of law rule, and structure that rule in such a way that a limited number of substantive state laws would govern the entire controversy. As we saw, state choice of law rules vary a great deal, and none inexorably lead to the equitable application of a limited number of rules. Moreover, to the extent that the cases are filed in federal court, *Klaxon* stand squarely in the way of such a solution. Does a state or federal court have the constitutional power and the institutional competence to overcome these difficulties?

The third option is to manipulate the present system. With the exception of the presently disfavored *lex loci* rules, most choice of law approaches used in states today are malleable, and there are usually no more than four or five (rather than fifty) views on the principles applicable to a particular controversy. In many cases enough squishiness exists in present choice of law rules to steer the case to the point where only a limited set of substantive principles applies to the case. Does such a result-oriented approach to choice of law adequately respect the reasons that we have choice of law rules in the first instance? Does it respect the policies behind the Full Faith and Credit clause and *Klaxon*? Does it give too much discretion to a judge to let the case come out in the way that she wants?

A final approach is to muddle along with the present system, being faithful to the Full Faith and Credit, due process, *Erie*, and doctrinal concerns explored in the last section. This approach preserves the maximal adversarial right of plaintiffs to select the best forum, even if it does sometimes create dysfunction or inefficiency, and even if it results in disparate treatment of similarly situated (but for the applicable law) victims.

This section examines some of the approaches that courts have used or commentators have recommended to handle state choice of law problems. The cases and commentaries fit into one or the other of the first three approaches that were just described. Do not, however, be misled. Nearly all complex cases opt for the final approach, the one that we examined in the last section. The cases and commentary you will read are the exceptions to the norm; but, as exceptions, they are vitally important. As you read these materials, you will also see some familiar themes: the bending of the usual rules of litigation to the needs of the complex or complicated case, the concern for judicial legitimacy, adversarialism, and equitable treatment of like persons and claims.

1. Manipulating Traditional Choice of Law Rules in Complex and Complicated Cases

IN RE AIR CRASH DISASTER NEAR CHICAGO, ILLINOIS ON MAY 25, 1979

644 F.2d 594 (7th Cir.), cert. denied, 454 U.S. 878 (1981)

■ SPRECHER, Circuit Judge. This case presents complex conflicts-of-law questions regarding the allowance of punitive damages in wrongful death actions arising out of an air crash disaster. The law of the place of the disaster, the law of the place of manufacture of the airplane, and the law of the primary place of business of the airline do not allow punitive damages; but, the law of the primary place of business of the manufacturer of the airplane and the law of the place of maintenance of the airline do allow punitive damages. We find that, under each of the applicable state choice-of-law rules, punitive damages cannot be allowed against either the manufacturer or the airline.

I

The stark facts of the tragedy resulting in this litigation are undisputed. On May 25, 1979, a DC-10 jet airplane, designed and built by McDonnell Douglas Corporation ("MDC"), operated by American Airlines ("American") was scheduled to fly from Chicago, Illinois to Los Angeles, California as American's Flight 191. Shortly after takeoff from O'Hare International Airport, however, the plane lost an engine and crashed in the immediate vicinity of the airport. All two hundred seventy-one persons aboard the plane, and two persons on the ground, were killed.

Now there are one hundred eighteen wrongful death actions arising out of the crash. These cases were originally filed in Illinois, California, New York, Michigan, Hawaii, and Puerto Rico.[1] Many of the complaints allege wrongful death counts which request awards of punitive as well as compensatory damages. The plaintiffs and their decedents are and were residents of California, Connecticut, Hawaii, Illinois, Indiana, Massachusetts, Michigan, New Jersey, New York, Vermont, Puerto Rico, Japan, the Netherlands, and Saudi Arabia.

The defendants in these cases are MDC and American. MDC is a Maryland corporation having its principal place of business, now and at the time of the accident, in Missouri. The plaintiffs contend MDC's conduct in the design and manufacture of the DC-10 was egregious. That alleged misconduct occurred in California. American is a Delaware corporation. American's place of business prior to 1979 was New York. During 1979, American moved its principal place of business to Texas. Some plaintiffs contend that, on the date of the crash, American's principal place of business was in Texas, but American contends that its principal place of business on that date was New York. The plaintiffs contend that American's conduct regarding the maintenance of the DC-10 was egregious. That alleged misconduct occurred in Oklahoma, site of American's maintenance base.

Both defendants moved in district court to strike the claims for punitive damages on the ground that such claims failed to state legally sufficient claims for relief. . . .

Using the choice-of-law rules of each state where these actions had originally been filed, the district court arrived at the following results. Under the Illinois "most significant relationship" test, the district court found that the law of the state of the principal place of business should prevail with regard to the issue of punitive damages. Finding that New York was American's principal place of business at the time of the crash and does not allow punitive damages, and that Missouri, MDC's principal place of business, does allow the equivalent of punitive damages, the court allowed the motions to strike punitive damage claims against American but not against MDC.

---

1. The cases have been transferred to the Northern District of Illinois for pretrial purposes by order of the Judicial Panel on Multidistrict Litigation.

Under the California "comparative impairment" test, the district court held that the policies of the state of the principal place of business would be impaired more than the policies of the state of misconduct if those policies were not applied. Thus, the court allowed the motion to strike punitive damage claims with regard to American but not with regard to MDC. The district court reached the same result with regard to the actions filed in New York, Michigan, Puerto Rico, and Hawaii.

Although generally agreeing with the district court regarding which states allow punitive damages and the choice-of-law theories to be used, we reach a different result in applying those theories. For the reasons discussed below, we find that the motions to strike claims of punitive damages should be granted with regard to both MDC and American.

II

At the outset, we must first determine whether we confront "real" rather than "apparent" conflicts between the laws to be applied. This requires a determination, first, of the law regarding punitive damages in the relevant states: Illinois, Missouri, California, Oklahoma, New York, Texas and Hawaii. After this determination, it will then be necessary to determine the conflict-of-law theories of the forum states and to apply those theories. . . .

[W]e find that the "line-up" of the states involved regarding the issue of punitive damages is as follows: Illinois, place of the injury, does not allow punitive damages. Missouri, MDC's principal place of business, does allow punitive damages, but California, place of MDC's conduct, does not. New York, one principal place of business of American, does not allow punitive damages while Texas, another principal place of business of American, does. Oklahoma, the place of American's conduct, does allow punitive damages. [The court deferred discussion of Hawaii law.] . . .

IV

We now confront the actual conflicts issues among the various states. It is not disputed that, since federal jurisdiction is based on diversity of citizenship, the choice-of-law rules to be used are those choice-of-law rules of the states where the actions were originally filed. Klaxon Co. v. Stentor Electric Mfg. Co., 313 U.S. 487 (1941); Van Dusen v. Barrack, 376 U.S. 612 (1964) . . . .

In general, we must attempt to determine which, if any, of the states having some relationship to the parties or to the crash has the most significant interest in the application of its own substantive law to the merits of the punitive damage issue. The application of choice-of-law rules is not a mechanical process of cranking various factors through a formula. Critical to conflicts analysis is the notion that we must examine the choice-of-law rules not with regard to various states' interests in general, but precisely, with regard to each state's interest in the specific question of punitive damages. Thus, we approve the concept of "depecage": the process of applying rules of different states on the basis of the precise issue involved.

. . .

V

We begin with the actions filed in Illinois. The Illinois courts apply the "most significant relationship" test of the Restatement (Second) of Conflict of Laws ("Restatement (Second)") to determine the applicable law in wrongful death actions. This test incorporates a presumption that the local law of the state where the injury occurred should govern, unless another state has a "more significant relationship" to the occurrence or to the parties....

A

Turning to defendant MDC, the precise issue, of course, is which state's law regarding the availability of punitive damages should apply. The states having contacts to be taken into account are: Illinois, place of injury, California, place of MDC's alleged misconduct; Missouri, MDC's principal place of business; and, if it can be determined, the states where the relationship between the parties is centered.

It is unclear where the relationship of the parties is "centered"....

We next turn to the interests of the states of domicile of the plaintiffs. The domiciliary states do not have an interest in disallowing punitive damages because the decision to disallow such damages is obviously designed to protect the interest of resident defendants, not to effectuate the interest of domiciliary states in the welfare of plaintiffs....

Nor do the domiciliary states have an interest in imposing punitive damages on the defendants.... Once the plaintiffs are made whole by recovery of the full measure of compensatory damages to which they are entitled under the law of their domiciles, the interest of those states is satisfied.

We thus turn to the interests of the three relevant states, Illinois, California, and Missouri....

[The Court then reviewed the interests of California and Missouri in applying their punitive damages law to this case and concluded:] Thus, we find that the balance on the scales of significant contacts is even: we cannot say that either California or Missouri has a "greater" interest in the decision whether to allow punitive damages against MDC. This situation involves a total and genuine conflict: one jurisdiction allows punitive damages, the other does not. There does not seem to be any way to arrive at a "moderate and restrained" interpretation of either policy so as to avoid a true conflict.

With the scales evenly balanced, we now turn to the interest of Illinois, the place of injury. The old rule in many jurisdictions, developed from torts other than air crashes, was that where there was nothing fortuitous about the fact that the injury occurred in a given state, great weight would be given to the law of the place of injury. But air crash disasters often present situations where the place of injury is largely fortuitous.... That the injury in our case occurred in Illinois can only be described as fortuitous. Had the DC-10's engine fallen off later, the injury might have occurred in one of any number of states. Because the place of injury is much more fortuitous than the place of misconduct or the principal place of business, its interest in and ability to control behavior by deterrence or punishment, or to protect defendants from liability, is lower than that of the place of misconduct or principal place of business. Also, merely as the place of injury, Illinois would not have strong interests in protecting nonresident defendants from excessive financial liability.

But the fact that the interest of the place of injury is less than the interest of the principal place of business and the interest of the place of alleged misconduct does not mean that Illinois has no interest in the punitive damages question. Illinois has very strong interests in not suffering air crash disasters and also in promoting airplane safety. . . .

Also, in this case Illinois is more than merely the place of injury. As noted before, many of the other contacts of significance were in Illinois. With regard to the actions filed in Illinois, all but two of the decedents resided in Illinois. As the home of O'Hare International Airport, one of the world's busiest airports, Illinois certainly has strong interests in encouraging air transportation corporations to do business in the state.

Because Illinois has such strong interests in promoting airline safety, it would have a strong interest in allowing punitive damages to deter corporate misconduct relating to air safety. But because Illinois also has such strong interests in having airlines fly into and out of the state, and having related air transportation companies do business within the state, it would have a strong interest in protecting air transportation companies by disallowing punitive damages. Thus, the decision made by the Illinois legislature must be accorded special weight.

As noted earlier, Illinois' choice-of-law law gives presumptive importance to the place of injury. The law of the place of injury is to be supplanted only when another state has a more significant relationship than the place of injury. Restatement (Second) § 175. Although either California or Missouri, taken separately, would have a greater interest than Illinois, the fact that the laws of these states are in absolute conflict indicates that neither state has an interest greater than the other's. Thus, in terms of a principled basis upon which a choice can be made, neither state has a "more significant interest" than Illinois. Since neither California nor Missouri can be chosen on a principled basis, the application of the "most significant relationship" test leads to the use of Illinois law.

Finally, application of Illinois law comports with the general criteria of the Restatement (Second) which emphasize certainty, predictability, uniformity of result, and ease in the determination and application of the law to be applied. In this case, it is important to resolve the conflict between states by a principled means. Determining that all other factors being equal, the law of the place of injury shall be used, provides a principled means of decision which also creates certainty. . . .

Our result also comports with the Restatement (Second)'s principle that choice-of-law rules should be relatively simple and easy to apply. Restatement (Second) § 6, at 10. We conclude, therefore, that under the "most significant relationship" test, the law of Illinois should apply. For the above reasons, we grant MDC's motion to strike punitive damages claims.

B

We now apply the Illinois "most significant relationship" test to American. The significant contacts to be examined are the place of injury, the place of alleged misconduct, the principal place of business, and the place where the relationship between the parties is centered. As discussed with regard to MDC, the place of injury is Illinois and the place where the relationship between the parties is centered is either Illinois or California. Neither of these states allows punitive damages. The place of American's alleged misconduct is Oklahoma, site of its maintenance base, which does allow punitive damages. [New York, which was American's principal place of business, does not allow punitive damages.]

Just as we concluded with regard to MDC, we conclude that the place of conduct and the principal place of business each have strong interests in having its law applied to the punitive damages question; we are unable to say that one state's interest is greater than the other. Thus, we follow the same analysis used above in concluding that, under the "most significant relationship" test, when the interests of the states of alleged misconduct and primary place of business are equal and in a true and total conflict, the law of the place of injury is to be used.

Again, we emphasize that this result in no way signifies a return to the mechanical, wooden law of *lex loci delicti*. Rather, it emphasizes the fact that there must be some principled method of decision when the standard "interest analysis" of conflicts law cannot settle the question. Moreover, as discussed above, the choice of Illinois law is particularly appropriate here. Illinois has strong interests in both protection of airline corporations and in the deterrence of wrongful conduct by those corporations. Therefore, we affirm the district court's decision to strike the claims for punitive damages against American with regard to the actions filed in Illinois.

VI

We now turn to the actions filed in California. California follows the "comparative impairment" approach to choice-of-law questions. . . . The resolution of conflicts under this test is as follows. First, the respective laws of interested states are examined to ensure that there is an apparent conflict. . . . There is such a conflict with regard to both MDC and American because, in both situations, the law of the place of alleged misconduct differs from the law of the principal place of business.

Second, when an apparent conflict is found to exist, the court reexamines the applicable laws and circumstances to see if a "moderate and restrained interpretation" of both the policy and the circumstances reveals that only one state has a legitimate interest in the application of its policy. . . . But as discussed with regard to the actions filed in Illinois, both the principal place of business and the place of alleged misconduct have strong interests in the protection of defendants and the deterrence of wrongful conduct. We see no restrained or moderate interpretation of either state's policy which can resolve this conflict.

When, as here, the reexamination of an apparent conflict reveals no way in which the conflict can be resolved by a restrained or moderate interpretation, the conflict is indeed a "true" conflict. The comparative impairment analysis "proceeds on the principle that true conflicts should be resolved by applying the law of the state whose interest would be the more impaired if its law were not applied." ... This approach does not involve the court in "weighing" the conflicting governmental interests in the sense of determining which law represents "better" social policies. Such an approach would vitiate the policies of federalism which, within constitutional limits, allow states to determine their own policies as they wish. ... Rather, the process used by the comparative impairment approach is "'essentially a process of allocating respective spheres of lawmaking influence.'" .... This process of allocation involves several steps. First, of course, the states with relevant interests must be identified. ...

[T]he principal place of business and the place of alleged misconduct have strong and equal relevant interests. These states have the interests of deterrence of misconduct or protection of local corporations .... Illinois, the state in which the injury occurred, also has an important interest in the application of its law because it is a state in which both the policies of protection of airline corporations and deterrence of misconduct are peculiarly important. Also as discussed with regard to the Illinois test, the domiciliary states of the plaintiffs and their representatives do not have significant interests in the punitive damages question.

The comparative impairment theory requires that the court attempt to determine the relative commitment by each interested state to the law involved. ... This examination of relative commitment examines two factors: (1) the current status of a statute and the intensity of interest with which it is held; and (2) the "comparative pertinence" of the statute: the "fit" between the purpose of the legislature and the situation in the case ....

A

Applying California's "comparative impairment" analysis to MDC, we begin with Missouri. [After reviewing the current status and "fit" of the conflicting interests of Missouri and California, the court concluded that] we are unable to say that either state's interest would be impaired less by the failure to apply its policy.

We now turn to the place of injury, Illinois. As discussed above, Illinois does have significant interests under the facts of this case. ...

Illinois was severely affected by this major disaster and Illinois also has strong interests in the protection of airplane-related industries. Because Illinois does have unique interests in both the awarding and the denial of punitive damages, the decision of its legislature to deny punitive damages must be given special attention. For these reasons, then, we find that, all other factors being equal, the interests of Illinois tip the scales against the allowance of punitive damages.

The use of Illinois' interests as the deciding factor regarding the substantive question of punitive damages also comports with principles of certainty and uniformity. Our result under current California choice-of-law law is consistent with our result under Illinois choice-of-law law, which requires the adoption of the law of the place of injury, unless another state has a greater interest in the application of its law. Although California choice-of-law law does not require this result, nothing in our approach is inconsistent with California law. . . .

For all of the foregoing reasons, therefore, we reverse the district court and grant MDC's motion to strike the punitive damage claims with regard to the actions filed in California.

B

We now consider the punitive damage claims sought against American, with regard to the actions filed in California. . . . [The Court then undertook an analysis of the interests New York and Oklahoma in the application of their law, and found that] there is a true and equal conflict between the punitive damage rules of the principal place of business and of the place of the alleged misconduct. Each state's interest will be equally impaired if the rule of the other state were used. . . .

As we did in the analysis regarding MDC, we now turn to the state with the next strongest relevant interest, Illinois. For the reasons discussed with regard to the claims against MDC, it seems proper that Illinois law, which does not allow punitive damages, should be the deciding factor. For the foregoing reasons, therefore, we hold that, with regard to the actions filed in California, the motions to strike punitive damage claims against American are granted.

[In Parts VII through X of its opinion, the court performed similar choice of law analyses for the cases filed against MDC and American in New York, Michigan, Puerto Rico, and Hawaii, concluding in each instance that Illinois law controlled either because of the conflict between the punitive damage rules of the principal place of business and the principal place of alleged misconduct or because of the *lex loci* rule of some states.]

XI

In conclusion, we agree with the district court's comments on the problems involved in determining choice-of-law issues in airplane crash cases. Airline corporations and airplane manufacturers are subject to uniform federal regulation in almost every aspect of their operations, except their liability in tort. As recently as 1978, a bill was introduced in Congress to establish a federal cause of action for injuries suffered through aviation activity. . . . If this bill, or any of its predecessors, had passed, those actions would all be governed by federal law, uniform as to liability and damages, rather than by the varying laws of a number of states. . . . Along with the district court, we conclude that it is clearly in the interests of passengers, airline corporations, airplane manufacturers, and state and federal governments, that airline tort liability be regulated by federal law. Of course, we are well aware of the fact that it is up to Congress, and not the courts, to create the needed uniform law.

For the foregoing reasons, the orders of the district court in denying the motions to strike punitive damage claims against MDC are reversed, while its orders granting such motions with regard to American are affirmed.

Notes and Questions

1. The result in the *Chicago Air Crash* case is both exceptional and famous. It is exceptional because, in most aggregated cases, the traditional method of applying the law of each relevant forum will lead to the application of different states' laws, some of which will be at odds with each other. Are you convinced that the Seventh Circuit's conclusion that all of the claims are governed by the same law is merely a happy fortuity resulting from the neutral, objective application of each state's choice of law rules? Or did the court's desire to simplify the litigation and make it manageable influence its holdings? If the individual cases in *Chicago Air Crash* had never been transferred by the MDL Panel to Illinois, do you think that all of the transferor forums would have concluded that the plaintiffs are not entitled to punitive damages? Did transfer actually affect the substantive law to be applied — despite the commands of *Klaxon* and *Van Dusen*?

The case is famous because of the court's herculean effort to wade through the conflicts rules of many states and apply them to a series of legal issues in dispute. The lengthy opinion, only a small portion of which is reproduced here, demonstrates the difficulty of the traditional, case-by-case approach to choice of law issues in complex or complicated cases. Moreover, the Seventh Circuit's opinion followed on the heels of an equally lengthy and detailed analysis of the same conflicts rules by the district court — which, using those same rules, had come to a different conclusion on the applicable law for half of the punitive damages issues!

The American Law Institute cited *Chicago Air Crash* as an example of what is wrong with the traditional choice of law approach in complex litigation. The Seventh Circuit's result, the ALI said, "underscores the lack of predictability in the choice of law regime as it is applied today." American Law Institute, Complex Litigation 307 (1994). Other academic commentary has been less restrained. Professor Lowenfeld has said that "the airplane cases in the 1970s and 1980s seem to have made a parody not only of the conflict of laws but of the law of torts in general." Andreas Lowenfeld, *Mass Torts and the Conflict of Laws: The Airline Disaster*, 1989 U. Ill. L. Rev. 157, 158. Professor Kramer has called the opinion "a virtual 'how-to' manual of ways to manipulate choice-of-law analysis." Larry Kramer, *Choice of Law in Complex Litigation*, 71 N.Y.U. L. Rev. 547, 555 (1996). Kramer was especially unimpressed by the "fancy footwork" the Seventh Circuit performed to say that domiciliary states had no interest in the application of their punitive damage rules and by its decision to break the tie between two interested states "by choosing the law of an avowedly less interested third state" — a result that impaired the interests of both states. Id. at 556-57. Kramer also criticized the Seventh Circuit's misreading of New York's choice of law rules and its "grotesque distortion" of Michigan's choice of law rules, although those discussions were edited out of the opinion you read. Id. at 557-59.

2. *Chicago Air Crash* is not alone. Other mass tort cases that were transferred to one federal court have undertaken similar analyses, with similar

outcomes: the application of one or of a limited number of laws. See In re Paris Air Crash of March 3, 1974, 399 F. Supp. 732 (C.D. Cal. 1975) (applying California law); In re Union Carbide Corp. Gas Plant Disaster, 634 F. Supp. 842 (S.D.N.Y.), *aff'd*, 809 F.2d 195 (2d Cir. 1986) (applying law of India under all approaches); In re Air Crash Disaster at Sioux City, Iowa, on July 19, 1989, 734 F. Supp. 1425 (N.D. Ill. 1990) (applying law of single jurisdiction to all claims against each of three defendants). See generally James A.R. Nafziger, *Choice of Law in Air Disasters: Complex Litigation Rules and the Common Law*, 54 La. L. Rev. 1001 (1994) (analyzing 62 state and federal cases decided between 1960 and 1993, and finding that single law was usually applied).

The same trend toward the manipulation of choice of law rules in order to select one or a limited number of laws can be seen in large-scale business litigation. See Harmsen v. Smith, 693 F.2d 932 (9th Cir. 1982), cert. denied, 464 U.S. 822 (1983) (creating presumption of applying forum law and requiring defendant to prove that other laws of other states are applicable and interests of other states would be impaired); In re Seagate Technologies Securities Litigation, 115 F.R.D. 264 (N.D. Cal. 1987).

3. Professor Nafgizer's analysis of choice of law decisions in airplane crash litigation makes an important point: Although the cases that we have studied in this chapter arose in federal court, the problem of applying multiple rules of substantive law, as well as the temptation to manipulate the state's choice of law rule to have a single law apply, also exist in state court. See Nafgizer, 54 La. L. Rev. 1065-84 (analyzing 22 state cases). One difference in the state and federal cases, however, is that the choice of law question in the state cases is more straight-forward: Subject only to the limitation imposed by *Allstate* and *Shutts*, the state court will adopt its own choice of law rule. The question in the federal system is complicated by the overlay of *Klaxon* and, in transferred cases, by the overlay of *Van Dusen* and *Ferens* as well. These latter problems do not exist in state court.

4. At the same time, it would be a mistake to think that every state and federal court has manipulated choice of law rules in order to make a single or a limited number of laws to apply. Many of the reported cases finding that differing choice of law rules require the application of different laws to different plaintiffs are class actions. Often these courts hold either that the multiple laws would make the class action unmanageable or that individual issues predominate over common ones; class treatment is, therefore, denied. See Ilhardt v. A.O. Smith Corp., 168 F.R.D. 613 (S.D. Oh. 1996), and cases cited in *Complex Litigation*, supra, at 347-48; but see In re: The Prudential Insurance Co. of America Sales Practices Litigation, 962 F. Supp. 450 (D. N.J. 1997) (finding differences in state law not to be so great as to make case unmanageable). To sidestep this problem, some courts conditionally certify the case as a class action without performing an in-depth choice of law analysis and reserve the right to decertify the class if choice of law concerns turn out to make the case unmanageable. See Maywalt v. Parker & Parsley Petroleum Co., 147 F.R.D. 51 (S.D.N.Y. 1993).

The class action cases remind us about what is at stake with regard to the choice of law question. An inability to limit the number of substantive laws that apply might not only make the case a nightmare to litigate and try, but it might also might lead a court not to aggregate a case at all.

5. Would there be anything wrong in admitting candidly that, when it is necessary to avoid dysfunction or inefficiency, courts can "bend" their usual state

choice of law principles to achieve the application of a manageable number of substantive state laws? Is this approach any different than simply creating special choice of law rules for complex or complicated cases? Since a change in choice of law principles might well be outcome-determinative, can the difference in treatment of routine and complicated cases be justified? Can the difference in treatment of routine and complex cases be justified?

One of the problems of such an approach is that it would need to be accomplished state-by-state, and it is unlikely that every state will agree that its choice of law principles need to bend or be changed in the face of complex or complicated litigation. Some of this difficulty could be eliminated by overruling *Klaxon* in complex and/or complicated litigation, permitting federal courts to adopt their own choice of law principles in such litigation, and requiring that these choice of law principles strongly prefer the application of a single state law or a manageable number of state laws. But that solution too would likely be inadequate, since it would drive parties that wanted a more favorable choice of law rule into the state courts and make the aggregation of related litigation more difficult.

6. An argument to sidestep these problems would be that state choice of law rules that require the adoption of an unmanageable number of state laws are unconstitutional. Could such an argument be made? It is difficult to see how it could be made with respect to complicated litigation; although the unmanageable number of state laws is causing inefficiency, there is probably no constitutional right to rules that guarantee more efficient litigation. With respect to complex litigation, however, the argument should by now be a familiar one. The due process clause guarantees rational adjudication (defined to mean the guarantee of a judgment, entered after reasoned application of the law to the facts, that provides an efficacious remedy for all similarly situated parties); the dysfunction caused by an unmanageable number of state laws threatens rational adjudication; therefore, the choice of law rules that require the adoption of an unmanageable number of state laws is unconstitutional. The weak spot in the argument is the first premise — particularly whether the due process clause makes the guarantee of reasoned judgment applicable to those not necessarily before the court. A second weak spot is that the elimination of dysfunction-causing state choice of law rules is not necessarily required. The constitutional right (if it exists) is a guarantee of rational adjudication; if other means that we have studied or will study can protect the right, a court would not in addition be able to change state choice of law rules.

Granting the last point to be true, how is a court to choose which method or combination of methods should be used to eliminate dysfunction? Should concerns for efficiency enter in at this point, so that the court should use the methods that lead to an efficient and speedy resolution of the case?

7. Using the analysis in the last Note, and accepting the assumption that *Chicago Air Crash* did in fact manipulate state choice of law rules to simplify the litigation, was the manipulation appropriate? The answer seems to be "No." *Chicago Air Crash* was not complex; the ability of parties and nonparties to obtain effective relief, based on reasoned judgment, was not in jeopardy. Nor is it obvious that *Chicago Air Crash* was complicated; although the elimination of the punitive damage issue streamlined the litigation, the maintenance of two tracks of claims (those entitled to receive punitive damages and those that were not) would not have created any significant inefficiencies in the litigation. What, then, drove *Chicago Air Crash* to manipulate the choice of law rules of the

relevant states? Was it simply that, as in *Korean Air Lines* (see p. 820, *supra*), the court could not stomach the dissimilar substantive treatment in one court of identically injured victims? However compelling that desire for substantive equality might have been in *Korean Air Lines*, which involved theoretically uniform federal law, isn't it an inevitable consequence of a federal system, in which different states can choose non-uniform substantive laws, that some identically situated victims will be treated differently than others? How much weight should be placed on federalism interests in complex litigation? Do they outweigh the constitutional interest in rational adjudication?

8. Even if manipulation or change of state choice of law rules is the most effective means of addressing a constitutional imperative of rational adjudication, a court still needs to determine the choice of law rules that should be applied to reduce the number of state laws to a manageable number. Should the rules be *lex loci*? Most significant contacts? Interest analysis of some form? Should the choice depend on the nature of the litigation. For instance, *Chicago Air Crash* was a single event mass tort — everyone was injured in the same place by the same conduct. There was one and only one state — Illinois, the state in which the injury occurs — that could legitimately assert an interest in everyone's claim. Assuming that *Chicago Air Crash* had been a complex case that was a legitimate candidate for choice of law manipulation, it is tempting to return in such circumstances to the old *lex loci* rule.

On the other hand, as Professor Juenger noted (see pp. 791-92, *supra*), the *lex loci* rule works less well in dispersed mass torts, such as DES or asbestos cases, in which the injuries occur in many different states. In these cases, choosing the law of the place of the wrongful conduct may better guarantee the use of a single law — although, even here, it does not work especially well when there are multiple defendants making products in different states. Moreover, if we adopt the law of the place of the wrong, we need to worry about the possibility that states with large manufacturing concerns have liability rules more favorable to manufacturers than to victims.

Is obtaining a single rule of law so important that we should tolerate these substantive effects? Rather than letting the law of any single state win, should we develop some new body of law to resolve the litigation? The following two subsections explore two different sources in which such a body of law might be grounded; after these subsections, we return to the question of developing choice of law principles that limit to a manageable number the state laws that might apply to a complex or complicated case.

2. Creating Federal Common Law

In *Chicago Air Crash*, the Seventh Circuit suggested that one way out of the state choice of law conundrum was to create uniform federal law to deal with the dispute. Two possible sources for this federal law exist: Congressional enactment or court-created federal common law. It is unrealistic in many situations to expect that Congress will pass legislation that both provides a rule of decision for a complex or complicated case already pending in court *and* pre-empts all state law remedies. Insofar as the parties and the court are concerned, the only realistic avenue for the application of federal law is federal common law. After *Erie*'s clear (and constitutionally derived) holding that there is no "federal general common law," however, is there any room for a court to create such law? Might the concerns of complex or complicated litigation be an adequate ground for a court's authority? If so, why should people in ordinary cases receive different legal rules than people in complex or complicated cases?

KOHR v. ALLEGHENY AIRLINES, INC.

504 F.2d 400 (7th Cir. 1974), cert. denied, 421 U.S. 978 (1975)

■ SWYGERT, Chief Judge. Defendants-appellants Allegheny Airlines, Inc. and the United States, appeal from the dismissal of their cross-claims and third-party complaints for indemnity and contribution against defendants-appellees Brookside Corporation (Brookside), Forth Corporation (Forth is a wholly-owned subsidiary of Brookside), and the estate of Robert W. Carey. The instant actions arise out of a mid-air collision on September 9, 1969, in the airspace over Fairland, Indiana between an Allegheny Airlines DC-9-31 jet aircraft and a Piper Cherokee aircraft piloted by Robert W. Carey and owned by Forth. . . .

As a result of the mid-air collision both aircraft were totally destroyed and all eighty-three occupants were killed.

[Wrongful death actions and suits for damage to the planes were filed in various federal courts on the basis of diversity of citizenship as to defendants Allegheny, Brookside, Forth, and the estate of Carey, and on the basis of the Federal Tort Claims Act as to the United States. The Judicial Panel on Multidistrict Litigation transferred the cases to the United States District Court for the Southern District of Indiana. In a move now prohibited by *Lexecon* (see p. 516, *supra*) the district court judge subsequently issued orders pursuant to 28 U.S.C. § 1404 transferring cases from the transferor forums to his court, and consolidated the cases with the companion cases that had been initially filed in his court. Allegheny and the United States then filed cross-claims and third-party complaints against Brookside, Forth, and the estate of Carey seeking indemnity and contribution.

[An agreement was arrived at between the United States and the liability insurers of Allegheny for a pro-rata formula to be utilized between them in disposing of all cases, whether by settlement or judgment. Under the settlement Allegheny and the United States retained their claims for indemnity and contribution against Forth, Brookside, and the estate of Carey. The court granted motions of Forth, Brookside, and the estate of Carey to dismiss these claims because Indiana law did not allow indemnity and contribution after settlement.]

Allegheny urges that a federal rule of contribution and indemnity should govern in the instant action. Failing the application of a federal law of contribution Allegheny contends that in view of the multiplicity of state jurisdictions involved, with the various plaintiffs instituting actions in numerous states other than Indiana, the trial judge should have conducted an evidentiary hearing to facilitate a proper choice of law analysis. Had the district judge done so, it is claimed that jurisdictions other than Indiana would be found to have a more substantial interest in having their laws on contribution and indemnity applied. In addition, Allegheny contends that even assuming Indiana law controls, the district court misapplied the rules on contribution and indemnity. . . .

Were it necessary, we would be inclined to agree with Allegheny that the district judge failed to engage in an adequate conflict of laws analysis and that he erred on the application of Indiana law on contribution and indemnity. We need not reach these issues, however, for we agree with Allegheny that there should be a federal law of contribution and indemnity governing mid-air collisions such as the one here. . . .

The basis for imposing a federal law of contribution and indemnity is what we perceive to be the predominant, indeed almost exclusive, interest of the federal government in regulating the affairs of the nation's airways. Moreover, the imposition of a federal rule of contribution and indemnity serves a second purpose of eliminating inconsistency of result in similar collision occurrences as well as within the same occurrence due to the application of differing state laws on contribution and indemnity. Given the prevailing federal interest in uniform air law regulation, we deem it desirable that a federal rule of contribution and indemnity be applied.

That the federal interest in regulating airways is predominant was long ago recognized by Justice Jackson in Northwest Airlines v. Minnesota, 322 U.S. 292, 303 (1944) . . . . With the passage of the Federal Aviation Act of 1958, 49 U.S.C. §§ 1301, et seq., Congress expressed the view that the control of aviation should rest exclusively in the hands of the federal government. In section 1108 of the Act, 49 U.S.C. § 1508(a), it is clearly provided that:

> (a) The United States of America is declared to possess and exercise complete and exclusive national sovereignty in the airspace of the United States . . . .

The explicit objective of the Act is to foster the development of air commerce. 49 U.S.C. § 1346. To that end, it has been recognized that the principal purpose of the Act is to create one unified system of flight rules and to centralize in the Administrator of the Federal Aviation Administration the power to promulgate rules for the safe and efficient use of the country's airspace. . . . When the notion of federal preemption over aviation is viewed in combination with the fact that this litigation ensues from a mid-air collision occurring in national airspace, that the Government is a party to the action . . ., and that this litigation has since its inception been subject to the supervision of the Judicial Panel created by the Multidistrict Litigation Act . . ., there is no perceptible reason why federal law should not be applied to determine the rights and liabilities of the parties involved. The interest of the state wherein the fortuitous event of the collision occurred is slight as compared to the dominant federal interest. Accordingly, the rights and liabilities of Allegheny and the United States are peculiarly federal in nature and are to be governed by a federal rule of contribution and indemnity. . . .

[The court then held that, under federal common law, the "better rule" of contribution and indemnity among joint tortfeasors was a rule "of contribution and indemnity on a comparative negligence basis."]

IN RE "AGENT ORANGE" PRODUCT LIABILITY LITIGATION

635 F.2d 987 (2d Cir. 1980), cert. denied, 454 U.S. 1128 (1981)

■ KEARSE, Circuit Judge. This appeal presents the question whether claims asserted by veterans of the United States armed forces against companies which supplied the United States government with chemicals that are alleged to have been contaminated and to have injured the veterans and their families, are governed by federal common law. Defendants-appellants Diamond Shamrock Corporation, Monsanto Company, Thompson-Hayward Chemical Company, Hercules Incorporated and the Dow Chemical Company were the manufacturers of various herbicides including "Agent Orange" (hereinafter collectively referred to as "Agent Orange") for use by the military as defoliants in the Vietnam War. The plaintiffs, veterans of that war and their families, allege that they have sustained various physical injuries by reason of the veterans' exposure to Agent Orange. Plaintiffs seek redress of those injuries under federal common law, and have invoked the "federal question" jurisdiction of the district court. 28 U.S.C. § 1331(a) (1976). Defendants contest the existence of a federal common law cause of action, and moved below to dismiss for want of jurisdiction. The United States District Court for the Eastern District of New York, George C. Pratt, Judge, denied their motion. Defendants obtained certification of the jurisdiction issue and took this appeal pursuant to 28 U.S.C. § 1292(b) (1976).

We agree with defendants that there is no federal common law right of action under the circumstances of this litigation. Accordingly, we reverse.

I

The present litigation began in late 1978 and early 1979, when several individual veterans and their families commenced actions in the Northern District of Illinois and the Southern and Eastern Districts of New York, claiming injury from the veterans' exposure to Agent Orange and purporting to represent several classes of injured persons and persons allegedly "at risk" of injury. . . . By order of the Judicial Panel on Multidistrict Litigation, thirteen such actions, involving thirty named plaintiffs, were transferred to the Eastern District of New York and assigned to Judge Pratt for coordinated or consolidated pretrial proceedings pursuant to 28 U.S.C. § 1407 (1976). Subsequently, additional actions were filed and were transferred to the Eastern District. It appears that there are presently more than 800 named plaintiffs in these proceedings. . . .

What marks these proceedings as somewhat extraordinary are the size of the plaintiff class and the scope of the relief that is sought. Plaintiffs purport to represent the 2.4 million veterans who served as combat soldiers in Southeast Asia from 1962 through 1971, as well as most of the families or survivors of those veterans. Fifteen plaintiff subclasses are identified; many of these subclasses consist of persons who are "at risk" of, but have yet to sustain, various physical injuries. Plaintiffs have alleged that "the combined liquid assets of the 'corporate defendants' will be insufficient to fully compensate the entire class of plaintiffs." Plaintiffs therefore seek, in addition to unspecified damages, a decree requiring defendants, upon a determination of liability, to establish

> a trust found out of the current earnings of the defendants in the nature of a reserve against the claims of all the individual members of the plaintiff class to insure that the compensation of any group of individual plaintiffs will not impair the rights of those not before the Court at that time.

Plaintiffs also seek a permanent injunction against further manufacture of Agent Orange. . . .

Plaintiffs argue that federal common law should be applied to their claims principally because of the unique federal nature of the relationship between the soldier and his government, relying chiefly on United States v. Standard Oil Co., 332 U.S. 301, 305 (1947) ("Perhaps no relation between the Government and a citizen is more distinctively federal in character than that between it and members of its armed forces."). They contend that this interest brings the case within the doctrine of Clearfield Trust Co. v. United States, 318 U.S. 363, 366 (1943), which held that, in order to ensure uniformity and certainty," [the] rights and duties of the United States on commercial paper which it issues are governed by federal rather than local law." Plaintiffs argue that the government similarly has an interest in having all of its veterans compensated by government contractors who manufactured or marketed Agent Orange, and that application of the respective state laws would impede recovery on a uniform basis.

The district court rejected the contention that *Clearfield Trust* stated the controlling principle, recognizing that the United States, a party to *Clearfield Trust*, is not party to the plaintiffs' claims here.[6] Rather, the court recognized that since the present action involves only private parties, the federal common law issue is controlled by the principles set forth in Miree v. DeKalb County, 433 U.S. 25 (1977), and Wallis v. Pan American Petroleum Corp., 384 U.S. 63 (1966). After reviewing the latter decisions, the district court applied a three-factor test to determine whether federal common law governs plaintiffs' claims:

> (1) the existence of a substantial federal interest in the outcome of a litigation; (2) the effect on this federal interest should state law be

---

[6]. We note that the defendants have impleaded the United States in the present action. It is clear, however, that the jurisdiction of the district court over the claims of the plaintiffs is not enhanced by third party complaints. Cf. Louisville & Nashville RR. Co. v. Mottley, 211 U.S. 149 (1908).

applied; and (3) the effect on state interests should state law be displaced by federal common law. . . .

[T]he district court ruled that plaintiffs had stated valid causes of action under the federal common law. The court therefore held that it had subject matter jurisdiction over the case, and denied defendants' motion to dismiss. This appeal followed.

II

Both plaintiffs and defendants accept the three-part test that the district court applied to the federal common law issue, and for purposes of discussion we accept that framework. But, focusing our consideration chiefly on the first factor of the test, *i.e.*, "the existence of a substantial federal interest in the outcome of the litigation," we disagree with the district court's analysis and conclude that the court gave insufficient weight to the Supreme Court's repeated admonition that

> [in] deciding whether rules of federal common law should be fashioned, normally the guiding principle is that a *significant conflict between some federal policy or interest and the use of state law in the premises must first be specifically shown.* . . .

Wallis v. Pan American Petroleum Corp., 384 U.S. at 68 . . . . Principally we reject the district court's conclusion that there is an identifiable federal policy at stake in this litigation that warrants the creation of federal common law rules.[11]

In considering plaintiffs' contentions, it is essential to delineate precisely the relation of the United States to the claims here at issue. These claims are brought by former servicemen and their families against private manufacturers; they are not asserted by or against the United States, and they do not directly implicate the rights and duties of the United States. They are thus unlike the claims in *United States v. Standard Oil Co., supra*, in which the government brought suit to recover for its payments to a soldier injured as a result of the defendant's negligence, and *Clearfield Trust Co. v. United States, supra*, in which the government brought suit to enforce its rights in commercial paper issued by it. In each of those cases the government was a party seeking to enforce its own asserted rights, and analysis reveals two federal concerns which are inherent in such cases. First, the government has an interest in having uniform rules govern its rights and obligations. Second, the government has a substantive interest in the contents of those uniform rules. The first interest prizes uniformity for its own sake and is content-neutral; it does not dictate the substance of the federal common law rule to be applied. Thus, in *United States v. Standard Oil Co., supra*, the Court applied federal common law, recognizing the government's interest in uniformity, but refused to impose the liability argued for by the United States as the substance of that law.

---

11. Since we conclude that there is not now an identifiable federal policy, we need not reach the second and third factors of the test and speculate as to how state law, if it were already developed, would affect the federal policy if it were identifiable — or vice versa.

The present litigation is fundamentally different from *Standard Oil* and *Clearfield Trust* with respect to both uniformity interest and substantive interest in the content of the rules to be applied. Since this litigation is between private parties and no substantial rights or duties of the government hinge on its outcome, there is no federal interest in uniformity for its own sake.... The fact that application of state law may produce a variety of results is of no moment. It is in the nature of a federal system that different states will apply different rules of law, based on their individual perceptions of what is in the best interests of their citizens. That alone is not grounds in private litigation for judicially creating an overriding federal law....

The second fundamental difference between the present litigation and the *Clearfield Trust* type of case is that in the latter, the government's substantive interest in the litigation is essentially monothetic, in that it is concerned only with preserving the federal fisc, whereas here the government has two interests; and here the two interests have been placed in sharp contrast with one another. Thus, the government has an interest in the welfare of its veterans; they have given of themselves in the most fundamental way possible in the national interest. But the government also has an interest in the suppliers of its material; imposition, for example, of strict liability as contended for by plaintiffs would affect the government's ability to procure materiel without the exaction of significantly higher prices, or the attachment of onerous conditions, or the demand of indemnification or the like.... [U]nlike a simple uniformity interest, neither the government's interest in its veterans nor its interest in its suppliers is content-neutral. Each interest will be furthered only if the federal rule of law to be applied favors that particular group.

The extent to which either group *should* be favored, and its welfare deemed "paramount" is preeminently a policy determination of the sort reserved in the first instance for Congress. The welfare of veterans and that of military suppliers are clearly federal concerns which Congress should appropriately consider in setting policy for the governance of the nation, and it is properly left to Congress in the first instance to strike the balance between the conflicting interests of the veterans and the contractors, and thereby identify federal policy. Although Congress has turned its attention to the Agent Orange problem, it has not determined what the federal policy is with respect to the reconciliation of these two competing interests....

We conclude that in the present case, while the federal government has obvious interests in the welfare of the parties to the litigation, its interest in the *outcome* of the litigation, *i.e.*, in how the parties' welfares should be balanced, is as yet undetermined. The teaching of *Wallis* and *Miree* is that before federal common law rules should be fashioned, the use of state law must pose a threat to an "identifiable" federal policy.... In the present litigation the federal policy is not yet identifiable. We conclude, therefore, that the district court erred in ruling that plaintiffs' claims were governed by federal common law. The order denying defendants' motion to dismiss for lack of subject matter jurisdiction is accordingly

Reversed.

■ FEINBERG, Chief Judge (dissenting).... That the present case is *sui generis*, and national in proportions, is evident from the complaint itself....

[T]hat the plaintiff veterans and the defendant contractors have opposing interests in this litigation hardly means that the paramount federal interest is somehow divided or self-contradictory.... [T]he United States' interest in the "welfare" of defendants cannot approach, either in magnitude or in quality, its interest in the welfare of the Agent Orange plaintiffs. In short, in the case before us the paramount interests of the United States are in the welfare of its veterans and in their fair and uniform treatment....

Having discerned a significant federal interest, we are next required to determine whether or not a "significant conflict" exists between that interest and the application of state law.... [I]f the laws of 30 or 40 state jurisdictions are separately applied, veterans' recoveries will vary widely — despite the fact that these soldiers fought shoulder to shoulder, without regard to state citizenship, in a national endeavor abroad. In sum, the federal interest here in uniformity would be defeated by the application of discrete and differing state laws.

The third and last factor involves the extent to which state interests would be affected, if state law were to be "displaced" by federal common law in the present case.... I agree with Judge Pratt's conclusion that the claims made by plaintiffs in this unique and unprecedented litigation do not fall within the developed area of state tort law.... [T]he states' product liability law is in flux; with respect to a case as novel as the one before us, a consistent and established body of state law is less discernible. Accordingly, I think Judge Pratt was correct in holding that that the application of federal common law would not "displace state law, because there is no substantial body of state law on this issue to be displaced. I thus conclude that all three factors, accepted by the majority as the proper analytical framework, point to the use of a federal common law rule in the present case, giving rise to federal question jurisdiction.

Notes and Questions

1. The creation of federal common law has a couple of significant advantages. First, as *Agent Orange* states, when federal common law governs a claim, federal courts have § 1331 "arising under" jurisdiction over the claim. See Textile Workers Union of America v. Lincoln Mills of Alabama, 353 U.S. 448 (1957). (The same would not be true if federal common law governed a defense, as opposed to a claim. See pp. 312-25, *supra*.) As we have seen, federal courts are often a better forum for the aggregation of related cases. Since the presence of a federal question makes it easier for a federal court to exercise jurisdiction over supplemental state law claims, since federal questions are always removable should the plaintiff choose to bring the case in state court, and since federal judges may have some limited powers of removal even when neither party chooses to remove the case (see pp. 348-60, 374, 388-89, *supra*), the existence of federal common law is a great aid in the reduction of joinder complexity or complication. Second, federal common law is *the* rule of decision

for the relevant claim or issue; although state law may still govern related claims or issues, federal common law displaces state law with respect to the precise claim or issue at stake. The displacement of fifty potentially different bodies of law with one reduces the number of issues that a court must address during the pretrial and trial phases, thus reducing or eliminating those forms of complexity or complication.

2. Can both *Kohr* and *Agent Orange* be right? Can they both be wrong? Are you satisfied that the law of indemnity and contribution in airplane crashes contains sufficient federal interests to create federal common law, and the law of product liability for harms done to our nation's soldiers in a foreign conflict contains insufficient federal interests to create federal interests? Is the outcome in *Agent Orange* determined by the holding in *Day & Zimmerman, Inc. Challoner*, 423 U.S. 3 (1975) (p. 805, *supra*) that state choice of law rules governed a product liability claim arising out of the Vietnam War, and the implicit assumption underlying that holding that non-federal law provided the rule of decision for the claim?

3. One way to "reconcile" the two cases is to place them in their historical contexts. *Kohr* was decided just two years after Illinois v. City of Milwaukee, Wisconsin, 406 U.S. 91 (1972), in which the Court authorized the use of federal common law to deal with the problem of interstate pollution. *Illinois v. Milwaukee* is probably the modern high water mark of the courts' power to create federal common law. After Miree v. DeKalb County, 433 U.S. 25 (1977), which was decided after *Kohr* but before *Agent Orange*, the power began to recede.

That recession continued in Texas Industries, Inc. v. Ratliff Materials, Inc., 451 U.S. 630 (1981), which was decided about six months after *Agent Orange*. In *Texas Industries*, the Court held that the courts had no federal common law power to create a rule of contribution for antitrust claims, even though those claims were based on federal law. *Texas Industries* suggests that courts can create federal common law only in circumstances "in which a federal rule of decision is 'necessary to protect uniquely federal interests,'... and those in which Congress has given the courts the power to develop substantive law." 451 U.S. at 640. The first category, the Court said, included cases that "only in such narrow areas as those concerned with the rights and obligations of the United States, interstate and international disputes implicating the conflicting rights of States or our relations with foreign nations, and admiralty cases." Id. at 641. The second category required that the congressional intent to permit courts "to create governing rules of law" be clearly expressed. Id. at 642.

Nonetheless, the tide seemed to have reversed itself, at least temporarily, in Boyle v. United Technologies Corp., 487 U.S. 500 (1988), in which the Court held that the existence and elements of the government contractor defense (which was also involved in *Agent Orange*) should be determined under federal common law. The Court stated that the circumstances under which state law would hold government contractors liable for work done at the federal government's behest involved "uniquely federal interests." Id. at 504. The Court also held that, in the context of this defense, "uniquely federal interests" were "a necessary, not a sufficient, condition for the displacement of state law. Displacement will occur only where... a 'significant conflict' exists between an identifiable 'federal policy or interest and the [operation] of state law,' or the application of state law would 'frustrate specific objectives' of federal legislation." Id. at 507. The Court found that a significant conflict existed because federal contractors might be liable for conduct for which the federal government, had it made the product in question, would have been immune from suit. The result is especially interesting because Congress had considered, and never enacted numerous bills that would have established a defense rather like the one that *Boyle* created through federal common law.

Because *Boyle* created a new type of "unique federal interest" not included within the categories listed in *Texas Industries*, it has been read as inconsistent with the narrower understanding of federal common law suggested by *Texas Industries*. See, *e.g.*, Michael D. Green & Richard A. Matasar, *The Supreme Court and the Products Liability Crisis: Lessons from* Boyle*'s Government Contractor Defense*, 63 S. Cal. L. Rev. 637 (1990). *Boyle* does not presently appear, however, to mark a new direction in courts' power to create federal common law; later cases have again receded to the basic categories suggested in *Texas Industries*. See Atherton v. Federal Deposit Insurance Corp., 519 U.S. 213 (1997); O'Melveny & Myers v. Federal Deposit Insurance Corp., 512 U.S. 79 (1994). But the trend is not entirely uniform. See Musick, Peeler & Garret v. Employers Insurance of Wausau, 508 U.S. 286, 292 (1993) (creating federal common law of contribution for Rule 10b-5 securities actions; since Rule 10b-5 actions were judicially created, courts could create "ancillary" common law rules for those actions).

4. Does the holding and analysis in *Texas Industries* strike a dagger through the heart of *Kohr*'s creation of a federal common law of contribution and indemnity, or does the involvement of the United States in *Kohr* or the result in *Musick, Peeler* save *Kohr*'s result? Cf. Overseas National Airways, Inc. v. United States, 766 F.2d 97 (2d Cir. 1985) (rejecting federal rule of contribution to be used by United States in aviation litigation). Does *Boyle* suggest that *Agent Orange* was wrong in not creating a federal law of liability to deal with the injuries of service personnel, or rather that the case was right? Could there be an insufficient basis for federal common law to govern the elements of the plaintiff's prima facie claim, but a sufficient basis for federal common law to govern the manufacturer's affirmative defense?

5. The ability of a federal court to create federal common law is not the last step in the analysis. Even when the *power* to create federal common law exists, courts still need to discern the *content* of the federal rule. In a number of situations, courts have, as a matter of discretion, chosen to adopt as the federal rule the relevant state rule. See DeSylva v. Ballentine, 351 U.S. 570 (1956); United States v. Kimbell Foods, Inc., 440 U.S. 715 (1979); *O'Melveny & Myers*, 512 U.S. 79. In *Kimbell Foods*, the Court described the appropriate analysis:

> Whether to adopt state law or to fashion a nationwide federal rule is a matter of judicial policy "dependent upon a variety of considerations always relevant to the nature of the specific governmental interests and to the effects upon them of applying state law." . . .
>
> Undoubtedly, federal programs that "by their nature are and must be uniform in character throughout the Nation" necessitate formulation of controlling federal rules. . . .Conversely, when there is little need for a nationally uniform body of law, state law may be incorporated as the federal rule of decision. Apart from considerations of uniformity, we must also determine whether application of state law would frustrate specific objectives of the federal programs. If so, we must fashion special rules solicitous of those federal interests. Finally, our choice-of-law inquiry must consider the extent to which application of a federal rule would disrupt commercial relationships predicated on state law. [440 U.S. at 728-29.]

For a defense of this approach, see Henry J. Friendly, *In Praise of Erie — And of the New Federal Common Law*, 39 N.Y.U. L. Rev. 383 (1964). For trenchant criticism, see Martha A. Field, *Sources of Law: The Scope of Federal Common Law*, 99 Harv. L. Rev. 881 (1986). In a multistate case in which state law is adopted as the federal rule of decision, whose state law should apply? Must a court (as in *Klaxon*) apply the choice of law rule of the forum? Does the possibility that these problems will arise make the use of federal common law even less desirable to use than state law?

6. The power to create federal common law and its content are difficult questions, both theoretically and practically. These notes skim over some very deep waters. For more detailed treatments, see Richard H. Fallon et al., Hart & Wechsler's The Federal Courts and the Federal System 744-810 (4th ed. 1996) and the sources cited; Symposium, 12 Pace L. Rev. 227 (1992).

7. Neither *Kohr* nor *Boyle* would appear to have been a complex case; *Agent Orange* was. Is one of the lessons of these cases that the question of complexity is irrelevant to the question of whether federal courts have the power to create federal common law? Or should another category be added to the *Texas Industries* list, so that courts have the power to create federal common law in cases whose complexity can be eliminated by federal common law? Exactly what would be the source of such power? Many of the circumstances involving "unique federal interests" are grounded in the Constitution; for instance, the power to create admiralty law or the law in State-to-State disputes derives from the federal courts' Article III jurisdiction to hear such cases, and the power to create law for international relations or with government contractors derives from the Article I and Article II powers. Could the same argument be made for complex litigation: that the due process clause guarantees rational adjudication and implies the power to make law that overcomes complexity? In order to avoid unnecessary clashes with the federalism and separation of powers concerns, should the courts' law-making power be restricted just to those cases in which no other means of avoiding dysfunction exist? If a federal court has power to create federal common law every time that a constitutional provision is implicated, how much state law will remain? See generally Jackson v. Johns-Manville Sales Corp., 750 F.2d 1314 (5th Cir. 1985) (no federal common law for punitive damages in asbestos cases); In re Joint Eastern and Southern Districts Asbestos Litigation, 129 B.R. 710 (E. & S.D.N.Y. 1991) (no federal common law for set off and contribution rights in asbestos settlement), vacated on other grounds, 982 F.2d 721 (2d Cir. 1992), modified, 993 F.2d 7 (2d Cir. 1993).

Even if such a power could be created in complex cases, could a similar power be made to create federal common law to reduce the inefficiencies associated with complicated litigation?

8. Although it was addressing a different point, the Supreme Court has expressed some hostility to the argument that the peculiar needs of particular litigation can lead to the creation of federal common law. In *O'Melveny & Myers*, 512 U.S. 79, the FDIC argued that it required a single, federal rule regarding a defense that persons might raise in suits brought by the FDIC as receiver of a failed bank. The Supreme Court held that here was an insufficient conflict between state and federal law to warrant the creation of a federal common law defense. Along the way, the Court observed:

> There is not even at stake that most generic (and lightly invoked) of alleged federal interests, the interest in uniformity. The rules of decision at issue here do not govern the primary conduct of the United States or any of

its agents or contractors, but affect only the FDIC's rights and liabilities, as receiver, with respect to primary conduct on the part of private actors that has already occurred. Uniformity of law might facilitate the FDIC's nationwide litigation of these suits, eliminating state-by-state research and reducing uncertainty — but if the avoidance of those ordinary consequences qualified as an identifiable federal interest, we would be awash in "federal common-law" rules. [Id. at 88.]

Does *O'Melveny & Myer* eliminate the ability to argue for federal common law in complex litigation? In complicated litigation?

9. *Texas Industries* also states that Congress can authorize courts to create federal common law. Should Congress legislate such authority in complex or complicated litigation? Will Congress be able to define the cases to which this power extends with enough clarity that the power will be neither underinclusive nor overinclusive? For a legislative proposal to extend the power of making common law to "mass torts," see Linda S. Mullenix, *Class Resolution of the Mass-Tort Case: A Proposed Federal Procedure Act*, 64 Tex. L. Rev. 1039, 1091, 1095 (1986). For a criticism that this approach would lead to uncertainty and lack of uniformity, see American Law Institute, Complex Litigation 314 (1994).

10. What might federal common law look like? Will the rules for large disputes be more favorable to corporate defendants? Will they give plaintiffs new powers to extort settlements from businesses? Is it desirable to apply one set of rules to small disputes and another set to large disputes? Since federal common law also guarantees access to a federal forum, will federal courts become the repository of "big" cases and state courts will become a backwater of minor litigation? Since "big" cases are often the ones that spur substantive and procedural reform, will state law stagnate and atrophy?

3. Creating National Consensus Law

If it is neither doctrinally possible nor theoretically desirable for courts generally to create federal common law, the affected states might achieve some of the advantages of federal common law by agreeing, as a matter of their own common law, to sacrifice their parochial interests in their own law and adopt a single consensus law. How likely is this scenario?

IN RE "AGENT ORANGE" PRODUCT LIABILITY LITIGATION

580 F. Supp. 690 (E.D.N.Y. 1984)

■ WEINSTEIN, Chief Judge. A considerable number of Vietnam war veterans resident in all or almost all states, Puerto Rico and the District of Columbia and a number of foreign countries, and members of their families, claim to have suffered injury as a result of the veterans' exposure to herbicides in Vietnam. Defendants produced those herbicides. Individual claims, originally filed in all parts of the country, were transferred for pretrial purposes to this court. Subject to some powers to opt out, common issues presented by plaintiffs' claims will now be tried together since a class has been certified pursuant to Rule 23....

As required by Klaxon Co. v. Stentor Elec. Mfg. Co., 313 U.S. 487 (1941), this court has examined the conflict of law rules of the states in which the transferor courts sit. Van Dusen v. Barrack, 367 U.S. 612 (1964). For the reasons set forth below, it is concluded that under the special circumstances of this litigation, all the transferor states would look to the same substantive law for the rule of decision on the critical substantive issues.

I. Introduction...

[G]iven the special facts of this litigation, under any approach utilized today, so far as can reasonably be predicted, the result would be the same: each state would probably apply the same law, that is to say either federal or national common law....

In view of a growing consensus about what the law governing manufacturer's liability is — a problem to be dealt with in a subsequent opinion — there is a convergence between the result required in the instant case under the separate state conflicts of law rules and the separate state substantive tort rules. Thus, the obviously sensible result of treating members of this nation's armed forces and their families in essentially the same way for any injuries suffered in a national war fought on foreign soil would, it is now provisionally found, be reached by each of the states....

Essentially, there are five different conflicts of laws methodologies widely used in this country. These may be summarized as (1) traditional or Restatement (First) based upon Professor Beale's work, (2) Restatement (Second) being in large part a pragmatic and conservative revision by Professor Reese of Professor Currie's interest analysis school, (3) governmental interest, (4) Leflar, and (5) forum. There is a sixth proposed approach that has some of the aura of Leflar, but which we treat separately as the von Mehren approach. Some states use a combination or variation of these techniques.... For purposes of this opinion, we have eschewed specific discussion of the effects of modern doctrine leading to renvoi ... or the increased likelihood of depecage ..., though, as will be seen, both doctrines are implicated in the present case. Finally, it is unnecessary to consider whether any state's conflict of law rule would deprive a litigant of due process, equal protection, or other constitutional right since each of the states whose conflict rule might apply has sufficient nexus with the matter through residence or the like....

III. *Conflict of Laws Rules*

While there are a number of analogous approaches and decisions, none is directly on point in connection with the special conflicts of law issue now posed. Accordingly, since "no clearly discernable and clearly applicable conflicts rule has been announced by the ... state, the rule must be hypothesized to correspond with all available indices of what the rule would be if presently formulated" by the state courts....

[The court examined how the approaches of the *Restatement (Second) of Conflicts*, governmental interest, LeFlar's better law, *lex loci*, and forum law would resolve the liability, government contract defense, and punitive damages issues in the case. After finding that these approaches generally supported the use of national consensus law in the unique circumstances of the case, the court turned to Professor von Mehren's approach.]

F. *von Mehren — Reconciling Conflicts*

The increasing incidence of conflicts of law problems result in large measure from the fact that the social, economic and technical worlds we live in far exceed in geographic scope the legal jurisdictions which establish and enforce controlling law.

One method of solving the conflict is for the forum state to create appropriate substantive law recognizing the policies of the various jurisdictions having an interest in the dispute. As von Mehren put it:

> The clash of values or policies that has arisen within the ad hoc community of concerned states is to be resolved not by considering what value or policy of the forum can be advanced but rather by determining how the forum would, in general, resolve the clash in question. The most obvious and general basis for making this determination is reasoning by analogy from the results reached in wholly domestic situations involving comparable clashes. Multistate situations involving true conflicts would thus present, just as do analogous domestic situations, the problem of deciding which among conflicting policies are, in general, to be preferred.

von Mehren, *Choice of Law and the Problem of Justice*, 41 Law and Contemporary Problems 34 (Spring 1977) . . . .

In most cases the choice of one jurisdiction's domestic law would suffice. But in some instances a molding of the conflicting substantive laws to achieve a viable alternative compromise acceptable to the larger overarching community would be sensible and just. One approach is that of compromise.

> . . . If a unitary source is not posited, compromises — designed to take competing views and policies into account and to advance harmony within a multistate order — can hardly be viewed as necessarily or inherently unjust. On the contrary, compromise as a principle of justice becomes understandable and attractive.

Id. at 38-39. And when the legislature does not act to make the necessary compromises, the courts must act. Id. at 39.

Most of the examples given by von Mehren involve two party cases that recur over and over again as a result of the use of our multistate road systems. How much more apt is the approach he posits where tens of thousands are involved in what is alleged to be a single and unique national disaster with repercussions in scores of jurisdictions.

There is much logical merit and conceptual appeal in von Mehren's suggestion of individually crafted compromise statements of substantive law to meet the choice of law problems where the domestic substantive law of none of the states having contacts with the parties and their disputes should control. In run-of-the-mill conflicts situations this approach would lead to excessive lack of predictability and cost. The burden on the system would be greater than the benefits in most cases since lawyers and judges would spend too much time on customizing the law in individual cases and there would undoubtedly be increased appeals and reversals when trial and appellate court judgments on what was sound in the particular case diverged. Nevertheless there are special cases with unique circumstances not likely to recur in the future where von Mehren's approach suggests the only sound method. Such a situation is now presented.

The overwhelming need for a uniform approach and a single substantive standard is obvious. Normally we would expect Congress to recognize this and provide a federal statute which would be all encompassing or which would leave lacunae to be filled by the federal court directly or through absorbtion of state law. Although it could do so under its commerce or war powers, Congress has not enacted such a statute.

Given a failure of the legislature and the executive, the federal courts could be expected to step in by creating federal common law to cover a national problem. But the Second Circuit has blocked that route by denying that federal substantive law controls of its own force. Thus, under *Klaxon*, we look to the states to accomplish the sound result. As a federal court we sit as a surrogate for the state courts, attempting to predict how pragmatic and wise state judges would address the problem.

It is entirely reasonable to assume that the state courts would recognize the strong national interest in a uniform national rule. A considerable number of states have already recognized the unique nature of the *Agent Orange* litigation problem. Given the strong state-federal interest in uniformity, the lack of a federal statute or of a uniform state statute, and the Second Circuit opinion denying that federal common law controls of its own force all substantive issues in *Agent Orange*, what would state courts do? Would they not look to the first court that dealt with the issue or to a neutral body to formulate the uniform rules they could all accept for this unique litigation? And is not a federal court charged with adjudicating all or nearly all the *Agent Orange* cases such a body? Professor von Mehren's analysis suggests that the answer to each of these questions is yes.

Once it is conceded, as we think it must be, that each of the jurisdictions involved would appreciate the overwhelming need for uniformity, to what single state's law could any state look to as controlling? Given the plethora of states and nations with contacts and the impossibility without a full trial of even knowing where the allegedly offending dioxin was produced, it becomes apparent that no acceptable test can point to any single state. Thus, the law is driven in this most unusual case to either federal or national consensus substantive law as the only workable approach.

G. *National Consensus Restated*

At most, a state's contacts in an "Agent Orange" suit would consist of the individual plaintiff veteran's residence in that state — a factor readily subject to change in our transient society — and the fact that one of the seven defendant companies is either incorporated, has its principal place of business or manufactured its Agent Orange in that state. At the risk of restating the obvious, those contacts are dwarfed by the national contacts in the case. The only jurisdiction with which all elements in the litigation undoubtedly have significant contacts, and the only unifying factor, is the nation. . . .

The application of a federal or national consensus common law to all substantive issues is consistent with the relevant decisions of the state courts and the federal courts sitting as state courts under *Erie* and *Klaxon*. Although the national and international contacts and interests present in this case are far greater, in both quantity and quality, than that of any heretofore decided, a number of state and federal courts have had occasion to deal with choice of law issues in mass tort situations where the interests of dozens of jurisdictions, including the United States, have been implicated.

In the litigation most clearly analogous to Agent Orange for present purposes, the federal court for the District of Columbia, sitting in a diversity case as a local District of Columbia court, had to decide the law applicable to claims arising out of the crash near Saigon of an Air Force C-5A carrying United States military and civilian personnel and 226 Vietnamese orphans. In re Air Crash Disaster Near Saigon, South Vietnam on April 4, 1975, 476 F. Supp. 521 (D.D.C. 1979). The specific issue before the court related to the survival of decedents' causes of action. It noted that the District of Columbia follows the "interest analysis" methods in choice-of-law. It analyzed the relevant interests as follows:

> The United States government (as distinguished from any state of the United States) carried on [the Vietnam] war and ended it for national foreign policy and military purposes. . . . It is a "paramount" interest and concern of the United States federal government that its courts provide a just and reasonable resolution of claims such as those on behalf of the estates of the deceased orphans. . . .

It applied District of Columbia law of survival to all parties despite the fact that plaintiffs resided all over the United States, and that Lockheed Aircraft Corp., a defendant with the United States, had its chief place of business and place of incorporation outside the District. District of Columbia law was really only a euphemism for a national substantive law of liability. Rejecting traditional conflicts of law, the court relied upon the *sui generis* nature of the case. . . .

Because of the *sui generis* nature of this litigation, it is not surprising that there are no cases directly on point. It is, however, common to find state courts and federal courts sitting as state courts under *Erie* applying federal law, because of the predominant federal interest in the litigation. . . . Thus, state courts will often look to federal law if they feel it is appropriate.

That neither New York nor, as far as we have ascertained, any state has had a case such as this one before us does not permit our throwing up our hands and refusing to decide the question. Perhaps it would have been better if certification rules permitted posing the conflicts question to the more than half-a-hundred jurisdictions involved. But no such procedure is presently in place. In the meantime, this court must ascertain the living state law as best it can. The "evolutionary growth" of the law of conflicts means that each "litigant, whether in the federal or the state courts, has a right that his case shall be a part of this evolution — a live cell in the tree of justice." . . .

IV. *Statutes of Limitation*

Statutes of limitations present special choice of law problems. Each state has developed precise and complex statutory criteria. The parties have been asked to brief this issue. A decision on the application of statutes of limitations and the effect of the rules respecting conflicts of laws awaits receipt of those briefs.

V. *Conclusion*

For the reasons noted, it is likely that each of the states would look to a federal or a national consensus law of manufacturer's liability, government contract defense and punitive damages. What is the nature of the national consensus or federal law is a subject for another memorandum.

We emphasize that this memorandum is a first general guide to the parties of the court's present thinking. It is subject to refinement and change as the legal issues, facts, and applicable law become clearer during the course of the pretrial and trial proceedings.

IN THE MATTER OF RHONE-POULENC RORER INC.

51 F.3d 1293 (7th Cir.), cert. denied, 516 U.S. 867 (1995)

■ POSNER, Chief Judge. [Manufacturers of certain blood products that were widely used by persons with hemophilia had allegedly failed to take adequate precautions with regard to screening blood donors. The effect of this failure was that thousands of persons with hemophilia, their spouses and lovers, and their children were infected with the human immunodeficiency virus (HIV). The Judicial Panel on Multidistrict Litigation consolidated the federal suits in the Northern District of Illinois, and the district court eventually certified a Rule 23(b)(3) class action. The manufacturers sought a writ of mandamus. The Seventh Circuit granted the writ for several reasons, two of which we study elsewhere in this book (see p. 540, *supra*.; p. 1283, *infra*.) A third reason was grounded in the fact that the district judge proposed to try the case by using a jury instruction on the issue of negligence that was, in the words of Chief Judge Posner, "a kind of Esperanto instruction, merging the negligence standards of the 50 states and the District of Columbia."]

[The district court] proposes to have a jury determine the negligence of the defendants under a legal standard that does not actually exist anywhere in the world. One is put in mind of the concept of "general" common law that prevailed in the era of *Swift v. Tyson*. The assumption is that the common law of the 50 states and the District of Columbia, at least so far as bears on a claim of negligence against drug companies, is basically uniform and can be abstracted in a single instruction. It is no doubt true that at some level of generality the law of negligence is one, not only nationwide but worldwide. Negligence is a failure to take due care, and due care a function of the probability and magnitude of an accident and the costs of avoiding it. A jury can be asked whether the defendants took due care. And in many cases such differences as there are among the tort rules of the different states would not affect the outcome. . . .

We doubt that it is true in general, and we greatly doubt that it is true in a case such as this in which one of the theories pressed by the plaintiffs, the "serendipity" theory, is novel. If one instruction on negligence will serve to instruct the jury on the legal standard of every state of the United States applicable to a novel claim, implying that the claim despite its controversiality would be decided identically in all 50 states and the District of Columbia, one wonders what the Supreme Court thought it was doing in the *Erie* case when it held that it was *unconstitutional* for federal courts in diversity cases to apply general common law rather than the common law of the state whose law would apply if the case were being tried in state rather than federal court. . . . The law of negligence, including subsidiary concepts such as duty of care, foreseeability, and proximate cause, may as the plaintiffs have argued forcefully to us differ among the states only in nuance, though we think not, for a reason discussed later. But nuance can be important, and its significance is suggested by a comparison of differing state pattern instructions on negligence and differing judicial formulations of the meaning of negligence and the subordinate concepts. . . . The voices of the quasi-sovereigns that are the states of the United States sing negligence with a different pitch.

The "serendipity" theory advanced by the plaintiffs . . . is that if the defendants did not do enough to protect hemophiliacs from the risk of Hepatitis B, they are liable to hemophiliacs for any consequences — including infection by the more dangerous and at the time completely unknown AIDS virus — that proper measures against Hepatitis B would, all unexpectedly, have averted. This theory of liability, which draws support from Judge Friendly's opinion in Petition of Kinsman Transit Co., [338 F.2d 708, 725 (2d Cir. 1964)], dispenses, rightly or wrongly from the standpoint of the Platonic Form of negligence, with proof of foreseeability, even though a number of states, in formulating their tests for negligence, incorporate the foreseeability of the risk into the test. . . . These states follow Judge Cardozo's famous opinion in Palsgraf v. Long Island R.R., 248 N.Y. 339, 162 N.E. 99 (1928), under which the HIV plaintiffs might (we do not say would — we express no view on the substantive issues in this litigation) be barred from recovery on the ground that they were unforeseeable victims of the alleged failure of the defendants to take adequate precautions against infecting hemophiliacs with Hepatitis B and that therefore the drug companies had not violated any duty of care to them.

The plaintiffs' second theory focuses on the questions when the defendants should have learned about the danger of HIV in the blood supply and when, having learned about it, they should have taken steps to eliminate the danger or at least warn hemophiliacs or their physicians of it. These questions also may be sensitive to the precise way in which a state formulates its standard of negligence. If not, one begins to wonder why this country bothers with different state legal systems.

Both theories, incidentally, may be affected by differing state views on the role of industry practice or custom in determining the existence of negligence. In some states, the standard of care for a physician, hospital, or other provider of medical services, including blood banks, is a professional standard, that is, the standard fixed by the relevant profession. In others, it is the standard of ordinary care, which may, depending on judge or jury, exceed the professional standard. . . . Which approach a state follows, and whether in those states that follow the professional-standard approach manufacturers of blood solids would be assimilated to blood banks as providers of medical services entitled to shelter under the professional standard, could make a big difference in the liability of these manufacturers. . . .

The diversity jurisdiction of the federal courts is, after *Erie*, designed merely to provide an alternative forum for the litigation of state-law claims, not an alternative system of substantive law for diversity cases. But under the district judge's plan the thousands of members of the plaintiff class will have their rights determined, and the four defendant manufacturers will have their duties determined, under a law that is merely an amalgam, an averaging, of the nonidentical negligence laws of 51 jurisdictions. No one doubts that Congress could constitutionally prescribe a uniform standard of liability for manufacturers of blood solids. It might we suppose promulgate pertinent provisions of the *Restatement (Second) of Torts*. The point of *Erie* is that Article III of the Constitution does not empower the federal courts to create such a regime for diversity cases.

Notes and Questions

1. Does *Agent Orange* put you in mind of Justice O'Connor's dissent in Sun Oil Co. v. Wortman, 486 U.S. 717, 740 (1988) (see p. 802, *supra*), in which she expressed concern that a choice of law rule will pass constitutional muster as long as a court can "invent a legal theory so novel or strange that the other State has never had an opportunity to reject it; [and] then, on the basis of nothing but unsupported speculation, 'predict' that the other State would adopt that theory if it had the chance"? Would *Agent Orange* pass constitutional muster under *Shutts* and *Wortman*?

2. Isn't there a lot of wisdom in the *Agent Orange* approach? By definition, the controversy was larger than any single jurisdiction, yet standard choice of law analysis requires that one state's law "win" and the other states' law "lose." Isn't it more sensible to try to compromise the interests of the relevant states? See Friedrich K. Juenger, Choice of Law and Multistate Justice (1993). Are courts in the best position to make the necessary compromises?

3. Isn't Judge Posner correct that this approach is essentially the creation of federal common law, and thus runs afoul of *Erie* and *Klaxon*? Judge Weinstein

might respond to the latter problem by suggesting that this approach is faithful to *Erie* and *Klaxon*, for it asks what law each state would adopt. But isn't it is unlikely in the extreme that all of the fifty states would agree on this approach? According to Professor Kramer, Weinstein's approach was deeply flawed:

> One problem with Chief Judge Weinsten's argument that every state would choose "national consensus law" . . . is that not a single court had ever suggested such a thing . . ., a fact Weinstein failed to note. . . .
>
> There is an even more fundamental flaw . . . . Who said that a single law had to be chosen? More importantly, where did Chief Judge Weinstein get the idea that the question was what a state court would do if faced with the class action? The appropriate question was, what would the various courts of origin have done if the actions remained dispersed? And there is absolutely no reason to think they would have made up some novel "national consensus law" in that circumstance.

Larry Kramer, *Choice of Law in Complex Litigation*, 71 N.Y.U. L. Rev. 547, 562-63 (1996).

4. Moreover, do the limits that Weinstein imposes on the use of national consensus law make it useful only in the most extreme cases? For instance, would it be possible to use a national consensus approach to choose the law in domestic product defect cases like the Dalkon Shield, DES, Bendectin, or breast implant litigation? Would it apply to state law fraud claims related to a federal securities claim? What limit could be placed on the national consensus approach — would it apply any time in which the case was larger than the interests of any given state? But isn't that every case that involves a choice of law question?

Agent Orange was a case that was complex at every stage that a case could be complex — at the joinder stage, the pretrial stage, the trial stage, and the remedial stage. Might it be possible to limit the national consensus approach just to cases involving complexity? How about complicated litigation too? How would the disparate treatment of these cases, in relation to other cases in which one state's law would "win," be justified? Couldn't the problems in this paragraph be avoided if a von Mehren-*Agent Orange* approach were applied to cases of all sizes? Is *Agent Orange* the hope of the future, and *Rhone-Poulenc* the curse of the past? If *Agent Orange* is the hope, then why hasn't a single court since 1984 adopted its rationale?

5. The use of a "national consensus" approach has important procedural consequences, one of which is that it makes it easier for a court to find the existence of common questions of law and fact among disparate plaintiffs. As we have seen, common questions of law or fact are necessary for numerous joinder and consolidation devices, including Rule 42 and multidistrict consolidation and Rule 20 and Rule 23 joinder.

Indeed, prior to this opinion, Weinstein had tentatively certified a Rule 23(b)(3) class of Agent Orange veterans on liability issues. To overcome the argument that the law of numerous states was different on critical liability issues, thus making individual rather than common issues predominate, Weinstein suggested that state-to-state differences on liability were small and that a "consensus" existed among states that provided a "national substantive rule governing the main issues in this case." In re "Agent Orange" Product Liability Litigation, 100 F.R.D. 718, 724 (E.D.N.Y. 1983). The defendants petitioned for a writ of mandamus against the decision, which the Second Circuit declined to give. In the course of its opinion, the Second Circuit observed:

> It is, of course, the law of this case that plaintiffs' claims arise under state law[,] In re "Agent Orange" Product Liability Litigation, 635 F.2d 987 (2d Cir. 1980), cert. denied, 454 U.S. 1128 (1981), and it is possible that the law of every state and Australia and New Zealand, including choice of law rules, will at some point come into play. While we will not disclaim considerable skepticism as to the existence of a "national substantive rule," we note Chief Judge Weinstein's declared intention to create subclasses as dictated by variations in state law. Given the unique aspects of this case arguably creating a need for a single dispositive trial on the common issues described above, we cannot say that the use of subclasses corresponding to variations in state law is a palpable error remediable by mandamus. . . .

In re Diamond Shamrock Chemicals Co., 725 F.2d 858, 861 (2d Cir.), cert. denied, 465 F.2d 1067 (1984).

Weinstein was aware of the Second Circuit's skepticism when, a month later, he proposed an even more dramatic use of national consensus law in the opinion you have just read. Was this latter opinion vague in its particulars and subject to revision in part to avoid a successful mandamus petition?

Shortly after issuance of this opinion, and on the eve of trial, *Agent Orange* settled; thus, the parties never challenged Weinstein's choice of law opinion. Nor did Weinstein ever issue an opinion describing exactly what the content of "national consensus" law would be. Might the uncertainty about exactly what law would govern the trial have been one of the reasons that the parties were willing to settle? Is that possibility a reason to give a judge the power to declare national consensus law or a reason not to?

On appeal from the settlement, the Second Circuit called the "national consensus" opinion "bold and imaginative," but noted that

> in light of our prior holding that federal common law does not govern plaintiffs' claims, every jurisdiction would be free to render its own choice of law decision, and common experience suggests that the intellectual power of Chief Judge Weinstein's analysis alone would not be enough to prevent widespread disagreement.

In re "Agent Orange" Product Liability Litigation MDL No. 381, 818 F.2d 145, 165 (2d Cir. 1987), cert. denied, 484 U.S. 1004 (1988).

6. Judge Weinstein himself declined to follow *Agent Orange* in a complex case involving the restructuring of the Manville asbestos trust fund. One of the issues in the restructuring involved the rights of certain persons to set offs or contribution from the fund. The laws of the various states disagreed about the rights of such persons. Weinstein rejected the argument that national consensus law applied to the controversy:

> This situation differs markedly from that presented by *Agent Orange*. . . . State tort law addressing questions of injuries caused by toxic exposure while serving in the armed services in Vietnam did not vary significantly from state to state leading the court to conclude that states faced with claims against government military contractors would refer to national consensus law. Here, the states have recently adopted statutes focusing on the precise issue covered by section H. The law in the several jurisdictions is in flux and ought to be defined in the first instance by the state courts.
>
> This is not to say that other state and federal courts ought not follow the rule adopted in the Settlement in the interests of consistent and equitable

treatment of all Trust beneficiaries to the extent that it does not violate a state's public policy. Emphatically, they should do so. But, when state public policy and the dictates of *Erie* prevent this sensible result, they cannot be compelled by the federal courts to do so.

In re Joint Eastern and Southern Districts Asbestos Litigation, 129 B.R. 710, 878 (E. & S.D.N.Y. 1991), vacated on other grounds, 982 F.2d 721 (2d Cir. 1992), modified, 993 F.2d 7 (2d Cir. 1993).

7. As with federal common law, national consensus law creates problems of content. How should the judge resolve differences between the states over the standards for punitive damages, the requirements for proving a product "defective," the measure of compensatory damages a plaintiff is due, the effect of negligence or assumption of the risk by the plaintiff, and so on? These tort standards are increasingly codified in statute; will a court be able to overlook or compromise legislation in creating national consensus law? Will the substantive rules favor plaintiffs, defendants, or neither? Why should some parties (those to whom national consensus law applies) receive one type of law, and others receive different, more traditional law?

8. As interesting a solution as national consensus law is, is it really workable? If not, are there other alternatives that are more workable?

4. Using the Law of the Most Restrictive Jurisdiction

The last two subsections have suggested two possible ways to get around choice of law limitations: federal common law or national consensus law. Although different, both approaches derive from a common idea — the selection of a single body of substantive law that applies to all cases. In this subsection, we consider a third method that provides a single law to dispose of the entire controversy.

IN RE SCHOOL ASBESTOS LITIGATION

977 F.2d 764 (3d Cir. 1992)

■ BECKER, Circuit Judge. [A group of school systems that had spent money to remove asbestos from their school buildings brought a nationwide class action seeking recovery on behalf of all similarly situated schools and school systems. More than fifty companies were named as defendants. In the first portion of the opinion, the court of appeals ordered the district judge removed from the case. See p. 961, *infra.*]

Throughout this litigation, an overriding concern of both the district court and this court has been the manageability of the class action. The defendants originally opposed class certification on the ground that because so many different state laws would have to be applied common issues could never predominate and the class action would be unmanageable. Counsel for the class plaintiffs repeatedly responded that the differences in state laws were not that great and that the plaintiffs were willing to prove their case according to the law of the "strictest" jurisdiction. Relying in part on those two representations, and on the possibility of certifying subclasses under Rule 23(c)(4), the district court certified the class [under Rule 23(b)(3)]. . . . We affirmed that certification, albeit with explicit doubts about manageability and with the caveat that the district court could revoke the certification if that seemed appropriate. . . .

[Shortly before trial of the cases was to commence, one of the defendants, Kaiser Cement, filed a writ of mandamus alleging] that the district court plans to try the case according to the law of the strictest state, rather than according to the law of each individual jurisdiction, and that the district court's approach runs afoul of the Supreme Court's ruling in Phillips Petroleum Co. v. Shutts, 472 U.S. 797 (1985).

Shutts held that due process requires that in a class action based on the laws of separate jurisdictions the adjudicating court must apply to any particular claim the substantive law of a jurisdiction having a significant interest in that claim. . . . Courts may not simply apply the law of the forum state or, presumably, a hybrid or composite of state laws. Thus, *Shutts* suggests that each plaintiff in this case has the right to have its claims judged according to the law of its jurisdiction, not according to that of a putative or imaginary strictest state.

At first blush, one might question why Kaiser Cement, a defendant, has standing to raise this objection. After all, the strictest-state standard appears to make the plaintiffs' case more difficult to prove, and, thus, to advantage the defendants. Kaiser Cement's concern, however, is that even if it wins against the class plaintiffs, and even if the *class plaintiffs* have waived their *Shutts* claim, its victory will be hollow because *absent class members* from more "lenient" jurisdictions will be able to challenge the judgment collaterally. Kaiser Cement notes that the opt-out notice did not inform the class members that they were waiving their right to have their claims adjudicated according to their own states' (possibly more lenient) laws, and that they therefore could claim inadequate representation by the class plaintiffs. According to the petition, the current trial plan binds Kaiser Cement if it loses, but does not bind absent plaintiffs if it wins. Kaiser Cement thus views trial as unwinnable from a practical standpoint and, hence, fundamentally unfair, in violation of both Rule 23 and the Due Process Clause.

We agree that Kaiser Cement has standing to raise this claim, but we do not believe that the issue is ripe for our adjudication. First, it is far from clear how the district court intended to resolve issues other than the standard of proof. Second, even if the district court had taken a clear position on what law to apply, a new district judge will now be presiding over the case. If the newly assigned district judge insists on holding the class plaintiffs strictly to their earlier representations, then they or the defendants may seek review from this court at that time.

We expect that that will not prove necessary, however. Despite the barbs that have been traded and the parties' penchant for painting each other with black hats, it appears that both the class plaintiffs and the defendants agree, for different reasons, that *Shutts* requires the district court to apply the law of the individual jurisdictions. The plaintiffs believe that the case will be manageable if issues are put to the jury according to special interrogatories with the district court later molding the verdict according to the law of each state. The defendants continue to believe that such an approach will be unmanageable, and they therefore desire to have the class action decertified. As we stated in our earlier opinion, however, we believe that the district court will be in a much better position to evaluate and handle such manageability concerns initially, and at this stage we again prefer to defer to its judgment. For now, we simply urge the incoming district judge to examine *Shutts* carefully before submitting the case to the jury according to the law of a hypothetical strictest state, even if the class plaintiffs once agreed to that approach.

Notes and Questions

1. Is the Third Circuit correct that absent class plaintiffs would be able to avoid an adverse judgment? Start with the court's analysis of *Shutts*. *Shutts* does not hold, as the court suggests, that "each plaintiff in this case has the right to have its claims judged according to the law of its jurisdiction." Rather, *Shutts* holds that it is unconstitutional to resolve an absent class member's claims under the law of a state that has no significant contacts with the class member. Therefore, according to *Shutts*, the *School Asbestos* plaintiffs that had no significant contacts with the state with the most restrictive law on an issue would not be bound on that issue. But it is impossible to know how many plaintiffs would be affected (and on what issues) until the court determined which law was most restrictive on each issue and how many plaintiffs had no significant contacts with that law. Whatever the exact number, it is certainly fewer than all of the absent class plaintiffs, as Kaiser Cement argued and the Third Circuit implied.

Was the Third Circuit's real point that absent plaintiffs would be able to argue inadequate representation if the class representatives acceded to a trial plan using the law of the most restrictive jurisdiction? But is that point necessarily true? Couldn't the class representatives, at least in some possible states of the world, rationally determine that the risks to absent class members of using the law of the most restrictive jurisdiction were outweighed by the efficiencies of a class trial? If they make a reasonable calculation to this effect, are they inadequate representatives?

Maybe the Third Circuit's point was that, at least insofar as the choice affected absent class members, the use of the law of the most restrictive jurisdiction violated *Klaxon*'s command to use the choice of law method of the forum state? But can't class representatives, rationally and without becoming inadequate representatives, waive *Klaxon*?

2. In any event, couldn't *School Asbestos* be avoided by any of three simple techniques: appointing an adequate class representative from each state and securing the agreement of each representative to the trial plan, creating separate subclasses for each state and again securing the consent of an adequate subclass representative for the plan, or providing a second notice describing the trial plan and an opportunity to opt out of the class action at that point? None of these three options guarantees that the same law will be applied to all; a class

or subclass representative may refuse to consent, or there may be a significant number of opt-outs. But at least the choice of law concerns would be reduced, wouldn't they? Should the Third Circuit have remanded with instructions to consider these alternatives?

Note that in a mandatory class action, only the first two options would be available. Should the concept of using the law of the most restrictive jurisdiction be unavailable in mandatory class actions?

3. The Third Circuit's concerns are clearly directed toward absent class members. Is there anything wrong with using a "most restrictive jurisdiction" approach in litigation that is not aggregated on a class action basis?

4. Unlike other methods that choose a single law, the "most restrictive jurisdiction" method is fairly consistent with a standard adversarial approach to litigation. The other methods that choose a single law seek to change the law (and thus the plaintiffs' lawyers' adversarial calculus) just for complex or complicated cases. This method accomplishes a similar goal, but it seems to require the consent of the plaintiffs (or their representatives) before the law can be changed. Since it leaves the ultimate decision about changing the law in the hands of the plaintiffs and their lawyer(s), the concern for autonomy that underlies an adversarial system is honored. Would it ever be appropriate for a judge to order the "most restrictive jurisdiction" approach over the objection of the plaintiffs? Do you worry that, once the method is recognized, a judge might "persuade" plaintiffs to consent, even when they do not wish to do so?

5. Unlike other methods that choose a single law, the "most restrictive jurisdiction" method chooses a law that clearly favors one side — the defendant. Should a choice of law method be so blatantly substantive? How likely is it that, in less mature torts, plaintiffs would concede to the defendants the ability to obtain the best possible legal standard?

5. Choosing a Single Law with a Right to Opt Out or Opt In

Another possibility — to which *School Asbestos* vaguely alluded — for reducing the complexity or complication associated with multiple state laws is to declare the law that will be applied to a consolidated set of cases, and then give the parties to whom that law would not otherwise have applied the right to opt out of the litigation. The obvious defect of this possibility is that it fails to establish a single law under which everyone's case will be tried; those who are entitled to have different, more favorable law applied are likely to opt out. To some extent the rush to opt out will be tempered by concerns for manageability (the lack of confusion that attends a single jury instruction may outweigh whatever marginal legal advantages the better law promises), efficiency (the streamlining of discovery and trial may also outweigh those advantages), and litigation dynamics (the likelihood of a successful result may be increased by the presence of additional claimants). But at least some plaintiffs, and many defendants, will undoubtedly opt out of the "single law" trial, thus reducing its utility as a device to secure a single law applicable to an entire controversy.

A related approach is to allow parties to opt into a trial that uses a particular state's law. The most famous case that used the opt-in approach was the Bendectin litigation before Judge Rubin. More than 900 Bendectin cases were either filed in, removed to, or transferred by the Judicial Panel on Multidistrict Litigation to the Southern District of Ohio, where Merrell Dow Pharmaceuticals, the manufacturer of Bendectin, was headquartered. Judge Rubin decided to conduct an initial trial on the issue of causation (see p. 1293, *infra*). Rubin then gave the cases that had been multidistricted to his court the opportunity to opt into the joint trial, which was to be held using the law of Ohio. Although Ohio law was arguably less favorable on certain points than the laws of other jurisdictions, a surprising number of MDL plaintiffs (261 out of about 850) opted into the joint trial.

The trial turned out badly for the plaintiffs: The jury found that Bendectin did not cause their injuries. On appeal the Sixth Circuit rejected the arguments of some of the multidistrict plaintiffs that this method of proceeding with the trial was inappropriate. In re Bendectin Litigation, 857 F.2d 290, 302-03 (6th Cir. 1988), cert. denied, 488 U.S. 1006 (1989).

In its decision, the Sixth Circuit noted, but did not base its holding on, the argument that the plaintiffs' consent to the use of Ohio law waives any claim that its use is unfair. Shouldn't the plaintiffs' consent be the end of the matter? Parties often negotiate about the law that is to be applied to interpretation of the contract, and such clauses are enforced as long as the law chosen has a reasonable relationship to the transaction and is not contrary to the public policy of any state with a materially greater interest. *See* U.C.C. § 1-105(1); Restatement (Second) of Conflict of Laws § 187; Eugene F. Scoles & Peter Hay, Conflict of Laws §§ 18.1-.12 (2d ed. 1992).

Should the Sixth Circuit have worried about *Shutts*? Surely, though, *Shutts* would allow the law of Ohio, which has a "significant contact or aggregate of contacts" with the *Bendectin* litigation, to apply. Should the Sixth Circuit have worried about *Klaxon*? Surely the rule of *Klaxon* can be waived by agreement of the parties. Should it have worried about forum shopping? About the extra pressure that an opt-out or opt-in tactic might put on the Judicial Panel for Multidistrict Litigation's decision to multidistrict a case and its decision about where to do so? About the pressure that the transferee judge might put on plaintiffs to opt into the joint trial? About the abuse of this tactic in cases in which no single state has an interest in the adjudication of all the claims? Could some of these latter concerns be overcome by limitations on the opt-out principle? Are any remaining concerns powerful enough to override the parties' consent?

6. Creating Federal Choice of Law Principles

This section began with the observation that any solution to the problem of choice of law in complex or complicated litigation would either need to change the choice of law rules used for ordinary lawsuits, or else change the underlying law itself. The approaches in the last four subsections have either pursued the second path or straddled the line between the first and second paths. All of approaches, however, resulted in the choice of a single law that governed a particular issue or claim. In this subsection, we pursue the first path, and examine whether a court in a complex or complicated case can develop special choice of law principles to select the appropriate law or laws. Unlike the prior approaches that we have examined, this approach does not necessarily result in the application of a single law that governs an issue or claim. Will this approach adequately reduce the problems of complexity or complication?

American Bar Association Commission on Mass Torts, REPORT TO THE HOUSE OF DELEGATES

1d, 4d (1989)

DRAFT FEDERAL LEGISLATION . . .

Sec. 101. Short Title.

This Act may be cited as the Federal Mass Tort Jurisdiction Reform Act.

. . .

Sec[.] 106. Choice of Law.

In consolidated mass tort litigation instituted, transferred, removed or maintained under this act, the district court shall determine the source or sources of applicable substantive law. Whenever State law supplies the rule of decision, the court may make its own determination in light of reason and experience as to which State(s) rule(s) shall apply to some or all of the actions, parties or issues.

American Law Institute, COMPLEX LITIGATION: STATUTORY RECOMMENDATIONS AND ANALYSIS

321-23 (1994)

§ 6.01. Mass Torts

(a) Except as provided in §6.04 through §6.06, in actions consolidated under §3.01 or removed under §5.02 in which the parties assert the application of laws that are in material conflict, the transferee court shall choose the law governing the rights, liabilities, and defenses of the parties with respect to a tort claim by applying the criteria set forth in the following subsections with the objective of applying, to the extent feasible, a single state's law to all similar tort claims being asserted against a defendant.

(b) In determining the governing law under subsection (a), the court shall consider the following factors for purposes of identifying each state having a policy that would be furthered by the application of its laws:

(1) the place or places of injury;

(2) the place or places of the conduct causing the injury; and

(3) the primary places of business or habitual residences of the plaintiffs and defendants.

(c) If, in analyzing the factors set forth in sub-section (b), the court finds that only one state has a policy that would be furthered by the application of its law, that state's law shall govern. If more than one state has a policy that would be furthered by the application of its law, the court shall choose the applicable law from among the laws of the interested states under the following rules:

(1) If the place of injury and the place of the conduct causing the injury are in the same state, that state's law governs.

(2) If subsection (c)(1) does not apply but all of the plaintiffs habitually reside or have their primary places of business in the same state, and a defendant has its primary place of business or habitually resides in that state, that state's law governs the claims with respect to that defendant. Plaintiffs shall be considered as sharing a common habitual residence or primary place of business if they are located in states whose laws are not in material conflict.

(3) If neither subsection (c)(1) nor (c)(2) applies, but all of the plaintiffs habitually reside or have their primary places of business in the same state, and that state also is the place of injury, then that state's law governs. Plaintiffs shall be considered as sharing a common habitual residence or primary place of business if they are located in states whose laws are not in material conflict.

(4) In all other cases, the law of the state where the conduct causing the injury occurred governs. When conduct occurred in more than one state, the court shall choose the law of the conduct state that has the most significant relationship to the occurrence.

(d) When necessary to avoid unfair surprise or arbitrary results, the transferee court may choose the applicable law on the basis of additional factors that reflect the regulatory policies and legitimate interests of a particular state not otherwise identified under subsection (b), or it may depart from the order of preferences for selecting the governing law prescribed by subsection (c).

(e) If the court determines that the application of a single state's law to all elements of the claims pending against a defendant would be inappropriate, it may divide the actions into subgroups of claims, issues, or parties to foster consolidated treatment under §3.01, and allow more than one state's law to be applied. The court also may determine that only certain claims or issues involving one or more of the parties should be governed by the law chosen by the application of the rules in subsection (c), and that other claims or parties should be remanded to the transferor courts for individual treatment under the laws normally applicable in those courts. In either instance, the court may exercise its authority under §3.06(c) to sever, transfer, or remand issues or claims for treatment consistent with its determination.

Notes and Questions

1. Although they have their differences, the ABA and ALI approaches agree on a basic premise: that the selection of a different choice of law rule, rather than the selection of different substantive law, is the appropriate way to handle the problem of mass torts and/or "complex" litigation (as defined by the ALI). Is this a better approach than an approach that selects a single law? The ALI argued that it was, for several reasons. First, "federal choice of law rules should not be designed with the objective of promoting substantive preferences for one party rather than the other." Second, using a federal choice of law rule, without allowing courts to develop an entirely new body of doctrine, helped "to maximize certainty and to assure that a uniform standard is applied"; as the ALI argued, "transferee courts should be released from state law constraints, but not allowed unbridled discretion." Third, the choice of law standards proposed by the ALI were both "sufficiently flexible to protect against arbitrary results and to accommodate varying state interests by authorizing the court to sever issues to be treated under differing state laws when appropriate." See *Complex Litigation, supra*, at 314-15, 318.

Do these advantages outweigh the basic problem of a choice of law approach — that differing state laws create complexity or complication? The first section of this chapter suggested that the real choice of law problems were (in descending order) different substantive laws, different choice of law rules, *Klaxon*, and *Van Dusen-Ferens*. The ABA and ALI approaches address the last three problems. But they do not address the first. Won't any solution that fails to address the first concern come up short in terms of reducing complexity or complication?

The ALI attempts to overcome this problem, at least to some degree, by urging that a single state's law apply. Is this preference consistent with the rest of the analysis in § 6.01? Recall that the ALI strongly criticized the result-oriented manipulation of choice of law rules in *Chicago Air Crash*, in which the court found a single law to apply to the entire controversy, because of its lack of predictability. See p. 841, *supra*. Isn't the ALI's proposal, which speaks in rather squishy terms such as "interests" and then loads on a "single law" presumption, subject to precisely the same criticism?

2. The ALI approach permits a court to make a choice of law determination on an issue-by-issue basis. Will this use of *dépeçage* make the court's task of finding a single law even more difficult?

3. The ALI's approach toward choice of law is more detailed and structured than the ABA's approach. Which approach is better — a more structured method or a more open-ended method? Does the answer depend on what the goal is — choice of a limited number of governing laws that can avoid complexity or complication, or predictability in the application of choice of law rules? The latter goal is more faithful to choice of law as its own field of law, but the former goal is more faithful to the concerns of complex or complicated litigation.

4. If a multi-factor approach is better, has the ALI identified the right factors? For a different list of factors, see H.R. 1857, 105th Cong., 1st Sess. (1997) (factors include "place of injury," "place of the conduct causing the injury," "principal place of business or domiciles of the parties," "danger of creating unnecessary incentives for forum shopping," and "whether the choice of law would be reasonably foreseeable to the parties").

5. The ABA Report and H.R. 1857 proposed a choice of law rule only for certain mass torts. The ALI proposal deals with all "complex" (and also complicated) litigation, and provides, in sections not included in this book, choice of law rules for contract cases, statutes of limitation, and compensatory and punitive damages. See *Complex Litigation, supra*, §§ 6.02-.06. It did not, however, provide choice of law rules for any other state law theories that might be invoked in a case. How would a court resolve the choice of law questions that these theories might pose? Wouldn't some sort of a catch-all provision be necessary? Why doesn't the ALI propose such a provision?

The use of separate choice of law principles for separate legal theories may seem inconsistent with a trans-substantive assumption that the same procedural rules should apply to all cases. As the old *lex loci* rules show, however, choice of law rules have never been trans-substantive. Should they be? Or is the choice of law inquiry so closely tied to substance that separating the rules from the substantive theory would be a bad idea? Are you happy with having one set of choice of law rules for complex tort cases, one for ordinary tort cases, one for complex contract cases, one for ordinary contract cases, and so on?

6. Does the ALI's proposal pass constitutional muster under *Shutts*? Does the ABA's proposal?

7. For a symposium largely dedicated to the ALI proposal's choice of law provisions, see Symposium, 54 La. L. Rev. 833 (1994). As might be expected, the views of contributors — including Professors Trautman, Symeonides, Juenger, Mullenix, Sedler, Seidelson, and Shreve — varied widely. Professor Sedler, for instance, thought the proposal's attempt to apply a single law to a defendant or issue more flexible and reasonable than earlier proposals that sought to provide a single law that governed the entire controversy, but still thought that the proposal "unjustifiably intrudes upon that state sovereignty which is so fundamental in the American constitutional system, and thus must be rejected." Robert A. Sedler, *The Complex Litigation Project's Proposal for Federally-Mandated Choice of Law in Mass Tort Cases: Another Assault on State Sovereignty*, 54 La. L. Rev. 1085, 1110 (1994). Professor Seidelson thought that § 6.01 was "jerry-built," and its subsections "don't work any better than they look." David E. Seidelson, *Section 6.01 of the ALI's Complex Litigation Project: Function Follows Form*, 54 La. L. Rev. 1111, 1111, 1137 (1994).

8. Both the ABA Report and the ALI proposal were written with the belief that the choice of law principles they espouse would be enacted by Congress. Could a court adopt a new choice of law approach without waiting for congressional action? Such an approach would appear to be inconsistent with *Klaxon*. When we explored the limits of the *Klaxon* rule, we questioned whether the rule should give way in complex or complicated cases. See pp. 808-09, *supra*. In at least one case, however, it appears that *Klaxon* may have already been replaced by a federal choice of law rule. In Gruber v. Price Waterhouse, 117 F.R.D. 75 (E.D. Pa. 1987), the court was faced with a securities case in which there were pendent state claims. The defendant argued that the class action would be unmanageable because different state laws would apply. Noting that "[r]ecently, several courts have concluded that the law of the forum governs the common law claims of the entire class in securities cases," the court stated that it intended to apply Pennsylvania law to the claims of all class members; thus, the choice of law problems did not make the class action unmanageable. Id. at 81. The court avoided *Shutts* by stating that Pennsylvania, in which many of the wrongful acts occurred, had significant contacts with the case.

The precedential authority of *Gruber* is, however, rather weak. First, it misread the case on which it had primarily relied — In re Pizza Time Theatre Securities Litigation, 112 F.R.D. 15 (N.D. Cal. 1986) — in which the court had not merely applied the forum's law, but had rather engaged in the analysis required under *Klaxon* and California choice of law rules, and then found California law to apply. *Pizza Time* had not, as *Gruber* implied, replaced *Klaxon* with a blatant *lex fori* rule. Second, after indicating that it would apply forum state law, *Gruber* actually applied the whole law of Pennsylvania, including its choice of law rule. Hence, despite dicta to the contrary, *Gruber* did not in fact depart from *Klaxon*.

Would a simple *lex fori* rule be a better choice of law principle, at least in cases in which the forum has significant contacts with the transaction? Or would this rule give plaintiffs too much leeway as masters of the complaint to secure the law they desire?

9. As we stated at the beginning of this chapter, choice of law issues are different than issues we have studied before. In the first place, they take us away from the "substance-neutral" procedural rules that we have studied thus far, and force us to think about procedural rules that directly control the substantive law that will apply. Second, choice of law issues affect not only the joinder decisions on which Part One of this book has focused, but also the pretrial, trial, and remedial decisions that are the subject of Parts Two, Three, and Four. As we now turn to the study of these subjects, the need to simplify the issues in the case will become apparent. Choice of law rules that limit the number of applicable laws are one way (though not the only) in which issues can be simplified.

PART TWO

PRETRIAL COMPLEXITY

At last the forum has been selected, the parties have been joined, and the law has been chosen. The next task is to begin the process of litigating the case. In our procedural system, this means shepherding the case through a pretrial phase in which relevant facts and issues are exposed; a trial phase in which the legal claims associated with those facts and issues are adjudicated; and a remedial phase in which the judgment is implemented or enforced. In this Part, we examine the pretrial phase.

The pretrial phase is what many students think of when they think of complex litigation. Mountains of paper, blizzards of motions, torrents of lengthy depositions — certainly all of these are aspects of most complex cases. But they can also be aspects of cases that most of us would regard as routine. So the first issue is whether there exists something called "pretrial complexity" that distinguishes the truly complex case from the more routine case whose pretrial process has run amok. If there is, then the second issue is what we can do about the problem.

Some people deny that we can fruitfully distinguish the pretrial problems of "complex" cases from those of other, more routine cases. The most famous expression of this view is that of the *Manual for Complex and Multidistrict Litigation*, which stated in 1970 that "[t]here are no inherently protracted cases, only cases which are unnecessarily protracted by inefficient procedures and management." Many practitioners and scholars disagree, arguing that there are peculiar pretrial problems associated with complex litigation. The most common description of "pretrial complexity" focuses on the "massive," "voluminous," or "extensive" amount of information that complex cases generate during discovery. A slightly different description focuses on the causes of large-scale discovery: the unusual multiplicity or difficulty of legal and factual issues in complex cases. Still another approach is to define pretrial complexity in terms of the consequences of massive discovery: the protraction of complex cases in relation to routine ones.

We too believe that the phenomenon of "pretrial complexity" exists, but we disagree that the usual descriptions, which seek a definition in symptoms, causes, and manifestations, appropriately define pretrial complexity. "Pretrial complexity" can be understood only against the backdrop of our modern American adversarial system. This system places the pretrial phase — primarily pleading, discovery, and pretrial motions — almost exclusively in the hands of lawyers, who gather the evidence, take the depositions, formulate the issues, and make the arguments. Other than supplying information and occasionally attending hearings or depositions, the parties have relatively little to do with the pretrial stage. Juries, obviously, have no role whatever. The judge is somewhat more involved, but the judge's role is primarily to resolve disputes regarding discovery, to rule on motions (brought by the lawyers, of course), and to set the deadlines within which the lawyers must complete the process of getting the case ready for trial. In the pretrial phase, however, the lawyers are the stars of the show.

Under our understanding of pretrial complexity, the lawyers are unable adequately to perform their adversarial task. The reasons for this inability are many, but three factual scenarios recur:

(1) The nature of the information that the lawyer must garner and marshal make it impossible for the lawyer to formulate adequate proofs and arguments. For instance, the information may be wide-ranging and extensive, costly to obtain, or, due to time lags, no longer in existence.

(2) The substantive law may be so open-textured and uncertain, and thus the information potentially relevant to various understandings of the law are so vast, that the lawyer's task of shaping the issues for trial becomes exceedingly difficult if not impossible.

(3) Lawyers who represent clients with the same or similar interests may be unable to frame the facts and issues in a way that narrows the case for trial. As a result, the trial threatens to become a Tower of Babel that makes rational adjudication based on adversarial proofs and arguments an impossibility. These internal disagreements among similarly situated parties about the conduct of the litigation can be particularly intense when limited assets lead the parties to compete for the greatest possible share of the assets, and consequently reduce the incentive for lawyers to cooperate.

Nonetheless, the existence of "lawyer dysfunction" is not, by itself, enough to make a case "complex" in the pretrial sense. We also believe that two additional elements are required: first, that the problem of lawyer dysfunction can be ameliorated by granting the judge more power in the pretrial process than the judge enjoys in the traditional adversarial model; and second, that the judicial solutions to pretrial complexity result in rules that are "non-trans-substantive" — *i.e.*, rules that do not treat like cases procedurally alike.

The following two chapters explore the themes of adversarialism and trans-substantivism in the context of pretrial complexity. Chapter Eight begins by examining the appropriate relationship between judicial officers and attorneys in complex cases, focusing on the rise of the "managerial judge" who is more active in pretrial matters. Chapter Nine examines the management concepts that such a judge might implement in order to overcome lawyer dysfunction and narrow the issues and facts for trial, focusing on whether the gains from case management in terms of efficient and speedier resolution outweighs the costs of less adversarialism and the disparate treatment of like cases. Chapter Nine also examines the issue of technology in complex litigation, focusing on whether modern computer technology might alleviate some of the problems of lawyer dysfunction and provide at least a partial solution to the vexing problems of pretrial complexity.

To some extent, the division of the pretrial phase in this manner is arbitrary, and creates artificially tidy distinctions. For instance, the use of a particular counsel structure (discussed in Chapter Eight) will have an important bearing on the types of case management techniques (discussed in Chapter Nine) that are available. On a larger scale, even the division of the pretrial phase from the joinder, trial, and remedial phases is arbitrary. For instance, whether or not a jury will ultimately hear the case (an issue discussed in Part Three) will have a tremendous bearing on the way in which the case will be managed during the pretrial phase (a Part Two issue), just as the size of the litigation (a Part One issue) affects both whether there will be a jury and how the case will be managed. We will occasionally make links between a particular pretrial issue and other pretrial, trial, remedial, and joinder issues; but time and space do not allow us to make all of the connections for all the issues. You should constantly ask yourself, as all good lawyers do, what ripple effects a particular position on a particular pretrial issue will have on other issues in the litigation.

CHAPTER EIGHT

SELECTING LAWYERS AND JUDICIAL OFFICERS FOR THE PRETRIAL STAGE

> Judicial management contemplates abandonment of the judge's traditionally passive umpireal role. But . . . [t]here is no necessary conflict between judicial management and the adversary system.
>
> William W Schwarzer

Like the issues in Part One, in which we set the court, the parties, and the law into place, the issues in this chapter are "table-setters." Before we can get to the "main event" — the processing of a complex case through discovery and trial — we still need to set the lawyers and the judicial official(s) into place. But what is there to set into place? The adversary system already tells us that the parties' own lawyers will discover the facts and develop the triable issues, and that the judge will intervene only to set timetables and resolve motions or disputes brought to her attention by the lawyers. So let's move on!

Unfortunately, we can't. The "active" lawyer and the "passive, umpireal" judge describe with some accuracy the roles expected of lawyers and judges in most bi-polar cases handled in most American courts today. In cases of pretrial complexity, however, the usual roles fail to work. Complex cases can involve thousands of parties, hundreds of discovery requests and depositions, and hundreds of motions. We cannot realistically expect each party to be represented by counsel of her choosing, nor adversaries to eschew a war of attrition when the stakes are so high and the legitimately discoverable information is so vast. We cannot realistically expect a judge to sit idly by and watch a litigation free-for-all that, if left in lawyers' hands, might drag on for five, ten, or twenty years. Nor can we expect a single judge with many other cases before her to rule in a timely way on each of the hundreds of pretrial motions and other disputes a complex case is likely to generate.

The usual response to these concerns is to suggest changes in the roles of lawyer and judge in complex cases — to assign the judge a more active role, and the lawyer a less active one, in "managing" the pretrial process. Necessarily, such changes affect the relationship between lawyer and client, lawyer and judge, and judge and polity. As you examine the changes that the roles of lawyer and judge undergo in complex cases, ask yourself whether you are comfortable with these new relationships.

A. SELECTING A COUNSEL STRUCTURE

1. The Initial Selection of Counsel

RICHARDSON-MERRELL, INC. v. KOLLER

472 U.S. 424 (1985)

■ JUSTICE BRENNAN, concurring. A fundamental premise of the adversary system is that individuals have the right to retain the attorney of their choice to represent their interests in judicial proceedings.... [I]f an attorney is adequately qualified and has not otherwise acted so as to justify disqualification, the client need not obtain the permission of the court or of his adversary to retain the attorney of his choice....

■ JUSTICE STEVENS, dissenting. Everyone must agree that the litigant's freedom to choose his own lawyer in a civil case is a fundamental right.

MANUAL FOR COMPLEX LITIGATION, THIRD

26-31 (1995)

Complex litigation often involves numerous parties with common or similar interests but separate counsel. Traditional procedures in which all papers and documents are served on all attorneys, and each attorney files motions, presents arguments, and conducts witness examinations, may result in waste of time and money, in confusion and indirection, and in unnecessary burden on the court. Special procedures for coordination of counsel are therefore needed and should be instituted early in the litigation to avoid unnecessary costs and duplicative activity.

In some cases the attorneys coordinate their activities without the court's assistance to eliminate duplication of effort, and they should be encouraged to do so. More often, however, the court will need to institute procedures under which one or more attorneys are selected and authorized to act on behalf of other counsel and their clients with respect to specified aspects of the litigation. . . .

20.221 Organizational Structures

Attorneys designated by the court to act in the litigation on behalf of other counsel and parties in addition to their own clients (referred to collectively as "designated counsel") generally fall into one of the following categories:

• Liaison counsel: charged with essentially administrative matters, such as communications between the court and other counsel (including receiving and distributing notices, orders, motions, and briefs on behalf of the group), convening meetings of counsel, advising parties of developments in the case, and otherwise assisting in the coordination of activities and positions. Such counsel may act for the group in managing document depositories and in resolving scheduling conflicts. Liaison counsel will usually have offices in the same locality as the court.

• Lead counsel: charged with major responsibility for formulating (after consultation with other counsel) and presenting positions on substantive and procedural issues during the litigation. Typically they act for the group — either personally or by coordinating the efforts of others — in presenting written and oral arguments and suggestions to the court, working with opposing counsel in developing and implementing a litigation plan, initiating and organizing discovery requests and responses, conducting the principal examination of deponents, employing experts, arranging for support services, and seeing that schedules are met.

• Trial counsel: serves as principal attorney for the group at trial in presenting arguments, making objections, conducting examination of witnesses, and generally organizing and coordinating the work of the other attorneys on the trial team.

• Committees of counsel: often called steering committees, coordinating committees, management committees, executive committees, discovery committees, or trial teams — may be formed to serve a wide range of functions. Because the appointment of committees of counsel can lead to substantially increased costs, they should not be made unless needed; a need is most likely to exist in cases in which the interests and positions of group members are sufficiently dissimilar to justify giving them representation in decision making. Committees may be assigned tasks by the court or lead counsel, such as preparing briefs or conducting portions of the discovery program, but should not be formed to accomplish tasks that one lawyer can perform adequately. Great care must be taken, however, to avoid unnecessary duplication of efforts and to control fees and expenses. . . .

The types of appointments and assignments of responsibilities will depend on many factors, the most important of which is achieving efficiency and economy without jeopardizing fairness to parties in the litigation. . . .

20.224 Court's Responsibilities

Few decisions by the court in complex litigation are as difficult and sensitive as the appointment of designated counsel. Because of the stakes involved, competition for appointment is often intense, and the judges need to be prepared to manage it appropriately.... At the same time, because appointments of designated counsel will alter the usual dynamics of client representation in important ways, attorneys will have legitimate concerns that their clients' interests be adequately represented.

For these reasons, the judge needs to take an active part in making the decision on the appointment of counsel. Deferring to proposals by counsel without independent examination by the court, even those that seem to have the concurrence of a "majority" of those affected, invites problems down the road....

Attorneys should not be appointed or approved by the court to serve as designated counsel unless they have the resources, the commitment, and the qualifications to accomplish the assigned tasks. They should be able to command the respect of their colleagues and work cooperatively with opposing counsel and the court. Prior experience in similar roles in other litigation may be useful, but past performance may also demonstrate that an attorney may have generated personal antagonisms that will undermine effectiveness in the present case or is otherwise ill-suited for the contemplated assignment. Although the court should move expeditiously and avoid unnecessary delay, an evidentiary hearing may be needed to bring all relevant facts to light, or to allow counsel to state their case for appointment and answer questions from the court about their qualifications (the court may call for the submission of resumes and other relevant information).... The court should inquire as to normal of anticipated billing rates, define recordkeeping requirements, and establish guidelines, methods, or limitations to govern the award of fees....

The court's responsibilities are heightened in class action litigation, where the judge must approve counsel for the class.

VINCENT v. HUGHES AIR WEST, INC.

557 F.2d 759 (9th Cir. 1977)

■ WALLACE, Circuit Judge. In consolidated cases arising out of a 1971 air crash disaster, the district court awarded attorneys' fees to four law firms that had comprised a plaintiffs' "committee of lead counsel" for discovery and other purposes. The award was to be paid out of the various settlements negotiated between the defendants, Hughes Air West, Inc. (Hughes) and the United States, and the next-of-kin of the crash victims. Some of the next-of-kin and their attorneys appeal, contending either that the district court had no authority to make the award or that the court erred in computing the award and designating the recipients....

I

[The case commenced in the Central District of California with the filing of several complaints against Hughes and the United States. In July 1972, the Judicial Panel on Multidistrict Litigation transferred to the Central District of California 11 cases arising out of the crash.] Soon thereafter, the district judge ordered all of the air crash cases consolidated for the sole purpose of determining liability. On the same day, August 30, he appointed John D. Miller of the Miller firm "liaison counsel between plaintiffs' counsel" and directed Miller to call a meeting of plaintiffs' counsel

> for the purpose of agreeing upon lead counsel or a committee of lead counsel, with Mr. Miller as Chairman, for all plaintiffs, to conduct all further discovery on liability and to try the case on liability, if that becomes necessary, and to voluntarily agree upon the contribution by non-members of such committee to a fund to be deposited with the Clerk from moneys paid by defendants resulting from the above-numbered lawsuits, to reimburse said committee members for such additional work as may result from the activities of said committee, and for compensation of fees to the members of said committee for work performed for the benefit of all plaintiffs. The members of the committee will keep accurate account of their time and expenditures as members of and for said committee.

At the ordered meeting of plaintiffs' counsel, a majority of those present selected four law firms to serve as a committee of lead counsel: the Miller firm [and three other firms].... A majority of those present also agreed to let the district court determine the method and amount of payment to lead counsel for their work. Some objected to this plan.

The proceedings of this meeting were presented to the district judge and on December 11, 1972, he confirmed the appointment of the committee of lead counsel.... The court then outlined both the responsibilities of lead counsel — "to conduct all further pre-trial proceedings, to bring or oppose all motions, and to prepare and conduct the trial on the issue of liability" — and the concurrent restrictions on plaintiffs' counsel not so designated (nonlead counsel), constituting generally a prohibition against initiating either further discovery proceedings or pretrial motions without first securing approval of lead counsel. The court did not grant lead counsel an absolute veto, however. Nonlead counsel disappointed with a decision of lead counsel could "apply to the Court for an order authorizing him to file [his proposed] motion or initiate [his proposed] discovery proceeding."

[Subsequently, the district judge approved lead counsels' plan for attorneys' fees. The plan required each class member to deposit five percent of any judgment or settlement with the clerk of the court. That five percent, known as the Special Class Fund, was to be taken from the contingent fee of the claimant's attorney to the extent that that fee exceeded 20 percent of the total recovery. The balance, if any, was to be paid from the claimant's portion of the recovery.]

As settlements were finalized and approved by the court and five percent of the recoveries deposited, the amount in the depository, generally referred to as the Special Class Fund, grew to over $450,000. In December 1973, the district court gave notice of a hearing to consider disbursement of the fund. The Miller firm and others commenced filing affidavits and other materials as proof of the time and costs they had expended on the liability issue. Some of the firms also filed pleadings and affidavits opposing the claims of various attorneys. . . .

[After four days of hearings the district judge] found that the work of lead counsel was competent and benefitted all claimants by removing the liability issue, that any services of nonlead counsel were not "for and on behalf of the entire Class," and that the value of lead counsel's services was between five and ten percent of the gross recoveries. Accordingly, the district judge awarded the entire Special Class Fund, minus the costs incurred by individual attorneys on the liability issue, to the committee of lead counsel. . . .

Most attorneys not on the committee acquiesced in the orders. Five groups of claimants and attorneys, however, have appealed . . . .

[The court first found that, because one plaintiff, Jewel Vincent, had negotiated a separate settlement using a lawyer working on an hourly basis, and because the clients of another lawyer, Demanes, had settled before appointment of lead counsel, neither could be forced to contribute to the Special Class Fund.]

IV

The remaining appellants (hereafter referred to jointly as "nonlead counsel" because all of the money at issue here came from the attorneys' portion of the settlements) can be treated as one for the purposes of this appeal; their cases cannot be distinguished on the basis of any material fact. To respond to the arguments of nonlead counsel, we turn first to one of the two asserted bases for the district court's orders in the present case: the federal courts' historic equity powers in class actions.

[The court held that, because the case could not be maintained as a class action, the district court could not use the powers of Rule 23 to justify its order regarding fees. It therefore turned to a second basis for the district court's order: the "common fund" doctrine, which requires the beneficiaries of a lawyer's efforts to create, discover, increase, or preserve a common fund to compensate counsel for those efforts. The court held that this doctrine, which prevents unjust enrichment, was a sufficient ground for the district court's order.]

We recognize that in this case the disparity in effort between lead counsel and nonlead counsel was effectively compelled by the district court's order of December 11, 1972, confirming lead counsel's appointment and imposing limits on the work of nonlead counsel. Nevertheless, the fact remains that lead counsel, according to the district court's findings, engaged in substantial work after their appointment that benefitted all claimants. On the basis of this finding we believe that the common fund doctrine permits fee shifting of the sort ordered by the district court. We are reinforced in this view by the fact that the district court's deposit formula operated to prevent a "double" payment of attorneys' fees by the claimants. ... Indeed, none of the claimants represented by nonlead counsel before us on this appeal (except Vincent) paid any of their portion of the recovery into the Special Class Fund. All deposits came from their attorneys' shares.

C

As noted above, the disparity in the efforts of lead and nonlead counsel was effectively compelled by provisions in the district court's order confirming the appointment of lead counsel. On this appeal, nonlead counsel make a frontal attack on the power of the district court to promulgate such an order, specifically to appoint lead counsel in multiparty litigation and to restrict the activities of nonlead counsel. We believe that the district court has such power and that the district court properly exercised it in these consolidated cases.

In recent decades, complex multiparty litigation has become an increasingly frequent occurrence in the federal district courts. The causes are many and include, in addition to the substantive laws underlying much of this litigation, the liberal joinder and intervention rules of the Federal Rules of Civil Procedure, Rules 19-20, 24, the provisions of Rule 42(a) permitting consolidation of actions, the provisions of 28 U.S.C. § 1404 permitting transfer by a single district judge, and the significant transfer authority granted to the Judicial Panel on Multidistrict Litigation by 28 U.S.C. § 1407. With this advent of complex multiparty litigation have come serious administrative problems, and the federal courts have found it necessary to develop innovative procedures to meet the problems. One of the earlier-devised procedures was the appointment of a "liaison counsel." The liaison counsel serves all parties on one side of the dispute. He is selected either by his colleagues or by the court, and his duties are generally ministerial. For example, he may receive and distribute to the parties on his side notices and other documents from the court or adverse parties, or he may call meetings where joint action is considered. The concept of liaison counsel was incorporated in an early edition of the Manual for Complex Litigation.

The limited scope of both liaison counsel's authority and his duties, however, sometimes created new problems, especially for plaintiffs in multidistrict aircrash cases. . . . Accordingly, proposals were advanced calling for creation of the role of "lead counsel," an attorney or group of attorneys with significant authority and a concomitant responsibility to conduct pretrial discovery and, if necessary, to litigate the liability issue. In 1972, the editors of the Manual for Complex Litigation incorporated many of these proposals in section 1.92 of the Manual.

Although some courts at an earlier time apparently doubted their power to create the role of lead counsel and oversee its filling, . . . by the time section 1.92 was added to the Manual for Complex Litigation the authority of the district courts regarding lead counsel was well-established. MacAlister v. Guterma, 263 F.2d 65 (2d Cir. 1958), represented "the first time that the power of the courts to order consolidation for the pre-trial stages and the appointment of general [lead] counsel to supervise and coordinate the prosecution of plaintiffs' case [was] presented to a federal appellate court." Defendants in a stockholders' derivative suit moved the district court for an order consolidating various related actions and appointing lead counsel for the consolidated plaintiffs. The district court refused. On appeal, the Second Circuit held that the district court had the "inherent powers" to consolidate and appoint lead counsel but that in that case, the district judge had not abused his discretion in refusing to do so. In support of its decision regarding the district court's authority to appoint lead counsel, the Second Circuit noted:

> The benefits achieved by consolidation and the appointment of general counsel, *i.e.* elimination of duplication and repetition and in effect the creation of a coordinator of diffuse plaintiffs through whom motions and discovery proceedings will be channeled, will most certainly redound to the benefit of all parties to the litigation. The advantages of this procedure should not be denied litigants in the federal courts because of misapplied notions concerning interference with a party's right to his own counsel. . . .

The authority recognized in *MacAlister* has never been seriously disputed. Indeed, many courts since that decision have explicitly reaffirmed their authority to appoint lead counsel and have exercised that authority. See, *e.g.*, Katz v. Realty Equities Corp., 521 F.2d 1354, 1356 (2d Cir. 1975) . . . .

We likewise hold that the district court had the authority to direct the appointment of a committee of lead counsel.[15] Further, we do not disapprove of the manner in which the district judge exercised that power in this case. The procedures leading to creation of the committee of lead counsel followed closely the guidelines set forth in the Manual for Complex Litigation § 1.92. Indeed, the purpose of that section — to insure the orderly disposition of the actions with economy of time, money and effort for the court, counsel and the parties — was largely fulfilled in this case.

Notes and Questions

1. When he appointed lead counsel, the district judge in *Vincent* did two things specifically discouraged in the *Manual, Third*: He allowed the plaintiffs' lawyers to choose the counsel structure for their side of the case, and he approved a committee of counsel rather than a single lead counsel. On both points, the *Manual, Third* takes a different position than the 1972 version of the *Manual for Complex Litigation*, which was in use at the time of *Vincent*. The 1972 *Manual* recommended that the court *not* select and appoint lead counsel, but allow the parties to do so; it also "encourage[d] the use of steering committees in appropriate cases." See Manual for Complex Litigation § 1.92

---

15. It is conceivable that the district court's authority to appoint lead counsel could serve as an independent basis for an order awarding lead or liaison counsel an extra fee for their services. We need not finally decide that question in this case, however. Regarding all the appellants but Vincent and Demanes, the traditional common fund doctrine is available to sustain the district court's orders. . . .

(1972). Might the problems in *Vincent* have been avoided if the judge had seized a firmer grasp of the counsel situation and the fee arrangements at the outset? Would you want a judge to exercise that much control over the decision about who will represent particular interests and how that representation will be funded? Does the contradictory advice found in the two Manuals make you more uneasy about giving a judge this control? Consider these questions in light of the following notes.

2. The *Manual, Third* suggests a number of counsel arrangements. If we take individual representation by a lawyer of the client's choosing as the ideal (as the adversarial system does), these different arrangements intrude on the ideal to varying degrees. The least intrusive is the liaison counsel arrangement, in which the individual's right to present her own proofs and reasoned arguments on the merits is unaffected. The most intrusive is the appointment of lead counsel by the court. A trial counsel arrangement, in which individual participation is guaranteed throughout the pretrial process, is a middle case, as are most committees of counsel.

3. As the *Manual, Third* suggests, there is no magical formula to figure out which type of arrangement will work best in a given case. Often judges will try to mix and match concepts. For instance, a judge may appoint trial counsel to handle the trial, and a committee of counsel to handle pretrial litigation. She may create a committee of counsel, and name one of its members liaison counsel and another member lead counsel. She may name one counsel to be both lead and liaison, divide the job of lead counsel among two or more "co-lead" counsel, or even appoint a non-lawyer with good organizational skills to be the liaison. Similarly, when a committee of counsel is appointed, committees may be broken down along procedural lines (*e.g.*, a discovery team, a trial team, a settlement team, a logistics team), along substantive lines (*e.g.*, one team working on statute of limitations issues, another on causation, another on damages, another on liability), or along interest group lines (*e.g.*, subclasses).

A review of reported decisions does reveal certain patterns. In cases in which plaintiffs are identically situated with regard to liability and remedy (for instance, a civil rights injunctive suit), the use of plaintiff lead counsel seems standard. The same is true for cases in which liability issues are essentially identical but remedial issues vary (for instance, securities fraud cases and single accident mass torts). When there are significant differences on liability issues among claimants (as in many dispersed mass torts), committees of plaintiff counsel are more common.

A final pattern is that judges seem more willing to appoint counsel for plaintiffs than for defendants. Indeed, the notion that a judge can appoint lead counsel or a committee of counsel to represent a group of plaintiffs is taken for granted today. It is quite rare, however, to see a judge do more than appoint a liaison counsel to coordinate matters among defendants. But see Active Product Corp. v. A.H. Choitz & Co., 163 F.R.D. 274 (N.D. Ind. 1995) (appointing defense steering committee); In re San Juan Dupont Plaza Hotel Fire Litigation, 1989 WL 168401 (D.P.R.) (appointing defense counsel to joint plaintiff-defendant discovery committee).

Taken as a whole, do these patterns suggest that defendants are better able than plaintiffs to hold onto the adversarial ideal of individual participation through proofs and reasoned arguments? If so, are there good reasons to accord different treatment to plaintiffs and defendants?

4. As the *Manual, Third* says, allowing the lawyers to select their own counsel structure is today a fairly discredited notion. The reason is explained by the infamous *Fine Paper* antitrust litigation, in which one plaintiffs' firm filed a complaint and then began circulating it among other potential plaintiffs' counsel. Some of these firms also filed suit. After consolidation of the cases, the various plaintiffs' firms later agreed on an Executive Committee arrangement with two co-lead counsel. The district court approved the arrangement, but after the attorneys requested hourly fees that amounted to 40 percent of the eventual settlement, the district court took a different view. It found that the initial group of plaintiffs' lawyers had planned "the distribution of patronage, that is, deciding to which firms the work assignments would be allocated," and that the committee structure "generate[d] wasted hours on useless tasks, propogate[d] duplication, and mask[ed] outright padding." In re Fine Paper Antitrust Litigation, 98 F.R.D. 48, 71, 75 (E.D. Pa. 1983), *aff'd* in part, *rev'd* in part, and remanded, 751 F.2d 562 (3d Cir. 1984) (approving most, but not all, of the district court's slashing of attorneys fees). See also John C. Coffee, Jr., *The Regulation of Entrepreneurial Litigation: Balancing Fairness and Efficiency in the Large Class Action*, 54 U. Chi. L. Rev. 877, 907-08 (1987) (likening consensual counsel arrangements to political conventions in which access to work is often traded for votes, resulting in "overstaffing and an acceptance of the free-riding or marginally competent attorney whose vote gave him leverage his ability did not"); In re "Agent Orange" Product Liability Litigation, 818 F.2d 226 (2d Cir.), cert. denied, 484 U.S. 926 (1987) (approving district court's dramatic cuts in attorneys fees of plaintiffs' committee because of duplication or lack of utility of counsels' efforts).

If lawyers cannot be trusted to select the counsel arrangement that best protects their clients' interests, who can be trusted? The standard answer today is that the judge must be actively involved in selecting lead counsel. But how is the judge to perform this task? Typically one or more of the existing counsel in a case will volunteer for the role. The *Manual, Third* describes the type of criteria that most judges then use to sift through the "applications" and choose the best counsel overall. Since one firm rarely comes out on top in all the relevant categories, judges often need to decide whether to select the firm with the most experience, the firm with the largest financial resources, the firm with the fee structure that is most attractive, or the firm that is likely to be most cooperative in the litigation process. The ultimate choice is likely to have a huge impact on the way the litigation is conducted and on the chances of recovery for the plaintiffs. Should we give judges this much discretion to influence the future course of the litigation? Isn't giving the judge discretion especially problematic when the judge's self-interest will lead her to favor counsel that will cause the judge the least difficulty in the management of the litigation?

5. Although as a practical matter lawyers for existing parties have an edge, a judge is not required to select any existing lawyers as liaison, lead, or committee counsel. In fact, in several recent securities cases, a court has resorted to putting the job of lead counsel up for nationwide bid. In re Oracle Securities Litigation, 132 F.R.D. 538 (N.D. Cal. 1990); In re Wells Fargo Securities Litigation, 157 F.R.D. 467 (N.D. Cal. 1994); In re Amino Acid Lysine Antitrust Litigation, 918 F. Supp. 1190 (N.D. Ill. 1996). Some of the existing counsel have bid for the position, but law firms with no prior connection to the case — or to any client in the case — have also submitted bids. The courts have examined the bids against both qualitative and quantitative considerations.

Qualitative considerations included experience, reputation, attorney and staff resources, familiarity with opposing counsel, proximity to court and witnesses, prior sanctions history, and willingness to keep litigation expenses to a minimum. Quantitative considerations focused on the firms' proposed fee arrangements, which varied from flat contingency fees to intricate sliding scale fees in which the firms' marginal rates of recovery depended on the length of the litigation and the amount of recovery. In assessing quantitative considerations, the court's stated objective was to find the fee that was most likely to maximize recovery to the plaintiffs. In light of the sliding scale fee structures, the court therefore needed to predict how long the case was likely to last and what the likely recovery was going to be in order to compare the merits of the various fees. Isn't there a danger that this type of analysis will lead the judge to prejudge the case? That the judge will do everything in her power to make the prejudgment come true, so that her choice of counsel will appear in retrospect to have been correct?

6. Since the bid system may result in the selection of a law firm that has no contact with any client in the case, you might think the proposal too radical. But it is not half as radical as the proposal of Professors Macey and Miller. Their perception is that, in large-scale, small-claim litigation like securities fraud cases, no plaintiff has much incentive to monitor the work of the attorney; other control mechanisms such as "bonding" of attorney to client are weakly present; and attorneys' fees arrangements provide incentives for lawyers either to run up the bill (the hourly fee arrangement) or to settle early to maximize attorney fees (the contingency fee arrangement). The result of these factors is that "plaintiffs' class and derivative attorneys function essentially as entrepreneurs who bear a substantial amount of the litigation risk and exercise nearly plenary control over all important decisions in the lawsuit." Jonathon R. Macey & Geoffrey P. Miller, *The Plaintiffs' Attorney's Role in Class Action and Derivative Litigation: Economic Analysis and Recommendations for Change*, 58 U. Chi. L. Rev. 1, 3 (1991). The authors' proposed solution is to auction off such large-scale, small-claim cases to the highest bidder. The proceeds from the auction are distributed among the plaintiffs. The winning bidder can then press the case against the defendant. Any amounts recovered in excess of the bid belong to the winning bidder as a profit; if the amount recovered is less than the bid, the bidder suffers a loss.

The advantages of such a proposal are that the litigation is placed in the hands of someone with a significant interest in monitoring the work of attorneys, that competitive forces will ensure that plaintiffs will recover the market value of their claims, that an asset (here, the plaintiffs' claims) will be directed toward its most efficient (*i.e.*, highest valuing) user, and that enforcement of small-claim cases will be increased. See id. at 108-10. Although the authors do not mention it, this approach will likely remove the judge from the process of selecting a counsel structure; presumably the winning bidder can decide for herself what the most efficient and effective counsel structure will be.

One of the fears that the Macey and Miller proposal raises is champerty. But in much complex litigation, plaintiffs' lawyers advance the litigation costs, which can run into the millions of dollars; and, in spite of what the attorney-client agreement says, the lawyers usually eat those costs if the defendants win. See Jack B. Weinstein, Individual Justice in Mass Tort Litigation 76 (1995). Thus, between costs and time, the lawyers often have an interest in the litigation that exceeds the interests of any client. Moreover, it is not unusual (although it is arguably unethical) for lawyers or judges to place on a steering committee some lawyers who act as investors that bankroll the litigation and who expect a significant return on their investment (the exact amount of which is often negotiated secretly) should a favorable settlement or verdict be reached. Id. at 77. At least the Macey and Miller proposal makes the financial interests of the lawyers open and obvious, and avoids the temptation to sell out the clients' interests as soon as the lawyers' investment and compensation interests are met.

For other drawbacks to the auction proposal, see 58 U. Chi. L. Rev. at 110-16; Randall S. Thomas & Robert G. Hansen, *Auctioning Class Action and Derivative Lawsuits: A Critical Analysis*, 87 Nw. U. L. Rev. 423 (1993) (sympathetically suggesting refinements to plan); Jonathon R. Macey & Geoffrey P. Miller, *Auctioning Class Action and Derivative Lawsuits: A Rejoinder*, 87 Nw. U. L. Rev. 458 (1993) (responding to suggestions).

7. Whatever you think of the Macey and Miller proposal, its basic point is not one that can be easily ignored: In large-scale cases lawyers often do operate with little client control. Some scholars claim that, even in more routine cases, clients have little contact with their lawyers and therefore exercise little effective control over their lawyers' decisions. See Deborah R. Hensler, *Resolving Mass Toxic Torts: Myths and Realities*, 1989 U. Ill. L. Rev. 89 (p. 124, *supra*). The anecdotal evidence in larger cases tells a similar tale. Most challenges to the appointment of lead counsel arise during arguments among law firms about which firm would make the best lead counsel, or, as in *Vincent*, during fee disputes in which the interested parties are lawyers, not clients. See In re Air Crash Disaster at Florida Everglades, 549 F.2d 1006 (5th Cir. 1977); Smiley v. Sincoff, 958 F.2d 498 (2d Cir. 1992); Walitalo v. Iacocca, 968 F.2d 741 (8th Cir. 1992). Only rarely is an appointment challenged because lead counsel is allegedly ignoring individual clients' interests, and even more rarely is such a challenge successful. See In re Ivan Boesky Securities Litigation, 948 F.2d 1358 (2d Cir. 1991) (rejecting class members' arguments that lead counsel improperly agreed to settle their claims and that settlement was unfair); Farber v. Riker-Maxson Corp., 442 F.2d 457 (2d Cir. 1971) (rejecting argument that order appointing lead counsel "den[ied] appellants an appropriate opportunity to participate in the litigation"); Arney v. Finney, 766 F. Supp. 934 (D. Kan. 1991) (rejecting argument that lead counsel ignored some class members), *aff'd* in part and dismissed in part, 967 F.2d 418 (1992).

Should we care about a party's autonomy to control the litigation? If parties in cases of all sizes have little control over their own litigation, then more formalized mechanisms by which client control is removed in complex cases — such as appointment of lead counsel or committees of counsel — are less problematic in fact than they seem to be in theory, aren't they? Or do the ideals of client autonomy and client control still have a critical value even when the reality falls short of the ideal? This is the assessment of Judge Weinstein:

> When we impose this adversarial model — the lawyer as fiduciary to the client — on the mass tort case, we find that the notion of the lawyer standing in the shoes of the client is somewhat ludicrous. In asbestos litigation, for example, some lawyers represent more than ten thousand plaintiffs.... The efficiency advantages due to economies of scale in such circumstances are obvious. Amassing large numbers of cases in the hands of relatively few specialized lawyers can greatly facilitate settlement and afford plaintiffs the benefit of attorneys experienced in complex cases.

But plaintiffs in mass cases pay a price for these advantages. Many of these lawyers do not maintain meaningful one-to-one contact with their clients, nor can they represent these people as individuals, each with his or her own needs and desires. The client becomes no more than an unembodied cause of action. Defendants . . . also pay a price in inflated recoveries for large numbers of questionable cases . . . .

At best these plaintiffs' lawyers construct small bureaucracies including paralegals, newsletters, and phone banks to maintain contact with their clients. At worst the lawyers neglect their clients. Injured persons may find that they have surrendered their rights to a system in which they have little or no input. Even with the best-intentioned lawyers, some alienation of the individual seems inevitable.

Weinstein, *supra*, at 54.

8. Subtle differences in legal, factual, and litigation positions often exist among parties with seemingly identical claims. Is it really possible for one counsel, or group of counsel, to represent vigorously all the different interests? How can counsel represent the interests of persons that counsel has never met? Isn't it likely that counsel will identify either with the interests of the client(s) that counsel has brought into the litigation, or else with counsel's own image of what an "average" client would want?

9. Other concerns are also raised by lead counsel or committee of counsel arrangements. In In re Thirteen Appeals Arising out of the San Juan Dupont Plaza Hotel Fire Litigation, 56 F.3d 295 (1st Cir. 1995), the court of appeals reversed a district court decision that ordered 70 percent of attorneys' fees to be given to the plaintiffs' steering committee and only 30 percent to be given to the lawyers who represented the individual plaintiffs. In the process of holding that a 50-50 split was more equitable, the court observed:

First, we are troubled by the implications of a scheme in which the trial judge selects a chosen few from many lawyers who volunteer, assigns legal tasks to those few (thereby dictating, albeit indirectly, the scope of the work remaining to be done by the many), and then, in awarding fees, heavily penalizes the very lawyers to whom he has relegated the "lesser" duties. . . . [Lead counsel] have no right to harbor any expectation beyond a fair day's pay for a fair day's work if a fee fund develops. . . .

Courts must also be sensitive to a second facet of economic reality: the power to appoint lead counsel gives the trial judge an unusual degree of control over the livelihood of the lawyers who practice before the court. . . . [T]he judge must attempt to avoid any perception of favoritism. . . .

Third, and relatedly, this case required the [individual attorneys] not merely to go along for a free ride but to earn their keep. They exhibited great versatility, counseling clients, researching medical histories, arranging for specialists to evaluate injuries, preparing the damages aspect of each case. . ., obtaining evidence . . ., responding to client-specific discovery, preparing for and attending clients' depositions, negotiating settlement values . . ., assisting clients with probate, insurance, and tax matters, and handling a bewildering array of idiosyncratic problems as they developed. . . .

We . . . are of the view that [the district judge] undervalued the worth of the client contact/counseling aspect of this litigation. . . . Despite their lack of visibility, . . . the mundane chores incident to client representation are particularly critical in a mass tort common fund case. [56 F.3d at 310.]

10. Professor Chayes believed the defining features of public law litigation to be an amorphous party structure and the broad participation of various interests. See p. 61, *supra*. Lead counsel, trial counsel, and committee arrangements reduce the amorphousness of that structure and aggregate interests in a way which inevitably reduces the ability of persons to participate fully. Professor Fuller predicted this result when polycentric disputes are "shoehorned" into the form of adjudication: Courts will be forced to ignore interests in an attempt to come to an acceptable result. See p. 108, *supra*. Does the rising use of lead counsel, trial counsel, or committees of counsel vindicate Fuller? Is this use of counsel consistent with a truly public law vision of litigation?

11. Do you now think that courts should freely appoint lead counsel, trial counsel, or committees of counsel in cases involving pretrial complexity? In cases not involving pretrial complexity, where such arrangements would nonetheless be an efficient management tool?

2. The Work and Structure of the Litigation Team

Whatever their theoretical problems, lead counsel and committee of counsel arrangements are likely to continue to be common in complex litigation. In this section we explore the types of tasks that such counsel can be expected to undertake during a complex case, and also the types of internal organizational structures that such counsel might adopt to perform these tasks efficiently and well.

IN RE: MGM GRAND HOTEL FIRE LITIGATION

660 F. Supp. 522 (D. Nev. 1987)

■ BECHTLE, District Judge. [A fire that broke out in the MGM Grand Hotel in Las Vegas killed 87 persons and injured more than 1,000. Suits were filed in state and federal courts against more than 100 defendants. The federal cases were transferred by the Judicial Panel on Multidistrict Litigation to the District of Nevada. The transferee judge appointed a "Plaintiffs' Legal Committee" (PLC) "to initiate, coordinate and conduct all pretrial liability and damage discovery on behalf of all plaintiffs" involved in the MDL proceeding. The case eventually settled for more than $205 million. At the outset of the case the PLC had agreed to take a contingency fee of 5 percent of the total recovery. After conclusion of the settlement, the PLC petitioned the court to increase its fees to 7 percent. In ruling on this request, the court described the many functions undertaken by the PLC.]

Many of the attorneys who ultimately became PLC members of the 12 member committee conducted an extensive on-site investigation at the MGM Grand Hotel in Las Vegas and hired, at their expense, experts to study the site before the demolition and rebuilding of the affected areas of the hotel. The PLC recovered over 6,000 objects from the fire site and stored and used them in a joint warehouse depository during the course of this litigation. It hired some of the best experts in the nation to test various products found in the hotel at substantial expense and retained an "in house" expert to coordinate all experts and supervise a substantial regimen of testing. The PLC established a document depository, reviewed (which included cataloguing and some microfilming) over 4,000,000 documents produced by the various defendants, and organized and catalogued all information gleaned by computer for retrieval by subject categories.

The PLC members participated in and supervised the taking of over 1,400 depositions, in "tracks" of up to 11 depositions in different cities at one time, and prepared summaries of all relevant depositions for the trial of the case. It reviewed every deposition transcript and designated each section expected to be used at trial. The PLC completed all aspects of all waves of discovery in accordance with the Manual for Complex Litigation.

The PLC filed pleadings on behalf of all plaintiffs, including original and amended complaints and all discovery pleadings in state and federal courts across the country and in the United States Court of Appeals for the Ninth Circuit. It was eventually successful in having all claims filed in this court thereby permitting claims which had originally been filed in many federal district and state courts to proceed together. The PLC reviewed and responded to thousands of items of correspondence and pleadings by the defendants and initiated substantial correspondence and hundreds of pleadings on behalf of all of the 1,000 or so plaintiffs. It prepared and filed extensive motions, applications, and briefs relative to . . . [all] aspects of this litigation. As noted above, the PLC prepared the single amended complaint for all plaintiffs' interests. It prepared agendas for and attended all pretrial conferences with this court including weekly and bi-weekly discovery and dispute hearings before the Magistrate, and prepared pleadings for and appeared at more than 225 pretrial hearings over the course of the litigation, including the handling of in excess of 1,000 motions dealing with discovery issues. The PLC coordinated the compilation of damage material in each individual case, participating in the preparation of answers and/or objections to all damage interrogatories.

The PLC was successful in having trial dates set in succession against various groups of defendants in order to conduct the trial in the most expeditious manner. It marshalled over 11,000 relevant documents for trial, prepared dozens of witnesses for trial, prepared an extensive pretrial order and jury trial books. It conducted a demographic jury poll to analyze the likelihood of success in the Nevada courts against selected defendants.

Prior to the "global settlement," claims in excess of $17,500,000.00 were consummated as a result of the PLC's efforts . . . . This agreement enabled the plaintiffs, via the PLC, to adequately conduct substantial discovery and other pre-trial functions. In addition, the members of the PLC advanced expense funds on behalf of the plaintiffs of over a million dollars during the pendency of this litigation. . . .

During the pendency of this action, the PLC, with the participation of the court, was able to confirm a sum of $134,887,992.00 as the amount needed to settle all of the claims of the 1,084 plaintiff interests. It then negotiated settlements with all of the remaining unsettled defendants, in order to fund this amount demanded as the aggregate settlement amount by the plaintiffs. The PLC drafted unique settlement agreements with all defendants that provided for almost every contingency, including indemnity from every plaintiff. The PLC drafted and/or reviewed all receipts and releases and coordinated the execution of those documents by all plaintiffs, including translation of many releases into other languages because of several hundred Spanish-speaking claimants and attorneys, and reviewed every release to ascertain that it had been properly executed. The total amount of the recovery produced by this effort, with interest, is in excess of $205,000,000.00 and was obtained from the various approximately 114 defendants. . . .

A distribution plan was established by the PLC and implemented by a reputable accounting firm hired by the PLC. Throughout this litigation the PLC took a very active part in monitoring the trust, including several hundred telephone calls, much correspondence, and many meetings with the Trustee and members of the accounting firm which the PLC had commissioned to conduct a full-scale audit of the trust.

The PLC has successfully distributed $168,365,198.93 . . . . A member of the PLC staff reviewed and confirmed every form and every check issued in the . . . distributions. . . .

This was clearly a risky and burdensome venture the PLC embarked upon and the principal beneficiaries have been the plaintiffs. In this effort, the PLC members, their partners, associates, paralegals and the support personnel expended over 77,500 hours in dedicated and competent service to all plaintiffs that produced an extraordinary result. The court has audited the hours submitted by the PLC members and finds that they are reasonable. The PLC made proper uses of staff to perform non-attorney functions. . . .

To the court's knowledge, the results of the PLC's efforts have never been equaled in any other mass disaster litigation. Indeed, of the dozens of mass disaster cases that were pending or begun during the pendency of this case, none of them have concluded except this one, and from the court's viewpoint, that says it all.

The court determines that an increase in the PLC fees from 5% to 7% of the "global" settlement is plainly warranted and promptly required.

Danny P. Richey, GUIDELINES AND TECHNIQUES FOR LEADING AND MANAGING THE LITIGATION TEAM

19 Ohio N. L. Rev. 23, 24-30, 33, 35, 37, 39, 48-49, 51 (1992)

One of the most important tasks in litigation is the selection and organization of the litigation team. The litigation team may be organized "loosely" or informally in small cases, while the litigation team tends to be "highly organized" in large or complex cases. In complex litigation, the team generally takes, or at least evolves into, a "cluster" format. Rigid vertical or horizontal hierarchies are generally not practical in organizing a litigation team for protracted litigation. Rather, the team, although formally organized, resembles a cluster organized according to activity. . . .

II. THE LITIGATION TEAM

Large, complex cases require a wealth of resources and personnel. The litigation team for a complex case usually consists of most or all of the following types of members:

1. *Trial or "lead" counsel.* Large cases are typically led and managed by the "lead counsel," who is usually a law firm partner. Occasionally, complex cases require that two or more attorneys assume lead counsel roles. However, cases involving more than one lead counsel run the risk of becoming too decentralized or fractionalized for proper management control. . . .

2. *The "second chair."* Lead counsel will often select a junior partner or senior associate to act as "second chair." In a sense, the second chair is a "lead counsel" in training. The second chair acts, in the fullest sense of the term, as the "right hand" of lead counsel. Usually, the second chair is very active in discovery, brief writing, assisting lead counsel in managing the case and the litigation team, developing case strategies, and handling various aspects of the trial.

3. *Other attorneys.* Often, other attorneys may be needed in a complex action for research, briefing, or discovery purposes.

4. *Local counsel.* If a case is pending in a district other than where lead counsel resides or in a court other than where lead counsel is admitted to practice, then it may be necessary to hire local counsel. Typically, local counsel plays a major role in scheduling court appearances, arranging for trial accommodations, and assisting in voir dire at trial. Additionally, local counsel's role may be expanded to include substantive areas, depending upon the case needs and the client's desires.

5. *Legal Assistants.* Legal assistants should be used to manage documents, assist discovery, organize and administer trial exhibits, and other projects. They can also be used for minor research projects, drafting written discovery, and attending depositions as either "note takers" or document organizers. . . .

6. *Secretaries.* Secretaries are responsible for maintaining the litigation files, handling communications, performing word processing, and assisting in the use of computerized management programs. Secretaries may also serve as their attorney's "right arm" for team coordination, information flow purposes, client coordination, and time scheduling. . . . Finally, a crucial task which may be assigned to a secretary is docket control and case scheduling.

7. *Client representative.* The client representative, if the client is a business entity, or the client himself or herself, comprises an integral part of the litigation team.... The client can be a valuable team member by providing background information and analyzing case strategies, particularly where the case involves technical or esoteric areas....

8. *Experts.* Experts can be utilized in many ways during the course of a case; early employment of experts and integration of the experts' talents into the team structure provides numerous benefits to the attorneys and clients....

9. *Litigation consultants.* Several types of litigation consultants are available to assist in preparing and trying a complex case. Litigation consultants seek to apply various aspects of social sciences to litigation. They may provide information about prospective jurors, conduct attitudinal surveys, conduct mock presentations of trials, provide feedback and suggestions to attorneys and witnesses regarding trial presentation and communication, prepare visual aids and trial exhibits, and provide trial monitoring and feedback.

10. *Document managers.* Several independent firms offer document management services to attorneys. The services available include document indexing, full text retrieval, and deposition abstracting.

11. *Third-party factual witnesses.* In addition to testifying, cooperative non-client factual witnesses may provide valuable resources during litigation. Generally, these resources will be similar to those provided by the client representative and the experts....

12. *Vendors, runners, and other team members.* During the course of litigation, several outside vendors may be employed as court reporters, graphic artists, video technicians, or the like. In addition, "runners" will be needed for errands....

III. SELECTING THE TEAM ...

In selecting team members, you should consider what the case requires in terms of staffing needs, whom does the case need, and when various team members need to become involved. Since you are limited by available personnel and their talents, you must select the most talented team from the available personnel pool while considering their diverse personalities and talents. Additionally, you must understand that too many team members can be as disastrous as not enough members. Therefore, select the best qualified members who are available for the entire litigation period, who possess the requisite individual and team skills, and who are capable or working together as a unit....

IV. THE ORGANIZATION AND STRUCTURE OF A LITIGATION TEAM ...

The usual litigation team structure is, strictly speaking, neither purely vertical nor a pyramid. A true vertical chain of command, designed similarly to a corporate hierarchy, would require vendors and runners to report to the second chair, and the second chair to report to the lead counsel. . . . Usually, a litigation team cannot be organized and managed by such a rigid chain of command.

Similarly, a pyramid structure has lead counsel at the top, other attorneys in descending order down the pyramid, with the pyramid spreading out at the base to include legal assistants, secretaries, and support personnel. . . . The pyramid structure is a form of vertical integration that does not generally reflect the practicalities of a litigation team. A more useful description of the realities of how a litigation team must function is the term "clustering."

A "cluster system" is organized, to a certain degree, both horizontally and vertically, but fluctuates with particular case projects and tasks, depending on the personnel involved and the allocation of responsibilities.

In a clustering system, personnel are organized into groups or clusters which revolve and evolve depending upon the needs of the organization and the tasks being performed. Within the clustering structure, personnel and tasks may be organized vertically or horizontally. Consider, for example, the taking of an expert's deposition . . . . The team members involved in this project are leading counsel who will attend the deposition and offer input; an expert witness who will assist in deposition preparation and also attend the deposition; a legal assistant who will gather and organize deposition exhibits and attend the deposition as a document manager; and a secretary who will schedule the deposition, arrange for a court reporter, and attend the deposition as a note taker. In this example, all members will generally report to lead counsel; however, at times, the client representative may talk directly with the expert, or the paralegal and secretary may deal directly in scheduling and organizational matters. Thus, while a cluster is formed around lead counsel, there is also some interaction between the other members. However, there is no rigid, vertical structure similar to the typical corporate chain of command. In the clustered litigation team, tasks are divided along functional lines. In other words, the nature of the task determines the team member who will be responsible for it: lead counsel takes the deposition, the expert and client representative offer input, a paralegal handles exhibits, and a secretary handles scheduling and note taking. The only meaningful overlap of tasks is between the expert and the client representative, both are involved for purposes of providing advice and technical expertise.

Essentially, the idea of organizing functional tasks in a horizontal fashion is to assign projects and organize the litigation team according to the function which must be performed. Hence, the team may be organized according to issues, witnesses, events, or a combination of the three. Another functional approach is to divide case assignments according to events or activities; for example, some members would be in charge of discovery, another group in charge of briefing, a third group in charge of document organization, and so on. The danger in dividing tasks according to events or activities is lack of continuity; no one may have the overall picture. Consequently, long-term case assignments should usually be structured according to issues and/or witnesses, rather than events or activities.

In sum, the litigation team should be organized in logical format but remain flexible so as to accommodate scheduling, available resources, and case needs. A clustering system organized somewhat vertically with assignments made horizontally according to functional needs usually provides the most practical structure for a litigation team....

VI. Delegation and Supervision

Two important leadership and management "tools" underlying the litigation team concept are supervision and delegation. It is particularly important for lead counsel and second chair to devote attention to the principles and practice of supervision and delegation.

Delegation is assigning tasks and authority to others; supervision is "overseeing" how tasks are performed and the authority is exercised. Stated differently, delegation is "the process of turning work over to subordinates"; supervision is the process of insuring that work is handled correctly by others. The two principles are, of course, intertwined.

Delegation should be a *planned process* whereby specific tasks and responsibilities are assigned to appropriate team members..... Assigning tasks due to a pending crisis reflects a *lack* of foresight and planning.... [D]elegation is a leadership and management tool; "dumping" is simply an emotional reaction to lack of leadership and management....

A litigation team cannot function effectively without clear, precise, timely assignments and allocations of responsibility. By following the basic principles of delegation and supervision, lead counsel can create a team environment directed toward a true spirit of cooperation and "togetherness."

Notes and Questions

1. Imagine yourself in the position of lead counsel who has to accomplish the types of tasks outlined in the *MGM Grand* case. What sort of team would you assemble? What would be your management philosophy?

Now imagine yourself as a young attorney working on the case. Which philosophy and style of management would you prefer?

Now imagine yourself as a paralegal or a secretary. Same question: How would you like to be treated?

2. Mr. Ritchie says that a cluster approach is *the* best approach. Do you necessarily agree? What are some of the weaknesses of such an approach?

3. Even within the cluster approach, many management decisions remain. One of the most crucial is how large your team should be. One model, which we might call the "large law firm" model, is to have a lead counsel, several junior counsel, and lots of young associates who are drawn out of an associate pool to research specific issues. The young associates do research for junior counsel, who blend the research into arguments under the direction of the lead counsel, who presents the argument in court. Another model, which we might call the

"government lawyer" model or "plaintiff" model, utilizes a lead counsel and a very small number of attorneys. All counsel, including the lead attorney, have responsibility for doing basic research, writing, and presentation of arguments in court. In which system would you rather work as lead counsel? As a young lawyer?

4. Do you think that law school has equipped you with the management skills necessary to be lead counsel? If not, how can you develop those skills?

5. One skill which Ritchie's article does not discuss, but which is absolutely vital to success as lead counsel, is the ability to interact with, and if necessary exploit, the litigation structures of the other parties in the litigation. This requires you to know something about how the other teams are set up and about the strengths and weaknesses of their structure in relation to yours. It also requires you to have good instincts about the personalities of those on the other teams: which persons are cooperative, which are truculent, which are trustworthy, which have real (as opposed to nominal) influence, which have private agendas, and so on.

6. So the only thing you need to be a good lead counsel is training in law, management, and psychology, and lots of years of practical experience. Other than that, it's easy!

3. Disqualification of Counsel

In an adversary system, the client's legitimate interests become those of the lawyer. In litigation this model requires the lawyer to present, zealously but within the bounds of the law, those proofs and arguments that advance a client's interests. The attorney-client privilege, which ensures the confidentiality of communications both to and from clients, helps the lawyer to accomplish this task. With that privilege, of course, comes a responsibility: Except in limited circumstances, lawyers can never use or disclose information obtained from a client for other purposes — especially not for the purpose of harming the client's interests.

Whenever a lawyer enters into an attorney-client relationship with one party, however, the possibility exists that the lawyer may have represented (or still be representing) another party with interests adverse to the present representation. Not only does this possibility divide the loyalty of an attorney between two clients, but it also raises the danger that the lawyer will use or disclose information obtained from one of the representations in a way that is detrimental to the other. To avoid these problems, lawyers will typically screen potential clients to avoid the representation of inconsistent interests. But sometimes these conflicts filter through the screen. A typical remedy in this situation is to disqualify the attorney from continuing one or the other representation.

As we have seen, complex litigation often involves many parties who have a welter of interests. Situations in which a lawyer has represented or is representing parties whose interests seemingly oppose each other are common, and the risk that confidential information will be used to harm one set of these interests is ever-present. The issue, therefore, is whether lawyers finding themselves with these actual or apparent conflicts of interest should be disqualified.

IN RE "AGENT ORANGE" PRODUCT LIABILITY LITIGATION

800 F.2d 14 (2d Cir. 1986)

KEARSE, Circuit Judge. Stephen J. Schlegel, Esq., a member of the Plaintiffs' Management Committee ("PMC") in the "Agent Orange" product liability litigation, moved in this Court for an order disqualifying the law firm of Ashcraft & Gerel ("Ashcraft") and the Law Offices of Benton Musslewhite ("Musslewhite"), Inc., from representing in the captioned appeals certain class members and other plaintiffs who challenge the settlement of the litigation approved by the district court. Schlegel contends principally that Ashcraft and Musslewhite, as a result of their prior representation of parties supporting the settlement, have conflicts of interest requiring their disqualification as appellate counsel. . . .

I. BACKGROUND

The Agent Orange lawsuits began in late 1978 and early 1979 when several individual veterans of the Vietnam War and their families brought suit in the Northern District of Illinois and the Southern and Eastern Districts of New York. Named as defendants were several chemical companies that had manufactured Agent Orange and other herbicides for use by the military as defoliants in the Vietnam War. The plaintiffs alleged that they had sustained various physical injuries by reason of the veterans' exposure to Agent Orange. [All cases were transferred to the Eastern District of New York by the Judicial Panel on Multidistrict Litigation. The district court certified a Rule 23(b)(3) opt-out plaintiff class consisting of members of the armed forces of United States, New Zealand, and Australia, and their spouses, parents, and children who were directly or derivatively injured as a result of the exposure.]

A. *Representation of Class Plaintiffs* . . .

Schlegel became counsel to various plaintiffs in the litigation as early as November 1978. He has been designated as one of plaintiffs' counsel of record throughout the Agent Orange litigation. Musslewhite became involved as plaintiffs' counsel in Agent Orange litigation as early as January 1979. He represents some 1,500 Vietnam veterans as individual clients. Ashcraft has represented plaintiffs in Agent Orange litigation on an active basis since early 1980. It represents more than 2,000 plaintiff class members, as well as 386 individuals who originally opted out of the class; 60 of those opt-outs later rejoined the class.

In 1980, after tentatively granting the class certification, the district court appointed Yannacone & Associates ("Yannacone"), a consortium of

New York-area lawyers, as lead counsel to the class. Thereafter, Ashcraft acted as class action counsel under an agreement with Yannacone. At the request of or by agreement with Yannacone in early 1983, Schlegel, Musslewhite, and Ashcraft became members of the PMC. All functioned for a time thereafter as class counsel. In addition, Schlegel and Musslewhite were designated by the court as lead counsel.

Ashcraft was never appointed lead counsel, but as a member of the PMC and as class action counsel, it undertook a number of tasks on behalf of the class, including attending depositions, reviewing documents obtained through discovery, and writing, filing, and opposing motions in the district court. During Musslewhite's tenure as a member of the PMC, he was listed as counsel of record in numerous filings with the district court and joined in motions concerning class certification, proposed forms of notice to class members, and other substantive issues in the litigation.

In September 1983, Yannacone moved for and was granted permission to withdraw as lead counsel and a member of the PMC. Ashcraft also withdrew from the PMC in September 1983. The order of the district court approving the withdrawal of Yannacone provided that the PMC would function as lead counsel. The PMC then consisted of Schlegel, Musslewhite, and the law firm of Baskin & Sears.

B. *The Settlement Agreement, the Pending Appeals, and the Present Disqualification Motion*

Prior to May 7, 1984, with the class actions scheduled to go to trial on May 7, the parties negotiated a settlement of the class actions. The agreement called for the defendant chemical companies to pay a total of $180 million in settlement to the members of the plaintiff classes.

As a member of the PMC, Musslewhite had participated in the negotiations that led to the settlement agreement; he voted in favor of that agreement and spoke in support of it in the fairness hearings conducted by the district court in August 1984. Thereafter, however, Musslewhite became disenchanted with the proposed settlement agreement, and in January 1985, he withdrew from the PMC.

In January, 1985, the district court found the settlement to be fair, reasonable, and adequate under the circumstances, . . . and in May 1985, it approved a distribution plan for the settlement fund . . . .

Following the entry of final judgments approving the settlement, Ashcraft and Musslewhite, on behalf of the thousands of plaintiffs they represent, filed appeals contending that the settlement should be set aside. Ashcraft, on behalf of its clients and on behalf of 21 law firms around the country claiming to represent some 3,000 additional class members, filed a brief challenging the fairness, reasonableness, and adequacy of the settlement and contending, in addition, that the district court lacked subject matter jurisdiction of the litigation and had denied individual claimants due process in certifying the class.

Musslewhite filed a brief adopting the arguments made in Ashcraft's brief and making additional challenges to the sufficiency of the notice given to class members and the adequacy of the approved settlement. In responding to the present motion, Musslewhite stated that his view of the adequacy of the settlement, which he initially had favored, was changed by information that came to light only after the agreement was negotiated, as to the number of class members who did not receive notice of the class action and the number of class members who have claims to be satisfied from the settlement fund. . . .

Schlegel, on behalf of the PMC as it is presently constituted, moved to disqualify Ashcraft and Musslewhite from representing parties on the pending appeals, principally on the grounds that the combination of (1) Ashcraft's representation of both class members and individuals who chose to opt out of the class, (2) Musslewhite's participation in the negotiation of the proposed settlement on behalf of the class, and (3) the prior roles of Ashcraft and Musslewhite as members of the PMC and class counsel, have given them "such a direct conflict of interest as to create a clear impropriety in violation of controlling standards of professional conduct." For the reasons below, we have concluded that the motion should be denied.

II. DISCUSSION

As a matter of professional responsibility, an attorney owes a duty of loyalty to his client. This duty encompasses an obligation to defer to the client's wishes on major litigation decisions, not to divulge confidential communications from the client, and not to accept representation of a person whose interests are opposed to those of the client. *E.g.*, A.B.A. Code of Professional Responsibility EC 7-1, 4-1, and 5-2.

These obligations do not necessarily end when the attorney-client relationship ends. *E.g.*, Cinema 5, Ltd. v. Cinerama, Inc., 528 F.2d 1384 (2d Cir.1976) . . . . Thus, we have ordered disqualification of a party's attorney where, as a result of his prior representation of another client, "the attorney is at least potentially in a position to use privileged information concerning the other side . . . thus giving his present client an unfair advantage." Board of Education v. Nyquist, 590 F.2d 1241, 1246 (2d Cir. 1979); *see, e.g.*, Fund of Funds, Ltd. v. Arthur Andersen & Co., 567 F.2d 225 (2d Cir. 1977); . . . In re Corn Derivatives Antitrust Litigation, 748 F.2d 157, 161 (3d Cir. 1984) ("*Corn Derivatives*") ("In litigation, an attorney may not abandon his client and take an adverse position in the same case. This is not merely a matter of revealing or using the client's confidences and secrets, but of a duty of continuing loyalty to the client."), *cert. denied*, 472 U.S. 1008 (1985).

Applying these traditional principles in non-class-action litigation, we have held that, in order to support a motion for disqualification, "'the former client [need] show no more than that the matters embraced within the pending suit wherein his former attorney appears . . . are substantially related to the matters or cause of action where the attorney previously represented him, the former client.'" *Funds of Funds, Ltd. v. Arthur Andersen & Co.*, 567 F.2d at 235 (quoting T.C. Theatre Corp. v. Warner Bros. Pictures, 113 F. Supp. 265, 268 (S.D.N.Y. 1953) (Weinfeld, J.)). Although disqualification has the immediate adverse effect on the present client of depriving him of the attorney of his choice, removal of the attorney in such circumstances may be "necessary to preserve the integrity of the adversary process." *Board of Education v. Nyquist*, 590 F.2d at 1246.

Class action litigation presents additional problems that must be considered in determining whether or not to disqualify an attorney who has represented the class and who seeks to represent thereafter only a portion of the class. . . . These problems are created by, *inter alia*, the facts that there are, by definition, numerous class members and that there is often no clear allocation of the decision-making responsibility between the attorney and his clients. Further, though there will be common questions affecting the claims of the class members, it is not unusual for their interests, especially at the relief stage, to diverge. Such a divergence presents special problems because the class attorney's duty does not run just to the plaintiffs named in the caption of the case; it runs to all of the members of the class. . . .

Automatic application of the traditional principles governing disqualification of attorneys on grounds of conflict of interest would seemingly dictate that whenever a rift arises in the class, with one branch favoring a settlement or a course of action that another branch resists, the attorney who has represented the class should withdraw entirely and take no position. Were he to take a position, either favoring or opposing the proposed course of action, he would be opposing the interests of some of his former clients in the very matter in which he has represented them. . . .

Nonetheless, as Judge Adams noted in his concurring opinion in *Corn Derivatives*, although automatic disqualification might "promote the salutary ends of confidentiality and loyalty, it would have a serious adverse effect on class actions." 748 F.2d at 164. When many individuals have modest claims against a single entity or group of entities, the class action may be the only practical means of vindicating their rights, since otherwise the expenses of litigation could exceed the value of the claim. In such class actions, often only the attorneys who have represented the class, rather than any of the class members themselves, have substantial familiarity with the prior proceedings, the fruits of discovery, the actual potential of the litigation. And when an action has continued over the course of many years, the prospect of having those most familiar with its course and status be automatically disqualified whenever class members have conflicting interests would substantially diminish the efficacy of class actions as a method of dispute resolution. This is so both because the quality of the information available to the court would likely be impaired and because even if a class member were familiar with all the prior proceedings, the amount of his stake in the litigation might well make it unattractive for him to participate actively, either on his own or through new counsel.

Our system of justice demands that the interests of all concerned be accommodated as fairly as possible, and this accommodation must include the preservation of the class action form of litigation without a wasteful multiplication of its cost. In order to proceed efficiently and fairly and to protect the interests of all members of the class, the court needs, insofar as is practicable, the benefit of the participation of attorneys who are familiar with the litigation. This need has been accommodated in many cases in which a technical conflict may exist, for the attorney for the class is normally allowed to oppose the contentions of class members who have appeared in court in opposition to a proposed settlement of the class action, . . . although technically the Code of Professional Responsibility would seem to prohibit his doing so. . . . In this case, for example, Schlegel, though moving to disqualify Ashcraft and Musselwhite for representing objectors in opposition to class members they formerly represented, himself represented as class counsel many of the objectors he now opposes.

Thus, we conclude that the traditional rules that have been developed in the course of attorneys' representation of the interests of clients outside of the class action context should not be mechanically applied to the problems that arise in the settlement of class action litigation. A motion to disqualify an attorney who has represented the entire class and who has thereafter been retained by a faction of the class to represent its interests in opposition to a proposed settlement of the action cannot be automatically granted. Rather, there must be a balancing of the interests of the various groups of class members and of the interest of the public and the court in achieving a just and expeditious resolution of the dispute.

Relevant considerations in determining whether the moving party has shown sufficient ground for disqualification of prior class counsel include "the amount and nature of the information that has been proffered to the attorney, its availability elsewhere, its importance to the question at issue, such as settlement, as well as actual prejudice that may flow from that information." *Corn Derivatives,* 748 F.2d at 165 (Adams, J., concurring). The court must consider as well the costs to the class members of requiring that they obtain new counsel, taking into account such factors as the nature and value of the claim they are presenting, the ease with which they could obtain new counsel, the factual and legal complexity of the litigation, and the time that would be needed for new counsel to familiarize himself with all that has gone before.

In the present litigation, we conclude that the weighing of the various interests requires that the motion to disqualify Ashcraft and Musslewhite be denied. First, we note that Schlegel in his moving papers has failed to allege any actual prejudice that would result if Ashcraft and Musslewhite were not disqualified. He has not indicated that client confidences were received by Ashcraft or Musslewhite from pro-settlement members of the class. Nor, if such confidences be assumed, has he indicated how or even whether such confidences would be violated by these firms' continued participation in the appeals. Schlegel's general allegations of conflict of interest are insufficient to warrant a finding of prejudice.

Several factors weigh against disqualification here. . . . If the thousands of objectors were now deprived of the services of Ashcraft and Musslewhite, all of the choices confronting the court would be unattractive. It could require the objectors to proceed promptly, which would mean that they would be unrepresented or would be represented by attorneys who are not fully familiar with the prior course of the litigation and the hundreds of thousands of documents turned up in discovery. In the context of the present motion, which was made to this Court in December 1985 in connection with appeals to be argued in April 1986, we doubt that new counsel could have been found who would have been willing and able to assimilate these documents in such a short period. Alternatively the court could allow the objectors time for their new attorneys to familiarize themselves with the proceedings and the documents. This, of course, would delay for the other thousands of class members who favor the settlement the receipt of compensation they deem adequate, or at least acceptable, for their injuries.

Finally, we note that the size of the proposed settlement in light of the large number of class members could itself constrain the ability or incentive of objecting class members to obtain new counsel who would fully familiarize themselves with the pertinent facts of the litigation. The settlement distribution plan approved by the district court provided for a maximum payment of $12,800 to any one class member, with an average payment of approximately $4,200. . . . Musslewhite's estimate as to individual recovery amounts is even lower, for he contends that there are some 243,000 claimants. If he is correct, the arithmetical mean share of the $180 million settlement fund, plus interest, would amount to approximately $850. . . .

In all the circumstances, we conclude that disqualification of Ashcraft and Musslewhite is not "necessary to preserve the integrity of the adversary process." *Board of Education v. Nyquist*, 590 F.2d at 1246.

Jack B. Weinstein, INDIVIDUAL JUSTICE IN MASS TORT LITIGATION

44, 46-47, 87-88 (1995)

It has been properly noted that "much of the intellectual effort in the field of legal ethics during the past quarter century has been an attempt to reevaluate the rules that emerged during the 'golden age' of the solo practitioner and the small firm." Yet, the current American Law Institute project on Restatement of the Law Governing Lawyers ignores mass torts and largely restates the old models of the one-lawyer, one-client relationship and the two-litigant case.

My own experiences on the bench have led me to conclude that we need to go beyond the rules of the past and provide more realistic guidance to today's lawyers and judges. . . . For the attorney, the viability is placed in question of such ethical imperatives as the duty to communicate with each client effectively, to maintain confidences, and to avoid conflicts of interest in client representation. . . .

Because of the political, sociological, economic, and technological implications of many mass tort cases, we must consider not only the individual litigant and lawyer, but entire communities. We assume, properly I believe, that dignity is enhanced by individual control of litigation for each person's benefit. . . . But just as individualism run riot can be damaging in social matters, so too may it need checking in mass litigations.

Each of us lives in many communities if we define this term as a group of people having common rights and privileges or common interests....

To deal with such groups it is helpful to consider some of the insights of communitarian ethicists. We need to look not only to the individual's hurt but also to similar harm suffered by others in the community, and suggested solutions for those who may be secondarily affected....

George Sharswood's work of the last century — upon which our current legal ethics codes are based — assumed a communitarian bent. He exhorted a "[h]igh moral principle [as] the [lawyer's] only safe guide, the only torch to light his way amidst the darkness and obstruction." The lawyer's primary obligation, as he perceived it, was to the common good. In balancing this "republican" role with the lawyer's adversarial role, Sharswood apparently understood that the system "could not require each individual lawyer to represent any client and to seek the greatest success for every client represented." Accordingly, he endorsed the view that "the lawyer was a public officer with duties to the public and the court as well as the client."
. . .

Once we recognize that large-scale representation in mass tort cases is both inevitable and desirable and accept the view that this form of representation makes the traditional one-on-one relationship between lawyer and client impracticable, we cannot avoid the need for a new formulation of the lawyer's ethical duty. Without such a new ethic, the lawyer will be too likely to be guided by his or her own interests where it becomes difficult to discern or follow the interests of the many clients.

A broader view of obligations to the public weal, approved by the profession and bench, would permit exercise of this goodwill without the inhibitions imposed by the narrow traditional rules restricting the lawyer to individual client interests. If the lawyer in the mass tort case understands his or her duty as running in part to the community to which clients belong, or the communities which may be affected by the result, individual needs may be better served. Such a communitarian ethic requires the lawyer to consider more than the optimal dollar recovery for the group. The lawyer must consider the impact of the benefit and harm on the community as a whole, in both the short and the long run. The lawyer should attempt to communicate with the communities as a whole to learn their needs and desires. The lawyer should understand that the significance of the case to a community will remain long after the lawyer has left the scene....

These suggestions are tentative at best. Many questions are raised. Is it possible to regulate such a communitarian ethic or would be have to rely on lawyers to listen to the better angels of their nature? Is such an understanding of the lawyer's role incompatible with an adversarial system of dispute resolution? Would we be better off with a system that relies on lawyers — somewhat moderated by judges — to represent the needs of the community? Or are we better off with a system constructed primarily on lawyer's and client's self-interest?

Notes and Questions

1. Disqualification of counsel can occur for reasons other than potential or actual conflicts of interest. For instance, disqualification may occur when an attorney is a material witness to an event in the litigation, see Kalmanovitz v. G. Heilman Brewing Co., 610 F. Supp. 1319 (D. Del. 1985), unless disqualification would impose an undue hardship on the client, see General Mill Supply Co. v. SCA Services, Inc., 505 F. Supp. 1093 (E.D. Mich. 1981), *aff'd*, 697 F.2d 704 (6th Cir. 1982). Disqualification will occur when a spouse or law partner of a lawyer is a named class representative, see Zylstra v. Safeway Stores, Inc., 578 F.2d 102 (5th Cir. 1978); when the attorney is a member of the class that the attorney represents, see id.; and when a lawyer is both a party *and* an attorney for another party, see United States v. Lenox, 1989 WL 143167 (E.D. Pa.). And disqualification is possible when an attorney engages in certain kinds of litigative misconduct, including subornation of perjury, see Addamax Corp. v. Open Software Foundation, Inc., 151 F.R.D. 504 (D. Mass. 1993); use of fact witness with access to confidential information as "trial consultants," see Rentclub Inc. v. Transamerica Rental Finance Corp., 811 F. Supp. 651 (M.D. Fla. 1992); false statements and misrepresentations to a court, see In re Wirebound Boxes Antitrust Litigation, 724 F. Supp. 648 (D. Minn. 1989); or *ex parte* communications with the judge, see id.

2. Although these other grounds are occasionally asserted, nearly all disqualification motions involve conflicts of interest. It would be foolish to pretend that we can teach everything that you need to know about recognizing and resolving potential conflicts in a few pages. We must leave that to courses in ethics and to your own sense of decency and fairness. Here we can hope only to raise some basic procedural and substantive issues surrounding disqualification motions, and show how those issues interact with the major themes of adversarial process, judicial discretion, and rational adjudication of complex cases.

3. Let's begin with the procedure of disqualification motions:

(a) *Burden of Proof.* Few cases focus on the exact burden of proof a party making a disqualification motion must meet. Some cases seem to imply that, as soon as the moving party comes forward and identifies a colorable conflict, the party resisting disqualification must then prove that no conflict exists. Nonetheless, the cases that focus on the issue hold that the moving party bears the burden of proving that disqualification is proper. See, *e.g.*, Duncan v. Merrill Lynch Pierce Fenner & Smith, Inc., 646 F.2d 1020 (5th Cir.), cert. denied, 454 U.S. 895 (1981). Some courts describe this burden as a "heavy" one requiring a "high standard of proof." Evans v. Artek Systems Corp., 715 F.2d 788, 791 (2d Cir. 1983); Alexander v. Primerica Holdings, Inc., 822 F. Supp. 1099 (D. N.J. 1993). It is commonly said that disqualification motions are viewed with "disfavor." See, *e.g.*, *Alexander*, 822 F. Supp. at 1114 (citing cases).

On the other hand, without apparently worrying about the mixed signals being sent, many of these same cases claim that "doubts are to be resolved in favor of disqualification." See, *e.g.*, *Alexander*, 822 F. Supp. at 1114; Cheng v. GAF Corp., 631 F.2d 1052, 1059 (2d Cir. 1980), vacated on other grounds and remanded, 450 U.S. 903 (1981). In addition, a series of presumptions (discussed in greater detail in Note 4, *infra*) help a party seeking disqualification to meet the burden of proof.

(b) *Source of Law.* The law that applies to a disqualification motion depends on the court in which the motion is filed. In state court, state law applies; and state law is determined largely by reference to the code of ethics promulgated by the state Supreme Court or bar association. See, *e.g.*, In re Complex Asbestos Litigation, 232 Cal.App.3d 572, 283 Cal.Rptr. 732 (1993). In federal court, the standards for disqualification are a matter of federal, rather than state, law. See, *e.g.*, In re American Airlines, Inc., 972 F.2d 605 (5th Cir. 1992), cert. denied, 507 U.S. 912 (1993); Manual for Complex Litigation, Third § 20.23 n.73 (1995). But federal courts usually adopt the code of ethics used in state court, see, *e.g.*, In re Corn Derivatives Antitrust Litigation, 748 F.2d 157 (3d Cir. 1984), cert. denied, 472 U.S. 1008 (1985), although some federal courts promulgate their own standards, see, *e.g.*, Dondi Properties Corp. v. Commerce Savings and Loan Associaton, 121 F.R.D. 284 (N.D. Tex. 1988). The *Erie* issues involved in using federal standards in diversity cases have received scant attention. See Linda S. Mullenix, *Multiforum Federal Practice: Ethics and* Erie, 9 Geo. J. Leg. Ethics 89 (1995). So has the issue of which state's ethics rules should be applied in multistate representations. See H. Geoffrey Moulton, Jr., *Federalism and Choice of Law in the Regulation of Legal Ethics*, 82 Minn. L. Rev. 73 (1997).

(c) *Need for Hearing.* An evidentiary hearing on a disqualification motion is typical, but not required. See *General Mill*, 697 F.2d 704; Analytica, Inc. v. NPD Research, Inc., 708 F.2d 1263 (7th Cir. 1983).

(d) *Appealability.* Neither the grant nor the denial of a motion to disqualify is appealable of right on an interlocutory basis. Richardson-Merrell, Inc. v. Koller, 472 U.S. 424 (1985); Firestone Tire & Rubber Co. v. Risjord, 449 U.S. 368 (1981). Certification of the issue under 28 U.S.C. § 1292(b) is possible, see Charles A. Wright et al., Federal Practice and Procedure § 3914.21 (1992), but rare. Mandamus is the only other route to obtain immediate appellate review of a district court's disqualification decision, but the high threshold of error required to grant mandamus makes mandamus a fairly ineffective route to appellate review. See In re Bushkin Associates, 864 F.2d 241 (1st Cir. 1989). Disqualification decisions are appealable after entry of final judgment.

4. The substance of disqualification motions divides into two categories. The first category accuses an attorney or law firm of an actual conflict of interest that involves representation of inconsistent interests or the potential disclosure of confidential matters. The second category accuses an attorney or firm not of an actual ethical violation but rather an "appearance of impropriety."

(a) *Actual Ethical Violations.* This first category can be subdivided into two types of claims: first, claims that an attorney or firm is *at the present moment* simultaneously representing clients with inconsistent interests; and second, claims that an attorney or firm has *in the past* represented a client whose interests oppose a client that the firm is now representing. Both categories involve the threat that a lawyer will use information gained in the course of a representation to the disadvantage of that client; the first circumstance also divides the loyalty of the lawyer between two present clients, making it difficult to believe that the interests of both clients will be fully advanced.

Courts seem to perceive this difference, and have developed somewhat different rules to deal with each type of conflict. Regarding simultaneous representations, one rule is easy: A single lawyer or firm cannot represent two clients in a lawsuit in which they have adverse interests. A more difficult case occurs when one client is adverse to the other in a lawsuit, but the attorney's or firm's representation of the first client has nothing to do with the lawsuit. (For instance, one lawyer in a firm may sue a company on a products liability claim, while another lawyer is advising the company on ERISA matters.) In this situation, the simultaneous representation of two clients is regarded as "prima facie improper." See Cinema 5, Ltd. v. Cinerama, Inc., 528 F.2d 1384, 1387 (2d Cir. 1976); International Business Machines, Inc. v. Levin, 579 F.2d 271 (3d Cir. 1978). The prima facie impropriety could be rebutted by a showing that the parties consented to or waived the conflict (see Note 6, *infra*); or presumably by a showing that the conflict does not exist. This latter showing, however, may be impossible to make. See United States v. Nabisco, Inc., 117 F.R.D. 40 (E.D.N.Y. 1987). Finally, a conflict occurs when an attorney or law firm represents a client that sues a party, and the firm also represents some group or association to which that adverse party belongs. See, *e.g.*, Glueck v. Johnathon Logan, Inc., 653 F.2d 746 (2d Cir. 1981); Westinghouse Electric Corp. v. Kerr-McGee Corp., 580 F.2d 1311 (7th Cir.), cert. denied, 439 U.S. 955 (1978); Nabisco, 117 F.R.D. 40. Here a "substantial relationship" test, which requires disqualification if the subject matter of the two representations is sufficiently related "as to create a realistic risk either that the [client involved in litigation] will not be represented with vigor or that unfair advantage will be taken of the [party related to the other client]," has been employed. *Glueck*, 653 F.2d at 749.

The second type of conflict occurs when a present representation appears inconsistent with a prior representation. As *Agent Orange* describes, the usual approach to this situation is to use the "substantial relationship" test. Due to the different concerns involved, however, the meaning of "substantial relationship" varies somewhat from its meaning in *Glueck*. Since the attorney or firm is at the present moment only representing one set of interests, *Glueck*'s concern about the attorney's or law firm's present loyalty or the vigor of the present representation is not directly at issue. Rather, the fear is that, in vigorously representing the present client's interests, the attorney or firm will betray confidences obtained from the previous client. Therefore, some courts have held that the relationship is "substantial" only when the information developed in the prior representation might be useful in the present case. See Bennett Silvershein Associates v. Furman, 776 F. Supp. 800, 804 (S.D.N.Y. 1991) (collecting cases); but see Government of India v. Cook Industries, Inc., 569 F.2d 737, 740 (2d Cir. 1978) (substantial relationship exists only if relationship between two representations is "patently clear," or actions are "identical" or "essentially the same").

Once the relationship is deemed substantial, the issue then becomes whether the attorney or law firm can overcome the prima facie grounds for disqualification by demonstrating that no confidential information was used or could be used in the present representation. Two distinct presumptions have been developed by courts for making this inquiry. The first presumption is that confidential information was actually shared by the prior client with the lawyer(s) in the firm who performed legal services for the prior client. The second presumption is that the lawyer(s) who received this information shared it with the other lawyers in the firm who are representing the present client. See Novo Terapeutisk Laboratorium A/S v. Baxter Travenol Laboratories, Inc., 607 F.2d 186 (7th Cir. 1979); In re Corrugated Container Antitrust Litigation, 659 F.2d 1341 (5th Cir. 1981). The combination of these presumptions makes it difficult for a law firm that has a substantial relationship to a former client to resist disqualification. Indeed, the only way to resist disqualification is to rebut one or the other of the presumptions.

That issue — whether the presumptions of disclosure can be rebutted — has been frequently litigated. The present consensus seems to be that the first presumption — confidential information was disclosed to the attorney — is irrebuttable. *Corrugated Container*, 659 F.2d at 1347 (collecting cases); but see United States Football League v. National Football League, 605 F. Supp. 1448, 1461-62 (S.D.N.Y. 1985) (leaving issue open); see also Decora Inc. v. DW Wallcovering, Inc., 901 F. Supp. 161 (S.D.N.Y. 1995) (allowing party to prove *ex parte* that confidential information was in fact disclosed rather than simply relying on presumption of disclosure). Whether the second presumption can be rebutted is a more difficult question. When the prior client is a long-standing, traditional client of the firm, the presumption of shared disclosure may well be irrebuttable, as some courts have held. See *Corrugated Container*, 659 F.2d at 1346; but see *Duncan*, 646 F.2d at 1029 (refusing to apply mechanical rule of disqualification even with long-standing prior client). When the prior client used a firm on a few occasions, however, the cases are mixed. Some cases say that the presumption is irrebuttable, see *Analytica*, 708 F.2d 1263; other cases allow a firm to prove that a confidence entrusted to one lawyer in the firm did not make its way to the lawyer(s) representing the second client, see *Corrugated Container*, 659 F.2d at 1346 ("this presumption of imputed knowledge may be unduly harsh in some circumstances"); *Bennett Silvershein*, 776 F. Supp. at 804-05 (using lack of disclosure as evidence that no substantial relationship existed). Finally, courts often apply a different rule when a lawyer whose old firm or government agency represented a client switches jobs into a firm that is representing a party with interests adverse to the former client. Most courts are willing to permit the second firm to prove that the laterally hired attorney either had no access to confidential information from the prior client or has not disclosed the confidential information he does possess. See, *e.g.*, *Cheng*, 631 F.2d 1052.

The strongest showing that a law firm can make to overcome the various presumptions (especially in the case of lateral hires) is that the firm took immediate and decisive measures to shield the attorney with confidential information from any contact with the present case and to shield the attorneys working on the present case from any contact with the lateral attorney on matters related to the present case. Courts often find such walls ineffective to ward off disqualification, but some arrangements do pass muster. The factors considered are the same as the factors used to decide if disqualification is prima facie appropriate: whether the lateral attorney's prior work is in the same field as the present representation; whether, during the prior representation, the lateral attorney was a partner involved in firm strategy or a young associate; whether the prior client was involved in a counseling or a litigation relationship (the assumption being that litigation involves representation of more discrete interests, thus making disqualification less likely); whether the lateral attorney had actual (not presumed) access to confidential information from the prior client in the prior job; whether the lawyer came from a different firm or from government practice (a lower Chinese wall may be required for laterally hired government lawyers); whether a different office of the firm was handling the present representation; whether the firm was large or small (the courts' assumption being that a Chinese wall is more difficult to erect in a small firm); whether the wall was immediately instituted; whether the attorney receives as compensation any money derived from the present representation; whether effective measures, such as the present representation being segregated and case-related communication with the lateral lawyer being curtailed, are taken; and whether the case of the second client is so complex that no other local firm would be willing or able to take the case on. See, *e.g., Cheng*, 631 F.2d 1052; Nemours Foundation v. Gilbane, Aetna, Federal Insurance Co., 632 F. Supp. 418 (D. Del. 1986); *United States Football League*, 605 F. Supp. at 1459, 1466-68; INA Underwriters Insurance Co. v. Nalibotsky, 594 F. Supp. 1199, 1210 n.8 (E.D. Pa. 1984) (citing cases on Chinese wall); In re Asbestos Cases, 568 F. Supp. 910 (E.D. Va. 1981); Lemaine v. Texaco, Inc., 496 F. Supp. 1308 (E.D. Tex. 1980); Larry S. Kaplan, Complex Federal Litigation §§ 2.07, 2.13 (1993); *Manual, Third* § 20.23 n.77.

(b) *Appearance of Impropriety*. A second claim — the appearance of impropriety — can sometimes serve as a ground for disqualification. This claim does not require that an actual ethical violation be shown; rather, it assumes that no ethical violation exists but that the lawyer's conduct nonetheless appears improper. It is fair to say that courts are far less willing to order disqualification for a mere appearance of impropriety. When the only apparent impropriety is an alleged violation of an ethical obligation (such as representation of conflicting interests or disclosure of confidential information), and the court has already refused to disqualify because the violation does not in fact exist, the court is very unlikely to disqualify because of the mere appearance. See, *e.g.*, Telectronics Proprietary, Ltd. v. Medtronic, Inc., 836 F.2d 1332 (Fed. Cir. 1988) (appearance of impropriety by itself is usually not sufficient basis for disqualification); *Bennett Silvershein*, 776 F. Supp. at 806 (appearance of impropriety standard "does not confer a roving moral commission to disqualify attorneys based on conduct specifically treated in other" ethical obligations); In re Coordinated Pretrial Proceedings in Petroleum Product Antitrust Litigation, 658 F.2d 1355, 1361 (9th Cir. 1981), cert. denied, 455 U.S. 990 (1982) (disqualification appropriate only with clear improprieties viewed from perspective of reasonable person); Woods v. Covington County Bank, 537 F.2d 804, 813 (5th Cir. 1976) (while there does not need to be "proof of actual wrongdoing," there must be "a reasonable possibility that some specifically identifiable impropriety did in fact occur").

5. Both types of impropriety require proof of one additional fact: an attorney-client relationship between the lawyer and the client whose interests are allegedly compromised by the present representation. The point may seem obvious, but it occasionally comes into play in disqualification decisions. The classic case is *Westinghouse*, 580 F.2d 1311. In *Westinghouse* one office of a law firm agreed to represent the American Petroleum Institute (API) in lobbying efforts. As part of that representation, the law firm was given access to confidential information from API members, including Kerr-McGee and Getty. The law firm then wrote a report concluding, among other things, that the uranium industry was competitive and therefore not in need of further regulation.

At the same time another office of the same firm agreed to represent Westinghouse in an antitrust claim against Kerr-McGee, Getty, and others. The allegation was that these defendants had conspired to monopolize the uranium industry — an allegation flatly inconsistent with the conclusions in the report of the firm's other attorney. When Kerr-McGee and Getty moved to disqualify the law firm in the uranium case, the law firm sought to avoid disqualification by arguing that it had never entered an attorney-client relationship with Kerr-McGee or Getty. The Seventh Circuit rejected the argument:

> [A]n attorney-client relationship does not arise only in the agency manner such as when the parties expressly or impliedly consent to its formation.... The professional relationship for purposes of the privilege for attorney-client communications 'hinges upon the client's belief that he is consulting a lawyer in that capacity and his manifested intention to seek professional legal advice.'... A fiduciary relationship may result because of the nature of the work performed and the circumstances under which confidential information is divulged. [580 F.2d at 1317, 1319-20.]

Because Kerr-McGee and Getty had supplied confidential information with the understanding that the law firm was working on behalf of their interests, the court found that an attorney-client relationship existed in fact, and disqualified the firm. The *Westinghouse* view that substance rather than form determines the existence of an attorney-client relationship has been widely followed. See, *e.g.*, Premium Products Sales Corp. v. Chipwich, Inc., 539 F. Supp. 427 (S.D.N.Y. 1982) (no attorney-client relationship when "client" could not reasonably believe that law firm was representing its interests).

    6. An attorney can overcome a disqualification motion by demonstrating that both the first and the second client have consented to the representation of the second client, or by showing that the first client waived the conflict. A court will not lightly find that consent exists. Consent must be actual, not constructive. See *IBM*, 579 F.2d 271. When it seems that no confidences of the first client will be disclosed, courts are willing to enforce the first client's consent to the second representation. See, *e.g.*, Interstate Properties v. Pyrmaid Co., 547 F. Supp. 178 (S.D.N.Y. 1982). When the risk of disclosure exists, however, courts insist that, at a minimum, the first client expressly consent to the use of its potential confidences against it (not a likely scenario); but even such consent is likely to be invalidated by a court that takes a dim view of attorney breaches of confidence. See, *e.g.*, Westinghouse Electric Corp. v. Gulf Oil Corp., 588 F.2d 221 (7th Cir. 1978). See generally *Manual, Third* § 20.23 nn.79 & 81.

    Implied waivers occur with greater frequency. The typical ground for finding a waiver is delay: The first client, well knowing of the existence of the conflict, waits until late in the case (often after the case starts to go badly) to move to disqualify. The risks of disclosure of confidential information are still significant, of course, but courts are unwilling to let such tactical gamesmanship by the first client carry the day. See, *e.g.*, *Alexander*, 822 F. Supp. 1099 (three year delay constitutes waiver); Jackson v. J.C. Penney Co., 521 F. Supp. 1032 (N.D. Ga. 1981) (fifteen months constitutes waiver).

    7. Even when a conflict exists, disqualification is not automatic. Some courts use a two-step inquiry: first, they look to see if there are adequate grounds for disqualification (in other words, an actual or apparent ethical conflict); and second, they ask whether "the likelihood of public suspicion or obloquy outweighs the social interests which will be served by a lawyer's continued participation in a particular case." *Woods*, 537 F.2d at 813 n.12. In striking that balance, relevant factors may include whether confidential information from the first client was actually passed (what about the irrebuttable presumption?); whether disqualification would significantly prejudice the second client, either in time or money; whether disqualification would significantly delay the progress of the case; whether the first client's conduct contributed to the conflict; and whether

the integrity of the judicial process was compromised. See Gould v. Mitsui Mining & Smelting Co., 738 F. Supp. 1121 (N.D. Ohio 1990); SWS Financial Fund v. Salomon Brothers, Inc., 790 F. Supp. 1392 (N.D. Ill. 1992).

Remedies other than disqualification are possible. One remedy is simply to have the law firm limit the scope of its second representation. (The second client must, of course, fully consent to such a limitation, and limitations are not always effective in removing the conflict.) See *Westinghouse*, 580 F.2d 1311; *Telectronics*, 836 F.2d 1332; Kaplan, *supra*, § 2.12. A second remedy, available in rare circumstances, is to allow the law firm to choose which client it wishes to continue to represent and which to drop. See *Gould*, 738 F. Supp. 1121. A third remedy is for the judge to report the conflict to the appropriate disciplinary board for disciplinary action against the attorneys involved. See id; *SWS Financial Fund*, 790 F. Supp. 1392.

8. Most disqualification issues arise from potential conflicts of interest or disclosures of confidential information by attorneys. But disqualification of a law firm can also be sought because other employees of a law firm — such as secretaries, paralegals, and law clerks — are in a position to reveal confidential information obtained from a party adverse to the firm's present client. These employees typically obtain the information from a prior job. See Fund of Funds, Ltd. v. Arthur Andersen & Co., 567 F.2d 225 (2d Cir. 1977); Riddell Sports, Inc. v. Brooks, 1994 WL 67836 (S.D.N.Y.); Kapco Manufacturing Co. v. C & D Enterprises, Inc., 637 F. Supp. 1231 (N.D. Ill. 1985).

9. In an adversarial system, disqualification motions are almost always made by an adversary, not by the court. An adversary has little incentive to make such a motion when opposing counsel is incompetent or unqualified; the adversary makes the motion when he sees a tactical advantage (whether replacing a highly qualified firm with a less qualified firm, delaying the litigation, or simply distracting the better firm). This tactical use (and abuse) has been noted by judges, who often do not disguise their dislike for disqualification motions. See, *e.g.*, Board of Education of City of New York v. Nyquist, 590 F.2d 1241 (2d Cir. 1979); *Addamax*, 151 F.R.D. 504; *SWS Financial Fund*, 790 F. Supp. 1392; *Bennett Silvershein*, 776 F. Supp. 800. But these motions also raise a theoretical issue that cuts to the heart of adversarial process. As Justice Brennan said:

> [T]he tactical use of attorney-misconduct disqualification motions is a deeply disturbing phenomenon in modern civil litigation. When a trial court mistakenly disqualifies a party's counsel as the result of an abusive disqualification motion, the court in essence permits the party's opponent to dictate his choice of counsel. . . . [T]his result is in serious tension with the premises of our adversary system . . . .

Richardson-Merrell, 472 U.S. at 441 (Brennan, J., concurring). This concern has led many courts to hold that one factor they consider in deciding whether to disqualify an attorney is the client's right to be represented by his or her own counsel. See, *e.g.*, Brennan's, Inc. v. Brennan's Restaurants, Inc., 590 F.2d 168, 172 (5th Cir. 1979); *Nyquist*, 590 F.2d 1241; *Alexander*, 822 F. Supp. 1099; *Bennett Silvershein*, 776 F. Supp. 800.

Nyquist arguably goes a step further. The court found a common thread uniting the cases that ordered disqualification: "we have utilized the power of trial judges to disqualify counsel where necessary to preserve the integrity of the adversary process in actions before them. . . . [U]nless an attorney's conduct tends to 'taint the underlying trial,' . . . courts should be quite hesitant to disqualify an attorney." 590 F.2d at 1246. Does this principle ultimately explain the complex system of disqualification rules we have just described? Should we replace the present system of rules with this one principle, as *Nyquist* arguably suggests?

10. Two questions of particular importance to complex litigation arise from *Nyquist*'s suggestion. First, isn't there an inconsistency between the courts' professed concern for a party's adversarial right to counsel of her choice at the disqualification stage and their lack of concern for that right at the stage of appointment of lead counsel? One principle along which this apparent inconsistency could be reconciled is that a court can and should determine how much deviation from vigorous representation of an individual client's interests is acceptable. Should the judge possess this power?

Second, as we have seen, complex cases cannot be adjudicated within the framework of the adversarial system. Is there any reason to apply disqualification standards that seek to preserve the integrity of a process that, by definition, is inappropriate for the case? Isn't this the basic question posed in *Agent Orange* and in the excerpts from Judge Weinstein: Why use ethical standards designed for one type of case when another type of case, in which those standards cannot work, presents itself? On the other hand, are you comfortable with the pragmatic assumption underlying the conclusions of the Second Circuit and Judge Weinstein: that ethical standards should vary with circumstance and context? (Put differently, with what principles or arguments can you justify the maintenance of two sets of ethical norms — one for routine cases and one for complex cases?) If you can justify separate systems, are you convinced that Judge Weinstein's communitarian ethic is the right ethical standard for complex cases? Does this standard give a roving commission to lawyers and judges to ignore the interests of individual clients, as Judge Weinstein himself worries? Do you think that plaintiff and defense lawyers will see the common good in the same way? Logically, couldn't a judge operating under Judge Weinstein's "common good" regime disqualify an attorney for failing adequately to protect the common good? Wouldn't this power make the judge the ultimate arbiter of the common good — an arbiter whose views the lawyer ignores at his peril? Should the judge possess this power?

On the other hand, isn't abandonment of traditional ethical notions in favor of a communitarian ethic inevitable once we authorize class actions and lead counsel arrangements?

11. One alternative ethical system to Judge Weinstein's system would be to say that the lawyer owes the usual duties of loyalty and confidentiality to the "client," but then to redefine the "client" to be the group rather than any individual in the group. While such a system is more in keeping with a traditional adversarial ethic, can it explain the result in *Agent Orange*? Can a lawyer more easily represent a group's interests than the common good? *Cf.* Richard B. Stewart, *The Reformation of American Administrative Law*, 88 Harv. L. Rev. 1669 (1975) (arguing against interest group model of administrative law). Would this ethical system mean that a lawyer cannot subsequently represent clients whose substantially related interests conflict with those of the group? Will the court need to become more active in overseeing the work of the lawyer? See David L. Shapiro, *Class Actions: The Class as Party and Client* 73 Notre Dame L. Rev. 913 (1998) (advocating model of "class as client," and suggesting expanded role for judicial supervision of class counsel).

12. The idea that lawyers in complex cases operate under ethical standards that look beyond individual interests to group or communitarian interests receives some support from the case law. First, there are cases like *Agent Orange*, in which class lawyers are allowed to represent some class members whose interests conflict with other class members; here, the usual concerns for disclosure of confidential information seem to evaporate. See also Bash v. Firstmark Standard Life Insurance Co., 861 F.2d 159 (7th Cir. 1988). Second, although authority is scant, it seems that a lawyer can represent interests adverse to a former client when the client was an unnamed member of a class that the lawyer had represented; the usual "substantial relationship" test and concomitant presumptions do not apply. See In re Fine Paper Antitrust Litigation, 617 F.2d 22 (3d Cir. 1980); *Manual, Third* § 20.23 n.69. Third, disqualifications of an attorney or law firm does not typically result in disqualification of co-counsel, even though the threat of shared information exists. See *Brennan's*, 590 F.2d 168; *Manual, Third* § 20.23 n.78; but see *Fund of Funds*, 567 F.2d 225 (disqualifying co-counsel). Finally, one court has held that an attorney can represent individual asbestos claimants in one set of cases and a class of future claimants in another, even though the limited funds of the defendants suggested a conflict of interest between present and future claimants and even though the settlements of the two sets of cases varied from each other. Georgine v. Amchem Products, Inc., 157 F.R.D. 246, 328 (E.D. Pa. 1994), *rev'd* on other grounds, 83 F.3d 610 (3d. Cir. 1996), *aff'd*, —U.S. —, 117 S.Ct. 2231 (1997). This aspect of *Georgine* has attracted some academic attention. Compare Susan P. Koniak, *Feasting While the Widow Weeps:* Georgine v. Amchem Products, Inc., 80 Corn. L. Rev. 1045 (1995) with Carrie Menkel-Meadow, *Ethics and the Settlement of Mass Torts: When the Rules Meet the Road*, 80 Corn. L. Rev. 1159 (1995).

Taken as a whole, are these doctrines more consistent with a "common good" ethic or an "interest group" ethic?

13. If we accept the argument that, in complex cases, we need to replace our traditional adversarial ethics, how can we legitimately claim that we should maintain an adversarial process for resolving complex cases? Conversely, if we feel the need in complex cases to replace an adversarial process with some other process, we cannot expect the lawyers involved in the new process to operate under an adversarial system of ethics, can we? Ethical questions lie at the very heart of complex litigation, and no proposed solution for complex litigation can be deemed adequate unless the solution works out its ethical implications. Thus far, none of the solutions we have considered in this book has done so.

4. Withdrawal of Counsel

Rather than waiting to be disqualified, an attorney or law firm can seek to withdraw voluntarily from the representation that creates the conflict. An attorney can also withdraw from a case for a host of other reasons. An attorney cannot, however, withdraw unilaterally; either the client must consent, or a judge must relieve the attorney of his obligations. When the client refuses to consent, the attorney must convince the judge that there is good reason for withdrawal. It should be apparent by now that undertaking the responsibilities of an attorney in complex litigation can be a taxing —

perhaps overtaxing — burden. We complete our look at the attorney's role in pretrial litigation by exploring the circumstances under which this burden can be lifted from the attorney's shoulders.

HAINES v. LIGGETT GROUP, INC.

814 F. Supp. 414 (D.N.J. 1993)

■ LECHNER, District Judge. Currently before the court is the motion of Budd Larner Gross Rosenbaum Greenberg & Sade, P.C. ("Budd Larner") to withdraw as counsel for M. Susan Haines ("Haines"), plaintiff in the above-captioned matter. For the following reasons, the motion is denied.

FACTS

A. *Background*

In the Spring of 1983, three New Jersey law firms — Budd Larner; Porzio, Bromberg & Newman ("Porzio"); and Wilentz Goldman and Spitzer ("Wilentz") — entered into an agreement (the "Litigation Agreement") whereby they agreed jointly to litigate cigarette-related health claims on behalf of smokers who developed lung cancer, allegedly from smoking. Ultimately, as a result of the Litigation Agreement, eight cases (the "Cigarette Cases") were filed against various cigarette companies, including . . . the instant case. . . .

The Litigation Agreement continued until March 1986, when Marc Z. Edell ("Edell") left Porzio to join Budd Larner. Thereafter, only Budd Larner and Wilentz litigated the Cigarette Cases, with the exception of *Haines*, the instant case. On 29 September 1988, Wilentz was disqualified in *Haines* by Magistrate Judge Ronald Hedges . . . . Since 29 September 1988, Budd Larner has assumed sole legal and financial responsibility for this case.

In each of the Cigarette Cases, including the present case, Budd Larner, Porzio and Wilentz entered into contingency fee agreements with the various plaintiffs. Pursuant to these contingency fee agreements, the expenses of litigation have been borne exclusively by Budd Larner and the other law firms. According to Budd Larner, "[n]o client has expended even a single dollar toward satisfaction of those costs; the expenses are recoverable only if plaintiffs prevail at trial — in which case those sums will be deducted from plaintiffs' share of the judgments."

At the present time, of the original eight cases filed under the Litigation Agreement, Budd Larner remains as counsel only in the present case and possibly one other.

B. *The Parties and Claims*

On 22 February 1984, this case was filed by Haines as administrator of the estate of Peter F. Rossi . . . . The defendants [are Liggett Group, Inc.,

Loew's Theatres, Inc., Phillip Morris, Inc., R.J. Reynolds Tobacco Co., and the Tobacco Institute.] Haines alleges, *inter alia*, that Rossi developed lung cancer and died on 28 May 1982 as a result of smoking cigarettes manufactured by Defendants. . . .

DISCUSSION

A. *Arguments by Budd Larner For Withdrawal*

Budd Larner argues it should be granted permission to withdraw from this case because litigation against the cigarette industry "has become an unreasonable financial burden." . . .

According to Budd Larner, the three firms have expended significant amounts of money and time in litigating these eight cases against the cigarette industry. Specifically, Budd Larner states:

> [T]he firms have incurred approximately $1.2 million in out-of-pocket expenses (not including the costs of more than one million Xerox copies made in house), of which Budd Larner has paid more than $500,000. The firms have also spent well over $5 million in lawyer and paralegal time, of which Budd Larner was responsible for the largest share -- approximately 75%.

Budd Larner does not specify how much money or time it has spent to date in litigating *Haines*.[7] Nevertheless, Budd Larner suggests that "[t]o approximate the costs of litigating the present case through trial, one need look no further than Budd Larner's experience in *Cipollone*." According to Budd Larner:

> From approximately the procedural point where *Haines* is today through trial, the *Cipollone* case cost more than $500,000 in out-of-pocket expenses and approximately $2 million in lawyer and paralegal time. There is no reason to believe that *Haines* could be tried any more quickly than *Cipollone*, which took four months to try. . . .

Budd Larner also suggests that *Cipollone* should serve as a model for the type of post-trial activity that can be expected in this case. According to Budd Larner:

> In *Cipollone*, almost half of the ten years since the case was filed was spent on post-trial matters. During that period, Budd Larner incurred approximately $150,000 in out-of-pocket costs and expended over $900,000 in attorney and paralegal time.

---

7. Budd Larner states, however, that in the eight cases as a whole, Defendants have taken two hundred twenty-two days of fact-witness depositions and seventy days of expert witness depositions, while plaintiffs have taken eighty days of fact-witness depositions and twenty-seven days of expert witness depositions. Budd Larner calculates that for every day of deposition in the eight cases, plaintiffs' attorneys "spent approximately one and a half days in preparation." Budd Larner thus estimates that, in total, "the deposition process has consumed approximately 1,000 days; translated into standard work weeks of Monday through Friday, that is approximately four years' worth of depositions." Finally, Budd Larner indicates that, in *Cipollone* alone, more than one hundred motions were filed.

As a final cost consideration, Budd Larner argues that "much remains to be done to prepare *Haines* for trial." Budd Larner anticipates five motions will be filed on behalf of Haines and eight motions will be filed by Defendants. Apparently, both Budd Larner and Defendants also plan to take additional discovery.

In light of these anticipated expenses, Budd Larner concludes: "[I]t has become apparent that the amount of recovery against the tobacco industry is not likely to exceed these costs." To support this claim, Budd Larner points to the fact that, even when it received a verdict favorable to a plaintiff in *Cipollone*, that verdict was only for $400,000.

Apart from cost considerations, Budd Larner argues that considerations of public policy have already been achieved by its work in this case and that such considerations do not require Budd Larner to remain as Haines' counsel in this case. Budd Larner states:

> Even though the present case has not yet been tried, many believe that these cases have substantially achieved one of the main goals of product liability law — to provide the public, courts and legislators with the truth regarding a manufacturer's or an industry's practices. Budd Larner's efforts have been widely credited with obtaining in discovery what no other attorneys had been able to obtain. . . . These revelations regarding the tobacco industry's practices, and the ability of Congress and the public in general to benefit from Budd Larner's efforts, will be unaffected by whether Budd Larner remains as counsel in *Haines* or any other case. *Nor does the public have any overriding interest in whether* Haines *or any other particular case proceeds to trial.* . . .

In fact, Budd Larner argues that "there is a strong public interest in discontinuing lawsuits when the aggregate costs of the litigation far exceed the potential benefit to an individual plaintiff. . . . [T]here is a public interest in refraining from — or discontinuing — suits that have no economic viability." . . .

B. *Arguments By Haines Against Withdrawal*

Haines begins by re-formulating the issue presented by this motion. She states:

> . . . The issue which *should* be addressed by the Court is not whether a comparison of projected legal expenses against potential recovery makes it ethical or permissible for Budd Larner to withdraw. Rather, the issue is whether this Court should permit the *[D]efendants* in this case to engage in pre-trial and trial conduct which generates such an imbalance.
>
> As long as any Court is willing to sit back and merely watch as the parties in tobacco litigation engage in a battle of attrition, the plaintiff will always run out of ammunition before the [D]efendants even begin to notice a diminution of their resources.

Haines discusses what she describes as "the Tobacco Industry Strategy" to defend against cigarette liability suits. According to Haines, the "tobacco industry has taken the position that its members will never settle a lawsuit which involves claims that tobacco has caused injuries to an individual." Moreover, she states, "the ability to outspend and over-litigate is . . . used to persuade those attorneys and their clients who were 'foolish' enough to file suit to voluntarily dismiss their claims." . . .

Haines recognizes that she "does not want this Court to force Budd Larner to spend hundreds of thousands of dollars in a vain effort to match [D]efendants' ability to spend." Instead, Haines argues that "this Court should take firm control of the litigation to ensure . . . that magnitude of the impact of the disparity in resources between these parties, plus the sophisticated and calculated exploitation of the situation by the [D]efendants, do not approach a denial of due process." . . .

C. *Standard of Review*

Rule 6 of the General Rules of District Court for the District of New Jersey (the "Local Rules") provides that members of the bar permitted to practice in this court are governed by the Rules of Professional Conduct of the American Bar Association (the "ABA"), as those rules have been revised by the Supreme Court of New Jersey, and subject to "such modifications as may be required or permitted by [F]ederal statute, regulation, court rule or decision at law." . . .

New Jersey Rule of Professional Conduct 1.16 ("RPC 1.16"), entitled "Declining or Terminating Representation," is the state ethical rule which governs this motion. RPC 1.16 states in pertinent part:

> A lawyer may withdraw from representing a client if withdrawal can be accomplished without material adverse effect on the interests of the client, *or* if . . . (5) the representation will result in an unreasonable financial burden on the lawyer or has been rendered unreasonably difficult by the client.

RPC 1.16(b) (emphasis added). Based on this language, RPC 1.16 has been interpreted by some commentators as providing for withdrawal under two circumstances: (1) for any reason, so long as no material adverse effect on the client occurs and (2) for good cause, such as financial hardship, even if withdrawal has a material adverse effect on the client. . . .

Even with these provisions, RPC 1.16 provides that withdrawal is entirely within the discretion of the court and a court may refuse to allow withdrawal despite a showing of good cause. . . . Specifically, the Rule states: "[A] lawyer shall continue representation *notwithstanding good cause* for terminating the representation" when so ordered by the court. RPC 1.16(c). The theory behind this provision is that, even if withdrawal is otherwise appropriate, other considerations must sometimes take precedence, such as maintaining fairness to litigants and preserving a court's resources and efficiency. . . .

Federal law does not expressly permit withdrawal by an attorney on the ground of financial hardship. Instead, Local Rule 18 provides that court permission is required before an attorney may withdraw from representation. Local Rule 18 states: "Unless counsel is substituted, no attorney may withdraw an appearance except by leave of Court. After a case has been first set for trial, substitution and withdrawal shall not be permitted except by leave of Court."

The comment to Local Rule 18 indicates that consideration of four criteria is appropriate for motions to withdraw: (1) the reasons why withdrawal is sought, (2) the prejudice withdrawal may cause to litigants, (3) the harm withdrawal might cause to the administration of justice and (4) the degree to which withdrawal will delay resolution of the case. . . . These criteria are consistent with the provisions of RPC 1.16.

1. *Good Cause For Withdrawal*

Budd Larner argues that it should be permitted to withdraw because it can no longer afford to maintain this action against Defendants and, therefore, by demonstrating financial hardship, it has demonstrated good cause for withdrawal. The issue, however, is not so simple.

Although there is no debating that the Cigarette Cases have cost Budd Larner a significant amount of money, this expense represents the aggregate expense to Budd Larner of *all* eight Cigarette Cases. . . . Haines should not lose her representation because Budd Larner has incurred significant expenses in other — similar but separate — matters.

Equally difficult to accept is Budd Larner's suggestion that *Cipollone* should be used as a yardstick for the determination of potential costs in this case. This case is not *Cipollone*. Whatever may have occurred in *Cipollone*, that case was not before this court. . . . The design of the Federal Rules, to ensure the "just, speedy, and *inexpensive* determination" of this action or any matter, Fed.R.Civ.P. 1 (emphasis added), cannot be ignored. . . .

Because of *Cipollone* and the other Cigarette Cases, much of the groundwork for trial of this case has already been set in place. Prior discovery, in the form of both documents and deposition testimony, can provide the parties with ready data which will decrease the amount of discovery necessary in this case. In addition, as a result of the holdings in *Cipollone*, the legal issues in this case have been narrowed and clarified; the parties are better able to focus their discovery requests.

In sum, while Budd Larner has demonstrated that it has expended a significant amount of resources in litigating the Cigarette Cases generally, it has not demonstrated a sufficient basis to permit withdrawal absent the consent of Haines.[25]

2. *Additional Bases For Denying Withdrawal*

a. Inability to Find Substitute Counsel

Contrary to the assertions of Budd Larner and their expert, Fred S. McChesney ("McChesney"), this motion for withdrawal implicates concerns

---

25. Budd Larner's motion is also based on the fact that, in *Cipollone*, the jury returned a verdict for only $400,000. This argument too is not persuasive.

other than money. At stake is the ability of citizens to bring and maintain suits for the purpose of vindicating rights and receiving compensation for injuries, as well the ability of clients to rely upon the representation of and the agreements with their attorneys.

When an attorney agrees to undertake the representation of a client, he or she is under an obligation to see the work through to completion. . . . This obligation is not disposed of easily. . . .

In cases when withdrawal would significantly impair a client's ability to find substitute counsel or to maintain the action, courts have refused to permit withdrawal despite the fact that representation has become unprofitable for the client's lawyers.[27] Such is the case here. If Budd Larner is permitted to withdraw from this case, it is unlikely that Haines will be able to find counsel to take Budd Larner's place. . . .

Even if Haines could procure substitute counsel, serious questions are raised as to whether such a transition could be effected without causing severe prejudice to Haines' interests. Put simply, Budd Larner is recognized as the leading law firm in the field of tobacco products liability litigation. . . . Budd Larner is uniquely aware of the facts, documents, expert testimony, litigation strategy, legal issues and legal authority which are necessary for effective representation in this case, given the complex legal and factual issues which it presents. . . .

To allow withdrawal under these circumstances would be inappropriate. When an attorney undertakes to represent a client, he or she has an obligation to fully protect his or her client's interests. . . . Given the inability of Haines to find any substitute counsel at all, let alone effective substitute counsel, it appears nothing can be done to protect her interests or minimize the harm of withdrawal. Without counsel, as Haines indicates, this action will not go forward. . . .

b. Contingency Fee Contract

Also significant to the question of withdrawal is the fact that Budd Larner's representation is premised upon a contingency fee arrangement. At the core of such an arrangement is "a contract between an attorney and client setting the formula for calculating the attorney's fee" in exchange for representation. Iskander v. Columbia Cement Co., 197 N.J.Super[.] 169, 174, 484 A.2d 353 (App. Div. 1984). This contract is binding. A "client may not disavow the formula after settlement on the thesis that the settlement

There simply is no way to predict the verdict which a jury in this case might render . . . .

27. For this reason, [In re "Agent Orange" Product Liability Litigation], 571 F. Supp. 481 [(E.D.N.Y. 1983)], is distinguishable. Although Budd Larner cites this case (and only this case) as an instance in which a law firm was allowed to withdraw for reasons of financial hardship, replacement counsel was available and ready and willing in *Agent Orange*. Moreover, *Agent Orange* was a class action where the private relationship with an attorney, as contracted for by Haines and developed by Budd Larner, was absent. To permit substitution or withdrawal in a situation such as this case, the threshold question is whether plaintiff consents.

was easier than average or quicker than anticipated." Id. at 174. The opposite of this principle is applicable here; an attorney must abide by the terms of the contract as well, particularly in this case in which withdrawal is sought because of (1) expenses incurred in other matters and (2) anticipated expenses that have not yet been incurred. . . . Simply put, Budd Larner is ill at ease because the contract it made may not be lucrative, as it hoped at the time the contingency fee agreement was formed. . . .

Budd Larner also argues that, if this were a contract case not involving legal representation, the agreement between Haines and the firm would be void on the ground of unilateral or mutual mistake. . . .

This argument is not compelling in the context of a contingency fee relationship which, by its nature, involves uncertainty and risk and requires the parties to make predictions as to (1) the likelihood of recovery, (2) the length of time until recovery and (3) the probable size of recovery. Given their litigation experience, lawyers are in a better position than clients to make these predictions. . . .

Finally, important public policy considerations which underlie contingent fee arrangements would be ill-served by permitting withdrawal in this case.. . .

If lawyers — after assessing the likelihood of recovery, negotiating a contingency fee and raising the expectations of their client — are permitted to withdraw when contingency fee representation becomes unprofitable or even costly, the purpose of contingency fee litigation will be defeated. Access to justice will not be broadened; it will be constricted. Moreover, as in this case, the contingency fee arrangement will actually have made matters worse.

When a lawyer is permitted to withdraw on the ground that maintaining the litigation has become too costly, finding substitute counsel may well prove to be difficult or even impossible. Individual claims, as well as entire classes of claims, may be stigmatized. As for plaintiffs, the disappointment at having been abandoned mid-stream is likely to undermine faith in the legal system and to reinforce the notion that access to the courthouse is a function of wealth. Simply put, the needs and obligations of the contingency fee system dictate that Budd Larner not be permitted to close the door to the courts which it has opened. To permit withdrawal would be to permit the nullification of any contingency fee contract which later turns out to be less profitable than originally thought.

Notes and Questions

1. How much burden is too much? Complex cases put severe financial pressure on attorneys. The tendency to consolidate cases, and then to assign the lawyering tasks to a lead counsel or small committee of counsel, intensifies the pressure. Obviously, if attorneys cannot be released from their responsibilities, even in the face of financial or personal ruin, they will be exceedingly reluctant to take on complex cases. On the other hand, the clients and the administration of justice suffer if an attorney can walk off the job as soon as a case starts to

become more trouble (from the attorney's viewpoint) than it is worth. This is especially true for lawyers that are doing an effective job.

Did *Haines* find the right balance between these concerns? In re Agent Orange Product Liability Litigation, 571 F. Supp. 481 (E.D.N.Y. 1983), intimated that the balance should be struck somewhat differently. There a loose consortium of attorneys known as Yannacone and Associates had operated as lead counsel for about four years. As the case was about to enter a critical stage of discovery, the consortium decided that it was "unable to absorb the enormous expense that continued prosecution of the litigation will inevitably entail." The court granted the consortium's motion to withdraw, noting that "[t]he court does not feel it would be appropriate to refuse to release Yannacone and Associates from their obligations as lead counsel in the face of their claim of inability to continue carrying the burdens of the litigation any longer." As *Haines* notes, a distinguishing feature in *Agent Orange* was the willingness of other counsel to step in and represent the plaintiffs. But the language and tone of *Agent Orange* reflect a greater sympathy for the overwhelming burdens that lead counsel sometimes face.

The same attitude can be seen in Portsmouth Redevelopment and Housing Authority v. BMI Apartments Associates, 851 F. Supp. 775 (E.D. Va. 1994), a routine environmental suit in which a law firm representing a defendant sought withdrawal because the firm had already rung up hourly fees of more than $260,000, only $44,000 of which had been paid by the client. The client's proposed payment schedule — $2,000 per month — would not have covered additional legal fees, much less have made up the existing unpaid balance. Although no replacement counsel had been found, the court allowed the law firm to withdraw. But see Gibbs v. Lappies, 828 F. Supp. 6 (D.N.H. 1993) (refusing to allow defense firm to withdraw when insurance company stopped paying fees for representing insured; defense of case did not impose undue burden on "experienced and successful" firm, especially when firm could have protected itself with large retainer).

Do you see any consistent principle running through these cases? That contingent fee cases are harder to withdraw from than hourly fee cases? That representations of groups are harder to withdraw from than representations of individuals? That $216,000 in uncompensated fees is sometimes enough, and that it sometimes isn't?

2. Undue financial burden is not the only ground for withdrawal. Among the other grounds, which can arise in but are not limited to complex litigation, are:

(a) The client commits perjury, see A Sealed Case, 890 F.2d 15 (7th Cir. 1989); the client demands that the attorney commit an act that violates F.R.Civ.P. 11, see Bayges v. Southeastern Pennsylvania Transportation Authority, 887 F. Supp. 108 (E.D. Pa. 1995); or, after clear and direct advice that the client's conduct is illegal, the client continues the conduct, and the attorney's services amount to a substantial factor aiding the conduct, see In re American Continental Corp./Lincoln Savings and Loan Litigation, 794 F. Supp. 1424 (D. Ariz. 1992).

(b) The client and attorney have fundamental disagreements on strategy, tactics, authority, or mutual obligations, see Lindsey v. Admiral Insurance Co., 804 F. Supp. 47 (N.D. Cal. 1992); the client and attorney have some other irreconcilable conflict, see Mekdeci v. Merrell National Laboratories, 711 F.2d

1510 (11th Cir. 1983); the client refuses to give the attorney the authority or funds to represent the client vigorously, see Stafford v. Mesnik, 63 F.3d 1445 (7th Cir. 1995), and Chemray Coatings Co. v. United States, 27 Fed.Cl. 470 (1993); communication between the client and attorney have irreparably broken down, or the client is otherwise non-cooperative, see Washington v. Sherwin Real Estate, Inc., 694 F.2d 1081 (7th Cir. 1982), and Marfia v. T.C. Ziraat Bankski, 874 F. Supp. 560 (S.D.N.Y. 1994); or the client refuses to accept the attorney's advice to settle the case, see *Washington*, 694 F.2d at 1087-88, and Spero v. Abbott Laboratories, 396 F. Supp. 321 (N.D. Ill. 1975). At least one case has indicated that a client's grant of authority to enter settlement negotiations, but refusal to allow the attorney to litigate the case, was not a disagreement necessarily justifying withdrawal. See Brand v. NCC Corp., 540 F. Supp. 562 (E.D. Pa. 1982).

(c) The client or the attorney becomes insane or suffers from other debilitating mental or physical health problems, see Green v. Forney Engineering Co., 589 F.2d 243 (5th Cir. 1979), and Donnelly v. Parker, 486 F.2d 402 (D.C. Cir. 1973). The stresses of complex litigation often cause such problems.

(d) The client consents to the attorney's withdrawal, or, as happens in some cases, fires the attorney, see Crabtree v. Academy Life Insurance Co., 878 F. Supp. 727 (E.D. Pa. 1995).

(e) The attorney has a conflict of interest. See p. 898, *supra*.

(f) The case lacks merit. See Harmon v. Adams & Sons Roofing Co., 120 F.R.D. 78 (N.D. Ind. 1987).

3. In the multidistrict Prozac litigation, the plaintiffs' lead counsel also represented another Prozac plaintiff in a state case. Near the end of that case, the plaintiff entered into a secret settlement with the defendant. Shortly thereafter the counsel moved to withdraw as lead counsel in the multidistrict case, all the while refusing to disclose the terms of the secret agreement. Would you have allowed him to do so without knowing more about the agreement? The district court did. Aspects of the withdrawal ruling have generated considerable satellite litigation. See Winkler v. Eli Lilly & Co., 101 F.3d 869 (7th Cir. 1996).

4. Even when an attorney has good grounds for withdrawal, the attorney usually cannot withdraw unilaterally; court approval is required. Court approval is hardly pro forma; in one case, a court refused to allow withdrawal even after the client had fired the law firm. See Ohntrup v. Firearms Center, Inc., 802 F.2d 676 (3d Cir. 1986). As *Haines* says, courts look at a host of factors in deciding whether to permit withdrawal. See, *e.g.*, *Portsmouth Redevelopment*, 851 F. Supp. 775; *Gibbs*, 828 F. Supp. 6; Federal Trade Commission v. Intellipay, Inc., 828 F. Supp. 33 (S.D. Tex. 1993); Beshansky v. First National Entertainment Corp., 140 F.R.D. 272 (S.D.N.Y. 1990); Akers v. Bonifasti, 629 F. Supp. 1212 (M.D. Tenn. 1985). Many courts have local rules that list the factors considered by that court. Some are comparable to the one discussed in *Haines*, which permitted withdrawal of counsel *without* court approval when there is a simultaneous appearance entered by new counsel. It is hard to believe, however, that Budd Larner could have automatically withdrawn three days before trial as long as Ms. Haines agreed to substitute as her counsel some warm body willing to try her case.

5. Courts can also put conditions on an attorney's withdrawal. The typical condition, mentioned above, is either that substitute counsel enter an

appearance or that the client clearly demonstrate a willingness and capacity to represent herself *pro se*. When the client does not consent to withdrawal, withdrawal can be accomplished only upon notice to the client of the motion to withdraw and its grounds. See Woodall v. Drake Hotel, Inc., 913 F.2d 447 (7th Cir. 1990). The withdrawing attorney may also be required to complete some litigation tasks that the new counsel would have difficulty accomplishing in a timely manner. See *Beshansky*, 140 F.R.D. at 274. Moreover, a court can insist that the attorney seeking withdrawal hand over the case files and cooperate with the new counsel. See Industry Network System, Inc. v. Armstrong World Industries, Inc., 54 F.3d 150 (3d Cir. 1995). When withdrawal is required because of a conflict of interest, the firm will need to screen its files to assure that no confidential information regarding another party is contained in the files; and in an appropriate case, a court may order that the withdrawing attorney receive no fees for the representation that created the conflict. See Esser v. A.H. Robins Co., 537 F. Supp. 197 (D. Minn. 1982).

6. One commentator has recommended that attorneys in complex cases specify in the original representation agreement the circumstances under which the client will permit the attorney to withdraw and the consequences of a withdrawal. Larry S. Kaplan, Complex Federal Litigation § 3.08. Suppose that, at the outset of the representation, Haines and Budd Larner had entered into an attorney-client agreement in which Haines consented to the withdrawal of Budd Larner if the case became an undue financial burden on the law firm. Do you think that such *ex ante* consent would have persuaded the district court to let Budd Larner withdraw?

7. A trial court decision to approve or deny a motion to withdraw is reviewed on appeal only for an abuse of discretion. *Stafford*, 63 F.3d 1445; Fleming v. Harris, 39 F.3d 905 (8th Cir. 1994). Once again, we must ask whether trial judges should have this much discretion to determine who will represent the interests of particular parties.

8. A critical issue is whether the standards for withdrawal vary between routine and complex cases. *Haines* suggests that attorneys will have a more difficult time withdrawing from cases with a public interest dimension — which most complex cases possess. The same theme was present in *Woodall*, in which class counsel sought to withdraw from their representation of two members of the class, while still representing the remaining members. After finding that the district court had abused its discretion in allowing withdrawal without requiring the attorneys to disclose the grounds for their motion, the court of appeals stated that "a court should be particularly circumspect in permitting counsel to withdraw from representing just a few plaintiffs in the context of a class action. . . . The likelihood is great that the excluded plaintiffs will not be able to retain new counsel." 913 F.2d at 450; see also id. at 449 (requiring "valid and compelling reason for the court to allow the withdrawal over objection" of class member); Securities and Exchange Commission v. International Scanning Devices, Inc., 415 F. Supp. 3 (W.D.N.Y. 1974) (withdrawal not allowed when counsel at outset was aware of complexity of case and public interest mandated that no further delay occur).

Indeed, many of the standard grounds for withdrawal — such as lack of communication with or cooperation from clients, disagreements about litigation strategy and tactics, potential conflicts of interest, huge financial burdens — are the norm in complex litigation rather than the exception. Unless some adjustments are made in the standard grounds, lawyers who want to find a reason to escape from a complex case will find it easy to do so. On the other hand, it is difficult to know who the "client" is or what the client's "consent" to withdrawal means in the context of a large multi-party case in which universal agreement among co-parties on any point is unlikely. Thus, lawyers who agree with most but not all of their clients that withdrawal is appropriate may find that they cannot withdraw.

Thus far, no court or scholar has systematically considered whether the usual rules for withdrawal, which were designed for two-party adversarial litigation, should change in complex litigation. It seems, however, that the answer to whether and how much the rules should change depends upon how we conceive of the lawyer's role and ethical responsibilities in complex cases. Whom does the lawyer represent: a group of individuals with individual interests, a group with an overall collective interest, or the public good? What is the lawyer's role in this representation: to present reasoned proofs and arguments on behalf of individuals, or to assure that the public interest is served? We have asked these questions in the prior sections concerning the selection and disqualification of counsel, where the literature on the ethical, social, and legal implications of a move away from the adversarial ideal is greater. The answers you formulated in those materials should inform your judgment on the issue of withdrawal.

9. One thing seems clear from *Haines*: The plaintiffs' lawyer is seen as having a loyalty not only to the client but also to the cause (here, holding tobacco companies accountable). But the lawyer, the court recognizes, cannot go it alone — at least in light of tobacco company tactics that are entirely legitimate when seen from the perspective of the traditional adversarial model. Hence, the judge also agrees to modify her role from the passive judge of adversarial process to an activist judge that interjects herself into the pretrial process to ensure that the client, and the cause, receive a fair hearing. In the following sections of this chapter and in the next chapter, we examine what this new judicial role might look like. After studying these materials, you might consider again whether you like the role that complex litigation increasingly expects lawyers to play.

B. SELECTING JUDICIAL OFFICERS TO MANAGE THE PRETRIAL PROCESS: JUDGES, MASTERS, AND MAGISTRATES

Throughout this book we have talked a great deal about a new role that judges in complex litigation are being required to assume. In this section we examine what that role entails in the context of pretrial proceedings. We begin by exploring the history, as well as some of the theoretical and practical concerns, that led judges in complex litigation to assume this new role as "case manager." We then turn to the question of choosing the judicial structure that best fulfills this role: In particular, we examine whether a single judge, a group of judges, a master, a magistrate, or some combination of judge, master, and magistrate serves as the best case manager. Finally, we look at the circumstances in which a judicial officer can be disqualified from a case, and ask whether those circumstances should change due to the demands of complexity.

The discussion in these materials proceeds at a fairly general level. In the next chapter we explore specific principles and solutions that judges and lawyers can employ in handling pretrial complexity. Only after you have seen the general debate about the new roles of lawyers and judges in pretrial litigation (the focus of this chapter), and then seen how that debate plays out in practical and specific terms (the focus of the next chapter), can you adequately assess whether the "case management" concept is the salvation or the curse of complex civil litigation.

1. Historical and Theoretical Perspectives on the Judge as Case Manager

REPORT OF THE JUDICIAL CONFERENCE OF THE UNITED STATES ON PROCEDURE IN ANTI-TRUST AND OTHER PROTRACTED CASES

(1951), reprinted in 13 F.R.D. 62, 65-66 (1953)

The person who must insure that a [complex case] is thoroughly prepared prior to the trial is the trial judge himself. . . . The actual work must be done by counsel. But one of the tasks of the trial judge in a case of this sort is to make certain, prior to setting the case for trial, that counsel are completely prepared and have efficiently organized their material. This is a task of inquiry and negotiation on the part of the judge and may require considerable patience and persistence. . . .

It is not practical to proceed in these cases as in a lawsuit of ordinary complexity and bulk; that is, to let the parties exhaust the cross fire of pleading, to conduct open-court pre-trial hearings, or to let counsel try the case as they please. The potential range of issues, evidence and argument is so great, and the necessities of adversary representation so compelling, that the activities of counsel will result in records of fantastic size and complexity unless the trial judge exercises rigid control from the time the complaint is filed.

HANDBOOK OF RECOMMENDED PROCEDURES FOR THE TRIAL OF PROTRACTED CASES

(1960), reprinted in 25 F.R.D. 351, 377, 383-85 (1960)

Recommendation: Each big case should be assigned in its entirety to one judge for all purposes, including all pre-trial motions. . . .

Recommendation: When a protracted case is identified, the assigned judge should, at the earliest moment, take actual control of the case. The judge should make himself available at all reasonable times, holding frequent pre-trial conferences, offering constructive suggestions and maintaining a firm but understanding attitude towards the parties, with the objective of organizing and simplifying the issues and of obtaining the stipulation of all possible facts and an accurate statement of the material issues concerning which there is a genuine disagreement. . . .

There can exist no question as to the power of the court to control the case . . . . The nature of the long or protracted case is such that strong control must be exercised from the time of filing to its disposition. The "remedy is for the trial judge to take the case in hand at the outset, study it, and act as his best judgment dictates." Judge Prettyman coined the expression "Iron hearted Judges" . . . . The phrases repeatedly found in the literature suggesting that the judge "take the case in hand at the outset," "gain control of the case in an early stage," take "full control of a case from the time of filing," and exercise "rigid control" all suggest that firmness and resolved required of the trial judge in undertaking the pre-trial of the protracted case. "A judge must be willing to assume his role as the governor of a lawsuit. He can't just be the umpire." . . .

As pre-trial proceeds, more and more will be required of the judge in order to be abreast of the case. Most of the actual work will be done by counsel, but it is the task of the trial judge to see that the work is done, the case organized and made ready for trial.

MANUAL FOR COMPLEX LITIGATION, THIRD

14-15 (1995)

§ 20.13 Effective Management

Effective judicial management generally has the following characteristics:

- **It is active.** The judge attempts to anticipate problems before they arise rather than wait passively for matters to be presented by counsel. Because the attorneys may become immersed in the details of the case, innovation and creativity in formulating a litigation plan may frequently depend on the court.
- **It is substantive.** The judge's involvement is not limited to procedural matters. Rather, the judge becomes familiar at an early stage with the substantive issues in order to make informed rulings on issue definition and narrowing, and on related matters, such as scheduling, bifurcation and consolidation, and discovery control.
- **It is timely.** The judge decides disputes promptly, particularly those that may substantially affect the course or scope of further proceedings. . . . Sometimes the parties may prefer that a ruling be timely rather than perfect.

- **It is continuing.** The judge periodically monitors the progress of the litigation to see that schedules are being followed and to consider necessary modifications of the litigation plan. The judge may call for interim reports between scheduled conferences.

- **It is firm, but fair.** Time limits and other controls and requirements are not imposed arbitrarily or without considering the views of counsel, and they are subject to revision when warranted by the circumstances. Once having established a schedule, however, the judge expects schedules to be met, and, when necessary, imposes appropriate sanctions . . . for derelictions and dilatory tactics.

- **It is carefully prepared.** Heavy-handed case management by an unprepared judge may often be counterproductive, while an early display of careful preparation sets the proper tone and can enhance the judge's credibility and effectiveness with counsel.

The judge's role in developing and monitoring an effective plan for the orderly conduct of pretrial and trial proceedings is crucial. . . . The attorneys — who will be more familiar than the judge with the facts and issues in the case — should play a significant part in developing the litigation plan and are primarily responsible for its execution.

Notes and Questions

1. Early in our own procedural history, when pleading was oral, the way to narrow a case to a triable issue was to have the lawyers appear before the judge at the medieval equivalent of a pretrial conference. See p. 33, *supra*. But we should not place too much emphasis on the similarities between the case manager and the judge of fourteenth century England. Today judges must manage discovery, many parties, and wide-ranging multi-claim complaints — all of which were unknown at common law. Moreover, the medieval judge expressed his views only on the legal sufficiency of the pleas; the lawyers had responsibility for suggesting the triable issue and developing the facts.

Recall that the flexibility of oral pleading eventually gave way to the rigidity of written pleading. Is it possible to maintain the flexibility of case management in the long run? What have the lessons of our own history taught us about whether, and how, we can avoid excessive rigidity in case management?

2. The modern history of case management can be traced to the *Report on Procedure in Anti-Trust and Other Protracted Cases*, commonly known as the Prettyman Report (after its principal author, Chief Judge E. Barrett Prettyman). The report was commissioned because a series of antitrust cases in the post-World War II era presented the federal courts with a large and unwieldy animal unlike any they had seen before. The Prettyman Report contended that one strategy that seemed to move these cases along was a strong judge. The report was quite short on the specifics of how the judge was to act, but a series of seminars during the 1950's put more flesh on the case manager's skeleton. See, *e.g.*, Seminar on Procedures Prior to Trial, 20 F.R.D. 485 (1957); Proceedings of the Seminar on Protracted Cases, 21 F.R.D. 395 (1957); Proceedings of the Seminar on Protracted Cases for the United States Judges, 23 F.R.D. 319 (1958). The culmination of these seminars was the publication of the *Handbook of*

Recommended Procedures, which made more concrete recommendations about what characteristics a case manager should have and what a case manager should do. The *Handbook* was replaced by the Manual for Complex and Multidistrict Litigation (1970). This *Manual* went through five interim editions, two supplements, and a re-titling (to the *Manual for Complex Litigation*) before being replaced by the Manual for Complex Litigation (Second) (1985). The *Manual (Second)* further refined the appropriate characteristics and conduct for a successful case manager. The Manual for Complex Litigation, Third replaced the *Manual (Second)*, but added little to the case manager framework.

In the next chapter we study the specific techniques that a judge can employ to manage a case well. Here we are focusing on the basic nature and qualities of a good case manager. Do you detect any change between 1951 and 1995 in the opinions about the nature and qualities of a good case manager?

3. What would you regard as the most important qualities for a good case manager? Do those qualities mesh with your sense of the qualities that are most important in a judge? If not, which set of qualities do you prefer (both generally and in the context of complex litigation)?

4. The rise of the case manager concept in complex litigation has had an important effect on routine litigation. Given the prevailing wisdom that early, active, and continuous intervention in complex cases was beneficial, some judges began to apply case management notions to more routine litigation during the 1970's. At the same time, concerns among the bench, bar, and public about the costs and delays of civil litigation were increasing. Therefore, in 1983, the drafters of the Federal Rules turned to a solution that seemed to be working: case management. Rules 16 and 26(b) were lengthened and Rule 26(f) was created in order to permit more case conferences and more discovery planning. Even greater authority for judges to manage federal cases (both complex and routine) was added by virtue of 1993 amendments to Rules 16 and 26. At present, the case management movement continues to grow.

5. The literature on case management also continues to grow. In addition to the materials cited above, see, *e.g.*, Federal Judicial Center, Manual for Litigation Management and Cost and Delay Reduction (1993); Bureau of Justice Assistance, Differentiated Case Management (1993); William W Schwarzer & Alan Hirsch, The Elements of Case Management (1991); Brookings Institution Task Force, Justice for All: Reducing Costs and Delays in Civil Litigation (1989); William W Schwarzer, Managing Antitrust and Other Complex Litigation (1982); American College of Trial Lawyers, Recommendations on Major Issues Affecting Complex Litigation, *reprinted in* 90 F.R.D. 207 (1981); Managing to Reduce Delay (National Center for State Courts 1980); Report of the National Commission for the Review of Antitrust Laws and Procedures (1979), *reprinted in* 80 F.R.D. 509 (1979); Todd Peterson, *Restoring Structural Checks on Judicial Power in the Era of Managerial Judging*, 29 U.C. Davis L. Rev. 41 (1995); Symposium, 29 Judge's J. 1 (Fall 1990); Robert F. Peckham, *The Federal Judge as a Case Manager: The New Role in Guiding a Case from Filing to Disposition*, 69 Cal. L. Rev. 770 (1981). For a stimulating article that examines case management from historical and theoretical perspectives and then concludes that managerial discretion is good and uniformity among cases is less valuable, see David L. Shapiro, *Federal Rule 16: A Look at the Theory and Practice of Rulemaking*, 137 U. Pa. L. Rev. 1969 (1989).

6. Fundamentally, pretrial case management shifts some power from lawyers to judges. Does case management reform the adversarial system or abolish it? If it is a reform, will an eventual, albeit unintended, consequence be the abolition of the adversarial system? Judge Schwarzer thinks not:

> Judicial management contemplates abandonment of the judge's traditionally passive umpireal role. But it does not call for the judge to take the case away from the lawyers and usurp the advocate's role, say by calling or extensively questioning witnesses.... [F]irm and sound management conducted by a well-prepared, demanding but fair judge will tend to strip the case to its essentials, and focus the lawyers' attention and effort on the issues on which decision should turn, thereby increasing the effectiveness of advocacy and enhancing the working of the adversary process.

Schwarzer, Managing Antitrust and Other Complex Litigation, *supra*, at 11-12. Do you agree?

Assuming that this shift in power is a good (or at least a necessary) thing for complex cases, is it wise to transplant the idea to routine litigation? Was the case manager of complex litigation created to reduce cost and delay, to make the rational adjudication of complex disputes possible, or both? If routine disputes can be adjudicated rationally without case management, the claim for case management in routine litigation is less compelling, isn't it?

The following three readings may help you answer these questions. Do they persuade you that a judge acting as case manager is a good thing, a bad thing, or a neutral thing in complex litigation? In complicated litigation? In routine litigation?

John H. Langbein, THE GERMAN ADVANTAGE IN CIVIL PROCEDURE

52 U. Chi. L. Rev. 823, 824, 858-62, 866 (1985)

My theme is that, by assigning judges rather than lawyers to investigate the facts, the Germans avoid the most troublesome aspects of our practice. But I shall emphasize that the familiar contrast between our adversarial procedure and the supposedly nonadversarial procedure of the Continental tradition has been grossly overdrawn....

Apart from fact-gathering, ... the lawyers for the parties play major and broadly comparable roles in both the German and American systems. Both are adversary systems of civil procedure. There as here, the lawyers advance partisan positions from first pleadings to final arguments. German litigators suggest legal theories and lines of factual inquiry, they superintend and supplement judicial examination of witnesses, they urge inferences from fact, they discuss and distinguish precedent, they interpret statutes, and they formulate views of the law that further the interests of their clients....

Important changes have occurred in recent years that [further] diminish the contrast between German and American civil procedure. Under the rubric of case management, American trial judges are exercising increasing control of the conduct of fact-gathering....

What makes [the case management approach] look "proto-Germanic" in the eyes of the comparative lawyer is the informal feel of "the conference method;" and the active judicial role in defining issues, promoting settlement, and fixing the sequence for fact-gathering. . . .

[Managerial judging] has reoriented pretrial procedure away from adversary domination; and in a legal system that actually tries only a tiny fraction of its civil caseload, judicial capture of pretrial could become more important than continuing adversary control of trial. . . .

On the other hand, the haphazard growth of managerial judging has not been accompanied by Continental-style attention to safeguarding litigants against the dangers inherent in the greatly augmented judicial role. The career incentives for our judiciary are primitive, and the standards of appellate review barely touch the pretrial process.

The trend toward managerial judging is irreversible, because the trend toward complexity in civil litigation that gave rise to managerial judging is irreversible. If we were to learn from the success of the long established German tradition of managerial judging, we would not only improve our safeguards, we would encourage more complete judicial responsibility for the conduct of fact-gathering. For example, we might have the judge (or a surrogate such as a master or a magistrate) depose witnesses and assemble the rest of the proofs, working in response to adversary nomination and under adversary oversight as in German procedure. We might then be able to forbid the adversaries from contact with witnesses — in other words, we could abolish the coaching that disgraces our civil justice. We would also be able to routinize the use of court-appointed experts. . . .

Regardless of where managerial judging is headed for the future, it has already routed adversary theory. I take that as further support for the view . . . that adversary theory was misapplied to fact-gathering in the first place. Nothing but inertia and vested interests justify the waste and distortion of adversary fact-gathering. The success of German civil procedure stands as an enduring reproach to those who say that we must continue to suffer adversary tricksters in the proof of fact.

Judith Resnik, MANAGERIAL JUDGES

96 Harv. L. Rev. 374, 376, 378, 408, 413, 417, 420-27, 430-31 (1982)

Until recently, the American legal establishment embraced a classical view of the judicial role. Under this view, judges are not supposed to have an involvement or interest in the controversies they adjudicate. Disengagement and dispassion supposedly enable judges to decide cases fairly and impartially. . . .

[T]he role of judges before adjudication is undergoing a change . . . . Judges have described their new tasks as "case management" — hence my term "managerial judges." As managers, judges learn more about cases much earlier than they did in the past. They negotiate with parties about the course, timing, and scope of both pretrial and posttrial litigation. These managerial responsibilities give judges greater power. Yet the restraints that formerly circumscribed judicial authority are conspicuously absent. Managerial judges frequently work beyond the public view, off the record, with no obligation to provide written, reasoned opinions, and out of reach of appellate review. . . .

Informal judge-litigant contact provides judges with information beyond that traditionally within their ken. [Pretrial conference] topics are more wide ranging and the judges' concerns are broader than either are when proceedings are conducted in court. The supposedly rigid structure of evidentiary rules, designed to insulate decision-makers from extraneous and impermissible information, is irrelevant in case management. Managerial judges are not silent auditors of retrospective events retold by first-person storytellers. Instead, judges remove their blindfolds and become part of the sagas themselves. . . .

[F]ew institutional [constraints] inhibit judges during the pretrial phase. . . . During pretrial supervision, judges make many decisions informally and often meet with parties *ex parte*, and appellate review is virtually unavailable. The judge has vast influence over the course and eventual outcome of the litigation. As a result, litigants have good reason to capitulate to judicial pressure rather than risk the hostility of a judge who . . . has ongoing responsibility for the case. During pretrial management, judges are restrained only by personal beliefs about the proper role of judge-managers. . . .

Proponents of managerial judging typically assume that management enhances efficiency in three respects. They claim that case management decreases delay, produces more dispositions, and reduces litigation costs. But close examination of the currently available information reveals little support for the conclusion that management is responsible for efficiency gains (if any) at the district court level, and strong reason to suspect that many of the purported efficiency gains in the district courts are illusory. . . .

Even when we find that some managerial trial courts do have faster dispositions than other trial courts, we have great difficulty identifying the causes of the difference. . . . Consequently, it is difficult to isolate and weigh the actual effect (if any) of managerial judging on the speed of trial court dispositions. Few researchers have even entered this thicket; management advocates rely instead on anecdote and intuition to support their claims. . . .

Management advocates also claim that judges' efforts to channel litigation into more "efficient" methods of dispute resolution, such as settlement, have improved the administration of justice by increasing the total number of dispositions. But again empirical moorings are wanting; no data firmly support the conclusion that judicial intervention results in more settlements than would otherwise have occurred.

Moreover, the claim that "the more dispositions, the better," raises difficult valuation tasks; decisionmaking must be assessed not only quantitatively, but also qualitatively. On any given day, are four judges who speak with parties to sixteen lawsuits and report that twelve of those cases ended without trial more "productive'" than four judges who preside at four trials? . . . Measuring judicial accomplishment is complex. Scales designed to measure achievement in other institutions cannot simply be imported into the courtroom. . . .

Management advocates assume that judicial supervision not only saves time and produces more dispositions, but also limits the ability of litigants to impose unfair financial pressure on their opponents and of attorneys to make excuses for excessive billing. Proponents therefore conclude that managerial judging reduces courts' and litigants['] costs. But no data exist to support this conclusion. If we rely instead on intuition, it is not obvious that judicial supervision averts costly adversarial decisions or attorney misconduct. . . . [S]upervision itself can present further opportunities for vigorous adversarial encounters. . . .

Moreover, judicial management itself imposes costs. The judge's time is the most expensive resource in the courthouse. Rather than concentrate all of their energy deciding motions, charging juries, and drafting opinions, managerial judges must meet with parties, develop litigation plans, and compel obedience to their new management rules. . . .

In the rush to conquer case loads, few proponents of managerial judging have examined its side effects. Judicial management has its own techniques, goals, and values, which appear to elevate speed over deliberation, impartiality, and fairness. Ironically, the growth of federal judges' interest in management has coincided with their articulation of due process values, their emphasis on the relationship between procedure and just decisionmaking. . . .

[N]o explicit norms or standards guide judges in their decisions about what to demand of litigants. What does "good," "skilled," or "judicious" management entail? . . . [How is the managerial judge] to determine, for the litigants and for the system as a whole, what was "better" or less "expensive"? . . .

Moreover, judges are in close contact with attorneys during the course of management. Such interactions may become occasions for the development of intense feelings — admiration, friendship, or antipathy. Therefore, management becomes a fertile field for the growth of personal bias.

Further, judges with supervisory obligations may gain stakes in the cases they manage. Their prestige may ride on "efficient" management, as calculated by the speed and number of dispositions. Competition and peer pressure may tempt judges to rush litigants because of reasons unrelated to the merits of disputes. . . .

Unreviewable power, casual contact, and interest in outcome (or in aggregate outcomes) have not traditionally been associated with the "due process" decisionmaking model. These features do not evoke images of reasoned adjudication, images that form the very basis of both our faith in the judicial process and our enormous grant of power to federal judges. The literature of managerial judging refers only occasionally to the values of due process: the accuracy of decisionmaking, the adequacy of reasoning, and the quality of adjudication. Instead, commentators and the training sessions for district judges emphasize speed, control, and quantity. . . . Case processing is no longer viewed as a means to an end; instead, it appears to have become the desired goal....

Proponents of management may be forgetting the quintessential judicial obligations of conducting a reasoned inquiry, articulating the reasons for decision, and subjecting those reasons to appellate review — characteristics that have long defined judging and distinguished it from other tasks.

E. Donald Elliott, MANAGERIAL JUDGING AND THE EVOLUTION OF PROCEDURE

53 U. Chi. L. Rev. 306, 315-17, 319, 321-26, 328, 334-35 (1986)

Some opponents of managerial judging, led by Professor Resnik, contend that managerial judging is ineffective — or at least that the effectiveness of managerial judging has not been demonstrated. Here I must respectfully part company with the loyal opposition. Both my personal experience as a litigator and the available published data convince me that at least some managerial techniques are effective in reducing the amount of time and effort invested in processing a given case....

Focusing on the effectiveness, rather than the fairness, of managerial judging diverts the debate from the more important issue of the ad hoc and potentially arbitrary nature of managerial judging. There *is* an undeniable potential for arbitrariness in any procedure that forecloses issues in litigation without adequate consideration of their merit.

The potential for arbitrariness inherent in managerial judging was clearly demonstrated in a unique controlled experiment .... The participating judges were divided into separate workshop sessions, each of which was asked to propose approaches for managing the same hypothetical case. The reports of the workshops disclosed dramatic differences in the ways that individual judges would have handled the case. Based on her intuition that the case had little merit, one trial judge would have required thousands of plaintiffs to file individual, verified complaints — a move that would have made it all but impossible for the plaintiffs' lawyer to pursue the cases. On the other hand, another trial judge confronting exactly the same hypothetical case would have ordered the defendants to create a multi-million dollar settlement fund....

[T]he problem that managerial judging aims to solve is, at base, structural: it results from a fundamental imbalance in the Rules between the techniques available for developing and expanding issues and those for narrowing or resolving them prior to trial....

To improve the issue-narrowing capacity of our present procedural system, we need to fill the gaping hole that now exists between the overly scrupulous standard for summary judgment and the essentially standardless procedures of managerial judging. If judges were permitted to find, from a preliminary assessment of the merits, that further development was unlikely to be worth its cost, narrowing of issues might be less arbitrary....

To say that managerial judging arose originally as a way of narrowing issues is not to say, however, that issue-narrowing is either its permanent or only function. On the contrary, once a legal idea or practice wins acceptance, it takes on a life of its own. Every established legal doctrine or technique becomes part of the raw material that judges can adapt creatively to new contexts. . . .

Only shortly after it achieved undisputed legitimacy, the institution of managerial judging has begun to undergo such a transformation. Managerial judging is evolving rapidly from a set of techniques for narrowing issues to a set of techniques for settling cases. . . .

The evolution toward greater use of managerial judging techniques to encourage settlement was predictable, if not inevitable. At base, the powers of managerial judging are the powers to impose costs, and thereby to increase the price of exercising the powers delegated to attorneys by the Federal Rules of Civil Procedure. There is good reason to believe, however, that the cost of litigation is one of the critical factors that affect decisions to settle. Thus, to the extent that managerial judging increases costs — and perhaps alters their timing and distribution as well — managerial judging can cause some cases to settle that would otherwise go to trial. . . .

It is true that litigants must ultimately accept a settlement "voluntarily" as in their best interests, but their choices are inevitably constrained by the shape of the playing field. When the shape of the playing field is not determined in advance, but altered by discretionary choices made by managerial judges for the purpose of encouraging settlement, it is at least debatable whether the essential conditions for procedural justice are satisfied.

On the other hand, in some circumstances changes in incentives as a result of managerial judging may promote just outcomes. . . . [W]hat the critics (and the supporters) generally have overlooked is that managerial judging can be justified not only in terms of reducing the procedural costs of civil litigation generally, but also by showing that managerial judging improves the quality of substantive justice received by litigants in particular cases. We lack sufficient data to make a definitive assessment of whether on balance managerial judging does in fact increase the quality of substantive justice. . . .

[Therefore,] the admission that there are costs to managerial judging in terms of real or perceived procedural unfairness should not by itself be dispositive. The proper issue is whether the benefits of managerial judging in enhancing substantive justice exceed its costs. At least in certain categories of cases, I believe that the benefits of managerial judging in enhancing substantive justice can exceed the costs in terms of procedural justice, and therefore I favor the judicious use of managerial judging despite the potential for arbitrariness which it admittedly entails. . . .

Whether managerial judging will actually have that effect, however, depends primarily on how accurately judges are able to detect and remedy particular distortions in incentives created by process costs. While in particular cases managerial judging may achieve results that are more just than would passive judging, there is no reason to be confident that judges will be able to perform this function consistently well. . . .

In the long run, . . . the disadvantages that arise from the ad hoc character of managerial judging cannot be eliminated, only reduced. More fundamental reform must proceed by addressing directly the system of incentives that creates the need for managerial judging in the first place.

Notes and Questions

1. Professor Langbein presents a generally favorable argument for case management, Professor Resnik presents a generally negative argument, and Professor Elliott presents a balanced argument. The success of each argument depends on certain assumptions: for Langbein, that German procedure (especially judicial fact-gathering) is better; for Resnik, that traditional adversarial procedure embodies and protects important values; for Elliott, that substantive justice can be put into a utilitarian balance with procedural justice, and that fostering settlement is good. Do you agree with their assumptions? For instance, if case management is a way station on the road to a Germanic system, and if you are troubled by continental-style civil procedure, you might be less sanguine than Langbein about the managerial judge. Likewise, if you think that efficiency trumps all concerns about adversarial notions like individual participation and neutral fact-finding, Resnik's critiques may ring hollow. If you believe in jury adjudication, or if you doubt the ability to balance substantive and procedural justice, Elliott's analysis may be unappealing. Once again, the theoretical, comparative, and historical materials with which we began this book are critical to an assessment of specific procedural choices.

2. Many of the arguments that have been made for or against case management are discussed in these three articles. Which set of arguments are most attractive? Do you have other arguments? These are not academic questions: In a real complex case in which you might become involved, you may need to persuade a judge to take a more (or less) active role than the judge initially intends. To do that, you will need command of all the arguments concerning case management, and then pick those arguments that are most likely to sway the judge. Are you comfortable with a system in which judges can choose their role on an ad hoc basis, and lawyers can seek to influence that choice to serve their clients' private ends?

3. Two arguments not raised in the articles were suggested in the earlier comparative and historical materials. First, recall Professor Damaska's thesis that a procedural system is a function of both the nature of the state and the nature of bureaucratic organization. See pp. 81-82, *supra*. An implication of this thesis is that any successful change in procedural paradigms must be accompanied by a compatible shift in political and organizational philosophy. Over the long term, can a case manager succeed in a state with diffuse judicial decisionmaking and a laissez-faire attitude toward governance? Second, our own procedural history and our comparative study of other procedural systems showed that procedural choices in one sphere often have a domino effect in other spheres. See pp. 27-82, *supra*. What might be the effect of the case manager on the right to jury trial? On a single, culminating trial event? On the rules of evidence? Of discovery? Of joinder? Langbein, Resnik, and Elliott discuss, or

at least hint at, what some of these changes might be. Do other changes that might flow from case management make you enthusiastic about the notion?

4. One theme of Resnik's article is an attempt to distinguish between pretrial and post-trial judicial activism, and to suggest that pretrial activism raises greater concerns. The judge active in posttrial proceedings is, of course, Professor Chayes' public law judge (see p. 61, *supra*). Wasn't an inevitable consequence of the judge's assertion of greater posttrial powers an effort to assert greater judicial power in other aspects of litigation? And is the consequence of this effort the judicial attempt to adjudicate polycentric disputes that, according to Professor Fuller, are incapable of adjudication? At a more practical level, has our own procedural history (especially our history of equity) shown us the dangers — and the ultimate futility — of allowing judges too much discretion?

5. Lost in all of these arguments may be a fundamental point. In complex cases, as we have defined them, lawyers are unable to accomplish the tasks the adversarial system has assigned them. By default, the judge must step into the vacuum in order to preserve rational adjudication. The preservation of rational adjudication provides not only the reason for, but also the structure of and the limitation on case management. Therefore, to the extent that we regard rational adjudication as a fundamental procedural norm, all non-fundamental concerns about case management for complex cases must give way. While case management might also be appropriate for routine litigation, this move would need to be justified by reasons that generate other structures and limitations on case management.

This point acknowledges that we are unable to treat all cases procedurally alike. But the preservation of rational adjudication provides a powerful reason to discriminate among cases — unless you regard trans-substantivism (*i.e.*, the like treatment of like cases) as equal to or more fundamental than rational adjudication. In more routine litigation in which adversarial process does not threaten rational adjudication, however, how do you justify the ad hoc, disparate treatment that case management accords like cases?

6. Until now we have been talking about the "case manager" or "judge" as if she were a single person. The more active the judge becomes, however, the less likely it is that she can handle all of the case management functions by herself. In the following section we examine how the role of case manager might be, and has been, divided among various judicial or quasi-judicial officials. The practical and theoretical concerns that this sharing of judicial power raises will provide additional arguments about the utility of case management.

2. Choosing the Judicial Officer(s) to Manage a Case

A judge managing a complex case needs to establish an appropriate organizational structure to help her accomplish her judicial tasks. A large part of that structure — law clerks and courtroom clerks — will already be in place. But the judge will often feel the need of additional assistance in the tasks of planning and adjudicating the many pretrial matters that arise.

Different types of assistance are possible. A judge might divide pretrial tasks among a group of judges. A second possibility is to appoint private citizens with particular expertise in handling pretrial matters as masters. A third possibility, which is a compromise between the first two, is to give some authority over pretrial matters to magistrate judges. We examine each option in turn.

a. Using Multiple Judges for Pretrial Matters

MANUAL FOR COMPLEX LITIGATION, THIRD

13 (1995)

All related cases pending or which may later be filed in the same court, whether or not in the same division, should be assigned at least initially to the same judge . . . . Pretrial proceedings in these cases should be coordinated and consolidated under Fed. R. Civ. P. 42(a). . . .

Although one judge should supervise the litigation, other judges may be requested to perform special duties, such as conducting settlement discussions . . . . Moreover, in the course of consolidated or coordinated pretrial proceedings, severable claims or cases may appear that could be assigned to other judges.

Notes and Questions

1. The first half of the *Manual's* advice is to consolidate related cases. This theme was the focus of the first part of this book. It has also been a primary tenet of case management since at least 1960, when the *Handbook of Recommended Procedures for the Trial of Protracted Cases* recommended that "[e]ach big case should be assigned in its entirety to one judge for all purposes, including all pre-trial motions." 25 F.R.D. at 377. The quoted language of the *Manual, Third* is the most recent version of this tenet.

2. The second half of the *Manual's* advice is to use other judges when appropriate. Doesn't this conflict with the idea that one judge should handle the entire case? The reasons for having a single judge handle all aspects of complex litigation include consistency, efficiency, appreciation of the big picture, scarcity of judicial resources, and finality. Aren't these reasons undercut by giving portions of the case to another judge to manage?

3. One reason to use another judge is to preserve the first judge's neutrality. For instance, the *Manual's* suggestion that other judges be used for settlement purposes reflects a long-standing practice of many judges, in cases both complex and routine. The standard rationale for this practice is that information learned during settlement negotiations may make it difficult for the judge to maintain neutrality during trial. This rationale is consistent with traditional adversarial theory. But in complex litigation managerial judges have already taken off the blindfold and stepped into the pretrial fray. So again we ask: What reasons justify one judge's sharing of adjudicatory authority with another judge?

4. Another reason for using different judges might be that the case cannot be consolidated before a single judge. A study of some recent examples of judicial cooperation in cases simultaneously pending in state and federal courts found, however, that coordination of judicial activity was the exception rather than the rule. Even when coordination occurred, one judge (typically the federal judge) tended to assert control over pretrial matters, and the other judge tended to acquiesce. Only in some cases and only for some occasions (usually regarding substantive law) did the judges divide the work according to their expertise. See William W Schwarzer, Nancy E. Weiss & Alan Hirsch, *Judicial Federalism in Action: Coordination of Litigation in State and Federal Courts*, 78 Va. L. Rev. 1689 (1992).

5. Perhaps the problems in the division of judicial responsibility could be avoided or ameliorated if we imposed a hierarchical system on judicial officers: using one "lead" judge who assembles other judicial officers around her to perform specific tasks. We have already seen this approach used in the context of lead counsel and committees of counsel. It would typically be difficult for one judge to be subservient to another, and it would be a waste of scarce judicial resources. But there are other judicial officers who could play the requisite role: special masters and magistrate judges.

b. Using Masters for Pretrial Matters

Rule 53 (a) of the Federal Rules of Civil Procedure authorizes a "court in which any action is pending [to] appoint a special master." Rule 53 (b) admonishes that "[a] reference to a master shall be the exception and not the rule." Aside from that advice, Rule 53 (b) establishes separate standards for the appointment of masters in jury-tried and judge-tried cases. In cases tried to juries, "a reference shall be made only when the issues are complicated." In cases tried to the bench, "save in matters of account and of difficult computation of damages, a reference shall be made only upon a showing that some exceptional condition requires it."

A fair reading of Rule 53 shows that the rule contemplates the use of masters for a trial on the merits, for the adjudication of technical remedial issues such as accountings, and for the resolution of related evidentiary issues. Nothing in Rule 53 expressly authorizes the use of masters in pretrial proceedings. On the other hand, nothing expressly precludes the use of masters. Should a judge should share the task of pretrial case management with a special master?

In re "AGENT ORANGE" PRODUCT LIABILITY LITIGATION

94 F.R.D. 173 (E.D.N.Y. 1982)

■ PRATT, District Judge. . . . With discovery about to begin under control of the court, the defendants requested the appointment of a special master to supervise discovery, and defendants have agreed to pay the entire cost of the special master. Plaintiffs have opposed appointment of a special master. The government, while not a party to the case, will no doubt be the target of the majority of the discovery sought, and the position of the government is that appointment of a special master at this stage would be premature.

After careful reflection, the court is satisfied that the magnitude of the case, the complexity of the anticipated discovery problems, the sheer volume of documents to be reviewed, many of which are subject to claims of privilege, the number of witnesses to be deposed, the need for a speedy processing of all discovery problems in order to meet the trial date established in this order, all argue in favor of using a special master to supervise discovery and prepare the pretrial order for purposes of the Phase I trial.  While the government is partially correct in pointing out the absence of serious discovery disputes thus far, defendants point out that there are an estimated four million government documents yet to be produced, and an estimated two thousand documents that the government has tentatively asserted are privileged. Discovery in these and other areas can be effectively and more efficiently handled through the constant attention of a readily available special master.

Accordingly,

1. Pursuant to Rule 53 of the Federal Rules of Civil Procedure, Sol Schreiber . . . is appointed special master with the powers and duties hereinafter set forth.

2. The special master shall be empowered and charged with the duty to:

(a) Rule upon all pending and future motions relating to discovery.

(b) Control the scheduling of all discovery.

(c) Rule on legal and factual disputes concerning the proper scope of discovery under FRCP 26(b) including, but not limited to, issues of discoverability, privilege, attorney work product, discovery of expert testimony and trial preparation materials.

(d) Issue or modify protective orders, where deemed appropriate, relating to discovery matters.

(e) Resolve disputes between the parties relating to answers to written interrogatories propounded pursuant to FRCP 33, including objections to written interrogatories and to the adequacy of any responses thereto and directing any party to answer or to supplement any answer to any interrogatory.

(f) Resolve disputes between the parties relating to the production, inspection and copying of documents and other items pursuant to FRCP 34.

(g) Resolve disputes between the parties relating to physical and mental examinations and depositions of in extremis plaintiffs.

(h) Resolve disputes between the parties relating to any request for admission propounded pursuant to FRCP 36, including the propriety of any requests and the adequacy of any responses thereto.

(i) Resolve disputes between the parties relating to the taking of depositions .... The special master may attend depositions upon a joint request by the parties or upon request of one of the parties when the special master deems it appropriate to attend the deposition. When the special master does not attend the deposition, he may be consulted by telephone to rule on disputes arising during the deposition.

(j) Regulate all proceedings in every hearing before him and to do all acts and take all measures necessary or proper for the efficient performance of his duties as set forth in this order.

(k) Require the attendance of counsel for conferences and place under oath witnesses and/or agents, officers or employees of the parties and examine them.

(l) Rule on all applications for any protective orders in this litigation and, in appropriate circumstances, grant requests for modification of, or exceptions to, such protective orders.

(m) Rule on any request for an order compelling discovery pursuant to FRCP 37 and for costs or expenses related thereto. The special master may also make assessments in appropriate situations as a penalty for noncompliance with discovery orders. Such penalties shall not be reallocated at the conclusion of trial.

3. In addition, the special master shall have all powers relating to discovery allowed to masters under Rule 53 of the Federal Rules of Civil Procedure, and all powers necessary and proper to effectuate Rules 16, 26 through 37, and Rule 45(a)-(d) of the Federal Rules of Civil Procedure, subject to review as hereinafter provided, and to do all other acts and to take all other measures that are necessary or advisable to supervise discovery in these cases and to assist the parties in any settlement negotiations and in the preparation of a pretrial order.

4. Any action taken or ruling made by the special master shall be subject to review by the court upon application of any party aggrieved by such action or ruling, provided that such application shall be served and filed with the court within 10 days after said action or ruling unless such time shall have been enlarged by the master for good cause....

5. If one of the parties shall so request in advance, or upon the direction of the special master, a court reporter shall be present at any proceeding before the special master....

8. The special master shall be compensated for his services at a fair and reasonable rate, which at the present time the court determines to be $180 per hour. The special master shall also be reimbursed for any necessary expenses, and he may use other people in his office to assist him in matters involving legal research, document and file review, service and filing, and such other matters as may be appropriate in the exercise of his duties. The compensation for such assistance shall be at the rate of $75 per hour for associates, and $45 per hour for legal interns. The special master shall periodically submit statements to counsel for defendant Dow with a copy to the court.

PRUDENTIAL INSURANCE CO. OF AMERICA v. UNITED STATES GYPSUM CO.

991 F.2d 1080 (3d Cir. 1993)

■ GARTH, Circuit Judge. Petitioners, Prudential Insurance Company of America and PIC Realty Corporation ("Prudential"), seek the issuance of a writ of mandamus that requires the review of an order of the district court appointing Dean Henry G. Manne of the George Mason University School of Law as a special master. Because the record before us does not satisfy the exceedingly high standard that must be met before the reference of a special master can be made pursuant to Fed.R.Civ.P. 53(b), we will grant the writ.

I.

The underlying dispute from which this petition arises involves several products liability actions brought by Prudential against the United States Gypsum Company [and other asbestos companies. Prudential sought recovery for remediation costs to thirty-nine Prudential properties located in eighteen different states.]

At a [1992] status conference before the magistrate judge, who had been handling discovery matters since the inception of the case [in 1987], all parties agreed that the litigation did not require the services of a special master and asked that the magistrate judge inform the district court of their determination.

The district court apparently did not agree with the litigants' conclusion. Citing "the complexity of both the legal claims and the factual scenario involved in the litigation," the district court appointed Dean Manne to serve as a special master in the litigation pursuant to Fed.R.Civ.P. 53. In his order dated July 31, 1992, the district court judge defined the role of Dean Manne as follows:

> A. To confer promptly with the parties regarding the status of this matter and determine what type and nature of proceedings are necessary for the master to become knowledgeable regarding the matters at issue herein and to carry out his duties as specified below;
>
> B. To consider and resolve expeditiously any and all future disputes between the parties relating to discovery and other nondispositive motions made prior to the time of trial;
>
> C. To fully consider and prepare reports to be submitted to the Court, including an exposition of all relevant facts and conclusions of law, concerning any and all future dispositive motions made prior to the time of trial.

The order specified Dean Manne's rate of compensation and provided that one-half of the master's bill was to be paid by Prudential and the other half by the Defendants....

By opinion dated October 13, 1992, the district court denied Prudential's motion to vacate the reference to the special master, and Prudential subsequently moved to certify the issue for immediate interlocutory appeal pursuant to 28 U.S.C. § 1292(b) and to stay the proceedings before Dean Manne pending appeal. The district court denied the motion . . ., and on November 3, 1992, Prudential filed the instant petition.

II. . . .

The Supreme Court has recognized that it is ultimately within the sound discretion of the court of appeals to issue writs of mandamus in cases such as the one before us. La Buy v. Howes Leather Co., 352 U.S. 249, 255 (1957). Since *La Buy*, mandamus has become "an accepted means to challenge a district court's order referring matters to a special master under Rule 53." In re U.S., 816 F.2d 1083, 1086 (6th Cir. 1987). See also In re Bituminous Coal Operators' Ass'n, Inc., 949 F.2d 1165, 1168 (D.C. Cir. 1991) (citing *La Buy*, 352 U.S. at 256) ("We grant the writ not because the district judge simply 'abused his discretion,' but because he has no discretion to impose on parties against their will 'a surrogate judge,' a substitute from the private bar charged with the responsibility for adjudication of the case."). We therefore turn to Prudential's petition.

III.

A.

The historical role of the special master informs our decision. Special masters were first utilized as judicial assistants to the court in the early years of the English chancery practice. See Kaufman, *Masters in the Federal Courts: Rule 53*, 58 Colum. L. Rev. 452, 452 (1958). Although the practice was continued in the United States, id. at 453, beginning in 1912 the rules of equity restricted the use of masters to situations where an "exceptional condition" required it. Silberman, *Masters and Magistrates Part II: The American Analogue*, 50 N.Y.U. L. Rev. 1297, 1322 (1975). . . .

As stated by Professor Silberman,

> There seems to be no official comment as to why the restriction [requiring an exceptional condition] was added. However, in Los Angeles Brush Mfg. Corp. v. James, 272 U.S. 701 (1927), the Court, per Chief Justice Taft, ascribed the rule's purpose to a shielding of equity litigants from the delay and expense that often accompanied reference to a master. . . .

Id. at 1325, n.161.[5]

It was not until the Federal Rules of Civil Procedure were adopted in December of 1937 that a clause was added to the rule that distinguished between jury trials and nonjury trials. . . . Although we have been unable to find any contemporaneous explanation as to why the Rules Committee saw

---

[5]. Although in more recent times this rationale seems to have taken a back seat to the Supreme Court's concern for the "abdication of the judicial function," *La Buy*, 352 U.S. at 256, there can be little doubt that Chief Justice Taft's concerns also inform the rule's purpose.

fit to add the "complicated" standard to actions involving juries, statements made during a 1938 symposium on the Federal Rules suggest that the new clause was not intended to depart in any substantial way from the [1912 Equity Rules]. . . .

B.

Ordinarily, in order to determine whether a reference to a special master is permissible, it is necessary to ascertain the type of action underlying the reference. . . . [I]f the case is to be tried by a jury, the issues involved must be "complicated" before a special master may be appointed. If, however, there is to be a nonjury trial, an "exceptional condition" is required before a special master may be authorized. We emphasize, however, . . . that in all cases a reference is to be "the exception and not the rule."

It is a matter of dispute between the parties as to whether the jury or nonjury standard applies in this case. Although Prudential's complaint in the underlying action seeks a jury trial, Prudential urges that the relevant standard to be applied at this stage of the proceeding is nevertheless the more demanding "exceptional condition" requirement. This is so because, as argued by Prudential, the determination of core issues, which must be decided prior to trial, must be tested under the nonjury standard of Rule 53, particularly since such issues are, and have always been, within the province and special competence of the appointed judiciary to decide.

Indeed, in this very case the matters consigned by the district court to the master involve proceedings having to do with motions to dismiss, motions to strike defenses, summary judgment motions and discovery. All of these proceedings must be resolved prior to trial and all universally and traditionally have been decided by judges without jury involvement. . . .

Moreover, rather than utilizing the special master to perform some specialized matters of account or difficult computation of damages, see Fed.R.Civ.P. 53(b), or some other time consuming or detailed tasks that the district court judge or a magistrate judge would be less efficient in accomplishing, the district court in this case merely appears to have substituted a master for the magistrate judge, who had been managing the case for five years with the approval of all parties. Indeed, the district court has neither given us specific reasons for appointing a special master nor has it called our attention to any particular, unique, special or exceptional circumstances with which a magistrate judge could not deal effectively or which would require that a magistrate judge be replaced by a special master.

Finally, the plain language of the rule supports Prudential's contention that the jury standard of Rule 53 is inapplicable to the instant petition. . . . Although, admittedly, Prudential has requested a jury trial in its complaint, the action currently before us is not yet a jury trial, nor is there any assurance, or even probability, that Prudential's claims ever will be presented to a jury. . . . Thus, in light of the pre-trial role that the district court assigned to the special master, we will measure the district court's appointment of a special master by the nonjury standard of Rule 53.

C.

The "exceptional condition" standard of Rule 53(b) has been addressed by a significant number of courts.[10] As noted, the seminal Supreme Court case regarding the application of the rule is La Buy v. Howes Leather Co., 352 U.S. 249 (1957), which involved two underlying antitrust actions affecting ninety-three plaintiffs and twelve defendants. Concerned by the complicated nature of the case, the time it would take to try and the congestion of the court calendar, the district court in *La Buy* referred the case to a special master, authorizing him to "take evidence and to report the same to [the] Court together with his findings of fact and conclusions of law." Id. at 253.

The Supreme Court affirmed the Seventh Circuit's issuance of the mandamus writ to withdraw the reference, holding, in part, that the complexity of the legal and factual issues did not warrant the appointment of a special master: "[o]n the contrary, we believe that this is an impelling reason for trial before a regular, experienced trial judge rather than before a temporary substitute appointed on an ad hoc basis and ordinarily not experienced in judicial work." Id. at 259. Therefore, according to *La Buy*, as the complexity of the litigation increases, so, too, does the need for the district judge's personal attention. A district court has no discretion to delegate its adjudicatory responsibility in favor of a decision maker who has not been appointed by the President and confirmed by the Senate. . . .

Given the constraints that *La Buy* places on Rule 53, we cannot say on the record before us, and on the various representations made to us on appeal based on the record, that Prudential's claims establish an exceptional case. As we have noted, the district court has not called our attention to any exceptional qualities of this case nor has it fashioned any findings of fact nor given us any compelling, specific reasons from which we could discern that this case is, indeed, exceptionally different from other cases that have presented complex legal and factual claims, but in which no special masters were sought or appointed. . . . Beyond the district court's generalized statement that Prudential's legal claims and the factual scenario developed are complex, it provides only the following explanation for the reference:

> [T]he volume of documents, the length of the proceedings, the number of the motions and the breadth of documents accompanying the motions, and the inherent complexity of an asbestos litigation all demonstrate that the matters encompassed in the reference in this case not only meet the "complexity" standard of the Rules but also are unique in their complexity.

Far from justifying the appointment of a special master, however, the factors listed by the district court have been specifically rejected by the

---

10. Because we conclude that the nonjury standard applies in this case, we need not reach the question of how, if at all, the Rule 53(b) jury standard differs from the nonjury standard. We note, however, that as a definitional matter, it is difficult to understand how a reference to a master may be the "exception," as required by the first sentence of Rule 53(b), and yet be made in the absence of an "exceptional condition."

Supreme Court as justifications for referring a case to a special master. Neither the volume of work generated by a case nor the complexity of that work will suffice to meet the "exceptional condition" standard promulgated by Rule 53. *La Buy*, 352 U.S. at 259.

Additionally, *La Buy* was decided more than a decade prior to the enactment of the Federal Magistrate's Act, 28 U.S.C. §§ 631-639 (West Supp. 1992) (originally enacted in 1968). Since the implementation of that Act, the analysis, reasoning and conclusions of *La Buy* are even more compelling in disfavoring the appointment of special masters. Much of the concern over docket congestion has been addressed by the appointment of magistrate judges who are expressly authorized by statute to assist the district court with pre-trial matters, including discovery and dispositive legal motions. 28 U.S.C. § 636(b)(1) (West Supp. 1992) . . . . It stands to reason, therefore, that any contemporary examination of the "exceptional condition" standard must be made in light of the Magistrate's Act and the current availability of magistrate judges to whom Congress has specifically authorized the referral of pre-trial matters.

Accordingly, we next turn our attention to the question of whether there is some exceptional aspect of the underlying proceedings giving rise to this petition that might require the appointment of a special master in lieu of a magistrate. . . . Again, nothing in the record informs us that Dean Manne is more qualified to recommend how the pre-trial motions in this case should be decided than is a magistrate judge who has been involved with the Prudential claims and the defenses thereto for more than five years and who has attended approximately forty status conferences. We are not persuaded that the academic credentials of Dean Manne, as impressive as they are, can justify replacing a federally appointed magistrate judge, who, by all accounts, has an excellent working knowledge of the facts and issues in the case and who has thus far ably supervised pre-trial activities. . . .

IV. . . .

In this case, . . . we can envisage no possibility that the applicable nonjury standard of Rule 53 can be satisfied. This being so, no order of reference defining or redefining the master's role, no matter how restrictive in scope, could be framed. The instruction of *La Buy*, the availability of a competent magistrate judge familiar with the earlier proceedings, the overwhelming preference of the Supreme Court and other case authorities for legal issues to be determined by Article III judges and, in particular, the absence of any exceptional conditions revealed by the record all persuade us that in this case, at this time, it would be both error and a waste of valuable judicial resources not to direct that the order of reference be vacated.

We will therefore issue a writ of mandamus directing the district court to withdraw and vacate its reference to the special master.

Notes and Questions

1. Can you reconcile *Agent Orange* and *Prudential*?

2. As *Prudential* says, the use of masters derives from equity practice. Masters, whose roots extend back at least into the early fourteenth century, were Chancery officials who performed numerous functions for the Lord Chancellor. Eventually their chief duty came to be the provision of assistance to the Chancellor in the hearing of and reporting on aspects of equitable suits — assistance necessitated by the fact that the Chancery became an intolerably slow one-man court (see pp. 44-47, *supra*). As the backlog grew, masters received more and more references to consider preliminary (and sometimes dispositive) motions, investigate factual claims, and account for funds. Masters reported their findings to the Chancellor, who retained final authority to decide the suit. See R.E. Ball, *The Chancery Master*, 77 L.Q. 331 (1961); Linda J. Silberman, *Masters and Magistrates Part I: The English Model*, 50 N.Y.U. L. Rev. 1070 (1975); 1 William Holdsworth, A History of English Law 416-21 (7th ed. rev. A.L. Goodhart & H.G. Hanbury eds. 1956); 9 Holdsworth, *supra*, at 360-65.

The abuses associated with Chancery masters were well-known. Masters eventually came to be compensated by charging the litigants for copies of their reports and by having the use of the funds in the suit. Hence, masters had little incentive to streamline issues or to process disputes quickly; and the lack of finality of their reports merely added delay. In 1382 one writer complained that masters were "over fatt both in bodie and purse and over well furred in their benefices, and put the king to verry great cost more than needed," 1 Holdsworth 426; in 1707 another writer complained of the "great charge and delay before the masters," 9 Holdsworth 360. Despite the criticisms, Chancery masters have survived, in a less corrupt and corpulent form, in modern Chancery practice. They continue to have significant responsibilities for pretrial matters, as well as a wide array of other matters. See Ball, *supra*, at 347-54.

English common law first used masters in the mid-nineteenth century to perform certain pretrial tasks. The role of these masters has slowly expanded, so that today in Britain, Queen's Bench masters have nearly complete control over pretrial management, and they even possess authority to decide certain pretrial motions (including dispositive motions) and try certain preliminary issues. See A.S. Diamond, *The Queen's Bench Master*, 76 L.Q. 504 (1960); Silberman, *supra*. The rationales for the use of Queen's Bench masters are to preserve judicial time for the trial of cases and to preserve judicial impartiality (in England, most cases are tried to a judge rather than a jury). Id.

3. Masters have been used in America since colonial times. The ancestry of the American master lies with the Chancery master, not with the later common law master. Irving R. Kaufman, *Masters in the Federal Courts: Rule 53*, 58 Colum. L. Rev. 452 (1958); Linda J. Silberman, *Masters and Magistrates Part II: The American Analogue*, 50 N.Y.U. L. Rev. 1297, 1321-22 (1975); Wayne D. Brazil, *Authority to Refer Discovery Tasks to Special Masters: Limitations on Existing Sources and the Need for a New Federal Rule*, in Managing Complex Litigation 305, 337 (Wayne D. Brazil et al. ed. 1983). In many American states and in federal court, however, masters were not government officials; they were drawn from the ranks of lawyers and, on occasion, the private citizenry.

4. The principal cases and foregoing history suggest that the use of masters for pretrial matters raises four distinct issues. The first is whether a court has

the constitutional power to refer some or all pretrial issues to masters. The second is whether the court has statutory or other authority to make these references. The third issue concerns the legal standards that determine when a reference is permissible. The final issue involves the prudential considerations that govern the decision to make a reference.

(a) *Constitutional Constraints.* Two constitutional constraints suggest outer limits on using masters in complex litigation. The first is the concern, reflected in *Prudential*, that the use of masters results in the entrustment of essential judicial functions to a non-Article III judicial officer. This concern is a variant of the arguments that you may have seen in other courses regarding the power of Congress to delegate adjudicatory responsibility to Article I courts, administrative agencies, and magistrate judges. See generally Erwin Chemerinsky, Federal Jurisdiction §§4.1-.5 (2d ed. 1994). The present, confused state of the law suggests that non-Article III officials can exercise "inherently judicial power" as long as they act as an adjunct to an Article III court and effective appellate review exists. See id. at § 4.5.4; United States v. Raddatz, 447 U.S. 667, 683 n.11 (1980) (analogizing magistrates to masters, and implying that use of masters to take evidence at trial is constitutional); Crowell v. Benson, 285 U.S. 22, 51-52 (1932) (observing in dicta that use of masters to aid juries was constitutional); Ex Parte Peterson, 253 U.S. 300, 312-14 (1920) (finding inherent power to appoint common law master). Therefore, although the Supreme Court has never held that the pretrial use of masters is constitutional, it likely would do so unless the reference amounted to an abdication of the Article III court's power to make findings of jurisdictional and constitutional fact, and its power to decide questions of law. Cf. In re Bituminous Coal Operators' Association, Inc., 949 F.2d 1165, 1168 (D.C. Cir. 1991) (stating that limits on orders of reference are "impelled by the character of federal courts functioning under Article III"); Jack Walters & Sons Corp. v. Morton Building, Inc., 737 F.2d 698 (7th Cir.) (describing constitutional limits in dicta), cert. denied, 469 U.S. 1018 (1984); United States v. Conservation Chemical Co., 106 F.R.D. 210 (W.D. Mo.), *rev'd*, 770 F.2d 103 (8th Cir. 1985) (analyzing Article III concerns).

The second obstacle is the Seventh Amendment, which preserves the right of jury trial in civil cases. Unless a pretrial reference effectively eliminated the right of a jury to make findings of fact, this provision is also unlikely to bar the reference. See *Peterson*, 253 U.S. at 309-12.

(b) *Sources of Authority.* A judge must also possess a source for the authority to order a pretrial reference to a master. In the federal system, the question would seem to be answered by Rule 53; in fact, this is the answer that *Prudential* assumes. The problem is that Rule 53 is found in the portion of the Federal Rules that deals with trials, and nearly all of the language of Rule 53 contemplates a master who acts at trial or during the remedial phase, rather than during pretrial.

Only a handful of cases (none from the Supreme Court) raise the issue about whether Rule 53 authorizes the use of masters in pretrial, and nearly all avoid the issue. See Brazil, *supra*, at 319-32. In contrast, Professor Brazil's detailed examination of the history of American masters and of the drafting of Rule 53 has led him to conclude that Rule 53 does not authorize the use of masters for pretrial tasks. See id. The few commentators who have squarely considered the issue share Brazil's doubts that Rule 53 can support pretrial references. See Kaufman, *supra*, at 462 ("[T]he operation of [Rule 53] in this area is doubtful"); Linda Silberman, *Judicial Adjuncts Revisited: The Proliferation of Ad Hoc*

Procedure, 137 U. Pa. L. Rev. 2131, 2135 (1989) (Rule 53 "does not quite fit the circumstances in which special masters are used today").

For Brazil and Kaufman, however, all is not lost; they contend that courts have an inherent power to appoint masters for pretrial tasks. Their bulwark of support is *Peterson*, a pre-Rule 53 case in which the Supreme Court held that federal courts "have (at least in the absence of legislation to the contrary) inherent power to provide themselves with appropriate instruments for the performance of their duties.... This power includes authority to appoint persons unconnected with the court to aid judges in the performance of specific judicial duties, as they may arise in the progress of a cause." 253 U.S. at 312. But *Peterson* involved a reference to an auditor who performed trial-like tasks of examining accounts and taking evidence. Moreover, even if we concede that *Peterson* confirms a court's inherent power, we run up against the Federal Rules' silence on, and apparent refusal to grant, authority for pretrial references to masters.

(c) *Limits of Authority*. The legal standards that govern pretrial references are equally murky. For those who believe that Rule 53 is the source of the authority to refer, Rule 53 also should provide the limits of that authority. As *Prudential* discusses, however, the text of Rule 53 is a puzzle. Do the phrases "exception rather than the rule" and "exceptional condition" mean something different? If not, why are both phrases used? Is it easier or more difficult to get a master under the "exception plus complicated issues" combination used for jury trials or the "exception plus exceptional condition" language of non-jury trials? For pretrial references, what difference should it make whether a jury trial or a non-jury trial awaits? Or, as *Prudential* holds, are all pretrial matters by nature non-jury, so that the "exception plus exceptional condition" standard applies?

Those who find the authority for pretrial references in the court's inherent power have a similar interpretive problem. Some, like Kaufman, believe that an "exception and not the rule" standard acts as the limit of the inherent power. Others, like Brazil, think that judges can use a master in complex disputes whenever a reference "would contribute substantially to the expedition or orderliness of case preparation." Brazil, *Authority to Refer, supra*, at 385. There is language in *Peterson* to support both the more restrictive view of Kaufman and the broader view of Brazil. See 253 U.S. at 312-14.

Look again at the readings. *Prudential* uses Rule 53's "exceptional condition" standard. *Agent Orange* holds that the reference would expedite the litigation; it makes no effort to show exceptional circumstances and never cites Rule 53. Which approach, if either, seems right?

Consider as well the following three well-known examples: *Armco*, 770 F.2d 103; (environmental dispute), In re United States, 816 F.2d 1083 (6th Cir. 1987) (same); and *Bituminous Coal*, 949 F.2d 1165 (pension litigation). In each case a district judge appointed a special master to oversee the entire discovery period, to make initial rulings on all motions (including dispositive motions regarding liability), and to hear evidence. In *Bituminous Coal* the master was also ordered to make recommended findings of fact and conclusions of law, while in *Armco*, the master was ordered to preside at trial. In *Bituminous Coal* the district judge justified the reference by citing to the complexity of the case and the press of other cases; in *United States* the judge stated that the complexity of the case, calendar congestion, possibility of a lengthy trial, extraordinary pretrial management, and the public interest in speedy resolutions of environmental matters justified the reference; and in *Armco* the factors justifying reference were nearly the same (see *Conservation Chemical*, 106 F.R.D. 210).

In each case, the appellate court issued a writ of mandamus to preclude the reference, at least in its broad form. In *Armco* the court thought that the master should not have been given authority to preside over trial, but then went on to hold that "the district court acted properly in granting the master the broad authority to supervise and conduct pretrial matters, including discovery activity, the production and arrangement of exhibits and stipulations of fact, the power to hear motions for summary judgment or dismissal and to make recommendations with respect thereto." 770 F.2d at 105. In *United States* the court rejected *Armco*'s apparent "distinction between referring the *trial* to the master and referring *pretrial* matters," noting that "dispositive, pretrial motions are more akin to the trial than to discovery matters" and that "even though the reference of nondispositive discovery matters may be justified in some nonjury cases, it will be the extremely rare case where the reference of a dispositive matter (be it a pretrial motion for summary judgment or the actual trial) will be appropriate." It then issued a writ against the use of the master to decide dispositive matters, but not otherwise to manage discovery. 816 F.2d at 1091. Finally, in *Bituminous Coal* the court of appeals found that the use of the master to decide dispositive issues of law and fact was inappropriate, but specifically rejected the defendant's argument that the reference of any issues to a master was inappropriate with the observation that it would be "reluctant to invoke the heavy artillery of [mandamus] to second guess the district court's judgment — informed by its experience in the litigation — that the assistance of a special master is required to ensure that *pretrial preparation* moves forward at a pace appropriate to the need for the expeditious resolution of the matters in controversy." 949 F.2d at 1169. See also Stauble v. Warrob, Inc., 977 F.2d 690, 695 n.6 (1st Cir. 1992) (stating in dicta that dispositive pretrial matters should not be referred to masters). Are any of these cases consistent with *Prudential*?

(d) *Pragmatic Factors.* Assuming that the judge possesses the power of pretrial reference, the judge is not required to exercise that power. Factors favoring a reference include the greater time that a master can devote to pretrial management, the quicker response that a master can provide, the expertise that a master can bring to certain types of specialized pretrial tasks, the freedom that a judge has to concentrate on major pretrial and trial tasks (both in this case and in others), the informality and flexibility that a master provides, the master's accessibility, and the preservation of the trial judge's impartiality. Negative factors include the cost of a master (note the hourly rate of the master in *Agent Orange*), the delay and duplication of effort that ensue when the master's decisions are appealed to the district judge and when the judge needs to become familiar with the case before trial, the district judge's inability to control the litigation, the private master's lack of expertise in managing pretrial matters, the different quality of justice that comes with informality, the possibility that the master's maintenance of a private practice will tempt the master to shape the law to favor his private interests, the potential for abuse of power, the master's lack of political accountability, and the lack of satisfaction and acceptance that clients may feel toward adjudication by a non-judicial officer. See, *e.g.*, Wayne D. Brazil, *Special Masters in Complex Cases: Extending the Judiciary or Reshaping Adjudication*, 53 U. Chi. L. Rev. 394 (1986); Report of the National Commission for the Review of Antitrust Laws and Procedures, *reprinted in* 80 F.R.D. 509, 530 (1980); American College of Trial Lawyers, Recommendations of Major Issues Affecting Complex Litigation, *reprinted in* 90 F.R.D. 207, 223-25 (1981); Wayne D. Brazil, *Special Masters in the Pretrial Development of Big Cases: Potentials and Problems*, in Managing Complex Litigation, *supra*, at 1; Robert C. McLean, *Pretrial Management in Complex Litigation: The Use of Special Masters in* United States v. AT&T, in Managing Complex Litigation, *supra*, at 275; Richard A. Posner, *Coping with the Caseload: A Comment on Magistrates and Masters*, 137 U. Pa. L. Rev. 2215 (1989); Seminar on Protracted Cases, 23 F.R.D. 319, 563-83 (1959) (debate among Judges Biggs, Clark, Graven, and Kaufman).

Agent Orange provides an interesting case study on some of these factors. After the appointment of Mr. Schreiber as master, more and more of the day-to-day running of pretrial devolved upon him. See Peter H. Schuck, Agent Orange on Trial 96-98, 102, 105-06 (1986). This "mission creep" ended abruptly when Judge Weinstein took over the case. Weinstein thought that discovery was moving too slowly, and within two months had replaced Schreiber with a federal magistrate because he wanted "someone who would be stationed in the courthouse at all times, whose cost would be borne by the government, and who would bring a fresh vigor to the case." Id. at 122. Within five months, Judge Weinstein and the new magistrate had pushed the case to the point of trial.

The attitude of the masters and their relationship to the judges in the *Agent Orange* case is also instructive. Schreiber is reported to have said: "You are paid like a lawyer, and called Judge." Id. at 83. David Shapiro, one of the settlement masters later appointed by Weinstein, said that he wore three hats: "the judge's man, the judge's buffer, and the judge's mediator. And . . . the special master must sometimes negotiate with the judge." Id. Shapiro told of an instance in which he had ordered the parties to do something, and represented to the parties that he had Judge Weinstein's authority to order it. In fact, he did not. The subsequent conversation between Shapiro and Weinstein went like this: "'Don't get sore, Judge,' Shapiro began, 'but this is what I've done and you've got to cover for me.' Weinstein burst out laughing. 'You tell them that that's my order.' Shapiro laughed even harder. 'I already did,' he said." Id. at 150.

Wouldn't the *Agent Orange* anecdotes have sounded familiar to a Chancery practitioner of the seventeenth century?

5. Whatever doubts we might have instilled in you regarding the legal authority for and wisdom of appointing masters, you should not be deceived. As *Agent Orange* and *Prudential* show, judges often order pretrial references without significant concerns about the authority to do so. The tasks for which masters today might be appointed include: (1) organizing the litigation, see In re Wirebound Boxes Antitrust Litigation, 128 F.R.D. 250 (D. Minn. 1989); (2) proposing case management orders, see In re Shell Oil Refinery, 136 F.R.D. 588, 592 (E.D. La. 1991), *aff'd* on other grounds, 979 F.2d 1014 (5th Cir. 1991); (3) helping define issues, see Geoffrey C. Hazard, Jr. & Paul R. Rice, *Judicial Management of the Pretrial Process in Massive Litigation*, *in* Managing Complex Litigation, *supra*, at 77, and Belfiore v. New York Times Co., 654 F. Supp. 842 (D. Conn. 1986), *aff'd* on other grounds, 826 F.2d 177 (2d Cir. 1987), cert. denied, 484 U.S. 1067 (1988); (4) overseeing depositions and reviewing them to see if prima facie claims are established, see In re Estate of Ferdinand E. Marcos Human Rights Litigation, 1994 WL 874222 (D. Haw. 1994); (5) presiding at scheduling and discovery conferences, see Roberts v. Heim, 1990 WL 306009 (N.D. Cal.); (6) ruling on privilege claims, see In re Sunrise Securities Litigation,

124 F.R.D. 99 (E.D. Pa. 1989); and (7) handling discovery disputes, see Baxter v. Coca-Cola Co., 47 F.R.D. 345 (S.D.N.Y. 1969), *aff'd* on other grounds, 431 F.2d 183 (2d Cir. 1970), cert. denied, 401 U.S. 923 (1971).

General pretrial references for all discovery matters still occur, see In re San Juan Dupont Plaza Hotel Fire Litigation, 1989 WL 168401 (D.P.R. 1989), but district courts are increasingly wary of them, see United States v. Hooker Chemical and Plastics Corp., 123 F.R.D. 62 (W.D.N.Y. 1988). See Manual for Complex Litigation, Third 16 (1995) (stating that referral of pretrial management to master is "not advisable," but advocating referral "for limited purposes requiring special expertise," such as devising "complex program for settlement needs. For case studies on the use of masters, see Wayne D. Brazil, *Special Masters in Complex Cases, supra* (describing appointment of masters in several complex cases); Francis E. McGovern, *Toward a Functional Approach for Managing Complex Litigation*, 53 U. Chi. L. Rev. 440 (1986) (same); (describing use of masters in AT&T antitrust litigation).

6. It is widely assumed that the constitutional, statutory, and pragmatic considerations we have been discussing apply only to references that one or more parties oppose. When all parties consent to a reference, the limits of the reference can be established by the parties themselves; and those limits can exceed the limits of a judge's power to order a reference. See Kimberly v. Arms, 129 U.S. 512 (1889) (delegation of trial tasks); Brazil, *Authority to Refer, supra*, at 307-14; Silberman, *Masters and Magistrates Part II*, 50 N.Y.U. L. Rev. at 1354.

Is this an accurate assumption? Doesn't the last sentence of Rule 53(b) imply that consensual references to *private* masters must still meet the stringent terms of Rule 53(b) (assuming, of course, that Rule 53 governs pretrial references at all)? Judge Kaufman thought that "the permissive scope of the reference is broadened" when the parties consented, but cautioned that even a consensual reference might be inappropriate "in those limited instances where the public interest demands retention of the initial inquiry by the court." Kaufman, 58 Colum. L. Rev. at 459. In Wilver v. Fisher, 387 F.2d 66 (10th Cir. 1967), the defendants had refused to answer certain interrogatories. The parties consented to refer the matter to a master, and further consented to give the master the power to restate the interrogatories and to recommend the answers — obviously powers that an adversarial judge does not enjoy. On appeal, the Tenth Circuit held that "[t]he parties, not a Master, ask the questions and give the answers. The court has control over and responsibility for the discovery procedures authorized by the rules. The order of reference here borders on an abdication of the judicial function and is not justified by the record." 387 F.2d at 69.

7. *Wilver* has been criticized, see, *e.g.*, Brazil, *Authority to Refer, supra*, at 312-14, but it raises an interesting issue: Whether a judge can order a master to perform tasks that a judge operating within standard jurisdictional, ethical, and adversarial bounds could not. Your immediate reaction is probably that such a reference would be inappropriate. But recent descriptions of the work of masters in complex cases make clear that masters in fact do certain things that traditional judges cannot, such as holding *ex parte* conversations with parties or coordinating related state and federal proceedings. See Hazard & Rice, *supra*, at 91-92; Brazil, *Special Masters in Complex Cases*, 53 U. Chi. L. Rev. at 420-22; Schuck, *supra*, 144-49, 259; In re DES Cases, 142 F.R.D. 58 (E.D.N.Y. & N.Y.Sup.Ct. 1992) (appointing joint settlement master for state and federal cases). Does such an arrangement let a judge have her cake and eat it too?

This last question raises the larger theoretical issues neglected in the standard discussions about the advantages and disadvantages of pretrial masters. Professor Brazil, who supports the use of pretrial masters, expressed one set of concerns in this way:

> [S]ome may fear that special masters will be used as instruments for transforming basic features of the established system and thus for attacking the values that system symbolizes and is presumed to promote. . . .
>
> Could the introduction of a special master during the discovery stage change the [standard adversary model in which attorneys control discovery]? The answer clearly is yes. A master with an assertive personality and broad authority to manage and monitor the discovery process could exercise considerable influence over its character. . . .
>
> [Moreover,] permitting a master to aggressively use his or her influence to manipulate or pressure lawyers or litigants into positions they otherwise would not adopt would represent a significant change in the adjudicatory system and would create significant opportunities for abuse of power.

Brazil, *Special Masters in Big Cases*, supra, at 71, 74.

Professor Silberman raises other, related concerns:

> [T]he trans-substantive premise of the [Federal Rules of Civil Procedure] is being eroded in numerous indirect ways. The *Manual for Complex Litigation* . . ., although not in formal rulemaking guise, adopt[s] a set of particularized procedures and recommendations for certain large and complex cases. . . . But by and large the erosion of trans-substantive rules has come via ad hoc, informal, customized procedures devised by judges and, often, their judicial adjuncts to cope with the difficulties posed by the modern caseload. . . . [D]evices such as special masters [and] judicial management . . . have made trans-substantive rules a concept in name only. . . .
>
> [Second,] it is partly due to our continuing delegation of process to judicial adjuncts that we have failed to make more comprehensive procedural reform. . . . Rather than confront the policy issue of whether litigation like *Agent Orange* should have something other than a judicial forum, there are sighs of relief that [innovative management] helped bring about the settlement of the case. Thus, the use of judicial adjuncts has pushed formalized procedure into retreat. . . .

Silberman, *Judicial Adjuncts Revisited*, 137 U. Pa. L. Rev. at 2175-77.

How do we respond to claims that the use of special masters threatens the two core assumptions of our modern American procedural system — adversarialism and trans-substantivism? Shouldn't those concerns be as relevant to a judge as the cost or delay of a master in a particular case? Indeed, who will act to protect the core values of a procedural system, if not the judge? On the other hand, the judge has little private (as opposed to public) reason to protect the system in this way. Is the answer to this problem simply to ban the pretrial use of masters? To trust that judges and masters will adequately factor into the balance these public concerns? Or to abandon adversarialism and trans-substantivism? (Silberman's solution, by the way, is precisely "to move away from trans-substantive procedural rules," see 137 U. Pa. L. Rev. at 2177.) Once again, practical procedural questions require us to consider fundamental procedural values.

8. One solution to the problem of masters is to recall the nature of complex litigation. By definition, complexity in pretrial litigation involves circumstances in which lawyers cannot perform adequately their adversarial tasks, but rational adjudication can nonetheless be preserved through judicial assistance at the pretrial stage. Thus, in complex litigation the concern that a master will harm the adversarial process is misplaced: The need to preserve rational adjudication trumps the desirability of adversarial process. Two corollaries follow from this conclusion. First, the reasons that a master might be necessary in complex litigation in no way justify a reference to a master in routine litigation — especially when the reference in the routine case causes harm to adversarial values. Second, a pretrial reference in complex litigation must satisfy a highly restrictive test: The master must possess abilities or qualities that will facilitate rational adjudication, while the judge does not possess those abilities or qualities.

This restrictive test for using masters does not, however, address Silberman's concern with trans-substantivism. In this book we have frequently talked about the value of treating like cases alike, but we have never decided exactly how fundamental a value it is. Should we allow a pretrial reference to a master create a process that leads to an outcome different than the outcome for other parties in the same or other cases?

9. Within the constraints discussed in the preceding materials, the decision to appoint a special master is committed to the judge's discretion, see Meeropol v. Meese, 790 F.2d 942 (D.C. Cir. 1986), and is not immediately appealable (although a liberal use of mandamus by some courts of appeal has made many references effectively appealable). The standard of review for pretrial decisions entrusted to a master is unclear. Regarding trial and remedial matters, Rule 53 provides that, in non-consensual cases, a master's findings of fact must be accepted unless clearly erroneous in a non-jury trial, and are mere evidence for a jury to consider in a jury trial; conclusions of law are subject to de novo review in both types of trial. F.R.Civ.P. 53(e)(2)-(3). Unless the parties otherwise stipulate, the same standards are applicable in consensual references. F.R.Civ.P. 53(e)(4). Some authority suggests that the non-jury standards of Rule 53 apply for pretrial decisions. See American Honda Motor Co. v. Vickers Motors, Inc., 64 F.R.D. 118 (W.D. Tenn. 1974). This result is consistent with *Prudential*'s logic.

10. In Chapter Eleven, we will examine the power of a district judge to appoint experts and technical advisors to assist in the trial of a case. It might also be possible for a judge to appoint experts or advisors to handle pretrial aspects of a case; in fact, there is some authority supporting their pretrial use. See Thomas E. Willging, Court-Appointed Experts 18-20 (1986); *Manual, Third, supra*, at 16; cf. Reilly v. United States, 863 F.2d 149 (1st Cir. 1988) (court appointed technical advisor for trial); In re Joint Eastern and Southern Districts Asbestos Litigation, 151 F.R.D. 540 (E. & S.D.N.Y. 1993) (court appointed advisor to select expert panel, and then appointed expert panel to estimate value of certain claims). Unlike a master, an expert or advisor would have no decision making power; they merely provide information that the judge can use in making her own decision.

The authority for the appointment of experts is Fed.R.Evid. 706. The authority for the appointment of technical advisors is, apparently, the inherent power of the court. See *Reilly*, 863 F.2d at 156. There do not seem to be any reported decisions in which district judges have appointed technical advisors to assist in case management functions. Would the use of advisors be a way to take the best of the master system while avoiding the worst? Or is the failure to provide decisionmaking authority to an advisor borrowing the worst of the system without extracting any countervailing benefits? Should we experiment and find out? Or should we be cautious about ad hoc procedural reform?

c. Using Magistrate Judges for Pretrial Matters

Remember that we are considering the ways that a district judge can assemble around her the resources necessary to fulfill her case management responsibilities. As *Agent Orange* and *Prudential* show, a judge has an intermediate choice between managing the pretrial phase herself and appointing a master to do the work. That choice is to use a magistrate judge. Predecessors to the magistrate judge have existed since 1789, but modern magistrate judges trace their history to 1968, when Congress created the office and assigned specific duties to magistrates. See 28 U.S.C. §§ 631 et seq. Magistrate judges are not Article III judicial officers; they serve a term of eight years, and are eligible for reappointment upon a majority vote of the relevant district judges and approval by the circuit's judicial council. § 631(e)-(f).

With regard to civil pretrial matters, § 636(b)(1)(A) permits a district court to designate a magistrate judge to "hear and determine any pretrial matter pending before the court, except a motion for injunctive relief, for judgment on the pleadings, for summary judgment, . . . to dismiss or to permit maintenance of a class action, to dismiss for failure to state a claim upon which relief can be granted, or to involuntarily dismiss an action." With regard to these excepted motions (which, other than the class action motion, are often dispositive), the district court can designate the magistrate judge "to conduct hearings, including evidentiary hearings, and to submit to a judge of the court proposed findings of fact and recommendations for the disposition." § 636(b)(1)(B). Appeals must be taken from a magistrate judge's ruling or report within ten days. Parties can also consent to have a matter (whether pretrial or trial) referred to a magistrate judge, in which case the magistrate judge exercises the same power as a district judge. § 636(c).

MANUAL FOR COMPLEX LITIGATION, THIRD

16 (1995)

The judge should decide early in the litigation whether to refer all or any part of pretrial supervision and control to a magistrate judge. In making that decision, the judge needs to consider a number of factors, including the experience and qualifications of the available magistrate judge, the relationship and attitude of the attorneys, the extent to which a district judge's authority may be required, the time the judge has to devote to the litigation, the novelty of the issues presented and the need for innovation, and the judge's personal preferences. Some judges believe that judicial supervision of complex litigation should ordinarily be exercised directly by them rather than by a magistrate judge, even in courts that routinely make such referrals for discovery or other pretrial purposes. They believe that referrals in complex cases may cause additional costs and delays when the parties seek review by the judge, weaken the impact of directions given to counsel during pretrial proceedings, diminish supervisory consistency and coherence as the case proceeds to trial, create greater reluctance to try innovative procedures that might aid in resolution of the case, and cause the judge to be unfamiliar with the case at the time of trial. Other judges have found that magistrate judges have the competence, experience, and authority to be able to provide effective case management during the pretrial stage, enabling the judge to devote time to more urgent matters.

Even if no general referral is made to a magistrate judge, referral of particular matters may be helpful. The judge may refer supervision of all discovery matters, or supervision of particular discovery issues or disputes, particularly those that may be time consuming or require an immediate ruling; examples include resolving disputes by telephone, ruling on claims of privilege and motions for protective orders, and conducting hearings on procedural matters, such as personal jurisdiction. Magistrate judges may also be called on to assist counsel with formulation of stipulations and statements of contentions, and to facilitate settlement discussions.

Notes and Questions

1. Magistrate judges provide an interesting counterpoint to special masters. As with masters, the use of magistrate judges raises constitutional concerns. For the most part, however, those concerns have been resolved in favor of magistrates. See Mathews v. Weber, 423 U.S. 261 (1976) (delegation of Social Security cases upheld); United States v. Raddatz, 447 U.S. 667 (1980) (delegation of hearing on suppression of evidence upheld); Peretz v. United States, 501 U.S. 923 (1991) (consensual use of magistrate to supervise felony jury selection upheld); Administrative Office of United States Courts, A Constitutional Analysis of Magistrate Judge Authority, *reprinted in* 150 F.R.D. 247 (1992). Today there seems to be little doubt that, given the review available from the district judge, the present delegation of pretrial tasks to magistrate judges is constitutional.

As with masters, the pretrial use of magistrate judges raises issues about the source of authority for appointment, the limits of a magistrate judge's power, and the pragmatic factors that influence the use of a magistrate judge. Contrary to the master's more ambiguous position, the source of authority for the pretrial use of magistrate judges is clearly defined: 28 U.S.C. § 636, supplemented by F.R.Civ.P. 72. Those same provisions clearly describe the limits of a magistrate judge's power, which varies with the consent of the parties and the dispositive or non-dispositive nature of the matter. Thus, the critical issue regarding the pretrial use of magistrate judges is typically the pragmatic one.

2. Let us explore that pragmatic issue. Since the magistrate judge, like the district judge, is likely to be a generalist, what exactly is the advantage of using

a magistrate judge to manage the pretrial aspects of a complex case? Can a magistrate judge do anything to promote the rational adjudication of a complex dispute that a district judge cannot? When time is of the essence (*i.e.*, the rational adjudication of a dispute will be impossible if the case is not adjudicated within a certain time frame), and when no single judge could perform all of the pretrial tasks within that time frame, there seems to be a clear need for another judicial officer. Likewise, if related cases within a single district are pending before different judges, their consolidation before a single magistrate judge helps to ensure the like treatment of like cases. But these circumstances are relatively rare: Time is not usually "of the essence," and consolidation before a single district judge obviates the need for resort to a magistrate judge to ensure like treatment. See In re Repetitive Stress Injury Cases, 142 F.R.D. 584 (E.D.N.Y. 1992) (cases consolidated before one district judge; magistrate judge oversaw discovery even after consolidation), vacated, 11 F.3d 368 (2d Cir. 1993).

Should a magistrate judge be used in other complex cases? The *Manual, Third* lists a number of additional factors — many of which are the same as the factors that animate a judge's decision to use a master (see pp. 950-51, *supra*) — that might lead to the use of a magistrate judge. Professor Silberman, on the other hand, sounds two cautionary notes not heard in the *Manual*:

> First, an uncensored, almost reflexive response to refer all pre-trial discovery to magistrates is developing. As a result, there may be a hydraulic effect on discovery, now that there is an "institutional setting" in which discovery disputes may flourish. Litigants are somewhat insulated from the judge, and to some degree the recent emphasis on strong and close judicial management is undercut because the magistrate and not the judge has control of the case. . . . Second, the institutional response — to take burdensome discovery away from judges and place it elsewhere in the system — may have relieved some of the pressure on the rulemakers to reassess the discovery rules more generally. Ad hoc attention to and discretionary-based treatment for different kinds of cases — in the form of magistrate supervision — continue to give sustenance to the myth that we operate in a system of trans-substantive procedure. Systematized, formal rules for particular cases may be an alternative that the creation of the magistrate system has allowed us to forsake.

Linda Silberman, *Judicial Adjuncts Revisited: The Proliferation of Ad Hoc Procedure*, 137 U. Pa. L. Rev. 2131, 2141 (1989).

The *Manual* also fails to mention other institutional concerns in the use of a magistrate judge. Recent studies of the magistrate judge system suggest that magistrate judges occupy one of three roles in particular cases: either as an additional judge, handling her own consensual caseload; as a specialist, handling a particular type of case on the docket and building an expertise in that field; or as a team player, helping the district judge out on pretrial matters in cases on the district judge's docket. See Carroll Seron, The Roles of Magistrates (1985). Moreover, magistrate judges often work for more than one judge, and district judges often do not accord magistrate judges the respect that they believe they deserve. See Christopher E. Smith, United States Magistrates in the Federal Courts (1990). Therefore, the resources of magistrate judges may already be spread into other areas, making it difficult for a magistrate judge to devote adequate time to the pretrial preparation of a complex case; and, unless both the district judges and the magistrate judges agree on and value the magistrate's role as team player, a magistrate judge may not have an adequate incentive to invest herself in the pretrial management of a case. See also James S. Kakalik et al., An Evaluation of Judicial Case Management under the Civil Justice Reform Act 77-80 (1996) (reporting that use of magistrate judges significantly increases attorney satisfaction, but does not significantly affect time to disposition, lawyers' work hours, or lawyers' view of fairness of process). Richard A. Posner, *Coping with the Caseload: A Comment on Magistrates and Masters*, 137 U. Pa. L. Rev. 2215 (1989) (noting concern that reliance on magistrate judges leads to excessive bureaucratization of federal judiciary).

Do the factors described in the *Manual* and elsewhere convince you that a district judge should delegate her responsibility to manage a case? Why would a district judge ever do so? Is the answer that a magistrate judge (except in limited circumstances described above) has no advantages in the complex case itself, but that the magistrate's work in the complex case allows a district judge to allocate her resources to other matters on her docket? Is that an adequate answer, given the judge's responsibility to ensure that complex disputes be adjudicated with as little damage as possible to our adversarial ideal and our trans-substantive aspirations?

3. Many district judges apparently do not share these reservations; they have delegated a wide range of pretrial tasks in complex cases to magistrate judges. Some judges have assigned all pretrial tasks, including management of discovery, to magistrate judges. See In re MGM Grand Hotel Fire Litigation, 570 F. Supp. 913, 917 (D. Nev. 1983) (excluding dispositive motions); In re San Juan DuPont Plaza Hotel Fire Litigation, 1989 WL 168401 (D.P.R.) (magistrate appointed as discovery master). Other judges have delegated discrete pretrial tasks, including the following: (1) appointing the members of a plaintiffs' committee of counsel, and establishing the committee's responsibilities and fee structure, see Smiley v. Sincoff, 958 F.2d 498, 499 (2d Cir. 1992); (2) helping parties prepare a discovery plan and entering a case management order, see Castano v. American Tobacco Co., 160 F.R.D. 544, 559 (E.D. La. 1995), *rev'd* on other grounds, 84 F.3d 734 (5th Cir. 1996), and Klein v. King, 132 F.R.D. 525 (N.D. Cal. 1990); (3) determining the relevancy of documents, see In re Harcourt Brace Jovanovich, Inc. Securities Litigation, 838 F. Supp. 109 (S.D.N.Y. 1993); (4) determining and applying the relevant law of privilege, see In re Combustion, Inc., 161 F.R.D. 51 (W.D. La. 1995), *aff'd*, 161 F.R.D. 54 (W.D. La. 1995); (5) ruling on motions to compel discovery, see Champion International Corp. v. Liberty Mutual Insurance Co., 129 F.R.D. 63 (S.D.N.Y. 1989); and (6) issuing or modifying protective orders, see Cipollone v. Liggett Group, Inc., 785 F.2d 1108 (3d Cir. 1986), and State of Florida v. Jones Chemicals, Inc., 148 F.R.D. 282 (M.D. Fla. 1993).

In all of these cases, the use of a magistrate judge is reported in a matter-of-fact way; none of the cases entertains any doubt about the power to assign these tasks to magistrate judges. The one case that might have raised your eyebrows was *Smiley*, involving the appointment of a committee of counsel. Would you, as a district judge, delegate this task to a magistrate judge?

4. Let us assume that, for whatever reason, a judge correctly decides that she needs another judicial officer to help her manage a complex case. Recall *Prudential*'s argument that pretrial references to special masters ought to be particularly suspect in light of the availability of magistrate judges. Note as well that 28 U.S.C. § 636(b)(2) and F.R.Civ.P. 53(b) allow a magistrate judge to be appointed as a special master; upon the consent of the parties, the magistrate judge can even be appointed without meeting the usual "exception and not the

rule" requirements of Rule 53. In light of these two facts, when should a district judge appoint a magistrate judge and when should she appoint a master?

Part of the answer is legal: The constraints of Rule 53 (assuming it applies) and § 636 differ, and generally make it easier to delegate pretrial responsibilities to a magistrate judge. Hence, legal standards may determine a judge's choice. When both a master and a magistrate judge remain permissible options, however, the choice is a pragmatic one. Magistrate judges and masters have different strengths. Since the salary of a magistrate judge is not borne by the parties and the fees of a master are, this fact favors the magistrate judge. Concerns for ethical improprieties and institutional commitment to the quality of adjudication are less acute with magistrate judges. On the other hand, a generalist magistrate judge carries a significant caseload of other matters, thus reducing the speed with which she can act in the complex case; the magistrate judge may not have the substantive expertise or familiarity with informal procedures that a master does; and the closer bond of the magistrate judge to the institution of the court may reduce the magistrate judge's effectiveness, creativity, and flexibility. See Margaret G. Farrell, *The Role of Special Masters in Federal Litigation*, in 1 Civil Practice and Litigation in Federal and State Courts (Sol Schreiber ed. 1994). Likewise, a master's ability to develop a consistent pretrial strategy for related cases that cannot be joined in one forum makes a master an appealing option when all of the judges in the various forums can agree on a single master.

One option for a judge is to use a combination of master and magistrate judge. That is the arrangement upon which Judge Weinstein finally settled in the *Agent Orange* case, in which he gave general responsibility for discovery to a magistrate judge and responsibility for specific tasks to a series of masters. Judge Greene initially adopted a somewhat different arrangement in the *AT&T* litigation, granting general responsibility for pretrial to a magistrate and delegating only the task of ruling on claims of privilege and work product to the masters. United States v. American Telephone & Telegraph Co., 461 F. Supp. 1314, 1348 (D.D.C. 1978). Subsequently, however, the court gave the special masters the authority to handle the most significant pretrial matters, and virtually cut the magistrate out of the picture. In post-mortem analysis, the special masters concluded that the original division of responsibility was wrong and the latter division correct:

> [I]t is a mistake to have a horizontal division of responsibility between judge and magistrate or magistrate and special master. By horizontal division, we mean a coordinate division of responsibility over subject matter. In *United States v. AT&T* the division had discovery go to the magistrate, privilege claims to the special master, and everything else to the judge.... [T]he swirl of pretrial does not categorize so easily, and coordination by these means is slow and rigid. As things evolved, there emerged a vertical division of responsibility. We as special masters became responsible for almost all of the pretrial under the judicial authority and administrative superintendence of the judge. This allowed a division of labor between the judge and subordinate judicial officers but put the judge and us in a position to see and guide the case as [a] whole. The result was much closer coordination of the court responses to various parts of the case.

Geoffrey C. Hazard, Jr. & Paul R. Rice, *Judicial Management of the Pretrial Process in Massive Litigation, in* Managing Complex Litigation 77, 84 (Wayne D. Brazil et al. ed. 1983). What is the difference between the "horizontal" and "vertical" arrangements other than the elimination of the magistrate from the picture? Hazard and Rice make a case for not slicing pretrial responsibility into too many pieces, but do they make a case for giving masters the largest slice?

5. When matters (typically dispositive) under § 636(b)(1)(B) are involved, the statute requires the district judge to "make a de novo determination of those portions of the report or specified findings or recommendations to which objection is made," and the district judge may even receive further evidence. This fact reduces the utility of using magistrate judges for dispositive pretrial matters. See Report of the Federal Courts Study Committee 80 (1990) ("De novo review can be so time-consuming and costly for both court and litigants that in many cases referral of a matter ultimately requiring such review may be inefficient."). When non-dispositive matters under § 636(b)(1)(A) are involved, however, the standard of review is "clearly erroneous or contrary to law." The deference due a magistrate judge's ruling on these non-dispositive motions, which include most pretrial rulings, sometimes poses problems for a district judge. In Haines v. Liggett Group, Inc., 975 F.2d 81 (3rd Cir. 1992), a district judge delegated part of the responsibility for deciding a non-dispositive discovery matter to a magistrate judge and another part to a master. The magistrate judge resolved his part in a way generally favorable to the defendants. The plaintiff sought review from the district judge, who resolved the issue in a way more favorable to the plaintiffs. As part of the judge's decision, he relied on evidence that had not been presented to the magistrate judge, but that the judge was aware of from related litigation he was handling. On mandamus, the court of appeals held that, because the matter delegated to the magistrate was non-dispositive under § 636(b)(1)(A), the district judge acted improperly in considering additional evidence. In large-scale litigation involving supervision by both a district and a magistrate judge, isn't it almost inevitable that the district judge will have information that the magistrate judge does not? After *Haines*, will judges be less inclined to use magistrate judges?

6. In addition to the sources cited above, discussions of the magistrate judge system can be found in Carroll Seron, The Roles of Magistrates in Federal District Courts (1983); Philip M. Pro & Thomas C. Hnatowski, *Measured Progress: The Evolution and Administration of the Federal Magistrate System*, 44 Am. U. L. Rev. 1503 (1995); R. Lawrence Dessem, *The Role of the Federal Magistrate Judge in Civil Justice Reform*, 67 St. John L. Rev. 799 (1993); Shira A. Scheindlin, *Discovering the Discoverable: A Bird's Eye View of Discovery in a Complex Multidistrict Class Action Litigation*, 52 Brook. L. Rev. 397 (1986); Linda J. Silberman, *Masters and Magistrates Part II: The American Analogue*, 50 N.Y.U. L. Rev. 1297 (1975).

3. Recusal of a Judicial Officer

Recusal is the judicial equivalent of a lawyer's disqualification: A judge is removed ("recused") because of some actual or apparent impropriety. Like disqualification, recusal forces us to consider whether complex litigation, which alters the traditional adversarial roles of lawyers and judges, requires us to adjust the ethical norms that the adversarial system expects of judges. The answer to these questions are critical, for no judge can ultimately be a more creative case manager than her ethical norms allow her to be.

IN RE SCHOOL ASBESTOS LITIGATION

977 F.2d 764 (3rd Cir. 1992)

BECKER, Circuit Judge. . . . Before us are eight petitions for mandamus brought by various defendants shortly before trial was scheduled to begin in this nationwide products liability class action. The trial, which has been stayed pending resolution of these petitions, will concern over 30,000 school districts' claims that the defendants are liable for expenses incurred in eliminating the alleged danger caused by asbestos-containing products in their school buildings. . . .

Petition No. 91-1887, filed by Pfizer, Inc. and supported by numerous other defendants, challenges the refusal of the district judge, the Honorable James McGirr Kelly, to disqualify himself from the case. . . .

Two companion petitions, No. 91-1943 filed by ACandS, Inc. and No. 91-1981 filed by Asten Group, Inc., argue additionally that specific rulings adverse to them, which were issued after defendants first requested Judge Kelly to disqualify himself are tainted by the appearance of partiality and must be vacated. . . .

IV. THE PETITIONS RELATING TO DISQUALIFICATION . . .

A. *Mandamus as a Means to Review a District Judge's Failure to Disqualify Himself or Herself*

Initially, we must determine whether a mandamus petition is a proper means for a court of appeals to review a district judge's refusal to disqualify himself or herself from a case. . . .

Section 455 is addressed directly to judicial officers, requiring them to act *sua sponte* when confronted with situations requiring their disqualification. Subsection (a) provides:

> Any justice, judge, or magistrate of the United States shall disqualify himself in any proceeding in which his impartiality might reasonably be questioned.

Subsection (b), in turn, lists a number of specific circumstances in which a judge is required to disqualify himself or herself. Most relevantly, disqualification is required when there is "a personal bias or prejudice concerning a party, or personal knowledge of disputed evidentiary facts concerning the proceeding." 28 U.S.C. § 455(b)(1). While the parties may, after full disclosure on the record, waive the grounds of disqualification under subsection (a), a judge may not accept a waiver of the grounds listed in subsection (b).

The petitioners urge us to adopt the consensus position of our sister circuits and hold that mandamus is a proper means of challenging a district judge's refusal to disqualify himself or herself under section 455. . . . [W]e agree with the petitioners. . . .

B. *The Facts Surrounding the Conference on the Hazards of Asbestos in Place*

We now describe the facts of this case so as to determine whether section 455 "clearly and indisputably" required the district judge to disqualify himself and hence requires us to issue a writ of mandamus directing him to do so.

The origins of this controversy date to November 1986, at which point Judge Kelly had been presiding over this litigation for more than three years. Dr. Irwin J. Selikoff of the Mt. Sinai School of Medicine in New York City, a noted expert on asbestos-related diseases, invited Judge Kelly to attend a scientific conference on diseases caused by inhaling asbestos. Asbestos-related cases constitute a large percentage of the civil docket in the Eastern District of Pennsylvania, and Judge Kelly took the admirable view that judicial education about the scientific aspects of these cases would improve judicial case management. Because of docket pressures, Judge Kelly declined that invitation. He did, however, express to Selikoff an interest in attending a similar conference in the future.

By Pretrial Order 137, dated August 8, 1988, the district court established a process by which it would approve the class plaintiffs' use of certain escrowed funds from prior settlements to pay for litigation expenses. Under that procedure, the class plaintiffs would apply under seal for installments of up to $50,000. Further distributions would not be authorized until the court had approved an accounting, also filed under seal, for the previous $50,000.

By late fall 1989, the plaintiffs' executive committee had become unhappy with the asbestos industry's sponsoring of what the committee perceived to be one-sided scientific conferences on the dangers of asbestos in place. As a result, the executive committee contacted Selikoff, who agreed to supervise an alternative conference on the dangers of asbestos in buildings and low-level asbestos exposure generally (hereinafter the "Third Wave Conference"). According to Selikoff's proposal, the conference would be conducted under the auspices of the nonprofit Collegium Ramazzini, a society of environmental and occupational health scientists of which Selikoff was president, and speakers would not be paid honoraria.

On December 1, 1989, the class plaintiffs applied under seal (and thus without the defendants' knowledge) for $50,000 from the settlement fund to help finance the proposed conference. The plaintiffs indicated that the conference was to be coordinated by Selikoff and that it would be helpful in supporting the plaintiffs' case. They emphasized that Selikoff was a world-renowned expert, yet a neutral in asbestos litigation, in addition to their belief that "a balanced view of issues concerning asbestos in buildings is not being presented to the public or scientific community at this time." On December 6, in sealed Pretrial Order 201, Judge Kelly granted the plaintiffs' request. Shortly thereafter, a $50,000 check was issued, which became the seminal source of funding for the conference.

On February 2, 1990, the plaintiffs' executive committee wrote to Selikoff and encouraged him to send a notice or invitation to Judge Kelly "so that he is advised of the progress and details." . . . [O]n February 15, 1990, Selikoff invited Judge Kelly, on Collegium Ramazzini stationery, to attend and enclosed an announcement describing the conference. The invitation mentioned neither the plaintiffs' role in the conference nor the court's earlier approval of funding for the conference. . . . On February 20, 1990, Judge Kelly accepted Selikoff's invitation. According to Judge Kelly, he had forgotten that the conference was supported by the plaintiffs' settlement funds; rather, he believed that Selikoff was extending a follow-up to his 1986 invitation.

In March and April 1990, the plaintiffs' executive committee supplied the Collegium Ramazzini with the names and research materials of various scientists whom the plaintiffs proposed to call as expert witnesses at trial. Many of these experts were then invited to speak at the Third Wave Conference. The plaintiffs' executive committee also supplied the Collegium Ramazzini with the names of various state and federal judges who had been handling asbestos matters. The Collegium Ramazzini in turn invited many of these judges, including Judge Kelly, to attend the conference as guests of the sponsors. Their registration fees were to be waived and their hotel accommodations provided; the judges, however, would have to pay for their own transportation and meals. A number of judges, including Judge Kelly, expressed an interest in attending the conference. On May 2, 1990, the Collegium Ramazzini confirmed to Judge Kelly that it would waive his registration fee and pay for his hotel room.

The Third Wave Conference took place in New York City from June 7 to June 9, 1990, and was attended by Judge Kelly and fourteen other judges. There were fifty-six presentations, with each day's proceedings lasting eight to ten hours. The views expressed were overwhelmingly consistent with the plaintiffs' position, although opposing views were not actively suppressed. Representatives of numerous defendants attended, but did not speak. It is not clear which presentations Judge Kelly attended, although according to his later recollection he was primarily interested in personal injury questions rather than in the property injury questions that are at the heart of the school asbestos litigation. While Judge Kelly spoke with Selikoff, he did not converse with any other conference speakers. Regardless, it is clear that the Collegium Ramazzini (and hence the plaintiffs' settlement fund, at least indirectly) paid for Judge Kelly's registration fee and two nights' lodging.

In addition, the Collegium Ramazzini issued promotional literature and numerous press releases that trumpeted the appearance of the judges. It also informed the media and the public that the conference was supported by a "grant" approved by a federal court. In late July 1990, counsel for one of the defendants, W.R. Grace, began inquiring about the court "grant." About that time, the plaintiffs filed their list of eighteen expected expert trial witnesses, thirteen of whom had spoken at the Third Wave Conference. If Judge Kelly noticed the overlap, he made no mention of it to the parties. On September 14, 1990, counsel for W.R. Grace wrote to Judge Kelly on behalf of numerous defendants to request an in camera meeting to discuss his role in approving the funding for the conference. On September 19 and

20, 1990, Judge Kelly responded in writing, with copies to all counsel of record, candidly detailing the events as he recalled them, but declining a meeting.

Eventually, through hard-fought discovery and over the course of more than six months, the full details about the conference, including the formerly sealed documents, were revealed. . . .

On April 18, 1991, twelve defendants moved for Judge Kelly's disqualification on the grounds that his partiality could reasonably be questioned and that he had personal knowledge of disputed evidentiary facts. . . . Judge Kelly saw his choices as three: (1) disqualify himself; (2) deny the motion and proceed as if nothing had happened; or (3) deny the motion, but, to assuage fears of taint, refuse to allow conference participants to appear as witnesses at trial. On June 17, 1991, in Pretrial Order 318, he selected the third option. . . .

C. *Disqualification — Appearance of Partiality*

The petitioners argue, as they did before the district court, that the above circumstances required Judge Kelly to disqualify himself under both 28 U.S.C. § 455(a), because "his partiality might reasonably be questioned," and 28 U.S.C. § 455(b)(1), because he has "personal knowledge of disputed evidentiary facts concerning the proceeding." Because we conclude that subsection 455(a) mandated disqualification, we do not decide the more difficult question whether subsection 455(b)(1) also required disqualification.

We emphasize at the outset the nature of our inquiry. . . . Our role is not to ascribe blame to anyone. Rather, we must determine whether a reasonable person, knowing all the acknowledged circumstances, might question the district judge's continued impartiality.

We are convinced that a reasonable person might question Judge Kelly's ability to remain impartial. To put it succinctly, he attended a predominantly pro-plaintiff conference on a key merits issue; the conference was indirectly sponsored by the plaintiffs, largely with funding that he himself had approved; and his expenses were largely defrayed by the conference sponsors with those same court-approved funds. Moreover, he was, in his own words, exposed to a Hollywood-style "pre-screening" of the plaintiffs' case: thirteen of the eighteen expert witnesses the plaintiffs were intending to call gave presentations very similar to what they expected to say at trial. We need not decide whether any of these facts alone would have required disqualification, for, as we shall explain, we believe that together they create an appearance of partiality that mandates disqualification.

Congress enacted subsection 455(a) precisely because "people who have not served on the bench are often all too willing to indulge suspicions and doubts concerning the integrity of judges." Liljeberg v. Health Services Acquisition Corp., 486 U.S. 847, 864-65 (1988). In high profile cases such as this one, the outcome of which will in some way affect millions of people, such suspicions are especially likely and untoward. A reasonable person might suspect that Judge Kelly's plaintiff-subsidized attendance at the "preview" of the plaintiffs' case would have predisposed him toward the plaintiffs' position. Alternatively, others may reasonably believe that because he now knows that the plaintiffs indirectly paid his way, he might be angry at them for compromising him and might overreact to their prejudice.

Any such (perceived) bias could manifest itself in a number of ways. Although Judge Kelly correctly noted that a jury trial has been demanded, section 455 properly makes no distinction between jury and nonjury trials. The district judge in a jury trial must still make numerous pretrial rulings, including crucial summary judgment rulings, and will doubtlessly be called on to make numerous rulings on the qualification of witnesses and on evidentiary matters, not to mention post-trial motions. . . .

We underscore that we are not intimating that Judge Kelly actually harbors any illegitimate pro-plaintiff bias. The problem, however, is that regardless of his actual impartiality, a reasonable person might perceive bias to exist, and this cannot be permitted. See In re Murchison, 349 U.S. 133, 136 (1955) . . . .

We find it significant that . . . Judge Kelly recognized that some people could reasonably suspect a taint. . . . Moreover, invoking what he later described . . . as his "'inherent power' to remedy Plaintiffs' counsels' disregard of the integrity of the judicial process," he excluded the expert testimony of conference participants. . . . Section 455, however, clearly requires that judges *shall* disqualify themselves where such a taint appears, rather than attempt creative, alternative remedies such as disqualification of witnesses. In any event, we believe that a reasonable person might still suspect a prospective taint notwithstanding the district court's nonstatutory remedy.

The Code of Conduct for United States Judges points to the same result. The language of section 455 was based on the nearly identical language of Canon 3C of the Code, which is reprinted in II Guide to Judiciary Policies and Procedures at I-7 to I-9. . . . This fact suggests that appearances of partiality are likely if conduct is inconsistent with the related canons of judicial ethics regarding judges' out-of-court associations with actual and potential litigants.

Opinion No. 67 of the Judicial Conference's Advisory Committee on Codes of Conduct interprets Canon 5C(4) (regarding the receipt of gifts) and advises judges that they should not attend educational seminars related to a litigation issue if the sponsor or source of funding is involved, or likely to be involved, in the litigation. . . .

Likewise, Advisory Opinion No. 17, interpreting Canons 2B (regarding external influence on judges) and 6B (regarding expense reimbursement) of the Canons of Judicial Ethics of the American Bar Association, observes that an appearance of impropriety may arise if lawyer organizations identified with a particular viewpoint regularly advanced in litigation pay for a judge's hotel and travel expenses. . . .

That Judge Kelly was unaware in 1990 of the circumstances creating the appearance of impropriety cannot change our conclusion. The Supreme

Court has squarely held that a judge need not have had actual knowledge of facts creating an appearance of partiality to violate subsection 455(a). *Liljeberg*, 486 U.S. at 859-61. . . . Thus, we cannot assume that a reasonable person would believe that Judge Kelly simply forgot the connection between Selikoff, the conference, and the source of funding for the conference. Even making that assumption, however, we cannot further assume that a reasonable person would believe that this episode will have no prospective effect on the litigation.

We suspect that Judge Kelly chose not to disqualify himself because he felt duty-bound to shepherd this extraordinarily complicated and protracted litigation to its conclusion and out of concern about creating additional delay. These are both laudable sentiments, and we must acknowledge that the newly assigned district judge will face a gargantuan task in becoming familiar with the case. We also recognize that the delay may disadvantage the plaintiffs, although that result is, to some degree, of their own doing. Nevertheless, a district judge has no "duty to sit," and under 28 U.S.C. § 455 he or she may not sit where his or her partiality may reasonably be questioned and the parties refuse to waive that objection. . . . If Judge Kelly were to continue presiding, the outcome of this massive, important, and widely followed case would be shrouded with suspicion. Accordingly, we are compelled to order Judge Kelly to disqualify himself.

D. *Remedy — Vacatur of Past Rulings?*

It does not follow, however, that this litigation must return to square one, or even to where it stood on June 6, 1990, the day before Judge Kelly attended the Third Wave Conference. As Justice Stevens wrote for the Supreme Court in *Liljeberg*, "[t]here need not be a draconian remedy for every violation of § 455(a)." 486 U.S. at 862. The Court observed that "[a]lthough § 455 defines the circumstances that mandate disqualification of federal judges, it neither prescribes nor prohibits any particular remedy for a violation of that duty. Congress has wisely delegated to the judiciary the task of fashioning the remedies that will best serve the purpose of the legislation." Id. at 862.

In *Liljeberg* itself, the Court . . . suggested that in deciding whether to vacate a judgment, courts should "consider [(1)] the risk of injustice to the parties in the particular case, [(2)] the risk that the denial of relief will produce injustice in other cases, and [(3)] the risk of undermining the public's confidence in the judicial process." Id. at 864. . . .

Although we are not considering a Rule 60(b) motion [as in *Liljeberg*], we believe that a similar balance should inform the decision as to which prior rulings to vacate. We will therefore consider both prejudice to the litigants — the likelihood of actual bias and the harm from upsetting and delaying this massive litigation — and systemic interests — including the likely extent of lost public confidence in the district court's rulings, and the strong public interest in avoiding unnecessary, costly duplication of work and in propelling this case to a speedy and just conclusion. . . .

Cases from other circuits . . . suggest that, especially in complex litigation, vacatur of rulings ought to be as limited as possible while remaining consistent with the purposes of section 455. . . . We agree.

In this case, we have a wide range of options. We could vacate all orders after the date on which the appearance of partiality arose, which presumably is June 7, 1990 — the date on which the Third Wave Conference began. Alternatively, we could vacate all orders after the date on which Judge Kelly was informed of the facts creating the appearance of partiality (and hence should have disqualified himself), which would be approximately September 14, 1990 — the date on which several defendants notified him of most of the details. We could also vacate all orders after the date on which certain defendants moved for disqualification, April 18, 1991. Or we could choose to vacate orders qualitatively, rather than chronologically — according to the nexus between the order and the subject of the Third Wave Conference. Finally, we could, as several petitioners suggest, combine the qualitative and chronological approaches. For the following reasons, however, we choose not to vacate any of the district court's orders at this time.

Preliminarily, we note that we do not believe that leaving Judge Kelly's orders in place will cause any serious injustice to the parties in this case. To the contrary, vacatur of more than a handful of orders would upset tremendously this huge yet fragile litigation, to the severe disadvantage of the plaintiffs and numerous defendants. For example, approximately seventy pretrial orders have been entered since the original disqualification motion was filed. . . .

Most of the controversial pretrial orders since the Third Wave Conference have dealt with two types of subjects: summary judgment motions and trial structure. Even if any of the summary judgment rulings were affected by unintentional bias, those rulings will be subject to plenary review upon final judgment. To vacate all those rulings now and to order full reconsideration by the incoming district judge would entail enormous cost to the parties and to the judicial system with little corresponding gain. Accordingly, we will not do so, especially since we believe that none of Judge Kelly's orders were infected with actual bias.

The largely discretionary orders affecting trial structure are more problematic. Deferential review after final judgment might not cure any prejudice in this regard in the unlikely event that it occurred. We do not think, however, that wholesale vacatur of these rulings is in order. Instead, we will authorize, but not require, the incoming judge to reconsider earlier rulings on these matters at his or her discretion. We believe that this is appropriate in any case since the new judge may bring a different perspective to the case and may have different ideas about how it should be tried. To prevent undue delay, however, the parties should file any motions for reconsideration within thirty days of the assignment of the new district judge.

Finally, we return, as we must, to the keystone of section 455: public confidence in the judicial system, both in the particular case and in general. Our prospective disqualification of Judge Kelly should guarantee public confidence in the critical trial and post-trial rulings. The availability of later plenary review of the disposition of summary judgment motions and our authorization of reconsideration of discretionary trial structure motions should be adequate to assure public confidence in past rulings without needless disruption of this very important litigation. Vacatur of hundreds of past rulings might arguably be the most cautious course, but we believe that that is unnecessary and would be undesirable in these circumstances.

Jack B. Weinstein, INDIVIDUAL JUSTICE IN MASS TORT LITIGATION

50, 111-12 (1995)

The judge in mass tort as well as public institution cases has an obligation to assist both attorneys and clients. . . . But the court also needs to consider how what is done affects the larger community. Mass cases require us to rethink the obligation of the judge in our society. . . .

Judges who remain passive and rely solely on the parties to drive the litigation and protect the rights of all those affected will be more likely to fail, I believe, in their duty to society as a whole as well as to the individual parties. Judges should reach out and embrace what competent and neutral help they can secure in the difficult task before them. . . .

This broadening of responsibility has its costs. In place of the relatively hard-edged and tested ethical rules of traditional one-on-one cases, the court has broader and less well-defined responsibilities. One way of clarifying those responsibilities and ethical rules is by engaging in a more open discussion of what is happening in the courts and in the real world of mass torts. . . .

I have suggested that forms of communitarian and communicatarian ethics might help guide lawyer and judge through these largely uncharted waters. Since the law is both eclectic and pragmatic, all the traditional ethical rules and jurisprudential approaches, from Aristotelian to Posnerian, need to be mined for their wisdom and insights.

Many will have different ideas about what sort of ethics should control the conduct of those who participate in mass forms of justice. Most, if not all, I trust, will agree that the old models at least need reconsideration in the area of mass torts.

Notes and Questions

1. "To decide when a judge may not sit is to define what a judge is. To define what a judge is is to decide what a system of adjudication is all about." John Leubsdorf, *Theories of Judging and Judicial Disqualification*, 62 N.Y.U. L. Rev. 237, 237 (1987). What theory of adjudication underlies the *School Asbestos* opinion? What theory underlies Judge Weinstein's proposals? (Hint: Weinstein thought that Judge Kelly's disqualification "represent[ed] questionable policy.

If error there was, it was not significant in view of the huge cost of requiring the parties and courts to educate a new judge to replace [an] outstanding jurist[] who had devoted years to understanding [a] complex litigation[]." Weinstein, *supra*, at 108.)

2. Before we pick up on the argument that judicial ethics (and thus the standards for judicial disqualification) should be transformed in light of the needs of complex cases, it would be wise to understand the basic law of recusal. The purposes of recusal are to remove a judicial officer who is unduly biased or prejudiced against a particular party or proceeding, see Liteky v. United States, 510 U.S. 540 (1994), and to ensure public confidence in the integrity of the administration of justice, see Liljeberg v. Health Services Acquisition Corp., 486 U.S. 847 (1988). Three sets of sources provide specific rules and standards regarding disqualification. The first is the due process clause of the Constitution (and, for state judges, similar provisions of the state constitution). Second, statutes may establish standards for recusal; in the federal system, the statutes are 28 U.S.C. §§ 144 and 455. Third, the applicable judicial code of conduct, which describes the ethical obligations of judges, might call for recusal for the violation of certain ethical norms. In federal court, the determinative sources are usually §§ 144 and 455, which establish a line for impermissible judicial conduct lies well within the due process boundary and which closely track judicial codes of conduct. Aiken County v. BSP Division of Envirotech Corp., 866 F.2d 661 (4th Cir. 1988); In re International Business Machines Corp., 618 F.2d 923 (2d Cir. 1980); In re Wirebound Boxes Antitrust Litigation, 724 F. Supp. 648 (D. Minn. 1989); see In re Ronald Parr, 13 B.R. 1010, 1019 (E.D.N.Y. 1981) (due process clause "may be invoked in situations where the statutes do not technically apply").

3. As with lawyer disqualification, the disqualification of judges raises a series of procedural, substantive, and remedial issues. This note describes the procedural issues concerning recusal.

(a) *Scope.* Obviously the disqualification rules apply to judges. By their terms § 455 and the Code of Judicial Ethics also apply to magistrates; § 144 and the due process clause do not expressly apply, although there is little doubt that magistrates are covered by these provisions. For those contemplating a position as law clerk, the rules also apply to you; you must disqualify yourself from a case when one of the applicable sources requires it, and depending on the circumstances, your judge might need to recuse herself because of your recusal. See In re Allied-Signal, Inc., 891 F.2d 967 (1st Cir. 1989), cert. denied, 495 U.S. 957 (1989); Parker v. Connors Steel Co., 855 F.2d 1510 (11th Cir. 1988), cert. denied, 490 U.S. 1066 (1989).

Should a special master be governed by the same code of conduct? Neither § 144, § 455, nor the due process clause expressly mentions masters, but the Code of Judicial Ethics does (with some exceptions not pertinent here). At least one court has found that § 455 applies to masters. United States v. Conservation Chemical Co., 106 F.R.D. 210 (W.D. Mo.), *rev'd* on other grounds, 770 F.2d 103 (8th Cir. 1985). On the other hand, masters often engage in *ex parte* communication — in some cases, at a level that would be disqualifying for a judge or magistrate. See Margaret G. Farrell, *Special Masters*, in Reference Manual on Scientific Evidence 575, 606-09 (1994); Note 7, *infra*. Should we allow masters the freedom to range beyond present ethical norms for judges, while at the same time limiting judges to a more traditional set of ethical norms? Might this arrangement create the type of "exceptional circumstance" that justifies the use of masters in complex cases?

(b) *Mechanics*. The method for bringing and resolving a recusal motion under 28 U.S.C. § 144 are specified in the statute. A party who believes that the judge "has a personal bias or prejudice either against him or in favor of any adverse party" is required to file an affidavit stating the facts and reasons for the belief. Unless excused for good cause, the affidavit must be filed "not less than ten days before the beginning of the term at which the proceeding is to be heard" (in other words, with due diligence), and must be accompanied by a certificate of counsel stating that the affidavit is made in good faith. The affidavit is submitted to the judge handling the case; if she determines that the affidavit is "timely and sufficient," she must recuse herself. Only one such motion may be brought in any case. See Charles A. Wright et al., Federal Practice and Procedure § 3551 (1984).

The mechanics of recusal motions based on § 455 or other sources are less certain. It is clear that § 455 requires self-policing, so that a judge whose conduct fits within its terms must disqualify herself even when no motion is made. If a party makes the motion, no affidavits need accompany it. Typically the judge who is the subject of the motion will hear it herself, although in extraordinary circumstances she may ask another judge to decide the matter. See id., § 3550; Chitimacha Tribe of Louisiana v. Harry L. Laws Co., 690 F.2d 1157 (5th Cir. 1982), cert. denied, 464 U.S. 814 (1983). The judge need not hold a hearing on the matter, although a court of appeals will accept as true any well-pleaded allegations in the event that a hearing is not held. United States v. Heldt, 668 F.2d 1238 (D.C. Cir.), cert. denied, 456 U.S. 926 (1981). There is no express limit on the number of motions that may be filed, although the law of the case doctrine will bar repeated motions on the same point. National Auto Brokers Corp. v. General Motors Corp., 1978 WL 1386 (S.D.N.Y.) (barring second motion brought in one case and further barring first motion brought in severed but related case).

(c) *Burden of Proof*. The burden of proof rests with the party seeking recusal. Pope v. Federal Express Corp., 974 F.2d 982 (8th Cir. 1992). Some cases say that there is a presumption of judicial even-handedness, see Fero v. Kerby, 39 F.3d 1462 (10th Cir. 1994), cert. denied, 515 U.S. 1122 (1995); that the evidence must be compelling to warrant recusal, see id.; that the requirements of § 144 will be strictly construed, see United States v. Sykes, 7 F.3d 1331 (7th Cir. 1993); and that the judge's entire conduct, and not just an isolated incident, will be considered, see *Wirebound*, 724 F. Supp. 648, and In re Federal Skywalk Cases, 680 F.2d 1175 (8th Cir.), cert. denied, 459 U.S. 988 (1982). On the other hand, other courts state that a "reasonable factual basis" for doubting the fairness of the court is all that must be shown, see *Parr*, 13 B.R. at 1019, and that close questions must be resolved in favor of recusal, see United States v. Dandy, 998 F.2d 1344 (6th Cir. 1993), cert. denied, 510 U.S. 1163 (1994).

Statistical evidence that the judge has ruled against a party on a large percentage of motions can be used to demonstrate undue prejudice, but it is given neither conclusive nor strong weight. See *IBM*, 618 F.2d 923; City of Cleveland v. Cleveland Electric Illuminating Co., 503 F. Supp. 368 (N.D. Oh. 1980).

(d) *Appealability*. There presently exists a great deal of disagreement about when, and even if, a judge's decision to recuse herself becomes appealable. See

Wright et al., *supra*, § 3553. Similar disagreement exists about the proper method of seeking appellate review of a judge's decision not to recuse herself. Most circuits hold that these decisions can be reviewed by interlocutory appeal, by appeal after entry of judgment, or by mandamus; the Seventh Circuit, however, says that only mandamus review is available, while the Sixth says that mandamus is never appropriate. See id. Whatever the method of appellate review, decisions on recusal motions are committed to the sound discretion of the trial judge, and they can be overturned only for abuse of discretion. *Pope*, 974 F.2d 982.

In limited circumstances, federal courts can review state court recusal decisions. The Supreme Court can review on certiorari claims that a state judge's failure to recuse amounted to a due process violation, see Aetna Insurance Co. v. Lavoie, 475 U.S. 813 (1986), and lower federal courts can review the same constitutional claim through habeas corpus petitions. *Fero*, 39 F.3d 1462. Claims that state judges violated state statutes or judicial codes of ethics, however, lie beyond the federal courts' purview. See id.

4. When a case must be remanded after appeal for further proceedings, a court of appeals retains the authority to order that the case be assigned to a different judge. 28 U.S.C. § 2106; United States v. Microsoft Corp., 56 F.3d 1448 (D.C. Cir. 1995); Haines v. Liggett Group Inc., 975 F.2d 81 (3d Cir. 1992). Since such an order has the effect of disqualification, appellate courts apply the substantive standards for disqualification to their decision to re-assign.

5. The substantive law of recusal is similar to that of lawyer disqualification: judicial disqualification occurs either when a judge commits an actual impropriety or when an appearance of impropriety requires recusal.

(a) *Actual Impropriety*. Section 455(b) lists five specific situations in which a judge must recuse herself. Since these situations encompass all of the actual improprieties to which other statutes, judicial codes of ethics, and the due process clause might reach, we can use § 455(b) as the framework for discussion:

(1) *"Where [a judge] has a personal bias or prejudice concerning a party, or personal knowledge of disputed evidentiary facts concerning the proceeding."* This language, quoted from § 455(b)(1) and nearly identical to the language of § 144, goes to the heart of the meaning of impartial adjudication. Every judge comes to a case with a lifetime of experiences that color her perspective, and as she handles the present litigation she necessarily begins to form impressions of the parties, the lawyers, and the merits of the case. Indeed, the very nature of decision making requires that certain biases be created; and in the world of case management, judges create those biases at an early stage in the litigation. Hence there is a need to distinguish between permissible biases and those that threaten impartiality.

Section 455 tries to solve this problem by requiring a "personal" bias. The term is nowhere defined, but, prior to *Liteky*, it had come to be closely associated with something called the "extrajudicial source" doctrine. This "doctrine" holds that a judge might need to be disqualified when she possesses biases or prejudices that derive from an "extrajudicial source" — *i.e.*, some source other than the sources to which a judge is exposed in her judicial duties. When the biases and prejudices are formed as a result of her duties in this and other cases, however, there is no ground for recusal.

The problem with the "extrajudicial source" test, as *Liteky* observed, is that it is both too broad and too narrow:

The fact that an opinion held by a judge derives from a source outside judicial proceedings is not a *necessary* condition for "bias or prejudice" recusal, since predispositions developed during the course of a trial will sometimes (albeit rarely) suffice. Nor is it a *sufficient* condition for "bias or prejudice" recusal, since *some* opinions acquired outside the context of judicial proceedings (for example, the judge's view of the law acquired in scholarly reading) will *not* suffice. Since neither the presence of an extrajudicial source necessarily establishes bias, nor the absence of an extrajudicial source necessarily precludes bias, it would be better to speak of the existence of a significant (and often determinative) "extrajudicial source" *factor*, than of an "extrajudicial source" *doctrine*, in recusal jurisprudence. . . .

It is enough for present purposes to say the following: First, judicial rulings alone almost never constitute valid basis for a bias or partiality motion. . . . Almost invariably, they are proper grounds for appeal, not for recusal. Second, opinions formed by the judge on the basis of facts introduced or events occurring in the course of the current proceedings, or of prior proceedings, do not constitute a basis for a bias or partiality motion unless they display a deep-seated favoritism or antagonism that would make fair judgment impossible. Thus, judicial remarks during the course of a trial that are critical or disapproving of, or even hostile to, counsel, the parties, or their cases, ordinarily do not support a bias or partiality challenge. They *may* do so if they reveal an opinion that derives from an extrajudicial source; and they *will* do so if they reveal such a high degree of favoritism or antagonism as to make fair judgment impossible. . . . A judge's ordinary efforts at courtroom administration — even a stern and short-tempered judge's ordinary efforts at courtroom administration — remain immune. [510 U.S. at 554-56.]

On the need to recuse a judge with knowledge of disputed facts, see United States v. State of Alabama, 828 F.2d 1532 (1987), cert. denied, 487 U.S. 1210 (1988) (recusal ordered when judge, as state legislator, had actively participated in and made factual findings regarding events involved in civil rights suit); In re Beard, 811 F.2d 818 (4th Cir 1987) (recusal not required when judge said president of defendant corporation was "a neighbor" and "a fine man").

(2) *Prior Representations.* Judges must also recuse themselves when, in prior private practice, they or a lawyer associated with them represented a party in the present controversy, or were material witnesses in the matter. See § 455(b)(2). Recusal is also required when the judge had, while in prior government employment, acted as counsel, adviser, or material witness in a proceeding, or expressed an opinion regarding its merits. § 455(b)(3).

(3) *Financial or Other Interest.* A third classic ground for recusal is a judge's personal financial interest in the case. That interest could be direct, in that the judge might profit from the outcome of the case, or indirect, in that the judge might profit because the decision in the case will affect another case or matter in which the judge has an interest. See § 455(b)(4); *Lavoie*, 475 U.S. 813 (due process clause). Section 455(b)(4) requires that the judge "know" of interest involved, and also expands the types of interests that require recusal to include fiduciary interests, cf. *Liljeberg*, 486 U.S. 847, the interests of the judge's spouse or minor children residing in her house, and non-financial interests "that could be substantially affected by the outcome of the proceeding."

This commonsensical rule can create problems in complex litigation. Obviously a judge involved in a massive antitrust case might benefit, as all consumers will, from the breakup of a monopoly; or a company in which a judge owns a few shares might benefit. To deal with the former problem, there has developed a rule that a judge who will merely benefit as a member of the public need not disqualify herself. See In re New Mexico Natural Gas Antitrust Litigation, 620 F.2d 794 (10th Cir. 1980). The latter problem has proven more intractable. In In re Cement Antitrust Litigation (MDL No. 296), 688 F.2d 1297 (9th Cir. 1982), *aff'd* in absence of quorum, 459 U.S. 1191 (1983), the court of appeals upheld the decision of a judge whose wife owned stock in seven of the 210,000 class members to recuse himself, even though the case was had entered its fourth year and the judge had been actively involved in its management. But see In re Industrial Gas Antitrust Litigation, 1985 WL 2869 (N.D. Ill.) (judge refused to recuse herself in 172,000 member class action where husband owned stock in two class members, husband divested himself of stock after learning of situation, and little activity had occurred in case).

A novel argument for recusal of Judge Weinstein was rejected in the *Agent Orange* litigation. Some purported plaintiffs argued that Weinstein's fiduciary obligations to the Agent Orange settlement fund created a conflict of interest. The Second Circuit held that Weinstein's "legally-imposed duties qua judge with regard to the settlement funds are not a 'fiduciary' obligation within the meaning of section 455(b)(4), and do not mandate disqualification from cases which may involve the fund." In re "Agent Orange" Product Liability Litigation, 996 F.2d 1425 (2d Cir. 1993), cert. denied, 510 U.S. 1140 (1994).

Would a judge who was an investment partner with an attorney involved in the litigation be required to recuse herself? See In re Allied-Signal Inc., 891 F.2d 974 (1st Cir. 1989) (no); *Beard*, 811 F.2d at 830-31 (no).

(4) *Close Relationship*. A judge also must disqualify herself when a spouse or a "person within the third degree of relationship to either of them, or a spouse of such a person," is a party or an officer, director, or trustee of a party; is a lawyer in the case; is known to have an interest that could be substantially affected by the outcome; or is known to be a material witness. § 455(b)(5). Wouldn't strict enforcement of this rule cripple large-scale class actions? See *State of Alabama*, 828 F.2d 1532 (judge not required to recuse himself even though his children were members of civil rights class action, when their interest in discrimination-free schools was no greater than that of other children).

(b) *Appearance of Impropriety*. The due process clause, judicial canons of ethics, and recusal statutes also require recusal when there exists an appearance of partiality. See *Lavoie*, 475 U.S. 813; ABA Code of Judicial Conduct, Canon 3(c); 28 U.S.C. § 455(a). Since neither lawyers nor other judges are wont to accuse a judge of actual improprieties, you might expect — correctly — that most cases involve this somewhat less opprobrious standard: Even if the judge entertains no actual bias, a judge must disqualify herself if a reasonable person might doubt that she could decide the case impartially.

Rather than creating an entirely new set of expectations for judges, this standard has acted largely as a penumbra around the more specific situations, listed above, that require recusal. For instance, conduct that did not create an actual bias under § 455(b)(1), like Judge Kelly's conduct in attending the seminar, might still appear to do so, and thus require recusal under § 455(a). Consistent with this penumbral notion, the Supreme Court has read into

§ 455(a) the "extrajudicial source" factor, so that apparent biases created during the performance of judicial duties can rarely serve as grounds for recusal. *Liteky*, 510 U.S. 540.

(c) *Factors Influencing the Disqualification Decision.* Other factors sometimes enter into the disqualification equation. One is the concern that a liberal attitude toward recusal encourages satellite litigation. See *Wirebound*, 724 F. Supp. at 653. A related concern is that parties are using recusal motions for strategic reasons (in other words, they are shopping for a better judge, often after a critical decision has gone against them). See In re Sam M. Antar, 71 F.3d 97, 101 (3d Cir. 1995); In re Cargill, Inc., 66 F.3d 1256, 1262-63 (1st Cir. 1995), cert. denied, 517 U.S. 1156 (1996). Third, courts sometimes consider waste of resources, burden upon the transferee judge, and prejudice to the parties — particularly in cases that have been ongoing for some time. *City of Cleveland*, 503 F. Supp. at 382; *Parr*, 13 B.R. at 1019. A fourth factor, which we take up in Note 7, *infra*, is the complexity of the case and the need for an innovative judge.

These factors seem most frequently to color the court's view of a recusal motion in cases of an appearance of partiality, rather than in cases of actual impropriety. See *Cement Antitrust Litigation*, 688 F.2d 1297 (upholding recusal for financial conflict in spite of concerns for future of litigation and for class action practice generally).

(d) *Defenses.* Aside from these factors, there are two related "defenses" that permit denial of a recusal motion. The first is timeliness. As mentioned, Section 144 contains an express timeliness requirement. Most courts have read into § 455 a comparable requirement of due diligence, although an untimely motion involving a § 455(b) ground might still be entertained. See United States v. York, 888 F.2d 1050 (5th Cir. 1989); Wright et al., *supra*, § 3550 n.9. The second defense is waiver. Under § 455(e), parties may waive their right to recusal when only an appearance of partiality is involved and when the judge makes full disclosure of the facts on the record, but they may not waive their right when an actual impropriety under § 455(b) is involved. See *Cargill*, 66 F.3d 1256 (waiver by local counsel).

6. When grounds for disqualification exist, the next issue is the remedy. Two separate remedial issues are posed: first, the appropriate prospective remedy to prevent future conflicts, and second, the appropriate retrospective remedy to undo any wrongful effects of past rulings. With respect to prospective relief, the remedy required under §§ 144 and 455 is recusal; the same is true of a due process claim or claim of violation of judicial ethics. With respect to retrospective relief, the appropriate remedy should be vacation of the judgment or tainted rulings. Nonetheless, since vacation forces a judgment or settled rulings to be reopened, it is not a desirable option. The three factors announced in *Liljeberg* and applied in *School Asbestos* seek to balance the interests in impartial justice and the needs of finality and certainty. See *Allied-Signal*, 891 F.2d at 973 (1st Cir. 1989) (declaring mistrial in mass tort case would needlessly "threaten to undo matters of considerable importance previously decided"); Rohrbach v. AT&T Nassau Metals Corp., 902 F. Supp. 523 (M.D. Pa. 1995) (undoing summary judgment), and 915 F. Supp. 712 (M.D. Pa. 1996) (modifying vacatur ruling). *Liljeberg* itself involved an appearance of impropriety that was discovered more than a year after judgment; hence, the Court needed to reconcile the policies of § 455 and F.R.Civ.P. 60(b), which provides limited exceptions to the finality of judgments. When Rule 60(b) is not involved, or when an actual impropriety is found, is there ever reason to allow the judge's rulings to stand?

Might other remedies be appropriate? In *Industrial Gas*, 1985 WL 2869, the judge's husband divested himself of holdings in two plaintiffs at a loss of something less than $1000. The judge held that this remedy obviated the need to recuse herself. She never considered whether any past rulings should have been vacated.

7. We have seen that complex litigation changes the conduct that we expect of judges. This fact raises an important descriptive question regarding whether the changed nature of the judge has changed the grounds for recusal. The answer seems to be a qualified "yes." See *Federal Skywalk*, 680 F.2d at 1184 (noting, in context of declining to order recusal, "the complexity of the issues" and commending district judge for "his creative efforts" in pretrial); *Allied Signal*, 891 F.2d at 972 (refusing to order recusal, in part because "need for judicial management by the district court counsels caution prior to intervention by an appellate court" in "large, complex, and time consuming" cases).

Moreover, at a practical level, it seems that recusal motions premised on the overly managerial attitude of the judge are rarely successful. In *Agent Orange*, 996 F.2d at 1439, plaintiffs sought to recuse Judge Weinstein because he possessed "some traits of megalomania, of having a 'systematic interest in retaining excessive judicial powers over mass tort cases.'" Brushing the claims aside, the court said it had previously approved of these powers, and went on to praise Weinstein for his "'innovations' and 'innovative managerial skills' in such large-scale litigation." Weinstein also refused to recuse himself in DES cases when defendants claimed that he had improperly obtained information about DES litigation while sitting as a settlement judge in state cases, noting that such a requirement would severely hamper the effectiveness of the judge as case manager. See Bilello v. Abbott Laboratories, 825 F. Supp. 475, 479-80 (E.D.N.Y. 1993). Other cases have refused to disqualify a judge even when the judge solicits a class representative by means of an *ex parte* contact with the plaintiff's lawyer in which the judge also promised to appoint the lawyer assistant class counsel, see *Federal Skywalk*, 680 F.2d 1175; or when the judge has *ex parte* contacts with litigants and lawyers, see *Beard*, 811 F.2d 818; *Aiken*, 866 F.2d 661; *Microsoft*, 56 F.3d at 1464; *Wirebound*, 724 F. Supp. 648; *Parr*, 13 B.R. 1010.

8. The classic story of a strong managerial judge is Judge Miles Lord, whose conduct in an antitrust case included aggressively questioning a witness at a deposition he attended and later opining on the truthfulness of the witness, attempting to block a settlement agreement with the Justice Department because it upset his "'game plan' for managing the case," soliciting new class plaintiffs to continue the litigation when a settlement of the private class action appeared imminent, and calling the Patent Office "the sickest institution . . . ever invented." The court of appeals thought that Lord's characterization of the Patent Office was "injudicious," but saw nothing in the case that manifested a personal bias or prejudice toward defendants. Pfizer Inc. v. Lord, 456 F.2d 532 (8th Cir.), cert. denied, 406 U.S. 976 (1972). *Pfizer* was decided prior to passage of § 455.

The famous counter-example to *Pfizer* is the story of Judge H. Lee Sarokin, who had shepherded the first of a series of tobacco products liability cases through trial and was just turning his attention to the remainder. In ruling on a discovery motion, Sarokin opened his opinion with a three-sentence lamentation about the culture of concealment in American industry, followed by the sentence: "As the following facts disclose, despite some rising pretenders, the tobacco industry may be the king of concealment." While refusing to order

Sarokin's recusal, and praising him for his "magnificent abilities," the court of appeals thought that the remarks created an appearance of partiality and exercised its supervisory powers to order that the case be handled by a different judge on remand. *Haines*, 975 F.2d 81. Nowhere did the court of appeals mention the effect that this removal might have on the management of the remaining cases. Subsequently Sarokin recused himself in the other tobacco cases as well. See Cipollone v. Liggett Group, Inc., 799 F. Supp. 466 (D.N.J. 1992).

Sarokin developed his opinion of the tobacco industry from his contacts in court. *Liteky*, which was decided two years later, said that recusal for in-court bias should be rare. Did *Haines* meet *Liteky*'s standard? Can you account, except on the historical ground that *Haines* was post-§ 455 and pre-*Liteky*, for the difference in treatment of Judges Lord and Sarokin? For an interesting panel discussion regarding the Sarokin affair, see *Disqualification of Judges (The Sarokin Matter): Is It a Threat to Judicial Independence?*, 58 Brook. L. Rev. 1063 (1993).

9. Prescriptively, the question is whether we should adjust our standards for disqualification in complex litigation. As Professor Leubsdorf says, one way to answer this question is to ask what adjudication is fundamentally about; we cannot allow judges to act in a way inconsistent with their adjudicatory role. There are also certain features that we find desirable in our adjudicatory system, and, all things being equal, we want judges to conduct themselves in accordance with those features as well. But we can forsake the desirable features when there is adequate cause. For example, if we view rational judgment as an essential component of adjudication, and an adversarial approach to adjudication as a desirable feature, we would never allow a judge who is actually biased to decide a case; but when the needs of the case are strong enough, we might allow the judge to engage in conduct inconsistent with the judge's adversarial role. On the other hand, if we viewed adversarial process as an essential aspect of adjudication, conduct inconsistent with the judge's adversarial role would be barred.

Is this analysis sound? If so, is an adversarial system essential or merely desirable?

To recognize a theoretical avenue through which a judge might depart from the ethical conduct expected of an adversarial judge is, however, only a part of the answer. As Judge Weinstein says, it is still incumbent on us to draft a code of conduct for judicial officers involved in a non-adversarial adjudicatory process. Presumably those rules would flow from the reasons that we are departing from an adversarial approach and would authorize conduct consistent with the particular non-adversarial process we have designed. Until such a code is developed, do you think it wise to allow judges to free-lance away from their adversarial obligations?

CHAPTER NINE

NARROWING ISSUES AND DISCOVERING FACTS

> Obviously the question of issue definition versus discovery activity is a "chicken and egg" problem.
>
> James R. Withrow and Richard P. Larm

Having established the roles of the pretrial players, it is time to begin the process of making the case ready for trial. As the above quote suggests, any successful pretrial process accomplishes, to some degree at least, two things: first, it defines the claims and issues that will be tried, and second, it develops the factual information that proves or disproves these claims and issues. As the quote also suggests, a tension exists between these two functions — at least if each is to be performed modestly well. It is impossible to know whether the right claims and issues have been selected for trial until the relevant facts are discovered, but it is impossible to know what the relevant facts are until the claims and issues have been defined. Hence the "chicken and egg" problem of pretrial procedure.

Different systems of procedure feel this problem more or less acutely. In a continental system, aspects of pretrial and trial are intermingled, so that the tasks of issue definition, factual discovery, and issue resolution proceed together somewhat seamlessly. See Chapter 1.C, *supra*. Our procedural system has faced a harder struggle. For all the advantages that the denouement of the Anglo-American trial possesses, the pretrial narrowing of issues and discovery of facts takes on a heightened, indeed critical, importance. As we have seen, common law procedure handled the tension between issue definition and factual discovery rather bluntly; it focused almost exclusively on the narrowing of a claim to a single triable issue, and it did so by means of pleadings. See Chapter 1.B, *supra*. At least until equity was eventually enlisted in the waning days of common law procedure, the parties had no ability to discover relevant information, and were left to whatever private resources for investigation they possessed.

The persons who devised our modern procedural system earlier in this century shifted strongly away from this common law model, swinging toward, and in some instances beyond, the continental-like procedures of our system of equity. Pleadings were short, designed merely to give notice rather than to delineate and narrow issues. A wide range of discovery devices — including interrogatories, requests for production, and depositions — were authorized, all with the belief that, once the full range of facts was known, the parties would be able to determine the relevant issues in dispute and proceed to trial. The emphasis was on factual discovery; issue definition and narrowing were secondary concerns. Moreover, although some devices for issue resolution (such as motions to dismiss and motions for summary judgment) were built into the pretrial process, the pretrial tasks of issue definition and factual discovery were fairly well divorced from the trial task of issue resolution; like common law, there remained, at least typically, an all-encompassing trial event at the end of the day.

For routine cases this new system of procedure has worked well enough. More cases are decided on their merits and fewer on procedural traps and technicalities. With better factual information parties are able to make better judgments about the value of their cases and better equipped to settle amicably. There are occasional, and probably deserved, complaints about the costliness of discovery, the mean-spiritedness of the lawyers, and the potential for frivolous lawsuits. Nonetheless, given our modern procedural sensibilities, what we have seems superior to what preceded it.

In complex cases, however, this modern system of pretrial procedure does not work. The factual information is immense; the claims and issues are sprawling and amorphous; the temptation of the adversaries to win by attrition is irresistible. An obvious solution is to change the modern pretrial balance, and once again to put a greater emphasis on early issue definition and narrowing. In so doing, discovery can be focused on particular matters. If the initial matters are chosen wisely, cases might be resolved through settlement or dismissal without the difficulties of full-fledged discovery and trial, thus making the process of discovery less burdensome.

Yet there remains a nagging fear. These cases are amorphous, and often involve the rights of thousands of people. As we limit issues, and consequently discovery, are we foreclosing access to information that might have changed a defeat into a victory, or a nuisance-value settlement into an appropriate one? What justifies such different, possibly outcome-determinative treatment between plaintiffs in complex cases and plaintiffs in routine disputes? Can we trust judges to strike, on a case-by-case basis, the proper balance between issue definition and discovery? Perhaps we could avoid these concerns if we moved pretrial procedure in all cases in the direction of early issue definition and narrowing. But haven't we tried that experiment already, and hasn't it failed? Is there a third way?

These are the questions we address in this chapter, as we examine the ways in which a managerial judge can push a complex case through the pretrial process. We begin by exploring the devices that the judge can use to define and narrow claims and issues, and then turn to some novel devices that can be used to discover evidence relevant to whatever issues remain.

A. ISSUE NARROWING TECHNIQUES

Perhaps the best way to understand what is at stake with issue narrowing devices is to look at the library shelves that contain the Federal Reporter, 2d series. There are 999 volumes in the series, comprising a total of 1.25 million pages (give or take a few thousand). Now, if you assume that you spent 6 seconds a page, which is enough time to scan the page and get a very rough sense of its contents, it would take you nearly 2,100 hours (an entire year's worth of billable hours!) to read the entire series. It is not unusual for a complex case to contain as many as 10 million pages worth of documents — in other words, eight complete sets of Federal Reporter, 2d Series, or eight years worth of scanning. Comprehension time, of course, would be extra.

Suppose now that devices were available that made it unnecessary to read three-quarters of the documents — you'd be all for it, wouldn't you?

That, in a sense, is what is at stake with regard to devices that define and narrow issues at an early stage: the opportunity to forestall, and perhaps forever eliminate, vast amounts of discovery. Most of the devices that we will study permanently eliminate issues or claims, making discovery regarding those issues unnecessary. Other devices, however, merely postpone certain issues in the hope that, after discovery on the early issues or claims is completed, litigation on the remaining issues and claims will be either unnecessary or else greatly abbreviated.

As we have set this problem up, it is hard not to like issue-defining and issue-narrowing techniques. But consider the problem from another perspective. Suppose that somewhere in the pages of discovery that was obviated by an issue-narrowing technique is a smoking gun that proves that the defendant is liable on a theory that has either been eliminated from the case or not yet raised. Suddenly issue-narrowing techniques act like the bad old pleading rules of common law procedure, cutting off relevant matters and thwarting substantive justice. Add into the mix the fact that the judge is active in wielding the tools that define and narrow the issues. Can we trust the judge to conduct herself in an even-handed way, or will she too become a partisan player in the defining and narrowing of issues?

1. Pleading Requirements in Complex Cases

a. Pleading with Heightened Specificity

The first opportunity to define and narrow issues occurs at the stage of the initial pleadings. The basic pleading rule of the Federal Rules of Civil Procedure, Rule 8, is one of the linchpins of our present procedural system. Rule 8(a) provides for "notice pleading," under which a plaintiff is required to provide only a "short and plain statement" of jurisdiction, "a short and plain statement of the claim showing that the pleader is entitled to relief," and "a demand for judgment for the relief the pleader seeks." The defendant is to respond similarly, stating "in short and plain terms the party's defenses" and admitting or denying "the averments upon which the adverse party relies." F.R.Civ.P. 8(b). The pleadings are to be "simple, concise, and direct. No technical forms of pleading . . . are required." F.R.Civ.P. 8(e)(1). Only with regard to some matters — most notably fraud and mistake — must a party's allegations "be stated with particularity." F.R.Civ.P. 9(b). Moreover, Rule 18 permits a plaintiff to join as many claims as she has "against an opposing party," and Rule 13 allows parties to assert counterclaims and cross-claims as well.

These rules are premised on the assumptions that an entire factual transaction or related series of transactions should be joined together, that pleading technicalities should not stand in the way of resolutions on the merits, and that the discovery process can winnow the triable issues from the chaff. Whether these assumptions hold true in complex cases is far from clear. If they are not accurate, should we change the pleading rules in complex cases so that they serve, as they had at common law, issue-defining and issue-narrowing functions?

NAGLER v. ADMIRAL CORP.

248 F.2d 319 (2d Cir. 1957)

■ CLARK, Chief Judge. This is an antitrust and price-discrimination action for injunction and damages by thirteen retailers in the Greater New York area of radio, television, and electrical appliances. It is brought against twenty-six defendants, of whom twenty-four are "suppliers," i.e., manufacturers, wholesalers, and distributors, and two are retailers operating chain stores in this area. The case is founded upon the allegation that these two defendant-retailers, Davega Stores Corporation and Vim Television and Appliance Stores, Inc., received special price concessions from the supplier defendants. The complaint is in twenty-nine paragraphs and three counts, or "causes of action" as they are labeled. The first cause is for "Defendants' Discrimination Against Plaintiffs in Violation of the Robinson-Patman Act," 15 U.S.C. § 13; while the other causes, reincorporating the allegations of the first, are for violations of the Sherman Act, 15 U.S.C. §§ 1, 2. Ten of the defendants joined in a motion to dismiss for improper pleading under Fed.Rules Civ.Proc., rule 8(a) and (e), and for misjoinder of parties; alternatively they asked for relief under F.R. 10(b), 12(e) and (f), i.e., for separate statements as to each defendant, for a more definite statement, and for striking parts of the complaint. . . . The court, in a substantial opinion, granted dismissal on the grounds urged and dismissed the complaint as to all the defendants. This appeal followed.

The drastic remedy here granted for pleading errors is unusual, since outright dismissal for reasons not going to the merits is viewed with disfavor in the federal courts. . . . And this has been true generally in both English and American law and legal history, for cases are not finally disposed of on mere points of pleading alone. Courts naturally shrink from the injustice of denying legal rights to a litigant for the mistakes in technical form of his attorney. Moreover there are, or would be, serious questions of *res judicata* .... For are the plaintiffs merely relegated to initiating a new action or are they permanently barred? ... We are clear, therefore, that the case must go back for some less final disposition at least permitting the plaintiffs to amend. But because of their practical importance in routine litigation, we think some elaboration of both the pleading and the joinder issues is desirable.

It is true that antitrust litigation may be of wide scope and without a central point of attack, so that defense must be diffuse, prolonged, and costly. So many defense lawyers have strongly advocated more particularized pleading in this area of litigation; and recently the judges in the court below have treated it as accepted law that some special pleading — the extent is left unclear — is required in antitrust cases. But it is quite clear that the federal rules contain no special exceptions for antitrust cases. When the rules were adopted there was considerable pressure for separate provisions in patent, copyright, and other allegedly special types of litigation. Such arguments did not prevail; instead there was adopted a uniform system for all cases — one which nevertheless allows some discretion to the trial judge to require fuller disclosure in a particular case by more definite statement, F.R. 12(e), discovery and summary judgment, F.R. 26-35, 56, and pre-trial conference, F.R. 16. ...

In asserting a special rule of pleading for antitrust cases, [certain district judges have] in terms rejected the "modern 'notice' theory of pleading" as here insufficient and said that an antitrust complaint must "state a cause of action instead of merely stating a claim." But while these essentially nebulous concepts often creep into pleading discussions, they are no part of the rules themselves, but were in fact rejected for more precise formulations. It is well to go back to the rules themselves and their intended purpose. To this end we accept as definitive the precise statement formulated by the Advisory Committee in the light of both purpose and experience to answer criticisms based on some dispute in the interpretation of the rules. ... The following extracts therefrom are directly pertinent to our present discussion: "The intent and effect of the rules is to permit the claim to be stated in general terms; the rules are designed to discourage battles over mere form of statement and to sweep away the needless controversies which the codes permitted that served either to delay trial on the merits or to prevent a party from having a trial because of mistakes in statement.... It is accordingly the opinion of the Advisory Committee that, as it stands, the rule adequately sets forth the characteristics of good pleading; does away with the confusion resulting from the use of 'facts' and 'cause of action'; and requires the pleader to disclose adequate information as the basis of his claim for relief as distinguished from a bare averment that he wants relief and is entitled to it."

Turning to the complaint before us, we remark that in outward form at least it is an imposing document consisting of twelve or more printed pages. ... The complaint is filled with the pleading of conclusions of both fact and law; it is far from that lean and terse allegation in sequence of events as they have happened which we have stressed. But we are not conducting exercises in pleading; we must look beyond the mere mountain of words to the meaning sought to be conveyed. So looking we can have no doubt that plaintiffs say the supplier defendants have given their favored customers Vim and Davega price discounts and other special favors (listed in some detail) which have lost sales to the plaintiffs, destroyed their capacity to compete, and forced some of them out of business.

In testing whether this is a sufficient statement of claim upon which to base a lawsuit, we ought practically to consider the alternatives, both what can be expected and asked of antitrust plaintiffs and what can be accomplished by compulsive orders. Here seems to be the rock upon which [cases that attempt] to achieve more particularized pleading have definitely foundered; for the judges' directions double the bulk without increasing enlightenment, while they delay the cause and exhaust the time of several judges. So in this case the district judge has stated several requirements which would seem either not feasible or not such as to advance the case toward adjudication. Most of them relate to details either not pertinent to the legal point or covered generally, such as addresses and location of defendants, the territory involved (the "Greater New York area"), the time (necessarily the period permitted by the applicable statutes of limitation to the date of filing of the complaint), and so on. Perhaps the nub of all this is the conclusion that by "stating the claims of all the plaintiffs against all the defendants collectively, they have deprived the defendants of notice of the precise nature of the claims that each will be required to meet." But we note that a similar order in a companion case has resulted only in a complaint doubled in length, with separate paragraphs of iteration in general form of action by individual plaintiffs against individual defendants — a formal compliance, with no gain in useful information that we can perceive.

It is to be noted that this complaint meets certain difficulties sometimes adverted to in other cases, such as allegations as to interstate commerce or public injury occasionally found wanting. It does lack a direct allegation that the defendants conspired together, although it assumes the defendants' "combinations and conspiracies" and the resulting damage to plaintiffs. But as to this the trier of facts may draw an inference of agreement or concerted action from the "conscious parallelism" of the defendants' acts of price cutting and the like, as the Supreme Court recognizes. . . . It would seem therefore that the plaintiffs have set forth a prima facie case which, if proved, will force the defendants to their proof in rebuttal.

In criticizing these complaints the trial judges have tended to see willful violations of precise instructions. We doubt if this is a profitable approach in any event; however willful seeming, lawyers must represent their clients in what they conceive the most effective way in the light of their knowledge, which must include that neither English nor American experience lends support to mere pleadings as a substitute for trial. But as we try to visualize practical substitutes we question the adverse implication. For actually this demand seems to come to a call for specific instances, as that Admiral made such and such a discount sale of specified goods to Davega on a particular day at a particular place. Anything short of this, as the practice below is demonstrating, will permit of the vagueness the judges are finding troublesome. And yet such pleading of the evidence is surely not required and is on the whole undesirable. It is a matter for the discovery process, not for allegations of detail in the complaint. The complaint should not be burdened with possibly hundreds of specific instances; and if it were, it would be comparatively meaningless at trial where the parties could adduce further pertinent evidence if discovered. They can hardly know all their evidence, down to the last detail, long in advance of trial.

The sad truth is that these cases are likely to prove laborious in any event and that there is no real substitute for trial, although pre-trial conferences and orders may greatly speed the result. But a considerable part of federal litigation is of a lengthy and burdensome nature and we are not justified in frowning on a Congressional policy so definitely cherished as is this, a policy which is, after all, the cause of our troubles. And while as appellate judges we would help our brethren at the crucial trial stage where we could, the experience, as generally noted, shows that attempts at special pleading are definitely not the remedy. This has a bearing on the alternative relief here asked, that of a more definite statement under F.R. 12(e). Trial judges should of course have some discretion to attempt improvements in particular pleadings before them where they have the available time and energy to do so. Yet it seems clear that "motions for particulars will not serve that purpose" of particularizing antitrust issues, Procedure in Anti-Trust and Other Protracted Cases, A Report Adopted by the Judicial Conference of the United States, September 26, 1951, page 10, and "Orders for more definite statements ordinarily do not result in furtherance of the solution of the big case." Resolutions Adopted at Seminar on Long Cases in New York, August 26-30, 1957, No. 8. The real solution — so far as there is one short of trial — would appear to be that recommended in these important and informed authorities, viz., continuing pretrial conferences under the direction of a single judge who may thus avoid the duplicating efforts of various judges we have noted above.

[The court then went on to hold that plaintiffs had adequately alleged facts to permit joinder under Rules 20 and 23 of the Federal Rules of Civil Procedure.]

NORTHLAND INSURANCE CO. v. SHELL OIL CO.

930 F. Supp. 1069 (D.N.J. 1996)

■ ROSEN, United States Magistrate Judge.... Presently before the court is the [plaintiffs'] motion . . . to vacate the RICO case management order pursuant to Fed.R.Civ.P. 8.... [T]he motion shall be denied.

BACKGROUND

[Northland Insurance filed a putative class action on behalf of insurers that asserted subrogation rights against three defendants that manufactured allegedly defective polybutylene plumbing systems. Northland and the other class members paid the claims of policyholders whose property was damaged by the defective systems. Eventually the defendants settled policyholders' claims on a classwide basis.

[The basic theory of the plaintiff's Amended Complaint — which was, in the court's words, "painted with extraordinarily broad strokes" — was that this settlement between the defendants and policyholders usurped the plaintiffs' subrogation rights against the policyholders. Included in the plaintiffs' seven-count complaint were Counts V and VI, alleging violations of 18 U.S.C. §§ 1962(c) and 1962(d), which are part of the Racketeer Influenced and Corrupt Organizations Act (RICO).]

Substantively, the complaint makes only generalized and vague allegations against the defendants. For example, . . . Count V, the RICO count, does not describe with specificity the factual bases to support the elements for a RICO fraud claim. Rather, after a series of general and conclusory statements regarding the defendants' activities, the plaintiff refers the defendants and this court to the RICO statute itself for a description of the allegedly violative activity, stating:

> 75. Plaintiffs and the class were directly injured in their business and property by defendants' participation in this pattern of unlawful activity, *as more fully described in 18 U.S.C. §§ 1961(1), (5).*

(Complaint ¶ 75) (emphasis added). . . .

On February 22, 1996, following a status and case management conference during which the parties both recognized the certain complexity of the case, this court exercised its discretion under Rule 15B.6, General Rule for the District of New Jersey (hereinafter "Local Rule"), to order preparation of a RICO Case Statement. . . . The present motion followed.

The plaintiff has advanced several arguments in support of vacating the order[, including] that the complaint, as amended, is pled with sufficient specificity for the purposes of Fed.R.Civ.P. 8, thus the RICO Case Statement is unnecessary; . . . and that the notice requirements for federal pleading prohibit the RICO Case Statement. Essentially, the plaintiff argues that the court has no authority to require the entry of the RICO Case Statement. In support of the plaintiff's assertions, Northland analogizes the Statement to either a heightened pleading requirement, violative of Supreme Court jurisprudence under Leatherman v. Tarrant County Narcotics Intelligence [and Coordination] Unit, 507 U.S. 163 (1993) . . . .

Conversely, the defendants assert that the Federal Rules, Local Rules and Acts of Congress are replete with authority to support the RICO Case Statement practice. The defendants rely upon the Judicial Improvements Act, 28 U.S.C. § 2071, et seq., Federal Rules 83, 12(e), 9(b) and 16, and Local Rules 1A and 15.

DISCUSSION

The rule-making authority of local federal courts is primarily located in the Judicial Improvements Act, 28 U.S.C. § 2071, et seq., and Federal Rule of Civil Procedure 83. Section 2071 provides that:

The Supreme Court *and all courts established by Act of Congress* may from time to time prescribe rules for the conduct of their business. Such rules shall be consistent with Acts of Congress and rules of practice and procedure prescribed under section 2072 of this title.

28 U.S.C. § 2071(a) (emphasis added). . . . Federal Rule of Civil Procedure 83 incorporates the dictates of Section 2071, providing in relevant part that:

> Each district court, acting by a majority of its judges, may, after giving appropriate public notice and an opportunity for comment, make and amend rules governing its practice. A local rule shall be consistent with — but not duplicative of — Acts of Congress and rules adopted under 28 U.S.C. §§ 2072 and 2075[.]

Fed.R.Civ.P. 83(a) . . . .

The Civil Justice Reform Act of 1990, 28 U.S.C. § 471, et seq., (hereinafter "CJRA") referenced in Local Rule 1A provides further guidance for district court rule promulgation and practice. . . . Congress contemplated that courts — particularly local courts — would utilize the CJRA as a basis for promulgating procedures for management of complex cases. With respect to the CJRA, Congress made the following findings: . . .

> (5) Evidence suggests that an effective litigation management and cost and delay reduction program should incorporate several interrelated principles, including —
>
> (A) the differential treatment of cases that provides for individualized and specific management according to their needs, complexity, duration, and probable litigation careers; [and]
>
> (B) early involvement of a judicial officer in planning the progress of a case, controlling the discovery process, and scheduling hearings, trials, and other litigation events . . . .

28 U.S.C. § 471 . . . .

In accordance with the mandates of the CJRA[,] the Judicial Improvement Act[,] and the Federal Rules, the District of New Jersey continuously scrutinizes its existing rules, refining and modifying them when deemed appropriate. . . . By amendment in 1991, the District of New Jersey formally adopted the RICO Case Order as it appears in Appendix O to Local Rule 15B.* The order was designed to aid plaintiffs in framing their claims with particularity sufficient for the requirements of the RICO

---

* Local Rule 15B.6 authorized a judge or magistrate judge, in a civil RICO action, to "require a RICO case statement to be filed and served." Appendix O, which described the case statement as "equivalent to a supplemental pleading, required the plaintiff to provide details to 20 specific questions, many of which had sub-parts. Among the information required was the identity of each defendant, "the alleged misconduct and basis of liability of each defendant," the identity and alleged misconduct of all other wrongdoers who were not defendants, a description "in detail [of] the pattern of racketeering activity or collection of unlawful debts alleged for each RICO claim," a description "in detail [of] any alleged conspiracy," a description of the effects of the conduct on interstate commerce, and a description of injury and damages sustained. — ED.

statute, 18 U.S.C. §§ 1961-1968. . . . Significantly, the order of a RICO Case Statement under Local Rule 15B.6 is discretionary, not mandatory.

Although approximately one dozen districts have adopted and routinely employ RICO Case Statements similar to that of the District of New Jersey, the plaintiff supplies no case which has held the RICO Case Order improper. Moreover, the Third Circuit and the United States Supreme Court have relied upon the RICO Case Statements filed by parties in various cases for a full statement of the plaintiff's claim. See, *e.g.*, National Organization of Women, Inc. v. Scheidler, 510 U.S. 249 (1994) (noting without pejorative comment that the plaintiffs "later amended their complaint, and pursuant to local rules, filed a 'RICO Case Statement' that further detailed the enterprise, the pattern of racketeering, the victims of the racketeering activity, and the participants involved"); Jaguar Cars, Inc. v. Royal Oaks Motor Car Co., Inc., 46 F.3d 258, 264 (3d Cir. 1995). . . .

Certain of the Federal Rules have been recognized as more specific authority for the RICO Case Statement. One example is Federal Rule 12(e), which authorizes federal courts to order plaintiffs to provide more definite statements of their claims. Courts have upheld the case statement tool in RICO cases in response to allegations of vagueness. See Old Time Enterprises, Inc. v. International Coffee Corp., 862 F.2d 1213, 1217 (5th Cir.1989) . . . . However, the federal rule providing the strongest authority for the RICO Case Statement is Rule 16.

This court has recently re-affirmed its commitment to ardent enforcement of Rule 16 and its emphasis on case management. . . . Subsection (c)(12) provides that:

> [a]t any conference under this rule consideration may be given, and the court may take appropriate action, with respect to . . . (12) the need for adopting special procedures for managing potentially difficult or protracted actions that may involve complex issues, multiple parties, difficult legal questions, or unusual proof problems[.]

Fed.R.Civ.P. 16(c)(12) (as amended 1993). . . . [In this case] the procedural history and primary issues promise to be involved, costly and complicated. Further, the parties do not dispute that RICO claims generally involve complex issues.

In contradistinction to all the above referenced authority, the plaintiff offers Leatherman v. Tarrant County Narcotics Intelligence Unit, 507 U.S. 163 (1993) . . . .

In *Leatherman*, the Court found the "heightened pleading standard" applied to civil rights cases brought under 28 U.S.C. § 1983 violative of the "notice pleading" adopted by the Federal Rules. 507 U.S. at 168. The plaintiff urges this court to apply the reasoning of *Leatherman* to the instant case, arguing that Rule 8(a)'s notice pleading prohibits practices such as the RICO Case Statement. However, *Leatherman* does not apply to RICO cases for two primary reasons. First, RICO cases often involve allegations of fraud, which, under the federal rules, require pleading with specificity pursuant to Federal Rule 9(b). While not all RICO claims contain allegations of fraud, the plaintiff's amended complaint clearly asserts fraud as a basis for certain claims. Finally, it is significant that the Supreme Court relied upon the RICO Case Statement for a complete statement of the claim in the *NOW v. Scheidler, supra*, in 1994, a full year after the *Leatherman* decision.

Second, *Leatherman* did not consider a local court's interpretation of a local rule or a local order. Rather, the Court addressed a Fifth Circuit practice of requiring heightened pleading in Section 1983 cases notwithstanding the basis of the claim or its relative complexity. Id. at 166-168. As noted above, none of the parties suggest that RICO cases are commensurate to section 1983 cases as regards complexity or vastness. Moreover, the RICO Case Statement does not constitute a heightened pleading standard. Although the Statement is considered "equivalent to a supplemental pleading" (Local Rule 15, Appendix O), the statement is not required in every case. Rather, a judicial officer may order the statement's entry in appropriate cases. Local Rule 15.B.6. Thus, the statement serves as a case management tool. . . . Consequently, this court declines to extend the reasoning in *Leatherman* to civil RICO Case Statements.

Further, in this particular case, the RICO order was advisable as the only federal claim within the suit is the RICO claim. Federal courts are under a continuing obligation to assure that subject matter jurisdiction has been appropriately asserted. . . . Although the plaintiff also has asserted jurisdiction on the grounds of diversity of citizenship, the amount in controversy element of diversity will become a critical factor in review of the class certification issue. Any parties who cannot individually meet the amount in controversy requirement may wish to rely upon federal question jurisdiction. This enhances the court's need to review federal question subject matter jurisdiction early on in this complex and potentially costly litigation. The RICO Case Order can provide a useful tool for such a review.

Notes and Questions

1. *Nagler* is an old case, but an influential one. Its author, Judge Clark, was one of the primary drafters of the Federal Rules of Civil Procedure, and one of the passionate advocates of notice pleading. See, *e.g.*, Charles E. Clark, Handbook on the Law of Code Pleading (1928). *Nagler* itself was a practical application of Clark's fervent beliefs, previously articulated in Charles E. Clark, *Special Pleading in the "Big Case,"* 21 F.R.D. 45, 47-48 (1957), that "strict special pleading has never been found workable or even useful in English and American law" and that "in federal pleading no special exceptions have been created for the 'Big Case' or for any other particular type of action."

2. The Supreme Court has never wavered in its support of notice pleading. In Conley v. Gibson, 355 U.S. 41 (1957), the Court held that a complaint passes muster under Rule 8 as long as it gives defendant "fair notice of what the plaintiff's claim is and the grounds upon which it rests," 355 U.S. at 47; a complaint cannot be dismissed "unless it appears beyond doubt that the plaintiff can prove no set of facts in support of his claim which would entitle him to relief," id. at 45-46. Despite occasional dissenting suggestions that the majority has been unduly insensitive to this liberal pleading philosophy, see *e.g.*, Renne

v. Geary, 501 U.S. 312, 347 n.5 (1991) (Marshall, J.,dissenting), and Baldwin County Welcome Center v. Brown, 466 U.S. 147, 164 (1984) (Stevens, J., dissenting), the Court's opinions all endorse the approach. See, *e.g.*, Schiavone v. Fortune, 477 U.S. 21, 27 (1986) (Federal Rules have "rejected an approach that pleading is a game of skill in which one misstep may be decisive"); Foman v. Davis, 371 U.S. 178, 181 (1962) ("It is too late in the day and entirely contrary to the spirit of the Federal Rules of Civil Procedure for decisions on the merits to be avoided on the basis of 'mere technicalities.'").

Most recently, in Leatherman v. Tarrant County Narcotics Intelligence and Coordination Unit, 507 U.S. 163 (1993), the Court had a chance to insist on heightened pleading requirements. *Leatherman* was a § 1983 case against police officials in which the defense of immunity was likely. In prior cases the Supreme Court had suggested that such immunity defenses should be resolved as soon as possible. See Harlow v. Fitzgerald, 457 U.S. 800 (1982). In general furtherance of this goal, the Fifth Circuit in *Leatherman* had required of § 1983 plaintiffs that their "complaints state with factual detail and particularity the basis for the claim which necessarily includes why the defendant-official cannot successfully maintain the defense of immunity." Leatherman v. Tarrant County Narcotics Intelligence and Coordination Unit, 954 F.2d 1054, 1057 (5th Cir. 1992) (citation omitted). The Supreme Court reversed:

> We think that it is impossible to square the "heightened pleading standard" applied by the Fifth Circuit in this case with the liberal system of "notice pleading" set up by the Federal Rules. . . .
>
> Rule 9(b) does impose a particularity requirement in two specific instances. It provides that "[i]n all averments of fraud or mistake, the circumstances constituting fraud or mistake shall be stated with particularity." Thus, the Federal Rules do address in Rule 9(b) the question of the need for greater particularity in pleading certain actions, but do not include among the enumerated actions any reference to complaints alleging municipal liability under § 1983. *Expressio unius est exclusio alterius.* . . .
>
> Perhaps if Rules 8 and 9 were rewritten today, claims against municipalities under § 1983 might be subjected to the added specificity requirement of Rule 9(b). . . . In the absence of such an amendment, federal courts and litigants must rely on summary judgment and control of discovery to weed out unmeritorious claims sooner rather than later. [507 U.S. at 168-69.]

Cf. Crawford-El v. Britton, — U.S. —, 118 S.Ct 1584 (1998) (suggesting that courts could order Rule 7(a) reply or Rule 12(e) motion for more definite statement to obtain additional specificity in qualified immunity cases).

3. Although the Supreme Court has never met a complaint that fell below the standards of Rule 8, presumably at a certain point a complaint would fail to clear its hurdle. At what point would that be? One commentator has thought that *Conley*'s "fair notice" requirement implied that "the rules do contemplate a statement of circumstances, occurrences, and events in support of the claim being presented." 5 Charles A. Wright & Arthur R. Miller, Federal Practice and Procedure § 1215 (1990). On the other hand, "fair notice" has not been thought to require that a plaintiff plead facts on each element of a cause of action. Id. § 1216; see also Atchison, Topeka and Santa Fe Railway Co. v. Buell, 480 U.S. 557, 568 n.15 (1987) ("Under the Federal Rules of Civil Procedure, respondent had no duty to set out all of the relevant facts in his complaint.").

4. None of the Supreme Court's Rule 8 decisions involved complex cases. Do you believe that the Court would create a heightened pleading requirement in complex cases? If not, how can *Northland* be explained? Is it true, as the magistrate judge says, that the notice pleading requirements of Rules 8 and 9 must be read against Rule 16(c)(12), the Civil Justice Reform Act, and local rulemaking authority? None of those factors was present in *Nagler*; neither Rule 16(c)(12) nor the CJRA had yet been promulgated, and there was no local rule authorizing heightened pleading. Granting that to be true, can either Rule 16(c)(12) or the CJRA, which talk only in general terms about case management, overcome the specific language of Rules 8 and 9? Can a local rule in New Jersey overcome Rules 8 and 9, when F.R.Civ.P. 83(a)(1) requires that local rules be consistent with the Federal Rules of Civil Procedure? Other courts have found authority for comparable RICO Case Statements in Rules 11 and 12(e). Does anything in either of these rules overcome the specific language of Rules 8 and 9?

One way to justify *Northland* is to view it as a Rule 9(b) case, in which the allegations of fraud require heightened pleading. While this is a possible justification, most courts have insisted on a little bit more, but not very much more, specificity in fraud allegations; Rule 9(b) is not thought to require anything approaching the kind of detail contemplated in *Northland*'s RICO case statement. See Wright & Miller, *supra*, §§ 1297-98 (stating that allegations of time, place, and identity of wrongdoer, together with basic elements of fraud, are sufficient; noting, however, a trend in some courts to require greater specificity in securities fraud and RICO cases); Vicom, Inc. v. Harbridge Merchant Services, Inc., 20 F.3d 771, 777 (7th Cir. 1994) (purposes of heightened pleading under Rule 9(b) are "(1) protecting a defendant's reputation from harm; (2) minimizing 'strike suits' and 'fishing expeditions'; and (3) providing notice of the claim to the adverse party").

5. So we return to the basic question: Is complexity an adequate reason to require more by way of pleading? The advantage of requiring more, of course, is that more pleading can narrow the issues considerably; discovery can be tailored; and a plan for managing the case can be more easily developed. The disadvantages are the different treatment accorded different cases and the possibility that failing to uncover facts or issues might make a difference in the ultimate outcome.

Assuming that a rule requiring greater specificity in complex cases is desirable, is it possible to develop a rule that gives this concern any concrete meaning? Would it have to be a discretionary rule, allowing the judge to insist on additional pleading when the constellation of factors of the particular case so dictate? Or could we develop hard-and-fast rules, requiring more of plaintiffs in particular types of actions (such as RICO, antitrust, securities, CERCLA)? Does the first solution give too much power to the judge? Does the second solution destroy the trans-substantive aspirations of our pleading rules, and harbinge a return to the days of common law pleading? Under either approach, how much more specificity is appropriate?

6. A few cases seem to have adopted the first approach, stating that "[t]he more complex the litigation the greater the amount of detail required in the pleadings." Electronic Laboratory Supply Co. v. Motorola, Inc., 1989 WL 113127, *1 (E.D. Pa.). The highwater mark for this approach is probably Associated General Contractors of California, Inc. v. California State Council of Carpenters, 459 U.S. 519 (1983). In *Associated General Contractors*, the plaintiff's complaint

made only vague references to the existence of coercion, which was a necessary element of its successful Sherman Act claim. The Court indulged the assumption that coercion existed, but stated in dicta:

> Had the District Court required the Union to describe the nature of the alleged coercion with particularity before ruling on the motion to dismiss, it might well have been evident that no violation of law had been alleged. In making the contrary assumption for purposes of our decision, we are perhaps stretching the rule of Conley v. Gibson, 355 U.S. 41, 47-48 (1957), too far. Certainly in a case of this magnitude, a district court must retain the power to insist upon some specificity in pleading before allowing a potentially massive factual controversy to proceed. [459 U.S. at 528 n.17.]

In a similar vein, some courts have suggested that the amount of specificity required in the pleadings depends upon a range of factors that as a practical matter would require heightened pleading in complex cases. For instance, Boston & Maine Corp. v. Town of Hampton, 987 F.2d 855, 865 (1st Cir. 1993), the court suggested that the following three factors should influence the degree of specificity required:

> First, a complaint that is too general will not "give the defendant fair notice of what the plaintiff's claim is and the grounds upon which it rests." . . . Accordingly, some distinction must be made between an adequate complaint and one that is too general. Second, rising litigation costs (and the associated impact of an improper threat of litigation) speak for requiring some specificity before permitting a claimant "to drag a defendant past the pleading threshold." . . . Third, the burgeoning caseload crisis in the district courts weighs in favor of earlier disposition of baseless claims.

See also Sutliff, Inc. v. Donovan Companies, Inc., 727 F.2d 648 (7th Cir. 1984) ("The heavy costs of modern federal litigation, especially antitrust litigation, and the mounting caseload pressures on the federal courts, counsel against launching the parties into pretrial discovery if there is no reasonable prospect that the plaintiff can make out a cause of action from the events narrated in the complaint."); but see Hammes v. Aamco Transmissions, Inc., 33 F.3d 774, 778 (7th Cir. 1994) (Posner, J.) (stating that *Leatherman* "scotched" efforts such as those described in *Boston & Maine* to insist on heightened pleading). Should other factors be the aid that heightened pleading can provide to rational adjudication and the availability of other pretrial devices that adequately narrow issues and facts?

7. The second pleading approach in complex cases is to establish specific rules of heightened pleading for particular types of complex cases or claims. The usual approach, reflected by *Nagler*, is to resist heightened pleading requirements in specific subject areas. See In re Commercial Explosives Litigation, 945 F. Supp. 1489, 1491 (D. Utah 1996) ("Complex antitrust litigation is not subject to any greater pleading requirements than Rule 8(a)(2) requires of ordinary litigation."); Wright & Miller, *supra*, §§ 1297-98 (no additional requirements in securities cases); Warwick Administrative Group v. Avon Products, Inc., 820 F. Supp. 116, 121 (S.D.N.Y. 1993) (no heightened pleading requirements in environmental cases). Nevertheless, as *Northland* shows, one type of claim that often results in heightened pleading requirements is the RICO claim, for which many district courts insist on a RICO case statement. Such insistence rarely invokes negative comment on appeal. See Word of Faith Outreach Center Church v. Sawyer, 90 F.3d 118 (5th Cir. 1996), cert. denied, — U.S. —, 117 S.Ct. 1248 (1997); DeJesus v. Sears, Roebuck, Inc., 87 F.3d 65 (2d

Cir. 1996), cert. denied, — U.S. —, 117 S.Ct. 509 (1997); Lightning Tube, Inc. v. Witco Corp., 4 F.3d 1153 (3d Cir. 1993); but see McLaughlin v. Anderson, 962 F.2d 187, 194 (2d Cir. 1992) (RICO allegations not involving fraud should be judged under Rule 8(a) pleading standard).

Despite the general acceptance of *Nagler's* rule, courts facing securities, antitrust, and environmental claims sometimes seem to impose *de facto* heightened pleading requirements. Securities claims, of course, usually involve allegations of fraud, so the heightened pleading standards of Rule 9(b), which sometimes are interpreted to require exquisite amounts of specificity, pertain. See Richard L. Marcus, *The Revival of Fact Pleading under the Federal Rules of Civil Procedure*, 86 Colum. L. Rev. 433, 447-49 (1986); Wright & Miller, *supra*, § 1297, esp. nn. 11 & 15; id. § 1298, esp. nn. 24 & 25. In 1995, the Private Securities Litigation Reform Act established specific pleading requirements for allegations of misleading statements and for state of mind. See 15 U.S.C. §§ 78u-4(b)(1)-(2). Next, with regard to antitrust claims, the Supreme Court once observed that "where a bona fide complaint is filed that charges every element necessary to recover, summary dismissal . . . can seldom be justified." United States v. Employing Plasterers' Association, 347 U.S. 186, 189 (1954). Some courts have inverted this observation into a requirement that an antitrust complaint contain factual allegations on each element of a cause of action — a return to the world of code pleading from which notice pleading sought to escape. See pp. 50-53, *supra*; *Sutliff*, 727 F.2d 648; Faulkner Advertising Associates, Inc. v. Nissan Motor Corp., 905 F.2d 769, 772 (4th Cir. 1990); see also Oregon Natural Resources Council v. Mohla, 944 F.2d 531, 539 (9th Cir. 1991) (requiring heightened pleading in antitrust case in which allegations threatened to chill First Amendment rights). There is also some support for heightened pleading in the environmental area. See Cash Energy, Inc. v. Weiner, 768 F. Supp. 892, 900 (D. Mass. 1991); cf. B.F. Goodrich Co. v. Murtha, 815 F. Supp. 539 (D. Conn. 1993) (authorizing defendants to file third party complaints only against hazardous waste generators whose potential liability was substantiated enough to pass Rule 11 muster; 1151 potential third party defendants reduced to less than 50).

In any event, with the exception of sometimes lengthy RICO case statements, most of the cases that have imposed heightened pleading have not insisted on a great deal more by way of pleading — certainly not enough to cause significant amount of issue- and fact-narrowing in the pleading process.

8. An indirect method to require more pleading in complex cases is to use Rule 12(e), which permits a party to file a motion for a more definite statement. As a general matter, Rule 12(e) is not a favored rule; it applies only to a rare group of cases in which the pleading is adequate for Rule 8 purposes but is so "vague and ambiguous that a party cannot reasonably be required to frame a responsive pleading." See 5A Charles A. Wright & Arthur R. Miller, Federal Practice and Procedure §§ 1374-77 (1990). In at least some complex cases, courts have been willing to grant the motion. See Wildman v. Wills, 81 F.R.D. 588, 590 (E.D. Pa. 1978) (granting motion with observation that "adequacy of a complaint for purposes of withstanding a motion to dismiss does not establish its adequacy as a foundation for complex litigation"). Even in highly complex litigation, however, a motion for a more definite statement is rarely successful. See In re Hanford Nuclear Reservation Litigation, 780 F. Supp. 1551 (E.D. Wash. 1991); In re Arthur Treacher's Franchise Litigation, 92 F.R.D. 398 (E.D. Pa. 1981); Gilbert v. Bagley, 492 F. Supp. 714, 719 (M.D.N.C. 1980) (Merhige, J.) ("Pretrial

discovery is preferable to a more definite statement."); cf. In re Jackson Lockdown/MCO Cases, 568 F. Supp. 869 (E.D. Mich. 1983) (denying motion until completion of first round of discovery).

9. Remember that the purpose of heightened pleading requirements in complex cases is to narrow the issues during pretrial. In order for pleading rules to accomplish this purpose, they must not only demand more at the outset but also preclude the parties from amending the pleadings to add new issues during pretrial. Such a stingy attitude toward amendment is inconsistent with the liberal amendment philosophy of F.R.Civ.P. 15(a), which authorizes parties to amend a pleading once as a matter of course before a responsive pleading is filed and instructs the trial judge to "freely give[ ]" leave to amend after expiration of this period "when justice so requires." In Foman v. Davis, 371 U.S. 178, 182 (1962), the Court stated:

> If the underlying facts or circumstances relied upon by a plaintiff may be a proper subject of relief, he ought to be afforded an opportunity to test his claim on the merits. In the absence of any apparent or declared reason — such as undue delay, bad faith or dilatory motive on the part of the movant, repeated failure to cure deficiencies by amendments previously allowed, undue prejudice to the opposing party by virtue of allowance of the amendment, futility of amendment, etc. — the leave sought should, as the rules require, be "freely given."

Foman was not a complex case, so we once again need to consider whether the usually liberal philosophy of pleading should be adjusted in complex litigation. For the most part the answer appears to be that complex litigation does not change this philosophy. A number of cases take the complexity of a case into account in declining to permit amendment, but in nearly all of the cases other *Foman* factors — most typically, either the last-minute nature of an amendment, the inclusion of new theories or parties that would cause great prejudice to existing parties, or the futility of amendment — also came into play. See, *e.g.*, Duchon v. Cajon Co., 791 F.2d 43 (6th Cir. 1986); Ross v. Houston Independent School District, 699 F.2d 218 (5th Cir. 1983); Chitimacha Tribe of Louisiana v. Harry L. Laws Co., 690 F.2d 1157 (5th Cir. 1982), cert. denied, 464 U.S. 814 (1983). See generally Manual for Complex Litigation, Third § 21.32 (encouraging court to establish firm schedule for finalizing all pleadings in order "to avoid later enlargement of issues and expansion or duplication of discovery").

10. If negative consequences, such as refusal to entertain claims pleaded with insufficient detail, will not work, perhaps positive inducements to plead with more particularity will. One such inducement is found in F.R.Civ.P. 26(a)(1)(A) and (B), which requires parties automatically to disclose certain types of discoverable information (such as the identity of witnesses and the location of documents) to other parties when that information is "relevant to disputed facts alleged with particularity in the pleadings." We will return to examine these provisions, and their possible impact on complex cases, later in this chapter. See pp. 1094-98, *infra*. For now, it is enough to know that the information disclosed under Rule 26 would be discoverable in any event upon request by a party; Rule 26 merely accelerates the process and obviates the need to make the request. Do you anticipate that a carrot such as this would generate enough specificity to significantly narrow the issues in the case? Could you think of other carrots that would do a better job?

11. Sometimes there are reasons for a party to provide a great deal of specificity in a complaint. Triggering the automatic disclosures of Rule 26 is one

reason; others might be to make a statement about the strength of the case, to reach an external audience (media, prospective clients, other potential defendants), or to influence the judge. Such complaints violate Rule 8's "short and plain" requirement, but courts usually treat Rule 8 as a floor and not as a ceiling on pleading. Still, some complaints are so lengthy that courts feel compelled to do something — including, perhaps, dismissing the complaint. For instance, in *Vicom*, 20 F.3d 771, the plaintiffs filed a "119-page, 385-paragraph less-than-coherent amended complaint" that included RICO allegations. The district court toyed with dismissing the complaint on Rule 8 grounds, but ultimately dismissed it on the merits. On appeal, the Seventh Circuit affirmed on the merits, but not before pausing to observe:

> Under Rule 8, a complaint "'must be presented with intelligibility sufficient for a court or opposing party to understand whether a valid claim is alleged and if so what it is.'" Wade v. Hopper, 993 F.2d 1246, 1249 (7th Cir.) (citations omitted), cert. denied, 510 U.S. 868 (1993); see also Jennings v. Emry, 910 F.2d 1434, 1436 (7th Cir. 1990) . . . . A complaint that is prolix and/or confusing makes it difficult for the defendant to file a responsive pleading and makes it difficult for the trial court to conduct orderly litigation. . . . . Thus, courts should not allow plaintiffs to "plead[ ] by means of obfuscation." *Jennings*, 910 F.2d at 1436.
>
> Because it is difficult to file a pleading in response to a prolix and confusing complaint, doing so also can be costly. The Ninth Circuit discussed the expenditure of a defendant's resources, as well as the costs to nonparty litigants, when it affirmed the district court's dismissal with prejudice of a plaintiff's verbose and confusing amended complaint . . . .
>
> Many plaintiffs attempt to excuse lengthy and confusing complaints by pointing to the type of claim or theory under which they are pleading. . . . However, the caselaw is clear that, although RICO complaints often might need to be somewhat longer than many complaints, RICO complaints must meet the requirements of Rule 8(a)(2) and Rule 8(e)(1). . . .
>
> Vicom's confusing, redundant, and seemingly interminable amended complaint violated the letter and the spirit of Rule 8(a). [20 F.3d at 775-76.]

See also Maryland Staffing Services, Inc. v. Manpower, Inc., 936 F. Supp. 1494, 1497 (E.D. Wis. 1996) (suggesting that prolix complaint could have been dismissed under *Vicom*).

b. Ordering Consolidated Pleadings

Problems of prolixity can arise not only from a single long complaint but also from the number of complaints filed in related actions. Different complaints may name different defendants and allege different theories of recovery. When the cases are consolidated in a single forum, the cacophony of complaints makes it very difficult to keep track of who is suing whom, and for what. The filing of responsive pleadings, in which different admissions might be made and defenses might be raised to each complaint, adds to the confusion. These problems, in turn, make it exceedingly difficult to manage the pretrial process: Trying to figure out which discovery is relevant to which complaint, who can attend which deposition, and who may file or respond to which motion can be a great headache.

In theory, of course, this problem is not insurmountable, but it would be far easier, more tidy, and more economical if the array of pleadings could be replaced by a single consolidated pleading for each side. That simple solution, however, carries a significant drawback: Parties are no longer "masters of their complaints," and lose control of the proofs and arguments that they wish to make. In prior chapters we have seen that a party may be joined in a forum not of her choosing and may be represented by counsel not of her choosing. When she also loses the ability to control who she sues and on what theories, the assault upon the traditional adversarial model is nearly complete.

For a time after the Supreme Court's decision in Johnson v. Manhattan Railway Co., 289 U.S. 479 (1933), it was believed that a federal court could not order consolidated pleadings. In *Johnson*, which involved a question of whether an attack on a judgment was direct or collateral, the Court observed that consolidation of cases "does not merge the suits into a single cause, or change the rights of the parties, or make those who are parties in one suit parties in another." 289 U.S. at 496-97. A consolidation that did not accomplish some streamlining of parties or claims would be pretty useless, but any consolidation of pleadings that added (or deleted) parties or claims would appear to run afoul of *Johnson*. See Garber v. Randall, 477 F.2d 711 (2d Cir. 1973) (refusing to authorize consolidated complaint that alleged wrongdoing by law firm, when law firm was peripherally involved, firm had been sued in only one of three cases by only one of fifteen plaintiffs, and other plaintiffs had dissociated themselves from allegations). In 1975, however, the world changed.

KATZ v. REALTY EQUITIES CORP. OF NEW YORK

521 F.2d 1354 (2d Cir. 1975)

■ WATERMAN, Circuit Judge. This appeal concerns an order of a district judge requiring the filing and service of a single consolidated complaint for pretrial purposes upon defendants in a number of related securities cases. We affirm the order which, under the circumstances present, was a proper exercise of the trial judge's authority in the management of complex multiparty litigation.

[An insurance company, Republic National Life Insurance, had invested heavily in Realty Equities, and then allegedly conspired with Realty to fraudulently conceal Realty's shaky financial condition from the public. The Securities and Exchange Commission filed a complaint in the Southern District of New York against Republic, seven of Republic's directors and officers, Realty, two of Realty's officials, and the auditors of both companies. Shortly afterwards, twelve private complaints were filed in the Southern District of New York, and five in other federal district courts. The Judicial Panel on Multidistrict Litigation consolidated all the cases in the Southern

District of New York. In two of the consolidated cases, two additional auditors of Realty — Klein, Hinds & Finke ("KHF") and Alexander Grant & Co. ("Grant") — were named. Although both were peripherally involved in the dispute, there were no allegations that either participated in the real estate and financial transactions that formed the basis of the SEC complaint against Republic and Realty. Indeed, the SEC complaint did not name either KHF or Grant as a defendant.

[The district judge, Judge Pollack, began by appointing lead and liaison counsel. Then, "in the exercise of discretion . . . to foster the efficient and proper conduct of the claims asserted in the individual complaints," Pollack ordered that a "single consolidated complaint, supplemented and amended, shall be prepared and served herein by liaison counsel which shall set forth the claims for relief asserted in the constituent actions, collated into separately stated counts by class and derivative categories as to each kind of securities holders and at the head of each count shall specifically designate by name or other convenient reference the defendants against whom such count is asserted." He further ordered "that the answer of each defendant to the consolidated complaint 'shall be deemed' to have asserted cross-claims in the nature of contribution and indemnification against all other defendants." Pollack also made clear that this complaint was for pretrial purposes, "without prejudice . . . to whether or not there will be a consolidated trial and without prejudice to the use of the individual complaints as they now stand at a consolidated trial, and certainly without prejudice to their use in individual trials if that should eventuate."

[In the consolidated complaint that followed, twenty-one plaintiffs, representing five separate classes of investors, sued thirty-nine defendants. KHF and Grant were named in three of the thirty counts. Therefore, as a result of the consolidation order, KHF and Grant found themselves facing twenty-one plaintiffs, most of whom had not previously asserted claims against them, and thirty-nine defendants, each of whom was now deemed to have a cross-claim against them.

[Obviously chagrined, KHF and Grant took an immediate appeal from the consolidation order. After holding that such an order is immediately appealable, the Second Circuit turned to the merits of the appeal.]

It is axiomatic that consolidation is a procedural device designed to promote judicial economy and that consolidation cannot affect a physical merger of the actions or the defenses of the separate parties. . . . There is here, however, no indication that the court below intended a physical merger of claims or that one was accomplished despite the court's intent. Rather, it is evident that the district court limited the use of the consolidated complaint to the controversies' pretrial stages in order to prevent unnecessary duplication and in order to reduce the potential for confusion. . . .

The use of the consolidated complaint here has significant attractions in keeping the preliminary stages of these cases within reasonable bounds. There are seventeen actions pending against thirty-nine defendants; many of the defendants are sued in most of the actions, some in but a few. A separate answer from each defendant to each complaint in which that defendant is named would involve literally hundreds of answers. As noted previously, all the complaints in the private actions track the SEC complaint, and the answers to each complaint would be substantially the same. The benefits of collecting, for example, sixteen identical answers in each of sixteen cases from one defendant is not readily discernible. It is true that those defendants named in only a small number of complaints, for example Grant and KHF, would not be overly burdened, but, nevertheless, the overall economies in reducing the proliferation of duplicative papers warrant the trial judge's efforts in the present circumstances. Moreover, it is apparent that a consolidated complaint also aids the consolidated discovery process which all parties, including the appellants, favor. Directing discovery to one complaint, rather than to seventeen complaints, avoids the possible confusion and the possible problems stemming from the situation where each plaintiff pursues his individual complaint. While it is true that carefully supervised and coordinated discovery proceedings would reduce the potential for chaos, the use of a consolidated complaint promotes the desired objective. . . .

[T]he validity of a consolidated order must be examined with reference to the special underlying facts prompting the order, and with close attention alike to the potential economies of the consolidation on the one hand, and the threatened prejudice to a party or parties, on the other hand. . . . Without a firm conviction that prejudice will result, we are most reluctant to interfere, and perhaps disrupt, the efforts of the district court which, without sacrificing the rights of the various parties, seeks to expedite this complex litigation.

The appellants claim that they have been prejudiced in two ways: the expansion of the classes in the consolidated complaint; and the deeming of cross-claims amongst the defendants during the discovery process. As noted *supra*, the [original complaints against KHF and Grant] were brought on behalf of purchasers of common stock of Realty and Republic respectively, while the consolidated complaint alleges claims on behalf of purchasers of securities in the companies. This expansion of the classes, for which there is no authority in the district court order, would of course increase the potential liability of Grant and KHF in the event that the consolidated complaint was used at trial. This is not the physical merger of claims, which the caselaw forbids, but rather an expansion of classes, which is also troubling. However, the classes have not yet been defined by the district court, and the appropriate place for appellants to object to the proposed definition of the proposed classes is before the district court.

The appellants did not appeal from that portion of the district court order which deemed the answer of each defendant to assert cross-claims for indemnification and contribution against all other defendants. . . .

The appellants' fear, perhaps substantial, that because of their peripheral involvement in the principal transactions involved in the litigation they will suffer prejudice, does not result from the consolidation of the complaints. . . . [In the original complaints against KHF and Grant] the appellants are also peripheral defendants. At the preliminary hearing the district court expressly invited Grant and KHF to move for dismissal of the complaint. In addition, the use of the consolidated complaint for pretrial purposes does not impair appellants' subsequent recourse to the timely motion for severance. At present appellants' fears of prejudice are wholly speculative: if the classes are defined along the present lines, if a motion to dismiss is denied, if a motion for severance is denied, and if the consolidated complaint is used at trial, then appellants' right to their separate defenses may be jeopardized. This possibility is too remote to justify appellate intervention into the pretrial stages of this litigation . . . .

Notes and Questions

1. Since *Katz*, other courts have also authorized the use of consolidated pleadings, usually with little to none of the trepidation reflected in *Katz* itself. See, *e.g.*, In re Prudential Securities Inc. Limited Partnerships Litigation, 158 F.R.D. 562 (S.D.N.Y. 1994); In re Wirebound Boxes Antitrust Litigation, 128 F.R.D. 262 (D. Minn. 1989); In re Storage Technology Corp. Securitites Litigation, 630 F. Supp. 1072 (D. Colo. 1986); In re Equity Funding Corp. of America Securities Litigation, 416 F. Supp. 161 (C.D. Cal. 1976). Indeed, the use of consolidated complaints today is so routine that appellate and district courts mention them almost in passing, without a thought that they might be problematic. See, *e.g.*, In re Donald J. Trump Casinos Securities Litigation, 7 F.3d 357 (3d Cir. 1993), cert. denied, 510 U.S. 1178 (1994); In re Newbridge Networks Securities Litigation, 926 F. Supp. 1163 (D.D.C. 1996). The Manual for Complex Litigation, Third (1995) also take consolidated complaints as a given. See § 33.32.

2. Why the shift in attitude? Is it because there is no prejudice in the procedure? But isn't there prejudice, both to the parties and to the procedural system? Start with the potential harm to defendants. *Katz* avoids the hard questions of prejudice to defendants KHF and Grant by suggesting that some of the prejudice could be avoided by contesting the class certification motion and any remaining prejudice had not been adequately preserved on appeal. Do you find this resolution satisfactory? Aren't KHF and Grant harmed just by having to argue about the shape of the classes and by the risk that the certification decision might be adverse to their interests? See In re AM International, Inc. Securities Litigation, 108 F.R.D. 190, 198 n.11 (S.D.N.Y. 1985) (rejecting defendants' claim that single class inappropriate); *Equity Funding*, 416 F. Supp. at 177 n.11 (severing claims against some defendants). If the issue had been preserved adequately on appeal, how could the Second Circuit have avoided finding harm to KHF and Grant in the district court's decision to "deem" that thirty-eight other defendants had filed cross-claims against each of them?

3. Switch now to the plaintiffs' side. Might there be prejudice to the plaintiffs that chose not to include claims against KHF and Grant? What if these plaintiffs did not want their lawsuits complicated by the inclusion of weak yet expensive-to-litigate peripheral claims? In *Wirebound Boxes*, two plaintiffs in a multidistricted proceeding moved to dismiss a consolidated complaint that was filed by plaintiffs' lead counsel and named them as parties. The plaintiffs complained that they would be prejudiced because the consolidated complaint "alleges a broader plaintiff class and names more defendants than do their individual complaints." 128 F.R.D. at 264. Judge Murphy refused to dismiss the complaint, holding that the consolidated complaint's "anticipated, and already proven, benefits greatly outweigh any potential prejudice to the parties." Id.

Murphy stressed that the complaint operated only for pretrial purposes; she would "undertake appropriate measures to preserve for trial and judgment, if proper, the individual identities of these actions." Id.; see also *Storage Technology*, 630 F. Supp. at 1074 (allowing lawyers who objected to consolidated complaint to "disavow the inclusion of their clients' claims within" — in other words, to opt out of — "the amended consolidated complaint").

4. In a subsequent article, Judge Murphy stated that consolidated complaints could have significant effects on the course of the litigation and thus on the rights of both plaintiffs and defendants. Among those effects were (1) the possibility that dispositive motions directed at the consolidated pleading might lead to dismissal of certain claims that would have previously survived, or lead to the defeat of motions that might previously have succeeded; (2) the streamlining of discovery disputes; (3) the elimination of conflicting classes and subclasses, and the consequent streamlining of class certification disputes; (4) the possibility that multidistricted cases may be more difficult to remand for trial purposes; (5) the expansion of the liability exposure of smaller defendants that must now defend against all cases; and (6) the potential that consolidation would affect choice of law issues. Diane E. Murphy, *Unified and Consolidated Complaints in Multidistrict Litigation*, 132 F.R.D. 597 (1991). Murphy also questioned whether courts really could fashion pretrial orders "that would preserve the separate identity of consolidated cases for trial and judgment," and acknowledged that, "to the extent a unified complaint encourages and facilitates a broad class action which would be continued through trial, it appears to consolidate the actions into one for more than pretrial purposes." 132 F.R.D. at 603, 607. On balance, Murphy thought that consolidated pleadings had "pros and cons as a case management device." 132 F.R.D. at 598. See also Joan Steinman, *The Effects of Case Consolidation on the Procedural Rights of Litigants: What They Are, What They Might Be Part II: Non-Jurisdictional Matters*, 42 UCLA L. Rev. 967, 974 (1995) (mentioning effect of consolidated pleadings on jury trial demands and settlement prospects).

5. Judge Murphy's article shows that consolidated pleadings also raise larger, systemic issues. The first is the substantive and procedural effect of consolidated pleadings. How can the disparate treatment of like cases — one with a consolidated complaint and one without — be justified? Since the parties' own support for or opposition to consolidated pleadings is likely to be driven by their private interests, who will protect the trans-substantive aspirations of our procedural system if not the judge? Can the judge be trusted to protect these aspirations adequately when the siren call of streamlined pretrial proceedings beckons?

6. A second, related concern is the effect of consolidated pleadings on the adversarial ideal. In routine cases, the parties' lawyers shape the party structure and the claims. In complex cases using consolidated pleadings, however, the party and claim structure is often different than the structure that the party faced in the original complaint or sets of complaints; almost invariably, these pleadings are "kitchen sink" pleadings in which all of the parties and all of the theories of the individual pleadings are tossed in. Professor Steinman observes:

> If something is new here, it is not that amended pleadings can make such changes, but the odds that decisions so to amend will be beyond the control of claimants. This change is largely a function of the consolidation of large numbers of claims and of the typically concomitant appointment of

lead counsel and executive or steering committees, whom the courts afford considerable freedom to act without regard to the wishes and directions of individual claimants whom counsel have been appointed to represent.

The forces that isolate parties from the lawyers handling their claims, which may first be manifest in connection with pleadings, continue to operate throughout the litigation. These indirect effects of consolidation change, if not the procedural rights of litigants, at least the realities of the litigation process for them.

Steinman, *supra*, 42 UCLA L. Rev. at 974-75. Steinman is clearly correct that the appointment of lead counsel or committees of counsel makes consolidated pleadings more likely. Does this fact make you more or less sanguine about such appointments? See pp. 879-91, *supra*. More generally, should the damage to the adversarial process be considered in decisions to use consolidated pleadings?

We should not, of course, overstate the damage. The pleadings are drafted by a person charged with the task of representing a party's interests, and consolidated pleadings are sometimes filed with the consent of all interested persons. See Murphy, *supra*, 132 F.R.D. at 601-02 (recognizing that court order to consolidate pleadings is more problematic than consensual consolidation). So the victory of the inquisitorial process is not complete. Should the next step be taken, and actually permit the judge to draft the pleadings herself? If not, then how do we justify Judge Pollak's decision in *Katz* to "deem" that all defendants asserted cross-claims against each other. Does a judge who "deems" pleadings to be filed impermissibly cross the case management line into forbidden territory? See *Manual*, *supra*, §§ 21.32, 41.52 (suggesting that judge enter order "deeming" certain pleadings to be filed in cases later brought into litigation).

7. A third systemic cost derives from the "kitchen sink" nature of consolidated pleadings. As more claims are asserted against more parties, the pleadings no longer perform an issue-narrowing function; rather, they perform an issue-expanding function. This means greater costs to the litigants, and sometimes to the court, during pretrial.

8. Granting that consolidated pleadings create, in at least some cases, both private and systemic costs, are those costs significant enough to prevent the use of consolidated pleadings? Since it ignores or sidesteps the various costs of consolidated pleadings, *Katz* itself is unclear about what sort of calculus should be used when these costs are present. It clearly implies, however, that a balancing test that weighs the harm caused by consolidated pleadings against the benefits of the procedure should be used. See also *Wirebound Boxes*, 128 F.R.D. at 264. Can the systemic costs of consolidated pleadings be adequately weighed in a cost-benefit analysis? If not, how do we value these costs in relation to the efficiency gains of consolidated pleadings? Should the judge, who might have an incentive to value efficiency gains more highly, be entrusted with such a calculation?

9. What is the source of the judge's power to order consolidated pleadings? The cases do not usually focus on the question. Some of the authority may derive from F.R.Civ.P. 42(a), which authorizes a court to consolidate cases and to "make such orders concerning proceedings therein as may tend to avoid unnecessary costs or delay." What about cases not consolidated under Rule 42(a) (for instance, cases consolidated under 28 U.S.C. § 1407)? Does the judge have an inherent power to order consolidated pleadings? What are the limits on this power?

10. Whatever the source of the power, the decision to order consolidated pleadings is typically regarded as a matter within the trial judge's discretion. *Equity Funding*, 416 F. Supp. at 175.

11. Our study of present pleading rules should leave us feeling pessimistic about the ability of pleadings to narrow the legal and factual issues in a way that might overcome pretrial complexity. At the same time, we have seen that some of the pleading changes occasioned by complex litigation create significant friction with our adversarial and trans-substantive procedural aspirations. Whether there are other pretrial devices that can better accomplish the issue-narrowing function with less friction is the subject to which we now turn.

2. Narrowing the Issues after the Initial Pleadings

In this section of the chapter we examine a host of post-pleading techniques that can be used to narrow the factual and legal issues. As you shall see, some of these devices are specifically designed to accomplish issue-narrowing, while such narrowing is an indirect by-product of others. Some are party-initiated; others are judicially driven. Some derive clearly from the Federal Rules of Civil Procedure; others seem to emanate from an inherent reserve of judicial power. It is highly unlikely that all of the devices will be used in one case; but it is highly likely that some combination of them will be used during the litigation. We lay them out in the order in which they are usually encountered. Before pretrial commences, however, the lawyer must be aware about each device and about different ways to combine and time their use. As you consider these devices, ask whether any of them does an adequate job in the context of complex litigation, whether other devices not yet adopted might do better, and whether these devices grant too much (or too little) power to the managerial judge.

a. Clearing Away the Deadwood: Motions to Dismiss and Other Early Dispositive Devices

In complex cases, a complaint often invokes an immediate motion to dismiss. These motions can be based on a number of perceived flaws in the complaint: lack of subject matter jurisdiction, lack of personal jurisdiction, improper venue, insufficiency of process or of service of process, failure to state a claim on which relief can be granted, and failure to join indispensable parties. See F.R.Civ.P. 12(b). All but the next-to-last motion, called a Rule 12(b)(6) motion, deal with deficiencies unrelated to the complaint's merits, and therefore do not act as issue-narrowing devices (although they may be case-dispositive devices). The Rule 12(b)(6) motion may also be a case-dispositive device, but even when it cannot dispose of the entire case, it still has potential to trim the case to the claims worth disputing.

The issue-narrowing potential of a Rule 12(b)(6) motion hinges on the standard under which such motions are decided. According to *Conley v. Gibson*, 355 U.S. 41, 45-46 (1957), the threshold for granting a motion to dismiss is high: "[A] complaint should not be dismissed for failure to state a claim unless it appears beyond doubt that the plaintiff can prove no set of facts in support of his claim which would entitle him to relief." This seems a nearly impossible standard to meet, prompting Arthur Miller to observe: "It is a wonderful tool on paper, but have you ever looked at the batting average of the Rule 12(b)(6) motions? I think it was last effectively used during the McKinley Administration." Arthur R. Miller, The August 1983 Amendments to the Federal Rules of Civil Procedure: Promoting Effective Case Management and Lawyer Responsibility 7-8 (1984).

Stephen Calkins, SUMMARY JUDGMENT, MOTIONS TO DISMISS, AND OTHER EXAMPLES OF EQUILIBRATING TENDENCIES IN THE ANTITRUST SYSTEM

74 Geo. L.J. 1065, 1104-08, 1127-30, 1137 (1986)

IV. MOTIONS FOR SUMMARY JUDGMENT AND MOTIONS TO DISMISS . . .

The Georgetown Project data base [a database that tracked outcomes in 1,946 antitrust cases — ED.] provides a unique opportunity to explore the use of these pretrial motions [to dismiss and for summary judgment] in antitrust cases. . . . The data indicates that even before [1985] pretrial motions for summary judgment and motions to dismiss for failure to state a claim were highly successful and played an important role in antitrust litigation . . . . A consistent, if sometimes unspoken, recent theme is that disposal of antitrust cases prior to trial is encouraged. . . .

A. CONVENTIONAL WISDOM ON MOTIONS TO DISMISS

1. In General

The motion to dismiss is scorned by the leading civil procedure authorities. . . . Charles Wright cites a 1962 sampling for the Advisory Committee on Civil Rules that "suggests that [Rule 12(b)] motions are made in only about 5% of all cases, and that in fewer than 2% of all cases do such motions lead to a final termination of the action." The leading Supreme Court discussion of the standard for dismissing complaints continues to be *Conley v. Gibson* . . . .

However, whatever past experience indicates, it may not accurately forecast the future. . . . Inevitably, the concern over litigation excesses is changing thinking about motions to dismiss.

2. In Antitrust Cases

At one time antitrust complaints were held to a more stringent standard than other complaints, and motions to dismiss antitrust complaints enjoyed a warm reception by the courts. In part this was a response to the perceived greater complexity and burden of antitrust cases....

As all antitrust litigators know, this rigorous approach to antitrust complaints gradually died out, or at least courts asserted it did. The same pleading standards are said to apply in antitrust as in other cases. Indeed, support can be found for the proposition that more relaxed standards apply to pleadings in antitrust cases, because of the difficulty of proof....

Benjamin DuVal's investigation of Chicago class actions conflicts with this generally accepted wisdom. DuVal reviewed all antitrust treble damages actions filed in the Northern District of Illinois from July 1, 1966, through June 30, 1973, that were not subsequently transferred out of the district. DuVal found that 10.8% of all terminated nonclass action suits and 17.3% of all terminated class action suits were "involuntarily dismissed." DuVal cautioned that his numbers were small. He also speculated that the greater success of defendants in class suits may be attributable to the tenuous nature of many class actions where lawyers are lured by the prospect of rich rewards or hope to coerce settlement of nonmeritorious suits, or to judges' interest in dismissing class suits to avoid requiring the giving of notice....

C. FINDINGS FROM THE GEORGETOWN DATA SET

The Georgetown data set provides a rich, though flawed, collection of information on the use of summary motions in antitrust cases....

The data set shows that the most important motions are defendants' motions for summary judgment and motions to dismiss for failure to state a claim. Accordingly, unless otherwise specified the data presented herein are limited to these two defendants' motions....

1. Frequency

If the data set is a fair guide, prospects for a plaintiff seeking summary relief are bleak....

For defendants, the picture is much brighter. Pretrial "motions for dismissal" of one kind or another (including summary judgment) were granted or partially granted in 900 cases. This would be 46.2% of the data set's 1,946 cases, but obviously it involves double counting.

Motions to dismiss for failure to state a claim were granted in 142 cases (7.3%), and granted or partially granted in 179 cases (9.2%).... By comparison, fewer than 6% of all cases were tried. Success rates for motions to dismiss for failure to state a claim also were quite high. Motions were granted in 44.0% of cases in which they were filed and were granted or partially granted in 55.4%....

Given the traditionally expressed hostility toward summary relief in antitrust cases,... [t]he importance of motions to dismiss for failure to state a claim is especially remarkable. The frequency with which motions are filed and granted is much higher than the figures suggested for all cases by Charles Wright; however, the frequency with which they are granted is comparable to results in the Chicago antitrust class action study.... Since high quality information about current use of summary procedures outside of antitrust cases is lacking, one cannot be certain that these procedures are used more commonly in antitrust cases than elsewhere. But it seems unlikely that they are used less commonly.

2. Over Time

Defendants have been markedly more successful in winning summary relief in recent years. In both regressions, the parameter coefficients for date of last docket entry, the nearest approximation for decision date, were positive and statistically significant (1% confidence level for summary judgments, 5% confidence level for dismissals).

Dismissal for failure to state a claim was ordered at less-than-average rates before 1980 (although the differences were not statistically significant), except for cases with last docket entries in 1977 . . . . From 1980 to 1983, the last complete year surveyed, motions were filed in increasing numbers (in 25% of all cases ending in 1982-1983). Although success rates were somewhat inconsistent, motions were granted in increasing percentages of cases, rising to 11.2% of all cases ending in 1982 (significant at 5% confidence level) and 15.6% of all cases ending in 1983 . . . (significant at 1% confidence level). There is a sharp drop in all percentages for cases with last docket entries in 1984. This appears to be an aberration, but it was only partially caused by inclusion of pending cases. . . .

8. Jury Suits

Although commentators suggest that summary procedures are used more frequently in nonjury cases, antitrust litigation does not fit this pattern. Instead, summary procedures are used more frequently in jury cases than nonjury cases . . . . [M]otions to dismiss were granted more commonly but not significantly so. . . .

10. Appeals Over Time

An overwhelming majority of summary dispositions are affirmed if appealed. This is contrary to the conventional wisdom. Of 57 appeals of dismissals for failure to state a claim, only 9 were granted (15.8%) and 5 were partially granted (total: 24.6%).

Notes and Questions

1. Motions to dismiss and the pleading rules that we studied in the last section are related. The usual method by which allegedly insufficient pleadings are challenged is the Rule 12(b)(6) motion. Thus, a complaint must state enough facts both to give adequate notice of the claim and to demonstrate an entitlement to relief.

The Rule 12(b)(6) motion is also closely related to two other Rule 12 motions: the motion to strike, Rule 12(f), and the motion for judgment on the pleadings,

Rule 12(c). See generally 5A Charles A. Wright & Arthur R. Miller, Federal Practice and Procedure §§ 1367-72, 1380-83 (1990). The motions do have some differences, among them their timing. A motion to strike must be filed within twenty days of the pleading sought to be stricken; a motion for judgment on the pleadings must be made after the close of the pleadings "but within such time as not to delay the trial"; and a motion to dismiss may be prior to filing a responsive pleading, raised in the responsive pleading as a defense, or made at any time prior to or during trial. The Rule 56 motion for summary judgment can also be used at the outset, and has the advantage of a more favorable standard for a defendant. But summary judgment motions are rarely granted before some period of discovery. See pp. 1066-68, *infra*. Therefore, motions to dismiss, to strike, and for judgment on the pleadings are typically brought at the outset of the case; motions for summary judgment are brought later during pretrial.

2. Professor Calkins' study of antitrust cases looked at both motions to dismiss and motions for summary judgment. We will examine motions for summary judgment later in this section. See pp. 1047-71, *infra*. The basic distinction is that a motion to dismiss for failure to state a claim is decided on the basis of the plaintiffs' complaint; all well-pleaded factual allegations are deemed to be true, and the issue is whether, in the hypothetical world that the plaintiff has described, the plaintiff has a legal remedy against the defendant. A motion for summary judgment relies not on the allegations but on the facts as they have been disclosed through discovery or affidavit. Courts rarely grant motions for summary judgment until an adequate period for discovery has passed. Therefore, motions for summary judgment are not usually effective as an initial tool to narrow issues.

3. Conversely, motions to dismiss are horrible vehicles for narrowing issues when the complaint states a set of facts that the law recognizes as actionable — regardless of how false those "facts" might be in reality. The problem derives from the fact that the Rule 12(b)(6) motion can be used only to eliminate "claims" upon which no relief can be granted; the motion is not capable of narrowing other factual and legal issues that are not "claims." Therefore, as a theoretical matter, a motion to dismiss is useless as an issue-narrowing technique when: (1) A complaint states an adequate claim for relief, and the real dispute between the parties is whether the legal rule should be construed broadly to grant a lot of relief or narrowly to grant very little relief; (2) The real issue is whether the facts in the complaint actually occurred; or (3) The parties' approach to the litigation will vary a great deal depending on whether one possible set of facts or another is true.

As a practical matter, however, motions to dismiss are sometimes tactically useful. Lawyers view every contact as an opportunity to educate the judge about their clients' case. Some — indeed, a great many — motions to dismiss are primarily "educational" in nature; the lawyer does not expect to win the motion, but hopes to color the judge's perspective, to suggest indirectly to the judge how to manage the case, and to obtain significant concessions from the plaintiff's response to the motion. For instance, suppose the complaint alleges as true a fact that seems somewhat preposterous, but that is essential to the plaintiffs' recovery. Since the court will need to assume as true the preposterous fact, a motion to dismiss will likely lose. But the motion will have served its purpose: The judge now understands that the plaintiff can prevail only if this fact is true, and is entertaining doubts about whether it can be true. That may well influence the judge's decision about how to organize the pretrial process (perhaps requiring discovery on the preposterous issue first), as well as influence the judge about the proper outcome when the matter returns on a motion for summary judgment. Of course, the lawyer must balance these gains against the risks that the judge will be alienated by needing to decide a motion lacking merit, that the lawyer will be sanctioned, and that the other side will have an opportunity through its responsive brief to do some "counter-coloring." The lawyer also needs to consider his ethical obligations to the system of justice.

Should a motion to dismiss be constrained to its stated purpose? Can you think of any practical way to do so? If we do constrain the motion to dismiss, should we design other rules to (1) eliminate factual issues and (2) provide authoritative rulings on disputed legal issues of importance to the litigation? If such rules are developed, won't advocates use them, just as they have used motions to dismiss, for their own tactical purposes? (Put differently, do the problems with the effectiveness of motion to dismiss lie with the nature of the rule, with the adversary system, or with both?)

4. Calkins' description of the academic attitude toward the motion to dismiss is accurate: It is regarded as a motion with very few teeth. Whether you think that it should have even fewer teeth (indeed, perhaps even be eliminated) or should have more teeth depends, at least to some extent, on whether you accept the modern procedural assumption that full factual development and resolution of cases on the merits is good. But a more vigorous use of motions to dismiss also threatens a number of other valued assumptions: that jury trials have an inherent political value, that open and sustained discussion in public law litigation (a category into which most complex cases fall) is important, and that we should try to do justice between the parties. On the other hand, these assumptions have their own significant costs, nowhere more so than in complex litigation.

Does the last paragraph suggest to you that we should have two different attitudes about motions to dismiss, one for routine litigation and one for complex litigation? Does the Georgetown data, as interpreted by Professor Calkins, demonstrate that different attitudes already exist? Assuming that such attitudes either do or should exist, how would they be translated into the language of a rule? How about this rule: "In complex litigation, dismissal of a claim is required unless the likelihood of recovery and the importance of the right sought to be vindicated exceed the probable expenditure to the parties and court in the prosecution of the claim." Do you like the idea of an economically-oriented dismissal rule that overtly balances a party's right to individual adjudication against its costliness to the system? Do you like the idea of having separate rules in routine and complex cases? If so, what definition are we to use of "complex litigation"? Do you like the idea of the judge being the person who makes the decisions about whether a case is "complex" and whether the likely success of a claim outweighs its costs? How is the judge to make these decisions without a great deal of information about the claim that she does not possess at the outset of the litigation?

5. Aside from being limited to "claims" and having a high threshold, a motion to dismiss suffers from a third "flaw" as an issue-narrowing device: It relies on the initiative of the parties. This "flaw" is consistent with adversarial theory, in which the parties make the tactical and strategic choices about the conduct of the litigation. Throughout this book, however, we have seen judges in complex cases assume some of the powers reserved to the lawyers under adversarial theory. Must a judge managing a complex case wait for a party to

decide, for whatever tactical reasons, that now is the time to bring such a motion? Or should a judge have the inquisitorial power to eliminate certain issues at the outset when it is necessary to the case's effective management? Compare F.R.Civ.P. 12(f) (authorizing judge to strike "insufficient defenses" and "redundant, immaterial, impertinent, or scandalous matter" on "the court's own initiative") with F.R.Civ.P. 12(b)(6) or Rule 12(c) (no comparable "initiative" mentioned).

What would be the source of this power? Perhaps the answer is F.R.Civ.P. 16(c)(1). Rule 16, which we shall study in more detail shortly, is the primary rule authorizing case management. A central feature of case management is the pretrial conference between the judge and the lawyers. According to F.R.Civ.P. 16(c): "At any conference under this rule consideration may be given to, and the court may take appropriate action, with respect to" sixteen case management matters. The first such matter, described in Rule 16(c)(1), is "the formulation and simplification of the issues, including the elimination of frivolous claims or defenses." Therefore, Rule 16(c)(1) seems to grant authority to a judge to eliminate "frivolous" claims or defenses without awaiting a motion from a party.

The real issue is how "frivolous" the claim or defense must be. Is the standard the same as the standard for a motion to dismiss (*i.e.*, the pleading fails to demonstrate any set of facts that might entitle the pleader to relief)? Should it be set even higher (if that is possible), on the theory that the judge ought not become an advocate in the case and can therefore dismiss only claims or defenses that are clearly and utterly ridiculous? Or should we set the standard lower, giving judges the power to eliminate marginal claims or defenses which are not so frivolous that relief is impossible, but whose likelihood and magnitude of success are outweighed by their costliness to the litigation? Should we set the standard lower only for complex cases in which judicial issue narrowing is needed to overcome lawyer dysfunction?

6. Thus far, these questions have received surprisingly scant exploration. The 1983 Advisory Committee Notes on Rule 16 suggest a fairly liberal attitude toward the exercise of the (c)(1) powers:

> The references in Rule 16(c)(1) to "formulation" is intended to clarify and confirm the court's power to identify the litigable issues. It has been added in the hope of promoting efficiency and conserving judicial resources by identifying the real issues prior to trial, thereby saving time and expense for everyone. . . . The notion is emphasized by expressly authorizing the elimination of frivolous claims or defenses at a pretrial conference. There is no reason to require that this await a formal motion for summary judgment. Nor is there any reason for the court to wait for the parties to initiate the process called for in Rule 16(c)(1).

If the committee notes are an accurate interpretation, the standard for a Rule 16(c)(1) dismissal appears to be equivalent to that of summary judgment. We shall study the summary judgment standard — as well as its meaning in complex litigation — at pp. 1047-71, *infra*. For now, it is enough to know that the summary judgment standard permits dismissal of a claim when the evidence demonstrates the lack of a genuine issue as to any material fact.

The problem that we are addressing, however, is whether we can use Rule 16(c)(1) to dismiss a claim or defense at the outset of the litigation, prior to the costly development of evidence. Can a judge enter a Rule 16(c)(1) dismissal prior to discovery when the asserted claim or defense has no *legal* merit? See United

States v. Kramer, 953 F. Supp. 592 (D.N.J. 1997) (Rule 16(c)(1) can be used by court to rule on pure issue of law when ruling will help shape subsequent pretrial proceedings). Can a judge use Rule 16(c)(1) to accomplish dismissals of *factually* suspicious claims or defenses at the outset of the litigation? In virtually all of the (relatively few) reported decisions involving Rule 16(c)(1) dismissals, the dismissal occurred after some period of discovery. See Berkovitz v. Home Box Office, Inc., 89 F.3d 24 (1st Cir. 1996) (judge can enter Rule 16(c)(1) dismissal of claim lacking factual support only after ensuring both adequate opportunity for discovery and adequate opportunity to present relevant evidence to court). Therefore, Rule 16(c)(1) is sometimes used to narrow legal issues at the outset of the litigation; it is not used to narrow factual issues at the outset.

7. Although "early-in-the-litigation" dismissal devices can sometimes dispose of entire claims, they often do not. Moreover, neither pleadings nor "out-of-the-box" dismissals achieve any significant narrowing of factual issues. Necessarily, therefore, the parties and the judge must use other pretrial devices to perform the claim-narrowing and issue-narrowing tasks. It is to these devices that we must now turn.

b. Common Case Management Techniques: Herein of the Case Management Order

As we saw in Chapter Eight, the idea of the American judge "managing" a case originally developed in response to complex cases. Since the 1951 Prettyman Report, from which the concept of case management derives, it has been understood that a central feature of case management is a series of pretrial conferences between judge and lawyers. Report of the Judicial Conference of the United States on Procedures in Anti-Trust and Other Protracted Cases (1951), reprinted in 13 F.R.D. 62 (1952); see also *Handbook of Recommended Procedures for the Trial of Protracted Cases*, 25 F.R.D. 351 (1960). The idea of pretrial conferences is today ingrained in the litigator's psyche, and institutionalized in F.R.Civ.P. 16. Yet the pretrial conference remains a recent phenomenon — and one that does not co-exist easily with a classical system of adversarial justice.

Often there are many pretrial conferences during the course of a complex case. Typically, the first few conferences are devoted to the issue of organizing the pretrial proceedings, in terms of both the issue-narrowing devices that will be employed and the discovery plan that will be implemented. The outcome of the conference(s) is usually an order or series of orders that operate collectively as a case management plan for the case.

MANUAL FOR COMPLEX LITIGATION, THIRD

41-43 (1995)

The primary objective of the conference is to develop (subject to later revision and refinement) a plan for the "just, speedy, and inexpensive determination" of the litigation. The plan should include procedures for identifying and resolving disputed issues of law, identifying and narrowing disputed issues of fact, carrying out disclosure and conducting discovery in an efficient and economical manner, and preparing for trial if the case is not resolved by settlement or summary judgment.... Following is a checklist of topics relevant to the development of case-management plans ....:

- identification and narrowing of issues of fact and law...;
- deadlines and limits on joinder of parties and amended or additional pleadings...;
- coordination with related litigation...;
- severance of issues for trial...;
- consolidation of trials...;
- the possibility of referring some matters to magistrate judges, special masters, or other judges...;
- appointment of lead/liaison/trial counsel and special committees...;
- plans for prompt determination of class action questions...;
- management of disclosure and discovery, including such matters as:
  — preservation of evidence...;
  — use of document depositories and computerized storage...;
  — informal discovery and other cost-reduction measures...;
  — protective orders and procedures for handling claims of confidentiality and privilege...;
  — sequencing and limitations, including specific scheduling and deadlines...;
- schedules and deadlines for completion of various pretrial phases of the case and the setting of a tentative or firm trial date...;
- consideration of any unresolved issues of recusal or disqualification ...;
- any other special procedures that may facilitate management of the litigation.

Rule 16(e) requires that following the conference the court enter an order reciting any action taken. The order should address the various matters on the agenda and other matters conducive to the effective management of the litigation. It should memorialize all rulings, agreements, or other actions taken, and it should set a date for the next conference or other event in the litigation.

Notes and Questions

1. Samples of a standard case management order and of specialized orders on matters sch as appointment of counsel and masters can be found in the *Manual, Third* §§ 41.30-.39. According to Rule 16(e), such orders "shall control the subsequent course of the action unless modified by a subsequent order."

2. In many ways the list of possible conference topics mentioned in the *Manual, Third* mirrors the lists of topics found in Rules 16(b) and (c). Rule 16(b) requires judges to enter a scheduling order that fixes dates for joining parties, filing motions, and completing discovery, and authorizes a court to include in the order "any other matters appropriate in the circumstances of the case." Rule 16(c) contains a 16-item laundry list of possible matters to which "consideration may be given" and on which "the court may take appropriate action" at a pretrial conference. Among these matters are the formulation, simplification, and elimination of issues; the amendment of pleadings; the obtaining of admissions of fact; limitations on cumulative proof; the "appropriateness and timing of summary adjudication under Rule 56"; references to magistrate judges or masters; and establishing a structure for trial in which issues or claims might be tried separately. Of particular import is Rule 16(c)(12), which authorizes the court to consider and act with respect to "the need for adopting special procedures for managing potentially difficult or protracted actions that may involve complex issues, multiple parties, difficult legal questions, or unusual proof problems." Does Rule 16(c)(12) act as a *carte blanche* to judges to use *any* pretrial procedure that leads to a more efficient resolution? If not, what are its limits? What procedural powers, if any, does Rule 16(c)(12) provide to a judge that the more specific powers listed in Rules 16(b) and (c) do not already provide?

3. A comparable laundry list of case management practices is contained in the Civil Justice Reform Act of 1990 ("CJRA"), which Congress passed in order to combat the twin problems of cost and delay in civil litigation. 28 U.S.C. §§ 471 et seq. The CJRA required each federal district court to develop a plan to reduce cost and delay in the district. Although not requiring that any of these principles or techniques be adopted as a part of the plan, the CJRA directed district courts to consider the possibility of implementing six specific case management principles and six specific case management techniques. Id. at §§ 473(a)-(b). Among the principles and techniques are: differential case management (see Note 4, *infra*); early and ongoing judicial intervention in the pretrial process (particularly, the establishment of limitations on the time for and amount of discovery); the encouragement of cost-effective means of discovery; and "careful and deliberate monitoring through a discovery-case management conference or series of conferences" in complex cases. As aspects of this "monitoring" in complex cases, courts were required to consider the possibility of settlement; the "identifi[cation] and formulat[ion of] the principal issues in contention"; "the staged resolution or bifurcation of issues for trial"; a discovery plan with "presumptive time limits"; other discovery procedures that limit the volume of discovery and phase discovery into stages; and deadlines for filing all motions. Id. at § 473(a)(3).

Therefore, to the extent that such principles and techniques have found their way into the cost and delay reduction plans of individual district courts, the CJRA provides another impetus for, and another source of authority for the adoption of, case management principles in complex litigation.

4. Both Rule 16(c)(12) and the CJRA assume that it is possible to distinguish between complex and non-complex cases, yet neither defines the term "complex." If special case management principles and techniques (or at least special applications of those principles and techniques) are necessary for complex cases, shouldn't the establishment of a definition be a critical first step? Some early authorities understood this fact, and consequently provided easy-to-apply definitions of complex cases. See pp. 83-84, *supra*. The modern idea of

differential case management likewise creates separate management "tracks" — and therefore different levels of case management — for cases that meet various criteria. One of the "tracks" is usually a "complex case" track, in which complexity is determined by judicial designation, by attorney designation, or by readily discernible, objective criteria such as the presence of a class action, a certain number of plaintiffs or defendants, or certain legal theories (such as products liability, securities fraud, or RICO). See Maureen Solomon & Holly Bakke, *Case Differentiation: An Approach to Individualized Case Management*, 73 Judicature 17 (June/July 1989); James S. Kakalik et al., An Evaluation of Judicial Case Management under the Civil Justice Reform Act 47-50 (1996) (reporting generally unsuccessful results with differential case management).

Do you agree that objective criteria can adequately distinguish complex from non-complex cases? Is it better to leave the decision about what is "complex" to the discretion of the trial judge, as Rule 16 and the CJRA seem to contemplate? Should the lawyers make the decision? Is the definition of "pretrial complexity" that we proposed (see p. 876, *supra*) a better alternative?

5 Whatever the source of the court's case management power, the number of case management tools that a court can employ is great. We have already explored several of these tools. In the remainder of this Chapter we examine many of the other tools that can narrow issues and streamline discovery. As we examine them, ask yourself whether these case management tools are adequate to meet the demands of complex litigation and whether other case management devices make more sense. Also keep in mind that various management techniques can often be used together, and ask yourself whether certain combinations of techniques depart too radically from the adversarial method. Finally, keep in mind that the context in which the application of these devices will often be debated is the case management conference, and the vehicle through which they will be given life is the case management order.

i. Establishing Early, Firm Deadlines

One method of reducing the lawyer's problems in collecting and distilling information into legally and factually relevant issues is to limit the amount of time within which information can be obtained. Time limits are an indirect means of narrowing issues; they force the parties to concentrate their attention on the issues and information that are critical to their case. But time limits also threaten to preclude the development of relevant issues, and may work to the disadvantage of parties who either are not well-enough financed to afford a pretrial blitzkrieg or have less access to information.

IN RE FINE PAPER ANTITRUST LITIGATION

685 F.2d 810 (3d Cir. 1982), cert. denied, 459 U.S. 1156 (1983)

■ ALDISERT, Circuit Judge. These consolidated appeals present several procedural issues arising from a complex antitrust proceeding. Ten states, plaintiffs below, appeal from judgments entered on a jury verdict in their actions for treble damages alleging a nationwide price-fixing conspiracy in violation of § 1 of the Sherman Act. The defendants did not offer any evidence at trial, but rested at the close of the plaintiffs' case; the jury then found in favor of all defendants. On appeal, the plaintiffs assert numerous procedural errors, generally contending that the district court unduly limited their opportunity to develop and present their case. We are not persuaded that the district court either abused its discretion or erred in its selection, interpretation, or application of the controlling legal precepts, and therefore we will affirm its judgment in all respects.

I.

This case has a complicated procedural history, owing in part to the number of parties. Named as defendants were manufacturers and merchants of "fine paper," which the states buy in large quantity. Some of the merchants are owned by the mills themselves and some are independent. Beginning in 1977, following the initiation of ultimately inconclusive investigations by the Federal Trade Commission and the United States Department of Justice, several states and private plaintiffs brought a total of 37 individual actions alleging that the mills and merchants had participated in a nationwide price-fixing conspiracy. Pursuant to 28 U.S.C. § 1407, the Judicial Panel on Multidistrict Litigation transferred the cases to the Eastern District of Pennsylvania for coordinated pre-trial proceedings, assigned to Judge Joseph L. McGlynn. . . .

The district court divided the plaintiffs into three groups: a class of private plaintiffs, "minority states," and "majority states." The minority states alleged only a horizontal conspiracy among the mill defendants; the majority states, the present appellants, alleged both a horizontal conspiracy among the mill defendants and vertical conspiracies involving mills and merchants. In addition to certifying a class of private plaintiffs, the court certified each minority state and its respective government entities as a separate plaintiff class, but it refused to do the same for the majority states because the added factor of vertical conspiracy made those actions less susceptible to generalized proof. . . .

Following a pre-trial conference on March 7, 1979, the court established discovery deadlines and set a tentative trial date of January 2, 1980. The next few months were occupied with discovery and related motions. On September 27, 1979, plaintiffs asked for an extension of the trial date because of the number of depositions they wished to take, but the court expressed reluctance to deviate from its schedule. At a conference on December 4, 1979, the court rejected plaintiffs' proposal that trial not begin until October 1980, but it rescheduled the trial for the "certified plaintiffs" (the private plaintiffs and the minority states) to September 22, 1980, barring a "nuclear holocaust." The court did not fix a trial date for the majority states, but it established July 3, 1980, as the discovery cut-off date in all of the cases.

On January 15, 1980, the court decided it could resolve the litigation more efficiently if trial on the majority states' claims were conducted in advance of the certified plaintiffs' trial. It then set for the majority states a trial date of June 16, 1980, and a revised discovery deadline of May 30. Appellants vehemently protested that they still had 300,000 documents to review and more than 100 depositions to take, and that the court's revised schedule left inadequate time for discovery and trial preparation. The court denied their motion for reconsideration. . . .

In early June 1980, in contemplation of a June 16 trial, the majority states submitted a 200-page pre-trial memorandum. Defendants moved to dismiss, contending that the memorandum was unacceptable because it presented only conclusory allegations rather than the specific enumeration of facts the court had required. The court did not grant defendants' motion, but it ordered plaintiffs to prepare a memorandum by July 25 "which outlines the case chapter and verse as to each defendant." Plaintiffs moved for a continuance, again complaining that they had not been allowed enough time for discovery. The court stated that the majority states' actions would be tried with or after the certified plaintiffs' trial. It did not modify the discovery schedule, but it did allow some additional depositions.

The certified plaintiffs settled their cases shortly before trial. On September 25, 1980, the court announced that the majority states' trial would begin on October 6, 1980 — nine months after the tentative trial date and four months after the trial date set on January 15, 1980. Although they had been on notice since January 17, 1980, that the court wished to try the cases itself, the plaintiffs objected that they would have insufficient time to set up a Philadelphia office and to transport their files across the country. The court considered these arguments but concluded that October 6 was a realistic date.

On September 29, 1980, over plaintiffs' objections, the district court, pursuant to 28 U.S.C. § 1404(a), formally transferred all of the majority states' cases to the Eastern District of Pennsylvania for trial, which began on October 6, 1980. Following plaintiffs' four-week presentation, which consisted primarily of reading depositions to the jury, the defendants rested without offering any evidence. The jury returned a verdict in favor of all defendants on December 2, 1980. . . .

III.

Appellants' primary argument is that they were afforded too little time for discovery and trial preparation. Appellants have a heavy burden to bear, however, as matters of docket control and conduct of discovery are committed to the sound discretion of the district court. . . . We will not interfere with a trial court's control of its docket "except upon the clearest showing that the procedures have resulted in actual and substantial prejudice to the complaining litigant." Eli Lilly & Co. v. Generix Drug Sales, Inc., 460 F.2d 1096, 1105 (5th Cir. 1972). Similarly, we will not upset a district court's conduct of discovery procedures absent "a demonstration that the court's action made it impossible to obtain crucial evidence, and implicit in such a showing is proof that more diligent discovery was impossible." Id.

We find no abuse of discretion by the district judge in his scheduling of discovery or of the trial. After considering all of appellants' contentions and examining the 16-volume appendix that they have supplied to this court, we are not persuaded that the pre-trial rulings of the district court prejudiced the preparation or presentation of their case. The trial of their antitrust claims followed fifteen months of discovery, including approximately 270 depositions and production of nearly two million documents. The trial commenced four months after conclusion of discovery and one month after the date appellants had earlier set as the date on which they would be ready for trial.

When discovery ended on May 30, 1980, the majority states sought a continuance and further discovery. The court allowed them to depose some additional witnesses and, relying on their representation that they would need until September 1 to prepare for trial, advised them that their trial would commence with or after the certified plaintiffs' trial, scheduled for September 22, 1980.

Upon settlement of the certified plaintiffs' cases, the court on September 25, 1980, notified appellants that their trial would commence on October 6. Appellants again requested a continuance, but the district court responded:

> Every time I set a deadline I get the same problem arising from the Majority States. They're never ready. They can't go to trial, the case is going to be prejudiced. The same thing happened in June, the same thing when I asked you to file answers to these interrogatories and you didn't have the time. The same thing happened when I asked you to file your pretrial memorandum. You said you didn't have the time, you needed more time, you wanted to supplement. I gave you time to supplement. It hasn't even been supplemented yet, except for a couple of states. It's just constant.

... Having reviewed the record, we consider the district court's observations to be accurate. Moreover, we do not share the view expressed by appellants' counsel at oral argument that antitrust cases involving price fixing are generically complex. It has been our experience that the legendary complexity is due largely to the parties' inability or unwillingness to simplify their presentations. Our independent review of the record persuades us that the trial court in this case was firm but fair. It deferred the trial date from January 2 to June 16 to October 6, 1980 and it accommodated appellants' requests whenever feasible. The appellants have not shown that "the court's action made it impossible to obtain crucial evidence"; nor have they made a clear showing that the court's conduct "resulted in actual and substantial prejudice." We find no abuse of discretion.

James S. Kakalik et al., AN EVALUATION OF JUDICIAL CASE MANAGEMENT UNDER THE CIVIL JUSTICE REFORM ACT

1, 52, 54-55, 63-66, 91-92 (1996)

RAND's Institute for Civil Justice evaluated the pilot program of the Civil Justice Reform Act of 1990 (CJRA), at the request of the Judicial

Conference of the United States. The general objective of the evaluation was to identify effective approaches to cost and delay reduction for civil cases in federal district courts. The specific objective was to evaluate the implementation and effects of the CJRA case management principles and techniques in ten pilot and ten comparison districts.

This document describes the evaluation of the effects of the CJRA case management principles and techniques on time to case disposition, litigation costs, and participants' satisfaction and views of fairness in pilot and comparison districts. . . .

[Among the case management principles and techniques evaluated were early case management — which included the setting of a trial date early in the pretrial process — and the setting of a short discovery schedule.]

Early management is statistically significant in predicting shorter time to disposition. For cases that survive at least nine months, the estimated reduction in the median time to disposition is 1.5 to two months if any judicial case management took place within six months of filing.

We explored the component procedures of early management separately. Setting a schedule for trial early was the most important component of early management in terms of significantly reducing time to disposition. Cases in which a trial was set before day 180 had statistically significant shorter times to disposition. We estimate that if a trial schedule is set as part of the early management package, the median time to disposition is reduced by an *additional* 1.5 to two months. . . .

Early management is associated with reduced time to disposition, but at a cost. Early management is significantly related to increased lawyer work hours per litigant. For cases that survive at least nine months and receive early management, we estimate approximately a 20-hour increase in the lawyer work hours. . . .

The costs to litigants were also higher in dollar terms, and in litigant hours spent, when cases were managed early . . . .

We again explored the component procedures of early management separately. If a trial schedule is set as part of the early management package, lawyer work hours per case fall by seven, but this is not a statistically significant difference. There are also no statistically significant differences for any of the other components of early management. . . .

In our explorations of attorney satisfaction, we found that early management and setting a trial schedule early in the case — the early management policies that had the greatest effects on time to disposition and lawyer work hours — had no statistically significant effect on lawyer satisfaction. Litigant data showed mixed results for satisfaction with early management, higher in the pre-CJRA sample and lower in the post-CJRA sample . . . .

We found no consistent statistically significant effects of early judicial management on attorney views of fairness. A very high percentage of attorneys (93 percent in 1992-93 and 91 percent in 1991) report that case management was fair. . . .

[The report then turned to the use of tools to manage discovery, including the entry of discovery cutoff dates.] A district's median days to discovery cutoff is a statistically significant predictor of time to disposition. Analysis of our data predicts that the longer the time from the setting of a discovery schedule to the discovery cutoff date, the longer the time to disposition of the case. We estimate approximately a 1.5-month reduction in the median time to disposition for cases that survive at least nine months if the district median for discovery cutoff is reduced from 180 days to 120 days....

Of all the policy variables we investigated as possible predictors of reduced lawyer work hours, only judicial management of discovery seemed to produce the desired effect. Reported lawyer work hours significantly decrease as the district median time to discovery gets shorter, using the 1992-93 data. We estimate approximately a 17-hour reduction in lawyer work hours for cases that survive at least nine months if the district median is reduced from 180 days to 120 days. When we use the 1991 data, we also see a reduction in lawyer work hours, but the reduction is not significant. The data on costs to litigants in dollar terms, and in litigant hours spent, appear consistent with the data on lawyer work hours....

We find no statistically significant relationship between the district median days to discovery cutoff and attorney satisfaction. Litigant data also show little difference in satisfaction between shorter and longer discovery cutoff....

We find no statistically significant effects between early disclosure and reported views on the fairness of case management....

These findings suggest a package of case management policies with the potential to reduce time to disposition without changing costs, attorney satisfaction, and views of fairness. The package includes discovery control, the only CJRA case management practice that seemed to be effective in reducing costs.

If early case management and early setting of the trial schedule are combined with shortened discovery cutoff, the increase in lawyer work hours predicted by early management can be offset by the decrease in lawyer work hours predicted by judicial control of discovery. We estimate that under these circumstances, litigants in general civil cases that do not close within the first nine months would pay no significant cost penalty for a reduced time to disposition of approximately four to five months — about 30 percent of their current median time to disposition. And as we have seen, none of these policies has any significant effect on lawyers' satisfaction or perception of fairness.

Our analysis suggests that the following approach to early management of general civil litigation cases should be considered....

- For cases that have issue joined [*i.e.*, the pleading stage has closed], wait a short time after the joinder date, perhaps a month, to see if the case terminates and then begin judicial case management.

- Include setting of a firm trial date as part of the early case management package, and adhere to that date as much as possible.

- Include setting of a reasonably short discovery cutoff time tailored to the case as part of the early management package.

Notes and Questions

1. Rules 16(b)(3) and (b)(5) give the courts authority to set timetables for completing discovery and setting the date of trial. It is difficult to argue against the idea that the judge should possess both powers. Indeed, it may be difficult to see why setting timetables is regarded as a case management strategy tool. The answer lies in the linchpin of these powers: the establishment of an *early, firm* trial date. Both adjectives are important. First, the trial is set to occur as early as soon as reasonably possible. This necessarily means that the period for discovery will be limited; discovery cannot continue past the end of trial. Second, the trial date is firm; knowing that they cannot receive extensions of the trial date, the parties will focus on completing discovery and readying the issues for trial within the allotted time. If a judge establishes an early trial date that is not firm, or a firm trial date that is not early, the focus of the parties on the case at hand dissipates.

The early discovery cutoff follows from the idea of the early, firm trial date. Certainly discovery can — and often does — occur up to and even during trial. But in order to narrow the factual and legal issues for trial, it is necessary to call a halt to critical discovery at some point before trial. If the trial is set for an early date, then the discovery cutoff will need to occur even earlier. An early cutoff further shrinks the opportunity for the development of evidence and therefore forces the parties to come to the heart of the case quickly.

2. Indirectly, therefore, setting an early trial date and setting discovery cutoffs in advance of that date do have the potential to narrow issues and shorten discovery. Indeed, both techniques have developed considerable support in the literature. See, *e.g.*, Manual for Complex Litigation, Third §§ 20.13, 21.422, 21.61 (1995); Brookings Institution, Justice for All (1989); Report to the President and Attorney General of the National Commission for the Review of Antitrust Laws and Procedures 28-30 (1979), reprinted in 80 F.R.D. 509, 534-36 (1979). Although aggrieved parties sometimes complain, the judicial power to establish time limits also passes without serious question in the cases. See, *e.g.*, In re Air Crash Disaster, 86 F.3d 498, 517-18 (6th Cir. 1996) (court appropriately adhered to discovery cutoff when failure to do so would have forced change in established trial date); Whittaker Corp. v. Execuair Corp., 736 F.2d 1341, 1347 (9th Cir. 1984); Stewart v. Walbridge, Aldinger Co., 162 F.R.D. 29 (D. Del. 1995). The recent RAND findings that an early trial date reduces median disposition times (and perhaps attorney hours as well) and that a discovery cutoff reduces attorney hours make the combination seem almost irresistible.

3. So is there a credible case against early, firm trial dates or discovery cutoffs? Judge Schwarzer raises a number of difficulties:

> [T]ime limits restrict the ability of the parties to obtain information, to prepare for trial and to present their case at trial. Unless carefully fashioned, they may handicap one side more than the other. They should also be set and administered with due regard for each party's right to a fair trial.

William W Schwarzer, Managing Antitrust and Other Complex Litigation § 4-1 (1982). Other concerns also exist. First, early trial dates and discovery cutoffs grate against the spirit that animated the Federal Rules of Civil Procedure — a spirit reflected in Roscoe Pound's statement that "[e]xcept as they exist for the saving of public time and maintenance of the dignity of tribunals, . . . rules of procedure should exist only to secure to all parties a fair opportunity to meet the case against them and a full opportunity to present their own case." See p. 54, *supra*. There is something of the ancient writ system in these cutoffs, with the straitjacket of the writ having been replaced by the straitjacket of time. The consequence of failing to fit within the straitjacket is in both cases the same: the sacrifice of possibly valid legal claims. For instance, in Harleysville Mutual Insurance Co. v. Sussex County, Delaware, 831 F. Supp. 1111 (D. Del. 1993), aff'd, 46 F.3d 1116 (3d Cir. 1994) (Table), the district court refused to certify a critical question of state law to the Delaware Supreme Court for a definitive ruling; the court's only stated reason for denying certification was that it would take too long, and thereby thwart the court's Civil Justice Reform Act plan to try all cases within 18 months.

Next is the concern that judges, and not the adversaries, are determining the flow and cost of the litigation. In the "old" days preceding the 1983 amendments, the lawyers often worked up a case until they were ready for trial. Continuances of the court-established trial date (assuming that the court established a date at all) were nearly automatic, as long as all parties consented; and judges became involved only when the lawyers disagreed about whether or for how long a continuance should be granted. Today the lawyers suggest to the judge what the discovery cutoff and trial dates should be; the judge makes the decision, often with little information about the particulars of the case. If the RAND report is correct, the earlier that such a decision is made, the better; but presumably the judge has the poorest information about the case in its early stages.

Finally, discovery cutoffs and early trial dates may not treat all cases fairly. For instance, an across-the-board discovery cutoff of six months will give the parties plenty of time in a simple slip-and-fall case, but will make impossible the full development of issues in a massive antitrust case. Once a judge tries to tailor the cutoff to the type of case, however, other problems arise. In order for a cutoff to be a useful means of forcing the parties to cut to the quick, it must provide the parties with adequate time to address central issues but inadequate time to fully develop all issues. How much inadequacy should a judge tolerate in a slip-and-fall? How much inadequacy should a judge tolerate in an antitrust case? Do you like the idea of giving the judge the case-by-case power to decide the amount of time that is adequate? How can the judge make the judgment about which issues are central, and which are not? Should the judge possess the power to order cutoffs in routine cases but not complex ones, or vice versa?

4. Therefore, the economy and efficiency of cost and delay reduction can be costly to other procedural values. Should we limit the use of discovery cutoffs and early, firm trial dates to cases in which rational adjudication is threatened if the adversaries are left to develop the factual issues fully (*i.e.*, "complex" cases, as we define that term)? For instance, if the reason for pretrial complexity is a party's lack of adequate financing, the cost savings of cutoffs and trial dates might justify their use. Likewise, when complexity arises from the possible loss of critical evidence due to the passage of time, delay-reducing early trial dates are defensible. On the other hand, when complexity is not due to financial or

time-sensitive factors, can our general preference for cheaper and faster justice justify the harm that cutoffs and early, firm trial dates cause to our adversarial and trans-substantive procedural aspirations and to the "equitable" spirit of the Federal Rules? If cutoffs and trial dates in fact cause this harm, can we ever justify their use in routine litigation?

5. Another way to consider the problem is to look at *Fine Paper*, which is a leading case enforcing discovery and trial deadlines. Clearly the plaintiffs' lawyers in the case had not yet completed discovery and had not been able to organize the issues adequately for trial. Let us assume that the reason for the lawyers' inability lay beyond their control, and that the reason was neither financial nor time-sensitive (perhaps, for instance, the amount of evidence was simply too voluminous or technical). In this circumstance, discovery cutoffs and early, firm trial dates do not act as an aid to overcome the lawyers' inability to perform their adversarial task; they actually help to cause it by reducing even further the available time to define and develop the issues.

This does not mean that a judge should use cutoffs or early trial dates only to overcome lawyer dysfunction. If the lawyers are incompetent or unwilling to perform their pretrial tasks in a timely and cost-effective way, then cutoffs and early, firm trial dates trim needless fat from the pretrial process. If this trimming can be done without cutting into the lawyers' ability to fulfill their adversarial roles, then there is a lot to like about cutoffs and early, firm trial dates. But what happens when the judge, in applying the whip, sets the discovery cutoff or trial date so early that it now becomes impossible even for competent counsel to perform the pretrial and trial tasks adequately? Should a judge ever be able to apply a case management technique that *creates* lawyer dysfunction simply in order to achieve other goals? Is this what occurred in *Fine Paper*?

6. Therefore, an important lesson of *Fine Paper* may well be that case management techniques do not necessarily eliminate the lawyer dysfunction that lies at the heart of complexity; they may in some circumstances cause complexity. An equally important lesson is that discovery cutoffs and trial dates do little, in and of themselves, to cure complexity unrelated to excessive cost or delay. The judge does not assume the lawyers' adversarial tasks; she simply gives the lawyers less time within which to perform these tasks. When cutoffs and trial dates are used in cases that are complex for non-financial or non-time-sensitive reasons, must the judge also use positive case management techniques that will aid the lawyers in the discharge of their pretrial tasks? In other words, do such deadlines demand even greater judicial involvement at other points in the pretrial process?

7. The RAND study did not distinguish between complex cases and routine ones. Would you expect that discovery cutoffs would have greater cost savings in complex cases? Would early, firm trial dates lead to the same (or greater) savings in complex cases? If greater time or cost savings existed, would you favor these devices despite their potential to cause lawyer dysfunction?

8. The RAND study also made no direct effort to measure the value of discovery cutoffs and early, firm trial dates as issue-narrowing devices, either in complex cases or in routine ones. To the extent that a reduced time to disposition is correlated with issue-narrowing — and that correlation is far from clear — it would appear that an early, firm trial date and a discovery cutoff can help to narrow issues. Should the RAND study have focused explicitly on the issue-narrowing and dysfunction-reducing aspects of early trial dates and

discovery cutoffs? Probably not, since the study was done in response to the CJRA, which was focused on the cost- and delay-reducing potential of case management. But the study does show that what you test for determines the conclusions you reach. Based on your reading so far, are you convinced that the reduction of cost and delay are the goals on which we should concentrate in complex litigation?

9. Judges usually order deadlines for the completion of tasks other than discovery and the start of trial. Among the more common deadlines incorporated into case management orders are dates for filing amended pleadings, dates for the joinder of additional parties, dates for the filing of various motions, and dates for the filing of other pretrial submissions such as proposed pretrial orders. See F.R.Civ.P. 16(b). Some dates are keyed to other dates; typically, for instance, the due date for a motion for summary judgment or for a proposed final pretrial order is a certain number of days after the date for close of discovery.

10. What is the consequence for failing to comply with one of these deadlines? The consequence for failing to show up for trial is obvious, and too painful to consider. What if a lawyer continues to try to discover information after the discovery cutoff? Other parties can usually get a protective order against such discovery, and the court is also likely to preclude any evidence accumulated in the post-cutoff period. See *Stewart*, 162 F.R.D. 29; cf. *Whittaker*, 736 F.2d 1341 (court improperly excluded post-cutoff evidence obtained during discovery in related case; if discovery in related case was being used to circumvent discovery cutoff, court in related case could issue protective order).

11. You may have noted that the RAND study found no savings in expense or time from the other case management principles and techniques it examined. Although we have suggested in these notes that such savings are not the critical issue in complex cases, the RAND findings are nonetheless important. If case management principles and techniques do not reduce cost and delay, why do we use them? Maybe the answer is that we still need to use them in complex cases, to the extent that these principles and techniques reduce lawyer dysfunction. But is there any justification for their use in routine litigation? Keep these questions in mind as we turn to other common case management ideas, and see the extent to which they can overcome pretrial dysfunction.

ii. Bifurcating Pretrial Issues

The next case management device we consider is a court order that organizes pretrial issues in a sequential order, and forces parties to complete pretrial proceedings on one issue before proceeding to the next. When the pretrial process is split into two, we often say that the pretrial proceedings have been "bifurcated"; when split into three sets of issues, "trifurcated"; and when split into more than three sets of issues, "polyfurcated." For convenience, we will refer to this pretrial issue-splitting only as "bifurcation."

The theory underlying bifurcation is simple: the early development and resolution of certain critical issues may lead to an early resolution of the entire controversy (whether by settlement or by dispositive motion). This resolution in turn eliminates the need to engage in pretrial proceedings for the remaining issues. Thus, like early, firm trial dates and discovery cutoffs, bifurcation of issues does not directly narrow the issues for trial; but if the issues are chosen wisely, bifurcation may avoid the need to develop and discover many issues. On the other hand, this device contains some very large "ifs." Suppose that the evidence on the initial issues fails to resolve the case; in this case, bifurcation may slow down rather than speed up the pretrial process. Or suppose that the initial issues are the very issues that create pretrial complexity; depending on the type of pretrial complexity involved, deciding these issues first will do little to overcome the problems of complexity that the case poses. Moreover, the judicial decision to bifurcate pretrial issues brings the judge into a task classically reserved to the advocate: how best to develop the proofs and arguments for trial.

IN RE "AGENT ORANGE" PRODUCT LIABILITY LITIGATION

506 F. Supp. 762 (E.D.N.Y. 1980)

■ PRATT, District Judge. Plaintiffs, Vietnam war veterans and members of their families claiming to have suffered damage as a result of the veterans' exposure to herbicides in Vietnam, commenced these actions against the defendant chemical companies. Defendants, seeking indemnification or contribution in the event they are held liable to plaintiffs, then served third party complaints against the United States. [The veterans' cases were transferred to the Eastern District of New York by the Judicial Panel on Multidistrict Litigation. The court then entered a stay of further discovery until various motions to dismiss, motions for summary judgment, motions for class certification, and other preliminary pretrial matters were resolved.

[The court dismissed the third party claims against the United States. It then turned to the plan for managing the remainder of the litigation.]

III. THE CASE MANAGEMENT PLAN

There have been pending for some time motions by various parties urging the court to make various orders affecting the overall management of this action, including such matters as class action treatment, summary judgment, discovery, and division of the action into various parts for pretrial and trial purposes. The court has reserved decision on all these motions pending resolution of two major questions that greatly affect how the case might be managed efficiently: (1) whether the United States was to be a party to the action, and (2) whether jurisdiction lies under federal common law or whether the principles and consequences of diversity jurisdiction must be considered. Now that both of these questions have been answered,[30] it is

---

30. The first question is answered by the earlier part of this memorandum and order. The second question was answered by a decision and order of the Second Circuit Court of Appeals .... which held that this litigation should not be governed by federal common law, but rather must be controlled by the laws of the several states applied under diversity of citizenship principles. [See p. 847, *supra*.]

time to get on with orderly discovery and ultimate disposition of the litigation.

In developing the case management plan described in this section, the court has weighed and considered many problems presented by this litigation. Some of them are:

1. There are a large number of plaintiffs and potential plaintiffs who claim to have been injured by exposure to Agent Orange. There are now approximately 167 suits pending in the Eastern District of New York involving over 3,400 plaintiffs. The court has been informed that there are many thousands more who have, at the court's request and pending decision of the class action motion, refrained from bringing individual actions.

2. There are numerous chemical companies named as defendants. The fact that they may have had differing degrees of involvement in manufacturing and supplying Agent Orange for the government may or may not cause differing levels of responsibility for the effects of Agent Orange on plaintiffs.

3. The present plaintiffs come from most of the 50 states and from Australia. This may require consideration of varying standards of conduct, rules of causation and principles of damages that may substantially affect the results in individual cases.

4. The causation issues are difficult and complex. Clearly this is not the "simple" type of "disaster" litigation such as an airplane crash involving a single incident, having a causation picture that is readily grasped through conventional litigation techniques, and presenting comparatively small variations among the claimants as to the effects upon them of the crash. With the Agent Orange litigation, injuries are claimed to have resulted from exposure to a chemical that was disseminated in the air over southeast Asia during a period of several years. Each veteran was exposed differently, although undoubtedly patterns of exposure will emerge. The claimed injuries vary significantly. Moreover, there is a major dispute over whether Agent Orange can cause the injuries in question, and there are separate disputes over whether the exposure claimed in each case did cause the injuries claimed. The picture is further complicated by the use in Vietnam of other chemicals and drugs that also are claimed to be capable of causing many of the injuries attributed to Agent Orange.

5. The litigation presents numerous questions of law that lie at the frontier of modern tort jurisprudence. Among them are questions of enterprise liability, strict products liability, liability for injuries that appear long after original exposure to the offending substance, and liability for so-called genetic injuries.

6. Many of the people exposed to Agent Orange may not even yet have experienced the harm it may cause.

7. Numerous scientific and medical issues are presented, and there are serious questions of whether there is adequate data to reach scientifically sound conclusions about them. There is the further question of whether legally permissible conclusions may nevertheless be reached on data that would not permit "scientific" conclusions.

8. Various agencies of the government have expressed concern but as yet have shown little tangible action about the problems claimed to have been caused by the government's use of Agent Orange.

9. There are important and conflicting public policies that run as crosscurrents through many phases of both the substantive and procedural problems of this litigation.

10. There is a wide choice available among the many procedural devices that could be used for addressing and ultimately deciding this controversy.

All of these problems are compounded by the practical realities of having on one side of the litigation plaintiffs who seek damages, but who have limited resources with which to press their claims and whose plight becomes more desperate and depressing as time goes on, and having on the other side defendants who strenuously contest their liability, who have ample resources for counsel and expert witnesses to defend them, and who probably gain significantly, although immeasurably, from every delay that they can produce. . . .

Out of these and other problems it is this court's task as the transferee judge in this multidistrict litigation to supervise and manage the action so as to bring it to a "just, speedy and inexpensive determination", Rule 1 FRCP, either in this court, or if that is not possible, then in the transferor courts after completion here of as much of the litigation as may fairly and reasonably be resolved under the supervision of this single judge.

With the foregoing and other problems in mind, the court has considered a variety of possibilities for managing this multidistrict litigation. Each possibility has both advantages and disadvantages. Among the numerous possibilities are the following:

1. Transfer all actions to the Eastern District of New York for trial before this court. . . .

2. Supervise all discovery, prepare a pretrial order, and then remand the cases for separate trials in the transferor districts around the country. . . .

3. Coordinate discovery and other pretrial work, consolidate the actions for trial of the common issues of fact and law, and then remand to the transferor districts for separate trials of the individual issues such as specific causation and damages. . . .

4. Certify the litigation as a class action, using all the flexibility of that device, including subclasses, to determine common issues before this court and ultimately determine the individual issues either under the direct supervision of this court or after remand to other courts. . . .

After considering the submissions and arguments of the parties and after weighing all of the foregoing and many other considerations, the court has developed the following plan for management of the Agent Orange litigation assigned to it under MDL No. 381:

1. Class action. The Agent Orange litigation will be certified as a class action under F.R.C.P. 23(b)(3). . . .

3. *Separate trials of some issues.* Whenever common issues are presented, a common trial should be had, if practicable. These trials will be held as promptly as possible in the Eastern District of New York, preserving at all times the parties' right to a jury trial when properly demanded. Plaintiffs have moved for so-called "serial" trials, describing in some detail the issues they would like tried and the order in which they should be tried. Except insofar as plaintiffs' plan is adopted by this decision, that motion is denied. As appears in the discussion below entitled "Summary Judgment" there is an issue that can be separately tried at the threshold of this action: whether the defendants are protected by the "government contract defense". The court intends to try that issue separately. After that, if needed, there may be an additional trial addressing liability questions such as negligence, product liability, and general causation, where a jury will be able to hear all of the evidence relating to the development, manufacture and use of Agent Orange, and the scientific and medical evidence relating to its potential effects, and report its findings in carefully drafted special verdicts. Those special verdicts can then serve as a framework for later disposition of the issues of individual causation (whether a particular veteran was exposed, to what degree, and with what results) and damages. The court has not yet determined whether the individual issues can be best resolved under the direct supervision of this court or by remand of subclass actions to transferor courts for processing in ways appropriate to the circumstances of the subclasses. Those determinations necessarily must be made at a later date.

4. *Discovery.* Until now the court has stayed all discovery except that conducted voluntarily. That stay will now be lifted, and mandatory discovery shall now proceed according to the plan described in the section below entitled "Discovery"....

V. SUMMARY JUDGMENT

[After conditionally certifying the case as a class action, the court then turned to the defendants' motions for summary judgment, which were premised on the "government contractor defense." In general terms, this defense would have absolved the manufacturers of Agent Orange and other Vietnam-era herbicides procured by the military from any tort liability for injuries caused by the herbicides. Whether such a defense existed at all, and what the elements of such a defense would be, were both uncertain questions in 1980.]

Having considered all the authorities cited and the arguments of counsel, the court is satisfied that a government contract defense exists and has possible application to the facts at bar. Plaintiffs are correct, however, to the extent that they argue the presence of fact issues which preclude summary judgment since any application of the government contract defense in this context will require that defendants prove that their relationship with the government and performance under the government contract was essentially as they describe it. In short, whatever the minimum showing necessary to support a finding for defendants on the government contract defense may be, allegations with respect to their contract performance and relationship with the government present issues of fact requiring trial.

Resolution of the fact issues by separate trial will determine whether defendants have a complete defense to the claims asserted against them. This is the reason the court has chosen the government contract defense for the Phase I trial as discussed in section III above. The elements of the defense will be uniquely adapted to consideration and adjudication, separate and apart from the issues of liability, causation and damages. As a practical matter, discovery as to these discrete issues will be rather narrow compared to the discovery that some of the other fact issues presented by this action may require....

[T]he court believes that early resolution of this potentially dispositive issue will serve the interests of justice and judicial efficiency. Although justice is always served by the efficient management of any action, this is especially true in this case where any other procedure adopted might subject the parties to years of discovery and trial only to have later generations of judges, lawyers, and litigants discover that an early trial of the government contract defense might have preempted the need for almost all of the discovery undertaken and saved thousands of person-hours and millions of dollars associated with those unnecessary efforts. The parties here are entitled to have this action handled as efficiently and expeditiously as possible and, in the court's considered view, the approach here outlined balances the numerous interests in a way that will best serve those goals.

VI. DISCOVERY

Under the case management plan set forth in section III of this pretrial order, it is appropriate for discovery to proceed now as efficiently and expeditiously as possible on all Phase I issues....

The first wave of Phase I discovery is to commence immediately, and the stay is vacated, but only for this purpose.... At [the next pretrial] conference the court will hear argument about the various proposals and soon thereafter will establish a comprehensive discovery and trial schedule to govern the remainder of Phase I.

IN RE LOVE CANAL ACTIONS

145 Misc.2d 1076, 547 N.Y.S.2d 174 (N.Y. Sup. Ct. 1989),
modified, 161 A.D.2d 1169, 555 N.Y.S.2d 519 (A.D. 1990)

■ DOYLE, Justice. Motion by Occidental Chemical Corporation (Occidental defendants), Board of Education of the City School District of the City of Niagara Falls, New York, the City of Niagara Falls, New York, and the County of Niagara, New York for an order amending the four coordinated discovery orders previously granted in these Love Canal actions (entered 8/7/81, 2/4/83, 9/25/84 and 9/25/84) by granting a superseding coordinated discovery order:

1) so that, prior to allowing a plaintiff to further prosecute a personal injury claim after service of a summons and complaint in these Love Canal actions, each plaintiff shall provide:

a) *Exposure.* Evidentiary documentation, showing the factual basis, including street addresses for each plaintiff's exposure to a chemical at or from the old Love Canal landfill.

b) *Injury.* Reports of physicians and other medical experts documenting the existence of each injury claimed to have been caused by exposure to chemicals from the old Love Canal landfill.

c) *Causal Relationship.* Reports or affidavits of a physician or other qualified expert demonstrating that each injury of a plaintiff was, in fact, caused by the plaintiff's exposure to chemicals at or from the old Love Canal landfill.

d) And dismissing so much of plaintiffs' claims for alleged personal injury who fails to substantiate, within the time established by this Court's order, a *prima facie* showing pursuant to a), b) and c) above. This motion is opposed by all plaintiffs.

Hooker Electrochemical Company, later known as Hooker Chemicals and Plastics Corporation and now known as Occidental Chemical Corporation used a partially excavated canal for disposal of industrial waste from 1942 to 1953. [The old canal property was transferred in 1953 to the Board of Education of the City of Niagara Falls. A school was subsequently built on land adjacent to the canal, as were many homes. Portions of the canal land were subsequently obtained by the City of Niagara Falls and the State of New York.]

In 1977, area residents started to complain that chemicals were migrating from the old landfill site. On August 22, 1978, after a surge of publicity regarding Love Canal, the State of New York began installation of an eight-foot-high chainlink fence enclosing the old landfill, which subsequently was extended to include the first and second rings of homes, all of which were demolished except for two in the second ring. The old landfill was sealed during 1978 and 1979 with a three-foot thick clay cap, eliminating even the possibility of the risk of any chemical exposure to persons after late 1979.

[After significant litigation, the original wave of cases brought against the defendants by area residents were settled. A second wave of actions was commenced in 1985 on behalf of 216 plaintiffs, and 689 named plaintiffs commenced a third wave of 432 separate actions in 1986 and 1987.]

While defendants have not moved for summary judgment ... and have explicitly advised this Court that such is not the basis for the present motion, they have nonetheless, presented numerous affidavits, studies, opinions, citations of cases, and arguments to persuade this Court that in view of what they describe as newly developed information, plaintiffs will be unable to prove the necessary causation between plaintiffs' alleged exposure to chemicals and the injuries claimed. Likewise, plaintiffs, while acknowledging that the present motion is not for summary judgment, nonetheless provide this Court with a number of studies which causally relate health injuries sustained by these plaintiffs as a result of exposure to Love Canal chemicals; concluding, that in any event, questions of fact have been raised as to the issue of causation. Clearly, this evidence is not addressed to the specific issues raised on the instant motion, namely . . . should this Court exercise such authority under the circumstances now presented.

Plaintiffs contend in opposition: (1) this Court has no power to compel disclosures absent formal motions for summary judgment, (2) New York law does not authorize this Court to grant the relief requested, (3) that this Court is without explicit authority to order disclosure of discovery within a reasonable time after commencement of these actions. However, plaintiffs do agree that evidence as to exposure and injury is subject to pretrial discovery. Also, plaintiffs agree that evidence of causation is a most relevant issue which will be presented at the time of trial. Nor do plaintiffs dispute that without such evidence, they cannot recover under any theory of law. Thus, evidence of exposure, injury and causation is "material and necessary" in these actions, and any facts relating to these issues are discoverable . . . .

Clearly, plaintiffs will have to reveal during discovery stages evidence upon which their causation expert will base his or her opinion. Additionally, plaintiffs are obligated to provide medical reports from attending and treating physicians with respect to the injuries alleged in plaintiffs' lawsuits before trial. . . .

As to the issue of this Court's authority, the provisions of CPLR § 602[a] provide in pertinent part as to actions before it, ". . . the court . . . may make such other orders concerning proceedings therein as may tend to avoid unnecessary costs or delay . . .". Plaintiffs acknowledge that the large number of cases required "special procedures" by the Court to manage these actions. Also, plaintiffs recognized the court's *inherent powers* pursuant to CPLR 602[a] to "consolidate and coordinate all pretrial proceedings." Thus, the parties agree the Court has broad inherent powers. In this regard, CPLR 3103(a) provides in pertinent part:

 The court may at any time on its own initiative, or on motion of any party or witness, *make a protective order denying, limiting, conditioning or regulating the use of any disclosure device.* Such order shall be designed to prevent unreasonable annoyance, expense, embarrassment disadvantage, or other prejudice to any person or the courts. ([E]mphasis added).

Defendants, here, propose an amendment to the [court's discovery orders] "regulating" the discovery process to require disclosures of exposure, injury and causation before trial so as to avoid the expenses and delay of discovery and the expenditure of the Court's time in those cases where plaintiffs are unable to present sufficient evidence of causation. Obviously, where evidence of exposure, injury and causation are sufficiently demonstrated, further disclosure proceedings will be ordered and conducted. . . . Moreover, New York requires attorneys in all actions to investigate the legal and factual basis for an action before commencing litigation . . . .

Plaintiffs' counsel, here, having been involved in these Love Canal cases for nearly 10 years, with the knowledge that expert's opinion is a necessary concomitant to proof of causation cannot now claim prejudice or hardship if such evidence of causation must be produced prior to the time of trial. Further, "a court may invoke its inherent authority to deal with cases before it (as here) in any appropriate manner, even in the absence of any direct grant of legislative or administrative power".... Inherent powers consist of all powers reasonably required to enable a court to perform efficiently its judicial functions and to make its lawful actions effective.... Every court has inherent power to do all things that are reasonably necessary for the administration of justice within the scope of its jurisdiction....

The court in Lore v. Lone Pine Corp., # L3306-85 (N.J.Super.Ct., Monmouth County, Nov. 18, 1986), 1 Tox Law Rpt (BNA) 726, granted the exact relief sought here. The court in *Lone Pine* issued a case management order requiring plaintiffs' counsel to produce evidentiary documentation on behalf of each plaintiff in that case who claimed personal injury arising from the Lone Pine landfill. After submission of information by plaintiffs, the court rejected it as inadequate. On motion, the court dismissed all claims with prejudice....

[T]he uncontradicted facts stated by defendants' counsel are (1) that the complaints used by the [plaintiffs'] firms in all waves of these Love Canal actions are "form" complaints containing 13 alleged causes of action. The only meaningful variance in such complaints is the names and addresses of the various plaintiffs, (2) and the Bill of Particulars served by plaintiffs are ambiguous and misleading in that the form response made by each plaintiff to defendants' inquiry as to specific addresses and dates of visits by plaintiffs to areas where chemicals and waste products were allegedly deposited, is not only unresponsive but inaccurate where concededly, access to most of the region between 97th and 99th Street (rings 1 and 11) was prohibited by the erection of an eight-foot fence in 1978. Yet plaintiffs state that some plaintiffs not even born until 1980 frequented the above indicated area from October, 1980 through November, 1980....

Accordingly, prior to any further prosecution of a personal injury claim in these Love Canal actions, within six months from the service of an order herein, each plaintiff shall provide the following documentation to defendants: ...

(a) Facts, including street addresses for each plaintiff's exposure to a chemical at or from the old Love Canal landfill,

(b) reports of treating physicians and medical or other experts, supporting each individual plaintiff's claim of injury and causation thereof by exposure to chemicals from the old Love Canal landfill.

Plaintiffs' actions shall not be dismissed absent prior application to this Court.

If so desired, a case management conference as to implementation of this order, may be scheduled on some mutually convenient date.

Notes and Questions

1. *Agent Orange* shows the close relationship between bifurcating pretrial proceedings and bifurcating trial. Indeed, one of the best reasons to bifurcate the pretrial issues is that the court has decided to bifurcate the case for trial; in this situation, it is logical, and often efficient, for discovery to be conducted just on

the issues that will be tried. We will examine the costs and benefits of trial bifurcation in Chapter Eleven, see p. 1273, *infra*. Suffice it for now to say that trial bifurcation is controversial. When you study that material, you will gain additional insight into the issue of whether pretrial bifurcation is appropriate.

Love Canal, however, demonstrates that there is not a necessary correlation between pretrial and trial bifurcation. In *Love Canal*, the court did not seem to contemplate that the trial of the case would be conducted just on the individual causation issues that were segmented for pretrial purposes. Rather, the court staged the development of the issues because it thought that the evidence uncovered in this stage might avoid the need for a trial at all. Therefore, there are reasons — usually grounded in the value of pretrial bifurcation as an issue-narrowing device — to bifurcate the pretrial proceedings regardless of whether it makes sense to bifurcate the trial. It is this use of pretrial bifurcation as an issue-narrowing device on which this chapter is focused.

2. *Agent Orange* and *Love Canal* also differ on the question of bilateral, as opposed to unilateral, bifurcation. Typically, a certain issue or set of issues is carved off from the rest of the case, and full discovery by both parties is conducted with respect to those issues. This is what occurs in *Agent Orange*. But *Love Canal* shows that a court can force just one side to disclose information, making bifurcation an entirely one-sided affair. Is the court's order in *Love Canal* functionally distinct from a heightened pleading requirement? Is it the toxic-tort equivalent of a RICO case statement? See pp. 990-91, *supra*.

Unilateral disclosure is designed to make sure that the one side has enough of a case to make the pretrial process worthwhile. Another way of accomplishing the same goal is to enter a stay of discovery until the one side demonstrates the existence of a good faith dispute. See W. Cole Durham & Johnathan A. Dibble, *Certification: A Practical Device for Screening Spurious Antitrust Litigation*, 1978 B.Y.U. L. Rev. 299; Blair v. Source One Mortgage Services Corp., 1997 WL 79289 (E.D. La.) (declining to stay merits discovery while class discovery proceeded).

3. A third difference between the two cases is that the issue selected in *Agent Orange* was — at least relative to much more difficult state law issues of causation and liability — fairly straight-forward. In *Love Canal* the issue chosen — individual causation — was one of the most difficult and complicated in the case.

4. From an issue-narrowing perspective, a judge would love to find an issue that blended a bit of *Agent Orange* with a bit of *Love Canal*. The bifurcated issue should not be complicated; one party should possess all the relevant information; there should be a high probability that the issue can be resolved without need for trial; and there should be a high probability that the issue will dispose (or at least significantly narrow) the case. As you might imagine, however, such a perfect issue is hard to come by. When no perfect candidate emerges, how is the judge to choose among the imperfect contenders? Should she choose an issue that is complicated but that has great potential to end the litigation during pretrial; or should she choose a discrete issue that is less likely to be case-dispositive? Among such imperfect contenders, isn't there a great risk that the bifurcation of issues will ultimately not avoid a trial on all issues? If so, won't this device actually delay the litigation and create additional expense?

Given these risks, do you worry that the judge's choice will become a self-fulfilling prophesy? Does the fact that the judge chooses to focus on a particular issue already signal that the judge regards a particular issue as the weak link in the chain? How can the judge — without the benefit of evidence — come to this conclusion? Will the judge feel pressure to rule in a case-dispositive way in order to justify her decision to bifurcate and in order to avoid the inefficiency and delay that will occur if that first issue turns out not to be case-dispositive?

5. The answers to some of these questions could probably be found in empirical data about the effect of pretrial bifurcation on the outcomes of cases. We are unaware of any direct data that has addressed these matters. There is, however, a body of data, which we consider in Chapter Eleven, suggesting that *trial* bifurcation results in a significantly higher chance for a defense verdict, but also leads to significant savings in terms of trial time. To the extent that pretrial bifurcation acts as an aid to trial bifurcation, as in *Agent Orange*, pretrial bifurcation would presumably change the calculus in a similar way: more defense verdicts, but less expense. It seems intuitively likely — although we emphasize that we do not have supporting data — that the same types of results are likely when bifurcation is used primarily as a pretrial issue-narrowing device. If these data and intuitions are correct, how do we justify the use of potentially outcome-determinative procedures in some, but not all, cases?

6. Pretrial bifurcation is not an uncommon phenomenon, although few reported cases discuss it. (For instance, note that the case on which *Love Canal*-style bifurcation was based — *Lore v. Lone Pine Corp.* — was not published in an official reporter, although it quickly became famous by word of mouth.) See, *e.g.*, United States v. Shell Oil Co., 1992 WL 144296 (C.D. Cal.) (denying pretrial trifurcation); In re Data General Corp. Antitrust Litigation, 490 F. Supp. 1089 (N.D. Cal. 1980) (describing prior order to bifurcate pretrial); cf. In re Data General Corp. Antitrust Litigation, 510 F. Supp. 1220 (J.P.M.L. 1979) (transfer under § 1407 appropriate even when transferee court has bifurcated previously transferred proceedings to hear antitrust claims before trade secret claims, and when present proceedings relate primarily to trade secret claims); In re Sugar Industry Antitrust Litigation, 427 F. Supp. 1018 (J.P.M.L. 1977) (multidistrict panel "bifurcated" § 1407 transfer so that some parts of case were heard in one district, and other parts in another district). One reason that there are so few reports is that pretrial bifurcation is usually accomplished in a pretrial order, few of which are ever published.

7. What exactly are the sources of the judicial power to bifurcate? Curiously enough, although judges have bifurcated pretrial proceedings for years, the answer to that question is not entirely clear. The source is not F.R.Civ.P. 42(b), which authorizes a court only to order separate *trials*. Nor does F.R.Civ.P. 16, the fountainhead of case management authority, explicitly mention pretrial bifurcation, although several of its provisions could be read to imply such a power. See F.R.Civ.P. 16(c)(1) ("formulation and simplification of the issues"); (c)(12) ("special procedures for managing difficult or protracted actions"); (c)(13) ("order for a separate trial"); (c)(14) ("order directly a party or parties to present evidence early in the trial"). Nevertheless, the best textual sources for bifurcation orders may be F.R.Civ.P. 26(f)(2) — which requires a discovery plan to consider "whether discovery should be conducted in phases or be limited to or focused upon particular issues" — in conjunction with F.R.Civ.P. 26(c)(2) — which authorizes a court to issue a protective order "that the disclosure or discovery may be had only on specified terms and conditions, including a designation of the time and place." But note that Rule 26 seems to put much of the onus for proposing bifurcated pretrial proceedings on the

lawyers; and if they do not ask in a Rule 26(f) discovery plan for bifurcated treatment, the court must tease out its authority to bifurcate from other sources.

8. The Manual for Complex Litigation, Third (1995) seems to have a rather lukewarm attitude toward pretrial bifurcation. In its list of techniques for pretrial narrowing of issues, pretrial bifurcation does not rate a mention. See *Manual*, § 21.33; cf. § 21.632 (discussing separate trials, and suggesting that a separate trial on an early issue might affect "the scope of [later] discovery"). In its discussion of discovery plans, it acknowledges pretrial bifurcation, see § 21.421, but it makes no endorsement of the idea. Its strongest favorable statement is contained in § 21.422:

> For effective discovery control, . . . the court should direct initial discovery at matters — witnesses, documents, information — that appear pivotal. As the litigation proceeds, this initial discovery may render other discovery unnecessary or provide leads for further necessary discovery. Initial discovery may be targeted at information that may facilitate settlement negotiations or provide the foundation for a dispositive motion . . . . Targeted discovery may be nonexhaustive, conducted to rapidly produce critical information on one or more specific issues. In permitting this kind of discovery, the court must balance the potential savings against the risk of later duplicative discovery should the deposition of a witness or the production of documents have to be resumed.

Why the reluctance to embrace pretrial bifurcation? Is the idea of targeting discovery at critical issues — even when those issues may not be dispositive in themselves or lead to a dispositive trial event — a better way of approaching pretrial issue-narrowing? See p. 1117, *infra*.

9. Recall that one of the great differences between Anglo-American and continental procedure is that continental procedure lacks a definitive trial event, proceeding instead through a series of hearings on various issues. See pp. 68-74, *supra*. Pretrial bifurcation of issues is one of the clearest examples of the shift in complex litigation away from the classic Anglo-American form of adversary trial. In your judgment, does this fact speak well or ill of pretrial bifurcation?

iii. Forcing Pretrial Stipulations

Another way to reduce the number of factual and legal issues in a case is to develop mechanisms that force the parties to stipulate to certain facts, thereby eliminating the need for discovery with regard to those facts. There exists in the Federal Rules of Civil procedure one such device — the Rule 36 request for admission. But Rule 36 requests for admission are party-initiated, and the consequences for failing to admit — the assessment of the costs of proving the issue at trial in the event that the failure was both of "substantial importance" and not based in "reasonable ground" — are not particularly ominous. See F.R.Civ.P. 37(c)(2). Moreover, a party can often escape answering a request for admission when the "information known or readily obtainable by the party is insufficient to enable the party to admit or deny" the request, F.R.Civ.P. 36(a); thus, admissions often work best at the end of the discovery process to reduce trial issues, rather than in the early stages of the discovery process to reduce pretrial issues.

The real issue, therefore, is whether the trial judge enjoys an authority independent of Rule 36 to force the parties to stipulate to certain matters that will eliminate the need for certain discovery. Once again, we find that the need for efficient resolution of complex cases is pitted against fears of increased judicial power and the potential for dissimilar treatment of similar cases.

UNITED STATES v. AMERICAN TELEPHONE & TELEGRAPH CO.

461 F. Supp. 1314 (D.D.C. 1978)

■ GREENE, District Judge. The motions before the Court address the Court's jurisdiction and they raise fundamental issues concerning the discovery that should govern the future path of this antitrust litigation. . . .

The complaint was filed on November 20, 1974. It alleges violations of Section 2 of the Sherman Act, 15 U.S.C. § 2, by the American Telephone and Telegraph Company (AT&T), Western Electric Company, Inc. (Western Electric), and Bell Telephone Laboratories, Inc. (Bell Labs). . . .

The complaint explains that the defendants are violating the antitrust laws by various monopolistic practices . . . . It is further alleged that, as a consequence of these practices (1) defendants have achieved and are maintaining a monopoly of telecommunications service and equipment; (2) competition in these areas has been restrained; and (3) purchasers of telecommunications service and equipment have been denied the benefits of a free and competitive market. Among other relief, the action seeks the divestiture by AT&T of all Western Electric stock; the separation of some or all of the Long Lines Department of AT&T from the Bell Operating Companies; the divestiture by Western Electric of its manufacturing and other assets sufficient to insure competition in the manufacture and sales of telecommunications equipment; and such relief against Bell Labs as the Court may find appropriate. . . .

Shortly after the filing of the complaint, in November of 1974, and while [jurisdictional] issues were being litigated, the parties began to engage in discovery. Defendants served a request for production of documents upon the government, as well as a comprehensive set of interrogatories. The government, for its part, filed numerous discovery requests upon defendants and each of the operating telephone companies in which AT&T holds a majority interest, and it began fairly extensive third party discovery. Disputes arose almost immediately, however, with each side accusing the other of making unduly broad requests and of engaging in obstructive conduct in relation to opposing requests.

These controversies became moot in relatively short order, as the course of discovery was stayed pending resolution of the jurisdictional issues. Eventually, and contemporaneously with its ruling on these issues, the Court issued an order vacating the stay that had been in effect for almost 22 months[,] and shortly thereafter, pursuant to stipulation of the parties, it issued a number of other pretrial orders, which established machinery for the recommencement of discovery. Almost immediately upon the entry of these orders, defendants sought review of the Court's ruling on the jurisdictional issues by petitioning both the U.S. Court of Appeals and the U.S. Supreme Court for writs of certiorari, and during the pendency of these petitions in the appellate courts, all proceedings in this Court, including discovery, were again stayed, this time, with one brief interruption, from January 25, 1977, to November 28, 1977.

When the last certiorari petition was denied, and the stays were dissolved, the parties filed a number of proposed orders concerning pretrial discovery, and the Court, by its order of February 7, 1978, referred the case to Magistrate Lawrence S. Margolis to direct the preparation of a discovery schedule....

Pursuant to the authority vested in him by the Court, Magistrate Margolis on April 27, 1978, issued two discovery orders. Defendants objected to the second of these orders, and appealed it to the Court (28 U.S.C. § 636(b)(1)(A)) which approved a provision establishing a mechanism for the voluntary production of documents from government agencies, but otherwise stayed the effect of the order. Since that time, there has been little activity,[15] and such discovery as has been attempted has been the subject of intense controversy.

[After dealing with preliminary matters regarding jurisdiction and whether the entire United States government should be deemed the "plaintiff" for purposes of discovery, the court turned to the remaining issues, including "the future course of this action, including the scheduling of proceedings and the authority of the Magistrate and the Special Masters."]

IV

The complaint herein was filed in November of 1974, and the answer in February of 1975. During the three and one-half years since then, all proceedings were effectively halted for a total of 31 months.... During the infrequent periods lasting no more than a few months at a time when the proceedings were not under a stay order, relatively little discovery was being carried on. Thus, in spite of its age, this case has not come close to going to trial....

However, in view of the Court's decision today on all major outstanding issues, the time is ripe for sketching out a procedural plan to move this litigation expeditiously along toward its disposition without doing violence to the legitimate rights of the parties....

The complaint, as defendants have pointed out, is sweeping, broad, and vague. This has not only had the effect of making it difficult for defendants to formulate their defenses, but it has also been an obstacle to discovery.

---

15. However, on June 29, 1978, the Court, acting pursuant to Rule 53, F.R.Civ.P., and the still viable Pretrial Order No. 7 to which the parties had stipulated, appointed Professors Paul Rice of American University and Geoffrey Hazard of Yale University as Special Masters to deal with claims of privilege in the discovery process....

Absent greater precision and specificity with respect to the government's claims, discovery is likely to remain so unfocused as to be both unduly expensive and unmanageable. Moreover, it is generally agreed that one key to the swift disposition and firm management of cases such as this is a narrowing of the issues.[94] Thus, it is essential that this relatively amorphous complaint be shaped as quickly as possible into specific allegations, and that a continuing mechanism be established for identifying and narrowing the issues and specifying the evidence to be relied upon by both plaintiff and defendants.

After considering defendants' request for greater specificity, plaintiff's offer to submit a preliminary order of proof, and the need for expeditious processing of this litigation and an appropriate limitation on discovery, an order to govern pretrial proceedings (Pretrial Order No. 12) is being entered this date.[98]

In essence, that order provides that the parties shall file four successive Statements of Contentions and Proof over the next eighteen months, each to become progressively more specific than the last, and each to be followed by a special pretrial conference. The filing of the final statements shall signal the close of discovery.

Thus, by November 1, 1978, plaintiff shall file a Statement of Contentions and Proof, in which it shall describe, with specificity, each of the government's legal and factual contentions, including the activities of the defendants it expects to rely upon to prove its charges of violation of Section 2 of the Sherman Act. Under the heading of each factual contention, the statement shall list the witnesses and the documentary and other evidence which will be used to support the claim that such activity was carried on to effect unlawful combinations in violation of the antitrust laws, or which will otherwise support the allegations of the complaint. The statement shall describe the extent to which such evidence is presently in the possession of the plaintiff, or where, in the government's view, it may be found.

Defendants shall then have until January 1, 1979, to file their first Statement of Contentions and Proof in which they shall state their factual and legal contentions in response to plaintiff's claims, the factual and legal basis for their affirmative defenses, if any, and the documentary or other proof they expect to rely upon in support of each factual contention. Defendants' statement shall be organized in a manner similar to that of plaintiff and it shall be similarly detailed.

Within thirty days thereafter, a special pretrial conference shall be held before the Magistrate in accordance with Rule 16, F.R.Civ.P. and 28 U.S.C. § 636, for the principal purposes of narrowing and simplifying the issues,

---

94. See, *e.g.*, . . . Manual for Complex Litigation, para. 1.20; J. Withrow and R. Larm, *The "Big" Antitrust Case: 25 Years of Sisyphean Labor*, 62 Cornell L. Rev. 1, 42-3 (1976) . . . .

98. The order is based on the Court's authority under Rules 16 and 26, F.R.Civ.P. At the same time, the Court recognizes that in a lawsuit of this magnitude, pretrial mechanisms must not merely follow the literal language of the Rules but should also take account of the logistics of dealing with proof of potentially enormous proportions. . . .

arriving at stipulations of uncontroverted facts, and reducing further unnecessary discovery.

Each of the parties shall file three additional Statements of Contentions and Proof, and three additional special pretrial conferences shall be held successively thereafter .... Some of these pretrial conferences, particularly the later ones, may be conducted by the Court rather than the Magistrate. On April 1, 1980, contemporaneously with the submission of the final statements, all discovery shall be closed.

If the issues are to be narrowed and this case is to be brought to trial within a reasonable period of time, it is essential that the parties be bound by their Statements of Contentions and Proof. Accordingly, after a party has filed a statement, it will be restricted to discovery within the limitations of the issues identified by that statement and the contemporaneous opposing statement. Likewise, with the exceptions noted below, subsequent statements may not enlarge upon or add to contentions previously made, and they will have as their purpose not the inclusion of matters neglected or overlooked in earlier statements, but the further narrowing and tightening of matters in dispute between the parties.

Discovery will also be restricted to data relevant to proof of propositions which are material, as distinguished from merely generally relevant conduct, periods of time, or areas . . ., and proof at trial will be limited to the issues framed by the final statements and the last pretrial order.

To be sure, in the early stages of this process the parties may not be able to be fully definitive as to either the evidence or the specific contentions that will be based on that evidence. Accordingly, upon leave of the Magistrate, which will be freely granted with respect to a request based upon new discovery, the second statement may enlarge upon the first, either by broadening existing contentions or by adding new contentions. Cf. Rule 15, F.R.Civ.P. Thereafter, however, the burden to justify a departure from previous statements shall become progressively heavier. After the parties file their second statements, an enlargement will be allowed only upon good cause shown, and after the third statements are filed, any amendment, other than by way of limitation, will be granted only to prevent manifest injustice. . . . These procedures will be enforced and administered to achieve a narrowing of the issues, to apprise opponents and the Court of the status of the case, and to effect appropriate limitations on discovery.

To a substantial extent, the development of discovery and the definition and clarification of issues present a classic "chicken and egg problem," *i.e.*, "to be manageable, discovery ought to be confined to framed issues, but to be framed carefully, issues must be based on concrete knowledge." Antitrust Commission, Briefing Paper on Expediting Complex Antitrust Cases, p. 15; 62 Cornell L. Rev., *supra*, at 27. The authorities differ on how this dilemma should be resolved, that is, in what sequence and by what methods discovery and issue definition should take place. Some writers advocate that, in order to avoid the unnecessary production of documents and the taking of depositions which ultimately may not prove to be helpful, all discovery should be stayed until the issues have been clearly specified. . . . The highly respected Manual for Complex Litigation, on the other hand, takes the position that the issues cannot be defined until all discovery has more or less been completed; [*Manual,*] para. 1.20; 1.70.

In my judgment, in a suit of this magnitude it would be self-defeating either to let discovery continue on an almost unlimited basis, until the parties are prepared fully to define the issues, or to freeze discovery indefinitely in the illusory hope that the parties without the benefit of discovery will somehow acquire the capability to give concrete shape to the generalized issues raised by the complaint and the answer. Either course can lead only to procrastination. The short of the matter is that "the need to settle every conceivable dispute and to have every conceivable theory and fact presented must be balanced by the need for final resolution." 62 Cornell L. Rev., *supra*, at 24. The procedures specified herein are designed to move the case along while seeking to escape the adverse consequences inherent in the several contending methods of handling the pretrial process. Discovery and issue definition will go hand in hand. Initially this will entail a certain amount of discovery that will have to be disregarded later but as the issues are narrowed further, less and less irrelevant discovery should take place. Concomitantly the ongoing discovery process should provide the information necessary to narrow the issues.

If mutually fair, appropriately complete, and expeditious discovery is to be effected, and if the real issues are to emerge at an early date, it is essential that the parties cooperate in good faith with each other, the Magistrate, the Special Masters, and the Court. Counsel will be expected to meet informally with each other whenever appropriate to attempt to iron out discovery disputes, and only when controversies are so genuine and substantial that they cannot be resolved informally shall they be submitted to the Court.

The parties are in agreement that the details of discovery must be closely supervised by a judicial officer if this case is to move expeditiously to a disposition on the merits. There is some difference of opinion as to whether these supervisory functions would best be exercised by the Court, the Magistrate, or the Special Masters . . . .

[I]t appears that broadening the responsibilities of the Special Masters to include ruling on all discovery disputes, as suggested by defendants, would be inappropriate. The Special Masters will have an enormous responsibility, with respect to both volume and sensitivity, in passing upon claims of privilege advanced by defendants and many government departments. Moreover, each of the Special Masters is carrying a full teaching load, while the Magistrate has no additional responsibilities other than those arising out of litigation in this Court. The Magistrate, unlike the Masters, has his office in this courthouse where he may be deemed to be available both to the parties and to this Court at all times. Further, the legislation creating the post of Magistrate contemplated that persons occupying the position would undertake precisely such responsibilities.

For these reasons, the Magistrate is hereby designated to supervise pretrial discovery and to consider and deal with all discovery disputes, other than those matters which by Pretrial Order No. 7 have been delegated by the

Court to the Special Masters, and except as may hereafter be ordered otherwise by the Court. . . .

Important substantive issues are raised in this action, and the parties are entitled to a judicial process which will fairly, impartially, and expeditiously resolve these issues. It is the Court's purpose to provide them with such a process.

Notes and Questions

1. In spite of its radical-sounding nature, Judge Greene's response to the pretrial demands of the *AT&T* case established a framework that still let the parties develop the relevant issues and proof of facts. Indeed, wasn't the stipulation process just a throwback to common law procedure, in which the swapping of increasingly specific pleadings framed the issues for trial? One difference is that the parties also engaged in discovery to help refine the pleadings; the common law had no discovery devices. But equity did. So is the *AT&T* stipulation really all that radical? Wasn't Greene's response essentially consistent with the adversarial model's traditional judicial role, in which the judge takes no active role in shaping the case for trial?

The stipulation process did cause real damage to the principle of transsubstantivism — the like treatment of like cases. But this too is familiar, since common law pleading also used different forms of procedure for different types of cases. Given the problems that common law pleading encountered, how would you predict that the *AT&T* stipulation process actually fared?

2. This is what happened. Shortly after the process commenced, it became apparent that the limited judicial role envisioned by Judge Greene was inadequate. The centerpieces of the plan were the Statements of Contentions and Proof, and the parties had bogged down. The second round of Statements resulted in 1,872 pages filed on behalf of the plaintiff, and 2,147 pages filed on behalf of the defendants. They amounted to "a concatenation of conclusory allegations with ambiguous factual contentions. Hyperbole was rampant. . . . [The process of going through each allegation and its underlying documentary support] generated thousands of pages of worksheets, required the expenditure of tens of thousands of man-hours over a six-month period of exchanges, and resulted in agreement on only a few paragraphs of factual contentions. And a substantial number of contentions had not even been addressed." Geoffrey C. Hazard, Jr. & Paul R. Rice, *Judicial Management of the Pretrial Process in Massive Litigation: Special Masters as Case Managers*, in Wayne D. Brazil et al., Managing Complex Litigation 103 (1983).

Consequently, in a larger departure from the adversarial ideal, Greene put the stipulation process in the hands of the special masters, to whom he had initially declined to give this role. The masters convinced the parties to divide the case into episodes. The parties identified 82 discrete episodes at issue, many of which "constitute[d] major antitrust disputes in their own right." United States v. American Telephone & Telegraph Co., 88 F.R.D. 47, 51 n.21 (D.D.C. 1980). The masters met on a regular basis with the lawyers to continue negotiations over the stipulations regarding each episode. The "negotiation process was long, arduous, and costly. It lasted for 13 months, ultimately involving 19 negotiating teams for each side and a heavy cost in manpower and supporting services." Hazard & Rice, *supra*, at 105.

Aside from this stipulation process, enormous discovery problems existed. Hundreds of depositions needed to be coordinated, and the information from these depositions and from millions of pages of documents needed to be digested for inclusion in the stipulations. At one point shortly before trial commenced, the government indicated that, just to complete its deposition program (in which multiple attorneys would be taking different depositions simultaneously), it would need 36 more weeks. Greene took an increasingly active role in managing the pretrial process, and ultimately set a firm trial date of January, 1981 — even though he realized that discovery could not possibly be completed by that time.

If efficiency is the measure of benefit, the stipulation process ultimately had some beneficial effects. Many factual contentions — estimated by Hazard and Rice at 80 to 85 percent — were agreed upon. The United States agreed to abandon 14 of the episodes, leaving a mere 68 episodes for trial. The deposition testimony of many witnesses became part of the Statements of Contention and Proof, so that at trial direct examinations were eliminated or drastically reduced.

Despite all the limits placed on traditional party control of discovery, the trial itself lasted nearly a year. The government "presented close to 100 witness, many thousands of documents, and additional thousands of stipulations. . . . [Defendants] presented approximately 250 witnesses and tens of thousands of pages of documents." The parties settled before the conclusion of the trial, and entered into a consent decree in whose shadow we still live. United States v. American Telephone & Telegraph Co., 552 F. Supp. 131 (D.D.C. 1982), aff'd, 460 U.S. 1001 (1983).

3. In your judgment, would a 17% decrease in the number of triable episodes be worth the energy and expense of the stipulation process? Would the elimination of 80-85% of the factual issues make the process worthwhile? Even if the stipulation process was not particularly successful in narrowing pretrial issues, would the process still be worth the energy and expense if the trial itself was simplified? (Note that, as with pretrial bifurcation, see pp. 1019-30, *supra*, a pretrial case management technique might be justified not so much for its ability to resolve problems of pretrial complexity as for its ability to reduce problems of trial complexity.)

Now for the hard question: Assuming that the pretrial stipulation process is indeed worth the energy and expense devoted to it, are the gains in terms of reducing pretrial and trial complexity worth the harm that the process causes to adversarial and trans-substantive ideals?

4. The special masters themselves thought that the departure from the adversary ideal was not only warranted, but essential:

> Historically judges have assumed a formal and distant roles in their relationship with the litigants and the management of the litigation. This has been thought to be essential to preserve both the appearance and the reality of impartiality. Whether this is justified is not clear. What is clear, however, is that this judicial posture severely inhibits the type of supervision needed to resolve expeditiously, if not avoid altogether, the myriad disputes that give rise to delay. Given this role for the presiding judge, what is needed is a new type of supervising judicial officer, possessing the power of the presiding judge but serving more in the role of judicial case manager — an intensely active and substantially less formal position. This

is the role we assumed in the government litigation against AT&T, a role we have concluded is vital to the most successful management of litigation.

Hazard & Rice, *supra*, at 91.

One of *AT&T*'s lead attorneys in the case was less sanguine; he noted some problems with the informality of the process, frequent *ex parte* communications, counterproductive supervision of the stipulation process, costliness of the masters, and the possibility (not present in the *AT&T* case itself) of masters of marginal competence or commitment. His conclusion: " . . . Hazard and Rice may be attempting to draw universal conclusions from an unusual situation. . . . [A]ny attempt to impose such a system automatically in all or even most complex cases would be fraught with danger and could very easily increase the cost of complex litigation substantially without any concomitant improvement in quality." Robert D. McLean, *Pretrial Management in Complex Litigation: The Use of Special Masters in United States v. AT&T*, in Managing Complex Litigation 275, 279-80; see also pp. 939-55, *supra* (discussing benefits and drawbacks of masters). Professor (now Dean) Sherman has raised still other questions with the stipulation procedure:

> Does this portend a move away from the traditional Anglo-American notion that oral testimony elicited through direct and cross examination of a witness observed by the factfinder is the preferred form of evidence? Does it mean that our trial process will move closer to the "dossier-trial" system of European continental countries, in which the entire case is put into a dossier on which the factfinders will base their conclusions? If so, how will this change the discovery and trial strategy of attorneys?

Edward F. Sherman, *Restructuring the Trial Process in the Age of Complex Litigation*, 63 Tex. L. Rev. 721, 746 (1984).

5. In hindsight, does Greene's solution to the complexity of the *AT&T* litigation — pretrial stipulation plus special master — seem like the best one? It is hard to believe that each of the 68 episodes remaining for trial received the type of consideration it would have received if it had been the only allegation at stake; indeed, with only five months to try its case, the government needed to prove the illegal dimensions of a new episode every other day (and that includes time for defendants' cross-examination). Would a better option have been to separate for pretrial and trial a few of the major episodes, to allow traditional discovery on those episodes, and to move along (if necessary) to other episodes as the earlier ones were resolved? Of course, with that approach, the parties might have been litigating the case into the next century, and much relevant information would have been lost, forgotten, or destroyed in the meantime. Which is worse: inadequate but early participation on all issues, or full participation on some issues and the risk of little to no participation on the rest?

Did Judge Greene have any other options for managing the *AT&T* pretrial process?

6. Greene refers to the "chicken and egg" problem of any pretrial management alternative: In order to streamline discovery and make it manageable, the lawyers and the court need to know which issues are relevant, but they cannot know which issues are relevant until the facts have been discovered. By now it should be obvious that there is no easy answer to the problem. Greene's stipulation plan created a fairly rigid pretrial procedure useful for identifying the issues but less helpful for uncovering the facts and resolving factual disputes. In *AT&T*, much historical evidence was contained in

documents, and there were few disputes concerning historical fact. Would the stipulation process work less well in cases in which significant evidentiary disputes exist?

Moreover, the *AT&T* litigation was ultimately tried to the bench. Could we have expected a jury to keep the facts and issues straight with the type of whirlwind presentation of stipulations and evidence that occurred in the *AT&T* trial? If not, would the stipulation process be less useful in a jury-tried case? Does it concern you that we might use different procedural rules to handle the pretrial phases of jury-tried and bench-tried cases? Or use different rules to handle cases with few evidentiary disputes and cases with many evidentiary disputes?

7. Aside from these theoretical issues, there was a very practical matter that confronted Judge Greene: the source of his power to order and enforce pretrial stipulations. Ultimately he located the power in Rules 16 and 26 of the Federal Rules of Civil Procedure. The then-current versions of Rules 16 and 26 did not make even the remotest mention of this power. That situation, however, has changed; the 1983 amendments to Rule 16 now give the judge authority to "formulat[e] and simplif[y]" the issues, to consider methods that will lead to "the possibility of obtaining admissions of fact and of documents which will avoid unnecessary proof," and to "adopt[ ] special procedures for managing potentially difficult or protracted actions that may involve complex issues." F.R.Civ.P. 16(c)(1), (c)(3), (c)(12). Even more to the point, the Manual for Complex Litigation, Third (1995) recommends as both an issue-narrowing device and a trial-expediting device the party presentation of "a detailed statement of their contentions, with supporting facts and evidence." § 21.33; see § 21.641. See also William W Schwarzer, Managing Antitrust and Other Complex Litigation § 2-2(C)(3) (suggesting use of statements of contention and proof to "identify and clarify issues").

Despite this authority, few cases have used the *A&T* stipulation process — at least in its pure form. The reported cases have all been antitrust actions, and none has explained in detail the reasons for using the procedure. See Southern Pacific Communications Co. v. American Telephone & Telegraph Co., 556 F. Supp. 825 (D.D.C. 1982), *aff'd*, 740 F.2d 1011 (D.C. Cir. 1984); Greater Rockford Energy and Technology Corp. v. Shell Oil Co., 790 F. Supp. 804 (C.D. Ill. 1992), *aff'd*, 998 F.2d 391 (7th Cir. 1993), cert. denied, 510 U.S. 1111 (1994); Ralph C. Wilson Industries, Inc. v. American Broadcasting Co., 598 F. Supp. 694 (N.D. Cal. 1984), *aff'd*, 794 F.2d 1359 (9th Cir. 1986); In re Ampicillin Antitrust Litigation, 88 F.R.D. 174 (D.D.C. 1980).

8. In another sense, however, the *AT&T* stipulation process has carried the day. Recall that Rule 16 and Rule 26 authorize the court to hold a series of pretrial conferences. Often the court will order the parties to prepare separate or joint statements concerning the matters to be covered in the conference, and after the conference, the court is supposed to prepare a pretrial order reciting the actions taken. See F.R.Civ.P. 16(e), 26(f)(4). Especially as the pretrial conferences approach the end of the litigation, the court puts pressure on the parties to agree on certain factual or legal issues in their pretrial submissions, and memorializes their agreements in a pretrial order that "control[s] the subsequent course of the action unless modified by a subsequent order." F.R.Civ.P. 16(e). "Courts generally hold stipulations, agreements, or statements of counsel made at the pretrial conference binding for purposes of the trial." 6A Charles A. Wright et al., Federal Practice & Procedure § 1527 (1990). They also

"may require the parties to reveal the theories underlying their claims or defenses, and then preclude a party from introducing evidence on a claim or defense that is not revealed." Id.; see also In re Control Data Corp. Securities Litigation, 933 F.2d 616 (8th Cir.), cert. denied, 502 U.S. 967 (1991); Smith v. Gulf Oil Co., 995 F.2d 638 (6th Cir. 1993).

At the end of the pretrial process, there will usually be a final pretrial conference, for which the parties are typically required to submit a proposed final pretrial order. F.R.Civ.P. 16(d). This proposed order will contain the matters on which the parties agree, the legal issues remaining in dispute, the factual issues remaining in dispute, a list of the documents that each side will use to prove its case, and a list of the witnesses that each side will call. See *Manual, supra*, § 21.67. After the final pretrial conference, the court then either signs the proposed order or prepares its own. As a practical matter, the final pretrial order acts as a new pleading.

According to Rule 16(e), this final pretrial order can "be modified only to prevent manifest injustice." Parties will usually be precluded from introducing evidence concerning legal or factual issues not listed in the order, and cannot use documents and witnesses not listed in the pretrial order. The only exception — the existence of "manifest injustice" — is a decision committed to the trial court's sound discretion. The cases suggest that courts should read "manifest injustice" liberally, in order to prevent "a return to the old sporting theory of justice." See Clark v. Pennsylvania Railroad Co., 328 F.2d 591, 594 (2d Cir.), cert. denied, 377 U.S. 1006 (1964); Wright et al., *supra*, § 1527. On the other hand, the hallways of courthouses are littered with lawyers whose inability to demonstrate "manifest injustice" led to the loss of an opportunity to present important evidence. See, e.g., *Control Data*, 933 F.2d 616; Phoenix Canada Oil Co. v. Texaco, Inc., 842 F.2d 1466 (3d Cir.), cert. denied, 488 U.S. 908 (1988) (enforcement of pretrial orders particularly important in complex litigation).

9. Courts are not bound by parties' stipulations. "A court, for example, is not bound to accept stipulations regarding questions of law, . . . nor may the parties create a case by stipulating to facts that do not exist. . . . A district court may also disregard a stipulation if it would be manifestly unjust to enforce the stipulation." Sinicropi v. Milone, 915 F.2d 66, 68 (2d Cir. 1990).

10. An indirect method of forcing pretrial stipulations is the "contention interrogatory." Interrogatories allow one party to ask another party written questions. See F.R.Civ.P. 33. Within 30 days, the other party is supposed to respond. Interrogatories can be used to elicit many types of information, among them the factual and evidentiary bases of a particular claim or defense. The usual form of such a contention interrogatory is: "Do you contend that [defendant] is liable for [some specified conduct]? If so, state every fact that supports or refutes your contention, every witness with information relevant to each fact, and every document that supports or refutes your contention." See Larry S. Kaplan, Complex Federal Litigation § 16.11 (1993). If the interrogatories are well-drafted and specific, and if they are answered fairly by the other side, this device achieves most of what the court sought to do in the *AT&T* stipulation process. As a practical matter, however, responding parties tend to stonewall such interrogatories when they are asked too early in the pretrial process, and tend to give vague and evasive answers when they are asked later on. Rather than engaging in an extensive stipulation process like *AT&T*, should a court simply encourage the litigants to use contention

interrogatories, and then make sure that the parties' disclosures are real and substantive?

11. From the perspective of issue-narrowing, stipulations and pretrial orders are weak devices. The native caution of adroit counsel usually prevents early stipulations on issues of significance. The final pretrial order does narrow issues, but it comes at the end of the discovery process. While the final pretrial order helps to streamline the trial process, and can therefore be useful in dealing with problems of trial complexity, it does not alleviate problems of pretrial complexity.

Moreover, in order for the stipulation process to work, the parties must stipulate to something. As the *AT&T* experience suggests, however, parties are unlikely to stipulate to very much unless a judicial officer rides herd, cajols, and generally makes life unpleasant for recalcitrant parties. Unless a court is committed to the use of judicial adjuncts, it is unlikely that the court has the time and resources to devote to this task.

Therefore, if a judge is significantly to narrow issues, the judge must possess the authority to resolve pretrial issues on which the parties cannot agree. We have already explored the court's power to dismiss claims or issues at the pleading stage — a power that we have seen to be less than completely effective. See p. 1000, *supra*. We now turn to the court's power to eliminate factual and legal issues after the commencement of pretrial discovery.

Before we do so, however, keep in mind one point. To a certain extent, all the case management devices we have explored, as well as the ones we are about to explore, harken back to a single question: If the case cannot be managed by the parties' lawyers through the traditional adversarial process, should the case be adjudicated at all? Here again, Fuller's point about polycentrism is critical. See pp. 16-17, *supra*. Certainly the breakup of AT&T was a far more polycentric problem than the examples that Fuller cited in his article as not being proper subjects of adjudication. All Americans had, and still have, a stake in the outcome of the case. We did not all have, however, an opportunity to participate in the case through reasoned proofs and arguments. There were many sides of the *AT&T* problem that lay beyond the ability of the court to know, to affect, or to control. Should cases such as this be dismissed because they ask of our courts something that our sense of due process does not permit? Or is adversarial process — and in particular the judicial role within that process — merely a presumption, so that such cases can be adjudicated even when they take us far afield from that presumption?

Justice Rehnquist noted a part of this problem when the *AT&T* consent decree came before the Supreme Court. Prior to a court's entry of a consent judgment in an antitrust case like *AT&T*, 15 U.S.C. § 16(b) requires the district court to "determine that the entry of such judgment is in the public interest." Judge Greene so found. On appeal, the Supreme Court upheld this determination summarily. Justice Rehnquist suggested that the role forced upon the judge by § 16(b) was unconstitutional:

> The question assigned to the district courts by the Act is a classic example of a question committed to the Executive. "The province of the courts is, solely, to decide on the rights of individuals, not to inquire how the executive, or executive officers, perform duties in which they have a discretion." Marbury v. Madison, 1 Cranch 137, 170 (1803). . . . There is no standard by which the benefits to the public from a "better" settlement of a

lawsuit than the Justice Department has negotiated can be balanced against the risk of an adverse decision, the need for a speedy resolution of the case, the benefits obtained in the settlement, and the availability of the Department's resources for other cases. . . . Even though Congress may by statute impose such a duty on the federal courts, they may not perform it.

Maryland v. United States, 460 U.S. 1001, 1005-06 (1983) (Rehnquist, J., dissenting).

iv. Adjudicating Disputed Issues

As we have seen earlier in this chapter, a judge possesses a power to dismiss claims and defenses that are truly frivolous. That power is a limited one — it applies only to claims and defenses, and the standard for dismissal is a very high one. Even this limited power of dismissal was controversial. One of the main objections was that immediate dismissals might foreclose discovery that might have demonstrated the existence of a valid claim.

Of course, that objection would no longer be valid if, after an opportunity for discovery had been extended to the parties, the facts simply did not support the particular claim or defense. Should the judge therefore possess a power to dismiss claims or defenses once the pretrial process is underway? If so, should the standard for such a dismissal be the same as a dismissal at the pleading stage, or should it be lower? Moreover, should a judge have the power to adjudicate on a pretrial basis not only claims and defenses, but also non-dispositive factual and legal issues that might significantly narrow the remaining discovery and trial? If a judge can determine these factual issues, however, discovery and trial can be artfully pruned, and the parties' attention can be tightly focused on the critical matters at hand.

The power to adjudicate claims and defenses on a pretrial basis moves our procedural system closer to a continental-style continuous trial, and away from the culminating event of a common law trial. It also moves the system away from the use of juries to resolve factual disputes. Should it be the judge's job — as opposed to the lawyers' — to decide which issues are worth pursuing? Should it be the judge's job — as opposed to the jury's — to decide whether a factual claim is unsupported? Will the judge's active involvement in the pretrial process make it impossible for her to distinguish an artful pruning from a hatchet job? Should these concerns, which are grounded in constitutional guarantees of due process and jury trial, trump a judge's attempt to overcome pretrial complexity? Or should the concern for rational adjudication prevail? If so, should the power to prune pretrial issues be the same in complicated cases? In routine cases?

These questions are most troublesome with regard to disputed factual issues; no one would doubt the power of a judge to decide on a pretrial basis the disputed legal issues in a case with no factual disputes. We begin our discussion with a device that provides a judge with an indirect, and quite limited, power to resolve disputed factual issues; we then move to more direct methods by which a judge can resolve factual disputes during pretrial.

NATIONAL HOCKEY LEAGUE v. METROPOLITAN HOCKEY CLUB, INC.

427 U.S. 639 (1976)

■ PER CURIAM.

This case arises out of the dismissal, under Fed.Rule Civ.Proc. 37, of respondents' antitrust action against petitioners for failure to timely answer written interrogatories as ordered by the District Court, 63 F.R.D. 641. The Court of Appeals for the Third Circuit reversed the judgment of dismissal, finding that the District Court had abused its discretion, 531 F.2d 1188. The question presented is whether the Court of Appeals was correct in so concluding. Rule 37 provides in pertinent part as follows:

> "If a party ... fails to obey an order to provide or permit discovery ... the court in which the action is pending may make such orders in regard to the failure as are just, and among others the following: ...
>
> (C) An order striking out pleadings or parts thereof, or staying further proceedings until the order is obeyed, or dismissing the action or proceeding or any part thereof, or rendering a judgment by default against the disobedient party."

This Court held in Societe Internationale v. Rogers, 357 U.S. 197, 212 (1958), that Rule 37

> "should not be construed to authorize dismissal of [a] complaint because of petitioner's noncompliance with a pretrial production order when it has been established that failure to comply has been due to inability, and not to willfulness, bad faith, or any fault of petitioner." ...

The District Court, in its memorandum opinion directing that respondents' complaint be dismissed, summarized the factual history of the discovery proceeding in these words:

> "After seventeen months where crucial interrogatories remained substantially unanswered despite numerous extensions granted at the eleventh hour and, in many instances, beyond the eleventh hour, and notwithstanding several admonitions by the Court and promises and commitments by the plaintiffs, the Court must and does conclude that the conduct of the plaintiffs demonstrates the callous disregard of responsibilities counsel owe to the Court and to their opponents. The practices of the plaintiffs exemplify flagrant bad faith when after being expressly directed to perform an act by a date certain, *viz.*, June 14, 1974, they failed to perform and compounded that noncompliance by waiting until five days afterwards before they filed any motions. Moreover, this action was taken in the face of warnings that their failure to provide certain information could result in the imposition of sanctions under Fed.R.Civ.P. 37. If the sanction of dismissal is not warranted by the circumstances of this case, then the Court can envisage no set of facts whereby that sanction should ever be applied." ...

The Court of Appeals, in reversing the order of the District Court by a divided vote stated:

"After carefully reviewing the record, we conclude that there is insufficient evidence to support a finding that M-GB's failure to file supplemental answers by June 14, 1974 was in flagrant bad faith, willful or intentional." . . .

The Court of Appeals did not question any of the findings of historical fact which had been made by the District Court, but simply concluded that there was in the record evidence of "extenuating factors." The Court of Appeals emphasized that none of the parties had really pressed discovery until after a consent decree was entered between petitioners and all of the other original plaintiffs except the respondents approximately one year after the commencement of the litigation. It also noted that respondents' counsel took over the litigation, which previously had been managed by another attorney, after the entry of the consent decree, and that respondents' counsel encountered difficulties in obtaining some of the requested information. The Court of Appeals also referred to a colloquy during the oral argument on petitioners' motion to dismiss in which respondents' lead counsel assured the District Court that he would not knowingly and willfully disregard the final deadline.

While the Court of Appeals stated that the District Court was required to consider the full record in determining whether to dismiss for failure to comply with discovery orders, see Link v. Wabash R. Co., 370 U.S. 626 (1962), we think that the comprehensive memorandum of the District Court supporting its order of dismissal indicates that the court did just that. That record shows that the District Court was extremely patient in its efforts to allow the respondents ample time to comply with its discovery orders. Not only did respondents fail to file their responses on time, but the responses which they ultimately did file were found by the District Court to be grossly inadequate.

The question, of course, is not whether this Court, or whether the Court of Appeals, would as an original matter have dismissed the action; it is whether the District Court abused its discretion in so doing. . . . Certainly the findings contained in the memorandum opinion of the District Court quoted earlier in this opinion are fully supported by the record. We think that the lenity evidenced in the opinion of the Court of Appeals, while certainly a significant factor in considering the imposition of sanctions under Rule 37, cannot be allowed to wholly supplant other and equally necessary considerations embodied in that Rule.

There is a natural tendency on the part of reviewing courts, properly employing the benefit of hindsight, to be heavily influenced by the severity of outright dismissal as a sanction for failure to comply with a discovery order. It is quite reasonable to conclude that a party who has been subjected to such an order will feel duly chastened, so that even though he succeeds in having the order reversed on appeal he will nonetheless comply promptly with future discovery orders of the district court.

But here, as in other areas of the law, the most severe in the spectrum of sanctions provided by statute or rule must be available to the district court in appropriate cases, not merely to penalize those whose conduct may be deemed to warrant such a sanction, but to deter those who might be tempted to such conduct in the absence of such a deterrent. If the decision of the Court of Appeals remained undisturbed in this case, it might well be that *these* respondents would faithfully comply with all future discovery orders entered by the District Court in this case. But other parties to other lawsuits would feel freer than we think Rule 37 contemplates they should feel to flout other discovery orders of other district courts. Under the circumstances of this case, we hold that the District Judge did not abuse his discretion in finding bad faith on the part of these respondents, and concluding that the extreme sanction of dismissal was appropriate in this case by reason of respondents' "flagrant bad faith" and their counsel's "callous disregard" of their responsibilities. Therefore, the petition for a writ of certiorari is granted and the judgment of the Court of Appeals is reversed.

■ MR. JUSTICE BRENNAN and MR. JUSTICE WHITE dissent.

■ MR. JUSTICE STEVENS took no part in the consideration or decision of this case.

Notes and Questions

1. Sanctions are not usually available for merely failing to comply with a discovery request; a party must first violate a court order that compels discovery. See F.R.Civ.P. 37(b). Thus, the first step that a party who fails to obtain discovery must take is to file a motion to compel. F.R.Civ.P. 37(a). Unless the opposition to the motion to compel is "substantially justified," the court will award, as a first level of sanctions, the reasonable expenses that the moving party incurred in prosecuting the motion to compel. F.R.Civ.P. 37(a)(4)(A). (If the motion to compel is not substantially justified, the court will assess reasonable expenses against the moving party. See F.R.Civ.P. 37(a)(4)(B).) Once the court enters an order granting the motion, and the party from whom discovery is sought still fails to comply, then a second level of sanctions kicks in.

It is this second level of sanctions that is at stake in *National Hockey League*. In that case the district judge imposed the ultimate sanction — the death penalty for the plaintiffs' case. But Rule 37(b)(2) provides a host of permissible sanctions. Among them are:

"(A) An order that the matters regarding which the order [on the motion to compel] was made or any other designated facts shall be taken to be established for purposes of the action . . .;

"(B) An order refusing to allow the disobedient party to support or oppose designated claims or defenses, or prohibiting that party from introducing designated matters in evidence;

"(C) An order striking out pleadings or parts thereof, or staying further proceedings until the order is obeyed, or dismissing the action or any part thereof, or rendering a judgment by default against the disobedient party; [and]

"(D) In lieu of any of the foregoing orders or in addition thereto, an order treating as a contempt of court the failure to obey any orders except an order to submit to a physical or mental examination."

There are also exceptional circumstances that allow the imposition of the second level of sanctions without a prior order compelling discovery. First, when a party refuses to serve answers to interrogatories or to respond to requests for production, or fails to appear at a deposition, a court can impose any of the sanctions listed in Rules 37(b)(2)(A)-(C), but not the contempt sanction of Rule 37(b)(2)(D). See F.R.Civ.P. 37(d). Second, Rules 26(a) and 26(e)(1) may impose an obligation to disclose certain types of information about witnesses and documents. See pp. 1094-98, *infra*. When a party fails "without substantial justification" to disclose this information, that party "shall not, unless such failure is harmless, be permitted to use as evidence at a trial, at a hearing, or on a motion any witness or information not so disclosed." See F.R.Civ.P. 37(c)(1).

2. Aside from Rule 37(b), there are a number of other sources for sanctions. Among them are Rule 37(g), permitting sanctions for failure to participate in good faith in the framing of a discovery plan; Rule 16(f), permitting sanctions for failing to "obey a scheduling or pretrial order," or failing to appear or be adequately prepared for a pretrial conference; Rule 56(g), authorizing sanctions for summary judgment affidavits presented in bad faith; Rule 11, permitting sanctions for filing frivolous pleadings and motions; 28 U.S.C. 1927, permitting sanctions for unreasonable and vexatious multiplication of proceedings; and the court's inherent power. All of these sources authorize a court to award as sanctions the reasonable expenses of the aggrieved party. Rule 16(f) also authorizes a court to impose the additional sanctions provided for in Rules 37(b)(2)(B)-(D). It is not certain which additional sanctions a court may impose as a matter of its inherent power, although they include both the power to dismiss a case for failure to appear at a pretrial conference and the power to award attorneys' fees. Link v. Wabash Railroad Corp., 370 U.S. 626 (1962); Chambers v. NASCO, Inc., 501 U.S. 32 (1991).

3. From the lawyer's viewpoint, the heart of complex litigation is the discovery process, and the hardest part of that process is extracting information from the other side. Consequently, filing and responding to motions to compel (as well as their converse — Rule 26(c) motions for a protective order) are a crucial part of the complex litigator's stock in trade. For an exploration of some practical aspects of these motions, see Larry S. Kaplan, Complex Federal Litigation §§ 16.15-.16, 18.37, 20.17 (1993).

4. Our purpose is not to work through the details of these motions or of the law of sanctions, but rather to focus on the potential of such motions and sanctions to narrow pretrial issues. In *National Hockey League* the district court accomplished the ultimate in issue-narrowing — no issues survived the sanction. But lesser sanctions can also accomplish a fair degree of issue-narrowing. For instance, facts can be taken as conclusively established, claims or defenses can be either conclusively established or tossed out of the case, and discovery into certain evidence can be precluded. See Insurance Corp. of Ireland v. Compagnie des Bauxite de Guinee, 456 U.S. 694 (1982) (upholding sanction that conclusively established personal jurisdiction when defendant refused to answer discovery and comply with discovery orders relevant to issue of personal jurisdiction).

Although sanctions can narrow pretrial issues, it should be evident that they are a rather unsatisfactory means of achieving this goal. First, they require a certain type and level of contumacious conduct — usually violation of a court rule or order, or else outright failure to participate — before they can be used. Second, the point of sanctions is not to narrow issues for trial; the point is to punish and deter bad pretrial conduct. There must be a degree of proportionality between the offense and the sanction; a judge (in theory, anyway) cannot impose a sanction merely because it is the most desirable from the standpoint of case management. Third, even when the case-narrowing sanctions of Rule 37(b)(2) are available, it is clear that a district court need not impose them; instead, district courts retain broad discretion, and often temper their justice with mercy. See 8A Charles A. Wright et al., Federal Practice & Procedure § 2284 (1994). Finally, when a sanction is imposed, a court usually (and sensibly enough) decides to preclude facts or claims that are related to the matter that is the subject of the sanction. But this matter may not lie at the heart of the controversy, and even if it does, sanctions can be imposed only after discovery on the issue has begun — rather than before discovery commences.

Therefore, we must move along to more direct, and hopefully better, methods for resolving factual disputes on a pretrial basis. We do so, however, with both regret and a word of caution. The regret is that we have skimmed very lightly over the top of deep water. We must leave to other courses such difficult issues as the various sources of sanctions, the precise conduct that invokes each sanction, the factors that courts consider in choosing appropriate sanctions, and appellate attitudes about sanctions.

The word of caution is that it is easy in complex litigation to have a "hardball" attitude that seeks to stonewall legitimate discovery requests. The inefficiency and unpleasantness of hardball lawyering is, however, one of the great justified criticisms of the adversary system, as well as one of the reasons that we have seen so many courts engaging in case management experiments. A hardball attitude distorts the adversary process. Adversaries should play tough, but they must also play fair. And that means, among many other things, giving opposing parties the information to which they are legitimately entitled in a timely fashion and in a professional and courteous manner. When a judge can be assured of professional conduct, she has less reason, except in truly complex cases in which the lawyers cannot perform their adversarial tasks, to take the development of proofs and arguments out of the lawyers' hands.

You might think that it is easy for a couple of law professors who no longer litigate complex cases for a living to say this sort of thing. So if you need further incentive, just remember *National Hockey League*. The conduct of the plaintiffs' lawyer may have been wilful, and arguably in bad faith, but other lawyers have done far worse. In today's litigation world, with all its emphasis on efficiency and case management, *National Hockey League* tells district judges that, at least every once in a while, it is OK to shoot a hostage.

POLLER v. COLUMBIA BROADCASTING SYSTEM, INC.

368 U.S. 464 (1962)

■ MR. JUSTICE CLARK delivered the opinion of the Court.

The question involved here is whether this treble damage action based on alleged violations of the restraint of trade and monopoly sections of the Sherman Law was rightly terminated by a summary judgment of dismissal. The petitioner, Lou Poller, is the assignee of the Midwest Broadcasting Company, a dissolved corporation. In 1954 Midwest was the owner and operator of WCAN, an ultra high frequency (UHF) broadcasting station located in Milwaukee. The station was affiliated with the Columbia Broadcasting System network and was of the alleged value of $2,000,000.

Poller charged that the respondents in 1954 entered into an unlawful conspiracy to eliminate WCAN from the broadcast field in Milwaukee. [The conspiracy centered around CBS's agreement with Thad Holt. Holt assigned his option to buy another UHF station (WOKY) to CBS. CBS then canceled its contract with WCAN, and WCAN was forced out of business. Poller claimed that the overall purpose of CBS was to destroy UHF broadcasting in order to protect its interest in VHF stations throughout the United States. In his complaint, Poller also alleged that CBS ultimately acquired WCAN and its broadcasting equipment at a loss of $1,450,000 to Midwest.]

At the hearing on the motion for summary judgment the trial judge held that the injury suffered was *damnum absque injuria*, stating that CBS had a right to purchase WOKY, subject to Federal Communications Commission approval, and to cancel its affiliation contract with WCAN. . . . The Court of Appeals affirmed . . ., and we granted certiorari . . . . We now conclude that there was a genuine issue as to material facts and that summary judgment was not therefore in order.

I.

Summary judgment should be entered only when the pleadings, depositions, affidavits, and admissions filed in the case "show that (except as to the amount of damages) there is no genuine issue as to any material fact and that the moving party is entitled to a judgment as a matter of law." Rule 56(c), Fed. Rules Civ. Proc. This rule authorizes summary judgment "only where the moving party is entitled to judgment as a matter of law, where it is quite clear what the truth is, . . . [and where] no genuine issue remains for trial . . . [for] the purpose of the rule is not to cut litigants off from their right of trial by jury if they really have issues to try." . . . We now examine the contentions of the parties to determine whether under the rule summary judgment was proper.

II.

The respondents in their motion for summary judgment depended upon the affidavits of four persons. The first is Richard Salant, Vice President of CBS; another, Jay Eliasberg, Director of its Research Division; a third, Lee Bartell, who made the sale of WOKY to CBS at a $50,000 profit; finally, Thad Holt, a codefendant who received $10,000 from the transaction. These were supplemented by material taken from petitioner's depositions of Salant and CBS President Stanton. It is readily apparent that each of these persons was an interested party. . . .

III. . . .

Poller submitted a deposition of Holt, an exhibit to which showed CBS had furnished Holt a complete analysis in writing of the Milwaukee market and the ownership and affiliation of the TV stations there, including WCAN. The deposition revealed that Holt had knowledge that the obvious purpose and necessary effect of the plan would be to eliminate independent UHF in

Milwaukee and that he had a personal stake in its success. This included, *inter alia*, Holt's statements that he met with top CBS officials in New York for a briefing on his role, that he was a close friend of these officials, and that he would have retained the option for himself if unused by CBS. The latter admissions . . . suggest that the alternative plan was to let Holt exercise the option and take the affiliation if CBS could not. Likewise, Bartell's affidavit, barely a page and a half in the record, does not negative the allegations of conspiracy. Unquestionably, after knowing that Holt had in truth been acting for CBS and that the sale would prove disastrous to WCAN, he did file certain papers with the Federal Communications Commission requesting approval of the sale of WOKY. Poller had no opportunity to cross-examine him although he was a key witness to respondents' theory of the case. . . . It might be that on a trial Poller could substantiate his claims of conspiracy even against Bartell, although this would not be necessary to his case.

Respondents' answer to the charge that one of the purposes of the alleged conspiracy was to exert a restraining effect upon the development of UHF is that this is a "fantastic assumption — for which there is not a shred of evidence." . . .

The record indicates that Poller had built up a profitable UHF operation, which was recognized as "the most successful" in the United States. Even CBS officials pointed to it as an example of how "a vigorously and aggressively managed new UHF station in that community can do well." In the short period of a year its public acceptance in Milwaukee was so great that 90% of the 260,000 TV sets in the area had been modified, at an expense of some $20 to each owner, so as to be able to receive UHF signals. While CBS had refused to enlarge the six-month cancellation clause, at no time prior to the alleged conspiracy did it indicate an intention to cancel the WCAN affiliation. It was, Poller claims, only pursuant to the conspiracy that CBS came into the Milwaukee market and eliminated both WCAN and WOKY. Since that time the total number of commercial UHF stations in the United States has steadily declined from 121 at the end of 1953 to 94 by midyear 1956. At the close of 1957 the number was only 88. In 1958 CBS itself abandoned a UHF station in Hartford, and in 1959 the very station in controversy here was likewise abandoned, leaving Milwaukee with no commercial UHF service. Instead, CBS has switched to VHF, affiliating with a Storer Broadcasting Company station which was authorized there the same year. It will be remembered that Mr. Storer is the same prospect who, Poller claims, indicated he would pay $2,000,000 for WCAN when [a proposed FCC] rule was adopted but who cooled after a CBS warning. All of this may not be sufficient to warrant the finding that Poller contends for on this charge, but it does indicate more than fantasy, particularly in the light of the testimony of CBS Vice President Salant in his deposition that "it would be the kiss of death to UHF if either NBC or CBS abandoned a UHF station."

It may be that upon all of the evidence a jury would be with the respondents. But we cannot say on this record that "it is quite clear what the truth is." Certainly there is no conclusive evidence supporting the respondents' theory. We look at the record on summary judgment in the light most favorable to Poller, the party opposing the motion, and conclude here that it should not have been granted. We believe that summary procedures should be used sparingly in complex antitrust litigation where motive and intent play leading roles, the proof is largely in the hands of the alleged conspirators, and hostile witnesses thicken the plot. It is only when the witnesses are present and subject to cross-examination that their credibility and the weight to be given their testimony can be appraised. Trial by affidavit is no substitute for trial by jury which so long has been the hallmark of "even handed justice." . . .

■ MR. JUSTICE HARLAN, with whom MR. JUSTICE FRANKFURTER, MR. JUSTICE WHITTAKER and MR. JUSTICE STEWART join, dissenting.
. . . [T]he draftsmen of [Rule 56] of course did not intend to cut off a litigant's right to a trial before the appropriate fact-finder if triable issues remained unresolved after the pleadings were closed and pretrial discovery had. . . . On the other hand, it is equally clear that their purpose was to obviate trials which would serve no useful purpose. In administering the Rule, the availability of pretrial discovery, as well as matter actually discovered, is a factor to be considered in determining whether a "genuine issue as to any material fact" is open. . . . Further, the Rule does not indicate that it is to be used any more "sparingly" in antitrust litigation . . . than in other kinds of litigation, or that its employment in antitrust cases is subject to more stringent criteria than in others. On the contrary, without reflecting in any way upon the good faith of this particular lawsuit, having regard for the special temptations that the statutory private antitrust remedy affords for the institution of vexatious litigation, and the inordinate amount of time that such cases sometimes demand of the trial courts, there is good reason for giving the summary judgment rule its full legitimate sweep in this field. . . .

[Petitioner] should not be permitted to proceed to trial just on the hope that in the more formal atmosphere of the courtroom witnesses will revise their testimony or that a clever trial tactic will produce helpful evidence. Courts do not exist to afford opportunities for such litigating gambles.

MATSUSHITA ELECTRIC INDUSTRIAL CO. v. ZENITH RADIO CORP.

475 U.S. 574 (1986)

■ JUSTICE POWELL delivered the opinion of the Court.

This case requires that we again consider the standard district courts must apply when deciding whether to grant summary judgment in an antitrust conspiracy case.

I . . .

A

Petitioners, defendants below, are 21 corporations that manufacture or sell "consumer electronic products" (CEPs) — for the most part, television sets. Petitioners include both Japanese manufacturers of CEPs and American firms, controlled by Japanese parents, that sell the Japanese-manufactured products. Respondents, plaintiffs below, are Zenith Radio Corporation (Zenith) and National Union Electric Corporation (NUE). Zenith is an American firm that manufactures and sells television sets. NUE is the corporate successor to Emerson Radio Company, an American firm that manufactured and sold television sets until 1970, when it withdrew from the market after sustaining substantial losses. Zenith and NUE began this lawsuit in 1974, claiming that petitioners had illegally conspired to drive American firms from the American CEP market. According to respondents, the gist of this conspiracy was a "'scheme to raise, fix and maintain artificially *high* prices for television receivers sold by [petitioners] in Japan and, at the same time, to fix and maintain *low* prices for television receivers exported to and sold in the United States.'" . . . These "low prices" were allegedly at levels that produced substantial losses for petitioners. . . . The conspiracy allegedly began as early as 1953, and according to respondents was in full operation by sometime in the late 1960's. Respondents claimed that various portions of this scheme violated §§ 1 and 2 of the Sherman Act, § 2(a) of the Robinson-Patman Act, § 73 of the Wilson Tariff Act, and the Antidumping Act of 1916.

After several years of detailed discovery, petitioners filed motions for summary judgment on all claims against them. The District Court directed the parties to file, with preclusive effect, "Final Pretrial Statements" listing all the documentary evidence that would be offered if the case proceeded to trial. Respondents filed such a statement, and petitioners responded with a series of motions challenging the admissibility of respondents' evidence. In three detailed opinions, the District Court found the bulk of the evidence on which Zenith and NUE relied inadmissible.

The District Court then turned to petitioners' motions for summary judgment. In an opinion spanning 217 pages, the court found that the admissible evidence did not raise a genuine issue of material fact as to the existence of the alleged conspiracy. At bottom, the court found, respondents' claims rested on the inferences that could be drawn from petitioners' parallel conduct in the Japanese and American markets, and from the effects of that conduct on petitioners' American competitors. . . . After reviewing the evidence both by category and *in toto*, the court found that any inference of conspiracy was unreasonable, because (i) some portions of the evidence suggested that petitioners conspired in ways that did not injure respondents, and (ii) the evidence that bore directly on the alleged price-cutting conspiracy did not rebut the more plausible inference that petitioners were cutting prices to compete in the American market and not to monopolize it. Summary judgment therefore was granted on respondents' claims under § 1 of the Sherman Act and the Wilson Tariff Act. Because the Sherman Act § 2 claims, which alleged that petitioners had combined to monopolize the American CEP market, were functionally indistinguishable from the § 1 claims, the court dismissed them also. Finally, the court found that the Robinson-Patman Act claims depended on the same supposed conspiracy as the Sherman Act claims. Since the court had found no genuine issue of fact as to the conspiracy, it entered judgment in petitioners' favor on those claims as well.

B

The Court of Appeals for the Third Circuit reversed. The court began by examining the District Court's evidentiary rulings, and determined that much of the evidence excluded by the District Court was in fact admissible. . . .

On the merits, and based on the newly enlarged record, the court found that the District Court's summary judgment decision was improper. The court acknowledged that "there are legal limitations upon the inferences which may be drawn from circumstantial evidence," but it found that "the legal problem ... is different" when "there is direct evidence of concert of action." . . . [T]he Court of Appeals concluded that a reasonable factfinder could find a conspiracy to depress prices in the American market in order to drive out American competitors, which conspiracy was funded by excess profits obtained in the Japanese market. . . .

II

We begin by emphasizing what respondents' claim is not. Respondents cannot recover antitrust damages based solely on an alleged cartelization of the Japanese market, because American antitrust laws do not regulate the competitive conditions of other nations' economies. . . . Nor can respondents recover damages for any conspiracy by petitioners to charge higher than competitive prices in the American market. Such conduct would indeed violate the Sherman Act, . . . but it could not injure respondents: as petitioners' competitors, respondents stand to gain from any conspiracy to raise the market price in CEPs. . . . Finally, for the same reason, respondents cannot recover for a conspiracy to impose nonprice restraints that have the effect of either raising market price or limiting output. Such restrictions, though harmful to competition, actually benefit competitors by making supracompetitive pricing more attractive. Thus, neither petitioners' alleged supracompetitive pricing in Japan, nor the five-company rule that limited distribution in this country, nor the check prices insofar as they established minimum prices in this country, can by themselves give respondents a cognizable claim against petitioners for antitrust damages. The Court of Appeals therefore erred to the extent that it found evidence of these alleged conspiracies to be "direct evidence" of a conspiracy that injured respondents.

Respondents nevertheless argue that these supposed conspiracies, if not themselves grounds for recovery of antitrust damages, are circumstantial evidence of another conspiracy that is cognizable: a conspiracy to monopolize the American market by means of pricing below the market level. The thrust of respondents' argument is that petitioners used their monopoly profits from the Japanese market to fund a concerted campaign to price predatorily and thereby drive respondents and other American manufacturers of CEPs out of business. Once successful, according to respondents, petitioners would cartelize the American CEP market, restricting output and raising prices above the level that fair competition would produce. The resulting monopoly profits, respondents contend, would more than compensate petitioners for the losses they incurred through years of pricing below market level. . . .

The issue in this case thus becomes whether respondents adduced sufficient evidence in support of their theory to survive summary judgment. We therefore examine the principles that govern the summary judgment determination.

III

To survive petitioners' motion for summary judgment, respondents must establish that there is a genuine issue of material fact as to whether petitioners entered into an illegal conspiracy that caused respondents to suffer a cognizable injury. Fed.Rule Civ.Proc. 56(e) . . . . This showing has two components. First, respondents must show more than a conspiracy in violation of the antitrust laws; they must show an injury to them resulting from the illegal conduct. Respondents charge petitioners with a whole host of conspiracies in restraint of trade. Except for the alleged conspiracy to monopolize the American market through predatory pricing, these alleged conspiracies could not have caused respondents to suffer an "antitrust injury," because they actually tended to benefit respondents. Therefore, unless, in context, evidence of these "other" conspiracies raises a genuine issue concerning the existence of a predatory pricing conspiracy, that evidence cannot defeat petitioners' summary judgment motion.

Second, the issue of fact must be "genuine." Fed.Rules Civ.Proc. 56(c), (e). When the moving party has carried its burden under Rule 56(c), its opponent must do more than simply show that there is some metaphysical doubt as to the material facts. . . . In the language of the Rule, the nonmoving party must come forward with "specific facts showing that there is a *genuine issue for trial*." Fed.Rule Civ.Proc. 56(e) (emphasis added). . . . Where the record taken as a whole could not lead a rational trier of fact to find for the non-moving party, there is no "genuine issue for trial." . . .

It follows from these settled principles that if the factual context renders respondents' claim implausible — if the claim is one that simply makes no economic sense — respondents must come forward with more persuasive evidence to support their claim than would otherwise be necessary. . . .

Respondents correctly note that "[o]n summary judgment the inferences to be drawn from the underlying facts . . . must be viewed in the light most favorable to the party opposing the motion." . . . But antitrust law limits the range of permissible inferences from ambiguous evidence in a § 1 case. . . . To survive a motion for summary judgment or for a directed verdict, a plaintiff seeking damages for a violation of § 1 must present evidence "that tends to exclude the possibility" that the alleged conspirators acted independently. . . . Respondents in this case, in other words, must show that the inference of conspiracy is reasonable in light of the competing inferences of independent action or collusive action that could not have harmed respondents. . . .

Petitioners argue that these principles apply fully to this case. According to petitioners, the alleged conspiracy is one that is economically irrational and practically infeasible. Consequently, petitioners contend, they had no motive to engage in the alleged predatory pricing conspiracy; indeed, they had a strong motive not to conspire in the manner respondents allege. Petitioners argue that, in light of the absence of any apparent motive and the ambiguous nature of the evidence of conspiracy, no trier of fact reasonably could find that the conspiracy with which petitioners are charged actually existed. This argument requires us to consider the nature of the alleged conspiracy and the practical obstacles to its implementation.

IV

A

A predatory pricing conspiracy is by nature speculative. Any agreement to price below the competitive level requires the conspirators to forgo profits that free competition would offer them. The forgone profits may be considered an investment in the future. For the investment to be rational, the conspirators must have a reasonable expectation of recovering, in the form of later monopoly profits, more than the losses suffered. . . . Moreover, it is not enough simply to achieve monopoly power, as monopoly pricing may breed quick entry by new competitors eager to share in the excess profits. The success of any predatory scheme depends on *maintaining* monopoly power for long enough both to recoup the predator's losses and to harvest some additional gain. . . . For this reason, there is a consensus among commentators that predatory pricing schemes are rarely tried, and even more rarely successful. . . .

Two decades after their conspiracy is alleged to have commenced, petitioners appear to be far from achieving this goal: the two largest shares of the retail market in television sets are held by RCA and respondent Zenith, not by any of petitioners. Moreover, those shares, which together approximate 40% of sales, did not decline appreciably during the 1970's. Petitioners' collective share rose rapidly during this period, from one-fifth or less of the relevant markets to close to 50%. Neither the District Court nor the Court of Appeals found, however, that petitioners' share presently allows them to charge monopoly prices; to the contrary, respondents contend that the conspiracy is ongoing — that petitioners are still artificially depressing the market price in order to drive Zenith out of the market. The data in the record strongly suggest that that goal is yet far distant.

The alleged conspiracy's failure to achieve its ends in the two decades of its asserted operation is strong evidence that the conspiracy does not in fact exist. Since the losses in such a conspiracy accrue before the gains, they must be "repaid" with interest. And because the alleged losses have accrued over the course of two decades, the conspirators could well require a correspondingly long time to recoup. Maintaining supracompetitive prices in turn depends on the continued cooperation of the conspirators, on the inability of other would-be competitors to enter the market, and (not incidentally) on the conspirators' ability to escape antitrust liability for their *minimum* price-fixing cartel. Each of these factors weighs more heavily as the time needed to recoup losses grows. If the losses have been substantial — as would likely be necessary in order to drive out the competition — petitioners would most likely have to sustain their cartel for years simply to break even....

B

[C]ourts should not permit factfinders to infer conspiracies when such inferences are implausible, because the effect of such practices is often to deter procompetitive effect.... [M]istaken inferences in cases such as this one are especially costly, because they chill the very conduct the antitrust laws are designed to protect....

[The] economic realities [that make predatory pricing typically unsuccessful] tend to make predatory pricing conspiracies self-deterring: unlike most other conduct that violates the antitrust laws, failed predatory pricing schemes are costly to the conspirators.... [U]nlike predatory pricing by a single firm, *successful* predatory pricing conspiracies involving a large number of firms can be identified and punished once they succeed, since some form of minimum price-fixing agreement would be necessary in order to reap the benefits of predation. Thus, there is little reason to be concerned that by granting summary judgment in cases where the evidence of conspiracy is speculative or ambiguous, courts will encourage such conspiracies.

V

As our discussion in Part IV-A shows, petitioners had no motive to enter into the alleged conspiracy. To the contrary, as presumably rational businesses, petitioners had every incentive *not* to engage in the conduct with which they are charged, for its likely effect would be to generate losses for petitioners with no corresponding gains.... The Court of Appeals did not take account of the absence of a plausible motive to enter into the alleged predatory pricing conspiracy. It focused instead on whether there was "direct evidence of concert of action."... The Court of Appeals erred in two respects: (i) the "direct evidence" on which the court relied had little, if any, relevance to the alleged predatory pricing conspiracy; and (ii) the court failed to consider the absence of a plausible motive to engage in predatory pricing.

The "direct evidence" on which the court relied was evidence of *other* combinations, not of a predatory pricing conspiracy. Evidence that petitioners conspired to raise prices in Japan provides little, if any, support for respondents' claims: a conspiracy to increase profits in one market does not tend to show a conspiracy to sustain losses in another. Evidence that petitioners agreed to fix *minimum* prices (through the check-price agreements) for the American market actually works in petitioners' favor, because it suggests that petitioners were seeking to place a floor under prices rather than to lower them. The same is true of evidence that petitioners agreed to limit the number of distributors of their products in the American market — the so-called five company rule. That practice may have facilitated a horizontal territorial allocation, . . . but its natural effect would be to raise market prices rather than reduce them. Evidence that tends to support any of these collateral conspiracies thus says little, if anything, about the existence of a conspiracy to charge below-market prices in the American market over a period of two decades.

That being the case, the absence of any plausible motive to engage in the conduct charged is highly relevant to whether a "genuine issue for trial" exists within the meaning of Rule 56(e). Lack of motive bears on the range of permissible conclusions that might be drawn from ambiguous evidence: if petitioners had no rational economic motive to conspire, and if their conduct is consistent with other, equally plausible explanations, the conduct does not give rise to an inference of conspiracy. . . . Here, the conduct in question consists largely of (i) pricing at levels that succeeded in taking business away from respondents, and (ii) arrangements that may have limited petitioners' ability to compete with each other (and thus kept prices from going even lower). This conduct suggests either that petitioners behaved competitively, or that petitioners conspired to *raise* prices. Neither possibility is consistent with an agreement among 21 companies to price below-market levels. Moreover, the predatory pricing scheme that this conduct is said to prove is one that makes no practical sense: it calls for petitioners to destroy companies larger and better established than themselves, a goal that remains far distant more than two decades after the conspiracy's birth. Even had they succeeded in obtaining their monopoly, there is nothing in the record to suggest that they could recover the losses they would need to sustain along the way. In sum, in light of the absence of any rational motive to conspire, neither petitioners' pricing practices, nor their conduct in the Japanese market, nor their agreements respecting prices and distribution in the American market, suffice to create a "genuine issue for trial." Fed.Rule Civ.Proc. 56(e)

On remand, the Court of Appeals is free to consider whether there is other evidence that is sufficiently unambiguous to permit a trier of fact to find that petitioners conspired to price predatorily for two decades despite the absence of any apparent motive to do so. The evidence must "ten[d] to exclude the possibility" that petitioners underpriced respondents to compete for business rather than to implement an economically senseless conspiracy. . . . In the absence of such evidence, there is no "genuine issue for trial" under Rule 56(e), and petitioners are entitled to have summary judgment reinstated. . . .

■ JUSTICE WHITE, with whom JUSTICE BRENNAN, JUSTICE BLACKMUN, and JUSTICE STEVENS join, dissenting. . . . The Court's initial discussion of summary judgment standards appears consistent with settled doctrine. . . . But other language in the Court's opinion suggests a departure from traditional summary judgment doctrine. . . . Such language suggests that a judge hearing a defendant's motion for summary judgment in an antitrust case should go beyond the traditional summary judgment inquiry and decide for himself whether the weight of the evidence favors the plaintiff. . . .

If the Court intends to give every judge hearing a motion for summary judgment in an antitrust case the job of determining if the evidence makes the inference of conspiracy more probable than not, it is overturning settled law. If the Court does not intend such a pronouncement, it should refrain from using unnecessarily broad and confusing language. . . .

[T]he Third Circuit is not required to engage in academic discussions about predation; it is required to decide . . . whether, viewing the evidence in the light most favorable to respondents, a jury or other factfinder could reasonably conclude that petitioners engaged in long-term, below-cost sales. I agree with the Third Circuit that the answer to this question is "yes."

Samuel Issacharoff & George Loewenstein, SECOND THOUGHTS ABOUT SUMMARY JUDGMENT

100 Yale L.J. 73, 87, 91-93, 95-96, 98-100, 103-07 (1990)

[The authors began by discussing *Matsushita* and two other summary judgment decisions decided by the Supreme Court later in the same term — Celotex Corp. v. Catrett, 477 U.S. 317 (1986), and Anderson v. Liberty Lobby, 477 U.S. 242 (1986).] As a consequence of the trilogy, the Court appears to have transformed summary judgment from a mechanism for assuring a modicum of genuine dispute in cases set for trial to a full dress-rehearsal for trial with legal burdens and evidentiary standards to match those that would apply at trial. Indeed, the trilogy can be read to "endorse summary judgment as a substitute for trial."[75] Neither the dress-rehearsal analogy nor the trial analogy should obscure the critical difference between summary judgment and trial: there is no jury sitting as trier of fact and only plaintiffs are at risk of adverse final judgment. . . .

Any assessment of the actual impact of the summary judgment trilogy in the lifestream of litigation should look beyond the doctrinal level to see how the alterations have played out in the district courts. To this end, we have reviewed all the published federal court opinions in the first quarter of 1988 that refer to *Celotex*, a total of 192 opinions. We eliminated 52 of the 192 on the grounds that they involved cross-motions for summary judgment where, of necessity, the parties have represented to the court that legal issues predominate and there are no issues of material fact in dispute. This left 140 contested summary judgment motions from which the following observations may be drawn:

1. Summary judgment is a defendant's motion. Of the 140 motions, 122 were made by defendants and 18 by plaintiffs.

2. The courts are encouraging the filing of summary judgment motions. Although our analysis is limited to reported cases in which a higher proportion of granted summary judgment motions would be

---

75. [Richard L.] Marcus, *Completing Equity's Conquest? Reflections on the Future of Trial under the Federal Rules of Civil Procedure*, 50 U. Pitt. L. Rev. 725, 740 (1989).

expected, the unmistakable message to the bar is that district courts are highly receptive to summary judgment motions and, indeed, that such motions are being freely granted. Thus, summary judgments were awarded defendants in whole or part in 98 cases and denied in only 24 (including one in which the complaint was dismissed on other grounds). Summary judgments were awarded to plaintiffs in 16 cases and denied in 2.

3. At the doctrinal level, courts are not reviewing the sufficiency of the defendant/movant's production. In 59 of the 98 cases (60%) in which judgment was entered for defendant, the district court granted summary judgment without any discussion of the sufficiency of the defendant's production in support of the summary judgment motion. Moreover, the courts in 12 of these cases did not discuss any evidence or documentation introduced by defendants in support of the summary judgment motion; instead, they based awards solely on the perceived insufficiency of plaintiffs' production.

This review of the 1988 district court caselaw is fully consistent with a recent study of all reported antitrust conspiracy decisions in the aftermath of *Matsushita*. The study found that summary judgment was entered for defendants in 64 cases, that it was denied in only 13 cases, and that in no case was summary judgment entered for plaintiffs; the study reported no decisions entered after trial on the merits in an antitrust conspiracy case.

In sum, as revealed by the doctrinal and empirical reviews of the lower courts, the increased availability of summary judgment alters the balance of power between plaintiffs and defendants in the pretrial phases of litigation by raising both the costs and risks to plaintiffs at the summary judgment stage while diminishing both for defendants. By matching the doctrinal analysis of the courts with their practices as revealed through published opinions it becomes evident that the summary judgment trilogy allows for summary judgment without supporting affidavits, documents or other forms of evidence of record, so long as the assertion of the absence of material facts in dispute is made by the party not bearing the ultimate burden of proof — typically the defendant.

The consequences of such summary judgment procedures are [several], as we will elaborate in the economic analysis that follows. . . .

For illustrative purposes we track a hypothetical suit involving specific monetary amounts . . . . Our illustrative case involves a one million dollar claim in which the plaintiff has an eighty percent chance of success on the merits and in which both parties agree on this likelihood of plaintiff's success. Plaintiff's trial expenses are $75,000; defendant expenses are $50,000. We assume that settlement prior to trial or to the filing of summary judgment motions is cost-free.

When we introduce the summary judgment option, we assume that the defendant incurs no expenses at the summary judgment stage, while the plaintiff is assumed to spend $50,000. Furthermore, we assume half of plaintiff's expenses in defense of the summary judgment motion ($25,000) to be recoverable costs, which will carry forward to trial as expenses that would have been incurred regardless of the summary judgment motion, and half

($25,000) to be independent costs which would be incurred in defending against the summary judgment motion proper. Thus, having spent $50,000 on summary judgment, the plaintiff will only spend $50,000 on trial. Together with these levels of expenditures, we assign to the defendant a ten percent chance of prevailing on summary judgment. . . .

With no summary judgment, the parties' willingness to settle prior to trial will depend upon the expected value of the claim to each party. These values are defined by the minimum amount the plaintiff would accept in lieu of pressing charges on the one hand, and the maximum amount the defendant would pay on the other; the range of mutually accepted bargains between these amounts is the settlement zone. These values, delineating the settlement zone, depend on the award to be recovered if the plaintiff prevails, discounted by the probability of prevailing. In our example, assuming that both parties are risk neutral, the one million dollar claim in which the plaintiff has an eighty percent chance of success has an expected value of $800,000. From that $800,000 figure, we must subtract, for each party, the cost of litigating the claim. Taking account of trial expenses, the plaintiff's expected value of going to trial is $725,000 ($800,000 - $75,000); the defendant's expected loss is $850,000 (-$800,000 - $50,000). The plaintiff would prefer any settlement that provided a payment greater than $725,000 and the defendant would prefer any settlement that provided a payment less than $850,000. By definition, the settlement zone is the range between $725,000 and $850,000. We will adopt the common assumption that parties will settle at the midpoint of the settlement zone — in this case at $787,500. . . .

The introduction of summary judgment complicates the situation considerably. With summary judgment, the initial value of the claim to both parties depends on: (a) whether the defendant will, in fact, move for summary judgment; (b) the probability that such a summary judgment motion will succeed; and (c) the "recoverability" of plaintiffs' costs (defined as the degree to which plaintiff's costs incurred at the summary judgment stage are recoverable costs that carry over to trial).

Let us begin by examining the last of these three factors, the impact of which is least obvious. Suppose that the defendant has moved for summary judgment, that the motion has failed, and that both parties are now contemplating settling prior to trial. The plaintiff has already spent $50,000, $25,000 of which applies to trial, reducing her trial expenses from $75,000 to $50,000. The zone of agreement now runs between $750,000 ($800,000 - $50,000) and $850,000 ($800,000 + $50,000). The midpoint of the settlement zone is now $800,000 instead of $787,500. The reason for the shift in the settlement zone is that the plaintiff has less incentive to settle prior to trial as a result of having already invested a substantial portion of her expected trial costs and therefore faces reduced future litigation expenses. It is straightforward to show that the settlement zone will shift upward as the percentage of plaintiff's expenses that are recoverable increases.

When the defendant decides whether to move for summary judgment, two considerations are relevant: the likelihood of prevailing and the increase in the expected value of settlement should the bid fail as a result of the plaintiff's reduced incentive to avoid trial. . . . If the defendant fails to move for summary judgment, she . . . can expect to settle at the midpoint of the settlement zone: $787,500. If she does move for summary judgment, she has a ten percent chance of losing nothing, and a ninety percent chance of losing $800,000, the midpoint of the settlement zone after an unsuccessful summary judgment bid, as calculated above. Her expected loss given summary judgment is $720,000, well below the expected loss without a summary judgment option. Thus, given the award amount, probabilities of success, and legal expenses in our example, we would expect the defendant to move for summary judgment. The plaintiff's expected gain is equal to $670,000, calculated as the likelihood that she prevails at summary judgment times the expected settlement following summary judgment (.9 x 800,000) minus her legal expenses ($50,000) which are borne regardless of whether summary judgment succeeds or fails. The settlement zone prior to summary judgment, therefore, lies between $670,000 and $720,000. If the two parties settle prior to summary judgment, we would anticipate a settlement value of $695,000, a substantial reduction in defendant's exposure from the baseline of no summary judgment where defendant's expected exposure was $787,500. . . .

The shifting of the settlement zones and the introduction of an additional period of negotiations produced by summary judgment has diverse consequences for the process and outcome of a legal dispute. First, it is likely to alter settlement rates and aggregate legal expenses. By introducing two periods of negotiation, summary judgment might be expected to increase the likelihood of settlement. However, the settlement zone during each of these periods is usually smaller [than] that prevailing during the single period of negotiation that occurs in the absence of summary judgment. . . .

[W]e find that the likelihood of settlement following an unsuccessful motion for summary judgment is less than the likelihood of settlement prior to trial if summary judgment has not occurred. But the overall impact of summary judgment, taking into account opportunities for settlement prior to summary judgment and prior to trial, is indeterminate. Even taking into account the likelihood that a successful summary judgment motion will terminate some cases, it is not at all clear that the expansion of summary judgment yields the intended consequence of decreasing the likelihood of trial. Furthermore, the expansion of summary judgment will likely increase aggregate legal expenditures, thus producing a corresponding deadweight loss to society. . . .

Although not an intended consequence of the liberalization of summary judgment, perhaps the most striking and unambiguous impact of the trilogy is a transfer of wealth from plaintiffs to defendants. This is illustrated in our hypothetical by the reduction in the anticipated settlement value from $787,500 to $695,000 with the introduction of the summary judgment option. . . . [T]he introduction of summary judgment will never increase, and will often decrease, the value of the suit for plaintiffs and will correspondingly benefit defendants for any award amounts, probabilities, and levels of legal expenditures. . . .

The impact of summary judgment is most pronounced for cases that have a high ratio of anticipated costs to anticipated recovery. This is the result of the adverse impact of summary judgment on the expected value of litigation for plaintiffs. As a result, the chilling effect on the initiation of lawsuits is particularly pronounced for marginal or nonmeritorious lawsuits ("strike suits") in which the expected value of the plaintiff's claim does not cover anticipated legal expenses. It is precisely the "in terrorem" value of such suits that has long concerned the Supreme Court and has motivated various proposed procedural reforms.

By increasing the anticipated costs, summary judgment discourages a broad spectrum of plaintiffs from entering the litigation arena. This effect can be seen in three categories of cases: first, cases in which liberal summary judgment will deter the filing of novel legal claims as a result of the low probability of success; second, cases where the higher costs associated with defending against summary judgment will deter filing of well-established legal claims because the anticipated reward is too small to justify suit; and, third, cases where summary judgment will allow defendants to more effectively withstand strike suits. Of these three groups of discouraged cases, only strike suits are a proper target for removal from the judicial system. By definition, these are cases that neither expand the realm of positive law nor vindicate pre-existing legal rights. . . .

[S]ummary judgment under the trilogy remains a powerful but blunt instrument; while it will no doubt excise strike suits, liberal summary judgment is not sufficiently finely-honed to distinguish sharply between, on the one hand, genuine strike suits and, on the other, cases of limited monetary value or cases seeking to establish novel legal claims.

Notes and Questions

1. The analysis by Issacharoff and Loewenstein shows that the existence or non-existence of summary judgment has significant consequences on litigation. Since Rule 56 does exist, however, the analysis in the article is to some extent jousting with windmills. The critical issue regarding summary judgment — and the issue that arguably divides *Poller* from *Matsushita* — is whether such motions should be stingily or liberally granted. On that question, the analysis by Issacharoff and Loewenstein has some indirect implications, since a stingily-granted motion approaches a world without summary judgment, while a liberally-granted motion may make the defendant's chance of success higher than the hypothesized 10%. Thus, the sorts of effects that Issacharoff and Loewenstein describe are relevant to the debate about whether summary judgment should be stingily or liberally granted; the magnitude of those effects, however, may be different from the magnitude detailed in the article.

2. Much has been written and said about whether the Supreme Court's 1986 trilogy of summary judgment cases has effectively changed the law of summary judgment — and if so, by how much. It is hard to read *Matsushita* against the earlier *Poller*, or to read Celotex Corp. v. Catrett, 477 U.S. 317 (1986) against the earlier Adickes v. S.H. Kress & Co., 398 U.S. 144 (1970), without thinking that the Supreme Court's attitude about summary judgment shifted in 1986. It is not our purpose here, however, to recount all aspects of this summary

judgment debate. See generally Jack H. Friendenthal, *Cases on Summary Judgment: Has There Been a Material Change in Standards?* 63 Notre Dame L. Rev. 770 (1988); Jeffrey W. Stempel, *A Distorted Mirror: The Supreme Court's Shimmering View of Summary Judgment, Directed Verdict, and the Adjudication Process*, 49 Ohio St. L.J. 95 (1988). Nor do we involve ourselves with the intricacies of what is a "genuine issue as to any material fact," with the details of how a motion for summary judgment is filed, with the problems of determining which depositions, interrogatory answers, and documents are admissible for purposes of summary judgment, or with the various burdens that plaintiffs and defendants bear in trying to win or defeat a motion for summary judgment. These are matters which you probably studied in a basic procedure class, and which occupy hundreds of pages in leading treatises. See, *e.g.*, 10 & 10A Charles A. Wright et al., Federal Practice & Procedure §§ 2711-42 (1983); Edward J. Brunet et al., Summary Judgment (1994). Rather, our focus is on two interrelated matters: the use of summary judgment as an integral part of an overall case management strategy, and the question whether the nature of complex litigation should affect the way in which the device is used.

3. Our goal has been to find case management strategies through which pretrial issues can be identified and resolved early in the litigation in order to avoid the problems of lawyer dysfunction in the accumulation and organization of proofs and arguments. Thus far, however, we have not found the ideal issue-narrowing device; the issue-narrowing effect of each device we have studied has been either too indirect, too insignificant, too laborious and expensive, too one-sided, too draconian (in the sense of frustrating resolutions on the merits), or too overbearing (in the sense of providing expansive and unchecked judicial power).

Summary judgment provides a case management tool that seems, at first glance, to survive this gamut of concerns. Unlike some of the issue-narrowing devices we have explored, summary judgment is specifically designed to eliminate claims and defenses on a pretrial basis. Unlike some, it does not limit the parties' access to information. Unlike most of the devices, summary judgment examines the merits of the case. It is also a device equally available (in theory at least) to both sides. See F.R.Civ.P. 56(a) (summary judgment for claimant), 56(b) (summary judgment for defending party). Moreover, the lawyers remain firmly in charge of the proofs and arguments in a summary judgment motion. Summary judgment can even make other issue-narrowing pretrial devices more effective; for instance, when combined with pretrial bifurcation, summary judgment serves as a device by which trials in complex cases can be narrowed or eliminated, and unnecessary discovery can be avoided.

Not surprisingly, therefore, summary judgment is now regarded as an integral part of pretrial case management. Cf. *Celotex*, 477 U.S. at 329 (summary judgment is "not . . . a disfavored procedural shortcut, but rather . . . an integral part of the Federal Rules"). Rule 16(c)(5) specifically authorizes the court at a case management conference to consider and take action with regard to "the appropriateness and timing of summary adjudication under Rule 56." Likewise, the Manual for Complex Litigation, Third (1995) devotes a section to the use of summary judgment to narrow issues. See § 21.34; see also Brunet et al., *supra*, § 1.06 (discussing critical role of summary judgment in complex litigation).

Nonetheless, the endorsement of summary judgment by the *Manual* and by much other case management literature, although favorable, is qualified. An even greater reluctance to embrace summary judgment is found in *Poller* and in the article from Issacharoff and Loewenstein. What is there about summary judgment that leads to a somewhat lukewarm appraisal? Here are some main concerns:

(a) *Infringement on the Right to Jury Trial.* At the time of the Seventh Amendment's adoption in 1791, neither common law nor equity had a procedure comparable to summary judgment. Summary judgment was a nineteenth century invention, used in Britain as a type of summary collection device to handle certain commercial disputes in which the debt was clearly owed and the damages were liquidated. It was transplanted to this side of the Atlantic early in the twentieth century, when several states (often with tight restrictions on its use) adopted the idea. See John A. Bauman, *The Evolution of the Summary Judgment Procedure*, 31 Ind. L.J. 329 (1956); Charles E. Clark, Code Pleading § 88 (2d ed. 1947).

From these humble beginnings, the drafters of the Federal Rules of Civil Procedure developed the present Rule 56. Since summary judgment has no common law roots, and since it substitutes the judge for the jury as a factfinder in some jury-triable cases, the constitutionality of Rule 56 might seem doubtful. Those doubts, however, have been resolved in favor of Rule 56. See Fidelity & Deposit Co. of Maryland v. United States, 187 U.S. 315 (1902) (upholding District of Columbia summary procedure); Sartor v. Arkansas Natural Gas Corp., 321 U.S. 620, 627 (1944) ("[T]he purpose of the rule is not to cut litigants off from their right of trial by jury if they really have issues to try."); 10 Charles A. Wright et al., Federal Practice & Procedure § 2714 (1983).

Nonetheless, the jury trial issue colors summary judgment. Although *Celotex* and Anderson v. Liberty Lobby, 477 U.S. 242 (1986), make clear that summary judgment should never be granted when a jury-triable issue exists, the fear remains that live testimony at trial might reveal nuances to the jury that a cold record of interrogatory answers, documents, and deposition transcripts might not reveal to the judge. Nor is it certain that a judge and a jury share the same set of values, so that switching from a jury to a judge might well change the trial outcome. (This point, of course, assumes that juries tend to be more plaintiff-oriented factfinders than judges. In fact, the available empirical evidence suggests that judges and juries agree on the outcomes of most cases, and when they do disagree, judges actually tend to be more pro-plaintiff. See pp. 1216-17, 1238, *infra*.) Finally, there are inherent political values that jury trial promotes and that summary judgment defeats.

Since the Seventh Amendment right to jury trial does not attach to equitable claims, and since the judge is going to be the factfinder in any event, should a judge in a bench-tried case grant summary judgment more liberally? Because Rule 56 makes no distinction between jury and non-jury cases, many courts have refused to "vary [the rule] with this circumstance." Farmland Industries, Inc. v. Grain Board of Iraq, 904 F.2d 732, 738 (D.C. Cir. 1990). Other courts, however, have noted a somewhat more liberal attitude toward summary judgment in non-jury proceedings:

> [W]here the ultimate fact in dispute is destined for decision by the court rather than by a jury, there is no reason why the court and the parties should go through the motions of a trial if the court will eventually end up deciding on the same record. However, just as the procedural shortcut must not be disfavored, courts must not rush to dispose summarily of cases — especially novel, complex, or otherwise difficult cases of public importance — unless it is clear that more complete factual development could not

possibly alter the outcome and that the credibility of the witnesses' statements or testimony is not at issue.

Transworld Airlines, Inc. v. American Coupon Exchange, Inc, 913 F.2d 676, 684-85 (9th Cir. 1990); see Coats & Clark, Inc. v. Gay, 755 F.2d 1506 (11th Cir.), cert. denied, 474 U.S. 903 (1985); see generally William W Schwarzer et al., The Analysis and Decision of Summary Judgment Motions 39-41 (1991) (collecting cases). Even if a court sitting in equity feels less constrained because of a lack of a jury, however, other concerns with summary judgment still exist.

(b) *The "Continentalization" of American Procedure.* Related to the jury trial concern is a concern for a loss of the classically Anglo-American form of trial — the single, culminating event in which all issues are definitively decided through the immediacy of live testimony and the drama of cross-examination. See p. 34, *supra*. Especially when it is used as a part of an overall case management strategy of narrowing issues, summary judgment moves the American procedural scene much closer to a continental form of trial, in which the "trial" is actually a continuous set of hearings that resolve discrete issues. See pp. 68-74, *supra*. Indeed, we have already seen how the more activist judge and the case management movement may already be harbingers of the "continentalization" of American procedure. In many ways, some sort of summary judgment procedure is the linchpin of this shift; without it, as we have seen, judges would often be unable to resolve issues on a pretrial basis and would still be forced to resort to a more formal trial method to adjudicate issues. Cf. Wallace v. SMC Pneumatics, Inc., 103 F.3d 1394 (7th Cir. 1997) (noting that trend to increased use of summary judgment "must be resisted unless and until Rule 56 is modified (so far as the Seventh Amendment permits) to bring federal practice closer to the practice in the legal systems of Continental Europe").

Of course, you might prefer a more continental approach to litigation and therefore regard summary judgment, as well as the active judge it portends, as positive developments. If you do, then let us raise some concerns that suggest that summary judgment may not go far enough as a case management tool.

(c) *Party Control.* Rule 56 contemplates that "a party . . . move . . . for summary judgment." F.R.Civ.P. 56(a), 56(b). It does not put in the judge's hands the decision about how and when to adjudicate issues, nor does it put into the judge's hands the decision about which arguments and which evidence to employ. While the judge can influence these decisions by means of pretrial orders directing that motions for summary judgment on certain matters be filed within certain time frames, see F.R.Civ.P. 16(c)(5), the decision whether to file and the details of the arguments and evidence are still party-controlled.

From an adversarial viewpoint, this is precisely as it should be. For persons desiring stronger judicial control over pretrial issue development, however, this remains something of a drawback in Rule 56.

(d) *Limitation to Claims and Defenses.* By the terms of Rule 56(c), summary judgment can be granted only when "the moving party is entitled to judgment as a matter of law." Typically, this has been thought to mean that Rule 56 cannot resolve particular factual issues unless the resolution of those issues leads to a judgment on a claim or defense. There is a limited exception to this rule, so that "summary judgment, interlocutory in character, may be rendered on liability alone although there is a genuine issue as to the amount of damages." F.R.Civ.P. 56(c). But that exception seems only to emphasize that non-dispositive factual issues are generally inappropriate for summary resolution.

This is a problem of enormous significance. If the issues are to be narrowed during pretrial, a judge must act as a surgeon delicately resolving discrete factual disputes. If we handicap the judge by allowing her this power only when judgment can be rendered on an entire claim or defense, we deny her much of her needed power to put collateral issues to rest. In turn, this denial can put pressure on the judge to distort the facts and law in order to render a dispositive judgment. It is a bit like telling a surgeon to operate with a meat-ax instead of a scalpel; we should not be surprised if the result is an occasional botched job.

The standard response to this problem has been to concede the flaw in Rule 56, but to find textual ways around it. Two avenues hold some promise. First, Rule 56(d) provides that, when summary judgment "is not rendered upon the whole case or for all the relief asked and a trial is necessary," the court "shall if practicable ascertain what material facts exist without substantial controversy" and "make an order specifying the facts that appear without substantial controversy." At the trial, the "facts so specified shall be deemed established, and the trial conducted accordingly." Second, Rule 56(a), dealing with motions by the claimant, states that the moving party may move for summary judgment "in the party's favor upon all or any part thereof"; Rule 56(b), dealing with motions by a defending party, states that the moving party may move for summary judgment "in the party's favor as to all or any part thereof." Some commentators have argued that the word "part" in these sections also authorizes the judge to adjudicate disputed factual issues on summary judgment, even when those issues do not lead to the dismissal of an entire claim or defense. See Brunet et al., *supra*, § 1.05; Schwarzer et al., *supra*, at 69-73.

The problem with the Rule 56(d) approach is that it requires a party to file a motion seeking summary judgment on an entire claim or defense. See City of Wichita, Kansas v. United States Gypsum Co., 828 F. Supp. 851 (D. Kan. 1993). If genuine disputes exist with respect to some of the elements of the claim or defense, the party is between a rock and a hard place: either file the summary judgment motion and hope to avoid Rule 11 sanctions for a frivolous motion, or file nothing and lose the chance to eliminate certain factual disputes. The argument from Rules 56(a) and 56(b) does not suffer this problem, but it still fails to address the language of Rule 56(c) that summary judgments can be *granted* only when the moving party is entitled to judgment as a matter of law.

There is a division of authority about whether Rule 56 authorizes these "partial summary judgments" (perhaps a better phrase would be "pretrial factual adjudications" or "partial summary adjudications"). The more liberal trend is represented by cases such as Archer-Daniels Midland Co. v. Phoenix Assurance Co. of New York, 936 F. Supp. 534 (S.D. Ill. 1996), in which an insured suing on an insurance contract had been filing motions that sought to establish, one at a time, each of the elements necessary to prove its entitlement to insurance coverage. The court rejected the non-moving party's arguments that such motions, none of which resulted in a judgment *per se*, were improper:

> "Summary judgment motions can help define, narrow, and resolve issues[ ]" prior to trial. Manual for Complex Litigation (Third) § 21.34 (1995) . . . . As the Seventh Circuit has noted, the label "'partial summary judgment' is, of course, consistent with section (d) of Rule 56, which allows a court to establish facts prior to trial over which there is no 'substantial controversy.'" ODC Communications Corp. v. Wenruth Invs., 826 F.2d 509,

515 (7th Cir. 1987). . . . [W]hereas a grant of partial summary judgment may not resolve a separate claim . . ., it is an appropriate mechanism for resolving separate issues prior to trial. [936 F. Supp. at 536-37.]

See also Brunet et al., *supra*, § 1.05 ("A pragmatic reading of the text of Rule 56 together with the 1983 revision of Rule 16 yields a conclusion that courts should be flexible about narrow motions for summary judgment on less than an entire claim. The movement towards judicial management embodied in amended Rule 16 grants the court considerable discretion to manage the case."); but see id. n.109 (collecting cases declining to use partial summary judgment); Capitol Records, Inc. v. Progress Records Distributing, Inc., 106 F.R.D. 25 (N.D. Ill. 1985) (refusing to grant partial summary judgment); *City of Wichita*, 828 F. Supp. 851 (same); Schwarzer et al., *supra*, at 69-73 (collecting cases on both sides of issue).

Partial summary adjudications have certain problems. For instance, resolving selective non-dispositive issues might waste the court's time on ultimately collateral matters. See Brunet et al., *supra*, § 1.05; *Capitol Records*, 106 F.R.D. 25. Would the summary judgment problems described by Issacharoff and Loewenstein also be exacerbated by partial summary adjudications? Would American procedure become too continental?

During the late 1980's, the Advisory Committee on the Federal Rules of Civil Procedure considered amendments to Rules 56(d) and (e) that would clearly have permitted a court to entertain a motion to "establish" law or facts. That proposal was not ultimately adopted. See Paul D. Carrington, *Making Rules to Dispose of Manifestly Unfounded Assertions: An Exorcism of the Bogy of Non-trans-substantive Rules of Civil Procedure*, 137 U. Pa. L. Rev. 2067 (1989). Does the lack of adoption suggest that courts do not possess the power to summarily adjudicate non-dispositive issues, or that they already do? Cf. E. Donald Elliott, *Managerial Judging and the Evolution of Procedure*, 53 U. Chi. L. Rev. 306 (1986) (p. 934, *supra*).

(e) *Lack of Finality*. Even assuming that the power to enter a partial summary adjudication exists, such an adjudication would not be a final judgment. Therefore, it is always subject to revision if later discovery warrants the change. While this power is in many regards appropriate, it does make summary adjudications difficult to rely on. The same problem exists with regard to summary judgments that decide a claim or defense but less than the entire case; unless the judge enters an order directing entry of final judgment, the judgment is subject to revision. See F.R.Civ.P. 54(b); Anixter v. Home-Stake Production Co., 977 F.2d 1533 (10th Cir. 1992), cert. denied, 507 U.S. 1029 (1993).

(f) *High Threshold and Need for Discovery*. The goal in our search for the ideal issue-narrowing device has been to find a device that can avoid massive discovery by resolving pretrial matters early in the litigation. In order for this device to be truly effective, a court must be able to eliminate factual issues with a relatively low evidentiary showing (*e.g.*, a simple preponderance standard) and without the need for complete discovery on the issue. Of course, a low evidentiary threshold and incomplete discovery would inject a higher degree of error into the issue-narrowing decision and move the court away from a resolution on the merits.

On both evidentiary threshold and discovery grounds, summary judgment is far from ideal. First, the threshold for granting a summary judgment motion — "no genuine issue as to any material fact" — is high. According to *Anderson*:

[S]ummary judgment will not lie if the dispute about a material fact is "genuine," that is, if the evidence is such that a reasonable jury could return a verdict for the nonmoving party. . . . [A]t the summary judgment stage the judge's function is not himself to weigh the evidence and determine the truth of the matter but to determine whether there is a genuine issue for trial. . . . If the evidence is merely colorable, . . . or is not significantly probative, summary judgment may be granted. . . . [But the] evidence of the non-movant is to be believed, and all justifiable inferences are to be drawn in his favor. [477 U.S. at 248-50, 255.]

See also Eastman Kodak Co. v. Image Technical Services, Inc., 504 U.S. 451, 456 (1992). Although terms such as "evidence for a reasonable jury, "colorable," "not significantly probative," and "justifiable inference" are hardly self-defining, they clearly point toward something higher than a "preponderance of the evidence" standard. Exactly how much higher is a matter of some dispute; cases like *Poller* and *Adickes* seem to say "A lot higher," while cases such as *Matsushita*, *Celotex*, and *Anderson* seem to say "Higher, but not really, really high." Whatever the precise line, judges cannot use summary judgment to decide factual disputes on which reasonable minds can differ, so that the issue-narrowing potential of summary judgment is less than ideal.

Summary judgment is also sub-optimal in the sense that it cannot be granted until an adequate period for discovery on the relevant issue has occurred. Even "pro-summary judgment" cases like *Celotex* and *Anderson* make this clear. See *Anderson*, 477 U.S. at 250 n.5 (summary judgment inappropriate "where the nonmoving party has not had the opportunity to discover information that is essential to his opposition"); *Celotex*, 477 U.S. at 322 ("Rule 56(c) mandates the entry of summary judgment, *after adequate time for discovery* and upon motion, against a party who fails to make a showing sufficient to establish the existence of an element essential to that party's case, and on which that party will bear the burden of proof at trial") (emphasis added). Likewise, in *Eastman Kodak*, which the Court described as "yet another case that concerns the standard for summary judgment in an antitrust controversy," 504 U.S. at 454, the Court emphasized that antitrust determinations are not to be made on the basis of presumptions and legal fictions, but rather on the realities of market power. Judge Schwarzer, the district judge in *Eastman Kodak*, had granted summary judgment after very limited discovery; the defendant had filed the motion prior to discovery, after which Judge Schwarzer had "permitted respondents to file one set of interrogatories and one set of requests for production of documents and to take six depositions." Id. at 459. Although its decision to reverse did not hinge on the fact, the Court was troubled by the thin factual record. See William W Schwarzer & Alan Hirsch, *Summary Judgment after* Eastman Kodak, 45 Hast. L.J. 1, 14 (1993). *Eastman Kodak* can be read at least two different ways — either broadly as a cutback on *Matsushita* and a return to *Poller*, or narrowly as an unwillingness "to accept [defendant's] theory as a matter of law on a record based on only truncated discovery." Id. at 14.

The need for discovery can be particularly problematic in areas in which relevant scientific or technical studies are still being conducted. For instance, in In re Breast Implant Cases, 942 F. Supp. 958, 961 (E. & S.D.N.Y. 1996), the defendants demonstrated that certain of the plaintiffs' claims of injury were not supportable on the basis of present scientific studies. The courts nonetheless declined to enter summary judgment, holding that "dismissal of plaintiffs' cases now would be unfair since scientists are still developing relevant information."

The combination of high threshold and need for discovery contribute to summary judgment's problems as a pretrial issue-narrowing device. Do not misunderstand — summary judgment is granted with some degree of frequency. See Stephen Calkins, *Summary Judgment, Motions to Dismiss, and Other Examples of Equilibrating Tendencies in the Antitrust System*, 74 Geo. L.J. 1065, 1129 (1986) (in data set of 1946 antitrust cases, summary judgment or equivalent motions granted for plaintiffs in 0.8% of cases, and "granted for defendants in 6.9% of all cases and granted or partially granted in 9.1%"); William P. McLauchlan, *An Empirical Study of the Federal Summary Judgment Rule*, 6 J. Leg. Stud. 427 (1977) (in data set of 1984 cases pending in one district during 1970, summary judgment was sought in 4.0% of all cases and granted in 2.3%); Joe S. Cecil & C.R. Douglas, Summary Judgment Practice in Three District Courts (1987) (summary judgment was used in 16% of the cases filed in three districts under study, and was granted in 28% and partially granted in 7% of those cases). The successful use of summary judgment was on the rise even before the Supreme Court's 1986 trilogy, see Calkins, *supra*, at 1130-31; and the work by Issacharoff and Loewenstein suggests that this trend has continued since 1986. But see Cecil & Douglas, *supra* at 11 (summary judgment motions, while filed as often, were granted less in 1986 than in 1975). Nonetheless, summary judgment works best as an issue-narrowing device for *trial*, rather than as an issue-narrowing device that avoids pretrial complexity. To be effective as a pre-trial device, it must be used in conjunction with other case management tools, such as bifurcation or a factual stipulation process, that allow the court to resolve issues on summary judgment prior to completion of discovery.

(g) *Cost and Time Considerations*. Issacharoff and Loewenstein hypothesize that summary judgment results in wasted expenditures for plaintiffs. McLauchlan's well-known empirical work tempers this concern to a degree. His statistical analysis suggested that cases in which summary judgment was granted took between 233 and 243 days to reach a final disposition (whether judgment or settlement), compared to an average of 286 days for cases settled at the stage of the final pretrial conference. When summary judgment was denied, however, the average time for disposition increased to 309 days, 23 days more than the average disposition for cases settled at the stage of the final pretrial conference.

Cost factors are less clear. McLauchlan's figure of a 58.3.% success rate for summary judgment motions (and 73.4% success rate if partial grants are considered) corresponds well to Calkins' reports that pre-*Matsushita* summary judgment motions were successful in 53.6% of antitrust cases, and fully or partially successful in 68.0%. McLauchlan, *supra*, at 436; Calkins, *supra*, at 1129. Obviously, in each of the successful cases, the expenses of all (or at least part) of a trial were avoided. In the cases in which the motion was denied, some of the labor by the court and the parties would be expended in vain, but some of it would not be. Given the fairly high success rates for these motions, it seems intuitively correct that they reduce costs, but we are unaware of data that confirms this intuition.

The cost issue with summary judgment, however, may be a distributive more than an allocative question. First, summary judgment motions often accelerate costs and sometimes waste resources. Thus, it can be used by well-financed parties (often defendants) to make it more difficult for poorly financed parties (often plaintiffs) to litigate. Second, Issacharoff and Loewenstein show that the burden of summary judgment falls more on plaintiffs than defendants. This is true both because plaintiffs spend more in non-retrievable costs in responding to the motion and because the existence of the motion creates a wealth transfer effect in favor of defendants. Should we use rules that can so dramatically skew trial outcomes in favor of one party? Or do all procedural rules skew trial outcomes? How do you decide how much distributional effect you want summary judgment to have? Is it possible to decide where to set the standard for summary judgment without determining this question?

(h) *Lopsided Use and Strategic Behavior by Defendants.* Although in theory summary judgment is available to both sides, in practice it is a defendant's motion. In McLauchlan's study of summary judgment cases between 1938 and 1968, summary judgment was sought by plaintiffs in only 21.7% of the cases in which a summary judgment motion was filed, and by defendants in 58.1% (the remainder being cases in which both parties or third party defendants sought summary judgment). McLauchlan reported that plaintiffs won 54.3% of their motions, while defendants won 70.0% of theirs. McLauchlan, *supra*, at 441-42. Calkins' data in antitrust litigation found plaintiffs seeking summary judgment only half as often as defendants and enjoying a strikingly less successful rate of success (16.8% rate for plaintiffs, 53.6% rate for defendants). Calkins, *supra*, at 1129; see also Cecil & Douglas, *supra*, at 5-6 (summary judgment used by plaintiffs 27% of the cases and by defendants in 70%; success rates for plaintiffs and defendants not listed). The data of Issacharoff and Loewenstein also show a much heavier use by defendants, although plaintiffs enjoyed a high degree of success in the cases in which they filed the motion. See pp. 1057-58, *supra*; see also *Wallace*, 103 F.3d at 1397 (noting "drift in many areas of federal litigation toward substituting summary judgment for trial").

The lopsided use (and success rate) of summary judgment heightens the distributional issues that we raised in the last note. So does another, real-world aspect of summary judgment: its strategic use by defendants. Every defense lawyer knows that some of the primary goals of litigation are to pin the other side down to a particular theory, to extract useful concessions, and to avoid revealing the defense's lines of attack. In each regard, summary judgment is ideal. In a summary judgment motion, the defense lawyer pokes holes in the plaintiffs' case; the motion need not reveal the defense's affirmative strategy. The defense can also force the plaintiff to commit to or abandon certain theories, and can garner useful factual concessions. The defendant can also instill in the court doubts about the plaintiffs' case. Other than the cost of making the motion and the possibility of Rule 11 sanctions, there is very little downside to the motion from the defendant's viewpoint — even if the motion is unlikely to be successful. In short, summary judgment is often a "unilateral rule" transferring information from plaintiffs to defendants; "[g]iven the value of this information, strategic misuse of summary judgment must be considered a real possibility." Issacharoff & Loewenstein, *supra*, at 111.

4. Considering both the benefits and drawbacks of summary judgment, do you think that it should be used more frequently in complex cases than in routine ones? Less frequently? Or at the same rate? Put differently, should the problems of lawyer dysfunction make a judge more willing, less willing, or equally willing to use summary judgment to narrow issues?

The standard debate on these questions has focused on *Poller, Matsushita,* and *Eastman Kodak* — three cases that, by virtue of their antitrust pedigree, are usually regarded as complex. *Poller* was sometimes read to mean that summary judgment was virtually forbidden in complex litigation, making the device less useful in such cases than in routine litigation. See *Wallace*, 103 F.3d at 1397; 10A Wright et al., *supra*, §§ 2732-32.1; see also Kennedy v. Silas Mason Co., 334 U.S. 249, 256-57 (1948) ("summary procedures, however salutary where issues are clear-cut and simple, present a treacherous record for deciding issues of far-flung import"); but see Calkins, *supra* (data showed rising use of summary judgment in antitrust cases even before *Matsushita*). After *Matsushita*, however, some courts have indicated that summary judgment should be granted more liberally in complex cases than in routine ones. See Collins v. Associated Pathologists, Ltd., 844 F.2d 473, 475 (7th Cir.) ("Contrary to the emphasis of some prior precedent, the use of summary judgment is not only permitted by *Matsushita* but encouraged . . . in antitrust cases."), cert. denied, 488 U.S. 852 (1988). The more typical interpretation of *Matsushita*, however, is well-represented by Thompson Everett, Inc. v. National Cable Advertising, L.P., 57 F.3d 1317, 1322-23 (4th Cir. 1995):

> While Rule 56 is to be applied to antitrust cases no differently from how it is applied to other cases, that is not to say that the summary judgment device is not an appropriate and useful tool for resolving antitrust cases. On the contrary, because of the unusual entanglement of legal and factual issues frequently presented in antitrust cases, the task of sorting them out may be particularly well-suited for Rule 56 utilization. . . . The summary judgment practice does not become disfavored simply because a case is complex. Rather, it is favored as a mechanism to secure the "just, speedy and inexpensive determination" of a case, see Fed.R.Civ.P. 1, when its proper use can avoid the cost of trial. . . .
>
> Moreover, the inferences which may be drawn vary from one substantive area of the law to another.

Is this just double-talk that tacitly admits that summary judgment is in fact a favored device in complex litigation? Indeed, has *Matsushita*'s emphasis on the policy arguments that supported its summary judgment decision made the wider use of summary judgment in complex cases inevitable? Cf. B.F. Goodrich v. Betkoski, 99 F.3d 505, 521 (2d Cir. 1996) (in CERCLA cases, summary judgment is "'powerful legal tool" that can "avoid lengthy and perhaps needless litigation"; nonetheless, "showing required to survive summary judgment also remains the same"); but see *Manual*, *supra*, at § 21.34 (although "standard for deciding a summary judgment motion is the same in all cases," need for discovery and complicated issues may make complex cases less "susceptible to resolution" on summary judgment).

5. In their efforts to reconcile *Poller* and *Matsushita*, courts may have overlooked a significant point: *Poller* may not have been a complex case. The basic issue to be decided in *Poller* — Was there a conspiracy? — was relatively simple. The evidence needed to prove a conspiracy was limited. Moreover, although difficult issues of market power existed, the size of the market was limited. Is there any reason to think that, in this situation, the lawyers were unable to marshal proofs and arguments? On the other hand, *Matsushita* was one of the largest and most difficult antitrust cases ever filed. See In re Japanese Electronic Products Liability Litigation, 631 F.2d 1069 (3d Cir. 1980) (p. 1223, *infra*) (describing proof problems in *Matsushita*). Can the difference in attitude between *Poller* and *Matsushita* be explained by the fact that the former was not complex, and therefore did not require the application of non-traditional

judicial power to overcome lawyer dysfunction, while the latter case was complex?

If that is the best explanation of the two cases, then two additional questions arise. The first is whether it is appropriate for a judge in complex litigation to assume powers that she might not assume in more routine litigation. Is this violation of trans-substantivity justifiable? If not, in which direction should our procedural system move: back toward a limited role for summary judgment, or forward toward a broader role?

The second question is whether the broader use of summary judgment suggested in *Matsushita* is the full extent of the judge's power to narrow pretrial issues. We have seen several flaws in summary judgment as an issue-narrowing device. Can a judge act *sua sponte*, without waiting for a party to file a summary judgment motion? Can a judge adjudicate facts that are not dispositive of claims or defenses? Can a judge use a lesser evidentiary threshold when she exercises her prerogative to adjudicate these facts? If the answer to any or all of these questions is "Yes," should we limit the judge's power to complex cases, or extend it to routine litigation? These are the questions taken up in the next set of materials.

PORTSMOUTH SQUARE, INC. v. SHAREHOLDERS PROTECTIVE COMMITTEE

770 F.2d 866 (9th Cir. 1985)

■ CANBY, Circuit Judge. Portsmouth Square, Inc. appeals from an adverse judgment on its claim against the Shareholders Protective Committee — a group of Portsmouth Square minority shareholders — and the individual members of the Committee. Portsmouth Square seeks injunctive and declaratory relief under section 13(d) of the Securities and Exchange Act of 1934, 15 U.S.C. § 78m(d). After several years of litigation, the district court dismissed Portsmouth Square's suit *sua sponte* at the final pretrial conference. Portsmouth Square now challenges both the procedure by which the court entered judgment and the conclusion of law on which the judgment rests. We affirm the district court in all respects....

We begin by addressing Portsmouth Square's attack on the procedure by which the district court dismissed its claim. At the final pretrial conference, Judge Schwarzer raised *sua sponte* the question whether the plaintiff had stated a section 13(d) claim. He did not specifically notify the parties in advance that he intended to raise the issue. At the conference, the court pressed counsel for Portsmouth Square to show how the facts set forth in the plaintiff's proposed Findings of Fact stated a section 13(d) claim. After a lengthy dialogue with plaintiff's counsel, the court denied a motion for a continuance and indicated that it would enter judgment for the defendant. In its Amended Order and Judgment, the court labelled its action a "judgment on the pleadings treated as a Motion for Summary Judgment under Rules 12(c) and 56 of the Federal Rules of Civil Procedure." For purposes of the judgment, the court accepted the plaintiff's proposed Findings of Fact as true. It concluded that neither those facts nor the evidence set forth in the pretrial conference materials established a cause of action under section 13(d).[1]

Portsmouth Square argues that the district court had no power to enter a summary judgment *sua sponte*. It also claims that the court violated Rule 56(c), which requires at least 10 days notice of a hearing on a summary judgment motion, and Local Rule 220-2 of the Northern District of California, which requires 28 days notice. Furthermore, Portsmouth Square tells us, the court denied it an opportunity to respond with affidavits and other evidence in support of its claim. Portsmouth Square implies that the district court and opposing counsel have obscured the absence of due process by characterizing the result as a Rule 12(c) judgment on the pleadings treated as a summary judgment. We reject all of these arguments. We are satisfied that the district court proceedings met the requirements of the Federal Rules and the demands of due process.

Under certain limited circumstances a district court may issue summary judgment on its own motion. For example, *sua sponte* summary judgment is appropriate where one party moves for summary judgment and, after the hearing, it appears from all the evidence presented that there is no genuine issue of material fact and the *non-moving* party is entitled to judgment as a matter of law.... We have also allowed summary judgment where a district court, on its own initiative, converted a Rule 12 motion to dismiss into a summary judgment motion by considering pertinent documents that the parties had not presented with their pleadings or motions....

We believe that the district court has similar limited authority to grant summary judgment *sua sponte* in the context of a final pretrial conference. One purpose of the Rule 16 pretrial conference procedure is to promote efficiency and conserve judicial resources by identifying litigable issues prior to trial....[2] If the pretrial conference discloses that no material facts are in dispute and that the undisputed facts entitle one of the parties to judgment as a matter of law, a summary disposition of the case conserves scarce judicial resources. The court need not await a formal motion, or proceed to trial, under those circumstances.

Where the district court grants summary judgment in the absence of a formal motion, we review the record closely to ensure that the party against whom judgment was entered had a full and fair opportunity to develop and present facts and legal arguments in support of its position... A litigant is entitled to reasonable notice that the sufficiency of his or her claim will be

---

1. The pretrial conference materials, submitted by both parties pursuant to a pretrial order, included trial memoranda stating the facts expected to be proved at trial and the law applicable to those facts. The parties also submitted statements summarizing the expected testimony of all witnesses; copies of all exhibits that they planned to introduce; and citations to relevant portions of interrogatories and deposition testimony.

2. Professor Wright notes that summary judgment is directed toward ending litigation before trial, while the pretrial conference generally facilitates trial. 6 Wright and Miller, Federal Practice and Procedure: Civil § 1529 (1971). But he also believes that "the use of Rule 16 to determine whether there are any issues remaining in the case that justify proceeding to a full trial on the merits is not inconsistent with the general purpose of Rule 16." Id. at 622-23.

in issue.... Reasonable notice implies adequate time to develop the facts on which the litigant will depend to oppose summary judgment.... Having reviewed this record, we conclude that Portsmouth Square was afforded a full and fair opportunity to make its case.

Although it would have been preferable for the district court specifically to notify the parties that it intended to consider granting a summary judgment at the pretrial conference, Portsmouth Square was adequately notified that it might have to defend the sufficiency of its claim. The merits of the parties' claims and defenses are a legitimate subject of discussion at a pretrial conference. Fed.R.Civ.P. 16(c)(1). Throughout the course of this litigation the parties have disputed whether Portsmouth Square states a section 13(d) cause of action, and counsel should not have been surprised that the issue arose at the conference. Portsmouth Square also had a full opportunity to develop the facts in support of its case. Its discovery was complete at the time of the pretrial proceedings....

Moreover, Portsmouth Square had a full opportunity to present to the district court its section 13(d) theory and the facts supporting that theory. The court made clear from the outset of the pretrial conference that it intended to explore the merits of the plaintiff's claim, and that it was specifically concerned about whether the corporation could establish a violation of section 13(d). In that connection the court considered all the evidence that Portsmouth Square planned to present at trial. It repeatedly pressed Portsmouth Square's counsel to show that a genuine issue of material fact remained for trial, or that the facts set forth in the proposed Findings stated a claim. The court reached its decision only when it had become clear that counsel could not make the necessary showing.

[The court went on to hold that Portsmouth Square had not established a claim under section 13(d), and affirmed the judgment.]

FIDELITY AND DEPOSIT CO. OF MARYLAND v. SOUTHERN UTILITIES, INC.

726 F.2d 692 (11th Cir. 1984)

■ GODBOLD, Chief Judge. In this case, in which a jury trial was demanded, the district court... granted a "directed verdict" without a trial and in circumstances where summary judgment was not appropriate. It must be reversed.

Southern Utilities, Inc. is an electrical contractor insured by Fidelity & Deposit Co. (F & D) under a "Comprehensive Dishonesty, Disappearance and Destruction Policy." The policy covered Southern for employee dishonesty for losses up to $1 million.... Southern notified F & D of its claim that Hayworth, Southern's former vice-president, acquired and converted construction materials worth $261,685.01. F & D refused to pay. Southern brought suit in Missouri state court to recover the loss plus interest, damages, and attorney's fees... for F & D's vexatious refusal to pay. F & D removed that action to the U.S. District Court W.D. Missouri and filed a third-party complaint against Hayworth seeking indemnity for any sum F & D was required to pay to Southern. Prior to that removal F & D filed a complaint in the U.S. District Court M.D. Georgia, seeking a declaration that F & D had no liability to Southern and that Hayworth would be liable to F & D for any sum it paid Southern. The Missouri action was transferred to M.D. Georgia and the two cases consolidated.

Prior to trial the district court expressed doubt whether Southern could present sufficient evidence to submit the case to a jury. The court utilized plaintiff's trial brief, a narrative statement of evidence required of plaintiff, and a further summary of plaintiff's evidence given at a pretrial conference. It considered this material as though it had been presented in court before a jury and a motion for directed verdict had been made by defendant, and the court then granted a "directed verdict" for F & D and dismissed without prejudice F & D's third-party claim against Hayworth.

The court recognized that the case was not appropriate for summary judgment and that the procedure it used was outside the provisions of the Federal Rules of Civil Procedure. The court based its action on two grounds: (1) judgment may be ordered following a pretrial conference pursuant to Rule 16 if there is no triable issue left at the end of the discussion, and (2) the procedure is analogous to directing a verdict after an opening statement describing the evidence to be presented.

Rule 16 by its terms does not confer special powers to enter judgment not contained in Rule 56 or the other rules. The Second Circuit aptly described the relation between Rule 16 and Rule 56 in Syracuse Broadcasting Corp. v. Newhouse, 271 F.2d 910, 914 (2d Cir.1959):

> . . . Rule 16 confers no special power of dismissal not otherwise contained in the rules. Rule 12(b) and Rule 12(c) provide that summary judgment, under Rule 56, is mandatory when matters outside the pleadings are considered in disposing of a motion to dismiss for failure to state a cognizable claim, or for judgment on the pleadings. Disposition under Rule 56 would appear to be no less mandatory when analogous motions are considered at the pre-trial stage.

See also 6 C. Wright & A. Miller, Federal Practice and Procedure § 1525, at 592-93 (1971) (although judgment may be ordered "at the conference if there is no triable issue left at the end of the discussion," the pretrial judge lacks power "to determine disputed issues of fact or to render a decision after all the issues have been presented" (footnotes omitted)). Some of Southern's evidence of employee dishonesty was disputed, and conflicting inferences could be drawn from it. A triable genuine issue of material fact remained after the pretrial conference. Rule 16 did not authorize entry of judgment.

Likewise, the court's ability to direct a verdict after an opening statement did not allow entry of judgment. Best v. District of Columbia, 291 U.S. 411, 415 (1934), allows the court to direct a verdict after opening statement if the statement shows the plaintiff has no right to recover. . . . Pretermitting whether this power is available before trial, we hold that the court may not direct a verdict where "the opening statement leaves doubt as to the facts or permits conflicting inferences." *Best*, 291 U.S. at 415. Where fair-minded men may draw different conclusions from the evidence, "the question is not one of law but of fact to be settled by the jury." Id. . . .

[The court then found that Southern had presented sufficient evidence to make a jury question out of Hayworth's alleged dishonesty.]

Notes and Questions

1. The source and extent of a court's power to adjudicate disputes *sua sponte* have been debated for a long time. One of the earliest cases to find such a judicial power is Holcomb v. Aetna Life Insurance Co., 255 F.2d 577 (10th Cir.), cert. denied, 358 U.S. 879 (1958). In *Holcomb*, the critical issue was whether Aetna had converted certain property of a deceased policyholder or whether, instead, the property had been paid to Aetna as consideration for an insurance policy. The beneficiaries of the policy brought an action in Oklahoma state court, and Aetna brought an interpleader action in federal court. The beneficiaries refused to "tender" (*i.e.*, provide any factual basis or evidence relating to) the issue of conversion to the federal court during a pretrial conference. As a result, the court, acting on its own authority, "found that no issue of fact existed . . . and rendered summary judgment accordingly." 255 F.2d at 580. The beneficiaries' appeal challenging the right of a federal court "to determine a question of fact at pretrial" was rejected:

> The purpose of pre-trial conferences is to simplify the issues and eliminate waste of time and money by avoiding unnecessary proof at trial. . . . Where at pre-trial admissions and pleadings show that no issue of fact remains to be determined, the court has the power to decide the questions of law and enter summary judgment thereon . . . .
>
> A pre-trial conference is more than a mere conference at which the court seeks to eliminate groundless allegations or denials and the court has the power to compel the parties to agree to all facts concerning which there can be no real issue. [255 F.2d at 580.]

The court then went on to hold that the trial court's ruling was correct.

Likewise, in Fox v. Taylor Diving & Salvage Co., 694 F.2d 1349 (5th Cir. 1983), the plaintiff's Jones Act claim hinged on whether he was indeed a "seaman" within the meaning of the statute. At trial, the plaintiff elicited testimony from an economist, who calculated the plaintiff's wage loss on the basis of plaintiff's on-shore (*i.e.*, non-seaman) employment. The next witness, the plaintiff himself, then began to testify in a way that suggested that he was a seaman. The court immediately called a halt to the trial, held a hearing in chambers at which the court determined that the plaintiff was not a seaman, and dismissed the Jones Act claim. On appeal, after finding that the plaintiff was not a seaman, the Fifth Circuit held in the alternative that the district court's action was within its powers:

> We find no impropriety. In reaching this conclusion, we begin by recognizing that a district court judge has both discretion and responsibility to aid in narrowing the issues to be presented at trial. Fed.R.Civ.P. 16. A groundless contention, one in which both the facts and the law are to the contrary, need not be heard in the district court. In this case, the facts were abundantly clear that Fox was an onshore management worker at the

shipyards. The expert testimony relied upon this status. Fox's adoption of the testimony sealed the book of judgment on this issue.

The trial judge properly recessed the court when this question arose and held an in-chambers conference to evaluate the evidence regarding Jones Act status. Fox's attorney was unable to make a showing that he could present any credible evidence to support a Jones Act claim. The trial judge, therefore, was not obliged to allow Fox to continue with a Jones Act theory, and indeed made such a ruling on his return to the bench. . . . To promote the "[c]onservation of precious court and judge time", . . . summary disposition of unsupportable claims is within the broad discretion of the trial judge, even if those same claims survived the scrutiny of a pre-trial order. [694 F.2d at 1356-57.]

Holcomb and *Fox* are not ideal cases if you are trying to argue that a judge has a *sua sponte* pretrial power to determine disputed issues. In *Holcomb*, the judge made the ruling after the plaintiff declined to provide evidence on a disputed question; in *Fox* the judge's determination occurred during trial, long after pretrial proceedings had been concluded. In both cases, the appellate court treated the procedural propriety of summary adjudication as an alternate holding, and independently found that the factual determination was correct. Neither case provided the exact standard that a court should use to decide disputed factual issues. Finally, in both cases the factual issue that the court resolved disposed of one of the plaintiff's claims; hence, the power of a judge to decide factual issues that were not dispositive of claims was never considered.

Nonetheless, *Holcomb* and *Fox* are important cases, often cited for the proposition that the judge does enjoy a *sua sponta* power to determine disputed factual issues. See, *e.g.*, Manual of Complex Litigation, Third § 21.33 n.102 (1995). See also Pifcho v. Brewer, 77 F.R.D. 356 (M.D. Pa. 1977) (using Rule 16 to dispose of case on *sua sponte* basis).

2. *Holcomb* and *Fox* ground the power to determine factual disputes on Rule 16. It was far from clear that the then-extant Rule 16 — which provided only that "the court may in its discretion direct the attorneys for the parties to appear before it for a conference to consider . . . [t]he simplification of the issues . . . [and such] other matters as may aid in the disposition of the action" — authorized pretrial adjudication. Likewise, the trial judge in *Fidelity and Deposit* entered his ruling prior to the 1983 amendments to Rule 16. *Portsmouth Square*, on the other hand, occurred after the 1983 amendments that completely overhauled and invigorated Rule 16. In particular, the 1983 amendments added Rule 16(c)(1), which authorizes a court to "take appropriate action, with respect to . . . . the formulation and simplification of the issues, including the elimination of frivolous claims or defenses." Although this language is not an outright endorsement of *sua sponte* pretrial adjudication, it is a step in that direction. Do the 1983 amendments explain the difference between *Portsmouth Square* and *Fidelity and Deposit*, or does the disagreement run deeper? See Williams v. Georgia Department of Human Resources, 789 F.2d 881 (11th Cir. 1986) (in case decided after 1983 amendments to Rule 16 became effective, adhering to *Fidelity and Deposit* when trial judge that had decided *Fidelity & Deposit* again entered "directed verdict").

3. A different source for judicially-initiated factual adjudication was suggested by Celotex Corp. v. Catrett, 477 U.S. 317 (1986). In the course of explaining its generally favorable attitude toward summary judgment, the Court observed:

Our conclusion is bolstered by the fact that district courts are widely acknowledged to possess the power to enter summary judgments *sua sponte*, so long as the losing party was on notice that she had to come forward with all of her evidence.... It would surely defy common sense to hold that the District Court could have entered summary judgment *sua sponte* in favor of petitioner in the instant case, but that petitioner's filing of a motion requesting such a disposition precluded the District Court from ordering it. [477 U.S. at 326.]

Although Rule 56 does not by its terms authorize judicially-initiated summary judgments, this dicta has not gone unnoticed. Courts now discuss the *sua sponte* power to enter a Rule 56 summary judgment as a given. See, *e.g.*, B.F. Goodrich v. Betkoski, 99 F.3d 505 (2d Cir. 1996); Berkovitz v. Home Box Office, Inc., 89 F.3d 24 (1st Cir. 1996); Goldstein v. Fidelity and Guaranty Insurance Underwriters, 86 F.3d 749 (7th Cir. 1996); O'Keefe v. Van Boening, 82 F.3d 322 (9th Cir. 1996).

4. Does it make a difference whether a *sua sponte* power of dismissal is located in Rule 16 or in Rule 56? In particular, are the procedures or standards different in the two rules? Following the suggestion of *Celotex*'s dictum, courts have generally required that a judicially-initiated summary judgment under Rule 56 provide both notice of the judge's intent to entertain summary judgment and an adequate opportunity to conduct discovery. See *B.F. Goodrich*, 99 F.3d at 522; Hubbard v. Parker, 994 F.2d 524 (8th Cir. 1993). With regard to the element of notice, some courts have required that a judicially-initiated summary judgment meet the 10-day notice rule of Rule 56(c). See id. at 522-23; but see Madewell v. Downs, 68 F.3d 1030, 1047-49 (8th Cir. 1995) (lack of notice was harmless error). As *Portsmouth Square* reflects, the procedural requirements for a Rule 16(c)(1) dismissal appear to be the same. See also *Berkovitz*, 89 F.3d at 29-30 (using same factors of notice and opportunity to discover, and reversing summary adjudication because "district court failed to give the plaintiff adequate notice of the basis for the action that the court ultimately took").

Similarly, there seems to be no distinction in the standard under which Rule 16 or Rule 56 summary adjudication will occur. The standard under Rule 56 is that there be "no genuine dispute as to any material fact," thus entitling a party to judgment as a matter of law. See *B.F. Goodrich*, 99 F.3d at 521. *Portsmouth Square* applies an identical standard to Rule 16 dismissals. See also *Berkovitz*, 89 F.3d at 29 (same).

5. Recall that party-initiated summary judgments suffered from certain issue-narrowing weaknesses, including the inability to resolve factual issues that are not dispositive of a claim or defense, a high threshold, and a need for adequate factual development. See pp. 1064-68, *supra*. If the latter two weaknesses are replicated in judicially-initiated summary judgments, as the last Note suggests, is it also true that the first weakness is replicated?

Portsmouth Square's dictum seems to answer that question in the affirmative. So does dictum in *Berkovitz*. See 89 F.3d at 29 n.5 ("A district court also may grant partial summary judgment *sua sponte*, removing some (but fewer than all) of the parties' claims or defenses from the case."). But in these cases the factual matter in dispute was claim-dispositive; the courts had no occasion to consider whether they could resolve factual disputes that were not dispositive.

Should a court possess the power to resolve non-dispositive factual disputes? Surprisingly, despite a lot of discussion about a court's power to grant *sua sponte* partial summary judgments, the cases have never focused the issue of adjudicating non-dispositive facts. See David L. Shapiro, *Federal Rule 16: A Look at the Theory and Practice of Rulemaking*, 137 U. Pa. L. Rev. 1969, 1989 (1989) (raising issue in passing). Recall that one of the concerns with permitting non-dispositive factual adjudications on a party's motion was the potential waste of court resources that many such motions would entail. See p. 1066, *supra*. Since the judge will presumably invoke the power only in cases in which the case management payoff is worth the cost, is this concern still applicable? Moreover, recall that there is a fitful trend to permit parties to request summary adjudication of non-dispositive factual disputes. See pp. 1064-66, *supra*. If that trend continues, is there any reason not to grant a comparable authority to the judge?

The answer to this question may depend, once again, on your attitude toward the adversarial system. Once we grant a judge the power to decide non-dispositive factual disputes *sua sponte*, and combine that power with the power to bifurcate pretrial issues, we have moved well along the way to a continental system of continuous trial in which the lawyers are relegated to a lesser role in the development of proofs and arguments. Of course, as long as the threshold for granting such motions remains high, the movement will not be complete. But the common law ideal of a single dispositive trial event will have disappeared.

6. *Fidelity and Deposit* seems fairly hostile to the notion of *sua sponte* summary adjudication, and even *Portsmouth Square* hedges on its endorsement with some pretty serious qualifiers like "limited authority," "final pretrial conference," "no material dispute," claim-dispositive issue, and conservation of "scarce judicial resources." Other cases express a similar caution. For instance, in *Goldstein*, the Seventh Circuit observed:

> We do not want to encourage district courts to consider summary judgment *sua sponte* because the procedure warrants "special caution," and it's often inappropriate.... It is also largely unnecessary, as a district court can always invite a nonmoving party to file a motion for summary judgment in its favor. But while we do not express resounding approval of *sua sponte* summary judgment, it is not always wrong for a district court to resolve certain cases in this fashion. It's just a bit risky. [86 F.3d at 751.]

Does *Goldstein* publicly profess reluctance about, yet secretly bless, *sua sponte* summary adjudication? Or is its reluctance genuine? What might be the source of reluctance? Is it an unwillingness to push the case management role too far into the adversarial task of prosecuting and defending claims? If judicially-initiated summary adjudication of factual disputes can advance the efficiency of the pretrial process, should we care about the damage it does to the adversarial ideal?

7. Thus far, we have not discussed whether the complexity of the litigation ought to influence the use of *sua sponte* summary adjudication. The cases themselves make no distinction between complex and routine. Does the fact of complexity nonetheless explain the difference between *Portsmouth Square* (an arguably complex case) and *Fidelity and Deposit* (a routine case)?

In complex cases there may be less reason to care about the damage that *sua sponte* adjudication does to the adversarial ideal, since, by definition, the adversarial system does not work well. But that fact does not necessarily argue for an expanded role for summary adjudication in complex cases. Given all the inroads on judicial neutrality that case management devices such as *sua sponte* adjudication make, is it wise to give the judge the ultimate power to dispose of disputed factual issues? Wouldn't the judge's public incentives (she has already adjudged this issue as particularly weak) and private incentives (she wants to dispose of issues and cases) lead the judge to dispose of issues and claims that lie in the gray area between the clearly frivolous and the clearly triable? Are case management devices that involve the judge less in the prosecution of defenses and claims preferable? If those devices are inadequate to the case management task, should we then permit *sua sponte* summary adjudication? If so, do we need to extend any *sua sponte* authority to routine cases in which adversarial presentation remains adequate? If not, is our only option to seek resolution of the dispute through mechanisms other than litigation?

Once again, we find that complex litigation puts our procedural system between a rock and a couple of hard places: either maintain two different and unequal systems of procedure, abandon the adversarial system in cases in which it functions perfectly well, or muddle along with procedures that are inadequate to the task of rational adjudication. Does this range of choices make more attractive the option of handling of complex cases outside of the adjudicatory system?

v. Using Prior Judgments

In Chapter Two we learned the ways in which claim or issue preclusion can be used to overcome problems of joinder complexity. See pp. 155-239, *supra*. Lying on the frontier of legal thought, this use of preclusion doctrines was highly controversial and still largely theoretical. Concerns for loss of individual control over litigation and lack of adequate representation seems to have fairly well doomed the venture, at least for the present.

There is also a different — and time-honored — use of preclusion doctrines: to eliminate, or at least limit, certain claims or issues in subsequent litigation. In this capacity, preclusion doctrines can act as issue-narrowing devices. When claim preclusion (res judicata) kicks in, an entire claim can be stricken. When issue preclusion (collateral estoppel) kicks in, factual issues that were actually litigated and necessarily decided in the prior lawsuit are conclusively established for purposes of the second suit. Since preclusion usually presents a clean legal issue that can be resolved early in the case without extensive discovery, the doctrines seem to be an ideal remedy for some of the ills of pretrial complexity.

The problem, of course, is that preclusion doctrines are hard to satisfy. Claim and issue preclusion traditionally could be invoked in a second lawsuit only between the parties (or those with whom they were in privity) to the first lawsuit. At least with respect to issue preclusion, that limitation is giving way, and defensive and offensive uses of collateral estoppel are now permitted. But even here, the party against whom preclusion is asserted in the second suit must have been a party in the first suit; with few exceptions, it is not enough to say that the factual issues of Defendant B's liability are conclusively determined merely because Defendant A, whose conduct was identical, was found liable in a prior lawsuit. Moreover, even when

Defendant B was a party in the prior suit, numerous exceptions hedge in the availability of collateral estoppel in the second suit. See pp. 164-65, 194-207, *supra*.

Having explored the preclusion doctrines in Chapter Two, we do not intend to re-examine the doctrines in detail here. Rather, we present a single case that shows how the issue-narrowing potential of preclusion can be joined with other case management techniques to eliminate or limit problems of pretrial complexity.

COLUMBIA STEEL FABRICATORS, INC. v. AHLSTROM RECOVERY

44 F.3d 800 (9th Cir.), cert. denied, 516 U.S. 864 (1995)

■ KLEINFELD, Circuit Judge. The district court granted summary judgment *sua sponte* against plaintiffs, even though the defendant had not yet appeared. Another defendant had won summary judgment on the same grounds, and the court found the case to be frivolous. We affirm.

Facts

Ahlstrom was the general contractor building a boiler for Louisiana Pacific Corporation. Ahlstrom hired Stevens Equipment for steel fabrication, and Stevens contracted with its affiliate Columbia Steel for materials. Ahlstrom hired Aaro Kohonen Oy (AKO), in Finland, for engineering.

Stevens and Columbia made a number of claims against Ahlstrom, including that the engineering was bad and late, costing them more money. Stevens sued Ahlstrom in California state court, and then arbitrated its claims on its own and Columbia's behalf. Stevens prevailed in arbitration, but not on the claims related to the case at bar. After the arbitration award was reduced to judgment in state court, Columbia and Stevens brought this diversity suit.

In this federal case, AKO, the engineering subcontractor in Finland, never appeared. It had been served, but Stevens and Columbia had not filed proof of service, or requested entry of default, so when the district court granted summary judgment, the judge inferred from the record that AKO had not been served. As we analyze the case, the judge's erroneous belief that AKO had not been served does not matter.

Ahlstrom moved for summary judgment. The district judge decided, after full consideration of the submissions on this contested motion, that Ahlstrom was entitled to judgment on alternative independent grounds, res judicata and statute of limitations. She also made an express finding that the lawsuit was "frivolous and vexatious," because all the claims at issue had been before the arbitration panel and had been considered by the arbitrators, were considered again by the arbitrators on Stevens' and Columbia's motion for reconsideration, and were considered again by the state court before it entered judgment based on the arbitration award. Because of the finding of frivolousness and vexatiousness, the district court granted Rule 11 sanctions against Columbia, Stevens, and their attorneys. Columbia and Stevens have settled with Ahlstrom, so the judgment for Ahlstrom, and the Rule 11 sanctions, are not before us on appeal.

At oral argument in district court, when counsel for Columbia and Stevens pointed out that the district court judge's grant of summary judgment to Ahlstrom left open the claims against AKO, the judge said that both defenses applied equally to AKO, and that summary judgment in favor of AKO was appropriate as well. Columbia and Stevens did not object, suggest that any different legal or factual considerations might apply to their claim against AKO, or ask for additional time to make any submission.

Analysis

Columbia and Stevens argue that the district court could not properly grant summary judgment in favor of a defendant who did not appear in the case or move for summary judgment. This proposition may generally be correct, but not always, and not here.

We have upheld dismissal with prejudice in favor of a party which had not yet appeared, on the basis of facts presented by other defendants which had appeared. . . .

We have also upheld *sua sponte* summary judgment. Portsmouth Square v. Shareholders Protective Comm., 770 F.2d 866, 869 (9th Cir.1985) . . . . We have specifically upheld *sua sponte* consideration of the res judicata effect of a prior judgment. . . .

These cases do not necessarily control. They do not go so far as to uphold *sua sponte* summary judgment based on res judicata in favor of a party which has not appeared. Nevertheless, the factual distinctions which might be drawn make no difference here. The reasoning of these earlier authorities applies fully to the case at bar.

Columbia and Stevens correctly note that AKO was not a party to its arbitration with Ahlstrom. But collateral estoppel does not require that the party benefitting have been a party to the earlier litigation. Stevens presented against Ahlstrom in the arbitration all claims which it could have presented against Ahlstrom's engineering subcontractor, AKO. The arbitrators found that Stevens did not prove damages caused by the alleged error and delay. This basis for the arbitration award compelled the conclusion, inferred by the district court, that even if Ahlstrom's subcontractor AKO was responsible for whatever error and delay there was, Stevens had exhausted its opportunity to prove damages. It is well established that collateral estoppel can operate in favor of a party which did not litigate the earlier case, in appropriate circumstances. . . . Columbia and Stevens have not demonstrated why they would not be precluded by the arbitration award and judgment in favor of Ahlstrom, which was in privity of contract with AKO. . . .

Res judicata doctrine preserves scarce judicial resources, as well as protecting litigants from multiple lawsuits, . . . so courts have an independent interest in raising it, even if a party does not.

Sua sponte summary judgment in favor of a nonappearing party should not be routine. We noted in Portsmouth that the circumstances for such dismissal on the merits are "limited." *Portsmouth*, 770 F.2d at 869 . . . . It is a dangerous case management technique, because of the increased risk of error in the absence of full adversarial development of the facts and law. But it is not a prohibited technique under the circumstances of this case.

This case was appropriate for *sua sponte* summary judgment for the nonappearing party, AKO. Several circumstances justified the relief. Columbia and Stevens had a full and fair opportunity to brief and present evidence on the issues raised by Ahlstrom. . . . These were the same issues controlling the AKO determination. The court held oral argument before granting summary judgment for AKO. Columbia and Stevens brought up AKO's presence as a party, and did not suggest to the district court that their case against AKO would require any additional or different evidence or briefing from their case against Ahlstrom. They still have not demonstrated why their case against AKO would not be controlled by the decision in their case against Ahlstrom. They did not ask the district judge for time to consider whether their case against AKO would be different, or to submit any additional papers. Nor did they object to summary disposition at the time and in the manner it was made. The district judge found that the case was frivolous. Our *de novo* review reveals no genuine issue of fact or entitlement against AKO as a matter of law, and affords some protection against defects which might have resulted from surprise. . . .

Under these circumstances, *sua sponte* summary judgment avoided what would have otherwise been a considerable and needless burden on AKO and the judicial system in a frivolous case.

Notes and Questions

1. Res judicata and collateral estoppel are affirmative defenses that must be asserted at the pleading stage. F.R.Civ.P. 8(c).

2. Chapter Two examined the use of preclusion doctrines to overcome joinder complexity. Here we are considering the use of preclusion doctrines to overcome pretrial complexity. Should these different uses lead to different interpretations of preclusion doctrines in the two contexts, or should the doctrines remain constant regardless of the use to which they are put? If you think that the doctrines should be interpreted in light of the circumstances of their use, are the problems of joinder and pretrial complexity different enough to justify different interpretations? Don't both types of complexity grow from the same root: lawyer dysfunction?

3. *Columbia Steel* involved both res judicata (in favor of Ahlstrom on Ahlstrom's motion) and defensive collateral estoppel (in favor of AKO *sua sponte*). Should a court be able summarily to invoke offensive collateral estoppel? Should it be able summarily to invoke defensive collateral estoppel against a plaintiff who was not involved in the other litigation but whose interests with respect to the finding are substantially identical to those of other plaintiffs who lost the same issue against the defendant (or, even more broadly, against other, similarly situated defendants)? Should a court be able summarily

to invoke offensive collateral estoppel against a defendant who was not involved in the other litigation but whose interests with respect to the finding are substantially identical to other defendants who lost the same issue against the plaintiff (or, even more broadly, against other, similarly situated plaintiffs)?

In Chapter Two we learned that, when a party files a motion, the answers to the three questions in the last paragraph are "Sometimes," "No," and "No." Unless the judge is given greater *sua sponte* powers, the answers should presumably be the same when the judge acts summarily. But this series of questions does show the issue-narrowing potential of preclusion doctrines — if the doctrines are construed more broadly than they are at present. You might wish to reconsider the wisdom of restrictive preclusion rules now that you have seen a second use to which they can be put. Or you might not; there are powerful constitutional and political reasons not to tamper with the law of preclusion.

Even if preclusion doctrines were to be broadened, would summary adjudication of such issues be a desirable outcome? On the one hand, *Columbia Steel* shows that summary adjudication on these matters is a powerful case management tool that can narrow issues significantly early in the litigation. On the other hand, were the plaintiffs' claims against AKO so patently frivolous that an adversarial presentation of the matter would have been pointless? *Columbia Steel* seems to straddle the line on this question, professing in its language the "dangerous" and "limited" nature of judicially-initiated summary adjudication, yet approving in its holding a technique that efficiently resolved the case. Should the court's inquisitorial power become narrower if preclusion doctrines expand, or should it be the same regardless of the scope of preclusion law?

4. *Columbia Steel* does not appear to be a complex case. Should the court have greater powers to use preclusion doctrines summarily in complex cases, even if that power is not enjoyed in more routine litigation?

vi. Providing (or Withholding) Advice

Until now we have examined case management options that are authoritarian and authoritative — judgments, orders, forced stipulations, sanctions, and the like. We have also seen that it is often not possible for a judge to demand that the parties do that which is the most sensible from a case management standpoint. As any lawyer will tell you, however, most judges are also very good at "persuading" parties to do things voluntarily that the judge could not order them to do. A great deal of this persuasion is "an iron fist in a velvet glove"; judges have tremendous discretion to manage pretrial issues, and can make a recalcitrant party's life difficult.

By this point, you should not be shocked by this fact. The existence of judicial discretion, especially in complex litigation, is a fact. Any system that imbues significant discretion in the judge creates the risk of abuse of power. But discretion also carries the promise of achieving justice. Whether the risk of abuse outweighs the benefit of ensuring justice has been a central question of this book.

In this section, we focus on a particular aspect of the trial judge's discretion: the giving of non-authoritative judicial "advice." It is often the case, and nowhere moreso than in complex litigation, that the parties need to know the judge's feelings about a particular legal, evidentiary, or factual issue in order to make certain strategic and tactical decisions. At the same time, an authoritative ruling in the context of a motion to dismiss or a motion for summary judgment is clearly not appropriate.

Therefore, authorizing the judge to opine on a preliminary, non-authoritative basis about legal and factual issues can serve a valuable case management function. The authority for issuing such preliminary opinions, however, is not entirely clear. Rule 56 does not specifically authorize it; neither does Rule 16. It does, however, seem to be a power that fits as easily within the penumbra of Rules 16(c)(1), (c)(4), (c)(12), and (c)(16) as some of the other powers that we have seen judges assert. One of the original purposes of the pretrial conference authorized under Rule 16 was precisely to give the lawyers the opportunity to exchange ideas about the case's progress with the judge. In a Rule 16 conference the judge and lawyers are free to discuss ideas. Often the lawyers will toss out ideas, and measure the judge's response. If the judge's response is negative, the idea might need to be discarded or at least refined; but at least a lot of wasted time has been avoided. If the response is positive, more legwork must be done; but potentially the pretrial issues have been significantly streamlined.

This type of judicial guidance occurs all the time, in cases both complex and routine. Rarely, however, does it come to the public eye. The judge's advice is almost never put into a published decision; indeed, the advice may not even be transcribed into the record. Only on a few occasions has an advisory opinion come into the limelight. See In re "Agent Orange" Product Liability Litigation, 580 F. Supp. 690 (E.D.N.Y. 1984) (p. 855, *supra*) ("preliminary memorandum" on choice of law issue).

There are risks associated with the use of such non-binding guidance. There is the cost factor, as well as the possibility that the guidance will ultimately be unnecessary to the resolution of the case. Moreover, without the impetus of a definitive motion before her, the judge may not pay as careful attention to the issue as she should, and may even erroneously prejudge the controversy. Finally, on some occasions the best response to the parties' need for advice is not to give it, but rather to keep them in the dark in order to give them a mutual incentive to work out the problem on their own.

This last objection suggests that, at least in some situations, the best case management tool is not to give advice but to withhold it. Withholding advice might also be appropriate with regard to definitive motions; the uncertainty created by a failure to rule may maintain a tension that is helpful to the resolution of the case. Indeed, withholding advice or a definitive ruling has been singled out as a significant case management tool:

> [S]ome trial courts have successfully attempted to promote settlement of mass tort claims by *withholding* decisions on these crucial questions in order to maintain a high level of uncertainty — and, consequently, risk — for both sides of the litigation....
>
> The *Agent Orange* litigation offers repeated examples of the court's strategic manipulation of uncertainty. Throughout the litigation, Judge

Weinstein avoided issuing final decisions on potentially dispositive issues. Instead, he issued statements of preliminary decisions or indications of how he might rule on those issues. Judge Weinstein finally ruled on critical issues . . . only after the litigation had been settled. Weinstein's opinion on the fairness of the settlement turned on his conclusion that plaintiffs' cases were so weak as to have little value. . . . If these opinions had been issued prior to the settlement, the defendants would have had no incentive for settling the litigation. . . .

Courts' attempts to decide . . . complicated issues entail hard intellectual labor, certain criticism, and the risk of reversal, all of which can be avoided if litigation is resolved by settlement before the court is forced to decide. Postponing resolution of these complicated questions pressures parties toward settlements, which may relieve the judge from ever having to decide the issues. In short, trial courts faced with mass tort lawsuits often find it in their interests to fail to articulate and address legal issues.

Mark A. Peterson & Molly Selvin, *Mass Justice: The Limited and Unlimited Power of Courts*, 54 Law & Contemp. Prob. 227, 240-41 (Summer 1991). This withholding of advice or decision is hardly an isolated phenomenon; in one study, no action was recorded with respect to 34% of the summary judgment motions filed in three courts during 1986. Joe S. Cecil & C.R. Douglas, Summary Judgment Practice in Three District Courts 5-6 (1987) (noting that in many of these cases, "the case settled soon after the motion was filed").

Should a judge have discretion not to judge? Would your answer depend on whether the failure to judge served a legitimate case management purpose? How could you (or an appellate court) distinguish a "legitimate" purpose from an "illegitimate" one?

The literature on case management rarely mentions — much less legitimates — the practice of refusing to rule. Indeed, principles of case management — such as the need for just, speedy, and inexpensive resolution of disputes, the need for prompt, firm, and fair judicial management, and the need to define and narrow factual and legal issues as soon as possible — point in the opposite direction. *See* 28 U.S.C. § 473(a)(3)(D) (in complex litigation, district courts should consider development of plans that "set[ ], at the earliest practicable time, deadlines for filing motions and a time framework for their disposition"); Manual for Complex Litigation, Third § 20.13 ("The judge promptly decides disputes, particularly those that may substantially affect the course or extent of further proceedings.")

The best-known case discussing the "failure to judge" issue took a dim view of the practice. In In re School Asbestos Litigation, 977 F.2d 764 (3d Cir. 1992), Georgia Pacific and W.R. Grace were among the more than fifty defendants sued by a plaintiff class in a massive asbestos case. On September 5, 1991, the trial court issued a pretrial order that limited the initial trial to the issues of conspiracy and fraud. Shortly afterwards, on October 25, 1991, the court further limited the initial trial to ten defendants. The court's list contained Georgia-Pacific but not W.R. Grace.

Five days later, Georgia-Pacific filed a motion for summary judgment on conspiracy and fraud. On November 8, 1991, W.R. Grace filed a comparable motion. On November 29, 1991, the district court issued a pretrial order, founded on its "discretionary powers," that dismissed as untimely Georgia-Pacific's motion. The court explained that all defendants had long been on notice that the time for filing motions concerning the initial trial "would soon come to an end," and that consideration of the motions would unduly delay the trial. On December 16, 1991, the district court dismissed the motion for summary judgment of W.R. Grace for similar reasons.

W.R. Grace and Georgia-Pacific then filed petitions for writs of mandamus asking that the Third Circuit direct the district court to consider and decide their summary judgment motions on the merits. The Third Circuit first held that mandamus was an appropriate remedy because "a district court's failure to consider the merits of a summary judgment motion is a failure to exercise its authority when it has the duty to do so." 977 F.2d at 793. The court of appeals then turned to the merits of the petition:

> [I]n this case the district court had set no explicit deadline for summary judgment motions, nor a specific trial date. These factors make all the difference. The district court may well have been correct that resolution of these motions in December 1991 would not have advanced the litigation from an overall perspective. [The initial trial] would still have had to proceed with the other defendants, and if the district court had had to deal with more than a handful of these motions, trial might have been delayed. But fairness to defendants is as much a policy of Rule 56 as are fairness to plaintiffs and the convenience to the district court....
>
> Under the policy of Rule 56, movants are entitled to avoid the expense and tribulations of trial if they can prove that there is no triable issue.... [W]here, as here, parties are not given any deadline and do not violate the ten-day limitation of Rule 56(c), they cannot be said to have waived their right or to have been unfair to their opponents. District courts are entitled to broad deference regarding timeliness restrictions, but they are entitled to that deference only if they state those deadlines explicitly. [977 F.2d at 793-95].

Would mandamus have been appropriate if, instead of denying the motions for summary judgment, the judge had simply failed to rule on them? Can the Third Circuit's decision be reconciled with the following observation:

> Neither do we suggest that the trial courts should act other than with caution in granting summary judgment or that the trial court may not deny summary judgment in a case where there is reason to believe that the better course would be to proceed to a full trial.

Anderson v. Liberty Lobby, Inc. 477 U.S. 242, 255 (1986).

B. DISCOVERY TECHNIQUES

In the first section of this chapter you explored many of the case management techniques for narrowing issues during pretrial. Hopefully you can now appreciate some of the concerns — such as efficiency, effectiveness, discretion, jury trial, adversarial or inquisitorial participation, and trans-substantivism — that surround these case management techniques. The same concerns surround the other half of the "chicken-and-egg" problem: the control of pretrial discovery.

Pretrial discovery, which had been available in a limited fashion in equity, became a feature of all civil actions after the adoption of the Federal Rules of Civil Procedure in 1938. The drafters of the Federal Rules hoped that the discovery rules would make the trial run more efficiently and avoid "trial by ambush." Whether these goals were best accomplished by affording the parties nearly unlimited access to their opponents' storehouses of information is certainly debatable. Moreover, the costliness of discovery has to some degree replaced trial by ambush with another merits-frustrating problem: the "blackmail" of strike suits in which a defendant settles a meritless suit in order to avoid discovery costs. Moreover, even assuming that discovery was capable of meeting its goals, there was a strong theoretical objection to it: It forced lawyers to reveal to their opponents proofs and, at least indirectly, arguments that they had accumulated in the discharge of their adversarial responsibilities.

Although criticism of discovery has continued unabated since 1938, discovery is not only an inveterate feature of our procedural system, but also the central feature of the system. Fewer than 10% of all cases at the federal level come to trial; the remainder are either settled or dismissed. In many of these cases, settlement or dismissal follows a period of discovery. The shift from trial to discovery is so complete that an entire branch of the legal profession is no longer "trial practice"; it is "litigation practice."

In complex litigation, discovery often poses a significant problem of gathering, sifting, and organizing relevant evidence. Indeed, it was this very problem that led to the search for issue-narrowing devices. But, as we have seen, issue-narrowing devices are often unavailable until some discovery has occurred; and even when discovery is successfully avoided on some issues, these may not be the issues that require intensive discovery. Massive discovery is the most common and obvious symptom of pretrial complexity.

At the same time, a generous right of discovery is one of the main procedural causes of pretrial complexity. We do not wish to overstate the case; there are numerous other procedural and substantive causes as well. Nevertheless, if lawyers were not entitled to the extensive discovery that modern rules permit, then the problem of lawyer dysfunction in the pretrial setting — i.e., the inability of the lawyers to adequately marshal evidence and formulate arguments — would be reduced or eliminated. (Of course, that reduction would likely be offset, at least to some degree, by an increase in problems of trial complexity.)

All of these considerations suggest that we might wish to think about changing our usual rules of discovery in complex cases. The changes can occur in one of two ways: either restrictions can be placed on the quantity or quality of information to which the parties have access, or the judge can become more actively involved in the process of gathering, sifting, and organizing information. Neither change is an unadulterated blessing. For instance, as access to information declines, the chance of reaching the correct decision on the merits declines. The chance of holding governmental and corporate entities accountable declines. The chance of settling or dismissing lawsuits declines; indeed, without an adequate opportunity for discovery, devices such as summary judgment may no longer be available. Finally, the chance for a crisply presented trial may decline.

Conversely, if the discovery rules are changed in such a way that the judge has more control over the development of proofs and arguments, a conflict with the system's adversarial ideal ensues. Granting the judge a more active role in discovery and significant discretion to decide whether and how to restrict access to information presupposes the consistent and wise use of that authority. Moreover, if similar steps are not taken in more routine cases, changes in discovery in complex litigation might create a two-tiered pretrial system in which a party's prospects for success might hinge on whether the case is "complex" or "routine."

These are the major matters that will occupy us in this section. We begin with a quick look at the concept of the discovery plan, which is an integral aspect of the case management plan. We then examine some changes and adjustments that have been made in traditional discovery to accommodate the information overload of complex litigation. We end with a look at non-traditional means of discovering information.

1. The Discovery Plan

Rule 26(f), which was added in 1980 and amended in 1993, requires parties to meet "as soon as practicable and in any event at least 14 days before a scheduling conference is held or a scheduling order is due under Rule 16(b)," and at that meeting "to develop a proposed discovery plan." The plan must include the parties' views on numerous discovery matters, including (1) any changes that should be made to the mandatory disclosures and to other limitations that the discovery rules impose, see F.R.Civ.P. 26(f)(1) and (f)(3); (2) "the subjects on which discovery may be needed, when discovery should be completed, and whether discovery should be conducted in phases or be limited to or focused upon particular issues," see F.R.Civ.P. 26(f)(2); and (3) the appropriateness of any protective orders under Rule 26(c) or other orders under Rules 16(b) and (c), see F.R.Civ.P. 26(f)(4). Within 10 days of the meeting, the parties must submit the plan to the court.

By tying the discovery plan to the initial Rule 16(b) pretrial conference, Rule 26(f) seeks to ensure that both issue narrowing and discovery techniques are included in the case management plan. Assuming that case management is a good thing, this tying arrangement is theoretically correct. Given the "chicken-and-egg" relationship between issue development and discovery, case management that focused solely on issue development, without understanding how various approaches would affect and be affected by discovery, would be partially effective at best. A comprehensive case management plan must address both issue development and discovery.

Rule 26(f) puts the onus for proposing such a plan squarely on the lawyers' shoulders. Rule 16(b) then requires a judge, "after receiving the report from the parties under Rule 26(f)," to enter a scheduling order limiting the time for discovery, and permits the judge to include in the scheduling order "modifications of the times for disclosures under Rules 26(a) and 26(e)(1) and of the extent of discovery to be permitted." Rule 16(c)(6) further authorizes the court, at the pretrial conference, to consider and "take appropriate action, with respect to . . . the control and scheduling of discovery, including orders affecting disclosures and discovery pursuant to Rule 26 and Rules 29 through 37."

In a sense, therefore, the real issue is not whether the judge can be active in developing a discovery plan, but rather how active the judge can be.

MANUAL FOR COMPLEX LITIGATION, THIRD

55-56 (1995)

A discovery plan should be designed to facilitate the orderly and cost-effective acquisition of relevant information and materials and the prompt resolution of discovery disputes. No single format is appropriate for all cases; the discovery plan should be tailored to the circumstances of the litigation. While the court needs to take responsibility for the adoption of a discovery plan, its development and implementation must necessarily be a collaborative effort with counsel. Because the lawyers will be more familiar with the case, the court should call on them initially to propose a plan. Agreement among counsel is, of course, desirable, and joint recommendations should be given considerable weight. Nevertheless the judge should not accept them uncritically and may need to place limits on discovery even if agreed on by counsel. The judge's role is to oversee the plan and to provide guidance and control, always recognizing that the litigation is conducted by the lawyers and not the court. In performing that role, the judge, while recognizing his or her limited familiarity with the case, should not as a result abdicate the responsibility for control. Judges should not hesitate to ask counsel why particular discovery is needed and whether needed information can be obtained more efficiently and economically by other means. Regular contact with counsel through periodic conferences will enable the court to monitor the progress of the plan, ensure that it is operating fairly and effectively, and from time to time adjust it as needed.

Notes and Questions

1. Does the *Manual* give you a good sense of how active the judge is supposed to be in developing and modifying a discovery plan? There seems to be language on which both the aggressive case manager and the more detached judge could seize. Is it even possible to state the appropriate level of judicial activity in the development of a discovery plan?

2. Should the judge necessarily have the same level of activity with respect to every plan, or should the nature of the case determine the judge's involvement? If the nature of the case is relevant, which factors should lead a judge to be more active? Should the need to streamline litigation be a factor? The cooperativeness of the lawyers? The inability of the lawyers to perform their discovery responsibilities without judicial assistance? If involvement varies from judge to judge and from case to case, and if discovery is the critical period in litigation, how can there be any consistency in result among cases?

3. With the exception of cases exempted under local rules, every case must in theory have a proposed discovery plan. This is a marked shift from the original Rule 26(f), which merely authorized the court to hold a discovery conference on either a party's motion or the court's own initiative; the upshot of such a conference was an order that established a discovery plan. According to one unscientific survey of published decisions, fewer than 50 discovery conferences were held between 1980 and 1987. See Union City Barge Line, Inc. v. Union Carbide Corp., 823 F.2d 129 (5th Cir. 1987). Undoubtedly this figure understated the actual use of discovery plans, but the figure indicates that lawyers and judges did not perceive a tremendous need to interject the judge into discovery planning in all cases.

The 1993 amendments to Rule 26(f) made the proposed discovery plan mandatory. To some extent, the shift was necessitated by contemporaneous changes in Rule 16(b) that required the court to enter orders concerning completion of discovery and extent of discovery; as the Advisory Committee stated in its notes, "[b]efore entering such orders, the court should consider the views of the parties." But that logic merely ducks the real issue: Why should a judge become so intimately involved in the discovery process? The Advisory Committee Notes on the 1993 amendments to Rules 16 and 26 are unhelpful, with the Note to Rule 26(f) stating only that "[t]he desirability of some judicial control of discovery can hardly be doubted." Is that true? If it is, is it necessarily true that the best way to exercise this authority is by means of mandatory discovery plans? Can the revisions to Rule 26(f) nonetheless be defended on trans-substantive grounds — that discovery plans were needed in some cases, and extension of the process to all cases was necessary to ensure like treatment of all cases? If so, wouldn't this argument logically require that there be consistency with regard to both the level of judicial involvement in developing plans and the content of the plans themselves? See generally Discovery and Disclosure Practice, Problems, and Proposals for Change 31-32 (Federal Judicial Center 1997) (reporting that 60% of attorneys actually met to develop discovery plan, and that majority of attorneys reported that meeting had no effect "on litigation expenses, disposition times, fairness, or the number of issues in the case").

4. When related cases cannot be consolidated in a single forum, one way to achieve many of joinder's advantages is to file a joint discovery plan in each relevant forum. For examples of such plans in the state-federal context, as well as for a sample order, see James G. Apple et al., Manual for Cooperation Between State and Federal Courts 18-19, 131-36 (1997).

5. The *Manual* states that a discovery plan must be monitored by the judge and adjusted as appropriate. This seems sensible enough. Presumably the vehicle for accomplishing the adjustment is a subsequent pretrial conference held pursuant to Rule 16. Suppose, however, that, after the entry of a discovery plan, the case is multidistricted to another forum. Can the multidistrict judge

amend the discovery plan, or does it act as law of the case? Likewise, suppose that the original discovery plan was adopted by a multidistrict transferee judge after transfer, and after completion of multidistrict proceedings, the case is remanded to the transferor forum. Can the transferor judge amend the discovery plan, or does the plan act as the law of the case? See In re Multi-Piece Rim Products Liability Litigation, 653 F.2d 671 (D.C. Cir. 1981).

6. Neither Rule 16 nor Rule 26 authorizes the judge to become the lead player in the gathering, sifting, or organizing of information; they merely authorize the judge to become a more active participant in shaping the lawyers' work of gathering, sifting, and organizing. It is important to think in the abstract about how active the judge should become in the discovery planning process. Before you commit to an answer, however, you might wish to have a bit more information about exactly what a judge can do in a discovery planning order. This is the question to which we now turn, first by examining the judge's powers within the confines of traditional discovery and then by examining non-traditional approaches to the discovery of relevant information.

2. Traditional Discovery: Problems and Possible Solutions

The traditional methods of discovery — interrogatories, document production requests, and depositions — create problems for complex litigation. Even after 45 years of experience with big case litigation, it remains an open issue whether traditional methods can handle the informational needs of complex cases in a fair and efficient manner. It is also an open question whether alternatives to traditional discovery — such as increased judicial involvement in fact gathering or non-traditional fact-gathering techniques — can do any better. If no method works well, would it be better to handle complex litigation through non-litigative means?

a. Traditional Discovery Devices: A Review

There are four, or arguably five, discovery devices provided for under the Federal Rules of Civil Procedure: oral and written depositions (Rules 30-32), interrogatories (Rule 33), requests for inspection of documents and other tangible things (Rule 34), physical and mental examinations (Rule 35), and, arguably, requests for admission (Rule 36). Of these devices, three (interrogatories, examinations, and admissions) can be sought only from parties; depositions and production of documentary evidence can be obtained from both parties and non-parties. See F.R.Civ.P. 45. All of the discovery devices are subject to Rule 26, which limits the scope of discovery to "any matter, not privileged, which is relevant to the subject matter involved in the pending action." F.R.Civ.P. 26(b)(1). But the "information sought need not be admissible at the trial if the information sought appears reasonably calculated to lead to the discovery of admissible evidence." Id.

The most common devices are depositions, interrogatories, and requests for inspection. Each relies upon the others to attain full effectiveness.

Fleming James, Jr. et al., CIVIL PROCEDURE

238-39, 242-44 (4th ed. 1992)

The most widely used discovery device is the oral deposition. . . . The greatest advantage of an oral deposition over other methods of discovery is the flexibility it affords in probing a witness by requiring immediate, on-the-spot answers to oral questions (without the chance to rehearse responses that written interrogatories would afford) and to allow the examiner to frame successive questions in the light of the answers given. Moreover, the examiner can elicit a preview of the witness's line of testimony as the witness will give it at trial. . . .

The greatest disadvantage of the oral deposition is the expense. In some cases the deposition may have a more limited reach than interrogatories addressed to a party, because . . . interrogatories require a party to respond with any available information — not merely what can be recollected at the time of the question. . . .

Interrogatories to parties enjoy wide use; the device is almost as popular as the oral deposition. . . . [I]t is much less expensive, and, although it lacks the flexibility of the oral deposition, it is often used to pave the way for more economical and effective use of the deposition procedure (by ascertaining the names and addresses of witnesses) and for the disclosure of documents (by ascertaining their identity and whereabouts). Claims of abuse of the interrogatory procedure, however, are frequent. The questioner can easily frame questions requiring great effort to answer; the answerer can submit vague and evasive answers. . . .

Rule 34 permits a party to obtain inspection of physical objects, including documents and data in a computer, and to enter on land or other property to make inspections. In connection with the inspection, the party may make copies, photographs, measurements, and tests. . . .

This device requires a specification of the things to be inspected. . . . A document does not have to be turned over or made available to the other party unless it is requested; hence, attorneys have an incentive to interpret discovery requests narrowly to avoid damaging disclosures. This in turn requires the requests to be drafted with meticulous care . . . . If the party seeking discovery lacks information sufficient to make the specification, the information must first be obtained through preliminary use of other discovery devices such as depositions or interrogatories.

Notes and Questions

1. As you might expect, many of the weaknesses of the traditional discovery methods are exacerbated in complex litigation. There are likely to be

hundreds of depositions, the costs of which can be staggering. For instance, if each deposition lasts two hours, each attorney spends two hours preparing for the deposition, each attorney charges $150 per hour, and only three attorneys attend the deposition, then a single deposition costs $1800 in attorneys fees — and this does not include witness, travel, transcription, or digesting costs. These assumptions probably underestimate the actual costs. Therefore, it is not unusual for a full program of depositions in a large case to cost hundreds of thousands, and sometimes millions, of dollars. All of this to generate information that may not deliver perfect, or even particularly adequate, information about the facts of the case.

The problems of excessive use, evasion, and ultra-literalist interpretation that infect interrogatories and requests for inspection are not peculiar to complex litigation. Once again, however, the stakes of the case and the resultant willingness of clients to spend large sums for small tactical advantages make such conduct more likely. Exactly how likely is not, however, certain. The last thirty years of our procedural history are full of anecdotes about abusive discovery practices, and the idea that discovery is widely abused has become a commonplace part of our legal and popular lore. See, *e.g.*, Herbert v. Lando, 441 U.S. 153, 176-77 & n.26 (1979). Whether the lore is in fact true is hard to determine. Compare Frank H. Easterbrook, *Discovery as Abuse*, 69 B.U. L. Rev. 635 (1989) (discovery is used to both discover information and impose costs on other side; "impositional" discovery is common) with Jack B. Weinstein, *What Discovery Abuse: A Comment on John Setear's* The Barrister and the Bomb, 69 B.U. L. Rev. 649, 653-54 (1989) ("I am skeptical that 'discovery abuse' is really a problem in our courts, for in most instances it appears to be absent").

A recent empirical study of discovery practices, which was based on attorney surveys, found that discovery costs represented about 50% of all litigation costs, that unnecessary discovery problems averaged about 9% of total discovery costs and 4% of total litigation costs, that total discovery costs were strongly associated with the amount at stake in the case, and that "[h]igh levels of discovery problems and high expenses were more likely to occur in cases with high stakes, high levels of contentiousness, high levels of complexity, or high levels of discovery activity." Discovery and Disclosure Practice, Problems, and Proposals for Change 2 (Federal Judicial Center 1997). The study also found that "[t]he *percentage* of unnecessary discovery expenses attributed to problems did not vary with the total amount of discovery expenses, suggesting that the higher incidence of problems and greater absolute cost in larger or more complex cases may simply be in proportion to the greater amount of discovery in such cases." Id. at 5.

2. Whether accurate or not, the perception of discovery abuse and inefficiency led to amendments to the discovery and case management rules in 1980 and 1983, and spawned a host of local rules, ad hoc experiments, and academic proposals to cut down on the problems. Among the proposals were discovery limitations (for instance, limiting a party to a certain number of interrogatories or a certain number of depositions) and court-ordered or court-encouraged disclosure of the identity of relevant witnesses and documents. See, *e.g.*, Local Rules for the Eastern District of Virginia (1988) (restricting number of interrogatories and depositions); Marvin E. Frankel, *The Search for Truth: An Umpireal View*, 123 U. Pa. L. Rev. 1031, 1057 (1975) (proposing mandatory disclosure of relevant, non-privileged information); William W Schwarzer, *The*

Federal Rules, the Adversary Process, and Discovery Reform, 50 U. Pitt. L. Rev. 703 (1989) (same).

Many of the experiments occurred in complex cases, in which judges were encouraged to impose "explicit and implicit controls . . . on the discovery process" and otherwise to help the lawyers "conduct discovery in ways that minimize delays, costs, and inconvenience to their clients, to opposing counsel and parties, and to others involved in the discovery process." Manual for Complex Litigation (Second) §§ 21.421-.422 (1985). But there was also considerable objection and hostility to such local rules and experiments. Among the most telling criticisms was the argument that such limitations were neither authorized by the rules nor consistent with the founding philosophy of broad and open discovery.

3. This argument is considerably more difficult to make after the 1993 amendments to the Federal Rules, which were enacted shortly after the last edition of Professor James's treatise. The 1993 amendments added certain mandatory disclosure requirements. Rule 26(a)(1) now requires each party, "without awaiting a discovery request, to provide to other parties" four matters, including the identity of witnesses "likely to have discoverable information relevant to disputed facts alleged with particularity in the pleadings," a copy or description of all documents and other physical things "relevant to disputed facts alleged with particularity in the pleadings," a computation of damages, and any pertinent insurance agreements. Similarly, Rule 26(a)(2) requires, again without request, disclosure of expert opinions, and Rule 26(a)(3) requires, without request, disclosure of witnesses, transcripts, and documents likely to be used at trial. The initial disclosures of Rule 26(a)(1) must be made "at or within 10 days after" the discovery planning meeting called for under Rule 26(f); the expert disclosures of Rule 26(b)(2) must be made "at the times and in the sequences directed by the court," but at least 90 days before trial; and the trial disclosures must be made at least 30 days before trial. The sanction for a failure to disclose that is not "harmless" is to preclude the blameworthy party's use of the witness or information during trial, hearings, and motions. F.R.Civ.P. 37(c)(1).

Second, the 1993 amendments established new limitations on discovery. Rule 30(a)(2)(A) imposed a 10-deposition limit for each side, and Rule 33(a) imposed a 25-interrogatory limit for each party. Under Rule 26(b)(2), a court can also by local rule or order "limit the length of depositions under Rule 30 and the number of requests under Rule 36."

Neither the disclosures nor the discovery limitations are utterly inflexible. With respect to the mandatory initial disclosure, Rule 26(a)(1) permits a district to opt out of the mandatory disclosure device either by local rule or by order in an individual case. About half of the federal districts have opted out by local rule. See Donna Stienstra, Implementation of Disclosure in United States District Courts, With Specific Attention to Courts' Responses to Selected Amendments to Federal Rule of Civil Procedure 26 (1997) (Rule 26(a)(1) in effect in 49 districts, in effect with revisions in 7, and not in effect in 45). Despite the lack of clear authority to do so, a few districts have also opted out of the Rule 26(b)(2) and (b)(3) requirements. Id. (12 districts opted out of Rule 26(b)(2), 18 out of Rule 26(b)(3)). With respect to discovery limitations, Rule 26(b)(2) authorizes courts by order or local rule to alter the discovery limitations. Moreover, both Rule 30(a)(2)(A) and Rule 33(a) allow parties in individual cases to seek leave to exceed the deposition or interrogatory limitation; leave is to be granted "to the extent consistent with the principles stated in Rule 26(b)(2)," which in essence requires that discovery be cost-effective and non-dilatory.

4. Note the incentive that initial disclosure under Rule 26(a)(1) gives the plaintiff to plead with more particularity. Is this indirect movement away from notice pleading an appropriate trade-off for greater issue narrowing? Or will particularized pleading be utilized most by plaintiffs who wish to impose high front-end discovery costs on their opponents?

5. What is the justification for mandatory disclosure? Traditionally the lawyers have decided what information to obtain, and when to obtain it. Mandatory disclosure alters this adversarial model, so that the court initially dictates to the parties the information that is to be discovered. Of course, the victory of the inquisitorial model is far from complete; the court does not yet sift the data that is disclosed. But why make a change at all?

One commentator has suggested that mandatory disclosure is necessary to change the "litigation culture" of discovery abuse and "the profession's unquestioning acceptance of the partisan tradition." Charles W. Sorenson, Jr., *Disclosure under Federal Rule of Civil Procedure 26(a) — "Much Ado about Nothing?"* 46 Hastings L.J. 679, 796 (1995). Do you agree that discovery abuse is an inevitable consequence of an adversarial system? If not, why weaken the adversary system merely to avoid discovery abuse? Conversely, will initial disclosure prevent discovery abuse? Are there other, less intrusive alternatives to prevent discovery abuse? Should a weakening of our partisan tradition be a goal of our procedural system generally?

The Manual for Complex Litigation, Third (1995) suggests that the reasons for initial disclosure are "to avoid the cost of unnecessary formal discovery and to accelerate the exchange of basic information useful to the planning and conduct of discovery and to settlement negotiations." § 21.13. Assuming that these goals will be accomplished, we confront, in yet another context, the question whether efficiency gains are worth the loss of adversarial process.

Now question the assumption: Will the *Manual's* stated goals be accomplished? In cases that use bifurcated discovery as an issue-narrowing device, see p. 1019, *supra*, initial disclosure partially destroys the utility of the device. More generally, Professors Issacharoff and Loewenstein have performed a detailed economic analysis of mandatory disclosure, and have concluded that disclosure is appropriate only in those cases at risk of discovery abuse. Samuel Issacharoff & George Loewenstein, *Unintended Consequences of Mandatory Disclosure*, 73 Tex. L. Rev. 753 (1995). In their judgment, the "allure of trans-substantive procedure" that permitted a rule appropriate for this minority of cases to be adopted in all cases was not "worth the anticipated problems with mandatory disclosure." Id. at 782. Among the likeliest problems of disclosure that they identified were "an increase in litigation costs, an increase in strike suits, and a greater difficulty in reaching efficient settlements." Id. at 786.

Two recently completed empirical studies of mandatory disclosure did not support the fear of Issacharoff and Loewenstein that discovery costs would rise, but they provided little solace for proponents of disclosure either. According to the first study, early mandatory disclosure did not result in a significantly different time to disposition, nor did it affect lawyer work hours or litigation costs or the litigants' sense of fairness with the litigation process. James S. Kakalik et al., An Evaluation of Judicial Case Management under the Civil Justice Reform Act (1996). The second study reached somewhat different conclusions. According to the second study, 37% of surveyed attorneys reported problems with initial disclosure; the most common problem, reported by 19% of attorneys, was incomplete disclosure. Problems with initial disclosure occurred "more frequently in cases involving large stakes and expenses or that were characterized as complex or contentious." Although some attorneys thought the opposite, more attorneys thought that initial disclosure "decreased litigation expense, time from filing to disposition, the amount of discovery, and the number of discovery disputes," and also thought that initial disclosure "increased overall procedural fairness, the fairness of case outcome, and the prospects of settlement." Analysis of docket information confirmed that "initial disclosure is associated with a reduction in time from filing to disposition." It did not, however, "confirm attorneys' perceptions that initial disclosure was linked to a decrease in their clients' litigation costs." *Discovery and Disclosure Practice, Problems, and Proposals for Change, supra,* at 6.

6. Mandatory disclosure may well be the most controversial procedural device adopted in the last 15 years. For an interesting three-sided debate, see Griffin B. Bell et al., *Automatic Disclosure in Discovery — The Rush to Reform*, 27 Ga. L. Rev. 1 (1992); William W Schwarzer, *In Defense of Automatic Disclosure in Discovery*, 27 Ga. L. Rev. 655 (1993); Carl Tobias, *In Defense of Experimentation with Automatic Disclosure*, 27 Ga. L. Rev. 665 (1993). For other reading, see American Bar Association, Mandatory Prediscovery Disclosure: A First Look (1994); Rochelle C. Dreyfuss, *The What and Why of the New Discovery Rules*, 46 Fla. L. Rev. 9 (1994); Rogelio A. Lasso, *Gladiators Be Gone: The New Disclosure Rules Compel a Reexamination of the Adversary Process*, 36 B.C. L. Rev. 479 (1995). As of this writing, the entire system of discovery, including mandatory disclosure, is undergoing an intensive study by the Advisory Committee on the Federal Rules of Civil Procedure.

7. It should be evident that initial disclosures under Rule 26(a)(1), as well as discovery limitations under Rules 26(b)(2), 30(a)(2)(A), and 33(a), are going to run into problems in complex cases. Begin with the requirement of initial disclosure. In a truly complex case, it is impossible to identify, much less to disclose, all the relevant information within 10 days after the discovery planning conference; moreover, it is often impossible to know within this time frame what the disputed facts actually are. See Bell et al., *supra*, at 39-40. Rule 26(e), which imposes a limited duty on parties to supplement or correct initial disclosures, eases some of the problems, and suggests that a good-faith effort is all that can be expected in the initial disclosure. Cf. In re TMI Litigation Cases Consolidated II, 922 F. Supp. 997 (M.D. Pa. 1996) (discussing good faith idea with regard to expert disclosures); Sierra Club v. Cedar Point Oil Co., 73 F.3d 546 (5th Cir.) (discussing factors to use in striking testimony of expert witnesses), cert. denied, — U.S. —, 117 S.Ct. 57 (1996). Nonetheless, with the sanction of evidentiary preclusion looming, the stakes for initial disclosure are high, and satellite litigation over the good faith of initial disclosure can be anticipated.

Given these anticipated problems in complex cases, should the process of initial disclosure be suspended in complex litigation? The *Manual*'s answer is "Quite possibly":

> The [initial disclosure] rule should be administered to serve [its] purposes . . . . In complex litigation, the application of this rule may therefore have to be modified or suspended entirely.
>
> The scope of disputed issues and relevant facts may not be sufficiently clear from the pleadings to enable parties without further clarification to make the requisite disclosure. . . . To the extent agreement cannot be reached by the parties at the [Rule 26(f)] conference, disclosure should be deferred until after the Rule 16 conference, at which the court can fashion

an appropriate order defining and narrowing the factual and legal issues in dispute and, on the basis of that order, establish the scope of disclosure.

Manual, Third, supra, § 21.13. This advice is particularly telling because a principal drafter of the *Manual* was Judge Schwarzer, who was also one of the moving forces behind the idea of initial disclosures.

But the *Manual's* advice seems to conflict with some cases — admittedly dealing with expert disclosures rather than initial disclosures — that have suggested that "[c]ompliance with the disclosure requirements is particularly important in complex cases." In re Ford Motor Co. Bronco II Products Liability Litigation, 1996 WL 28517 (E.D. La.) (striking experts for class certification motion when non-disclosure occurred without "substantial justification"); *TMI,* 922 F. Supp. at 1005 (observing that, "[w]ere the instant action a less complex lawsuit, the court would be more inclined to find Plaintiffs' Rule 26 violations harmless"). Will the issue-narrowing allure of sanctions for non-disclosure be too strong for a court in a complex case to resist? Is there any justification for treating disclosure in complex and complicated cases more or less flexibly than disclosure in routine cases?

One way to think about initial disclosure in complex cases is to use a functional analysis. Lawyer dysfunction in complex cases does not usually occur in the process of asking for information; that is one area in which lawyers — even in complex cases — excel. The problem occurs in the retrieval, comprehension, and organization of information. Mandatory initial disclosure does nothing to help this problem; indeed, by accelerating discovery, it makes more difficult the lawyer's task of digesting information at a steady, controlled pace. If this is true, and if the *Manual* is correct that the goals of initial disclosure are less likely to be met in complex cases, then complex cases return by default to a traditional adversarial approach to discovery. What possible reason is there to maintain a less adversarial system in routine litigation than in complex litigation?

8. A limit of 25 interrogatories and 10 depositions is clearly insufficient for complex litigation. Cf. *Manual, Third, supra,* § 21.422 ("[L]imitations should be imposed only after the court has heard from the attorneys and is able to make a reasonably informed judgment about the needs of the case."). Does this suggest that the 1993 discovery amendments were not designed with complex cases in mind? Since the pre-1993 discovery rules already gave the parties a right to relief when discovery became excessive, see F.R.Civ.P. 26(b)(1), (c) (West 1992 ed.), the import of the 1993 amendments was to shift the presumption from an entitlement to discovery to a non-entitlement (beyond the limitations at least). Will it ultimately be more inefficient for the parties to have to petition the judge for relief from discovery limitations than for parties to petition the court for relief from excessive discovery? Once again, why the shift from a system in which lawyers are in charge of discovering information to a system in which judges micro-manage discovery decisions? In complex cases, is it appropriate to give a judge, with all the issue-narrowing pressures that she feels, an easy way to preclude discovery and thereby narrow the issues?

9. To some extent, the point of both initial disclosure and discovery limitations is to make the discovery process run more efficiently. They do so in somewhat different ways: Initial disclosure seek to streamline the process of requesting information, while discovery limitations seek to ensure access only to information that is worth the cost of disclosure. This basic distinction —

between streamlining discovery procedures and streamlining the substance of discovery itself — is the framework that we follow in the following two sections.

b. Making the Process of Discovery Efficient in Complex and Complicated Cases

There are several techniques by which a judge can make standard methods of discovery work more efficiently. The first three methods — identification, preservation, and centralization of documents — are fairly straight-forward and applicable to most complex cases. The last method — staging or targeting of discovery — is more controversial, and less likely to achieve efficiency in every complex case.

MANUAL FOR COMPLEX LITIGATION, THIRD

74-75 (1995)

Complex litigation usually involves the production and handling of voluminous documents. Efficient management during discovery and trial requires careful planning and ongoing attention to the documentary phase of the litigation by the attorneys and the judge from the beginning of the litigation.

21.441 Identification System . . .

At the outset of the case, before any documents are produced or used in depositions, the court should direct counsel to establish a single system for identifying all documents produced (by any procedure) or used in the litigation. To reduce the risk of confusion, each document should be assigned a single identifying designation that will be used by all parties for all purposes throughout the case, including depositions and trial.

Usually consecutive numbering is the most practicable; blocks of numbers are assigned to each party in advance to make the source of each document immediately apparent. Every page of every document is Bates-stamped consecutively. . . . To avoid later disputes, a log should be kept recording each document produced and indicating by, to whom, and on what date production was made.

21.442 Preservation

Before the commencement of discovery — and perhaps before the initial conference — the court should consider whether to enter an order requiring the parties to preserve and retain documents, files, and records that may be relevant to the litigation. Because such an order may interfere with the normal operations of the parties and impose perhaps unforeseen burdens, the judge should discuss with counsel at the first opportunity the need for a preservation order and, if one is needed, what terms will best serve the purposes of preserving relevant matter without imposing undue burdens. A preservation order may be difficult to implement perfectly and cause hardship when records are stored in data-processing systems that automatically control the period of retention. Revision of existing computer programs to provide for longer retention, even if possible, may be prohibitively expensive (though print-out and retention of hard copies, or duplication of databases at periodic intervals before deletions occur, may be feasible). Such an order should ordinarily permit destruction after reasonable notice to opposing counsel; if opposing counsel objects, the party seeking destruction should be required to show good cause before destruction is permitted. The order may also exclude specified categories of documents whose cost of preservation is shown to outweigh substantially their relevance in the litigation. . . . If relevance cannot be fairly evaluated until the litigation progresses, destruction should be deferred. As issues in the case are narrowed, the court may reduce the scope of the order. The same considerations apply to the alteration or destruction of physical evidence. . . .

21.444 Document Depositories

Central document depositories can help meet the need for efficient and economical management of voluminous documents in multiparty litigation. Requiring that all discovery materials be produced to and stored at one or more convenient locations, where they can be inspected and copied by parties seeking discovery, may reduce substantially the expense and burden of document production and inspection. Use of a depository also facilitates determination of which documents have been produced and what information is in them, minimizing the risk of later disputes.

On the other hand, the cost of establishing and maintaining a central document depository may be substantial; before ordering one, the court should satisfy itself that the cost is justified by the anticipated savings and other benefits. The court, in consultation with counsel, will need to allocate costs fairly among the parties . . . . Special arrangements for less affluent parties may be needed to ensure fair access.

It may be necessary to appoint an administrator to operate the depository, with the cost allocated among the parties. . . . Where significant costs are involved, the court should consider periodic assessments to fund operations, usually beginning with the order establishing the depository.

IN RE THREE ADDITIONAL APPEALS ARISING OUT OF THE SAN JUAN DUPONT PLAZA HOTEL FIRE LITIGATION

93 F.3d 1 (1st Cir. 1996)

■ SELYA, Circuit Judge. . . . These appeals commemorate the latest flight of the phoenix that rises repeatedly from the ashes of the tragic fire that engulfed the San Juan Dupont Plaza Hotel a decade ago. Today, we review the district court's actions following the remand that we ordered in an earlier opinion. See In re Two Appeals Arising Out of the San Juan Dupont Plaza Hotel Fire Litigation, 994 F.2d 956 (1st Cir.1993). . . .

I. BACKGROUND . . .

The sprawling litigation that burst forth from the smoldering embers of the charred hotel encompassed wrongful death, personal injury, property damage, and other claims brought by more than 2,000 plaintiffs against more than 200 defendants. In an effort to tame this behemoth and to orchestrate the proceedings, the district court devised an innovative case-management system. The system included the appointment of liaison counsels (to facilitate interactions both between the court and the legion of lawyers linked to the litigation as well as among the lawyers themselves); the formation of a Joint Discovery Committee ("JDC") to coordinate discovery initiatives; and the creation of a Joint Document Depository ("JDD") as a resting place for all pleadings, discovery materials, and the like. . . . To pay for this case-management system, the trial judge imposed mandatory assessments on all litigants.

The appellants (whom we shall call "the pre-fire insurers") comprise thirteen insurance companies that had issued liability policies to firms which eventually became defendants in the underlying litigation. The quondam insureds settled with various claimants and then sued the pre-fire insurers for indemnification, notwithstanding that all the policies had expired prior to the conflagration. Not to be outdone, the original plaintiffs joined the pre-fire insurers as direct defendants. Though they had been brought late into the fray, the district court levied an assessment against each pre-fire insurer for a standard "defendant's share" (which, over time, amounted to roughly $41,500). Like all such assessments, these funds were slated for use in defraying the expenses associated with the case-management scheme.

Fairly early in the game, the pre-fire insurers moved for summary judgment on all claims against them. After a lengthy interval, the district court granted their motions but ordered *sua sponte* that they bear their own costs. The court afforded the pre-fire insurers no opportunity to be heard. Moreover, it did not specifically mention the cost-sharing assessments.

The pre-fire insurers appealed the denial of costs. In deciding those appeals, we ruled, *inter alia*, that a trial court has the power to reallocate monetary assessments imposed as part of a case-management system. See [994 F.2d] at 965. Because the district court did not give the pre-fire insurers a fair chance to seek reallocation of those costs, we remanded so that they might ask the district court to determine whether the circumstances warranted some redistribution of the payment burden. See id. at 969. The pre-fire insurers made the request, but, in the end, it went unrequited. See In re San Juan Dupont Plaza Hotel Fire Litigation, MDL-721, Order No. 581 (D.P.R. Aug. 17, 1995).

On appeal, the pre-fire insurers contend that the district court ignored the guideposts we erected in *Two Appeals* for evaluating case-management cost-reallocation claims. They also contend that the lower court failed to recognize that they had established a prima facie case for reallocation. Finally, they complain that they did not receive any benefit from the case-management system, and that, therefore, the court improperly refused to relieve them from the standardized assessments.

II. DISCUSSION

Because the district court has spelled out an acceptable basis for its cost-sharing orders and for its refusal to grant a special dispensation to the pre-fire insurers, we affirm principally on the strength of its rescript, adding only a few amplificative comments.

First: The pre-fire insurers have incorrectly identified the legal standard applicable to appellate review of Order No. 581. They insist that plenary review is appropriate here because the trial judge ignored and/or mishandled the general guides for evaluating cost-reallocation claims that we limned in *Two Appeals*, thereby committing an error of law. This argument elevates form over substance.

In *Two Appeals* we delineated several factors that might be considered in mulling whether to reallocate court-ordered case-management expenses. . . . [W]e made it very clear that the trier's judgment is inevitably a critical element in determining which factors have relevance in a particular case, what other factors may be pertinent, and what weights to assign to various factors. . . .

This issue is fact-sensitive, and even a cursory reading of the record reveals that the district court stayed well within the broad contours of the inquiry that we had suggested. Stripped of rhetorical flourishes, the pre-fire insurers' real complaint is not that the judge misunderstood the relevant factors but that he weighed them haphazardly. . . . In circumstances where, as here, a matter is committed to the trial judge's equitable discretion, . . . deference is due. . . .

Second: The pre-fire insurers misconstrue our comment that they had previously established "at least a prima facie case for some reallocation of the assessments." *Two Appeals*, 994 F.2d at 968. They interpret this language as signifying that on remand the appellees had a burden to proffer evidence sufficient to rebut this prima facie case, and that the district court should have responded in terms both to the prima facie case and to the lack of any formal rebuttal. This self-serving reading of *Two Appeals* injects more into the quoted comment than the context will bear.

Third: The district court's finding that the pre-fire insurers did in fact receive a significant benefit from the existence of the case-management system withstands review under an abuse-of-discretion test. The pre-fire insurers assert that they received no benefit from the devices because (1) discovery already had been completed at the time they were brought into the case, (2) they were perfectly capable of doing for themselves what the JDD accomplished for them, and (3) they did not need to rely on the material in the JDD since they sought (and were granted) summary judgment as a matter of law on the claims lodged against them. We agree with the district court . . . that these assertions stem from an overly simplistic view of the pre-fire insurers' situation. . . .

The fact that discovery had been concluded was a two-edged sword. While it meant that the pre-fire insurers did not have to use the JDD to keep track of ongoing discovery, it also meant that they "had available to them in a single location all pleadings, discovery, service lists, pretrial documents, records of all court proceedings, trial transcripts, evidence utilized at trials, memoranda, as well as docket reference[s] as to all that had transpired up to that time."

For another thing, it is of no moment that the pre-fire insurers might have preferred to go it alone. The case-management system that the district court so painstakingly devised could not have operated on a voluntary basis. It depended on the court's authority to order all parties both to participate and to share the associated costs. Since the court acted within the scope of its case-management powers in establishing the overall paradigm, see . . . In re Recticel Foam Corp., 859 F.2d 1000, 1004 (1st Cir. 1988), we give short shrift to the notion that the pre-fire insurers would have been better off conducting their defense in more traditional surroundings.

Finally, the district court found specially that the materials in the JDD were of significant benefit to the pre-fire insurers. . . . This finding is also supportable. After all, the allegations against the pre-fire insurers developed during, and arose from the results of, the discovery process. Thus, materials in the JDD had to be searched, and some were directly relevant to the claims asserted and/or to the pre-fire insurers' defenses. As the district court put it, "upon being served with [a] copy of the claims asserted against them — two or three years after the initial complaint [in the underlying litigation] had been filed — [the pre-fire insurers] could, through the availability of a well-organized and efficient Joint Document Depository, ascertain the status of the proceedings and have readily available all documentation pertinent to their case." . . .

Although the pre-fire insurers ultimately proved themselves able to defeat the claims without relying on discovery materials, simple prudence required them carefully to check those materials (if for no other reason than to guard against the possible denial of their Rule 56 motions), and it was to their advantage that the materials were pre-assembled, catalogued, cross-indexed, and readily accessible. In a similar vein, the compilation of those materials necessarily assisted in the processing of their motions.

Furthermore, as the district court explained, previous litigation of other issues earlier in the trial (including extensive discovery) had framed the issues, thereby enabling the court to resolve the claims against the pre-fire insurers with relative ease. . . .

Fourth: The pre-fire insurers refuse to recognize the extent to which the size and complexity of the underlying litigation affected the district court's evaluation of the relative benefits and burdens imposed by the case-management system. In our judgment, it is this blind spot that explains their contention that the district court failed adequately to compare relative costs and benefits between and among the parties.

To be sure, we stated in *Two Appeals* that the principle which "dominates the constellation of factors bearing on the decision to reallocate" is that a district court should consider reallocating case-management assessments if and when "it determines that a party or group of parties has significantly failed to derive the expected benefits from burdens imposed under cost-sharing orders entered earlier in the litigation, or has derived those benefits to a significantly greater or lesser extent than other similarly situated parties." *Two Appeals*, 994 F.2d at 966. But at the same time we emphasized that "the relative weight and impact of relevant considerations will vary from situation to situation." Id. at 967. Even though comparative benefits are always a salient aspect of the reallocation calculus, see id. at 966, district courts cannot be expected to measure benefits and burdens with the precision of a micrometer in an antiseptic laboratory setting.

This vastly complicated case (or, more accurately put, compendium of cases) — which involves upwards of 2,000 plaintiffs whose claims have run the gamut of imaginable and unimaginable theories of liability — illustrates the need for a flexible standard. In such circumstances, it is simply not practicable to contrive a clean matrix of benefits and burdens. The best that a trial court can do is to determine, as a matter of rough remedial justice, whether significant disparities in the distribution of benefits and burdens demand readjustment of a generic formula.

Notes and Questions

1. Things become more controversial as we move from document identification to document preservation to document depositories. Only the most ardent believer in secrecy would object to a single system of document identification; the practical benefits of a single system are too great. In theory, document preservation is also not objectionable, but it becomes a more difficult matter in practice. The costs of preservation can sometimes be quite high, and the utility of the preserved information can be quite low. Since a preservation order is costless to the party obtaining the order, it can also become a device by which discovery costs are unilaterally imposed by the seeking party on the party in possession of information. Such unilateral costs skew the settlement range and the incentives of the parties to settle. Some of these concerns are moderated if both sides have information properly subject to preservation orders, but the preservation of potentially relevant information has clear drawbacks.

Document depositories are costly, and probably unjustified in all but the largest cases. Since most lawyers prefer to keep working copies of documents in their own offices, depositories to some extent constitute a duplication of resources. When the number of lawyers in the case is great enough, however, sending the documents to a single place becomes more efficient than making multiple copies for each lawyer or accommodating multiple document inspections. As with document preservation, however, the court must be sensitive to the cost factor, in order to ensure that a depository does not become a vehicle for imposing outcome-affecting litigation costs.

2. Since document preservation and document depositories can impose litigation costs, they pose the risk of changing the litigation's outcome. With a document depository, the judge can, in theory at least, apply a fairly simple test

to avoid cost distortions: Does a depository save more money than it costs? But this cost-reduction test masks an outcome-distorting potential. On the one hand, as *Three Additional Appeals* demonstrates, costs may be allocatively efficient, but the possibility of reallocation to the losing party creates distributional consequences that put pressure on the parties (especially poorer parties) to settle. On the other hand, if costs are not reallocated, reducing overall costs advantages the poorer party (an effect that may be difficult to care about when overall efficiency is enhanced — unless you represent the better-funded party); cost reduction also reduces the settlement range. Do the two sets of effects cancel each other out, or does a depository change the parties' litigative calculus?

In the context of a document preservation order, it is difficult to know if preservation even leads to allocative efficiency: How is a court to balance the unknown value of destroyed information against the often uncertain cost of preserving information? Unlike a document depository, document preservation forces the court to make judgments not just about the costs of discovery's procedures, but also about the value of discovery's output.

3. Document depositories can sometimes eliminate the need to send out requests for inspection. Parties operate under an informal agreement, or sometimes a court order, that requires relevant documents to be sent automatically to the depository. Even if such an agreement or order does not exist, courts will sometimes order the parties to tailor their requests so as not to duplicate requests for information already contained in the depository. See In re Aircrash Disaster at Stapleton International Airport, Denver, Colorado, on November 15, 1987, 1988 WL 243502 (D. Colo.). The existence of a depository can also lead to the denial of a request to conduct discovery of information that could have been gleaned from the documents in the depository, and defeat a claim that a party has not had adequate opportunity to conduct discovery. See City of Detroit v. Grinnell Corp., 495 F.2d 448 (2d Cir. 1974); City of New York v. Exxon Corp., 697 F. Supp. 677 (S.D.N.Y. 1988).

4. Does *Three Additional Appeals* satisfy you that a court has the authority to order parties to pay for a document depository? From precisely what source does such authority derive? Certainly not from the Federal Rules of Civil Procedure (unless the penumbra of Rules 16(c)(12) and (c)(16) casts its shadow this far). Prior to 1993 amendments to the Federal Rules of Civil Procedure, Rule 26(f) gave the district court the authority to enter an order, following a discovery conference, "determining such other matters, including the allocation of expenses, as are necessary for the proper management of discovery." In the first *San Juan Dupont Plaza* decision to deal with the allocation of case management expenses, the First Circuit seemed somewhat uncertain about the source of the authority to allocate the case management expenses. Citing Rule 26(f), however, it observed that "we are skeptical that a district court's authority to impose reasonable cost-sharing orders in multi-district litigation is much in doubt." In re Reticel Foam Corp., 859 F.2d 1000, 1004 (1st Cir. 1988). By the time that it considered the issue again, in In re Two Appeals Arising out of the San Juan Dupont Plaza Hotel Fire Litigation, 994 F.2d 956 (1st Cir. 1993), the same court had convinced itself not only of the court's power to impose such costs but also to reallocate those costs at the end of discovery; it cited Rule 16 (which never mentions such expenses), Rule 26(f), and the court's inherent power. 994 F.2d at 965-66 & n.15.

After the 1993 amendments, however, the quoted language from Rule 26(f) was deleted, and was not relocated (as other parts of Rule 26(f) were) into Rule

16. What inference should be drawn from this fact? That courts do not have such authority? Or that such authority was too evident even to mention? Note that *Reticel Foam* relied, at least in part, on the multidistrict nature of the case. Should the court have the authority in non-MDL cases?

5. An indirect way to achieve cost sharing for a document depository is to get some parties to agree to share the cost, and then to deny access to parties that fail to enter the agreement. See Case v. Continental Airlines Corp., 1992 WL 201080 (10th Cir.). Can a court subsequently assess a portion of the cost of the depository to a party who refuses to enter an agreement, on the theory that the party indirectly benefitted from the work of those who had access? At least on the facts of the case, *Case* thought the argument "tenuous, conclusory, and without merit," and reversed a district court order assessing costs against a non-participating plaintiff.

6. Should the location of a document depository affect a decision about whether and where to transfer a case to a new venue? See Armco Steel Co. v. CSX Corp., 790 F. Supp. 311 (D.D.C. 1991).

7. What happens when a party ignores or overlooks a document preservation order? In In re the Prudential Insurance Co. of America Sales Practices Litigation, 169 F.R.D. 598 (D.N.J. 1997), a defendant whose agents inadvertently destroyed documents subject to a preservation order found out the hard way. The defendant had developed a document destruction policy in 1994, and put the policy into a manual in 1995. It also developed a document retention policy, which it communicated through an e-mail system. At about the same time, some of the defendant's policyholders commenced class actions alleging deceptive sales practices; the cases were then multidistricted. On September 15, 1995, the transferee judge ordered the parties to retain all documents "containing information potentially relevant" to the litigation. The plaintiffs' repeated claims that the defendant was ignoring the order led ultimately to an investigation in which it was discovered that the court's order had not been specifically disseminated to company employees; rather, some general references had been made in e-mail communications about the need to preserve documents for the litigation. In part because most employees did not have e-mail, some documents were destroyed in four branch offices.

Although unintentional, the court found the document destruction "inexcusable," 169 F.R.D. at 615, and further found that it "has hindered and burdened the administration of justice," id. at 616. The court then issued sanctions pursuant to Rule 16(f) and the court's inherent authority. After imposing the expected sanctions of ensuring that the preservation order was communicated properly and that each office certify its compliance with the order, the court came to the heart of the matter: the payment of plaintiffs' attorneys fees plus $1,000,000 payable to the Court. See also National Association of Radiation Survivors v. Turnage, 115 F.R.D. 543 (N.D. Cal. 1987) (sanctions included attorneys' fees, a $15,000 fine, and appointment of special master to assure defendant's compliance with discovery); Alexander v. National Farmers Organization, 687 F.2d 1173 (8th Cir. 1982), cert. denied, 461 U.S. 937, 938 (1983) (in case of wilful destruction, sanction was to draw adverse factual inferences with respect to matters in destroyed documents; dicta suggested that dismissal of party's own claims and default judgment against party with respect to claims against it would have also been appropriate).

Other "sanctions" may also exist. One of the hottest new torts is "spoliation of evidence," which provides that a party that destroys evidence relevant to a lawsuit may be liable to the plaintiff for the value of the suit. Spoliation can also be set up as a defense to a claim when the plaintiff destroys evidence, or as a ground for deeming certain facts or claims established. See generally Robert L. Tucker, *The Flexible Doctrine of Spoliation of Evidence: Cause of Action, Defense, Evidentiary Presumption, and Discovery Sanction*, 27 U. Tol. L. Rev. 67 (1995).

8. The *San Juan Dupont Plaza* cases have provided most of the interesting decisions on document depositories. Two other holdings in the cases are also of interest: (1) The prevailing party's pro rata share of establishing and maintaining a document depository cannot be taxed as costs against the losing party under Rule 54(d) and 28 U.S.C. § 1920, see *Two Appeals*, 994 F.2d at 964; and (2) Discovery expenses that ordinarily would have been taxable against the losing party might not be taxed if the expenses could have been avoided by using the depository, see In re San Juan Dupont Plaza Hotel Fire Litigation, 142 F.R.D. 41, 46-47 & n.21 (D.P.R. 1992).

9. Sample case management orders for document identification, document preservation, and document depositories can be found in the *Manual*, §§ 41.2, 41.30, 41.34, 41.35. For the order describing the workings of the document depository, the responsibilities of the parties with respect to the depository, and the functions of the depository administrator in the *Dupont Plaza* case, see In re San Juan Dupont Plaza Hotel Fire Litigation, 1989 WL 168401, *20-24(D.P.R.).

10. Technology may eventually solve many of the problems of document identification, preservation, and depositories. Today, great quantities of information can be stored and retrieved in media easily accessible by computer. We explore this issue more generally at p. 1173, *infra*.

11. Through procedures such as document preservation orders and document depositories, judges have a limited power to change the usual distributional effects of discovery. We have also seen that this power is largely discretionary. Do you have confidence that the judge will exercise the power only to achieve allocative efficiency, or do you fear that the judge, who is by now deeply involved in managing the case, will impose costs in a manner consistent with the predispositions that she has begun to develop?

UNITED STATES v. AMERICAN TELEPHONE & TELEGRAPH CO.

461 F. Supp. 1314 (D.D.C. 1978)

■ GREENE, District Judge. [The basic facts of this antitrust dispute, in which the United States alleged that AT&T had engaged in a long-standing pattern of seeking to monopolize the telecommunications industry, are set out at p. 1031, *supra*. It turned out that the United States was not alone in its views of AT&T's practices. Several other companies — including MCI Communications Corp. (then a fledgling long-distance company) and Litton Systems, Inc. — had also sued AT&T on antitrust grounds.]

III

Discovery Order No. 2, entered by Magistrate Margolis on April 27, 1978, requires *inter alia* that defendants produce for inspection and copying all microfilm copies of documents, transcripts, and exhibits produced in connection with a number of antitrust actions brought by private parties against AT&T in other districts. Defendants have appealed this order to the Court, contending that, for a number of different reasons, such a requirement is inconsistent with the spirit, if not the letter, of the Federal Rules of Civil Procedure.

It is appropriate initially to articulate precisely what is currently at issue between the parties with respect to Discovery Order No. 2. The order may be read to include three types of documents generated in seven other court proceedings: (1) documents (or microfilm copies of documents) produced by AT&T to the private plaintiffs, and selected for use by the private plaintiffs, (2) documents produced by the private plaintiffs to AT&T, and (3) documents produced by third parties to AT&T, to the private plaintiffs, or to both. According to the United States, however, it seeks only those documents in the first of these three categories. Moreover, it has actively pursued its request for production with respect to documents produced in only two of the other court proceedings. Thus, the question before the Court is whether defendants should be required in this proceeding to produce to plaintiff here copies of documents previously produced and selected for use in the lawsuits brought against defendants by Litton Systems, Inc. and MCI Communications Corp. in the Southern District of New York and the Northern District of Illinois, respectively. . . .

As a defendant in this litigation, AT&T's duty to produce is squarely resolved by Rules 26 and 34, F.R.Civ.P., which provide for the production of relevant documents within a party's possession, custody, and control. The documents here sought are, and always have been within defendants' possession, since they are defendants' own documents. Conceptually it makes no difference under the Rules whether as such they represent the product of some process of selection worked out between the parties in the other actions or whether that process never took place.

Defendants here do not and cannot dispute that in the normal course of discovery in this litigation the government would be entitled to production of the same 12 million pages of documents (subject to claims of relevancy and privilege) they produced in the *Litton* and *MCI* lawsuits. What plaintiff is seeking to do is to obtain some lesser number of documents, perhaps some 2.5 million,[75] by eliminating for purposes of production in this case all those which the attorneys for Litton and MCI have already determined to be irrelevant. The only effect of the procedure requested by plaintiff, then, is to exclude the bulk of the records from even being considered for production here. The Court can find no basis for concluding that AT&T is suffering legal injury as a result of such a narrowing of the volume of the documents to be produced.

If anyone would have a legitimate complaint concerning this procedure, it would be the plaintiffs in the private lawsuits, who could conceivably assert a work product privilege. . . . Yet, not only have these plaintiffs not

---

75. It is estimated that defendants produced 7 million pages of documents in the *MCI* suit from which plaintiff selected 1.5 million for copying; and 5 million pages in the *Litton* suit, from which plaintiff selected 1 million for copying.

asserted that privilege, but they have affirmatively agreed with the procedure proposed by the government. Defendants have cited no authority for what would appear to be a startling proposition: that they may assert a work product privilege claim on behalf of their opponents in other lawsuits.

To be sure, to the extent that the government will not need to review the millions of documents generated by AT&T at the request of the private plaintiffs and may confine itself to the more limited number of records which those plaintiffs found useful, it will ease the government's discovery burden and speed this litigation along. But defendants have no legal interest in making the government's accumulation of proof more difficult or in delaying a trial on the merits. The intricacies of common law pleading and procedure, whereby a party could, through artifice, prolong litigation or avoid adjudications on the merits, have long given way to more sensible, merit-oriented processes. As one court has noted, "one of the purposes of the Federal Rules of Civil Procedure was to take the sporting element out of litigation, partly by affording each party full access to evidence in the control of his opponent." Martin v. Reynolds Metals Corp., 297 F.2d 49, 56 (9th Cir. 1961).... It would not advance but defeat the purpose of the Rules to require plaintiff in this case to proceed laboriously, and possibly at the cost of several years' delay, to duplicate the document selection process conducted by the plaintiffs in *Litton* and *MCI* when the fruits of that process are readily available and in the possession of a party to this very litigation, and when those who conducted the search do not object.

Defendants next argue that unspecified portions of the requested documents might be irrelevant to this litigation, or privileged, and that therefore the Court may not order their production until (1) the government has made specific designations of classes of documents in terms of their relevancy to this action, and (2) the defendants have screened the documents to eliminate privileged materials. These contentions will be considered *seriatim*....

To be sure, neither the confluence of issues in the private lawsuit with those in this lawsuit, nor the findings of relevancy made in those private actions, are determinative, and some of the documents produced by AT&T in *Litton* and *MCI* may ultimately be found to be outside the range of relevancy within the meaning of this action. But the discovery rules do not require absolute precision, and no order of production can serve as a guarantee that every document produced will be relevant. If the purposes of the Rules, and of pretrial discovery generally are to be effectuated, actual discovery must be expected to be somewhat of a "fishing expedition," particularly in antitrust and similarly complex litigation.

It is difficult to envision what prejudice could ensue from the production of documents, a small number of which might turn out not to be relevant to this lawsuit. To the extent that any irrelevant documents are produced, defendants will be amply protected by this Court's protective order, which will maintain the confidentiality of all documents produced, and order the return of any irrelevant documents to the defendants.

This Court is not required to compel plaintiff to engage in a time-consuming reenactment of the discovery process engaged in by the

Litton and *MCI* plaintiffs, with the result that eventually, that is, several years later, essentially the same documents will be produced. The Court clearly has the authority under the Federal Rules to order production of documents which are on any reasonable interpretation of that concept relevant, and through a process which fully protects the legitimate interests of defendants. There is no basis in the law or common sense to prescribe the more cumbersome procedure.

This, then, leaves only defendants' claims as to privilege. In this regard, defendants are entitled to a mechanism (1) for honoring appropriate claims of privilege and (2) for insuring, by means of an appropriate protective order, that any privileged documents produced to plaintiff will not be used improperly. . . .

Accordingly, the Court has this day entered Pretrial Order No. 11 which requires defendants to produce by November 1, 1978, all of the approximately 2.5 million documents produced by them in *Litton* and *MCI* and selected for use by those private plaintiffs. Documents as to which defendants wish to assert a claim of privilege are to be segregated and delivered to the Special Masters by that date. To the extent that defendants are unable to determine by that date all claims of privilege they wish to assert, they shall, in the manner prescribed in Pretrial Order No. 7, deliver the documents to plaintiff and assert appropriate claims of privilege subsequently. Pretrial Order No. 11 further directs plaintiff to bring this Order to the attention of the U.S. District Court for the Southern District of New York and the U.S. District Court for the Northern District of Illinois, and to request leave from those courts for the production of such documents notwithstanding any protective orders that may have been entered therein.

Notes and Questions

1. As we have discovered in earlier chapters, it is often true that related cases are spread across a number of forums. Having access to discovery proceedings from other cases can significantly streamline the discovery process, as long as the allegations in the two sets of cases are closely related and the lawyers in the first set of cases are competent. Cf. In re Temporomandibular Joint (TMJ) Implants Products Liability Litigation, 113 F.3d 1484, 1489 (8th Cir. 1997) (noting that district court had ordered parties to use document depository created in related litigation, and had permitted additional discovery only upon leave of court).

Are there any reasons not to allow the lawyers in the second set of cases access to the earlier work? From a litigant in AT&T's shoes, the answer may be "Yes" for at least six reasons. First, the litigant may simply be trying to impose additional costs on the opponent, making it more difficult for the opponent to maintain the litigation. Second, the litigant may have handed over some of the documents in the prior litigation under the terms of a confidentiality order (see pp. 1149-52, *infra*), and therefore has a legitimate expectation of privacy. Third, public disclosure may cause embarrassment or financial loss to a party. Fourth, the litigant may have been forced to turn over the documents after an adverse ruling from the first court, and may want a chance to convince the second court not to permit discovery or use of the previously disclosed material. Fifth, the litigant may be the subject of a grand jury or other governmental investigation, and legitimately fear that granting access to the government would become a shortcut in that investigation. Sixth, the litigant may fear that disclosure will jeopardize the possibility of a fair trial. A court might also be reluctant to order access for two reasons: First, access to the earlier material reduces the opponent's litigation costs, and therefore reduces the settlement range and likelihood of settlement; and second, access might make parties in other cases less willing to enter into confidentiality orders. Finally, the parties that obtained the information in the prior litigation might object for two reasons: either that their work product is being invaded or that they have bestowed a benefit on other parties without receiving compensation.

Which, if any, of these concerns are legitimate reasons for depriving a party of access to materials from prior litigation? For each reason that you regard as legitimate, how would you balance that interest against the interest in streamlining the discovery process? Note that Rule 26(c) authorizes a court to tailor a protective order to accommodate some of these reasons; for instance, a court could presumably condition disclosure of previously obtained information on the payment to the original party of a fair portion of the cost of obtaining that information.

2. The lawyers for AT&T continued to resist the disclosure of the materials from the *Litton* and *MCI* litigations, ultimately pressing their arguments all the way to the Supreme Court. AT&T's basic argument was that it had agreed to disclosure of certain sensitive documents in the *MCI* litigation with the understanding that they would be used only in that litigation, that the district court had entered a protective order to that effect, and that any modification of the protective order violated its legitimate expectations and caused it prejudice. It began its campaign by filing a writ of mandamus against Judge Greene in the Second Circuit (in which the *Litton* case was pending). The writ was apparently transferred to the District of Columbia Circuit, which refused to issue a writ. AT&T then applied for a writ of certiorari and a stay of Greene's order from the Supreme Court; the stay was briefly granted, but ultimately removed when the Supreme Court denied certiorari. See American Telephone & Telegraph Co. v. United States, 439 U.S. 962 (1978).

AT&T continued its fight in the *MCI* litigation. It agreed to hand over the relevant documents, but argued that the protective order in *MCI* should not be modified to include disclosure of deposition transcripts and MCI's analyses of data. Judge Grady, who was handling the *MCI* litigation, modified the protective order to permit the disclosure of all the material that the government sought. AT&T then filed an appeal and a conditional writ of mandamus in the Seventh Circuit. The court of appeals affirmed Grady's order:

> [W]here a protective order is agreed to by the parties before its presentation to the court, there is a higher burden on the movant to justify the modification of the order. . . . [N]onetheless this Court cannot conclude that the district court erred in permitting modification of the protective order. The exceptional considerations warranting the alteration of an agreed protective order exist in the present case. The government filed its antitrust complaint eight months after the filing of the MCI complaint. Since the government filed its complaint against ATT nearly four years ago, there is no showing that the government seeks to exploit *MCI v. ATT* in the prosecution of *USA v. ATT*. In addition, there is no showing that any claim of privilege was waived or that anything discovered by MCI would be

protected from a long and costly discovery process in the District of Columbia case. . . . We are impressed with the wastefulness of requiring government counsel to duplicate the analyses and discovery already made.

American Telephone & Telegraph Co. v. Grady, 594 F.2d 594 (7th Cir. 1978). The Supreme Court again denied certiorari. 440 U.S. 971 (1979).

3. Later in this section we examine more generally the idea of using protective orders as a way of streamlining the discovery process. See p. 1136, *infra*. On the assumption that such orders are generally beneficial, do you agree with *Grady* that they should be modified to permit disclosure in subsequent litigation only on a showing of "exceptional considerations"? Shortly afterwards, the Seventh Circuit thought that this phrase was "an unfortunate choice of words," Wilk v. American Medical Association, 635 F.2d 1295, 1300 (7th Cir. 1980), and consequently modified the *Grady* test so that "where an appropriate modification of a protective order can place private litigants in a position they would otherwise reach only after repetition of another's discovery, such modification can be denied only where it would tangibly prejudice substantial rights of the party opposing modification," id. at 1299. Given that discovery is presumptively a public process, see F.R.Civ.P. 5(d) and *Grady*, 594 F.2d at 596, is the *Wilk* reformulation a better test?

Perhaps not. Richard Marcus, a leading scholar in the field of complex litigation, has worried that a near-automatic modification of protective orders in prior litigation will greatly reduce parties' willingness to enter into such orders and "increases the risk that parties fearing repeated claims may fight discovery more vigorously." Richard L. Marcus, *Myth and Reality in Protective Order Litigation*, 69 Corn. L. Rev. 1, 43 (1983). Instead, Professor Marcus suggests this test:

> First, in order to obtain access to materials produced under a protective order in litigation number one, the party involved in litigation number two should demonstrate that he would have the right to obtain them in the second action. Otherwise one risks subverting the substantive policies justifying nondisclosure in litigation number two. But if the party to litigation number two has a right to obtain such materials in that case, denying him access simply increases his expense. Second, a court should ordinarily deny nonparty access if all the parties to litigation number one oppose it, even though it may increase the nonparty's expenses. Finally, a court should set aside confidentiality orders entered in connection with settlements only in extraordinary circumstances. This is a form of party autonomy that is critical to the reliability of such orders; in most situations they should not be disturbed. [69 Corn. L. Rev. at 43-44.]

For a somewhat different set of factors, arguably making disclosure even more difficult, see Arthur R. Miller, *Confidentiality, Protective Orders, and Public Access to the Courts*, 105 Harv. L. Rev. 427 (1991). See also Manual for Complex Litigation, Third § 21.432 (1995) (listing 8 relevant factors for lifting confidentiality orders).

4. The strongest cases denying access to discovery materials from prior litigation arise in the context of government investigations. In the leading case on the issue, GAF Corp. v. Eastman Kodak Co., 415 F. Supp. 129 (S.D.N.Y. 1976), the Antitrust Division of the Department of Justice sought to modify a protective order in order to obtain from GAF certain documents that it had received from Eastman Kodak in an ongoing private antitrust suit. The

government's purpose in wanting these documents was unclear, but it appeared that Eastman Kodak was the subject of an antitrust investigation. Judge Frankel began by citing dictum to the effect that "the discovery procedures 'are designed to be used solely for the purpose of obtaining information for use in the federal court action in which they are employed.'" 415 F. Supp. at 131 (quoting Beard v. New York Central Railroad Co., 20 F.R.D. 607, 609 (N.D. Ohio 1957)). He then observed that many documents had been given by consent and that "[t]here has been throughout an explicit understanding between the parties that discovery was being demanded and given solely for use in, and preparation of, this case. . . . All the positions taken over the years have had presumably in view the understanding that discovery was for the party receiving it, not for strangers to the case, public or private." Id. Finally, he came to the heart of the matter: "The Government as investigator has awesome powers, not lightly to be enhanced or supplemented by implication. . . . [I]ts inquisitorial powers are great, and certainly as great as Congress has determined they should be." Id. at 132. The first two reasons suggest a very limited power to permit disclosure of any materials accumulated in prior litigation; the last suggests that the power is limited only when the government is acting in an investigatory capacity. Are these reasons persuasive? See Martindell v. International Telephone & Telegraph Co., 594 F.2d 291 (2d Cir. 1979) (denying government access to depositions given under assurance of protective order when government wished to use them for criminal investigation).

GAF was itself subsequently limited in United States v. GAF Corp., 596 F.2d 10 (2d Cir. 1979), in which the government again sought access to some of the same materials. In the meantime, however, its hand had been strengthened by the passage of legislation that broadened the government's power to issue "civil investigative demands" in antitrust cases. As a result, the Second Circuit held that the government was entitled to obtain the material that it sought — not by means of a modification of the discovery order but by means of a civil investigative demand. See *Martindell*, 594 F.2d at 296 n.6 (leaving open issue of government's ability to seek deposition transcripts by means of subpoena). Does *GAF* show the futility of Frankel's original position?

5. Protective orders can sometimes have other consequences. For instance, a witness with a legitimate Fifth Amendment self-incrimination claim might waive the privilege in a private suit on the condition that his testimony not be disclosed in any other proceeding. If the government can subsequently enter the litigation and obtain the testimony, the witness will obviously be chagrined and future witnesses will not be so cooperative. See Marcus, *supra*, at 44 n.188 (proposing that Fifth Amendment objection should not automatically bar disclosure to government).

6. Can a private litigant turn the tables on the government and obtain files from the government's prior litigation? If the government is a civil litigant in the first suit, and if no peculiar governmental privileges are at stake, there seems to be little reason not to permit access to materials in the government's possession on the same terms as access would be granted to materials in a private litigant's possession. When the government acts as a prosecutor in the first action, however, different concerns may be present. Of course, when the material sought is publicly available (such as transcripts or exhibits from the criminal trial), questions of access usually do not exist. Cf. *Manual, supra*, § 31.2 (suggesting that criminal case should usually take priority over related civil case); but cf. In re Residential Doors Antitrust Litigation, 900 F. Supp. 749 (E.D.

Pa. 1995) (refusing to stay civil discovery until completion of criminal investigation). But what happens when a party wants access to the government's investigatory files or the materials or testimony considered by a grand jury?

With respect to investigatory materials, there exists a "law enforcement privilege" that may block disclosure unless a significant need for the material is demonstrated. See Black v. Sheraton Corp. of America, 564 F.2d 531 (D.C. Cir. 1977); In re Department of Investigation of City of New York, 856 F.2d 481 (2d Cir. 1988); Torres v. Kuzniasz, 936 F. Supp. 1201 (D.N.J. 1996); Morrissey v. City of New York, 171 F.R.D. 85 (S.D.N.Y. 1997). With respect to grand jury materials, the matter is more complicated. The operations of grand juries have historically been shrouded in secrecy. Today Rule 6(e)(2) of the Federal Rules of Criminal Procedure guards that secrecy, providing that government attorneys, grand jurors, stenographers, and those assisting the investigation "shall not disclose matters occurring before the grand jury, except as otherwise provided for in these rules." The major exceptions provided in the rules are disclosures "permitted by the court at the request of the defendant" seeking dismissal of an indictment, disclosures to other grand juries, disclosures to appropriate state law enforcement officials, and disclosures "directed by a court preliminarily to or in connection with a judicial proceeding." F.R.Crim.P. 6(e)(3)(C).

7. The Supreme Court has considered the applicability of Rule 6(e) — and particularly the "judicial proceeding" exception of Rule 6(e)(3)(C) — in a series of cases in which a party in civil litigation has either sought access to grand jury materials or claimed that the government improperly disclosed grand jury materials to government lawyers handling a related civil litigation. See, *e.g.*, United States v. John Doe, Inc., I, 481 U.S. 102 (1987); United States v. Baggott, 463 U.S. 476 (1983); United States v. Sells Engineering, Inc., 463 U.S. 418 (1983); Douglas Oil Co. of California v. Petrol Stops Northwest, 441 U.S. 211 (1979). The basic rules for disclosure of matters occurring before the grand jury seem to be: (1) Application for an order for access to grand jury information must be made before the court in which the grand jury sat, although this court may consult with the court in which the civil case is pending, *Douglas Oil*, 441 U.S. 211; (2) The disclosure must be "related fairly directly to some identifiable litigation, pending or anticipated"; "it is not enough to show that some litigation may emerge from the matter in which the material is to be used, or even that litigation is factually likely to emerge," *Baggott*, 463 U.S. at 480; (3) A government lawyer who handled the grand jury investigation can use information obtained during these proceedings in a subsequent civil action as long as she is careful not to disclose the processes of the grand jury itself, see *John Doe*, 481 U.S. 102; and (4) Disclosure of information to any other person — whether to another government lawyer handling the civil litigation or to private lawyers or litigants — can be made only upon a showing of "particularized need," id.; *Douglas Oil*, 441 U.S. 211.

Most of the attention in the Supreme Court and lower court opinions has been directed at the issue of "particularized need." In *Douglas Oil*, the Court suggested a three-part test for demonstrating particularized need:

> Parties seeking grand jury transcripts under Rule 6(e) must show that the material they seek is needed to avoid a possible injustice in another judicial proceeding, that the need for disclosure is greater than the need for continued secrecy, and that their request is structured to cover only material so needed.... [I]n considering the effects of disclosure on grand

jury proceedings, the courts must consider not only the immediate effects upon a particular grand jury, but also the possible effect upon the functioning of future grand juries. . . . [T]he interests in grand jury secrecy, although reduced, are not eliminated merely because the grand jury has ended its activities. [441 U.S. at 222.]

The burden of establishing "particularized need" rests on the person seeking disclosure. Id. at 223; see *Sells Engineering*, 463 U.S. at 443 (requiring "strong showing of particularized need").

The Court has emphasized that the "particularized need" calculus of *Douglas Oil* "is a highly flexible one, adaptable to different circumstances and sensitive to the fact that the requirements of secrecy are greater in some situations than in others." *Sells Engineering*, 463 U.S. at 445. It is generally easier for government attorneys to make a "particularized need" showing than for private litigants and lawyers to do so. Id.; *John Doe*, 481 U.S. at 112-13. But this is not always true; "in weighing the need for disclosure, the court could take into account any alternative discovery tools available by statute or regulation to the agency seeking disclosure." *Sells Engineering*, 463 U.S. at 445; *John Doe*, 481 U.S. at 113. The availability of discovery would presumably affect a private litigant's right to disclosure of grand jury materials, and make it more difficult to obtain grand jury materials when the same information is obtainable by other means. On the other hand, *John Doe* emphasized that cost savings and reduced delay in the second litigation are valid considerations in permitting disclosure. 481 U.S. at 115-16; see In re Grand Jury Investigation, 55 F.3d 350, 354 (8th Cir.) (same), cert. denied, — U.S. —, 117 S.Ct. 917 (1996).

8. According to the wording of Rule 6(e)(2), witnesses themselves (unless they fit into one of the forbidden categories) can disclose their own grand jury testimony. See *Sells Engineering*, 463 U.S. at 425; cf. Butterworth v. Smith, 494 U.S. 624 (1990) (witness has First Amendment right to disclose testimony after conclusion of state grand jury proceedings). Witnesses probably cannot be forced to reveal the questions asked of them by investigators assisting the grand jury or by the grand jury itself, nor can they be forced to reveal the exact contents of their testimony to an investigator or grand jury. They must, however, respond to discovery requests that seek to elicit evidence that was also provided to an investigator or grand jury. In re Potash Antitrust Litigation, 896 F. Supp. 916 (D. Minn. 1995); cf. In re Shopping Carts Antitrust Litigation, 95 F.R.D. 299 (S.D.N.Y. 1982) (corporate defendant needed to answer interrogatories seeking identity of employees that testified before grand jury without showing of "particularized need"); In re Wirebound Boxes Antitrust Litigation, 129 F.R.D. 34 (D. Minn. 1990) (same).

In Pillsbury Co. v. Conboy, 459 U.S. 248 (1983), certain corporate officials had testified before a grand jury with regard to an alleged price-fixing scheme. Their testimony, for which they were willing to invoke a Fifth Amendment privilege against self-incrimination, had been compelled by a grant of "use immunity." In the related civil case, the same officials continued to assert their Fifth Amendment protections. As a result, the multidistrict judge found that the plaintiffs had demonstrated a "particularized need" for the grand jury testimony, and ordered that the plaintiffs be given access to the deponents' testimony. See In re Corrugated Container Grand Jury and Corrugated Container Anti-trust Criminal and Civil Litigation, 659 F.2d 1330 (5th Cir. 1981), cert. denied, 456 U.S. 937 (1982); In re Corrugated Container Antitrust Litigation, 556 F. Supp. 1117 (S.D.Tex. 1982) (ordering disclosure with respect to certain additional witnesses). The plaintiffs then deposed the witnesses, essentially reading back to them their grand jury testimony in question form. One of the witnesses, John Conboy, again invoked his Fifth Amendment privilege, and the district judge found him in contempt. *Conboy* held that a witness like Conboy could not be compelled to give testimony. *Conboy* noted, in passing, that "[t]he propriety of the District Court's release of grand jury materials to the civil parties is not before the Court." 459 U.S. at 250 n.1.

Was the district court right to have authorized release of the transcripts? Given the outcome in *Conboy*, is there any reason to permit the disclosure of grand jury transcripts to parties in other litigation? Cf. Baxter v. Palmigiano, 425 U.S. 308, 318-19 (1976) (in civil proceedings, adverse inference can be drawn from invocation of Fifth Amendment privilege).

9. The recent Supreme Court decisions deal with the discovery of testimony and other materials prepared specifically in conjunction with grand jury proceedings. Should documents produced pursuant to a grand jury subpoena or otherwise provided to a grand jury be subject to the same showing of "particularized need"? In In re Grand Jury Proceedings, 851 F.2d 860, 863 (6th Cir. 1988), the court surveyed the various positions of the federal courts, and found four different answers to the question: (1) A *per se* rule that such documents are never "matters occurring before a grand jury," and are always subject to disclosure; (2) An opposite *per se* rule that documents are "matters occurring before a grand jury," and therefore are subject to disclosure only on a showing of "particularized need"; (3) A rule that such documents are subject to disclosure unless the purpose of the discovery request is to find out what transpired before the grand jury; and (4) An individualized determination that seeks to determine if the effect (rather than the purpose) of disclosure will be to reveal grand jury secrecy. The court of appeals then adopted a fifth resolution of the issue:

> The general rule ... must be that confidential documentary information not otherwise public obtained by the grand jury by coercive means is presumed to be "matters occurring before the grand jury" just as much as testimony before the grand jury. The moving party may seek to rebut that presumption by showing that the information is public or was not obtained through coercive means or that disclosure would be otherwise available by civil discovery and would not reveal the nature, scope, or direction of the grand jury inquiry, but it must bear the burden of making that showing, just as it bears the burden of showing that there is a "particularized need."
> [851 F.2d at 866-67.]

See also *Grand Jury Investigation*, 55 F.3d at 354 (suggesting that "particularized need" must be shown for all documents, but that "particularized need" is sliding scale depending on nature of document and needs of grand jury secrecy).

10. Should the existence of pretrial complexity influence a court's decision about whether to permit disclosure of prior materials accumulated in other litigation or in a grand jury investigation? In Cipollone v. Liggett Group, Inc., 113 F.R.D. 86 (D.N.J. 1986), mandamus denied, 822 F.2d 335 (3d Cir.), cert. denied, 484 U.S. 976 (1987), plaintiffs' attorneys that were operating under a protecive order asked that they be allowed to share the non-confidential discovery with the public and with plaintiffs prosecuting similar claims against tobacco companies. The tobacco defendants raised a host of arguments against disclosure, including "1) that defendants will suffer financial and other

embarrassment; 2) that fairness at trial will be compromised; 3) that plaintiffs are estopped from disseminating this material by a prior agreement of plaintiffs' counsel; 4) that discovery in this case will be facilitated; [and] 5) that dissemination constitutes an abuse of the discovery process." 113 F.R.D. at 89. The court rejected each argument:

> [D]efendants' showings simply do not establish that substantial rights will be so tangibly prejudiced that injustice will result unless the discovery obtained in this litigation is limited to it. Indeed, no direct purpose can be discerned from their position except to discourage future identical actions against them by maintaining the costliness of the discovery involved to other plaintiffs. . . .
>
> So long as the initial litigation has not itself been instituted in bad faith for the purpose of obtaining documents for other actions, and so long as the interests of those represented in the initial litigation are being fully and ethically prosecuted, the Federal Rules do not foreclose the collaborative use of discovery. [113 F.R.D. at 91.]

Cipollone presented a classic case of pretrial complexity: The volume and expense of discovery made it impossible for the lawyers in the later litigation to perform their adversarial tasks. From the viewpoint of complexity, therefore, the court was certainly correct to permit disclosure. Moreover, the interest in efficient management of litigation also pulled in the direction of authorizing disclosure.

The real question is whether the other considerations mentioned in these notes can overcome the combined interests in reducing complexity and increasing efficiency. In *Cipollone* itself, the tobacco companies had made only general and unsubstantiated claims of harm. Suppose that they had instead made specific, substantiated claims of financial harm. See Tavoulareas v. Washington Post Co., 111 F.R.D. 653 (D.D.C. 1986) (claim that disclosure would harm specific business deal was reason not to permit modification of confidentiality order). Suppose that the right to a fair trial in the first litigation was put in somewhat greater jeopardy than was true in *Cipollone*. Or suppose that the relevant materials were contained in grand jury transcripts in a still ongoing criminal investigation. At what point do these other interests deprive the judge of her power to prevent pretrial complexity and thereby preserve the hope for rational adjudication in the later cases? Does the answer depend on whether the right to rational adjudication is an interest of constitutional stature?

11. As we observed earlier, these issues are felt most acutely in cases in which the material from the first litigation is disclosed in secrecy (hence, the emphasis in these materials on confidentiality orders and grand juries). When such secrecy does not exist, lawyers representing similar interests often collaborate and share information. When the litigation is large enough (for instance, tobacco or asbestos litigation), formal networks are often established for the purpose of sharing information. With some types of litigation, there are specialized media that cover important developments in individual cases. There have even been a few instances in which attorneys have sold briefs, transcripts, and other materials to other attorneys representing similar interests. See Marcus, *supra*, at 41-42. When market forces are working to provide the free flow of information, should the judge ever step in to require disclosure in subsequent litigation?

KLEIN v. KING

132 F.R.D. 525 (N.D. Cal. 1990)

■ BRAZIL, United States Magistrate. [Plaintiffs, who were shareholders in a company called Informix, brought a class action complaint against certain defendants after Informix merged with a company called Innovative. After a discovery planning conference and hearing, the court entered the following discovery planning order on September 14, 1990.]

1. *Class certification.*

   A. Defendants shall have no more than *90 calendar days* from the date this Order is filed to complete all discovery related to class certification issues *and* to file and serve any objections/challenges/opposition to plaintiffs' motion for class certification. Because, with one limited exception noted below, it is not clear what the principled basis might be for resisting the class certification motion, the Court expects defendants to consider in good faith the possibility of not formally opposing the motion. . . .

   C. Plaintiffs and their counsel are ordered to respond promptly to the document production requests and interrogatories that defendants have served with respect to the class certification issues.

   D. Without a stipulation from plaintiffs' counsel or an order from this court, defendants may take no more than three depositions, each of no longer than one day, as part of the discovery they conduct with respect to the class certification issues. . . .

   E. Without a stipulation from plaintiffs' counsel or an order from this court, defendants may serve no additional interrogatories or document requests with respect to the class certification issues. . . .

4. *Staged discovery with respect to the core aspects of the case.*

   The Court has considered carefully defendants' creative suggestions about staging discovery by time periods and about using 90 day interval iterations of issues to focus, discipline and limit the discovery process. We have concluded not to endorse either of these proposals as made, in part because we have formulated an alternative plan that we hope will deliver more to all the interests involved here. We decline to adopt the staging by time periods approach because we feel that there is considerable overlap in evidence, and sources of evidence, relating to the periods suggested, and because it is arguable that the center of the case rests in the second period, a period which the parties would not aggressively explore, under defendants' plan, for many months. We do not want to put exploration of the center of this case on hold. Instead, we want the parties to go to the center first and try to settle this case before they spend unjustifiable amounts of their clients' resources dotting every discovery "i" and crossing every discovery "t". The "issue iteration" proposal also carries several risks. It would require investment of considerable lawyering resources that might well be better spent finding out what the essential underlying facts are. While there is a lot of fancy verbiage about a case like this, in essence it is about facts: what was the state of the company at various points, and who knew or should have known what about that state. We want the parties to focus on these major factual matters, because once they are explicated good lawyers ought to have a pretty good idea about where the case is going to end up. The issue iteration proposal also would create a considerable risk of friction between lawyers and lots of unproductive and perhaps inconclusive satellite litigation. . . .

A. A general outline of the Court's discovery plan.

The plan the Court hereby imposes contemplates dividing discovery into two or three stages (the parties, at a juncture to be described, will have a great deal to say about whether there are two or three stages). The purpose of the first stage will be to get as efficiently on the table as possible the core information that the parties need in order to value the case sensibly for settlement purposes. In this stage we will focus primarily on documents, and on those documents that shed the most light on the most important facts. After core document production, and a limited number of depositions, the parties will participate in Court-ordered settlement negotiations, hosted by a special master or team of special masters of their choosing (assuming they can agree on nominees in whom the Court has confidence). The Court expects the parties to make a very hard run at settlement at this juncture. If that hard run fails, they will have two options. The first option would be to conduct limited additional discovery, for about two months, for the purpose of explicating matters that surfaced as obstacles to settlement in the negotiations held at the end of the first stage. That discovery would make up stage two of the pretrial process. It would be followed by another, final round of settlement negotiations, again hosted by the special master(s). If settlement could not be achieved, the parties would move into stage three of the pretrial period, during which they would be permitted to complete the document, deposition, and other discovery necessary to prepare the case for trial. If the parties, with inputs from the special master, conclude after the settlement negotiations at the end of stage one that there is no point in returning after two months or so of additional discovery for further settlement negotiations, they would skip what we are labelling stage two and move directly into the broader additional discovery necessary to dispose of the case by trial (what we are calling the final discovery stage).

If the parties elect to pursue focused discovery for a couple of months after completing the first stage and before giving up on the settlement process (at least until the trial looms more real), the court will permit the parties to decide what discovery to do during this interim period. If counsel cannot agree what discovery to conduct during this limited period, the Court will resolve their differences.

For the discovery in the final period, the Court will require submission of detailed discovery plans and will enter another discovery planning order.

Under this plan, no party will be permitted to file a motion for summary judgment or any motion under Rule 12 or Rule 16 until the completion of stage one discovery. This restriction is imposed for several reasons. First, we want all counsel to focus in this first period on learning the facts necessary to understand the center of the case and to value it for settlement. We do not want resources devoted during this early stage to motions that are unlikely to completely derail or substantially re-configure this case. Moreover, we believe that the discovery we contemplate for stage one would have to be done in any event before the Court is likely to be in a position to rule on a motion that would change the basic shape of this litigation. . . .

    B. Stage One.

(1) *Documents.*

In this stage the discovery will focus almost exclusively on documents. Counsel for all parties shall work together to identify the documents (wherever located) that are most likely to shed light on the *facts* on which disposition of this litigation will turn. In particular, counsel are ordered to focus their initial document examinations and productions on the papers that show, at various junctures, how Informix and, to a lesser extent, Innovative, were in fact doing . . . .

There is no justification for forcing opposing counsel to use interrogatories to acquire basic information about the nature, organization, and location of discoverable documents; counsel shall work together to identify, at least by category, the documents most likely to provide reliable information about the factual matters that are at the center of this action. . . . *The initial productions by defendants shall be made no later than 60 days after the filing of this order.* The court does not expect these initial productions to be exhaustive, even as to "essential" or core documents. But the court does expect a substantial production. After this initial substantial production, defendants shall make additional productions, on a schedule whose specifics the court leaves to counsel to work out, of the remainder of the core documents, i.e., documents needed to sensibly value the case for settlement purposes. *The production of the stage one documents shall be complete by March 1, 1991.* . . .

Counsel are reminded that the court does not expect the stage one document production to be exhaustive. Additional opportunities to complete production of documents that are clearly less central to assessing the case for settlement purposes but that are necessary for trial will be afforded in stages two or three.

(2) *Interrogatories.*

During stage one, interrogatories may be used for only one purpose: to ascertain the "identity" of persons with knowledge of relevant matter. During this stage no party may serve more than 35 interrogatories . . . . Because counsel are ordered to work cooperatively to fashion appropriate document production requests, there is no need to use interrogatories to learn the nature, organization or location of documents.

Any interrogatories used during stage one shall be served no later than January 15, 1991, and shall be answered fully within 30 days. The Court has selected these dates to give counsel an opportunity to use information learned in the first core document productions to frame interrogatories seeking the identity of individuals with knowledge of important matters disclosed in those documents. Counsel may want to depose some such people toward the end of stage one. . . .

(3) *Depositions.*

Unless the parties otherwise stipulate, plaintiffs will be permitted to take no more than 12 and defendants no more than 6 depositions during stage one. Absent stipulations to the contrary, none of these depositions may consume more than two days.

Because the purpose of discovery in this first stage is not to probe exhaustively every dimension of each area of knowledge that each deponent might have, but to get to the center of things efficiently, the Court does not expect counsel to "complete" each deposition noticed in this stage. Thus, if the parties fail to settle the case, or to dispose of it by motion, the Court will entertain requests by counsel to re-convene in the final stage of discovery some depositions that were taken in stage one. In any deposition that is re-convened, however, the Court will limit questioning to matters not covered in the first deposition. . . .

Counsel shall complete the taking of the depositions permitted here (stage one) by no later than May 1, 1991. . . .

(5) *Requests for Admission.*

No party may serve requests for admission during stage one. . . .

(7) *Settlement negotiations at the close of stage one.*

During May, 1991, the parties shall engage in intensive, good faith settlement negotiations. . . .

C. Stage Two Discovery. (Optional)

(1) As noted above, if the parties fail to reach a settlement during the negotiations at the close of stage one but feel that some limited, well-focused additional discovery (or other process of generating information) might improve appreciably the odds of reaching agreement, the Court will permit counsel to submit plans for developing or sharing the necessary information over a limited period, e.g., two months, to be followed promptly by a second intensive round of settlement negotiations. It is possible that during the first round of settlement negotiations counsel will identify a few key areas of disagreement or ignorance that seem to be serving as real impediments to one or more of the parties making the final settlement-valuation decisions that must be made to determine whether settlement is possible. If such "informational" obstacles to settlement exist (as opposed to differences of opinion about inferences a trier of fact will draw from evidence that is already on the table or about the legal implications of such evidence), it

might well make sense to attack those obstacles through focused discovery, investigations, or information exchanges, then return to the bargaining table with the "informational" excuses removed. . . .

(3) At the close of this second stage, the parties again shall engage in intensive settlement negotiations. . . .

D. Motions.

Any party may file motions directed to the merits of the case, e.g., a motion for summary judgment or partial summary adjudication, at any time after the completion of stage one discovery, i.e., any time *after May 1, 1991.*
. . .

E. Final Stage Discovery.

If neither settlement negotiations nor motions have resolved this case after the close of the first and second stages of discovery, the parties shall submit proposed plans for completing the discovery that is necessary to prepare for trial. The plans submitted for final stage discovery shall describe the discovery already completed, identify with particularity the discovery that still needs to be done, justify that discovery and the methods to be employed to conduct it, suggest and defend discovery limitations, and set forth proposed timetables. . . .

The parties shall submit these plans either by June 17, 1991 (if the parties decide not to engage in second state discovery for purposes of follow-up settlement efforts) or by September 10, 1991 (if follow-up discovery and settlement are pursued).

Notes and Questions

1. Magistrate Judge (formerly Professor) Brazil is among the best-known authorities on case management. His discovery planning order in *Klein* therefore makes an interesting study, as he blends several efficiency-enhancing discovery techniques and rejects others. In brief, this is what he does (and does not) order:

- He *targets* discovery at a particular issue — here, the class certification issue.

- He *phases* discovery into two (possibly three) separate segments, with the hope of concluding the case after the first phase. He rejects, however, the idea of phasing discovery by time periods, instead permitting discovery of the dispute and relying on the next three discovery control devices to prevent unregulated discovery.

- His timetable for first-phase discovery strongly encourages the parties to *sequence discovery according to form* — in other words, to engage in one form of discovery (document production) first, followed by another form of discovery (interrogatories), and then another form (depositions). As part of this sequencing, requests for admission are temporarily suspended.

- He limits the amount of second-wave (interrogatories) and third-wave (deposition) discovery permitted during the first phase.

- He rejects the proposal to use "issue iteration," which sounds a lot like the *AT&T* stipulation method, to narrow issues. Instead, he keeps discovery from running amok by imposing another issue-narrowing device we have examined — stringent time limitations.

2. *Klein*'s penultimate device — limiting the amount of discovery — will be examined in detail in the following subsection. See p. 1126, *infra*. The ideas of "issue iteration" and discovery cutoffs have already been examined. See pp. 1010, 1030, *supra*. In this section, we examine the concepts of targeted discovery, phased discovery, and discovery sequenced according to form. As we have stressed throughout and as *Klein* shows, judges often mix and match different techniques in an attempt to strike the right balances between issue definition and discovery, and between full discovery and cost-effectiveness.

3. We use the term "targeted discovery" to refer to discovery that is directed to particular legal issues. Often these will be critical issues that, once explored, will narrow the case considerably or lead to its outright dismissal. In this regard, there is a strong affinity between targeted discovery and issue bifurcation (see p. 1019, *supra*). There are some differences, among them the lack of a formal bifurcation order and the flexibility that the judge retains to adjust the case management plan and permit discovery on other matters in the targeted discovery process.

We use the term "phased discovery" to refer to discovery that is broken into a sequence of smaller segments. Targeted discovery is a special type of phased discovery; it segments discovery by legal issues. But discovery can be phased in other ways for other reasons. Phasing can be used, as in *Klein*, to facilitate settlement; it can be used to control the development of information according to time periods, geographical areas, conduct, or party; or it can be used to uncover the basic information necessary to determine how to structure further case management and discovery plans.

Finally, we use the term "discovery sequenced according to form" to refer to the seriatim use of each form of discovery. Typically, this means that document production precedes interrogatories, which precede depositions, which precede requests for admission. Other orderings of discovery are also possible. A variant of this formal sequencing is called "wave" discovery, in which the first wave is geared to identifying witnesses and relevant documents, and a second wave is geared to deposing witnesses and completing other discovery aimed at the merits.

4. In general terms, the Manual for Complex Litigation, Third § 21.422 (1995) endorses targeted, phased, and sequenced discovery. The *Manual* cautions, however, that these tailored discovery plans also have risks to which the court must be sensitive, including the risk that such discovery devices will actually cause more inefficiency than they prevent. This is particularly true when discovery on certain targeted issues is intertwined with discovery on non-targeted issues; for instance, if *Klein* did not settle after the first two stages, discovery against some deponents might need to be re-commenced. Likewise, forcing all document production to occur at the outset may be less efficient than permitting document production and deposition testimony to be woven together.

In this regard, the *Manual* is more flexible than some of its ancestors. The grandparent of the present *Manual*, the Manual for Complex and Multidistrict

Litigation (1970), flatly asserted that, "in the absence of rare and exceptional circumstances," discovery should be conducted in two to three waves. §§ 0.5, 1.5, 2.3. The Manual for Complex Litigation (Second) § 21.421 (1985) tempered this enthusiasm for wave discovery, stating only that "[d]iscovery generally proceeds in a more orderly fashion" if discovery is conducted in waves. On the other hand, the ideas of targeted and phased discovery did not even rate a mention in the 1970 and 1985 *Manuals*.

Why the progressive weakening of enthusiasm for wave discovery? Is it because other methods of discovery control and issue narrowing have proven more effective? Is it that mandatory initial disclosure has dispensed with the need for most of the first wave of discovery? Conversely, why the increasing interest in targeted and phased discovery?

5. The default rule of the Federal Rules of Civil Procedure is there is no targeting, phasing, or sequencing of discovery; decisions about discovery order are left to the lawyers. Nonetheless, the judge has clear, ample authority to target, phase, or sequence discovery. See F.R.Civ.P. 16(b)(6), (c)(6), 26(b)(2), 26(c); 28 U.S.C. § 473(a)(3)(C)(ii) (authorizing district courts to develop CJRA plans that "phase discovery into two or more stages" in complex cases). Reported cases usually mention such discovery controls in passing; they do not question the ability of the court to enact such controls. See, *e.g.*, In re Dennis Greenman Securities Litigation, 94 F.R.D. 273, 287 (S.D. Fla. 1982); In re "Agent Orange" Product Liability Litigation, 506 F. Supp. 762, 797 (E.D.N.Y. 1980) (p. 1024, *supra*) (ordering wave discovery within phased discovery).

6. Courts do not, however, automatically impose such controls, even when they clearly think them a good idea. See Adsani v. Miller, 1996 WL 531858 (S.D.N.Y.); DeWit v. Firstar Corp., 904 F. Supp. 1476, 1529 (N.D. Iowa 1995) (inviting briefs on issue). It is also fair to say that judges in complex cases do not usually order targeted, phased, or sequenced discovery. Our anecdotal sense is that, when they are left to their own devices, lawyers often engage informally in sequenced and wave discovery, first obtaining documents and the identity of witnesses and then proceeding with depositions. Likewise, when grounds for a dispositive motion exist, defense lawyers often target their early discovery at the plaintiffs' weak spot.

If true, these observations come to the core of a critical question: whether and when a judge should exercise her authority to target, phase, or sequence discovery. The *Manual* suggests that the issue should resolve itself through an efficiency calculus: Is targeting, phasing, or sequencing likely to lead to more cost-effective discovery? On efficiency grounds, it is not clear how frequently the court should exercise its power. From one perspective, courts should be willing to impose controls, since lawyers act consistently with these controls in any event. From another perspective, courts should be reluctant to impose controls, since lawyers are perfectly capable of determining, and indeed are in the better position to determine, the most efficient way to conduct discovery. The only occasions on which the court should need to act are the times of "market distortion," *i.e.*, times when one party is using uncontrolled discovery primarily to impose costs on an opposing party rather than to obtain information.

But is efficiency the sole issue that should concern a court faced with the option of controlling the order of discovery? What other concerns might, or should, weigh into the balance? One concern might be a general preference for adversarial procedure. A second might be a concern that controlling the order of discovery could skew the outcome of the case in relation to other, similar cases in which discovery is not controlled. The first concern highlights once again the tension that can exist between the drive for cost-effective procedure and the desire to maintain adversarial procedure; the second worries that the drive for efficient adjudication is overlooking the critical importance of the like procedural treatment of like cases.

There is a dearth of data about these techniques of discovery control. There is evidence that bifurcation of issues for trial purposes can significantly affect outcomes in the defendants' favor, see pp. 1284-87, *infra*; thus, targeted discovery, to the extent that it acts to bifurcate issues, may be a pro-defense device. To our knowledge, phased, sequenced, and wave discovery have not been studied to determine what changes, if any, they might have on our adversarial system and the neutrality of judges.

Does it concern you that we are proceeding with these discovery control devices without first analyzing the 30 years of experience that lawyers have with these devices?

7. One non-empirical reconciliation of the competing interests in efficiency, adversarialism, and trans-substantivism can be found in a functional analysis. With pretrial complexity, the problem lies in the lawyers' inability to perform their adversarial tasks of gathering and marshaling evidence and then organizing the evidence into relevant arguments. If this is the problem which the judge must address, then the use of discovery controls such as targeting, phasing, and sequencing makes sense when the lawyers, left to their own devices, are unable to gather information in an orderly fashion.

That said, it is not certain how frequently such situations arise. As a general proposition, the decision to use sequenced or wave discovery seems to be a decision that the lawyers can make on their own, without the need for judicial intervention; indeed, they are probably in the best position to make such a decision. Put differently, lawyer dysfunction is unlikely to occur in the lawyers' decision about the order in which to use discovery devices to gather information. Of course, lawyers representing different parties wish to order discovery in differing ways to serve their clients' best interests. This type of disagreement is not the same as lawyer dysfunction; it is merely the adversarial system at work. Presumably the judge can solve the disagreement by applying notions of efficiency and fairness.

Targeted and phased discovery are a different matter. Both have close connections to issue-narrowing; both can be used to help overcome lawyer dysfunction in the management of information by narrowing the amount of information that the lawyer must consider at one time. If lawyer dysfunction is the problem, the court should apply targeting and phasing with an eye to avoiding the circumstances causing dysfunction; efficiency is not the critical variable in deciding how to target or phase discovery. This does not mean that efficiency is irrelevant. First, if different targeting or phasing methods can equally overcome the dysfunction, efficiency can be used to help break the tie. Second, in cases in which lawyer dysfunction does not exist (*i.e.*, cases in which there is no pretrial complexity), efficiency, along with fairness, can certainly help the court to resolve disagreements among the parties about which discovery control (if any) to use.

8. The analysis in the last note does not exhaust the situations in which discovery controls should be used. Until now, we have assumed that the lawyers were acting in good faith, but were having difficulties or disagreements

concerning the best method of ordering discovery to obtain information. That assumption is not always true; lawyers sometimes engage in discovery primarily to impose costs on their opponents. In other words, lawyers sometimes abuse discovery.

The use of rules (such as discovery rules) for purposes other than their intended use is an inevitable side effect of any system of rules. That side effect is exacerbated in the context of an adversarial system, which in theory operates without this behavior but which in practice must deal with it. Hence, a court must sometimes impose discovery controls in order to prevent discovery abuse. It is important to note, however, that this use of discovery controls, as well as the type of controls which might be appropriate, are distinct from the use and type of controls to prevent pretrial complexity. Under a functional analysis, the nature of the lawyers' problem determines the nature of the judge's response. In this book, our primary interest lies in the judicial response to overcome the problem of lawyer dysfunction — the inability, rather than the unwillingness, of lawyers to perform their adversarial tasks.

9. Was *Klein* a case of either lawyer dysfunction or potential discovery abuse? If it was not, was there a reason for Magistrate Brazil to have entered the order that he did? How well would you have expected the plan in *Klein* to work? There are no more reported decisions in the case, but one of the participants in *Klein* has reported to us that he did not think that the discovery controls were particularly effective. The stated reason is that one set of lawyers balked at the system, and made it difficult for the plan to work as intended. The same participant said, however, that essentially the same plan had worked extremely well in other, more routine litigation. This anecdote shows that, at least in some cases, even the best-laid discovery plans cannot overcome the external forces — whether created by market pressures or by irrational behavior — that resist logical, efficient, and orderly discovery.

10. Sometimes you will hear lawyers in complex litigation refer to "discovery tracks." One meaning of this phrase is that lawyers are conducting discovery on different issues simultaneously. Thus, one team of plaintiffs' and defense lawyers may be conducting discovery with regard to one time frame or one issue in the litigation, while another team of plaintiffs' and defense lawyers conduct discovery on another time frame or issue. Tracks can help to overcome lawyer dysfunction when there is a concern that a considerable mass of critical evidence will dissipate before the usual discovery process can obtain it. It is more frequently used, however, by parties faced with a discovery cutoff too short to conduct full discovery on all issues. The first use of tracks helps to avoid pretrial complexity; the latter does not, and in fact defeats to some extent the issue-narrowing potential of discovery cutoffs.

There are certain inefficiencies built into the track system, since it is often difficult for any single lawyer on either side to keep track of all the information that is being generated. The system also requires that each side have enough lawyers available to handle all the tracks. Because of these problems, and because tracks can be used to impose significant costs on less well-funded parties, judges may be called in to approve of the tracking concept. Cf. In re MGM Grand Hotel Fire Litigation, 660 F. Supp. 522, 526 (D. Nev. 1987) (p. 891, *supra*) (mentioning use of 11 discovery tracks to take 1,400 depositions).

11. The devices on which this section has focused — such as document identification, document depositories, shared discovery, and targeted or phased discovery — are not the only means by which discovery can be streamlined.

Among the other devices that the *Manual* recommends are telephonic depositions, group depositions, use of joint discovery requests and responses, coordination of discovery in related cases, and modification of discovery requests to provide equivalent information in a different form. See §§ 21.423, 21.455. Indeed, the range of such devices is limited only by the lawyers' and judge's imagination. Like other streamlining devices, however, these devices raise tactical concerns for the lawyers; they also raise larger issues about the roles of efficiency, adversarialism, and equal treatment in complex litigation.

c. Imposing Limitations on the Quantity of Discovery

Another way to make traditional discovery run more efficiently is to limit the amount of discovery in which the parties can engage. This method is controversial, since critical information about a case is sometimes found in unlikely places. If the amount of discovery is limited, the parties will need to maximize the potential return on their discovery investment, and therefore overlook some of the nooks and crannies in which critical information might be located. Whether the overall saving in terms of reduced discovery costs is worth the occasional failure to uncover critical information is difficult to measure in an empirical way. General attitudes about the value of a resolution of the merits versus the costliness and abuse of discovery often fill the empirical gap.

Discovery limitations are becoming more popular, and the authority for them is becoming more explicit. We have already seen the court's power, first articulated in 1980, to limit the time for discovery as a means of indirectly limiting access to information. See p. 1010, *supra*. Following the trend of a number of comparable local rules, the 1993 amendments to the Federal Rules of Civil Procedure limited the number of depositions to 10 and the number of interrogatories to 25. See p. 1094, *supra*. The same amendments gave the courts the power to limit the number of requests for inspection and requests for admission, F.R.Civ.P. 26(b)(2), and refined a judge's general power, first articulated in the 1983 amendments, to ensure that discovery is not unduly burdensome or expensive in relation to "the needs of the case, the amount in controversy, the parties' resources, the importance of the issues at stake in the litigation, and the importance of the proposed discovery in resolving the issues," F.R.Civ.P. 26(b)(2)(iii). These powers derive from the even more general power of Rule 26(c), which allows the entry of protective orders that prevent "annoyance, embarrassment, oppression, or undue burden or expense" in discovery.

The relevant facts in complex cases cannot be discovered within draconian limitations like 10 depositions and 25 interrogatories. On the other hand, the vast quantities of information that are potentially discoverable make the need for some judicial check on the amount of discovery particularly pressing — at least when the discovery of every relevant fact threatens to make the lawyers' task of gathering and organizing information difficult or impossible. How broad should the judge's power be — just enough to permit the lawyers to perform their task, or as much as is necessary to ensure that the likelihood of obtaining useful information exceeds the expected cost of discovery? The following case forces us once again to squarely confront whether a concern for efficient procedure should trump other basic values in our procedural system

MARRESE v. AMERICAN ACADEMY OF ORTHOPAEDIC SURGEONS

726 F.2d 1150 (7th Cir. 1984) (en banc),
rev'd on other grounds and remanded, 470 U.S. 373 (1985)

■ POSNER, Circuit Judge. These consolidated appeals present important questions relating to the scope of the doctrine of res judicata in our system of dual state and federal courts, and to the responsibilities of federal district judges in controlling pretrial discovery.

In 1976 the American Academy of Orthopaedic Surgeons, a private association, rejected the plaintiffs' applications for membership, without a hearing or a statement of reasons. The plaintiffs sued the Academy in an Illinois state court, claiming among other things that the common law of Illinois and the Illinois constitution required the Academy to grant a hearing on their applications and to use reasonable standards in deciding whether to accept the applications. The plaintiffs made no claim under Illinois antitrust law; nor did they, at that time, bring a federal antitrust suit.

The Illinois Appellate Court ordered Dr. Treister's complaint dismissed for failure to state a claim. . . .

Dr. Marrese was not a party to the appeal, but his suit was stayed pending Treister's appeal and was dismissed after Treister lost his appeal.

After losing in the Illinois Appellate Court, Dr. Treister (joined by Dr. Marrese) brought this suit in federal district court for damages and injunctive relief under section 1 of the Sherman Act, 15 U.S.C. § 1. The complaint alleged that the Academy is "a monopoly in its field, possessed of substantial power to control the market for orthopaedic surgical services," and that the plaintiffs were refused membership because they compete too vigorously with existing members of the Academy. The Academy moved to dismiss the complaint on the ground that the judgment in the plaintiffs' state-court action against the Academy was res judicata in the present suit. The motion was denied. [After further maneuvering] pretrial discovery began. The plaintiffs asked the Academy to produce its files relating to all denials of membership applications between 1970 and 1980. The Academy refused. When it persisted in its refusal after the district judge issued an order to produce, the judge held the Academy in criminal contempt and fined it $10,000. See Fed.R.Civ.P. 37(a)(2), 37(b)(2)(D).

No. 81-2671 is the Academy's appeal from the contempt judgment. . . .

[In a holding later reversed by the Supreme Court, the court of appeals held that principles of res judicata barred the plaintiffs' federal antitrust claims, and ordered dismissal of the federal case. That holding did not, however, solve the problem of contempt, which occurred while the case was pending in the district court. The court of appeals began consideration of this issue by holding that the validity of the discovery order was presented on appeal, and that the criminal contempt sanction exceeded the trial judge's authority since the lawsuit was not properly pending before him.]

We need not rest our decision in No. 81-2671 (contempt) entirely on [res judicata]. The argument made in No. 81-2671 that whether or not the entire case should have been dismissed on res judicata grounds the contempt judgment should be reversed because the discovery order violated Rule 26 of the Federal Rules of Civil Procedure has been fully briefed and argued to us, was discussed at length in both panel decisions, and is ripe for decision.

Rule 37(a)(2), authorizing discovery orders, must be read in light of Rule 26(c), which empowers the district court to "make any order which justice requires to protect a party or person from annoyance, embarrassment, oppression, or undue burden or expense, including . . . that discovery not be had . . .," and Rule 26(d), which empowers the court, "upon motion, for the convenience of parties and witnesses and in the interests of justice," to control the sequence and timing of discovery. Of course the effective management of complex litigation requires that the district judge be allowed a broad discretion in guiding the discovery process, . . . and hence in deciding whether to limit discovery in accordance with Rules 26(c) or (d). But his discretion is not unlimited; if we have a firm conviction that he has made a mistake, we must reverse. . . . This was the test suggested by Justice Stewart, in his opinion dissenting from the second panel decision, for reviewing the discovery order in this case. See 706 F.2d at 1498.

A motion under Rule 26(c) to limit discovery requires the district judge to compare the hardship to the party against whom discovery is sought, if discovery is allowed, with the hardship to the party seeking discovery if discovery is denied. He must consider the nature of the hardship as well as its magnitude and thus give more weight to interests that have a distinctively social value than to purely private interests; and he must consider the possibility of reconciling the competing interests through a carefully crafted protective order. He must go through the same analysis under Rule 26(d) except that an order merely postponing a particular discovery request obviously should be granted more freely than one denying the request altogether.

In an effort to show that more than purely private interests are at stake the Academy argues that its membership files are protected by the First Amendment. If meant to establish a complete immunity from pretrial discovery of these materials the argument is untenable . . . . Even if the Academy were engaged in advocating controversial views and the publication of its internal files would expose members to retaliation for those views, it would not have an absolute privilege against discovery, though the plaintiffs would then have the burden of showing that the information sought was essential to their case and unobtainable by other means that would be less likely to discourage such advocacy. . . .

Yet there is in this case, if not a First Amendment right, at least a First Amendment interest, which the discovery sought by the plaintiffs would impair and which differentiates this case from the usual antitrust case, where discovery is sought of invoices or salesmen's reports or the minutes of a board of directors' meeting. In NAACP v. Alabama, 357 U.S. 449 (1958), a case involving resistance to pretrial discovery of membership lists, the Supreme Court recognized a First Amendment right of association for the purpose of expressing ideas. The American Academy of Orthopaedic Surgeons is not the NAACP, but neither is it a country club or a trade association; it is a professional association and a forum for exchanges of information about surgical techniques and related matters of substantial public interest. . . . If the Academy has to reveal its membership files, members may be reluctant to offer candid evaluations of applicants, and the atmosphere of mutual confidence that encourages a free exchange of ideas will be eroded.

The Constitution to one side, one does not have to be a student of Aristotle and de Tocqueville to know that voluntary associations are important to many people, Americans in particular, and that voluntary professional associations are important to American professionals (the premise of the plaintiffs' antitrust suit, as it was of their Illinois suits). Since an association would not be genuinely voluntary if the members were not allowed to consider applications for new members in confidence, the involuntary disclosure of deliberations on membership applications cannot but undermine the voluntary character of an association and therefore harm worthy interests, whether or not those interests derive any additional dignity from the First Amendment. . . .

The other side of the coin is that barring the plaintiffs or their counsel from all access to the membership files would probably make it impossible for them to prove their antitrust case. But there were various devices that the district judge could have used to reconcile the parties' competing needs. For example, he could have examined the membership files himself *in camera*, a procedure described by the Supreme Court in a related context as "a relatively costless and eminently worthwhile method to insure that the balance between petitioners' claims of irrelevance and privilege and plaintiffs' asserted need for the documents is correctly struck." Kerr v. United States District Court, 426 U.S. 394, 405 (1976). We are told the membership files may be voluminous. No doubt the files in all cases between 1970 and 1980 where applications for membership in the Academy were refused are voluminous, but the place to start an *in camera* examination would be with the files on Drs. Marrese and Treister. If the judge found no evidence in those files of any anticompetitive purpose attributable to the Academy, he would not have to look at any other files. This is not a class action; the plaintiffs are not suing as the representatives of other orthopaedic surgeons who have been denied membership in the Academy.

Better yet, the judge might have followed the procedure discussed in this court's recent decision in EEOC v. University of Notre Dame Du Lac, 715 F.2d 331, 338-39 (7th Cir. 1983). There we ordered the files of faculty tenure deliberations edited ("redacted") to remove the names of the deliberating faculty members and any other information that might enable them to be identified, and we directed that on remand the redaction be reviewed *in camera* by the district judge, who would have the originals before him to compare with (and thereby assure the accuracy of) the redactions. Had the same procedure been followed here, the plaintiffs' counsel would have been able to read the files personally. If the files had turned out to contain evidence or leads to evidence of anticompetitive conduct, the plaintiffs' counsel could then have requested the judge to order names revealed to counsel so that the relevant individuals could be deposed. We do not think that only universities should be entitled to such consideration. . . .

Rule 26(d) (control of the sequence and timing of discovery) provided another method of accommodating the competing interests here with minimal damage to either. If there is other discovery that a plaintiff must complete in order to be able to resist a motion by the defendant for summary judgment, and thus a significant probability that his case will fail regardless of what the internal files he is seeking may show, the district judge has the power under Rule 26(d) to require the plaintiff to complete the other, nonsensitive discovery first. . . . And in an appropriate case he has the duty. . . .

Assuming discovery would not be at an end when the files were turned over and any leads contained in them were tracked down, Rule 26(d) could have been used to schedule the sensitive discovery last.

We do not hold that all files of all voluntary associations are sacrosanct; we do not even hold that the membership files of an association of medical professionals are sacrosanct. They are discoverable in appropriate circumstances, subject to appropriate safeguards. But we may not ignore as judges what we know as lawyers — that discovery of sensitive documents is sometimes sought not to gather evidence that will help the party seeking discovery to prevail on the merits of his case but to coerce his opponent to settle regardless of the merits rather than have to produce the documents. . . . "Unnecessary intrusions into the privacy of the individual, high costs to the litigants, and correspondingly unfair use of the discovery process as a lever toward settlement have come to be part of some lawyers' trial strategy." Erickson, *The Pound Conference Recommendations: A Blueprint for the Justice System in the Twenty-First Century*, 76 F.R.D. 277, 288 (1980).

Many other judges and commentators have voiced concern over the use of discovery to force settlement in groundless cases. See, *e.g.*, Blue Chip Stamps v. Manor Drug Stores, 421 U.S. 723, 741 (1975); Herbert v. Lando, 441 U.S. 153, 176 (1979) . . . . There is at least a hint of predatory discovery in this case in the fact that the plaintiffs did not seek access to the federal court system with its liberal discovery rules till after they had lost their state-court suit, and in the determination expressed by Dr. Marrese's counsel to use the Academy's membership files as the basis for deposing the individuals who voted against his client's membership application.

There are so many ways in which Judge Shadur could have prevented the plaintiffs from abusing the discovery process, without denying them any information essential to developing their case, that we are left with the firm conviction that the discovery order he issued, when he issued it, was erroneous. Our conclusion is consistent with the evolving concept of the district judge's managerial responsibility in complex litigation. Although amended Fed.R.Civ.P. 26(b)(1), which expands that responsibility, did not take effect until August 1, 1983, after the discovery order in issue here was issued, the Advisory Committee's Note indicates that the purpose of the amended rule is in part to remind federal district judges of their broad powers — and, we believe, correlative responsibilities — under Rule 26.

This case illustrates the pathological delays that are all too frequent in modern litigation. After nearly eight years of state and federal litigation, the case remains stalled in the earliest stages of discovery. It has gone on long enough. In No. 81-2671, the contempt judgment is reversed with directions to dismiss the contempt proceeding. . . .

■ HARLINGTON WOOD, Jr., Circuit Judge, with whom CUMMINGS, Chief Judge, and CUDAHY, Circuit Judge, join, dissenting. . . . When a party objects to discovery of confidential information, the trial court must weigh the interests of the parties and of public policy to arrive at an appropriate discovery compromise. . . . Generally, broad discovery is available under the Federal Rules of Civil Procedure. See Fed.R.Civ.P. 26(b)(1). Privileges excluding relevant evidence are construed narrowly because they constrict the fact-finding process. . . . Further, in the antitrust area, there is a strong public policy interest in open competition and private enforcement of the antitrust laws. . . . With these principles forming the backdrop, we now turn to analysis of the discovery order in this case. . . .

An asserted freedom of association does not raise a privilege against all discovery in the early stages of antitrust litigation, but requires a balance of the interests in confidentiality and disclosure to reach a discovery compromise. The trial judge endeavored to achieve that balance by working with the parties. I believe that the discovery order reasonably protected the Academy's confidentiality interests to at least a minimum extent while granting plaintiffs access to information without which, both Judge Posner's opinion and the district court agree, they probably would be foreclosed from proving their case.

Upon questioning at oral argument, counsel for the Academy labeled plaintiffs' suit a "fishing expedition," an attempt to gain access to otherwise unavailable information. Under the circumstances, however, plaintiffs' pursuit of the files and plan to seek further discovery using leads from the files were within the bounds of appropriate discovery. The discovery record in this case evidences not the slightest abuse, harassment, or coercion to pressure a settlement. Judicial concern about discovery abuse is always legitimate, but such arguments are gratuitous in the context of this case. The abuse of discovery here instead is the Academy's obstinate defiance of the trial court, which now is sanctioned by this court.

Although not condemning any one omission as an abuse of discretion, the discovery majority is left with the "firm conviction" that the district court's discovery order was erroneous. I am not. The district court sought and received proposed protective orders from the parties, and mediated negotiations on this issue. Bifurcation of discovery was not mandatory in this case, and the court reasonably provided for the Academy's confidentiality concerns through the protective order. The Academy should not now reap a windfall from reversal of the discovery order because the order did not incorporate certain provisions that the Academy still would refuse to accept....

Although the discovery order could have been improved, the district court's fashioning of the terms was not an abuse of discretion under the circumstances of this case. What the merits of this case would have turned out to be, we now will never know.

Notes and Questions

1. *Marrese* is an unusual discovery opinion, in the sense that issues of constitutional stature influenced the case's outcome. Such issues are not, however, infrequent in complex litigation, and they demonstrate an important point: that matters of substantive policy can influence the scope of discovery. This reality makes the idea of the like procedural treatment of all cases more difficult to achieve in practice.

2. Easily lost in the constitutional aspect of *Marrese* is its initial holding that judges can limit the amount of discovery by balancing the relative hardships to each side. What do you think of this cost-benefit approach? In the adversarial system, lawyers are the ones who engage in this balance, deciding whether the expected benefit of certain information outweighs its cost. The judge's role is to police the process, resolving complaints of the parties that the requested information is irrelevant, is privileged, is extravagantly expensive in relation to its importance, or is being sought primarily to impose costs on the opponent (this last concern often being evidenced by problems with one or more of the first three).

Marrese suggests a considerably more active role for the judge: She is now the one that makes the cost-benefit analysis about whether information should be sought in the first instance. The same suggestion can be found in the 1983 and 1993 amendments to Rule 26. Although the parties will often be the ones to raise the issue, the court has an independent obligation to ensure that cost-effective discovery is occurring. See also 28 U.S.C. §§ 473(a)(2)(C), (a)(3)(C)(i) (requiring courts to consider CJRA plans that "control[ ] the extent of discovery").

3. Is the judge really in the best position to make the cost-benefit determination? According to classical economic theory, discovery is efficient as long as the marginal expected benefit from the information exceeds the marginal cost of obtaining the information. See Robert Cooter & Daniel Rubinfeld, *An Economic Model of Legal Discovery*, 23 J. Leg. Stud. 435 (1994). This equation is a variant of the Hand Formula. But the Hand Formula assumes a rational decisionmaker operating with perfect information. See Richard A. Posner, Economic Analysis of Law § 6.1 (4th ed. 1992). Can a judge that has been exposed to the case during the case management process put aside her biases and resolve the matter based only on the rational economic outcome? Does she have adequate information about the parties' legal theories (which the parties often wish, for strategic reasons, to keep secret) to know exactly when the marginal cost exceeds the marginal benefit? And how is she to quantify marginal costs and benefits precisely enough to make sure that her ruling leads to an efficient level of discovery? Isn't such valuation particularly hard in complex cases? (Think, for instance, about assigning a value to the competing First Amendment and antitrust enforcement interests in *Marrese*.)

One response to this criticism is to suggest that the parties are not in the best position to make these determinations; they often tend to undervalue public goods and interests (such as a speedy and current docket) and overvalue their own private interests. On the other hand, won't judges tend to overvalue public resources and undervalue private interests?

4. Is the classical economic analysis of limitations on discovery even the right way to think about the problem? Operating from within an economic paradigm, Professor Hay believes that a case-by-case focus on the optimal amount of discovery neglects the social welfare perspective. This perspective recognizes that the ultimate goal of a legal system is to minimize the sum of accident costs, accident prevention costs, and the costs of running the legal system. Bruce L. Hay, *Civil Discovery: Its Effects and Optimal Scope*, 23 J. Leg. Stud. 481, 509 (1994). Hay suggests that discovery which is not efficient from the perspective of the particular case may still be efficient if the extra discovery leads to a more optimal level of precaution by potential wrongdoers *and* if the savings in terms of reduced injuries exceeds the combined costs of extra discovery plus extra costs of taking precautions. But he concedes that it is often difficult to apply this test, or to know if it leads in concrete instances to a more efficient outcome than the case-specific test suggested in *Marrese* and in Cooter & Rubinfeld, *supra*. When he considers the settlement-inducing effects of discovey, he becomes even more pessimistic, stating that even a "rule allowing an apparently ideal amount of discovery may backfire if it leads the parties to settle without undertaking discovery." Hay, *supra*, at 514. He concludes that "[f]inding the best approach to discovery control — a hardy perennial on the litigation reform agenda — will not be easy." Id. at 515.

Also using economic analysis, Professor Kaplow puts still another spin on the discovery problem. He suggests that parties often have "an excessive incentive to provide information in adjudication." Louis Kaplow, *The Value of Accuracy in Adjudication: An Economic Analysis*, 23 J. Leg. Stud. 307, 384 (1994). He therefore suggests that methods of reducing these incentives — including but not limited to limitations on the amount of discovery — are necessary to achieve efficiency in the adjudicatory process.

5. Judge Schwarzer, who favors both mandatory disclosure and strong discovery limitations, once observed that, with mandatory disclosure, "on occasion, some information helpful to a party that exhaustive discovery would uncover will not come to light. But the question must be asked whether the marginal value of preventing such occasional failures is worth the great cost of unrestrained discovery." William W Schwarzer, *Slaying the Monsters of Cost and Delay: Would Disclosure Be More Effective Than Discovery?* 74 Judicature 178 (1991). Is there any way to answer this question other than with a personal belief about the value (or lack of value) of party-controlled discovery?

6. In light of its present indeterminacy, is economic analysis even the right analysis to use in thinking about these questions? A different, albeit out-of-fashion, alternative is to analyze the situation in functional terms. We begin with the adversarial system. This system assigns the function of requesting and gathering information to the lawyers. As long as the lawyers are capable of (1) making decisions about which information to seek, (2) gathering that information, and (3) organizing it into proofs and arguments, there is no functional reason to change the system. (There may be other reasons, of course, but that is a different matter.) Only when the lawyers are stymied does a functional reason for making changes exist.

As we have said before, lawyers, even in complex cases, do not usually have difficulty during the first stage of seeking information; their problems lie in the second and third stages of obtaining and assimilating information. These are the places at which the judge arguably needs to step into the process to assist the lawyers. Restricting the flow of information is one way in which the judge can reduce or eliminate these second and third stage difficulties. But what test is the judge to use to restrict information? Certainly, no information vital to the lawyers' ability to present proofs and arguments can be restricted. Nor could the judge even restrict access to all non-essential information. Rather, the judge can only limit access to the minimal amount of non-essential information necessary to make the lawyers' adversarial functions once again achievable.

There are certain problems with this analysis. First, the test, while easy enough to understand in theory, is difficult to implement in practice. How is the judge to know what is "essential" and what is 'non-essential"? And how is she to know what is the minimal amount of non-essential information? Second, in any case there is usually a fair amount of useful but non-essential information. If a judge restricts access to the non-essential information in Pile A, the case will take on one hue; if she restricts access to information in Pile B, it takes on a slightly different hue. These shadings might well affect the outcome of the case. In making the choice between Pile A and Pile B, a functional analysis does not give a judge much guidance. What neutral principle will she use to decide whether to restrict access to Pile A and to Pile B? A cost-benefit test? Whose cost-benefit test — Cooter and Rubinfeld's, or Hay's?

One thing to keep in mind is that restricting access to information is one way to overcome lawyer dysfunction in the pretrial process, but it is not the only way. Nor is it necessarily the best way. Throughout these last two chapters we have seen other alternatives, and we still have a few more to go. Does the difficulty of finding, and then applying, an appropriate test for limiting information suggest to you that limiting access to information is one of the worst alternatives? Or are others even less attractive?

7. There are other practical problems of limiting the quantity of discovery. Among them are whether to suspend the 10-deposition and 25-interrogatory limits of Rule 30 and 33; whether to replace those limits with similar hard-and-fast numbers or to be more open-ended; whether to limit the length of depositions; whether to limit attendance at depositions; whether and under what circumstances to permit second depositions of some witnesses; whether to require high-level corporate officials to testify; and whether additional discovery into some issues would be probative or abusive. See Manual for Complex Litigation, Third §§ 21.422, 21.451 (1995); Tri-Star Pictures, Inc. v. Unger, 171 F.R.D. 94 (S.D.N.Y. 1997); Bonnie & Co. Fashions, Inc. v. Bankers Trust Co., 945 F. Supp. 693, 732 (S.D.N.Y. 1996). Does any theory of general applicability tell the judge how to address these specific matters? If not, how useful can the theory be? Conversely, how can a judge set any limits without some sense of what she is trying to accomplish? Do the standards of Rules 26(b)(2) and 26(c) establish the appropriate mix of generality and specificity?

8. You can test your sense of how to handle discovery limitations by considering a common problem area in complex litigation: discovery against unnamed class members. Sometimes defendants claim that they need, or at least want, to discover information from these plaintiffs. The great fear of allowing them to do so, of course, is that defendants are merely trying to impose costs on their opponents, either making it too costly for them to maintain the

case as a class action or else securing the dismissal of the claims of class members that would prefer not to be involved in the discovery process. How should the problem be addressed?

The leading case on the problem is Brennan v. Midwestern Life Insurance Company, 450 F.2d 999 (7th Cir. 1971), cert. denied, 405 U.S. 921 (1972), in which the district judge dismissed the claims of absent class members that ignored repeated efforts and court orders to answer interrogatories that the defendant had propounded. The court of appeals affirmed, noting that the "requests were not designed solely to determine the identity and amount of the class members' claims, but were also directed at obtaining information relating to certain defenses raised by Midwestern in the principal trial" and that "there is nothing in the record to suggest that the discovery procedures were used as a tactic to take undue advantage of the class members or as a stratagem to reduce the number of claimants." 450 F.2d at 1005. Then-Circuit Judge Stevens dissented, arguing that plaintiffs that did not wish to respond should have been given the opportunity to opt out. *Brennan* was arguably limited in its own circuit by Clark v. Universal Builders, Inc., 501 F.2d 324 (7th Cir.), cert. denied, 419 U.S. 1070 (1974), in which the court both found that the requested discovery sought information already known to the defendants, and suggested that the requested discovery was a ruse to limit the size of the class. An even greater inroad on *Brennan's* attitude toward class discovery is Cox v. American Cast Iron Pipe Co., 784 F.2d 1546 (11th Cir.), cert. denied, 479 U.S. 883 (1986). In *Cox*, the court thought that the requested discovery probably did not meet the *Brennan-Clark* test, but then went on to hold that the threat of dismissal effectively made answering discovery an "affirmative 'opt-in' device — that is, it requires passive class members to take positive action to stay in the suit. The Advisory Committee specifically rejected the practice of forcing absent class members to opt into a Rule 23 class action to secure its benefits." 784 F.2d at 1556.

9. Can a court to whom multidistrict proceedings have been transferred for pretrial purposes enter orders that limit the number of witnesses that might be used at trial, once the multidistricted cases have been remanded to the transferor forums? One MDL court has so held, slashing the number of potential expert witnesses that the defendant wished to place on the witness list from 137 to just 24. The court noted that this restriction was necessary in order to keep the pretrial deposition schedule in the case manageable. It further found that "Rule 16 applies to multidistrict proceedings the same as it applies to individual cases, and the transferee court may exercise the authority granted under Rule 16(c)(4) to limit the number of expert witnesses to be called at trial." In re Factor VII or IX Concentrate Blood Products Litigation, 169 F.R.D. 632, 637 (N.D. Ill. 1996). The court acknowledged that individual transferor judges might need to make adjustments to the list of 24 experts in particular cases. Id. at 637. If so, how effective is the transferee judge's power of limitation?

10. According to Rule 29, "[u]nless otherwise directed by the court, the parties may by written stipulation . . . modify . . . limitations placed upon discovery." There is an exception to this power when such a stipulation would interfere with the time set for completion of discovery, a hearing, or trial. Granting that the "unless otherwise directed" clause gives the court the ultimate power to quash a mutiny, how effective can the judge's decision to limit discovery be when the parties rebel?

11. The language of Rule 26 seemingly gives courts ample authority to impose limitations on the quantity of discovery. Not surprisingly, it is generally

thought that district courts have wide discretion in setting appropriate discovery limitations. See Gile v. United Airlines, Inc., 95 F.3d 492 (7th Cir. 1996); Stagl v. Delta Airlines, Inc., 52 F.3d 463, 474 (2d Cir. 1995) (discretion abused under facts of case).

12. The *Manual* acknowledges that limitations on the length and amount of discovery is sometimes an appropriate means of controlling discovery, but it is nonetheless cautious in its appraisal. It suggests that "limitations should be imposed only after the court has heard from the attorneys and is able to make a reasonably informed judgment about the needs of the case" and that limitations "are best applied sequentially to particular phases of the litigation, rather than as aggregate limitations." § 21.422; see also §§ 21.451, 21.462. Moreover, the *Manual* lists limitations on quantity as merely one option among several (including discovery cutoffs and phased, sequenced, and targeted discovery).

The *Manual* also suggests an interesting check when discovery limitations are imposed: "When limits are placed on discovery of voluminous transactions or other events, statistical sampling techniques may be used to measure whether the results of the discovery fairly represent what unrestricted discovery would have been expected to produce." Id. We will shortly look at the ideas of sampling and surveys as alternative to traditional discovery. See p. 1153, *infra*. Note how the *Manual* suggests a blend of the traditional (ordinary discovery), the newer case management techniques (discovery limitations), and the non-traditional (sampling and surveys).

Likewise, in *Marrese* the Seventh Circuit suggested that the district court use one of a number of devices — such as an *in camera* inspection or the creation of redacted copies of critical documents — in conjunction with its discovery limitation. These techniques are, of course, specific applications of the principles of phased and targeted discovery, see p. 1122, *supra*, which are tailored to deal with the problem of sensitive information. Once again, limitations on discovery quantity are joined with other case management techniques to ensure that a party is not being "case managed" out of a valid claim.

Are blends of traditional discovery with case management techniques and non-traditional discovery the best hope for handling the problems of information management that complex cases create? Do these blends suggest that strict quantity limitations on non-abusive discovery, without checks to guarantee an acceptable degree of disclosure, are unfair and unworkable? Or, like the dissent in *Marrese*, do you worry that even these blends move us too far away from our prior baseline of fairness — party-initiated, party-controlled discovery?

13. *Marrese*'s suggestion of using *in camera* screening or redaction of copies can also be helpful techniques for streamlining a last, and important, part of the traditional discovery process: the resolution of discovery disputes regarding entitlement to particular information. It is to that task that we now turn.

d. Resolving Discovery Disputes Effectively

Many of the discovery techniques that we explored in the last two subsections have the effect of limiting the amount of information that parties receive. While we have evaluated these devices on their own merits, they also have (if successful) an indirect and beneficial consequence: They reduce the number of occasions on which the parties will engage in disputes over the scope of discovery. Theoretically, complex litigation poses no peculiar issues with regard to such disputes. As a practical matter, however, the opportunities for friction are often much greater in complex cases. For one thing, the stakes are greater, so the incentives to "shade" discovery requests and responses are greater. Moreover, the amount of information available in complex cases increases the likelihood that claims of privilege exist, and also increases the absolute number of documents or responses arguably subject to such a claim. Finally, the very cost of resolving significant numbers of these disputes might price some lawyers out of the case, thus creating pretrial complexity.

Therefore, if the traditional discovery process is to have any chance of working efficiently in complex cases, some expeditious means of handling discovery disputes must be developed. In the following materials, we explore some of the methods that courts have used to resolve, or at least keep to a minimum, the number of discovery disputes. Although these techniques are applicable in all cases, the main issue here is whether they reduce the chances for dispute or streamline the dispute resolution process enough to make traditional discovery feasible in complex cases.

MANUAL FOR COMPLEX LITIGATION, THIRD

62-65 (1995)

Discovery disputes, with their potential of breeding satellite litigation, are a major source of cost and delay. Few aspects of litigation management are more important than bringing about the prompt and inexpensive resolution of such disputes. The mere availability of such a procedure — and the court's insistence that it be adhered to — will deter counsel from the kind of conduct that often obstructs discovery, since no advantage can be gained from it. . . . Such procedures are equally effective where discovery management is referred to a magistrate judge.

A discovery plan should therefore include specific provisions, such as the following, for the fair and efficient resolution of discovery disputes. . . .

No dispute or request for relief should be submitted to the court until after the parties have met and attempted to resolve it. Rules 37(a) and 26(c) condition the right to make a motion to compel or for a protective order upon certification that the movant in good faith conferred or attempted to confer with the opponent to resolve the matter without court action. . . . It is advisable, however, for the discovery plan to specify the ground rules for such conferences, such as requiring that the party requesting the conference send the opponent a clear and concise statement of the asserted deficiencies or objections and the requested action. . . .

Although opinions differ, many judges believe that by making themselves available to resolve such disputes informally, disputes are in fact discouraged and those that are submitted are resolved quickly. . . . [W]hen the attorneys know that the judge (or magistrate judge) is readily available by telephone and the opponent can obtain prompt relief, the incentive for unreasonable behavior is reduced. . . .

If informal procedures fail or are rejected, the court should adopt procedures to minimize the activity needed to resolve disputes. Motions, memoranda, and supporting materials should be restricted in length, replies normally barred, and time limits for submission set. At times, of course, discovery disputes involving issues having a significant impact on the litigation, such as rulings on privilege, may require substantial proceedings. . . .

Special masters have been successfully used to oversee discovery, particularly where there are numerous issues, such as claims of privilege to resolve. Because appointments of special masters can increase substantially the cost of litigation (though the resulting efficiencies could result in offsetting savings), they should not be made except in cases where the parties can afford the cost, and preferably not over the parties' objections. . . .

Submission of certain discovery disputes may be made to a judge outside of the district. A motion to compel or to terminate a deposition held outside a district where the action is pending, or for a protective order, may be presented either to the judge before whom it is pending or to a judge in the district where the deposition is being held. In complex litigation, particularly if procedures have already been established for expedited consideration, it may be well to require all such matters to be presented to the assigned judge. Fed.R.Civ.P. 37(a)(1) requires that motions to compel be presented to the court where the action is pending if directed at a party; only if directed at a nonparty must it be presented to a court in the district where discovery is taken. When a dispute is presented to a deposition-district court, however, the assigned judge may have or be able to obtain authority to act also as deposition judge in that district, and indeed may be able to exercise those powers by telephone. In multidistrict litigation under 28 U.S.C. § 1407(b), "the judge or judges to whom such actions are assigned . . . may exercise the powers of a district judge in any district for the purposes of conducting pretrial depositions." In other cases, arrangements may sometimes be made for an interdistrict or intercircuit assignment, enabling the judge to whom the case is assigned to act as deposition judge in another district. . . .

Whatever procedure is adopted, the court should expedite the resolution of discovery disputes. While such disputes remain pending, they tend to disrupt the discovery program and result in additional cost and delay. It is generally more important to the parties that the dispute be decided promptly than that it be decided perfectly.

Notes and Questions

1. Most of these principles are hard to disagree with, at least most of the time. Moreover, the court seems to have clear authority to adopt them; the Federal Rules (often supplemented by local rules) require counsel to seek an informal resolution in good faith, see F.R.Civ.P. 26(c), 37(a)(2), 37(d), and the

other devices lie comfortably within the boundaries of the court's inherent power to control litigation. Although some areas of disagreement remain about the means of implementation (for instance, whether the judge should informally seek to resolve disputes), the streamlining of discovery disputes has also long been perceived as an appropriate goal. See, *e.g.*, Brookings Institution, Justice for All (1989); 28 U.S.C. § 473(a)(5). This goal seems especially unobjectionable for discovery disputes that involve attempts by one party to impose costs on another party, since these disputes frustrate, rather than advance, the proper functioning of an adversary system.

Nevertheless, many of the *Manual's* principles are honored in the breach. Discovery plans or case management orders rarely include dispute resolution provisions. Good faith conferences often yield little agreement, yet invariably add another layer of expense. Discovery that seeks primarily to impose costs on opponents, as well as discovery motions that seek to do so, are endemic. In many courtrooms, discovery motions languish, and, when decided, simply spawn satellite litigation regarding sanctions. See pp. 1043-47, *supra*. Special masters and magistrate judges can also create certain problems. See pp. 939-60, *supra*.

2. Discovery disputes are probably inevitable in a system in which (a) the parties are required to disclose information on a pretrial basis to the opposing party; and (b) the parties' lawyers are in charge of interpreting opposing lawyers' discovery requests and supervising the disclosure of information. But how different would the result be if the judge were in charge of making discovery requests? Don't factors (a) and (b) still apply? Perhaps factor (b) would be somewhat muted, for a lawyer might not wish to incur a judge's wrath. But a considerable amount of evasion would still occur. Is it best just to accept that a certain amount of evasion and nastiness will occur during discovery, and rely on discovery controls and the threat of sanctions to keep the amount within bounds? How are these bounds to be determined? Are there any other alternatives?

One (unthinkable?) alternative is to return to the common law mode of trial, in which factors (a) and (b) simply did not apply. Another (idealistic?) alternative is to inculcate in the bar the professional responsibility to assure that discovery runs properly. A third (inadequate?) alternative is to attack factor (b), and to bring the court more into the process of garnering and supervising disclosure of information. Does the court have the resources to undertake this last task? Even if it does, should it?

3. It may be impossible to answer these questions without also considering the ways in which discovery disputes arise. Discovery disputes usually fit into one of three genres: (1) there is some defect in the discovery request itself — too vague, too mean-spirited or argumentative, too repetitive of prior requests; (2) there is some reason that the requested information should not be provided — the material is irrelevant, the material is privileged, or the material, while relevant and non-privileged, is too burdensome, costly, or embarrassing to disclose; or (3) the party, without justification, is simply stonewalling the disclosure of information. Judicial intervention to establish the appropriate parameters of a discovery request is likely to be successful with regard to the first genre. Even then, however, the party may still refuse disclosure for the second or third reasons.

How successful is judicial intervention likely to be with regard to the second genre? The following case examines the kinds of disputes that can arise concerning discovery requests, and some ways in which those claims might be resolved through more activist judicial intervention in the discovery process. As you read the case, ask yourself whether even this degree of intervention can avoid the third genre of stonewalling.

IN RE "AGENT ORANGE" PRODUCT LIABILITY LITIGATION

97 F.R.D. 427 (E.D.N.Y. 1983)

■ PRATT, Circuit Judge. In this multidistrict litigation, plaintiffs, Vietnam war veterans and members of their families, seek to recover for injuries allegedly suffered as a result of the veterans' exposure to various herbicides, which defendants manufactured and supplied to the government for use in the Vietnam war. On April 29, 1982, the court appointed Sol Schreiber as special master pursuant to F.R.C.P. 53, to supervise all pretrial discovery for the Phase I trial on the government contract defense, scheduled to commence on June 27, 1983. . . .

Since most of the defendants' documentary discovery on the government contract defense centers on documents which are in the possession of various government agencies and which may be subject to executive privilege claims, the special master submitted to the court a report entitled "Recommended Procedures for Assertion of Executive Privilege" . . . . Defendants have submitted a letter with attached exhibits in support of their objection to portions of the special master's recommendation, and the government has submitted a memorandum in support of the recommendation with suggestions for two modifications. . . .

The government cannot be required to produce in litigation material which falls within the "deliberative process" privilege, Kinoy v. Mitchell, 67 F.R.D. 1, 10-11 (S.D.N.Y. 1975), or the "state secrets" privilege, United States v. Reynolds, 345 U.S. 1, 6 (1953). The former protects communications to the executive for purposes of decision making; the latter protects material which contains national security or state secrets. The special master recommended different procedures for handling these two categories of materials and discussed them separately in his report.

I. *Deliberative Process Privilege*

In his report to the court, the special master thoroughly discussed the rationale for the deliberative process privilege and the factors to be considered in determining whether the privilege should apply. . . . Whether or not such a privilege will apply to particular documents or testimony must await the specifics of a particular claim, when and if it is made. As to the procedural side of the problem, now before the court, without expressing any view as to the scope or extent of the privilege, the court concludes that the special master has recommended a practical and efficient method for handling possible assertions of the privilege by the government, and the court adopts these procedures in full.

The deliberative process privilege satisfies the need for protecting the government's policy-making processes in that the evaluations, expressions of opinions, and recommendations on policy matters of government officials "are held confidential to preserve the free expression, integrity and independence of those responsible for making the determinations that enable government to operate." *Kinoy v. Mitchell*, 62 F.R.D. at 11 (footnote omitted). Briefly stated, the special master recommends that the following procedures be adopted for handling discovery of these materials:

1. *Documents* — If the government objects to production of a document on the basis of the deliberative process privilege, it shall submit an affidavit by an official of the agency having custody of the document describing the document in general terms, why the privilege should apply, and the harm which would result from disclosure. In addition, the government shall make the document available to the special master for *in camera* inspection. The party seeking disclosure shall have seven days to submit to the special master and the government a statement of litigative need. After the special master has ruled on the privilege claim, the parties and the government may appeal his decision within ten days to this court.

2. *Depositions* — If the government asserts the privilege with respect to a witness at a deposition, the party seeking a response has seven days to submit to the government and the special master a copy of the unanswered questions, together with a detailed statement of litigative need. Seven days after that submission, the government must submit to the parties and the special master an affidavit by an official of the agency on whose behalf the privilege is asserted, stating why the privilege applies and what harm disclosure of the response would cause. In addition, the government must submit to the special master a detailed summary of the responses the witness would have made absent the privilege. The appeal procedure from the special master's ruling is the same as that with respect to documents.

No party has objected to the recommended procedures for assertion of the deliberative process privilege. However, the government recommends that the procedures be modified in two respects. First, it suggests that the special master determine whether a document is relevant to the litigation before requiring the government to assert the privilege formally. Second, it requests that the government be permitted to submit a more detailed affidavit to the special master in lieu of the requirement of automatic *in camera* review.

The special master considered the possibility of making a relevance finding prior to formal assertion of the deliberative process privilege and rejected it. In doing so, he noted that he will consider relevance in determining whether the privilege should apply, and the court agrees with his reasoning on this issue.

The court also concludes that the provision for automatic *in camera* inspection of a document at issue is fair. Courts have often employed this method to determine whether the privilege should apply. . . . It enables the special master to make a speedy determination as to whether the document should be protected, thereby expediting discovery; at the same time, the government's burden is lessened because the affidavit it must submit in support of its claim of privilege need not be as detailed. . . .

Because of the limited time remaining before the commencement of trial and because of the parties' need to conduct full discovery, the court concludes that *in camera* inspection provides the best method for determining whether the privilege is applicable. . . .

II. *State Secrets Privilege*

Material containing information concerning national defense, military secrets, or international relations is protected by the state secrets privilege. . . . Unlike the deliberative process privilege, which is qualified and may be overcome by a showing that the interests in disclosure outweigh the interests in non-disclosure, *see Kinoy v. Mitchell*, 65 F.R.D. at 11, the state secrets privilege is absolute and will not be overcome by a demonstration of litigative need, *United States v. Reynolds*, 345 U.S. 1, 11 (1953) . . . . In addition, while *in camera* review of documents claimed to be protected by the deliberative process privilege is routinely utilized, . . . *in camera* inspection is not routine in cases where the state secrets privilege is invoked, *see United States v. Reynolds*, 345 U.S. at 10 . . . .

The special master . . . recognized that the case law indicates that, for assertion of the privilege, there must be a formal claim of privilege by the head of the department or agency in control of the matter after personal consideration by that officer, *United States v. Reynolds*, 345 U.S. at 7-8; he also recognized, that, in view of the large number of documents at issue here, a requirement that the government formally assert the privilege for all documents, including those which are not relevant to the litigation, may be oppressive and burdensome. In addition, he recognized, as do the government and all parties to the litigation, that the imminence of the trial date requires a speedy and efficient method of resolving privilege claims.

Briefly stated, the special master's recommended procedures for assertion of the state secrets privilege are as follows:

1. *Documents* — If the government believes that a document is protected by the privilege but is not relevant to the litigation, it shall supply to the parties and the special master an affidavit by one with knowledge of the document indicating why it is not relevant. The government shall also either (a) submit the document to the special master for *in camera* review, or (b) submit a more detailed affidavit on the issue of relevance. A party seeking disclosure has seven days to submit a statement showing why the document is relevant. If the special master determines that the document is relevant and the government asserts the privilege, it shall then submit to the parties and the special master an affidavit by the head of the agency having control over the matter describing the document in general terms, stating that the affiant has personally examined the documents and describing the harm which would result from disclosure. The party seeking disclosure has seven days to submit a statement of litigative need. The government may also submit the document to the special master for *in camera* inspection, or an affidavit describing it in more detail. After the special master rules on the privilege claim, the parties and the government may appeal his ruling to the court.

2. *Depositions* — If the government asserts the privilege with respect to a witness at a deposition, the party seeking a response has seven days to submit to the government and the special master a copy of the unanswered questions and a detailed statement of relevance and litigative need. The government has seven days to submit to the special master and the parties an affidavit of nonrelevance and a summary of the responses the deponent would have made if the privilege were not asserted. If the special master determines that the questions are relevant, and the government asserts the state secrets privilege, it has seven days to submit to the parties and the special master an affidavit by the head of the agency having control over the matter stating that the affiant has personally reviewed the questions and the responses, and stating the harm resulting from disclosure. The government may also submit to the special master a summary of the responses for *in camera* inspection. The parties and the government may appeal the special master's ruling on the privilege claim to the court.

Defendants object to the recommended procedures on the ground that the government as a nonparty has no standing to object to discovery requests on relevance grounds. They argue that the government should be required to assert the state secrets privilege formally with respect to all documents requested, whether or not relevant to the issues in this case. The government, on the other hand, argues that to require it to assert the privilege formally with respect to each and every document, whether or not relevant to this litigation, may be burdensome and oppressive.

While it is not clear that a nonparty has standing to object on the ground of relevance, . . . the special master determined that his recommendation that relevance be considered prior to assertion of the state secrets privilege "accommodate[s] the needs of the parties while protecting sensitive materials and minimizing the burden on the government."

The defendants' position is that permitting the government to assert a relevance claim before formally asserting the state secrets privilege inserts an additional step in the discovery proceedings that unduly prejudices defendants. They argue that, with less than four months before the commencement of the Phase I trial, they should not be required to show that documents are relevant before the government formally asserts the state secrets privilege.

This argument is disingenuous, to say the least. In its memorandum, the government outlined the procedures it is required to follow if it wishes to assert the state secrets privilege formally. [The procedures involved a four-step review process by a privilege committee and high-ranking officials in two agencies.]

These procedures are obviously cumbersome and time consuming, but the issue now facing us is not the efficiency or validity of the government's established procedures. The issue, instead, is: how can this case be fairly and efficiently prepared for trial, given such governmental obstacles to releasing potentially relevant information? Requiring the government to follow these procedures for every document it believes should be protected by the state secrets privilege, whether or not relevant to this litigation would entail a much longer time than will be required by the special master's examination of the documents for relevance prior to formal assertion of the privilege. . . .

With respect to the defendants' argument that the government lacks standing to object to the relevance of requested discovery, the court agrees with the special master that, in view of the large number of documents at issue here, a prior determination of relevance will tend to decrease the burden on the government. In addition, all parties, if they have not done so already, should inform the special master, in detail, of the nature of the information they believe is relevant in order to assist him in making his relevance prior to formal assertion of the privilege. Contrary to defendants' position, the special master's recommended procedures are designed to enable defendants to obtain quickly all of the relevant documents and testimony not subject to privilege. . . .

Indeed, in view of the procedures the government must follow before asserting the state secrets privilege formally, a requirement that the government formally assert the privilege with respect to every document it believes mat be protected, whether or not relevant to this litigation, appears to be both burdensome and oppressive. . . .

The special master's recommended procedures provide an orderly method through which the defendants can obtain materials relevant to the Phase I trial without unduly burdening the government. . . . The procedures . . . are adopted in full.

Notes and Questions

1. The standing issue in *Agent Orange* — whether a non-party can object on relevance grounds — has never been definitively resolved. Rule 45, which governs the subpoena of information from non-parties, underwent significant changes in 1991. These changes generally provided more protection for non-parties. The rule allows non-parties to move to quash subpoenas on a range of grounds, such as the existence of a privilege "or other protected matter," "undue burden," or "a trade secret." F.R.Civ.P. 45(c)(3)(A)(iii), (c)(3)(A)(iv), (c)(3)(B)(i). Curiously, however, the rule does not mention relevance as a ground for quashing subpoenas. Prior to the amendment, there were some cases that suggested that non-parties could not assert a relevance objection. See Ghandi v. Police Dept. of City of Detroit, 74 F.R.D. 115 (E.D. Mich. 1977); Cooney v. Sun Shipbuilding and Drydock Co., 288 F. Supp. 708 (E.D. Pa. 1968). Nonetheless, like *Agent Orange*, most cases have permitted non-parties to assert a relevance objection. See 9A Charles A. Wright & Arthur R. Miller, Federal Practice & Procedure § 2459 (1995). One case reasoned that a non-party's relevance objection can be accounted for under the "undue burden" prong of amended Rule 45. Compaq Computer Corp. v. Packard Bell Electronics, Inc., 163 F.R.D. 329, 335-36 (N.D. Cal. 1995).

2. *Agent Orange* demonstrates the range of issues that can arise in discovery disputes: relevance, privilege, and burdensomeness. We examined the general problem of burdensomeness in the last subsection, and relevance is a fact-specific inquiry about which it is difficult to generalize. Many discovery disputes, however, involve claims of privilege, and here some generalizations are possible.

(a) *Source of Privilege Law.* The Federal Rules of Civil Procedure do not themselves list the applicable privileges; that task is left to the Federal Rules of Evidence. The basic privilege rule is F.R.E. 501, but it is not particularly helpful. It states that, when state law provides the rule of decision, then the privilege "shall be determined in accordance with State law"; while privilege rules in other cases "shall be governed by the principles of the common law as they may be interpreted . . . in the light of reason and experience." What happens when a case involves both federal question and state law claims? See von Bulow v. von Bulow, 811 F.2d 136 (2d Cir.), cert. denied, 481 U.S. 1015 (1987) (federal law of privilege controls)

(b) *Types of Privilege.* As *Agent Orange* shows, there are two basic structures to privileges: absolute privileges, which cannot be overcome, and qualified privileges, which can be overcome when a great enough need is shown. Among the absolute privileges are the attorney-client privilege, the portion of the work-product privilege that protects an attorney's mental impressions, the doctor-patient privilege, the marital communication privilege, the clergy privilege, the state secrets privilege, and the Fifth Amendment privilege against self-incrimination. See generally John W. Strong, McCormick on Evidence §§ 78-143 (4th ed. 1992); 23 Charles A. Wright & Kenneth W. Graham, Jr., Federal Practice & Procedure §§ 5425-31 (1980); F.R.Civ.P. 26(b)(3). (The "absoluteness" of the Fifth Amendment privilege is debatable; while it cannot be overcome, certain negative consequences can follow from its invocation. See pp. 1112, 1114-15, *supra*.) Among the qualified privileges are the deliberative process privilege and the portion of the work-product privilege that protects materials prepared in anticipation of litigation. F.R.Civ.P. 26(b)(3); Hickman v. Taylor, 329 U.S. 495 (1947). In addition, a First Amendment privilege for journalists is sometimes recognized, either absolutely or with qualification. Wright & Graham, *supra* § 5426. Other qualified First Amendment "privileges" that permit persons not to disclose certain information (such as membership lists of an organization) also exist. See, *e.g.*, *Marrese*, p. 1127, *supra*.

Since the basic content of the absolute and qualified privileges does not vary with the complexity of the case, we leave to other courses the task of examining the details of these privileges. Let us make just one observation. We have seen throughout these materials that the adversarial process has adjusted to accommodate the needs of complex cases. Should the privileges that undergird the adversary system — in particular, the attorney-client privilege, the absolute protection given to mental-impression work product, and the conditional impression given to other forms of work product — also be changed, and perhaps even eliminated, in complex cases? After all, if the reason for the rule no longer obtains, the rule is an empty formality. Would the prospect of changes in these privileges make you more skeptical about making changes in adversarial procedure?

(c) *Waiver.* Privileges can be waived. Under classical waiver theory, a voluntary waiver of a privilege with respect to some information or documents acted as a waiver with respect to all privileged information or documents on the same subject matter. It also acted as a waiver against the entire world; once one person had seen the information, any other litigant (even a litigant in another case) could demand to see the information as well. See 8 Wright et al., *supra*, § 2016.2.

These classical waiver rules ill fit the needs of complex and complicated litigation. First, in a document production involving thousands of documents, it is almost inevitable that some privileged documents will be disclosed inadvertently. The traditional waiver rule would force a party in a million-document case to expend enormous sums and energy ensuring that no waiver occurred, and might also force the party to assert an objection every time the privilege issue is debatable. This latter fact would then require the court to sort through motions to compel on numerous documents. See Transamerica Computer Co. v. International Business Machine Corp., 573 F.2d 646, 648 (9th Cir. 1978) (describing "herculean effort" to find privileged documents in document production comprising 17 million documents); Richard L. Marcus, *The Perils of Privilege: Waiver and the Litigator*, 84 Mich. L. Rev. 1605, 1609-15 (1986). Second, in a case with numerous co-parties, it is sometimes advantageous to share confidential information with litigation allies. If this disclosure constitutes a waiver, then litigation adversaries are also entitled to the information — a result that would make collaboration among parties with similar interests more difficult and information-sharing with witnesses less likely.

Taking the second problem first, a number of courts have developed a "joint defense" or "common interest" doctrine that permits parties with a common litigative interest to share certain privileged information without the sharing constituting a waiver. See, *e.g.*, United States v. American Telephone & Telegraph Co., 642 F.2d 1285 (D.C. Cir. 1980) (p. 1188, *infra*); Marcus, *supra*, at 1637-42. The exact scope of this doctrine is, however, unclear. Some courts limit the doctrine to the situation in which information is shared by parties represented by the same lawyer; other courts use the doctrine whenever the parties have a common interest in a joint defense; and still other courts arguably permit the doctrine to be invoked when the parties do not have a common legal strategy but do have a "community of interests." See Bank Brussels Lambert v. Credit Lyonnais (Suisse), 160 F.R.D. 437 (S.D.N.Y. 1995) (adopting middle position).

The first problem — the inadvertent disclosure of privileged material — has also been addressed through three different approaches. The first approach is that such disclosure amounts to a waiver; all communications relating to the same subject matter must be disclosed. See, *e.g.*, In re Sealed Case, 877 F.2d 976, 980-81 (D.C. Cir. 1989). The second approach is precisely the opposite; it holds that inadvertent disclosure does not amount to a waiver under any circumstances. See Georgetown Manor, Inc. v. Ethan Allen, Inc., 753 F. Supp. 936, 938 (S.D. Fla.1991) (attorney-client privilege is held by client and cannot be waived by attorney's mistake). The third approach lies between the others; it eschews *per se* rules in favor of a test that focuses on whether the disclosing party took reasonable steps to prevent the disclosure. "Reasonableness" is often determined by application of a balancing test that examines such factors as "(1) the reasonableness of the precautions taken to prevent inadvertent disclosure, (2) the time taken to rectify any error, (3) the scope of discovery, (4) the extent of the disclosure, and (5) overriding issues of fairness." See *Bank Brussels*, 160 F.R.D. at 443 (noting that "[t]his regimen best reconciles the principles underlying the attorney-client privilege with the realities of document production in complex litigation"). As another way of loosening the usual rules of waiver, some courts have taken the position that disclosure pursuant to court order is not "voluntary" and therefore not a waiver. See *Transamerica Computer*, 573 F.2d at 651 (no voluntary waiver when judge imposed "extremely rigorous schedule for discovery" and significant measures to prevent inadvertent disclosure were taken).

There also exists another perplexing waiver problem: whether disclosure of privileged information to potential witnesses constitutes a waiver. This problem still lies largely in uncharted water. When privileged information is shown to a witness and the witness relies on the information to refresh his or her testimony or to form an opinion, other parties are entitled to have access to this information. See Sporck v. Peil, 759 F.2d 312, 315 (3rd Cir.), cert. denied, 474 U.S. 903 (1985); F.R.Civ.P. 26(a)(2)(A), (b)(4). It is not clear, however, whether disclosure of information that did not refresh a witness's memory or aid in formulation of an opinion would constitute a waiver, or whether the waiver (if any) is limited just to the information shared with the witness or expert. See Marcus, *supra*, at 1642-48 (arguing that disclosure should be required only upon a showing of "substantial need").

Do any of the many permutations on the waiver rules adequately address the problems of discovery in the complex case? Should an entirely new set of rules be developed to deal with the problem? If lawyer dysfunction is the cause of complexity, should the rules be limited just to those cases in which the use of the classical waiver rules would generate such costs for a lawyer that it might make it impossible for the lawyer adequately to perform his other litigation tasks?

(d) *Reprivileging*. What happens when a document is disclosed to another party, but the court does not deem that the disclosure amounts to a waiver of the privilege? Does the party to whom disclosure was made at least get to keep and use the disclosed document? This problem can set off a battle between the parties about whether the document should be "reprivileged," so that the receiving party must return the document and make no further reference to it. See Lloyds Bank PLC v. Republic of Ecuador, 1997 WL 96591 (S.D.N.Y.) (granting protective order reprivileging virtually all documents); Milford Power Ltd. Partnership v. New England Power Co., 896 F. Supp. 53 (D. Mass. 1995) (same). The Manual for Complex Litigation, Third (1995) recommends that parties come to an agreement that all parties will return (without copying or further reference) privileged material that was inadvertently disclosed. § 21.431; but see 8 Wright et al., *supra*, § 2016.2 (questioning whether such agreements might still constitute a waiver of privilege against other entities). Since this is the rule to which the parties would likely have agreed before the inadvertent disclosure, should an "automatic return and reprivileging" rule be the default rule?

Assuming that reprivileging occurs, can the attorney to whom the document was disclosed be disqualified for looking at the privileged material? Would other sanctions be appropriate? See *Milford Power*, 896 F. Supp. at 58-59 (refusing to disqualify counsel or dismiss portions of complaint related to privileged material).

3. Identifying the documents that may be irrelevant, privileged, or otherwise not subject to production is just the first step in the process. The other side may not agree (indeed, is quite unlikely to agree) with the party's decisions about which documents should be withheld from production. Since these disputes often affect many hundreds or thousands of documents, courts must develop assembly-line strategies for resolving the disputes. *Agent Orange* describes three techniques: entrusting decisions about particular documents to a judicial adjunct such as a special master, using *in camera* screening, and forcing the parties to articulate more precisely their legal theories. A fourth common tactic is to require the party claiming protection to prepare an index

that provides the basic identifying information and subject matter of each document withheld. In *Marrese*, pp. 1129-30, *supra*, we saw a fifth possible tactic: requiring the party (or the court) to redact sensitive material from documents. And in *AT&T*, p. 1109, *supra*, we saw reference to a sixth approach: using confidentiality orders. Each tactic is used in complex litigation, sometimes in combination with other tactics; each has benefits and drawbacks.

(a) *Judicial Adjuncts.* One of the most common uses of judicial adjuncts, and particularly masters, is to resolve disputes concerning particular documents. Typically the court develops the basic framework for deciding claims of relevance, privilege, or burdensomeness; the adjunct then applies the framework to the specific documents. (Note, however, that in *Agent Orange* the master both developed and applied the framework. Is this wise?) This approach frees up the judge to work on larger case management issues, and also keeps the judge from becoming too familiar with certain segments of the case in advance of trial.

On the other hand, use of a judicial adjunct may delay the litigation if a significant number of appeals are taken from the adjunct's decisions, and may also prevent the judge from getting a feel for the litigation she is supposed to be managing. Moreover, a master may impose significant costs on the parties. The use of judicial adjuncts does not obviate the need for document-by-document review of non-disclosure claims; it merely substitutes one reviewer for another. Other theoretical concerns, which we explored at pp. 939-60, *supra*, are also applicable.

(b) *In Camera Review.* Often used in conjunction with judicial adjuncts when the volume of documents is voluminous, *in camera* review allows the court to review contested documents in order to determine if a privilege has been properly asserted. One problem with *in camera* inspection is that it may prejudice the judge, particularly in a non-jury case; indeed, the *Manual* recommends in such cases that another judge or judicial adjunct be used to review the relevant documents. *Manual, supra,* § 21.431. Moreover, with respect to some types of claims (such as a state secrets privilege with respect to highly classified information), *in camera* inspection may not be an option. In *Agent Orange*, the special master received a security clearance from the government to avoid the problem. But the security classification of some documents may exceed the clearance of the master.

Moreover, *in camera* review does not preclude the need for document-by-document review; indeed, automatic *in camera* review is very labor-intensive. Selective *in camera* review of representative documents or particularly sensitive documents avoids some of the labor, but still requires the judge to find ways to deal with the remaining documents.

(c) *Detailing Legal and Factual Theories.* Forcing the parties to develop their legal and factual theories in detail is one of the least invoked powers for resolving discovery disputes. It makes particularly good sense with respect to relevance claims, but it would also be helpful in assessing the degree of need for qualified privilege claims. This technique has the happy side-effect of acting as an issue-narrowing tool akin to the forced stipulation process explored at p. 1030, *supra*. Unfortunately, document discovery, as well as the assertion of relevance or privilege claims, often occurs in the early stages of the litigation, just when the parties are least able to provide a helpful degree of detail concerning their cases. Waiting to rule on objections until more discovery has occurred may obviate that problem, but if the documents are ultimately released, a certain amount of discovery may need to be repeated.

(d) *Indexing.* The 1993 amendments to Rule 26 require that a party withholding information under a claim of privilege or work product "shall describe the nature of the documents, communications, or things not produced or disclosed in a manner that, without revealing the information itself privileged or protected, will enable other parties to assess the applicability of the privilege or protection." F.R.Civ.P. 26(b)(5). The idea of generating such lists of documents first developed in the Freedom of Information Act context, in which the government was required to describe documents withheld pursuant to a FOIA request. See Vaughn v. Rosen, 484 F.2d 820 (D.C. Cir. 1973), cert. denied, 415 U.S. 977 (1974). But the concept quickly spread into complex civil litigation; indeed, at least in complex cases, Rule 26(b)(5) merely codified an already common practice. See Manual for Complex Litigation (Second) § 21.432 (1985). Such a list, which usually contains the author and addressee, date, title, and brief description of the document, is commonly called a "privilege log" or "*Vaughn* index." See *Manual, Third, supra*, § 21.431.

Indexing should, in theory, reduce the number of documents about which there will be legitimate disputes, and should provide the court with basic information concerning each document. Because indexing is expensive, it should also, in theory, discourage profligate objections. On the other hand, the process imposes a significant additional cost on a party legitimately entitled to withhold information.

(e) *Redaction.* Sometimes a document is objectionable only in part. In these situations, the party or the court can edit out the potions of a document that are privileged, and produce the remainder. From the court's viewpoint, it is usually preferable for the party to do the editing, although there is the problem that the party might have an incentive to do a bit too much redaction. Redaction often occurs in conjunction with an *in camera* inspection of a privileged document. See In re Braniff Insolvency Litigation, 153 B.R. 941 (Bankr. M.D. Fla. 1993).

A leading example of the use of redaction is Equal Employment Opportunity Commission v. University of Notre Dame Du Lac, 715 F.2d 331, 337 (7th Cir. 1983), in which the defendant refused to produce, in response to an administrative subpoena, the personnel files of faculty members involved in an allegedly discriminatory tenure decision. The court of appeals found that the identity and other revealing characteristics of the faculty members were subject to a qualified privilege. The court of appeals ordered the defendant to redact the personnel files to eliminate identifying information, and further ordered the district court to review the redactions *in camera* to ensure that the redactions were "reasonably necessary" to protect the faculty's identity. It allowed the plaintiff an opportunity to obtain more information from the files upon a showing of "substantial need." Id. at 337-38; see also Roberts v. Heim, 123 F.R.D. 614 (N.D. Cal. 1988) (ordering sanctions against lawyer that failed to produce non-privileged aspects of document, despite special master's order authorizing lawyer to produce redacted version).

(f) *Confidentiality Orders.* Each of the prior methods usually requires a degree of document-by-document review by the court. A very different idea, which obviates the need for such review, is the confidentiality order. Under this approach, the parties operate under a court order that designates as confidential certain categories of documents, or in some cases all documents. Typically, the order authorizes the designated documents to be disclosed to a limited group of individuals (usually the lawyers, their staffs, and sometimes their clients), and further orders that the documents be used solely for purposes of the litigation; further re-disclosures and all other uses are forbidden. The orders also usually apply only to pretrial disclosure; the parties reserve their rights to argue about disclosure at trial. Nonetheless, the hope is that the case will settle or that most documents will turn out to be tangential; in either event, a ruling on the document can be avoided.

Confidentiality orders come in two flavors: "umbrella orders" — like that found in *AT&T* — which protect documents without an individualized determination of confidentiality from the court, or document-specific orders that protect only documents specifically designated by the court. The *Manual, Third*, describes the following advantages and disadvantages of each type of order:

Umbrella orders. When the volume of potentially protected materials is large, an umbrella order will expedite production, reduce costs, and avoid the burden on the court of document-by-document adjudication. Umbrella orders provide that all assertedly confidential material disclosed (and appropriately identified, usually by stamp) is presumptively protected unless challenged. The orders are made without a particularized showing to support the claim for protection, but such a showing must be made whenever a claim under an order is challenged. Some courts have therefore found that umbrella orders simply postpone, rather than eliminate, the need for the court to closely scrutinize discovery material to determine whether protection is justified, thereby delaying rather than expediting the litigation.[141]

Applications for umbrella orders, usually presented to the court by stipulation of the parties, should specify the following matters: . . . the categories of information subject to the order; . . . the procedure for determining which particular documents are within protected categories; . . . the procedure for designating and identifying material subject to the confidentiality order; . . .the persons who may have access to protected materials; . . . the extent to which protected materials may be used in related litigation; . . . the procedures for maintaining security; . . . the procedures for challenging particular claims of confidentiality; . . . the exceptions, if any, to the general prohibitions on disclosure; . . . the termination of the order after the litigation or at another time; . . . the return or destruction of materials received; and . . . the court's authority to modify the order, both during and after conclusion of the litigation.

Particularized protective orders. A person from whom discovery is sought may move under Fed. R. Civ. P. 26 (c) for a protective order limiting disclosure or providing for the confidentiality of information produced. . . . [T]he parties should address the subject of protective orders in their proposed discovery plan. . . .

In fashioning the order, the court should balance the movants' legitimate concerns about confidentiality against the needs of the litigation, protecting individual privacy, or the commercial value of information while

---

141. . . . The problems of preserving protection for documents produced under umbrella orders are aggravated by the understandable tendency of counsel to err on the side of caution by designating any possibly sensitive documents as confidential under the order. The time saved by excessive designations, however, may be more than offset by the difficulties of later opposing some request for access or disclosure. . . .

making it available for legitimate litigation use. The objective should be to protect only materials for which clear and significant need for confidentiality has been shown; this will reduce the burdensomeness of the order and render it less vulnerable to later challenge. [§ 21.432.]

For cases using umbrella orders, see Cipollone v. Liggett Group, Inc., 785 F.2d 1108, 1121-22 (3d Cir 1986), cert. denied, 484 U.S. 976 (1987); Grundberg v. Upjohn Co., 137 F.R.D. 372 (D. Utah 1991); Zenith Radio Corp. v. Matsushita Electric Industrial Co., 529 F. Supp. 866, 914-15 (E.D. Pa. 1981) ("nothing other than a blanket order can meet the manageability concerns present in a complex case"); see also In re Ford Motor Co. Bronco II Products Liability Litigation, 1996 WL 428114 (E.D. La.) (agreeing with concept of umbrella order but denying order until certain changes made). For a proposed form of an umbrella order, see *Manual, Third, supra,* § 41.36.

Typically, umbrella orders apply only to certain types of privileged information, such as "trade secrets, special formulas, company security matters, customer lists, financial data, projected sales data, . . . data which touch upon the topic of price," and other types of business information. See *Manual, Third, supra,* at 459. Thus, confidentiality orders at best limit, rather than eliminate, the use of other methods for handling objections. Moreover, with umbrella confidentiality orders, a party can always challenge the designation, and the party that designates the material as confidential must show good cause why the designated material should remain confidential. See, *e.g., Cipollone,* 785 F.2d at 1122; id. at 1122 n.17 (suggesting that sanctions are appropriate for improper designations). Again, individual determinations are not always avoided.

4. Confidentiality orders are controversial. Much of the controversy surrounds subsequent attempts to modify the confidentiality order in order to permit others to gain access to the materials covered by the order. We have already explored an aspect of this question when we examined the ability of parties in related litigation to obtain access to materials produced in prior litigation. See p. 1106, *supra.* But parties in other cases are not the only ones who request modification of confidentiality orders; sometimes public advocacy groups, the press, or the public requests access. We saw that, in the context of similar parties, courts were often disposed to modify the confidentiality order to permit access. But advocacy groups, the press, and the public stand on a different footing. Is there ever a reason to modify a confidentiality order to permit access for public interest reasons?

In Seattle Times Co. v. Rhinehart, 467 U.S. 20 (1984), the Supreme Court answered part of that question. In *Seattle Times,* a newspaper involved in litigation with a religious group had obtained through discovery certain information about the group that it wished to publish. The state trial court issued a protective order against its publication. The newspaper alleged that this order was a prior restraint that violated the First Amendment's right to freedom of the press and speech. The Supreme Court disagreed, noting that civil pretrial discovery had traditionally been regarded as a private rather than a public matter, that the newspaper could publish the information if it obtained it from other sources, and that there was good cause to enter the order.

Seattle Times held only that the First Amendment did not require a judge to grant access to materials produced under a confidentiality order; it did not state whether or when a judge could grant access. That issue — whether confidentiality orders can be modified to grant public access to information that had been treated as confidential — has led to a significant amount of litigation.

The leading case is In re "Agent Orange" Product Liability Litigation, 821 F.2d 139 (2d Cir.), cert. denied, 484 U.S. 926 (1987), in which a public advocacy group sought access to documents produced in the *Agent Orange* litigation. Although one of defendants' express conditions in entering a $180 million settlement was that all discovery materials produced to plaintiffs be returned, Judge Weinstein ordered the material unsealed. He also rejected the defendants' claim that they were entitled to renege on the settlement. The Second Circuit affirmed; it found that the public had a presumptive right to discovery material, that the order did not violate the settlement agreement, but that, if it did, the modification was merely "incidental." Id. at 144. See also Jepson, Inc. v. Makita Electric Works, Ltd., 30 F.3d 854 (7th Cir. 1994); Public Citizen v. Liggett Group, Inc., 858 F.2d 775 (1st Cir.1988), cert. denied, 488 U.S. 1030 (1989); see generally Arthur R. Miller, *Confidentiality, Protective Orders and Public Access to the Courts*, 105 Harv. L. Rev. 427 (1991). The proper procedure for a person seeking access to discovery information is to permissively intervene in the case. See Beckman Industries, Inc. v. International Insurance Co., 966 F.2d 470 (9th Cir.), cert. denied, 506 U.S. 868 (1992).

5. When one court enters a confidentiality order, are other courts required to abide by the order? Compare Keene Corp. v. Caldwell, 840 S.W.2d 715 (Tex. Ct. App. 1992) (notions of comity and Full Faith and Credit Clause required state court to defer to protective order of federal court) with Thomas v. General Motors Corp., — U.S. —, 118 S.Ct. 657 (1998) (full faith and credit principles did not require federal court to defer to Michigan state court injunction prohibiting testimony of witness).

6. The inefficiencies of traditional discovery and the inevitable disputes that it entails might have led you to wonder whether there are better ways of obtaining information in complex and complicated cases. We turn to that issue next. As you read the following materials, ask whether these non-traditional devices will better resolve the relevance, privilege, and burdensomeness concerns that inhere in the traditional discovery process.

3. Non-Traditional Discovery Techniques

In this section, we examine discovery techniques that lie beyond the standard methods — depositions, interrogatories, requests for inspection (or its equivalent for non-parties, the Rule 45 subpoena of tangible things), physical examinations, and requests for admission — provided in the Federal Rules of Civil Procedure. In 1985, the Manual for Complex Litigation (Second) urged courts to consider an array of "informal discovery" techniques and the lawyers to consider stipulations that amended the usual methods of conducting discovery. § 21.422. In 1995 the Manual for Complex Litigation (Third) continued the call for lawyers and judges to consider non-traditional discovery methods. § 21.423. Indeed, the automatic disclosure requirement now in effect in many districts (see pp. 1094-98, *supra*) is an outgrowth of this desire for more cost-effective, informal discovery.

This idea of non-traditional discovery raises two questions: first, the source of authority to use non-traditional means, and second, the nature of the devices. On the first issue, since *Manuals* are not themselves sources of authority, the power must be found elsewhere. Two sources exist: the Civil Justice Reform Act ("CJRA") and Rule 29. The CJRA, passed in 1990, ordered courts to consider the possibility of creating plans that encouraged "cost-effective discovery through voluntary exchange of information among litigants and through the use of cooperative discovery devices." 28 U.S.C. § 473(a)(4). Few districts, however, appear to have adopted plans providing explicitly for alternative methods of discovery. Rule 29 provides that, "[u]nless otherwise directed by the court, the parties may by written stipulation . . . modify other procedures governing or limitations placed upon discovery," as long as the modification does not interfere with the time set for completion of discovery, a hearing, or trial. Note that Rule 29 places this power of modification entirely in the parties' hands; the judge cannot order *sua sponte* a non-traditional means of discovery.

The following materials address the second question: the types of non-traditional devices that might be used. As you read the materials, ask whether and when all parties to the litigation might have a mutual incentive to agree under Rule 29 to use non-traditional devices, and whether the judge can force the parties to adopt a device in the absence of consent.

a. Interviews and Surveys in Lieu of Depositions and Interrogatories

One non-traditional method of discovering information is to substitute for the lawyers a neutral information gatherer that conducts interviews or performs surveys to garner information for both sides. Aside from providing initial directions or suggestions to the neutral party, the lawyers are cut out of the information-gathering process. When the third party is the judge, we have the Germanic style of pretrial procedure. See pp. 70-73, *supra*. Might it be possible to entrust the fact-gathering function to other third parties? Or is the use of third parties too great a breach of the adversarial spirit?

Francis E. McGovern & E. Allen Lind,
THE DISCOVERY SURVEY

51 Law & Contemp. Prob. 41, 41-49, 57-62, 66, 69, 72-73 (Autumn 1988)

There is a pervasive assumption that information gathered under fire or in the crucible of the adversarial process is superior to any possible alternative. Virtually no effort is expended to determine whether there are more timely, efficient, or accurate methods of gathering information; attorneys can become oblivious to the blind spots created by looking at the world through adversarial lenses. . . . They generally assume that information has value as long as there is some perceived advantage for further discovery; lower quality but more efficient surrogates are often seen as poor substitutes for 100 percent certainty, regardless of cost.

This article will discuss a lawsuit involving approximately 10,000 plaintiffs in which the court and the parties tested several assumptions regarding discovery in the context of actual litigation. The plaintiffs in the case were allegedly exposed to a pesticide released by the defendant corporation. [The pesticide, DDT, had been manufactured on an Army base near the Tennessee River by Olin Corp. and its predecessor in interest. Olin's manufacturing processes had led to the deposit of more than 400 tons of DDT in the Tennessee River and two of its tributaries. Residents in small towns between Huntsville and Decatur relied heavily on the waterways and river for food, commerce, and recreation. The lawsuits, named after the lead plaintiff in one of the cases, were collectively known as the *Wilhoite* cases. The defendants were Olin, some of its employees, and the Tennessee Valley Authority. A subset of the plaintiffs also sued the United States, but this action was severed under F.R.Civ.P. 42(b) and did not use the discovery procedures described in this article.[*]]

There was nothing particularly complex about the case except for the vast number of named plaintiffs and the technical evidence concerning a correlation, if any, between DDT exposure and the plaintiffs' health. United States District Judge U.W. [Clemon] and the parties concluded that the case needed additional attention, and the judge appointed a special master to develop and implement a case management plan.[5] ...

Olin contended vehemently that there was no evidence that DDT causes harm to humans. Thus, *Wilhoite* falls into a category of mass tort cases, like the Agent Orange litigation, where the central legal and factual issues are related to causation. . . .

Aside from the causation issue, the difficulties facing the special master in devising a case management plan were twofold: (1) efficiency — how to ensure that such a large number of cases could be resolved without clogging the docket for the Northern District of Alabama; and (2) fairness— how to address the efficiency concern without using a procedure that would bias the outcome toward one side or the other. Counsel for the parties did not agree on the issue. Attorneys for the plaintiffs suggested that they should select a small number of their clients and proceed immediately to trial on a first come, first served basis. The defendants proposed that there be a separate trial on the issue of causation alone. . . .

Notwithstanding this apparent conflict in the parties' interests, there were areas of joint concern — but the parties were unable to find them. . . . Unable to communicate candidly with each other out of a concern that one side would take advantage of the other in adversarial gamesmanship, the negotiations resembled a traditional zero sum game. Neither side wanted to try a large number of cases, and it was unnecessary to decide how cases would be tried until there was more information. . . .

An "onion peel" approach to case management seemed advisable: a quick and inexpensive method of paring back each layer of uncertainty in

---

[*] One of the authors of this book was lead counsel for the United States in the severed action. — Ed.

[5] One of the authors of this paper, Francis E. McGovern, was appointed special master. . . .

the lawsuit until only those plaintiffs, if any, who could raise a factual issue remained. Only then would it be possible to select truly representative plaintiffs for trial or to reach a settlement on the values of the cases....

Active mediation by the special master broke down many of the communication barriers, and the parties agreed on a case management plan that had three tracks. The first track involved general discovery of all the named plaintiffs. The second track was an in-depth discovery of twenty randomly selected plaintiffs who were subject to pretrial discovery under the traditional adversarial model. The third track was reserved for legal issues to be resolved prior to trial. All three tracks were pursued concurrently so that, upon completion, the court could decide how the cases would be tried.

The general discovery track was designed to elicit information from each named plaintiff on issues relevant to the case. The parties could then develop an accurate overview of the plaintiffs as a whole. Upon completion of the general discovery it would be possible to select representative, rather than random, plaintiffs for trial. This need to collect information from thousands of plaintiffs stimulated the development of the discovery survey ....

The discovery survey consisted of a questionnaire jointly drafted by plaintiffs and defendants through a series of negotiations. Once the common discovery instrument was completed, neutral third parties, paid for jointly by plaintiffs and defendants, were hired to administer the survey and make the information available to all the parties....

Plaintiffs were notified by mail that they were required by the court to attend an interview session and complete a questionnaire or their cases would be dismissed. They were also required to bring any relevant personal and medical records with them to refresh their memories. By requiring plaintiffs to appear physically at an interview center, it was anticipate that a large number of marginally interested plaintiffs would drop out of the case....

There were lengthy discussions concerning the ability of the plaintiffs to comprehend and answer the questions in the questionnaire. Because of a suspected high illiteracy rate among the plaintiffs, the parties decided to have an interviewer read the questionnaire to each plaintiff and record the answers. The interviewer was instructed to press for answers when plaintiffs appeared unable or reluctant to respond.... There was also some concern that the plaintiffs would be unable to answer detailed questions unless they had access to extensive personal documents to refresh their memory. The interviewers were restricted from providing any additional assistance to plaintiffs unless supplementary comments had been approved in advance by the special master. Attorneys were allowed to oversee the interview process but were not permitted to speak to their clients once they entered an interview center....

The negotiations themselves concerning the questions to be included in the questionnaire occasionally created additional problems.... [T]he lawyers were sometimes more concerned with the tactical and legal ramifications of questions than their lucidity. They reached agreement on the wording of several questions at the cost of virtually guaranteeing confusion . . . .

The problem became particularly acute in the context of decisions concerning the use of open-ended or closed-ended questions and answers and the use of prompting to obtain full answers. Generally, the defendants desired to have open-ended questions without prompting, whereas the plaintiffs preferred more tightly structured questions and answers. By virtue of extensive negotiations, compromises were reached on all of these issues. . . .

By January 1986, 10119 plaintiffs had been scheduled for the discovery survey, 6731 had completed a questionnaire, 300 had answered interrogatories, 20 had been deposed, and 3068 had been dismissed. . . . The case settled for approximately $15 million in May of the same year [as a Rule 23(b)(3) settlement class action]. . . . There were three opt outs and 5968 opt ins. In addition, the 3068 plaintiffs who had been dismissed for failure to attend interview sessions were allowed to join the settlement. All persons who had not completed questionnaires were sent a blank questionnaire form, the so called "mailed discovery survey," and were required to return them to the court. Six thousand eighteen plaintiffs completed the mailed discovery survey.

The settlement also provided that the special master allocate the settlement funds among the plaintiffs based upon each individual plaintiff's blood DDT level, exposure to Olin DDT, diseases or injuries, and other relevant factors. The special master scheduled all plaintiffs in the settlement class to attend a session where they could have their blood sampled and complete an updated form of the discovery survey entitled "survey update." This survey was significantly shorter than the previous survey, contained primarily closed-ended questions, and concentrated more on the needs of the providers and end-users of the data being collected, and less on the tactical concerns of the attorneys. The survey update was self-administered . . . .

Wilhoite v. Olin provides a unique opportunity for an empirical comparison of alternative discovery devices. The multiple information-gathering instruments used in the case offer the possibility of comparing traditional discovery devices and the various forms of the discovery survey with respect to their costs in time and money, the quality and quantity of information they collected, and evaluations of the devices by plaintiffs, attorneys, and experts. . . .

A. Timeliness and Cost . . .

The negotiation of the original questionnaire was abnormally long. . . . Experiences in other cases suggest that negotiating an instrument is difficult and time-consuming but can possibly be accomplished within several months with a total cost of $25,000. . . .

The time and cost figures for the depositions and interrogatories contained in Charts 2 and 3 were obtained from interviews with attorneys and clients and from a review of the documents themselves. This comparison suggests that the discovery survey has a potential role in discovery, at least in the kind of cases illustrated by *Wilhoite*.*

CHART 2
COST OF DISCOVERY DEVICES

DISCOVERY DEVICE	CREATION (TOTAL)	ADMINISTRATION (PER PLAINTIFF)	PROCESSING (PER PLAINTIFF)	TOTAL COST
Deposition	$ 20,000	$1000	$100	$7,720,000
Interrogatories	$ 10,000	$ 200	$ 50	$1,760,000
Discovery Survey	$150,000	$ 16	$ 5	$ 297,000
Mailed Discovery Survey	$150,000	$ 3	$ 5	$ 206,000
Survey Update	$ 50,000	$ 8	$ 2.50	$ 123,500

CHART 3
TIMELINESS OF DISCOVERY DEVICES

DISCOVERY DEVICE	CREATION (TOTAL)	ADMINISTRATION (PER PLAINTIFF)	PROCESSING (PER PLAINTIFF)	TOTAL TIME
Deposition	200 hours	5 hours	4 hours	63,200 hours
Interrogatories	100 hours	3 hours	2 hours	35,100 hours
Discovery Survey	1500 hours	45 min.	40 min.	11,416 hours
Mailed Discovery Survey	1500 hours	1 hour	40 min.	13,166 hours
Survey Update	500 hours	15 min.	10 min.	3416 hours

B. Information Quantity and Quality . . .

The major finding with respect to the quantity or completeness of information was that the discovery survey performed as well as did the traditional discovery devices — interrogatories and depositions — when it

---

* The "Total Cost" and "Total Time" columns in the ensuing charts were obtained by assuming that the case contained 7,000 plaintiffs, and then applying the following formula: [Column 1 ("Creation") + [Column 2 ("Administration") + Column 3 ("Processing")] × 7,000 = Column 4 ("Total Cost" or "Total Time"). — ED.

was administered under controlled circumstances. The mailed self-administered discovery surveys were not as good.... Finally, the information quantity analysis showed that the survey update performed at least as well, and perhaps better, than the traditional discovery devices.

Three measures of the quality of information produced by the various discovery devices were examined. The first measure of quality of information is called its internal *reliability*.... With the exception of the mailed discovery survey, all of the devices are good, and all are about equally good on this test of information quality.

The other two measures of information quality used the information from the survey update to test the consistency of information across time. ...

On the basis of these results, it appears that the discovery survey and the survey update were at least as successful as the more traditional procedures of interrogatories and depositions. The surveys yielded information that was by and large as complete and consistent as the information produced by the traditional procedures....

These findings are very favorable indeed for the discovery survey methods, especially when one considers the low cost of these instruments relative to more traditional discovery procedures. If similar levels of information quality and quantity can be obtained with substantially less costly discovery devices, the devices are certainly worth considering.... If surveys are administered in person by trained interviewers, or even if they are self-administered under close supervision, as was the case with the survey update, there is little reason to doubt that survey methods can produce information as good as that supplied by interrogatories and depositions....

C. Plaintiff Evaluations ...

The findings with respect to the plaintiffs' reactions to the various discovery procedures are interesting. The plaintiffs might be described as uncomplaining in their assessment of the discovery procedures. They almost never saw the procedures as unfair, and they were seldom unwilling to tolerate even relatively burdensome procedures such as interrogatories or depositions.... [P]laintiffs' responses do show that they experienced some trouble with depositions. They apparently had a good deal of difficulty in understanding the questions and responding with the right information.... The plaintiffs who were deposed were less likely to think that they had been treated well in the course of the discovery process.

D. Satisfaction of Attorneys

The general reaction of the attorneys to the discovery survey was favorable, with time and cost being the major pluses. Attorneys also showed substantial appreciation for the ability to get an overview of the entire range of plaintiffs. Initial concerns that the neutral interviewers would interject some types of bias into the information were not realized. Expectations that some attorneys would manage to take tactical advantage of the situation also did not materialize.

At the more detailed level, concern remains about the possibility of potential bias and unfairness resulting from the precise wording of the questions. . . .

There was unanimity that redundancies and excesses existed in the original questionnaire. In retrospect, the limited inquiries in the survey update were probably sufficient. . . . Perhaps if there had been more discovery prior to the design of the questionnaire, it would have been possible to agree upon an abbreviated format. . . .

[T]he discovery survey — a negotiated questionnaire administered and processed by neutrals — can be a useful addition to the development of data in a case involving large numbers of plaintiffs. Short-term tactical advantages sought by attorneys in discovery can be neutralized, and massive amounts of information can be gathered quickly at relatively low cost. . . . Straightforward questions calling for objective, verifiable information and persistent monitoring by neutrals can result in accurate and complete responses. Carefully controlled answers can be readily processed by computer. The satisfaction of clients, attorneys, and experts with respect to the discovery survey can be maintained at a higher level than it can with respect to more traditional discovery techniques.

Notes and Questions

1. Professor McGovern and Mr. Lind make strong claims for the efficacy of discovery interviews or surveys conducted under the auspices of neutral parties, and beyond the reach of the parties' lawyers. Note, however, that McGovern's stated concern as a special master was to design a system that was both efficient and fair, with fairness being measured by the outcome-distorting potential of the process. While the efficiency claims for the discovery survey are manifest, is it obvious that the survey is fair in the sense that McGovern describes? Assuming that they had not been allowed to re-enter the lawsuit to share in the settlement, would the 3,068 plaintiffs who found themselves out of court under the discovery survey have thought the system was fair? Can you defend on fairness grounds the use of a non-traditional discovery device with the potential to change the outcome of the lawsuit for nearly one-third of the entire group of plaintiffs? Obviously, one way to avoid this unfairness is to use the discovery survey without the consequence of dismissal for non-appearance. But would the defendants, who were better-financed than the plaintiffs, have agreed to the survey procedure without the dismissal provision?

If the defendants had objected to the use of a discovery survey without a dismissal provision, would the court have had the authority to order the survey? One court has held that it had the authority under Rule 23(d) to require class members to file proof of claim forms drafted by the parties prior to commencement of the damages phase of the litigation. Biben v. Card, 789 F. Supp. 1001 (W.D. Mo. 1992). That position is controversial. See 7B Charles A. Wright et al., Federal Practice & Procedure § 1787 (1986). Moreover, the purpose of the form in *Biben* was merely to obtain damages information for settlement purposes; the request did not involve any significant expenditures to employ neutral third parties to obtain information. In any event, the arguable power under Rule 23(d) does not extend to non-class actions such as *Wilhoite*. Might the catch-all case management powers of Rules 16(c)(12) and 16(c)(16) be an appropriate source of authority in non-class-action cases? If not, would the court have the inherent power to order a discovery survey over the objection of one or more of the parties? Would such an inherent power also permit a court to order objecting parties to pay a portion of the cost of the survey?

2. The efficiency of the discovery survey may distort the outcome in another way. Without the survey, traditional discovery of the plaintiffs would have cost, according to the calculations of McGovern and Lind, about $9,480,000. If we assume that the defendants would have borne about two-thirds of those costs, traditional discovery would have imposed $6,320,000 in costs on the defendants and $3,160,000 in costs on the plaintiffs. Under the survey method, the costs of discovery were about $525,000, shared equally by the parties. All other things being equal in the two discovery processes, we can use the same type of economic analysis used by Issacharoff and Loewenstein, see pp. 1058-61, *supra*, and discover that the defendants' mid-range settlement point was $1,508,000 higher under traditional discovery than under the survey method. Since the case settled for $15,000,000, the discovery survey reduced the expected gross recovery to the plaintiffs by almost exactly 10%. Whether it would have reduced the net recovery would have depended on whether the plaintiffs' lawyers could have made a claim for extra fees against the 10% additional recovery and the amount of discovery expenses that would actually have been incurred prior to the settlement. As a general proposition, however, the discovery survey would seem to result in a lower expected net recovery if the plaintiffs settled before intensive discovery of individual plaintiffs occurred, but a greater expected net recovery if the case settled after such discovery. Given that judges possess case management tools, such as bifurcation, to defer intensive plaintiff discovery, is the case for the efficiency of the discovery survey as clear as McGovern and Lind suggest? On this matter, it might be relevant to know that the United States, which declined to participate in the discovery survey process, won a bifurcated trial on liability issues, thus avoiding the cost of plaintiff discovery entirely.

From the perspective of overall social costs (which is the approach taken by Professor Hay, see p. 1133, *supra*), the additional cost of traditional procedure ($9,480,000 versus $525,000) is a wasted expenditure, at least as long as the value of the information obtained in both methods is equivalent and there are no other costs attached to the survey. Note how the private incentive of the plaintiffs (to obtain a larger settlement) may come into conflict with the social incentive (to reduce overall litigation costs). Does this suggest that the judge (who can be more sensitive to such social costs), rather than the lawyers (who seek to obtain their clients' private goals), should make the decision about whether to use a survey?

3. Both the last Note and the analysis by McGovern and Lind rest on the assumption that adversarial procedure has no value. If it does, then the damage that the discovery survey did to the adversarial system must be factored in as a cost of the discovery survey. But how are we to value adversarial procedure? One test is to use the *Wilhoite* numbers. If the calculations of McGovern and Lind are accurate, the discovery survey cost $8,965,000 less than traditional discovery would have cost. Is the parties' right to control the accumulation of evidence worth that much?

Since the lawyers in *Wilhoite* acceded to the discovery survey, the answer that the lawyers gave was "No." Would the 10,000 plaintiffs themselves have given the same answer? Is the solution to the valuation issue to leave the decision about the value of adversarial process in the parties' hands, and to allow the use of surveys only when they all agree to use it? Will parties undervalue public goods for private gain? On the other hand, if we leave the decision about using the discovery survey in the judge's hands, we again have the problem of valuing adversarialism and the related problem that different judges might value it to different degrees.

A different way to think about valuing adversarialism is to re-read Professor Langbein's descriptions of, and arguments for, Germanic procedure. See pp. 70, 930, *supra*. Although the use of trained interviewers is somewhat different than the use of the judge to discover relevant facts, the basic similarities between the discovery survey and Germanic pretrial process are striking. How comfortable are you with converting our system into a more Germanic one, knowing that the cost savings of doing so are potentially significant? Would you be comfortable if the procedure were used in routine cases as well as complex? If not, are there features of complex cases that justify the discovery survey's departure from adversarial process? Is the departure justified only when the savings from the survey eliminate a lawyer's financial inability to gather information?

Yet another way to think about adversarialism's value is to recall the caveat that McGovern and Lind placed on the use of the discovery survey: that the survey was useful to obtain routinized, identical background information on issues of damage. Would you be comfortable with using trained interviewers to discover the facts from critical liability or damages witnesses? If not, the discovery survey may be a useful device only in the limited number of cases in which many individual, identifiable plaintiffs have been joined *and* the plaintiffs' lawyers are willing to concede the dismissal of plaintiffs who fail to come in for an interview.

4. The discovery survey may not even be useful in all of these cases. In *Wilhoite* the discovery survey became appealing because the parties could not agree on a different method of handling pretrial and trial. Had they been able to agree on, or had the court insisted on, a bifurcated pretrial and trial plan (see p. 1019, *supra*, p. 1273, *infra*), the entire expense of surveying the plaintiffs might have been eliminated. One of the issues that McGovern and Lind fail to explore is whether the discovery survey, while a potential savings over traditional discovery, was nonetheless wasteful in relation to other case management solutions for the case.

5. The *Wilhoite* survey, which sought to survey an entire litigant population through court-annexed means, is unique. Other surveys are more common. Surveys are often conducted in the ordinary course of business, and as long as they are relevant and non-privileged, they can be used in the litigation. Surveys conducted for purposes of litigation also occur with some frequency. For instance, surveys based on representative sampling are sometimes used in areas such as trademark, securities, and antitrust. See, *e.g.*, Bath & Body Works, Inc. v. Luzier Personalized Cosmetics, Inc., 76 F.3d 743, 750 (6th Cir. 1996) (trademark survey conducted after discovery cutoff inadmissible); Piper Aircraft Corp. v. Wag-Aero, Inc., 741 F.2d 925 (7th Cir. 1984) (trademark survey admissible); In re Airline Ticket Commission Antitrust Litigation, 918 F. Supp. 283 (D. Minn. 1996) (permitting sampling survey of plaintiff class). Party control of these surveys is typical; there are only a few examples of surveys not

controlled by the parties, and, with the exception of *Wilhoite*, they were designed only to obtain representative information of a plaintiff class. See, *e.g.*, *Biben*, 789 F. Supp. 1001; In re Fibreboard Corp., 893 F.2d 706 (5th Cir. 1990) (p. 1294, *infra*) (Special Master McGovern surveyed 3,031 plaintiffs to advise jury of basic demographics of entire group; approach rejected by Fifth Circuit); Hilao v. Estate of Ferdinand Marcos, 103 F.3d 767 (9th Cir. 1996) (p. 1299, *infra*) (special master used claim form of representative sample of 137 plaintiffs to estimate damages for entire group).

Indeed, although it has been ten years since McGovern and Lind wrote their article about discovery surveys, to our knowledge *Wilhoite* remains the only successful example of its type. What does this fact say about the discovery survey? About the attitudes of lawyers and judges toward party control of information gathering?

6. For a description of methodological concerns that surround the admissibility of sampling evidence, see Manual for Complex Litigation, Third § 21.493 (1995); see generally Federal Judicial Center, Reference Manual on Scientific Evidence (1994).

7. Party-controlled surveys may need to be tightly monitored in order to prevent abuse. In the *Airline Ticket* litigation, for example, a defendant allegedly used its contacts with the unnamed class members to convince the members to settle their claims individually. If true, the conduct might be a sanctionable breach of professional ethics. In re Airline Ticket Commission Antitrust Litigation, 1996 WL 585301 (D. Minn.).

8. The idea underlying the *Wilhoite* discovery survey — the control of discovery by persons not aligned with the parties — is a reality for many lawyers who find themselves engaged in discovery in foreign jurisdictions. We now turn to this issue.

b. Discovery in Foreign Legal Systems

Discovery involving foreign parties raises four interrelated issues. The first is how to conduct discovery against a foreign citizen who is a party to litigation in an American court and whose discoverable information is located in the United States. The second is how to conduct discovery against a foreign party when the information is located outside the United States. The third is how to conduct discovery against a foreign non-party with information located within the jurisdiction of American courts. The fourth is how to conduct discovery against a foreign non-party with information located in a foreign country. With the rise of a global economy, the importance of knowing the limits of discovery in each of these scenarios should be evident. Because broad discovery and party control of evidence gathering are peculiarly American phenomena, a brief study of these issues may suggest some practical alternatives for parties wishing to create a less adversarial structure for their litigation.

The answers to these issues lie in the intersection of American law, conventional law (*i.e.*, treaties and the like), and the domestic law of the relevant foreign jurisdictions. To begin with American law, a number of rules and statutes deal with aspects of taking discovery in foreign countries. See, *e.g.*, F.R.Civ.P. 28(b) (depositions in foreign countries); 28 U.S.C. §§ 1781-84 (receipt of letters rogatory and subpoena of persons in foreign countries). These rules and statutes, however, deal with specific situations and do not provide a general approach to the problem of foreign discovery. Section 442(1)(a) of the Restatement (Third) of Foreign Relations Law of the United States (1987) reflects the more general approach of American courts to the problem of discovery involving foreign persons. It provides that a "court or agency in the United States, when authorized by statute or rule of court, may order a person subject to its jurisdiction to produce documents, objects, or other information relevant to an action or investigation, even if the information or the person in possession of the information is outside the United States." In deciding whether to order such production, § 442(1)(c) states that a court should balance a number of factors, such as "the importance to the investigation or litigation of the documents or other information requested; the degree of specificity of the request; whether the information originated in the United States; the availability of alternative means of securing the information; and the extent to which the request would undermine important interests of the United States, or compliance with the request would undermine important interests of the state where the information is located."

The notes to § 442 make clear that non-parties are not treated differently than parties (except to the extent that F.R.Civ.P. 45, dealing with non-party discovery, is more restrictive than F.R.Civ.P. 26-36, dealing with discovery from parties); the critical issue is whether the court has jurisdiction over the person from whom disclosure is sought. The notes also make clear that a court can require a party subject to its jurisdiction to produce information kept in a foreign country, although they acknowledge that the court "should scrutinize a discovery request more closely than it would scrutinize comparable requests for information located in the United States." See § 442, Comment *a*. There has been a fair degree of litigation concerning whether certain information is really in the possession or control of the person subject to the court's jurisdiction, and particular rules have been developed to deal with discovery from foreign subsidiaries of American corporations, foreign parents of American subsidiaries, and foreign managing agents, directors, officers, or employees of corporations subject to American jurisdiction. See Gary B. Born & David Westin, International Civil Litigation in American Courts 355-57 (2d ed. 1994).

The balancing approach of the *Restatement (Third)* has been subject to criticism, largely on the ground that there is no general reason to make discovery discretionary for any person subject to American jurisdiction. See John B. Houck, Restatement of the Foreign Relations Law of the United States *(Revised): Issues and Resolutions*, 20 Int. Law. 1361, 1373 (1986); cf. Reinsurance Co. of America, Inc. v. Administratia Asigurarilor de Stat, 902 F.2d 1275 (7th Cir. 1990) (Easterbrook, J., concurring) (suggesting that balancing under § 442(1)(c) is almost impossible). From another perspective, the *Restatement (Third)*'s approach could be criticized for its apparent conflict, at least with regard to evidence located in a foreign country, with the Hague Convention on the Taking of Evidence Abroad in

Civil or Commercial Matters. 23 U.S.T. 2555, reprinted at 28 U.S.C.A. § 1781 (1994).

The Hague Convention is the primary source of conventional law for dealing with discovery in the international arena. The United States has been a party to the Convention since 1972; 26 other countries, mostly from Western Europe, have also signed.* The Hague Convention requires each signatory country to designate a Central Authority. When a court in Country A wishes to conduct discovery of information located in Country B, the court sends a letter of request to the Central Authority of Country A, and that Central Authority transmits the letter to the Central Authority in Country B. The Central Authority in Country B is then required either to provide the evidence unless (1) the person from whom the evidence is sought has a "privilege or duty to refuse to give the evidence" under the law of either Country A or Country B, see Article 11; (2) "the execution of the Letter does not fall within the functions of the judiciary" of Country B, see Article 12(a); or (3) Country B "considers that its sovereignty or security would be prejudiced," see Article 12(b). At the time of ratification, each signatory country could declare "that it will not execute Letters of Request issued for the purpose of obtaining pretrial discovery of documents as known in Common Law countries," see Article 23. Australia, Cyprus, Denmark, France, Germany, Italy, Luxemburg, Monaco, Portugal, and Spain have declared that they will not execute such letters, while Finland, Mexico, the Netherlands, Norway, Singapore, Sweden, and the United Kingdom will execute letters only on limited terms.

When Country B agrees to provide information, the Convention provides three methods for taking evidence. The first is that the Central Authority may itself obtain it, see Article 13. Second, a diplomatic officer or consular agent of the requesting state may take the evidence, see Articles 15 and 16. Third, "a person duly appointed as commissioner for the purpose" may take the evidence, see Articles 17. When the Central Authority obtains the evidence, the collection of information is usually performed by a judicial authority that "appl[ies] its own law as to the methods and procedures to be followed," see Article 9. When an officer, agent, or commissioner is used, she is authorized to "take all kinds of evidence which are not incompatible with the law of the State where the evidence is taken or contrary to any permission granted" by the Central Authority; she cannot, however, take evidence by means forbidden by the law of this State, and the person from whom evidence is sought enjoys the Article 11 "privilege or duty" to refuse to provide the evidence. See Article 21. Finally, an officer, agent, or commissioner may obtain such information only by voluntary means; she cannot compel its production. Should compulsion be required, she must request "appropriate assistance" from the Central Authority of the country in which she is taking the evidence. See Article 18.

From a theoretical and comparative perspective, the Hague Convention provides a wonderful contrast to American procedure: Information sought

---

* A second, more limited source is the Inter-American Convention on Letters Rogatory, reprinted at 28 U.S.C.A. § 1781, to which the United States has been a signatory since 1988.

must be specifically designated, and it is obtained by someone other than the party's own lawyer. The Convention was an attempt to compromise between the civil law and common law methods of pretrial process, and also an attempt to deal with the nearly universal fear (or contempt) of American-style pretrial discovery. Does it seem a better process than the process that we have been studying in this chapter? Doesn't it become harder to defend our system of pretrial process when so much of the Western world both (a) adopts different procedures and (b) is appalled by our procedures? Nothing in adversarial theory requires that we use the type of pretrial process which we have adopted. Adversarial theory guarantees the right of the parties to control the presentation of proofs; it does not create a free-ranging right to obtain such proofs in advance of trial.

From a practical perspective, the Hague Convention presents some real problems. International discovery in complex litigation is a fairly common phenomenon. The Hague Convention procedures seem quite lengthy in comparison to American discovery, and they may not garner the information necessary to achieve a rational resolution of the dispute — in short, they threaten to create lawyer dysfunction and pretrial complexity. Is resort to the Hague Convention mandatory? Clearly the answer is "No" with respect to discovery sought in countries that have not signed the Convention. Equally clearly, the answer is "No" with regard to information contained within the United States that is relevant to an American lawsuit; the Convention applies only to information located in another country. But must the Hague Convention, rather than the Federal Rules of Civil Procedure, be followed when information relevant to an American lawsuit is located in another signatory country and the party is subject to American jurisdiction?

In Societe Nationale Industrielle Aerospatiale v. United States District Court, 482 U.S. 522 (1987), the Court held that the Hague Convention did not establish an exclusive method for obtaining foreign discovery, nor was a party in an American lawsuit required to use the Hague Convention before resort to discovery under the Federal Rules. In an approach remarkably similar to that of § 442(1)(c), the Court found that a federal court should engage in a comity analysis that considered the nature of the discovery request, the "particular facts" of the litigation, "the likelihood that resort to [Convention] procedures will prove effective," and the "claims and interests of the parties and the governments whose statutes and policies they invoke." 482 U.S. at 544, 546. It did urge that courts be sensitive to "the danger that unnecessary, and unduly burdensome, discovery may place [foreign litigants] in a disadvantageous position," id. at 546, but ultimately upheld the trial court's decision to permit American-style discovery of the foreign defendant to occur. Four dissenters thought that first resort should have been made to the Convention's procedures. See also Joseph F. Weis, *The Federal Rules and the Hague Convention: Concerns of Conformity and Comity*, 50 U. Pitt. L. Rev. 903 (1989) (urging amendments to Federal Rules to make first resort to Convention mandatory). Would a first resort merely result in additional delays when it appears likely the country from which information is sought will not provide it?

Certain matters were left unresolved by *Aerospatiale*. The first is its applicability to state courts. One line of thought contended that state courts would be required to resort to the Hague Convention; an opposing line of thought contended that *Aerospatiale*'s comity principle was a matter of federal law that did not bind state courts. Neither view seems to have prevailed, and the *Aerospatiale* analysis is usually employed by state courts. See Born & Westin, *supra*, at 437; In re Asbestos Litigation, 623 A.2d 546 (Del. Super. 1992). Second, *Aerospatiale* involved a case in which the discovery sought was interrogatories, requests for production, and requests for admission. It was possible, therefore, for the defendant to respond to discovery "in" the United States. The deposition of a foreign person or inspection of a foreign facility must, however, physically occur "in" the foreign country. Must the Hague Convention be used in these situations? There is some authority to this effect. See Born & Westin, *supra*, at 432; but see *Aerospatiale*, 482 U.S. at 541 ("text of the Convention draws no ... sharp line between evidence that is 'abroad' and evidence that is within the control of a party subject to the jurisdiction of the requesting court").

Third, *Aerospatiale* did not state how courts should balance the relevant factors; indeed, the majority consciously chose "not [to] articulate specific rules to guide this delicate task of adjudication." 482 U.S. at 546. For instance how would you balance the *Aerospatilae* factors in *Asbestos Litigation*, in which a Finnish defendant presented an affidavit from a Finnish judge that stated, in essence, that in Finland "[t]he judiciary can permit private evidence-gathering, but would regard any attempt by the parties to do so on their own initiative as an offense to the Court's jurisdiction" and that "the Finnish government perceives an important sovereign interest in the regulation of the taking of evidence in Finland and regards the Hague Convention procedures as the proper means of taking evidence in Finland by foreign litigants," 623 A.2d at 550? The judge in *Asbestos Litigation* ordered American-style discovery. If *Asbestos Litigation* is right, can you ever imagine a set of circumstances in which a judge would order use of the Convention procedures?

Fourth, in *Aerospatiale* the discovery was sought against a litigant subject to the trial court's jurisdiction; the Court did not focus on the appropriate response to requests for discovery from non-litigants. How should discovery from non-litigants be handled? *Aerospatiale* observed that "the text of the Convention draws no distinction between evidence obtained from third parties and that obtained from the litigants themselves." 482 U.S. at 541. Certainly, however, foreign persons not subject to the jurisdiction of an American court cannot be reached by other means, and resort to the Hague Convention is necessary. What about foreign non-litigants subject to American jurisdiction? In Orlich v. Helm Brothers, Inc., 160 A.D.2d 135, 560 N.Y.S.2d 10 (1990), a plaintiff sought discovery from Mercedes Benz, the West German manufacturer of an allegedly defective car but a non-party in the case. The court held that, "[w]hen discovery is sought from a non-party in a foreign jurisdiction, application of the Hague Convention, which encompasses principles of international comity, is virtually compulsory.... Since fact gathering is a judicially controlled process in civil law nations such as West Germany, the non-judicial taking of evidence located within their territory is regarded as an affront to their sovereignty. Such an exercise would be particularly offensive where, as here, the entity being subjected to the court-ordered fact gathering, . . . is not even a party to the litigation."

Even after the right to use American-style discovery has been secured (whether under a § 442(1) analysis or, in the case of the Hague Convention, an *Aerospatiale* analysis), a litigant is not yet in the clear. In response to the needs for commercial secrecy and the perceived excesses of American discovery, many foreign nations have enacted "blocking laws" that make it illegal to disclose certain information in litigation. See American Bar Association, Obtaining Discovery Abroad (1990). In such a situation, a person from whom discovery is sought is caught between a rock and a hard place. Sometimes the person can ease the tension by negotiating with authorities in the blocking country to permit disclosure. If disclosure is still precluded, the person generally has no choice but to refuse disclosure. That act disadvantages an American litigant, since the refusal to provide discovery might be sanctionable. See pp. 1043-47, *supra*. Given that both the party seeking disclosure and the party holding the information are innocents, how should a court resolve the problem? In Societe Internationale Pour Participations Industrielles et Commerciales v. Rogers, 357 U.S. 197 (1958), the owner of assets seized by the United States under the Trading with the Enemy Act sought their return. The United States asked the owner to produce certain bank records maintained in a Swiss bank in an attempt to establish that the assets had in fact been owned by an "enemy." After extensive efforts to do so, the owner was able to obtain a waiver of Swiss bank secrecy laws with regard to many documents, but not all. As a result of the owner's inability to comply fully with the production request, the district court dismissed the case.

The Supreme Court reversed, holding that the owner's good faith precluded the entry of the ultimate sanction of dismissal. The Court did, however, recognize that the court had a range of other sanctions available, including the court's ability to "draw[ ] inferences unfavorable to petitioner as to particular events." 357 U.S. at 213. See also *Restatement (Third)*, *supra*, § 442(2) (essentially codifying *Rogers* result); *Aerospatiale*, 482 U.S. at 544 n.29 (stating that French blocking laws in case did not require first resort to Hague Convention procedures); Richmark Corp. v. Timber Falling Consultants, 959 F.2d 1468 (9th Cir.), cert. dismissed, 506 U.S. 948 (1992) (upholding contempt sanction of $10,000 per day and award of attorneys' fees for failure to comply with discovery orders in proceeding to execute default judgment against corporation owned by Chinese government, despite fact that information sought was regarded as classified by government).

During the preceding discussion you might have wondered about whether parties in foreign litigation are entitled to use American discovery procedures. That subject lies generally beyond the scope of this work, although you might be interested to know that a number of courts have refused to permit a foreign litigant to take advantage of American discovery procedures unless the law of their own country makes the same information discoverable. See, *e.g.*, In re Application of Asta Medica, S.A., 981 F.2d 1

(1st Cir. 1992); contra, In re Application of Aldunate, 3 F.3d 54 (2d Cir.), cert. denied, 510 U.S. 965 (1993); see also In re Letter of Request from Amtsgericht Ingolstadt, Federal Republic of Germany, 82 F.3d 590 (4th Cir. 1996) (American court should not second-guess foreign court's determination that information is not discoverable under laws of foreign country). Doesn't such a requirement advantage Americans, who, after *Aerospatiale*, get the advantage of American procedure for some information in foreign countries even when the foreign country's procedures would not permit disclosure but who do not have to disclose American-based information in foreign litigation when the foreign country would not permit it?

More generally, do you find that the attitude in *Aerospatiale* and *Rogers* smacks of Yankee superiority? Suppose that a foreign jurisdiction did not have an attorney-client or work product privilege, and ordered your client to disclose information protected by these privileges. Isn't that exactly how French or German people must feel as they see the juggernaut of American discovery invading their personal privileged zones? Should we be less provincial about our procedural system, and more willing to search for some middle ground? Are complex and complicated litigation, whose emphasis on judicial activism has already moved American procedure toward a civil law model, the place to begin that search?

Whatever the ultimate answers to these questions, discovery from foreign persons or in foreign countries is undeniably a difficult and tricky area. We have sought here to provide only a brief overview of some basic points. Hopefully this overview has shown a number of intersections between international discovery and the main theme of this book: the future course of American procedure.

c. Alternative Means of Obtaining Information from Governmental and Private Sources

Like everyone, lawyers usually return to that with which they are familiar. When it comes to discovering relevant information, that means turning to the tried-and-true methods of interrogatories, requests for inspection, and depositions. But these are specialized devices for obtaining information. When a private person wants to get information, she does not enjoy recourse to these devices. But she usually does get the information she wants — through phone calls, tips, books, news and print media, Internet searches, and so on. Successful litigators never forget that there are many ways to find out information, and the inability to find it in one way (for instance, through discovery) is not the end of the matter but rather a challenge to be more creative in the search process.

This is all fairly obvious; the hard parts are figuring out what methods should be used to get the information, and then having the tenacity to get it. As a general matter, however, efforts to find out information through devices other than the traditional discovery methods travel under the names of "pretrial investigation" or "informal discovery." See Thomas H. Hart, III,

Case Preparation in Federal Court: Informal Discovery, Case & Comment 22 (July-August 1987). Such efforts are critically important to the successful prosecution or defense of most complex (and also most non-complex) cases.

At the risk of overlooking other important sources of information, let us mention three that should always be considered. The first is your client. You might think it impossible that a lawyer would overlook a client as a source of information, but it happens all the time. Some studies suggest that lawyers and clients have little contact with each other during the course of a lawsuit. See Deborah R. Hensler, *Resolving Mass Toxic Torts: Myths and Realities*, 1989 U. Ill. L. Rev. 89. Moreover, law firms are often large institutions that fit into a certain hierarchical relationship with their large institutional clients. Lawyers, whether in the law firm or the corporation's general counsel's office, do not talk frequently with middle management or rank-and-file employees in the company. Yet these people, if they can be found, often possess a wealth of relevant information.

Second, the government must never be overlooked. Government agencies have a great deal of information about matters within their jurisdiction. Under the Freedom of Information Act, 5 U.S.C. § 552, and comparable state statutes, governments must, subject to some exceptions, disclose documents or information upon proper request. Moreover, the government often employs some of the best, most knowledgeable people in particular fields, so government employees are often a gold mine of information. Of course, ethical rules might forbid contact with the employees when the government is an actual or contemplated opposing party, and many agencies have regulations that preclude testimony or the release of information by employees except under certain circumstances. See United States ex rel. Touhy v. Ragen, 340 U.S. 462 (1951); but see In re Bankers Trust Co., 61 F.3d 465 (6th Cir. 1995) (federal regulations cannot prevent disclosure of government information that falls into hands of private litigant), cert. dismissed, 517 U.S. 1025 (1996).

Third, a new age of information technology is upon us. Although lawyers may not entirely understand the capabilities of the Internet, it is the source of a tremendous and ever-growing mountain of information. Lawyers who do not themselves use the Internet must either learn, or at least seek the services of experts who can conduct the searches for them. Likewise, a wealth of information is often found in e-mail files or in other electronic methods of storing and transmitting data. Indeed, there are now experts in the field of "computer forensics" who specialize in the retrieval of lost or deleted information from computer databases.

Until now, we have talked about informal discovery as if it were an entirely private process, controlled by a party's lawyer. In this regard, informal discovery is a supplement to, rather than a substitution for, traditional discovery. An interesting question is whether the parties might agree to the use of such informal methods in lieu of formal discovery. See 28 U.S.C. § 473(a)(5) (encouraging courts to consider "cost-effective discovery . . . through the use of cooperative discovery devices"). In a complex case, in which a great deal was at stake for your client, would you agree to substitute a FOIA request for a more formal subpoena of records from a governmental agency? Would it depend on whether the information was critical to the case, or merely background? See Friedman v. Bache Halsey Stuart Shields, Inc., 738 F.2d 1336 (D.C. Cir. 1984) (information unavailable under FOIA may nonetheless be available through discovery). Would you trust an Internet search to do the work of a Rule 34 request for inspection or a Rule 45 subpoena? If not, are these tools destined to remain adjuncts to the litigator's standard arsenal, rather than tools that can substitute for that arsenal?

Can you think of other adjuncts to traditional discovery? Would your ideas end up treating different sets of litigants (those getting your proposal and those getting traditional discovery) so differently that the outcomes in the two sets of cases might be different? Do your ideas swing strongly away from party control of the discovery process, or are they more in line with standard adversarial notions?

Often it is hard to think of such ideas in the abstract, but once you start to work on actual cases, never lose sight of suggesting alternative means of gathering information. (Indeed, the discovery survey discussed by McGovern and Lind, p. 1153, *supra*, was precisely such an alternative means.) As we have seen throughout this chapter, a court has a strong reserve of Rule 16 and/or inherent powers to manage litigation. Even if a court cannot order the parties to use it, a court has a strong ability to "influence" recalcitrant parties to agree to an alternative proposal. Sometimes at least, the race in complex litigation belongs not to the swift or the rich, but to the creative.

d. Alternative Means of Obtaining Opinions from Experts

Complex litigation almost invariably involves the use of expert testimony. Traditionally the parties have chosen their own experts. After the 1993 amendments to Rule 26, parties are required to provide the identity, opinions, and reports of their expert witnesses "who may be used at trial," and the other parties have the right to depose such experts. F.R.Civ.P. 26(a)(2), (b)(4).

The handling of expert testimony can be one of the most challenging aspects of the pretrial process. Claims are often made that one party's experts are using unreliable data or assumptions, or that their conclusions are not supported by the data. If a party can succeed in preventing an opposing party's expert from testifying, the opponent may lack evidence on one or more critical issues in the case, thus making the case ripe for summary judgment. See, *e.g.*, In re Agent Orange Product Liability Litigation, 611 F. Supp. 1290 (E.D.N.Y. 1985), *aff'd* on other grounds, 818 F.2d 210 (2d Cir. 1987), cert. denied, 484 U.S. 1004 (1988) (discarding opinions of plaintiffs' experts and entering summary judgment against opt-out class members); see generally Daubert v. Merrell Dow Pharmaceuticals, Inc., 509 U.S. 579 (1993) (describing appropriate test for exclusion of expert testimony); General Electric Co. v. Joiner, — U.S. —, 118 S.Ct. 512 (1997) (clarifying and applying *Daubert*).

The many strategic aspects of the pretrial "battle of the experts" are a course of study in their own right. In this section, however, we focus on a few ways in which creative uses of experts in complex litigation have shifted the battleground.

The appointment of an expert under Federal Rule of Evidence 706 provides the courts with an alternative to the parties' use of their own experts. Because the main use of such experts is to present testimony at trial, we examine in depth this power of appointment, and some of its problems, in Chapter Eleven. See p. 1347, *infra*. Here we mention, in a much briefer fashion, the potential of such appointments to streamline the pretrial process

In theory, the parties could all stipulate to abide by the court-appointed expert's conclusions, thus reducing a major source of dispute in the case and significantly narrowing the discoverable issues. It is unlikely, however, the parties will surrender control over some of the most critical evidence that can be presented on their clients' behalf. If the parties do not assent, does the court nonetheless possess the power — inherently or under Federal Rule of Civil Procedure 16(c) — to appoint an expert that supplants the parties' experts? Should the judge at least possess the power in cases in which the problems of coping with expert testimony create lawyer dysfunction? How many such cases are there?

Assuming that the judge does not possess the power to replace the parties' experts with the court's own, for what reason might a judge nonetheless wish to appoint an expert to provide pretrial testimony? First, as we shall see in more detail in Chapter Ten, the verdict or judgment frequently falls in line with the testimony of the court-appointed expert. Therefore, a court could use the threat of an appointment as leverage to force the parties to settle the case.

Furthermore, a court appointment of an expert might streamline the trial. A leading example is the appointment of experts in the multidistricted *Silicon Gel Breast Implant Litigation*. In this litigation the plaintiffs alleged, among other things, that leaking implants damaged the immune system and caused other long-term health effects. The defendants bitterly disputed the allegations, attacking the plaintiffs' expert testimony both as inconsistent with basic principles of scientific methodology and as inadmissible under *Daubert*. The MDL transferee judge, Judge Pointer, appointed a panel of experts under Rule 706 to help determine which, if any, of the plaintiffs' theories were viable. See Order No. 31, In re Silicone Gel Breast Implant Litigation, No. 92-CV-10000-S (N.D. Ala., May 31, 1996). Judge Pointer contemplated that members of the expert panel would be subject to deposition and their testimony thus made available for trial in individual cases.

Additionally, a court-appointed expert can also help streamline pretrial issues. In another breast implant case, Judge Robert Jones appointed a panel of expert advisors (as opposed to experts) and used their advice to help him make rulings at a *Daubert* hearing on the admissibility of the opinions of plaintiffs' experts. Hall v. Baxter Healthcare Corp., 947 F. Supp. 1387 (D. Or. 1996). After receiving their advice, Jones held that many of the plaintiffs' expert opinions were inadmissible, and consequently found that many of the plaintiffs' legal theories were subject to dismissal. He nonetheless held the dismissal of claims in abeyance until the MDL's panel of experts had finished its work. Of course, the use of a court-appointed expert or panel of experts is limited to resolving legitimate factual disputes between the parties; a court-appointed expert cannot turn a genuine issue of material fact into an issue susceptible to summary judgment.

Therefore, from the judicial perspective, a court-appointed expert may lead to certain reductions in pretrial or trial complexity. Given the outcome-determinative potential of such experts, however, the judge needs to ensure that such experts are highly qualified. Suppose that the best expert is unwilling to testify. Can a judge force a recalcitrant expert to testify? In its antitrust case against IBM, the government sought to obtain the testimony of two experts with knowledge of the computer industry. The experts refused to testify voluntarily. Their testimony, however, related to their existing expertise, and did not require new testing or the development of new opinions. On a mandamus petition, Judge Friendly upheld the court's order requiring the testimony:

> Since there is . . . no federal rule giving expert witnesses any privilege that can be formulated as a principle of law, petitioners are really asking us to utilize mandamus to set standards that should guide a trial judge in exercising his power to grant dispensation to an expert witness from the general principle of testimonial compulsion and then to hold that the district court violated such standards here. . . . [T]he utmost we could do would be to list a variety of factors appropriate for consideration by a trial judge in determining whether the exercise of compulsion upon an expert would constitute such a misuse of the court's processes that, despite the lack of any general privilege, the expert should nevertheless be excused from testifying in the particular case. Appropriate factors for consideration some pointing against a dispensation and some for one would be the degree to which the expert is being called because of his knowledge of facts relevant to the case rather than in order to give opinion testimony; the difference between testifying to a previously formed or expressed opinion and forming a new one; the possibility that, for other reasons, the witness is a unique expert; the extent to which the calling party is able to show the unlikelihood that any comparable witness will willingly testify; the degree to which the witness is able to show that he has been oppressed by having continually to testify; and, undoubtedly, many others. But, as this discussion shows, the end result is that dispensation would represent an exercise of discretion by the trial judge, and mandamus could not issue unless there had been "clear abuse of discretion," . . . a showing that would not be remotely approached here.

Kaufman v. Edelstein, 539 F.2d 811, 822 (2d Cir. 1976). See also Carter-Wallace, Inc. v. Otte, 474 F.2d 529, 536 (2d Cir. 1972), cert. denied, 412 U.S. 929 (1973) ("[A]lthough it is not the usual practice, a court does have the power to subpoena an expert witness and, though it cannot require him to conduct any examinations or experiments to prepare himself for trial, it can require him to state whatever opinions he may have previously formed."); but see Krumme v. West Point-Pepperell, Inc., 735 F. Supp. 575 (S.D.N.Y. 1990) (noting in dicta that, under *Erie*, experts may not be forced to testify in diversity case when New York state law forbade compelled testimony of experts). It is not clear whether *Krumme* is still good law; in 1991 new language was added to Rule 45 that authorized a party to subpoena and procure testimony from unretained experts, although the party needed to demonstrate "substantial need" and "undue hardship," and further needed to agree to compensate the witness. F.R.Civ.P. 45(c)(3)(B)(ii). The advisory committee notes state that the factors listed in *Kaufman* should guide the court's decision to quash or modify the subpoena.

Rule 45(c)(3)(B)(ii) still contemplates that a party, not the court, will subpoena the unwilling expert. Should a court be able to force an unwilling expert to accept a court appointment? Or does a discretionary, compulsory, *and* court-controlled system of expert testimony sound too inquisitorial? Which (if any) troubles you the most — the discretion, the compulsion, or the court control? (Note that *Kaufman* itself involved only two of the elements; court control was lacking.) Would such a system be even more problematic if the court also forbade the use of party-selected experts?

We return to some of these issues in greater detail in Chapter Ten, when we explore problems of trial complexity. For now, let us revert to the question with which we opened this section: In how many cases is it necessary to appoint experts to reduce problems of *pretrial* complexity?

C. INFORMATION TECHNOLOGY: THE SOLUTION TO PRETRIAL COMPLEXITY?

Throughout the materials on pretrial complexity we have talked about the problems of lawyers gathering and comprehending information. We have also looked at a variety of solutions that would either reduce the number of issues that a court must consider and streamline the discovery process for the issues that remain. If the problem of pretrial complexity is a problem of harnessing information for effective use, you might wonder whether advances in information technology might make the problem of pretrial complexity disappear. In the materials in this section, we give you a brief overview of what is technologically possible today, as well as some of the legal issues surrounding the use of information technology.

1. A Primer on Automated Litigation Support

Using computers and other information technology to assist in the gathering, storage, retrieval, and analysis of discovery material is referred to by various names, such as "litigation support," "automated litigation support," "information management," and "computerized management." Among the first decisions lawyers must make in a case are to develop an "information management plan" and to select the technology best suited to that plan. This plan is also one of the most important decisions in the case; if it is designed without adequate flexibility, the lawyers may be hamstrung by an information retrieval system that does not give access to relevant documents as the case turns in new directions. If the information retrieval system thus dictates what the lawyers can prove, rather than the lawyers' proof dictating what the system retrieves, then the system has failed.

The first critical decision is how to capture and reproduce relevant documents and other litigation materials. The next decision is how to make those materials readily accessible to the lawyers. The first two readings discuss the reproduction of relevant materials. The next three excerpts discuss the primary technological methods by which litigation materials can be made accessible to lawyers. After a few brief notes, we close with a look at how the court can be brought into the information management picture.

Phyllis V. Deets & Gowan Deets, THE APPLICATION OF EIM/OCR TECHNOLOGY TO LITIGATION CASE MANAGEMENT

29-30, in Advanced Litigation Support & Document Imaging (V. Mital ed. 1995)

Photocopying is of course the most familiar process [of document reproduction].... Costs are dependent on volume and document preparation considerations. Cost advantages diminish as document populations grow. Why? Document control considerations require that each page reflect a unique identifying number (LDC) to maintain the integrity of the documents and facilitate accurate reference and retrieval. With photocopying, this numbering task must be manually performed, and labor is expensive. Also, it is important to maintain the integrity of the documents and their respective location within the filing system, another labor intensive endeavour. The danger of misfiling or otherwise compromising the system's integrity is high.

Then too, customary case management practices dictate that the originals, or first generation copies of other parties' documents, remain secure, protected from destruction or loss, thus necessitating additional working copies, adding cost and increasing demand for extra storage capacity.

The advantages of microfilming are immediately obvious. A roll of microfilm, typically 3 x 3"[,] contains approximately 2500 pages. Space efficiency is coupled with overall cost savings. Microfilm costs only pennies more per page with hardcopy reproduction (copyflo) additional. But, the camera can generate the important unique identifying number — the LDC number discussed above — for each page filmed, thereby combining tasks in a cost effective application. Once filmed, the integrity of the documents can only be compromised if the film is lost or damaged.

With either of the above methods, significant labor cost and time delays can be associated with retrieving needed copies. For example, you must manually search for, retrieve and reproduce all documents responsive to a database query. This task is generally performed by a case clerk but can eat up a lot of your budget. Either method requires each party to have its own set of documents or film or send an individual to the document depository to obtain needed copies.

Instead, visualize "looking" at the documents responsive to your database query on your computer monitor, and immediately printing a laser quality copy of any document of interest. Or responsive documents could be automatically printed in whatever sort order you choose. Most important, for shared database situations, electronic imaging allows for instantaneous communication of document based information and multiple, simultaneous viewing (or printing) of documents.

Attractive concept? Efficient? What is the real cost? One U.S. imaging service estimates the cost of scanning at $.15 to $.20 [per page,] with a penny per page for duplication. This cost is roughly twice to comparable microfilming services. Sequential LDC numbers are applied to each image and a rudimentary index to facilitate later searches for documents is included. But, the critical cost factor here depends on your pre-existing platform, i.e. what hardware/software combinations and capacities does your firm presently utilize. Currently, a single work-station, consisting of a microcomputer, high-resolution monitor, optical disk drive, scanner, printer and related software can cost between 10,000 and 70,000 U.S. dollars depending on the configuration required. . . .

Obviously, then, cost is an important factor in determining the appropriate reproduction methodology. Imaging may look more costly, but it contains real cost savings in terms of labor intensive "retrieval" of the actual documents. To know what is truly costly, and what is actually cost-effective, requires a thorough knowledge of the needs of the case.

James G. Apple et al., MANUAL FOR COOPERATION BETWEEN STATE AND FEDERAL COURTS

21 (1997)

The use of new technologies, such as CD-ROM and laser disk storage and retrieval technology, may reduce costs associated with document depositories as well as enhance access to these materials for interested parties. The breast implant cases, for example, have generated over one million documents. To make document retrieval more manageable, Chief Judge Sam C. Pointer (U.S. N.D. Ala.) placed the defendants' discovery documents (including complaints, tests and studies, research and development, outlines, laboratory notebooks, insurance policies, letters, memos, contracts, patents, and inspection procedures and protocols) on CD-ROM. The 15,000 documents stored on CDs were made available to plaintiffs for a $25 charge — immensely cheaper and more efficient than requiring attorneys to travel to a central depository to inspect and copy documents.

Phyllis V. Deets & Gowan Deets, THE APPLICATION OF EIM/OCR TECHNOLOGY TO LITIGATION CASE MANAGEMENT

30-31, in Advanced Litigation Support & Document Imaging (V. Mital ed. 1995)

The decision of how best to reproduce documents in a particular case is but one aspect of the case management plan, providing as it does a particular way to access relevant documents. Of critical concern, however, is getting information about the document — what does the text of the document say, who wrote it, who received it, who saw it, in what chain of command, who commented on it, etc. The functional ability to retrieve information is what most attracts lawyers to computerized litigation support systems.

Effective retrieval requires the creation of a database which captures pertinent information according to the dictates of the case plan.

James L. Stengel & Andrew M. Calamari, COMPLEX LITIGATION

4-3 to -6 (1994)

Perhaps the most basic litigation management technique is "full-text" search and retrieval, a process that involves creating a database containing the entire text of relevant documents.... Using full-text retrieval software, the attorney can search within the entire collection of transcripts or other documents for particular words, combinations of words, or words within a specified proximity to other words in much the same way that a Lexis or Westlaw search is conducted....

A full-text retrieval system has the advantage of providing the attorney with the actual text of the deposition but, like any other system of document management, it has certain limitations.... The creation of a database requires a means of inputting data into the system. With depositions, this is a relatively simple matter since most court reporters record testimony both on tape and computer diskette.... But documents usually can be input into the system in only one of two ways — by manually typing the verbatim text of the document into the system or by scanning the document through imaging techniques. Manual input is impractical in most situations, and scanning or imaging, while quite effective, is also expensive.

Another limitation of full-text retrieval is that it usually offers no way to organize testimony along subject or topic lines. Some software does provide some capability of this type. Other software even includes artificial intelligence, which can examine the search criteria and find related topics and documents that are worded differently. But without these capabilities, the effectiveness of a full-text retrieval system generally depends upon the attorney's ability to select the proper search terms. . . .

While a full-text retrieval system without more may be enough to satisfy the attorney's needs in some cases, subject matter or topic search capability is usually desirable. . . . Once the database is established, the attorney can retrieve information by inputting subject matter terms into the system. A pure indexing system does not provide the attorney with the full text of the relevant record excerpts but with record references . . . .

Indexing is equally applicable to [depositions and to] documents, which can be indexed by objective criteria, such as author, recipient and date, and by subjective criteria, *i.e.*, according to a more detailed, issue-based outline. As with depositions, the index can include a summary of the key issues in the document. . . . A more specific catalogue of features can be created for highly relevant documents.

Depending upon how extensive an indexing program the attorney decides upon, the mechanics of indexing the documents and depositions can be time-consuming and expensive. The more sophisticated the subject matter outline, the more likely that lawyers will be needed to perform the indexing task.

Phyllis V. Deets & Gowan Deets, THE APPLICATION OF EIM/OCR TECHNOLOGY TO LITIGATION CASE MANAGEMENT

31-32, in Advanced Litigation Support & Document Imaging (V. Mital ed. 1995)

Typically, coding [or indexing] services are performed in-house by paralegal staff, or by an outside service. Because coding is generally the single most expensive line item on a litigation support budget, careful consideration should be given to the selection of what documents deserve this treatment.[5]

In a particular case, or for some portion of the relevant documents population, the advantages of FTR [full-text retrieval] may be compelling. Instead of, or in addition to, a minimal abstract of each document, full text can be captured by utilizing optical character reader (OCR) technology. By digitally "reading" the characters of the text of the documents, OCR conversion automates, and theoretically streamlines, the information capture process to the obvious relief of already time-constrained lawyers. Secondly, OCR technology can be incorporated into the imaging process, allowing the lawyers to combine the information search and document access without additional database training.

---

5. In our experience, we have found that generally only 40-50% of all produced documents merit objective coding and only 40-60% of that population merits subjective or FTR [full-text retrieval] treatment.

OCR is a tremendously exciting technology where major advances may be expected within the next few years. However, at present, this application should be viewed with caution in the filed of computerized litigation support. The caution here has to do with the accuracy of the text actually converted. OCR is best at recognizing computer generated laser quality print and standardized printed text, and requires more highly specialized, expensive equipment to reliably capture handwriting and graphics. The condition of the document itself is significant — is it first generation, wrinkled, old, faded? . . . All additional handling and specialized equipment add considerably to an already expensive proposition.

Cost is of course of paramount consideration and runs, generally[,] $.50 to $1.50 per standardized page, assuming 1,000 character[s] per page, with an accuracy rate of 95%. An accuracy rate of even 95% leaves questions about 1 of every 20 characters or perhaps 5-7 words a page. Accuracy drops dramatically when measuring the ability to capture handwritten comments, or other marginalia. Overseas high volume keying operations in places such as Taiwan, Korea and Jamaica, with verification controls, can be purchased at rates ranging from $1.30 to $2.50 per 1000 characters, but with accuracy rates at 99.5 percent. . . .

OCR is, however, a truly amazing technology to watch. It will undoubtedly revolutionize the methods by which we presently search for, use and control information. It is fascinating to watch the technology as it grapples with its ability to "read" and constructs "dictionaries", "thesauri", and other techniques to combine the talents of artificial and creative intelligence to build reliability and increase confidence.

Notes and Questions

1. As you know, the cost of information technology is constantly falling. A computer system considerably more powerful than the one about which Ms. and Mr. Deets wrote three years ago can now be purchased for considerably less than the $10-70,000 they stated. As technology advances and becomes more cost-efficient, the movement away from manual reproduction or microfilming techniques will undoubtedly continue. For now, however, some hurdles must still be overcome. One is storage of scanned information. For instance, it takes about 50 kilobytes (KB) of space to store the image of each page of a document, or about 20 pages per megabyte (MB). With those kinds of numbers, it is obviously impossible to store information on a hard drive if a significant number of documents exist. Hence, optical disks must be used; a 5.25" disk will hold 10-12,000 pages, and a 12" disk will hold 100-120,000 pages. See Joseph M. Howie, Jr., *Applying Imaging: A Survey of the U.S. Law Office Scene* 35, 37-38, in Advanced Litigation Support and Document Imaging (V. Mital ed. 1995). A second problem is image quality; although better than CD-ROM image quality, laser disk image quality is not as crisp as print media. See Manual for Complex Litigation, Third §§ 34.33-.34 (1995).

A far more significant problem is cost; the upfront cost of 15 cents per page for scanning is considerably more than the upfront cost of hard copy reproduction or microfilming. Storage costs and costs of retrieval might make up for some (or all) of this differential at the back-end, but it is risky to spend a lot of money on scanning when the case may go away on a motion or may head in a direction that makes much of the scanned information irrelevant.

2. The greatest drawback of scanning technology, just as it is of photocopying or microfilming, is that it does not permit the database to be searched for relevant terms or persons. There are three options discussed in the readings for creating a search capability: manual sorting, coding, and full-text retrieval (this being done either with manual keying of documents into the database or through the use of OCR technology). Manual sorting is very time-intensive and (especially given the storage requirements) very costly. Coding is also costly; it becomes more costly as more information is captured from each document. OCR technology is also costly (between 50 cents and $1.50 per page), with an even heftier charge for high levels of accuracy. The total price suggested by Deets & Deets for foreign OCR firms of $1.30 to $2.50 per page is low. Among domestic firms, the quality control needed in order to make OCR 95% accurate costs at least $1.00 per page and to make OCR 99.5% accurate may cost as much as $4.00 per page, thus making the total price for OCR somewhere between $1.50 and $5.50 per page. See Stengel & Calamari, *supra*, at 4-9.

Even when OCR technology is used to create a full-text retrieval system, the database suffers from all the limitations of any full-text retrieval system. The lawyer must use the right terms to search the documents, and misspellings can lead the computer to skip over critical documents. (Think, for instance, about your own experience with LEXIS or Westlaw — do your searches always capture the entire universe of relevant information?) Artificial intelligence may eventually overcome some of these problems, but the technology is still too new to be practical in many applications.

Until these problems are solved, coding remains an attractive option. Although coding does not permit full-text retrieval, it does convey basic information about a document. If you wish to spend more money, coding can even capture some basic subject matter areas, thus permitting a narrower search of documents only in particular subject areas. Moreover, when joined with scanning technology, coding allows documents on relevant subject areas to be accessed with a few strokes of a keyboard. Coding too has its problems; it relies on the talents and judgment of the person doing the coding, and it is inflexible if later developments in the case suggest that the subject areas are too narrow, too broad, or irrelevant.

3. One danger of costly technology is that it may simply replace one form of dysfunction with another: The lawyer's physical inability to retrieve and digest information is replaced by the lawyer's financial inability to afford the technology needed to retrieve and digest information. In either event, however, the outcome is the same: The lawyer cannot perform the task required of him in the adversarial system.

Should a court consider a lawyer's technological wherewithal (or at least his financial wherewithal to afford the technology) in making a decision about which lawyer to appoint as lead counsel? The days when the "best lawyer" meant the most skillful litigator are fading; today the "best lawyer" may well be the person with the best blend of management, technological, and litigating capabilities.

4. Will cost of technology drive a further wedge between the "haves" and the "have-nots" in litigation, and make it even more difficult for the poor to receive a fair hearing? Should the court level the playing field? How?

5. The previous readings discussed the in-house use of technology to help the lawyers harness vast quantities of information. The following case discusses how technology can help the judge manage the case and avoid dysfunction in the courthouse.

ACTIVE PRODUCTS CORP. v. A.H. CHOITZ & CO.

163 F.R.D. 274 (N.D. Ind. 1995)

■ LEE, District Judge.... On July 19, 1995, a 131-page complaint under the Comprehensive Environmental Response, Compensation and Liability Act of 1980, as amended by the Superfund Amendments and Reauthorization Act of 1986, was filed by twenty-three (23) named plaintiffs on behalf of themselves and some sixty-six (66) other parties who had assigned their rights to the named plaintiffs. Named as defendants are 1,181 individual and corporate entities. The caption of the cause alone spans some twenty-one and one-half (21½) pages, single spaced. Even among "Superfund" cases, this action is very substantial, ... particularly when one considers that as the action is presently pending, it accounts only for the primary defendants and does not take into account the possibility of third- and fourth-party complaints against other potentially responsible parties.

The logistics involved in managing this litigation, which involves such a large array of parties, leads this Court to conclude that a detailed Case Management Order needs to be entered. The need for such an Order, apart from the salutary purpose of managing what promises to be time-consuming litigation, arises from the fact that while this case is pending, this Court must still maintain its regular docket and provide all other litigants in this Court with prompt and efficient consideration....

It would be impossible for this Court to manage a case of this magnitude utilizing traditional methods and preserve any kind of currency for the rest of its docket while also providing the litigants in this case a prompt and cost-effective administration. Accordingly, this Court will employ ... an electronic filing, docketing, and service system to assist in the administration of this case....

This case will utilize a system of electronic filing and service known as Complex Litigation Automated Docket (CLAD). CLAD is a system that provides for the electronic filing and retrieval of full-text pleadings and related documents. CLAD has been used in several complex cases to significantly reduce the time typically required by the Court and lawyers to store and distribute filings by essentially creating a paperless docket and file.

CLAD is being used successfully in a complex DES product liability case currently being litigated in the Northern District of Ohio. In the Ohio case, attorneys pay $18.00 to file each document and $.15 per page for text downloaded into their own computers.... Robin Weaver, lead defense counsel in the case, noted, "It's an unbelievable convenience. Before we got it, sending a simple notice of deposition to 200 people cost $3,000 and tied up my secretary for an entire afternoon. Now it costs $18 and takes a couple of minutes." In addition to the filing cost benefits, advantages of the system include, among others, the following:

- providing instant access to the full text of the case docket;
- reducing or eliminating hardcopy filing and retrieval costs;
- establishing an electronic database of filings for conducting computer-assisted legal research;
- enhancing communications by enabling the Judge to issue orders and decisions electronically;
- providing users with option for automatic fax "notification of filing" service; and
- allowing more focus on legal issues by eliminating the administrative burdens.

Users of CLAD need to have a personal computer, modem, and phone line. When Court-authorized users wish to file a document with the Court, they simply access the CLAD toll-free telephone number and enter their CLAD filing ID and password. A series of on-screen prompts leads the user through the filing process. Filings are available immediately to all authorized users. Because filing pleadings, briefs, and other documents requires masses of paper, reducing paper ultimately means more efficient management of the court's docket and the attorneys' case. An electronic system means that authorized users can file documents easily and sort through a large volume of materials to locate specific information, enabling lawyers to spend more time "lawyering" and less time managing paper.

To simplify the filing process, the computer leads the way by asking a series of questions or giving prompts. Basically, the user enters an ID number and a name for the document to be filed. The user then sends the document from the user's personal computer in a pre-determined format, such as WordPerfect or ASCII. After confirmation, the filing is instantly available.

Users will be provided with free training and toll-free customer service. CLAD can be accessed at anytime and from any location. As noted earlier, all the users need is a personal computer, modem, phone line, and CLADTRAN software, which is provided to users free of charge. Users incur costs for filing documents ($4 to $25 per document), downloading documents ($.15 to $.55 per page), and the optional fax notification service ($.50 per page; notices generally one page in length). Additional costs can be incurred for counsel using the Private Database to conduct LEXIS-type searches ($12 per search) and downloading such documents ($2 per document to download/print).

Utilizing CLAD in this litigation is in keeping with the spirit of Rule 1 of the Federal Rules of Civil Procedure, which emphasizes the importance of the "just, speedy, and inexpensive determination of every action." Fed.R.Civ.P. 1. CLAD will be a great boon to all attorneys involved in this case. Further, CLAD will enable the court to operate most efficiently and will relieve the Clerk's small staff (whose resources are already stretched to the limit) from thousands of hours of work. In fact, if CLAD is not used in the present action, it is clear that additional personnel will need to be hired simply to handle all of the filings that are necessary in a case of this magnitude.

In spite of all of the obvious advantages to everyone using CLAD, this Court is aware that concerns have been expressed with regard to its use of CLAD. These concerns have primarily arisen with respect to Rule 79 of the Federal Rules of Civil Procedure which provides that the Clerk of the Court keep a "civil docket." It has been suggested that if the docket is kept automatically by the CLAD system, rather than manually by the Clerk's office, the Clerk may be subject to some form of liability if, for example, a document is not filed or is filed incorrectly.

Additionally, concerns have been expressed regarding 28 U.S.C. § 1914, which prescribes the fees which the Clerk may collect. The specific concern is that, even though the Clerk does not actually collect the fees that are paid for the use of CLAD (LEXIS/NEXIS charges and collects all relevant fees), the implication might arise that the Clerk is exceeding his statutory authority.

This court considers the above concerns to be, at most, *de minimis*. Rule 79 does not prohibit use of an electronic filing system, and Rule 5(e) specifically envisions such a system of filing. . . .

Likewise, the matter of collecting fees appears to be a non-issue. . . . The CLAD system will actually facilitate the functioning of the Clerk's office and the ability of the parties and counsel to secure information. Furthermore, the Clerk is not collecting any fees in relation to CLAD, as LEXIS/NEXIS collects such fees.

Nevertheless, in an effort to address the concerns discussed above, this court will solicit the consent of all parties to this case to the use of CLAD as the formal, official docket, and a waiver of any claims against the Clerk of the Court (or his staff) that may arise out of the use of CLAD. The failure of any party to object to the use of CLAD before the April 18, 1996 pretrial conference will be found to be both a consent to its use and a waiver of any and all claims against the Clerk of the Court.

Notes and Questions

1. The use of an electronic filing system eases the task of the court and the lawyers. Since it also makes the filing, service, and retrieval of documents less costly in cases with significant numbers of parties, it seems to be a "win-win" technology. Of course, the numbers of parties must justify the expense.

2. The control of papers filed with the court is a huge concern from the court's viewpoint, but a relatively minor concern from the viewpoint of parties who must grapple with thousands of documents obtained during discovery. After a party has chosen a particular means of controlling these documents, should it share its efforts with the court? There are both benefits and drawbacks of

allowing the court free access to the documents themselves. A benefit is that the court can become educated about the case and, if a full-text retrieval system is used, can pull up relevant documents at hearings or conferences. A drawback is that the lawyer loses control over the selection and presentation of evidence to the court; the court can perform its own searches for information responsive to motions or other matters, thus making it easier for a judge to move into an inquisitorial mode. As a lawyer, how do you respond when the judge asks for access to the optical disks on which your case documents are stored? As a judge, would you ask for access?

2. Legal Issues Involving Automated Litigation Support

The critical legal issue in computerized litigation support is whether other parties can gain access to the data. In a sense, this question divides into two parts: access to data that existed in computerized form prior to the litigation, and data or databases that were created especially for the litigation itself. The following two cases explore the circumstances under which each type of data may be protected from discovery, as well as the legal effect of sharing otherwise protected data with parties that have common litigation interests.

SANTIAGO v. MILES

121 F.R.D. 636 (W.D.N.Y. 1988)

■ FISHER, United States Magistrate. This is a class action pursuant to 42 U.S.C. § 1981 and § 1983 on behalf of black and hispanic prisoners at the Elmira Correctional Facility. Plaintiffs allege intentional discrimination in the assignment of housing, in the assignment of programs, and in the administration of discipline by defendants who are employees of the New York State Department of Correctional Services at Elmira Correctional Facility....

Left for decision is the motion to compel discovery of computer generated material. Samples of the printouts have been submitted *in camera*, and they fall within two categories. The first set of documents was directed to be prepared in early 1987, after this lawsuit began, by Assistant Attorney General Richard Barrantes, then an assistant counsel with the Department of Correctional Services. In response to the filing of the lawsuit, Barrantes met with Elmira Correctional Facility officials and then developed a computer program with another unspecified DOCS employee which generated these documents.

Barrantes describes this process as follows: "The purpose of these meetings was to discuss the present 42 U.S.C. § 1983 civil rights action, relevant case law and the data, to wit: statistical analysis[ ] deponent considered necessary in preparation of a defense to this action." The unnamed DOCS employee "transmitted" printouts in this first category directly to Barrantes. Included in these documents are a "statistical analysis" of the disparity in job assignments by ethnicity and "raw data pertaining to the ethnic distribution of inmates in preferred assignments."

For awhile, these same printouts were also sent to officials at Elmira because the "raw data facilitated the preparation of . . . ethnic distribution reports . . . by Richard Cerio at Elmira Correctional Facility." Since September of 1985, these ethnic breakdown lists had been prepared at the facility. The computer material sent to Elmira was later "modified to exclude, among other things, the statistical analysis and the programs not regarded as preferred." Barrantes admits that the computer documents in this second category were used by Cerio for business purposes, but contends that, because "[a]ll of the information contained in Exhibit B [the second category] . . . is derived from the information contained in Exhibit A [the first category] . . ., both of these documents should be considered as work product and deemed privileged."

Defendants have consented to discovery of Cerio's monthly/weekly ethnic breakdown lists, but they resist discovery of the computer generated documents. The latter differ in that both sets of computer generated material contain a "cross-tabulation . . . showing the statistical significance of any disparity in the distribution of job assignments by ethnicity."

Analysis of defendants' attorney work-product objection to discovery of these documents begins with an examination of Fed.R.Civ.P. 26(b)(3) . . . .

There can be little doubt that the printouts produced from a computer program developed by counsel and another government employee in response to the filing of this lawsuit are "documents and tangible things . . . prepared in anticipation of litigation or for trial" within the meaning of Rule 26(b)(3). The documents in the first category are therefore subject to the qualified immunity provided for in the rule, and plaintiffs do not seriously dispute this proposition. The issue in this case is whether defendants may avoid discovery, even in the face of plaintiffs' asserted showing of substantial need, because an examination of the printouts would involve "disclosure of the mental impressions, conclusions, opinions, or legal theories of an attorney or other representative of a party concerning the litigation." Fed.R.Civ.P. 26(b)(3).

The computer printouts, produced from a program developed by counsel for this very litigation, contain raw data not protected by the attorney work product doctrine. However, the printouts themselves reflect, because of counsel's participation in developing the computer program, an attorney's "selection process [which] itself represents defense counsel's mental impressions and legal opinions as to how the evidence in the documents relates to the issues and defenses in the litigation." Sporck v. Peil, 759 F.2d 312, 315 (3rd Cir. 1985), cert. denied, 474 U.S. 903 (1985). As stated in *Sporck*, "We believe that the selection and compilation of documents by counsel in this case in preparation for pretrial discovery falls within the highly-protected category of opinion work product." Id., 759 F.2d at 316. Accord, Shelton v. American Motors Corporation, 805 F.2d 1323, 1329 (8th Cir. 1986); James Julian, Inc. v. Raytheon Company, 93 F.R.D. 138, 144 (D.

Del. 1982); Berkey Photo, Inc. v. Eastman Kodak Company, 74 F.R.D. 613, 616 (S.D.N.Y. 1977).

The Second Circuit has recognized the selection and compilation doctrine as a "narrow exception" to the general rule that documents received by lawyers from their clients, "which would not be protected if they remained in the clients' hands, would not acquire protection merely because they were transferred" to the lawyer. Gould Inc. v. Mitsui Mining & Smelting Co., Ltd., 825 F.2d 676, 679-80 (2d Cir. 1987). However, the circuit court held that application of this narrow exception "depends upon the existence of a real, rather than speculative, concern that the thought processes of . . . counsel in relation to pending or anticipated litigation would be exposed." Id., at 680. In addition, the court stated that application of the *Sporck* exception may depend on the equities of the case, which includes consideration whether "the files from which documents have been culled by . . . [counsel] were not otherwise available to . . . [the party] or were beyond the reasonable access to [the party]." Id., 825 F.2d at 680.

The discussion of the equities of the case might, at first glance, suggest a retreat from the nearly "absolute" protection afforded mental impression work product under Fed.R.Civ.P. 26(b)(3). . . . The Supreme Court has made "clear" that mental impression "work product cannot be disclosed simply on a showing of substantial need and inability to obtain the equivalent without undue hardship." Upjohn Company v. United States, 449 U.S. 383, 401 (1981) (reversing a Magistrate's discovery order upon such a showing). The Court refused, however, to decide whether mental impression "material is always protected by the work-product rule," and instead simply stated that "a far stronger showing of necessity and unavailability by other means" is made applicable to mental impression work product than is made applicable to other work product by Fed.R.Civ.P. 26(b)(3). Upjohn Company v. United States, 449 U.S. at 401-02. . . .

Accordingly, this court considers the Second Circuit's statement in the *Gould* case, suggesting that the equities of whether the material is "not otherwise available" or is "beyond the reasonable access" of a party, as but an application of *Upjohn* . . . .Access to mental impressions, if ever to be permitted, may occur "only on a strong showing 'of necessity and unavailability by other means.'" . . .

If the computer program was modified to generate a discrete set of documents for Cerio (see below), it may clearly be modified to generate a printout containing the raw data plaintiffs need, i.e., a printout showing all of the work locations at Elmira and the ethnicity of inmates in those locations. A request for raw information in computer banks is proper and the information is obtainable under the discovery rules. Daewoo Electronics Company, Ltd. v. United States, 650 F. Supp. 1003, 1006 (C.I.T. 1986); Bills v. Kennecott Corporation, 108 F.R.D. 459, 461-62 (D. Utah 1985); National Union Electric Corporation v. Matsushita Electric Industrial Co., Ltd., 494 F. Supp. 1257, 1260-62 (E.D. Pa. 1980).

Therefore, with respect to the first category of computer printouts, it is appropriate to apply the *Sporck* doctrine to this case. There can be little question on this record, which establishes that then assistant counsel

Barrantes participated in the design of the computer program generating this material in connection specifically with preparing a defense to this lawsuit, that disclosure of the first set of documents would violate the *Hickman v. Taylor* doctrine and Fed.R.Civ.P. 26(b)(3). . . . As to these documents the motion to compel is denied, and the cross-motion for a protective order is granted.

The second category of computer generated materials presents a more difficult problem. As a preliminary matter, the fact that documents in the first category were, for a brief time, forwarded to Richard Cerio at the facility for assistance in preparing the monthly/weekly breakdown reports does not deprive them of their character under the rule as attorney work product. Simply delivering attorney work product revealing counsel's mental processes to a governmental client's subordinate employees is a fortuitous circumstance in the work product analysis unless such delivery "has substantially increased the opportunities for potential adversaries to obtain the information." 8 Wright & Miller, Federal Practice and Procedure § 2024 p. 210 (1970). . . . As stated in In re Doe, 662 F.2d 1073 (4th Cir. 1981), cert. denied, 455 U.S. 1000 (1982), "the forfeiture or waiver must be consistent with a conscious disregard of the advantage that is otherwise protected by the work product rule." Id., 662 F.2d at 1073.

> Disclosure to a person with an interest common to that of the attorney or the client normally is not inconsistent with an intent to invoke the work product doctrine's protection and would not amount to such a waiver. However, when an attorney freely and voluntarily discloses the contents of otherwise protected work product to someone with interests adverse to his or those of the client, knowingly increasing the possibility that an opponent will obtain and use the material, he may be deemed to have waived work product protection.

Id., 662 F.2d at 1081. . . .

Because the disclosure here was to a DOCS employee and there is no reason to believe that delivery of the work product to Cerio was "deliberately employed to prepare — and thus, very possibly, to influence and shape — testimony, with the anticipation that these efforts should remain forever unknowable and undiscoverable[,]" Berkey Photo, Inc. v. Eastman Kodak Company, 74 F.R.D. at 616, or to "interlac[e]" discoverable fact "with core work product[,]" Bogosian v. Gulf Oil Corporation, 738 F.2d 587, 595 (3rd Cir. 1984), there is no waiver of the work product immunity for those few documents in the first category which were delivered to Cerio. Disclosure to Cerio was made for the sole purpose of "facilitating" his preparation of the monthly/weekly ethnic breakdown reports which defendants have now turned over to plaintiffs while steadfastly maintaining the confidentiality of the computer material itself. United States v. Gulf Oil Corporation, 760 F.2d 292, 295-96 (Em.App. 1985).

After an initial period when the printouts sent to Barrantes were forwarded to Cerio at Elmira, the central office modified the format sent to Cerio. This second category of documents was not sent to Barrantes; indeed Barrantes has only second hand information concerning how the program was modified. Barrantes does not specify who made the modification or for what purpose, but he admits that the second category of printouts are "presently transmitted to the Elmira Correctional Facility."

That the computer printouts in the second category were prepared for Cerio's use in the preparation of his monthly/weekly ethnic breakdown reports concerning preferred job assignments is a critical fact, because the monthly/weekly breakdown reports were not prepared in anticipation of litigation. As Barrantes stated in his original affidavit, they "were being prepared on a monthly basis since September, 1985," well before initiation of the lawsuit. And as defendant Donald McLaughlin testified at a deposition, these reports were conceived as part of a program developed at Elmira which responded to inmate administrative grievances concerning program assignments....

Cerio "looked at" the monthly/weekly reports as they came in, "and balance[d] . . . [them] against our ethnicity percentages." Cerio then referred the data, or his interpretation of it, to "the program committee" headed by defendant McLaughlin with appropriate recommendations concerning any disparity. According to Barrantes, the process of examination intensified when the lawsuit was filed (e.g., by preparation of weekly reports), but this basic scenario had been in place several months before the lawsuit commenced or even was envisioned by defendants.

The generally accepted test of whether a document falls within the work product doctrine was set forth in *United States v. Gulf Oil Corporation*, 760 F.2d at 296:

> Our inquiry should be to determine the "primary motivating purpose behind the creation of the document." . . . If the primary motivating purpose behind the creation of the document is not to assist in pending or impending litigation, then a finding that the document enjoys work product immunity is not mandated. . . .

The court finds that Cerio's original preparation of the monthly/weekly reports was in the ordinary course of the business of the Elmira Correctional Facility to facilitate inmate relationships with DOCS officials by prompt response to administrative inmate complaints.

Defendants[ ] have offered no reason to suppose that Cerio's preparation of the weekly/monthly reports is now any less related to the admitted business purpose for their creation simply because of the institution of this lawsuit. In this case, the computer printouts in the second category which assisted Cerio in this endeavor are, upon the court's *in camera* examination, . . . wholly different in form and somewhat different in content from the printouts in the first category sent to Barrantes. While there is ample reason to assume that the second category printouts used by Cerio are now prepared with the pending litigation in mind, the primary motivation for their creation concerns the on-going effort in the normal course of business at Elmira, begun well prior to litigation and not in contemplation of it, to appropriately respond to inmate grievances presented through the Inmate Liaison Committee. The nature of these second category printouts thus preclude any work product doctrine protection. . . .

The motion to compel discovery of the computer material sent to assistant counsel Barrantes is denied, and a protective order is hereby granted as to it. The motion to compel discovery of the computer material of the second category sent to Richard Cerio is granted as indicated herein.

UNITED STATES v. AMERICAN TELEPHONE AND TELEGRAPH CO.

642 F.2d 1285 (D.C. Cir. 1980)

■ WILKEY, Circuit Judge. Appellants MCI Communications Corp. and MCI Telecommunications Corp. (hereinafter collectively "MCI") seek reversal of an interlocutory discovery order of the district court, issued in the course of a civil antitrust suit brought by the United States against the American Telephone and Telegraph Company (AT&T). The district court's order would require the United States to accede to AT&T's discovery request for certain documents which the Government earlier received from MCI, and in which MCI claims a work product privilege. We have stayed the district court's discovery order pending our decision on this appeal.

Shortly before the district court handed down its discovery order, MCI moved to intervene for the purpose of asserting its claim of work product privilege in the documents requested by AT&T. The district court denied this motion. MCI now appeals both the district court's denial of its intervention motion and the district court's interlocutory discovery order, and in the alternative seeks a writ of mandamus to prevent the transfer of the documents from the Government to AT&T. We hold that MCI should have been allowed intervention as of right, that the denial of intervention is appealable, and that MCI has not waived any work product privilege that it might have in the requested documents. . . .

The controversy in this appeal arises from two antitrust suits with closely related issues, filed against AT&T in two different federal district courts. The first suit was filed against AT&T by MCI in the United States District Court for the Northern District of Illinois on 6 March 1974. MCI charged AT&T with monopolizing and attempting to monopolize the market for long-distance telephone communications. The second suit, which directly concerns us in this appeal, was filed as a civil antitrust action by the United States against AT&T on 20 November 1974 in the United States District Court for the District of Columbia. In claims overlapping those made by MCI, the Government charged AT&T with monopolizing, attempting to monopolize, and conspiring to monopolize markets for telecommunications services and equipment.

Discovery in the District of Columbia suit has extended over a several year period, interrupted at times pending appeals on various issues. The first stage of the controversy that resulted in the present litigation occurred in 1978, when a magistrate supervising the discovery process required AT&T to produce for the Government all materials previously given by AT&T to private plaintiffs in the discovery stage of several private antitrust actions. [That decision was ultimately affirmed by the court of appeals. See pp. 1110-11, *supra*.]

At the same time, the United States pursued a second approach to benefit from MCI's earlier discovery efforts against AT&T. Upon a motion by the United States in the Northern District of Illinois, the judge presiding there over MCI's antitrust suit against AT&T granted a modification of an existing protective order to allow MCI to make available to the United States all discovery materials it had acquired from AT&T in the case, including documents, deposition transcripts, and exhibits referred to in depositions. In addition, this order permitted MCI to furnish to the Department of Justice "any explanatory material or information which would be helpful to an understanding of the items produced." To preserve the confidentiality of any material provided by MCI pursuant to the order, the order prohibited the Government from using such materials for any purpose other than its case against AT&T in the District Court for the District of Columbia. It is this latter, explanatory material, which is in issue in the case at bar.

Following the Seventh Circuit's affirmance of this modification of the protective order, MCI furnished the Government the documents, depositions, and exhibits that MCI had discovered from AT&T. MCI also furnished certain documents pertaining to a "database" consisting of computerized abstracts of documents, deposition transcripts, and exhibits received from AT&T during discovery. MCI's counsel had prepared the database for the Northern District of Illinois litigation. The "database documents" furnished by MCI and at issue in the current appeal describe the structure of the database and explain how information can be entered and retrieved. MCI claims to have maintained strictly the secrecy of the database documents from AT&T....

Since AT&T had already given microfilm copies to the Government for documents selected by MCI in discovery, the major additional effect of the modification of the protective order was to permit MCI to produce their depositions and analyses of data for Government counsel's use. Much of this analysis of data and documents was contained in MCI's computerized litigation support system, to which the now disputed database documents pertain. Unlike the documents and data themselves, none of the analytical or descriptive material in the database documents is admissible as evidence. But the database documents enable the United States to gain access to the analysis contained in the computerized support system, and might well enable AT&T to determine which documents a plaintiff's counsel would consider important, why counsel might consider them to be important, and what portions of those documents counsel might think are most important for the issues in this suit.

[The Special Masters and the district court overruled the claim of privilege, and further denied MCI's right to intervene in the suit for purposes of appealing the order. After holding that MCI should have been granted the right to intervene, the court turned to the issue of the database.]

The [district court's] ground of decision turns on whether MCI waived any work product privilege it might otherwise have had when it handed the database documents to the United States. Rule 26(b)(3) of the Federal Rules of Civil Procedure, as amended in 1970, defines the scope of the work product privilege. Documents can come within this privilege if they were "prepared in anticipation of litigation or for trial by or for another party or by or for that other party's representative (including his attorney, consultant, surety, indemnitor, insurer, or agent)." Any claim of work product privilege can be overridden by a "substantial need of the materials" on the part of the requesting party.

MCI claims that the database documents at issue in this case were prepared by or for MCI's attorneys specifically in anticipation of litigation in MCI's antitrust suit against AT&T in the Northern District of Illinois. On such facts the work product privilege would attach to the documents in the Northern District case and they could not be discovered by AT&T in that case without a showing of substantial need. The question for our consideration is whether the work product privilege applies also in the case between AT&T and the United States in the District of Columbia.

A number of district court opinions have considered whether the work product privilege is waived when a party that created documents in anticipation of litigation provides those documents to another party for use in litigation in a related case. Several of the decisions have turned on whether the transferor has "common interests" with the transferee. In applying this standard courts have held the work product privilege not to be waived by disclosures between attorneys for parties "having a mutual interest in litigation," or between parties which were potential co-defendants to an antitrust suit, or between attorneys representing parties "sharing such a common interest in litigation, actual or prospective," or between parties one of whose interests in prospective litigation may turn on the success of the other party in a separate litigation. The earlier opinions in this line of decisions tended to employ a narrow definition of "common interests," restricted to situations in which the relationship of the parties was similar to that between co-parties in a suit.

One such decision found the work product privilege to be waived in circumstances similar to the present case. In D'Ippolito v. Cities Service Co., [39 F.R.D. 610 (S.D.N.Y. 1965),] the plaintiff in a private suit raised the work product privilege to prevent disclosure of an exhibit, but conceded that it had voluntarily disclosed the exhibit to attorneys in the Antitrust Division of the Department of Justice. Observing that the government was not a party to the lawsuit, the court found that "the disclosure of the document cannot be termed as an interchange of information between counsel on the same side of the litigation." Consequently, the court held the privilege to be waived. This narrow concept of "common interests," limiting it to co-parties, parallels the strict standard applied for waiver of the attorney-client privilege, which we will discuss below.

In contrast to *D'Ippolito*, a more recent decision from the same court, the Southern District of New York, held the work product privilege not to be waived by disclosure of trial preparation documents by a private antitrust plaintiff to the government. The court in GAF Corp. v. Eastman Kodak Co., [85 F.R.D. 46 (S.D.N.Y. 1979),] found that despite voluntary disclosure of the documents to persons not on the same side of the litigation, the privilege remained intact.... [T]he court held that disclosure to a third party does not waive the privilege "unless such disclosure, under the circumstances, is inconsistent with the maintenance of secrecy from the disclosing party's adversary." Waiver would occur, the court elaborated, only if the disclosure "substantially increases" the possibility of an opposing party obtaining the information. Since the disclosure had occurred under a statutory guarantee of confidentiality on the part of the government, the court held the conditions for waiver not to be satisfied.

The opinions in *GAF Corp.* and *D'Ippolito*, both arising out of cases very similar to the present one, follow quite different standards. We do not consider the strict standard of waiver in the attorney-client privilege context, as reflected in *D'Ippolito*, to be appropriate for work product cases. The attorney-client privilege exists to protect confidential communications, to assure the client that any statements he makes in seeking legal advice will be kept strictly confidential between him and his attorney; in effect, to protect the attorney-client relationship. Any voluntary disclosure by the holder of such a privilege is inconsistent with the confidential relationship and thus waives the privilege.

By contrast, the work product privilege does not exist to protect a confidential relationship, but rather to promote the adversary system by safeguarding the fruits of an attorney's trial preparations from the discovery attempts of the opponent. The purpose of the work product doctrine is to protect information against opposing parties, rather than against all others outside a particular confidential relationship, in order to encourage effective trial preparation. . . . A disclosure made in the pursuit of such trial preparation, and not inconsistent with maintaining secrecy against opponents, should be allowed without waiver of the privilege. We conclude, then, that while the mere showing of a voluntary disclosure to a third person will generally suffice to show waiver of the attorney-client privilege, it should not suffice in itself for waiver of the work product privilege.

We do not endorse a reading of the *GAF Corp.* standard so broad as to allow confidential disclosure to any person without waiver of the work product privilege. The existence of common interests between transferor and transferee is relevant to deciding whether the disclosure is consistent with the nature of the work product privilege. But "common interests" should not be construed as narrowly limited to co-parties. So long as transferor and transferee anticipate litigation against a common adversary on the same issue or issues, they have strong common interests in sharing the fruit of the trial preparation efforts. Moreover, with common interests on a particular issue against a common adversary, the transferee is not at all likely to disclose the work product material to the adversary. When the transfer to a party with such common interests is conducted under a guarantee of confidentiality, the case against waiver is even stronger.

In the present case, MCI shares common interests with the United States, in the sense that they are proceeding on overlapping antitrust issues against a common adversary, AT&T. The United States and MCI shared common interests in developing legal theories and analyses of documents on which to proceed on those issues where they both made the same antitrust claims against AT&T. Moreover, the Northern District of Illinois court order authorizing the transfer of the database documents also ordered the Government to maintain their confidentiality. This transfer is consistent with the promotion of trial preparation within the adversary system. Further, because of the Government's interests adverse to AT&T on these issues, the transfer poses very little likelihood of AT&T gaining access to the documents through the United States....

We believe our holding on the waiver issue furthers the purpose of the work product privilege by protecting attorneys' preparations for trial and encouraging the fullest preparation without fear of access by adversaries. The work product privilege rests on the belief that such promotion of adversary preparation ultimately furthers the truth-finding process. For MCI to contribute the fruit of its analysis to the Government on those issues common to their two cases will further the Government's preparation for trial and eliminate some duplication of effort. The advantages of such sharing led the judge in MCI's Northern District of Illinois case against AT&T to remark, "we believe the court should not only encourage the sharing of discovery in cases with common fact questions but order it on its own motion even where the parties do not suggest it."

We recognize that the truth-finding process might be further enhanced in the short term in this particular case if AT&T gained access to the documents in question. In the long run, however, this would discourage trial preparation and vigorous advocacy and would discourage any party from turning over work product to the government.

We hold therefore that MCI has not waived its work product privilege by disclosing the database documents to the Government, and that MCI as intervenor can raise its claim of work product privilege to defend against AT&T's discovery request. Accordingly the district court's order granting AT&T access to the database documents must be vacated....

Finally, the work product privilege is a qualified privilege which may be overridden by a showing of substantial need by the requesting party. The district court[ ] ... did not include a consideration of substantial need by AT&T. On appeal AT&T has asserted the district court's discretion concerning the applicability of this qualified privilege, but AT&T has made no showing of substantial need on the record. On remand it is of course open to the district court to consider the substantial need argument if AT&T raises such allegation, and if the district court finds that allegation to be raised in timely fashion.

Notes and Questions

1. The basic rules in *Santiago* and *AT&T* are simple and sensible enough. Behind these rules lie some significant ambiguities. As *Santiago* shows, it is not always easy to determine whether something is prepared in the ordinary course of litigation or for the purposes of litigation. As *AT&T* shows, there is some disagreement about how much commonality of interest two parties must possess before they can deny shared information to other parties.

Perhaps the most significant ambiguities, however, concern the changes in information technology. For instance, the bone of contention in both *Santiago* and *AT&T* was information that had been prepared after litigation started; in *Santiago*, the initial confrontation involved data manipulation done to assist the attorney handling the case, and in *AT&T*, it was the coding of the documents themselves that was the center of contention. It is easy to see why such information should be protected in an adversarial system, but what should the rules be with regard to access to scanned copies of information or full-text database of documents? Like *Santiago* and *AT&T*, such databases are prepared with litigation in mind, but unlike *Santiago* and *AT&T*, they contain no mental impressions of the attorneys. Can a judge order a party to hand over its database because the purpose of the work product rule — the protection of attorneys' mental impressions — is not implicated? Or should the judge enforce the letter of the rule, and deny access because the information was prepared (at least in computerized format) in anticipation of litigation?

Presumably the usual reason that one side would not wish the other side to have such information is economic: The other side may be unable to afford the technology, and the one side is unwilling to even up the sides. Should the court consider this factor in deciding whether or not to order disclosure? Is it the court's job to even up economic disparities among parties? Can the court do so as long as the other side agrees to pay its fair share of the cost?

2. In complex and complicated cases, should the court respect work product claims in which standard adversarial procedures have created unilateral dysfunction (*i.e.*, dysfunction among one side's lawyers), and which can be cured simply by ordering disclosure? Or will such an order discourage litigants from investing in such technology in the first place, thus transforming unilateral dysfunction into multilateral dysfunction that will require even stronger judicial intervention? Should the judge's role be to mediate the dispute and hope for voluntary agreement? Wouldn't it be best if the entire matter were resolved before one party invested significant funds to computerize data? Cf. Manual for Complex Litigation, Third § 21.12 (1995) (suggesting that court take measures at start of case to establish master file for litigation); id. at 393 (suggesting early establishment of ground rules for technology).

3. Work product privileges can be lost not only when technology is shared with other parties; it can also be lost when it is shared with experts or witnesses. In Pearl Brewing Co. v. Jos. Schlitz Brewing Co., 415 F. Supp. 1122, 1134-41 (S.D. Tex. 1976), experts retained by the plaintiff in an antitrust suit developed a computer model. The computer experts themselves were not going to testify, but their model was going to be relied on by the expert economic witness that was going to testify. The plaintiff offered to make available the data that the model developed, but balked at providing the model itself. The defendant contended that, without the model, its expert could understand the data only by spending a great deal of time and money and that this process would further delay discovery. Finding that these facts were "exceptional" enough to override the work product protection accorded to expert testimony and materials, the court held that the reliance of the plaintiff's expert economist on the computer model required its disclosure to the defendant. The court further required that the computer experts themselves be subject to limited depositions that would help interpret the computer program, and that the defendant pay the costs of copying the program and deposing the experts. It did not, however, require that alternative model designs rejected by the computer experts be disclosed.

Likewise, in Sporck v. Peil, 759 F.2d 312 (3d Cir.), cert. denied, 474 U.S. 903 (1985), a defendant's lawyer preparing the defendant for his deposition had shown the defendant certain documents. At the deposition, the plaintiff asked whether the defendant had examined any documents. When the witness answered in the affirmative, the plaintiff asked for copies. The defense objected, arguing that its choice of which documents to show the defendant was a matter of work product. On mandamus, the Third Circuit agreed, but stated that the work product protection for the documents could be overcome if the defendant had relied on and been influenced by the documents.

Pearl Brewing and *Sporck* suggest that litigation support systems might lose their protection if the systems are disclosed to experts or witnesses who rely on the systems for their testimony. It would be a real stretch of the two cases to suggest, however, that a litigation support system is discoverable merely because an expert or witness was shown documents or given information that had been obtained by searching the system. Rather, it would seem that the system itself must have been disclosed to the expert, or the expert must have relied on data that the system processed.

4. Unlike *Pearl Brewing* or *Sporck*, National Union Electric Corp. v. Matsushita Electric Industrial Co., 494 F. Supp. 1257 (E.D. Pa. 1980), suggests that, at least in some circumstances, the disclosure of information obtained through use of a litigation support system might make portions of the system discoverable. *National Union* involved one of the early skirmishes in the highly complex antitrust case that culminated in *Matsushita* (p. 1050, *supra*). The defendants had asked interrogatories concerning sales and other information, and the plaintiff had responded with the information in a computer printout format. The plaintiff generated the printout by using a litigation support system specially prepared for the litigation. The underlying information that had been entered into the litigation support system and reproduced on the printout was factual in nature; no one disputed that it was discoverable. After receiving the printout, however, the defendants requested the same information in a computer-readable format, so that they could save the expense of creating their own database. The defendants even offered to pay all the expenses of creating the tape. The plaintiff objected, stating that the database contained the mental impressions of the lawyers that made decisions about which information to collect, that they could not be forced under the Federal Rules to create a document (the computer tape) not already in existence, and that the defendants could create their own database from the information supplied.

How would you decide the case? Judge Becker ordered the plaintiff to create and supply the tape.

5. Many of the issues raised in the preceding notes were also implicated in Fauteck v. Montgomery Ward & Co., 91 F.R.D. 393 (N.D. Ill. 1980), an employment discrimination class action. Early in the litigation the defendant's lawyers had prepared a computer analysis of the plaintiff class. The plaintiffs sought access to the analysis, and also sought access, in computer-readable form, to some of the underlying data (such as name of employee, social security number, education, performance rating, and salary) in this analysis. The defendant was unwilling to provide either set of information, arguing that each had been prepared in anticipation of litigation. The defendant was, however, willing to provide plaintiffs with the personnel records from which the plaintiffs could construct their own data and analysis.

Despite recognizing "the convenience and economies that will result from granting [plaintiffs'] request," id. at 397, the court refused to give access to the analysis, at least until it had been disclosed to and relied upon by experts. It did, however, require the defendant to turn over the basic data in computer-readable form. Rejecting defendants' assertion that the disclosure of which data to encode would reveal the thought process of attorneys, the court found that "the judgments entailed in database compilation are essentially statistical in nature and that the methodology of computerizing personnel records for litigation purposes is well established in the field." Id. at 399. Believing the cost and delay of forcing the plaintiffs to encode the data was pointless, the court ordered disclosure of the data in computerized form. The court did require the plaintiffs to pay 50% of the defendant's costs of compilation, and also suggested that the plaintiffs had a reciprocal obligation to share information with the defendants.

Does *Fauteck* seem like the right resolution of the problem? Or does it tear too large a hole in the work-product doctrine? Would you be as inclined to computerize relevant information if you knew that the other side could gain access to the factual components of your database merely by handing over a check for half of your costs? Doesn't *Fauteck*'s logic suggest that scanning, OCR, or manual full-text retrieval databases, which are inherently "factual" in nature, are automatically discoverable? On the other hand, is a 50-50 split of costs such a bad rule? Isn't it the rule to which the parties would have likely negotiated before one side spent the money to computerize the relevant information?

6. The saga in *Fauteck* continued for another round when the plaintiffs filed a discovery request for access to the defendant's computerized database, including access to all relevant codes. The defendants did not provide all the relevant code books, and the information on the tape was not usable without the codes. The court was not amused by the defendant's position that plaintiffs needed to ask separately for each code and were not entitled to the code books themselves. It awarded sanctions in the amount of the costs and attorneys' fees the plaintiffs had incurred. See Fautek [sic?] v. Montgomery Ward & Co., 96 F.R.D. 141 (N.D. Ill. 1982).

7. Do the results in *National Union* and *Fauteck* suggest that, to the extent they capture and organize basic factual and historical information, computerized litigation support systems will enjoy little protection from discovery? Do the results also demonstrate that a judge has the ability to override rules (including, but not limited to, the work-product rule) that are designed to protect the adversary system when the judge is faced with problems of lawyer dysfunction and pretrial complexity? Is this the ultimate lesson of our study of pretrial complexity?

PART THREE

TRIAL COMPLEXITY

The following two chapters explore some of the issues that surround the trial of complex cases. Few complex cases, however, come to trial. Many are disposed of by pretrial motion or voluntary dismissal. Most others are settled.

You might, therefore, wonder whether this material on the trial of complex cases is particularly important. It is, for three reasons. First, trial remains the default option when other dispute resolution methods fail. Second, it is nearly impossible to determine early in the case whether the case will settle or go to trial. Despite the inefficiencies involved, every case must be prepared as if it were the one going to trial, not one of the twenty going away before trial. Third, and most important, recall our historical and comparative studies in Chapter One. We learned that the form of trial strongly influences the type of pretrial preparation in which the parties will engage. For instance, if the trial consists of a single event in which all issues will be decided by a jury, the pretrial process will need to produce evidence on all issues, and the evidence and issues will need to be packaged in a form comprehensible to lay persons. On the other hand, if the trial involves a judge as factfinder, the judge would be able to divide the trial up into a series of discrete hearings or segments, thus dictating a different pretrial process. Good judges and lawyers make their joinder and pretrial management decisions with an eye to the form of trial that awaits. Hence, the trial issues that we discuss here are vitally important to the joinder and pretrial issues that arise in all cases.

As always, we begin our examination of these issues by asking exactly what trial complexity is; and, as always, we answer that question by looking at the roles the adversarial system assigns to various players. As with pretrial, the adversarial system expects the lawyers to be the central players: They define the issues in dispute, present the oral and documentary evidence, and make the arguments about how the evidence applies to the law. As with pretrial, the parties themselves do little. Unlike pretrial, however, the adversarial system gives the decision maker important responsibilities during trial: The decision maker needs to rule on the admissibility of evidence, to find the facts, to declare the law, to come to a decision by applying the facts to the law, and, if necessary, to establish a remedy. The functions of the decision maker can be accomplished by one person or it can be divided among various persons or groups.

Cases are "complex" in the trial sense when either the lawyers or the decision maker(s) are incapable of performing adequately their expected roles, when a stronger, non-adversarial application of judicial power will preserve the rational adjudication of the dispute, and when that application results in the disparate treatment of like cases. Among the circumstances that make the lawyers and decision makers(s) unable to perform their tasks are:

(1) The nature of the information that the lawyer must garner and marshal make it impossible for the lawyer to formulate adequate proofs and arguments. For instance, the information may be wide-ranging and extensive, costly to obtain, or, due to time lags, no longer in existence.

(2) Lawyers who represent the same or similar interests may be unable to frame the facts and the issues in a way that clarifies the case for the decision maker.

(3) The factfinder may be incapable of using reasoned judgment to resolve the case. This incapacity can arise from different sources: The factfinder may lack the intellectual ability to understand the evidence, either because it is esoteric, technical, or overwhelmingly voluminous; the factfinder may be unable to understand the law; the factfinder's life experiences may make it impossible for her to make the necessary factual or legal inferences; or the length of trial may put inordinate demands on the factfinder's ability to deliberate.

You might have noticed that the first two types of dysfunction are nearly identical to two of the types of dysfunction we used to define pretrial complexity (see p. 876, *supra*). The difference is that the lawyers' difficulty in organizing and presenting proofs manifests itself at trial, rather than during pretrial. Many cases that are complex in the pretrial sense will be complex in the trial sense. This is not, however, invariably true; strong pretrial measures may make the lawyers' adversarial task at trial manageable, or, conversely, the lawyers' difficulties may surface only after a jury enters the picture.

The third type of dysfunction is new; it involves the decision maker. Our definition of trial complexity encompasses only the decision maker's tasks in finding and applying the facts to the law. As long as persons learned in legal analysis find the law (as judges, with the aid of lawyers, do in our adversarial system), we do not believe that legal issues, however intricate and complicated, create enough "complexity" to threaten reasoned judgment. The declaration of remedies can be complex, but we deal with that issue in

Part Four. Therefore, the only matter that concerns us in trial complexity is the inability to use reasoned judgment to find and apply the facts.

With trial complexity, the use of expansive judicial power to overcome lawyer and factfinder dysfunction raises difficult issues. Most obviously, if the factfinder cannot rationally find the facts, and if the judge is the factfinder, the use of additional judicial power is unlikely to solve the problem. In addition, apparent solutions to trial complexity rub against important constitutional protections. If a judge cannot rationally find the facts but a special master can, we run into the problem that reference to a special master may violate Article III; if a jury cannot rationally find the facts but a judge can, the Seventh Amendment's right to jury trial may preclude the judge from assuming the factfinder role herself; if factfinding can be rationally accomplished only with inquisitorial or non-traditional trial methods, the judge may be prevented from adopting these methods by the due process clause. Hence, the judge may be more constrained in dealing with trial complexity than with other forms of complexity — a problem that squarely raises the question of how our system should respond to lawsuits that cannot be adjudicated rationally.

Chapter Ten begins the exploration of these issues by examining the ability of the judge to replace the factfinder (whether herself or a jury) in order to obtain a factfinder that can rationally resolve the dispute; it also looks at the judge's power to select counsel to overcome lawyer dysfunction. Chapter Eleven then examines non-traditional trial techniques (other than replacement of factfinders or lawyers) that a judge might adopt in order to preserve rational adjudication. As with pretrial complexity, however, the issues of who fills particular roles and what techniques can be used are integrally related; for instance, the use of some trial techniques (a Chapter Eleven issue) might allow us to preserve the right to jury trial (a Chapter Ten issue). Moreover, as we said earlier in this introduction, the availability (or non-availability) of jury trial (a Part Three issue) will have important consequences for parties making joinder decisions (a Part One issue) and pretrial organization decisions (a Part Two issue). Civil procedure truly is a seamless web.

CHAPTER TEN

SELECTING LAWYERS, FACTFINDERS, AND JUDICIAL OFFICERS FOR TRIAL

> I see the effect on the lawyers when the jury is out of the box.
> When the scalpel goes out, the shovel comes in.
>
> Patrick E. Higginbotham

An implicit assumption in the first two Parts of this book was that, after aggregation and aggressive pretrial management, there awaited a trial process that could rationally resolve all the claims of all the claimants. Now we must put that assumption to the test. If it turns out to be inaccurate, we will need to reform our attitudes about aggregation and pretrial, our trial process, or both.

We can begin to explore this issue by examining the roles that the standard trial process assigns to each player. The parties provide evidence and ideas; otherwise, they are passive. A judge is the lawgiver. A jury is the factfinder in cases at law, while the judge is the factfinder in suits in equity. Finally, the lawyer for each party is responsible for the presentation of proofs and arguments on the party's behalf. For the most part, lawyers are in charge; judge and jury are a *tabula rasa* upon whom the lawyers write their stories.

This process is adequate to ensure the rational adjudication of routine cases. Unfortunately, it ill serves the web of issues and voluminous, technical facts found in most million-member class actions and ten-million-document lawsuits, and makes the attainment of rational adjudication problematic. Therefore, just as complexity forced the trial judge to make adjustments in the standard roles during the joinder and pretrial phases, we now must consider whether complex litigation also requires judges to adjust the trial responsibilities of lawyers, judges, and juries.

As you read the materials in this chapter, keep three things in mind. First, consider the material on its own merits: Why has the standard trial model allocated responsibility to lawyers, judges, and juries in the way that it has; do the problems of trial complexity persuade you of the need to re-allocate responsibility; and how can we perform needed re-allocations without damaging a host of constitutional provisions, statutes, rules, and traditions? Second, consider the material against the problems of joinder and pretrial complexity: If we are unable or unwilling to re-allocate trial responsibilities, what effect will that fact have on aggregation and pretrial management decisions in complex cases? Third, consider the possibility of less draconian adjustments in the trial process: Might we be able to preserve rational adjudication through adoption of non-traditional trial techniques, thus avoiding the all-or-nothing re-allocations that this chapter explores?

A. SELECTING TRIAL COUNSEL

In Chapter Eight, we examined the power of the trial judge to appoint lawyers other than a party's own to represent the party during a complex case. Our focus there was on the power of the court to appoint lead, liaison, or committees of counsel to handle pretrial tasks; but we did learn in passing that courts also claim the power to appoint counsel who will try the case on behalf of a group of plaintiffs. Here we examine more specifically this latter power, and the reasons behind it. Our goal is limited. We do not address issues such as the selection process for trial counsel, conflicts of interest and disqualification of trial counsel, or withdrawal of trial counsel. Those issues are vitally important, but they have already been addressed in Chapter Eight. In this section the focus is on the arguments for and against the judge's ability to alter one of the — if not *the* — quintessential rights in an adversary system: the right to have a lawyer of your own choosing present the proofs and reasoned arguments on your behalf.

MANUAL FOR COMPLEX LITIGATION, THIRD

133 (1995)

The proliferation of counsel in multiparty cases can lead to delay and confusion. The court should therefore consider appropriate procedures, including the following:

- assigning primary responsibility for the conduct of trial to a limited number of attorneys, either by formal designation of trial counsel . . . or by informal arrangements among the attorneys, taking into account legitimate needs for individual representation of parties; . . .

- providing that objections made by one party will be deemed made by all similarly situated parties unless expressly disclaimed — other counsel should be permitted to add further grounds of objection, again on behalf of all similarly situated parties unless disclaimed . . . .

IN RE AIR CRASH DISASTER AT DETROIT METROPOLITAN AIRPORT ON AUGUST 16, 1987

737 F. Supp. 396 (E.D. Mich. 1989)

■ COOK, Chief Judge. [The case arose out of an airline crash that killed more than 250 people. Previously, the Judicial Panel on Multidistrict Litigation had ordered that all federal suits be consolidated before Chief Judge Cook. Judge Cook subsequently ordered the transfer of the cases to himself for trial, and then consolidated the cases. In the order,] this Court notified the parties that it intended to appoint the Plaintiffs' Steering Committee (PSC) to serve as the lead counsel for the purpose of prosecuting the joint liability trial which began on October 2, 1989. . . .

The only objection to the proposed lead counsel designation was submitted by the Plaintiff in [one of the consolidated cases]. . . . [S]he essentially maintains that (1) this Court has no authority to appoint the PSC to serve as the lead counsel in a joint liability trial, and (2) such a designation would abridge her right to representation by counsel of her choice. . . .

In In re Bendectin Litigation, 857 F.2d 290, 297 (6th Cir. 1988), cert. denied, 488 U.S. 1006 (1989), the Sixth Circuit Court of Appeals upheld the lower court's decision to appoint a "lead counsel committee" that would serve as counsel for the plaintiffs in a multidistrict litigation case. Despite the protestations of some plaintiffs that such an appointment would "den[y] them the right freely to choose counsel," the *Bendectin* Court concluded that "[i]n complex cases, it is well established that the district judge may create a Plaintiffs' Lead Counsel Committee." Id. at 297 (citations omitted).

In addition, the Fifth Circuit Court of Appeals also determined that the district court has the authority to appoint lead counsel to conduct pretrial discovery and to litigate liability issues which are common to all plaintiffs. In In re Air Crash Disaster at Florida Everglades, 549 F.2d 1006 (5th Cir. 1977), the district court appointed lead counsel to conduct all pretrial matters and to prosecute the issues of liability on behalf of all plaintiffs. In recognizing the authority of the trial court to make such an appointment, the *Florida Everglades* Court noted:

> The need for a court to exercise its inherent managerial powers as expressed in rule 42(a) may take precedence over desires of counsel. . . .
>
> It is not open to serious question that a federal court in a complex, consolidated case may designate one attorney or a set of attorneys to handle pre-trial activity on aspects of the case where the interests of all co-parties coincide. MacAlister v. Guterma, 263 F.2d 65 (2d Cir. 1958), is perhaps the leading case on the court's power to appoint and rely on lead counsel. Chief Judge Kaufman's opinion contains these pertinent passages on the issue of judicial power:
>
>> "The purpose of consolidation is to permit a trial convenience and economy in administration. Toward this end Rule 42(a) in addition to providing for joint trials in actions involving common questions of law and fact specifically confers the authority to 'make such orders

concerning proceedings therein as may tend to avoid unnecessary costs or delay.'...

"An order consolidating ... actions during the pre-trial stages, together with the appointment of a general counsel may in many instances prove the only effective means of channeling the efforts of counsel along constructive lines and its implementation must be considered within the clear contemplation of the rule....

"The advantages of this procedure should not be denied litigants in the federal courts because of misapplied notions concerning interference with a party's right to his own counsel...."

Id. at 1014-15 (footnote and citations omitted).[5]

Despite the Plaintiff's objections, this Court concludes that it does have the authority to appoint and designate the PSC to serve as lead counsel for the Plaintiffs for the purpose of prosecuting the common issues in a joint liability trial. See also Vincent v. Hughes Air West, Inc., 557 F.2d 759 (9th Cir.1977); ... In re Swine Flu Immunization Products Liability Litigation, 89 F.R.D. 695, 699 n.3 (D.D.C. 1981).

Roger H. Trangsrud, MASS TRIALS IN MASS TORT CASES: A DISSENT

1989 U. Ill. L. Rev. 69, 74-76, 82-83, 87-88

Until recently, our system treated [catastrophic human tragedies] and the tort claims they created with uncompromised due process. This we should continue to do.

Underlying our tradition of individual claim autonomy in substantial tort cases is the natural law notion that this is an important personal right

---

5. The Plaintiff maintains that the *MacAlister* decision, which was relied upon in the *Florida* court, does not support the proposition that the district court may appoint lead counsel to try a case on behalf of all plaintiffs.... However, the Plaintiff fails to mention that the Second Circuit Court of Appeals subsequently clarified *MacAlister* by noting that its decision was not intended to preclude a trial court from designating lead counsel to conduct pretrial matters and to prosecute the case on behalf of all plaintiffs in complex cases. ... Farber v. Riker-Maxson Corporation, 442 F.2d 457, 459 (2d Cir. 1971) ....

6. This Court further reasons that the source of authority which supports this appointment may emanate from (1) the inherent power of a federal district court to "'control the disposition of the causes on its docket with economy of time and effort for itself, counsel and for litigants,'" In re FTC Line of Business Report Litigation, 626 F.2d 1022, 1027 n. 29 (D.C. Cir. 1980) (quoting Landis v. North American Co., 299 U.S. 248, 254 (1936)), or (2) the terms of Rule 42(a) of the Federal Rules of Civil Procedure, see *Florida*, 549 F.2d at 1014-15.

This Court also notes that, contrary to the Plaintiff's position, it has not precluded non-PSC members from participating in the joint liability trial. Certainly, the non-PSC members may offer assistance and suggestions to lead counsel during the course of the proceedings. However, the conduct of this trial would become chaotic and totally unmanageable if the Court permitted the counsel for each Plaintiff to present his position or theory of the case to the jury.

of the individual. While much less celebrated than other natural rights, such as the right to practice one's own religion or to think and speak freely, the right to control personally the suit whereby a badly injured person seeks redress from the alleged tortfeasor has long been valued here and in England. . . . It was not the duty of the government or some third party to initiate such a suit, nor could the government or some third party interfere in the prosecution of the action.

This jealous protection of the individual's absolute right to control his own tort claim was respected for practical as well as philosophical reasons. . . . Unless control of such tort claims was left with the injured party, a "litigious person could harass and annoy others if allowed to purchase claims for pain and suffering and pursue the claims in court as assignees." There was also the risk of overreaching, deception, and other misconduct by the party seeking to acquire the right to bring a tort claim on another's behalf. These remain major concerns today, as evidenced by the methods used by attorneys . . . to obtain control over the cases of nonclients by bringing class actions or becoming lead counsel in huge consolidated tort cases. . . .

Other traditional justifications for individual claim autonomy remain important today in mass tort cases. From a purely economic point of view, our system operates mainly on the assumption that economic decisions are best made by the true owner of property rather than by any other person. . . . If others assume control over their claim, then [the best outcome from the plaintiff's standpoint] is less likely to happen because these strangers will often not be aware of the special circumstances attending this claim or will have a divided loyalty because the stranger will often be responsible for many other substantial tort claims as well. . . .

Avoiding mass trials and protecting individual claim autonomy also helps mute the serious conflict-of-interest issues that characterize tort litigation in general, but mass tort litigation in particular. For example, the standard contingency fee contract creates a tension between the attorney who wishes to accept an early settlement offer . . . and the client who may benefit by his attorney putting more hours into the case before settling it or trying it. This conflict of interest is greatly exacerbated if a mass trial is ordered because the costs to the attorney of preparing such a case are very high and the risks of failure at trial are substantial. . . .

In such circumstances, how can the plaintiff lawyer's advice to settle be regarded as independent and objective professional counsel? The inherent tensions of contingency fee representation have been intensified to such an extent by the mass trial that the adversary system may break down. The individual plaintiff must trust that the trial court will not approve the settlement if it is unfair or collusive. The trial judge, however, cannot know the strengths and weaknesses of particular claims as well as the lawyer for an individual plaintiff. The judge is also the actor who stands to benefit the most from settlement rather than trial of the claims. The usual checks and balances that regulate professional conduct in the ordinary tort case are weakened when mass trials are ordered. . . . A mass trial profoundly alters the traditional relationship between tort plaintiff and her representative . . . .

Conflicts of interest of this type are particularly troubling in a mass tort case where a mass trial is ordered because the individual plaintiff is in a poor position to exercise influence over lead counsel for the plaintiff group or the course of the complex litigation. . . .

Our civil justice system owes a twelve-year-old girl born with foreshortened limbs after her mother took [Bendectin] the same due process it owes a thirty-two-year old man paralyzed when the brakes on his Chevrolet fail and his automobile slams into a tree. In the latter case, the man's claim would be tried in its entirety to one jury, in the venue of the man's choosing, represented by a lawyer of the man's choosing . . . . So long as we rely on private compensation to redress private wrongs and on juries to hear all the facts of a case and to do justice consistent with common sense and our community norms, we owe the young girl the same procedure we routinely afford the victims of the many automobile accidents that are tried every year.

Notes and Questions

1. *Detroit Metropolitan* is a very rare case. To our knowledge, it is the only published decision, state or federal, during the last twenty-five years in which a party squarely challenged the court's power to appoint trial counsel. In In re Air Crash Disaster at Stapleton International Airport, Denver, Colorado, on November 15, 1987, 720 F. Supp. 1505 (D. Colo. 1989), a plaintiff who had received an unfavorable verdict on a liability issue challenged the court's trial plan. Under that plan, appointed trial counsel had presented liability and damages evidence for two plaintiffs and only liability evidence for the remaining plaintiffs. The objecting plaintiff did not squarely challenge the right of the court to appoint trial counsel; rather, the plaintiff generally attacked "the procedures applied pursuant to the trial plan." The trial court held that the "standard of review applied to determine whether trial procedures applied in complex litigation have combined to deny a party's rights to due process and fair trial is one of actual prejudice to the substantial rights of that party." 720 F. Supp. at 1513. Without specifically addressing the appointment of trial counsel, the court found no actual prejudice in the trial procedures.

Should "denial of due process and fair trial" be the standard used to determine if the appointment of trial counsel is appropriate? Was it the standard used in *Detroit Metropolitan*? Or did *Detroit Metropolitan* use a standard of convenience and economy? Did it use any standard at all?

2. Could a court appoint a single trial counsel to represent two pedestrians slightly injured in a simple car accident whenever it would be convenient and economical to do so? Wouldn't the attorneys for each pedestrian want to avoid alienating the jury, and thus cooperate in the presentation of testimony? Wouldn't the same "market forces" keep multiple counsel in complex cases from presenting needless evidence? Should judges step in and appoint trial counsel only when these market forces are likely to be distorted? Under what circumstances would they be distorted? Was *Detroit Metropolitan* one of these cases? Might other techniques (such as limited time for each attorney to question witnesses) correct the distortions without the need for trial counsel?

3. Professor Trangsrud's article raises serious philosophical, economic, and pragmatic difficulties with the use of trial counsel. Focus on the last difficulty: the loss of trans-substantivity that use of trial counsel in some, but not all, cases entails. What is the reason that we do not accord litigants in complex cases the same adversarial rights that litigants in simpler cases enjoy? Which set of claimants (if either) deserves more vigorous individual representation?

In thinking about these questions, consider the potential outcome-determinative effects of the appointment of trial counsel. First, a single counsel can press only a single theory of the case. Details of the individual litigants must be boiled down to a generic description good enough to serve for all. Multiple counsel, on the other hand, can provide judge and jury with particularized perspectives, potentially increasing the chances of striking a responsive chord in the factfinder. Second, the use of trial counsel almost inevitably requires the trial of common issues first. In most cases, the common issues concern liability rather than damages. As we shall learn in the next chapter, the bifurcation of liability and damage issues, with liability issues being tried first, increases the chances of a defense verdict (see pp. 1284-87, *infra*).

Outcome-determinative procedures do more than threaten an abstract procedural value like trans-substantivity; they also create advantages and disadvantages for real litigants. Shouldn't courts seriously consider these consequences before they appoint trial counsel?

4. What is the precise source of the court's authority to appoint trial counsel? In class actions, the sources are thought to be Rule 23(a)(4) and Rule 23(d)(1). In cases that are consolidated for trial, the authority is thought to reside in Rule 42(a). *Detroit Metropolitan* also locates the authority in the court's inherent power. These sources grant broad discretion to trial judges. Do you agree that they permit the appointment of trial counsel over a party's objection? If they do, is it wise to invest such authority in a judge who has private incentives to use the power in a wide range of cases? Should the rules be more specific about the factors a judge must consider before appointing trial counsel?

5. How much of the standard adversarial model does the due process clause incorporate? In particular, would a party be bound by an unfavorable judgment obtained by trial counsel to whom the party has not consented? See generally Phillips Petroleum Co. v. Shutts, 472 U.S. 797, 812 (1985) (holding that minimal due process needed to bind absent class plaintiff included "notice plus an opportunity to be heard and participate in the litigation, whether in person or through counsel"); Goldberg v. Kelly, 397 U.S. 254 (1970); Note, *The Right to Retain Counsel in Civil Litigation*, 66 Colum. L. Rev. 1322, 1325-27 (1966).

Could Rule 23, which binds class members to judgments obtained by class counsel, survive a due process "right" to trial counsel of a party's choosing? Perhaps. Rule 23 contains procedural safeguards that ensure the adequacy of the representation of a class representative and her lawyer (Rule 23(a)); guarantee a party's right to opt out except in constrained circumstances where the parties' interests are aligned (Rule 23(b)); permit any member of an opt-out class to "enter an appearance through counsel" (Rule 23(c)(2)(C)); and authorize intervention of unnamed class members (Rule 23(d)(2)). None of these protections, of course, exists when trial counsel is appointed pursuant to Rule 42(a) or the court's inherent powers. Cf. Joan Steinman, *The Effects of Case Consolidation on the Procedural Rights of Litigants: What They Are, What They Might Be Part II: Non-Jurisdictional Matters*, 42 UCLA L. Rev. 967, 978 (1995) (Rule 23 protections should be extended to counsel chosen in consolidated cases).

One reply to a party's "right" to individual trial counsel is to argue that the crux of due process is rational adjudication. When individual counsel threatens rational adjudication, the court must have the authority to suspend adversarial process in order to protect the more fundamental interest in reasoned judgment. But in how many cases can it really be said that reasoned judgment is threatened by the participation of each party's lawyer? Couldn't the threats in this subset of cases usually be dealt with through other mechanisms?

A second, and simpler, response is to deny that the due process clause guarantees the participation of an individual's selected counsel. This is Professor Fiss's position. Fiss seeks to distinguish between a right of participation and a right of representation. In contexts in which "particular individuals have been singled out," "the value of individual participation ranks very high, maybe even supreme.... But in structural litigation no individual is singled out .... Accordingly, the value of participation, understood in its individualist form, loses some of its force." See Owen M. Fiss, *The Allure of Individualism*, 78 Iowa L. Rev. 965, 978 (1993). In these structural cases, the concept of due process requires "not a representation of individuals but a representation of interests.... If an individual's interest has been adequately represented then he or she has no further claim against the decree." Id. at 972.

Once again we return to one of the central issues with which we opened this book: Is a Fulleresque right of individual participation essential to the nature of adjudication? Even Fiss seems to think that it might be critical in simple cases. If so, what is so unique about the structural reform case that it eliminates a right guaranteed in routine litigation? Would Fiss regard a mass tort case as a case in which individuals have been singled out, or a structural reform case in which the collective right of a social group is at stake?

6. The academic musings in the last five notes should not be mistaken for the present state of the law: Courts claim the power to appoint trial counsel, and they use it. Indeed, the popularity of appointing trial counsel appears to be growing. When the *Manual for Complex and Multidistrict Litigation* was published in 1970, it did not suggest that trial counsel was an option. Within two years, the revised *Manual* suggested the possibility of trial counsel; and soon thereafter, the use of trial counsel received its first appellate imprimatur. In re Air Crash Disaster at Florida Everglades on December 29, 1972, 549 F.2d 1006, 1015 (5th Cir. 1977). Today such appointments are fairly routine. See, *e.g.*, In re San Juan Dupont Plaza Hotel Fire Litigation, 768 F. Supp. 912 (D.P.R. 1991) ("Full participation by each individual plaintiffs' counsel would likely result in numerous attorneys each vying for the attention of the Court, zealously representing the interests of their individual cases and possibly leading to the presentation of confusing and conflicting theories. Clearly, this would be detrimental to the interests of the larger group of plaintiffs.").

7. The 1985 predecessor to the *Manual, Third* — the *Manual for Complex Litigation (Second)* — contained the following admonition: "Other counsel should be afforded an opportunity to conduct supplemental examination, particularly on matters unique to their clients not already covered in prior examination." The *Manual, Third* deleted this sentence, inserting in its place the phrase "taking into account legitimate needs for individual representation of parties." Perhaps, however, the changed language in the *Manual, Third* was more descriptive than normative. Professor Steinman has noted that "courts sometimes have uttered reassurances about the ability of nonlead counsel to participate, but increasingly they have acknowledged the substantial

disenfranchisement of nonlead counsel." Steinman, *supra*, at 976. Might we have predicted this progression once a discretionary power of appointment was granted to trial judges?

8. Typically, a court will issue a written order confirming a lawyer's status as trial counsel. See *Manual for Complex Litigation (Second)* 435 (1985) (sample order). What happens if the court never makes a formal designation, but an attorney acts as *de facto* trial counsel? In Central Illinois Public Service Co. v. Allianz Underwriters Insurance Co., 158 Ill.2d 218, 633 N.E.2d 675 (1994), two sets of defendant insurers had identical interests with respect to certain dispositive issues. During pretrial, all the defendants ran a single defense on these issues, fully participated in discovery, shared litigation expenses, and even agreed on the experts that would be presented at trial. The trial, however, involved only one set of insurers; the other set of insurers was not put on trial. After the verdict went against the first set of insurers, the trial judge tried to bind the second set of insurers to the judgment on the theory that trial counsel had represented all common interests and therefore the first set of insurers were the "virtual surrogate" of the remaining insurers. The Illinois Supreme Court held that, because the second set of insurers had been barred from participation in the trial, they could not be bound by the judgment. A dissent argued that, although "perhaps it might have been more prudent if the trial court in the instant cause had formally appointed . . . lead counsel or trial counsel," the control exercised by the second set of insurers bound them to the judgment.

9. At one level, the court's power to appoint trial counsel seems more troublesome than the court's power to appoint lead counsel for pretrial purposes. At another level, since few cases ever reach the point of trial, the ability to appoint pretrial lead counsel is a power of considerably greater consequence. You might wish to revisit the wisdom of appointing lead counsel for pretrial purposes in light of the material contained in this section.

B. SELECTING THE DECISION MAKER(S) FOR TRIAL

In an adversary system, factfinding and lawgiving tasks are kept distinct from the task of presenting the proofs and arguments. In the American version of the adversarial system, factfinding and lawgiving tasks often are subdivided. With respect to factfinding, a judge bears certain factfinding responsibilities, a jury bears others, and judicial adjuncts such as masters may bear still others. With respect to lawgiving, judicial officers dominate, but in jury cases, juries have some ability to decide mixed questions of law and fact and may also, through their secret verdicts, refuse to follow legal rules with which they disagree.

A case can be complex when the factfinding task cannot be performed adequately by the player (judge or jury) entrusted with factfinding responsibility. As long as a person learned in the law is performing the lawgiving task, however, a case cannot be complex merely because of the intricacies of lawgiving. Therefore, in complex cases, we should expect to find that (1) a trial judge possesses the power to take the factfinding function away from the player who traditionally performs it and order it performed by another player more capable of the task; and (2) the judge possesses virtually no power to substitute another person for herself as lawgiver. The first of these expectations threatens to create a head-on collision with constitutional constraint, in particular the Seventh Amendment's right to jury trial and Article III's requirement that an Article III judge perform essential judicial functions. The following materials sort out these tensions, first in the context of factfinding and then in the context of lawgiving.

1. Selecting the Factfinder in Complex Cases

In complex trials, which may last a long time and involve sophisticated economic or scientific information, there is some reason to doubt that a jury can find the facts with an appropriate degree of rationality. Of course, there is also reason to doubt that a judge is an adequate factfinder. The following three sections examine the division of factfinding responsibility between judge and jury in the modern American system, the power of a judge to replace a jury as factfinder in circumstances of complexity, and the power of a judge to replace herself when she too might not rationally find the facts.

a. Background: The Right to a Civil Jury Trial

Even in routine cases, trying to understand which player(s) are responsible for factfinding, and the precise scope of their responsibilities, is a vexing task. Start with the federal courts. The Seventh Amendment provides: "In suits at common law, where the value in controversy shall exceed twenty dollars, the right of jury trial shall be preserved, and no fact tried by a jury, shall be otherwise re-examined in any Court of the United States, than according to the rules of the common law." The first half of this amendment has been interpreted to require the use of juries in actions at common law, but not to require juries in suits in equity. Even if a jury is not constitutionally required, Congress can by statute provide for jury trials, and it has done so with regard to a few types of claim.

Using juries to hear some but not all claims raises three concerns. First, some line of demarcation needs to be established between common law matters and matters sounding in equity. But the line between the common law and equity was always fluid, and has changed a fair amount during the course of Anglo-American history. Moreover, finding an answer to this historical question would do nothing to solve the problem of jury trial in cases involving modern statutory and administrative rights that have no ready analogue to common law or equity.

A second set of pressures arises from the modern tendency to join multiple claims in one proceeding. It is quite possible that one case might involve both jury-tried claims and judge-tried claims. Moreover, some disputed facts are likely to be relevant to both sets of claims. The problem, then, is how to allocate factfinding responsibility with regard to the overlapping facts.

Third, once we have sorted out basic factfinding responsibility both for claims and for overlapping facts within those claims, it becomes necessary to ask what judicial controls, if any, should be placed on the factfinder's authority.

Comparable issues arise in cases brought in state courts. The Supreme Court has never held that the terms of the Seventh Amendment are binding as a matter of due process on the state courts; most states, however, have a constitutional provision comparable to the Seventh Amendment, and in those states that do not, all but Louisiana at least indirectly provide for (and use) civil juries in actions at law. See Geoffrey C. Hazard, Jr., et al., Cases and Materials on Pleadings and Procedure 1118-20 (7th ed. 1994).

Your basic course in civil procedure might have addressed the ways in which American courts have resolved these issues. To take them in reverse order, the first issue is the extent of judicial control over the factfinding function. In the federal system, appellate courts act as a limited check on a judge's factfinding authority; a judge's findings of fact can be reversed when there is clear error. A jury's findings of fact are subject to similar appellate review, but they are also subject to additional controls, both direct and indirect. Directly, the trial judge can enter judgment as a matter of law (during or after trial) when she is convinced that no reasonable jury could find for a party on a particular issue. Indirectly, a judge can comment on the evidence, ask follow-up questions to elicit additional facts, instruct the jury, and order a new trial when she believes that the jury's verdict is against the weight of the evidence. None of these jury-control devices violates the Seventh Amendment. See Galloway v. United States, 319 U.S. (1943). For the most part, states have comparable controls, although a few states provide less control, and a few states provide more.

It is fair to say that the vigor with which these jury control devices have been employed has varied over time, with the twentieth century easing the more stringent judicial management of juries that occurred during the late nineteenth century. See Stephan Landsman, *The History and Objectives of the Civil Jury System*, in Verdict 22 (Robert E. Litan ed. 1993). Such a general statement, however, must be tempered by the qualification that summary judgment is a twentieth century invention; that judgment as a matter of law has been widely used in this century; and that the latter half of the century has seen important changes (such as six-member panels, non-unanimous verdicts, and segmented verdicts) in the structure and function of the jury. Moreover, many procedural reformers and legal realists of the early part of this century disliked jury trial, as do some modern law-and-economic advocates. See id. at 47-51,; Leon Green, Judge and Jury (1930); Jerome Frank, Courts on Trial (1950); Richard A. Posner, Economic Analysis of Law 549-50 (4th ed. 1992); George L. Priest, *Justifying the Civil Jury*, in Verdict, *supra*, at 103; Symposium, *The Role of the Jury in Civil Dispute Resolution*, 1990 U. Chi. L.F. 1. The proper scope of judicial management of the civil jury remains a hotly debated issue as we enter the twenty-first century.

The second issue — the allocation of responsibility to decide factual issues that overlap legal and equitable claims — has essentially been settled in the federal system by two cases, Beacon Theatres, Inc. v. Westover, 359 U.S. 500 (1959), and Dairy Queen, Inc. v. Wood, 369 U.S. 469 (1962). In *Beacon Theatres*, a potential antitrust defendant sought both a declaration that no antitrust violation had occurred and an injunction preventing the putative plaintiff (Beacon Theatres) from filing suit. Beacon Theatres filed a counterclaim for money damages based on the antitrust violation. A statute specifically required that antitrust violations like the one raised in the counterclaim to be tried to a jury. Following the practice prior to the merger of law and equity in 1938, in which the factfinder that first acquired jurisdiction decided overlapping facts, the trial judge held that he, and not a jury, would decide the facts common to both the original claim and the counterclaim. The court of appeals refused to grant a writ of mandamus from this order. After holding that mandamus was an appropriate vehicle to challenge the denial of a jury trial, the Supreme Court reversed:

> [T]he use of discretion by the trial court under Rule 42(b) to deprive Beacon of a full jury trial on its counterclaim and cross-claim, as well as on Fox's plea for declaratory relief, cannot be justified....
>
> If there should be cases where the availability of declaratory judgment or joinder in one suit of legal and equitable causes would not in all respects protect the plaintiff seeking equitable relief from irreparable harm while affording a jury trial in the legal cause, the trial court will necessarily have to use its discretion in deciding whether the legal or equitable cause should be tried first. Since the right to jury trial is a constitutional one, however, while no similar requirement protects trials by the court, that discretion is very narrowly limited and must, wherever possible, be exercised to preserve jury trial....
>
> [O]nly under the most imperative circumstances, circumstances which in view of the flexible procedures of the Federal Rules we cannot now anticipate, can the right to a jury trial of legal issues be lost through prior determination of equitable claims. [359 U.S. at 508-11.]

Beacon Theatres left issues open — in particular, its applicability in cases in which the equitable aspects of the case strongly predominated over the legal. *Dairy Queen* raised this issue. The plaintiff (owner of the Dairy Queen trademark) sued a franchisee that had allegedly breached its franchise agreement. The plaintiff styled its claim as one for an accounting of profits (traditionally an equitable claim) rather than for breach of contract (traditionally a legal claim). The plaintiff did not ask for a jury trial, but the franchisee did. The trial judge struck the request, holding that the case was either "purely equitable" or at best the legal issues were "incidental" to the equitable ones. Again on mandamus, the Supreme Court reversed:

> The holding in *Beacon Theatres*... applies whether the trial judge chooses to characterize the legal issues presented as "incidental" to equitable issues or not. Consequently, in a case such as this where there cannot even be a contention of... "imperative circumstances," *Beacon Theatres* requires that any legal issues for which a trial by jury is timely and properly demanded be submitted to a jury. There being no

question of the timeliness or correctness of the demand involved here, the sole question which we must decide is whether the action now pending before the District Court contains legal issues. . . .

Petitioner's contention . . . is that insofar as the complaint requests a money judgment it presents a claim which is unquestionably legal. We agree with that contention. . . .

The respondents' contention that this money claim is "purely equitable" is based primarily upon the fact that their complaint is cast in terms of an "accounting," rather than in terms of an action for "debt" or "damages." But the constitutional right to trial by jury cannot be made to depend upon the choice of words used in the pleadings. The necessary prerequisite to the right to maintain a suit for an equitable accounting, like all other equitable remedies, is, as we pointed out in *Beacon Theatres*, the absence of an adequate remedy at law. Consequently, in order to maintain such a suit on a cause of action cognizable at law, as this one is, the plaintiff must be able to show that the "accounts between the parties" are of such a "complicated nature" that only a court of equity can satisfactorily unravel them. In view of the powers given to District Courts by Federal Rule of Civil Procedure 53(b) to appoint masters to assist the jury in those exceptional cases where the legal issues are too complicated for the jury adequately to handle alone, the burden of such a showing is considerably increased and it will indeed be a rare case in which it can be met. But be that as it may, this is certainly not such a case. . . . The legal remedy cannot be characterized as inadequate merely because the measure of damages may necessitate a look into petitioner's business records. [369 U.S. at 472-73, 476-79.]

One effect of *Beacon Theatres* and *Dairy Queen* is that litigants receive the same procedure regardless of the order in which the equitable or legal claims are filed, or whether the legal claims are "incidental." Should the Supreme Court have relied explicitly on this trans-substantive rationale?

Perhaps not. There still remains the third issue judge-jury issue: the establishment of a line separating factual issues that are "legal" (*i.e.*, jury) from those that are "equitable" (*i.e.*, non-jury). Wherever that line is drawn, a plaintiff with a purely equitable claim will receive different procedures (and perhaps even a different outcome) than a plaintiff with a purely legal claim or with both an equitable and a legal claim. Although a solution to this trans-substantive problem is to legislate a jury trial for every case, including equitable ones, this solution has thus far generated no political enthusiasm. See Paul D. Carrington, *The Seventh Amendment: Some Bicentennial Reflections*, 1990 U. Chi. L.F. 33, 74-76.

So where should the line between jury and bench trial be drawn? In its dicta, *Dairy Queen* hints at a piece of the answer, suggesting that "legal" factual issues which are sufficiently complicated might be converted into "equitable" factual issues. The logical endpoint of this dicta, of course, is that the right to jury trial can be suspended in cases of complexity. The next case, probably the most famous of the Court's Seventh Amendment decisions, further explores these questions.

ROSS v. BERNHARD

396 U.S. 531 (1970)

■ MR. JUSTICE WHITE delivered the opinion of the Court.

The Seventh Amendment to the Constitution provides that in "[suits] at common law, where the value in controversy shall exceed twenty dollars, the right of trial by jury shall be preserved." Whether the Amendment guarantees the right to a jury trial in stockholders' derivative actions is the issue now before us.

Petitioners brought this derivative suit in federal court against the directors of their closed-end investment company, the Lehman Corporation, and the corporation's brokers, Lehman Brothers. They contended that Lehman Brothers controlled the corporation through an illegally large representation on the corporation's board of directors, in violation of the Investment Company Act of 1940, 54 Stat. 789, 15 U.S.C. § 80a-1 et seq., and used this control to extract excessive brokerage fees from the corporation. The directors of the corporation were accused of converting corporate assets and of "gross abuse of trust, gross misconduct, willful misfeasance, bad faith, [and] gross negligence." Both the individual defendants and Lehman Brothers were accused of breaches of fiduciary duty. It was alleged that the payments to Lehman Brothers constituted waste and spoliation, and that the contract between the corporation and Lehman Brothers had been violated. Petitioners requested that the defendants "account for and pay to the Corporation for their profits and gains and its losses." Petitioners also demanded a jury trial on the corporation's claims.

On motion to strike petitioners' jury trial demand, the District Court held that a shareholder's right to a jury on his corporation's cause of action was to be judged as if the corporation were itself the plaintiff. Only the shareholder's initial claim to speak for the corporation had to be tried to the judge. [On interlocutory appeal] the Court of Appeals reversed, holding that a derivative action was entirely equitable in nature, and no jury was available to try any part of it. . . .

We reverse the holding of the Court of Appeals that in no event does the right to a jury trial preserved by the Seventh Amendment extend to derivative actions brought by the stockholders of a corporation. We hold that the right to jury trial attaches to those issues in derivative actions as to which the corporation, if it had been suing in its own right, would have been entitled to a jury. . . .

However difficult it may have been to define with precision the line between actions at law dealing with legal rights and suits in equity dealing with equitable matters, some proceedings were unmistakably actions at law triable to a jury. . . . Whether the corporation was viewed as an entity separate from its stockholders or as a device permitting its stockholders to carry on their business and to sue and be sued, a corporation's suit to enforce a legal right was an action at common law carrying the right to jury trial at the time the Seventh Amendment was adopted.

The common law refused, however, to permit stockholders to call corporate managers to account in actions at law. The possibilities for abuse, thus presented, were not ignored by corporate officers and directors. Early in the 19th century, equity provided relief both in this country and in England.... The remedy made available in equity was the derivative suit, viewed in this country as a suit to enforce a corporate cause of action against officers, directors, and third parties. As elaborated in the cases, one precondition for the suit was a valid claim on which the corporation could have sued; another was that the corporation itself had refused to proceed after suitable demand, unless excused by extraordinary conditions. Thus the dual nature of the stockholder's action: first, the plaintiff's right to sue on behalf of the corporation and, second, the merits of the corporation's claim itself.

Derivative suits posed no Seventh Amendment problems where the action against the directors and third parties would have been by a bill in equity had the corporation brought the suit. Our concern is with cases based upon a legal claim of the corporation against directors or third parties. Does the trial of such claims at the suit of a stockholder and without a jury violate the Seventh Amendment?...

What can be gleaned from this Court's [pre-1938] opinions is not inconsistent with the general understanding, reflected by the state court decisions and secondary sources, that equity could properly resolve corporate claims of any kind without a jury when properly pleaded in derivative suits complying with the equity rules.

Such was the prevailing opinion when the Federal Rules of Civil Procedure were adopted in 1938. It continued until 1963 when the Court of Appeals for the Ninth Circuit, relying on the Federal Rules as construed and applied in Beacon Theatres, Inc. v. Westover, 359 U.S. 500 (1959), and Dairy Queen, Inc. v. Wood, 369 U.S. 469 (1962), required the legal issues in a derivative suit to be tried to a jury. DePinto v. Provident Security Life Ins. Co., 323 F.2d 826. It was this decision that the District Court followed in the case before us and that the Court of Appeals rejected.

Beacon and *Dairy Queen* presaged *DePinto*. Under those cases, where equitable and legal claims are joined in the same action, there is a right to jury trial on the legal claims which must not be infringed either by trying the legal issues as incidental to the equitable ones or by a court trial of a common issue existing between the claims. The Seventh Amendment question depends on the nature of the issue to be tried rather than the character of the overall action.[10] The principle of these cases bears heavily on derivative actions.

We have noted that the derivative suit has dual aspects: first, the stockholder's right to sue on behalf of the corporation, historically an equitable matter; second, the claim of the corporation against directors or

---

10. As our cases indicate, the "legal" nature of an issue is determined by considering, first, the pre-merger custom with reference to such questions; second, the remedy sought; and, third, the practical abilities and limitations of juries. Of these factors, the first, requiring extensive and possibly abstruse historical inquiry, is obviously the most difficult to apply....

third parties on which, if the corporation had sued and the claim presented legal issues, the company could demand a jury trial.... [L]egal claims are not magically converted into equitable issues by their presentation to a court of equity in a derivative suit. The claim pressed by the stockholder against directors or third parties "is not his own but the corporation's." The corporation is a necessary party to the action; without it the case cannot proceed. Although named a defendant, it is the real party in interest, the stockholder being at best the nominal plaintiff. The proceeds of the action belong to the corporation and it is bound by the result of the suit. The heart of the action is the corporate claim. If it presents a legal issue, one entitling the corporation to a jury trial under the Seventh Amendment, the right to a jury is not forfeited merely because the stockholder's right to sue must first be adjudicated as an equitable issue triable to the court. *Beacon* and *Dairy Queen* require no less....

Actions are no longer brought as actions at law or suits in equity. Under the Rules there is only one action — a "civil action" — in which all claims may be joined and all remedies are available. Purely procedural impediments to the presentation of any issue by any party, based on the difference between law and equity, were destroyed. In a civil action presenting a stockholder's derivative claim, the court after passing upon the plaintiff's right to sue on behalf of the corporation is now able to try the corporate claim for damages with the aid of a jury.... Under the rules, law and equity are procedurally combined; nothing turns now upon the form of the action or the procedural devices by which the parties happen to come before the court....

Thus, for example, before-merger class actions were largely a device of equity, and there was no right to a jury even on issues that might, under other circumstances, have been tried to a jury. Although at least one post-merger court held that the device was not available to try legal issues, it now seems settled in the lower federal courts that class action plaintiffs may obtain a jury trial on any legal issues they present....

In the instant case we have no doubt that the corporation's claim is, at least in part, a legal one. The relief sought is money damages. There are allegations in the complaint of a breach of fiduciary duty, but there are also allegations of ordinary breach of contract and gross negligence. The corporation, had it sued on its own behalf, would have been entitled to a jury's determination, at a minimum, of its damages against its broker under the brokerage contract and of its rights against its own directors because of their negligence. Under these circumstances it is unnecessary to decide whether the corporation's other claims are also properly triable to a jury. The decision of the Court of Appeals is reversed.

■ MR. JUSTICE STEWART, with whom THE CHIEF JUSTICE and MR. JUSTICE HARLAN join, dissenting.... Since, as the Court concedes, a shareholder's derivative suit could be brought only in equity, it would seem to me to follow by the most elementary logic that in such suits there is no constitutional right to a trial by jury. Today the Court tosses aside history, logic, and over 100 years of firm precedent to hold that the plaintiff in a shareholder's derivative suit does indeed have a constitutional right to a trial by jury. This holding has a questionable basis in policy[5] and no basis whatever in the Constitution....

[T]he derivative suit can, of course, be artificially broken down into separable elements. But so then can any traditionally equitable cause of action, and the logic of the Court's position would lead to the virtual elimination of all equity jurisdiction....

The fact is, of course, that there are, for the most part, no such things as inherently "legal issues" or inherently "equitable issues." There are only factual issues, and, "like chameleons [they] take their color from surrounding circumstances." Thus the Court's "nature of the issue" approach is hardly meaningful.

Notes and Questions

1. After *Beacon Theatres*, a court's denial of a jury trial demand is almost always immediately reviewable through a writ of mandamus. Only in cases in which the right to jury trial is debatable might mandamus be unavailable. See In re Pasquariello, 16 F.3d 525 (3d Cir. 1994). An erroneous grant of a jury trial, however, does not appear to be immediately appealable, and is often regarded as harmless error. See 11 Charles A. Wright et al., Federal Practice & Procedure § 2887 (1995).

2. Although the erroneous grant of a jury trial might be regarded as harmless error for appellate purposes, the existence of a jury is one of the most critical pieces of procedural information in a lawsuit. At a practical level, the "conventional wisdom" of trial lawyers will lead many lawyers to try cases to judges and to juries in different ways. Juries are often thought to be more sympathetic to the little guy, less careful with the law, and more open to bamboozlement. Thus, a jury often affect the parties' tactical trial choices in matters such as the arguments used and the level of theatrics, rhetoric, and surprise employed. Jury trials may also affect the quality and quantity of evidence presented; one veteran trial lawyer once observed that "the use of a jury helps shorten a trial.... [A] civil antitrust suit tried to a judge ... is the most uncontrolled, worst proceeding that can be conceived, and that's because the judiciary takes the attitude, let anything in. We will get it all, and it's going to be faster. In fact, it's much slower.... If we let go of the jury in this context, we are really going to have two elephants trying to get into that Volkswagen." See ABA Antitrust Section, Expediting Pretrials and Trials of Antitrust Cases 135 (1979) (comments of Joseph M. Alioto).

It is far from clear that all of the conventional wisdom about juries is accurate. Research suggests that judges and juries agree in eighty to ninety percent of cases, and that judges may on balance be more disposed toward plaintiffs than juries. See Harry Kalven, Jr., *The Dignity of the Civil Jury*, 50 Va. L. Rev. 1055 (1964); R. Perry Sentell, Jr., *The Georgia Jury and Negligence:*

---

5. See, *e.g.*, J. Frank, Courts on Trial 110-111 (1949). Certainly there is no consensus among commentators on the desirability of jury trials in civil actions generally. Particularly where the issues in the case are complex — as they are likely to be in a derivative suit — much can be said for allowing the court discretion to try the case itself...

The View from the Bench, 26 Ga. L. Rev. 85 (1991); Kevin M. Clermont & Theodore Eisenberg, *Trial by Jury or Judge: Transcending Empiricism*, 77 Corn. L. Rev. 1124 (1992); Audrey Chin & Mark A. Peterson, Deep Pockets, Empty Pockets (1985). Whatever the truth about juries, however, they do influence trial procedures.

But the most significant consequences of the jury may not be the jury's direct effect on trial procedures. As we learned in our study of common law pleading, see pp. 28-36, *supra*, the use of a lay jury as factfinder requires that all issues need to be resolved in a limited number of hearings, thus setting in motion the chicken-and-egg problem of narrowing of issues and discovering relevant facts (a problem that occupied us in Chapter Nine) and creating the possibility that trial outcomes will be skewed in relation to the continuous trial method (a problem that will concern us in Chapter Eleven). Moreover, as Damaska points out, the use of decentralized decision makers like juries dictates (or at least strongly counsels) an adversarial process.

3. Footnote 10 of *Ross* is one of the famous footnotes in Supreme Court history. The Supreme Court has refined the relationship among *Ross*'s three factors in a series of subsequent cases. The Court has applied the first two factors — the historical practice in 1791 and the nature of the relief sought — in every case. The first factor often requires an abstruse historical investigation. The second factor is more straight-forward: If the requested relief is injunctive, then the claim is regarded as "equitable"; if the requested relief is monetary, then the claim is regarded as "legal," unless the monetary relief can be regarded as restitutionary or "incidental to or intertwined with injunctive relief." Chauffeurs, Teamsters and Helpers Local No. 391 v. Terry, 494 U.S. 558, 570-71 (1990). In the event that the first two factors point in different directions, "[t]he second inquiry is the more important in our analysis." *Terry*, 494 U.S. at 565; see also Granfinanciera, S.A. v. Nordberg, 492 U.S. 33, 42 (1989) ("The second stage of the analysis is more important than the first."). The Court has apparently limited the third factor — the practical abilities and limitations of juries — to public rights cases that involve the determination of facts by administrative agencies or specialized courts. See *Granfinanciera*, 492 U.S. at 42 n.4; *Terry*, 494 U.S. at 575 n.2; Atlas Roofing Co. v. Occupational Health and Safety Review Commission, 430 U.S. 442 (1977).

Does this three-part test make sense? Our historical study in Chapter One revealed that the precise boundary between common law and equity was fluid, even in the eighteenth century. Is it logical to take a snapshot of the law-equity relationship as it existed in 1791 and freeze that moment into constitutional limit? Moreover, what do the twists, turns, and many mistakes of Anglo-American legal history have to do with deciding whether a jury can perform the factfinding function in modern America? Since the second factor outweighs the first in any event, should the historical inquiry be abandoned? See *Terry*, 494 U.S. at 574 (Brennan, J., concurring) ("I think it is time we dispense with [the historical test] altogether."); Martin H. Redish, *Seventh Amendment Right to Jury Trial: A Study in the Irrationality of Rational Decision Making*, 70 Nw. U. L. Rev. 486 (1975); Charles W. Wolfram, *The Constitutional History of the Seventh Amendment*, 57 Minn. L. Rev. 639 (1973); see also Markman v. Westview Instruments, Inc., 517 U.S. 370 (1996) (holding that patent infringement claim was triable to jury after examining only historical analogue).

On the other hand, what does the nature of the relief have to do with the decision about whether to give a case to a jury? As we learned in Chapter One, equity sometimes granted money damages and law sometimes granted injunctive relief (or its equivalent). Is there any reason to believe that juries are competent to decide the factual issues in cases in which the plaintiff wants money damages, but not in cases in which the plaintiff wants an injunction? Obviously, juries are better suited to award damages, which are a one-time form of relief, than to award injunctive relief, which requires particularized crafting and ongoing supervision. But is the jury less capable of finding the facts regarding liability in injunctive cases than in cases for money damage? Conversely, even in a "legal" case, parties do not necessarily have a right to a jury determination of the amount of damages. Compare Tull v. United States, 481 U.S. 412, 425-26 (1987) (no Seventh Amendment right to have jury "determine the remedy in a trial in which it must determine liability"; assessment of civil penalties "is not an essential function of a jury trial") with Feltner v. Columbia Pictures Television, Inc., — U.S. —, 118 S.Ct. 1279, 1287 (1998) (Seventh Amendment requires jury to determine amount of damages when damages "serve purposes traditionally associated with legal relief" and when juries had done so prior to 1791; distinguishing *Tull*).

4. *Tull* raises an important, and often overlooked, final step in the jury trial analysis: Even after a claim has been determined to be "legal," each issue within the claim must be examined to determine whether it should be tried to a jury. In *Tull*, for instance, the court held that it is constitutional not to permit the jury to decide on the appropriate amount of civil penalties for a legal claim. Likewise, in *Markman*, after holding that a patent infringement claim was a matter for jury trial, the Court held that the proper construction of the claim document, which is a critical step in deciding the infringement claim, is an issue for the judge. According to *Tull*, only the "substance of the common-law right of trial by jury" must be preserved; "[o]nly those incidents which are regarded as fundamental, as inherent in and of the essence of the system of trial by jury, are placed beyond the reach of the legislature." *Tull*, 481 U.S. at 426. *Markman* determined which issues went to the "substance" of jury trial by examining historical practices in 1791, prior precedent, "the relative interpretive skills of judges and juries and the statutory policies that ought to be furthered by the allocation." 517 U.S. at 384. Does this step make the Seventh Amendment analysis even more bizarre?

5. If the Supreme Court's test for determining the right to jury trial is suspect, with what should we replace it? One test would be to ask what values the jury promotes, and to preserve the jury in the cases that advance those values. Juries can promote two types of values. The first are political: the participation of citizens in governance; a check on abusive governmental power, legal elitism, and legal technicality; and the fostering of greater acceptance of legal judgments. The second set of values concerns the integrity of the trial process: twelve heads are better than one; the experience and common sense of jurors lead to a more accurate assessment of evidence; twelve people called together for trial cannot easily be bribed; and the prejudices developed during pretrial and during years on the bench can handicap a judge's impartiality. See Harry Kalven, Jr. & Hans Zeisel, The American Jury 3-9 (1966) (also describing counter-arguments to these values); *Developments in the Law — The Civil Jury*, 110 Harv. L. Rev. 1408, 1421-42 (1997) (discussing values of civil jury).

Another possible test would be to ask whether a jury is functionally capable of deciding the particular factual issue at stake. To some extent, this test is consistent with the history and nature of equity. Traditionally, equity assumed jurisdiction over "difficult" cases. See The Federalist No. 83 (Alexander Hamilton) ("The great and primary use of a court of equity is to give relief *in extraordinary cases*, which are the *exceptions* to general rules."). It is also a commonsensical approach: Figure out what types of fact a jury can find well, and what types of fact it cannot, and then call the former situations "legal" and the latter "equitable." See Carrington, 1990 U. Chi. L.F. at 73-74 (suggesting a functional analysis). Isn't this functional analysis the same as the third factor of *Ross*? Should this factor, and not the nature of the relief requested, be the pre-eminent factor in jury trial analysis? Should this factor share equal billing with a fourth factor, not even mentioned in *Ross*, of a jury's political value?

6. Assuming that the practical abilities and limitations of juries is a relevant factor in Seventh Amendment analysis, what are the types of cases in which we might doubt the jury's abilities to decide facts rationally? One set of cases would be lengthy trials, in which it might be difficult for a jury to serve. Another set would be cases in which the publicity of the case would make it difficult to obtain twelve representative jurors without bias. A third set would be cases in which fears of jury manipulation by slick or prejudicial presentations were significant. A fourth set would be cases in which the evidence was so voluminous or technical that a jury, operating with common sense and memory, could not accurately find the facts through the application of reasoned judgment.

We have just described the world of trial complexity. And so we now must face the critical question: To what extent does the trial judge have the ability to override the right to jury trial when the jury, due to the complexity of the case, cannot fulfill its adversarial function of finding the facts rationally?

b. The Power of the Trial Judge to Strike a Jury in Complex or Complicated Litigation

IN RE BOISE CASCADE SECURITIES LITIGATION

420 F. Supp. 99 (W.D. Wash. 1976)

■ SHARP, District Judge. Before the Court are defendants' motions to strike plaintiffs' jury demands in this securities fraud litigation. The question before the Court is whether these jury demands may be stricken without conflicting with the Seventh Amendment. The Court is of the opinion that the answer is in the affirmative.

[The case arose out of the acquisition of West Tacoma Newsprint Co. (Newsprint) by Boise Cascade Corp. (Boise) in November, 1969. In return for their shares in Newsprint, stockholders received shares of Boise with a per share market value of approximately $75. In 1971 and 1972 Boise was forced to write down its assets, which resulted in a reduction in the price of Boise's shares to approximately $12. Several shareholders in Newsprint brought civil actions alleging violations of federal and state securities laws by Boise, its accountant, and its directors and officers.

[In 1973, the Judicial Panel on Multidistrict Litigation ordered the cases consolidated for pretrial purposes. During the pretrial phase of the case, counsel expended more than 50,000 lawyer hours, and more than 900,000 documents were produced. In 1976, motions by defendants to sever the various cases for trial were denied. The court granted motions by plaintiffs to consolidate some, but not all, of the multidistrict cases for trial. The defendants then moved to strike the plaintiffs' demand for jury trial.

[The court began its analysis of this motion by listing a number of complicating factors presented by the consolidated trial. First was the number of plaintiffs. According to the court, "each plaintiff has a different measure of reliance and . . . it will be necessary to contain the proof of each plaintiff to that particular plaintiff" — a complicated task because the burden of disproving reliance varied according to the context of the transaction. The court then turned to other difficulties a jury would face:]

Other portions of the complaints present complicated concepts that will involve lengthy explanation and documentary evidence.

For example, the complaints allege that Boise failed to make proper provision for discount reserves with respect to its land sales. . . . The foundation for this will likely require proof that a market rate of interest existed with respect to the land sales in question; the rate or rates charged by Boise; the amount of time that the market rate exceeded the rate actually charged and the amount of interest outstanding at various times. It may also be necessary to present evidence regarding the reasonableness of the rate or rates charged by Boise as well as proof relating to usury laws and state regulations, if any, of land sales and installment purchase contracts.

As another example, plaintiffs claim that Boise chose improper bases for the valuation of assets acquired in corporate acquisitions effected under 26 U.S.C.A. § 334(b)(2). As a result, it is alleged that Boise failed to note that it could be liable for up to $5,000,000 in federal income taxes. One of the issues here would be whether Boise properly accrued potential judgments resulting from litigation with the Internal Revenue Service before a United States District Court and the United States Tax Court. . . .

Other portions of the complaints which present unique and difficult accounting concepts are the following:

Boise improperly allocated unit land costs to the costs of goods sold so as to understate the costs of goods sold for more desirable lots, overstate the value of the remaining land inventory, and consequently to overstate profits derived from the sale of recreational land.

And also:

Boise's quarterly financial statements for the first three quarters of each year, including 1969, failed to recognize ratably and proportionately various adjustments made in the fourth quarter and therefore overstated net income for the first three quarters accordingly. The effect of said fourth quarter adjustments was concealed by the device of pooling the financial results of profitable companies acquired by merger during the year.

In addition to the complex accounting and proof questions, there is the very real possibility of substantial prejudice to the defendants due to evidence that Boise settled numerous civil actions brought by the State of

California and others alleging improper land development and marketing practices. . . .

Finally, and most important, in order to determine whether liability exists, the fact finder will have to analyze the Boise accounting, not only of the accounts as they existed at the time of the merger, but as the plaintiffs claim they should have existed. It is anticipated that experts for each side will have to go through the accounting techniques and resulting figures in each of the areas complained of in [the complaint]. In all, assets and liabilities in excess of a billion dollars are involved and a period of more than five years will have to be examined. . . . [T]he truth or falsity of many of the allegations may have to be determined in the light of economic conditions as they existed a decade ago.

Competing theories of accounting will be presented for all of these matters. It has been suggested that more than one "generally accepted accounting principle" can be applied to a particular booking problem but that not all of those principles fairly reflect the financial condition of the corporation.

In sum, it appears to this Court that the scope of the problems presented by this case is immense. The factual issues, the complexity of the evidence that will be required to explore those issues, and the time required to do so leads to the conclusion that a jury would not be a rational and capable fact finder.

III

There can be no doubt that jury trials are favored in civil litigation in this country. The combination of the Seventh Amendment and the merger of actions at law and in equity into a single civil action under the Federal Rules of Civil Procedure encourages the use of juries to determine facts. See Ross v. Bern[h]ard, 396 U.S. 531 [1970] . . . .

However broad this policy may be, the Supreme Court has recognized that the use of juries is not without limits. In Ross v. Bern[h]ard, *supra*, the Court set forth three factors which determine the susceptibility of a claim to trial by jury:

> [First,] the pre-merger custom with reference to such questions; second the remedy sought; and third, the practical abilities and limitations of juries. Id. at 538 n.10.

No authority was cited for these three factors. As for the first two, Supreme Court precedent appears so clear as to be obvious. See *e.g.*, Parsons v. Bedford, 28 U.S. (3 Pet.) 443, 447 (1830) (Story, J.). The third part is not explicit from previous opinions.

The procedural safeguards inherent in our legal system provide the impression and fact of fairness to the litigants and society. This is necessary in order to assure obedience to judgments and resort to the legal system as the only sanctioned means of settling disputes in a complex civilized society. Indeed, under the Fifth and Fourteenth Amendments, the legitimacy of government action is measured in terms of fairness.

Central to the fairness which must attend the resolution of a civil action is an impartial and capable fact finder. A properly selected panel of veniremen must generally be presumed to yield an impartial and capable jury. However, at some point, it must be recognized that the complexity of a case may exceed the ability of a jury to decide the facts in an informed and capable manner. When that occurs, the question arises as to whether the right and necessity of fairness is defeated by relegating fact finding to a body not qualified to determine the facts. The third part of the analysis in footnote 10 to the majority opinion in Ross v. Bern[h]ard, *supra*, directly recognizes this....

Of course, the point at which a jury's limitations exceed its abilities is not precise nor is it easy of definition. No single factor alone can dictate that a jury should not hear a case. As in this case, a number of factors must combine to convince the Court that a jury would be incapable of fairly deciding the case.

IV

It must be apparent that any jury chosen to hear this case will not be a fair cross section of the community at large because of the estimated trial time of four to six months. It would not be unreasonable to excuse prospective jurors from serving in this civil case if they believe that service for that period of time would impair their employment. At the outset, then, the availability of employed persons to serve on this jury is limited. This suggests that at least the appearance of fairness would be diminished, if not eliminated, when a lengthy civil action involving millions of dollars in potential damages in a commercial setting would be heard by jurors who have not had exposure to a contemporary commercial or business environment. This should not be taken to mean that a non-employed person is somehow less able to determine facts. Rather, a basic purpose of the jury, the determination of facts by impartial minds of diverse backgrounds, is defeated if a sizable and significant portion of the community must be excluded from service.

Pointing out the limits of a jury to hear an extended civil action does not answer the problems presented by a particular case unless it can be shown that trial to the Court would be superior.

In addition to the Court's experience in presiding over other complicated cases involving commercial matters, the Court has available to it tools that are unwieldy in the possession of a jury. Among these tools are review of daily transcripts; admission of depositions into evidence instead of reading relevant portions aloud; review of selected portions of testimony from the reporter's notes and flexibility in scheduling trial activities. In addition, the Court is able to study exhibits in depth and carry on colloquies with witnesses, expert and non-expert alike, in an orderly and systematic manner. Of course, this is in addition to the Court's knowledge of the litigation resulting from its review of the record since the cases were filed.

In the light of the limitation of a jury to determine the facts in an informed manner and the ability of the Court to hear and review the evidence in an efficient and effective manner, the Court believes that it would be more capable of fairly deciding the facts.

V

The Court is of the opinion that the third part to footnote 10 in Ross v. Bern[h]ard, *supra*, is of constitutional dimensions. It must be seen as a limitation to or interpretation of the Seventh Amendment. Furthermore, the Court is of the opinion that there is no conflict in this case with any statutory policy favoring trial by jury, 28 U.S.C.A. § 1861, or the Federal Rules of Civil Procedure.

The explosion of litigation in the past two decades in terms both of number of filings and the complexity and scope of many of those cases has led thoughtful minds to wonder whether the judicial system as we now know it can cope with some of these cases. . . .

With these thoughts in mind, the necessity for the appearance and fact of fairness dictate that the motions now before the Court be granted.

Because of the effect of this Order, the Court hereby certifies this question for appeal under 28 U.S.C.A. § 1292(b). . . . The Court will retain jurisdiction of the remainder of this litigation.

IN RE: JAPANESE ELECTRONIC PRODUCTS ANTITRUST LITIGATION

631 F.2d 1069 (3d Cir. 1980)

■ SEITZ, Chief Judge. This certified interlocutory appeal from a pretrial order of the district court raises an issue that currently is the subject of much debate: In an action for treble damages under the antitrust and antidumping laws, do the parties have a right to trial by jury without regard to the practical ability of a jury to decide the case properly?

I.

This litigation began in the District of New Jersey with the complaint of National Union Electric Corp. (NUE). . . . NUE was a major domestic producer of television receivers until February 1970. The following December, it filed the first complaint of this litigation, charging several of its Japanese competitors with violations of the antitrust laws and the laws governing competition in international trade. The complaint names as defendants the Mitsubishi Corp., which is a Japanese trading company, and seven Japanese television manufacturers: Matsushita Electric Industrial Co., Toshiba Corp., Hitachi, Ltd., Sharp Corp., Mitsubishi Electric Corp., Sanyo Electric Co., and Sony Corp. Nine subsidiaries of these companies also are named as defendants in NUE's action.

NUE alleges that the defendants have sought to drive American television producers out of the American market by selling televisions at artificially depressed prices.... NUE seeks treble damages for injuries sustained between 1966 and 1970.... NUE also seeks injunctive relief.

[Zenith Radio Corp. filed a complaint in 1974, naming all of the defendants of the NUE action, a few additional subsidiaries, and two American companies: Motorola, Inc., and Sears, Roebuck, and Co.] The Zenith complaint repeats NUE's allegations of dumping, conspiracy, and intent to destroy domestic competititon in the American market, but Zenith's allegations are broader in two respects. First, Zenith seeks damages for injuries sustained over a longer period, from 1968 through 1977, as opposed to a period of 1966 through 1970 in NUE's complaint. Second, Zenith's allegations cover not only televisions but also radios, phonographs, tape and audio equipment, and electronic components. In addition, Zenith charges defendants with discriminating in price among American purchasers, in violation of the Robinson-Patman Act, 15 U.S.C. § 13(a) (1976). Finally, Zenith asserts that the Matsushita and Sanyo defendants have violated § 7 of the Clayton Act, 15 U.S.C. § 18 (1976), by acquiring interests in domestic producers of consumer electronic products previously held by Motorola and Sears. Like NUE, Zenith prays for treble damages and injunctive relief.

[Some of the defendants in *Zenith* filed counterclaims which alleged that Zenith and its distributors had violated the Sherman, Robinson-Patman, and Lanham Acts, and that Zenith and about 30 co-conspirators maintained a program of sham litigation against Zenith's competitors.

[Shortly after the filing of the Zenith action, the two suits were consolidated for pretrial proceedings in the Eastern District of Pennsylvania. Subsequently, the two suits were consolidated for trial.]

Both NUE and Zenith made timely demands for jury trial. Fourteen of the defendants moved to strike the demands, arguing that the case is too large and complex for a jury. The district court denied their motion, concluding that the seventh amendment does not recognize the complexity of a lawsuit as a valid reason for denying a jury trial. The court... certified its order for interlocutory appeal under 28 U.S.C. § 1292(b) (1976). We have permitted the appeal....

II.

Appellants argue that the proof of foregoing claims will be too burdensome and complicated for a jury. They have cited several dimensions of complexity.

The district court accepted one of appellants' basic contentions: the trial will be protracted. The court predicted that the trial would last a full year. It noted that the parties are nearing the end of discovery, which after nine years has produced millions of documents and over 100,000 pages of depositions. The court did not estimate how much of this evidence will be introduced at trial.

Beyond these observations of the district court, we have only the parties' divergent predictions of the proof that appellees' claims call for. We understand their primary disagreements to concern four general sources of complexity: proof of the Antidumping Act claims, proof of the alleged conspiracy, resolution of a number of financial issues, and understanding of several conceptually difficult legal and factual issues.

Under the Antidumping Act, appellees must prove that the defendants made sales of articles in the United States at a price lower than the price of "such articles" in Japan. 15 U.S.C. § 72 (1976). Appellants read the Act to permit price comparisons only for identical products sold in the two countries. During the relevant periods, defendants produced thousands of technically distinct models of the products covered by this litigation. They contend that to identify the products appropriate for price comparisons, the jury will have to review the technical features of thousands of different models and understand how differences between the models relate to cost of manufacture, product performance, and marketability. Appellees construe the Antidumping Act to permit price comparisons between functionally equivalent products, such as all portable color televisions with a particular screen size and VHF-UHF channel selection. They contend that a jury could identify such functionally equivalent products without massive or highly technical proof.

The conspiracy charged in this suit is massive. Appellees allege that it has lasted for at least 30 years, involved almost 100 firms around the world, and affected international trade in several consumer electronic products. Appellants argue that litigation of the existence and operation of this conspiracy will produce an enormous amount of evidence for the jury to consider. They see further difficulties in the fact that the alleged conspiracy involved Japanese businessmen and that its operations included restraint of trade in Japanese markets. Appellants fear that a jury might not understand the evidence due to the difficulty of understanding business practices and market conditions in Japan. Appellees respond that proof of the conspiracy and its operations will be simple because the facts are well established in unambiguous documentation. . . .

Some parts of the case will require the jury to resolve a series of financial issues. Appellants have highlighted three such parts. First, for the Antidumping Act claims, the jury will have to decide whether the price of an article sold in the United States is "substantially less than the actual market value or wholesale price" in Japan and whether a defendant has maintained differential pricing "commonly and systematically." 15 U.S.C. § 72 (1976). This inquiry may be complicated by several influences on prices that might have to be factored out before comparing prices, such as currency fluctuations and different marketing techniques in the two countries. Second, appellees allege that the conspirators disguised their artificially low prices in the United States by a series of complicated rebate schemes. Appellants say that the jury will be able to test this allegation only by reviewing the circumstances surrounding thousands of separate transactions. Third, appellees intend to show injury by proving that they lowered their own prices in response to defendants' artificially low prices and that they lost sales to defendants. These allegations will require evidence of appellees' transactions and may raise issues regarding appellees' pricing policies and marketing techniques and the quality of appellees' products.

Appellants contend that litigation of these three parts of the case will produce an enormous mass of financial documentation for the jury to work through. They also contend that the jury will need the assistance of substantial amounts of expert testimony on accounting, marketing, and other technical matters. Appellees reject this prediction, arguing that all the relevant financial evidence can be submitted neatly in computer printouts with accompanying summaries. They do not foresee great problems in the jury's understanding of the evidence.

Finally, appellants argue that the complexity of the suit will be compounded by the presence of some issues that conceptually are very difficult. The claims under both the Antidumping Act and § 2 of the Sherman Act will require proof of predatory intent. On the § 2 claims and on Zenith's claims under § 7 of the Clayton Act, appellees will have to prove relevant product markets, relevant geographic markets, and market shares. Zenith's claims under the Robinson-Patman Act will raise issues of whether products sold to different customers are of a "like grade and quality" and whether any price differences are cost justified. 15 U.S.C.§ 13(a) (1976)....

III.

[The Third Circuit held that the antitrust statutes at issue did not guarantee plaintiffs a jury trial.]

IV. ...

Suits for treble damages under the antitrust and antidumping laws, as a class, are plainly legal in nature. They seek relief in a form traditionally associated with courts of law: compensatory and punitive damages caused by legal wrongs....

Appellants dispute none of the foregoing .... They argue that the seventh amendment does not guarantee a right to jury trial when any particular suit, because of its extraordinary complexity, is beyond the ability of the jury to decide.

For the sake of clarity, we should state our understanding of complexity in this context. A suit is too complex for a jury when circumstances render the jury unable to decide in a proper manner. The law presumes that a jury will find facts and reach a verdict by rational means. It does not contemplate scientific precision but does contemplate a resolution of each issue on the basis of a fair and reasonable assessment of the evidence and a fair and reasonable application of the relevant legal rules.... A suit might be excessively complex as a result of any set of circumstances which singly or in combination render a jury unable to decide in the foregoing rational manner....

The third prong of the [*Ross v. Bernhard*] test plainly recognizes the significance, for purposes of the seventh amendment, of the possibility that a suit may be too complex for a jury. Its inclusion in the three prong test strongly suggests that jury trial might not be guaranteed in extraordinarily complex cases ....

The district court made no use of the *Ross* footnote, finding it too brief to authorize a major departure from the traditional construction of the seventh amendment. We also find it unlikely that the Supreme Court would have announced an important new application of the seventh amendment in so cursory a fashion. Yet, at the very least, the Court has left open the possibility that the "practical abilities and limitations of juries" may limit the range of suits subject to the seventh amendment . . . . With this understanding of *Ross*, we shall consider the merits of appellants' arguments for a complexity exception.

V.

Appellants' first argument relies on historical analysis to advance the proposition that the fact of extraordinary complexity renders a suit equitable in nature. Although complexity is not commonly recognized as a defining feature of equity, appellants argue that by the time of the adoption of the seventh amendment the chancellor's jurisdiction had extended to any suit that he found too complex for a jury. . . .

Whether or not [the chancellor used such power] is a question that may interest historians; we need not decide it here. We note that appellants' only support for the authority of a chancellor to remove difficult issues from juries in suits at law is a single decision of dubious authority. With this meager support, we cannot conclude that complexity alone ever was an established basis of equitable jurisdiction. . . .

IBM [an amicus participant] has presented the court with a related historical argument. . . .

We understand the essential terms of this argument as follows. In England in 1791, the chancellor controlled the boundary between law and equity. He exercised this control with a measure of flexibility, removing suits from trial at common law when the procedures of law were inadequate to do justice in a particular case. . . . In essence, the argument is a deduction of the likely reaction of the English chancellor to a hypothetical complex suit filed in 1791. . . .

We choose not to pioneer in this use of history. If the developments since 1791 have so changed the character of a suit at law to make trial of particular suits to a jury unjust, then perhaps the historically recognized boundary between law and equity should not govern the extent of the seventh amendment right. If so, then deviations from this approach to the seventh amendment should be based on the current policies and present circumstances of the federal courts. We see no persuasive reason for incorporating into the seventh amendment the policies and probable actions of the English chancellor of 1791.

VI.

Both appellants and IBM offer a second constitutional argument. They contend that the due process clause of the fifth amendment prohibits trial by jury of a suit that is too complex for a jury. They further contend that this due process limitation prevails over the seventh amendment's preservation of the right to jury trial.

Although no specific precedent exists for finding a due process violation in the trial of any case to a jury, the principles that define the procedural requirements of due process would seem to impose some limitations on the range of cases that may be submitted to a jury. The primary value promoted by due process in factfinding procedures is "to minimize the risk of erroneous decisions." Greenholtz v. Inmates of the Nebraska Penal and Correctional Complex, 442 U.S. 1, 13 (1979). See also Mathews v. Eldridge, 424 U.S. 319, 335 (1976). A jury that cannot understand the evidence and the legal rules to be applied provides no reliable safeguard against erroneous decisions. Moreover, in the context of a completely adversary proceeding, like a civil trial, due process requires that "the decisionmaker's conclusion . . . rest solely on the legal rules and evidence adduced at the hearing." Goldberg v. Kelly, 397 U.S. 254, 271 (1970). Unless the jury can understand the legal rules and evidence, we cannot realistically expect that the jury will rest its decision on them.

As we have noted, the law presumes that a jury will decide rationally; it will resolve each disputed issue on the basis of a fair and reasonable assessment of the evidence and a fair and reasonable application of relevant legal rules. We conclude that due process precludes trial by jury when a jury is unable to perform this task with a reasonable understanding of the evidence and the legal rules.

If a particular lawsuit is so complex that a jury cannot satisfy this requirement of due process but is nonetheless an action at law, we face a conflict between the requirements of the fifth and seventh amendments. In this situation, we must balance the constitutionally protected interests, as they are implicated in this particular context, and reach the most reasonable accommodation between the two constitutional provisions. . . .

The due process objections to jury trial of a complex case implicate values of fundamental importance. If judicial decisions are not based on factual determinations bearing some reliable degree of accuracy, legal remedies will not be applied consistently with the purposes of the laws. There is a danger that jury verdicts will be erratic and completely unpredictable, which would be inconsistent with evenhanded justice. Finally, unless the jury can understand the evidence and the legal rules sufficiently to rest its decision on them, the objective of most rules of evidence and procedure in promoting a fair trial will be lost entirely. We believe that when a jury is unable to perform its decisionmaking task with a reasonable understanding of the evidence and legal rules, it undermines the ability of a district court to render basic justice.

The loss of the right to jury trial in a suit found too complex for a jury does not implicate the same fundamental concerns. The absence of a jury trial requirement in equitable and maritime actions indicates that federal courts can provide fair trials and can grant relief in accordance with the basic justice without the aid of a jury. Moreover, the Supreme Court has consistently refused to rule that preservation of civil jury trial is an essential element of ordered liberty required of the states by the due process clause of the fourteenth amendment....

The district court asserted that the due process argument fails to account for the special benefits that juries bring to civil litigation. Because the jury is a representative of the community and can call upon the community's wisdom and values, the legal system has relied on it to perform two important functions. The first is "black box" decisionmaking. The jury issues a verdict without an opinion to explain or justify its decision. This feature allows juries to perform a type of "jury equity," modifying harsh results of law to conform to community values in cases where a judge would have to apply the law rigidly. The second function is to accord a greater measure of legitimacy to decisions that depend upon determinations of degree rather than of absolutes, such as whether particular conduct constitutes negligence. Certain decisions of this "line drawing" nature seem less arbitrary when made by a representative body like the jury.

In the context of a lawsuit of the complexity that we have posited, however, these features do not produce real benefits of substantial value.... [W]hen the jury is unable to determine the normal application of the law to the facts of a case and reaches a verdict on the basis of nothing more than its own determination of community wisdom and values, its operation is indistinguishable from arbitrary and unprincipled decisionmaking. Similarly, the "line drawing" function is difficult to justify when the jury cannot understand the evidence or legal rules relevant to the issue of where to draw a line.

The district court also noted that preservation of the right to jury trial is important because the jury "provides a needed check on judicial power." ... A jury unable to understand the evidence and legal rules is hardly a reliable and effective check on judicial power. Our liberties are more secure when judicial decisionmakers proceed rationally, consistently with the law, and on the basis of evidence produced at trial. If the jury is unable to function in this manner, it has the capacity of becoming itself a tool of arbitrary and erratic judicial power.

Therefore, we find the most reasonable accommodation between the requirements of the fifth and seventh amendments to be a denial of jury trial when a jury will not be able to perform its task of rational decisionmaking with a reasonable understanding of the evidence and the relevant legal standards. In lawsuits of this complexity, the interests protected by this procedural rule of due process carry greater weight than the interests served by the constitutional guarantee of jury trial. Consequently, we shall not read the seventh amendment to guarantee the right to jury trial in these suits.

VII.

The district court devoted most of its discussions of appellants' due process argument not to factors relevant to the balancing of interests set out in the foregoing section but to a number of practical objections to the argument. We shall consider those objections in this section.

First, the district court challenged the premise that a case could exceed a jury's ability to decide rationally[5] and asserted that a jury was at least as able as a judge, the only alternative factfinder, to decide complex cases. The court noted that a jury possesses the wisdom, experience, and common sense of twelve persons. It has a greater effect than a judge in disciplining attorneys to present their cases clearly and concisely. Furthermore, its capabilities can be enhanced by special trial techniques like the preliminary charge and interim charges on the law contemplated by the district court in this case. . . . On the basis of these observations, the court concluded that a jury "is brighter, more astute, and more perceptive than a single judge, even in a complex or technical case; at least it is not less so."

Any assessment of a jury's ability to decide complex cases should include consideration not only of a jury's particular strengths and the possible enhancement of its capabilities but also of the particular constraints that operate on a jury in complex cases. The long time periods required for most complex cases are especially disabling for a jury. A long trial can interrupt the career and personal life of a jury member and thereby strain his commitment to the jury's task. The prospect of a long trial can also weed out many veniremen whose professional background qualifies them for deciding a complex case but also prohibits them from lengthy jury service. . . . Furthermore, a jury is likely to be unfamiliar with both the technical subject matter of a complex case and the process of civil litigation. The probability is not remote that a jury will become overwhelmed and confused by a mass of evidence and issues and will reach erroneous decisions. The reality of these difficulties that juries encounter in complex cases is underscored by the experience of some federal district judges who have found particular suits to have exceeded the practical abilities of a jury. . . .

Given that a jury has both particular strengths and weaknesses in deciding complex cases, we cannot conclude *a priori* that a jury is capable of deciding a suit of any degree of complexity. A litigant might prove that a particular suit is too complex for a jury. Because of the important due process rights implicated, a litigant should have the opportunity to make that showing.

A general presumption that a judge is capable of deciding an extraordinary complex case, by contrast, is reasonable. A long trial would not greatly disrupt the professional and personal life of a judge and should not be significantly disabling. In fact, the judge's greater ability to allocate time to the task of deciding a complex case can be a major advantage in surmounting the difficulties posed by the suit. Although we cannot presume that a judge will be more intelligent than a jury or more familiar with technical subject matters, a judge will almost surely have substantial familiarity with the process of civil litigation, as a result of experience on the bench or in practice. This experience can enable him to digest a large amount of evidence and legal argumentation, segregate distinct issues and the portions of evidence relevant to each issue, assess the opinions of expert

---

5. The Ninth Circuit rejected a due process argument with a similar expression of doubt. In re U.S. Financial Securities Litigation, 609 F.2d 411, 427-31 (9th Cir. 1979), cert. denied sub nom., Gant v. Union Bank, 446 U.S. 929 (1980).

witnesses, and apply highly complex legal standards of the facts of the case. The judge's experience also can enable him to make better use of special trial techniques designed to help the factfinder in complex cases, like colloquies with expert witnesses. The requirement that a judge issue findings of fact and conclusions of law offsets the substantial tendency to overlook issues in order that a verdict might be reached in these difficult cases. Fed. R. Civ. P. 52(a). Finally, if after trial and during deliberation a judge finds himself confused on certain matters or unable to decide certain issues, he can reopen the trial for the purpose of obtaining clarification or additional evidence. Fed. R. Civ. P. 59(a).

A judge's abilities are, of course, not unbounded. It is conceivable that a case might be so complex that a judge could not decide it rationally and competently. However, the possibility of such a case cannot justify trial by jury, because the presence of a jury does not relieve the judge of the need to understand the issues disputed in a case and the relevance and strength of the evidence. . . .

The lawsuit that exceeds the ability of a judge to decide rationally and competently would challenge the basic capacity of our system of civil litigation to decide lawsuits by any means. It would call for adjustments far more fundamental than an allocation of issues between judge and jury. Prudence compels us to defer consideration of these adjustments until we face a real possibility of such a lawsuit. In the meantime, the best course to follow is to presume the judge's ability to decide a complex case and to focus inquiry on the jury's ability.

Finally, the district court feared that the authority to strike jury trial demands on case-by-case determinations of complexity would lead to the long-run dilution of the right to jury trial. This fear results in part from the seemingly broad discretion that district court judges will exercise when determining whether a jury is capable of deciding a case and in part from the difficulty that courts will have in applying the due process standard.

We do not believe that a due process limitation allows the district courts a substantial amount of discretion to deny jury trials. Because preservation of the right to jury trial remains a constitutionally protected interest, denials of jury trial on grounds of complexity should be confined to suits in which due process clearly requires a nonjury trial. This implies a high standard. It is not enough that trial to the court would be preferable. The complexity of a suit must be so great that it renders the suit beyond of the ability of a jury to decide by rational means with a reasonable understanding of the evidence and applicable legal rules. Moreover, the district court should not deny a jury trial if by serverance of multiple claims, thoughtful use of the procedures suggested in the Manual for Complex Litigation, or other methods the court can enchance a jury's capabilities or can reduce the complexity of a suit sufficiently to bring it within the ability of a jury to decide. Due process should allow denials of jury trials only in exceptional cases. . . .

■ GIBBONS, Circuit Judge, dissenting. First, I agree that this case is complex. Three objective manifestations of complexity are present: the predicted length of trial; the multiplicity of factual issues which may have to be resolved; and the conceptual difficulty of the governing law. However, all three manifestations of complexity are for the most part products of the liberal joinder rules of the Federal Rules of Civil Procedure and of the district court's ruling consolidating two multi-count cases for trial. Neither the liberal joinder rules nor the rule permitting consolidation for trial are required by any provision of the Constitution. The seventh amendment guarantees a jury trial of any separate claim for relief which would have been tried to a jury at common law. It does not guarantee that a single jury will decide multiple separate claims. If by virtue of joinder and consolidation a case becomes too complex for a single jury to handle, the remedy mandated by the seventh amendment is separate juries, as at common law. Thus we should not even consider the constitutional issue which the majority undertakes to decide in the form in which it has been presented here, because we are considering not the actual constitutional issue, but a hypothetical construction of a series of procedural rulings.

I have, however, a more serious disagreement with the majority.... The majority opinion attempts to objectify the factors that bear upon complexity, but in the end the factors which are identified will permit the exercise of trial court discretion. I fear that the exercise of that discretion will sometimes be influenced by unarticulated sympathies for or hostilities toward the underlying policies sought to be advanced in the lawsuit....

Part of my difficulty with the majority's position probably results from a perception of the nature of the judicial process and the role of juries in that process. It is often said that the judicial process involves the search for objective truth. We have no real assurance, however, of objective truth whether the trial is to the court or to a jury. The judicial process can do no more than legitimize the imposition of sanctions by requiring that some minimum standards of fair play, which we call due process, are adhered to. In this legitimizing process, the seventh amendment is not a useless appendage to the Bill of Rights, but an important resource in maintaining the authority of the rule of law. In the process of gaining public acceptance for the imposition of sanctions, the role of the jury is highly significant. The jury is a sort of ad hoc parliament convened from the citizenry at large to lend respectability and authority to the process. Judges are often prone to believe that they, alone, can bear the full weight of this legitimizing function. I doubt that they can. Any erosion of citizen participation in the sanctioning system is in the long run likely, in my view, to result in a reduction in the moral authority that supports the process.

ILC PERIPHERALS LEASING CORP. v. INTERNATIONAL BUSINESS MACHINE CORP.

Record 19, 490-91, reprinted in Note, The Right to a Jury Trial in Complex Civil Litigation, 92 Harv. L. Rev. 898, 908 n.60 (1979)

[The following exchange between the trial judge and the jurors came at the end of a lengthy antitrust case:]

The Court: ... Do you know what demand substitutability is, [Juror A]?

Juror [A]: Well, I would like to kind of look into that.

The Court: Okay. And how about the barriers to entry, [Juror B]?

Juror [B]: I would have to read about it. . . .

The Court: And [Juror D], what is software?

Juror [D]: It's software.

The Court: Well, what is software?

Juror [D]: That's the paper software.

The Court: What's the hardware?

Juror [D]: That's the wires and hardware.

The Court: And what is — do you know what an interface is?

Juror [D]: Yes.

The Court: What's that?

Juror [D]: The interface is the — I am not good in English, your honor.

The Court: No, that's all right.

Juror [D]: But it's the interface, you know.

The Court: Can you give me an example of that?

Juror [D]: Well, if you take a blivet, turn it off one thing and drop it down, it's an interface change; right?

Notes and Questions

1. *There you have it. Boise Cascade, Japanese Electronic,* and *ILC,* 458 F. Supp. 423, 444-49 (N.D. Cal. 1980) (granting motion for directed verdict; in dicta striking jury trial in the event of remand), are three of the six federal decisions that have struck a jury trial demand because of the complexity of the case. The others are Bernstein v. Universal Pictures, 79 F.R.D. 59 (S.D.N.Y. 1978); In re United States Financial Securities Litigation, 75 F.R.D. 702 (S.D. Cal. 1977); and an unreported decision in Cotten v. Witco Chemical Corp., (E.D. La.). Of this lot, *Cotten* and *U.S. Financial* were reversed on appeal, and *ILC* was affirmed on other grounds. Cotten v. Witco Chemical Corp., 651 F.2d 274 (5th Cir. 1981); In re U.S. Financial Securities Litigation, 609 F.2d 411 (9th Cir. 1979), cert. denied, 446 U.S. 929 (1980); Memorex Corp. v. IBM, 636 F.2d 1188 (9th Cir. 1980), cert. denied, 452 U.S. 972 (1981). Moreover, since *ILC* and *Boise Cascade* predated *U.S. Financial,* they should not be regarded as good law within their own circuit. Aligned against the two remaining "survivors" (*Bernstein* and *Japanese Electronic*) are a host of cases, federal and state, that have either declined to recognize a complexity exception to the right to jury trial, or else found that the case was not complex enough. See, *e.g.,* Soderbeck v. Burnett County, 752 F.2d 285 (7th Cir.), cert. denied, 471 U.S. 1117 (1985); SRI, Int'l v. Matsushita Elec. Corp., 775 F.2d 1107 (Fed. Cir. 1985); Pinemont Bank v. Belk, 722 F.2d 232 (5th Cir. 1984); City of New York v. Pullman, Inc., 662 F.2d 910 (2d Cir. 1981), cert. denied, 454 U.S. 1164 (1982); Brisk v. City of Miami Beach, 726 F. Supp. 1305 (S.D. Fla. 1989); Kian v. Mirro Aluminum Co., 88 F.R.D. 351 (E.D. Mich. 1980); Davis-Watkins Co. v. Service Merchandise Co., 500 F. Supp. 1244 (M.D. Tenn. 1980), affirmed on other grounds, 686 F.2d 1190 (6th Cir. 1982); Kenny v.

Scientific, Inc., 512 A.2d 1142 (N.J. Super. Ct., Law Div.) (striking jury demand), reversed, 517 A.2d 484 (N.J. 1986) (reinstating jury demand); S.P.C.S., Inc. v. Lockheed Shipbuilding & Construction Co., 631 P.2d 999 (Wash. Ct. App. 1981). Cf. Loral Corp. v. McDonnell Douglas Corp., 558 F.2d 1130 (2d Cir. 1977) (affirming striking of jury trial demand when case would have exposed jury to classified information and parties arguably waived right to jury trial in contract).

2. The idea of a "complexity" exception to jury trial reached its high water mark in the late 1970's and early 1980's. One of the reasons that it may no longer be a "hot" issue is the Supreme Court's subsequent handling of *Ross*'s "practical abilities and limitations" factor. Dicta in Granfinanciera, S.A. v. Nordberg, 492 U.S. 33, 42 n.4 (1989), limited this third factor to cases in which "Congress has permissibly entrusted the resolution of certain disputes to an administrative agency or specialized court of equity, and . . . jury trials would impair the functioning of the legislative scheme." This dicta was re-affirmed in more dicta in Chauffeurs, Teamsters and Helpers Local No. 391 v. Terry, 494 U.S. 558, 575 n.2 (1990). Obviously this narrow reading of *Ross*'s third factor is a strong signal that there is no complexity exception in the Seventh Amendment, at least until Congress creates a specialized court of equity.

Nonetheless, the Court has never squarely refuted the existence of a Seventh Amendment complexity exception, nor has the Court disowned the dicta in *Dairy Queen* concerning the lack of jury trial in "complicated" cases. See *Terry*, 494 U.S. at 583 (Stevens, J., concurring) (determining if issue was triable to jury in part by asking whether facts "are typical grist for the jury's judgment"). Markman v. Westview Instruments, Inc., 517 U.S. 370 (1996) (see pp. 1217-18, *supra*) may again fan the flames of the argument. Of particular note was *Markman*'s statement that "the relative interpretive skills of judges and juries and the statutory policies that ought to be furthered by the allocation" helped to determine whether a factual issue was jury-triable. 517 U.S. at 384. Moreover, because the issue of patent interpretation in *Markman* did not exist in 1791 and prior precedents provided no clear answer, the Court turned to "functional considerations [that] also play their part in the choice between judge and jury":

> The construction of written instruments is one of those things that judges often do and are likely to do better than jurors untrained in exegesis. . . . "The judge, from training and discipline, is more likely to give a proper interpretation to such instruments than a jury; and he is, therefore, more likely to be right, in performing such a duty, than a jury can be expected to be." . . . [A] jury's capabilities to evaluate demeanor . . . or to reflect community standards . . . are much less significant than a trained ability to evaluate the testimony in relation to the overall structure of a patent. [517 U.S. at 388-90.]

Finally, the Court held that the important policy "of uniformity in the treatment of a given patent [was] an independent reason to allocate all issues of construction to the court." Id. at 390.

It is too early to know whether *Markman* will revitalize the debate over a "complexity" exception to the Seventh Amendment. Cf. Warner-Jenkins Co. v. Hilton Davis Chemical Co., 520 U.S. 17 (1997) (indicating in dicta that application of patent doctrine of equivalents was jury issue despite concerns for jury's competence). But its focus on the functional capabilities of judges and juries breathes life into the third factor of *Ross* v. *Bernhard*, albeit in the new context of deciding which factual issues within a legal claim should be tried to a jury. So does *Markman*'s concern for uniform treatment. Might *Markman* ultimately create indirectly (through the device of assigning to judges the difficult factual issues within legal claims) the "complexity" exception that *Granfinaciera* seems to preclude directly?

3. Even if the Seventh Amendment and comparable state provisions do not recognize a complexity exception, the matter of due process remains. The due process clauses of the Fifth and Fourteenth Amendments do not mention rational adjudication. The Seventh Amendment, by contrast, is quite specific on the issue of jury trial. How can it reasonably be thought that the former supersedes the latter? See *SRI*, 775 F.2d 1107 (no due process trump); *U.S. Financial*, 609 F.2d 411 (same). One argument is that the trump is implicit in modern procedure. For instance, jury control devices — such as the power to order judgment as a matter of law and summary judgment — can be justified on the ground that the notion of rational decisionmaking inherent in due process overrides the jury trial guarantee of the Seventh Amendment. See Paul D. Carrington, *The Seventh Amendment: Some Bicentennial Reflections*, 1990 U. Chi. L.F. 33, 44-47. Viewed in this light, the due process obligation to strike juries in complex cases is not an extraordinary power, but rather the logical endpoint of the court's long-standing responsibility to supervise the work of juries. Moreover, since the due process clause, unlike the Seventh Amendment, applies to states, both state and federal judges must exercise this responsibility.

Remember, though, that jury trial is thought to advance not only the goal of rational and accurate adjudication; it also advances the political objectives of American democracy. From this perspective, it isn't so easy to sacrifice the voice of average citizens to our desire for rational adjudication, is it? Is it a particular problem that a due process limit to jury trial entrusts to a judge the decision about whether to allow common citizens to participate?

4. Would the decisions in *Boise Cascade* and *Japanese Electronic* have been necessary if the cases of multiple plaintiffs and defendants had not been consolidated? Rather than asking whether the due process clause trumps the Seventh Amendment, shouldn't the question be why the Federal Rules of Civil Procedure and other joinder devices trump the Seventh Amendment? Recall that *Beacon Theatres* said that "only under the most imperative circumstances, circumstances which in view of the flexible procedures of the Federal Rules we cannot now anticipate, can the right to a jury trial of legal issues be lost"? Has the flexibility of the joinder rules actually created that which *Beacon Theatres* thought unimaginable? Or must the flexibility of the Federal Rules be employed to preclude the joinder of related cases that create jury-endangering complexity? How do we resolve the dilemma created when joinder is needed to protect the ability to apply reasoned judgment to the claims of like claimants, but that very joinder makes it impossible for a jury to apply reasoned judgment?. Is the only way out of this box to substitute for the jury a factfinder who can use reasoned judgment? Is a legislative or administrative solution a better answer?

5. After remand in *Japanese Electronic*, the district court entered summary judgment for the defendants. The Supreme Court upheld that judgment in Matsushita Electric Industrial Co. v. Zenith Radio Corp., 475 U.S. 574 (1986) (see p. 1050, *supra*.) Would the Supreme Court have tolerated such an expeditious end to the case if the factfinder were a jury? Does *Matsushita*'s outcome argue for or against the power to strike juries in complex cases?

6. Until now, we have been assuming that the basic premise of *Boise Cascade* and *Japanese Electronic* is true: that some cases are so complicated that a jury cannot adjudicate them. Do you agree with this premise? Judge Sharp

did, using essentially the following line of thinking: (a) The trial is expected to take several months; (b) As a result, the type of people who have had the business experience to understand the issues at trial will be unable to serve on the jury; (c) Business experience is the experience that matters; (d) The lawyers will be unable to educate the people who will be able to serve on the jury; therefore, (e) Any jury that could be empaneled would simply be unable to comprehend the issues and facts of the case and render a rational verdict; and, finally, (f) The judge can comprehend the issues and the facts and render a rational judgment. The Third Circuit focused particularly on the fifth assumption, without getting very specific about exactly what might cause a jury to be unable to reach an acceptable verdict. Let us now examine these assumptions in more detail:

(a) *That the trial will last a long time.* Could Judge Sharp and the Third Circuit have developed pretrial strategies that greatly reduced the disputed issues and facts? Could they have developed trial strategies to shorten trial (such as splitting the trial into shorter segments, limiting the amount of time each side had to present its case, limiting the number of witnesses, or requiring the parties to present summaries of less important matters)? Or would such devices eviscerate the very essence of jury trial?

(b) *That a jury with the requisite business experiences could not be empaneled.* Do you accept Judge Sharp's statement that business persons had a valid reason to be excluded from a lengthy trial? Although jury service is an obligation of citizenship, judges often excuse potential jurors with significant business commitments. As a result, a recent study found that "[j]urors selected for service in lengthy trials [*i.e.*, more than twenty trial days] are more likely to be unemployed or retired, as well as unmarried. . . . Jurors in lengthy trials are also less likely to have a college education, . . . [and] jurors in lengthy trials are more likely to be women. These differences, although statistically significant, are relatively small in magnitude." Joe S. Cecil et al., Jury Service in Lengthy Civil Trials 1 (1987). Granting that some cases of extreme hardship might exist, should federal judges generally be unwilling to grant excuses from jury duty?

Such a solution would not, on its own, be enough. Lawyers frequently seek to strike (whether for cause or peremptorily) people with general backgrounds in the relevant field. See Note, *The Right to an Incompetent Jury: Protracted Commercial Litigation and the Seventh Amendment*, 10 Conn. L. Rev. 775 (1978). Should a judge deny lawyers the opportunity to strike qualified jurors? Or would this solution unduly impinge on the parties' adversarial rights?

(c) *That the lawyers will be unable to educate a jury about the relevant business practices.* Assuming that non-business people comprise the jury panel, is it true that they will be unable to comprehend the issues at stake in the case? Could the judge bring in neutral experts to teach the jury the basics of accounting and business practices? Cf. Laurens Walker & John Monahan, *Social Frameworks: A New Use of Science in Law*, 73 Va. L. Rev. 559 (1987) (discussing experts who educate jury about social milieu surrounding conduct at issue); Neil J. Vidmar & Regina A. Schuller, *Juries and Expert Evidence: Social Framework Testimony*, 52 Law & Contemp. Prob. 133 (Autumn 1989) (same). Couldn't the parties do the same thing? Is the lack of comprehension which Judge Sharp observed in prior business trials the failing of jurors, or of lawyers who were too incompetent to teach the jury what it needed to know? See Saul M. Kassin & Lawrence S. Wrightsman, The American Jury on Trial 127 (1988) ("I have never tried a complex case . . . all cases are reducible to the simplest of stories. . . . The problem is that we, as lawyers, have forgotten how to speak to ordinary folks.") (quoting Gerry Spence).

(d) *That business experience is the type of experience which matters.* Neglected in Judge Sharp's opinion are the important values that jury trial fosters. Is not the opinion of a homemaker about the dealings of a business enterprise as valuable as the schooled judgment of an accountant? See generally John Guinther, The Jury in America (1988).

(e) *That the jury cannot rationally adjudicate the facts.* Here we come to the linchpin of the argument for a complexity exception. The common lore is that juries are easily manipulated and often irrational. Glanville Williams is claimed to have said: "It is an understatement to describe a jury... as a group of twelve men of average ignorance." Valerie P. Hans and Neil Vidmar, Judging the Jury 114 (1986). When the trial is lengthy and the evidence complex, such pessimism about the jury's ability multiplies. On the other side, however, there are passionately committed proponents of jury trial who find civil juries a "sacred right of the common law" or a "palladium of liberty." 2 J. Kendall Few, Trial by Jury 466 (1993); Lloyd E. Moore, The Jury iii (2d ed. 1988).

Until quite recently, there was little empirical research to support or refute these anecdotes; the only, and often quoted, statistic was that of Kalven and Zeisel, who claimed that judges agreed with civil jury verdicts in about 78% of all cases. Harry Kalven, Jr. & Hans Zeisel, The American Jury 63-65 (1966). Such a statistic, of course, says only that judges and juries are equally rational (or irrational) in most cases; and unequally rational (or irrational) in the rest.

The last dozen years, however, has seen an upswing in empirical data on juries. Much of the data involves criminal rather than civil juries, and much of the civil data does not involve the comprehension problems of complex cases. See, *e.g.*, Larry Heuer & Steven Penrod, *Trial Complexity*, 18 Law and Human Behavior 29 (1994); Robert MacCoun, *Inside the Black Box: What Empirical Research Tells Us about Decisionmaking by Civil Juries*, in Verdict 137 (Robert E. Litan ed. 1993); Richard Lempert, *Civil Juries and Complex Cases: Taking Stock after Twelve Years*, in Verdict, *supra*, at 181; Michael S. Jacobs, *Testing the Assumptions Underlying the Debate about Scientific Evidence: A Closer Look at Juror "Incompetence" and Scientific "Objectivity,"* 25 Conn. L. Rev. 1083 (1993); Valerie P. Hans & William S. Lofquist, *Jurors' Judgments of Business Liability in Tort Cases: Implications for the Litigation Explosion Debate*, 26 Law & Society Rev. 85 (1992); Jane Goodman, *Jurors' Comprehension and Assessment of Probabilistic Evidence*, 16 Am. J. Trial Advocacy 361 (1992); Alan Reifman et al., *Real Jurors' Understanding of the Law in Real Cases*, 16 Law & Hum. Behav. 539 (1992) (analyzing criminal cases); Symposium, *Is the Jury Competent?*, 52 Law & Contemp. Prob. 1 (Autumn 1989); Inside the Jury (Reid Hastie ed. 1993); Hans & Vidmar, *supra*; Michael J. Saks, Small Group Decision Making and Complex Information Tasks (1981); Michael J. Saks, Jury Verdicts (1977); see also Walter F. Abbott et al., Jury Research (1993) (bibliography of approximately 1400 articles, many of which involve empirical studies).

Even if much of it was obtained in cases that were not complex or complicated, some of the data's findings are interesting to ponder:

- Twelve heads often are better than one in terms of decision making. The group decision, however, is usually worse than the decision to which the most competent member of the group would have come.

- It is not necessary that every member of a jury understand every point. As long as two or three members of a jury understand a matter, the deliberations of the entire group are advanced.

- Decision making tasks are better performed by individuals when the task does not lend itself to a division of labor, if organizational problems overwhelm the group, or if low performance standards are set.

- The decision making performance of groups is considerably less efficient than that of individuals, even if it is better.

- Juries are influenced by such extra-adjudicatory factors as the identity, age, wealth, and status of the parties, as well as by evidence that they have been asked to disregard, but the strength of the evidence at trial is a major — and perhaps the most important — determinant of the verdict.

- There is present disagreement among psychologists about how (and how well) a person or group understands evidence, makes inferences, and arrives at an ultimate decision. The emerging leader, however, is the "story model," which postulates that jurors seek to understand the evidence and reach a judgment by imposing a narrative story organization on trial information and choosing the verdict that best fits the story.

- Present research, which is sketchy, suggests that juries hold individuals and corporations to different standards, but they show considerable restraint in judging corporate accountability.

- Juries may fail to comprehend adequately as many as half of the judge's instructions regarding the law.

Some findings with particular relevance to complex litigation include:

- The length of trial does not seem to affect adversely a jury's ability to recall evidence or deliberate accurately about the facts.

- The joinder of parties does not lead to confusion, although the aggregation of plaintiffs may lead juries to find for plaintiffs more frequently.

- A great challenge for juries is understanding technical, scientific, or statistical evidence. The adversarial presentation of such evidence, usually through experts, often does little to clarify matters, and can lead to a jury's disregard of the testimony on both sides. On the other hand, some research suggests that jurors assimilate expert evidence fairly well, and are appropriately critical of difficult evidence — at least when the other side does not introduce opposing expert evidence that obfuscates the issues. Moreover, in comparison to judge-tried cases, lawyers in jury-tried cases work harder to make difficult concepts understandable.

- Juries in complex cases usually reach defensible decisions, and judges are typically satisfied with their performance. The level of judge-jury agreement in one study of complex civil cases was 63%, somewhat lower than Kalven and Zeisel's 78%. The authors noted that most of the 15% difference occurred when judges would have found for the plaintiff but the jury found for the defendant; and further noted that neither the complexity of the trial nor the trial procedures used to address complexity was significantly related to the level of judge-jury agreement.

Several of these studies found that certain techniques improved jury comprehension and decision making, thus making even less tenable the claim that juries cannot rationally decide complex cases. We will consider some of those techniques in the next chapter.

(f) *That judges are capable of rational adjudication even when juries are not.* This, of course, is the critical last assumption. Judge Sharp and the majority in *Japanese Electronic* assume that judges possess certain institutional advantages that will permit rational deliberation even when juries cannot so deliberate. Obviously, if the problem is difficulty in comprehending legal issues and jury instructions, the use of a judge overcomes the problem. But with regard to the other causes of trial complexity — length of trial and difficulty in comprehending evidence — the available research does not suggest that the substitution of a judge for a jury will improve rational decisionmaking. The length of trial does not seem to affect the quality of a jury's deliberation. Moreover, the presence of six (or twelve) jurors decreases the likelihood that important information will be neglected, a serious risk when only one person acts as adjudicator. Finally, judge-tried complex cases tend to take longer to try than jury-tried cases. Judges end up being bombarded with additional information, thus increasing the chances that vital evidence will be overlooked.

Similarly, no empirical evidence of which we are aware suggests that judges have less difficulty with complicated evidence than juries. Judges often seem to make the same mistakes, and share the same misconceptions, regarding statistical and other technical evidence. Compare William C. Thompson, *Are Juries Competent to Evaluate Statistical Evidence?*, 52 Law & Contemp. Prob. 9 (Autumn 1989) (juries tend to undervalue statistical evidence) and David L. Faigman & A.J. Baglioni, Jr., *Bayes' Theorem in the Trial Process: Instructing Jurors on the Value of Statistical Evidence*, 12 Law & Hum. Behav. 1 (1988) (same) with Gary Wells, *Naked Statistical Evidence of Liability: Is Subjective Probability Enough?*, 62 J. Personality and Soc. Psych. 739 (1992) (judges demonstrate same fallacious statistical reasoning as juries) and Lempert, *supra*, at 215-217 (anecdotal evidence and inferences from data suggest that judges have equal difficulty assessing difficult scientific evidence). Second, a judge does not possess the diverse background of a jury, so there is reason to doubt that the judge's one head will outperform the jury's six (or twelve) heads with any regularity, even in complex cases. See Robert MacCoun, Improving Jury Comprehension in Criminal and Civil Trials 3 (1995); Lempert, *supra*, at 217-19; Phoebe C. Ellsworth, *Are Twelve Heads Better Than One?*, 52 Law & Contemp. Prob. 205 (Autumn 1989); Saks, *Small Group Decision Making, supra.*

Finally, recall a primary concern of case management: that the managerial judge will form premature opinions regarding certain claims, evidence, and parties. A partial check against this bias is to assure that another entity makes factfinding decisions at trial. Therefore, to the extent that case management is a necessary incident of complex litigation, there is good reason to prefer that the jury find the facts. See Lempert, *supra*, at 219 ("If it is difficult to choose between bench and jury trials when rational factfinding is taken as a due-process requisite, it seems easier when the right to an impartial decisionmaker or the right to meaningful trial are the values that due process protects.")

7. On further reflection, were Judge Sharp and the Third Circuit correct in holding that the cases were beyond the ability of the jury? Is the real message of these opinions that the court did not find the right to jury trial worth the inconvenience of designing pretrial and trial techniques that would preserve the role of the jury?

8. Despite the paucity of case law, the potential conflict between complex litigation and the right to a jury trial has generated a flood of academic discussion. The most notable contribution is a debate between Lord Devlin and Professor Arnold concerning the use of juries in "complex" cases in 18th century Britain and post-revolutionary America. Patrick Devlin, *Jury Trial of Complex Cases: English Practice at the Time of the Seventh Amendment*, 80 Colum. L. Rev. 43 (1980); Morris S. Arnold, *A Historical Inquiry into the Right to Trial by Jury in Complex Litigation*, 128 U. Pa. L. Rev. 829 (1980); see James S. Campbell and Nicholas Le Poidevin, *Complex Cases and Jury Trials: A Reply to Professor Arnold*, 128 U. Pa. L. Rev. 965 (1980). For a sampling of other articles, see Franklin Stier, *Making Jury Trials More Truthful*, 30 U.C. Davis L. Rev. 85 (1996); Richard O. Lempert, *Civil Juries and Complex Cases: Let's Not Rush to Judgment*, 80 Mich. L. Rev. 68 (1981); Comment, *Complex Civil Litigation and the Seventh Amendment Right to a Jury Trial*, 51 U. Chi. L. Rev. 581 (1984); Note, *Preserving the Right to Jury Trial in Complex Civil Cases*, 32 Stan. L. Rev. 99 (1979); Note, *The Right to a Jury Trial in Complex Civil Litigation*, 92 Harv. L. Rev. 898 (1979); *Developments in the Law — The Civil Jury*, 110 Harv. L. Rev. 1408 (1997).

9. While the existence and utility of a "complexity" exception to jury trial may be debatable as both a legal and an empirical matter, the complexity of a case may still be a decisive factor when a trial judge has a discretionary power to grant a jury trial. The typical instance for exercise of this power occurs when the parties fail to file a jury trial demand within the time limits stated in F.R.Civ.P. 38. Under the terms of Rule 38(d), the parties are deemed to have waived their right to jury trial. The judge, however, still retains the discretion under Rule 39(b) to permit a jury trial. In Rutledge v. Electric Hose & Rubber Co., 511 F.2d 668 (9th Cir. 1975), an antitrust plaintiff failed to file an appropriate jury trial demand, and the trial judge refused to grant an untimely motion for jury trial. The Ninth Circuit held that the denial of a jury trial was not an abuse of discretion, in part because the plaintiff did not show "a good faith desire for jury trial," in part because the judge was "facing an avowed highly complex and prolonged trial involving great expense and months of judicial time," and in part because of "the public interest generally." 511 F.2d at 675.

NOTE ON THE SPECIAL JURY

One option that would preserve the right to jury trial while still ensuring jury competence would be trial before a group of expert factfinders. For instance, in *Boise Cascade* a jury of accountants and other business persons would possess the requisite expertise; trial to such a jury would presumably be relatively short and free of obfuscation; and Seventh Amendment concerns about striking the jury would be avoided. Great solution, right?

Such a jury is usually called a "special jury," a "blue ribbon jury," or a "struck jury," and it has a long lineage in Anglo-American history. In 1351 there is a report of a special jury comprised of cooks and fishmongers trying a person accused of selling bad food. Special juries of merchants were often used in mercantile disputes. In 1730 Parliament declared every litigant's entitlement, whether in civil or criminal cases, to a special jury upon motion and a willingness to pay the jury's expenses. See James B. Thayer, *The Jury and Its Development (Part II)*, 5 Harv. L. Rev. 295, 300-02 (1892). Lord Mansfield, Chief Justice of the King's Bench from 1756 to 1788, frequently used special juries, especially in commercial contexts. See Note, *The Case for Special Juries in Complex Cases*, 89 Yale L.J. 1155, 1164-65 (1980). Blackstone's view was that special juries were available "when the causes were of too great nicety for the discussion of ordinary freeholders; or where the sheriff [who was ordinarily responsible for the selection of jurymen] was suspected of partiality." 3 William Blackstone, Commentaries *357. Professor Thayer's assessment was that, "as among eligible persons, there seems always to have existed the power of selecting those especially qualified for a given service." Thayer, *supra*, at 300.

Special juries have been employed with varying degrees of frequency in American states. See Jeannette E. Thatcher, *Why Not Use the Special Jury?*, 31 Minn. L. Rev. 232, 251 (1947) (listing sixteen states that passed special jury statutes, and two that used special juries without legislative authorization). The Supreme Court has declared the special jury constitutional, albeit in criminal cases. See Moore v. New York, 333 U.S. 565 (1948); Fay v. New York, 332 U.S. 261 (1947). For our purposes, Delaware has the most interesting special jury statute. Originally modeled on the 1730 Act of Parliament, the statute authorized either party to request a special jury. The clerk of the court then assembled a list of forty-eight "indifferent and judicious citizens, qualified to serve as jurors," from which twelve jurors were selected through a series of strikes both peremptory and for cause. 10 Del.C. §§ 4541-43 (1974). In 1987, however, the Delaware General Assembly eliminated the automatic right of the parties to request a special jury, and substituted the following section:

> The court may order a special jury upon the application of any party in a complex civil case. The party applying for a special jury shall pay the expense incurred by having a special jury, which may be allowed as part of the costs of the case.

10 Del.C. § 4506 (1987). The new statute never defines "complex civil case" and therefore gives discretion to judges to determine when a special jury would be appropriate. See In re Asbestos Litigation, 551 A.2d 1296 (Del. Super. 1988) (upholding statute against constitutional challenge).

As a statutory matter, it seems unlikely that federal judges possess a similar power to constitute a special jury in complex cases. In the United States, the usual presumption, shared in all but a couple of states, is that special juries must be statutorily authorized. Not only do federal judges lack such express statutory authorization, but they also face precedential and statutory constraints that point in exactly the opposite way. For instance, in Thiel v. Southern Pacific Co., 328 U.S. 217 (1946), the Supreme Court, in the exercise of its supervisory powers, overturned the verdict of a jury in which the judge had systematically excluded daily wage earners from the jury lists, so that "business men and their wives" comprised 50% or more of the potential jurors. The Supreme Court found that "[j]ury service is a duty as well as a privilege of citizenship"; that "nothing in the federal statutes warrants such an exclusion"; and that "[t]he American tradition of trial by jury ... necessarily contemplates an impartial jury drawn from a cross-section of the community." 328 U.S. at 224, 222, 220. Even more to the point is the subsequently enacted Jury Selection and Service Act of 1968, 28 U.S.C. §§ 1861 et seq. It declares as "the policy of the United States that all litigants in Federal courts [are] entitled to trial by jury ... selected at random from a fair cross section of the community." § 1861. In § 1865(b), the Act states that every person is deemed qualified to serve on a jury unless the person (1) is not a citizen; (2) "is unable to read, write, and understand the English language with a degree of proficiency sufficient to fill out satisfactorily the juror qualification form"; (3) "is unable to speak the English language"; (4) "is incapable, by reason of mental or physical infirmity, to render satisfactory jury service"; or (5) is charged with or has been convicted of a felony. Arguably the second, third, and fourth exceptions demonstrate a congressional desire for jurors who are capable of understanding and rationally deliberating about the evidence. But could such a preference be turned into a license to constitute a special jury when the case is complex? Thus far, no reported decision has tried. See generally William V. Luneburg & Mark A. Nordenberg, *Specially Qualified Juries and Expert Nonjury Tribunals: Alternatives for Coping with the Complexities of Modern Civil Litigation*, 67 Va. L. Rev. 887 (1981) (describing how Jury Selection and Service Act could be amended to allow special juries in complex cases); Louis Harris & Associates, *Judges' Opinions on Procedural Issues: A Survey of State and Federal Trial Judges Who Spend at Least Half Their Time on General Civil Cases*, 69 B.U. L. Rev. 731, 747-48 (1989) (reporting that 52% of federal and 59% of state judges rejected limitations on use of jury in complex civil cases involving technical or scientific evidence; 60% of federal and 59% of state judges rejected limits in complex business cases; and 58% of federal and 66% of state judge rejected idea of minimal educational level for jury in complex cases).

A number of states that previously permitted special juries have moved in the same direction as the federal courts. As we saw, Delaware eliminated the right to a special jury in all but complex cases. New York went even farther in 1965, repealing in its entirety an oft-invoked special jury statute. Cf. Franklin Stier, *The California Judiciary on Trial Reform: A Survey*, 1 J. Pac. Sw. Acad. Leg. Stud. Bus. 63, 75 (1995) (reporting that only minority of California judges surveyed favored specially qualified juries).

Granted that the use of a special jury may presently face a high hurdle as a statutory matter, could its use be required as a matter of due process? After *Japanese Electronic*, the argument should be familiar: Due process requires a decision maker who can rationally adjudicate the facts. A jury comprised of a cross-section of the community will be unable to do so, but a jury derived from some subset of the community (business persons, economists, etc.) can rationally deliberate. In this circumstance, the due process clause trumps the cross-sectional requirement of the Jury Selection and Service Act. Unlike *Japanese Electronic*, this argument does not put the Seventh and Fifth Amendments on a direct collision course: The frequent use of special juries in 1791 suggests that they pass muster under the historical prong of *Ross* v. *Bernhard*; and since a jury, rather than a judge, will find the facts, the "nature of the relief" prong should also be satisfied.

An even more modest solution starts with recent jury research that suggests that, as long as two or three people understand a particular point, the decision making process of the entire jury benefits. See p. 1238, *supra*. Perhaps all that the due process clause requires is that the jury be "salted" with two or three persons with relevant experience; the remaining members could be drawn from a cross section of the community. This proposal deflects at least some of the anticipated criticism about the anti-democratic tendencies of special juries and the discretion that the power to appoint special juries gives to judges. See generally Jonathan D. Casper, *Restructuring the Traditional Civil Jury: The Effect of Changes in Composition and Procedures*, in Verdict 414, 428-32 (Robert E. Litan ed. 1993) (noting that "[e]xtensive experience with the use of special juries and research on their impact are lacking," but describing benefits and drawbacks — especially homogeneity — of special jury).

Are these criticisms telling enough to refuse to entertain the idea of a special jury? How do we justify different procedural treatment (and possibly different outcomes) for routine and complex cases? What about the damage that these proposals might cause to the adversarial system? Cf. Tracey L. Trager, *One Jury Indivisible: A Group Dynamics Approach to Voir Dire*, 68 Chi.-Kent L. Rev. 549, 560-61 (1992) (with "adversarial view, the goal of voir dire is to impanel a jury with a favorable attitude toward the client's case, although the statutory purpose of voir dire is to select fair and impartial jurors").

Even if you conclude that special juries cannot be empaneled in the absence of legislation akin to Delaware's, it seems that the parties have the ability to consent to a trial before a special jury if they want. In In re Richardson Merrell, Inc. "Bendectin" Products Liability Litigation, 624 F. Supp. 1212, 1217 (S.D. Ohio 1985), affirmed, 857 F.2d 290 (6th Cir. 1988), cert. denied, 488 U.S. 1006 (1989), the court sought to convince the parties to use either a "blue ribbon jury" comprised of people with greater formal education or a "blue, blue ribbon jury" comprised of people knowledgeable in the relevant field. The defendant was willing, but the plaintiffs were not; Judge Rubin therefore dropped the idea. Instead, Judge Rubin developed a trial plan, which we shall study at p. 1273, *infra*, that resulted in a defense verdict. Would it be proper for a judge to use her power to design an adverse trial plan as a stick to "convince" a recalcitrant party to accept a special jury? Or does that possibility convince you that the entire notion of a special jury is a bad idea?

NOTE ON VOIR DIRE

Assuming that a jury will be used in a complex case, the selection of the jury creates a number of peculiar problems. In understanding these problems, we might begin by describing the jury selection process in routine litigation. The selection process selection begins by issuing jury summonses to members of the relevant community. From those who have been summoned on a particular day, a "venire panel" (a group of prospective jurors usually consisting of forty to eighty people) is selected and ushered into the courtroom. At this point the process of "voir dire," in which members of the jury panel are asked a series of questions, begins. The theoretical point of voir dire is to make sure that potential jury members questions (1) are capable of serving on the jury; (2) do not know the parties; (3) do not know the events of the case and have formed no opinions about how such cases should come out; and (4) do not harbor other deep-seated convictions or possess other handicaps that would make it impossible for them to rationally deliberate about the case. After jurors who fail to pass through this filter are excused "for cause," each party is typically entitled to exercise a number of "peremptory challenges," which allow the party to strike some number of jurors for reasons other than race or gender.

At a practical level, voir dire is also the lawyers' first chance to tell their clients' stories, and to examine how potential jurors react. In an adversarial system, the lawyer's job is not to ensure that an impartial jury is selected; rather, it is to ensure that a jury as favorable to his client as possible is empaneled. Usually the lawyer is guided in his decisions about who to try to knock off the jury for cause and who to strike from the jury peremptorily by his or her intuition. See generally Larry S. Kaplan, Complex Federal Litigation §§ 23.03-.28 (1993).

In many state systems, the lawyers conduct the voir dire examinations. In the federal system, however, judges usually ask the lawyers to submit their proposed voir dire questions in writing. The judge then decides which questions to ask, and also asks the questions of the panel members. Sometimes lawyers are allowed to ask follow-up questions to particular answers; sometimes the court does so. See F.R.Civ.P. 47(a).

In complex cases, the usual processes often require modification. First, the court faces the problem of summoning a sufficiently large pool of potential jurors; if the case is notorious in the community, or has widespread remedial implications, several hundred people might need to be examined in order to find six to twelve jurors who can survive the filter of voir dire. The next problem is the actual examination of this mass of people. A third problem is the handling of peremptory challenges: in particular, whether each side should get more than the statutory number of challenges (three for each side in federal civil trials, see 28 U.S.C. § 1870), and whether each party or sub-grouping of parties should get its own set of challenges (e.g., should each defendant in a 20-defendant case get three challenges, for a total of 60 defense challenges). In addition, the court must decide on (1) the number of jurors who will sit on the jury (at present the minimal number in the federal system is six, but as many as twelve can be empaneled, see F.R.Civ.P. 48, and a comfortable margin in excess of the required six may be needed if the trial will last long); (2) the number of alternate jurors (at present, Rule 48 does not allow alternates in civil trials, but many states do); and (3) the need for unanimity of the verdict (again, Rule 48 requires a unanimous verdict unless the parties consent to a non-unanimous verdict, but many states permit non-unanimous verdicts).

Judges in complex cases often solve some of the former problems by pre-selecting hundreds of potential jurors and sending them questionnaires that "elicit basic information and identify jurors unable to serve." Manual for Complex Litigation, Third § 22.41 (1995). This method saves court time, but may cause a large number of potential jurors to ask to be excused from duty and cause other curious panelists to investigate the case. Hence, an alternative is to have jurors fill out these questionnaires after they arrive at the courthouse. Id.; see also William W Schwarzer, Managing Antitrust and Other Complex Litigation § 7-2(B)(1); Dennis Bilecki, *A More Efficient Method of Jury Selection for Lengthy Trials*, 73 Judicature 43 (June-July 1989). Some of the latter problems are solved by adding additional jurors (the *Manual, Third* recommends starting with eight for a two-month trial, ten for a four-month trial, and twelve for longer trials), and by allowing additional peremptory challenges to sub-groupings of parties whose interests diverge significantly.

The lawyers do not sit idly by while this process is occurring. To help select the "best" jury, lawyers often hire investigators or consultants that specialize in determining which kinds of jurors will be sympathetic or unsympathetic to their client. They also participate in the drafting of juror questionnaires, and analyze responses with a fine-tooth comb.

Given that lawyers seeking an adversarial edge have little incentive to seek an impartial jury, should a judge become more actively involved in the selection of the jury in a complex case? One partial solution is to eliminate peremptory challenges, which lessens the opportunity for adversarial gamesmanship. A different solution is to allow the judge to select the jury. See William W Schwarzer, *Reforming Jury Trials*, 132 F.R.D. 575, 581 (1991); (describing judge who used this method upon consent of parties); Managing Antitrust and Other Complex Litigation, *supra*, § 7-2(B)(1) (describing antitrust case in which, with consent of parties, judge was authorized to excuse prospective jurors who lacked adequate qualifications). Does a judge enjoy this power even when the parties do not consent? For instance, suppose the judge saw that the parties were deliberately passing over jurors with relevant knowledge, and the judge feared that the jury selected by the parties would be incapable of rational adjudication. Could the judge order that jurors with relevant knowledge be placed on the jury? Which is more important: the right to have your lawyer pick a jury favorable to your case or the system's need for rational adjudication? Should a judge have this authority when the only other alternative to preserve reasoned judgment is to strike the jury altogether?

c. The Power of the Judge to Appoint Alternate Factfinders in Complex or Complicated Bench Trials

As we saw in the last section, judges are not necessarily better equipped than juries to find the facts in the face of complex and technical evidence. Yet they too must act as factfinders in some complex trials. In this section we examine the ability of a judge, when she acts as the factfinder, to assign all or part of the factfinding role to specialized judicial adjuncts. Such authority to delegate, should it exist, is important. Most obviously, the nature of the pretrial and trial process might be altered if a specialized adjunct will determine the facts. In addition, if judges can delegate factfinding to competent adjuncts, then judges can better perform the factfinding tasks than juries. In turn, that fact would put pressure on judges to find some "complexity" exception or other doctrinal artifice to keep a jury away from the case.

One possible adjunct is the advisory jury, permitted under F.R.Civ.P. 39(c). Advisory juries, however, are just that — advisory; the judge must still find the facts for herself, without deference to the advice of the jury. See 9 Charles A. Wright et al., Federal Practice & Procedure § 2335 (1990). An advisory jury is also unlikely to solve the comprehension problem of complex evidence.

Of course, if a judge could appoint a jury comprised of knowledgeable persons — a "blue, blue ribbon jury," in the words of Judge Rubin — then the advisory jury would be of use to the judge. Rule 39 says nothing about the composition of advisory juries. Nor is it clear that the Jury Selection and Service Act, 28 U.S.C. §§ 1861 et seq., applies to advisory juries. See §§ 1861, 1862 (Act applies to "grand and petit" juries). To our knowledge, no cases or authorities have squarely addressed the point. Cf. United States v. Exum, 744 F. Supp. 803 (N.D. Ohio 1990) (suggesting that Rule 39 acts as independent authority, distinct from Jury Selection and Service Act, for summoning jurors); Manual For Complex Litigation, Third § 21.54 (1995) (suggesting "use of an advisory jury of experts in a nonjury case," but failing to analyze Jury Selection and Service Act issues). See generally James A. Martin, *The Proposed "Science Court,"* 75 Mich. L. Rev. 1058 (1977) (discussing pros and cons of advisory or binding scientific panels).

Apart from a formal advisory jury, might it be possible for a judge to work with a technical advisor who can provide the judge with the insight needed to understand and deliberate on the evidence? Such a technical advisor would be akin to a court-appointed expert witness, a subject we consider in the following chapter (see p. 1347, *infra*). Unlike an expert, however, the advisor would be able to have *ex parte* communications with a judge and would not be subject to the parties' cross-examination.

REILLY v. UNITED STATES

863 F.2d 149 (1st Cir. 1988)

■ SELYA, Circuit Judge. [Peter and Donna Reilly and their minor daughter, Heather, brought a medical malpractice action due to severe injuries that Heather suffered at birth. Liability was conceded.]

I. BACKGROUND . . .

After discovery [on damages] was completed, a 7-day bench trial ensued. Both sides introduced expert testimony as to the calculation of damages for lost earning capacity. Appellees also supplied expert testimony regarding expenses for Heather's future care, but "the government presented almost no factual argument against the necessity for and pecuniary valuation of the[se] itemized damages." [Reilly v. United States, 665 F. Supp. 976, 1000 (D.R.I. 1987).] The trial came to a halt on November 26, 1986 — but, as matters turned out, more evidence was to be taken at supplementary hearings.

During the interval between the trial and the resumed hearings, the district judge attempted to enlist an economist to assist him in respect to certain technical aspects pertinent to the calculation of a damage award. He approached several potential candidates. Professor Feldman, an economist at Brown University, disqualified himself because he had previously discussed the case with the plaintiffs' lawyer; others were contacted and one agreed to serve. The judge did not inform counsel of his search. By happenstance, the government learned of it when an assistant United States Attorney (AUSA), in an apparent effort to prepare for the supplementary hearings, called Professor Feldman. The academician forthrightly informed the AUSA that he had already worked on the case at the behest of plaintiffs' lawyer, and mentioned in passing that he had also been contacted by the judge.

The AUSA immediately requested a chambers conference. The session was held on April 10, 1987. The district judge recounted his conversations with the economists and made no bones about his intent to hire one as a technical advisor. He informed all counsel that he had already contacted the Administrative Office of the United States Courts to this end, and that he was awaiting approval from the Chief Judge of the First Circuit. The government voiced no contemporaneous objection to the procedure, did not ask the name of the economist whom the court intended to retain, did not ask that either the court's instructions to the expert or the expert's advice be reduced to writing, and did not request an opportunity to question him.

To make a tedious tale tolerably terse, the approvals were forthcoming, and the judge appointed Dr. Arthur Mead of the University of Rhode Island to act as a technical assistant to the court. The judge had two short conferences with Dr. Mead in the spring of 1987. During the same time frame, the court conducted supplemental evidentiary hearings on April 16 and May 5, 1987. On July 28, an opinion and order was issued awarding Heather Reilly $1,000,000 for pain and suffering, $1,104,641 for lost earning capacity, and $8,933,323 in respect to anticipated future care....

II. APPOINTING A TECHNICAL ADVISOR

The United States concedes that a district court has inherent authority to appoint an expert as a technical advisor.[4] It maintains, notwithstanding,

---

4. The court below held that it had both statutory and inherent authority to appoint a technical advisor. Because we agree that such power inheres generally in a district court, see, *e.g.*, Ex parte Peterson, 253 U.S. 300, 312-13 (1920), we need not explore — and express no opinion on — the lower court's view of the statutory mosaic. By the same token, we need not analyze the suggestion (eschewed

that (1) such power is strictly circumscribed by Fed.R.Evid. 706(a), a rule whose protocol the district court saw no need to obey; (2) the court abused its discretion in appointing an advisor at all in this case; (3) the court's appointee far exceeded the limited role of a technical advisor; and (4) the absence of meaningful procedural safeguards rendered utilization of the advisor fundamentally unfair. We examine these points seriatim.

A. *Rule 706*

Throughout its text, Fed.R.Evid. 706 refers not to "experts" generally, but to a more exclusive class: "expert witnesses." Because the plain language of a Civil Rule is the most reliable indicator of its meaning, we are constrained to conclude that the grasp of Rule 706 is confined to court-appointed expert witnesses; the rule does not embrace expert advisors or consultants. . . .

This conclusion is buttressed by the text of the advisory committee notes (Notes) accompanying Rule 706. As we read them, the Notes seem geared exclusively to expert witnesses as opposed to technical advisors. . . . Given the undeniable fact that, at common law, federal trial courts were empowered not only to designate expert witnesses, . . . but to appoint technical advisors as well, see, *e.g.*, Ex parte Peterson, 253 U.S. 300, 312-13 (1920) (Brandeis, J.), the omission of any language limitative of the latter power is, we think, telling.

We acknowledge that the question is not free from all doubt. The government, in support of its argument to the contrary, relies on a statement by two respected commentators that "the provisions of . . . Rule 706 operate as restrictions on the judge's common law power to appoint experts." 3 J. Weinstein & M. Berger, Weinstein's Evidence ¶ 706[02] at 706-15 (1988). Yet this statement, we suggest, can — and should — be interpreted to encompass only the appointment of expert witnesses. . . .

The substance as well as the language of Rule 706 comports with this interpretation. The rule establishes a procedural framework for nomination and selection of an expert witness and for the proper performance of his role after an appointment is accepted (*e.g.*, advising the parties of his findings, submitting to depositions, being called to testify, being cross-examined). By and large, these modalities — though critically important in the realm customarily occupied by an expert witness -- have marginal, if any, relevance to the functioning of technical advisors. Since an advisor, by definition, is called upon to make no findings and to supply no evidence, provisions for depositions, cross-questioning, and the like are inapposite. . . .

The finishing touch is in the caselaw. The United States, despite

by all of the parties to this case) that Fed.R.Civ.P. 53, which deals with the naming of masters, may be a fertile source of judicial power to retain necessary technical assistance. See, *e.g.*, Reed v. Cleveland Bd. of Educ., 607 F.2d 737, 746 (6th Cir. 1979) (authority to appoint "expert advisors or consultants" derives from either Rule 53 or court's inherent power); Hart v. Community School Bd., 383 F. Supp. 699, 764 (E.D.N.Y. 1974) (Rule 53 "is broad enough to allow appointment of expert advisors").

herculean efforts, has adverted to no reported cases binding the engagement of technical advisors with the strands of Rule 706. . . .

We conclude, therefore, that Rule 706, while intended to circumscribe a court's right to designate expert witnesses, was not intended to subsume the judiciary's inherent power to appoint technical advisors. The Civil Rules, after all, were never meant to become the sole repository of all of a federal court's authority. . . .

B. *Abuse of Discretion*

The government's immediate fallback position is that, even if literal compliance with Rule 706 was not essential, the district court nevertheless abused its discretion in appointing a technical advisor at all. We concur wholeheartedly that such appointments should be the exception and not the rule, and should be reserved for truly extraordinary cases where the introduction of outside skills and expertise, not possessed by the judge, will hasten the just adjudication of a dispute without dislodging the delicate balance of the juristic role. Cf. La Buy v. Howes Leather Co., 352 U.S. 249, 255-57 (1957) (discussing appropriate occasions for employment of special masters) . . . .

We wish to emphasize our strongly-held view that the appointment of a technical advisor must arise out of some cognizable judicial need for specialized skills. Appropriate instances, we suspect, will be hen's-teeth rare. The modality is, if not a last, a near-to-last resort, to be engaged only where the trial court is faced with problems of unusual difficulty, sophistication, and complexity, involving something well beyond the regular questions of fact and law with which judges must routinely grapple. Although a technical advisor can be valuable in an appropriate case, the judge must not be eager to lighten his load without the best of cause.

Despite the fact that the integument as we have shaped it is a narrow one, we believe that this litigation slips fittingly within it. The case involved esoterica: complex economic theories, convoluted by their nature, fraught with puzzlement in their application, leading to a surpassingly difficult computation of damages. Future-care expenditures and lost earnings had to be projected over a 70-year period — and for an infant with no proven financial track record. Plaintiffs' experts differed among themselves on some points. The stakes were demonstrably high. The government was of small help. Its submission on damages, amounting to little more than a lick and a promise, can best be characterized as feeble. The one-sidedness of the evidence itself lent encouragement to the use of a technical advisor to help the court understand the theories which were bruited about. All in all, the litigation was so far outside the mainstream that the judge, in our estimation, had good reason to energize his inherent power to bring a technical advisor on board. Cf. Manual for Complex Litigation, Second (MCL 2d) § 21.54 (1985) (court may consider appointing confidential advisor in "complex litigation" and "when complicated issues are involved"). Mindful of the trier's discretion in this regard, the charge of abuse simply will not wash.

C. *The Technical Advisor's Role*

Our decision that this was a seemly case for nominating a technical advisor and that the district court was not bound to comply with the requirements of Rule 706 in making the appointment does not end this phase of our inquiry. The government argues that, whatever may be said of the need for the appointment or its mechanics, the district court permitted Dr. Mead to roam far beyond the precincts to which a technical advisor must properly be confined. In the end, the government hints, the judge abdicated the factfinding function in favor of Dr. Mead, relying on him to resolve the merits. We find that the district court's use of its expert in this case was limited to appropriate technical assistance, and therefore reject the government's plea.

We start with a restatement of the principle derived from a watershed case anent technical advisors. In Ex parte Peterson, 253 U.S. 300 (1920), the Supreme Court recognized that trial judges in the federal system possessed "inherent power to provide themselves with appropriate instruments required for the performance of their duties," including the power to "appoint persons unconnected with the court to aid judges in the performance of specific judicial duties, as they may arise in the progress of a cause." Id. at 312. . . . Advisors of this sort are not witnesses, and may not contribute evidence. Similarly, they are not judges, so they may not be allowed to usurp the judicial function. See Kimberly v. Arms, 129 U.S. 512, 524 (1889) (court may not, through appointment of a master or otherwise, "abdicate its duty to determine by its own judgment the controversy presented") . . . . In fine, the advisor's role is to act as a sounding board for the judge — helping the jurist to educate himself in the jargon and theory disclosed by the testimony and to think through the critical technical problems.

In this case, it does not appear that the district judge stepped over the line. . . . [T]he judge wrote that he needed an expert in-house "to advise and instruct [him] on the myriad and arcane aspects of economic science necessary to a just adjudication of the . . . case." The judge reported to counsel at a chambers conference that he had explained to Dr. Mead the economist's role as being to function "in the nature of a law clerk," someone with whom the judge could engage in "freewheeling discussion." Judge Pettine specifically warned the advisor that if in their discourse "anything developed which I feel I want to use which is apart from the briefs, which may go into an area which the briefs did not discuss, . . . I am going to feel an obligation to let counsel know. . . . If they want to question you, that is up to them." It is readily apparent that the district court crafted the contours of the engagement with care. . . .

A second contention hawked by appellant is more troublesome. The government urges that because Dr. Mead received no written instructions and submitted no written report, it is unclear to what extent the district court may have allowed the boundaries to be overrun. We agree that it would have been better practice to document the interchange between jurist and advisor in some more readily retrievable fashion. Yet we perceive no fatal flaw. . . . Here, the record fully supports the judge's explanation of how he used Dr. Mead's services, and the government has offered no cogent reason to doubt this explanation. . . .

Appellant's complaint that it was deprived of any opportunity to cross-examine Dr. Mead appears asthenic. If, as the district court stated, the advisor was not an evidentiary source, there was neither a right to cross-question him as to the economics of the situation nor a purpose in doing so. And, to the extent that it might have profited the government to grill Dr. Mead about his role in the case, the short and simple response is that, after being informed at the April 10 chambers conference that the district court intended to hire a technical advisor, the prosecutors did not ask for written specification of the advisor's anticipated role or attempt to reserve a right of inquiry. . . . Having failed to raise that point below, the United States cannot raise it for the first time on appeal. . . .

D. *Procedural Safeguards*

Appellant has one remaining shot in its sling. It protests vigorously that, even where a technical advisor may appropriately be engaged by a trial judge outside the realm of Rule 706, fundamental fairness requires that the appointment be hedged about with a panoply of procedural safeguards. Among other things, appellant urges that the district court should have given advance notice to the parties of the expert's identity and how he was to be used; that written instructions should have been prepared regarding the expert's duties; and that Dr. Mead should have been required to file a written report. We are quick to acknowledge that these suggestions have some merit.

We think it advisable in future cases that the parties be notified of the expert's identity before the court makes the appointment, and be given an opportunity to object on grounds such as bias or inexperience. . . . We also think that there is much to commend the preformulation of a written "job description" for the advisor (or in lieu thereof, that the judge deliver comprehensive verbal instructions to the advisor, on the record, in the presence of all counsel). At the conclusion of his stint, the advisor should file an affidavit attesting to his compliance with the job description.[8] And we do not regard such matters as mere ritual; in an appropriate case, we would not hesitate to reverse if procedural safeguards were wholly inadequate.

Our belief in the value of such prophylactic measures, however, does not avail the government here. On April 10, the district court advised the parties that it had received permission from the paymasters in Washington to employ a technical advisor and that it had staged preliminary discussions with the intended appointee. The government did not inquire as to the expert's identity or express any objection to the court's use of an (unknown)

---

8. We disagree with the suggestion that a technical advisor should be required, as a matter of course, to write a report. The essence of the engagement, requires that the judge and the advisor be able to communicate informally, in a frank and open fashion. Given the freewheeling nature of the anticipated discourse, and the fact that the advisor is not permitted to bring new evidence into the case, requiring a written report in every case would serve no useful purpose.

expert; indeed, the United States Attorney, himself in attendance at the conference, appeared affirmatively to agree. Nor did the government request that any safeguards be set in place. The record makes manifest that appellant sat back and knowingly acquiesced in the court's unconditional hiring of an unidentified technical advisor. This was, we think, a waiver....

Appellant's last gasp on the point invokes the rubric of plain error. Concededly, we have the power to overlook many waivers or procedural defaults in cases where a gross miscarriage of justice would otherwise prevail or where the integrity of the judicial process is seriously threatened. This is not such an instance. The district judge has satisfactorily explained the reasons why he sought to engage a technical advisor, and they are proper reasons. There is no suggestion of bias or any other disqualifying characteristic on the expert's part. And the judge's account of the manner in which the advisor's services were employed comports with the appropriate dimensions of the role and matches what can fairly be deduced from the record. There is no sign that justice was thwarted.

Notes and Questions

1. As *Reilly* says, the fountainhead of authority for the use of technical advisors is Ex Parte Peterson, 253 U.S. 300 (1920). Justice Brandeis' dicta in the case is broad, stating that "[c]ourts have (at least in the absence of legislation to the contrary) inherent power to provide themselves with appropriate instruments required for the performance of their duties." 253 U.S. at 312. But *Peterson* itself involved the appointment of an auditor in a case at common law — a novel idea but hardly remarkable in light of the long history of using auditors in equity and the fact that the division between law and equity was eroding in 1920. Moreover, *Peterson's* auditor was supposed to narrow the disputed issues for trial, examine evidence and conduct a hearing on remaining disputed matters, and write a report with tentative findings of fact that were submitted to a jury. These tasks are rather different than the tasks assigned to the technical advisor in *Reilly*. See Hall v. Baxter Healthcare Corp., 947 F. Supp. 1387, 1392 n.8 (D. Or. 1996) (invoking F.R.Evid. 104 to appoint technical advisors appointed to assist with evidentiary hearing).

2. Technical advisors have long been used in admiralty cases. The first complex case in which an advisor of the *Reilly* type appears to have been used was United States v. United Shoe Machinery Corp., 110 F. Supp. 295 (D. Mass. 1953), affirmed *per curiam*, 347 U.S. 521 (1954), an antitrust case in which Judge Wyzanski employed an economist as advisor. Wyzanski and the economist were later reported to have regretted the appointment, believing that the economist should have (1) been appointed as an expert witness or as a special master, (2) written a report, and (3) been subject to cross-examination. See Samuel R. Gross, *Expert Evidence*, 1991 Wis. L. Rev. 1113, 1188 n.230. Nonetheless, the concept of a technical advisor took hold, was endorsed in the Handbook of Recommended Procedures for the Trial of Protracted Cases, reprinted in 25 F.R.D. 351, 420-21 (1960), and continues to receive a qualified recommendation in the Manual for Complex Litigation, Third § 21.54 (1995):

> [C]onsultation with a confidential adviser to the court may be considered in complex litigation. Unless specifically authorized by statute or agreed by

the parties, however, the court should be cautious in experimenting with such procedures in cases in which, if the judge is held to be in error, a lengthy and costly retrial might be required. The referrals to court-appointed experts, special masters, and magistrate judges authorized by statute or rule should be adequate in most cases to provide the needed assistance.... These procedures should ... be used not to displace the parties' right to a resolution of disputes through the adversary process, but rather to make that process fair and efficient when complicated issues are involved.

3. Assuming that the power to appoint an advisor exists, was *Reilly* sufficiently extraordinary to invoke the power? Obviously, making predictions regarding inflation, discount rates, worklife expectancy, and life expectancy are not the simplest tasks, but, as the Supreme Court has noted, the task need not become a "graduate seminar on economic forecasting." Jones & Laughlin Steel Corp. v. Pfeifer, 462 U.S. 523, 548 (1983). Judges and juries undertake this task every day, and, with appellate review available to catch any glaring errors, irrational damage computations seem an unlikely event. Note that an additional factor mentioned in *Reilly* was the fact that the United States had failed in its adversarial obligation to provide proofs and arguments of its position. Should *Reilly* therefore be limited to cases in which the judge needs to "even up" the sides in order to preserve reasoned judgment? Such a limitation would be consistent with the limited scope of a judge's power to alter traditional factfinding roles due to trial complexity. But is *Reilly* really a proper case for the exercise of this power?

One way to think about this question is to view the adversarial model as a dialectical method of finding truth: The factfinder discovers the truth from hearing the discussion of differing viewpoints. The use of advisors, however, is a didactic approach to truth-finding: The factfinder is taught the appropriate way to think about the facts by a knowledgeable person. See Bert Black et al., *Science and the Law in the Wake of* Daubert: *A New Search for Scientific Knowledge*, 72 Tex. L. Rev. 715, 791-98 (1994). As a general matter, American procedure is firmly committed to the dialectical approach. Under what circumstances, if any, should we depart from this approach in favor of a didactic method?

4. In a much-watched decision, Judge Jones appointed a panel of expert advisors to assist him in conducting an evidentiary hearing concerning the admissibility of controversial expert testimony by plaintiffs in a breast implant case. After the hearing and after consultations with the expert advisors, Jones tentatively excluded nearly all of the plaintiffs' opinion testimony on certain disease processes. See *Hall*, 947 F. Supp. 1387. As a general matter, however, the power to appoint a technical advisor has rarely been exercised. See Burton v. Sheheen, 793 F. Supp. 1329, 1339 (D.S.C. 1992) (redistricting); Renaud v. Martin Mariette Corp., 972 F.2d 304, 308 n.8 (10th Cir. 1992) (toxic exposure); Hemstreet v. Burroughs Corp., 666 F. Supp. 1096 (N.D. Ill. 1987) (patent); cf. In re Eastern & Southern Districts Asbestos Litigation, 151 F.R.D. 540 (E. & S.D.N.Y. 1993) (recognizing inherent power to appoint advisor, but choosing to treat consultant as court-appointed expert witness). Discussions of the proper scope of the advisor's authority are even rarer. An advisor was found to have exceeded his authority in Drexel Burnham Lambert Group, Inc. v. Galadari, 127 B.R. 87 (S.D.N.Y. 1991). In *Galadari*, an American lawsuit filed by Refco, a creditor of Galadari, had been stayed in favor of receivership proceedings in

Dubai, United Arab Emirates. The government of Dubai had created a Committee of Receivers to manage Galadari's affairs. The Committee was represented by an attorney, Asher, and by a British firm, Richards Butler. The creditor sought to lift the stay against the American proceedings, arguing that it had been denied due process in the proceedings in Dubai. The district court agreed, finding, among other violations, that the Committee of Receivers had delegated its decision-making authority to Asher and Richards Butler:

> To the extent that the Committee is a judicial body entrusted to adjudicate Refco's claim our notions of due process prohibit a judicial body from delegating to a person who is outside the court system the powers of fact-finding or ultimate decision making. See, *e.g.*, Kimberly v. Arms, 129 U.S. 512 (1889); Reilly v. United States, 863 F.2d 149 (1st Cir. 1988).
>
> The Committee's conduct in abdicating its decision making functions to biased "advisors" violates not only its own rules, but also United States law and public policy. Thus, the Dubai proceedings are not entitled to international comity. [127 B.R. at 104-05.]

5. In theory, the technical advisor would not need to be a single person specifically selected for the job. There are occasional proposals that a judge should be allowed to call upon a private or public agency with significant, relevant technical expertise or upon some other group of advisors. See, *e.g.*, Troyen A. Brennan, *Helping Courts with Toxic Torts*, 51 U. Pitt. L. Rev. 1 (1989); Black, *supra*, at 796; *Manual, Third* § 21.54.

6. Thus far there have been no proposals to allow juries to have access to technical advisors during their deliberations. Are there valid reasons for the difference between judges, who have access to advisors, and juries, who do not? Is the ability of a judge to use advisors in bench trials a reason to interpret the right to jury trial in a way that judges will be the factfinders in cases in which technical advisors will aid the rational resolution of factual disputes? Or should advisors be made available to juries?

7. One of the drawbacks (or is it strengths?) of a technical advisor system is that the advisor does not do the factfinding. You might wonder whether a court can actually delegate the factfinding responsibility to an expert. We examine this issue in the following materials.

LA BUY v. HOWES LEATHER CO.

352 U.S. 249 (1957)

■ MR. JUSTICE CLARK delivered the opinion of the Court.

These two consolidated cases present a question of the power of the Courts of Appeals to issue writs of mandamus to compel a District Judge to vacate his orders entered under Rule 53(b) of the Federal Rules of Civil Procedure referring antitrust cases for trial before a master. . . .

History of the Litigation. — These petitions for mandamus, filed in the Court of Appeals, arose from two antitrust actions instituted in the District Court in 1950. [The two cases, *Rohlfing* and *Shaffer*, involved 93 plaintiffs that were either operators of independent retail shoe repair shops or wholesalers of shoe repair supplies. Each case involved 6 defendants, who were manufacturers, wholesalers, retail mail order houses, and chain operators of shoe repair stores. The complaints asserted a Sherman Act conspiracy among the defendants "to monopolize and to attempt to monopolize" and fix the price of shoe repair supplies sold in interstate commerce in the Chicago area, and a price discrimination charge under the Robinson-Patman Act.] Both complaints pray for injunctive relief, treble damages, and an accounting with respect to the discriminatory price differentials charged.

The record indicates that the cases had been burdensome to the petitioner. In *Rohlfing* alone, 27 pages of the record are devoted to docket entries reflecting that petitioner had conducted many hearings on preliminary pleas and motions. The original complaint had been twice amended as a result of orders of the court in regard to misjoinders and severance; 14 defendants had been dismissed with prejudice; summary judgment hearings had resulted in a refusal to enter a judgment for some of the defendants on the pleadings; over 50 depositions had been taken; and hearings to compel testimony and require the production and inspection of records were held. It appears that several of the hearings were extended and included not only oral argument but submission of briefs, and resulted in the filing of opinions and memoranda by the petitioner. It is reasonable to conclude that much time would have been saved at the trial had petitioner heard the case because of his familiarity with the litigation.

The References to the Master. — The references to the master were made under the authority of Rule 53(b) of the Federal Rules of Civil Procedure. The cases were called on February 23, 1955, on a motion to reset them for trial. *Rohlfing* was "No. 1 below the black line" on the trial list, which gave it a preferred setting. All parties were anxious for an early trial, but plaintiffs wished an adjournment until May. The petitioner announced that "it has taken a long time to get this case at issue. I remember hearing more motions, I think, in this case than any case I have ever sat on in this court." The plaintiffs estimated that the trial would take six weeks, whereupon petitioner stated he did not know when he could try the case "if it is going to take this long." He asked if the parties could agree "to have a Master hear" it. The parties ignored this query and at a conference in chambers the next day petitioner entered the orders of reference sua sponte. The orders declared that the court was "confronted with an extremely congested calendar" and that "exception [sic] conditions exist for this reason" requiring the references. The cases were referred to the master "to take evidence and to report the same to this Court, together with his findings of fact and conclusions of law." It was further ordered in each case that "the Master shall commence the trial of this cause" on a certain date and continue with diligence, and that the parties supply security for costs. While the parties had deposited some $8,000 costs, the record discloses that all parties objected to the references and filed motions to vacate them. Upon petitioner's refusal to vacate the references, these mandamus actions were filed in the Court of Appeals seeking the issuance of writs ordering petitioner to do so. [The appellate court issued the writs.]

The Power of the Courts of Appeals. — . . . Since the Court of Appeals could at some stage of the antitrust proceedings entertain appeals in these cases, it has power in proper circumstances, as here, to issue writs of mandamus reaching them. . . . We pass on, then, to the only real question involved, *i.e.*, whether the exercise of the power by the Court of Appeals was proper in the cases now before us.

The Discretionary Use of the Writs. — It appears from the docket entries to which we heretofore referred that the petitioner was well informed as to the nature of the antitrust litigation, the pleadings of the parties, and the gist of the plaintiffs' claims. He was well aware of the theory of the defense and much of the proof which necessarily was outlined in the various requests for discovery, admissions, interrogatories, and depositions. He heard arguments on motions to dismiss, to compel testimony on depositions, and for summary judgment. In fact, petitioner's knowledge of the cases at the time of the references, together with his long experience in the antitrust field, points to the conclusion that he could dispose of the litigation with greater dispatch and less effort than anyone else. Nevertheless, he referred both suits to a master on the general issue. Furthermore, neither the existence of the alleged conspiracy nor the question of liability vel non had been determined in either case. These issues, as well as the damages, if any, and the question concerning the issuance of an injunction, were likewise included in the references. Under all of the circumstances, we believe the Court of Appeals was justified in finding the orders of reference were an abuse of the petitioner's power under Rule 53(b). They amounted to little less than an abdication of the judicial function depriving the parties of a trial before the court on the basic issues involved in the litigation.

The use of masters is "to aid judges in the performance of specific judicial duties, as they may arise in the progress of a cause," and not to displace the court. The exceptional circumstances here warrant the use of the extraordinary remedy of mandamus. . . .

The record does not show to what extent references are made by the full bench of the District Court in the Northern District; however, it does reveal that petitioner has referred 11 cases to masters in the past 6 years. But even "a little cloud may bring a flood's downpour" if we approve the practice here indulged, particularly in the face of presently congested dockets, increased filings, and more extended trials. This is not to say that we are neither aware of nor fully appreciative of the unfortunate congestion of the court calendar in many of our District Courts. . . . But, be that as it may, congestion in itself is not such an exceptional circumstance as to warrant a reference to a master. If such were the test, present congestion would make references the rule rather than the exception. Petitioner realizes this, for in addition to calendar congestion he alleges that the cases referred had unusual complexity of issues of both fact and law. But most litigation in the antitrust field is complex. It does not follow that antitrust litigants are not entitled to a trial before a court. On the contrary, we believe that this is an impelling reason for trial before a regular, experienced trial judge rather than before a temporary substitute appointed on an ad hoc basis and ordinarily not experienced in judicial work. Nor does petitioner's claim of the great length of time these trials will require offer exceptional grounds. The final ground asserted by petitioner was with reference to the voluminous accounting which would be necessary in the event the plaintiffs prevailed. We agree that the detailed accounting required in order to determine the damages suffered by each plaintiff might be referred to a master after the court has determined the over-all liability of defendants, provided the circumstances indicate that the use of the court's time is not warranted in receiving the proof and making the tabulation.

We believe that supervisory control of the District Courts by the Courts of Appeals is necessary to proper judicial administration in the federal system. The All Writs Act confers on the Courts of Appeals the discretionary power to issue writs of mandamus in the exceptional circumstances existing here. Its judgment is therefore affirmed.

■ [The dissenting opinion of MR. JUSTICE BRENNAN, with whom MR. JUSTICE FRANKFURTER, MR. JUSTICE BURTON, and MR. JUSTICE HARLAN joined, is omitted.]

Notes and Questions

1. In *LaBuy*, Judge LaBuy was apparently going to be the factfinder for all issues. It is not clear whether the parties had waived their right to jury trial, or whether LaBuy thought that he could suspend the right in view of the case's equitable aspects. *La Buy* was decided before *Beacon Theatres* and *Dairy Queen*, pp. 1211-12, *supra*. After these cases, a jury would have been required first to find the facts relevant to legal issues, as well as the facts relevant to overlapping legal-equitable issues.

Assuming that this had been a jury trial, could Judge LaBuy have appointed a master to serve as an aid to a jury? We will take up this use of a master in the next chapter, when we examine various devices to enhance jury comprehension. See p. 1347, *infra*. Here, we are concerned with a judge's power to substitute another factfinder for herself. On this question, *La Buy* remains the central case.

2. In a non-jury suit, the master's report, containing findings of fact and conclusions of law, is submitted to the judge, who must accept the findings of fact unless they are clearly erroneous. If a party objects to any part of the report, the judge must hold a hearing, at which the judge has the discretion, but not the duty, to receive additional evidence. F.R.Civ.P. 53(e)(2). Hence, even if a reference for factfinding is appropriate, the trial judge cannot entirely absolve herself of responsibility for factfinding. The master's conclusions of law, by the way, are reviewed *de novo* by the judge.

3. Is *La Buy* a constitutional holding, a holding about the scope of Rule 53, or both? In Chapter Eight we examined the text of Rule 53, and discovered that Rule 53(b) made a distinction between references to masters in jury trials and references in non-jury trials. In both types of trials, a "reference to a master shall be the exception and not the rule." In addition, in jury trials, "a reference shall be made only when the issues are complicated"; in non-jury trials, except for difficult accountings or damage issues, "a reference shall be made only upon a showing that some exceptional condition requires it." *La Buy* can certainly be read as saying that the combination of a congested docket, lengthy trial, and complicated issues did not amount to a sufficiently "exceptional condition." On the other hand, it can be read as saying that Article III demands that an Article III official resolve the basic factual issues in the case.

The proper interpretation of *La Buy* is more than an academic question. If it is a Rule 53 case, then congestion, trial length, and complicated issues might be enough to allow a reference to an expert master when combined with other factors, such as highly technical facts that are beyond the ability of the judge to comprehend adequately. (By the way, in *La Buy*, the judge referred the matter to an attorney, rather than to an economist. Might this have influenced the outcome of the case?) But if *La Buy* is a constitutional decision, and if Article III requires an Article III factfinder for basic issues, then a judge could not refer even this case to a master unless Article III contained some sort of "complexity" exception equivalent to the one we explored in the context of the Seventh Amendment.

4. Thus far, lower courts seem to treat *La Buy* more as a Rule 53 case, albeit one with significant Article III underpinnings. See In re Bituminous Coal Operators' Association, Inc., 949 F.2d 1165 (D.C. Cir. 1991); United States v. Conservation Chemical Co, 106 F.R.D. 210 (W.D. Mo.), reversed *sub nom.* In re Armco, Inc., 770 F.2d 103 (8th Cir. 1985); but see Stauble v. Warrob, Inc., 977 F.2d 690 (1st Cir. 1992) (analyzing Article III constraints inherent in Rule 53). See generally Erwin Chemerinsky, Federal Jurisdiction § 4.5 (use of legislative and administrative courts and magistrate judges as factfinders constitutional as long as they act as adjuncts to Article III courts). As a result, in addition to the Article III issue of abdication, all the standard concerns about using masters that we examined in Chapter Eight — concerns such as cost, delay, partiality, abuse of power, and loss of adversarialism and trans-substantivity — play into the decision about whether Rule 53 authorizes a particular reference for trial.

When all the concerns are added together, a reference to a master for factfinding ought to be an event that is, to use *Reilly*'s phrase, "hen's-teeth rare." And, in fact, it is. In non-jury cases, masters are appointed with some frequency to handle intricate matters of account or damages, and to handle other issues of remedial declaration or implementation. See Wright & Miller, *supra*, § 2605; pp. 1419, 1443, *infra*. But references for trial on critical issues of liability have almost never occurred, and when they have, appellate courts have had little trouble issuing writs of mandamus to prevent the reference. The leading quartet of cases, which we already discussed in Chapter Eight in connection with their views on pretrial references, are *Bituminous Coal*, 949 F.2d 1165, *Armco*, 770 F.2d 103, *Stauble*, 977 F.2d 690, and In re United States, 816 F.2d 1083 (6th Cir. 1987). All involved references to a master for, *inter alia*, a trial on liability issues; all agreed, in the words of *Bituminous Coal*, that "it is the function of the district judge, in a non-jury civil case, to decide dispositive issues of fact and law genuinely disputed by the parties. The judge may not impose on the parties . . . [a] master as a 'surrogate judge' to try the controversy and determine liability." 949 F.2d at 1169.

Among the few reported post-*La Buy* cases in which non-jury trial references were allowed are Rogers v. Societe Internationale, S.A., 278 F.2d 268 (D.C. Cir. 1960); United States v. Suquamish Indian Tribe, 901 F.2d 772 (9th Cir. 1990) (arguably reference for remedial matter); Loral Corp. v. McDonnell Douglas Corp., 558 F.2d 1130 (2d Cir 1977); and Olsen Associates, Inc. v. United States, 853 F. Supp. 396 (M.D. Fla. 1993) (reference of tax claim; no discussion of authority to make reference). See generally Irving R. Kaufman, *Masters in Federal Courts: Rule 53*, 58 Colum. L. Rev. 452, 459 ("With a few minor exceptions, references in non-jury cases run counter to the spirit and purpose of judicial administration in the federal courts."); Liptak v. United States, 748 F.2d

1254, 1257 (8th Cir. 1984) (noting that, outside of complicated pretrial matters, accountings, and damage calculations, "it is difficult to conceive of a reference of a nonjury case that will meet the rigid standards of the *La Buy* decision").

5. Would the use of a master with technical expertise meet *LaBuy*'s rigid standards when the judge was incapable of finding the facts with the degree of rationality required by the due process clause? If not, how are we to reconcile the requirements of Rule 53 and Article III on the one side with those of the due process clause on the other? Is the reconciliation the same as the balance between the Seventh Amendment and the due process clause (an issue we examined in connection with *Japanese Electronic,* see p. 1223, *supra*)? Or are the concerns of Rule 53 and Article III weightier than the concerns of the Seventh Amendment?

6. In the context of pretrial references to masters, we saw a respectable body of thought that courts retained an inherent power to appoint masters even when the reference did not comply with the terms of Rule 53. See pp. 948-49, *supra.* Does a judge possess a comparable inherent power to appoint a master for a non-jury trial, even when that reference would violate *La Buy*? See Ex Parte Peterson, 253 U.S. 300 (1920) (federal courts have inherent power to appoint adjuncts that aid in performance of judicial duties). Such power would presumably still be constrained by Article III, as adjusted by the due process clause.

7. Assuming that a judge retains some power to appoint a master to find the facts in a non-jury trial, we would still need to ask whether this power was the least restrictive alternative. First, we need to consider the possibility of using novel trial techniques that would assist the judge in coming to a rational conclusion without utterly displacing her. Many of these techniques will be explored in Chapter Eleven. But one we have already explored: the use of a technical advisor. Does the possibility of using a technical advisor make it even more difficult to justify factfinding references to a master? Or does the "on-the-record" nature of the master's work make the master a preferred option to a technical advisor?

A different option is to refer technical matters to a magistrate judge. Recall from Chapter Eight that some courts use magistrate judges as expert judges to resolve certain types of cases. See p. 955, *supra.* Presumably a system could be developed in which some magistrate judges are selected for their particular expertise. Thus, magistrate judges with advanced degrees in economics could be called upon to conduct the trial of a complex antitrust case, those with accounting degrees could hear securities cases, and those with science backgrounds toxic exposure cases. The magistrate judge would issue a report with proposed findings of fact and conclusions of law. Findings of fact would be reversible only for clear error. See Edward V. Di Lello, Note, *Fighting Fire with Firefighters: A Proposal for Expert Judges at the Trial Level,* 93 Colum. L. Rev. 473 (1993). Unless expert magistrate judges could be appointed as masters, see 28 U.S.C. § 636(b)(2), this system would require changes in the statutory responsibilities of magistrate judges, who at present are able to issue reports on dispositive motions but who can conduct trials only upon the consent of the parties. See 28 U.S.C. §§ 636(b)(1), (c)(1). Would such a system lead to overspecialization and narrowness of focus? Would expert magistrate judges be unable to adjudicate the dispute impartially? How could a judge distinguish between the complex case for which an expert magistrate judge is appropriate and the more routine case for which she is not?

A final option would be to appoint expert judges or to create specialized courts with a limited subject matter in which judges could soon become expert. There are a few expert courts in existence in our country. The most noteworthy are the Delaware Chancery Court, which handles a high volume of sophisticated business litigation; the Tax Court; the Bankruptcy Court; and the Federal Circuit, which has exclusive appellate jurisdiction over matters such as patents and government contracts. See Symposium, *The Sixth Abraham L. Pomerantz Lecture*, 61 Brook. L. Rev. 1 (1995) (favorably evaluating specialized courts in terms of accuracy, efficiency, and due process). Would it also be possible to appoint expert judges in courts of general jurisdiction? For instance, a judge with a strong business background could be appointed in the Southern District of New York, a court in which many securities cases are filed, but also be available for assignment in other districts to handle business litigation. See 28 U.S.C. §§ 291-97 (allowing reassignment of circuit and district judges). Would the concerns that we raised in connection with expert magistrate judges also apply here? See generally Richard L. Revesz, *Specialized Courts and the Administrative Lawmaking System*, 138 U. Pa. L. Rev. 1111 (1990).

8. One of the reasons that *La Buy* rejected the reference to the master was that a knowledgeable judge was being replaced by a master who knew little of the case. Assuming that this reason influenced the outcome in *La Buy*, it makes an interesting point: The more managerial and active the judge during pretrial, the less likely it is that the judge will be able to turn to judicial adjuncts at trial. Is this an argument against active case management in cases likely to be complex at trial? Or is it an argument for greater involvement of masters during the pretrial phase of such cases? Cf. *Stauble*, 977 F.2d 690 (requiring trial before judge even though master had been deeply involved in pretrial management).

9. The parties have the ability to consent to a trial before a master, even when a judge has no power to order the reference. See, *e.g.*, Turner Construction Co. v. First Indemnity of America Insurance Co., 829 F. Supp. 752 (E.D. Pa. 1993). If the parties so stipulate, the master's findings of fact can even be regarded as final. F.R.Civ.P. 53(e)(4).

10. As *La Buy* shows, it is often possible to obtain immediate appellate review of trial references to masters in non-jury matters through a writ of mandamus. Indeed, *Bituminous Coal, Armco,* and *United States* all arose on petitions for mandamus. It is also possible to secure review after trial; but a timely objection to the reference must have been made in the trial court. See *Stauble*, 977 F.2d 690 (reversing reference on post-trial appeal even though court of appeals had declined to issue writ of mandamus prior to trial); Madrigal Audio Laboratories, Inc. v. Cello, Ltd., 799 F.2d 814 (2d Cir. 1986) (failure to object to reference bars appeal on the issue).

11. As we close our examination into the selection of the appropriate factfinder in complex litigation, it should be obvious that the judge's power to substitute a factfinder capable of rational adjudication for one that may not be capable is significantly constrained by constitutional and procedural rules, as well as by our political vision for American society. It is important to understand that these constraints, as well as the slight wobble that we have discovered in them, have important effects on the joinder, pretrial, and remedial aspects of complex litigation. A plaintiff's lawyer that wants a jury may need to limit the number of claims or defendants he brings in order to avoid a "complexity" exception argument; likewise, in order to ensure a jury, he may file a damages claim, even though the distribution of damages creates significant remedial

problems. Similarly, a judge who knows that a jury will try the case is constrained in her management options, both during pretrial and at trial. See William W Schwarzer, *Reforming Jury Trials*, 132 F.R.D. 575, 577 (1991). In the materials that we have read, these considerations, which seek to fit the issue of the appropriate factfinder and lawgiver within the larger context of the needs of complex cases, are rarely mentioned. Should they be?

2. Selecting the Lawgiver in Complex Cases

In a traditional adversarial model, the judge bears the responsibility for declaring the applicable legal principles and determining the legal effect of the facts found at trial. Given that judges, by virtue of their legal training, are presumably expert in such matters, there is little reason to suspect that the judge needs the power to alter the standard division of adversarial responsibility and delegate this task to another player.

REED v. CLEVELAND BOARD OF EDUCATION

607 F.2d 737 (6th Cir. 1979)

■ LIVELY, Circuit Judge. This appeal is from an order of the district court making an interim allowance of fees to the special master and several experts appointed by the court in a school desegregation case. [A class action was filed, seeking a permanent injunction enjoining racial and economic segregation in the public schools of Cleveland, Ohio. After conducting a bench trial on the issue of liability, the district court found the defendants' operation of the school system to be in violation of the Constitution. Subsequently the district court appointed a special master, Daniel R. McCarthy, to assist with remedial issues. The court also appointed two "experts" to aid the master in his appraisal of various desegregation plans. One of the experts, Dr. Gordon Foster, was an expert in the field of school administration. The other expert, Edward A. Mearns, Jr., was a professor of constitutional law.

[Subsequently, the court ordered the defendants to pay the interim fees, which exceeded $500,000, of the masters and experts. Prof. Mearns' share of the fees was $66,330, representing 1105.5 hours of work. The defendants objected to the payment of the fees, and an appeal ensued.

[The court began by upholding the power of the district court to appoint expert advisors pursuant to Rule 53 or its inherent powers. It then approved the fees for Dr. Foster.]

The appointment of Professor Mearns presents the court with a more complex problem. In explaining the selection of Mr. McCarthy as special master the district court pointed out that he was experienced in accounting, business and finance, skills which the court itself did not possess. This same reasoning would support the appointment of Dr. Foster, whose expertise in educational matters was not shared by the special master or the court. On the other hand, Professor Mearns is primarily a teacher of constitutional law, an area with which the experienced trial judge in this case has been involved throughout his career. The use of masters is permitted because they improve the judicial process by bringing to the court skills and experience which courts frequently lack. However, courts are presumed to be informed on legal issues, and the determination of purely legal questions is the responsibility of the court itself. The court is not without assistance in performing this duty. The attorneys in a given case are required to inform the court of their views of the controlling law. Each district judge is provided at public expense with a staff which includes qualified law clerks. In addition, the United States was designated as *amicus curiae* in the present case and participated actively in the remedy phase, appearing through attorneys in its Civil Rights Division.

It is difficult to determine from the record exactly what duties Professor Mearns actually performed. He was appointed primarily to "assist with the evaluation of the plan to be submitted by the Cleveland Board of Education . . . ." Yet, on February 15, 1977 the district court directed Dr. Foster to assist in evaluating the plan to be submitted by the Cleveland Board as well as that of the State Board. There was no corresponding assignment of Professor Mearns to assist with evaluation of the State plan. The record discloses that Professor Mearns met with the court and the judge's law clerks on a number of occasions and that he wrote memoranda and drafted orders for the court. Our conclusion is that Professor Mearns functioned frequently as an advisor to the court on constitutional law issues. These activities and communications did not occur in open court and the parties had no opportunity to question Professor Mearns as a witness.

The use of masters in non-jury cases has been criticized on three main grounds: it causes delay in the proceedings, it adds to the expense of litigation and it often leads to an abdication of the judicial function. . . . The appointment of the master in this case does not appear to have caused delay. However, the appointment of two experts to advise the master has added significantly to the expense of this litigation. In view of Mr. McCarthy's lack of experience in educational matters, he clearly required the assistance of someone with Dr. Foster's qualifications. However, the same justifications did not exist for the appointment of Professor Mearns, and we do not approve the practice of appointing legal advisors to a master or the court. To the extent that the master was not qualified to make recommendations to the court because of a lack of experience in constitutional law, he should have submitted such legal issues to the court. The court could rely on his own experience and learning and the assistance of his staff and all counsel in the case. The District Judge clearly had no intention to abdicate his judicial responsibility in this case. Nevertheless, to the extent that he relied on advice received in chambers from a "legal expert" there was a partial abdication of his role. Whatever may have been the practice of Lord Mansfield the adversary system as it has developed in this country precludes the court from receiving out-of-court advice on legal issues in a case. He must depend on his own resources, which include the work of his staff and the offerings of counsel.

This court realizes that a case of the magnitude of the present one puts a severe strain on the resources of a district court. . . . In the absence of an express agreement by all the parties, however, a court may not avail itself of legal advice from one who is neither counsel in the case nor subject to the oath and discipline imposed on members of his staff. . . .

It is our conclusion that 322.5 hours [of Prof. Mearns's time] were spent on activities which . . . involved research for the court, meetings with the court and his staff and drafting orders and memoranda. These are not services for which defendant should be required to pay. . . . Thus, we conclude that Professor Mearns is entitled to be paid for 738 hours.[6]

Notes and Questions

1. *Reed* involved the appointment of a legal advisor for a remedial matter. As we shall see in more detail in Chapter Thirteen, the rules for the appointment of judicial adjuncts in the remedial stages are often more lenient. Hence, it is fair to assume that the court of appeals in *Reed* would have been even more concerned with the use of a legal advisor to assist the court in its lawgiving tasks on trial issues.

2. *Reed* assumes that the court and lawyers are capable of determining the relevant legal rules. This is entirely consistent with the basic assumption of the adversarial model. Once you factor in the judge's power to appoint trial counsel, can you envision any circumstance in which this assumption is wrong, and a court is incapable of rationally determining the applicable law? Cf. F.R.Civ.P. 44.1 (allowing judge to consider evidence, including testimony, regarding law of foreign country). If you cannot, then we should expect to find that the trial judge has no power to shift the task of law determination from herself to another person.

3. In fact, that expectation is largely fulfilled. Cases on the point are sparse, perhaps because the lawgiving function of the judge is so taken for granted. See, *e.g.*, Crowell v. Benson, 285 U.S. 22 (1932) (Article III requires that ultimate responsibility for lawgiving be retained by Article III official). The notion of using a legal advisor has fared badly in the few cases that have raised the idea. See Reilly v. United States, 863 F.2d 149, 157 (1st Cir. 1988) (stating in dicta that "judge may not, for example, appoint a legal advisor to brief him on legal issues"); Young v. Pierce, 640 F. Supp. 1476, 1485 n.9 (E.D. Tex. 1986) (appointing advisor but giving advisor no authority to advise on "what is a constitutionally permissible remedy, since that is a legal issue best handled by the court").

The same reluctance to delegate the lawgiving task at trial also exists for adjuncts other than legal advisors. While it is true that judges have the authority to delegate to magistrate judges the power to make conclusions of law when cases are referred to them, see 28 U.S.C. § 636(b)(1), magistrate judges are not authorized to conduct trials without the parties' consent, see 28

---

6. Since there was no objection to the appointment of Professor Mearns, all his work related to assisting the special master will be compensated. In the future, specific agreement will be required for the appointment of a legal advisor to a special master.

U.S.C. § 636(c)(1); therefore, the lawgiving task of magistrate judges at trial is narrow. Although masters can make conclusions of law in their reports, see F.R.Civ.P. 53(e)(1), these conclusions are not usually made available to the jury. See 9A Charles A. Wright & Arthur R. Miller, Federal Practice & Procedure § 2613 (1995). As we have seen, references to masters for non-jury trials are nearly impossible to obtain; even if a reference is permissible, the master's conclusions of law are entitled to no deference, and legal questions must be decided by the district court de novo. See F.R.Civ.P. 53(c)(2); Stauble v. Warrob, Inc., 977 F.2d 690 (1st Cir. 1992); Polin v. Dun & Bradstreet, Inc., 634 F.2d 1319 (10th Cir. 1980).

In one trademark case, a judge sought to delegate the lawgiving (and factfinding) task to a special master with the following blunt assessment of his capabilities:

> "I don't understand anything about the merits of any patent or trademark case. I'm not about to educate myself in that jungle. I appoint routinely Special Masters who know what this is all about. . . . I would have no confidence in my ability to do any justice in that thicket of patent and trademark, which I never understood when I was trying to practice law, and I wouldn't begin to understand it now. . . .
>
> "[Y]ou're not going to get any expertise from me in [the] field [of trademark law]."

The parties consented to the reference, one of them reluctantly so. On appeal, that party then sought to challenge the reference. The Second Circuit held that the party had waived its right to contest the reference because of its consent in the district court, but left no doubt about its views regarding the reference:

> We must express our firm disagreement with the district judge's concept of his duties. Having by his oath of office accepted the task of adjudicating all issues falling within the court's federal jurisdiction, he is obligated, whenever faced with unfamiliar factual or legal issues (including those involving trademark and copyright matters), to educate himself in those fields with the aid of counsel, colleagues on the bench, law clerks, and published texts and decisions. This has been the path traditionally followed by respected members of the federal judiciary. . . . "[T]he fact that 'the case involves complex issues of law or fact is no justification for reference to a Master, but rather a [com]pelling reason for trial before an experienced judge.'"

Madrigal Audio Laboratories, Inc. v. Cello, Ltd., 799 F.2d 814, 818 & n.1, 821 n.2 (2d Cir. 1986).

4. We should not put the matter too strongly. Through pretrial references of summary judgment and other motions, judges faced with difficult legal issues can glean useful legal advice from a magistrate judge or master; a master's conclusions of law contained in a report written pursuant to a trial reference can also be helpful. But the lawgiving function in complex litigation remains squarely on the judge's shoulders, precisely where our definition of "trial complexity" suggests that it should.

CHAPTER ELEVEN

TRYING A COMPLEX CASE

> New devices may be used to adapt the ancient institution [of jury trial] to present needs and to make of it an efficient instrument in the administration of justice. Indeed, such changes are essential to the preservation of the right.
>
> Louis D. Brandeis

Once the trial counsel, the factfinder, and the lawgiver have been set into place, the trial can begin. But exactly what form should the trial take? In a routine case to be tried to a jury, the jury is selected, the lawyers for the parties make an opening statement, the lawyers for each side present all their documentary and testimonial evidence at once (interrupted only by cross-examination of witnesses from other parties), each lawyer makes a closing argument, and the judge reads the instructions of law to the jury. The jury retires to deliberate, and returns with a verdict on which judgment is entered.

In this trial the presentation of evidence and arguments is adversarial, in the sense that the parties and their lawyers determine what witnesses to call, what documents to introduce, what questions to ask, and what arguments to make. The jury and the judge sit stone-faced, absorbing the proofs and arguments but not creating them. Moreover, this trial is a single trial on all issues; the jury does not decide one issue first, adjourn for a few days or weeks, and then move on to other evidence or other issues.

Routine judge-tried cases proceed in a similar way, but with some important differences. Opening statements are often dispensed with or greatly shortened; the judge may order the parties to submit trial briefs instead. Likewise, judges may not entertain any (or at least any lengthy) closing arguments, preferring to have the parties write post-trial briefs. Third, there are no jury instructions; post-trial briefs take care of arguing the law. Next, judges are somewhat more free to cut a trial into discrete segments, so that the parties might present evidence on some issues, take a break while the judge decides that issue or attends to other matters, and then return to present additional evidence, if needed. Finally, judges are often more willing to ask questions of witnesses. In short, a judge-tried case has somewhat more of the feel of the old proceedings in equity (in which most evidence was submitted in written form), and somewhat more of the feel of the civil law model (in which a "trial" is a continuous series of hearings on discrete issues, and judicial solicitation of evidence is common).

We saw in the last chapter that the traditional common law trial — lay factfinder, single trial on all issues, adversarial presentation — created difficulties for a factfinder trying to comprehend the factual issues in a complex case. We also learned that juries have a hard time understanding the legal instructions — a problem that makes it difficult for a jury rationally to apply the facts to the law in cases both routine and complex.

In this chapter we explore techniques that can help the factfinder overcome the problems of comprehending factual and, in the case of juries, legal issues. We begin by looking at the matter of physical plant: making sure that the courtroom facility is large enough, and technologically sophisticated enough, to allow the lawyers to put forth their best efforts in presenting proofs and arguments. We then move on to techniques that limit the amount of information that a factfinder needs to consider at one sitting. Finally, we examine a series of techniques aimed at increasing the comprehension of the information that is presented.

Most of the techniques we examine invest more discretion in the trial judge to affect outcomes than a pure adversarial model would tolerate. Nonetheless, most of the techniques operate loosely within the adversarial tradition, in which information is presented through dialogue and dialectic. Moreover, most of the techniques are designed to preserve jury trial and seek to ensure reasoned decision making in complex cases. You might want to ask yourself whether these techniques go far enough to guarantee comprehension, and whether even more radical solutions might be preferable. Conversely, you might want to ask whether these techniques are consistent with the standard trial format, whether these techniques are always necessary (as opposed to being merely novel and chic), and, when they are necessary, whether trial is the most sensible way to resolve the dispute. This is the great question of this chapter: Are the costs of preserving jury trial and reasoned judgment too high?

A. CREATING THE COURTROOM

We have already seen how technology can make easier the lawyers' task of storing, retrieving, and making effective use of quantities of information during pretrial proceedings. The same problems of storage, retrieval, and use occur during trial, in which immediate access to information is an invaluable aid to lawyers, judges, and juries. Before we examine techniques for enhancing trial comprehension, therefore, we should pause to consider how technology can help the lawyers and the court manage the quantities of information introduced at a complex trial and how to create a workspace within which the lawyers, the judge, and the jury can operate optimally.

Fredric I. Lederer, TECHNOLOGY COMES TO THE COURTROOM, AND ...

43 Emory L.J. 1095, 1097-1101, 1107-16, 1118-19, 1121 (1994)

Unveiled on September 13, 1993, Courtroom 21, The Courtroom of the 21st Century Today, is located in the McGlothlin Courtroom of William & Mary's Marshall-Wythe School of Law in Williamsburg, Virginia. The Courtroom is a joint project of William & Mary and the National Center for State Courts, and functions as an adjunct to the National Center's Court Technology Laboratory. . . . The public service goal of the Courtroom 21 project is to provide judges, court administrators, architects, lawyers, court reporters, and others concerned with courtroom activities with a functional model courtroom that they can examine in order to determine technological solutions to their unique needs. . . .

Currently, Courtroom 21's major technological capabilities include:

- Assisted listening device support;
- Remote two-way television arraignment and witness examination;
- Lexis and WestLaw legal research at bench and counsel tables with JuriSoft software support;
- Information storage and presentation via FolioViews;
- Concurrent (real-time) Stenograph court reporter transcription, including the ability for each lawyer to mark an individual computerized copy for later use;
- Recorded or real-time televised evidence display with analog optical disk storage using the Doar Presenter and Disk Partner system and the Litigation Sciences videodisc system, which features bar code indexing and light-pen control;
- Built-in video deposition playback facilities;
- Automatic Court Technologies microchip-controlled, multi-camera, multi-frame, video recording of proceedings using ceiling-mounted cameras and Shure Microphone voice-initiated switching; optional synchronization to the real-time transcript;
- Text, graphics, and TV-capable jury computers and monitors used to display floppy disk, CD-ROM, laser videodisc, videotape, or real-time live data and images, including multi-media computer animations and graphics, as well as more mundane documents;
- The A.D.A.M. simulation and display of the human body;
- Concurrent computer-displayed transcription for hearing-impaired witnesses, jurors, lawyers, and judges;
- Consecutive translation of up to 143 languages using AT&T's Language Line; and
- Teleconferencing via Teleconferencing Systems integrated telephone/audio system.

Evidence presentation was originally directed from the court clerk's master station ... Control is scheduled to be moved to counsel's podium.... The courtroom computers are connected via a specialized Stenograph Caseview network and a video network....

To the degree possible, Courtroom 21 uses software compatible with Microsoft Windows....

Although installation and long-term maintenance of much of the equipment requires technically trained personnel, operation of the equipment requires little or no technical training; a three- to five-minute explanation suffices for operation of most equipment....

II. Pretrial ...

Although on-line computer research is now commonplace and fundamental, courtrooms proper rarely have legal research capabilities.... The ability to have instant access to a case when unsure as to its applicability may greatly improve the accuracy of legal rulings. Indeed, the mere knowledge by counsel that they may be called on their legal authorities in public by the court may raise the standard of practice.

Legal research facilities at bench and counsel tables, however, raise two possible problems. The first is financial; who will pay the cost of access? ... The second is human; will a higher probability of courtroom confrontations over differing interpretations of legal text further increase the strain of litigation? ...

III. Trial Record

A. *Real-time Transcript*

Real-time transcription is the use of computer-aided transcription equipment (CAT) to obtain a useful transcript of testimony as that testimony is given. Real-time transcription provides near-instantaneous transcripts, both in traditional written form and in computer-searchable electronic form. In addition to providing the severely hearing-impaired lawyer, judge, juror, or witness with sufficient information to function, the transcript serves the usual roles extraordinarily well: disputes as to prior testimony can be resolved immediately, and judge and counsel have an immediate record from which to plan further witness examination and, when applicable, jury instructions....

The courtroom strength of real-time reporting, however, is not just the near-instantaneous production of a transcript with approximately 99% accuracy, it is the ability to electronically distribute the transcript, as it happens, to judge and counsel, each of whom may independently mark aspects on her or his own computer. The transcript may be searched electronically and may be taken back to chambers or the office in disk format for further trial preparation. In some cases, the electronic transcript may even be synchronized with videotape so that a computer may cue previously videotaped testimony....

Real-time transcription is substantially more efficient and useful than traditional reporting. Furthermore, real-time transcripts can be sent electronically over telephone lines to counsel's office or even to an appellate court....

B. *Video Records and Multi-Frame Video* ...

Ordinarily, two justifications are used for video records of trial: cost and scope of record. To the extent that video records are made on inexpensive tape by one or more cameras, the cost of which can be amortized over many cases, the cost of a videotape record is substantially cheaper than a traditional written transcript prepared by a court reporter. Because the tape can preserve demeanor, including voice and body language, it is potentially more comprehensive than the traditional written record.

Video records present, however, more complications than might initially seem apparent. One concern is technological quality, including whether the given system has adequate assurance of preserving everything said at trial, an audio requirement that can be technologically demanding. Another concern is whether the cameras themselves will adequately preserve the video record. How many cameras should be installed and who will operate them? Must every trial have a director? Multiple camera raw footage is wasteful, but human selection is risky. Will there be close-ups that risk undue emphasis or which will miss a critical event happening elsewhere in the courtroom? New technology permits installation of a multi-camera system, with each camera showing up in a small window on the television screen. This approach means that the entire courtroom can be preserved without need for a human operator. Further, voice-actuated switching can place the active camera picture in a large window for easier review later....

The ideal use of a video record is ... in conjunction with a synchronized real-time transcript. This would allow an appellate counsel or judge to use the electronic transcript to determine the key portion of a tape and to automatically cue the tape to the appropriate location....

Subject to concerns about finality, one might expect a full video record to render moot the long-expressed rule that in a bench trial the appellate court must defer to the trial judge's determinations of fact because of the judge's ability to observe the demeanor of the witnesses. It is by no means clear that this change in appellate procedure would open the appellate floodgates to a sea of reversals, however. In one study of Kentucky appeals, the National Center for State Courts found that appeals based on video records were more likely to yield affirmances than those based on written transcripts.

IV. INFORMATION PRESENTATION

A. *In General*

Communication is the heart of litigation; everything else is secondary. Evidence is meaningless if it cannot be transmitted effectively to the factfinder, and from the perspective of the litigator, evidence may be valueless if it is not transmitted persuasively.... Not surprisingly, therefore, trial lawyers are bringing to the courtroom an enormous variety of documents, photographs, recorded action (including "day-in-the-life" videotapes), spreadsheets, and computer graphics, including computer animations. Information enters the courtroom in traditional formats and on such innovative formats as videotape, laserdisc, floppy disk, CD-ROM, and analog disk, to mention only some of the options. Such high-technology information is in turn presented on television or computer monitor....

The use of television and computer-related information display systems is important because:

- They present a means of storing, organizing, and presenting vast quantities of information in a relatively inexpensive, simple format;
- Pictorial information can be conveyed in a more effective and often less expensive fashion than otherwise possible;
- Some information could not be presented, let alone in a meaningful form, absent use of computer-related output;
- Scientific studies indicate that visual data may be more likely to be persuasive and more likely to be remembered than other forms of information....

B. *Computer Graphics and Animations*

Normally, computer graphics, including computer animations, do not present unique problems. [The article then analyzed evidentiary concerns with computer graphics, a subject we consider at p. 1388, *infra*.]

C. *Remote Counsel Appearances and Remote Witness Testimony*

Teleconferencing has long been thought to be a significant way to reduce travel-related costs and delays. Conference call telephone sessions have their place, but the absence of video data limits full understanding and affects the comfort level of those involved. What is needed is television.... Although television hardware has developed to the point that effective teleconferencing is easily possible, bandwidth limitations have sharply limited the inexpensive transmittal of data.... The economics of teleconferencing, however, are in the process of change as consistent announcements concerning the information superhighway demonstrate. It would not be surprising if unscheduled video teleconferencing were routinely and economically available within the next five years. The question must then be considered, what useful courtroom purpose would be served by incorporation of that technology?...

[F]rom a courtroom perspective, video teleconferencing is desirable to permit appearances both by counsel and by witnesses, especially experts, and, perhaps, those witnesses in criminal trials or domestic relations cases who are afraid of being physically present in the same courtroom as another trial participant. Because remote appearance by counsel outside the trial proper does not appear to raise constitutional or practical problems, the better, and more difficult, question concerns the desirability and implications of remote witness testimony....

Arguably, the proposed procedure might be lacking in three particulars: (1) the factfinder might find the demeanor of the witness ... too difficult to evaluate; (2) the electronic media or the physical set up may impair some other sense or senses; or (3) perhaps the very use of remote testimony might suggest a lack of importance that would defeat the hoped-for tendency of direct confrontation, in-courtroom testimony to impel solemn truthfulness.

Indeed, these very concerns suggest the need for serious empirical research. Even if no legal objections to remote testimony arise, and none may in civil cases, to what extent, if at all, would a factfinder (judge or juror) find remote live testimony more or less persuasive than in-person testimony? Would the evaluation vary by the age of the factfinder or the factfinder's attitude toward or experience with technology? These questions are critical, for decreasing communications costs will rapidly lead to the use of remote testimony in courts, and having some idea of its practical effects would be helpful for refining and improving electronic courtroom technology.

Notes and Questions

1. Few people would dispute the fact that courtrooms need to be redesigned so lawyers and experts can use today's technology in order to teach both judge and jury. "We have built [judges] some nice wooden benches, but the places are not equipped for the fast transfer of complex information or data. Go into any courtroom today and it's hard even to find a blackboard or a grounded plug." Victoria Slind-Flor, *Tackling High Tech*, Natl. L.J., Oct. 19, 1992, at 1 (quoting Jack A. Russo).

2. Likewise, no one pretends that a technologically sophisticated courtroom is the answer to all the problems of trial complexity. But it can help lawyers, judges, and juries more easily harness and organize critical information. It can also make the presentation of evidence clearer and more compelling. Does technological packaging run the risk of overlooking critical information that is not easily captured in a technical format? Does it force lawyers and decision makers to think only in the categories made possible by the various software programs? Isn't it possible that clear and compelling evidence will also be misleading? In his article Dean Lederer calls for empirical studies on the effect of modern technology on the trial process. What might some of those effects be? Does it make you uneasy to think that judges have the discretion to implement this technology before the empirical studies have been conducted?

3. This technology costs money. Assuming that empirical studies showed that technology has a positive effect on litigation outcomes for those who use it, does it worry you that rich litigants will be able to buy a better outcome?

One way to avoid a monetary imbalance is to have the court spend the money to install the technology. But how is the court to finance the installation? Money for capital improvement projects in most courthouses is notoriously scarce. Perhaps the court could tax the parties for the costs of technological improvements, much as courts sometimes tax the parties for facilities such as document depositories (see p. 1099, *supra*). For instance, in the Dupont Plaza

Fire Litigation, Judge Acosta had a courtroom too cramped and technologically unsophisticated to accommodate the trial. He decided that the only way to accommodate the trial was to construct a new courtroom and related facilities. In a series of pretrial orders, he taxed each party $10,000 for the construction of the new courtroom. After the judge ultimately obtained authorization from the Administrative Office for United States Courts to build the courtroom with taxpayer dollars, he diverted the $10,000 to meet other litigation expenses. As a result, the judge's authority to order the parties to subsidize the construction of a "complex litigation friendly" courtroom was never squarely addressed. But the court of appeals at least intimated that the judge possessed this power, as well as the power ultimately to shift the costs of construction onto the losing party by means of awarding the prevailing party its costs of litigation. See In re San Juan Dupont Plaza Hotel Fire Litigation, 142 F.R.D. 41, 46 n.20 (D.P.R. 1992); In re Two Appeals Arising out of the San Juan Dupont Plaza Hotel Fire Litigation, 994 F.2d 956 (1st Cir. 1993) (holding that court has inherent power to re-allocate case management expenses as equity requires); cf. Manual for Complex Litigation, Third § 22.12 (1995) (describing need to arrange for larger and technologically appropriate physical space for trial, but not suggesting sources of funding). But see Kemner v. Monsanto Co., 217 Ill.App.3d 188, 576 N.E.2d 1146 (1991) (reversing award of costs against losing party for construction of courthouse annex used to store evidence).

Should a court have the power to force the parties to pay for courtroom facilities? If it doesn't have this power and if other capital improvement money is unavailable, what is the court to do? Hold the trial in a facility that is not conducive to the logical presentation of evidence? Let the lawyers for the parties into the courtroom only when it is their turn to examine witnesses? Might the limitations of the physical facility induce a judge to select a technologically unsophisticated trial counsel for a group of claimants, even when the judge knows that separate counsel who would develop lengthier and more sophisticated presentations of evidence would be a better alternative?

4. As the last note suggested, the concern is not merely about putting the right technology into the courtroom, but also about making the courtroom large enough to accommodate all of the lawyers, the parties, the evidence, and the equipment. Standard-sized courtrooms simply cannot do so. When the primary issue concerns the number of parties, one option is to conduct the trial in a regular courtroom, to broadcast the proceedings to a remote facility in which parties can watch the proceedings, and to provide electronic means by which the remote plaintiffs can communicate with their lawyers in the courtroom. This was the solution used in the multidistricted Bendectin trial, although Judge Rubin's primary motivation for doing so was to keep a parade of horribly disfigured children and adults from unduly influencing the jury on the causation issue. See In re Bendectin Litigation, 857 F.2d 290, 322-25 (6th Cir. 1988), cert. denied, 488 U.S. 1006 (1989) (upholding exclusion of plaintiffs from courtroom).

This solution will not, of course, work when the problem lies with the number of lawyers or the amount or size of the equipment and evidence. In these cases, the only solution is to find a larger physical facility. "Choices to consider include clubs, gymnasiums, National Guard armories and governmental offices, such as county board rooms and auditoriums." Illinois Manual for Complex Litigation 84 n.11 (1991). In past cases each counsel table has been equipped with a computer wired to the judge's bench, so that objections to questions could be instantaneously registered with the judge.

5. For other reading on courtroom design and technological innovation in the courtroom, see Jeffrey S. Wolfe, *Toward a Unified Theory of Courtroom Design Criteria: The Effect of Courtroom Design on Adversarial Interaction*, 18 Am. J. Trial Advoc. 593 (1995); Julie K. Plowman, Note, *Multimedia in the Courtroom: Valuable Tool or Smoke and Mirrors?* 15 Rev. Litig. 415 (1996); Jessica Copen, *Courts of the Future*, 77 A.B.A. J. 74 (June 1991).

B. TECHNIQUES TO LIMIT INFORMATION AT TRIAL

Having created a physical space conducive to the processing of information, the next task is to make the presentation of that information (at a minimum) adequate enough to ensure reasoned judgment and (hopefully) superior to other means of communicating information. There are two different, but not mutually exclusive, means of accomplishing this task. The first is to limit the amount of information that the decision maker needs to consider. The second is to enhance the decision maker's ability to comprehend the information that is presented. In this section we consider a number of ways to limit information. In Section C we will explore techniques to increase comprehension.

1. Limiting Issues and Claims

The most obvious way to limit trial information for the decision maker is to limit the number of factual disputes that need to be resolved in one sitting. We already have seen this technique used during pretrial, where a judge might order discovery of issues in stages (see p. 1019, *supra*). There is, however, no necessary correlation between division of issues during pretrial and division of issues at trial. Issues could be discovered in stages, but tried together; conversely, all issues could be discovered together, but tried separately. Moreover, during pretrial we were concerned primarily with the problems faced by lawyers in the accumulation and organization of evidence. Those concerns still plague the division of issues at trial, but here two new concerns are injected: first, the concern that the factfinder be able to comprehend the relevant evidence; and second, when the factfinder is a jury, the concern that too fine a parsing of issues into sub-trials may contravene the very nature of jury trial and hence the Seventh Amendment.

IN RE BENDECTIN LITIGATION

857 F.2d 290 (6th Cir. 1988)

■ ENGEL, Chief Judge. These actions were brought on behalf of children with birth defects against Merrell Dow Pharmaceuticals, Inc., alleging that their birth defects were caused by their mothers' ingestion during pregnancy of defendant's anti-nausea drug Bendectin. Immediately involved are eleven hundred eighty claims in approximately eight hundred forty-four multidistrict cases. These cases represent only a part of the Bendectin cases which have been brought in numerous federal and state courts around the nation. Although there are some differences among the complaints, most are virtually identical, requesting relief on the grounds of negligence, breach of warranty, strict liability, fraud, and gross negligence, and asserting a rebuttable presumption of negligence per se for defendant's alleged violation of the misbranding provisions of the federal Food, Drug and Cosmetic Act (FDCA), 21 U.S.C. § 301 et seq.

After twenty-two days of trial on the sole question of causation, the jury answered the following interrogatory in the negative: "Have the plaintiffs established by a preponderance of the evidence that ingestion of Bendectin at therapeutic doses during the period of fetal organogenesis is a proximate cause of human birth defects?" . . . Accordingly, the district judge entered judgment for defendant. . . .

I. BACKGROUND OF THE CASE

The unusually large number of individual cases involved here found their way to the United States District Court for the Southern District of Ohio in a variety of ways [including direct filings, removal from state court, and multidistrict transfers. In total, approximately 2200 cases were brought together.]

The court designated a five-member Plaintiffs' Lead Counsel Committee to act as the counsel for all plaintiffs. After the completion of discovery, on November 16, 1983, the district court consolidated under Rule 42(a) of the Federal Rules of Civil Procedure all Bendectin cases [originating in Ohio,] and set those cases for trial beginning June 4, 1984 on all common issues of liability. The original decision was to bifurcate the trial, and if the plaintiffs were successful in obtaining a verdict finding liability, the court would schedule individual damages trials. While consolidation for trial was mandated for all cases pending in federal court in Ohio, the trial judge also permitted consolidation upon the liability issues for any case which had been transferred to the Southern District of Ohio under MDL 486. 28 U.S.C. § 1404. Those cases would be returned to the originating district if the verdict in the first portion of the bifurcated trial was for the plaintiffs. The district judge indicated that under Erie Railroad Co. v. Tompkins, 304 U.S. 64 (1938), all claims which had been originally brought or removed to federal court in Ohio would necessarily be governed by Ohio law, and that plaintiffs who had originally filed in other districts and who voluntarily chose to participate in the common issues trial would consent to application of the law of Ohio by so agreeing to participate. A number of plaintiffs chose to leave the consolidated proceedings after the completion of discovery and this order, and the district court accordingly returned those suits to the district in which they had been originally filed. . . .

Because the parties could not agree which issues should be tried during the first phase of trial, the court itself decided that the common issues to be tried beginning on June 11, 1984, would be whether: (1) taken as prescribed,

Bendectin caused any of a list of birth defects; (2) Bendectin was unreasonably dangerous as defined by Ohio courts; and (3) Merrell Dow provided to the medical profession adequate warnings of the danger of the product. On April 12, 1984, the district court amended this order. Rather than bifurcating the trial on issues of liability and damages, the court instead decided to trifurcate the case, or bifurcate the liability question into liability and causation. Initially, a jury determination would be made on the causation question. If plaintiffs prevailed on the causation question, the jury would then consider the other liability questions. Conversely, if defendant received a favorable verdict on the causation issue, the trial would cease. Because the case would now be trifurcated rather than bifurcated, the district judge allowed any plaintiffs whose cases had been brought originally in courts outside Ohio to rescind their agreement to participate in the trial . . . .

The trifurcated trial commenced in February, 1985. . . . Following trial, judgment was entered for defendant upon the jury's negative answer to the question whether plaintiffs had proven that ingestion of Bendectin proximately causes birth defects. . . .

IV. TRIFURCATION

The plaintiffs challenge the district judge's decision to trifurcate this case by trying only the issue of proximate causation. They maintain that trifurcation violates their due process rights and Seventh Amendment right to trial by jury, and thus renders the decision an abuse of discretion. . . .

Plaintiffs raise many different arguments to support their claim that the district court judge abused his discretion in ordering trifurcation. First, they maintain that under the law of proximate causation as applied in this case, causation is not an issue capable of separation from issues of defendant's fraud, wrongful conduct, or negligence. Second, they object to the ruling because: the court's trifurcation decision came as a surprise and only *after* discovery had been completed; a different jury would have heard later stages of trial; proximate cause was a particularly difficult and improper issue to be independently decided by a lay jury; and trifurcation resulted in a sterile trial removed from plaintiffs' actual injuries. Third and finally, plaintiffs assert that the trifurcation ruling resulted in the exclusion of evidence that was vital to the determination of the single, causation issue.

Of all the issues on appeal, the validity of the trifurcation ruling has been most troubling to us. We reiterate that the standard of review is abuse of discretion. . . . "The decision whether to try issues separately is within the sound discretion of the court. . . . Abuse of discretion exists only where there is 'definite and firm conviction that the court below committed a clear error of judgment in the conclusion it reached upon a weighing of the relevant factors.'" Yung v. Raymark Industries, 789 F.2d 397, 400 (6th Cir. 1986) (citation omitted).

The standards for separating issues is set forth in the language of Fed. R. Civ. P. 42(b) . . . . "The Advisory Committee Note to the 1966 amendment, though cryptic, suggests that . . . the changes in Rule 42 were intended to give rather delphic encouragement to trial of liability issues separately from those of damages, while warning against routine bifurcation of the ordinary negligence case." 9 C. Wright, A. Miller & F. Elliott, Federal Practice & Procedure, § 2388 at 280 (1971 & Supp. 1987). It cannot seriously be argued that this is a routine case.

The principal purpose of the rule is to enable the trial judge to dispose of a case in a way that both advances judicial efficiency and is fair to the parties. . . . Neither Rule 42(b) nor the textual elaboration cited gives any precise guidelines for the trial judge in considering the propriety of ordering separate trials, probably because of the wide variety of circumstances in which it might come into play. Consequently, courts have adopted a case-by-case approach. . . . Courts, including our own, have measured trial court decisions to try issues separately by whether fairness was advanced in the particular case . . . .

In our case this same test applies to whether the decision is to try only one or more than one issue separately. Our opinion in In re Beverly Hills [Fire] Litigation, 695 F.2d 207 (6th Cir. 1982), approving trifurcation on the causation question, did not indicate any different standard of review than that applicable to bifurcation nor has our research led us to authority suggesting such a distinction. While few cases appear to have been trifurcated on the issue of causation, there are nonetheless numerous cases that have tried an individual issue separately under circumstances that, had the issue been decided in favor of the plaintiff, the trial would have had more than two phases to it. . . . It follows, therefore, that a decision to try an issue separately will be affirmed unless the potential for prejudice to the parties is such as to clearly demonstrate an abuse of discretion. *Beverly Hills*, 695 F.2d at 216.

Of course, the subject for review is not the abstract question of trifurcation generally, but the appropriateness of trifurcation in the context of the litigation at hand. It is to the specific facts of this case that we must apply the 42(b) standards for separating issues.

A. PROXIMATE CAUSATION AS A SEPARABLE ISSUE

Fundamental to plaintiffs' challenge of the trifurcation decision is their argument that the causation question in this case was not an issue which could be tried separately. In support of their claim, plaintiffs rely heavily on Gasoline Products Co. v. Champlin Refining Co., 283 U.S. 494, 500 (1931). There, the Court held that "where the practice permits a partial new trial, it may not properly be resorted to unless it clearly appears that the issue to be retried is so distinct and separable from the others that a trial of it alone may be had without injustice." The Court noted that the issue in that case could not be submitted independently of the others without creating jury confusion and uncertainty that would "amount to a denial of a fair trial." Id. Many courts consider the issue's ability to be tried separately, and without injustice, to be the standard for determining whether the Seventh Amendment has been violated by conducting a trial only on that one issue. Thus, they apply the *Gasoline Products* standard to initial determinations whether a district judge properly ordered a separate trial in the first instance. *Franchi Construction Co. v. Combined Insurance Co. of America*, 580 F.2d 1, 7 (1st Cir. 1978). While *Beverly Hills* did not cite *Gasoline Products*, our court in Helminski v. Ayerst Laboratories, 766 F.2d 208, 212 (6th Cir. 1985), cited *Gasoline Products* as the standard for determining whether the issues of liability and damages in that case were sufficiently separable to justify a separate trial. . . . We affirm the appropriateness of the *Gasoline Products* standard to the context of Rule 42(b).

Under this standard, many courts have upheld cases bifurcated between liability and damages because the evidence pertinent to the two issues is wholly unrelated, and as a logical matter, liability must be resolved before the question of damages. . . . By the same token, courts have refused to permit even bifurcation of liability and damages where these issues could not be tried separately. . . .

In the present case, plaintiffs argue that the *Gasoline Products* standard is violated because under the current standards and presumptions set forth in Ohio law, the issue of causation cannot be separated from the issue of defendant's tortious conduct. In their assertion of the nonseparability of these two issues, plaintiffs cite various tort theories that shift the burden of proof to defendants before causation has been proven more probable than not or weaken plaintiffs' burden of proof with regard to causation.

First, plaintiffs contend that in cases involving multiple possible causes, the courts must abandon any "but for" causation test in favor of the "substantial factor" test to be applied where plaintiff seeks to prove that the defendant's wrongful act is only one of several substantial factors bringing about the injury. Thus, it is argued, because the determination of wrongdoing affects which standard plaintiffs need prove, liability must be tried either before or contemporaneously with the determination of causation. Moreover, plaintiffs argue that the court should have charged the jury that the plaintiff need only show that Bendectin is a substantial contributing factor in causing birth defects and the burden of proof would then shift to the defendant to prove that Bendectin was not such a substantial factor. . . .

[After surveying Ohio law, the court concluded] that even if the cited Ohio cases were applied to the present case, plaintiffs would still have to prove "but for" causation rather than some weaker "substantial factor" standard. . . .

B. TRIFURCATION AS A POTENTIAL SOURCE OF UNFAIR PREJUDICE . . .

The plaintiffs . . . challenge the trifurcation order because even had they won this stage of the trial, the court gave no assurance that the same jury that heard the evidence on causation, and rendered them a favorable verdict, would decide the question of liability. Plaintiffs' attorney Chesley specifically repeated this assertion at oral argument. The facts are otherwise. In Mr. Chesley's presence, the district judge indicated "that if the plaintiffs prevailed . . . the same jury [would] be used for the next phase of the trial." Judge Rubin did, however, offer to impanel a new jury if both sides so requested. No objection was raised to either comment, and, in fact Mr. Chesley explicitly indicated that it would "not [be] impossible to seat a new jury." Even had such a procedure been contemplated, and we emphasize that it was not, the party challenging such a procedure was willing to accept it below. In his argument on behalf of plaintiffs on appeal, Professor Arthur Miller acknowledged that there is no constitutional prohibition against trying these issues before different juries. . . .

Plaintiffs' next challenge the decision to trifurcate on the proximate causation question because the issue trifurcated was the one which a lay jury would be least qualified to understand, evaluate, and decide. The district judge offered to try the case before a blue ribbon jury, but the plaintiffs rejected the idea. This was, of course, their right. In any event we conclude that if the issues were indeed difficult, their resolution was not rendered more difficult due to trifurcation. If anything, the narrowing of the range of inquiry through trifurcation substantially improved the manageability of the presentation of proofs by both sides and enhanced the jury's ability to comprehend the causation issue.

Plaintiffs' primary argument against trifurcation as unfairly prejudicial is that trying the question alone prejudiced plaintiffs by creating a sterile trial atmosphere. In *Beverly Hills*, we addressed similar concerns that trifurcation could possibly prevent the plaintiffs from exercising their right to present to the jury the full atmosphere of their cause of action, including the reality of injury:

> A strong argument can, it is true, be made against the bifurcation of a trial limited to the issue of causation. There is a danger that bifurcation may deprive plaintiffs of their legitimate right to place before the jury the circumstances and atmosphere of the entire cause of action which they have brought into the court, replacing it with a sterile or laboratory atmosphere in which causation is parted from the reality of injury. In a litigation of lesser complexity, such considerations might well have prompted the trial judge to reject such a procedure. Here, however, it is only necessary for us to observe that the occurrence of the fire itself, a major disaster in Kentucky history by all standards, was generally known to the jurors from the outset. Further, the proofs themselves, although limited, were nonetheless fully adequate to apprise the jury of the general circumstances of the tragedy and the environment in which the fire arose. As a result, we hold that the trial judge did not abuse his discretion in severing the issue of causation here.

Beverly Hills, 695 F.2d at 217. Judge Rubin considered this language when he denied the plaintiffs' motion for a new trial. On appeal plaintiffs also rely heavily on the same language. Sterility is not necessarily the inevitable consequence in a trifurcated trial merely because the jury may not hear the full evidence of defendant's alleged wrongdoing. It more properly refers to the potential danger that the jury may decide the causation question without appreciating the scope of the injury that defendant supposedly caused and without the realization that their duties involve the resolution of an important, lively and human controversy. It is with respect to this latter concern that the plaintiffs urge that they were unfairly prejudiced by the trifurcation. The record reveals that the district judge consciously worked to avoid the potential for unfair prejudice. For example, he instructed the jury:

> Let me suggest to you that what you are about to do may be one of the most important things you will ever do in your entire entire [sic] life. This is a significant case. It involves a lot of people. It involves not only the plaintiffs who are individuals, it involves people, scientists, people who have done experiments, people who are employees of the defendant company. The totality of this case involves people and while you will hear technical evidence, I do point out to you that at all times, you should keep in mind that on both sides, there are people involved.

The court was not alone in efforts to avoid the dangers of sterility. In his final argument, plaintiffs' attorney Eaton told the jury that the trial was not an academic exercise, and that the case involved many real people who sought justice, and who would, as children, be affected by the jury's verdict well into the next century.

Finally, plaintiffs argue that Judge Rubin failed to consider the caveats of Rule 42(b) in his trifurcation decision, and instead justified trifurcation only upon unsubstantiated claims of judicial efficiency, thus unduly prejudicing plaintiffs' case without good reason. We believe, however, that the district judge carefully made the necessary inquiry. In his final order the trial judge noted that Bendectin litigation could "substantially immobiliz[e] the entire Federal Judiciary. There have been only four cases involving Bendectin which have been individually tried. They required an average of 38 trial days." Judge Rubin calculated that if all 1100 cases were tried at that average length on an individual basis, they would be able to keep 182 judges occupied for one year. Contrary to the plaintiffs' claims that Judge Rubin never considered the language of Rule 42(b), he did correctly require plaintiffs to prove that the defendant's drug caused their injury, and would not allow plaintiffs to buttress a weak causation case with a strong negligence case. Thus, in line with the language of Rule 42(b), the trial judge considered the causation question to be a separate issue.

In reviewing the district court's decision to trifurcate we further note Rule 42 which "giv[es] the court virtually unlimited freedom to try the issues in whatever way trial convenience requires." C. Wright, A. Miller & F. Elliott, *supra*, § 2387 at 278. Thus, a court may try an issue separately if "in the exercise of reasonable discretion [it] thinks that course would save trial time or effort or make the trial of other issues unnecessary." Richmond v. Weiner, 353 F.2d 41, 44 (9th Cir. 1965). In this case, the district judge considered the time savings in trying this case in this fashion, and surmised that if the plaintiffs won on this issue, another eight weeks of trial would be necessary to resolve the other questions.

Many courts have in fact permitted separate issue trials when the issue first tried would be dispositive of the litigation. The courts do so because the efficiency of the trial proceedings is greatly enhanced when a small part of the case can be tried separately and resolve the case completely. For example, in *Yung v. Raymark*, 789 F.2d at 401, we recently approved the separate trial of the issue of statute of limitations because if that issue were resolved to bar recovery, the court would be spared the necessity of trying liability and damages. . . . Plainly, Judge Rubin had a massive case management problem to resolve, and chose to do so by trying the case on a separate issue that would be dispositive. . . .

To summarize, the three considerations we apply in reviewing a decision to try an issue separately are (1) whether the issue was indeed a separate issue, (2) whether it could be tried separately without injustice or prejudice, and (3) whether the separate trial would be conducive to judicial economy, especially if a decision regarding that question would be dispositive of the case and would obviate the necessity of trying any other issues. We hold that since the initial trial on the proximate causation issue was a separate issue, promoted efficiency, and did not unduly prejudice plaintiffs, trifurcating this case on the separate issue of proximate causation was proper. We need not decide whether this was the best or even the only good method of trying this case. We need only determine whether, under all of the circumstances before him, the trial judge's decision to trifurcate was an abuse of discretion. . . .

[W]e are not persuaded that the law in any American jurisdiction would preclude separation of the issues of causation and culpability in such complex cases as the present one. Therefore, we conclude that the district judge did not abuse his discretion in determining to try causation as a separate issue as to all plaintiffs over which that court had jurisdiction. . . .

In upholding the result here to the extent we have, it is at least deserving of note that a careful examination of the trial record itself reveals the management of the trial by a judge who does not appear at any time throughout to have sought consciously or unconsciously to have unfairly tipped the scales in favor of one side or the other, but who instead in his rulings appeared to be genuinely concerned with producing a trial that was as fair and free from error as human endeavor could make it. While we must always be conscious of the potential danger of making the trial a sterile exercise of scientific investigation by limiting issues and evidence too narrowly, it is quite evident, through several thousand pages of testimony, that the jury was presented with and bound to appreciate the seriousness of a very real issue of great importance to the parties at suit. In fact, to have broadened the issues beyond that of causation would have occasioned a real risk of overencumbering the jurors and impairing their ability to reach a knowledgeable and intelligent verdict based upon the evidence and upon the law applicable under the appropriate instructions. . . .

■ JONES, Circuit Judge, concurring in part and dissenting in part. . . . Although I have no problem with the approved trifurcation order in this court's *Beverly Hills* decision, I do become hesitant when that decision is applied, seemingly without reservation, to a case, such as this one, which is complex in nature. Because I find several distinctions between this case and *Beverly Hills*, I am reluctant to apply such reasoning wholesale. Thus, I find that if *Beverly Hills* is narrowly construed, several problems become apparent with the majority opinion.

First, all of the victims in the *Beverly Hills* litigation were affected by the same event, a disastrous and tragic fire. Thus, the issue of causation could, quite competently, be tried separately from the issues of liability and damages with only a small chance that the plaintiffs would be prejudiced. . . . Individual facts about the individual plaintiffs would therefore, have had little significance in regard to the question of causation.

The *Bendectin* litigation, however, is quite different. Over eight hundred plaintiffs, whose mothers took the drug at different times and places and under different circumstances, are involved. As such, a single, unique event such as a fire is replaced by over eight hundred distinct events that, in all likelihood, affected the individual plaintiffs in different ways. Although each distinct event involved the ingesting of the same drug, it is hard to believe that all eight hundred plus claims can be tied neatly into one package and satisfactorily resolved by the answering of one question, *i.e.*, did Bendectin cause the relevant birth defects? In tying all of these claims together, an argument could certainly be made as to prejudice. That is, by not allowing the plaintiffs to present evidence as to how they were individually affected by the drug could have resulted in prejudice to them in their attempt to establish the required elements of their case. . . . The majority opinion refers to the fact that the plaintiffs were not "unduly" prejudiced by the court's trifurcation order. I do not agree that this is the burden plaintiffs must meet to establish an abuse of discretion by the lower court with regard to a trifurcation order. Rather, my suggestion is that any prejudice to a plaintiff in the litigation of his or her case should be enough to hold that the lower court has abused its discretion. . . . Plaintiffs here simply failed to meet their burden to demonstrate any prejudice. That is, plaintiffs lost their case because they failed to establish any link between their birth defects and the drug Bendectin, not because of any prejudice to them resulting from the trifurcation order. . . .

Simply because a litigant shares his complaint with eight hundred other claimants is not a reason to deprive him of the day in court he would have enjoyed had he been the sole plaintiff. However, as the majority points out, a trifurcation order is authorized and necessitated at some point so as to allow a district court to manage and control the complexities and massive size of a case. The duty of this court, however, is to prevent such a case-management tool from becoming a penalty to injured plaintiffs seeking relief via the legal system.

Roger H. Trangsrud, MASS TRIALS IN MASS TORT CASES: A DISSENT

1989 U. Ill. L. Rev. 69, 80-82

Trifurcation of issues in a mass tort case is neither fair nor efficient. It is not fair because it robs the jury of its traditional flexibility in tort cases to balance uncertainties in the plaintiff's case on liability against strengths in the plaintiff's case on damages. Trifurcation of issues also inevitably leads to the sterile trial of technical issues related to causation divorced from the fact of the plaintiff's injury and a full account of the defendant's role in the tragedy....

The plaintiffs' argument [in *Bendectin*] that trifurcation had transformed an ordinary tort suit into a sterile and laboratory inquiry into causation was rejected on grounds that appear to be utterly implausible. The Sixth Circuit stated that this concern was adequately allayed by the trial judge's instruction to the jury that "[t]his is a significant case. It involves a lot of people" and by the closing argument of plaintiff's counsel that the trial was "not an academic exercise" and "involved many real people who sought justice." The suggestion that such remarks are an adequate substitute for the presence and testimony of the injured plaintiff and a full presentation of all of the alleged misconduct of the defendant pharmaceutical company is incredible on its face. This Bendectin jury was deprived of the evidence most tort juries would routinely hear regarding the totality of circumstances surrounding the plaintiff's injury in a manner likely to affect their deliberations in a substantial way.

Some commentators have argued all tort cases should be routinely bifurcated so that jury deliberation on liability issues would be unswayed by evidence of the nature and severity of the plaintiff's injury. Despite the apparent appeal of separating these issues, bifurcation is rare in ordinary tort litigation because for decades most courts have felt that the fusion of liability and damage issues by a tort jury is necessary to allow the jury to play its proper and traditional role as an institution that directly reflects current norms, concerns, and thinking. Sometimes legal doctrine falls behind jury wisdom....

If the Bendectin claims had been tried separately, it is possible that the defendant would have consistently prevailed. It is also possible, however, that juries presented with the entire case against the manufacturer of this drug would have awarded discounted damages to the plaintiffs before them, mindful of the serious character of the plaintiffs' injuries and the inconclusive evidence that the injuries were caused by the defendant's drug. Such an outcome would seem to be at odds with our current law of causation, but might anticipate reform of that law in the future. Perhaps the law is moving to allow a discounted recovery when a defendant's product increases the risk of disease or injury beyond natural levels, but strict causation cannot be proven due to the passage of time or the imperfect nature of our science.

In any event, it is wrong to take such options and flexibility away from those juries that hear mass tort trials and leave them only with the opportunity to give an opinion on an abstract question of causation. The plaintiffs in such cases are no less deserving of and entitled to full jury consideration of their case than are the victims of isolated torts.

IN THE MATTER OF RHONE-POULENC RORER INC.

51 F.3d 1293 (7th Cir.), cert. denied, 516 U.S. 867 (1995)

■ POSNER, Chief Judge. [The facts of this product liability action, brought by persons with hemophilia against the makers of HIV-infected blood products, are described at p. 540, *supra*. Briefly, plaintiffs in the multidistrict proceeding obtained certification of a (b)(3) litigation class. Defendants sought a writ of mandamus against the certification order. The court first found that irreparable harm might occur to the defendants if the writ of mandamus did not issue. It then turned to the issue of whether defendants were entitled to the writ because of the district court's clear abuse of discretion. After finding that the trial judge had erroneously granted class certification on two other grounds, see pp. 540, 860, *supra*, the majority turned to a third reason that mandamus relief against the certification order was appropriate.]

The third respect in which we believe that the district judge has exceeded his authority concerns the point at which his plan of action proposes to divide the trial of the issues that he has certified for class-action treatment from the other issues involved in the thousands of actual and potential claims of the representatives and members of the class. Bifurcation and even finer divisions of lawsuits into separate trials are authorized in federal district courts. . . . However, as we have been at pains to stress recently, the district judge must carve at the joint. Hydrite Chemicals Co. v. Calumet Lubricants Co., 47 F.3d 887, 890-91 (7th Cir.1995) . . . . Of particular relevance here, the judge must not divide issues between separate trials in such a way that the same issue is reexamined by different juries. The problem is not inherent in bifurcation. It does not arise when the same jury is to try the successive phases of the litigation. But most of the separate "cases" that compose this class action will be tried, after the initial trial in the Northern District of Illinois, in different courts, scattered throughout the country. The right to a jury trial in federal civil cases, conferred by the Seventh Amendment, is a right to have juriable issues determined by the first jury impaneled to hear them (provided there are no errors warranting a new trial), and not reexamined by another finder of fact. This would be obvious if the second finder of fact were a judge. . . . But it is equally true if it is another jury. Gasoline Products Co. v. Champlin Refining Co., 283 U.S. 494, 500 (1931) . . . .

The plan of the district judge in this case is inconsistent with the principle that the findings of one jury are not to be reexamined by a second, or third, or nth jury. The first jury will not determine liability. It will determine merely whether one or more of the defendants was negligent under one of the two theories. The first jury may go on to decide the additional issues with regard to the named plaintiffs. But it will not decide them with regard to the other class members. Unless the defendants settle, a second (and third, and fourth, and hundredth, and conceivably thousandth) jury will have to decide, in individual follow-on litigation by class members not named as plaintiffs . . ., such issues as comparative negligence — did any class members knowingly continue to use unsafe blood solids after they learned or should have learned of the risk of contamination with HIV? — and proximate causation. Both issues overlap the issue of the defendants' negligence. Comparative negligence entails, as the name implies, a comparison of the degree of negligence of plaintiff and defendant. . . . Proximate causation is found by determining whether the harm to the plaintiff followed in some sense naturally, uninterruptedly, and with reasonable probability from the negligent act of the defendant. It overlaps the issue of the defendants' negligence even when the state's law does not (as many states do) make the foreseeability of the risk to which the defendant subjected the plaintiff an explicit ingredient of negligence. . . . A second or subsequent jury might find that the defendants' failure to take precautions against infection with Hepatitis B could not be thought the proximate cause of the plaintiffs' infection with HIV, a different and unknown blood-borne virus. How the resulting inconsistency between juries could be prevented escapes us.

The protection of the right conferred by the Seventh Amendment to trial by jury in federal civil cases is a traditional office of the writ of mandamus. Beacon Theatres v. Westover, 359 U.S. 500 (1959) . . . . But the looming infringement of Seventh Amendment rights is only one of our grounds for believing this to be a case in which the issuance of a writ of mandamus is warranted. The others as we have said are the undue and unnecessary risk of a monumental industry-busting error in entrusting the determination of potential multi-billion dollar liabilities to a single jury when the results of the previous cases indicate that the defendants' liability is doubtful at best and the questionable constitutionality of trying a diversity case under a legal standard in force in no state. We need not consider whether any of these grounds standing by itself would warrant mandamus in this case. Together they make a compelling case.

Hans Zeisel & Thomas Callahan, SPLIT TRIALS AND TIME SAVING: A STATISTICAL ANALYSIS

76 Harv. L. Rev. 1606, 1607-08, 1616-17, 1624-25 (1963)

The way in which separation of issues may save court time is clear. In the traditional form of trial, the damage issue must be litigated even where the verdict will ultimately reject liability; separation would eliminate the need for trying the damage issue in those cases, comprising roughly 40 per cent of all personal injury jury trials. . . . There remained, however, the possibility that these savings might well be offset by a number of countervailing factors not so immediately obvious. . . . The crucial question for this study was, therefore, not so much whether but rather *how much* time would be saved by the separation of issues. . . .

[One] table provides further insights into the means by which time is saved through the separation process: Table 6 compares the stage and mode of termination of regular and separated trials. . . .

TABLE 6

STAGE AND MODE OF DISPOSITION OF PERSONAL INJURY JURY TRIALS

Stage of Termination	Settled	Verdict for Defendant		Jury Verdict for Plaintiff on Liability and Damages	Total
		Directed Verdict	Jury Verdict		

A. Regular Trials

Stage of Termination	Settled	Directed Verdict	Jury Verdict	Jury Verdict for Plaintiff on Liability and Damages	Total
During Plaintiff's Case	18%	..	..	..	18%
At End of Plaintiff's Case	3%	1%	..	..	4%
During Defendant's Case	..	..	..	..	..
After Full Trial	3%	2%	31%	42%	78%
Total	24%	3%	31%	42%	100%

B. Separated Trials

Stage of Termination	Settled	Directed Verdict	Jury Verdict	Jury Verdict for Plaintiff on Liability and Damages	Total
During Liability Trial	10%	9%	..	..	19%
At End of Liability Trial	15%	4%	43%	..	62%
During Damage Trial	4%	..	..	..	4%
After Full Damage Trial	3%	..	..	12%	15%
Total	32%	13%	43%	12%	100%

* * *

Separation of issues will save, on the average, about 20 per cent of the time that would be required if these cases were tried under traditional rules. The saving derives from the fact that in many cases separation makes the litigation of damages unnecessary. This group includes all cases in which liability is denied, but also the majority of cases in which liability is affirmed, because two out of three of these cases are likely to be settled without trial of the damage issue. There is no evidence that this saving is offset by a change in the settlement ratio prior to trial, in the frequency of jury waivers, or in the proportion of hung juries, any one of which factors — if affected — could increase the court's trial load.

It is not possible to sort out effectively in advance the cases in which separation would prove futile. Therefore, if a court wants to realize the maximum of potential time saving through separation, it should separate as frequently as possible. . . .

The introduction of the separation rule . . . raised other questions beyond its efficacy as a delay remedy. These questions concern the possible effect of separation on the substance of the jury verdicts. By depriving the jury of its joint verdict, it is argued, subtle influences operate to affect the verdict, and should therefore be included in an overall appraisal of the rule. We are now in the process of collecting data which might have a bearing on this problem; if findings prove significant, they will appear in a subsequent report.

Notes and Questions

1. Professor Zeisel and Mr. Callahan did not subsequently report any findings on the effects of trial-splitting on the substance of jury verdicts. They may, however, have overlooked the rather stunning effect intimated in Table 6. In cases with all issues tried together, 33% of the 78% of trials that reached completion ended in a defense verdict, for a 44% success rate. In bifurcated cases, 47% of the 62% of cases resulted in a defense verdict, for a 76% success rate. (A less dramatic, but equally accurate, way of interpreting the statistics is to say that 34% of all single-resolution cases brought to trial resulted in a defense verdict, while 56% of bifurcated cases resulted in a defense verdict.) Other commentators have noted the outcome-changing effect suggested by these statistics. See, *e.g.*, Charles A. Wright & Arthur R. Miller, 9 Federal Practice & Procedure § 2390 (1995); Doyle W. Curry & Rosemary T. Snider, *Bifurcated Trials*, 24 Trial 47 (March 1988).

Would you expect trifurcation of issues — especially trifurcation in which a "sterile" issue like scientific causation is tried first — to show an even more dramatic skew in defendants' favor? In one recent experiment, 25% of the mock juries that heard only causation found for plaintiffs, while a whopping 87.5% of the mock juries that heard all the evidence, but were asked to deliberate only on the causation question, found for the plaintiffs. The same study also showed, however, that the 25% of the plaintiffs who prevailed in the causation-only trial were awarded significantly higher damages than the 87.5% of the plaintiffs who prevailed in a full trial. See Irwin A. Horowitz & Kenneth S. Bordens, *An Experimental Investigation of Procedural Issues in Complex Tort Trials*, 14 Law & Hum. Behav. 269 (1990)

Would you also expect an order of bifurcation or trifurcation to have a spill-over effect and to result in settlements more favorable to defendants?

2. If the statistics of Zeisel and Callaghan or Horowitz and Borden are correct, under what circumstances would a trial judge be justified in using bifurcation or trifurcation? Are efficiency gains of 20 per cent enough? What if the efficiency gain is the avoidance of damages testimony for a 3,000 member class? What if the jury's ability to comprehend the case was threatened without trial splitting? Whatever the gain, can we justify the disparate treatment of similar Bendectin claimants, some of whom received the trifurcated procedure, and some of whom did not?

3. Indeed, is bifurcation between liability and damages a procedural rule, or a substantive rule that lies beyond the permissible limits of the Rules Enabling Act, 28 U.S.C. § 2072? Compare Eubanks v. Wynn, 420 S.W.2d 698

(Tex. 1967) (issue of liability cannot be bifurcated from issue of damages in tort cases) with Rosales v. Honda Motor Co., 726 F.2d 259 (5th Cir. 1984) (in Texas diversity case, liability properly divided from damages; Rule 42 bifurcation was procedural for purposes of Rules Enabling Act) and Simpson v. Pittsburgh Corning Corp., 901 F.2d 277 (2d Cir.), cert. dismissed, 497 U.S. 1057 (1990) (bifurcation not required even when state courts traditionally use bifurcation for similar cases).

4. A defense lawyer might respond to some of these concerns as follows: "Nothing in an adversarial system demands that a case be tried all together. The single-resolution form of trial was dictated by the needs of the common law — needs that, in light of modern communication and transportation, are no longer imperative. The problem is not that bifurcation skews the results in favor of defendants; the problem has always been that the common law form of trial skewed the results in favor of plaintiffs. If you worry about treating like cases alike, then bifurcate every case. But why in the world should you want to continue with an anachronistic procedure in which jury sympathy, rather than close regard for the facts, plays a decisive role?" Why indeed?

5. Rule 42 permits separate trials in any manner that furthers convenience or avoids prejudice; it does not require the liability-damages divisions that seems to stack the deck against the plaintiff. Some other possibilities include:

(a) *Multiple Bifurcations.* As the *Bendectin* litigation shows, a judge can split a trial into more than two parts. The term of art for a splitting into three parts is "trifurcation," and for more than three parts "polyfurcation." First used about ten years ago in the context of complex litigation, trifurcation is becoming increasingly common. It has been used in mass torts to divide liability from punitive damages from individual issues of causation and damages; in other tort cases to divide statute of limitations issues from other liability and from damages issues; in RICO cases involving supplemental state law claims to separate federal law from state law from damages issues; in third-party or counterclaim cases to separate liability, damages, and third party claims or counterclaims; in patent cases to divide infringement, validity, and damages from each other; and in equitable civil rights cases to divide up various aspects of violation and relief. Sanford v. Johns-Manville Sales Corp., 923 F.2d 1142 (5th Cir. 1991); Hilao v. Estate of Ferdinand Marcos, 103 F.3d 767 (9th Cir. 1996); Osei-Afriyie v. Medical College of Pennsylvania, 937 F.2d 876 (3d Cir. 1991); Yung v. Raymark Industries, Inc., 789 F.2d 397 (6th Cir. 1986); Tabas v. Tabas, 1996 WL 107848 (E.D. Pa.); Miller v. New Jersey Transit Authority Rail Operations, 160 F.R.D. 37 (D. N.J. 1995); Tec Air, Inc. v. Nippondenso Manufacturing USA, Inc., 1995 WL 470243 (N.D. Ill.); United States v. Yonkers Board of Education, 837 F.2d 1181 (2d Cir. 1987). Some courts have further subdivided issues into four or more phases. See *Miller*, 160 F.R.D. 37.

Multiple bifurcations often do not remove the problems of liability-damages bifurcation; indeed, they may enhance the problems. Multiple bifurcations also move American procedure closer to the continuous trial method of many of the world's procedural systems — systems with a high level of hierarchy and a more limited role for lawyers and trial judges. See Mirjan Damaska, The Faces of Justice and State Authority 51-52 (1986).

(b) *Bellwether, Exemplar, or Randomly Selected Plaintiffs.* One of the great concerns of bifurcation is that the jury will not get a flavor of the wrongs that the plaintiffs have suffered, and will therefore be unable to temper their justice with mercy. A partial solution to this problem is to try the liability issues for all the plaintiffs, but also to try the damages cases of a select handful of the plaintiffs. Not only does this solution avoid the sterile laboratory atmosphere that detractors of bifurcation fear, but it also provides the plaintiffs and defendant(s) with reasonably good information about the damage potential of remaining cases, thus enhancing the settlement prospects of those cases. Should the defendant prevail, the amount of wasted time of trying only some damage claims is significantly less than the amount of wasted time had each case been fully tried.

The plaintiffs who are selected to have their entire cases tried are typically called "bellwether plaintiffs," or sometimes "exemplar plaintiffs." The Supreme Court spoke approvingly of the use of bellwether plaintiffs in Affiliated Ute Citizens v. United States, 407 U.S. 916 (1972), and the concept has been used with some frequency. See, e.g., In re Shell Oil Refinery, 136 F.R.D. 588, 596 (E.D. La. 1991), affirmed, 979 F.2d 1014 (5th Cir. 1992), rehearing en banc granted, 990 F.2d 805 (5th Cir. 1993); Maenner v. St. Paul Fire and Marine Insurance Co., 127 F.R.D. 488 (W.D. Mich. 1989) (using class representatives as bellwether plaintiffs); In re Air Crash Disaster at Stapleton International Airport, Denver, Colorado, on November 15, 1987, 720 F. Supp. 1455 (D. Colo. 1988); Allen v. United States, 588 F. Supp. 247 (D. Utah 1984) rev'd on other grounds, 816 F.2d 1417 (10th Cir. 1987), cert. denied, 484 U.S. 1004 (1988); In re Ampicillin Antitrust Litigation, 88 F.R.D. 174 (D.D.C. 1980). But see In re Copley Pharmaceutical, Inc., 161 F.R.D. 456 (D. Wyo. 1995) (rejecting use of bellwether plaintiffs when this method would have delayed trial and class representatives already served as bellwether plaintiffs).

Not surprisingly, the use of bellwether plaintiffs creates a dispute among the parties over which plaintiffs are to be chosen. The plaintiffs want to use their most attractive cases, and the defendant(s) want the least attractive. Traditionally the plaintiff had the ability to nominate the bellwethers, but some courts have developed processes by which trial plaintiffs are randomly selected, selected after some neutral screening, or selected in part by the defendant. See, e.g., Meranus v. Gangel, 1991 WL 120484 (S.D.N.Y.); Blue v. United States, 567 F. Supp. 394 (D. Conn. 1983); Francis E. McGovern, *The Alabama DDT Settlement Fund*, 53 Law & Contemp. Prob. 61, 62-63 (Autumn 1990). If a court intends to use the trials of bellwether plaintiffs to create a judgment that binds all subsequent plaintiffs (a technique we consider in the following section), one court has held that "the sample must be one that is a randomly selected, statistically significant sample." In re Chevron U.S.A., Inc., 109 F.3d 1016, 1021 (5th Cir. 1997).

(c) *Reverse Bifurcation.* Courts in some mass torts, especially asbestos cases, have turned to "reverse bifurcation" (or "reverse trifurcation"), in which damages and causation issues are tried before liability issues. One rationale for such a procedure is that, in mature mass torts like asbestos, the parties have excellent information about the likelihood of success on liability issues; the real sticking points in settlement are the individual issues of causation and damage. Furthermore, by reversing the usual order, some of the "sterility" problems of liability-first bifurcation are removed, although the same jury will need to hear the liability case in order to overcome the problem altogether. See Angelo v. Armstrong World Industries, Inc., 11 F.3d 957 (10th Cir. 1993); Dunn v. Owens-Corning Fiberglass, 774 F. Supp. 929 (D. St. Croix 1991); United States v. Kramer, 770 F. Supp. 954 (D.N.J. 1991); but see Coates v. AC and S, Inc., 844 F. Supp. 1126, 1138 (E.D. La. 1994) (refusing to reverse bifurcate when plaintiff had prepared for single trial and reverse bifurcation had not, in court's experience, facilitated settlements); United States v. New Castle County, 116 F.R.D. 19 (D. Del. 1987) (refusing to trifurcate third party claims in environmental dispute).

(d) *Wave Trials.* In multi-plaintiff cases a court might try one set of plaintiffs first, and if necessary, another and then another. See *Shell Oil*, 136 F.R.D. at 596; Manual for Complex Litigation, Third § 33.28 (1995). These "wave trials" have two purposes. One is to make the factfinding task, which would be difficult if all of the cases of all of the plaintiffs were tried at once, more managable. If the early cases are chosen wisely, a second purpose of wave trials is to provide the general range of likely verdicts so that the parties can settle the latter cases without trial. (You might be wondering whether there is some way to circumvent the later trials. We take up that issue in the next subsection.)

(e) *Other Forms of Claim Bifurcation.* Other types of claim bifurcation are also possible. For instance, one asbestos case divided the trials according to the types of asbestos products to which the plaintiifs had been exposed. See Adams-Arapahoe School District No. 28-J v. GAF Corp., 959 F.2d 868 (10th Cir. 1992). Likewise, legal theories can be segregated; for instance, federal claims can be tried before state claims, or patent claims before antitrust ones. See *Tabas*, 1996 WL 107848; In re Innotron Diagnostics, 800 F.2d 1077 (Fed. Cir. 1986).

(f) *Background and Blueprint Trials.* Plaintiffs have sometimes proposed trials in which the first jury would decide the "background" issues that would then establish the factual framework for later discovery and trials. Other plaintiffs have suggested "blueprint" trials, in which the first jury would leave to later triers of fact only ministerial questions of fact. For instance, in a case like *Bendectin*, the first jury would decide not only whether Bendectin caused the injuries, but also what injuries, in what dosages, and under what circumstances Bendectin could cause such injuries. The only thing that later juries would need to decide would be whether the specific plaintiff was exposed to Bendectin, what the dosage was, and whether the plaintiff had a Bendectin-related injury.

Thus far, courts have not been overly receptive to either background or blueprint trials. See United States v. American Telephone & Telegraph Co., 83 F.R.D. 323, 335-36 (D.D.C. 1979) (no background trial, in part because parties could not agree on what was a background, and what was a central, issue); Payton v. Abbott Labs, 83 F.R.D. 382, 395 (D. Mass. 1979) (blueprint trial would lead to "confusion and uncertainty, which would amount to a denial of a fair trial"); but see Union Carbide and Carbon Corp. v. Nisley, 300 F.2d 561, 589 (10th Cir.), cert. dismissed, 371 U.S. 801 (1962) (approving antitrust trial plan in which first jury established formula for damages recovery for class members).

6. No studies comparable to the Zeisel and Callahan study have been performed on these other trial-splitting devices, so their time saving and outcome-determinative effects are unknown. A court is not restricted to just one of these issue-splitting devices; they can be combined, as long as the overall package of trials meets the terms of Rule 42 and the Seventh Amendment.

7. It should be obvious that the decision whether or not to segregate issues into separate trials will have a dramatic effect on trial strategy. See Curry & Snider, *supra* (discussing ways plaintiffs can win bifurcated trials). It also should be obvious that separate trials have an important effect on pretrial strategy, since discovery and issue-narrowing devices can (not must, but can) be tailored to the ultimate trials. As *Rhone-Poulenc* shows, the possibility and

nature of separate trials also has an effect on joinder decisions. For instance, many courts consider, in ruling on a class certification decision, the possibility of bifurcating the trial. See, *e.g.*, McCarthy v. Kleindienst, 741 F.2d 1406, 1415 (D.C. Cir. 1984) (a "district court should, of course, ordinarily consider such well-established methods as bifurcating the trial into liability and damages phases before denying class certification"); *Maenner*, 127 F.R.D. at 490-91 ("[I]n complex cases with complex issues, justice is often best served if issues are separated."); see also Celestine v. Citgo Petroleum Corp., 165 F.R.D. 463 (W.D. La. 1995) (finding case unmanagable as class action even with bifurcation), *aff'd*, — F.3d —, 1998 WL 244989 (5th Cir. 1998) (p. 599, *supra*); Boughton v. Cotter Corp., 65 F.3d 823 (10th Cir. 1995) (not abuse of discretion to refuse to certify class and instead to use bellwether plaintiffs); Cook v. Rockwell International Corp., 151 F.R.D. 378 (D. Colo. 1993) (use of bellwether plaintiffs rather than class action would be wasteful). See also Schneck v. International Business Machine Corp., 1996 U.S. Dist. LEXIS 10126 (D.N.J.) (considering problems of bifurcation in context of declining to order Rule 42(a) consolidation).

Perhaps the most creative use of trial splitting to aid a class certification decision occurred in *Copley*, which involved multidistricted cases of users of a prescription drug. In a nearly point-by-point refutation of *Rhone-Poulenc*, the transferee judge ordered a nationwide class certified just on common issues of liability and general causation. The judge then established a bifurcated trial plan in which these issues would be tried on a class basis; if liability existed, the individual cases were to be returned to their transferor districts for trial on issues of individual causation, damages, and defenses. 161 F.R.D. at 468-69. The opinion addressed the Seventh Amendment concerns raised by Judge Posner, but concluded that "the Seventh Amendment is not violated by the separation of common issues of liability for class treatment." Id. at 464. Is it an appropriate use of bifurcation to split the trials among numerous districts? Does this district-splitting technique raise Seventh Amendment concerns not found in standard bifurcation? Are those concerns overcome when "district-split" trials are necessary to prevent joinder complexity?

In short, trial splitting is more than a method by which information can be made more digestible for the factfinder. It is also a case management tool that can reduce or eliminate joinder and pretrial complexity, and consequently might be required even when trial complexity is not present. You would therefore expect that judges sensitive to the needs of case management would consider whether to split a trial at an early stage of the litigation. Often they do, but a surprising number of judges delay the decision on trial bifurcation until late in the pretrial process. Should a judge be required to make a bifurcation decision early in the case, subject to change only for new circumstances? See F.R.Civ.P. 16(c)(13). Does it concern you that a judge has the power to time a bifurcation decision in order to advance or retard certain interests?

8. Courts seem to differ on the exact standards or circumstances under which trial-splitting should occur. The most comprehensive list of factors is found in Kimberly-Clark Corp. v. James River Corp. of Virginia, 131 F.R.D. 607, 608-09 (N.D. Ga. 1989):

> In addition to the more general factors set forth in Rule 42(b); *i.e.*, (1) convenience; (2) prejudice; (3) expedition; and (4) economy; a court reviewing a motion for separate trials may properly consider (5) whether the issues sought to be tried separately are significantly different; (6) whether they are triable by jury or the court; (7) whether discovery has been directed to a

single trial of all issues; (8) whether the evidence required for each issue is substantially different; (9) whether one party would gain some unfair advantage from separate trials; (10) whether a single trial of all issues would create the potential for jury bias or confusion; and (11) whether bifurcation would enhance or reduce the possibility of a pretrial settlement.

Other courts look to the enhancement of juror comprehension of complex issues, the possibility that bifurcation may make the presentation of lengthy evidence unnecessary, and the lack of unfair prejudice, see Barr Laboratories, Inc. v. Abbott Laboratories, 978 F.2d 98 (3d Cir. 1992); prejudice, less confusion for the jury, convenience and economy, distinctness of the separated issues, possibility of eliminating unnecessary evidence, and lack of objection by parties, see In re Air Crash Disaster at Detroit Metropolitan Airport on August 16, 1987, 737 F. Supp. 391 (E.D. Mich. 1989); distinctness of issues, reduction of burden of trial preparation, possibility of settlement, and efficient consolidation, *Stapleton International*, 720 F. Supp. at 1459; the possibility of management problems with or without bifurcation, *Ampicillin Antitrust Litigation*, 88 F.R.D at 178; the ability of the court to organize the presentation of evidence and to focus the jury's attention in a limited direction, *Tec Air*, 1995 WL 470243; the avoidance of undue juror sympathy for severely injured plaintiffs, *Miller*, 160 F.R.D. at 40-41; and convenience and economy, separability of issues, and fairness, *Angelo*, 11 F.3d at 964-65. See also *Payton*, 83 F.R.D. at 394 ("Insuring a fair trial must take precedence over economy and convenience.").

Does the lack of a clear standard for bifurcation, and the use by different courts of related but different factors, concern you?

9. Trial splitting is hardly routine or automatic; courts and litigants have found a host of problems with trial splitting. Among them are: (1) the possibility that relevant evidence will be excluded, the possibility that plaintiffs are not similarly situated, and the possibility that, with one jury hearing general defenses and another hearing plaintiff-specific defenses, no jury will obtain a complete picture of the case, Rosen v. Reckitt & Colman Inc., 1994 WL 652534 (S.D.N.Y.) (ultimately rejecting arguments); (2) the possibility of inconsistent verdicts, see Lempel & Son Co. v. Boden, 1993 WL 256711 (S.D.N.Y.); (3) the possibility of unfairness if a party needs to reveal its theory of the entire case during the first trial, *Yung*, 789 F.2d at 400-01; (4) the problem of deciding how to try borderline issues that could legitimately be placed into either trial, *Ampicillin Antitrust Litigation*, 88 F.R.D. at 178-79; see Hydrite Chemical Co. v. Calumet Lubricants Co., 47 F.3d 887, 890 (7th Cir. 1994); (5) the related problem that evidence may need to be introduced and witnesses may need to testify twice, see *Miller*, 160 F.R.D. at 40; Beirne v. Security Heating — Clearwater Pools, Inc., 759 F. Supp. 1120, 1124 (M.D. Pa. 1991); In re New York Asbestos Litigation, 1990 WL 100811 (E. & S.D.N.Y.); (6) the ease and speed with which the case could be tried in a single sitting, *Beirne*, 759 F. Supp. at 1124-25; (7) the damage that trial splitting might do to a case management plan or to a party's trial strategy, Refac International, Ltd. v. Mastercard International, 758 F. Supp. 152 (S.D.N.Y. 1991); *Coates*, 844 F. Supp. at 1138; and (8) the ability of a party to use inconsistent legal theories in the two trials, thus maximizing their chance of recovery, *Angelo*, 11 F.3d at 965.

Aside from these specific concerns, there are a host of broader concerns that occasionally make their way into specific arguments about trial splitting. One that we have already explored is bifurcation's possible substantive effect. Another is the Seventh Amendment concern discussed in *Bendectin* and *Rhone-*

Poulenc. The common law jury system contemplated a single trial on all issues. The Seventh Amendment, of course, "preserve[s]" the common law right of jury trial. See also F.R.Civ.P. 42 (b) (trial splitting must "preserv[e] inviolate the right of trial by jury as declared by the Seventh Amendment"). A critical interpretive issue now arises: Does the Seventh Amendment guarantee the common law form of trial, or only that a jury will decide whatever factual issues are presented to it? As *Bendectin* and *Rhone-Poulenc* show, the tendency of the cases is to answer the question with reference to Gasoline Products Co. v. Champlin Refining Co., 283 U.S. 494 (1931). *Gasoline Products* dealt with the issue of how much of a case constitutionally needed to be retried after an order for a new trial. Nonetheless, its "distinct and separable" standard has been used in bifurcation cases as well, so that a court cannot bifurcate a case in a way that the findings in the first trial might preclude a subsequent jury from fully adjudicating the factual issues in the subsequent trial. See Franchi Construction Co. v. Combined Insurance Co., 580 F.2d 1 (1st Cir. 1978). If this is the constitutional standard for trial splitting, should we still seek to preserve the single trial method whenever possible? See Jennifer M. Granholm & William J. Richards, *Bifurcated Justice: How Trial-Splitting Devices Defeat the Jury's Role*, 26 U. Tol. L. Rev. 505 (1995).

One way in which courts have sought to lessen the tension between bifurcation and the Seventh Amendment is to retain the first jury for subsequent trials, so that the same jury will hear all the relevant evidence. See *Rosen*, 1994 WL 652534; *Detroit Metropolitan*, 737 F. Supp. at 395 (use of same jury will prevent sterile or laboratory atmosphere); *Maenner*, 127 F.R.D. at 491-92 (leaving open until after first trial whether same jury would need to be recalled because issues were constitutionally intertwined). Does the use of the same jury for each trial meet the Seventh Amendment concerns of *Gasoline Products*? Will this solution work in complex litigation?

A third general problem with trial splitting is that, in global terms, it may not have the efficiency gains that the method initially promises. A leading law-and economics scholar has performed an extensive economic analysis of trial-splitting techniques, the conclusion of which was that

> a sequential [*i.e.*, bifurcated] trial lowers the expected cost of litigation compared to a unitary trial for both the plaintiff and the defendant . . . . Consequently, a sequential trial (a) increases the plaintiff's incentive to sue, (b) increases the number of lawsuits, and (c) reduces the likelihood that the parties will settle out of court by narrowing the range of mutually acceptable settlements. Hence, sequential decision making may increase the aggregate cost of litigation even though it lowers the expected cost of litigating (as opposed to settling) a particular dispute.

William M. Landes, *Sequential versus Unitary Trials: An Economic Analysis*, 22 J. Legal Stud. 99, 100-01 (1993). Professor Landes did not determine whether the individual gains that typically result from trial splitting outweigh the aggregate losses, but opined that "a sequential trial may cost more than a unitary trial." Id. at 134. Landes further found that reverse bifurcation had effects roughly comparable to ordinary bifurcation. He also described a set of circumstances in which split trials gave incentives to parties to spend more than on a single trial, thus reversing the aggregate effects described above. See also George L. Priest, *Private Litigants and the Court Congestion Problem*, 69 B.U. L. Rev. 527, 552-54 (1989) (using economic analysis to show that bifurcation does little to improve court congestion, but may encourage settlement).

Fourth, given the outcome-determinative potential of trial splitting and the discretion of judges to implement it, we return to our primary concerns with trans-substantivism and adversarialism. The fact that those who are subject to trial splitting might receive a different result from those who are not creates a significant issue of fairness. Likewise, while adversarialism does not establish any specific trial method, it abhors a system of rules in which judges are given power that allows them to change the terms of the parties' participation at trial. Under what circumstances should a trial be split despite trans-substantive and adversarial concerns? Can these concerns be overcome when trial splitting is the only way to ensure rational adjudication? Or should such cases not be adjudicated?

Concerns for trans-substantivism and adversarialism could be addressed by making bifurcation the norm in all cases, both simple and complex. At present, however, routine bifurcation is discouraged. See Lis v. Robert Packer Hospital, 579 F.2d 819 (3d Cir.), cert. denied, 439 U.S. 955 (1978).

10. A few procedural points on trial splitting:

(a) *Burden of Proof.* The party who requests separate trials bears the burden of proving the need for the separation. Lowe v. Philadelphia Newspapers, Inc., 594 F. Supp. 123 (E.D. Pa. 1984).

(b) *Waiver.* A party can waive its right to object to a judge's trial-splitting decision. *Sanford*, 923 F.2d at 1145-46.

(c) *Standard of Review.* A trial judge's decision to separate issues for trial is committed to her discretion. In re Master Key Antitrust Litigation, 528 F.2d 5 (2d Cir. 1975); *Miller*, 160 F.R.D. at 40; *Lowe*, 594 F. Supp. at 125. The decision may be reversed only when an abuse of discretion and clear prejudice to a party are shown. 9 Wright & Miller, *supra*, § 2392. The decision is not appealable of right until the litigation is finished. *Master Key*, 528 F.2d at 14.

11. You might have wondered about the collateral estoppel effects of a separated trial when the cases of some parties are litigated to conclusion, and one of the parties to that litigation wants to use the factual findings of the litigation against other parties who did not participate in the trial. The few cases that have considered the issue have come to the unsurprising conclusion that the factual findings cannot be used against unrelated parties who did not participate in the trial. See *Lempel & Son*, 1993 WL 256711; see also *Tabas*, 1996 WL 107848 (no res judicata effect when federal and state claims are separated).

12. Judges polled on their opinions about trial splitting overwhelmingly supported bifurcation (94% of federal and 82% of state judges sometimes bifurcated cases, and 84% thought that it helped the process). Louis Harris & Associates, *Judges' Opinions on Procedural Issues: A Survey of State and Federal Trial Judges Who Spend at Least Half Their Time on General Civil Cases*, 69 B.U. L. Rev. 731, 743-45 (1989). 98% of federal judges and 88% of state judges also reported that their jurisdiction authorized bifurcation. Id.

The Harris Poll reflects an important point overlooked in the prior notes: State as well as federal courts use trial splitting techniques. See Braddy v. Nationwide Mutual Liability Insurance Co., 470 S.E.2d 820 (N.C. App. 1996); Myers v. Celotex Corp., 88 Md. App. 442, 594 A.2d 1248 (1991); Illinois Manual for Complex Litigation 81-82 (1991).

2. Trial by Statistics

Trial splitting does not avoid the factfinder's ultimate obligation to consider the individual liability and damages issues of individual claimants. Hence, even though trial splitting can limit the information that the factfinder must consider in one trial, it does not limit the information that the factfinder needs to consider overall (at least if plaintiff prevails). In this section we examine a controversial method in which the overall information that the factfinder needs to consider can be limited. That method is often called, sometimes disparagingly, "trial by statistics." The basic notion of such a trial is that the court conducts a survey of all claimants in order to obtain relevant information, selects an adequate sampling of individual claims to use as bellwether cases, and then allows the factfinder to extrapolate, based on the survey data and the bellwether cases, the appropriate remedy for the entire group of claimants. Sound fair? Read on.

IN RE FIBREBOARD CORP.

893 F.2d 706 (5th Cir. 1990)

PATRICK E. HIGGINBOTHAM, Circuit Judge. Defendants Fibreboard Corporation and Pittsburgh Corning Corporation, joined by other defendants, petition for writ of mandamus, asking that we vacate pretrial orders consolidating 3,031 asbestos cases for trial entered by Judge Robert Parker, Eastern District of Texas.

In 1986 there were at least 5,000 asbestos-related cases pending in this circuit. We then observed that "because asbestos-related diseases will continue to manifest themselves for the next fifteen years, filings will continue at a steady rate until the year 2000." That observation is proving to be accurate. In Jenkins v. Raymark, [782 F.2d 468 (5th Cir. 1986),] we affirmed Judge Parker's certification of a class of some 900 asbestos claimants, persuaded that the requirements of Rule 23(b)(3) were met for the trial of certain common questions including the "state of the art" defense. After that order and certain settlements, approximately 3,031 asbestos personal injury cases accumulated in the Eastern District of Texas.

The petitions for mandamus attack the district court's effort to try these cases in a common trial. In summary, and we will explain later in more detail, the district court has set these 3,031 cases for trial commencing February 5, 1990. The trial will proceed in three phases. Phase I is similar to the procedure approved in *Raymark* in which common defenses and punitive damages will be tried. In Phase II, and before the same jury, certain representative cases will be fully tried and the jury will decide the total, or "omnibus" liability to the class. In Phase III, any awarded damages will be distributed utilizing various techniques. Petitioners grumble over Phase I, conceding that it is no more than we have approved in *Raymark*, and focus their fire upon Phase II. . . .

The standard of review is familiar. We are to issue a writ of mandamus only "to remedy a clear usurpation of power or abuse of discretion" when "no other adequate means of obtaining relief is available." . . .

I

On September 20, 1989, Professor Jack Ratliff of the University of Texas Law School filed his special master's report in *Cimino v. Raymark*. The special master concluded that it was "self-evident that the use of one-by-one individual trials is not an option in the asbestos cases." . . . On October 26, . . . [t]he district court concluded that the trial of these cases in groups of 10 would take all of the Eastern District's trial time for the next three years, explaining that it was persuaded that "to apply traditional methodology to these cases is to admit failure of the federal court system to perform one of its vital roles in our society . . . an efficient, cost-effective dispute resolution process that is fair to the parties." The district court then consolidated 3,031 cases under Fed.R.Civ.P. 42(a) "for a single trial on the issues of state of the art and punitive damages and certified a class action under rule 23(b)(3) for the remaining issues of exposure and actual damages." The consolidation and certification included all pending suits in the Beaumont Division of the Eastern District of Texas filed as of February 1, 1989, by insulation workers and construction workers, survivors of deceased workers, and household members of asbestos workers who were seeking money damages for asbestos-related injury, disease, or death.

Phase I is to be a single consolidated trial proceeding under Rule 42(a). It will decide the state of the art and punitive damages issues. . . .

The district court also described the proceedings for Phase II in its October 26 order. In Phase II the jury is to decide the percentage of plaintiffs exposed to each defendant's products, the percentage of claims barred by statutes of limitation, adequate warnings, and other affirmative defenses. The jury is to determine actual damages in a lump sum for each disease category for all plaintiffs in the class. Phase II will include a full trial of liability and damages for 11 class representatives and such evidence as the parties wish to offer from 30 illustrative plaintiffs. Defendants will choose 15 and plaintiffs will choose 15 illustrative plaintiffs, for a total of 41 plaintiffs. The jury will hear opinions of experts from plaintiffs and defendants regarding the total damage award. The basis for the jury's judgment is said to be the 41 cases plus the data supporting the calculation of the experts regarding total damages suffered by the remaining 2,990 class members.

Class members have answered questionnaires and are testifying in scheduled oral depositions now in progress. Petitioners attack the limits of discovery from the class members, but we will not reach this issue. It is sufficient to explain that defendants are allowed a total of 45 minutes to interrogate each class member in an oral deposition. These depositions will not be directly used at the trial in Phase II. Rather, the oral depositions, with the other discovery from class members, provide information for experts engaged to measure the damages suffered by the class.

II

Defendants find numerous flaws in the procedures set for Phase II of the trial. They argue with considerable force that such a trial would effectively deny defendants' rights to a jury under the seventh amendment, would work an impermissible change in the controlling substantive law of Texas, would deny procedural due process under the fifth amendment of the United States Constitution, and would effectively amend the rules of civil procedure contrary to the strictures of the enabling acts. . . .

-A-

The contentions that due process would be denied, the purposes of *Erie* would be frustrated, and the seventh amendment circumvented are variations of a common concern of defendants. Defendants insist that one-to-one adversarial engagement or its proximate, the traditional trial, is secured by the seventh amendment and certainly contemplated by Article III of the Constitution itself. Defendants point out, and plaintiffs quickly concede, that under Phase II there will inevitably be individual class members whose recovery will be greater or lesser than it would have been if tried alone. Indeed, with the focus in Phase II upon the "total picture", with arrays of data that will attend the statistical presentation, persons who would have had their claims rejected may recover. Plaintiffs say that "such discontinuities" would be reflected in the overall omnibus figure. Stated another way, plaintiffs say that so long as their mode of proof enables the jury to decide the total liability of defendants with reasonable accuracy, the loss of one-to-one engagement infringes no right of defendants. Such unevenness, plaintiffs say, will be visited upon them, not the defendants.

With the procedures described at such a level of abstraction, it is difficult to describe concretely any deprivation of defendants' rights. Of course, there will be a jury, and each plaintiff will be present in a theoretical, if not practical, sense. Having said this, however, we are left with a profound disquiet. First, the *assumption* of plaintiffs' argument is that its proof of omnibus damages is in fact achievable; that statistical measures of representativeness and commonality will be sufficient for the jury to make informed judgments concerning damages. We are pointed to our experience in the trial of Title VII cases and securities cases involving use of fraud on the market concepts and mathematical constructs for examples of workable trials of large numbers of claims. We find little comfort in such cases. It is true that there is considerable judicial experience with such techniques, but it is also true we have remained cautious in their use. Indeed, as the district court stated in one massive Title VII case resting on math models:

> . . . [E]conometrics and statistics . . . push from the outside roles of tools for "judicial" decisions toward the core of decision making itself. Stated more concretely: the precision-like mesh of numbers tends to make fits of social problems when I intuitively doubt such fits. I remain wary of the siren call of the numerical display . . .

This concern is particularly strong in this case, where there are such disparities among "class" members.

The plaintiffs' answers to interrogatories and the depositions already conducted have provided enough information to show that if, as plaintiffs contend, the representative plaintiffs accurately reflect the class, it is a diverse group. The plaintiffs' "class" consists of persons claiming different diseases, different exposure periods, and different occupations. The depositions of ten tentative class representatives indicate that their diseases break down into three categories .... [In addition, the amount and timing of exposure to asbestos, the severity of the injuries, the nature and type of damage, the strength of the legal claims, and the allegedly responsible defendant(s) varied among class members.]

We are also uncomfortable with the suggestion that a move from one-on-one "traditional" modes is little more than a move to modernity. Such traditional ways of proceeding reflect far more than habit. They reflect the very culture of the jury trial and the case and controversy requirement of Article III. It is suggested that the litigating unit is the class and, hence, we have the adversarial engagement or that all are present in a "consolidated" proceeding. But, this begs the very question of whether these 3,031 claimants are sufficiently situated for class treatment; it equally begs the question of whether they are actually before the court under Fed.R.Civ.Proc. Rules 23 and 42(b) in any more than a fictional sense. Ultimately, these concerns find expression in defendants' right to due process.

-B-

These concerns are little more than different ways of looking at a core problem. The core problem is that Phase II, while offering an innovative answer to an admitted crisis in the judicial system, is unfortunately beyond the scope of federal judicial authority. It infringes upon the dictates of *Erie* that we remain faithful to the law of Texas, and upon the separation of powers between the judicial and legislative branches.

Texas has made its policy choices in defining the duty owed by manufacturers and suppliers of products to consumers. These choices are reflected in the requirement that a plaintiff prove both causation and damage. In Texas, it is a "fundamental principle of traditional products liability law . . . that the plaintiffs must prove that the defendant supplied the product which caused the injury." These elements focus upon individuals, not groups. The same may be said, and with even greater confidence, of wage losses, pain and suffering, and other elements of compensation. These requirements of proof define the duty of the manufacturers.

Plaintiffs say, of course, that these requirements will be met by the proposed procedures. This proof for 2,990 class members will be supplied by expert opinion regarding their similarity to 41 representative plaintiffs. Plaintiffs deny that they will be extrapolating a total universe from a sample. While we are skeptical of this assertion, plaintiffs' characterization is of little moment. The inescapable fact is that the individual claims of 2,990 persons will not be presented. Rather, the claim of a unit of 2,990 persons will be presented. Given the unevenness of the individual claims, this Phase II process inevitably restates the dimensions of tort liability.

Under the proposed procedure, manufacturers and suppliers are exposed to liability not only in 41 cases actually tried with success to the jury, but in 2,990 additional cases whose claims are indexed to those tried.

Texas has made its policy choices in its substantive tort rules against the backdrop of a trial. Trials can vary greatly in their procedures, such as numbers of jurors, the method of jury instruction, and a large number of other ways. There is a point, however, where cumulative changes in procedure work a change in the very character of a trial. Significantly, changes in "procedure" involving the mode of proof may alter the liability of the defendants in fundamental ways. We do not suggest that procedure becomes substance whenever outcomes are changed. Rather, we suggest that changes in substantive duty can come dressed as a change in procedure. We are persuaded that Phase II would work such a change.

The basic changes in the dynamics of trial caused by the rules of evidence and procedure have been particularly noted with respect to the use of expert testimony. A contemplated "trial" of the 2,990 class members without discrete focus can be no more than the testimony of experts regarding their claims, as a group, compared to the claims actually tried to the jury. That procedure cannot focus upon such issues as individual causation, but ultimately must accept general causation as sufficient, contrary to Texas law.... This type of procedure does not allow proof that a particular defendant's asbestos "really" caused a particular plaintiff's disease; the only "fact" that can be proved is that *in most cases* the defendant's asbestos *would have been* the cause. This is the inevitable consequence of treating discrete claims as fungible claims. Commonality among class members on issues of causation and damages can be achieved only by lifting the description of the claims to a level of generality that tears them from their substantively required moorings to actual causation and discrete injury. Procedures can be devised to implement such generalizations, but not without alteration of substantive principle.

We are told that Phase II is the only realistic way of trying these cases; that the difficulties faced by the courts as well as the rights of the class members to have their cases tried cry powerfully for innovation and judicial creativity. The arguments are compelling, but they are better addressed to the representative branches — Congress and the State Legislature. The Judicial Branch can offer the trial of lawsuits. It has no power or competence to do more. We are persuaded on reflection that the procedures here called for comprise something other than a trial within our authority. It is called a trial, but it is not.

The 2,990 class members cannot be certified for trial as proposed under Rule 23(b)(3), Fed.R.Civ.Pro. Rule 23(b)(3) requires that "the questions of law or fact common to the members of the class predominate over any questions affecting individual members." There are too many disparities among the various plaintiffs for their common concerns to predominate.... To create the requisite commonality for trial, the discrete components of the class members' claims and the asbestos manufacturers' defenses must be submerged. The procedures for Phase II do precisely that, but, as we have explained, do so only by reworking the substantive duty owed by the manufacturers. At the least, the enabling acts prevent that reading.

Finally, it is questionable whether defendants' right to trial by jury is being faithfully honored, but we need not explore this issue. It is sufficient now to conclude that Phase II cannot go forward without changing Texas law and usurping legislative prerogatives, a step federal courts lack authority to take.

III

We admire the work of our colleague, Judge Robert Parker, and are sympathetic with the difficulties he faces. This grant of the petition for writ of mandamus should not be taken as a rebuke of an able judge, but rather as another chapter in an ongoing struggle with the problems presented by the phenomenon of mass torts. The petitions for writ of mandamus are granted. The order for Phase II trial is vacated and the cases are remanded to the district court for further proceedings. We find no impediment to the trial of Phase I should the district court wish to proceed with that trial. We encourage the district court to continue its imaginative and innovative efforts to confront these cases. We also caution that defendants are obligated to cooperate in the common enterprise of obtaining a fair trial.

HILAO v. ESTATE OF FERDINAND MARCOS

103 F.3d 767 (9th Cir. 1996)

FLETCHER, Circuit Judge. The Estate of Ferdinand E. Marcos appeals from a final judgment entered against it in a class-action suit after a trifurcated jury trial on the damage claims brought by a class of Philippine nationals (hereinafter collectively referred to as "Hilao") who were victims of torture, "disappearance", or summary execution under the regime of Ferdinand E. Marcos. . . .

PROCEDURAL HISTORY

Shortly after Marcos arrived in the United States in 1986 after fleeing the Philippines, he was served with complaints by a number of parties seeking damages for human-rights abuses committed against them or their decedents. District courts in Hawai'i and California dismissed the complaints on the grounds that the "act of state" doctrine rendered the cases nonjusticiable. This court reversed in consolidated appeals. Trajano v. Marcos, 878 F.2d 1439 (9th Cir.1989). The Judicial Panel on Multidistrict Litigation consolidated the various actions in the District of Hawai'i.

In 1991, the district court certified the Hilao case as a class action, defining the class as all civilian citizens of the Philippines who, between 1972 and 1986, were tortured, summarily executed, or "disappeared" by Philippine military or paramilitary groups; the class also included the survivors of deceased class members. Certain plaintiffs opted out of the class and continued, alongside the class action, to pursue their cases directly. . . .

The district court ordered issues of liability and damages tried separately. In September 1992, a jury trial was held on liability; after three days of deliberation, the jury reached verdicts against the Estate and for the class and for 22 direct plaintiffs and a verdict for the Estate and against one direct plaintiff. . . .

The district court then ordered the damage trial bifurcated into one trial on exemplary damages and one on compensatory damages. The court ordered that notice be given to the class members that they must file a proof-of-claim form in order to opt into the class. Notice was provided by mail to known claimants and by publication in the Philippines and the U.S.; over 10,000 forms were filed.

In February 1994, the same jury that had heard the liability phase of the trial considered whether to award exemplary damages. After two days of evidence and deliberations, the jury returned a verdict against the Estate in the amount of $1.2 billion.

The court appointed a special master to supervise proceedings related to the compensatory-damage phase of the trial in connection with the class. In January 1995, the jury reconvened a third time to consider compensatory damages. . . .

IX. Methodology of Determining Compensatory Damages

The Estate challenges the method used by the district court in awarding compensatory damages to the class members.

A. District Court Methodology

The district court allowed the use of a statistical sample of the class claims in determining compensatory damages. In all, 10,059 claims were received. The district court ruled 518 of these claims to be facially invalid, leaving 9,541 claims. From these, a list of 137 claims was randomly selected by computer. This number of randomly selected claims was chosen on the basis of the testimony of James Dannemiller, an expert on statistics, who testified that the examination of a random sample of 137 claims would achieve "a 95 percent statistical probability that the same percentage determined to be valid among the examined claims would be applicable to the totality of claims filed". Of the claims selected, 67 were for torture, 52 were for summary execution, and 18 were for "disappearance".

1. Special Master's Recommendations

The district court then appointed Sol Schreiber as a special master (and a court-appointed expert under Rule 706 of the Federal Rules of Evidence). Schreiber supervised the taking of depositions in the Philippines of the 137 randomly selected claimants (and their witnesses) in October and November 1994. These depositions were noticed and conducted in accordance with the

Federal Rules of Civil Procedure; the Estate chose not to participate and did not appear at any of the depositions. (The Estate also did not depose any of the remaining class members.)

Schreiber then reviewed the claim forms (which had been completed under penalty of perjury) and depositions of the class members in the sample. On the instructions of the district court, he evaluated

> (1) whether the abuse claimed came within one of the definitions, with which the Court charged the jury at the trial . . ., of torture, summary execution, or disappearance; (2) whether the Philippine military or paramilitary was . . . involved in such abuse; and (3) whether the abuse occurred during the period September 1972 through February 1986.

He recommended that 6 claims of the 137 in the sample be found not valid.

Schreiber then recommended the amount of damages to be awarded to the 131 claimants. Following the decision in Filartiga v. Pena-Irala, 577 F. Supp. 860, 863 (E.D.N.Y.1984), he applied Philippine, international, and American law on damages. . . . The recommended damages for the 131 valid claims in the random sample totalled $3,310,000 for the 64 torture claims (an average of $51,719), $6,425,767 for the 50 summary-execution claims (an average of $128,515), and $1,833,515 for the 17 "disappearance" claims (an average of $107,853).

Schreiber then made recommendations on damage awards to the remaining class members. Based on his recommendation that 6 of the 137 claims in the random sample (4.37%) be rejected as invalid, he recommended the application of a five-per-cent invalidity rate to the remaining claims. He then performed the following calculations to determine the number of valid class claims remaining:

	Torture	Summary Execution	Disappearance
Claims Filed	5,372	3,677	1,010
Facially Invalid Claims	-179	-273	-66
Remaining Claims	5,193	3,404	944
Less 5% Invalidity Rate	-260	-170	-47
Valid Claims	4,933	3,234	897
Valid Sample Claims	-64	-50	-17
Valid Remaining Claims	4,869	3,184	880

He recommended that the award to the class be determined by multiplying the number of valid remaining claims in each subclass by the average award recommended for the randomly sampled claims in that subclass:

	Torture	Summary Execution	Disappearance
Valid Remaining Claims	4,869	3,184	880
x Average Awards	$51,719	$128,515	$107,853
Class Awards	$251,819,811	$409,191,760	$94,910,640

By adding the recommended awards in the randomly sampled cases, Schreiber arrived at a recommendation for a total compensatory damage award in each subclass:

	Torture	Summary Execution	Disappearance
Class Awards	$251,819,811	$409,191,760	$94,910,640
Sample Awards	$3,310,000	$6,425,767	$1,833,515
TOTALS	$255,129,811	$415,617,527	$96,744,155

Adding together the subclass awards, Schreiber recommended a total compensatory damage award of $767,491,493.

2. Jury Proceedings

A jury trial on compensatory damages was held in January 1995. Dannemiller testified that the selection of the random sample met the standards of inferential statistics, that the successful efforts to locate and obtain testimony from the claimants in the random sample "were of the highest standards" in his profession, that the procedures followed conformed to the standards of inferential statistics, and that the injuries of the random-sample claimants were representative of the class as a whole. Testimony from the 137 random-sample claimants and their witnesses was introduced. Schreiber testified as to his recommendations, and his report was supplied to the jury. The jury was instructed that it could accept, modify or reject Schreiber's recommendations and that it could independently, on the basis of the evidence of the random-sample claimants, reach its own judgment as to the actual damages of those claimants and of the aggregate damages suffered by the class as a whole.

The jury deliberated for five days before reaching a verdict. Contrary to the master's recommendations, the jury found against only two of the 137 claimants in the random sample. As to the sample claims, the jury generally adopted the master's recommendations, although it did not follow his recommendations in 46 instances.[9] As to the claims of the remaining class members, the jury adopted the awards recommended by the master. The district court subsequently entered judgment for 135 of the 137 claimants in the sample in the amounts awarded by the jury, and for the remaining plaintiffs in each of the three subclasses in the amounts awarded by the jury, to be divided pro rata.[10]

9. The jury awarded more than recommended to six torture claimants and less than recommended to five torture claimants; more than recommended for lost earnings to two execution claimants and less than recommended for lost earnings to nineteen execution claimants; more than recommended for pain and suffering to three execution claimants and less than recommended to one execution claimant; less than recommended for lost earnings to six "disappearance" claimants; and more than recommended for pain and suffering to one "disappearance" claimant and less than recommended for three "disappearance" claimants.

10. Although never expressly explained by the district court, the mechanics of this division, as represented by Hilao, are as follows: The 135 random-sample claimants whose claims were found to be valid would receive the actual amount awarded by the jury; the two sample claimants whose claims were held

B. Estate's Challenge

The Estate's challenge to the procedure used by the district court is very narrow. It challenges specifically only "the method by which [the district court] allowed the validity of the class claims to be determined": the master's use of a representative sample to determine what percentage of the total claims were invalid.

The grounds on which the Estate challenges this method are unclear. It states that to its knowledge this method "has not previously been employed in a class action". This alone, of course, would not be grounds for reversal, and in any case the method has been used before in an asbestos class-action case, the opinion in which apparently helped persuade the district court to use this method. See Cimino v. Raymark Indus., Inc., 751 F. Supp. 649, 659-667 (E.D. Tex.1990).

The Estate also argues that the method was "inappropriate" because the class consists of various members with numerous subsets of claims based on whether the plaintiff or his or her decedent was subjected to torture, "disappearance", or summary execution. The district court's methodology, however, took account of those differences by grouping the class members' claims into three subclasses.

Finally, the Estate appears to assert that the method violated its rights to due process because "individual questions apply to each subset of claims, i.e., whether the action was justified, the degree of injury, proximate cause, etc.". It does not, however, provide any argument or case citation to explain how the methodology violated its due-process rights. Indeed, the "individual questions" it identifies — justification, degree of injury, proximate cause — are irrelevant to the challenge it makes: the method of determining the validity of the class members' claims. The jury had already determined that Philippine military or paramilitary forces on Marcos' orders — or with his conspiracy or assistance or with his knowledge and failure to act — had tortured, summarily executed, or "disappeared" untold numbers of victims and that the Estate was liable to them or their survivors. The only questions involved in determining the validity of the class members' claims were whether or not the human-rights abuses they claim to have suffered were proven by sufficient evidence.

Although poorly presented, the Estate's due-process claim does raise serious questions. Indeed, at least one circuit court has expressed "profound disquiet" in somewhat similar circumstances. In re Fibreboard Corp., 893 F.2d 706, 710 (5th Cir.1990). . . . [*Fibreboard*] granted the petitions for mandamus and vacated the trial court's order, but it did so not on due-process grounds but because the proposed procedure worked a change in the parties' substantive rights under Texas law that was barred by the *Erie* doctrine.[14]

---

invalid would receive nothing. All remaining 9,404 claimants with facially valid claims would be eligible to participate in the aggregate award, even though the aggregate award was calculated based on a 5% invalidity rate of those claims.

14. *Cimino*, the district court case upon which the district court appears to have relied in choosing the procedure it followed here, was decided after *Fibre-*

On the other hand, the time and judicial resources required to try the nearly 10,000 claims in this case would alone make resolution of Hilao's claims impossible.... The similarity in the injuries suffered by many of the class members would make such an effort, even if it could be undertaken, especially wasteful, as would the fact that the district court found early on that the damages suffered by the class members likely exceed the total known assets of the Estate.

While the district court's methodology in determining valid claims is unorthodox, it can be justified by the extraordinarily unusual nature of this case. "'Due process,' unlike some legal rules, is not a technical conception with a fixed content unrelated to time, place and circumstances". Cafeteria and Restaurant Workers Union, Local 473 v. McElroy, 367 U.S. 886, 895 (1961). In Connecticut v. Doehr, 501 U.S. 1, 10 (1991), a case involving prejudgment attachment, the Supreme Court set forth a test, based on the test of Mathews v. Eldridge, 424 U.S. 319 (1976), for determining whether a procedure by which a private party invokes state power to deprive another person of property satisfies due process:

> [F]irst, consideration of the private interest that will be affected by the [procedure]; second, an examination of the risk of erroneous deprivation through the procedures under attack and the probable value of additional or alternative safeguards; and third, ... principal attention to the interest of the party seeking the [procedure], with, nonetheless, due regard for any ancillary interest the government may have in providing the procedure or forgoing the added burden of providing greater protections.

501 U.S. at 11. The interest of the Estate that is affected is at best an interest in not paying damages for any invalid claims. If the Estate had a legitimate concern in the identities of those receiving damage awards, the district court's procedure could affect this interest. In fact, however, the Estate's interest is only in the total amount of damages for which it will be liable: if damages were awarded for invalid claims, the Estate would have to pay more. The statistical method used by the district court obviously presents a somewhat greater risk of error in comparison to an adversarial adjudication of each claim, since the former method requires a probabilistic *prediction* (albeit an extremely accurate one) of how many of the total claims are invalid. The risk in this case was reduced, though, by the fact that the proof-of-claim form that the district court required each class member to submit in order to opt into the class required the claimant to certify under penalty of perjury that the information provided was true and correct. Hilao's interest in the use of the statistical method, on the other hand, is enormous, since adversarial resolution of each class member's claim would

board by the same district judge whose order had been vacated in *Fibreboard*. The main difference between the procedures disapproved in *Fibreboard* and those used in *Cimino* appears to be that while the *Fibreboard* process would have presented the 41 cases of the class representatives and allegedly "illustrative" class members to the jury and used those cases to determine an aggregate damage award for the class, the *Cimino* process presented to the jury a statistically significant random sample of class claims and awarded each of the non-sample claims the average of the damages awarded in the sample claims....

pose insurmountable practical hurdles. The "ancillary" interest of the judiciary in the procedure is obviously also substantial, since 9,541 individual adversarial determinations of claim validity would clog the docket of the district court for years. Under the balancing test set forth in *Mathews* and *Doehr*, the procedure used by the district court did not violate due process. . . .

■ RYMER, Circuit Judge, concurring in part and dissenting in part. Because I believe that determining causation as well as damages by inferential statistics instead of individualized proof raises more than "serious questions" of due process, I must dissent from Part IX of the majority opinion. Otherwise, I concur.

Here's what happened: Hilao's statistical expert, James Dannemiller, created a computer database of the abuse of each of the 10,059 victims based on what they said in a claim form that assumed the victim's torture. Although Dannemiller would have said that 384 claims should be examined to achieve generalizability to the larger population of 10,059 victims within 5 percentage points at a 95% confidence level, he decided that only 136 randomly selected claims would be required in light of the "anticipated validity" of the claim forms and testimony at the trial on liability that the number of abuses was about 10,000.

He selected three independent sample sets of 242 (by random selection but eliminating duplicates). Hilao's counsel then tried to contact and hold hearings or depositions with each of the claimants on the first list, but when attempts to contact a particular claimant proved fruitless, the same number in the next list was used. . . .

The persons culled through this process went to Manilla to testify at a deposition (which Dannemiller thought was "remarkable"). He opined that "this random selection method in determining the percentage of valid claims was fair to the Defendant" as "[a] random selection method of a group of 9541 individuals is more accurate than where each individual is contacted." Further, the statistician observed that "[t]he cost and time required to do 9541 would be overwhelming and not justified when greater precision can and was achieved through sampling." Finally, he concluded that "the procedures followed conformed to the standards of inferential statistics and therefore . . . the injuries of the 137 claimants examined are representative of the 9541 victims."

In accordance with the "computer-generated plan developed by James Dannemiller," the Special Master oversaw the taking of the 137 depositions in the Philippines. . . . Based on a review of the deposition transcripts of the 137 randomly selected victim claims, and a review of the claims, the Special Master found that 131 were valid within the definitions which the court gave to the jury; the Philippine military or para-military were involved in the abuse of the valid claims; and the abuse occurred during the period 1972 through February 1986. As a result, he recommended the amount of compensatory damages to be awarded to the valid 131 claimants, and for the entire class based on the average awards for torture, for summary execution . . ., and disappearance . . . . His report indicates that "for all three categories, moral damages as a proximate result of defendants' wrongful acts or omissions, Phil.Civ.Code §§ 2216, 2217 were weighed into the compensation."

Thus, causation and $766 million compensatory damages for nearly 10,000 claimants rested on the opinion of a statistical expert that the selection method in determining valid claims was fair to the Estate and more accurate than individual testimony; Hilao's counsel's contact with the randomly selected victims until they got 137 to be deposed; and the Special Master's review of transcripts and finding that the selected victims had been tortured, summarily executed or disappeared, that the Philippine military was "involved," that the abuse occurred during the relevant period, and that moral damages occurred as a proximate result of the Estate's wrongful acts.

This leaves me "with a profound disquiet," as Judge Higginbotham put it in In re Fibreboard Corp., 893 F.2d 706, 710 (5th Cir.1990). Although I cannot point to any authority that says so, I cannot believe that a summary review of transcripts of a selected sample of victims who were able to be deposed for the purpose of inferring the type of abuse, by whom it was inflicted, and the amount of damages proximately caused thereby, comports with fundamental notions of due process.

Even in the context of a class action, individual causation and individual damages must still be proved individually. . . . Sterling v. Velsicol Chem. Corp., 855 F.2d 1188, 1200 (6th Cir.1988).

There is little question that Marcos caused tremendous harm to many people, but the question is which people, and how much. That, I think, is a question on which the defendant has a right to due process. If due process in the form of a real prove-up of causation and damages cannot be accomplished because the class is too big or to do so would take too long, then (as the Estate contends) the class is unmanageable and should not have been certified in the first place. As Judge Becker recently wrote for the Third Circuit in declining to certify a 250,000-member class in an asbestos action: "Every decade presents a few great cases that force the judicial system to choose between forging a solution to a major social problem on the one hand, and preserving its institutional values on the other. This is such a case." Georgine v. Amchem Prod., Inc., 83 F.3d 610, 617 (3d Cir.1996).

So is this. I think that due process dictates the choice: a real trial. I therefore dissent.

Notes and Questions

1. The concept of trial by statistics is, in our opinion, one of the central matters in this book. It seeks to assure the like treatment of similarly situated claimants, which we generally regard as a good, but it does so at the expense of individual participation through adversarial process, which we regard as disturbing.

2. As *Hilao* says, *Fibreboard* was not the end of the asbestos saga in the Eastern District of Texas. Judge Parker, the district judge in *Fibreboard*, had been trying for a long time to find a creative solution to resolve the asbestos cases clogging his docket. Prior to *Fibreboard*, he had sought to get the

defendants to agree voluntarily on a market-share allocation of asbestos products in his district, an idea which went nowhere; he had attempted to use issue preclusion in order to find asbestos defective and unreasonably dangerous as a matter of law, which the Fifth Circuit rebuffed; he certified an opt-out class action for asbestos cases, which the Fifth Circuit did approve; and he created a voluntary alternative dispute resolution program for class members, which was set aside by the judges of the Eastern District of Texas sitting en banc. See Cimino v. Raymark Industries, Inc., 751 F. Supp. 649, 651 (E.D. Tex. 1990); Hardy v. Johns-Manville Sales Corp., 509 F. Supp. 1353 (E.D. Tex. 1981), reversed in part, 681 F.2d 334 (5th Cir. 1982); Jenkins v. Raymark Industries, Inc., 782 F.2d 468 (5th Cir. 1986). His next solution having failed in *Fibreboard*, Parker "was then back to the *Jenkins* procedure. However, *Jenkins* was flawed in that it could not accommodate the large number of cases that had accumulated on the Court's docket." See *Cimino*, 751 F. Supp. at 651.

Parker's dilemma was simple: In order to reduce joinder complexity, he had aggregated the cases, but the very aggregation now created an issue of trial complexity. In *Cimino* he returned to the drawing board and crafted a trial plan that began with a trifurcation of issues: Phase I resolved all common liability issues and the entitlement of the class to punitive damages; Phase II involved the issues of which asbestos products were used in which worksites during particular times, which crafts were sufficiently exposed to asbestos, and an apportionment of causation among defendants; and Phase III involved individual causation, defenses, and damages issues. The plan for the trial of Phase III was the controversial part. Parker divided the plaintiffs into five disease categories, and then randomly selected 160 plaintiffs (some from each disease category) for full trial. He used two juries, each of which heard five common days of medical testimony and then heard specific evidence in about eighty cases. Each of the 160 plaintiffs then received as his or her damages the amount of the jury's verdict. The process lasted eight months, involved more than 560 witnesses and 6,100 exhibits totaling 577,000 pages, and generated more than 25,300 pages of transcripts. Four judges and three magistrate judges were involved in the process.

As Parker later observed, "[i]f all that is accomplished by this [effort] is the closing of [160] cases, then it was not worth the effort and will not be repeated." *Cimino*, 751 F. Supp. at 653. But Parker went a step further: He averaged the various verdicts for each disease category, and awarded the arithmetic mean of these verdicts to each of the 2,138 class members who had not been involved in an individual trial. Thus, each of the 1,050 class members who suffered from asbestosis (one of the disease categories) but who had not received an individual trial received as their "verdict" the average of the awards given to the 50 class members with asbestosis who had received a full Phase III trial. Prior to the Phase III trial, Parker secured the consent of the 2,138 class members who did not receive an individual trial to this novel procedure.

In a post-trial ruling, Parker defended this arrangement against both policy and constitutional challenge:

>Acceptance of statistical evidence is now commonplace in the Courts. The following illustrations demonstrate the diverse legal contexts in which statistics, particularly random sampling, has been used. Statistical evidence occurs frequently in Title VII employment discrimination cases, most often demonstrating a pattern or practice of discrimination on the part of the employer. . . . Statistical evidence has been used in anti-trust cases

to project pre and post merger market share and market concentration. . . . In trademark infringement suits, statistical sampling is useful in determining consumer product identification and confusion regarding trademarks. . . . Statistical evidence frequently comes into play in civil rights cases. . . . Statistical data has also been used to prove up discrimination in jury selection cases. . . . Moreover, public opinion polls have been allowed in some state courts as evidence of community standards in obscenity cases. . . . In the area of torts, statistics have been used to prove both liability and damages. . . . Courts frequently permit evidence of life-expectancy or mortality tables when determining damages. . . .

The reasons the courts have come to rely on statistics are the same reasons that society embraces the science. It has been proved to provide information with an acceptable degree of accuracy and economy.

Departing from the area of statistical evidence, it is incumbent upon the Court to note that various courts have permitted, or even advocated, the use of formulas or models for damage awards in class action suits, rather than employing an individual-by-individual approach. . . .

Against this backdrop, defendants assert that statistical methodology is somehow inappropriate for mass tort cases. This contention fails when examined under the same microscope used in other cases. The method incorporated into Phase III produces a level of economy in terms of both judicial resources and transaction cost that needs no elaboration. . . .

The post-trial hearing held November 6, 1990, has persuaded the Court that the samples used were, in fact, representative. When setting the sample size for each disease category, the Court sought a confidence level of 95%, in other words ± 2.00 standard deviations. The testimony adduced at the post-trial hearing indicates that the actual precision level achieved by the samples exceeds that sought by the Court. Professor Ronald G. Frankiewicz . . . indicates that, with two minor exceptions, the samples on the whole achieved a 99% confidence level, or in other words, a standard deviation of ± 2.56.

The Court finds no persuasive evidence why the average damage verdicts in each disease category should not be applied to the non-sample members. The averages are calculated after remittitur and take into consideration those cases where plaintiffs failed to prove the existence of an asbestos-related injury or disease resulting in a zero verdict. Individual members of a disease category who will receive an award that might be different from one they would have received had their individual case been decided by a jury have waived any objections, and the defendants cannot show that the total amount of damages would be greater under the Court's method compared to individual trials of these cases. Indeed, the millions of dollars saved in reduced transaction costs inure to defendants' benefit.

This Court, during the inception and implementation of the plan, had one additional concern — a concern similar to one expressed by Judge Higginbotham . . . . The concern is that dispute resolution under our system cannot be reduced to formula. Computers cannot replace judges who bring to their tasks experience and sensitivity to due process as well as the basic fairness that is at the core of our judicial system. Careful scrutiny has persuaded this Court that, in this case, science has assumed its proper role, a role that is in aid of the court and not in replacement of it.

The siren call of numerical display has here too been resisted. It also cannot be said that this effort was not a trial. *Cimino* was a trial in the traditional sense. The 373 Orders entered and the numerous other rulings were the product of judicial opinion, not calculations. The liability verdicts and 160 damage awards were made by three juries in a traditional trial. . . .

Defendants, taking comfort in the language of *In re Fibreboard Corp., supra*, object to the Court's plan and assert that due process, even in the asbestos context, entitles defendants to a traditional one-on-one trial in each of the 2,298 cases. . . .

What remained [after the Phase I and Phase II trials] was the usual variables that are reflected by elements of damages in a personal injury case for a particular plaintiff. The Court addressed these variables by structuring a damages only trial in Phase III that was indistinguishable from a reverse bifurcation damage trial that defendants favor in many parts of the country. [The Phase III trial] produced a result to a 99% confidence level the average of which would be comparable to the average result if all cases were tried. If the existence of variables are the driving force behind defendants' due process argument, then due process has been served.

However, a due process concern remains that is very troubling to the Court. It is apparent from the effort and time required to try these 160 cases, that unless this plan or some other procedure that permits damages to be adjudicated in the aggregate is approved, these cases cannot be tried. Defendants complain about the 1% likelihood that the result would be significantly different. However, plaintiffs are facing a 100% confidence level of being denied access to the courts. The Court will leave it to the academicians and legal scholars to debate whether our notion of due process has room for balancing these competing interests.

Judges at both trial and appellate court levels seldom have the luxury of the time required for true reflection on the consequences of what we do and how we may do it better. All too often the constraints of time militate in favor of traditional methodology even when traditional methods consistently produce a result that is quite unacceptable to litigants, the courts, and to society. . . .

It is this Court's opinion that due process in the asbestos context should not be analyzed in the narrow, traditional, one-sided view of defendants, but should also encompass the impact on plaintiffs and even the obvious societal interest involved. To take defendants' argument is to embrace perfection as the benchmark; this Court submits that a confidence level of 99% will do. [751 F. Supp. at 660-66.]

What exactly is the difference between the procedure in *Fibreboard* and the procedure in *Cimino*? In *Fibreboard* the jury was to have heard the evidence of a non-representative (in statistical terms) sample of 41 class members and evidence about the characteristics of the remaining class members, and then awarded damages to the class as a whole. After such a trial, presumably, the trial court would then have needed to distribute the lump sum among the class, and presumably would have done so on a pro rata basis. In *Cimino* the jury heard evidence of a representative sample of class members and awarded individual damages in those cases, and the court then awarded the average award for comparable damages to the remaining members. Does the *Cimino* trial plan meet the primary objections raised in *Fibreboard* with respect to the class members whose cases were not tried? The *Cimino* defendants sought both a writ of mandamus and interlocutory appeal against the Phase III trial in *Cimino*, but the Fifth Circuit, without written opinion, refused the writ and further refused to accept interlocutory appeal. See Fibreboard Corp., No. 90-4199 (5th Cir. Mar. 29, 1990); Celotex Corp., No. 90-9060 (5th Cir. Mar. 29, 1990). As of this writing, the case is pending on appeal from the final judgment. How would you decide the appeal?

3. *Hilao*, which upholds a trial plan that was derived from *Cimino*, may help you answer this question. In several ways, *Hilao* is more radical than *Cimino*: It uses a judicial adjunct to advise the jury on appropriate damage awards, it authorizes a lump-sum jury award to non-sample plaintiffs, and it accepts a 95% (as opposed to 99% for most categories in *Cimino*) confidence level that the actual verdicts would have fallen within the sample's range.

The Fifth Circuit itself seems to have backtracked on the spirit, if not the letter, of *Fibreboard*. After *Fibreboard* another district court in the Fifth Circuit faced the problem of how to resolve a mass tort arising from an oil refinery explosion. The trial court certified a Rule 23(b)(3) class action containing more than 18,000 members. Its trial plan included a Phase 1 trial on common liability issues, including the class's entitlement to punitive damages. If an entitlement to punitive damages was established, then a Phase 2 trial would have tried the compensatory damage claims of 20 sample cases, and would have included testimony from a statistical expert on the compensatory damage claims of the class as a whole. The purpose of this Phase 2 trial was not, however, to award lump compensatory damages; it was merely to establish the proper ratio of punitive damages to compensatory damages for class members, for which the statistical evidence was intended as a guide. Phase 3 then was to try the remaining cases (selected on the basis of groupings suggested by a statistician) in waves of five. In Phase 4, the court was to allocate a share of the punitive damages to each recovering plaintiff in accordance with the jury's Phase 2 ratio. See In re Shell Oil Refinery, 136 F.R.D. 588 (E.D. La. 1991). On interlocutory appeal, the defendant challenged the trial plan as a violation of *Fibreboard*. The Fifth Circuit held that the use of a single jury to set the punitive damage ratio for the entire class passed muster:

> We find the instant case distinguishable from *Fibreboard* because the Phase 2 jury is to make a determination about punitive damages in a mass-disaster context, rather than compensatory damages in products liability litigation. . . . It hardly needs to be emphasized that the punitive damages inquiry — unlike that for compensatory damages — focuses primarily on the egregiousness of the defendant's conduct. . . . [T]he degree of culpability underlying a single act — and hence the propriety of imposing punitive damages as a result of that act — should not markedly vary in a setting such as is here presented . . . .
>
> More importantly, the Phase 2 jury is not to extrapolate punitive damages but, rather, is to determine a basis for assessment of punitive damages in the form of a ratio. . . . Unlike the plan in *Fibreboard*, Phases 2 and 3 appropriately enforce the Louisiana law requirement that a claimant must prove both causation and damage to recover punitive damages.
>
> Judge Parker had 3,031 cases consolidated in one action. Judge Henry Mentz has more than 18,000 plaintiffs in the case now before him. We express our admiration for the manner in which Judge Mentz . . . has woven our mass tort case law into an acceptable and workable trial plan.

Watson v. Shell Oil Co., 979 F.2d 1014, 1019, 1023 (5th Cir. 1992). The Fifth Circuit granted rehearing en banc in *Watson*, 990 F.2d 805 (5th Cir. 1993), but the case settled while awaiting rehearing, see In re Shell Oil Refinery, 155 F.R.D. 552 (E.D. La. 1993).

Likewise, in In re Chevron U.S.A., Inc., 109 F.3d 1016, 1021 (5th Cir. 1997), the Fifth Circuit granted a writ of mandamus against a trial plan in a case by 3,000 plaintiffs that sued Chevron for personal and property injuries due to Chevron's toxic dumping. The district judge allowed the plaintiffs to pick 15 bellwether plaintiffs and the defendant to pick another 15, and then proposed to bind the entire group of plaintiffs to the outcome. In a decision written by Judge Parker, who had been appointed to the Fifth Circuit, the Fifth Circuit held that, although a court could pick bellwethers in this fashion, the court could not "utiliz[e] the results of such a trial for the purpose of issue or claim preclusion." 109 F.3d at 1017. The court of appeals did, however, appear to permit a trial with preclusive effects as long as it met the *Cimino* conditions:

> This case is a classic example of a non-elastic mass tort, that is, the universe of potential claimants are either known or are capable of ascertainment and the event or course of conduct alleged to constitute the tort involved occurred over a known time period and is traceable to an identified entity or entities. When compared to an elastic mass tort where the universe of potential plaintiffs is unknown and many times is seemingly unlimited and the number of potential tortfeasors is equally obtuse, the task of managing the non-elastic mass tort is infinitely less complex. In the non-elastic context, the necessity for the obtainment of maturity as reflected by a series of verdicts over time is not required in order to test the viability of plaintiffs' claims or the defendant's defenses....
>
> The selected thirty (30) cases included in the district court's "unitary trial" are not cases calculated to represent the group of 3,000 claimants. Thus, the results that would be obtained from a trial of these thirty (30) cases lack the requisite level of representativeness so that the results could permit a court to draw sufficiently reliable inferences about the whole that could, in turn, form the basis for a judgment affecting cases other than the selected thirty. While this particular sample of thirty cases is lacking in representativeness, statistical sampling with an appropriate level of representativeness has been utilized and approved....
>
> We, therefore, hold that before a trial court may utilize results from a bellwether trial for a purpose that extends beyond the individual cases tried, it must, prior to any extrapolation, find that the cases tried are representative of the larger group of cases or claims from which they are selected. Typically, such a finding must be based on competent, scientific, statistical evidence that identifies the variables involved and that provides a sample of sufficient size so as to permit a finding that there is a sufficient level of confidence that the results obtained reflect results that would be obtained from trials of the whole....
>
> We recognize that in appropriate cases common issues impacting upon general liability or causation may be tried standing alone. However, when such a common issue trial is presented through or along with selected individuals' cases, concerns arise that are founded upon considerations of due process. Specifically, our procedural due process concerns focus on the fact that the procedure embodied in the district court's trial plan is devoid of safeguards designed to ensure that the claims against Chevron of the

non-represented plaintiffs as they relate to liability or causation are determined in a proceeding that is reasonably calculated to reflect the results that would be obtained if those claims were actually tried. Conversely, the procedure subjects Chevron to potential liability to 3,000 plaintiffs by a procedure that is completely lacking in the minimal level of reliability necessary for the imposition of such liability.

Our substantive due process concerns are based on the lack of fundamental fairness contained in a system that permits the extinguishment of claims or the imposition of liability in nearly 3,000 cases based upon results of a trial of a non-representative sample of plaintiffs. Such a procedure is inherently unfair when the substantive rights of both plaintiffs and the defendant are resolved in a manner that lacks the requisite level of confidence in the reliability of its result.

We recognize that our due process concerns seem to blur distinctions between procedural and substantive due process. However, our difficulty in compartmentalization does not detract from the validity of our concern that is ultimately based on fundamental fairness. [109 F.3d at 1018, 1020-21.]

Judge Jones, specially concurring, agreed that "the district judge's method of selecting 'bellwether' cases is fatally flawed," but seriously doubted "that bellwether trials can be used to resolve mass tort controversies." Id. at 1021, 1023. In particular, she thought that statistical trials raised Seventh Amendment, due process, and separation of powers concerns:

We are not authorized by the Constitution or statutes to legislate solutions to cases in pursuit of efficiency and expeditiousness. . . . Essential to due process for litigants, including both the plaintiffs and Chevron in this non-class action context, is their right to the opportunity for an individual assessment of liability and damages in each case. [Id. at 1023.]

4. Other cases seem to approach *Hilao* with great caution. See Arch v. American Tobacco Co., 175 F.R.D. 469, 493 (E.D. Pa. 1997) (finding class action unmanageable; rejecting *Hilao* as means of avoiding unmanageability because defendants did not consent to use of statistical approach and because each plaintiff's degree of injury varied significantly; further distinguishing *Hilao* because it was not an employment discrimination case and damages sought in *Hilao* exceeded assets of defendant). Were the injuries in *Hilao* all that similar, as *Arch* seems to suggest? Or does *Hilao* ultimately hinge on the failure of the defendant to object to the procedure? Or on the limited assets of the defendant? Note that each distinction of *Hilao* suggests a different rationale for its scope.

5. The due process analysis in *Hilao* and *Chevron* was influenced by an article written by Professors Saks and Blanck. See Michael J. Saks and Peter David Blanck, *Justice Improved: The Unrecognized Benefits of Aggregation and Sampling in the Trial of Mass Torts*, 44 Stan. L. Rev. 815, 827 (1992). Saks and Blanck strongly advocate the use of aggregate procedures, suggesting that such procedures better comport with both the instrumental values contained in the due process clause and non-instrumental values such as the appearance of fairness, equality, predictability, transparency, rationality, revelation, and participation. Saks and Blanck further argue that aggregate procedures are more accurate and more likely to provide both distributive and procedural justice to long queues of claimants than individual trials. Id. at 826-39. In order to make sure that these goals are met, however, they recommend that the random

sampling be performed accurately, that the sampling groups be designed appropriately, and that attention be paid to the appropriate number of juries to use in order to assure a more accurate set of verdicts. Id. at 841-50. In this regard they were critical of *Cimino*'s award of the actual verdicts to the 160 randomly selected plaintiffs; they thought that these plaintiffs too should have received the average award for the entire subgroup. Id. at 849.

Hilao picks up on only one piece of the multi-layered due process analysis of Saks and Blanck, considering the question solely in terms of a *Mathews v. Eldridge* balancing test. That test is essentially an economic one, and ignores a range of other procedural meanings that are sometimes understood to inhere in the notion of "due process" — including the notion of individual, adversarial participation at trial. See pp. 8-10, *supra*. Is it possible to weigh the plaintiffs' due process interest in a speedy adjudication against the plaintiffs' and defendant's due process interest in accurate individualized outcomes? Is it appropriate to throw onto the scale the court's interests in resolving cases expeditiously? Are these sorts of judgments better made through the legislative and administrative processes? How different are *Cimino* and *Hilao* from an administrative worker's compensation system?

6. *Fibreboard* raises, but does not decide, whether a trial by statistics violates the Seventh Amendment. The defendants in *Hilao* apparently failed to raise the issue in the court of appeals, but they did do so in the district court. The district judge dismissed the argument:

> The Seventh Amendment provides no formula for the procedures to be used in a trial by jury. Rather, it is the rules of evidence and procedure that impact jury trials. Pragmatic application of these rules, consistent with justice, is all that is necessary for the presentation of the facts necessary for a jury determination. To claim otherwise certainly raises form over substance to a new level in today's jurisprudential world.
>
> Here, the jury did determine the facts of the case, as the substance of the action was presented to the jury. There would be no benefit to either side in having the entire class testify given the repetition in the claims. Rule 23 of the Federal Rule[s] of Civil Procedure does not mandate the presence of each member of the class. Therefore, by choosing a random sample of 137 claimants in an aggregate trial, neither side was deprived of even the form of their right to a jury trial.
>
> In recent years, both complexity of cases and the concern of the length of trials have been the bases upon which several courts have refused jury trial demands. This Court did not go that far. Defendant was given its day in court with the jury, by procedures facilitating the presentation of evidence by use of random sampling in an aggregate damage trial.

In re Estate of Ferdinand E. Marcos Human Rights Litigation, 910 F. Supp. 1460, 1468-69 (D. Haw. 1995).

Does this Seventh Amendment analysis persuade you? Does the jury trial right contain not only a guarantee of a lay factfinder but also a guarantee of a trial method generally consonant with the individualized adversarial approach of the common law? Or is the latter guarantee, if it exists at all, solely a matter of due process? In Leverence v. PFS Corp., 193 Wis.2d 317, 532 N.W.2d 735 (1995), occupants of 222 defective homes sued the company whose faulty inspections led to bodily injuries and home repairs. Since the amount at stake in each case was small, the trial court adopted the *Cimino* plan of trying a sample of cases that generated a 95% confidence level and then applying the average verdict of the sample to the remaining cases. The Wisconsin Supreme Court reversed:

> [T]he aggregative procedure cannot be used, as it was here, in place of a party's right to a trial, unless all parties to the litigation consent.... [T]he right to a jury trial guaranteed by Art. 1, § 5 of the Wisconsin Constitution is not contingent upon (a) the amount of damages at stake in a given case or (b) the burden the litigation might place upon the court system. [532 N.W.2d at 740.]

See also Markeise v. Peck Foods Corp., 556 N.W.2d 326 (Wis. App. 1996) (remanding to consider whether trial plan in which jury would decide liability issue for 400,000 member class, while other "tribunal" would decide individual issues of causation and contributory negligence, violates defendants' right to jury trial).

7. The *Manual for Complex Litigation, Third* suggests a series of possible approaches for resolution of individual issues in mass tort cases, one of which sounds a great deal like the lump-sum damage award rejected in *Fibreboard* and another of which is exactly the average verdict approach of *Cimino*. It also recommends as possibilities two approaches akin to the Phase 4 trial in *Shell Oil* and the *Hilao* plan, in which "a stipulated procedure [is used] to resolve individual claims according to a formula or by a hearing before an arbitrator, special master, or magistrate judge." *Manual*, § 33.28.

8. As *Cimino* says, aggregate procedures for the award of relief are common in areas other than mass torts, especially in class actions. The oldest case of which we are aware is Union Carbide and Carbon Corp. v. Nisley, 300 F.2d 561, 589 (10th Cir.), cert. dismissed, 371 U.S. 801 (1962), in which Judge Murrah approved an antitrust trial plan in which a jury decided liability issues as well as the formula for damage suffered by each class member (*i.e.*, the number of cents per pound that the defendants' conduct caused the price of ore to drop). The trial judge then appointed a special master to determine the amount owed to each class member, an amount calculated by multiplying the jury's formula times the amount of ore that, according to defendants' own records, each class member had sold to the defendant. Emphasizing that any unresolved questions regarding the identity of class members or the amount of money due them would be resolved by a jury empaneled for that purpose, Murrah approved the plan. Cf. Tull v. United States, 481 U.S. 412 (1987) (no jury trial right to determine damages).

More recently, in Long v. Trans World Airlines, Inc., 761 F. Supp. 1320 (N.D. Ill. 1991), which involved a labor dispute, the court limited damages discovery to a sampling of class plaintiffs, despite the defendant's argument that it was entitled to individual discovery from each plaintiff in advance of trial. The court held that, since a class-wide damage award could be given, discovery of a sample of plaintiffs was adequate. It distinguished *Fibreboard* because individual issues of causation predominated in *Fibreboard*, because Texas law required individual proof, and because the 41 plaintiffs used in *Fibreboard* were not a random sample.

9. More generally, *Cimino* is also right that statistical evidence is increasingly used in American courts. See United States v. Shonubi, 895 F. Supp. 460, 513-18 (E.D.N.Y. 1995) (Weinstein, J.), vacated, 103 F.3d 1085 (2d Cir. 1997); Federal Judicial Center, Reference Manual on Scientific Evidence

(1994). Often this statistical evidence is used as proof of a defendant's wrongful conduct (for instance, statistics used to prove a pattern of racial discrimination) or causation (for instance, statistics used to prove the cancer-causing potential of a chemical). They are used to help answer a critical issue in dispute ("Was there discrimination?" or "Was there causation?"). In cases like *Cimino* and *Hilao*, however, statistics are not used to answer a question in dispute; they are used to avoid answering the critical questions ("Is *this* plaintiff entitled to damages, and, if so, how much?"). Until "the average verdict" is the legal standard for the award of damages to all plaintiffs, the statistics in *Cimino* and *Hilao* answer no legally relevant question.

Granting this to be true, what is wrong with using procedural devices to push the substantive law in bold new directions? A trial by statistics would feel and smell like a "real trial" if the relevant issue were group, rather than individual, harm. Besides, what is a "real trial," other than a bunch of procedures created by people long since dead to resolve a type of dispute that does not resemble mass controversies in the least? Once we clear our head of nostalgia and tradition, don't aggregate procedures based on valid statistical methods make the most sense?

10. Ultimately, is it possible to form an adequate opinion about aggregate procedures without turning to core procedural values? The identification of such values was the task with which we opened this book, way back in Chapter One. Do the core values that you identified as critical to an adjudicatory system permit aggregate trials? If not, are you willing to bend your values in light of the practical reality that individual trials might take a decade or longer to complete?

Two of the values we have discussed throughout this book are adversarialism and trans-substantivism. From an adversarial viewpoint, the lack of individual participation, control, and adjudication makes aggregate procedures unacceptable. From a trans-substantive viewpoint, the reaction is more mixed. Trans-substantivism requires only that the same procedures be applied to all cases; it clearly does not demand that the substantive outcome be identical in all cases, and is even suspicious of such outcomes. Moreover, while trans-substantivism can endorse the similarity of procedural treatment accorded claimants in a trial by statistics, it could be equally happy with procedures that guaranteed each plaintiff a one-on-one trial. What is troubling to the trans-substantive assumption is the use of disparate procedures that result in different outcomes for similarly situated persons. From this perspective, Judge Parker's disparate treatment of the sample cases (which received their actual verdicts) and the remaining cases (which received the average of all verdicts) is indefensible. More broadly, the fact that other asbestos plaintiffs in other federal districts in Texas, as well as those in Texas state court, received different procedures than the *Cimino* class plaintiffs is problematic; also worrisome (although less so) is the fact that other asbestos victims in the rest of the country received different procedures. Most broadly of all, the fact that other tort (and contract and antitrust and so on) plaintiffs still receive individual trials rather than aggregate verdicts of all similar trials is a problem.

Obviously, as we move from the disparate treatment of different *Cimino* plaintiffs to the disparate treatment of contract or antitrust plaintiffs, the force of the trans-substantive argument weakens. At what point along the chain might you say that trans-substantivism demands the same procedures, and at what point would the use of the same procedures be merely a desirable, but not an essential, goal of an adjudicatory system?

11. We have seen in other contexts that procedural developments in complex litigation are often harbingers of developments in routine litigation. Are we about to enter a brave new world of collective trials in all cases? After all, we have excellent information from our many court systems about the average verdicts in cases involving car accidents, slip-and-falls, and medical malpractice. Why not award every plaintiff this average amount (perhaps periodically adjusted for inflation or by means of a few sample trials conducted each year)?

Before you toss off the idea of awarding average verdicts, recall that this approach has been used in mass tort settlement class actions. See pp. 659-60, *supra*. Is it so crazy to move toward a general mandatory use of aggregate procedures? If you are reluctant to implement this strategy generally, can you still support the result in complex cases? Would an administrative law solution for complex cases make even more sense?

12. Until now we have assumed that the factfinder is capable of understanding statistical evidence. In fact, empirical data suggests that factfinders — including highly educated factfinders such as judges — routinely misunderstand statistical evidence even when it has been accurately explained to them. See William C. Thompson, *Are Juries Competent to Evaluate Statistical Evidence?* 52 Law & Contemp. Prob. 9 (Autumn 1989); Laurence H. Tribe, *Trial by Mathematics: Precision and Ritual in the Legal Process*, 84 Harv. L. Rev. 1329 (1971) (juries may overvalue statistical evidence); Michael J. Saks & Robert F. Kidd, *Human Information Processing and Adjudication: Trial by Heuristics*, 15 Law & Society Rev. 123 (1980-81) (critiquing Tribe and suggesting that juries undervalue or ignore statistical evidence). That's a telling argument against a trial by statistics, isn't it?

13. Aggregate "trial by statistics" procedures would be very difficult to implement if the court had no power to bifurcate and try common liability issues first. You might wish to consider again the proper scope of a court's power to bifurcate, now that you understand the cutting-edge consequences of that power.

14. For other literature on trial by statistics, see Robert G. Bone, *Statistical Adjudication: Rights, Justice, and Utility in a World of Process Scarcity*, 46 Vand. L. Rev. 561 (1993); Edward F. Sherman, *Aggregate Disposition of Related Cases: The Policy Issues*, 10 Rev. Litig. 231, 261-66 (1991).

3. Multiple Juries

Another way in which the amount of information that a jury must consider can be reduced is the use of more than one jury. We have seen the idea of multiple juries already. In the context of bifurcation, we saw that, at least when the issues are distinct and separable, two different juries can decide different factual issues in the case. In *Cimino* Judge Parker used two juries to hear the cases of 160 plaintiffs. In this section we consider a different use of multiple juries: Juries, each of which hears the bulk of the entire case, are given the task of deliberating just on certain parts of the case. The circumstances under which this technique might be useful are rare, but they do exist.

William W Schwarzer et al., JUDICIAL FEDERALISM IN ACTION: COORDINATION OF LITIGATION IN STATE AND FEDERAL COURTS

78 Va. L. Rev. 1689, 1727-31 (1992)

The most advanced stage of state-federal cooperation would involve a joint trial. The Manual for Complex Litigation encourages judges to consider this kind of arrangement, and the potential benefits are clear. Like joint hearings, joint trials may be more efficient because the parties are required to adduce evidence only once. A joint trial, like a joint hearing, would also enable judges to benefit from one another's insights and information.

Despite these advantages, none of the judges we interviewed conducted a joint trial, which suggests that such trials may be impractical. However, in several cases — the Hyatt Skywalk, Florida Everglades, and Brooklyn Navy Yard litigation — the state and federal judges considered conducting a joint trial. . . .

Assuming that joint trials are indeed feasible, they likely would encounter problems. The potential logistical and practical complications, for example, labor disputes arising from the assignment of court personnel, are manifold but stem mostly from the need for separate juries in the state and federal cases. Most of the judges who have contemplated joint trials envision two juries in the courtroom — one for the state cases and one for the federal cases. Judge Fay notes that the attorneys could stipulate that the same people may serve as both the state and federal jury, but the general view is that two separate juries are necessary. When conflicts between state and federal rules arise, all parties must be guaranteed the protection of the system in which their case is heard. The state rules may permit certain testimony that the federal rules do not. The use of two separate juries would allow the federal court to excuse the federal jury during such testimony. Having two juries ensures that the state and federal judges each retain control over their cases by allowing them to pursue different paths — through different instructions or admonitions, for example. With a single jury, one judge might have to defer to another's rulings or face unresolvable conflicts. In addition, although a federal jury must be unanimous to return a verdict, many states do not require unanimity.

A "two jury" approach creates complications of its own, however. Some are purely logistical matters — two juries may place a strain on the limited accommodations of a courtroom, and one juror's illness will cause delays in both jurisdictions. Numerous other problems stem from differences between state and federal law. State and federal jury selection procedures are often "worlds apart." As a result, it could take much longer for one court to select a jury than for the other, which would delay the trial in the faster court. Similarly, states may differ with the federal system as to the availability of interlocutory appeals during trial. Conflicts between state and federal rules of evidence may present the greatest difficulty. Although one jury may be sent out of the courtroom so that evidence can be introduced before the other jury, this process can cause confusion and delay. Further, the process of presenting different evidence to separate juries will not be uncontroversial. Even if one jury is dismissed while certain evidence is presented, the circumstances surrounding the jury's excusal may create an impression that influences that jury. This may result in additional appeals that frustrate the goal of greater judicial economy. . . .

The use of two juries also presents the risk of inconsistent verdicts. . . . Inconsistent verdicts reduce public confidence in the jury system by dispelling the notion that there is a single proper resolution to all issues that would be arrived at by any jury hearing a particular matter. In addition, such verdicts would be regarded as unjust by the parties adversely affected. . . .

Until joint trials are attempted, it is impossible to say whether they are viable and, if so, desirable. Even if they are regarded as unworkable, it does not follow that state-federal coordination cannot occur in the trial phase of litigation. . . .

Michael D. Green, THE INABILITY OF OFFENSIVE COLLATERAL ESTOPPEL TO FULFILL ITS PROMISE: AN EXAMINATION OF ESTOPPEL IN ASBESTOS LITIGATION

70 Iowa L. Rev. 141, 221-23 (1984)

An unusual trial conducted two years ago in the United States District Court for Eastern District of Texas provides striking corroboration of the inconsistencies generated when juries are faced with the difficult, indeterminate legal standards governing asbestos litigation. Five plaintiffs' cases were consolidated for trial against a total of twelve defendants. Five separate juries were impanelled, one assigned to each plaintiff's case. Each jury was present in the courtroom for all proceedings. . . .

[O]nly common questions bearing on liability were tried by the same attorneys using the same evidence in one courtroom. The judge instructed the five juries simultaneously. Each jury was given eight identical special interrogatories to answer. . . . Each of the juries also had a list of the products manufactured by all defendants in that jury's case.

Despite the procedural uniformity, the juries' findings on the evaluative issues were strikingly divergent. . . . Answers to the question inquiring when an asbestos manufacturer should have had knowledge of the danger ranged from 1935 to 1965, with 1946 and two 1964's as the other three findings. Three juries decided whether [one defendant's] products were defective in design; one jury found all nine were defective in design at some time, while two juries found none of the products was defective in design. Although all of the juries found at least some products were marketed at some time without adequate warnings, there was substantial disagreement as to which products required warnings, whether a subsequently provided warning was adequate, and, most significantly, the evaluative determination of whether the failure to provide an adequate warning rendered those products defective....

The attempt to resolve the asbestos backlog in the Eastern District of Texas by conducting five simultaneous test trials failed.

Notes and Questions

1. The use of multiple juries in the cases Judge Schwarzer and his co-authors describe was necessitated by the inability of the courts to achieve a single consolidation of all cases in one forum. Judge Parker used multiple juries in an effort to demonstrate that, if several juries had the same view of defendants' liability, collateral estoppel could be used against the defendants in order to reduce the issues for future trials. Thus, Judge Schwarzer's use of the multiple jury sought to overcome problems of joinder complexity, while Judge Parker's use sought to overcome problems of pretrial complexity. Neither use appears to have been especially successful, but they do highlight an important lesson: Novel trial techniques can be used not only to avoid problems of trial complexity but also to avoid problems of joinder or pretrial complexity.

2. Having noted that lesson, can you envision any situations in which the use of multiple juries will help to reduce or eliminate trial complexity? In theory, we could envision such situations, but how many cases like this exist in reality? However many there are, there is no way to avoid the possibility that the different juries will arrive at inconsistent verdicts. Do you regard that possibility as disqualifying? Does the preservation of rational adjudication require that a single, "correct" answer be achieved, or only that reasoned judgment be brought to bear on a factual problem capable of different resolutions?

3. If you thought that trial-splitting and/or trial by statistics were measures that exceeded the court's power, or were at least troubled by the breadth of these powers, multiple juries may be a way to accomplish some of the benefits of trial-splitting or aggregation while still preserving a more traditionally adversarial form of trial. Obviously multiple juries have their problems, and they do not work as efficiently as bifurcation or aggregation to limit information to a digestible bite; but they might nonetheless be a compromise in some cases.

4. Time Limits on Trial

MCI COMMUNICATIONS CORP. v. AMERICAN TELEPHONE AND TELEGRAPH CO.

708 F.2d 1081 (7th Cir.), cert. denied, 464 U.S. 891 (1983)

■ CUDAHY, Circuit Judge. In this extraordinary antitrust case, defendant American Telephone and Telegraph Company ("AT&T") appeals from a judgment in the amount of $1.8 billion, entered on a jury verdict, in a treble damage suit brought by plaintiffs MCI Communications Corporation and MCI Telecommunications Corporation (collectively "MCI") under section 4 of the Clayton Act, 15 U.S.C. § 15 (1976).

I. FACTS

MCI's original complaint, filed March 6, 1974, contained four separate counts: monopolization, attempt to monopolize, and conspiracy to monopolize — all under section 2 of the Sherman Act — and conspiracy in restraint of trade — under section 1 of the Sherman Act. MCI alleged that AT&T had committed twenty-two types of misconduct, classifiable into several categories including predatory pricing, denial of interconnections, negotiation in bad faith and unlawful tying. MCI claimed at trial, on the basis of a lost profits study originally prepared in part for financing purposes, that it had suffered damages of approximately $900 million as a result of AT&T's allegedly unlawful actions.

The case was tried to a jury between February 6 and June 13, 1980. After completion of MCI's case in chief, the district court directed a verdict in favor of AT&T on seven of the twenty-two alleged acts of misconduct. The remaining fifteen charges — all based on section 2 of the Sherman Act — were submitted to the jury. A special verdict form required the jury to make a separate finding of liability as to each of the fifteen charges, but permitted the jury to award damages in a single lump sum, without apportioning MCI's claimed financial losses among AT&T's various lawful and unlawful acts. The jury found in favor of MCI on ten of the fifteen charges submitted, and awarded damages of $600 million — a sum equal to two thirds the total damage figure claimed in MCI's aggregated lost profits study. The district court trebled this damage award, as required by section 4 of the Clayton Act, resulting in a judgment of $1.8 billion, exclusive of costs and attorneys' fees.
. . .

VII. THE CONDUCT OF THE TRIAL

AT&T argues that the manner in which the district court presided over the case amounted to a denial of due process. AT&T complains of the court's . . . imposition of a time limit upon the parties' presentations . . . .

We . . . reject AT&T's argument that the district court did not allow AT&T sufficient time to present its case in an intelligible manner. Originally, AT&T predicted that it would take approximately eighteen months to try the case. Understandably chagrined, the district court directed the parties to submit lists of their witnesses and a summary of the testimony of each, together with a more precise estimate of the time required for trial. MCI's list named seventeen witnesses and predicted that it would require twenty-six days to present its case-in-chief. AT&T's list, by contrast, named 162 witnesses and described a minimum of twenty-one more by category. At that time, AT&T predicted that trial of the entire case would take eight to nine months. The district court reviewed those materials and only then imposed a twenty-six day time limit on the presentation of each side's case-in-chief.[130] The district court did not place a limit on the time allotted for rebuttal or surrebuttal. . . . On appeal, AT&T argues that the limits which were imposed were wholly arbitrary and amounted to a denial of due process. We cannot agree.

Litigants are not entitled to burden the court with an unending stream of cumulative evidence. . . . As Wigmore remarked, "it has never been supposed that a party has an absolute right to force upon an unwilling tribunal an unending and superfluous mass of testimony limited only by his own judgment and whim. . . ." 6 Wigmore, Evidence § 1907 (Chadbourne Rev. 1976). Accordingly, Federal Rule of Evidence 403 provides that evidence, although relevant, may be excluded when its probative value is outweighed by such factors as its cumulative nature, or the "undue delay" and "waste of time" it may cause. Whether the evidence will be excluded is a matter within the district court's sound discretion and will not be reversed absent a clear showing of abuse. . . .

The time limits ordered by Judge Grady had the effect of excluding cumulative testimony, although in setting those limits the district court apparently fixed a period of time for the trial as a whole. This approach is not, *per se*, an abuse of discretion. This exercise of discretion may be appropriate in protracted litigation provided that witnesses are not excluded on the basis of mere numbers. . . . Moreover, where the proffered testimony is presented to the court in the form of a general summary, the time limits should be sufficiently flexible to accommodate adjustment if it appears during trial that the court's initial assessment was too restrictive.

The limits set by the district court were not absolute. As Judge Grady stated in his order, "[t]hese limits are subject to change if events at the trial satisfy the court that any limit is unduly restrictive. It is my intention to allow each party sufficient time to present its case; I have no interest in speed for the sake of speed." Similarly, at a pretrial hearing the court told the parties that there was "nothing absolutely hard and fast" about the limits. After MCI completed presentation of its case in fifteen and one-half days, the court expressed an unwillingness to permit AT&T to exceed its twenty-six day limit, yet it later tempered this by reminding the parties, "I want to make it very clear that nobody is being pushed to do anything that is inconsistent with what he perceives to be the best interest of his client." We cannot say that the district court was prepared to adhere strictly to its preliminary time limits without regard to possible prejudice to either party.

Insisting that the twenty-six day limit was too restrictive, AT&T cites SCM Corp. v. Xerox Corp., 77 F.R.D. 10 (D. Conn. 1977), where the court imposed a six-month limit on the plaintiff's presentation when the plaintiff had failed to make a *prima facie* showing of liability after fourteen weeks of trial. AT&T in effect suggests that whenever time limits are imposed in a complex case, the limits should involve months, not days. Although there may be some validity to this suggestion in most complex cases, we cannot

---

130.   . . . The record indicates that much of AT&T's proposed testimony would in fact have been repetitive. . . . AT&T also predicted that it would require between twenty-two and forty-six days to cross-examine MCI's witnesses who, by MCI's estimate, could be directly examined in twenty-six days.

say that it should necessarily control in the case before us. Obviously, there must be specific attention to the substance of the testimony and the complexity of the issues, but it does not follow that several weeks for each side will never suffice. The circumstances of each individual case must be weighed by the trial judge, who is in the best position to determine how long it may reasonably take to try the case. MCI was confident that it could establish liability in twenty-six days, and in fact finished eleven days ahead of schedule. We recognize, as did the district court, that presentation of a competent defense may require more time than presentation of a plaintiff's case-in-chief. In light of the substance of AT&T's proffered testimony, however, and the district court's considered view that an efficient, yet effective, presentation of AT&T's defense would take no longer than the time MCI used to present its case, we conclude that the district court did not manifestly abuse its discretion in limiting the time for AT&T's case-in-chief.

Notes and Questions

1. The point of time limits at trial is obvious: If you reduce the amount of time, you reduce the amount of information to which the factfinder can be exposed. That, in turn, makes it easier for the factfinder to recollect the evidence and to come to a judgment. According to Judge Leval, who ordered time limits in the "vast" *Westmoreland v. CBS* libel trial, there are other benefits as well:

> This technique has considerable benefits, primarily five: It requires counsel to exercise a discipline of economy choosing between what is important and what is less so. It reduces the incidence of the judge interfering in strategic decisions. It gives a cleaner, crisper, better-tried case. It gives a much lower cost to the clients. Finally, it will save months of our lives.
>
> All counsel in the *Westmoreland* trial have told me they believe they tried their case better as a result of the time limit, and that it was shorter by a half than it would have been.

Pierre N. Leval, *From the Bench*, 12 Litigation 7, 8 (Fall 1985).

2. There are several ways to impose trial limits. One way is to limit time for direct and cross examination on a witness-by-witness basis. See Rohrbaugh v. Owens-Corning Fiberglas Corp., 965 F.2d 844 (10th Cir. 1992) (30 minutes for direct, 45 minutes for cross, of each expert). A second way is to impose a limit on the number of days within which a party must rest its case. Under this approach, the plaintiff's case, including direct, cross-examination, re-direct, and so forth may take no more than "X" days (in *MCI*, 26 days). The third way is to allocate to each side "X" hours, which the party may use as it sees fit — in direct, cross-examination, re-direct, and so forth. There is no limit (other than the outside limit of "X" hours) within which the party must rest its case. If it does so quickly, it has more time for cross-examination of the other party's case. If it does so slowly, it may have little or no time left to contest the opponent's case. The allocation of time is a strategic decision left to counsel's discretion.

Leval thought the third method far preferable to the second. Since the evidence of each side is not necessarily of the same bulk, especially if the plaintiff has done a good job of laying the foundation, the "X days for each party's case" approach may leave too much time for defendants in relation to plaintiffs.

More significantly, this approach creates an incentive for each side to linger over its cross-examinations, making it difficult for the party to get in its evidence on direct. But the "X hours for each party" approach creates its own disincentives; a plaintiff may use most of its time on its case-in-chief and call lots of witnesses, trying to force the defendant to run out of time before it can even present its own case-in-chief. Id; cf. Duquense Light Co. v. Westinghouse Electric Corp., 66 F.3d 604 (3d Cir. 1995) (judge switched from "X hours" to "X days for each side's case" approach when judge thought that plaintiff was not moving quickly enough). Could the three approaches be combined? How? See CRS Sirrine, Inc. v. Dravo Corp., 213 Ga. App. 710, 445 S.E.2d 782 (1994) (limiting cross examinations to 4 hours each and defendant's overall trial time to 3 weeks). Isn't it an inevitable side effect of the adversary system that any set of rules, however benign and reasonable, will be exploited by parties seeking a private advantage?

3. Note that one of Leval's arguments for time limits is that it better preserves the adversary's right to present evidence as he sees fit: Having allocated the hours to a party, the judge no longer needs to worry as much about the presentation of cumulative evidence or interject herself to keep the trial moving; the lawyers for each party can present whatever case they want. As *Duquense Light* shows, however, busy judges may have a difficult time watching time being frittered away even after a certain number of hours have been allocated. More important, Leval glosses over the critical intrusion: the very power to set the number of hours or days for a party's case.

Four problems are apparent. First, how is the judge to determine how many hours are appropriate for the trial? If the judge has had little contact with the case during pretrial, she is not likely to have enough of a feel for the case to know how many hours are correct, and she will need to rely on the estimates of counsel. In most trials, however, one side is advantaged by a quick trial, and one side disadvantaged. Both counsel will want some negotiating room, so it is unlikely that the judge will get an accurate estimate from either party. A judge who manages a case during pretrial would get a better feel of the required time, but recall that the case manager often develops biases or predispositions. Will the judge be able to put these opinions aside when she allots the trial time?

Second, how is the judge to divide the time fairly among the parties? It is usually true that one side or the other needs longer to present its case. A judge, however, is hard pressed to allot more time to one side than the other, since it seems unfair. Thus, the judge is likely to give each side the same amount of time. But equal allocations will usually advantage one party at the expense of the other; they are not outcome-neutral. Nonetheless, the reported decisions seem to suggest that judges overwhelmingly use equal time allocations rather than time allocations tailored to achieve substantive fairness. See *Duquesne Light*, 66 F.3d at 608-09 (140 trial hours apiece, switched to 11 trial days apiece); General Signal Corp. v. MCI Telecommunications Corp., 66 F.3d 1500 (9th Cir. 1995) (28 hours apiece); Monotype Corp. PLC v. International Typeface Corp., 43 F.3d 443 (9th Cir. 1994) (nine trial days, divided equally); Deus v. Allstate Insurance Co., 15 F.3d 506 (5th Cir. 1994) (3 days apiece); Tabas v. Tabas, 166 F.R.D. 10 (E.D. Pa. 1996) (30 hours apiece); but see Flaminio v. Honda Motor Co., 733 F.2d 463 (7th Cir. 1984) (18 hours for plaintiff, 15 for defendant); McKnight v. General Motors Corp., 908 F.2d 104 (7th Cir. 1990) (11 for plaintiff, 10 for defendant).

A third problem is the equitable treatment of these cases in relation to cases that receive regular treatment. *MCI* remains one of the largest judgments ever rendered, yet it was set to be tried in a maximum of 52 days (less than 11 weeks). It is not unusual for medical malpractice cases to last 11 weeks. Can we justify time limits in some, but not all, cases? Moreover, the trial in the related antitrust action, *United States v. American Telephone & Telegraph*, lasted nearly one year. See pp. 1036-37, *supra*. Shouldn't we at least make sure that related cases receive the same type of procedural treatment?

The fourth, and most significant, problem is well-described in *McKnight*:

> [I]n this age of swollen federal caseloads district judges must manage their trials with an iron hand .... But to impose arbitrarily limitations, enforce them inflexibly, and by these means turn a federal trial into a relay race is to sacrifice too much of one good — accuracy of factual determination — to obtain another — minimization of the time and expense of litigation. [908 F.2d at 115.]

Was it really possible to present all the evidence necessary to determine AT&T's liability in a $1.8 billion case in just 52 days? See Newton Commonwealth Property, N.V. v. G + H Montage GmbH, 261 Ga. 269, 404 S.E.2d 551 (1991) (trial court erred in limiting trial time in complex case, where limit had "effect of prejudicing the parties and preventing a full and meaningful presentation of the merits of the case"). Don't these sorts of time limits encourage "throw mud against the wall" lawyering strategies? Can such strategies lead to rational adjudication? Perhaps it depends on what we mean by "rational adjudication." If we mean the ability to apply reason to a set of given facts and to make logical inferences from those facts, then rational adjudication can occur within short time frames, provided that enough evidence can be introduced for the logical inferences. On the other hand, if we mean the ability to apply reason to the universe of readily available information in order to ensure an outcome that is as accurate as possible, then rational adjudication is threatened by short time frames for trial. How important is it that a legal judgment be not only logically coherent but also accurate?

Clearly accuracy is an important value in rational adjudication, all other things being equal. Note, however, that this drive for accuracy — for complete disclosure of relevant information — comes into conflict with another aspect of rational adjudication — the need not to be so overwhelmed with information that the processes of logical inference and application of these inferences to legal standards becomes impossible. How is a judge to decide where to strike this balance? Would such a choice be best struck by the parties and their lawyers, who have the greatest access to information and the greatest incentive to achieve the optimal blend of accuracy and comprehension? Wouldn't a judge with a crowded docket have a private incentive to value comprehension (*i.e.*, brevity) more than accuracy? See United States v. Reaves, 636 F. Supp. 1575, 1580 (E.D. Ky. 1986) ("Setting a reasonable time limit forces counsel to conform their zeal to the need of the court to conserve its time and resources."); Patrick E. Longan, *The Shot Clock Comes to Trial: Time Limits for Federal Civil Trials*, 35 Ariz. L. Rev. 663 (1993) (arguing that parties and court value marginal costs and benefits of additional evidence in different ways).

4. *MCI* says that the use of time limits does not violate due process. But its due process analysis is quite thin. It never identifies the due process values at stake, much less analyze those values in terms of relevant precedent. Does the last note convince you that a credible due process claim exists? See *General Signal*, 66 F.3d at 1507-09 (rejecting due process argument because time limits

were "reasonable," "sufficiently flexible," and did not "sacrifice justice in the name of efficiency").

5. From what source does the power to order time limits derive? One court has described the following sources:

> Although the procedural rules governing federal litigation do not explicitly authorize a district court to set time limits for a trial, a district court has inherent power "to control cases before it," provided it exercises the power "'in a manner that is consistent with the Federal Rules of Civil Procedure.'" ... The rules repeatedly embody the principle that trials should be both fair and efficient. Thus, the Federal Rules of Civil Procedure "shall be construed and administered to secure the just, speedy, and inexpensive determination of every action." Fed.R.Civ.P. 1. Similarly, the Federal Rules of Evidence "shall be construed to secure ... elimination of unjustifiable expense and delay." Fed.R.Evid. 102. More particularly, Fed.R.Evid. 403 allows judges to exclude even relevant evidence because of "considerations of undue delay, waste of time, or needless presentation of cumulative evidence."

Duquesne Light, 66 F.3d at 609; see also *Reaves*, 636 F. Supp. at 1578 (citing Fed.R.Evid. 611 as additional source of power); F.R.Civ.P. 16(c)(15) (in pretrial conference, allowing court to "take appropriate action" with respect to "an order establishing a reasonable time allowed for presenting evidence"). Once again, the "inherent power" of the court comes to the rescue.

6. What happens when a party's time runs out? The answer may depend on the judge, and on her opinion of how well you have been trying your case. In *McKnight* the defendant had only 49 minutes left to put on the four witnesses in its case-in-chief. The judge gave the defendant an extra thirty minutes, but no more — a ruling which led to the spectacle of witnesses literally running to and from the stand to save time. 908 F.2d at 115. Likewise, in *General Signal*, the plaintiff used all of its time presenting its case-in-chief. It asked for additional time for cross-examination and for a rebuttal case. The court gave no time for rebuttal, and a whopping five minutes to do each cross-examination. It may not have helped the plaintiff that its attorney had earlier insisted on rigid enforcement of time limits against the defendant, and had ignored the judge's suggestion to save time for cross-examination with the comment that he asked only five questions of witnesses on cross. 66 F.3d at 1509. In M.T. Bonk Co. v. Milton Bradley Co., 945 F.2d 1404 (7th Cir. 1991), a judge also enforced the time limit against a lawyer who had neglected warnings to keep things moving.

Appellate courts seem most troubled by time limits when they detect a lack of flexibility on the trial judge's part. That concern, however, does not seem to translate into reversals. See *Flaminio*, 733 F.2d at 473 ("disapprov[ing] of the practice of placing rigid hour limits on a trial," but nonetheless upholding limits in case); *McKnight*, 908 F.2d at 115 (indicating that it would have reversed district judge for sticking rigidly to time allocations if defendant had preserved issue for appeal); *General Signal*, 66 F.3d at 1508-09 (upholding failure to give more time when plaintiff had mismanaged time and additional time would have been unfair to defendant that had abided by limits).

7. A party must preserve its objection to time limits if it intends to make an issue of the limits on appeal. *McKnight*, 908 F.2d at 115 (objection waived); *Monotype*, 43 F.3d at 451 (waiver when party failed to request additional time); Johnson v. Ashby, 808 F.2d 676 (8th Cir. 1987) (waiver); see *General Signal*, 66

F.3d at 1507 (no waiver when party tried to give offers of proof of excluded evidence and moved for additional time for rebuttal). It must also be able to show prejudice — in other words, that the excluded evidence might have made a difference in result. *Flaminio*, 733 F.2d at 473; *McKnight*, 908 F.2d at 115 (no reversible error when defendant failed to "show what it would have done with" extra time); *Deus*, 15 F.3d at 520; *Duquesne Light*, 66 F.3d at 611; *General Signal*, 66 F.3d at 1510.

8. Whatever the method used for time limits, time-keeping issues always arise. One issue is whether and how to count jury selection, opening and closing statements, rebuttal, objections, sidebar arguments, court breaks, partial trial days, and so on. Compare *Duquesne Light*, 66 F.3d at 608-09 (time included opening and closing arguments; partial trial days counted as full day) with *General Signal*, 66 F.3d at 1504 (time included rebuttal; breaks and delays charged equally to both sides) and *Tabas*, 166 F.R.D. at 12-13 (time included rebuttal, but not jury selection or opening and closing statements). When the "X hours" approach is used, someone constantly needs to be keeping track of the time, starting and stopping the clock depending on whose time is charged for various matters — a "method that [makes] the computation of time almost as complicated as in a professional football game." *Flaminio*, 733 F.2d at 473.

9. Time limits should usually be established before trial begins. It is possible, however, to establish time limits, to change the amount of previously allocated time during trial, and to change the method of calculating time in mid-trial. See Manual for Complex Litigation, Third § 22.35 (1995); *McKnight*, 908 F.2d at 114-15 (reducing number of hours during trial); *Duquesne Light*, 66 F.3d at 608-09 (switching from "X hours" to "X days for case-in-chief" during trial).

10. Witnesses running to and from the stand, timekeepers with stopwatches who must decide when and how to allocate time, lawyers managing their cases like football coaches nursing a lead as the clock winds down — is this a trial? Maybe the problem is that lawyers have forgotten how to try cases — how to achieve the optimal blend of accuracy and comprehension. Would a better solution be to create a barrister system, in which a small cadre of truly skilled lawyers handled complex cases?

5. Presenting Evidence in Summary or Narrative Form

A final method of limiting trial information is to require that evidence be submitted in some type of condensed or summary form. One form of evidence that easily lends itself to summary presentation is the deposition. The traditional practice concerning deposition testimony has been for the lawyer (often assisted by another reader) to read the questions and answers from the deposition to the jury. Unless you have Tom Cruise and Jack Nicholson playing the two roles, transcript reading is one of the most tedious parts of any trial; and it also puts the testimony at the mercy of the theatrical talents of the readers. These problem are increasingly being solved with the use of video-taped depositions in which the most salient aspects are played back. But even these techniques may not go far enough in some cases.

OOSTENDORP v. KHANNA

937 F.2d 1177 (7th Cir. 1991), cert. denied, 502 U.S. 1064 (1992)

■ FLAUM, Circuit Judge. Plaintiff Debra Oostendorp sued the defendants for negligence following gall bladder surgery in 1986. The jury found for the defendants. Oostendorp appeals, citing as error . . . the district court's order that the parties summarize in five pages or less any deposition testimony they wished to present at trial. . . .

The district court's order prior to the final pre-trial conference in this case stated, in part:

> Extensive (*i.e.*, more than 5 pages) reading from depositions will not be permitted. Rather, the proponent of a deposition must prepare a written narrative summary of a deposition the party intends to offer.

. . . Plaintiff's counsel objected to this procedure before trial, and refused to summarize the depositions of two witnesses, Doctors Michael Sarr and Myron Denney, he intended to present at trial. The district court therefore barred Oostendorp from introducing their deposition testimony at trial, a ruling she claims contravenes Fed.R.Civ.P. 32(a)(3)(B), the due process clause of the fifth amendment, and her seventh amendment right to a jury trial.

To begin, we note that Oostendorp did not attempt to comply with the district court's procedure. She made no attempt to show why the district court's requirement was unreasonable as applied to the depositions she wished to offer in this case, nor did she offer any objections to the content of the deposition summaries prepared by the defendants. As plaintiff's counsel confirmed at oral argument, he declined to propose any modifications to the district court's order because he objected to the requirement that depositions be summarized in any fashion. Plaintiff's beef, then, is not with the district court's application of the rule but with the rule itself; she makes a facial challenge to the district court's deposition summary procedure. Although we might question the validity of an overly rigid application of the district court's requirement (the district court should be willing to consider increasing the five-page limit in appropriate cases), we have not been presented with such a claim here. At oral argument, plaintiff's counsel rejected our invitation to cast the claim in terms of an abuse of discretion and we must therefore consider not whether it was reasonable to require Oostendorp to summarize the Sarr and Denney depositions in five pages, but only whether the district court may require such summaries as a general matter.

In this focus, plaintiff's claim is without merit. Rule 32 of the Federal Rules of Civil Procedure permits the use of depositions in civil cases, but contrary to the plaintiff's assertion that deposition testimony must be admitted when offered, the decision to admit deposition testimony is within the sound discretion of the district court. . . . It follows that the court may control the manner in which deposition testimony is presented; indeed, trial courts are charged to "exercise reasonable control over the mode and order of interrogating witnesses and presenting evidence so as to (1) make the interrogation and presentation effective for the ascertainment of the truth [and to] avoid needless consumption of time . . . ." Fed.R.Evid. 611(a). The district court adopted its rule to serve these objectives, and we agree that requiring deposition summaries can be a reasonable means of implementing the mandate of Rule 611. We therefore conclude that the district court's requirement was not an abuse of its discretionary authority to regulate the conduct of civil trials. . . .

Plaintiff's attempt to ground her objection in the Constitution borders on the frivolous. Neither the due process clause nor the seventh amendment requires courts to admit deposition testimony; indeed, the more common argument is that the Constitution forbids the substitution of depositions for the live testimony of witnesses. Jenkins v. McKeithen, 395 U.S. 411 (1969), on which plaintiff mistakenly relies, is just such a case. In *Jenkins*, the Court invalidated a state statute that created a commission empowered to investigate and make findings of fact concerning the possible violation of state and federal labor laws. The statute restricted the right of persons investigated to call witnesses to testify in their behalf in what amounted to a criminal proceeding, permitting only the presentation of written statements from such witnesses. That restriction violated due process. 395 U.S. at 429. *Jenkins* offers scant support, however, for plaintiff's position. She was not denied the right to call witnesses; rather, she opted to present deposition testimony rather than testimony from a witness in court. *Jenkins* imposes no requirement, constitutional or otherwise, that parties must be permitted to substitute verbatim deposition testimony for live testimony. Plaintiff's counsel conceded at oral argument that he knew of no case imposing such a requirement; we know of none either. The due process clause gives parties to litigation the right to present evidence; the seventh amendment gives them the right to do so in front of a jury. Neither provision, however, gives litigants license to prolong trials needlessly; neither deprives courts of their authority to regulate the conduct of the trial. As long as the procedures utilized by the trial courts are fair, there is no conflict with either constitutional provision. Since there is nothing inherently unfair in requiring the parties to summarize deposition testimony . . . we hold that the rule imposed by the district court in this case does not offend the due process clause or the seventh amendment.

Notes and Questions

1. The narrative summary of testimony changes the nature of trial from a dialectic (question-and-answer) approach to a didactic (lecture) approach. We saw a similar shift in the last chapter, when we studied the use of technical advisors who "lectured" to judges. See p. 1328, *supra*. Do these techniques suggest a shift in the nature of trial? As you have probably noted in law school, a lecture approach is more efficient at conveying quantities of information, but a question-and-answer approach may lead to a truer and deeper understanding of difficult points. Which approach seems more appropriate for complex cases?

Maybe the answer is a compromise: that some routine, fairly non-controversial information can be best conveyed in a didactic fashion, while other, more critical information is best conveyed in a dialectic fashion. This was the solution arrived at in In re Air Crash Disaster at Stapleton International Airport, Denver, Colorado, on November 15, 1987, 720 F. Supp. 1493 (D. Colo. 1989). The trial judge limited the use of narrative summaries to the presentation of "corroborative testimony on various issues, lessening the delay of repetitive testimony. Because the applicability of summary testimony is tempered by the court's preference for oral testimony in open court, the parties were neither requested nor allowed to present the testimony of key witnesses in summary form." 720 F. Supp. at 1503. How can the judge know which witnesses are central and which are peripheral? Do we again have the problem of a judge with either little knowledge of the case (if she has not managed the case aggressively) or a biased view of the case (if she has managed aggressively) making decisions about how much emphasis should be placed on certain information? Would the lawyers be better suited to the task of balancing undue repetition against appropriate emphasis? Should the judge step in only when the lawyers are incapable of performing this task due to trial complexity?

Is this compromise a better solution than requiring *all* deposition testimony to be summarized? It seems that the plaintiff's lawyer in *Oostendorp* believed that the two deposition witnesses were critical to the plaintiff's case. Should the Seventh Circuit have been sensitive, as the judge in *Stapleton International* was, to the need to allow important testimony to be delivered in dialectic fashion?

2. One important way in which *Stapleton International* is actually broader than *Oostendorp* is that the judge in *Stapleton International* ordered narrative summaries even of witnesses who could have appeared live at trial; in *Ooostendorp*, the doctors were apparently unavailable for trial. What is the exact source of the court's authority to order summaries of testimony from witnesses who could have testified in open court? The few courts that have considered the issue have found the authority either in Fed.R.Evid 611 or (once again) in the court's inherent power to control cases before it. Walker v. Action Industries, Inc., 802 F.2d 703, 713 (4th Cir. 1986), cert. denied, 479 U.S. 1065 (1987); United States v. Young, 745 F.2d 733, 761 (2d Cir. 1984), cert. denied, 470 U.S. 1084 (1985); *Stapleton International*, 720 F. Supp. at 1481; Nigh v. Dow Chemical Co., 634 F. Supp. 1513, 1519 (W.D. Wis. 1986). The latter source, Rule 611, merely allows a court to "exercise reasonable control over the mode and order of *interrogating* witnesses and *presenting* evidence" (emphasis added). The Advisory Committee notes on Rule 611 states that Rule 611(a)(1) "restates in broad terms the power and obligation of the judge as developed under common law principles," including "such concerns as whether testimony shall be in the form of a free narrative or responses to specific questions." The notes cite as support for a narrative approach McCormick's treatise on evidence. That treatise, however, clearly contemplates that it is the *witness* who will be doing the narrating; it does not suggest that the *lawyer* can narrate or summarize testimony on a witness's behalf. See John W. Strong, McCormick on Evidence § 5 (4th ed. 1992); but see Charles R. Richey, *A Modern Management Technique for Trials Courts to Improve the Quality of Justice: Requiring Direct Testimony to be Submitted in Written Form Prior to Trial*, 72 Geo. L.J. 73, 80 (1983) ("rule 611(a) read in light of rule 102 gives the trial judge authority not only to *control* but also to *devise* a *mode* of interrogation"). Is the court's inherent power the basis for the additional stretch to let the lawyers narrate?

We keep running across this inherent power, which seems to act as a reserve of authority allowing courts to do things that the rules of procedure and evidence do not exactly allow. What are the exact limits of this inherent power, anyway? What is the point of having rules if they can be superseded so easily? See Edward R. Becker & Aviva Orenstein, *The Federal Rules of Evidence after Sixteen Years — The Effect of "Plain Meaning" Jurisprudence, The Need for an Advisory Committee on the Rules of Evidence, and Suggestions for Selective Revision of the Rules*, 60 Geo. Wash. L. Rev. 857, 903 (1992) (since "neither [Rule 611] nor the accompanying Advisory Committee notes encourages [narrative] statements," the Federal Rules of Evidence should be amended to permit them).

3. *Stapleton International* actually used two different forms of narrative summaries. The court described the two methods as follows:

> The primary method of summary testimony involves summarization of the relevant portions of a deposition in a one or two page narrative, prepared by the offering attorney. Opposing counsel is given an opportunity to review the summary and the deposition for accuracy. The offering attorney then reads a stipulated narrative summary to the jury.
>
> The second method of summary testimony involves the reading of a narrative statement of a witness's direct testimony while the witness is in court, under oath. The presenting attorney reads a summary of direct examination. The witness is then asked to supplement or correct the attorney's statement, under oath, again in narrative form. Testimony then proceeds through traditional cross and redirect examination. This method of presenting evidence is most useful in presenting the testimony of witnesses who appear to corroborate the testimony of key witnesses. In this trial for example, two of several passengers testified to their observations of the aircraft, events and weather conditions [ ] through the modified summary form. [720 F. Supp. at 1503-04.]

The first technique, of course, is equivalent to the one used in *Oostendorp*. In some ways the first technique is more worrisome than the second; with the first technique, the deposition witness never had an opportunity to be present in court, to correct statements, or to be subject to cross-examination, all of which are important if the jury is to judge the witness's demeanor. But the second technique is also problematic; there may be good reason to require summaries of the testimony of witnesses who cannot be present, but to require a summary for a witness sitting on the stand deprives the court and jury of an opportunity to hear the story in the witness's own words and might make the cross-examination appear stronger or weaker than it should. Cf. Traylor v. Husqvarta Motor, 988 F.2d 729, 734 (7th Cir. 1993) (describing potential prejudicial effect of allowing witness to testify live on direct but through videotape on cross).

Nonetheless, the second technique has been used in many cases. The most notable example is *United States v. AT&T*. Recall that the pretrial process in *AT&T* used a series of stipulations to narrow issues for trial. See pp. 1031-37, *supra*. One part of the stipulation process was to set out remaining contentions between the parties. A consequence of these contentions was that the substance of the testimony of most witnesses was reduced to writing. Thus,

> abbreviated testimonial presentations were possible. The direct testimony of most witnesses [there were nearly 350 witnesses called altogether] was submitted in writing. Background and preliminary questioning of witnesses was entirely eliminated. The primary purpose of oral testimony on direct was not to convey information but to establish the credibility of the source. Such testimony was usually limited to a summary of the written

submission. The cross-examinations at trial were correspondingly short. The effect on trial was substantial, perhaps radical. Presentations that normally would be estimated to require half a day took an hour or less. . . .

[I]t was originally conjectured that the trial of the largest antitrust case in history might be the longest in the history of federal jurisprudence. However, . . . the trial took less than a year. That's not bad.

Geoffrey C. Hazard, Jr. & Paul R. Rice, *Judicial Management of the Pretrial Process in Massive Litigation: Special Masters as Case Managers*, in Wayne D. Brazil et al., Managing Complex Litigation 77, 107-08 (1983). See United States v. American Telephone & Telegraph, 83 F.R.D. 323, 339-40 (D.D.C. 1979) (describing process in detail). See also Saverson v. Levitt, 162 F.R.D. 407 (D.D.C. 1995) (ordering use of narrative direct testimony and citing cases); cf. F.R.Civ.P. 43(a) (requiring testimony to be taken in open court).

4. *Oostendorp* was not a complex case, at least as we use that term. Should a court have greater authority to use narrative or summary techniques in complex cases than in other cases? See *Stapleton International*, 720 F. Supp. at 1504 ("Development of techniques for the summary presentation of evidence is recommended in complex litigation."). Remember that a case is complex in the trial sense when reasoned judgment is threatened by lawyer or factfinder dysfunction. When such a threat exists, perhaps the overriding demand of rational adjudication requires that a judge act to change the usual form of trial to make the presentation of evidence more comprehensible. Judges could in theory do the same thing in cases that are not complex, but their reasons for doing so would be different. Are the efficiency gains that seem to underlie *Oostendorp* powerful enough a reason to change the traditional form of trial?

5. Perhaps there is more to plaintiff's due process and jury trial arguments in *Oostendorp* than the Seventh Circuit acknowledged. The use of narrative summaries makes our system of trial look both more continental (summaries of testimony, rather than verbatim transcripts, are often used in continental systems) and more equity-based (the Chancellor also relied on written summaries of testimony and evidence). The strength of the common law form of trial always lay in the immediacy and drama of the live presentation of testimony. See p. 34, *supra*. The use of narrative summaries of testimony would have been highly unusual, if even possible at all, when the Seventh Amendment was enacted in 1791. How much of that historical form of trial is of constitutional stature? More specifically, is the ability of the jury to hear the testimony of witnesses a matter of constitutional stature?

We opened this chapter with Justice Brandeis's observation that the form of jury trial must change with the times. Throughout the chapter we have seen how various information-limiting devices have changed the historical form of trial. Presumably, however, the Seventh Amendment must have some core content or group of elements not subject to change. Arguably the jury's need to hear each witness's own words does not lie within that core. But suppose that the judge ordered all the testimony to be submitted in narrative form, so that the jury heard only the lawyers. Or suppose that we start to pile novel procedure on novel procedure, so that we have a bifurcated trial-by-statistics with time limits and a requirement of narrative summaries for many witnesses. Have we now crossed the constitutional line? Does the Seventh Circuit's line — that there is no Seventh Amendment issue as long as the procedures are "fair" — adequately describe the constitutional concern or the constitutional limit? See *Stapleton*

International, 720 F. Supp. at 1481 n.14; 720 F. Supp. at 1504 (summarily dismissing argument that summaries violate right to jury trial).

Another way to think about this concern is to ask whether narratives help to preserve the right to jury trial or signal its demise. Lay people are pretty good at judging demeanor and making credibility assessments. When the evidence is a bunch of words on paper, however, the jury cannot claim special expertise in factfinding; indeed, the judge, who can reflect on the narratives in chambers, might claim an institutional advantage. As trials become more like hearings in equity, is there a need for the jury?

6. Are the jury trial concerns as acute when the second technique, which at least permits cross-examination of the witnesses, is used?

7. Of course, in cases not tried to a jury, such as *AT&T*, the jury trial concerns about narrative summaries disappear. Due process concerns still remain. Is the Seventh Circuit's assessment that narrative summaries are not "inherently unfair" an adequate due process analysis? Again we need to ask what values are critical to due process, and to decide whether a novel trial technique advances or defeats those values in the context of complex cases. Compare In re Burg, 103 B.R. 222, 225 (9th Cir. BAP 1989) ("[E]ssential [due process] rights of the parties may be jeopardized by a [narrative direct testimony] procedure where the oral presentation of evidence is not allowed, where the bankruptcy court's ability to gauge the credibility of a witness or evidence is questionable and where rulings on objections to the admissibility of all direct evidence, may be unclear") with Adair v. Sunwest Bank, 965 F.2d 777, 780 (9th Cir. 1992) ("We disagree with the *Burg* panel that [a narrative direct testimony] procedure raises significant due process concerns"). See generally William W Scwharzer, Managing Antitrust and Other Complex Litigation § 7-3(A) (recommending use of narrative direct testimony for non-controversial testimony in bench trials).

8. The same summary technique can be applied to evidence other than testimony. In complex cases, it is not unusual for thousands of documents, some of which run hundreds of pages, to be admitted. The salient points of these documents can, however, often be succinctly stated, either through significant redaction of the original text or through a lawyer's summary description of the document's contents. Courts encourage such summaries. In *Nigh*, for example, the court not only ordered short summaries of all deposition testimony, but it also ordered that exhibits not be read to the jury. Instead, the parties were allowed to introduce the exhibits, to quote or summarize pertinent parts of the exhibits when necessary to develop testimony, and to quote from exhibits at any length in the closing arguments. The court held that this procedure was authorized by Fed.R.Evid. 611(a). 634 F. Supp. at 1518; see also Manual for Complex Litigation, Third §§ 21.492, 22.32 (recommending use of summaries for voluminous or complicated data and for other exhibits).

9. What happens when the parties disagree about the content, accuracy, or fairness of a summary? One solution is to present the proposed summaries, as well as the full text of the transcript or exhibit, to the court for in camera review and ruling. Another is to allow opposing counsel to supplement the summary by reading portions of the actual transcript or exhibit to the jury. A third is to allow each side to submit, in heavily edited form, the exact portions of the transcript or exhibit that the party wants the factfinder to hear. See *Stapleton International*, 720 F. Supp. at 1503-04.

10. A final technique would be to require the lawyers to provide the jurors with the relevant portions of the deposition transcripts, and to let the jurors read the transcripts on their own time. This is not quite a summary, but presumably jurors with competent reading skills can glean the relevant information in a fraction of the time that it would take them to have the material read to them. Thus far, however, the practice of giving juries this type of homework has been disapproved. See Stine v. Marathon Oil Co., 976 F.2d 254, 267 (5th Cir. 1992).

11. A party can waive its objections to the use of a narrative summary. See *Walker*, 802 F.2d at 712; *Stapleton International*, 720 F. Supp. at 1504 (considering objection in spite of untimeliness).

12. On appeal, a judge's decision regarding the use of narrative summaries is reviewed for abuse of discretion. *Young*, 745 F.2d at 761. Once again, the trial judge has broad powers to determine the course and form of trial.

C. TECHNIQUES TO MAKE TRIAL INFORMATION MORE COMPREHENSIBLE

In the last section we examined ways to limit the amount of information that a factfinder must consider. A different way to make the factfinder's task of rational adjudication easier is to make the information more comprehensible. In this section we examine a number of comprehension-enhancing techniques that have been employed in complex cases. Our basic concerns remain the same: Do these techniques unduly infringe on the parties' rights to adversarial presentation, due process, and jury trial? How do we justify the use of these procedures in some but not all cases? Do the changes so distort the process of trial that the game of complex litigation is no longer worth the candle, and, if so, what are the alternatives for resolving these disputes?

1. Amending the Usual Order and Structure of Trial

MANUAL FOR COMPLEX LITIGATION, THIRD

143-44 (1995)

Jury recollection and comprehension in lengthy and complex trials may be enhanced by altering the traditional order of trial. Techniques that have been used include the following:

- **Evidence presented by issues.** Rather than have evidence presented in the conventional order, the court may organize the trial in logical order, issue by issue, with both sides presenting their opening statements and evidence on a particular issue before moving to the next.... This procedure, roughly equivalent to severance of issues for trial under Fed.R.Civ.P. 42(b), can help the jury deal with complex issues and voluminous evidence, but may result in inefficiencies if witnesses must be recalled and evidence repeated.

- **Arguments presented by issues/sequential verdicts.** If it is impractical to arrange the entire trial in an issue-by-issue format, it may still be helpful to arrange closing arguments by issue, with both sides making their closing on an issue before moving to the next. The entire case may be submitted to the jury at the conclusion of all argument, or the issues may be submitted sequentially.... The latter procedure may be advantageous if a decision on one issue would render others moot or if the early resolution of pivotal issues will facilitate settlement; on the other hand, it can lengthen the total time for deliberations and requires recurrent recesses while the jury deliberates.

- **Interim statements and arguments.** Some judges have found that in a lengthy trial it can be helpful to the trier of fact for counsel from time to time to summarize the evidence that has been presented or outline forthcoming evidence. Such statements may be scheduled periodically (for example, at the start of each trial week), or counsel may be allowed to make one when they think appropriate, with each side allotted a fixed amount of time to use as it sees fit. Some judges, in patent and other scientifically complex cases, have permitted counsel to explain to the jury how the testimony of an expert will assist them in deciding an issue. Although such procedures are often described as "interim arguments," it may be more accurate to consider them "supplementary opening statement" since the purpose is to aid the trier of fact in understanding and remembering the evidence and not to argue the case. The court should remind the jury of the difference between evidence and counsel's statements. Interim jury instructions ... may also be helpful.

Notes and Questions

1. The judge's power to change the usual structure of trial derives from Fed.R.Evid. 611, which lets a court exercise "reasonable control over the mode and order of interrogating witnesses and presenting evidence." We will return to the concept of the sequential verdict in a later section. See p. 1378, *infra*. Do the remaining ideas seem sensible?

2. Start with the idea of presenting all the evidence on one issue before proceeding to the next issue. If the judge instructed the jury and asked for a verdict on the first issue before proceeding to the next, we would have, of course, bifurcation, whose advantages and disadvantages we have already considered. See pp. 1273-93, *supra*. Perhaps issue-by-issue trial organization, which is a type of bifurcation, will soften some of the pro-defendant effects of bifurcation while still achieving some of bifurcation's benefits. Is it an experiment worth pursuing? On the other hand, does the inability of this procedure to end the litigation after the trial of a single dispositive issue make this procedure both less attractive than bifurcation and less efficient than a regular trial? Would the ping-pong match confuse the jury? Certainly the judge will need to warn the jury about what is happening, since this method probably will not be expected. Will the jury form preconceptions that will make it difficult for it to address later

evidence? Will the procedure unduly disrupt the flow of the plaintiff's and defendant's stories? Will it waste the time of witnesses who might need to be recalled? How discrete must the issues be in order for the procedure to work effectively? How will the judge decide which issues to try first, and which to try later? Should the judge possess this potentially significant power?

We are unaware of empirical studies that have directly addressed the issues raised in issue-by-issue trial organization. Cf. SCM Corp. v. Xerox Corp., 463 F. Supp. 983 (D. Conn. 1978), affirmed, 645 F.2d 1195 (2d Cir. 1981), cert. denied, 455 U.S. 1016 (1982) (judge who used this method in conjunction with special verdicts at end of each issue thought that procedure eliminated introduction of unnecessary evidence, promoted organized consideration of evidence, and reduced chance of retrial). In a study of potential relevance, however, Professors Borden and Horowitz examined the effects on outcomes and damage awards under various forms of unitary and bifurcated trials. One of the things that Borden and Horowitz did was to switch the order of evidence in the unitary and bifurcated trials; some juries heard the plaintiffs' evidence in the order of liability, causation, and damage, followed by the defendant's evidence on those issues, while others heard causation first, then liability and damages. The study found that the order of evidence presentation in both unitary and bifurcated trials had significant effects: In unitary trials in which causation was heard first, juries that returned verdicts for the plaintiffs "rendered higher average compensatory awards than juries hearing liability first," and in bifurcated trials, while defendants won most cases, the juries that did find the defendant liable awarded "significantly higher [compensatory damage awards] than their unitary counterparts." Irwin A. Horowitz & Kenneth S. Bordens, *An Experimental Investigation of Procedural Issues in Complex Tort Trials*, 14 Law & Hum. Behav. 269, 281 (1990). While this study does not squarely address the issue-by-issue trial plan, it would appear that the order in which the judge arranges the issues under such a plan will be tried *may* have an effect on the substantive outcome of trial and *will* have an effect on the amount of damages (if any) awarded. For a bibliography of psychological studies on the effect of order of presentation of evidence on a jury, see Walter F. Abbott et al., Jury Research 29, 183-85 (1993). Cf. United States v. Real Property Known as 77 East 3rd Street, New York, New York, 1994 WL 4276, *3 (S.D.N.Y.) (declining to switch order of proof to allow defendant to present its case first, but suggesting that court had power to do so when it was "logical and more efficient").

Should we await better empirical evidence before we embark on the course of trial reorganization? Does it make you uneasy that the *Manual* recommends this method of trial organization without empirical studies?

3. Interim arguments seem logical enough an idea: Let the lawyers put the past and upcoming evidence into context for the jury, thus helping the jury better focus on and comprehend the issues in the case. Such a technique, of course, takes time, and always carries the risk that the lawyers will overstep the line between focusing the jury and arguing the case. Interim arguments would seem to work particularly well in conjunction with an issue-by-issue trial plan, where there are natural breaks in the testimony both to summarize and to set the stage for upcoming issues. Does the idea have much utility in a standard unitary trial in which evidence is rarely broken up as discretely, and the defendant's evidence may be separated by weeks or months from the plaintiff's evidence on a particular point? Would a few short sentences from the judge be a more useful tool for focusing the jury? Does even a neutral focusing statement

create a risk that the jury will prejudge the case before all the evidence is introduced? Should we run some empirical studies to see how effective these interim arguments actually are in increasing comprehension, and what undesired substantive or remedial side effects they might have?

Anecdotally, in one asbestos case the court allowed the plaintiff and defendant 30 minutes of interim argument each week, and the cross-claim defendants 10 minutes of argument each week, to be used in whatever fashion the parties wished. The defendants eventually objected when it became apparent that the plaintiff was using the time to argue vociferously for punitive damages, thus trying to persuade the jury before the defendants' evidence came in. Since it found that punitive damages were not allowable for other reasons, the appellate court declined to reverse the decision to allow interim arguments. ACandS, Inc. v. Godwin, 340 Md. 334, 667 A.2d 116, 152-54 (1995). Do the *Godwin* facts show that interim arguments are a good idea, a bad idea, or a good idea only when accompanied by heavy-handed policing from the judge?

Among other cases authorizing interim arguments are In re Eastern & Southern Districts Asbestos Litigation, 772 F. Supp. 1380, 1386 (E. & S.D.N.Y. 1991), reversed in part on other grounds, 971 F.2d 831 (2d Cir. 1992); and In re New York Asbestos Litigation, 149 F.R.D. 490, 499 (S.D.N.Y. 1993). See also Cimino v. Raymark Industries, Inc., 1989 WL 253889 (E.D. Tex.) (master's report recommending use of interim arguments as part of trial plan); see also Brookings Institution, Charting a Future for the Civil Jury System 17 (1992) (recommending "mini-opening statements" throughout trial). But see Gray v. Phillips Petroleum Co., 1990 WL 62074 (D. Kan.) (declining to permit weekly interim arguments). See generally William W Schwarzer, *Reforming Jury Trials*, 132 F.R.D. 575, 595-96 (1991) (discussing pros and cons).

4. Pre-instructions and interim instructions seem another good idea whose empirical support is somewhat lacking. The touted benefits of such instructions are the establishment of an appropriate legal framework for the evidence and the multiple opportunities that the jury receives to understand the law in the case (such understanding being one of the jury's weakest points (see p. 1238, *supra*; p. 1376, *infra*)). The potential drawbacks are that the instructions may conform poorly to the evidence presented, that it may create prejudgment or bias in the jury, and that the judge might direct jurors toward testimony she finds relevant and away from testimony they find relevant. See Larry Heuer & Steven D. Penrod, *Instructing Jurors: A Field Experiment with Written and Preliminary Instructions*, 13 Law & Hum. Behav. 409 (1989); John Guinther, The Jury in America 216 (1988); Schwarzer, *supra*, 132 F.R.D. at 583-84; see also Robert MacCoun, *Inside the Black Box: What Empirical Research Tells Us about Decisionmaking by Civil Juries*, in Verdict 137, 151-52 (Robert E. Litan ed. 1993) (describing research suggesting increased comprehension due to preliminary instructions). Heuer and Penrod found no evidence of harmful consequences from their study and some limited evidence of better comprehension of legal standards. But they were cautious: Their research did not allow them to explore some of the more serious possible drawbacks of pre-instruction (such as the creation of initial biases), and did not show strong positive effects. See Heuer & Penrod, *supra*, at 426-27, 429-30. Other studies have mixed results:

> Some studies suggest pre-instructed jurors better recall testimony, while other report no such effect. There is little definitive evidence that pre-instruction improves the jurors' ability to recall judicial instructions. In terms of its effect on overall verdicts, the evidence is also mixed. [One study

found that, in criminal cases,] pre-instruction produces more not guilty verdicts because it predisposes jurors to favor the defendant. [Another study] found that pre-instructions had no effect on patterns of overall verdicts in criminal trials . . . .

Finally, it is worth noting that none of the research suggests that there are serious costs associated with the procedure. Fears that pre-instruction might be logistically cumbersome, promote premature decisionmaking, or encounter opposition from judges and attorneys do not appear to be borne out. Indeed, it appears that jurors are more satisfied with their experience when given pre-instructions and that judges and attorneys are pleased with the procedure. The evidence, however, does not come from complex cases. Under conditions of greater complexity, the efficacy of repetition and of a framework that facilitates jurors' ability to comprehend information might be expected to be greater. . . . [I]t seems worthwhile to employ it and to evaluate its efficacy further.

Jonathan D. Casper, *Restructuring the Traditional Civil Jury: The Effects of Changes in Composition and Procedures*, in Verdict 414, 445-46 (Robert E. Litan ed. 1993). Should we forge ahead with this device despite the lukewarm support and the chance that it *might* have an outcome-determinative effect?

5. Courts have fairly long-standing experience with the use of interim instructions in multi-defendant criminal cases, in which the court often needs to caution a jury to disregard evidence of other defendants' guilt. See, *e.g.*, United States v. Oxford, 735 F.2d 276, 280 (7th Cir. 1984). Pre-instructions have been similarly used in multi-plaintiff trials consolidated under Rule 42(a), as a means of ensuring that the jury focuses on each plaintiff individually rather than on the plaintiffs as a group. See Johnson v. Celotex Corp., 899 F.2d 1281, 1285 (2d Cir.), cert. denied, 498 U.S. 920 (1990) ("When considering consolidation, a court should also note that the risks of prejudice and confusion may be reduced by the use of cautionary instructions . . . ."); *Eastern & Southern Districts Asbestos*, 772 F. Supp. at 1386; *New York Asbestos*, 149 F.R.D. at 499. They have also been proposed as a means of "provid[ing] ongoing education for the jury as to the contentions of the parties and the applicable legal principles" in an antitrust trial expected to last a year. Zenith Radio Corp. v. Matsushita Electric Industrial Co., 478 F. Supp. 889, 953 (E.D. Pa. 1979), vacated on other grounds, 631 F.2d 1069 (3d Cir. 1980).

Interim instructions are, obviously, for the interim. The *Manual* recommends that the court caution the jury about their interim nature, and tell it that final instructions will be given prior to deliberations. *Manual*, § 22.433.

6. One type of pre-instruction that is difficult to disagree with on principle is a set of orientation instructions for jurors. Such instructions might explain to the jury the basic nature of the case, the burden of proof, their daily schedule and ultimate responsibilities in the case, the courthouse facilities, and so forth. See, *e.g.*, *Manual*, § 22.432; Schwarzer, *supra*, 132 F.R.D. at 583-84. Some commentators have suggested the preparation of a juror orientation handbook to cover some of these matters. See Arthur D. Austin, Complex Litigation Confronts the Jury System 101-02 (1984).

7. Note how trial techniques such as changed order of presentation, interim arguments, and pre-instructions are often more than a technique to increase trial comprehension. These techniques can be used to reduce joinder complexity by making it possible to achieve rational verdicts in joined cases.

2. Using High-Tech Demonstrative Evidence

Seeing is believing. The corollary to this adage, as any seasoned trial lawyer can tell you, is that seeing evidence in a dramatic or appealing fashion aids believing. A striking diagram or model can communicate in a second's glance information that minutes or hours of testimony would probably not convey as clearly. Today, the technology to create charts, diagrams, computer graphics, and even computer animation sits on every lawyer's desk. These high-tech jury aids might well presage a new era of trial. Nowhere would the impact be greater than in complex cases, in which the potential payback in terms of shortening trials and increasing factfinder comprehension is great.

Not surprisingly, litigation guides advocate the use of glossaries, indexes, time lines, charts and diagrams, data summaries and compilations, enlargements, and the like. See, *e.g.*, Manual for Complex Litigation, Third § 22.3 (1995); Larry S. Kaplan, Complex Federal Litigation §§ 25.01-26.22 (1993). But such technology is not an unadulterated good. What can lead to a true understanding can, in other hands, mislead and obfuscate. Moreover, the best technology also tends to be expensive, resulting in the possibility that an undeserving litigant can buy a verdict with a blinding technical display. Finally, the new era that this technology presages — a world of virtual reality disconnected from the actual events in dispute — may make traditionalists uncomfortable.

HINKLE v. CITY OF CLARKSBURG, WEST VIRGINIA

81 F.3d 416 (4th Cir. 1996)

■ RUSSELL, Circuit Judge. [Plaintiffs sued the City of Clarksburg and various police officers for violation of the civil rights of their decedent, Bea Wilson. Among the claims was that one police officer, Officer Lake, had used excessive force when he shot and killed the decedent. At trial, the judge allowed the defendants to introduce a computer-animated videotape showing their expert's opinion of the events leading up to the shooting. The jury returned a verdict for the defendants, and plaintiffs appealed.]

Appellants contend the district court erroneously admitted a computer-animated videotaped demonstration of the Appellees' theory of the case....

We review a district court's decisions whether to admit or exclude evidence for abuse of discretion....

At trial, Alexander Jason, a Forensic Animation Technologist, testified for the Appellees to a version of the shooting that was based on his interpretation of the evidence and was consistent with the police officers' testimony. To illustrate Jason's testimony, Appellees introduced a computer-animated videotape. The videotape depicted Wilson's apartment complex, the officers' position in relation to the open door to Wilson's apartment, and a step-by-step account of the incident. It showed an animated version of Officer Lake on the stairwell outside the apartment aiming his gun toward Wilson, who was moving toward the open door. It depicted Wilson raising his shotgun toward the doorway, Officer Lake firing the fatal shot, Wilson's body spinning around from the force of the shot, and his shotgun discharging into the stuffed chair in the back of the room. It then showed how the officers' version of the event was consistent with the physical evidence by concluding with a depiction of the trajectory of Officer Lake's bullet in-line with the wounds to Wilson's forearm, chest, back, and the bullet hole in the wall of the room.

Appellants assign as error the district court's denial of their motion in limine to suppress this evidence. Appellants contend the videotape was inadmissible because it was experimental evidence that attempted to recreate the events but failed to reflect conditions substantially similar to those existing at the time of the shooting.

Typically, demonstrations of experiments used to illustrate principles forming an expert's opinion are not required to reflect conditions substantially similar to those at issue in the trial. Gladhill v. General Motors Corp., 743 F.2d 1049, 1051 (4th Cir. 1984). We have, however, recognized the unique problems presented by the introduction of videotapes purporting to recreate events at the focus of a trial. In *Gladhill*, we noted the potential prejudicial effect of such evidence because the jury viewing a recreation might be so persuaded by its life-like nature that it becomes unable to visualize an opposing viewpoint of those events. Hence, we established a requirement that video taped evidence purporting to recreate events at issue must be substantially similar to the actual events to be admissible.

Obviously, the requirement of similarity is moderated by the simple fact that the "actual events" are often the issue disputed by the parties. Nonetheless, to the extent the conditions are not a genuine trial issue, they should be reflected in any videotaped recreation. In *Gladhill*, for instance, the plaintiff crashed his car into a utility pole. He sued General Motors in a products liability action, contending that the brakes were faulty. The parties agreed that at the time of the accident it was night, and plaintiff was driving down a hill at a sharp curve in the road when he struck the utility pole. General Motors introduced a videotaped recreation of the accident that was conducted at a test facility on a flat, straight, asphalt surface in daylight by an experienced driver. We rejected the use of this videotape, holding that "when the demonstration is a physical representation of how an automobile behaves under given conditions, those conditions must be sufficiently close to those involved in the accident at issue to make the probative value of the demonstration outweigh its prejudicial effect." . . .

We have not previously applied the requirement of "substantial similarity" to computer-animated videotapes that purport to recreate events at issue in trial. We fail to see a practical distinction, however, between a real-life recreation and one generated through computer animation; both can be a particularly powerful recreation of the events. Nonetheless, we need not explicitly decide this issue because we are satisfied the jury here fully understood this animation was designed merely to illustrate Appellees' version of the shooting and to demonstrate how that version was consistent with the physical evidence. The district court carefully instructed the jury on this point:

> [t]his animation is not meant to be a recreation of the events, but rather it consists of a computer picture to help you understand Mr. Jason's opinion which he will, I understand, be giving later in the trial. And to reenforce the point, the video is not meant to be an exact recreation of what happened during the shooting, but rather it represents Mr. Jason's evaluation of the evidence presented.

Although there is a fine line between a recreation and an illustration, the practical distinction "is the difference between a jury believing that they are seeing a repeat of the actual event and a jury understanding that they are seeing an illustration of someone else's opinion of what happened." Datskow v. Teledyne Continental Motors Aircraft Prods., 826 F. Supp. 677, 686 (W.D.N.Y. 1993). The jury understood that the very thing disputed in this trial was the condition under which the shooting occurred. In light of this fact and the court's cautionary instruction, there was no reason for the jury "to credit the illustration any more than they credit the underlying opinion." Id.

We are convinced Appellants suffered no undue prejudice as a result of this computer animation, and we will not disturb the broad discretion afforded trial judges in this area. In reaching this holding, however, we are not unmindful of the dramatic power of this type of evidence; hence, we encourage trial judges to first examine proposed videotaped simulation evidence outside the presence of the jury to assess its foundation, relevance, and potential for undue prejudice.

IN RE AIR CRASH DISASTER

86 F.3d 498 (6th Cir. 1996)

■ BOGGS, Circuit Judge. [In the legal aftermath of the crash of a Northwest Airlines jet, the Judicial Panel on Multidistrict Litigation transferred all cases to the Eastern District of Michigan for consolidated pretrial proceedings, and the district judge subsequently transferred all cases to himself for trial. The main defendants in the case, Northwest and McDonnell Douglas, settled with all plaintiffs before or during trial, but retained certain claims against each other for contribution and equitable apportionment. One of the main points in dispute was whether the pilots had turned off a circuit breaker for a warning beeper that would have alerted them to the problem that caused the crash. At the conclusion of an eighteen-month trial, the jury found Northwest 100% at fault for the crash, and further awarded McDonnell Douglas damages on its equitable apportionment claim. Northwest appealed, citing numerous errors in evidentiary rulings, including the introduction of a computer animation.]

[W]e now turn to Northwest's challenges to rulings that admitted evidence. Our standard of review is [that the] trial court has broad discretion, and we will not reverse a judgment unless we believe that errors at trial had a substantial effect on the final result. . . .

Northwest claims that the court erred in allowing Exhibit 3096, McDonnell Douglas's circuit breaker videotape, to be shown to the jury. Exhibit 3096 is a six-minute computer-animated videotape that depicts the operation of a TI 7274-55 circuit breaker. The videotape was used during the testimony of circuit breaker expert John Bryan Williamson to demonstrate the circuit breaker's inner workings. According to Northwest, the court's admission of the videotape violated the Brumby Rule [and] Rule 26(e)(2) of the Federal Rules of Civil Procedure . . . . Northwest also contends that the videotape was inadmissible under Rule 403 of the Federal Rules of Evidence.

Northwest maintains that admission of the videotape violated the Brumby Rule [and] Rule 26(e)(2) . . . because its contents were not disclosed during the deposition of any McDonnell Douglas witness prior to trial. Northwest argues that Williamson did not disclose during his deposition an intention to use a computer-animated videotape and that, when asked what else he planned to do in the case, he was misleadingly silent.

[Named after a witness in the case, the "Brumby Rule" was developed by the district court with the general agreement of both parties. In order to eliminate surprises at trial, the] Brumby Rule precluded experts from testifying about subjects and opinions not formed at the time of deposition. It did not bar opinions that were formed prior to, but not drawn out at, deposition. The videotape now at issue did not violate the Brumby Rule because it contained no new information. The video simply illustrated what Williamson said in deposition. Furthermore, the court, which had a better grasp of the parties' original intentions regarding their evidentiary agreements than we have now, did not interpret the Brumby Rule to apply to demonstrative evidence.

Rule 26(e)(2) requires that a party supplement a discovery response in certain circumstances. It does not require that a party volunteer information not fairly encompassed by the earlier request. Since Northwest did not depose Williamson concerning matters on the videotape, Rule 26(e)(2) does not preclude the later use of the tape, if otherwise proper. . . .

Northwest also contends that Rule 403 precluded admission of the videotape. Northwest argues that the videotape was inadmissible under Rule 403 because it suggested a similarity to actual events and illustrated MDC's argument that the crew pulled the circuit breaker. We agree that it did both of these things — but do not agree that it was improper. Use of the videotape was limited to demonstration, and the court instructed the jury about the limited basis of its admission. The district court found, and we cannot disagree, that the probative value of the videotape was not substantially outweighed by its prejudicial effect. . . .

The videotape was not, as Northwest contends, offered to simulate what had happened to the circuit breaker in the accident or to simulate the results of Williamson's examination of that circuit breaker. Northwest has not objected on appeal to the Williamson testimony that was the subject of Exhibit 3096. As McDonnell Douglas points out, Williamson could have drawn the same information on a sketch pad in front of the jury. Moreover, no less than six witnesses testified in defense of the circuit breaker design. The use of the tape was entirely proper.

RACZ v. R.T. MERRYMAN TRUCKING, INC.

1994 WL 124857 (E.D. Pa.)

■ TROUTMAN, Senior District Judge. [Plaintiff brought a wrongful death action for a car accident allegedly caused when one of the defendant's drivers veered into another lane. Whether the driver actually did so, however, was hotly disputed. The defendant's accident reconstruction expert developed a computer-animated simulation. The plaintiff moved to preclude the animation under Fed.R.Evid. 403.]

Relying upon the old adage, "seeing is believing," we conclude that the jury may give undue weight to an animated reconstruction of the accident. We are particularly concerned with the translation to visual representation of the discrepancy in the expert report noted in the discussion of the previous motion. The apparent decision of the accident reconstructionist to discount the testimony of a witness who reported seeing the trailer portion of the truck encroach into the decedent's lane of travel is magnified and given enhanced credibility when such decision becomes part of the data upon which an animated visual representation is based. It would be an inordinately difficult task for the plaintiff to counter, by cross-examination or otherwise, the impression that a computerized depiction of the accident is necessarily more accurate than an oral description of how the accident occurred. Because the expert's conclusion would be graphically depicted in a moving and animated form, the viewing of the computer simulation might more readily lead the jury to accept the data and premises underlying the defendant's expert's opinion, and, therefore, to give more weight to such opinion than it might if the jury were forced to evaluate the expert's conclusions in the light of the testimony of all of the witnesses, as generally occurs in such cases.

Based upon our conclusion that the relevance of the computer animation is outweighed by the danger of confusion and prejudice, we will grant plaintiff's motion to preclude the computer simulation.

VAN HOUTEN-MAYNARD v. ANR PIPELINE CO.

1995 WL 317056 (N.D. Ill.)

■ BOBRICK, United States Magistrate Judge. Before the court are a series of motions in limine . . . filed by defendant/third-party plaintiff ANR Pipeline Company ("ANR"). [The case involved a wrongful death claim made by Arlene Van Houten-Maynard, whose husband, a truck driver for

Jones Truck Lines, veered off the road and crashed into a natural gas metering station owned by ANR. After suit was filed, ANR impleaded Jones Truck Lines.]

ANR's motion in limine No. 35 seeks to bar the use of computer animation.

ANR had not received timely notice of plaintiff and Jones' intention to use computer animation with the filing of the pretrial order. ANR has thus been severely prejudiced in its ability to respond to the credibility, reliability, accuracy and materiality of this evidence. Additionally, this type of evidence can be highly influential upon a jury, well beyond its reliability and materiality, due to its documentary-type format presented in a "television" like medium. Additionally, we believe that computer animation evidence, by reasons of its being in a format that represents the latest rage and wrinkle in video communications and entertainment, may well have an undue detrimental effect on other more reliable and trustworthy direct-type evidence. We conclude this evidence has been untimely brought into the case, and thus should be excluded. We also find this evidence as being excludable under Fed.R.Evid. 403 by reasons of its great potential for being misleading and prejudicial.

Notes and Questions

1. Our definition of trial complexity requires three things: (1) Either an inability of counsel to present evidence or an inability of the factfinder to understand the presented evidence; (2) the ability of the trial judge, through changing the usual course of adversarial trial, to correct the problems of counsel or factfinder; and (3) the resulting disparate treatment of like cases. The use of high-tech evidence such as computer animation, as well as somewhat less high-tech evidence such as charts, test simulations, or videotape, does not necessarily fit within our understanding of trial complexity *per se*, because the lawyers are able, without judicial intervention, to create this type of evidence. We include a discussion of high-tech evidence partly to keep you apprised of how the cutting edge of technology might convert today's complex cases into tomorrow's routine cases, partly to suggest that technology might act as a savior of the adversarial system, and partly to raise the question whether the salvation technology promises is worth the price that must be paid.

In some circumstances, however, high-tech evidence can directly raise issues of trial complexity. First, suppose that a lawyer chooses not to use high-tech evidence that would avoid factfinder dysfunction. Can the trial judge require the parties use such evidence? If the lawyer refuses, can the judge put on this evidence herself? Would the source of this authority be Fed.R.Evid. 611 and the court's inherent power? Could a judge accomplish the same thing by putting her own witness on the stand and having that witness present the high-tech evidence? See p. 1347, *infra*. On these types of questions, the Manual for Complex Litigation, Third (1995) walks a fine line, recognizing that "the presentation of the evidence at trial is normally controlled by the strategies and tactics of counsel," but also observing that "the judge should nevertheless take responsibility for encouraging and directing the use of techniques that will facilitate comprehension and expedition, [including] use of visual and other aids." § 22.3. This amounts to a more ambitious role for the judge than the role outlined in the *Manual*'s predecessor, which stated that "[a]ctive involvement by the judge . . . need not and should not alter counsels' primary responsibility for collecting, organizing, and presenting the evidence." Manual for Complex Litigation (Second) § 22.24 (1985).

A second interaction with trial complexity occurs when a party uses high-tech evidence not to make comprehension easier, but to obfuscate the issues and make comprehension more difficult. The judge certainly has the evidentiary tools — notably, Fed.R.Evid. 402 and 403 — to prevent this sort of behavior, which was a primary concern in all four of the principal cases above. How is a judge to know when this type of evidence is an aid and when a ruse? Must she seek the guidance of a technical advisor? See p. 1245, *supra*; *Manual, Third* § 34.2 (suggesting that judges "call on independent experts for advice on questions pertaining to specific uses of technology"). Judges rule on the admissibility of technical evidence all the time; perhaps this isn't any more difficult a decision than any other. Or perhaps it is — judges might be more bowled over by glitzy graphics than by an outlandish scientific theory.

2. With the arguable exception of *Air Crash Disaster*, none of the principal cases was complex. Should the complexity of the case be a factor in a judge's decision whether to admit high-tech evidence? Which way does complexity cut — in favor of such evidence or against?

3. *Hinkle* and *Air Crash Disaster* describe a range of high-tech and low-tech demonstrative evidence: live or videotaped test simulations, videotaped re-enactments of events, even charts and diagrams. The demonstrative use of charts, diagrams, models, enlargements, and the like seem today to be beyond question, at least as long as they represent the matter being described with some semblance of fairness. In-court test simulations also enjoy a broad latitude of admissibility and, in many jurisdictions, need not be substantially similar to the actual events at issue; since the jury and the opposing lawyers can observe the test, the risk of bamboozling the jury is somewhat limited. See Veliz v. Crown Lift Trucks, 714 F. Supp. 49 (E.D.N.Y. 1989) (allowing live demonstration using fork lift that differed from fork lift at issue in significant ways; judge gave appropriate precautionary instructions). Out-of-court simulations, whether actual or computer-generated, create greater concerns about bamboozlement. *Hinkle* reflects the general rule that actual out-of-court simulations must be substantially similar to the events at issue in order to be admissible. See also Champeau v. Fruehauf Corp., 814 F.2d 1271, 1278 (8th Cir. 1987); Szeliga v. General Motors Corp., 728 F.2d 566 (1st Cir. 1984). "Admissibility, however, does not depend on perfect identity between actual and experimental conditions. Ordinarily, dissimilarities affect the weight of the evidence, not its admissibility." *Champeau*, 814 F.2d at 1278 (defendant proffered list of similarities and differences between experimental and actual conditions to jury).

Should computer-generated graphics, which can isolate (and possibly distort) particular aspects of an event to a greater degree than an actual videotape, be held to an even higher standard than "substantial similarity"? Before answering the question, you might wish to know about a recent study by Professors Kassin and Dunn. Using a mock case in which the victim fell from a rooftop, they created a pro-plaintiff version of the fall and a pro-defendant version of the fall, and developed a computer animation that accurately depicted each version. Using a control group that heard only oral testimony and experimental groups that were exposed to a computer animation that correctly depicted the fall, the results of the experiment "clearly supported the hypothesis that a computer-animated reconstruction can facilitate decision making by increasing the extent to which jurors render verdicts consistent with the physical evidence." Saul M. Kassin & Meghan A. Dunn, *Computer-Animated Displays and the Jury: Facilitative and Prejudicial Effects*, 21 Law & Hum. Behav. 269, 276 (1997). Then they flipped the experiment, and showed different groups a computer animation that inaccurately depicted the fall. In this condition, jurors rendered decisions contrary to the physical evidence at a greater rate when shown the misleading animation sequence than when they heard only oral testimony. The authors concluded that accurate computer animations can help to facilitate accurate decisions, but that misleading animations can lead to decisions that contradict the physical evidence. They hypothesized that both effects would be more pronounced in cases involving "complex physical events that the average juror does not understand as a matter of common sense" and in lengthy trials in which oral testimony tends to recede from the jury's mind. Id. at 279-80.

4. A "substantial similarity" (or other) test is designed to answer the question whether the probative value of particular demonstrative evidence outweighs its potential for undue prejudice. But there are other evidentiary hurdles that high-tech evidence must overcome. Obviously, it must be relevant (Fed.R.Evid. 402). Carlo D'Angelo, *The Snoop Doggy Dogg Trial: A Look at How Computer Animation Will Impact Litigation in the Next Century*, 32 U.S.F. L. Rev. 561 (1998). Moreover, until now, we have talked about high-tech evidence as "demonstrative" evidence — evidence that is used to help the factfinder understand underlying evidence that is admissible, but that is not admissible itself. It is, however, possible for high-tech evidence to be admitted as substantive evidence, so that the factfinder can use the videotape or computer simulation as a "fact" in its deliberations. To qualify as substantive evidence, several additional evidentiary hurdles must be overcome. First, the underlying data on which the high-tech evidence is based must either be admissible into evidence (hearsay and authentication are often the stumbling blocks), be the expression of an expert's opinion or the grounds for the expert's opinion, or be regarded as data derived from a method used and accepted within the relevant scientific or other community. Second, a ground for admitting the evidence itself (the usual route being Fed.R.Evid. 702 and 703, concerning expert testimony) must be found. Larry S. Kaplan, Complex Federal Litigation §§ 26.06-.11 (1993); Mario Borelli, Note, *The Computer as Advocate: An Approach to Computer-Generated Displays in the Courtroom*, 71 Ind. L.J. 439 (1996); Adam T. Berkoff, Comment, *Computer Simulations in Litigation: Are Television Generation Jurors Being Misled*, 77 Marq. L. Rev. 829 (1994); Commercial Union Insurance Co. v. Boston Edison Co., 412 Mass. 545, 591 N.E.2d 165 (1992). Third, an adequate foundation for the evidence must be laid. Cf. Bledsoe v. Salt River Valley Water Users' Association, 179 Ariz. 469, 880 P.2d 689, 692 (Ariz. App. 1994) (counsel could not use computer animation in closing argument when it had never been used during trial, no foundation had been laid for admissibility, and no opportunity for cross-examination existed); *Manual*, § 34.32 (describing foundational requirements).

5. Out-of-court videotapes, whether actual or computer-animated, come in two flavors; they are either a "reconstruction," in which the demonstration is based on evidence collected from the relevant past or present event and visually describes a person's opinion of what must have occurred, or a "simulation," in

which some past, present, or future event is depicted based upon theoretical data or formulas that pertain to the event. Kaplan, *supra*, §§ 26.01; Fredric I. Lederer, *Technology Comes to the Courtroom, and . . .*, 43 Emory L.J. 1095, 1116-17 (1994). Reconstructions are typically demonstrative in nature; we know of no case in which an actual or computer-animated videotape reconstruction was admitted as substantive evidence over a party's objection. See, *e.g.*, Datskow v. Teledyne Continental Motors Aircraft Products, 826 F. Supp. 677, 685-86 (W.D.N.Y. 1993). It is not unusual, however, for computer simulations to be used as substantive evidence of what occurred, is occurring, or might occur. See, *e.g.*, *Commercial Union*, 591 N.E.2d 165 (model used to determine how much utility had overcharged consumer for heat); PPG Industries, Inc. v. Costle, 630 F.2d 462 (6th Cir. 1980) (model used to predict future concentrations of pollutants). Those distinctions having been made, the line between "reconstruction" and "simulation" is a thin one, and the courts normally defer to the trial judge's discretion. See Lederer, *supra*, at 1117.

6. Computer animation and other forms of high-tech evidence allow the parties to create visual images of abstract concepts, and give tremendous creative control over the images. But there are also disadvantages to this type of evidence. One concern, mentioned in all of the principal cases, is that the medium of computer animation may overpower the message. The *Manual, Third* also raises several additional concerns: the high cost, the need for a "guide" to lead the factfinder through the program, the fact that "computer-animated images are ultimately human-created and thus susceptible to human biases," and the need to establish an adequate foundation for both the underlying data and the computer program. § 34.32; see also Berkoff, *supra* (raising similar concerns).

A final concern, mentioned in *Houten-Maynard*, is that the traditional form of trial, with its emphasis on live witnesses and direct presentation, will erode. Is this such a bad thing? Judge Marvin Frankel, a staunch critic of the adversarial system's status quo, probably would not think so. His observations on the use of television in the courtroom seem equally applicable to computer animation:

> The miracle of television, if it became widely known in American courts, could spare us some of the pressures and misfortunes of the live, continuous trial. . . . When both sides have recorded all their witnesses and other evidence, the jury can be selected and the entirety of the trial submissions can be given to the assembled jurors without recurrent delays and interruptions, combining the taped accounts of witnesses with the "live" offerings of counsel, documents, other evidence, and the judge's instructions. The process would consume a fraction of our standard trial time. The worries we have about prejudicial evidence inadvertently revealed will be eliminated by the TV "editor" (the editor being in this case the judge, resolving in standard manner of ruling on objections what should and what should not be placed before the jury).

Marvin F. Frankel, Partisan Justice 110 (1978). Frankel went on to describe several experiments with "TV trials," which, according to his account, were extremely successful. See also Walter F. Abbott et al., Jury Research 224-29 (1993) (describing empirical research, generally favorable, on jury trials that used videotape and computer graphics). Is the TV trial, with liberal use of computer graphics and other high-tech evidence to further aid understanding, the way to save the adversarial system while still assuring rational adjudication?

Or is this new world just a little too brave for you? Does the judge's role as "editor" worry you?

7. One point to be careful about is that evidence not be unfairly presented in dual media. For instance, in Traylor v. Husqvarna Motor, 988 F.2d 729 (7th Cir. 1993), an expert testified live on direct examination on a Friday, but, due to a schedule conflict, was unable to come back for cross-examination on the next Monday. The magistrate judge ordered that the cross-examination be videotaped on Saturday, and shown to the jury on Monday. While stating that this procedure was not by itself reversible error, the court of appeals was clearly troubled, since he felt that the direct testimony had more impact than the cross. After remanding on other grounds, the court ordered that both direct and cross be presented in the same medium. 988 F.2d at 734. If *Traylor* is right about the extra impact of live testimony, will TV trials become even more a battle of the lawyers (who will present live openings and closings) and not of the evidence?

8. Obviously, in order for computer animation or other high-tech evidence to be useful, the courtroom must be high-tech-friendly. See pp. 1266, *supra*; see generally Brookings Institution, Charting a Future for the Civil Jury System 17, 22 (1992) (strongly advocating videotape and computer presentations).

9. Computer graphics are usually used in conjunction with the testimony of expert witnesses, as an aid to explain their often difficult and technical opinions and bases for opinions. In the next section we turn directly to the subject of the use and control of expert opinion in complex litigation.

3. Handling Expert Testimony, Court Appointed Experts, and Masters

Nearly all complex cases require the use of expert testimony. Lay witnesses who observe events simply cannot explain or describe the technical and scientific issues in these cases — at least with the degree of accuracy that is necessary for reasoned judgment. A functional adversary system in complex cases would be unimaginable without expert testimony.

On the other hand, the scientific or technical community may be divided on a particular issue, meaning that the trial becomes another forum in which that community engages in a debate that no lay factfinder can adequately resolve. Moreover, the adversary system also has certain built-in incentives that lead to abuse of expert witnesses. One side might have a reason to cloud the scientific issues rather than to clarify them, and through skillful examination lead the factfinder away from rather than toward the truth. Likewise, a wealthy party might be able to buy the testimony of "hired gun" experts who will willingly arrive at whatever opinion the holder of the checkbook desires, or else buy up all of the best experts in a field.

Much could be written on the subject of using expert witnesses in complex litigation: how you pick them, how you pay them, how you prepare them, how you persuade the jury to accept their opinions on direct examination, how you poke holes in those opinions on cross-examination. Indeed, much has been written. (For a tiny smattering of the discussion of legal and practical issues, see Federal Judicial Center, Reference Manual on

Scientific Evidence (1994); 2 Civil Practice and Litigation in Federal and State Courts (6th ed. Sol Schreiber ed. 1994); American Bar Association, Trying Mass Toxic Tort Cases (1989).) For the most part, these issues are not dramatically different in simple and complex cases, and they are better addressed in evidence and trial advocacy courses. Hence we will not be examining them in these materials. Instead, our focus will be, as it has been throughout, on the judge's power to influence the standard operation of the adversary system. This focus leads us to the court's power to appoint its own experts or special masters who present evidence solicited not by the parties but by the judge.

HIERN v. SARPY

161 F.R.D. 332 (E.D. La. 1995)

■ JONES, District Judge. Pending before the Court is defendants' motion for appointment of a special master, or, alternatively, for appointment of an expert. Having reviewed the memoranda of the parties, the record and the applicable law, the Court DENIES the motion.

Background

This litigation arises from a long-term business relationship between plaintiff Livingston S. Hiern and defendant A. Lester Sarpy. Hiern and Housemaster Corp. filed this lawsuit in March 1994 alleging violations of RICO, legal malpractice, breach of fiduciary duty, securities violations and other state law claims in regard to transactions between Hiern and Sarpy and their related businesses. Allegedly the illegal transactions occurred between the mid-1970s and the early 1990s. [The transactions involved loans from Sarpy's to Hiern's company in order that Hiern could purchase real estate. These loans typically carried an interest rate of 24 to 30 percent per annum. When Hiern sold the land, he took a mortgage for part of the sales price. He then sold the mortgages to Sarpy for about 50% of their face value. Sarpy would credit the proceeds of these sales against the money Hiern owed on existing loans.]

The dispute revolves around whether these loans from defendants to plaintiffs were ever paid off, whether defendants ever gave plaintiffs a proper accounting, and whether subsequent transactions after the loans were allegedly paid off inured to the benefit of defendants instead of plaintiffs. Defendants also allege that various compromise agreements between the parties occurred due to the difficulty of keeping track of the balances due.

Both parties contend that since the lawsuit was filed they have worked to exchange documents to try to narrow the issues and the amounts allegedly due from one party to the other. Needless to say, they still disagree.

Defendants move for an appointment of a special master pursuant to Fed.R.Civ.P. 53(b), or, alternatively, for appointment of an expert pursuant to Fed.R.Evid. 706. Defendants desire the appointment of a special master to unravel the alleged mystery of the complex real estate and loan transactions. In their amended motion defendants deleted their request that the special master determine if fraud occurred, conceding that this is a jury question. However, defendants contend that, because each side's expert will put his own gloss on the issues at trial, a special master is needed to evaluate the documents and testimony of each party and present an independent opinion. Otherwise, the jury will be hopelessly confused at trial.

Alternatively, defendants seek appointment of an expert pursuant to Fed.R.Evid. 706. Defendants argue that an objective expert would be able to examine the accounting, real estate and loan documents at issue and provide findings and opinions that would better aid the jury in reaching a conclusion because each side's hired experts are only interested in helping his own clients. . . .

Law and Application

A. Appointment of Special Master

According to Rule 53(b), as a general proposition the reference to a special master is the exception rather than the rule. In a jury trial the reference should be made only when the issues are "complicated." "The minimum required is a demonstration that over and beyond a mere numerical quantitative analysis, the case is intrinsically complex." In re Tom Watkins, 271 F.2d 771, 774 (5th Cir.1959). Citing *Watkins*, the Supreme Court has stated: "Even this limited inroad upon the right to trial by jury 'should seldom be made, and if at all only when unusual circumstances exist.'" Dairy Queen, Inc. v. Wood, 369 U.S. 469, 478, n. 18 (1962), quoting La Buy v. Howes Leather Co., 352 U.S. 249, 258 (1957). . . .

In the present case, although there seem to be numerous financial transactions and records at issue, the record does not show an inordinate number to be in dispute. Indeed, according to the unrebutted assertion of plaintiffs in their memoranda, only about 40 of these transactions are in contention. . . . [T]he issues are for a jury as factfinder to decide. Beyond a mere quantitative analysis, there has been no showing that the case is so intrinsically complex as to require a special master's aid.

Moreover, the fact that the experts disagree is not sufficient reason to require intervention of a special master. . . . [R]esolution of expert disagreement is within the province of the factfinder. The use of masters should aid, not displace, the jury as factfinder. *La Buy*, 352 U.S. at 256. See also *Watkins*, 271 F.2d at 775 (reference to special master "nullifies the right to an effective trial before a constitutional court").

Additionally, although defendants concede that appointment of a special master is improper in fraud actions, the appointment of a special master to determine non-fraud issues rather than all issues runs the risk of confusing the jury more than helping it.

Therefore, the Court finds that defendants have failed to show that this case is so complicated that reference to a special master is necessary.[4]

B. Appointment of Expert

Rule 706(a) of the Federal Rules of Evidence provides, in pertinent part:

> The court may on its own motion or on the motion of any party enter an order to show cause why expert witnesses should not be appointed. . . .

Such an appointment by the court is within its discretion, but "the mere fact that the parties' retained experts have expressed divergent opinions does not necessarily warrant that the Court appoint an expert to aid in resolving the conflict." Mallard Bay Drilling, Inc. v. Bessard, 145 F.R.D. 405, 406 (W.D. La. 1993). See also Applegate v. Dobrovir, Oakes & Gebhardt, 628 F. Supp. 378, 383 (D.D.C. 1985) (appointment of expert appropriate only in "compelling" circumstances).

In this case, while the experts apparently disagree heartily on the outcome of the case (one claims that the plaintiffs owe defendant $1.6 million and the other expert claims that defendants owe plaintiff $1.9 million), plaintiffs contend that this disagreement arises largely from the treatment of pre-1978 transactions, specifically interest on those transactions. Additionally, plaintiffs maintain that both side's experts use the same accounting methodologies and agree on the treatment of many transactions. Where they disagree, according to plaintiffs, is on the treatment of key transactions, the amount of damages and the existence of fraud.

Notwithstanding the cause of the disagreement, plaintiffs correctly argue that defendants have not shown specifically how the appointment of an expert will help the jury to comprehend the evidence to be presented at trial. Absent such a showing, the court's appointment of an expert would just add an additional witness, who may testify in favor of one side or the other. Whether or not the jury is informed that the third expert was appointed by the court,[6] a danger exists that the appointed expert would side with either of the other experts, giving one side an inappropriate numerical advantage. As the Magistrate Judge stated in *Mallard Bay Drilling*, "it is axiomatic that the weight of evidence is not to be determined by the number of witnesses that testify." 145 F.R.D. at 406.

Further, the parties are free at trial to examine and cross-examine the

---

4. As to plaintiffs' contention that reference to a special master would cause financial hardship because of the costs associated with the special master's fees, the Court notes that at least one court has refused to appoint a special master when financial burdens would be imposed on the plaintiff, Fraver v. Studebaker [Corp.], 11 F.R.D. 94 (W.D. Pa. 1950). . . . [I]n this case, where each side apparently has experts, and where the parties have worked diligently on narrowing the disputed issues, the Court also finds there is no reason to impose additional costs on either party.

6. It is within the court's discretion whether or not to tell the jury that the court appointed the expert. Fed.R.Evid. 706(c).

experts, testing their theories and reasoning, such that a jury will be able to decide the issues.

Defendants quote extensively from the Manual for Complex Litigation on the necessity for appointment of an expert, but they fail to quote the following sentence: "Even in complex litigation, [appointment of an expert] is the exception and not the rule." Manual for Complex Litigation, § 21.5. Indeed, as the *Manual* states, the objective of the appointment of an expert is "a more understandable trial, not a shorter one." Id. at § 21.51. Defendants have not specifically shown how appointment of an expert would make this trial more understandable....

Therefore, the Court finds that defendants have not made a sufficient showing as to the need for a court-appointed expert.[7]

GATES v. UNITED STATES

707 F.2d 1141 (10th Cir. 1983)

■ PER CURIAM. This is an appeal from the judgment of the district court dismissing plaintiff's action against the United States for personal injury allegedly caused by the swine flu vaccination administered during the National Swine Flu Immunization Program of 1976, 42 U.S.C. § 247b(j)-(l) (1976) ("Swine Flu Act"). The sole issue was whether the swine flu vaccine received by plaintiff (Fae L. Gates) was the proximate cause of the Guillain-Barre Syndrome ("GBS") she suffered in the fall of 1977. The district court held that plaintiff had failed to prove causation by a preponderance of the evidence....

Before trial, the parties stipulated that plaintiff had GBS. According to the Final Pretrial Order, she did not have to establish a theory of liability to win her case; she had only to prove the existence of a causal nexus between the swine flu vaccination and her GBS.

·In advance of [the non-jury] trial, the district court appointed a panel of three medical experts to assist the court in resolving the complex medical issues involved. The panel submitted its findings to the court in a report which was admitted into evidence....

On appeal plaintiff raises . . . [w]hether the trial court's appointment of a panel of experts was error . . . .

Plaintiff challenges the make-up of the panel of experts appointed to assist the trial court because, plaintiff argues, the panel of three experts consisted of two specialists in neurology and one expert witness with a strong predilection to a neurological bias.

---

7. Defendants also state that they would be willing to pay the cost of a court-appointed expert. Fed.R.Evid. 706(b) specifically provides that the court may apportion the costs of an appointed expert among the parties and at such time as the court directs. However, because the Court declines to appoint an expert for the reasons stated, the Court does not reach the issue of who should pay for a court-appointed expert.

The panel consisted of C.H. Milliken, M.D., professor of neurology at the University of Utah; Stanley H. Appel, M.D., professor of neurology at Baylor College of Medicine; and Leonard T. Kurland, M.D., professor of epidemiology and medical statistics at the Mayo Clinic. All members of the panel had had previous experience in diagnosing GBS. The panel was empowered to conduct physical examinations of plaintiff, consider medical literature submitted by the parties, and review past medical records of plaintiff. Two members of the panel conducted separate examinations of plaintiff. The panel was unanimous in its conclusion that plaintiff suffered from GBS but that the time interval between the inoculation and onset of GBS, which the panel determined to be approximately eleven months, was too great for a causal nexus to exist.

Plaintiff argues that the diagnosis and treatment of GBS crosses a broad spectrum of medical disciplines and, therefore, the appointment of a panel of experts consisting of two neurologists and one epidemiologist was erroneous in that the experts' backgrounds in neurology constituted a bias in their conclusions and findings.

The trial judge has broad discretion in regulating trial procedure, including the appointment of a panel of experts to assist the trial court in understanding complex matters. See Fugitt v. Jones, 549 F.2d 1001, 1006 (5th Cir.1977). [The court then quoted Fed.R.Evid. 706.]

Before the appointment of the advisory panel, the trial court directed the parties to discuss whether such a panel should be appointed. The parties were allowed to offer a proposed order for appointment and to suggest up to five potential panel members. The panel members were required to be available for trial and for deposition. Plaintiff deposed two of the panel members, and the depositions were admitted into evidence.

The diagnosis and treatment of GBS is primarily committed to specialists in neurology. In undertaking its nationwide study of the incidence of GBS following the swine flu vaccination program, the [Center for Disease Control] contacted neurologists for the collection of data with regard to the number of cases of GBS occurring in the population. The experts appointed by the trial court are well qualified in their fields. Moreover, plaintiff has failed to show the existence of any bias on the part of this panel. Under these circumstances, we find no abuse of discretion in the trial court's appointment of the panel.

Joe S. Cecil & Thomas E. Willging, ACCEPTING *DAUBERT'S* INVITATION: DEFINING A ROLE FOR COURT-APPOINTED EXPERTS IN ASSESSING SCIENTIFIC VALIDITY

43 Emory L.J. 995, 1004, 1041, 1043-45, 1069-70 (1994)

Many commentators have mentioned that the use of court-appointed experts appears to be rare, an impression based on the infrequent references to such experts in published cases. To obtain an accurate assessment of the extent to which court-appointed experts have been employed, we sent a one-page questionnaire to all active federal district court judges.[33] . . .

[E]ighty-six judges, or 20% of those responding to the survey, revealed that they had appointed an expert on one or more occasions. The figures indicate that, taken together, these judges made approximately 225 appointments, far more than suggested by the paucity of published opinions dealing with the exercise of this authority. . . .

Our interviews revealed that juries and judges alike tend to decide cases consistent with the advice and testimony of court-appointed experts. We asked, "Was the disputed issue resolved in a manner consistent with the advice or testimony of the 706 expert?" Of fifty-eight responses, only two indicated that the result was not consistent with the guidance given by the expert. Both of these cases involved bench trials in which the judge pursued a legal analysis that was independent of the technical issues. [In five other cases, the expert either did not render an opinion or was regarded merely as useful in shaping a resolution.]

In the remaining fifty-one cases, including seven jury trials, the outcome was consistent with the expert's advice or testimony. Whether the advice of the expert influenced the outcome is, of course, another matter. Twenty-one of the judges who indicated consistent outcomes also volunteered the information that the experts' opinions were not the exclusive, or even the most important, factor in determining the outcome of their cases. . . .

One final question when the case involved a jury trial was, "Did the testimony of the court-appointed expert appear to overwhelm the expert testimony offered by the parties?" In a dozen jury cases, it appears that the testimony of court-appointed experts dominated the proceedings. In general, the testimony of the court's expert affirmed the testimony of one of the parties' experts, thereby overcoming contrary evidence. . . .

We are wary of overstating the strength of these findings in light of the inability of social psychologists to demonstrate greater deference to appointed experts by jurors in controlled laboratory settings.[132] . . .

When viewed in the light of circumstances leading to an appointment, perhaps it should come as no surprise that the outcome of a case is greatly influenced by the testimony of the appointed expert. . . . The primary reasons for appointment of an expert were either a failure of the parties to offer credible expert testimony or an actual or anticipated conflict in the testimony of the parties' experts that defied resolution through traditional means. Regarding the failure of advocacy cases, . . . [g]iven a void of evidence on a critical issue, the court-appointed expert's testimony would necessarily be influential.

Similarly, in cases with an unresolvable conflict among the parties' experts, the equipose in the evidence prior to appointment renders the court-

---

33. Questionnaires were sent to 537 active federal district court judges; 431 responded (a response rate of 80%).

132. See, *e.g.*, Nancy J. Brekke et al., *Of Juries and Court-Appointed Experts: The Impact of Nonadversarial versus Adversarial Expert Testimony*, 15 Law & Hum. Behav. 451 (1991) . . . .

appointed expert likely to tip the scale to one side or the other. Any other result would raise significant questions about whether there had been a need for an outside expert. These reasons tend to explain and qualify our findings. Nonetheless, the central finding is clear: judges who appointed an expert indicated that the final outcome on the disputed issue was almost always consistent with the testimony of the appointed expert....

Appointment of an expert by the court represents a striking departure from the adversarial process of presenting information for the resolution of disputes. But such an appointment should not be regarded as showing a lack of faith in the adversarial syatem. We learned that judges who appointed experts appear to be as devoted to the adversarial system as those who made no such appointments. Most appointments were made after extensive efforts failed to find a means within the adversarial system to gain the information necessary for a reasoned resolution of the dispute. Appointment of an expert was rarely considered until the parties had been given an opportunity and failed to provide such information. We find it hard to fault judges for failing to stand by a procedure that had proved incapable of meeting the court's need for information; to insist, in such a circumstance, that the court limit its inquiry to inadequate presentations by the parties is a poor testament to the adversarial system and the role of the courts in resolving disputes in a principled and thoughtful manner.

Notes and Questions

1. In Chapters Eight and Ten we examined other uses to which a master could be put — specifically, as the director or assistant director of the pretrial show, as a substitute factfinder, and as a substitute lawgiver. Here we explore yet another role for the master: as an aide to the factfinder. Court-appointed experts, about whom we have not studied, serve essentially the same role, providing testimony and evidence to the factfinder. In theory, there are differences between the master and the court-appointed expert. One is the standard under which masters and experts are appointed. References to masters are "the exception and not the rule," and can occur in jury trials only when the "issues are complicated" and in non-jury trials when some "exceptional condition requires it." F.R.Civ.P. 53(b). Experts can be appointed whenever there is "cause." Fed.R.Evid. 706(a). In reality, however, the standards tend to blend; as both *Hiern* and the research of Cecil and Willging suggest, judges are reluctant to appoint experts unless the parties have failed in their adversarial task or a court-appointed expert is seen as necessary to reasoned decisionmaking. Thus, the use of experts is also the exception rather than the rule.

A second difference involves the tasks to which masters and experts are put. An expert is used, in theory, to provide opinion testimony that will assist the factfinder. See Fed.R.Evid. 702. A master has a broader range of responsibility. A master can hear testimony and receive other evidence, can rule on its admissibility, and conduct trial-like hearings. See F.R.Civ.P. 53(c), (d). Unlike an expert, a master makes findings of fact; in non-jury cases, the findings of fact in the report must be accepted unless clearly erroneous, and in jury cases, the master's findings are "admissible as evidence of the matters found and may be read to the jury." F.R.Civ.P. 53(e)(1)-(3). At least in jury trials, however, these differences may be less than they seem. As *Gates* shows, experts often investigate and accumulate information to render an opinion. Moreover, the findings of fact of a master are used merely as evidence by the jury, and therefore are entirely equivalent to an expert's testimony.

A third difference is the form of the end-product. A master is to write a report; an expert is to give testimony. But the form too can be overstated; masters can testify at trial, cf. Crateo, Inc. v. Intermark, Inc., 536 F.2d 862 (9th Cir.), cert. denied, 429 U.S. 896 (1976) (not reversible error not to require master to read findings personally or to be subject to cross-examination), and experts often prepare written reports that form the basis of their oral testimony, see Cecil & Willging, 43 Emory L.J. at 1035-36.

There are other differences as well. Overall the master is a more flexible tool capable of performing a range of pretrial and trial tasks. But in terms of the specific function that we are considering here — making the factfinder's task of comprehension easier — there are strong similarities. Should there be a single set of standards and procedures for these "comprehension assistants," rather than two? If so, should the high threshold of the master's reference or the nominally lower threshold of the expert's appointment be adopted? Cf. In re Estate of Ferdinand E. Marcos Human Rights Litigation, 1994 WL 874222 (D. Haw.) (single person was appointed to act as master for some trial tasks and court-appointed expert for others).

2. In previous chapters we explored some of the problems, including cost, delay, bias, and dissimilar treatment of like cases, that masters generate. How many of those problems carry over to the master as a "comprehension assistant"? Would the same problems infect the court-appointed expert? See Manual for Complex Litigation, Third § 21.51 (stating that disadvantages of court-appointed expert include cost, delay, potential harm to neutrality of court, lack of neutrality of expert, and problems of timing appointment; advantages are "great tranquilizing effect" on contentious experts of parties, facilitation of settlement or issue narrowing, and increase in comprehension).

3. Like masters, court-appointed experts have a long history in Anglo-American procedure. A court-appointed expert appears to have been used as early as 1345, and by the 1600s the use seems to have become routine. See Learned Hand, *Historical and Practical Considerations Regarding Expert Testimony*, 15 Harv. L. Rev. 40, 42-47 (1901); Hart v. Community School Board of Brooklyn, 383 F. Supp. 699, 762-63 (E.D.N.Y. 1974) (Weinstein, J.). Prior to the creation of Rule 706, federal courts claimed, not surprisingly, that they possessed an "inherent power" to appoint expert witnesses. Scott v. Spangler Brothers, Inc., 298 F.2d 928 (2d Cir. 1962).

4. The title of the Cecil and Willging article refers to the Supreme Court's decision in Daubert v. Merrell Dow Pharmaceuticals, Inc., 509 U.S. 579 (1993), which held that expert testimony was admissible as long as it was relevant and scientifically valid but which then suggested that, in deciding whether to admit such testimony, the judge "should also be mindful of other applicable rules [including] Rule 706." 509 U.S. at 595. We should not read too much into a passing suggestion, but the Supreme Court's reference to Rule 706 indicates that Rule 706 is not utterly disfavored in high places. Cf. In re Joint Eastern and Southern Districts Asbestos Litigation, 151 F.R.D. 540, 545 (E. & S.D.N.Y 1993) (Weinstein, J.) (suggesting that *Daubert* requires "trial court to take an active role in the presentation of expert evidence").

5. The Cecil and Willging article that we excerpted is a somewhat condensed version of their manuscript on court-appointed experts. See Joe S. Cecil & Thomas E. Willging, Court Appointed Experts (1993). This manuscript covers a great deal of ground that we need not re-trace here in detail. Some of this information includes how judges pick experts (usually from nominations from the parties, but not always), what kinds of cases experts are useful in (patent cases topped the list, followed by product liability and antitrust cases), when appointments are made (usually early in the litigation, but many were appointed on the eve of trial), how experts are used (frequently to testify, but often to perform advisory or other non-testimonial functions), and how experts are paid (usually the cost is split equally among parties, with the possibility that the judge will award the prevailing party its share of the fee as a cost of litigation under 28 U.S.C. § 1920(6)). Let us focus on three points of larger significance:

(a) *Reasons for Appointment*. Judges appointed experts either to aid decision making or to help the parties settle. Cecil & Willging, 43 Emory L.J. at 1009-15. The latter reason was infrequently cited. Concerning the former reason, judges saw two benefits in appointments: either to provide testimony where the lawyers had failed, or to provide testimony when the parties' experts made comprehension difficult. These two circumstances, of course, correspond in our vocabulary to problems of lawyer dysfunction and factfinder dysfunction — one or the other of which is the first element in trial complexity.

It is doubtful, however, that judges confine their appointments only to cases of true dysfunction — *i.e.*, cases in which the lawyers or factfinder were truly incapable of performing their adversarial tasks. For instance, a party may simply have incompetent counsel. In cases that do not involve true dysfunction, is there an adequate reason to appoint an expert? In answering this question, you might want to know that Cecil and Willging found that four-fifths of the cases in which a court-appointed expert testified were bench trials. Unless we are to assume that judge-tried cases are inherently more complex or that judges are less competent to make factual findings, something is going on here. Are judges appointing experts in bench trials even when lawyer or factfinder dysfunction does not exist? Cf. Kian v. Mirro Aluminum Co., 88 F.R.D. 351, 356 (E.D. Mich. 1980) (refusing to appoint expert in jury trial when facts "are within the comprehension of laypersons").

(b) *Non-adversarial Presentation*. The judicial appointment of an expert clearly fulfills the second element of trial complexity: the non-adversarial use of judicial power to overcome lawyer or factfinder dysfunction. Most judges, however, soften the non-adversarial nature of the court-appointed expert through various devices designed to make the witness appear less authoritative, and more like a regular witness. Three devices, required by Rule 706(a), are that any party may take the expert's deposition, that any party may call the expert as a witness at trial, and that any party may cross-examine the expert at trial. See DeAngelis v. A. Tarricone, Inc., 151 F.R.D. 245 (S.D.N.Y. 1993); cf. *Asbestos Litigation*, 151 F.R.D. at 544-46 (refusing to allow depositions of panel of experts, but allowing opinions to be disclosed at court-supervised pretrial hearing). A fourth device, mentioned in *Hiern*, is that the court has the discretion not to advise the jury of the expert's court-appointed status. Fed.R.Evid. 706(c); but see Cecil & Willging, 43 Emory L.J. at 1038-39 (jury was told of the expert's court-appointed status in 6 of 7 trials). But these devices do not return the trial to an adversarial status quo.

Another breach of adversarial etiquette occurs when the judge communicates with the expert. In an adversarial system, contacts between judge and witness must be kept to a minimum in order to prevent bias. With a court-appointed expert, some contacts are inevitable. The research of Cecil and Willging suggested that some judges limited their *ex parte* communications to procedural matters such as recruiting the expert, describing the task, and answering questions about the appointment. Many judges, however, also communicated "on at least some occasions to elicit technical advice," to review draft opinions, or to review documents; judges varied widely regarding how much, if any, of these conversations they revealed to the parties. Id. at 1032; see also id. at 1065-67 (recommending guidelines for *ex parte* communication). In bench trials, is it possible to avoid prejudgment when *ex parte* communications occur?

How do you feel about this non-adversarial application of judicial power? Is it generally justifiable? Is it at least justifiable in complex cases? Does your answer depend on whether an expert or master might increase the accuracy of the verdict or judgment? In Contini v. Hyundai Motor Co., 149 F.R.D. 41, 41-42 (S.D.N.Y. 1993), Judge Broderick addressed a number of these themes in the course of ruling that he expected to appoint an expert in a products liability case:

> Concern about the impact of presentation to lay juries (who cannot study background written materials and ask extensive questions of experts to assure understanding of complex concepts) of testimony given by biased experts is increasing. This reflects the-ever-more technical nature of issues presented in product liability and similar intricate litigation. . . .
>
> This phenomenon may be especially troubling where, for example, a significant part of the livelihood of an expert is drawn from testimony favorable to a particular side of a controversy, or where an expert is dependent upon income from an industry closely connected to the interests of one side or another. Requiring the fullest disclosure of potential sources of partiality of expert witnesses represents an important if incomplete response to this problem.
>
> With proper cross-examination generalist factfinders may be able to assess experts' credibility. This does not assure generalists' ability to reach correct affirmative conclusions with respect to controverted obscure technical issues, a challenge deserving of continuing attention.

See also In re Joint Eastern and Southern Districts Asbestos Litigation, 830 F. Supp. 686, (E.& S.D.N.Y. 1993) (noting that appointment "is not commonplace," but that "work of such experts is especially critical in dealing with complex mass tort problems such as" complex and interdependent scientific issues, thousands of parties, equitable treatment, and strong and conflicting interests in character of relevant data); J & M Turner, Inc. v. Applied Bolting Technology Products, Inc., 1997 U.S. Dist. LEXIS 1835 (E.D. Pa.) (declining to appoint expert for unclear and complicated issue when parties could retain own experts and court appointment would cloak one expert with aura of judicial imprimatur).

(c) *Dissimilar Treatment of Similar Cases.* The final element of trial complexity is that the judge's non-adversarial use of power results in dissimilar outcomes in similar cases. Undoubtedly you noticed the striking correlation reported by Cecil and Willging between the expert's testimony and the outcomes of the cases. Although a judge is unlikely to know which way the appointment will cut, a judge must realize that the appointment is likely to influence the outcome in a significant percentage of cases. See *Kian*, 88 F.R.D. at 356 ("The presence of a court-sponsored witness, who would most certainly create a strong, if not overwhelming, impression of 'impartiality' and 'objectivity,' could potentially transform a trial by jury into a trial by witness."). Other research suggests another potential outcome-determinative effect of court-appointed experts. As we discussed when we examined the judge's power to amend the usual order of proof, the placement of evidence within a trial can sometimes affect the outcome. See p. 1335, *supra*. The exact placement of the court-appointed expert's testimony can, therefore, have a dramatic effect. If it is placed near the end, the jury might regard it as the most compelling evidence in the trial; if it is placed in the middle, its impact will be much less. See Cecil & Willging, 43 Emory L.J. at 1040 ("The timing and sequence of the testimony may have serious effects on the jury's recollection of the evidence and may distort the normal primacy and recency benefits that accompany the opening and closing presentations during trial.").

So how can such an appointment be justified in some, but not all, cases? Granting that appointments are necessary to preserve the opportunity for reasoned adjudication, this justification explains appointments only in those cases in which reasoned judgment is threatened. Is there any justification for appointing experts in other cases? If appointments are limited just to those cases in which reasoned judgment is threatened, "complex" and "routine" cases receive different, outcome-determinative procedural treatment? If we require court-appointed experts in all cases, we have made an inroad on the adversarial system when it is not essential. If we refuse to permit experts in any cases, we condemn the subset of complex cases to irrational adjudication. Is an administrative or legislative solution for complex cases the only other alternative?

6. As *Gates* shows, a court appointment is not limited to one person; a panel of experts with different relevant areas of expertise can sometimes be appointed. See *Asbestos Litigation*, 151 F.R.D. 540 (expert panel on remedial issue); In re Swine Flu Immunization Products Liability Litigation, 495 F. Supp. 1185 (W.D. Okla. 1980). Experts can also be used in conjunction with other trial techniques. See Cimino v. Raymark Industries, Inc., 1989 WL 253889 (E.D. Tex.) (special master report recommending appointment of experts to testify at planned "trial by statistics").

7. In Young v. Pierce, 640 F. Supp. 1476, 1478 (E.D. Tex. 1986), a judge appointed a special master who was specifically authorized to seek the advice of a court-appointed expert. Does Rule 706 allow the appointment power to be exercised by judicial adjuncts? Does a self-perpetuating bureaucracy concern you, or do the needs of complex cases justify the risk? (You might harken back to the lessons of equity from Chapter One.)

8. As *Gates* says, the trial judge's decision to appoint an expert is reviewed for abuse of discretion. See also Fugitt v. Jones, 549 F.2d 1001 (5th Cir. 1977). Again we come up against the trial judge with broad discretion to make potentially outcome-determinative procedural moves.

9. Whatever their actual merit, court-appointed experts are sometimes touted as a solution to problems of jury comprehension. See, *e.g.*, ABA Antitrust Section, Expediting Pretrials and Trials of Antitrust Cases 52-59 (1979); ABA Commission on Mass Torts, Report to the House of Delegates 62-63 (1989); Samuel R. Gross, *Expert Evidence*, 1991 Wis. L. Rev. 1113, 1187-1208.

10. A judge's power to appoint and call witnesses is not limited to experts. Judges also enjoy a common law power to call and interrogate fact witnesses. See 9 Wigmore's Evidence § 2484 (James H. Chadbourn ed. 1981). That power has been codified in Fed.R.Evid. 614(a), which provides that the court "may, on its own motion or at the suggestion of a party, call witnesses, and all parties are entitled to cross-examine witnesses thus called"; Rule 614(b) gives the judge the power to interrogate such witnesses. One of the reasons that judges first assumed this power was the common law rule that a witness could not be impeached by the party who called the witness. Although that rationale no longer exists, see Fed.R.Evid. 607, the drafters of Fed.R.Evid. 614(a) thought that such a rule was still valuable so that "the judge is not imprisoned within the case made by the parties." See Fed.R.Evid. 614 advisory committee's note.

We know of no study or survey comparable to that of Cecil and Willging concerning the frequency with which courts call non-expert witnesses. From the reported decisions, it seems to be a rare event. Among these rare cases, nearly all are criminal rather than civil. See, *e.g.*, United States v. Agajanian, 852 F.2d 56 (2d Cir. 1988). Is the sense of an adversary system stronger in civil cases? In complex civil cases, should the judge be more willing to call additional witnesses who can help the jury comprehend the issues?

The court's power to call expert or lay witnesses implies, and Rule 614(b) confirms, that the court has the power to interrogate such witnesses. Rule 614(b), however, is actually broader; in full text, it says: "The court may interrogate witnesses, whether called by itself or by a party." We turn to this power of interrogation in the following section.

4. Questioning and Commenting by Judge and Jury

An obvious solution to comprehension problems is to let the person who is having difficulty in comprehension either ask questions of the persons providing information or make comments that show the present level of understanding to those persons. We do this every day in class, at home, and at work. In an adversarial system, which hinges on party control of the information that the decision maker hears, this obvious solution has obvious drawbacks. Do questions and comments from judge and jury provide an easy solution to comprehension problems, or does this technique create more problems than it solves?

RESERVE MINING COMPANY v. LORD

529 F.2d 181 (8th Cir. 1976)

■ Opinion of the Court by Circuit Judge LAY, Circuit Judge BRIGHT, Circuit Judge ROSS, Circuit Judge STEPHENSON, Circuit Judge WEBSTER and Circuit Judge HENLEY.... The matter now comes to us on a petition for mandamus seeking to enjoin the district judge, the Honorable Miles Lord, from interference with state administrative hearings.

Petitioners also seek to recuse the district judge from further proceedings in this case.

[Reserve Mining was polluting both the air in and about Silver Bay, Minnesota and the water of Lake Superior with its discharge of taconite tailings. Judge Lord, one of the more colorful jurists in American history, had ordered the plant to shut down; but, in a prior appeal, the court of appeals had found that Reserve's discharges, while posing a danger to the public health, did not pose imminent enough a danger to justify such a remedy. One of the reasons for the court of appeal's decision was Reserve's commitment to complete abatement procedures within approximately three years after approval by the State of Minnesota of a tailings disposal site. But this commitment hinged on actions not yet taken by Minnesota on Reserve's application for a disposal site.

[After remand, on November 10, 1975, Judge Lord convened a hearing on Minnesota's motion to order the Corps of Engineers to continue water filtration. The court continued the matter until November 14. On November 14, Judge Lord required United States Marshals to serve a letter on members of the Minnesota Pullution Control Agency and the hearing officer appointed to oversee selection of the disposal site. The letter requested all these state officials to come to the November 14 hearing. On November 14 all of the state officials summoned were present. The court took a roll call of those present. After hearings on Friday, November 14 and Saturday, November 15, the court ordered Reserve to pay the City of Duluth $100,000.00 by Monday morning.]

Reserve had no notice of any motion to assess damages against it at the proceedings held on November 10, 14, 15 and 19. Reserve was afforded no opportunity to be heard or to cross-examine any witnesses. For the most part the proceedings constituted a review of the evidence relating to air pollution. The court called witnesses and testified himself. Early in these proceedings the court announced:

> I have dispensed with the usual adversary proceeding here, because I simply do not have time to spend, as I did, nine months in hearing, six months of which was wasted by what I find now, and did find in my opinions, to be misrepresentations by Reserve Mining Company. Six out of nine months.

Ordinarily, when unfair judicial procedures result in a denial of due process, this court could simply find error, reverse and remand the matter. Recusal would be altogether inappropriate. However, the record in this case demonstrates more serious problems. The denial of fair procedures here was due not to good faith mistakes of judgment or misapplication of the proper rules of law by the district court. The record demonstrates overt acts by the district judge reflecting great bias against Reserve Mining Company and substantial disregard for the mandate of this court.

It is urged that the district court's actions were nothing more than a judge acting upon his deep convictions formed after nine and one-half months of trial. No one can doubt that Judge Lord does have deep convictions in this matter or that such convictions largely influenced his actions. However, the record reveals more than a trial judge merely acting in accord with his prior judgment. In the November proceeding Judge Lord called and examined the witnesses and interspersed testimony of his own; the trial judge announced on the record that witnesses called by Reserve could not be believed, "that in every instance Reserve Mining Company hid the evidence, misrepresented, delayed and frustrated the ultimate conclusions"; and that he did not have "any faith" in witnesses to be called by Reserve. He further announced that the court would have to take depositions since the lawyers opposing Reserve "did not know anything about it."

Judge Lord seems to have shed the robe of the judge and to have assumed the mantle of the advocate. The court thus becomes lawyer, witness and judge in the same proceeding, and abandons the greatest virtue of a fair and conscientious judge — impartiality.

A judge best serves the administration of justice by remaining detached from the conflict between the parties. As Justice McKenna stated long ago, "[T]ribunals of the country shall not only be impartial in the controversies submitted to them but shall give assurance that they are impartial . . . ." Berger v. United States, 255 U.S. 22, 35-36 (1921). When the judge joins sides, the public as well as the litigants become overawed, frightened and confused. . . .

In our prior opinion, we encouraged the State of Minnesota and Reserve to "exercise zeal" to arrive at an appropriate on-land disposal site in order to protect public health, to continue employment of several thousand people and to continue production in an important segment of the nation's steel industry. We specifically stated that selection of the land site was not within the federal court's jurisdiction since issuance of permits for land and water discharge was governed by provisions of Minnesota laws. . . .

None of the proceedings in any way related to providing proper filtration of the drinking water. The proceedings on November 14, which Judge Lord himself branded as "unusual," instead were a broad consideration of the overall health evidence. Evidence was adduced by the court for the "educational" benefit of the state officials and the hearing officer on selection of an on-land disposal site.

Although Judge Lord states that this proceeding was within his jurisdiction to develop new health evidence, it is obvious that the court below acted in defiance of this court's previous mandate, and that Judge Lord continues to attempt to influence the state administrative process concerning the feasibility and location of the on-land disposal site. Requesting the hearing officer and members of the Minnesota Pollution Control Agency to attend this court was for the precise purpose of exerting improper influence. . . .

Equally significant, however, is the damaging effect the overall proceedings, since issuance of our mandate, must have on the administration of justice. . . .

Our system of government is premised upon subservience to the rule of law. If a judge in the exercise of judicial power loses sight of these principles, the result is autocratic rule by lawless judicial action. . . .

[T]aking cognizance of the record which discloses a deliberate denial of due process to the parties, a gross bias exhibited against defendant Reserve Mining Company, and an intentional violation of the mandate of this court, we order corrective measures *sua sponte*. In the exercise of this court's supervisory power over this litigation and in order to protect the integrity of this court's mandate we ... request that the remaining issues be assigned to a new judge or to the Chief Judge himself if he chooses.... We urge that the assignment be made with great expedition.

IN RE INTERNATIONAL BUSINESS MACHINES CORP.

618 F.2d 923 (2d Cir. 1980)

■ MULLIGAN, Circuit Judge. More than a decade ago, on January 17, 1969, the United States of America, by its attorneys, acting under the direction of the Attorney General, filed a complaint in the United States District Court for the Southern District of New York which alleged that International Business Machines Corporation (IBM), commencing in or about 1961, had monopolized and attempted to monopolize the market for general purpose electronic digital computers in violation of Section 2 of the Sherman Act (15 U.S.C. § 2). In addition to injunctive relief the Government sought such "divorcement, divestiture and reorganization" of IBM as might be appropriate to restore competitive conditions. On January 26, 1972, Hon. David N. Edelstein, Chief Judge of the Southern District, assumed control of the case. After extensive pretrial discovery, the bench trial was commenced on May 19, 1975. Counsel for the Government estimated that its case would take two to three months and IBM's counsel predicted that its defense would take six to eight months.

These estimates in fact proved to be grossly erroneous. The Government's direct case lasted for almost three years, ending on April 26, 1978. IBM's defense began on that date and it continues as of this writing. Eleven years have elapsed since the filing of the initial complaint, pre-trial depositions commenced some eight years ago, and more than four and one-half years of trial time have been consumed. A mammoth record of trial transcript and exhibits has been assembled. To the best of our knowledge no litigation has taken so much time and involved such expense.

On July 19, 1979, IBM filed an application requesting Chief Judge Edelstein to recuse himself on the grounds that he has a "personal bias and prejudice against IBM and in favor of plaintiff, that his impartiality in this action may reasonably be questioned, that he has a bent of mind that will prevent impartiality of judgment, and that his bias and prejudice could not have come from any source other than an extrajudicial source." IBM therefore urged his recusal under 28 U.S.C. §§ 144, 455 and the due process clause of the Fifth Amendment. In addition IBM argued that resumption of the trial before a new judge would be inappropriate until the record has been "purged of the effects of the Chief Judge's bias."

On September 11, 1979, Chief Judge Edelstein filed a written opinion in which he denied the request for recusal as both untimely and legally insufficient.... On September 13, 1979 IBM filed in this court a Petition for a Writ of Mandamus pursuant to 28 U.S.C. § 1651 and Fed.R.App.Pr. 21.... Argument on the merits of the petition was heard in this court on October 16, 1979. As of that time more than 90,000 pages of testimony had been transcribed, almost 9,000 documents had been received into evidence, several hundred witnesses deposed, and some seventy trial witnesses called. In the argument counsel for IBM suggested that the case might take five more years of trial time to complete, putting the case into 1984, an appropriately Orwellian denouement....

IBM's petition recognizes that the alleged prejudice of the trial judge must be extrajudicial, that it must arise by virtue of some factor which creates partiality arising outside of the events which occur in the trial itself. ...

IBM has not shown and does not purport to establish or identify any personal connection, relationship or extrajudicial incident which accounts for the alleged personal animus of the trial judge. IBM's claim of prejudice is based completely on Chief Judge Edelstein's conduct and rulings in the case at hand. These we have repeatedly held form no basis for a finding of extrajudicial bias....

A reading of the cases supporting the general proposition that the bias which requires recusal must be personal and cannot rest upon trial rulings or conduct, reveals two practical considerations which have influenced the courts. The first is quite obvious. As the Supreme Court noted in Ex parte American Steel Barrel Co., 230 U.S. 35, 44 (1913), "[The recusal statute] was never intended to enable a litigant to oust a judge for adverse rulings made, for such rulings are reviewable otherwise...." ...

This brings us to the second policy consideration underlying the rule that the bias necessary for recusal must be extrajudicial and not based upon what the judge has learned in this case. Chief Judge Edelstein is the sole finder of the fact here. His role is not that of a passive observer. His obligation is to determine the facts in a field which is exceedingly complex and technical....

We have examined the affidavits of the nine IBM witnesses, all of whom state that his conduct demonstrates an unidentified personal bias. Much of this is not discernible from the record. Many complain of his "stares," "glares" and "scowls." One urges that the Chief Judge "would often glower at me, scowl and then turn and make bold notes on a pad of paper, as if threatening me with the contents."

There is no question but that these witnesses have felt that the judge's conduct was intimidating. However, the burden of IBM is to establish clearly and convincingly that his attitude can only be attributed to his personal prejudice. [T]he trial judge has the obligation to form judgments as to the veracity of the witnesses before him. His asperity and incivility may well be due to his feeling that a witness is not forthright, that he is trying to protect a position, or is otherwise attempting to obfuscate the fact finding process. IBM complains, for example, that Chief Judge Edelstein has asked its witnesses too many questions, has required them to draw meaningless charts and diagrams, to answer questions "yes" or "no" when they are not susceptible to such simplistic solutions. He has, we are assured, interrupted plaintiff's 52 witnesses "only 846 times and has interrupted IBM's first 19 witnesses over 1200 times." Accepting all of these contentions at face value we do not find them to be of the stuff upon which one can sensibly premise extrajudicial bias.

What may be a simple technical issue to the expert witness or even to IBM counsel, who have been given technical training in preparation for this litigation, may well be arcane to the jurist. His questioning, his interruption, his insistence on clarification may well be prompted by his struggle to determine the truth in a field in which he is not sophisticated. His asperity may well be prompted by a feeling that the witnesses for IBM (three are long time employees) are dissembling. We do not know and cannot on this record determine whether his conduct has been guided by what he has learned during the trial, in which case his reaction is licit, or whether it is due to a personal prejudice which is clearly impermissible. The point is that IBM has not met its burden of showing that the Chief Judge is personally biased against the petitioner.

There is of course another factor at play here — the seemingly interminable length of the trial. The IBM witnesses did not begin to testify until almost three years of trial time had elapsed. Even the most stoic might well lose patience in these circumstances. The judge's allegedly hostile attitude to IBM witnesses as compared to Government witnesses may be due to the natural factor of fatigue in a case of this difficulty and duration. At any rate, while the duration of trial is certainly the responsibility of the trial judge, the marathon here is as wearing on the Government as it is upon IBM and cannot constitute evidence of extrajudicial bias against IBM....

In sum we conclude that the rulings and conduct of the trial judge complained of here are legally insufficient to warrant recusal under Title 28, §§ 144, 455 or under the due process clause of the Fifth Amendment of the United States Constitution.

DeBENEDETTO v. GOODYEAR TIRE & RUBBER CO.

754 F.2d 512 (4th Cir. 1985)

■ MICHAEL, District Judge. Deborah Samluck Drier and Melissa E. DeBenedetto (by her guardian ad Litem, Frances DeBenedetto) appeal from the jury verdict in favor of the defendant Goodyear Tire & Rubber Company (Goodyear) in these consolidated product liability cases....

The second assignment of error is based on the trial court's decision allowing jurors to question witnesses.[1] Appellants maintain that since the

---

1. In his opening comments to the jury, the trial judge expounded his policy of permitting questions by jurors. After counsel completed their examination of a witness, the court allowed jurors to direct questions to the bench. If the trial judge

Federal Rules of Evidence do not explicitly permit this practice, it is error for a trial court to permit it.

First, as an important point in the ultimate decision on this issue, we note that appellants did not object during the trial either to the policy of allowing questions by jurors or to any specific juror question. . . . Where there is no objection in trial below, this court ordinarily does not consider the issue. Nevertheless, because of the way we view this matter, we address the merits of this issue.

The Federal Rules of Evidence neither explicitly allow nor disallow the practice of permitting jurors to question witnesses. The only guidance to be found is in Fed.R.Evid. 611(a) which instructs the court to "exercise reasonable control over the mode and order of interrogating witnesses . . . ." Those courts considering the propriety of juror questions have concluded that it is a matter within the discretion of the trial judge. See, *e.g.,* United States v. Callahan, 588 F.2d 1078 (5th Cir.), cert. denied, 444 U.S. 826 (1979); United States v. Witt, 215 F.2d 580 (2d Cir.), cert. denied, 348 U.S. 887 (1954). . . .

While we agree that allowing juror questions is a matter within the discretion of the trial court, we do not agree that such questions are analogous to or even comparable to questioning of witnesses by the judge. Suffice it to say that the judge is not "an umpire or . . . moderator at a town meeting," but he sits "to see that justice is done in the cases heard before him." United States v. Rosenberg, 195 F.2d 583, 594 (2d Cir.), cert. denied, 344 U.S. 838 (1952) . . . . One simply cannot compare the questioning by the trial judge — who is trained in the law and instructed to "see that justice is done" — with the questioning by members of the jury — who are untutored in the law, and instructed to sit as a neutral fact-finding body. Thus, we believe that juror questioning and questioning by the trial judge are clearly and properly distinguishable, although both forms of questioning are matters within the trial court's discretion.

Notwithstanding our belief that juror questioning is a matter within the trial court's discretion, we believe that the practice of juror questioning is fraught with dangers which can undermine the orderly progress of the trial to verdict. Our judicial system is founded upon the presence of a body constituted as a neutral factfinder to discern the truth from the positions presented by the adverse parties. The law of evidence has as its purpose the provision of a set of rules by which only relevant and admissible evidence is put before that neutral factfinder. Individuals not trained in the law cannot be expected to know and understand what is legally relevant, and perhaps more importantly, what is legally admissible.

Since jurors generally are not trained in the law, the potential risk that a juror question will be improper or prejudicial is simply greater than a trial court should take, absent such compelling circumstances as will justify the exercise of that judicial discretion set out above.

---

deemed the question proper, he instructed the witness to answer it. Counsel were given the opportunity to re-question each witness after all inquiries from the jury were resolved.

While the procedure utilized in the trial below permitted screening of the questions before an answer was given, the statement of the question itself was in the hearing of the other jurors, bringing with it the unknown, and perhaps unknowable, mental reactions of those other jurors. In the case where such a question is rejected, not only the questioning juror but the other jurors are likely to retain whatever mind-set has been generated by the question, leaving the court and counsel to ponder, under the stress of trial, how much influence a juror question, answered or unanswered, may have had on the perceptions of the jury as a whole.

Although the court can take remedial steps once such an improper or prejudicial question is asked, it is questionable how effective remedial steps are after the jury has heard the question, as noted *supra*. More importantly, the remedial steps may well make the questioning juror feel abashed and uncomfortable, and perhaps even angry if he feels his pursuit of truth has been thwarted by rules he does not understand. Under the tension and time pressure of a trial, such a reaction is all the more likely. Of course, under the worst case, a juror question may emerge which is so prejudicial as to leave only a declaration of mistrial as an appropriate remedial step, with all the waste that flows from a mistrial.

One further aspect of this practice deserves comment. Human nature being what it is, one or two jurors often will be stronger than the other jurors, and will dominate the jury inquiries. Indeed, this appears to have happened in this case, as discussed *infra*. Moreover, since these questions are from one or more jurors, the possibility that the jury will attach more significance to the answers to these jury questions is great. Every trial judge has noted the development in most lengthy trials of a cohesiveness in the jury as the trial goes on, coming eventually almost to a spirit of camaraderie, in which the actions and reactions of any individual juror are perceived by the jurors as those of the whole jury. In such a setting, the individual juror's question, and the answer elicited, almost certainly will take on a stronger significance to the jury than those questions and answers presented and received in the normal adversarial way.

To the extent that such juror questions reflect consideration of the evidence — and such questions inevitably must do so — then, at the least, the questioning juror has begun the deliberating process with his fellow jurors. Certainly, this is not by design, but stating the question and receiving the answer in the hearing of the remaining jurors begins the reasoning process in the minds of the jurors, stimulates further questions among the jurors, whether asked or not, and generally affects the deliberative process.

With these concerns in mind, we examine the record to determine whether in this instance appellants were prejudiced by the jurors' questions.

There were some 95 questions by jurors during this three-week trial; over half of the questions were asked by the foreman. As noted *supra*, the foreman's number of questions indicates that he was one of the stronger, more vocal members of the jury. Appellants claim that if nothing else, the sheer volume of juror questions indicates a loss of control by the court, thereby prejudicing the appellants' rights.

We have examined carefully each of the questions propounded by jurors and we perceive no bias in any of the questions. The vast majority of the juror questions were technical in nature and reflect a commendable degree of understanding and objectivity by the jury. That such a salutary conclusion is to be reached in this case does not by any means assure that the same or a similar result would come about with other juries.

Because we detect no prejudice to any party, and because appellants did not object to the procedure at the time of trial, we do not find error in the use of juror questions in this case. However, for the reasons set out above, such juror questioning is a course fraught with peril for the trial court. No bright-line rule is adopted here, but the dangers in the practice are very considerable.

Notes and Questions

1. Three separate strands weave their way through these cases. One strand is whether a group of people not trained in the law ought to be asking questions. A second strand is whether a factfinder — judge or jury — ought to be asking questions. A third strand is whether the judge ought to be asking questions when she is not the factfinder. When a jury asks questions, as it did in *DeBenedetto*, the first and second strands are implicated. When a judge asks questions in a case in which she is the factfinder, as the judges did in *Reserve Mining* and *IBM*, only the second strand is implicated. There is also a third strand, which is not directly implicated in any of the cases: Whether a judge should ask questions in an action in which the jury serves as the factfinder.

Should our response to these three scenarios be different? At one level, they all raise the same basic question: Does questioning by persons other than the parties' lawyers threaten to destroy the factfinder neutrality upon which the adversary system insists? At another level, the scenarios are different: The competence of the questioner, as well as the directness of the threat to neutrality, do vary among the three situations.

2. Start with the third scenario: judicial questioning in a jury trial. "This just exercise of [the judge's] function was never doubted at common law.... One of the natural parts of the judicial function, in its orthodox and sound recognition, is the judge's power and duty to *put to the witnesses* such *additional questions* as seem to [the judge] desirable to elicit the truth more fully." 3 Wigmore's Evidence § 784 (James H. Chadbourn ed. 1970); see also Fed.R.Evid. 614(b) ("The court may interrogate witnesses, whether called by itself or a party."). The dangers in this scenario are similar to the dangers of the court appointment of an expert in a jury-tried case: The judge's questions may exert an undue influence on the jury, they may suggest to the jury that the judge is leaning in a particular way, and they may hamper the ability of the parties to control the proofs and arguments. In addition, there is no guarantee that such questions will in fact aid the jury's comprehension, since the judge has no greater knowledge of the jury's level of comprehension than the parties and their lawyers do.

On the other hand, if the judge is confused on a particular point, the jury is likely to be confused as well. Judicial questioning is a useful check on the tendency of the adversary system to devalue truth. It can also assist the orderly presentation of evidence and prevent unnecessary repetition. Fears of jury tampering can be assuaged through standards that prohibit biased questioning.

On balance, limited judicial questioning of witnesses in jury-tried cases seems tolerable as long as it impartially seeks to clarify testimony or bring out important facts not elicited by the parties. It is a common practice, both in criminal and in civil cases. See Michael H. Graham, Federal Practice & Procedure § 6602 (interim ed. 1992); United States v. Evans, 994 F.2d 317, 323 (7th Cir.), cert. denied, 510 U.S. 927 (1993) (clarifying questions may be particularly useful in "lengthy and complex trial" or when lawyers cannot competently perform adversarial tasks); Warner v. Transamerica Insurance Co., 739 F.2d 1347, 1351 (8th Cir. 1984) (judge may "take active role in . . . developing the evidence," but may not "assume the role of advocate"). Reversals for inappropriate judicial questioning are exceedingly rare, although they do occur. See United States v. Saenz, 134 F.3d 697 (5th Cir. 1998); United States v. Edwardo-Franco, 885 F.2d 1002 (2d Cir. 1989) (judge's questions failed to maintain "appearance of impartiality and detachment"); United States v. Mazzilli, 848 F.2d 384, 388 (2d Cir. 1988) (judge's skeptical questions played "overly intrusive role"); Champeau v. Fruehauf Corp., 814 F.2d 1271 (8th Cir. 1987) (new trial proper when judge — Judge Lord, in fact — interrupted and questioned defendant's expert 145 times). It is advisable for the court to instruct the jury that it should draw no inferences from the judge's questions. Van Leirsburg v. Sioux Valley Hospital, 831 F.2d 169 (8th Cir. 1987); William W Schwarzer, *Reforming Jury Trials*, 132 F.R.D. 575, 591-93 (1991) (providing sample instruction).

3. Now to the more difficult questions: should the judge or jury, when acting as factfinder, be entitled to ask questions of the witnesses. The reasons to do so, which are detailed to some extent in *IBM*, should be obvious. The risks, which are described in *DeBenedetto* and displayed in *Reserve Mining*, should be equally obvious. To a large extent, your attitude about jury questioning is likely to be shaped by your views on the merits of the adversary system. If you believe that truth-seeking at trial is paramount, and if you doubt that the adversary system finds the truth with any degree of regularity, then questioning by the factfinder is not problematic. This attitude underlay United States v. Gray, 897 F.2d 1428 (8th Cir. 1990), in which the court approved juror questioning in a criminal case:

> A trial is a search for truth, subject to the burdens of proof imposed upon the parties and the requirements prescribed by the Constitution and the law. Trial judges must have substantial latitude in overseeing this search and they should be reversed on matters of trial procedure only when prejudice to one party or the other affects the outcome of the litigation. [897 F.2d at 1429.]

See also State v. Hays, 256 Kan. 48, 883 P.2d 1093, 1099-1102 (1994) (analyzing issue in truth-seeking vs. adversarial terms; holding that, "[i]n keeping with this court's view of trial as a quest for the truth, we elect to . . . permit the practice of juror questions").

On the other hand, if you believe that party control of proofs and arguments is a critical value, or if you think that the adversary system is an effective engine of truth-seeking, you will be skeptical of factfinder questioning. This attitude is reflected in Chief Judge Lay's concurrence in United States v. Johnson, 892 F.2d 707 (8th Cir. 1989), an en banc decision that affirmed the use of juror questioning:

The fundamental problem with juror questions lies in the gross distortion of the adversary system and the misconception of the role of the jury as a neutral factfinder in the adversary process. Those who doubt the value of the adversary system or who question its continuance will not object to distortion of the jury's role. However, as long as we adhere to an adversary system of justice, the neutrality and objectivity of the juror must be sacrosanct.

Allowing juror questions disrupts neutrality, because even a seemingly innocuous response to a seemingly innocuous juror question can sway the jury's appraisal of the credibility of the witness, the party, and the case. The factfinder who openly engages in rebuttal or cross-examination, even by means of a neutral question, joins sides prematurely and potentially closes off its receptiveness to further suggestions of a different outcome for the case. . . .

The neutrality of the jury is crucial to reaching the truth in an adversary trial. Truth in the adversarial process emerges from the presentation of competing points of view about the events in question. The jury's role, in essence, is to select the more plausible theory of the case or "story." A lawyer's success in presenting a convincing story often depends on his ability to question the obvious, in order to demonstrate the truth of initially unlikely facts. Every effort must be made to ensure that the jury will not close its mind to these unlikely possibilities before counsel has had the opportunity to fully develop and present them. . . .

To reach the truth requires skillful advocacy before a neutral factfinder willing to listen to the argument. If the juror begins to match his interrogation skills with the lawyer all of that is lost. [892 F.2d at 713-14.]

Accord United States v. Bush, 47 F.3d 511, 515 (2d Cir. 1995).

4. In trying to assess the merits of these concerns, we are not without empirical data. One set of data is comparative: As we learned in Chapter One, many procedural systems use an inquisitorial mode in which the factfinder (usually a judge) asks questions. See pp. 68-74, *supra*. Another set is historical: In suits in equity, the Chancellor or his deputies also solicited evidence by asking questions of witnesses. See p. 39, *supra*.

A third set of data comes from Professors Heuer and Penrod, who used actual trials to determine the advantages and disadvantages of juror questions. Two sets of trial conditions were created, one in which jurors were instructed that they could ask questions and one in which they were not allowed to do so. In the former set, judges were asked to fill out forms analyzing each question, and in both sets jurors, lawyers, and judges were surveyed at the end of trial. Jurors asked a total of 88 questions in 33 cases (2.7 questions per trial); 67% of the questions were directed toward the witnesses of the plaintiff (or prosecution), and 18% were objected to by the lawyers for one or both sides. The surveys revealed that juror questions (1) did not "uncover important issues in the trial," (2) did not "increase the jurors' satisfaction with the procedure," (3) did "serve to alleviate juror doubts about trial testimony," (4) did "provide[] the lawyers with feedback about the jurors' perception of the trial," (5) did not "slow the trial," (6) did not "upset the lawyers' strategy," and (7) did not become "a nuisance to the courtroom staff." In addition, lawyers were not embarassed to object to questions, and jurors did not report feeling embarrassed or angry when their questions were objected to. Lawyers reported that the juror questions had no great benefit, but seemed to do no harm. Significantly, however, the study of Heuer and Penrod did not examine whether "[j]uror questions would cause the jurors to become overinvolved in the trial, thus losing their objectivity. Because of the difficulty of measuring this possible consequence of juror questions, we were unable to test this hypothesis." See Larry Heuer & Steven Penrod, *Increasing Jurors' Participation in Trials: A Field Experiment with Jury Notetaking and Question Asking*, 12 Law & Hum. Behav. 231 (1988); see also Leonard B. Sand & Steven A. Reiss, *A Report on Seven Experiments Conducted by District Court Judges in the Second Circuit*, 60 N.Y.U. L. Rev. 423 (1985) (reporting on smaller experiment with juror questioning).

Do these various pieces of data make you optimistic about question-asking? Pessimistic? Would you prefer to have more data before you made up your mind? In particular, would you like to know whether the outcomes in cases with factfinder questioning were different than in cases without such questioning? If the outcomes were different, how could we reconcile our interests in rational adjudication, adversarial process, and like treatment of like cases?

5. In the last few notes we have been concerned with the consequences of factfinder questioning without regard to the identity of the factfinder. There are also some unique concerns associated with allowing either a judge or a jury to ask questions. When the judge is the factfinder, as in *Reserve Mining* and *IBM*, we face the problem of questions being asked by a judge who has been very likely intimately involved in shaping and managing the case. If biases begin to develop during the case management process, doesn't question-asking make it even harder for the judge to resolve factual disputes neutrally? Are *Reserve Mining* and *IBM* the inevitable consequence of managerial judging? Does this mean that a judge should not be as active a manager when she foresees the need to ask questions at trial, or that she should engage in case management but refrain from significant, substantive questioning?

Different factfinder-specific concerns may come into play when the jury asks questions. Many of them are discussed in *DeBenedetto*. A different concern is whether question-asking so changes the nature of the jury that it violates the constitutional right to jury trial or the role of the jury in our constitutional structure. Cf. Duncan v. Louisiana, 391 U.S. 145, 156 (1968) ("Providing an accused with the right to be tried by a jury of his peers gave him an inestimable safeguard against the corrupt or overzealous prosecutor and against the compliant, biased, or eccentric judge."); *Johnson*, 892 F.2d at 715 (Lay, C.J., concurring) ("When the jury becomes an advocate or inquisitor in the process, it forsakes its role of arbiter between the government and its citizens."). *Duncan* and *Johnson* were criminal cases. Are their concerns equally applicable in civil cases? See Spitzer v. Haims & Co., 217 Conn. 532, 587 A.2d 105 (1991) (rejecting constitutional arguments); Mark A. Frankel, *A Trial Judge's Perspective on Providing Tools for Rational Jury Decisionmaking*, 85 Nw. L. Rev. 221, 225 (1990) (by enhancing jury's factfinding powers, jury questioning "foster[s] the democratic ideals embodied in the jury system").

6. The general run of academic commentary cautiously favors the use of questioning by factfinders. See, *e.g.*, Manual for Complex Litigation § 22.42 (1995); Richard Lempert, *Civil Juries and Complex Cases: Taking Stock after Twelve Years*, in Verdict 181, 222-23, 226 (Robert E. Litan ed. 1993); Stephen A. Saltzburg, *Improving the Quality of Jury Decisionmaking*, in id. 341, 358-59; Brookings Institution, Charting a Future for the Civil Jury System 20 (1992); Valerie P. Hans & Neil Vidmar, Judging the Jury 123-24 (1986); Schwarzer,

supra, 132 F.R.D. at 591-93; Steven I. Friedland, *The Competency and Responsibility of Jurors in Deciding Cases*, 85 Nw. L. Rev. 190 (1990). In the reported cases, judicial questioning of witnesses is almost taken for granted when the judge is the factfinder. See United States v. Witt, 215 F.2d 580 (2d Cir.), cert. denied, 344 U.S. 838 (1952). The federal cases, many of them decided in the criminal context, reflect a more cautious response to juror questioning. See, *e.g.*, United States v. Ajmal, 67 F.3d 12, 14-15 (2d Cir. 1995) (questions should be allowed only in "extraordinary or compelling circumstances"); *Bush*, 47 F.3d 511 (permitting questioning but "strongly discourag[ing] its use"); United States v. Cassiere, 4 F.3d 1006, 1018 (1st Cir. 1993) (allowing questions but warning that "the practice should be reserved for exceptional situations, and should not become the routine, even in complex cases"); United States v. Lewin, 900 F.2d 145, 147 (8th Cir. 1990). Is there a reason to be less cautious in complex *civil* cases?

Most states have resolved the issue in favor of factfinder questioning. See Spitzer v. Haims & Co., 217 Conn. 532, 587 A.2d 105, 112 n.8 (collecting cases); *Hays*, 883 P.2d at 1098-99 (same); State v. Graves, 907 P.2d 963 (Mont. 1995) (allowing questioning).

7. Because of the concerns about questioning, most courts have adopted certain precautions to accompany their use. Some of the standard precautions are "(1) the questions should be factual, not adversarial or argumentative, and should only be allowed to clarify information already presented; (2) the questions should be submitted to the court in writing; (3) counsel should be given an opportunity to object to the questions outside of the presence of the jury; (4) the trial judge should read the questions to the witness; and (5) counsel should be allowed to ask follow-up questions." *Graves*, 907 P.2d at 967. Other possible precautions include these: "The district court should inform counsel at the earliest possible time of its intention to use this technique and allow counsel the opportunity to object. The court should instruct the jurors that they should limit their questions to important points, that at times the rules of evidence will dictate that the court not ask a question, and that the jurors should draw no implication from the court's failure to pose a juror-proposed question to the jury. . . . [I]n its charge, the court should include a prophylactic instruction . . . ." *Cassiere*, 4 F.3d at 1018.

Since the trial judge has broad discretion over factfinder questioning, courts of appeal have upheld the process even in the absence of one or more of these safeguards. See United States v. Groene, 998 F.2d 604 (8th Cir. 1993) (affirming conviction even when jurors asked questions directly); *Hays*, 883 P.2d at 59-60 (affirming conviction even when prosecutor asked jurors' questions, and when jurors deliberated and asked group questions). Appellate courts appear to focus "on the effect of the questions on the trial, not the number of questions, in and of itself." *Cassiere*, 4 F.3d at 1018; see United States v. Thompson, 76 F.3d 442 (2d Cir. 1996). A party can waive the issue by failing to object seasonably during trial to factfinder questioning. *Bush*, 47 F.3d at 514 (must show prejudice or plain error to overcome lack of objection); *Groene*, 998 F.2d at 606 (same).

8. Related to the notion of judicial or jury questioning is the judge's ability to comment on or summarize the evidence. Comments are a two-edged sword. They interject the judge's impression of evidence that has been received, and can therefore act as an aid to the factfinder in the process of comprehension. On the other hand, comments may also lead to premature judgment.

The power of a judge to comment on, and thereby to seek to bring the jury around to her view of, the evidence has been an integral part of the common law system of trial for centuries; indeed, it "must be regarded historically as an essential and inseparable part of jury trial." See 9 Wigmore on Evidence § 2551 (James H. Chadbourn ed. 1981). Nonetheless, American judges have always been far more loathe to comment on the evidence than their British counterparts. Jack B. Weinstein, *The Power and Duty of Federal Judges to Marshall and Comment on the Evidence in Jury Trials and Some Suggestions on Charging Juries*, 118 F.R.D. 161, 162 (1988). The leading case on judicial commentary remains Quercia v. United States, 289 U.S. 466, 468 (1933), in which the Supreme Court reversed a conviction when the trial judge said that a witness's demeanor meant that nearly everything the witness said "was a lie." The Supreme Court said that a judge commenting upon testimony "may not assume the role of a witness. He may analyze and dissect the evidence, but he may not either distort or add to it." 289 U.S. at 470.

Judge Weinstein also recommends the use of judicial summaries of the evidence, in which the judge marshals the relevant evidence on each of the points that the jury is to consider. In one case, according to Weinstein, the judge even drew up charts that laid out the evidence relevant to each element of the case. See Weinstein, *supra*, 118 F.R.D. at 172-73. You could imagine a technologically sophisticated judge using computer graphics to create high-tech summaries.

Judicial commentary or summary is authorized in federal court, see, *e.g.*, *Van Leirsburg*, 831 F.2d at 173 (comments on defendant's record-keeping system, "although gratuitous, . . . did not destroy the overall fairness of the trial"), but it is rarely used. Many states forbid judicial comments on or summaries of the evidence, believing that these devices unduly impinge on the right to jury trial. See Weinstein, *supra*, 118 F.R.D. at 169 & nn. 17-18 (listing 20 states that do not permit comment or summary, and 17 more that permit only summary).

Judge Weinstein finds the American reluctance to comment on the evidence "unfortunate, . . . particularly in complex and technically oriented trials which are difficult for juries to follow." According to Judge Weinstein, "a judge's summary and comment on the evidence can increase the jury's ability to understand the proceedings it has attended, and thus increase the accuracy of verdicts." Id. at 166. Comments also "can serve to clarify what may have been distorted by the bias of counsel's arguments"; indeed, Weinstein suggests that the mere power to comment might keep lawyers' tactics in line. Id. at 166-67. Finally, Weinstein suggests that judicial summary of and comment on the evidence in complex cases is less "radical and disadvantageous" than other proposals such as abolition of juries, use of special juries, and even juror notetaking. Id. at 168.

Do you agree with Judge Weinstein? Doesn't the case for judicial commentary and summary hinge on the hypothesis that the judge is more capable of understanding and neutrally describing the evidence than the jury? In the famous jury study by Professors Kalven and Zeisel, the authors found that, when summaries and commentary were not used, judges disagreed with the jury verdict in 4% to 26% of all cases. When summaries or commentary were used, disagreement dropped to less than 1%. Their conclusion was that "the jury's revolt [against the law] is never enough to carry the jury beyond both the evidence and the judge." Harry Kalven, Jr. & Hans Zeisel, The American Jury 417-27 (1966). In a field experiment on complex cases, Professors Heuer and Penrod found that judicial comments and summaries were not helpful to jurors, and that "judges' efforts were least helpful when the evidence was particularly complex." Larry Heuer & Steven Penrod, *Trial Complexity*, 18 Law and Hum. Behav. 29, 50 (1994). Their conclusion, which was tentative due to a small sample size, was that "judges are exercising sound discretion in their reluctance to comment or summarize." Id.

9. One way to avoid judicial tampering with the jury's factfinding function would be to allow jurors to comment on the evidence directly. This technique could both increase comprehension and, if the comments were disclosed to the lawyers, help the lawyers to present additional evidence more clearly. Traditionally, jurors have not been allowed to comment on or discuss the evidence until they enter the jury room for deliberation; the reason for this prohibition was to protect the jury from external influence and premature judgment. There has been some discussion of moving away from this rule, particularly in complex cases. One present proposal is to allow jurors to engage in preliminary deliberations during trial as a way of "reveal[ing] areas of misunderstanding that jurors could then clarify by questioning the witnesses or the judge." Schwarzer, *supra*, at 594. Judge Schwarzer thought the proposal might ease tensions among jurors and force jurors to keep an open mind if they discover that others disagree with them. Id.

Some have tentatively endorsed the idea, see Saltzburg, *supra*, at 362-63, but others have opposed it, see Brookings Institution, *supra*, at 20; *Hays*, 883 P.2d at 1101-02 (finding jury deliberations that resulted in jury asking questions of witnesses to be "troubling"). This device might not be available in states that have constitutional or statutory provisions precluding early deliberations by juries. Cf. *Spitzer*, 587 A.2d at 109 (mentioning constitutional prohibition); *Hays*, 883 P.2d at 1102 (statute does not preclude deliberations). Do you think that this proposal will increase factfinder comprehension?

5. Jury Notetaking

Another way potentially to increase comprehension is to allow the factfinder to take notes during the trial. This idea is hardly a novel one in bench trials; judges have long taken notes when they are the factfinder. But courts have traditionally been reluctant to extend this privilege to jurors. Numerous reasons have been cited: Undue emphasis might be placed on the notes by jurors who take them; jurors might make errors in their notes, and trust their notes excessively; notetaking jurors might exert an undue influence in jury deliberations; notetaking jurors might be less willing to change their minds or to engage in discussions with other jurors; notetaking might favor plaintiffs, since juries are might tire of notetaking as the trial goes on; notetaking might be distracting to other jurors, the lawyers, and the judge; and notetaking might make the juror miss other, crucial information. See Larry Heuer & Steven Penrod, *Increasing Jurors' Participation in Trials: A Field Experiment with Jury Notetaking and Question Asking*, 12 Law & Hum. Behav. 231, 234-36 (1988); William W Schwarzer, *Reforming Jury Trials*, 132 F.R.D. 575, 590-91 (1991); Larry Heuer & Steven Penrod, *Juror Notetaking and Question Asking during Trials: A National Field Experiment*, 18 Law & Hum. Behav. 121 (1994).

Imagine, however, trying to sit through a four-month class that meets for six to eight hours a day without being able to take a note, only to find that you are expected to have perfect recall of the information at the end of the class. This is exactly the position in which jurors in lengthy trials find themselves. Notetaking might result in a jury better informed about the evidence and the law — in other words, aid jury comprehension. According to proponents of notetaking, it also might increase the level of juror involvement in the trial and increase the jurors' satisfaction with the trial outcome and their level of confidence in the verdict. See Heuer & Penrod, *Increasing Jurors' Participation, supra*, at 233-34; Heuer & Penrod, *Juror Notetaking, supra*, at 123.

Studies on the effectiveness of notetaking have come to different conclusions. The most comprehensive studies, which also nicely summarized the findings of previous studies, were those of Professors Heuer and Penrod. Their studies examined actual trials, some of which permitted jurors to take notes and some of which did not. Afterwards they surveyed jurors, judges, and lawyers in both settings, and gave jurors some basic comprehension tests. The conclusions of Heuer and Penrod were that notetaking did not seem to increase juror comprehension or serve as a useful memory aid, but that none of the feared drawbacks of notetaking materialized either. Since notetaking did increase (weakly, but somewhat) the level of juror satisfaction, and since judges and lawyers seemed favorably impressed with the idea, the authors concluded that notetaking "deserve[d] serious consideration by the judicial system." Heuer & Penrod, *Increasing Jurors' Participation, supra*, at 257. These conclusions dovetailed with three other studies conducted in two federal courts and one state court, none of which found significant problems with notetaking. Schwarzer, *supra*, at 591; John Guinther, The Jury in America 68-69 (1988). Although the studies did not single out complex cases in particular, the second study by Heuer and Penrod involved a fairly large number of cases that the authors considered complex. See Heuer & Penrod, *Juror Notetaking, supra*, at 149.

In another study of immediate relevance, Heuer and Penrod reported some counter-intuitive data on juror notetaking in complex federal cases. Although the judges in the complex federal cases did not perceive any difference between notetaking and non-notetaking juries, notetaking jurors in complex cases reported feeling less well-informed than jurors who were not allowed to take notes; notetaking juries further reported more difficulty in reaching a verdict than non-notetaking juries. See Larry Heuer & Steven D. Penrod, *Trial Complexity*, 18 Law & Hum. Behav. 29 (1994); see also Richard Lempert, *Civil Juries and Complex Cases*, in Verdict 181, 225-26 (Robert E. Litan ed. 1993) (suggesting as an alternative that jurors be provided with daily transcripts of testimony).

A somewhat stronger endorsement of juror notetaking can be found in Lynne ForsterLee et al., *Effects of Notetaking on Verdicts and Evidence Processing in a Civil Trial*, 18 Law & Hum. Behav. 567 (1994). Using a simulated complex tort case and mock jurors, the researchers found that notetaking jurors were better at correctly differentiating weak cases from strong ones, and at awarding appropriate levels of compensation for deserving plaintiffs. Interestingly, the study found that jurors who used their notes during deliberations did no better than jurors who were not allowed to refer to their notes; apparently the value of notetaking came from the process of writing the information down. The authors concluded that notetaking in complex cases "holds some promise as a competence enhancing aid for jurors." Id. at 577.

In spite of tepid empirical support, many commentators have jumped on the notetaking bandwagon in complex litigation. See, *e.g.*, Manual for Complex Litigation, Third § 22.42 (1995); Robert MacCoun, Improving Jury Comprehension in Criminal and Civil Trials (1995); Stephen A. Saltzburg, *Improving the Quality of Jury Decisionmaking*, in Verdict, *supra*, 341, 359; H. Lee Sarokin & G. Thomas Munsterman, *Recent Innovations in Civil Jury Trial Procedures*, in id. 378, 386-88; Jonathan D. Casper, *Restructuring the Traditional Civil Jury: The Effects of Changes in Composition and Procedures*, in id. 414, 444. In the real world notetaking is becoming increasingly common, both in complex cases and in routine ones. See United States v. Polowichak, 783 F.2d 410 (4th Cir. 1986) (trial judge has discretion to authorize notetaking when case was complex and when judge gave instruction to jury on use of notes); United States v. Wild, 47 F.3d 669 (4th Cir. 1995) (within judge's discretion to allow only one juror to take notes); In re Brooklyn Navy Yard Asbestos Litigation, 971 F.2d 831 (2d Cir. 1992); Zenith Radio Corp. v. Matsushita Electric Industrial Co., 478 F. Supp. 889, 955 (E.D. Pa. 1979). But notetaking is far from universally endorsed; many of the potential drawbacks still worry judges, and they either refuse to allow notetaking or place restrictions on the use of notes. See United States v. Darden, 70 F.3d 1507, 1536 (8th Cir. 1995) (notetaking is "not a favored procedure," especially in complex cases; judge properly let jury take notes on exhibits, but not on testimony); United States v. Baker, 10 F.3d 1374 (9th Cir. 1993) (within judge's discretion not to allow jury to take notes when judge thought jury would be distracted, would record evidence selectively, and would rely on inaccurate notes); United States v. Porter, 764 F.2d 1, 12 (1st Cir. 1985) (within judge's discretion to allow use of notes only during opening and closing statements and jury instructions); Clemmon v. Sowders, 34 F.3d 352 (6th Cir. 1994) (within judge's discretion not to permit notes to be taken into jury room).

Notetaking is a small step, compared to many of the more radical trial innovations we have explored. It does raise certain practical problems, such as providing security for juror notebooks during the trial and the proper disposition of the notebooks after trial. See *Zenith*, 478 F. Supp. at 955; Gray v. Phillips Petroleum Co., 1990 WL 62074 (D. Kan.). In terms of the larger themes of this book, there is nothing wrong with allowing jurors to take notes as long as notetaking does not distract lawyers, make it more difficult for jurors to comprehend the evidence, and change substantive outcomes in relation to similar cases in which notes are not taken. The issue is whether there is anything "right" with letting jurors take notes — whether, in other words, notetaking can avoid resort to more radical trial innovations that do implicate these larger concerns.

6. Fashioning Comprehensible Jury Instructions

In Chapter Ten we learned that juries, by and large, perform the factfinding task as well as, if not better than, a judge. See pp. 1237-39, *supra*. The one area in which juries were demonstrably weak was the comprehension of jury instructions. Two separate problems are presented. One is recall: The jury is usually read the instructions by the judge, and jurors are expected to remember the instructions when they retire to the jury room. According to one study, individual jurors recalled half or less of the jury instructions, and jurors as a whole were able to recall the instructions with about 80% accuracy. See Reid Hastie et al., Inside the Jury 78, 81 (1983); see also id. at 137 (jurors who had not completed high school recalled only 25% of some instructions). The second problem is the ability of the jury to understand the instructions they have remembered. A great deal of psychological and linguistic evidence has been accumulated during the past twenty years that suggests that "given the convoluted language and special legal terms, jurors' comprehension of instructions is often very low." See Valerie P. Hans & Neil Vidmar, Judging the Jury 121 (1986). One study of criminal instructions suggests that juries correctly referred to the law only 51% of the time, and incorrectly or unclearly referred to the law the other 49%. Deliberation did nothing to clear up these errors; some jurors who began with the correct understanding of the law changed to an incorrect one during deliberation. See Phoebe C. Ellsworth, *Are Twelve Heads Better Than One?*, 52 Law & Contemp. Prob. 205, 218-23 (Autumn 1989); see also Amiriam Elwork et al., Making Jury Instructions Understandable (1982) (also reporting 49% error rate in understanding of criminal instructions). Indeed, in one famous study, juries that received no jury instruction on the issue of negligence performed exactly as well as juries that received the Michigan pattern jury instruction. Amiriam Elwork et al., *Juridic Decisions: In Ignorance of the Law or in Light of It?*, 1 Law & Hum. Behav. 163 (1977). Other studies are equally pessimistic. See, *e.g.*, Robert P. Charrow & Veda R. Charrow, *Making Legal Language Understandable: A Psycholinguistic Study of Jury Instructions*, 79 Colum. L. Rev. 1306 (1979); Alan Reifman et al., *Real Jurors' Understanding of the Law in Real Cases*, 16 Law & Hum. Behav. 539 (1992); Arthur D. Austin, Complex Litigation Confronts the Jury System 55-62 (1984); cf. Joe S. Cecil et al., Jury Service in Lengthy Civil Trials 33-34 (1987) (finding that jurors in lengthy trials were more likely to find judge's instructions difficult to understand).

In theory, the judge can solve the problem of recall — without any damage to the adversarial system — simply by delivering the instructions in an interesting and informative way, see William W Schwarzer, Managing Antitrust and Other Complex Litigation § 7-2(C)(2) (1982), by letting the jury take notes on the instructions, see United States v. Porter, 764 F.2d 1, 12 (1st Cir. 1985), or by providing the jury with written (or taped) copies of the instructions, see Manual for Complex Litigation, Third § 22.434 (1995); Austin, *supra*, at 104. This last option has attracted some attention. The most extensive study, again by Professors Heuer and Penrod, found that written instructions did not help the jury better understand, remember, or apply the judge's instructions, did not make the jury more satisfied with the process, did not decrease jury deliberation time, and did not reduce the number of disputes regarding the meaning of the instructions. On the other hand, the use of written instructions did not have any drawbacks, such as jurors spending too much time reading them, jurors not focusing on the evidence, or judicial personnel being burdened. Since written instructions did seem useful in settling disputes about the meaning of the judge's instructions, and since judges seemed to think the trial process was fairer, Heuer and Penrod ultimately concluded that written instructions were worth serious consideration. See Larry Heuer & Steven D. Penrod, *Instructing Jurors: A Field Experiment with Written and Preliminary Instructions*, 13 Law & Hum. Behav. 409 (1989); cf. United States v. Quilty, 541 F.2d 172, 177 (7th Cir. 1976) (decision to use written instructions rests in judge's sound discretion). In fairness, Heuer and Penrod's study, and hence their less than ringing endorsement of written instructions, involved civil and criminal cases, most of which were not complex. Would the advantages of written instructions be greater in complex cases?

As Heuer and Penrod noted, the provision of written instructions cannot solve the more serious problem of juror comprehension; if the instruction is incomprehensible when it is heard, it will usually remain incomprehensible when it is read. The only solution is to rewrite the jury instructions in a simpler, clearer, more comprehensible form tailored to the case at hand. Judges, however, are reluctant to create such special instructions. First, judges are not linguists, and there is no guarantee that a clearer instruction will emerge. Second, institutional pressures favor pattern jury instructions; the judge knows that, if she uses the pattern instruction already approved by the court of appeals, she will not be reversed. On the other hand, special instructions tailored to the case carry the risk that the court of appeals will find a fatal flaw. Third, even simple stylistic changes often will change, perhaps subtly, the meaning of a particular phrase. Changes in the language might, perhaps subtly and perhaps dramatically, effect changes in the substantive law. Finally, some evidence suggests that clearer instructions in criminal cases favor the prosecution, making the writing of clearer instructions a potentially outcome-determinative event. See generally Stephen A. Saltzburg, *Improving the Quality of Jury Decisionmaking*, in Verdict 341, 356 (Robert E. Litan ed. 1993) (describing objections to simplified instructions); Jane Goodman & Edith Greene, *The Use of Paraphrase Analysis in the Simplification of Jury Instructions*, 4 J. Soc. Behav. & Personality 237 (1989) (suggesting that clarification of jury instructions may raise conviction rates).

Despite these concerns, field research suggests that jurors who receive clearer instructions perform better in terms of jury comprehension. See Elwork, *Juridic Decisions, supra*. Indeed, a study by Heuer and Penrod of complex federal cases reported that jurors had less confidence in their verdicts when the judge stuck closely to the pattern jury instructions. Larry Heuer & Steven D. Penrod, *Trial Complexity*, 18 Law & Hum. Behav. 29 (1994). As with written instructions, there has been a strong academic movement in the direction of creating simpler jury instructions. See, *e.g.*,

Saltzburg, *supra*, at 355-58; Schwarzer, *supra*, § 7-2(C)(2) (describing rules to follow in drafting such instructions); Brookings Institution, Charting a Future for the Civil Jury System 24 (1992); see also Robert MacCoun, Improving Jury Comprehension in Criminal and Civil Trials (1995) (endorsing idea in theory, but recognizing need for more empirical research). Thus far, the movement has played less well in the courts, although it might well be complex cases which ultimately force courts to reform the antiquated and indefensible world of jury instruction. See Peter M. Tiersman, *Reforming the Language of Jury Instructions*, 22 Hofstra L. Rev. 37, 55-59 (1993).

Perhaps a judge could avoid some of the concerns of revised jury instructions by appointing a psychologist or linguist to work with her in drafting the instructions, see Austin, *supra* at 104, and by allowing the parties to review the instructions for legal accuracy, see Hans & Vidmar, *supra*, at 122. Is there any way, however, for the judge to avoid the possibility that the tailor-made instructions will skew the outcome in relation to a trial with pattern instructions?

7. Changing Deliberation Patterns: Special Verdicts, Verdicts with Interrogatories, and Sequential Verdicts

Jonathan D. Casper, RESTRUCTURING THE TRADITIONAL CIVIL JURY: THE EFFECTS OF CHANGES IN COMPOSITION AND PROCEDURES

in Verdict 414, 432-44 (Robert E. Litan ed. 1993)

The traditional general verdict has long been criticized as an impediment to rational decisionmaking in civil cases. Two related concerns lie at the center of most of the critiques. The first focuses on the fact that juries are often called on to make several legally discrete decisions on the basis of different evidence. By asking the jury for a single answer, the general verdict procedure fails to assist the jury in organizing the evidence and legal principles in appropriate ways. Second, the general verdict in civil cases is often said to promote compromise verdicts, conflating legally separate issues and producing results that may appear just to jurors but that are inconsistent with the policies of the legislatures or appellate courts fashioning the legal rules. . . .

Such concerns about the general verdict have led to many suggestions for modifying the jury's tasks, some experimentation with such innovations, and a small body of research assessing the consequences of such change. Three alternatives have been most frequently discussed: special verdicts, bifurcated verdicts, and general verdicts with interrogatories.

SPECIAL VERDICTS. Both special verdicts and interrogatories are authorized by Rule 49 of the Federal Rules of Civil Procedure. Under a special verdict procedure, the judge submits to the jury a series of specific questions dealing with factual issues and requires the jury to deliberate and provide answers to them. The judge then applies the law to these findings to decide the case.... The questions the jury answers often involve some mixture of law and fact, for they require the application of legal concepts such as negligence, but the decisions are made separately, and it is usually suggested that jurors not be told the consequences of their verdicts.

Several variants of the special verdict procedure have been suggested and sometimes used in complex trials....

An alternative has been called the "periodic, segmented special verdict." Under this procedure, judges can separate various questions that are at issue in the case, allowing the jury to hear testimony and reach a special verdict on each at the conclusion of each segment of the trial. In one complex antitrust case, the district court divided the presentation of evidence into three phases.... After each stage, the jury returned a special verdict. As a result, evidence about claims rejected in prior segments did not have to be presented in subsequent segments. The trial judge concluded that the format promoted organized consideration of evidence and decreased the likelihood of a retrial.

BIFURCATED TRIALS.... A closely related procedure is the bifurcated or split trial....

GENERAL VERDICTS WITH SPECIAL INTERROGATORIES. A closely related procedure involves retaining the general verdict but adding special interrogatories that require the jury to make additional specific factual determinations. Like special verdict procedures, these interrogatories permit the judge to insure that the jury's verdict is the product of appropriate factual determinations and provide a way for the jury to structure its deliberations. Under this procedure, the jury reaches its general verdict, but the judge oversees the process by examining the relationship between the jury's factual findings and its decision.

Advantages of Alternative Verdict Procedures

Proponents of such modifications to jury verdict procedures cite a variety of advantages they may provide when compared with the traditional general verdict.

ORGANIZING AND SIMPLIFYING JURY TASKS.... [S]pecial verdicts or special interrogatories may provide a useful framework within which the jury can organize testimony, particularly when the facts and law are complex.... Moreover, when special verdicts or interrogatories are submitted during a trial that involves large numbers of witnesses and exhibits, they may improve jurors' ability to recall testimony.

SIMPLIFYING JUDICIAL INSTRUCTIONS. Special verdicts or interrogatories may simplify judicial instructions in [at] least two ways. If the periodic, segmented special verdict is employed, jurors will receive judicial instructions and the accompanying verdict questions in smaller packets delivered at intervals during the testimony.... Some proponents have also claimed that jury instructions are likely to be simpler when special verdicts are employed because fewer legal concepts will have to be accurately conveyed to the jury.... It is clear from prior research that understanding judicial instructions is one of the most difficult tasks faced by the traditional jury. But the frequent assertion that special verdicts will solve this problem may be too optimistic.... If a special verdict asks about negligence or causation, for example, these concepts must be explained to the jury and understood before the special verdict question can be adequately answered.

ENCOURAGING SETTLEMENTS AND REDUCING THE LENGTH OF TRIALS.... If a special verdict question is answered in a way that clearly favors one side — if, for example, a defendant is found liable — this interim result may encourage the losing party to seek a settlement rather than continue the trial....

EFFECTIVE SUPERVISION OF JURIES BY TRIAL AND APPELLATE JUDGES. By requiring juries to make specific factual determinations during the trial itself or at the end, special verdicts or interrogatories can facilitate the ability of judges to monitor how well juries comply with legal principles. ... Moreover, "the special verdict enables errors to be localized so that the sound portions of the verdict may be saved."...

AVOIDING COMPROMISE VERDICTS. Special verdicts or interrogatories may also reduce the possibility of compromise verdicts. If jurors are not informed of the legal consequences of their answers to special verdict or interrogatory questions, an if the questions are sufficiently opaque that their implications are not readily discernible by the jurors, legal principles may be more appropriately applied....

Disadvantages of Alternative Verdict Procedures ...

JUROR EVALUATION OF WITNESSES. Juror judgments about credibility and persuasiveness of witnesses are presumably formed over the course of the whole range of testimony.... The early closure caused by the requirement of a series of special verdicts over the course of the trial may inappropriately affect the ability of jurors to evaluate witnesses and their testimony....

SYSTEMATIC BIASES ASSOCIATED WITH SPECIAL VERDICTS. Richard O. Lempert and others discuss a number of unexplored but plausible systematic biases that could be associated with the move from the general verdict to special verdicts, some operating against the plaintiff and some against the defendant. In terms of possible bias against the plaintiff, two important elements stand out: the requirement that the jury find for the plaintiff on all issues and the increased number of decisions that special verdicts require the jury to make. Lempert notes, "As the number of issues that the factfinder considers increases and the evidence on each issue becomes closer, it becomes likely that chance will at some point lead the factfinder to hold for the defendant."[76] Posing another possibility, Lempert suggests that a majority that has prevailed over a minority on several issues

---

76. [Richard O. Lempert, *Civil Juries and Complex Cases: Let's Not Rush to Judgment*, 80 Mich. L. Rev. 68, 113 (1981).]

may eventually defer to the minority on a later issue in a spirit of compromise, inadvertently causing the defendant to win....

Elizabeth C. Wiggins and Steven J. Breckler suggest that the move to special verdicts might have unfavorable consequences for the defendant as well. They argue that in cases with multiple claims or alternative theories, special verdicts give the plaintiff greater opportunities to prevail because jurors are more likely to compromise when the evidence is seen as relatively even across the two sides.[78] ...

DIFFICULTIES IN FORMULATING SPECIAL VERDICT QUESTIONS.... In practice, though, questions [for special verdicts and interrogatories] are not easy to frame.... [S]pecial interrogatory and verdict questions in complex cases often involve mixed issues of fact and law, making such questions difficult to formulate; in addition, many of the problems with judicial instructions in general may plague special verdict or interrogatories as well....

THE JURY AS REPRESENTATIVE OF COMMUNITY VALUES. Special jury verdicts or interrogatories may reduce the ability of the jury to bring its own sense of justice, rightness, or equity to its decision....

The use of special interrogatories along with a general verdict may appear to offer the best of both worlds: a technique that focuses jurors on the critical issues while still allowing the jury's sense of justice to play a role in its verdict. This does not, however, appear to be the aim of those urging the use of special interrogatories along with general verdicts....

The Effects of Changes in Verdict Structure

The available empirical evidence on the effects of changes in verdict structures remains quite small but intriguing. The sketchy anecdotal evidence from practitioners who have employed innovative verdict procedures and from post-trial interviews with jurors conducted by journalists and academics is quite mixed. Judges who have employed special verdicts or interrogatories tend to find that they were helpful, while evidence from jurors suggests that problems with comprehension and organization of testimony are not always solved. Systematic evidence suggests that the ways in which verdicts are structured may affect jury decisions. [Here the article discusses the study on bifurcation conducted by Zeisel and Callahan, as well as the study conducted by Horowitz and Borden, which we examined pp. 1284-86, 102-03, *supra*.]

In a recent study of the effect of special verdict procedures, Elizabeth C. Wiggins and Steven J. Breckler examined the effects of both special and general verdicts in a simulation study of juror decisions in a defamation case. The verdict procedure had no effect on decisions about defendant's liability, with some two-thirds of all jurors in both verdict conditions finding for the plaintiff. Jurors making special verdicts gave significantly higher compensatory damage awards than those making only general verdicts,

---

78. [Elizabeth C. Wiggins & Steven J. Breckler, *Special Verdicts as Guides to Jury Decision Making*, 14 Law and Psychology Rev. 1 (1990).]

although there were no differences in the size of punitive awards or in total awards....

Finally, on the issue of the relationship between verdict structure and juror comprehension, Wiggins and Breckler did not find that alternative structures had a strong effect on jurors' ability to understand the evidence and testimony.... [W]hen Wiggins and Breckler tested juror understanding of the appropriate relationship between answers to special verdict questions and a finding for the plaintiff or defendant, they found no difference across the verdict procedure conditions and very low accuracy rates overall.

There is clearly much still to be learned about the effects of changes in verdict procedures. Many quite plausible consequences have been advanced, and the early work done thus far to examine how variations in verdict procedures play out suggests that the consequences are likely to be quite complex and unpredictable.

Notes and Questions

1. We began our survey of novel jury techniques with the bifurcated or split trial. We now conclude that survey by coming nearly full circle to special verdicts and general verdicts accompanied by interrogatories. These devices do not physically split the trial into segments, but they do mentally segment the trial.

2. Professor Casper provides a balanced presentation of the advantages and disadvantages of these procedures, and of the paltry state of empirical research on the subject. Does his presentation persuade you that these procedures are a good idea? A bad idea? That some of the devices are better than others? That we need better data before we rush to embrace any of these devices? See Larry Heuer & Steven Penrod, *Trial Complexity*, 18 Law and Hum. Behav. 29 (1994) (reporting on field experiment in which special verdict forms were found useful in some, but not all, complex cases; forms were most useful in cases with large quantities of information).

3. Aside from the segmented special verdict procedure, none of these devices is a means to limit trial information. Their strongest claim for adoption, then, is that they increase juror comprehension of the evidence, or that they otherwise advance reasoned decisionmaking. How can special verdicts or interrogatories increase the level of jury comprehension, when they are not even provided to the jury until after the evidence has been heard? Given the problem of wording verdict or interrogatory questions, under what circumstances is it likely that these devices will lead to a more reasoned decision?

The segmented special verdict procedure does limit trial information, and it also might enhance juror comprehension because all of the testimony on a particular point is heard within a shorter time frame. But this procedure falls prey to the outcome-determinative concerns that we studied in the context of bifurcation. See pp. 1284-87, *supra*. One possibility would be to treat each segmented verdict as preliminary, subject to reconsideration when the jury retires for final deliberations. Of course, if the verdict is treated merely as preliminary, one of the great advantages of this segmenting — that some of the later testimony can be eliminated — will no longer exist.

4. As Casper says, some commentators like the general verdict accompanied by interrogatories, because it tries to preserve a measure of jury discretion while providing a measure of jury control. A practical drawback of this procedure, which arises with some frequency, is that the jury's general verdict is not always consistent with its answers to interrogatories. In such cases F.R.Civ.P. 49(b) instructs the trial court either to enter judgment in accordance with the answers, to return the case to the jury for further consideration, or to order a new trial. When the answers are also inconsistent with each other, Rule 49(b) permits only the latter two options. See generally 9A Charles A. Wright & Arthur R. Miller, Federal Practice & Procedure §§ 2510, 2513 (1995). Trial and appellate courts, however, sometimes go to great lengths to make answers consistent. For instance, in Watkins v. Fiberboard Corp., 994 F.2d 253 (5th Cir. 1993), a jury found in answer to one interrogatory that plaintiff's exposure to asbestos products had caused no disease, but then went on to answer another interrogatory that plaintiff should be compensated for his injuries resulting from asbestos exposure. The court of appeals said that, due to somewhat different definitions of "disease" and "injury" in the judge's instructions, the jury could have legitimately understood "disease" and "injury" to be different things.

Sometimes, however, even inventive interpretation cannot create consistency, leaving a judge with the choice between further deliberation or a new trial. If a new trial is ordered, can the judge limit the trial just to those aspects on which there was an inconsistency? In In re New York Asbestos Litigation, 155 F.R.D. 61 (S.D.N.Y. 1994), a jury found that one defendant's asbestos was a proximate cause of harm, but then allocated 0% of the responsibility to that defendant. The trial judge ordered a new trial limited just to the issue of the relative percentage of that defendant's responsibility. Does such a limited trial pass Seventh Amendment scrutiny? See Gasoline Products Co. v. Champlain Refining Co., 283 U.S. 494 (1931); pp. 1283-84, *supra*.

5. Special verdicts or interrogatories have enjoyed many champions, including judges such as Jerome Frank and John Brown; other judges, such as Charles Clark and Learned Hand, were more cautious. See Wright & Miller, *supra*, § 2505. Commentators today tend to endorse the idea, especially in complex cases. See, *e.g.*, Manual for Complex Litigation, Third § 22.451 (1995); Stephen A. Saltzburg, *Improving the Quality of Jury Decisionmaking*, in Verdict 341, 360-62 (Robert E. Litan ed. 1993); Larry S. Kaplan, Complex Federal Litigation § 28.03-.11. But these devices are not frequently used, even in complex cases, suggesting that some of the concerns mentioned by Casper weigh heavily on trial judges. See Wright & Miller, *supra*, §§ 2502, 2505; William W Schwarzer, *Reforming Jury Trials*, 132 F.R.D. 575, 586 (1991).

6. Not surprisingly, the decision to use a special verdict or interrogatories, as well as the form of the questions, lie within the discretion of the trial judge. See Wright & Miller, *supra*, § 2505, 2508, 2511-12.

D. CONCLUDING THOUGHTS

One of the main purposes of this chapter was to explore techniques by which both the demand for rational adjudication and the right to jury trial could be preserved. You have now seen a wealth of alternative trial structures and formats. There are many other ideas — such as juror notebooks, the use of daily transcripts, the provision of glossaries, the use of flow charts, the creation of juror orientation materials, and so on — on which we did not touch or touched only briefly. Imaginative lawyers and judges will always be coming up with new ideas and new technologies; perhaps you have come up with a few of your own.

These various devices can often be used in conjunction with each other. If they all were used, the result would be a trial that resembles the trial of our common law tradition in name only. See Sims v. ANR Freight Systems, Inc., 77 F.3d 846, 849 (5th Cir. 1996) (suggesting that combination of detailed stipulations of fact, judicial comment on evidence and questioning of witnesses, and setting of rigorously enforced time limits "adversely impacted on the comprehensibility of the evidence to the point that [plaintiff] was denied a trial," but nonetheless finding error harmless). Maybe a new form of trial is not a bad thing. As one commentary argues: "Fundamentally, trial procedures and evidentiary rules should be changed and simplified to embrace modern communication methods as well as modern knowledge of how we, as human beings, think and make decisions." Brookings Institution, Charting a Future for the Civil Jury System 16 (1992). This was also Justice Brandeis's point in the quote with which we began this chapter. Now that you have seen the range of possibilities, you need to ask yourself whether you are willing to make compromises with tradition in order to keep alive the aspiration of reasoned decisionmaking and jury trial. How many compromises will you make? The minimum that are necessary to preserve reasoned judgment and jury trial? The most that are constitutionally permissible?

If you are not willing to make the sorts of compromises that this chapter suggests, would it be better to eliminate the jury? Would it be better not to have created joinder and discovery rules that put such enormous pressures on our trial system? Would it be better to handle cases that generate this type of complexity through some administrative system?

In Chapter One, we suggested that the trial structure of a procedural system dictates many other procedural and substantive choices. You have just explored some possible worlds of trial structure for complex cases. Now it is time for you to choose one for yourself, understanding that in making this choice you are also dictating an entire procedural and substantive world.

PART FOUR

REMEDIAL COMPLEXITY

The parties have been joined, the pretrial proceedings have finished, and the settlement or trial has been concluded. Assuming that the defendants are not absolved of responsibility, the case now enters into its final phase — the remedial phase. In many ways, this phase is the most important. Plaintiffs and their lawyers don't often litigate to obtain empty victories; they litigate to obtain a concrete remedy. If, for some reason, that remedy cannot be obtained or can be obtained only with undue difficulty, it is unlikely that most plaintiffs will bother to litigate in the first place. Furthermore, at least in large-scale litigation, the remedial phase of the case is often more protracted and contested than the liability phase. For instance, in *Brown v. Board of Education*, the liability phase lasted only a few years, and was essentially completed by 1954. The remedial phase, however, lasted more than forty years. Likewise, in latent-injury mass torts, the settlement or judgment often comes after three to five years of litigation; the implementation of the remedy may last for twenty to thirty years.

In an adversarial system, the basic principle for providing a remedy is, to use Professor Laycock's term, "restoring the plaintiff to his rightful position." See Douglas A. Laycock, Modern American Remedies 11 (2d ed. 1994). Whether through damages for harm that has already occurred or through an injunction to prevent harm that has not yet occurred, the principle attempts to place the plaintiff in the position that he or she would have enjoyed in a counterfactual world without wrongful behavior. There is a nice corrective correspondence between the plaintiff and the defendant; the defendant did a wrong to the plaintiff, and now must provide a remedy to that plaintiff. Plaintiffs' rights and defendants' remedies are mirror images.

That nice corrective correspondence between plaintiff and defendant, and between right and remedy, does not exist in complex litigation. The defendant may be a large institution that engaged in a long-standing pattern of wrongdoing, so that it is impossible either to match the wronged plaintiffs and the wrongdoing defendants or even to know exactly what the rightful position actually is. The costs of providing the traditional one-to-one remedy may be so high that the delivery of the remedy will leave plaintiffs with little to no compensation. Nonparties may exert such influence that the party that is to provide the remedy may be unable effectively to implement the remedy. The first situation concerns the problem of declaring the remedy. The second and third situations concern the problem of implementing the remedy.

The following chapter examines some of the problems in declaration and administration of equitable and monetary remedies in complex cases. In some ways, this chapter marks a shift in approach. The three prior forms of complexity — joinder, pretrial, and trial — involved situations in which the cause of complexity was often the lawyers' inability to perform the tasks that the adversarial system had assigned to them. In the final stage of litigation — the remedial stage — the lawyers' role is rather small. The central players are the court, which must declare and enforce the remedy, and the parties, who must implement the remedy. The emphasis in this chapter, therefore, is on the court and the parties and on their dysfunction.

Despite these surface differences, a common theme runs through this Part and the three prior Parts. Throughout the book we have seen that complex litigation makes it difficult for the relevant "player" to fulfill his or her function in the rational adjudication of the dispute, but that the assignment of portions of the function to the judge permits rational adjudication to proceed. Following this analysis, remedial complexity exists in situations in which either the judge of the adversarial model is unable to perform her adversarial responsibility to declare the remedy, or else the parties are unable to implement the remedy. Further following our prior analysis, these forms of dysfunction can be overcome at the price of taking power away from the parties and/or providing more power to the judge.

Whether and in what circumstances an increase in judicial power can either help the judge to declare the remedy or help the parties to implement the remedy is the central question of the following chapter. At the same time, several subsidiary themes emerge: Is the loss of our adversarial ideal worth the benefit of more efficacious remedies? Should we maintain a dual system of remedial principles — one set of rules for ordinary litigation and another for complex cases? Does the more powerful judge required to assure adequate declaration and implementation accord with our notions of the judicial function in American society? Given that many complex remedies involve federal courts, does the more powerful role accord with our notions of the appropriate scope of *federal* judicial power? If the price of entertaining complex litigation is the creation of remedial bureaucracies, should complex litigation be handled through non-adjudicative means?

Remedies may lie at the end of the line in complex litigation, but the answers to these questions necessarily affect and define all that precedes it.

CHAPTER TWELVE

DECLARING AND IMPLEMENTING REMEDIES

> [N]o judge is likely to decree more than he thinks he has the power to accomplish. . . . He will strive to lessen the gap between declaration and actualization. He will tailor the right to fit the remedy.
>
> Owen M. Fiss

This chapter examines the problems of declaring and implementing remedies in complex litigation. A separate section is devoted to each of these two problems. Within each section, the problems are examined first from the viewpoint of injunctive relief and then from the viewpoint of relief for money. After the basic problems are described, each section examines ways in which a more powerful judicial role might overcome the remedial complexity that the courts and parties face, as well as the limits on that judicial power.

A. DECLARING THE REMEDY

Declaring the remedy may seem to be one of the easiest tasks in the entire lawsuit. Under the "rightful position" principle (or, as Professor Fiss calls it, the "tailoring principle"), once the nature of the wrong has been determined, the remedy follows ineluctably — the wrongdoer places the plaintiff in the position that the plaintiff would have enjoyed but for the wrong. Guided by the lawyers' proofs at trial, the remedy-declarer (whether judge or jury) should be able to declare the remedy with some ease. There is no need of special judicial authority to assist in this task — indeed, when the judge is the remedy-declarer, is it even sensible to talk about how expanded judicial power might make the task of declaration easier? In fact, difficulties do exist, and solutions to them are not obvious.

1. Injunctive Relief

BROWN v. BOARD OF EDUCATION

349 U.S. 294 (1955)

■ MR. CHIEF JUSTICE WARREN delivered the opinion of the Court.

These cases were decided on May 17, 1954. The opinions of that date, declaring the fundamental principle that racial discrimination in public education is unconstitutional, are incorporated herein by reference. All provisions of federal, state, or local law requiring or permitting such discrimination must yield to this principle. There remains for consideration the manner in which relief is to be accorded. . . .

Full implementation of these constitutional principles may require solution of varied local school problems. School authorities have the primary responsibility for elucidating, assessing, and solving these problems; courts will have to consider whether the action of school authorities constitutes good faith implementation of the governing constitutional principles. Because of their proximity to local conditions and the possible need for further hearings, the courts which originally heard these cases can best perform this judicial appraisal. Accordingly, we believe it appropriate to remand the cases to those courts.

In fashioning and effectuating the decrees, the courts will be guided by equitable principles. Traditionally, equity has been characterized by a practical flexibility in shaping its remedies and by a facility for adjusting and reconciling public and private needs. These cases call for the exercise of these traditional attributes of equity power. At stake is the personal interest of the plaintiffs in admission to public schools as soon as practicable on a nondiscriminatory basis. To effectuate this interest may call for elimination of a variety of obstacles in making the transition to school systems operated in accordance with the constitutional principles set forth in our May 27, 1954, decision. Courts of equity may properly take into account the public interest in the elimination of such obstacles in a systematic and effective manner. But it should go without saying that the viability of these constitutional principles cannot be allowed to yield simply because of disagreement with them.

While giving weight to these public and private considerations, the courts will require that the defendants make a prompt and reasonable start toward full compliance with our May 17, 1954 ruling. Once such a start has been made, the courts may find that additional time is necessary to carry out the ruling in an effective manner. The burden rests upon the defendants to establish that such time is necessary in the public interest and is consistent with good faith compliance at the earliest practicable date. To that end, the courts may consider problems related to administration, arising from the physical condition of the school plant, the school transportation system, personnel, revision of school districts and attendance areas into compact units to achieve a system of determining admission to the public schools on a nonracial basis, and revision of local laws and regulations which may be necessary in solving the foregoing problems. They will also consider the adequacy of any plans the defendants may propose to meet this problems and to effectuate a transition to racially nondiscriminatory school system. During this period of transition, the courts will retain jurisdiction of these cases. The [cases are remanded to the lower courts] to take such proceedings and enter such orders and decrees consistent with this opinion as are necessary and proper to admit to public schools on a racial nondiscriminatory basis with all deliberate speed the parties to these cases.

BRADLEY v. MILLIKEN

540 F.2d 229 (6th Cir. 1976), *aff'd*, 433 U.S. 267 (1977)

■ PHILLIPS, Chief Judge. When this school desegregation case was filed in August 1970, Ronald Bradley, one of the black plaintiffs, had been assigned to enter the kindergarten of a Detroit school whose enrollment was 97 per cent black. There have been numerous court proceedings since that time, culminating in the opinion of the Supreme Court in Milliken v. Bradley, 418 U.S. 717 (1974) . . . . The Supreme Court remanded with directions for "prompt formulation of a decree directed to eliminating the segregation found to exist in Detroit city schools, a remedy which has been delayed since 1970." 418 U.S. at 753.

This court now reviews appeals and cross-appeals from various orders and decisions of the District Court . . . .

In September 1976 Ronald Bradley is scheduled to enter the sixth grade of the Clinton School, which now is more than 99 per cent black. The decisions of the District Court which we now review do nothing to correct the racial composition of the Clinton School. They grant no relief to Ronald Bradley nor to the majority of the class of black students he represents.

Nevertheless, this court finds itself in the frustrating position of having to leave standing the results reached by the District Judge on the issue of assignment of students, although we disagree with parts of his opinions and orders. Our affirmance is found to be necessary for the simple reason that reversal would be an exercise in futility under the situation now existing in the Detroit school system and the law of this case as established by the Supreme Court in *Milliken v. Bradley*. . . .

[The district court concluded that *de jure* segregation existed in the Detroit public school system, and that both the State of Michigan and the City of Detroit's Board of Education had causally contributed to this segregation. It concluded by noting that the Supreme Court's 1974 decision in *Milliken* did not "disagree with or disturb in any way the findings of unlawful segregation with respect to the Detroit school system."]

II. The Remedy . . .

The principal question to be resolved on the present appeal involves the remedy. . . .

a) Previous Efforts to Effect a Remedy

After his finding of *de jure* segregation, Judge Roth grappled with the problem of fashioning a remedy in accordance with Swann v. Board of Education, 402 U.S. 1 (1971), Monroe v. Board of Commissioners, 391 U.S. 450 (1968), Green v. County School Board, 391 U.S. 430 (1968) and Brown v. Board of Education, 349 U.S. 294 (1955). Initially he contemplated a "Detroit only" solution. A motion was made to add other school districts as parties defendant. Judge Roth reserved a decision on this motion pending submission and consideration of desegregation plans. . . .

Judge Roth required the school board defendants, Detroit and State, to develop and submit plans of desegregation, "designed to achieve the greatest possible degree of actual desegregation, taking into account the practicalities of the situation." Three "Detroit only" desegregation plans were submitted by the plaintiffs and by the Detroit Board of Education. Judge Roth found that:

> [While] plaintiffs' plan would accomplish more desegregation than now obtains in the system, or which would be achieved under Plan A or C of the Detroit Board of Education submissions, none of the plans would result in the desegregation of the public schools of the Detroit school district. . . . [Relief] of segregation in the Detroit public schools cannot be accomplished within the corporate geographical limits of the city. . . .

[On interlocutory appeal from this decision, the court of appeals] held that it would be within the equity power of the District Court to adopt a plan of desegregation extending beyond the boundaries of the Detroit School District. We remanded the case to the District Court for the taking of additional evidence because several of the suburban school districts had not been heard or had an opportunity to be heard. We held that as a prerequisite to the implementation of a plan affecting any school district, "the affected district must be made a party to this litigation and afforded an opportunity to be heard." 484 F.2d at 250-52.

The Supreme Court reversed the decision of this court, holding that no remedy involving any school district other than Detroit would be within the equitable power of the District Court without evidence that the suburban district or districts had committed acts of *de jure* segregation. . . .

b) The Remedy at Issue on Present Appeals

District Judge DeMascio[, who handled the case after Judge Roth's death,] was faced with an extremely difficult (if not impossible) assignment, confronted as he was with the responsibility of formulating a decree which would eliminate the unconstitutional segregation found to exist in the Detroit public schools, without transgressing the limits established by the Supreme Court. . . .

The plan adopted by the District Court became effective as of the beginning of the winter-spring semester, 1976. As of September 26, 1975, the Detroit public schools enrolled 247,774 students, 75.1 per cent of whom were black. In broad outline the plan adopted by the District Court required the reassignment of 27,524 students, of whom 21,853 would require bus transportation. The plan changed the racial balance in 105 schools out of approximately 300 zoned schools in the system. Prior to the implementation of the plan approximately 80 schools had enrollments of a majority of white students. Under the District Court's plan, 67 of these schools received black students through transportation and rezoning. The result of the student reassignments is that no school in Detroit, with two marginal exceptions, will have an enrollment of less than 30 per cent black students. Moreover, 47 of the previously white schools have become more than 40 per cent black.

In addition, 38 schools, the majority of which previously were at least 80 per cent black, received white students via transportation and rezoning. Under the plan 25 of these schools became 45 to 55 per cent black. Furthermore, at least 23 of Detroit's schools, enrolling approximately 22,599 students, contain a substantial mix of black and white students without any student reassignment. . . .

Finally, the District Court ordered the closing of certain antiquated schools, the establishment of vocational centers available on a non-racial basis to all qualifying students, and certain Educational Components, hereinafter discussed in further detail. . . .

Although some improvements have been accomplished by the District Court, the plan contains glaring defects that could never pass constitutional muster and would not be countenanced by this court in a different factual situation. . . .

Notwithstanding the reassignments effected by the District Court, the percentage of black students in each of the eight regions remains substantially unchanged under the adopted plan. Only twelve of the 157 zoned schools with previous enrollments over 90 percent black have become under 90 percent black. Approximately half of Detroit's schools remain more than 90 percent black. Moreover, the three regions which contain the highest concentration of black students, regions 1, 5 and 8, remain virtually untouched. This means that approximately 83,000 students are granted no relief from unconstitutional *de jure* segregation. . . .

We recognize that the overwhelming number of black students in Detroit and their concentration in the inner city undoubtedly makes some one-race schools unavoidable under any "Detroit only" remedy. However, when the Detroit School Board virtually eliminated regions 1, 5 and 8 from both its initial plan and the plan finally adopted, it assumed the heavy burden of justifying its elimination of the schools located in these three regions. . . .

The Board's burden of justification is particularly heavy in this case because the three regions which the Board has left untouched, in the inner city, are in the area most affected by the acts of *de jure* segregation of which both the Detroit and State defendants have been found guilty.

The records discloses no adequate justification for excluding regions 1, 5 and 8 from the plan. The principal testimony pertaining to the reasons for excluding the inner city from student reassignments came from Merle Henrickson, Director of Planning and Building Studies for the Detroit

Board. Mr. Henrickson stated that the inner city "was beyond the limits of possible treatment." Exclusion of the inner city was necessary, in his view, in order to maintain "the racial mix of desegregated schools." The result of desegregating the inner city, he predicted, would be white flight. . . .

Even though we do not approve of that part of the District Court's plan which fails to take any action with respect to schools in Regions 1, 5 and 8, this court finds itself unable to give any direction to the District Court which would accomplish the desegregation of the Detroit school system in light of the realities of the present racial composition of Detroit. . . .

Recognizing the absence of alternatives, we affirm the judgment of the District Court on the issue of assignment of students in areas other than Regions 1, 5 and 8. . . . We must, however, remand the case for further consideration in regard to the three central regions of the City of Detroit which both the school board and the District Judge excluded from their proposed remedial plans. We cannot hold that where unconstitutional segregation has been found, a plan can be permitted to stand which fails to deal with the three regions where the majority of the most identifiably black schools are located.

We recognize that it would be appropriate for us at this point to supply guidelines to the District Judge as to what he should do under this remand. Omission of such guidelines is not based on any failure to consider the problem in depth. It is based upon the conviction which this court had at the time of its en banc opinion in this case — and for the reasons carefully spelled out therein — that genuine constitutional desegregation can not be accomplished within the school district boundaries of the Detroit School District.

MISSOURI v. JENKINS

515 U.S. 70 (1995)

■ CHIEF JUSTICE REHNQUIST delivered the opinion of the Court.

As this school desegregation litigation enters its 18th year, we are called upon again to review the decisions of the lower courts. In this case, the State of Missouri has challenged the District Court's order of salary increases for virtually all instructional and noninstructional staff within the Kansas City, Missouri, School District (KCMSD) and the District Court's order requiring the State to continue to fund remedial "quality education" programs because student achievement levels were still "at or below national norms at many grade levels."

I

A general overview of this litigation is necessary for proper resolution of the issues upon which we granted certiorari. This case has been before the same United States District Judge since 1977. . . . In that year, the KCMSD, the school board, and the children of two school board members brought suit against the State and other defendants. Plaintiffs alleged that the State, the surrounding suburban school districts (SSD's), and various federal agencies had caused and perpetuated a system of racial segregation in the schools of the Kansas City metropolitan area. The District Court realigned the KCMSD as a nominal defendant and certified as a class, present and future KCMSD students. The KCMSD brought a cross-claim against the State for its failure to eliminate the vestiges of its prior dual school system.

After a trial that lasted 7½ months, the District Court dismissed the case against the federal defendants and the SSD's, but determined that the State and the KCMSD were liable for an intradistrict violation, *i.e.*, they had operated a segregated school system within the KCMSD. . . . Furthermore, the KCMSD and the State had failed in their affirmative obligations to eliminate the vestiges of the State's dual school system within the KCMSD. . . .

In June 1985, the District Court issued its first remedial order and established as its goal the "elimination of all vestiges of state imposed segregation." . . .

The District Court, pursuant to plans submitted by the KCMSD and the State, ordered a wide range of quality education programs for all students attending the KCMSD. First, the District Court ordered that the KCMSD be restored to an AAA classification, the highest classification awarded by the State Board of Education. . . . Second, it ordered that the number of students per class be reduced so that the student-to-teacher ratio was below the level required for AAA standing. . . . The District Court also ordered programs to expand educational opportunities for all KCMSD students: full-day kindergarten; expanded summer school; before- and after-school tutoring; and an early childhood development program. . . .

The KCMSD was awarded an AAA rating in the 1987-1988 school year, and there is no dispute that since that time it has "'maintained and greatly exceeded AAA requirements.'" . . . The total cost for these quality education programs has exceeded $220 million. . . .

In November 1986, the District Court approved a comprehensive magnet school and capital improvements plan and held the State and the KCMSD jointly and severally liable for its funding. Under the District Court's plan, every senior high school, every middle school, and one-half of the elementary schools were converted into magnet schools. The District Court adopted the magnet-school program to "provide a greater educational opportunity to *all* KCMSD students," and because it believed "that the proposed magnet plan [was] so attractive that it would draw non-minority students from the private schools who have abandoned or avoided the KCMSD, and draw in additional non-minority students from the suburbs." . . . Since its inception, the magnet school program has operated at a cost, including magnet transportation, in excess of $448 million. . . .

In June 1985, the District Court ordered substantial capital improvements to combat the deterioration of the KCMSD's facilities. In formulating its capital-improvements plan, the District Court dismissed as "irrelevant" the "State's argument that the present condition of the facilities

[was] not traceable to unlawful segregation." . . . Instead, the District Court focused on its responsibility to "remed[y] the vestiges of segregation" and to "implemen[t] a desegregation plan which w[ould] maintain and attract non-minority members." . . . The initial phase of the capital improvements plan cost $37 million.

In September 1987, the District Court adopted, for the most part, KCMSD's long-range capital improvements plan at a cost in excess of $187 million. . . . The plan called for the renovation of approximately 55 schools, the closure of 18 facilities, and the construction of 17 new schools. . . . The District Court rejected what it referred to as the "'patch and repair' approach proposed by the State" because it "would not achieve suburban comparability or the visual attractiveness sought by the Court as it would result in floor coverings with unsightly sections of mismatched carpeting and tile, and individual walls possessing different shades of paint." . . . As of 1990, the District Court had ordered $260 million in capital improvements. Missouri v. Jenkins, 495 U.S. 33, 61 (1990) (*Jenkins II*) (KENNEDY, J., concurring in part and concurring in judgment). Since then, the total cost of capital improvements ordered has soared to over $540 million.

As part of its desegregation plan, the District Court has ordered salary assistance to the KCMSD. In 1987, the District Court initially ordered salary assistance only for teachers within the KCMSD. Since that time, however, the District Court has ordered salary assistance to all but three of the approximately 5,000 KCMSD employees. The total cost of this component of the desegregation remedy since 1987 is over $200 million. . . .

The District Court's desegregation plan has been described as the most ambitious and expensive remedial program in the history of school desegregation. . . . The annual cost per pupil at the KCMSD far exceeds that of the neighboring SSD's or of any school district in Missouri. Nevertheless, the KCMSD, which has pursued a "friendly adversary" relationship with the plaintiffs, has continued to propose ever more expensive programs. As a result, the desegregation costs have escalated and now are approaching an annual cost of $200 million. These massive expenditures have financed

> "high schools in which every classroom will have air conditioning, an alarm system, and 15 microcomputers; a 2,000-square-foot planetarium; green houses and vivariums; a 25-acre farm with an air-conditioned meeting room for 104 people; a Model United Nations wired for language translation; broadcast capable radio and television studios with an editing and animation lab; a temperature controlled art gallery; movie editing and screening rooms; a 3,500-square-foot dust-free diesel mechanics room; 1,875-square-foot elementary school animal rooms for use in a zoo project; swimming pools; and numerous other facilities." *Jenkins II*, 495 U.S., at 77 (KENNEDY, J., concurring in part and concurring in judgment).

Not surprisingly, the cost of this remedial plan has "far exceeded KCMSD's budget, or for that matter, its authority to tax." Id., at 60. The State, through the operation of joint-and-several liability, has borne the brunt of these costs. . . . [T]he District Court "has gone to great lengths to provide

KCMSD with facilities and opportunities not available anywhere else in the country." . . .

II

With this background we turn to the present controversy. First, the State has challenged the District Court's requirement that it fund salary increases for KCMSD instructional and noninstructional staff. The State claimed that funding for salaries was beyond the scope of the District Court's remedial authority. Second, the State has challenged the District Court's order requiring it to continue to fund the remedial quality education programs for the 1992-1993 school year. The State contended that under Freeman v. Pitts, 503 U.S. 467 (1992), it had achieved partial unitary status with respect to the quality education programs already in place. As a result, the State argued that the District Court should have relieved it of responsibility for funding those programs. . . .

Because of the importance of the issues, we granted certiorari to consider the following: (1) whether the District Court exceeded its constitutional authority when it granted salary increases to virtually all instructional and noninstructional employees of the KCMSD, and (2) whether the District Court properly relied upon the fact that student achievement test scores had failed to rise to some unspecified level when it declined to find that the State had achieved partial unitary status as to the quality education programs. . . .

III . . .

Almost 25 years ago, in Swann v. Charlotte-Mecklenburg Bd. of Ed., 402 U.S. 1 (1971), we dealt with the authority of a district court to fashion remedies for a school district that had been segregated in law in violation of the Equal Protection Clause of the Fourteenth Amendment. Although recognizing the discretion that must necessarily adhere in a district court in fashioning a remedy, we also recognized the limits on such remedial power:

> "[E]limination of racial discrimination in public schools is a large task and one that should not be retarded by efforts to achieve broader purposes lying beyond the jurisdiction of the school authorities. One vehicle can carry only a limited amount of baggage. It would not serve the important objective of Brown [v. Board of Education, 347 U.S. 483 (1954)] to seek to use school desegregation cases for purposes beyond their scope, although desegregation of schools ultimately will have impact on other forms of discrimination." Id., at 22-23.

Three years later, in Milliken [v. Bradley, 418 U.S. 717 (1974) (*Milliken I*)], we held that a District Court had exceeded its authority in fashioning interdistrict relief where the surrounding school districts had not themselves been guilty of any constitutional violation. . . . We said that a desegregation remedy "is necessarily designed, as all remedies are, to restore the victims of discriminatory conduct to the position they would have occupied in the absence of such conduct." Id., at 746. "[W]ithout an interdistrict violation and interdistrict effect, there is no constitutional wrong calling for an interdistrict remedy." Id., at 745. . . .

Three years later, in Milliken v. Bradley, 433 U.S. 267 (1977) (*Milliken II*), we articulated a three-part framework derived from our prior cases to guide district courts in the exercise of their remedial authority.

> "In the first place, like other equitable remedies, the nature of the desegregation remedy is to be determined by the nature and scope of the constitutional violation. . . . The remedy must therefore be related to 'the *condition* alleged to offend the Constitution . . . .' *Milliken I*, 418 U.S., at 738. Second, the decree must indeed be *remedial* in nature, that is, it must be designed as nearly as possible 'to restore the victims of discriminatory conduct to the position they would have occupied in the absence of such conduct.' Id., at 746. Third, the federal courts in devising a remedy must take into account the interests of state and local authorities in managing their own affairs, consistent with the Constitution." Id., at 280-281 (footnotes omitted).

We added that the "principle that the nature and scope of the remedy are to be determined by the violation means simply that federal-court decrees must directly address and relate to the constitutional violation itself." Id., at 281-282. In applying these principles, we have identified "student assignments, . . . 'faculty, staff, transportation, extracurricular activities and facilities,'" as the most important indicia of a racially segregated school system. Board of Ed. of Oklahoma City Public Schools v. Dowell, 498 U.S. 237, 250 (1991).

Because "federal supervision of local school systems was intended as a temporary measure to remedy past discrimination," *Dowell, supra*, at 247, we also have considered the showing that must be made by a school district operating under a desegregation order for complete or partial relief from that order. In *Freeman*, we stated that

> "[a]mong the factors which must inform the sound discretion of the court in ordering partial withdrawal are the following: [1] whether there has been full and satisfactory compliance with the decree in those aspects of the system where supervision is to be withdrawn; [2] whether retention of judicial control is necessary or practicable to achieve compliance with the decree in other facets of the school system; and [3] whether the school district has demonstrated, to the public and to the parents and students of the once disfavored race, its good-faith commitment to the whole of the courts' decree and to those provisions of the law and the Constitution that were the predicate for judicial intervention in the first instance." 503 U.S., at 491.

The ultimate inquiry is "'whether the [constitutional violator] ha[s] complied in good faith with the desegregation decree since it was entered, and whether the vestiges of past discrimination ha[ve] been eliminated to the extent practicable.'" Id., at 492 . . . .

Proper analysis of the District Court's orders challenged here, then, must rest upon their serving as proper means to the end of restoring the victims of discriminatory conduct to the position they would have occupied in the absence of that conduct and their eventual restoration of "state and local authorities to the control of a school system that is operating in compliance with the Constitution." 503 U.S., at 489. We turn to that analysis.

The State argues that the order approving salary increases is beyond the District Court's authority because it was crafted to serve an "interdistrict goal," in spite of the fact that the constitutional violation in this case is "intradistrict" in nature. "[T]he nature of the desegregation remedy is to be determined by the nature and scope of the constitutional violation." *Milliken II, supra*, 433 U.S., at 280. . . . The proper response to an intradistrict violation is an intradistrict remedy . . . .

Here, the District Court has found, and the Court of Appeals has affirmed, that this case involved no interdistrict constitutional violation that would support interdistrict relief. . . . Thus, the proper response by the District Court should have been to eliminate to the extent practicable the vestiges of prior *de jure* segregation within the KCMSD: a system-wide reduction in student achievement and the existence of 25 racially identifiable schools with a population of over 90% black students.

Instead of seeking to remove the racial identity of the various schools within the KCMSD, the District Court has set out on a program to create a school district that was equal to or superior to the surrounding SSD's. Its remedy has focused on "desegregative attractiveness," coupled with "suburban comparability." . . .

The District Court's remedial plan in this case . . . is not designed solely to redistribute the students within the KCMSD in order to eliminate racially identifiable schools within the KCMSD. Instead, its purpose is to attract nonminority students from outside the KCMSD schools. But this interdistrict goal is beyond the scope of the intradistrict violation identified by the District Court. In effect, the District Court has devised a remedy to accomplish indirectly what it admittedly lacks the remedial authority to mandate directly: the interdistrict transfer of students. . . .

Respondents argue that the District Court's reliance upon desegregative attractiveness is justified in light of the District Court's statement that segregation has "led to white flight from the KCMSD to suburban districts." The lower courts' "findings" as to "white flight" are both inconsistent internally, and inconsistent with the typical supposition, bolstered here by the record evidence, that "white flight" may result from desegregation, not *de jure* segregation. . . .

The District Court's pursuit of "desegregative attractiveness" cannot be reconciled with our cases placing limitations on a district court's remedial authority. . . . This case provides numerous examples demonstrating the limitless authority of the District Court operating under this rationale. . . .

Nor are there limits to the duration of the District Court's involvement. The expenditures per pupil in the KCMSD currently far exceed those in the neighboring SSD's. . . .

The District Court's pursuit of the goal of "desegregative attractiveness" results in so many imponderables and is so far removed from the task of eliminating the racial identifiability of the schools within the KCMSD that we believe it is beyond the admittedly broad discretion of the District Court. In this posture, we conclude that the District Court's order of salary increases . . . is simply too far removed from an acceptable implementation of a permissible means to remedy previous legally mandated segregation.

Similar considerations lead us to conclude that the District Court's order requiring the State to continue to fund the quality education programs because student achievement levels were still "at or below national norms at many grade levels" cannot be sustained. . . .

In reconsidering this order, the District Court should apply our three-part test from *Freeman v. Pitts, supra,* 503 U.S., at 491. The District Court should consider that the State's role with respect to the quality education programs has been limited to the funding, not the implementation, of those programs. As all the parties agree that improved achievement on test scores is not necessarily required for the State to achieve partial unitary status as to the quality education programs, the District Court should sharply limit, if not dispense with, its reliance on this factor. Just as demographic changes independent of *de jure* segregation will affect the racial composition of student assignments, . . . so too will numerous external factors beyond the control of the KCMSD and the State affect minority student achievement. So long as these external factors are not the result of segregation, they do not figure in the remedial calculus. . . .

The District Court also should consider that many goals of its quality education plan already have been attained: the KCMSD now is equipped with "facilities and opportunities not available anywhere else in the country." Minority students in kindergarten through grade 7 in the KCMSD always have attended AAA-rated schools; minority students in the KCMSD that previously attended schools rated below AAA have since received remedial education programs for a period of up to seven years.

On remand, the District Court must bear in mind that its end purpose is not only "to remedy the violation" to the extent practicable, but also "to restore state and local authorities to the control of a school system that is operating in compliance with the Constitution." *Freeman, supra,* 503 U.S., at 489.

The judgment of the Court of Appeals is reversed.

■ [The concurring opinion of JUSTICE O'CONNOR is omitted.]

■ JUSTICE THOMAS, concurring. The Constitution extends "[t]he judicial Power of the United States" to "all Cases, in Law and Equity, arising under this Constitution, the Laws of the United States, and Treaties made . . . under their Authority." Art. III, §§ 1, 2. I assume for purposes of this case that the remedial authority of the federal courts is inherent in the "judicial Power," as there is no general equitable remedial power expressly granted by the Constitution or by statute. As with any inherent judicial power, however, we ought to be reluctant to approve its aggressive or extravagant use, and instead we should exercise it in a manner consistent with our history and traditions. . . .

Motivated by our worthy desire to eradicate segregation, however, we have disregarded this principle and given the courts unprecedented authority to shape a remedy in equity....

Our willingness to unleash the federal equitable power has reached areas beyond school desegregation. Federal courts have used "structural injunctions," as they are known, not only to supervise our Nation's schools, but also to manage prisons, see Hutto v. Finney, 437 U.S. 678 (1978), mental hospitals, Thomas S. v. Flaherty, 902 F.2d 250 (C.A. 4), cert. denied, 498 U.S. 951 (1990), and public housing, Hills v. Gautreaux, 425 U.S. 284 (1976). . . . Judges have directed or managed the reconstruction of entire institutions and bureaucracies, with little regard for the inherent limitations on their authority....

Such extravagant uses of judicial power are at odds with the history and tradition of the equity power and the Framers' design. The available historical records suggest that the Framers did not intend federal equitable remedies to reach as broadly as we have permitted....

Two clear restraints on the use of the equity power — federalism and the separation of powers — derive from the very form of our Government. Federal courts should pause before using their inherent equitable powers to intrude into the proper sphere of the States.... A structural reform decree eviscerates a State's discretionary authority over its own program and budgets and forces state officials to reallocate state resources and funds to the desegregation plan at the expense of other citizens, other government programs, and other institutions not represented in court.... When District Courts seize complete control over the schools, they strip state and local governments of one of their most important governmental responsibilities, and thus deny their existence as independent governmental entities....

The separation of powers imposes additional restraints on the judiciary's exercise of its remedial powers. To be sure, this is not a case of one branch of Government encroaching on the prerogatives of another, but rather of the power of the Federal Government over the States. Nonetheless, what the federal courts cannot do at the federal level they cannot do against the States; in either case, Article III courts are constrained by the inherent constitutional limitations on their powers. There simply are certain things that courts, in order to remain courts, cannot and should not do. There is no difference between courts running school systems or prisons and courts running executive branch agencies....

[T]he District Court retained jurisdiction over the implementation and modification of the remedial decree, instead of terminating its involvement after issuing its remedy. Although briefly mentioned in *Brown II* as a temporary measure to overcome local resistance to desegregation, 349 U.S., at 301 ("[d]uring this period of transition, the courts will retain jurisdiction"), this concept of continuing judicial involvement has permitted the District Courts to revise their remedies constantly in order to reach some broad, abstract, and often elusive goal. Not only does this approach deprive the parties of finality and a clear understanding of their responsibilities, but it also tends to inject the judiciary into the day-to-day management of institutions and local policies — a function that lies outside of our Article III competence. Cf. Fuller, The Forms and Limits of Adjudication, 92 Harv. L. Rev. 353 (1978)....

To ensure that district courts do not embark on such broad initiatives in the future, we should demand that remedial decrees be more precisely designed to benefit only those who have been victims of segregation. Race-conscious remedies for discrimination not only must serve a compelling governmental interest (which is met in desegregation cases), but also must be narrowly tailored to further that interest.... In the absence of special circumstances, the remedy for *de jure* segregation ordinarily should not include educational programs for students who were not in school (or were even alive) during the period of segregation. Although I do not doubt that all KCMSD students benefit from many of the initiatives ordered by the court below, it is for the democratically accountable state and local officials to decide whether they are to be made available even to those who were never harmed by segregation....

Even if segregation were present, we must remember that a deserving end does not justify all possible means. The desire to reform a school district, or any other institution, cannot so captivate the Judiciary that it forgets its constitutionally mandated role. Usurpation of the traditionally local control over education not only takes the judiciary beyond its proper sphere, it also deprives the States and their elected officials of their constitutional powers. At some point, we must recognize that the judiciary is not omniscient, and that all problems do not require a remedy of constitutional proportions.

■ JUSTICE SOUTER, with whom JUSTICE STEVENS, JUSTICE GINSBURG, and JUSTICE BREYER join, dissenting. . . . The attractiveness of the Court's analysis disappears . . . as soon as we recognize two things. First, the District Court did not mean by an "intradistrict violation" what the Court apparently means by it today. The District Court meant that the violation within the KCMSD had not led to segregation outside of it, and that no other school districts had played a part in the violation. It did not mean that the violation had not produced effects of any sort beyond the district. Indeed, the record that we have indicates that the District Court understood that the violation here did produce effects spanning district borders and leading to greater segregation within the KCMSD, the reversal of which the District Court sought to accomplish by establishing magnet schools. Insofar as the Court assumes that this was not so in fact, there is at least enough in the record to cast serious doubt on its assumption. Second, the Court violates existing case law even on its own apparent view of the facts, that the segregation violation within the KCMSD produced no proven effects, segregative or otherwise, outside it. Assuming this to be true, the Court's decision that the rule against interdistrict remedies for intradistrict violations applies to this case, solely because the remedy here is meant to produce effects outside the district in which the violation occurred, is flatly contrary to established precedent.

We did not hold [in *Milliken I*] that any remedy that takes into account conditions outside of the district in which a constitutional violation has been committed is an "interdistrict remedy," and as such improper in the absence of an "interdistrict violation." To the contrary, by emphasizing that remedies in school desegregation cases are grounded in traditional equitable principles, ... we left open the possibility that a district court might subject a proven constitutional wrongdoer to a remedy with intended effects going beyond the district of the wrongdoer's violation, when such a remedy is necessary to redress the harms flowing from the constitutional violation. ...

Today's decision therefore amounts to a redefinition of the terms of *Milliken I* and consequently to a substantial expansion of its limitation on the permissible remedies for prior segregation. ...

■ [The dissenting opinion of JUSTICE GINSBURG is omitted.]

Notes and Questions

1. The liability phase in *Brown* itself was relatively simple and straightforward; the case was filed in 1951, and the issue of liability ended for all practical purposes in 1954. The remedial phase is another story. A 1955 desegregation plan proposed by the school district was approved by the district court, but the plan made little progress in remedying the past effects of segregation. Not until a lawsuit in 1973 and threats by the Department of Health, Education and Welfare to withhold funds in 1974 were any significant efforts undertaken by the school board to remedy past problems.

In 1979, Linda Brown Smith, the schoolgirl who was the named plaintiff in the case, returned to court as the mother of children in the Topeka school system, seeking to reopen the 1955 desegregation order on the grounds that the school system continued to have vestiges of illegal segregation. Brown v. Board of Education, 84 F.R.D. 383 (D. Kan. 1979). The court re-opened the case, ending with the admonition that "[i]f we find that [the school district] is not in full compliance with all constitutional requirements, we intend to enter and enforce the orders necessary to obtain such compliance and then close the case." *Brown*, 84 F.R.D. at 405. After trial, the district court ultimately concluded that the Topeka school system showed no evidence of "illegal, intentional, systematic, or residual separation of the races," and refused to modify the 1955 decree. Brown v. Board of Education, 671 F. Supp. 1290 (D. Kan. 1987). In a 2-1 decision, the court of appeals disagreed, and ordered further remedial action. Brown v. Board of Education, 892 F.2d 851 (10th Cir. 1989). That judgment was vacated for consideration in light of other decisions by the Supreme Court. 503 U.S. 978 (1992). On remand, the court of appeals, in another 2-1 decision, affirmed its earlier order with some minor modifications, 978 F.2d 585 (10th Cir. 1992), cert. denied, 509 U.S. 903 (1993). Forty-two years after the case was commenced, the remedy still had not been agreed upon. Will *Brown* reach its fiftieth birthday without full implementation of the promised remedy? Is this "all deliberate speed"?

2. In *Bradley*, the Supreme Court subsequently affirmed the Educational Components of the district court's proposed remedial plan. Milliken v. Bradley, 433 U.S. 267 (1977). It did not, however, review the student re-assignment portions of the plan. On remand, the district court sought to follow the court of appeals' instructions to do something about the student re-assignment portions of the plan, but finally held that there were no lingering effects of *de jure* desegregation in Detroit because the few neighborhoods in which intentional

segregation had once occurred were now entirely African-American. Hence, the district court concluded, there was nothing left to remedy.

The court of appeals reversed as clearly erroneous the finding of no lingering effects. Again it ordered that the inner city regions be integrated, but said that it might be enough to integrate a few of the inner city schools by bringing in white students from other regions. Milliken v. Bradley, 620 F.2d 1143 (6th Cir.), cert. denied, 449 U.S. 870 (1980). Further remedial issues arose as the district court tried to remove aspects of the remedial plan, including a Monitoring Commission which oversaw implementation of the remedy. Bradley v. Milliken, 585 F. Supp. 348 (E.D. Mich. 1984), vacated, 772 F.2d 266 (6th Cir. 1985). Efforts by other interested parties to intervene during later remedial stages and attorneys fees issues occupied the Sixth Circuit until 1990 — nineteen years after the case was filed. See Bradley v. Milliken, 828 F.2d 1186 (6th Cir. 1987); Bradley v. Milliken, 918 F.2d 178 (Table), 1990 WL 177183 (6th Cir. 1990).

In the *Bradley v. Milliken* decision from which we excerpted, the Sixth Circuit is remarkably candid about the issue of impracticality. In essence, the court of appeals said, "District court, you have not restored the plaintiffs to their rightful position, and you must. Of course, we do not have a clue about how you can do so, but you need to keep trying."

If you were the plaintiff's lawyer in *Bradley*, would you have taken the case if you knew that the most immediate victims in the case (those discriminated against in Regions 1, 5, and 8) would receive virtually no remedy at all? Ethically you should explain the risks as well as the benefits of litigation to your client. Would your client be likely to press the case if you said that practical problems like those described in *Bradley* might preclude an effective remedy? The issue of what you actually get, as opposed to what you are entitled to get in a perfect world, is very important, is it not?

3. Obviously, if we shake our allegiance to the rightful position principle, we can avoid the problems of declaration and implementation that haunt *Bradley*. That suggestion was one of Professor Chayes's main points: We should no longer conceive of remedies as retrospective, two-party efforts which precisely correct past wrongs. See pp. 61-64, *supra*. Chayes appears to replace the rightful position principle with a principle of "equity" (in the modern and not in the historical sense; even in its heyday, equity practice was designed to restore, or to keep, plaintiff in the rightful position). Yet Chayes's notion of "doing good for the polity" is not without its problems.

The first problem is a legal one: *Missouri v. Jenkins* seems firmly committed to the rightful position principle as the *maximum* remedial authority of a federal court in institutional reform litigation. Over the years, the Court has wavered on whether the rightful position principle, as opposed to a principle of "doing good," was the appropriate principle in these cases. See Swann v. Charlotte-Mecklenburg Board of Education, 402 U.S. 1, 15-16 (1971) (stating both that "[o]nce a right and violation have been shown, the scope of a district court's equitable powers to remedy past wrongs is broad" and that "[a]s with any equity case, the nature of the violation determines that scope of the remedy"); Dayton Board of Education v. Brinkman, 433 U.S. 406, 420 (1977) (desegregation order should correct only the "incremental segregative effect" of illegal discrimination); Dayton Board of Education v. Brinkman, 443 U.S. 526 (1979) (endorsing a nearly irrebuttable presumption that discrimination in a few schools means discrimination in the entire school system). With *Missouri v. Jenkins*, the Court seems to have put that issue to rest, at least for the time; the rightful position principle is the principle that district courts must use. Presumably, if a court simply cannot figure out how to restore the plaintiffs to that position, as in *Bradley v. Milliken*, the case will need to be dismissed for the plaintiffs' failure to demonstrate an entitlement to a remedy.

Second, although the issue is downplayed in *Missouri v. Jenkins* itself, the court has also made clear in the recent past that other constraints — notably the separation of power and federalism constraints that Justice Thomas emphasizes in his concurrence — may prevent a court even from restoring plaintiffs to their rightful position. In Board of Education of Oklahoma City Public Schools v. Dowell, 498 U.S. 237 (1991), the district court dissolved an injunction requiring desegregation. African-American parents argued that an injunction could be dissolved only upon a showing of a "grievous wrong invoked by new and unforeseen conditions," which was the standard the Court had imposed on the dissolution of an antitrust injunction in United States v. Swift & Co., 286 U.S. 106 (1932). The Court held that *Swift* was an improper standard to use in school desegregation cases, in part because of "[c]onsiderations based on the allocation of powers within out federal system." 498 U.S. at 248. The Court also stated that a relevant consideration in dissolving the injunction was "whether the vestiges of past discrimination had been eliminated to the extent practicable." Id. at 250. In the last paragraph of the majority opinion in *Missouri v. Jenkins*, the Court seems strongly to suggest that the constitutional limitations of separation of powers and federalism, as well as the pragmatic constraint of practicability, both operate in the initial declaration phase as well.

Third, there are other practical difficulties with abandoning a rightful position approach to remedies in favor of a "do good" approach:

> Chayes's approach[ ] would put the judge in a difficult personal position. The judge in street clothes is in principle an equal of the parties. What justifies the power of the judge in robes is that the judge speaks of the law. Regarding findings of liability, judges can readily respond to a defendant's rebuke "how dare you find me liable" with "the law made you liable." This answer is inadequate, however, when the defendant challenges the judge's authority to issue an injunction because the judge must exercise discretion in shaping the injunction to fit the case. . . . [B]y turning the judge into a policy maker, Chayes's approach fails to offer constraints to both legitimate the exercise of equitable discretion and allow the judge to cast at least some of the blame for the injunction's consequences onto the law.

David Schoenbrod, *The Measure of an Injunction: A Principle to Replace Balancing the Equities and Tailoring the Remedy*, 72 Minn. L. Rev. 627, 656-57 (1988).

4. The rightful position principle is highly consistent with an adversarial approach to litigation, in which each plaintiff controls her own claims and is entitled to receive only as much remedy as she personally deserves; if she receives more, she may infringe on another's right to receive what he deserves. The rightful position principle is also, however, one of the causes of lawyer dysfunction in the joinder area, for the inability of the court to "do good" means that early-filing claimants seeking a remedy restoring them to their rightful position might disadvantage late-filing claimants seeking a remedy restoring the late filers to theirs. Now we see that the principle can also cause judicial dysfunction by making it impossible, at least in some cases, to declare a remedy. It can also create constitutional friction.

Is the rightful position principle normatively required by the form of adjudication? If it is not, is it nonetheless required by the due process clause, which embodies the fundamental aspects of the American form of adjudication? If the rightful position is not compelled, why shouldn't we abandon it in complex cases, just as we have seen courts abandon other adversarial principles when faced with other forms of dysfunction? Is one reason that whatever principle we select to replace the rightful position — whether it be Chayes's "do good" concept or some other notion — will have its own problems of declaration and implementation? Perhaps we should not abandon the rightful position until we analyze the complexities into which the alternatives lead us.

5. Might a departure from the rightful position principle be justified by some sense of distributional fairness? For instance, in *Brown*, the generations of black school children in Topeka prior to 1955 — to whom significant constitutional harm occurred — were not the ones who would receive the benefits of the remedy. How, forty years after the fact, could any judge undo the effects of an inferior education and its many consequences in terms of employment and missed opportunities? Might the provision of some "extra" benefits to the next generation of school children, which is arguably what the district court did in *Missouri v. Jenkins*, therefore be justified? Might the provision of extra benefits be justified on the theory that Topeka or Kansas City spent less on African-American education for generations, and the provision of "extra" remedies was an attempt to disgorge the unjust enrichment that the taxpayers of these cities enjoyed? Might it be possible to reach across district lines in Detroit or Kansas City on the same theory — that the white flight caused by illegal patterns of discrimination artificially swelled the tax bases of suburbs, and it is unjust for the suburbs to retain the benefits of this wrongful behavior?

6. As *Dowell* states, a court guided by the rightful position principle must both exercise only the amount of power necessary to correct the precise violation and discontinue the use of that power as soon as it is no longer necessary. The Court discussed in detail the latter requirement of dissolution of an injunction in Rufo v. Inmates of the Suffolk County Jail, 502 U.S. 367 (1992), and in Freeman v. Pitts, 503 U.S. 467 (1992).

2. Monetary Relief

DOUGHERTY v. BARRY

869 F.2d 605 (D.C. Cir. 1989)

■ RUTH BADER GINSBURG, Circuit Judge. [Plaintiffs were eight white firefighters alleging reverse discrimination on the part of the District of Columbia Fire Department and its former Administrator Elijah B. Rogers. Specifically, plaintiffs argued that the Department had discriminated on the basis of race by promoting two black firefighters to deputy fire chief. Five of the plaintiffs brought suit under section 1981. After the EEOC reversed its determination that there was no cause to support the charges of race discrimination, the five, accompanied by three other firefighters, also filed a Title VII action. The actions were subsequently consolidated. The district court held that the defendants violated Title VII and section 1981. It then awarded each plaintiff an amount of backpay and benefits to compensate for the full value of the promotion.]

I. . . .

The [district court] explained why an order directing promotion of any or all of the plaintiffs to deputy chief would be inappropriate. Only two positions had been open, meaning six plaintiffs definitely would not have been promoted even absent discrimination; promotions were based on subjective as well as objective factors, which made it difficult to evaluate plaintiffs against each other; and plaintiffs did "not comprise the entire group of officers eligible for promotion to deputy" at the time.

Nevertheless, the court awarded full monetary relief to each plaintiff in the form of back pay and an annuity adjustment, *i.e.*, for monetary award purposes, each plaintiff was to be recompensed as though he had been promoted to one of the two deputy positions. The court reasoned that defendants could not show "that any particular plaintiff would not have been promoted absent discrimination." Dividing the monetary value of the two promotions eight ways would not make plaintiffs whole, the district court believed, for they had lost the opportunity to gain a large, albeit intangible, benefit — the "pride and respect of one's colleagues which accompany a hard-earned promotion." The District of Columbia and Rogers appealed, challenging the district court's decision only with regard to the timeliness of the Title VII claim and the scope of the relief granted.

II.

[The court concluded that appellees' Title VII action should be dismissed because it was not timely filed and therefore the three firefighters who were party only to the Title VII action were not entitled to any relief.]

III.

Turning to the question of monetary recovery, we reject appellants' argument that appellees are not entitled to any relief because two other whites [not party to this suit], Joseph R. Granados and Harry H. Shaffer, would have gotten the promotions absent discrimination. As the district court held, once appellees proved they had been subjected to disparate treatment, the burden shifted to appellants to show by clear and convincing evidence that each appellee was not entitled to relief because he would not have received one of the promotions even absent discrimination. . . .[8] Appellants failed to carry that burden in this case. . . .

---

8. A court may impose classwide relief for a group of individuals subjected to discrimination where it is impossible to determine which particular individual would have received the benefit but for the discrimination without falling "into 'a quagmire of hypothetical judgments.'" . . . Once the group establishes liability, as the district court found appellees did, there is a presumption that each member is entitled to relief; the burden is on the defendant to "rebut that presumption in each

Although appellees are entitled to monetary relief, the extent of that relief granted by the district court was overly generous. We are unaware of any support for the district court's decision to award full recompense to each appellee as though each had been promoted. Rather, precedent favors dividing the monetary value of the two promotions among appellees pro rata....

Dividing the value of the promotions among appellees more closely approximates the goal of " 'recreat[ing] the conditions and relationships that would have been had there been no' unlawful discrimination." ... If the district court had been able to determine with certainty which two of the appellees would have received the promotions, the proper course would have been to award those two appellees full relief and the others none.... Because the court was unable to do so, however, one must assume that each appellee enjoyed less than a one hundred percent chance of being promoted. By awarding each appellee full back pay, however, the district court treated each as though he possessed a one hundred percent chance of receiving one of the promotions, counter to that court's own conclusion that one could not determine for certain which appellees, if any, would have been promoted. Thus, in order to restore appellees to the position they would have occupied absent discrimination, . . . the district court should have awarded each appellee a fraction of the promotions' value commensurate with the likelihood of his receiving one of the promotions.

Because the relief awarded by the district court thus put appellees in a better position than they would have occupied absent discrimination, we vacate the award and remand the matter to the district court. The district court has already stated that it is unable to evaluate appellees against one another; on remand, then, the district court may simply divide the monetary value of the two promotions equally among appellees.[10]

KYRIAZI v. WESTERN ELECTRIC CO.

465 F. Supp. 1141 (D.N.J. 1979), *aff'd*, 642 F.2d 388 (3d Cir. 1981)

■ STERN, District Judge. At the conclusion of "Stage I" of this Title VII litigation — the liability phase — this Court found that Western Electric

---

each individual case." Although this case does not involve a class action, the same principles apply because all of the appellees were eligible for the promotion, and the district court was unable to determine which of them would not have been promoted. Furthermore, although cases establishing this allocation of burdens generally involve Title VII, we see no reason — and neither party offers any — to treat section 1981 differently in this regard. Dismissing the Title VII claim therefore does not affect the allocation of burdens.

10. We need not consider the thornier question of whether the fraction due each appellee should in fact be smaller because other battalion chiefs not party to this suit were eligible for the promotions. Appellants have made no claim that the other qualified battalion chiefs should be considered in devising the share due each appellee, and appellants' counsel specifically conceded at oral argument that if we rejected the argument that Granados and Shaffer would have received the promotions, the value of the two promotions should be divided among appellees.

discriminated against its female employees, applicants and former employees in the areas of hiring, promotion, participation in job training programs, layoffs, wages and opportunities for testing. We now enter "Stage II", the damage phase. Stage II requires adjudication of the claims of thousands of class members. . . .

1. *Burden of Proof*

The Supreme Court has made clear that once there has been a finding of class-wide discrimination, the burden then shifts to the employer to prove that a class member was not discriminated against; that is, a finding of discrimination creates a rebuttable presumption in favor of recovery. . . .

Accordingly, the sole burden upon class members will be to demonstrate that they are members of the class, that is, that now or at any time since June 9, 1971, they were either employed by Western, applied for employment at Western or were terminated by Western. . . . The Court will not require individual class members to specify the manner in which they were discriminated against. . . . Thus, once an individual demonstrates that she is a class member, the burden will then shift to Western to demonstrate that the individual class member was not the victim of discrimination. . . .

3. *Computation of Back Pay Awards*

The courts have adopted a number of approaches in connection with the computation of back pay awards. One approach, the "pro rata" formula . . ., looks to the difference between the salary of the class members computed collectively and that received by employees of comparable skills and seniority, not the victims of discrimination. The class member then receives his pro rata share of that collective difference, based upon his salary differential and the number of competitors for the position. Another approach is the "test period" approach, . . . in which the court awards class members the difference between the pay they receive after implementation of the Title VII decree and the pay they received while the discriminatory policies were in force. [The court then described two variants of the "test period" approach. In one, class members were awarded "the difference between the pay they receive after implementation of the Title VII decree and the pay they received while the discriminatory policies were in force." In another, class members were awarded "the difference between their own actual earnings and the earnings of the skilled trade opportunity jobs from the effective date of Title VII."]

The Court finds none of these approaches appropriate here. As we found in connection with Stage I, we deal with discrimination which manifests itself in a number of ways. . . . It is, therefore, apparent that a backpay award must take into account the fact that a male and a female entering Western with comparable skills would, over a period of time, take dramatically divergent paths.

While this approach will not yield an exact measure of damages, neither could any other approach. However, the law is clear that where one has been damaged by the wrong of another, the victim is not to be denied any recompense merely because the exact measure of damages is uncertain.... The approach we adopt at least gives individual consideration to each claimant and, if not precise, it is no more imprecise than lumping claimants into groups and extracting averages, or otherwise depersonalizing victims of discrimination by running them through a mathematical blender....

According to Western, if there were three women who should have been considered for one promotion and none were, and if we cannot now determine which of the three women should have received the promotion, then each one receives one-third of the benefits. As Western notes, this approach does shield Western from having to pay three increases when only one was actually possible, but it also unjustly penalizes the one woman who was entitled to *all* — not just one-third — of the benefits of that promotion. Under Western's approach, two of the claimants get a windfall while the actual victim receives only one-third of the back pay to which she is statutorily entitled. If we know that all three claimants were discriminated against in that they were not considered for promotion but that only one — which, we do not know — would have actually received the promotion, then all three should get the full benefit of the promotional opportunity. Where it is proved that an employer unlawfully disregarded women for promotion, it is better that it pay a little more than to permit an innocent party to shoulder the burdens of the guilty. Western *will* be permitted to demonstrate that the promotion would have gone to one class member, rather than the others. However, if Western cannot demonstrate which claimant would have received the promotion, Western cannot divide the benefits of the one job. It is no more unreal to construe three promotions out of one, than to divide the salary increase of one promotion among three prospects. Either smacks of some artificiality but the latter protects the wrongdoer at the expense of the innocent....

[I]n an effort to assure back pay awards on as individualized basis as possible, where appropriate class members will be compared to the male employee with comparable skills upon initial hire and comparable seniority. The class member will then be awarded the difference between her salary and that received by the male counterpart, including bonuses and any other fringe benefits.

Notes and Questions

1. Is it equitable to give the individual plaintiff who would have been promoted absent discrimination only a partial remedy because the defendant's misconduct has made it difficult to determine which individual would have been promoted? Is it unfair to the defendant to pay the value of five promotions when only two were in fact available? Is it significant that *Dougherty* is a "reverse" discrimination case, and *Kyriazi* is not? To what extent should substantive preferences influence the rightful position principle? Cf. United States v. City of Warren, Michigan, 138 F.3d 1083, 1099 (6th Cir. 1998) (distinguishing *Dougherty* and awarding full backpay when it was likely that African-American applicant would have been selected for position). Can the difference between *Dougherty* and *Kyriazi* be explained by the courts' different conceptions of the victim — the entire class (*Dougherty*) or a group of individuals (*Kyriazi*)?

2. Should the amount of backpay distributed among the *Dougherty* plaintiff group be discounted because not all white firefighters eligible to compete for the promotion were before the court? *Dougherty* leaves this "thornier" question open. Suppose that no discount occurred. Would a later-filing claimant be precluded from obtaining a remedy? If he or she is precluded, don't we have a classic form of lawyer dysfunction that we studied in the context of joinder complexity (see p. 88, *supra*)? Assuming that the defendant's assets are sufficient to satisfy both claims, is there any dysfunction if the latter lawsuit is permitted to proceed? Are there any problems in declaring the remedy when both suits are permitted? Is it unfair to make a defendant possibly pay twice for a single wrong? How much weight should these factors be given in determining the answer to the "thorny" question? See Meredith v. Beech Aircraft Corp., 18 F.3d 890 (10th Cir. 1994) (later-filing plaintiff could not be precluded from litigating her entitlement to the promotion based on judgment entered in favor of earlier-filing claimant because she was not a party to earlier suit).

Obviously, the "thorny" issue disappears if our rules mandated the joinder of all interested parties in the first litigation. But complete joinder creates the declaration problem faced in *Dougherty* and *Kyriazi*. How do we resolve the conflict between one form of complexity (joinder) and another (remedial)?

3. As *Kyriazi* shows, these troubling issues are magnified when litigation is brought as a class action, since the risks of unfairness to the defendant or inequitable remedies within the plaintiff class become more pronounced. Should this fact make courts reluctant to certify class actions?

4. Comparable declaration problems can sometimes arise in two other situations. First, in toxic tort litigation in which the relationship between exposure to a chemical and certain disease processes is unclear, a court faces a difficult task of declaring the portion of a settlement or judgment fund that should be allocated to each claimant. Because of the strong implementation overtones of this situation, we reserve until the next section the exploration of this issue. See p. 1435, *infra*. Second, the declaration of punitive damages, at least in widespread litigation, might raise declaration difficulties. Some courts have suggested, and one has held, that there exists an absolute limit on the amount of punitive damages and the number of times that a defendant might be punished through punitive damages for the same pattern of conduct. See Juzwin v. Amtorg Trading Co., 705 F. Supp. 1053 (D.N.J. 1989), vacated, 718 F. Supp. 1233 (D.N.J. 1989). Most courts have disagreed with *Juzwin*, see, *e.g.*, Dunn v. HOVIC, 1 F.3d 1371 (3d Cir.), modified, 13 F.3d 58 (3d Cir.), cert. denied, 510 U.S. 1031 (1993); but at least three states (Georgia, Missouri, and Kansas) have passed statutes that permit punitive damages to be awarded in only one case, see Ga. Code § 51-12-5.1; Mo. Stat. Ann. § 510.263(4); Kan. Civ. Proc. Code Ann. § 60-3701(e)-(f); see also Mack Trucks, Inc. v. Conkle, 263 Ga. 539, 436 S.E.2d 635 (1993) (upholding Georgia statute as constitutional). Assuming the correctness of *Juzwin*, how should a court respond to the problem of declaring and distributing a single punitive damage award? Should it certify a mandatory class action? See p. 593, *supra*.

5. Do the questions in these Notes, as well as the similar questions in the subsection on injunctive relief, convince you that we should abandon the rightful position principle in complex litigation? What effect would an abandonment have on the problems of joinder, pretrial, and trial complexity? Put differently, how many of the problems of complex litigation are spawned by the rightful position principle? With what principle might the rightful position principle be

replaced? What problems would be spawned by a substitute principle? In light of *Missouri v. Jenkins* (p. 1392, *supra*), is it even possible for federal courts to abandon the principle? Consider these questions as you read the next case.

DEMOCRATIC CENTRAL COMMITTEE OF THE DISTRICT OF COLUMBIA v. WASHINGTON METROPOLITAN AREA TRANSIT COMMISSION

84 F.3d 451 (D.C. Cir. 1996)

■ PER CURIAM.

[In a lawsuit commenced in the 1960s, the bus company (D.C. Transit) that provided service to riders in Washington, D.C. was found to have charged excessive fares. The fare increases had been ordered by the Washington Metropolitan Area Transit Commission (WMATA), but those orders were later overturned in litigation. The bus riders then sought restitution of the excessive fares. Eventually the litigation resulted in the creation of two funds: the "Bebchick Fund" — which contained, after certain distributions, $1,461,756 in 1974 and which had risen in value to $6,560,588.17 in 1996 — and the "Riders' Fund" — which contained $4,850,459.80 plus certain unliquidated assets. A trustee was appointed for the Riders' Fund; no trustee was ever appointed for the Bebchick Fund.]

II. DISCUSSION

Of the many recommendations submitted to the court regarding the disposition of the restitutionary funds, none suggested giving the farepayers an opportunity to prove and collect the amounts they were overcharged by D.C. Transit. Although a proof-of-claim procedure might usually be considered the most precise and direct method of compensation, the parties, special interest groups, and individual citizens that submitted recommendations correctly recognized that using such a procedure in this case would not be feasible. More than a quarter of a century has passed since D.C. Transit collected the excessive fares; identifying, locating, and notifying all those overcharged after so much time would be very difficult, if not impossible. The prohibitive cost of notification, together with the cost of distribution, would greatly reduce, or even exceed, the total amount of the funds. Even if such an opportunity were given, it is doubtful whether any of the overcharged farepayers would avail themselves of it; many would likely consider the potential of recovering a small award not worth the considerable effort of establishing a claim arising out of numerous minor transactions that occurred 25 years ago.... Because of the great cost and likely failure of a proof-of-claim procedure, another method of distributing the restitutionary funds is needed to benefit the overcharged farepayers.

In class actions, some courts have applied the equitable doctrine of cy pres to undistributed damage or settlement funds. See State v. Levi Strauss & Co., 41 Cal.3d 460, 224 Cal.Rptr. 605-611, 715 P.2d 564, 570 (1986). That doctrine permits such funds to be distributed to the "next best" class when the plaintiffs cannot be compensated individually. The object of applying the funds to the "next best" class is to parallel the intended use of the funds as nearly as possible by maximizing the number of plaintiffs compensated. . . . In the context of class actions, the cy pres doctrine is referred to as "fluid recovery."[2] The "next best" class in this case would be the current bus riders in the service region from which the excessive fares were collected. . . .

Fluid recovery offers four approaches to the distribution of unclaimed settlement or damage funds: (1) reduction of the defendant's prices, (2) escheat to a governmental body for either specified or general purposes, (3) establishment of a "consumer trust fund," and (4) "claimant fund sharing." See *Levi Strauss*, 224 Cal.Rptr. at 612, 715 P.2d at 571. Under the price reduction approach, the price of the defendant's product or service is lowered until the funds are completely distributed. Id. This approach is "particularly effective for remedying overcharges on items which are repeatedly purchased by the same individuals." Id. . . . Because of the inability to predict or control its effect on a market, the price reduction approach is most appropriate in cases where the defendant is a monopoly. See *Levi Strauss*, 224 Cal.Rptr. at 613, 715 P.2d at 572 . . . . None of the recommendations submitted to the court suggested this approach for distributing the restitutionary funds.

There are two forms of the governmental escheat approach: the specified or "earmarked" escheat and the general escheat. *Levi Strauss*, 224 Cal.Rptr. at 613, 715 P.2d at 572. Under the former, funds are disbursed to a particular governmental agency for the purpose of benefiting a group of persons who approximate the injured class; the details of the distribution are left to the agency. See id. The advantage of the earmarked escheat is that it utilizes governmental agencies to administer the fund. Id. Under the general escheat, the funds are unconditionally deposited into the treasury of a governmental body for the benefit of the public at large. Id. Because this approach provides the least focused compensation to the injured class, it is used only when a more precise method cannot be found. Id. 224 Cal.Rptr. at 613-14, 715 P.2d at 572-73 . . . . Of the recommendations submitted to the court, five suggested that all of the restitutionary funds should escheat to WMATA; one suggested that WMATA should only get the liquid assets. None of the recommendations suggested a general escheat.

2. Implementing fluid recovery, also referred to as "fluid class recovery," in federal class actions is controversial. . . . In Eisen v. Carlisle & Jacquelin, 479 F.2d 1005 (2d Cir.1973), vacated on other grounds, 417 U.S. 156 (1974), the Second Circuit held that the class-wide damage assessment utilized in fluid recovery violates due process and that reading fluid recovery into Rule 23 of the Federal Rules of Civil Procedure improperly alters substantive rights in violation of the Rules Enabling Act. The Fourth and the Ninth Circuits have relied on *Eisen* to disallow fluid recovery distribution methods in class actions. See Windham v. American Brands, Inc., 565 F.2d 59, 72 & n. 41 (4th Cir. 1977), cert. denied, 435 U.S. 968 (1978); Kline v. Coldwell Banker & Co., 508 F.2d 226, 233-34 (9th Cir. 1974). Others have argued that the use of separate trials for liability and damages in fluid recovery deprives defendants in class actions of their seventh amendment right to trial by jury. . . . State courts, in particular California, have been more hospitable to fluid recovery in class actions. This case, however, is not a class action; the constitutional challenges mentioned above are not at issue here.

The third available approach is the establishment of a "consumer trust fund." *Levi Strauss*, 224 Cal.Rptr. at 614, 715 P.2d at 573. Like the governmental escheat, the consumer trust fund can be arranged in two ways: the foundation method or the existing organization method. Under the former, the court appoints a board of trustees and deposits the funds with them. Id. The trustees then create an organization through which it finances projects beneficial to the injured consumers and those similarly situated. Id. The second method of establishing a consumer trust fund is to provide funding to an existing organization to support new and ongoing projects. . . . Like the earmarked escheat, the advantage of this second method is that it minimizes administrative costs by utilizing existing programs. *Levi Strauss*, 224 Cal.Rptr. at 614, 715 P.2d at 573 . . . . Two recommendations suggested the creation of committees to oversee the distribution of restitutionary funds; one suggested distributing a portion of the restitutionary funds to two existing transportation public interest groups.

The final approach is "claimant fund sharing," which allows class members who submit claims to divide the funds pro rata. *Levi Strauss*, 224 Cal.Rptr. at 614, 715 P.2d at 573. While this approach compensates all who submit legitimate claims, unidentified class members do not receive any compensation, even indirectly. Id. The larger the number of unidentified class members, the greater the likelihood that those submitting claims will receive a windfall. This approach is, therefore, most appropriate where a large proportion of the class members participate and submit accurate claims. Id. . . . None of the recommendations suggested this approach.

In determining which of the four approaches to employ, we consider the following factors: (1) the amount of compensation to class members, (2) the proportion of the class members sharing in the recovery, (3) the extent to which nonclass members will benefit, and (4) the cost of the administration. *Levi Strauss*, 224 Cal.Rptr. at 614, 715 P.2d at 573 . . . .

Our initial conclusion is that we should not use the general escheat or the claimant fund sharing approaches to distribute the restitutionary funds; the former because a more precise distribution approach is available, the latter because of the notification and proof difficulties discussed earlier. After evaluating the remaining approaches, we further conclude that an earmarked escheat to WMATA to implement its January 19, 1996 proposal is the best method of distributing the restitutionary funds to the "next best" class, the current bus riders. . . .

Using WMATA to distribute the funds makes sense: it has been providing bus transportation for over twenty years; its experience in serving the intended beneficiaries of the restitutionary funds is unparalleled; it is experienced in overseeing and administering large sums of money; it has an administrative infrastructure capable of beginning distribution immediately; and because virtually all of the funds will go to the benefit of the bus riders, the cost of administering the restitutionary funds will be negligible.

Distributing the restitutionary funds through the consumer trust fund approach would not be as effective or efficient. Any trustees the court could appoint would lack WMATA's experience in, and knowledge of, bus transportation services. In addition, administrative costs of creating a new organization, relative to WMATA's administrative costs, would be substantial.... The existing public interest groups, MetroWatch and ACT, also lack WMATA's experience and knowledge.

Distributing the restitutionary funds through the price reduction approach would effectively deliver the funds to the current bus riders. The benefit, however, would be extremely diffused and could be difficult to administer because WMATA would have to determine the precise point the funds would be exhausted.

Two recommendations argue that the interests of WMATA conflict with the interests of the bus riders and that the restitutionary funds should not, therefore, be transferred to WMATA. We find no conflict.... The interests of the riders conflicted with those of the transit operators, but not with the interests of the [WMATA and its predecessor, the Public Utility Commission]. Indeed, this court stated that "the Commission, in administering the [settlement fund] acts more nearly as a trustee to implement judicial directives concerning the use of the fund than in the statutory regulatory powers."... Like its predecessors, WMATA shares the riders' interest in safe, adequate, and inexpensive public transportation but not the transit operators' conflicting interest in making a profit. [The] separate counsel and segregated property [of WMATA] might well be characteristic of parties whose interests conflict, but they do not, in and of themselves, establish that a conflict exists.

Finally, both ACT and MetroWatch expressed concern that applying the funds to WMATA's operating budget would result in a commensurate decrease in the contributions from the jurisdictions that fund WMATA. The conditions to which the escheat is subject should allay their concerns....

[T]o assure that the restitutionary funds are used in a manner that most closely serves their original purposes, the escheat to WMATA is subject to the following two conditions. First, the restitutionary funds cannot be the basis for any reduction in the contributions due from the jurisdictions that fund WMATA. Second, with two exceptions mentioned below, WMATA must use the funds, as it has proposed, exclusively for "the purchase of new buses for use in the affected service area."... As WMATA explained, purchasing new buses would provide

> widespread, long-lasting and tangible benefits for the farepaying public, ... [including] improved service, increased safety, reduced operating costs, lower maintenance costs, improved environmental performance, and standard features to aid the elderly and disabled.

While the funds must be spent primarily for new buses, we recognize that WMATA will inherit responsibilities from the current Riders' Fund trustee, the Bank of New York. Accordingly, we also authorize WMATA to use a reasonable portion of the restitutionary funds to cover the cost of (i) liquidating the real property assets in the Riders' Fund (including the cost of such legal and real estate services as it may deem appropriate to help realize the assets' potential value) and (ii) prosecuting the judgment the Riders' Fund has against D.C. Transit.

III. CONCLUSION

We conclude that the Riders' Fund and the Bebchick Fund should be consolidated pursuant to Article Two of the Riders' Fund Trust Agreement, . . . and that all the assets of the restitutionary funds, both liquidated and unliquidated, be transferred to WMATA, subject to the conditions described above. WMATA is directed within sixty days to submit implementing orders to the court.

Notes and Questions

1. *Democratic Central Committee* was not a class action. Most of the cases in which the issue of "fluid recovery" has been considered, however, have been class actions. In class actions, one of the effects of the "fluid recovery" concept is that it makes the distribution of the remedy manageable, and thus makes the class action as a whole more manageable. Because manageability is a central concern in the decision to certify class actions (see pp. 545-46, *supra*), the ability to use fluid recovery may make or break class certification. Whether this makes fluid recovery more or less appealing may depend, therefore, on your view of class actions as an aggregation device. Note how, once again, issues of remedial complexity and issues of joinder complexity merge.

2. Because the persons that are injured and the persons that receive a remedy do not perfectly correspond, fluid recovery seems difficult to reconcile with the rightful position principle. Can it be justified on the theory that the essential nature of adjudication is not to restore plaintiffs to their rightful position but rather to ensure that defendants' wrongful conduct is adequately deterred? After *Missouri v. Jenkins* (p. 1392, *supra*), is it nonetheless true that, whatever the essential nature of adjudication might be, the essential nature of the American form of adjudication requires the use of the rightful position? If so, is there any other argument that can justify fluid recovery, or must we simply permit defendants to retain their ill-gotten gains?

3. On a related point, to what extent were the remedies that were often ordered in school desegregation cases a form of fluid class recovery: The persons that had been harmed were generations of African-Americans educated in the "separate but equal" days, it was impossible to provide a remedy for these persons, and the "next best" group to obtain the remedy were the present children in the school system? By unhinging the school system's obligation from the present children's entitlement, a case could be made for remedies that exceed the rightful position of the present children. Should the scope of injunctive remedies in desegregation cases and monetary remedies in fluid recovery cases be the same? If not, in which area should courts have more power to create a remedy unrelated to the rightful position of the present plaintiffs?

4. How different is the concept of fluid recovery from the concept of trial by statistics, which we examined at p. 1294, *supra*? Aren't both devices an attempt to avoid the problem of individual proof of damage? Cf. Nelson v. Greater Gadsden Housing Authority, 802 F.2d 405, 409 (11th Cir. 1986) ("The objections to fluid recovery appear to relate to the use of this system to relieve plaintiff classes of the burden of proving individual damages or to avoid the dismissal of unmanageable class actions. Neither problem exists here."). Should the two concepts rise or fall together? Which is superior?

5. In thinking about the questions in the last three Notes, you might wish to know that most federal courts have rejected the use of a fluid recovery procedure to relieve class members of the burden of proving individual damages on the basis that the Rules Enabling Act prohibits procedural devices from modifying substantive rights. See Windham v. American Brands, Inc., 565 F.2d 59 (4th Cir. 1977), cert. denied, 435 U.S. 968 (1978); In re Hotel Telephone Charges, 500 F.2d 86 (9th Cir. 1974). The Second Circuit has gone even further, concluding that fluid class recovery as a method of assessing damages violates the procedural due process provisions of the Constitution. See Eisen v. Carlisle & Jacquelin, 479 F.2d 1005 (2d Cir. 1973), vacated on other grounds, 417 U.S. 156 (1974).

In perhaps the most well-known fluid recovery case, however, the Seventh Circuit has adopted an ad hoc approach to the use of a fluid recovery procedure to assess class damages:

> Plaintiffs apparently contend that the harmed individuals cannot be identified and therefore a fluid recovery should be utilized. Strictly speaking, plaintiffs' contention proves too much. . . . Indeed, to accept plaintiffs' position would be to ignore the requirements of Rule 23, such as whether an identifiable class exists and whether notice to the class can be executed. Therefore, we reject any approach which would automatically utilize a fluid recovery mechanism as a procedural alternative to class action disposition.
>
> At the other extreme is the position that a fluid recovery mechanism is unconstitutional. The argument raised is that it violates defendant's right to trial by jury. . . .
>
> We need not adopt either of the two extreme positions — that is, whether a fluid recovery always can be used to surmount problems in the going forward of a class action or whether a fluid recovery is per se unconstitutional. Rather we believe that a careful case-by-case analysis of use of the fluid recovery mechanism is the better approach. In this approach we focus on the various substantive policies that use of a fluid recovery would serve in the particular case. The general inquiry is whether the use of such mechanism is consistent with the policy or policies reflected by the statute violated. This matter can be more particularized into an assessment of to what extent the statute embodies policies of deterrence, disgorgement, and compensation.

Simer v. Rios, 661 F.2d 655, 675-76 (7th Cir. 1981), cert. denied, 456 U.S. 917 (1982). *Simer* went on to hold that, on the facts of the case (which involved erroneous deprivations of government assistance), the policies of deterrence and disgorgement weighed against the use of fluid recovery, while the policy of compensation generally favored fluid recovery. On balance, the court of held that the former policies outweighed the latter, and declined to permit the use of fluid recovery.

6. Even though courts typically remain cautious about the use of fluid recovery as a substitute for the award of individualized damages, many courts approve the use of fluid recovery to distribute damages that are unclaimed by plaintiffs that are entitled to them. For instance, in Six (6) Mexican Workers v. Arizona Citrus Growers, 904 F.2d 1301 (9th Cir. 1990), the Arizona Citrus Growers and two of its members were found to have violated the Farm Labor Contractor Registration Act. Statutory damages of $1,846,500 were awarded in

favor of a class of undocumented Mexican farm workers, most of whom could not be located. The district court permitted class members to assert claims against the fund, and decided to award all unclaimed portions the fund to the Inter-American Fund for use in areas of Mexico in which class members might have lived. On appeal, the defendants argued both that the class should not have been certified because of the manageability problems of awarding damages and, more directly, that the district court's distribution order was wrong.

The court of appeals held that the class was properly certified, and further held that the unclaimed damages could be distributed either through pro rata distribution to identified class members, cy pres or fluid distribution, escheat to the government, or reversion to the unclaimed funds. After stating that "[f]ederal courts have broad discretionary powers in shaping equitable decrees for distributing unclaimed class action funds," that "[t]he district court's choice among distribution options should be guided by the objectives of the underlying statute and the interests of the silent class members," and that "we do not generally disapprove of cy pres," 904 F.2d at 1307-08, the court held that the use of cy pres or fluid distribution in the case itself was improper:

> The district court's proposal benefits a group far too remote from the plaintiff class. Even where cy pres is considered, it will be rejected when the proposed distribution fails to provide the "next best" distribution. . . . The district court's plan permits distribution to areas where the class members may live, but there is no reasonable certainty that any member will be benefited.
>
> The tool for distribution, the IAF, is not an organization with a substantial record of service nor is it limited in its choice of projects. Under such circumstances, any distribution plan should be supervised by the court or a court appointed master to ensure that the funds are distributed in accordance with the goals of the remedy. . . . The plan does not adequately target the plaintiff class and fails to provide adequate supervision over distribution. We therefore set aside the court's cy pres application as an abuse of discretion. [Id. at 1308-09.]

See also Beecher v. Able, 575 F.2d 1010 (2d Cir. 1978) (allowing distribution of unclaimed amounts to certain subclasses); Van Gemert v. Boeing Co., 553 F.2d 812 (2d Cir. 1977) (rejecting argument that identified class members are automatically entitled to receive pro rata distribution of unclaimed fund, and suggesting that reversion to defendant is only way to ensure that plaintiffs have adequate incentive to inform unnamed class members); Wilson v. Southwest Airlines, Inc., 880 F.2d 807, 813 (5th Cir. 1989) (ordering reversion of unclaimed portions of settlement fund, after deduction for fees and expenses of class counsel, because "the fund, pursuant to the consent decree, achieved the remedial purposes of Title VII"; further declining to award entire unclaimed amount to class counsel); In re Folding Carton Antitrust Litigation, 744 F.2d 1252 (7th Cir. 1984), cert. dismissed, 471 U.S. 1113 (1985) (ordering escheat to government of unclaimed funds).

7. As *Six Mexican Workers* demonstrates, courts sometimes decide to give a portion of the funds to an organization or charity that has some relationship to the plaintiffs in the litigation. The two most famous cases in which this tack was taken are *Folding Carton*, 744 F.2d 1252, and In re "Agent Orange" Product Liability Litigation, 818 F.2d 179 (2d Cir. 1987), cert. denied, 487 U.S. 1234. In *Folding Carton*, the district court proposed to use unclaimed amounts to

establish a tax-free foundation to study complex antitrust litigation and substantive antitrust law. The court of appeals reversed, holding that

> the establishment of the proposed Foundation would be carrying coals to Newcastle. There has already been voluminous research with respect to multidistrict antitrust litigation and the substantive and procedural aspects of the antitrust laws by judges, lawyer specialists, law schools, bar associations, Congressional committees, the Department of Justice and the Federal Trade Commission, and it is a continuing project of all those concerned. In our view, establishing an unneeded Foundation for these purposes from the reserve fund would be a miscarriage of justice and an abuse of discretion. [818 F.2d 1254-55.]

Note that *Folding Carton* did not entirely reject the idea of the use of a foundation. In *Agent Orange*, the idea was taken a bit further. The parties agreed to a $180 million settlement, but made no decisions about how the money was to be allocated. The district judge, Judge Weinstein, conducted fairness hearings and proposed to use one-quarter of the settlement

> to support a "class assistance foundation" that would "serve as a national focus for Vietnam veterans who are class members to mobilize themselves and others to deal with their medical and related problems." The "broad mandates" of the foundation were defined as "to fund projects to aid children with birth defects and their families and alleviate reproductive problems" and "to fund projects to help meet the service needs of the class as a whole."
> . . .
>
> The court offered a number of examples of the sorts of programs for which the foundation might provide financial support. The projects that might be funded for children with birth defects included "[p]rotection and advocacy services," "[a] public hotline and referral service," "[g]rants to hospitals and clinics," "insurance programs," "vocational training projects," "grants to establish peer support groups to enable children with birth defects to discuss their problems openly among themselves," and "[g]rants or loans ... to families in grave financial need to help pay for essential medical services." Other possibilities "for funding of classwide services" enumerated by the court included projects to "help class member veterans better obtain and utilize VA services and to monitor the VA and other federal and state services to ensure that they are responsive to the needs of the class," to "increase public awareness of the problems of the class," to provide health information and social service assistance to the class, and to "help members of the class become a more integrated part of society."

In re "Agent Orange" Product Liability Litigation, 818 F.2d 145, 158-59 (2d Cir. 1987), cert. denied, 484 U.S. 1004 (1988). Note that, unlike *Folding Carton*, *Agent Orange* proposed to use a portion of the actual settlement proceeds to establish the foundation, rather than only the unclaimed amounts.

Although stating that such a use of a portion of the settlement would not necessarily contravene the bar in *Eisen*, 479 F.2d 1005, and *Van Gemert*, 553 F.2d 812, against fluid recovery, the court of appeals nonetheless reversed the district court's order:

> We are unwilling for several reasons to permit the distribution of any settlement proceeds to a largely independent foundation. First, while a district court is permitted broad supervisory authority over the distribution of a class settlement, . . . there is no principle of law authorizing such a

broad delegation of judicial authority to private parties. We perceive no assurance that the "self-governing and self- perpetuating" board of directors of the class assistance foundation, or any other such body that might be devised by the court, will possess the independent, disinterested judgment required to allocate limited funds to benefit the class as a whole. One of the district court's prime functions in distributing such a fund is to protect the less vocal and less activist members of the class. The proposed foundation is not well designed to perform that function. Moreover, given the very evident discord among various veterans as to the use of the settlement fund, we see great hazards in transferring that discord to a foundation having permanent control over portions of that fund. There is a great danger that the fund would be expended in ways that generate more controversy than benefits and would create even more frustration among a group already frustrated enough by perceived political and legal setbacks. However unique it may be, this is an action for personal injuries, and we believe that only direct judicial supervision can assure that the settlement fund is expended for appropriate purposes. . . .

Moreover, we are concerned that the broad mandate given the class assistance foundation, which must remain an arm of the court however loosely connected, would permit settlement proceeds to be expended on activities inconsistent with the judicial function. For example, activities to "help class member veterans better obtain and utilize VA services" and to "increase public awareness of the problems of the class," might include political advocacy. We do not believe that the proceeds of a court-administered settlement ought to be used for such a purpose.

Finally, we are concerned that, even given the expressed intention to allow the foundation great latitude, the district court and this court would repeatedly be asked to intervene in foundation decisions alleged not to benefit the class. When such claims are made, they call for greater scrutiny than is contemplated by the district court's exercise of only a "modest supervisory role." In addition, endless legal argument over the disbursement of the settlement fund would simply prolong the suffering and frustrations of the class.

We explicitly note, however, that the district court may in the exercise of its discretion and after consultation with veterans' groups undertake to use portions of the fund for class assistance programs that are consistent with the nature of the underlying action and with the judicial function. Accordingly, the district court on remand may designate in detail such programs and provide for their supervision. A reserve fund for as yet undefined programs may be established. Alternatively, the court may reallocate any or all of the funds earmarked for the class assistance foundation to augment the awards to individual class members. [818 F.2d at 185-86.]

On remand, the district court decided to allocate $40 million to a "Class Assistance Program" administered and monitored by the court. In re "Agent Orange" Product Liability Litigation, 689 F. Supp. 1250 (E.D.N.Y. 1988). Do such foundations or programs take the court too far afield from its traditional adversarial role? Can they be justified as being necessary to overcome declaration problems in the remedial process? If not, how can they be justified?

8. More generally, fluid recovery can be used as a device both to overcome problems of joinder complexity (when fluid recovery makes possible a class

action, and a class action prevents joinder complexity) and problems of remedial complexity (when the declaration of the "rightful position" remedy for individual litigants is impossible). Again we face the questions of how central the rightful position principle actually is, and whether we can abandon it when faced with problems of lawyer or judicial dysfunction in a traditional adversarial system. Does the rightful position principle enjoy a status equivalent to the guarantee of rational adjudication of the defendants' obligations?

9. As a lawyer, what are your ethical obligations with respect to a request for fluid recovery? Must you advise your client at the outset that you might be seeking relief that benefits people other than him, and may leave him undersompensated? Does the existence of fluid recovery demonstrate that the truly interested parties in many complex disputes are the lawyers?

10. For a further general discussion of fluid class recovery procedures, see Glen O. Robinson, *Collective Justice in Tort Law*, 78 Va. L. Rev. 1481 (1992); Kerry Barrett, Note, *Equitable Trusts: An Effective Remedy in Consumer Class Actions*, 96 Yale L.J. 1591 (1987); Natalie A. DeJarlais, Note, *The Consumer Trust Fund: A Cy Pres Solution to Undistributed Funds in Consumer Class Actions*, 38 Hastings L.J. 729, 730 (1987); Anna L. Durand, Note, *An Economic Analysis of Fluid Class Recovery Systems*, 34 Stan. L. Rev. 173 (1981).

11. A problem related to fluid recovery is the "passing-on" doctrine in antitrust litigation. Under this doctrine, when a distributor or retailer passes on the cost of a good sold to it under anti-competitive conditions, and thus suffers no economic harm, the distributor or retailer cannot obtain recovery for the violation. See Hanover Shoe, Inc. v. United Shoe Machinery Corp., 392 U.S. 481 (1968); State of West Virginia v. Chas. Pfizer & Co., 440 F.2d 1079 (2d Cir.), cert. denied, 404 U.S. 871 (1971). If they did obtain a recovery, distributors and retailers could presumably pass along the savings to a "next best" class — the present purchasers of comparable products. Does the unwillingness to permit recovery in this situation affect your views on fluid recovery more generally?

Conversely, state attorneys general are often able to maintain *parens patriae* actions on behalf of their citizens that are victimized by a defendant's conduct. See In re Baldwin-United Corp., 770 F.2d 328 (2d Cir. 1985) (p. 401, *supra*); cf. *State of West Virginia*, 440 F.2d at 1089 (discussing theory but refusing to rely on it). Isn't recovery by a state attorney general a form of fluid recovery, in which the court delegates to the "next best" attorney general the task of distributing a settlement or judgment fund to individuals? Does the use of attorneys general in this way affect your views on fluid recovery more generally? Could the *parens patriae* idea be used as the foundation for a privatized model in which courts would enter contracts with private organizations that would agree, in return for a percentage of the recovery, to distribute the funds to deserving claimants? Cf. pp. 888-89, *supra* (discussing auctioning of small individual claims to single highest bidder).

3. Using Judicial Adjuncts to Assist in the Process of Declaring a Remedy

The declaration of a remedy is a function that is typically performed by the judge with respect to injunctive relief, and the jury with respect to monetary relief. When the case settles, the parties themselves "declare" the relief. In the prior two subsections, we saw that the declaration of relief can often be difficult, since the exact scope of appropriate relief cannot readily be determined. In the other Parts of this book, we saw that, when the person to whom a specific function has been assigned cannot capably perform it, an expanded exercise of judicial power — often by judicial adjuncts — helped to overcome the incapacity. To what extent might the use of judicial adjuncts help in the declaration phase of a complex case?

Special masters have long been used to assist in the declaration process in cases involving complex questions of accounting or assessment of damages in admiralty, patent, copyright, or trademark litigation. 9A Charles A. Wright & Arthur R. Miller, Federal Practice & Procedure § 2605 (1995). Such references are not automatic; as we saw in Chapter Eight, the usual rule is that the appointment of a master is "the exception and not the rule." F.R.Civ.P. 53(b); pp. 939-55, *supra*. In jury cases, this "exception" requirement is further supplemented by the requirement that the issues referred to the master must be "complicated." F.R.Civ.P. 53(b). In non-jury cases, the "exception" requirement is supplemented by the element that "some exceptional condition requires" the reference. Id. In 1966, however, Rule 53 was amended to make explicit the power to refer to masters in non-jury cases "matters of account and of difficult computations of damage" without the need to meet the "exceptional condition" requirement. Does this amendment suggest that references for "difficult computations of damage" should be easier to obtain in non-jury cases than it jury cases? Should the fact that the master's findings of fact are mere evidence for the jury to consider, while the master's report is binding on the judge in a non-jury action unless it is clearly erroneous, see F.R.Civ.P. 53(e)(1)-(3), influence the court's decision to order a reference?

Recall the use of the special masters in the declaration phase of the "trial by statistics" cases, Hilao v. Estate of Ferdinand Marcos, 103 F.3d 767 (9th Cir. 1996) and Cimino v. Raymark Industries, Inc., 751 F. Supp. 649 (E.D. Tex. 1990). (See pp. 1299-1310.) Were these appropriate cases for reference, given that both were tried to juries? Couldn't the court itself have performed the same function? Was there nonetheless an advantage in using a master, who would appear to a jury less authoritative than the court, who could help to preserve the court's impartiality, and who could free up the court to concentrate on larger issues of managing the litigation?

One of the more unusual uses of a master in the declaration phase of a case seeking damages occurred in the *Agent Orange* litigation. In a master-brokered settlement, the parties agreed to a lump-sum settlement without agreeing to specific allocations of damages to specific class members. The district court then referred to another special master the issue of determining an appropriate allocation and allocation mechanism for the fund. As it turned out, many class members disliked the allocations ordered by the district court, and no one adverse to these plaintiffs was willing to defend the district court's decision. As a result, the court of appeals requested the special master to defend the district court's distribution order, which was based on the master's recommendations, "essentially in the role of an amicus curiae." In re "Agent Orange" Product Liability Litigation, 818

F.2d 179, 180 (2d Cir. 1987), cert. denied, 487 U.S. 1234 (1988). Are the various roles of the special masters appropriate roles for a judicial adjunct, or does the use of masters in *Agent Orange* suggest that the court has strayed too far from its traditional adversarial role?

With respect to the declaration of injunctive relief, it might seem that the need for judicial adjuncts such as masters is less compelling; the court should be able to determine the appropriate terms of injunctive relief. Nonetheless, some courts have found various uses for masters in the declaration phase of difficult institutional reform litigation. Masters have been used to negotiate with the parties about the appropriate scope of the remedy. See Special Project, *The Remedial Process in Institutional Reform Litigation*, 78 Colum. L. Rev. 784, 809 (1978). They have been used to gather information from the community. Curtis J. Berger, *Away from the Court House and into the Field: The Odyssey of a Special Master*, 78 Colum. L. Rev. 707 (1978). They have also proposed to the court the terms of the injunction. Id.; Special Project, *supra*, at 805.

Aside from masters, courts have turned to others for assistance in the declaration of remedies. In some cases, the adjunct has been a receiver placed in charge of an institution. See Peretz v. Boston Housing Authority, 379 Mass. 703, 400 N.E.2d 1231 (1980). Sometimes the adjunct has acted more as an expert or advisor to the court. See Bradley v. Milliken, 402 F. Supp. 1096, 1104 (E.D. Mich. 1975) (commissioning three desegregation experts as officers of the court, but not masters), modified on other grounds, 540 F.2d 229 (6th Cir. 1976), *aff'd*, 433 U.S. 267 (1977). Courts need to be careful about their contacts with such receivers, experts, or consultants. For instance, in *Bradley*, the plaintiffs filed a motion to recuse the judge, partly because of his *ex parte* contacts with the experts. The Sixth Circuit refused to order recusal, but expressed concern about the judge's conduct:

> The plaintiffs also complain that Judge DeMascio's conduct violated Canon 3 A(4) of the Code of Judicial Conduct:
>
>> (4) A judge should accord to every person who is legally interested in a proceeding, or his lawyer, full right to be heard according to law, and, except as authorized by law, neither initiate nor consider *ex-parte* or other communications concerning a pending or impending proceeding. A judge, however, may obtain the advice of a disinterested expert on the law applicable to a proceeding before him if he gives notice to the parties of the person consulted and the substance of the advice, and affords the parties reasonable opportunity to respond. . . .
>
> [T]he plaintiffs argue [that] Judge DeMascio's use of experts violated Canon 3 A(4). By order of April 15, 1975, Judge DeMascio appointed three educators as experts to assist him in gathering background information, soliciting the views of community groups and educators, and evaluating the Educational Components of the Board's remedial plan. The plaintiffs do not question the court's authority to utilize experts. Rather, they complain the court's experts did not file reports of record and were never subject to cross-examination, but submitted their views *ex parte*.

We do not believe Judge DeMascio's use of experts, or his receipt through them of community and expert views on how best to approach the problems of desegregating Detroit schools, required recusal. We are concerned with the plaintiffs' charge that the reports of these experts were not placed in the record nor made available to the parties. Accordingly, we expressly direct that if any experts are employed to advise the district court on any further matters in this litigation, they shall prepare written reports, copies of which shall become part of the record and shall be made available to all parties or their attorneys.

Bradley v. Milliken, 620 F.2d 1143, 1157-58 (6th Cir.), cert. denied, 449 U.S. 870 (1980). See also *Peretz*, 400 N.E.2d at 1253 ("[W]e think it was understood, and was in fact provided in the consent decree itself (although not with entire clarity), that there could be private consultations between the judge and master.").

For an innovative article suggesting that (1) district courts should use "expert neutral judges" during the declaration process, (2) the judges that will hear the appeal should consult with the district court prior to the declaration of the remedy, and (3) the district court should be able to provide input to the appellate court after the case is on appeal, see Frank M. Coffin, *The Frontier of Remedies: A Call for Exploration*, 67 Cal. L. Rev. 983 (1979).

Are the uses of judicial adjuncts and the changes that it signals in traditional adversarial roles consistent with your view of the proper functioning of the judiciary? For a negative answer, see Donald L. Horowitz, *Decreeing Organizational Change: Judicial Supervision of Public Institutions*, 1983 Duke L.J. 1265, 1297-1302. For a more optimistic answer, see Berger, *supra*, 78 Colum. L. Rev. 707.

4. Methods of Declaring the Remedy that Reduce Intransigence

The traditional adversarial approach assumes that the judge or jury will declare the remedy in an authoritative fashion. In many complex cases, especially in institutional reform cases in which state institutions are subject to the scrutiny of a federal court, an authoritative pronouncement is often counterproductive, and can breed hostility among the very people (whether plaintiffs, defendants, or both) on whom the court must depend for support in the implementation of the remedy. Although we discuss the problem of intransigence in implementation in the following section, it is worthwhile to note that the way in which a court declares the remedy can sometimes influence the way in which that remedy is accepted. As Professor Fiss's quote with which we opened this chapter suggested, judges are typically savvy persons with an acute political sense and a sensitivity to the way in which to best effectuate the remedy.

Aside from the traditional authoritative pronouncement, the court has a number of alternative method to declare the remedy. The one most closely aligned with the traditional approach is to ask the parties for their input and suggestions before declaring the remedy. See Special Project, *The Remedial Process in Institutional Reform Litigation*, 78 Colum. L. Rev. 784, 802-05 (1978). A second possibility is "remedial abstention," in which the court directs the defendant to suggest the proper remedy and then evaluates those proposals. "Remedial abstention has been most important in reapportionment cases, in which relief is sometimes initially denied to permit purely legislative correction," Special Project, *supra*, at 797, but it has also been used in desegregation and prison reform litigation. The court may provide the defendant some guidelines to assist in this process. Id. at 798. A third alternative approach, mentioned by Professor Chayes (p. 64, *supra*), is to require the parties to negotiate over the terms of the remedy. See Morales v. Turman, 383 F. Supp. 53, 126 (E.D. Tex. 1974), *rev'd* on other grounds, 535 F.2d 864 (5th Cir. 1976), *rev'd* and remanded, 430 U.S. 322 (1977). A fourth approach, which we examined in the last subsection, is to use judicial adjuncts to assist in the remedial process, although this approach does not typically create less friction than a straight judicial declaration. Finally, a court can itself appear at various community forums to hear different opinions and to garner support for the proposed remedy. See Bradley v. Milliken, 620 F.2d 1143, 1157 (6th Cir.), cert. denied, 449 U.S. 870 (1980); Jay Tidmarsh, Mass Tort Settlement Class Actions 85 (1998) (describing television and personal appearances of judge to answer questions of class members concerning settlement proposal).

Are these alternative methods of attempting to declare a remedy consistent with the judicial role? See *Bradley*, 620 F.2d at 1157 (refusing to order recusal of judge for his appearance at community forums; noting that "[a]lthough perhaps a bit unorthodox, Judge DeMascio's actions appear to us to have been judicial activities"). We continue to examine this question as we turn to problems in the implementation phase.

B. IMPLEMENTING THE REMEDY

In adversarial litigation, the court declares a simple remedy with which it is easy to comply. Implementation of this remedy is essentially the parties' responsibility. Although courts have available writs of execution and contempt powers to "nudge" the recalcitrant party, these powers often prove unnecessary.

Complex litigation, in contrast, often involves one of two implementation difficulties that contrast sharply with the traditional model. In the first place, the expectations or rights under the remedy that has been declared may not be clearly defined, and the implementation process requires further work to deliver the general declaration to the deserving claimants. (This first difficulty could also be viewed as a problem in the declaration process, but we treat it as an implementation problem. It makes no analytical difference if it is treated the other way.) Second, the parties may in good faith simply be unable to comply with the ordered remedy. Often the reason for this inability to comply is that the relevant parties may be under legal constraints that make full implementation impossible. In other cases, the parties depend for the ultimate power to implement the remedy on other persons that refuse to assist in the process of implementing the remedy, and indeed may even be attempting to block the implementation of the remedy.

As in the last section, we examine these issues in the context of both injunctive and monetary relief, then examine the ways in which an expansive role for judicial adjuncts might assist the implementation process, and finally examine the powers of the court to overcome the intransigence of nonparties who threaten to undermine the implementation of the remedy.

1. Injunctive Relief

MISSOURI v. JENKINS

495 U.S. 33 (1990)

■ JUSTICE WHITE delivered the opinion of the Court.

The United States District Court for the Western District of Missouri imposed an increase in the property taxes levied by the Kansas City, Missouri, School District (KCMSD) to ensure funding for the desegregation of KCMSD's public schools. We granted certiorari to consider the State of Missouri's argument that the District Court lacked the power to raise local property taxes. For the reasons given below, we hold that the District Court abused its discretion in imposing the tax increase. We also hold, however, that the modifications of the District Court's order made by the Court of Appeals do satisfy equitable and constitutional principles governing the District Court's power.

I

In 1977, KCMSD and a group of KCMSD students filed a complaint alleging that the State of Missouri and surrounding school districts had operated a segregated public school system in the Kansas City metropolitan area. The District Court realigned KCMSD as a party defendant, and KCMSD filed a cross-claim against the State, seeking indemnification for any liability that might be imposed on KCMSD for intradistrict segregation. After a lengthy trial, the District Court found that KCMSD and the State had operated a segregated school system within the KCMSD.[3]

The District Court thereafter issued an order detailing the remedies necessary to eliminate the vestiges of segregation and the financing necessary to implement those remedies. The District Court originally estimated the total cost of the desegregation remedy to be almost $88 million over three years, of which it expected the State to pay $67,592,072 and KCMSD to pay $20,140,472. The court concluded, however, that several

---

3. The District Court also found that none of the alleged discriminatory actions had resulted in lingering interdistrict effects and so dismissed the suburban school districts and denied interdistrict relief.

provisions of Missouri law would prevent KCMSD from being able to pay its share of the obligation. The Missouri Constitution limits local property taxes to $1.25 per $100 of assessed valuation unless a majority of the voters in the district approve a higher levy, up to $3.25 per $100; the levy may be raised above $3.25 per $100 only if two-thirds of the voters agree. Mo. Const., Art. X, §§ 11(b), (c). The "Hancock Amendment" requires property tax rates to be rolled back when property is assessed at a higher valuation to ensure that taxes will not be increased solely as a result of reassessments. Mo. Const., Art. X, § 22(a); Mo.Rev.Stat. § 137.073.2 (1986). The Hancock Amendment thus prevents KCMSD from obtaining any revenue increase as a result of increases in the assessed valuation of real property. "Proposition C" allocates one cent of every dollar raised by the state sales tax to a schools trust fund and requires school districts to reduce property taxes by an amount equal to 50% of the previous year's sales tax receipts in the district. Mo.Rev.Stat. § 164.013.1 (Supp.1988). However, the trust fund is allocated according to a formula that does not compensate KCMSD for the amount lost in property tax revenues, and the effect of Proposition C is to divert nearly half of the sales taxes collected in KCMSD to other parts of the State.

The District Court believed that it had the power to order a tax increase to ensure adequate funding of the desegregation plan, but it hesitated to take this step. It chose instead to enjoin the effect of the Proposition C rollback to allow KCMSD to raise an additional $4 million for the coming fiscal year. The court ordered KCMSD to submit to the voters a proposal for an increase in taxes sufficient to pay for its share of the desegregation remedy in following years.

[In further proceedings, the court of appeals ordered that the State and KCMSD split the costs of the plan equally, and the district court] approved KCMSD's proposal to operate six magnet schools during the 1986-1987 school year. The court again faced the problem of funding, for KCMSD's efforts to persuade the voters to approve a tax increase had failed, as had its efforts to seek funds from the Kansas City Council and the state legislature. Again hesitating to impose a tax increase itself, the court continued its injunction against the Proposition C rollback to enable KCMSD to raise an additional $6.5 million.

In November 1986, the District Court endorsed a marked expansion of the magnet school program. It adopted in substance a KCMSD proposal that every high school, every middle school, and half of the elementary schools in KCMSD become magnet schools by the 1991-1992 school year. It also approved the $142,736,025 budget proposed by KCMSD for implementation of the magnet school plan, as well as the expenditure of $52,858,301 for additional capital improvements....

The District Court then held that the State and KCMSD were 75% and 25% at fault, respectively, and ordered them to share the cost of the desegregation remedy in that proportion. To ensure complete funding of the remedy, the court also held the two tortfeasors jointly and severally liable for the cost of the plan.

Three months later, the District Court adopted a plan requiring $187,450,334 in further capital improvements. By then it was clear that

KCMSD would lack the resources to pay for its 25% share of the desegregation cost. KCMSD requested that the District Court order the State to pay for any amount that KCMSD could not meet. The District Court declined to impose a greater share of the cost on the State, but it accepted that KCMSD had "exhausted all available means of raising additional revenue." Finding itself with "no choice but to exercise its broad equitable powers and enter a judgment that will enable the KCMSD to raise its share of the cost of the plan," ibid., and believing that the "United States Supreme Court has stated that a tax may be increased if 'necessary to raise funds adequate to . . . operate and maintain without racial discrimination a public school system,'" (quoting Griffin v. Prince Edward County School Bd., 377 U.S. 218, 233 (1964)), the court ordered the KCMSD property tax levy raised from $2.05 to $4.00 per $100 of assessed valuation through the 1991-1992 fiscal year. KCMSD was also directed to issue $150 million in capital improvement bonds. A subsequent order directed that the revenues generated by the property tax increase be used to retire the capital improvement bonds.

The State appealed, challenging the scope of the desegregation remedy, the allocation of the cost between the State and KCMSD, and the tax increase. [The court of appeals upheld the scope of the desegregation order and the allocation of costs.]

Turning to the property tax increase, the Court of Appeals rejected the State's argument that a federal court lacks the judicial power to order a tax increase. . . .

Although the Court of Appeals thus "affirm[ed] the actions that the [District] [C]ourt has taken to this point," it agreed with the State that principles of federal/state comity required the District Court to use "minimally obtrusive methods to remedy constitutional violations." The Court of Appeals thus required that in the future, the District Court should not set the property tax rate itself but should authorize KCMSD to submit a levy to the state tax collection authorities and should enjoin the operation of state laws hindering KCMSD from adequately funding the remedy. The Court of Appeals reasoned that permitting the school board to set the levy itself would minimize disruption of state laws and processes and would ensure maximum consideration of the views of state and local officials. . . .

II

[The Court first held that it had jurisdiction to entertain the appeal.]

III

We turn to the tax increase imposed by the District Court. The State urges us to hold that the tax increase violated Article III, the Tenth Amendment, and principles of federal/state comity. We find it unnecessary to reach the difficult constitutional issues, for we agree with the State that the tax increase contravened the principles of comity that must govern the exercise of the District Court's equitable discretion in this area.

Appeals held that the District Court in the future should authorize KCMSD to submit a levy to the state tax collection authorities adequate to fund its budget and should enjoin the operation of state laws that would limit or reduce the levy below that amount.

The State argues that the funding ordered by the District Court violates principles of equity and comity because the remedial order itself was excessive. As the State puts it, "[t]he only reason that the court below needed to consider an unprecedented tax increase was the equally unprecedented cost of its remedial programs." We think this argument aims at the scope of the remedy rather than the manner in which the remedy is to be funded and thus falls outside our limited grant of certiorari in this case. As we denied certiorari on the first question presented by the State's petition, which did challenge the scope of the remedial order, we must resist the State's efforts to argue that point now. We accept, without approving or disapproving, the Court of Appeals' conclusion that the District Court's remedy was proper. . . .

The State has argued here that the District Court, having found the State and KCMSD jointly and severally liable, should have allowed any monetary obligations that KCMSD could not meet to fall on the State rather than interfere with state law to permit KCMSD to meet them. Under the circumstances of this case, we cannot say it was an abuse of discretion for the District Court to rule that KCMSD should be responsible for funding its share of the remedy. The State strenuously opposed efforts by respondents to make it responsible for the cost of implementing the order and had secured a reversal of the District Court's earlier decision placing on it all of the cost of substantial portions of the order. The District Court declined to require the State to pay for KCMSD's obligations because it believed that the Court of Appeals had ordered it to allocate the costs between the two governmental entities. Furthermore, if the District Court had chosen the route now suggested by the State, implementation of the remedial order might have been delayed if the State resisted efforts by KCMSD to obtain contribution.

It is true that in *Milliken v. Bradley*, 433 U.S., at 291, we stated that the enforcement of a money judgment against the State did not violate principles of federalism because "[t]he District Court . . . neither attempted to restructure local governmental entities nor . . . mandat[ed] a particular method or structure of state or local financing." But we did not there state that a district court could never set aside state laws preventing local governments from raising funds sufficient to satisfy their constitutional obligations just because those funds could also be obtained from the States. To the contrary, 42 U.S.C. § 1983, on which respondents' complaint is based, is authority enough to require each tortfeasor to pay its share of the cost of the remedy if it can, and apportionment of the cost is part of the equitable power of the District Court. Cf. *Milliken v. Bradley*, supra, at 289-290.

We turn to the constitutional issues. The modifications ordered by the Court of Appeals cannot be assailed as invalid under the Tenth Amendment. "The Tenth Amendment's reservation of nondelegated powers to the States is not implicated by a federal-court judgment enforcing the express

It is accepted by all the parties, as it was by the courts below, that the imposition of a tax increase by a federal court was an extraordinary event. In assuming for itself the fundamental and delicate power of taxation the District Court not only intruded on local authority but circumvented it altogether. Before taking such a drastic step the District Court was obliged to assure itself that no permissible alternative would have accomplished the required task. We have emphasized that although the "remedial powers of an equity court must be adequate to the task, . . . they are not unlimited," Whitcomb v. Chavis, 403 U.S. 124, 161 (1971), and one of the most important considerations governing the exercise of equitable power is a proper respect for the integrity and function of local government institutions. Especially is this true where, as here, those institutions are ready, willing, and — but for the operation of state law curtailing their powers — able to remedy the deprivation of constitutional rights themselves.

The District Court believed that it had no alternative to imposing a tax increase. But there was an alternative, the very one outlined by the Court of Appeals: it could have authorized or required KCMSD to levy property taxes at a rate adequate to fund the desegregation remedy and could have enjoined the operation of state laws that would have prevented KCMSD from exercising this power. The difference between the two approaches is far more than a matter of form. Authorizing and directing local government institutions to devise and implement remedies not only protects the function of those institutions but, to the extent possible, also places the responsibility for solutions to the problems of segregation upon those who have themselves created the problems.

As Brown v. Board of Education, 349 U.S. 294, 299 (1955), observed, local authorities have the "primary responsibility for elucidating, assessing, and solving" the problems of desegregation. See also Milliken v. Bradley, 433 U.S. 267, 281 (1977). This is true as well of the problems of financing desegregation, for no matter has been more consistently placed upon the shoulders of local government than that of financing public schools. As was said in another context, "[t]he very complexity of the problems of financing and managing a . . . public school system suggests that 'there will be more than one constitutionally permissible method of solving them,' and that . . . 'the legislature's efforts to tackle the problems' should be entitled to respect." San Antonio Independent School District v. Rodriguez, 411 U.S. 1, 42 (1973) . . . . By no means should a district court grant local government *carte blanche*, cf. Swann v. Charlotte-Mecklenburg Bd. of Education, 402 U.S. 1 (1971), but local officials should at least have the opportunity to devise their own solutions to these problems. . . .

The District Court therefore abused its discretion in imposing the tax itself. The Court of Appeals should not have allowed the tax increase to stand and should have reversed the District Court in this respect. . . .

IV

We stand on different ground when we review the modifications to the District Court's order made by the Court of Appeals. . . . [T]he Court of prohibitions of unlawful state conduct enacted by the Fourteenth Amendment." 433 U.S., at 291. "The Fourteenth Amendment . . . was avowedly directed against the power of the States," Pennsylvania v. Union Gas Co., 491 U.S. 1, 42 (1989) (SCALIA, J., concurring in part and dissenting in part), and so permits a federal court to disestablish local government institutions that interfere with its commands. . . .

Finally, the State argues that an order to increase taxes cannot be sustained under the judicial power of Article III. Whatever the merits of this argument when applied to the District Court's own order increasing taxes, a point we have not reached, a court order directing a local government body to levy its own taxes is plainly a judicial act within the power of a federal court. We held as much in *Griffin v. Prince Edward County School Bd.*, 377 U.S., at 233, where we stated that a District Court, faced with a county's attempt to avoid desegregation of the public schools by refusing to operate those schools, could "require the [County] Supervisors to exercise the power that is theirs to levy taxes to raise funds adequate to reopen, operate, and maintain without racial discrimination a public school system . . . ." *Griffin* followed a long and venerable line of cases in which this Court held that federal courts could issue the writ of mandamus to compel local governmental bodies to levy taxes adequate to satisfy their debt obligations. See, *e.g.*, . . . Von Hoffman v. City of Quincy, 4 Wall. 535, 18 L.Ed. 403 (1867); Board of Commissioners of Knox County v. Aspinwall, 24 How. 376, 16 L.Ed. 735 (1861).[20]

The State maintains, however, that even under these cases, the federal judicial power can go no further than to require local governments to levy taxes as authorized under state law. In other words, the State argues that federal courts cannot set aside state-imposed limitations on local taxing authority because to do so is to do more than to require the local government "to exercise the power that is theirs." We disagree. This argument was rejected as early as *Von Hoffman v. City of Quincy, supra.* . . .

It is therefore clear that a local government with taxing authority may be ordered to levy taxes in excess of the limit set by state statute where there is reason based in the Constitution for not observing the statutory limitation. In *Von Hoffman*, the limitation was disregarded because of the

---

20. The old cases recognized two exceptions to this rule, neither of which is relevant here. First, it was held that federal courts could not by writ of mandamus compel state officers to release funds in the state treasury sufficient to satisfy state bond obligations. The Court viewed this attempt to employ the writ of mandamus as a ruse to avoid the Eleventh Amendment's bar against exercising federal jurisdiction over the State. . . . This holding has no application to this case, for the Eleventh Amendment does not bar federal courts from imposing on the States the costs of securing prospective compliance with a desegregation order, . . . and does not afford local school boards like KCMSD immunity from suit . . . . Second, it was held that the writ of mandamus would not lie to compel the collection of taxes when there was no person against whom the writ could operate. . . . This exception also has no application to this case, where there are state and local officials invested with authority to collect and disburse the property tax and where, as matters now stand, the District Court need only prevent those officials from applying state law that would interfere with the willing levy of property taxes by KCMSD.

Contract Clause. Here, the KCMSD may be ordered to levy taxes despite the statutory limitations on its authority in order to compel the discharge of an obligation imposed on KCMSD by the Fourteenth Amendment. To hold otherwise would fail to take account of the obligations of local governments, under the Supremacy Clause, to fulfill the requirements that the Constitution imposes on them. However wide the discretion of local authorities in fashioning desegregation remedies may be, "if a state-imposed limitation on a school authority's discretion operates to inhibit or obstruct the operation of a unitary school system or impede the disestablishing of a dual school system, it must fall; state policy must give way when it operates to hinder vindication of federal constitutional guarantees." North Carolina Bd. of Education v. Swann, 402 U.S. 43, 45 (1971). Even though a particular remedy may not be required in every case to vindicate constitutional guarantees, where (as here) it has been found that a particular remedy is required, the State cannot hinder the process by preventing a local government from implementing that remedy.

Accordingly, the judgment of the Court of Appeals is affirmed insofar as it required the District Court to modify its funding order and reversed insofar as it allowed the tax increase imposed by the District Court to stand. The case is remanded for further proceedings consistent with this opinion.

■ JUSTICE KENNEDY, with whom THE CHIEF JUSTICE, JUSTICE O'CONNOR, and JUSTICE SCALIA join, concurring in part and concurring in the judgment.

In agreement with the Court that we have jurisdiction to decide this case, I join Parts I and II of the opinion. I agree also that the District Court exceeded its authority by attempting to impose a tax. The Court is unanimous in its holding, that the Court of Appeals' judgment affirming "the actions that the [district] court has taken to this point," must be reversed. This is consistent with our precedents and the basic principles defining judicial power.

In my view, however, the Court transgresses these same principles when it goes further, much further, to embrace by broad dictum an expansion of power in the Federal Judiciary beyond all precedent. Today's casual embrace of taxation imposed by the unelected, life-tenured Federal Judiciary disregards fundamental precepts for the democratic control of public institutions. I cannot acquiesce in the majority's statements on this point, and should there arise an actual dispute over the collection of taxes as here contemplated in a case that is not, like this one, premature, we should not confirm the outcome of premises adopted with so little constitutional justification. The Court's statements, in my view, cannot be seen as necessary for its judgment, or as precedent for the future, and I cannot join Parts III and IV of the Court's opinion.

I . . .

By the time of the order at issue here, the District Court's remedies included some "$260 million in capital improvements and a magnet-school plan costing over $200 million." And the remedial orders grew more expensive as shortfalls in revenue became more severe. As the Eighth Circuit judges dissenting from denial of rehearing in banc put it: "The remedies ordered go far beyond anything previously seen in a school desegregation case. The sheer immensity of the programs encompassed by the district court's order — the large number of magnet schools and the quantity of capital renovations and new construction — are concededly without parallel in any other school district in the country."

The judicial taxation approved by the Eighth Circuit is also without parallel. Other Circuits that have faced funding problems arising from remedial decrees have concluded that, while courts have undoubted power to order that schools operate in compliance with the Constitution, the manner and methods of school financing are beyond federal judicial authority. . . .

Any purported distinction between direct imposition of a tax by the federal court and an order commanding the school district to impose the tax is but a convenient formalism where the court's action is predicated on elimination of state-law limitations on the school district's taxing authority. As the Court describes it, the local KCMSD possesses plenary taxing powers, which allow it to impose any tax it chooses if not "hinder[ed]" by the Missouri Constitution and state statutes. This puts the conclusion before the premise. Local government bodies in Missouri, as elsewhere, must derive their power from a sovereign, and that sovereign is the State of Missouri. . . .

II

Article III of the Constitution states that "[t]he judicial Power of the United States, shall be vested in one supreme Court, and in such inferior Courts as the Congress may from time to time ordain and establish." The description of the judicial power nowhere includes the word "tax" or anything that resembles it. This reflects the Framers' understanding that taxation was not a proper area for judicial involvement. "The judiciary . . . has no influence over either the sword or the purse, no direction either of the strength or of the wealth of the society, and can take no active resolution whatever." The Federalist No. 78, p. 523 (J. Cooke ed. 1961) (A. Hamilton). . . .

The nature of the District Court's order here reveals that it is not a proper exercise of the judicial power. The exercise of judicial power involves adjudication of controversies and imposition of burdens on those who are parties before the Court. The order at issue here is not of this character. It binds the broad class of all KCMSD taxpayers. It has the purpose and direct effect of extracting money from persons who have had no presence or representation in the suit. For this reason, the District Court's direct order imposing a tax was more than an abuse of discretion, for any attempt to collect the taxes from the citizens would have been a blatant denial of due process.

Taxation by a legislature raises no due process concerns, for the citizens' "rights are protected in the only way that they can be in a complex society, by their power, immediate or remote, over those who make the rule." . . . The citizens who are taxed are given notice and a hearing through their representatives, whose power is a direct manifestation of the citizens' consent. A true exercise of judicial power provides due process of another sort. Where money is extracted from parties by a court's judgment, the adjudication itself provides the notice and opportunity to be heard that due process demands before a citizen may be deprived of property.

The order here provides neither of these protections. . . . The taxes were imposed by a District Court that was not "representative" in any sense, and the individual citizens of the KCMSD whose property (they later learned) was at stake were neither served with process nor heard in court. The method of taxation endorsed by today's dicta suffers the same flaw, for a district court order that overrides the citizens' state-law protection against taxation without referendum approval can in no sense provide representational due process. No one suggests the KCMSD taxpayers are parties. . . .

The confinement of taxation to the legislative branches, both in our Federal and State Governments, was not random. It reflected our ideal that the power of taxation must be under the control of those who are taxed. This truth animated all our colonial and revolutionary history. . . .

The operation of tax systems is among the most difficult aspects of public administration. It is not a function the Judiciary as an institution is designed to exercise. Unlike legislative bodies, which may hold hearings on how best to raise revenues, all subject to the views of constituents to whom the Legislature is accountable, the Judiciary must grope ahead with only the assistance of the parties, or perhaps random *amici curiae*. Those hearings would be without principled direction, for there exists no body of juridical axioms by which to guide or review them. On this questionable basis, the Court today would give authority for decisions that affect the life plans of local citizens, the revenue available for competing public needs, and the health of the local economy.

Day-to-day administration of the tax must be accomplished by judicial trial and error, requisitioning the staff of the existing tax authority, or the hiring of a staff under the direction of the judge. The District Court orders in this case suggest the pitfalls of the first course. See App. to Pet. for Cert. 55a (correcting order for assessment of penalties for nonpayment that "mistakenly" assessed penalties on an extra tax year) . . . . Forcing citizens to make financial decisions in fear of the fledgling judicial tax collector's next misstep must detract from the dignity and independence of the federal courts.

The function of hiring and supervising a staff for what is essentially a political function has other complications. As part of its remedial order, for example, the District Court ordered the hiring of a "public information specialist," at a cost of $30,000. The purpose of the position was to "solicit community support and involvement" in the District Court's desegregation plan. This type of order raises a substantial question whether a district court may extract taxes from citizens who have no right of representation

and then use the funds for expression with which the citizens may disagree.
. . .

At bottom, today's discussion seems motivated by the fear that failure to endorse judicial taxation power might in some extreme circumstance leave a court unable to remedy a constitutional violation. . . . I do not think this possibility is in reality a significant one. More important, this possibility is nothing more or less than the necessary consequence of any limit on judicial power. If, however, judicial discretion is to provide the sole limit on judicial remedies, that discretion must counsel restraint. Ill-considered entry into the volatile field of taxation is a step that may place at risk the legitimacy that justifies judicial independence. . . .

IV . . .

James Madison observed: "Justice is the end of government. It is the end of civil society. It ever has been, and ever will be pursued, until it be obtained, or until liberty be lost in the pursuit." The Federalist, No. 51, p. 352 (J. Cooke ed. 1961). In pursuing the demand of justice for racial equality, I fear that the Court today loses sight of other basic political liberties guaranteed by our constitutional system, liberties that can coexist with a proper exercise of judicial remedial powers adequate to correct constitutional violations.

Notes and Questions

1. The Court's 1990 decision in *Missouri v. Jenkins* authorizing the district court to enjoin the enforcement of Missouri law has to some degree been superseded by the Court's 1995 holding that the remedial measures that the district court was attempting to fund exceeded the permissible scope of the remedy (see p. 1392, *supra*). Nonetheless, the 1990 decision in *Missouri v. Jenkins* is significant, for it may well be that, in some cases, a defendant institution cannot fund the remedy required under the rightful position principle. The court must then face the question about the extent of its powers to implement the remedy.

2. The traditional power of the court to deal with the problem of a party that failed to implement an injunctive decree was contempt. See International Union, United Mine Workers of America v. Bagwell, 512 U.S. 821 (1994). When the party itself holds the key to implementing the remedy, contempt can often be effective, although sometimes the contempt sanction needs to be significant to make an institution act. See Spallone v. United States, 493 U.S. 265 (1990). In a remedially complex case like *Missouri v. Jenkins*, however, holding the school district in contempt is unlikely to accomplish very much, since they were perfectly willing, but legally unable, to implement the remedy ordered by the court.

In this situation, how much power should a court have? Does your answer depend on whether the court is a state court as opposed to a federal court? On whether the defendant is a private actor or a public institution? On whether the defendant is attempting to act in good faith, or instead is intransigent? On whether the court is seeking to exercise powers (or at least remove the operation of legal constraints) that are typically performed by other branches of government?

3. It is difficult to generalize about the exact scope of a court's power to assure adequate implementation of a remedy; it may depend on the facts and the fine balance of factors present in each case. For instance, in some cases, courts have placed an institution into receivership; in others, courts have ordered the marshals to assure that adequate compliance will occur. One way to think more generally about the limits of a court's power is to use the theory of remedial complexity. Under this theory, remedial complexity can occur when the parties are unable to fulfill their obligations under adversarial system to implement the remedy. A prevailing party that cannot receive the remedy to which he or she is entitled obtains a hollow victory. The defendant has not been forced to meet its obligations, nor has the plaintiff been made whole. Regardless of whether the enforcement of obligations or the rightful position principle is the principle that inheres in the form of adjudication, doesn't it seem that the form of adjudication requires that the court have some power to remove the stumbling block to implementation? Indeed, isn't that the reason that courts claim the power to find parties in contempt? If some judicial power to overcome difficulties in implementation exists in the nature of adjudication, is it also true that this power is grounded in the due process clause's guarantee of rational adjudication? If this line of analysis is accurate, then how would this due process power compare to the separation of powers and federalism concerns — which also have a constitutional foundation — in a case like *Missouri v. Jenkins*? See Donald L. Horowitz, *Decreeing Organizational Change: Judicial Supervision of Public Institutions*, 1983 Duke L.J. 1265. If the analysis cannot provide an answer to this very practical question, how helpful is it?

4. Of course, the existence of a power to remove stumbling blocks to the implementation of a decree does not mean that the court must use the power. There are all sorts of reasons to hold at least some of the power in reserve. As a pragmatic matter, isn't the majority in *Missouri v. Jenkins* right that the court should apply less power rather than more as long as it appears that less power will do the job? Removing the taxation stumbling block, rather than ordering a tax itself, is more than a mere formalism, isn't it? As a matter of sound judicial administration, as well as a matter of entrusting those with the expertise and the accountability to try to do the job in the first instance, wouldn't this be the appropriate course (assuming that the remedy was necessary and that the court's power was not diminished by separation of powers and federalism concerns)?

5. Contempt and decrees like the one in *Missouri v. Jenkins* are classic examples of "command and control" responses. Traditionally, this has been how the adversarial system, and the judge within that system, operate. But this traditional approach might not always be the best way to overcome implementation problems. For instance, a judge may attempt to enter into negotiations with the parties, or perhaps with legislators or others that hold the key to implementation, in order to obtain voluntary implementation. Likewise, the judge may go out into the community to garner political or community support for her desired remedy. Do these departures from the judge's traditionally neutral and passive role seem appropriate?

6. There is a wealth of literature — ranging from the anecdotal to the highly theoretical — on the problems of implementing consent decrees. For a small sampling, see Owen M. Fiss & Doug Rendleman, Injunctions 1-58, 528-827

(2d ed. 1984); Owen M. Fiss, The Civil Rights Injunction (1978); Donald L. Horowitz, The Courts and Social Policy (1977); Barry Friedman, *When Rights Encounter Reality: Enforcing Federal Remedies*, 65 S. Cal. L. Rev. 735 (1992); Susan P. Sturm, *A Normative Theory of Public Law Remedies*, 79 Geo. L.J. 1355 (1991); Note, *Implementation Problems in Institutional Reform Litigation*, 91 Harv. L. Rev. 428 (1977). See generally Fiss & Rendleman, *supra*, at 827-30 (bibliography of literature on structural injunctions).

2. Monetary Relief

In routine litigation, the jury or judge determines the exact amount of damages that each plaintiff deserves, or the parties negotiate the exact amount that each plaintiff is to receive. In some complex cases, however, the parties negotiate a lump-sum (or global) settlement without deciding exactly which plaintiffs should get a recovery, and exactly how much they should get. When this occurs, what should the court's role be?

IN RE COMBUSTION, INC.

978 F. Supp. 673 (W.D. La. 1997)

■ HAIK, District Judge. [Plaintiffs worked at or lived near a waste oil recycling site that operated for 18 years. Eventually significant contamination was discovered on and around the site. Individual tort and environmental cases were commenced in Louisiana state court. The state court certified the case as a class action. Subsequently, the case was removed to federal court, which maintained the case as a class action. Ultimately the case contained more than 10,000 plaintiffs and 450 defendants. After 11 years of litigation, the case settled against all but one defendant for more than $20 million. The settlement did not, however, provide a method of allocating the settlement among plaintiffs. After the court preliminarily approved the settlement as fair, adequate, and reasonable, it ordered a special master to establish specific criteria for distributing the settlement to class members. The master submitted a report recommending a distribution plan for the 10,000 claimants.]

On August 15 and 18, 19 and 22, 1997, this Court conducted a hearing ("Hearing") that represented the culmination of more than five month's work by the Special Master and his staff, the Plaintiff Steering Committee (PSC), and this Court toward the ultimate goal of disbursing funds to the Claimants. The purpose of the Hearing was to consider the recommendations of the Special Master and the Court-appointed-disbursing-agent, ("CADA"), regarding the allocation process and Claimant allocation schedule, to consider individual objections, and in general, to clear the last major hurdle in the long-awaited disbursement of funds.

For the reasons stated below, the Court adopts the Report of the Special Master RE: Combustion Litigation Claims Allocation Methodology of June

26, 1997 as amended July 3, 1997, ("Report I"), the Special Master's Report Regarding Prehearing Conferences, ("Report II"), and the amended Claimant allocation schedule submitted under seal as CADA # 3.

Each Claimant who elected to maintain his objection after consideration by the Special Master and then by the Court at the Hearing was issued an individual Final Judgment, entered by the Clerk of Court at that time. By the Final Judgment issued in conjunction with this Ruling, the Court dismisses all objections by Claimants who timely filed but failed to appear at both the Special Master's conferences and before the Court at the Hearing, by claimants who filed timely objections and appeared before the Court but did not show just cause for failing to follow the Special Master's protocol and failing to appear at the Special Master's conferences, by Claimants who maintained their objections after the Special Master's conferences but who failed to appear at the Hearing, and by Claimants who failed to timely object but who appeared at the Hearing and did not show just cause for such derelict behavior. Finally, the Court dismisses all other claims asserted by Class members who appeared at the Hearing.

Background

The partial distribution process began in March of this year when the Court ordered the Special Master to write and submit a report "as to the nature and amount of any and all maximum reserves to be established in order to determine the amount of the Claimants' Fund available for partial distribution." The Court also ordered that notice be sent to the Claimants regarding the report and that a hearing be set for April 18, 1997 to consider the recommendations of the Special Master.

After the April 18, 1997 evidentiary hearing, the Court issued extensive reasons adopting the Special Master's report and ordering him to proceed with his work toward disbursement.

Accordingly, the Special Master enlisted a staff of attorneys and a medical expert board certified in pathology and internal medicine to assist evaluating all the reports of the medical and toxological experts filed in this case, and in reviewing each Claimant's file, including all medical records and property claims. Only after an exhaustive review of the information available to him did the Special Master recommend to the Court a methodology upon which individual allocations were based and a schedule of the individual allocation for each Claimant. See Report I. Report I was amended by Motion of July 3, 1997 because of clerical error, but the amendment did not affect the allocation schedule. The Court gave preliminarily approval to Report I by Order, June 25, 1997, (filed June 26, 1997). The allocation schedule was filed under seal.

Methodology

The cornerstones of the Special Master's methodology were exposure and medical problems. Using expert reports and the state court's geographical class definition, the Special Master determined that the site had no impact on people living beyond 3 miles from a center point lying between two portions of the site. Thus, personal injury recovery was limited exclusively to Claimants who lived, worked, or attended school within the 3 mile radius. Enhancement factors were proximity, duration, and degree of lethal activity at the site during the Claimant's time within the creditable radius. Once a Claimant's exposure points were calculated, each point was valued at $3.00, with the product yielding a total exposure award.

To this award was added the compensation for medical problems determined by the medical expert to be associated with the site. The expert evaluated and classified each Claimant's medical problem by studying the symptoms, the age of the Claimant, and the date of diagnosis. Enhancing factors included the nature and severity of the condition, the probability of a causal link to the site, the relationship of the medical claims to each other, and the effect on the life of the Claimant. Categories A, B, C, and D classified diseases or clinical courses according to severity from "unusual or unexpected major diseases and/or clinical courses" to "chronic effects to include birth defects and deformities." Other categories were used simply as a formality, but only these four classifications earned dollar credits.

The maximum awards for these four categories ranged from $1,000,000 to $15,000. After it was determined that a claimant belonged in category A, for example, that Claimant's maximum possible medical award was tapered to fit his actual circumstance.

First, the Special Master set up four "rejection of medical claim" categories. Medical claims were not allowed for Claimants who were diagnosed prior to January 1, 1968, or who moved from the site prior to January 1, 1968, or who were diagnosed after moving outside the 3 mile radius.

Causation was factored into the medical award for the claims that survived the rejection threshold. The actual medical award was the product of the maximum dollar amount for that Claimant's illness category and the ratio of that Claimant's actual exposure points to his maximum possible exposure points calculated as if he had lived at the site throughout all relevant time beginning with his date of birth. The sum of the medical award and the exposure point award was each Claimant's personal injury allocation.

Minimum compensation awards ranging from $250-$20,000 were allotted to Claimants whose exposure points fell into one of six categories but whose corresponding total allocation was lower than the corresponding minimum amount set by the Special Master. As a baseline rule, an allocation of $250 was allotted to the Claimants who lived outside the three mile radius and never attended school or worked within the radius and who had no other creditable exposure or property damage but who participated in the Class action as instructed by the many newsletters and legal notices.

Property damage was determined in increments of one-quarter mile from the site up to one mile from the site. The dollar amount was based on the Assessor's rolls for Claimants who owned the property when the suit was filed in July 1986. Reimbursement ranged from 100% to 25% of "actual value," calculated to be greater [than] the assessed value by the factor of ten.

Other categories were compensated. Business losses were considered on a case by case basis because of the relatively few claims of this nature. Compensation to class representatives, bellwether plaintiffs, and other claimants who participated in depositions, medical examinations, and generally contributed to the development of the case was awarded because of the extra time and effort and work of these Claimants during the course of the law suit.

In addition to individual awards to the Claimants, the Special Master also recommended establishing a medical monitoring fund for annual medical check-ups, including blood work, for five years free of charge to the Class members. He recommended $1.5 million for this service. This service had been requested by claimants in letters to the Court in conjunction with the April 18, 1997 hearing. Finally, the Special Master reported the intervention by the State of Louisiana asserting liens for recovery of medical and related expenses incurred by the State hospital facilities.

Protocol

On June 26, 1997, the Court gave preliminary approval to Report I and allocation schedule and ordered a hearing pursuant to Federal Rule of Civil Procedure, (FRCP), 23(e). The individual allocation letters and the Important Notice of Hearing were mailed to each Claimant beginning June 26, 1997. Incorporated in the Important Notice of Hearing was the procedure that dissatisfied Claimants were ordered to follow to object to their allocations. The notice also included the methodology to be used by the Special Master and his staff to review each objection. The Report of the Special Master was made available for inspection at the Special Master's office and the Clerk of Court in Livingston Parish, and for inspection and duplication at the Joint Document Depository.

Each objector was instructed to file by hand, U.S. mail, or fax his written objection by midnight July 21, 1997, an equitable extension to the FRCP 53(d)(2) ten-day deadline. Objectors were expressly instructed that they "must respond [to any communication from the Special Master] as directed . . ." regarding their objection. And "[if the Claimant fails] to comply with any of the above requirements, [the Claimant's] objection will not be considered and will be overruled by the Court."

Approximately 1600 objections were received timely. Each objector's file was studied and re-evaluated. The Special Master scheduled individual appointments for every objector and notified each one of the appointment in writing and by phone. Each objector was encouraged to submit additional records in support of his objection even though the Court-ordered deadline for supplementing records was November 15, 1996.

For eleven days, beginning July 29 through August 12, 1997, the Special Master and his staff held individual conferences with each objector who appeared in person, beginning at 8:00 a.m. and continuing until 9:00 or 10:00 p.m., in an effort to satisfy each Claimant's concerns. The court-appointed medical expert was available at all times, either by phone and fax or personally, to evaluate additional medical records submitted by the objectors. All parties were placed under oath, and transcriptions of all conferences with the Special Master were filed into the record under seal at the Hearing.

More than $1 million dollars in adjustments were made as a result of the conferences. Claimants who were satisfied with the adjustments signed written statements withdrawing their objections. Claimants who maintained their objections were scheduled to appear at the Hearing and encouraged to bring additional documentation to support their positions.

On August 14, the Special Master presented to the Court the Report II along with the consultation reports of the Court-appointed physician. The Special Master also presented an amended allocation schedule incorporating the adjustments resulting from the prehearing conferences.

Court Hearing

Claimant's who maintained their objections, including several who received upward adjustments but wished to present their case in Court, appeared at the Hearing. For each objection presented, the Court read and reviewed that objector's complete file, the transcript of his conference with the Special Master, and an additional evaluation of the claimant's medical records provided by the court-appointed physician. The objector was given another opportunity to present to the Court additional evidence not presented to the Special Master.

As each Claimant appeared and after consideration of additional evidence introduced to the Court by the Claimant, the Special Master presented his revised recommendation. The Court then ruled on each objection from the bench. Those objectors who maintained their objections after the ruling by the Court were issued Final Judgments pursuant to FRCP 54(b). The individual Judgments were entered by the Clerk of Court on the dates they were issued.

In addition, Claimants who had not complied with the objection process but appeared at the Hearing and presented to the Court just cause for not complying with the Special Master's protocol were allowed to present their objections to the Special Master or an attorney on his staff and proceed through the same process at that time. The Court was also provided complete files for these claimants. Those Claimants who did not withdraw their objections after meeting with the Special Master and appearing before the Court were issued Final Judgments.

Claimants who failed to show just cause for not following the Special Master's objection protocol were dismissed with prejudice as were persons who appeared but who had not filed proof of claim forms, a matter already concluded by the Court in September 26-29, 1995.

A total of $1.6 million in adjustments was made as a result of this extraordinary effort by the Special Master and his staff and by the Claimants. These adjustments reflect errors in data entry as well as additional credit for new medical records indicating a more serious category of disease than previously shown in the Claimant's file. After considering almost 1,800 objections, the Court issued only sixty-three (63) Final Judgments, less than 4% of the original number [of objections] filed.

Analysis

A district court shall accept the report of a master unless clearly erroneous. F.R.C.P. 53(e)(2). This Court finds no clear error in either of the reports submitted by the Special Master.

As repeatedly stressed by the Special Master in the conferences and in Court, the thesis of his methodology was fairness and parity to the Class as a whole, "an imperative consideration in a case of this kind." The Court whole-heartedly agrees and applauds the tireless efforts of the Special Master and his staff for holding firm to the equity touchstone of the distribution model and for taking the time to explain the methodology to every single objector who attended a conference.

The Court now focuses on several key findings made by the Special Master, as these determinations form the cornerstones of the Special Master's methodology. First is his determination that claims recovery should be limited to a radius of 3 miles from the site. This conclusion was based on his knowledge of the case through the tens if not several hundred settlement conferences he conducted, through the exhaustive review he made of the reports of the plaintiffs' and defendants' medical and toxicological experts, and through the extensive consultations he had with the court-appointed physician.

Further, the Court has not received credible evidence to the contrary. The class territory was initially defined to extend to 2.5 miles from the center of the site, though on remand the state court judge included the entire Parish of Livingston. This original effort coupled with the Special Master's experience led him to conclude that the impact of the site beyond 3 miles was *de minimis*, except possibly the fear and fright of harmful effects from the site.

However, in keeping with equitable considerations, the Special Master set a minimum award of $250 for Class member who filed a valid proof of claim but who had no creditable exposure within the 3 mile radius. The purpose of this award was to account for considerations such as inconvenience, fear, fright, and medical conditions of these Claimants.

The Court will not repeat the lengthy analysis on causation set out in the Ruling of June 4, 1997, except to state that establishing a causal link between the chemicals at the site and the various personal injury claims alleged by Class members was the acknowledged Achilles Heel of the Plaintiffs' case. Defendants' experts concluded that harmful exposure, if any, expended only a matter of yards from the site. At least one site worker testified at the August 15 hearing that the extent of his medical problems was a collapsed lung, determined not to be related to chemicals at the site. The Court finds no clear error with the 3-mile radius determination or with the $250 minimum award for Claimant's having no other creditable points.

Next, the Special Master credited only residency, employment, and schooling within the three mile radius and did not allow double recovery.

Notably omitted were those claims based on time spent hunting, fishing, and otherwise visiting within the creditable radius. The Special Master found that the transient nature of these types of visits created too much variation and uncertainty as to sufficiency of damaging exposure. The Court finds no clear error in this determination.

The Special Master also found that no credit would be given for lost wages or medical expenses. This latter decision was based on the extreme subjectivity and difficulty with proof that chemical exposure caused a missed day of work during the time period from 1968-1994. In addition, almost every Claimant listed medical expenses in the proof of claim form. The Special Master determined that reimbursement of these expenses together with the expense required to verify each claim would itself exhaust the Claimant's fund. Therefore, the decision to eliminate recovery for medical expenses was due to the limited amount of time, personal, and funds available. Furthermore, as stated in the Report I, inclusion of these expenses as a consideration distinct from the exposure point considerations "would skew the allocation in such a way that would be generally unsatisfactory to the large majority of persons involved." The Court finds no clear error in this decision.

The remaining findings of the Special Master regarding allocations for property claims, class representative participation and other incentive awards, and business loss appear to be well reasoned in the Report I, and the Court finds no clear error with those findings.

The Special Master's recommendation that $1.5 million be set aside for medical monitoring to Class members free of charge for five years has been requested by Claimants and is wholeheartedly supported by the Court. This service will include annual physical examinations and connected laboratory work. . . .

[T]he State of Louisiana has intervened in these proceedings, asserting liens for recovery of medical and related expenses incurred by the State through the Department of Health and Hospitals, all State Hospital facilities, and Louisiana medicaid participants. The Special Master reports that the State negotiated a payment of $1.2 million with possible enhancement of up to $300 thousand, at the discretion of the Court, after other expenses and costs are paid. The Court finds no clear error in the Special Master's recommendation to accept this compromise.

Finally, the Special Master set aside a portion of the Claimants' Fund to account for adjustments made during this entire allocation process. From this pool was drawn the funding for the $1.6 million increases in allocations made as a result of the objection process. This safety mechanism is prudent accounting, is fair to the Class as a whole, and the Court finds no clear error in this recommendation.

Notes and Questions

1. Based on your earlier reading of the class action cases, is fairness to the class as a whole the appropriate touchstone for award of relief? If it is not, and

if the individuality of claims remains important in class actions seeking individualized monetary relief, is *In re Combustion* fatally flawed in its decisions regarding the distribution of the remedy? Suppose that *In re Combustion* were not a class action. Can the outcome in the case be reconciled with the rightful position principle?

2. To what extent is the implementation problem in *In re Combustion* created by the lack of clear scientific evidence indicating causal relationships between the injuries of plaintiffs and the toxic substances? To what extent is the problem caused by the parties' decision to settle for a lump sum without working out the details of the distribution? Doesn't the lump-sum settlement create inevitable conflicts of interest among different groups of claimants? Should the court, rather than the parties, be forced into the role of resolving these conflicts and determining in the first instance the proper amount of the settlement for individual claimants? Or should a court force the parties to resolve the conflicts and to negotiate precise terms for the payment schedule, with the court playing a more judicial role of ensuring that all claimants have received adequate representation in the negotiation process?

From the viewpoint of defendants, sometimes there is an advantage in settling for a sum certain, rather than negotiating a payment schedule under which its obligations remain uncertain; indeed, in some cases, a defendant may refuse to enter into an open-ended settlement. Should that reality be factored in by the court in deciding whether to take on the parties' usual role of allocating settlement proceeds? Should it make a difference that the case would present intractable problems of joinder, pretrial, or trial complexity if the case were not settled? If so, why should a court be able to have greater allocational powers in complex cases than in cases that are not complex? Was *In re Combustion* complex?

3. How much leeway should the court have in making allocational decisions among claimants? In perhaps the most famous case involving allocational decisions, Judge Weinstein ordered the distribution of the $180 million *Agent Orange* settlement to Vietnam veterans that had died or were totally disabled; veterans with less than total disability received no awards. See In re "Agent Orange" Product Liability Litigation, 689 F. Supp. 1250 (E.D.N.Y. 1988). Among the problems that faced Weinstein were the lack of good evidence of duration or amount of exposure and the lack of scientific evidence that Agent Orange and other herbicides caused any injuries whatsoever. Do the solomonic solutions in *Agent Orange* and *In re Combustion* convince you that providing the judge with the power to make allocational decisions is wise? Or do they convert the court into a quasi-administrative social service agency whose functions a court is incapable of performing well?

4. *In re Combustion*'s use of a master to create a payment schedule and a court-appointed distribution agent to handle the actual disbursements turns the court into something of a mini-bureaucracy or, to use Professor Minow's phrase, a "temporary administrative agency." Martha Minow, *Judge for the Situation: Judge Jack Weinstein, Creator of Temporary Administrative Agencies*, 97 Colum. L. Rev. 2010 (1997). The bureaucracy in *In re Combustion*, however, pales in comparison to the bureaucracies that have been set up to deal with some of the larger mass torts, such as *Agent Orange, Dalkon Shield,* asbestos, and silicone gel breast implants. Some of these bureaucracies existed, or will exist, for more than a decade, cost millions of dollars to operate, and employ a staff of dozens. For a series of articles examining the operations of some of these claims

resolution facilities, see Symposium, *Claims Resolution Facilities and the Mass Settlement of Mass Torts*, 53 Law & Contemp. Prob. 1 (Autumn 1990). One of the articles in the symposium did a comparative study of operation and costs of several such facilities, and concluded that they worked best when "modest money is given to claimants who have legally questionable claims." Conversely, "[t]he success of claims facilities is more clouded when their objectives are more ambitious, that is, where the facility has been substituted for litigation of great stakes to claimants." Mark A. Peterson, *Giving Away Money: Comparative Comments on Claims Resolution Facilities*, 53 Law & Contemp. Prob. 113, 135 (Autumn 1990). Moreover, claims facilities often differ in numerous ways, including the type of resolution procedures under which claimants can appeal adverse claims decisions and the ability of claimants to opt out of the resolution process. See id.; Jay Tidmarsh, Mass Tort Settlement Class Actions (1998).

Are the creation of such bureaucracies appropriate? In thinking about this question, you might wish to re-read Justice Kennedy's dissent in *Missouri v. Jenkins* (p. 1430, *supra*). Assuming that the creation of a claims resolution bureaucracy is appropriate, should courts strive to routinize the process, so that claimants in different settlements do not receive markedly different methods of claims handling? How can different courts ultimately agree on a routinized process? Should there be a legislative solution? Does the possibility of such a solution suggest that the entire enterprise of creating judicial bureaucracies to implement monetary recoveries is illegitimate? Are the alternatives to such bureaucracies — dismissal of claims or endless re-litigation of related claims — worse than the problems that the bureaucracies create?

5. The existence of judicial bureaucracies suggests that courts cannot implement complex remedies without assistance from judicial adjuncts. We turn more generally to the use of adjuncts in the implementation phase in the next subsection.

3. Using Judicial Adjuncts to Assist in the Process of Implementing a Remedy

RUIZ v. ESTELLE

679 F.2d 1115 (5th Cir. 1982), amended in part, vacated in part on other grounds, 688 F.2d 266 (5th Cir. 1982), cert. denied, 460 U.S. 1042 (1983)

■ RUBIN, Circuit Judge. [A class action was brought on behalf of the 33,000 prisoners housed in prisons operated by the Texas Department of Corrections (TDC). The district court found that prisoners were confined in violation of the Eighth and Fourteenth Amendments. It ordered a series of remedial measures to correct the violations. Among the orders was the appointment of a special master and monitors to ensure that the TDC was implementing the remedy. The court of appeals affirmed most of the findings of constitutional violation and of remedy, but reversed certain parts of the judgment. It then turned to the district court's decision to use a master and monitors.]

IX. APPOINTMENT OF SPECIAL MASTER

The district court's order of reference appoints a special master and provides for the appointment of "several monitors" to help the special master. It imposes on the special master the responsibility of seeing that the district court's decree is implemented, and empowers him to hold hearings, find facts, and make recommendations to the district court concerning TDC's compliance with the decree. As authority for the appointment the district court invoked both Fed.R.Civ.P. 53 and its inherent power as a court of equity.

TDC contends that the appointment of a special master was improper because the district court failed to comply with rule 53, which, according to TDC, codifies and limits a court's authority to appoint a special master. Rule 53(b) states that a district court may appoint a special master "only upon a showing that some exceptional condition requires" the appointment.[235]

The district court stated several reasons for its decision to make the appointment: the difficulty of superintending the implementation of "a comprehensive, detailed plan for the elimination of the unconstitutional conditions found to exist in the Texas prison system"; TDC's "record of intransigence toward previous court orders requiring changes in TDC's practices and conditions"; the "strained" working relations between TDC's lawyers and the plaintiffs' lawyers; TDC's failure to acknowledge even "completely evident" constitutional violations; and TDC's failure to conform its actual practices to its written policies and procedures. The district court did not, as TDC implies, simply rely on the "mere complexity" of the case. Moreover, the court was not required to await the failure or refusal of TDC to comply with the decree before appointing an agent to implement it. Noncompliance may constitute one "exceptional condition" under rule 53, but it is not exclusive.

Furthermore, rule 53 does not terminate or modify the district court's inherent equitable power to appoint a person, whatever be his title, to assist it in administering a remedy. The power of a federal court to appoint an agent to supervise the implementation of its decrees has long been established. Such court-appointed agents have been identified by "a confusing plethora of titles: 'receiver,' 'Master,' 'Special Master,' 'master hearing officer,' 'monitor,' 'human rights committee,' 'Ombudsman,'" and others. The function is clear, whatever the title.

The district court's opinion stated the reasons for the appointment of the special master and his monitors. As it noted, we have previously approved the appointment of such agents to oversee compliance with continuing court

---

235. One article argues that rule 53's "exceptional conditions" requirement, as interpreted in La Buy v. Howes Leather Co., 352 U.S. 249 (1957), does not even apply in cases like this one. . . . Special Project, [*The Remedial Process in Institutional Reform Litigation*, 78 Colum. L. Rev. 784, 807 (1978).] This article does, however, state that "the use of masters in such cases must nonetheless meet the general rule 53 (b) requirement that references to masters be the exception and not the rule." Id. at 808 . .

orders. Insofar as the special master is to report on TDC's compliance with the district court's decree and to help implement the decree, he assumes one of the plaintiffs' traditional roles, except that, because he is the court's agent, he can and should perform his duties objectively....

The special master is also given powers that are quasijudicial. He is permitted to hold hearings and is directed to find facts "concerning the defendants' compliance with the provisions of the Court's Orders and the need, if any, for supplemental remedial action." The order also establishes rules of procedure: the monitors are to make reports of factual observations and to submit them to the special master and the parties. If any party objects, the special master is to hold a hearing, then make his report to the district court. No objection may be filed to the special master's report that could have been filed to the monitor's report preceding it. The special master's findings of fact are to be accepted by the court unless clearly erroneous. In addition, the special master may hold hearings *sua sponte* without a preliminary monitor's report; and in such instances factual findings in his reports are to be credited unless clearly erroneous. He may, moreover, submit reports based on his own observations and investigations without conducting a hearing. The order of reference does not distinguish between the credit to be given such reports and those submitted after hearings and accompanied by an evidentiary record.

To fulfill his responsibilities, the special master is given sweeping powers, including "unlimited access" to TDC premises and records as well as the power to conduct "confidential interviews" with TDC staff members and inmates, and to require written reports from any TDC staff member. These powers are unconfined save by the following instructions: he is not to intervene in the administrative management of either TDC or any of its units and he is not to direct the defendants or any of their subordinates to take or to refrain from taking any specific action to achieve compliance.

The order of reference does not make clear that, in conducting investigations and hearings, the special master and the monitors are not to consider matters that go beyond superintending compliance with the district court's decree. Such an express constraint is appropriate because of the danger that the special master or the monitors may entertain inmate complaints that convert the remedial process into a surrogate forum for new § 1983 actions. In the interests both of prison administration and sound judicial procedure, it should be made clear to the plaintiffs, the special master, the monitors, and the TDC staff that the special master is not an inmate advocate or a roving federal district court. As we have pointed out before, the powers of the court's appointed agents should not intrude to an unnecessary extent on prison administration.

In one respect, the order of reference is too sweeping. It permits the special master to submit to the district court "reports based upon his own observations and investigations in the absence of a formal hearing before him." This not only transcends the powers traditionally given masters by courts of equity, but denies the parties due process.

Accordingly, the order of reference shall be amended as follows: (1) it should be made clear that the special master and the monitors do not have the authority to hear matters that should appropriately be the subject of separate judicial proceedings, such as actions under § 1983, and that their duties are restricted to those set forth in the order of reference; and (2) unless based on hearings conducted on the record after proper notice, the reports, findings, and conclusions of the special master are not to be accorded any presumption of correctness and the "clearly erroneous" rule will not apply to them.

Finally, the reduction in the scope of the district court's decree directed by this opinion should occasion further inquiry by the district court to determine whether or not there is a continuing need for a staff of six monitors to assist the special master.

Notes and Questions

1. *Ruiz v. Estelle* is perhaps the most famous case regarding the use of masters and judicial adjuncts such as monitors in the implementation phase of institutional reform litigation. It is best known for its acceptance of the use of monitors rather than its use of masters; even though the use of masters in the implementation phase is a recent occurrence, it is generally accepted today that, in appropriate circumstances, masters can be used for these purposes. See also Hoptowit v. Ray, 682 F.2d 1237, 1263 (9th Cir. 1982); Williams v. Lane, 851 F.2d 867 (7th Cir. 1988), cert. denied, 488 U.S. 1047 (1989).

There are, however, instances in which courts thought that the use of monitors intruded too deeply into the prerogatives of the institutional defendant. The most well-known may be Newman v. Alabama, 559 F.2d 283, 288-90 (5th Cir. 1977), cert. denied, 438 U.S. 915 (1978), in which the Fifth Circuit (which later decided *Ruiz*) held that the district court had abused its discretion when in appointed a 39-member "Human Rights Committee" to monitor compliance. Among other things, the Court noted that the committee members had not been shown to have expertise in monitoring, the number of members made the committee unwieldy, the mandate of the committee was too broad, and the committee had apparently functionally taken over the administration of the prison. See also Women Prisoners of the District of Columbia Department of Corrections v. District of Columbia, 93 F.3d 910, 930 (D.C. Cir. 1996) (reversing order that authorized monitors to "perform the functions of local authorities" and therefore "effectively usurp[ed] the executive functions of the District"), cert. denied, — U.S. —, 117 S.Ct. 1552 (1997).

2. In structural reform litigation, masters can play other roles than an enforcer. For instance, masters have been appointed to "to cope with anticipated resistance to the decree; . . . to negotiate with actors whose cooperation would be necessary to secure implementation; to advise and assist the defendant organization; to monitor the conduct of the organization and provide intelligence to the judge about its behavior; to be alert to the need to amend the decree; and to resolve disputes over the meaning of the decree." Donald L. Horowitz, *Decreeing Organizational Change: Judicial Supervision of Public Institutions*, 1983 Duke L.J. 1265, 1298. As we saw in the last subsection, masters and other adjuncts can also be used in cases involving monetary relief to propose the terms of a settlement distribution, to determine which claimants are eligible to receive benefits, and to run the mini-bureaucracy needed to distribute the funds.

3. Courts tend to assume that the general language of Rule 53 — that the appointment of a master be "the exception and not the rule" — controls in the implementation setting as well. See *Women Prisoners*, 93 F.3d at 930. Some federal courts have also found that an appointment of a master to monitor compliance can be grounded in the All Writs Act, 28 U.S.C. § 1651. National Organization for the Reform of Marijuana Laws v. Mullen, 828 F.2d 536 (9th Cir. 1988).

Assuming that the power to make the appointment exists, what factors should a court use in determining whether to appoint a judicial adjunct? One of the factors that often weighs heavily in the determination of an "exception" is the lack of the defendant's prior good faith compliance, see id.; *Williams*, 851 F.2d 867; presumably, because of the size of the institution, it may be difficult for a court alone to monitor the defendant's future compliance. What other factors should enter into the decision? Does the answer depend on the function that the adjunct is being asked to perform? For instance, in *Ruiz v. Estelle*, why can't the district court adjudicate complaints of non-compliance? Likewise, does a master have any special expertise in creating a payment schedule or determining eligibility in a case like *In re Combustion*? If not, how can the use of the master be justified? If the logic of LaBuy v. Howes Leather Co., 352 U.S. 249 (1957) (p. 1254, *supra*) applies to appointments in the implementation phase, the mere complexity of the task or the burden on the court is not an adequate reason to pass off the job. Would the effect of a reduction in the ability to appoint masters be a reduction in the willingness of judges to approve lump-sum settlements or to order sweeping relief? Would this result be so bad? Or should a reduction in remedies that are already too tightly cabined make a judge more willing to order appointments?

4. Professor Horowitz, a staunch critic of much institutional reform litigation, sees still other problems with the use of a master:

> Precisely because masters sense the need to act unconventionally, they test the boundaries of judicial propriety. They sometimes engage in what would clearly be improper *ex parte* communications if engaged in by the judge. If they rely more heavily on one side or the other for information or for cooperation in drafting a plan, they risk the appearance or the reality of lost neutrality. If they hire subordinate personnel, they delegate some part of their function, thus removing the judge a second step from the action taken. If they use their power to interview staff members, to recommend staff changes, or to give orders to staff on operational matters, they may intrude unduly into administration and raise questions of organizational accountability and lines of authority. If, in monitoring a decree, they commit themselves to a certain view of who is responsible for shortfalls in implementation, they risk partisan commitment, in which they may also entangle the judge if he accepts their view of the matter, even after a formal hearing.
>
> Perhaps unsurprisingly, then, it turns out that appointing courts occasionally disown what the master has done or proposed. The unconventional character of the initial appointment leads to unconventional behavior, for organizational change cases are different from the normal run of cases. What masters propose sometimes appears too ambitious or too risky or too politically entangling to the judges who appointed them.

Horowitz, *supra*, at 1298-99. Do you agree with this assessment?

5. As we noted above, the use of masters or monitors in institutional reform litigation is often a response to problems of intransigence by the party subject to the decree. As we saw in *Missouri v. Jenkins* (p. 1424, *supra*), sometimes parties are only too willing to comply, but they face external constraints. When those constraints are placed on the party by the actions of nonparties, a different situation presents itself. In the final subsection, we examine a court's power to deal with nonparties that threaten the effectiveness of a remedy.

4. Removing Roadblocks to the Implementation of the Remedy: Nonparty Intransigence

Sometimes the parties' ability to implement a remedy is threatened by nonparties whose actions might disrupt the remedy. What should be the extent of the court's power to prevent third parties from thwarting the remedy? In yet another context, we face the problem of the court's power over persons that are not parties to the litigation, but nonetheless hold a key to the court's ability to adjudicate successfully the case before it.

UNITED STATES v. HALL

472 F.2d 261 (5th Cir. 1972)

■ WISDOM, Circuit Judge. This case presents the question whether a district court has power to punish for criminal contempt a person who, though neither a party nor bearing any legal relationship to a party, violates a court order designed to protect the court's judgment in a school desegregation case. We uphold the district court's conclusion that in the circumstances of this case it had this power, and affirm the defendant's conviction for contempt.

On June 23, 1971, the district court entered a "Memorandum Opinion and Final Judgment" in the case of Mims v. Duval County School Board. The court required the Duval County [Jacksonville], Florida school board to complete its desegregation of Duval County schools, in accordance with the Supreme Court's decision in Swann v. Charlotte-Mecklenburg Board of Education, 1971, 402 U.S. 1, by pairing and clustering a number of schools which had theretofore been predominantly one-race schools. This order culminated litigation begun eleven years before . . . . This Court affirmed the district court's order in Mims v. Duval County School Board, 5 Cir. 1971, 447 F.2d 1330. The district court retained jurisdiction to enter such orders as might be necessary in the future to effectuate its judgment.

Among the schools marked for desegregation under the plan approved by the district court was Ribault Senior High School, a predominantly white school. The plan directed pairing of Ribault with William E. Raines Senior High School, a predominantly black school, so that the black enrollment would be 59 percent at Raines and 57 percent at Ribault. After the desegregation order was put into effect racial unrest and violence developed at Ribault, necessitating on one occasion the temporary closing of the school. On March 5, 1972, the superintendent of schools and the sheriff of Jacksonville filed a petition for injunctive relief in the *Mims* case with the district court. This petition alleged that certain black adult "outsiders" had caused or abetted the unrest and violence by their activities both on and off the Ribault campus. The petition identified the appellant Eric Hall, allegedly a member of a militant organization known as the "Black Front", as one of several such outsiders who, in combination with black students and parents, were attempting to prevent the normal operation of Ribault through student boycotts and other activities. As relief the petitioners requested an order "restraining all Ribault Senior High School students and any person acting independently or in concert with them from interfering with the orderly operation of the school and the Duval County School system, and for such other relief as the court may deem just and proper."

At an *ex parte* session on March 5, 1972, the district court entered an order providing in part:

1. All students of Ribault Senior High School, whether in good standing or under suspension, and other persons acting independently or in concert with them and having notice of this order are hereby enjoined and restrained from

(a) Obstructing or preventing the attendance in classes of students and faculty members; [or]

(e) Committing any other act to disrupt the orderly operation of Ribault Senior High School or any other school of the Duval County School System;

2. Until further order of this Court, no person shall enter any building of the Ribault Senior High School or go upon the school's grounds except the following:

(a) Students of Ribault Senior High School while attending classes or official school functions;

(b) The faculty, staff, and administration of Ribault Senior High School and other employees of the Duval County School Board having assigned duties at the school;

(c) Persons having business obligations which require their presence on the school's premises;

(d) Parents of Ribault Senior High School students or any other person who has the prior permission of the principal or his designee to be present on the school's premises;

(e) Law enforcement officials of the City of Jacksonville, the State of Florida or the United States Government.

The order went on to provide that "[a]nyone having notice of this order who violates any of the terms thereof shall be subject to arrest, prosecution and punishment by imprisonment or fine, or both, for criminal contempt under the laws of the United States of America. . . ." The court ordered the sheriff to serve copies of the order on seven named persons, *including Eric Hall*.

Hall was neither a party plaintiff nor a party defendant in the *Mims* litigation, and in issuing this order the court did not join Hall or any of the other persons named in the order as parties.

On March 9, 1972, four days after the court issued its order, Hall violated that portion of the order restricting access to Ribault High School by appearing on the Ribault campus. When questioned by a deputy United States marshal as to the reasons for his presence, Hall replied that he was on the grounds of Ribault for the purpose of violating the March 5 order. The marshal then arrested Hall and took him into custody. After a nonjury trial, the district court found Hall guilty of the charge of criminal contempt and sentenced him to sixty days' imprisonment.

On this appeal Hall raises two related contentions. Both contentions depend on the fact that Hall was not a party to the *Mims* litigation and the fact that, in violating the court's order, he was apparently acting independently of the *Mims* parties. He first points to the common law rule that a nonparty who violates an injunction solely in pursuit of his own interests cannot be held in contempt. Not having been before the court as a party or as the surrogate of a party, he argues that in accordance with this common law rule he was not bound by the court's order. Second, he contends that Rule 65(d) of the Federal Rules of Civil Procedure prevents the court's order from binding him, since Rule 65(d) limits the binding effect of injunctive orders to "parties to the action, their officers, agents, servants, employees, and attorneys, and . . . those persons in active concert or participation with them who receive actual notice of the order by personal service or otherwise." We reject both contentions.

I.

For his first contention, that a court of equity has no power to punish for contempt a nonparty acting solely in pursuit of his own interests, the appellant relies heavily on the two leading cases of Alemite Manufacturing Corp. v. Staff, 2 Cir. 1930, 42 F.2d 832, and Chase National Bank v. City of Norwalk, 1934, 291 U.S. 431. In *Alemite* the district court had issued an injunction restraining the defendant and his agents, employees, associates, and confederates from infringing the plaintiff's patent. Subsequently a third person, not a party to the original suit and acting entirely on his own initiative, began infringing the plaintiff's patent and was held in contempt by the district court. The Second Circuit reversed in an opinion by Judge Learned Hand, stating that "it is not the act described which the decree may forbid, but only that act when the defendant does it." 42 F.2d at 833. In *Chase National Bank* the plaintiff brought suit against the City of Norwalk to obtain an injunction forbidding the removal of poles, wires, and other electrical equipment belonging to the plaintiff. The district court issued a decree enjoining the City, its officers, agents, and employees, "and all persons whomsoever to whom notice of this order shall come" from removing the equipment or otherwise interfering with the operation of the plaintiff's power plant. The Supreme Court held that the district court had violated "established principles of equity jurisdiction and procedure" insofar as its order applied to persons who were not parties, associates, or confederates of parties, but who merely had notice of the order....

This case is different. In *Alemite* and *Chase National Bank* the activities of third parties, however harmful they might have been to the plaintiffs' interests, would not have disturbed in any way the adjudication of rights and obligations as between the original plaintiffs and defendants. Infringement of the *Alemite* plaintiff's patent by a third party would not have upset the defendant's duty to refrain from infringing or rendered it more difficult for the defendant to perform that duty. Similarly, the defendant's duty in *Chase National Bank* to refrain from removing the plaintiff's equipment would remain undisturbed regardless of the activities of third parties, as would the plaintiff's right not to have its equipment removed by the defendant. The activities of Hall, however, threatened both the plaintiffs' right and the defendant's duty as adjudicated in the *Mims* litigation. In *Mims* the plaintiffs were found to have a constitutional right to attend an integrated school. The defendant school board had a corresponding constitutional obligation to provide them with integrated schools and a right to be free from interference with the performance of that duty.... Disruption of the orderly operation of the school system, in the form of a racial dispute, would thus negate the plaintiffs' constitutional right and the defendant's constitutional duty. In short, the activities of persons contributing to racial disorder at Ribault imperiled the court's fundamental power to make a binding adjudication between the parties properly before it.

Courts of equity have inherent jurisdiction to preserve their ability to render judgment in a case such as this. This was the import of the holding in United States v. United Mine Workers of America, 1947, 330 U.S. 258. There the district court had issued a temporary restraining order forbidding a union from striking, though there was a substantial question of whether the Norris-La-Guardia Act had deprived the district court of jurisdiction to issue such an order. The Supreme Court upheld the defendants' contempt conviction for violation of this order. As an alternative holding the Court stated that the contempt conviction would have been upheld even if the district court had ultimately been found to be without jurisdiction. This holding affirmed the power of a court of equity to issue an order to preserve the status quo in order to protect its ability to render judgment in a case over which it might have jurisdiction....

The integrity of a court's power to render a binding judgment in a case over which it has jurisdiction is at stake in the present case. In *Mine Workers* disruptive conduct prior to the court's decision could have destroyed the court's power to settle a controversy at least potentially within its jurisdiction. Here the conduct of Hall and others, if unrestrained, could have upset the court's ability to bind the parties in *Mims*, a case in which it unquestionably had jurisdiction. Moreover, the court retained jurisdiction in *Mims* to enter such further orders as might be necessary to effectuate its judgment. Thus disruptive conduct would not only jeopardize the effect of the court's judgment already entered but would also undercut its power to enter binding desegregation orders in the future.

The principle that courts have jurisdiction to punish for contempt in order to protect their ability to render judgment is also found in the use of in rem injunctions. Federal courts have issued injunctions binding on all persons, regardless of notice, who come into contact with property which is the subject of a judicial decree.... A court entering a decree binding on a particular piece of property is necessarily faced with the danger that its judgment may be disrupted in the future by members of an undefinable class — those who may come into contact with the property. The in rem injunction protects the court's judgment. The district court here faced an analogous problem. The judgment in a school case, as in other civil rights actions, inures to the benefit of a large class of persons, regardless of whether the original action is cast in the form of a class action.... At the same time court orders in school cases, affecting as they do large numbers of people, necessarily depend on the cooperation of the entire community for their implementation.

As this Court is well aware, school desegregation orders often strongly excite community passions. School orders are, like in rem orders, particularly vulnerable to disruption by an undefinable class of persons who are neither parties nor acting at the instigation of parties. In such cases, as in voting rights cases, courts must have the power to issue orders similar to that issued in this case, tailored to the exigencies of the situation and directed to protecting the court's judgment. The peculiar problems posed by school cases have required courts to exercise broad and flexible remedial powers. See Swann v. Charlotte-Mecklenburg Board of Education, 1971, 402 U.S. 1, 6, 15. Similarly broad applications of the power to punish for contempt may be necessary, as here, if courts are to protect their ability to design appropriate remedies and make their remedial orders effective.

II.

The appellant also asserts that Rule 65(d) of the Federal Rules of Civil Procedure prevents the court's order from binding him. He points out that he was not a party to the original action, nor an officer, agent, servant, employee, or attorney of a party, and denies that he was acting in "active concert or participation" with any party to the original action.

In examining this contention we start with the proposition that Rule 65 was intended to embody "the commonlaw doctrine that a decree of injunction not only binds the parties defendant but also those identified with them in interest, in 'privity' with them, represented by them or subject to their control." Regal Knitwear Co. v. NLRB, 1945, 324 U.S. 9, 14. Literally read, Rule 65(d) would forbid the issuance of in rem injunctions.... But courts have continued to issue in rem injunctions notwithstanding Rule 65(d), since they possessed the power to do so at common law and since Rule 65(d) was intended to embody rather than to limit their common law powers....

Similarly, we conclude that Rule 65(d), as a codification rather than a limitation of courts' common-law powers, cannot be read to restrict the inherent power of a court to protect its ability to render a binding judgment. ... We hold that Hall's relationship to the *Mims* case fell within that contemplated by Rule 65(d). By deciding *Mims* and retaining jurisdiction the district court had, in effect, adjudicated the rights of the entire community with respect to the racial controversy surrounding the school system. Moreover, as we have noted, in the circumstances of this case third parties such as Hall were in a position to upset the court's adjudication. This was not a situation which could have been anticipated by the draftsmen of procedural rules. In meeting the situation as it did, the district court did not overstep its powers.

We do not hold that courts are free to issue permanent injunctions against all the world in school cases. Hall had notice of the court's order. Rather than challenge it by the orderly processes of law, he resorted to conscious, willful defiance. See Walker v. Birmingham, 1967, 388 U.S. 307.

It is true that this order was issued without a hearing, and that ordinarily injunctive relief cannot be granted without a hearing. . . . But we need not hold that this order has the effect of a preliminary or permanent injunction. Rather, the portion of the court's order here complained of may be characterized as a temporary restraining order, which under Rule 65(b) may be issued *ex parte*. The prohibition directed to restricting access to the school grounds nowhere purported to be an injunction. Moreover, Hall's violation occurred within four days of the issuance of the order, well within the ten-day limitation period for temporary restraining orders. . . .

We hold, then, that the district court had the inherent power to protect its ability to render a binding judgment between the original parties to the *Mims* litigation by issuing an interim ex parte order against an undefinable class of persons. We further hold that willful violation of that order by one having notice of it constitutes criminal contempt. The judgment of the district court is affirmed.

IN RE U.S. OIL AND GAS LITIGATION

967 F.2d 489 (11th Cir. 1992)

■ HATCHETT, Circuit Judge. In this case of first impression in this circuit, we affirm the district court's imposition of a settlement bar order and establish the standard of review to be abuse of discretion.

FACTS AND PROCEDURAL HISTORY

In the late 1970s, the U.S. Oil and Gas Corporation, Eagle Oil and Gas Corporation, and the Stratford Company (the Companies) began selling an advisory service to investors seeking to bid on federal oil and gas leases. The Companies obtained customers through telephone solicitations. The investments were extremely high risk because customers obtained no return on their investment unless they were successful in the lease auctions. In an effort to serve customers who were willing to pay more for lower risk, the Companies developed a "money back guarantee" program. Essentially, the program required the purchase of a master insurance policy for participating investors.

The Companies contacted an insurance broker, Alexander and Alexander, Inc. (A & A). After domestic insurance companies refused to participate in the program, A & A obtained a policy from Pinnacle Reinsurance Company, Ltd. (Pinnacle), a Bermuda corporation. Pinnacle issued a $1 million annuity contract in exchange for a $525,000 premium.

By 1983, the Companies had sold their services to some 8,000 customers. They had also attracted the attention of United States postal authorities and the Federal Trade Commission (FTC). The FTC filed an enforcement action against the Companies in the United States District Court for the Southern District of Florida, and the court appointed a receiver to protect the interests of the Companies' customers. In 1985, the receiver filed a complaint on his behalf and instituted a class action on behalf of the customers alleging securities fraud and RICO violations.

The complaints named A & A, Pinnacle, and ninety-four others as defendants. As the plaintiffs state, the litigation became "breathtakingly complex." Between 1984 and 1990, the court held 50 hearings, the plaintiffs attended 260 depositions, and discovery produced hundreds of thousands of relevant documents. As trial approached, plaintiffs stipulated that more than 700 issues of fact remained unresolved.

Near the end of 1990, the possibility of a long, complicated, and expensive trial began to produce settlements. The Morgenstern defendants, a group which had provided legal services to the Companies, entered into the first major settlement with the plaintiffs. On January 26, 1991, pursuant to the settlement agreement, the district court entered a series of orders. These orders approved the fairness of the Morgenstern settlement, dismissed the receiver's and the class's claims against the Morgenstern defendants, and barred "all claims" by non-settling defendants against settling defendants, or by settling defendants against non-settling defendants, related to the subject matter of the litigation. This last order, the Morgenstern settlement bar, drew no serious objections from Pinnacle, which had no cross-claims pending against the settling defendants.

Pinnacle did, however, object to the settlement bar order which is the subject of this appeal. In 1988, Pinnacle filed a cross-claim against A & A alleging indemnity, breach of fiduciary duty, fraud, and negligence. Pinnacle claimed that A & A knew of the Companies' fraudulent activities, but wrongfully withheld that information from Pinnacle when it brokered the annuity contract. Throughout the litigation, Pinnacle sought to preserve this claim against A & A, even while it sought settlement with the plaintiffs.

Pinnacle's desire to preserve its cross-claim eventually conflicted with the plaintiffs' desire to achieve a favorable settlement with A & A. . . . When Pinnacle and plaintiffs agreed to settle for $500,000, a settlement bar order was not part of the bargain.

A & A, however, was still engaged in settlement negotiations with plaintiffs and was not willing to settle its liability without a bar order protecting it from Pinnacle's pending cross-claim. Although A & A and plaintiffs disputed in the district court whether a settlement bar order was a condition precedent to the effectiveness of their settlement agreement, they both agreed that the district court should enter such an order. Plainly,

A & A was unwilling to disburse an eight and a half million dollar [$8,500,000] settlement without the assurance that it would be protected from further claims for contribution or indemnity. Even more plainly, plaintiffs weighed A & A's eight and a half million dollar settlement against Pinnacle's five hundred thousand dollar settlement and saw the light of supporting A & A's insistence on a bar order.

By the beginning of 1991, the plaintiffs and a large number of defendants had entered into settlement agreements. On January 30, 1991, the district court conducted a hearing to resolve outstanding issues among the settling parties. Chief among these outstanding issues was A & A's insistence on a settlement bar order, plaintiffs' support of such an order, and Pinnacle's opposition to it. The court afforded each party an opportunity to fully argue its position on the settlement bar issue. The court asked Pinnacle whether it sought to withdraw from its settlement with plaintiffs now that plaintiffs and A & A were jointly urging the court to adopt a settlement bar order. Pinnacle stated emphatically that it did not seek to withdraw from the settlement. . . .

On April 12, 1991, the district court entered a settlement bar order extinguishing all claims related to the litigation against the settling defendants. The court reviewed the law supporting settlement bar orders generally and then applied those principles to the facts of the present case. The court recognized and addressed Pinnacle's objections to the order. Nonetheless, it concluded that the order was justified: "If litigation of cross-claims were allowed, the resources of the court, class members, class members' counsel, and defendants' counsel would continue to be expended, because it would be impossible to try cross-claims without addressing the complex facts underlying this litigation. . . . Settlements in complex cases cannot satisfy their ultimate purposes unless they conclude the litigation in its entirety." . . .

ISSUES

The issues presented are: (1) whether the district court erred in entering the settlement bar order; and (2) whether the district court denied Pinnacle due process in entering the order.

DISCUSSION

The Bar Order

Public policy strongly favors the pretrial settlement of class action lawsuits. . . . Complex litigation — like the instant case — can occupy a court's docket for years on end, depleting the resources of the parties and the taxpayers while rendering meaningful relief increasingly elusive. Accordingly, the Federal Rules of Civil Procedure authorize district courts to facilitate settlements in all types of litigation, not just class actions. See Fed.R.Civ.P. 16(a), (c) . . . . Although class action settlements require court approval, such approval is committed to the sound discretion of the district court. . . .

Modern class action settlements increasingly incorporate settlement bar orders such as the one at issue in this case. See, e.g., In re[ ] Jiffy Lube Securities Litigation, 927 F.2d 155 (4th Cir. 1991); Franklin v. Kaypro Corp., 884 F.2d 1222 (9th Cir. 1989), cert. denied sub nom[.] Franklin v. Peat Marwick Main & Co., 498 U.S. 890 (1990) . . . . The reason for this trend is that bar orders play an integral role in facilitating settlement. Defendants buy little peace through settlement unless they are assured that they will be protected against codefendants' efforts to shift their losses through cross-claims for indemnity, contribution, and other causes related to the underlying litigation. . . . Thus, in the present case, A & A expressed a strong unwillingness to pay eight and a half million dollars to the plaintiffs unless it was assured that Pinnacle's cross-claims would not subject it to further liability. In short, settlement bar orders allow settling parties to put a limit on the risks of settlement.

We believe that these principles strongly support the district court's decision to enter a settlement bar order in this case. We note, however, that this case involves unique features which distinguish it from the precedents cited above. In particular, this case presents a settling defendant's challenge to a settlement bar order. In all of the cases previously cited, nonsettling defendants challenged the bar order as prejudicial to their rights. In the typical case involving a nonsettling defendant, the court is concerned with calculating the proper "offset" to ensure that plaintiffs do not enjoy a double recovery against nonsettling defendants in any subsequent litigation of outstanding claims. See, e.g., *Jiffy Lube*, 927 F.2d at 160-62; *Franklin*, 884 F.2d at 1230-32. We express no opinion in this case regarding the proper method to be applied in calculating such "offsets." Because Pinnacle agreed to settle, it risked no further liability from plaintiffs. Thus, the district court was not faced with the difficult task of determining the proper offset to ensure that plaintiffs did not gain a "double recovery" in subsequent judgments against nonsettling defendants.

A second distinctive feature about this case, related to the first, is the severability of the settlement bar order. At oral argument and in its brief, A & A repeatedly questioned Pinnacle's right to appeal the bar order. We agree that in many cases, a settling defendant's appeal of a bar order would be problematic. To the extent that the bar order is an integral part of the settlement, the settling defendant may have waived the right to object to it. Where the parties have stipulated that the bar order is integral to the settlement, this court may not consider the order in isolation. . . . Thus, as a general rule, we may not consider an appeal of a bar order separately from the entire settlement.

In the present case, however, Pinnacle preserved its right to challenge and appeal the bar order, despite its agreement to the settlement as a whole. The final settlement stipulation provides that "Pinnacle's execution of this stipulation is not a waiver of its right to appeal [the settlement bar order]." The stipulation further provides that the settlement "shall be unchanged if . . . the bar order is ever modified or vacated by any order of an appellate court, or by any order of the district court after proceedings required by a remand from an appellate court." Knowing that this circuit had never addressed the propriety of settlement bar orders in class action lawsuits, the parties plainly intended that their settlement should remain in effect, even if this court invalidated the bar order as a matter of law. Because Pinnacle carefully reserved its rights, it was entitled to both the benefit of the settlement and a continuing challenge to the bar order on appeal.

We now address the merits of Pinnacle's specific challenge. Seeking to distinguish this case from the numerous precedents upholding the validity of settlement bar orders, Pinnacle argues that the district court erred as a matter of law when it barred Pinnacle's claims for indemnity, fraud, and negligence against A & A. According to Pinnacle, settlement bar orders have been entered only in cases where a nonsettling defendant sought to preserve contribution claims against settling defendants. Pinnacle argues that independent claims and indemnity claims cannot be precluded through a settlement bar order.

Pinnacle . . . offers this court not a shred of logic upon which we could base a principled distinction between bar orders against contribution, on the one hand, and orders against indemnity or so-called "independent claims," on the other. Pinnacle places primary reliance instead upon its argument that most, if not all, of the prior federal cases supporting bar orders dealt exclusively with contribution claims.

Pinnacle's legal argument is unavailing. First, several federal courts have approved of settlement bars against indemnity claims. See, *e.g.*, *Jiffy Lube*, 927 F.2d at 158; *Franklin*, 884 F.2d at 1225 & 1225 n.2 . . . . In addition, as the district court noted, the substantive weakness of Pinnacle's indemnity claim supported the entry of the settlement bar against it. Indemnification claims are not cognizable under the Securities Acts of 1933 and 1934. . . . Because Pinnacle's cross-claim was largely an attempt to seek indemnity from A & A for the federal securities law violations alleged against Pinnacle in the complaints, it was unlikely to survive even the most cursory adjudication on the merits. . . .

The settlement bar order is also effective against Pinnacle's allegedly independent causes of action for fraud and negligence. These claims were not, in fact, independent of Pinnacle's or A & A's liability to the plaintiffs. For example, Pinnacle stated in its cross-claim that it "seeks damages against A & A and Riley to the extent that it is liable to any of the plaintiffs herein." . . . Pinnacle's fraud and negligence claims "are nothing more than claims for contribution or indemnification with a slight change in wording." . . . Because Pinnacle's fraud and negligence claims were integrally related to plaintiffs' claims against both A & A and Pinnacle, the district court properly extinguished those claims in the settlement bar order.

The propriety of the settlement bar order should turn upon the interrelatedness of the claims that it precludes, not upon the labels which parties attach to those claims. If the cross-claims that the district court seeks to extinguish through the entry of a bar order arise out of the same facts as those underlying the litigation, then the district court may exercise its discretion to bar such claims in reaching a fair and equitable settlement. That is precisely what the district court did in this case.

Due Process

At oral argument in this case, the court inquired as to whether, when, and to what extent Pinnacle was aware of the district court's intent to enter a bar order. Pinnacle argued that it did not know about the settlement bar order when it settled. A & A argued that the parties appended the bar order to early drafts of the settlement stipulation, and therefore, Pinnacle was fully aware of it.

Our review indicates that Pinnacle did not contemplate the entry of a bar order at the time it reached its settlement with plaintiffs.... [P]laintiffs' counsel conceded in the district court that the bar order was not a part of plaintiffs' settlement discussions with Pinnacle. Our review further indicates, however, that by the time the district court entered the bar order several months later, Pinnacle was fully aware that the order had become part of the settlement....

A district court may issue a settlement bar order against a nonsettling defendant after it makes a reasoned determination that it is fair and equitable to do so. See, *e.g.*, *Jiffy Lube*, 927 F.2d at 158-60; *Franklin*, 884 F.2d at 1232. Surely, then, the district court may enter a settlement bar order against a defendant who has participated fully in settlement negotiations and utilized every opportunity to preserve its rights within those negotiations. In the end, Pinnacle has gotten exactly what it had a right to expect in this case: a binding settlement with plaintiffs and a full opportunity to challenge, at both the trial and appellate levels, the propriety of the settlement bar order.

CONCLUSION

For the foregoing reasons, the judgment of the district court is affirmed.

Notes and Questions

1. The Supreme Court has cited *Hall* with apparent approval on several occasions. See, *e.g.*, Golden State Bottling Co. v. National Labor Relations Board, 414 U.S. 169, 180 (1973); Washington v. Washington State Commercial Passenger Fishing Vessel Association, 443 U.S. 658, 693 n.32 (1979) (respondents were "probably subject to injunction under . . . the rule that nonparties who interfere with the implementation of court orders establishing public rights may be enjoined, *e. g.*, United States v. Hall, 472 F.2d 261 (CA5 1972), cited approvingly in Golden State Bottling Co. v. NLRB, 414 U.S. 168, 180"). But the Court has not viewed such orders as automatic. In Spallone v. United States, 493 U.S. 265 (1990), the district court faced a city that refused to abide by an agreement requiring integrated housing. One of the reasons for the refusal was that the city council did not pass the necessary implementing legislation. The district court held both the city and the legislators, who were not parties to the litigation, in contempt. After a standoff of several weeks, during which the city was driven into bankruptcy and the recalcitrant council members were threatened with imprisonment, one of the members of the council changed his vote, and the legislation passed. In an opinion heavily laced with

concerns for federalism and separation of powers, the Court held that the district court had erred in acting against the nonparty legislators. The Court hinted that such action might have eventually been appropriate had the direct sanctions against the city not worked.

2. The logic of *Hall* should be very familiar by now: The parties' ability to obtain a meaningful remedy is threatened by the actions of nonparties, and the court must have the power to deal with the problem. This is precisely the logic that we have suggested throughout this book is a compelling ground for departure from a standard adversarial model, under which the court usually can act only on the parties before it. Taken out of the specific context that gave rise to its holding, does *Hall* suggest that courts possess — or should possess — a power to guarantee an effective remedy for the parties when standard adversarial processes cannot? Or is *Hall* limited, as *Washington State Commercial Passenger* suggests, just to public law litigation? If so, what about public law litigation makes it different than private litigation? Should we maintain different procedural rules for different cases, or should we strive to hold onto our modern trans-substantive aspiration?

3. One way to test some of these questions is to consider *U.S. Oil and Gas*. The case is not a public law case, at least in the typical understanding of that phrase. Nor does it present a situation in which Pinnacle, who was a nonparty to the relevant settlement agreement, threatened the ability of the plaintiffs to obtain any remedy at all. Do these facts mean that *U.S. Oil and Gas* is wrong? See TBG, Inc. v. Bendis, 36 F.3d 916, 924 (10th Cir. 1994) (disagreeing with *U.S. Oil and Gas* "that the interest in settlement can give courts the power to bar statutory contribution claims" because "[c]ourts may not extinguish such rights in order to facilitate settlement unless the statute authorizes them to do so"; further holding that the All Writs Act, 28 U.S.C. § 1651, may provide a source of authority to enter bar orders in appropriate cases).

The two cases can be reconciled on different grounds. First, even though the court's logic does not seem to limit itself to this fact, Pinnacle was a party in *U.S. Oil and Gas*. Second, the equities in *Hall* and *U.S. Oil and Gas* are different; in *Hall*, the nonparty was attempting to disrupt the remedy, while in *U.S. Oil and Gas* the "nonparty" had obtained a comparable bar order itself. Third, in both cases, the "nonparty" had knowledge of the relevant order that sought to effectuate the remedy. Does this knowledge, combined with the desirability of obtaining a litigation-ending remedy for present parties, justify the result in *U.S. Oil and Gas*? What are the limits of this power?

4. These questions — what is the court's power to deal with those who sit on the sidelines, what is the relevance of notice and opportunity to participate, can a court act in a non-adversarial way only when there exists a threat to rational adjudication, what about the need to prevent needless litigation of claims, what about the like procedural treatment of like claims — return us full circle to the place where this book began. As we have remarked before, complex civil litigation is truly a seamless web. Like all webs, there are no easy solutions that permit a quick escape. Ultimately, complex litigation is the story of a procedural system wrestling with the unavoidable difficulties that its chosen rules have caused. This quest for an unattainable justice gives complex litigation both its fascination and its peculiar bite.

INDEX

ABSTENTION (See also **STAYS**)
By federal courts, 426-37
By state courts, 437-42

ADVERSARIAL SYSTEM
Alternatives to, 60-82
Justifications for, 13-27
Relationship to complex litigation, 2, 85-86

ALL WRITS ACT
Anti-suit injunction and, 401-12
Removal and, 388-89
Bankruptcy and, 724, 741
Use in remedial stage, 1447, 1459
Venue transfers and, 524

AMICUS CURIAE, 154-55

ANTI-SUIT INJUNCTIONS
Among courts of coordinate jurisdiction, 467-72
Anti-Injunction Act and, 393-401
In international context, 472
In state-federal context, 393-412
Interpleader and, 419

ASBESTOS LITIGATION
Bankruptcy and, 702-03, 749-51, 755-56, 765-87
Class actions
    Litigation, 632-36
    Settlement, 658-89
Consolidation of, 473-81
Masters in, 942-46
Multidistrict transfers of, 498-509
Trial of, 1294-99, 1306-10
Venue transfers of, 487-89

ATTORNEYS' FEES (See **LAWYERS**)

AUTONOMY
As procedural value, 10, 12-20, 120-26,
In class action decisions, 535-39
In joinder decisions, 120-26
In selection of counsel, 879, 889-90
Master of the complaint rule and, 92, 115, 127

BANKRUPTCY
Advantages as aggregation device, 703-09
Limits of
    Aggregation of other defendants, 730-52
    Aggregation of future claims, 752-69
    Requirement of "related to" jurisdiction,
Modification of bankruptcy plan, 769-78
Relationship to class actions, 778-87
Relationship to interpleader, 787

BIFURCATION
Pretrial, 1019-30
Trial, 1273-93

BILL OF PEACE, 423-25

CASE MANAGEMENT
Advantages and disadvantages of, 925-39
Comparative perspectives on, 70-74, 930-31
History of, 926-30
Techniques to narrow issues
    Dispositive motions (See **SUMMARY ADJUDICATION**)
    Early, firm deadlines, 1010-19
    Pretrial stipulations, 1030-42
    Providing advisory opinions, 1083-86
Techniques to enhance discovery (See **DISCOVERY**)
Use of judicial adjuncts (See **JUDICIAL ADJUNCTS**)

CHOICE OF LAW
Basic principles, 791-97
Class actions and, 641-42, 860-62
Constitutional limitations on choice of law rules, 797-804
Effect of transfer on
    Federal questions, 819-32
    State law issues, 809-19
Erie and, 805-09
State law issues
    Generally, 805-19
    Methods of avoiding choice of law rules
        Federal choice of law principles, 869-74
        Federal common law, 844-55
        Manipulation of choice of law principles, 833-44

Most restrictive jurisdiction, 865-68
National consensus, 855-65
Single law with opt-out right, 868-69

CLASS ACTIONS
Advantages and disadvantages as aggregation device
    Autonomy, 535-39
    Deterrence, 539-45
    Doctrinal advantages and disadvantages, 531-34
    Ethical considerations, 546-49
    Manageability, 545-46
    Trans-substantivism, 549-50
Anti-suit injunction and, 393-412, 533, 614-17
Appeal of certification decision, 553-54
Attorneys fees, 554-55
Bankruptcy and, 778-87
Choice of law and, 641-42, 860-62
Civil rights and, 564-70, 599-606
Commercial litigation and, 570-74, 585-89, 621-30
Defendant class actions, 689-92
Jury trial and, 617-20, 642-43, 1283-84
Litigation class actions, 555-647
Mass torts and, 574-79, 589-95, 606-07, 630-47
Notice to class members, 552-53
Preclusive effect of judgment, 174-94, 534
Remedies and, 1410-19
Reform of, 693-98
Requirements of
    All class actions, 556-83
        Commonality, typicality, and adequacy, 564-83
        Existence of class, 556-59
        Membership in class, 559
        Numerosity, 559-64
    Mandatory class actions, 584-620
        (b)(1)(A) and (b)(1)(B) classes, 584-98
        (b)(2) classes, 598-613
    Opt-out class actions, 620-47
Settlement class actions, 647-89
Settlement of class action, 553
Statute of limitations in, 553
Subject matter jurisdiction, 331-40, 349-60, 532
Territorial jurisdiction, 532-33
Venue, 533

COMPARATIVE LAW
Discovery in foreign systems, 1162-68
General comparison, 60-82
    Procedures in alternate adversary systems, 61-68
    Procedures in civil law systems, 68-74
    Procedures in socialist systems, 74-82

COMPLEX LITIGATION
Definitions of, 83-86
Forms of complexity,
    Joinder, 87-90
    Pretrial, 875-77
    Trial, 1197-99
    Remedial, 1385-85

COMPLICATED LITIGATION
As distinguished from complex litigation, 88-89

CONSOLIDATION (See also TRIAL BY STATISTICS), 473-525

COOPERATION BETWEEN STATE AND FEDERAL COURTS
Generally, 442-48
Trial cooperation, 1317-18

COUNSEL (See LAWYERS)

DISCOVERY
Discovery of class members, 1132-34
Discovery plan, 1088-91
Privileges
    Generally, 1140-52
    Common defense privilege, 1188-92
    Waiver, 1145-47
Resolving discovery disputes, 1136-52
Sanctions in, 1043-47
Special discovery techniques in complex litigation
    Confidentiality orders, 1149-52
    Document depositories, 1099-1103
    Document preservation orders, 1098, 1103-06
    Expert witnesses, 1170-72
    Limiting discovery, 1126-36
    Obtaining discovery from other sources
        Government, 1112-16, 1170-72
        Grand jury, 1113-16
        Other litigation, 1106-17, 1188-92
        Private sources, 1168-70
    Phased discovery, 1117-26
    Targeted discovery, 1117-26
    Wave discovery, 1117-26
Surveys and interviews, 1153-62
Traditional methods of discovery, 1092-98

DISMISSAL OF CLAIMS (See SUMMARY ADJUDICATION)

EFFICIENCY
As procedural value, 8-10
In case management and discovery, 1095, 1132-34

Of discovery surveys, 1160
Summary judgment, 1057-61

ELEVENTH AMENDMENT, 360-62

EQUITY (See also **INJUNCTIONS**)
History of, 36-47
Equitable remedies and joinder complexity, 88
Equitable remedies and remedial complexity, 1386, 1388-1404, 1324-35

ERIE **DOCTRINE**, 640-41, 805-09

EXPERT WITNESSES
Court appointed experts
  Pretrial, 1170-73
  Trial, 1347-59
Expert panels, 1171-72, 1351-52

FLUID RECOVERY, 1410-19

FORUM NON CONVENIENS (See **STAYS**)

FUTURE CLAIMANTS
Bankruptcy and, 752-87
Mootness of claims, 369-72
Ripeness of claims, 371, 685
Settlement class actions and, 658-89
Standing to bring claims, 363-68, 370-72, 685

HISTORY
English civil procedure
  Common law, 27-36
  Equity, 36-47
American civil procedure, 47-60

INJUNCTIONS
As means to stay related litigation, 389-442, 467-72
Remedial difficulties with, 1388-1404, 1424-35

INTERPLEADER
Distinction between statutory and rule, 417-19
Stays in, 397, 416, 419
Subject matter jurisdiction, 325-27, 418
Territorial jurisdiction, 416, 418
Venue, 418-19454

INTERVENTION
Of right, 136-53
Permissive, 153-55
Preclusion after notice and opportunity to intervene, 239-57

JOINDER
Joinder complexity defined, 88
Rule 19, 116-32
Rule 20
  Joinder of plaintiffs, 93-109
  Joinder of defendants, 109-15
Rule 22 (see **INTERPLEADER**)
Rule 23 (see **CLASS ACTIONS**)
Rule 24 (see **INTERVENTION**)

JUDGE
As factfinder at trial, 1208-09, 1239, 1245-61
As lawgiver at trial, 1261-64
Role of judge in case management (See also **CASE MANAGEMENT**),
Role of judge in public law litigation, 61-64

JUDICIAL ADJUNCTS
Advisors, 1246-54, 1421-22
Magistrate judges, 955-60
Masters
  In pretrial, 939-60
  At trial, 1254-61
  During remedial stage, 1421-23, 1443-48

JUDICIAL PANEL ON MULTIDISTRICT LITIGATION (See **MULTIDISTRICT LITIGATION**)

JURISDICTION
Subject matter jurisdiction
  Bankruptcy and, 704-05
  Diversity jurisdiction, 325-40
  Eleventh Amendment, 360-62
  Federal question jurisdiction, 312-25
  Mootness, 369-72
  Removal jurisdiction, 373-
  Ripeness, 371
  Special rules in complex litigation, 322-23, 331-32, 339-40360
  Standing, 363-68, 370-72
  Supplemental jurisdiction, 340-60
Territorial jurisdiction
  Bankruptcy and, 706
  Class actions and, 613-14
  Generally, 260-310
  Interpleader and, 416, 418
  Over plaintiffs, 293-310
  Over defendants, 262-93
  Pendent personal jurisdiction, 274
  Special rules in complex cases, 276-78, 291, 306-07

JURY TRIAL
Blue-ribbon juries, 1240-43
Comprehension problems in complex cases, 1237-39

Comprehension-enhancing techniques
   Enhancing comprehension (See **TRIALS** — Techniques to increase comprehension)
   Limiting information (See **TRIALS** — Techniques to limit information)
Effect of right to jury trial on class actions, 617-20, 642-43
Effect of right to jury trial on procedural system, 29, 32, 35
Generally, 1209-45
History of, 28-29
Seventh Amendment and, 617-20, 642-43, 1209-19, 1283-84
Special juries, 1240-43
Striking jury demand in complex cases, 1219-40
Use of multiple juries, 1316-19
Voir dire in complex cases, 1243-45

LAWYERS
Adequacy of counsel in class actions, 573-74, 581-83
Committees of counsel, 886, 891-93
Disqualification of, 898-914
Dysfunction in
   Joinder, 88
   Pretrial, 876
   Remedies, 1386
   Trial, 1198
Fees
   Bids for, 887-89
   Generally, 891-93
   In class actions, 554-55
Lead counsel in pretrial, 885-86
Lead counsel at trial, 1201-08
Liaison counsel, 886
Role in adversary system, 13-27
Role in complex litigation (See **LAWYERS** — Dysfunction)
Selection of counsel, 879-91
Structure of litigation team, 891-98
Withdrawal of counsel, 914-925

MAGISTRATE JUDGES (See **JUDICIAL ADJUNCTS**)

MANAGEMENT OF LITIGATION (See **CASE MANAGEMENT**)

MASTERS (See **JUDICIAL ADJUNCTS**)

MASTER OF THE COMPLAINT RULE
Generally, 87, 92, 258
Limitations on, 127, 147, 388, 437
Problems of rule in complex cases, 258, 310-11, 360

MATURITY OF LITIGATION
Generally, 235-36
In class actions, 642

MOOTNESS, 368-72

MULTIDISTRICT LITIGATION
Advantages of, 495
Choice of law in
   Diversity, 817
   Federal question, 819-32
Disadvantages of, 495, 525
Generally, 494-525
Judicial Panel on Multidistrict Litigation, 494-95
Remand of transferred cases, 516
Selection of transferee judge, 514-15
Standards for transfer, 509-12
Trial transfers and, 516-25

NOTICE
As central procedural value, 58
In class actions, 552-53
Preclusion after notice as alternative to joinder, 239-57

OUTCOME-DETERMINATIVE EFFECTS OF AGGREGATION, 102-03, 235-36

PERSONAL JURISDICTION (See **JURISDICTION** — Territorial Jurisdiction)

PHASED DISCOVERY (See **DISCOVERY**)

PLEADING
Common law pleading, 31-36
Pleading in complex cases
   Generally, 979-93
   Use of consolidated complaints, 993-1000

PRECLUSION
As issue-narrowing technique, 1079-83
Full faith and credit of judgments, 167-70
Generally
   Claim preclusion, 156-60, 166-73
   Issue preclusion, 160-73
Nonparty preclusion in complex litigation, 207-39
Party preclusion in complex litigation, 174-207
Preclusion after notice as alternative to joinder, 239-57

PRETRIAL PROCEEDINGS (See **CASE**

MANAGEMENT; DISCOVERY; JUDICIAL ADJUNCTS; LAWYERS; SUMMARY ADJUDICATION)

PROCEDURAL THEORY, 3-27

REMEDIES
Declaration problems in complex litigation
    Injunctive remedies, 1388-1404
    Monetary remedies, 1404-19
Implementation problems in complex litigation
    Injunctive remedies, 1424-35
    Monetary remedies, 1435-43
Non-party interference with
    Injunctive remedies, 1448-53, 1458-59
    Monetary remedies, 1453-59
Remedial complexity defined, 1385-86
Rightful position principle defined, 1385
Use of judicial adjuncts, 1419-22, 1443-48

REMOVAL JURISDICTION
Generally, 373-89
Sua sponte removal power, 388-89

RIPENESS, 370

SANCTIONS (See DISCOVERY — Sanctions)

STAGED DISCOVERY (See DISCOVERY — Staged discovery)

STANDING, 363-68, 370-72

STAYS
Federal stay in favor of other federal forum, 467-70
Federal stay in favor of state forum (See also ABSTENTION),
Forum non conveniens dismissal or stay, 458-67
State stay in favor of federal forum, 437-42
State stay in favor of other state forum, 470-72
Stay in favor of foreign forum, 472

SUBJECT MATTER JURISDICTION (See JURISDICTION — Subject matter jurisdiction)

SUMMARY ADJUDICATION
Motion to dismiss
    Generally, 1000-07
    Sua sponte power of court to dismiss, 1005-07
Summary judgment
    Generally, 1047-71

    Jury trial and, 1063-64
    Sua sponte power of court to enter summary judgment, 1071-79

SUMMARY JUDGMENT (See SUMMARY ADJUDICATION — Summary judgment)

SURVEYS (See DISCOVERY — Surveys and interviews)

TECHNOLOGY
Pretrial technology
    Methods of information control, 1173-80
    Privileges to prevent disclosure to opposing parties, 1183-95
    Use to assist in filing and serving documents, 1180-83
Trial technology, 1266-73, 1338-47

TRANSFERS (See MULTIDISTRICT LITIGATION; VENUE — Aggregation)

TRIAL
Techniques to increase comprehension
    Changing the order of trial, 1333-37
    Demonstrative evidence, 1338-47
    Experts and court appointed experts, 1347-59
    Jury notetaking, 1373-75
    Questioning or commenting by judge and jury, 1359-73
    Revising jury instructions, 1376-78
    Using special verdicts and sequential verdicts, 1378-84
Techniques to limit information
    Bifurcation, 1273-93
    Limiting time for trial, 1319-26
    Narratives or summaries, 1326-33
    Trial by statistics (See TRIAL BY STATISTICS)

TRIAL BY STATISTICS, 1294-1316

VENUE
Aggregation in a single venue
    Injunctions (See INJUNCTIONS)
    Stays (See STAYS)
    Transfers
        Transfers for all purposes under § 1404, 487-94
        Transfers for pretrial multidistrict purposes (See MULTIDISTRICT LITIGATION)
Ancillary venue, 455
Consolidation of cases in a single venue (See CONSOLIDATION)

General rules, 56
Local action rule, 455-56
Stays in favor

VERDICTS (See **TRIAL** — Techniques to increase comprehension)

WAVE DISCOVERY (See **DISCOVERY**)

WRIT SYSTEM, 29-31